A DICTIONARIE OF THE FRENCH AND ENGLISH TONGUES

Compiled by

RANDLE COTGRAVE

Reproduced from the first edition,

London, 1611

with introduction by

WILLIAM S. WOODS

UNIVERSITY OF SOUTH CAROLINA PRESS
COLUMBIA

PUBLISHED IN COLUMBIA, S. C., BY
THE UNIVERSITY OF SOUTH CAROLINA PRESS, 1950
2ND PRINTING, 1968

LIBRARY OF CONGRESS CATALOG CARD NUMBER: 51-4027
MANUFACTURED IN THE UNITED STATES OF AMERICA

INTRODUCTION

Concerning the life of Randle Cotgrave, the compiler of the *Dictionarie of the French and English Tongues,* we have very few facts.

The *Dictionary of National Biography* gives a little information about him. He may have been Randle, son of William Cotgrave of Christleton in Cheshire. He was admitted to St. John's College, Cambridge, on November 10, 1587, on the Lady Margaret Foundation. He became secretary to William Cecil, Lord Burghley, eldest son of Thomas, the first Earl of Exeter.

He presented a copy of the *Dictionarie* to Prince Henry, eldest son of James I, and received a gift of ten pounds. The first edition of this work appeared in 1611 and it is probable that Cotgrave saw the second edition through the press in 1632. There are extant two letters from Cotgrave to M. Beaulieu, secretary of the British Ambassador in Paris, which are concerned with various details of the dictionary project. The first of these, dated November 27, 1610, relates to the progress that was being made with the printing of the dictionary, in the preparation of which he says that he had received valuable help from Beaulieu himself and from a Mr. Limery. In the other letter Cotgrave states that he has sent his correspondent two copies of his book, and requests payment of twenty-two shillings, "which they cost me, who have not been provident enough to reserve any of them, and therefore am forced to be beholden for them to a base and mechanicall generation, that suffers no respect to weigh down a private gain."

It appears from these letters that Cotgrave was still in Lord Burghley's service. It is probable that he married Ellinor Taylor of Chester and had four sons by her, William, Randolph, Robert, Alexander, and a daughter, Mary. If this Randle Cotgrave is the compiler of the *Dictionarie,* he was at that time registrar to the Bishop of Chester. Cooper's *Memorials of Cambridge* gives the date of his death as 1634.

However, Dr. V. E. Smalley has shown in *The Sources of a Dictionarie of the French and English Tongues* that this statement is erroneous. The entry reads: "Randle Cotgrave, author of a french and english dictionary, flourished 1634 (?)."

The dedication of the *Dictionarie* (1611) is to Sir William Cecil, Lord Burghley. This William Cecil was born in 1566. He went to Paris with his tutor, a Mr. Bird, at the age of seventeen, and two years later was traveling in Italy, when he visited Rome, contrary to his father's express commands. In 1589 he married Elizabeth Manners, Baroness of Roos, or de Ros, daughter of the Earl of Rutland. She was only thirteen years old, and being a ward of the Crown could not marry without a license, which she had not obtained. For this offense she and her husband were fined six hundred pounds. She died in 1591, after giving birth to one son, William, who became Lord Roos.

William Cecil was knighted in 1603 when his father entertained King James at York. He took part occasionally in the functions at court but did not distinguish himself in any way. He succeeded his father as Lord Burghley in 1605, and as Earl of Exeter in 1623. His second wife was Elizabeth Drury of Halstead, and by her he had three daughters. He was Lord Lieutenant of Northampton, a member of the Privy Council, and a Knight of the Garter. He died in July 1640 and was buried in Westminster Abbey.

The first edition of the *Dictionarie* came out in 1611 and, as it is considered the best, it is being reproduced here. In the supplementary material, following the dictionary itself, small portions of five pages from the second edition have been used, but these do not differ from the corresponding pages in the first edition.

The four later editions, all containing some alterations, are as follows:

II. Part I. *A Dictionarie of the French and English Tongues* Compiled by Randle Cotgrave. Whereunto is also annexed a most copious Dictionarie, of the English set before the French. By R. S. L. London, Printed by Adam Islip, Anno 1632.

Part II. *Dictionaire, Anglois et François,* pour l'utilité de tous ceux, qui sont desireux de deux Langues. *A Dictionarie English and French;* Compiled for the commoditie of all such as are desirous of both Languages. by Robert Sherwood Londoner. London, Printed by Adam Islip. Anno 1632.

III. Part I. *A French-English Dictionary,* compil'd by Mr. Randle Cotgrave: with Another in English and French, Whereunto are newly added the *Animadversions and Supplements,* &c. of *James Howell* Esquire. *Inter Eruditos* Cathedram *habeat* Polyglottes. London. Printed by W. H. for *Humphrey Robinson,* and are to be sold at his shop at the signe of the three Pigeons, in *Pauls* Church-yard: 1650.

Part II. *Dictionaire Anglois et François,* pour l'utilité de tous ceux, qui sont desireux de deux Langues. *A Dictionary English and French;* Compiled for the commoditie of all such as are desirous of both Languages. by Robert Sherwood Londoner. London, Printed by Susan Islip. 1650.

IV. Part I. *A French and English Dictionary.* Composed by Randle Cotgrave with another in English and French Whereunto are added sundry Animadversions, with Supplements of many hundreds of words never before printed; with accurate castigations throughout the whole work, and distinctions of the obsolete words from those now in use. Together, With a large Grammar, and a Dialogue consisting of all Gallicismes, with additions of the most usefull and significant Proverbs, with other refinements according to Cardinall Richelievs late Academy. For the furtherance of young Learners, and the advantage of all others that endeavour to arrive to the most extant knowledge of the French Language, this work is exposed to publick. By James Howell Esqr. Inter Eruditos Cathedram habeat Polyglottes. London. Printed by William Hunt in Pye-corner, 1660.

Part II. *A Dictionarie Anglois et François,* pour l'utilité de tous ceux, qui sont desireux de deux Langues. *A Dictionary English and French;* compiled for the commodity of all such as are desirous of both the Languages. By Robert Sherwood Londoner. Printed by William Hunt, 1660.

V. Part I. *A French and English Dictionary*. Composed by Mr. Randle Cotgrave with another in English and French Whereunto are added Sundry Animadversions, with Supplements of many hundreds of Words never before Printed; With Accurate Castigations throughout the whole *Work*, and Distinctions of the Obsolete Words from those that are now in Use. Together with A large *Grammar*, and a *Dialogue* consisting of all Gallicismes, with Additions of the most Usefull and Significant Proverbs, with other Refinements according to Cardinall Richelieu's late Academy. For the furtherance of young Learners, and the advantage of all others that endeavour to arrive to the most exact knowledge of the French Language, this work is exposed to Publick, by *James Howell* Esq.; *Inter Eruditos* Cathedram *habeat* Polyglottes. London. Printed for *Anthony Dolle* and are to be sold by *Thomas Williams* at the *Golden Ball* in *Hosier Lane*, MDCLXXIII.

Part II. *A Dictionaire Anglois et François*, pour l'utilité de tous ceux, qui sont desireux de deux Langues. *A Dictionary English and French;* compiled for the commodity of all such as are desirous of both *Languages*. By Robert Sherwood Londoner. London. Printed in the year, MDCLXXII.

In her study of the sources of Cotgrave's *Dictionarie*, Dr. Smalley concluded that it represents the effort of a group of men working under the direction of an editor, presumably Cotgrave himself. This conclusion is suggested by the fact that he acknowledged having received help from at least two other persons, M. Beaulieu and Mr. Limery. It is further substantiated by the general uneven quality of the work, which shows a mixture of careful and accurate scholarship with rather glaring errors both in translation and in choice of material.

Dr. Smalley also concludes that the *Dictionarie* was probably a business venture rather than a scholarly project. As to the sources of the work, she finds that the idea for a French-English dictionary probably came from Claudius Holyband's (or Claude de Sainliens) *The Treasurie of the French Tong* (London, 1580) and *A Dictionaire French and English* (London, 1593). The dictionary to which Cotgrave was most indebted was Nicot's *Thresor de la langue françoise* (Paris, 1606). Among other dictionary sources for his work were Gabriel Meurier's *Dictionaire françoys-flameng* (Antwerp, 1562), César Oudin's *Tesoro de las dos lenguas francesa y española* (Paris, 1607), John Palsgrave's *Lesclarcissement de la langue françoise* (London, 1530), John Barrett's (or Baret) *An Alvearie, or quadruple dictionary in English, Latin, Greeke, and French* (London, 1580), the Latin-English dictionaries compiled by Elyot, Cooper, and Thomas, the *Worlde of Words* of Florio, and Minsheu's *A Dictionarie in Spanish and English*. Along with these and others Cotgrave utilized many literary, social, and scientific documents for collecting and illustrating the entries in his *Dictionarie*.

The genesis and development of the project which led to Cotgrave's work can be traced in the following entries taken from the Registers of the Company of Stationers of London:

(i) 166b 22 july 1567 - 22 July 1568

L. Haryson Recevyed of Lucas haryson for his lycense for the pryntinge of a boke intituled a Dyxcionary ffrynshe and englesshe &c. . . . . .xij d.

(ii) 149 Thomas Woodcock

Decimo quinto Die July / 1578

Licensed unto him theis Copies hereafter menconed which are sold by mistress *harrison* wief unto master *Luke Harrison* Deceased and which aperteined unto master *harrison* in his lief Tyme......................

......vijj s.

master Deeringes lectures
master Knewestubbes lectures
....
Dictionarie Ffrenche and English

(iii) paule Lynley

7b

9 ffebruarij 1596

Assigned over unto him from mistress *woodcocke* by consent of the Company all her Interest in and to the pryntinge of all and every bookes and partes of bookes whatsoever Which Laufully apperteyned to her late husband Thomas woodcocke and after his Decease to her..............

......x s.

(iv) John flasket

26 Junij 1600

Entred for his copies by consent of our Maister and Master Man Warden these bookes and partes of Bookes folowynge whiche were Paule Lynlayes ....

......viij d.

....
master Deringes Lectures
Master Knewestubbes Lectures
Holybandes Dictionary French and Inglishe
....

(v) 169 John Bill Assigned over to hym from John Flasket

7 Junij 1608

A Dictionarie in Ffrenche and Englishe Collected first by C. Holyband and sythenc(e) Augmented or Altered by Randall Cotgrave/ The whiche is nowe by Master fflaskettes Assent and agrement entred for Master Billes copie...

......vj d.

John fflaskett

(vi) 194b Adam Islip/ Assigned over unto him from Master Byll, and by Master Bylls consente and agrement nowe entered for the sayd Adam Izlipps copy, by consente of a Courte of the master wardens, and assistantes.

27 mo Aprilis/1610

A dictionary in Ffrenche and Englishe collected first by Claudius Holyband, and sithence augmented or altered by Randall Cotgrave which copye was assigned over from John fflaskett to master Byll and Entred for master Bills Copy the vij of January(June) 1608 Anno 6-to Regis.....

......vj d

John Bill

Dr. Smalley points out that the form of the Cotgrave *Dictionarie* is a decided improvement over earlier French lexicons, principally because the vocabulary is arranged in strictly alphabetical order, whereas Estienne and his followers had used an etymological order for the words. English lexicographers had used the alphabetical order from the first half of the sixteenth century and Cotgrave followed their example. Cotgrave's vocabulary is almost twice as long as that of Nicot's *Thresor,* the total number of items being computed by Dr. Smalley as nearly 48,000. She also states his contributions to French lexicography as follows (p. 219) "some twenty thousand new items added to the vocabulary of French dictionaries, exclusive of variants and derivates of words already in the dictionaries; the establishment of a new type of material as legitimate stuff for dictionary vocabularies, i.e., technical and popular words in far greater numbers than had ever appeared in a French dictionary; the use of old legal and literary popular texts as source material instead of romances, poetic works, or classics of French literature, so that many dialectal and popular expressions are preserved in the *Dictionarie;* the use of proverbs and popular expressions as illustrative material in his *Dictionarie;* and the first serious attempt to incorporate in a dictionary, if not all, at least as many as possible of the variant forms that existed in French of the 16th and early 17th centuries. These are all substantial contributions to the history of French lexicography."

The need for a reprint of the first edition of Cotgrave's *Dictionarie of the French and English Tongues* has long been felt. Professor Levy says of it: "This dictionary is a necessity for reading French texts of (the) fifteenth century. Wit and richness of definition, breadth of interest and accuracy, make this one of the world's great books . . . There is need for a modern reprint of an early edition." Lazare Sainéan has made the following statement about the work: "C'est le répertoire lexicographique le plus complet qu'on possède sur le XVIe siècle. Il embrasse à la fois la langue parlée, pour laquelle Cotgrave mit à contribution le *Thrésor* de Nicot (1606), et la langue littéraire, pour laquelle il dépouilla tous les auteurs contemporains, grands ou petits, bons ou médiocres . . . La phraséologie de Cotgrave est la plus riche qu'on ait jamais enregistrée; le nombre des proverbes, locutions et idiotismes qu'il cite est unique dans son genre." The work has become the chief lexicographical source of our knowledge about Middle and Renaissance French. It is of great worth in the study of Old French vocabulary and that of the early seventeenth century. The first edition of this great work is almost unobtainable and the volumes which are accessible have reached the category of rare books. That a work of such importance to the scholarly and general public is not readily available does not reflect credit on our sense of values.

The University of South Carolina Press has earned the gratitude of the scholarly world for making accessible again a work of such magnitude and importance. Special thanks should be expressed to Dr. Urban T. Holmes and to Dr. Robert W. Linker of the University of North Carolina, who through the years have tried with unrelenting zeal to encourage a project for the reprinting of the *Dictionarie.* Without their help and suggestions the realization of this undertaking would have been impossible.

William S. Woods
Newcomb College
Tulane University

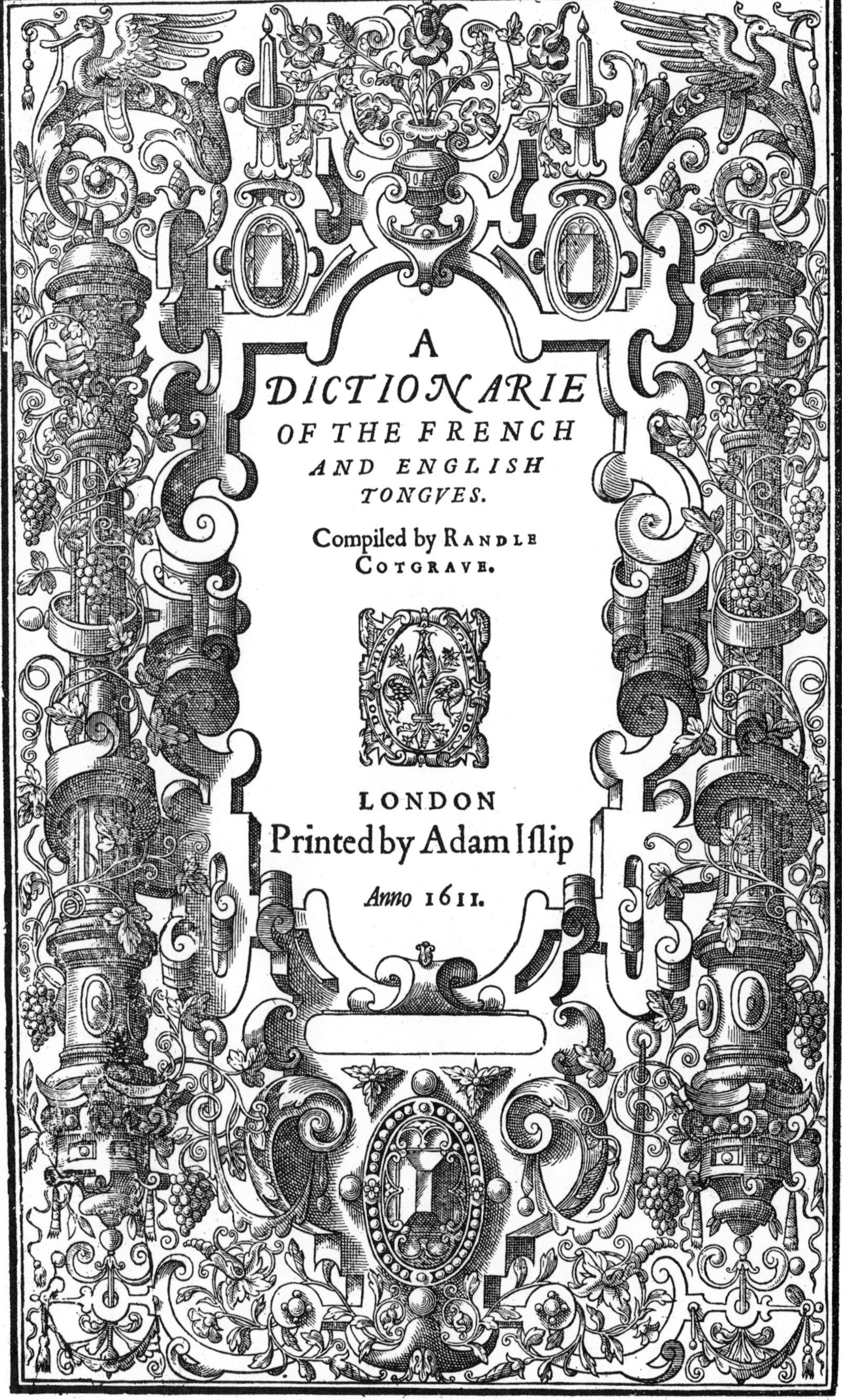

A DICTIONARIE OF THE FRENCH AND ENGLISH TONGVES.

Compiled by RANDLE COTGRAVE.

LONDON
Printed by Adam Islip
Anno 1611.

TO THE RIGHT HONO-rable, and my very good Lord and Maiſter,

Sir WILLIAM CECIL *Knight*, *Lord* Burghley, *and ſonne* and heire apparant vnto the Earle of Exceter.

Here preſent vnto your Lordſhips view an Account of th'expence of many houres, which in your ſeruice, and to mine owne benefit might haue beene otherwiſe imploied: for ſloth, howſoeuer, had not conſumed them; ſomewhat I muſt haue done the whileſt; nor could I haue beſtowed them on a Worke of leſſe vſe for your Lordſhip, the French being alreadie ſo well vnderſtood by you, and all yours. In which regard, as I am particularly bound to acknowledge your Lordſhips goodneſſe, bearing with my humor to follow, and allowing me time to finiſh it; ſo haue all they, to whom it ſhall proue of any worth, iuſt cauſe to honour in your Lordſhip that goodneſſe, continued a long time vnto their, and the common good. No priuat conſideration was fit to make your Lordſhip often to diſpence with th ordinarie attendance of an ordinarie ſeruant. But this is one of the leaſt of your Lordſhips reſpects to the Publicke; and I would be loath to ingage your Judgement, or Honour, on the ſucceſſe of ſo meane a Peece. My deſires haue aimed at more ſubſtantiall markes; but mine eyes failed them, and forced me to ſpend much of their vigour on this Bundle of words; which though it may be vnworthie of your Lordſhips great patience, and perhaps ill ſorted to the expectation of others, yet is it the beſt J can at this time make it, and were, how perfect ſoeuer, no more then due to your Lordſhip, to whom I owe, for what I haue beene many yeres, whatſoeuer I am now, or looke to be hereafter.

Your Lordſhips

most bounden ſeruant,

Randle Cotgraue.

Au favorable Lecteur François.

LEcteur, l'Auteur de ce livre (Gentilhomme Anglois, à qui son propre Pays &, sur tout, le notre ont vne obligation particuliere, qu'ilz ont à peu d'autres) apres avoir peniblement veillé & travaillé par plusieurs ans, sur cet œuvre, non moins, certes, ingrat que laborieuz; En fin est contraint de le laisser partir de ses mains, plutot vaincu de l'importunité de ses Amis, & de la necessité que le Public en a, que satisfait en son ame de son propre ouvrage. Et t'assure que si on l'eut voulu croire, il fût encore apres à se tourmenter, pour trouver la signification de telz mots, qui, possible, ne seront jamais plus ouyz en ce monde, (quoy que luz) & dont, ie croy, il n'y a personne qui ait ouy parler depuis cent ans, que luy; tant sa curiosité a eté grande & exacte à lire toute sorte de livres, vieuz & nouveauz, & de tous noz dialectes. A cette cause, peur, possible, qu'ayant égard à ce que tu voys, non à ce que tu ne voys pas, tu l'accuses plutot de ce qu'il a dit, que de ce qu'il a eté contraint de laisser; qui toutefois seroit vn tresor inestimable, s'il eût pu trouver, ou pardeça, ou en France mesmes (où il a eté si curieuz d'envoyer expres) qui l'eut pu, ou voulu resoudre de ses doutes; Il te suplie bien fort, si tu trouves icy quelques mots qui te sonnent mal auz oreilles, ou mesme qui n'y ayent encore iamais sonné, de croire, qu'ilz ne sont point de son invention, mais recueilliz de la multitude & diversité de noz Auteurs, que possible tu n'auras pas encore luz, & qui, tant bons que mauvais, desirent tous d'estre entenduz. Il pouvoit bien citer le nom, le livre, la page, & le passage; mais ce n'eut plus icy eté vn Dictionaire, ains vn Labirinte. Ceuz qui ne les sauront pas, les aprendront; Ceuz qui les sauront, jugeront bien que l'ignorance, possible, d'vn seul mot, soit substanciel, metaforique, inusité, ou tiré de la varieté des Ars, peut souvent obscurcir tout vn sens, & rendre barbares les conceptions les plus gentilles. Permis à qui voudra d'en vser, ou de les laisser; Bien entendu, toutefois, que ce ne seroit pas le pis qui nous pût arriver, que de remettre suz, certains mots sur-annez, que nous avons mieuz aimé laisser perdre, quoy que trespropres & significatifs; Et autres de notre propre cru, bien que de divers terroir, allans plutot mandier chez les Etrangers pour nous exprimer, ou bien nous taisans du tout, ou parlans par vn long contournement de paroles, que d'ouvrir vn peu la bouche pour en prononcer quelques vns qui sembloyent trop revesches pour la douceur du palais de noz Damoiselles, ou grater l'oreille delicate de Messieurs noz Courtisans de ce tems-cy. Quant auz fautes de l'Impression, l'Autheur ne les peut totalement prendre sur soy, ne niant pas qu'il n'en soit eschapé assez, comme aussi possible en quelques endroits, quelque impropre interpretation; esperant bien toutefois, que les vnes ny les autres ne seront pas si grandes que ta courtoisie n'y puisse bien suppleer. A tant, Il recomande son œuvre à ta bonne reception, & moy ie demeure

Ton tresaffectionné Patriotte,

I. L'OISEAV de Tourval, Parisien Δ.

To the Reader.

HVmanum est errare, *say the Latinists, to whom verie many (too much men in their much erring) haue beene exceedingly beholden for an excuse vpon iust accusations. I (who am no God, nor Angell) either to preuent, or to profit, others, am willing ynough to accuse my selfe; and therefore haue caused such ouerslips as haue yet occurred to mine eye or vnderstanding, to be placed neere the forhead of this Verball creature; as lesse afraid so to disgrace it, then to deceiue those that shall harbor it; and chusing rather to publish mine owne errors, then to be guiltie of other mens; I will not presume to affirme that these be all, no more then I will acknowledge, or giue any account for, such, as the malicious and ignorant shall captiously pinch, or fondly point, at: but my hope is, that as I haue dealt freely in the discouerie of these, so all that be iudicious will vse me friendly in their corrections of the rest.*

Errata.

A

IN *the first Page,* col. 1. Il a gaigne, *for,* Il y a gaigné. volunte, *for,* volonté. *and* col. 2. *an Adiectiue, for a Nowne. whose tone foot is, for, who hath one foot. and* Abbaisse, *for,* Abbaissé.

Adouber, *for* Adouber.

dessus, *for* dessous; *in a phrase vnder* Aile.

Aoriste. *A Tense; is, more particularly, a Tense of time indefinitely, or betweene Perfect and Imperfectly, passed.*

Appensensement, *for* Appensement.

La Perche *vnder* Arpent; *the la superfluous, and false; for* Perche *is masculine.*

B

Balise, & Balisse *(tearmed about* Orleans Baslis;) *is more properly, a causey in a riuer for the turning of the streame vnto a Mill, &c.*

Bannier, *for* Banniere; *vnder* Banniere.

Bardechiser, *for* Bardachiser.

Basse.contre, *for* Basse-contre.

Baston cornu, *a Battleaxe; is rather, a staffe tipped at both ends with horne; and heretofore vsed in publicke Duelloes, or Combats.*

pigue, *for* figue; *in* Batre à froid, *vnder* Batre.

Belitresse, *for* Belistresse.

Bisac, *for* Bissac.

hnnoeur, *for* honneur; *vnder* Blesser.

Bord, *is more properly an edging, or binding about the edge, of a garment, &c, then either welt, or hemme: and* Border *much more properly to edge, or bind, or compasse with an edging or binding lace, &c, then either to gard, or to border.*

le cueillier, *for* la cueillier; *in a Prouerbe vnder* Bouche; *and (in the most Copies) vnder* Cuillier.

se Bride, *for* se Brider; *vnder* Brider.

C

19, *for* 192, *in* Carat.

Carlin, *worth* 40 Quadrins; *is to be vnderstood of the Florentine* Quattrino, *worth no more then halfe the French* Quadrin.

Carminatif. *Wind-voiding, &c; is rather, cutting or dissoluing, and thereby refining and thinning, grosse humors.*

An ounce, in stead of a graine; in Carrube.

Ceincture de dueil (*vnder* Ceincture) *referred vnto* Dueil, *where it was forgotten: but you shall find it expounded in the word* Littre.

Brusler la chandelle. par (*vnder* Chandelle) *the full point superfluous.*

festes, *for* fesses; *in a Prouerbe vnder* Charité.

levrier, *for* levriers; *in a Prouerbe vnder* Chasse.

repend, *in stead of* repent; *in a Prouerbe vnder* Chat, *and in another vnder* Despendre.

le chevre, *for* la chevre; *in a phrase vnder* Chevre.

Chicambaut, *the Luffe-blocke, should be, the Bumkin.*

old, *for cold, in the word* Cigale.

poules, *for* poulets; *in a Prouerbe vnder* Cimitierre.

loye triste & coeur; *in a Prouerbe vnder* Coeur, *the* & *superfluous.*

dammages, *for* dommages; *vnder* Conclusion.

Comforter, *in stead of* Conforter; *in a phrase vnder* Conforter.

Contrechange, *for* Contreschange.

chausteau, *for* chasteau; *in a Prouerbe vnder* Corps.

Coquiol, *for* Coquiole, *and a superfluous comma in that line.*

Couäné, *and in some words that follow it, the Dieresis ill placed ouer the* a.

grand, *for* grands; *in a Prouerbe vnder* Coup.

Grattant, *for* gratant, *in a phrase vnder* Cul.

D

Dardiller *(a frequentatiue to* Darder) *signifies, to dart, or throw darts, verie fast.*

Decicif, *in stead of* Decisif.

things,

things, for thinkes, in the last line of Discretion.
Resve, *in stead of* Resuë; *in* Domaine forain, *vnder* Domaine.
Douves d'un tonneau. *Be as well the side-staues, as the head-peeces, of caske.*
Dragme: m. *for* Dragme: f.
Daulerie, *for* Draulerie.
pon wants (to the making of vpon) in the beginning of the third line of Droict de Registre, ou contentor *(vnder* Droict.)

E

Mitaines engantées, *were better; banded, or put on the bands, like gloues.*
Esraigne, *for* Escraigne.
Escruoëlle, *for* Escrouëlle.

F

Fanné, *read* Fanne.
Foret. *Is rather a Drill, then either a Gimlet, or Piercer.*
breaker, for breaker; in Fracteur: *And,* Aujourd'uy, *in stead of* Aujourd'huy; *vnder the same word.*
Franchemulle de mouton. *(which should be* Franchemule) *may verie well be that in a Weather, which* Franche mule*(vnder* Mule) *is in an Oxe.*

G

Gaigne-pain. *Is most properly (in the last sence) an old-fashioned shield stucke thicke with the teeth of Horses or Moyles.*
In Generalité, *say I, there be 21 generall Receiptes,* &c; *(whereof the Printer hath ouerslipped one,* viz. Rion, *in the reckoning) wherein I followed a late English Author of good worth: But now find in the later French (as the last edition of the Comment vpon* Code Henrie, *and* l'Oiseau *his booke of Orders) and by the report of a iudicious Gentleman, verie lately imployed in France, that there be but 20; whereof* Rion *is one, and* Moulin*(the last in my computation) none.*
Gouldron, Gouldronné, & Gouldronner; *referred vnto* Gouderon, &c; *in stead of* Goderon, &c.
sound, for found; vnder Gracieux.
32, *for* 16; *in* Gros.
La guinderesse de la misaine. *The mizzen hallyards; belongs rather to the foresaile.*

H

also, as Hayreux; *forgotten in* Haireux.
paine, *for* peine; *vnder* Har.
In Hipothequer *(a little before which,* Hipotheque; *as* Hypotheque, *was ouerslipped) and in* Hypotheque, *the word immouables might haue beene spared.*
Houille. *Is a kind of sea-coale.*

I

Dicu, *for* Dieu; *vnder* Iambe.
Ibix, *for* Ibex; *in* Ibice.

L

Legion *(say I) consisted of 6830 souldiers; which was the full, and perfect Legion, sayes Thomas Thomasius out of* Vegetius. *In Cæsars time the full Legion contained but 5000; And though sometimes before the number were greater, as when Scipio went into Affricke, 6500, and after the Macedonian warre 6300; yet both before and after those times the most vsuall rate was either that, or but 4200.*

M

In Manganese, *a superfluous, or.*
Mareschaux de France. *Now there be 10, say I, following therien my English Author, who writ aboue 10 yeares agoe: Since when there haue beene 12 at one time, and now I doe not heare of aboue 9.*
Veine, *for* Veines; *in* Mesaraïque.
Müiere, *for* Mieüre.
Mouelle; *as* Moelle. Mouette, & Mouettes; *as* Moette, & Moettes, *want each of them a* Dieresis *ouer the first* e.

N

Soubs peine nisi, *for* sous peine de nisi *(in most bookes.)*

P

Panceron. *Is rather a little, then a great, paunch.*
boale, *for* boüle; *in a phrase vnder* Pied.
Pillorier, *for* Pilorier.
Pressuirier, *for* Pressurier; *vnder* Pressurier.

R

A comma wanting after Tradesmen; in the phrase vnder Robon.

S

Gurnet, *for* Garnet; *in* Spinelle.
old Metellus, *for* Paulus Æmilius; *in a Prouerbe vnder* Soulier.

V

Veinec oronale, *for* Veine coronale; *vnder* Veine.
meseraïques, *for* mesaraïques; *in the same page.*

A Dictio-

¶ A DICTIONARIE OF THE French and English Tongues.

The first letter of all Alphabets, is (as it is a letter) a Substantiue: whence; Il est marqué à l'A: *he is a right honest man: or, one in whom there is as much vertue, as great worth, as can be in any man: (From the monie of France; euery sort whereof hath stamped on it a particular letter, denoting the place wherein it was made; now, that which is coined in Paris hath on it an* A, *and is, commonly, of the best mettall.)*

A. *The third person singuler of the verbe* Avoir, *signifies (of it selfe) hath, holdeth, possesseth, enioieth; as,* Assez a qui bon credit a: *also (when it hath the local Adverb* y *before it) is; as,* Assez y a si trop n'y a: *But when it precedes a Participle in the preterperfect Tense of another verbe, it is restrained vnto the first signification, hath; as,* il a gaigne ce qu' il a peu: *In all which (and otherwise, onely as it is a letter) it is written without Accent.*

'A. *an Article, set before a proper name, or Nowme, signifies, in matters of possession, of; as,* La maison à Pierre, La femme à Robert: *But where the verbe* Estre *goes before, it signifies To, or, Vnto; as,* La maison est à Pierre, *belongs to Peter: So doth it also when it followes verbes that require a Datiue case; as,* Ie l'ay donné à toy; cela appartient à moy; *or that signifie motion to a place; as,* Ie m'en iray à Londres, à ma metairie.

'A. *an article, or Preposition; signifieth sometimes, As, or For;* Il est tenu à perdu; à sot; à fable: *sometimes only, For;* à cette cause: *sometimes, At; as,* Tu me trouveras à Paris; à loisir; à vostre commandement: *also In, or, At; as,* à temps, & lieu: *sometimes In, or, Before; as,* à la presence du Roy: *sometimes By; as,* à l'adventure; à cœur; à droit; à tort: & *(as in old Authors)* à dieu le veu, *in stead of* par dieu ie le veux: *sometimes On, or Vpon; as,* à lundi; il monte à cheval: *sometimes To; as,* à propos; à point: *also Agreeable, or, According to; as,* à l'ordonnance des Arbitres: *also, Like vnto; After the manner, or fashion of; as,* vestu à l'Italienne; vne espée à l'Espagnole: *sometimes, With; as,* à peu de perte; à banniere desployée; vne chaire à accoudoirs; & *(in Blazon)* Il porte de Synople à trois Lyons d'argent: *also, With, or Among; as,* à nous tel fait est bien vilain; Il est à nous grande vinée.

'A la mienne volunte, *If I might haue my will: or, I would to God.*

Dont il est à grande ioye, *Whereof he is very glad; which makes him very merrie.*

Ils se faisoient tenir à douze; *They made themselues be held by twelue: or, were so fierce that twelue were faine to hold them.*

A. *preceding the Infinitiue mood of a verbe, signifies, to, seruing to, for to, of purpose for; as,* S'il a chose à dire; vn clou à pendre des sacs. *Somtimes it either giues the verb a participiall sence, as,* Il est à dormir, *he is sleeping, or new, or neere asleepe; or, the verb being present, it denotes the future, as,* I'ay cela à faire, *I am to doe that hereafter.*

'A. *before an Adiectiue, sometimes makes it admit of an Aduerbiall interpretation; as,* à droict, à tort; *rightfully, wrongfully.*

'A, *is sometimes not expressed, but vnderstood; as,* Si Dieu plaist, *for,* s'il plaist à Dieu.

Aachée: f. *a dolefull crie, lamentation, Ay-mee.*

Aage: m. *age, yeares, dayes; also, an age; time, season.*

De grand aage; *very old, a grandsire, a gray-beard, whose tone foot is alreadie in the graue.*

De petit aage; *very yong, a child, an infant, an innocent, an vnderling.*

Avoir de l'aage, *to be strong and lustie: also to be well in yeares, or well stricken in yeares.*

Aagé: m. aagée: f. *aged, old; of age, of years; of full age, of great yeares.*

Abaissé; & Abaissement; *as,* Abbaissé; & Abbaissement.

Abaisser; & Abaisseur; *as,* Abbaisser; & Abbaisseur.

Abandon: m. *bandon, free licence, full libertie for others to vse a thing; The quitting, abandonment, or prostitution of a thing vnto others; whence;*

Mettre sa forest en abandon; *to lay it open, or make it common, for all men that will gather wood, or graze their cattell, in it.*

Abandon fait larron; Prov. *Things carelesly left, layd vp, or looked vnto, make them theeues that otherwise would be honest: we say, fast bind fast find.*

Qui faict nopces, & maison, il met le sien en abandon; Prov. *The building of houses and making of feasts, are vnlimitted wasters of a mans substance.*

Abandonné: m. née: f. *abandonned, forsaken, forgone, quitted, giuen ouer, cast off; layd open, left at randome; prostituted vnto, made common for, any man; also proscribed, outlawed.*

Cheval abandonné sur la bride. *hanging vpon the hand.*

Chose trop abandonnée. *thats vnrecouerable, or in very desperat tearms.*

Abandonnement:m. an abandonning, quitting, forsaking, leauing off, giuing ouer, laieng open for, prostituting vnto, others; also a proscribing or outlawing.

Abandonnement de raison. a wilfull defection, reuolting, or swaruing, from reason.

Abandonnement. at randome, dissolutely, licenciously, profusely, with full libertie.

Abandonner. to abandon, quit, forsake, forgoe, waiue or giue ouer, shake or cast off, lay open, leaue at randome, prostitute vnto, make common for, others; also, to outlaw.

Abandonner la vie de tel au premier qui le pourra tuer. to proscribe a man; (is euer to be vnderstood of a Soueraigne, or such a one as, next vnder God, hath absolute and vncontrowlable power ouer his life.)

s'Abandonner à plaisirs. sensually to yeeld, or become a slaue, vnto pleasure; wholy to captiuat, or deuote, his thoughts to delights.

Fille qui donne s'abandonne; Pro. A maid that giueth yeeldeth.

Il commence bien à mourir qui abandonne son desir; Pro. he truly begins to die that quits his chiefe desires.

Abandonneur: an abandonner, leauer, quitter, forsaker, forgoer, giuer ouer, prostitutor of.

Abaque: m. a Plinth, or flat square stone, on the Capitell of a pillar.

Abastardi: m. ie: f. adulterated, sophisticated, bastardized, counterfeited; marred, corrupted, depraued; degenerat, changed out of it owne kind; made worse, growne worse and worse.

Abastardir. to bastardise, adulterat, sophisticat, counterfeit; to change out of it owne kind into a worse; to depraue, corrupt, viciat, spoile, marre, make worse; also, to degenerat, wax naught, grow worse & worse: (In which sense it hath, most commonly, the Passiue note, Se, before it.)

Abastardissement: m. an adulterating, sophistication, counterfeiting; a corrupting, marring, deprauing; a making worse, or changing out of it owne kind into a worse; also a degenerating.

Abastardisseur: m. an adulterator; sophisticater, counterfeiter; a corrupter, deprauer, spoiler of things; also, a bastard-maker.

Abatis; Abatre; & Abatu. Looke Abbatis; Abbatre; and Abbatu.

Abayement; Abayer; & Abayeur. Looke, Abbayement; Abbayer; and Abbayeur.

Abbais. as Abbois.

Abbaissé: m. ée: f. debased, deiected, humbled, prostrated; bent, or brought downe; made, or growne low; decreased, fallen, stooping.

Abbaissement: m. a debasing, abasing, deiecting, humbling, prostrating; bending downewards, bringing downe, making low; also, a stooping; decreasing, falling, waxing low.

Abbaissement de courage. faintheartednesse, or the growing fainthearted; a failing in courage; the falling of the crest; also, lowlinesse of mind.

Abbaissement de son estat. an impairing, diminution, or abatement, of his means.

Abbaisser. to debase, abase, abate, humble, depresse, deiect; bend downwards, bring downe, make low; also, to stoope; decrease, fall, or wax low.

Abbaisser la Maiesté d'un Prince. to disgrace, disparage, violate, infringe, or tread vnder foot, the Maiestie of a Prince.

s'abbaisser à. to humble or prostrat himselfe before; also, to yeeld or submit himselfe, vnto.

Abbaisseur: m. an abaser, debaser, deiecter, depresser, humbler, bringer downe of.

Abbandon; & Abbandonné; as Abandon; and Abandonné.

Abbandonnement; & Abbandonner; Looke Abandonnement; & Abandonner.

Abbatement: m. a felling, a beating, or breaking, a violent bearing, or bringing, downe; also, an abatement; also, the thing thats felled, beaten, or borne, downe.

Abbateur. a feller, ouerthrower, beater, breaker, or bearer, downe of.

Grand abbateur de bois. a sore fellow, horrible swaggerer, terrible bugbeare; one that ouerthrowes all he meets with; (Ironically.)

Abbateure: f. as Abbatement.

Abbateures. the boughs, leaues, or sprigs, which a Deere breakes and beares downe with his head in rushing through a thicket.

Abbatial: m. ale: f. Abbotlike, Abbay-like; of, or belonging to, an Abbot, or Abbey.

Abbatis: m. an ouerthrow; or ouerthrowing; as Abbatement; Also, an vtter defeature, execution, or slaughter of men.

L'abbatis d'une forest. wind-falls; or the wood, or trees, grubd vp, felled, or fallen downe.

L'abbatis d'une maison; the ruines of a house.

Abbatre. to fell; to beat or breake downe; violently to beare, or bring downe; to ruine, ouerthrow, cast to the ground; also to defeat vtterly, discomfit wholy.

Cela abbat l'yvresse. that quels, allaies, abates drunkennesse; or, makes a man sober againe.

Fort est qui abbat, & plus fort qui se releue; Pro. Seeke, Releuer.

Abbatu: m. uë: f. felled; beaten, or broken downe; violently borne, or brought down; quelled, ruined, ouerthrowne, cast to the ground.

Il a le coeur tout abbatu. his mind is vtterly deiected, courage abated, heart gone; hee is wholy crestfallen; there is no further life, no mettall, no spirit, left in him.

L'abbatu veut tousiours luicter; Prov. sayd of an obstinat fellow, whom no foile can make leaue a Contention, or suit, begun.

Chasteau abbatu est à demy refaict; Pro. A house puld downe is halfe built vp againe.

Abbay: m. a barking, or baying of dogges; Looke Abbois.

Tenir en abbay. to hold at bay; also, to delay, or driue off, with false hopes.

Abbayant. sub. as Abbayeur; a barker, &c.

Abbayant. part. barking, baying; railing.

Abbaye: f. an Abbay, Monasterie, Religious house.

Abbayé: m. ée: f. barked at; railed on.

Abbayement: m. a barking or baying of dogs; also, a lowd, extreame, and passionat reuiling of, skoulding at, rayling on.

Abbayer, to barke, or bay at; also, to reuile extreamly, lowdly to raile on.

Il abbaye contre la Lune. he barks at the Moone; sayd of one that obstinatly striues to falsifie, or disgrace the truth; wherein he spends his indeauors most ridiculously, vnprofitably, miserably.

Chien qui abbaye ne mord pas; Pro. The barking dogge bites little; and, He that sayest most, commonly does least.

Qui sert commun nul ne le paye, & s'il defaut chascun

Chascun l'abbaye; Pro. *He that serues a Communaltie is controlled by euery one, rewarded by none.*

Abbayeur: m. *a barker, a rayler.*

Abbé: m. *an Abbot.*

Face d'abbé. *a jollie, fat, and red face; a fierie facies.*

Pas d'Abbé. *a leasurely walking, slow gate, Aldermans pace.*

Table d'Abbé. *a plentifull, or well furnished, table.*

Il iure comme vn Abbé. *he sweares like an Abbot, viz. extreamely.*

Abbé, & Convent ce n'est qu'un, mais la bourse est en divers lieux: Pro. *Though an Abbot, and Couent haue but one bodie, yet haue they seuerall meanes (and minds.)*

Homme ne connoit mieux la malice que l'Abbé qui a esté Moine: Pro. *No man can play the knaue better than an Abbot that hath beene a Monke.*

Abbec: m. *a bait, for fish.*

Abbeché *fed, as a yong bird by the old; also, instructed; or, inueigled, as a nouice.*

Abbechement: m. *a beakefull of; also, a feeding, or putting into the mouth of; also, an instructing; or, inueagling.*

Abbecher. *to feed, as birds doe their young, or faulkeners their hawkes; to put into the mouth of: hence, to instruct a young one, and, to inueagle, allure, intice, a nouice.*

Abbée: f. *a hole, or ouverture, for the passage of some part of a streame thats held in by a damme, sluice, &c.*

Abbeille: f. *a Bee; the little hiue-bee, or honnie-bee; Looke,* Abeille.

Abbesse: f. *an Abbesse.*

Abbois: m. *barkings, bayings.*

Abbois de l'estomac. *the gnawing of the stomach, in extreame hunger.*

Aux derniers abbois. *at his last gaspe, or, breathing his last; also, put to his last shifts, driuen to vse his last helpes: A metaphor from hunting; wherein a Stag is sayd,* Rendre les abbois, *when wearie of running he turnes vpon the hounds, and holds them at, or puts them to, a bay.*

Abbonnement. *as* Abonnement.

Abbordé; Abbordée; & Abborder: *as* Abordé; Abordée; *and* Aborder.

Abbougri: m. ie: f. *growne crooked, or withered in the top, as an ill-thriuing tree.*

Abbougrir. *to hinder from growing, to keepe from rising, to let from thriuing; also, to grow crooked, or wither in the top, like an ill-thriuing tree.*

Abbougry. *as* bbougri.

Abboyé: m. ée: f. *barked at, bayed at.*

Abbras. *the name of a terrible Gyant in the old Romants; whence,*

Ce fier abbras, *this kill-cow, skar-crow, bugbeare, swashbuckler, horrible backster.*

Abbregé: m. *an Abridgment, Abstract, Epitome, Summarie, Compendium, short course, or discourse.*

Abbregé: m. ée: f *shortened, abridged, curtalled, abbreuiated, epitomised; also, briefe, short, compendious.*

Abbregemént: m. *a shortning, abridging, epitomising, abbreuiating; also, an abridgement.*

Abbregément. *shortly, briefly, succinctly, compendiously, by abridgement.*

Abbreger. *to shorten, abridge, abstract, abbreuiat, epitomise, curtall, cut short.*

Abbreuiateur: m. *an abbreuiator; a maker of breefs; or of writs.*

Abbreuiature: f. *a Breuiat; Abbreuiation, Abbreuiature; a short note.*

Abbreuvé: m. ée: f. *watered, steeped, soked, seasoned in, throughly wet, or moistned with, liquor; also shrunk, as cloth, in water.*

Abbreuvé d'une opinion. *whose thoughtes are wholly possest with, or fully persuaded in, an opinion.*

Abbreuver. *to water, as a horse, &c; throughly to wet, or moisten with water; steepe, soke, or season, in liquor: also, to shrinke, as Fullers do their cloth, by water.*

Abbreuver de quelque opinion. *to imbue, possesse wholly, with an opinion; to imprint, or fix it in the mind; to breed in the thoughts an assured persuasion, or full beleefe, thereof.*

Abbreuvoir: m. *a watering place for horses.*

vn abbreuvoir à mousches. *an open wound, or hurt; (whereat flies, if they may quietly, drinke their fill.)*

Abbruti: m. ie: f. *beastly, brutish; or, made beastly, become brutish.*

Abbruver. *as* Abbreuver.

Abderois. *of* Abdera; *the ancient name of a towne in Thrace; & of another, now called Almeria, in Spaine; and of a certaine Island neere vnto Samothrace.*

Rire Abderois: Prov. *A continuall or vncessant laughter; such as the Philosopher Democritus (who was of the first* Abdera*) is sayd to haue vsed.*

Abdiquer. *to abdicate; to refuse, reiect, forsake; resigne, giue ouer; cast off, expell, put out of fauour; also. to abrogate, or disanull; also, to prohibit the vse of.*

Abducteur. *a leader out, or away; a withdrawer, or puller away.*

Abecé: m. *an Abcee, the Crosse-row, an Alphabet, or orderly list, of all the letters.*

Abecedaire: com. *in his Abcee: that but beginnes to learne his Abcee: hence also, childish, young, simple, ignorant.*

Abechement. *as* Abbechement.

Abecher. *as* Abbecher.

Abequeter. *to pecke at.*

Abedissimon *a serpent of the kind of dragons.*

Abeillanne. *the white muscadine grape.*

Abeillaud: m. *a Dorre, or Drone-bee;* ¶ Langued.

Abeille: f. *a Bee; the little hiue, or honnie-bee.*

Les abeilles ne deuiennent point frelons; Prov. *Good, or well-bred, spirits neuer degenerat.*

Abeillon: m. *a neast, or swarme, of Bees.*

Abequer. *as* Abbecher.

Abesté: m. ée: f. *mounted on horsebacke; or, that hath an horse to ride on.*

Abesti: m. ie: f. *made, or become beastly; full of, or besotted with beastly humors.*

Abestin. *perpetually burning.* ¶ Rab.

Abestir. *to make a beast, or beastly; to bring into beastly courses; to besot with beastly humors; to fill with sauage, or bruitish, conditions.*

Abhorrant: m. *an abhorrer, detester, loather; Or, as* Abhorrent; *and hence;*

Ie ne suis trop abhorrant de cette opinion; *I differ not much from, I am not altogither against, this opinion.*

Abhorré: m. ée: f. *detested, abhorred, loathed.*

Abhorrent. *abhorring, detesting, loathing; abhorrent from, vtterly disagreeing in nature, and humor; also, vnusuall, vnaccustomed, out of course.*

Abhorrer. *to abhorre, detest, loath extreamely, haue in abomination; vtterly disagree from, wholly shunne, flie,*

flie, hate the company of.
Abhorrir; *as* Abhorrer.
Abhorrissant; *abhorring, detesting, loathing.*
Abiect: m. ecte: f. *abiect, base, vile, contemptible, outcast, of no value; despised, cast off, or away; lowly deiected, out of courage, out of conceit with himselfe.*
Abiection: f. *abiection, vilenesse, abiect lowlinesse; basenesse of heart, faintnesse in courage, ouermuch humilitie, or vndervaluing of himselfe.*
Abier: m. *a faulcon gentle.*
Abile; & Abiller, *as* Habile; *&* Habiller.
Abisme; & Abismer, *as* Abysme; *&* Abysmer.
Abismé: m. ée: f. *ingulfed.*
Abiuré: *abiured, denied by oath; forsworne.*
Abiurement: m. *an abiuring, forswearing, denying with an oath.*
Abiurer. *to abiure, forsweare; denie with an oath.*
Ablatif: m. *the ablatiue Case.*
Ablation: f. *a taking away, or from.*
Ablayé; terres ablayées de bled; *Corne ground; land whereon Corne growes, or wherin it hath beene sowed.*
Ablays: m. *Corne growing, or insheaues.*
Able: f. *a blay, or bleake, fish.*
Ableret: m. *a kind of small fish-net.*
Ablette: f. *a little blay, or bleake.*
Abloquié. Edefices abloquiez; viz. baillez par le seigneur direct en Emphyteose, & Censiue.
Ablution: f. *a washing away.*
Abois: m. *as* Abbois.
Aboli: m. ie: f. *abolished, rased, defaced, put out, abrogated, extinguished, annihilated, foredone, disanulled.*
Abolir; *to abolish; to rase, deface, blot, or put, out; to abrogate, annihilate, extinguish, foredoe, disanull.*
Abolissement: m. *an abolishment, or abolishing; a rasing, defacing, abrogating, disanulling.*
Abolition: f. *an abolishment, annihilation, abrogation, extinguishment; And in law, The leaue giuen by the king, or iudges, vnto a criminal accuser, to desist from further persecution: In Chancerie, An absolute, or generall, pardon.*
Abolition de creances, & vieilles scedules; *a generall, release,* Quietus est, *or forgiuenesse of olde debts.*
Lettres d'abolition *An absolute pardon granted by the Prince vnto a whole Countrie, Towne, or Village, that hath offended:* ¶ Nicor. *Yet others, more generally, meane by* Abolition, *any absolute or generall pardon.*
Abominable: com. *Abbominable, execrable, detestable.*
Abomination: f. *an Abbomination, a detestation, a horrible, or execrable thing.*
Abominer; *To detest, abhorre, loathe extreamely; to haue in abbomination.*
Abondamment. *abundantly, copiously, fully, plentifully, enough and enough againe.*
Abondance: f. *Store, abundance, plentie, fulnesse, copiousnesse.*
Abondant. *Abundant, plentifull, plentious, copious, very full, exceeding much.*
D'abondant, (Aduerbially) *Ouer and besides, moreouer.*
Abonder. *To abound, or ouerflow with; to be rich in; to be full, or haue store, of.*
Abonnage; *as* Abornement; *Also, an exchange, or alienation of rents, duties, or seruices.*
Abonnassé *Calmed, quieted, appeased, pacified.*
Abonné: m. ée: f. *Compounded for, or with; agreed for before hand; at a certaine rate with; made good with, exchanged for.*
Abonnement: m. *A compounding with, or for, an agreeing for, a being at a certaine rate with, beforehand; a making good of one thing with another; also an exchanging, or aliening of one thing for another.*
Abonner. *To compound with, or for; to agree beforehand, or bee at a certaine rate, with; for a thing; to make good one thing with another; also to alien, or exchange, one thing for another.*
Abonneur. *An alienor, exchanger; Also, as* Acquereur.
Abonni: m. ie: f. *Made good; Also as* Aborné.
Abonnir. *To make good; also to doe good vnto; Also, as* Aborner.
Abord: m. *An arriuall, an approach; a boording, abbording, drawing neere vnto.*
De doux abord. *Gentle, courteous, affable: of open accesse, easie to be spoken with, or come vnto.*
Abordable: com. *Affable, abbordable, approachable, boordable.*
Abordade: f. *as* Abordée.
Abordé. *Approached, abboorded, accoasted, boorded, drawne neere vnto; also arriued, or landed at.*
Abordée: f. *An approach, boording, abboording, accoasting, drawing neere vnto; also, an arriuall, arriuing, or landing at.*
D'abordée. *At first, at first sight; as soone as they touched, incountred, or came, togither.*
Abordement; *as* Abordée.
Aborder. *To approach, accoast, abboord; boord, or lay aboord; come, or draw neere vnto; also, to arriue, or land at.*
Abornage; *as* Abournage.
Aborné: m. ée: f. *Limitted, stinted, bounded, knowing his bounds, or what hee must trust vnto; hence, compounded with, or for; agreed beforehand for; at a certaine rate with, vpon a former agreement.*
Abornément. *A limiting, bounding, stinting; also, a composition, or compounding; a setting of a certaine price on, or a standing at a certaine rate for; a receiuing, or paying for, things, otherwise than in kind.*
Aborner. *To limit, bound, stint; also, to compound with, or for; to set a certaine rent on; to stand at a certaine rate for; to receiue, or deliuer, by former agreement, any thing otherwise than in kind.*
Abortif: m. iue: f. *Abortiue, vntimely, still-borne, bred, borne, or brought forth, before a due time.*
Oeuf abortif. *An addle egge, or, an eg whose shell is not yet hard.*
Abouchement: m. *A parley, or conference.*
Aboucher. *To parley, treate, conferre with by word of mouth; to speake face to face vnto.*
Abouchon; d'ab: *Groueling, layd on his face, or on all foure; also, stooping; hauing, or holding, the face downward.*
Abouquement: m. *A heaping vp, as of new made sault.*
Abouquer. *To heape, or pile vp.*
Abourionner. *To bud, sproute out, put forth.*
Abournage: m. *A composition, a certaine rate, or valuation of, a beforehand agreement for, things.*
Abournement; & Abourner, *as* Abornement; Aborner.
Abouter; *To bring, or draw to an head, or end.*
Abouti: m. ie: f. *Growne ripe, drawn to a head, brought to an end; also, abutted, affronted, confined, come neere*

neere vnto,met at,the end.

Aboutir. *To wax ripe,or draw to a head, as an impostume; also,to end; to approach,or grow, towards an end; to meet at their end; also to touch, affront, abut vpon, confine,or be neere, vnto in the head,foot, front,bottome, top, or end of; also, to approach, or make towards.*

Aboutir en pointe. *To end sharpe, or pointed; to grow smaller,and smaller towards the toppe, head, or end.*

Aboutissans d'une maison. *Th'vtmost ends or parts of a house,at the front and backeside thereof.*

Aboutissans d'une heritage. *The vtmost bounds, or limits of an inheritance,at both ends thereof.*

Aboutissant. *Drawing, or comming,vnto a head, or end; also affronting,abutting,confining vnto at the top or bottome,head or foot, or at either end; also, making,or approching, towards.*

Aboutissement. *A drawing to a head, a growing towards an end: a meeting at their end,a touching, affronting,abutting vpon,a confining, or neerenesse,at either end.*

Aboutissement d'os. *as*,Epiphyse.

Aboutissement de terres. *The vtmost boundes, marches,limits,or ends of lands.*

Abouvier. *To vnyoke Oxen;* ¶Norm.

Abradant. *Paring, shauing,scraping,rasing; wearing away.*

Abregé:m. *An Abridgement,&c;as* Abbregé.

Abregé. *Abridged,abbreuiated,shortened, curtalled.*

Abregement. *as* Abbregement.

Abri.m. *A couert, shrowd,shelter,or shadie place; a lee-shore,shead, seat,or corner, whereto neither wet, nor wind,can come: Hence,a sanctuary,place of suretie,or of safe retreit,in aduersitie.*

Vn port de bon abri pour les nauires. *A safe harbor for shipping, in all weathers.*

Abricot:m. *The Abricot,or Apricocke plum.*

Abricotier. *An Apricocktree.*

Abrier d'Arbeleste:m. *The tree of a Crossebow.*

Abrier. *To couer, shrowd, shelter, shadow.*

Abrogation:f. *An abrogation, abolishment; repealing, disanulling.*

Abrogé:m.ée:f. *Abrogated,abolished, disanulled, repealed.*

Abroger. *To abrogate,abolish,disanull,repeale.*

Abroton:m. *The hearbe Sothernwood.*

Abruption:f. *An abruption; a breaking off, a bursting asunder.*

Abruption d'os. *An entire seperation of some part of a bone from the rest,which thereby suffers a manifest want.*

Abruti:m.ie:f. *Made beastly,growne brutish.*

Abrutir. *To make beastly,or brutish.*

Abruvé:m.ée:f. *Watered,wet throughly; seasoned, steeped,or shrunk in; filled, furnished,or stored with, water,&c.*

Abruver. *as* Abbreuver.

Abruvoir. *as* Abbruvoir, *A watering place for horses.*

Abry:m. *Looke* Abri.

Abscez:m. *An impostume,botch,or swelling ful of mattar; a course of ill humours running out of their veins and naturall places,into the emptie spaces betweene muscles.*

Abscis:m.ise:f. *Cut off,diuided,seperated from.*

Absconse:com. *Hidden,obscure,darke,secret, couert, lurking, concealed.*

Absconsé:m.ée:f. *Hidden, obscured, concealed, kept close.*

Absconsement:m. *A hiding,obscuring,concealing.*

Absconser. *To hide, conceale, obscure,keepe close, or secret.*

Abscynte:m. *Woormewood; Looke* Absynthe.

Abscyntien:m.enne:f. *Belonging to Wormwood, bitter as Wormewood,tasting of Wormwood.*

Absence:f. *Absence.*

Absent. *Absent,missing,wanting,out of the way.*

Absenté:m.ée:f. *Absented; sent,had,or kept,got, flit, or fled,out of the way.*

Absenter. *To absent,to send,keepe, get, or haue out of the way.*

S'absenter. *to flit,be gone,flie his countrie,play least in sight,keepe out of the way. (Vsed most commoqly in the worst sence.)*

Absince. *as* Absinte.

Absinte:m. *Wormwood; Looke*,Absynthe.

Absinthe. *as* Absinte.

Absolte:f. *An absolute pardon,a generall absolution, forgiuenesse,remitment of offences.*

Absolut:m.ute:f. *Absolute. Whence;*

Ieudy absolut. *Maundie-Thursday, Sheere-Thursday.*

Absolution:f. *An absolution; a forgiuenesse or forgiuing; a discharge of, or deliuerie from; an abolition of debts,wrongs,offences.*

Absolutoire:com. *Absoluatorie,pardoning,forgiuing.*

Lettre absolutoire; *A Pardon signed.*

Absorbé:m.ée:f. *Supped,or drunke wholy vp; deuoured, swallowed.*

Absorber. *To sup,or drinke vp all: to deuour,swallow, consume.*

Absoudre. *as* Absouldre.

Absouldre, *To absolue, to forgiue absolutely,pardon wholy; to remit offences vnto, to discharge, deliuer, quit from all danger.*

Absouls; *as* Absous.

Absoulte; *as* Absolte.

Absous:m.oute:f. *Absolued,pardoned, forgiuen,quit, cleerely discharged of, or deliuered from, the danger of iudgement.*

Absoute:f. *as* Absolte; *or, A generall absolution, pardon, forgiuenesse,remitment of offences.*

Abstenir. *To abstaine, forbeare, temper himselfe, refraine,withhold from medling with.*

Soustenir,& abstenir. *To temporise it; to bear with, or apply himselfe vnto the time.*

Abstersif:m.iue:f. *Abstersiue, cleansing, or wiping away.*

Abstinence. *Abstinence,refraining,forbearance.*

Abstinence de guerre. *A truce,or surceasing from warre.*

Abstraction. *An abstraction,a drawing out, or away.*

Abstraict:m. *A seperation,disunition,disunction.*

Abstraindre. *To bind fast, to knit hard, to wrap in bands.*

Abstrus:m.use:f. *Close,hidden, shut vp,darke, secret, wrapped vp in obscuritie,hard to be knowne, or vnderstood.*

Absurde:m. *An absurditie; a grosse, vnlikely, or vnreasonable matter.*

Absurde:com. *Absurd,sottish,grosse,foolish,vnlike,abrupt,without reason,out of order.*

Absurdement. *Absurdly,grosly,vnorderly,abruptly.*

Absurdité:f. *An absurditie,grossenesse,foolishnesse,an abrupt, or sottish part, an vnlikely thing, vnreasonable dealing.*

Absynce; & Absynte; *as* Absynthe.

Absynthe: m. Wormewood.

Absynthe marin. Sea Wormwood, is of three kinds; one called white sea-wormwood; the second, broadleaued sea-wormwood; the third, Mugwoort wormwood, or, Sothernwood wormwood.

Absynthe Pontique. Ponticke Wormwood; whereof there be two kinds, the ordinarie broadleaued, and the small Ponticke Wormewood: Some also call the white sea wormewood Absynthium Ponticum; others confound the Ponticke with the Roman; and it seemes (by them) that, that which heretofore was termed Ponticke, is now turned into Roman.

Absynthe Romain. Romane Wormewood, French Wormwood, small-leaued Wormwood, Garden or Cypres Wormewood; called also Wormewood gentle, by reason of the sweet smell, which, contrarie to all the other kinds, it yeelds.

Absynthe de Sainctongne, ou Santoniq;. The same; or small white Wormewood; (some call the second Ponticke, and others the white sea Wormewood, Absynthium Santonicum, but not so properly.)

Petit absynthe; as Absynthe marin; especially the first, and last, kinds thereof.

Abus: m. An abuse; deceit, imposture, disappointment, fallacie, gullerie; also, a misspending, or disorderly imploiment of.

Abusé: m. ée: f. Abused, misused, wronged: also, misspent, or disorderly bestowed: also, deceiued, mistaken, in an error, beguiled, gulled.

Abusement: m. An abusing, or misusing; a misspending, or disordered bestowing of; also, a deceiuing, disappointing, mockerie, beguiling.

Abusement de l'œil, ou, de veuë. A mistie dimnesse in the eyes, which causeth them to mistake one thing for another, and is the auauntcourror of blindnesse.

Abuser. To abuse, misuse, wrong, misspend, or bestow disorderly; also to deceiue, disappoint, gull, cousine, beguile.

s'Abuser. To mistake, or be in error; to wrong himselfe; also, to loose time.

Abuseur: m. An abuser, a misspender of; also, a deceiuer, imposter, beguiler.

Abuseux: m. euse: f. Full of abuses; deceitfull, guilefull.

Abusif: m. iue: f. Abusiue, deceitfull, guilefull; also, against custom, cleane out of order, or from the vse of.

Abusion: f. An abusing, an error, fallacie, imposture, guile, deceit.

Abusiuement. Abusiuely, most vnorderly, cleane from the right vse, or sence of.

Abutter. To aime, or, to shoot, at.

Abysme: m. An Abysmus; a bottomlesse hole, or pit; an infinit, immense, or vnmeasurable depth; a whirlepoole, or swallowing gulfe.

Abysmé: m. ée: f. Abismed, ingulfed; throwne into, or swallowed, by a whirlepoole, bottomlesse pit, or hole of an vnknowne depth; also beaten, or thrust so flat vnto, or far into, another, that it seemes lost, or appeares no more; also, sunke, vndone, throwne downe, ouerthrowne, become on a suddain of most rich most poore: and hence;

Il a abysmé son ennemy. He hath wholy suppressed, or vtterly ruined, his enemie.

Abysmer. To abisme, or ingulph; to swallow vp in an infinit, and vnmeasurable depth; to cast into a bottomlesse hole, or pit; to throw downe from a great heighth vnto the bottome; also, to beat, or thrust one thing so flat vnto, or far into, another, that it seeme lost, or appeare no more; and (by metaphor) vtterly, and on a sudden, to destroy, ruine, vndoe, ouerthrow.

Abysmeux: m. euse: f. Gulphie, full of whirlepools; also bottomlesse, of an infinit, or vnmeasurable, depth.

Acablé. as Accablé; Also, made fast with, or vnto, a Cable.

Acabler. To fasten with, or vnto, a Cable; also, as Accabler.

Acace: f. A certaine thornie plant, of two kinds; a greater, growing most in Egypt, & a lesse, in Pontus; also, as;

Acacie: f. A medecinall iuice, or liquor, drawn from the seed of the Egyptian thorne Acacia; in steed whereof, (saies Gerard) the German Apothecaries both vse, & call so, the iuice of Sloes.

Academié: m. ée: f. Besotted, puzled, or plundered, with too much skill, or studying.

Acaire. A proper name for a man; and the name of a saint, vnto whome furious, hastie, and harebraind people are sent in Pilgrimage.

Acamusé: m. ée: f. Flatted; made, or beaten, flat; blunt, or flat pointed; like a flat nose.

Acalli: m. ie: f. Hardned, enured, accustomed vnto; that hath got a habit of, &c.

Acanthe: m. The smooth thistle called, Brankvrsin, and Beares-breech.

Acaré: m. ée: f. Affronted, confronted; set before, presented vnto, the face of.

Acarement: m. An affronting, or confronting.

Acarer. To affront, confront, set face to face, or before the face of; bring neere vnto, or, together.

Il luy acara son Arquebuse à l'estomac: He presented his Peece vnto the others stomack.

Acariastre: com. Harebraind, rash, brainlesse, hastie, furious, vnreasonable, inconsiderat; one that is violently swaied by his owne mad will, and franticke humour.

Acariastreté: f. Franticke obstinacie, mad wilfulnesse, harebraind furie, opinionat rashnesse.

Acaser. To inhabit, soiourne, lodge, dwell, or house himselfe, in.

Acazer. To rent, or let out vpon a yearely rent.

Accablé: m. ée: f. Ouerthrowne, ouerwhelmed, beaten, or borne, downe with blowes, &c; Oppressed by much waight, or ouer-heauie burthens; confounded, vtterly ruined.

Accabler. To ouerthrow, beat, or beare, downe with blowes, &c. Oppresse by much waight, or ouerheauie burthens; ouerwhelme, ruine, confound vtterly.

Accagnardement: m. Sloath, idle sensualitie.

Accagnarder. To grow lazie, sloathfull, idle, woorthlesse.

Accaration: f. as Acarement.

Accariastreté. as Acariastreté.

Accasané. Louing home, euer within doores, a housedoue, mued vp, neuer stirring abroad.

Accasement. as Accoisement.

Accelerateur. A speeder, hastner, dispatcher.

Muscle accelerateur. A certaine muskle whereby the vrine and seed are ierted out.

Acceleration. Hast, or speedmaking; an acceleration.

Acceleré: m. ée: f. Accelerated, hastened; dispatched.

Accelerer. To accelerat, hasten, speed, make hast, dispatch.

Accence: m. as Acence.

Accensement. Il tient cela par ac: He holds that by lease, or at a certaine yearely rent; or is to pay an yearly Cens for it; Looke Acensement.

Accensissement: m. A holding by lease, or in farme, or

or the paying of an yearely rent, or Cens *for any thing held.*

Accent: m. *An Accent; also, the raising, or letting fall, of the voice in pronunciation.*

Accent aigu. *A sharpe accent, marked thus, ́, & much vsed.*

Accent circonflex, ou contourné. *The bowed accent is marked thus ^, or thus ~, and is not much vsed in French.*

Accent graue. *is marked thus, ̀, & set ouer the words* à, où, là, &c.

Accentué: m. ée: f. *Accented; noted, or pronounced, with an accent.*

Accentuer. *To marke, note, or pronounce, with an accent.*

Acceptable: com. *Acceptable, gracious, pleasing, fit, or worthy, to be entertained.*

Acceptation: f. *An acceptation, intertainment, receipt, allowance of.*

Accepté: m. ée: f. *Accepted: receiued, or intertained in good part.*

Accepter. *To accept, intertaine, receaue in good part; admit, approue, allow of.*

Acceptilation: f. *A paiment; or, an imaginary discharge of a debt, made from a Creditor vnto a Debtor in this forme;* Tiens tu pas pour eu, & receu ce que ie t'ay promis? *(saies the Debtor; wherto the other answers)* Ouy, Ie le tiens.

Acception: f. *An acception, accepting, receauing, taking; an admission, or intertainment of; also, a respect, or distinction of persons, in Iudgement.*

Accessible: com. *Accessible, familiar, courteous, gentle, of easie accesse.*

Accessif: m. iue: f. *Accessible, accessiue, easie to come vnto.*

Accession. *An accession, or addition; also, an accesse or comming vnto.*

Accessoire: com. *A circumstance; an accession, increase, augmentation, ouerplus, vantage ouer and besides the due or principall; also, a danger, great mischiefe, or trouble; also, an error, or disorder.*

Accessoire: com. *Accidentall, or accessarie; happening, or comming in, or making one by chance.*

Accessoirement. *Accessarily, accidentally.*

Accez: m. *An accesse, an entrie, or passage vnto, a comming vnto a place, or matter.*

Accez de fiebvre. *A fit of an ague.*

Accident. *An accident, a circumstance; also, a misfortune, mishap, calamitie, mischance; also, any accident, or casualtie.*

Accidental: m. ale: f. *Accidentall, Casuall.*

Accidentalement. *Accidentally, casually, by fortune, by meere chance.*

Accidentellement. *as* Accidentalement.

Acclampé. *Fastened, pinned, pegged;* ¶Norm.

Acclamper. *To fasten, to pin, or peg;* ¶Norm.

Accodepot. *A Triuet; the prop, or supporter, of a seething pot.*

Accoeuiller. *To benum, or besot, with sencelesnesse.*

Accoinct, *or* Accoint; *Acquainted, or familiar with; also, neat, compt, fine, spruce in apparell, or otherwise.*

Accointable: com. *Acquaintable, easie to be acquainted, or familiar, with.*

Accointance: f. *Acquaintance, conuersation, or commerce, with.*

Accointement. *as* Accointance; *(An old word.)*

Accointer. *To make iollie, peart, quaint, comely, gallant, gay; to pranke, decke, tricke vp: also, to seeke, or affect, the acquaintance of; In which sence it is most vsed passiuely, or with the passiue article; as;*

S'accointer de. *To wax acquainted, grow familiar, with; or, to get, or desire, the acquaintance of.*

Accoisé: m. ée: f. *Quieted, calmed, pacified, appeased, quallified, assuaged, allaied, eased.*

Accoisement. *A quieting, pacifieng, appeasing, qualifying, easing, assuaging, abatement of paine or passion.*

Accoiser. *To quiet, pacifie, appease, calme, assuage, ease, mittigat, quallifie, abate, allay.*

Accolite: m. *A nouice, or yoong proficient, also the boy that ministers to the priest at masse-time.*

Accollade: f. *A colling, clipping, imbracing about the necke; Hence, the dubbing of a knight, or the ceremonie vsed therein.*

Accollé. *Colled, clipped, imbraced about the necke; in blazon, collared.*

Accollée: f. *as* Accollade.

Accoller. *To embrace, coll, or clip about the necke.*

Accolleer. *To make meet, or fit for the necke; Also, to strike in the necke, as men kill conies.*

Accommodable. *Fittable, aptable, appliable.*

Accommodation. *A fitting, apting, applying, accommodating, furnishing.*

Accommodé. *Fitted, apted, applied; furnished, accommodated; also, helped, assisted; also coursed, or cudgelled.*

Accommoder. *To accommodat, fit, apt, applie, frame vnto, or for; to furnish; also, to assist, helpe, succour; also, to course, beat, cudgell, vse a knaue in his kind.*

Accommoder vne femme. *To vse a woman.*

s'accommoder au temps. *To serue the time; to follow the swinge, course, or fashion, of the present world; to doe as others doe.*

Accompagnable: com. *Companable, sociable, easie to bee conuersed with.*

Accompagné. m. ée: f. *Accompanied, associated, consorted, kept with; hauing the company, or fellowship, of.* Mieux vaut estre seul que mal accompagné. Pro. *It is better to be alone than with idle, or ill sorted, companie.*

Accompagnement. *A companying, or accompanying; a fellowship, societie, association.*

Accompagner. *To accompanie, associat, consort, keepe, or hold, fellowship with; also, to follow (in courtesie.)*

Accomparageant. *Comparing, matching with, resembling vnto.*

Accomparager. *To compare, match, equall, confer one thing with another.*

Accomparer. *as* Accomparager.

Accompli: m. ie: f. *Accomplished, atchieued, finished, performed, fulfilled; also, furnished, supplied, indued, with.*

Cent ans accomplis. *Full a hundred yeares.*

Accomplir. *To accomplish, finish, fulfill, performe, atchieue; supplie or furnish what lacketh.*

Accomplissement. *A fulfilling, accomplishment, atchieuement, full performance of; also, a supplie, or furnishing.*

Accomplisseur. *a fulfiller, atchieuer, performer, accomplisher, finisher, supplier, full furnisher.*

Acconditionné: m. ée: f. *Giuen, or granted, vpon condition.*

Acconditionner. *To giue, or graunt, vpon condition.*

Acconduire. *To lead, or bring to; to conduct, or guide vnto.*

Acconsuyvre. *To ouertake, or attaine vnto; to reach, in iourneying, or going.*

Ie ne scauroy acconsuyvre par paroles le grand plaisir. *I cannot expresse or comprehend, in any words,* the

the great,&c.

Accopper. *as* Achoper.

Accoquiné. *Made tame, inward, familiar; also, growne as lazie, sloathfull, idle, as a beggar.*

Accoquiner. *To make tame, inward, familiar; to reclaim a wild thing.*

s'Accoquiner. *To wax as lazie, become as idle, grow as sloathfull, as a beggar.*

Accord: m. *Accord, agreement, concordance, consent; also, a contract, composition, bargaine agreed on; also, the deed whereby that contract, &c, is made, or passed; also an accord, or concord in musicke.*

Accordable. *Compoundable, accordable, agreeable; fit, or easie, to be agreed.*

Accordailles: f. *The betrothing, or making sure of a man and woman together.*

Accordance: f. *An accord, or agreement; a concord, or concordance in musicke.*

Accordant. *Agreeable, accordant, concordant; well fitting vnto: compounding, or consenting, with.*

Accordé. vn ac: *A man betrothed to a woman.*

Accordé. *Accorded, agreed, concurred with; consented, graunted, yeelded vnto; chaffered, bargained, compounded for; attoned, compounded, reconciled together.*

Figure accordée. *Looke* Figure.

Accordée. Vne accordée. *A woman that's handfast with, or betroathed vnto, a man.*

Accordement: m. *An according, concurring, or agreeing with; a yeelding, or graunting vnto; also, a bargaining, or compounding for; also, a reconciliation, or composition of differences; an agreeing vpon.*

Accorder. *To accord, concur, consent, agree, with; to yeeld, or graunt vnto; also, to attone, compound, reconcile differences, or parties in difference; also, to bargain, chaffer, compound for; also, to agree vpon.*

Accorder vne fille. *To handfast, affiance, betroath himselfe vnto a maiden.*

Deux chiens ne s'accordent point à vn os: Prov. *We say, Two cats and a mouse, two wiues in one house, two dogs and a bone, neuer agree in one.*

Accorné: m. ée: f. *Horned, hauing, or wearing horns: (In Blazon) attired.*

Accort: m. te: f. *Discreet, headie, warie, aduised, circumspect, foreseeing, aware; of a good spirit, quicke wit, notable reach, that hath an excellent forecast; also, wilie, subtill, cunning.*

Accortement. *Warily, discreetly, heedfully, circumspectly, aduisedly; wittily, subtilly, cunningly.*

Accortesse: f. *Circumspection, warinesse, heedfulnesse, discretion, aduisednesse, a great reach, or forecast, subtiltie of spirit, quicknesse of wit.*

Accortise: f. *as* Accortesse.

Accostable: com. *Accoastable; fit, or easie, to be accoasted.*

Accosté: m. ée: f. *Accoasted, approached, or drawne neere vnto; growne familiar with; also, affronted, braued, vrged.*

Accoster. *To accoast, or ioine side to side; to approach, or draw neere vnto; also, to wax acquainted, or grow familiar, with; also, to affront, vrge, braue (to his face.)*

Accoté: m. ée: f. *Vnderset, vnderpropped; whose sides are held vp; supported, sustained, staied from shaking, or slipping; also, reared, or leaned, against.*

Accotement: m. *An vndersetting, vnderpropping; supporting, sustaining, staying vp; also, a prop, shore, supporter.*

Accotepot: m. *A prop, or stay, for a (seething) pot; properly, a thicke peece of yron, (made somewhat like a halfe moone) wherewith the one side of a pot is supported.*

Accoter. *To vnderset, vnderprop, or hold vp the sides of; to sustain, support, shore, buttresse, beare vp; to stay from shaking, or slipping.*

s'Accoter contre. *To reare himselfe, or leane, against.*

Accouché: m. ée: f. *Laid downe, got into bed.*

Accouchée. *A woman that lies in childbed.*

Accouchement: m. *A lying downe in bed; also, a womans being brought to bed; or her being in childbed.*

Accoucher. *To lie downe in, to get himselfe, to bed; also to be brought to bed, as a woman of a child.*

Accoudement: m. *A leaning on the elbow.*

s'Accouder. *To leane, rest, or stay, on his elbow.*

Accoudoir: m. *A forme, bench, rayle, &c, whereon one leanes with his elbow; a rest, a stay, a leaning stocke.*

Vne chaire à accoudoirs. *A chaire with elbowes.*

Accoulpé: m. ée: f. *Blamed for, charged with, accused of, a crime.*

Accouplable: com. *Yoakeable, coupleable, fit to be coupled with.*

Accouplage: m. *A coupling, or coniunction; a yoaking, or vniting together, or vnto.*

Accouplé. *Coupled, yoaked, ioyned together, or vnto.*

Accouplement. *as* Accouplage.

Accoupler. *To ioyne, vnite, couple, yoake together, or vnto.*

Accouragé: m. ée: f. *Incouraged, hartened, imboldened; that hath mettle put into him.*

Accourager. *To hearten, incourage, imbolden.*

Accourber; & Accourbir. *To bow, crooke, or bend inwards, or towards.*

Accourci: m. ie: f. *Shortened, abridged, curtalled, contracted, clipped, or cut short.*

Accourcir. *To shorten, abridge, curtall, clip, or cut short.*

Accourcissement. *An abridging, shortening, curtalling, contracting; a clipping, or cutting short.*

Accourement: m. *A concourse, comming, or running of many men together to one place; an assemblie, or hastie gathering of people from many places vnto one.*

Accourir. *To run, hast, or hie together in flocks, or troups, vnto a place.*

Accours. *as* Accourement; *Also, a chase.*

Accousiné. *Taken as, acknowledged for, a kinsman.*

Accousiner. *To make, acknowledge, or take, for his cousin.*

Accoustement: m. *A hearkening, or listening too; a drawing neere with his eares, or vnto the eare of.*

Accouster. *To hearken, listen, giue eare to, draw neere vnto the eare of, or, with his eares.*

Accousteur: m. *A hearkener; one that listens, or giues eare, vnto another.*

Accoustré: m. ée: f. *Dressed, attired, arraied, apparelled, trimd, decked.*

Accoustré à la Tigresque. *Cruelly handled, horribly bethwacked, or bescratched.*

Il m'a mal accoustré. *He hath vsed me very hardly, he hath dealt most badly with me; or, he hath brought me to much misfortune, a poore estate, an ill passe.*

Accoustrement: m. *A dressing, attiring, appavelling, decking, trimming; also, a garment, raiment, habilimẽt, suit of apparell, suit of cloathes.*

Accoustrer. *To cloath, dresse, apparell, attire, array; deck, trimme.*

O comme il accoustre les gens. *Oh how vilely he disgraces, how badly he reports of, how filthily hee handles, how skuruily he deales with, all men.*

Il s'accoustre bien. *He stuffes himselfe soundly, hee lines his iacket throughly with liquor; The like is;*

Il

Il s'accouſtre pour aller au guet. *He takes his liquor kindly, freely, fully; (from the cuſtome of thoſe that are to watch.)*

Le Roy s'accouſtra de telle cruauté, & furie. *The king put on ſuch crueltie, entered into that furie.*

Accouſtumance: f. *Cuſtome, vſage, woont; alſo, an accuſtoming.*

Accouſtumé: m. ée: f. *Accuſtomed, vſed, woonted, enured vnto; alſo vſuall, or much vſed: and hence;*

Choſe accouſtumée n'eſt pas trop priſée: Pro. *We ſeldome prize whats ordinarie.*

Accouſtumer. *To accuſtome, vſe; enure vnto, practiſe in.*

Accoutré; Accoutrement; & Accoutrer: *as* Accouſtré; Accouſtrement; *&* Accouſtrer.

Accoutumance; Accoutumé; & Accoutumer: *as* Accouſtumance; Accouſtumé; & Accouſtumer.

Accouvé: m. ée: f. *Brooded; ſet cloſe on, crowded ouer; alſo, couered, hidden, ouerſhadowed.*

Accouver. *as* Accouveter.

Accouveter. *To brood, ſit cloſe, or crowding, as a henne ouer her egges, or Chickens; (and hence) alſo, to ouerſhadow, couer, hide.*

Accravanté. *as* Accrevanté.

Accravanter. *as* Accrevanter.

Accrazer. *To breake, burſt, craze; bruize, cruſh.*

Accreſté: m. ée: f. *Creſted, copped; hauing a great creaſt, or combe, as a Cocke; alſo, cockit, proud, ſaucie, ſtately, luſtie, creaſt-riſen.*

Accreſter. *To wax cockit, grow proud, become ſaucie, liuely, ſtately, to ſtrout it, or ſtand vpon high tearms.*

Accreu: m. uë: f. *Growne, increaſed, enlarged, augmented, amplified; alſo, multiplied.*

Accrevanté. *Violently burſt, furiouſly broken.*

Accrevanter. *To burſt, or breake violently.*

Accrevanter les villes. *To raſe, ouerthrow, deſtroy, whole townes.*

Accruë: f. *A growth, increaſe, eeking, augmentation.*

Accrever. *To burſt, or thruſt out the guts of.*

Accroché: m. ée: f. *Hooked; claſped, grapled, faſtened vnto; alſo, graſped; alſo, ſtayed, or delaied, as a ſuit; whence;*

Le procés eſt accroché. *Hangs by the wall.*

Accrochement. m. *A hooking, claſping, grapling; a faſtening to, or hanging on, a hooke; a graſping, reaching, or catching at, a drawing to, by a hooke; alſo, a ſtaying, delaying, or foreſlowing, of a Suit.*

Accrocher vn procés. *To ſtay a ſuit from further proceeding; to delay, or leaue off, for a time, the proſecution of it.*

Accroire. *To entruſt, to commit vnto the keeping of in truſt; alſo, to lend (as monie) vpon truſt.*

S'en faire accroire. *To thinke well, or be well conceited, of himſelfe; to take too much, or very much, vpon him; hence, to preſume on, or make himſelfe ſure of, a matter; to ouer-rule it, diſpoſe of it, preuaile in it, make it go on his ſide, or be for his purpoſe; to commaund abſolutely, or (as we ſay) to rule the roaſt; alſo, to ſpread far in reputation; increaſe mightily in credit; get or grow into great authoritie, by a thing.*

Accroiſſance: f. *Increaſe, augmentation, growth, eeking.*

Accroiſſement: m. *An increaſing, augmenting, amplifying; a making or growing, bigger and bigger; alſo, a multiplying.*

Accroiſt. *as* Accroiſſance.

Accroiſtre. *To increaſe, augment, amplifie, enlarge, make bigger and bigger; alſo, to multiplie, or wax many.*

Tel cuide vanger ſa honte qui l'accroiſt: Pro. *Some, thinking to redeeme their ſhame, redouble it.*

Accroitre. *as* Accroiſtre.

s'Accroſter. *To graſpe, claſpe, grapple, or buckle together.*

Accroüé: m. ée: f. *Drooping, as a bird that ſits with hir feathers looſe, or ſtaring, about hir.*

Accroupi: m. ie: f. *Crouched, cooped, ſtooped, or ſet ſtooping; bent, or bowed forward; ſquat vpon the taile.*

s'Accroupir. *To ſtoope, crouch, coope, bend, leane, or bow, forward; ſit, bending forward, vpon the taile, or knees.*

Accruës: f. *as* Accreuës.

Accubes: f. *Couches, lodgings; reſting places; Cabins to lie, or to reſt, in.*

Accueilli: m. ie: f. *Intertained, receiued; welcommed; alſo, arriued, or gathered together in a place; alſo, taken, ouertaken; or ſtricken, as with thunder.*

Accueillir. *To entertaine, receiue, or welcome (kindly;) alſo, to reach, ouertake; or ſtrike; alſo, to come, gather, flocke together, or (as wormes, &c,) breed, in a place.*

Accueillir ſa voye vers. *To trauell, journey, wend, or go, towards.*

Accueuré. *Sicke, or ill, at the heart.*

Accul: m. *A ſtop, or ſtay; any action, or thing, that plunges, or hinders from proceeding; a ſetting, or ſitting on the taile; alſo, the bottome, end, or furtheſt part of a foxes, or badgers earth, where ſitting on his taile, he defends himſelfe againſt the Terriers.*

Acculé: m. ée: f. *Ouerthrowne, or ſet on his taile; brought vnto a ſtrait, or into tearms of vnauoidable danger; alſo, ſtopped, or ſtayed, from further proceeding.*

Acculé en ſon opinion. *Setled, or obſtinat, in his opinion; not to be moued, not to be drawne, from it.*

Ils l'ont acculé de toutes parts. *They haue beſet him round, they lay hard vnto him on all ſides; (from the wild Bore, who brought vnto a bay ſets him on his Gammons, and turning thereon, is forced to defende himſelfe againſt both dogs, and men, on euery ſide aſſailing him.)*

Acculer. *To throw downe, or ſet on his taile; alſo, to beſet round, lay hard vnto, bring into a ſtrait, or vnto tearms of vnauoidable danger; (in arguing) to put to his plunges, or driue vnto a nonplus; alſo, to ſtop, or ſtay from further proceeding.*

Acculer vn ſoulier. *To tread, or weare, a ſhoe downe at the heeles.*

Accullé; *as* Acculé.

Accumulateur: m. *An accumulator; a heaper, or piler; a hoorder, or gatherer; a ſauing, or thriuing, fellow.*

Accumulation: f. *An accumulation, or accumulating; a heaping, or piling vp; a hoording, or gathering into heapes.*

Accumulé: m. ée: f. *Accumulated; heaped, or piled vp; hoorded, or gathered into heapes.*

Accumuler. *To accumulat, heape, or pile vp; to hoord, or gather into heapes; to increaſe mightily; to lay on load.*

Accuſant: m. *An accuſant, or accuſer.*

Accuſant. (partic.) *Accuſant, accuſing.*

Accuſateur: m. *An accuſer, plaintife, informer, faultfinder.*

Accuſatif: m. *The Accuſatiue Caſe.*

Accuſation: f. *An accuſation; a complaint made, an information brought, againſt; an imputation caſt on.*

Accuſatrice: f. *An accuſatrix, or accuſereſſe.*

Accuſé: m. ée: f. *Accuſed, appeached, complained of, informed againſt, charged with a crime; alſo, diſcloſed, or bewraied.*

Accuſement: m. *An accuſing, a complaining of, or informing againſt; a finding fault withall; alſo, a diſcloſing, or bewraying.*

Ac-

Accuser. *To accuse, or appeach; to complaine of, informe against, charge with a crime; cast an aspersion, lay an imputation, on; also, to bewray, disclose, or discouer, a secret.*

Tel s'excuse qui s'accuse: Pro. *Looke* Excuser.

Accuvé: m. ée: f. *Put into a fat; let stand, or let worke, in a fat.*

Accuver. *To put into a fat; to let stand, or let worke, in a fat.*

Acence; *or,* Acense: m. *A farme, or lease.*

Acensé: m. ée: f. *Leased, or let out to farme.*

Acensement. m. *A farming; a letting, or taking, to farme.*

Acenser. *To let, or take, to farme.*

Acenseur: m. *A farmer; a letter out, or taker, to farme.*

Acensivé: m. ée: f. *Let out for (an yearely)* Cens.

Acensivement: m. *A letting out for* Cens; *the creating of a* Censiue, *or of a Tenure by* Cens.

Acensiver. *To giue, or let out, for (an yearely)* Cens; *To create a* Censiue, *or a Tenure by* Cens.

Acerbité: f. *Acerbitie, sharpenesse, sourenesse.*

Aceré: m. ée: f. *Steeled; forged or made of, tempered, or strengthened with, Steele.*

Acerer. *To steele; to forge or make of, temper or strengthen with, Steele.*

Acertement. *as* Acertenement.

Acertené. *Certefied, assertained, assured.*

Acertenement. *A certifying, ascertaining.*

Acertener. *To certifie; ascertaine, assure, affirme boldly, informe confidently.*

Acertes. (Adverb.) *Of a certaine, in very deed; in good earnest; also, hartily, affectionatly, without faigning.*

Acetabule. *as* Cotyledon; *Also, an ancient measure containing about six spoonfuls of liquid things; & two ounces and a halfe of drie; or (according to our waight) an ounce, 3 quarters, 2 Carats, 12 grains and a halfe.*

Aceteuse: f. *The hearbe Sorrell.*

Aceteux: m. euse: f. *Sharpe, sourish; of the substance, or hauing the tast, of Vinegre.*

Acetosité. *Sharpenesse, sourenesse; the substance, or tast, of vinegar.*

Ach. *An Interiection of sorrow, as, Oh; and of sorrowfull exclamation, as, Ah; vsed also in Imprecations, as, Ha.*

Achalandé: m. ée: f. *Customed; frequented by chapmen, or customers.*

Achalander. *To allure chapmen, get customers, draw custome.*

Achancri: m. ie: f. *Cankered; made, or growne, cankred.*

Achantique. Mastic achantique: *A sweet tasting Masticke, or Gum, bred on the top of the Calthrop, or Star-thistle.*

Achapt: m. *as* Achet; *A purchase, &c.*

Achapt passe louage. *Seeke* Louage.

Achapter; & Achapteur; *as* Acheter; *and* Acheteur.

Acharné: m. ée: f. *Fleshed with, or vpon; also, fed, or baited with, affected vnto, flesh; also felly minded, cruelly bent against, prosecuting extreamly, bloudily persecuting, pursuing vnto death without remorce, or mercie.*

Acharnement; m. *A fleshing; a feeding, or baiting with flesh; a laying of flesh vpon; also, an entering in, or prouocation vnto, crueltie.*

Acharner. *To flesh on; to lay flesh vpon; to feed, or bait, with flesh; to enter, or traine vp, in blood; also, to prouoke, or egge vnto all cruell and bloodie courses against.*

Acharner vn Leurre. *To tie flesh vnto a Lure.*

S'acharner sur. *To be felly minded, or cruelly bent against; to prosecute extreamly, pursue most hatefully, persecute without remorce, or mercie.*

Achasser. *To driue, or chase, towards.*

Achat. m: *as* Achet.

Achate. *The pretious stone Achates; (makes the wearer gracious, and keepes him from idlenesse.)*

Ache: m. *The letter H; also, the hearbe Smallage.*

Ache femelle. *Female Smallage.*

Ache des Iardins. *Parseley.*

Ache large. *Great Parseley, Alexanders.*

Ache de marais. *Marsh, or marish, Parseley, water-Parsley, Smallage.*

Ache de risée. *Is either the Crowfoot of Illiria, or, the Crowfoot of the fallow field.*

Ache rustique. *Smallage, marsh, or marish, parseley.*

Ache de Sardaigne. *The same.*

Ache sauvage. *Wild parseley.*

Grand ache. *The hearbe Alexanders.*

Achées: m. *Grubs, ground-worms.*

Achelois: m. ise: f. *Of, or belonging to the famous Grecian riuer Achelous; also, waterie; and hence;*

Bruvage Achelois. *Water; or waterie drinke.*

Achemé: m. ée: f. *Decked, attired, adorned, dressed, with.*

Achemer. *as* Achemmer.

Achemeresse. *as* Achemmeresse.

Achemes: m. *as* Achées; *Also, attires, deckings, ornaments for women.*

Acheminé: m. ée: f. *Put, or set, in the way; addressed vnto, directed in, a course; begun, entered into.*

Acheminement: m. *A setting, or directing, in the way; an entring; a shewing of the way vnto; also, an addresse, introduction, entrie, ingression; way, passage, means, vnto a thing.*

Acheminer. *To addresse vnto, put into, set, or direct in, the way; to enter; to shew the way vnto; also, to commence, begin, set forward; breake the ice, giue an entrie, make an ouerture, vnto.*

Il persuadoit, & acheminoit tant qu'il pouvoit, à. *He persuaded, and laboured all he could, to.*

S'acheminer. *To wend, go, take his way, beginne his iourney, set forward.*

Achemmer. *To decke trim, adorne; dresse, array, attire.*

Achemmeresse: f. *A woman that makes profession of dressing, or decking of Brides; hence also, any waiting-woman, or chambermaid, that hath that office about hir Ladie, or mistresse.*

Achenal: m. *A channell.*

Achepter. *as* Acheter.

Acher. *To set the teeth on edge.*

Acheramin: m. *A kind of Smallage, or Crowfoot resembling Smallage.*

Acheron. *The name of one of the riuers faigned to be in Hell.*

Acheronté: m. ée: f. *Plunged in Acheron, drowned in Hell; also, hellish, or bred in Hell; and (thence) most cruell, fell, hideous.*

Acherontide. Ames Acherontides. *Damned soules.*

Achesmes. *as* Achemes; *Tires, or ornaments, for women.*

Achet: m. *A bargaine, or purchase; a thing bought, or purchased; also, buying, or purchasing.*

Acheté: m. ée: f. *Bought, purchased; gotten, or procured, for money.*

Acheter. *To buy, to purchase; to get, or procure, by bargaining, or for money.*

Acheter chat en poche. *To bargaine vnaduisedly; to buy a pig in the poke; to buy one knowes not, or sees not, what.*

Achete maison faitte. Pro. *Buy a house readie made; (for many haue vndone themselues by building;) The like is;*

Il faut acheter maison faitte,& femme à faire:Pro. *Buy a house made,and a wife vnmand.*

A trop acheter n'y a que revendre: Pro. *Wares ouerbought are sildome returned without losse; nor doe many things (on the getting whereof we haue bestowed much time or toile) gotten, quit the cost wee were at about them.*

Il faut acheter vigne deserte; Pro.*Buy ground that lies vntilled.*

Qui bon l'achete bon le boit;Pro.*He that wil pay, or take pains,for good things,enioies good things.*

Trop achete le miel que sur espines le leche; Pro. *He that lickes honnie of thornes paies too deere for it.*

Acheteresse: f.*A woman that buies,or purchases.*

Acheteur: m.*A buier,a purchaser.*

Achetiver; *as* Chetiver. *Also,to inthrall,or captiuat.*

Achevé: m.ée:f.*Atchieued,ended,effected,finished,concluded,consummated,compassed,accomplished.*

Son honneur est achevé de perdre; *His honour is wholy,his reputation fully,lost.*

Achevement: m. *An atchieuement,or atchieuing; a perfecting,or bringing to perfection; a full ending,effecting,or finishing; a consummating, or accomplishment.*

Achever.*To atchieue; to end, finish, conclude (fully;) to dispatch, effect, performe (throughly;) to perfect, consummat,accomplish,go through-stitch, with.*

Cela servira pour l'achever de peindre; *There wants but that to fill vp the measure of his ill fortune; that being once done,he is vndone.*

Achilles: m. *(The well-knowne name of a most valiant Greeke; vsed sometimes,by the French,to signifie) a defender,protector, supporter, propugnator, warrant, assurance; buckler,fortification.*

Achoise: f.*An occasion,an oportunitie.*

Achoison: f.*The same; also,election, or choise; also,an accusation.*

à petite achoison le Loup prend le Mouton; Pro. *The Woolfe takes any small occasion to seize on the Sheepe.*

Achoisonner.*To accuse,to picke a quarrell against.*

Achommer. *To rest, or make Holyday; also, to stay, or attend.*

Achon.*A kind of long Axe.* ¶ Bourbonnois.

Achopé: m.ée: f. *Stumbled at,or on.*

Achopement.*A stumbling; offence giuen,or taken.*

Achoper.*To stumble at,or on.*

Acide: com.*Sower,eager,tart,sharpe.*

Acidité.*Eagrenesse,sharpenesse, sourenesse,tartnesse.*

Acier: m.*Steele.*

Acierer.*Seeke* Acerer.

Aclamper; *as* Acclamper.

Acné.*A witlesse,and gracelesse,fellow.*

Acoint; Acointer; *Seeke* Accoint.

Acollé; *as* Accollé.

Acolyte, *as* Accolite. *Hee that ministers to the Priest whyle he sacrifices or sayes Masse.*

Aconduire; *Seeke* Acconduire.

Aconit: m.Aconitum,*a most venemous hearbe; of two principall kindes,*viz.*Libbards-bane,and Wolfe-bane.*

Aconsuyvre; *as* Acconsuyvre.

Acope: m.*A medecine compounded of heating, & mollifying Simples.*

Acoquiner; *as* Accoquiner.

Acore: m.Calamus aromaticus,*the sweet Cane.*

Acorné: m.ée: f.*Horned; hauing hornes.*

Vache acornée; *(in Blazon) Armed.*

Acort; *as* Accort.

Acoster.*Looke* Accoster.

Acoter.*Seeke* Accoter.

Acoucher.*as* Accoucher.

Acouhardir. *To accowardize, effeminate, make faint-hearted.*

Acoup.*Quickly, shortly, speedily, suddainly, in a trice, in a minute, in a moment.*

A-coup-venant.*The name of a faire ruddie Apple.*

Acouter.*as* Accouter; *or as* Escouter.

Acquerement: m.*A purchasing,obtaining,getting,procuring; or,as* Acquest.

Acquereur: m.*A purchaser,getter,gainer; one that increases his substance by buying; also, a challenger, or claimer of,one that pretends a title vnto,land.*

Acquerir. *To acquire; to get, obtaine, procure a thing sought for; to purchase,or gaine by purchasing; also,to claime,challenge,or pretend title vnto,land.*

Acquest:m.*A purchace,a thing procured,got,or bought; also,a getting,procuring,purchasing; also,profit, gain, commoditie,gettings,increase of substance.*

Acquests.*Purchases made,or things bought, by the vnmaried; or by,or for,only one. (Therein different from* Conquests.)

Nouveaux acquests.*Purchases of inheritances feodal, allodial, or censuel, &c, made by Churchmen, Corporations,Fraternities,&c, after they haue procured letters of Mortmaine (for other things;) whereof the King informing himselfe by Commission or otherwise,they are summoned to void out of the lands, &c, so purchased, within a yeare; by the end whereof if they haue not paid the fine, whatsoeuer, imposed on them by his Officers, the lands are immediatly, and without recouerie,seized into his hands.*

Droict de nouvel acquest. *A Priuiledge of fining, at certaine times, the ignoble Tenant that possesses, or purchases,a noble Tenement,or inheritance; Looke* Droict.

Il n'y a point d'acquest en luy. *He is but a drie fellow,there is nought to be got by dealing with him.*

En grand fardeau n'est pas l'acquest; Prov. *The greatest burthens are not the gainfullest; or, The goodnesse of a thing rests not in the greatnesse of it.*

Acquesté: m.ée: f.*Purchased,acquired; gotten,gained; procured,obtained.*

Acquester.*To purchase,get,gaine,acquire, procure, obtaine.*

Acquesteresse: f.*A woman that purchaseth.*

Acquesteur: m.*A purchaser,getter,gainer; a thriuing fellow; one that encreaseth his substance by buying.*

Acquests.*Looke* Acquest.

Acquiescement: m.*Quietnesse; also,an agreement; a yeelding,or comming to agreement before iudgment; also,an approuing of,or a submitting himselfe vnto, a iudgement passed against him.*

Lettres d'acquiescement. *A letter of Atturney, whereby a Client giues his Counsellor,Atturney,or Solicitor,authoritie to agree with his Aduersarie.*

Acquiescer.*To yeeld,or agree vnto; come to an agreement,be at quiet,striue,or stir,no more.*

Acquiescer a la sentence dont est appel. *To approue, or submit himselfe vnto,a sentence, though against him; to pursue no further appeale.*

Acquis: m.ise: f. *Got, purchased, obtained,acquired, bought with money.*

Acquisiteur: m.*A purchaser.*

Acquisition.*An acquisition,a purchasing,a purchase.*

Acquit: m.*A discharge,acquittance,*Quietus est,*a deliuerie,dispatch,riddance,from a trouble,or charge.*

Droict d'acquit. *Looke* Droict.

Par forme d'acquit seulement. *Sleightly, carelesly, onely for a fashion; more of necessitie, or for feare, then from the heart, or in any good will.*

Acquité: m. ée: f. *Acquitted, discharged, freed, cleered, rid of, deliuered from; also, performed, acted, effected, dispatched.*

Acquiter. *To quit, acquite, free, cleere, discharge, rid of, deliuer from.*

Acquiter marchandise. *To custome, or pay custome for, merchandise.*

Acquiter vne terre. *To quit, or quiet a peece of land; to rid it from suits, trouble, and controuersie, by recouering, or deliuering, it from such as vsurped it; to cleere the title thereof.*

S'acquiter de son deuoir. *To doe his dutie, to play an honest mans part.*

S'acquiter de sa promesse, ou serment. *To performe his promise, to fulfill his oath.*

Qui s'acquite s'enrichit: Prov. *He that gets out of debt growes rich; or, Hee that keepes touch enriches himselfe.*

Acquoiser; *as* Accoiser. *To pacifie.*

Acravanter. *Looke* Accravanter.

Acre. *An aker of land;* ¶Norm. *(It is most commonly larger than the Arpent.)*

Acre. Azur d'acre. *Looke* Asur.

Acre: com. *Eager, sharpe, tart, sower, vnripe; also, earnest, vehement.*

Acredité: m. ée: f. *put, or got, into credit.*

Acrediter. *to put, or get, into credit.*

Acresté. *Crested, copped; also, cocket, lustie, proud, stately, highminded, crest-risen.*

Acreu; *as* Accreu.

Acrimonie. *Eagernesse, sharpenesse, tartnesse, sowernes.*

Acroamatie: f. *Melodie harmonie; a pleasing discourse; a plausible action.*

Acroamatique. *Musicall, harmonious, delightsome, pleasing, plausible; to the eare.*

Acroc: m. *A hooke, a claspe, a stay; any thing to hang another thing on.*

Acromion. *The shoulder pitch, or point, wherewith the hinder, and fore, parts of the necke are ioyned together.*

Acrotaires; *as* Acroteres.

Acroteres: m. *Promontories, hilles, or Elbowes of high ground, lying out into the sea, and seene afar off at sea; also, the extreame parts of the bodie; also, Pillasters, or Pedistalles for Statues in the forefront of Buildings.*

Acroupi: m. ie: f. *Whose hinder parts are drawne vp, or gathered together.*

s'Acroupir. *A Horse to knit, or draw vp, or gather togither, his hinder parts; and withall, to beare himselfe vpon them.*

Acroupissure: f. *A Horses strong knitting, drawing vp, or gathering, together of his hinder parts; any such action, motion, or posture of his.*

Acte: m. *An act, fact, exploit, or deed; also, an Act; an authenticall writing, or Instrument, entered, or set downe as a Record, or President, in Court; a Testimoniall, or (short) order of Court; also, an Act, or Pause in a Comedie, or Tragedie; also, a quantitie, or measure, of ground, containing 120 feet.*

Les derniers exploicts, & actes de possession. *Are (in an Assise of* Nouel disseisin*) the Plaintifs averment, and proofe, that he had quiet possession a whole yeare before the Disseisin.*

Actif: m. iue: f. *Actiue, quicke, stirring, busie, diligent, laborious, euer doing, neuer idle.*

Debtes actiues. *Debts that be owing, or due, vnto vs.*

Vasselage actif. *The right of fealtie, due by euery Vassall vnto his Lord.*

Actifs. *An Order of Friers, that weare tawnie Habits, and feed on naught but roots.*

Action: f. *An action, deed, exploit, enterprise; also, an action in Law; a plea, or right to plead.*

Action de graces. *Thankesgiuing.*

Actionné. *Indited, impleaded, sued; also, acted, effected.*

Actionner. *To sue, indict, implead; also, to worke, acte, effect.*

Activité. *Actiuitie, quicknesse, nimblenesse; readinesse.*

Actourné: m. *An Atturnie;* ¶Norm.

Actournée: f. *A Warrant, or letter of Atturnie;* ¶Norm.

Actuel. *Readie, speedie, present, dispatching, effectuall.*

Cautere actuel. *An actuall Cauter. See* Cautere.

Actuellement. *Presently, quickly, speedily, out of hand, without delay, or attendance for.*

Acuité: f. *Acuitie, sharpenesse, keenenesse; piercing, subtiltie.*

Acuré. Oiseau acuré; *That hath had casting giuen hir.*

Acutelle. *The hearb Camocks, Rest-harrow, Pettie whin, Ground furres.*

Adage: m. *An adage, prouerbe, ould-sayd-saw; wittie saying.*

Adagial: m. ale: f. *Prouerbiall, or full of adages.*

Adam. *Adam (the first man that euer was;) also, the Adam peare (whereof excellent Perrie is made.)*

Baston d'Adam. *The weapon wherewith Adam vsed to fight with Eue.*

Morceau d'Adam. *The head of the windpipe, or throat, composed of three little gristles, or peeces of flesh.*

Pomme d'Adam. *Adams apple; a certaine yellow fruit that resembles a small Cowcumber; also, the Assyrian apple, or Assyrian Citron, (round, and twice as big, as a big Orange.)*

Adanté. *Lying on his face, groucling; leaning on his teeth: Looke* Adenté.

Adaptation. *An adapting, fitting, or suiting of one thing to another.*

Adarce: f. *A salt foame that cleaues vnto reeds, & other marsh hearbs, in drougth, and drie weather.*

Adayé. *Prouoked, vrged, incensed, egged, moued vnto wrath:* ¶Pic.

Adayement. *An vrging, incensing, prouoking, egging, mouing vnto wrath:* ¶Pic.

Adayer. *To prouoke, incense, vrge, egge, stir vp, moue vnto wrath:* ¶Pic.

Adayeur: m. *A prouoker, a quarreller, a contentious person:* ¶Pic.

Adcense: f. *A Lease, or estate in farme.*

Adcensement. *A leasing, or letting out to farme.*

Adcensivement. *A fee farme.*

Addenté. *Looke* Adenté.

Additament: m. *An addition, increase, eeking, augmentation, aduantage.*

Additaments mammillaires. *The part of the braine that lies toward the forehead, and next vnto the nose, as whence our smelling is deriued; also the two processes of the Temple-bones.*

Addition. *An addition, appendix, increase, eeking, augmentation, aduantage, accesse of more.*

Addition beccue. *The bone of the elbow (so tearmed by some Anatomists.)*

Additions mammillaires; *as* Addittaments mammillaires.

Addomestiqué: m. ée: f. *tamed, reclaimed, made gentle, inward,*

inward, familiar, housall, acquainted with vs.

Addomestiquer. *To tame, reclaime, make gentle, inward, familiar, housall; to acquaint with vs; to entertaine, or bring into our house.*

Addonné: m. ée: f. *Giuen, bent, affected, addicted, inclined, applied, deuoted vnto.*

s'Addonner à. *To giue, bend, addict, affect, apply, deuote, incline, render, yeeld himselfe vnto.*

Le lieu s'addonne ainsi; *such is the nature, or qualitie of the place; for such purposes only it serues, or is fit.*

Selon que les choses s'addonnent. *As our affaires succeed, as those matters come to passe; or, as those affaires, those matters permit, or come to purpose.*

Addorsé. *Indorced; or, set backe to backe; a tearme of Blason.*

Addossé. *as* Adossé.

Addouber. *To dresse, patch, mend; to set fitly together; also, to arme at all points, or with all his peeces, for the fight.*

Addoubeur: m. *A dresser; patcher, mender.*

Addoubeur de mauuaises causes. *A crafty Lawyer; one that prolongs ill causes by shifts, cauils, and delayes.*

Addouci: m. ie: f. *Sweetned; assuaged, mitigated, qualified, appeased, pacified; softened; smoothed.*

Addoucir. *To sweeten; smooth; assuage, temper, qualifie; appease, pacifie, mitigate; soften, mollifie.*

Addoucissement: m. *A sweetning; smoothing; softning; assuaging, tempering, qualifying; appeasing, pacifying.*

Addouez homme à homme. *Fastened, clasped, grapled; or, coaped, bustled, scuffled, together.*

Addoulci; Addoulcir, &c, *as* Addouci, Addoucir, &c.

s'Addressant. *Directing, addressing; fashioning himself vnto; medling with.*

Addresse. *as* Adresse.

Addresser. *Seeke* Adresser.

Adduire. *To bring forth; or, to bring vnto.*

Adebtz. *A kind of Seigniorall dutie, within the iurisdiction of S.* Omers.

Adelantade: m. *A Lord Deputie, President, or Lieutenant for a Prince in a countrey; (we commonly take it for, an Admirall.)*

Adeneré. *Prized, valued, set to sale for money; or for which money is made.*

Adenerer. *To prize, value, rate; to make money of, to set to sale for money.*

Adenes. *Little kernels in the mouth, or throat, and diseasing either of them.*

Adenet. *(The diminutiue of* Adam) *little* Adam.

Adent: m. *A mortaise, notch, or indented hole in wood.*

Adenté: m. ée: f. *Mortaised; fastened, or ioyned by Mortaise.*

Adenté tout plat à bas. *Fallen down flat on his face; layed groueling, lying on his teeth.*

Adenter. *To mortaise, to fasten or ioyne by Mortaise; to enchace one thing within another.*

Adenter vne eschelle à vn mur. *To fasten; or settle a ladder vnto a wall, by the yron hookes which are at the top of it.*

Ades. *Presently, out of hand, by and by, incontinently, immediatly.*

Adeser. *To touch, or handle slightly.* ¶Picard.

Adestre: com. *Quicke, readie, nimble, actiue, agile; also, comely, gracefull, handsome in; able, fit, apt, for any thing he vndertakes.*

Adestrer. *To make fit, able, apt for; quicke, readie, nimble in; to instruct, teach, traine, or frame vnto; also, to fit, adapt, accommodate; also, to accompanie, or follow the humor of.*

Adevancer. *To preuent, fore-stall, ouer-run; to goe, or get before one.*

Adeuillé. *as* Adeullé.

Adeullé: m. ée: f. *Heauie, dolefull, sad, wofull, mournefull; in mournefull weeds, in mourning array.*

s'Adeuloir. *To be sad, heauie, dolefull; to mone, to mourne.*

Adex. *as* Adeptz.

Adextre. *as* Adestre.

Adextrer. *as* Adestrer.

Adfiliation. *An adopting, an adoption.*

Adfilié. *Adopted.*

Adfirmation. *as* Affirmation.

Adglutinatif: m. iue: f. *Glewie; clammie, cleauing, or sticking vnto euery thing; also, glewing.*

Adglutinement. *A glewing; a ioyning, closing, or fastening vnto, or together, as with glew.*

Adglutiner. *To glew; to ioyne, close, or fasten vnto, or together, with glew.*

Adgression. *Looke*, Aggression.

Adherant: m. *An adherent, an accessarie, partener, or partaker.*

Adherant: m. ante: f. *Adhering, cleauing, or sticking fast vnto; also, partaking, siding, taking part with.*

Adherdre. *Seeke*, Aherdre.

Adherer. *To adhere; cleaue, or sticke fast vnto; also, to side, or take part with.*

Adheritance. *A possession; a Liuerie and seisin.*

Adherité. *Inseisined, put into possession of.*

Adheritement: m. *A giuing possession, a making of Liuerie and seisin vnto.*

Adheriter. *To aduest, to put into possession, to giue possession vnto, to make Liuerie and seisin of an inheritance.*

Adhesion: f. *An adhering, cleauing, sticking fast vnto.*

Adhorer. *To come at a good houre, or in due season.*

Adjancé: m. ée: f. *Fitted, apted, adapted, adiusted; ordered; trimmed, decked; featly placed, handsomely ioyned, suteably matched together.*

Adjancement: m. *A fitting, apting, adapting, adiusting, accommodating; a comely trimming, dressing, or decking; a iust placing, handsome ioyning, suteable matching of things together; also, handsomenesse, aptnesse, agreeablenesse.*

Adjancer. *To fit, apt, adapt, adiust; accommodate; proportion, order, decke, trim; set fitly, ranke featly, ioyne finely, match duly, put handsomely together.*

Adiante: m. *Venus haire, maidens haire, our Ladies haire (an hearbe.)*

Adjection: f. *An adiection; an addition, or casting, vnto.*

Adience. *as* Adiante.

Adjoinct: m. *An Adiunct; an Assistant, Associate, fellow, companion in a charge, commission, function, or office; also, a ioynt heire; and a iointenant; also, one that ioynes with another in a suit, or action.*

Adjoinct: m. cte: f. *Adioyned; knit, coupled, set, added, (also) neere, vnto; neere hand touching.*

Adjoindre. *To adioyne; set, adde, put, applie, or knit vnto; to couple, vnite, associate, match together.*

Adjoint. *as* Adjoinct.

Adjonction: f. *An adiunction, addition, or ioyning vnto; also, a partaking with an accuser, or plaintife; also, an association in office, or charge.*

Adjour: m. *A Commission of Summons, or Adiurnement; also, the report, or the returne thereof, made by the Sergeant, or Summoner.*

Adjourné: m. ée: f. *Adiurned, cited, summoned, warned to appeare at a certaine day.*

Adjournement: m. *A citing, summoning, warning to appeare at a day; also, the Summons, or Processe, whereby a partie is so warned; also, a growing towards day.*

Adiournement Libellé. *Seeke* Libellé.

Adiournement personnel. *A personall arrest, or seisure of the bodie.*

Adjourner. *To cite, summon, warne to appeare; to serue a proces of apparance on; also, to make day, or turne into day; or, as;*

s'Adjourner. *To wax day, or grow towards day.*

Adjourneur: m. *A citer, or summoner; one that warns, or serues a processe on, another to appeare.*

Adjousté: m. ée: f. *Added, put, or set vnto; also, encreased, augmented, inlarged.*

Adjoustement: m. *An adding, putting, or setting vnto; also, an increasing, augmenting, eeking.*

Adjouster. *To adde, adioyne, set, or put vnto; also, to increase, augment, eeke; also, as* Adjuster; *and hence;*

Adjouster vn horologe. *To wind vp a clocke.*

Adipeux: m. euse: f. *Fattie, full of fat; also, breeding fatnesse.*

Veines adipeuses. *Looke,* Veine.

Adire: m. *A difference.*

Adiré: m. ée: f. *Wanting, wandered, missing, astray, out of the way; also, left, abandoned, bid farwell vnto.*

Adirer. *To wander, goe astray, be missing, or out of the way; also, to leaue, abandon, forsake, bid farewell vnto.*

Adisme: m. ée: f. *Tythed, on which a tythe is set, for which tythe is payed.*

Adismer. *To tythe; to set a tythe on, exact a tythe from.*

Adjudicataire: m. *He to whom a thing is adiudged, or deliuered by iudgement.*

Adjudication: f. *An adiudication; an adiudging, or giuing, or deliuerie vnto, by iudgement.*

Adjugé: m. ée: f. *Adiudged; giuen, or appointed, vnto, by iudgement.*

Adjuger. *To adiudge; to giue, passe, or appoint, vnto, by iudgement.*

Adjurateur: m. *An adiuror, or earnest swearer; also, one that exacts an oath.*

Adjuration: f. *An adiuration, or coniuration; an earnest swearing vnto; also, th'exaction of an oath from others.*

Adjuré: m. ée: f. *Adiured; coniured; sworne; or deposed vnto; from whom an oath is exacted.*

Adjurer. *To adiure; or coniure; to sweare earnestly vnto; also, to exact an oath of, to put vnto his oath.*

Adjusté: m. ée: f. *Adiusted; iustly placed, euenly couched, fitly or aptly set, orderly disposed.*

Adjustement: m. *An adiusting, iust placing, apt setting, euen couching, fit ioyning, handsome ordering, orderly disposing of seuerall things.*

Adjuster. *To adiust, place iustly, set aptly, couch euenly, ioyne handsomely, match fitly, dispose orderly, seuerall things together.*

Adjutoire. *The vpper bone of the arme toward the shoulder; so called by some Anotamists.*

Admener. *To lead, or bring vnto.*

Admeneur. *Looke,* Ameneur.

Admettre. *To admit, receiue, intertaine, bring or let in; permit, suffer; approoue, allow of.*

Admignoter. *as* Amignoter.

Adminicule: m. *An aid, helpe; support, prop.*

Administrateur. *An administrator, gouernour, manager of affaires for another.*

Administration: f. *An administration; gouernment, or charge; a guiding, or disposing of busines for another.*

Administratoire: com. *Administratorie; administring, or ministring vnto.*

Administrer. *To minister, or administer; to guide, rule, gouerne, manage, handle, dispose of, a charge, or businesse.*

Admirable: com. *Wonderfull, admirable, maruellous, miraculous, aboue custome, or expectation.*

Admirablement. *Admirably; wonderfully, beyond expectation, or wont, maruellously, miraculously; excellently well.*

Admiral: m. *An Admirall; a Princes Lieutenant on the sea.*

Admirale: f. *An Admiralesse (The late Admirall* Chastillons *wife is called so in a Historie of some accompt among the French.)*

Admiratif: m. *Th'admiratiue point, or point of admiration (and of detestation) marked, or made, thus !*

Admiration. *Admiration, wonder, maruelling.*

Admirauté: f. *An Admiraltie; the office of an Admirall; also, th'Admirall Court.*

Admiré: m. ée: f. *Admired; wondered at.*

Admirer. *To wonder, admire, maruell at.*

Admis: m. ise: f. *Admitted, intertained, receiued, brought or let in; suffered, permitted; approoued, allowed of.*

Admissible. *Admittable; admissible; fit to be admitted, receiued; allowed of.*

Admodiateur. *A Lessor; he that letteth out land to halues, by great, or for part of the crop, increase, or profit thereof; also, (and more properly) a Lessee, or Farmer, one that takes lands on those conditions.*

Admodiation. *A leassing, letting out to the halues, or for part of the crop, increase, or profit.*

Admodier. *To leasse, farme, or let out land by great, vnto halues, or for part of the crop, increase, or profit thereof.*

Admonesté: m. ée: f. *Admonished, warned, aduised, aduertised.*

Admonestement. *A warning, admonishment, aduertisement, aduisement; a shewing, a putting in mind of.*

Admonester. *To admonish, warne, aduertise; exhort, aduise; to shew, to put in mind of.*

Admonesteur. *An admonisher, warner, aduiser, exhorter, aduertiser.*

Admonition. *An admonition, exhortation; as* Admonestement.

Admorti. *Looke,* Amorti.

Admortir. *To dead, stint, quaile, abolish, extinguish, make cease; make disappeare; to mortaise, or ioyne by mortaise.*

Admortir la foy, &c; vne rente; *Looke* Amortir.

s'Admortir. *A weake, aged, or sickly person, or (by the custome of* Chalons*) a villain, to giue himselfe, & all his goods vnto another, on condition that he shall maintaine him, and discharge his debts.*

Admortissable. *as* Amortissable.

Admortissement. *A mortaising; a disappearing, or loosing it selfe within another; as in the parts of pillars that are ioyned to other pieces; or in pillars made so, as many seeme to be ioyned in one; also, Mortmaine; and, a licence to hold in Mortmaine.*

Admortissement de foy, & homage. *An exchanging of them for other seruices; an extinguishment of them.*

Admortissement d'heritage. *A passing, or giuing of land in Mortmaine.*

Admortissement real. *A certain priuiledge, whereby the bishop of* Theroanne *hath all kinds of iurisdiction vnder the king.*

Admortissement de rente. *A redeeming, or buying out, an extinguishment, of rent.*
Adnection. *A knitting, fastening, ioyning, annexing to.*
Adnuicter. *Seeke* Annuicter.
Adobber. *as* Addouber.
Adolescence: f. *Youth, or young age.*
Adolescent: m. *A youth, or young man.*
s'Adolorer. *To grieue, sorrow, take griefe, be aggrieued, pensiue, or full of heauinesse.*
Adombré: m. ée: f. *Shadowed, ouercast, couered.*
Adombrement: m. *A shadowing, ouercasting, couering; and among Painters, a shadowing, or bare pourtraying of a thing.*
Adombrer. *To adumbrate, shadow, ouercast; cast a mist, or fog ouer; to pourtray, or draw a resemblance grossely, as Painters do in their first lines.*
Adomestiqué: m. ée: f. *Tamed, reclaimed, made gentle, inward, familiar, housall, acquainted with; also, intertained, brought into, made as one of the house.*
Adomestiquer. *To tame, reclaime, make gentle, inward, familiar, housall; to acquaint with; to intertain, bring into, vse as one of the house.*
Adonc. *Then, or at that time.*
Adonin. face Adonine. *a faire sweet face, such a one as* Adonis *had.*
Adoniser. *To Adonize it; to resemble* Adonis; *to imitate, or counterfeit the graces, or beautie of* Adonis.
Adopté. *Adopted; appointed, or chosen to be another mans child.*
Adopter. *To adopt; to take, or chuse for his child one that in nature is not so.*
Adoptif: m. iue: f. *Adoptiue; fit to be adopted; chosen by adoption.*
Adoption. *Adoption.*
Adorable: com. *Adorable; worthie, or fit to be adored.*
Adorateur. *A worshipper; an adorer; one that prayeth to, or beareth himselfe towards, another with all reuerence.*
Adoration: f. *Adoration, worship, reuerence in the highest degree; a giuing of all honour vnto.*
Adorer. *To adore, worship; reuerence, or honour in the highest degree.*
Adossé: m. ée: f. *Leaning, or set against; also, set backe to backe; also, backed; strengthened on the backe part.*
Adossement. *A backing; a leaning against with the backe; a setting backe to backe; a strengthening backeward.*
Adosser. *To backe, to set backe to backe; to strengthen on the backe-side.*
s'adosser contre. *To set his backe against; to leane against with his backe.*
Adot: m. *A blow, bumpe, or thumpe; also, much adoe, trouble, or businesse; also, a kind of fish.*
Il luy donna des adots; *he gaue her the gentle thump.*
Adoüber. *Seeke* Addouber.
Adoulcir. *as* Addoucir.
Adoulcissement. *Seeke* Addoulcissement.
s'Adouloir; &, s'Adoulourer; *as,* s'Adolorer.
Adpropriance. *Looke,* Appropriance.
Adquiescement; &, Adquiescer; *Seeke* Acquiescement; *&* Acquiescer.
Adressant. *Adressing, directing; leading, instructing, shewing the neerest way vnto.*
Adressé: m. *The meeting of crosse-wayes.*
Adresse: f. *An adresse, a direction; a compendious, and short course; a neere, direct, and readie way; also, a seamarke.*
Ie sçay les adresses de la maison. *I know all the priuat corners in, or priuie wayes vnto, the house.*
Ie seray là mis pour venir aux adresses. viz. pour me trouver au besoing.
Les vignes ont eu adresse. *The vines haue flourished, or taken kindly.*
Adresé: m. ée: f. *Adressed, directed; instructed; set in the neerest, and readiest way.*
Adresement. *An adressing, directing; instructing, or setting in the neerest, and readiest course.*
Adreser. *To adresse, direct; lead; instruct; set in, shew the neerest, or the readiest way vnto.*
s'Adreser à. *To resort vnto, make towards; meddle with, haue a fling at.*
Adroict. *as,* Adroit; *or, as* Adestre.
Adroit: m. ite: f. *Handsome, nimble, wheeme, readie, or quicke about; apt or fit for, any thing; also, fauourable, propitious, prosperous.*
Adscrire. *To ascribe, attribute, impute, referre; also, to inroll, register, accompt, reckon among others.*
Adscrit. *Ascribed, attributed; inrolled, reckoned among.*
Adsigné. *as* Assigné.
Advaluation: f. *A valuing, rating, or setting of a price on.*
Advalué: m. ée: f. *Valued, rated.*
Advaluer. *To value, rate, set a price on.*
Advance. *Looke,* Avance.
Advancé. *Forwarded, aduanced, hastened; payed before hand.*
Advancement. *Looke,* Avancement.
Advancer. *Seeke* Avancer.
Advantage. *Seeke* Avantage.
Advantagement. *A furthering, forwarding, profiting, aduantaging.*
Adueillé: m. ée: f. *Heauie, sad, mournefull, pensiue, aggrieued, full of sorrow.*
Adveillé. *Watchfull; wakefull; awaked.*
Advenamment. *Comely, handsomely, gracefully, decently, properly, sightly.*
Advenant. l'ad. *The lawfull and contingent portion of inheritance, and patrimonie wherein a daughter may succeed her intestate father; also, a sufficient part of an inheritance, reserued by a vassal, or tenant, of purpose to preserue from homage-doing him that hath purchased the rest.*
Advenant bien faict. *A portion of inheritance giuen by an elder vnto his younger brother, in recompence of th'vnpartable dignitie which himselfe retaines.*
Le plus que l'advenant. *A fourth part of the daughters part, before mentioned, which a father and mother (being noble) may, before the mariage of their eldest sonne, bestow in frank-mariage with their eldest, or first maried, daughter.*
Advenant. *Handsome, proper, comely, decent, neat, gracefull, well-fashioned, well-behaued; conuenient, well-beseeming, fitly-fitting, sight-fitting.*
à l'advenant. *Both, to boot, moreouer, besides, ouer and besides; also, proportionably, or, according vnto.*
Logis advenant. *A conuenient house which the heire of a gentleman, according to the means left him, is to allow vnto the widow.*
Advenement: m. *A chance, or hap; an arriuing, or comming to.*
Advenir. *To happen, chance, betide, come to passe, fal out, befall.*
Cela n'y pourra advenir. *That cannot fit, nor furnish it, cannot attaine vnto it; that must faile, or come short of it.*
Ia n'advienne que. *God forbid that.*

s'advenir. *To be fit, suitable, handsome; to become, to sit featly, to beseeme.*
Adventif: m. iue: f. biens adventifs. *Goods comming, or giuen, by chaunce; had of another, or of a stranger; not got by his owne industrie, nor from his own parents; casualties, vnlikely and vnlooked for windfals.*
Advents de Noël. *The time of Aduent; before Christmas.*
Adventure: f. *An aduenture, chaunce, hap, lucke, fortune, hazard.*
à l'adventure cela n'est point. *I doubt me whether; tis a question whether yea or no; or, perhaps that is not.*
d'adventure. *Casually, by meere chaunce, haply, as hap was, as it happened, by hap hazard.*
En adventure gisent grands coups: Pro.
Qui sçauroit les adventures il ne seroit iamais pauvre: Pro. *Could men foresee mishaps, th'would not be poore; wee say, He that did know what would be deare, might grow full rich within a yeare.*
s'Adventurer. *To aduenture, ieopard, hazard, expose himselfe vnto danger; to trie his fortune.*
Qui ne s'adventure n'a cheual ny mule: Pro. *Nothing venture nothing haue, say we.*
Qui trop s'adventure perd cheual & mule: Prov. *But he that ventures too farre, looses all: (Now the question will be, in these two prouerbes, Whether is better for a man, to loose nothing though he get nothing, and to keepe his skin whole; or, to loose that which he hath gotten, and only haue left him a skin full of holes.)*
Adventureusement. *Hazardously, aduenturously.*
Adventureux. *Hazardous, aduenturous; that feares no colours.*
Adventurier. *An aduenturer; one that freely and without compulsion, or charge goes to the warres; also, a free-booter, or boot-haler.*
Vn Adventurier vagabond. *An idle loitering rogue; a hedge-creeper, henne-killer, sheet-stealer.*
Adventurier: m. ere: f. *as* Adventureux.
Advenu: m. uë: f. *Chaunced, happened, betided, come to passe.*
Vne fille bien advenuë. *Well prooued, well growne, well come on, well prospered; well hatned, or batled.*
Advenuë. *An accesse, passage, or entry vnto a place; also, a hap, chaunce, euent, accident.*
Adveré. *Auerred, verified; Looke* Averé.
Adversaire. *An aduersarie; opponent, enemie; the aduerse, or contrarie partie.*
Adversité: f. *Aduersitie; afflictions, crosses, mishaps, misfortunes.*
Adverti: m. ie: f. *Aduertised, informed, certified, warned, admonished, aduised; signified vnto; hauing notice, or intelligence, of.*
Advertir. *To informe, certifie, aduertise; warne, admonish, aduise; to send word of; to signifie, giue notice, or intelligence, vnto.*
Advertissement: m. *An aduertisement, signification, information, intelligence, notice; a warning, aduise, monition, admonishment; (In Law,* C'est vn motif de faict ou de droict, que la partie baille par escript sur vn incident, ou debat survenu en la cause, ou apres les escritures principales, premieres & secondes additions, ou quand le different est petit. ¶Ragueau.)
Advertissemens. *The Bill, Answere, and rest of the Pleadings, or Bookes put into the Court both by plaintiffe and defendant, thereby fully to informe the Iudges of the state of the cause, and of the points and reasons alledged on both sides.* ¶Nicot.
Advertisseur. *An aduertiser, informer, intelligencer, certifier; warner, admonisher, aduiser.*
Advest: m. *An aduesture, inuesture; a Liuerie and seisin.*
Advestir. *To aduest, inuest, cloth with; giue possession of; make Liuerie and seisin vnto.*
Advesture: f. *An aduesture, an inuesture; a cloathing, or possessing with; a deliuering ouer, a making of Liuerie and seisin vnto; also, fruit hanging by the root, or standing on the ground; whence;*
Advesture de bled. *Corne standing; or sprung, and put vp to a good height, thereby cloathing the ground all ouer.*
Adveu: m. *An aduowing, or auouching; an approuing; an acknowledging as, or taking for, his owne; a warranting; pawning of the word, passing of credit vpon; also, a contract, bargaine, agreement; also, a Suruey; or (more properly) a protestation, or confession made by a tenant (in words, or in writing) that he holds the things, mentioned in his suruey, of the lord vnto whom he deliuers it.*
Adveu du pere; ou du mari. *Signifies (in some passages of the French Lawes) the good-will, or consent of the father; or husband.*
Adveu du vassal; *as before in* Adveu; *or, a profession, confession, or acknowledgement, of tenure.*
Blasme d'adveu. *Looke,* Blasme.
Gens sans adveu. *Vagabonds, rogues, masterles men; such as none will owne, or challenge interest in.*
Matiere d'adveu. *A suit, action, or bill of complaint for moueables.*
Au sceu, & adveu de tout le monde. *Before the face, in the sight, or presence, of all men.*
Faictes cela à mon adveu. *Doe that on my word, I will be your warrant for it; also, follow my humour in that, or, doe as I would haue you in it.*
Adveu emporte l'homme. *When a prisoner alledges that he is the vassall, or vnder the iurisdiction, of a lord, and desires to be tried before him, he is commonly sent vnto him, if the Lord will; or may, by his priuiledges, take notice of the case.*
Advis: m. *Aduise, opinion; counsell; sentence; iudgement; also, an information, intelligence, notice, aduertisement, or inckling giuen of.*
Assene & advis: *Looke,* Assene.
Il m'est advis; ou; il me semble aduis, que. *Me thinkes; it seemes vnto me; I am of opinion, or of mind, that.*
Advisagé: m. ée: f. *Beheld earnestly in the face.*
Advisager. *To looke in the face; to behold earnestly, wistly to eye, the visage of.*
Advisé: m. ée: f. *Aduised; warie, discreet, considerat, heedfull, circumspect; also, told, informed, warned, admonished.*
Mal advisé n'est pas sans peine: Pro. *He thats vncircumspect wanteth no trouble.*
Advisemént: m. *Aduisement, heed, warinesse, discretion, consideration, circumspection; also, an aduising, warning, telling, informing; admonishing.*
Advisément. *Aduisedly, heedily, warily, discreetly, considerately, circumspectly.*
Adviser. *To aduise, marke, heed, consider of, looke to, attend vnto, regard with circumspection; to thinke, imagine, iudge; also, to aduise, counsell, warne, tell, informe. Looke,* Aviser.
Adulateur: m. *A flatterer, cogger, smoother, soother, fawner, claw-backe.*
Adulation. *Adulation, flatterie, fawning, soothing, cogging, smoothing, blandishment.*

Adulatoire : com. *Adulatorie, belonging to flatterie, full of cogging.*
Adulte: com. *Growne to full age*; adultus, *past breeching.*
Adultere : m. *An adulterer*; *also, adulterie.*
Adulterer. *To commit adulterie, to play the adulterer, to adulterize it*; *also, to adulterate, viciate, corrupt.*
Advocassé : m. ée : f. *Pleaded for.*
Advocasseau : m. *A Petti-fogger*; *a simple, or poore-spirited Aduocat, or Councellor at Law.*
Advocasser. *To play the Aduocate, to plead, or argue, for.*
Advocasserie : f. *A pleading, or playing of the Aduocate.*
Advocat : m. *An Aduocate, or Counsellor at Law.*
Disner d'advocat. *A large dinner (eaten, not bestowed.)*
Tousiours ouvert, comme la gibbeciere d'un advocat. *Sayed of any thing that is alwaies open, and apt to receiue.*
A l'advocat le pied en main : Prov. ascauoir, de perdris, faisans, chappons &c; *to grease his fist withall.*
Bon advocat mauvais Voisin : Pro. *a good Lawyer an euill neighbour.*
De ieune advocat heritage perdu : Pro. *The young (or vnexperienced) Lawyer hazards what he pleads for.*
Longuement proceder est à l'advocat vendenger: Pro. *Long suits are Lawyers haruests.*
Advocatie: f. *An Aduocateship*; *the dutie, or place, of an Aduocate*; *also, the countenance, assistance, or support of a great person in a suit.*
Advoerie : f. *as* Advoeson.
Advoeson : f. *Gard, protection, defence, charge, ouersight of*; *an answering, or vndertaking for, another.*
Advoison : f. *The same.*
Advolé : m. ée : f. *Fled vnto*; *run quickly towards.*
Advolée : f. *A flight, or flying vnto*; *also, a place to light on after flying.*
Advolement : m. *A flying vnto*; *a swift, or quick running towards.*
Advoler. *To flie vnto, run speedily to, come apace towards.*
Advouäison: f. *An aduowing, auouching*; *a taking into protection*; *an answering, or vndertaking for*; *an ouersight, or charge of.*
Advouäteur : m. *An aduower, auoucher*; *answerer, vndertaker for*; *also, one that acknowledges, and challenges his beast, taken dammage-fesant.*
Advoué: m. *An adopted child*; *also, a Patron, Guardian, Protector*; *a defender of, or chiefe dealer for, a Church, Prouince, Towne, &c*; *also, an Atturney, or one that in Court vndertakes, or answeres, for a Clergie man, widow, priuiledged citizen, &c*; *also, one that answeres, as champion, a publicke challenge for another.*
Advoué : m. ée: f. *Aduowed, auouched*; *approoued, allowed of*; *warranted, authorized, taken into protection*; *answered, or vndertaken for.*
Advouër. *To aduow, auouch*; *approoue, allow of*; *warrant, authorize*; *defend, protect*; *vndertake, answer for*; *owne*; *acknowledge, confesse to be, take as, or for, his owne.*
Advouër l'espave. *To own, & claime, a waife, or stray.*
Advouër vne rente en son fief: *To acknowledge, and yeeld a rent out of his inheritance.*
Ie vous advoue en cela. *I approoue your carriage, or proceeding in that*; *or, I will beare you out in it.*
Advouerie : f. *Adoption*; *also, the defence, patronage, protection of*; *vndertaking, or answering for*; *ouersight, or charge ouer, another.*
Advourie. *The same.*
Advoyer. *A principall Ouerseer, Aduocate, Agent, Patron, or Protector of*; *vndertaker for, &c*; *as* Advoué.
Aduré : m. ée : f. *Hardened, stiffened, enured vnto.*
Adurer. *To harden, stiffen, make strong, enure vnto.*
Aduste : com. *Adust*; *parched, burned, rosted, or tosted (in the Sunne.)*
Adustible : com. *Adustible*; *burneable, wasteable, parcheable.*
Adustion: f. *An adustion, burning, parching, rosting, or tosting (in the Sunne, &c.)*
Aeditue : m. *A Church-warden, or Sexton*; *the Officer who is to looke vnto a Church, and the Church goods.*
Aele. *A wing*; *Seeke* Aile.
s'Aeler. *To be winged*; *or to get wings.*
Aemorrhoïde. *A kind of serpent, by which he thats bitten, bleeds to death*; *also, the Hemrods, or Piles in the fundament.*
Aeré: m. ée: f. *Ayrie, of ayre*; *also, aired.*
Aereux: m. euse: f. *Ayrie, full of ayre.*
Aerien : m. enne: f. *Ayrie, of ayre*; *also, of, or belonging vnto, Brasse.*
Aerin. *as* Airain.
Aerolle: f. *A blister, or wheale.*
Aeromantie. *Diuination by the ayre.*
Aerugineux : m. euse : f. *Full of, or, like vnto, Verdigrease.*
Cholere aerugineuse. *Looke,* Cholere.
Afaire. *as* Affaire.
Afaner. *To get hardly, or with much toyle*; *to take exceeding paines for, to sigh in the laborious getting of.*
Affabilité: f. *Affabilitie*; *a kind fashion of speaking to, a gentle garbe in hearing of, others.*
Affable: com. *Affable*; *gentle, courteous, gracious, in words, of a friendly conuersation, easily spoken to by, willingly giuing eare to, others.*
Affablement. *Affably*; *gently, graciously, courteously (in speech, or conuersation.)*
Affaçonner. *Looke* Affassonner.
Affadi : m. ie : f. *Made or growne vnsauorie, tastlesse, wallowish, waterish*; *weake*; *witlesse.*
Affadir. *To make or grow tastlesse, wallowish, waterish*; *weake*; *vnsauorie*; *witlesse.*
Affadissant. *Making wallowish, growing tastlesse, yeelding an vnsauorie, weake, or waterish tast.*
Affadissement: m. *Wallowishnesse, vnsauorinesse, tastlesnesse*; *weakenesse of sauor, waterishnesse of tast.*
Affaicté : m. ée : f. *Trimmed, tricked, decked, curiously dressed*; *refined*; *reclaimed, ciuillized*; *made inward, or gentle*; *tamed*; *throughly manned.*
Affaicter. *To trim, tricke, decke, dresse curiously, make neat, spruce, fine*; *to refine*; *also, to tame, reclaime, breake, make gentle, bring to ciuilitie.*
Affaicter vn oiseau. *To man a hauke throughly.*
Affaicterie : f. *A trimming, tricking, decking, neat, quaint, or fine dressing*; *also, neatnesse, nicenesse, curiositie, quaintnesse*; *also, a breaking, taming, reclayming, ciuilizing, making gentle*; *(hence) also, the through manning of a hauke, &c.*
Affaire : m. *An affaire, businesse, imployment*; *worke, matter, somewhat to doe*; *also, a labour, trouble*; *charge.*

Qui ueut entretenir son ami n'ait nuls affaires auec luy: Prov. *Let him that will hold a friend, haue little to doe with him.*
Affairé: m. ée: f. *Full of businesse, much employed; busie, euer doing of somewhat.*
Affaireusement. *Very busily, as one thats full of imployments.*
Affaireux. *as* Affairé.
Affaisement. *Looke,* Affaissement.
Affaissé: m. ée: f. *Shrunke, sunke, weighed down, ouerladen, pressed downe, as low as it can goe, as flat as it can be; setled in the bottome of.*
Affaissement: m. *A quelling; a sinking, shrinking, or yeelding vnder a great burthen; a weighing downe; a setling in the bottome of; hence, also, the grounds, or dregs in the bottome of liquor, &c.*
Affaisser. *To bow, presse, or weigh downe.*
s'Affaisser. *To be ouerladen; to quell, sinke, shrinke, or yeeld vnder a great burthen; also, to settle, as a heauie thing in the bottome of.*
Affaitté. *as* Affeté.
Affaitter. *as* Affaicter.
Affaitterie. *Looke* Affaicterie.
Affaitteur de cuirs. *A Skinner, or Leather-dresser.*
Affamé: m. ée: f. *Famished, starued, very hungry, hunger-starued.*
Intestin affamé. *The second small-gut of the Ventricle; alwaies emptie (by reason of the many midriffe veines which passe from it vnto the Liuer) and therefore tearmed, the Hungrie gut.*
Ventre affamé n'a point d'orielles: Pro. *The hunger-starued belly wanteth eares.*
Vilain affamé demy enragé: Pro. *A hungry Boore is halfe a bedlam.*
Affamement: m. *A famishing, staruing, hunger-staruing.*
Affamer. *To famish, to starue, to hunger-starue.*
Affan: m. *Extreame toyle, or griefe: as* Ahan: ¶Lang.
Affassonner. *To forme, or fashion; to bring into good proportion; to make handsome, fit, and readie for the purpose.*
Affaytement: m. Oiseau de doux affaytement. *A hauke thats gentle, and easie to be made, or manned; a well natured hauke.*
Affayter. *as* Affaicter.
Affeager. *To create a tenure in fee simple; to passe, alien, or graunt in fee, or, a fief.*
Affeblir. *as* Affoiblir. *To weaken.*
Affectateur: m. *An affector; one that (curiously) imitates a fashion, or takes on him a habit, which either becomes, or befits, him not.*
Affectation: f. *Affectation; ouer-curious imitation; a foolish desire, or following of, what one hath not, or is not, by nature; also, a publicke or legall assignement, or appointing of a thing vnto; a fastening or tying it on; a binding it for, the maintenance, or assurance of another.*
Affecté: m. ée: f. *Affected, fancied, desired, coueted; aspired vnto, sought after; also, affectioned, bearing good will, or wishing well, vnto; also, affectiue; or, as* Affeté; *also, especiall, or of purpose; also, affected; fastened or tyed on, destinate for, assigned or appointed vnto.*
Affecter. *To affect, fancie; desire, couet; seeke after, aspire vnto; also, to wish well, or beare good will to; also, to affect; fasten, or tye on; destinate (or bind) for; assigne, or appoint vnto.*
Affecterie: f. *as* Afteterie; *also, affectation; or, a curious imitation of.*
Affection: f. *An affection, liking, loue, good will vnto; a desire of, or longing after; also, a passion, perturbation, or trouble of mind; (and hence) also a sicknesse, disease, or imperfection (of mind, or bodie.)*
Affectionné: m. ée: f. *Affectionate, or affectionated; hauing an affection, bearing a good will, to; giuen, addicted; excited, animated, vnto; also, beloued, esteemed, affected.*
Affectionnément. *Affectionately, with great affection.*
Affectionner. *To affectionate; beget a liking, breed an affection; excite, incite, or animate, vnto.*
s'Affectionner à. *To affect, or loue; to addict, or deuote himselfe; to giue his mind, vnto.*
Affectueusement. *Most affectionatly; desirously, heartily; greedily, couetously.*
Affectueux: m. euse: f. *Most affectionate; heartie; desirous of; full of affects, or of affection; full of good will; also, bearing a great affection, or much good will, vnto.*
Affené: m. ée: f. *Fed, or inseamed, with hay; stall-fed.*
Affener. *To feed or inseame with hay; to stall-feed.*
Afferant. *(The Participle of the Impersonall* Affiert) *beseeming, or becomming; also, concerning, or belonging to.*
Affermable: com. *Affirmable, auoucheable; also, farmeable, leaseable, lettable.*
Afferme: f. *A farming; leasing, letting out.*
Affermé: m. ée: f. *Farmed; let or leased out; also, as* Affirmé.
Affermement: m. *as* Afferme; *also, an affirming.*
Affermer. *To farme; lease; or let out vnto farme; also, to affirme, &c; as in* Affirmer.
Affermi: m. ie: f. *Strengthened, confirmed, fortified; assured; compacted, consolidated, setled, hardened, stiffened, closed, fastened; made firme.*
Pain affermi. *Stale bread.*
Affermir. *To strengthen, fortifie, confirme; assure; compact, consolidate, settle, harden, stiffen, close, fasten; make firme.*
Affermissement: m. *A strengthning; compacting, consolidating, closing, setling, stiffening, hardening.*
Affermisseur: m. *A strengthner; compactor, closer, setler, fastener, stiffener, hardner.*
Afferrer. *as* Enferrer.
Affertilé: m. ée: f. *Fertilized, made fertile.*
Affertiler. *To fertilize; to make fertile, or fruitfull.*
Affessé. *as* Affaissé.
s'Affessir. *To grow wearie; to wax lumpish, or heauie.*
Affesté: m. ée: f. *Set, setled, or pearched on the top of.*
s'Affester. *To pearch, to set, or settle it selfe, on the top of.*
Affetardi: m. ie: f. *Made, or become slouthfull, drowsie, negligent; slow, dull; faint-hearted; ouglie to the sight.*
Affetardir. *To make slouthfull, drowsie, lazie; dull, slow, cowardly, faint-hearted; also, to make loathsome, or ouglie to the sight.*
Affeté; ou, Affetté: m. ée: f. *Craftie, subtile, slye, wylie, dissembling; also, nice, curious, daintie, quaint, precise.*
Affeter. *as* Affaicter.
Affeterie. ou, Affetterie. *Craft, subtiltie, slynesse, wylinesse, dissimulation, guilefulnesse; also, nicenesse, daintinesse, curiositie, precisenesse, quaintnesse.*

Affeu-

Affeublage: m. *Looke* Affublage.
Affeubler. *Looke* Affubler.
Affeurage: m. *as* Afforage; *also, a rating, or setting of a price on things.*
Affeurer. *To rate, value at a certaine rate, set a certain price on*; *Looke* Afforer.
Affeurré. *Foddered, (with straw.)*
Affeurrer. *To fodder (with straw.)*
Affiche: f. *A Siquis; a bill set vp; or pasted, or fastened, on a post, doore, gate, &c.*
Affiché: m. eé: f. *Fastened vpon, fixed, or affixed vnto; also, caught, or laid fast hold on; also, performed, or made good.*
Affichement: m. *A fastning; a fixing, or affixing vnto; also, a catching, or laying fast hold on; also, a making good of a promise, or word.*
Afficher. *To fasten vpon; to fix, or affix vnto; also, to seize, catch, or lay fast hold on; also, to make good a promise, or word.*
Affiĉter. *To annex, or giue, for a time.*
Affidé: m. eé: f. *Ingaged; that hath past his faithfull promise; that hath pawned his faith, and credit.*
Affié: m. eé: f. *Assured, assied, confirmed, affirmed; also, planted, set, or graffed; affixed, fastened.*
Tous mes biens te sont affiez par droit; *All my goods belong, or are assigned, to thee by right; they be all tyed on thee.*
Affiement. *An assuring, affirming, confirming; also, a setting, planting, graffing; affixing, fastening.*
Affier. *To affie, assure, affirme on his word; to pawne his faith, and credit on; also, to strengthen, or confirme; also, to plant, set, or graffe; affix, fasten.*
Affiert. *(A Verbe Impersonall) it becommeth, or beseemeth; also, it concerneth, or belongeth to.*
Affieux: m. *A good fellow, a boone companion.*
Affilé: m. eé: f. *Sharpened, whetted, that hath an edge set on it; also, decked, dressed, or stiffened with wire.*
Affilement: m. *A whetting, sharpening, or setting of an edge on; also, a dressing, or stiffening with wire.*
Affiler. *To whet, sharpen, set an edge on; also, to decke, dresse, or stiffen with wire.*
Affileur: m. *A whetter, or sharpener of edg'd tooles.*
Affileure: f. *as* Affilement; *Also, the edge, or sharpenesse of a toole.*
Affiliant: m. *An adopter.*
Affiliation: f. *Adoption; or an adopting.*
Affilié: m. eé: f. *Adopted.*
Affilier. *To adopt.*
Affiloire: m. *A whetstone.*
Affin: m. *A kinsman, or Ally; one with whom affinitie is had, or contracted.*
Affin. Aduerb: *That, to the end that.*
Affinage: m. *A fining; or a refining, of mettals.*
Affiné: m. eé: f. *Deceiued, cosened, beguiled; also, brought vnto an end; also, fined, purified, refined.*
Affinement. *A cousening, deceiuing, beguiling; also, a fining of mettals.*
Affiner. *To cousen, deceiue, beguile; also, to bring to end, or effect; also, to refine, or fine, as mettals; to purifie, or improue them* (c'est rendre haut, & fin l'Or, &c, qui est bas, selon le tiltre qu'il faut; *sayes a French man.)*
Affineur. *A deceiuer, beguiler, cousener; also, a refiner, or finer of mettals; a purifier, or improuer of them.*
Affinité: f. *Affinitie; kindred, allyance; neerenesse.*
Affiniter. *To ally; to make of affinitie, or kindred, with;*
Affinoire: m. *A fining house; the roome, shop, or place, wherein gold, or siluer is vsually fined.*

Affiquet: m. *Any prettie toy, trinket, or trifle of small value; as a little brooche, flower, button, aglet, &c, stucke on the hat, head, hood, or elsewhere; and worne (especially by a woman) for ornament.*
Affirmateur. *An affirmer, soother, auoucher, ascertainer, auower.*
Affirmation. *An affirmation, asseueration, assertion, ascertaining.*
Affirmé: m. eé: f. *Affirmed; auouched, soothed, auowed; assured, ascertained, stood vnto.*
Affirmer. *To affirme, sooth, auouch, auow; assure, ascertaine, stand vnto.*
s'Afflaquir. *To wax flaggie, limber, feeble; to become loose ioynted; to faint.*
Afflat: m. *A blast, breath, wind, inspiration, blowing in.*
Afflater. *To flatter, blandish; allure, or intice with faire speeches; to cog, or glose with, to fawne on.*
Affleurir l'eau. *To go close by the water, as the lee-side of ships in a strong side-wind; Seeke* Effleurer.
Afflictif: m. iue: f. *Afflictiue, grieuing, molesting, tormenting.*
Peines afflictiues de corps. *corporall punishments.*
Affliction. *Affliction, molestation, calamitie, crosses, vexation, trouble, woe, persecution.*
Affligé: m. eé: f. *Afflicted, vexed, tormented; exceeding much grieued, molested, troubled.*
Affliger. *To afflict, vex, torment, molest, grieue, trouble, exceeding much.*
Afflouï: m. ie: f. *Blurred, blunted; and hence;*
Diamant afflouï. *That hath lost it point.*
Afflouïr. *To blurre; also, to blunt.*
Affluence: f. *Affluence, plentie, store, flowing, fullnesse, aboundance.*
Afflux: m. *An afflux, or affluence; plentifull accesse; or, as* Affluence.
Affoiblement. *as* Affoiblissement.
Affoibli: m. ie: f. *Weakened, enfeebled; decayed in strength; also, allayed, delayed, or abated, as the value of coine.*
Affoiblir. *To weaken, enfeeble, make infirme, depriue of strength, take away the force, or vigour of; also to delay, allay, or abate the value of coine.*
Affoiblissement: m. *A weakening, enfeebling, depriuing of force, power, strength; also, an allaying, or abating of the value of coine.*
Affoisonnement: m. *An increase, or increasing of store.*
Affolé: m. eé: f. *Foyled, bruised, wounded, sore hurt; spoiled; vndone, ruined; also, gulled, or besotted.*
Affolé d'une iambe, d'un pied, &c; *Lame, or maymed, of a leg, foot.*
Affolement: m. *A foyling, bruising, wounding (by strokes;) also, a spoyling, ruining, vndoing; also, a gulling, besotting, befooling.*
Affoler. *To foyle, wound, bruise, or hurt sore with blows; also, to spoyle, ruine, vndoe; also, to besot, gull, befoole.*
Affolure: f. *A foyle, bruise, wound, sore hurt; a spoyling, ruining, vndoing; an extreame impression, or aggrieuance.*
Affoncer. *To thrust farre, or deep, into, &c. as* Enfonser.
Affondé: m. eé: f. *Sunke down to the bottome, or lying (as a heauie thing) at the bottome, of.*
Affonder: ou; s'Affonder. *To sinke, fall, or go downe to the bottome; as, a heauie thing, thats cast into the water.*
Affor: m. *A piercing, or broaching of wine, &c.*

Afforage:

Afforage: m. *The same.*
Droict d'afforage. *Two pots of wine, &c; paied vpon the broaching of euerie vessell retailed; one to the Land-lord, his right for the standing thereof on his ground, and for his leaue to sell it; another vnto the Magistrat for allowance of the liquor, and for the rate set on it.*
Afforagé: m. eé: f. *pierced, or set abroach; also, rated, or whose price is set downe; licenced, or allowed (as good, and wholesome wine, &c;) to be sould, by a Magistrat, or Land-lord.*
Afforer. *To pierce, or set abroach a vessell of wine, &c; or (rather) the Magistrat to set a rate on, and the Landlord to giue a licence for, the retaile thereof; or, to take a rate from the Magistrat, and a licence of the Land-lord, for the retaile thereof.*
Affouchié: m. eé: f. *Put into, layed among, fearne.*
Sanglier affouchié. *Thats busily rooting for fearne roots; or, that in searching for fearne roots, plowes vp the ground with his snowt.*
Affouler. *as* Affoler; *And (particularly) a woman to miscarrie, cast her child, or be deliuered before her time, by the violence of blowes (or a fall) receiued.*
Affourrager. *as* Affourrer. *To fodder cattell.*
Affourrer. *To serue, or fodder, cattell with straw, &c.*
Affranchi: m. *A freed man, free man, or one that is made free.*
Affranchi: m. ie: f. *Franchised, made free; discharged, released, deliuered from bondage; also, reclaimed, tamed; seasoned, sweetened.*
Affranchir. *To affranchise, free, make free; giue libertie vnto; deliuer, or discharge, from seruitude; release, or rid from charge, or annoyance; also, to reclaime, season, or sweeten; to make tame, in season, or fit for vse what was wild, rammish, or harsh.*
La verge anoblit, & le ventre affranchit: Prov. *Looke* Ventre.
Affranchissement: m. *An affranchising, or freeing; a discharging of, or deliuering from, seruitude; also, a seasoning, sweetening; taming, reclaiming.*
Affranchisseur: m. *An affranchiser, freer, freedome-giuer.*
Affrequane: f. *A Tygre; (because bred in Affrica.)*
Affres. Ie luy ay donné vne mauuaise affres. *I haue frighted, scarred, affrayed him exceedingly; or, I haue put him into his dumpes.*
Affreté: m. eé: f. *Fastened, clasped; or, clung'd vnto.*
Affreusement. *Gastly, terribly, horribly, as one that hath beene scarred; also, grimly, sternely, sowerly; fell, frowardly, frowningly, vnder the browes.*
Affreuseté: f. *Gastlinesse, terriblenesse, horrour in the countenance; sternnesse, grimnesse, felnesse; frowning, lowring, sowernesse, or churlishnesse of looke.*
Affreux: m. euse: f. *Gastly, horride, fearefull, terrible in looke; grim, sterne, fell, sower, frowning, lowring, looking big on; of a spightfull, churlish, and vnpleasant countenance.*
Affriandé: m. eé: f. *Liquorous, or made liquorous, of; set in a longing after; (hence) also, allured, inticed, inueagled, tolled, or drawne on by plausible or fayre meanes.*
Affriandement: m. *A making liquorous of; also, an alluring, inticing, or tolling on, by plausible, or sweet meanes.*
Affriander. *To make liquorous of, or, set in a longing after; also, to allure, inueagle, intice, draw, or toll on, by faire, sweet, or plausible meanes.*
Affriolé. *as* Affriandé.
Affriolement: m. *An alluring, or allurement.*
Affrioler. *as* Affriander.
Affriquain. *African, of Affricke.*
Vent Affriquain. *The Southwest wind.*
Affrodille: m. *Th'Affodill, or Asphodill flower; also, the plant that beares it; also, the bulbed root thereof.* *Looke* Aphrodille.
Affronitre: m. *as* Aphronitre; *Salt-peeter.*
Affront: m. *An affront, brauadoe, wrong, or abuse, offered to a mans face; an impudent, and iniurious gullerie; a bold, scuruie, or cosening part, played a man openly.*
Affrontailles: f. *Th'ends, or corners of a peece of land abutting vpon other lands, which belong vnto diuers Lords, or owners.*
Affronté: m. eé: f. *Affronted; encountred, set vpon; contested, swaggered with; abused, gulled, openly, or to his face.*
Affrontement: m. *as* Affront; *also, an affronting; incountring, assaulting of.*
Affronter. *To affront; or lye affront of; to come before, or face to face; also, to incounter, assault, set vpon; contest, quarell, swagger with; braue; wrong, abuse; cosen, gull, deceiue, impudently, openly, or to the face of.*
Affronteur: m. *A brauer, affronter, abuser of people to their faces; a common swaggerer, an impudent, or bold companion; also, an open, or publique deceiuer, beguiler, cheater, cogging mate; cousening merchant.*
Affublage: m. *A cloathing, cladding; muffling, or enwrapping in; a hiding, or shrowding vnder, (clothes;) also, garments, raiments, apparell, clothes.*
Affublé: m. eé: f. *Clad, or clothed; muffled, or enwrapped in; couered, or attired with; hid, or shrowded vnder (clothes.)*
Affublement: m. *as* Affublage.
Affubler. *To cloath, clad, put on; to attire, or couer with, muffle, or enwrap in, hide, or shrowd, vnder clothes.*
Il ne faut estre loup, ny en affubler la peau. Prov. *We must neither be, nor seeme, naught.*
Affuir. *To flie, or recourse vnto for helpe, and succour.*
Affuler. *as* Affubler: ¶Pic.
Affust: m. *The frame, or cariage of a peece of ordnance; also, as* Toile baptiste.
Affusté: m. eé: f. *Stocked, fitted with a stocke; or staffe; mounted, as artillerie; furnished with a frame, or carriage.*
Affuster. *To stocke; fit with a stocke; or staffe; to mount artillerie; to furnish (it) with a frame, or carriage.*
Affutage: m. *Frames, carriages, or stockes for artillerie.*
Afiliation: f. *Adoption, or the conferring on fremme children all aduantages belonging to naturall ones.*
Afrodille. *as* Affrodille.
Afrodisiace: f. *A kind of stone, or minerall of a whitish colour mingled with red.*
Afrolitre: m. *A kind of light, brittle, and purple coloured Niter.*
Afronitre. *The same.*
Afuselé: m. eé: f. *Pointed, or made small towards the point, as a spindle; fashioned like a spindle.*
Afuselement: m. *A fashioning of things like spindles.*
Afuseler. *To fashion, point, or make small towards the end, like a spindle.*
Afyer. *as* Brouiller; *or, as* Tromper.
Aga, mon amy; *See, looke friend; (spoken in mirth, or mockerie.)*
Agacé. *Egged, vrged, incensed, prouoked, exasperated; also,*

also, set on edge, as a tooth; also, blunted, as a weapon.

Agaceant. *Egging, vrging, angring, prouoking, exasperating; also, setting on edge, the teeth; blunting weapons.*

Agacement: m. *An egging, vrging, angring, prouoking, exasperating; also, a setting of the teeth on edge; also, a dulling, or blunting of weapons.*

Agacer. *To egge, vrge, prouoke, anger, vex, exasperate; also, to set the teeth on edge; also, to blunt, or dull a weapon, &c.*

Agache. *as* Agasse.

Agaillardé: m.eé: f. *Growne liuely, iocond, blithe, frolicke.*

s'Agaillarder. *To be iocond, liuely, blithe, frolicke, merrie.*

Agalloche: m. *The sweet wood called, Lignum Aloes.*

Agamber. *To step, or stride ouer.*

Aganni: m.ie: f. *Withered, faded, consumed, growne fruitlesse, depriued of force.*

Agannir. *To consume, wither, vade, faile, grow fruitlesse, loose all vigour, and force.*

Agaric: m. *Agaricke; a white, and soft mushrome, or excrescence growing vpon the Larch tree; also, a root in Sarmatia, that helpes disgestion.*

Agaric noir. *A heauie, poisonous, and blackish kind of Agaricke; full of little sinewie threads.*

Agart. *Looke* Hagard.

Agasse: f. *A Pie, Piannet, or Magatapie.*

Agassé: m.ée: f. *as* Agacé.

Agasser. *as* Agaçer.

Agasseté: f. *Bluntnesse in an edged toole.*

Agasseur: m. *An egger, vrger, prouoker, exasperater.*

Agassin. *A corne, or agnele in the feet, or toes; also, the lowest bud, or braunch of a vine.*

Agassure. *as* Agasseté; *and, as* Agacement.

Agathe. *An Agate.*

Agathonien: m.enne: f. *Wanton, lasciuious, bawdie, full of ribaldrie; (of* Agatho, *the name of a certaine wanton Minstrell.)*

Agay: m. *The marrow of fowle; (a Faulconers tearme.)*

Agazer. *as* Agacer.

Ageancé: m. ée: f. *Fitted, adapted, adiusted, set handsomely, placed orderly.*

Ageancement. *Seeke* Agencement.

Ageancer. *as* Agencer.

Agelaste: com. *Sad, sullen; that neuer laugheth:* ¶Grec.

Agember. *as* Agamber.

Agencé: m. ée: f. *Fitted, apted, adapted, adiusted, proportioned, accommodated; ordered; dressed, trimmed, decked, handsomely; fitly disposed, finely placed, featly suited, rightly matched, iustly applied.*

Agencement: m. *A fitting, apting, iust placing, setting in order; an adapting, accommodating; a trimming, dressing, decking; also, sutablenesse, handsomnesse, good proportion.*

Agencer. *To fit, apt, adapt, adiust, proportion, accommodate; also, to dresse, trim, decke; to dispose fitly, set featly, place finely, sute rightly, match iustly, ioyne handsomely together.*

Agenouillé: m.ée: f. *Kneeled; on his knees, kneeling.*

Agenouiller. *To kneele.*

A la quenouille le fol s'agenouille: Pro. *The foole submits himselfe to his proud wife.*

Agenouillon. *Kneeling, or vpon his knees.*

Agent: m. *An Agent, a dealer, Negotiator, Embassador.*

Agesimos. *A wondering voyce, or exclamation.*

Aggere: m. *A heape of stones, earth, or turues; and hence, a bulwarke, mount, rampier, made for the defence of a fort, or campe; also, a fort, or blockehouse; also, a causey, banke, damme, sea-wall, hill of earth raysed against, or seruing to keepe out, waters.*

Agglué: m.ée: f. *Glued; ioyned close vnto, or together.*

Aggluer. *To glue; to ioyne, as with glue; to close vnto, or together.*

s'Aggluer à: *To cleaue, or sticke fast vnto.*

Agglutinatif: m.iue: f. *Of power, or propertie, to glue, or close together.*

Agglutinement: m. *A gluing, or closing vnto, or together.*

Agglutiner. *as* Aggluer.

Aggraffe: f. *A hooke, a grapple; a haspe, or claspe.*

Aggraffement. *A hooking, clasping, buckling, grapling to; a hasping; seizing, or taking hold of.*

Aggraffer. *To grapple, or claspe with; to hooke vnto; to buckle, to haspe; to seize, gripe, take hard, or violent hold of.*

Aggrandi: m.ie: f. *Greatened, inlarged; augmented, increased; preferred, aduanced.*

Aggrandir. *To greaten, augment, inlarge, increase, make great, preferre, aduance.*

Aggrandissement: m. *A greatning, inlarging, increase; preferment, aduancement.*

Aggrandisseur: m. *An inlarger, increaser, augmenter; preferrer, aduancer.*

Aggravanté: m.ée: f. *Aggrauated, exasperated.*

Aggravanter. *To aggrauate, exasperate, make more hainous, or grieuous.*

Aggravation: f. *An aggrauation, or aggrauating; also, a curse, excommunication, or execration denounced against an obstinat offendor.*

Aggravé: m.ée: f. *as* Aggravanté; *also, made heauy, surcharged, swayed, or borne downe, by ouer-much weight; also, grauelled, or, as a ship, fast on the ground.*

Aggravé des pieds. *Surbated, foundered, foot-beaten.*

Aggravé de somme. *Fast asleepe, in a dead sleepe.*

Aggraver. *To aggrauate, exasperate, make more hainous, or grieuous than it was; also, to make heauie, surcharge, oppresse; to sway, or beare downe, by weight.*

s'Aggraver. *To be grauelled; to sticke fast on ground, or in the grauell.*

Aggreable com. *Agreeable, acceptable, gracefull, gracious, delectable, welcome, well liked.*

Aggréer. *To agree, or sute with; to be acceptable, welcome, or pleasing vnto.*

Aggregé: m.ée: f. *aggregated, congregated; ioyned, added vnto.*

Aggreger. *To assemble, aggregate, congregate, gather together; also, to adde, or ioyne vnto a societie; also, to aggrauate.*

Aggrené: m. ée: f. *Fed, filled, or inseamed, with corne, or graine.*

Aggrener. *To feed, or fill with with corne, or graine; to take vp a horse, or coult from grasse, and inseame him with corne or prouender;* Seeke Agrener.

Aggresé: m. ée: f. *Assaulted, assailed, set on.*

Aggressement. *An assaulting, or setting on.*

Aggresser. *To assaile, assault, set on.*

Aggresseur. *An assayler, or assaulter; he that giues the onset, or first layes hands on his weapon, to doe another violence.*

Aggression. *An aggression, assault, incounter, or first set-*

setting on.

Aggriffer. *as* Aggripper; *or, as* Griffer.

Aggripper. *To gripe, seize hard, lay sure hold on.*

Agian : m. *A bearing cloth for a child; also, a beere-cloth for a dead corps.*

Agiaux. *Ceremonies; Looke* Agios; *or the Plurall to* Agian.

Agiers : m. *The steps, wayes, or turnings to be obserued for the readie comming vnto a house, or place.*

Agile : com. *Nimble, agile, actiue; quicke, prompt; of supple members, or parts; of a readie stirring.*

Agilement. *Nimbly, actiuely, with agilitie; quickely, promptly, supplely, readily.*

Agilité : f. *Agilitie, nimblenesse, actiuitie; promptnesse, readinesse, quicknesse, dexteritie; supplenesse of members, or of parts.*

Agiographe. *A holy writing; holy Writ.*

Agios. *Sacred, holy;* ¶Grec. *hence;*
Faire beaucoup d' agios. *To be verie scrupulous, or ceremonious; or, rather, to vse many blessings, crossings, or superstitious gestures in the doing of any thing.*

Agiotare : m. *A holy and blessed man.*

Agir. *To sue, implead, plead, commence suit, bring an action against; also, to worke, operate, worke effect, haue an operation in.*

Agitant. *Tossing, much mouing, reuoluing, wagging, stirring vp and downe.*

Agitation. *An agitation, stirring, great motion, much exercise, reuolution, working, wagging.*

Agité : m. ée : f. *Tossed, wagged, agitated, much moued, stirred, exercised, reuolued.*

Agiter. *To tosse, agitate; wag, stir, moue often; to reuolue, worke, exercise, verie much.*

Agnafile *A kind of Moorish Trumpet.*

Agnation : f. *Kindred by the fathers side; also, (but lesse properly) adoption; also, a thing that growes beside, or aboue, the course of nature.*

Agneau : m. *A Lambe.*
Blanche d' agneaux. *The furre called, white Lambe, or, white Budge.*
Autant maniable comme vn agneau. *as meeke as a Lambe.*
Brebis trop apprivoisée de trop d'agneaux est tetteé: Prov. *The gentle Ewe is suckt by too many Lambs; (appliable to an ouer-kind, or too familiar, woman.)*
De mal est venu l'agneau & à mal retourne la peau: Prov. *To naught it goes that came from naughtinesse.*

Agnelé : m. ée : f. *Lambed.*

Agnelement : m. *A lambing; a falling of Lambs.*

Agneler : m. *The same; and thence;*
A l'agneler verra on lesquelles sont prains: Prov. *At lambing time we find what Ewes were full.*

Agneler. *To lambe.*

Agnelet : m. *A little Lambe; a Lambkin, or young Lambe.*

Agnelette. *as* Agneliere.

Agneliere : f. *Th'inmost of the three membranes which enwrap a wombe-lodged infant; called by some Midwiues, the Coyfe, or Biggin of the child; by others, the childs shirt.*

Agnelin : m. *Lambes furre, Budge.*

Agobilles : f. *Trifles, nifles, trinkets, trash, trumperie, paultrie stuffe.*

Agonarque : m. *A Master of the Reuels; a President, or chiefe Iudge; a principall author, or directer, of publick exercises, playes, or games.*

Agonie : f. *Agonie, griefe, perplexitie, anguish, anxietie, vexation of mind.*

Agoniser. *To grieue extreamely; to be much perplexed, full of agonie, fraught with anguish.*

Agoranome : m. *The Clearke, or Comptroller, of a Market.*

Agoubilles. *as* Agobilles.

Agoué : m. ée : f. *Halfe choked, wel-nigh stifled (as one that hath a bone, or gobbet in his throat, which will neither vp, nor downe;) also, cloyed, saded, ouer-glutted, ouer-full.*

Agoure de lin. *(The weed) Dodder.*

Agouster. *To haue a smacke, or tast of.*

Agoutter. *To drop, as raine from a house eaue.*

Agouttis : m. *The eauings of a house.*

Agrandir. *as* Aggrandir.

Agraffe. *as* Agraphe.

Agrailir. *Looke* Agreslir.

Agrailissement. *A lessening; a making thinne, small, slender.*

Agraphe : f. *A claspe; hooke; brace; grapple; haspe.*

Agrapher. *To buckle, grapple, haspe, claspe; to hooke vnto; to seize, gripe, or take hold of.*

Agraphiner. *To seize, gripe, lay his clawes on, take hold of.*

A-gré. *Willingly, with a good will.*

Agreable. *as* Aggreable.

Agreableté : f. *Agreeablenesse, acceptablenesse; comelinesse, gracefulnesse.*

Agreation : f. *An agreement, concord, assent, consent; also, an agreeing.*

Agrené. *Inseamed, fed, or, filled, with corne.*

Agrener. *as* Aggrener.
Agrener le moulin. *To fill the mill hopper (with corne.)*

Agrerer. *To chuse, part, or lay out his part of the fruites of his land let out to parts.*

Agreslir. *To make, or become thin, leane, small, slender; to lessen, to narrow.*
Agreslir la voix. *To squeale, or squeake; to sing in a high pitch; to rise in singing.*

Agresśé : m. ée : f. *Assaulted, set on.*

Agresseur. *as* Aggresseur.

Agreste : com. *Sower, tart, or sharpe, as verges; also, rude; clownish, rusticall, vngentle, boorish.*

Agricole : m. *A husbandman, plowman, countrey Farmer.*

Agriculture. *Tillage, husbandrie.*

Agrier : m. droit d'agrier. *as* Terrage.

Agriere : f. *Seeke* Terrage.

Agrimenseur : m. *A Surueyor, or measurer of land.*

Agrimoine. *as* Aigremoine.

Agriotat. *The iuyce, or syrop of tart cherries.*

Agriotte : f. *The ordinarie sharpe, or tart cherrie; which we also call, the Agriot cherrie.*

Agripauline. *The hearbe Motherwort.*

Agrippine. poudre Ag. *Meat that prouokes lust; leacherous stuffe.*

s'Agrouper. *A horse to knit, and gather himselfe close together, carrying himselfe vpon his hinder parts, and drawing them vp, as if hee would yearke out behind.*

Agu : m. uë : f. *Keene, sharpe, small-topped, or pointed; piercing; smart; subtile, wittie, ingenious; eagre, vehement.*

Aguafile : f. *A kind of Moorish Trumpet.*

Aguard. *as* Hagard.

Aguelette. la tunique a. *A thinne soft skin, or shirt, wherein children are wrapped in the matrix, besides their bed, or after birth, which is more grosse.*

Aguement. *Sharply, keenely; smartly; wittily, piercingly.*

Aguerriment. *Martiall order, warlike discipline; also, a making, or becomming warlike; a training vp in warfare.*

Aguerrir. *To make warlike, or fit for the wars; to traine vp in martiall discipline.*

Aguerrissant. *Making warlike, training vp in warfare.*

Aguet: m. *An ambush, or lying in wait for.*

Aller d'aguet en ses affaires. *To go warily to worke; to proceed leasurely, to take him leasure in his businesse.*

Aguetté. *Dogged; watched, waited; lien for.*

Aguetter. *To watch, dog, lye in wait, or ambush for.*

Aguigner. *To leuell, or ayme at; to leere, winke, or looke with one eye at.*

Aguillade. *A long, ash-coloured, great eyed, big-bellied Dog-fish, that hath two sharpe and strong prickles, on her back; and thereof may be tearmed, (as she is by the Germanes) a Thorne-hound.*

Aguillan-neuf. *An old word compounded of 4 words;* au-guy-l'an-neuf. *Seeke* Auguillanneuf.

Aguillat. *A kind of Dog-fish; as* Aguillade.

Aguille: f. *A needle; also a long small fish, called a Hornebacke, or Horne-fish; Looke* Aiguille.

Aguillette. *A point; Seeke* Esguillette.

Aguilletter. *To tye points.*

Aguillier: m. *A needle case.*

Aguillon. *A pricke, a goade, a sting; Looke* Esguillon..

Aguillonnement: m. *A pricking, or stinging; an instigation, mouing, prouoking, inciting, or setting forward.*

Aguillonner. *To pricke, sting; prouoke, moue, incense, instigate, incite, egge, vrge forward.*

Aguillonneur: m. *A pricker, or prouoker forward.*

Aguiner. *as* Aguigner.

Aguisé: m.ée: f. *Whetted, sharpened.*

Aguisement: m. *A whetting, sharpening, or setting an edge on.*

Aguiser. *To whet, sharpen, grind, or set an edge on.*

Pierre à aguiser. *as* Pierre Aguisoire.

Aguisoire. pierre ag. *A whetstone; a grindstone.*

Aguyon: m. *A gentle, pleasant, or calme wind; called so among Brittish, and Normand Mariners.*

Agyos. *Looke* Agios.

Ahan: m. *The lowd sighing, and paine-expressing time, which wood-cleauers, heauie-loden porters, &c, keepe, with their voices, vnto the blowes they giue, or steps they make; hence, extreame labour, great trauell, exceeding toile of body, much anguish, vexation, affliction of mind; or any loud, painfull, & short expression therof.*

Ahané. *Extreamly toiled, trauelled, payned, vexed, perplexed; also, ploughed.*

Ahaner. *To sigh out; to keepe time with lowd sighes vnto his toylesome strokes, or painfull steps; also to labor, toyle, trauell exceeding hard; also, to plough, or breake vp a stiffe peece of ground.*

Ahannable. terre ahannable. *Rich, & tough earable; land that yeelds great encrease, but requires much labor, or puts the laborer to much toile, in the tilling of it.*

Ahannant. *Toyling extreamly, sighing often through the great paine his worke puts him to.*

Ahanner. *as* Ahaner.

Ahanneux: m. euse: f. *Toylesome, painefull, most laboursome, verie troublesome; full of affliction, vexation, trauell, anguish.*

Ahen. *as* Ahan; *also, a plough.*

Ahennage: m. *A ploughing, or breaking vp of (a stiffe peece of) ground.*

Ahenner. *as* Ahaner.

Aherdre. *To snatch, or plucke; to catch, gripe, or take by violence.*

Aheurté: m.ée: f. *Stiffe, wilfull, obstinate, that wil forward how deere so euer it costs him.*

Aheurtement: m. *Obstinacie, wilfulnesse, or selfewill; stiffenesse in opinion, stubbornnesse, headinesse.*

s'Aheurter. *To be wilfull, obstinate, headie, selfewilly, stiffe, in a bad matter.*

Ahocquer. *as* Accrocher: ¶Pic.

Ahonti: m. ié: f. *Abashed, dasht out of countenance; made ashamed.*

Ahontir. *To make ashamed; to abash; to dash out of countenance.*

Ahurir. *To affright, scare; appall, astonish, amaze, dismay exceedingly; to make ones haire stand annend, or bring him to his wits end, by frighting, or amazing of him.*

Ahurté. *as* Aheurté.

Ahy. *Out alas (an Interiection of feare.)*

Aj. *Oh; ay me; (an Interiection expressing sence of pain, or of smart;) or as* Ahy.

Aidant: m. ante: f. *Aiding, helping, succouring, assisting, releeuing, furthering, forwarding.*

Dieu aidant. *By the helpe of God, if God prosper my proceedings, or spare me life and health; and God wil, if God say amen.*

Aide: m. *An aidant, helper, second, assistant; Looke* Aides.

Vn Aide à Masson. *A Masons boy, or seruant, that reaches him stone, and morter as he workes.*

Aide: com. *Aide, helpe, assistance; reliefe, succour; support; furtherance, a forwarding; (also, a subsidie, lone, custome, taxe; a prestation due from subiects to their Soueraigns, and from tenants to their land-lords; generally, any money thats leuied by either (ouer and aboue their ordinarie reuenue) for the warres, or other extraordinarie imployments.*

Aides (as in Aide) *All kind of Subsidies, lones, taxes, tithes, pecuniarie subuentions; and particularly, the ordinarie imposition of twelue pence in the pound* Tour. *vpon all sorts of fruites, prouision, and marchandise, sold in any part of France (if they belong not to such persons as are priuiledged by custome, or charter from the King;) also, light-armed souldiours imployed for seconds; and the forces or troupes which one friend, or colleague, sends to the ayde of another.*

Aides cheuels. *Three pecuniarie, and casuall aydes, or dueties, yeelded in Normandie, by euery tenant in fee vnto his Land-lord (if he be noble) the first when his eldest sonne is knighted; and thus is tearmed,* Aide de chevalerie; *the second, towards the mariage of his eldest daughter, called* Aide de mariage; *the third, to helpe to pay his ransome, when he is prisoner in a warre, wherein he serued the king by reason of his owne tenure; and this they call,* Aide de rançon: *By the customes of* Amiens, *and in some other places, onely the two first (and those but once during a tenants life) are yeelded: within* Ponthieu *(and in many other parts of Fraunce) the two first whensoeuer they accrue, the last (most commonly) but once during a lords time. The most common proportion is, ten pounds* Parisis *for euery fee held in Peeredome, and for euery whole Knights fee, 60.s'. and so ratably, when they are to be apportioned.*

Aides coustumiers. *The same; and called so in the auntient customes of Normandie.*

Aide de l'ost. *Looke* Ost.

Aide de reliefe. *The fine paid by euerie tenant vnto his new mesne Land-lord, presently after the death of the old one, & towards the reliefe, which hee is to pay vnto the lord Paramount.*

La Cour des Aides. *as in* Cour.

Droit d' aide. *as* Aides chevels; *called so in the customes of* S.Paul, Arthois, Amiens, Beauquesne, Doulens, *& of some other places: In both the Burgundies the same proportion is due, by this title, vnto lords for their voyages into the Holy land.*

Loyaulx aides. *as* Aides chevels; *tearmed so within the dominion of* Tours, Lodunois, Poictou, *and* Lille.

Bon droict a bon mestier d'aide: Prov. *Good right hath (in our dayes) great need of fauour.*

Aidé: m. ée: f. *Aided, helped, assisted, releeued, succoured; supported; fauoured; furthered, forwarded.*

Aider. *To aid, helpe, assist; releeue, succour; second; support; fauour; forward, further.*

Bon est le dueil qui apres aide: Prov. *Good is that sorrow which at length does good; happie the griefe which in the end makes vs happie.*

Fortune aide à celuy qui se veut aider: Pro. *Fortune helpes him that's willing to helpe himselfe.*

Ajencement, & Ajencer. *Looke* Agencement, & Agencer.

Ajetter vn oiseau. *To cast, or whistle, off a hawke; to let her go, let her flie.*

Aiglantier: m. *An Eglentine, or sweet-brier tree.*

Aiglas: m. *Eaglets, yong Eagles.*

Aigle: f. *An Eagle.*

Aigle de mer. *An Osprey; water Eagle, sea Eagle.*

Petite aigle noire. *A Saker.*

Pierre d'aigle. *An Eagle-stone; found in the Eagles nest; applyed to the thigh of a woman that is in labor, hasteneth her deliuerie.*

Aigleron: m. *An Eaglet, or yong Eagle.*

Aiglesse: f. *An Eaglesse; a henne Eagle.*

Aigneau: m. *a Lambe; Seeke* Agneau.

Aigneaux. *Mannacles; fetters for the hands.*

Aignelé: m. ée: f. *Lambed.*

Aignelement. *A lambing.*

Aigneler. *To lambe; Seeke* Agneler.

Aignelet: m. *A Lambkin, a little, or yong, Lambe.*

Aignelette, & Aigneliere. *as* Agneliere.

Aignelin. *White Budge, white Lambe.*

Aigras: m. *Veriuyce; (an old word.)*

Aigre. *A kind of Grub-axe, or instrument wherewith roots, and shrubs are plucked vp.*

Aigre: com. *Eagre, sharpe, tart, biting, sower; also, brittle, or easily broken (with a hammer.)*

Aigre halleine. *A stinking (which wee also call a sower) breath.*

Mal aigre. *A disease of Hawkes, by wormes that breed in their gorge.*

Aigrebel-heur. *The name of a certaine sower apple.*

Aigre-douce: f. *A ciuile Orange; or, Orange, that is betweene sweet and sower.*

Aigre-doux: m. douce: f. *betweene sweet and sower, or, halfe sweet, halfe sower.*

Aigre-fin: m. *A certaine Turkish coyne; also, a fish that resembles a Whiting; and may be called (according to the Latine* Iecorarius*) the Liuer fish.*

Aigrement.. *Eagrely, sharpely, tartly, bitingly, sowerly; seuerely.*

Aigremoine: f. *The hearbe called Agrimonie, or Egrimonie; and by some Liuerwort, (because it is good for a diseased liuer.*

Aigremoine Sauvage. *Wild Tansie, Siluer-weed.*

Aigret: m. ette: f. *Somewhat tart, sharpe, or eagre.*

Syrop aigret. *Syrop of vinegar.*

Aigrette. *(A foule verie like a Heron, but white;) a criell Heron, or dwarfe Heron; also, the hearbe Sorrell.*

Aigrettes d' Heron. *Heron-tops.*

Aigreur: f. *Sharpnesse, tartnesse, eagrenesse, sowernesse.*

Aigri: m. ie: f. *Sharpened; exasperated, aggrauated, grieued, galled; incensed, prouoked vnto anger.*

Aigrir. *To sharpen, sower; exasperate; aggrauate; to grieue, gall, stirre vp, or prouoke to anger.*

s'Aigrir. *To wax eagre; sharpe, tart; angrie.*

Aigrissant. *Gauling, incensing, exasperating, aggrauating.*

Aigrun. *Any thing that increases, or exasperates, a disease, or sore.*

Persil aigrun. *Great water Parsley; Looke* Persil.

Aiguade: f. *A watering, a taking in of fresh water; also, a place of watering, for shippes.*

Aigue: f. *Water; also, a Mare.* ¶Lang.

Aigue-marine. *Sea-water-greene colour.*

Aigueux: m. euse: f. *Waterish; or, full of water.*

Aiguier: m. *A sinke, or washing stone, in a kitchin; or, as* Ayguier.

Aiguiere: f. *An Ewer, or Lauer.*

Aiguillat. *as* Aguillat.

Aiguille: f. *A needle; also, a Horne-backe, Piper-fish, Gane-fish, or Horne-fish; also, the lesse of the two legbones; also, a spire steeple; or Obeliske.*

Aiguilles. *Short worms that breed in a Hawke, and bring her, without speedie helpe, vnto her death; some call them, Back-wormes.*

Aiguille de berger. *as* Aiguille de pasteur.

Aiguille de chariot; &c. *The draught tree of a Chariot, &c.*

Aiguille musquée. *Musked Pinkneedle, musked Storks-bill, or Cranes-bill; Muscata.*

Aiguille de pasteur. *Three seuerall hearbs are called so; the first, our Shepheards needle, wild Cheruill, mocke Cheruill, Ladies combe; the second, Storkes bil, Cranes bill, Hearons bill, Pinkneedle, (whereof there be many kinds;) the last, Hearbe Robert, (a stinking hearbe.)*

De fil en aiguille. *Euery iot of it, from point to point, from one end to the other.*

Enfiler son aiguille. *Seeke* Enfiler.

Fourni de fil & d'aiguille. *Readie for any imployment; also, neuer to seeke for an answer.*

On ne cache point aiguilles en sac: Prov. *Looke* Sac.

Aiguillé: m. ée: f. *Of a needle; full of needles; like a needle; wrought, or pricked, with needles.*

Aiguillette: f. *A point; Seeke* Esguillette.

Aiguillettes d'armes. *The hearbe, or grasse, called Ladies laces, white Cameleon grasse, painted, or furrowed grasse.*

Aiguilletter. *To trusse, or tye, poynts; also, to whip, or lash, with points.*

Aiguillier. *A needle case.*

Aiguillon. *Looke* Esguillon.

Aiguillonné: m. ée: f. *Pricked, stung; sharp, sharpened, small-pointed, as a pricke or sting.*

Aiguisement: m. *A whetting, sharpening, or setting of an edge on.*

Aiguiser. *as* Aguiser.

Aigument. *Sharpely, piercingly; subtilely, wittily, quickly.*

Ail: m. *Garlicke, poore-mans Treacle;* *Seeke* Aulx.

Ail masle. *The whole-headed Garlicke.*

Ail d'ours. *Ramsons, Ramsies, Bucke rammes, Beares garlicke.*

Ail porreau. *Great mountaine Garlike.*

Ail Sauvage. *Wild Garlicke, Crow Garlicke, Hearts Garlicke, Stags Garlicke, Snakes Garlicke.*

Ail de Serpent. *The same.*

Il amassé la disme de l'ail. *Hee hath beene soundly cudgeled; (a* Poictevin *Prouerbe.)*

Aile: f. *A wing; also, the brimme, or brerewood of a hat.*

Les ailes d'un forest. *The sides or skirtes of a Forest.*

Les ailes du nez. *The nose-thrils.*

Les ailes de poissons. *The finnes of fishes.*

'A tire d'aile *With force of wing; as fast as hee can flye.*

Batre de l'aile. *To smell ranke, or strong, especially from the arme-holes.*

Il ne bat plus que d'une aile. *Hee is become lame, hee is halfe vndone, he hath but one string left to his Bow; also, hee is wellnigh dead, or a dying.*

Chausser les ailes. Il leur chaussa les ailes aux pieds. *Hee gaue wings to their feet; hee made them flye as if fire had beene at their tayles.*

Rongner les ailes à. *To weaken, pull downe, bring vnder, hold short, keepe low.*

Tirer de dessus l'aile. *Cunningly to steale, purloin, conuey away a thing that was hid, couered, kept close, or warily looked vnto.*

Il en tirera pied, ou aile. *See* Pied.

Voler de haulte aile. *To carrie himselfe proudly, loftily, ambitiously; to beare a high sayle, to stand on high points, to flye a high pitch; to meddle with no meane matters.*

Ils veulent voler sans ailes. *They would compasse great matters without meanes; also, they would be held Masters before they haue serued halfe a Prentiship.*

Ailé: m. ée: f. *Winged; swift, flying.*

Ailées. bailler les ailées à vn cheval. *To giue a horse the head, that he may run the faster.*

Ailer. *To giue wings vnto, or set wings vpon.*

Ailerette. *as* Aileron.

Aileron. *A little wing; or the end of a wing.*

Ailerons grands. *as* Landies.

Aileron petit. *as* Nymphe.

Ailerons de poissons. *The finnes of fishes.*

Ailes: f. *Wings; also, as* Aissel les; *The arme-holes; also, (in Anotamie) the sides of a womans priuities.*

Ailette: f. *A little wing.*

Aileures: f. *Two beames that runne along the hatches of a Shippe, and with the* Trauersins *make a long-square hole, whereat the Ship-boat is let downe into the hold; our Ship-wrights name them, Comings, or Carlings.*

Aillade: f. *Garlicke sawce; also, the smell of Garlick; whence;*

Il sent l'aillade. *He smells of, or like vnto, Garlicke; he smells as if he had eaten Garlicke.*

Aillasse: f. *A great wing.*

Ailler: m. *A Quaile-net.*

Ailleurs. *Elsewhere, somewhere else, otherwhere, in another place, or matter.*

Ailloignon: m. *Great Garlicke.*

Ail-porreau: m. *Great mountaine Garlicke.*

Aimable. *as* Amiable; *also, loueable.*

Aimant: m. *A louer, a seruant, a sweet-heart; also, the Adamant, or Load-stone.*

Aimant: m. ante: f. *Louing, affecting, delighting, pleasing himselfe in.*

Aimantin: m. ine: f. *Adamantine; like an Adamant; strong as the Adamant; Iron-drawing; belonging to the Adamant.*

Aimé: m. ée: f. *Loued, affected, beloued, well liked; delighted, or pleased with.*

Ils ont aimé mieux. *They had leauer, they chose rather.*

Bien a en sa maison qui de ses voisins est aimé: Prov. *He finds all well within, who is beloued without, doores.*

Le dernier venu est le mieux aimé: Prov. *Hee is best thought of that comes last; a new friend makes the old forgotten; the last Suiter wins the wench.*

Aime-bal. *Liuely, actiue, daunce-louing.*

Aime-carnage. *Cruell, butcherly, bloudie minded, well pleased with slaughters.*

Aime-esbats. *Gamesome, sportfull, sports affecting.*

Aime-humains. *Gentle, charitable, sociable, men-affecting, mankind-louing.*

Aime-loix. *Iust, Iustice-louing, Lawes-affecting.*

Aime-lyre. *Musicall, Harpe-louing, Lyre-affecting.*

Aime-maistre. *Obsequious, dutifull, seruiceable.*

Aime-mars. *Martiall, warlike, warre-affecting.*

Aime-noise. *A brabler, vnquiet fellow, contentious companion, wrangling marchant, brawling makebate; one that loues to see, or set, others together by the eares.*

Aime-noveauté. *Inconstant, humorous, fantasticall, new things louing, nouelties affecting.*

Aime-paix. *Peaceable, mild, quiet, peace-louing, rest-affecting.*

Aime-pleurs. *Cruell, pitilesse; also dolefull, teares-louing, much giuen, or affected, vnto weeping.*

Aimer. *To loue, affect, like well of; to delight, or be pleased in.*

Et l'aime de vous. *And I loue it because it was yours.*

Aimer & sçavoir n'ont mesme manoir: Prov. *Loue and knowledge liue not together.*

C'est trop aimer quand on en meurt: Prov. *They loue too much who dye for loue; We say, loue me little and loue me long.*

Iamais grasse geline n'aima chapon: Prov. *A fat wife neuer loued a faint husband.*

Iamais tigneux n'aima le pigne: Prov. *Neuer did Scabd iade loue the currycombe; nor a corrupt heart correction.*

Les folles femmes n'aiment que pour pasture: Pro. *Whoores affect your purse, not you; or, loue you not if you feed them not.*

Le paresseux aime bien besongne faitte: Prov. *The sluggard loues alife things done to his hands.*

Onques n'aima bien que pour si peu hait: Prov. *He neuer loued well, that hated for a trifle.*

Onques mastin n'aima Levrier: Prov. *A churle neuer cared for gentleman.*

Qui aime Bertrand aime son chien: Prov. *Loue me loue my dog (say we.)*

Qui bien aime bien chastie: Prov. *He throughly punishes that loues throughly.*

Qui bien aime tard oublie : Prov. *Sound loue is not soone forgotten.*

Qui mieux aime autruy que soy, au moulin il meurt de soif : Pro. *He that loues another better than himselfe, starues in a Cookes shop.*

Tel cuide aimer qui muse : Prov. *Some thinke they loue who do but dote; or, some, though they thinke they loue, but dreame of loue.*

Aime-silence. *Still, husht, silence-louing, noyse-hating.*

Aime-tout. *Most kind, most louing, most charitable, all-affecting; or, none (because all) affecting.*

Ain. *as* Haim.

Ainçois. *But, rather; before, ere, or eve.*

Aines : f. *The grine, or groyne of man or woman.*

Ains. *as* Ançois.

Ainsi. *So, as, euen so, euen as, like as, as it were.*

Ainsi comme ainsi. *Howsoeuer, though it had not beene so; also, bee it as it bee will; as well as we may; so so.*

Ainsi que. *The whilest, iust when, at the time that; also, as much, as well as, like as, euen as.*

Par ainsi. *Therefore, for this, or for that, cause.*

On luy dit qu'ainsi fust que &c. *One told him, that the signe or token thereof was, that, &c; or that if it fell out, that, &c.*

Ainsin. *as* Ainsi. ¶Parisien.

Ainsné. *Looke* Aisné.

Ajoindre. *To ioyne, adde, put, or applie vnto.*

Ajoint : m. inte f. *Adioyned, added, put, applyed vnto.*

Adjolié : m. ée : f. *Pranked, trickt vp, set forth, made fine.*

Ajolier. *To pranke, tricke vp, set out, make fine.*

Ajoliver. *To be merie, buxome, iolly, iocond; to make much of himselfe; also, to pranke, or tricke vp himselfe, to put on his holyday face, to set the better leg before.*

Ajourner. *To be neere day, to grow towards day;* (vieil mot.)

Ajous : m. *Furze, Gorse.*

Air : m. *The aire, breath, wind which we sucke vp; also the element ayre; also, a small blast, breath, or puffe of wind; aire; also, a tune, sownd, or ayre in Musick; also, the forme, or species of a thing; also, the fauour, grace, good opinion of men; also, the aspect, presence, apparance of man; also, a good grace, handsomenesse, or becomming of what one does;* (Il danse d'un bel air :) *In horsemanship, a doing, or stirring manage, or manage raised aboue ground.*

L'air de l'oratoire; l'air de uos lettres. *The neatnesse, aptnesse, delicacie, decorum, pleasantnesse thereof.*

à demy air. *A certaine curuet, or manage, wherin the halfe of a horse is in the aire, the other on the ground.*

Il donna air à ses entreprises. *He published, reuealed, divulged them, gaue a passage or vent vnto them.*

Aïr : m. *Anger (a word of two sillables.)*

Airaigne : f. *A Spider, or Spinner; also, a net of wire set before, and on the out-side of, the glasse windowes of Churches, &c.*

Airaigneux. *Looke* Araigneux.

Airain. *Brasse; Looke* Arain.

Aire : m. *An ayrie, or nest of Haukes.*

De bon aire. *Gentle, mild, courteous, debonaire, without gall, that beares no man any malice.*

Aire : f. *A flat, euen, leuell, peece or plot of ground; (hence) also, the floore of a house, or barne; also, the whole superficies, or superficiall compasse, of a plot, or floore; also, a bed, plat, or quarter, in a garden; also, as* Heulet; *also, the halfe-pace, or landing place of a halfe-pace staire.*

Aire des poils. *The gristlie brimme, or edge of the eyebrowes.*

Aire de vent. *An opposition of winds, as of the South to the North, &c; a gush of contrarie winds, at sea.*

Couppé à tire & à aire. *Cut close by the ground, or cleane away; and (in the sale of vnderwoods) cut close by the stocke, or wholly away from it.*

Airé : m. ée : f. *Angrie, chollericke, in a chafe.*

Aireau : m. *A Plough.*

Airée : f. *A floore-full, or bed-full of.*

Airelles : f. *Whortle berries, or winberries.*

Airer. *To ayrie; to make a nest, or ayrie.*

Aïrer. *To chafe, or be angrie.*

Aireste. *as* Areste.

Airin : m. ine : f. *Ayrie; full of ayre; abounding with ayre.*

Airon. *A Herne, or Heron :* ¶Savoyard.

Airure : f. *The earing, or plowing of land.*

Ais : m. *A planke, or boord.*

Compter les aix & solieueaux. *To trifle out the time, or loose it altogether.*

Aisance : f. *Ease, facilitie, readinesse, easinesse; conuenienciе, opportunitie, commoditie; also, an ease, or easefull thing.*

Aisances. *(In the Plurall number) A Priuie, or house of office.*

Aisceau : m. *A Chip-axe, or one-handed plane-axe, wherewith Carpenters hew their timber smooth.*

Aiscellaire. *as* Axillaire.

Aiscette : f. *A little planing axe.*

Aise : m. *Ease, leasure; facilitie; commoditie; delight, pleasure, full content.*

L'on endure tout fors que trop d'aise : Prov. *Wee say, all things may be suffered sauing wealth.*

Qui à aise tend, aise luy faut : Prov. *Hee that studies his contentment ouermuch, euer wants it.*

Aisé : m. aisée : f. *easie, easefull; gentle, facile; free; soft; pliant; pleasant; delightfull; also, rich; whence;*

Aisé en son mesnage. *Of good estate, well lined, well to liue; well furnished with all houshold prouision.*

Chose aisée croyable : Prov. *Ordinarie things are easily beleeued.*

Aise : com. *Cheerefull, glad; contented, in fulnesse of delight, with great satisfaction, at much ease; whence;*

Ils estoyent à table aises comme Peres. *(A phrase, whose Author by* Peres *meant Abbey-lubbers.)*

Ils repaissent aises comme à nopçes. *They feed as freely (or cheerefully) as if they were at a wedding.*

Chascun n'est pas aise qui danse : Prov. *Euerie one is not merie that dances (viz. that seemes merie)*

Il n'est pas aise qui est courroucé : Prov. *Anger, and hearts-ease, are vtter enemies.*

Il n'est vie que d'estre bien aise : Prov. *Hee onely liues that liues contented; or, a lif's no life, without store of contentments.*

Aiseément. *Easily, lightly, expediently, with facilitie.*

Aisément. *The same.*

Aisements. *as* Aisances.

Aiser. *To be lazie, easefull, sensuall; to take ease, to loue, or liue at, ease.*

Aisle. *Seeke* Aile.

Aisler. *Seeke* Ailer.
Aisleron. *Looke* Aileron.
Aisné. *Eldest, first-borne.*
Charge, debte, rente &c, aisnée. *The most auntient, formost, or first in date.* ¶Normand.
Aisneage: m. *Eldership.*
Droict d'aisneage. *as* Droict d'aisnesse.
Aisnesse: f. *Eldership, eldestship, the being eldest, or first borne.*
Droict d'aisnesse. *The right, and prerogatiue of the eldest child; the portion due, by prime birth, vnto him; which is, the principall house, and garden, with the inclosure thereof; and if there be no garden, the* Arpent *of ground lying next vnto the house, or, as farre as a Capon can flye from it; In the rest he hath but an equall share with the younger: This is his due in many parts, and places of Fraunce; in some others they deale otherwise, and seuerally, according to their seuerall customes.*
Aissade: f. *An instrument wherewith Gardeners open, or breake vp, the ground.*
Aisseau. *as* Aisseul; *Also, the verie middle, or centre of a pillar from the top to the bottome thereof.*
Aisseliere. *The veine which passeth along the arme-hole.*
Aissellaire. *as* Aisseliere.
Aisselle: f. *An arme-hole; also, a little planke, boord, or shingle of wood.*
Aisseul: m. *An axletree; also, one of the poles whereon (some say) the world is turned.*
Aissi. *as* Aissil.
Aissieu: m. *An axletree, &c. as* Aisseul.
Aissil: m. *A single, or shingle of wood, such as houses are, in some places, couered withall.*
Aistres. *as* Agiers.
Aitiologie: f. *A yeelding, or shewing, of a reason, or cause.*
Ajusté: m. ée: f. *Adiusted; Looke* Adjusté.
Ajuster. *To adiust; Looke* Adjuster.
Alabandique. pierre Alabandique. *A kind of black stone, mingled with purple.*
Alachi: m. ie: f. *Slackened; hung flagging; fallen downe by weakenesse out of it right place; decayed, quailed, faded, failed, growne feeble, or loose.*
Alachir. *To slacken; to hang flagging downeward; to slip, or fall downe, by weakenesse, out of it place; to quaile, fade, fayle, decay in strength; growe loose, feeble, weake.*
Alachissement: m. *A slackning; a loosenesse, or slacknesse; a quailing, a growing loose, or feeble; a flagging, or falling downe, through feeblenesse; a decaying, fading, or fayling in vigor, strength, force.*
Alaigre: com. *Cheerefull, blithe, iolly, merie, ioyfull, glad, buxome, iocond; also, nimble, actiue, lustie.*
Alaigre comme vn papillon. *As merie as a cricket (say we.)*
Alaigrement. *Cheerefully, iocondly, blithely, gladly, ioyfully; also, lustily, nimbly, actiuely.*
Alaigresse: f. *Alacritie, cheerefulnesse, mirth, or merinesse, iocondnesse, or ioyfulnesse of heart; lustinesse, nimblenesse,*
Alaigreté. *as* Alaigresse; *also, nimblenesse, actiuitie, readinesse, promptnesse.*
Alaine. *as* Haleine; *Breath, or breathing.*
De son alaine. *Of his faction, or side; that is of his owne humour, or applies himselfe to it; a bird of his owne feather.*
Alainer la langue. *To hold out the tongue, as a bird, or beast, that in extremitie of heat breathes for ayre.*
Alaire. *Seeke* Allaire.
Alaitté. *as* Allaicté.
Alambic. *as* Alembic; *A Limbeck, or stillitorie.*
Alambiqué. *Extracted, distilled, drawne out; also, worne, wasted, consumed.*
Alambiquer. *To extract, distill, draw out.*
s'Alambiquer. *To consume, wast, pine, weare away.*
Alampers. *A kind of Peach.*
Alan. *Seeke* Allan.
Alandäal. trocisque al. *A Trociske made of Coloquintida.*
Alangouri: m. ie: f. *Languishing, fainting, feeble; wearie; lazie, sluggish, lither; also, languished, fainted, infeebled; wearied.*
s'Alangourir. *To languish, faint, grow feeble, or wearie, faile in strength, decay in vigour; also, to grow lazie, sluggish, lither, idle.*
Alantir. *as* Allentir.
Alarme: m. *An Alarum.*
Alaterne: m. *Fruitlesse, or barren Priuet.*
Albacore. *A certaine fish in the Indian sea, which is verie good meat.*
Albanois. *An Albanian, an inhabitant of* Albania; *also, a light horseman wearing a high-crowned hat; or (more particularly) the Albanian light horse, imployed by Popes in their ordinarie garrisons.*
Albanois: m. oise: f. *Albanian; of* Albania; *belonging, or like, vnto an Albanian; and hence;*
Chapeau fait à l'Albanoise. *An hat with a crowne like a sugarlofe; an high-crowned hat.*
Albassan: m. *A kind of white and hard stone, whereof lime may be made.*
Albastre. *Alleblaster.*
Albastrin. *White as Alleblaster; like Alleblaster; of Alleblaster.*
Albazzan. *as* Albassan.
Albe. *as* Able.
Albereau: m. *A verie hard white free-stone, that resembles th'Albassan.*
Albergame. *The amorous apple, apple of loue, golden apple.*
Albergation. *A kind of alienation in fee farme, and for a fine, or income.*
Alberge. *A kind of small Peach.*
Alberger: m. *A kind of small Peach tree.*
Alberger. *To alien in fee farme; (as before in* Albergation.
Albette. *as* Ablette. ¶Rab.
Albrenner. *To hunt the yong wild Ducke, or the old one when she mootes; to go a ducking.*
Albrent: m. *A young wild Ducke; also, (a mooter, or moulter,) the old one when shee mootes, or hath cast her feathers; also, a Pochard; or, as* Sarcelle.
Albugine: f. *An extraordinarie, or vicious whitenesse in the eye; a whitish filme in, or ouer, an eye.*
Albugineux: m. euse: f. *Whitish, or resembling the white of an egge.*
Alcali. Sel Alcali. *Looke* Sel.
Alcange. *The hearbe Alcakengie, or Winter Cherrie.*
Alcharacte. *A Scorpion.* ¶Rab.
Alchechange, *or* Alchequange. *Alkakengie, red Nightshade, Winter Cherries.*
Alchermes. *A graine wherewith Crimzons are dyed; or, as* Alkermes.
Alchimille: f. *Lions foot, Ladies mantle, great Sanicle (an hearbe.)*
Alcibienne: f. *Vipers hearbe, Vipers Buglasse, Snakes buglasse,*

buglasse, the lesse wild buglasse.
Alcofribas. *A greedie glutton; a great deuourer.*
Alcoran: m. *Mahomets Alcoran; (The word signifies a true Law; and is therefore most vnfit for that most false one.)*
Alcret: m. *as* Halecret.
Alebastre. *Alleblaster.*
Alebastrin. *Of Alleblaster; white as, like or belonging to, Alleblaster.*
Alebrenne. *A Salamander.*
Alebromantie. *Diuination by barley meale mixed with wheat.*
Alectoire. *The Cocke stone; a Christall coloured stone (as big as a beane) found in the gyzerne, or maw of some Cockes.*
Alectorophoneme. *The song, or crowing of a Cocke.*
Alectryomantie: f. *Diuination by a Cocke; or by the Cocke stone.*
Alegerir. *To lighten, or make light.*
Alegerir vn cheval à la main. *To bring, or cause a horse to be light borne.*
Aleine. *as* Haleine.
Aleiner. *Seeke* Halener.
Aleman: m. *An Almaine, German, High-Dutchman; also, the Almaine, or German language.*
Peigne d'Aleman. *The hand; or foure fingers and a thumbe.*
Querelle d'Aleman. *A quarell, or brable, entred into vpon a sleight, or drunken, occasion.*
Theriaque des Alemans. *The iuyce of Ginepar berries, extracted according to art; called so, both because it is good against poison, & because the Germans haue vsed to take it much.*
Il n'en entend que le haut Aleman. *Tis Greek vnto him; he vnderstands no part of it; hee is neuer a whit the wiser by it.*
Alembic: m. *A Limbeck, or Stillitorie.*
Alembiqué: m. ée: f. *Distilled, or extracted, by Limbecke, &c; Seeke* Alambiqué.
Alembiquer. *To extract, or distill by Limbecke; or as* Alambiquer.
Alemelle d'espée. *as* Alumelle.
Alenois. Cresson Alenois. *Kers, garden Cresses, towne Kars, towne Cresses.*
Alenti: m. ie: f. *Slackened; loosened; softened; allayed, appeased; growne remisse; not so hastie, or violent as it was; also, weakened, enfeebled.*
Alentir. *To slacken, loosen; soften; be allayed, or appeased; wax tractable; grow remisse; or not so hastie, hard, nor violent as it was; also, to be weakened, or enfeebled.*
Alentissement: m. *A slackening; loosening, softening; allaying, appeasing; a weakening, enfeebling.*
Aleron. *A little wing; also, a twig, sprig, or smal branch.*
Alesne: f. *An awle; or (Shoomakers) bodkin; also a spotted, and long snowted Ray, or Thornebacke, tearmed by some, the sharpe-snowted Ray.*
Alesnes. *Cockle, Corne-rose, field Nigella, wild Nigella.*
Aleu: m. *Libertie, freedome, franchise, immunitie; also free tenure which holds of no man, and for which no seruice, nor fine is due to any; (it hath commonly the addition of,* franc; *and* franc-aleu *is also, a free subiect, or tenant.)*
Franc aleu noble. *High iurisdiction, and Seigniorie, held without homage, fealtie, fine, or seruice.*
Franc aleu roturier. *A tenure without iurisdiction (whereunto it is subiect) but otherwise (as the other) exempted from all seruices, rents, fines, &c.*

Aleve. *The wild Pine tree; so called in* Dauphinois.
Aleuf. *as* Aleu.
Alexandre. *Alexander; a proper name; also, the hearb great Parsley, Alexanders, or Alisaunders.*
Pied d'Alexandre. *The hearbe Bartrane, Bertrain, Pellitorie of* Spaine.
Alexandrin. *A verse of 12, or 13 sillables.*
Alexandrin: m. ine: f. *Of Alexandria, or belonging to Alexander.*
Persil Alexandrin. *The hearbe Alexanders.*
Alexitere. *A preseruation against poyson.*
Alezan. *A sorrell horse; or the sorrell colour of horses.*
Alezan toustade. *A darke reddish colour, as of mettall burnt in the fire; a burnt sorrell.*
Algame. *Mixtion of gold, and quicksiluer.*
Algarade: f. *An vnexpected incursion, assault, or brauadoe of horsemen, seamen, or other souldiours against their enemies; any swaggering and sudden florish, rauage, tumult, vprore.*
'Algarie: f. *A kind of instrument wherewith Chirurgians prouoke vrine; some tearme it, a Catheter.*
Alge: f. *Sea-weed, sea-grasse, Reets; a kind of wrinckled, and broad leaued weed, that grows on rocks in the sea.*
Algebre: f. *The art of Equation; or of figuratiue numbers; an Art consisting both of Arithmetick and Geometrie; also, a breach, fracture, diuision, solution of continuitie, especially in bones.*
Algisé. *The Lote, or Nettle tree.*
Algorisme: m. *The Art, or vse of Cyphers, or of numbring by Cyphers; Arithmetick, or a curious kind therof.*
Fol d'Algorisme. *A foole by figure, an Asse in grain.*
Algousant: m. *A Lieutenant.*
Alhatrat *(In* Rabelais, *is* Auicennaes Alhatraf) *a Dragon, or Serpent, whose biting wounds, but impoisons not.*
Alhidade. *as* Alidade.
Aliage. m. *The stiffening, allaying, or imbacing of gold, or siluer, by mingling them with other mettals.*
Aliayre. *The hearbe, called Iack of the hedge; Looke* Alliaire.
Alibi. *The being in another place then was obiected.*
Alleguer son alibi. *A prisoner to alledge for his iustification his being elswhere when the fact was committed.*
Alibi-forains. *Crafty shifts, cunning euasions, or appeals, vsed for the auoiding of an accusation, or delaying of an action.*
Alibis forains. ¶Rab. *All the corners.*
Aliboron. *A Polypragmon, medler; busie-bodie; one that hath his hand in euery dish, an oare in euery boat; also, one that pretends skill in all things, and indeed knowes nothing.*
Alicacubut. *The hearbe Alkakengie, or winter cherrie.*
Alican. Bossu alican. *Looke* Bossu.
Alicté. *In bed, layed a bed; bedred.*
Alictement. *A lying sicke in bed; a lying bedred.*
s'Alicter. *A sicke man to get himselfe to bed; or to lye sicke in bed; or to lye bedred.*
Alidade d'un Astrolabe. *Th'Albidada of an Astrolabe; the rule which turneth on the backe thereof.*
Alié: m. ée: f. *Allayed, or stiffened, as gold, or siluer, by other mettals.*
Alienation: f. *An alienation; a selling, putting, or making away of; also, an estranging, turning, or withdrawing from.*
Aliené: m. ée: f. *Aliened; alienated, altered; sold, or made away; estranged, or withdrawne from.*
Aliené de son entendement. *Distraught, franticke, sick-braind, out of his little wits.*
Aliener. *To alien; alienate; alter; to sel, put, passe, or make away;*

away; also, to estrange, turne, draw, or withdraw from.
Alier tremaillé. *A Trammell net, or double net.*
Alier. *To allay; to stiffen, or imbase gold, &c, by mingling it with other mettals. Looke* Allier.
Aligné: m. ée: f. *Made straight, as a line; set in a iust, and direct file, or line; drawne, or squared out by line, and leuell.*
Homme bien aligné. *Well featured, well shapen, well proportioned, as straight as a line.*
Alignement: m. *A card, a draught, or thing drawne by line and leuell; also, a peece of ground in a street, or by the side of a high way, let by a lord vnto his tenant, (to be inclosed, or built on) by line and measure, to the end that the publique may not be incroached on; also, a making straight as a line; a setting in a iust line; a drawing, or squaring out by line, and leuell; also, the ligning of a bitch, &c.*
Aligner. *To make straight as a line; place in direct file, set in a iust line; draw or square out by line and leuell; also, to ligne, as a dog, or the dog wolfe, a bitch; also, to ioyne, or couple one plant vnto another, by graffing, &c.*
Aliment: m. *Food, sustenance, nourishment.*
Alimenté. *Fed, nourished, sustained, fostered, dietted, cherished.*
Alimenter. *To feed, nourish, diet, sustaine, foster, cherish.*
Alimenteux: m. euse: f. *Much feeding, very nourishing, full of nourishment.*
Alimonner. *To put into, or fasten vnto, the thill of a cart, &c.*
Alipte: m. *He that, in old time, annoynted wrastlers before they exercised.*
Aliqualement. *Indifferently, after a sort, so so.*
Alis: m. ise: f. *Solide, compacted, hard wrought, close layed together; in which there appeare no maner of holes, or pores.*
Alise: f. *The (sweet and wholsome) fruit, or berrie of the Lote tree; also as* Alize.
Alisier: m. *The Lote, or Nettle tree.*
Alisier gris. *The gray Lote.*
Alisier rouge. *The red Lote; both (and all the kindes thereof) strangers in England.*
Aliter. *as* Alicter.
Alize. *Any solide, well compacted, or close wrought thing.*
Alkali. *A medicinable salt made of the ashes of diuers sorts of hearbes, but most especially of Glassewort. Looke* Sel.
Alkatim. *The most eminent part of the buttockes.* ¶Rab.
Alkerenge. *The hearbe Nightshade, or Alkakengie.*
Alkermes. *A confection made of the decoction, and infusion of silke into the iuice of the graine* chermes; *(a soueraigne remedie for all swondings.*
Allagant. *Washing, watering.*
Allaicté: m. ée: f. *Suckled; fed with milke.*
Allaictement: m. *A giuing of sucke, or milke vnto.*
Allaicter. *To sucke; to giue sucke, or milke vnto.*
Allaire. *A little walk, or alley, in a wood; or, a tree growing therein.*
Allambre. *Copper. (In Spanish.)*
Allan: m. *A kind of big, strong, thicke headed, and short snowted dog; the brood whereof came first out of* Albania, *(old* Epirus.*)*
Allan de boucherie. *Is like our Mastiue, and serues Butchers, to bring in fierce oxen, and to keepe their stalls.*
Allan gentil. *Is like a Grayhound in all properties, and parts, his thicke and short head excepted.*
Allan vautre. *A great, & ougly curre of that kind (hauing a big head, hanging lips, and slowching eares) kept onely to bait the Beare, and wild Boare.*
Allanguir. *To make languish, pine, or wast away.*
Allant: m. *A goer, a gadder; also, a subtile, craftie, wilie; or, a cousening, deceitfull, cheating, fellow.*
Allant: m. ante: f. *Going, walking, wending, pacing, marching, trauelling, iourneying; proceeding, departing.*
Allantoïde. Membrane al. *Looke* Membrane.
Allarme: m. *An alarum.*
Allarmé: m. ée: f. *Roused, or affrighted, by an Alarum.*
Allarmer. *To giue an Alarum vnto; also, to rouse, prepare, or affright, by Alarums.*
s'Alaschir. *as* s'Alachir.
Allayé: m. ée: f. *Allayed; stiffened, or imbased, as gold, or siluer (coyne) by the mixture of other mettals.*
Or allayé au blanc, ou sur le blanc. *Gold allayed with siluer.*
Or allayé au rouge, ou sur le rouge. *Gold allayed with copper.*
Allayer. *To allay, or mix gold, or siluer with baser mettals.*
Alle: f. *(The old drinke of England) Ale. Seeke* Alles.
Allé: m. ée: f. *Gone, walked, went, iourneyed, departed.*
C'est bien allé. *Matters are in good tearmes; the businesse goes well forward, goes well on.*
Alleage: m. *as* Aliage.
Alleboteur: m. *A grape gleaner.*
Allebouter. *To rake, gather, or gleane after; Looke* Halleboter.
Allebrent. *as* Albrent.
Allechant. *Bayting, alluring, tempting, inueagling, inticing.*
Allecher. *Looke* Allicher.
Allecter. *To wamble, as a queasie stomacke doth.*
Allée: f. *A going, walking, wending, pacing; a gate, walke, iourney, march, pace; also, an alley, gallerie; walke, walking place, path, or passage.*
Il eut l'allée pour le venir. *Hee got his trauell for his paines; he might euen as well haue stayed.*
Allegation: f. *An allegation, alleadgement, alleadging.*
Allege: m. *An ease, lightning, disburdenment, easement, helpe towards the bearing of a burthen; a refreshment; asswagement; comfort, solace; any thing that lightens, or lessens a charge, care, griefe, or mischiefe.*
Allege: f. *A lyter (boat.)*
Allegé: m. ée: f. *disburdened, lightened, eased; helped; refreshed; asswaged; mitigated; solaced; also, lessened, diminished, extenuated.*
Allegeance. *as* Allege.
Allegement: m. *A lightning, disburdening, easing; a lifting vp, or helping to beare, a thing that lyes heauie on; a refreshing; asswaging; mitigating; allaying; solacing; also, a lessening, or impayring of.*
Alleger. *To lighten, disburden; ease, or discharge, of part of a burthen; to lift vp, or helpe to beare, a loade; to refresh, asswage, mitigate, allay; solace; also, to lessen, diminish, extenuate.*
Allegorie: f. *An Allegorie.*
Allegorique: com. *Allegoricall.*
Allegoriser. *To allegorize it; To vse Allegories.*

Allegué: m. ée: f. *Alleadged; produced, uttered, brought forth.*
Alleguer. *To alleadge; to urge, or produce reasons, arguments, euidence, or authoritie for the proofe of.*
Alleinée: f. *A breath, ayre, puffe; a breathing, or puffing.*
Allelyon: m. *A little spread Eagle, or other bird, in blazon, wanting beake, feet, and legs.*
Alleman. *Looke* Aleman.
Allenée. *as* Alleinée.
Allentir. *as* Alentir.
Aller. *To goe, walke, wend, march, pace, tread; proceed, iourney, trauell, depart.*
Aller par ambages, ou en ambagoye. *To use many circumstances, to goe about the bush.*
Aller en appoinctant. *as* Aller en poincte.
Aller à S. Bezet. *To rest in no place; continually to trot, gad, wander up and downe.*
Aller au change. *Looke* Change.
Aller de cholere contre quelqu'un. *To raile upon, inueigh against.*
Aller au deuant de. *To preuent; meet; present himselfe before.*
Aller au deuant par derriere. *To take a wrong, to go a contrarie, course.*
Aller à l'encontre. *To resist, withstand, repugne; also, to meet.*
Aller à l'entour du pot. *To use idle circumstances, needlesse ceremonies; we say, to go about the bush.*
Aller eschais. *To shale, to straddle.*
Aller par escuelles, tout y va par escuelles. *There is cheere in bowles; or, the house is throwne out at the windowes.*
Aller d'une fesse. Il n'y va que d'une fesse. *Hee workes by halues; he goes but slackly, or unwillingly, to worke.*
Aller de guet à ses affaires. *To go slowly, or sleepily about his businesse.*
Aller long. *To haue a squirt, to squatter out behind.*
Au long aller. *At length; in continuance, or processe of time, after much ado.*
Aller aux meures sans crochet. *Looke* Meure.
Aller du pair auec. *To goe cheeke by iowle with; to equall, match, keepe play, hold tacke, with.*
Aller & parler. Il sçait aller, & parler. *He is an industrious, discreet, well-behaued person; he knowes when to speake, how to carrie himselfe; any imployment fits, any fashion becomes, him.*
Aller le pas. *To pace it, or goe a foot-pace.*
Aller à pas menu. *To tread gingerly, to mince it like a maid.*
Aller de l'un pied sur l'autre. *To affect, or mince it, in gate, pace, or treading.*
Aller du pied comme un chat maigre. *To be swift, or light, affoot; also, to tread softly, or gingerly.*
Aller en poincte. *To grow lesse and lesse; to lessen towards the top, as a spire, Pyramides &c.*
Aller quant & quant quelqu'un. *To hold equall pace; or, go cheeke by iowle, with.*
Aller à la raison. *To incline unto reason, to speake somewhat reasonably.*
Aller à la rengette. pour se laisser al. *For running riot, flying out; for giuing her lustfull appetite more scope than became her; for playing a whoorish tricke or two.*
Aller aux requestes. *Looke* Requeste.
Aller en rond. *To turne round, or wheele about; also, to be of a round forme.*
Aller au saffran. *To fall to decay, to grow bankrupt in estate, to go downe the weather.*
Aller de plus grande singlée. *A Shippe to make the greater way, or to beare the more sayles, for speed.*
Aller tousjours son train. *To keep alwayes one place; to hold on the old course still.*
Aller à travers champs. *To wander; to goe roaming out of the high, out of the road, out of the right, way.*
Aller à la veuë. *To goe lodge a Bucke, or harbour a Stagge; (mornings worke for woodmen.)*
Au fort, ou, au pis aller. *At worst, if the worst fall out, and the worst come to the worst.*
Au long aller. *Seeke* Aller long.
Au mieulx aller. *Howsoeuer, whatsoeuer fall out; or, at the best, although the best befall.*
Au par aller. *At the length.*
S'en aller. *To depart, flit, auoid, be gone; also, as* Aller.
S'en aller au haut & au long. *To runne his Countrey.*
S'en aller à la moustarde. Tout le monde s'en va à la moustarde. *Tis common vulgar, divulged all the world ouer; (of a booke) wast paper is made of it, mustard pots are stopped with it, (so much the world esteemes it.)*
S'en aller de paire. Ie m'en uay de paire. *I will be unlaid againe.*
S'en aller à un. *To agree, consent, accord; to come all to one.*
On s'en peut bien aller. *You may be gone, you may depart when you will; you may goe shake your eares; the matter is dispatched, our businesse at an end, here is no more to be done.*
Il m'y va de. *It touches, or concernes; it depends upon, my.*
Aller & parler peut on, boire & manger non: Pro. *One may visit a friend sometimes, but must not if hee looke to bee welcome (another time) stay long with him.*
Aller & venir font le chemin peler: Pro. *Much trauelling makes bad wayes.*
C'est grand peine d'aller à cheval, & une mort d'aller à pied: Prov. *Tis a great trouble to ride, and a death to foot it. (Some lazie fellow, belike, inuented this prouerbe.)*
Va ou tu peux, meurs ou tu dois: Pro. *Trauel whither thou canst, but dye where thou oughtest; see as many countries as thou wilt, so thou dye in thine owne.*
Ainsi va qui mieux ne peut: Prov. *He poorely goes that cannot richly goe; hee barely liues that cannot brauely liue; euen so goes he that cannot better goe.*
Il ne va pas du tout à honte qui de demie voye retourne: Prov. *He neuer goes through for shame, that turned backe when he was halfe way.*
Qui va il lesche, qui repose il seiche: Prov. *He that bestirres him gets somewhat, whereas he that lyes still doth starue.*
Qui n'y va n'y chet: Prov. *He incurres no daunger that comes not where tis; come not among blows, your skin will be whole ynough.*
Qui par tout va par tout prend: Prov. *He that goes far gaines much.*
Alleran. *as* Alezan.
Allerion. *as* Allelyon.
Alles. Ils eurent alles. *They had a reputation; or, they passed*

passed currantly.

Alleud: m. Free hold, free tenure; as Aleu; also, inheritance that comes freely, and by discent, not by purchace; and which one leaues, or may leaue, vnto his heire.

Alleuf. as Aleu; ¶Poicteuin.

Alleure: f. as Allure.

Alleut. A free hold, or free tenure; or, as Alleud.

Alleutier. A free holder, or, free tenant.

Alleyer. A Marchant to declare (vpon his oath) vnto a Toll-gatherer, through whose libertie he passes, what, & how much, ware, and chaffer he caries along with him. ¶Gasc.

Alliage: m. as Aliage.

Alliaire. Sauce alone, Iacke of the hedge; (an hearbe.)

Alliance: f. Alliance; confederation, fellowship, combination; agreement, consent; a league of friendship.

Alliances. Gimmoules, or Gimmoule-rings.

Alliance Theutonique. The Companie, or Corporation of Marchants of the Hanse.

Alliché: m. ée: f. Allured, inueagled, inticed, tempted, drawne, tolled, or brought on by flattering, and faire meanes.

Allichement: m. An allurement, inueaglement, inticement, bait; a temptation, or flatterie; or, an alluring, inticing, inueagling, tempting, drawing on by flattering meanes.

Allicher. To allure, inueagle, intice, tempt, toll, draw on, bring vnto, by flatterie, or faire meanes.

Allichoir. as Allichement; (in the first sence.)

Allidade. as Alidade.

Allie: m. An allie, kinsman; confederate; a companion, mate, associate; also, an accessarie, or fellow in an offence.

Allié: m. ée: f. Allied; confederate with; ioyned, coupled, knit, neere vnto in fellowship, and friendship; also, accessarie, or, as farre in as another; also, allayed, or stiffened; as gold, &c.

Allier. To allie, ioyne, knit, couple in fellowship, and friendship; to associate, accord, confederate together; also, as Alier; to stiffen, or mingle gold, or siluer with other mettals.

Allignée: f. A Vine tyed to, or coupled with, an Elme tree, braunch, or stake.

Allignement. as Alignement.

Alligner. as, Aligner.

Allitti: m. ie: f. Bedred; or, layd sicke in bed.

Allochons d'un rouët. The teeth, or toothing, of a wheele, in a clocke, &c.

Allode: f. Free possession, free tenure; or, as Alleud.

Allodial. terres allodiales. Free lands, for which no rents, fines, nor seruices are due; of whose soyle there is no lord; which are held immediatly from God; (yet are they (vnlesse they be noble) subiect vnto iurisdiction.)

Alloigné: m. ée: f. Driuen, chased; gone, got, farre from, or farre before.

Alloigner. To chase, or driue farre from, or before.

s'alloigner de sa maison. To abandon, or get far from his house.

Allonge. as Alongement.

Allongement; &, Allonger; as Alongement, & Alonger.

Allotement: m. A parting, diuiding; an allotting, or laying out, vnto euery one his part.

Allotir. To diuide, or part; to allot, or lay out, vnto euery one his part.

Allou. as, Allodial; ¶Namur.

Alloué. as Alleut; also, a Seneschals Lieutenant.

Allouër. To allow, aduow, approue, like well of.

Allouette. Seeke, Alouëtte.

Allouvi: m. ie: f. As hungrie as a Wolfe; also, fleshed, or, cruell, as a Wolfe.

Alloyandier. ¶Rab. A roster of short ribbes of beefe; seeke Aloyau.

Alloyé: m. ée: f. Seeke Allayé.

Allumé: m. ée: f. Lighted, kindled, set on fire, or on a flame.

Allumelle. Seeke Alumelle.

Allumement: m. A lighting, a kindling, inflaming, a setting on a flame.

Allumer. To lighten, kindle, set on a fire, or on a flame.

Vieilles amours, & vieux tisons s'allument en toutes saisons: Prov. Old loue and brands are kindled in all seasons.

Allume-sang. Bloud-inflaming.

Allumetier: m. A maker, or seller, of matches for tinder-boxes.

Allumettes: f. Matches for tinder-boxes.

Allumeur: m. A kindler, inflamer, or setter on fire.

Allure: f. A gate, pace, traine, treading, or going.

D'une allure. At once; at one, or of equall, length, or motion; also, with one continued gate, motion; breath, or length.

Allusion: f. An allusion, or likening; an alluding, or applying of one thing vnto another.

Alluvion: f. A still increase, rising, or swelling of waters, which in time, and by degrees, growes to a deluge, or inundation.

Alluz. All out; or, a carouse fully drunke vp.

Almadie: f. as Almande; A kind of boat.

Almanach: m. An Almanacke, or Prognostication.

petits Almanacs. The flowers called Pinks.

Almande: f. An Amande; Also, a little, narrow, and long boat, made of the barke of a tree; and in vse among the sauages of Africke, and India.

Almandine: f. A certaine stone like a Rubie; or a Rubie of the coursest; (for it is much browner in the eye, and rougher in handling, then the best.)

Alme: com. Faire, beautifull, cleere; calme; gracious, propitious; nourishing.

Alme-beau. Goodly, gracious; most cleere, most beautifull, fairely-propitious.

Almicantarat. as Almucantarath. ¶Rab.

Almoire. An ambrie; cup-boord; box. Looke Armoire.

Almucantaraths. Are, in an Astrolabe, certaine circles denoting the heights that be aboue our Hemisphere.

Alocation. An allocation, placing; fitting with, setting in, a place.

Alo; & Alod; as Aleu; ¶Lang.

Alode. Free possession, free tenure.

Alodial. as Allodial.

Aloë: m. as Aloës.

Aloë: f. A Larke.

Aloës: m. The hearbe Aloes, sea houseleeke, sea aigreene; also, the bitter iuice thereof congealed, and vsed in Purgations.

Aloës Cicotrin. The best, most liuer-coloured, most cleere, and most transparent kind of Aloes; called so, of th'Island Succotora, whence it comes.

Aloës hepatique. Looke, Hepatique.

Aloës de vessie: as Aloës Cicotrin; Tearmed so, because it is ordinarily kept in bladders.

Bois d'aloës. The sweet, and precious wood called, Lignum Aloës.

Alogique: com. Vnreasonable, imprudent, inconsiderat.

Aloine.

Aloine. *as* Alvine.
Alonge: m. *as* Alongement.
des alonges. *Haukes Lunes.*
Alongé: m. ée: f. *Lengthened; extended, wire-drawn; prolonged, delayed, driuen off.*
Alongeail: m. *as* Alongement.
Alongement: m. *A lengthning, drawing out in length, extension, prolonging, delaying, driuing off.*
Alonger. *To lengthen, draw out in length, extend, wire-draw, prolong, proroge, deferre, delay, driue off.*
Alonger la courroye. *To lengthen out a matter, to prolong a suit.*
Alonger les estriers. *Looke* Estrier.
Alonger les ss. *To play false in accompts; as, to set downe an* f *(which stands for a* franc*) in stead of an* ſ, *which stands but for a* sol.
Alongissement. *as* Alongement.
Alopecie. *The foxes euill; a disease causing the haire of the head, or beard to fall of.*
Alors. adverb. *Then; at that time.*
Alose: f. *A Shad (fish.)*
Aloser. *To colour, or cloake a matter.*
Aloud. franc al. *as* Aleu. ¶Bourgongnois.
Alouër. *as* Allouër; *Also to let out to hire; also, to appoint, or set downe a proportion for expence, or for any other imployment.*
Alouette. *A Larke.*
Alouette de la gorge. *The flap that couers the top of the wind-pipe.*
Alouette huppée. *as* Cocheuis.
Alouette de mer. *The little sea foule called, a Purre.*
Alouette de pré. *The chit, or small meddow-larke.*
Petite alouëtte. *as* Alouette de pré.
Pied d'alouette. *The hearbe, larks spurre, larks claw, larks heele, larks toes, Monks hood.*
Donner la bourde de l'alouette. *To misse-lead, or traine along from the place he would find; (from the larke, which euer flies fromward her neast, when shee sees any bodie eyes her.)*
Il pense que les alouettes luy tomberont en la bouche toutes rosties; *He vainely thinkes, that good fortune will come a wooing to him.*
Alourdi: m. ie: f. *Dulled, besotted, made blockish.*
Alourdir. *To dull, besot, make blockish.*
s'Alouser. *To praise, or commend himselfe; to brag, or boast, of himselfe.*
Aloy: m. *Th'allay of gold, or siluer, coyne; the (mixed) matter, or mettall whereof it is made; also, fine bell-mettall; also, a kind of larke; also, as* Aleu.
Aloyau de bœuf. *A short rib of beefe, or the fleshie end of the rib, diuided from the rest, and rosted; a little piece of (rosted) beefe hauing a bone in it.*
Aloyne. *as* Alvine..
Alozer. *as* Alouser; *(An old word.)*
Alpes. *The Alpes; the mountaines which are betweene France, and Italie.*
Alpestre: com. *Mountainous, craggie, wild, hillie.*
Alphe: m. *A morphue, or stayning of the skin.*
Alphitomantie. *Diuination by barley meale.*
Alphonsin. *A coyne of gold, worth about seuen shillings Sterl.*
Alquemie. *Alchumie, Alcumistrie.*
Faire l'alquemie des dentes, ou, auec les dents. *To fast.*
Alquequanges. *The hearbe Night-shade, Alkakengie, Winter-cherries.*
Alte. *as* Halte.
Alteratif: m. iue: f. *Thirst-breeding, thirst-increasing.*
Alteration: f. *An alteration, change, or changing; also, thirst, or drouth.*
Altercateur. *A brabler, brawler, brangler, wrangler, contentious, or litigious person.*
Altercation: f. *Altercation; brabling, brawling, wrangling, brangling; strife, debate, contention in wordes; contentious proceeding, litigious pleading of one against another.*
Altere: m. *A poise of lead, which dauncers on ropes hold in their hands for a counterpeise; also, a piece of lead to lift vp, for exercise.*
Alteré: m. *The spotted, and small-headed Viper* Dipsas, *whose biting causeth an extreame, and vnquenchable thirst.*
Alteré: m. ée: f. *Altered, changed, varied, different from what it was; falsified, sophisticated; also, drie, athirst, almost dried vp; also, extreamely passionat, exceedingly angred, or moued; in a chafe, in a fume.*
Alterer. *To alter, change, varie, turne from what it was; also, to adulterate, falsifie, sophisticate; also, to breed, or increase thirst, or drouth; to make drie, or adrie; to drie vp.*
s'alterer. *To grow drie, or athirst; also, to fall in a chafe, or grow into choler.*
Alteres: f. *Vehement passions of the mind; strange, and doubtfull conceits floating in the thoughts; also, diuine furie; or, inspirations from aboue, rauishing, and transporting the spirit out of her proper seat; extasies, transportations of spirit.*
Alternatif: m. iue: f. *Alternatiue, interchangeable, succeeding in course, done by turnes, or immediatly one after another.*
Alternation: f. *An alternation; a succession by turne; an interchange; a variation of one immediately after another.*
Alternativement. *Interchangeably; by course, or turns, one presently after another; one in the necke of another; one for another.*
Alterner. *To interchange, to doe by course, or turnes.*
Alterquer. *To brabble, wrangle, brawle, chide, brangle, contend in words; to plead one against another.*
Altesse: f. *Highnesse; (the title of a Soueraigne, Duke, or Prince.)*
Altier: m. ere: f. *Proud, loftie, stately, disdainefull, haughtie.*
Altitonant. *Thundering from high, or from aboue.*
Alveole. *The pit, or hollow part of the iaw, whereinto a tooth is fastened.*
Aluette. *The Vuula; a little piece of flesh in the roofe of the mouth, like a cockes spurre; See* Gargatte.
Alueux, ou Aluex. *as* Aleu.
Alvine: f. *Wormewood; Looke* Absynthe *for the seuerall kinds thereof.*
Alvineux: m. euse: f. *Bitter as Wormewood; of Wormwood; full of, or fraught with, Wormewood.*
Alumelle: f. *The blade of a sword, or knife.*
Alumette. *Seeke* Allumette.
Alumineux: m. euse: f. *Full of Allum; belonging vnto Allum.*
Eau allumineuse. *Allum water.*
Alun: m. *Allum.*
Alun d'escaille. *A kind of Allum thats made of the transparent stone called,* Miroir d'Asne.
Alun de glace. *Roche Allum; See* Glace.
Alun de plume. *A hard, and white Allum, full of streakes, or flakes; we call it, stone Allum, or itching pouder; Looke* Plume.
Alun saccharin. *That is as white as sugar; or, as*

Alun succrin.

Alun succrin. *An Allum compounded of Rose water, whites of egges, and roche Allum; Italian women vse it much in their cleansing, or whitening, imployments.*

Aluté: m. ée: f. *Bedaubed, beplaistered, bemyred, or besmeared all ouer with clay, durt, or loame.*

Aluyne: f. *Wormewood.*

Aluyne Pontique; & Romaine; *as* Absynthe Pontique, & Romaine.

Petite aluyne. *Sea Wormewood; especially the white one; and that which is called Sothernwood Wormewood.*

Alys. *Smooth, sleeke, polished; an old word.*

Alysson. *The hearbe Madwort, Moonewort, healedog.*

Alzan. *as* Alezan.

Alzatin. ¶Rab. *The fat cawle, or kell, wherein the bowels are lapt.*

Amadées: m. *A certaine Order of Cordeliers, or gray friers.*

Amadis. Pinsegreneur d'Amadis. *A neat, spruce, affecting speaker.*

Amadizé: m. ée: f. *Quaint, spruce, affected, prankt with fine words, full of gay tearmes.*

Amadoüé. *Flattered, smoothed; woon, or inueagled by pleasing tearmes; pacified, or appeased with good, or faire, words.*

Amadoüement: m. *A flattering, smoothing, inueagling, tickling, or lulling asleepe the mind and affection with pleasing tearmes; a pacifying, appeasing, or sweetning of an angrie, or harsh spirit, with good words.*

Amadoüer. *To flatter, to smooth, to gloze with; to allure, intice, inueagle, win, with flattering speeches; to tickle, delight, or lull asleepe the mind, and affection with pleasing tearmes; also, to sweeten, or appease a harsh, or angrie spirit with faire words.*

Amadoüeur: m. *A flatterer, smoother, glozer, faire speaker.*

Amafrose. *Blindnesse caused by the obturation of the Opticke sinew.*

Amaigri: m. ie: f. *Macerated; made, or growne leane, meagre, thinne, slender; shrunke, fallen away.*

Amaigrir. *To macerate, make leane, meagre, thin.*

s'amaigrir. *To grow leane, wax meagre, shrinke, or fall in flesh, fall away.*

Amainer. *To strike sayle; (a sea tearme.)*

s'Amaisonner. *To lodge, house, or harbour himselfe.*

s'Amalader. *To fall sicke.*

Amalgame. *A mixture, or incorporation of quick siluer with other mettals.*

Amalgamer. *To mix, or incorporate, &c; a Chimicall tearme.*

Amanché. *as* Emmanché.

Amande: f. *An Almond; also, the kernell of a plumstone, cherry-stone, &c.*

Amandé: m. ée: f. *Of Almonds; mingled, or seasoned with Almonds.*

Amandier. *An Almond tree.*

Amandin. *A kind of reddish marble.*

Amanite. *The name of a wholesome toadstoole.*

Amanoté: m. ée: f. *Manacled; also, furnished with a handle.*

Amanoter. *To manacle; to handfast, or bind the hands fast, with manacles.*

Amantelé: m. ée: f. *Cloaked; couered with a cloake, or mantle; Seeke* Emmentelé.

Amaphrose. *as,* Amafrose.

Amaranthe: f. *The flower gentle, Floreamour, Flower valure, purple veluet flower.*

Amareur: f. *as* Amaritude.

Amaritude: f. *Bitternesse; also, extreame harshnesse; extreame anguish.*

Amarrage: m. *The great cordage, or tackle of a ship.*

Amarré. *Moored; fastened, bound, or tied fast with great ropes.*

Amarrer. *To tye, bind, fasten, or make fast with cables, or great ropes; to moore.*

Amarres: f. *Great anchor-cables; or, ground Tackle.*

Amarri: m. *The wombe, or matrix of a woman.*

Amas: m. *A heape, or pile; a great number, sort, crue, rout; also, a Moone-calfe, or Tympanie in a womans wombe; as* Mole.

Amase. *A messuage, or tenement.* ¶Wallon.

Amasé: m. ée: f. *Housed, or hauing a tenement on it.*

Amasement: m. *A messuage, tenement, building.*

Amassé: m. ée: f. *Piled, heaped, gathered together; also, taken vp, or, stooped for.*

Amassement: m. *A collection; a heaping, or gathering together; a piling one vpon another; also, a taking, or gathering vp.*

Amasse-miel. *Honnie-getting, sweets-gathering.*

Amasser. *To pile, heape; gather, collect together; also, to take vp; also to stoope for.*

s'amasser. *To assemble, meet, or swarme, together in troupes.*

Amasser la disme de l'ail. *To be well and soundly cudgelled; or, to doe that for which he is sure of a cudgelling; (a* Poicteuin *phrase.)*

On ne sçait pour qui on amasse: Pro. *Men know not who shall spend their gettings, or, God onely knowes who shall enioy those heapes.*

Amasseresse: f. *A woman that piles, heapes, gathers; takes vp, or stoopes for.*

Amasseur: m. *A piler, heaper, gatherer; a taker vp of, or stooper for, things.*

à pere amasseur fils gaspilleur: Prov. *See* Pere.

Mieux vaut bon gardeur que bon amasseur: Pro. *A warie keeper is better than a carefull getter.*

Amastiné: m. ée: f. *Made, or become dogged, surly, churlish, currish.*

s'Amastiner. *To become dogged, surly, currish, churlish.*

Amateur. *A louer, affecter; wooer; an amorous companion.*

Amathyste. *The precious stone called an Amatist.*

Amati: m. ie: f. *Mated, amated, quayled, abated, allayed; decayed; mortified; faded, vpon withering; also, enured, accustomed, trained vp vnto.*

Amatir. *To enure, accustome, traine vp vnto; or, as* Ematir; *to mate, amate, &c.*

Amatrice: f. *An Amatrix, a she louer.*

Amaurote. *A Moore, or one of Mauritania.*

Amazé. *as* Amasé.

Ambages, *or* Ambageois. *Ambages; circuits, compasses, or circumstances in wordes; a going about the bush.*

Ambagieux: m. euse: f. *Full of ambages, or friuolous circumstances.*

Ambagoye. Aller en ambagoye; *Seeke* Aller.

Amballage: m. *Package; Looke* Emballage.

Ambarvales: m. *Rogation, or Gang, weekes; religious feasts, or walkes, wherein the fruits of the earth are prayed for.*

Ambassade: f. *An Embassage, an Embassie, an Embassadorship; also, a troupe, or companie of ioint Embassadors sent together from a Prince.*

Am-

Ambassadeur. *An Embassadour.*
Ambe. *With, together with, in companie of.* ¶Gasc.
Ambezatz. *Ambes ace, or two aces at dice.*
Ayant faict ambezatz. *Hauing buttered the connie; hauing had that chaunce that no wise man would nicke.*
Ambi. *A certaine woodden instrument of two peeces, vsed for the putting of a shoulder into ioynt.*
Ambier. *To goe;* (Barrag;) *also, to compasse, or goe about; also, to sue for an Office, labour for promotion, canuas for a place.*
Ambigu: m. üe: f. *Ambiguous, doubtfull, vncertaine, double; which may be taken in diuers sences, or diuers wayes.*
Ambigüement. *Ambiguously; doubtfully, vncertainely; of diuers sences, with double vnderstanding.*
Ambigüité: f. *Ambiguitie; doubtfulnesse, vncertainetie.*
Ambitieux: m. euse: f. *Ambitious; greedie of honors; desirous of promotion.*
Ambition: f. *Ambition; excessiue desire of honor, preferment, or promotion.*
Amblant. *Ambling, pacing, racking.*
Amble: f. *An amble, pace, racke; an ambling, or racking pace; a smooth, or easie gate.*
Aller l'amble, ou, les ambles; *as* Ambler.
Mettre aux ambles. *To make a man readie to doe, or speake, a thing before he know, or be aware, how he was drawne vnto it; also, to bring to reason, or persuade vnto reasonable tearmes, one, that before was froward, or vnreasonable.*
Et plus la mettoit en cett' amble. *And put her more into that humor, or, set her forward in that veine.*
Il y perdit les ambles. *That madded him, or made him loose all patience; also, that was beyond his reach, out of his proper element.*
Ambler. *To amble, pace, racke; to go easily, and smoothly away.*
Ambligone. *A blunt angle; or, a triangle one of whose angles are blunt.*
Ambliopie: f. *Dulnesse, or dimnesse of sight.*
Ambouchouer. *Seeke* Embouchouer.
Ambre: m. *Amber.*
Ambre blanc. *White Amber; one kind therof (thrown by the floating sea on the Pruthian shore) which being giuen to drinke, in wine, vnto a fasting wench, will force her to pisse, if she haue lost her maidenhead.*
Ambre crud. *Raw Amber; Amber as it growes, or as it is, before it be prepared, polished, and made transparent (by the fat of a sucking Pig.)*
Ambre gris. *Ambergreece, or gray Amber; (the best kind of Amber) vsed in perfumes.*
Ambre noir. *Blacke Amber (the worst kind of Amber) vsually mingled with Aloes, Labdanum, Storax, and such like aromaticall simples, for Pomander chains, &c.*
Ambre de Patenostres. *Bead-amber; the ordinarie yellow Amber.*
Ambroisie. *Ambrosia; the food of the gods.*
Ambrosie: f. *The same; also, the hearbe called Oke of* Cappadocia; *and another, called Oke of* Ierusalem.
Ambrum. (Rab.) *Seeke* Lambrum.
Ambulatif: m. iue: f. *Ambulatiue; euer walking, or stirring on each side; whence;*
Vlcere ambulatif. *An vlcer, which continually spreading it selfe, gnaws, frets, and consumes the sound parts next vnto it.*
Ambulatoire: com. *Ambulatorie; vnsetled, remouing from place to place; whence;*
Parlement ambulatoire. *The Iudges circuit; or, a Court, or Terme, that oft remoues.*
Ame: f. *The soule, or spirit; also, a spirit, or ghost; also, the mould that is within the bore of Artillerie when tis cast.*
Ameiller. *To milke; or sucke.*
Amelette. *A little prettie soule.*
Amelioré: m. ée: f. *Bettered, improoued, mended; amended, recouered.*
Ameliorement: m. *A bettering, mending, improuing; amending, recouering.*
Ameliorer. *To better, mend, improue; amend, reforme, recouer.*
Amelot. *A kind of small bitter-sweet apple.*
Amenage: m. *Carriage; or, the bringing of.*
Amendable: com. *Amerceable, fineable; that deserues to be fined, or may be amerced; also, mendable, amendable.*
Amendaye: f. *A groue, or orchard, of Almond trees.*
Amende: f. *A penaltie, fine, mulct, amerciament; an amends made by an offendor to the law violated, or partie wronged; also, a certaine engine, or net to catch fish with.*
Amendes arbitraires. *Fines imposed at the pleasure of the Court, and different from* Amendes coustumieres, *which are limitted by the peculiar lawes, and customes of euery Countrey, and Court.*
Amende du cas de Nouvelleté: *60 pound* Tour. *due vnto the king vpon euery writ, or action, of* Nouel disseisin.
Amende de la Cour. *is in some places vii. s. vi. d.* Tour. *in others, but v. s.*
Amendes coustumieres. *Looke,* Amendes arbitraires.
Amende curiale. *An amercement of an inferiour Court; or, as* Amende de la Cour.
Amende enflambée. *Whereby an offendor is enioyned to hold a burning torch in his hand while he asketh forgiuenesse.*
Amende de fol appel. *is xx. l.* Parisis, *after a iudgement giuen, and before, x. l, or more, if need be, at the discretion of the Iudges, and in recompence to the party interessed by the delaying of the suit.*
Amende de gage. *is vii. s. vi. d.* Tour. *due by euery vassale that hath not deliuered vnto his Lord a sufficient suruey of the peeces he holds (by the customes of* la Perche.)
Amende grosse. *is vi. s. sterling; or a greater summe, rated according to the qualitie of the offence, or omission, for which it is inflicted.*
Amende honorable. *A most ignominious punishment inflicted vpon an extreame offendor; who must goe through the streets bare foot, and bare headed (with a burning linke in his hand) vnto the seat of Iustice, or some such publicke place; and there confesse his offence, and aske forgiuenesse of the partie hee hath wronged.*
Amende de loy. *is vii. s. vi. d.* Tour.
Amende ordinaire. *as* Amende grosse.
Amende simple. *vi. d, or at most, ix. d. sterling: the vsuall fine, or amerciament, for small faults, or sleight omissions.*
Amende statutaire. *as* Amende coustumiere; *for which looke* Amende arbitraire.
Amende de tost-entrée. *is a fine of vi. s'.* Paris. *set on the head of euery new Lord of an inheritance* Roturier, *or* Allodial, *if he enter into it before he haue been orderly*

orderly inuested, and put into possession by such as haue iurisdiction in the place, or territorie, wherein it lyes (by the customes of Rheims.)

La grande amende. *is vi.s. sterl.*

La petite amende. *is in some places ix. d, in others, but vi.d. sterl.*

Droict d'amende. *Looke* Droict.

Il est de Lorry, ou le battu paye l'amende; (&, C'est la loy du païs de Bearn, que le battu paye l'amende: Pro.) *He beares away the blowes, and yet must pay for the bloudwipe.*

Amendé: m. ée: f. *Mended, amended, bettered; satisfied, made amends for.*

Amendement: m. *A mending, amendment; amends, recompence.*

Amender. *To correct, amend, better; also, to satisfie, recompence, make amends for.*

Ie le vous amende. *I crie you mercie; Looke,* Ployer.

Amendeur. *A mender, amender, corrector.*

Amené: m. ée: f. *Brought, led, fetched in, or vnto.*

Amenée: f. *The walke, or circuit of a Sergeant, or Baylife, wherein he may arrest, summon, or adiourne; also, an arrest; summons, or adiournement, executed by him.*

Amenement: m. *A leading, or bringing vnto.*

Amener. *To bring, or lead, vnto; to fetch in, or to.*

Amener l'eau au moulin. *To draw in gaine, to bring in commoditie; to furnish with needfull, and profitable things.*

Amener les voiles. *To strike sayle, or to take in the sayles.*

Ameneur. *A bringer, or fetcher vnto; also, a kind of Sergeant, or Baylife in some parts of France, belonging to particular Lords.*

Amenité: f. *Amenitie; pleasantnesse, delectablenesse, delightfulnesse.*

Amenuisant. *Lessening; or, growing lesse and lesse; or, making little.*

Amenuisé: m. ée: f. *Lessened; made little; growne lesse and lesse.*

Amenuisement: m. *A lessening; a making little.*

Amenuiser. *To lessen; to make little; also, to grow little, or lesse and lesse.*

Ameos: m. *Hearbe William, Ameos, Ammi, Bull-worte, Bushops-weed.*

Amer: m. *The gall of a beast; &c.*

Amer: m. ere: f. *Bitter; also, full of anguish; or harshnesse; also, most despightfull.*

Amer-doux. *A bitter-sweet apple.*

Amerement. *Bitterly; most harshly; most despightfully.*

Ameret. *Cyder made of bitter apples.*

Ameril: m. *Corruptly for* Emeril; *an Emrod.*

Amerine: f. Agnus castus, *Abrahams balme, chast or hempe tree, Parke-leaues.*

Ameriquain: m. *The Neapolitane, or French disease; called so, because it first came from* America.

Amertume: f. *Bitternesse; also, anguish of mind; also, extreame despightfulnesse.*

Amertumer. *To make bitter.*

Amesnagé: m. ée: f. *Managed, gouerned, ordered, setled, as a houshold; husbanded, or well handled, as an estate.*

Amesnager. *To gouerne, rule, order, settle, a houshold; to manage, handle, husband, or dispose of, an estate.*

Amesson. *as* Hameçon; *a hooke.*

Amessonné: m. ée: f. *Hooked, hookie, like a hooke.*

Amessures. cas d'am. *The reuiling, slandering; striking, or fetching bloud, of a man; or, the suspition of an offence, whose punishment is but pecuniarie.*

s'Amesurer. *To keepe within his bounds; to liue within his compasse; to hold an euen measure in his actions; to be sober.*

Ameté: m. ée: f. *Bounded, limitted; meted, or measured out.*

Ametiste. *The precious stone called an Amethist.*

Amette. *A little soule, spirit, or ghost.*

Amettre. *as* Admettre.

Ameubler. *as* Ammeubler; *and as* Emmeubler.

Ameubli: m. ie: f. *Mooueable; or, which may be remooued.*

Ameuri: m. ie: f. *Ripened, made ripe.*

Ameurir. *To ripen, to make ripe.*

Ameuté. Chasse ameutée. *A close running, or hunting, of dogs, together; Looke,* Amuté.

Ameuter. *To semble dogs in hunting, to hold them vp close together; also, to agree together, as well-sorted dogs, in hunting; also, to run, or hunt very close together.*

Amezeau: m. *A Trunke, or Pipe of wood, through which the sea-water (whereof salt is made) passes, eyther from the receptacles, tearmed* Conches *(or* Couches*) vnto another that is called* Forans; *or, from the first, and greatest receptacle, tearmed* Iard, *into the said* Conches.

Ami: m. *A friend; a louer, a Paramour; a louing mate, a deere companion.*

Vne beauté faicte à l'ami; &, Cheveux affotez à l'ami. *Daintily, quaintly, curiously.*

Il en est bien mon bel ami. *He is farre in loue withall, he likes it passing well; and, he would faine haue it, or, be owner of it.*

Vn ami veille pour l'autre: Prov. *One friend euer watches, or cares, for another.*

à rich homme n' en chaut qui ami luy soit: Prov. *The rich man needs no friends; or needs not care who he takes to friend; or (which is most ordinarie, and the most true) respecteth no mans friendship.*

Bien part de sa place qui son ami y laisse: Pro. *He fitly leaues his place, that leaues his friend to keepe it; or (if it was good) that helpes his friend vnto it.*

Il n'y a meilleur miroir que le vieil ami: Pro. *Seeke,* Miroir.

La mort n'a point d'ami, le malade n'a qu'un demi: Pro. *The dead haue no friends, the sicke but faint ones; or, when a man is dead his friends forsake him, and while he is sicke they care not greatly for him; or, no man loues death, or fully loues the diseased.*

Longue demeure fait changer ami: Pro. *Long absence alters affection, breeds forgetfulnesse, weakens constancie, brings in change.*

Mieux vaut avoir ami en voye qu'or ny argent en courroye: Pro. *We say (but with some difference) better a friend in court then a penny in the purse.*

On ne peut avoir trop d'amis: Pro. *One cannot haue too many (faithfull, and discreet) friends.*

Parens sans amis, amis sans pouvoir, pouvoir sans vouloir, vouloir sans effect, effect sans profit, profit sans vertu, ne vaut vn festu: Prov. *Kinred without friends, friends without power, power without will, will without effect, effect without profit, profit without vertue, is not worth a fescue.*

Qui preste à l'ami perd au double: Prov. viz. *both friend and money; To which purpose wee haue a certaine (triuiall, but true-meaning) Ryme, which begins with, I lent my money to my friend, and ends with,*

with, I lost both money, and my friend.

Qui veut entretenir son ami n'ait nuls affaires avec luy: Prov. *Looke,* Affaire.

Tenir ne faut pour bon voisin vn ami de Table, & de vin: Pro. *(For when you haue need of him, or when your Table growes needie, he will be sure to giue you the slip.)*

Viande d'ami est bientost preste: Pro. *A friends meat is soone readie; (for giuing it willingly, he prouides it quickly; or, one thinkes it not, or must not seeme to thinke it, long in comming.)*

Amiable: com. *Amiable, louely; friendly; comely, gracious, exceeding handsome.*

Amiablement. *Amiably, friendly, louingly, gently, graciously; gracefully.*

Amiableté: f. *Friendlinesse, louingnesse, amiablenesse.*

Amict: m. *An amict, or Amice; part of a massing priests habit.*

Amidon. *as* Amydon.

Amidonner. *To starch.*

Amie: f. *A loue, a lemman, a she-friend, a sweet-heart; also, a certaine skalesse fish, like the Bonito, which hauing swallowed a hooke, sheeres the line asunder with her teeth, and so escapes.*

Nous verrons au Ieu qui aura belle amie: viz. *who shall get the victorie; a Metaphor, from such as fight for their mistresses.*

Ia couard n'aura belle amie: Pro. *We say, faint heart neuer woon faire ladie.*

Amieller. *To sweeten; intice, allure, inueagle with honied words; to delight, win, or toll on, by honie, or any sweet meanes.*

Amielleure: f. *A liniment, or oyntment, of the thicknesse, and colour, of honie.*

Amiette: f. *A little loue; young mistresse, lemman, or sweet-heart.*

Amigdale: f. *An Almond; Looke,* Amygdales.

Amignarder. *To pranke, trim, or, to cocker, feddle, make a wanton of; make much of.*

Amignotant. *Pampering, cockering, pranking; also, stroaking, flattering, fawning on, making much of.*

Amignotement: m. *A pampering, cockering, pranking; also, a stroaking, flattering, fawning, making much of.*

Amignoter. *as* Amignarder; *also, to stroake; flatter, fawne on.*

Amiot. *A little friend, also a kind of Peare wherof most excellent perrie is made.*

Amiral. *Seeke* Admiral.

Amission: f. *A losse, leesing, or loosing,*

Amitié: f *Amitie, friendship, loue, kindnesse, good will; concord, correspondencie.*

Bonne amitié seconde parenté: Pro. *Sound friendship a second affinitie.*

Ammaires. *as* Ammares, *or* Amarres.

Amman: m. *A Maior, or Bourgomaister (among the Swizzers.*

Ammares: f. *Great, or strong ropes; anker-cables; also, haspes of yron, or cleytes of wood, &c. as in* Auche.

Ammenteller. *as* Emmenteler.

Ammeubler. *To make moueable; also, as,* Emmeubler.

Ammi. *as* Ameos.

s'Ammignonner. *To wax pretty, fine, feat, minion; to pranke, tricke vp, set out, himselfe.*

Ammitonne. *Lapt in furre like a cat.*

Ammodite. *A creeping vermine like a viper, but of a sandie colour, and full of blacke spots.*

Ammoniac: m. Ammoniacum *(in shops) the iuice, or gumme of th'African hearbe,* Agasillis, *or of the Cyrenian ferula, or fennell-gyant.*

Sel ammoniac. *Looke,* Sel.

Amnestie: f. *Forgetfulnesse of things past.*

Amnie. *as* Aguelette.

Amobilié. *Moueable, remoueable, to be remoued.*

Amobilier. *To remoue, to make moueable.*

Amoderer. *To moderate, assuage, temper, qualifie; measure; also, to slope, cut slope, take downe.*

Amodiateur. *A farmer.*

Amodiation. *A farming, a letting to hire, or to halues; Looke,* Admodiation.

Amodier. *as* Amoderer; *also, as* Admodier.

Amoindri: m. ie: f. *Diminished, lessened, extenuated, impaired, appaired; abated; allayed.*

Amoindrir. *To lessen, diminish, appaire, extenuate, impaire; abate; allay.*

Amoindrissant. *Lessening, abating, diminishing.*

Amoindrissement. *A lessening, diminishing, impairing, extenuating; abating; allaying.*

Amoitir. *To moisten.*

Amolir. *To remoue, or put away hardly, with paine, or much adoe; also, to depart, or goe away.*

Amolli: m. ie: f. *Softened, mollified; pacified, appeased; effeminated.*

Amollir. *To soften, mollifie; make tender, gentle, pliant; also, to pacifie, appease, quiet; also, to effeminate.*

Amollissable: com. *Fit, or apt to be softened, mollified, made tender.*

Amollissant. *Softing, mollifying, effeminating; quieting.*

Amollissement: m. *A softing, mollifying, making tender; or quiet.*

Amome: m. *A small, and thicke aromaticall shrub, whose blossomes resembled white violets, and leaues those of the wild Vine: This true* Amomum *of th'Ancients, is not found, or not discerned, at this day:* Plinie *cals thus, tree Nightshade; others (erroniously) call so the Rose of Ierusalem, or our Ladies Rose; and some as wisely, hearbe Robert; but the most,* Vita longa, *or, Ethyopian pepper; which (though it be not the right) is now the most currant,* Amomum.

Amomite. Encens Amomite. *A whitish kind of incense, which, in handling, becomes soft as Masticke.*

Amomon. *as* Amome.

Amoncelé: m. ée: f. *Heaped, piled, compacted, packed, or trussed up in a heape.*

Amoncelement: m. *A heaping, piling, compacting, packing; a gathering together into a heape.*

Amonceler. *To heape, accumulate, pile, compact; to gather, packe, make up into a heape; to lay on a heape, to lay heape to heape.*

Amonestement. *as* Admonestement.

Amont. *Vpwards.*

Païs d'amont, *is, among people which dwell neere to riuers, the countrey that lyes neerer then theirs vnto the heads, or Source, thereof.*

Vent d'Amont. *The East wind.*

Amoraye. *A coyne vsed at* Ferara, *and worth twelue* Quadrins.

Amorce: f. *A bayt; also, the touch-hole of a peece; or powder for the touch-hole; also, as* Esmorche.

Amorcé: m. ée: f. *Bayted; allured, inticed, drawn on.*

Vne beste amorcée. *A mankind beast.*

Amorcement: m. *A baiting; alluring, inticement.*

Amorcer. *To bayt; also, to allure, beguile, inueagle, intice.*

Amorceure: f. *A bait; a baiting.*

Amorcher. *To put pouder into the touch-hole of a peece.*

Amorti: m. ie: f. *Deaded, quenched, quayled, extinguished, ceased, abolished; also, redeemed, or bought out, as a rent charge, &c; also, graunted, or passed away in Mortmaine; also, exchanged by agreement, as, one seruice for another; also, disappearing, dead, gone, or lost, as the part of a piller thats closed within a wall; or, the piece of timber that is, by mortaise, ioyned vnto another piece.*

Censiues amorties. *Which are not held by homage, and fealtie.*

Heritages amorties. *Which owe neither homage, fealtie, rent, nor seruice; or, which are held of the church, or by Mortmaine; or, passed away in Mortmaine.*

Amortir. *To dead, quench, quayle; abolish, dissolue; also, to extinguish; redeeme, or buy out, as a rent charge, &c; also, to graunt, alien, or passe away, in Mortmaine; also, to exchange by agreement, as, one seruice for another; also, as* Admortir; *to mortaise, or ioyn by mortaise.*

s'amortir. *as* s'Admortir; *also, to disappeare.*

Amortissable: com. *Quenchable, stintable, dissolueable, abolishable, extinguishable; redeemeable.*

Amortissement. *Mortmaine; also, a licence of, or passing in Mortmaine; also, a deadding, quenching, dissolution, extinguishment, vtter ceasing of; also, a disappearing, or loosing it selfe within another; also, a mortaising, or ioyning by mortaise.*

Amortisement de foy, &c; de Rente. *Looke* Admortissement.

Lettres d'amortisement. *A licence of alienation, or of purchase, in Mortmaine, graunted vnto churchmen, corporations, guilds, fraternities, &c; and must be procured by them vpon euery new purchase (generall letters not being sufficient) otherwise th'Imposition* de nouveaux Acquests *is layd on them, once in euery kings time: And this is good onely from the king, of whomsoeuer the land be held; and for this, a third part of the value is to be allowed him.*

Amour: com. *Loue, kindnesse, charitie; good will, good liking, affection; also, the name of a certaine Italian sport; for which looke,* Iouër.

Amours. *The spermaticke vessels of beasts; called so by those that vse to lib, or geld, them.*

Estre en amour. *(Said of birds that bill, tread, or breed.)*

Ie le feray pour l'amour de vous: viz. *For your sake, or for the respect I beare you.*

Amour de garse, & saut de chien ne dure si l'on ne dit, tien: Prov. *Whores and dogs fawne on a man no longer then he feeds them; or, a whores loue, and a dogs leaping continue but while they are fed.*

Amour de muge: Pro. *Faithfull loue of a wife to her husband; (The female Mullet will rather be caught by fishermen then abandon her Make.)*

Amour de putain feu d'estoupe: Pro. *(Th'exposition followes)* qui luit fort, & dure peu.

Amour de seigneur est ombre de buisson: Prov. *The loue of a great man is of small continuance, and dangerous consequence.*

Amour, & seigneurie ne se tindrent iamais compagnie: Prov. *Loue, and lordlinesse neuer held companie together; a friend, and a lord are incompatible.*

Amour apprend les asnes à danser: Prov. *Looke* Danser.

Amour fait beaucoup, mais argent fait tout: Prov. *Loue does much, but money does all.*

L'amour, la tousse, & la galle ne se peuvent celer: Pro. *We say, Loue, and the Cough cannot be hidden.*

Amour vainc tout fors que coeur felon: Pro. *Loue ouercomes any thing but a froward, or spightfull, heart.*

En amour est folie, & sens: Prov. *In loue there is both dotage, and discretion.*

Argent faict rage, & amour mariage: Pro. *Money breeds rage, loue mariage.*

Au batre faut l'amour: Pro. *By beating (the beloued) loue decayes.*

D'oiseaux, de chiens, d'armes, & d'amours pour vn plaisir mille douleurs: Prov. *Who follow haukes, hounds, armes, or are in loue, for one delight a thousand sorrowes proue.*

En cent livres de plaid n'y a pas vn maille d'amour: Pro. *In a hundred pound of law there's not a halfepenny weight of loue.*

Fy d'avoir qui n'n ioye & d'amours sans monnoye: Pro. *Looke* Fy.

Il n'est que les premieres amours: Prov. *The first loue is the fastest; there is no loue to the first.*

Oncques n'y eut laides amours ny belle prison: Pro. *Neuer seemd mistresse foule, nor prison faire.*

Veilles amours, & vieux tisons s'allument en toutes saisons: Pro. *Looke* Allumer.

Amoureau: m. *A little loue; also, the little god of loue.*

Amourescher. *To woe (an old word.)*

Amourettes: f. *Loue-tricks; wanton loue-toyes, ticking, ticklings, daliances; also, the grasse tearmed, Quakers, and Shakers, or quaking grasse.*

Aussi bien sont amourettes soubs bureau, que soubs brunettes: Pro. *Loue bides in cottages, as well as in Courts.*

Amoureusement. *Amorously; louingly, affectionately, kindly; gently, courteously.*

Amoureux: m. *A louer, one that is in loue; a woer.*

Amoureux de Quaresme. *A Lenten louer; a bashfull, modest, or maidenly, woer.*

Amoureux de triqueniques. *A paltry louer, a fond woer, a trifling paramour.*

Amoureux: m. euse: f. *Amorous, in loue, affecting, affectionate, full of loue.*

Muscles amoureus. *Two muscles (a great one, and a lesse) belonging to the eye, the which they turne round.*

Amoustillé: m. ée: f. *Seasoned, sweetened, furnished; intertained, or made drunke, with new sweet wine.*

Amoustiller. *To sweeten, season, or furnish (also, to intertaine guests, or welcome friends) with Must, or new sweet wine.*

Amparlier. *as* Emparlier; *a Pleader.*

Ampes: f. *Raspises.*

Ampeser. *To starch.*

Amphibie: com. *Liuing both in water, and on the land.*

Amphiblistroïde. *The fift thin membrane of th'eye, bringing inward light vnto the Christaline humour.*

Amphibole: com. *Ambiguous, vncertaine, doubtfull, subiect to controuersie, of a double sence, or meaning, which may be taken sundry wayes.*

Amphibolie. *as* Amphibologie; *(and the better word.)*

Amphibologie: f. *A doubtfull, or double, meaning in one, or many words.*

Amphisbeine: f. *Th'Amphisbæna; a small, spotted, and worme-like Serpent, that hath a head at both ends, and biteth, and goeth, both wayes: yet* Mathiolus *and* Greuin *hold, that she hath but one head; onely she seemes to haue two, because her tayle resembles her head: the more probable opinion; for no serpent (saith* Gesner) *hath, naturally, more heads then one.*

Amphitrite: f. *The Sea.*

Amphore. *An auncient measure of about 36 quarts; it was commonly of earth, had two eares, and was a foot square euery way.*

Amphytane. *A square, and golden-coloured stone, of the nature of a Loadstone; or more powerfull; for it also drawes gold vnto it.*

Ample: com. *Full, ample, wide, large, scopefull, spacious, of great compasse; also, copious, abundant; sumptuous; huge.*

Fief ample. *A whole fief, or knights fee; for a Heriot whereof the Landlord takes his deceased tenants best horse, and part of his armour, or if he had no horse, lx. s.* Tournois.

Amplement. *Amply, largely, widely, spaciously; fully; copiously, aboundantly; sumptuously; hugely, verie greatly.*

Ampliateur: m. *An amplifier, inlarger, increaser.*

Ampliation. *An inlarging, amplification, increase, augmentation.*

Amplié: m. ée: f. *Amplified, inlarged; augmented, increased.*

Amplier. *as* Amplifier.

Amplificateur. *An amplifier, inlarger; augmenter, increaser.*

Amplification: f. *Amplification, inlargement; augmentation, increase.*

Amplifier. *To amplifie, inlarge; augment, increase.*

Ampois: m. *Starch.*

Ampoule: f. *A small blister, wheale, powke, or rising of the skin; Looke,* Empoule.

Ampoulé: m. ée: f. *Beblistered; full of water-poukes, or wheales.*

Amprise. *as* Entreprise; *(corruptly;) An enterprise.*

Amputation. *An amputation, a cutting away; or paring about; a ridding, or taking away.*

Amputé: m. ée: f. *Cut away; pared about; rid, or taken away.*

Amputer. *To cut away, or pare about; to rid, or take away, superfluities.*

Amuletier: m. *A counter-charmer, wisard, or good witch.*

Amulette: f. *A counter-charme.*

Amurer. *as* Amarrer; *also, to wall vp.*

Amusé: m. ée: f. *Amused; put into a muse, driuen into a dumpe; held, stayed, or delayed by a discourse, question, &c.*

Amuse-fol: m. *One that with vaine pratling, or toying, holds fond people at gaze.*

Amuseller. *To muzzle; to close, or couer the mouth with a muzzle.*

Amusement: m. *An amusing, or amusement.*

Amuser. *To amuse; to make to muse, or thinke of; wonder, or gaze at; to put into a dumpe; to stay, hold, or delay from going forward by discourse, questions, or any other amusements.*

s'amuser sur la vinaigrette. *To stand on trifles.*

Amuseur. *An amuser of people; one that holdeth folkes at gaze, or putteth them into dumps.*

Amusoire: m. *A thing to wonder at; a gazing stocke; a subiect, or cause, for amusement.*

Amusse. *as* Aumuce.

Amuté. Chasse amutée. *A close running, or hunting of dogs together; or, dogs that be sembled, or held vp close together; also, a well-sorted crie of dogs.*

Amy. *as,* Ami.

Amydon: m. *Fine wheat flower steeped in water; then strained, and let stand vntill it settle at the bottome; then drained of the water, and dried at the Sunne; vsed for bread, or in brothes it is very nourishing; also, starch made of wheat.*

Amye: f. *Looke,* Amie.

Amygdales. *Kernels rising in the necke, or vnder the root of the tongue; also, Almonds.*

An: m. *A yeare, a tweluemonth.*

Ans vieux. *Old age, decrepit yeares.*

En cent ans civiere, en cent ans banniere: Prov. *Sometimes a wheelebarrow, sometimes a banner; those that are poore now, may be potent hereafter; no family holds very long at one stay.*

Le mal an entre en nageant: Pro. *Th'ill (or vnseasonable) yeare comes swimming in;* viz. *begins with much raine.*

Anacampserote. *A certaine hearbe whose touch renueth decayed loue betweene man and man (as some haue imagined.)*

Anacarde: m. *Th'East-Indian fruit called* Anacardium, *or Beane of* Malaca.

Anacardin: m. ine: f. *Of* Anacardium; *whence;*

Miel anacardin. *A certaine venomous, and caustike oyle found, between the kernell, and outward rinde, of th'*Anacardium.

Anacephaleose: f. *A briefe rehearsall, a recapitulation of things spoken.*

Anachorete: m. *The Hermit called an Ankrosse, or Anchorite.*

Anafile. *as* Agnafile.

Anagal: m. *The hearbe Pimpernell.*

Anagnoste: m. *A reader; a Clarke that reades to a writer; a boy that reades to his master, &c.*

Anagrammatiser. *To make an Anagram; to frame a conceit, or sentence, of the letters of a name set together.*

Anagrammatisme. *A making of Anagrams; or the art of making Anagrams.*

Anagramme: m. *An Anagram; a Sentence, Poesie, or pretie conceit framed of the letters of a name.*

Anagyre. *The plant called Beane Trifolie, or Pescod tree.*

Analemme: m. *An instrument whereby the course, and eleuation of the Sunne is fouud.*

Analogie: f. *An Analogie, example, proportion, similitude, conformitie, correspondencie, comparison.*

Analogique: com. *Analogicall; conformable vnto some other thing; answering in proportion vnto another thing; correspondent.*

Analogiser. *To compare, conforme, and ioyne, by affinitie or proportion, one thing with another.*

Anangé. *Fatall, or of destinie.*

Anaphore. *An ascention of the planets from the East, by daily course of the firmament; also, a figure called Repetition, when two verses begin with one word.*

Anaporique. *A kind of circular dyall for the Winter.*

Anaquil. *as* Anafile.

Anarche: com. *Without kingdome, or commaund; without Prince; without beginning; licentious, vnbrideled, vnruled, vnruly.*

Anarchie: f. *An Anarchie; a Commonwealth without a head, or Gouernour; a confused state, wherein one is as good as another; also, want of gouernment, libertie, licentiousnesse, dissolutenesse.*

Anarchique: com. *Belonging to an Anarchie; without rule, gouernment; beginning, or order; dissolute, licentious.*

Anastomose: f. *The communication of veines with arteries, whereby they helpe one another.*

Anate:

Anate. *A ducke, or drake.*
Anatematization. *as,* Anathematisation.
Anathematisation: f. *An anathematisation, extreame cursing; vowing, or deuoting vnto the diuell.*
Anathematisé: m. ée: f. *Anathematized, cursed vnto the pit of hell.*
Anathematiser. *To anathematize, deuote vnto the diuell, curse vnto the pit of hell.*
Anatheme: m. *A gift bestowed, or offering made in a church; also, a solemne curse of the church.*
Anatheme: com. *Execrated, excommunicated, most accursed.*
Anatomie: f. *Anatomie; a section of, and looking into, all parts of the bodie; also, an Anatomie, or carkasse cut vp.*
Anatomique: com. *Anatomicall; of, or belonging to, Anatomie.*
Anatomiste: m. *An Anatomist.*
Anatomizer. *To anatomize; to cut vp, and looke into, the parts of the bodie.*
Ancelle: f. *A hand-maid, or maid-seruant.*
Ancestres: m. *Auncestors, predecessors, forefathers.*
Anche: f. *The little pipe, tongue, or tenon, which is the mouth of a Trumpet, Hoeboy, &c; also, as* Enche.
Anchois; ou Anchoies; *The fish Anchoveyes.*
Ancholie: f. *The Columbine (hearbe, or flower.)*
Anchoyes. *as* Anchoies; *The fish Anchoveyes.*
Anchraige: m. *Ankorage, ankoring.*
Anchre; & Anchré. *as* Ancre; *and* Ancré.
Anchuses: f. *Wild Buglosse, Orchanet, Alkanet.*
Ancien: m. enne: f. *Old, auncient; stale; of long continuance, of good antiquitie.*
Anciennement. *Auncientl; oldly, stalely; of old, in old time, in time past.*
Ancienneté: f. *Auncientnesse, oldnesse, stalenesse.*
Ancoigner. *To driue, or thrust, into a corner.*
Ancoigneure: f. *A corner, or cone; any thing thats cornered, like a wedge.*
Ancon: m. *A long, and heauie axe, which in old time souldiors vsed to throw at their enemies either before, or iust at, their ioyning together in battell.*
Ancraige: m. *as* Anchraige.
Ancre: f. *An ankor.*
Estre à l'ancre. *To be idle, or at leisure; to stand, or lye still; to haue nought to doe.*
Iecter l'ancre sacrée. *To employ their last, or chiefest remedies; to fall vnto prayer, or implore the diuine assistance, when all other meanes doe faile.*
Mouiller l'ancre. *To cast ankor.*
Ancré: m. ée: f. *Ankored, hauing cast ankor; at an ankor; also, made, or fashioned like an ankor; and hence;* Croix ancrée.
Ancrer. *To ankor, to cast ankor.*
Ancrier: m. *An inkehorne.*
Ancrier: m. ere: f. *Of, or belonging to an ankor; or, to an inkehorne; also, inkie, yeelding inke, blacke as inke; whence;*
Seiche ancriere. *Obscuring the water with her black, or inkie, spume.*
Ancrouëlle. pie an. *A Shrike; Ninmurder, Wariangle.*
Andabatisme: m. *A commotion, vprore, hurrie.*
Andain: m. *A stride; or as much ground, or space, as a man can comprehend by striding.*
Andains. *Rewes of new-mowed hay, &c, lying on the ground, about a pace asunder.*
Andoille. *as* Andouille.
Andoillers: m. *The brow-anklers, or first branch of a Deeres head.*
Andosseure: f. *The backe, or back-part of; (hence) also, the ridge, or couering of the ridge, of a house, &c; also, an indorsement, or indorsing of.*
Andouille: f. *A linke, or chitterling; a big hogges gut stuffed with small guts (and other intrailes) cut into small pieces, and seasoned with pepper and salt.*
Il luy rend le nez aussi plat come vne andouille; *Hee shames him vtterly; hee dashes him cleane out of countenance.*
Andouillers. *as* Endouillers, *or* Andoillers.
Andouillois: m. ise: f. *Of linkes, or chitterlings.*
Andousseure: *as* Andosseure.
Andrin. *An ill fauoured blacke colour of a horse.*
Androginé: m. ée: f. *Made of both sexes; growne both man and woman.*
Androgyne: com. *An Hermaphrodite; one thats both man and woman; or hath the priuities of both.*
Aneanti: m. ie: f. *Annichilated, abrogated, made void, brought vnto nothing; also, weakened, enfeebled, made forcelesse; ruined, vndone; and hence, deiected, imbased, abased, despised, respected as nought, or but as a thing of nought.*
Aneantir. *To abrogate, annichilate, make void, or nothing of; also, to weaken, enfeeble, make forcelesse; ruine, vndoe, bring vnto nothing; and hence, to deiect, imbase, abase, despise, respect as nothing.*
s'Aneantir. *To disesteeme himselfe; also, to languish, or pine away, to grow not worth the ground hee goes on.*
Aneantisant. *Annichilating; bringing to nought; also, abasing, despising, disesteeming, deiecting; also, weakening, enfeebling.*
Aneantisement: m. *An abrogating, annichilating, making void, or nought of; also, a weakening, enfeebling; ruining, vndoing; bringing to nought; and hence, a deiecting, abasing, despising, respecting as nought.*
Aneau. *Seeke* Anneau.
Anelet. *as* Annelet.
Anematiser. *To anathematize, or curse.*
Anemoné. *The wind-flower.*
Anemoné double. *The double scarlet wind-flower.*
Anemoné simple. *The purple wind-flower.*
Anemophilace. *An obseruer of heauenly rules.*
Anestie: f. *The season.*
Anet: m. *The hearbe called Anet, and Dill.*
Anet sauvage. *Wild Dill; also, yellow, or little, barrow.*
Aneth. *as* Anet.
Anetin: m. ine: f. *Of the hearbe Dill.*
Anette *A Ducke, or Dig.* ¶Pic.
Aneurisme: m. *A soft swelling ingendred by the relaxation, or dilation, of an Arterie.*
Aneurisement: m. *An vlcer, or vlceration, in the skin of a sinew.*
Anforge: f. *A leatherne wallet; a double male, or budget, to be carried behind a man on horsebacke.*
Anfractueux: m. ée: f. *Full of turnings, compasses, inuolutions.*
Anfractuosité: f. *Anfractuositie; a manifold (and vneuen) circuit, compasse, inuolution, turning, or winding about.*
Angar: m. *An open shed, or houell, wherein husbandmen set their ploughes &c. out of the Sunne, and weather.*
Angarie: f. *Personall seruice, or drudgerie; that which a man is forced to performe in his owne person.*

Angarié: m. ée: f. *Toyled, vexed, harried; oppressed with continuall seruices, charges, exactions; forced, or put, vnto much drudgerie, or trauell.*

Angarier. *To toyle, vex, harrie, hurrie; to oppresse, or weare out, with continuall imployments, exactions, charges; to force vnto any drudgerie, or excessiue trauaile.*

Ange: m. *An Angell; Gods immediate messenger; our* Genius, *or the spirit (whether good, or euil) that haunts, and accompanies vs.*

Ange de Greue. *One that hangs in chaynes, or on a gibbet, a good while after he is dead.*

Ange de mer. *The great, long, rough, and hard-skind, skate-fish.*

Bouque d'ange. *Conserue, or Sucket, made of the stalkes of Lettuce.*

Eau d'ange. *A kind of delicat compound water.*

Aile d'ange, & voix de Diable: Prov. *An Angels wing, and deuils voice (the stile of a Peacocke.)*

Au prester ange, au rendre Diable. *A prouerbe expressing the ingratitude, and ill nature, of some borrowers, who honour a man when he supplies them, and hate him when they are to pay him.*

Angele: f. *A she Angell; a woman Angell.*

Angelique: f. *The hearb Angelica; also, a kind of white, long, and great fig.*

Angelique sauvage. *Wild Angelica, whose root wants that sweet odour which the right one hath.*

Angelique: com. *Angelicall, Angell-like, belonging to an Angell.*

Angellet; &, Angellette: f. *A little, or pretie, Angell.*

Angelot: m. *The cheese called, an Angelot; also, an English Angell; also, a young, or little, Angell.*

Angelot à la grosse escaille. *An old Angell; and, by Metaphor, a fellow of th'old, sound, honest, and worthie, stampe.*

Angelot de mer. *as,* Ange de mer.

De jeune Angelot vieux Diable: Pro. *Of a young Angell an old deuill; many that (while they were yong) seem'de wonderous pure, are (now they be aged) most prophane.*

Angine: f. *The Squinsie, or Squinancie.*

Anglantine: f. *An Eglantine, or sweet brier; also, a certaine wittie game (vsed at* Tholouse*) wherein onely Poets contend, and to the best doer a siluer Eglantine, to the second a Marigold, is giuen.*

Angle: m. *An angle, cone, or corner.*

Angler. *To shut vp in a corner, bring into a strait, inclose within a narrow roome.*

Anglet: m. *An anglet, or angle; a corner.*

Grand anglet. *The corner of the eye towards the nose.*

Petit anglet. *Th'outward corner towards the Temples; tearmed so by Anotamists.*

Angleux: m. euse: f. *Full of angles, or corners; like an angle; corner-wise.*

Noix angleuse. *A nut that hath a thicke shell, and small kernell.*

Anglois. *An Englishman; also, a creditor, that pretends he hath much money owing, which is neuer like to be payed him.*

Anglué: m. ée: f. *Looke* Englué.

Angoisse: f. *Anguish, griefe, sorrow, agonie, perplexitie, vexation of mind, or bodie.*

Pommes d'angoisse. *Choaking apples.*

Angoissé: m. ée: f. *Vexed, grieued, perplexed, filled with anguish.*

Angoisser. *To vex, grieue, afflict, perplex, fill with anguish, almost choake with sorrow.*

Angoisseusement. *Most painefully, most sorrowfully, with great anguish, and agonie.*

Angoisseuseté: f. *Much anguish, choaking sorrowfulnesse, great vexation, or painfulnesse; extreame affliction, agonie, or perplexitie of spirit.*

Angoisseux: m. euse: f. *Full of anguish, fraught with sorrow, most perplexed; extreamely afflicting; paine-procuring.*

Angonailles: f. *Botches, (pockie) bumps, or sores.*

Angonnages: *In stead of* Angonailles.

Angoüé: m. ée: f. *as* Agoué.

Angoulevent. *A swallow-wind; one that deuoures wind, as the Cameleon.*

Angourie: f. *A kind of cowcomber, somewhat longer then the ordinarie one; or, as* Angurie.

Angouste. *A locust, or grassehopper.*

Angué. *The hearbe, Wallwort.* ¶Langued.

Anguiliere: f. *A pond, or place to keepe Eeles in.*

Anguillade: f. *A whipping, lash, or blow, with an Eele, or, with an Eeles skin.*

Anguille: f. *An Eele.*

L'Anguille. *The name of the tyde-boat which passes betweene* Blaye, *and* Bourdeaux.

Anguille de bois. *as* Anguille d'haye; *or, the bush Adder, or wood snake.*

Anguille fine. *The female Eele; so called in* Languedoc.

Anguille d'haye. *The hedge, or dunghill, Adder; blackish of colour, and not very venomous.*

Escorcher les anguilles par la queue. *To doe a thing cleane kamme, out of order, the wrong way.*

Il y a bien de l'anguille sous roche. *There is some misterie, some hidden matter in it; some pad in that straw; or, more then all the world can discerne.*

Rompre l'anguille au genouil. *To attempt an impossible matter; or, to labour in vaine.*

Anguilles de Melun (qui crient avant qu'on les escorche:) Pro. *Cowardly apprehenders of a mischiefe before it happen; such as yeeld before the danger, or crie before their paine approch them.*

à grand pescheur eschappe anguille: Prov. *Seeke* Pescheur.

Par trop presser l'anguille on la perd: Prov. *Wee often loose things by too much looking to them; or, the faster you meane to hold a slipperie thing, the sooner it ouerslips you.*

Anguillette: f. *A Grig, or little Eele.*

Anguillonneux: m. *A craftie fellow, slye mate, subtill marchant.*

Angulaire: com. *Angular, of a corner, that hath corners; placed, or set in a corner.*

Anguleux. *as* Angleux.

Angurie: f. *The great long Pompion.*

Anguste: com. *Strait, narrow, pinching, scant, scarce, of a small compasse.*

Angustie: f. *Straitnesse, narrownesse; pinching, scarcitie, scantnesse; also, distresse, perplexitie, griefe.*

Anhelé: m. ée: f. *Breathed on; also, drawne (as the breath) with difficultie; also, much longed for, greatly desired, greedily aspired vnto.*

Anheler. *To breath on; also to fetch wind, or draw breath with difficultie; also, to be verie greedie, or desirous of; to aspire vnto with great indeuour.*

Anhelit: m. *Difficult breathing.*

Ani. *Seeke,* Anis.

Anichiler. *Seeke,* Annichiler.

Aniler. *To abate; also, to darken.*

Anille. *The mill-rind of a mill-stone; in Blazon; an inkmolyne.*
Anilles: m. *Crutches for impotent persons.*
Animadversion: f. *An animaduersion; a marking, or heeding; a consideration; a iudgement; also, a warning, censure, chiding, reprehension.*
Animal: m. *An animall; a creature that hath life, spirit, and sence; (more particularly) a beast; (wee sometimes call a blockhead, or gull, an Animall.)*
Anime: f. *A fashion of easie (because large-plated, and large-iointed) armour; also, the name of an aromaticall East-Indian gumme.*
Animé: m. ée: f. *Animated; quickened, inspired with life, or breath; also, heartened, incouraged; incited, incensed.*
Animelles: f. *The stones, cods, or cullions of Lambes, &c.*
Animer. *To quicken, giue life vnto; inspire breath, infuse a spirit into; also, to animate, incourage, hearten, imboulden; incite, incense.*
Animeusement. *Couragiously, stoutly, resolutely, with a great stomacke.*
Animeux: m. euse: f. *Stout, hardie, resolute, couragious, full of heart, mettall, spirit; of a bold, and great stomacke; that will take no wrong, that will carrie no coales.*
Animosité: f. *Animositie, stoutnesse, courage, mettall, boldnesse, resolution, hardinesse.*
Anir. *The name of an Indian hearbe, vsed much by Dyers.*
Anis: m. *The hearbe Anise; also, the seed thereof, Aniseed; also, as* Engeance; *and hence;*
Petis anis. *A troupe of little children.*
Anis: f. Annis, *or* Nanne *(a proper name for a woman.)*
Anisé: m. ée: f. *Seasoned, or sweetned with Ani-seed; also, multiplied, in brood.*
Aniser. *To season, or sweeten with Aniseed; also, to increase, or multiplie.*
Aniveller. *To measure, leuell, or square by plumbe-line, or plumbe-rule.*
Anizé. *as,* Anisé.
Annales: f. *Annales; annuall Chronicles; yearely relations.*
Annaliste: com. *An Annalist; a writer of yearely Chronicles, a relator of annuall occurrences.*
Annate. *The first fruits of a Benefice; the profit of a whole yeare after the remooue, or death, of th'Incumbent.*
Anneantir. *Seeke,* Aneantir.
Anneau: m. *A ring, or signet for a finger; or (more generally) any ring; also, the ligament that incircles the wrist, in forme of a hoope-ring.*
L'Anneau d'une clef. *The bow (or vpmost part) of a key.*
à l'anneau. *Vpon the marriage.*
Il a mis en son doigt anneau trop estroict; *He hath vndertaken a matter, which is most vnworthie of him; or which will turne much to his preiudice.*
Année: f. *A yeare; a yeares time; the season within a yeare; also, a yeares crop, or increase; whence;*
La bonne année en peu de temps s'en va, la petite se garde: Prov. *Good haruests makes men prodigall, bad prouident.*
Annelé: m. ée: f. *Ringed, full of rings, made like a ring, set, or decked with rings; marked with round, or with ring-like, spots.*
Cheueux annelez. *Haire frizeled, curled, or twirled round, or into round knots.*
Anneler. *To ring; to curle, or twirle round like a ring; to hooke, hang, claspe, close, decke, or furnish, with rings.*
Annelet: m. *A gimmew, or little ring for the finger; also, a hawther; also, a mayle, or a ring of mayle; any annelet, or small ring, vsed about apparell, or armour.*
Annellé. *as,* Annelé.
Annexe: f. *An annexation, or thing annexed.*
Annexé: m. ée: f. *Knit, annexed, linked, ioyned, coupled, added, vnto.*
Annexer. *To annex, knit, linke, ioyne, couple, adde, vnto.*
Annicher. *To nestle, or put into a nest.*
Annicheur: m. *A nestler; a nest-maker; a putter of things into nests; a setter of birds on nests; and hence;*
Docte annicheur de poules. *An excellent, or learned, cotqueane.*
Annichilé: m. ée: f. *Annichilated, annulled, brought vnto nothing.*
Annichiler. *To annull, annichilate, bring vnto nothing.*
Annion. Priviledge d'annion. *An yeares protection graunted by the Prince, or Magistrate, vnto a debtor.*
Anniversaire: m. *An yearely Obit, Trentall, or seruice said, at a time certaine, for the dead.*
Anniversaires: m. *The winds which ordinarily blow about the dog-dayes.*
Annombré: m. ée: f. *Counted, reckoned, numbred, told out, or ouer.*
Annombrer. *To reckon, number, count, tell out, or ouer.*
Annoncé: m. ée: f. *Declared, shewed, aduertised, informed, signified vnto.*
Annonce-iour. *Day-denouncing, light-proclaiming.*
Annoncement: m. *A shewing, declaring, signifying, aduertising.*
Annoncer. *To announce, or denounce; to proclaime; declare, shew, signifie, bring newes, aduertise, carrie tidings vnto.*
Annonce-salut. *Health-declaring.*
Annonceur: m. *An announcer, declarer, proclaimer, signifier, aduertiser; a bringer of newes, a carrier of tidings, vnto.*
Annonchali: m. ie: f. *Disesteemed, neglected, carelesly handled, ill looked vnto; also, pined, wasted, worne away, growne carelesse of himselfe, not worth the ground he goes on, by his owne carelesnesse.*
s'Annonchalir. *To grow carelesse of himselfe, or of his own health; (and thereby) to wast, pine, languish, weare away.*
Annonciation: f. *An annunciation, a denouncement.*
Annone. *A kind of white, soft, sweet, sauourie, and kernellie Indian fruit; also, meslin, or grudgins; the corne whereof browne bread is made for the meynie.*
Annotation: f. *An annotation; a marke, note, obseruation; title, register; or, a marking, noting; intitling.*
Annotation de biens. *A seisure of the goods of offendors that appeare not in person, or by Atturny, within a yeare after they haue beene summoned.*
Annoté. *Marked, noted, obserued; intitled; registred; also, whose goods are seised; as in* Annotation.
Annoter. *To marke, note, obserue; intitle; register.*
Annuel: m. elle: f. *Annuall, yearely, done euerie yeare.*
Annuellement. *Annually, yearely, euerie yeare, from yeare to yeare.*
Annulaire: m. *The Chauncellor of Fraunce; tearmed so in old time, when the Kings signet was his great Seale.*

Annulaire : com. *Annular; of a ring; like a ring; round.*

Doigt annulaire. *The ring finger, or wedding-ring finger; the third finger, or, that which is next vnto the little one.*

Ligament annulaire. *A certaine muskle, or fleshie band, which compasses th'vpper part of th'instup, and receiues, vnder it, the tennons of the muskles belonging to the fore-part of the leg.*

Annullé : m. ée : f. *Disannulled, annulled, annihilated.*

Annuller. *To annull, disannull, annihilate; abrogate, cancell, make void, or of no effect.*

Anobli : m. ie : f. *Ennobled, made noble, ingentilized, made a gentleman.*

Anoblir. *To ennoble, make noble, ingentilize, make a gentleman.*

La verge anoblist, & le ventre affranchist; *Looke* Verge.

Anoblissement : m. *An ennobling, or ingentilizing.*

Anodin. Remedes anodins. *Medicines which (by procuring sleepe) take from a Patient all sence of paine.*

Anoirci : m. ie : f. *Blackned; made, or become, blacke.*

Anoircir. *To blacken; to make, or grow, blacke.*

Anomal: m. ale: f. *Inequall, rough, or not euen; also, irregular.*

Anombrer. *as* Annombrer. *To number, count, reckon, tell out, or ouer.*

Anoncement. *as* Annoncement.

Anoncer. *as* Annoncer.

Anonces. *The banes of Matrimonie.*

Anonchallanti : m. ie : f. *Neglected, carelesly handled; also, languishing; also, out of sale, out of request, out of custome, or, which no customers will deale for.*

Anonchaly. *Neglected; or, as* Annonchali.

Anonciade. *as* Annonciation; *whence,* Ordre de l'a: *An Order of knighthood, instituted in the yeare 1350, by a duke of Sauoy.*

Anonexie : f. *Looke* Anorexie.

Anorexie : f. *Inapetencie; the want, or weakenesse of appetite; the loathing of all meat; queasinesse of stomacke.*

Anoüé : m. ée : f. *Almost choaked, or stifled, by letting downe too great a morsell.*

Anoüer. *(Almost) to choake, stifle, strangle with greedie eating, or by deuouring too great a morsell.*

Ansarot : m. *A certaine bitter Gumme; Looke* Sarcocolle.

Anse : f. *The handle, or eare of a pot, cup, &c. whereby we take hold thereof; (hence) also, an oportunitie, or occasion; also, a creeke, nooke, bay, gulfe, or arme of the sea; Looke,* Anses.

Les bras courbez en anse. *With armes a-kemboll.*

Vn pot à deux anses: Pro. *An equiuocation; a word, &c, of double meaning, or whereof a double construction may be made.*

Ansé : m. ée : f. *Eared; or that hath an eare, or handle.*

Ansée: f. *A kind of basket hauing two handles, or eares, to be carried betweene two.*

Anses : f. *Handles, &c, as in* Anse *(whereof this is the plurall) also, th'ends of ropes tyed snare-wise, or made into nooses.*

Anseté. *as* Ansé.

Ansette. *A little handle, or eare of a pot, &c.*

Ansouple : m. *Looke,* Ensouple.

Ansule : f. *A little handle.*

Antartique. *The circle in the Sphere called the South, or Antarticke, Pole; which, by reason of th'earths opposition, we cannot, in these parts of the world, discerne.*

Ante : f. *as* Tante; *an aunt; also, the cheeke, or iaumbe of a doore; also, as* Ente.

Antecesseurs : m. *Predecessors, auncestors.*

Anteines : f. *The sayle-yard; the crosse peece whereto the sayle is fastened.*

Anten. *The last yeare.*

Des anten. *A twelue-month agoe.*

Ie te crains aussi peu que les neiges d'anten. *I feare thee as much as nothing; I dread thee not at all.*

Antenais: m. *Shoots, or sprigs of a yeares growth.*

Antenne : f. *A Sayle-yard.*

Antenois : m. *A hog, an yearling, or yeare-old sheepe; a lambe of the last yeare.*

Anterieur : m. eure : f. *Anterior, fore, former, or that is before the former; that goeth, or is set, before.*

Anterieurement. *Before, formerly, in the fore-part, or former place.*

Anthere. *The yellow tuft in the middle of a Rose.*

Anthoine. Anthonie; *a proper name.*

Feu S. Anthoine : *A swelling full of heat, paine, and rednesse; we call it also,* S. Anthonies *fire.*

Porcelet de S. Anthoine. *The vermine called, a Ches-lop, or Wood-louse.*

Anthosat. *Made of Rosemarie.*

Anthracite. *A precious stone, wherein there seeme to be flames, or sparkes of fire.*

Anthromantie. *Diuination by the raysing of dead men.*

Anthropopathie : f. *Humane, or mans, passion.*

Antiborée : f. *That kind of dyall, which (contrarie to all others) is to be turned towards the North; a North dyall.*

Antibust. Ceinct à l'antibust. *Girt loosely, carelessely, or after the great-belly fashion, the girdle riding ouer the middle of the bosome; also, girt back-wards.*

Antichambre : f. *The chamber of Presence in a Princes Court; the great Chamber in a great mans house; any outward chamber which is next, or neere vnto, the bed-chamber.*

Anticipant : m. *A preuenter, forestaller, anticipator.*

Anticipant : m. ante : f. *Anticipating, preuenting, forestalling.*

Anticipation : f. *Anticipation, preuention, forestallment; also, the naturall knowledge one hath of a thing before he see, or heare, it.*

Lettres d'anticipation; *The Kings letters, or Commission, mentioned in* Appel anticipé.

Anticipé : m. ée : f. *Anticipated, preuented, forestalled; taken, or gotten before.*

Appel anticipé. *Th'Appealant preuented; and vrged by the Kings letters, or a speciall Commission (procured by th'Appealee) to shew cause for his appealing sooner then otherwise he would, or should, haue done.*

Partie anticipée. *The same.*

Anticiper. *To anticipate, preuent, forestall; take, or get before.*

Anticiper les quatorzaines des criées. *A Sergeant to make Proclamation before the day appointed for it.*

Antidate : m. *An Antidate.*

Antidaté : m. ée : f. *Antidated.*

Antidater. *To antidate.*

Antidore. *A requitall, a remuneration; one good turn for another.*
Antidotaire : com. *Antidotarie; seruing for a counterpoison; treating of counterpoisons.*
Antidote : m. *An Antidote, or counterpoison; a preseruation against poyson, or euill ayre.*
Antidoté. *Furnished with preseruatiues, forearmed with Antidotes, assured from poysons with counterpoisons.*
Antidoter. *To furnish with preseruatiues, to preserue by Antidotes, to arme, or assure against poyson with counterpoison.*
Antienne : f. *An Antem, or supplication.*
Antifortunal : m. *An opposition, or crosse vnto fortune; somewhat against fortune.*
Antille de bois. *A woodden latch of a doore; or, the ring that serues both to lift vp the latch, and pull the doore too.*
Antimoine : m. *Antimonie; a certaine white stone, or imperfect mettall (the beginning of siluer, and lead) found in siluer mines; and good for the eyes.*
Antimonie : f. *Contrarietie, or opposition of two Lawes.*
Antinormies. *Enormous contrarieties.*
Antipathie : f. *An antipathie; a contrarietie of naturall humours; a naturall, and extreame disagreement of dispositions; crossing, or contrarie inclinations of seuerall persons, without manifest cause knowne to themselues for it.*
Antipelargie : f. *The reciprocall loue of children to their parents; or (more generally) any requitall, or mutuall kindnesse.*
Antiperistase : f. *A mutuall, or generall cohibition, compression, or repulsion of humors, &c, whereby they become the stronger, and the more strongly possesse the parties they are in.*
Antiphones : f. *The reciprocall voyces, aunsweres, or chaunting of two companies that sing by turnes, as in a Quier.*
Antiphonnier : m. *The booke of Anthems, (In a Cathedrall Church.)*
Antipodes : m. *The Antipodes; the people which goe directly against vs, or with the soles of their feet against ours.*
Antipodium : m. *A surplusage, ouerplus addition, or aduantage aboue measure.*
Antiporte : f. *An outward gate; or, a gate that is iust opposite vnto another.*
Antiquaille. *The Anticke; an Anticke; also, an auntient monument.*
Antiquaire : m. *An Antiquarie; one that professes, or delights in, the search, or knowledge of Antiquities.*
Antiquaire : com. *Old, auntient, stale.*
Antique. Taillé à Antiques. *Cut with Antickes, or with Anticke workes.*
Antique : com. *Auntient, antique, old, stale.*
Antiquement. *Auntiently, after the old maner.*
Antistrophe : f. *An Antistrophe; or alternall conuersion of two things, which be somewhat alike.*
Antonnoir. *as* Entonnoir.
Antonomasie : f. *A Pronomination; the vsing of an Epithite, or propertie, in stead of the proper name wherunto it belongs.*
Antonomatic : m. ique : f. *Excellent.*
Antore : f. *Yellow Monkes-hood, Aconits Mithridate.*
Antrac : m. *A Carbuncle (stone, or sore.)*
Antract. *Looke* Entract.
Antre : m. *A caue, denne, grot, cauerne, hole, or hollownesse, vnder the ground.*

Anubet : m. *The name of an apple, wherof excellent cyder is made.*
Anui. *To day; all this day.*
Anuicter. *To deferre, stay, or keepe vntill night; also, to benight, make night, turne into night.*
s'Anuicter. *To wax night, to grow late, or towards night.*
Anuiter. *as* Anuicter.
Anulaire : m. *The Keeper of the Kings Ring, or Signet, called so in old time: Or, as in,* Annulaire.
Anulaire : com. *Annular; of, or belonging to a ring; Looke* Annulaire.
Anullé : m. ée : f. *Annulled, disannulled, annihilated, made effectlesse, made voide.*
Anullement : m. *An annulling, disannulling, annihilating.*
Anuller. *To annull, disannull, annihilate, abolish, bring to nothing, make effectlesse, make voide.*
Anuot : m. *A Blind-worme.*
Anxieté : f. *Anxietie, anguish, vexation, perplexitie, care, carke, sorrow of mind.*
Any : m. *The hearbe Anise; also, (the seed thereof) Anny-seed.*
Aoriste. *A Tense:* ¶Grec.
Aornement. *An ornament, attire, imbellishment, adornment; as* Ornement.
Aorner. *as* Orner; *To decke, imbellish, adorne, attire.*
Aorolat. *as* Rolat. *(In the customes of* la Bourt.)
Aorte. artere aorte. *One of the three principall Arteries of the bodie, issuing from the left Ventricle, and broad, end of the heart, whereunto first it giues two others, tearmed* Coronales: *Some call it the mother of Arteries.*
Aouillé : m. ée : f. *Cloyed, saded, full gorged, filled that his belly strouts withall.*
Aourser. *To burne at, or to, the bottome, as a pot, or stuffe in a pot, wherein there wants liquor.*
Aoust : m. *(The Moneth) August; also, Haruest-time.*
Double d' aoust. *An ordinarie tax or subsidie payed euery August vnto lords by their villeines, or such as hold land of them by a seruile tenure.*
Vallet d' Aoust. *A Reaper, or Shearer; a Hind, or Hireling, for the time of Haruest onely.*
En Aoust les gelines sont sourdes: Prov. *In August Hennes are deafe.*
Aousté : m. ée : f. *Reaped; also, ripened.*
Aouster. *To reape, or mow, as men doe in August; also, to ripen, as fruit, or corne does in Summer.*
Aousteron : m. *A Reaper; or as,* vallet d'Aoust.
Aousteux : m. euse : f. *Of, or belonging to, August; also, full ripe, as most fruit is in August.*
Aparier. *Seeke* Apparier.
A-part. *Apart, alone, singly, solely, priuatly, by himselfe; assunder, one from another.*
Apast. *Seeke* Appast.
Apaster. *as* Appaster.
Apedeftes. *Ignorant people:* ¶Rab.
Apens. de guet apens. *Wittingly, willingly, of set purpose, with a full intent.*
Apensement: m. *A full purpose, determination, or intent to do a thing.*
Apenser. *To purpose, intend, or determine beforehand; to doe a thing willingly, wittingly, or of set purpose.*
Apentis : m. *A Penthouse; also, an open gallerie, (made round about a Court &c.)*
Apercher. *To pearch; to set, or sit on a pearch, or branch.*

Aperitif: m.iue: f. *Of an opening power, or qualitie.*
Apert. *Apparant, open, euident, plaine, manifest.*
Loy aperte. *as* loy apparente.
Apert. *See* Appert.
Apertement. *Openly, plainely, manifestly, euidently; apparantly, without dissimulation.*
Apertise. *Seeke* Appertise.
Apetissant. *Daintie; whetting, or inuiting the appetite.*
Aphairese: f. *The figure* Aphæresis; *the taking of a letter or sillable from the beginning of a word.*
Aphorisme: m. *An Aphorisme (or generall rule in Physicke.)*
Aphorretique: com. *Doubtfull, vnsetled in opinion, whose mind, or iudgement is at oddes with it selfe.*
Aphrodille: m. *The Affodill, or Asphodill flower; also, the plant that beares it; also, the budded root thereof.*
Aphrodille blanc. *The white Asphodill, Dutch Asphodill.*
Aphrodille femelle. *The Onion Asphodill, roundbulbed Asphodill, female Asphodill: Some also call so, the Kings-speare Asphodill, or little yellow Asphodill.*
Aphrodille masle. *The white Asphodill, male Asphodill.*
Aphronitre. *Salt-peeter.*
Aphyer. *as* Afyer.
Apier: m. *A place where Bees are kept, and tended.*
Apilé. fort, & apilé. *Strong; well set, well trust, well knit, well heaped, together.*
Apistolé: m. ée: f. *Cousened, guld; cuckolded, made a wittall; also, baited, nipped, taunted.*
Apistoler. *To cousen, or gull; also, to bait, nip, taunt, afflict with bitter girds; also, to hornifie, or giue the blow that smarts not.*
Apitoyer. *To take pitie, to haue compassion, of.*
Aplanir. *Seeke* Applanir.
Aplanoyer. *as* Applanir; *also, to qualifie, tame, calme, make as mild as a Lambe.*
Aplegement: m. *Suretiship; Looke* Appleiger.
Aplet: m. *A kind of great draw-net, vsed in the fishing for Herrings, Mackerels, &c.*
Aplomb: m. *A perpendiculer, or downe-right fall, seat, or forme; a plumpe descent.*
s'Aplomber. *To fall, or sinke downe plumpe, by reason of it owne weight.*
Apocalypse: f. *The Apocalipse, or Reuelation of S. Iohn; and (more generally) any Reuelation; patefaction, denudation.*
Apocryphe: m. *Th'Apocrypha; Scripture thats not Canonicall; also, (most properly) an obscure place, lurking hole, or corner, secret thing.*
Apogée: m. *A shrowd, or denne vnder th'earth; also, the point of heauen wherein the Sunne, or any Planet, is furthest from the center of th'earth.*
Apoinct: m. *as* Appoinct; *opportunitie, fitnesse, &c.*
à son apoinct. *Fitly, for his purpose or turne; after his mind, according to his humour.*
Apointé: m. ée: f. *Pointed, or, sharpened at the point; also, referred, or appointed ouer; as a cause, vnto hearing.*
Apointement. *as* Appoinctement.
Apointer. *Looke* Appoincter.
Apointi: m. ie: f. *Pointed; made with a point; sharpened, or smalled, at the point.*
Apointir. *To point, or make with a point; to sharpen, or make small, at the point.*
s'Apoitronner. *To play the coward; also, to grow lazie, or slothfull.*
Apollinaire: f. *Henbane.*
Apologie: f. *An Apologie, defence, purgation, excuse.*
Apologue: m. *A (prettie and significant) fable, or tale, wherein bruit beasts, or dumbe things, are fained to speake.*
s'Apoltronner. *as* s'Apoitronner; *(and the better word) to grow cowardly; or, lazie.*
Aponeurose. *The Sinewie seperation of the muscles.*
Apophthegme: m. *An Apothegme; a short and pithy sentence.*
Apophyse: f. *An eminent production, or outstanding of some true, and inseperable part of a bone beyond the naturall places confining vnto it; Anotamists call it, a Processe.*
Apoplectique. *One that hath an Apoplexie.*
Apoplexie: f. *An Apoplexie, or dead Palsie.*
Aporetique: com. *Euer doubting, neuer certaine in, or assured of, any thing; (the custome, or humor of a Pyrrhonian Philosopher.)*
Aposeme: m. *A Decoction of medicinable hearbes, in water.*
Apostasie: f. *An Apostasie; a reuolting, or falling away from a Religion, duetie, or purpose, formerly professed.*
Apostasier. *To play th'Apostata, to Apostatise it; or, to fall away from his religion, duetie, or purpose.*
Apostat. *An Apostata.*
Apostater. *as* Apostasier.
Apostatizer. *as* Apostasier.
Aposté: m. ée: f. *Suborned; set; appointed.*
Aposteine. *Seeke* Apostume.
Aposteiner. *To swell, or grow vnto an impostume.*
Aposter. *To suborne, &c; as* Apposter.
Apostil: m. *as* Appostile.
Apostile, & Apostiler; *Seeke* Appostile, & Appostiler.
Apostolat: m. *A Apostleship; the office of an Apostle.*
Apostoles: f. *Letters missiue from a prince; also, writs, or letters of Appeale sent by the Iudge appealed from, to him that is appealed vnto; (A tearme (at this day) of Ecclesiasticall Courts.)*
Apostolique: com. *Apostolicall, Apostle-like, belonging to an Apostle; Seeke* Notaire.
Souliers a l'Apostolique. *Sandalls.*
Apostolizer. *To play the Apostle.*
Apostre: m. *An Apostle; Embassadour; Messenger; also, the Popes Deleguate for the receiuing of appeals in a forreine Prouince.*
Apostres. *Apostles; also, as* Apostoles.
Apostrophé: m. ée f. *Auerted, wryed, turned aside; also, reuoked, recalled; also, apostrophised; cut off by an Apostrophe.*
Apostropher. *To auert, wry, turne aside; also, to reueke, or call backe; also, to apostrophise; to cut off (by an Apostrophe) the last vowell of a word.*
Apostume: f. *An Impostume; an inward swelling full of corrupt matter.*
Apostumé: m. ée: f. *Impostumed, or impostumated; mattered, suppurated, inwardly.*
Apostumer. *To impostumate, or impostume; to rise in, or grow to, an impostume; to suppurate, or matter, inwardly.*
Apotherapie. *Pastime, recreation; any exercise, or manner of good gouernment after exercise.*
Apothicaire: m. *An Apothicarie.*
Apothicairaisse: com. *Of an Apothecarie, made, or ministred by an Apothicarie; Apothecarilike.*

Apothicairerie: f. *Apothecariship; the trade, or skill of Apothecaries.*
Apoué: m. ée: f. *Saded, so full as he can eat no more.*
Apovrir. *To impouerish; Looke* Appovrir.
Apozeme, *or* Apozime. *A decoction, of water with diuers sorts of hearbes and spices, vsed in stead of a syrop.*
s'Appaillarder. *To spend his life in, or giue himselfe wholly to, whoorisme; to turne leacher, smell-smocke, bitch-hunter, whooremunger.*
Appaisé: m. ée: f. *Appeased, pacified, quieted, calmed, qualified.*
Appaisement: m. *An appeasement, or appeasing; a pacification, quieting, calming, qualifying.*
Appaiser. *To appease, pacifie, calme, quiet, qualifie, asswage, content.*
Assez peut pleurer qui n'a nul qui l'appaise: Pro. *He may weepe his eyes out that hath none to still him.*
Appaiseur: m. *An appeaser, pacifier, peace-maker; calmer, quieter, qualifier, contenter.*
Appali: m. ie: f. *Growne, or made, pale.*
Appalir. *To wax pale; also, to make pale.*
Appanage. *Seeke* Appennage.
Appanager. *as* Appennager.
Appané: m. ee: f. *That hath had a portion; that hath receiued a childs part; that is alreadie bestowed, or prouided for.*
Appaner. *To giue a younger sonne his portion, or childs part.*
Appanner. *The same.*
Appaouvri: m. ie: f. *Beggared, impouerished, made poore.*
Appaouvrir. *To beggar, impouerish, make poore.*
Apparagé: m. eé: f. *Fitly matched, well paired.*
Fille apparagée suffisamment, ou deüement. *A maid thats maried vnto her equall, or, thats not disparaged.*
Apparat: m. *A preparation, decking, prouision, furniture.*
Grand apparat. *Great coyle, stirre, or adoe; much preparation for.*
Apparcevoir. *Seeke* Apperceuoir.
Appareil: m. *Preparation, prouision, readie-making; a decking, dressing, trimming; cooking, seasoning.*
Haut appareil. *A Gorget; also, a Corslet.*
Appareillé: m. ée: f. *Prepared, prouided, made readie, trimd vp for; also, dressed; cooked, or seasoned, (as meat) also, armed at all points.*
Appareillement: m. *A preparing, prouiding, readie-making, trimming vp for; a dressing; a cooking, a seasoning; also, an arming.*
Appareiller. *To prepare, prouide, or trimme vp for; to fashion, or make readie; to make fit for vse, or shew; also, to dresse, cooke, or season (meat;) also, to arme, or put on armour.*
Appareilleur: m. *A preparer, prouider, trimmer vp for; one that makes things readie for vse, or shew; a dresser; fashioner; seasoner.*
Appareilleuse: f. *A waiting woman, or chamber-maid, that vses to dresse her Mistresse; also, a Bawde.*
Apparemment. *Apparently, euidently, manifestly, openly, plainely, to full view; also, seeming, or to the shew.*
Apparence: f. *An apparance, or appearance; a shew, seeming, signe, signification.*
Apparent. *Apparant, euident, manifest, open, plaine; also, excellent, notable, notorious, of great marke, much eminencie.*
Apparenté: m. ée: f. *Of kin, or neere kinsman, vnto.*
Bien apparenté. *Well allyed, of a good house; that hath many, or great, kinsfolkes.*
Apparenter aucun. *To challenge, or acknowledge any one for a kinsman.*
s'Apparesser. *as* s'Apparessir.
s'Apparessir. *To grow idle, wax lazie, become sluggish.*
Apparfondir. *Seeke* Approfondir.
Appariation: f. *A matching, or pairing; also, a perpetuall association, or correspondencie of iurisdiction betweene the king and a lord Spirituall, or Temporall; or betweene a lord Spirituall, and a Temporall, neighbours.*
Apparié: m. ée: f. *Paired, coupled, matched; equalled; conioyned; compared.*
Apparier. *To paire, couple, match, equall; ioyne, conioyne, compare, together.*
s'Apparier. *To couple, or match; as birds doe in the Spring, or a little before they would breed.*
Apparietaire. *as* Apparitoire.
Apparissant. *Appearing; or, as* Apparent.
Appariteur: m. *An Apparator, Sumner, Pursuyuant; also, a hangman.*
Apparition: f. *An Apparition, Vision, Phantasma; also, an appearing, or manifestation.*
Apparitoire: f. *Pellitorie of the wall.*
Apparoir. *To appeare, seeme; be seene, or shew it selfe, on a sudden; also, to be apparant, manifest, plaine, euident.*
Apparoissance: f. *An appearance, or appearing; a seeming, shewing, or shew; also, an eminencie, a passing or standing aboue others.*
Apparoistre. *as* Apparoir.
Appartenance: f. *An appurtenance, an appendant; a proprietie; a due, or thing that belongs vnto.*
Il est de nostre appartenance. *He is one of our house, familie, or followers.*
Appartenant. *Pertaining, appertaining, belonging vnto.*
Appartenir. *To pertaine, appertaine; belong, or be due vnto; also, to beseeme.*
Apparu: m. uë: f. *Appeared, manifested, seen, or shewne on a sudden.*
Appast: m. *An appast, bait; allurement, inticement; also, a repast, or meale.*
Appastant. *Bayting; also, alluring, or inticing by baits; also, feeding.*
Appasté: m. ée: f. *Bayted; also, allured, or inticed, as by a bait, or by the bait of; also, fed.*
Appastelé: m. ée: f. *Fed with the hand; also, as* Appasté.
Appasteler. *To feed by hand, or with the hand; or, as a bird feeds her yong; also, as* Appaster.
Appaster. *To bait; also, to allure, or intice, by a bait, or by the bait of; also, to feed.*
Appasteux: m. *An alluring, inticing, or cousening mate.*
Appasteux: m. euse: f. *Full of allurements, fraught with inticements.*
Appeau: m. *as* Appel; *also, a bird-call; the reed, or little pipe wherewith fowlers call sillie birds to their destruction.*
Appeaux. *Chymes; or, the chiming of bells; also, Appeales, and, the Court of Appeales.*
Appel: m. *An Appeale (from an inferior Court, or Iudge, vnto a superiour.)*
Appel comme d'abus. *An appealing by a temporall person from th'Ecclesiasticall Court, or by an Ecclesiasticall person from a temporall Court, vnto the king, in his high Court of Parliament.*

Appel volage. *An antient forme of Appeale vsed by such defendants as pretended disturbance in the possession of their inheritance.*

Fol appel. *An idle, or litigious Appeale; which is finable; Seeke* Amende de fol appel.

Contre la mort n'y a nul appel: Prov. *Death admits no Appeale; or, none can appeale from death.*

Appelant: m. *An Appealant, or Appealer, one that appeales; also, a caller, or crier vnto; (and hence do Fowlers name a Finch,* Appelant; *) also, an appeacher, or accuser.*

Visage d'appelant. *A heauie looke, sorrowfull visage, pitifull countenance.*

Appelant. *Calling; appealing; appealant; spelling; accusing.*

Appelé: m. ée: f. *Called, named, tearmed, cleeped; also, appealed from; also, spealed; also, accused, appeached, charged with.*

Appeler. *To call; name, tearme, cleape; whoope for, cry vnto; also, to appeale from, or vnto; also, to speale, or set letters together; also, to accuse, appeach, or charge with.*

Appeler comme d'abus. *Looke* Appel.

Appeler omisso medio. *To appeale vnto a higher Iudge than him before whom th'Appeale was by due course to haue beene brought; as when one appeales from a Preuost vnto a Presidiall Iudge, baulking the* Bailli, *who is betweene both, and who (excepting against th'Appeale) may draw the matter to bee heard before himselfe: Otherwise, it is in Appeales made vnto a Court of Parliament, the proceedings wherof cannot be interrupted by an inferiour iurisdiction; nor is there any great need they should; for the reuerend Iudges of those high Courts remaund the most part of those causes vnto their due places, and fine th'Appealants.*

Appeler du rolle. *To read, or call, ouer in court, the roule, or catalogue of causes which are to be heard.*

Appellant. *as* Appelant.

Appellation: f. *A calling, or crying vnto; a naming, or tearming; also, an Appeale, or appealing; wherof Lawyers make two (generall) kinds.*

Appellation extrajudiciaire. *An appealing from acts done out of the Court; as, from a publicke Seisure, Execution, &c.*

Appellation iudiciaire. *Is from th'Acts, Iniunctions, or Orders passed in Court; and must be done by speech, and writing; both in these two words,* I'appelle.

Appellatoire: com. *Appellatorie; appealing.*

Appellé. *as* Appelé.

Appellement: m. *A calling, naming; spealing.*

Appeller. *as* Appeler.

Appelleur: m. *A caller, or spealer; also, the Plouer which in flying leadeth all the rest.*

Appelourder. *To counterfeit, adulterate, falsifie, sophisticate; also, to pollute, soyle, steine, blemish.*

Appendice: f. *An appendix, addition, labell, hang-by.*

Appendicule: f. *An appendicle, or little appendix.*

Appendre. *To hang vp, or on high, as offerings to the gods in temples (or vnto Saints in churches) also, to depend on, hang by, appertaine, or belong vnto.*

Appennage: m. *The portion of a younger brother of Fraunce; the lands, Dukedomes, Counties, or countries assigned by the king vnto his younger sonnes, or brethren, for their intertainment; also, any portion of land, or money, deliuered vnto a sonne, daughter, or kinsman, in lieu of his future right of succession to the whole, which he renounces, vpon the receit thereof; or, (as* Nicod.*) the lands, and lordships giuen by a father vnto his younger sonne, and to his heires for euer, a childs part.*

Terres tenues en appennage. *As it were to vse only; for the propertie of them is in the crowne; and therefore they cannot be aliened; nor inherited by a woman.*

Appennager. *To assigne, or deliuer ouer vnto a younger sonne his portion, or childs part.*

Apenné. *That hath alreadie his portion, that hath receiued his childs part; alreadie prouided for.*

Appenner. *as* Appennager.

Appens. de guet appens. *Deliberatly, of set purpose, wittingly, willingly; See* Guet.

Appensé: m. ée: f. *Determined, meant, or thought of before hand; wittingly, and of set purpose entred into.*

Appensement. *A bethinking himselfe of a matter before he do it; also, a full purpose, meaning, or determination to do it.*

Iour d'appensensement, & d'aduis. *A time to consult, or deliberate, of a matter.*

s'Appenser. *To deliberate, pause, or bethink himselfe of a thing before he do it; also, to determine, or meane it before hand.*

Appentis: m. *The Penthouse of a house.*

Apperceu: m. euë: f. *Perceiued, discerned, marked, noted, heeded, espied.*

Appercevable: com. *Perceiuable, to be perceiued.*

Appercevance: f. *A knowledge, perceiuing, or inkling of a matter; an appearance, or marke.*

Appercevoir. *To perceiue, discerne; marke, note, behold, espie.*

Appert: m. ee: f. *Expert, readie, dexter, prompt, actiue, nimble; feat, handsome, in that he does.*

Appert *(a Verbe Impersonall)* il appert. *It appeareth, or seemeth to be so; also, it is manifest, apparant, certainly so.*

Appertement. *Expertly, readily, promptly; with good facilitie, nimblenesse, dexteritie, featnesse.*

Appertise: f. *Expertnesse, facilitie, readinesse, dexteritie, promptnesse, actiuitie, nimblenesse; featnesse, handsomenesse; also, prowesse, valour, good skill, great abilitie in warlike matters.*

Appesanti: m. ie: f. *Made heauie, or vnweldie (by weight that is layed on it) much burthened, sore laden; pressed, or weighed downe.*

Appesantir. *To make heauie, or vnweldie (by laying a great load on;) to weigh, or presse downe; to aggrauate, burthen, load extreamely.*

s'Appesantir. *To wax heauie, lumpish, vnweldie, dull, slow.*

Appesantissement: m. *A making heauie, or vnweldy, a weighing, or pressing downe.*

Appeté: m. ée: f. *Coueted, lusted for, longed after; fancied, affected, much desired.*

Appetence: f. *Appetencie, appetite; a desire of, or stomacke vnto, meat, &c.*

Appeter. *To couet, long for, lust after; haue an appetite, stomacke, or humour vnto; affect, fancie, desire, much.*

Appetissé: m. ée: f. *Lessened, diminished, abated; impaired, extenuated; also, in appetite, hauing a good stomacke; also, affected, coueted, desired, with an appetite.*

Appetissement: m. *A lessening, abating, diminishing; impairing, extenuating.*

Appetissement de mesure. *Looke* Mesure.

Appetisser. *To lessen, diminish, abate; impaire, extenuate; also, as* Appeter.

Appetit: m. *An appetite, coueting, desire of, lust after; fancie, affection, humor, stomacke vnto.*

Appetit de chien. *Looke* Chien.

En mangeant l'appetit se perd: Prov. *Eating, better than any thing, quells appetite, or abates the stomacke.*

En mangeant l'appetit vient; Prov. *One shoulder of mutton drawes downe another.*

Appetitif: m. iue: f. *Appetitiue; full of appetite; much wishing for; also, breading an appetite, or desire vnto it.*

Appetits: m. *as* Eschalotes; *Ciues, or Chiues.*

Appieceter. *To peece, patch, mend; to set a peece, or clap a patch vnto.*

Appigres. *The nets, hookes, or other implements vsed, by fishers, or fishermen; whence.*

Messieurs n'y trouverent pas grand appigres. *They saw there was not much good to be got, much fish to be caught.*

Appiler. *To heape, or pile together.*

Applané: m. ée: f. *Planed, leuelled, smoothed, euened, made plaine.*

Applaneur: m. *A planer, leueller; layer, or maker of things euen.*

Applaneur de draps. *The Cloathworker; who with his thistly cards doth smooth, and stroake down clothes.*

Applani: m. ie: f. *Planed, smoothed, euened, leuelled.*

Applanier. *To smooth; also, to sooth, or flatter.*

Applanieur. m Applanisseur.

Applanir. *To plaine, plane, euen, leuell, smooth; to make of equall pitch.*

Applanissement: m. *A planing, euening, leuelling, smoothing, making equall.*

Applanisseur: m. *A planer, euener, leueller, smoother; and more particularly, the Cloathworker, who with his cards of tazle smoothes, and stroakes downe clothes.*

Applany. *Looke* Applani.

Applati: m. ie: f. *Flatted; flat, flatting; made plaine, or euen; squashed downe; also, sunke, or shrunke in.*

Applatir. *To flat, or flatten; to make plaine, or euen; to squash downe.*

s'Applatir. *To fall, sinke, or shrinke in.*

Applatissant. *Sinking, shrinking in; making flat, or plaine.*

En applatissant. *Flatling.*

Applatissement. *A flatting, a making flat; also, flatnesse.*

Applaudir. *To applaud, commend, praise highly; or, to clap the hands, or stampe with the feet, in signe of ioy taken in, or liking had vnto, a thing done.*

Applaudissement: m. *An applause, commendation, approbation, or congratulation, expressed by clapping of the hands, or stamping with the feet.*

Applaudisseur. *An applauder, commender; flatterer.*

Applausement. *as* Applaudissement.

Applege: f. *A reall complaint, or bill of complaint for land.*

Applegé: m. ée: f. *Pledged, ingaged, obliged, bound, in bonds, become suertie for; vndertaken, or warranted to be good.*

Applegement. *as* Appleigement.

Appleger. *as* Appleiger.

Appleige: f. *as* Applege.

Appleigé: m. ée: f. *Impledged, obliged, in bonds for &c; as* Applegé.

Appleigement: m. *A pledging, gaging, pawning, vndertaking, entring into bonds for; also, a reall complaint, or bill of complaint for land.*

Appleiger. *To become pledge, giue a gage, deliuer a pawne, be suertie, enter into bond for; also, as* s'Appleiger.

Appleiger son marche. *To assure, warrant, or become bound for the goodnesse of, or the goodnesse of his right in, the thing he sels.*

s'Appleiger. *To complaine; to present vnto, or put into the court a bill of complaint for land.*

Application. *An application, apposition, applying, or laying vnto; an inclination, bending, or bowing to; also, a relation, conforming, comparing, with.*

Appliqué. *Applied, put, set, or laied vnto; inclined, disposed, bent, or bowed to; also, conformed, or compared, with.*

Appliquer. *To applie, incline, bend, bow vnto; to dispose, put, set, or lay to; also, to conforme, compare, associate, with.*

s'Appliquer à. *To apply, &c, himselfe to; also, to leane; or adhere vnto; also, to humor, or follow the humor of.*

Applommé de sommeil. *In a sound, heauie, or dead, sleepe; fast asleepe.*

Applommer de sommeil. *To lay, or lull, fast asleepe; to bring, or cast into a heauie, or dead sleepe; also, to make heauie, lumpish, drowsie, sleepie.*

Appoinct: m. *Fitnesse, opportunitie; a thing for ones purpose, after his mind, according to his humour; such an occasion, or time, as were it in his choyce, hee would appoint no other.*

Appoincté. *as* Appointé.

Appoinctement: m. *A composition, agreement, reconciliation, league, peace, made betweene friends fallen out; also, a sentence, decree, order, or Iniunction, for the possession of a thing in controuersie; also, an appointing, assigning, or graunting ouer vnto; or, an assignement, or grant, of a thing; also, a pointing, or sharpening at the point; also, a rule giuen by a Iudge vpon contestation; and hence;*

Appoinctement de faict, ou, en droict. *Is (when a suit cannot be iudged presently, or vpon the first hearing thereof; by reason that the contrarie allegations, or crosse pleadings of the parties require further prooues from them, or deliberation of the Court) the referment of a cause vnto a further deliberation, or hearing.*

Appoincter. *To determine, order, decree, decide; finish, end, a controuersie; to accord, attone, agree, reconcile, make a league, or composition betweene, parties in controuersie; also, to appoint, assigne, or grant ouer vnto; also, to point, or sharpen at the point; also, to referre a cause ouer vnto a further deliberation, or hearing; to giue a rule in a cause.*

Appoint: m. *as* Appoinct.

Appointant: m. ante: f. *Determining, deciding, finishing, ending controuersies; agreeing, reconciling parties in controuersie; also, appointing, or assigning ouer vnto; also, pointing, or sharpening at the point.*

Appointé: m. ée: f. *Determined, ordered; compounded; ended, finished, as a controuersie; agreed, accorded, reconciled, at a point, or peace with; also, appointed, assigned, or granted vnto; also, pointed, or, sharpened at the point; also, referred ouer vnto a further deliberation.*

Appointez. *Gentlemen of Companies; such as receiue better pay than th'ordinary Sentinels, or soldiors.*

Appointé du Roy de 500 escus par an. *Hauing 500 Crownes a yeare pension, or entertainment of the king.*

Appointement, & Appointer. *as* Appoinctement; & Appoincter.

Appointir. *To point; to sharpen, or make small, at the end, or point.*

Appointusant. *Growing narrow, sharpe, or small, towards*

wards the end,point,or top.

s'Appointuser. *To grow narrow, sharpe, or small, towards th'end,point,or top.*

Appoissonné:m.ée:f.*Stored,furnished,or fraught,with fish.*

Appoissonnement: m. *A storing,furnishing,or fraughting with fish.*

Appoissonner. *To store, furnish,or fraught,with fish.*

Apport:m.*A carriage,or bringing vnto;also,an arriual, or approach; also,a landing place; also,a resort,a trouping,or comming to in troups; also,the reuenew,gaine, or profit which a thing brings in to it owner.*

l'Apport d'une fiancée. *The portion in mouables,or immouables brought by a woman contracted, vnto her future husband,ouer and besides her dowrie; also, the goods come vnto her by succession from the time of the contract; also, the mariage gifts bestowed on her by him,or others,before the mariage be fully solemnized.*

Apporté: m.ée: f.*Caried; or brought vnto; also, arriued at,or,come neere to,the hauen,or shore.*

Apportement: m.*A carrying; or,bringing to; also,an arriuing at,or drawing neere vnto, the hauen,or shore.*

Apporter.*To carie, bring,or beare vnto; also,to arriue, or approach neere to the hauen,or shore.*

Chasque demain apporte son pain: Prov. *God so prouides for all his creatures, that they need not care much for the morrow.*

Qui vient est beau;qui apporte encores plus beau: Prov.*Faire is he that comes,but fairer he that brings; no emptie hand lookes so well as a full one.*

Trop tost vient a la porte qui mauvaise nouvelle apporte: Prov. *Looke* Nouvelle.

Apportionner.*To apportion; to giue a portion,or childs part.*

Apposé: m.ée: f. *Layed,put, set on, or neere to,added vnto; assigned,or expresly appointed for.*

Apposer. *To lay,to set on,or neere to; to put,or adde vnto; to destinate,appoint,or make to serue for.*

Apposition. *An apposition; an adding,or putting to; a setting on,or neere to.*

Apposté: m.ée: f.*Apposted, suborned,procured vnderhand; put into,appointed vnto, a businesse, of set purpose, or,to a place for the purpose.*

Apposter. *To apposte, suborne, procure vnderhand; to put into,or appoint vnto, a place,or businesse,of set purpose,or for priuate purposes.*

Appostile. *An answer vnto a petition, set downe in the margent therof; and,generally,any small addition vnto a great discourse in writing.*

Appostiler. *To amplifie, enlarge,or adde vnto a writing; to answer a petition in the margent thereof.*

Appovri: m.ie: f. *Beggared,impouerished,made poore; vndone.*

Appovrir. *To impouerish,beggar,make poore; vndo.*

Appovrissement: m. *An impouerishment, beggaring, vndoing.*

Appreci. *A price,rate,value set on things; or, as* Appreciation.

Rentes à l'appreci. *Looke* Rente.

Appreciateur. *A priser,rater,valuer,praiser.*

Appreciation: f. *A praising,or prising; a rating,valuation,estimation of.*

Apprecier.*To rate,esteeme,prise, value, hold at, set a price on.*

Apprehendre. *To apprehend,conceiue,vnderstand;perceiue,discouer, spie out.*

Apprehensif: m.iue: f.*Apprehensiue; wittie,of a quick conceit,or nimble vnderstanding.*

Apprehension: f. *An apprehension, or comprehension; vnderstanding,wit,conceit,or conception; a quick discouerie of matters.*

Apprenant: m.ante: f. *Learning,conning,comprehending.*

Apprendre.*To learne,comprehend,conne; also,to teach, or (as we say also) to learne one a thing; whence;*

Apprendre aux poissons à nager. *To teach fishes to swimme; (an idle, vaine, or needlesse labour) we say, to teach his grandame to grope ducks.*

Apprenti: m. *A Prentise; learner, new beginner; scholler.*

Vn apprenti de S. Crispin. *A Shoomaker.*

Nouveau apprenti n'est pas Maistre: Prov. *A new Prentise is no Master; (and therfore a great difference is to be put betweene them, whether it be for vse, or in estimation.)*

Apprentisage: m. *A Prentship.*

Apprest: m.*A preparation,dressing,prouision,making in a readinesse for.*

Apresté: m.ée: f.*Dressed,prepared, prouided, made readie for.*

En bonne maison l'on a tost apresté: Prov. *All things are soone prepared in a well ordered house.*

Apprester. *To prepare,dresse,prouide,make readie for.*

Apprimer. *To initiate,or giue the first direction vnto;to enter; imbolden,or flesh a yong one vpon a thing which before it durst not meddle with.*

Apprins. *as* Appris.

Appris: m.ise: f. *Taught,instructed; nurtured,trained vp; also,learned; conned; comprehended.*

À peine endure mal qui ne l'a appris: Prov. *Hee hardly beares affliction that neuer tried any.*

Envis meurt qui appris ne l'a: Prov.*Vnwillingly he dies,that hath not thought of death; or,that hath not learnt to die.*

Apprivoisé: m.ée: f.*Tamed, reclaimed,made inward, growne familiar, gentle, tractable; housall.*

Brebis trop apprivoisée de trop d'agneaux est tettée: Prov. *Looke* Agneau.

Apprivoisement: m.*A taming, reclaiming,making inward,tractable,gentle; housall.*

Apprivoiser. *To tame, reclaime, make inward, gentle, tractable, familiar; housall.*

Approbatif: m.iue: f. *Approbatiue,approuing.*

Approbation: f. *An approbation, allowance; confirmation of.*

Approchant. *Approaching,drawing neere vnto; arriuing almost at.*

Approche: f. *An approach,a drawing neere vnto.*

Approché: m.ée: f. *Approched, drawne neere to; almost arriued at; (also,adiourned,cited,or serued with proces to appeare:* ¶Norm.*)*

Approchement. *An approaching, drawing nigh, arriuing toward,or almost at.*

Approcher. *To approach; to come,or draw neere vnto; to arriue towards,or almost at; (also,to adiourne, cite, or summon to appeare,by proces:* ¶Norm.*)*

Approfité: m.ée: f. *Benefited,profited by; turned,or imployed vnto the profit of; also,receiued,or gathered, as the reuenew,or fruits of an inheritance.*

Approfitement: m.*An aduantaging,profiting,bringing of profit vnto; a turning,or imploying vnto the profit of; also, a receiuing,taking,or gathering of the reuenew,profits,or fruites of an inheritance.*

Approfiter. *To profit,or thriue by; to make profit, or gaine of; to bring profit vnto; to turne,or imploy vnto profit; also,to receiue,take,or gather the reuenew,profit,*

fits, or fruits of an inheritance; (In which sence the Normand, and Piccard, Lawyers vse it much.)
Approfondir. *To deepen; or, to make more deepe, and hollow; to dig further into.*
Appropriance: f. *An appropropriation, or appropriating; a taking, or conuerting a thing vnto his owne vse.*
Approprié: m. ée: f. *Appropriated, conuerted vnto his owne vse; also, fitted, apted, applied, matched, conformed, accommodated.*
Appropriement: m. *A fitting, conforming, accommodating; also, as* Appropriance.
Approprier. *To fit, match, conforme, approper, accommodate; also, to appropriate, or conuert vnto his owne vse.*
Approsse. de grosse approsse. *Violently, vehemently, with great strength.*
s'Approvisionner. *To furnish himselfe with, to prouide himselfe of, necessaries.*
Approuvé: m. ée: f. *Approued, allowed, auowed; soothed, confirmed, found good, consented vnto.*
Approuvement: m. *An approuing, allowing, auowing; a soothing; a confirming, a consenting vnto.*
Approuver. *To approue, allow, auow, find good, like well of, confirme, sooth, consent vnto.*
Appui-pot: m. *Any thing that stayes, or sustaines, a pot on the fire.*
Appuré: m. ée: f. *Cleered, cleansed, purged, clarified, purified; also, discharged, as a debt; passed, or fully made, as an account.*
Appurement: m. *A cleering, purging, clarifying, purifying; also, the discharging of a debt; the passing, or full-cleering of an account.*
Appurer. *To cleanse, purge, clarifie, purifie.*
Appurer vn compte. *To cleere an account, to passe a reckoning, to procure a* Quietus est.
Appurer vne debte. *To discharge a debt.*
Appurer vn emende. *To rate, assesse, or tax, an Amerciament.*
Appuy: m. *A stay, buttresse, prop, rest, or thing to leane on; also, as* Appuye.
Appuy d'amis. *Support, store, or strength of friends.*
Appuy de la bouche, ou de la bride. *(In horsemanship) the rest vpon the hand; and hence;*
Cheval de bon appuy. *A horse of a temperate, and sweet rest vpon the hand.*
Appuyal: m. *A leaning stocke.*
Appuye: f. *An open, and outstanding terrace, or gallery, set on th'outside with railes to leane vpon.*
Appuyé: m. ée: f. *Stayed, propped, supported, sustained, held vp; also, rested, or leaned, on; built, or depended vpon.*
Appuyer. *To stay, prop, support, sustaine, vnderprop, hold, or beare vp.*
s'Appuyer. *To rest, or leane on; to build, or depend vpon.*
Aprelle. *Seeke* Asprelle.
Apres. *After; following; next vnto.*
En apres. *Afterwards, hereafter; moreouer furthermore; consequently; so then.*
Il estoit tousiours apres le Roy, &c. *Hee daily solicited the King; he was euer in hand, or earnest with him, to.*
Appresdisnées: f. *The fees, dueties, or profit accruing vnto Presidents, or Iudges, and their assistants, by giuing of afternoone Orders; or the afternoone sittings, or hearings, wherein they are giuen by them.*

Apres-germain. vn cousin apres-germain. *A cousin germaine remoued.*
Apresté. *as* Appresté.
Aprique: com. *Sunnie, or that lyeth open to the Sunn*
Aprisonner. *To imprison, or take prisoner.*
Apron. *Seeke* Aspron.
Apte: com. *Apt, fit, sutable, agreeable, well fitting; meet, conuenient.*
Aptitude: f. *Aptitude; abilitie; also, aptnesse, meetnesse, fitnesse, conueniencie, sutablenesse.*
Apvril: m. *Aprill; Seeke* Avril.
Aquatil: m. ile: f. *Aquatile, waterie, lying in the water.*
Aquatique: com. *Waterish; of, or belonging to, the water; liuing in water.*
Aqueduct: m. *An Aqueduct, or conduit of water.*
Aqueux: m. euse: f. *Waterie, waterish, full of water.*
Argent aqueux. *Quick-siluer.*
Humeur aqueux. *A humour in the forepart of the eye, of consistence almost like the white of an egge, and set there, to bridle the impetuositie of colours descending vpon the eye, and somewhat to stay the first violent incounters of obiects.*
Aquiescer. *as* Acquiescer.
Aquilin: m. ine: f. *Of an Eagle, like an Eagle; as,* nez Aquilin; *a Hawke nose; a nose like an Eagle.*
Pierre aquiline. *The Eagle stone; a certaine stone, (found in an Eagles nest) which applied vnto the thigh of a woman that is in labour, is held to giue her much ease.*
Aquilon: m. *The Northerne wind.*
Aquilonal: m. ale: f. *Cold, Northerly, subiect vnto the North.*
Aquilonien: m. enne: f. *Of the North; belonging to the North.*
Aquoest. *This; or (altogether as rudely) thilke:* ¶Gasc.
Aquosité: f. *Aquositie, waterishnesse.*
Ar. Deux & ar. *Deuse ace:* ¶Rab.
Arabe: m. *An Arabian.*
Arabesque: f. *Rebeske worke; a small, and curious flourishing.*
Arabesque: com. *Arabian-like.*
Arabic: m. ique: f. *Arabian, of Arabia.*
Gomme Arabic. *Gumme Arabicke; issues from the shrub* Acacia, *th'Egyptian thorne.*
Arable: com. *Earable, ploughable, tillable.*
Aracte. *The greene, most venimous, and bloud-sucking Serpent,* Cenchris.
Aragnoïde. *A small, thinne, and splendant membrane of the eye (not much vnlike a Spinners web) which serues to vnite, and retaine (as the leaden foyle of a looking glasse) the formes receiued.*
Aragon. *An oyntment made of Brionie roots, wild Cowcumber roots, and other things; good against Crampes and Conuulsions.*
Araigne: f. *A Spider; a Spinner.*
Araigne de mer. *as* Maie; *The greatest kind of crab; also, as* Viue.
Le pertuis de l'araigne. *A certaine hole in an Astrolabe, that represents the Pole of the world, and with a nayle in the middle thereof, ioynes together all the tables belonging to the Astrolabe.*
La toile de l'araigne. *A cobweb.*
Les araignes ont fait leurs toiles sur nos dents. *Our idle teeth by long fasting, are growne full of cobwebs.*

Araignée : f. *A cobweb* ; *or as* Araigne.
Araigneux : m. euse f. *Full of spiders, spinners* ; *or of cobwebs* ; *also, hunting, or feeding on, spiders* ; *whence.*
Souris araigneuse. *A Shrew mouse.*
Araignier : m. ere : f. *Spiderie* ; *of, or like, a spider, or cobweb.*
Tunique araigniere. *as* Aragnoïde.
Arain : m. *Brasse.*
Oeil d'arain. *A red, fierce, fierie, or sparkling eye, such as a Lion hath.*
Pierre d'arain. *Red Vitrioll* ; *the stone wherewith Brasse is tried.*
Il pense que nuës sont pailles d'arain. *(Wee say of such an Idiot* ; *) hee thinkes the Moone is made of greene cheese.*
Araïre. *A plough.* ¶Lionnois.
Araisonner. *Seeke* Arraisonner.
Araisonner la marchandise. *To set a rate, or price on it.*
Aramne. *A fine, or amerciament set on a plaintifes, or defendants head, for not appearing.*
Aransor ; *as* Harenc-sor ; *A red herring.*
Araroye. *A round, and skreene-like ornament of feathers, worne by the West-Indian Sauages at their backes.*
Arasser. *as* Frayer.
Arbaleste : f. *A Crosse-bow* ; *also, a Bow-net* ; *also, the sinewie Crosse-bow, wherewith a man shoots, not deere, but his deerest.*
Arbaleste à boulet. *A Stone-bow.*
Arbaleste à gelais. *The same.*
Arbaleste de passe. *The greatest, or longest kind of Crosse-bow* ; *or as in* Passe.
Arbalestier : m. *A Crosse-bow-man, one that shoots in, or serues with, a Crosse-bow* ; *also, a Crosse-bow maker.*
Arbalestrage : m. *The shooting in a Crosse-bow.*
Arbalestrier. *as* Arbalestier.
Arban : m. *A dayes worke in euerie weeke, due by some Vassalls, that hold by Villenage, vnto their Lords.*
Arbausier : m. *Th'Arbute, or Strawberrie tree.*
Arbaux. *Looke* Herbaux.
Arbenne : f. *A kind of white Partridge (of a Pigeons bignesse) thats rough legd, and footed like a Hare* ; *some hold, that she is browne in Summer, and onely in Winter, white* ; *others, that one kind (which liues in plaines, and vallies) is euer browne* ; *and another (which lurkes on the shadowie sides of snowie mountaines) alwayes, and all-ouer, white.*
Arbitrage : m. *An award, or arbitrement* ; *the sentence, determination, authoritie, or Office, of an Arbitrator.*
Arbitraire : com. *Arbitrable* ; *arbitrating* ; *also, at the will, and pleasure of another* ; *and hence* ;
Amende arbitraire. *Looke* Amende.
Arbitrateur : m. *An Arbitrator, vmpier, stickler* ; *a friendly compounder of differences (according to equitie.)*
Arbitre : m. *An Arbitrator (who is to iudge by the strict rules of Law) also, will, pleasure, fancie* ; *scope of mind, libertie of iudgement, freedome of thought.*
Arbitré : m. ée : f. *Arbitrated, stickled* ; *awarded* ; *compounded, agreed* ; *iudged, or adiudged, by award.*
Arbitrer. *To arbitrate, stickle* ; *award* ; *compound, agree* ; *iudge, or adiudge, by award.*
Arborateur. *A planter, primer, dresser, breeder of trees.*
Arboré : m. ée : f. *Stucke downe, fixed, or planted, as an ensigne into the earth* ; *set vpright.*
Arborer. *To fix, plant, or sticke downe into the earth* ; *to set, as a tree, vpright.*
Arborise. *A kind of white free stone.*
Arboriser. *To studie the nature, to obserue the properties, of trees.*
Arbosier : m. *An Arbute, or Strawberrie tree.*
Arbouce ; ou, Arbouse : f. *The harsh red berrie, called an Arbute, or tree-Strawberrie.*
Arbousier. *as* Arbosier.
Arboutan. *as* Arc boutant. ¶Rab.
Arbre : m. *A tree.*
L'arbre fourchu. *A standing on the head, or on the hands, with out-spread legs.*
Arbre marin, ou de mer. *The greatest of Starre-fishes* ; *called so, because she spreads her selfe abroad, like a full-branched tree.*
l'Arbre d'un moulin. *Th'Axletree* ; *the beame that caries the wheele of a water-mil, and sailes of a windmill.*
l'Arbre d'un nauire. *The Maste.*
Arbre de Paradis. *The tree of Paradise* ; *growes in Ægypt, and beares many blossomes, all at the top, and yeelding all but one fruit* ; *which resembles a Pineapple, and tasts most delicately.*
l'Arbre d'un pressoir. *The beame, tree, or timber of a presse* ; *the thickest, and longest peece of wood belonging to it.*
Arbre de vermilion. *The Scarlet Oke, or Scarlet Holme Oke.*
Arbre de vie. *An Aromaticall tree, so called.*
Arbre trop souuent transplanté ne porte pas fruict à planté. *Looke* Planté.
L'arbre ne tombe pas du premer coup : Prov. *Though a little man can fell a great Oke, yet falls it not at the first blow* ; *Rome was not built on a day* ; *nor are great matters atchieued as soone as attempted.*
De l'arbre d'un pressoir le manche d'un Cernoir : Prov. *(We say of one that hath squandered away great wealth) hee hath thwitten a mill-post to a pudding pricke.*
De doux arbre douces pommes. *A sweet tree yeeldeth sauourie fruit.*
Arbreau : m. *A shrub, or small tree.*
Arbret. *A little tree.*
Arbrier : m. *The Tillar of a Crosse-bow.*
Arbrisseau : m. *A shrub.*
Arbrisselet. *A little shrub.*
Arbrisselet d'aigreur. *The red Gooseberrie shrub.*
Arbuste : m. *A shrub* ; *also, a groue of trees that are lopt, and cut.*
Arbuster. *To plant a ground with thicke rankes of shrubs.*
Arbustif : m. iue : f. *Shrubbie* ; *also, running, or growing vp by the side of a shrub* ; *as Iuie, Vines, &c.*
Arc : m. *A bow* ; *a hand-bow, or long-bow* ; *also, a vault, or arch in building* ; *also, the circle that enuirons the ball, or apple of the eye* ; *the bow, or Iris of the eye.*
Arc boutant. *An arch, bowing pillar, buttresse, or post, that serues to shore, support, or vnderset a building* ; *also, the arke, or arch of a vault* ; *the couer of a cradle* ; *the tilt of a boat, &c.*
L'arc au ciel. *The Rainebow.*

Arc à gelet; ou, à jallet. *A stone-bow.*

L'arc du jour. *The whole day, from Sunne rising to the setting thereof.*

Arc Turquois. *The Turkish long bow.*

Il a plusieurs cordes à son arc. *He hath many strings to his bow (viz. many trades, meanes, helpes, dependancies, or assurances, to rely on.)*

Passer par l'arc S.Bernard. *To be beshitten; to beray himselfe.*

Desbander l'arc ne guerist pas la playe: Prov. *The bows vnbending healeth not the wound (it hath made;) the withdrawing of forces is no amends for the wrongs or harmes, which they haue done.*

Arcade: f. *An arch, or halfe circle.*

Mettre les mains en arcade sur les costes. *To set his hands a kenbow.*

Arc-agelet. *Looke* arc.

Arcanne: f. *Rudle, red chaulke, red oaker.*

Arcasse: f. *The Counter (in the Poope) of a Ship,*

Arc-boutant. *Looke in* Arc.

Arceau: m. *A little bow; bought; arch; also, a Sadle-bow; also, a Carpenters yard, or workehouse.*

Arceler. *Seeke* Harcelet.

Arcenal: m. *An Arcenall; an Armorie; a storehouse of Armour; Artillerie; Shipping, or Ships.*

Archade. *as* Arcade.

Archail. *as* Archal.

Archal &; fil d'archal. *Yellow laten wire; or copper wire.*

Archant: &; Archat; *as* Archal.

Arche: f. *A cofer, chest; hutch, binne; also, an Arke; whence,* l'arche de Noë; *also, the arch of a bridge, &c; also, the well of the Pumpe of a Ship.*

Archecapelein de toute Flanders. *The Arch-chaplaine (or as some thinke) the Chauncellour of Flanders.*

Archediaconé: m. *An Archdeaconrie.*

Archediacre: m. *An Archdeacon.*

Crotté en Archediacre. *Dagd vp to the hard heeles; (for so were the Archdeacons in old time euer woont to be, by reason of their frequent, and toylesome, Visitations.)*

Archeé: f. *A bow-shoot; or, the reach of a bow; as far as a bow will carrie.*

Archelette: f. *A little arch, or arke; also, a womans eare-wire.*

Archenocher: m. *A chiefe Mariner; the Pilot, or Master of a ship.*

Archeprestre: m. *An Arch-priest, High-priest, head-priest, chiefe-priest.*

Archer: m. *An Archer, or Bowman; also, a Yeoman of the (Kings) Gard; also, one of the Prouost Marshalls attendants, or gard; also, a Warder in a Towne, or fortresse; (whose ordinarie weapon, at this day a Halberd, was in old time a bow, and arrowes;) also, a horseman, who in seruice euer accompanies the* Gendarme des Ordonnances; *to whom though he be somewhat inferiour, and though he haue but halfe as much pay (about twentie pounds sterl. a yeare) yet is he to be a Gentleman of birth and breeding; or such a one as hath beene Captaine, Lieutenant, Ensigne, or Sergeant Maior, of a foot companie six yeares together: and whosoeuer will be a* Gendarme *must formerly haue beene an* Archer *of at the least a yeares continuance (if the ordinances be duely obserued.)*

Archers du guet. *The ordinarie watchmen of the towne of* Paris; *(who are not Burguers, but a kind of Souldiours; both appointed, and payed by the King.)*

Franc archer. *Looke* Franc.

Archerie: m. *A match of shooting; also, a field, or ground, to shoot in.*

Archerot: m. *A little Archer, a young Bow-man.*

Archet: m. *The bow of a Viol, &c.*

Archetype: m. *A principall type, figure, forme; the chiefe patterne, mould, modell, example, or sample, whereby a thing is framed; an authenticke, or originall draught.*

Archiatre: m. *A principall Physitian.*

Archidiacre. *An Archdeacon.*

Archiduc. *An Archduke.*

Archier: m. *as* Archer.

Archifs: m. *The Rolls (for the Crowne) or, a place wherein all the Records, Charters, and Euidences that concerne the King, or belong vnto the Crowne, are kept in chests, and boxes.*

Archimandrite: m. *An Abbot; a Generall, or Gouernour of Hermits; a Superintendent, or Ouerseer, of such as reside in desart caues, and dennes.*

Archimarmitonerastique: m. *An Abbey-lubber, or Arch-frequenter of the Cloyster beefe-pot, or beefe-boyler.*

Archimbaud. *A proper name for a man.*

C'est la famille d'Archimbaud, plus y en a & pis vaut: Prov. *(Said of a state, or family, thats pestered with rakehels.)*

Architecte: m. *An Architect; a Gouernour, Ouerseer, director; a chiefe deuiser, contriuer, or framer, of buildings; a worke-master, or master workman, in points of Architecture.*

Architecté: m. ée: f. *Built, contriued, framed, fashioned; set, or made vp, as a house, &c.*

Architecter. *To gouerne, ouersee, direct, a building; also, to contriue, deuise, frame, fashion; make, or set vp, artificially, a building, &c.*

Architectonique: com. *Architectiue; belonging to an Architect, or Architecture.*

Architecture: f. *Architecture; the Art, or Science of building; the framing, or building of a house, &c; also, the frame of a house, or building; an edifice, or building.*

Architrave: m. *The Architraue (of pillars, or stone-worke;) the reason peece, or master beame (in buildings of timber.)*

Archives. *as* Archifs.

Archool. *Dust; (of* Alchool, *an Arabian word.)*

Archure: f. *A mill-hoope, or mill-case; the open chest that holds the mill-stones.*

Arçoir. *as* hier au soir. *Yesternight; (a rusticall word.)*

Arçon: m. *The arson, or bow of a sadle.*

Faire vuider les arçons. *To cast off horsebacke, or out of the sadle.*

Arçon: f. *A burning, or setting on fire.*

Arçonné: m. ée: f. *Set on horsebacke, or betweene the sadle bowes; setled, or set fast, in a sadle.*

Arçonner. *To fasten, setle, or set sure; as, the breech betweene the bowes of a sadle.*

Arçonner vne vigne. *To vnderprop a vine both before and behind.*

Arçonneux: m. euse: f. *Of, or belonging to, a sadle bow; also, fit to hang, or to be carried at, a sadle bow; whence;*

Malette arçonneuse. *A capcase; male, budget, &c.*

Arçonnier: m. ere: f. *as* Arçonneux.

Arcotic: m. ique: f. *Benumming, stupifying.*
Arcou: m. *A kind of laten, or copper, whereof kettles are made.*
Arctique: com. *Northerne, or Northerly.*
Cercle Arctique. *A Circle in our Hemispheare, called, the Pole Articke.*
Arcture: m. *The starre* Boötes *(which followeth Charls waine.)*
Arcuer. *To arch; bow, bend; grow compasse, or crooked, like an arch.*
Arcure: f. *An arching, bought, or bow; compasse, or bowing.*
Ardamment. *Ardently, hotly, feruently; earnestly, eagrely, vehemently; with great heat; passion, or desire.*
Ardans: m. *S. Hermes fires; the flittering, or going fiers, flashes, or flames, which be seen by night, and neere vnto waters.*
Ardant: m. ante: f. *Ardent, hoat, burning; feruent; eagre, earnest, greedie, vehement, most affectionate.*
Chambre ardante. *Looke* Chambre.
Eau ardant. *Aqua, or Aquauitæ.*
Feu ardant. *White Vine, white Bryonie, wild Nep, Tetterberrie; The Wallons, sayes* Gerard, *call Garden Nightshade,* feu ardant.
Vin ardant. *Aquauitæ.*
Ardent. *as* Ardant.
Ardentement. *as* Ardamment.
Ardeur: f. *Ardour; heat, burning; feruencie; eagrenesse, earnestnesse, vehemencie; greedinesse; exceeding affection, extreame passion.*
Ardid. *as* Ardit.
Ardille: f. *Clay, loame, tough mold.*
Ardillé: m. ée: f. *Dawbed, or done ouer, with clay.*
Ardiller. *To clay; to dawbe, or doe ouer, with clay.*
Ardillier: m. ere: f. *Clay, clay-like; of clay.*
Terre ardilliere. *Tough earth, or clay, whereof brick, and tyle may be made.*
Ardillon: m. *The toung of a buckle.*
Ardit: m. *as* Liard; *A coyne thats worth* iij.d. Tourn. ¶Gascon.
Ardoir. *To burne, or be on fire; to be inflamed, or kindled; (hence) also, to be verie earnest; or hot, in a matter; to loue exceedingly; desire feruently, couet vehemently, long for verie much; also, to inflame, or set on fire; as in the Prouerbe,*
L'argent ard gent.
Ardoise: f. *A slate.*
Ardoisé: m. ée: f. *Slated, couered with slates; also, slatie, or of slates.*
Ardoiseux: m. euse: f. *full of, or, filled with, slates.*
Ardoisiere: f. *A slate-pit, slate quarrey, ground full of slates.*
Ardoisin: m. ine: f. *Slatie, or, of slate.*
Ardoüe: f. *A little brooke, or reyne, that gently runnes along a field.*
Ardre. *as* Ardoir.
Ardu: m. uë: f. *Hard; painefull, difficult; great, ample, high, steepe, daungerous; hard to get on, or come to.*
Ardy. *as* Ardit.
Arechal. fil d'arechal. *as* Archal.
Areille. *as* Oreille: ¶Norm.
Arene: f. *Sand; grauell.*
Aréne. *A Theatre for Fencers; a place to iust in, strowed with grauell; and hence was that stately Amphitheatre of Nismes, called,* des Arenes.

Areneux: m. euse: f. *Sandie, grauelly; full of sand, or of grauell.*
Arenger. *Seeke* Arranger.
Areniere: f. *A sand-pit, or grauell-pit; a plot whereout sand, or grauell is digged.*
Arentelles: f. *Gossymere; the long, white, and cobweblike exhalation, that flyes on the ayre in Summe, and Summer, dayes.*
Arenuleux: m. euse: f. *Full of small grauell, or sand.*
Arer. *To plough, till, eare, the ground.*
Arere: f. *A plough.*
Ares-metys. *Presently, euen now, by and by:* ¶Gasc. ¶Rab.
Areste: f. *The small bone of a fish; also, the eyle, awne, or beard of an eare of corne; also, the edge, or outstanding ridge of a stone, or stone-wall.*
Areste du dos. *The backe-bone; or, the ridge of the backe.*
Areste d'un espee &c. *The Crest, of a sword, &c; a sharpe rising in the middle thereof.*
Aresteux: m. euse: f. *Full of small bones, as a Fish.*
Areteuse: f. *The Hearbe Sorrell.*
Arez. *Now, presently, by and by:* ¶Gasc. ¶Rab.
Arfie: f. *A Hornefish, Hornebeake, Snacotfish, Ganefish, Pipe fish.*
Argalice: f. *A Raddish root.*
Argalie: f. *A (Chirurgions) squirt, or siringe; or the instrument wherewith he searcheth the passages of the vrine, or bladder.*
Arganete. *A Wire-drawers bench.*
Argatile. *A kind of titling, or titmouse.*
Arge. *A lightning, which blasteth, and maketh black.*
Argenocher. *as* Arche-nocher; *Or, one of the Argonauts, who sayled with Jason for the Golden Fleece.*
Argent: m. *Siluer; also, money, coyne, chinkes, gilt; also, Argent, in Blason.*
Argent aqueux. *Quick-siluer.*
Argent de cendrée. *Fine, or purified siluer, of* xj.d. *eighteene grains finenesse; thus the finors make at first into wedges, and marke them with their puncheons, thereby vndertaking for the goodnesse, and value thereof.*
Argent comptant. *Readie money; whence;*
Argent comptant porte medicine: Prov. *Readie money is a readie medicine; or, procures any medicine.*
Argent de Cour. *Siluer of* xj.d. *allay (twelue grains baser than* Argent le Roy*) heretofore the proportion for all kind of Goldsmithes worke.*
Argent mignon. *as* Argent comptant.
Argent le Roy. *The Kings siluer; the siluer thats vsed, now adayes, for coyne, and Goldsmithes worke; six graines in the pennie weight baser than* Argent de Cendrée; *(it comes to* 47. s. 6. d. Tournois *the ounce.)*
Faire de l'argent avec les dents. *To grow rich by faring hard; by staruing the bellie to stuffe the purse.*
'A beau ieu bel argent. *Roundly, in good earnest, without faining, dalliance, or delay; also, as good as is brought, one for another.*
Du temps qu'on se cacha. pour prester de l'argent. *In good old times when men were loath to publish their owne goodnesse, or the necessities of others.*
I'en puis parler pour mon argent. *I knewe it to my*

my cost; I can speake of what I haue paid for.
Il veut avoir drap & argent ensemble. *He wil haue both my cloath and his owne coine; (applyable to an vnreasonable chapman, hard bargainer, sore dealer.)*
Le terme vaut l'argent. *The Terme is worth the money; (a phrase most vsed by those whom the benefit of a little time makes to neglect the paiments, or punishments whereto they be subiect.)*
Argent ard gent: Prov. *Mony burnes many;* (viz. *the loue thereof enflames their hearts.)*
Argent contant porte medicine: Prov. *Ready money is a readie medicine.*
Argent faict guerre: Prov. viz. *It moues men to begin, and enables them to follow, it.*
Argent faict perdre, & pendre gent: Prov. *Looke* Perdre, or Pendre.
Argent faict rage, & amour mariage: Prov. *Coyne moues men vnto rage, loue vnto mariage.*
Argent faict tout: Prov. *All (earthly) things are commanded, and compassed, by it.*
Argent frais, & nouveau ruine le Iouvenceau: Pro. *Th'aboundant, or free vse of money ruines youth.*
l'Argent quand l'orge: Prov. *One for another: when we haue their ware let them haue their money.*
Argent receu le bras rompu: Prov. *Looke* Bras.
C'est argent qu'argent vaut: Prov. *Nothing but money is money-worth.*
En argent soit le capital de celuy là qui le veut mal: Prov. *(Belike, because the keeping of it is both sinfull, and casuall.)*
Quand argent faut tout faut: Prov. *He that wants money wants all things.*
Qui a argent a des chapeaux: Prov. *Most men salute the monyed man; or, he that hath money hath most things.*
Qui n'a argent en bourse ait du moins du mel en bouche: Prov. *He that cannot pay let him pray.*
Amour faict beaucoup, mais argent faict tout: Pro. *Loue is potent, but money omnipotent.*
Bon marché tire l'argent hors de la bourse: Prov. *Good cheape commodities are notable picke-purses.*
Desolation paroist tost en argent avancé, &c: *Looke* Desolation.
Femme, argent, & vin, ont leur bien, & leur venin: Prov. *Money, wine, and women, haue good and bad things in them.*
Mieux vaut avoir ami en voye qu'or n'argent en courroye: Prov. *A friend on the way is better than a penie in the purse.*
Nul n'a trop pour soy de sens, d'argent, de foy: Prov. *Looke* Foy.
Quelque sçavoir que soit on l'hommes, s'il n'a de l'argent, on s'en mocque: Prov. *The skilfullest, wanting money, are but scorned.*
Qui combat avec les armes d'argent est asseure de vaincre: Prov. *He that doth fight with siluer armes is sure to ouercome.*

Argentangine: f. *The siluer Squinzie; a disease wherwith many besides Demosthenes (to whom it was first obiected) haue beene troubled.*
Argenté: m. ée: f. *Siluered ouer; couered with, or enchaced in, siluer.*
Astre Argenté. *The Moone.*
Argenter. *To siluer ouer; to gild, or couer with siluer, tinne, or lead; also, to enchace or inclose, in siluer.*
Argenterie: f. *The Mastership of the Wardrobe; also, a banke of exchaunge; also, a siluer myne; also, any stuffe, plate, or Iewels of siluer; as (in churches) cups, chalices, crosses, &c; siluer stuffe; also, a vestrie, presse, or chest, wherein siluer stuffe, or plate is kept; also, a cupboord of siluer plate.*
Argenteux: m. euse: f. *Siluerie; of siluer; full of money, or siluer; that hath store of siluer.*
Argentier: m. *A Steward, Purse-bearer, or other Officer, that layeth out money for his Master, or hath the charge of his Masters money; also, a Banker, one that lendeth, or exchangeth, money for gaine; also a Cup-bearer.*
Argentier du Roy. *The Master of the Wardrobe; Or Gentleman of the Robes; an Officer that keepes, and giues an account of all the Robes, garments, and clothes made for the kings owne wearing, for his Wardrobe, or chamber, or to be giuen away.*
Agentiere: f. *The place wherein mettalls are tried, before coyne be made of them.*
Argentin: m. ine: f. *Argentine, siluerie, of siluer, siluerlike.*
Chardon argentin, *Argentine, Siluer-Thistle, Oat-Thistle, Gumme-Thistle, Cotton-Thistle, the wilde white Thistle.*
Argentine: f. *Wild Tansie, Siluer weed.*
Argerite. *The (Siluer-coloured) foame of tried lead.*
Argilier: m. *The Ponticke* Acatia; *(a Thornie shrub.)*
Argiliere: f. *A clay-pit; or, a plot wherein Potters clay is gotten.*
Argille: f. *Potters clay; fat mould; a fattie, or clammie earth, whereof pots, &c, may be made.*
Argillette: f. *Fine clay, or mould.*
Argilleux: m. euse: f. *Clayish: full of a fat mould, or clay; made of a clammie, or fat clay; clammie, or fat, as Potters clay.*
Arglantier: m. *An Eglantine tree, or plant.*
Argolet: m. *A light horseman.*
Argot: m. *The Spurre of a Cocke; the deaw-clawe of a dog, &c; the heele, or talon of a hog.*
Argoté: m. ée: f. *Hauing spurres; armed, or furnished, as a Cocke, with spurres; also, brabled, contended, contested, wrangled.*
Argoter. *To spurre; to fight with spurres; also, to brable, contest, wrangle, contend with.*
Argoteur: m. *A wrangler, brabler, cauiller, contentious person.*
Argoteure. *as* Ergoture.
Argoteuse: f. *A scould; a wrangling, or cauilling house-wife.*
Argoüil: m. *A ring of yron.*
Argousin. *The Lieutenant of a Gallie.*
Argu. la teste pleine d'argu. *Full of anger, perplexitie, displeasure; fraught with fretfull proclamations.*
Tu ne me parles que d'argu. *Thy words are nought but cauils, thou doest nothing but brable with me.*
Argué: m. ée: f. *Argued, pleaded, reasoned; reproued, rebuked, chidden.*
Arguër. *To argue, plead, reason; dispute; discusse, or examine by argument; also, to chide, reproue, reprehend, rebuke; also, to incense, vrge, or prouoke vnto anger.*
Argueur: m. *An arguer, or pleader.*
Arguillonneux: m. euse: f. *Litigious, contentious; full of subtile cauilling.*
Argument: m. *An argument; reason, or proofe; a subiect to write, reason, or speake, of; also, the summe of a written matter; the summarie, or substance of a Booke, or Chapter; also, a coniecture,* pre-

presumption; iust occasion, sure token.
Arguties: f. *Sharpe quirkes, or subtilities, subtill words, wittie sayings.*
Argyrite. *Looke* Argerite.
Ari: m. ie: f. *Dryed vp, full soaked, wholly drained; withered; without sap, or humor; whose naturall moysture is spent, or consumed.*
Aride: com. *As* Ari. *Dry, withered, without sap.*
Aridelle: f. *A leane, or carrian tit; an ill fauoured fleshlesse iade; also, an Anotamie, or bodie whereon there is nought left but skin, and bone.*
Aridité: f. *Drinesse; witherednesse; want of humour, lacke of moisture.*
Arietant. *Ramming, jurring, leacherous; euer fighting, or leaping; as a Ramme, at rut.*
Arignée. *Seeke* Araignée.
Arigot. *as* Argot; *also, a (musicall) Recorder.*
Aristocratie: f. *An Aristocratie; the gouernment of Nobles; or of some few of the greatest men in a State.*
Aristocratique. *Aristocraticall, ruled by Nobles, gouerned by some few great men.*
Aristocratiquement. *Lordly, Aristocratically.*
Aristolochie: f. *Hartwort, Birthwort.*
Aristolochie clematite. *Climing Birthwort.*
Aristolochie longue. *Long Birthwort, or male Birthwort.*
Aristolochie ronde. *Round, or female Birthwort.*
Arithmeticien: m. *An Arithmetician.*
Arithmetique: f. *Arithmeticke; the art of numbers, or of numbering.*
Armaire: com. *A Cupboord, Ambrie, little presse; any hole, or box contriued in, or against, a wall; any small hollow roome, or place, wherein things may be set, laid vp, and kept;* Looke Armoire.
Armaison: f. cecy est plus d'armaison que cela. *This is more strong, better armed, fitter for fight, or to endure a fight, than that.*
Armateur: m. *An Armer, a prouider of armes, or weapons for; whence;*
Armateurs de navires. *Such as vndertake to furnish shipping with powder, bullets, nayles, chaine-shot, wild-fire, &c.*
Arme: f. *A weapon; Looke* Armes; *also, as* Ame; *(in* Languedoc.*)*
Armé: m. ée: f. *Armed, harnessed; furnished with arms, prouided of weapons; fortified, fenced.*
Poisson armé. *A shell-fish.*
Armée: f. *An armie, or hoast.*
Armelin: m. *The (hate-spot) Ermelin, or Ermin.*
Armement: m. *An arming; also, warlike prouision, as powder, bullets, chaine-shot, wild-fire, &c, for shipping.*
Armer. *To arme, or harnesse; to put on, or clad in, armour; to furnish with armes, or weapons; to strengthen, fortifie, fence; to prouide for, or against warre.*
Cheval qui s'arme. *That armes, or defends himselfe, (by clapping his bit vnto his breast, whereby the curbe hath little or no power ouer him.)*
Contre la nuict s'arment les Limaçons: Prov. viz. *Put forth their hornes.*
Armeries. *as* Armoires.
Armes: f. *Harnesse, armour; weapons; armes offensiue, and defensiue; also, Armes; Cognisances, or Scutcheons of armes; also, the two great tuskes, or tushes of a wild Boare.*
Armes d'ast. *Any weapons, that are vsually hurled, or cast at an enemie; or, as;*
Armes d'hante, ou d'haste; *(most properly) such weapons as haue long heads, and handles; as darts, iauelins; pikes, or speares, &c.*
Cotte d'armes. *A Coat-armour; also, a Heraulds coat.*
Espée d'armes. *Looke* Espée.
Faicts d'armes. *Acts, or feats of Chiualrie; deeds of prowesse; warlike, or valourous atchieuements.*
Homme d'armes. *A man of armes; one that serues in compleat armour, on a great horse.*
Faire armes. *To fight; also, to fight most valiantly.*
Il en parla comme vn escolier d'armes. *Hee spake of it ignorantly, improperly, impertinently, or he knew not what.*
D'oiseaux, de chiens, d'armes, & d'amours, pour vn plaisir mille douleurs: Prov. *Who fall in loue, or follow Hawkes, hounds, armes, for one delight sustain a thousand harmes.*
Armet: m. *An Helmet, or (horsemans) head-peece.*
Armeurerie: f. *Armorie; armor; armes.*
Armeures. *as* Armures.
Armilles: f. *Th'yron rings, or braces, wherein the gudgeons of a (wheeles) spindle turne; also, certaine little round members in pillars, &c.*
Arminette: f. *as* Erminette.
Armoire: com. *as* Armaire; *An ambrie; cupboord; box; little booke-presse; &c; (and hence) also, the Pix wherein the Sacrament is kept.*
Armoire tournant. *The round, and turning box (contriued in a Nunnerie wall) whereby the sisters receiue (vnseene) either gifts, or necessaries.*
Armoires: f. *The flowers called Sweet-Iohns, or Sweet-Williams, Tolmeyners, and London tufts.*
Armoirie: f. *An armorie, or store-house for armes.*
Armoiries. *Armes, Cognisances, Scutcheons, coats of armes; also, as* Armoires.
Armoirié: m. ée: f. *Grauen, or charged with armes; set thicke with Scutcheons of Armes; bearing armes.*
Armoise: f. *The hearbe called Mugwort, or Mothewort.*
Armoise mince-fueilles, ou à petites fueilles; *thinleaued Mugwort.*
Petite armoise. *The same, and a third, or lesse kind thereof.*
Armoisin: m. *Taffata.*
Armoisin: m. ine: f. *Of Taffata; silken.*
Armoisine: f. *as* Armoisin: m.
Armoniac. *Armoniacum; a Gumme issuing from the Cyrenian* Ferula, *or* Fennell-giant.
Armoniac. *Of, or seasoned with, Armoniacum.*
Sel Armoniac. Looke Sel.
Armonie: f. *Seeke* Harmonie.
Armorial: m. ale: f. *Belonging vnto armor; or expressing, or setting out ones armes.*
Armorier: m. *An Armorer, or Harnesse-maker.*
Armories. *as* Armoires.
Armottes: f. *A broth, or pap, made of meale steeped in liquor, and sodden vntill it be thicke.*
Armoux. choux armoux. *A kind of greene Coleworts whose leaues are of an ouall forme.*
Armoyer. *To tip, or decke the heft of a knife, or handle of a sword, with any worke:* (vieil mot.)
Armoyse. *Mugwort; Looke* Armoise.
Armoysine. *as* Armoisine.
Armure: f. *Harnesse, or Armour for the bodie.*
L'armure d'un poisson. *The shell, or scales of a fish.*
Armures. *(As vsuall as in the Singular number) arms, harnesse, armour for the bodie.*

Arné:

Arné: m. ée: f. *Weake-backed, feeble-rained, loose-ioynted; vnfit, or vnable to please a woman.*

Arneat. *The rauenous bird, called a Shrike, Nynmurder, Wariangle.*

Arnement: m. *A weakening, strayning, or breaking the reines of.*

Arner. *To weaken, enfeeble, straine, crush, breake the reines, or backe, of.*

Arnoglosse. *Plantaine, Waybred.*

Arollé: m. ée: f. *At it, at worke, whose hand is in.*

Aromat. *as*, Aromatique.

Aromates. *Spices, fragrant Simples.*

Aromatic rozat. *A certaine sweet pouder, good for the stomacke and heart.*

Aromaticité: f. *Sweet sauour, pleasant smell, pleasing tast; as, of spices.*

Aromatique: m. *An aromaticall Simple, or compound.*

Aromatique gariofilé. *A certaine composition wherein there are cloues; good for the passions of the heart.*

Aromatique: com. *Aromaticall, spicie, odoriferous, fragant, sweet-smelling.*

Aromatizé: m. ée: f. *Perfumed, aromatized, spiced; seasoned, or sweetened with spices.*

Aromatizer. *To aromatize; to perfume, season, or sweeten with spices, or fragrant Simples.*

Aron. *The hearbe Aron, Calues foot, Ramp, Starchwoort, Cuckoe-pint, Priests pintle.*

Aronde: f. *A tronke to shoot in; also, as* Arondelle.

Arondeau: m. *A young Swallow.*

Arondelet. *as*, Arondeau.

Arondelle: f. *A Swallow.*

Arondelle de mer. *The flying fish called the sea Bat, or sea Swallow; also, a kind of mullet, called otherwise,* Faulcon de mer.

Arondelle de riuage. *Looke*, Hirondelle.

La grande arondelle. *The great, blacke, and scriching, Martin.*

L'herbe d'arondelles. *Celandine, great Celandine, Swallowort, Tetterwort.*

Queuë d'arondelle. *See* Queuë.

La venuë des arondelles. *is about the two and twenteith of March.*

Aroy: m. *A plough.*

Arpailleur: m. *A seller of old trinkets, or of old yron; also, a finer of mettals, or gold-finer.*

Arpent: m. *An acre, or furlong of ground; the most ordinarie one called (sometimes)* L'arpent de France, *is 100 perches square (or euery way) after 18 feet to the perche.*

L'arpent de bois; *containes, in most places, two roods and a halfe; the rood 40 perches; the perch 24 feet; and the foot 24 ynches.*

L'arpent de bois de Bourgoigne. *containes 440 perches.*

L'arpent de Clermont. *is in most places 100 Verges, in others but 70; after 26 feet to the verge.*

L'arpent de Dunois. *is of 100 perches, after 20 feet to the perch.*

L'arpent de France. *as before, in* Arpent.

L'arpent de Nevers. *is foure quarters square; the quarter tenne fadomes; the fadome six ordinarie feet.*

L'arpent de Paris. *is 100 perches square after 22 feet to the perche; (yet is not this proportion of the Perche generall; for in some places about* Paris *it containes 25 feet, and in others (after the ordinarie rate) but 18.)*

Arpent de la Perche. *contains 100 perches, the perch 24 feet, the foot 13 ynches.*

Arpent de Poictou. *is 80 paces square.*

L'arpent Romain. *was 240 feet long, and 120 feet broad.*

Arpentage: m. *A suruey taken of land.*

Arpenté: m. ée: f. *Surueyed, or measured, as land; also, runne.*

Arpentement. *A surueying, or measuring of land.*

Arpenter. *To measure, or suruey land; also, to run.*

Arpenterie: f. *A surueying, or measuring of land.*

Arpenteur: m. *A surueyor, or measurer of land.*

Arpilleux: m. *Rauenous, deuouring.*

Arquebousade. *as* Arquebusade.

Arquebouse, & Arquebousier. *as* Arquebuse, *and* Arquebusier.

Arquebusade: f. *The shot of a caleeuer, or harquebuse.*

Arquebuse: f. *An harguebuse, caleeuer, or handgunne.*

Arquebuse de chasse. *A fowling peece.*

Arquebuse à croc. *An harguebuse a-crocke (somewhat bigger then a musket.)*

Arquebuse à fusil. *A Snap-haunce.*

Arquebuse à grand ressort. *A French harquebuse.*

Arquebuse à rouët. *A fire-locke, or Peece that goes with a fire-locke.*

Arquebusier: m. *An harquebusier, or small-shot; one that serues with an harquebuse, or caleeuer.*

Arquemie. *Seeke*, Alquemie.

Arquer. *To arche; to bend, crooke, or bow like an arch, or bowe.*

Arrabler. *To rape, and rend; to rauine, rob, spoile; to get by hooke or by crooke; (an old word.)*

Arraché: m. ée: f. *Rooted vp; drawne, torne, plucked out, or vp by the root; pulled away by violence.*

Arrachement: m. *A rooting vp; a drawing, tearing, plucking, vp by the root; a pulling away by violence.*

Arrachement d'une voulte. *The root, bottome, or beginning of a vault; as* Tas de charge.

D'Arrache-pied. *Continually, without intermission, without discontinuance, together.*

Arracher. *To root vp; to draw, teare, plucke vp by the root; to pull away by violence; to plucke out.*

Il arrache les bonnes herbes, & plante les mauvaises. *He reuiles the good, and flatters the bad; or, he supplants vertue, to support vice.*

Arracheur: m. *A puller, tearer, rooter vp.*

Arrachis: m. *as* Arrachement.

Arrager. *as* Emager.

Arraisonné: m. ée: f. *Reasoned, talked, discoursed, fallen in speech with.*

Arraisonnement: m. *A reasoning, talking, discoursing with.*

Arraisonner. *To reason, conferre, talke, discourse, fall in speech, enter into tearmes, with.*

Arramir. *To sweare.*

Arrangé: m. ée: f. *Ranked, ranged, disposed, ordered, arrayed, digested, sorted, set in it place.*

Arrangement. *An ordering, sorting, ranging, ranking.*

Arranger. *To ranke, range, dispose, order, sort; array; digest; set in it right place, rowe, or array.*

Arrapant. *Suddenly, and violently plucking, or snatching away.*

Arraper. *To take by violence; to snatch away; to gripe, or plucke away on a suddaine.*

Arrassade. *A Salamander.*

Arré: m. **ée**: f. *Bespoken, or, for which earnest hath beene giuen.*

Arre: com. *Tart; or, choaking, as a wild peare.*

Arrecer. *as* Arresser; *also, as* Frayer.

Arreche. *as* Areste.

Arréement: m. *Good array, order, equipage.*

Arrement: m. *A giuing of money in earnest, or before-hand.*

Arremens. Ce sont les dernieres expeditions, & Actes de Iustice faicts entre parties litigantes. ¶Ragueau.

Arrené: m. **ée**: f. *Reined; borne vp (as a horse) by his reines.*

Arrengé: m. **ée**: f. *Ranged, ranked, ordered, disposed.*

Arrengement. *Looke* Arrangement.

Arrenté: m. **ée**: f. *Rented; let, or taken, vpon rent.*

Arrentement: m. *A renting, or letting out vpon an yearely rent.*

Arrenter. *To rent, to let out for rent; also, to take at a rent.*

Arrer. *To giue in earnest, in hand, or beforehand; also, to giue earnest for; to buy, or conclude a bargaine, by giuing of earnest.*

Arrerage: m. *An arrerage; remainder, &c; as* Arrierage.

Arrerager. *To fall, grow, come, into arrerages.*

Arrerailles: f. *Lateward seed; corne thats sowed late in the yeare, or in the Spring.*

Arres. *Earnest; mony giuen for the conclusion, or striking vp, of a bargaine.*

Reprenons nos arres. *Looke* Erres.

Arressement. *The rising, or stiffenesse of the yard; prick-pride; a standing.*

Arresser. *The yard to rise, and grow, stiffe, or to stand.*

Arrest: m. *An Arrest, Sentence, Decree, Order, or finall iudgement of a Court; also, an arrest; a seisure of, or execution serued vpon, a mans person, or goods; also, the Rest whereon a man of armes setleth his lance; and generally, any rest, stop, or stay for a thing.*

Arrest de pont. *An Engine that goes with a vice, and hinders a draw-bridge, once downe, from being pulled vp againe.*

Tu n'as non plus d'arrest qu'un ieune veau. *Thou art as giddie as a sucking calfe.*

Arreste: f. *as* Areste.

Arresté: m. **ée**: f. *Stayed, stopped, arrested; setled; also, detained, with-held from; also, decreed, determined, resolued.*

Arreste-bœuf. *The hearbe Rest-harrow, pettie-Whinne, graund furze, Cammocke.*

Arrestement: m. *A stopping, arresting, staying; setling; determining.*

Arreste-nef. *Ship-staying, bark-stopping, boat-arresting.*

Arrester. *To stay, stop, arrest; settle; also, to determine, decree, resolue of; also, to detaine, or with-hold from.*

s'arrester. *To stay, rest, stop at, abide in, a place; also, to pawse on; also, to resolue.*

Arrhemens. *as,* Erres, *or* Erremens.

Arrierage: m. *An arrerage; the rest, or the remainder of a payment; that which is vnpayed, or behind.*

Arrieré: m. **ée**: f. *Cast, come, or fallen, behind; behind-hand.*

Arriere. *Behind, backward; also, aloofe, or farre from; also (imperatiuely) backe, or get you backe; also, Againe! Yet more! What, so often? or, Will you neuer haue done? (said in anger vnto an importunate repeater of vnpleasing motions) also, moreouer, furthermore, besides, ouer and besides.*

Pour vn petit n'avant n'arriere. *A little breakes no square; It makes no matter though wee misse a little.*

Arriereban: m. *A Proclamation, whereby those that hold of the king by a mesne tenure, are summoned to assemble, and serue him in his warres; different from* Ban, *whereby such are called as hold immediately of him; (also, the whole troupe of those mesne tenants, or vnder-vassals so assembled)* ¶Ragueau; *The Author of* Guidon general des financiers *holds, the contrarie, that* Ban *is for mesne, and* Arriereban *for immediat, tenants; Others imagine, that* Ban *summons* Roturiers, *or yeomen;* Arriereban, *gentlemen, or such as hold noble* fiefs; *Some say, that* Ban *is the first summons,* Arriereban, *a second, vnder penaltie; Others by* Ban *vnderstand ordinarie seruice, by* Arriereban *extraordinarie; and, in old time, such as were called by the* Ban, *serued at their owne charges fortie daies; during which, or afterwards, vpon vrgent occasions, th'* Arriereban, *or a second Proclamation was made, enioyning them to serue in that manner fortie daies more; Howsoeuer, at this day, these two words are most commonly ioyned together, and comprehend both the gentleman, and yeoman; th'immediate, and the mesne, tenant. Looke* Ban.

Arriere-boutique. *A back-shop; or back-roome, vsed for priuat wares, or working in.*

Sans arriere-boutique. *Plainely, openly; wholly; without flinching, dodging; dissembling, or double-dealing.*

Il a vne arriere-boutique; &, Il se reserue vne arriere-boutique. *He dissembles, or suppresses as yet his courage, or cunning; he reserues, or spares them for a last cast, or for his last effort.*

Arriere-censive: f. *A mesne tenure in an estate, or land, that is* Roturier, *or held by a* Roturier; *or, held by* Cens; *a mesne* Censive.

Arriere-chambre: f. *A backe-chamber; an inner, or withdrawing chamber.*

Arriere-coin: m. *A backe corner; a small, priuat, hidden, or inner roome; or, a hidden roome in a backe corner.*

Arriere-court: f. *A backe-yard, or base-Court.*

Arriere-demandé. *Sleightly demaunded, slowly asked, or, long before he were asked for.*

Arriere-fais: m. *The secondine, or after birth; the three skins wherein an infant lyes wrapped while it is in the wombe, or when it comes into the world.*

Arriere-feudal. Seigneur ar. *A mesne Lord.*

Arriere-fief: m. *A mesne* fief; *a fief that is held of, or depends on, another, or higher fief. Looke* Fief.

Arriere-foin: m. *A latter mathe; or, lateward hay.*

Arriere-foncier. *as* Surfoncier.

Arriere-fossé: m. *A backe ditch, or dike; an outward dike; also, as* Reffiron.

Arriere-garde. *The reregard of an armie; also, the wardship of one that holds by Knights seruice of a ward.*

Arrieregarend. C'est le garend du garend; ¶Ragueau.

Arriere-main: m. *A blow giuen backward, or with the backe of the hand; also, the profit made of an Office (besides fees) by secret bribes, and exactions; priuat vayles.*

Arriere-nepveu: m. *A great graund-child, the sonne of a graund-child.*

Arriere-ouvert: m. **erte**: f. *Wide open.*

Arriere-poinct: m. *A backe-stitch.*

Arriere-poinƈté: m. ée: f. *Back-stitched, wrought with back-stitch.*
Arriere-poinƈter. *To worke back-stitch; to set a back-stitch.*
Arrierer. *To goe backward; also, to set backe.*
Arriere-saison. *Later math; a late haruest, a lateward yeare.*
Arriere-taille: f. *A second, or later tax; a further imposition.*
Arriere-vassal. *An vnder-vassall; a vassall vnto a vassall.*
Arriere-uasseur. *An vnder-vassall; or, an vnder-villaine; a vassall, or villaine vnto a vassall, or villaine.*
Arrigateur: m. *A waggoner, or chariot-driuer.*
Arriger. s'ar. *To rise, or stand vp stiffe, as the yard.*
Arrivé: m. ée: f. *Arriued, abboorded, come vnto.*
Arrivée: f. *An arriuall, accesse, abboord, or comming to.*
Arrivement: m. *An arriuing, or comming to.*
Arriver. *To arriue, abboord, or come vnto.*
Arrobe: f. *A iarre; a vessell, or measure, which, in the weight of ordinarie marchandise, comes to twentie fiue pound.*
Arroches. *Orache, Orage, golden hearbe.*
Arroches de mer. *A certaine hoarie, gray, or mealie-coloured plant, called sea Orage.*
Arroches sauvages. *Wild Orage, All-seed.*
Arrogamment. *Arrogantly, presumptuously.*
Arrogance: f. *Arrogancie; presumption; vaunting, pride, ouer-weening.*
Arrogant: m. ante: f. *Arrogant; presumptuous; ouer-weening; proud, or, that proudly attributes too much vnto himselfe.*
s'Arroger. *To arrogate, or ascribe too much vnto himselfe; to presume, or boast, more of himselfe then hee should.*
Arrollé: m. ée: f. *At worke, or, whose hand is in.*
s'Arroller. *To fall, or set himselfe, to worke; to be at worke, or be willing to worke.*
Arrondir. *To round, make round, turne round.*
Arrondir les esperons. *To spurre a horse in turning, most on the side whereon he turnes.*
Arrondissement: m. *A rounding, making round, or turning round.*
Les Arrondissemens d'un habillement. *The pieces, or shreds that are cut off in the rounding of a garment.*
Arrosé: m. ée: f. *Bedeawed; besprinkled; gently wet, or moistened; a little watered.*
Arrosement: m. *as* Arrousement.
Arroser. *as* Arrouser.
Arroseur: m. *A bedeawer; a besprinkler; a gentle waterer of.*
Arrouë. *as* Arrobe.
Arrouler. *To rowle, or tumble towards; to bring with rowling.*
Arrousable: com. *Fit to be watered, besprinkled, bedeawed.*
Arrousage: m. *as* Arrousement.
Arrousé: m. ée: f. *Bedeawed, sprinkled, moistened, gently wet, or watered.*
Arrousement: m. *A bedeawing, sprinkling, moistening; gentle wetting, watering.*
Arrouser. *To bedeaw, besprinkle; wet, moisten, water gently.*
Arrousoir: m. *A watering pot.*
Arrouter. *To set in the way, put into the way.*
s'Arrouter. *To assemble in troupes, to gather together in routs, to make a riot.*
Arroy: m. *Order, array; equipage, furniture.*
Arroyé: m. ée: f. *Arrayed; furnished, in full equipage.*
Arroyer. *To array; furnish; put in order, equipage.*
Arrudir. *To make rude, clownish, vnciuile, barbarous.*
Arrumé: m. ée: f. Carte arrumée. *A sea-card, wherein all the quarter winds, or trauers boords, are delineated.*
Arrumer. *To delineate, or set out, in a sea-card, all the* Rums *of winds.*
Arruner. *To ranke, sort, range, dispose, put in order, set in array.*
Arry avant. *On afore, away there hoe; (from the Carters cry,* Arry, & hori ho.*)*
Ars. les ars: m. *The breast, or brisket of a horse.*
Ars: m. arse: f. *Burnt; scorched, parched; consumed with heat, or fire.*
Arsacide: m. *as* Assassin.
Arseirole: f. *A little, red, sower, and peare-like fruit, that comes of a Hawthorne grafted on a Quince.*
Arsel. *as* Arzel.
Arsenic: m. *Arsenicke, Orpiment, Orpine (the naturall one is of two sorts; th'one red, th'other yellow; whereas;)*
Arsenic crystallin; *is compounded of salt, and little pieces of Orpiment, and thus tearmed, because it is, as Christall, transparent.*
Arson: m. *as* Arceau; *or, as* Arçon.
Art: m. *An art, science; trade, craft, misterie, occupation; also, skill, cunning, workmanship; also, craft, subtiltie, deceit, guile.*
Arts de vents. *as* Rumbs.
L'homme qui a de l'art possede sa part: Prov. *He that hath wit, will haue a share in euery thing.*
Qui sçait l'art serre la boutique: Prov. *Th'enuious workeman often hides his cunning.*
Qui ne sçait l'art serre la boutique: Pro. *The bungler, to seeme cunning, makes it daintie.*
Artail: m. *as* Orteil.
Artemon: m. *The mizen Maste, or sayle, of a ship.*
Artere: f. *An Arterie, pulse, panting veine; a skinnie, round, and hollow vessell, whereby the vitall spirit, mixed with bloud, is conueyed from the heart vnto all parts of the bodie.*
Artere aorte. *The great Arterie, mother Arterie, or mother of Arteries. Looke* Aorte.
Artere axillaire. *Th'arme-hole-Arterie; or, a left branch of th'* Aorte*, from which it ascends obliquely towards th'arme-hole; where after it hath sent it branches to the higher ribs, and other adiacent parts, it descendeth downe to the bought of the cubit.*
Artere carotide. *Issues from th'*Axillaire*, and is diuided into two branches; th'inward, and greater, which goes vnto the braine; the outward, which passeth vnto the* Larinx*, tongue, nose, eyes, and muscles of the temples.*
Artere cervicale. *An Arterie in the nape, or hinder part, of the necke; issues from the* Sousclaviere*, and goes thence through the neck-bone vnto the braine.*
Artere cœliaque. *Issues from the bodie of the great Arterie, and is diuided into three branches; Looke* Cœliaque.
Arteres coronales. *Two little branches of the great arterie, and left by it vnto the left ventricle, and broad end, of the heart.*
Artere crotaphique. *See,* Crotaphique.

Artere crurale. *Th' arterie of the thigh, among whose muscles it diuides it selfe.*
Artere cubitale. *The cubitall arterie, a branch of th'* Axillaire.
Artere cystepatique. *A branch of the* Cœliaque; *goes vnto the liuer, and the gall.*
Artere diaphragmatique. *Issues from the trunke of the great arterie, and thence goes vnto the* Diaphragma.
Artere Epigastrique. *A branch of the Iliacke arterie; distributes it selfe among the muscles of th'* Epigastre.
Artere Gastrepiploique. *A branch of the* Cœliaque, *whence it goes vnto the ventricle, and th'* Epiploon.
Arteres gemelieres. *The twin arteries; two small ones, which descend vnto the ioint of the knee betweene the processes of the thigh bones.*
Artere grande. *as,* Aorte.
Artere honteuse. *Issues from the great arteries descendent branch, and bestowes it selfe among the priuities.*
Artere hypogastrique. *A branch of th' Iliacke; distributes it selfe among the parts of th'* Hypogastre.
Artere Iliaque. *Th' Iliacke arterie, or, descendent branch of the great one.*
Arteres intercostales. *Two arteries; an vpper; which bestowes it selfe among the muscles that be between the foure highest ribs; and, an vnder one, which goes vnto euery muscle that is betweene the rest of the ribs.*
Arteres Lumbaires. *The loyne-arteries; issue from th'* Aorte *vnto all the parts of the loynes, giuing life vnto the marrow of the backe bone, and sending as many branches vnto the ioints thereof as there be holes in it.*
Artere Mamillaire. *The pap-arterie; issues from the trunke of th'* Aorte.
Arteres Mesenteriques. *Looke,* Mesenterique.
Arteres Planteres. *Two branches of the thigh arterie (the which they diuide in the middle of the leg) an inward one, which descends to the ioint, or setting on of the foot, and passing along the sole, ends in fiue branches, whereof two serue for the great toe, two for the second toe, and one for the middle toe; Th' outward (as th' inner) ends also in fiue branches; two whereof it bestowes on the little toe, two on the next vnto it, and one on the middle one.*
Artere de poulmon. *The wind-pipe.*
Artere radiale. *A second branch of th' arme-hole-arterie, whence it bestowes it selfe on the* Radius, *or the vpper, and greater bone of the arme.*
Artere renale. *The kidney arterie; issues out of the* Aorte, *and enters into the kidney, bringing vnto it the serositie of th' arteriall bloud.*
Artere sacrée. *A branch of the great arteries descendent branch; goes vnto the marrow which is in the* Os sacré.
Artere sousclaviere. *Th' ascendent branch of the great arterie.*
Artere spermatique. *The spermaticke arterie; goes from the bodie of th'* Aorte *vnto the testicles, and there ioynes with the veine that gouernes those parts.*
Artere splenitique. *The spleene arterie, or greatest branch of the* Cœliaque, *whence it goes vnto the spleene, and therein ends.*
Artere temporelle. *Th' arterie of the temples.*
Artere thorachique. *The breast arterie; issues out of the great arteries ascendent branch, and goes vnto the anterior muscles of the breast.*
Artere veineuse. *The veinie arterie; one of the three principall ones of the bodie; issues from the left ventricle of the heart, and carries thence to the lungs bloud for their nourishment.*
Aspre artere. *The wind-pipe.*
Trachée artere; *or,* Trachiartere; *the same; called also, the pipe of the lungs; is one of the three principall arteries in the bodie; and th' instrument of breath, and voice; it begins at the* Larinx, *and ends at the lungs, or lights.*
Arterial: m. ale: f. *Of, or belonging to, arteries.*
Arterieux: m. euse: f. *Full of arteries.*
Veine arterieuse. *Looke,* Veine.
Arteriotomie: f. *An incision of arteries.*
Arthetiques: f. *Cowslips, or Oxslips.*
Arthritique. Ive arthritique. *Hearbe Iue, ground Pine, field Cypres, Forget-me-not.*
Arthrodie: f. *An halfe coniunction of two bones; the head of the one being but halfe lodged within the cauitie of th' other.*
Artialiser. *To make artificiall; or, to make an art of.*
Artichau, & Artichaud. *as,* Artichault.
Artichauliere: f. *A Bed, or Plot set with Artichockes.*
Artichault: m. *An Artichocke.*
Artichault sauvage. *The wild Artichocke, or prickly Artichocke; also, the white thistle, milke thistle, our Ladies thistle.*
Artichaut. *as* Artichault.
Article: m. *An article; a head, principall clause, title, or point of a matter; also, a Summe, or* Item *of a Summe, in accounts; also, a ioint, or knuckle.*
Articulaire: com. *Of, or in, the ioints; belonging to a ioint.*
Douleur articulaire. *Paine, or ache in the ioints; and (more particularly) the Gout.*
Articulation. *A growing, springing, or shooting vp from knot to knot, from ioint to ioint; also, the hurting, or bursting of young ioints; the slaring of trees, whose yong shoots are beaten of by tempest, or hurt, and bruised by rude, and vnskilfull handling.*
Articulé: m. ée: f. *Articulated, articled; set downe in, reduced vnto, articles; distinguished, summarily handled, particularly, and precisely described; also, iointed, or knotted.*
Voix articulée. *A distinct voice, a voice thats easie to be vnderstood.*
Articuler. *To articulate, article, reduce into articles, diuide, or distinguish by seuerall heads, titles, or summes; precisely, and particularly to describe, or point out.*
Artien: m. *An Artist; or one that studies, or professes, artes.*
Artiere: f. *The Sharpling, Stickling, or Sticklebacke; (a small fish.)*
Artifice: m. *Skill, cunning, workmanship; also, craft, subtiltie, guile, deceit.*
Artificiel: m. elle: f. *Artificiall, skilfull, cunning, workmanly, workemanlike.*
Artificiellement. *Artificially, cunningly, workmanly.*
Artificieux: m. euse: f. *Artificiall, full of art.*
Artifier. *Artificially to forge; to make by art, or craft.*
Artiller. *To furnish with Ordnance, or Artillerie.*
Artillerie: f. *Artillerie, Ordnance.*
Artillerie cardinale. *is (among sea-men) a peece of Ordnance of a very wide bore.*
Artillier: m. *A Bowyer, or Bow-maker; also, a Fletcher; or one that makes both bowes, and arrowes.*
Artillier du Roy. *The Kings Bowyer, or Fletcher; an officer*

officer in ordinarie; who makes not onely these instruments of shooting, but also, all manner of artificiall fireworkes.

Artinion. *A little sayle, called otherwise,* Trinquet.

Artiron: m. *A little, round, and greenish worme, not much vnlike a lowse, and ordinarily cleauing, in great numbers, to the leaues of Coleworts, and other plants, the which in time they deuour.*

Artisan: m. *An artificer, workman, handicrafts man; also, an artist, or artisan.*

Artison. *as* Artiron; *also, a kind of moth; also, a woodworme; also, as* Teigne, *the skurfe of a scald head; so tearmed, because the part infected with it seemes to be moth-eaten, or worme-eaten.*

Artisonné. *Moth-eaten, worme-eaten.*

Artiste: m. *as* Artisan; *also, an artist, or Master of art.*

Artistement. *as* Artificiellement.

Artoir: m. *The great toe.*

Artre: f. *A moth; also, a kings-fisher.*

Artres des boulengiers. *A kind of butterflies, or great white mothes, which liue altogether in bake-houses, or mylls.*

Artre grise des bois. *The vermine called, a Woodlowse.*

Artrose: f. *A naturall, and moueable connexion of bones.*

Artuson. *A corne-deuouring Weeuill; or, as* Artison.

Arzel: m. *A horse with a white foot on the right, or further side.*

As. *An Ace at dice, or cards.*

Demeurer entre deux & as. *To rest on vncertaine tearmes, to bee doubtfull of his successe; not to know what will betide him.*

Respondre entre deux & as. *Looke* Deux; *or,* Az.

Asare: m. *The hearbe Folefoot, Haslewort,* Asarabacca.

Asarine: f. *Italian* Asarabacca.

Asarole: f. *A kind of small, and prickly medlar tree, bearing a lesse, and harder fruit then the ordinarie one; Seeke* Azarole.

Asbetin. *of* Asbestinum; *a kind of line, or flax, that wil not be burned, and yeelds a cloth which fire scoures better then water.*

Ascalabe. *The venomous beast called* Stellio, *or, the starrie Lizard.*

Ascalaue, & Ascalavette. *as* Ascalabe.

Ascaride: f. *A kind of small round worme, which breeds in the bowels.*

Asçavanté. *Instructed, fully informed, made skilfull in, or throughly acquainted with.*

Asçavanter. *To informe, or instruct throughly, to let know, giue to wit, make skilfull in, or fully acquainted with.*

Asçavoir. *To wit, that is to say.*

Ascendant: m. *A kinsman in ascent; as the vnkle is to the nephew, &c.*

Asche: f. *The hearbe Smallage; Looke,* Ache.

Aschée. *A ground-worme, or grub.*

Aschet. *as,* Aschée.

Ascite. *A kind of Dropsie, which makes the belly sound like a bottle, when one strikes on it.*

Ascles: f. *Shiuers, or splinters of wood, breaking.* ¶Langued.

Ascouter. *as* Accouter; *or, as* Escouter.

Aserches: f. *Wild prickmadam, stone-crop, wormegrasse.*

Asereiner. *To cleere, or cheere, vp.*

Asgrandissement. *as,* Aggrandissement.

Asinin: m. ine: f. *Asse-like; of, or belonging to an Asse.*

Chardon asinin. *The white thistle, milke thistle, our Ladies thistle.*

Concombre asinin. *The wild, or spirting, Cowcomber.*

Asmatique: com. *Pursie, short-winded, breathing with difficultie.*

Asme: m. *Difficultie of breathing, short-wind; a painfull, or hard drawing of the breath, accompanied with a wheezing, puffing, or pursinesse.*

Asne: m. *An Asse; also, a little fish with a great head, called, a Bull head, or Millers thumbe; also, a dunce, blockhead, sot, loggarhead, dull-pated fellow.*

Asne d'Inde. *The beast* Rhinoceros; *or (as some will haue it) th'Vnicorne.*

Coq à l'asne. *A Libell, Pasquine, Satire.*

Cul d'asne. *The name of a daintie fish.*

Dos d'asne. à dos, ou, en dos d'asne. *Ridgill-backed; bowed, boughtie, or bowing; highest in the middle.*

Miroir d'asne. *A kind of tender, and transparent white stone; as* Talc.

Oreille d'asne. *Th'hearbe Comfrey, knit-backe, knitwort, blackewort.*

Oreille d'asne: Pro. *The part, or dutie of a seruant; to heare all his angrie master sayes without replying; from the nature, and custome of an Asse, that (whatsoeuer noise is made about him) only claps downe his eares, and followes on his way.*

Pas d'asne. *The hearbe Folefoot, Coltsfoot, Horsefoot, and Hallfoot; also, a certaine ring, or hoope, of yron in the forecastle of a ship; also, a fashion of a Port, or Vpset in the mouth of some bits.*

Persil d'asne. *Wild Cheruill, mocke Cheruill, great Cheruil, Asse parsely,* Myrrhis *Cashes, Caxes, or Kexes.*

Pont aux asnes. *Any shift, euasion, helpe at a pinch for th'ignorant; any ease, or direction vnto dull, or vnlearned people, for the resolution of difficulties which otherwise they cannot conceiue; as, a Dictionarie; and, in Logicke, the conuersion of Propositions.*

Avoir de l'asne. Il y aura icy de l'asne. *Here will be some foolish coyle, some idle sturre, or other.*

Braire avec les asnes. *To follow the fashion, or doe what others doe, how absurd, or sottish soeuer it be.*

Brider l'asne par la queuë. *To do things out of order; to goe the wrong way to the wood, or to worke.*

Cholere comme vn asne à qui l'on attache vne fusée aux fesses. *As angrie as an Asse with a squib in his breech.*

Demander de la laine à vn asne. *To aske for a thing where tis not to be had.*

Desferrer l'asne. *To vnshoe the Asse; wee say, to ride the wild mare.*

Faire de l'asne pour avoir du bran. *Looke,* Bran.

Laissons aux asnes les chardons. *Let Asses feed on thistles, dunces on dull stuffe, dull wits on drie matters.*

Mener l'asne. *To be laughed at, or little accounted of by all men that see, or meet him.*

Monter sur l'asne. *To breake, become bankrupt, renounce his owne goods: (A Phrase deriued from an auncient custome, whereby such as broke were compelled to ride backward on an Asse through the towne they dwelt in, holding his tayle in their hands, in stead of a bridle.)*

On y va comme asnes desbastez: *(Of those that meet at stollen lecherie) they goe to it hotely, furiously, with a terrible appetite; (for Asses discharged of their burthens, vnsadled, and set at libertie, are the friskest creatures aliue.)*

Saulter du coq à l'asne. *To digresse from the matter, or, to leape suddainely, and disorderly, from one matter to another.*

Tirer pets d'un aſne mort. *To make a dead aſſe fart; to worke impoſſibilities.*
Aſne d'Arcadie broute chardons,& ortie,&c. Pro. *Looke*,Ortie.
L'aſne qui brait le plus, eſt celuy qui mange le moins: Prov. *Th'aſſe that brayeth moſt eateth leaſt.*
Vn aſne n'entend rien en Muſique: Pro. *An aſſe is but a bad Muſician; or,cannot iudge of Muſicke.*
à lauer la teſte d'un aſne on ne perd que le temps, & la lexive: Pro. *In vaine one ſtriues to make learned a ſottiſh,or make honeſt a graceleſſe, perſon.*
à la preuve l'on eſcorche l'aſne: Prov. *Looke* Eſcorcher.
à qui eſt l'aſne ſi le garde: Prov. *Let him that owes a thing looke to it.*
à qui eſt l'aſne ſi le tienne par la queue: Prov. *See* Queue.
à rude aſne rude aſnier: Pro. *A ſtubborne ſeruant needs a froward maſter; a curſt wife a curbing husband; a rebellious ſubiect a rigorous Soueraigne.*
à vilain charbonnée d'aſne: Prov. *A churle would haue churles fare, groſſe meats,courſe entertainment.*
Amour apprend les aſnes à danſer: Prov. *Looke* Danſer.
Aſſez va au moulin qui ſon aſne y envoye: Prov. *He may be ſaid to doe a thing that ſets his man about it.*
Chantez à l'aſne il vous fera des pets: Prov. *The ignorant blockhead ſcornes both Muſicke,and the Muſes; or,as wee ſay, Claw a churle by the breech, and he will beray your fiſt.*
Deux orgueilleux ne peuvent eſtre portez ſur vn aſne: Prov. *One poore aſſe cannot carrie two proud ones.*
Il ne faut pas lier les aſnes auec les cheuaux: Pro. *Churles are not to be matcht, or ſorted, with gentlemen.*
On n'aura ia bon aſne vieil: Pro. *A ſlugg,or dullard growne old is worſe then naught.*
On ne fait boire à l'aſne quand il ne veut: Prov. *Men force not th'aſſe (but aſſes men) to drinke.*
Plus d'un aſne à la foire a nom Martin: Prov. *We ſay (with a ſmall reſemblance of ſence) there be more maids then Malkin, or, more maids then one be called Malkin.*
Pour vn poil Martin perdit ſon aſne: Pro. *The puniſhment, or taxation of thoſe that vpon a ſmall occaſion enter into a great contention; as thus poore man did,who laying a wager that his aſſe was all white,was ſhewed a blacke haire on him,and ſo,like an aſſe,loſt his aſſe,which was the wager.*
Pour vn poinct Martin perdit ſon aſne: Prov. *A ſmall omiſſion,or error may turne a man to much preiudice; Looke*,Poinct.
Qui à aſne tend à aſne vient: Prov. *He that will, may,ſoone ynough,proue an aſſe.*
Qui femme croit, & aſne mene, ſon corps ne ſera ia ſans peine: Prov. *He that beleeues a woman, and leads an aſſe,will neuer be in quiet.*
Sous ombre d'aſne entre le chien au Moulin: Pro. *(So many a knaue ſneakes into good places in companie, or vnder the pretext,of honeſt men.)*
Tel aſne tel aiguillon: Prov. *Such as the aſſe, his goad.*
Aſnée: f. *An Aſſe-load of.*
Aſne-fueille. *A kind of Origan,which Aſſes loue exceeding well.*
Aſnerie: f. *Sottiſhneſſe, dulneſſe, ignorance, doltiſhneſſe, blockiſhneſſe; any impertinent, or Aſſe-like, pranke.*
Aſneſque: com. *Aſſe-like; ſottiſh, dull, ignorant, blockiſh.*
Aſneſſe: f. *A ſhee Aſſe.*
De petit eſguillon poinct on bien grande aſneſſe: Prov. *Great beaſts are pricked forward with ſmall goads.*
Aſnichon: m. *A young aſſe.*
Aſnichons. *Two little ſtarres in the ſigne* Cancer.
Aſnier: m. *One that driueth,or dreſſeth,Aſſes.*
Gros aſnier. *A ioltbead, blockhead, loggarhead; a fellow of a heauie mettall, groſſe capacitie, dull ſpirit.*
A rude aſne rude aſnier: Pro. *A rude knaue is to be awed by a rough controller.*
A l'hoſpital les bons ouvriers, en dignité les gros aſniers: Pro. *Looke* Ouvrier.
Aſnier. *To ride vpon an Aſſe.*
Aſnon.*as* Aſnichon. *A young Aſſe; alſo,the little watervermine called,a Bull-head.*
Aſnonner. *To fole,or bring forth,an Aſſe.*
Aſoté: m. ée: f. *Sotted, beſotted, doting on. Looke*,Aſſoté.
Aſoter. *To ſot, beſot,make dote on,bring too farre in loue with.*
Aſpalathe: m. *A kind of prickly ſhrub, whoſe maſſiue, ruddie, and aromaticall wood is vſed by Perfumers: ſome, erroniouſly,haue thought it to be red Saunders; others the Rhodian wild Oliue tree; and Gerard cals Engliſh Galingale,*Aſpalathum.
Aſpalier. *as* Eſpallier.
Aſparge. *as* Aſperge.
Aſpect: m. *An aſpect,regard,ſight; the viſage,or countenance.*
Aſperer. *To ſharpen,exaſperate,aggrauate,make rough, churliſh,angrie.*
Aſperge: m. *The hearbe Sparage,or* Sparagus; *alſo,the young,and tender ſprig,or ſhoot of any plant.*
Aſperge de marais. *Marſh Sparage.*
Aſperges montagnars. *Mountaine* Sparagus; *a kind of wild one.*
Aſperge paluſtre. *as* Aſperge de marais.
Aſperges pierreus. *Stone Sparage, wild* Sparagus.
Aſperge ſauvage. *The ſame.*
Aſpergement: m. *A beſprinkling; a poudering, or bepoudering.*
Aſperger. *To beſprinkle; pouder, bepouder; to ſprinkle, or ſtrew water,or duſt vpon.*
Aſperget: m. *A holy-water ſprinkle.*
Aſpergiere: f. *A bed of* Sparagus.
Aſpergoutte: f. *The hearbe Featherfew, Feuerfew, Whitewort.*
Aſpergoutte menuë,ou mineur. *Starrewort, Cudwort, Sharewort.*
Aſpergule: f. *Clauer, Gooſegraſſe.*
Aſperſé: m. ée: f. *Beſprinkled,or bedeawed with.*
Aſperſion: f. *A beſprinkling,or bedeawing; an aſperſion.*
Aſperſoie: f. *A holy-water-ſprinkle made of briſtles.*
Aſpertule: f. *Clauer, Gooſegraſſe.*
Aſphalthe. *as* Bitume.
Aſphodile. *The Daffadill, Affodill, or Aſphodill flower; alſo,the root,or bulbes thereof.*
Aſphrodille. *as* Aſphodile; *or,as* Aphrodille.
Aſpic: m. *The Serpent called,an Aſpe.*

Aſpic

Aspic cornu. *A sand-coloured Serpent, full of blacke spots; his head (with muzzle vpturned) is bigger then a vipers; in all other parts he is very like her.*

Aspic sourd. *(Th'Aspe, sayes* Gesner, *by reason of her exceeding drought, is also accounted deafe; although she be very quicke of hearing.)*

Aspic: m. *The hearbe Spikenard, or Lauander Spike; especially the common, or blew-floured one.*

Aspic Celtique. *French Spikenard, mountaine Spikenard.*

Aspic d'outre mer. *Indian Spikenard; or, the true Spikenard; for th'others (especially the French one) are but bastards.*

Aspiration: f. *An aspiration; a blowing, breathing, drawing of breath.*

Aspiré: m. ée: f. *Breathed, blowne; also, desired, aspired vnto; also, noted, or pronounced with an aspiration.*

Aspirer. *To breath, blow, fetch wind, draw breath; also, to desire, couet, ayme at, aspire vnto.*

Aspre. *A Turkish coyne of siluer, in value little more then our penny, or iust as the French* Sous; *for 60 of them goe to a* Seraph, *which is worth about a French Crowne.*

Aspre: com. *Sharpe, tart; harsh, vnpleasant in tast; rude, rugged, rough, in handling; biting, pricking, or grieuous to be felt; churlish, austere, surly, seuere, vntractable, rigorous, in proceeding; fierce, eager, earnest, vehement, very hot, or forward, in any matter.*

L'aspre artere. *The wind-pipe.*

Lieu aspre. *A craggie, ill-fauoured, vneuen place; a place ill to be gone in, traueld on, passed ouer.*

Asprelle: f. *Horse-tayle, Shaue-grasse (an hearbe.)*

Asprement. *Sharpely, eagerly, tartly; harshly, vnpleasantly; roughly, ruggedly; seuerely, rigorously, austerely, vntractably; surlily, churlishly; vehemently, earnestly, ardently, fiercely.*

Aspresse: f. *as* Aspreté.

Aspreté: f. *Sharpenesse, eagernesse, tartnesse; harshnesse, vnpleasantnesse; roughnesse, ruggednesse; austeritie, rigor, seueritie; surlinesse, vntractablenesse, churlishnesse; fiercenesse, vehemencie, earnestnesse, extreame desire to doe a thing.*

Asprir. *To sharpen; exasperate, aggrauate, incense; to make rough, harsh; churlish, angrie.*

Asprissement. *A sharpening, exasperating.*

Aspron: m. *A little, rough-finned, and Gudgeon-like fish, found onely in that part of the* Rosne *which is betweene* Vienne, *and* Lyons.

Assablé: m. ée: f. *Grauelled; filled with sand; also, stucke in, or run on, the sand.*

Assabler. *To grauell, to stick in the sand; to fill with sand; to take in sand, as a boat.*

Assablissement. *A shole, shelfe, or hill of sand, appearing aboue water.*

Assagi: m. ie: f. *Become wise, growne discreet.*

Assagir. *To make wise, discreet, sage.*

Assagissement: m. *A becomming, or making, wise.*

Assaieret. Pillules d'assaieret. *Pills made of* Hiera, *Masticke, Mirablans,* Aloës, *and the syrrup of* Stœchas; *(tearmed so by the Arabian Phisitions, and from them by all others.)*

Assaillant: m. *A Challenger at Tilting, &c; also, an Assailant, or Assailer; whence;*

Rien ne vaut l'assaillant s'il n'est fort, & vaillant: Prov. *It boots not to assaile, if strength, or courage, faile.*

Assaillant. *Assayling, setting on.*

Assailli: m. ie: f. *Assaulted, assayled, set vpon; also, challenged at Tilt, &c.*

Homme assailli à demi vaincu: Pro. *He thats assayled is halfe ouercome (tis good therfore to be before-hand with an enemie.)*

Assaillir. *To assayle, assault, or set vpon; also, to challenge at Tilt, Barriers, &c.*

Assaisonné: m. ée: f. *Seasoned, made sauourie.*

Assaisonnement: m. *A seasoning, tempering, making sauourie, giuing a good tast vnto.*

Assaisonner. *To season, temper, make sauourie, giue a good tast vnto.*

Assaisonneur. *A seasoner.*

Assassin: m. *An apponsted manslayer, cut-throat, murtherer; one that kils another for gaine, or vpon hope, or promise, of reward.*

Assassinat: m. *A murther, or murtherous act committed for gaine, or in hope of a reward; also, a suddaine assault, made of set purpose, and with a murtherous intent, although th'assaulted be not killed.*

Assassinateur. *as* Assassin.

Assassiné. *Murthered, slaine, killed; also, assaulted, or set on with a murtherous intent.*

Assassinement: m. *A killing, slaying, murthering; also, an assaulting with a murtherous intent.*

Assassiner. *To slay, kill, murther for gaine, or vpon hope, or promise, of reward; also, to assaile, or set on with a murtherous intent.*

Assation: f. *A rosting, or concoction by a forraine, or outward, and drie heat.*

Assavanter. *To instruct, informe, certifie, let know, giue to wit, make fully acquainted with.*

Assault: m. *An assault, assayling, setting on.*

Assavoir. *as* Asçavoir. *To wit; that is to say.*

Assauvagi: m. ie: f. *Made wild, become rude, growne sauage.*

Assauvagir. *To make wild, skittish, or wood.*

Asse: m. *Th'ancient Romanes* As; *a copper coyne worth somewhat more then a pennie sterl.*

Asse douce. *The sweet gumme that issues from the scarified, or cut stalks, and roots of th'African and Cyrenian* Laserpitium, *or Laserworte.*

Asse fetide. *The stinking iuyce, or gumme, which issues from the Laserwort that growes in* Syria, Media, Armenia, *and* Lybia: *Apothecaries call it,* Asse fœtida.

Assecher. *as* Asseicher.

Assediacre. *An Archdeacon; Ironically.*

Assée: f. *A Woodcocke.*

Asséeur: m. *A cessor, in matter of taxes, &c.*

Asseiché: m. ée: f. *Dried, growne or made drie.*

Asseicher. *To drie; to make, or wipe, drie.*

Asseller. *To goe to the stoole.*

Assemblage: m. *An assembling; a setting, closing, ioyning, couching of many pieces together; also, the worke made of many pieces so ioined; in-layed worke; also, the whole furniture of a roome, &c.*

Assemblé. *Assembled, gathered, met, flocked, trouped; incountred, come, drawne together; ioyned, couched, closed, set, put, pegged; heaped, packed, compacted together.*

Assemblée: f. *An assembly, congregation, companie; a meeting, or drawing of people together, as at a hunting; (hence) also, a hunting, or a troupe of hunters; also, a Proclamation, publicke Summons of, or commaund vnto, souldiors, to meet, or make their* Rendevous *at a certaine place, and thence to goe into the field; also, the fight, coaping, or incounter of two armies.*

Assemblement: m. *as* Assemblée; *also, a ioyning, setting, gluing, packing, or couching of things together.*
Assembler. *To assemble, draw, get, or gather together; to ioyne, put, set, couch, close, glue, peg, packe, or compact, together.*
s'Assembler. *To assemble, meet, flocke, troope; draw, gather, or come, together.*
Assembler vne Armée. *To raise an armie.*
Assembler le Conseil. *To call a counsell.*
Assembler à l'ennemy. *To fight, buckle, coape, or incounter, with th'enemie.*
Ce qu' assemble pille pille desassemble tire tire: Prov. *That which rapine gathers, reuelling disperses.*
Assemblure: f. *as* Assemblement.
Assence. *Assent, consent. (An old word.)*
Assencement; &, Assenceur. *as* Acensement, & Acenseur.
Assene: m. *An assignation, or laying out of a dower, or ioynter, for a widow, or wife.*
Assene, & advis. *A portion, or gift bestowed by a father on his younger sonnes, or on his daughters, for their preferment.*
Assené: m. ée: f. *Strucken, hit, raught, or touched home; also, proportioned, squared, measured out; also, seised on, taken into his owne hands.*
Assenement: m. *A striking, hitting, reaching, touching home; also, a proportioning, squaring, or measuring out; also, a seisure, or seising.*
Assener. *To hit, strike, reach, or touch home; also, to proportion, measure, or square out; also, to seise, or take into his owne hands.*
Assenne. *as* Assene.
Assenner. *as* Assener.
Assens: m. *A certaine profit made of forrests, and high-growne woods; as the Pawnage, Mastage, &c.*
Assentation: f. *Assentation, flatterie, colloguing.*
Assentatoire: com. *Flattering, soothing, colloguing.*
Assentement: m. *An assent, or consent; also, the sent of a hunted beast, a sent in hunting.*
Assenti: m. ie: f. *Assented, agreed, accorded vnto; also, sented, smelt, winded.*
Assentir. *To assent, agree, accord vnto; also, to sent, or wind; to take the wind, or sent, of.*
Asseoir. *To set, settle, place, plant; also, to cesse, or tax.*
s'Asseoir. *To sit, or set him downe.*
Asseoir son iugement sur. *To giue his opinion, or interpose his iudgement, on.*
Asseral. *A kind of Turkish drug.*
Asseré: m. ée: f. *Steeled; made of, tempered with, Steele.*
Assermenté: m. ée: f. *Sworne, bound by oath; or, put vnto his oath.*
Assermenter. *To sweare, put vnto an oath, bind by oath, take th'oath of.*
Asserrer. *as* Serrer.
Asserteur: m. *A claimer, or challenger; also, a maintainor, protector, defendor, of another.*
Assertion: f. *An assertion, affirmation, auerment; also, a demonstration, or document.*
Assertivement. *Affirmatiuely, demonstratiuely, resolutely, as one that will stand to what he sayes.*
Asservagi: m. ie: f. *Inthralled, subiected, submitted vnto, tyed in seruile bonds.*
Asservagir. *To inthrall, or subiect vnto; to make slauish, or seruile; to bring vnto bondage, or tye in seruile bonds.*
Asservi: m. ie: f. *Subiected, inthralled, submitted; made seruant vnto, or the slaue of.*
Asservir. *To subiect, inthrall, submit; make seruant vnto, or the slaue of.*
Asservisage: m. *Thraldome, or, an inthralling of; and hence, land bound for a debt; or, such a binding thereof.*
Asservissement: m. *An asseruanting, subiecting, inthralling; a subiection.*
Assesseur: m. *A Iudge Laterall, or, an Assistant vnto a Iudge; one that sits in Court, as an associate with, or an aduisor of, him; and more particularly, an Assistant vnto a Prouost Marshall, or Litutenant criminell.*
Assessoriat: m. *Assistance, or by-sitting; th' office, dutie, or place, of a Iudge Laterall, Assistant, or* Assesseur.
Asseulé: m. ée: f. *Abandoned, forsaken, left solitarie, or alone.*
Asseuler. *To abandon, forsake, leaue without companie, leaue alone.*
Asseur. *For,* Asseuré; *as;*
Qui a peur il est asseur: Prov. *He that feares, is assured; hee that feares false ground, treads surely; or, false measure, workes safely.*
Asseurance: f. *Surenesse, assurance, trust, confidence, securitie; boldnesse, hardinesse; also, as* Asseurement.
Asseuré: m. ée: f. *Bold, fearelesse, hardie, dreadlesse; confident, secure; stable, firme, constant, certaine; also, assured, setled, confirmed; also, affirmed.*
Il n'est pas asseuré qui trop haut est monté: Prov. *He is not safe thats got too high; hee sits not sure that sits too high.*
Asseurement: m. *The Peace, or good behauior graunted vnto one against another, who, if he breake it, commits felonie (by some customes in* France;*) also, protection, safegard, or safeconduct.*
Asseurément. *Boldly, assuredly, confidently, securely, trustfully, dreadlesly, without flinching, or feare; certainely, stably, firmely, constantly.*
Asseurément chante qui n' a que perdre: Prov. *Looke* Chanter.
Asseurer. *To assure, settle, confirme, fasten; resolue; to giue securitie vnto; also, to protect, safegard, safeconduct; graunt the Peace against; also, to lay vp in a safe, or sure place; also, to vndertake for the safetie, or suretie of; to warrant; also, to ascertaine; affirme, auouch.*
Asseurer vn oiseau. *To make, or man a hauke throughly;* L'asseurer au Iardin &c; *To set her out in a garden &c. to weather.*
Asseureté: f. *as* Asseurement.
Assez. *Inough, sufficiently; very well, as much as needs; also, a competent quantitie, or number, of.*
Assez a qui bon credit a: Pro. *A good name is wealth sufficient.*
Assez a qui se contente: Pro. *He hath ynough thats pleased.*
Assez y a si trop n'y a: Prov. *Inough is as good as a feast; or, too much of any thing is good for nothing.*
Assez boit qui a dueil: Pro. *He drinks ynough that mournes; (yet we say, Sorrow is drie.)*
Assez consent qui ne dit mot: Pro. *He that gainesayes not, giues his full consent; (of the same vessell is;)*
Assez octroye qui mot ne dit.
Assez demande qui se plaind: Pro. *He that bemones his wants, hath begd sufficiently.*
Assez demande qui bien sert: Pro. *A faithful seruant asks ynough; what his words do not aske, his worth doth.*
Assez dort qui rien ne fait: Pro. *As good sleepe altogether as doe nothing.*

Assez en dit qui apporte bonnes nouvelles: Prov. *He that hath told good newes, needs tell no more.*
Assez escorche qui tient le pied: Pro. *Looke* Pied.
Assez gaigne qui malheur perd: Prov. *He gets ynough that balkes ill lucke; or, that looses nothing.*
Assez ieusne qui pauvrement vit: Prov. *He that feeds barely fasts sufficiently.*
Assez parens assez tourmens: Prov. *The more kinsmen the more afflictions.*
Assez peut pleurer qui n'a nul qui l'appaise: Pro. *He may weepe till his heart ake, that hath no bodie to appease him.*
Assez sçait qui sçait vivre & se taire: Prov. *Looke* Sçavoir.
Assez va au moulin qui son asne y envoye: Prov. *He's guiltie ynough of an offence that appoints his man to commit it.*
Assez veille qui bien fait: Prov. *Looke* Veiller.
De petit petit, & d' assez assez: Prov. *From much take much, from little take a little.*
Rien n'a qui assez n'a: Prov. *He that hath not ynough hath nothing; or, he that couets more then he hath enioyes not what he hath.*
Assidu: m. uë: f. *Daily, frequent, oft, continuall; diligent, serious, laborious.*
Assiduellement. *Daily, continually, frequently, commonly, often.*
Assiduement. *as* Assiduellement.
Assiduité: f. *Assiduitie, frequencie, oftennesse, diligence, continuance in.*
Assiegé: m. ée: f. *Besieged, beleaguered.*
Assiegement de ville. *A besieging, or beleaguering, of a towne; a siege, or leaguer.*
Assieger. *To besiege, to beleaguer.*
Assiegeur: m. *A besieger, a beleaguerer.*
Assiement: m. *A sitting.*
Assier: m. *Steele.*
Assiete. *as* Assiette.
Assiette: f. *A trencher-plate; also, the seat, scite, or scituation of a house, or place; also, a plot for, or the platforme of, a building; also, a couch, bed, course, or laine of stone, &c, in building; also, a sitting; also, land surueyed and set out to th' vtmost rate; or th' vtmost rent raised, and extent layed, vpon land, for the payment of a debt, &c.*
Assiette à dorer. *Size to gild with, gold size.*
Assiette de taille. *A cessement, or cessing of a tax.*
Monnoye de bonne assiette. *Of a good forme.*
Pastez d'assiette. *Small Pasties, or Pies, serued in, at the first course, vpon Plates.*
Vin vendu en assiette. *Wine vttered, and drunke, by pints, or quarts, &c, in a tauerne.*
Assignal: m. *Land assigned, or layed out vnto a woman for her iointer, or dower; and which she enioyeth vntill she haue leuied as much as she brought with her.*
Assignal de rente. *Rents assigned vnto a woman for the same purpose.*
Assignat: m. *An assignation, or appointment; a distribution of, a limitation, or allotment, vnto; also, a day giuen, or place appointed.*
Assignation: f. *An assignation, assignement, appointment; a distribution; an assigning, or appointing ouer; a distributing.*
Se donner assignation. *(Two, or more) to appoint a certaine place for their meeting.*
Assigné: m. ée: f. *Assigned; appointed, ordained, or deputed, for; allotted, layed out, set or put, ouer vnto; also, seised, or taken, as forfeited, into his owne hands.*
Assigner. *To assigne; appoint, ordaine, or depute, for; to allot, lay out, set or put, ouer (also, to giue day) vnto.*
Assigner sa main au fief de son vassal; &, Assigner à son fief les terres de son vassal; *To seize, enter vpon, or take into his owne hands, as forfeited, th' inheritance of his vassall.*
Assillonnement: m. *A making of baulkes in plowing.*
Assillonner. *To baulke, or plow vp in baulkes.*
Assimenter. *To cement, close, or glue together.*
Assimilation: f. *A comparing, likening, resembling; an application, or applying of things, together.*
Assimilativement. *By comparison, semblably, in like manner.*
Assimilé: m. ée: f. *Likened, resembled, compared, vnto.*
Assimiler. *To compare, liken, resemble, apply things together.*
Assis: m. *Assessements; or, impositions.*
Assis: m. ise: f. *Set, sitting; seated, placed, setled, fixed, planted; also, limitted, appointed; also, taxed, cessed, or assessed.*
Oiseau trop haut assis. *Whose stalkes (or legs) are too long.*
Il a le cœur assis en bonne part. *He is honest, faithfull, resolute, valiant.*
Il n'y a pas bien assis ses lunettes. *He hath mistaken the matter; or, he hath not looked into it so throughly as he might, so diligently as he should, haue done.*
Assise: f. *An Assise, or Sessions (a word most vsed, as our Assises, in the plurall number) also, the customarie fine thats taken, in* Brittanie *only, for certaine beasts found dammage fesant; also, as* Assize.
Assises de Iustice. *Are, by the customes of* Normandie, *assemblies of knights, and other discreet, and substantiall men, in companie of a* Bailly, *at a place, and for a time, certaine.*
La grande assise. *is held by a Seneschall, or* Bailly.
La petite assise. *is held by a Preuostall, or inferior, Iudge.*
Droict d'assise de six deniers. vj.d. Tour. *Due vnto the towneship of* Tournay *vpon euery pottle of wine retayled within it.*
Assises: f. *The solemne, or ordinarie Assises, Sessions, or sittings of Iudges; also, as* Assis, *substan.*
Assistance: f. *Assistance, helpe, support, countenance, presence of men in helpe of their friends; a standing to in extremitie.*
Assistant: m. *An assistant; a helper; a stander by.*
Assisté. *Assisted, helped, aided, defended; stood by, or vnto.*
Assisté de plusieurs autres. *Accompanied with, or followed, by many others.*
Assister. *To assist, helpe, defend, aid, countenance; also, to accompanie, associate, be at, or be present at, stand by, or vnto.*
Assize: f. *as* Assise; *also, a course of stones, or bricks, in building.*
Associable: com. *Companable, sociable, associable, fit to hold fellowship with.*
Association: f. *An accompanying, association, societie, fellowship.*
Associé: m. ée: f. *Associated, accompanied, consorted, kept much with.*
Associer. *To associate, accompanie, hold societie, or fellowship, consort, or keepe much, with.*
Assode: com. *Wasted, or much broken by sicknesse; forlorne, wearie of his life, carelesse of himselfe.*

Assolé: m. ée: f. *Sunned; seasoned, hardened, or dried in the Sunne; also, setled, (as a horse, &c,) vpon all his feet.*

Assoler. *To sunne; to season, harden, or drie in the Sun.*

s'Assoler. *To settle himselfe vpon all his feet.*

Assommeiller. *To cast into a slumber.*

Assommé: m. ée: f. *Felled, stricken, or knocked, downe; also, cast into a heauie sleepe; also, cast vp, or summed, as a reckoning.*

Assommer. *To fell, strike, or knocke downe; to ouerbeare with blowes; also, to cast into a heauie sleepe; also, to summe, or cast vp a reckoning.*

Assommeresse. main as. *A heauie, or dead hand, that knockes or fels downe whatsoeuer it strikes.*

Assommeur: m. *A knocker, feller, or beater, downe.*

Assopi: m. ie: f. *Layed, brought, lulled, asleepe; cast into a sleepe; also, dulled, benummed, made sencelesse, as one that sleepes; also, quieted, pacified, appeased; qualified, calmed, asswaged; also, repressed, suppressed, extinguished.*

Assopir. *To lay, bring, or lull, asleepe; also, to benumme, dull, make sencelesse, as one that is asleepe; also, to quiet, pacifie, appease, calme, asswage; also, to suppresse, represse, extinguish, put vnder foot.*

Assopissement: m. *A laying, bringing, or lulling asleep; also, a dulling, benumming, making sencelesse; also, a quieting, pacifying, appeasing, asswaging; also, a repressing, suppressing, extinguishing.*

Assorbir. *To drinke, soke, or sucke, vp.*

Assortable: com. *Sortable, suitable; fit to sort, or to be suited, withall.*

Assorti: m. ie: f. *Sorted, assorted, suited, matched; also, furnished, or garnished fully.*

Assortiment. *as* Assortissement.

Assortir. *To sort, assort, suit; match, equall; dispose, order seuerall things handsomely; also, to furnish, or store with all sorts of.*

Assortissement: m. *Stuffe, or furniture; also, a sorting, or suiting of things together; disposition; also, a furnishing, or storing with all sorts of.*

Assoté: m. ée: f. *Sotted, besotted, doting on, too farre in loue with.*

Il en est plus assoté qu' un coquin de sa bouteille: *Sayd of one that foolishly affects a thing too much.*

Il en est plus assoté qu' un fol de sa Marotte. *The same.*

L'Assotée de. *A mans Sweet-heart, or Mistris, on whom the foole dotes.*

Assoter. *To sot, besot, make dote on, bring too farre in loue with.*

s'Assoter de. *To dote on, or, be extreamely in loue with.*

Il n'est si bon qui femme n'assote: Prov. *The best man may be gulled by a woman.*

Assotir. *To make, or become, sottish, doltish, foolish.*

Assotter. *as* Assoter.

Assoubjectir. *To assubiect, make subiect, subdue, bring vnder.*

Assouchement: m. *A genealogie, stocke, progenie.*

Assoupir. *as* Assopir.

Assoupli: m. ie: f. *Supplied, maccrated, made soft, or pliant.*

Assouplir. *To supple, macerate, make soft, tender, pliant.*

Assourdi: m. ie: f. *Deafened; made, or growne, deafe.*

Assourdir. *To deafen, or make deafe.*

Assourdissement: m. *A deafening, or making deafe.*

Assouvager. *To asswage; quiet, still, pacifie.*

Assouvi: m. ie: f. *Filled, contented, satiated, satisfied; also, glutted, saded, cloyed.*

Assouvir. *To fill, content, satiate, satisfie; also, to cloy, glut, sade.*

Assouvissement: m. *A filling, contenting, satiating, satisfying; also, a glutting, sading, cloying.*

Assubjectir. *as* Assoubjectir.

Assuefaction: f. *An accustoming, enuring; or continuance in a thing.*

Assumpter. *To take vp from below vnto a high place; to take vp into heauen.*

Assumption. *An assumption, or taking vp into a high place; also, the* Minor *in a Syllogisme.*

L'assumption nostre Dame. *A solemne holiday kept by the Church of Rome the 15 of August; wee tearme it our Ladie day in haruest.*

Assus. (Adverb.) *On, or vpon; whence;*

Mettre assus vne trahison à. *To accuse of, or charge with, treason; to lay treason to the charge of.*

Ast. Armes d'ast. *Weapons to be cast; as darts, &c; looke* Armes.

Astace: m. *A Lobster.*

Astalabote. *as* Ascalabe. ¶Rab.

Astelles. *as* Attelles.

Astellier: m. *A Stall.*

Asterion: m. *The name of a certaine hound-fish, or dog-fish, whose coat is full set with starre-like spots.*

Asterique: com. *Starrie, starre-like; of, or belonging vnto, a starre.*

Asteure. *as,* à cett' heure; *Presently, euen now.*

Asthmatic: m. ique: f. *Pursie, short-winded, that often and with paine fetcheth breath.*

Asthme: m. *Pursinesse, short-windinesse; an often, painefull, or difficult breathing, or breath-drawing.*

Astillier: m. *A worke-house for Masons; a Carpenters yard.*

Astipulateur: m. *A Record, or Witnesse; also, an accorder with, or assenter vnto, another; also, an assistant, helper, fauourer.*

Astivité: f. *Craft (in buying and selling;) mechanicall subtiltie.*

Astour. *Seeke* Atour.

Astragale: m. *A buckle-bone, or bonket; the first bone of th'instup; also, the Game thats played with buckle-bones; also, a smal, and round member in Architecture, sometimes plaine, sometimes wrought, sometimes wrythen; and tearmed by our workemen, an Astragall, or small Boultell; also, the Plant, or Pulse, called, the Milke vetch.*

Astragalomantie. *Diuination by buckle bones.*

Astraict: m. *as* Abstraict.

Astrantie: f. *The hearbe Maisterwort.*

Astrapade: f. *The Strappado.*

Astre: m. *A Starre, a Planet; also, destinie, fate, fortune, hap.*

Astre argenté. *The Moone.*

Astre cornu. *The same.*

L'Astre du iour. *The Sunne.*

Astreinct: m. cte: f. *Bound, tyed, or knit hard; in sure bonds; also, costiue, or belly-bound; also, forced, compelled, constrained.*

Astreindre. *To bind fast; to tye, or knit hard; to wrap in sure bonds; also, to make costiue, or belly-bound; also, to force, compell, constraine.*

Astrelabe. *Looke* Astrolabe.

Astringeant. *Astringent, astrictiue; binding, making costiue.*

Astro-

Aſtrolabe: m. An Aſtrolabe; a flat-round inſtrument, whereby the ſeuerall motions of heauenly bodies, and the length, height, and breadth of any other thing, may be diſcerned and found out.

Aſtrologie: f. Aſtrologie; a reaſoning, or ſpeculation of heauenly motions.

Aſtrologien: m. as Aſtrologue.

Aſtrologue: m. An Aſtrologer; a skilfull diſcourſer, or ſtudious beholder, of celeſtiall motions.

Aſtronome: m. An Aſtronomer; a teacher, or profeſſor, of the knowledge of ſtarres, or heauenly motions.

Aſtronomie: f. Aſtronomie; knowledge, or, profeſſion of the knowledge, of ſtarres.

Aſtronomien. as Aſtronome.

Aſtrucier: m. An Oſtridger; one that keepes or catches, Oſtridges.

Aſtruſer. To preſſe, or keepe downe.

Aſtuce: f. Craft, ſubtiltie, guile, deceit, couſenage.

Aſtut: m. ute: f. Aſtute, craftie, ſubtill, wylie, guilefull.

Aſur: m. Azure; skie-colour, or, the ſtuffe whereof tis made.

Aſur d'Acre. Naturall Azure, as it is taken out of the Mine.

Aſur d'Alemaigne; Germane Azure; is an exhalation of ſiluer Mines; from the tops and ſides of whoſe ſtones it is choicely ſcraped, and gathered.

Aſur de Levant. as Aſur d'outre mer.

Aſur d'outre mer. Beyond-ſea Azure; the beſt kind of Azure, made of Lapis Lazuli, and reſiſting both fire, and water.

Cendrée d'aſur. The whiteſt kind of Azure.

Pierre d'aſur. Lapis Lazuli; or, the Lazull ſtone.

Vert aſur. A colour betweene a blonket, and a greene; found in mines of the copper which is mingled with ſiluer; and an excellent purger of melancholie.

Aſurer. To dye, paint, ſtaine, or colour, with azure.

Aſurin: m. ine: f. Skie-coloured; cleere as the skie; blew, or wanne like azure; of, or belonging to, azure.

Aſyle: m. A Sanctuarie; a priuiledged place; a place of refuge for the afflicted, or offendor; a place of libertie, franchiſe, freedome.

Aſymbole: com. Shot-free, or ſcotfree; that payeth nothing for his victuals.

Atabal. as Attabale; alſo, a tymbrell, or little braſen drumme, to daunce by.

A-tant. Forthwith; incontinently.

Ataraxie: f. Reſolution, conſtancie, vnmoueableneſſe of iudgement; alſo, tranquilitie, or quietneſſe of mind.

A-tard. Late, ſlowly.

Ataſtre. The plaine part, or face of an Architrave; alſo, a large fillet, or bend in a pillar, &c.

Atedier. Seeke Attedier; to wearie.

Atelles. as Attelles.

Atermoyé. as Attermoyé.

Atermoyement: m. A giuing of dayes for the payment of a ſumme.

Aterrer. To throw, or ouerthrow, to daſh, or caſt downe, to the earth; alſo, to couer, or ouerwhelme, with earth; alſo, to ruine, oppreſſe, wrong extreamely.

s'Aterrer. To grow earthie, or full of earth; to be ouergrowne, or choaked vp, with earth.

Athanaſie. The hearbe Tanſie.

Athaner. To kill. ¶Bourg.

Athée: m. An Atheiſt; one that beleeues there is no God.

Atheïſme: m. Atheiſme; infidelitie; the denying of, or not beleeuing in, God.

Atheïſte. as Athée.

Atheïſterie. as Atheïſme.

Athelan: m. A very ſmall fiſh in the riuer Laiz neere Montpellier.

Atheronne. A little painleſſe impoſtume, whoſe mattar is like vnto pap.

Athle: m. A miſerable, wretched, or languiſhing fellow.

Athlete: m. A champion, at wraſtling, running, and ſuch other common games of ſtrength, actiuitie, or ſleight.

Athletique: com. Champion-like, belonging to a champion; ſtrong, ſwift, actiue, as a champion.

Atifer. Seeke Attifer.

Ativelles: f. Trinkets, tyres, or attyres.

Atizer. Seeke Attiſer.

Atome: m. A moate in the Sunne; a thing ſo ſmall, that it cannot be diuided.

Atour: m. An attire; alſo, a French hood.

Toile d'atour. Lawne.

Atourneresſe: f. as, Attourneresſe.

Atout. With, together with.

Atrabiliaire: com. Subiect, or belonging to melancholy, or blacke choller; or, as Atrebiliaire.

Atrainer. To traile, drag, or draw along vnto.

Atre: m. A harth.

Il n'y a rien en ſa maiſon ſi froid que l'atre. Hee keepes a very poore houſe; his cheere is as cold as his chimney (in which there came no fire this ſeuen yeare.)

Qui a Maraſtre a le diable en l'atre: Prov. As good haue a diuell to his dam as a ſtepdame.

Atrebiliaire: com. Compoſed of melancholy, and blacke choller; or, as Atrabiliaire.

s'Atriſter. To mourne, wax heauie, become ſorrowfull, grow ſad.

Atroce: com. Moſt cruell, pittileſſe, fell; fierce, terrible, horrible to behold; alſo, outragious, hainous, extreame.

Atrocement. Moſt cruelly, pittileſly; felly, fiercely, terribly, horribly; alſo, outragiouſly, hainouſly, extreamely.

Atrocité: f. Atrocitie, great crueltie, fierceneſſe, felneſſe; terribleneſſe, horribleneſſe; alſo, outragiouſneſſe, extremitie, hainouſneſſe.

Atrophe: com. In a conſumption; one with whom his meat dowes not, or to whom it does no good.

Atrophie: f. A conſumption that comes by a fearefull eating of too little, or a greedie deuouring of too much.

Atrophié: m. ée: f. One thats in ſuch a conſumption; or as Atrophe.

s'Atrophier. To conſume, waſt, pine, grow leane, weare away.

Atruander. Seeke Attruander.

Atſens. Bounds, meeres, limits; ¶Wallon.

Attabale. A kind of brazen drumme, vſed by the Mooriſh horſemen.

Attache: f. A thing faſtened on, or tyed vnto, another thing; as a Libell, Proclamation, or publicke Edict paſted on the corner-poſtes of ſtreets, or ſet vp in open places, that all perſons may take notice thereof.

Attache d'un cheual. The ſtanding, or tying vp of a horſe in an Inne (or any ſuch like place) for which ſome ſmall conſideration is to be giuen to the Inne-keeper, or owner.

Levrier d'attache. An Iriſh, or great, greyhound.

Attaché: m. ée: f. Faſtened, tyed, clapt vpon; ſet, annexed, knit; alſo, grapled, vnto; alſo, medled, quarrelled, brabled; fought with.

Attaché par les carrefours. *Publikely excommunicate; or, outlawed by proclamation; also, defamed by libels set vp on euery post.*

Attachement. *A tying, fastening, annexing, binding, knitting, setting vnto.*

Attacher. *To tye, fasten, claspe, knit, bind, annex, vnto, to sticke, or set vp, to hang, or clap vpon, a post, wall, &c.*

s'attacher à. *To coape, deale, meddle, scuffle, grapple, quarrell, fight, brabble with.*

Attainct. *Seeke* Attaint.

Attaincte. *as* Attainte.

Attaindre. *To reach, or attaine vnto; to touch; hit, or strike, in reaching; also, to ouertake, or fetch vp, in going &c; also, to get, procure, obtaine; bring to passe; also, to attaint, or conuict; also, to appeach, accuse, or charge with.*

Attaint: m. te: f. *Raught, attained vnto; touched; hit, strucken; ouertaken, fetched vp; also, gotten, procured, obtained; also, tainted, attainted, conuicted; also, appeached, accused of, charged with.*

Il est attaint. *He is taken; he's farre in loue; he is but a gone, or is no more his owne, man.*

Attainte: f. *A reach; hit, home touch; blow, or stroke; also, a designement, intention, purpose, pretence; also, a gentle nip, quip, or iert; a sleight gird, or taxation.*

Tirée d'attainte. *A shot within reach, or leuell.*

Nul n'y osoit donner attainte. *None durst attempt it, or deale with it; no one durst venture on it.*

Attalenté: m. ée: f. *as* Entalenté; *or, prouoked vnto, put into a longing of.*

Attalenter. *To egg, prouoke; put into a longing; to set the desire on worke, to giue it an edge, or appetite.*

Attaque: f. *An assault; incounter, skirmish, fight; a violent meeting of two armies, or enemies.*

Attaqué: m. ée: f. *Incountred, scuffled or medled with; assaulted, or set on.*

Attaquer. *To assault, or set on; to incounter, coape, scuffle, any way to meddle with.*

Attavanat: m. *A horse thats flye-bitten onely on the flanke, or on the necke.*

Attayne: f. *Moodinesse, anger, testinesse, pettishnesse,* (vieil mot.)

Attayneux: m. euse: f. *Moodie, angrie, froward, pettish, testie.*

Attediation: f. *A toyling, wearying; cloying, or troubling with too much of one thing; also, a loathing, wearisomenesse, tediousnesse.*

Attedié: m. ée: f. *Toyled, wearied; cloyed, or troubled with too much of.*

Attedier. *To toyle, wearie; annoy; make loath; cloy, or trouble with too much of one thing.*

Atteinte. *Looke* Attainte.

Attelage: m. *Harnesse for a Draught, or Teame, &c, or for the cattell that draw it; all the furniture vnto it, or them, belonging; also, a Licence graunted, by th'officers of a forrest, vnto a Potter, Glasier, Tyler, Turner, Smith, Ash-maker, &c, for the taking of Earth, Wood, or Minerals, for their seuerall vses.*

Attelé: m. ée: f. *Spanged, or fastened, as a horse, &c, vnto a Plough, Chariot, Coach, Cart, &c.*

Attelements: m. *Th'attirals, harnesse, geeres, or furniture, belonging to draught horses, or oxen; or vnto that which they draw.*

Atteler. *To spang, yoake, or fasten a Horse, Ox, &c, vnto a Chariot, Plough, Coach, or Cart; to put them into it; also, to harnesse them for it.*

Attelier: m. *A worke-house, or shop for an artificer.*

Attelle: f. *A splent, or sticke to make a splent of.*

Attelles: f. *The haumes of a draught horses collar; the two flat sticks that incompasse it.*

Attenance: f. *A dependancie vpon, a belonging vnto; also, as* Attente; *hope, expectation.*

Attenant: m. ante: f. *Belonging, or appertaining to; adioyning vnto; depending on; holding, or cleauing, by.*

Attendant: m. *An attendant, retayner, waiter.*

Attendans. *Ashlers; binding stones, (in Masonrie.)*

Attendant: m. ante: f. *Attending, waiting on; expecting; tarrying, staying, for.*

Attendant que. *Whilest that.*

Attendre. *To attend, wait, stay, tarrie; expect, looke for; to daunce attendance on.*

s'attendre à. *To trust, rest, relye, depend, vpon.*

Attendre la venue du boiteux. *To stay for Iohn Long the Carrier; to tarrie long for that which comes but slowly.*

De ce que tu pourras faire n'attends autruy: Pro. *Bid not another doe that which thou canst do thy selfe; or, build not, relye not, on anothers doing of that which &c.*

Pour neant recule qui malheur attend: Prov. *In vaine he retires that attends mishap (which if it must come, hurts least being met with.)*

Qui attend il a fort temps: Prov. *He that attends hath time ynough; or to him that waits all time seemes tedious.*

Qui s'attend à l'escuelle d'autruy il disne souvent bien tard: Prov. *He that waits on another mans trencher, makes many a late dinner.*

Qui bon maistre sert bon loyer en attend: Prov. *Hee that serues a good master, hopes for a good reward.*

Qui fol envoye fol attend: Pro. *He that imployes a foole, expects a foole.*

Tout est fait negligemment là où l'un à l'autre s'attend: Prov. *Nothing is well done where one altogether trusts vnto, or relyes vpon, another.*

Tout vient à point qui peut attendre: Prov. *He that can stay his time, shall compasse any thing.*

Attendrir. *To soften, mollifie, make tender, gentle, plyant.*

s'attendrir. *To grow tender, soft, gentle; nice, faint, effeminate.*

Attendrissement: m. *A softening, mollifying, making tender.*

Attendu: m. uë: f. *Attended, waited, stayed on; expected, looked, tarried for.*

Attendu que. *Seeing that.*

Petit disner longuement attendu n'est pas donné, mais cherement vendu: Pro. *We buy too deerely meat we stay long for; or, a little meat long stayed for's deerely bought; (The like may be said of any benefit, or fauor.)*

Attendue: f. *An attendance, or attending.*

Attenir. *To retaine, detaine, with-hold, keepe, or stay, backe.*

s'attenir à. *To belong vnto; to depend vpon; also, to be linked, or ioyned in consanguinitie with.*

Attentat: m. *A proceeding in suit notwithstanding an appeale; also, a taking (by the plaintife, or defendant) to his owne vse part of a thing which the Court hath wholly sequestred; any attempt made, or course held on, contrarie to a publicke Order.*

Attente: f. *Expectation; hope, desire of; an attending, staying, tarrying for; also, a preiudicate opinion.*

Attente d'un edifice. *Th'inchoation, or vnperfect beginning of a building, giuen ouer before it be finished.*

Laissons celuy la en attente. *Let vs leaue him alone (to his hopes; or, to picke strawes, or pull daysies.)*

Sans autre attente. *Incontinently; without more tarrying, delay, or ado.*

Attentes d'une muraille, &c. *Denting parts, or peeces of a wall &c.*

Table d'attente. *A plate of copper, &c, whereon some notable inscription, or other thing, is engrauen; also, a flat peece of marble, &c, charged with the like stuffe, and set (as the other, most commonly) on the outside of a roome, or building.*

Attenté: m. ée: f. *Attempted, enterprised; essayed, proued, put vnto triall.*

Attenter. *To attempt, enterprise; essay, proue, begin, put into triall; also, a plaintife, or defendant to conuert vnto his vse or benefit part of the thing in suit, notwithstanding a former sequestration thereof made by the Court.*

Attenter au prejudice l'appel. *To goe on with his suit notwithstanding the Appeale of the aduerse partie.*

Attentif: m. iue: f. *Attentiue, listening, heedfull carefull, diligent; vigilant; earnestly bent vnto, exceedingly set vpon.*

Attentiuement. *Attentiuely, carefully, heedfully, wistly.*

Attenu: m. uë: f. *Bound, or beholden to.*

Attenuation: f. *An attenuation, or extenuation; a lessening, impairing, diminishment; a making thinne, slender, weake.*

Respondre par attenuation. *Looke* Respondre.

Attenué: m. ée: f. *Diminished, lessened, impaired, wasted, extenuated; made thinner, smaller, slenderer; weaker.*

Attenuer. *To lessen, diminish, impaire, appaire, wast; extenuate; to make thinner, slenderer; weaker.*

Attenuri: m. ie: f. *Made thinne, slender, small; or as* Attenué.

Attenurir. *To make thinne, slender, or small; to minish, extenuate, lessen, impaire.*

Atterissement: m. *An ouerthrowing to the earth; a couering with earth; a surrounding, or ouerwhelming by the earth.*

Attermoyé: m. ée: f. *That hath a terme, or time granted for the paiment of a debt; also, put off from terme to terme, from time to time.*

Atterrasseur: m. *An ouerthrower (to the earth;) a ruiner, vndoer, oppressor.*

Atterré: m. ée: f. *Couered with, ouerwhelmed, ouerthrowne to, the earth; ruined; oppressed.*

Atterre-espi. *Corne-burying, eare-ouerwhelming.*

Atterrer. *To couer, or ouerwhelme with earth; to ouerthrow vnto the earth; or, as* Aterrer.

s'Atterrir. *To rot vnto earth; or, by lying on the earth, or by rotting on the earth; to become as earth; also, to fall vnto the earth.*

Atterrissement. *as* Atterissement.

Attestation: f. *An attestation; affirmation, calling to witnesse; a iustification by witnesses.*

Attesté: m. ée: f. *Attested; protested, auouched, affirmed; testified, witnessed, iustified by witnesse.*

Attester. *To attest; auouch, affirme, protest, call to witnesse; also, to testifie, witnesse, confirme by witnesse.*

Atteyner vn chien sur. *To set a dog at, or turne a dog vpon.*

Attiedi: m. ie: f. *Warmed, made luke-warme.*

Attiedir. *To warme; to make luke-warme.*

Attifté: m. ée: f. *Decked, pranked, tricked, trimmed.*

Attiffement: m. *A pranking, decking, tricking, trimming of.*

Attiffer. *To decke, pranke, tricke, trim, adorne.*

Attiffets: m. *Attires, or tires, dressings, trickings, attirals.*

Attiler. *as* Attiffer.

Attiltré: m. ée: f. *Suborned, appoasted; instructed beforehand, taught the matter he hath to say.*

Attiltrer. *To suborne, or appoast, instruct, or teach before hand; to informe, or forewarne of, the matter he is to deliuer.*

Attiné: m. ée: f. *Prouoked, vrged, irritated, incensed; also, fleshed, or fastened on.*

Attiner. *To prouoke, vrge, irritate, incense against; also, to flesh, or fasten on.*

Attinté: m. ée: f. *Decked, tricked, trimmed, pranked; also, fine, spruce, compt, neat; also, fitted, set right; or (as an arrow on the bow-string) nocked.*

Attinter. *To decke, pranke, tricke, trimme; also, to fit well, set right, place iust.*

Attiquets: m. *Little notes, or tickets.*

Attirail: m. *A great mans retinue, traine, attendants, followers.*

Attirantons: m. *An Artificers tooles, or instruments.*

Attiraux: m. *Plough-geeres; the tooles, or instruments belonging to a plough.*

Attiré: m. ée: f. *Drawne to; tolled on; inuited, inticed, allured vnto.*

Attirement: m. *A drawing to; a tolling on; an inuiting, inticing, alluring vnto.*

Attirer. *To draw, or bring to; to toll, or lead on; also, to inuite, intice, allure vnto.*

Attisé: m. ée: f. *Kindled, or stirred, as fire.*

Attise-feu: m. *A fire-kindler, or fire-stirrer; and (metaphorically) a stirrer vp of strife, a firebrand of contention, a raiser of sedition.*

Attise-querelle: m. *A brabling make-hate; a renewer, a reuiuer of old, and ouer-worne quarels.*

Attiser. *To kindle (a fire;) to stirre the fire; to lay one cole, or brand neere vnto another.*

Attiser le feu avec l'espée. *To prouoke an angry person extreamely.*

Attisonné: m. ée: f. *Scorched, or halfe burnt; blackish, or duskie-coloured, as a firebrand, &c.*

Attisonner. *as* Attiser.

Attorné: m. ée: f. *Dressed, attired, trimmed, decked, adorned.*

Attorner. *To attire, dresse, decke, adorne, trimme, trick, pranke, set out.*

Attouche: f. *A gentle touch; also, a glaunce at, or short mention of.*

Attouché: m. ée: f. *Gently touched, handled, or felt softly; lightly, or slightly mentioned.*

Attouchement: m. *A gentle touching, light handling, soft feeling of; also, as* Attouche.

Attoucher. *To handle gently, touch lightly, feele softly; also, to mention briefely, glaunce at sleightly; meddle, or deale with but a little, any way.*

Attour: m. *A French-hood; also, any kind of tire, or attire, for a womans head.*

Damoiselle d'attour. *The waiting woman that vses to dresse, or attire, her mistresse.*

Attouré: m. ée: f. *Tired, dressed, attired, decked, trimmed, adorned.*

Attour-

Attournance : f. *An Atturneyship ; or, the following of a cause by an Atturney ; also, as* Attournement.
Attourné : m. ée : f. *as* Attouré ; *also, atturned, as a tenant.*
Attournée : f. *as* Attournement ; *Also, a letter of Atturney.*
Attournement : m. *An attiring, dressing, decking ; also, the Atturnement of a tenant.*
Attourner. *To attire, decke, dresse ; also, to atturne, as a tenant.*
Attourneresse : f. *A waiting-woman, or chamber-maid, that vses, or helpes, to attire her mistresse.*
Attourneur : m. *A Groome of the Chamber ; one that waits in the chamber, to dresse his Master, or Mistresse.*
Attrabilaire. *as* Atrabiliaire.
Attractif : m. iue : f. *Attractiue ; inticing, alluring ; of power, or propertie, to draw vnto.*
Attraction : f. *An attraction ; a drawing to.*
Attrahiere : f. *Escheatage ; or, an Escheat ; Looke* Estrayeres.
Attraict : m. *An attraction, or attractiue ; a bait, allurement, inticement, inueaglement.*
Attraiement : m. *An attracting, or drawing vnto ; also, an alluring, inticing, inueagling.*
Attraire. *To attract, or draw vnto ; also, to allure, intice, inueagle, toll on ; moue, or prouoke vnto, by faire meanes.*
Attraire tesmoins. *To produce witnesses.*
Vn dormir attrait l'autre : Prov. *One sleepe draws on another.*
Attrament. *Inke ; or bleach for Shoomakers.*
Attrapé : m. ée : f. *Caught, intrapped, apprehended ; ouertaken ; taken tardie, or in the manner.*
Tost attrapée est la souris qui n'a pour giste qu'un pertuis : Prov. *Looke* Souris.
Attraper. *To intrap, catch, apprehend ; ouerreach, ouertake, take tardie, or in the manner.*
Attraperie : f. *A catching, intrapment, intrapping.*
Attrapoire : m. *An intrapping, or catching ; also, a trap, the instrument, or meanes, whereby one is intrapped.*
Attrayamment. *Attractiuely, alluringly, inticingly.*
Attrayant. *Attracting, attractiue, leading, or drawing vnto ; alluring, inticing.*
Attrayement. *as* Attraict ; *or, as* Attraiement.
Attrayeres : f. *Escheats ; Looke* Estrayeres.
Attrectation : f. *A soft, and often handling, touching, feeling.*
Attrempance : f. *Sobernesse, temperance, modestie, staiednesse, gouernment ; moderation in behauiour, or humour.*
Attrempé : m. ée : f. *Tempered, moderated, well gouerned ; of a temperate, or stayed humour ; also, moistened, soaked, well steeped in liquor ; also, mixed, or seasoned with.*
Attrempement : m. *A temper, moderation, euen measure, iust proportion, modestie, moderate disposition, staied behauiour ; also, a moistening, steeping, or soaking in liquor.*
Attrempément. *Temperately, moderately, modestly ; patiently ; stayedly, cooley, faire and softly, soberly.*
Attremper. *To temper, moderate, vse a iust, and euen measure ; also, to mix, or season ; also, to moisten, soke, or steepe in moisture.*
Attribué : m. ée : f. *Attributed, imputed, giuen, or laied, vnto ; charged with ; put vpon.*
Attribuer. *To attribute, impute, or put vpon ; to charge with ; to giue, or lay vnto.*
s'Attribuer. *To challenge, assume, or take vpon him.*
Attributif : m. iue : f. *Attributiue ; attributing.*
Attristé : m. ée : f. *Agrieued, growne sad, made sorrowfull.*
Attriste-coeur. *Heart-sadning, thoughts-grieuing.*
Attrister. *To agriene, make sad, heauie, sorrowfull.*
Attrit : m. ite : f. *Rubd, fretted, wasted, worne away.*
Attrition : f. *A rubbing, fretting, wearing.*
Attroupé : m. ée : f. *Trouped, in troupes.*
s'Attrouper. *To assemble in troupes, or companies ; to troupe together.*
s'Attruander. *To loyter, grow lazie, become sluggish, wax an idle truant.*
Aturré à vn' opinion. *Resolute, or obstinate in, an opinion ; fully bent to defend, or follow it.*
Au *(a Masculine Article ; or, a Preposition bearing th'energie of a Masculine Article) is euer set before Masculine Nownes that begin with a consonant, and signifies, In the ; to the ; at the ; on the ; &c, as in* 'A.
Avachi : m. ie : f. *Loosened, slackened ; quailed, faded, growne flaggie ; failed in liuelinesse, vigour, vehemencie.*
s'Avachir. *To loosen, slacken, grow flaggie ; quaile, fade, faile of it former liuelinesse, vigour, and vehemencie ; to wax faint, feeble, heartlesse ; to hang downe the head.*
Avail : m. *A wild Boare.*
Availlon : m. *A kind of shell-fish.*
Avaindre. *To take, or draw out ; to bring, or lead forth ; also, to touch, to reach vnto.*
Aval. *Downe, or downeward.*
Vent d'aval. *A West-South-West wind ; or a Westerly wind that somewhat inclines to the South.*
Avalanche. *as* Avallanche.
Avalisque. *Auant, be gone ; fie vpon it :* ¶Langued.
Avallage : m. *A letting, putting, or laying, downe ; also, a swallowing, or swilling downe ; also, a fall, or a falling downe, as of riuers, or other waters ; also, a Porters hire, for the laying of wine downe into a sellor.*
Avallanche : f. *A great falling, or sinking downe, as of earth &c.*
Avallasse : f. *An inundation ; also, a swallowing gulfe, or deepe swallow.*
Avallé : m. ée : f. *let, put, layed, cast, felled, fallen, downe ; swallowed, swilled, gulped, downe ; also, cut off, or cut downe.*
Boyau avallé. *The disease called, Bursting.*
Avallé en tetasse de vieille. *Swagging, like an old wiues dug.*
Les cheveux nonchalemment avallez. *Their haire hanging carelesly about their eares.*
Avallement : m. *A letting, putting, or laying downe ; a letting fall downe ; also, a supping vp, a swallowing, or swilling downe ; also, a cutting off, or downe.*
Avaller. *To let, put, lay, cast, fell, downe ; to let fall downe ; also, to sup, or gulpe vp ; to swill, or swallow downe ; also, to cut off, or downe ; whence ;*
Il luy avalla l'espaule d'un coup d'espée. *He claue one of his shoulders from his bodie ; or, at one blow he stroke off one of his shoulders.*
Il luy avalla sa robbe de dessus les espaules. *He pulled, or plucked his gowne ouer his shoulders.*
La lice avalla son ventre. *The Bitch growes big with whelpe ; or, the whelpes within her make her belly almost touch the ground.*
Avaller gros, & mascher dru : Prov. *(As we say,) to stumble at a straw, and leape ouer a blocke.*
Avalleur : m. *A letter, layer ; feller, cutter, downe ; a gulper,*

gulper, swiller, or swallower, downe of.

Avalleur de biens. *A prodigall glutton; one that consumes his owne, or other mens estate, by immoderat eating, and drinking.*

Avalleur de frimats. *An idle fellow; a man of small worth, or capacitie; a carelesse companion.*

Avalleurs de pois gris. *Looke* Pois.

Availoire. *A hole, trap-doore, window, &c, to let a thing downe by into a lower roome.*

Avallouëre. *as* Avalloire.

Avalluation: f. *A valuation, or valuing; a rate, price, or value set downe.*

Avalluer. *To value, rate, prise; to set a price on; to hold at a rate.*

Avaluement: m. *as* Avalluation.

Avance: d'avance. *In hand, giuen before hand, or in part of a greater summe.*

Faire avance. *To further, to forward; to get, or set, forward.*

Avancé: m. ée: f. *Forwarded, forward, in good forwardnesse, got, or put, forward; furthered, aduanced, accelerated, hastened, shortened by hast; also, giuen in hand, or before hand; also, thriven in, or profited by.*

Avanceant. *Forwarding, furthering, setting forward, putting out, or on; aduancing, hastening, accelerating; giuing in hand, or before hand.*

Avancement: m. *A forwarding, setting forward, putting on, or out; a giuing in hand, or before hand; a hastening, or accelerating; also, an aduancing, a getting, or going forward, a proceeding, progression, passing on; also, aduancement, preferment, promotion.*

Avancer. *To forward, set forward, further, put on; also, to hasten; and, to shorten, or cut off by hast; also, to aduance, prefer, promote.*

s'Avancer. *To proceed, go on, get forward; also, to thriue, increase, preuaile in, profit by.*

Avancer argent. *To giue money in hand, or aforehand.*

Avancer le doigt. *To put forth, or stretch out, a finger beyond his fellowes.*

Avancer vn terme de louage. *To pay before the day, or giue before hand.*

Le iour s'avance. *The day approaches, or breakes.*

Avanceur: m. *A forwarder, aduancer; hastener, accelerater; also, a foregoer.*

Avanchaye: f. *A groue of Oziers, or of such like trees.*

Avanger. *To satisfie, suffice, serue the turne; to furnish throughly, to beare the whole charge of.*

Vous n'avanger rien. *You goe no whit forward.*

Nous avons tant de vin que nous ne pouvons avanger à boire. *We haue more wine than we are able, or know how, to drinke.*

Avant: m. *The time of Aduent; which is about a moneth before Christmas.*

Avant. *Is some times an Aduerbe of time; and then signifies, before, or ere, and forward; and sometimes of place, (then commonly following,* bien*) and signifies; forth, forward, inward, deepely in, farre in.*

Avant la main. *In hand, or before-hand.*

Avant que proceder. *A prolonging, or deferring of sentence, or of proceeding when the suit is readie for sentence.*

Estre bien avant de feste. *To liue merily, or in iollitie.*

Mettre en avant. *To aduance, put forward, preferre; also, to propound, open, declare, what he hath to say.*

Venir en avant. *To come, aduance, or step forth; to grow, increase, thriue, preuaile, proceed, come forward in the world.*

Pour vn petit n' avant n' arriere: Prov. *A little breakes no square; no matter for a little.*

Avantage: m. *An aduantage, oddes; ouerplus; addition, eeking; a benefit, furtherance, or forwarding; also, a mounting-blocke; a blocke to get on horsebacke by.*

'A l'avantage. *Excellently, or exceeding well.*

D'avantage. *Moreouer, further, furthermore, else, besides, ouer and besides, aboue and besides, with odds, more than measure.*

Avantagé: m. ée: f. *Aduantaged, hauing the aduantage of; also, benefited, priuiledged; aduanced, furthered.*

Bien avantagé en nez. *Nosed with aduantage, well nose-growne, hauing a Gnomicall, or goodly long, Nose.*

Avantager. *To aduantage, giue aduantage vnto, further, set forward; aduance, benefit, doe good vnto.*

Avantageusement. *Aduantageously, with great aduantage; easefully, profitably, well for a man.*

Avantageux: m. euse: f. *Aduantageous, easefull, commodious, behouefull; also, verie forward, full of forwardnesse.*

Avant-bras. *A vambrace; armour for an arme; also, the part of the arme that extends from the elbow to the wrist; also, the vnderbone of that part.*

Avant-chien. *The lesser dog-star, which appears when dog-dayes begin.*

Avant-conceu: m. euë: f. *Fore-conceiued, formerly deuised.*

Avant-cour. *An outward, or little, Court before the portall, or gate, of a great house.*

Avant-courement. *A forerunning; preceding, foregoing.*

Avant-coureur: m. *A forerunner, Auantcurror.*

Avant-coureux: m. *as* Avant-coureur.

Avant-coureux: m. euse: f. *Forerunning, precedent.*

Avant-garde. *The Forward, or vauntgard, of an armie.*

Avant-hier. *The day before yesterday; two dayes agoe.*

Avant-jeu: m. *An assay, triall, or proofe before a game begin.*

Avantin: m. *The arme, or braunch of a vine, climing, or brought along, from tree to tree.*

Avantjoüeur. *A Prologue, he that beginneth, or playeth before, the game, Enterlude, or Commedie.*

Avant-iugé. *as* Preiugé.

Avant-logis: m. *A roome, or lodging in the forepart of a house, standing alone; an outward gate with lodgings in it; also, a Court-yard, or comming in; and, a Court, Porch, or Portall, before a house.*

Avant-main. *The forepart of the hand; or, that part which is betweene the wrist, and the knuckles.*

Avant-mur: m. *An auantmure; fore-wall, out-wall, or outward-wall.*

Avant-parleur: m. *A fore-speaker; or one that is too forward to speake.*

Avant-pas: m. *The start, or an aduantage, in a race, or Course.*

Avant-penser. *To premeditate, or bethinke himselfe before-hand of.*

Avant-perse. *The greatest kind of Abrecocke; or as;*

Avant-pesche. *Th'Auant-peach, or hastie peach; russet on one side, and red to the Sunne-ward, yet bigger than th'ordinarie red Peach; it comes timely, and eats delicately; and therefore some call so, the greatest kind*

kind of Abrecocke.
Avant-pied. *The part of the foot thats next to the toes, and consisteth of fiue bones.*
Avant-poignet. *So much of the hand as is betweene the wrist and the knuckles.*
Avant-portail: m. *A foreporch; an outward portall; a porch at the vtter doore of a house.*
Avant-propos: m. *A Prologue.*
Avant-proumenoir: m. *An open lodge, or close walke for suitors, &c, before the doore of a great house.*
Avant-toict. *An house-eaue, or easing; as* Severonde.
Avanture. Avanturer. Avantureux. Avanturier. *Seeke* Adventure, &c.
Avare: com. *Auaricious, greedie, couetous, vnreasonably desirous of, vnsatiably thirsting after, money, &c.*
Avarement. *Auariciously, greedily, couetously.*
Avarice: f. *Auarice, couetousnesse; an vnreasonable desire of, an insatiate thirst after, money, &c.*
Avarice fait petit monceau: Prov. *Small is the heap that auarice affoords (when wealth comes either to be displayed, or distributed.)*
Avarice rompt le sac: Prov. *Looke* Sac.
Quand tous pechés sont vieux avarice est encores ieune: Prov. *The loue of wealth continues yong when all sinnes else grow old.*
Avaris: m. *Decay of wares, or marchandise; leckage of Wines; also, the charges of the cariage, or measuring thereof; also, the fees, or veiles of a Cooke, &c.*
Avaritieusement. *Auariciously, couetously, greedily.*
Avaritieux: m. euse: f. *Auaricious, full of auarice.*
Avau l'eau. *Downe the water.*
Aubades. *Morning Musicke; such as fidlers play vnder chamber windowes.*
Les vieilles gens qui font gambades, à la mort sonnent des aubades: Prov. *Looke* Vieil.
Aubain: m. *An alien, stranger, forreiner; properly such a one as is borne in a countrey so neere ours, as notice may conueniently be taken of his originall, and name; therein differing from* Espaue, *who comes one knowes not whence.*
Aubain: m. ine: f. *Strange, forreine, of another countrey; also, casuall; due, comming, or falling by escheat.*
Aubaine: f. *Escheatage; also, an Escheat; land, or substance falling to the King, or Lord, by the death of strangers, or illigitimation of bastards; any such casualtie; (but especially, the first) also, forreinnesse, strangenesse; the estate, or condition of a forreiner, or straunger;* (Anciennement aucuns ont prins le mot d'aubaine pour desherance: ¶Ragueau.)
Droict d'aubaine. *Escheatage; the right of succession in the estate of all strangers dying in France, without naturalization, and French-borne issue: (This right is, or should be onely the Kings; yet diuers Lords incroach vpon it; and some, who haue high iurisdiction, challenge thereby the goods of all, though naturall Frenchmen, which haue dwelt within their libertie as forreiners, or not free thereof.*
Aubaineté: f. *Escheatage.*
Aubanité. *The same.*
Aubans: m. *The shrowds, of a ship.*
Aubarede: f. *A groue, small copse, or small wood.*
Aube: f. *The dawning, or breake of day; Seeke* Aubes.
L'aube d'un bast. *Is, the same in a packsadle, that* Arçon *is in a great sadle.*
L'aube d'un prestre. *A Priests Albe.*
'A l'aube des mousches. *Some two or three houres after Sunne-rise; or, when the Sunne beginnes to bee hot.*

En mes aubes. *In my infancie, or swathing clothes; when I was in my cradle.*
Aubeau: m. *The white Poplar, or Peplar tree.*
Aubec: m. *The pith, sap, or heart of wood, and timber;* ¶Bourdelois.
Aubeine. *as* Aubaine; *Also, a kind of grape.*
Aubel. *as* Aubeau.
Aubeliere: f. *A huffler, a nifle, a whin-whau.*
Aubenable: com. *Subiect vnto Escheatage; or vnto* Droict d'Aubaine.
Aubenage: m. *Escheatage; as* Aubaine.
Droict d'aubenage. *as* Droict d'aubaine; *Or a kind thereof; and is, in some parts of Fraunce, a new purse, and iiij. d. in it; in others a pound of wax due vnto the Lord Iusticer of the Bailiwike, Libertie, or Mannor wherein a stranger, or forreiner dyes: In some places this duetie is leuied foure and twentie houres after the stranger is buried; in others, before he be carried vnto buriall.*
Auber. *To flit, stirre, shift, remoue from place to place; (a rusticall word.)*
Aubere: m. *A Dapple-gray horse; also, a hobbie.*
Aubereau: m. *The hawke tearmed a Hobbie; also, a kind of Eagle.*
Auberet. *as* Aubereau: ¶Savoyard.
Aubergade. *as* Queste.
Auberge: f. *A kind of small Peach also, a lodging house, or dwelling place; also an Inne.*
Aubergé: m. ée: f. *Lodged, housed, harboured, inned.*
Aubergeon. *as* Haubergeon.
Auberger: m. *Th' Auberge Peach tree.*
Aubert: m. *Money, coyne, siluer, chinkes:* ¶Barrag; *also, as* Haubert.
Aubes: f. *The short boordes which are set into th' outside of a water-mills wheele; we call them, ladles, or aueboords.*
Aubespin: m. *The White-thorne, or Hawthorne.*
Aubicon: m. *A kind of great fig; which, being sooner ripe, is more esteemed, than any other.*
Aubier: *The pith, sap, or whitest and softest part of timber, subiect vnto worme-eating.*
Aubifoin: m. *A Turkish stone; also the weed Blew-bottle, Blew-blaw, Corne-flower, Hurtsickle.*
Grand aubifoin. *The great Blew-bottle.*
Petit aubifoin. *The common Blew-blaw, or Blew-bottle.*
Aubin. *as* Aubier; *Also, the white, or gleare, of an egge.*
Aubinage. *as* Aubaine; *or* Aubenage.
Aubour. *as* Aubier.
Aubourt: m. *A kind of tree tearmed in Latine,* Alburnus; *(it beares long yellow blossomes, which no Bee wil touch.)*
Aubun d'œuf. *The white of an egge.*
Aucaigne. *as* Ocaigne; *Dogs leather well dressed.*
Auche: f. *A round haspe of yron, or cleit of wood, wherin the barrell of a windles turneth.*
Aucteur. *Seeke* Autheur.
Auctorisation. *Looke* Authorisation.
Auctorisé. *Authorised; established, set in authoritie.*
Auctoriser. *as* Authoriser.
Aucun. *Some bodie, some one; any, any one.*
Aucunement. *Somewhat; after a sort, in a manner; so, so.*
Aucunesfois. *Sometimes; now and then; otherwhiles; at one time or other.*
Audace: f. *Audacitie, boldnesse, hardinesse, courage, mettall, stomacke; also, rashnesse; presumption, saucinesse,*

cineſſe,audaciouſneſſe.

Audacieuſement. *Boldly,aduenturouſly, couragiouſly, hazardouſly,daringly; audaciouſly; raſhly, preſumptuouſly,ſaucily.*

Audacieux: m.euſe: f. *Bold, ſtout, hardie, aduenturous, hazardous, couragious, full of mettall, ſtomacke, valour; alſo, audacious, daring, ſaucie, malapert, preſumptuous; raſh.*

Audience: f. *An audience, or hearing; a report, or examination of letters patents,&c, in Chancerie; alſo,the reuenue of the Chancerie ſeale.*

Tenir l'audience. *To examine, or heare read, letters patents,&c, before they bee ſealed, or abſolutely paſſed.*

Audiencé: m.ee: f. *At a hearing, come to a hearing; alſo, examined, or heard read, as a letters patents, &c. before th'inſealing, or abſolute paſſing thereof.*

Audiencier: m. *A hearer, or giuer of audience; alſo, an Officer in the Chancerie, that examines, or heares read, all letters patents,&c, before they paſſe the ſeale, and deliuers them out, being ſealed; he alſo receiues the fees of the ſeale, and thereout payes all wages, and ſtipends aſſigned vnto the Offices, and defrayes all the ordinarie charges, of that Court; (an Vſher, or Cryer is alſo, in ſome Courts, tearmed* Audiencier, *but with the addition of* Huiſſier.*)*

Le grand audiencier de France. *The chiefe Audiencier of France, and chiefe paimaſter of all Chancerie Officers; for vnto him the inferiour* Audiencier *(in each Parliamentall Chancerie one) payes ouer, euerie halfe yeare, that which he hath receiued.*

Auditeur: m. *An Auditor, hearer, hearkener, liſtener; alſo, an Auditor, or Examiner of Accompts, in th'Exchequer; (of whom looke* Auditeur des Comptes;*) Alſo, a Magiſtrat, or Officer, before whom all contracts of ſale, or aſſignation of rents, are (in ſome places) acknowledged, paſſed, and authoriſed.*

Auditeurs du Chaſtelet de Paris. *Certaine pettie Iudges, who determine finally, and without oppoſition, or appeale, of ſuch perſonall cauſes as are brought before them, and exceed not the value of* xx.l. Pariſis, *beſides coſts of ſuit.*

Auditeurs des Comptes. *Are ſixteene in the Exchequer, or Chamber of Accompts eſtabliſhed at* Paris; *and fewer in the reſt of the Parliamentall Exchequers: Theſe muſt take no manner of gift of any Accomptant; nor, without expreſſe order from the court, examine, or make report of, two accompts for one thing. The Court being ſet, they muſt not goe forth (nor at any time out of the towne) without leaue, vnleſſe it be when a kinſman, or ally of theirs giues in his accompt, for then they muſt ariſe, and be gone without bidding: The Court being riſen, they are the laſt that ſtay, and are not to leaue any bodie in the chambers thereof behind them.*

Auditif: m.iue: f. *Auditiue; of a hearing propertie, or facultie.*

Audition: f. *A hearing.*

Audition, & cloſture des comptes. *Th'examination, and allowance, of Accompts by an Auditor.*

Auditoire: m. *An audience, auditorie; aſſembly, or companie of hearers; alſo, a Court, or hall of audience; a Seſſions houſe, or Shire hall.*

Auditoire des maiſtres des Requeſtes. *The Court of Requeſts; or, the Court wherein the titles of Offices are determined.*

Audroict. *With, or towards; alſo, ſtraight by, directly vpon, or all along through.*

Ave. *as* Have; *Dry, leane, witherrd.*

Avec. *With, withall, together with.*

Avec le temps. *At length, in time, in th'end.*

D'avec. *From.*

Aveille: f. *The hiue-Bee, or hony-Bee.*

Aveindre. *Seeke* Avaindre.

Aveine. *as* Avoine; *Oats.*

Pain d'aveine. *Iannocks; or, oaten bread; alſo, the name of a certaine Bourrough in* Normandie.

Avelaignier: m. *A Filbeard tree.*

Avelaine: f. *A Filbeard.*

Avelaine des Indes. *The drunken date; a medicinable fruit; called by th'Arabians (and in ſome ſhops)* Faufel.

Avelaine rouge. *The red-skinned Filbeard; the right Ponticke Filbeard.*

Avelane. *as* Avelaine: ¶Langued.

Avellaine. *as* Avelaine.

Aven. *as* Avoir. *Wealth, ſubſtance, goods, riches.*

Avenage: m. *Certaine quarters, or a quantitie, of oats paied vnto a Lord, or Land-lord in lieu, or acknowledgment, of ſome other dutie; Alſo, as* Aubenage.

Bourgeoiſie d'avenage. *Looke* Bourgeoiſie.

Avenages. *Oats, prouender.*

Avenaire: com. *An alien, ſtranger, forreiner.*

Avenant. *Seeke* Advenant.

Avenat: m. *Oat-meale; or, oat-meale flower.*

Avene. *as* Avoine; *Oats.*

Avenement. *as* Advenement.

Aveneray. *as* Aveneron.

Aveneri: m. *Oaten ſtraw, or ſtubble.*

Aveneron. *Wild oats, barren oats, hauer, or oat graſſe.*

Aveneux. *Strangers, forreiners; (an old word.)*

Avenger. *Seeke* Avanger.

Avenier: m.ere: f. *Oatie, belonging to oats; feeding on oats.*

Avenir. *as* Advenir.

Aventure. *as* Adventure; à l'avent: cela n'eſt point. *I doubt, or, tis a queſtion, whether that be; or, perhaps that is not.*

Avenue. *as* Advenue.

Averé: m.ée: f. *Auerred, aduouched, affirmed, verified; witneſſed; alſo, ſearched, or ſifted out.*

Averément: m. *A iuſt eſtimation of things; alſo, an averring, auouching, verifying; alſo, a ſearching, or ſifting out.*

Averer. *To auerre, auouch, verifie, witneſſe; alſo, to ſearch, or ſift out.*

Averlan: m. *A good fellow, a mad companion, merie Greeke, ſound drunkard.*

Avernal: m. ale: f. *Helliſh, of hell pit.*

Averne: f. *Hell; or, (as we ſay) the pit of hell.*

Averon. *as* Aveneron.

Averroncation: f. *A purging, or weeding; a turning, putting, or taking away, of euill things; a diuerting of miſchiefes; alſo, an appeaſing.*

Averronquer. *To purge, or weed; to turne, put, or take, away euill; to diuert miſchiefes; alſo, to appeaſe.*

Avertin: m. *Frenzie, lunacie; giddineſſe, dizzineſſe; a turning round about, or a lunacie, in beaſts, manifeſted by their often turning; alſo, ſtubbornneſſe, obſtinacie, ſullenneſſe, wilfulneſſe, diſobedience.*

s'Avertiner. *To become giddie; franticke, lunaticke; ſullen, ſelfe-willy, ſtubborne.*

Avertineux. *Dizzie, giddie; franticke, lunaticke, fantaſticall; alſo, moodie, humorous; wilfull, obſtinate, ſtubborne, ſullen.*

Aveſprement: m. *A drawing towards euening; the eue-*

euening-tide.

Avesprer. *To draw towards euening, to grow neere night.*

Il Avesprit. *Th'euening approches; it growes almost, or it drawes towards, night.*

Avet: m. *A Fyrre tree.*

Avette. *A little Bee.*

Aveu. *Seeke* Adveu.

Aveuëment: m. *A view; the first appearance, representation, or comming in sight of.*

Aveugle: com. *Blind, sightlesse, without eyes, depriued of sight, or of his eyes; also, ignorant, or in an errour.*

Il en parle comme vn aveugle de couleurs. *Hee speakes of it like a blind man of colours;* viz. *ignorantly, at randome, he knowes not what.*

Vn aveugle meine l'autre en la fosse: Prov. *An ignorant Pastor leads an ignorant sheepe headlong into hell.*

Vn borgne est Roy au païs des aveugles: Prov. *An ordinarie scholler is held a great Doctor by the ignorant multitude; and a meere swaggerer a tall souldiour by women, and children.*

Aveuglemént: m. *Blindnesse, darkenesse, want of sight; also, ignorance, errour; also, a blinding of the eyes, a darkening of the vnderstanding.*

Aveugler. *To blind, hudwinke, depriue of eyes, or sight.*

Aveuglété: f. *Blindnesse; as* Aveuglement.

Aveuglette. à Aveuglettes. *Blindly, blindfold, in ignorance, at randome.*

Aufegue: f. *(A kind of) pale-red wheat.*

Auge: m. *A trough; also, a manger; also, a Plaisterers tray.*

C'est vn porc à l'auge. *He commonly feeds till he be readie to burst withall.*

Augée: f. *A trough-full, manger-full, or trayfull of.*

Auget: m. *A little trough, manger, or tray.*

Augibis. *(The name of) a grape, whereof an excellent raisin is made.*

Augive: f. *An ogiue; a wreath, circlet, round band, in Architecture.*

Branches d'augives. *Branches ogiued; or, limmes with ogiues.*

Augmentatif: m. iue: f. *Augmentatiue; able, fit, or easie, to increase.*

Augmentation: f. *Augmentation, increase; amplification; an increasing, augmenting; amplifying.*

Augmentateur. *An increasor, augmentor; inlarger, amplifier.*

Augmenté: m. ée: f. *Augmented, increased; inlarged, amplified.*

Augmenter. *To augment, increase; amplifie, inlarge.*

Augué. *as* Hieble; *Wallwort:* ¶Langued.

Augure: m. *Diuination, soothsaying, or coniecture of things to come, by birds; also, a fore token, presage, prophecie, forewarning.*

Augurement: m. *A diuining, soothsaying, auguring.*

Augustins. *The Austine Friers; or blacke Friers, of the order of S.* Austine.

Au-guy-l'an-neuf. *The voyce of country people begging small presents, or new-yeares-gifts, in Christmas; (An ancient tearme of reioycing, deriued from the Druides; who were woont, the first of Januarie, to goe vnto the woods, where hauing sacrificed, and banqueted together, they gathered Misletow, esteeming it excellent to make beasts fruitfull, and most soueraigne against all poison.)*

s'Aviander. *To feed, or victuall himselfe.*

Avictuaillé: m. ée: f. *Victualed; furnished with, prouided of, victuals.*

Avictuaillement. *A victualling.*

Avictuailler. *To victuall; to furnish, or store, with victuals.*

Avide: com. *Greedie, couetous, hungrie, rauenous, gluttenous, vnsatiable; eagar, desirous.*

Avidement. *Greedily, hungrily, eagarly, rauenously.*

Avidité: f. *Greedinesse, couetousnesse; extreame lust, ardent affection, eagar desire.*

Avier. *To set in the way; also, as* Aviver.

Avignon. vent A. *as* Aguyon.

Avigouri: m. ie: f. *Vigorous, lustie, able, strong; also, enabled; made lustie, strong, vigorous.*

Avilé: m. ée: f. *Imbased, disesteemed, made vile; grown cheape, fallen in price.*

Avilener. *To disgrace, dishonest, or do a villanie vnto.*

Aviler. *To despise, disesteeme; imbase, make vile, or cheape; to pull downe the price of, to bring to a low price.*

Avili: m. ie: f. *as* Avilé.

Aulier. *To fill vp wine vessels, which by working haue eiected part of their liquor.*

Avilissement: m. *An imbasing, disgracing, disesteeming*

Avillonné. *for* Environné; ¶Poictevin; *also, affronted; vexed, molested, harried.*

Avillonnement: m. *An affronting; vexing, harrying, molesting.*

Avillonner. *To affront; vex, harrie, trouble, molest.*

Aviné: m. ée: f. *That hath taken too much wine; also, giuen to drinking of wine; also, winie; or tasting like wine; or, turned into the nature of wine; also, filled, or seasoned, with wine.*

Aviner vn vaisseau. *To fill, or season, a vessell with wine.*

Aujourd'huy. *To day; this day; also, now, at this time.*

Aujourd'huy caissier, demain cassé: Prov.
Aujourd'huy en chere, demain en biere: Prov.
Aujourd'huy facteur, demain fracteur: Prov.
Aujourd'huy marchant, demain meschant. Prov.
Aujourd'huy marié, demain marri: Prov.
Aujourd'huy monsieur, demain moucheur: Pro.
Aujourd'huy Roy, demain de rien: Prov.
Aujourd,huy Seigneur, demain singe ord: Prov.
Aujourd'huy Thresorier, demain tresarriere. *A Prouerbe expounded, as all the rest, elsewhere.*

Aviron: m. *An oare, or skull.*

Avironner. *To row with oares; (an old word.)*

Avis. *Looke* Advis.

Avisé: m. ée: f. *Aduised, warie, considerate, heedfull, discreet, circumspect; also, tould, warned, informed, hauing notice, or intelligence of.*

Avisement: m. *Aduisement; heed, warinesse, forecasting, discretion, circumspection, consideration; also, an aduising, warning, telling, informing.*

Avisément. *as* Advisément.

Aviser. *To marke, heed, see, looke to, attend vnto, regard with circumspection; to consider, aduise of, take aduice on; to thinke, imagine, iudge; also, to aduise, counsell, warne, tell, informe, do to wit, giue to vnderstand.*

On y avisera. *We will thinke of it; we will consider, or see, what may be done in it.*

De tout s'avise à qui pain faut: Prov. *Hunger makes men industrious; want makes them looke narrowly, and throughly, about them.*

On s'avise tard en mourant: Prov. *When death approaches,*

proches, had-I-wist comes too late.
Qui bien se cognoit peu se prise, qui peu se prise Dieu l'avise: Prov. *Looke* Priser.
Vn fol avise bien vn sage: Pro. *Looke* Sage.
Avision nocturne. *A nightly dreame, or vision.*
Avitaillé. *as* Avictuaillé.
Avitin. Biens avitins. *Goods that come by inheritance, and whereunto the eldest succeedeth; heire-loomes.*
Avivé: m. ée: f. *Quickned, reuiued, made liuing, whereinto breath is put; whereunto spirit is giuen.*
Aviver. *To quicken, make liuing, put breath into, giue spirit vnto.*
Avives. *The Vives; a disease in horses.*
Avivre vn corps. *as* Aviver.
Aul. vn aul; *as* ail; *Garlicke*; *Seeke*, Aulx.
Aulbain. *Looke* Aubain.
Aulbereau. *as* Albereau. *A kind of hard white stone, fit for building.*
Aulberge. *as* Auberge.
Aulbespin: m. *The white thorne, or hawthorne.*
Aulbin: m. *An alien, stranger, forreiner*; *as* Aubain.
Aulbinage: m. *as* Aubenage.
Aulmosne. *Seeke* Aumosne.
Aulmosné. *as* Aumosné.
Aulnage: m. *Ell-measure, the measuring with an ell; also, measure.*
Aulnaye. *An Alder-groue, or place to plant Alders in.*
Aulne: m. *An Aller, or Alder tree.*
Aulne: f. *An Ell; the measure so called; (The most common one in* France *is three foot, seuen ynches, and eight lines in length.)*
Aulne de Bourdeaux. *is foure foot, and (very neere) a halfe, long.*
Aulne de Dijon. *is but two foot, and a halfe.*
Aulne des marchans de draps de soye; *is halfe an ynch shorter then the common, or ordinarie, Ell.*
Aulne de Paris. *is three foot, & two thirds of an ynch, and about the fiftieth part of a foot, long; (this is the iust length of it at this day; heretofore, as appeares by some Customes, it hath bin 3 foot, 8 ynches, and 4 lines long.)*
Aulne de Provins; *as* Aulne de Dijon; *two foot, and a halfe.*
L'Aulne du Roy. *is (as th' ordinarie one) three foot, seuen ynches, and eight lines.*
Au bout de l'aulne faut le drap. *There is but iust measure, or, no more then needs.*
Il a vn'aulne de boyaux vuides pour festoyer ses parens. *He is a hungrie, or greedie starueling.*
Il mesuroit le peril à l' aulne de la peur. *His feare made the danger seeme the greater.*
Il prenoit la mesure de leurs habits d' une dure aulne. *He cudgelled them soundly; or, dealt extreamly with thē; (we say, when one hath lamd another, he hath taken the measure of his shoulders with a good cudgel.)*
Il sçait combien en vaut l'aulne. *He knowes well ynough whereof they are made, what worth they are of, what stuffe there is in them.*
Tout au long de l' aulne. *Fully, wholly, soundly, throughly; whence;*
Ie vous en bailleray tout le long, ou, tout du long de l'aulne. *I will pay you home; (euer spoken angrily, and in euill part.)*
Aulné: m. ée: f. *Measured by the Ell.*
Aulnée: f. *Helicampane, Scabwort, Horseheale.*
Aulnée champestre. *Wild, or field, Helicampane.*
Aulner. *To measure by the Ell.*
Aulneur: m. *A measurer by the Ell.*
Aulnoye: f. *An Alder groue.*

Aulonnes: f. *Ouldernes, Medrinacks, Pouledauies; the canuas whereof sayles for ships are made.*
Aulonnier: m. *A certaine shrub that beares a fruit like vnto, but somewhat bigger then, a Raspis, or Strawberrie; and therefore I thinke it may safely be called, the Strawberrie tree.*
Aulvent. *as* Auvent.
Aulx: m. *Garlicke; Looke* Ail.
Herbe aux aulx. *Sauce alone, or, Iacke of the hedge.*
Le mortier sent tousiours les aulx: Pro. *Th' ill impressions made by nature, or bad habit got by custome, are seldome, or neuer, worne out.*
Aulx; *as* Autres; *others.* ¶Gasc.
Aulx-oignon. *Great garlick; or, great mountain garlick.*
Aumaille: f. *Great cattell; or any kind of Neat, as Oxen, Kine, &c.*
Aumelette d'œufs. *An Omelet; or pancake made of egs.*
Vireurs d'aumelettes. *Idle fellowes, vaine companions, or, cotqueanes; people that busie themselues, or loue to be medling, in base, or vnworthie imployments.*
Aumoire: m. *A cupboord; ambrie; almes-tub.*
Aumonner. *as* Aumosner.
Aumosne: f. *An almes; a deuotion; a gift bestowed, with a charitable respect, on the poore.*
Pure aumosne. *That which in our Law is called* Frankalmoine.
Esprit tousiours à l'aumosne, & à l'hospital. *A most beggarly, and lame wit.*
Aumosné. *Giuen in almes, bestowed to charitable vses.*
Aumosner. *To bestow in almes, or free gift; to giue a charitable almes, or vnto charitable vses.*
Aumosnerie: f. *An Almes-house.*
Aumosnier: m. *An Almner, or Amner; also, an almesgiuer; in old time a Legatarie was called so.*
Aumosnier: m. ere: f. *Charitable, almes-giuing, good or liberall to the poore.*
Aumosniere: f. *An almes-purse; or little purse wherein we carrie small money for the poore.*
Aumuce: m. *An ornament of furre worne by Canons.*
Aumusse. *as* Aumuce.
Aumussé. *Wearing an* Aumuce.
Aunaye: f. *An Alder groue, or thicket of Alders.*
Aune: m. *An Aller, or Alder tree.*
Herbe de l'aune. *Helicampane, Scabwort, Horseheale.*
Aunée: f. *as* Herbe de l'Aune.
Auner. *To make one, or, to ioyne in one; (an old word.)*
Aunir. *To close, or shut vp.*
Aunon. *A Keeling (fish.)*
Aunoye: f. *as* Aulnaye; *an Alder groue.*
Avoie: f. *A sloe-worme, or blind-worme.*
Avoier. *as* Advoué.
Avoine: f. *Oats.*
Avoine folle. *Wild oats, barren oats, hauer, oat grasse.*
Avoine sauvage. *Barren oats, wild oats.*
Avoine sterile. *Red darnell, wall barley, way Bennet.*
Poures avoines. *as* Avoine folle.
Bailler de l'avoine pour du foing. *To returne a good turne with vsurie; or, to be better then his word.*
Fais luy bien gaigner son avoine. *Put him to it roundly, make him come off lustily, take your full penniworths out of him.*
Elles ne hennissoient apres autre avoine. *That only was their desire, they longed for nothing more, their minds ran vpon nothing else.*
Manger son avoine en son sac. *To snudge it; or churlishly to eat all his meat all alone; (from Moyles, who haue bags of prouender hung so close to their noses, that none but themselues can come at it.)*

Il ne perdra point l' avoine à faute de brailler. *He will want no commoditie which clamorous, or importunate, words can get him.*

Avoine touillée croist comme enragée: Pro. *Looke* Touillé.

Avoir: m. *Wealth, substance, meanes, goods, riches, possessions, abilitie.*

Fy d'avoir qui n'a ioye, & d'amours sans monnoye: Pro. *Looke* Fy.

Avoir. *To haue; to hold, occupie, vse, possesse, enioy; also, to containe; also, to be.*

Avoir beau. *Looke afterwards; or, in* Beau.

Avoir bec. Ils n' ont que le bec. *They are nothing but words; or the best thing in them is but a little talke; or, they haue no more of a man in them but the face, outside, presence.*

Avoir bon bec. *To speake discreetly, or warily; to be circumspect in his speeches; to heed well what he sayes (especially in a time of danger, or during an examination.)*

Avoir le bec gelé. *To play mumbudget; to be tonguetyed; to say neuer a word.*

Avoir le bond. *To be cosened, cheated, gulled; to haue the gentle thumpe.*

Avoir bouche à Cour. *To eat and drinke scotfree; to be in ordinarie at Court.*

Avoir bonne bouche. *To be secret.*

Avoir la bouche fraiche. Tant vous avez la bouche fraiche! *Good Lord what quaint tearmes, what goodly words you vse! Ironically.*

Avoir son Cardinal; ou, son cas. *A woman to bee troubled with her monthly flux.*

Avoir sa chemise; &, ce qu' elle doit avoir. *The same.*

Avoir le cœur net de. *To be fully satisfied in, throughly resolued of.*

Avoir son compte. *To be merrie, liuely, iolly, light hearted, at ease; as one that hath past a troublesome accompt, or is cleere of a combersome reckoning, and knowes alreadie what he is to trust vnto.*

Avoir les dents à machecoulis. *Looke* Dent.

Avoir le feu à la feste. *To be hot, hastie, cholericke, fierce, furious; forward, hazardous, aduenturous.*

Avoir le filet. *To be tongue-tyed.*

Avoir du foin aux cornes. Il a du foin aux cornes; *He beares hay in his hornes; he is a shrewd, fierce, curst, or dangerous fellow to meet with; See,* Foin.

Avoir froid. *To be cold.*

Avoir froid aux pieds. *To be iealous; or, as in* Froid.

Avoir haine à. *To hate, or beare hatred vnto.*

Avoir les mains derriere le dos. *To be lazie, idle, negligent, carelesse, retchlesse, not to passe, not to care, how the world goes.*

Avoir sa male semaine. *A woman to haue her flowers.*

Avoir son Marquis. *The same.*

Avoir son mois. *The same.*

Avoir le Moyne. Nous avons le Moyne. *We haue ill lucke; or, we are cosened, guld, poopt.*

Avoir du nez. S'il a du nez. *If the . be any sence, conceit, or iudgement in him.*

Cela n'a point de nez. *There is no wit, no sauour, no garbe at all in that.*

Avoir la salle. *To be whipt in publicke, as breeching boyes are sometimes in the hals of Colledges.*

Avoir son temps. *A woman to be troubled with her monthly disease.*

Avoir la teste prez du bonnet. *To be hot, hastie, cholericke; also, to be craftie, subtill, wylie.*

Avoir vent en pouppe. *To prosper, to proceed happily, to lead the world in a string, to haue the world at will.*

Avoir bon vent. *To be long-breathed; also, to haue a readie wit; quicke sent; perfect smelling.*

Avoir leur vin. Avoir son vin. *Looke* Vin.

Avoir la vogue. *To beare sway, to rule the roast.*

Il n'a garde de faire cela. *Hee cares not greatly for doing that; or, I beleeue he will take heed how he does it.*

Il y a bien Monsieur pour toy. *I might be Master (or Lord) in thy mouth well ynough.*

Il y a de l'oignon. *There is a pad in that straw; somewhat is amisse among them.*

Qu' auez vous à plorer? *What ayles you, or, what cause haue you, to weepe?*

Il y aura icy de l'asne. *We shall be troubled with some foolish coyle, or vaine businesse.*

I'ay beau attendre! *Here's goodly tarrying sure! I stay to much purpose indeed! (Ironically) also, as in;*

Ils l'avoient beau flatter. *They were faine to speake him faire.*

Assez a qui se contente: Prov. *Contentment is treasure ynough; nor needs he more thats pleased with what he hath.*

Assez a qui bon credit a: Prov. *A good report is a sufficient portion.*

Assez y a si trop n'y a: Prov. *There is ynough where there is not too much; (a difference betweene sufficiencie, and superfluitie.)*

Bien a en sa maison qui de ses voisins est aimé: Prov. *Well doth he liue within, who is beloued without, dores.*

Il faut avoir mauvaise beste par douceur: Prov. *A mischieuous, froward, or curst beast must be reclaymed, caught, or woon, by faire meanes.*

Qui a argent a des chapeaux: Pro. *Looke* Argent.

Qui a bon voisin a bon matin: Prov. *Good neighbors affoord kind salutations, vse friendly greetings, giue good dayes, or the time of the day.*

Qui a compagnon a maistre: Prov. *He that hath a fellow-ruler, hath an ouer-ruler.*

Qui n'a argent en bourse ait du moins du miel ou bouche: Prov. *Let him that cannot spend freely speake faire.*

Qui n'a cœur ait iambes: Prov. *Let him that dares not fight vse flight.*

Le frere veut que sa sœur ait, mais que rien du sien n'y ait: Pro. *The brother loues to see, but not to make, his sister rich.*

Mieux vaut vn tenez que deux vous l'aurez: Pro. *Better is one thing in possession then two in expectancie.*

s'Avoisiner. *To approch, draw neere, seat himselfe hard by, be neighbor vnto.*

De grasse cuisine pauvreté s'avoisine: Pro. *A great housekeeper is next dore to a beggar.*

Avoye: f. *A Blind-worme.*

Auque: m. *A Goose.* ¶Langued.

Aure: f. *as the Latine,* Aura; *a soft, gentle, coole wind, or aire.*

Aureille: f. *An eare. Seeke* Oreille.

Aureillons: m. *The Mumpes.*

Aurelles: f. *Whoortle berries, Wyn-berries, Bill-berries, Bull-berries.*

Aurelles rouges. *Red Whoorts, red Whoortle-berries.*

Aureole. *Seeke* Laureole.

Auriculaire: com. *Auricular, of the eare.*

Doigt auriculaire. *The little finger.*
Veine auriculaire. *The eare veine; runs vp along by the kernels which are vnder the eare, and is there diuided into two branches, the one whereof mounts vp before the eare, and the other behind it; Surgeons open it against the deafenes, pain, & vlcerations of the eares.*
Auriflamme. *as* Oriflambe.
Avril: m. *Aprill.*
Poison d'Avril. *A Mackerell (fish;) also, a young baud, or, a Page employed by his maister in baudie seruices.*
Aurillage: m. *An imposition layed (in some parts of* France) *vpon the profit thats made of Bees.*
Auriol: m. *The greatest kind of the fish* Turdus; *on the backe of a ruddie, on the bellie of a leaden, colour; and full of blacke, and wan spots all ouer; some hold it to be the Goldenie.*
Auriou: m. *as* Auriol.
Auripeaux: m. *the Mumpes.*
Aurislage. *as* Aurillage.
Auroesne. *The hearbe Sothernwood.*
Avron: m. *Wild Oats, barren Oats.*
Auron: m. *as* Auronne.
Auronne: f. *The hearbe Sothernwood.*
Auronne femelle. *Female Sothernwood, great Sothernwood, mountaine Sothernwood; some also call so, dwarfe, or sweet, Sothernwood.*
Auronne de jardin. *Garden Sothernwood.*
Auronne masle. *Male Sothernwood, champian Sothernwood, the lesse Sothernwood.*
Aurore: f. *The morning.*
Aurorin: m. ine: f. *Of, or belonging to, the morning; also, early.*
Ausé. *Looke* Osé.
Auspice: m. *A signe, token, signification, or presage of future things by the flight, or other motion, of birds; also, fortune, lucke; or, a luckie beginning of matters.*
Aussi. *Also, likewise, as, euen as.*
Aussi bien ne faittes vous rien. *For, or because, you doe nothing.*
Austere: com. *Austere, seuere, sterne, rigorous; rude, rough, soure or harsh of disposition, pitilesse.*
Austerement. *Austerely, sternely, seuerely, rigorously; rudely, roughly, sourely, harshly, without pitie.*
Austerité: f. *Austerenesse, austeritie, sternenesse, rigour, seueritie; sourenesse, roughnesse, rudenesse, harshnesse of disposition; want of pitie.*
Austerons. *as* Aousterons; *also, the fruits of August, or haruest; corne.*
Austour: m. *as* Autour.
Austral: m. ale: f. *Southerly; of, or belonging to, the South.*
Austre: m. *as* Austrie.
Austrie. *The South, or Southerne, wind.*
Austrin: m. ine: f. *Of the South; warme as the South.*
Austruche: f. *An Austridge, or Ostridge.*
Autan: m. *A Southerne wind.*
Autant. *as much; as well; so, so much, so well; as many; so many.*
Il n'en falloit plus qu'autant. *He wanted, or, there wanted, but as much more.* ¶Rab.
Il se retira avec autant de nez. *He got him away with shame ynough; (a speech wherein this word is expressed with the hand;) Looke* Nez.
Autel: m. *An Altar.*
Authentique: com. *Authenticke, authenticall, of good authoritie; approued, or allowed, by authoritie.*
Seel authentique. *Looke* Seel.
Authentiqué. *Authorized, made authenticall.*
Authentiquer. *To make authenticke; to authorize, or giue authoritie vnto.*
Autheur: m. *An author, actor, causer, founder; th'originall inuentor, the first deuiser, of a thing; also, an author, or writer of bookes; also, he that sels with warrantie.*
Tel autheur tel œuvre: Prov. *Looke* Oeuvre.
Authorisation: f. *An authorization, or authorizing; an allowing by authoritie.*
Lettres d'authorisation. *Letters patent, whereby a woman is authorized, in th'absence, or vpon the refusal, of her husband, to follow his suits, & manage his estate.*
Authoriser. *To authorize, allow by authoritie, put in authoritie, giue authoritie vnto.*
Authorité: f. *Authoritie, sway, power; credit, reputation, dignitie, estimation; also, reuerence, grauitie.*
Authrice: f. *An Autrix, Authoresse, or Actresse.*
Autins: m. *Vines which grow vp along trees, or, as hops, twining about long Poles.*
Autographe. *Written with his owne hand, or, by him that sent it.*
Autoin. *as* Automne.
Vent d'Autoin. *The South wind.*
Automate. *Any thing that goes by a vice, or peise, yet seemes to moue of it selfe.*
Automnal: m. ale: f. *Of Autumne, beloging vnto haruest.*
Rose automnale. *A Muske Rose.*
Automne: m. *Autumne, or haruest time.*
Violette d'Automne. *The Paunsie.*
Automnel. *as* Automnal.
Autour: m. *is (generally) a short-winged hauke; and particularly, the Goshauke.*
Demy Autour. *A kind of leane, little, and cowardly goshauke, or short-winged hauke.*
Autour. *About, round about, in a round.*
Autre. *Another, other, ought els, any besides; different from the former (but in some especiall, not any generall, respect.)*
L'autre d'apres. *The second, or next.*
'A l'autre. *Now shall I be troubled againe; or, this fellow comes to trouble me as much as the former did.*
Autrement. *Otherwise, els, on other termes; except that, if not on any other condition.*
Autres-fois. *Heretofore, in times past; sometime; at another time; Looke,* Fois.
Autruy. *Another mans, belonging to another; also, other men, others.*
Faire d'autruy cuir large courroye. *To cut a large thong of another mans leather.*
Robbe d'autruy ne fait honneur à nulluy: Prov. *No apparrell can truly grace him that owes it not; or, as in* Robbe.
Tout a esté à autruy, & sera à autruy: Prov. *All came from, and shall goe to, others.*
Autumnal. *as* Automnal.
Autumne. *Seeke* Automne.
Auvent: m. *A penthouse of cloth, &c, before a shop window, &c.*
Auvernas. *A kind of blacke grapes; tearmed otherwise (by reason of their hue)* Morillons.
Auviez. *as* Alesve; *A kind of wild Pine.*
Avulse: com. *Plucked away, pulled of.*
Auxerrois: m. *as* Megle.
Auxiliateur: m. *A helper, aider, assister.*
Axillaire: com. *Of, or belonging to, th'arm-hole; whence;*
Artere axillaire. *Th'arm-hole Arterie; Looke* Artere.
Veine axillaire. *The liuer veine; or, a great branch of the hollow veine conueyed vnder the cannell bone, and through th' arme-hole into th' inner part of th' arme, where tis dispersed.*

Axionomantie: f. *Diuination by a hatchet, and ieat burnt.* ¶Rab

Axonne: f. *as* Axunge.

Axunge: f. *Tallow, fat, seame, grease (properly of swine;) also, oyntment (thereof.)*

Ayant. *(The Participle of* Auoir*) hauing; holding; enioying.*

Ayde. *as* Aide; *helpe, aid, assistance.*

Ayeul: m. *A grandfather.*

Ayeule: f. *A grandmother.*

Aygue: f. *Water.* ¶Langued.

Ayguier: m. *A gutter, sinke, or sewer.* ¶Langued.

Ayguiere: f. *An Ewer, or Lauer.*

Aymant; *as,* Aimant; *an Adamant, or Loadstone.*

Aymer; *as,* Aimer; *To loue, &c.*

Aynets: m. *Little rods, or twigs, wherein herrings are threaded, and layed on hurdles to be redded.*

Ayré: m. **ée**: f. *Ayred.*

Aysement: m. *A Iakes, or Priuie.*

Aysle: f. *as,* Aile; *a wing.*

Az. *An ace at cards, or dice.*

Demeurer entre deux & az. *Looke,* As.

Respondre entre deux & az. *To frame such a cunning answer betwixt yea and no, that a man cannot tel what to make of it; a* Metaphor *taken from a dye that stands edgeling, so as tis doubtfull what chance it will yeeld.*

Azagaye. *as* Zagaye.

Azarole: m. *A small Medlar tree, called, the three-graind Medlar, or Neapolitane Medlar tree.*

Azaron. *An hearbe; as,* Cabaret.

Azez, gayes: *in stead of,* Azagayes. ¶Rab.

Azile. *as* Asyle. *A Sanctuarie.*

Azime: com. *Sweet, vnleauened, without leauen; sincere.*

Azimuth. *An* Azimuth, *or Verticle circle, which discends from the* Zenith.

Azur. *Seeke* Asur.

Azuré. *A certaine blewish, and long-legd spider, full of poyson, and very dangerous.*

Azuré: m. **ée**: f. *Azured, of azure, painted or coloured with Azure.*

Azurer. *To make Azure; to paint, or colour with Azure.*

Azurin: m. **ine**: f. *Azurie, blonket, skie-coloured, Azure-like.*

B

B *The letter,* B. *In Musicke, the Note, or Cliffe, called Befabeemie; whence;*

De b carre en b mol: Prov. *In discourse, to shift often, idly, and on a suddaine, from one subiect vnto another.*

Baaillant. *Gaping, yawning.*

Baaillement: m. *A gaping, or yawning; wide opening, or going asunder.*

Baailler. *To gape, to yawne; to open, or spread wide.*

Baaillon: m. *A gag.*

Baaillonner. *To gag.*

Ba-bat: m. *A panting, or often beating.*

Babaye: f. Faire la babaye. *To gape, or make a mouth at.*

Babbiner. *See* Babiner.

Babeurre: m. *Whig, or butter-milke.*

Babil: m. *Bable, tatle, pratle, chat; babling, iangling, chattering, ouer-much talking.*

Babillard: m. *A babler, tatler, prater, pratler, chatterer, iangler, word-monger; talkatiue companion; one whose tongue neuer lyes (and yet he often lyes.)*

Babillard: m. **de**: f. *Babling, tatling, talkatiue.*

Babillarde: f. *A title-tatle; a pratling gossip; a babling houswife; a chatting, or chattering Minx.*

Babiller. *To bable, pratle, tatle, chatter, iangle, talk ouermuch, vse too many words.*

Babillerie: f. *as* Babil.

Babillons: m. *The players that hang to the port of a bitt.*

Babine: f. *The lip of a beast, as of a dog, beare, horse, cow, &c.*

Babiner. *To play with the lips; to pratle, or talke hard.*

Babiole: f. *A trifle, whimwham, guigaw, or small toy, for a child to play withall.*

Babioles. *Trifles, nifles, trinkets, toyes; also, faire (but deceitfull) teares.*

Babion: m. *A Babion, or Baboone.*

Baboin: m. *as* Babion; *also, a trifling, busie, or craftie knaue; a crackrope, waghalter, vnhappie rogue, retchlesse villaine.*

Baboiner. *as* Babouïnner.

Baboles. *as* Babioles.

Babort. *The Larboord of a ship.*

Babote: f. *A certaine little blacke Caterpiller, which in drie seasons breeds on the hearbe* Saint-foin.

Babou. Faire la babou. *To bob, or, to make a mow at.*

Babouin. *as* Baboin; *also, a frozen place, whereon boyes vse to slide; a sliding place.*

Baiser le babouin. *See* Baiser.

Babouïnner. *To baboonize it; to play the Monkey; to vse apish or foolish tricks, waggish or knauish prankes; also, to deceiue, cosen, gull.*

Babouïnnerie: f. *Apishnesse, fopperie, foolerie, childish trifling, baboonizing; also, an vnhappie tricke, waggish part, knauish, wilie, or busie pranke; also, a deceit, cosenage, gullerie.*

Babouleur: m. *A babler; a reporter of trifles, a teller of lyes.*

Baboye: f. *A fib, or fable; a foolish tale ill-fauoredly told.*

Baboyer. *To blabber with the lips; to famble, to falter; also, to fib, fable, tell foolish tales.*

Bac: m. *A great ferry-boat, or horse-boat; also, an open vessell of Copper, and full of water, for wine-pots to stand in at meale times.*

Droict de bac. *Ferriage; the money thats due at a ferrie vnto the Lord, or Owner, of the boat.*

Bacbuc. *A bottle.* ¶Rab.

Baccal: m. *A Weesill.*

Baccar. *Th'hearbe Haslewort, Folefoot, Asarabacca.*

Bacces: f. *Berries.*

Bacchanaleries: f. *Bacchanals,* Bacchus *feasts, shrouing, wakes, feasts.*

Bacchanales. *as* Bacchanaleries.

Bacchanaliser. *To rage, play mad pranks, fare like mad men; (as the priests of* Bacchus *were wont to do when they celebrated his feasts.)*

Bacchanisante: f. *An enraged, or furious, woman.*

Bacchante. *as* Bacchanisante.

Bacche. *A kind of wild Peare.*

Bacchique: com. *Belonging vnto* Bacchus.

Bacclé: m. **ée**: f. *Barred, or boulted on the inside (with a short woodden boult.)*

Baccler. *To barre, boult, or shut close, on th'inside (with a short boult of wood.)*

Baccolant. *Playing at titter totter; riding the wild Mare; tottering, swinging, often lifting vp and downe.*

Baccoler. *To play at titter totter, or at totter-arse; to ride the*

the wild Mare; as children who sitting vpon both ends of a long Pole, or Timber-log (supported only in the middest) lift one another vp and downe; hence, also to tottar, swag, swing, lift, or heaue often vp and downe.
Bacées: f. *as* Brisées.
Bacelle. *as* Chastelleine. *An old word.*
Bachat: m. *A Bassa; a chiefe Commaunder, Gouernour, or Officer, vnder the great Turke.*
Bachelage: m. *Bachelership, prentishood.*
Bachelerie: f. *A bachelership; the degree, estate, condition of an Esquire, or Bacheler.*
Bachelette: f. *A young, and marriageable girle, maid, or wench.* ¶Pic.
Bachelier: m. *A bacheler; a youth of sixteene, or eighteene yeares of age; also, he that hath passed Master in a trade, but is not yet sworne of the Companie; also, a Batcheler of Art; also, a title of gentrie inferiour to* Banneret, *and superiour to* Escuyer; *a young gentleman that aspires vnto Knighthood, and the priuiledge of bearing a Banner in the field; also, the Lord of a castle, fort, great house, or Place, that is deriued from (but in iurisdiction equall with) an Earledome, Vicountie, or Baronie.*
Bachelier en busche. *A woodden loggarhead.*
Bachelier: m. ere: f. *Bachelerly, bacheler-like; of, or belonging to, a bacheler.*
Chevalier bachelier. *Marched vnder other mens colours, and had twice as much pay as th'Esquire.*
Bachevaleureux. *as* Chevaleureux.
Bachot: m. *A wherrie; or small ferry-boat.*
Bachoüe: f. *A kind of flat-sided basket, of wicker, close wouen, and pitched in th' inside; vsed in time of Vintage.*
Bacille: f. *The hearbe Sampire; or, as* Bassille.
Bacilles doubles. *The double Crowfoot, or Bachelers buttons.*
Bacinet. *as* Bassinet. *The hearbe Crowfoot.*
Baclé: m. ée: f. *Close bolted; shut, or made vp on the inside.*
Bacler. *To bolt, close, or shut close, on the inside, with a short woodden bolt.*
Bacon: m. *Bacon, or (the fat of Bacon) Lard.*
Bacquaige. *as* Bagage.
Bacquet: m. *A pale, or bucket; also, a small and shallow tub, vsually set vnder a wine vessell, or the spout, or cocke of a fountaine, to receiue the liquor that distils, or descends, from it.*
Bacqueter. *To lade, or draine a riuer, or other water, with pales, or buckets.*
Bacquier: m. *A hog fed in the stye; a stye-fed hog.*
Bacul: m. *A Crupper for an Asse, or Moyle.*
Bacule: f. *A square, and heauie dore (commonly) hanging, and held vp, by chaynes, a pretie distance without the maine gate of a fortresse, and let fal (as a Portcullis) in a trice, with a whurrie, and to the confusion of them it reaches, or lights on; also, as* Bascule.
'A la bacule. *The riding of the wild mare; also, the punishment of misses in some games, to be clapt on the bumme with a batting-staffe.*
En bacule. *Hanging aslope, as the* Bacule.
Baculer. *To bumpe on the* Posteriorums *with a Bat; or, as* Baccoler.
Badauderie: f. *Sottishnesse, fopperie, doltishnesse.*
Badaudise. *as* Badauderie.
Badault: m. *A foole, dolt, sot, fop, asse, coxcombe; gaping hoydon.*
Badé: m. *A crie, as of hounds.* ¶Breton.
Badecoquille: f. *The name of a small shell-fish.*

Badelaire: m. *A short, and broad back-sword, bending towards the point like a Turkish scimitar.*
Badelori: m. *as* Badault.
Badelorié: m. ée: f. *Besotted; made a gull, or foole.*
Badigoines: f. *The great, and hanging lips, or slowching chaps of beastes (especially horses) or of beastly fellowes.*
Badin: m. *as* Badault; *also, a Iugler; Tumbler; or any such sport-maker.*
Badin enfariné; & Badin sans farine. *A notable coxcombe, an Asse in graine; also, a foole, or Vice in a play.*
Aller en badin. *To goe slowly, as one that seemes to count the steps he sets.*
Escholier babillard prez le feu, & badin hors la classe: Prov. *Looke* Escolier.
Badinage: m. *Foolerie, fopperie; toying, tumbling, iugling; any kind of apish gambolling.*
Il est fait au badinage. *He hath his part readie, his lesson at his fingers end; he hath got the tricke of it; he is throughly instructed how to handle the matter, how to carrie the complot.*
Badinement. *Foolishly, apishly, sottishly, foppishly.*
Badiner. *To play the foole, or Vice; to vse apish trickes, and toyes; to tumble, or iuggle; to trifle it any way.*
Badiner les perdris. *To driue Partridges into a Tunnell.*
Badinerie: f. *as* Badinage.
Baditin: m. *The water Lillie, or water Rose.*
Badoüiner. C'est, Besongner come vn Asne. ¶Rab.
Baffoüé: m. ée: f. *Hoodwinked; also, deceiued; also, besmeared; also, baffled, disgraced, vnworthily handled, iniuriously vsed, reuiled, reproched.*
Baffoüer. *To hoodwinke; also, to deceiue; also, to besmeare; also, to baffle, abuse, reuile, disgrace, handle basely in tearmes, giue reprochfull words of, or vnto.*
Baffray. *as* Baffroy.
Baffroy: m. *A Beacon; or a watch-tower of timber, &c; also, an Allarum Bell; and, the greatest Bell in in a Church; and chiefest clocke in a Towne; also, a Bastile of timber, whereout besiegers beat the besieged.*
Bafoüé. *as* Baffoüé.
Bagage: m. *The cariage of an armie; luggage, bag, and baggage; also, the carters, boyes, and Mulettiers, that looke vnto it.*
Bagagier: m. *A carrier of souldiors baggage, or luggage.*
Bagasse: f. *A Baggage, Queane, Iyll, Punke, Flirt.*
Bagatelle: f. *A toy, trifle, nifle, thing of small value.*
Bagatelleries: f. *Triflings, toyings, idle trickes, or, tricks of Legerdemaine.*
Bagateur: m. *A maker of playing cards.*
Bagatin: m. *A base Italian coyne of Brasse; worth about the sixteenth part of our penny.*
Baglon: m. *as* Baillon; *a gag.*
Bagnoire. *as* Baignoire.
Bagois: m. *Gibridge, fustian, strange talke; idle tatle.*
Bagos: m. *A man-baud; a Ribauld.*
Bague: f. *(is properly) a ring, or iewell set with one precious stone, or more; also, the Ring whereat gallants run with launces; (whence,* Courir la bague; *to run at the Ring;) also, the reward bestowed on, or prize gained by, him that does the best in a publicke Game, or Exercise; as tilting, wrestling, running, leaping, &c; (and hence;)*

Il a gaigné la bague. *He hath woon the spurres, or carried away the Prize; the victorie, or day, is absolutely his.*

Bagues. *(The plurall) is taken, sometimes for iewels, or any ornament of gold, or siluer belonging to, or worne by, a woman; and sometimes for our whole substance, or stuffe; hence;* moy, mes gens, & mes bagues; *my selfe, my people, and goods; hence also,*

Bagues sauves. *With bag and baggage, safe and sound, scotfree; without the losse, wast, or expence, of any thing.*

Bagué: m. ée: f. *Beiewelled; inriched, adorned, or furnished, with iewels; also, tucked, or trussed, vp.*

Baguenaude: f. *A (forme of) ridiculous ryming, or versifying vsed (and thus named) in old time.*

Baguenaudes. *Bladder nuts,* S. Anthonies *nuts, wild Pistachoes; also the cods, or fruit of bastard Sene; also (the fruit of red Nightshade, or* Alkakengie) *red Winter cherries; (all which being of little, or no value, cause this word to signific) also, trifles, nifles, toyes, paltrie trash.*

Baguenauder. *To trifle, toy, dally with, idle out the time.*

Baguenaudeur: m. *A trifler, toyer, dallier, loyterer, lingerer; a vaine, or idle, companion.*

Baguenaudier: m. *The Sene tree, or bastard Sene; a shrub which hath bin mistaken for the true Sene; most improperly; for it onely resembles it, and is not (howsoeuer we name it) any kind thereof, sayes* Gerard.

Baguer. *To inrich, adorne, or furnish, with iewels; also, to trusse, or tucke, vp; (whence;)*

Trousser, & baguer. *To packe vp (his) bag, and baggage.*

Baguette: f. *A wand, switch, riding rod, whisking rod; also, a (houshold) stewards, or principall officers, white rod; also, a little iewell; also, the (sleight) cloth Pennistone; also, a small brasse coyne in* Gasconie.

Baguette d'arquebuse. *The scouring sticke.*

Baguette de Veneur. *A hunting Pole.*

Commander à baguette. *To commaund (like a steward) absolutely, peremptorily, or with authoritie.*

Si tu veux cognoistre vn villain baille luy la baguette en main: Pro. *The way to discerne a (knaue, or) clowne, is to giue him authoritie.*

Baguetté. *Beaten with a rod, or wand; also, commaunded, ouer-ruled, awed.*

Baguetter. *To commaund like a steward; also, to strike with a sticke, or wand.*

Baguetteux: m. euse: f. *Wandie, full of rods, wands, or switches.*

Baguier: m. *The male Bay-tree (so tearmed about* Montpellier.)

Bahu: m. *A trunke (to carrie, or keepe, things in.)*

Bahutier: m. *A trunke-maker.*

Bahutier: m. ere: f. *Of, or belonging to, a trunke; whence;*

Cheual bahutier. *A Sumpter-horse, or trunkehorse.*

Bai; &, Baiard; *See* Bay; *&,* Bayard.

Baie: f. *A berrie; See,* Baye.

Baigner. *To bathe; wet, moisten; wash.*

Il se baigne en ces nouvelles. *These newes doe him good at the heart; he battles with them; he takes exceeding delight in them.*

Baignerie: f. *A bathe; a priuat roome to bathe in.*

Baigneur: m. *A bather; wetter, moistener.*

Baigneux: m. euse: f. *Bathing; or, that vseth much bathing.*

Baignoire: m. *A bathing-tub; also, any great and open vessell made like a bathing-tub; and (hence) the tub whereinto new wine fals out of the Presse.*

Baignolet: m. *A little bath; bathing house; or, bathing tub.*

Bail: m. *A guardian, or gouernour, of a Ward, or (as a husband) of a wife; also, such a wardship, tuition, gouernment; also, the Deed, Instrument, or Lease, whereby a thing is passed, or let, vpon a certaine rent; also, a giuing, graunting, yeelding, passing ouer in farme, or by lease; See,* Garde.

Bail à ferme. *A lease for yeares; especially such a one, as giues the lessor power to reenter for non-payment of the rent.*

Bail à ferme d' heritage. *A fee-farme; (with like clause of reentrie.)*

Bail de Iustice. *The publicke magistrats letting, or setting of land, &c, (seised by order of Law) or of Wards lands; or of the rights of the kings Demaine; or of the profits of his woods, and forrests.*

Bail à louage. *A chattell, or moueable hired out for a certaine time, and with clause of reentrie, as before.*

Bail de mariage. *The wardship, or gouernment which a husband hath* (de Iure) *of his wife, and of her whole estate.*

Bail naturel. *The wardship a father or mother hath of their child.*

Tenir le Royaume en bail. *To be Protector of the Kingdome; or to haue the Regencie, or Gouernment thereof.*

Bail: m. baille: f. *Bay (of colour.)*

Baile: m. *The Bailife, or Magistrate of a village;* ¶Langued. *also (in* Gasconie) *a Iaylor; or one that lookes to a Prison; or an Officer that hath power onely to apprehend, and keepe, malefactors.*

Baile: f. *A nurse.* ¶Langued.

Bailif: m. *as,* Bailli.

Baillarge. *A kind of small barly.*

Baille: m. *A Steward, or Ouerseer of; a Solicitor, Atturney, or vndertaker for, a Church, Towne, Corporation, Communaltie, &c; also, as,* Bailli; *also, an ordinarie Bailife, or Sergeant.*

Baillé: m. ée: f. *Giuen, graunted, conferred, bestowed; yeelded ouer, passed away; also, presented, offered, exhibited vnto.*

Il luy l'a baillé belle. *He hath payed him soundly, he hath giuen it him home; or, hee hath serued him a touch indeed; also, he hath faire and mannerly cousened him.*

Baillement: m. *A giuing, graunting, bestowing; dealing, deliuering, conferring; also, a presenting, or exhibiting vnto.*

Bailler. *To giue, bestow, conferre, graunt; yeeld ouer, deliuer, deale, or passe away; also, to present, offer, exhibite vnto.*

Bailler à aucun tout du long de l'aulne. *To course one soundly, to handle him shrewdly, to pay him home.*

Bailler de l' avoine pour du foin. *To returne a benefit with vsurie, to be better then his word.*

Bailler balliuernes. *To cog, foist, lye.*

Bailler belle; Baille luy belle *(of one that hath done, or spoken foolishly) faire befall him; let him euen haue it a Gods name.* Ironically.

Bailler bonne. vous la baillez bonne; *(neere the sence of* bailler belle) *True Roger, wisely brother Timothie; See,* Bon.

Bailler le boucon. *To poyson.*

Baillér le bouquet. *To bid one do in his turne that which others haue done before him (In some parts of* France, *when a feast is ended, whereat neighbours haue met, and beene merrie together, the master thereof deliuers vnto some one of the company a nosegay, & thereby tyes him to make the next.)*
Bailler bris contre Robert. *Looke* Bris.
Bailler des canards à la moitié. *To cousen, beguile, conicatch; to play the mountebanke.*
Bailler des cassades. *To flout, frumpe; lye, cog; deceiue, gull, well-meaning people.*
Bailler des plus cornues. *Looke* Cornu.
Bailler la Diane. *Souldiours to rouze their enemies with a hot mornings allarum; to giue a* Camisadoe.
Bailler vne entorce. *To offer hard measure, to giue a shrewd wring, a cruell pinch, a vile blowe vnto.*
Bailler des febues à my-croist. *To deceiue, cousen, gull, conycatch; to play th'impostor.*
Bailler le fil. *To flatter, cog, smooth, glose with;* (à vn couteau; *to set an edge on it.)*
Bailler foin en corne. *To giue one the boots, to sell him a bargaine.*
Bailler du foin à la mule. *To deceiue, beguile, gull, conycatch.*
Bailler griefs. *To open ones griefes, to complaine of wrongs done him, before a Court, or assembly; to exhibit vnto the Court a relation, or complaint of these things.*
Bailler la haire. *To play a shrewd tricke, ill pranke, hard part; to serue an euill touch.*
Bailler par les ioues de. *To lay sure hold on; also, to enter deepely; imbarke himselfe farre; plunge at first into the middle of.*
Bailler la main. *To reach a hand; Looke* Main.
Bailler le moine. *To crampe; also, to bring ill lucke vnto.*
Bailler le Moine par le col. *To hang, or twitch vp.*
Bailler mornifle sur les levres du Roy. *To coine false money.*
Baillér sur le mouffle. *To lay on the lips, to pash on the snout, to giue a dash on the mouth.*
Bailler sur le nez du Roy. *To coyne false money.*
Bailler vne oeillade. *To winke, or cast a wanton eye, at.*
Bailler du plat de la langue. *To sooth, smooth, flatter, cog with.*
Bailler vne mauvaise secousse à vn. *To shake, or swing one cruelly; to do him a mischieuous turne.*
Baillet: m. *A pale red, or flesh colour; also, a horse that hath a white spot, or starre, in his forhead.*
Baillet: m. Baillette: f. *Of a pale red, or flesh colour.*
Vache baillette. *A pide cow, red and white.*
Vin baillet. *A pallet, or pale Claret, wine.*
Baillette: f. *A Pochard, or Widgion; or, a little water-fowle, that somewhat resembles the Teale; also, a lease, or graunt; and, a leasing, or letting to farme.*
Bailleur: m. *A giuer, granter, bestower; dealer, distributer, deliuerer; presenter, exhibiter.*
Bailleur de bons iours. *An ordinarie saluter of euery one he sees, or meets; a fawning, or populer fellow; a cogging, or glosing companion.*
Bailleur de Canards à la moitié; ou, de febues à my-croist. *A cousening Iacke; a mountebanke; a deceiuer, imposter, conycatcher.*
Bailleures. *Looke* Baillieures.
Bailli: m. *A Bailife (but of much more authoritie than ours) a Magistrat appointed within a Prouince, or precinct certaine, to execute iustice, maintaine the peace, and preserue the people from oppression, vexation, and wrong: To which end he takes notice of treasons committed, false money coyned; robberies, and murthers done; rebellions, or seditions raised; vnlawfull, or populer assemblies made; Armes borne, or souldiours leuied, without warrant; Protections, or Sanctuaries violated; Pardons, and Charters abused; Faires, markets, freedomes, and other priuiledges vsurped, or vniustly stood on: Hee makes proclamations in his owne name; he calls the* Ban, *and* Arriereban; *leads those that be raised by it; and appoints th'ordinarie musters of his Prouince: hee determines Appeales from the sentences of Prouosts, and other inferior Iudges, at Assises, whereof he is the principall Iudge; and is thereby held the most proper Iudge for Gentlemen, who haue euer pretended that their causes must bee decided at Assises; and yet for all this, (and though hee may haue a Lieutenant) he is but a Deputie, either vnto the king, or vnto some lord; euery one whereof (vnto the* Chastellain) *hath, or may haue, a* Bailli *within his territories.*
Baillis de France. *Were but foure in old time, when the French kings had ioyned to their demains but foure townes, viz.* Vermendois, Sens, Mascon, *and* S. Pierre de Moustier *(all other the townes, and Bailiwikes of* France *being then in the possession of Dukes, or Earles) and therefore the Bailies of those townes are to this day called,* les 4 anciens Baillis de France, *thereby to differ somewhat from the rest of the Bailifes royall, whereof there are now very many.*
Baillis de Prouinces. *The Bailifes of Prouinces, or of superiour Bailiwikes; The Bailifes of Dukes, Marquesses, and Earles; called so in difference from those that belong to Vicounts, Barons, and* Chastellains; *which are inferiour vnto, and oftentimes depend on, the other.*
Baillis Royaux. *The Bailifes Royall, whereof (as I haue said) there be very many (by reason of the reunion vnto the Crowne of th'ancient Dukes, and Earles estates; and otherwise by new erections,) who besides other prerogatiues challenge th'entire decision of royall, and priuiledged, cases.*
Grands baillis. *as* Baillis de Prouinces.
Le grand bailli d'Henault. *The chiefe Iustice of that countie.*
Bailliage: m. *A Bailiwike; the office, iurisdiction, or authoritie of a* Bailli; *also, the Prouince, or precinct wherein he gouernes; and sometimes (absolutely) a Prouince; In some old authors, and customes it also imports, as much as, protectiue iustice; and euer holds a more honourable ranke than simple, or ordinarie iurisdiction.*
Bailliage du Palais. *Is (at* Paris) *a iurisdiction ouer Marchants, & Tradesmen, which owe for their wares within that citie, and the liberties thereof.*
Droict de bailliage. *Power to keepe Assises; or to haue vnder him a* Bailli, *and a superiour seat, or Court, of iustice for the decision of such great causes as, in due course, belong not to an ordinarie iurisdiction; This power euerie Lord of dignitie (from the Duke to the* Chastellain) *hath; and had withall (for the decision of smaller causes) a Court of ordinarie iurisdiction, and a Iudge thereof called* Iuge, *or* Garde de iustice, *vntill the yeare* 1573; *when by an ordinance (made at* Paris, *but confirmed at* Roussillon) *they were enioyned to content themselues with onely one iurisdiction in one place; which though it bee gouerned, almost in one forme, by one, and the same Iudge, yet keepes hee still*

two seuerall Courts, or Sessions; an ordinarie one, and the Assises.

Bailliager: m. ere: f. *Attending on, or, belonging to, a Bailife, or Bailywike.*

Baillie: f. *Seigneurie, gouernment, authoritie, rule ouer, protection of; also, a Bailiwike, or country Iusticeship; the place, function, charge of a Bailife, or countrey Iustice; administration of iustice; and (as* Bailliage) *the Shire, Prouince, precinct, and compasse of countrey wherein he gouernes.*

Lettres de baillie. *Are (according to the stile of* Normandie) *letters, writs, or obligations, authorizing him to whom they are directed, to proceed to execution upon the goods, or possessions, of another.*

Baillif: m. *A Bailife; or, as* Bailli.

Baillisseur. *A Guardian, Tutor, Gouernor of a Ward; he that hath the Wardship of a Gentleman.*

Baillistre: m. *as* Baillisseur; *especially, one that is a collaterall kinsman to the Ward; or his mother, or grandmother againe maried.*

Baillistrerie: f. *The wardship, tuition, or gouernment of an heire within age.*

Bailliveau. *as* Baliveau.

Baillon: m. *A gag.*

Baillonner. *To gag; and sometimes as* Baailler; *to yawne.*

Baillot: m. *A trough.*

Bailly. *as* Bailli.

Baimaux. (En l'ordonnance du Roy Charles 5, de l'an 1376; faicte pour le reiglement des forests) *False printed for,* Balliueaux; *Standers; trees left standing in forests for increase.*

Bain: m. *A bath.*

Bain de Marie. *Maries bath; a Cauldron, or Kettle full of boyling water; or, a distilling by the heat thereof.*

Chevalier des bains. *Looke* Chevalier.

Baïocque: m. *A small Italian coyne worth two (Italian) pence.*

Baïoque. *as* Baiocque.

Bair. *as* Vair; *A kind of furre; or, that which in Blason is called* Verrie.

Bairer. *as* Baiser.

Baisé: m. ée: f. *Kissed, smouched; smacked.*

Baise-main: m. *A kissing of the hand, in courtesie, or signe of submission; also, a fine, or (in lieu thereof) a peece of money (greater, or lesse, as the custome is) paid vnto a Lord, at the sealing, or making, of a lease; also, the spirituall reuenue of the Church, as offerings, &c.*

Baisement. *A kissing.*

Baise-nue. *High, tall, cloud-kissing, reaching to the clouds.*

Baiser: m. *A kisse.*

Baiser. *To kisse, to smoutch, to smacke.*

Baiser le babouïn. *Basely to submit himselfe, doe reuerence, or yeeld respect, vnto an vnworthy thing.*

Baiser la porte, ou la serrure, ou le verrouil de l'huis du fief. *A vassall to kisse the gate, &c, of the principall Mannor house of his absent Lord, in lieu of the homage he should otherwise haue done him, had he bin present.*

Baiseret: m. *A little kisse, or prettie smacke.*

Baiseur: m. *A kisser, smoutcher, smacker.*

Baisler. *as* Baailler.

Baisotté: m. ée: f. *Often kissed.*

Baisotter. *To kisse often.*

Baissant. *Humbling, stooping, inclining, bowing or bending downewards.*

Baissant la teste. *Holding downe his head; also, preparing himselfe vnto, or being readie for, the combat.*

Baisse de marest. *A low bottome which the water hath turned vnto a marish; a bog, or quagmire.*

Baissé: m. ée: f. *Stooping, inclining, declined, bowed downe, humbled; deiected, abased, brought low; let fall.*

'A teste baissée. *Desperatly, headlong, without care what may betide him, or whether hee sinke, or swim; also, resolutely, or with prepared force.*

Baissement: m. *A bowing downe, laying downe, bringing low, letting fall; an humbling, stooping, inclining, declining.*

Baisser: m. *An humbling, &c; as* Baissement.

Baisser. *To bow downe, lay downe, bring low, let fall, humble, deiect, abate, abase.*

Se baisser. *To stoope, to bow downe, decline, bend, or incline downewards.*

Baisser bois. Ils baisserent bois. *They put their launces in their rests.*

Baisser ses cornes. *To humble himselfe, to let fall his crest; or, as* Baisser la teste.

Baisser le front. *To hold, or bow downe, the head, in signe of humblenesse, or of submission.*

Baisser la teste. *The same; also, to settle, or prepare himselfe vnto an exploit, or combat; (from the custome of horned beasts, that bow downe their heads, when they are to meet an enemie) hence, also;*

Tu ne doibs ia baisser la teste. *Thou shouldest not be so resolute, so hardie, so forward for the matter.*

'A la hausse qui baisse. *Looke* Hausse.

Le iour se baisse. *The day growes old; it waxes late, or farre on the day.*

Baissieres: f. *The grounds, or lees of wine; also, any drinke when it drawes low; the dregges of any such liquor.*

Bal: m. *A daunce; a dauncing; Reuels, or, a Reuelling.*

Balade. *A ballet.*

Baladin: m. *A common dauncer of galliards, and other stirring, or liuely Ayres.*

Balaffre: &c; *as* Balafre; &c.

Balafre: f. *A slash ouer the face; a king Harry cut; a gash, or wipe, ouer the snowt.*

Balafré. *Slashed, or cut ouer the face.*

Balafrer. *To slash, or cut ouer the face.*

Balafreux. *A cutter, swaggerer, swashbuckler.*

Balafrure: f. *A slashing; or, as* Balafre.

Balaine: f. *A Whale, or, the Whirlpoole, (a kind of Whall.)*

Balan: m. *As the latine* Balanus; *any kind of Acorne; or, any thing made like an Acorne.*

Balan myrepsique. *Th'aromaticall, and oyly nut, or Acorne, called,* Ben.

Balance: f. *A ballance; a paire of weights, or ballances; also, one of the twelue signes in the Zodiacke.*

Estre en balance. *To doubt, wauer, totter in opinion; be vncertaine, or in suspence, what to say, or thinke, what way to hold, what course to take.*

Peser en seuere balance. *To examine very strictly.*

Balancé: m. ée: f. *Ballanced, weighed, peised, pondered; also, shaken, or tottered.*

Balancer. *To ballance, weigh, peise; ponder; also, to stagger, or wauer betweene two opinions; (any way) to shake, or totter.*

Le cerf balance. *So say French Hunters, when a Stag runs first one way, and then another, without any certain, or outright course in his flight; we say, he beats vp and downe, or flies round.*

Balanceur. *A balancer; a weigher of things in a ballance.*

Balanceux: m.euse: f. *Belonging to a ballance; also, full of ballances.*
Balancier: m. *A ballance maker; also, the ballance of a clocke.*
Balancier: m.ere: f. *Of, or belonging to, a ballance.*
Balancieur: m. *as* Balanceur; *Or th'Officer that weighes money as soone as it is coyned.*
Balancines: f. *The lifts; two small cords belonging to the sprit saile of a ship.*
Balane: f. *Any kind of Acorne; or thing made like an Acorne; as the top of a mans yard, &c;* See Balan.
Balauste. *The blossome, or flower of the wild Pomegranet tree.*
Balay: m. *A broome, or beesome; also, a Balleis Rubie.*
Donner trois tours de balay par la cheminée. *Look* Baley.
Nettoyer au balay. *To make cleane worke, to sweepe all away.*
Balayer. *To sweepe, or make cleane, with a broome.*
Balayeures: f. *as* Balieures.
Balayeuse: f. *A drudge, or sweeping wench.*
Balbucie: f. *A stutting, or stammering.*
Balchon: m. *A Balcone; a little Terrace on the top of a house, ouer a gate, or before a window.*
Balcon. *as* Balchon.
Baldachin: m. *The Canopie thats caried ouer a prince; or, a cloath of estate.*
Baldaquin. *The same.*
Baldaquin: m. *An yron, and open cresset, full of pitched wreathes.*
Bale: f. *A bullet; also, a ball; also, a packe, as of marchandise; also, the chaffe of wheat, or other corne; hence;*
Pain de bale. *Chaffe bread, vnraunged bread, the coursest kind of bread.*
Baleine: f. *A whall.*
Balenchoüeres. *The childish game called, titter totter.*
Balenes: f. *Whall bones; Whall-bone bodies; French bodies.*
Baler. *To daunce.*
Balestrier: m.ere: f. *Crossebow-like, of a crossebow.*
Balet: m. *A beesome, or broome.*
Four balet. *A maulkin.*
Balevolter. *as* Baleuoter.
Balevoter. *To wag, wauer, flicker, as a streamer in the wind.*
Baleustres: m. *Looke* Balustres.
Baley. *as* Balet; *A broome beesome.*
Donner trois tours de baley par la cheminée. *To swing a broome three times about a chimney (a ceremonie vsed by witches a little before they go vnto their diuellish assemblies.)*
Balié: m. ée: f. *Swept, or made cleane, with a broome.*
Balier. *To sweepe; or make cleane, with a broome.*
Balieure: f. *A sweeping, or making cleane, with a broome.*
Balieures. *Sweepings; the filth, or dust thats swept out of a roome; (hence) also, any trash, outcast trifles, or things of no value.*
Balievres: f. *The chaps (of a man, or beast.)*
Baligaut: m. *An vnweldie lubber, great lobcocke, huge luske, mishapen lowt, ill fauoured flabergullion.*
Balise. *as* Balisse; *Or, a certaine marke set vp, for the direction of saylers in a nauigable riuer.*
Balisse. *A Beacon.*
Baliste: f. *An ancient engine, or kind of ordnance, wherout stones, were throwne.*

Balivaginer. *To prattle, or babble; to vse too many words.*
Baliveaux. *Standers; trees left in a wood for th'increase, and preseruation thereof.*
Baliverne: f. *A lye, fib, gull:* (bailleur de balivernes. *Looke* Bailleur) *also, a babling, or idle discourse.*
Baliverner. *To cog, foist, lye, talke idle, vainely, or to no purpose.*
Balladin. *A dauncer; as* Baladin.
Balladiner. *To daunce high, or liuelily.*
Balladinerie: f. *High, or liuely dauncing, as, of galliards, Corantoes, or Jigges.*
Ballay. *A balleys Rubie.*
Balle. *as* Bale.
Balles. *Twelue times twelue dozen; or twelue grosse.*
Ballet: m. *A cape of a clocke; also, as* Appentis; *also, a dauncing.*
Balletrou: m. *A sweepe-hole;* Membre viril: ¶Rab.
Ballié: m.ée: f. *Swept, cleansed, made cleane.*
Ballier. *To sweepe; to make cleane (with a broome, &c.)*
Ballieur: m. *A sweeper.*
Ballieures. *Looke* Balieures.
Balliveaux: m. *Standers, or trees left standing after a wood sale.*
Balliverne. *as* Baliverne.
Ballizer vne Riviere. *To rake, scowre, or cleanse a riuer.*
Ballocher. *To totter; as one that goes on a rope, or narrow bridge.*
Ballon: m. *A fardle, or small packe.*
Ballot: m. *A little packe.*
Ballotage. *A rifling, or lotterie; a casting of lots; a chusing by lots.*
Ballote. *as* Balotte; *Also, blacke Horehound, stinking horehound.*
Ballottement: m. *A casting of lots; a triall of matters by lotterie.*
Ballotter. *To cast lots; to chuse officers, and magistrats; to passe, or dash lawes propounded; to condemne, or absolue th'accused, by lots, or lotterie.*
Ballouëtter. *To tosse, as a ball; to turne, or tumble a thing often, and into sundrie places.*
Balluque: f. *Gold ore, or gold vnfined; also, a vessell whereinto gold is powred.*
Ballustres: m. *as* Balustres.
Balme. *Looke* Baulme.
Balme: f. *A caue, denne, hole, grot.*
Baloffe: f. *A course bed, or mattresse filled onely with chaffe, straw, and such like; or, as* Balouffe.
Baloié: m. ée: f. *Swept; or, made cleane, with a broome.*
Balon: m. *A little ball; or packe; also, a football, or baloone.*
Balong. (Sub.& Adiec.) *See* Barlong.
Balongue: f. *A trough, or vessell, ground, plot, or figure, which is much more long than broad.*
Balongue cornue. *Is of vnequall forme, and vnlike both in the length of the sides, and breadth of the ends.*
Balongue droicte. *Is more long than broad, but of equall proportion both in length and breadth.*
Balorde: com. *as* Balourde.
Balorderie: f. *Sottishnesse, blockishnesse, dull folly, ignorant fopperie.*
Balot: m. *A little packe, or fardle.*
Balotade: f. *A bounding, or bounsing; as, of a football, or high-going horse.*
Baloté: m.ée: f. *Bounded, or bounsed high from the ground;*

ground; also, tossed, as a football.
Baloter. *To bound, or bounse high from the ground, like a football; also, to tosse, as a football.*
Balotte: f. *A little bullet, or pellet; also, a small button, or ball, in the mouth of a bit; also, one of those little stones, partie coloured beanes, or marked balls, which heretofore were, and (as at* Venice *the balls yet) are, vsed for lots, in the election of Magistrats; and hence;*
Donner sa balotte à. *To giue his voyce to, yeeld his consent vnto.*
Balotter. *as* Ballotter.
Balouffe: f. *The chaffe of oates, or barley; or, as* Baloffe.
Balourde: com. *Sottish, blockish, foolish.*
Baloyer. *as* Ballier. *To sweepe.*
Balroter. *To froth in bubbles.*
Balsamine: f. *The Balsam apple (whose oyle doth close vp wounds like Balme.)*
Balsane: f. *as* Balzane.
Balser. *To bound.*
Balthée: m. *A belt; arming girdle, or sword girdle.*
Balustre: f. *as* Balauste.
Balustres: m. *Ballisters; little, round, and short pillars, ranked on the outside of Cloisters, Terraces, Galleries, &c.*
Balzan: m. *A horse that hath a white leg, or foot.*
Balzane: f. *The white of a horses leg, or foot; also, (more generally) a white spot, or marke in any part of his bodie.*
Bambelotier: m. *as* Bimblotier; *Or, a Brooch maker.*
Ban: m. *A Proclamation by voyce, or with sound of trumpet; an edict, or ordinance published; the pleasure, or commaundement of a Lord proclaimed; also, a Proscription, Outlawrie, Banishment; or, a Proclamation of Outlawrie, or of banishment; generally any publike Summons, Conuocation, Notification, or Denouncement; also, a Fief, or Mannor, within the territorie whereof the Lord may cause Proclamations to be made; also, the territorie, precincts, liberties, or limits of iurisdiction, belonging to a towne.*
Bans arbans. *as* Bians.
Ban & Arriereban. *A Proclamation whereby all (except some priuiledged Officers, and citizens) that hold their lands of the Crowne, are summoned to meet at a certaine place, there to attend the king whithersoeuer, and against whom soeuer he goes; (Looke* Arriereban*) (At this day those that list not attend him in person (which in old time they were tied to do) may for a small fine stay at home.)*
Ban de moulin; four; &c. *as* Bancage.
Ban de vendanger. *A Proclamation for the beginning of Vintage; which is (commonly) appointed, and limited by the publike Magistrate.*
Cloche du ban. *The common bell, whereby the people is assembled.*
Droict de ban à vin. *Looke* Vin.
Vn four, ou moulin à ban. *A common ouen, or mill whereat all men may, and euerie tenant and vassall must, bake, and grind.*
Seigneur du ban. *The Lord of* [illegible] *an ouen, or mill.*
Trois bans francs, à Namur. *A priuiledged time, during which no debtor may be arrested, nor goods attached, but for contracts made within that time.*
Donner au ban. *To prostitute; make common for, expose vnto the vse of, euery bodie.*
Mettre au ban. *To banish, or outlaw by proclamation; also, as,* Donner au ban; *or, to giue a thing in pray to any one that will take it.*
Banc: m. *A bench, banke, forme, seat; (and particularly) the seat of a rower in a Gally, or Barge; also, a long shole, shelfe, or sandie hill in the sea, against which the waues doe breake.*
Bancs. *Crosse walls of stone made (in vineyards which be planted on the steepe sides of hills) to keepe the earth from falling; also, the Banes of Matrimonie.*
Ie n'en iray pas du banc au feu. *I will not stirre an inch, I will not mooue a iot, I will not goe one foot, for it.*
Bancage: m. *The circuit of countrey within which the inhabitants are bound to repaire vnto one certaine mill, ouen, wine-presse, &c, paying a fee for their seuerall vses vnto the Lord thereof; also, the Royaltie, or priuiledge of hauing such a mill, &c; also, the reuenue, or benefit made of it.*
Bancelle: f. *A little bench, forme, seat, or banke.*
Bancquage. *as* Bancage.
Bandage: m. *A binding; also, a swath-band; also, the gaffle of a crossebow; also, a truckle for a pully; also, a bending, as of a bow.*
Bande: f. *A band; properly, a long and narrow peece of any stuffe; hence, a welt, or gard; a fillet, or haire lace; a swathing band for a child; a fascia, swath-band, or tye-band, for a wound; a bend in Armorie; the streak of a cart wheele; also, a band, or companie of souldiours; a troupe, or crue; a faction, or combination, of any other persons.*
Vne bande de larde. *A flitch, or side of bacon.*
Clou à bandes. *A streake nayle.*
Bandé: m. ée: f. *Bent, as a bow; bound, swathed, or tied with strings, laces, bands; filletted; also, garded, or welted; also, bandied, or combined together.*
Bandeau: m. *A fillet, head-band; little band.*
Bandée: f. *as* Ban de vendanger: ¶Bourbonnois.
Bandelette. *A little band, or string; also, a small troupe; a handfull of men.*
Bander. *To bend a bow, &c; also, to bind, swaddle, swath, tye with bands, fasten with strings; also, to bandie, at Tennis; also, to gard, or welt a garment.*
'A Bander & à racler. *By hooke, or crooke; in all extremitie.*
Coucher tout à bander, & à racler. *To set all on sixes and seuens; to set his whole rest vpon a desperat game.*
Iouër à bander & à racler contre. *To bandy against, at Tennis; and (by metaphor) to pursue with all insolencie, rigour, extremitie.*
Se bander contre. *To bandie, or oppose himselfe against, with his whole power; or to ioyne in league with others against.*
Ils se bandent à faire vn entreprise. *They are plotting a conspiracie together.*
Banderet. *A Captaine of a quarter in a good towne.*
Banderolle: f. *A little flag, or streamer; a Penon worne on the top of a launce by a horsman that would be gallant.*
Banderolle de Monfaucon. *One that hangs on a paire of gallowes.*
Bandie. *as* Bancage; *also, a priuiledge of some Lords, to forbid all the inhabitants of such a circuit all maner of selling their wines, for fortie dayes together, that in the meane while they may the better vent their owne;* (la Marche.)
Bandier. *The Lord, or owner of th'aforesaid Royaltie.*
Bandier. four bandier. *as* four à ban.
Bandiere. *as* Banniere.
Bandiment. *as* Ban; *Or a proclaiming; outlawing; bani-*

banishing.

Bandon : m. *Leaue, libertie, licence, sufferance, free scope to do a thing.*

A bandon. *At large, roaming, roauing, at randome.*

Prinse de bestes à bandon. *The suffering other mens cattell, for hire, to graze all ouer his pastures.*

Grand bandon grand larron : Prov. *Much libertie brings men to the gallowes ; or, great libertie breedes much theeuerie.*

Bandouilleres : f. *A musketiers bandooleers; or charges, like little boxes, hanging at a belt about his necke.*

Bandouillier : m. *A robber by the highway side ; also, any one that beares a scrip, or wallet ; or his girdle scarfe wise ; also, a musketier.*

Bani : m. ie : f. *Banished, exiled ; confiscated ; Looke* Banni.

Banie : f. *An exile, or banishment ; also, a confiscation ; Looke* Bannie.

Banier. four, ou, moulin banier ; *as* four à ban. *Looke* Bannier.

Baniere. *as* Banniere.

Banir. *To banish, exile, relegate ; also, to proscribe ; confiscate, seize. Looke* Bannir.

Banissement : m. *A banishment, exile ; exiling, banishing ; seizing, confiscating.*

Banlieuë : f. *The circuit of a league (or thereabouts) from a towne, or Mannor house (being the precinct, and liberties thereof) within which, if it be the kings, the ordinarie Iudge of that place, if a Lords, he, or his ordinarie officer, may make Proclamations, and exercise what other iurisdiction they haue.*

Banlieuë de moulin. *The compasse of ground whose inhabitants must carrie their grist vnto a common, or Lords mill : (In* Brittaine *it contains* 120 *cords length from the mill, and euerie cord* 120 *foot.)*

Bannage : m. *A Proclamation, or publike crie for a thing; also, as* Bancage.

Bannal : m. ale : f. *Common ; which any one may, and euerie one (residing within that libertie, or precinct) must, vse, and pay for the vse of ; Looke* Bannier.

Bannalité : f. *The reuenew, or benefit of a common Ouen, Mill, Wine-presse, &c ; also, the libertie, or circuit of countrey wherein a Lord hath any of those, or the like royalties ; also, the royaltie it selfe.*

Banners : m. *Ground keepers ; those that are appointed to looke vnto, and keepe beasts out of grounds, at times wherein they are not to be eaten :* ¶Bourgognois.

Banne : f. *A Maund, Hamper, Flasket, or great Basket.*

Bannée : f. Droict de bannée ; *as,* Bancage : ¶Pic.

Banneret : m. *A Banneret, or Knight banneret (inferiour to a Baron, and better than an ordinarie Knight) a title (the priuiledge whereof was to haue a banner of his own for his people to march, & serue vnder) giuē by the kings of* France *to such as had ten Vassals, and means to maintaine a troupe of horse ; or vnto any gentleman that had valiantly carryed himselfe in two royall battels ; neglected, after that* Charles *the sixth had made* 560 *of them at the siege of* Bourges.

Banneret : m. ette : f. *As* Bannal : (¶Wallon) *also, belonging to a Knight banneret ; whence ;*

Dame bannerette. *The widow, or inheritrix of a Knight banneret.*

Bannerie : f. *Base, or low, iurisdiction ; (an old word.)*

Droict de bannerie. *The royaltie of a common ouen, mill, presse, &c, whereto tenants of, and dwellers within, a libertie, or Mannor, are to resort.*

Bannerolle. *as* Banderolle.

Banneux. *Of, or belonging to a flasket, or hamper.*

Banni : m. ie : f. *Banished, exiled ; confined ; also, outlawed ; also, seized, or confiscated ; also, published, cried, or proclaimed ; whence ;*

Contract banni. *A contract published in Court.*

L'ost banni. *as* Ban, & Arriereban : ¶Norm.

Bannie : f. *as* Ban ; *Or, a seisure, confiscation, interdiction, outcrie of goods, &c ; or, the banishment, or outlawrie, of a man, proclaimed.*

La bannie d'une ville. *The territorie, or extent and compasse of territorie, belonging to a towne.*

Droict de bannie. *as* Bannalité.

Le temps des bannies. *The season wherein common medowes are not to be eaten by any cattell.*

Vignes estans en bannie. *The Vintage whereof is proclaimed by the Lord of the iurisdiction.*

Bannier : m. ere : f. *as* Bannal ; *Common, &c.*

Seigneur bannier. *A Lord that hath the royaltie, or priuiledge of a common mill, ouen, presse, &c ; or, that may prescribe vnto his vassals, tenants, and any other within his libertie, their time of vintage, and of sale for their wines.*

Subjects banniers. *Such as are bound to grind at a Mill, or to bake in an Ouen belonging to another.*

Taverne banniere du Seigneur. *The place, or house wherein a Lord may (as he may in most parts of* France) *retaile his wine fortie dayes before any other (that dwels in the same libertie) his.*

Taureau bannier. *A common, or town, bull; for whose leacherie the Lords of* France *(who loue to haue their owne freely) exact a fee of their poore tenants.*

Banniere : f. *A Banner, square Ensigne, or Standard ; also, a rag, or shread of cloth, &c ; (In old time certaine Lordships, or Mannors were tearmed* Bannieres.)

Banniere d'Orleans. *A ragged coat, or torne garment.*

Cheualier à banniere, ou, de bannier. *A Knight Banneret.*

Droict de banniere. *as* Droict de bannerie.

En cent ans civiere en cent ans banniere : Prov. *In one hundred yeares a Banner, in the next a wheelebarrow ; the family which at this day is held rich and noble, may within an age become both poore in estate, and meane in account.*

Bannir. *To banish, exile, expulse ; outlaw, proscribe ; seize, confiscate, by publicke act, or proclamation.*

Bannissement. *A banishment, exilement, relegation, expulsing ; proscribing, outlawing ; seizing, confiscating.*

Bannon. *as* Banon.

Banon : m. *The season wherein the cattell belonging to a whole towne is turned out into, or may feed all ouer, common pastures :* ¶Norm.

Cela est en banon. *That is common, or for euery bodies vse.*

Banoyement : m. *A proclaiming, or publishing, by sound of Trumpet, &c.*

Banquage. *as* Bancage ; *also, as* Bandie.

Banque : f. *A bank, where money is let out to vse ; or lent, or returned by exchange ; also, the table whereon such money is told.*

Banquerotier. *A bankrupt.*

Banqueroutte : f. *A breaking, or becomming bankrupt.*

Banqueroutier. *A bankrupt.*

Banquet : m. *A banket ; also, a feast ; also, part of the cheeke of a bit.*

Apres grand banquet petit pain : Prov. *After feasting*

sting fasting.
Il n'est banquet que d'homme chiche: Prov. *Looke* Chiche.
Banqueté: m.ée: f. *Banketted, feasted.*
Banquetement: m. *A banketting, or feasting.*
Banqueter. *To banket, or feast it.*
Banqueterie: f. *as* Banquetement.
Banqueteur: m. *A banketter; or feaster.*
Les grands banqueteurs font rarement de beaux faits d'armes: Prov. *Great banketters doe seldome great exploits.*
Banqueteux: m.euse: f. *Full of, or belonging to, bankets, or feasts.*
Banquetterie. *as* Banquetement; *or, a banquet.*
Banquier: m. *A Banker, an Exchanger; also, a bench-cloth, or a carpet for a forme, or bench.*
Banquier: m.ere: f. *as* Bannal.
Bans. *The banes of Matrimonie; also, as* Rangs.
Baptesme: m. *Baptisme.*
Baptisé: m.ée: f. *Christened, baptised; also, appointed, ordained; also, taxed, limited.*
Baptiser. *To Christen, to baptise; also, to appoint, or ordaine; also, to tax, or limit.*
Baptiser son appellation. *An appealant to publish his grieuances, and vnto what Iudge he will appeale, before he proceed actually in the appeale.*
Baptiser possessions contraires. *A defendant in a suit of* Novel disseisin *to propound, oppose, & alleadge his possession against the complaint of his aduersarie.*
Baptismal: m.ale: f. *Baptismall; of, or belonging to, baptisme.*
Baptistaire. *as* Baptistere.
Baptiste. S. Iean Baptiste. *S. Iohn Baptist.*
Baptiste. Toile bap. *Cambrick; or, a kind therof, much worne by Nunnes in their vailes.*
Baptistere: m. *A font; also, a Christening, or Baptizing; also, as* Papier baptistere.
Baptistere: com. *Belonging to a font, or, vnto Christening.*
Papier baptistere. *The Church booke wherein Christenings be recorded.*
Baque: f. *A berrie.*
Baquelette: f. *A yong wench, mother, girle:* ¶Pic.
Baquet: m. *A pale, or bucket; also, a small, shallow, and open tub; See* Bacquet.
Baqueter. *as* Bacqueter.
Bar: m. *The fish called, a Base.*
Baradon: m. *A drone, or dorre-bee.*
Baragant: m. *Dutch Grogeran, or Valentien Grogeran.*
Barat: m. *Cheating, deceit, guile, cousenage, lying, or falshood, in bargaining; also, a barter, scourse, trucke, exchange.*
Baratelle: f. *as* Cagnole.
Barater. *To cheat, cousen, beguile, deceiue, lye, cog, foist, in bargaining; also, to trucke, scourse, barter, exchange.*
Barateur: m. *A deceiuer, cheater, cousener; cogger, foister, lyer, (in bargaining;) also, a barterer, trucker, exchanger.*
Barateux: m.euse: f. *Deceitfull, craftie, cheating, full of lyes, or of slie deuises, in bargaining.*
Barathre: m. *An Abisme, or deepe gulfe, whence there is no returning; (hence) also, Hell.*
Baratier: m.ere: f. *as* Barateux.
Baratte: f. *A churne.*
Barbacane: f. *A casemate; or a hole (in a parrapet, or towne wall) to shoot out at; some hold it also to be, a Sentrie, Scout-house, or hole; and therupon our* Chaucer *vseth the word Barbican for a watch-tower, which in the Saxon tongue was called, a Bourough-keaning.*
Barbaïan. *The great horne owle.*
Barbare: com. *Barbarous, rude, vnciuile, rusticall, ignorant.*
Barbarement: m. *Barbarously; rudely, vnciuilely, ignorantly.*
Barbaresque. *as* Barbare; *Or, clowne-like, like a barbarous fellow.*
Barbaresquement. *Barbarously, vnciuilely, rudely, clownishly; without manners, respect, or knowledge.*
Barbarie: f. *Barbarie (a part, or Prouince, of Affricke;) also, barbarisme; also, the trade of a Barber.*
Barbarie de Biscay. *The name of a great bitter-sweet apple.*
Cancre de Barbarie. *See* Cancre.
Pomme de Barbarie. *A kind of faire, sappie, & well tasting, apple.*
C'est vne vache de Barbarie, qui ne recognoit que son propre veau: Prov. *Applied vnto such, as respect, or know not any, but their own family, friends, and kindred; a rude, ignorant, barbarous humor.*
Barbarin: m. *A small riuer Barbell; also, the sea Barbell, bearded Mullet, or sore Mullet.*
Barbarine: f. *A peece of coyne worth about six Sous.*
Barbarisme: m. *Barbarisme, inciuilitie, inhumanitie; a rude word, an vngentle deed.*
Barbasse: f. *A filthie great, or goat-like, beard.*
Barbassé. vn bouc barbassé. *A bearded goat.*
Barbaude: f. *Beere; Brewers liquor.*
Barbaudier: m. *A Brewer.*
Barbe: m. *A Barbarie horse.*
Barbe: f. *A beard; also, that part of a horses nether iaw whereon the curbe doth rest.*
Barbes. *Looke after* Barberousse.
Barbe de bouc. *The hearbe Goats-beard; called also, Starre of Jerusalem, Josephes flower, Noone-tide, and Goe-to-bed-at-Noone (for the flower thereof euer closes about noone.)*
Barbe de chevre. *Meadswort, Meadsweet, Queene of the medowes, (an hearbe.)*
La barbe d'vn coq. *A Cockes rattles, or waddles.*
Barbe de forests. *Water Plantaine; (some hold, that Sopewort, or Brusewort is called so, but they are in an errour, sayes Mathiolus.)*
Barbe de Iupiter. *Knee holme, Butchers broome.*
Barbe de prestre. *as* Barbe de bouc.
Barbe regnard. *Goats-thorne; the shrub whose root yeeldeth Gumme dragagant.*
'A sa barbe. *To his teeth, in his presence, before his face; also, mauger his beard, in despight of him; also, to his disgrace.*
Faire barbe. *To assemble together in troupes (as bees doe before, or about, the doore of their hiue a little before they swarme) a phrase in vse among the boores of* Languedoc.
Faire barbe de foarre à. *To deceiue, delude, abuse; depriue of his due; (especially in matters of religion wherein this phrase is most, and best, vsed; but then in stead of* Barbe *there must be* Gerbe; *Looke* Gerbe.*)*
Faire la barbe à. *To barbe, trimme, shaue; also, to beard, affront, or braue to the teeth; to resist, make head against, withstand publikely.*
Mettre en barbe à. *To oppose vnto, confront with, set against.*
Reprenons nostre chevre à la barbe. *Let vs take hold*

where we left; or, let vs returne to our matter againe.
Trouver en barbe. *To meet in the teeth with.*
Barbe de fol: Prov. *See* Fol.
Barbe rase, pied ferrat: Prov. *Cleerely, all charges borne, all things discharged, and done.*
Barbé: m. ée: f. *Bearded, hauing a beard.*
Rouget barbé. *A sea Barbell; or, sore Mullet.*
Barbeau: m. *The riuer Barbell; and* (at Bourdeaux) *the sea Barbell; also, a little beard.*
Barbecane. *as* Barbacane.
Barbel: m. *as* Barbeau.
Barbelé. *Bearded; also, full of snags, snips, iags; notches; whence;*
Flesche barbelée. *A bearded, or barbed, arrow.*
Barbelotte: f. *A hedge Toad, a land Toad.*
Barbelu: m. uë: f. *Bearded, beardie; or, as* Barbelé.
Barber. *To barbe, shaue, trim; to cut the beard off.*
Se Barber. *To grow bearded, or to get a beard; also, to (begin to) root, or, to get small haire-like sprigs in growing, at the root.*
Barberie: f. *Barbing; the act, or art, of Barbing; also, a Barbers shop; also, (the name of) a certaine round, great, and good apple.*
Barberies: f. *Pinks, or sops in wine, feathered Gillovers, small Honesties.*
Barbaries sauvages. *Wild Williams, marsh Gillovers, Cuckow Gillouers.*
Barberiot. *The name of an apple thats lesse, and yeelds better cyder, than* la Barberie.
Barberousse: m. *A red bearded fellow.*
Barbes: f. *Pushes, or little bladders, vnder the tongues of horses, and cattell, the which they kill if they be not speedily cured.*
Barbes aux veaux. *The barbles; a white excressence which, like the pip in chickings, growes vnder the tongues of calues, and hinders them from sucking.*
Barbet: m. *A little, young, or budding beard; also, a small riuer Barbell; also, a water-spanell, or any shag-haird dog.*
Pour Venus advienne barbet le chien. *Looke* Venus.
Barbet: m. ette: f. *Rough, or shag-haired, like a water-dog.*
Barbeter. *To grunt, mutter, murmure; or as* Barboter.
Barbette: f. *A small beard; also, a water-bitch, or shag-haired bitch.*
Barbidant. *Part of a womans, &c.*
Barbier: m. *A Barber, also, a Chirurgion; also, a certain fish, as* Poisson sacré.
Vn barbier rait l'autre: Prov. *One knaue trimmes; excuses, helpes; soothes, or flatters, another.*
Ieune barbier, & vieil medecin: Prov. *A young Chirurgian, and an old Physitian, (are commonly the best.)*
Au sanglier le barbier: Prov. *Looke* Sanglier.
Barbiere: f. *A Barbers wife; a barbaresse; a woman, or she, Barber.*
Barbillon: m. *A little Barbell; also, the beard of an eare of corne; also, the lesse fin of a fish; also, the barbe of a broad-arrow head, or any the like iagged thing.*
Barbillons. *The Frounce; (a disease bred in the tongues of hawkes by a cold rhewme.)*
Barbillonné: m. ée: f. *Bearded, barbed; iagged, rough by the iagges, or notches it hath on it.*
Dard barbillonné. *A dart that hath a forked, or barbed, head.*
Barbin: m. *A little beard.*
Barboire: m. *A maske, or mummerie; also, a visard.*
Barbolle. *Part of a womans, &c.*
Barbon: m. *A Barbell fish.*
Barbot: m. *The wallowing of a seething pot.*
Barbotage: m. *A confused fumbling, or mumbling vp of words.*
Barbote: f. *An Eele-powte; or, as* Lote d'eau douce.
Barboté: m. ée: f. *Mumbled, or muttered, as words betweene the teeth.*
Espice barbotez. *Bearded eares of corne.*
Barboter. *To mumble, or mutter words betweene the teeth; also, to wallow like a seething pot.*
Barboter de peur, ou de froid. *(The teeth) to shake, or quake for feare; to chatter, or didder for cold; to say an Apes Paternoster.*
Barbotin: m. ine: f. *Beardie, or bearded.*
Barbotine: f. *Wormeseed.*
Barbotte: f. *The chinne peece of an helmet.*
Barbouillage: m. *A rude mingle mangle, gallymaufrey, or confused hotchpot; also, as* Barbouillement.
Barbouillé: m. ée: f. *Confusedly iumbled, or hudled together; also, spotted, blotted, beraied, besmeared, begrimed all ouer.*
Barbouillement: m. *A confused iumbling of sundrie things together; also, a besmearing, beraying, bedashing.*
Barbouiller. *To iumble, confound, huddle, or mingle ill fauouredly; also, to blot, spot, smut, besmeare; bedash all ouer.*
Barbouilleries: f. *Trash, riffraffe; sundry things of small value iumbled, or hudled together.*
Barbouilleur: m. *A disorderly iumbler, hudler, mingler; also, a blotter, spotter, smutter, besmearer of.*
Barbuteur: m. *A Sicophant, a picketbanke, a priuie whisperer, a close detracter, a secret tale-teller.*
Barbu: m. uë: f. *Bearded; beardie; hauing a beard; full of, or ouergrowne with, beard.*
If barbu. *Looke* If.
Homme roux, & femme barbuë de cinquante pas les saluë, *(vne pierre ou poing, followes; because they are held verie dangerous people.)*
Barbuë: f. *The hearbe Gith, or garden Nigella; also, a kind of lesse Turbot, or Turbot-like fish, called by some, a Dab, or Sandling.*
Barbu-marsés. *Amelcorne, Starchcorne; or, as* Escourgeon.
Barbute: m. *A man of Armes; tearmed so in old time, because he ordinarily wore a Barbute.*
Barbute: f. *A riding hood; a Montero, or close hood, wherewith trauellers preserue their faces and heads from frost-biting, and weather-beating, in Winter; also, the beaver of an helmet; also, a Bay berrie; also, the hearbe Nigella; or, the seed thereof; also, a stopple, bung; or spigot.*
Barc: m. *A kind of smooth red earth, whereof vessells were made in old time.*
Barce. *as* Berche.
Barchaux: m. *Great barkes, or, the great boats called, lyters.*
Barche: f. *A little barke, or pinnace.*
Bardable: com. *Barbable; fit, or able to beare a barbed furniture, or armor.*
Bardache: m. *An Ingle; a youth kept, or acccompanied for Sodomie.*
Bardechiser. *To commit Sodomie; to bugger, to ingle.*
Bardacoculé. *Seeke* Bardococulé.
Bardane: f. *The Clote, burre-docke, or great burre; also, the noisome, and stinking vermine, called, a Punie.*

Bardane la grande. *The burre-dock, clote bur, great burre.*

Petite bardane. *The louse-burre, ditch-burre, lesse burre docke.*

Barde: f. *A long saddle for an Asse, or moyle, made onely of course canuas stuffed with flockes.*

Iavelin de barde. *A barbed Jauelin, for a horseman.*

Bardé: m. ée: f. *Barbed, or trapped, as a great horse; also, bound, or tied ouer, and acrosse.*

Barde: com. *Blunt, blockish, dull-witted, hard-headed, sottish.*

Bardeau: m. *A shingle, or small boord, such as houses are couered with.*

Bardelle: f. *A Bardello; the quilted, or canuas saddle, wherewith coults are backed.*

Barder. *To barbe, or trap, horses; also, to bind, or tye acrosse, ouercrosse, or ouerthwart.*

Bardes: f. *Barbes, or trappings, for horses of seruice, or of shew.*

Bardeure: f. *A trapping of a horse; also, an ouerthwart binding, or tying.*

Bardococulage: m. *A being armed, or couered all ouer, with cowles; Monkerie; or a Monkish habit.*

Bardococulé: m. ée: f. *Dressed or armed in, adorned or couered with, a cowle, or Monkes hood.*

Bardou: m. *A sot, a blockehead, a dull fellow; (an old word.)*

Baretter. *as* Bariner; *To churne.*

Barge: f. *A certaine fowle, that hath no spleene; shee is onely somewhat lesse than a Curlue, but otherwise resembles her; also, the banke of a riuer, or water.*

Barguignard. *A bargaining, or chaffering person; or as* Barguigneur.

Barguigne: f. *A bargaine; or a wrangling, and dodging in bargaine-making.*

Barguigner. *To chaffer; to bargaine; or (more properly) to wrangle, dodge, haggle, brabble, in the making of a bargaine.*

Apres besongne faitte le fol barguigne: Prov. *The foole beginnes to wrangle when his worke is ended; or, When worke is ended fooles fall out about it;* (viz. *for want of agreeing before hand.)*

Barguigneur: m. *A dodger, or hagler, a wrangling bargainer; one that vses to cheapen much, and buy nothing; or, vses many words about a thing, but comes not neere the price of it.*

Baricaue: f. *as* Barricave.

Baricquer. *To bray like an Elephant.*

Baril. *as* Barril.

Barillet. *A little barrell.*

Barillier: m. *A maker of barrels; also, an officer that tends, and lookes to, the caske of a great mans sellor.*

Bariner. *To churne butter.*

Bariquade: f. *as* Barriquade.

Barique: f. *The halfe of a Queuë, or Poinson; a vessell somewhat bigger than our barrell.*

Bariqué: m. ée: f. *Barricadoed.*

Bariquelle: f. *A skiffe, or little boat, like a Wherrie, or scull.*

Bariteau: m. *A Siue made of haire.*

Baritonnant. *Wagging, dangling; also, braying.*

Baritonner. *To wag, or dangle, vp and downe; also to bray like an Elephant.*

Barizel: m. *A Captaine, or leader of Catchpoles; an ordinarie Prouost Marshall.*

Barlong: m. *A vessell, plot, or proportion thats of more length than breadth; See* Balongue.

Barlong: m. gue: f. *More long than broad; or, longer in one place than in another.*

Barlonguer. *To make; or grow, or be, more long than broad.*

Barluë: f. *A glimmering; or a dimme, duskie, or imperfect light; also, pur-blindnesse.*

Barme: f. *The banke of a riuer, &c.*

Barnabé: m. *(A proper name)* Barnabie.

`A la S. Barnabé la faux au pré: Prov. *(That is about the eleuenth of June.)*

Barnage: m. *All the traine, stuffe, and equipage of a great person carried, and going, along with him in a progresse, or iourney. Looke* Bernage.

Barnez. *The Nobilitie, or Barons; (an old, and seldome vsed, word.)*

Barocco. *Barocco; the name of a Syllogisticall mood in Logicke; Hence (with an equiuocall allusion to the word* Broc) *The Tiplers phrase;*

Conclure in Barocco. *To draw a moist conclusion out of a Tankerd, or Flagon; to conclude by quaffing, or with a carouse.*

Baron: m. *A husband (*Pic. *and in our Law;) also, a Baron, or Lord Baron: In which sence it hath two significations; one generall, for an immediate vassall of the Crowne, (whether he be Duke, Marquesse, Earle, or Prince,) that hath not any right, or priuiledge, of Souevaigntie; (whence,* les Barons de France:) *Another speciall, for a Baron, or the Lord of a Baronie (see* Baronnie) *whose ranke is (as in England) next below a* Vicounts; *(if their tenures be equall; for otherwise a Baron that holds immediatly of the King, or of a royall Countie, &c, goes before a Vicount that holds of a Countie, &c, which is not royall;) and howsoeuer next aboue a Lo.* Chastellains. *In old time* les Barons *were th'ordinarie Magistrats of* France; *and the title grew so common, that all* Hauts Iusticiers *(especially such, as had incroached vpon* le Droict de Ressort) *vsurped it: At this day (no lesse commonly) the eldest sonne to the Lord of a village, is in many Prouinces tearmed,* le Baron; *And no better than the Burghers of some priuiledged townes, as* Bourges, &c, *do stile themselues* Barons; *(which degrees of Barons very often deserue to be Englished, Bare-ones;) The Lo. Baron may, of himselfe wall and fortifie the principall village of his Baronie; and keepe the keyes of the gates thereof whether th'inhabitants will or no; and in time of daunger, appoint a Captaine therin; but this with their consents.*

Parez vn herisson il semblera Baron: Prov. *Good, (or gay) clothes will make a Monkie seeme a Monsieur.*

Baron: m. onne: f. (Sain & baron) *Of the male kind; also, manly, hardie, strong.*

Barone: f. *A Baronesse; the Ladie of a Baronie, or wife of a Lo. Baron.*

Baronie: f. *as* Baronnie.

Baronnie: f. *A Baronie; a Lordship of dignitie, superiour to a* Chastelenie, *and inferiour to a Vicountie; Some define it, Any chiefe Seigneurie, next vnto the Soueraigne, held immediately of the Crowne,; Others, A title peculiar to certaine Seigneuries that are held onely of the King, and haue no other title; which definition agrees best with the moderne, and th'other with the ancient, French Baronies, wher of originally there were but three,* viz. Bourbon, Coucy, *and* Beaujeu; *all held immediatly of the Crowne, and at length made Dutchies, Marquessates, or Earledomes; so that they haue left almost no markes of, nor matches to, themselues behind them: For all, or the most of the*

the moderne Baronies are but the members of some Dutchie, or Countie (vnited, a good while agoe to the Crowne; or of later time erected, by the King) and are held (those by a direct, these by a dependant, Tenure) onely of the king, as, or in respect of, one of them: yet are they but little inferiour to th'ancient ones in other points; for being erected at first in emulation, or by the patterne, thereof, either by the old Dukes, or Earles (who hauing vsurped the absolute soueraignitie of their territories, would also haue their Barons as well as the King had his) or since the reunion of their estates to the Crowne, by Kings, they conferred on them all kind of (subalterne) iurisdiction, and authoritie; which they still retaine; and in the right thereof haue (or should haue) each of them a Bailli, *&c; as also, a walled, or fortified towne, and the gouernement thereof; a colledge, or Collegiate Church; an Abbey, or Priorie; an Hospitall; Forest; Faires, or Markets; a* Travers, *or Through-toll; a publicke seale for contracts, and diuers other priuiledges belonging to them: At this day, an inheritance, or Lordship, worthie of this title, must comprehend at the least three* Chastellenies, *all vnited together, that they may be held by one homage of the King.*

Barque: f. *A barke, little ship, great boat.*

Barquerot: m. *A sayler, or skipper in, a steeresman vnto, a barke.*

Barquette: f. *A little barke; a boat.*

Barrage: m. *as* Barriquade; *Also, a passage toll, or through-toll; so tearmed of the barre that ordinarily stands on the way wherein tis payable.*

Barragoüin. *Pedlars French, fustian language; any rude gibble-gabble, or barbarous speech; (tis compounded of two Brittish words,* barra, *bread; and* goüin, *wine.)*

Barragoüiner. *To speake fustian; to vse a language that no bodie vnderstands.*

Barraté: m. ée: f. *Churned; or, tossed, as butter is in the churning.*

Barraut: m. *A little barrell; or vessell, holding (most commonly) 36 Parisian pintes; and therefore not much different from our kilderkin, or beer-firkin of 36 quarts; also, a water bag, or budget.*

Barre: f. *A barre, or sparre, for a doore; also, the crosse-barre thats on the head of a peece of caske; generally, any barre; also, a hawkes pearch; also, the part of a horses nether iaw wheron his bit resteth (a little aboue his tushes.)*

Barres. *The martiall sport called Barriers; also, the play at Bace; or, Prison Bars; also, (in the stile of pleading) defences, and exceptions (whether dilatorie, or peremptorie) propounded in order; or, as we say, pleaded in barre.*

La barre de parlement. *The barre without which Aduocates, or Councellors do plead; (hence it seems are ours called Vtter-barresters.)*

La barre du timon. *The whip of the Rudder (of a ship.)*

Le barre d'vne ville. *The barres of a towne.*

Auoir barre sur. *To haue the aduantage, or get the start of; to be before handwith;* Prendre barre sur. *The same.*

Donner barres à. *To stop, to stay the course, or current of.*

Planter à la barre. *To plant the slips of vines in order, either two together, or one against another, or one by one, as we set willowes.*

Retraict de barre, ou de Cour. *Looke* Retraict.

Barré: m. ée: f. *Barred, sparred; boulted; grated, lattised.*

Os barré. *Looke* Os.

Barreau. *A little barre, or sparre; a boult; also, the bar of a Court whereat Lawyers plead.*

Barreaux. *Grates, or strong lattises (of wood, &c,) in a house, prison, or ship.*

Le barreau des Pairs. *The most honourable barre in the Court of the Parisian Parliament* (celuy qui est pres la cheminée de la Chambre dorée) *whereat the Aduocates of a Peere of* France *do plead.*

Les Gens de barreau. *Barresters, Aduocates, Councellors, pleading Lawyers.*

Barrer. *To barre, or sparre; to boult; also, to lattice, or grate vp.*

Barres. *Looke* Barre.

Barretade: f. *Cap-courtesie, hat-reuerence; the vailing of the bonnet; the putting off of the hat, or cap, in a salutation, &c.*

Barrette: f. *A cap, or bonnet.*

Parler à sa barette. *To expostulate with him face to face; to speake home, and to his teeth, vnto him.*

Barrez. *The Carmes, or White Friers were called so in old time, by reason of certain clokes (crosse garded with white, and blacke) which then they wore.*

Barricade. *See* Barriquade.

Barricadé: m. ée: f. *Barricadoed; stopped vp by a barricado.*

Barricave: f. *A hole, pit, or hollow place aboue ground; also, a low bottome, steepe valley; or deepe path, in a wood, or valley.*

Barriere: f. *A rayle, or barre; also, a stop, or let.*

Barrieres. *The rayles, or lists within which a Tilting, Turnay, &c, or single combat is to be performed.*

Barriere de Charpentier. *A great peece of timber borne vp, gibbet-like, by two posts, and set before the doore of a great house to the streetward.*

Faire barriere à. *To stop, hinder, let; also, to backe; also, to shrowd, or shield.*

Barril: m. *The (French) barrell; a vessell which (holding 72 Parisian pintes) comes neere to the Beere kilderkin, (which holds 72 of our quarts.)*

Nourri dans vn barril. *Brought vp in a Tub (a speech vsed to the disgrace, or as a description, of a simple, ignorant, vnexperienced, and home-bred hoydon.)*

Barrillet: m. *A little barrell; a firkin, or halfe barrell.*

Barriquade: f. *A barricado; a defence of barrels, timber, pales, earth, or stones, heaped vp, or closed together; and seruing to stop vp a street, or passage, and to keepe off shot, &c.*

Barrique: f. *The halfe of the* Queuë, *or* Poinson; *a vessell thats somewhat bigger than our barrell.*

De Corsaire à Corsaire n'y pend que barriques rompuës: Prov. *Nought's to be got of a roauer but trash, or blowes.*

Barriqué: m. ée: f. *Barricadoed; stopped, fortified, or defended by barricadoes.*

Barriqueau: m. *A firkin; or, halfe of the* Barrique.

Barriquer. *To barricadoe; to stop, fortifie, or defend with barricadoes.*

Barrit: m. *The braying, or cry of an Elephant.*

Barroir: m. *A Turrell; th'Oager wherewith Coopers make holes for the barre-pinnes of a peece of caske.*

Barrot: m. *A firkin, or barriket.*

Barroyements: m. *Delayes in Law, vsed for the better instruction, furnishing, or strengthening of a cause.*

Barroyer. *To vse delayes (as in* Barroyements.)

Barry. *as* Barrill; *also, a kind of fireworke in a woodden case, fashioned (like a spindle, or caske) thicke in the middle, and small at both ends.*
Bas: m. *The base, bottome, depth, or lowest part of; also, as* Bast; *a packesaddle.*
Vn bas de chausses. *A stocking, or netherstocke.*
Le bas de la Couverture d'vne maison. *The eaues, or casings of a house.*
Vn bas de manches. *An halfe sleeue.*
Le plat du bas. (viz. *Of the lower end of the table*) est tousiours le primier vuide: Prov. *Looke* Plat.
Bas: m. **Basse**: f. *Low, base; humble; deepe, vnder; deiected, abiect.*
Bas bord, ou, bord bas. *The larbord, or left side of a ship.*
Basse heure. assez basse heure. *Verie late, farre in the night.*
Basse Iustice. *Looke* Iustice.
Bas de poil. *Of poore estate, of small meanes; of little authoritie.*
Chambre basse. *A priuie, or house of office.*
Cour basse. *A base Court; or the Court of a Lord, who hath no other than base, or low iurisdiction.*
Facultez basses. qui a les facultez basses. *Poore, of meane estate; whose fortunes are at a great ebbe.*
Main basse. *A bad hand, course chance, &c; Looke* Main.
Bas (Aduerb.) *Vnder, low, below.*
Haut & bas la cheminée. *The ordinarie cry of chimney-sweepers in* France.
Taillables haut & bas. *Taxable at the will and pleasure of their Lord.*
Vole bas de peur des branches. *Looke* Branche.
Basane. *Looke* Bazane.
Basané: m. ée: f. *Duskie, swart, blackish, of a tawnie hue; also, smutched, beduske d.*
Basaner. *To bleake, smutch, beduske, make swart, browne, or blackish.*
Basanne: f. *A sheepes skin tawed; See* Bazane.
Basard: m. *A market place, wherein things are sold.*
Basauchieux. *Lawyers Clerkes; or as,* Basochiens,
Baschat: m. *A Bassa; a chiefe commaunder vnder the Turke; also, a kind of vaulted sinke.*
Baschelier. *for* Bachelier: ¶Rab.
Basclé. *Barred; stopped, shut vp; See* Baclé.
Bascule: f. *A swipe, scoope, or put-gally to draw vp water withall; also, as* Bacule.
Basculer. *To set vpon his taile; to bump, or beat on the taile; to giue an arseposse vnto; also, as* Baccoler.
Basculle: f. *as* Bascule.
Bas-de-fesses. *Low buttockt; arse-fallen.*
Base: f. *A base, or basis; a foot, ground, foundation, vnto.*
Base du coeur. *The flat, or broad part thereof; which in the bodie stands vpward.*
La base de la teste. *The root, or bottome of the head; or, as* Os basilaire.
La base des yeux. *The root of the eyes.*
Baselic: m. *A Basiliske, or Cockatrice; also, the (long) peece of ordnance called, a Basiliske; also, the hearbe Basill; (for which looke* Basilic.)
Basenne. *as* Bazane; *also, as* Bassenne.
Basenné: m. ée: f. *Duskie, swart, browne, blackish, darke-tawnie; also, smutched, bedusked, made swart, &c.*
Basennier: m. *A marchant, seller, or dresser, of coloured sheepes skinnes; as in* Bazane.
Basennier: m. ere: f. *as* Basenné *(in the first sence.)*

Basilaire. Os Basilaire. *The nape, or nuke (bone) the cuneall, or fundamentall bone of the head; Looke* Os.
Basilic: m. *The hearbe Basill; also, as* Basilisc.
Basilic citronnier. *Middle Basill, or Citron Basill.*
Basilic d'eau. *Water basill, fish basill; beares a white blossome, and a small blacke seed of a sharpe tast; the whole plant yeelds a milkie, and sweet iuyce.*
Basilic gentil. *Basill gentle, bush basill, some also call stone basill so.*
Basilic gyrofflé. *Bush basill, fine basill.*
Basilic menu. *The small wild basill, called by Herbalists,* Acynos.
Basilic sauvage. *Basill mint, wild basill, vnprofitable basill.*
Grand basilic. *Great garden basill, basill royall.*
Petit basilic. *as* Basilic gentil.
Basilique. *A royall palace; a princes court, honour, house; also, a shire-hall, guild-hald, or spacious place in a citie, wherein Councels be held, and Iustice administred, by the publick Magistrates.*
Basilique. veine bas. *The liuer veine.*
Basilisc: m. *A Basiliske, or Cockatrice.*
Basique: com. *Low, fundamentall, belonging to the basis, or bottome of.*
Basine: m. *Balme, balsamum; or, more properly, the balsamum tree, from which distils our balme (or* Opobalsamum; *for little, or no true balme is now adayes brought into these parts of the world.)*
Basoche: f. *The whole troupe, or companie of Lawyers Clearks in the palace of* Paris, *hauing among them a king, and their peculiar lawes; hence also, reuell, misrule (for these fellowes are none of the soberest) also, a certaine baudie Court, wherein wiues that beat their husbands, are censured.*
Fief de la Basoche. Il tient du fief de la B. *He is a pratling, or iangling Lawyer; or (as a Lawyers Clerke) an vnruly copesmate; or, his wife is his master.*
Roy de la Basoche. *The Master of Misrule, or chiefe man among the Clerkes, when they make their shewes.*
Basochiens: m. *Reuellers, or associates vnto Masters of Misrule; and, Lawyers Clerkes (who for the most part are verie vnruly) or, such as belong vnto the baudie Court aforesaid. (in* Basoche.)
Basquain: m. *as* Basque *(in the first sence onely.)*
Basque: m. *A Biscayan; one that dwells, or was borne, in* Biscay, *or about* Bayonne, *neere* Biscay; *also, a Lackey, or foot-boy; so called, because many that are of that profession in* France *come from that countrey; also, a bastard.*
Tour de Basque. *Cleanly conueyance, legerdemaine; a nimble tricke, deceitfull part, cheating pranke.*
Basque: f. *as* tour de Basque; *Also, a sudden affright, or scarring.*
Basque de pourpoint. *The skirt of a doublet.*
Basquine. *A Vardingale of the old fashion; or a Spanish Vardingale; See* Vasquine.
Basquinier. *See* Vasquinier.
Basse: f. *A basis; the base, or foot of a pillar; also, a bottome, or low ground; also, a great Salt bag.*
Les basses de la mer. *The shallowes, flats, and fallings of tides, in the sea.*
Basse. contre. *The base-part in Musicke; also, hee that sings, or beares it.*
Basse-cour: f. *A base Court, a backe Court for the houshold, or for horshold vses; an inner yard, or barton, wherein poultrie is (or may be) kept.*
Bassecule. *as* Bascule.

Basse-danse: f. *A measure.*

Bassement. *Basely, lowly, deiectedly, humbly, poorely; also, vnder, low, below.*

Bassenne: *The mizzen saile of a ship.*

Bassesse: f. *Basenesse, lowlinesse, abiect humblenesse; also, lownesse.*

Basset: m. *A terrier, or earthing beagle; also, a low stoole; also, a dwarfe, or very low man.*

Basse-taille: f. *Raised, or imbossed imagerie, wherin the representation is made, not of, but vpon, the whole peece.*

Bassetè: f. *Basenesse, abiection; too much humilitie.*

Basseur: f. *Humblenesse, lowlinesse.*

Bassier: m. *The tub that receiues tap-droppings; or, a tub to put lyes, or the dregs, or bottomes of wine, &c, in.*

Bassiere: f. *The same.*

Bassieres. *The bottomes, grounds, or lees of wine; dregs that be setled in the bottome of wine, &c.*

Bassille: f. *Rocke Sampire, Crestmarine.*

Bassin: m. *A bason to wash in; also, a scull; or sleight, & bason-like headpeece, vsed at barriers.*

Des Bassins. *as* Basinets; *Crowfoot.*

Bassin à selle percée. *The pan of a close stoole.*

Bassin d'vne balance. *The scowle of a balance.*

Cracher au bassin. *To lay out, or pay downe readie coine; also, to giue fees; or bestow a reward in hand; also, as in* Cracher.

Bassine: f. *A deepe, or bason-like, and footlesse, posnet, vsed most by Conseruers, or Comfet-makers.*

Bassiné: m. ée: f. *Warmed, fomented; rubbed, or chafed vntill it grow warme; also bathed, or washed with warme liquor.*

Bassinement: m. *Warming, a fomentation, or fomenting; a rubbing, chafing, or heating; a bathing, or washing, in warme liquor.*

Bassiner. *To warme, foment; rub, chafe, hug, heat a thing vntill it be full warme; also, to bath, wash, or heat in warme liquor.*

Bassinet. *(The hearbe) Looke* Bassinets.

Bassinet. *A little bowle, a small bason; also, the scull, sleight helmet, or headpeece, worne, in old time, by the French men of armes; and hence, a man of Armes (in which sence it is euer vsed in the Plurall number.)*

Le bassinet d'vne 'arquebuse. *The Firepan, or touchpan.*

Le bassinet d'un reschaut. *The pan of a chafing dish.*

Bassinets: m. *The flower Crowfoot, King-cob, gold crap, yellow craw, butter flower; There be many kinds of it, & that which we call, Batchelers buttons, is one (the double one) of them.*

Bassinets blancs. *White Crowfoot, Vrchin Crowfoot.*

Bassinets d'eau. *Water Crowfoot, marsh, Crowfoot.*

Bassinets de marais, ou, des prez. *The marsh Marigold.*

Petis bassinets. *Little Celandine, Pilewort, Figwort; so called, because the flower of it somewhat resembles the Crowfoot; otherwise, no kind thereof.*

Bassinoire: f. *A warming pan.*

Bast: m. *A pannell, or packsaddle.*

'A bast vuide. renvoyé à b. *Emptie handed; with a flea in his eare; as wise as he came; without effecting, or getting what he went for.*

De quelque costé que le bast vire. *Howsoeuer matters be carried, in what sort soeuer they be handled.*

Ventru à plein bast. *Swagbellied, gorbellied, full paunched.*

Bastage: m. *A certaine toll exacted by some country Lords for euery horse that passes by them sadled with a packesaddle, though he carrie nothing else; for if hee doe, they take toll both for his saddle, and his burthen.*

Bastance. *Sufficiencie; what is ynough.*

Bastard: m. *A bastard; the brood of a whoore; the son of the people; one that came in at the window; also, a course bowlter for cheat bread; also, as* Bastardeau.

Bon bastard c'est avanture, mais meschant c'est de nature: Prov. *A bastard may bee good, but nature makes him bad.*

Bastard: m. de: f. *Bastardly, base borne, misbegotten; false, adulterate, counterfeit; not rightly bred; vnlawfully begotten.*

Couleur bastarde. *A weake, faint, pale, wan, decaied colour.*

Espée bastarde. *A short sword; or a sword that is not long ynough.*

Fenestre bastarde. *A false window.*

Bastardage: m. *Bastardie, bastardisme.*

Bastardaille: f. *Bastardie; also, bastards, or, a crue, or knot of bastards.*

Bastarde: f. *A demie Cannon, or demie Culuerin; a smaller peece of any kind.*

Bastardeau: m. *A damme, or water-stop, made of piles, &c.*

Bastardie. *as* Bastardise: ¶Norm.

Bastardiere: f. *A seed plot, nurse garden, or nurserie, wherein yong trees are set to bee afterwards remooued.*

Bastardise: f. *Bastardie, bastardisme; the breeding; state, condition, qualitie, of a bastard; also, the succession of bastards, or that which falls to the king by the death of a bastard.*

Baste: f. *A wily sleight or subtiltie, a craftie pranke; an odde tricke, or shrewd turne; also, the skirt of a doublet, &c.*

Basté: m. ée: f. *Sadled with a packesaddle.*

Baste. *(A Verbe Impersonall;) No more, tis ynough, it sufficeth, be how it be will.*

Basteau. *as* Bateau.

Bastelé: m. ée: f. *Jugled; buffoonized; tumbled; idly talked; also, tossed vncertainely vp and downe.*

Basteler. *To iugle, or tumble; also, to play the buffoone, or foole; to talke verie much, and verie idly; also, to tosse, or wander vncertainely vp and downe.*

Bastelerie: f. *Jugling; tumbling; puppet-playing; any such foolish pastime, or legerdemaine; also, buffoonisme.*

Bastelet: m. *A little boat.*

Basteleur: *A iugler, tumbler, puppet-player, one that professeth any of those arts; also, one that leades bears, apes, baboones, or dauncing dogges about the countrey, and gets a scuruie liuing by them.*

Basteleuse: f. *A woman that makes a profession of Jugling, Tumbling, and such other idle, or base exercises.*

Basteliere: f. *as* Bateliere.

Baster. *To saddle with a pannell, or packesaddle; also, to looke, or gaze, as out of a window; also, to serue, or suffice.*

Tant que l'ame me bastera au corps. *Whilest I haue breath in my bodie.*

Basti. *Looke* Basty.

Bastier: m. *A maker of packesaddles; also, a base lubberly fellow.*

Bastier: m. ere: f. *Vsually bearing, or sadled with, a packesaddle.*

Bastilde: f. *The fortresse, or fortification tearmed a bastillion, or bastile.*

Bastille. *as* Bastilde; *or, a fortresse, or castle furnished with towers, donion, and ditches; (in* Paris, la Bastille *is as our Tower, the chiefe prison of the kingdome.)*

Bastillon: m. *A bastillon, or little fortresse.*

Bastiment: m. *A building, frame, house, or edifice; also, a composition, or compaction of many things together.*

Bastine: f. *The skirt of a doublet, or coat; also, a pad; also, as* Bardelle; *also, a packsaddle.*

Bastion: m. *(The fortification tearmed) a Bastion, or Cullion-head.*

Bastionner. *To fortifie with Bastions.*

Bastir. *To build, make, frame, erect; raise, or set vp; also, to compose; contriue, deuise.*

Bastir à quelqu'vn son roulet. *To teach one before hand what he shall say or doe.*

Denier sur denier bastit la maison: Prov. *Pennie vpon pennie builds the house; by little and little great matters are effected, great workes finished.*

Bastissage: m. *A frame, a composition; a building, making, framing.*

Bastissant: m. **ante**: f. *Building, framing, making, rearing, erecting; composing; contriuing.*

Baston: m. *A staffe, bat, cudgell, trunchion; club; also, a sword, and (more generally) any weapon of offence; also, a Battune, in blazon; also, a stay, prop, supporter.*

Baston d'Adam. *Adams weapon; a mans yard.*

Baston cornu. *A battle-axe.*

Baston à deux bouts. *A quarter staffe; or, a staffe which hath a pike at both ends.*

Baston à feu. *A Harquebuse, Caleeuer, musket, &c.*

Baston pastoral. *Water plantaine; or as* Verge à berger.

Baston de potence. *Looke* Potence.

Baston rompu. à bastons rompus. *A cutting, pinking, lacing, &c, crosse billet fashion.*

Baston royal. *A kingly Scepter.*

`A dague & baston. *Large measure, heaped measure, measure with aduantage.*

Le tiers coup de baston. *The third (and last) knock of the Cryers staffe in an Outrope; and hence (metaphorically) that action, or effect, which absolutely carries a matter.*

Par rain, & baston. *By a bough and a bat; (a fashion of Liuerie and Seisin vsed in some places.)*

Estourdi de baston. *Looke* Estourdi.

Entendre le ru du baston. *To be a cunning Fencer, old beaten souldior; of much experience in the world.*

Faire mordre au baston. *To make the more eagar; or make to bite at the offered bait.*

Mettre la main au baston. *To dispossesse himselfe of an inheritance, by the deliuerie of a little rod or sticke to him vnto whom he passes it.*

Saulter le baston. *To do the deed; or, to performe, with resolution, an ineuitable exploit.*

Sçauoir bien le tour du baston. *To be subtile, craftie, cunning, of great experience; to know well how things are to be carried, or, how the world goes.*

Tirer au baston. *To struggle, wrastle, tug, striue, contend; also, to fight, or lay about him.*

Baston porte paix quant & soy: Prov. *A good bat makes peace where it comes; The like is:*

Comme vn faquin porte faix, ainsi le baston la paix.

Autant vaut aller à pied, que de cheuaucher vn baston maigre: Prov. *As good go a foot as ride on a leane iade.*

Qui de mastin fait son compere plus de baston ne doit porter: Prov. *He that makes a mastiue his gossip need not carrie a cudgell about him.*

Tel porte le baston dont à son regret le bat on: *Many a one prouides a rod for his owne taile, or wears a bat wherewith himselfe is beaten.*

Bastonnade: f. *A bastonadoe; a banging, or beating with a cudgell.*

Bastonnadé: m. **ée**: f. *Banged, bethwacked with a cudgell.*

Bastonné. *as* Bastonnadé; *Cudgelled.*

Bastonneau. *A little staffe, trunchion, cudgell, bat; a sticke, or great rod, or wand.*

Bastonnée: f. *The stroake of a pumpe in a ship.*

Bastonnement: m. *A beating, or banging with a cudgell.*

Bastonner. *To strike, beat, bang, bethwacke with a cudgell; to giue the bastonadoe vnto.*

Bastonnet. *as* Bastonneau; *Also, the bastonet of a bridle.*

Bastonnier: m. *A staffe-bearer, or Vergier; also the carrier of the Crucifix in Processions; also, a great man in any company.*

Bastonnier: m. **ere**: f. *Of, or belonging to, a staffe, &c; also, bearing a staffe; and hence,*

Sergent bastonnier. *A Mace-bearer, or Sergeant of the Mace.*

Basty: m. *A territorie, or demesne, belonging to a place.*

Basty: m. **ie**: f. *Builded, made, framed, composed, reared, or set vp.*

Bat: m. *A stroake, or beating.*

Batable: com. *Beatable; batterable; worthy, fit, or apt, to be beaten; which will indure hammering, as mettall; or may be battered with cannon, as a fortresse; &c; also, quarelsome, contentious, litigious; (for such a one comes by many a knocke, and wil, now and then, put vp all he comes by.)*

Batail de cloche. *A mill clapper.*

Bataille: f. *A battell, or fight betweene two armies; also, a battell, or maine battell; the middle battallion, or squadron of an armie, wherein the Prince, or Generall, most commonly, marcheth; also, the whole army; and sometimes also, any squadron, battallion, or part, thereof.*

C'est belle bataille de chiens, & de chats; chascun a des ongles: Prov. *The fairest battels are performed with edged tooles: (but that is onely when the combatants are not worth keeping.)*

Bataillé: m. **ée**: f. *Battelled, fought; also, clappered, or hung with a clapper.*

Batailler. *To battell, wage battell; fight, striue, contend.*

Bataillon: m. *A battallion, or squadron (of footmen.)*

Batallier: m. **ere**: f. *Battelling; for battels; of, or belonging to, battells.*

Batalogie: f. *Effeminate, obscene, or scurrile, discourse.*

Batans d'vn poisson. *The gill of a fish.*

Batant. *as* Batail; *A bell clapper; also, a batant; the peece of wood, that runnes all along vpon the edge of the lockeside of a doore, gate, or window.*

Vne port à deux batans. *A fowlding, or two leaued, doore.*

Batant. (partic. *of* batre;) *beating; battering; thrashing.*

Il arriua tout batant vers. *He came verie hastily, or very lately, towards; or (as in this phrase)* Ie viens de là encores tout batant: *I come thence but euen now; or, or,I pant still through the hast I made thence; or,it may be seene by my panting what hast I made, how lately I came, from thence.*

Il les chassa tout batant. *Hee pursued them verie hard*; &,Il les a mené batant iusques dans les portes de la ville. *He gaue them a hot,and bloudie chace, euen vnto the gates of the towne.*

Bat-beurre: m. *A Churne-staffe.*

Bate: f. *A Rammer; a Pauers beetle; a Dawbers beater; th'instrument wherewith floores of earth are setled,and beaten leuell.*

Bateau: m. *A boat.*

Bateau mere. *Looke* Mere.

Estourdi de bateau. *Extreamly benummed,and therby vnfit,or vnreadie,for a suddaine imployment.*

Nous menerons le bateau d'un'autre sorte.*We will handle the businesse,or carrie the matter,after another manner.*

Batelage: m. *Iugling,Legerdemaine.*

Batelée. vne batelée de,&c; *a boatfull of.*

Batelleresque: com. *Iugling,or Iugler-like.*

Batelerie: f. *as* Bastelerie.

Batelet: m. *A little boat,or skiffe.*

Bateleur. *as* Basteleur.

Batelier: m. *A boatman,shipman,skipper.*

Bateliere: f. *A ferrie-woman,or boat-woman.*

Batellé. *Clappered; said of a Bell; in* Blason.

Batemare: f. *A wagtayle,or water Swallow.*

Batement: m.*A beating,thwacking,lamming,bumping, swindging,battering; also, a threshing.*

Le batement de la mer. *The working of the sea; also, the ebbing thereof.*

Baterie: f. *A beating; or batterie.*

Bateur: m. *A beater, cudgeller, swindger; also, a thresher.*

Bateurs d'estrade.*The forragers,or forerunners of an Armie.*

Bateur d'or. *A gold-drawer,or gold-layer.*

Bateur de pavez. *An idle, or continuall walke-street; a ietter abroad in the streets; one that sees the towne serued when honest men are in bed; a lasciuious, or vnthrifty,night-walker;generally,any loose or mad youth, dissolute or disorderly yonker.*

La grange est prés des bateurs. *(Said of a Nunnerie thats neere vnto a Fryerie;) the Barne stands neere the Threshers.*

Batisé. *as* Baptisé.

Batiture de fer. *The skales that flye from yron in the hammering thereof.*

Batoir: m. *A rammer,or pauing beetle; also, a Launderesses batting staffe; also,a threshing floore,or threshing place; also,a fulling Mill.*

Batre: m. *(Substantiuely) a beating; and hence;*

Au batre faut l' amour: Prov. *Much loue is lost by them that beat their loues.*

Batre.*To beat;thwack,bumpe,swindge,cudgell,belamme; also,to batter.* (Frapper est d'un coup donné,batre de plusieurs coups iterez. Nicot.)

Batre de l' aile. *To smell ranke, or strong; (especially at th'arme-holes.)*

Ne batre plus que d'une aile. *To be halfe vndone; to rest but vpon one only assurance; to haue but one helpe left him.*

Batre le beurre. *To churne.*

Batre le bled. *To thresh.*

Batre aux champs. *To forrage, to make a road,to seek for bootie,or a prey abroad.*

Batre les chemins. *To belay the way, as pursetakers and boothalers doe.*

Batre le chien devant le Lyon. *To punish a meane person in the presence,and to the terror,of a great one.*

Batre sa coulpe. *See* Coulpe.

Batre les draps. *To full clothes.*

Batre l'eau. *To loose his labour, or imploy his time to no purpose.*

Batre les eaux. *A Deere to take soyle.*

Batre leur eau.*To disgest,or shake down,their drinke, (by exercise) as horses which be ridden two or three miles after they haue beene watered.*

Batre les flancs. *To pant hard for want of breath.*

Batre à froid.*To worke out a thing with great paines, or toyle,as a Smith,that frames a thing out of cold yron; also,as* Bransler la pigue.

Batre la laine. *To leacher,to haire-beat it.*

Batre la lictiere. *A horse to rest,or continue long,in the stable.*

Batre le pavé. *See* Pavé.

Batre à tout poulmon. *To pant extreamely, to be almost out of breath.*

Batre les rues. *To reuell,iet,or swagger vp and down the streets,a nights.*

Batre le tambour avec les dents.*To chatter,didder, say an Apes Paternoster.*

Se batre. *To fight, combat, bicker, goe to it (at sharpe.)*

S'en batre les ioues. *To repent throughly, or afflict himselfe cruelly, for.*

Ils se faisoient batre à credit. *They got themselues a cudgelling without any purpose; or, being out of loue with their ease, they would needs take vp a cudgelling on their credits.*

Occasion trouve qui son chat bat: Pro.*He that will beat his cat,inuents a cause for't.*

Qui ueut batre son chien trouve assez de bastons: Prov. *(Almost of the same sence; or as we say;) Tis an easie matter to find a staffe to beat a dog withall.*

Tel porte le baston dont à son grand regret le bat on: Prov. *Many a one carries about him a cudgell for his owne shoulders.*

Bat-sain. *A rude allarum giuen to a whole countrey by ringing,and beating of pots,kettles,basons,&c.*

Battans d'un poisson. *The gylls of a fish.*

Batte: f. *The boulster of a Saddle.*

Les battes d'une porte. *as* les Batans.

Battecul: m. *A great linnen vaile,such as Nunnes weare.*

Batteler. *To iugle,&c; as* Basteler.

Battelerie: f. *as* Bastelerie.

Battelessisue: f. *The little yellow water-wagtaile.*

Battequeuë. *The same.*

Batterie: f. *as* Baterie; *also, a Platforme for batterie.*

Batteur. *See* Bateur.

Battier: m. *A hackney,or hired iade.*

Battre. *Looke* Batre.

Battu. *Looke* Batu.

Battue: f. *A beating, or stroke with the feet, in a setled, and proportioned time; (a tearme of horsemanship.)*

Batture: f. *A stripe,a stroke; a beating.*

Batture de bronze. *The skales that flye from brasse while it is hammered.*

Battus. *Looke* Batus.

Batu: m. uë: f. *Beaten; knocked, thwacked, bumped; swindged, belammed, cudgelled; also, battered; also, threshed; also,churned.*

Batu de mauuais vent. *Vnfortunate, vnhappie, disgracefull; euer hinderd, or crossed by one mischiefe or other.*
Le batu paye l'amende. *Looke* Amende.
De telles verges ils sont tous batus. *The same disease afflicts, or sicknesse infects, them all.*
Autant pleure mal batu que bien batu: Pro. *As much weepes he thats but sleightly, as he thats shrewdly, beaten; (whereunto agrees;)*
Mal batu longuement pleure: Prov.
Tel menace qui est batu: Prov *One may threaten, and be well swindged whe he hath done; (we say, threatened folkes liue long.)*
Batuë: f. *as* Battuë.
Bature. *A beating; stripe &c; as* Batture; *or,* Batement.
Batus. *An order of Friers, which in their nightly Processions whip their owne backes extreamely; (A sect of people bearing this name, and whipping themselues twice in the day, and once in the night, were driuen out of* Germanie *by* Charles, *sonne to the Emperor* Henry *the seuenth.)*
Bau. La nauire a tant de pieds de bau. *The ship is so many foot broad, or wide.*
Bau de bite. *The forepike; the part of a ship wherein the Bitts are placed.*
Bavard: m. *A driueller, or slauerer; also, a babler; also, a flouter.*
Bavarder. *To driuell, or slauer; also, to bable; also, to scoffe, or flout at.*
Bavardise: f. *Slauering; also, a babling; also, a mockerie, gullerie, flout, or ieast.*
Bavasse: f. *An idle tale, vaine tatle, bible bable.*
Bavasser. *To prattle, tattle, bable, se many words.*
Baubance: f. *Looke* Bobance.
Baube. *A pratler, babler, iangler, tatler.*
Bauboyant. Parolle tremblante, & bauboyante; *Faultring.*
Bauc: m. *A sot, asse, doult, dull-pated noddipeake, heauieheaded cokes, grosse-headed coxcombe.*
Baucal, *or* Baucale: m. *A glasse-violl, water-glasse, or cruze; (great bellied, long necked, and narrow mouthed.)*
Bauch. *as* Bauc.
Bauche: f. *A rew, ranke, lane, or course, of stones, or bricks, in building.*
Baucher. *To chip, hew, or square, timber, &c; also, to ranke, order, array; lay euenly.*
Baucheron: m. *A cleauer, chipper, or squarer of timber; he that doth the first work thats to be done vpon a piece of timber.*
Baucie: f. *The root of a Parsenip, or Carrot.* (v.m.)
Baud: m. baude: f. *Bold, insolent, impudent.* (v.m.)
Baude: com. *Merrie, blithe, iocond, iolly, cheerefull, glad, full of glee.*
Baude-bite. *Looke* Bau.
Baudement. *Merrily, iocondly, blithely, iollily, in all freedome, and fulnesse, of ioy.*
Baudere d'une sallade. *The beauer.*
Baudet: m. *An asse; or a tearme for an asse; whence, a blockhead, a sot, a doult, a dull fellow.*
Baudiner. *Two to ride vpon one asse, or horse; also, to teach, vnskilfully, one knowes not what; to do, any way, like an asse.*
Baudir. *To gladden, hearten, reioyce, exhilerate, cheere vp.*
Baudoüinage. *Asse-leacherie; th'act of generation performed by an asse.*
Baudoüiner. *To doe, leacher, or ingender, like an Asse.*
Baudrayer. *as* Baudroyer.
Baudrayeur. *as* Baudroyeur; *also, a belt, or baudricke, maker.*
Baudrer. *as* Bailler. (v.m.)
Baudri. *as* Baudrier, substan.
Baudrié. *Curried, and coloured, as a Cow-hide.*
Baudrier: m. *A hide, skin, or peece, of dressed, curried, and coloured Cowes-leather; also, a belt, baudricke, or sword-girdle of that leather.*
Baudrier. *To dresse; currie, and colour, the hides of kine, &c; also, to make belts, or baudricks.*
Baudroy: m. *A rauenous, and ougly fish, called, the Seatoad.*
Baudroyer. *To dresse, or currie leather, &c; as* Baudrier.
Baudroyerie: f. *(Th'art of) dressing, or currying of leather; also, baudrick-making; also, a place, or street, wherein curriers, or belt-makers, dwell.*
Baudroyeur: m. *A leather-dresser; a currier, and colourer of leather; also, a maker of belts, or baudricks.*
Baudryeur. *as* Baudroyeur.
Bauds: m. *A kind of white hounds; Looke* Souilliard.
Bauduffle: f. *The great rush wherewith poore houses are thatched; also, litter, or bedungued straw.*
Bave: f. *Foame, froath; slauer, driuell.*
Baver. *To foame, froath; slauer, driuell at the mouth; also, to famble, or falter in speaking; also, to toy, dally, trifle, ieast.*
Baverelles: f. *The players of a horses bitt.*
Baverette: f. *A bib, mocket, or mocketer to put before the bosome of a (slauering) child.*
Baverette à babillons. *The plate whereat a bitts players hang; the flap to hang the players at.*
Baverie: f. *A foaming, froathing, slauering, or driuelling at the mouth; also, a trifling, toying, ieasting; idle talking; flouting, mocking.*
Baverole: f. *A bib; as* Baverette.
Baverotte. *as* Baverette.
Bavesche: f. *The socket of a candlesticke, &c.*
Bavette. *as* Baverette.
Baveur. *as* Bavard.
Baveuse: f. *A certain skalelesse fish, that couers her selfe when she lifts with her owne foame.*
Baveusement. *Foamingly, slaueringly, froathily.*
Baveux: m. euse: f. *Froathie, foamie, foaming.*
Plus baveux qu'un pot à moustarde. *We say, foaming at the mouth like a boare.*
Bauffrer. *To rauine, deuour, eat greedily.*
Bauffreur: m. *A rauener, deuourer, glutton, greedie feeder.*
Bauffreure: f. *A rauening, deuouring, greedie feeding.*
Apres les premieres baffreures. *After the first bits greedily let down; or, after we had stayed our stomacks with a snatch or two.*
Bauffroy: m. *A watch-tower; or, as* Beffroy.
Bauge: m. *Dawbing, or morter, made of clay, and straw; also, a heape of durt, or of mud; also, a Slough; or, the place wherein a wild bore hath wallowed, or lien.*
Retirer les hommes des bauges. *To withdraw men from sensualitie, beastly liuing, or filthie humors.*
Baugeart: m. *A scowndrell; a scuruie, or beastly companion.*
Baviere: f. *A bib, &c; as* Baverette; *also, a Germane Dukedome, called* Baveere.
Baviere d'un armet. *The beauer of a helmet.*

Faire le voyage de Baviere. *To get the Pockes; or, to trauell for them.*
Bauldrier. *as* Baudrier.
Bauldrieur. *Looke* Baudrieur.
Bauldroy: m. *The sea-toad, or diuell of the sea; an ougly, and rauenous fish.*
Baulme: m. *Baulme; also, Balme-mint, Speare-mint, Garden-mint.*
Baulme crespu. *Crispe balme, crosse mint, curled mint.*
Baulme sauvage. *Horse-mint, wild mints, water-mints.*
Baulme: m. *Baulme, or* Balsamum. *Looke* Basme.
Baulme de Iesus Christ. *An excellent balme, made of the best oyle, and old wine.*
Bois de baulme. *The sweet wood of the Balsame tree.*
Baume: m. *as* Baulme.
Baume: f. *A hole, denne, caue, grot.*
Bavois: m. *A Table, or Paper, containing th' estimate of the rights of* Seigneuriage, Foiblage, *and* Brassage, *according to the seuerall rates of gold, siluer, and bullion, then currant, or made currant by the kings Ordinances.*
Bavoler. *To wag, wauer; flicker, or flye low, like a gnat in Vintage time.*
Bavolet: m. *A Billiment, or head-attire, worne by the women of* Picardie; *also, a Shittle-cocke.*
Bavoleté. Chambriere bavoletée. *A shittle-braind, or giddie-headed wench; also, one that weares a* Bavolet.
Bavon: m. *A bib, mocket, or mocketer, for the bosome of a slauering child, &c.*
Bavouer. *as* Bavois.
Bauracineux: m. euse: f. *Salt; or clammie; (from the minerall* Borax; *which the Arabians tearme* Baurach.)
Baus: m. *as* Bauds; *also, the beames, or floore-timbers, of a ship; the great pieces of timber that lye from side to side, within the Hould.*
Bausme: m. *The Baulme tree, or Balsame tree; also, Baulme it selfe; Looke* Baulme.
Bausouïns: m. *Streamers (in ships, &c.)*
Baut: m. Baude: f. *as* Baude; *iocond, merrie, blithe.*
Bay: m. Baye: f. *Bay, of colour.*
Le bay à miroir. *A bright-dapled bay.*
Bayard: m. *A man that gapes, or gazes earnestly at a thing; a flye-catcher, a greedie and vnmannerly beholder.*
Bayarde: f. *A woman that earnestly beholds, greedily eyes, eagerly lookes, and in looking gapes, at a thing; a gazing houswife.*
Bayart: m. *as* Bayard; *also, a basket, or dosser, vsed for the carrying of earth, and fastened, for the same purpose, about the necke with two leatherne thongs.*
Bayart: m. arde: f. *as* Bay, *(whence wee also tearme a bay horse, a bayard.)*
Baybaye: f. *A scornefull moe, or mouth made.*
Baye: f. *A lye, fib, foist, gull, rapper; a cosening tricke, or tale; also, a berrie; also, the cloth called Bayes; also, a bay of land.*
Repaistre de bayes. *Looke* Repaistre.
Bayer. *To gape, or open the mouth very wide; also, to stand gaping, and gazing about, as home-bred hoidons doe when they come into an honourable presence; (hence) also, to behold wistly; also, to couet greedily, eagerly to gape after; Looke* Béer.
Bayeul: m. *as* Bahu; *a Trunke.*
Bayeure: f. *A gaping, or yawning; a holding, or setting of the mouth wide open.*
Bayle: m. *as* Bailli, *or as* Baile; *a Bayliffe.* ¶Gasc.
Bayonnette: f. *A kind of small flat pocket-dagger, furnished with kniues; or a great knife to hang at the girdle, like a dagger.*
Bayonnier. *as* Arbalestier. *(an old word.)*
Bazane: f. *Sheepes leather dressed like Spanish leather, and coloured red, greene, or yellow, &c, for shoes, or the couerings of bookes.*
Bazaner. *as* Besanner; *also, to blot, staine, or besmeare, (as with blacking;) to bleake, to beduske.*
Se bazaner. *To wax bleake, tawnie, swart, blackish.*
Bazanne. *as* Bazane.
Bazaveresque: f. *The name of a delicate Italian Peare thats ripe in August.*
Baze: f. *A Basis, or Base; the ground, foundation, root, or foot of a thing; Looke* Base.
Bazenne. *as* Bazane.
Bazette. Toile baz. *(Linnen) cloth which is but halfe white, or hath not beene throughly whitened.*
Bazilles: f. *Rocke Sampire, Crestmarine.*
Bazoche. *Looke* Basoche.
Beant: m. ante: f. *Gaping, opening the mouth wide; also, gazing wistly, vnmannerly, or affectionately at.*
Bearn. *A Prouince of* Aquitaine, *seated at the root, or foot, of the Pyrenean mountaines.*
Cape de Bearn. *See* Cape.
C'est la loy du pays de Bearn que le batu paye l'amende: Prov. *The custome of* Bearne *is, that he thats beaten shall pay for the bloudwipe.*
Beat: m. ate: f. *Happie, blessed, holy, sacred; perfect; excellent.*
Beat pere. *as* Beaupere.
Habit de beat, ongles de chat: Prov. *A wolfe in a sheepes skin.*
Beatifié: m. ée: f. *Beatified; made blessed.*
Beatifier. *To beatifie; to make blessed, sacred, or happie.*
Beatiles: f. *as* Beatilles.
Beatilles: f. *Trinkets, or vaine toyes, wherewith finicall people decke themselues; trifles, nifles, odde attires, also, women of a low stature.*
Beatitude: f. *Beatitude, blessednesse, happinesse, felicitie, fulnesse of perfection, perfect goodnesse, or tranquilitie.*
Beau: m. *as* Beauté; *(whence;)*
Quand beau vient sur beau, beau perd sa beauté: Prov. *Beautie set off by beautie lookes beastly; or, beautie vsed as a foyle to beautie soyles it.*
Beau: m. belle: f. *Beautious, faire, beautifull; seemely, comely; proper, handsome, gracefull; of a goodly presence, of a sweet aspect, of a pleasing dye, or hue.*
Belle dame. *A kind of Dwale, or sleeping Nightshade.*
Tout beau. *Take you leisure, soft and faire, not too fast; hold there hoe; ynough's as good as a feast.*
'A beau ieu bel argent. *Round play, in good earnest, in good proportion; to good purpose; or, one for another; as in;*
'A beau ieu beau retour. *A tit for a tat, a tut for a tush, as good euery whit as was brought.*
I'ay beau attendre. *I stay to much purpose; here's goodly tarrying sure; I shall but loose my labor, how long soeuer I tarrie.*
Il a beau faire chois de. *He hath good leaue to chuse.*
Il a beau se leuer tard. *He may lye long ynough; he may get vp as late as he will. Seeke* Leuer.
Ils l'avoyent beau flatter. *They were glad, or faine, they held it their best course, to flatter him.*

Baillez

Baillez luy belle. *Goodly betide him; some bodie spit in his mouth, for now he hath hit it sure.*
Il luy l'a baillé belle. *He hath sold him a bargaine, he hath giuen him the boots, a gleeke, or gudgeon.*
Il l'avoit failli belle. *He scaped faire, or missed it narrowly; he was very neere it, he was very like to haue had, or hit, it.*
Beau chanter souvent enuye: Prov. *Sweet singing often loathes vs.*
Belle chere &c. *Looke* Chere.
Belle chose est tost ravie: Pro. *A goodly thing is quickly snatched vp.*
Belle femme mauvaise teste: Pro. *Faire women either curst, or cruell, be.*
Les beaux hommes au gibet: Pro. *The gibbet makes an end of proper men.*
Petites pucelles sont ensemble belles: Prov. *Looke* Pucelle.
Qui viẽt est beau, qui apporte encores plus beau: Prov. *No man's esteemd so faire as he that comes full-handed.*
Beaucoup. *Much, greatly, a great deale; also, many.*
Beaucoup offrir à vn qui peu demande, c'est luy nier tout à plat sa demande: Prov. *To offer much to him that asketh little, is flatly to denie him the little he asketh.*
Trois beaucoup, & trois peu destruisent l'homme: Pro. viz. *To speake much, and know but little; to spend much, and haue but little; to presume vpon much, and deserue but little.*
Beau-fils: m. *A step-sonne, or sonne in law; Seeke* Fils.
Beau-frere: m. *A brother in law.*
Beau-pere: m. *The title of a Frier which is a Confessor; also, a father in law; also, a father that hath bestowed all his children in mariage.*
Beaupré. *The sprit-sayle of a ship.*
Beauregard: m. *A Summer house, or Graunge; a house for pleasure, and recreation.*
Beauté: f. *Beautie, fairenesse, sweetnesse of fauor; comelinesse, goodlinesse, gracefulnesse.*
Beauté Grecque. *See* Grec.
Beauté sans bonté est comme vin esventé: Prov. *Beautie without goodnesse is like wine that hath taken wind.*
Beauté de femme fascheux resveille-matin: Prov. *A (wanton) womans beautie breeds a restlesse morning.*
Beauté & folie vont souvent de compaigne: Prov. *Beautie and folly are often matcht together.*
Fy de ieunesse, & de beauté desgarnie d' humilité: Pro. *Looke* Fy.
Quand beau vient sur beau beau perd sa beauté: Pro. *Beautie layed on beautie lookes beastly.*
Beauvois. *The name of a fruitfull red Vine.*
Bec: m. *The beake, or bill of a bird, &c; also, a Point of land at which two riuers meet.*
Bec à broüet. *A little pratling peart girle; a prattle-basket.*
Bec d'Asne. *A toole belonging to a Mason.*
Bec de Cane. *A kind of Pinsers, made like a duckes beake; and toothed within to hold a bullet (for the drawing out whereof it is vsed) the more firmely; See* Cane.
Souliers à bec de cane. *Old-fashioned shoes hauing long peakes, like beakes, sticking out for their toe-peece.*
Bec de Cicoigne. *The hearb Storks-bill, Pink-needle, Cranes bill, Hearons bill.*
Bec de Corbin. *A Pensioners halberd, or pollax; also, a Surgeons toole made like the beake of that bird; also, the anterior production of the shoulder blade; (so tearmed by some Anatomists.)*
Bec de cigne. *A Swans-bill; a Pinser, or Instrument, wherewith Surgeons pull bullets, &c, out of the bodie.*
Bec de faulcon. *A fashion of Pollax borne by the Peeres of* France, *and by the French kings Pensioners; Looke* Faulcon.
Bec de grue. *as* Bec de Cicoigne; *also, a Surgeons toole made like a Cranes bill.*
Bec iaulne. *See* Bejaune.
Bec de la lampe; *The socket, or snuffe of the lampe.*
Bec large. *as* Bec de Cane.
Bec de lezard. *An instrument wherewith Surgeons draw out bullets, and the splents of bones.*
Bec de lieure. *An vpper lip cleft vp to the nose.*
Bec d'oye. *Wild tansie, siluer weed; also, the Porpoise, or Sea-hog.*
Bec de perroquet. *A Parrats beake; a Pinser which opens, and shuts with a Vice; and serues to pull splints of bones, and other hard things, out of the bodie.*
Coup de bec. *A peck, bob, iob, or stroke with the beake of an angrie bird; and (metaphorically) a flout, scoffe, gird, nip, cut; also, a mischiefe, iniurie, or ill turne, done; also, a kisse.*
Oiseau de bec. *A Parasite, or Buffoone.*
Tour de bec. *A kisse; also, a word of the mouth.*
Avoir bon bec. *To speake discreetly, answere warily, aduisedly, or cunningly.*
Avoir le bec gelé. *To be tongue-tyed, silent, husht, as if his lips were frosen together.*
Elles n'ont que le bec. *They are all tongue, they can doe nought but prate, bable, tatle; or, they are but a little snout-faire, all their rest is not worth looking at.*
Il a bien d'autre paille au bec. *There's other kind of stuffe in him; he is another manner of man, then you thinke of.*
Faillir par le bec. sa cause ne faillira par le bec. *His matter will not be lost for want of words.*
Faire le bec à vn. *To teach one before hand what he shall say.*
Il luy passa la plume par le bec. *He drew his penne through his lips; he baffled, rid, gulled, abused him.*
Tenir le bec en l'eau. *To dally with; to delay, amuse, or hold in suspence.*
Il n'a pas tenu le bec en l' eau. *A man may safely say, he is drunke; but he that sayes, with water, wrongs him.*
Becasse: f. *A Woodcocke; See* Beccasse.
Becasseau, Becassine, & Becasson. *A Snite, or Snipe.*
Beccane. *A kind of blacke grape which yeeldeth an excellent wine.*
Beccard. *The female Salmon.*
Beccasse: f. *A Woodcocke.*
Beccasse de mer. *The sea Pie; also, a kind of fish.*
Beccasse petite. *A Snite, or Snipe.*
Beccassé: m. ée: f. *Gulled, abused, woodcockised, made a woodcocke.*
Beccasseau: m. *A Snite; also, a little Woodcocke.*
Beccassine: f. *as* Beccasseau; *a Snite, or Snipe.*
Beccasson: m. *The same.*
Beccu: m. ue: f. *Beaked; hauing a beake; beake-like; sharpe, or hooked, as a birds bill.*
Addition beccuë. *The elbow; tearmed so by some Anatomists.*

Beccusse: f. *A tumult, vprore, hurrie, hurliburly.*
Becdasse. ¶Rab. *as* Beccasse.
Becdoye. *A Dolphin.*
Becfigue. *The daintie little bird, called by some, a Gnat-snapper, or Fig-eater; (I rather thinke, that wanting the bird, as we doe, we want also a name for it.)*
Beche: f. *An instrument of Husbandrie, &c, hauing a crooked, or in-bending, and beake-like, head; and vsed for the opening, or breaking vp, of hard, or stony ground, whereinto the* Besche *(or spade) cannot enter.*
Bechebois: m. *A Speight, or Wood-picker.*
Bechée: f. *A beake-full, or bill-full of; also, the pecking of an angrie bird.*
Becher. *as* Bescher.
Bechet. *as* Brochet; *A Pike-fish.*
Bechevet. teste à teste Bechevet. *The play with pins, called, heads, and points; also, the lying of two in a bed, the one right, the other with his head at the feet; See* Beschevet.
Becheur. *as* Bescheur.
Bechique: f. *A medicine for the Cough.*
Bechistre. *A tempest, or storme.*
Bechu: m. uë: f. *Beaked; hauing a beake, like a bird, hooked, or sharpe, as a beake.*
Bechus. *A kind of deformed thing in the sea, thats neither fish, nor plant, yet seemes to moue of it selfe.* ¶Langued.
Becquade: f. *A pecke, iob, or bob with a beake.*
Becque: f. *A ditch, or trench made vpon the high way; (also, as* Beche. ¶Norm.)
Becqué. *Beaked; a tearme of Heraldrie.*
Becquebo. *A Woodpecker, or Highaw.*
Becquée. *as* Bechée.
Becquefigue. *as* Becfique.
Becquer. *To pecke, or bob with the beake.*
Becquet. *The name of an apple thats good to be eaten raw; also, a Pike (fish;) Looke* Bequet.
Becquetant: m. ante: f. *Pecking, as a bird; also, nodding with the head; also, playing, or checking, like a horse, with the mouth.*
Faim **becquetante**. *Biting, or pricking, hunger.*
Becqueté: m. ée: f. *Pecked, or iobbed at.*
Becquetement: m. *A pecking; also, a nodding; also, a checking with the mouth.*
Becqueter. *To pecke, like a bird; also, to nod with the head; also, a horse to play, or checke with the mouth.*
Becquillon: m. *A little beake, or bill.*
Becu. *as* Bechu.
Bedacier: m. ere: f. *Beadle-like; of, or belonging to, a Beadle.*
Bedaine: f. *A short barre of steele, or of yron; also, a forked arrow for a Crosse-bow; also, ill lucke; also, a fat guts, or gorbellie; also, the belly; and hence;*
Prendre **bedaine** sur la plaine. *To take the measure of his belly on the ground; or, to fall on his belly.*
Bedat. bois b. ou vedat. *An inclosed wood; a wood that lyes not open, or, is not common.*
Bedaud: m. *A fedle, minion, fauourite; a dilling, or darling.*
Mon petit **bedaud**. *My pretie ape, my little bullie.*
Bedeau: m. *A Beadle; a Verger; also, (in* Normandie, *and other places) an vnder Bayliffe, or yeoman to a Sergeant; or Catchpole inferior to the Sergeant.*
Bedegar: m. *Our Ladies thistle.*
Bedengue. *A certaine apple, that yeelds most excellent cyder.*
Bedier: m. *A doult, sot, cokes, ninnie, noddie.*
Deniers avancent les **bediers**: Prov. *Money aduanceth Meacockes.*
Bedon: m. *A Tabret; also, the belly.*
Mon **bedon**. *My pretie rogue, my sweet bully.*
Ce que dit le **bedon**, a de credit son: Prov. *The belly must also be listned vnto; the appetite beares great sway in all humane actions.*
Bedondaine: f. *That part of the belly which is between the nauell, and priuities.*
Bedonner. *To play vpon a taber.*
Bedoual. *as* Bedouau.
Bedouau. *A young Brocke, or Badger; also, a sea-cob, or sea-gull.*
Bedoue. *A Gray, Brocke, Boson, Badger.*
Bée: f. *The bleating of a sheepe; also, a hole, ouerture, or opening, in the wall, or other part, of a house &c.*
Bée. gueule **bée**. *Gaping, with an open mouth.*
Beelant. *A sheepe.* ¶Barr.
Beellement: m. *A bleating; or, the crie of a sheepe.*
Beeller. *To bleat, or crie, like a sheepe.*
Beement: m. *A gaping.*
Been: m. *An Arabian Plant, of two kinds,* viz. *a white, and a red one; (which difference is bred onely by their roots.)*
Been blanc. *The white (Arabian) Bene; Some of our moderne Herballists call frothie Poppie, or spatling Poppie, white Bene.*
Been rouge. *The red (Arabian) Bene; the same Herballists call, red Valerian, or Cow-basill; and others, Limeworte, or Catch-flye, red Bene; all improperly.*
Béer. *To gape, or open the mouth very wide; Looke* Bayer.
Béer contre vn four. *is, in effect, as much as, To halt before a criple, or speake Latine before clerkes.*
Befflé: m. ée: f. *Deceiued, mocked, gulled.*
Beffler. *To deceiue, mocke, or gull, with faire words, &c.*
Beffleries: f. *Fooleries, mockeries, gudgeons, gulleries.*
Beffroy: m. *A Beacon, or, a Watch-tower, from which things may be discerned farre off; also, an Allarum bell; also, a suddaine feare; also, a place wherein wild beasts are kept; Looke* Baffroy.
Begauder. *To loyter.*
Begayement: m. *A fambling, or maffling in the mouth; and (most properly) the imperfect pronunciation of a child, that begins, or but learnes, to speake.*
Beguayer. *To famble, fumble, maffle in the mouth; to speake imperfectly, or, as a child, that but begins to speake.*
Begude: f. *A Cote, Cottage, thatched shed, or shelter.*
Begue: f. *A Sea-mew.*
Begue: com. *Fambling, fumbling, maffling in the mouth; imperfectly, or childishly, speeking.*
Navire **begue**. *A ship whose stemme, beake, or nose is pointed with yron, or brasse.*
Beguée: m. *as* Beguer.
Beguer: m. *A Sergeant, or Officer, that executes the Commaundements giuen, and Commissions sent out, by the publicke Magistrate.* ¶Bearnois.
Begueyement. *as* Begayement.
Begueyer. *as* Beguayer.
Beguin: m. *A Biggin for a child.*
Beguines: f. *An Order of Nunnes, or religious women, who commonly be all old, or well in yeares.*
Beguiner. *To put on a Biggin.*
Beguoyement. *as* Begayement.
Behen. *A very cordiall root; of two sorts; white, and red; Looke* Ben.
Behistre. *A horrible storme, or tempest in the aire.* ¶Pic.

Be-

Behistreux: m. euse: f. *Tempestuous, raging, stormie.*

Behourd: m. *A Iuste, or Tourney of many together with launces, and battleaxes; also, a bustling, or blustering noyse.*

Behourdir. *To iust together with launces, &c, to make a bustling, or blustering noise.*

Behourdis: m. *A bustling, rombling, iusting of many men together; also, a blustering of winds.*

Feu de behourdis. *A bone-fire.*

Bejaunage: m. *Simplicitie, want of experience, lacke of knowledge, vnskilfulnesse; doltishnesse, sottishnesse.*

Bejaune: m. *A nouice; a late prentise to, or yong begin-ginner in, a Trade, or Art; also, a simple, ignorant, vnexperienced, Asse; a rude, vnfashioned, home-bred hoydon; a sot, ninnie, doult, noddie; one thats blankt, and hath nought to say, when hee hath most need to speake.*

Payer son bejaune. *To pay his welcome; a fee exacted, by schollers, of such as are newly admitted into their societie.*

Bejaunerie: f. *as* Bejaunage.

Bejaunise: f. *Simplicitie, young ignorance, vnskilfulnesse, want of experience; sottishness, doltishnesse.*

Beignet; *Corruptly, for* Bignet. ¶Rab.

Beille. *as* Begue.

Beillottes: f. *Akornes; or, Oake-apples.*

Beisle: m. *Th'Orelop, or vnder-hatches, of a ship.*

Bel: m. belle: f. *Faire &c; as* Beau.

Belaud. *as* Bedaud; *or, a fedle, minion, fauourite.*

Belenne. *A certaine little, skale-lesse, great-headed, small-mouthed, and sharpe-beaked, fish of the Mediterranean, or Grecian sea; and there but rare; in our sea neuer seene.*

Beler. *as* Beeller. *To blayte.*

Beleter. *as* Beeller.

Belette: f. *A Weesill.*

Belette Ictide. *Authors agree not what beast this is; The old ones, and most of their interpretors hold it to be the Ferret; others, a Fitch, or Fullmart; others (least probably) an Otter, or water Weesill.*

Beliard: m. *A Ramme.*

Belic. *A kind of red, or gueules, in* Blazon.

Belier: m. *A Ramme; also, th'ancient Engine of batterie so called.*

Belier marin. *The sea Ramme; a great, and rauenous fish, enemie to fishermen.*

Beliers d'un pressoüer. *The branches; the two greatest beames of a Presse.*

Chiches de belier. *Rammes Citches, blacke Citches.*

Couille de belier. *A ball made of a Rammes cod.*

Belin. *as* Belier. *A Ramme.*

Mascher en belin. *To mumble, as one that wants teeth.*

Beliné: m. ée: f. *Rammed; also, cosened, beguiled, gulled.*

Beliner. *To ramme; also, to cosen, beguile, deceiue, gull.*

Belinge: m. *as* Tiretaine. ¶Norm.

Belistraille: f. *A crue of beggars; a base, or beggarly crue.*

Belistre: m. *A beggar, vagabond, scowndrell, ragamuffian, poore knaue, needie rogue.*

Belistreau: m. *A little, or young beggar.*

Belistréement. *Beggarly, beggingly, basely, vagabond-like.*

Belistrer. *To beg from dore to dore; to play the beggar, or base fellow.*

Belistrerie: f. *Begging, beggarie, beggarlinesse; also, a leud, base, or filthie act; also, a thing of little, or no worth.*

Belistresse: f. *A woman Beggar; a Doxie, Morte, base Queane.*

Belitresse. *(Adiectiuely) begging, importunate, beggar-like, or beggarly.*

Belitraille. *as* Belistraille.

Belitre. *as* Belistre; *a beggar; &c.*

Belitrer. *as* Belistrer; *to beg; &c.*

Belitrerie. *as* Belistrerie.

Bellastre: com. *Fairish, reasonably faire, passable, so so, somewhat like.*

Bellateur: m. *A Warrior; a professed Souldior.*

Bellatrice: f. *A* Virago, *or Warrioresse.*

Belle. *The feminine of* Bel, *or of* Beau; *Looke* Beau.

Belle-dame. *Great Nightshade; or, a kind of Dwale, or sleeping Nightshade.*

Belle-fille: f. *A step-daughter; (Looke* Fille;) *also, the name of a certaine great, and white sweet apple.*

Bellement. *Fairely, beautifully; also, softly, gently, easily, at leisure, by little and little.*

Belle-mere: f. *A step-mother, or (most properly) a mother in law; as, the wiues mother, in regard of the husband, &c.*

Belleque: f. *A Coot.*

Bellette. *as* Belette.

Bellettement. *Pretily; also, faire and softly; at leisure, by little and little.*

Belle-vidcre. *The flower called Blew bells; or, as* Belvedere.

Bellic. *as* Belic.

Bellin. *as* Belin.

Belliqueusement. *Martially, warlikely; warfaringly.*

Belliqueux: m. euse: f. *Warlike, martiall, valorous, full of prowesse, valiant in armes; warfaring, fit for warre.*

Belliric: m. *A round Mirabolan plumme, somewhat lesse then the* Chebule.

Bellistrandie: f. *Beggarie, vagabondrie, roguerie.*

Bellistrandier: m. *A beggar, a great needie rogue.*

Bellocier. *A Bullace tree, or wild Plum-tree.*

Bellot: m. otte: f. *Prettie, iolly, somewhat faire, neat, handsome.*

Ma Bellotte. *My prettie Pigsnie.*

Belluge: f. *as* Belugue.

Belotte. *as* Belette. *A Weesill.*

Belouze: f. *The lower hazard in a Tenis-court.*

Belvedere. *A certaine shrub which growes to a mans height, in the proportion of a faire tree, full of pleasant greene boughes resembling branches of Hysope; it may very well be Broome tode flax, which by Italians is called,* Belvidere.

Belugue: f. *A sparke, or sparkle of fire;* (Provenç.) *also, as* Milan marin.

Belusteau: m. *A boulter, or boulting cloth.*

Belutage: m. *A sifting, or boulting of meale.*

Beluteau: m. *A boulter, or boulting cloth.*

Belutement. *as* Belutage.

Beluter. *To boult; also, to swiue.*

Belzoin. *as* Asse douce; *or, as* Benjoin.

Bemol. B *flat; (a tearme of Musicke;) Seeke* B.

Ben. *(of one syllable) an aromaticall nut, or akorne, whereof the Perfumers oyle of Benne is made; some call it, the oylie Akorne.*

Be'n. *(of two syllables) a certaine Arabian Plant, of two kinds, the one bearing a white, the other a red root; both vsed, and held very cordiall; some (improperly) call spatling, or frothie Poppie, white Bene; and red Valerian,*

Valerian, or red cow-Basill, Behenrubrum; *See* Been.
Benarric. *The little black-headed bird called, a Gnat-snapper.*
Bende; Bendelette. *See* Bande *&* Bandelette.
Bender. *as* Bander.
Bene. *A measure of coales, worth about three* sous.
Benedict: m. te: f. *Blist, happie, blessed.*
Huile benedict. *Oyle extracted by distillation from tyles, or brickes, which haue beene steeped some time in very old oyle.*
Benediction: f. *A benediction, benison, blessing; a wishing of all good lucke vnto.*
Benefice: m. *A benefit, fauour, pleasure, good office, good turne; also, a Benefice; also, a Prize, or Billet in a Lotterie; (in old time a* fief *was also called,* Benefice.)
Benefice à simple tonsure. *The place of a Prebend, or Canon; any Benefice, or spirituall liuing, that is without a charge of soules.*
Beneficence: f. *Liberalitie, bountie, beneficence, pleasure-doing.*
Beneficial: m. ale: f. *Belonging to a Benefice.*
Beneficié. *An Incumbent, or beneficed man; one that hath a Benefice.*
Beneficience: f. *Beneficence, liberalitie; a bestowing of fauours, a conferring of benefits, a doing of pleasure any way.*
Beneficier: m. *as* Beneficié.
Beneficier. *To giue a Benefice; also, to conferre benefits, bestow fauors, doe pleasures, good offices, good turnes.*
Beneſt. *as* Benet.
Benestier: m. *A holy-water pot, or stocke.*
Benet: m. *A simple, plaine, doltish fellow; a noddipeake, a ninnyhammer, a pea-goose, a coxe, a sillie companion.*
Benevole: com. *Well-willing, friendly, kind, gracious, fauourable; gentle, courteous.*
Benevolence: f. *A well-willing, or good will; a fauour, kindnesse, beneuolence.*
Benict: m. icte: f. *Blessed, holy, blissefull; See* Benist.
Benignement. *Benignely, gently, courteously, fauourably, graciously, kindly; liberally, bountifully.*
Benigneté: f. *Benignitie, humanitie, gentlenesse, courtesie, grace, fauour, kindnesse, bountie, goodnesse.*
Bening: m. Benigne: f. *Benigne, gentle, courteous, gracious, fauourable, kind, good, liberall, bountifull.*
Benjoin: m. *The aromaticall gumme, called* Benjamin, *or* Benzoin.
Benjoin francois. *The hearbe Maisterworte, or false Pellitorie of Spaine.*
Benir. *To blesse; to wish well vnto.*
Benir la table. *To say grace.*
Benisson. *A blessing, or benison.*
Benist: m. Beniste: f. *Holy, blessed.*
Eau beniste de Cave. *Good drinke.*
Eau beniste de Cour. *Good words. Looke* Eau.
Pain benist. *Holy bread. Looke* Pain.
Benistre. *as* Benir.
Benne: f. *A Binne; or, as* Banne; *also, a great sacke for corne, or coales; also, the head, or horns of a Stag.*
Bennel: m. *A Tumbrell, or close cart; a dung-cart, or dung-pot.*
Bennerie: f. *Base, or low iurisdiction (called so in old time.)*
Benoict: m. *Bennet (a mans name;) also, as* Benet.
Benoict: m. cte: f. *Looke* Benist.
Benoicte: f. *Hearbe Auens, Bennet, or blessed.*
Benoist. *as* Benet, *&* *as* Benoict.
Benoistier: m. *A holy-water pot, or stocke.*
Benoitte. *as* Benoicte.
Benzoin. *as* Benjoin.
Bequarre, *b, sharpe, (a terme of Musicke.)*
Beque: f. *A sea-cob, or Sea-gull.*
Bequée. *as* Bechée.
Bequebo: m. *A wood-pecker, or highawe.* ¶Pic.
Bequenauld: m. *A prattle-basket; a prating boy.*
Bequenaulde: f. *A pratling girle.*
Bequer. *as* Becquer.
Bequeru: m. *A weeuell, or little blacke, and corne-deuouring vermine.*
Bequerut. *A kinde of Oliue.*
Bequet: m. *The fish called a pike; also, the name of a sowrish aple; as* Becquet.
Bequet de mer. *A daintie, little, and long-nosed rock-fish; not very common, nor aboue sixe fingers long.*
Bequilles: f. *Crutches, for lame persons.*
Bequillon: m. *A little beake, or bill of a bird, &c.*
Bequu. *as* Bechu.
Ber. *An old word, signifying as much as,* haut Seigneur; *or Baron, also, as* Berceau; *a cradle; and, hence;*
Apprins au ber dure iusques au ver: Pro. *Men loose not till they dye the dy their youth sets on them.*
Berangene: f. *A certaine Spanish fruict, that resembles a peare, and growes neere the ground like a Melon.*
Berberis. *The barberie tree.*
Bercail: m. *A flocke, as of sheep, &c.*
Bercé: m. ée: f. *Rocked, shogged, or wagged vp and downe, as in a cradle.*
Ie suis tout bercé de cela. *I am throughly acquainted with that; Looke,* Bersé.
Berceau: m. *A cradle; also, an arbor, or bower in a garden; also, a case of tinne, wood, barke, &c; wherein a broken member is inclosed, thereby to repose it, and keep it in the iust forme which it hath pleased the Surgeon to giue it.*
Bercement: m. *A rocking; shogging, swinging.*
Bercer. *To rocke in a cradle, also, to shog, or swing; See* Berser.
Berche: f. *The peece of ordnance called, a Base.*
Bercherie: f. *Prouision, or Store, of Bases (in a ship.)*
Berchot: m. *The little wrenne; our Ladies henne.*
Berdin: m. *The shell-fish called, a Lympyne, or a Lempet.*
Berée: f. *A spinke, sheldaple, chaffinch.*
Bergamasque. Il boucle sa feme à la Bergamasque. *As the (Italian) Bergamasks, who buckle vp their wiues &c. with a deuice like a trusse for a burst man.*
Bergamotte: f. *A yellow peare with a hard rind, good for perrie; also, the delicate* Italian *small peare called, the Bergamotte peare.*
Berger: m. *A shepheard.*
Bourse de berger; *as* Malette de berger.
Malette de berger. *The herbe shepheards purse, shepheards scrip, picke-purse, toywood, coosewced, or caseweed.*
Verge à berger. *The tazle, or fullers thistle; also, water plantaine.*
Vn berger à peu de bruit gardant les brebis à la Lune. *sayd, of one that hangs in chaynes.*
Bergere: f. *A Shepheardesse.*
Bergerette: f. *A drinke made of old hard wine, and honnie.*

Bergerie: f. *A sheepe-fold, sheepe-coat, or sheepe-house; also, the skill, or trade, of keeping, feeding, and grasing of sheepe.*
Bergerolle: f. *A young shepheardesse.*
Bergeronnette: f. *The little bird called a Wagtaile; also, a young, or little, shepheardesse.*
Bergerotte. *as* Bergerolle. *A young shepheardesse.*
Bergier. *as* Berger.
Bergiere: f. *A shepheardesse.*
Berichot. *as* Berchot. *A Wren.*
Bericles. *Corruptly for* Besycles. *A paire of Spectacles.* ¶Rab.
Beril. *as* Berille.
Berille: m. *A Berill; a six-square precious stone, of an oylie, or sea-greene, colour.*
Berlaffe: f. *A slash, gash, deepe cut, great wound.*
Berlaffé: m. ée: f. *Slashed, gashed, wounded extreamely.*
Berlaffer. *To slash, gash, wound extreamely.*
Berlan: m. *A common tipling house; a house of gaming, or of any other disorder.*
Compaignons du berlan. *Pot-companions, ale-knights; disordered vnthrifts; a knot of idle, and gracelesse fellowes, that, ouer a pot, vse to censure, and deride all Estates.*
Berla dier. *An ordinarie haunter of dicing, or tipling houses; also, the keeper, or owner, of one of them.*
Berle: f. *The great water Parsenip, great water Parsely, or salade Parsely; called also, Belders, and Bell-rags.*
Berlin. *as* Berdin.
Berlingasse: f. *A peece of coyne worth about* vj. d. *sterling.*
Berlingue. *as* Berlingasse.
Berlong. *as* Barlong.
Berluë: f. *The being sand-blind, or purblind; dulnesse, or dimnesse of sight.*
Berlué. *Purblinded, made sand-blind.*
Berluement: m. *Purblindnesse; or, as* Berluë.
Berluquer. *To trifle out the time (a word sometimes vsed at Play.)*
Bernadet: m. *A kind of small-headed, great-eyed, wide-mouthed, rough and thick-skinned, dog-fish.*
Bernage: m. *The carriage, prouision, houshold-stuffe, equipage, furniture, traine, followers of a princes court, or campe; also, the necessarie carriage, baggage, or luggage belonging to an armie, or any other companie; also, noblenesse, courtesie, gallantnes of humor, open-heartednesse; also, Meslin, or seuerall sorts of corne mingled; whence;*
Bled bernage; *Looke* Bled.
Bernagoë: f. *A Carpenters Wimble, or Dible.*
Bernaque. *The foule called a Barnacle.*
Bernard. *A proper name; Bernard; also, a light-braind, or shittle-headed fellow.*
Bernard l'hermite. *A kind of small, and (of it selfe) naked Crabfish, or Crayfish; as* Branchuë.
Passer par l'arc S. Bernard. *To beray himselfe.*
Berne: f. *A Siue, or Vanne; also, a great kettle; also, a kind of Moorish garment, or such a mantle as Irish gentlewomen weare.*
Berné: m. ée: f. *Vanned, or winnowed, as corne; also, canuassed, or tossed in a Siue; also, mocked, flouted, ridden, abused, ieasted at.*
Il a esté berné. *He hath beene soundly tossed, throughly canuassed; (a phrase most commonly applied to an ignorant, or dull-headed fellow, that hath prouoked a learned penne, or tongue, to fall aboord him.)*
Berner. *To vanne, or winnow corne; also, to canuasse, or tosse in a Siue; (a punishment inflicted on such as commit grosse absurdities;) also, to flout, mocke, deride, ride, abuse, ieast, scoffe at.*
Bernie: f. *Rug; also, a mantle thereof.*
Berretin: m. *A little cap, or bonnet.*
Berröette: f. *A Wheelebarrow.*
Bers. *as* Ber (vieil mot) *or, as* Berceau; ¶Vandom.
Bers de chariot. *The sides, rackes, or rayles of a chariot, or waggon.*
Bersaut: m. *A Quintaine, or Whintaine, for countrey youths to run at.*
Bersé. *Rocked in a cradle; Seeke* Bercé.
Il l'a si longuement bersé qu' il l'a endormy en son opinion. *He hath by his faire words, and long persuasions, layed asleepe his iudgement, and woon him to be of his opinion.*
Berseau. *A little cradle; or as* Berceau.
Berser. *To rocke, in a cradle; to shog, or swing vp and downe.*
La teste luy berse en gondolle. *His head totters like a boat in a storme.*
Bertaudé: m. ée: f. *Curtalled; also, notched, or cut vneuenly.*
Bertauder. *To curtall a horse; to cut off his eares and taile; also, to notch, or cut the haire vneuenly.*
Berthe: f. *The name of a French queene, which was an excellent housewife; whence the Prouerbe,*
Au temps passé Berthe filoit. *The greatest women did in old time spin.*
Bertonneau. *A Bret, or Turbot.* ¶Norm.
Bertouder, *or* **Bertourder**. *as* Bertauder.
Bertouser. *The same.*
Bertrand: m. *Bertrand (a proper name for a man.)*
Os Bertrand. *The share-bone; or, the coniunction of the great bones which flanke the sides, and whereunto the thigh-bones are fastened.*
Roy Bertrand. *The (little) Wren.*
Deschausser Bertrand. *To be drunke, mellow, cupshotten; to whip the cat, shoo the goose, or see the deuill.*
Qui aime Bertrand aime son chien: Pro. *Loue me, loue my dog.*
Beryl. *as* Beril.
Besace: f. *A wallet, scrip, satchell, bag, pouch, or poake.*
Mettre à la besace. *To beggar, impouerish, vndoe, ouerthrow the estate or fortunes of, turne out of house and harbour.*
Qui plus despend qu'il ne pourchasse il ne luy faut pas de besace: Prov. *(Although the vnthrift needs no pocket, yet may he, in good time, carrie a wallet.)*
Besacier: m. *The bag-bearer, or wallet-bearer of a begging, or beggarly companie.*
Besaguë: f. *A (double-tounged) mattocke.*
Besanner. *To giue leather a graine, in dressing; or to dresse a sheepes skin like Spanish leather; also, as* Bazaner.
Besant: m. *A Besant; an auncient peece of golden coyne (worth fiftie pounds* Tourn.*) thirteene whereof the French kings were accustomed to offer at the Masse of their Consecration in* Rheims; *to which end* Henry *the second (after some discontinuance of that custome) caused the same number of them to be made, and called them* Bysantins; *but they were not worth aboue a double duckat the peece.*
Besas. *Aumes-ace, on the dice.*
Besch: m. *A Southwest wind.* ¶Rab.
Beschage: m. *An opening, or digging vp, of the ground (with a* Besche.*)*

Besche: f. *A Spade.*
Besché: m. ée: f. *Pecked, or picked at; also, digged, opened, or broken vp, as the earth (by a* Besche.)
Besche-bois: m. *The bird called a Speight, Heigh-haw, or Wood-pecker.*
Beschement: m. *A digging, opening, or breaking vp of the earth; also, a pecking, or picking at.*
Bescher. *To pecke, or picke, as a bird; also, to dig, open, or breake vp the earth (with a* Besche.)
Beschevet: m. *as much as* Double chef, *or* Double chevet; *Looke* Bechevet.
Beschéur: m. *A digger, or deluer; a labouring man.*
Beseau: m. *That side of a loafe which in the ouen cloue to another loafe, and thereby wants crustinesse.* (¶Parisien.)
Besfler. *as* Beffler.
Besiale. champ b. *A common field, ground, or pasture; a Common; Looke* Bosialle.
Besicles. *as* Besycles; *a paire of Spectacles.*
Besiclier. *A Spectacle-maker.*
Besier: m. *The hearbe Orage.*
Besle: m. *as* Beisle.
Besinus: m. *A sot, a doult, gull, woodcocke, lobcocke, asse.*
Besoche: f. *as* Hoyau; *Looke* Bezoche.
Besoing: m. *Need, necessitie, want, or great vse, of.*
Besoing fait vieille trotter: Pro. *Need makes the old wife trot.*
Qui a besoing de feu le cerche avec le doigt: Pro. *Looke* Feu.
Besoing. *Needfull, behoofefull, expedient, necessarie.*
Besongnant. *Working, labouring, trauelling; busying himselfe.*
Besongne: f. *Worke, businesse, an affaire; labour, trauell.*
Besongnes de nuict. *Ones night-geere.*
Besongne taillée. *Seeke* Taillé.
Le temps des besongnes. *Haruest time, reaping time.*
Apres besongne faitte le fol barguigne: Pro. *Wise men doe the worke, and fooles agree for it.*
Apres besongne repos & denier: Prov. *Ease and wealth succeed labour; Seeke* Denier.
Le paresseux aime bien besongne faitte: Pro. *The sluggard loues to find worke done to his hands.*
Nul ne fait si bien la besongne que celuy à qui elle est: Prov. *No man followes a businesse so well as he to whom it belongs.*
Besongné: m. ée: f. *Wrought, laboured, trauelled in, busied, occupied, fully employed.*
Besongner. *To worke, labour, trauell in; to busie, occupie, vse, or imploy throughly; also, to doe, or leacher with.*
'A peu parler bien besongner: Pro. *The most work's done with fewest words; or, the fewer words the more worke.*
Besongnette: f. *A little worke, small businesse, trifling affaire.*
Besot. *A dilling, or swill-pough; the last, or yongest child one hath.*
Besq. *as* Visc.
Besquée. *as* Bechée.
Besse: f. *A shouell headed with yron; or as* Besche.
Bessieres: f. *The tiltings, dregs, or bottomes of low-running wine &c.*
Besson: m. *A twinne.*
Besson: m. Bessonne: f. *Twinne, twin-like, borne together, both of a birth.*
Amande bessonne. *Two almonds in one shell.*
Bestail. *Cattell; See* Bestiail.
Beste: f. *A beast; also, a sot, luske, doult, lurdaine, loobie, blockhead; heauie, or dull, fellow.*
Bestes blanches. *Sheepe, Goats, &c.*
Bestes de compagnie. *Troupes of wild Swine, consisting of the Sowes, and young Bores, who follow their dams vntill they be about 18 months old.*
Beste douce, ou fauve. *a fallow Deere, red Deere, Roe, Goat; any harmelesse game; (Our huntsmen call the Buck, Doe, Rayndeere, Elke, Beare, Otter, and Martron, beasts of the Chase of the sweet foot.)*
Beste legiere; *a Stag, Hind, Buck, Doe, Roe, Rayndeere.*
Bestes mordantes. *The Wolfe, Bore, Otter, Fox &c.*
Beste noire. *A wild Swine.*
Beste puante. *A Fox, Otter, Badger, Polecat, &c; any vermine; (Our huntsmen call the Roe, Fox, Gray, Fulmart, Fitch, Polecat, Squirrell, and white Rat, beasts of the Chase of the stinking foot.)*
Beste rouge. *as* Beste douce; Beste rousse; *the same.*
Bestes de somme. *Horses, Cammels, Moyles, Asses.*
Bestes de voiture. *Carriers, or cart-horses; draught-horses, or oxen; pack-horses.*
Faire la beste à deux dos ensemble. *To leacher.*
Prendre du poil de la beste. *To take a remedie for a mischiefe from that which was the cause thereof; as to go thin clothed when a cold is taken; or in drunkennes to fall a quaffing, thereby to recouer health, or sobrietie; neere vnto which sence our Ale-knights often vse this phrase, and say, Giue vs a haire of the dog that last bit vs.*
Vivre en beste. *Looke* Vivre.
Bonne beste s'eschauffe en mangeant: Pro. *We say, quicke at meat quicke at worke; or, he that eats apace, commonly, works apace.*
Telle beste telle teste: Pro. *Looke* Teste.
C'est folie de se prendre aux femmes, & aux bestes: Pro. *Tis but a folly to quarrell with women, and beasts.*
En vieille beste n'y a point de ressource: Pro. *Of an old beast there is no recouerie; when an old man runs into errors, or looses the vigour of his spirit, there is no hope in him either of amendment, or of reinforcement.*
Il faut avoir mauvaise beste par douceur: Pro. *Look* Avoir.
Le loup sçait bien que male beste pense: Prov. *One knaue knowes well the thoughts, or shifts, of another.*
Besteau: m. *as* Batail. *The clapper of a Bell.*
Bestelette. *A little beast.*
Bestement. *Beastly, filthily; witlesly; heartlesly; dully, heauily, luskishly, lurdaine-like.*
Besterie. *as* Bestise.
Bestiail; *or,* Bestial: m. *Beasts, or cattell of any sort, as Oxen, Sheepe, &c.*
Bestiail privé. *The beasts which we feed, and put into the house a nights; tame cattell; as Oxen, Kine, Calues, Sheepe, Hogs, &c.*
Bestial: m. ale: f. *Beastly, filthie; sensuall, vicious, rude.*
Bestialité: f. *Beastlinesse, filthinesse, sensualitie, rudenesse.*
Bestiole: f. *A little beast.*
Bestion: m. *as* Bestiole.
Bestise: f. *Sottishnes, dulnes, blockishnes, want of spirit.*
Bestocquer. *To stab, foyne, thrust, giue a stoccado vnto; (an old word.)*
Bestourner. *To amaze, astonish, make dizzie; (an old word.)*
Besycle, *or* Besycles: f. *Spectacles.*
Besyclier: m. *A Spectacle-maker.*

Besyn. *Well nigh whittled, almost drunke, somwhat ouer-seene.* (v. m.)
Bete. *Looke* Bette.
Betelle: f. *A certaine Indian Sallate hearbe, that resembles the Gilliflower plant; or, bastard Pepper, called among th'Indians* Betle, & Betre.
Betoine: f. *Betonie,* Sarxiphagon *(an hearbe.)*
Betoine coronnaire, ou de couronnes. *The Cloue Gilliflower.*
Betoine sauvage, *as* Armoires; *sweet Williams.*
Beton: m. *Beest; the first milke a female giues, after the birth of her young one.*
Betosne. *as* Betoine.
Betourne: com. *Dizzie, or giddie in the head.* (v.m.)
Betrescher. *To trim, tackle, make tight, a ship, &c; also, to decke, adorne, tricke vp; set, ranke, or dispose things orderly, or handsomely; (an old word.)*
Bette: f. des bettes. *The hearbe Beet, or Beets.*
Bette blanche. *The common white Beet, or best kind of Beets.*
Bette estrangere. *The Roman, or strange, red Beet.*
Bette noire. *The blacke Beet, or worst kind of Beets;* (Mathiolus & Dodoneus *call the common red Beet* Beta nigra.)
Bette des prez. *as* Bette sauvage.
Bette rouge. *The common red Beet; also, as;*
Bette Romaine. *The Roman, or strange, red Beet.*
Bette sauvage. *Hearbe Pirola, Winter-greene, wild Beets.*
Bette-rave. *A kind of delicate red Parsenip, which, boyled, yeelds a sweet vermillion sap.*
Bettes. *Beets, &c, (as before in* Bette;) *also, tipling, sipping, bowsing, quaffing; and hence;*
Entrer en bettes. *To grow merrie, or mellow in drinking; or to fall a chattering, as gossips do when they haue drunke hard, together.*
Beturre: f. *A sinke-hole.*
Beu: m. beuë: f. *Drunke, bowsed, bibbed, tipled, swilled, quaffed; sucked vp; receiued, or soaked in.*
Apres beu dodo: Prov. *After drinke rest.*
Beuf: m. *An Oxe, a Beefe; Beefe; Looke* Bœuf.
Beuffroy: m. *A watch-tower, or high place fit for discouerie; See* Beffroy.
Beufle: m. *A Busle, Bugle, or wild Oxe.*
Prendre vn beufle par le museau: Pro. *To performe a hard, or hazardous, exploit.*
Beugler. *as* Bugler.
Beur. moyne beur. *A lubberly Monke; or in stead of* Beuveur; *a quaffing Monke.*
Beuratte: f. *A Churne.*
Beurée. *The name of a very tender, and delicat Peare.*
Beurichon. *A Wrenne.*
Beuriere: f. *A Churne; also, as* Beurriere.
Beurre: m. *Butter.*
Bas de beurre. *Buttermilke.*
Tour de beurre. *One of the three famous towers of S.* Maries *church in* Roan; *built with the mony that was payed by those of that diocesse, for a dispensation to eat butter in Lent.*
Vn Seigneur de beurre combat bien vn vassal d'acier. *A Prouerbe expressing the great oddes a lord hath of his tenant.*
Beurrette: f. *A Churne.*
Beurreux: m. euse: f. *Butterie; fattie; greasie; full of butter.*
Beurrier: m. *A butter man.*
Beurrier: m. ere: f. *Of, or belonging to, butter.*
Vn pot beurrier. *A butter pot.*

Beurriere: f. *A butter woman.*
Beuvailler. *To drinke excessiuely, or very often; to swill, quaffe, tiple.*
Beuvande: f. *Small wine, houshold wine, seruants wine.*
Beuvereau: m. *A sipper; a small drunkard.*
Beuverie. *Excessiue drinking, swilling, quaffing, bowsing, trolling of the bowle.*
Beuveron. *A riuer in the Prouince of* Solongne; *called so, because in Summer it is all drunke vp by the earth; also, a drench, or mash for a horse.*
Beuveter. *To drinke, to sip, to sup.*
Beuvette. *See* Buvette.
Beuveur: m. *A drinker, swiller, quaffer; a tosse-pot.*
Cela sent son beuveur d'eau. *One may well discerne by that how strict, spare, or poore, a diet he keepes; or, that sauors of a poore, or starued, spirit.*
Prodigue, & grand beuveur de vin, n'a du sien ne four, ne moulin: Pro. *The tipling vnthrift keepes nor myll, nor ouen.*
Beuvoire de Venus. *The fullers thistle, or tazle.*
Beuvrage: m. *Beuerage, drinke.*
Bezanne. *as* Bazane.
Bezant: m. *An auncient coyne of gold; Looke* Besant.
Bezans. *Besants, in* Blason; *(they must euer be round, whole, and of mettall.)*
Bezanté d'or. *Bezanted Or; or, charged with Besants; a tearme of* Blason.
Bezarder. *To dye.* ¶Barrag.
Bezer. *A Cow to run vp and downe, holding vp her taile, when the brizze doth sting her.*
Bezet. Aller à Sainct Bezet. *To trot, gad, runne, or wander vp and downe, like one that hath a brizze in his tayle.*
Bezoard: m. *A Beazar stone; (breeds in the maw of the Goat called, a Beazar.)*
Bezoche: f. *is, in some countries, the instrument of Husbandrie, tearmed in others,* Hoyau. *Looke* Hoyau.
Bezole: f. *The name of a certaine fish, thats found (only) in the Lake of* Geneva.
Biains. *as* Bians *(in* Anjou.)
Biais: m. *Byas, compasse, a slope, or sloping.*
Biais passé. *(So do workmen call) a gate, or dore made byas.*
Ie ne le prends pas de ce biais. *I meane it not this way, I take it not in this manner.*
Il ne s'y print pas de bon biais. *He went not the right way to worke; he tooke not a right course in the matter.*
Biaisant: m. ante: f. *Crooking, byasing, sloping, fetching a compasse.*
Biaisément. *Crookingly, obliquely, byas-wise, aslope, with a compasse.*
Biaiser. *To crooke, stand aslope, fetch a compasse, go awry, make about; or, as* Bihayser.
Biaiseure: f. *Slopenesse, byasnesse, compasse, obliquenesse, or obliquitie.*
Bians: m. *Daies works both of men, and beasts, due vnto Landlords by all tenants (who are no gentlemen) within the Countie of* Poictou.
Biaque. *Ceruse, or white lead, wherewith women paint.*
Biarn: m. *A white cloth of course wooll with interwouen streakes of blew, whereof the countrey people about* Languedoc *make cloakes.*
Biaut. *A kind of Brittish course garment, or iacket, worne loose ouer other apparrell.*
Bibaille: f. *A present, fayring, New-yeares gift.*
Bibelots: m. *Hucklebones; or, the play at hucklebones.*

Biberon: m. *A tipler, quaffer, bibber, sucke-spiggot; also, an Ewer; also, an instrument wherewith Surgeons draw milke from womens breasts; also, a tap, or faucet.*
Bibet: m. *A Gnat.* ¶Norm.
Bibette: f. *A wheale, or blister.*
Bible: f. *A Bible.*
Bibliopole: m. *A Booke-seller, or Stationer.*
Bibliotheque: f. *A Librarie.*
Biblot: m. *as* Bibelot; *or a small square peece, in checker-worke, or whereof checker-worke is made.*
Bibul: m. *The stalke of great Hemlockes, vsed by the country people of some places in stead of a canne, or pot, to drinke in.*
Bibule: f. *Blotting, or browne, paper.*
Bicarne: m. *The great Veriuice grape.*
Bichard: m. *A Hind calfe; or, a red Deere calfe.*
Biche: f. *A Hind; the female of a Stag.*
Biche de mer. *as* Cabrole.
Pied de biche. *The gafle of a Crosse-bow; or, the end thereof.*
Il a mangé de la biche blanche. *Said of one that is light-witted, shittle-headed, giddie-brain'de.*
Bichecoter. *To leacher it.*
Bichecoterie: f. *A leacherous tricke, a lasciuious part; firkerie, an odde pranke, or ierke, in whoorisme.*
Bichet: m. *A measure for corne, &c, holding about two Parisian bushels, or rather (according to th'vncertainetie of measures) of no certaine scantling; for in the countrey neere* Lyons *it weighs about 70 pound; in other places but 54; and,*
Bichet de marrons. *(a sacke full of great Chestnuts) weighs but 36 pound.*
Bicheteau: m. *A little Hind calfe.*
Bichette de Lyon. *The halfe of the* Bichet; *or, a iust bushell of* Paris.
Bichot. *as* Bicheteau; *also, a measure for corne vsed in* Burgundie, *and containing about fiue of their bushels.*
Bichotterie; *as* Bichecoterie.
Bicle; *as* Bigle. ¶Rab.
Bicoque: f. *A little paltrie towne, hold, or fort; not strong ynough to hold out a siege, nor so weake as to be giuen vp for words.*
Bicorne: com. *Double-horned, hauing two hornes.*
Bicornu: m. uë: f. *as* Bicorne.
Bicque: f. *A Goat; or, as* Biche.
Bidault de calebute; *See* Bidet de, &c.
Bidaulx: m. *Cowardly straglers after an armie; or, as* Bidaux.
Bidaux. *Footmen, souldiors.* (veil mot.)
Bidenté. *Double-toothed; that hath two teeth.*
Bidet: m. *A little nag, or curtall; also, a small Pistoll.*
Bidet de culebute. Membre viril.
Bidon: m. *A great cage, or open basket to keepe, or feed, pullein in.*
Bidonne: f. *A kind of sea Purslane that growes in great plentie on the Venetian shores.*
Biece: f. *A spade; or as* Beche.
Biecer. *To digge, delue, or open the ground with a spade, or* Besche.
Bien: m. *Wealth, substance, cheuisance, riches, possessions, goods; a patrimonie; also, a benefit, pleasure, fauor, good office, or good turne; also, goodnesse, honestie, vertue, sinceritie; also, a good thing.*
Biens au soleil. *Lands, leases, houses, cattell; such goods, or possessions as lye without dores. Looke* Soleil.
Biens vacans. *Waifes, strayes, wrecks; a purse, or treasure found; any land, or thing, that neuer had owner; or hath beene lost, or abandoned, by the owner.*
Gens de bien. *Honest, and (among souldiors) valiant people.*
Cela sent son bien. *That is comely, seemely, decent, orderly, well done, euen as it should be.*
C'est du bien de vous. *This is of your courtesie or fauour sir.*
Bien perdu bien connu: Prov. *Goods lost good knowne; we discerne not the worth of things vntill we be depriued of them.*
Les biens de fortune passent comme la lune: Pro. *Fortunes goods are flitting like the Moone.*
Vn bien acquiert l'autre: Prov. *One good thing begets another.*
De bien commun on ne fait pas souvent monceau: Prov. *Men often grow not rich by publicke treasure.*
Grand bien ne vient pas en peu d'heure: Pro. *Great matters are not compast in a moment.*
Nul bien sans haine: Prov. *No good thing vngrudged at.*
Quand les biens viennent les corps faillent: Pro. *When goods encrease the body decreases; most men ere they grow rich are old.*
Qui le bien voit, & le mal prend, fait folie en bon escient: Prov. *He that discernes the good, and chuses the bad, merits a bable.*
De gens de bien vient tout bien: Prov. *From good men comes all goodnesse.*
Les gens de bien font tousiours bien, ont tousiours bien, sont tousiours bien: Prov.
Dieu donne biens, & bœuf, mais ce n'est pas par la corne: Pro. *Looke* Bœuf.
On doit dire du bien le bien: Prov. *Of good things we must giue good words.*
Bien. adverb. *Well, good, right, content; fitly, aptly, commodiously; fully, throughly; in good case, with good reason, as it should be.*
Bien de par Dieu. *On then; to it I pray you; in Gods name be it.*
Bien à faire. *Much to doe.*
Bien au net. *Exactly, perfectly.*
Bien que. *Although, albeit that; suppose, or put the case that.*
Aussi bien ne faittes vous rien. *For, or because, you doe no good in it.* ¶Rab.
Et bien. *Well then, agreed, I will then; also (interrogatiuely) Will you? What meane you? What say you? What doe you purpose to doe?*
Ou bien. *Or else; otherwise.*
Que bien que mal. *Indifferently, reasonably, so so, one way or other; I know not how.*
Estre bien ensemble. *To agree wel, to be good friends.*
Il leur print bien que. *They had good luck, they might thanke God, or, it fell out well for them, that.*
Cela sent son bien. *That is comely, seemely, decent, orderly, well done, euen as it should be.*
Bien a crié la loup qui sa proye rescoult: Pro. *He complaines to some purpose that recouers what he complaines for.*
Bien a en sa maison qui de ses voisins est aimé: Pro. *He liues well at home that is beloued abroad.*
Bien courroucé de peu pleure: Prov. *He that is angred throughly sheds few teares.*
Bien de sa place part qui son ami y laisse: Prov. *He fitly leaues his roome that leaues a friend in't.*

Bien poussé longuement chancelle: Prov. *Looke* Chanceller.

Qui bien aime chastie: Prov. *He that loues throughly punishes throughly; or, he that loues well, payes home when he punishes.*

Qui bien aime tard oublie: Pro. *Seeke* Aimer.

Qui bien est ne se bouge: Prov. *He thats well had best hold him so; or, let not things fitly placed be remoued.*

Qui bien fera bien trouvera: Prov. *He that does well shall speed well.*

Qui bien gaigne, & bien espargne deuient tantost riche: Prov. *He that gets much, and spares much, will soone be rich.*

Qui bien tire deux en a: Prov. *Looke* Tirer.

Qui bien veut mourir bien viue: Prov. *He that would die well had need to liue well.*

Qui bien veut parler bien doit pourpenser: Prov. *Looke* Pourpenser.

Qui bien veut payer bien se doibt obliger: Prov. *He that meanes to pay truly giues good securitie.*

Biendisance: f. *Eloquence, well-speaking.*

Bien-en-allée: f. *A farewell;* ¶Parisien.

Bienfaict: m. *A benefit, good turne, pleasure, kindnesse, fauour.*

Bienfaict n'est iamais perdu: Pro. *One neuer looses by doing courtesies.*

Bienfaicteur. *A benefactor; a beneficiall friend; one that doeth a good turne, or great pleasure.*

Bienheuré. *Happie, prosperous, fortunat.*

Bienheurer. *To make happie, prosperous, fortunat.*

Bienheureté: f. *Blessednesse, happinesse, felicitie, prosperitie.*

Bienheureux: m. euse: f. *Happie, fortunat, prosperous, blisse-full, blessed*

Bien-public: m. *The Commonwealth; also, a faire title giuen to a foule rebellion of the Earle of* Charrolois, *and other French Lords, against* Lewis *the eleuenth.*

Biens. *Looke* Bien.

Bienseamment. *Comelily, agreeably, well-beseemingly, with good correspondencie.*

Bienseance: f. *A comelinesse, becomming, seemelinesse, agreeablenesse; also, congruitie, correspondencie.*

Estre à la bienseance de. *To lye fit for; as land &c.*

Bienseant: m. ante: f. *Comely, seemely, agreeable, well-beseeming, well-becomming; also, congruous, or correspondent; befitting, or well fitting.*

Bienveigner. *To welcome, receiue gladly, intertaine kindly.*

Bienvenement: m. *A welcome, or welcomming.*

Bienvienner. *To welcome; as* Bienveigner.

Bienvenuë: f. *A welcome; hence,* Payer sa bienvenuë. *To pay his welcom, as schollers do at their first entrance, or admission, into a schoole.*

Bienvoulu: m. uë: f. *Well beloued, well thought of, exceedingly well liked.*

Bienvueillance: f. *Fauor, good liking, heartie good will.*

Bienvueillant: m. ante: f. *Well-willing, fauourable, courteous, friendly, bearing good will, or affection vnto.*

Biere: f. *A coffin for a dead corpes; also, the drinke, Beere.*

Aujourd'uy en chere, demain en biere: Pro. *To day a man, to morrow none; (say we.)*

Au cerf la biere, au sanglier le barbier: Prov. *(For those beasts hard layed too, lay hard about them.)*

Biés. *Byas; Looke* Biais.

Bieure: m. *The beast called a Beauer; also, the water-horse; also, a kind of goose-like water-foule, that spoyles much fish, and is but very course meat.*

En petite eau souvent on trouve grand bieure: Prov. *Great worth is often found in things of small apparance.*

Biez. *as* Biais. *Bias.*

Bise. *A counterfeit iewell; also, as* Bisse.

Bisé: m. ée: f. *Rased, defaced, blotted, or put out.*

Bisement: m. *A rasing, defacing, blotting, or wiping out.*

Bisse: m. *A foole, asse, doult, woodcocke, coxcombe, ninnyhammer; also, as* Bise; *or one that seemes, or would seeme wise, and yet is, and euer will be, foolish.*

Bisser. *To deface, blot, rase, wipe out.*

Bisserie: f. *A defacing, rasing, wiping, or blotting out; also, any thing, that though it looke faire, is of little worth.*

Bisseure: f. *A rasing, defacing, or blotting out.*

Biforme: com. *Double-formed; that hath, or is of, two seuerall formes, or shapes.*

Biformité: f. *Biformitie, double forme, a duple or two-fold shape.*

Bifourché: m. ée: f. *Double-forked; diuided into, or consisting of, two (forked) parts.*

Bifre: m. *as* Bievre.

Biforcation: f. *A biforcation; a forking; a forked partition, diuision, or forme.*

Bigame: m. *Twice married, who hath had two wiues.*

Bigarré: m. ée: f. *Diuersified, varied, mingled, of many colours, of sundrie hues, motley-like.*

Oeil bigarré. *Looke* Oeil.

Bigarreans. *A kind of cherries, which be halfe white, halfe red.*

Bigarremént: m. *A variation, or diuersifying, as in colours.*

Bigarrément. *Diuersly, of sundrie colours, motley-like.*

Bigarrer. *To diuersifie, varie, mingle, or make, of sundrie colours.*

Bigarrer ses propos. *To discourse of diuers and sundrie matters at once; or, to run odly, and fantastically, from one matter vnto another.*

Bigarreure: f. *Varietie, or diuersitie, as of sundry colours mingled together.*

Bigarruge: f. *Motley colour.* (v. m.)

Bigaut: m. *An asse, foole, noddie, ninnie; or as* Bigot.

Bigearre, *or* Bigerre: com. *Odde, humorous, fantasticall.*

Bigearrement. *Odly, humorously, fantastically.*

Bigearrer. *as* Bigarrer.

Bigearrure. *as* Bigarreure; *also, odnesse of humor, fantasticalnesse.*

Bigerrerie: f. *A difference, or varietie of colours, fashions, or opinions, in one subiect; also, fantasticalnesse, or odnesse, of humor.*

Bigle: com. *Skenning, squinting, looking askew, or nine waies at once.*

Biglement. *Squintingly, skenningly, askew.*

Biglesse: f. *A squinting wench.*

Bigne: f. *A bumpe, knob, rising, or swelling after a knocke.*

Bigne: com. *Club-footed, or crump-footed.*

Bignets: m. *Little round loaues, or lumpes made of fine meale, oyle, or butter, and reasons; bunnes, Lenten loaues; also, flat fritters made like small pancakes.*

Bignoter. *as* Binoter.

Bigorne. *A Smiths anuile hauing two horne-like nookes, or corners.*

Bigorneau. *A Periwincle; or, as* Nerite; (¶Breton.

Bigornet. *as* Bigorneau.

Bigot. *(An old Norman word (signifying as much as,* De par Dieu; *or our, for Gods sake) made good French, and signifying) an hypocrite, or, one that seemeth much more holy than he is; also, a scrupulous, or superstitious fellow.*

Bigotage: m. *Hypocrisie, holines only in shew; also, scrupulous curiositie, superstitious deuotion.*

Bigotation. *as* Bigotage, *or* Bigotise.

Bigotie; *or,* **Bigotise:** f. *Hypocrisie; superstition, too much curiositie, or scruple of conscience.*

Bigotte. Chauses à la bigotte. *Close, or strait venitians tyed below the knee; Priests breeches.*

Bigotté: m. ée: f. *Turned hypocrite, or, made full of scruple.*

Bigotter. *To make superstitious, to fill with hypocrisie; or, to infect with too much scruple of conscience.*

Biguarruge. *as* Bigarruge.

Bihay. de bihay. *Bias, awry, crooking, obliquely, aslope, with a compasse; Looke* Biais.

Bihayser. *To crooke; to go by bias, fetch a compasse, stand aslope, turne awry; also, to place bias, put compasse, make aslope, set awry.*

Bihore. *A word, or voice wherewith French carters hastica on their horses.*

Bihoreau: m. *A kind of little Heron, which haunteth rocks, and hilly places, and hath a peake of feathers falling backward on the hinder part of his head.*

Bijon: m. *Liquid rozen; tarre.*

Bile: f. *Choller, gall; anger, fretfulnesse; melancholy intermixed with choller.*

Bileux: m. euse: f. *Angrie, chollericke, teastie, full of gall, full of rancor.*

Billard. *as* Billart.

Billard. pied billard. *A splay foot.*

Billardier: m. ere: f. *Baker-legd; that hath crooked legs, or goes in at the knees.*

Billart: m. *A short and thicke trunchion, or cudgell; hence, the cudgell in the play at trap; and, a billard, or the sticke wherewith we touch the ball at billyards; also, a baker-legd fellow.*

Bille: f. *A small bowle, or billyard ball; also, a young stocke of a tree to graft on; also, a lingot, wedge, or gad of mettall; also, money, coine, chinkes;* (Baragoüin) *also, a kind of sea fish, that hath a white line running along from her gills to her taile; otherwise, resembling a Pearch.*

Danser en bille. *To daunce verie lustily.*

Ce n'est bille pareille. *This is no euen match; the coin is not of like allay.*

Cela courra bille pareille. *That shall run the same course, vndergo the same hazard; that shall tast, or be partaker, of whatsoeuer betides the other.*

Billebarré: m. ée: f. *Crosse barred.*

Billeboquet: m. *A cord, or line (hauing at either end, and in the middle, a sticke fastened vnto it) wherewith Gardeners measure out their beds, and borders; also, a Bob; a bullet hanging by a line from the middle of a stick hollowed at the one end, or both, for the receiuing thereof.*

Biller. *To play at Billiards; also, to fasten the rope of a boat to the wood which runs ore-crosse the hammes of the horses that are to draw it.*

Billeron. la Maille billeron; *Looke* Maille.

Billet. *A little bill, note, or ticket (stucke vp on a post, or doore;) as* Etiquet.

Billette: f. *A billet of wood; also, a little bowle, somewhat longer than an ordinarie one; also, a passage toll, or through-toll; so called of a little log thats hung on a tree for a signe, or to giue warning, therof.*

Billettes d'une espieu. *Crosse barres of yron, or steele, somewhat aboue the head of a boare speare, to keepe it from running too farre, and therby the beast from comming too neere him that assailes him.*

Bille-vezées: f. *Trash, trifles, toyes, nifles.*

Billion: m. *A million of millions.*

Billon: m. *A twig, or shute of a full yeares growth; also, base, cried downe, or called in, coyne, which either hath no siluer in it, or not so much as it should haue; also, the mettal wherof base coyn is made; whence,* Monnoye noire *is also tearmed,* Monnoye de billon; *& the siluer that hath aboue a sixt part of* Empirance, *or allay in it, is held no better than* Billon.

Billonnage: m. *A melting, or making of* Billon; *also, (more particularly) a changing of one peece of coine for another, or of one kind of coyne into another; an vnauthorised altering, melting, or imbasing of coyne.*

Billonné: m. ée: f. *Melted, or made into,* Billon; *also, changed, as a bad peece of coine for a good one, or, as a good one into a bad one; altered, melted, and (in the melting) imbased, as coyne (without warrant for it.)*

Billonnement: m. *as* Billonnage.

Billonner. *To make of, or melt into,* Billon; *also, (more particularly) to change a bad peece of coyne for a good one, or a good one into a bad one; to alter, melt, & (in the melting) to imbase, the kings coyn, without any warrant for it.*

Billonneur: m. *An ordinarie melter of coine, or mettal into* Billon; *also, a changer of bad coyne for good, or of good into bad; one that without authoritie, and to make a gaine to himselfe, alters, or melts, and (in melting) imbases, coine.*

Billos. *Certaine imposts leuied vpon wines:* ¶Breton.

Billot: m. *A billet, blocke, or log (of wood;) also, a wedge, lingot, or lumpe (of mettall;) also, as* Piece à pommette.

Homme neuf, & de billot. *A rude, or vnfashioned; a raw, or vnexperienced, fellow.*

Bimauve: f. *The marsh mallow, moorish mallow, white mallow.*

Bimauve sauvage. *Mouse mallow, wild mallow, Veruine mallow, cut mallow, Simons mallow.*

Bimbeloté: m. ée: f. *Furnished with paultrie ware, or pedling stuffe.*

Bimblotier: m. *A paultrie Pedler; or, as* Brimblotier.

Binage: m. *as* Binement.

Binaire. nombre binaire. *The number of two.*

Binarchie. *The ioynt rule, or equall authoritie, of two Princes in one countrey.*

Binart: m. *A wry-neckt fellow.*

Biné: m. ée: f. *Digged, laboured, or weeded, as a vine; turned vp as the ground in a vineyard, the second time.*

Binement: m. *A labouring, digging, or grubbing vp of weeeds, &c; the second worke done in vineyards as soone as the vines haue branched, and put forth their clusters.*

Biner. *To labour, or turne vp, the ground; to digge, or grub vp, weedes, &c, in vineyards, the second time; (especially in May; when commonly the vines haue put forth.)*

Bineur: m. *A labourer, digger, turner vp of the ground, grubber vp of weeds, in vineyards.*

Bingu. *Troubled, molested, vexed:* ¶Gascon.

Binoire. *as* Bisnoire.
Binotage: m. *The second tilth, earing, or digging of soyle.*
Binotement. *as* Binotage.
Binoter. *To till, eare, dig, land, or vineyards, the second time.*
Binotis: m. *as* Binotage.
Bios. *God:* ¶ Gasc. ¶ Rab.
Bipartient. *Parting, or diuiding into two.*
Bipedal: m. ale: f. *Double footed; also, two foot long, or wide.*
Biquoquet: m. *The peake of a Ladies mourning hood.* (v. m.)
Birer. *as* Virer: ¶ Gasc.
Birrasque: f. *A high-going sea, or tempest at sea, caused by whirle-winds, and accompanied with gustes of raine.*
Bis: m. bise: f. *Browne, duskie, swart, blackish.*
Pain bis. *Rye bread, course bread, browne bread.*
Pierre bise. *Looke* Pierre.
Roche bise. *A hard, and blewish rocke, or quarrey, of stone.*
Ou à bis, ou à blanc. *By hooke or by crooke, one way or another.*
Bisacquier: m. *A scrip-carrier, or wallet-bearer.*
Bisaguë. *as* Besaguë.
Bisantin. *as* Besant: *So tearmed of* Bysantium, *or* Constantinople, *where it was first currant, as it is also at this day in most parts of* Asia.
Bisarme: f. *as* Guisarme.
Bisayeul: m. *A great great grandfather.*
Bis-blanc. *Wheaten, or cheat bread.*
Biscantine: f. *Drinke made of Bullas, or sloes.*
Biscapit. *is (among Exchequer men) a double imploiment of one summe, in an account, &c.*
Biscaye: f. *A vantage at Tennis.*
Bischard. *A fawne, or hind-calfe.*
Bischet. *as* Bichet.
Bisclant. *Squinting, looking askew.*
Biscle. *as* Bigle.
Biscoter. *To swiue.*
Biscuit: m. *A bisket; bisket bread.*
S'embarquer sans biscuit. *To goe abroad without bisket; to enter into an action without sufficient prouision; to vndertake that which he wants meanes, or abilitie, to performe.*
Manger avec vne faim de biscuit. *To eat very greedily.*
Biscuteau: m. *Small, or fine bisket bread.*
Bise: f. *A North wind.*
Bise traverse. *A North-west, or North-east wind.*
Bise: f. *A delicate Italian fruit that resembles the* Naveau.
Bise. *(The feminine of* Bis; *) Looke* Bis.
Biseau: m. *A bezle, bezeling, or scuing; such a slopenesse, or slope forme, as is in the point of an yron leauer, chizle, &c.*
Le bord de la fosse se ravallera en biseau. *Shall bee made scarfing.*
Biset. *as* Bizet.
Biseté: m. ée: f. *Wrought, or stript with plate, as some kind of stuffes be.*
Bisette: f. *Plate (of gold, siluer, or copper,) wherewith some kinds of stuffes are stripped.*
Bisexte: m. *The Bisext, or leape yeare; which comes by one day added in foure yeare.*
Bisner. *as* Biner.
Bisneur. *as* Bineur.

Bisnoire: f. *A grubbing forke, or grubbing axe; a forked, or double tongued mattocke, or pick-axe.*
Bison: m. *The Bison; a kind of hulch-backt, rough-maned, broad-faced, and great eyd, wild Oxe, that will not be taken as long as he can stand, nor tamed after he is taken.*
Bisongne. *as* Bison; *Also, a filthie knaue, or clowne; a raskall, bisonian, base humored scoundrell.*
Bisoüart: m. *A paultrie Pedlar, who in a long packe, or maund (which he carries, for the most part open, and hanging from his necke) before him) hath Almanacks, Bookes of newes, or other trifling ware, to sell.*
Bisque: f. *A fault, at Tennis.*
Bisac: m. *A wallet.*
Bisse: f. *An Adder.*
Manier en bisse. *as* Serpeger; *When a horse manages as an Adder goes, wrigling, wagling, or gliding.*
Bissestre. *Ill lucke; (from* Bissexte, *which is held vnluckie.)*
Bissexte: m. *The Bissext; the leape yeare; or, one day added in foure yeare.*
Bissines. *Silken words, spruce tearmes.*
Bissole: f. *as* Bizole.
Bistarde: f. *The great bird called, a Bustard.*
Bistorie: f. *A kind of crooked, sharpe-pointed, and double-edged launcet, vsed by Chirurgians in th'opening of sores, &c.*
Bistorié: m. ée: f. *Crooked, hooked, boughtie, awrie.*
Bistorin. *as* Bistorie.
Bistorte: f. *Bistort, Britannica, Snakeweed, Pashiens, Oisterloit.*
Bistorte grande. *Female Adderwort, or Snakeweed.*
Bistorte petite. *Male Adderwort, or Oisterloit, small Snakeweed.*
Bistortier: m. *A rolling pin, or pestle, of wood.*
Bite: f. *The hearbe called Beets; Looke* Bete.
Prendre du potage de la bite. *To take in some oyle of man; to do that a maid should not do.*
Bites: f. *The bits; two great wootden pegs whereto the cable is fastened when an anker is let fall.*
Bitume: m. *Bitumen, held by some to bee a fast, and clammie earth, lome, or clay, somewhat resembling pitch, and of the nature of brimstone; by others, (more probably) a fat skum, or fome driuen by the wind, and waues, on the bankes of the Palestinian lake,* Mare Mortuum; *whence commeth onely the best (for other waters also yeeld Bitumen) though verie rarely: Our ordinarie shop Bitumen is but a composition of Pitch, Petriolum, and some other such like simples, howsoeuer Apothecaries would make men beleeue it is the Palestinian Bitumen* (¶ Mathiolus.)
Bitume Apollonien. *Apollonian Bitumen (inferiour to the Palestinian) is also, the fome of a certaine water, thats neere vnto the citie* Apollonia *(now* Valonia) *in* Epirus.
Bituminer. *To annoint, besmeare, or mingle with Bitumen.*
Bitumineux: m. euse: f. *Full of Bitumen; also, glewie, slimie, clammie, fast cleauing, as Bitumen.*
Treffle bitumineux. *Clauer gentle, Treacle Clauer, Pitch Trefoyle, stinking Trefoyle.*
Bivet. faire bivet. *To take the end of a low-burnt candle out of the socket, and with a drop of tallow make it sticke vpon the edge of the candlesticks nose.*
Bizarderies: f. *Fantasticall trickes, odde parts, humorous*

rous

rous prankes; also, trash, nifles, trifles, toyes.

Bizarre: com. *Fantasticall, toyish, odde, humorous, giddie headed, selfe conceited, haire braind; also, diuers, or diuersified in fashion, or in colour; and hence;*

Habillement bizarre. *A garment of motley, or of sundrie colours, distinguished by seuerall peeces.*

Bizarrément. *Odly, fantastically; of sundrie fashions, of diuers colours.*

Bizarrerie: f. *Fantasticalnesse, toyishnesse, humorousnesse; also, a conceited toy, an odde pranke, a fantasticall tricke.*

Bizarreure: f. *Diuersitie of colours, or fashion in one subiect.*

Bizart. *as* Bizarre.

Bize. *as* Bise; *The North wind; also, a kind of small Tunnie, or fish like a Tunnie.*

Bizeau d'une pinse de fer. *The sloping point, end, or tongue of an yron leauer;* Looke Biseau.

Bizet: m. *A kind of small Stockedoue, or Queest, resembling a Partridge, but much worse meat.*

Bladier: m. *A Marchant, or Ingrosser of corne.*

Bladier: m. ere: f. *Of, or belonging to, corne.*

Blaffard: m. arde: f. *Pale, wanne, lew, bleake of colour, of a decayed hue.*

Oeil blaffard. *Looke* Oeil.

Blaffastre: com. *Somewhat pale, wanne, or decayed in colour.*

Blaier. Seigneur blaier. *The Land-lord that may amerce all such forreiners, as turne their cattell into the wast grounds, or* vaines pastures, *belonging vnto his Lordship; which without his permission (payed for) they ought not to haue done.*

Blaime: com. *Pale, wanne, bleake, whitish, dead coloured.*

Blaimeur: f. *Palenesse, wannesse, bleakenesse; a dead, or whitish colour.*

Blaimir. *To wax pale, bleake, wanne, white.*

Blaireau: m. *A Badger, Gray, Boason, Brocke.*

Blairie. Droict de blairie. *A Lords power to fine any forreiners, that turne their cattell into the* vaines pastures *of his Manor, without his leaue, and permission; or as in* Blayrie.

Païs de blairie. *A corne countrey; a countrey abounding in corne, or that hath great store of corne growing in it.*

Blanc: m. *A blanke, white, whitenesse, or white thing; the white, or marke of a paire of buts; a blanke of paper; a blanke in a lotterie; also, whitelime, or whiting for walls, &c; also, the halfe of a* Sol, *a peece of money which we call also, a blanke; also, the whiter side of a skinne of parchment; or, that side which cloue to the flesh.*

Blanc de chapon, perdris &c. *The brawne of a Capon, &c.*

Blanc d'eau. *The white water Lillie, water Rose, white Nenuphar.*

Blanc d'Espaigne. *Ceruse, or white Lead, wherewith women paint.*

Blanc de plomb. *The same.*

Blanc de Pouille. *The same.*

Grand blanc. *Is worth a* Sol, *or two ordinarie ones.*

Allayé au blanc. Or allayé au blanc. *Gold allayed with siluer.*

Armer à blanc. *To arme with white, and compleat armor.*

Ou à bis, ou à blanc. *By hooke or by crooke, by right or by wrong, one way or another.*

Celuy qui n'a point de blanc en l'oeil. *The Diuell; also, a cleane Gentleman; one that hath neuer a crosse to blesse him with.*

Mettre à blanc. *To strip into his shirt; to rifle of, or turne out of, all.*

Mettre haut le blanc à la butte. *To hold a vendible thing at a high rate; also, to propound vnto one a matter, which is aboue his reach, or capacitie.*

Toucher au blanc. *To strike the white; to hit the naile on the head.*

Blanc: m. Blanche: f. *White; also, hoarie.*

Blanc bois. *Box, Poplar, Aspe, Alder, and other such trees, whose wood is no timber.*

Bois blanc. *Priuet, Pimprint:* ¶Lionnois.

Blancs yeux. gens aux blancs yeux. *Cowards, dastards, faint-hearted, white-liuered, meale-mouthed fellowes.*

Carte blanche. *A blanke. See* Carte.

Dimanche de blanches. *Palmes-Sunday.*

Espée blanche. *A naked, or vnsheathed (also, a bloudlesse, or peaceable, sword;) whence;*

Cela ne se fait point à l'espée blanche. *That thing's not done without sound bobs, or bloudwipes.*

Fievres blanches. *The Agues wherewith maidens, that haue the greene sickenesse, be troubled.*

Fleurs blanches. *The Whites (a feminine disease.)*

Iournée blanche. *A Holy-day, or play-day.*

Ligne blanche. *The lower part of the bellie where the muscles thereof doe end (a tearme of Anotomie.)*

Menton blanc. *(Whence)* la vertu ne fut iamais à menton blanc. *Neuer had white, or hoarie chin,* viz. *neuer decayed, or grew old.*

Monnoye blanche. *White money; coyne of brasse, or copper, siluered ouer.*

Nihil blanc. *Seeke* Nihil.

Oeuvre blanche. *The making of all kind of yron tooles, as wedges, hedging bils, hatchets, &c, wherwith wood is cut.*

Pieds blancs. Il a les pieds blancs. *He passes euery where freely, or without paying ought, (from a custome they haue in* France, *to take no toll for such horses as haue foure white feet.)*

C'est le cheval aux quatre pieds blancs. *May from the same reason beare the same signification; yet is it most vsed to expresse, a Companion that promises much, and performes nought; or such a one as fails his friend at a pinch; (Looke* Cheval.)

Pomme blanche. *A pale apple.*

Solz, ou livres blancs. *As before, in* Monnoye blanche. *Siluer Sous, or two shilling peeces of siluer.*

Tunique blanche. *One of th'eyes principall tunicles; comes from th'inner skinne of th'eye lids, imbraces all the eye, and bindes it vnto the parts that bee about it.*

Blanc-doux. *A white sweeting; (an apple whereof excellent cyder is made.)*

Blance: f. *White wheat, square eared wheat.*

Blanchards: m. *An order of Friers, who goe ordinarily in white sheets, and weare neither hats nor shooes.*

Blanchastre: com. *Whitely, whitish; pale, wan, somewhat white, inclining to white.*

Blanche: f. *as* Blance; *Also, the Queene Dowager, so called of the people of* France, *because she euer mourned in white; a fashion altered at the funerall of* Henrie *the second by the late Queene Mother: also, whiting, or whiteliming.*

Des blanches. *A kind of the fish, called Bleaks.*

Blanche d'aigneaux. *White lamme, or white budge.*

Blancheastre. *as* Blanchastre.

Blanche-puce. *The Sea ground-Pine (a whitish hearb.)*

Blanche-putain. *The hearbe Ranke-goat, or stinking Motherwort.*
Blanche-pute. *as* Blanche-puce.
Blanche-queuë. *The rauenous Kite called, a Ringtaile.*
Blanchet: m. *A blanket for a bed; also, white wollen cloth; also, a peticote thereof; also, the apple called, a white sweeting.*
Blanchet: m. ette: f. *Whitish; or, a little white.*
Blanchette: f. *Fine white flower of wheat.*
Blancheur: f. *Whitenesse.*
Blanchi: m. ie: f. *Blanched, whited, whitened; also, sorted, or shifted, with cleane linnen.*
Blanchiment. *as* Blanchissage.
Blanchir. *To blanch, white, whiten, make white; also. to whiten, or grow white; also, to sort, suite, or shift, with cleane linnen.*
Blanchissage: m. *A whitning; a whiting, or white-liming; a pargetting white; also, a blanching.*
Blanchisseur: m. *A white dauber, or white limer; also, a whitener of clothes.*
Blanchisseuse: f. *A Laundresse, or woman that vses to whiten clothes.*
Blancque: f. *A blanke in rifling, or, in a lotterie; and hence;*
Ieu de la Blanque. *A rifling, or lotterie.*
Blancs-manteaux. *White cloakes; an order of begging Friers; Looke* Manteau.
Blanculet: m. *A Whittaile; or bird of her bignesse, thats verie fat, and very good meat.*
Blande: f. *A Salamander; called so of her slow, or soft, gate.*
Blandi: m. ie: f. *Blandished, flattered, soothed, smoothed, glozed with, fawned on; allured, inueagled with faire words.*
Blandices: f. *Soothings, flatterings, blandishments; allurements, inticements.*
Blandir. *To blandish, flatter, sooth, glose with, fawne on, make faire weather vnto, please, delight, or tickle the affection with faire words; also, to inueagle, allure, intice, by gentle tearmes, or meanes.*
Blandissant. *Soothing, smoothing, glozing with, pleasing, flattering, fawning on; inueagling, alluring, inticing, with faire words.*
Blandissement: m. *A blandishment; a soothing, smoothing, tickling of the mind, and affection with tearmes of flatterie; a clawing, a glozing with; an inueagling, alluring, inticing by faire words.*
Blandisseur: m. *A blandisher, gloser, soother, smoother, flattering sycophant, or claw-backe; also, an allurer, inticer, inueagler (by words, &c.)*
Blandureau: m. *The white apple, called (in some part of* England) *a Blaundrell.*
Blanque. *as* Blancque; *Also, a coyne thats worth about a penie* Tour.
Blanquet. *A kind of the best white wine of* Languedoc.
Blanquette. *The name of a delicate white Summer peare.*
Blaphard; & Blaphastre. *as* Blaffard; & Blaffastre.
Blareau. *as* Blaireau.
Blasmable: com. *Blamable, rebukeable, reproouable; worthie to be censured, or found fault with.*
Blasme: m. *Blame, rebuke, a checke; a censure; a reproofe, chiding, reprehension, redargution; also, an imputation, ill report, or discommendation.*
Blasme d'adveu. *The faults, omissions, errours, abuses found, or quoted by a Lord in the Survey deliuered him by his tenant.*
Blasmé: m. ée: f. *Blamed, rebuked, chidden, taxed, shent, reproued, censured, condemned; disallowed, discommended, accused, found fault with.*
Blasmer. *To blame, rebuke, checke, taxe, chide, reproue, reprehend; censure; accuse, disallow, discommend, condemne, find fault with.*
Blasmer l'adveu. *A Lord to disallow of, wrangle about, or, vtterly to refuse as faultie, or defectiue, the survey deliuered him by his tenant.*
Blason: m. *Armes, or, a coat of Armes; also, the scutchion, or shield wherein Armes are painted, or figured; also, Blazon, or the blazing of Armes; also, prayse, commendation, &c.*
Blason funebre. *A funerall Oration.*
Blasonnant: m. ante: f. *Blazing Armes; also, praising, extolling, commending; also, (the contrarie) reproching, dispraising, detracting from.*
Blasonné: m. ée: f. *Blazed, as a coat, or scutchion of Armes; also, praised, extolled, commended; also, (the contrarie) dispraised, reproached, detracted from.*
Blasonner. *To blaze Armes; also, to praise, extoll, commend; or, to publish the prayses, diuulge the perfections, proclaime the vertues of; also (the contrarie) to reproue, dispraise, derogate, or detract from; (In which sence we also vse the word, blaze.)*
Blasonneur: m. *A Herauld; or, skilfull blazer of Arms; also, a reuiler, detracter, euill speaker, foule mouthed fellow.*
Blasphemateur: m. *A blasphemer; a reuiler of God; a railer on goodnesse.*
Blasphematoire: com. *Blasphematorie, blasphemous.*
Blaspheme: m. *Blaspemie; an opprobrious reuiling of God, or goodnesse; any horrible execration, or great, and causelesse oath, wherein Gods name is abused.*
Blasphemé: m. ée: f. *Blasphemed.*
Blasphemer. *To blaspheme, curse, reuile God, or his workes, (as they be his.)*
Blasser. *To foment, moysten, or, bath gently with the hand a hurt (especially about a horse.)*
Blatir. *To knit, contract, gather vp, draw, or shrinke in, himselfe.*
Blattaire. *Mothe-mulleyn (an hearbe.)*
Blatte: f. *A certaine moath which gnawes both cloth, and bookes; also, a beetle; also, a kind of red wheat; also, a silkeworme; also, as* Belette.
Blatte bysance. *The small, smooth, and long shell of a certaine fish, vsed in perfumes, and called in shops,* Onyx, &, vnguis odoratus.
Blattier: m. *A marchant, or ingrosser of corne.*
Blavée: f. *Corne land; or, land which hath corne growing on it.*
Blavelles. *as* Blaveoles.
Blaveoles: f. *Blew bottles, Blew blawes, Corne flowers.*
Blaves. *as* Blaveoles; *Or, wild Poppie.*
Blavier: m. ée: f. *Of, or belonging to corne, or corne land.*
Sergent blavier. *An Officer that watches, and looks vnto corne grounds vntill they be reaped, or cut.*
Blaureau. *as* Blaireau.
Blayer. Seigneur blayer. *A Lord that hath* Droict de blayrie.
Blayeries: f. *Corne lands, corne grounds, corne countries.*
Blayrie: f. *A corne ground, or corne countrey; also, the*

feeding of cattell vpon corne lands, a raking with cattell ouer corne lands; also, the season (from th'Annunciation to th'end of Haruest) wherein cattell may, in some places, be turned, by some priuiledged persons, into common corne grounds.

Droict de blayrie. *Libertie, to turne his cattell a grazing into common corne grounds; or, as in* Blairie.

Blé. *as* Bled.

Blece-esprit. (*For,* Blesse-esprit) *Soule-hurting, spirit-wounding.*

Bleceure: f. *as* Blessure.

Bleche: com. *Flaggie, ouer soft; puft vp with an vnsound fulnesse.*

Blecque. pomme blecque. *An apple thats too ripe, or too mellow.*

Bled: m. *(Any manner of) corne; and particularly (or when tis vsed without addition) wheat.*

Bled barbu. *A kind of Panicke, tearmed by some, Turkie Hirse, by others, out-landish Panicke, or bearded wheat; also the ordinarie bearded wheat.*

Bled bernage. *Meslin, or moulture corne; Wheat, Rie, and Barley mingled; also, corne that grew on a mans owne land, or in his owne soyle; corne of that countrey, or of a certaine countrey.*

Bled frime. *Horse-flower, Oxe-wheat, Cow-wheat; Blacke-wheat.*

Bled d'Inde. *as* Bled de Turquie.

Bled leger. *Spelt, or Zea; a corne which makes light and sauorie, but not verie nourishing, bread.*

Bled locar. *Saint Peters corne; (a kind of wall Barley.)*

Bled mestail. *Meslin; Wheat, Rye, and Barley, mingled.*

Bled Marsés. *March corne; any corne thats vsually sowed in March; also, as* Excourgeon.

Bled mouture. *Moulture corne; or Meslin.*

Bled noir. *Blacke wheat, Cow-wheat, Oxe-wheat.*

Bled poullart, & poullé. *as* Bled locar.

Bled rouge. *Ordinarie red wheat; called by some Kentishmen, Duck-wheat, and* Normandie *wheat.*

Bled Sarrasin. *French wheat, Bucke-wheat, Bolymong (a verie course graine;) also, as* Bled de Turquie.

Bled tremés. *March corne, Summer corne; such corne as is ripe within three moneths after it is sowen.*

Bled turguet. *Amelcorne, Starch-corne.*

Bled de Turquie. *Turkie corne, Turkie wheat; (whereof there be diuers kinds, differing in colour.)*

Traite de bleds. *An imposition of iij. pounds x. shillings* Tour. *vpon euerie tunne of wheat (and ratably, vpon all sorts of graine) transported.*

Manger son bled en herbe. *To turne his cattell into his corne before it be eared; or, to sell his corne on the ground, and spend the money before it be ripe; to spend his rents before they be due, his reuenew before it come in; wastfully to consume, or send packing, his patrimonie.*

Prendre entre la haye, & le bled. *To surprise, or take vnprouided.*

'A quelque pris qu'est le bled. *How deere soeuer it cost me, how hardly soeuer I come by it, what price soeuer I giue for it.*

En petit champ croist bien bon blé: Prov. *Small fields haue good corne growing in them.*

On seme les bleds à l'auanture: Prov. viz. *Not knowing whether they will come vp or no.*

Bledier: m. ere: f. *Of, or belonging to, corne.*

Terre blediere. *Corne ground; land that beares corne, or abounds therein.*

Bleme. *as* Blesme.

Blemy. *Growne pale, wan, bleake, white.*

Blepharoïde. Tunique ble. *One of the eyes little tunicles, whereby the waterie humour is distinguished from the glassie one.*

Blereau. *as* Blaireau. *A Badger.*

Blesme: com. *Pale, wanne, bleake, whitish, dead coloured.*

Se loger sur le blesme. *Seeke* Loger.

Blesmet: m. ette: f. *Somewhat pale, a little wan.*

Blesmi: m. ie: f. *Growne pale, wan, bleake.*

Blesmer. *To looke pale, grow wan, wax bleake, whitish, dead coloured.*

Blesmissement: m. *Palenesse, wannesse, bleakenesse; also, a looking, or waxing, pale, wan, bleake.*

Blesmisseure: f. *as* Blesmissement.

Blessable: com. *Woundable.*

Blessé: m. ée: f. *Hurt, wounded; vlcerated; whose flesh is cut, or bruisd; whose skin is fretted off.*

Blesser. *To wound, or hurt; (whether by a bloudwipe, dry blow, or bruise) to vlcerate, or fret off, the skin.*

Blesser l'hnnoeur de. *To depraue, or detract from; to blemish the reputation of.*

Tel tue qui ne pense que blesser: Prov. *Some kill such as they would but hurt.*

Blessure: f. *A wound, or hurt; an (offensiue, or painfull) blow, cut, bruise, or skarre; also, a wounding, or hurting.*

Blet: m. *A blocke, doult, luske, sot, hoydon, lobcocke.*

Blete: f. *A turfe, or peat:* ¶Norm.

Blette: f. *The hearbe called Blite, and Blits; also, as* Belette.

Blette blanche. *The great, or ordinarie (white) Blite.*

Blette d'Espaigne. *Spanish Beets; or th'ordinarie Blites; (an hearbe that hath neither sauour, tast, nor store of qualities.)*

Blette grande. *The great red Beet, or Blite.*

Blette noire. *as* Blette rouge.

Blette rouge. *Th'ordinarie red Blite.*

Blette. poire blette. *An ouer-ripe peare; a peare thats rotten, or vnsound at the heart.*

Bleu: m. bleuë: f. *Blew.*

Bleüastre: com. *Blewish, or somewhat blew.*

Bleüet: m. *Blew-bottle, Blew-blaw, Corne-flower, Hurt-sickle.*

Blistres. *as* Belistres; *Also, the hearbe called Bleets.*

Bloc: m. *A grosse, great, or generalitie; the whole of; or a heape of diuers wares hudled together; also, a block, or log.*

En bloc. *Summarily, by great, in the whole.*

En bloc, & en tasche. *One with another, tag and rag, all together.*

Blocaille: f. *Rubbish, shards, ragged stones; any grosse stuffe, whereof rude walls (or morter for stone walls) are made.*

Bloccage: m. *as* Blocaille.

Bloccageux: m. euse: f. *Full of shards; rubbish, &c.*

Bloccaille. *as* Blocaille.

Bloccailleux. *as* Bloccageux.

Blocul: m. *The chiefest pole that vpholdeth a tent; also, a little fort, or block-house.*

Blond: m. blonde: f. *Light yellow, straw coloured, flaxen; also, (in hawkes, or stags) bright tawnie, or deer-coloured.*

Blondelet: m. ette: f. *Yellowish, pale yellow, somewhat flaxen haired.*

Blondir. *To grow light yellow, flaxen, or straw coloured.*

Blondoré : m.ée : f. *Of a golden yellow.*
Blondoyement : m. *A making, or becomming light yellow.*
Blondoyer. *as* Blondir.
Blondurel. *The Blaundrell apple.*
Bloquaille. *as* Blocaille.
Bloquer. *To ſhut in, or block vp; to beſiege, beſet, or compaſſe on all ſides; alſo, to conclude, or make vp a bargaine.*
Bloquil. *as* Blocul *(in the firſt ſence.)*
Bloſse. poire bloſſe. *An ouer mellow peare; a peare ſo ſoft as it is readie to rot.*
Blot. *as* Bloc.
Bloti : m.ie : f. *Squat, skowked, hidden; lying, or kept cloſe.*
Blotir. *To ſquat, skowke, or lye cloſe to the ground, like a daring Larke, or affrighted fowle; alſo, to hide, or keepe, cloſe.*
Blotte. *as* Bloutre.
Blotter. *To blot, ſtaine, blemiſh, defile.*
Bloty : m.ye : f. *Squat; laid cloſe; kept cloſe.*
Blouquette. *See* Bouclette.
Blouse : f. *A cloſe Tennis court, or a Tennis court in a hall, hauing a houſe on either ſide to ſerue on; ſo called at* Orleans.
Bloutre : f. *A clod, or clot of earth.*
Bloutré : m. ée : f. *Cloddie; full of clods.*
Bloutroer : m. *A Rowler; the round woodden inſtrument wherewith allyes are ſmoothed; walkes planed; and clods broken.*
Bloutroir. *as* Bloutroer.
Bluard : m.arde : f. *Gray, skie coloured, blewiſh.*
Bluet : m. *Blew-blaw, Blew-bottle, Corne-flower, Hurtſickle.*
Bluette : f. *A little ſtreake, or ſparke of heat, in the aire, when the ſeaſon is verie hot; and, more generally, any ſparke, or ſparkle of a flame.*
Bluetter. *To ſparke, or ſparkle; to caſt out, or yeeld forth ſparkes, or ſparkles.*
Blute. *as* Bluet.
Bluté : m. ée : f. *Boulted, alſo, toſſed, or ſwungd vp & downe.*
Bluteau : m. *A boulting cloth.*
Bluter. *To boult meale; alſo, to ſwing vp and downe, as a Baker doth his boulting cloth.*
Bluterie : f. *A boulting tub; alſo, a boulting.*
Bluteur. *A boulter of meale.*
A bon bluteur May propice : Prov. *A wooer ſpeeds (oft times) the better for his weapon.*
Bluttage : m. *A boulting of meale, &c.*
Bluttement : m. *A boulting; alſo, a ſwinging vp and downe.*
Blutté. *as* Bluté.
Blutteau. *as* Bluteau.
Blutter. *as* Bluter; *To boult, &c.*
Blutteur. *A boulter of meale; Seeke* Bluteur.
Bluttis. *A boulting tub; or a roome to boult meale in.*
Bluttoir : m. *The ſame.*
Bo. *as* Bois; *Wood:* ¶Pic.
Boage : f. *A place in Abbies, &c, full of drawers, wherein they lay vp Copes, &c.*
Bobance : f. *Riot, luxurie, vnthriftneſſe, exceſſiue ſpending, immoderate expence; (and becauſe that humour is commonly accompanied with pride, it ſignifies) alſo, inſolencie, ſurquedrie, proud or preſumptuous boaſting.*
Bobancer. *To Riot, ſquander, waſt, outlaſh; alſo, to boaſt.*
Bobancier : m. *An vnthrift, riotous waſter, ſuperfluous ſpender, immoderate ſtroy-good, luxurious or exceſſiue ſquanderer; (And becauſe ſuch a one is, commonmonly, proud of his (as he preſumes) liberalitie, it ſignifies) alſo, a proud, ſaucie, boaſting, or inſolent, aſſe.*
Bobans : m. *Riot, luxurie, waſting, vnthriftineſſe, exceſſiue ſpending, ſuperfluous, or immoderat expence; or as* Bobance.
Bobelin : m. *A patch, botch, peece, ſet on a ſhooe, or garment.*
Bobeline : f. *An old patched ſhooe, or garment.*
Bobeliner. *To cobble, patch, botch, or mend an olde thing.*
Bobelineur : m. *A cobler, botcher, patcher, mender of old things.*
Bobine : f. *A quill for a ſpinning wheele; alſo, a skaine, or banke of gold, or ſiluer thread.*
Bobulaire : com. *Big, huge, vnweldie like an Oxe.*
Bobulaires : f. *Toyes, traſh; dotings, doltiſh things.*
Bocage : m. *A groue, thicket, or ſmall wood; a place thats ſtored, or ſet thicke with trees; whence;*
Païs de bocage. *A wood-land countrey.*
Bocager : m.ere : f. *Grouie, wooddie; of, or belonging to groues, thickets, woods; alſo, frequenting, or affecting thickets, groues, or woods.*
Bocageux; *as* Bocager; *Or, full of thickets, groues, or woods.*
Bocagier : m.ere : f. *Wooddie, grouie; &c; as* Bocager.
Bocal : m. *A Viol; or any ſuch (big-bellied, long-necked, and ſmall-mouthed) veſſell, of earth, or (the more properly) of glaſſe; for water, wine, &c.*
Boccabrevé : f. *The name of a certaine apple.*
Boccaner. *as* Boucaner.
Boccaſin : m. *Boccaſin; or, a kind of fine buckeram, that hath a reſemblance of taffata, and is much vſed for lining; alſo, the ſtuffe Callimanco.*
Boce. *Looke* Boſſe.
Bochaſſe. *A wild Cheſtnut.*
Bocie : f. *A lymbecke, or ſtillitorie.*
Boclus. *Looke* Bouclus.
Bocon. *as* Boucon.
Bocque : f. *A kind of great-eyed Cackerell fiſh, the which hath on her back many golden, and ſiluer-hued ſtreaks running along from her neck to her taile; alſo, a floudgate, or ſluce.*
Bocquer. *To butte, or iurre.*
Bocquet : m. *A groue, or thicket; a little wood.*
Bode : m. *A young Bull.*
Boëſſeau : m. *as* Boiſſeau.
Boëſſelet. *as* Boiſſelet. *A little buſhell.*
Boëte; & Boëtte; *Looke* Boiſte; *alſo, ſmall, or houſehold wine.*
Boëtouyer. *To limpe, hault, be lame.*
Boëttelette : f. *A little box.*
Boeuf : m. *An Ox; a Beefe; alſo, beefe.*
Boeuf bran, ou brane. *A kind of wild Oxe in* Prouence, *and* Langued. *vnreclaimable, and onely good for the ſhambles.*
Boeuf de dieu. *A Wren.*
Boeuf de mer. *The Seale, or Sea-calfe; alſo, a ſea monſter that reſembles an Oxe.*
Langue de boeuf. *The leſſe, and rougher, kind of Bugloſſe, called Oxe-tongue, and* Lang-de beef.
Mort aux boeufs. *A certaine hearbe whereof if an Oxe do eat he dies immediately of the ſquinſie; and therefore we may call it Oxebane.*
Mouche aux boeufs. *A brizze, gadbee, Oxe flie.*
Oeil de boeuf. *An out-ſtrouting, or great-goggle eye; alſo, the hearbe Oxe-eye; alſo, the hearbe called fooliſh Mathes,*

Mathes, vnsauorie white Cotula, and white vnsauorie Camomill; *Seeke* Oeil.
Pennache de boeuf. *A goodly paire of hornes.*
Teste de boeuf. *A ioulthead, iobernoll, cods-head, grouthead, logerhead; one whose wit is as little as his head is great.*
Homme de porc, & de boeuf. *A grosse, base, rude, vnciuile, or vnmanerly, churle; a clunch, a clusterfist.*
Prendre vn boeuf par les cornes. *To vndertake a dangerous exploit.*
Quiter vn boeuf pour prendre vn oeuf. *To quit an Oxe for an egge; or, as our fenne-men, rather catch a ducke than feed an Oxe.*
Tourner la charrue contre les boeufs. *We say, to set the cart before the horse; Looke* Tourner.
Le boeuf las marche souef: Prov. *The wearie Oxe goes slowly; men that are beaten to the practise of the world are calme, and moderate in their proceedings.*
Le boeuf par la corne, & l'homme par la parole: Prov. Se lient, *is vnderstood; (for in forreine countries Oxen are yoked by the hornes.)*
Le boeuf salé faict trouver le vin sans chandelle: Prov. *The salt beefe-eater needs no candle to find his liquor withall; or salt beefe is your onely lantorne in a darke sellar.*
Le grand boeuf apprend à labourer au petit: Pro. *The old Oxe teaches the young to draw; wee say (with some small difference) the young cocke croweth, as he the old heareth.*
Les grands boeufs ne font pas les grandes iournées: Pro. *The greatest Oxen rid not most worke; we say, the greatest crabs are not all the best meat.*
Au pauvre vn oeuf vaut vn boeuf: Prov. *An egge is as deere to a poore man, as an Oxe to a rich; or, a poore man is as well content with an egge as with an Oxe.*
Dieu donne biens & boeuf, mais ce n'est pas par la corne: Prov. *God giues things plentifully and without perill.*
Il ne faut iouër au boeuf: Prov. *An Oxe is no fit, or no safe, play-fellow.*
Mieux vaut en paix vn oeuf qu' en guerre vn boeuf: Prov. *Seeke* Oeuf.
On a beau mener le boeuf à l'eau s'il n' a soif: Pro. *In vaine is an Oxe led to the water if he be not athirst; we say (with some difference of sence) a man may lead his horse to the water, but cannot make him drinke vnlesse he list.*
Pas à pas le boeuf prend le lievre: Pro. *A patient, & moderat proceeding, effects great matters.*
Bogue. *as* Bocque; *Also, the bunch, top, tuft, or huske wherein the seeds of hearbs are inclosed; (whence) also, the rough, or prickly rind of a greene chestnut.*
Bogue ravel. *Seeke* Ravel.
Bohade. *as* Bouäde: ¶Auvergnois.
Bohourd. *as* Behourd.
Bohourder. *as* Behourder.
Bohu. *Emptie, vacant*: ¶Rab.
Boicheron: m. *A wood-cleauer, or wood-feller.*
Boie: f. *A kind of great water-snake, that vses to sucke whole heards of kine.*
Boiffer. *To bungle vp, or slubber ouer, things in hast.*
Boiffeur: m. *A bungler vp, or slubberer ouer, of things in hast.*
Boileau. *An ordinarie drinker of water.*
Boiler. *as* Vouloir; *To will*: ¶Gasc.
Boilesve. *as* Boileau.
Boire: m. *Drinke, beuerage.*
Il se sent vn peu de boire. *He is somewhat mustie, a little mellow, almost ouerseene (in drinke.)*
Boire. *To drinke, bouse, bib, swill, quaffe, tipple; to sucke, or swallow vp; to receiue, or soke in; also, to smell, or vent, an ill sauour.*
Boire sa bride. *A horse to draw vp his bit into his mouth with his tongue.*
Boire la goutte sur l'ongle. *To leaue but one onely drop in the cup.*
Boire a-lut. *To drinke all out, all vp; to leaue iust nothing.*
Boire son mors. *as* Boire sa bride.
Boy le vin comme Roy, boy l'eau comme Taureau: Pro. *For th'one vses not to drinke much, th'other will drinke no more than he needs.*
Assez boit qui a dueil: Prov. *He hath drinke ynough that hath sorrow ynough; or, as in* Dueil.
'A petite fontaine boit on à son aise: Prov. *In a meane estate most ease.*
Aller & parler peut on, boire ensemble & manger non: Pro. *A man may visit, & conuerse with a friend, but must not, if he meane to keepe him, feed with him; the best way to preserue a friend, is, not to be verie inward with him.*
Apres compter il faut boire: Prov. *The reckoning ended we must drinke together; (a Dutch conclusion.)*
Apres tout dueil boit on bien: Pro. *(So tipling succeedeth teeene.)*
Celuy de bon sens ne jouït, qui boit & ne s' en resjouït: Pro. *He that in drinking feels no pleasure, his wits be surely out of measure.*
Qui a fait la faute si la boive: Prov. *Let him that did amisse be punished.*
Qui bon l'achepte bon le boit: Pro. *He that buyes good wine drinks good wine.*
Qui n'a laine bovie à la fontaine: Pro. *Let him that hath no wealth drinke at the well.*
Tel est petit qui boit bien: Pro. *Though he be little he can tipple.*
Tel fait la faute qu'un autre boit: Pro. *One commits the fault which another is blamed for.*
Vne fois l'année l'on s'appreste à boire: Pro. *Once in a yeare a man prepares himselfe to drinke; (viz. of his owne wine, in vintage time.)*
Bois: m. *Wood; also, a wood; also, a staffe, launce, or speare; also, the head, or hornes of a deere.*
Bois d'aloë. *th'aromatical wood called* Lignũ Aloes.
Bois de baulme. *The sweet wood of the Balsam tree.*
Bois bedat. *Looke* Bedat.
Bois blanc. *Priuet; (called so at* Lyons) *also, as* Blanc bois.
Bois de brin. *Round, or vnclest-small-wood (of what kind soeuer.)*
Bois de carde. *Small billets; or wood thats like, but lesse than, billets.*
Bois chablis. *Windfalls; Looke* Chablis.
Bois de charpente. *Timber.*
Bois pour charrons. *Yple plankes.*
Bois de coupe. *See* Coupe.
Bois cuict. *Charcoale.*
Bois debout. *The branch (of a vine) left growing (whẽ all the rest are lopped) for a future yeares increase.*
Bois de deluge. *Okẽ trees, or timber, which hauing bin lõg orewhelmed in water, are become as black as Ebony*
Bois d'escaille. *The heart of wood, or of timber (so called by Ioyners.)*
Bois d'esquine. *The knottie, and medicinable root of a certaine (Indian) bullrush.*
Bois à faucillon. *Brush wood, small wood.*

Bois flotte. *A float-boat; of wood, or timber, fastened together, and conueied down a streame vnto the place where it is to be sold or vsed.*
Bois flotté. *The same.*
Bois fruictier. *The branch of a tree, or plant, which beareth fruit; a fruit-bearing branch.*
Bois de fustée. *Branchlesse wood; naked, or powld, trees.*
Bois gentil. *The plant Mezereon, Germane Oliue-spurge, Dwarfe-Bay.*
Bois de haute fustaye. *High trees, tall & great trees, goodly woods; properly, such as haue not beene cut, nor lopped of at the least 30 yeres before; Looke* Fustaye.
Bois Hierosme. *The name of a certaine tender and delicate peare.*
Le bois d'une lict. *A bedstead.*
Bois mort. *All kind of dead, and drie wood in forrests; firewood.*
Bois moslé. *as* Bois de moulle; *especially in the last sence.*
Bois de moulle. *Billets; logs; or log-wood; great firewood of a certaine size; or any wood that hath beene assized by a* Mouleur.
Bois d'oeuvre. *Great timber, or wood, squared, and readie for vse, or worke.*
Bois puant. *Stinking beane-trefoile; (a shrub.)*
Bois de quartier. *Quarters of timber; or timber for quarters.*
Bois revenant. *A copse, or yong wood.*
Bois sainct. *Gwacum, Pock-wood.*
Bois de sap, ou de sapin. *Deale planks, deale boords.*
Bois de serpe. *Wood of ten yeres growth, or vpwards.*
Bois taillis. *Copse-wood, vnder-wood; such wood as is felled, or cut euery seuen or eight yeares.*
Bois de touche. *A holt, groue, or thicke Tuft of high trees (growing neere a house, & gracing the seat therof.)*
Bois vedat. *as* Bois bedat; *Looke* Bedat.
Blanc bois. *Box, willow, Poplar, Aspe, & other smaller trees, whose wood is not fit for timber-worke.*
Gentil bois. *Wild line, wild flax.*
Long bois. *A pike, launce, or speare.*
Mort bois. *Willow, Thorne, Alder, Broome, Ginepar; generally, all trees that either beare no fruit, or no profitable fruit.*
Grand abbateur de bois. *A great bugbeare, kill-cow, scarre-crow.*
Ie cognois bien de quel bois il se chauffe. *I know well ynough what helps he vseth, what meanes he relies on; or, I know very well what stuffe there is in him, what matter he's made of; what course hee followes, what maner of life he leads.*
Il est du bois dont on le fait. *Said of a dull fellow, or of one that is no other than he is made, or hath nothing but what is put into him.*
Faire de bois flesches. Il ne sçait plus de quel bois faire flesches. *He is at the last cast, at his wits end, at his vtmost; he knowes no longer what course to take, what meanes to vse, what shift to make.*
Faire de tout bois flesches. *To vse euery thing, or entertaine any thing, that serues his turne, or makes for his purposes.*
Faire haut le bois. *Souldiors to stop and make a stand, aduancing their pikes; also, to drinke hard, carouse lustily, quaffe apace.*
Faire visage de bois à. *To shut, or clap to, a doore against; in stead of a welcome to shut out of doores.*
Pour fendre le bois il fit des coings du bois mesme *He made the mans owne meanes &c, the instruments of his ruine.*
Mettre le doigt entre le bois, & l'escorce. *To intrude himselfe, or looke too far into, the businesses, or controuersies, which are betweene two neere friends; also, to set them at ods, or together by the eares.*
L'oeil tendu au bois. *Warily, watchfully, circumspectly; aduisedly; as one that tends, heeds, or lookes well to, his charge, or businesse.*
Vn oeil au bois l'autre à la ville. *Seeke* Oeil.
Porter bien son bois. *(A horseman) to carrie, or wield his staffe with a good grace.*
Elle porte bien son bois. *She is of a comely, stately, gallant carriage; or, shee hath a tall, straight, or vpright bodie, and as well she beares it.*
Porter des fueilles au bois. *To carrie leaues to the wood; to powre water into the sea.*
Retourner au champ du bois. *To fall vnto his former ill course, or pace; to returne to his old haunt, or vomit.*
La victoire sera comme il plaira au bois qui aura bonne beste. *He shall win the victorie that can best bestirre himselfe, or lay about him.*
Bois laid, & inutile porte le fruict pretieux: Prov. *(Meant of the vine) so may a foule, and foolish mother beare an excellent daughter.*
Bois ont oreilles, & champs oeillets: Prov. *Some heare, and see him, whom he heareth, nor seeth not; but fields haue eyes, and woods haue eares, ye wot;* (¶Heywood.)
Le bois acquiert le plain. *Seeke* Plain.
Tout bois vaut busches: Prov. *All wood is worth logs.*
'A conseil de fol cloche de bois: Prov. *For woodden consultations woodden bells.*
Il fait mauvais aller au bois quand les loups s'entremangent: Prov. *Tis ill going to the wood when wolues (are so hungrie, that they) eat one another.*
La faim chasse les loups hors du bois: Prov. *Hunger driues wolues out of the wood; or (as we say) breaks downe stone walls.*
Pour neant va au bois qui marrein ne cognoist: Pro. *To no purpose he vndertakes a businesse that vnderstands not the substance, effect, or end, of it.*
Boise: f. *A log, or great peece of wood; and (more particularly) a brace, of timber.*
Boissé: m. ée: f. *Hafted, or trimd with box.*
Boisseau: m. *The (French) bushell; (and the 12 part of a* Septier) *is somewhat lesse than our London pecke, & a halfe; for a* Boisseau *of wheat weighes 20 pounds; our pecke of wheat meale, 14.*
Boissel d'ozier. *A weele, or weere of Ozier twigs.*
Boisselet: m. *A small (French) bushell; or, the halfe of a* Boisseau.
Boisselier: m. *A maker, or seller of* Boisseaux.
Boissiere: f. *A hedge, thicket, or plot of Box trees.*
Boisson: f. *Drinke; any liquor wherewith our thirst is quenched; and particularly, small houshold wine.*
Boissonnerie: f. *Excessiue drinking; swilling, quaffing.*
Boiste: f. *A box; pix; forset; little casket; also, a chamber for a peece of ordnance; also, as* Auche.
Boiste de gouvernail. *The socket of a Rudder.*
La boiste d'un os. *The hollow panne wherein a buckle-bone is lodged.*
Lance à boiste. *A launce with a blunt, or burre head; a tilting staffe.*
Es petites boistes met on les bons onguens: Prov. *Sweet ointments are in little boxes put.*

Boiste-

Boistelette : f. *A little box, or pix.*
Boistemént : m. *A limping, halting, lamenesse, of a leg.*
Boistément. *Limpingly, haltingly, lamely.*
Boister. *To limpe, hault; be lame, vnperfect, maimed of a leg.*
Boisteux : m. euse : f. *Limping, cripple, halting, lame of a leg.*
Attendre la venue du boisteux. *To expect a matter thats slow, or long in comming.*
Clocher deuant les boisteux. *See* Clocher.
Boistusant, *Limping, halting.*
Boite. *as* Boiste.
Ce vin est en sa boite. *This wine is drinkable, in season to be drunke, fit to be drawne.*
Boitement. *A limping, or halting.*
Boiter. *To limpe, to halt.*
Boiteux. *as* Boisteux.
Boitouser. *To limpe, halt; be lame of a leg.*
Boitte : f. *as* Boiste; &, *as* Boite.
Boitte de foing. *A bottle of hay*; (v.m.)
Bovin : m. *A wine drinker; one that drinks nothing but wine, or wine for the most part.*
Bol : m. *Th'astringent, and medicinable red earth, or minerall, called* Bolearmenie; *also, as* Bolus.
Bol Oriental; &, Bol Armenien Oriental. *Oriental Bolearmenie; the best, and truest kind of Bolearmenie, ministred (with good effect) against all poisons, and in pestilent diseases; and more red than the ordinarie one, which should rather bee tearmed Sinopian red earth than Bolearmenie; Looke* Rubrique Sinopique.
Bolar : m. *A kind of Aspe-resembling tree; called thus about* Tours.
Bolarmene. *Bolearmenie.*
Bole d'Armenie. *The same.*
Bolet : m. *A little mushrome, or toadstoole; as,* Bolete.
Bolete : f. *A little toadstoole, or mushrome; white without, red within, and the best meat of all others.*
Bolieure : f. *A lip, or chap.*
Boline : f. *The Boline; a rope vsed when a ship sayls with a side wind, or goes neere a wind; whence;*
Vent à la boline. *A side, or scant wind.*
Boliner. *To sayle by a wind, or close vpon a wind; to lay tacke aboord.*
Bolleau. *as* Bouleau.
Bollettes de Cypres. *Cyprus nuts, or Clogs.*
Bolouër : m. *A bulwarke.*
Bolus : m. *A gobbet; morsell, mouth-full; as much as one can let downe at once; also, clay which hath no minerall substance in it.*
Bombance : f. *as* Bobans; *Also, a bragging, or vaunting.*
Bombarde : f. *A Bumbard, or murthering peece.*
Bombarder. *To discharge a Bumbard; to batter, or murder with Bumbards.*
Bombardier, *A Bumbardier, or gunner that vseth to discharge murthering peeces; and, more generally, any gunner.*
Bombasin : m. *The stuffe Bumbasine; or any kind of stuffe thats made of cotton, or of cotton, and linnen.*
Bombycine : f. *The second, and worse kind of the Leuant Manna, being also, commonly, sophisticated.*
Bon : m. *The goodnesse, good, or best of a thing; the height, principall part, or point, of a matter.*
Le bon de l'argent. *The surplusage, or ouerplus of the money.*
Le bon fut. *The best, or, onely sport of it, was.*
Au bon du coup. *When most good may be done in the matter; or, when it is time to do a mans best in it.*
Avoir du bon. Il veut tousiours avoir du bon. *He will euer be in the right; in dispute he must alwayes be yeelded vnto.*
Faire bon avec. Il faict bon avec luy. *He is a good master, his seruice (or companie) is worth the hauing.*
Faire bon pour. *To answer, or giue his word for; also, to play the game of.*
Tenez moy bon. *Hold me play, keepe me tacke, stand to me, continue with me.*
Bon : m. Bonne : f. *Good, honest, vertuous, vpright, sincere; also, apt, orderly, meet, fit; right; currant; holesome, plausible; fauourable, gracious, propitious; also, valiant, hardie, couragious; also, able, durable; sufficient.*
Bon homme; & bonne femme. *A title commonly bestowed on an old man, or woman in reuerence of their age; whereupon some will merily answer to such as thinke to grace them with that title,* Ie ne vas pas encores au baston.
Bon temps. *Prosperitie; also, merriment; or, time spent in merriment.*
Bailler bonne. Il luy l'a baillé bonne. *He hath plagued him throughly, he hath tickled him soundly, he hath paid him home, he hath dealt extreamly with him; also, he hath giuen him a notable gudgeon.*
Vous la baillez bonne. *True Roger; now you haue hit it; now you pay it home; Ironically.*
Estre en ses bonnes. *To be in a good mood, plausible humor, pleasant vaine; also, to be kindly disposed.*
Il la luy garda bonne. *He owed him a good turne; also, (the contrarie) he bore him a grudge, a long time after, for it.*
Tenir bon. *To hold good, to continue faithfull, or constant in a matter.*
Iouer à bonne veuë. *To play sure play, stand on safe tearmes, hazard little or nothing, know well ynough what he does.*
Tout à bon. *Throughly, fully.*
Trouver bon. *To approue, applaud, like, allow of.*
Bon Advocat mauvais voisin : Prov. *A good Councellor an ill companion.*
Bonne beste s'eschauffe en mangeant: Prov. *A good beast eats apace; or, as we say, good at meat good at worke.*
Bon charron tourne en petit lieu : Prov. *A skilfull carter turnes in a narrow corner.*
Bon chasteau garde qui sçait son corps garder : Pro. *He is a sufficient warder that can defend his own bodie.*
Bon coeur ne peut mentir: Pro. *An honest heart cānot, a worthy heart wil not, vtter, or be th'author of, vntruthes.*
Bon droict a bon mestier d'aide : Prov. *Good right hath need of great helpe; (so much ado haue men (in this vniust age) to recouer, or keepe, their owne.)*
Bon est le dueil qui apres aide : Prov. *Happie is that sorrow which is rewarded with happinesse.*
Bon est le lievre dont la peau couste cent sols: Pro. *Seeke* Lievre.
Bon est le medecin qui se sçait guarir : Prov. *He is a good Physitian that can heale his owne infirmitie.*
Bon gaignage fait bon potage : Pro. *Look* Potage.
Bon gré mal gré va le prestre au Sené : Prov. *(Some will expound this by a prouerbe of ours; he must needs go whom the diuell driues.)*
Bon guet chasse malaventure: Pro. *Good watch preuents misfortune; (fast bind fast find, say we.)*
Bonne iournée fait qui de fol se delivre: Pro. *he does an excellent dayes work that rids himselfe of a foole.*
Bonne la maille qui sauve le denier : Prov. *Well is*

is that halfepenie spent that saues a penie.
Bon marché tire l'argent de la bourse: Prov. *A cheape commoditie picks a customers purse.*
Bons mots n'espargnent nul: Prov. *A good mans words are no way partiall; good words pay home.*
Bonne mule mauuaise beste: Prov. *A good huswife is commonly no sheepe.*
Bons nageurs sont à la fin noyez: Prov. *Looke* Nageur.
Bon païs mauuais chemin: Pro. *In a fruitfull ground there is filthie going; in the best soyle the worst way.*
Bonne parole bon lieu tient: Prov. *Good speech finds good entertainment; wins great preferment.*
Bon sang ne peut mentir: Prov. *A worthy nature cannot conceale it selfe. Looke* Mentir.
Bon vin bon vinaigre: Prov. *Good wine (yeelds) good vinegar.*
Bon vin mauuaise teste: Pro. *Strong wine makes a weake braine; or, makes a man apt to brabble; (for we say of those that after drinking fall to swagger; their wine begins to worke.)*
'A bon chien bon os: Prov. *A good dog merits a good bone; Looke* Chien.
'A bon demandeur bon refuseur: Prov. *A bold asker is best matched by a resolute denier.*
'A bon entendeur ne faut qu'une parole: Pro. *The wise vnderstand a man by one word.*
'A bon iour bon oeuvre, & bonnes paroles: Pro. *A good day would be solemnized with good works, and good words.*
'A bon vin il ne faut point d'enseigne: Prov. *Good wine draws customers without any help of an Iuy-bush.*
Apres bon vin bon cheval: Pro. *Looke* Cheval.
Aux bons meschet il: Prov. *The honester man the worse lucke.*
De bon terroir bon vin: Prov. *A good soyle yeelds good fruit.*
En bonne maison l'on a tost apresté: Pro. *In an orderly, or plentifull house all things are soone made readie; or, we seldome tarie for our victuals.*
Femme bonne qui a mauuais mary a bien souvent le coeur marry: Pro. *Looke* Femme.
Il n'est si bon qu'aussi bon ne soit: Prov. *The best man hath his match; the purest his Peere; one may be euerie way as good as another.*
Il n'est si bon que femme n'assotte: Prov. *The wisest man's assotted by a woman.*
Il n'est si bon qui ne faille: Pro. *The best men commit faults; the wisest, errors.*
Le mauuais emporte le bon. *Seeke* Mauvais.
Qui bon l'achepte bon le boit: Pro. *He that will go to the price of, or take pains for, good things, may enioy good things.*
Qui bons lopins mange bons lopins le suyvent: Pro. *Prouision followes him that loues to fare well.*
Qui bon maistre sert bon loyer en attend: Pro. *He that serues a good master looks for a good reward.*
Qui bon vin boit il se repose: Prov. *He that drinks good wine takes good rest.*
Qui a bon voisin il a bon matin: Pro. *Look* Matin.
Tel a bonne cause qui est condamné: Prov. *A iust cause may be ouerthrowne by an vniust sentence.*
Toute chose qui est bonne à prendre est bonne à rendre: Pro. *Any thing thats good to be taken may wel be restored.*
Bonace: f. *as* Bonasse.
Bonace: com. *Calme, quiet, still, faire.*
Bonadies. *A good-morrow, good-day, good euen.*
Vn donneur de bonadies. *One thats sent vp and downe to carie salutations, or complements; also, a populer, or liberall, saluter of euery one he meets.*
Bonadres, *for* Bonadies. ¶Rab.
Bonasse: f. *A calme; faire, still, or quiet, weather at sea,*
Bonasse: com. *Calme, still, quiet; faire.*
Bon-crestien. poire de b. *A delicate Winter peare, in shape resembling our bastard warden.*
Bond: m. *A bound, a rebound; a hop, skip, leape, iumpe from the earth.*
Auoir le bond. Il eut doucement le bond. *He had the gentle thumpe.*
Donner le bond à. *In wrastling to ouerthrow, or giue a fall vnto.*
Faire vn faux bond; Elle a faict vn faux bond. *She hath got a crack; she hath plaid false, or trod her shooe awry.*
Il m'a faict vn faux bond. *He hath dealt falsly, or trecherously, with me.*
Perdre la volée pour le bond. *To loose an opportunitie, by neglecting it, vpon a hope that it will returne.*
Que de bond que de volée: Pro. *By hooke or crook; by right or wrong; any way; by any meanes; no matter how so we haue it; or, what by one means and another.*
Bonde: f. *A bung, or stopple; also, a sluce, or floudgate; and hence, also, the yate-stang, or beame thats pulled vp, when a mill is to be set agate.*
Lascher la bonde à. *To giue libertie, or free passage, vnto a violent thing.*
Bondelle. *A kind of fish thats not much vnlike a great Smelt; or, the least kind of the fish* Vmble, *well known by those of* Geneua, *in whose lake it breeds.*
Bondener. *To reason, argue, dispute; also, to grumble.*
Bondi: m. ie: f. *Bounded, rebounded; leaped, iumped, ierted, skipped (suddenly, and swiftly) vpward.*
Bondir. *To bound, rebound; to leape, iumpe, iert, skip, rise (suddenly, and swiftly) vpward.*
Bondissement: m. *A bounding, rebounding, leaping, iumping, ierting, skipping vpwards.*
Bondon: m. *A bung, or stopple.*
Bondonné: m. ée: f. *Shut, or stopped vp with a bung, or stopple.*
Bondonner. *To shut, or stop vp with a bung, or stopple.*
Bondrée: f. *A kind of short winged Eagle, that preyes altogether vpon fish, frogs, rats, and serpents; some call her, a Harrower.*
Bone: f. *as* Borne: ¶Pic.
Bon-enten-tu. *A good conceit, readie iudgement, ripe wit, quicke vnderstanding.*
Bon-Henry. *The wild sorrell called, Roman sorrell, round sorrell, and Tours sorrell; also, the hearbe, good Henry, good king Harry, and Allgood.*
Bonhort. *as* Behourd; *A Iust, or Turney, wherein many runne together.*
Bonifié: m. ée: f. *Made good; also, benefited, inriched, made wealthie.*
Bonifier. *To make good; to do good vnto, or vpon; to benefit, inrich, make wealthie.*
Boniton: m. *The fish called, a Bonitoe; seene most commonly playing in troups before a tempest.*
Bonnage. *as* Bornage.
Bonnaire: com. *Gentle, courteous, affable; mild; without malice, faithfull, sincere.*
Bonnairement. *Gently, mildly, courteously; sincerely, faithfully, with an open heart.*
Bonnaireté: f. *Gentlenesse, mildnesse, courtesie, humanitie, affabilitie, good nature; also, sinceritie, faithfulnesse, plaine dealing, openheartednesse.*

Bonne. *as* Borne.
Bonne-grace: f. *Th'vppermost flap of the down-hanging taile of a French-hood; (whence belike our Boongrace.)*
Bonnement. *Well, fitly, aptly, handsomely, conueniently, orderly, to the purpose.*
Bonnes-dames. *The hearbe Orage, or golden hearbe; also, Beets.*
Bonnet: m. *A bonnet, a cap.*
Bonnet à la cocarde. *See* Coquarde.
Bonnet à croppiere. *a square cap; a three cornerd cap*
Bonnet de fer. *An yron scull, or sallade.*
Bonnet à la Marabaise. *A flat cap.*
Bonnet de Prestre. *Spindle-tree, Prick-wood, Prick-timber; or as;*
Bonnet quarré. *The wild cherrie which groweth on the tree whereof Butchers make their pricks.*
Bonnet à quatre braguettes, ou gouttieres. *A (four-cornered) square cap.*
Bonnet verd. *A fashion of greene cap which Cessionarie bankrupts were, not long ago, enioyned to weare in publique assemblies, thereby to be the better knowne and auoyded.*
Du temps des hauts bonnets. *In old time, when men being rude and sillie, had not the wit to apparell themselues handsomely; and hence;*
Langage du temps des bonnets, ou des hauts bonnets. *An old wiues tale; or a stale, obsolete, or ouer-worne language; a fashion of speaking thats old, and quite out of fashion.*
La teste prés du bonnet. Avoir la teste prés, &c; *To be hot, hastie, chollerick; also, to be craftie, subtile, cunning.*
Prendre le bonnet. *To commence Master of Arts, or take a degree; (hence) also, to take on him the gouernment of himselfe; to waiue all tutorly Iurisdiction; to refuse, or haue no need of, further tutoring.*
Rire sous le bonnet. *To laugh in the sleeue.*
Bonneter. *To put off his cap vnto.*
Bonnetier: m. *A Capper, or Bonnet-maker; a knitter of caps, a cap knitter.*
Bonneton. *A little cap, or bonnet.*
Bonnette: f. *The bonnet of a sayle.*
Bonnette traineresse. *A drabler; a peece added vnto the bonnet, when there is need of more saile.*
Bonniere: f. *A proportion, or measure of land, not much differing from th'* Arpent.
Bon-lieu. *The name of a Priorie in* Burgundie.
Bons-enfans. *(The name of) a most ancient colledge in th'Vniuersitie of* Paris; *first called in all congregations, & hauing the first, or highest, place in all assemblies.*
Bons-hommes. *An order of Friers; as* Minimes.
Bonté: f. *Goodnesse, honestie, sinceritie, vertue, vprightnesse; also, bountie, liberalitie; also, valour, prowesse, courage.*
Beauté sans bonté est comme vin esventé: Pro.
Booie. *The water Serpent Boas; which vseth, to sucke kine, as long as they are milch, and afterwards to deuoure them.*
Boolingue. *as* Boulingue.
Boote. *Bootes; a slow mouing starre, seated in the North Pole, neere vnto Charles waine, the which it followes.*
Boque. *as* Bocque.
Boquet: m. *A groue, or small thicket of trees.*
Borax: m. *Borax, greene earth; Looke* Borrais.
Borborigme: m. *The rumbling, or croaking of the guts; also, the murmuring noise yeelded by running waters.*
Bord: m. *The welt, hem, or seluedge, of a garment; (and hence) the welt, or turneouer of a corke shoe; also, the side, edge, brinke, brim, shore, of a pit, of a hole, of a riuer, of a water, of the sea; also, th'end, conclusion, or last cast of a matter.*
Bords. *Ribbons; thicke boords nailed to th'outside of the floore-timbers of a ship.*
Bord bas, ou bas bord. *The larboord, or left side of a ship.*
Bord plat, or, plat bord. *In a ship, is the edge of the bridge, from the maine mast vnto the fore-castle, vpon which the great ordnance is placed.*
Grain sur bord. *Scant measure; hard striken measure, of corne, or salt.*
Oultre bord. *Excessiuely, beyond measure.*
Il est sur le bord de la fosse. *He is a drooping, old, decrepit creature; he is alreadie at the pits brinke; hee hath alreadie one foot in his graue.*
Prendre bord. *To take land, to go ashore.*
Bordage. *as* Bord; *Also, a base, drudging, or seruile tenure; villenage.*
Droict de bordage. *The drudgerie, or base seruices, reserued by some Lords vpon the letting of their cottages, or small tenements; which cannot be giuen, sold, nor engaged by the poore slaues that haue taken them.*
Borde: f. *A little house, lodging, or cottage of timber, standing alone in the fields, especially one thats built on wheeles, & may be quickly remoued from field to field; also (more generally) any scattered house, lodge, or village in the countiy; and (in some parts of* France) *any messuage, farme, or farme-house; also, a stalke of pilled hempe.*
Bordé: m. ée: f. *Bordered, garded, welted; also, imbrodered; also, stopped, or stayed; whence;*
Nous sommes bordez à midy. *We left work at noon; (rustically.)*
Bordeau: m. *A brothell, or bawdie-house; the Stewes.*
Bordelage: m. *Brothelling, wenching, whoore-hunting.*
Bordeler. *To hunt whoores, to hannt baudie houses.*
Bordelier: m. *A wencher, whoore-munger, whoore-hunter, haunter of baudie houses; also, as* Bourdelier.
Bordeliere: f. *A certaine fresh-water fish, that resembles a Breame, and hath neither teeth, nor tongue.*
Bordelois. *The name of a verie great grape.*
Border. *To border, gard, welt; also, to imbroder; also, to stay, stop, leaue off, giue ouer; whence;*
Border les avirons. *To hold vp the oares, or to surcease rowing.*
Bordereau: m. *A note, breefe, ticket; also, an accompt; a bill, or booke, of accompts.*
Borderie: f. *A quantity of earable ground furnished with competent medow and pasture, and containing altogether, in most parts of* Poictou *but two, and in fewer foure, Oxe-gates, or Oxe-gangs.*
Bordeur: m. *An Imbroderer.*
Autant pour le bordeur. *So much for that; yea marrie sir now you haue hit it; Or, one good turne requires another; or, I would I were able to requite you sir; all ironically; and the last the most proper; this phrase (wherin there is an allusion to* Bourdeur, *a lyer) being fitly vsed, as a wish, by those, that could find in their hearts to pay a lyer in his owne money.*
Bordeux: m. euse: f. *Full of, seruing for, or belonging to, hemmes, edges, brimmes.*
Bordier: m. *A villaine, or cottager; one that holds by a seruile, base, and drudging, tenure; also, a farmer.*
Bordieux: m. *Small tenements, little cottages, cotes.*
Bordonné. *Looke* Bourdonné.
Bords. *Looke* Bord.
Bordure: f. *A border, welt, hemme, or gard of a garment; and*

and particularly, the turneouer, or side betweene the sole and vpper-leather of a corke shooe.

Borée. *The North-east wind.*

Borgne: com. *One eyed, or, that hath but one eye.*

Vne chambre borgne. *That hath but one window, and is thereby with the darkest.*

Esguillette borgne. *A point that hath but one tag.*

Intestin borgne. *The blind gut; the first of the three great guts in the belly, seated on the right side, a little vnder the kidney; and so full of turnings, & foulds, that it seemes endlesse.*

Veine borgne. *Looke* Veine.

Ie le vous envoyeray par le borgne. *I will send it by Iohn Long the Carrier; you shall haue it when I know not what else to do with it.*

Vn borgne est Roy au païs des aveugles: Prov. *He that sees but little ouerrules them that see nothing.*

Borgner. *To winke with one eye, and looke with another; as those, that would discerne a thing through a narrow hole; or, as* Borgnoyer.

Borgnesse: f. *A woman that hath but one eye.*

Esguillette borgnesse. *as* Esguillette borgne.

Borgnet: m. ette: f. *Halfe blind; almost blind, or hauing wellnigh lost the vse of one eye.*

Borgnoyer. *To want an eye; to looke, or see but with one eye; to winke with, or faine himselfe blind of, one eye; also, to glow, glote, or loure.*

Borgue. *as* Nasse; *A weele, for fish.*

Borlet. *See* Bourlet.

Bornage: m. *The bounds, or limits, of; whence;*

Bornage de Hercules. *The straits of* Giblaltarre.

Droict de bornage. *The royaltie, or priuiledge of placing meeres, appointing limits, laying out bounds for other mens lands.*

Bornal de miel: m. *A hony combe.*

Borne: f. *A bound, limit, meere, march; the end, or furthest compasse of a thing.*

Mais là ne faut faire but ne borne. *But there wee must not stop, nor pause; thats no place to settle in, stay at, or dwell on.*

Au bout la borne: Prov. *Th'end tryes all; at length we shall see what will be done.*

Borné: m. ée: f. *Bounded, limited; apportioned; proportioned; stinted; whose part or portion is appointed him.*

Borner. *To limit, bound, assigne marches, appoint meeres vnto; to apportion; stint, proportion; to sort out a part for; to allot, or lay out a certaine portion, or proportion, which is not to be exceeded.*

Borneur: m. *A limiter, bounder; apportioner; stinter, proportioner.*

Bornion à miel. *A honie combe; or, bees nest full of honie.*

Borrache. *A Spanish borachoe, or bottle of leather.*

Borrais, ou Borras: m. *Borax, or greene earth; a hard and shining minerall, or humor congealed in mynes; There is also an artificiall one, made of Roche Allum, Armoniac, and other things; both vsed by Goldsmiths.*

Borras blanc. *White Borax; found (as* Mathiolus *thinks) in siluer mynes.*

Borras iaulne. *Yellow Borax, found in gold mynes, and fittest for Goldsmithes.*

Borras noir. *Blacke (and the worst) Borax; found, most commonly, in leaden mines.*

Borras Pierreux. *Vnrefined Borax, as it comes out of the rocke, or mine.*

Borras verd. *Greene Borax; the best, and most medicinable kind thereof; found (especially that which is of a darke greene colour) in brasse mynes.*

Borrasque. *as* Bourasque.

Borret: m. *A yearing, or young beast thats about a yeare old:* ¶Auvergnois.

Borrette: f. *A heyfer, or fillie, thats about a yeare old.*

Borriere. vache borriere. *A cow that hath a calfe running after her.*

Borrugat. *The sea fish called otherwise,* Maigre, ¶Baionnois.

Bortiere: f. *(Corruptly, for* Portiere*) the female Salmon, greater, and fuller of red spots than the male, and hauing the end of her nether iaw hooked, or bending vpwards, whereas his is straight.*

Bos. *as* Bois: ¶Pic.

Bosc. *The name of a drie sower apple; also, as* Bois: ¶Pic.

Boscage. *as* Bocage.

Boscal. *A little wood, or forest.*

Bosialle. champ b. *A peece of ground, or common (without any house vpon it) wherein diuers haue certaine, and seuerall parts.*

Bosne: f. *as* Borne.

Bosné. *Bounded, limited.*

Bosquet: m. *A thicket, groue, or little wood.*

Bosquillon: m. *A wood-feller, billet-maker, hedge-mender; a labouring man that fells wood, makes billets, &c, and mends, or lookes vnto, the hedges, or inclosures of a wood.*

Bossé d'une roue. *The naue of a wheele. Seeke* Moyeu.

Bosse: f. *A bunch, or bumpe; any round swelling, vprising, or puffing vp; hence, a wen, botch, bile, or plague-sore; also, a hulch in the backe; also, a knob, knot, or knurre in a tree; also, a hillocke, molehill, small hill, or barrow of ground; also, a bosse, or imbossing in workemanship; also, the first putting out of a deeres head formerly cast; which our wood-men call, if it bee a red deeres, the burle, or seale, and, if a fallow deeres, the button; (the which is also applied vnto the other.)*

Bosse de terre. *as* Truffe.

Sot en bosse, & platte peinture. *A foole in print, asse in graine, compleat coxcombe, absolute hoydon.*

La male bosse. *A plague-sore, pestilent botch, contagious bile.*

Desrobber la bosse à S. Roc. *To filtch, or steale any thing (how meane soeuer) that comes in his way.*

Bossé: m. ée: f. *Swollen, risen, bunchie, hulched, puffed vp; knobbie, bulked, or bumped out.*

Bosseler. *To dindge, or bruise, to make a dint in vessell of mettall, or in a peece of plate.*

Bosselure: f. *A bruise, dindge, or dint, in a peece of plate, or mettall.*

Bossetier: m. *A bosse-maker; a stud-maker.*

Bossette: f. *A little bunch, or knob; also, a little heape, rising, or swelling of earth; also, a bosse, or bullion set on a booke; also, a stud on any part of a horses furniture.*

Bossis: m. *High grounds; or, little hills raised by the hands of men.*

Bossu: m. uë: f. *Hulch backt, crump-shouldered; knobbie, knappie; swelling, puffed vp, rising vneuenly, crookedly, vnhandsomely.*

Mesnage bossu. *A disordered family wherein all is confounded, or awry.*

De nouveau Medecin cimitiere bossu: Prov. *A new Physitian breeds a fat churchyard.*

Veau mal cuit, & poulets cruds font les cimitieres bossus: Prov. *Raw veale, and chickens fill churchyards.*

Bossuër. *To make hulch, crumpe, or crooked; to swell, or puffe*

puffe vp vneuenly,and vnhandsomely.
Bot: m. *A woodden shooe,or patten.*¶Poict. *also,as* But. ¶Norm. *also,a luncheon,or (illfauored) big peece of.*
Bot. *Illfauoredly-round*; *whence*;
Pied bot. *A stumpe or club foot.*
Botaige. temps de botaige. *is from the ninth of Octo-ber to the last of Nouember.*
'Botanique: com.*Hearball*; *of,or belonging to hearbes, or,to skill in hearbs.*
Botanomantie: f. *Diuination, or witchcraft by the vertue of hearbes.*
Botargues: f. *The hard rowes of the* Murene, *or of a kind of Mullet,salted,and then dried,and eaten to pro-uoke drinking.*
Bote: f. *A boot*; *also,a faggot,a bundle*; *a bottle.*
S'ils pensent ainsi ils bruslent leurs botes. *They are farre wide,or much too blame,if &c*; *or (as we say) I smell them hither.*
Tous les deux y laisseront les botes. *They can nei-ther of them scape with life,they will both miscarrie, or die,in the place.*
Boté. *Booted*; *See* Botté.
Boteau. *A bundle,or bottle,as of hay,&c.*
Boteler. *To botle, or bundle vp*; *to make into botles, or bundles.*
Boteleur: m. *A maker of botles,or of bundles.*
Boter. *To boot,pull on boots,or put boots on*; *also,to prune, or cut of the superfluous branches of a tree.*
Bothoral: m. ale: f. *Whealie, poukie,pushie.*
Botine: f. *A buskin,or Summer boot.*
Botineur: m. *A buskin-maker*; *also,one that continually weares boots,or buskins*; *as a Monke,or any such crea-ture, who being not satisfied with wearing them aliue, will needs be buried in them,dead.*
Botryte: f. Cadmia *in grape-like clusters, gathered from the roofes of copper-houses, or ouer the furnaces wherein copper is ordinarily melted,or made.*
Botte: f. *The vessell which wee call, a Butt*; *also, as* Bote.
Botté. *Booted.*
Gens bottez de foin. *Silly clownes, rude swaynes, ignorant boores,home-bred hinds.*
Botteler. *as* Boteler.
Botter. *as* Boter.
Botterol: m. *A Toad.* (vieil mot.)
Bou. *A boyling, or bubling.*
Bouade: f.*The worke of two oxen,or vse of a small cart, due certaine daies in Summer by tenants (that hold by socage,or villenage) vnto their landlords,for the labou-ring,and dressing of their vineyards.*
Bouban,& Boubance. *Looke* Bobance.
Boubax. *The name of a kind of Oliues.*
Bouc: m. *A male Goat,or hee Goat*; *also,the engine of batterie called a Ramme*; *also,a harsh,hard,and thicke Spunge.*
Bouc d'estain. *The Alpian,and long-hornd wild goat, or beast like a goat,called (in Latine)* Ibex.
Barbe de bouc. *Goats-beard, Starre of* Ierusalem, *Noone-tide, Goe-to-bed at noone*; *(an hearbe.)*
Couillon de bouc. *See* Couillon.
Espine de bouc. *Goats-thorne (whose root yeeldeth Gum-dragagant.)*
Langue de bouc. *Wild buglosse, wall buglosse, snakes buglosse,Vipers buglosse, Vipers hearbe.*
Oeil de bouc. *The little shell-fish called,a Lympine,or Lempet*; *Seeke* Oeil.
Yeux de bouc. *Gogle eyes*; *rolling eyes.*
De bouc estourdi. *Rashly,turbulently,with a hurrie.*

Traire les boucs. *To loose time, or spend it fruit-lesly.*
Boucal: m. *as* Bocal; *also,a vent for the fire,or heat, of a furnace.*
Boucan: m.*A woodden gridiron,whereon the Cannibals broile peeces of men,and other flesh.*
Boucané: m. ée: f. *Ridden by a goat*; *also,rosted,broy-led,or scorched on a woodden gridiron.*
Boucaner. *To doe like a goat*; *to imitate the goat*; *also, to broyle,or scorch on a woodden gridiron.*
Boucanier: m. ere: f. *Old,stale,past date,out of vse,out of season.*
Boucassin. *as* Boccasin.
Bouccaiart: m. *Plaine Chamlet,vnwater Chamlet*; *or,as* Moncaiart.
Bouchard. *A kind of great-eared browne wheat.*
Boucharde: f. *A Masons hammer,or picke,pointed at both ends like a diamond.*
Bouchasses: f. *Wild,or bastard,Chestnuts.*
Bouche: f. *A mouth*; *also,a passage, entrie, entrance,or ouerture,into.*
Bouches à feu. *Spit-fires*; *Artillerie,Ordnance.*
Bouche fresche. *Looke* Frez.
La bouche,& les mains. *Homage,and fealtie*; *or,the ceremonies vsed in the doing thereof.*
De broc en bouche. *Immediatly,speedily,suddainly, out of hand,in a trice,while tis hot.*
Avoir bouche à Court. *To eat and drinke scotfree*; *to haue budge-a-Court, to be in ordinarie at Court.*
Avoir la bouche fraiche. *Looke* Fraiche.
Avoir la bouche à pleine main. *A horse to be nei-ther too hard,nor too sensible, of mouth*; *thereby giuing the hand a full rest.*
Avoir bonne bouche. *To be secret*; *to keepe coun-sell.*
Elle a la langue en la bouche non en la bourse *(of a pratling huswife) her tongue is euer at hand I war-rant you.*
Dire de bouche. *To tell, or vtter expressely, to make especiall mention of in speech,to declare vnto in plaine, and open tearmes.*
Faire la bouche à.*To instruct,or giue a man his lesson, beforehand.*
Faire la petite bouche.*To simper*; Il ne faisoit point la petite bouche. *He neither dissembled,nor was loth to vtter it*; *he spoke it openly,plainly, freely ynough.*
On y doit fermer la bouche, & ouvrir la bourse; viz. *When almes are to be giuen.*
Garder pour la bonne bouche.*To reserue a thing as the best for the last bit*; *to keepe it long of purpose to make vp his mouth withall.*
Gouverner bien la bouche. *To be temperat in diet.*
Large de bouche, & estroict de ceincture. *That promises,or offers,much,but put vnto it,will part with little or nothing.*
Moderer sa bouche. *To feed moderatly,to eat soberly,or no more then shall doe him good.*
Parler de quelqu' un en bonne bouche. *To speake well,or giue a good report of one*; en male bouche; *to reproch,raile on,reuile one.*
Tromper vn corbeau à bouche beante. *See* Cor-beau.
Venir l'eau à la bouche. Cela luy fit venir l' eau à la bouche. *That made his teeth water, or, set him on a longing.*
Bouche fresche pied sec: Prov. *He that would liue a long time, must keepe both his mouth coole,and moist, and his feet warme, and drie.*

De la main à la bouche se perd souvent la soupe: Prov. *Betweene the hand and lip the morsell's lost.*
Entre la bouche & le cueillier souvent advient grand destourbier: Prov. *Betweene the cup and the lip (say we, with the Latine Poet) many mischances happen.*
Qui n'a argent en bourse ait du moins du miel en bouche: Prov. *Looke* Avoir.
Selon ta bourse gouverne ta bouche: Pro. *Gouerne thy mouth by thy meanes.*
Table sans sel, bouche sans salive: Prov. *A table without salt, and a mouth without sap;* *Looke* Table.
Bouchée: f. *A morsell, or mouth-full of.*
Bouchelette: f. *A little mouth.*
Bouchement. *See* Bouschement.
Boucher: m. *A Butcher, or slaughter-man.*
Boucher. *To stop;* *See* Bouscher.
Boucherie: f. *A Butchers shambles, stall, or shop; also, a butcherie, slaughter, dismembring, or renting asunder of a liuing creature.*
Droict de boucherie. *Looke* Droict.
Boucheron. *See* Bouscheron.
Bouchet: m. *A kind of broth for a sicke bodie; also, the sweet drinke, Hydromel; or, a drinke made of water sweetned with sugar and cinnamon; or as;*
Eau de bouchet. *A certaine compound water, which with that of Corianders, makes a kind of Hipocras.*
Bouchette: f. *A little mouth.*
Bouchier: m. *A Butcher, or slaughter-man.*
Bouchimbarbe: f. *Goats beard, Iosephs flower, Starre of* Ierusalem, *Noone-tide, Goe-to-bed-at-noone; (an hearbe.)*
Bouchon: m. *A stopple; also, a wispe of straw, &c; also, the bush of a tauerne, or alehouse.*
Bouchons. *The little knots which be in fine wooll, or fall from it in spinning.*
Bouchons de Chenilles. *Clusters, or bunches of Caterpillers.*
'A bouchon. *Groueling; lying with his teeth downeward; or, couched vpon his face; as he is that lyes down at the play called Hot-cockles.*
Il me donna le bouchon d'une bouteille. *He gaue me a very trifle, or a thing not worth taking.*
Se mettre à l'ombre des bouchons. *To get him into a Tauerne; to take shelter, or sanctuarie, in a Taphouse.*
Bouchonné: m. ée: f. *Rubbed, wiped, or stuffed, as a horse with wispes of straw.*
Bouchonner. *To rub, wipe, or stuffe, as a horse, with wispes of straw.*
Bouchonnet: m. *A little wispe, or stopple.*
Bouchonneux: m. euse: f. *Full of stopples; wispes of straw; tauerne-bushes; woollie knots; bunches, clusters.*
Bouclas: m. *Birche.*
Boucle: f. *A buckle; also, a buble made by seething liquor.*
Tenir sous boucle. *To restraine, hold in awe, keepe vnder, or in order.*
Bouclé: m. ée: f. *Buckled; fastened, closed, ioyned, as with a buckle; also, rung, as a mare; also, cuffed, buffetted; also, swolne, bulching, rising, or bearing out, in the middle, as a buckle.*
Cela est serré, & bouclé. *That matter is fully ended.*
Boucler. *To buckle; to close, or fasten, as with a buckle; also, to ring a mare, thereby to keepe her from the horse; (also, to buffet, or cuffe) also, to swell, rise, or beare out in the middle; also, to finish, end, performe, shut vp.*
Il boucle sa femme à la Bergamasque. *Looke* Bergamasque.
Bouclette: f. *A small buckle.*
Bouclier: m. *A buckler.*
Bouclier Barcelonnois. *A footmans targuet, or shield.*
Bouclier de l'estomac. *The triangular gristle that growes to the bottome of the breast-bone, and from the middle thereof hangs ouer the stomacke.*
Levée de bouclier. *A great stirre about a small matter; huge preparation for a sleight action; much adoe about little or nothing.*
Faire bouclier de. *To trust in the defence; relie on the protection of; to saue, shaddow, shrowd, or shelter himselfe vnder.*
Bouclure: f. *A buckling; also, a swelling, or bearing out, in the middle; also, a buffetting.*
Bouclus: m. *Trenches, or ditches.*
Boucon: m. *A bit, morsell, mouthfull; especially such a one as is empoisoned; and hence,*
Bailler le boucon. *To poyson.*
Bouconnier: m. *A poysoner, one that giues an inuenomed bit.*
Boucque. *as* Bouche. ¶Pic. *whence;*
Boucque du haut ventre. *The mouth, or hole of the stomacke, next vnder the breast bone.*
Boucquet: m. *as* Bouquet.
Boucquine. *A rammish, or lasciuious queane.*
Bouc-soufflé. *as* Boursoufflé.
Boudin: m. *A pudding.*
Boudinal: m. ale: f. *Of, or belonging to, a pudding.*
Boudine: f. *The nauell.*
Boudrée. *as* Bondrée.
Bouë: f. *Durt, mud, mire; filth, dung, ordure; healing, mattar.*
Bouë de fer. *The small flakes that flye from hot yron when tis beaten.*
Bouée: f. *A Boy for an anchor.*
Bouër. *To heale, to mattar; also (among Mintmen)* C'est refrapper les carreaux pour les arrondir.
Bouerande: f. *The weed Cammocke, Rest-barrow, petie Whinne, ground Furze.*
Bouëte: f. *as* Bonnette.
Bouëtte: f. *A little box; also, as* Brouëtte.
Bouëur: m. *A scauinger; one that carries away the sweepings, and durt of streets, in carts.*
Bouëux: m. euse: f. *Durtie, myrie, slymie, muddie; filthie, full of mattar, healing, ordure.*
Boufage. *as* Bouffage.
Boufément. *Puffingly, swellingly, outstrouting.*
Boufeux: m. *A great eater, a greedie feeder; one whose cheekes are swolne by excessiue diet, or swell exceedingly whensoeuer he diets.*
Bouffage: m. *Any meat that (eaten greedily) fils the mouth, and makes the cheekes to swell; cheeke-puffing meat.*
Bouffancs: m. *Puffes in a garment, &c.*
Bouffant. *Puffing, blowing; swelling vp, strouting out; also, burgenning, or waxing big.*
Bouffard: m. arde: f. *Often puffing, much blowing, swelling vp, strouting out; also, swelling with anger; or, in a great chafe, in a monstrous fume.*
Bouffe: f. *The part of our cheekes which we puffe vp in blowing, or feeding; a swollen, or swelling cheeke.*
Bouffé: m. ée: f. *Puffed, blowne; swollen vp, or out; growne big.*
Bouffée: f. *A puffe; a suddaine, violent, and short blast;*

a berrie, or gust of wind; also, a short, and violent fit.

Bouffée de feu. *A flash of fire; such a one as comes out of the mouth of a canon, &c, when it is shot off.*

Bouffemént: m. *A puffing; blowing; swelling vp, or out; a bourgeonning, a waxing big.*

Bouffément. *as* Boufément.

Bouffer. *To puffe, blow; swell vp, or strout out; to burgen, or wax big.*

Bouffer de courroux. *To swell with anger; to be in his fumes.*

Bouffeux. *as* Boufeux.

Bouffi: m. ie: f. *Swollen, puffed vp, strouting out.*

Hareng bouffi. *A full-roed herring.*

Oeil bouffi. *An extreamely swolne eye that mooues with difficultie, and hath lost it naturall and liuely colour.*

Bouffiné: m. ée: f. *Eaten greedily, or with full and puft-vp cheekes.*

Bouffir. *To puffe, or blow vp; to make to swell, or strout out; or, as* Bouffer.

Bouffissure: f. *A swelling, or puffing vp, a strouting out; also, a kind of dropsie.*

Buffon: m. *A buffoon, ieaster, sycophant, merrie foole, sportfull companion; one that liues by making others merrie.*

Danser les buffons. *To daunce a morris.*

Bouffonner. *To buffoonize it; to play the foole, ieaster, Buffoone; basely to get a liuing by ieasts, or ieasting.*

Bouffonnerie: f. *Bouffoonisme, ieasting.*

Bouffonnesque. *Buffoone-like.*

Bouffonneur. *as* Bouffon.

Boufron: m. *A Cuttle-fish.*

Boug: m. *The little, and venomous greene frog, or hedge toad.*

Boug coupé. *A Tortoise.*

Bouge: m. *A swelling, strouting, or standing out in a flat peece of worke; hence, the bosse of a buckler; and, a belly, or out-leaning in the middle of a wall, &c; and, a little roome, or closet, built without the wall of a chamber.*

Bouge: f. *A budget, wallet, great pouch, male, or case of leather, seruing to carrie things in behind a man on horsebacke.*

Il a bien remply ses bouges. *He hath gained excessiuely, he hath feathered his neast exceedingly.*

Bougé: m. ée: f. *Stirred, budged, remoued, parted from.*

Bougeon: m. *A bolt, or arrow with a great head.*

Bouger. *To stirre, budge, flit, remoue, part from.*

Rasibus; qui bouge? *The words of a certaine game; Looke* Rasibus.

Qui bien est ne se bouge: Prov. *Let not him budge that finds himselfe well seated.*

Tel pense voler qui ne sçauroit bouger: Prov. *He meanes to flye, yet cannot moue a wing; (said of an ouerweening ambition, which though it want all meanes attempts all matters.)*

Bougeron. *as* Bougre.

Bougetier. *A budget-maker; or, a maker of little wooden coffers &c. as in* Bougette.

Bougette: f. *A little coffer, or trunke of wood, couered with leather, wherewith the women of old time carried their iewels, attires, and trinkets at their saddle bowes, when they rid into the countrey; now gentlemen call so, both any such trunke; and the box, or till of their Cabinets wherein they keepe their money; also, a little male, pouch, or budget.*

Bougie: f. *A searing candle; also, a size, or small round candle vsed in churches; Looke* Poincte.

Bougié. *Seared with a wax-candle.*

Bougier. *To seare with a wax-candle.*

Bougiron: m. *A Buggerer, a Sodomite.*

Bougironné: m. ée: f. *Buggered, abused by a Sodomite.*

Bougironner. *To bugger; to commit (horrible) Sodomie.*

Bougnette: f. *The smooth and long-tailed Ray, called the Forkfish.*

Bougoir: m. *A long candlesticke (of mettall) for a size, or (small) wax-candle.*

Bougonner. *To bungle.* ¶Orleannois.

Bougonneur: m. *A bungler.*

Bougrande: f. *Cammocke, Rest-harrow, ground Furze, pettie Whinne.*

Bougre: m. *as* Bougiron.

Bougrerie: f. *Buggerie, Sodomie.*

Bougrin: m. ine: f. *Buggering; or, fit for buggerie; whence;*

Chausses à la bougrine. *Strait venetians, without codpeeces.*

Bougrisque: com. *Buggering, committing Sodomie.*

Bouhourd. *as* Behourd.

Bouhourdi premier & second. *The first and second Sunday in Lent.*

Bouillamment. *Hotly, eagerly, feruently, with a boyling desire.*

Bouillant: m. ante: f. *Boyling, scalding hot.*

Bouilli: m. *Any broth, or boyled meat.*

Bouilli: m. ie: f. *Boyled, sodden.*

Bouillir. *To boyle, or seeth; also, to buble in seething.*

Bouillon: m. *Mullein, Wooll-blade, Long-wort, Hightaper, Torches, Long-beard, Bullocks Long-wort, Haresbeard.*

Bouillon blanc. *Base white Mullein, whereof there be two kinds, one with broad, the other with narrow, leaues.*

Bouillon Lychnite. *Candle-weeke Mullein.*

Bouillon noir. *Base blacke Mullein.*

Bouillon sauvage. *Wild Mullein; hath leaues like Sage, and yellow shining flowers.*

Bouillon: m. *A boyling, bubling, or buble; also, a broth, or boyled meat; also, durt, myre; and, a plashing, or dashing; also, oaten grout; a kind of small drinke made of Oats; also, a great and long ship-nayle; also, a studde; any great-headed, or studded, nayle.*

Bouillons. *Puffes, in a garment, &c.*

Bouillon de fleurs, & fruicts. *A thicke bunch, or cluster of sundrie leaues, fruits, and flowers, seeming to grow altogether out of one stalke.*

Bouillon de fumée. vn gros b. *A cloud of smoake.*

Bouillon de sang. *A clot of bloud.*

Bouillonné: m. ée: f. *Boyled, bubled; surged; also, trimmed, or set out, with puffes.*

Bouillonnement: m. *A boyling, a bubling, a surging, a seething ouer.*

Bouillonner. *To boyle, buble, surge, seeth ouer; also, to make puffes in a garment.*

Bouillonneux: m. euse: f. *Boyling, or bubling; also, durtie, myrie, plashie; also, full of puffes.*

Bouillu. *as* Bouilli.

Boujon: m. *A boult; an arrow with a great, or broad, head.*

Bouïotte: f. *A pigeon-hole in a doue-cote.*

Bouis: m. *Box; or the Box tree.*

Bouïs d'asne. *The Box thorne, prickly Box, Asse Box tree.*

Bouïs espineux, ou piquant. *The same.*
Grand bouïs. *Great Box, or, the Box tree.*
Petit bouïs. *Dwarfe Box, ground Box.*
Bouïssiere: f. *A Box-plot; a banke, or ground set, or stored, with Box.*
Boukimbarbe. *as* Bouchimbarbe.
Boulanger. *as* Boulenger.
Boular: m. *The little round neast of a Martin, Titmouse, &c.*
Boulay: m. *A Birch tree.*
Bouldure d' un moulin. *The conduit, or fall-trough, wherein the wheele goes.*
Boule: f. *A Bowle (to play with; or to drinke in.)*
Boule veuë. *A certaine play at Bowle-casting, wherein if the Bowle be at any time out of sight, the caster looses; whence;*
Iouër à boule veuë. *To deale surely, worke on sure grounds, make a warie bargaine, meddle with that for which he sees good warrant.*
Le coup valoit bien la boule. *See* Coup.
Tenir pied à boule. *To apply his businesse; to hold hard, or keepe close to it.*
Bouleau: m. *Birche; also, a small Bowle; and hence,*
Les bouleaux d'un vis. *The circles, or circling of a Scrue.*
Boulengé: m. ée: f. *Baked, made into bread.*
Boulenger. *To bake, make bread; or make into bread.*
Boulengerie: f. *A baking; also, a bakehouse.*
Boulengier: m. *A baker.*
Pet de boulengier. *A fart in syrrup.*
Boulengiere: f. *A woman baker; also, as* Boulengerie; *a bakehouse.*
Bouler. *To bowle.*
Boulerot: m. *A little round, blackish, and fennie Gudgeon, that liues continually in mud.*
Boulesche: f. *A great fish-net, called a Scene, or Seyne.*
Boulet: m. *A bullet; also, as* Bolete; *a Mushrome.*
Boulet noir. *A heauie, poysonous, and blackish kind of the Excrescence, called* Agaric.
Arbaleste à boulet. *A Stone-bow.*
Boulette: f. *A little Bowle.*
Boulettes de Cyprés. *Cypres nuts, or clogs.*
Boulever; ou, Bouleverd: m. *A Bulwarke.*
Bouleverse: f. *A subuersion, ouerturne, ouerthrow.*
Bouleversé: m. ée: f. *Subuerted, ouerturned, ouerthrowne.*
Bouleversement: m. *An ouerturning, subuerting, ouerthrowing.*
Bouleverser. *To ouerturne, or turne topsie turuie, to subuert, to ouerthrow.*
Bouleverseur: m. *An ouerturner, subuerter, ouerthrower.*
Boulevert: m. *A Bulwarke.*
Boule-veuë. *Seeke* Boule.
Boulge, & Boulgette. *as* Bouge, *&* Bougette.
Boulie: f. *Pap, or broth, for children.*
Cela sent sa boulie, viz. *is childish, fond; raw, rude.*
Boulieux: m. euse: f. *Full of, or belonging to, pap; also, feeding much on, or fed very much with, pap.*
Boulime: m. *as* Boulimie.
Boulimie: f. *A greedie hunger, an vnsatiable appetite, by disease, proceeding from the coldnesse of the stomacke.*
Boulin: m. *A pigeon-hole in a doue-cote.*
Boulinage: m. *A sayling with a side wind; a laying of tacke aboord.*
Bouline: f. *A Boline, or Tacke; also, as* Boulingue.
Aller à la bouline. *To sayle with a side wind.*
Boulingue: f. *A top-sayle.*
Boullause: f. *A Poute, or Eele-poute.*
Bouller. *To cog, foist; beguile, deceiue, cousen; also, to box, or pommell, with the fists.* (v. m.)
Boulligni. *An Italian coyne worth about* ij.d. *sterl.*
Boullon. *as* Boulon.
Boullonné: m. ée: f. *Puffed, or drawn out with puffes.*
Bouloers d'vn vis. *The circles, or circling of a Scrue.*
Bouloirs. *as* Bouloers.
Bouloire: f. *A bowling alley.*
Boulon. *A long, big, and big-headed peg of wood, wherewith Carpenters ioyne great peeces of timber together.*
Boulon de fer. *A great pin of yron, such as tradesmen shut in their shop-windowes withall.*
Boulongnois. *as* Boulligni.
Boulouër: m. *A bulwarke, fortresse, or strong hold.* (v. m.)
Boulture: f. *A seething, a boyling, a bubling.*
Bounc. *as* Borne.
Bouquanier. *as* Boucanier.
Bouqué: m. *as* Bouquet.
Bouque d' Ange: f. *Conserue, or sucket, of Lettice stalkes.*
Bouquer. *To kisse another mans thumbe; to take, or giue, a tucke, or kisse; also, to strike sayle, or pay custome, as ships, in passing by some places, are bound to doe.*
Bouquet: m. *A nosegay, or posie of flowers, &c; also, a lock of wooll; also, a buckle-bone; (also, a great Prawne,* Norm.) *also, a loope-hole in a wall.*
Bransle du bouquet. *The nosegay daunce, or kissing daunce (for there is much kissing in it.)*
Bailler le bouquet. *See* Bailler.
Elle a mis le bouquet sous l' oreille. *(Of a widow) she would faine be had, woon, or married; (of a whore) she may (for money) be had, woon, or vsed; (In* France, *when they ride, or lead, out horses, which they would sell, they vse to sticke posies vnder their eares.)*
Bouquetier: m. ere: f. *Of, or belonging to, nosegayes, nosegay-like.*
Bouquetiere: f. *An hearbe-wife; such a one as vses to sell, or to present, nosegayes.*
Bouquin: m. *A Kid; also, the hairie bush, or* Pubes.
Cornet à bouquin. *A (Musicall) Cornet.*
Vn vieux bouquin. *An old booke; also, an old scholler; or, one that hath red ouer many old bookes.*
Bouquin: m. ine: f. *Leacherous, lasciuious; also, ranke, rammish, goat-like.*
Bouquiner. *To grow hairie about the priuities; also, to be as lasciuious, or smell as ranke, as a goat; also, to be bookish, or, to read much in old bookes.*
Bourache: f. *A* Borrachoe; *or bottle (of leather) also, a candle-case; also, an engine (like a candle-case) wherewith fish is caught.*
Bourachon: m. *A small* Borrachoe; *a little candle-case; also, a drunkard, or Tosse-bottle.*
Bouras: m. *The towe of hempe; the coursest part of any such like stuffe.*
Bourasque: f. *A storme, tempest, gust, or flaw of wind.*
Bourasse: f. *A* Borrachoe, *or (Spanish) bottle of leather.*
Bourbe: f. *Mud, myre, durt; also, as* Bourbier.
Bourbelier: m. *The breast, or Essay of a wild Swine.*
Bourbeter. *as* Bourbetter; *also, to mutter, grunt, murmure.*
Bourbeteux: m. euse: f. *Louing the mud, as a ducke, &c; also, full of mud.*

Bour-

Bourbette. *A small fresh water fish, that altogether liues on, and lyes in, mud.*

Bourbetter. *To wallow in mud; to paddle, or pudder, in the myre.*

Bourbeux: m. euse: f. *Muddie, or full of mud; filth, durt.*

Bourbier: m. *A muddie place, a slough, or puddle full of durt, and mud.*

Bourblier: m. *as* Bourbelier.

Bourbonnois: m. oise: f. *Of* Bourbon.

Tarte Bourbonnoise. *A deepe slough, bog, or quagmire; a stable (of ill intertainement) for a horse.*

Bourboulenc. *The name of a Vine.*]

Bourcier. fiet bourcier. *as* fiet boursal; (par la Coustume des Chartres.)

Bourdaine: f. *A certaine low, and vpright-branched (French) hedge-tree, whose wood is very weake, and light, bearing a berrie (of the bignesse of a haw) first pale, then red, at length blacke; exceedingly loued by Stags.*

Bourdant: m. ante: f. *Iesting, bourding; trifling, toying; foisting, cogging with, gulling of, people.*

Truffant bourdant. *Betweene ieast and earnest.*

Bourde: f. *A east, fib, tale of a tub.*

Donner la bourde de l'Alouette. *Seeke* Alouette.

Bourdé: m. ée: f. *Grauelled, as a cart, &c.*

Bourdelage: m. *A tenure in the dominion of* Neuers, *whereby the tenant is bound to pay vnto his Landlord an yearely rent in money, corne, and feathers, or in any two of them; which if he omit three yeares together, he forfets his estate; In* Bourbonnois *it is as* Taille Réelle.

Bourdelais. *A certaine Vine, or grape that yeelds very soure wine; and therfore is it vsually set about arbors, more for the shadow, then for the fruit, it yeelds.*

Bourdelasier. *Full of ieasts, or of tales.*

Bourdelier. *Let out, or held in* Bourdelage; *also, holding by, or subiect vnto, it.*

Seigneur bourdelier. *The Lord vnto whom* Bourdelage *is due.*

Bourder. *To toy, trifle, dally, bourd, or ieast with; also, to cog, foist, gull, sell a bargaine, giue a gudgeon vnto; also, to quip, gird; mocke, scoffe at.*

Bourdereau. *as* Bordereau.

Bourdes: f. *Sybs, fibs, rappers, lyes; toyes to mocke apes; tales to gull asses with; also, scoffes, ieasts, gibes, cuts quips; and hence;*

Ce sont les pires bourdes que les vrayes: Pro. *The truest ieasts sound worst in guiltie eares.*

Bourdeur: m. *A mocker, ieaster; cogger, lyer; foister, guller of people.*

Bourdican: m. *A begging frier.*

Travailler en bourdican. *To trudge vp and down, to trot to and fro, to toyle like a horse, neuer to rest.*

Bourdin: m. *The shell-fish called a Limpin, or Lempet.*

Bourdon: m. *A Drone, or Dorre-bee; also, the humming, or buzzing of bees; also, the drone of a Bagpipe; also, the big end of a club, &c; also, a Pilgrims staffe; also, a walking staffe hauing a sword, &c, within it; (sometimes) also, a Pike, or Speare.*

Le bourdon d'un moulin à vent. *A wind-mill post.*

Chanter en faux bourbon; *See* Faux-bordon.

Demeure à bourdon planté. *A fixed dwelling, a setled residence in a place.*

Bourdonnasses: f. *A fashion of great hollow launces vsed in old time.*

Bourdonné: m. ée: f. *Furnished with, or made like to a Pilgrims staffe; also, buzzed, or hummed.*

Bourdonnement: m. *A buzzing, or humming, as of Drones, &c.*

Bourdonner. *To buzze, or humme like a Drone, &c.*

Bourdonnesque: com. *Humming, buzzing, Dronelike.*

Bourdonneur: m. *A hummer, a buzzer; also, one that playes on a Bagpipe.*

Bourdonniere: f. *The gudgeon thats in the top of the barre, or hindge-band, of a gate.*

Bourelet. *as* Bourlet.

Bourellé: m. ée: f. *Tormented, tortured, extreamely vexed.*

Bourellement: m. *A torture, torment, cruell racking; extreame vexing.*

Bourellément. *Most cruelly, with much torment.*

Boureller. *To torture, torment, vex horribly.*

Bourellerie: f. *as* Bourellement, *or* Bourrelerie.

Bouret. *A kind of shell-fish.*

Bourg: m. *A Borough, or great Towne (without wals, or ditches.*

De bourg en bourg. *Wandering, like a rogue, from borough to borough, or, from one good towne to another.*

Bourgade: f. *A village, hamlet, small borough.*

Bourgage: m. *A towneship, or boroughship; the inhabitants of houses in lands belonging to a towne, or borough; also, an estate, or tenure in burgage, held either of the king (as our Borough English) or of other Lords of the Borough, and subiect to no other then the customarie and accustomed rents, or seruices thereof.*

Bourgalois: m. *A Spanish coyne worth about* xviij.d. *sterl.*

Bourgamaistre: m. *A Mayor, or Burgamaster; the principall Magistrate, or Officer, in a citie, or good towne.*

Bourgeois: m. *A citizen, townes-man, burguer, burgesse; also, a freeman, in any place.*

Bourgeois d'Amphitrite. *A fish; a freeman of the sea.*

Bourgeois du Comte de Nevers. *His freed men; who payed vnto him an yearely rent of* xij d. Tourn. *and in regard of their freedome vnder him, were to renounce all other lords.*

Le Bourgeois d'un Navire. *The owner of a ship.*

Bourgeois du Roy. *The kings burgesse, or freeman; a lay, and true-borne, yeoman, (for neither gentleman, clerke, nor bastard must he be) at first of a seruile, now of a free, condition; yet subiect vnto all proceedings of Iustice, though with some priuiledge; for, in many parts of* France, *he must not be impleaded in any Court but the Kings; and elsewhere (in inferior courts) onely vpon reall actions.*

Francs bourgeois. *Free Burgesses; those that pay no yearely fines for their freedome, nor so many ordinarie amerciaments of courts as others; though they doe some other seruices, and yeeld other contributions, as others, vnto their lords.*

Selon la ville les bourgeois: Prov. *Such towne such townesmen.*

Bourgeois: m. ise: f. *Burguerly, citizen-like; belonging to a citizen, burgesse, burguer.*

Caution bourgeoise. *Citie securitie, or securitie of rich, and resident citizens.*

Pain bourgeois. *Crible bread; bread thats betweene white and browne; See* Pain.

Bourgeoisie: f. *A burguership, or burgesseship; the estate, or condition, of a burguer, or burgesse; also, burguers,*

guers, burgesses, freemen, townesmen, citizens; or a crue, or the whole companie thereof; also, a boroughship; and, the liberties, freedome, or priuiledges belonging to a towne, or borough.

Bourgeoisie d'avenage. *A certaine quantitie of Oats leuied to the kings vse, of those, who are made free of the towne of* Mehun sur Eure *in* Berry.

Droict de bourgeoisie. *Freedome; also, an yearely dutie, or fine of* xij d. Paris: *payed vnto the king by free burgesses; who in lieu thereof may refuse to answer in any court, but his, any personall action, or complaint whatsoeuer; except it be for an offence committed at that present, or three months before their freedome obtained. (This Dutie is also called,* Devoir de bourgeoisie.)

Droict de bourgeoisie de la Bassée sous Lille. *An yearely rent, or dutie of* iiij d, *payed by euerie freeman.*

Droict de bourgeoisie de la Chastre en Berry. *A certain yeerely summe, and a henne, payed by euery freeman vnto the lord of that place.*

Droict de bourgeoisie de Sedan. *is* xx d. *a yeare; and when he is made free (if he be the sonne of a freeman)* ij s. vj d; *or (if a forreiner)* v s. *payed vnto the Duke of* Buillon.

L'entrée de la bourgeoisie de Calais. *A dutie of* xxv francs, *payed by euery one that is made a burgesse, or freeman, of* Calis.

Bourgeon: m. *The young bud, sprig, or putting out, of a Vine; also, a pimple in the face.*

Bourgeon de laine. *A locke of wooll.*

Bourgeons. *Writlings, or critlings; the smallest, and most vntimely apples or peares; tearmed so by the Normane Fruiterers.*

Bourgeonné: m. ée: f. *Budded, burgeonned; put, sprung, sprouted out.*

Bourgeonnement: m. *A springing, budding, putting out.*

Bourgeonner. *To bud, spring, or sprout out; to burgeon, put, or shoot out.*

Bourgeonneux: m. euse: f. *Full of buds; richly set with pimples.*

Bourget: m. *A round stoole.*

Bourgrain: m. *Buckeram.*

Bourgespine: f. *Buck-thorne, Way-thorne, laxatiue Ramme.*

Bourguignon: m. *A Burgonian, one of Burgundie; also, the name of a Vine, whereof there bee diuers kinds.*

Bourguignon blanc. *The most fruitfull of all white Vines.*

Bourguignon cinquain. *as* Foirard.

Bourguignon noir. *as* Neraut.

Bourguignotte: f. *A Burganet, Huskin, or Spanish Murrion.*

Bourjassotte: f. *The name of a certaine figge.*

Bouringue. *as* Boulingue.

Bourjon. *as* Bourgeon; *a bud, &c.*

Bourjonner. *as* Bourgeonner.

Bourlesque: com. *Ieasting, merrie, pleasant, flouting, gibing.*

Bourlet: m. *A wreath, or a roule of cloth, linnen, or leather, stuffed with flockes, haire, &c; also, the Hood worne by Graduats, Lawyers, and Citizens, at their assemblies; also, a supporter (for a Ruffe &c) of Sattin, Taffata &c, and hauing an edge like a roule.*

Cerveaux à bourlet. *Hooded braines, or, such as haue better-stuffed hoods then heads; and (more particularly) ignorant Lawyers, vnskilfull plodders, Pettifoggers.*

Bournage. *as* Bornage.

Bournal: m. *A bonny-combe.*

Bournois. *as* Bournal; *or, a Bee-neast, or Bee-hiue, full of bonny-combes.*

Bourrabaquin: m. *A great carousing glasse, fashioned like a Cannon, Horne, or in some other anticke manner; (sometimes) also, a Bourrachoe.*

Bourrache. *as* Bourroche.

Bourrachiere. Corneille bour: *A Roiston Crow.*

Bourrachon: m. *A tipler, quaffer, tossepot, whip-canne; also, a little Bourrachoe.*

Bourrade: f. *A tempest, or storme; also, the cuffing, or ruffling of a bird by a hauke; also, the tossing, or muzzling of a hare by a greyhound before he beare her.*

Bourranflé. *Puffed vp, strouting out, with flocks, &c.*

Bourraquin. *as* Bourrabaquin; *or, a Bourrachoe.*

Bourras: m. *as* Borrais; *also, silke-rash; also, grosse, or course, canuas.*

Bourrasser. *To bastinade, beat, belamme, bethwacke.*

Bourre: f. *Flockes, or lockes of wooll, haire, &c, seruing to stuffe saddles, bals, and such like things; also, the downe, or hairie coat wherewith diuers hearbes, fruits, and flowers are couered; also (lesse properly) any such trash, as chaffe, shales, huskes, &c; also (least vsually) the couering, clothing, or backe-part, of a man.*

Bourre de soye. *Towe of silke, or the coursest silke; comes of the balls which the wormes haue pierced.*

Raisins qui sont encores en bourre. *Grapes that are as yet in the blossome, or, so young as they haue no forme.*

Faire bourre voler. *To play much at Tennis (the ball being meant by* bourre, *wherewith it is stuffed) also, to vse much, or spend much at, any costly game, pastime, or exercise.*

Bourre. *A Ducke.* ¶Norm.

Bourré: m. ée: f. *Stuffed, or stopped with haire, flockes, &c; also, beaten, thumped, cudgelled; also, stopped.*

Bourreau: m. *An executioner; a hangman.*

Bourrée: f. *A bauin, or faggot, of twigs; a bundle of any such like stuffe.*

Bourrelé: m. ée: f. *Tortured, tormented; executed; extreamely vexed.*

Bourreler. *To torture, torment; execute; vex extreamely; See* Bourreller.

Bourrelerie: f. *A torturing, tormenting; executing; th' office of a hangman; also, an extreame vexation.*

Bourrelet. *See* Bourlet.

Bourrelier: m. *A maker of horse-collars.*

Bourrelier: m. ere: f. *Tormenting, torturing, executing with crueltie; vexing extreamely.*

Bourreller. *To torture, torment, execute cruelly; vex extreamely.*

Il bourrelle la besongne. *(Said of a bungling artificer) he spoyles both worke and stuffe.*

Bourrer. *To stuffe with flocks, and haire; also, to beat, or thumpe; also, to stop.*

Bourrette: f. *The vppermost part of the clue, or ball of silke yeelded by the silke-worme; the coursest of silke.*

Bourreux: m. euse: f. *Full of flockes, &c.*

Herbe bourreuse. *Cudweed, Chaffeweed, Cottonweed.*

Bourrier: m. *as* Bourre; *also, weeds; and generally, any filth; as sweepings, or vnprofitable, and house-defiling, trash.*

Il y a de bourriers en sa fluste. *All is not well with him; somewhat's amisse in the matter.*

Bour-

Bourriquet: m. *A kind of tombrell, or dung-cart; also, such a title for an Asse as Iade is for a horse; and hence;* Harry bourriquet. *Words wherewith the Millers, &c. in* France *driue forward their Asses.*

Bourroche: f. *Bourrage.*

Bourru: m. uë: f. *Flockie, hairie, rugged, high-napped.*

Vin bourru. *New sweet wine; such as is not yet setled after vintage; or, new, thicke, vnfined (white) wine.*

Bourry. Moyne bourry. *as* Moyne beur.

Bours de cheures. *Stables, or pennes, for goats.*

Boursal: m. *A younger brother.*

Boursal: m. ale: f. *Of a younger brother; whence;* Fief boursal. *The inheritance, or portion of inheritance, belonging to a younger brother.*

Boursalement. Tenir b. *By the title of youngership; different from that of the elder brother, who is to do homage vnto the Lord for the whole inheritance.*

Boursavit: m. *A prick-purse, or purse for a pricke; also, a kind of big leatherne purse, worne by many right before their codpeeces.*

Boursaul: m. *The Cane Withie, or, Cane Willow.*

Boursaut: m. *A little purse.*

Boursaux: m. *Younger brethren.*

Bourse: f. *A purse; also, a bag, satchell, pouche; also, a case; any thing made of leather to put, or keepe tooles, or other implements in; also, a ballocke, or, the outward skin wherein the cod is contained; also, a purse-net; also, the place of a Pentioner in a Colledge (we call it a Schollership, or Fellowship;) or in the Chancerie, or Exchequer; also, the Pension it selfe; so tearmed, because it is commonly deliuered in a Purse vnto the partie that hath it.*

Bourse de berger. *Shepheards purse, poore mans Parmacetie, Toyworte, Pickpurse, Coeseweed.*

Bourse Coustumiere. *A yeoman, or customarie tenant; or, a purchase made by a yeoman, or customarie tenant.*

Bourse de Curé. *as* Bourse de berger.

Bourse desliée. *Readie money; or, money disbursed, or payed downe for a thing.*

Bourse de Pasteur. *as* Bourse de berger.

Clameur de bourse. *An action brought for the recouerie of an aliened inheritance.* ¶Norm.

Demarche de bourse. *The same.*

Rouge bourse. *A Robin red breast; (called so in* Savoy.*)*

Elle a la langue en la bouche, non en la bourse. *(Said of a tatling huswife, whose Clicket is euer wagging) she is not tongue-tied, I warrant you.*

Faire bourse à part. *To keepe house, or make a household, apart, and without any communitie of goods, or of estate with others.*

Tous les prisonniers s' en sont fuys de sa bourse. *Looke* Prisonnier.

Venir entre la bourse & les deniers. *To preuent, forestall, come betweene and home. Seeke* Venir.

Abbé & convent ce n'est qu'un; mais la bourse est en divers lieux: Pro. *Looke* Abbé.

Belle hostesse c'est un mal pour la bourse: Pro. *A faire hostesse brings in a foule reckoning.*

Le petit gain emplit la bourse: Prov. *Wee say, light gaines make heauie purses.*

Qui biengaigne, & bien despend, ne luy faut bourse à mettre argent: Pro. *He needs no purse, that spends, as well as gets, much; or, that spends as much as hee gets.*

Qui n' a argent en bourse ait du moins du miel en bouche: Pro. *Looke* Argent.

Selon ta bourse gouverne ta bouche: Prov. *Measure thy appetite by thy abilitie.*

Boursé: m. ée: f. *Pursed, impursed; inclosed, or shut vp, as in a purse; bulching, or bearing out, as a full purse; bunted.*

Bourseau. *A little blister, bumpe, or swelling, such as rises of a knocke, or after nettling.*

Bourselle: f. *A Mariners Compas, or Dyall.*

Bourser. *To purse, impurse; inclose, or shut vp, as in a purse; also, to gather, make bulch, or beare out, as a (full) purse; to bunt, or leaue a bunt in a sayle.*

Bourseron. *A little purse; bag, pouche.*

Bourset de devant. *The fore-sayle.*

Bourset de hune. *The top-sayle of a ship.*

Bourseteux: m. euse: f. *Purse-like; belonging to a purse; full of purses.*

Boursette: f. *A little purse.*

Boursettes de la semence. *The seed vessels; as* Parastates.

Ietter la boursette. *A hauke, taken out of the Mue, to be fully cleansed, and purged before she be flowne.*

Bourseux. *as* Bourseteux.

Boursicouter. *To make a purse, gathering, or collection.*

Boursier: m. *A Pentioner; or, one that hath an yearely Pension in a Colledge; or out of the fees comming in by a Court of Iustice; (and such are the Kings Secretaries, and Clerkes of the Chancerie, whose intertainment is payed them out of the profit made by the Great Seale.)*

Boursiller. *To contribute euery one his pennie; to make a purse, or lay their monyes together, as Mummers, &c, vse to doe; also, to put his hand into his purse, or take somewhat out of his purse.*

Boursillon: m. *A little purse.*

Boursin. *A certaine little rope that serues to fetch in the sprit-sayle.*

Bourson: m. *A little purse; case; bag.*

Boursoufflade: f. *Windie pride, idle vanitie.*

Boursoufflé: m. ée: f. *Swolne, puffed, or blowne vp, as with wind.*

Boursouffler. *To swell with wind, to puffe, or blow vp.*

Boursouffleure: f. *A swelling of the guts, or of any other part, by windinesse; any swelling, puffing, or blowing vp.*

Bousant: m. *A Buzzard, or bauld kyte.* ¶Savoyard.

Bousat. *as* Bousant.

Bouschement: m. *A stopping, estoppell, obstruction.*

Bouscher. *To stop, obstruct, shut vp; also, to hoodwinke.*

Les fruicts se bouschent. *Said when the blossomes of a tree are closed (or nipped) by cold, so that no fruit comes of them.*

Bouscheron. *A bill-man; also, a faggot-maker.*

Bouschon: m. *A stopple; See* Bouchon.

Bouse de vache: f. *The dung of a Cow; a Cow-turd, or Cow-shard.*

Bousée: f. *The same.*

Bouset. petit bouset. *A little odious fellow; a paltrie crop of a Cow-turd.*

Bousfler. *To puffe vp, or blow wind into.*

Bousille: f. *(perhaps as* Bousin*) daubing, or stuffe to daube with.*

Bousiller: m. *A dauber.*

Bousiller. *To daube; also, to bugle, or slubber a thing ouer.*

Bousin: m. *A soft, and mouldering, substance, that cleaues to the outside of free-stone, in Quarries; and is vsually taken, or pilled, from the stone before it be wrought.*

Bousinier.pierres bousinieres. *Soft, and mouldering, or melting away in water, or by weather; (for those be properties of the* Bousin.)

Boussade: f. *The rot, or plague, among sheepe.* ¶Langued.

Bousse: f. *The bunch of a Cammels backe; or (generally) as* Bosse.

Boussin: m. *A bit, cantill, mammocke, morsell.* ¶Gasc.

Boussole: f. *A Pilots Dyall, Compasse, or Quadrant.*

Boussu. *as* Bossu.

Boust: m. *A tombe, sepulchre, graue; a place wherein a dead bodie hath beene buried, or burned.*

Boustargues. *as* Botargues.

Bout: m. *The end, head, point, top, or tip, the extreame, or vtmost, part (in the length) of a thing; hence, the chape of a scabberd; the head of an arrow, &c.*

Les bouts des costez. *Stitches in the sides.*

Baston à deux bouts. *A Quarter-staffe; or, a Lope-staffe, wherewith Low-countrey men leape ditches.*

Vne corde à trois bouts. *A threefold rope.*

Bout cy bout là. *Bungarly, disorderedly, slouenly; here a peece, and there a patch.*

'A chaque bout de champ. *Still, euermore, euerie where, in each place, at all times.*

Du bout des levres seulement. *Sleightly; nicely, daintily; from the teeth outward, onely with the tip, edge, or outside, of the lips.*

Tout à bout. *On euery side, at euery turning, euerie where.*

Il est au bout de sa corde. *He can doe no more, he can goe no further; he may put vp his pipes, goe shake his eares.*

Ils sont au bout de la roye. *They are at their wits end, at their last helpes; they haue spent their pouder; they haue no more to say.*

Gaigner le haut bout. *To take, or set himselfe in, the highest place of a table; also, (in contentions, or trials) to get the vpper hand, carry away the best prize, win the spurres.*

Il ne peut au bout de l'an nouër les deux bouts de sa serviette ensemble. *Hee liues very barely; hath nought but from hand to mouth; cannot spare a dogge a bone, at the yeares end.*

Recerchons le bout de nostre fusée. *Let vs returne to our matter.*

Il ne regarde plus loing que le bout de son nez. *He is a carelesse, idle, lazie, dull, improuident fellow.*

Se tenir sur le bon bout. *To stand vpon his good parts, behauior, or birth.*

Se tenir sur le haut bout. *To stand vpon his pantofles, or on high tearmes.*

Au bout la borne: Pro. *At length we shall resolue, or settle, vpon somewhat.*

Au bout de l' aulne faut le drap: Prov. *Seeke* Aulne.

Boutade: f. *A starting; a suddaine, violent, and vnexpected passion, or stirring; also, as* Boutée.

Boutage. droict de boutage. *A certaine dutie, or fee, exacted by the Lord of* Breci *(a member of* Bourges) *for the wine retayled within his iurisdiction.*

Boutant: m. *A Buttresse, or shore-post.*

Boutant: m. ante: f. *Thrusting, putting, forcing, pushing forward; also, budding, or putting forth.*

Arcboutant. *Looke* Arc.

Boutargues. *as* Botargues.

Bouté: m. ée: f. *Thrust, forced, pushed forward; also, budded, or put forth.*

Boute-cul: m. *A Monke, or Frier, thats but a nouice, or newly entred into Orders; called so by the common people.*

Travailler en boute-cul. *as* Travailler en Bourdican; *Looke* Bourdican.

Boutée: f. *A put, push, thrust; a iert, brunt; shocke; violent attempt, vehement essay; also, a putting, spurting, sprouting, or budding, forth.*

'A boutées. *as* par boutées; *also, by heaps, or troupes.*

Par boutées. *By fits, or pushes; not all at once; eftsoones, now and then.*

Par plusieurs boutées. *Many and sundry times one after another; by diuers efforts made one in the necke of the other.*

Boute-feu: m. *A Boutefeu; a wilfull, or voluntarie firer of houses; also, a firebrand of sedition, a kindler of strife and contention; one that loues to set, and see, men together by the eares.*

Boutefoire. *A certaine shitten yew-game.*

Boute-hors: m. *The play called, Thrust out the harlot; (wherein the weakest euer come to the worst.)*

Bon boute-hors. *A good wit, conceit, vnderstanding; or, a good vtterance, a ready tongue, a quicke deliuerie.*

Bouteille: f. *A bottle; also, a buble raised on the water, by a drop of raine, &c.*

Il en est plus assotté qu' un coquin de sa bouteille. *He is more fond of it then a beggar is of his dish.*

Il m'a baillé le bouchon d'une bouteille. *See* Bouchon.

Il s'enyvre de sa propre bouteille. *He is too farre in loue with his owne good parts; or, he abuses them to his great shame, and confusion.*

Terre loing de soy n' apporte que flascons & bouteilles: Pro. *Grounds lying a farre off, breed nought but flaggons and bottles; (viz. extraordinarie expences.)*

Bouteillerie: f. *A cupboord, or table, to set bottles on; also, a cupboord, or house, to keepe bottles in.*

Bouteillette: f. *A small bottle, or buble.*

Bouteillier: m. *A butler; also, a bottleman, or yeoman of the bottles; also, a bottle-maker.*

Grand bouteillier. *The great Butler of* France; *an honourable Officer, but out of date, euer since* Charles *the seuenths time.*

Bouteilliere: f. *A Tympanie in, or swelling of, the lower part of the bellie, by reason of much water, or waterish humor, gathered together in it.*

Boutement: m. *A thrusting, putting, pushing forward.*

Boutement des feu. *A malicious firing of houses.*

Bouter. *To thrust, put, force, push, forward; also, to haue a strong breath (a faulconers tearme) also, to bud, or put forth, as a tree in the Spring; also, to roote, as a Swine.*

Bouter cap à la mer. *To cast about to sea-ward; a ship to make towards the maine.*

Bouter de loo. *To lay tacke aboord.*

Bouter selle. *To saddle; to clap a saddle on a horses backe.*

Bouter au vent. *To beare roomeward; or, to fill the sayles with wind.*

Bouter vent devant. *To goe too neere the wind.*

Bouter vent en penne. *To bring a ship vpon the Lee.*

Bouter en la vie. *To sayle directly into a port, or barred hauen.*

Si boute tel feur telle vente. *The thing is so'd as it was bought, let goe as it came; or (more carelessely) no matter, tis well ynough, let be how't will, come on't what can.*

Bouterolle: f. *The chape of a sheath, or scabberd.*

Boute-selle. *(The word for horsemen to prepare themselues) to horse.*
Boute-vent des Alchymistes; *a hole, or vent, in the top of their furnaces.*
Bouteufle: f. *A buble.*
Bouteure: f. *as* Boutture.
Bouticle. *as* Boutique; *also, a well, or lepe, for fish.*
Bouticlier: m. *A shop-keeper; or, he that looketh to a shop.*
Boutiffle: f. *A buble of water, &c.*
Boutignan. *The name of a kind of Oliue.*
Boutilier. *as* Bouteillier.
Boutine: f. *The nauell.*
Boutique: f. *A shop.*
Courtant de boutique. *A Prentice, or shop-boy.*
La grande boutique. *The Law; or, the profession thereof; or the Hall (as ours at Westminster) wherein it is practised; (called so, belike, because many things may be had in it for money.)*
Madamoiselle de la boutique. *Seeke* Madamoiselle.
Qui sçait l'art serre la boutique. *A prouerbe taxing th'enuie, or squeamishnesse of cunning Artists, who, for the most part, conceale from the world their excellent gifts.*
Qui ne sçait l'art serre la boutique: Prov. *(Imperatiuely) let him that hath no skill shut vp his shop; (so vnfit, and vnsafe a thing it is for a man to deale in a trade which he knoweth not;) or, as in* Art.
Qui tient boutique doit parler à chascun: Prov. *Shopkeepers must be courteous; or, such as haue ware to sell must haue words at will.*
Boutis: m. *The rooting of a wild Bore; also, as* Boutement.
Boutoir: m. *A Farriers Buttresse.*
Bouton: m. *A button; also, a bud of a Vine, &c; also, a locke of wooll.*
Bouton de feu. *An actuall cautere headed like a button.*
Boutons à queuë. *Long buttons; such as are laid on clokes &c.*
Bouton de verolle. *A pockie botch; or a high, and eminent pimple, bursting out in any part of a bodie infected with the pockes.*
Cauteré à bouton. *See* Cautere.
Serrer le bouton à. *To restraine, keepe short, or beare a hard hand ouer.*
Boutonné: m. ée: f. *Buttoned; budded; cauterized; set thicke with pimples, or pockie botches.*
Boutonnement: m. *A buttoning; a budding; a cauterizing.*
Boutonner. *To bud, spring, or sprout out; also, to button, or claspe; also, to cauterize, or seare with an actuall cauter.*
Boutonnerie: f. *A buttoning, or clasping; also, a budding, or sprouting out; also, a cauterizing.*
Boutonnet: m. *Rupture-wort, Burstwort; (an hearbe.)*
Boutonneur: m. *A Buttoner; or an instrument wherewith buttons are pulled through their ouer-strait holes.*
Boutonniere: f. *A button-hole.*
Boutouër: m. *The snout of a wild Swine.*
Bouts. *A great bottle; or, as* Oudre. (v.m.)
Boutticé. *An ashler, or binding stone (in building.)*
Boutton. *Looke* Bouton.
Boutture: f. *The slip of an hearbe; the sprig of a plant; a budding, or putting out, in either.*
Bouvaux. *The name of a kind of figs.*
Bouveau: m. *A bullocke; a little Oxe, or Bull.*
Bouvelt: m. *A young Bull, or Bull-calfe.*
Bouvi. qui sent le bouvi. *Smelling like an Ox.*
Bouvier: m. *A Cow-heard, a Neat-heard; a keeper of Oxen.*
Bouviere: f. *A small, round, bright-coloured, little-mouthed, and toothlesse, fish, of the riuer* Seine; *seldome eaten, because very bitter.*
Bouvillon. *as* Bouveau.
Bouvine: f. *All kind of Oxen; Neat, Oxen.*
Bouyau. *A bowell, gut, intestine; See* Boyau.
Bouys: m. *The shrub, called Box.*
Bouys d' asne. *Box-thorne, prickly Box, Asses-Box, thorne Box.*
Bouys espineux. *The same.*
Bouys poignant. *Kneehull, Kneeholme, Pettigree, butchers Broome.*
Bouze. *as* Bouse; *Cow-dung.*
Bouzine: f. *A rusticall Trumpet, or wind-instrument, made of pitched barke.*
Boyau: m. *A bowell, gut; entrall, intestine.*
Boyau avallé. *Bursting, or burstnesse; (the bowels being fallen downe into the cods.)*
Boyau culier, ou cuillier. *The right gut, or arse-gut (one of the three principall guts.)*
Boyau gasté. *The hurt of the draught gut (a disease among Oxen.)*
Gras boyau. *as* Boyau culier; *In beasts called, the Inche-pinne, or Inne-pinne.)*
Le long boyau. *The long gut; the third gut from the Ventricle; the thin, or small gut, wherein the* Chylus *waxing thicker, beginneth to rest; also, the name of a fertile plaine in the Isle of* France.
La Maison de Monsieur boyau. *Said of a house thats slated before, and thatched behind.*
Il a vn aulne de boyaulx vuides pour festoyer ses parens. *He hath a monstrous stomacke, a terrible appetite, a hungrie gut of his owne.*
Boye: m. *An Executioner, a Hangman.*
Bozel: m. *A thicke, or great boultell (commonly) in, or neere vnto, the Basis of a pillar.*
Bozine: f. *as* Bouzine.
Braailler. *as* Braire; *to bray like an Asse.*
Braçal. *See* Brassal.
Braçats: m. *Brasses, or Vambrasses; armor for the armes.*
Brace: f. *A measure of fiue foot; or, as* Brasse.
Bracelet: m. *A bracelet; also, the wrist of the arme.*
Bracelets. *Short linkes, and buttons, set to either side of the vpset, or port, of a bitt; or, the watering chaine of a bitt.*
Brachet: m. *A kind of little hound.*
Brachial: m. ale: f. *Of, or belonging to, an arme.*
Brachialement. *With maine force of armes; with all the strength he hath.*
Brachieux. *as* Brachial.
Braconnier: m. *A hunter.*
Bracque. *The name of a field neere* Paris, *wherein the schollers of the Vniuersitie vse to solace thẽselues.* ¶Rab.
Bracqué. *Looke* Braqué.
Bradypepsie: f. *Slow concoction; or, a painfull, and but halfe digestion, of meat.*
Bragard: m. arde: f. *Gay, gallant, flaunting; vain; also, pert, or dapper; also, braggard, bragging, braggadochio-like.*
Bragardement. *Gayly, gallantly, flauntingly; vainely; also, pertly; also, braggardly, braggingly, vauntingly.*
Bragarder. *To braue, or flaunt it; to weare gay attire, to goe gay; also, to brag, vaunt, swagger.*
Bragardise: f. *Brauerie, gaynesse, flaunting, proud vanitie; also, bragging, vaunting, swaggering.*

Bragmarder. *To draw, or imploy, his whineyard; to leacher.*

Brague: f. *A kind of Mortaise, or ioyning of peeces together.*

Bragues. *Short (and close) linnen breeches worne next vnto the thighes.*

Braguer. *To flaunt, braue; brag, or iet it.*

Braguerie: f. *Wanton tricking, lasciuious brauerie, or pranking; also, flaunting; bragging, swaggering.*

Braguesques: f. *Large venitians hauing codpeeces, and gathered, or full of stuffe, at the knees.*

Braguette: f. *A codpeece.*

Bonnet à quatre braguettes. *A square, or foure-cornered, cap.*

Bragueur. *as* Bragard.

Brahiers. *as* Brayers; *Linnen breeches.*

Brailler. *as* Braire. *To bray like an Asse, &c.*

Il ne perdra point l'auoine à faute de brailler. *He will not loose any commoditie for want of words.*

Brain: m. *The branch of a tree.*

Braire: m. *An Asse-like braying; a roaring, rude yelling, loud balling, vnmeasureable crying out.*

Braire. *To bray like an Asse; to bawle, yell, cry out loudly; rudely, vnmeasureably.*

Braire avec les asnes. *To follow the fashion, how rude soeuer it be.*

Braise: f. *A burning coale; quicke fire of coales; or hot imbers; also, a kind of inflamed swelling, full of rednesse.*

Saulter de la poile, & se ietter dedans les braises. *From ill to worse; from the frying-pan into the fire.*

Braisier: m. *A liue-coale; or, burning coales.*

Braisillonner. *To rost, or seeth vpon quicke coales, or imbers; or, as* Brasillonner.

Braisiner. *as* Bramer; *to roare.*

Braisset. *as* Graisset; *the greene toad.*

Brame: f. *A Breame.*

Brame de mer. *The sea Breame (called so at* Paris, *where it is ordinarie) also, the Guilt-head, or Goldennie (and diuers other fishes of that kind are also called so by the inhabitants of the sea coasts.)*

Bramé: m. ée: f. *Brayed, roared, yelled, cried out with a harsh voice.*

Bramer. *To bray, roare, yell, or crie out with a harsh voice.*

Bran: m. *The branne of Wheat; also, as* Bren; *a turd.*

Bran de Iudas. *Freckles in the face.*

Faire de l'Asne pour avoir du bran. *To play the foole, or make an asse of himselfe, in hope of gaine, or victuals.*

Farine du Diable n'est que bran: Prov. *Looke* Farine.

Tousiours truye songe bran: Pro. *The filthie glutton still dreames of his belly.*

Truye aime mieux bran que Roses: Prov. *The Sow loues draffe better then delicacies.*

Bran. bœuf bran. *A kind of vnreclaimeable wild Oxe, in* Provence, *&* Languedoc.

Branc d'acier: m. *A cuttleasse, or courtelax.*

Brancal: m. *The sides of a wagon, the shafts of a litter; the two beames, or poles, whose fore-part makes the Thill; also, a horse-litter, or close litter; and (generally) any such thing that hath armes, or out-bearing side-beames, and is to be carried by, or betweene, two; also, as* Brancar.

Brancar. *as* Brancal; *also, a branch of Corrall; also, the crosse-barre of a hilt.*

Brancas: m. *as* Brancal.

Brance. *Bearded red wheat.*

Branchage: m. *Branchinesse; thicknes, or store of branches; also, branches, boughes; also, Linage; or the branch of a Pettigree, &c; as* Branche.

Branchages. *as* Branchieres.

Branche: f. *The branch, or bough of a tree; also, the gill of a fish; also, the cheeke of a bit; also, a collaterall degree, or side, of kinred; Linage; or, a branch, or line, of a Pettigree.*

Branche d'augiues. *Looke* Augive.

Branche hircine; *as,*

Branche vrsine. *Brank-ursin, Beares-foot, Beares-claw, Beares-breech (an hearbe.)*

Droict de branche de Cyprés. *Looke* Cyprés.

Il se tient seulement à l'estoc sans s'amuser aux branches. *He holds him onely to the substance, without respecting circumstances.*

Vole bas de peur des branches. *Flie low, or be stopt by the branches; beare a low saile, or bee run vnder water; a middle, or moderate course is little subiect vnto enuious crossings.*

Brancheage: m. *as* Branchage.

Brancher. *To sit vpon a branch; to light vpon a bough; to take a tree; to take stand in a tree, as a hauke; to pearch, as a phesant.*

Brancher vn larron. *To twitch a theefe vp at a bough, to hang him vp at a tree.*

Tant que tige faict souche elle ne branche iamais. *As long as there are any heires of an elder Prince of the bloud, the younger cannot inherit the crowne.*

Branchet. Espervier branchet. *A brancher, or young hauke, newly come out of the neast.*

Branchette: f. *A little branch.*

Branchier: m. ere: f. *Haunting, or liuing among, branches; pearching, or sitting, on boughes; also, of, or belonging to, a branch, or bough.*

Espervier branchier. *A brancher, or young hauke, newly come of the neast.*

Branchiere: f. *A Passage-toll, or through-toll; so called, because the little log thats a signe therof (as in* Billette*) hangs on the branch of some tree or other.*

Branchieres. *The out-places, or parts of the high way, wherein the said logs, or billets, haue beene, a long time, hung vp.*

Branchillon. *A little branch.*

Branchu: m. uë: f. *Branchie, branched, full of branches, or boughes.*

Branchuë: f. *A kind of small red Cray-fish, which bred without a shell of it own, seises on some other, and therein continues, getting at length a resemblance of the fish it belonged vnto.*

Branchure: f. *A branch.*

Brand. *as* Branc.

Brandes: f. *Heathie grounds.*

Brandif: m. iue: f. *Brandishing, shaking, flourishing; lustie, liuely, stirring.*

Il mangea vn gigot de mouton tout brandif, viz. *wholly, or all whole.*

Brandillé: m. ée: f. *Brandled, tottered, wagged, shaken, swong, swagged; also, glistened, or flashed.*

Brandillement: m. *A swinging, wagging, swagging, shaking, tottering vp and downe; also, a glistening, or flashing.*

Brandiller. *To brandle, wag, shake, swing, totter; also, to glisten, or flash.*

Brandilloir: m. *A swing.*

Brandilloire: f. *The same.*

Brandir. *To cast, or hurle with great force, or violence; to make a thing shake, or quauer, by the force it is cast with; also, to brandish; to shine, or glister with a gentle shaking, or soft mouing.*

Brandon: m. *A torch, firebrand, great cresset, lanterne, or light set vp; also, the bush of a Tauerne, or Alehouse; also, a staffe topped with straw, and pitched down by a Landlord into his tenants ground, in signe of an arrest, or seisure for seruices omitted, or his rent vnpayed.*

Brandon doré. *The Sunne.*

Brandonné: m. ée: f. *Stucke downe, as a staffe of straw, on land, in signe of an arrest, or seisure; or, seised, as land by that ceremonie.*

Brandonner. *To seise land by pitching downe into it a staffe topped with straw; as before in* Brandon.

Brane. bœuf brane. *A kind of wild and vnreclaimeable Ox in the countries of* Languedoc, *&* Provence; *fit onely for the Shambles.*

Branlage: m. *A kind of toll, or tax.*

Branler. *See* Bransler.

Branquar. *as* Brancar; *also, the edge of the decke of a ship.*

Branque vrsine. *Brankursin, Beares-breech, Beares foot, Beares claw (an hearbe.)*

Branque vrsine sauvage. *Wild* Acanthus, *wild Beares-breech.*

Branqueté: m. ée: f. *Rifled, ransacked; oppreßed.*

Branqueter. *as* Bransquetter.

Branque-vrsine. *Brank-ursin, Beares-breech (an hearbe.)*

Branscat: m. *Spoyle, rauage, ransacking; oppression, extreame wrong.*

Branslant: m. ante: f. *Brandling; shaking, swinging; tottering; shogging, wagging; reeling, staggering; wauering.*

Chariot branslant. *Looke* Chariot.

Bransle: m. *A totter, swing, or swindge; a shake, shog, or shocke; a stirring, an vncertain and inconstant motion; also, a brandling, &c; as in* Branslement; *also, a brawle, or daunce, wherein many (men, and women) holding by the hands sometimes in a ring, and otherwhiles at length, moue all together.*

Le bransle contrainct. *The shaking of the sheets.*

Le bransle de la corde. *A swing in a halter; or, the rope-swing (which few men take with a good will.)*

Aller de grand bransle. *To moue apace, to goe very fast.*

Il est en bransle si. *Tis doubtfull, or vncertaine whether yea or no; the matter hangs in suspence, or is yet in the ballance.*

Sonner les cloches en bransle. *To ring out the bels.*

Bransle: m. ée: f. *Brandled; tottered; shaken, swung; shogged, wagged; reeled, staggered; waued, wauered; often stirred, or moued from side to side; also, trembled, quaked.*

Branslement: m. *A brandling; tottering; shaking, swinging; shogging, wagging; reeling, staggering; wauering; often, and vncertaine mouing from side to side; also, a trembling.*

Branslement des dents. *Loosenesse of the teeth.*

Bransler. *To brandle; totter; shake; swing; shog, wag, reele, stagger; waue, wauer; nod often, stirre apace, moue vncertainely, or inconstantly, from side to side; also, to tremble, or quake.*

Bransler au manche. *To be loose in the helue, or heft; to stagger, wauer, shake, or flinch, vpon a triall; to want courage, or grow faint-hearted, in a time, or at the point, of execution; resolution to faile a man when he hath most need of it.*

Bransler la pique. *To frig, to wrigle it.*

Bransler la teste. *To shake the head, in signe of contempt, scorne, mockerie, or discontentment.*

La teste luy bransle. *Said of one that is much afraid; and of one whose head by drinking is become too heauie for his bodie.*

L'Armée bransle. *The army begins to giue, or to loose, ground; begins to totter, or to fall into disorder.*

Bransloire: com. *Any thing that shakes, shogs, or swings a man vp and downe; any thing that makes him reele, totter, or stagger; also, a brandling, &c; as in* Branslement; *and hence;*

Bransloire d'enfans. *A fashion of tottering vsed by schoole-boyes, vpon one forme layed (with the feet vpwards) ouercrosse another.*

Bransquetter. *To rifle, rauage, ransacke; to spoyle, or take in a towne by violence; to oppresse, wrong, or grate vpon, extreamely.*

Braque: m. *A kind of short-tayled setting dog; ordinarily spotted, or partie-coloured.*

Braqué. *Bent, leuelled, or planted, as Artillerie, against a place; also, braked, as hempe.*

Braquemar. ou, **Braquemard.** *A woodknife, hangar, whineyard.*

Braquer (l'artillerie) contre. *To leuell; bend; or plant (artillerie) against.*

Braquer du chambre. *To brake hempe.*

Braquer vn chariot. *To turne, set, or bend, a chariot on the right, or left hand.*

Bras: m. *An arme, of the bodie; of a riuer, of the sea; also, the foreleg of a horse.*

Bras (plural.) *The two small ropes that passe through the end of the Bolt-sprit yard, and serue to hale in the sayle; our mariners name them, Clulings.*

Bras de l'antenne. *The Tyes; the tackling that holds, and stayes the sayle-yard.*

Le bras seculier. *Secular authoritie, lay iurisdiction; ciuill magistracie, or the ciuile magistrate.*

Les bras d'un Scorpion. *The cleyes, or clawes, of a Scorpion, &c.*

Chaire à bras. *A chaire with elbowes.*

Grand bras. *The whole arme, and hand.*

Homme de bras. *An artificer, labourer, handicrafts man; one that gets his liuing by the labour of his hands.*

Petit bras. *The vpper part of the arme from the elbow to the shoulders.*

Vallet à bras. *Looke* Vallet.

Bras à bras. *Arme in arme; louingly, or equally, together.*

Les bras croisez. *Idly, lazily, slouthfully, negligently, carelesly.*

Bras dessus & bras dessous. *Freely, affectionatly, with strict, or earnest imbracements, most familiarly.*

'A tour de bras. *Throughly, fully, soundly; with maine strength, or confident authoritie.*

Se laisser aller sous les bras d'autruy. *To relie vpon another.*

Canonizé gros comme le bras. *Canonized as sure as a club. (Ironically.)*

Il iette la pierre, & cache le bras. *He does the most mischiefe, and would be least seene in it.*

Bras à la poictrine, iambe en gesine: Prov. *Those parts, being hurt, must haue rest; the one in a scarfe; the other in bed, or on a stoole.*

'A l'or le feu fort, au fort bras la luicte: Prov. *The worth of gold is tried by fire, the strength of an arme by wrestling.*

Argent receu le bras rompu: Prov. *He that payes for worke beforehand, lames his workeman; or, hath it but lamely done.*

Braser. *To skue, or chamfret, viz. to slope the edge of a stone, as Masons doe in windowes &c, for the gaining of light.*

Braser l' argent; C'est, la repasser vn peu sur la braise.

Brasier: m. *A burning coale, quicke fire of coales; hot embers.*

Brasillé: m. ée: f. *Rosted, broyled, or boyled with a quicke fire; also, broyled, or heated much.*

Brasiller. *To rost, broyle, or boyle on quicke coales, or hot embers; also, to broyle, or heat much.*

Brasillonner. *To broyle, or boyle with a very quicke fire; also, to broyle extreamely, burne out, or be on a light fire.*

Brassage: m. *The fee which the Masters of the Mint haue out of euery sort of money coyned; as out of euery* marc *(or eight ounces) of gold* xxv s. Tourn. *and vpon euery* marc *of* Douzains vj s. vj d. Tour. *out of which they allow a certain proportion, in respect of euery sort, vnto the Grauers, Monyers, and other workmen; which proportion of theirs is also tearmed* Brassage.

Brassal: m. *An Archers bracelet, or bracer; also, a vambrace, or peece of armour for the arme; also, the wooden cuffe, or bracer worne by Balloone-players.*

Brassart. *as* Brassal.

Brassat. *The same.*

Brasse: f. *A fadome, or arme-full; or measure of fiue foot.*

Brasse de foing. *is to be fiue foot square euery way.*

Pain de brasse. *A great houshold loafe (of course bread) a loafe as big as one can fadome.*

Brassé: m. ée: f. *Brewed; also, deuised, plotted, contriued.*

Brassée: f. *A fadome, an arme-full, as much as one can hold within, or carrie in, his armes.*

Brasselet: m. *A bracelet, wrest-band, or bracer; also, an arming gantlet, that reaches vp almost to the elbow; also, the wrist.*

Brasser. *To brew, or make beere; also, to plot, contriue, deuise.*

Il ne sçavoit pas quel brouët se brassoit, avec vn autre. *He knew little, what priuat match was in making, what secret bargaine was a beating, what an odde pranke was a forging, with another.*

Brasserie: f. *A brewing; also, a contriuing.*

Brasseur: m. *A Brewer; also, a plotter, contriuer, deuiser.*

Brassier: m. *A Brasier; also, a sling; also, a cudgell; also, the tub that receiues the droppings of a tap; also, a labouring man.*

Brassiere: f. *A wast-coat, for a woman; or a child; also, (but lesse properly) the doublet some women doe weare in childbed; also, the arme, or branch of a riuer; also, a brace; one of the staues whereby men turne the beame of a Crane, &c.*

Brassin: m. *A brewing.*

Brassique: f. *Cole, or Coleworts.*

Brassique marine. *The sea Cole, or sea Colewort; mistaken by some for sea Bindweed, or Scottish Scuruie-grasse.*

Brater vn chariot. *as in* Braquer.

Bravache. (soldat bravache) *A Roister, Cutter, Swaggerer, Swash-buckler; one thats euer vaunting of his owne valour.*

Bravacherie: f. *An vnseemely, or vnseasonable, cutting, roisting, swaggering; also, a fond boasting, vaunting, bragging of his owne valour.*

Bravade: f. *A brauado; a swaggering pike, or quarrell; a boastfull affront; a glorious shew of challenge, or daring.*

De bravade. *(also) in a brauerie.*

Brave: m. *The reward, or prize for him that hath done best in playes, or games.*

Brave: com. *Braue, gay, fine, gorgeous, gallant (in apparrell;) also, proud, stately, loftie; braggard; magnificall, sumptuous; also, valiant, hardie, stout, couragious, that will carrie no coales.*

Faire le brave. *To stand on tearmes, or vpon his pantofles; to boast of his owne worth; to preferre himselfe before others.*

Bravement. *Brauely, gallantly, finely, gaily; sumptuously, gorgeously; magnifico-like; also, proudly, haughtily, loftily; also, stoutly, valiantly, couragiously; also, discreetly.*

Braver. *To braue, abuse, affront, swagger with.*

Se braver. *To braue it, or play the Gallant; also, as* Faire le brave.

Braverie: f. *Brauerie, gallantnesse, gorgeousnesse, or costlinesse in apparrell; also, as* Bravade.

Braveux: m. *He that giues the prize to the best doers in an exercise.*

Bray: m. *Ship-pitch, or a kind thereof; also, Mault.*

Brayant: m. ante: f. *Braying, yelling, or crying, like an Asse; also, braying, pounding, brusing.*

Brayart: m. *A braying, yelling, roring, or crying Asse.*

Braye: f. *A close linnen breeke, or vnder-slop (Looke* Brayes*) also, a trusse, a swathell, or halfe-slop of linnen, or leather; worne by such as are burst; also, a clout for a childs backside.*

Brayes. *Short (and close) breeches, drawers, or vnderhose, of linnen, &c, worne for cleanlinesse, &c, next vnto the skin; also, Barnacles for a horses nose.*

Braye à chausse. *A kind of fish-net, made somewhat like a breeke, or slop.*

Braye de cocu. *A Cowslip, or Paigle.*

Fausse braye. *A false-bray, or out-wall, in a fortresse.*

Faulses brayes. *The straps that hang downe on either side of a horses furniture.*

Brayé: m. ée: f. *Brayed, pounded, bruised; kneaded, as dough; braked, as hempe; grauen, as a ship.*

Brayement: m. *A braying, pounding, bruising; braking; also, an Asse-like braying, yelling, or crying out; also, a grauing, or pitching of a ship.*

Brayer: m. *as* Braye.

Le brayer d' une Chevre. *The Vdder of a shee Goat.*

Le brayer d' un oiseau. *The Brayle, or pannell of a hauke.*

Brayer. *To bray, poune, bruise; also, to knead dough with a staffe; also, to bray, yell, or crie, like an asse.*

Brayer du lin. *To brake, or dresse flax.*

Brayer vn navire. *To graue, picke, or pitch, a Ship.*

Brayere: f. *A Flax-wife.*

Brayes. *Looke* Braye.

Brayette: f. *as* Braguette; *also, the tryall, tongue, or cocke, of a Ballance.*

Brayetter. La langue me brayette. *My tongue trips, or falters.*

Brayetter la chemise. *To accommodate the skirt betweene the legs (passing the fore-skirt behind, and the binder before) that it be not cumbersome.*

Bray-

Brayeul: m. *The parts, or feathers, about a hawkes fundament, called by our Faulconers the brayle in a short-wingd, and, the pannell in a long-wingd, hauke.*
Breant. *The bird called, a Siskin.*
Brebiail: m. *Sheepe; Ewes.*
Brebiaille: f. *The same.*
Brebiette: f. *A little sheepe, or ewe.*
Petite brebiette tousiours semble ieunette: Pro. *The little sheepe seemes euer yong.*
Brebis: f. *A sheepe; properly, an ewe.*
Brebis de rebut. *An old, or diseased sheepe, thats not worth keeping; wee call such a one, a drape, or culling.*
Courage de brebis (le nez en terre, *followes) To it hearts; courage my Lads; (an irronicall, or sportfull phrase of encouragement.)*
Brebis contées mange bien le loup: Pro. *The wolfe eats counted, as well as vncounted, sheepe; (appliable vnto a beastly fellow, that respects nothing but the glutting of his filthy appetite.)*
Brebis trop apprivoisée de trop d'agneaux est tettée: Prov. *An ouer-kind man, or woman get more followers, than it stands with his ease, or her honestie to keepe.*
Ou brebis sont laine est: Prov. *Where sheepe are wooll is.*
Depuis que la brebis est vieille le loup la mange bien: Prov. *A wolfe can eat a sheepe though shee bee old.*
Deux loups mangent bien vne brebis: Prov. *Two wolues deuour one sheepe with ease.*
En la peau de brebis ce que tu veux y escris: Pro. *One may write what he will in a sheepes skin; (sheepe endure any thing.)*
Entre Beaucaire, & Tarascon ne paist ne brebis, ne mouton: Prov. *Looke* Tarascon.
Il n'est pas tousiours saison de brebis tondre: Pro. *Sheepe-sheering is not euer in season; silly people must haue some time allowed them to thriue in; so will their fleeces, at length, be worth clipping.*
Pendant que les chiens s'entregrondent le loup deuore la brebis: Prov. *Church-mens contention is the diuels haruest.*
Qui se fait brebis le loup le mange: Prov. *Those that will needs be sheepe the wolfe deuours; hee that like a sheepe carries himselfe, like a sheepe shall be fleeced, foulded, and fed on.*
Tandis que la loup muse la brebis entre au bois: Prov. *While the wolfe studies the sheepe escapes; while the cruell consult, the innocent ouerslip them; (hereby is also noted th'inconueniencie of an opportunitie neglected; and their slownesse, or dulnesse taxed, who go to councell when they should fall to action.)*
Breborions: m. *Old dunsicall bookes; also, the foolish charmes, or superstitious prayers, vsed by old, and simple women, against the tooth-ache, &c; any such thredbare, and mustie, rags of blind deuotion.*
Breche: f. *A bracke, or breach in a wall, &c.*
Breché: m. ée: f. *Breached; full of brackes, full of breaches; or hauing a breach made in it.*
Brechedent: m. *A tooth-gaper; one that wanteth diuers teeth; or, as* Breschedent.
Brechet: m. *The brisket.*
Brecheure d'une riviere. *A breach in a riuer.*
Bredaille: f. *A great paunch, or belly:* ¶Pic.
Bredailler: m. *A gorbelly, gorrell, gulch, fatguts.*
Brediner. *as* Bredouiller.
Bredouillard: m. arde: f. *Faultering, gabling, maffeling, imperfectly speaking.*
Bredouille: f. *A lurch at cards, or tables.*
Estre en bredouille. *To be tipled, or tipsie.*
Ma petite bredouille. *My prettie rogue, my little knaue (a tearme vsed much by the nurses of* France.)
Bredouillement: m. *A faultering, or maffling; an ill-fauoured speaking, imperfect pronounciation.*
Bredouiller. *To maffle, or faulter; to speake, or pronounce imperfectly.*
Bref: m. *as* Brevet; *A breefe, note, short writing; also, as* Brief; *a writ, &c.*
Droict de Brefs. *Certaine pecuniarie duties paid vnto the Kings Receiuers, or farmors in the Ports of* Brittaine, *euer since the yere 1566, when they were granted by a prouisionall Arrest of the Parliament there, in regard (as it seemes) of the Kings writs, licencing the passage of vessels out of those Ports; hence;*
Bref d'année. *Is for vessels of the burthen of fiue Tunnes and vnder; which pay* vij.s.vj.d.Tour.
Bref de conduicte & de victuailles. *Is giuen for vessels that be of burthen from nine to nineteene Tunnes; These pay* 50.s.Tour.
Bref de victuailles. *Is for vessels that be from fiue to nine Tunnes burthen; and these yeeld* 17. s. 6. d. Tour.
Tous briefs. *Must be had for such vessels as be of* 19 *Tunnes, or vpwards; and for them,* 110.s.*paid.*
Bref. *See* Brief; *Short, &c.*
Brefve: f. *Looke* Breve.
Bregmatis: Os bregmatis. *(Latine words vsed much by French Anatomists:) Looke* Os.
Brehaigne: f. *A barren woman, or female; or, (Adiectiuely) barren, sterill.*
Brei: m. *as* Bret *(The fowlers engine.)*
Breil de forest. *A thicke growne wood, or corner of a forrest, wherein great wild beasts vse to lurke.*
Breits. *as* Bray.
Brelafé. *Looke* Balafré.
Brelan: m. *A house of gaming, tipling, or of any such disorder; Looke* Berlan.
Brelandier: m. *An ordinarie haunter of gaming, or tipling houses; also, the master, or keeper of such an vngodly house.*
Brelengue. *as* Brelingue.
Brelingue: f. *A peece of coyne worth about eight pence sterling.*
Breller. *To batfowle; to catch birds by batfowling; also, to twinkle, or glitter.*
Brelles. *Ciues, chiues; or, ciuet, and sweth.*
Breluë. Il a la breluë. *His eyes are dazled; See* Berlue.
Bremant. Il n'a enfant ne bremant. *Hee hath nor child, nor chicke to care for; he liues without any manner of charge.*
Bremer. *as* Bramer.
Bremine: f. *as* Brame; *A Breame.*
Bren: m. *A turd, mans dung, excrement, ordure; Looke* Bran.
Brenasserie: f. *Scuruie shitten sturre, or stuffe.*
Breneux: m. euse: f. *Beshitten, all-to-berayed; full of turd, filth, ordure.*
Bresche. *The name of a verie hard, and sundrie coloured, marble.*
Brésché: m. ée: f. *as* Breché.
Breschedent. *An irronicall allusion to* President; *or, as* Brechedent.
Bresil: m. *The wood Brasill; also, beefe long salted, and hung by the fire till it become red; Martlemas beefe.*

Bre-

Bresillé: m. ée: f. *Made red, as, or with, Brasilewood.*
Boeuf bresillé. *as in* Bresil; *Martlemas beefe.*
Bresin: m. *The hooke of a crane; and, in a ship, the canne-hooke.*
Bressaudes: f. *The crispie mammocks that remaine of tried hogs grese.*
Bressaux. *A kind of fine cakes, or wafers; or, as* Pain de Quinque.
Bresse: f. *as* Broisse; *A brush; also, a thinne leafe, or cake, as, of wax, &c.*
Bresseron: m. *The Sow-thistle.*
Bressille des yeux: f. *The twinkling of the eyes.*
Bressiller. *To twinkle with the eyes.*
Bret: m. *A little engine (made of two stickes ioyned together) wherewith fowlers catch small birds, the whilst they wonder at an Owle, thats set of purpose to amaze them; also, as* Bray.
Bret. Estre, ou parler, bret. *To stammer, stut, or speake indistinctly.*
Bretaudé. *Curtalled.*
Bretauder. *To curtall; See* Bertauder.
Breteler. *To brabble, chide, brawle, scowld, berate.*
Breteleur: m. *A brabler, chider, brawler, or wrangler; a litigious, or vaine talker.*
Bretelles d'une hotte. *The arms, or handles of a basket, or maund; (In* France *they are commonly made of a peece of a girth.)*
Breteque. *as* Bretesque.
Bretesche. *The same.*
Bretesque. *A publicke place in a towne, wherein outcries, and proclamations are ordinarily made; also, a port, or portall of defence, in the rampire, or wall, of a towne.*
Brethecque. *The same.*
Breton. *A Britan; An Inhabitant of Britanie.*
Breton Bretonnant. *The low Britan, who speakes halfe Welsh, halfe Saxon, all barbarously.*
Breton Gallo, ou Gallot. *The high Britan, who speakes French, but verie corruptly.*
Saut de Breton. *Looke* Saut.
Bretonnant. *Speaking thicke and short; also, (but lesse properly) stammering, faultering, maffling in the mouth.*
Breton bretonnant. *Looke* Breton.
Bretonner. *To speake thicke and short; or, as wee say, nine words at once; also, to stammer withall.*
Brette: f. *A (Fencers) foyle.*
Bretté: m. ée: f. *Notched, indented, iagged, or toothed, like a saw.*
Brettesé: m. ée: f. *Imbattled; adorned, garnished, or furnished with battlements.*
Brettesse: f. *The battlements of a wall.*
Bretture: f. *An indenting, iagging, notching.*
Bretueil: m. *Th'yron peece called a Fowler, or Portpeece.*
Brevade: f. *as* Brevet.
Breve: f. *The mettall which is, at one time, deliuered vnto a Coyner, or money-maker, to be wrought; called thus, because the quantitie thereof is briefely specified in a Ticket.*
Brevet: m. *A breefe, note, breuiate, little writing, short declaration, ticket; or bill of ones hand; also, as* Brief; Sub.
Estre enferré aux brevets des marchands. *To bee farre in their bookes.*
Hausser le brevet. *To come off more liuely, to stretch the purse strings.*
Brevetade. *as* Brevet.
Breveter. *To abreuiate, epitomize, reduce into breefes, or breuiates.*
Breviaire: m. *A Breuiarie, or Masse booke; also, a breuiarie, summarie, compendious abridgement.*
C'est matiere de breviaire. *Tis holy stuffe I tell you; irronically:* ¶Rab.
Il est au bout de son breviaire. *He is at a plunge, or nonplus; he hath no more to say; (from ignorant Priests, that can say no more than they find in their Seruice booke.)*
Il est clerc iusques aux dents, il a mangé son breviaire. *He makes a shew of learning, but indeed hath none in him; or, as in* Clerc.
Breuil: m. *A thicke growne forrest, wood, or groue, haunted by great wild beasts.*
Breulet: m. *An engine of two sticks (gouerned by a small cord) wherewith Fowlers catch little birds.*
Breusse: f. *A dish, or footlesse cup, or bowle, of Tinne.*
Breusté: *for* Brousté; *Broosed, or knapped off.*
Breuvage. *as* Bruvage.
Breuvoer: m. *Liquor; or, any liquid stuffe, thats fit to be made into drinke.*
Breze. *as* Braise.
Brezil. *as* Bresil.
Breziller. *To twinkle, or glitter; as the Sunne beames in a hoat season.*
Bribe: f. *A peece, lumpe, or cantill of bread giuen vnto a begger.*
Il n'est vie que de coquins quand ils ont assemblé leurs bribes: Prov. *There is no life (no mirth) to that of a company of beggers, hauing laied their scrips together.*
Briber. *To beg his bread; also, to rauine, deuoure, eate greedily; (from the sound made by the lips of a horse that eats prouender.)*
Bribeur: m. *A begger, a scrap-crauer; one that begs victuals from doore to doore; also, a greedie deuourer, a rauenous feeder.*
Bribonner ses oraisons. *To mumble vp his prayers, like an old man.*
Briborions. *Prayers mumbled vp; or, as* Breborions.
Bric. prendre au bric. *To take at aduantage; to catch hold of an vnaduised word, and make thereof a confession; also, to giue a dead lift, or sore blow at the last.*
Brichet: m. *The brisket, or breast-peece.*
Bricole: f. *A bricke wall; a side-stroake at Tennis (wherein the ball goes not right forward, but hits one of the walls of the Court, and thence bounds toward the aduerse partie) also, a kind of engine wherewith, in old time, they beat downe walls; also, as* Bricolle.
Il m'a ioué d'une bricole. *He hath played mee sore, or foule, play; offered me hard, or odde, measure; dealt extreamly, or cunningly, with me; also, he hath deceiued, or disappointed, me.*
Bricoler. *To tosse, or strike a ball sideways; to giue it a bricke wall (at Tennis;) also, as* Bricoller; *also, to banke, at bowles.*
Bricolle: f. *as* Bricole; *Also, a kind of toyle for wild beasts.*
Bricoller. *To tosse, or strike a ball sideways; to giue it a bricke wall, at Tennis; (Hence) also, to reele, stagger, or make indentures, in going; and, to be violently carried ouerthwart, or sideways; also, to turne short (as a Swallow, &c, does, in flying;) also, to leacher.*
Bricot: m. *The stumpe of a shrub, or little tree; an vpsticking stub of a late cut shrub, or tree.*

Bricoteau. *A quoyte of stone* (v.m.)
Bridaveaux : m. *Hollow, round, and wreathed cracknels of fine flower, sugar, salt, and yoalkes of egs, incorporated together with water, and white wine.*
Bride : f. *A bridle; also, a border, or carkanet of gold, and pearle for a womans head, (in the hinder part whereof tis closed;) also, a kind of drinking vessell.*
Bride de Chapeau. *A stay, for a hat; a string put vnder the hat-band.*
Bride à oeilleres. *Looke* Oeillere.
Bride de Soulier : *as in* Souliers à bride.
Brides à veaux. *Fopperies; gulleries; grosse tricks, or lyes; vnlikely tales, or things; also, halters; also as* Bridaueaux.
Souliers à bride, ou à brides. *Sandals; or woodden pattins held vnto the foot by one, or more strings (tearmed* brides*) which fastened on both sides of their sole, thence runne, and rayne, ouer th'instup.*
'A bride avallée: *As fast as he can driue; as fast, or as much, as he can.*
Abandonné sur la bride. *Hanging vpon the hand; (a Horsemans phrase.)*
Fort en bride. *Stout, headstrong, stubborne; surly; vnruly.*
Lascher la bride à. *To carrie a gentler hand vpon; to afforde more scope, o giue more libertie, vnto.*
Ie vous en mets la bride sur le col. *I giue you full power ouer it; I abandone it wholy vnto you.*
Tenir en bride. *To restraine, to hold in.*
Bridé : m. ée : f. *Bridled; bitted; restrained, ruled, moderated, held vnder, kept in order.*
Brider. *To bridle, bit; restraine, moderate, rule, hold-under, keepe in order.*
Brider l'asne, ou, son cheual par la queuë. *To goe the wrong way to worke, to doe a thing by contraries.*
Brider la mule à. *To waite on, attend the leasure of, or doe base offices for.*
Se Bride de serment. *Looke,* Serment.
Bridon : m. *A snaffle.*
Bridoye : *A goose-bridler; (a nickname for a Lawyer* ¶Rab.
Brief : m. *A writ, or breefe; a short mandamus, iniunction; commission &c.*
Brief de Iudgement; *as* Dicton de Iudgement.
Brief d'obligation & de debt. *The first copie, note, or scedule of an obligation, deliuered in paper vnto a creditor by the notarie that drew it.*
Droit de briefs. *Looke* Bref.
Brief : m. brieue : f. *Breef, short, succinct, compendious, of little length, of small continuance.*
Le plus brief est le meilleur : Pro. *The shorter the better (in bad things.)*
Brief. Adverbially; *as,*
'A brief parler. *To be short; in a word; the summe of all is; not to trouble you with many words, not to hold you ouer long.*
De brief. *Shortly, anon, forthwith, incontinently, by and by, within a while, ere it be long.*
En brief. *Briefly, shortly, succinctly, compendiously, in few words.*
Briemart : m. *Poore folkes drinke, made of branne, leauen, and water.*
Briere. *as* Bruyere.
Brievement. *Breefely, shortly, succinctly, compendiously; straitly, in a narrow compasse, in a little roome.*
Brieveté : f. *Breuitie, shortnes, succinctnes, compendiousnes.*

Brifaut : m. *A hastie deuourer, a fast eater, a rauenous feeder, a greedie glutton.*
Brifeau. *as* Brifaut.
Brifée : f. *A morsell, bit, snatch, mouthfull (eaten greedily.)*
Brifer. *To deuoure, eate hastily, feed rauenously, or like a hungrie glutton.*
Brifeur. *as* Brifaut.
Briffaux : m. *Rauenous feeders, hastie deuourers.*
Briffeur : m. *as* Brifaut.
Brigade : f. *A troope, crue, or companie.*
Brigader. *To accompany, or associate, one another; to troope, or keepe companie, together.*
Brigaille : m. *A noteable smel-smocke, or muttonmungar, a cunning solicitor of a wench.*
Brigand : m. *A footman armed, or seruing, with a brigandine (In old time when those kind of souldiors marched, they held all to be good prise that they could purloyne from the people; and thereupon this word now signifies) also, a theefe, purse-taker, high-way robber.*
Brigandage : m. *A robbing, theeuery, purse-taking, bootehaling, vniust pillage.*
Brigande : f. *as* Brigade (v.m.)
Brigandeau : m. *A yong, or small theefe; a filcher, a pilferer.*
Brigander. *To rob, to take a purse; to theeue it by the highway silde.*
Brigandereau. *as* Brigandeau.
Briganderie : f. *A theeuing; purse-taking; robberie by the highway.*
Brigandin. *as* Brigantin.
Brigandine : f. *A Brigandine; a fashion of (ancient) armor, consisting of many iointed, and skale-like, plates, very plyant vnto, and easie for, the bodie; (some, lesse properly, confound it with* (Haubergeon) *a coate, or shirt, of mayle.)*
Brigant. *as* Brigand.
Brigantin : m. *A low, long, and swift Sea-vessell; bigger then the fregat, and lesse then a foist, and hauing some 12 or 13 oares on a side: we call it also, a Brigantine.*
Brignon : m. *The name of an excellent plum, whereof there be two kinds, a bigger and a lesse.*
Brigue : f. *A canuas, priuate suite, vnder-hand labouring for an offise, &c; (hence) also, debate, contention, altercation, litigious wrangling about any matter.*
Brigue de Metz. *A peece of coyne worth* 10 *pence* Tourn.
Brigué : m. ée : f. *canuased, or laboured for, vnderhand; also quarrelled, contended, wrangled about.*
Briguer. *To canuas, make priuate suite, labour vnderhand, for an office, &c; also, to quarrell, contend, wrangle about matters; also, to sharke, or take purses by the high-way side.*
Briguerie : f. *A priuate canuasing, secret labouring, vnderhand suing for an office, &c; also a litigious debating, wrangling, or contending for matters; also, a sharking, robbing, purse-taking.*
Briguet : m. *A mungrell; whence (also) a man thats nobly borne but of one side.*
Brigueur : m. *One that priuately labours, or vnderhand sues, for the assistance, or fauor of others; hence; a canuaser for an office, &c; also, a quarrelsome, contentious, or ligitious, person; also, as* Brigand.
Brihat : m. *One that is hot, and loud.*
Bril : m. *A glitter, sparkle, twinkle; or glittering &c.*

Brillant. les brillants des femmes. *The iewels which they weare in their haire; and their glistering petticoats of changeable colours.*
Brillant. *Glittering, sparkling, twinkling, shining.*
Brillement: *A glittering, sparkling, twinkling, as of the stars; also, a batfowling.*
Briller. *To glitter, twinkle, sparkle, as a starre, or like a good diamond; also, as* Breller, *to batfowle.*
Briller apres. *Greedily to couet, or lust after.*
Les chiens brillent bien. *Said of lustie, or well-metled hounds, which nimbly cast about, or (as in French)* Sont legiers à la queste.
Brillonner. *as* Briller.
Brimbalatoire. *See* Brimballatoire.
Brimbalé: m. ée: f. *Tumbled headlong; throwne down topsie-turuie; also, shaken, swagegd, quagged.*
Brimbaler. *To tumble downe headlong, to fall downe topsie-turuie; also, to shake, swag, or quag, as a great dug, or th'vnsound flesh of a foggie person.*
Faire brimbaler les cloches. *To set the bells agate.*
Brimbales: f. *The bells worne by cart, or carriers, horses.*
Brimballatoire: com. *Swagging, wagging, shaking, or quaking, ill-fauouredly, or loathsomely.*
Brimballer. *as* Brimbaler.
Brimballotier. *See* Brimblotier.
Brimbeur: m. *A paultrie pedler.*
Manteau de brimbeur. *A mantle, or cloke of rug, or course frize.*
Brimblotier: m. *A paultrie pedler; one that hath nought but trash to sell; also, a spangle-maker.*
Brimborions. *as* Breborions; *also, the knackes, iagges, nifles, bawbles, wherewith fooles caps, &c, are garnished.*
Il dit ses brimborions; *(for* Breviaire*) He sayes ouer his whole Psalter; or, he mumbles to himselfe his fond, and superstitious, deuotions.*
Brimboter. *To mumble, putter, mutter, grumble, or babble vnto himselfe.*
Brin: m. *A (little) slip, or sprig, of an hearbe, &c; also, a corne of salt; and more generally, any small substance, deale, or bit of a thing.*
Bois de brin. *Round, or vncleft wood.*
Brin à brin. *by peece-meale; or by little and little.*
Il n'est vn seul brin estonné. *He is not a iot, not a whit, not at all, astonished.*
Brindelles de balay. *The sprigs, or twigs, of a beesome.*
Bringue: m. *A drinking to.*
Bringuenarder. *To swiue.*
Bringuenarilles. *Wide nosethrils:* ¶Rab.
Bringuenaudée: f. *A common hackney, a wench thats often swiued.*
Brioche: f. *A brake for hempe; also, a rowle, or bunne, of spiced bread:* ¶Norm.
Brioler. *To glide, or slide, on the yce.*
Brionie: f. *Brionie, white vine, wild nep, tetter berrie;* See Bryonie.
Brique: f. *Bricke; also, a plate, leafe, or wedge of mettall fashioned like a bricke.*
Laver vne brique. *To labour in vaine; or, to loose both time, and labour.*
Briquer. *To set, or lay brickes; to worke, build, or fortifie with bricks.*
Briquetie: f. *A brick kill; a house, or place wherin brick is made.*
Briquet: m. *as* Briguet; *Also, a yong hare.*
Briqueterie: f. *Brick-worke, laying of bricks; also, a brick kill.*
Briquetier: m. *A Bricklayer.*
Briquettes: f. *Nifles, trifles, little toyes.*
Briqueux: m. euse: f. *Brickie; full of bricks; fit for brickes.*
Briquier. *A brick-maker; bricke-seller.*
Bris: m. *A bracke, breach, or great leake, in a ship.*
Droict de bris. *Th'Admiraltie of a sea coast; which giues a man all wrackes, or shipwracks.*
Bailler bris contre Robert. Ie luy bailleray bris &c. *I will call him Iacke if he call me Gill; I will giue him altogether as good as he brings.*
Courir au bris. *To run to wracke, to bee in danger of shipwracke.*
Ie feray tel bris de toy que tu as merité. *I will make that shipwracke of thy reputation, or estate, which thy lewdnesse deserues.*
Brisable: com. *Burstable, breakeable, brayable.*
Brisans: m. *The foamie breaking of the sea against rocks, or banks of sand.*
Brisant: m. ante: f. *Breaking, bursting, beating, braying into peeces.*
Quartiers brisans. *The quarters of the Moone, in the waine.*
Brische: f. *A bush made of lime twigs, and a stale hung at it to draw birds vnto it.*
Briscoter. *To leacher.*
Brise: f. *A peece of ground, thats new broke vp for tillage; (and hath lien long vntilled.)*
Brisé: m. ée: f. *Broken, burst; brayed, beaten in peeces; also, rent, or torne off; also bruised or crushed extreamly; (in Blason, oppressed, or charged with;) also, interrupted; also, infringed, or violated.*
Chaire brisée. *A foulding chaire.*
Saisine brisée. *Th'occupation, and vse, of an inheritance taken by the tenant, notwithstanding the seisure thereof made by the Lord.*
Somme brisée. *A broken summe with odde money; or, a whole summe with ouerplus.*
Vis brisée. *A staire that hath foure or fiue steps vpright, then turnes, and hath as many forward another way; or, a straight staire with halfe paces.*
Brisée: f. *A breach, brack, rupture; also, a step, track, or footing.*
Brisées. *Boughes rent by hunters from trees, and left in the view of a deere, or cast ouerthwart the way wherin he is likely to passe, therby to hinder his running, and to recouer him the better; Our wood-men call them, Blinkes.*
Reprenons nos brisées. *Let vs returne vnto our former way, businesse, discourse, &c.*
Retournons par nos brisées. *The same.*
Ie ne vay plus sur vos brisées. *I trace you no more, I follow your footing no longer; or, I am no longer your competitor, concurrent, corriuall.*
Brise-grain. *Corne-breaking, graine-crushing.*
Brise-gueret. *Fallow-breaking, mold vp-tearing.*
Brisement: m. *A breaking, breying, beating to peeces; a rending, or tearing off; sore crushing, or bruising; a violating, infringing; an interrupting.*
Brise-ponts. *Bridge-breaking (of a riuer) all downe-breaking.*
Briser. *To burst, breake; bray; beat in peeces; also, to plucke, rend, or teare off, or vp; also, to crush, or bruise extreamely; also, to interrupt, or breake off; also, to violate, or infringe.*
Briser le fer aux dents. Il pense briser le fer aux dents.

dents. *He strugling against too strong an opposition, thinks to performe impossibilities.*

Brise-tour. *Tower-breaking, tower-splitting.*

Brisette: f. *A little scale, or buske; a little splint, or shiuer, broken off any thing.*

Briseur: m. *A burster, breaker; brayer, beater in peeces; a tearer off, a plucker vp; a violater, an infringer.*

Briseure. *as* Brisure.

Briseux: m. euse: f. *Breaking, braying, crushing, bursting asunder.*

Dents briseuses. *The tuskes, tushes, or dogs teeth.*

Brisgoter. (¶Rab.) *as* Briscoter.

Brisseures: f. *Broken peeces.*

Brisure: f. *A breach, burst; breaking, or beating in peeces; also, a plucking, renting, tearing off, or vp; also, an extreame crush, bruise, crushing, or bruising; also, a broken peece of; also, an addition, in armorie, for the distinction of brothers; as, a Labell, halfe Moone, Mullet, &c.*

Brit. prendre au b. *Looke* Bric.

Britanique: f. *Brittannica, Bistort, Snakeweed, Pashions, Oisterloite; (an hearbe.)*

Brive: f. *A bridge.* (v.m.)

Britascher. I'ay oüi britascher d'une telle chose. *I haue heard some such muttering.*

Briz: m. *A bracke, breach, or leake, in a ship, &c; Looke* Bris.

Brize. *for* Bize. *The North wind:* ¶Rab.

Brizer. *as* Briser.

Broc: m. *A steane, great flagon, tankard, or pot; holding (most commonly) twelue Parisian pintes.*

De broc en bouche. *Suddenly, incontinently, while tis hot.*

Brocar: m. *Satin stript, or purfled, with gold.*

Brocard: m. *A quip, gird, or cut; a ieast, flout, scoffe, gibe, mocke; also, as* Brocar; *and as* Brocart.

Brocardé: m. ée: f. *Quipped, cut, or ieasted at; scoffed, mocked, flouted, gibed.*

Brocarder. *To quip, cut, gird, reach ouer the thummes; ieast at; flout, mocke, scoffe, deride, or gibe at.*

Brocarderie: f. *A cutting, quipping, nipping; ieasting at; flouting, mocking, scoffing, deriding, gibing at.*

Brocardeur: m. *A quipper, scoffer, mocker, flouter, derider, giber, or ieaster at.*

Brocart: m. *A two-yeare-old Deere; which if he bee a red Deere, we call a Brocket; if a fallow, a Pricket; also, a kind of swift stag, which hath but one small branch growing out of the stemme of his horne; also, as* Brocard.

Brocatel: m. *Tinsell; or thin cloth of gold, or siluer.*

Brocelles. *as* Brossailles.

Brochant: m. ante: f. *Broching, spitting, stitching.*

Brochant sur le tout. *Ouer all; (spreading, or displaying it self, is meant, but omitted, by our Blasonners.)*

Brochard: m. *A peg, or pricke, of wood.*

Broche: f. *A broach, or spit; also, a (great) stitch.*

Broches. *The piles (in the fundament;) also, the tusks, or tushes, of a horse; or wild bore.*

Broche de mer. *The Spit-fish.*

Couper broche à. *To preuent, or take away th'occasion of.*

Vendre vin à broche. *To retaile, or draw wine; to vtter, or sell it, by pot-fuls, &c.*

Broché: m. ée: f. *broached, spitted; also, (grosely) stitched; sowed, or set with (great) stitches.*

Brocher. *To broach, to spit; also, to stitch (grossely) to set, or sowe with (great) stitches.*

Brocher vn cheval des esperons. *To spurre him, to strike him with spurres; also, to spurre him hard, almost to sticke him with spurring.*

Brochereux: m. *Little Pickerels.*

Brochet: m. *A Pike (fish;) also, a faucet, or quill for a wine vessell.*

Brochet de mer. *The sea Pike, the Cod-fish; also, the Spit-fish; or, as* Bequet de mer.

Ils iettent les gardons pour tirer des brochets. *They forgoe an egge to gaine an Oxe; or, small, for great, matters.*

Brocheton: m. *A Pickerell, or small Pike (of the length of a foot, or vnder.)*

Brochette de bois, &c; *A pricke, or peg of wood, &c.*

Brochette d'argent. *A little wedge of siluer.*

Brochoir: m. *A (Farriers) shooing hammer.*

Brode: m. *Broth, pottage, brue.*

Brode: f. *A blacke, swart, or Sunne-burnt, wench.*

Pain de brode. *Browne bread.*

Brode. langage brode. *A loose, laskie, squattering, scuruie; also, an effeminate, language, or speech.*

Brodé: m. ée: f. *Imbrodered.*

Robbe d'argent brodé de merde. *Iustinians Institutes; (called so because of the filthie Commentaries made on them.)*

Brodequin: m. *A buskin.*

Les brodequins. *Buskins, or bootes (filled with hoat oyle, &c,) whereinto the legs being put are extreamely tormented.*

Broder. *To imbroder.*

Brodes. *A cloke, or mantle, of leather.*

Brodeur. *as* Bordeur.

Brodeure. *as* Bordure.

Brodier: m. *The arse, bumme, taile:* ¶Norm.

Broisse. *A brush; Looke* Brosse.

Bronmart: m. arte: f. *Drowsie.*

Broncher. *as* Bruncher.

Bronchique. muscle b. *One of the foure muscles which open the Larinx.*

Brondes: f. *Greene boughes, or branches, of trees; browzing for cattell; or browze-wood.*

Bronze: m. *Brasse.*

Bronzé: m. ée: f. *Brason, brassie, made of, or couered with, brasse.*

Bronzer. *To Braze; to make of, or couer with, brasse.*

Brossailles: f. *Little bushes of thornes; also, little bundles of twigs, or stickes fashioned like bauens, or fagots; also, little loose stickes remaining in a place where fagots, or bauens haue beene laded, or layed.*

Brossailleux: m. euse: f. *Full of little bushes, or loose stickes.*

Brossant. *Threeding a wood, rushing through it; also, brushing.*

Brosse: f. *A bush; also, a bushie ground, or thornie groue; also, the head-brush thats of a whitish, or straw-coloured heath, (now most in vse among the better sort;) also, a brush of wire; also, a flax-combe, or hetchell.*

Brosser. *To threed a wood, runne through bushes, rush through thickets; also, to brush, or make cleane with a brush; also, to combe, or hetchell flax, &c.*

Brosser bien vn cheval aux Tournois. *To manage a horse gallantly in Turneyes.*

Brossettes: f. *Small heath whereof head-brushes are made.*

Brot. *as* Broc; *A flagon, or great tankard.*

Vn brot de vigne. *The bud of a vine.*

Brotonne. *Male Sothernwood.*

Brou: m. *The outward huske of a greene wallnut.*

Remascher son brou. *To chaw the cud.*
Brouailles: f. *Washings of dishes; also, guts, and garbage of fowle; any such outcast trash.*
Brouaz: m. *as* Brouhaha.
Broudier. *as* Brodier.
Broue: f. *A little white clowde.*
Brouée: f. *A mist, or fog; also, as* Brouhaha; *or* Boutade; *a blustering or violent passion, or perturbation.*
Brouer: m. *as* Bronée *(in the first sence.)*
Brouet: m. *Potage, or broth; also, any liquor, podge, or sauce, of the thicknesse, or consistence of that whereof our pruine-tarts are made.*
Bec à brouët. *A little peart, and pratling girle.*
Il ne sçavoit pas le brouët qui se brassoit auec vn autre. *(Poore man) he knew not that he was bought and sould by others; or, what crosse match was in hand vnder-hand with others.*
Brouëter. *To set a wheelebarrow a-gate; to labor with, or carrie things in, a wheelebarrow.*
Brouëtte: f. *A wheelebarrow; also, a tacke-nayle.*
Brouëtteur: m. *One that workes with a wheelebarrow.*
Brouffer. *To snurt, or snifter with the nose, like a horse.*
Brouhaha: m. *A bluster; hurry, hurlyburly.*
Brouhoux: m. *Stormes, blusters; hurlyburlies.*
Brouil: m. *as* Brou.
Brouillar: m. *A cold mist, or fog.*
Brouillard: m. arde: f. *Confounding, iumbling, disordering, shuffling, or hudling matters in an vnquiet, or ilfauored, manner.*
Papiers brouillars. *Blotting, or wast papers; loose papers, wherein we write things carelesly, or at randome.*
Brouillas: m. *A mist, or fog.*
Brouillasser. *as* Brouiller (extremement.)
Brouillasseur: m. *as* Brouilleur *(in the highest degree.)*
Brouillé: m. eé: f. *Iumbled, confounded, il-shuffled, disorderly hudled, hurryed, troubled; marred in the mingling.*
Oeil brouillé. *An eye wherein, by some great wound or inflammation, all the humors are mingled, and iumbled together; which causeth the ball, or aple, to appeare of diuers colours.*
Oeufs brouillez. *Whose substance is mingled, & beaten together with a little vargis; and so vsed, eyther for sauce, or as an* Omelet.
Brouiller. *To iumble, trouble, disorder, confound, marre by mingling together; to hudle, tumble, shuffle, things il-fauoredly; to make a troublesome hotchpotch; to make a hurry, or great hurliburly.*
Brouiller les cartes. *To disorder, confound marre businesses; also, to keepe a foule coyle, a filthy stirre.*
Il ne fait que brouiller. *(Of one that playes on an Instrument) he doth but fumble, or slubber ouer the lesson he playes.*
Brouillerie: f. *A confusion; a troublesome, or disordered shufling, iumbling, hudling, tumbling of things together.*
Brouilleur: m. *A confounder, iumbler, hudler, disorderly shuffler, or mingler of things together; a troublesome, or vnquiet person; one that by ouerdoing marres whatsoeuer he does.*
Brouillis: m. *A confusion; a confounding; a iumbling; a disorderly hudling, il-fauored shuffling, vnquiet tumbling of things together; an il-compounded mixture; confused pesterment; intricate or perplexed hurry, trouble, hurlyburly.*
Brouillis de procez; *Pettifoggerie; a disordering, or intangling, of causes to make them the more litigious.*

Brouillon. *as* Brouilleur; *also, one that broaks in euery thing, whereby he may get but a pennie.*
Broüiné: m. eé: f. *Blasted, or burnt with mists.*
Broüir. *To rumble, rustle, bluster; also, to humme.*
Broüissement. *as,* Bruiement; *also, a humming.*
Brouser. *To brouze, knap, nible off, leaues, buds &c.*
Broussaille: f. *A thornie, bushie, or bryerie, ground, plot, or groue.*
Broussin: m. *A bunch, or knurre, in a tree.*
Broust: m. *A brouzing, nibling, knapping off of buds, sprigs, leaues, &c; also, brouze-wood; or a sprig, tendrel, bud, &c; a yong branch, or shoote, fit to be brouzed on.*
Qui suit le broust. *A smel-feast, or trencher-friend; one that daily hauntes other mens well-furnished tables.*
Brouster. *as* Brouter.
Brout. *as* Broust.
Broute: f. *The roote of the box-tree, seasoned, and fit for vse.*
Broutement: m. *A brouzing.*
Brouter. *To brouze; to knap, or nible off the sprigs, buds, barke &c. of plants; also, as* Brouëter.
Où la Chevre est liée faut qu'elle broute: Pro. *Looke* Chevre.
Brouteur: m. *A brouzer; also, as* Brouëtteur.
Brouteur: m. eure: f. *Brouzing; nibling, knapping of sprigs, buds &c.*
Brouteure: f. *A brouzing.*
Broutilles: f. *Beggars scraps.*
Broutique: f. *A monkey.* (v.m.)
Broutonner. *as* Boutonner; *to bud.*
Brouy: m. ie: f. *Burned, parched; withered by extreame heat.*
Brouyr. *To parch, burne, wither with scorching heate.*
Broyé: m. eé: f. *Pounded, brayed, beaten small, broken into little peeces.*
Broyement: m. *A braying, pounding, beating small.*
Broyer. *To pound, bray, beate small, breake into little peeces.*
Broyer de l'eau en vn mortier. *To loose labour.*
Broyeur: m. *A brayer, pounder, beater of things vntill they be broken small.*
Bru: f. *A daughter in Law; a sonnes wife.*
Bruant: m. *A certaine little beautifull, and dul-sighted bird; enemy to horses, whose neighing he counterfeits; some call him, a yellow-hammer, or yowlring.*
Bruchet: m. *The craw-bone, or merrie thought, of a bird.*
Bruel: m. *The Brayle, or Pannell of a hauke.*
Brueil. *The same.*
Bruge-espine: f. *Buck-thorne, way-thorne, laxatiue ramme.*
Brugier. *To bellow, yell, roare, make a hideous noise.* (v.m.)
Brugne: f. *A fashion of Corselet, or Brigandine, vsed in old time.*
Bruiant. *as* Bruant.
Bruiement: m. *A rumbling, rustling, blustering; clattering, creaking, cracking, crashing.*
Bruiment. *The same.*
Bruine: f. *A hot mist that blasteth, and burneth, plants.*
Bruiné: m. eé: f. *Blasted, or burned with mist; also, hoarie, as a thing thats couered with a mistie ryne; and hence;*
Friteaux bruinez de succre-candy. *Glazed ouer with sugar candy.*

Bruine-

Bruinement: m. *A blasting, or burning with hot mists; also, a glazing ouer.*
Bruiner. *To blast, or burne with hot mists; also, to glaze, or set a hoarie glosse on.*
Bruineux: m. euse: f. *Full of hot blasting mists.*
Bruire. *To rumble; rustle; bluster; clatter, crash; to sound very lowd, and very harshly; to make a lowd humming noise; also, as* Brugier.
Comme l'on bruit. *As the bruit is, as the world reports, as the talke goes.*
Bruit: m. *A bruit; a great sound, or noise; a rumbling, clamor, cracking, creaking; also, a rumour, common tale, publike voice, fame, reputation, report, the talke of people, the speech abroad.*
L'un a le bruit, l'autre lave la laine: Prov. *Th'one hath the credit, th'other the trouble; or, th'one gets the credit, th'other takes the paines.*
Qui a bruit de se lever matin peut dormir iusques au soir: Prov. *He that is thought to rise betime, may lye abed till noone.*
Brule-langue. *See* Brusle-langue.
Brulure: f. *Blight, Brancorne; (an hearbe.)*
Brumal: m. ale: f. *winterie; winter-like; Northerne; done on, or like to, the shortest winter-day.*
Bruman: m. *A sonne in law; the husband of a daughter.*
Brumbay. *Browne bay, or darke bay.*
Brume. *The shortest day in the yeare; also, the middest of winter; also, winter.*
Brumestre. *The name of a kind of vine.*
Brun: m. brune: f. *Browne, duskie, swart; obscure, or darke of colour.*
Brunchement: m. *A tripping, or stumbling.*
Bruncher. *To trip, or stumble.*
Brune: f. *A browne wench, a louely nut-browne woman; also, the euening twylight, or edge of the euening; cock-shoot time.*
Bruneau. Clos Bruneau. *The bumme, arse, nockeandroe.*
Brunet: m. ette: f. *Brownish, somewhat browne,*
Fille brunette est de nature gaye, & nette: Prov. *A nut-browne girle is neat, and blith, by nature.*
Brunette: f. *A nut-browne girle; also, a kind of small bird, like an Owsell; also, fine blacke cloth; whence;*
Aussi bien sont amourettes soubs bureau que sous brunettes: Prov. *Loue playes his prankes as well in Cotes as Courts.*
Brun-fauve: com. *Deere-coloured; or of a darke lyon-tawnie.*
Bruni. le b. d'un Cerf. *The burnishing of a Stags head.*
Bruni: m. ie: f. *Burnished, furbished, pollished; also, obscured, bedusked, made browne.*
Brunie: f. *as* Brugne. (v.m.)
Brunir. *To burnish, furbish, or polish; also, to beduske, obscure, make browne.*
Brunisseure: f. *A burnishing, or burnishment; a furbished neatnesse, or polished brightnesse.*
Brunissoir: m. *A burnishing brush, or sticke; or, a burnisher, polisher, furbisher.*
Brunissure: f. *A burnishing, furbishing, polishing.*
Brusc: m. *Butchers-broome, Pettigree, Knee-holme, Knee-huluer, (a shrub.)*
Brusc: m. usque: f. *Looke* Brusque.

Bruslable: com. *Burnable; fit, or easie to bee burned.*
Bruslant: m. ante: f. *Burning, firing, inflaming.*
Bruslé: m. ée: f. *Burnt, fired, inflamed; singed, scaulded, scorched.*
Brusle-fer. *Iron-burning (an ordinarie nickename for Smiths.)*
Brusle-grain. *Corne-burning, graine-firing.*
Brusle-langue. *Tongue-scorching, tongue-inflaming.*
Bruslement: m. *A burning, firing, inflaming; scorching, singing, scaulding; a being on fire; a consuming with fire.*
Brusler. *To burne, fire, inflame; singe, scauld, scorch; to be on fire; to consume with fire.*
Brusler la chandelle par les deux bouts. *Disorderedly to wast, and consume his substance; to spend hee cares not how, nor what; also, (contrarily, but lesse properly) to wire-draw it, play the micher, make a thing goe too too farre.*
Ils bruslent leur bottes s'ils pensent ainsi. *They are in a foule error, forget themselues too much; or, they runne into a great inconuenience, by thinking so.*
Se brusler à la chandelle; &; Il se vient brusler à la chandelle; *Looke* Chandelle.
De trop prez se chauffe qui se brusle: Prov. *Hee warmes himselfe too neere that burnes himselfe.*
Tel se cuide chauffer qui se brusle: Prov. *Some thinking but to warme, doe burne, themselues.*
Brusleur: m. *A burner, fyrer, inflamer, scorcher, scalder.*
Habillé comme vn brusleur de Maisons. *Dressed like a tattered, and desperat, rogue.*
Bruslure: f. *A burning; or burnt place; also, as* Brulure.
Brusque: com. *Briske, liuely, quicke; also, rash, haire-braind, headie; also, wild, fierce, rude, barbarous, vnciuile, harsh.*
Mesure brusque. *A swift measure, or fast time in Musicke.*
Vin brusque. *wine of a quicke, sharpe, or smart tast.*
Brusquement. *Quickly, liuely; rashly, headily; fiercely, wildly; rudely, harshly.*
Brusquet: m. ette: f. *Somewhat briske, &c.*
Vin brusquet. *Very small, and sharpe wine.*
Brut. argent brut. *Foule, ragged, and rough siluer, as it comes out of the mine.*
Caverne brute. *A rude, craggie, shapelesse, denne.*
Diamond brut. *A Diamond that neuer was cut, or is newly taken out of the rocke; a rough Diamond.*
Brutal: m. ale: f. *Beastly; wild, rude, sauage, brutish filthie.*
Brutalement. *Brutishly, beastly, wildly, rudely, sauagely; filthily, foulely.*
Brutalité: f. *Brutishnesse, beastlinesse, rudenesse, luskishnesse; filthinesse.*
Brute-bonne. *A certaine great, and soone-ripe peare, of an ill-fauoured shape, but of an excellent tast.*
Brutesse. *as* Brutalité.
Bruthier: m. *A Buzzard, or Bauld-kite.*
Iamais tu ne feras d'vn bruthier vn esperuier: Prov. *A bald, and beastly kite will neuer proue good hawke.*
Brutif. *as* Brutal; *Also, rash, rechlesse, heedelesse.*

Qui parle brutif. *One that falters, maffles, fambles; or speakes so thicke, and fast, that few can vnderstand him.*
Brutivement. *Brutishly, rudely, sauagely; also, faulteringly, ill-fauouredly; also, rashly, heedlesly, rechlesly.*
Bruvage: m. *Drinke, beuerage.*
Bruy. *as* Brouy.
Bruyan: & Bruyant: m. *A yellow hammer; or, as* Bruânt.
Bruyant: m. ante: f. *Rumbling, rustling, blustering; also, roaring, skreaking, yelling.*
Faisan bruyant. *The great blacke Moore-cocke; or, as* Coq de bois.
Bruyement. *as* Bruiment.
Bruyere: f. *Heath, ling, hather, whereof brushes bee made (in which sence tis commonly Plurall;) also, a heath, or heathie ground; also, the great Ægyptian Tamariske, the fruit whereof resembles Galls.*
Bruyere sauvage. *The lesse, and fruitlesse Tamariske of Ægypt.*
Bruyereux: m. euse: f. *Full of heath, ling, or hather.*
Bruyné. *Looke* Bruiné.
Bryonie: f. *Brionie, white vine, wild nep, tetter berrie.*
Bryonie noire. *The wild vine, blacke Brionie, our Ladies seale.*
Bryonie sauvage. *The same.*
Bryonnier: m. ere: f. *Of, or belonging to, Brionie; and hence;*
Vigne bryonniere. *as* Bryonie.
Bu. *as* Beu.
Apres bu dodo: Prov. *After liquor lazinesse.*
Buanderie: f. *A Laundrie; a place to wash bucks in.*
Buandiere: f. *A laundresse, or buck-washer.*
Bubailer. *To gape, to yawne.*
Bubbe. *as* Bube.
Bube: f. *A push, wheale, blister, waterie bud, bunch, or bumpe.*
Bube sauvage. *A malignant scabbie push (in quality resembling a Carbuncle) which makes the skin red, and at length eats, and frets it extreamely.*
Buberiges. *Dogs leekes; or, the hearbe that beares the purple starrie Jacint.*
Bubelette: f. *A little red bunch, or pimple on the nose, &c.*
Bubette: f. *A little wheale, push, or blister.*
Bubon: m. *A great bunch, push, botch; a plague-sore; pock sore, winchester-goose.*
Buc: m. *A buske; plated bodie, or other quilted thing, worne to make, or keepe, the bodie straight; See* Busq, *or* Buste.
Bucail. *The course mill, or graine, called French wheat.*
Buccail. *as* Bucail.
Buccinateur: m. *A Trumpeter.*
Buccine: f. *A Cornet, or Trumpet for the warre; also, the horne of a cowheard, or swineheard; also, the shellfish called, Venus-shell.*
Sasse bonne farine sans trompe ne buccine: Prov. *Doe not publish, nor boast of, the good things you enioy; vnlesse you meane that greatnesse, enuie, or too much companie, shall depriue you of them.*
Buce: f. *A certaine wine vessell, containing about halfe a pipe; or, as* Busse.
Buche de bois. *A logge, backe stocke, or great billet; See* Busche.
Droict de buche. *Looke* Droict.
Bucheron: m. *A wood-cleauer, or wood-feller; one that makes fagots, bauens, or billets, in woods for hire.*
Bucheronner. *To cleaue, or cut downe, wood; to make fagots, &c, in woods.*
Buchettes: f. *Sprigs, twigs, little sticks.*
Buchier: m. *A stalder, wood-house, or wood-pile.*
Buchs. *The name of a Gascon countrey (not farre from* Bourdeaux, *and) full of Rosen-Pine-trees; whence;*
Chandelles de Buchs. *Candles of Rozen, vsed by the poorer inhabitants both of that countrey, & of* Armignac.
Bucine. *as* Buccine.
Buclandere: f. *A kind of Dutch boat, or barke.*
Bucolic: m. ique: f. *Heardman-like; of, or belonging to, a heardsman, or a heard of neat.*
Bucoliquement. *Heardman-like.*
Bucquer. *as* Buquer; *Also, to butte, or iarre.*
Buée: f. *Lye wherewith clothes are scowred; also, a buck of clothes.*
Buer. *To wash a bucke; to scower with lye.*
Buffe: f. *A buffet, blow, cuffe, boxe, or whirret on the eare, &c.*
Buffeline: m. ine: f. *Buffe-like; of, or belonging to, a Buffle.*
Buffer. *To puffe, or blow hard; also, to spurt, or spout water on.*
Buffet: m. *A court-cupboord, or high-standing cupboord; also, a cupboord of plate; (Hence) also, as much plate as will furnish a cupboord.*
Buffeté: m. ée: f. *Wrought rough, or shagge, like Buffe; also, buffeted, or well cuffed; also, deaded, as wine that hath taken wind, or hath beene mingled with water.*
Buffeter. *To make rough, or shagge, like buffe; also, to buffet, or cuffe; also, to marre a vessell of wine by often tasting it before it be broached; or, to fill it vp with water, after much wine hath beene stollen, or taken, out of it.*
Buffeteurs de vin. *Such Carmen, or boatmen, &c, as steale wine out of the vessels they haue in charge, and afterwards fill them vp with water.*
Buffetolt: m. *The fish called a Lumpe, or paddle, or sea-Owle.*
Buffle: m. *The buffe, buffle, bugle, or wild oxe; also, the skin, or necke, of a buffe, See* Beufle.
Bufflée: f. *as* Buffe. (v.m.)
Buffler. *To deceiue.*
Buffroy. *as* Baffroy; *or,* Beffroy.
Bufon: f. *A toad.*
Bugie. *The barke of a Barbarie tree; (a tearme vsed by Simplists.)*
Bugle: m. *Bugle, middle Consound, middle Comfrey; (an hearbe.)*
Qui a du bugle, & du Sanicle, fait au Chirurgien la nique: Prov. *So excellent are those hearbes in the closing, and curing of wounds.*
Buglement: m. *A lowing, or bellowing.*
Bugler. *To low, or bellow.*
Le ventre me bugle de faim. *My belly croakes, or cries out, through hunger.*
Bugleux: m. euse: f. *Often, or much lowing; full of bellowing.*
Buglosat. *Of Buglosse; made of buglosse.*
Buglosse: f. *(Garden) Buglosse.*
Buglosse sauvage. *Wilde Buglosse; whereof there*

there bee diuers kinds; as, Alkanet, or Orkanet; and stone Buglosse; and Snakes Buglosse, Vipers Buglosse, or wall Buglosse.
Bugnets. *as* Bignets.
Bugrande; ou, Bugrane: f. *Rest-harrow, Cammocke, pettie whinne, ground Furze.*
Bugrate. *as* Bugrande.
Bugrunde. *The same.*
Buie: f. *A water-pot, or pitcher.*
Buire: f. *An oyle glasse, violl, or cruze.*
Buirette: f. *A cruet, or little violl.*
Buisart: m. *A Buzzard, or Bald-kite.*
Buisine: f. *A little pipe; a conduit pipe; a water pipe.*
Buissart. *as* Buisart; *Also, the vessell called (otherwise)* Poinson; *Looke* Poinson.
Buissine: f. *as* Buisine.
Buisson: m. *A bush; thorne, brier; also, a groue, couert, thicket, bushie ground.*
Buisson à connils. *A (priuat) warren for conies, neere vnto, and for the prouision of, a mans house.*
Meure de buisson. *A blacke-berrie, or bramble berrie.*
Rose de buisson. *The dogges Rose, wild Rose, bryer Rose.*
La beste a là son buisson. *There the beast vseth to lodge, or laire.*
Tirer le serpent du buisson. *Looke* Serpent.
Amour de Seigneur est ombre de buisson: Prov. *The loue of a great man is either momentarie, or dangerous.*
En petit buisson trouve on grand lievre: Prov. *A little bodie (oft) harbours a great heart; and a small head much wit.*
Il n'y a si petit buisson qui ne porte ombre: Prov. *The least bush hath it shadow.*
Buissonnages: m. *Bushes; or, bushie grounds, bushie plots, bushie places.*
Buissonnailles: f. *Bushes; thornie groues.*
Buissonné: m. ée: f. *Bushie; thicke with, or full of, bushes; also, lodged in, retired into, or withdrawn among, bushes, or bushie places.*
Buissonner. *To dog, watch, or lye in wait for, (also, to lodge) among bushes.*
Buissonnet: m. *A little bush; thorne; groue, thicket.*
Buissonneux: m. euse: f. *Bushie, thornie, full of bushes.*
Buissonnier: m. ere: f. *Of, or belonging to bushes; frequenting, or haunting, bushes; liuing, or lurking, among bushes; and hence;*
Faire l' eschole buissonniere. *To play the truant, or seeke birdes nests when hee should bee at schoole.*
Buissonniere: f. *A bushie groue, plot, or ground; a thicket of bushes, bryers, thornes.*
Bulbe: m. *A Bulbus; a bulbed, or onion, root; (generally) a root that is round, and hath many pills, or diuisions, one ouer the other, as th'onion, leeke, saffron, &c. (and particularly) the scallion.*
Bulbe sauvage. *Dogs-bane, Corne-leeke, wild or medow Saffron.*
Bulbe vomitif. *The root of the muskie Grape-flower; some also call so, Narcissus, or the white Daffadill; others, the rush Daffadill (Though the bulbed roots of all Daffadils might as well bee called so; for all of them prouoke vomit.)*
Bulbeux: m. euse: f. *Bulbed; round headed like an onion, &c.*
Bule: f. *A blister; or bubble.*
Buler. *as* Bugler; *Also, the Pope to write, grant, or send a Bull; to execute, or excommunicate, by Bull.*
Buletin. *as* Bulletin.
Buliste: com. *Of, or belonging to a Bull; or, as* Bulliste.
Bullage: m. *The sealing of cloath; the marking thereof with a seale of lead.*
Bulle: f. *A Bull; a Writ, Commission, or letter sealed with lead, and sent from the Pope; any such Papall, and leaden, dispatch.*
Bullé: m. ée: f. *Sealed with lead, as a Bull; stamped, as the leaden seale of a Bull; also, that hath obtained the Popes Bull for some particular aduancement, or priuiledge to himselfe.*
Bulleteau: m. *A boulter, or boulting cloth.*
Bulleter. *as* Bluter. (v. m.)
Bulletin: m. *A bill, ticket, cocket; a billet in a Lotterie.*
Bulletins: m. *(Among the Gray Friers are) such as haue beene reformed by the Popes Bulls.*
Bullette: f. *as* Bulletin.
Bullettes. *Such bubbles, or bobs of glasse as women weare for Pendants at their eares.*
Bulliste: m. *A writer, or a maker of Bulls; or as* Buliste.
Bullonner. *To runne, boyle, or burst, out in great aboundance; (an old word.)*
Bullot. *A certaine great, yellow, and sower, apple.*
Buon: m. *The beake of an Ewer, or pot; the mouth of a cruet, violl, &c; also, a little oyle pot.*
Bupreste. *The venomous blacke flie called, a long-leg, or wag-leg.*
Buquer. *To knocke, or to rap, at a doore.*
Bur: m. *as* Bureau.
Bur: m. Bure: f. *Browne, russet, darke coloured.*
Burail: m. *as* Burat; *Silke-rash.*
Burail croisé. *Silke say.*
Burail simple de Flanders, & vni. *Silke Moccadoe.*
Burat: m. *Silke-rash; or any kind of stuffe thats halfe silke, and halfe worsted.*
Burat basin. *Silke Bombasie.*
Burat crespu. *Silke Curle; or Curle.*
Burate: f. *That which remaines in a churne after the best butter is taken out; which strained through a linnen cloath, and well salted, and wrought vntill it grow verie thicke, is kept in earthen pots for the vse of the meynie; also, as* Burat.
Burbarin. *An allusion to* Bustarin: ¶Rab.
Bure: f. *as* Bureau; *(in the first sence.)*
Bureau: m. *A thicke and course cloth, of a browne russet, or darke mingled, colour; also, the table thats within a court of Audit, or of Audience (belike, because tis vsually couered with a carpet of that cloth) also, the Court it selfe; also, the hearing, or decision, of causes in (such a) Court, whence;*
Ventre de bureau. *One that feeds grosely.*
Le prochain bureau. *The next day of hearing.*
Mettre sur le bureau. *To fall a talking of; or to bring vpon the stage.*
Mettre le proces sur le bureau. *To bring the suit vnto a hearing.*
Aussi bien sont amourettes sous bureau que sous brunettes: Prov. *Loue trickes are played (loues rites performed,) as well by poore as rich, folkes; (or) as well in poore as rich, clothes.*

Ventre de velours, robbe de bureau: Prov. *A veluet belly clads the backe in rug.*
Bureau: Adiect. *Browne russet; or, darke browne, as the cloth,* Bureau.
Burellé d'argent & d'azur; *(We blaze it thus) he bears so many clossets argent, and azur.*
Buret: m. *The purple-fish:* ¶Langued.
Burette: f. *A little cruet, violl, or bottle for oyle, or vinegar.*
Burette: m.ée: f. *(In stead of* Beluté*) boulted.*
Burez: m. *as* Buret.
Burgan: m. *A welke, winkle, periwinkle; or, a generall tearme for most of those snaile-like shell-fishes.*
Burgrave: m. *The Captaine, or Gouernour of a fortresse.*
Burguespine. *as* Bourguespine.
Burin: m. *A grauing sticke, or yron.*
Buriné: m.ée: f. *Carued, ingrauen, intailed; also, pierced.*
Buriner. *To carue, graue, intayle; also, to pierce.*
Burineur: m. *A caruer, grauer, intailer.*
Buriot: m. *A yong duckling newly crept out of the shel:* ¶Norm.
Burler. *as* Hurler; *Also, to ieast with; or flout at:* ¶Rab.
Burlesque: com. *Jeasting, or in ieast, not serious; also, mocking, flouting.*
Burne: f. *The solitarie place, or corner, wherein an Owle sits in the day time.*
Burnie. main-burnie. *Ward, gard, custodie.* (v.m.)
Buron: m. *A poore cottage.*
Burre. *as* Beurre. *Butter.*
Burré. *Buttered.*
Burrer. *To butter.*
Burrier: m. *A seller of butter; also, a great eater of butter; a butter-box.*
Burriere: f. *A butter-wife; a wench that sels, or eats, much butter.*
Bursauli: m. *Cane-withie, with the yellowish barke.*
Busard: m. *A Buzzard.*
Busc: m. *A buske; or, as* Buc; *Seeke also for* Busq; *and,* Buste.
Buschailles: f. *Small twigs, or sprigs.*
Busche: f. *A log, a backe stocke; a great billet.*
Droict de busche. *Looke* Droict.
C'estoit vne busche en son oeil. *That was a beame in his eye, a blocke in his way; a great impeachment to his plots; a hinderance to his proceedings.*
Tortue busche faict droit feu: Prov. *A crooked log makes a straight fire.*
Tout bois vaut busches: Brov. *Any wood is as good as a log.*
Verde busche faict chaud feu: Prov. *A greene log makes a hot fire.*
Buscheron. *as* Bucheron.
Buscheter. *To gather stickes for the fire.*
Buschettes: f. *Small stickes, or sprigs.*
Buschilles: f. *Little sticks, twigs, or sprigs.*
Buschoier. *To gather stickes; get wood.*
Buse: f. *A hole; also, a Buzzard.*
Busine: f. *The pipe of a Cesterne, or conduit; (See* Buisine;*) also, a bagpipe; or as* Buzine.
Busq. *as* Buc.
Au vieux busq. *After the old cut.*
Busque: f. *Fortune, chance, lucke; or, as th'Italian* Busca; *a shifting, filching, prowling, catching by hooke or crooke; also, a buske; or buste.*
Busquer. *To shift, filtch; prowle, catch by hooke or crook.*
Busquer fortune. *To go seeke his fortune.*
Bussart: m. *The vessell called, otherwise,* Poinson; *Looke* Poinson.
Busse de raisins. *A drie-fat, or great (and hogs-head-like) vessell wherein Raisins bee put, or transported.*
Bust. *as* Busc; *or, as* Buste *(in the first sence.)*
Bustarin: *A great lubber, thicke druggell; cowardly luske, dastardly slaberdegullion.*
Buste: m. *as* Buc; *Or, a bust; the long, small, (or sharp-pointed) and hard-quilted belly of a doublet; also, the whole bulke, or bodie of a man from his face to his middle; also, a tombe, or sepulchre.*
Bustofer: m. vngros b. *A luske, loggerhead, lowt, slowch.*
Bustuaire: com. *Burnt, as a dead bodie; or, crauing, expecting, affecting, the sacrifice of mens bodies:* ¶Rab.
But: m. *A but, or marke; (and particularly, the pricke thats in the middest of the* Carreau *in a bowling alley) also, a scope, reach; purpose, end.*
But à but. *Of equall estate, on like tearmes, at euen hands, without any oddes at all.*
Mais là ne faut faire but, & borne. *But there wee must not pause; thats no place to stop at, or settle in.*
Buté: m.ée: f. *Touched at, or by, th'end of.*
I'ay buté à vne pierre. *I haue knockt, bit, struck my foot against a stone.*
Buter. *To touch at th'one end; to abut, or ioyne vnto, by th'end; also, to put, or thrust, away.*
Buteux. *Of, or belonging to, a but; full of buts.*
Butin: m. *A bootie, prey; or spoile, taken.*
Butinant. *Bootehaling, preying, making spoyle of.*
Butinement: m. *A boote-haling, preying on, making spoyle of.*
Butiner. *To prey, get bootie, make spoyle of, to bootehale it, to liue, or gaine by pillage.*
Butineur. *A bootehaler, preyer, pillager; one that liues of the spoile.*
Butineux. *Full of prey, spoyle, bootie; , or as* Butinant.
Butoesne: f. *Hearbe Bettonie.*
Butor: m. *A Bittor.*
Butte: f. *A but, or marke, to shoot at; also, a place appointed in open market for the sale of goods in execution.*
Mettre haut le blanc à la butte. *To demaund of one the resolution of a matter which is aboue his capacitie; also, to set a high price on a thing that would be sold.*
Buttet: m. *as* Hotte; *Sauing that it is made of a courser Ozier, called* du Plomb, *or* Plion; *and th'*Hotte *of a finer Wicker close wrought.*
Buvable: com. *Drinkable; fit to be drunke of.*
Buvage: m. *as* Bruvage.
Buveau: m. *A kind of Squire, or Squire-like Instrument, hauing mooueable, and compasse, branches; or, th'one branch compasse, and th'other straight; some call it a Beuell.*
Buvereau: m. *A bibber, supper, or sipper; one that drinks little, and often.*
Buverie: f. *A drinking; bibbing, sipping, bowsing.*
Buveter. *To bib, sip, sup; drinke but a little and often; or, but a little at once; or, by little and little.*
Buvetier: m. *A certaine Officer, that gathers money for the Iudges Collations.*
Buvette: f. *Small houshold wine.*

Buvettes.

Buvettes. *Sippings, tiplings; and particularly the Iudges drinkings, or Collations.*
Buvetter. *as* Buveter.
Buvotter. *The same.*
Buxolle: m. *The diall, or compasse, whereby a ship is guided.*
Buydon: m. *Such a cage, coupe, or open basket (of wicker) as Poulters keepe, and feed their chickens, or other fowle in.*
Buye. *as* Buie. *A water pot, or pitcher.*
Buyele: m. *as* Buxolle.
Buyer. *A Box-tree, or shrub.*
Buyrette: f. *as* Burette.
Buys: m. *Box;* *Looke* Bouïs.
Buysé: m. ée: m. *Bored, full of holes; or, that hath holes made into it.*
Buyser. *To bore, pierce, make holes into, or make full of holes.*
Buysine. *as* Buisine.
Buytronne: f. *A furnace to melt, and fine, siluer in.*
Buyzart. *Looke* Buisart.
Buzart. *A Buzzard, or Bald-kite.*
Buze. *A Buzzard, or Bald-kite; also, as* Buse.
Buzine: f. *A bagpipe; or, a clownes trumpet; a clownish instrument, made of pitched barke, and sounding like a trumpet:* ¶Gasc. *also, as* Busine.
Byble: f. *as* Bible.
Byrrasque: f. *A turbulent, and high-going sea, or horrible tempest at sea; as* Birrasque.
Byrantin. *A peece of coyne worth a double ducket, or thereabouts; Looke* Besant; & Bisantin.
Byze. *The sea-fish, Bonito.*

C

CA. *Is sometimes an Aduerbe of Place, and signifies, hither, to this place, this way; sometimes an Interiection of calling, or commaunding; where one bids another come vnto him, (and then signifies, approach, draw neere, come hither;) or to giue him somewhat; (then signifying, lets see there, giue me that, reach hither;) or to follow him (and then signifies, follow hoe, come after, &c.) This* Ca *is pronounced as* Sa.
ça en arriere. *Formerly, in former times, heretofore.*
ça & là. *Diffusedly, scatteringly, now here now there, hither and thither; in scattered troups, loose companies.*
Caable. *as* Cable. *A wind-fall.*
Cabab: m. *The chucking, churring, or iouking of a Partridge.*
Cababezancé. *Loaden with bags, and wallets; also, commented on; (a word coyned by* Rab.)
Cabaçet: m. *as* Cabasset.
Cabal: m. *The money, or marchandise which one takes of another, to yeeld him the halfe, or third, or fourth, part of the gaine thats made thereof.*
Cabalanizer. *To drinke like a horse; to swill, gull, quaffe, tipple extreamely.*
Cabale: f. *The Jewes Caball; or, a hidden science of diuine mysteries, which the Rabbies affirme, was reuealed, and deliuered, together with the Law, vnto Moses, and from him deriued, by successiue relation, vnto posteritie; (yet is it, in truth, no better than a vaine rabble of their owne traditions.)*
Tenu secret comme Cabale. *Concealed as a speciall mysterie.*
Cabalin: m. ine: f. *Of, or belonging to, a horse.*
Ongle cabaline. *Seeke* Ongle.
Cabaliste: m. *A Cabalist; a professor, or vnderstander, of the Iewes traditions.*
Cabalistique: com. *Cabalisticall; of, or belonging to, the Iewish Caball, or Iewish traditions.*
Caban: m. *A gabardine, or cloake of felt.*
Cabane: f. *A cote, or cottage; also, a shed, or cabin made of boughes.*
Cabaret: m. *An Ale-house; a tipling, and victualling house, tent, or booth; also, the hearbe Haslewort, Folefoot, Cabaret, Asarabacca.*
Suppost de cabaret. *An Ale-knight, Ale-house-haunter, lick-spigot, common tipler, ordinarie drunkard.*
Cabaretier: m. *A sutler, common victualler, Ale-house-keeper; also, as* suppost de Cabaret.
Cabaretter. *To frequent Ale-houses.*
Cabas: m. *A fraile (for raisins, or figs.)*
Vn vieil cabas. *An old fraile wherein figs, &c, haue beene; also, an old, or decayed woman, that hath been a good fellow in her dayes.*
Cabassé: m. ée: f. *Frayled; put, or packed vp in a frayle; heaped, or hoorded vp together, as in a frayle.*
Cabasseau. *as* Cubaseau.
Cabasser. *To fill a fraile with raisins &c; to put, or pack vp, in a frayle; also, to heape, or hoord vp together, as raisins, &c, in a fraile.*
Cabasset: m. *A sleight helmet, or casket.*
Cabasset de papier. *A long hood, or Myter, of paper.*
Cabasson: m. *A certaine little, toothlesse, and great headed, fish.*
Cabat. *as* Cabas.
Cabau. *as* Cabal.
Cabeillau: m. *Fresh cod.*
Cabeçon. *as* Caveçon.
Cabestan: m. *The Capstane of a ship.*
Cabilaud: m. *The Cheuin; (tearmed so by French Purueyors.)*
Cabillau: m. *Fresh cod.*
Cabinet: m. *A cabinet, or casket, for iewels, &c; also, a closet, little chamber, or wardrobe, wherin one keeps his best, or most esteemed, substance; also, an arbor in a garden.*
Cabinet d'Allemagne. *A kind of standish; or a small cabinet seruing for, or hauing in it, a standish.*
Le cabinet du Roy. *The priuie chamber.*
Cabirotade. *as* Capirotade.
Cabirots: m. *The sperme, or spawne, of Sturgeons, spread vpon bread, and eaten with vinegar, oyle, and pepper.*
Cable: m. *A cable, or great rope.*
Cable: f. *A wind-fall; a tree ouerthrowne by wind, or tempestuous weather.*
Cabochard: m. arde: f. *Headie, wilfull, obstinate; giddie, fantasticall, haire-braind.*
Caboche: f. *The Head:* ¶Pic.
Caboche bien tymbrée. *A well-garnished head-peece, well-tackled braine-panne, a stayed, or discreet pate.*
Cabochenu. *as* Cabochard.
Caboches. *A rebellious crue of Parisians in Charles the sixts time; called so of their captaine, whose name was* Simonet Caboche.
Cabocheux. *as* Cabochard; *Or, whose head is full of toyes; whose courses are wholly guided by the fond deuises of his owne braine.*
Cabochon de pierre precieuse. *The beazil, collet, head, or*

or highest part of a ring, or iewell, wherein the stone is set; also, the bosse, or rising of the stone it selfe; also, a fooles hood.
Cabot: m. *The Gull-fish, Bull-head, Millers-thumbe.*
Cabote: f. *as* Cabot; *Or, (more properly) a Gurnard.*
Cabre: f. *A Goat.*
A la cabre morte. *Vpon his necke.*
Cabrer. *To reare, or stand vpright on the hinder feet; to rise high before; as a Goat, or Kid that brouzes on a tree.*
Cabrer sur le devoir. *To bee restie, or backward in duetie (from a iade that reares vp when he should goe forward.)*
Cabril: m. *A yong Kid.*
Cabriole. *as* Capriole.
Cabriolé: m. ée: f. *Capered.*
Cabrioter. *To caper, to cut a caper.*
Cabrol: m. *An issue made for a fistula.*
Cabrole: f. *A certaine blew-backed, white-bellied, and small-mouthed fish.*
Cabucé: m. ée: f. *Headed, like a cabbidge.*
Caburlaut: m. *A Gull, Bull-head, Millers-thombe:* ¶Tholosain.
Cabus: m. uce; ou, usse: f. *Headed, round headed; great headed; and, hence,*
Choux cabus. *A Cabbidge.*
Laictuës cabuces, ou cabusses. *Leaued, or headed Lettuce.*
Cabusser. *To cabbidge; to grow to a head; or, grow round and close together, as a Cabbidge.*
Cacaber. *To chucke, or iouke, as a Partridge; to counterfeit the voice of a Partridge.*
Cacassement de poule. *The cackling of a hen.*
Cacasangue: f. *The bloudie flix.*
Cache: f. *as* Chasse: ¶Pic. *Also, a hiding hole, hidden corner; or nooke out of the way.*
Caché: m. ée: f. *Hidden, concealed, kept secret; in couert, in corners; lurking in some odde nooke or other; conueied away.*
Il est mal caché à qui le cul paroist: Prov. *Hee is ill hid whose taile appeares; he worse dissembles whose worst parts appeare.*
Mal est caché à qui l'on voit le dos: Prov. *Hee ill conceales himselfe that shewes his backe; or as the former.*
Cachebugade: f. *Æthiopian Hartwort, Seseli of Æ*thiopia; *(A shrub thats alwayes greene.)*
Cache-col. *A veluet attire, or ornament for the necke; much worne by the women of* France, *in ancient time when their gownes were cut low before.*
Cachectique: com. *In a consumption; that pineth away, nothing he eateth doing him good.*
Cachelaid: m. *A maske, or muffler.*
Cachelet. *as* Cachelaid.
Cachemaille: f. *A money box.*
Cachement: m. *A hiding, concealing, or keeping close.*
Cachément. *Closely, priuily, couertly, vnder-hand.*
Cachemi-tula. *A play wherein one must keepe a thing priuately deliuered him, and another find out the keeper among many others; which doing he is rewarded, otherwise punished.*
Cache-museau. *A kind of flawne; or, as* Cassemuseau; *also, a muffler, or maske, for the face.*
Cache-nez. *A maske, or muffler.*
Cacher. *To hide, conceale, keepe secret; conuey away; to couer, to suppresse; (also, as* Chasser: ¶Pic.)
Cacher en la mer. *To send into the sea; a ship to go so low before, that at euerie push forward she is like to thrust her nose into the sea.*
Il iette la pierre, & cache le bras. *He does mischiefe, but will not be seene, nor seeme, to haue any hand in it.*
Du temps qu'on se cachoit pour prester de l'argent. *In time of honest simplicitie, and innocent confidence; when men were more carefull to conceale others necessities, than to secure their owne debts.*
On ne cache pas aiguilles en sac: Pro. *Needles are not hidden, or laid vp in sacks.*
Cachereau. *as* Chartulaire.
Cachet: m. *A seale, or signet.*
Cachet du Roy. *The priuie signet; wherein is not, as in ours, any seale vsed, but onely the kings name stamped in characters of siluer, and afterwards couered with inke by one of the Secretaries; (this stampe is most commonly kept by the Constable; sometimes by a fauorite.)*
Cacheté: m. ée: f. *Sealed.*
Cacheter. *To seale, as a letter.*
Cachette: f. *A lurking hole, or corner; a close nooke, secret place, hiding hole; also, a denne, or couert.*
En cachette. *Priuily, closely, secretly, couertly, hiddenly, vnder-hand, in hugger mugger.*
Cacheur: m. *A hider, concealer; suppresser.*
Cachexie: f. *An euill disposition of the bodie (gotten by long sicknesse, ill diet, or bad physicke;) which makes the patient no whit the better for any thing he eates.*
Cachile. *Sea-rocket.*
Cachoire. *as* Chassoire: ¶Pic.
Cachot. *as* Caquot; *Also, a couert for Deere, or denne for a rauenous wild beast.*
Cachotte: f. *as* Cachette; *Or, the hole in a prison; sometimes also, a graue; and hence;*
Il a esté mis aujourd'huy en sa cachotte. *Hee was buried to day.*
Cachotté: m. ée: f. *Layed in the hole, of a prison.*
Cachry: m. *Rosemarie seed* (Mot Barbare.)
Cacidoine. *The pretious stone called, a Calcedonie.*
Cacochymie: f. *Euill disgestion; or, ill iuyce in the bodie.*
Cacoëthe: m. *A kind of most venomous, and incurable bile, or sore; or, a bile, or sore thats ill to bee cured.*
Cacolique. *(An ironicall allusion to* Catholique; *otherwise of little or no sence.)*
Cacologie: f. *Euill speech; railing, reproach, reuiling, detraction.*
Cacophonie: f. *An ill, harsh, or vnpleasing sound (in words;) a vitious vtterance, or pronounciation.*
Cacque. *as* Caque; *A cag.*
Cacqueter. *as* Caqueter.
Cacquetoire. *See* Caquetoire.
Cad d'eau: m. *A great fall, or showre of raine.*
Cadaliec. *as* Chaslit; *A bedstead:* ¶Langued.
Cadarce pour faire capiton. *The tow, or coursest part of silke, whereof sleaue is made.*
Cadastre. *An auncient rent-roll, Register, or Suruey, specifying what lands be* Roturiers, *and thereby subiect vnto the (kings)* Taille.
Cadavre: m. *A carkasse, or dead bodie.*
Cadavreux: m. euse: f. *Carkasse-like; leane, skraggie, fleshlesse; also, putrified, stinking, rotten.*
Cade: f. *The crimzon, or prickly Cedar:* ¶Langued.
Cadeau: m. *A great capitall, or text, letter; also, as;*
Cadel: m. *A castling, a starueling; one that hath need much of cockering, and pampering.*

Cadelé: m. ée: f. *Cockered, pampered, fedled, cherished; much made of.*
Lettres cadelées. *Great, capitall, or text letters.*
Cadeler. *To cocker, pamper, fedle, cherish, make much of; also, to write a Text hand; or, make a capitall letter, or great letters.*
Cadenat: m. *A Padlocke.*
Cadence: f. *A cadence; a iust falling, round going, of words; a proportionable time, or euen measure, in any action, or sound.*
'A chacune cadence. *At euery turne, euer and anon.*
Cadene: f. *An yron chayne.*
Cadett m. *A younger brother (among Gentlemen.)* ¶Poict.
Cadmie: f. *Cadmia; is either minerall, or artificiall; the first, of two kinds; the one, a stone, participates of no mettall (though it be needfull to the parting of some mettals) the other hath some affinitie with copper, or with siluer. The artificiall one comes of the smoake, or sparkles, that arise from furnaces wherein copper is melted, and made; and hereof there bee diuers kinds.*
Cadran. *as* Quadran.
Caducité: f. *Frailtie, weakenesse, aged feeblenesse.*
Caduque: com. *Fraile, caduke, feeble, ruinous, readie to fall, vnable to support it selfe.*
Eaux caduques. *Water that runs ouer a Poole; or, out of the wast pipes, or spouts of Conduit heads.*
Cæsarien: m. enne: f. *Looke* Cesarien.
Cafard: m. *An hypocrite; a counterfeiter of, or dissembler in, religion, deuotion, pietie; one that seemes, but is not, holy; especially, a Preacher, or preaching Frier; who in his teaching respects his owne, or his Orders, profit, more then his auditors; also, as* Caffard.
Cafard: m. arde: f. *Hypocriticall, dissembling, seeming holy, pious outwardly, deuout onely in shew.*
Cafarde. à la cafarde. *Hypocritically.*
Cafarder. *To pretend deuotion, play the hypocrite, seeme godly, counterfeit holinesse; looke demurely, precisely, religiously, and speake piously, but meane impiously; to preach often, but more to profit himselfe, or his Order, then his auditors.*
Cafardie: f. *Hypocrisie, outward holinesse, pretence of zeale, shew of conscience, counterfeiting of deuotion; often preaching for priuat respects.*
Cafardise: f. *The same.*
Cafas. *A kind of course Taffata.*
Cafetin. succre cafetin. *Refined Sugar.*
Cafezate. *A certaine little, reddish, most venomous, and malignant serpent, that lurkes (most commonly) among the leaues of trees, and thence flies at any man, or beast, that passes vnder them.*
Caffard. *A moath, or beetle that flyes by night; also, as* Cafard.
Caffardise. *as* Cafardie. *Hypocrisie.*
Cagade: f. *A vaine, and effectlesse flourish; a scuruie, shitten, idle boast, or boasting.*
Cagarel, ou Cagaret. *A Cackerell (fish.) Looke* Iuscle.
Cagarole de mer. *A Periwincle.* ¶Langued.
Cagasangue. *as* Cacasangue.
Cage: f. *A Cage.*
Cage d'osier. *A wicker cage; also, a Lattice window of wicker.*
Mieux vault estre oiseau de bois que de cage: Pro. *(The difference betweene libertie, and thraldome.)*
Cageois: m. *A countrey clowne, hynd, boore; a cottager, or one that dwels in a rusticall cote.*
Cageoler. *To prattle, or iangle, like a Iay (in a cage;) to bable, or prate much, to little purpose.*
Cageoleur: m. *A great, and idle, pratler; one that (like a Iay in a cage) iangles much to no purpose.*
Cagerotte: f. *A Chesforde, or Cheesfatt (of wicker.)*
Cagnard, Cagnardier, &c. *See* Caignard, &c.
Cagnasse: f. *A great bitch.*
Cagne: f. *A bitch.*
Cagnesque, Parler cagn. *To speake doggerie.*
Cagnole: f. *The rauenous, and ougly dogfish, called (of the fashion of her head) the Mallet-fish.*
Cagnot. *A little dog; and particularly, a kind of little dog-fish, that hates men extreamely.* ¶Lang.
Cagnot blau. *Another, of a light blew colour; otherwise much resembling the former; the blew dog-fish.*
Cagot: m. *An hypocrite, or dissembler; also, a white leaper.*
Cagoterie. *Hypocrisie; also, white leprosie.*
Cagouille: f. *A deaw-snayle.*
Cagoulle: f. *A Monks hood, or Cowle.* ¶Norm.
Caguemaille: m. *A filthie snudge, greedie wretch, miserable scrape-good, couetous hylding.*
Caguerasse: m. *A base micher, scuruie hagler, lowsie dodger; or, a cruell extortioner, greedie catch-good, rauenous oppressor.*
Cahin cahau. *as* Qu-'a-hu qu-'a-ha.
Cahier. *as* Cayer. ¶Rab.
Cahot: m. *The iumpe, hop, or iog of a coach, &c, in a rugged, or vneuen, way.*
Cahoter. *To iumpe, iog, or hop, as a coach in vneuen way.*
Cahuaille. *A companie of Owles; an Owlish companie.* ¶Rab.
Cahuët. *as* Cahot; *also, the backe point, or flap, of a friers Cowle.*
Cahuette: f. *A little cottage; also, as* Luette.
Cahuot. *as* Cahot.
Cahute: f. *A little house, cote, or cottage.*
Cahutelle: f. *The same; (or a diminutiue thereof.)*
Caiche: m. *As the Italian,* Catzo; membre viril. ¶Rab.
Caignard: m. *A lazie vagabond, lowsie hedgecreeper, slothfull scowndrell; tottered, or beggarly, rogue.*
Caignarder. *To play the idle rogue; or (like a nastie and slothfull beggar) lye, and lowse himselfe, vnder a hedge, or in the Sunne.*
Caignardier: m. *as* Caignard.
Caignardiere: f. *A hedge-whore, lazie queane, lowsie trull, filthie curtall, Doxie, Morte.*
Caignart: m. *as* Caignard; *also, a nastie, and filthie place, or corner, wherein beggars lye in the Sunne, or lowse themselues; the haunt of idle vagabonds; and hence, are some bridges about* Paris *(vnder which such rogues are wont to lurke) so called.*
Caigne: f. *A bitch.*
Caigne *(an Interiection of wonder) tush! Gods me! Gogs my wounds! is it possible?*
Caignon: m. *The chyne, or hinder part of the necke; (an old word.)*
Caignot. *as* Cagnot; *also, a little dog, a fysting curre.*
Cailhete: m. *A cockney.*
Caillat. *as* Caillé.
Caillé: m. *Curds; curded milke, or, the curds of milke.*
Caille: f. *A Quayle; also, a round bead &c; as in* Cailles *(next after* Cailler.)
Caille coiffée. *A woman.*
Herbe aux cailles. *Plantaine, Weybred.*
Mere des cailles. *A Rayle.*

Roy des cailles. *The same.*
Chaud comme vne caille. *(Of a very hot complexion) as hot as a Quayle.*
Caillé: m. ée: f. *Curded, curdled; coagulated, congealed, thickened.*
Enfant caillé. *A fat pursie fellow.*
Caillebotes: f. *Curds; the curds of milke.*
Cailleboteux: m. euse: f. *Full of curds.*
Lieux caillebotеux. *Craggie, stonie, rockie, or flintie places; places made vneuen, or vneasie, by manie stones.*
Caillement: m. *A curding, curdling, coagulating, congealing, thickening.*
Cailler. *To curd, or curdle; to coagulate; congeale as, turne into, curds.*
Cailles. *Round beads, wherewith Frenchmen play at* Trou-madame; *and whereof the* Trou-madame *is tearmed* Passe-caille.
Cailleteau: m. *A chackestone, or little flint stone.*
Caillette: m. *A foole, ninnie, noddie, naturall.*
Caillette: f. *A Rammes cod; also, the outward skin of the cods; also, a small bead; as in* Cailles; *or the diminutiue of* Caille.
Cailloeux. *as* Cailloteux.
Caillon: m. *A dot, clutter, clot, or congealed lumpe of flegme, bloud, &c.*
Caillorosat: m. *A Lording apple; also, a certain greene, and great peare of a pleasant tast.*
Caillotè: m. ée: f. *Curded, curdled; clotted, congealed, thickened, turned.*
Cailloter. *To curd, or curdle; to congeale, thicken, or turne; as milke, &c.*
Cailloteux: m. euse: f. *Flintie; full of hard, and sharpe little stones.*
Caillou: m. *A flint stone.*
Caillouët. *The name of a very sweet peare.*
Caillouëux: m. euse: f. *Flintie; full of small, hard, and sharpe stones.*
Caimand: m. *A beggar; one that goes a begging, or craues almes, from dore to dore.*
Caimander. *To beg; to go a begging, to beg from dore to dore.*
Caimanderie: f. *Extreame pouertie, beggarlinesse, beggarie, the state of a beggar; the art, action, or vse, of begging.*
Caimandise. *as* Caimanderie.
Caioler. *as* Cageoler.
Cajollerie: f. *A iangling, prating, babling, chattering.*
Caïon. *A young, or little hog.* ¶Lyonnois.
Caire: f. *The visage, countenance, looke, aspect, representation of the face.*
Cairin: m. *A Turkie Carpet; such a one as is brought from* Caire *in* Ægypt.
Caisne: f. *A bitch.*
Caisne. *as* Caigne.
Caissans. *The side-teeth, called, the Grinders.* ¶Languеd.
Caisse. *as* Casse; *also, a drumme; also, the pit, or trench, wherein stones gathered of corne-lands are buried; See* Quaisse.
Caissier: m. *A chest-maker; also, a chest-keeper, or treasurer; whence;*
Aujourd'huy caissier demain cassé: Prov. *To day in cash, to morrow cashiered.*
Cal: m. *A thicke, and vnsensible skin, or brawnie hardnesse of skin, comming on the much-vsed parts of the hands, or feet.*
Le cal de la conscience. *Hardnesse of heart, an obdurate spirit, a seared conscience.*
Calabace: f. *as* Calebasse.
Calage: m. *The caulking of a ship; also, Ockam, or the towe, wherewith it is caulked.*
Calamar: m. *A Pennar; also, the Calamarie, or sleeuefish.*
Calame: m. *A cane, reed; wheaten, or oaten straw; pipe, flute; &c. as the Latine* Calamus.
Calame aromat. *The sweet Arabian reed, or cane, tearmed,* Calamus odoratus, *or the Aromaticall reed.*
Calament: m. *The hearbe Calamint.*
Calament aquatic. *Water Calamint; (hath a larger stalke, greater branches, and longer leaues, but lesse vertue, then the other kinds.)*
Calament d'eau; ou, de marais. *The same.*
Calament de montagne. *Mountaine Calamint, bush Calamint, hoarie Calamint.*
Calament sauvage. *Wild Calamint, corne Calamint, wild Penniryall, wild Pollie.*
Calamenthe: f. *as* Calament.
Calaminaire. pierre Calaminaire. *A yellowish minerall, or stone, whereby copper is turned into brasse; or, as* Calamine.
Calamine: f. *A certaine yellow minerall substance, which fire consumes, but melts not; mixed with copper, it changes it into a fine brasse, that lookes like gold; also, the heauier foyle of brasse, or copper; which comes of the sparkles, and smoake that arise from the furnace, and cleaue to the roofe, and vpper sides, of the house, wherein it is melted; also, a kind of apple.*
Calamistrer. *To frizle, curle, or crispe the haire.*
Calamite: m. *The Adamant, Loadstone, or Magnesstone; also, a kind of Cadmia, or the stuffe that cleaues vnto the yron rods wherewith melting copper is stirred.*
Calamité: f. *Calamitie, miserie, wretchednesse, great trouble, much woe; misfortune, aduersitie; mischiefe, extreame hurt, or damage.*
Calamite. *Of, or belonging to, reeds; or kept in reeds; whence;*
Storax calamite. *The best kind of Storax, brought from* Aleppo, *and kept in canes, or in the leaues of reeds.*
Calamiteusement. *Wretchedly, miserably, mischieuously, to his great trouble, much woe, extreame hurt.*
Calamiteux: m. *A wretch, poore snake, miserable person, most vnfortunate fellow.*
Calamiteux: m. euse: f. *Wretched, miserable, wofull; mischieuous; most vnfortunate, fraught with troubles, full of calamitie.*
Calande. *A Weeuell, or Mite, among corne.*
Calandre. *as* Calendre.
Calandré: m. ée: f. *as* Calendré.
Calangement: m. *An accusing, an appeaching; a challenging for, a charging with, faults.*
Calanger. *as* Chalanger, *or* Calenger.
Calar. *as* Caler; *also, to be silent, leaue talking, desist from babling.* ¶Gascon.
Calate: f. *A gentle, or easie descent in ground; also, a peece, or plot of ground so descending, so declining.*
Calathe: m. *A basket, pannier, or hamper of oziers; also, a vessell to bring milke, or cheese to market in; also, a cup for sacrifice.*
Calcante: m. *Vitrioll.*
Calcination: f. *A calcination, or calcinating; a reducing of mettals vnto pouder by the fire; a purifying of mettals, or minerals, by fire.*

Calcinatoire: com. *Calcinatorie, calcinating; or, which calcinateth.*
Calciné: m. ée: f. *Calcinated, burnt vnto dust, reduced by fire, vnto pouder.*
Calcinement: m. *as* Calcination.
Calciner. *To calcinate; burne to dust, reduce vnto pouder, by fire, any mettall, or minerall.*
Calcioler. *To beat, or stand much on a matter; to repeat, or vrge a thing often, thereby to make it the better vnderstood, or remembred.*
Calcite. *as* Chalcite.
Calcitrer. *To kicke, spurne, wince, fling, let flye, yerke out behind, or with the heeles; also, to be stubborne, disobedient, obstinate, or, obstinate in disobedience.*
Calçons: m. *Short, and close linnen breeches, drawers, vnder-slops.*
Calcul: m. *A calculation, computation, reckoning; an accompt, or casting of accompts; also, the Stone in the bladder, or (more properly) in the reines.*
Calculateur: m. *A reckoner, calculator, caster of accompts.*
Calculatoire: com. *Calculatorie, calculating.*
Calculement: m. *A calculating, reckoning, accompting.*
Calculer. *To calculate, reckon, accompt; number, make a computation.*
Calderon. *A kind of long, and round Whall.*
Cale: f. *A Bay, or Creeke of the sea, entring, or eating, into the land; also, a kind of little cap; also, a little peece of wood put vnder a log, or peece of timber, thereby to make it lye the better.*
Calebasse: f. *A bottle made of an emptied gourd; or, as* Callabasse.
Calemar. *as* Calamar.
Le calemar d'un retraict. *The funnell of a priuie.*
Calendes: f. *Calends; the first day of euery moneth.*
Calendre: f. *The corne-deuouring Mite, or Weeuill; also, the Calander, or greatest kind of Larke; in* Paris *the great Thrush is (erroniously) called so.*
Calendré: m. ée: f. *Gnawne, or deuoured, as corne by Weeuils; also, sleeked, or smoothed ouer, as linnen cloth, &c.*
Calendrer. *To sleeke, smooth, plane, or polish (linnen cloth, &c.)*
Calendreure: f. *A sleeking, smoothing; planing, polishing.*
Calendrier: m. *An Almanacke, or Calender.*
Calendrine. pierre calendrine. *A Sleeke-stone.*
Calenge. *A claime; a challenging of, or making title vnto; also, a challenge; also, a complaint, accusation, or vrging of an offence against; also, an arrest, or apprehension of a man by a Sergeant; also, a seisure of, or complaint against, beasts that are found Damage fesant.*
Calengé: m. ée: f. *Claymed; challenged; accused, appeached, complained of, charged with an offence, or trespasse; also, arrested, apprehended; seised.*
Calenger. *To clayme, challenge, demaund, make title vnto; also, to challenge; accuse, appeach, complaine, charge with, call in question for, an offence, crime, or trespasse; also, to arrest, apprehend; seise, attach.*
Calengié. *as* Calengé. ¶Wallon.
Calepinages: m. *Dictionaries.*
Calepiner. *To interprete, or translate, exactly, or word by word.*
Calepinerie: f. *A true, iust, and precise interpretation, or translation of euery single word.*
Caler. *To loosen, or let downe, a hard, or high-stretched thing; and hence;*
Caler les voiles. *To strike sayle; and (metaphorically) to yeeld, submit, or accommodate himselfe vnto the season.*
Calessons. *as* Calçons.
Calfactif: m. iue: f. *Heating, or warming; of propertie, or power to heat, or to warme.*
Calfat: m. *An officer in a Galley that lookes to the caulking thereof.*
Calfater. *as* Calfeutrer.
Calfaterie: f. *The caulking of a ship; the stopping of the holes and chinkes thereof with Ockam, or Towe; or a stopping in of Ockam, or Towe betweene each boord, or planke, on the outside thereof.*
Calfateur. *as* Calfat; *or, the caulker of a ship.*
Calfatin: m. *The seruant of a* Calfat, *or caulker of a galley.*
Calfeutrage: m. *The caulking of a ship; or as* Calage.
Calfeutré: m. ée: f. *Caulked; whose chinkes are stopped, or the distances of whose plankes are filled, with Ockam, or Towe.*
Calfeutrer. *To caulke a ship; to stop, or fill the rifts, or chinkes thereof with Ockam; or to stop in Ockam &c. betweene each planke thereof.*
Calfeutreur de Navires. *A caulker of ships.*
Calfourchons. à cal. *as,* à cheuauchons. *Astraddle, or, bestriding.*
Calfreter. *as* Calfeutrer. ¶Rab.
Calibistris. *The priuie parts, or members.*
Calibre: f. *A qualitie, state, or degree; or, as* Qualibre.
Calibrer, se calibrer à. *To equall, compare, set himselfe in the ranke of, peize himselfe in balance with; esteeme himselfe as good, value himselfe as much, rate himselfe as high as.*
Calice: m. *A Challice, or drinking cup.*
Le Calice d'une rose. *The Calix, or cup of a rose; whereby the yellow part, and leaues of the flower are contained, and held in together.*
Calicules. *Little cups, or goblets; also, the rough shells of Chestnuts; also, the parings of a Corne, or Kernell; also, little skins vpon the eye, liuer, or any other tender part of the bodie.*
Caliditė: f. *Heat, warmth, hotnesse.*
Caliges: f. *Stockings, or netherstockes; also, greaues, legharnesse, or armour for the legs; forefold startups, being full of nayles in the bottome; also, breeches, or slops; and hence;*
Faire caliges, ou caligas. *To beray his hose; or to lay somewhat in them that should not be there.*
Caligineux: m. euse: f. *Dimme, obscure, mistie, almost darke.*
Caliginosité: f. *Obscuritie, dimnesse, blindnesse, darkenesse.*
Calimini. à cal. *Secretly, closely, priuily, in huggermugger.*
Calin: m. *A beggarly rogue, or lazie vagabond, that counterfeits one disease, or other, in hope that men will pitie him, and giue him somewhat.*
Calinaire. *A loue, leyman, or sweet heart.* ¶Provenç.
Caliot. *The name of a certaine Peare.*
Callabasse: f. *A great gourd; also, a bottle made thereof.*
Callafater. *as* Calfeutrer. ¶Rab.
Calland. *A customer vnto a shop.* ¶Pic.
Callate: f. *A descending, or declining plot; a sideling, or sloping peece of ground; the side (in the descent) of a hill.*

Calle: f. *A Bay, or Creeke of the sea, &c*; *as* Cale; *also, the hold of a ship.*

Callebasse: f. *A great Gourd; also, a bottle made of the emptied rinde thereof.*

Callebotes. *Curds; or, as* Caillebotes.

Calleboute: m. ée: f. *Curded, or beestie, as the milke of a woman thats newly deliuered.*

Calle-feutré: m. ée: f. *Caulked, or full rigged; See* Calfeutré.

Caller. *as* Caler; *also, to kittle, as a cat.*

Calles. *as* Cal; *or, Cornes in the feet, or toes.*

Calleux: m. euse: f. *Hard, or thick-skinned, by much labouring.*

Callibordes: f. *Crutches.*

Callifourchons. *as* Calfourchons.

Callique: f. *A certaine fish, that resembles a little shad; and is taken most about* Montpelier.

Callosité: f. *Callositie, or, a brawnie hardnesse of the skin.*

Calmar. *as* Calamar.

Calme: com. *Calme, still, quiet, peaceable, faire; gentle, vnmoued; without storme, without surges.*

Calmement. *Calmely, quietly, peaceably; stilly, fairely, gently.*

Calmer. *To calme, appease, pacifie, quiet, still.*

Caloches. *as* Galoches; *Woodden shooes, or pattens.*

Calomniateur. *A calumniator, malicious detractor, craftie, and false accuser.*

Calomnie: f. *A calumnie; false accusation, forged imputation, spightfull detraction; malicious inuention, or surmise deuised for the trouble, or disgrace of another.*

Serment de calomnie. *An Oath taken, sometimes, in personall actions, both by the plaintife that he sues not, and the defendant that he answeres not, with any purpose to calumniate, or vex his aduersarie, but because he imagines himselfe in the right.*

Calomnié: m. ée: f. *Calumniated; accused falsely, charged maliciously, appeached wrongfully, reuiled iniuriously; vniustly reproached, slaundered, or detracted from.*

Calomnier. *To calumniate; slaunder, detract from; to reproach vniustly, accuse falsely, charge maliciously, appeach wrongfully; to impeach the credit, blemish the fame, indanger the fortune of another, by forged imputations.*

Calomnieusement. *Calumniously; slanderously.*

Calomnieux: m. euse: f. *Calumnious, detracting, reproachfull, slaunderous; full of malice, falsehood, or forgerie in accusations.*

Caloniere: f. *A pot-gunne made of a Quill, or Elder sticke.*

Calosité. *as* Callosité.

Calote. *as* Calotte.

Calotte: f. *The paper, or cloth which women put about their flax on the distaffe; also, a Coife, or halfe Kerchiefe for a woman; also, a little light cap, or night-cap, worne vnder a hat.*

Calquas. *as* Carquois; *a Quiuer.* (v.m.)

Calsons: m. *Close linnen breeches.*

Calvainier. *as* Calvanier.

Calvaire: m. *The (bare) skull, or skalpe of the head.*

Calvanier: m. *A hynde, or hireling, for the time of haruest.*

Calvatré: m. ée: f. *Laid all along (like a lozell, or lubber) on his backe.*

Calvau. pomme de Calvau. *A certaine apple, that hath a blackish rinde.*

Caly: m. *A kind of hearbe; as* Kali.

Calyce: m. *as* Calice. *A cup, or chalice.*

Calyce. *Chalice-like; or, made like a chalice.*

Calyphe: m. *A Caliph; a name, or title of Office, and of Dignitie, in* Ægypt; *(in old time the Caliphes were Lords of* Caire; *now they are but subiects.)*

Camail: m. *A hood to couer the head in foule weather; also, a ribbon, lace, or string to tye vp the haire with; or, such a ribbon as one of our knights of the Order weares about his necke; also, a blacke, or purple Ornament, (somewhat resembling a captaines Gorget) worne by a Pontifical Bishop aboue his Rochet, and reaching as low as the bending of his arme.*

Camamine: f. *The hearbe Cameline, or Treacle Mustard.*

Camar. *as* Camard; *or, borne with a flat nose.*

Camard. nez camard. *A flat nose.*

Camarine: f. *A filthie, and stinking lake in Sicilie; also, a certaine stinking hearbe, that prouokes vomit.*

Camarre: f. *A Martingale for a horse; or, as* Camorre.

Camayeu: m. *The precious stone called a Sardonix; also, a brooche.*

Camayeux antiques. *Medals; or, old, and auncient images of mettall, molten, and cast into the forme of brooches.*

Cambouy. *as* Camboy.

Camboy: m. *The blacke, and oylie grease, of a wrought cart-wheele; some call it, the Gome.*

Cambray, ou, Toile de Cambray. *Cambricke.*

Cambre: com. *Crooked, boughtie, bowed, cambrell-like; vaulted, arched, bent or built arch-wise.*

Cambré: m. ée: f. *The same.*

Souliers cambrez. *Shooes which haue hollow, raised, or Polonian, heeles.*

Cambrer. *To bow, crooke, bend; vault, arch, or build arch-wise.*

Cambreure: f. *A bought, vault, arch; or, as* Cambrure.

Cambrure: f. *A bowing, crooking, or bending; a vaulting, or building arch-wise; or as* Cambreure.

Cameau. *as* Chameau; *a Cammell.*

Cameleon: m. *A Camelion; a beast, which (as many thinke) feeds on nought but the ayre.*

Camelin. aller le camelin. *To pace like a Cammell: the right, and left foot behind following the left, and right before.*

Camelin. sauce cameline. *A certaine daintie Italian sauce.*

Cameline: f. *The hearbe Cameline, or Treacle Mustard.*

Camelot: m. *Chamlet; also,* Lisle *Grogeram.*

Camelot à ondes. *Water Chamlet.*

Camelot plenier. *Vnwater Chamlet.*

Cameloté: m. ée: f. *Of Chamlet; waued like water Chamlet.*

Se Cameloter. *To grow rugged, or full of wrinckles; to become waued, like Chamlet.*

Camemine: f. *The hearbe Cameline, or Treacle Mustard.*

Camerade: f. *A Camerade, or chamberfell; a companie that belongs to, or is euer lodged in, one chamber, tent, cabin.*

Cameraire: m. *A chamberlaine; a groome of the chamber.*

Cameriste: m. *A Camerade; or, chamberfellow.*

Camessine: f. *A kind of Peare.*

Camiere: f. *(The name of) a certaine sweet Apple.*

Ca-

Camille. *A Messenger (in the Hetrurian tongue.)* ¶Rab.
Camin. *as* Chemin. ¶Pic.
Caminée. *as* Cheminée. ¶Pic.
Camion: m. *The small, and short Pinne wherewith women pinne in their ruffes, &c; also, a kind of little cart vsed by the vinegar-makers of* Paris; *also, a small Muserole for a horse.*
Camisade: f. *A Camisado, canuas, or cold Pie; a suddain assaulting, or surprisall of the enemie (so tearmed, because the souldiors that execute it, most commonly weare shirts ouer their armours, or take their enemies in their shirts;) also, the thin filme, or skin, which inwraps a child in the bed, or after-birth.*
Camisole: f. *A Wastcoat (for a man;) also, a certaine robe, or garment of linnen, worne by the French kings at their coronations.*
Camomille: f. *The hearbe Camamell, or Camomill.*
Camomille blanche. *White sweet Camomill, or garden Camomill.*
Camomille à fleur purpurée. *Red Camomill, red Maithe, Rosearubie,* Adonis *red flower.*
Camomille jaulne. *Yellow sweet Camomill; also, yellow Mayweed, or, golden* Cotula.
Camomille saffranée. *Golden corne-flower, yellow corne-flower; the wild, or corne Marigold.*
Camomille sauvage. *Wild Camomill, May-weed, stinking Maithes; some also call so, the hearbe Horehound.*
Camomille vulgaire. *The common, or wild Camomill; like vnto, but nothing so sweet as, garden Camomill.*
Camorre: f. *A sharpe, and double-edged Caueson of yron, for an vnruly horses nose.*
Camote: f. *The name of an Indian root, which rosted, is very good meat.*
Camouärd: m. *An ougly flat-nosed fellow.*
Camoufflet: m. *A Snuft, or cold Pie; a smoakie paper held vnder the nose of a slug, or sleeper.*
Camp: m. *A Campe; an Hoast, or Armie lodged; a Field.*
Camp arresté. *A fortified, setled, or standing campe, abiding still in one place, whether it be to keepe the field, or to besiege a fort.*
Camp clos. *Looke* Champ.
Camp ouvert. *A plaine or open place, wherein a battell or combat hath beene, or may be, fought.*
Camp volant. *An armie of light horse, or light armed footmen, kept for, and imploied in, rodes.*
Le camp luy est demeuré. *He hath gotten the victorie; the field is his.*
Campagne: f. *A plaine field, large plaine, wide and leuell peece of ground.*
Campaignard: m. arde: f. *Fieldie; keeping, or liuing in; of, or belonging to, the fields.*
Campaigne: f. *A plaine field, &c. as* Campagne.
Campal: m. ale: f. *Campall; of, in, or belonging to, a campe, or field.*
Campane: f. *A bell; also, the hearbe Elycampane; also, a Limbecke, or Stillitorie; or the vpper part thereof, which resembles a Bell.*
Mettre la campane au chat. *To make a iarre, to set at oddes, to begin a quarrell, to bring together by the eares.*
Campanel: m. *A Campanell, or Bell-fashioned rowle in the mouth of a bitt; also, a Bell bitt.*
Campanelle: f. *as* Campanel; *also, a little tinging bell.*
Campanelle à cul de bassin. *A Campanell, made compasse like the breech of a cannon, or outside of the bottome of a bason.*
Campanelle à cul plat. *A Campanell, whose broad end is made flat, and plaine.*
Campanette: f. *Withiewind; Bindweed, hedge-bels; also, the Peach-bell, or, Steeple-bell flower; also, the white Daffadill, or* Narcissus.
Campanettes blanches. *White Peach-bels, or Steeple-bell-flowers; also, great smooth Bindweed, or Hedge-bels.*
Campanotte jaulne de Bourgongne. *The yellow Daffadill.*
Campart. *as* Champart.
Campeger. *To incampe, or pitch a campe; also, to reside, or dwell in the fields.*
Camper. *To campe, to incampe, to pitch a campe.*
Camphre: m. *The gumme tearmed, Camphire.*
Camphre artificiel. *Artificiall Camphire, is such, as hath beene refined, and whitened in the Sunne, or by fire.*
Camphre en rose. *Naturall Camphire, is such, as hath not beene touched by fire.*
L'odeur de camphre chastre l'homme: Pro. *(Such power hath that Simple, diuers wayes, to make a man chast.)*
Camphré: m. ée: f. *Camphired; made of, or mingled with, Camphire; and hence;*
Eau camphrée. *Camphire water.*
Camphrer. *To make of Camphire; to dresse, mingle, or annoint with, Camphire.*
Campiger. *as* Campeger.
Campole. *The name of a certaine white grape, which hath very white kernels.*
Campoles: f. *The Tendrels, or twyning sprigs, of plants.*
Campos. *The leaue to play, or a vacation time, for schollers.*
Il a prins campos. *He hath betaken him to the wide, and broad fields; or, he is flatly run away.*
Camus: m. camuse: f. *Flat-nosed.*
Il fut rendu bien camus. *He was very much ashamed, extreamely out of countenance, exceedingly put downe; whence;*
Des harangueurs bien camus. *Blanked, grauelled, or driuen to a Non-plus.*
Camuser. *To flatten, or quash downe, the nose; to breake the bridge of the nose; to make flat-nosed.*
Camuserie: f. *The being flat-nosed.*
Camuset: m. ette: f. *Somewhat flat-nosed.*
Camusette: f. *A little flat-nosed Elfe.*
Canabassement: m. *A canuassing; or, a curious examination, searching, or sifting out, of matters.*
Canabasser. *To canuasse; or curiously to examin, search, or sift out, the depth of a matter.*
Canabasserie: f. *as* Canabassement.
Canabel: m. *A kind of earth (like vnto the smallest sand) which (as Arabians report) fals with raine from the skie.*
Canadelle: f. *The smallest of rock-fishes, beautified with spots of sundry colours, and very good meat.*
Canaille: f. *Dogs; a kennell, or companie of dogs, a knot of curres; also, a base crue, roguish troupe, rascall companie of scoundrels; the dregs, or offalls, of the people; persons of no worth, value, nor vertue.*
Canal: m. *A channell, kennell, furrow, gutter; also, a conduit pipe.*
Le canal de la bouche d'un cheval. *The hollow part wherein his tongue lyes.*

Le canal de colomnes. *A hollow creuise, or strake, grauen in pillars; a chamfring, or channell, in pillars.*
Canaliere: f. *A delicate Italian peare thats ripe in the beginning of Iune.*
Canard: m. *A Drake.*
Pied de canard. *The hearbe Goosefoot, or wild Orache.*
Vendeur de canards à moitié. *A cousener, guller, cogger, foister, lyer.*
Canarin: m. *A Canarie bird.*
Canart. *as* Canard.
Grace de S. Canart: Prov. *A gift of that which the giuer cannot keepe.*
Cancame: m. *as* Lacque; *an Armenian gumme vsed by Dyers.*
Cancelaresque: com. *Chancerie-like; of, or belonging to, the Chancerie.*
Cancelation: f. *A cancellation, or cancelling; a defacing, effacing, rasing, blotting, or crossing out of (a thing written;) also, a forgetting.*
Cancelé: m. ée: f. *Cancelled, razed; effaced, crossed, or blotted out.*
Canceler. *To cancell, crosse, raze; deface, efface, blot or put out.*
Cancelle: m. *as* Branchue.
Canceller. *as* Canceler.
Cancre: m. *A crab-fish; also, the signe in the Zodiacke, tearmed* Cancer; *also, a canker; or, a hard, and vneuen swelling, of an ougly, blackish, or blewish colour; also, an ancient engine of batterie, whose strong and yron head was made like a crab.*
Cancre de Barbarie. *The greatest kind of crab, round, and very rough-shelld, short-legd, slow a land, very swift in the water; and by old authors tearmed* Mæa, *or* Maia.
Cancre squinade. *Looke* Squinade.
Cancre! *(an Interiection of denying, or forbidding) fie; warre that; what a pox meane you; &c.*
Candelabre: m. *A candlesticke.*
Candelette. *A Suppositarie.* ¶Langued.
Candeur: f. *A bright, or shining whitenesse; also, courtesie, gentlenesse, integritie, sinceritie, faire dealing, vprightnesse.*
Candidat. *A flatterer, soother, smoother; one that euer makes it faire weather.*
Candide: com. *White, faire; bright, orient; also, prosperous, happie, fortunate; also, gentle, courteous, faire conditioned; also, vpright, sincere, innocent.*
Candidement. *Whitely, fairely, in white; fauourably, gently, mildly; faithfully, vprightly, sincerely, without fraud, malice, or enuie.*
Se Candir. *To candie, or grow candide, as sugar after boyling.*
Cane: f. *A ducke; also, a measure for cloth, being a yard, or thereabouts; also, a canne, or such like measure for wine; also, a measure of fiue foot and tenne ynches, for land.*
Cane de bois à brusler. *A certaine quantitie of, or scantling for, firewood.*
Cane d'une campane. *The lowest part of a bell, whereon commonly there is a wreath, border, or line made.*
Cane d'Inde. *is bigger then our ordinarie ducke, and differs from it in colour, and figure (the drake somewhat resembling a Turkie cocke, especially in the head) as also from all other fowle, in being dumbe.*
Cane de mer. *A sea-fowle that resembles a young, or small, goose; and hauing a white ring about her necke, is also tearmed,* Cane au colier blanc.
La petite cane. *The wild duck, lesse then the tame one.*
Bec de cane. *See* Bec; *also, a little instrument vsed in grafting* en escusson.
Estonnez comme canes. *Skared like a companie of duckes.*
Faire la cane. *To ducke, like a coward, when a blow is in comming; to play least in sight when blowes are a dealing; to hide, or absent himselfe, from a bickering, or battell, wherein he is much interessed.*
Canebasse. *as* Calebasse; *a bottle made of a gourd.*
Canelé: m. ée: f. *Channelled, fluted, furrowed, straked.*
Caneler. *To flute, strake, furrow, channell; to cut hollow rewes, or gutters into (stone, or timber.)*
Caneleure: f. *A fluting, channelling, straking, furrowing; gutter-worke (in stone, or timber.)*
Caneliere: f. *A reed-plot; a ground thats full, or set full, of reeds.*
Canelle: f. *(Our moderne Cannell, or Cinnamon; (Looke* Cinnamome) *also, the faucet, or quill of a wine vessel; also, the cocke, or spout of a conduit.*
Canellé: m. lée: f. *Of Cinnamon, of a Cinnamon colour; also, made of, or seasoned with, Cinnamon.*
Canelline: f. *A little cannell, pipe, or hollow rod.*
Canelure: f. *A channelling, or furrowing in stone, or in timber; a fluting.*
Canepetiere: f. *A certaine daintie land-fowle, that resembles a Bustard, or the Partridge called* Arbenne; *onely shee is not so big as that, nor rough-footed as this.*
Il fait de la canepetiere. *He (cowardly) hides himselfe in euerie hole; or ducks at the appearance of euery danger.*
Canepin: m. *The thinne inner rind of the barke of the Linden, and th'outward of the coat of a Birch, tree, written on in old time in stead of paper; also, th'outward thinne, and white pilling, of a dressed sheepes skin.*
Canepineuse. *The barke, or inner part of a sugar cane.*
Caner. *To squirt.*
Canet. *A yong ducke; or, a wild ducke.*
Caneter. *To waddle, or goe, like a ducke; also, to breed yong duckes.*
Canetier: m. ere: f. *Of a ducke, like a ducke; catching duckes; feeding, or preying, on duckes.*
Canetille: f. *(Gold, or siluer) Purle; also, a small purle of needle-worke; or, a small edging (bone) lace; also, a freckle, or, the frecklednesse of a face.*
Canetillé: m. ée: f. *Set, wrought, or inriched, with purle; also, edged with a small (needle-worke) purle, or bone lace; also, freckled.*
Caneton: m. *A duckling; yong ducke, or drake.*
Canette: f. *A little ducke; yong ducke; wild ducke; also, a little canne, or cruse; also, the quill of a spinning wheele.*
Canette d'estang. *A kind of small wild ducke, that haunts meares, and great standing waters.*
Canevas; ou, Canevers: m. *Canuas.*
Canjar. *as* Caniard.
Caniard: m. *A Sea-cob, or Sea-gull.*
Canichon. *A little ducke, or drake; a duckling.*
Caniculaires. (les jours ca.) *The dog-dayes.*
Canidé. *A certaine bird, whose backe and taile is blew, necke and belly yellow.*
Canif: m. *A pen-knife.*
Canin: m. ine: f. *Dogged, doggie, of dogs, dog-like.*
Convulsion canine. *The crampe of the mouth; or, a forced, and painfull wrying of the mouth.*

Dents canines. *A mans tushes; or, the teeth wherewith he breakes his meat.*
Rose canine. *A wild Rose. Looke* Rose.
Canisse: f. *A little table, or hurdle, of reeds, whereon fruits are dried, or silkewormes fed.*
Canivet: m. *A Penknife.*
Cannamelle: f. *The sweet cane, or sugar cane.*
Canne: f. *A reed, or cane; also, an Hebrew measure of nine foot; (the ordinarie one; for,* Canne du Sanctuaire, *was tenne) also, a kind of long Pipe vsed in distillings.*
Spodon de canne. *Looke* Spodon.
Canneau du col: m. *The nape of the necke.*
Cannelle. *as* Canelle.
Canne petiere. *See* Cane petiere.
Cannetille. *as* Canetille.
Cannisade: f. *A cage, or basket, of reeds.*
Cannisse: f. *as* Canisse.
Cannoniquement. *See* Canoniquement.
Cannule: f. *A little cane, reed, pipe, or hollow straw, through which one may sucke, blow, or conuey, any moisture, smoake, pouder, &c.*
Cannule parfumatoire. *as* Canon parfumatoire.
Cannulé. *Hollowed like a reed, or cane; or, as* Canelé.
Canolle: f. *A haukes Narell; one of the little holes whereat she drawes in, and lets out, her breath.*
Canon: m. *A Law; a Rule, Decree, Ordnance, Canon of the Law; also, a publicke, and authenticall Rowle, or Catalogue; also, the Gunne tearmed, a Canon; also, the barell of any Gunne; and (more generally) any Instrument, or thing, that is long, and hollow, as the barell of a Gunne; also, the sound-boord of an Organ; also, a Grasse; (Seeke,* Enter en Canon;*) also, a Canon-bitt for a horse; also, a little Ducke, or Drake.*
Canon de Casse. *The cod, or pipe of* Cassia fistula.
Canons de Chausses. *Cannyons.*
Canon parfumatoire. *A long funnell (strait, or crooked, as the parts for which it is to be vsed) wherewith Surgeons perfume, bathe, or moisten the Narrels, eares, fundament, &c.*
Canon pevier. *A Canon Peuier, or Perrier; a great murthering Peece of a wide Bore, and thin barell, charged (most commonly) with a stone.*
Canon de suls. *A Kex, or Elder sticke; also, a Potgunne made thereof.*
Bailler le canon. *To deceiue, gull, cousen.*
Canonicat: m. *A Canonship, or Canons place, in a Cathedrall church.*
Canonique: com. *Canonicall, authenticall; orderlie, according vnto rules; also, receiued, or put into the Roll, Catalogue, or List of.*
Canoniquement. *Canonically, authentically; also, orderly, in due forme, true season, right manner.*
Canoniste: m. *A Canonist; a Professor of, or Practiser in, the Canon Law.*
Canonization: f. *A canonization, or canonizing.*
Canonizé: m. ée: f. *Canonized, made holie, or a Saint; receiued, or put into the catalogue of Saints; also, made Canonicall.*
Canonizer. *To canonize; to make holie, or a Saint; to receiue, or put into the catalogue of Saints.*
Canonner. *To shoot at, or beat, with a Canon; also, as* Enter en Canon.
Canonnier: m. *A Canoneer, or maister Gunner.*
Canonniere: f. *A loope-hole, or port-hole, for a peece of Ordnance; also, a Potgunne.*
Canore: com. *Shrill, ringing; harmonious, melodious, of a pleasant, or pleasing sound.*

Canteau. *as* Chanteau. ¶Pic.
Canthare. *A certaine duskie, and muddie sea-fish, that neuer changes her mate; also, a great Iug, or Tankard.*
Cantharide: f. *The venomous greene flye Cantharides; (which breedes in the tops of the Ash, and Oliue, trees.)*
Cantharidise: f. *A confection of Cantharides.*
Canthenot: m. *A certaine tawnie, and vnsauorie, sea-fish.* ¶Langued.
Canthon. *as* Canton.
Canthonniere. *as* Cantonniere.
Canton: m. *A corner, or crosse way, in a street; also, a Canton, or Hundred; a Precinct, or circuit of Territorie, wherein there be diuers good townes, and villages; (This word is proper to* Helvetia, *or Switzer-land; which, at this day, consists of thirteene such Cantons.)*
Cantonné: m. ée: f. *Cantonned, or cantonnized; seuered from the rest of their fellows, and fortified, or quartered apart.*
Se Cantonner. *To canton, or cantonnize, it; to seuer themselues from the rest of their fellowes, or from the bodie of a State, and fortifie, quarter, or erect a new State, apart.*
Cantonniere: f. *A Doxie, common hackney, hedge-whore; one that will lye downe vnder any stall, or in any corner of a street.*
Canule: f. *A little cane, reed, or pipe. See* Cannule.
Canus. *A kind of strong-toothed, and pearch-like sea-fish, purple on the backe, and on all other parts of a colour, between red, and yellow; liues altogether among rocks, and stones; and is very good meat.*
Cap: m. *A Promontorie, Cape, hill, or nooke of land outstretched into the sea; a head of land lying out into the sea; also, the head, or niple of a ripe Imposthume.*
Cap d'Escadre, ou d'Escouärde. *A Corporall.*
Cap de mouton. *(in a ship is) a certaine flat peece of wood bored full of holes, and seruing to stiffen, or stretch out, the maine sheate; we call it, the Rammes-blocke.*
Bouter, ou faire cap à la mer. *To put backe into the maine, for feare of running vpon shallowes, or comming too neere the shore.*
Capable: com. *Capable, sufficient; large, big, wide; apt to receiue, or take into it; able to hold, or containe within it; also, of good capacitie, apprehension, understanding.*
Capacité: f. *Capablenesse, largenesse, receiueablenesse; also, capacitie, wit, vnderstanding; sufficiencie.*
Caparasson: m. *A Caparison.*
Caparassonné: m. ée: f. *Caparisoned; furnished with, prouided of, attired in, a Caparison.*
Caparassonner. *To caparison; to furnish with, prouide of, dresse or attire in, or put on, a caparison.*
Caparis: m. *The Caper tree, or shrub.*
Capdastre. *A Subsidie booke; a Register of taxes, or of tributes; or, as* Cadastre. ¶Langued.
Cap-descadre: m. *A Corporall.*
Capdeul: m. *A gentlemans chiefe house; falling (almost euery where) vnto the share of the eldest heire.*
Cape: f. *A Mariners gowne; or, a short, and sleeuelesse cloake, or garment, that hath, in stead of a cape, a capuche, behind it; also, a hood, or large, and square peece of water Chamlet, &c, wherewith women preserue their heads from wind and raine. See* Cappe.
Cape de Bearn. *A short, and sleeuelesse gown of course white cloth, vsually worne by the poorer inhabitants of that countrey.*
Capeau: m. *(in some of the outward parts of* France*) as* Chapeau; *and hence;*

Capeau carnu, ou charnu. *The sea-Nettle; called so about* Marseillis.
Capéer. *as* Cappéer.
Capel: m. *A little hat; or as* Chapeau. ¶Norm.
Capelan: m. *A Chapleine; or, the poore Curate of a Chappell; also, the Codfish; or, a kind thereof.*
Capelettes: f. *The heads of Cloues.*
Capelin: m. *as* Capeline.
Capeline: f. *A little flat, round, and narrow-brimd hat, vsually worne by shepheards, messengers, footmen, &c; In old time souldiours wore yron sculs of that fashion, and name, which bred the Phrase;*
Il est homme de capeline. *He is a man of action, full of courage, fit for an enterprise; he is a worthie, or gallant fellow.*
Capellan. *as* Capelan.
Capeluchon. *as* Coqueluchon.
Capendu. pomme de cap. *A certaine apple which is lesse, and more delicious, then the Pepin.*
Caperasson: m. *A Caparison.*
Capesolde. *as* Capesoulde.
Capesoulde: m. *A Gentleman of a Companie; or one that hath extraordinarie Lendings; also, extraordinarie Lendings, or entertainment.*
Capettes: m. *The poore Schollers of* Montagu *Colledge in* Paris.
Caphard; &, Capharder. *See* Cafard, *&* Cafarder.
Copharde: f. *An hypocriticall wench.*
Capharderie. *as* Cafardie; *Hypocrisie.*
Caphetan: m. *A kind of course, or grosse, Taffata; also, a long cassocke of the same.*
Capietrement. *Priuily, closely; theeuishly, stealingly, by stealth.*
Capifou. *A play which is not much vnlike our Harryracket, or Hidman-blind.*
Capilaire: com. *Hairie, full of haire, belonging to haire.*
Capilament: m. *A haire, little streake, or flaw, in a stone, &c.*
Capillaire: f. *The hearbe* Venus *haire, Maiden haire, or, our Ladies haire.*
Capillaire. *as* Capilaire.
Capirotade: f. *A Capirotadoe; or, stued meat, compounded of Veale, Capon, Chicken, or Partridge, minced, spiced, and layed vpon seuerall beds of Cheese.*
Capiscos: m. *Schoolemaisters, Regents, of Schooles.* ¶Gasc.
Capitaine: m. *A Captaine, Leader, or Commaunder of a companie of souldiors; or of a ship of warre; also, a Ring-leader.*
Capitaines du charroy de l'Artillerie. *Be twentie; (chosen out of the frontier Prouinces, or as neere them as may be) who are to prouide, vpon occasion of seruice, foure thousand draught horses, a thousand carters, and fiue hundred carts, or chariots, each in a like proportion; The yearely entertainment of euery one of them is two hundred pounds* Tour. *which he hath (as well in peaceable times as in warlike) payed him by the Receiuer of the* Tailles *of the Election wherein he resides: In time of seruice he hath also fiftie shillings* Tour. *a day, for himselfe, and twentie shillings for his deputie, towards the defraying of euery cart prouided by him; and this from the* Thresorier des frais extraordinaires de l'Artillerie.
Capitaine de la Porte. *The Gentleman Porter, Groome Porter, or chiefe Porter, of the Kings houshold.*

Capitaine du Roy, ou du Royaulme. *A title of dignitie bestowed onely vpon Princes; as Dukes, Marquesses, Earles.*
Le grand capitaine des gens de pied. *See* Colonel general de l'Infanterie Françoise.
Capitainerie: f. *A Captaineship; the Authoritie, Office, or Place, of a Captaine.*
Capitainesse. *An Admirall Galley, or Ship.*
Capital: m. *Wealth, worth; a stocke, a mans principall, or chiefe, substance; also, a captaine, or commaunder.*
En argent soit le capital de celuy là qui te ueut mal: Prov. *Let money be thy enemies whole stocke; Looke* Argent.
Capital: m. ale: f. *Chiefe; capitall; mortall, most hainous, deadly, death-meriting; worthie of disgrace, or of great punishment.*
Lettres capitales. *Text letters, great letters.*
Capitalité: f. *Capitalnesse; or, a capitall fact, or offence.*
Capitation: f. *Head-siluer, Pole-money; a subsidie, tax, or tribute, payed by the Pole.*
Capitau: m. *A Captaine, or Commaunder.* (v.m.)
Capitaux. *are numbred, in the 75 Article of the Customes of* Bourdeaux, *among Earles, Vicounts, and Barons.*
Capite. *A Cabbin in a ship.*
Capitel: m. *A strong compounded Lye, whereof cauters and other violent remedies are made.*
Eau de capitel. *A strong corrosiue made of that Lye.*
Capiton: m. *Capiton; course sleaue (silke.)*
Se Capitonner de. *To couer his head with.*
Capitouls: m. *are (in* Tholouse*) twelue principall magistrats; whereof the first is to be a Gentleman (of that Prouince) the rest Lawyers, and substantiall Marchants.*
Capitouls d'Orleans. *The Sheriffes of* Orleans; *or, as,* les Eschevins.
Capitulaire: m. *A capitular decree, a capitall Ordinance.*
Capitulaire: com. *Capitular; of, or belonging to, a chapter; also, capitall.*
Assemblée capitulaire. *A Chapter held, by the officers of a Cathedrall church.*
Capitulairement. *Capitally; also, in Chapter, or, with full consent of the Chapter.*
Capitulant: m. ante: f. *Hauing a voice in Councels, Assemblies, Conuocations, Chapters; also, capitulating.*
Capitulation: f. *A capitulation; an article of agreement.*
Capitulé: m. ée: f. *Capitulated; agreed vpon, distinguished by Articles, or Chapters.*
Capituler. *To capitulate; agree vpon articles; to distinguish by Articles, or Chapters.*
Capituleur: m. *A capitulator.*
Capnomantie: f. *Diuination by smoake rising from an altar, whereon Incense, or Poppie seed, is burned.*
Capolie: f. *A certaine Indian fruit much like a Cherrie.*
Caporal: m. *The Corporall of a band of souldiors.*
Capot: m. *A White Leaper; also, as* Cappot.
Cappe: f. *A short cloake, or loose, and sleeuelesse garment, which hath in stead of a Cape, a Capuche behind it; also, a kind of long, and Muskle-like shell-fish; also, the name of a small, round, and ruddie apple. See* Cape.
Cappe à femme. *A large hood of water Chamlet, &c, worne by citizens wiues, &c, in foule weather.*
Singler à la Cappe. *as* Cappéer.

Cap-

Cappé: m. ée: f. *Hooded; or, that hath a short, and capuched, cloake on.*
Pigeons cappez. *Ruffed Pigeons; the top of whose neckes is enuironned with a ruffe, or border, of feathers.*
Cappéer. *A ship to lye a-try; also, to goe very neere the wind.*
Cappet. noirs cappets. *Looke* Chapeaux noirs.
Cappette: f. *A little hood; or cloake, hauing a capuche in stead of a cape.*
Cappiettement. *for* Capietrement. ¶Rab.
Cappot: m. *A countrey cloake, or course, and scantie cloake; also, as* Capot.
Cappres. des cap. *The fruit Capers.*
Cappres d' Alexandrie. *Egyptian Capers; the best Capers; brought from Alexandria.*
Cappier: m. *A plot set with Caper shrubs; or, as* Caprier.
Capres: f. *(The fruit) Capers.*
Caprice: f. *A humor, caprichio, giddie thought, fantasticall conceit; a suddaine will, desire, or purpose to doe a thing, for which one hath no (apparent) reason.*
Capricieux: m. euse: f. *Capricious, humorous, fantasticall, conceited, giddie-headed.*
Capricorne: m. *Capricorne; one of the twelue Signes, (containing twentie starres.)*
Caprier: m. *A Caper shrub, or Caper plant.*
Capriere: f. *A Caper plot, bed, or ground.*
Caprifice: m. *A wild Figge-tree.*
Caprimulge: m. *A Goat-milker; an vnluckie, and Gull-resembling Night-bird, that suckes Goats, and mortifies their vdders.*
Caprin. le caprin. *Goats; the kind, or nature, of Goats; also, Goats flesh.*
Caprin: m. ine: f. *Goatie; of a Goat; like a Goat.*
Capriole: f. *A caper in dauncing; also, the* Capriole, *sault, or Goats leape (done by a horse;) also, the hearbe Manna-grasse, or Deaw-grasse; also, as* Pied de Corneille.
Capriot: m. *A caper in dauncing.*
Caprioter. *To caper, to cut a caper.*
Capse: f. *A coffer, chest; box; case.*
Capsetin: m. *A little coffer, or chest; a casket, or box.*
Capsoos: m. *The rights, and royalties belonging to the Lord of a Place.* ¶Bearnois.
Capsule: f. *A little chest, or coffer; a casket, box, or forsett.*
La capsule du cœur. *The skin* Pericardium; *wherein the heart lyes; and hence;*
Le cœur me tremble dans sa capsule. *I am afraid at the very heart.*
Captieusement. *Captiously, cauillingly; ouer-curiously; also, craftily, deceitfully, cautelously.*
Captieux: m. euse: f. *Captious, cauilling; too curious; also, deceitfull, craftie, fraudulent, cautelous.*
Captif: m. iue: f. *Captiue; taken in, imprisoned by, warre; also, seruile, subiect, that hath lost his libertie.*
Captiuer. *To captiuate; take in, imprison by, warre; also, to restraine of libertie, bring into seruitude, make a slaue of.*
Captiuité: f. *Captiuitie, thraldome; imprisonment; losse of libertie.*
Capture: f. *A capture, or taking; an arrest, or seisure; an arresting, or seising; also, a bootie, or prey; also, little or small gaine.*

Capuchon: m. *A Capuche; a Monks Cowle, or Hood; also, the hood of a cloake; also, one of the six muscles whereby the shoulder-blades are moued.*
Capucin: m. *A Capucine Frier (of S.* Frances *Order) weares neither shirt, nor breeches.*
Capucinage: m. *The Profession, Order, Estate, or life of a Capucine.*
Capulaire: m. *A coffin for a corse.*
Caputions: m. *Monkes; or, Capucine Friers.*
Caque: m. *A Cag; or, the fourth part of a* Muid; *(a barrell, or vessell, wherein saults-meats, pitch, rosen, &c, are vsually carried, or kept.)*
Caqueduc: m. *A niggard, micher, miser, scrape-good, pinch-pennie, penny-father; a couetous, and greedie wretch.*
Caquerel. *A sprat, or pickled herring; or as* Cagarel.
Caqueroles: f. *The shels of Snayles, Periwincles, and such like.* ¶Rab.
Caquerolierie: f. *A shore full of little shels.* ¶Rab.
Caquerotier: m. *A catcher, eater, or owner, of shellfish.*
Caquesangue: f. *The bloudie flix.*
Caquet: m. *Pratling, tatling, babling, tittle tattle, much talking.*
Caquetard: m. *A pratler, babler, tatler, long-tongue.*
Caqueté. *Tatled, pratled, babled, chattered.*
Caqueter. *To tatle, bable, pratle, chatter, prate, vse many words.*
Caquetereau: m. *A pratle-basket, a tatling iacke.*
Caqueteur. *as* Caquetard.
Caqueteuse: f. *A pratling huswife.*
Caquetiere: f. *The same.*
Caquetoire: m. *A place wherein women meet, and pratle together; as a myll, an ouen, a gossips feast, &c; also, the seat whereon they vse to sit at such a meeting.*
Caquettement: m. *A tatling, cackling, babling, pratling.*
Ca-queue: f. *The hearbe Horse-tayle, Shaue-grasse, Pewter-wort.*
Caquots: m. *White Leapers, infected inwardly; (for their faces are very cleere, and faire.)*
Car: m. *A Carre, Cart, or Waine.* ¶Picard.
Car. *For, because; (also) insomuch as, considering that, seeing it is as it is.*
Carabasse: f. *as* Callabasse; *a Gourd; or a bottle made thereof; (also, a Grit, Grampell, Pungar-fish.* ¶Marseillois.)
Carabassé: m. ée: f. *Much vsed, or carried vp and downe, as a Gourd-bottle is.*
Carabe: f. *A Corracle, or little round Skiffe, made of Ozier twigs wouen together, and couered with raw hides; also, yellow Amber.*
Carabin: m. *A Carbine, or Curbeene; an Arguebuzier armed with a morrian, and breast-plate, and seruing on horsebacke.*
Carabinage: m. *An assault made, or action performed, by Carbines.*
Carabiner. *To shoot, hit, or knocke, with a Petronell, or horsemans Peece.*
Caracol: m. *A Snayle; (whence;)*
Faire le caracol. *(Souldiors) to cast themselues into a Round, or Ring.*
Caractere: m. *A Caracter; letter, figure, or forme of writing; also, a marke, token, signe, seale, impression, or print in a thing.*
Caracteré: m. ée: f. *Caractered, or caracterized; imprinted,*

printed, stamped with a (peculiar) marke, figure, letter.

Caracterer. *To caracter, or caracterize; to make, or print, characters, letters, figures; also, to imprint, stampe, set, fix a marke, or signe on.*

Caraffe: f. *A certaine summe of money, payed as a Passage Toll, or dutie, vnto th'Arabian boot-halers, by such as trauell, without a strong* Caravan, *towards the Holy land, &c.*

Caramot: m. *A Prawne; or, as;*

Caramote: f. *The greatest kind of Prawne; somewhat resembling, and little lesse then, our Creuice.* ¶Marseillois.

Carance: f. *Want, or lacke of.*

Carance de biens. *A Note, or Testimoniall (vnder diuers hands) signifying, that such a one hath no goods nor chattels in such a place.*

Caraque. *See* Carraque.

Carasse: f. *A huge, or great face.*

Carat: m. *A Carrat; among Goldsmiths, and Mintmen, is the third part of an ounce; among Iewellers, or Stone-cutters, but the 19 part; for eight of them make but one Sterlin, and a Sterlin is the 24 part of an ounce.*

Fol à 25 carats (dont les 24 font le tout.) *An egregious foole, a foole beyond all proportion; (the finest gold being but of 24 Carrats.)*

Carathement. *A charming of a mans child-getter.*

Caravane: f. *A* Carauan, *or Conuoy of Souldiours, for the safetie of Marchants that trauell by land.*

Caravelle: f. *A Caruell; (the little shippe so called.)*

Clou à Caravelle. *See* Clou.

Caravellon: m. *A small Caruell.*

Caravene: f. *A little Boat, or Skiffe, made like a Trough, and (most commonly) of one piece.*

Caravirée: f. *A wry-mouthed, or wry-faced wench; or one that often makes wry mouthes, or ill fauoured wry faces.*

Carbassat: m. *Wet sucket, made of the vpper part of the long white Pompion, cut in slices.*

Carbasse: f. *The Crab-fish tearmed, a Pungar.*

Carbau: m. *The Cabot fish.*

Carbonade: f. *A Carbonadoe, a rasher on the coales; also, a slash ouer the face, which fetcheth the flesh with it.*

Carboucle. *A Carbuncle.*

Carcaillon: f. *A corne-deuouring Mite, or Weeuill.*

Carcamousse: f. *The battering Engine, called a Ramme.*

Carcan: m. *A Carkanet, or collar of gold, &c. worne about the necke; also, an yron chaine, or collar, wherein an offendor is tyed by the necke to a post, and (in that posture) exposed vnto publicke view.*

Carcant. *The same.*

Carchiophe: m. *An Artichoke.*

Carcinome. *A canker; See* Cancre.

Carcois: m. *as* Carquois; *also, the head, or vpper part of a Mast, where the cords that hold the sayle vnto the yard, passe through certaine Pullies.*

Cardaire. *A kind of Thornebacke, full of small prickles.* ¶Langued.

Cardamome: m. Cardamomum; *Graines, or Graine of Paradise; also, Ethyopian Pepper.*

Cardamome moindre. *The least kind of Graines.*

Cardanalizé. *See* Cardinalisé.

Carde. *A thistle Finch; also, the white thistle, whereof some kinds of Cardoons are made; also, the Cardoon it selfe.*

Cardes. *Cards for wooll, &c; working cards.*

Carde de montagne. *The white Carline thistle.*

Bois de carde. *See* Bois.

Cardé: m. ée: f. *Carded (as wooll, &c.)*

Carder la laine. *To card wooll.*

Cardeur de laine. *A wooll-carder.*

Cardiaque: com. *Heartie, heart-easing, cordiall, comforting the heart; also, pained in the stomacke, wrung at the heart; also, in a consumption, and continuall sweat, by the indisposition of the heart, and parts about it.*

Cardier: m. *A Card-maker.*

Cardinal: m. *A Cardinall, of the Church of Rome.*

Cardinal en Greve. *One thats beheaded in the* Greue *at* Paris.

Elle a son Cardinal. *She hath her flowers.*

Il a esté fait Cardinal sans s'en aller à Rome. *He hath got a red cap without a Cardinallship;* viz. *hee hath lost his head.*

Cardinal: m. ale: f. *Chiefe, principall, of the first ranke.*

Artillerie cardinale. *Ordnance of the widest bore; or, as* Cardinale.

Vent cardinal. *One of the foure principall winds; as East, West, North, or South.*

Vertus cardinales. *Cardinall vertues;* viz. *Wisdome, Iustice, Fortitude, and Temperance.*

Cardinalat: m. *A Cardinallship.*

Cardinale: f. *A kind of Artillerie for shipping, lesse then the Culuerine, and deuised at first by the Cardinall of Lorraine.*

Cardinalin: m. *A little, or young Cardinall.*

Cardinalisé: m. ée: f. *Red, redded, made of a red or skarlet hue; in a red or skarlet habit, such as Cardinals weare.*

Cardons: m. *Cardoones; the stalkes of Artichokes, or of the white thistle, buried in the ground, or otherwise vsed, to get them a whitenesse; (excellent meat.)*

Caré: m. *as* Ableret.

Care: m. *A certaine disease that benummes the head, and makes the whole bodie more sencelesse then an Apoplexie; or, a deepe sleepe, or sleepinesse, ioyned with weaknesse of the braine, sences, and motion.*

Care: f. *The face, visage, countenance, looke, aspect.*

Carence: f. *Want, lacke of; See* Carance.

Carene: f. *The Keele of a ship.*

Caresme: m. *Lent.*

Caresme entrant. *Shroue-tuesday.*

Caresme prenant. *Shrouetide; Fastnes; or Shrouetuesday.*

Plaidoyé de caresme prenant. *A wanton, baudie, lasciuious plea, or argument.*

Amoureux de caresme. *A Lenton louer; a bashfull, modest, or maidenly woer; one thats afraid to touch his mistresse.*

Figue de caresme. *A drie figge, Frayle figge, Lenten figge.*

Sainct de caresme. *Looke* Sainct.

Violette de caresme. *The ordinarie blew, or March Violet.*

I'y ay presché sept ans pour vn caresme. *I know the place well, and am still well knowne there.*

Caresme-entrant, &, Caresme-prenant. *See* Caresme.

Ca-

Caresse: f. *A cheering, cherishing, welcomming, friendly intertainment, hugging, blandishment, kind vsage, making much of.*

Caresser. *To cherish, hug, make much of, intertain friendly, vse kindly, make good cheere vnto.*

Caret. fil de caret; *Packthread.*

Carfou: m. *The peale which we also tearme Curfue, being of one bell, and about eight or nine of the clocke at night.*

Cargade: f. *as* Cargaison.

Cargaison: f. *The fraight, fraught, or lading, of a ship.*

Cargue: f. *A charge, or onset, giuen on an enemie.*

Carguer. *To charge; also, to lade; also, to leane all on one side; (in which sence it is most vsed by Mariners.)*

Cariage. Le c. *The carriage, luggage, baggage; all the necessarie prouision of an armie, &c, carried with, or after, it.*

Caribe. *The most biting kind of Indian pepper.*

Caribot: m. *A lunchion, or big peece, as of bread, &c.*

Carie: f. *Rottennesse, or putrifaction in wood by long continuance; a worme in wood; corruption in any thing.*

Se Carier. *To rot, putrifie, corrupt.*

Carieux: m. euse: f. *Rotten, putrified, worme-eaten; corrupted.*

Carillon: m. *A chyming of bels; a knell.*

Ie te frotteray à double carillon. *I will beat thee like a stockfish, I will swinge thee while I may stand ouer thee.*

Carillonné: m. ée: f. *Chymed, or knowled.*

Carillonner. *To chyme, or knowle, bels.*

Carillonneur: m. *A chymer, or knowler, of bels.*

Carimari carimara. ¶Rab. *See* Carymari.

Carine: f. *The keele of a ship.*

Cariol: m. *as* Cariole.

Cariole: f. *The root of a horses tayle, or the bone thereof; the rumpe-bone.*

Cariophillate: f. *Hearbe Auens, Bennet, or blessed.*

Carisi. *The name of a certaine Peare; also, the perrie made thereof.*

Carizé. *Kersie.*

Carler. *as* Carreler.

Carlin. *An Italian coyne worth fortie* Quadrins.

Carline: f. *The Carline, or Carline thistle; erroniously confounded, by some Authors, with our Ladies thistle.*

Petite carline. *The low, or little, Carline (thistle.)*

Carlingue: f. *The step of a Mast; the peece of timber whereinto the foot thereof enters.*

Carlonne. Vivre à la Carlonne. *To deale plainly.*

Carlure: f. *as* Carrelure.

Carmaignole: f. *An Apricocke.*

Carme: m. *A verse; also, a charme; also, the hornebeame, or yoake tree; also, a white Frier.*

Carmelitains: m. *The Carmelites; an Order of white Friers.*

Carminatif: m. iue: f. *Wind-voiding, wind-dissoluing, windinesse-correcting; also, flesh-taming, lust-abating.*

Carminificateur. *A versifier; a maker of verses.*

Carmoussal: m. *A kind of Turkish ship.*

Carnacier: m. ere: f. *Fleshie, of flesh; bloudie, cruell; flesh-deuouring, bloud-affecting; liuing, or feeding on flesh; also, as* Carnassier.

Carnage. *Flesh time, the season wherein tis lawfull to eat flesh;* ¶Pic: *also, a slaughter, butcherie, killing, slaying, murther of men.*

Carnages. *Flesh, flesh-meat, flesh ware, prouision of flesh.*

Carnagier. *as* Carnacier.

Carnassage: m. *as* Carnage; *a killing; a slaying; a slaughter; especially of beasts; as in* Carnaller.

Carnaller. *To kill, butcher, slay, slaughter; especially beasts found damage-fesant (which the partie dammaged in some places, and cases, may lawfully do) and eat, or sell their flesh.*

Carnasseries: f. *Fleshie matters.*

Carnassier: m. ere: f. *Plumpe, fleshie, full, well batled, well fed; also, as* Carnacier.

Carnaval: m. *Shrouetide; also, a licentious, or dissolute season.*

Carnavalée: f. *A wench thats growne as licentious, or is, vsed as licentiously, as the* Carnaval; (ou, qui est chevauchée tout le long du Carnaval.)

Carne: f. *An edge, or corner.*

Carne de testons. *A quarterne of Testons, consisting of foure, or of fortie.*

Carneau: m. *A battlement (of a wall.)*

Carnelé: m. ée: f. *Imbattled; hauing battlements.*

Carnelle: f. *The stampe of a peece of coyne.*

Carneller. *To stampe, or coyne, a peece of coyne.*

Carnet. *as* Cayer.

Carniforme: com. *Of a fleshie substance, or forme; like flesh.*

Carnosité: f. *Carnositie, Fleshlinesse, fulnesse of flesh.*

Carnu. *Looke* Charnu.

Carobe. *as* Carrobe, *or* Carrube.

Carocher. *A coachman.*

Carolle: f. *A kind of daunce wherein many daunce together; also, a Carroll, or Christmas song.*

Caroller. *To daunce, to reuell it; to sing carrols.*

Carolus: m. *A peece of white mony, worth* x d. Tour. *or a iust English penny.*

Carolus de Bezançon. *A siluer coyne; and is worth about* ix d. *sterl.*

Carolus de Flandres. *Another, worth about* iij s. *sterl.*

Carooler. *To inroule.*

Carosse: f. *A carosse, or caroach.*

Carote: f. *The Carrot (root, or hearbe.)*

Carote sauvage. Daucus, *wilde Carrot, birds neast.*

Carotes. *The hearbe Carroway, and Carroway seed;* ¶Dodoneus.

Carotide. *A branch of the great Arterie; which after it hath mounted a little by the side of the necke, diuides it selfe into two branches; one (inward and the greater) goes vp to the braine; the other (outward) bestowes it selfe on the Larinx, tongue, nose, eyes, and muscle of the temples.*

Carouges: f. *Carobs, or Carob-beanes, and Carob-beane cods; tearmed also, S. Iohns bread.*

Carous. *A carousse of drinke.*

Carousser. *To quaffe, swill, carousse it.*

Carozze. *as* Carosse; *a caroach, or great coach.*

Carpase: m. *A certain plant, whose iuice, being drunke, procureth sleepe, and in sleeping strangleth; (A report of auncient Herbarists; for the moderne ones either make no mention of it, or, confesse they know it not.)*

Carpe : m. *The wrist, or first part of the palme of the hand.*
Carpe : f. *A Carpe (fish.)*
Carpe de mer. *The sea-Carpe; somewhat blacker then the freshwater one, but otherwise very like vnto her.*
Saut de la carpe. *A turning top ouer tayle.*
Carpeau : m. *A young Carpe.*
Carpendu. pomme de car. *The apple called, a Shorte-start.*
Carpie : f. *The yoke tree, horne-beame, hard beame, yoke Elme, Witch hasell; (also, as* Charpie, ¶Pic.)
Carpion : m. *A kind of long-headed, slender-bodied, blacke-backed, and white-bellied Trout; hauing very small scales poudered (especially towards the backe) with blacke and red spots; and growing not to aboue a foot in length.*
Carpionne : f. *as* Carpion.
Carpir. *as* Charpir. ¶Pic.
Carpobalsame : m. *The fruit of the Balsamum, or Balsame, tree.*
Carpot. *The halfe, or part, of the fruit, or profit of a vineyard, yeelded as a rent by the tenant, vnto the lord, thereof.*
Carquan : m. *A carcanet; a (rich) chaine for the necke.*
Carquant. *The same; or (both) as* Carcan.
Carquasse : f. *A carkas, or dead corpes; the dead bodie of any creature; and hence, a Catch, Pelt, or dead bird, to take downe a Hauke withall.*
Carquois : m. *A quiuer for arrowes.*
Carquois : m. ise : f. *Of a quiuer, belonging to a quiuer, kept in a quiuer.*
Carrabin. *as* Carabin.
Carracon : m. *A small (but strong) carricke.*
Carraque : f. *The huge ship tearmed a carricke.*
Carraquon. *as* Carracon.
Carrat de bois à bastir. *A certaine quantitie of timber.*
Carré. *A Square; a square peece in Cutworke, or Networke; a square bed in a garden.*
Oeil de carré. *A side, or leering eye; also, a proud, surlie, statelie, big looke.*
Carre. le Carre d'un rocher. *The edge, or corner of a rocke.*
Carre : f. *as* Caire.
Carré : m. ée : f. *Squared; square.*
Carre : com. *Square; broad.*
B carre. *B sharpe (in Musicke.)*
De b carre en b mol. *Inconstantly, or vncertainely; from one subiect to another.*
Carreau : m. *(is generally) a little Square; (particularly) a Diamond, or Picke at cards; also, a cushion; also, a bed in a garden; also, the square of a Pillar (or as* Plinthe;) *also, a pauing tyle; also, a coping, or planchet of mettall, before it be rounded, or coyned; also, a taylors pressing-yron; also, a square stone layed in leuell with, and at each end of, a bowling alley, and in the middest thereof a pricke set, as the marke whereat (in* France) *they bowle; See* Quarreau.
Carreaux. *The bends, or wales, of a ship.*
Franc du carreau. *A certaine boyish Game, for counters.*
Frizer les carreaux. *To strike a ball vnder the Line, at Tennis.*
Carrefour : m. *as* Quarrefour.
Carreler. *To paue with square tyles, or brickes; also, to sole, or coble, shooes.*
Carrelet : m. *A (kind of broad, and short) Plaice; also, a sea-fish that resembles a herring, and is (most) seene before a dearth, or plague.*
Carrelure : f. *A sole; or, the soling of a shoo.*
Carrelure de ventre. *Meat, belly-timber, belly-cheere.*
Carrer. *To square; to make broad, or square.*
Se Carrer. *To square it; to looke stately, surly, or bigge on't.*
Carreure : f. *A square; also, breadth, or squarenesse; also, a squaring; also, a making broad, or square.*
Carrier : m. *A finder of stones, or quarries of stones; also, a stone-digger, a quarrey-man, a worker in Quarries.*
Carriere : f. *An high way, rode, or street* (Langued.) *also, a quarrey of stones; also, a Careere, on horsebacke; and (more generally) any exercise, or place for exercise, on horsebacke; as, a horse-race, or, a place for horses to run in; and, their course, running, or full speed therein.*
Carriere de Valois. *is eight foot broad.*
Lance de carriere. *Seeke* Lance.
Donner carriere à son esprit. *To recreate his spirit; or, to set his wits a running, his conceit a gadding, his thoughts on a gallop.*
Se donner carriere. *To raunge, flye out; giue himselfe scope; or to recreate himselfe; to run himselfe out of breath.*
Faire le loup à la carriere. *See* Loup.
Parfaire sa carriere. *To finish his careere, to run out his course, to end his race.*
Prendre bien sa carriere. *To part readily from the hand into a strait, and swift, careere.*
Carrillon : m. *A chyming, or knowling of bels. See* Carillon.
Carrillonner. *To chyme, or knowle bels; to make a knell.*
Carrobe : m. *The Carob, Carob-beane, or Carob-beane cod, S. Iohns bread; also, as* Carrube.
Carroce; &, Carroche. *As* Carrosse; *a Carroche.*
Carrochier; ou, Carrocier. *as* Carrossier.
Carrosse. *A caroach, or great coach.*
Carrossier. *A caroach-driuer; a coachman.*
Carrot de Galien. *Looke* Cerat.
Carrote : f. *as* Carote.
Carroube : m. *as* Carrobe; *also, as* Carroubier.
Carroubier : m. *The Carob tree, or Beane tree.*
Carrouge. *as* Carrobe.
Carrouselle : f. *A little hollow reed.*
Carrozze : f. *A caroach.*
Carrozzier : m. *A caroach-man, a coachman.*
Carrube : m. *as* Carrobe; *also, a small weight (among Mintmen, and Goldsmiths) making but the 24 part of an ounce.*
Cartame : m. *Bastard-Saffron, Mocke-Saffron, wild Saffron, Saffron Dorte.*
Cartame sylvestre. *Wild bastard Saffron.*
Cartasonne. *The Indian, whole-hoofed, and black-horned, Vnicorne.*
Carte : f. *A paper, or peece of paper; also, a card; also, a childs Horne-booke, or Abcee; also, a Pickadill, or supporter, of Pasteboord couered with linnen.*
Carte blanche. *A Blanke; and hence;*
Donner la carte blanche à. *To offer to receiue, or submit himselfe vnto, any conditions.*
I'en laisse la carte blanche à eux. *I leaue them to debate*

debate it; I leaue the decision, (or disposall) thereof to them.

Brouiller les cartes. *Looke* Brouiller.

Le premier en carte. *Th'eldest, or, the first thats dealt vnto, at cards.*

Cartée: f. *A (letter of) defiance, or challenge, for a (single) combat.*

Cartel: m. *as* Cartée.

Carteranche: f. *A certaine measure for salt.*

Carthame: m. *Bastard Saffron, wild Saffron, mocke Saffron, Saffron dort.*

Carthame sauvage, ou syluestre. *Wild bastard Saffron.*

Carthellages. *Square peeces of free stone.*

Cartibe. *A square table of stone, but somewhat more long than broad.*

Cartibes d'vn moulinet. *The ferrels, or bands of yron whereby the ends of a windlesse are strengthened.*

Cartilage: m. *A gristle, or tendrell of the eare, or nose; or such a skin as is betweene the toes of geese, duckes, &c.*

Cartilagineux: m. euse: f. *Gristly; full of tendrels, or gristles.*

Cartisannier: m. *A maker of (playing) cards.*

Cartoche. *as* Cartouche; *also, a Cartridge, or roll (in Architecture.)*

Carton: m. *The thicke paper whereon Painters draw sometimes; and that whereof some fannes are made; also, a square peece thereof, or of pastboord; (also, a Carter, or carre-man:* ¶Pic.*)*

Cartons d'une Selle. *The skirts of a saddle.*

Cartophilaces. *Law-bookes, auncient Records, authenticall writings; also, the roome, chest, or presse, wherein such writings be kept.*

Cartouche: f. *The cornet of paper whereinto Apothecaries, and Grocers put the parcels they retaile; also, a Cartouch, or full charge, for a pistoll, put vp within a little paper, to be the readier for vse; also, a peece of pastboord, or thicke paper, stuffed (in a round, or puddinglike forme) with bullets, &c, and to be shot out of a great peece; also, as* Cartoche.

Cartoufle. *(The name of) a shrub, that beares a Mushrome-like fruit; also, the fruit it selfe.*

Cartuche. *as* Cartouche.

Cartulaire. *A great paper-booke; or, as* Chartulaire; *also, as* Resve.

Cartulaire: com. *Cartular; of, or in, paper; proper vnto paper, or paper-bookes.*

Iuges cartulaires. *Iudges that giue their sentences in writing.*

Carvi: m. *Carowayes, or Caroway seed.*

Carvi sauvage. *Wild Cheruill, or wild Carowayes.*

Caruncule: f. *A little peece of flesh.*

Carymari carymara. *Fained words expressing a great coyle, stirre, hurlyburly, or the confused muttering of a rude companie.*

Caryote: f. *A Date.*

Cas: m. *A Case, cause, matter, thing; also, a crime, offence; fact; also, esteeme, account, reckoning of; also, the priuities (of man, or woman.)*

Cas fortuit. *A hap, or chance.*

Cas previlegiez. *as* Cas royaux.

Cas royaux. *Royall cases; causes wherein the king is interessed for the preseruation of his rights, or the maintenance of his authoritie; such as bee Treasons of all sorts against (humane) Maiestie; the violation of pasports, or of protections, granted by himselfe, or by the Officers of the Crowne; disturbance offered vnto any of his Officers, in the execution of their charges, or vnto any that goe vp and downe about his businesse; Violence vsed, riots committed, or armes borne, in vnlawfull assemblies; all causes that concerne his rights, reuenue,* finances, *coyning, officers, ordinarie seruants; Churches Cathedrall, or others of royall foundation, or therwise priuiledged; the execution of letters patents, & of Commissions, or Iniunctions vnder the great seale; and generally, all causes that depend on* les droicts royaux; *for which, looke* Droict.

Avoir son cas. *A woman to be in her flowers.*

Ce sera bien vostre cas. *This will fit you well, or bee for your turne.*

Cas sur cas n'a point de lieu. *(A ground in law) if a thing be seised by one, it cannot bee reseised by another, vntill the former haue tried his title vnto it.*

Cas: m. casse: f. *Hollow, or broken sounded; hoarse like a bell that hath got a craze, or the voyce of one that hath got a cold.*

Casal: m. *A huge, or great house; a Mannor house; also, a village, or hamlet.*

Casanier: m. *A house-doue, or home-bred sluggard; one that neuer stirres out of his owne doores.*

Casaque: f. *A cassocke, mandilian, long coat.*

Casard: m. arde: f. *Home-bred, house-louing, euer keeping within doores; also, tame, or kept about a house.*

Cascaret: m. *A furious, and boyling tide, or sea, that sometimes comes in (betweene* Bourdeaux *and* Rochel*) surging, and roaring, and ouerturning the barkes which be in the way thereof.*

Cascavelle: f. *A roundelay, or countrey song.*

Case: f. *(Is properly) a poore house, tenement, or cottage; (and sometimes) any house, or dwelling place.*

Doublet en case. *A corner point taken with two men at Tables.*

La Case monstre le Messer: Prov. *as,* La Maison fait cognoistre le Maistre.

Caseiforme: com. *Made (round, and flat) like a cheese.*

Casemate: f. *A case-mate; a loope, or loope-hole, in a fortified wall.*

Caseret: m. *A cheese-fat, or chesford, to make a cheese in.*

Casette: f. *A little house; a cote, or small cottage.*

Casier. *as* Caseret.

Casine: f. *A cote, a little cottage, or country house.*

Casois: m. *A countrey clowne, boore, clunch, hinde; a home-bred hoydon; a rusticall house-doue, an ignorant, or idle clusterfist.*

Casole: f. *A posnet; also, a kind of narrow-mouthed pot, somewhat like a perfuming pot.*

Casque: f. *The head-peece tearmed a caske, or casket.*

Casquet: m. *The same; or, a little one.*

Cassable: com. *Fraile, brittle, easie to be broken.*

Cassade: f. *A gudgeon, frumpe, mocke, flout, gull, cousening part, cheating pranke, deceitfull tricke; whence;*

Avoir la cassade. *To be gulled; or, to swallow a gudgeon.*

Cassant: m. ante: f. *Frayle, brittle, easie to be broken; also, quashing, cassing, breaking, infringing.*

Estoffe cassant. *Rending stuffe.*

Cassard: m. *A chest-like couer, a case-like receptacle; also, a Buzzard.*

Cassation: f. *A cassation; a quashing, cassing, breaking; abrogating, annulling, infringing.*

Cassaudes

Cassaudes: f. *Daisies; or, Bruizewort.*
Casse: f. *The drug, or spice tearmed* Casia; *or as;*
Casse aromatique. *The aromaticall wood, barke, or bastard Cinnamon, tearmed* Casia.
Casse de bois. *The same.*
Casse des iardins. *A sweet hearbe; which is held to be Lauender spike.*
Casse laxative. Casia fistula, *Pudding pipe.*
Casse nigre. *as* Casse laxative.
Casse: f. *A box, case, or, chest, to carrie, or keepe wares in; also, a Marchants cash, or counter; also, any chest, casket, or cabinet; also, a coffin, or shrine; also, a dripping-pan; also, an open mouthed pan, or vessell of earth, &c, fit to boyle things, or set plants, in; also, the hollow part of the sole of a horse-foot.*
Casse pointuë. *A fashion of a small boyling panne, which hath a narrow, or pointed bottome.*
Cassé: m. ée: f. *Broken, burst, quasht in peeces; also, cassed, casseered; cancelled; also, decayed, worne, or broken with age.*
Voix cassée. *A weake, hoarse, or whizzing voyce.*
Aujourd'uy caissier demain cassé: Prov. *To day in request, to morrow cassed.*
Casse-loix. *Lawes-infringing, disorderlie, exorbitant, outragious.*
Casse-moeurs. *Manners-breaking, rude, sauage, vnciuile.*
Casse-mussaux. *Cheese-cakes; or, a kind of thick, and three-cornered, or horned cakes, made of butter, egges, and cheese.*
Casse-noix: m. *A cracke-nut, or nut-cracker; also, a kind of little mountaine Daw, speckled, as an old Starling, all ouer with white.*
Casse-pot: m. *A sport wherein (the gamesters standing in rowes) one tosseth an earthen pot at another, who if he catcheth it not, falling it breakes, and hee forfeyteth.*
Casser. *To breake, burst, crash in peeces, quash asunder; also, to casse, casseere, discharge, turne out of seruice, depriue of entertainment; also, to infringe, annull, cancell, abrogate.*
Casser la noisille. *To cracke the nut; also, to cogge a Dye.*
La langue humaine n'a point d'os, & casse poictrine & dos. *A Prouerbe expressing the force of a malicious, enraged, or infected tongue.*
Qui a des noix il en casse, & qui n'en a il s'en passe: Prov. *Many, when they haue superfluities, can vse them, and when they haue none, can want them.*
Casserie: f. *A breaking, or quashing; a discharging; an infringing, or cancelling.*
Casserins: m. *Tills, drawers, or boxes in a presse, or cabinet.*
Casseron: m. *The Sleeue, or Calamarie; a fish, thats somewhat longer than the Cuttle, or Sea-cut, but otherwise resembles her; also, a vessell somewhat like a posnet, but without feet.*
Cassetin: m. *A little chest, casket, or cabinet; small forcer, cash, or counter; box, till, or drawer.*
Cassette: f. *A little shallow box, case, or vessell made of boords to put flowers, or branches of small trees in; also, a small casket, chest, cabinet, or forcer; also, a box, till, drawer; also, a small coffin, or shrine; also, a little trough for birds meat; also, a little frying pan.*
Casseur: m. *A breaker, burster, quasher; casser; canceller.*
Casseure: f. *The battering, or cracking of a vessell; any breaking, or bursting in peeces; also, a cassing, discharging, cancelling.*
Cassidonie: f. *A Cassidonie; a base, and brittle stone, of small value, though it shine like fire; also, a kind of excellent marble.*
Cassier. *The tree that beares the fruit* Casia.
Cassignon: m. *A pump, or thin-soled shooe.*
Cassine: f. *A banketing house; a graunge, out-house, or Summer-house in the fields; also, a little ware-house; also, a little Terrace-garden, or garden before a window.*
Cassoire: f. *A whip:* ¶Pic.
Cassole: f. *A coffin, box, or casket for perfumes; &c; also, as* Casole.
Cassolette. *A little chest, coffin, box, or casket to put sweet, or precious things in; also, a kind of smal pot with a narrow mouth, resembling a perfuming pot; also, a little pipkin, or posnet.*
Cassolle. *as* Casole; *or* Cassole.
Casson: m. *A great chest, binne, hutch, or standard.*
Cassonade: f. *Powder Sugar; especially, such as comes from* Brasile.
Cassure. *as* Casseure.
Castadour: m. *A Pioner.*
Castagnettes: f. *Finger-knackers, wherewith Players, &c, make a prettie noyse in some kind of daunces.*
Castagneux: m. *The little water-fowle, called a Dobchicke, or Dydopper.*
Castagnole: f. *A big finned, and chestnut-coloured sea-fish, in season about the Spring time, but then withall so common, that the better sort of people care not for it:* ¶Marseillois.
Castagnon. *A certaine fish that maketh a nest in the water; See* Roquau.
Castaign: m. aigne. *Chestnut-coloured; of, or like a chestnut.*
Castaigne: f. *A scallop-like peece of yron in the midst, or mouth, of an old fashioned bit.*
Castaloigne. *A Spanish couerlet, or rug.*
Caste. *Looke* Chaste.
Castillan: m. *A Spanish waight proportionable vnto the* Peso, *which in gold comes to viij.s. sterling, in siluer to iiij.s. or thereabouts.*
Castillaniser. *To imitate or affect Spanish fashions, or humors; to play the Spaniard; (hence) also, to speake big, stand on proud tearmes, take verie much vpon him.*
Castille: f. *Castile (the noblest part of Spaine;) also, contention, debate, brabling, altercation; whence,* Ils sont en Castille. *There is a iarre betwixt them; and;*
Prendre la castille pour autruy. *To vndertake another mans quarrell.*
Pierre de castille. *Lime-stone.*
Castillier: m. *The wild Gooseberrie shrub.*
Caston: m. *The beazill, collet, or head of a ring, &c; wherein the stone is enchaced.*
Castor: m. *The beast called a Beuer.*
Castorée: m. *as* Castoreum.
Castoreum. *The stinking oyle of Beuers stones; or rather an oylie liquor, contained in two pouches which cleaue vnto either side of the Groine of both male, and female, Beuers; (each of those pouches being as big as a large henne egge, whereas the stones of the male are no bigger than a cocks stones, and one fastened vnto his backbone.)*
Castrametation. *The pitching, or measuring out, of a campe.*
Castromantie. *Read* Gastromantie: ¶Rab.

Casuel : m. elle : f. *Casuall, accidentall; vncertaine, transitorie; happening by chance.*
Parties casuelles. *The sale of Offices, or the reuenue which the king makes thereof; Seeke* Partie.
Casuellement. *Accidentally, casually, by hap, or hab-nab; vncertainly; transitorily.*
Casuiste : m. *A casuist; one that writes of the cases of conscience.*
Catachrese : f. *The abuse, or necessarie vse of one word for lacke of another more proper.*
Catachrestique. *Abusiue; or vsed, though improper, for want of that which would be more proper.*
Catadoupes. *as* Catadupes.
Catadupes. *The falls of Nilus; or, certaine high places where that riuer violently falling, makes a roaring, or horrible noise.*
Cataglottiser. *To kisse with the tongue.*
Cataglottisme. *A kisse, or kissing with the tongue.*
Catagmatique : com. *Of, or belonging to broken bones, or the breaking of bones; also, healing, or closing such breaches.*
Catalepsie : f. *A disease comming of the braine, distempered with drinesse, and cold.*
Catalogue : m. *A Catalogue, list, rowle, Register, Kalender, enumeration, recension, recitall of names, matters, &c.*
Catalongne : f. *A (white) Spanish rug; or, a course couerlet of* Catologna.
Cataminy. *Womens flowers.*
Cataplasme : m. *A cataplasme, or poultis; a (soft, or moist) plaister.*
Cataplasme de chair de vautour avec les vifs. *Wee say, a plaister of warme guts (wherein leacherie is meant.)*
Catapuce grande. *The hearbe Kicke, or Ticke,* Recinus, Palma Christi.
Catapuce petite. *Garden Spurge.*
Catapulte : f. *A sling, or warlike engine, whereout great arrowes, or darts were shot.*
Cataracte : f *A violent fall of waters from a high and steepe place; also, a strong yron-bound chest, open in the top, and set with pikes in the bottome, thereby to sticke fast, and steadily where it is to stand; (vsed especially in water-workes;) also, a Cataract, or web in the eye.*
Catarré. *See* Catarrhé.
Catarrhe : m. *A rhewme, or catarre.*
Catarrhé : m. ée : f. *Troubled with rhewme.*
Catarrheux : m. euse : f. *Rhewmaticke, full of catarres, or of the rhewme.*
Catastre. *as* Cadastre.
Catastrophe. *A Catastrophe, conclusion, last act, or part of a play; the shutting vp of a matter; also, th'vtter ruine, subuersion, destruction, fatall, or finall, end of.*
Cateclisme. *A deluge, illuvion, or inundation :* ¶Rab.
Catefique : com. *Sad, heauie, sorrowfull, in melancholie, full of pensiuenesse, and hanging downe the head withall; (vsed in my Author (by one that would haue spoken learnedly) for short winded, or troubled with the Tisicke.)*
Catagide. *An ayrie inflamation :* ¶Rab.
Categorique : com. *Cathegoricall; plaine, authenticall, alreadie resolued on.*
Categoriquement. *Cathegorically, plainely, roundly, without wrangling, to the purpose.*
Catel. *A chattell; or, a thing, which (though of it selfe it be immouable) is diuided, deuised, and held, as a mouable; or as* Cateud.
Catelongne : f. *as* Catelonne.
Catelonne : f. *A white Spanish rug; or, a course, and rough couerlet of* Catalogna *(in Spaine.)*
Catepleure : f. *A crosse sayle; (such as is vsed in Carauels, Gallies, Hoyes, &c;) a smacke, or mizzen sayle.*
Caterolle : f. *A rabbets nest; or, the hole wherein a (Doe) conie keeps, and feeds her yong ones.*
Caterve : f. *A rout, crue, band, troupe, vncertaine number, confused multitude.*
Cateud. *A chattell; or, not onely a mouable (which may follow a bodie, and be remoued from place to place) but also, any immouable, that is no inheritance.*
Cateul. *as* Catel.
Cathartique. *A purgatiue, or euacuatiue; a purging medicine.*
Cathechiser. *To catechise.*
Cathedral : m. ale : f. *Cathedrall; of, or belonging to, a Cathedrall church; and hence;*
Esglise cathedrale. *A Minster, or Cathedrall church.*
Cathedrant : m. ante : f. *Sitting as Iudge, or moderator.*
Cathedratique. *A certaine fee, or duetie, belonging to a Bishop when he is first inuested into his sea.*
Cathegorie : f. *A predicament.*
Cathelane. *The name of an excellent plum; whereof there are three kinds, the greene, white one, and violet one.*
Cathene : f. *A chaine; whence;* Mat de cathene. *A furious, or enraged foole.*
Catheretique : com. *Eating, or gnawing away superfluous, and ouer-eminent flesh, or skin.*
Catherinaire. *The hearbe Tobacco.*
Catherine. *The bramble berrie, blacke-berrie; dewberrie; the berrie of the haire bramble, or heath bramble.*
Catherinettes : f. *Certaine prettie flowers (lesse than pinkes) growing in clusters, or many together on one stalke.*
Cathet : m. Cathete : f. *Perpendicular, plumpe downe*
Catheux. *A kind of mouables, although they adhere to the soyle, or be fastened to a house.*
Catholicon. *A certaine composition in Physicke, so tearmed, because it purges all kind of humors.*
Catholique : com. *Catholicke, vniuersall, generall.*
Catholisation : f. *The being, or becomming a Catholicke.*
Catholizer. *To catholikize it, play the Catholicke, become a Catholicke.*
Cati : m. ie : f. *Clapped close vnto, thrust hard together; hard, or close wouen; (for it is a weauers tearme.)*
Catilinisme. *Catilinisme, conspiracie.*
Catimini. *In corners, vnder-hand, in bugger mugger.*
Catir. *To close, to settle, to thrust hard together, in weauing; (for it is a weauers tearme.)*
Catoblepe : f. *A kind of Basiliske, or venomous worme, which with her sight kils a mile off.*
Catoire. *A bee-hiue.*
Catonien : m. enne : f. *Graue, seuere; grim, austere; censuring euery bodie.*
Catons. des ca. *Catkins, cattails, aglets, or aglet-like blowings of nut-trees, &c.*
Catopromantie : f. *Diuination by a looking glasse.*
Catouiller. *as* Chatouiller; *To tickle :* ¶Pic.
Cattel. *A chattell, or mouable :* ¶Wallon.

Droict

Droict du meilleur cattel. A Heriot: the best beast a Tenant hath, at the time of his death, due vnto his Landlord.

Cavailler. as Cavallier.

Cavain: m. A hole, caue, hollownes, hollow place, hollow way.

Cavalcade: f. A riding, or, a road of horse; whence; Faire la cavalcade. To course, or raunge vp & downe on horsebacke.

Cavalcador. A Horseman, a Rider.

Cavale: f. A mare.

Cavaler. To staulke, to dog; See Cavaller.

Cavalet: m. A long hollow sticke, through which they vse, in some places, to blow the fire, in stead of bellowes.

Cavalier: m. A horseman, or man of armes; a caualeere; also, a gallant; a noble, or worthie, fellow.

Cavalin: m. A litle horse.

Cavalle: f. A mare.

Cavalié: m. ée. f. Ridden; trauelled on; toyled; also, staulked, or dogged.

Caváller. To ride; also, to trauell, toyle, vse like, or as, a horse; also, to staulke, or dog.

Cavallerie: f. Horsemanship; also horsemen.

Cavallet des planches. The highest, or most-raised, part of garden-beds.

Cavallette. A kind of Locust.

Cavallier: m. A high platforme in a fortresse, to plant great peeces on; also, as Cavalier.

Cavallin. as Cavalin.

Cavalot. A certein coyne worth about iij.s. also, a nag, or little horse.

Caubare: m. A sandie coulored and verie venomous serpent, of a cubits length.

Caucheaux. Taxes payed vnto Lords in Henault towards the maintaining of common bankes, or causeyes.

Cauchemare. The disease called the Night-mare.

Cauche-poulet, or Cauche-vieille, as Cauchemare.

Caucher. To hatch, or sit on; to broode, or sit ouer; as hennes do their chickens; or, as Cauquer; to tread a henne.

Cauciage. as, Caucheaux.

Caudataire: com. A traine-bearer; one that beares vp the traine of a great person.

Caudelée: f. A cawdell: (in la Beausse.)

Cauderet: m. A hot bath; called so in the countrey of Bearn, where Chaude is pronounced, Caude.

Caudice: m. The stocke, stumpe, or bodie of a tree, or shrub.

Cave: f. A caue, cellar, vault, or hollow place in the ground.

Eau beniste de cave. Wine; strong drinke.

Marier la cave & le puis. To mingle wine and water together.

Cauë: f. A Chough, or Iacke-daw: ¶Pic.

Cavé. Hollowed, made hollow; digged into.

Caveau: m. A litle caue, or sellar.

Cavechure: f. A haulter; or, thing to haulter with: ¶Pic.

Caveçon: m. A cauechin, or cauesson, for a horses nose.

Cavedal: m. The principall summe lent out to vse.

Cavelade: f. A kind of ray-fish of a verie hard substance, (and therefore none of the daintiest.)

Cavelot: m. A prop, stay, or tresse: ¶Pic.

Cavement: m. A hollowing, or making hollow; an excauation; a digging into.

Cavenne de bergier: f. a Shepheards cote; litle cottage, or cabine made of turues, straw, boughes, or leaues.

Caver. To hollow, or make hollow; to dig into.

Cavereau: m. A little caue, or sellar.

Caverne: f. A denne, cauerne, grot; hollow place; lurking hole, priuie corner.

Caverneau: m. A little caue, or cauerne.

Caverneux: m. euse: f. Hollow, full of dennes, caues, holes; also, dwelling in caues, abiding in dennes, lurking in holes.

Cavesanne: f. A cauesan, false-raine, or head-straine (commonly of silke) to lead, or hold, a horse by.

Cavesche: f. The head (barbarously.)

Cavesne. Frowardly. (v.m.)

Cavesot: m. A Pole-head, or Bull-head; the little black vermine whereof toads, and frogs do come.

Cavessane. as Cavesanne.

Cavessine: f. A martingale for a horse.

Cavesson. as Caveçon.

Cavette: f. A little sellar; also, a little caue, denne, vault, hole, vnder ground.

Caüette: f. A Chough, or Jack-daw: ¶Pic.

Caveure: f. A hole, a hollow; a hollowing.

Cauhare. See Caubare.

Cavier. Seigneur c. A Landlord, or Lord of the soyle, who hath low iurisdiction ouer his tenants.

Cavillateur: m. A wrangler, cauiller, contentious fellow.

Cavillation. A cauill; a wrangling proposition, ouerthwart reason; also, a cauilling.

Cavillatoire. Wrangling, cauilling.

Caviller. To cauill, wrangle, reason crossely, speake ouerthwartly.

Cavillon. A kind of little Mullet.

Cavin: m. A hollow way, or dry brooke.

Cavine: f. The bottome of the mouth wherein the root of the tongue is.

Cavité: f. A cauitie, hollownesse; hollow way; or hollow place.

Caule: m. The stalke, or stemme of an hearbe; also, the hearbe Colewort.

Caulebasse: f. A gourd; or, a bottle made of the rind thereof.

Caulodis: m. Cabbidges.

Cault. as Chaud; Hot: ¶Pic. also, as Caut; craftie.

Caumas. Hot: ¶Gasc.

Cauné. The name of a kind of vine.

Caune. A certaine fish, not much vnlike vnto a Pearch.

Cauny. as Peneux (at Tours.)

Cauque: f. A tent (for a wound;) and hence;

Quand la fille pese vn auque on luy peut mettre la cauque: Prov.

Cauqué: m. ée: f. Trodden, as a henne; tented, as a wound.

Cauquemare. as Cauchemare: ¶Pic.

Cauquer. To tread a henne, as a cocke doth: ¶Norm. also, to tent a wound: ¶Gasc.

Cauquier. as Cauquer: ¶Pic.

Causaian: m. A wrangler, brangler, brabling or litigious person.

Causateur: m. A Suiter, a partie contending; a partie in a suit, or in law.

Causativement. Litigiously; also, causatiuely, or, for a cause.

Cause: f. A cause, reason, or occasion; also, a case, matter, businesse, or suit in law.

Tel a bonne cause qui est condemné: Pro. *A good cause often speeds but badly; or right sometimes is condemned as wrong.*

Causer. *To cause; bring, or be the occasion of; also, to contend, wrangle, brawle, striue together in words; also, to prattle, babble, talke idly, reason foolishly, vse much speech to little purpose.*

Causeresse: f. *A scowld, a brabling woman; also, a tatling huswife, pratling gossip.*

Causerie: f. *A pratling, talking, babling; idle speech, vaine talke, tedious discoursing.*

Causeur. *as* Causaïan; *also, a babler, pratler, tatler, iangler, idle talker; one whose tongue neuer rests; also, in old law-bookes) as* Causateur; *a partie in a suit, or in law.*

Causeuse: f. *as* Causeusse.

Causse d'vn Aysement. *The bottome of a iakes; the roome, or place wherein th'ordure lyes.*

Caustique: com. *Causticke; burning, scaulding, scorching the skinne; also, smacking of salt, or, of a sharpe tast.*

Caut: m. caute: f. *Craftie, subtile, wilie, sly; warie, aduised, cunning, circumspect.*

Cauteleusement. *Cautelously, subtily, cunningly, slily, craftily, deceitfully, ouerreachingly.*

Cauteleux: m. euse: f. *Cautelous, deceitfull, guilefull, craftie, cousening; full of sleights, wiles, fetches, reaches.*

Cautelle: f. *A wile, cautell, sleight; a craftie reach, or fetch, guilefull deuise or endeuor; also, craft, subtiltie, trumperie, deceit, cousenage.*

Cauteller. *To deceiue, beguile, cousen, ouerreach.*

Cautement. *Slily, craftily, cunningly, subtily, warily, circumspectly, aduisedly.*

Cautere: m. *A cauter; a searing hot yron; or, (more generally) any thing thats applied to burne, and is burning, or boyling, hot.*

Cautere actuel. *An actuall cauter; such a one as burnes actually, and incontinently; as, scaulding oyle, red-hot mettall; wood through-burnt, &c.*

Cautere à bouton. *The button cauter; smooth, and headed like a button; fit to cauterize a part, whereof the skinne is onely to be opened for an issue.*

Cautere circulaire. *The circular cauter; is made of fiue pointed buttons, set round, or in a ring, thereby to worke the more effectually.*

Cautere claval. *A certain cauter that goes little deeper than the skinne.*

Cautere cultellaire. *The knife cauter; is like a knife with a thicke back, which holding the heat long makes it in working the more effectuall.*

Cautere dactilaire. *The date cauter; so called, because fashioned like a date stone.*

Cautere dorsal. *The backe cauter; or, that kind of knife-like cauter which cuts but on th'one side.*

Cautere emporte-piece. *The wimble-cauter; round, hollow, and cutting; and fit to cauterize, with least flux of bloud, the skinne of the head when tis to be opened by a Trepane.*

Cautere ensal. *The sword-cauter; made like the point of a two-edged sword.*

Cautere olivaire. *The oliue cauter; tearmed so, because made like an oliue stone.*

Cautere à platine. *The plate cauter; a kind of flat cauter, wherewith members cut off are seared, to preuent corruption, and Gangrenes.*

Cautere potentiel. *A potentiall cauter; is any causticke, or burning medicine, salue, or compound, and is tearmed otherwise* Ruptoire, *and* Vesicatoire.

Cautere punctual. *The punctuall, or pointed cauter; is almost square, and altogether sharpe pointed, and fit to open impostumes.*

Cauterisation: f. *A cauterisation, or cauterizing.*

Cauterizé: m. ée: f. *Cauterized; burned, seared, or closed vp with fire, or fierie medicines.*

Cauterizer. *To cauterize; to seare, burne, or close vp with fire, or fire-hot instruments, yrons, oyntments, medicines, &c.*

Cautesse: f. *as* Cautelle.

Caution: f. *A caution; a suertie, pledge, or bayle for; also, bailing, suertiship, securitie.*

Caution bourgeoise. *Looke* Bourgeois.

O la bonne caution: ¶Iron. *He is an honest man sure; I would not take his word for a button.*

Cautionnage. *as* Caution; *Bailing, suertiship.*

Cautionné: m. ée: f. *Bayled, bound with suertie, that hath put in suerties.*

Cautionner. *To be bound, become suertie, enter into baile.*

Cautionneur: m. *A suertie, pledge, baile.*

Cauvette. *A Chough, or Jacke-daw:* ¶Pic.

Cay. *as* Quay; *Also, a Semy-colon; vsed in the end of an imperfect period, and marked thus* |;|.

Cayer: m. *A quire of written paper; a peece of a written booke diuided into equall parts.*

Caymander. *as* Caimander.

Caymanderie. *as* Caimanderie.

Caymant: m. *A certaine great Lizard, or Crocodile that liues in hot riuers.*

Cayreux: m. euse: f. *Worme-eaten, or moath-eaten.*

Caysseron. *A little chest, or coffer of wood:* ¶Langued.

Caysson: m. *A wooden chest, or coffer:* ¶Langued.

Cazole. *as* Casole.

Cazot: m. *A cote, or small house.*

Ce. *(A Pronowne demonstratiue) this; also, that; also, it; and, (going before any (plurall) termination of the Verbe* Estre) *these, or those: Put after that Verbe, in a question, tis as the Latine Interrogatiue* Ne; *as,* est ce ma femme? sera ce demain qu'il viendra? *Is this my wife or no? or, Is not this my wife? What? will he come to morrow? or, Will he not come to morrow? Looke* Cet.

Ceans. *Here within; in this place; in this house.*

Cebo: m. *A little bulch-backt, mishapen, or ill-fauoured starueling.*

Ceci. *as* Cecy.

Ceciliane: f. *The water chaine of a bit.*

Cecilie: f. *The blindworme, or sloworme.*

Cecine: f. *Beefe growne drie, & red with long hanging by the fire; Martlemas beefe.*

Cecité: f. *Blindnesse, darkenesse; vncertaintie.*

Cecy. *(A Pronowne demonstratiue) this, this here, euen this, this very thing.*

Ceder. *To yeeld, grant, or giue place to; to giue, grant, or make ouer vnto; To leaue, or part with.*

Cedre: m. *The Cedar tree.*

Cedre aigu. *The crimzon, or pricklie Cedar.*

Cedre Lycien. *The rough Cedar of* Lycia.

Cedre Phoenicien. *as* Cedre aigu.

Cedre sapin. *The Cedar of* Libanus; *the great cone-bearing Cedar.*

Grand Cedre. *The same.*

Petit Cedre. *The little, or low Cedar; the crimzon, or pricklie Cedar.*

Cedrelate: m. *The great Cedar.*

Cedriac. *A kind of Pome-citron, called so in* Prouence.

Cedride: f. *The fruit, or berrie of the low Cedar.*

Cedrie: f. *The rozen, or pitch that issues from the great Cedar.*

Cedrin: m. *The siskin; a little yellowish bird that resembles the Canarie bird; but sings more, and more sweetly, than she.*

Cedule: f. *A cedule; a scrowle, hand-writing, or priuat instrument in writing; a bill, obligation, acquitance, &c, signed onely with his hand that passeth it; also, an addition, or scrowle annexed vnto a Testament, or other deed.*

Ceguë: f. *Hemlocks.*

Ceinct: m. *A girdle; a band, or string to hold a thing in with.*

Ceinct: m. cte: f. *Girt, begirt, beset about; enuironed, incompassed, inclosed, held, or hemd, in on all sides.*

Ceinctes: f. *The bends, or wales of a ship; the thicke ledges that compasse th'outsides thereof.*

Ceincture: f. *A girdle; also, the wastband of a hose, or doublet.*

Ceincture ardente. *The fierie Zone, seated betweene the two Tropickes, and ordinarily called*, Torrida Zona.

Ceincture à bourse. *A large, and double belt, &c, vsed in old time, both as a purse, and a girdle.*

Ceincture à crouppiere. *A belt, arming girdle, or sword girdle of the old fashion.*

Ceincture dorée. *A golden girdle; (in former times worne onely by such as went for honest women; for noted whoores were forbidden it; yet,*

Bonne renommée vaut mieux que ceincture dorée: Prov. *A good report excells all ornaments.*

Ceincture de dueil. *See* Dueil.

La ceincture de la Royne. *A certaine pecuniarie right, or taxe due vnto the Queene of France; Looke* Royne.

Abandonner sa ceincture. *A woman to giue ouer the administration, or disposition of her deceased and indebted husbands goods; (a phrase appliable also vnto any Administrator; See* Quiter la ceincture; *apres.)*

Iecter sa ceincture à terre. *Looke* Iecter.

Les mains pendues à leur ceincture: Ils pensent qui leurs femmes tiennent les mains, &c. *They thinke their wiues liue peakingly at home, and pull strawes, plucke daisies, picke rushes, or blow their fingers; generally the phrase imports, an idle, and lazie fashion, or posture.*

Parler dessous la ceincture. *A certaine tricke in prisons; Looke* Parler.

Large de bouche, & estroict de ceincture. *Open mouthed, but close handed.*

Il a perdu sa ceincture. *He hath neither money, nor meanes left him; all is gone.*

Les pouces à la ceincture. *Idly, sloathfully, carelesly; or, as* Les mains penduës à leur ceincture.

Quiter la ceincture. *To breake, to fall bankrupt, to giue ouer his trade, to shut vp his shop windowes; (In old time when men wore their gownes close girt about them (as the Romanes did, and of latter dayes our countrey-men) bankrupts were forbidden wearing of girdles, that the decay of their estate being made notorious, their deceitfull fetches might be preuented; And euen in these times, if a man want a girdle, some will merily demaund, if he be not bankrupt.)*

Ceincturé: m. ée: f. *Girt.*

Ceincturer. *as* Ceindre; *To gird, or put on a girdle.*

Ceincturette. *A little girdle.*

Ceincturon. *Looke* Ceinturon.

Ceindre. *To gird, begird; enuiron, incompasse, hold, or hem, in on all sides.*

Ceint: m. te: f. *Looke* Ceinct.

Ceinture. *Looke* Ceincture.

Ceinturier: m. *A girdle-maker.*

Ceinturon: m. *A short, or small girdle; also the strap, or side-peece of a paire of hangers.*

Ceisan. *A vassall, or subiect vnto a Lord:* ¶Bearnois.

Cela. *(A Pronowne demonstratiue of the second, and third person) that, euen that; also, the act you wot of.*

Celade: f. *A Sallate, or headpeece.*

Cele. *A kind of preserue.*

Celé: m. ée: f. *Hidden, concealed, kept secret; couered, dissembled.*

Celebration: f. *A celebration, solemnizing, celebrating; also, a renowning; a making famous, or glorious.*

Celebre: com. *Famous, renowmed, glorious, honourable.*

Celebré: m. ée: f. *Celebrated, or solemnized with great assemblies; also, magnified, renowmed, exceedingly honoured.*

Celebrer. *To celebrate, or solemnize, with great assemblies of people; also, to magnifie, make renowmed, spread abroad the reputation, or fame of.*

Celebrité: f. *Celebritie; glorie, honour, renowme, famousnesse, a good name, a great report in the world.*

Celément. *Secretly, couertly, hiddenly, priuily, by stealth.*

Celer. *To hide, conceale, keepe secret, couer, cloake, dissemble.*

Celerier: m. *The Yeoman of a sellar.*

Celerin: m. *A little, yellow-headed, and white-bodied fish, liuing in the sea (and in some lakes) and resembling the Sardinos so neere, that many take it to bee the same.*

Celerité: f. *Celeritie, speedinesse, hast, swiftnesse, lightnesse, nimblenesse.*

Celeste: com. *Celestiall, heauenly, diuine.*

Paön celeste. *A wild Peacocke.*

Celestiel: m. elle: f. *Celestiall, heauenlie.*

Celeume. *The showt, or noyse that Mariners make when they weigh anker, or do any other office in the ship with ioyned strength; an encouraging sound.*

Celiac: m. aque: f. *Whence;* Le flux celiac. *A continuall thinne flux caused by the weakenesse of the stomacke, and accompanied with fretting, or paine in the belly.*

Maladie celiaque. *An extreame weakenesse, and disabilitie of digestion, in the stomacke, accompanied with a most thinne, or waterie flux.*

Celiaque: com. *Troubled with belly-ache, or fretting, and a continuall flux proceeding from the weakenesse of the stomacke.*

Celibat: m. *Single-life; the condition, or estate of an vnmaried person.*

Celibe: com. *Vnmaried, single; solitarie, alone.*

Celidoine: f. *The hearbe Celandine, Tetterwort, Swallowort; Looke* Chelidoine.

Celier: m. *A sellar, or (more properly) a roome, aboue ground, to lay wine in; for your vault vnder-ground, is better expressed by,* Cave.

Celique. *as* Celeste.

Celivage: com. *Heauen-faire; heauen-affecting; wending,*

-ding, or bending, towards heauen.

Celle : f. *The house, or mansion of, and a communitie of goods among, villeines, or persons of a seruile condition; their children also, being at schoole, or in seruice, by their parents appointment, are said to be,* en la Celle.

Celle. *The feminine of* Celuy; *she.*

Cellerage. *Sellerage; a duetie payed for the laying of wine into sellars.*

Cellerier : m. *A Butler, Drawer; Yeoman of the Sellar.*

Celoce. *A kind of swift Brigantine, or Pinace, deuised, at first, by the Rhodians :* ¶Rab.

Celsitude : f. *Celsitude, highnesse, excellencie; (tearmes conferred on Princes.)*

Celuy : m. celle : f. *The same.*

Celuy-là. *That same (man, &c.)*

Cement : m. *Cement; a strong, and cleauing morter, made (for the most part) of tyles, potshards, glasse, flint, the drosse of yron, &c, beaten to dust, and incorporated with lime, oyle, grease, rozen, and water; Looke* Ciment.

Cemetiere : m. *A churchyard.*

De nouveau medecin cemetiere bossu : Prov. *An vnexperienced Physitian fattens the churchyard.*

Veau mal cuict, & poules creuds font les cemetieres bossus : Prov. *Raw veale, and chickens make fat churchyards.*

Cemiterre. *A Scimitar, or Turkish sword.*

Cenacle. *Looke* Senacle.

Cencer. *To recken, esteeme, account among his reuenue; to number, tell, muster; also, to rate, assesse, taxe, value, prize.*

Cenchre : m. *A greenish Serpent, or Snake, whose bodie is couered all ouer with skales, and spots resembling Millet seeds; (those that be stung by him fall into a Letargie, and sleeping, die;) or as;*

Cenchrite. *A greene, and swift-gliding Serpent, big about the head, verie small towards the tayle, and full of Mill-resembling spots (onely) on the bellie; or as* Cenchrè.

Cenchryne. *as* Cenchrite.

Cencive. *as* Cens; *Also an inheritance held by, or subiect vnto,* Cens; *also, the title of, or a Tenure by,* Cens.

Cendre : f. *Ashes; cynders; imbers.*

Cendre gravelée. *Ashes made of the burnt lees, or dregs of wine.*

Cendre des Orfevres. *as* Cendrées des Orfevres.

Le jour des Cendres. *Ashwednesday.*

Quittons les cendres. *Lets quit our vnworthie stay, or sluggish life, at home.*

Cendré : m. ée : f. *Ashie, ash-like; of ashes; also, ash-coloured.*

Cendrée : f. *A melting, or purifying of siluer, &c, in ashes; also, a wedge, barre, lumpe, or ball of siluer, &c, so melted; also, an ash-heape; and, a place, or thing, burnt vnto ashes.*

Cendrées, & laveures des Orfevres. *The ashie mammockes, or bits of mettall, and drosse found, after a melting, in a Goldsmithes furnace, and among the sweepings of his shop; These the Finor puts into a vessell, and hauing washed them, pickes out that which is worth ought from among them.*

Argent de cendrée. *Fine, or purified siluer (of* xj.d. *eighteene grains finesse) which the finors make at first into wedges, and marke them with their puncheons, thereby vndertaking for the goodnesse, and value thereof.*

Cendrée sauvage. *Wild Marierome, groue Mariorome, Organ, Origanie.*

Cendreux : m. euse : f. *Ashie, full of ashes; also, pale, wanne, lew, of a dead, colour or complexion; also, lither, sluggish, idle; whose nose is euer hanging ouer the fire; and hence;*

Au Chat cendreux jamais ne tombe rien en gueule : Prov. *The idle house-doue neuer getteth ought.*

Cendrier : *A maker, or seller of ashes; also, a place to keepe, or corner to throw, ashes in; also, a sluggard, slowbacke, idlesbie; house-doue; one that sits lurking in the chimney corner.*

Cendroyé : m. ée : f. *Burnt vnto, or turned into, ashes.*

Cendroyer. *To burne vnto, or turne into, ashes.*

Cene : f. *A supper; (a word not much vsed but by those of the Religion, who thereby meane, the Lords Supper.)*

Cenglade : f. *A yerke, lash, or stripe with a girth.*

Cengle : f. *A girth (for a horse;) Looke* Sangle.

Il en avoit tout le long des cengles. *Hee was coursed, cudgelled, or chidden soundly; also, hee had taken in his full lading of liquor.*

Cenglé : m. ée : f. *girt, girded.*

Cengler. *To gird, or girth.*

Cenotaphe : m. *A monument, hearse, or emptie tombe erected in memorie, or to the honour, of a great Person.*

Cens : m. *Rent of Assise, Quit rent, old rent, chiefe rent; the first pecuniarie charge thats layed on conquered, or vnrented land, as a signe, or in acknowledgement, of the direct Seignorie of him that grants it : This charge had it originall from the first conquest of* Gallia *by the French; whose Princes giuing whole territories vnto their Captaines, they made a diuision thereof among their souldiours, and the naturall inhabitants of the countrey, on condition, that those should assist, and attend them in the warres (which condition, being a trust, they intitled,* Fief) *and that these should till their land, and pay vnto them for it such yearely rents, or tributes, as they had formerly yeelded the Romanes (by whome those rents, &c, were tearmed* Census;) *and thus this charge imposed at first as a resemblance of former seruitude, continues to this day a marke of a base, or seruile, Tenure.*

Cens capital. *A chiefe, or capitall* Cens; *chiefe rent.*

Cens à cherchage. *Which must bee demaunded by Lord* Censuel, *or his deputie, of the Tenant, or detayner of the inheritance, that yeelds it; therein different from that* Cens *which is payable at a place, and day, certaine.*

Cens à cher pris. *A racked* Cens, *which verie neere counteruailes the yearely reuenue of the land, and which being extraordinarie, and chargeable to the tenant he is thereby discharged of the* Ventes, *and* Relevoisons, *which the ordinarie* Cens *carries with it.*

Cens à iour nommé. *Looke* Nommé.

Cens mort. *A* Cens *seck, or dead* Cens; *a Quit rent; which, besides it selfe, yeelds the Lord no manner of profit, or aduantage, at the death, or change of the tenant; (This* Cens *is no signe of direct Seignorie.)*

Cens à queste, ou requerable. *as* Cens à cherchage.

Cens rogo. *The same.*

Cens truant. *A* Cens *secke, or dead* Cens; *a Quit* Cens, *or Quit rent; of no profit, or aduantage (other than what comes by it selfe) to the Lord, or owner thereof.*

Chef Cens. *A chiefe* Cens, *or chiefe rent.*

Cher cens. *Looke* Cens à cher pris.

Droict cens. *The first, capitall, or chiefe* Cens; *tearmed so belike, because tis a marke of direct Seignorie.*

Gros cens. *A surcharge of* Cens *vpon a second grant of land, which by reason thereof stands doubly charged;* viz. *both with the first* Cens, *which euer followes it; and with this, which euer exceeds the first; and is proportionable in some respects vnto a Fee-farme rent.*

Menu cens. *The first, capitall, or chiefe* Cens; *tearmed so because tis commonly payed by pence, and halfepence; or exceeds not a verie small proportion.*

Premier cens; &, pur cens. *The same; or, a Quit rent, a chiefe rent; a* Cens *of Assise.*

Censable: com. *For which, or to whom,* Cens *is due; also, which may be charged with* Cens.

Cense: m. *as* Cens; *also, a generall, and publicke valuation of priuate mens goods, and possessions.*

Cense: f. *A farme; also, Fee-farme.*

Censé: m. ée: f. *Reckoned, esteemed, accounted; numbred, mustered, among; also, rated, sessed, taxed, valued, prized.*

Censeable: com. *For which, or to whom,* Cens *is due; also, which may be charged with a* Cens.

Censer. *To reckon, esteeme, account among his reuenue; to number, tell, muster; also, to rate, assesse, taxe, value, prize.*

Censeur: m. *A Censor; or Comptroller; a Master of discipline, reformer of manners, punisher of disorders.*

Censier: m. *A farmer, or Fee-farmer; one that payes a Quit rent, or chiefe rent for the land he holds; (generally) one that holds by the title of* Cens.

Censier: m. ere: f. *Of* Cens; *yeelding* Cens; *or, to whom* Cens *is due.*

Iustice censiere. *as* Iustice Censuelle.

Censif: m. *An inheritance, or estate in land thats held by* Cens; *also, the Seigneurie thereof.*

Censif: m. iue: f. *Censiue; held by the title of* Cens; *or for which* Cens *is due.*

Censive: f. *as* Cens; *Also, an inheritance held by, or subiect vnto,* Cens; *also, the title of, or a tenure by,* Cens.

Censivement. *By* Cens; *by the title of* Cens.

Censivier. *A farmer, or fee-farmer; one that payes a Quit rent, or chiefe rent for the land he holds; (generally) one that holds by the title of* Cens.

Censorin: m. ine: f. *Censor-like, censorious; austere, seuere, controlling, vnpartially correcting.*

Censuel: m. elle: f. *Censuall; of, or belonging to* Cens; *held by the title of* Cens; *whereto* Cens *is due; in regard whereof* Cens *is paied.*

Iustice censuelle. *Base, or low iurisdiction, belonging to a Lord by reason, or for the recouerie, of his* Cens, *and Censuall rights.*

Retraict censuel. *Seeke* Retraict.

Censure: f. *A censure; admonition, animaduersion, reproofe, reprehension (that includes a punishment;) a denouncement, or sentence, of punishment.*

La censure tourmente les Pigeons, laissant aller les Corbeaux libres: Prov. *Censure tormenteth Doues, and freeth Rauens (so comes weake innocencie to the blocke, whilest powerfull wickednesse is winked at.)*

Censurer. *To censure, controll, admonish, reproue with authoritie; to pronounce, or denounce a heauie sentence against (an offendor.)*

Cent. *A hundred.*

Centaure: m. *A Centaure; one that is halfe a man, and halfe a horse.*

Centaurée. *The hearbe Centorie.*

Centaurée majeur. *Great Centorie.*

Centaurée mineur. *Small Centorie, common Centorie.*

Petite centaurée. *The same.*

Centeine: f. *A hundred; the number, or proportion of a hundred; a Band, or companie of a hundred.*

Par centeines. *By hundreds, hundred by hundred, in great number, many together.*

Centenaire: com. *Of a hundred, containing the number of a hundred, of a hundred yeares continuance, a hundred yeares old.*

Centenier: m. *A Centurion, a Captaine, or Commaunder of a hundred souldiors, &c.*

Centesimer. *To count, or cull out, by hundreds.*

Centidoine: f. *Centinodie; Knot-grasse, Way-grasse, Birds-tongue, Swines-grasse, Bloud-wort, S. Innocents hearbe.*

Centiesme: m. *A hundreth; a rate, or proportion, of a hundreth; a bundle, or troupe, containing a hundreth.*

Droict de centiesme. *The hundreth part of a subiects goods, or the value thereof, exacted by some Soueraigne Lords.*

Centiesme: com. *The hundreth of.*

Centine d'une rouë: f. *The boxe (or hole) of the naue of a wheele.*

Centoire: f. *The hearbe Centorie; as* Centaurée.

Centon: m. *A rapsodie; a confused heape, or collection of many different things; a mingle mangle of many matters in one booke.*

Centonifique: com. *Confusedly heaping, or hudling many seuerall things together; making one worke of many different peeces.*

Centre: m. *A center; the verie middest, or point in the middest, of any round, or circled thing.*

Centurie: f. *A centurie, or hundreth of; also, a certaine quantitie of, or measure for, ground, amounting to two hundreth* Iugera, *or furlongs.*

Cep: m. *The stocke of a tree, or plant; also, a log, or clog, of wood; such a one as is hung about the neck of a ranging curre.*

Des ceps. *A paire of Stockes for malefactors; also, (but lesse properly) shackles, boults, fetters, &c.*

Cepée: f. *An hearbe thats verie like vnto Brooke-lime, or water Pimpernell (if it be not the same.)*

Cependant. *Neuerthelesse, yet notwithstanding, yet for all that;* Cependant que. *The whilest that.*

Ceper vne muraille. *To vndermine, dig, breake, or cut downe a wall, at the foot.*

Cephale: m. *The Pollard fish.*

Cephaleonomanie. *Diuination by an asses head broyled on coles:* ¶Rab.

Cephalique: com. *Good for the head, curing a diseased head; of, or belonging to, the head.*

Veine cephalique. *The head Veine; Locke* Veine.

Cepier: m. *A goaler; one that lookes to the stocks; or hath charge of them, or of those that are in them.*

Cepride: m. *Baulme.*

Ceramite. *Potters earth*: ¶Rab. *also, a pretious stone of the colour of a tyle.*

Ceranvienne: f. *A certaine pretious stone thats alwaies verie moist, and seemes to sweat.*

Ceraste. *A most venomous serpent, called otherwise (and the more properly in French)* Serpent cornu; *See* Cornu.

Cerat: m. *A Plaister made of Waxe, Gummes, &c, and certaine oyles; wee also, call it, a Cerot, or Searecloth.*

Cerat sandlin. *The purple clout wherewith Cookes dye their Gellie; or, a Searecloth made of Saunders.*

Ceraunobule. *Thundering with Bulls; as the Pope.*

Cerceau: m. *A circle, ring; hoope; a round, or a round compasse; also, the Sercell, or Sarcell (feather) of a hawkes wing.*

Cerceau craquetant. *The ierting circle which a Peacocke makes with his taile, or a Turkie-cocke with his wings.*

Cercelé: m. ée: f. *Hooped; incircled; compassed with a round or circle; streaked, or scored round as a circle.*

Cerceler. *To hoope, incircle; compasse with a round, or circle; streake, or score, round as a circle.*

Cercelle: f. *(The water-fowle called) a Teale.*

Cerceller. *as* Cerceler.

Cercerelle: f. *A rattle, clicket, or clapper; also, a kastrell, fuckwind, steingall; also, a Teale.*

Cercereulle. *as* Cercerelle *(in the last sence.)* (v.m.)

Cerche: f. *A search, inquisition, inquirie, seeking after.*

Cerche ralongée. *Th'instrument wherewith Masons round, and fashion, pillars.*

Cerché: m. ée: f. *Searched, sought; hunted, inquired after; felt, groped, sounded; traced.*

Cerchefi. *Looke* Sercifi.

Cerchement: m. *A searching, seeking, hunting, inquiring after; also, an inquisition, or examination.*

Cercher. *To seeke, search, hunt, looke, or inquire after; to trace, feele, grope, sound.*

Cercher le broust. *To hunt after feasts, to play the parasite, or smell-feast.*

Cercher chappe cheute. *Looke* Chappe.

Cercher midi ou il n'est qu'onze heures. *To looke for a thing which is not, or, before it is, to bee had; also, to make faults of trifles; also, to seeke after his owne hurt, or to purchase his owne harme.*

Cercher en vn mouton cinq pieds. *Curiously to looke for more at a mans hands than hee is able to performe.*

Cercher noises pour noisettes. *To pick a quarell out of trifling occasions.*

Qui m'aura perdu ne m'aille cercher en ce païs là. *(A phrase, whereby one signifies his vtter mislike of a countrey.)*

Chacun cerche son semblable: Prov. *Euerie person seekes his Peere.*

Il cerche trop bas la charité qui fouille prez des fesses: Prov. *The charitie is too base that stoopes so low as the buttockes; or, hee lookes too low for charitie that gropes about the buttocks.*

Le fol cerche son malheur: Prov. *The foole indeuors to make himselfe vnhappie; or, the foole studies his owne mishap.*

Qui a affaire de feu le doit cercher; &; qui a besoing de feu le cerche avec le doigt: Prov. *We say, (with some little difference) Let them that bee acold blow at the cole.*

Cercheur: m. *A seeker, searcher; inquirer, tracer, hunter, looker after; a feeler, groper, sounder.*

Cercle: m. *A circle; a compasse, a round; also, a hoope for caske; Looke* Cicle.

Cercle finissant. *Th'Orizon; a circle that diuideth the visible part of heauen from that which to vs is inuisible.*

Cercle vertical. *Seeke* Vertical.

Il y quarre le cercle. *His squaring is there out of square.*

On ne cognoist point le vin aux cercles: Pro. *The goodnes of wine is not known by the fashion, or strength of the hoops that begird it.*

Cerclé: m. ée: f. *incircled, compassed; begirt; bound, or hooped about.*

Cerclet: m. *A little circle; round, compasse; hoope; also, a small wreath of Ozier twigs, to set vnder a dish on a table.*

Cerclet à feu. *A wreath, or circlet of wild-fire; a fire-worke made like a wreath, or circlet.*

Cerclouëre: f. *A paire of weeding tongues.*

Cercot: m. *A sauegard.*

Cercueil: m. *A coffin; also (but not so properly) a beere; also, a tombe, graue, sepulchre.*

Cerebelle, *for* **Cervelle**: f. *The hinder part of the head wherein the memorie is lodged.*

Cerebrin: m. ine: f. *Headie, rash, giddie, according to his owne braine, after his owne fancie, or humor.*

Cerelle: f. *A kind of pleasant perrie, made of the peare* Carisi.

Ceremonial: m. ale: f. *Ceremoniall; of, or belonging to, ceremonies.*

Ceremonie: f. *A ceremonie; a rite, custome, or fashion in, or about, religion.*

Ceremonieusement. *Looke* Cerimonieusement.

Ceremonieux. *Ceremonious; full of ceremonies.*

Cerf: m. *A stag, a red deere; a hart.*

Cerf ramé. *A raine deere.*

Cerf volant. *The great horned beetle, or bull-flie.*

Corne de cerf. *Hartshorne, Sandwort, Buckehorne plantaine, Crowfoot plantaine, hearbe Iuie, or Eve.*

L'herbe au cerf. *Harts-fodder; supposed to bee a kind of wild Parsenip.*

Langue de cerf. *The hearbe Harts-tongue, or stone Harts-tongue; ordinarily mistaken for, and made all one with,* Scolopendria.

Oeil de cerf. *A kind of wild Parsenip, that beares a red flower, and is not ill to be eaten.*

Poil de cerf. *The dunne, sandie, or deere, colour of some horses &c.*

Ronce de cerf. *Rough Bindweed.*

Faire le cerf de. *To passe a thing sleightly ouer, to make no conscience, nor account, of it.*

Au cerf la biere, au sanglier le barbier: Prov. *(So dangerous a beast is an enraged stag.)*

Cerfouëtte. *Looke* Serfouëtte.

Cerfouïr. *To dig the ground about the roots of trees; or as* Sarfouïr.

Cerfueil: m. *The hearbe Charuell, or Cheruill.*

Cerf-volant. *The great horned beetle, or bull-flie.*

Cerille: f. *A small tittle, or addition to the foot of a* C (as

C *(as in ç) which makes it be pronounced as an* S.
Cerimonialement. *Ceremonially, reuerently, religiously.*
Cerimonie. *A ceremonie; a rite, custome, or fashion in, or about, religion.*
Cerimonieusement. *Ceremoniously, with great reuerence, many ceremonies, much ado.*
Cerimonieux: m. euse: f. *Ceremonious; affecting, following, or full of, ceremonies.*
Cerin: m. *as* Serin. *A small bright-greene bird.*
Cerin-perse. *A bright skie-colour.*
Cerisaye: f. *A cherrie garden; an orchard of cherrie trees.*
Cerise: f. *A cherrie.*
Cerises d'outre mer. *The berries of the hearbe Nightshade, called by our Hearbarists, winter cherries.*
Faire d'une cerise trois morceaux. *To eat nicely, feed daintily; to mince it, or make it goodlie.*
C'est folie de manger cerises avec son seigneur: Prov. *No wise man will be very familier with one that is much better, or mightier than himselfe; besides, hee that eates cherries with his master gets not many good ones.*
Le Pigeon saoul trouve les cerises ameres: Pro. *Looke* Pigeon.
Cerisée: f. *The reuenue that comes in, or profit thats made, by cherries.*
Cerisier: m. *A cherrie tree.*
Cerisier bas, ou petit. *The dwarfe cherrie tree.*
Cerisin: m. *The little bird called a Siskin.*
Cerne: m. *A circle, round, compasse; inclosure; a turning round, fetching a compasse, wheeling about.*
Cerné: m. ée: f. *Incircled, compassed with a circle; inuironed, or inclosed round about; also, rounded, compassed, or wheeled about.*
Cerneau: m. *The kernell of a nut, &c.*
Cerneau d'aulx. *A cloue of garlick.*
Cerner. *To incircle, compasse with a circle; inuiron, or inclose round about; also, to make a round, fetch a compasse, wheele about.*
Cerner les arbres. *To make a round slit, or incision into the barkes of trees; to open or cut them round about.*
Cerner des noix. *To crack Wallnuts; or, to open them, and picke out their kernels, with a* Cernoir.
Cernoir: m. *A little blunt, and hulch-backt yron toole, or knife, (of some two fingers length, & hauing a woodden handle about an inch thick, and three fingers long) wherewith countrey people cut ripe wallnuts in two (while they are yet in the shale) and picke out the kernels.*
De l'arbre d'un pressoir le manche d'un cernoir: Prov. *To make of a verie great, a verie small, thing, by often handling, or altering, & euer cutting away, some peece or other, of it.*
Ceroesne. *as* Ceroine.
Ceroine: f. *Any ointment, or plaister, whereof rozen, or wax are the principall ingredients.*
Ceromantie: f. *Diuination, or soothsaying, by wax put into water.*
Cerot: m. *A seare-cloth; or plaister made of wax, gum, or other cleauing simples.*
Cerouënne: f. *Any ointment, or plaister, whereof wax or rozen are the chiefe ingredients.*
Cerquemage. *as* Cerquemanage.
Cerquemanage: m. *An assignement of bounds, a limitation of marches, an appointment of meeres betweene the lands of seuerall (priuate) men; or betweene priuat mens lands, and those which belong to the publike; as commons, high-wayes, riuers; &c.*
Cerquemané: m. ée: f. *Bounded, limited, whose marches are appointed, whose meeres assigned, and set, by publicke Officers.*
Cerquemanement: m. *An assigning of bounds, an appointing of marches, a setting of meeres betweene land and land.*
Cerquemaner. *To limit, assigne, or set meeres, appoint marches, lay out the bounds of land.*
Cerquemaneurs: m. *Certaine sworne Officers, who haue authoritie to set, or plucke vp, meeres and bounds betweene seuerall mens possessions; and to examine, & reforme incroachments made vpon high-wayes, commons, riuers, &c.*
Cerre: m. *Th'vnprofitable wild oke, tearmed, the Holme oke.*
Cerres: f. *as* Serres; *A hawkes talants; also, the pulse called great Chichlings, or flat peason; Looke* Pois Cerre.
Cerres sauvages. *Wild Chichlings, milke Vetches.*
Cerresine: f. *Gumme; or, liquor becomming like rozen, or gumme.*
Certain: m. *A certaintie, certaine truth, surenesse, assurednesse.*
Tesmoing de certain. *A witnesse that assures, or saies he knowes, all he sayes.*
Certain: m. aine: f. *Sure, doubtlesse, vnauoidable; assured, most true, vnfained; approued; cleere, manifest; appointed, determined; firme, steadie, fast; constant, faithfull, trustie.*
Certaines personnes que. *Certaine, or some persons that, &c.*
Certainement. *Certainly, doubtlesly, surely, assuredly, verily, in truth, questionlesse; vnauoydably; cleerely, manifestly.*
Certaineté. *as* Certitude.
Certe. à la certe. *Certainly, doubtlesly, questionlesse.*
Certeau à deux-testes. *The name of a verie tender and delicate peare.*
Certes. *Surely, verily, truly, &c; as* Certainement.
`A certes. *In sooth, in earnest, roundly, throughly, to purpose, without dalliance, or delay.*
Certificateur: m. *A certifier, ascertainer, assurer; also, an Informer, or notice-giuer.*
Certification: f. *A certificat, a passeport; also, a certification, ascertaining, assuring of.*
Certifié: m. ée: f. *Certified, assured, ascertained; informed, or aduertised of; made acquainted with.*
Certifier. *To assure, auouch, ascertaine; also, to certifie, informe, aduertise, or send word of; giue notice, or intelligence, vnto.*
Certioré: m. ée: f. *Certified, informed, aduertised of, made acquainted with.*
Certitude: f. *A certaintie; an assured notice, or true knowledge of.*
Cerve: f. *A Hind.*
Cerveau: m. *The braine.*
Cerveaux à bourlet. *Ignorant Lawyers, dunsicall pleaders, pettifoggers.*
Cerveaux enfroquez. *Monkes, or Fryers.*
Cerveau mal cuict. *A light, giddie, rash, humorous, fantasticall, or ill-digested disposition.*
Petit cerveau. *as* Cervelet.
Avoir le cerveau vn peu gaillard. *To be humorous, toyish, fantasticall, new-fangled.*

Estre

Estre en cerveau. *To be in his right wits; to be stayed, well-aduised, and out of aduise, resolute, or secure; to be prouided against all chances, armed for all essayes, readie for whatsoeuer shall befall.*

Ceruelat: m. *An excellent kind of dry saucidge that resembles our blacke pudding, but that it is somewhat thicker, and shorter; and is eaten could in slices.*

Ceruelet: m. *The hinder part of the braine, next to the nape of the necke; makes but a tenth of the whole, and is diuided from the rest by* Dura, & pia, Mater.

Ceruelin: m. ine: f. *Brainlesse, headdie, wilfull, giddie, fantasticall, harebraind.*

Ceruelle: f. *The braine; or, hinder part of the head wherein the memorie is lodged; the seate of the memorie.*

Ceruelle à double rebras. *A dunce, blockhead, iobernoll, ioulthead, thicke-skinne, dull fellow; one that is obstinately sottish; one into whom no wit can be beaten, no vnderstanding driuen.*

Gens de cervelle, ou (qui sont) bien en cervelle. *Wise, or stayed people; such as haue sound braines, or good heads.*

Tenir en cervelle. *To keepe in awe, or in play; to arme with heed by often allarums; to harrie, hould buisied or in breath.*

Cervelliere: f. *A scull, or sallet, of iron.*

Cervical: m. ale: f. *Belonging to the nape, or hinder part, of the necke.*

Artere ceruicale. *Seeke,* Artere.

Veine cervicale. *A branch of the* Sousclauiere, *which passing along by the transuerse processes of the neck-ioynts, goes vnto the membrane called,* Dura mater, *and ends in it.*

Cervier. Loup Cervier. *See* Loup-cervier.

Cervinespine. *The shrub way thorne, buckthorne, laxatiue ram.*

Cervoise. *Beere*: f.

Ceruse: f. *Ceruse, or, white lead, wherewith women paint; differs from Lithargie (called also, white lead) for this is made of the grossest lead, as it is in the mine; that, of lead refined, out of the mine.*

Ceruseux: m. euse: f. *Full of Ceruse; beplaistered all ouer with fard.*

Ces: m. *A stay, cessing, leauing, forbearing; also, a putting to silence, or forbidding to proceed.*

Ces (*The plurall of* Ce:) *Theis.*

Cesarien: m. enne: f. *Cesar-like; of, or belonging to* Cesar.

Enfantement Cesarien. *The birth of a child, by cutting him out of his mothers womb, without the death of eyther.*

Section Cesarienne. *Such a cutting.*

Cesarine. Tondu à la Cesarine. *Cut or powled round with, or like a dish; (an old fashion yet in vse with some old men.)*

Cesolfié: m. eé: f. *Sad, pensiue; troubled, perplexed, vexed in mind;* ¶Rab.

Cessation: f. *A cessation, ceasing, stay, pause, intermission, discontinuance, resting, or leauing off for a time; a vacation; also, lingering, slacknesse, loitering, sloath.*

Cesse: f. *The same.*

Sans cesse. *Vncessantly, without stint or ceasing, perpetually, continually; also, excessiuely, immoderately, out of all cesse and crie.*

Cessé: m. ée: f. *Ceased, surceased, left off, discontinued, intermitted, forborne, stayed, held backe, or giuen ouer for a time; also, lingered, slackened, loitered.*

Cessement: m. *Looke* Cessation.

Cesser. *To cease, forbeare; stop, stay, pawse, leaue off, giue ouer; to surcease, discontinue, intermit, rest a while, hold backe for a time; also, to linger, loyter, slacken, play the sluggard.*

Cessible: com. *Yeeldable, resignable, abandonnable.*

Cession: f. *Yeelding vp, or giuing ouer; an abandonment of, or departure from; and particularly, a giuing of place.*

Cession des biens. *An abandonment of his owne goods, or a renouncement of his title to another mans, thereby to bee but out of the reach, or danger, of creditors; This must bee done (especially in the first case) by the debtor himselfe (vngirt, and bare headed) in the presence of a full Court: After which hee is not constraynable to pay his creditours more than can bee raysed by the sale of his goods.*

Cessionnaire: com. *A cessionarie; one that abandons, or giues vp his goods as aforesayde (in* Cession de biens) *who though hee looseth his credit thereby, yet is hee not held so base as a bankrupt.*

Cessiouner. *To eat betweene meales; to take an afternoones repast:* ¶Norm.

Cest: m. ceste: f. *as* Cet.

Ceston: m. *A studded girdle, which (in old time) the Bridegroome put about his Bride as soone as they were maried, and tooke off when they went to bed, together.*

Cestrin. *A kind of yellow stone whereof beads are made.*

Cestuy. (*A Pronowne Demonstratiue*) *this man; also, hee.*

Cestuycy. (*With addition of that locall Aduerbe*) *this man here; this verie man, this same man.*

Cesue: f. *The sap of trees; Looke* Seve.

Cesure: f. *A cutting, section, diuision.*

Cet: m. cette: f. *This; that; it; as* Ce; *but with this difference; that whereas* Ce *is put before words that begin with a consonant, or* H *pronounced (as in naturall French it is)* Cet *precedes those which begin with a vowell, or with* H *vnpronounced (as in words derived from the Latine.)*

Cetacé. poisson cetacée. *Of the kind of Whales.*

Cete. *as* Cette; *The feminine of* Cet.

Ceterach: m. *The hearbe Scale-fearne, Stone-fearne, Finger-fearne, Miltewast.*

Cethin. *A kind of wood that corrupts not.*

Cetier de bled. *A quarter of corne; or as* Septier.

Ceton: m. *A rowell for a bruised, or impostumed horse.*

Cetuy. *Looke* Cestuy.

Cevadere: f. *The sprit saile of a ship.*

Ceucheter. *To whisper in the eare.*

Ceve: f. *A whetstone.*

Ceves: f. *Chiues, chibols.*

Cevotes. *The same.*

Chaas. (Monosillab.) *Is the space, and length betweene beame and beame, wall and wall, in building; or a bay of building; also, the lust of kine after the bull; also, Weauers starch.*

Chabins: m. *The sheepe of* Berry *(whose wooll is verie thicke, and as long as goats haire.*

Chable : m. *A cable, or great rope.*
Chable : f. *as* Cable, fem.
Chablis. bois chablis. *Wind-falls; the trees, or branches of trees, which the wind hath ouerthrowne.*
Chabot : m. *The little fish called a Gull, Bullhead, or Millers-thumbe; also, the little water vermine called, a Bullhead.*
Chabre : m. *The Cray-fish tearmed, a Pungar.*
Chabrer. *To reare vpright; or, to rise high before; as a goat that would reach to a bough.*
Chace. *Looke* Chasse.
Chacer. *as* Chasser; *To hunt &c.*
Chaceur. *A hunter, &c; Looke* Chasseur.
Chacie : f. *Blearednesse, or bleare-eyednesse; a running, or waterishnesse of the eyes, accompanied with a painefull shooting, and rednesse.*
Chacieuseté. *as* Chacie *(In extremitie.)*
Chacieux : m. euse : f. *Bleare-eyed; whose eyes are full of water, and bloud-shot.*
Chacun. *(Looke* Chascun*) each one, euerie man.*
Chacunerie : f. *Euery ones owne; that which particularly concernes, or belongs vnto, euery one.*
Chacun à sa chacunerie. *Euerie one to his owne home, or about his owne businesse.*
Chaffauder. *To scaffold, or set vp scaffolds; also, to set vpon scaffolds; or shew vpon a scaffold.*
Chaffault : m. *A scaffold.*
Chaffourré : m. ée : f. *Disguised, blotted, blurred, besmeared, marred; scribled.*
Chaffourrer. *To disfigure, blot, blurre, marre, besmeare; also, to scribble, or write ill-fauouredly.*
Se chaffourrer. *To disfigure, &c, himselfe; also, to be drunken.*
Chafouyn : m. *A Polecat.*
Chafourrer. *Looke* Chaffourrer.
Chagrigner. *Looke* Chagriner.
Chagrin : m. *Carke; melancholie, care, thought; perplexitie, heauinesse, anxietie, pensiuenesse, vexation, or anguish of mind; also, a disease, or maladie; especially, such a one as comes by melancholie.*
Chagrin : m. ine : f. *as* Chagriné; *Or pensiue, heauie, sad, melancholike, out of quiet.*
Chagriné. *Vexed, grieued, perplexed, disquieted.*
Chagrinement. *Pensiuely heauily, sadly, carkingly, carfully, in melancholie.*
Chagriner. *To vexe, disquiet, grieue, trouble, perplex, fill with care, heauinesse, melancholie, anguish.*
Chagrineux : m. euse : f. *Carefull, carking; pensiue perplexed, heauie, sad, ful of anxitie, fraught with anguish, all melancholie.*
Chahuant. *as* Chathuant.
Chaine : f. *A chaine; Looke* Chene.
Chaine de drap, ou de Tisserand. *The woofe of cloth; the thread which in weauing runs ouercrosse it.*
Chaine de S. Philibert. *A counterfeit chaine.*
Chainette. *A little chaine.*
Chainon d'une chaine. *A linke of a chaine.*
Le chainon du col. *The naupe, or (more properly) the chine-bone, of the necke; Looke* Chesnon.
Chair : f. *Flesh.*
La chair dure. *The hard, and white part of an oyster, which cleaues to the shell, and is couered with fish; the root of an oyster.*
Il y a plus de chair que de sauce. *Their companie growes fulsome; there's much more flesh than sauce among them.*
Perdre la chair pour les os. *To loose essentiall, for idle, things, the flesh for the bones.*
Prendre chair. *To battle, get flesh, wax fleshie, grow into good liking, become fat and faire.*
Tremblant entre cuir, & chair. *As vnder* Cuir.
Amour se nourrit de ieune chair : Prov. *Yong flesh is food for loue, loue battles with yong flesh.*
Ieune chair, & vieil poisson : Prov. *Yong flesh, and old fish (are daintiest.)*
Plus prés est la chair que la chemise : Prov. *Our women say, neere is my petticoat but neerer is my smocke.*
Toute chair n'est pas venaison : Prov. *All flesh is not venison; euery man is not to be affected, esteemed, trusted, or vsed; euery saying is not sooth, euery worke not of worth.*
Chair-bouillé : m. *A sodden fellow; or one whose flesh doth looke as if it had beene sodden.*
Chair-bouillé : m. ée : f. *Like sodden flesh; or, sodden as flesh.*
Chaircuicterie : f. *The market, or place, where bacon, or any kind of hogges-flesh may bee had readie boyled.*
Chaircuictier : m. *A Cooke that selleth all kind of bacon, porke, or hogges-flesh readie boiled; also, a bungler; an vnskilfull workeman, or tradesman.*
Chaircuiterie; &; Chaircuitier. *as* Chaircuicterie; &; Chaircuictier.
Chaircuté : m. ée : f. *Hacked, hewed, malled; cut as small as flesh vnto the pot.*
Chaircuter (à coups d'espées.) *To hew, cut, hacke, or chop as small as flesh to the pot.*
Chaire : f. *A chaire; also, a pulpit for a Preacher.*
Chaire brisée. *A foulding chaire.*
Chaire percée. *A close-stoole.*
Dire en chaire. *To preach.*
En defaut de sage le fol monte en chaire : Prov. *A foole, for want of wiser, steps into the roome.*
Chaise, or Chaize : f. *A pulpet.*
Chaiz. *Low warehouses, or sellars to lay marchandise in:* ¶ Bayonnois.
Chalamine. *as* Calamine.
Chalan : m. *A wood-boat, or barge; a kind of midling boat, vsed (most) in the carrying of wood vp & downe riuers.*
Chaland, ou Chalant. *A customer vnto a Marchant, or shop.*
Chalandise : f. *Custome, customing, vsuall trading vnto one shop.*
Chalanger. *To claime, challenge, make title vnto, set in foot for; also, to accuse of, charge with, call in question for, an offence; &c; as* Calenger.
Chalant : m. *A great barge; a Westerne barge; or, as* Chalan.
Chalant de. *Caring, passing, carking, taking thought for.*
Chalcide. *A kind of spotted Lezard which is very venomous, and yet being taken in drinke, healeth the hurt she made.*
Chalcidique. Lisard Chalcidique. *The same.*
Chalcite. *The recrement of brasse, cleauing to the sides of the furnaces wherein tis purified; (This is artificiall* Chalcitis; *for there is also, a naturall one, a caustícke, and corrosiue minerall, that somewhat resembles brasse; is full of long, and shining veines; growes commonly next vnder* Misy *(another minerall) and is of much vse in eye-medicines; against corrosiue vlcers, inflamations of the iawes, and offensiue tumors in other parts.)*
Chalemeler. *To play on a little pipe.*
Chalemelle : f. *A little pipe made of a reed, or of a wheaten,*

ten,or oaten,straw.

Chalemie: f. *as* Chalemelle.

Chalenée: f. *A boat-full,or barge-full of.*

Chalenger. *as* Chalanger.

Chaleur: f. *Heat,warmth,hotnesse; boyling; vehement passion,fierie affection.*

Faire venir en chaleur. *To make a bitch proud, or sault.*

Chaleureux: m. euse: f. *Hot,fierie,scalding,burning; feruent; full of heat; full of hotnesse.*

Chalibé: m. ée: f. *Steeled; done ouer with steele; wherein steele is quenched; belonging vnto steele.*

Chalict. *Looke* Chaslit.

Chaline: f. *A little thunder,in a morning;* ¶Poict: *also, drynesse,drought,or drie weather.* (v.m.)

Chalissier: m. *A maker of Bedsteads.*

Challer. *A hare to be bagd,or breed young; also,to shale, or vnshell,Nuts,&c.*

Chaloir. se cha. de; *to passe,care,take thought for.*

Ne te chaille. *Care not,be of good cheere man,take no thought for the matter.*

Qui peut il chaloir quant a la dispute? *What of that,what skils it,what matter makes it,of what consequence,or importance can it be,in the disputation?*

Chalon: m. *as* Chalan; *also,a kind of fish-net.*

Chaloppes: f. *The huskes,parings,or shalings,of a nut, or nut-kernell.*

Chaloupe: f. *A Shallop,or small boat.*

Chaluc. *A kind of Mullet which delighteth much in her owne tayle.* ¶Lang.

Chalumeau: m. *A small reed,or cane; also, the stemme of an hearbe; also,a wheaten,or oaten straw; or,a pipe made thereof.*

Chalumeux: m.euse: f. *Knottie,or full of knots, as a reed,or the staulke of some hearbes.*

Chamade: f. *The sounding of Trumpets; a call,or summon by the sound of Trumpets; and hence;*

Sonner la chamade. *To sound a parley; also, to summon,challenge,call on.*

Chamæcisse: f. *Spurge time.*

Chamaeleon blanc. *The Carline,or Carline thistle.*

Chamaeleon noir. *The blacke Chameleon thistle.*

Chamailler. *To strike,hacke,hew, slash with swords, or other weapons vpon armour,or armed men.*

Chamailleur: m. *A slasher, hackster, swash-buckler.*

Chamaillis: m. *The resounding of stroakes, or blowes, or the clashing sound of blowes,in a battell, or skirmish of armed men; also,such a battell, fight,bickering,skirmish.*

Chamaras: m. *The hearb* Scordium,*water-Germaunder,Garlicke Germaunder.*

Chamarier: m. *A certaine Officer,at* Lyons.

Chamarre: m. *A loose,and light,Gowne (and,lesse properly, a cloake) that may be worne aswash, or skarfewise; also,a studded garment.*

Chamarré: m. ée: f. *Laced thicke,all ouer; aslope,orecrosse, or billet-wise; also, studded, or set thicke with studs.*

Chamarrer. *To lace thicke,all ouer; aslope,orecrosse,or billet-wise.*

Chamarreure: f. *A thicke lacing aslope, ouercrosse, or billet-wise; also, a studding, or setting thicke with studs.*

Chamarrier. *as* Chamarier.

Chambellage: m. *An Income; a dutie,or fine payed,of course, vnto a Landlord vpon euery change of tenant; also, a fee thats due vnto the chiefe vsher of the Chamber of Accompts,vpon euery homage made by one of the Kings tenants.*

Chambellan: m. *A Chamberlaine; also,a Gentleman, Groome, or Vsher of the Chamber (especially the first; for the other two are more properly tearmed,* Valets de Chambre.)

Chambellenage. *as* Chambellage. ¶Breton.

Chambre: m. *Hempe.*

Chambre: f. *A Chamber; Lodging,Roome,in a house; also, a Law-Court, or Court of Iustice; or the Roome wherein tis vsually kept; also, the box of the naue, or stocke,of a wheele.*

Chambre aisée. *A Priuie, Iakes, house of Office; a Cabinet,or little corner to set a close stoole in.*

Chambre ardente. *A chamber, or court (in euery Parliament one) wherein those of the Religion haue bin censured,and adiudged vnto the fire.*

Chambre des Aydes. *The roome wherein the Court of* Aydes *is kept (In* Paris *there be two of them.)*

Chambre basse. *as* Chambre aisée.

Chambre des Comptes. *The court of Accompts, or of the Exchequer; In euery towne of Parliament there is one of them; and in that of* Paris,*two roomes,and a double* Bureau: *In old time there was but one in* France *(at* Paris) *and then certaine Lords,Officers of the Crowne,and of the priuie Councell, (two whereof, a Clarke,and a lay Lord, sate as Presidents) were appointed to looke vnto the Accompts: Afterwards it was made (as now it is) an ordinarie, and soueraigne Court, consisting of Presidents, and their Assistants,* Maistres des Comptes *(in other Courts tearmed Counsellors) and other Officers, peculiar to it selfe:* Montpellier *was the next towne of Parliament that got one; and after it the rest, at sundrie times, got theirs.*

Chambre du Conseil. *A soueraigne and extraordinarie Court, consisting of two Presidents, and eight or tenne Counsellors (halfe whereof belong to the Court of Parliament, and the other halfe to the chamber of Accompts) who heare, and determine finally such complaints as are made by suitors against the arrests, and decrees of that chamber;and otherwise take order,that the proceedings thereof be not,without great cause,hindered, or oppugned.*

Les Chambres de la Cour. *are as well,all the inferior Officers,Counsellors, or Commissioners that belong to a Court, as the roomes wherein it is vsually kept.*

Chambre aux deniers. *as* Chambres des monnoyes.

Chambre du Domaine. *A Court whereto Appeales are made from la* Chambre du Thresor.

La Chambre dorée. *The principall chamber, or Court,of the Parliament,wherein the chiefe Presidents heare and determine the weightiest causes; tearmed so,because the vpper seeling thereof is gilt.*

Chambre de l'Edict. *as* Chambre mipartie; *called so from an Edict (of the yeare 1594) whereby it was established.*

Les Chambres des Enquestes. *The Chambers, or Courts of Enquests; whereof there be diuers in the Parliament of* Paris, *for the examination,and triall of ciuill causes, and appeales, by witnesses,and other euidences.*

Chambre de femmes. *A Nurserie, or priuat roome onely for women.*

Chambre haute. *A dining chamber.*

La Chambre mipartie. *A Court of Iustice established in diuers good townes of* France, *in fauour, and for the righting,of them of the Religion, whereof the one halfe of the Iudges are, and the other halfe Papists.*

Chambre des monnoyes. *A Soueraign Court, wherin the currantnesse, weight, and value of moneyes are examined; and the disorders, faults, and offences of Mintmen, Coyners, Clippers, &c, punished. This Court hath two Presidents, and eight generall (assistant) counsellors (besides inferiour Officers) belonging to it; and pretends it selfe as auncient as the court of accompts, or to haue beene incorporated into the same (whereto there yet belongs a roome that hath a furnace within it, and is tearmed* La Chambre des monnoyes.) *In old time moneyes were made in 25 French townes, and all they called* Chambres des Monnoyes; *but there are not so many at this day.*

La Chambre nouvelle. *A certaine late-erected Court of Iustice, consisting of twentie Presidents, and Counsellors, besides inferior Officers.*

Chambre des Requestes. *The Court of Requests; whereof there be two; the one of good antiquitie; the other (consisting of two Presidents, and eight Counsellors, &c.) erected in the yeare* 1580.

La Chambre Royale. *A Court erected of purpose for the examination of the dealings and carriage of Financiers, or Exchequer men.*

Chambre du Thresor. *Was in old time a place of generall Receit for the reuenue of the Kings demeane, attended on by* le Changeur du Thresor, *a Controller, and two clarkes; Now tis a court wherein the Treasurers of France, assisted by eight Counsellors, heare and determine all suits that concerne, or happen by reason of, the said demeane; also, the Rolls; or the place wherein all the principall Charters, and Euidences of France are kept.*

La Chambre des vacations. *An ordinarie court (kept euery vacation) by certaine select Iudges for the determining of pettie causes.*

Arriere chambre. *Looke* Arriere-chambre.

La grande chambre des Enquestes. *The great, or principall chamber of Enquests.*

La grande chambre du plaidoyé. *as,* La Chambre dorée.

La nouvelle chambre des Enquestes. *The new, or last-erected, Court of Enquests.*

Robbe de chambre. *A night-gowne.*

Vuides chambres font Dames folles: Pro. *Emptie chambers make women play the wantons.*

Chambrée: f. *A Camerade; a chamberfull of; a companie that belongs to, or lyes in, one chamber.*

Chambrerie: f. *A Chamberlaineship; the estate, place, or office of a Chamberlaine.*

Chambrette: f. *A little chamber, a small roome.*

Chambreux: m. euse: f. *Much louing, or liuing in, a chamber.*

Chambrier: m. *A Chamberlaine in an Abbey, or in an Inne; also, a Chamberlaine, or one of the chamber, vnto a Prince.*

Grand Chambrier. *The Lord Chamberlaine (whose Office was by* Francis *the first suppressed, and the fees, profits, rights, and iurisdiction thereof annexed vnto the demeane of the Crowne,* Anno 1545.)

Chambriere: f. *A chamber-maid, or maid-seruant, (most commonly) one of the meanest ranke, and of basest imployment; or one that serues as a drudge, or kitchin-wench, in a house.*

En Moissons Dames chambrieres sont: Prov. *Ladies are but drudges, or wait on themselues, as long as Haruest lasts.*

Chambrillé: m. ée: f. *Chamberie; full of inner roomes, or chambers.*

Chambrillon: m. *A little roome, small chamber.*

Chambrillon: f. *A little, or young chambermaid, or kitchin-wench.*

Chameau: m. *A Cammell.*

Pasture de chameau. *The reed, or rush, tearmed Camels hay, and Squinant.*

Donner le fardeau selon le chameau. *To proportion a load vnto his strength that is to beare it.*

Chamedrée: f. *Germander, English Treacle (an hearbe.)*

Chamelée: f. *Widow-wayle (a shrub.)*

Chameleon: m. *Looke* Chamaeleon.

Chamelier: m. *A Camell-keeper; or, Camell-driuer.*

Chame. *A kind of cockle, or small, and round shell-fish, the which in eating inflames the mouth like Pepper.*

Chamion: m. *A little dray, without wheeles, whereon the vinegar-makers of Paris drag along their Lees.*

Chamois: m. *A wild Goat, or Shamois; also, the skin thereof dressed, and called ordinarily Shamois leather.*

Champ: m. *A field, land; open, or plain peece of ground; and (by metaphor) any large, and copious subiect for discourse; also, as* Camp.

Champ de bataille. *A place of battaile between two armies, or of combat betweene two champions.*

Champ bosialle. *A common field. See* Bosialle.

Champ clos. *A place rayled in, or inclosed, as a Tilt-yard, for single combats.*

Champ ouvert. *A plaine, and open field, or place, wherein a battaile hath beene, or may be, fought.*

Champ de relais. *A fallow ground, a lay land; a field that lyes a yeare together plowed, but vnsowed.*

Champ verré. Velours champ verré. *A Verry-coloured, or partie-coloured, Veluet.*

La clef des champs. *Libertie; Seeke* Clef.

La porte des champs. *The backe-dore of a countrey house.*

Sur le champ. *Presently, immediately, incontinently, forthwith, out of hand, at that very instant.*

Le champ luy est demeuré. *He hath got the victorie, woon the field; (for he that after a battaile keepes the field, though he haue lost the more men, is held the maister.)*

`A chasque bout de champ. *Still, euer, in each place, which way soeuer one turne him.*

Assez de champ pour faire glane. *Roome sufficient for many to helpe themselues in; aduantages enow for them to take hold of; stuffe good store for them to gaine by; matter ynough to be wrought on, gathered, or picked out, after others haue done withall.*

Aller aux champs. *To goe into the countrey.*

Ayant vn oeil aux champs, & l'autre à la ville. *Seek* Oeil.

Courir les champs en pourpoint. *To run like a bedlam, to course vp and downe like a mad man.*

Donner les champs à. *To giue libertie vnto.*

Donner la clef des champs à. *To dismisse, let go, send out, giue libertie vnto.*

Gaigner les champs. *To shew a faire paire of heeles, to flye his countrey, to run away.*

Mettre quelqu' un aux champs. *To prouoke one to anger, to put him into a chafe, to put him into choler, to make him as mad as a March hare; also, to set one aflote, to put him into a great conceit of himselfe; to make*

make him goe the faster on, or giue the more forward; also, to dismisse him, put him forth, or send him abroad, into the world.

Se mettre aux champs. *To braue it in shew, to put the better leg before; to set cocke a hoope, or himselfe out to the vtmost; also, to giue himselfe scope, libertie, roome ynough.*

Bois ont oreilles, & champs oeillets: Prov. *Woods haue their eares, and fields their eyes; so apt, and able is euery place to detect close villanie.*

En petit champ croist bien bon bled: Prov. *Good corne growes very well in little fields; or (better) verie good corne growes in little fields; excellent spirits are often lodged in exile, or small, bodies.*

Champagne. *The name of a Prouince in France.*

Droict de Champagne. *The fees due vnto the Officers of the Chamber of Accompts, out of farmes let in that Prouince;* viz. *two shillings sterl. out of such as are worth a hundred pounds, or lesse; and foure shillings for those that exceed that rate.*

Champaigne. *as* Campaigne; *also, a field, in armourie; whence;*

Champaigne potencée. *is that which our Blasoners tearme, a Barre miere.*

Champar, ou champart. *Field-rent; halfe, or part, or the twelfth part, of a Crop due, by bargaine, or custome, vnto a Landlord, and taken off the ground for him, before the farmer lead any; also, a field, or close; also, a greene lying before a countrey house.*

Champarter. *To diuide a field (or the crop of a field) by euen, or due, parts; to lay out vnto euery one his portion therein.*

Champarteresse. grange ch. *whereinto, the part of a crop due by the right of* Champart, *is layed.*

Champarteur. *A diuider of fields, or field-rent; one that shares out vnto euery one his due part of, or portion in, a crop.*

Champartir. *as* Champarter.

Champayage: m. *A running, or grazing of cattell in the fields; whence;*

Vn tel a champayage en tel lieu. *Hath going for his beasts in such a place.*

Champayer. *To reside, or continue among fields; also, to wander in, or walke ouer, the fields; also, to field it, or carrie abroad into the fields; also, to run, feed, graze, or pasture in fields; also (actiuely) to put cattell on a ground, or turne them into the fields, to let them goe therein.*

Champé d'asur. *Azure, or, the field Azure.* (Blason.)

Champestre: com. *Fieldie, plaine, champian; of, or belonging to, the fields; also, clownish, rusticke, boorish, homelie; bred in the countrey, liuing among fields; also, wild, rude, sauage, hagard, vnreclaimed, vnciuile, barbarous.*

Champeyer. *as* Champayer.

Champi: m. Champisse: f. *Bastard, or base-borne;* ¶Bourbon. *also, cousening, cheating, nimble-fingered; also, seeming, but not being, honest.*

Champicerie; vn tour de champicerie; *a cheating pranke; a tricke of nimble knauerie, or of Legierdemaine.*

Champignon: m. *A Mushrum, Toadstoole, Paddockstoole.*

Champignons de pourceaux. *The white, or yellowish mushrums, which may be eaten; In Latine they are also called,* Fungi suilli; *and by Latine Physitions,* porcini; *we may therefore lawfully call them, Hogs Mushrums, or Swines Mushrums.*

Champion: m. *A Champion; one that fights a publicke combat in his owne, or another mans, quarrell.*

Champis. *Looke* Champi *(the plurall whereof it is.)*

Champleure. *as* Chantepleure.

Champoyer. *as* Champayer; *to continue in the fields, &c.*

Chance: f. *A chance, hap, aduenture, hazard; also, the game at dice called Mumchance, or such another.*

Il n'est chance qui ne retourne: Pro. *All chances doe returne one time or other.*

Chanceler. *Looke* Chanceller.

Chancelerie: f. *A Chauncerie Court; the Chauncerie; the Seale Office, or Court of euery Parliament, and Presidiall Seat.*

Les Chancelleries Presidiales. *The meanest Courts of Chauncerie in France; whose seales are different from, and lesse then, the seales of other Chanceries; and are not imployed but in some few Writs, or Letters, for causes that be vnder the value of* 250 *pounds* Tourn. *Nor is any suitor tyed to vse them, but may procure his Writs to be sealed either in the great Chauncerie, or in that which belongs to the Parliament, within the iurisdiction whereof he liues.*

La grande Chancelerie. *The great Chancerie; euer attendant on the Kings person, and gouerned by the Lo. Chancelor of France.*

Les petites Chanceleries. *The Chanceries of Parliaments, and Presidial seats, are indifferently tearmed so, in difference of* la grande Chan. *The seales of these Chaunceries are gouerned by* les Gardes des seaux *in absence of the Maisters of Requests, who in their Circuits, assigned them by the Lord Chancellor, visit, at least, once a yeare, euery one of these Chanceries.*

Chancelier: m. *A Chancellor: The Lord Chancellor is the principall Magistrat of France (as ours of England) and is, in his iudgements, exempted from the iurisdiction, or censure of Parliaments (as ours vncontroulable by the common Law;) On him depends the ordering, and disposition of Iustice; the establishment of good, and sacred Lawes; the reformation of superfluous, and abrogation of vnprofitable, Edicts; and the putting downe of all Offices that be offensiue to the People, or chargeable to the State: He hath the keeping of the kings (great) Seale; and by the vertue thereof either passes, or may put backe, such Letters Patents, and Writs, as are presented vnto him.*

Chancelier de Geneviefve. *An Officer in the Vniuersitie of Paris, who hath authoritie to examine, and licence, Maisters of Art.*

Chancelier de nostre Dame. *Another, who hath authoritie ouer Diuines, Lawyers, Physitions, &c, and punishes vnrulie schollers, of what degree soeuer.*

Chanceliere: f. *A Chancelors wife.*

Chancellant: m. ante: f. *Staggering, reeling; stutting, stammering.*

Chancellement: m. *A staggering, reeling, wauering in gate; a stutting, stammering, faultering, in speech.*

Chanceller. *To reele, stagger; wauer, make indentures; also, to stammer, stut, faulter in speech.*

Bien poulsé longuement chancelle: Pro. *He staggers long thats thrust with a strong hand.*

Il vault mieulx tresbucher vne fois, que toujours chanceller: Prov. *Better fall at once, then stagger alwayes; better to erre altogether, then alwaies to wauer; better to step in for once, on the wrong side, then*

still

still to doubt what side he shall follow.

Chancellerie. *as* Chancelerie.

Chanceux: m. euse: f. *Fortunate, hapfull; successiue.*

Chanci: m. ie: f. *Mustie, fustie, stinking, or vnsauourie with age, or ill-keeping.*

Chancisseure. *Looke* Chansisseure. *Fustinesse.*

Chancre: m. *A Canker; a painefull, hard, ouglie, and vneuen swelling which blackens, and inflames, the veines that are about it.*

Herbe au chancre. *Turnesole, Wartworte, Heliotropium.*

Chancreux: m. euse: f. *Cankarie, cankared; full of Cankers.*

Bosse chancreuse. *A cankered byle; pockie sore, Winchester goose.*

Chandeleur. La feste de la Chandeleur. *Candlemas day; the Purification of the blessed Virgin.*

Chandeleuse. la Chan. *The same.*

Chandeleux: m. euse: f. *Full of candles, of a candle, belonging to a candle.*

Chandelier: m. *A Candlesticke; also, a Chaundler, or Candle-maker, or Candle-seller; also, Candlemas day.*

Mis au chandelier. *Intertained, receiued, accepted of; vsed, imployed, set on worke.*

Il en tuera dix de la chandelle, & vingt du chandelier. *Looke* Chandelle.

Aujourd'huy Febvrier demain Chandelier: Prov. (*For Candlemas day is euer the second of Februarie.*)

Chandelier: m. ere: f. *Belonging to a Chaundler, Candle, or Candlesticke.*

L'herbe chandeliere. *The Colewort is called so by some; by others (perhaps more properly) the hearbe Mullein; Seeke* Herbe.

Chandelle: f. *A candle, a size; a light, or taper.*

Chandelles de Buchs. *Rosen candles, vsed by the poorer sort of people neere vnto Bourdeaux.*

'A la chandelle; *By candle-light; in extremitie, or at the point of death, when a man is readie to giue vp the ghost (for then the Romanists light candles, vpon a conceit that euill spirits are driuen away thereby.)*

'A la chandelle allumée. *The same; or, before all be gone; while there is time, or any life in it; whilest it is in handling, or may be had.*

'A la chandelle esteincte. *Too late; when a thing is past recouerie; after all is gone, or the businesse done; (This Phrase, and the former, seeme deriued from Outropes; wherein after the first offers made, a candle is lighted at the bidding of more; after which, that being put out, another is also lighted, when a third part more is bidden; and when twice as much, another; which once put out, the thing is instantly deliuered ouer.)*

Brusler la chandelle. par les deux bouts. *To wast, or spend, things disorderedly; to squander hee cares not how, nor what; also (but lesse properly) to play the micher, nigardize it, goe very neerely to worke.*

Se brusler à la chandelle. *Sayd of one that giues so much for a farme &c. of the Kings (which is let by Outcrie, who will giue most, while three pound of Wax candles last lighted) that he looses verie much by it; This Phrase is also taken otherwise, as in that which followes.*

Il se vient brusler à la chandelle. *The light he hath receiued, ruines him; or, that which might haue directed, comes to ruine, him; also, he hath disclosed his own knauerie, he hath bewrayed himselfe.*

Emporter à la chandelle. *To carrie a thing cleere away by offering the most for it. (Looke in* 'A la chandelle esteincte.)

Gaster vne chandelle pour trouver vn petit mouchon. *To spoyle much in search after a little.*

Il en tuera dix de la chandelle, & vingt du chandelier. *Hee will doe wonders, hee will cut them into many peeces, hee will make minced meat for Crowes of their carkasses; no man will be able to stand before him, hee is growne so fell, fierce, or furious; (Ironically.)*

Le jeu ne vaut pas la chandelle. *It will not quit cost; there will be nothing got by him that toyles, or deales, in it.*

Il y avoit à chaque Sainct sa chandelle. *There was for euery Saint his candle; euerie one had somewhat, more or lesse, bestowed on him.*

Monter au grenier sans chandelle. *To light in a turd.*

'A la chandelle la Chevre semble Damoiselle: Pro. *By candle-light a shee Goat seemes a Gentlewoman; (where, by the candle, is meant a mans owne affection, or the opinion of another; either of which followed wholly in the choice of a wife, hath often proued erronious.)*

Au plus debile la chandelle en la main: Prov. *(We say) he that worst may holds the candle.*

Il n'y a si petit Sainct qui ne desire sa chandelle: Prov. *There is no man in authoritie, how small soeuer, but lookes for the respect thats due vnto him.*

Chanes. le grand chanes. *May-weed, wild Camomill, stinking Maithes.*

Chanfrain de Cheval d'armes. *The front-stall, head-peece, or forhead-piece, of a barbed horse.*

Chanfrain (creux.) *A chanfering; or, a channell, furrow, hollow gutter, or streake, in stone-worke, &c.*

Chanfron: m. *The name of an Italian coyne, worth about xx d.*

Change: m. *Sumacke, leather Sumacke, or Curriers Sumacke. (a shrub.)*

Change: m. *A change, transformation, metamorphosis; exchange; alteration, innouation; conuersion; also, a Banke of Exchange, or Place wherein money is exchanged, and commodities bartered for; also, a wrong Deere (in hunting,) or the heard whereinto a pursued Deere is gotten.*

Aller ou change: Il va au ch. *is said of a married man, or fornicator, that leaues his owne wife, or wench, and frequents the companie of other women.*

Garder le change. *Hounds to pursue onely the game they began with; hounds to sticke to their owne, or old game; to run, or hunt, their owne.*

Prendre le change. *Hounds to riot, or to run riot; to flye out at a wrong Deere, and leaue that which was first rowsed.*

Changé: m. ée: f. *Changed; transformed, metamorphosed, altered, varied; conuerted; innouated; also, exchanged, interchanged, chopped, bartered, scoorsed.*

Changeant. *Changing, transforming; altering, varying, exchanging, interchanging.*

Changement: m. *A changing, transforming, altering, varying; conuerting; innouating; also, an exchanging, interchanging, chopping, scoorsing, bartering; also, a kind of shadowing; Looke* Nuage.

Changer. *To change, transforme, alter, varie; innouate, conuert; also, to exchange, interchange, trucke, scoorse, barter, chop with.*

Changer de main. *To shift a thing out of one hand into*

into another; and (in matters of inheritance) to haue a new Lord, or owner.

Changer de note. *Looke* Note.

Changer de poil. *To mend his manners, to alter his former disposition, to become a new man.*

Tel change qui ne gaigne pas: Pro. *Many change for the worse.*

Changeur: m. *A changer, exchanger, banker; also, a tole-taker, or gatherer of tribute.*

Changeur du Thresor. *The Kings Receiuer generall, called so in old time; at this day,* Thresorier du Domaine.

Chanoine: m. *A Canon in a Cathedrall Church.*

Chanoinerie: f. *as* Chanoinie.

Chanoinie: f. *A Canonship; the place of a Canon.*

Chansi: m. ie: f. *Mustie, fustie; almost rotten, putrified; vnsauourie through age, or long keeping; also, mouldie, hoarie, vinewed.*

Chansisseure: f. *Mustinesse, fustinesse; putrefaction; also, hoarinesse, mouldinesse, vinewednesse.*

Chanson: f. *A Song; Ayre; Ballade; Lay, Roundelay, Virelay; also, a Poeme, or Discourse, in Meeter.*

Chanson de Ricochet. *A Song, Play, Tale, or Discourse, thats endlesse, and hangs ill together; or, whereof one part confutes, or contradicts, another.*

Chanson de Robin. *A merrie, and extemporall song, or fashion of singing, whereto one is euer adding somewhat, or may at pleasure adde what he list; hence, also, any tedious, or endlesse discourse, &c.*

Ces chansons procedent de la mesme cornemuse. *All these matters haue but one head, all these businesses but one originall.*

On luy demanda la chanson. *(Spoken ieastingly of one thats but newly come out of prison, where hauing been (as a bird in a Cage) inclosed, he may perhaps haue learnt to sing.)*

En vne chanson n'y a qu'un bon mot: Prov. *And thats the last (in the opinion of harsh, and barbarous, people.)*

Chansonet: m. *A Canarie bird; or as* Sansonet.

Chansonnette: f. *A little song, a prettie aire; a sleight, or light note, or tune.*

Chansonneur: m. *A great singer of songs.*

Chansonnier: m. ere: f. *Alwaies singing, full of songs.*

Chansons. *Colombine flowers.*

Chanstié: m. *as* Chantier; *a Gauntrie, or Stilling.*

Chant: m. *A Song, Ayre; Caroll, Ballade; Lay, Roundelay, Virelay; also, a Poeme, or Discourse, in Ryme.*

Chant Royal. *A kind of ancient Poeme dedicated to the honour of Jesus Christ, or of his Mother; and concluding with some fiue or six verses, commending, or directed vnto, one Prince or other, not formerly mentioned.*

Chanté: m. ée: f. *Sung, chaunted; warbled; crowed; resounded; commended, or described in Meeter, or in Verse.*

I'ay chanté à son han. *I haue spoken with him.* ¶Barrag.

Chanteau: m. *A corner-peece, or peece broken off from the corner, or edge of a thing; (and hence) also, a gobbet, lumpe, crust, or cantell of bread, &c; also, a quarter, or the quarter-peece, of a garment.*

Le Chanteau part le vilain: Pro. *See* Vilain.

Chantel. *as* Chanteau. ¶Lang.

Chantellage: m. *A certaine fee due vnto some Lords for the Gauntries whereon wine that is sold hath stood.*

Chantelle. Les quattre deniers de chantelle. *Foure pence payed euery yeare, within* Bourbonnois, *by certaine villains vnto their Lords, in acknowledgement of their seruile Tenures.*

Chantement: m. *A singing, resounding, chaunting; warbling; crowing.*

Chantepleure: f. *A garden Pot, or Gardeners watering Pot; also, the cocke of a cesterne; also, a certaine deuice, or Engine, for the emptying of a water-vessell; made of two Lattin pipes (of equall bignes, and length) ioyned together at the one end, and thence diuiding themselues, into the forme of a forke.*

Chantepoulet: m. *The lesser Centorie, Earth-gall, Feauerworte;* (Iunius.)

Chantepoulets. *as* Armoires; *Sweet Williams, Tollmeyners, London Tufts.* (Mathiolus.)

Chanter: m. *A singing, or chaunting; whence;*

Beau chanter souvent ennuye: Prov. *Euen choice delights are often tedious.*

Chanter. *To sing; resound; chaunt it; warble, as a bird; crow as a cocke, &c; also, to describe, or commend, in verse.*

Chanter en faulset. *To faine; also, to sing louder and louder, or higher and higher; to rise from note to note, in singing.*

Chanter deuant la feste. *To triumph before a victorie.*

Chanter l'hymne du Cigne. *To sing, speake, or vtter, his last.*

Chanter pouilles. *To scold, reproch, reuile, raile on.*

Chantez à l'asne, il vous fera des pets: Prov. *Sing you to an Asse, and he will fart vnto you; bestow any good thing on a churle, and if he do requite it, it shall be in one filthie manner or other.*

Asseurement chante qui n'a que perdre: Prov. *He boldly chaunts it that hath naught to loose; wee say; and who doth sing so merrie a note as he that cannot change a groat? (This Prouerbe will also affoord worthier expositions.)*

On se lasse de bien chanter: Pro. *Seeke* Lasser.

Tel chante qui n'a ioye: Pro. *Many a one sings that is full sorrie; (Those that, against their wils, ride vp Holborne, oft verifie this Prouerbe.)*

Chanterelle: f. *The treble, in singing; also, a treble string, or bell; also, a small bell for a chyme.*

Chantereme: f. *A greene frog, land toad, hedge toad.*

Chanteresse: f. *A Chaunteresse; a woman that sings, or sings much.*

Chanterie: f. *Chaunting, singing; Musicke; also, a Chaunterie; the place, degree, or office, of a Chaunter.*

Chanterre: m. *An ordinarie Poet, rymer, or versifier, so tearmed in old time.*

Chanteur: m. *A singer, a Chaunter; also, a small, white-breasted, and red-bellied forrest-bird that sings very much.*

Chantier: m. *A Wood-mongers, or Tymber-sellers, yard; also, a Staulder, or Wood-pile; also, a Vine-supporting pole, or stake (whether it stand vpright, or lye, as a crosse barre, ouerthwart; and (hence) also, as* Treillis, *or a rayle for the same purpose; also, a Stoope, or Pile, vnderpropping the banke of a riuer; also, a Gauntrie, or Stilling, for Hogs-heads, &c, to stand on; also, a Tresle to saw Tymber on.*

Chantier de bois. *A staulder, woodstacke, pile of wood.*

Leurs Nauires estoyent en chantier. *Their ships were on the stockes, or in the docke.*

Chan-

Chantillonné: m. ée: f. *Chaunted; sung roundly, or merrily.*
Chantillonner. *To chaunt it; to sing roundly, or merrily.*
Chantonner. *as* Chantillonner.
Chantourné: m. ée: f. *Turned round, as the shell of a snayle; or often in and out, as the course of a brooke in a meddow.*
Chantournement: m. *The wriggling, eddie, or often, and vncertain turning in and out of the course of small riuers.*
Chantourner. *To wryth, or turne often in and out, like a small streame in a plaine field, or meddow.*
Chantre: m. *A chaunter, a singer; also, a Chaunter in a Queere, or Cathedrall Church; also, as* Chavassine; *also, a white-breasted, and red-bellied forrest-bird that vses to sing very much.*
Chantrerie. *as* Chanterie.
Chanure: m. *Hempe.*
Chanure sauvage. *Bastard Hempe, wild Hempe, Nettle Hempe.*
Chanureux: m. euse: f. *Hempen, Hempie; of Hempe; full of Hempe.*
Chanurier: f. *A Hempen close, or, yard wherein Hempe is sowed.*
Chaos: m. *A Chaos; a confused, or disorderly heape; a huge, immense, and formelesse Masse, or mingle-mangle of sundry things hudled togetber.*
Chape: f. *A Cope; also, the locket of a dagger, &c; Looke* Chappe.
Chapeau: m. *A hat; hood, or bonnet for the head; also, a garland of flowers, &c.*
Chapeau à l'Albanoise. *A high-crowned hat; a hat with a crowne like a sugar-loafe; or of the Spanish blocke.*
Chapeaux blancs. *A multitude of seditious, and mutinous Rebels of Flanders, in* Charles *the sixts time.*
Chapeau cornu. *A certaine deformed, and pricklie fish, called, the great sea Nettle.* ¶ Provençois.
Chapeau de mer. *The same.*
Chapeaux noirs. *The flowers of* Lonchitis *(an hearb, whereof both* Dioscorides *and* Pliny *make mention; yet* Mathiolus *protests he neuer could find it, nor heare of any that of late had found it.)*
Chapeau de Roses. *Looke* Chapel.
Chapeau rouge. *A Cardinals hat; also, the bloudie necke of a headlesse carcas; whence;*
On luy a fait porter le chapeau rouge. *They haue cut off his head.*
Chapeau de triomphe. *A round garland worne about his head that triumphed.*
Qui a argent a des chapeaux: Pro. *He that is rich is reuerenced; or, he that hath money wants neither hat, nor hood; he that hath store of coyne hath store of all needfull commodities.*
Chapel. *as* Chapeau; *a hat; a garland.*
Chapel de Roses. *A sleight, incompetent, or lesse-then due Portion, giuen a maid by the father vnto her mariage.* ¶ Lodunois.
Chapelain: m. *A Chaplaine; also, the Curate of a Chappell.*
Chapelainie: f. *A Chaplainship; also, the cure, or charge of a Chappell; also, the liuing, or glebe, that belongs thereto.*
Chapelé: m. ée: f. *Chipped, as bread; or, as* Chapplé.
Chapeler (du pain) *To chip (bread;) also, as* Chappler.

Chapelet: m. *A Chaplet; garland, wreath for the head; also, a couer, copping, or topping (made like a Chaplet) for any thing; (Hence) also, a nayles head; also, a haukes hood; also, a paire of beads; also, a wreath, or circlet of wicker, &c, to set vnder dishes at meale-times; also, the breech of a Gunne.*
Chapelet du genouil. *The ball of the knee.*
Chapelet du iarret. *The bought of the hamme; the cambrell hogh of a horse.*
Danser en chapelet. *To daunce in a round, ring, or circle.*
Chapelier: m. *A Hat-maker; also, a maker of Garlands.*
Chapelier: m. ere: f. *Of a Chaplet, hat, or garland; becomming, or doing well in, a Chaplet, hat, or garland.*
Chapeliere: f. *A woman that makes hats, or garlands.*
Chapeline. *as* Capeline.
Chapelis. *Looke* Chapplis.
Chapelle: f. *A Chappell, Oratorie; little Church; also, also, a Lymbecke, or Stillatorie.*
Chapelures: f. *Chippings of bread.*
Chaperon: m. *A hood, or French hood (for a woman;) also, any hood, bonnet, or lettice cap.*
Chaperon à bourlet. *Such a hood as Lawyers and citizens weare on their shoulders vpon solemne dayes.*
Chaperon de fou. *A fooles cap set out with hornes, eares, ill faces, and other such fopperies.*
Le Chaperon d'une Trepane. *The head, or hood of a Trepane, whereby it is hindered from entring further then he lifts that holds it.*
Vn Chaperon fait à l'en veux *A notable whipster, or twigger; a good one I warrant her.*
Le moule à chaperon. *A womans pate.*
Deux testes en vn chaperon. *Two men of a like, or the same, humor, will, and disposition; two mindes, or hearts, agreeing in one.*
Il bailla à sa femme dronos, & chaperon de mesme. *Hee bangde, belammed, thumped, swadled, her.*
Qui n'a point de teste, n'a que faire de chaperon: Prov. *He that hath no head needs no hood.*
Chaperonné: m. ée: f. *Hooded, hauing a hood on.*
Pigeon chaperonné. *A ruffed, or copped, Pigeon.*
Chaperonner. *To be bare, or vncouer his head before; to cap, or put off his cap vnto; also, to hood, or put a hood on.*
Chaperonnier: m. *Looke* Chapprennier.
Chaperonnier: m. ere: f. *Hooded; hooding.*
Herbe chaperonniere. *wild Larks-heele; or, Monks-hood with the purple flower.*
Chaperonniere: f. *Looke* Chapperoniere.
Chaperonnieze: f. *A poore slut, a draggle-tayle.*
Chapiteau: m. *The top, head, or chapter, of a Pillar; also, the vpper part of a Limbecke.*
Chapitre: m. *The Chapter of a booke; also, a Chapter, or assemblie of the Deane, Prebends, Canons, & other Officers, of a Cathedrall Church.*
Pain de Chapitre. *Looke* Pain.
Avoix voiv en chapitre. *To be heard with much attention, and respect; to beare great sway in an assemblie,*
Chapitré: m. ée: f. *Schooled, censured, checked, reproued,*
Chapitrer. *To schoole, correct, reproue, checke, take vp; also (lesse properly) to beat, bruise; chop, & cut in peeces.*

Cha-

Chapitreur de foin: m. *A skarre-crow, bugbeare; one that threatens much, and does but a little.*
Chapler. *as* Chapeler; *to chip bread; or, as* Chappler.
Chaplis. *as* Chapplis; *also, bread-chippings; also, the small peeces that flye from stones in the hewing; we call them rags.*
Chapon: m. *A Capon; also, as* Chappon.
Chapon de mer. *The Rochet; or, a kind of red Gurnard.*
Vol d'un chapon. *is the Aker, or* Arpent *(or such a like proportion) of land, that lyes next vnto a Mannor house, or capitall Messuage, and fals euer (if there bee not a competent garden &c.) together with it, vnto the share of the eldest sonne. Looke* Cheze; & Vol.
Coucher en chapon. *To goe verie soone to bed a-nights; or, to get him to bed as soone as he hath supped.*
A qui chapon mange chapon luy vient: Pro. *He that eates good meat shall haue good meat.*
Iamais putain n'ayma preud hom, ny grasse geline chapon: Pro. *Neuer did whore loue honest man, nor wanton wife her weake man.*
Iamais tigneux n'ayma le pigne, ny chapon crester geline: Prov. *See* Crester.
Si tu te trouves sans chapon sois content de pain & d'oignon: Prov. *If thou hast not a Capon, feed on an Onyon.*
Chaponné. *Guelt, made a Capon; cut, as a Capon.*
Chaponneau: m. *A Caponet, or young Capon.*
Chaponner. *To cut Capons; to gueld.*
Chapoté: m. ée: f. *Hacked, or whitled; also, hagled, or dodged about the price of; busied in manie things to small purpose.*
Chapoter. *To hacke, or whitle; also, to hagle, paulter, trifle, or dodge, about the price of; also, to piddle, meddle, or busie himselfe in many things, and doe nothing well.*
Chappe: f. *A (Churchmans) Cope; also, a Iudges Hood; also, the helme (or head) of a Limbecke; also, the chape, or locket of a scabberd; also, the top, or crowne, on the top, of a Bell; also, a Mill-hoope, or Mill-case; the open chest wherein the stones do run.*
Cercher chappe cheute. *To picke, or be desirous of, a quarrell; to looke, or spie, what fault he may find.*
Debatre de la chappe à l'Evesque. *To contend, or brable about trifles; or for things which belong vnto others. Looke* Debatre.
Chappel: m. *A Hat; a Garland.* ¶Auvergnois.
Chappel d'argent; *as,* Garlande d'Argent.
Chappelainie: f. *A Chaplaineship; the estate, or place of a Chaplaine, or of the Curate of a Chappell.*
Chappelet. *Looke* Chapelet.
Chappelier: m. *A maker of Hats; or, of Garlands.*
Chappelier: m. ere: f. *Looke* Chapelier.
Chappeliere: f. *A woman that makes Hats; or Garlands.*
Chappelet: m. *Looke* Chapelet.
Chapperon. *as* Chaperon.
Chapperonniere: f. *A chambermaid, spinster, kitchinmaid, meane wench, homelie huswife.*
Chappier: m. *A Cope-maker.*
Chappins: m. *Choppines; a kind of high slippers for low women.*
Chapplé: m. ée: f. *Hacked, hewed, slashed; also, chipped; as bread.*
Chappler. *To hacke, hew, slash vpon, or in pieces; also, to chip; as bread.*
Chapplis: m. *The hacking, hewing, and slashing thats among armed men when they incounter; also, bread-chippings; and, the chipping of bread.*
Chappon: m. *A slip, small twig, or shoot of a plant, or tree.* ¶Bourg. *also, as* Chapon.
Chappoté: m. ée: f. *Dodged, paultred, hagled; also, hacked, or whitled.*
Chappron. *as* Chaperon. *A hood.*
Chappronner. *as* Chaperonner.
Chappronniet. Faulcon bon chappronnier. *That takes the hood gently, or will easily be hooded.*
Chappuis. *Looke* Chapuis.
Chapron. *as* Chaperon; *and (in* Rabelais) *a hooded foole.*
Chaptel. *A lease of a beast, and of the whole increase thereof, made for a certaine time, and price; or, a beast let out to the halues.*
Chaptels deniers. *The principall summe, and charges a purchaser hath payed, and beene at, for land which the next of kinne offers to redeeme.*
Chapuis: m. *A Carpenter; one that deales with tymber, or with tymber-worke.* ¶Dauph. & Lionnois.
Chapuiser. *To play the Carpenter; to worke Carpenters worke; to deale with tymber.*
Char: m. *A Carre, Waggon, Wayne, or Chariot.*
Characie. *Garden Spurge.*
Charactere. *A Caracter; Figure; &c; See* Caractere.
Charadrien. *A certaine bird, which earnestly beholding one that is sicke of the Iaundice, or beheld by him, heales him.*
Charanson. *as* Charanton.
Charansonné: m. ée: f. *Gnawed, eaten into, or eaten vp, by Weeuils.*
Charanton: m. *A Mite, or Weeuill.*
Charaveau: m. *A Beetle.*
Charbon: m. *A coale; also, a Carbuncle, or Plague-sore.*
Le charbon. *The first lines, or lineaments of a picture; (tearmed so, belike, because most Painters draw them with a peece of Charcoale.)*
Charbon blanc. *A kind of coale made of the wood of the Crimson, or pricklie, Cedar.*
Charbon de terre. *Sea-coale, or Pit-coale.*
Faire charbon de tout bois. *To imploy, or make vse of, euerie thing.*
D'un sac à charbon ne peut sortir que de la poussiere noire: Prov. *A coale-sacke yeeldeth nothing but blacke dust; Blacke thoughts can none but balefull acts produce.*
Charbonné: m. ée: f. *Painted, marked, written, with a coale; collowed, smeered, blacked with coales; (hence) also, darkened.*
Charbonnée: f. *A Carbonado, or collop of, &c.*
A vilain charbonnée d'asne. *Looke* Asne.
Charbonner. *To paint, marke, write, or smeare, with a coale; to collowe; to bleach, or make black, with a coale.*
Si vous ne le voulez croire charbonnez-le. *See* Croire.
Charbonnerie: f. *A Coale-pit, or, Coale-mine; also, a Coale-house.*
Charbonnesque: com. *Coalie, of Coales.*
Charbonneux: m. euse: f. *Coalie, full of coales, all to becollowed; also, full of Carbuncles, or Plague-sores.*
Charbonnier: m. *A Collier.*
Ce sont sacs de charbonniers qui se noircissent l'un l'autre: Pro. *These fellowes corrupt, by accompanying, one another.*
Charbonniere: f. *as* Charbonnerie; *also, a Colliers wife, or wench.*
Charbot: m. *A Beetle.*

Charbot de bœuf. *The venomous blacke, and beetle-like flye called, a long-leg, or wag-leg; a deadly morsell to the beast that lickes him vp.*

Chardon: m. *A thistle; also, a Cardoone, or the staulke of an Artichoke, which buried in the earth in the end of August, proues excellent meat towards Christmas.*

Chardon argentin. *Oat-thistle, Gumme-thistle, Cotton-thistle, wild white thistle, Argentine, or siluer, thistle.*

Chardon asinin. *The white thistle, wild Artichoke, or our Ladies thistle.*

Chardon benoict. *Holy thistle, blessed thistle,* Carduus benedictus.

Chardon à cent testes. *The hundred-headed thistle, field* Eringus, *Leuant sea Holme, Champian sea Hollie; (a stranger, as yet, in England.)*

Chardon estoillé. *The stone thistle, Caltrop, starre thistle.*

Chardon à foullon. *The Tazell, Fullers thistle, Card Tazell,* Venus *bason.*

Chardon franc. *The Artichoke.*

Chardon marin. *The sea thistle, sea Hollie,* Eringus.

Chardon de nostre Dame. *Our Ladies thistle, white thistle, milke thistle.*

Chardon pignolat. *Fullers thistle.*

Chardon roullant. *as* Chardon à cent testes.

Chardon sauvage. *as* Chardon argentin; *or, the ordinarie wild thistle.*

Chardon testu. *The hundred-headed thistle, or field* Eringus.

Chardons de treillis de fer. *A kind of yron defence, made thistle-like, or full of prickles, to keepe a wall from being scaled.*

Laissons aux asnes les chardons. *Let Asses feed on thistles; leaue vnto poorer spirits dull conceits.*

Qui seme les chardons recueille des espines: Pro. *He that sowes thistles reapes thornes.*

Chardonner le drap. *To raise, or lay the nap thereof, to dresse it, with the Tazell.*

Chardonnereau: m. *The barre of a dore; the peece, band, or plate, that runnes along on the hindge-side of some dores.*

Chardonneret: m. *A Goldfinch, or thistle Finch.*

Chardonnerette: f. *The thistlie, or pricklie Artichoke.*

Chardonnet: m. *Our Ladies thistle, milke thistle, white thistle; also, a Goldfinch.*

Chardonnette: f. *The wild, or pricklie, Artichoke; also, a kind of sauce for Kid.*

Formage à la chardonnette. *Cheese, whose milke was curded with the iuice of the wild Artichoke; or, a Lenten cheese, made of egges, and the spawne of fishes, and curded with the iuice of that thistle.*

Chardonniere: f. *A plot, or garden of Thistles, Artichokes, or Tazels; also, as* Chardonnereau.

Chardous: m. *Chardoones; or, the staulkes of Artichokes.*

Chardousse: f. *The white Cameleon, or white Carline, thistle.*

Chardousse noire. *The blacke Cameleon thistle.*

Chardrier. *as* Chardonneret.

Charée. *as* Charrée.

Charenson: m. *The (corne-deuouring) Mite, or Weeuill.*

Charesse; &, Charesser. *See* Caresse, *&* Caresser.

Chareti: m. *A waggon-house; a houell to set carts vnder.*

Charetier: m. *A Carter, or Carman.*

Charetin. *as* Chareti.

Charette: f. *A Chariot, or Waggon.*

Charevastre: m. *An Ash-cloth, Nash-cloth, or Buckcloth.*

Terny comme vn charevastre. *As pale as an Ashcloth.*

Chargais: m. *A certaine vnluckie bird of a browne, and (in some parts) of a white, colour.* ¶Savoyard.

Charge: f. *A Load, Burthen, Fardle; also, a charge, hinderance, or cause of extraordinarie expence; an Office, Commission; Dignitie, Estate; Place, or Imployment, of charge; a businesse, or matter giuen in charge; also, the charge of a Gunne; also, a charge giuen vpon the enemie; also, an accusation, imputation, or fault layed to the charge of; also, a Poultis, or moist plaister.*

Charge Palatine. *The Stewardship of an imperiall Court.*

Charge Vilaine. *as* Roture *(called so in old time.)*

Tas de charge. *Looke* Tas.

Chevaucher sa charge. *To ride circuit, as a Iudge, &c.*

Chargé: m. ée: f. *Charged, loaden, burthened, onerated; put vnto charges; assaulted, or charged, as an enemie; accused, or charged, as an offendor; also, that hath charge of.*

Chargé à poids de marc. *Throughly tipled, soundly whittled, that hath taken his liquor to purpose; that hath his full load, or carriage of it.*

Chargé de la plus fine. *The same; or delicately cupshotten; or as in* Fin.

Le cerf a chargé sa venaison. *The Stag is verie fat.*

Cheval chargé de teste, ou de col. *A heauie-headed, or hard-borne, horse.*

Couleur chargée. *A verie deepe colour.*

Temps chargée. *A gloomie, cloudie, ouer-cast, and raine-threatening season.*

Laisser passer les plus chargez. *To take no thought, passe the time merrily, let the world slide; (whilest others pine away through care;) or, suffering others, the whilest, to busie, charge, and torment themselues with cares.*

Chargeant: m. ante: f. *Heauie, burthensome, troublesome, expensiue; also, charging, loading, burthening.*

Charger. *To charge, burthen, onerate, load; lye heauie on, lay on, or lay load vpon; also, to trouble, charge, or put vnto charges; also, to giue charge vnto, bestow a charge on; also, to charge, assault, or set on.*

Charger toutes les voiles. *To clap on all the sayles.*

Ie ne charge de rien. *I will take nothing vpon me.*

Qui n'a cheual, ne chariot, il ne charge pas quand il veut: Prov. *He loads not when he lists that wants both horse, and cart.*

Chargnure: f. *as* Charnure.

Chargue: f. *as* Chargue.

Chariage: m. *Carriage; Carriages, Carts, or Waggons laden with prouision.*

Charier. *To Cart; to carrie, or conueigh in a Cart.*

Charier droit. *To tread straight, to take a right course; to behaue himselfe honestly, sincerely, vprightly; or, discreetly, warily, aduisedly.*

Chariot: m. *A Chariot, or Waggon; also, the seuen starres, or* Charles *wayne.*

Chariot branslant. *The Waggon, Coach, or Caroache, that hangs by leathers; a hanging Chariot.*
Compagnon bien parlant vaut en chemin chariot branslant: Prov. *Agrees with the Latine,* Comes facundus in via pro vehiculo est.
Qui n'a cheval ne chariot, il ne charge pas quand il veut: Pro. *Hee often wants of his will, that wants wherewithall.*
Chariotage: m. *Waggonnage; the riding in, or carrying by, wagons, &c.*
Chariotte: f. *A small Chariot, or toy that runs on wheeles, and teaches, or helps young children to goe; also, a kind of Litter borne vp by an axletree, and two wheeles; vsed heretofore by citizens wiues, who were not able, or not allowed to keepe ordinarie Litters.*
Charitable: com. *Charitable; bountifull to the poore, liberall to the needie, mercifull to those in miserie; good vnto all.*
Charitatif: m. iue: f. *as* Charitable; *also, doing charitable deeds; or, inclining vnto charitie.*
Charité: f. *Charitie, loue, mercifulnesse; pitie on, goodnesse vnto, the afflicted, or poore; also, loue, or good will vnto, agreement or concord with, neighbours; heartie friendlinesse maintained, good offices continued vnto, or among, all; also, a bad word giuen, imputation cast on, ill turne done one; and hence;*
Ce sont des charitez qu' il m' a monstré. *Such are the fauors, and friendlie offices which he hath done me in my absence; (Ironically.)*
Il cerche trop bas la charité en fouillant si prés des festes. *Charitie is too high a vertue to be looked for so low as the buttocks.*
Charité oingt, & peché poinct: Pro. *Charitie comforteth, sinne afflicteth.*
Charivaris: m. *A publicke defamation, or traducing of; a foule noise made, blacke* Santus *rung, to the shame, and disgrace of another; hence, an infamous (or infaming) ballade sung, by an armed troupe, vnder the window of an old dotard married, the day before, vnto a young wanton, in mockerie of them both; also, a manner of catching, or killing of Stockdoues by night.*
Charivaris de poelles. *The carting of an infamous person, graced with the harmonie of tinging kettles, and frying-pan Musicke.*
Charlaïde. *Stout, valiant, warlike; resembling, or holding of,* Charles; *(a name, wherein the French (by reason of the worth of some kings of theirs) do very much glorie.)*
Charlatan: m. *A Mountebanke, a cousening drug-seller, a pratling quack-saluer, a tatler, babler, foolish prater, or commender of trifles.*
Charlataner. *To cousen, beguile, gull; cog, foist; play the Mountebanke; to prattle, bable, tattle foolishly.*
Charlatanerie: f. *Cousening, or gulling speech; cogging, foisting, lying; extreme commendation of a trifle, thereby to make it the more saleable.*
Charlater. *Looke* Charlataner.
Charlaterie: f. *Charlatisme; or, as* Charlatanerie.
Charlot: m. *A Curlew.*
Charme: m. *The Yoake tree, Yoake Elme, Horn-beame, Witch-hasell, Hard-beame; also, a Charme, Spell, Incantation, Enchantment; also, a Stuble ground.*
Charmeau: m. *A young, or little Yoake tree.*
Charme-cœur. *Rauishing, heart-charming, thoughts-inchaunting.*
Charme-peine. *Griefe-charming, ache-inchaunting, paine-appeasing.*
Charmer. *To charme; to inchaunt.*
Charmeresse: f. *An Inchauntresse, Witch, or Wizard.*
Charme-soing. *Care-inchaunting, paines-allaying.*
Charme-souci. *Comforting, care-charming, cark-appeasing.*
Charmeur: m. *A Charmer, an Inchaunter, a Wizard.*
Charmeusement. *Charmingly, inchauntingly.*
Charmoye: f. *A groue of Yoakes, or of Horne-beame trees.*
Charnage: m. *Flesh-time; the season wherein flesh is eaten; also, flesh, or flesh-meat.*
Charnalité: f. *Sensualitie, fleshlinesse, carnallnesse.*
Charnaut: m. *Flesh-time; the season wherein flesh may be eaten.*
Charnié: m. *A stake, prop, stay, pole, to support a Vine.*
Charnie: f. *A Plaine, Downe, open, or vninclosed, ground.*
Charnier: m. *A Churchyard, or chanell house; a place wherein dead bodies are layd, or their bones kept; also, a little stake, pole, or prop; also, a poudering tub; and hence;*
Plus rouillé que la claveure d'un vieil charnier; &, Le visage leur reluisoit comme la claveure d' un charnier. *Seeke* Claveure.
Il fera trembler le lard au charnier. *He will doe wonders; or, he will terrifie them wonderfully. (Ironically.)*
Charniere: f. *A hindge; also, a knuckle, or turning ioynt; also, a certaine Deuice, or Engine, whereby a woodden leg, or arme is made to moue; also, as* Chardonnereau.
La charniere des genoux. *The whall-bone, or whirle-bone, of the knees.*
Charnu: m. uë: f. *Fleshie; grosse, corpulent, quarrie, thicke.*
Capeau charnu. *The sea Nettle.*
Charnure: f. *Brawne, fleshinesse, fulnesse of flesh, the substance of bonelesse flesh; the fleshie parts of the bodie.*
La charnure d' herbes. *Their pith, or pulpe; or the knottie, or big swelling of (some of) their staulkes, and rootes.*
Charongne: f. *A carrion; a stinking carkas; putrified flesh.*
Charongneux: m. euse: f. *Full of carrion; stinking of raw, and putrified, flesh.*
Charongnier: m. ere: f. *Affecting, or feeding on, carrion; as Kites, Curres, &c.*
Charopper. *To boyle one sort of liquor nine or ten times ouer; (a word most vsed by Syrrop-makers.)*
Charpentailler. *To cut, hack, hew; as a Carpenter doth Tymber.*
Charpentaire: f. *as* Herbe au Charpentier; *also, the sea-Onyon.*
Charpente: f. *A frame of Tymber (for a house, &c.)*
Bois de charpente. *Tymber.*
Charpenté: m. ée: f. *Wrought, or built, by a Carpenter; made, or framed of Tymber; also, cut, or hewed, as Tymber by a Carpenter; and hence; hacked, slashed, mangled, or wounded (in manie places of the bodie.)*
Charpenter. *To play the Carpenter, worke Carpenters worke; make, build, or frame, of Tymber; also, to cut, or hew as Carpenters doe Tymber; and hence; to hacke, slash, mangle, or wound in many places of the bodie; also, to rumble, or make a great noise in a roome, by remouing of heauie things.*

Charpenterie: f. *Carpentrie, Carpenters worke; the trade of a Carpenter; Architecture of tymber.*
Charpentier: m. *A Carpenter, a Wright.*
Herbe au charpentier. *Prunell, Carpenters-hearbe, Sickle-worte, Hooke-heale, Selfe-heale; also, Kibworte, Lambes tongue, small Plantaine, &c; Looke* Herbe.
Charpi: m. *Lint, or downe (of linnen.) Looke* Charpy.
Charpi: m. ie: f. *Tosed, or towsed; vncluttered, or pulled out (as a thicke locke of wooll;) also, drawne gently, as wooll, in the spinning; also, hatchelled, or hackelled; refined on the hatchell, or flaxcombe.*
Charpie: f. *as* Charpi. *Lint.*
Charpir de la laine. *To tose, or towse it; to pull out, or asunder, the thicke locks thereof; also, to draw it (gently) in spinning.*
Charpir du lin. *To hackle, or hatchell flax; to refine it, by hatchelling, or on the flaxcombe.*
Charpy: m. *Lint.*
Charpy de Nature. *A Cobweb.*
Charrau: m. *A Cart-way; Rutt-way.*
Charrée: f. *Buck-ashes, the ashes whereof Lye hath bin made; also, a little twelue-footed water-worme, much hunted after by Trowtes, and therefore vsed by fishers as a bayt for them.*
Charreton: m. *A little chariot.*
Charette: f. *A Chariot; a Wagon.*
Chasse à la charrette. *is by a Chariot (and the driuer thereof couered with leauie boughes) whereinone lyes, readie with a Peece, or Bowe, to shoot at Deere, while they gaze at the sight, or stop at the noyse, of the wheeles.*
Mangeur de charrettes ferrées. *A terrible cutter, swaggerer, bugbeare, swashbuckler; one that will kill all he sees, and eat all he kils.*
Charriable: com. *Carriable; which may be carried on waynes, or in waggons.*
Charrié: m. *A Bucking cloth, or Nash-cloth.*
Charrié: m. ée: f. *Carried, conueyed by cart, &c.*
Charrier: m. *as* Charrié.
Charrier. *To carrie, or conuey by cart, waine, chariot, or waggon. Looke* Charier.
Charriere. *as* Carriere.
Charron: m. *A Waggon-maker, Cart-wright, or Cart-maker; also, a Waggon-man, Wayne-man, or Carreman; one that driues, or goes with, a Cart, Wayne, or waggon; whence;*
Bon charron tourne en petit lieu: Prov. *A good carter turnes in a narrow corner; a wise fellow quits himselfe well in time of extremitie, or, shifts himselfe easily out of an extremitie.*
Charronnerie: f. *Cart-worke, Cart-making; Carre-directing, or driuing.*
Charroy: m. *Carriage, Portage, Waynage, Wagonnage; the carrying of things by Wayne, Cart, or Waggon; also, a cart, or other cariage; also, a Cart-load, Chariot-load, or Wagon-load of.*
Charroyer. *To carrie in, or transport by, a Wayne, or Cart.*
Charruage: m. *The furniture belonging to a plough; the plough-geeres; also, tilled, or plowed land.*
Droict de charruage. *as* Suitte de disme.
Charruë: f. *A Plough.*
Tourner la charruë contre les bœufs. *To doe things preposterously.*
Charruë de chien ne vaut rien: Prov. *The plough that a dog drawes is not worth the driuing.*
Charrué: m. ée: f. *Tilled, plowed.*
Charruër. *To till, eare, plow.*
Charte: f. *as* Carte; *also, the Charter of a Towne, or Corporation.*
Charté: f. *as* Cherté. *Deerenesse, &c.*
Charté: m. ée: f. *Hauing a Charter, holding, or held by Charter.*
Chartée: f. *A Cart-load, or, Cart-full of.*
Chartepartie: f. *A Charter-partie, or bill of lading.*
Charterie: f. *A carterlie, or churlish, tricke; also, a Houell to set carts vnder.*
Chartier: m. *A Carter, Carreman; Waine-man, Waggonman.*
Il iure comme vn chartier. *He sweares like a Carter; (we say, like a Tinker.)*
Il n'est si bon chartier qui ne verse: Pro. *The best of them sometimes ouerturnes his cart; or, (as we say) the best Cart may orethrow.*
Chartil: m. *The frame of a Cart, Wayne, or Waggon, without the wheeles.*
Chartin. *The same.*
Charton: m. *A Waggoner, or Chariot-driuer.*
Chartre: f. *A Charter (&c, as in* Chartres;) *also, a Prison; or, the darkest, or worst roome in a Prison; the Hole, or Dungeon; also, a Consumption; whence;*
Deuenir, ou estre en chartre. *To fall into, or be in, a consumption; to languish, pine, waste, or wither away; (Metaphorically, from such as hauing beene long pent vp in a close prison, looke, for the most part, most pitifully on it.)*
Chartres: f. *Charters; auncient Rolls, publike Records, Pleadings, Deeds, Instruments, or Euidences, concerning either the Crowne, or Countrey; or, a Comminaltie, or Corporation.*
Tresor des chartres. *The Rolls.*
Chartrier: m. *A Iaylor; also, a prisoner.*
Chartulaire: m. *A Terrier, or Coucher-booke.*
Charvi. *Looke* Chervis.
Chas. *Looke* Chaas.
Chas. à chas vn; *Scarce one, but one, onely one.*
Chascun: m. une: f. *Euerie one, all, each; Looke* Chasque.
Chascun a sa guise. *Euery one as he likes, &c.*
Chascun a son tour: Pro. *Euery one hath his turne, course, time.*
Chascune: f. *Looke* Chacunerie.
Chascunerie, *or* Chascuniere. *Looke* Chacunerie.
Chaseret: m. *A Chessfat, or Cheese-fat.*
Chasereux: m. euse: f. *Belonging to the Chessfat.*
Chasier: m. *A Cheese-presse; or as* Chasiere; *a Cheese-hecke.*
Chasiere: f. *A Cheese-hecke; the long and round racke whereon cheese is dryed; and the great, or grated Saue hung by a pulley, to the top of a Dayrie-house, or Store-house; and seruing to keepe cheese, white-meates, and other belly-timber in.*
Chaslict: m. *A Bedstead.*
Chasmate: f. *A Casemate in fortification; a murthering house placed in the ditch, to plague the assaylants, of a fortresse.*
Chasque: com. *Each; or as* Chascun; *(but with some difference; for this goes euer before a Substantiue; as,* chasque chose, chasque livre, chasque lieu, &c; *the other is most commonly, as a Substantiue, alone;* chascun le voit; chascun à part. &c.
'A chasque mercier son panier: Pro. *Euery one must looke to his owne charge; or, beare his owne burthen.*

Chassable: com. *Chaseable; fit to be chased, pursued, hunted after.*

Chasse: f. *A hunting; a chase, pursuit, or following of; a search for, inquirie after; also, a chase at Tennis; also, a Millers walke, or circuit, wherein he may lawfully fetch grist vnto his Mill; also, (in water-workes) that which forceth the water out, or giueth it force to burst out; any violent expulsion, expression, putting forth, driuing out; also, a Shrine for a Relicke, or other (held) sacred thing; also, that thing, or part of a thing, wherein another is enchased; and hence;*

La chasse d'un Raisor. *The handle of a Rasor.*

La chasse d'une Rose. *The greene sprigs on the bottome, or backside, of a Rose.*

La chasse des souldes. *Looke* Soulde.

La chasse d' un trebuchet. *The shrine of a paire of gold weights; the hollow wherein the Cocke, Tongue, or Tryall playeth.*

Arbaleste de courte chasse. *That carries, or shoots, leuell but a little way.*

Harquebouse de chasse. *A fowling peece.*

En chasse. *A bulling; as a Cow thats wanton.*

Marquez bien cette chasse. *Heed well that passage, marke well the point, whereof I haue informed you.*

Retourner ses chasses. *A hauke, when she hath flown out, at her height, to come in againe.*

C'est vne Chasse ou le veneur est prins: Pro. *Said of the ill (but deserued) successe of a false Accusation; or of any Enterprise, that proues hurtfull to the vndertaker, or deuiser of it; wee say of such a one; hee hath made a rod for his owne tayle.*

Il n'est chasse que de vieux levrier: Prov. *An old dog hunts surest, bites sorest, holds what he catches, kils what he reaches.*

Chassé: m. ée: f. *Chased, pursued; hunted after; put to flight; driuen away; reiected, or cast off; expelled out of.*

Chasse-bosse. *Hearbe-willow, or Willow-hearb, Loosestrife.*

Chasse-chien: m. *The Clarke, or inferiour Officer, of a Church; who (besides his authoritie ouer dogges) distributes the holie-bread, and begs for the (massing) Priest.*

Chasse-corneille: f. *A kind of small fowling peece.*

Chasse-crainte: com. *Feare-expelling.*

Chasse-diable. *Saint* Iohns *worte, Saint* Iohns *grasse.*

Chasse-ennui. *Care-expelling, cheering vp.*

Chasse-erreur. *Error-expelling, zealous of truth.*

Chasse-fievre: f. *Germaunder, English Treacle; an hearbe.*

Chasse-mal. *Mischiefes-expelling, ill-things out-driuing.*

Chasse-marée: m. *A Rippier.*

Chasse-messe: f. *A fire-locke; or horsemans peece that goes off by a fire-locke, and is charged with Quarter-shot of steele; so tearmed, because first vsed by them of the Religion.*

Chasse-monstre: com. *Monster-pursuing (an Epithite for* Hercules.)

Chasse-mort: com. *Preseruatiue, death-expelling.*

Chasse-nuë. *Skie-cleering.*

Chasse-ordure: com. *Cleansing, purging, filth-expelling, filthinesse out-driuing.*

Chasse-pape. *as* Chasse-messe. *(A word deuised in the late ciuile warres.)*

Chasse-peine. *Toyle-expelling; cares-excluding; as wine, and gold, &c.*

Chasse-peste. substan. *as* Chasse-bosse.

Chasse-peste. adject. *Plague-expelling.*

Chasse-poulx. *Wild blacke Ellebore, or Beares-foot.*

Chasser. *To chase, or driue away; to expell, reiect, cast off, or put away; also, to hunt; or, follow after; to pursue, or giue chase vnto.*

Chasser apres les mouches. *To spend the time most vainely, idly, foolishly; to as little purpose as may be; or, to loose time altogether.*

Autant vaut celuy qui chasse & rien ne prend, comme celuy qui lit & rien n'entend: Pro. *As good hunt and take nought, as read and vnderstand nought.*

Chasse-rage. *The hearb wild Cresses; or, Dittanie, Dittander, Pepper-wort.*

Chasse-rat. *A certaine harmelesse Serpent, called so, because she, commonly, feeds on Rats.*

Chasseresse: f. *A huntresse.*

Chasseret: m. *A little hunter.*

Chasserie: f. *Hunting; a chasing.*

Chasserot: m. otte: f. *Much giuen to hunting.*

Chasseteron. *A verie small chest, or coffer, of wood.*

Chasseton: m. *A Scrichowle; also, a little chest of wood.*

Chasseur: m. *A hunter, a chaser; one that seeketh, or traceth out, others.*

Chasseur de mouches. *A kill-flye; a Braggadochio; also, a vaine or idle fellow.*

Desjuner de chasseur. *A large, or great, breakefast (eaten.)*

Messe de chasseur. *A short, or soone-sayed, Masse.*

Chassie. *Looke* Chacie.

Chassieuseté: f. *Extreame bleare-eyednesse.*

Chassieux: m. euse: f. *Bleare-eyed; whose eyes doe runne continually.*

Chassis: m. *A frame of wood for a window; (hence) also, a woodden, paper, or linnen, window; and, the bands, or borders that are on either side of a dore, gate, or window; also, a Printers Tympane.*

Chassissé. Fenestre chassissée. *A window that is couered with Paper, or Linnen cloth, in stead of glasse.*

Chassitier: m. *A maker of woodden, or paper, windowes; or of frames, for paper, or linnen, windowes.*

Chassoire: f. *A Carters whip, or whip to driue horses.*

Chassot: m. *The Gull, Bull-head, or Millers thumbe; (a fish.)*

Chastaigne: f. *A Chesnut.*

Chastaigne chevaline. *The horse Chesnut; or, a kind of great blacke Chesnut; rounder and sweeter, but lesse sauourie, then the ordinarie one.*

Chastaigne d' eau. *The water Nut, Saligot, water Caltrop.*

Chastaigne femelle. *The small, or wild Chesnut.*

Chastaigne marine. *The sea Vrchin (a little shell-fish;) some also call so, the water Caltrop.*

Chastaigne masle. *as* Marron; *the great, or domesticall Chesnut.*

Chastaigne de mer. *The sea Vrchin.*

Chastaigne de riviere. *as* Chastaigne d'eau.

Il en plumera la chastaigne. *Hee will smart, or pay deerely, for it; it will cost him deerely; Seeke* Plumer.

Chastaigneraye: f. *A Groue, Plot, or Orchard of Chestnut trees.*

Chastaignier: m. *A Chessen, or Chestnut, tree.*

Chastain. *Chestnut-colour, Liuer-hue.*

Chaste: com. *Chast, lustlesse, continent, honest of bodie; pure, vndefiled; inuiolated, not distained with filth, or any (vnlawfull) Venerie.*

Chasteadun. *The chiefe towne of the Countie of* Dunois; *whose inhabitants being as rash, as quicke spirited, gaue beginning to the prouerbiall phrase.*

Il est de Chasteadun. *He replies too hastily; he is too quicke of conceit; presuming he vnderstands all ones meaning by one word, he often mistakes all.*

Chasteau: m. *A castle (is properly, a house furnished with towers, incompassed by walls, and ditches; and strengthened by a Mount, or Donjon in the middest; yet the French Courtiers tearme so any house of the kings;) also, a Rooke at Chesse.*

Chasteau deuant. *The fore-castle of a ship.*

Faire des chasteaux en Espaigne. *To build castles in the aire (say we;) to muse he knowes not about what; to bestow the time in friuolous contemplations; to bee full of wandering, and vain imaginations; to propound vnto himselfe, or others, most idle, or impossible, exploits; (for there are but few Castles in the main land of Spain; or if more were to be built, who hath to do withall but the Spaniard?)*

Chasteau abbatu est à demi refaict: Prov. *A castle once throwne downe is halfe repaired.*

Bon chasteau garde qui sçait sont corps garder: Prov. *A good fort guards he, that himselfe can guard.*

Chastel: m. *as* Chasteau; *also, a kind of Peare whereof excellent Perrie is made; also, a chattell; or, stuffe, goods, moueables.*

Deniers chastels. *Looke* Chaptels.

Chastelain: m. *A Lord Castellain; the Lord, or owner of a castle, or of a fortified house; or of a territorie, vnto which Castle-like Iurisdiction, and Royalties, belong; inferiour to a Baron in ranke (though in few points of Rights) and the meanest Lord of dignitie that is; also, the Gouernour, Captaine, Constable, or Iudge, of a Castle, or of a Towne that hath, or hath had, a castle in it; such as be, at this day,* Les Chastelains des villes de Dauphiné, Auvergne, *and* Poictou; *as also those of the countrey of* Forests *(wherein there be Iudges of this name, whose Iurisdiction exceedes not matters of threescore shillings value;) And as now in these Prouinces* Les Chastelains *are, euen so heretofore in all others they were, but Officers, (Captaines, or Iudges) placed by Dukes, or Earles (that had large Territories) within their principall, and most remote Bouroughes, to containe the inhabitants in obedience, or to administer Iustice vnto them, in ordinarie matters (for they were allowed to exercise no other then* basse Iustice *in villages, and* moyenne *in townes;) Thus hauing the commaund of Places, and being farre from their Lords, they incroached, by degrees, on the Inheritance, and Seignorie thereof, and so became of Officers, absolute Lords; turning all duties, and rights, which formerly they yeelded vnto their founders, into a bare Tenure; or holding (as vassales, or tenants) that of them, which at first (as Ministers, or Deputies) they held vnder them: And afterwards not contented with* La Basse *or* moyenne Iustice, *they vsurped* La haute; *and (more then that) all such extraordinarie, or two-fold Iurisdiction as the Barons of those times had; and held it vntill the yeare* 1573. *(Looke* Droict de Bailliage;) *Also, the Iudge, or Steward of a Lord Castellains Courts.*

Grand chastelain. *A Lord Baron; called so in many places, from the conformitie that is betweene the Estates of a Baron, and a* Chastelain, *who hath vsurped (almost) all Baron-like Rights, and Royalties.*

Chastelain: m. aine: f. *Of, or belonging to, a Castle; Castleship, Castlewicke, or Castleward.*

Chastelainerie: f. *as* Chastellenie; *or the Stewardship of a Lord Castellains courts.*

Chastelet: m. *A little Castle, Fort, or Hould; also, a Court, or Auditorie, of Iustice; a Guild-hall, or (ordinarie) Sessions house, within a citie, wherein both ciuile, and criminall causes are heard, and determined by a Lieutenant, or Prouost (royall) and certaine Assistant* Conseillers; *also, a prison (for great persons;) also, the childish game Cobnut; or (rather) the throwing of a Ball at a heape of Nuts, which done, the thrower takes as many as he hath hit, or scattered.*

Le petit Chastelet. *The name of a prison.*

Chastellain. *Looke* Chastelain.

Chastellé: m. ée: f. *Castellated (a tearme of* Blason.)

Chastellenie: f. *A Castle-wicke, or Castleship; the Tenure, or Honour of a Castleship; the Estate, Iurisdiction, or Dignitie of a Lord Castellain; a kind of Seigniorie thats held of some other then the king, or not directly of the Crowne, and hath all (subalterne) Iurisdiction annexed vnto it. (In respect whereof,* Toutes les Iustices ayans plein Territorie, & entier commandement sont appellées Chastellenies; *and in old Law-bookes this word often signifies,* L'enclaue, & distroict de toute pleine, & entiere Iustice, *sayes a learned Frenchman;) And though it be inferiour to a Baronnie in point of dignitie, and sometimes subiect in Tenure (some* Chastellenies *being held of Barons) and haue a farre lesse Territorie belonging to it (for a Baronnie should containe at least three* Chastellenies) *yet doth it resemble it in all Priuiledges, and Royalties; except that of the walled, or fortified towne; in stead whereof, the Lord Castellain may haue a castle, or fortified house; and hath power to debarre any one from building such another within his Territorie, though the King haue graunted the other a Licence to doe it.*

Droict de chastellenie. *So is* Droict de Bailliage *called in the custome of* Meaux; *because it belongs vnto Lords Castellains.*

Chastellerie. *as* Chastellenie.

Chastement. *Chastly, continently, honestly, modestly, without lust.*

Chasteneraïe: f. *A plot, or ground full of Chestnut trees.*

Chasteté: f. *Chastitie, continencie, lustlesnesse.*

Chastiable: com. *Chasticeable; fit to be chastised.*

Chastié: m. ée: f. *Chastised, punished; corrected.*

Chastier. *To chastise, punish; correct.*

Qui bien aime bien chastie: Prov. *He that loues throughly, payes home when he punishes.*

Qui ne chastie culot ne chastie culasse: Prov. *He that censures not small faults, ouersees great ones; or, he that will not amend small faults, cannot amend great ones.*

Chastieur: m. *A Chastiser, Punisher; Corrector.*

Chastiment: m. *Chasticement, punishment, correction.*

Chasti-villain. *A whip, scourge, or cudgell for a knaue; also, a Castle, or Citadell in, or neere, a good Towne.*

Chastrable: com. *Geldable; fit to bee gelt, speyed, or splayed.*
Chastré: m. ée: f. *Gelt, speyed, cut, lib'd, splayed.*
Vn arrest chastré. *Part whereof is reuoked by way of interpretation, or declaration of the Court that made it.*
Porc chastré. *A hog, or barrow hog.*
Chastrement: m. *A gelding, libbing, speying, splaying.*
Chastrer. *To geld, lib, cut, spey, splay.*
Chastrer les arbres. *To pierce them at the foot, therby to make them void th'ill humors which are in their stocke, and branches; also, to discharge them of noysome, and superfluous branches, or buds.*
Chastrer les mousches à miel. *To driue a hiue (of Bees.)*
Chastrer le parc. *To cull th'oldest sheepe out of a flocke, and furnish it with as many yong ones.*
Chastreur: m. *A gelder, libber, speyer.*
Chastrure: f. *as* Chastrement; *Also, the art, or manner of gelding.*
La chastrure d'un saulx. *The superfluous buds, or twigs which haue beene cut, or pulled, from it.*
Chasuble: f. *A chasuble, a fashion of cope thats open onely in the sides; and is worne at Masse both by the Priest (who hath it round) and his assistant Deacon, and Subdeacon, who haue it square, in the bottome.*
Chat: m. *A cat, a pusse.*
Chat fourré. *A Pettifogger, or paultrie Lawyer.*
Chat garanier. *Looke* Chat-garanier.
Chat huant. *An Owle, or Madge-howlet; Looke* Chat-huant.
Chat de mer. *The smallest (kind of) Dog-fish.*
Herbe au chat, ou, de chat. *Nep, or Nip, cats Mint.*
Herbe aux chats. *The same; also, as* Ortie puante.
Oeil de chat. *Calues-snowt, Snapdragon (an hearbe;) also, a certaine white gemme; (Looke* Oeil*;) also, a cats-eye; or sight that is as good by night as in the day; also, a great, and out-strouting eye.*
Patte de chat. *Ground iuie, cats-foot, alehoose, tunehoose, Gill creepe by the ground.*
Pied de chat. *A kind of port, or vpset of a bit, made like a Cats foot.*
Poil de chat. *A whitlow in the finger; also, the festering sore, tearmed a cats-tayle.*
Poire chat. *The name of a wholsome, sweet-smelling, and sharpe-tasting peare.*
Sault du chat. *The cat-leape; a certaine tricke done by Tumblers, and vaulters vpon a table set aslope against a wall.*
Acheter chat en poche, ou en sac. *We say, to buy a pig in a poke.*
Aller du pied comme vn chat maigre. *To be light, or swift of foot; also, to tread lightly, nicely, softly, gingerly, as if he went on egs.*
Avoir vn oeil à la poisle l'autre au chat. *To heed as well what will decrease, as what doth encrease, his gaine.*
Donner à manger au chien, & au chat. *To keepe a plentifull house.*
Entendre le chat sans dire minon. *To haue a good conceit, quicke apprehension, readie vnderstanding; to know without telling what is to be done.*
Esveiller le chat qui dort. *To incense an angrie bodie when he is at quiet; to set th'ill minded on mischiefe; to rub a hidden sore; to remember a forgotten fault.*
Plus esveillé qu'un chat qu'on fouette. *More quick, or nimble, than a whipped cat.*
Iecter le chat aux iambes à. *To cast an imputation, to lay the whole blame, and shame of an offence, on.*
Mettre la campane au chat. *To begin a quarell, to raise a brabble, make a iarre, set at oddes, or together by the eares; we say also, in the same sence, to hang the bell about the cats necke.*
On ne prend pas tels chats sans mouffles. *(Sayed of a strong towne, or stout person;) they will not bee forced, or fetched in easily; they will scratch those that offer to catch them, and therefore go prouided for them.*
Vous l' eussiez fait passer par le trou du chat. *You had made him doe wonderfull matters; or any thing. (ironically.)*
Chat eschaudé craint l'eau froide: Prov. *The scaulded cat feares water though't be cold.*
Le chat a faim quand il ronge du pain: Pro. *The cat is hungrie when a crust contents her.*
Au chat cendreux iamais ne tombe rien en gueule: Prov. *An idle house-doue neuer gets preferment.*
Au chat lescheur bat on souvent la gueule: Prov. *The lickorous cat hath many a rap.*
'A bon rat bon chat: Prov. *Two knaues well met, or matched.*
Celuy a bon gage du chat qui en tient la peau: Prov. *Hee's sure of a cat that hath her skin.*
C'est belle bataille des chiens, & des chats, chacun a des ongles: Prov. *Looke* Bataille.
Les rats se promenent à l'aise là ou il n'y a point de chats: Prov. *Where cats are wanting rats in freedome walke.*
Occasion trouve qui son chat bat: Prov. *Wee say (with some difference) a man may easily find a staffe to beat his dog.*
Tant dort le chat qu'il se resveille: Prov. *See* Resveiller.
Trop tard se repend le rat entre les pattes du chat: Prov. *When punishment's inflicted repentance comes too late.*
Chat-chastel, ou chateil. *A defensiue engine of warre, somewhat resembling the Roman* Testudo, *and grown (as it) altogether out of vse.*
Chate: f. *A she-cat, or doe-cat; also, a certaine Engine, wherewith fish is (forbidden to be) caught.*
Chatel: m. *A chattell, or mouable:* ¶Norm.
Chatemite. *An hypocrite; a counterfeiter of holinesse, religion, deuotion.*
Chatemiterie: f. *Hypocrisie; a faining of zeale, a counterfeiting of holinesse, religion, or deuotion.*
Chatemitiquement. *Hypocritically.*
Chatemitte. *Looke* Chatemite.
Chatepeleuse: f. *A corne-deuouring mite, or weeuell.*
Chat-fourré: m. *A Lawyer; or Pettifogger (who commonly weares a gowne furred with wild cat:* ¶Rab.
Chat-garanier: m. *A Polecat; or, a kind of wild Cat that haunts warrens.*
Chat-huant: m. *The great (rough-legd) Owle; also, the Horne-coot, or Horne-owle.*
Chat-huant plombé. *A small, and leaden-coloured Owle, very common in* Lorraine.
Petit chat-huant. *An Owlet, or the little (rough-legd) Owle.*
Chatillons: m. *Small fresh-water Lampreyes; called so at* Tholouse.
Chaton: m. *The Beazill, Collet, head, or broadest part of a ring, &c, wherein the stone is set; also, the paulme, or flower of a willow; Looke* Chatton.
Chaton de l'oeil; *as* Orbite.
Chatonner. *To kittle, or bring forth yong cats.*
Chatonnie: f. *A waggish tricke, a knauish or vnhappie pranke;*

pranke; also, th'art of pilfering, or nimming.

Chatouille: f. *A (certaine) fish, thats verie full of small bones, and therefore dangerous meat.*

Chatouillé: m. ée: f. *Tickled; gently, or with pleasure, touched; also, flattered; soothed, pleased with prayses.*

Chatouillement: m. *A tickling; a pleasant, or gentle touching, a delightfull mouing; also, flatterie, a soothing, praising, smoothing.*

Chatouiller. *To tickle, to touch gently,; to glad, or ioy by touching; to moue with pleasure, to prouoke with delight; also, to flatter, claw, smooth, praise, please with faire words.*

Se chatouiller pour se faire rire. *To flatter, and please himselfe with fond hopes, and vaine imaginations; also, to forge idle, and vnseasonable ieasts for himselfe to laugh at if others will not.*

Chatouilleux: m. euse: f. *Ticklish; tickle; quaint, nice, daintie, precise; loath, backward; odde, preposterous; wayward, froward; keene, soone cutting, dangerous to be touched, ill to be handled, hard to be dealt with.*

Chatouilleux à la pointe. *Quicke on the spurre, or, quickly answering the spurre.*

Chatouilloir: m. *Any ticklish part of the bodie, especially the side.*

Chatrin: m. *A Goaler (an old word.)*

Chat-rocher. *A kind of Doggefish.*

Chatte: f. *A she cat, or doe cat.*

Toute chatte a son febvrier: Pro. *Euerie man hath his madding fit; or, a season there is, wherein many women may be wooed, if not wonne.*

Chattement: m. *A kitling; a breeding, or bringing forth kitlings, or yong cats.*

Chattemiterie. *Looke* Chatemiterie.

Chatton: m. *A kitling, or yong cat.*

Des chattons. *The Catkins, Cattails, aglet-like blowings, or bloomings, of nut-trees, &c.*

Chatus. *A kind of vine.*

Chauäns: m. *Howlets, little Owles.*

Chavassine: f. *A measure, or quantitie, of land, containing in length 120 foot, and in breadth 30; an Oxegang, or dayes worke for two plough-Oxen; also, the end of a close, or furrow, where the plough turneth.*

Chauce. *as* Chausse.

Chauceaux. *Taxes paied, or fees allowed, vnto some Lords in* Henault, *for the maintenance of the common bankes, or causeyes.*

Chaucée. *Looke* Chaussée.

Chauchage. *Looke* Chaussage.

Chauché. *Troden on; troden downe; also, troden, as a henne by a cocke.*

Chauche-mare. *The disease tearmed the Nightmare.*

Chaucher. *To tread, as a cocke doth a henne; & hence, to tread on, or downe.*

Chaud: m. *A heat, hot season, hot place.*

Chaud: m. de: f. *Hot; feruent, ardent; also, teastie, cholericke, in a chafe, in a fume; also, vehement, violent, fierce, eagar, earnest; hastie, furious.*

Chaud mal. *A continuall feauer; or, burning Ague.*

De fievre en chaud mal. *From ill to worse; out of the frying pan into the fire.*

Fer chaud. *A marking yron, searing yron, red-hot yron.*

'A chaude colle. *In anger, in choller, while the bloud is hot, or vp; also, looke* Chaude-colle.

Il a les pieds chauds. *Hee is lustie, liuelie, gamesome, frolicke, wanton; also, he babbles, or brabbles, much.*

Il ne trouve rien de chaud; *Or,* Il ne trouve rien trop chaud, ny trop pesant. *He will take, or vndertake any thing; nothing (whereof profit may be made) comes amisse vnto him.*

Chaude: f. vne chaude. *A heating, as of yron in the fire; also, a fierce onset, a violent assault.*

'A la chaude. *In a chafe, in heat, in choller.*

Chaudeau: m. *A Caudle; or, warme broth.*

Chaude-colle: f. *Saltnesse, leacherousnesse, geereitch.*

'A chaude-colle. *Hotly; Looke in* Chaud.

Chaudement. *Hotly; ardently, feruently; angrily, fiercely, furiously; eagarly, earnestly, vehemently; roundly, in hast, in great heat.*

Chauderon: m. *A Cauldron, or kettle.*

Le chauderon machure la poisle; *one friend, or kinsman defames, disgraces, or detracts from, another.*

Convercle digne du chauderon. *Like maister like man; or bad intertainment for a bad guest; the punishment his leudnesse deserued.*

Chauderonnée: f. *A cauldron-full of.*

Chauderonnerie: f. *Flesh (or fish) thats ordinarily boiled in cauldrons, or kettles.*

Chauderonnier: m. *A Copper-smith; Kettle-maker; Tinker.*

Chaudet: m. *A warme place.*

Chaudiere: f. *A great cauldron, or kettle.*

Chaudot: m. *A heat, or hot thing.*

Chaudron: m. *A kettle, or cauldron; Looke* Chauderon.

Chaudronnée. *A kettle-full of.*

Chaudronnier. *Looke* Chauderonnier.

Chaveniere. *for* Cheneviere. *A hempe-yard, or hempen close.*

Chauet. *in stead of* Cahuët: ¶Rab.

Chauffage: m. *Fewell; heating stuffe, or stuffe to heat with; also, a heating.*

Droict de chauffage. *A certaine quantitie of fewell, due vnto diuers officers of the (French) kings woods, (but denied by the last king, vnto some of them.)*

Chauffe-cire: m. *A Chafe-wax (in the Chauncerie, &c.)*

Chauffe-con. *as* Chauffe-dos; *(called so because homelie women vse to warme their nether parts before such poore chimneyes;) or a stoue; such a one as a Dutch woman, in Winter-time, sets betweene her legs as she sits.*

Chauffe-dos: m. *A fashion of small, and low chimney, which hath but a hole, in stead of a funnell, for the voiding of smoke.*

Chauffe-pied: m. *A foot-stoue; a little and low stoue that serues to keepe the feet warme.*

Chauffer. *To heat, warme, chafe.*

Chauffer la cire. *To endure a long expectation of a benefit, or fauour, promised.*

Ie cognois bien de quel bois il se chauffe. *I know him as well as he that made him; I know well ynough what ayles him, what he would haue, what hee can doe.*

De trop pres se chauffe qui se brusle: Prov. *Hee stands too neere the fire that burnes himselfe.*

Tel se cuide chauffer qui se brusle: Prov. *Some, thinking but to warme, do burne, themselues.*

Chaufferette, *or* Chauffette: f. *A chafing-dish.*

Chauffour. *Looke* Chaufour.

Chauffourrer.

Chauffourrer. *To soyle, blot, marre, disfigure, bismeare; Looke* Chaffourrer.
Chaufour: m. *A lime kilne; a hole wherein lime hath beene made, or, whence the stuffe that makes it hath bin digged.*
Chaufournier: m. *A lime burner, or lime maker; also, one that works onely with lime, and chalke.*
Chaufrain. *as* Chanfrain.
Chauguette. *as* Eschaugette; *A watch-tower.*
Chauld. *Looke* Chaud.
Chaulde. *Looke* Chaude.
Chauliere: f. *A plot, or bed, of cabbidges in a Garden.*
Chaulmage: m. *The cutting, or mowing of straw, or stubble.*
Chauline: f. *Straw; or the stemme of corne.*
Chaulmer. *To picke, or gather vp straw; also, to cut, or mow, stubble.*
Chaulmeur: m. *A gatherer, or picker vp, of straw; a cutter, or mower of stubble.*
Chaulsepot. *A certaine little bird.*
Chaulx: f. *Lime.*
Chaulx metallique. *Is made (especially that kind whereof Ennamell is compounded) of two parts of lead, and one of Cornewall Tinne, well calcinated together in an ouen of reuerberation.*
Chaumeny: m. ye: f. *Mustie, mouldie, vnseasonable:* ¶Gasc. ¶Rab.
Chaumer. *as* Chaulmer; &, *as* Chommer.
Chaumes. *Desart, or vntilled, grounds; lay lands; or, as* Terres Chaumieres.
Chaumier: m. ere: f. *Strawie, of straw.*
Terres chaumieres. *Stubble grounds.*
Chaumin: m. ine: f. *Stubblie; made of, or, couered with stubble.*
Chaumine: f. *A thatched cote, or cabbin.*
Chaumoufflet: m. *Dunghill put into a cornet of paper, then kindled, and the smoke thereof put into the nosethrils of a sleeper; wee call it, a choaking pie, or cold pie.*
Chaussage: m. *Shooe-money; expence in shooes; (also, in hose) also, hosen, or shooes.*
Chaussant: m. ante: f. *Shooing, putting on shooes.*
Marroquin chaussant. *Gentle, yeelding, retching.*
Chausse: f. *A hose; a stocking, or netherstocke* (Bas de Chausse) *also, a breeke, or breech; (in which sence it is most commonly plurall)* Haut de chausses.
Chausse d'un aysement. *The bottome of a iakes; the roome, or hole, whereinto the ordure falls.*
Chausses à la bigotte. *Looke* Bigotte.
Chausses à la bougrine. *Strait Venitians without codpeeces.*
Chausse de clistere. *A glister bag.*
Chausses à la Garguesque. *Gregges, or Gallogaskins.*
Chausses à la gigotte. *A fashion of very close Venitians; old fashioned Venitians.*
Chausse d'hypocras. *The felt or cloth, through which that wine is distilled.*
Chausses en poincte. *Peeces of cloth wherewith Apothecaries clarifie their syropes; vsed in stead of the felt.*
Chausses à queuë de merlus. *Round breeches with strait cannions; hauing in the seat a peece like a fishes tayle; and worne by old men, schollers, and such like niggardlie, or needie, persons.*
Chausses à Tabourin. *Big, out-standing, or out-strouting, breeches; or the Swisse round hose, whose panes resemble the outside of a Taber.*
Braye à chausse. *A kind of fish-net made somewhat like a wide hose.*
Courtes chausses. *Women; (belike, because many of them weare short breeches, and few of them long stockings.)*
Tirer les chausses. *To kicke vp the heeles; to make a dye.*
'A courte chausse longue laniere: Prov. *(So that what wants in the one may bee supplied by the other.)*
Le vin va sans chausses: Prov. *Wine weares no breeches; a drunkard conceales nothing.*
Chaussé: m. ée: f. *Hosed; shod; that hath hose, or shooes on, or put on.*
Chaussée: f. *A woman that weares breeches; also, the causey, banke, or damme, of a pond, or of a riuer; also, the leuell, or superficies of the earth, whereout a wall first appeares aboue ground; (Looke* Rez.)
Tel mur est abbatu à rez de chaussée. *Is ouerthrowne flat, or made leuell to th'earth.*
Chausse-pied: m. *A shooing horne.*
Chausse-pot. *Looke* Chaulse-pot.
Chausser. *To shooe, to shod, to serue, fit, or furnish with shooes; also, to hose; to put on, or fit with, hose; or (lesse properly) gloues.*
Chausser les ailes aux pieds, ou, les esperons aux talons à. *To course, or giue hard chace vnto; also, to make to scud, runne, or flie a mayne; also, to make forward, or earnest, in pursuite of.*
Il me chaussa bien les esperons enuers le Roy. *He made me, by the tales I heard he had told of me, hye me towards the King.*
Il y chaussa bien mal ses lunettes. *He mistooke exceedingly, or was much ouerseene, therein.*
Il me chausse à moins de poincts que. *He makes me inferior vnto; or makes lesse to serue my turne then.*
Chaussetier: m. *A hosier, or hose-maker.*
Chaussetrape: f. *A Caltrop; or iron engine of warre, made with foure pricks, or sharp points, whereof one, howsoeuer, it is cast, euer stands vpward; also, the starre-thistle; (called (also) the Calthrop) also the water Calthrop, water Nut, Saligot; also, a Trapdoore.*
Chausse-trappe. *The same.*
Chaussettes: f. *Short linnen breeches, drawers, or vnder-hose.*
Chaussettes à estrier. *Stirrup stockings.*
Chausseure: f. *A hosing, or shooing; also, hosen, or shooes; Looke* Chaussure.
Chausson: m. *A litle hose; also, a socke.*
Chaussure: f. *A hosing, or shooing; also, hosen, or shooes.*
Ils ont rencontré chaussure à leur pied. *They haue met with stuffe for their purpose; or, they haue met with their matches;* Ils ont trouvé ch: &c: *The same.*
Le vin n'a point de chaussure: Pro. *Wine euer goes bare breeched; the drunkard discouers all thats within, or about, him; any man may see his hart, and (if he haue a mind) his arse.*
Chauve: com. *Bauld, bauld headed, bauld pated.*
Chauve d'esprit. *Bauld-spirited: that hath as little wit in, as he hath haire on, his head.*
Chauver. *To wax bauld.*
Chauver des oreilles. *To clap downe the eares, as a horse, or asse doth, when he is angrie, or intendeth mischieue; also, to make a signe with the eares.*

Chauvesouris: m. *A Batt, Flittermouse, Reremouse.*
Chauvesourissier: m. *The bat-wing bone (in the lower part of the head) so called, because it spreads, or is made like the wing of a bat.*
Chauveté: f. *Bauldnesse; bauld-patednesse (and hence) also, the barenesse of a place whereon nothing growes.*
Chauvir. *To wax bauld.*
Chauvissant. *Waxing bauld; also, smiling, or smoyling.*
Chauvisser. *as* Chauvir; *Also, to smile, or smoyle.*
Chaux: f. *as* Chaulx; *Lime.*
Chaziere: f. *Looke* Chasiere.
Cheant. *Falling, or tumbling downe.*
Cheau: m. *A whelpe, or cub.*
Chebule. *The biggest kind of the Mirabolan plumme; (is long, and somewhat like a peare, or a small leymon.*
Chedins: m. *The chiefe, or head men of the parish; called so by the barbarous peasant.*
Chef: m. *The head (of a man or woman;) also, a Chiefe, or Generall; a head, or principall Commaunder; also, the end of a place, time, or businesse; also, as* Chef lieu.
Le chef des armes d'une maison. *Is, the eldest brother of a house, or the most ancient house in a familie, which giues th'armes thereof without any difference.*
Chef d'oeuvre. *A Maister-peece, or Maisters peece; any principall peece of worke, or of workemanship.*
Fief en chef. *A Fief held in Chiefe, or in Capite.*
La piece du chef. *A French coyfe.*
'A chef de piece. *In th'end, at length; also, as one would wish it.*
Venir à chef d'un' affaire. *To compasse, finish, or ouercome, a businesse.*
Venir à chef de son intention. *To obtaine, or attaine to, his purpose; to compasse, or accomplish his desire.*
Venir à chef d'un mauvais marchand. *To fetch ouer or preuaile against, an euill customer.*
Le pied saisit le chef. *Looke* Pied.
Chef. *Chiefe, principall; capitall; paramount; Hence;* Chef cens; chef lieu; chef mets; chef seigneur, &c.
Chefcier: m. *The Threasurer, or keeper of a Vestrie.*
Chef-gros: m. *Shoomakers thread.*
Chef mois: m. *A chiefe Mannor house:* ¶Norm.
Cheintre: f. *A baulke, or swathe of grasse, along a hedge, or high-way.*
Chegros: m. *Shoomakers great thread.*
Chelhydre. *Looke* Chelydre.
Chelidoine: f. *Celandine; (an hearbe, whereof there be two kinds.)*
Chelidoine la grande. *Celandine the greater, common Celandine, Tettarwort, Swallowort, Swallowes hearb.*
Chelidoine mineure. *Little Celandine, or, Celandine the lesse, Pilewort, Figwort.*
Cheline: m. *A knaue, a skellam.*
Chelsydre. *Looke* Chelydre.
Chelydre. *A most venomous, and stinking Snake, or Serpent; rough-scaled, broad headed, and of a darke tawnie colour.*
Chemage: m. *The passage toll, or through-toll, thats payed at* Sens.
Chemard: m. arde: f. *Sad, pensiue, melancholicke, pining away by thought, and carefulnesse.*
Cheme. *An ancient measure holding about two spoonefuls.*
Chemer. *To decrease, or be (as the Moone) in the wane; to languish, grow leane, wast, pine, or fall away through care, thought, griefe, anguish, or anxietie of mind.*
Chemicher. *To whimper.*
Chemier: m. *The eldest, or chiefe heire in a discent; who is to do homage, and such other primarie dueties for the whole land that is discended.*
Chemin: m. *A way; a tract, or path to go in; a street, or causey to trauell in; a road; rut; passage; course, traine; iourney.*
Chemin chastellain (de Boullenois.) *Is 20 foot broad.*
Chemin de Clermont. *Is 32 foot broad.*
Chemin d'escole. *The longest, or furthest way.*
Chemin forain de Boullenois. *Is fifteene foot broad.*
Chemin S. Iacques. *The white streake in the skie, tearmed,* Via lactea, *or, the Milkie way.*
Chemin Royal. *The Kings high-way; which by the customes of some places may be made 60 foot broad; in others it is to be narrower; as;*
Chemin Royal de Vallois. *Is but 30 foot broad in arrable grounds, and 40 in woods.*
Chemin vicomtier (de Boullenois.) *Is thirtie foot.*
Chemin voisinal. *Is to be eight foot broad.*
Le grand chemin. *The ordinarie high-way; (which by the customes of* Tours, Lodunois, *and other places, must be sixteene foot broad; in some countries much more; as;*
Le grand chemin de Boullenois. *Must be sixtie foot broad.*
Le grand chemin de Bourgongne. *Is to bee thirtie foot broad.*
Le grand chemin peageau. *By the custome of* Anjou, *and* Maine, *must bee foureteene foot broad.*
Le grand chemin Royal de Boullenois. *Is sixtie foot broad.*
Le grand chemin Royal de Clermont. *Is to bee 64 foot broad.*
Tout d'un chemin. *All vnder one.*
Batre les chemins. *To way-lay, or lie in wait for, passengers; to rob on the high-way.*
Couper chemin à. *To barre, stop, crosse, preuent, forestall.*
Gaigner chemin. *To make speed, go fast, ride hard, rid away apace.*
Il nous faut despescher de cela, comme d'un mauvais chemin. *We must rid that as wee would an ill way; we must rid our hands of that as we would our feet of ill way; such worke should as quickly be rid off, as ill way would be rid ouer.*
Aller & venir font le chemin peler: Prov. *Seeke* Aller.
Il ne se tort pas qui va plain chemin: Prov. *Hee goes not much awry that keepes the high road way.*
Qui a florin, roussin, & Latin par tout il trouve le chemin: Prov. *He that hath store of money, a learned tongue, and a good horse, cannot misse his way.*
Qui trop se haste en cheminant, en beau chemin se fourvoye: Prov. *Hee that goes too fast failes in a faire way; we say, faire and softly goeth far.*
Semelles, & du vin passent chemin: Pro. *Shooes, and wine rid way.*
Cheminant. *Walking, wending, iourneying, trauelling.*
Qui trop se haste en cheminant en beau chemin se fourvoye: Prov. *The ouer-hastie traueller misses a a plaine way; we say, the hastie man seldom wants woe* (now

(now a greater woe than the misse of way cannot befall him that hath cause to make hast.)

Cheminé : m.ée : f. *Walked, went, gone, trauelled, iourneyed.*

Cheminée : f. *A chimney; also, a chimney-peece of Tapistrie; or of Masons worke.*

Haut & bas la cheminée. *Chimney-sweepe; the crie of chimney-sweepers.*

Licentié sous la cheminée. *An vnlearned Graduate; one that does his acts in* tenebris, *or steales a degree.*

En petite cheminée fait on bien grand feu : Prov. *In little chimneyes good big fires are made.*

Cheminer. *To walke, wend, go; trudge, iourney, trauell.*

Cheminer en pas d'Abbé. *Looke* Abbé.

Autant chemine vn homme en vn iour comme vn Limaçon en cent ans : Prov. *A man goes as far in a day as a snaile in an age; some men can dispatch more businesse in one day than others in many.*

Chemineux : m.euse : f. *That walkes much; also, belonging to a way; or to a chimney; or full of chimneyes.*

Cheminier : m.ere : f. *Of, or belonging to, a Chimney.*

Chemise : f. *A shirt, or smocke.*

Chemise de cloche. *The mould wherein a bell is cast.*

Chemise de drap. *A wastcoat.*

Chemise de necessité. *An inchaunted shirt which (as some superstitious people imagine) preserues men from all hurt in battailes, and eases women in their trauell.*

Avoir sa chemise. *A woman to haue her flowers (for* tachée de sang *is vnderstood.)*

Il leur porta vne chemise blanche. *He brought them a cleane shirt;* viz. *hee raised them with a mischiefe, rowsed them with a vengeance; he gaue them a sound camisadoe.*

Il m'en souvient autant que de ma premiere chemise. *I remember it as well as the houre I was borne in.*

Torcher à autruy le cul de sa chemise. *To giue one a pig of his owne sow; to affoord him helpe out of his owne meanes; (we vnderstand by the action expressed in this phrase, the doing of a good, and a bad turne together; because though one thing be wiped another is berayed.)*

Il faut discerner la peau de la chemise : Prov. *Wee must distinguish things which bee neere, from those which be further off, vs.*

Plus pres est la chair que la chemise : Prov. *Looke* Chair.

Chemisette : f. *A little shirt, or smocke; also, a wastcoat; also, a couering for a booke.*

Chemissant. *Whimpering.*

Chenal : m. *A channell, or gutter.*

Chenant : fleur de chenant. *A certaine flower wheron Camels vse to feed.*

Chenarde : f. *Wild Saffron.*

Chene. *as* Chaine. *A chaine; also, a Corbell of stoneworke.*

Chenets : m. *Andirons.*

Chenevel : m. *The name of a certaine fresh-water fish.*

Chenevi : m. *Hempseed.*

Cheneviere : f. *A hempe-yard, or hempen-close; also, a hempen staulke; also, a hempe countrey, or place wherein much hempe growes.*

Chenevilles : f. *The broken staulkes, or stemmes of hempe.*

Chenovette : f. *A hempen staulke, or stemme.*

Chenil : m. *A dog-kennell.*

Chenillaux : m. *Yong Caterpillers.*

Chenille : f. *A Caterpiller.*

Chenille de mer. *A sea Caterpiller; (of two kinds th'one a verie great fish, th'other, a small, and footlesse Insect.)*

Chenille de pins. *A little, reddish, and hairie worme, that breeds in the tops of Pine branches.*

Chenilles veluës. *Certaine great, hairie, and darkered wormes, or caterpillers, that feed altogether vpon the roots of corne, and hearbes.*

Chenille de vigne. *The little hairie, and many-footed worme, called the Vine-fretter.*

Chenillé : m. ée : f. *Of, or belonging to, Caterpillers; also, Caterpiller-like; also, full of, or wrought with, Caterpillers; and hence;*

Taffetas chenillé. *A kind of stript, or waued, Taffata.*

Chenillier : m. *An instrument wherwith Gardners pull downe Caterpillers.*

Chenin : m. *as* Chenil; *A dog-kennell.*

Chenin : m. ine : f. *Dog-like; of, or belonging to, a dog.*

Raisins chenins. *A kind of great red grapes, fitter for medicines than for meat.*

Taisson chenin. *A kind of Badger, that is footed, and snowted like a dog, and willingly feeds on flesh, and carrion, as a dog.*

Chenu : m.uë : f. *Gray, hoarie, white-headed, old.*

Vin chenu. *Mustie wine.*

Cheoir. *To fall; to tumble downe; also, to happen, chance, or fall vnto, as an inheritance, or escheat.*

C'est tout vn de cheoir, & de trebucher: Pro. *A man had as good fall outright as stumble.*

Qui n'y va n'y chet: Prov. *He that climbes not fals not; he that ventures not failes not.*

Qui plus haut monte qu'il ne doit de plus haut chet qu'il ne voudroit: Prov. *He that climbes higher than he should falls lower than he would.*

Qui rien ne porte rien ne luy chet: Prov. *He that carries nothing looses nothing; or, nought falls from him that hath nought.*

Chepage : m. *A Goaler; or, Goalership.*

Chepier : m. *A Goaler.*

Cher : m. ere : f. *Deare, leefe, well-beloued, best-affected, much esteemed, verie acceptable, or precious vnto; also, deare, costlie, of a great rate, or price, for which much is paied.*

I'aimerois aussi cher. *I had as leue, I would as soone, I could be as willing;* plus cher; *rather, sooner, with a better will.*

Fille trop veuë, robbe trop vestuë, n'est pas chere tenue : Prov. *A maid oft seene, and a garment oft worne are meanely alike esteemed of.*

Chercée : f. *A kind of earth-Alpicke.*

Cherchage. *A seeking, or searching for; an inquirie after.*

Cens à cherchage. *Looke* Cens.

Cherche ralongée. *Looke* Cerche.

Chercher. *Looke* Cercher.

Chercuictier. *Looke* Chaircuictier.

Chere : f. *The face, visage, countenance, fauour, looke, aspect of a man; also, cheere; victualls, intertainment for the teeth.*

Chere lie. *Seeke* Lie.

Faire bonne chere à. *To intertaine kindly, vse friendly, welcome heartily, make good cheere vnto.*
Faire grande, ou ioyeuse chere. *To be passing merie; to liue most pleasantly, and plentifully; to make great cheere.*
Faire mauvaise chere. *To frowne, powt, lowre, sell sowse, hold downe the head; also, to liue barely, feed meanely; make put poore, or course cheere.*
Belle chere, & coeur arriere: Prov. *A willing looke, and vnwilling heart.*
Belle chere vault bien vn mets: Prov. *A heartie welcome is worth halfe a feast.*
La belle chere amende beaucoup l' hostel: Prov. *The ill-fauoured house is much amended by the well-fauoured owner.*
Aujourd'huy en chere demain en biere: Prov. *To day glad, to morrow dead.*
Il n'est vie que de faire bonne chere, mais la fin n'en vaut rien: Prov. *The life spent in good cheere hath a faire beginning but a foule end.*
Cherer. *To cheere, to cherish, &c;* Looke Cherir.
Chereté. *as* Cherté.
Cherfueil: m. *The wood-bind, or honie-suckle.*
Cherissable: com. *Cherishable, fit to be cherished.*
Chernaye: f. *A wood of scarlet oakes; also, as* Charmoye.
Cherme. *The scarlet oake, or scarlet holme oake; also, as* Charme.
Chermes. *The scarlet-berrie, or scarlet graine.*
Chermisin. *as* Chermes.
Chernine: f. *The fruit, or berrie, of the scarlet oake.*
Cherpi: m. *A rag, or clout of linnen; or as* Charpie.
Cherquemmage. *as* Cherquemanage.
Cherrée: f. *Buck-ashes; or, as* Charrée.
Chersydre. *An Adder; or (more especially) the land Adder.*
Cherté: f. *Deerenesse, dearth, scarcitie, want of.*
Cherubin: m. *A Cherubin.*
Rouge comme vn cherubin. *Red-faced, Cherubin-faced, hauing a fierie facies like a Cherubin.*
Chervis: m. *The root Skirret, or Skirwicke.*
Chervis grand. *A Parsnip.*
Chervis sauvage. *The wild Parsnip; or wild Skirret.*
Petit chervis. *The ordinarie Skirret root.*
Chesaux: m. *The rubbish of decayed houses; or, (the Plurall of* Chesal*) mansions, houses.*
Chesiner. *To decrease, wane, lessen, abate, grow to want; pine, languish; decay, fall away.*
Chesnaye: f. *A wood, groue, or thicket of oakes.*
Chesne: m. *An oake; also, as* Chaine.
Chesne forchu. *The standing on the head:* ¶Rab.
Chesne vert. *The barren scarlet oake, holme oake, or French oake; a tree thats euer greene.*
Petit chesne. *The hearbe Germaunder, English Treacle.*
Petit homme abat grand chesne: Prov. *A little man fells a great oake; (so may a meane person ruine a mightie prince.)*
Chesneau: m. *A kind of water-snake, mortall enemie to oakes; also, a yong oake.*
Chesneteau: m. *A little yong oake.*
Chesnette: f. *as* Petit chesne; *Germaunder; also, a little chaine.*
Chesneux: m. euse: f. *Of oake; or, full of oakes.*
Chesnon: m. *The chine.*
Chestif. *Looke* Chetif.
Chestivement. *Wretchedly, miserably, vnfortunately; poorely, needily, basely, beggerly; also, scarcely, scantly; with much paultring, or pinching; also, knauishly, curstly, shrewdly; badly, naughtily, lewdly; caytiue-like.*
Chestiveté: f. *Miserie, wretchednesse, vnfortunatenesse, or, a forlorne estate; poorenesse, beggerie, barenesse, needinesse; also, want, scarcitie, pinching, scantinesse; also, curstnesse, knauerie, shrewdnesse; badnesse, lewdnesse, naughtinesse.*
Chestreux: m. euse: f. *Poore, miserable, in ill array.*
Chestron. *as* Chetron.
Chet-doux. *Gently-falling.*
Chete: f. *The height, or depth of a ship from the vpper decke to the keele; Hence;* Le navire a tant de pieds de chete. *The ship is so many foot deepe in hold.*
Chetif: m. iue: f. *Caitiue, wretched, miserable, vnfortunate, forlorne, poore, needie, bare, beggerlie; also, scarce, little, paultrie, scantie, small; also, knauish, curst, shrewd; naughtie, bad, lewd; and hence;*
Qui envoye chetif à la mer, il n'en rapporte poisson ne sel: Prov. *He that sends a bad seruant to sea, hath small returne of his venture.*
Chetivement. *Poorely, barely; wretchedly, miserably, as one that is forlorne; also, badly, lewdly, naughtily; also, curstly, shrewdly; also, scantly, scarcely, with much pinching.*
Chetiver. *To pine, make wretched, bring to want; lay miserie, inflict pouertie, on.*
Chetiveté: f. *Looke* Chestiveté.
Chetivoison: f. *Wretchednesse, miserie, pouertie.*
Chetron: m. *The till of a coffer, or chest.*
Cheu: m. Cheuë: f. *Fallen, tumbled downe; in the lapse; also, happened, chanced, fallen vnto; also, shrunk, diminished; growne lesse.*
Chevage. *An yearely duetie, fine, or fee of 12.d. Parisis paied to the kings vse, within the iurisdiction of* Vermandois, *and elsewhere, by euerie bastard, stranger, forreiner, and affranchised person, whether he be, or haue beene, maried.*
Cheval: m. *A horse.*
Cheval aquatique. *A certaine beast that liues in the riuer* Nilus *(in his backe, mane, and voice, resembling a horse, and therefore so tearmed.)*
Cheuaux de couble. *Paires, or couples of horses; Coach-horses, &c.*
Cheval courant. *A running horse; whence;*
Cheval courant est vn sepulchre ouvert: Prov. *(So much danger is his necke in that rides him.)*
Cheval fondu. *A kind of play like our trusse.*
Cheval Hongre, ou chastré. *A gelding.*
Cheval de haras. *A Stallion.*
Cheval de louäge. *A hackney.*
Cheval marin, ou de mer. *The Sea-horse (a great and long-footed fish; also, a kind of small sea Insect, or fish, whose foreparts are somewhat like a horses.*
Cheval de paille. *That feeds on straw in stead of hay; whence;*
Cheval de paille cheval de bataille: Prov. *For such horses are commonly the hardest, and hardiest.*
Cheval qui porte derriere. *A double horse, or double gelding.*
Cheval de poste. *A Post-horse; also, a dunce, lobcock, or loggerhead.*
Cheval aux quatre pieds blancs. *A horse that hath foure white feet; A marke which diuers vtterly mislike; and hence;*
C'est le cheval aux quatre pieds blancs. *He promises*

ses much, and performes little; or he failes at a pinch; he giues it ouer when there is most need of him; (Looke Blanc.

Cheval du Regne. *A courser of Naples.*

Cheval de rencontre. *Looke* Rencontre.

Cheval de riviere. *The water horse; &c, as* Hippopotame.

Cheval de selle. *A saddle horse; or, a readie horse; a horse that may safely bee backed, ridden, trauelled on.*

Cheval de seruice. *A great horse, or horse of seruice; Looke* Seruice.

Vassal à plein cheval de seruice. *One that enioyes, or holds by, a whole Knights fee.*

Cheval sommier, ou de somme. *A Sumpter horse.*

Cheval teste de more. *A roane, or dapple-gray horse with a blackish head.*

Cheval de traict. *A drag-horse, draught-horse, cart-horse, coach-horse; &c.*

Chevaux trauersans. *Looke* Trauersant.

Cheval de trompette. *One thats not afraid of shadowes; one whom no big, nor bugs words can terrifie.*

Cul de cheval. *The ouglie fish called a Sea Nettle.*

Dragée aux chevaux. *Blocke-wheat, or bolimong; See* Dragée.

Fer de cheval. *A horse-shooe; also, a kind of axseed, or the small pulse called horse-shooe.*

Pas de cheval. *The hearbe fole-foot, coults-foot, horse-foot, hallfoot, bullfoot, horse-hoofe.*

Queuë de cheval. *The hearbe horse-willow, cats-taile, horse-taile, shaue-grasse; See* Queuë.

Sergent à cheval. *Looke* Sergent.

Brider son cheval par la queuë. *To goe the wrong way to worke; or, to do a thing cleane kamme.*

Estre à cheval. Il est à cheval. *He rides, or is on horsbacke; also, he stands on hautie tearmes; or, hee is set on cockehorse; hee is all a hoight, hee now begins to flaunt it.*

Estre bien à cheval. *To ride comely, to sit a horse with a good grace.*

Il n'est si bon cheval qui n'en deviendroit rosse. *It would anger a Saint, or iade the best man that liues, to be thus troubled.*

Monter sur ses grands chevaux. *To swagger exceedingly, to beare himselfe hautily, to stand vpon his pantofles, to vse loftie tearmes; to be presently on the top of the house with a man.*

Parler à cheval. *To speake vpon aduantage, on good ground, or, as one that is sure of the better end of the staffe; (hence) also, to vse proud, scornefull, or disdainfull words.*

Prendre vn cheval par les crins. *To worke wonders, doe great matters, performe (almost) impossibilities.*

Cheval faict, & valet à faire: Prov. *A made horse, and a man vnmard, are fittest for vse: The like is;*

Cheval faict, & femme à faire: Prov.

Cheval Roigneux n'a cure qu'on l'estrille: Prov. *A scabd horse loueth not the curricombe; (nor an infected heart, correction.)*

`A grand cheval grand gué: Prov. *A great horse must haue a great foord.*

`A l'aise marche à pied qui mene son cheval par la bride: Prov. *Troubles are but trifles vnto them, that haue meanes enow to ease, or strength enough to ouercome, them.*

`A ieune soldat vieil cheval: Prov. *Looke* Soldat.

Apres bon vin bon cheval: Prov. *The pot hath made him valiant, and of a free humour; now that he hath drunke hard he dare swagger with any man, or censure euerie man.*

Il n'est cheval qui n'ait son meshain: Prov. *There is no creature perfect; euerie one is in some part, or point faultie, or defectiue; The like is;*

Il n'est cheval qui n'ait sa tare: Prov. &;

Il n'y a cheval si bien ferré qui ne glisse: Prov. *The best-shod horse doth slip sometimes.*

Iamais coup de iument ne fit mal à cheval: Prov. *When women strike men it is not to hurt them; or, men seldome-times catch hurt by womens blowes.*

Il ne faut pas lier les asnes avec les chevaux: Pro. *Asses must not be tied vp among horses; nor vnworthie people consorted with the worthie.*

Les maladies viennent à cheval, & s'en retournent à pied: Prov. *Seeke* Maladie.

Les mouches vont tousjours aux chevaux maigres: Prov. *Flies are euer most busie about leane horses; so are Puruevors, and Promooters with the poorest, or least powerfull, ranke of people.*

On touche tousjours sur le cheval qui tire: Prov. *We say, folke alway call on the horse that will carrie; the willingest are sorest laied vnto.*

Oncques bon cheval ne devint rosse: Prov. *Seldome hath a good horse turned iade; a worthie fellow will neuer prooue coward, nor knaue; no age can weaken, no daunger appall, no paine afflict, no offer infect, him.*

Ouvrier mediocre a cheval: Prov. *Seeke* Ouvrier.

Qui n'a cheval ne chariot il ne charge pas quand il veut: Pro. *He cannot do what he would that wants wherewithall; beggers must not be chusers.*

Qui ne s'adventure n'a cheval ny mule: Prov. *He that hazards nothing winneth nothing; faint heart neuer got faire Ladie.*

Qui trop s'adventure perd cheval & mule: Prov. *Seeke* Adventurer.

Trop presser fait le cheval restif: Prov. *To take too much of, or presume too much on, a friend, is the way to make him loath you, and to make you loose him; or, as in* Presser.

Chevaler. *To watch, espie, obserue, or dog; to hunt, or follow after; also, to checke, chide, reprooue, schoole, course; also, in horsemanship, to incavalar, or, a horse to lap one leg ouer another.*

Chevaleresse. *Knighlie; knight-like; also, of, or belonging to, a Knight.*

Chevalereusement. *Valiantly, valourously, doughtily, stoutly, manfully, couragiously; knight-like.*

Chevalereux: m. euse: f. *Cheualrous, doughtie, valourous, valiant, couragious, manfull, stout bold.*

Chevalerie: f. *Knighthood; th'order of Knighthood; also, cheualrie, doughtinesse, valour, prowesse; also, a bold attempt, hardie enterprise, manlie, or gallant act.*

Aide de Chevalerie. *as in* Aides chevels.

Droict de chevalerie. *The priuiledge of Knighthood, or being made a Knight; due vnto some Officers, and Magistrates in France, as here vnto the Lord Maior of London.*

Chevalet: m. *A Nagge, or little horse; also, the Bridge of a Lute, Violl, &c; also, the woodden logge whereon a Tanner scrapes his hides; (wee call it, his beame;) also, a sawing Tresse; also,*

also, a kind of racke, or stretching torture.

Chevaleter. *as* Chevaler; *To dog,&c.*

Chevaleureux. *Looke* Chevalereux.

Chevalier : m. *Signifies properly, a horseman; one that rides, or is, on horseback (and hence, also, a* Gendarme, *or man of Armes;) but particularly, and more commonly, a Knight, or Cavaleere; (In France the title of* Chevalier *is, often, a bare title of honour, and ordinarily conferred on great Officers (whether of the short, or long, Robe,) and on the Lords of great, and meane Seignories; All which may qualifie, and stile themselues Knights, as well as ordinarie Gentlemen may tearme themselues Esquiers:) Also, a daintie water-fowle, as big as a Stockdoue, and of two kinds, the one red, the other blacke; Also, the Knight-apple, somewhat bigger than an egge, and streaked all ouer with red; Also, a raising, or small heap of earth, or of clods; a ridge made by a stradling labourer, that fetches, with his mattock, &c, the earth betweene his legs, to such a height, that he seemes on horsebacke; also, a small & whitish crab, somewhat spotted with red, and so swift, as a footman can hardly ouertake her.*

Chevalier Bachelier. *A Knight Batchler; Looke* Bachelier.

Chevalier des bains. *A Knight of the Bath; so called, because bathing is the principall ceremonie of his admittance into that order.*

Chevalier banneret. *Looke* Banneret.

Chevalier de Cornovaille. *A Cuckold.*

Chevalier au drappeau quarré. *A Knight Banneret; called so in mockage.*

Chevalier errant du Royaulme de Logres. *A Knight errant of England; or one of King Arthures Knights.*

Chevalier du guet. *The Captaine of the watch; as in* Guet.

Chevalier honoraire. *In difference from a Knight of any one of the orders; Looke* Honoraire.

Chevalier des loix. *A Lawyer, or meere Scholler knighted.*

Chevalier de S. Martin. *The little spotted flie, called Ladie-henne, or, a Ladie-cow.*

Hier vachier, huy chevalier : Prov. *Looke* Vachier.

Pour l'amour du chevalier baise la Dame l'Escuyer : Prov. *The Ladie kisses her man for his Masters sake.*

Chevalin : m. ine : f. *Of, or belonging to a horse; whence;*

Bestes chevalines. *Horses, mares, or coults, of what kind soeuer.*

Chastaignes chevalines. *A kind of great, round, and blackish chestnuts; called so, because they are good for short-winded horses.*

Orges chevalines. *A kind of Winter barlie; called so, because the blades thereof in the Spring are good to purge, and fatten, horses.*

Chevaline : f. *The hearbe called Horse-taile, or shaue-grasse.*

La chevaline. *Horses, horse-flesh, or, the kind of horses.*

Chevalot : m. *A tressle, or prop of wood; &c; as* Chevalet; *also, a coyne of Guelderland, worth about* iij.s. sterl.

Chevance : f. *Cheuisance, wealth, substance, riches, goods.*

Chevauchable : com. *Rideable; easie to be rid on; fit to be rid in.*

Chevauché : m. ée : f. *Rid, bestrid, ridden, rid on; rid ouer, or vnto; and hence;*

Terre chevauchée est a demy mangée : Prov. *The reuenue of land thats often rid vnto is halfe consumed in riding charges.*

Chevauchée : f. *A riding, trauelling, iourneying, a road or course, a coursing to and fro, on horsebacke; (hence) also, a Princes progresse; a Judges circuit, &c; also, a furnishing with horses to ride on.*

Les chevauchées des Prevosts des Mareschaux de France. *The roads made by them ouer hills, through dales, narrow passages, and other suspected places, thereby to cleere the countrey, and high-wayes of rogues, and robbers, whom as soone as they take they trusse vp.*

Droict de chevauchée. *Looke* Droict.

Chevauchement : m. *A riding; or, as* Chevauchée.

Chevaucher. *To ride, or bestride a horse; to travell on horsebacke; also, to make a road, or iourney with forces of horse and foot, against an enemie; also, to swiue a woman.*

Chevaucher sa charge. *To ride circuit, as a Judge, &c.*

Chevaucher la chevre en la vallée. *To vndertake a dangerous taske, or matter which he is most like to fayle in; Looke* Chevre.

Chevaucher la corde. *The ball (at Tennis) to hit the line, and to get ouer it (but with much adoe.)*

Chevaucher à la genette. *To ride with verie short stirrups; to sit squirting on horsebacke with legs drawn vp almost vnto the saddle.*

Chevaucherie : f. *A riding; a swiuing.*

Chevaucheur : m. *A horseman; a rider; also, a Post-maister, or one, that keepes post-horses; whence;*

Chevaucheurs d'escuyrie. *Postes for the Packet;*

Sergent chevaucheur. *A certaine Officer in the kings forrests.*

Chevauchon. à chevauchons. *Astraddle, stradling, or bestriding, as a man, a horse.*

Chevecerie : f. *The Vestrie, or Treasurie of a church; the place wherein the lights, and ornaments vsed in it, are layed vp, and kept.*

Cheveche : f. *An Owle, or Madge-howlet; th'ordinarie rough-footed, and short-taild Owle.*

Chevecher : m. *The Keeper, or Treasurer of a Vestrie; a Sexton; or, as* Chevecier.

Chevecherie : f. *The Vestrie; or, as* Chevecerie.

Chevechier. *as* Chevecier.

Chevecier : m. *The Treasurer, or Keeper of the Vestrie in a Cathedrall, or Collegiat Church; an Officer that hath charge of the wax, lights, and ornaments vsed therein.*

Chevedage. feu, & che. *A dwelling house, or household.*

Cheveil. *as* Chevel.

Chevel. *Chiefe, principall:* ¶Norm.

Aides chevels. *Looke* Aide.

Fief chevel. *A noble inheritance held in* Capite, *and capable of iurisdiction.*

Lieu chevel. *A Mannor house, or chiefe house.*

Cheveler. *To sprig, or sprigle; to root, or put forth a hairie, or small, root.*

Cheveliere : f. *A haire-lace; also, a dressing of haire.*

Chevelu : m. uë : f. *Hairie, full of haire, rugged with haire, wearing long haire.*

Estoille cheveluë. *A blazing starre.*

Loy cheveluë. *A Law forbidding all men to weare long haire, except the Princes of the bloud, and their posteritie;*

posteritie; It was made by king Clodion *the hairie; continued vnto King* Pepins *time, and then disannulled.*

Chevelue: f. *A sucker; a small imp of a plant springing from the root thereof, or of itselfe rooted.*

Chevelure: f. *A hairie bush, or locke; hairinesse, long haire; also, the fibers or hairie threeds that hang at the roots of plants.*

Chevesche: f. *An Owle; as* Cheveche.

Chevesne: m. *The Cheuin, or Pollard-fish.*

Chevestre: m. *A rope, halter, coller for the head; a head-stall; or head-straine (especially for a cow, calfe, &c; for* Licol *is more proper to horses, moyles, &c, and more vsed.)*

Chevestreux. licol chevetreux. *Binding, or strayning the head.*

Chevet: m. *A boulster (for the head.)*

Hausser le chevet de &c. *To raise the price of a thing; to bid more for it, or value it higher, than before.*

Chevetain: m. *A Captaine, Commaunder, Leader; a Chiefetaine.*

Chevetain: m. ine: f. *Chiefe, commaunding ouer; aboue, or ouer others:* ¶Norm.

Chevetier. *Looke* Chevecier.

Cheveul: m. *The haire of a mans, or womans head; also, a locke, bush, or tuft of haire.*

Cheveux de Venus. *Venus haire, our Ladies haire, true maidens haire, blacke maiden haire; (an hearbe.)*

Faire les cheveux à. *To powle, barbe, trimme; cut the haire.*

Vouloir prendre vn homme ras par les cheveux. *To hope for more from a man than hee hath meanes to get, or th'other to giue.*

Cheuf. *as* Chetif; *An old word.*

Chevi: m. ie: f. *Compassed, preuailed with, shifted withall, done goood vpon; tamed, reclaimed, subdued, brought in or vnder; also, compounded, or agreed withall.*

Chevillage: m. *A pegging, or pinning; peggage, pinnage.*

Cheville: f. *A peg, or pinne of wood; also, a botch in a verse.*

Cheville du pied. *Th'ankle-bone.*

Compter des chevilles. *To attend long in hope of a good turne, or preferment promised; See* Compter.

Pendre son manteau à foible cheville. *To aske aduice of a foole, almes of a begger; or, to trust in, or depend on, vaine hopes, weake helps.*

'A chasque trou vne cheville: Pro. *For euerie fault an excuse, for each obiection an answer; for any mischiefe a remedie, helpe, euasion.*

'A tel pertuis telle cheville: Prov. *Said of any thing thats fitted, or suited in it kind.*

Chevillé: m. ée: f. *Pegged, pinned; fastened with pegs, ioyned with pinnes.*

La teste d'un cerf bien chevillée. *A Stags head, wel furnished, set, pinned.*

Cheviller. *To peg, to pin; to fasten, ioyne, or close with pegs, or pinnes.*

Chevilleur: m. *A pegger; also, a sorcerer, that holding his finger in a hole, and muttering certaine superstitious words, will hinder a man from pissing, vntill his finger be remoued.*

Chevilleure: f. *A pegging; a fastening with pegs.*

Chevilleures. *The broches of a Deeres head; all the pegs aboue the two lowest.*

Chevillures. *as* Chevilleures.

Cheviniau: m. *A Cheuin.*

Chevir. *To compasse, preuaile with, shift withall, doe good vpon; also, to tame, reclaime, ouerrule, bring in or vnder; also, to compound, make an end, come to an agreement, with.*

I'en cheviray bien. *I will bring him to reason, to my bent, vnto my will; I shall do well ynough with him.*

Ils ne pouvoyent tous chevir en la maison. *They could not all be lodged, or there was not roome ynough for them all, in the house.*

Chevissance: f. *An agreement, or composition made; an end or order set downe, betweene a creditor, and debtor.*

Chevolée: f. *A sprig, twig, or small imp of a plant; also, a fiber, or haire-like thread growing vnto the root of a plant.*

Chevoler. *To sprig; to put forth sprigs, or haire-like fibers, as the roots of plants do.*

Chevre: f. *A she-goat; also, a bag-pipe; also, the engine called by Architects, &c, a Fearne.*

Barbe de chevre. *Meadeswort, meadesweet, Queene of the medowes (an hearbe.)*

L'herbe aux chevres. *Shrub-trefoyle, milke trefoile,* Citisus *bush, tree trifolie.*

Laictues de chevre. *A kind of wild lettuce, called Lambes-lettuce, and corne-sallade.*

Oeil de chevre. *An eye full of white spots; or, one that hath too much white, or a pearle in it; a wall eye.*

Pied de chevre. *The end of a gaffle of a crossebow; also, the stay, or prop of a ladder, whereby tis both held steadie, and kept from leaning too hard on what tis set against; also, a leauer pointed like the foot of a goat.*

Verd de chevre. *A kind of sand whereof Painters make their greenes.*

'A la chevre morte. *With heeles, or bellie, vpwards.*

'A pied de chevre. *Aslope, or bias.*

Cheuaucher la chevre en la vallée. *To vndertake a dangerous taske, or enter into a businesse which he is verie like to faile in; (for he that rides downe a hill on a goat (a beast that stoops, and hath short legs before) can hardly come, without tumbling, to the bottome of it.)*

Il luy a mis les chevres en sa court. *He hath put him in a terrible feare.*

Prendre le chevre. *To take pepper in the nose; to take a thing in dudgeon, or in snuffe.*

Reprenons nostre chevre à la barbe. *Let vs returne vnto our former discourse; worke, matter, businesse.*

'A la chandelle la chevre semble belle: Prov. *Hee that chuses a wife by candle-light, or by other eyes than his owne, may perhaps be fouly deceiued.*

Ou la chevre est liée faut qu'elle broute: Prov. *The goat must brouze where she is bound; where a man is setled he is to seeke meanes to liue.*

Tant gratte la chevre que mal gist: Prov. *He keeps such a stur, he makes so much ado, to be well, that he is the worse for it: In old time a certaine goat painfully scraping the earth to get her selfe an easefull couch, turned vp a knife, wherewith presently after her throat was cut in a sacrifice; (This prouerbe is fittest applied vnto such, as ruine, or incommodate thẽselues by being too busie, or too curious, in what kind soeuer.)*

Chevreau. *A Kid, or yong Goat.*

Chevreaux. *Certaine starres which rise about the eight and twentieth of September, and get them gone againe towards the euening of the nine and twentieth.*

Chevreau sauvage. *A Roe.*

Chevre-fueille: f. *The wood-bind or honie-suckle.*
Chevre-pied. *Clouen-hooued, goat-footed; an Epithite for a Satyre.*
Chevreté: m.ée: f. *Kidded; fallen as a yong kid; also, enraged, horne-mad, almost wood.*
Chevreter. *To kid, or bring forth yong kids; also, to be in a rage, almost wood, or horne-mad; to grow madde with anger, and despight; (from a goat, which in his time of heat is madde for lust.)*
Chevrette: f. *A little goat; also, a wild goat; also, a great prawne; also, a little and low andiron; also, a Robinet, or small peece of ordnance, of a size betweene the Fauconnet, and Arguebuze a crocke.*
Chevreul: m. *A Roe, or a Roe-bucke; also, a wild goat; (which is also called;)*
Chevreul sauvage. *A Shamois, or wild goat.*
Chevrie: f. *A bag-pipe.*
Chevrier: m. *A Goat-heard, one that keepeth, or looketh vnto, goats.*
Chevrin: m.ine: f. *Goatie; goat-like; of a goat.*
Cheurme: f. *Looke* Chiorme.
Chevron: m. *A Kid; a Chevron (of timber in building;) a rafter, or sparre.*
Chevronde. *Looke* Severonde.
Chevronneau: m. *A small rafter, little chevron.*
Chevronot: m. *The same.*
Chevrot: m. *A Kid; a yong, or little Goat; Roe; or Shamois.*
Chevrotin: m. *Kids-leather.*
Tirer au chevrotin. *To eat, or drink exceeding much; also, to vomit (by that excesse.)*
Chevrottement: m. *The breeding, or bringing forth of Kids.*
Chevrotter. *To breed, or bring forth (as a she-Goat) a Kid.*
Cheusson: m. *A corne destroying mite, or weeuell.*
Cheute: f. *A fall, a lapse; an ouerthrow.*
Cheute de l'oeil. *The fall of the eye; is, when it is cleane out of it hollow seat; especially, if either an issue, or blow hath beene the cause thereof.*
De grand vilain grande cheute: Prov. *The greater a bad man is the more scandalous, and hurtfull are his vices, and therefore, the more headlong, and infamous, his fall.*
Chez. chez moy. *With me, at, or in my house.*
De chez moy. *From me.*
Chezal: m. *A chiefe Mansion, or Mannor house.*
Cheze: m. *The part or portion of an inheritance of course belonging vnto the eldest heire, ouer and besides his share in the rest; which is by the customes of* Tours, *the two* Arpens *of ground lying next without the wals, and ditches of a Gentlemans castle, or chiefe house; and foure* Arpens *so lying about the castle, or house of an Earle, Vicount, or Baron; by the customes of* Lodunois *it is otherwise called,* Le vol d'un Chapon; *and is as farre as a Capon can flie from the chiefe Manor house of a Gentleman; and the three* Septerées *of ground lying next without the ditches of a Barons castle.*
Chezeau: m. *A Gentlemans chiefe house; houshold, or familie.*
Chi. *as* Ci: ¶Pic.
Chiabrena. *A shitten come shite; a paultrie shitten fisgig; a nice, and scuruie wench.*
Chiappon: m. *A kind of port in the mouth of a bit; as* Pas d'Asne.
Chiard: m. *A shitten fellow; a stinking rogue; a scoundrell; a scuruie companion.*
Chiasse: m. *Drosse, dregs, froath, of mettall.*
Chiasser. *To shite; also, to be too curious.*
Chic. de chic à chic. *From little to little.*
Chicambault: m. *The luffe-blocke; a long, and thicke peece of wood, whereunto the foresayle, and spritsayle are fastened when a ship goes by the wind.*
Chicaner. *To wrangle, or pettifog it; to spoyle, or perplex a cause with craftie, and litigious pleading; also, to write a verie fast hand.*
Chicanerie: f. *Wrangling, pettifogging; litigious, or craftie pleading; the perplexing of a cause with trickes; or the pestering thereof with (subtile, but) impertiment, words.*
Chicaneur: m. *A wrangling Atturney, or Pettifogger; a busie, craftie, litigious, and verball, follower of causes.*
Chicaneus; &, Chicanous. *The same.*
Chichard. *as* Chiche.
Chicharou: m. *Bastard Mackerell:* ¶Saintongnois.
Chiche: com. *Miserable, niggardlie, niggish, neere, pinching, sparing, hard, strait-handed.*
Vn chiche. *A wretch, pinch-pennie, pennie-father, couetous hilding; one that would not part with the paring of his nayles.*
Autant despend chiche que large: Prov. *The wretch consumes as much as the great spender.*
Ce que chiche espargne large despend: Prov. *That which the micher spares the waster spends.*
Homme chiche iamais riche: Prov. *Looke* Riche.
Il n'est banquet que d'homme chiche: Prov. *Wee say, there is no feast to the misers; and by a misers feast we meane, a plentifull, though a rare, one.*
Chiche-face: m. *A chichiface, micher, sneake-bill, wretched fellow; one out of whose nose hunger drops.*
Chiche-maille. *A dodger, niggard, pinch-pennie, pennie-father; one that will stand whole houres hagling about a halfe-pennie.*
Chichement. *Miserably, niggardly, hardly, couetously, with a strait, or close hand.*
Chiches: m. *Ciches, chiches, red cich. sheepes-cich-peason; a pulse thats somewhat lesse than the ordinarie small pease.*
Chiches de belier. *Small blacke ciches fashioned like Rammes heads, and thereupon called, Rammes ciches, and, blacke cich.*
Chiches colombins. *White ciches.*
Chiches de montaigne. *Milke vetches, mountaine ciches.*
Chiches noires. *Rammes ciches, blacke ciches.*
Chiches rouges. *Red ciches, &c; as* Venereïques.
Chiches sauvages. *Wild ciches; also, milke vetches.*
Chiches venereïques. *Red ciches (the most lust-prouoking kind of them all.*
Chicheté: f. *Niggardlinesse, miserie, hardnesse, pinching, too much dodging, needlesse parsimonie, thrift, or sparing.*
Chichorée: f. *Succorie; Looke* Cichorée.
Chicot. *A stub, or stumpe; or as* Chiquot.
Chicotin. *The hearbe Orpin, Liblong, or Liuelong.*
Chicotrin. *as* Chicotin; *or, as* Cicotrin.
Chief. *Chiefe, principall, capitall; Looke* Chef.
Chien: m. *A dog; also, a base, filthie, or shamelesse, fellow; also, the Snaphaunce of a Pistoll.*
Chien d'Artois. *A Terrier.*
Chien de bergier. *A shepheards curre.*
Chien cerf. *A hart-hound.*
Chien de chasse. *A grey-hound.*
Chien couchant. *A setting dog.*

Faire le chien couchant. *To play the coward, or base fellow; to humble, or deiect himselfe too much in the presence of another.*
Chien courant. *A great hound, bucke-hound, barrier; any hound.*
Chien de damoiselle. *A pupsie, little dogge, fisting curre.*
Chien dogue. *A mastiffe.*
Chiens greffiers. *as* Bauds.
Chien de S. Hubert. *A kind of strong, short-legd, & deepe-mouthed hound, vsed most for the hunting of the Fox, Badger, Otter, &c.*
Chien de mer. *The Sea-hound, or Dog-fish that (somewhat) resembles a Lamprey.*
Chien de metairie. *A bandog, or countrey curre.*
Chiens muts. *The hart hounds* Bauds, *tearmed so, because being crossed by a change, they neuer open till they light on their first game.*
Chiens d'oiseaux. *Spaniels.*
Chiens publiques. *So were in old time those called, who had the letting, and setting of the subsidies granted, and taxes due, vnto the king.*
Chien terrier. *as* Basset; *A Terrier.*
Appetit de chien. *A most vnsaciate appetite; a stomacke which, though it lay in vnto vomiting, still would haue more.*
Chose de chien. *A paultrie thing; a matter of no value, or consequence; a trifle; trash, trumperie.*
Chou de chien. *Dogs Cole, wild Mercurie, dogs Mercurie.*
Couillon de chien. *See* Couillon.
Dent au chien. *Harts-horne Plantaine, Crowfoot Plantaine; also, (and the more properly) Cooch-grasse, Quitch-grasse, Dog-grasse; Looke* Dent.
Dent de chien. *Cooch-grasse, Quitch-grasse, Dogs-grasse; also, the hearbe Dandelion, Priests crowne, Pisseabed; also, grudge, repinning, ill meaning.*
Dents de chien. *A mans tuskes, or tushes; on either side two, next vnto the foure fore-teeth.*
Disner de chien. *A meale made onely of bread, & water; or wherein there is nothing drunke but water.*
Esguillettes de chien. *Course leather points, made of a dogs skin.*
Herbe à chien. *Dogs-grasse, Cooch-grasse, Quitch-grasse; or, (as some interpret it) the hearbe Dogs-tongue, or Hounds-tongue.*
Langue de chien. *The hearbe Dogs-tongue, Hounds-tongue, Hounds-pisse.*
Mort aux chiens. *Medow Saffron; also, the hearbe Dogs-bane.*
Mouche à chien. *A ticke, or tike.*
Oignon de chien. *A bastard kind of the starrie Jacinth, called, Dogs-leeke; also, as;*
Porreau de chien. *Leeke of the vine, wild Leekes, French Leeke, dogs Leekes.*
Ris de chien. *A disloyall, or treacherous, ieering; a laughing on him whose throat he wishes cut.*
Ronce de chien. *The Hep-tree; Looke* Ronce.
Teste de chien. *Calues-snowt, Snapdragon; also, Fleawort.*
Testicule de chien. *The hearbe Dogs-stones, Dogs-cullions, Dogs-testicles, Standle-wort, Stander-grasse, bastard Satyrion.*
Entre chien & loup. *In twilights, or cock-shoot time, (when a man can hardly discerne a dog from a wolfe.)*
'A vn autre chien avec cet os. *Make that offer to, bestow that kindnesse on, some other.*
Aussi tost prest qu'un chien auroit sauté vn eschalier. *As soone as dog would haue leaped ouer a doore-sill; or, as in* Eschalier.
Batre le chien devant le lion. *To punish a meane man in presence of, and for an example vnto, the mightie.*
Donner à manger au chien & au chat. *To keepe a bountifull house.*
Dormer en chien. *To sleepe fasting in the Sun when it is at the highest; or to sleepe immediately before dinner, or supper.*
Iecter son lard aux chiens. *To spend his fortunes idly, vnworthily, wastfully; to bestow much on hungrie, base, and scuruie, people; to lauish it vnreasonably, to squander all away.*
Il veut beaux chiens à peu de pain. *Hee would bee well attended on for little wages.*
Oster les chiens pour venir à bout du troupeau. *Looke* Troupeau.
Personne ne luy demanda, es tu chien es tu loup. *No man saluted, eyed, respected, him; no man asked him what, nor whither, he would; no man spoke to him, no one tooke notice of him.*
Tirer du foin aux chiens. *To vomit, spue, cast, sell oakes, pull hay for dogs.*
Tout d'une venue comme la iambe d'un chien. *We say, All of a bignesse, like a post; or a churne.*
Chien enragé ne peut longuement vivre: Prov. *A madde dog cannot long time liue.*
Chien eschaudé craint l'eau froide: Pro. *The scaulded dog feares euen cold water; (somewhat like our, A burnt child dreads the fire.)*
Chien hargneux a tousiours les oreilles deschirées: Prov. *A common brabler comes by many a knock; quarelsome lads are seldome without blacke eyes, broken pates, or scratcht faces.*
Chien qui abbaye ne mord pas: Prov. *The dogge that barkes much bites little; a great prater, a weake performer.*
Chien sur son fumier est hardi: Prov. *A dog (we say, a cocke) is valiant on his owne dung-hill.*
'A bon chien bon os: Prov. *A good dog deserues a good bone; a good seruant good intertainment; but;*
'A vn bon chien n'escheut onques bon os: Pro. *A good dog neuer lights on a good bone; or, the worst bones euer fall to the best dogs share; the honest man hath still the worst lucke.*
De toute taille bon chien: Pro. *There are some able men of all sorts, and sizes.*
Deux chiens ne s'accordent point à vn os: Prov. *Two dogs neuer agree about one bone; churles will not part, nor part with, any thing.*
Mauvais chien iamais ne veut compagnon en cuisine: Prov. *Greedie, or ill-natured people cannot indure competitors, or companions.*
Mauvais chien ne trouve ou mordre: Prov. *No place affoords a liuing to a curre; the slothfull knaue, or bungler, thriues no where.*
'A mauvais chien ne peut on monstrer le loup: Prov. *An ill dog hates to looke on a wolfe.*
'A mauvais chien la queuë luy vient: Prov. *An ill weed growes apace.*
Souvent à mauvais chien tombe vn bos en gueule: Prov. *An vnworthie fellow oft lights on worthie fortunes; or, the verier knaue the better lucke.*
'A meschant chien court lien: Prov. *A froward curre must be tied short; a currish fellow well fettered; (so will they doe least hurt.)*

'A petit chien petit lien: Prov. *Weake passions need but weake restraints.*

'A rude chien dur lien: Prov. *Violent humors must be stopped by hard curbs; churlish people awed with curst vsage.*

Vn vieil chien iamais ne jappe en vain: Prov. *The old dog neuer barketh (aged experience neuer aduiseth,) in vaine.*

Il n'est chasse que de vieux chiens: Prov. *There is no hunting to the old dogs; or, no dog hunts like the old one.*

Charruë de chien ne vaut rien: Prov. *Looke* Charruë.

En lict de chien n'y a point d'oingture: Prov. *Looke not for ciuet in a dogs kennell.*

'A chair de loup sauce de chien: Prov. *The best sauce for course meat is hunger (or) the fittest intertainment for a knaue, a cudgell.*

C'est belle bataille de chiens & des chats; chacun a des ongles: Prov. *Looke* Bataille.

D'oyseaux, de chiens, d'armes, & d'amours, pour vn plaisir mille douleurs: Prov. *The pleasure got by hawkes, hounds, loue, and armes, are deerely bought with millions of harmes.*

Eau, & pain est la viande du chien: Pro. *Bread and water is meat good ynough for a dog (though not for a man.)*

En fin les loups tuent le chien qui tue les loups: Prov. *At length the busie bodie comes vnto his bane.*

Nature fait chien tracer: Prov. *Looke* Tracer.

Pendant que les chiens s'entregrondent le loup deuore la brebis: Prov. *While Churchmen brabble, Satan feeds on soules.*

Quand vn chien se noye chascun luy offre à boire: Prov. *When a dog's a drowning euerie one offers him drinke.*

Qui a le loup pour compagnon porte le chien sous l'hocqueton: Prov. *Let him thats matcht with a knaue go well prouided for him.*

Qui aime Bertrand aime son chien: Prov. *Loue me loue my dog; (say we.)*

Qui se couche avec les chiens, se leue avec des puces: Prov. *They that lye downe with dogs rise vp with fleas; In filthie companie what can one gaine but filth?*

Qui veut avoir bon chien il faut qu'il le nourisse bien: Prov. *He that will haue a good dog must feed him well; he that desires a good seruant must vse him well.*

Qui veut batre son chien trouve assez de bastons: Prov. *It is an easie matter to find a staffe wherewith to beat a dog.*

Qui veut tuer son chien luy met la rage sus: Prov. *When a bad Prince would be rid of a good subiect, or seruant, the tricke is, to lay treason to his charge.*

Sous ombre d'asne entre le chien au moulin: Pro. *(So gets the knaue admittance where otherwise hee should be excluded.)*

Tandis que le chien chie le loup s'en va: Prov. *While the dog scummers the wolfe scuds away.*

Tandis que le chien crie le loup s'enfuit: Prov. *While the dog bawles the wolfe escapes; (thus by delaying and tatling an enemie oreslips him, and many aduantages others.)*

Tel le chien nourrit qui puis mange la courroye de son soulier: Prov. *Some breed vp those that proue their bane.*

Tel seigneur tel chien: Pro. *Like master like man.*

Chien-cerf. *A hart-hound.*

Chien-dent. *Couch-grasse, Quich-grasse, Dogs-grasse; also, a noble stinker; a loose, dissolute, or idle good fellow.*

Chien-dents. *as* Dents de chien; *The tushes.*

Chienesse: f. *Dogs; a brood, or number; the kind, or nature, of dogs.*

Chien-lict. *A shitcabed; a shitten fellow, beastlie companion, filthie scoundrell, stinking iacke, scuruie mate.*

Chienne: f. *A bitch.*

Chiennée: f. *The hearbe Dogs-bane, or, medow Saffron; also, a litter of whelpes.*

Chienner. *To whelpe.*

Chiennerie: f. *A dog-house, or dog-kennell.*

Chiennesse: f. *Dogs; a brood, litter, or number; the kind or nature, of dogs.*

Chiennet: m. *A little dog.*

Chienneté. *Whelped.*

Chienneter. *as* Chienner. *To whelpe.*

Chienneterie: f. *Doggishnesse; the kind, or nature of dogs.*

Chiennetier: m. *A dogge-keeper; yeoman fewterer, Groome of the Hunt, one that lookes vnto hounds.*

Chiennette: f. *A yong, or little, bitch.*

Chien-rage. *The hearbe Dogges-bane; or medow Saffron.*

Chier. *To shite, cacke, scummer, vntrusse the points, goe to the stoole, doe that which no bodie can doe for him.*

Chier dans le panier, pour le mettre sur la teste. *To disgrace a thing, of purpose, to obtaine it the easier; to intertaine on neere tearmes that whereof one hath formerly giuen most vile tearmes.*

Autant chie vn boeuf que mille moucherons: Pro. *As much dungs one oxe as a thousand flies; one rich man may spend more than many poore ones.*

Tandis que le chien chie le loup s'en va: Prov. *While the dog scummers the wolfe escapes.*

Chietins. *as* Theatins; *An order of Priests, in credit about Pope Clement the seuenths time; and of more antiquitie, by some few yeares, than the Iesuites.*

Chifetier: m. *A seller of old stuffe, clothes, clouts; or, one that cries vp and downe such trumperie to bee sold:* ¶Norm.

Chiffe: f. *A clout, old rag, ouer-worne, or off-cast, peece of stuffe.*

Chifflant. *Whizzing; hissing; whistling.*

Chifflement.: m. *A whizzing; whistling; hissing.*

Chiffler. *To whistle; hisse, or whizze.*

Chiffon: m. *A little clout, rag, or peece, of ouer-worne stuffe.*

Chiffre. *as* Chifre; *Also, an engine to catch fish with (forbidden.)*

Chiffrer. *Looke* Chifrer.

Chifre: m. *A Cypher; a figure, or number; the figures of 1, 2, 3, 4, &c; also, a strange caracter, figure, or forme of writing, not (easily) vnderstood by any but him that inuented it, and such as he hath acquainted with it.*

Le Chifre d'un Prince. *The list, or catalogue of a Princes Cyphers, deliuered (and expounded) vnto such as he would haue to vnderstand him.*

Chifré: m. ée: *Cyphered; written in cyphers, or in strange and vnknowne caracters; also, calculated, or examined, as an accompt, by cyphering.*

Chifrer. *To cypher; to write in cyphers; to expresse his meaning in strange, and vnknowne caracters; also,*

also, to calculate, or examine, an accompt, by cyphering.
Chignon: m. *The chyne, or chyne-peece of the necke; also, a knot, or knurre in a peece of Wood, or Tymber.*
Chigros: m. *Shoomakers thread; or, a tatching end.*
Chil. *as* Chile.
Chilagogue: f. *A choler-purging medicine.*
Chile: m. *The Chilus, or white iuice (of disgested meat) whereof our bloud commeth. Looke* Chyle.
Chilifier. *To concoct, disgest, or turne into a milkie, or white iuice.*
Chiller. *To seele, or sow vp the eyes; as* Siller.
Chilleure: f. *A seeling, or sowing vp of the eyes.*
Chilonique. à la Chilonique. *Briefely, succinctly, compendiously; (from one of the Grecian wisemen,* Chilo, *who in all his speeches, and writings was verie short.)*
Chimagrée: f. *A wry-mouth, &c. Looke* Simagrée.
Chimeres: f. *Chymeraes, idle conceits, friuolous thoughts, fond wishes, fruitlesse imaginations, castles in the ayre, things that neuer were.*
Chimeric: m. ique: f. *Imaginarie, altogether in fancie, that neuer was nor will be, onely in conceit.*
Chimie: f. *Melting; or Extraction; the second part of Alchymie.*
Chimique: com. *Chimicall, or Alchymisticall; extractiue, melting.*
Chimolie. terre chimolie. *A kind of earth that is good against burning, and hot impostumes.*
Chinage. *as* Chemage.
Chinchille: f. *A little, Indian, and Squirrell-like beast, which hath a verie smooth, and wholesome, skin.*
Chine: f. *A red, and spungious Indian root, good against the Gout.*
Chinfreneau: m. *A slampe, iert, wipe; thumpe, knocke, bob.*
Chinon du col: m. *The nape of the necke; or as* Chignon.
Chinquer. *To quaffe, swill, tiple, carouse, drinke extreamely.*
Chiolé: m. ée: f. *Whelped.*
Chiorme: f. *A banke of Oares; or, the whole companie of slaues, Rowers (in a Galley;) also, the noise they make in rowing; also, (in a ship) the Saylers; and, the noise they make, in weighing of ankers, and hoising vp of saile-yards.*
Chiot: m. *A whelpe, or little dog.*
Chipault. il est tout chipault. *He is all to be ragged, and rent.*
Chipoter. *To dodge, miche, paulter; trifle; &c; as* Chapoter.
Chipoterie: f. *Dodging, miching, paultering; trifling, fidling, foolish medling.*
Chipoutou: m. *A niggard; a micher, dodger, paulterer; a miser, pinch-pennie, scrape-good, pennifather.* ¶Gasc.
Chippe. *A barke, or ship; also, an old clout, ragge, or patch.*
Chiquaner. *Looke* Chicaner.
Chiquanique: com. *Wrangling, litigious, pettifogger-like.*
Chiquanourris. peuple ch. *Craftie pleaders, or pettifoggers; wrangling, or litigious followers of causes.*
Chiquanous. *A litigious pleader, craftie pettifogger.*
Chiques. *as* Chiches. ¶Picard.
Chiquenaude: f. *A fillip; flirt, or bob giuen with the finger, or nayle.*
Chiquenaudé: m. ée: f. *Fillipped; flirted; bobbed with the finger.*
Chiquenauder. *To fillip; to flirt, or bob, with the finger.*
Chiquenie. *as* Squenie.
Chiquetant. *Cutting, shredding, iagging; cutting into shreds, gashes, iags.*
Chiqueté: m. ée: f. *Cut, gashed, iagged, hacked.*
Chiqueter. *To cut; gash, iag, hacke.*
Chiqueteur: m. *A cutter.*
Chiquetteres: f. *Cuttings, iags, or shreds of cloth.*
Chiqueture: f. *A cutting; a gash, cut, garse; a launcing, shredding, slitting.*
Chiquot: m. *A scale in the root, or end of a nayle; also, a sprig, or shoot of a tree; also, the stumpe of a tooth.*
Chiquoter. *To sift, search, or secke out; also, to hacke, with a knife, &c.*
Chiragre: f. *Hand-gout; the gout in the hands.*
Chiroacte. *Nimble of hand, quicke fingered.* ¶Rab.
Chiroaine. *Looke* Ciroesne.
Chirographaire. Creancier chirographaire. *That hath for his assurance a Bill, or Note vnder the debtors hand.*
Chiromantie. *Palmistrie; a guessing at ones fortune by the markes, or making, of his hand.*
Chiromantien. *A Palmister, a Fortune-teller.*
Chiron. *as* Ciron.
Chirurgial: m. ale: f. *Belonging vnto Surgerie.*
Chirurgie: f. *Surgerie.*
Chirurgien: m. *A Surgeon.*
Choc: m. *A shocke, a brunt; a bustling, or hurrying together; a violent incounter, or coping of armed, and angrie, souldiors.*
Chocailler. *as* Chocquailler.
Chochepierre. *A kind of Nowpe, or Bullfinch, that feeds most on the kernels of Cherristones.*
Chocquailler. *as* Choquer; *(especially in the last sence) to drinke, tiple, quaffe, &c.*
Chocquer. *Looke* Choquer.
Choenes. porteurs de choenes. *So doe surueyors and measurers of land call those that goe before them, and carrie their lines, or chaines, and rods wherewith they measure.*
Choerin: m. *A shoate, or barrow pig.*
Choëur: m. *The Quire of a Church; also, a round, ring, or troope of singers, or dauncers; or of Auditors, or Spectators of those, or the like Exercises.*
Enfans de choëur. *Quirresters.*
Choier. *Looke* Choyer.
Choine: m. *A loafe of white bread.* ¶Norm.
Choir. *Looke* Cheoir.
Chois: m. *A choice, election, picking, or culling out; also, store, abundance, Gods plentie, good choice.*
Choisi: m. ie: f. *Chosen, elected; culled, picked out from others; also, seene, or discerned, a farre off.*
Choisir. *To chuse, elect; cull, or picke out; also, to see, or discerne, a farre off.*
Il ne choisit pas qui emprunte: Prov. *Borrowers must not be chusers.*
Qui avec son seigneur mange poires, il ne choisit pas des meilleures: Pro. *Looke* Poire.
Choison: f. *Opportunitie, occasion; also, as* Foison.
Choisne: m. *A loafe of white bread.* ¶Norm.
Cholagogue: f. *The thin, or small gut, wherein the Chilus*

Chilus thickening beginneth to rest; or (adiectiuely) of, or belonging thereto.
Chole: f. *Choler, anger, gall, ire.*
Cholere: f. *Choler, anger, fuming, testinesse, chafing, stomacke, moodinesse; also, the complection, or humor, tearmed, choler.*
Ronger vne cholere en son esprit. *To fret.*
Cholére: com. *as* Cholerique.
Cholereux. *as* Cholerique; *or full of choler.*
Cholerique: com. *Cholericke, angrie, testie, fuming, chafing, pettish, irefull, in a rage, as hot as a toast.*
Cholique: f. *The Collicke; a painfull windinesse in the bellie, or stomacke.*
Cholique pierreuse. *A paine like the Collicke, and caused by the Stone in the Kidneyes.*
Choliqueux: m. euse: f. *Full of, or much troubled with, the Collicke.*
Chomer. *Looke* Chommer.
Chommable. iour chommable. *A day of rest, a play day.*
Chommage: m. *A ceasing from worke, a resting, a making holyday; a lying idle, and out of vse, as money which is not currant.*
Chommer. *To make hollyday, cease from worke; play for want of worke; rest, lye idle, and out of vse; also, as* Manquer; *or, to want; whence;*
Nous en chommerons encor de pareil. *Wee shall not haue the like in hast.*
Chondrille: f. *Gum-Succorie.*
Choner. *as* Chommer, *or* Chopiner. ¶Rab.
Chonquetage: m. *A Round gone about, or View taken of, the Kings Woodsales, by the principall officers of his forrests, thereby to come to the knowledge of the offences (if any) committed by those that haue been put in trust withall.*
Choper. *To trip, or stumble; to be faultie; erre, or misse in footing.*
Qui chope & ne tombe, adjouste à son pas: Pro. *He that stumbles without falling, gets the more forward.*
Chopine: f. *A Chopine; or the Parisien halfe pint; almost as big as our whole one; (At S.* Denis, *and in diuers other places about Paris, three of them make but one pint.)*
Approbation faitte sur chopine. *An allowance giuen, or passed, ouer the pot.*
Chopiner. *To tiple, quaffe, swill, plie the pot, drinke all day, or whole dayes, long.*
Chopinette: f. *A small cup, or Chopine.*
Choppe. Poire choppe. *Which by ouerripenesse grows soft, and is almost vnsound at the core.*
Choppement: m. *A stumbling, a tripping.*
Chopper. *Looke* Choper; *also, a peare to grow soft, or almost vnsound at the core.*
Choquar. *A Chough; or, Cornish Chough.* ¶Valesien.
Choquer. *To giue a shock; violently, & with a hurrie to cope, knocke, incounter, bustle, or ioyne battell, together; also, to quaffe, carouse, tiple, tosse the pot.*
Choquer sa teste contre la muraille. *To runne his head against the wall.*
Chorage: m. *A keeper of Players garments.*
Chorde. *See* Corde.
Chordé. *as* Cordé.
Chore: m. *A companie of singers, or dauncers; any number, assembly, or whole companie; as the Chorus between euerie Act in a Tragedie.*
Choreal: m. ale: f. *Frequenting, or belonging to, a Queere.*
Choret: m. *A shote, or barrow pig; a young hog.*
Choriaux: m. *Queeremen, singingmen, quirresters.*
Chorion. *as* Arrierefaix; *or, the outmost of the three skins, whereof the Secundine consists.*
Choriste: m. *A Chorist; a singing man in a Queere.*
Chormes des naufs. *The Saylers, or Mariners. Looke* Chiorme.
Chose: f. *A thing; a matter; a cause; meane; case, affaire, deed; also, stuffe, geere, substance, goods, possessions.*
Chose accoustumée n'est pas trop prisée: Prov. *We prize not much the thing w' are vsed vnto.*
Chose bien donnée n'est iamais perduë: Prov. *A thing discreetly giuen is neuer lost.*
Chose faitte conseil prins: Prov. *When a thing is done aduise comes too late; a thing once done cannot be vndone; the care is alreadie taken.*
Chose qui plaist est à demy venduë: Prov. *Ware that doth please is halfe sold (when tis seene.)*
Petite chose de loing poise: Prov. *We say, Light burthen farre heauie; a little thing borne farre growes heauie.*
Chou: m. *The hearbe Cole, or Coleworts.*
Chou blanc. *as* Chou cabu.
Chou cabu. *Cabbage, white Colewort, headed Colewort, leafed Cabbage, round Cabbage Cole.*
Chou cabu rouge. *Red Cabbage Cole.*
Chou de chien. *Dogs Cawle, Dogs Mercurie, wild Mercurie.*
Choux crespus. *Curled garden-Coles; ragged, crisped, wrinckled Coleworts.*
Choux fleuris, fleurs, & floris. *The Collyflorie, or Cypres Colewort.*
Chou griseastre. *A kind of gray-leaued Colewort that seldome closes, and is of little worth.*
Chou marin. *The sea Cole; (the sea Withywind, sea-Solefoot, and Scottish Scuruie-weed is tearmed so by verie manie writers; but most improperly; for the right sea Colewort differs verie much from it, or anie kind of Bindweed.)*
Chou naveau. *The rape Colewort.*
Chou noir. *The blacke, or swart Cole.*
Chou petit. *The small, and slender Cole.*
Chou pommé, ou à pommes. *The ordinarie Cabbage.*
Chou rouge. *The bitter red Cole; or, the garden red Colewort.*
Choux de Savoye. *Ruffed, or curled Sauoy Coleworts; (there is also a smooth kind of them, tearmed, Sauoy Coles.)*
Chou sauvage. *The wild Colewort, or, wild sea-Cole.*
Choux tannez. *Wild red Coleworts; (fitter for medicine then for meat.)*
Choux verds. *Wrinckled, or ruffed greene Coleworts.*
Petit chou. *as* Chou petit. *Also, a puffe-cake, or loafe, made of butter, cheese, fine meale, and yolks of egges; (There be two kinds of them; one round, and plumpe like an apple; the other also round, but much flatter.)*
Chou pour chou. *One good turne for another.*
Ie n'en donneroye pas vn chou. *I value, or weigh it not; I care not for it; I would not giue a rush, a figge, a chip, for twentie such.*
Il en fait ses choux gras. *Hee gets well by it, makes his aduantage of it, feathers his neast with it.*

Souffler les choux en dormant. *To puffe in sleeping.*

Quand le chou passe le cep le vigneron meurt de soif: Prov. *Looke* Passer.

Chou. *An Interiection expressing a sence of a suddaine and extreame heat, or cold; also, a voice wherewith we driue away Pulleine.*

Choüan: m. *A Pollard, or Cheuin fish.* (Angevin.)

Choüans: m. *as* Chauäns.

Choüart. *Winsing, kicking, fluissing, flying out; and hence;*

Maistre Iehan Choüart. *A mans yard.*

Chouca. *A Chough, or Iacke Daw.*

Chouchette: f. *The Chough, Cadesse, Daw.*

Choüé: m. ée: f. *Disappointed, frustrated, deceiued.*

Chouëtte: f. *An Owlet; or, the little Horne-Owle; (a theeuish night-bird;) also, a Chough, Cadesse, Daw, Iack-Daw.*

Chouëtte rouge. *The Cornish Chough; the red-legd Chough.*

Choul: m. *as* Chou. *Cole.*

Chouquet: m. *A blocke.*

Chouquette: f. *A Chough, Cadesse, Iacke Daw.*

Chou-rave. *The rape Colewort.*

Chourme: f. *Looke* Chorme, *or* Chiorme.

Chouzer. *To swyue; (a countrey word.)*

Choyer. *To spare, forbeare, saue, not to vse; to refraine, abstaine, withhold himselfe from; to preserue, cherish, haue a great care of.*

Chraies: f. *Wild Peares, choake Peares.*

Chran: m. *A small kind of the fish* Glaucus, *couered with little shining skales of a golden blew colour.* ¶Marseillois.

Chras. *as* Chraies.

Chresme. *See* Cresme.

Chresmer. *To annoint with holie oyle.*

Chrestien: m. *A Christian.*

Poire de bon Chrestien. *A great Winter Peare, called by some, the Eusebian Peare. Looke* Poire.

Parlez Chrestien. *Speake plainely, or so as wee may conceiue you; deliuer your mind in some language which we vnderstand.*

Chrestien: m. enne: f. *Christian; of a Christian, professing Christianitie.*

Chrestienné: m. ée: f. *Christened, baptised.*

Chrestiennement: m. *A christening, or baptising.*

Chrestiennément. *Christianly, Christianlike.*

Chrestienner. *To christen, or baptise.*

Chrestienté: f. *Christendome, or Christianitie.*

Chrisocolle. *as* Chrysocolle.

Christ. *Christ, Sauiour.*

Baume de Iesus Christ. *Looke* Baume.

Herbe de Christ. *Blacke-Hellebore, Christs wort, Christs hearbe.*

Paulme de Christ. *The hearbe Kicke, Ricinus,* Palma Christi.

Christe-marine. *Sampire, rocke Sampire, Crestmarine.*

Christianisme: m. *Christianitie.*

Christianizé. *Christianized, christened, made a Christian.*

Christodin: m. *A new Christian, poore Christian, simple Christian.*

Chronique: com. *Temporall, or, returning at a certaine time.*

Chroniques: f. *Chronicles, Annales; generall, or yearelie relations of the chiefe matters acted, or happening, in a countrey.*

Chroniqueur: m. *A Chronicler, Annalist, Historiographer.*

Chroniste. *as* Chronicleur.

Chronographie: f. *A description of the times.*

Chronologie: f. *A Chronologie; a description, or numbring, of time.*

Chronologiste: m. *A Chronologist, or Chronicler; a describer of times.*

Chrysocolle: f. *Gold-solder; Borax, greene earth, (whether artificiall, or minerall) as* Borrais.

Chrysocome. *Gold flower, Gods flower, Goldylockes, golden Stechados (an hearbe.)*

Chrysogone: com. *Gold producing.*

Chrysolaine: f. *Orage, Orache, golden hearbe.*

Chrysolite: m. *A Chrysolite; a kind of Iasper of a golden lustre, or colour.*

Chrysopase: f. *A Chrysopase; a greene precious stone that yeelds a golden lustre.*

Chrysopatie. *The same.*

Chuat: m. *A whelpe.*

Chucas. *as* Chouca; *a Chough.*

Chucas rouge. *A Cornish Chough.*

Chucheté: m. ée: f. *Whispered.*

Chucheter. *To whisper in the eare.*

Chuchoté. *Looke* Chucheté.

Chue: f. *A Chough, Daw, Cadesse.* (Savoyard.)

Chupper. *To sup, or sucke, vp.*

Churle: f. *The white field Onyon, or Starre of Bethelem.*

Churquette: f. *A mouse-trap.* ¶Pic.

Chut. *as* Cheu.

Chyle: m. *The Chylus, or white iuice of disgested meat; the matter whereof our bloud is made: (The word originally signifies, a iuice concocted by heat vnto a consistence that holdes both of moisture, and drynesse.)*

Chylose: f. *An expression, confection, or disgestion of sap, or iuice; also, a thicke, or creamie sap, expressed.*

Chymerique: com. *Fond, vaine, imaginarie, onely in conceit, Chymericall, Chymera-like.*

Chymie: f. *The second part of Alchymie; melting; Extraction; (much vsed for Alchymie it selfe.)*

Chymique: com. *A Chymist, or Alchymist; a Melter; or an Extractor, of Quintessences.*

Chymique: com. *Chymicall; melting; extractiue, quintessentiall; whence;*

Sel chymique. *Salt made of the quintessence, or finest substance, of any thing.*

Chymistique: com. *Chymisticall, quintessentiall.*

Chyst. *as* Kyst.

Ci. *Here, in this place, in this matter.*

Ci pris ci mis. *Done speedily, presently, incontinently, quickly, out of hand; as soone done as spoken, no sooner said but done.*

Ciané: m. ée: f. *Azure, bright-blue of colour.*

Ciathe: m. *A small cup, or measure, among the auncient Romans, containing foure spoonefuls: about the weight of it Authors disagree; some saying it was twelue drammes; others, that it was but tenne; and others, (the most probably) that it was two Carrats, and fifteen graines (of our weight) more then tenne.*

Ciboile. *as* Ciboire.

Ciboire: m. *A Pix; the box, or cup wherein the Sacrament is put, and kept in Popish churches.*

Ciboule: f. *A Chiboll, or hollow Leeke.*

Cicatrice: f. *A Cicatrice, a skarre; a skin bred vpon*

a

a wound, sore, or vlcer.
Cicatricé. *Looke* Cicatrizé.
Cicatricer. *as* Cicatrizer.
Cicatrisatif: m. iue: f. *as* Cicatrizé; *also, cicatrizing, skarre-breeding, skinne-bringing.*
Cicatrizé: m. ée: f. *Cicatrised; skinned; skarred; also, full of skarres; that beares about him the markes of many wounds.*
Cicatrizer. *To cicatrize; to skinne; to skarre; to set a a skinne, make a skarre on; bring to a skinne, heale vp to a skarre.*
Cicerolles: f. *Small Cichlings, or Chichlings; small pettie Ciches; In Latine they are tearmed* Cicera, *which* Gerard *holds to be, yellow wild Fitches.*
Cices: f. *Ciches, Chiches, red Cich, Sheepes Cich peason; Looke* Chiches.
Cicharou: m. *Looke* Chicharou.
Cichenie. *Looke* Sequenie, *or* Squenie.
Ciches: f. *Ciches, Chiches, red Cich, Sheepes Cich peason; Looke* Chiches.
Cichorée: f. *The hearb Succorie.*
Cichorée blanche. *White Succorie; also, garden Endiue.*
Cichorée des champs. *Field Succorie, wild Succorie.*
Cichorée de Iardin. *Garden Succorie; or, as* Scariole, *garden Endiue.*
Cichorée iaulne. *Yellow Succorie (a wild kind thereof) also, Haukeweed; also, Dandelion, Succorie Dandelion, Pissabed.*
Cichorée sauvage. *Wild Succorie; whereof there be diuers kinds.*
Cichorée verrueuse. *Gumme Succorie; or, a kind thereof, that hath a blackish, and Rampion-like root; and takes away warts, being eaten in Salades.*
Cicle: m. *A Sheicle; an Hebrew coyne, or weight of two drammes, worth about fourteene pence sterling.*
Cicle du Sanctuaire. *Was twice as much as the ordinarie one; foure drammes in weight; in value, two shillings foure pence sterl.*
Cicle: m. *A Circle, Compasse, Round.*
Cicle Lunaire. *The Golden Number; or, full course, or compasse of the Moone, performed in nineteene yeares.*
Cicle solaire. *The reuolution, or full course of the Sunne, performed in, and consisting of, eight and twentie yeares.*
Cicogne: f. *A Storke; also, a Swype, or Scoope to draw water out of a Pit, or shallow Well.*
Bec de cicogne. *Hearbe Pinke-needle, Storkes-bill, Cranes-bill, Hearons-bill.*
Contes de la cicogne. *Idle histories; vaine relations; tales of a tub, or, of a rosted horse.*
Cicogneau: m. *A young Storke.*
Cicoigne; &, Cicoigneau; *as* Cicogne, *&* Cicogneau.
Cicotrin. *The hearbe Orpin; Liblong, Liuelong.*
Aloës cicotrin. *The best kind of Aloes; of a cleere, shining, and browne-yellow colour, tearmed so of the Island* Succotora, *whence it comes.*
Cicotriné. *Looke* Cicrotiné.
Cicrotin: m. *A kind of extraordinarie fine searce.*
Cicrotiné: m. ée: f. *Verie finelie searced.*
Cicutaire: f. *Mocke Cheruill, wild Cheruill, great Cheruill, Asse Perseley,* Mirrhis *Cash, Cax, or Kex; also, Hemlockes.*
Cidrage: m. *Ciderage, Peachwort, dead Arsesmart, dead Culerage.*
Cidre: m. *Cyder; drinke made of apples.*
Cie, *for* Scie; *a Saw.*
Ciel: m. *Heauen; also, the Skye, Welkin, Firmament; (in the plurall number* Cieux) *also, a canopie for, and, the Testerne, and Valances of, a Bed; also, the canopie that is carried ouer a Prince as he walkes in state; also, the inner roofe of a roome of State; (In all which sences, &c, the plurall is,* Ciels.)
Cielin: m. ine: f. *Heauenlie, of heauen, diuine; also, belonging to the Firmament; or to a Canopie, Testerne, or vpper seeling.*
Cier. *as* Scier. *To sawe.*
Cierge: m. *A big wax candle. Seeke* Poincte.
Cieure: f. *Saw-dust. Looke* Sieure.
Cigale: f. *A thicke, broad-headed, and mouthlesse flye, which ordinarily sits on trees, & sings (after her skreaking fashion) both day and night; liuing onely of the dew of heauen, which shee drawes into her by certaine tongue-like prickles, placed on her breast; she hath both old, and cold countries; and therefore we neither haue her, nor name for her.*
Cigale de mer. *A gray-eyed, thin-shelled, white, and (almost) transparent fish (of the kind of Creuises or Insects of the sea) hauing two crimson, and eye-like spots vpon her (broad) tayle, and on either side of the vpper part of her bodie three feet, besides a long arme, the cley whereof is so hard, that picktooths are oftentimes made of it.*
Babillard en cigale. *Pratling like a Parrat (say we.)*
Ferrer les cigales. *To spend the time in trifles; to take vpon him foolish businesses; to labour vainely, or in vaine.*
Cigaler. *To chirpe, sing, chatter, like a* Cigale.
Cigne: m. *A Swan.*
L'herbe du cigne. *The Swans hearbe; growes (by* Cardans *report) in a Scottish lake tearmed* Morania, *and neuer rots.*
Chanter l'hymne du cigne. *To sing his last.*
Cignean: m. anne: f. *Swan-like; of a Swan.*
Cigogne. *as* Cicoigne. *A Storke.*
Ciguë: f. *Hemlocke, Homlocke, hearbe Bennet, Kex.*
Cil: m. *The brimme (or the single ranke of haire that growes on the brimme) of an eye-lid; the haire of an eye-lid; also, the twinckling, or nimble motion, of the eye-lids; and sometimes (but lesse properly) an eye-lid.*
Cil. *(vsed sometimes, in stead of* Celuy) *he, that same man, that verie man.*
Cilindre: m. *A Rowler; a round and long instrument of wood, wherewith husbandmen breake clods, and Gardeners smooth their alleyes, &c.*
Cillement: m. *A winking, twinckling, or beckening with the eye; also, a seeling, or hoodwinking of the eyes.*
Ciller. *To winke often; to twinckle with the eyes; to becken, or make a signe, by mooning the eye-lids; also, to seele, or sow vp, the eye-lids.*
Cillier. faulcon c. *Whose eyes are seeled, or sowed vp; a seeled Hauke.*
Cillier. *To seele, or sow vp the eye-lids.*
Cimaise. *Looke* Cymaise, *or* Cymace.
Cimasulte. *Caruing that resembleth rowling waues.* ¶Rab.
Cimbale: f. *A Cymball. Seeke* Cymbale.
Cime: f. *The top, or knap, of a Plant.*
Ciment. *Cement; a strong, and cleauing morter, made (most*

(most commonly) of Tyles, Potshards, Flint, Glasse, the drosse of yron, &c, beaten to dust, and incorporated with lime, oyle, grease, rosin, and water.

Ciment royal. *An excellent Cement, or Solder, vsed by Goldsmiths; (heretofore Mintmen compounded a Cement for the tryall of gold, and tearmed it so.)*

Cimenté: m. ée: f. *Cemented; soldered, closed, or ioyned by Cement.*

Cimenter. *To cement; to solder, close, or ioyne together with Cement.*

Cimet: m. *as* Cime; *the top of a plant, or tree.*

Cimeterre: m. *A scymitar, or smyter; a kind of short, and crooked, sword, much in vse among the Turks.*

Cimettes. *Looke* Cymettes.

Cimier: m. *The vpper part of a rumpe of Beefe, &c, next, or neere, vnto the chine.*

Iouër du cimier. *To leacher.*

Cimitiere: m. *A Churchyard.*

De nouveau medecin cimitiere bossu: Prov. *An vnexperienced Physition fattens the Churchyard.*

Veau mal cuict, & poules cruds font les cimitieres bossus: Pro. *Raw Veale, and Chickens make fat churchyards.*

Cimmerique. Tenebres Cimmeriques. *Cimmerian (viz. perpetuall, or continuall) darknesse.*

Cimolée. terre Cimolée. *as* Terre Cimolie.

Cimolie. terre Cimolie. *Fullers earth; a kind of chalk; in lieu whereof (at this day not found, or not knowne) men foist in the thickened grounds, or bottome of the water of Grindlestones.*

Cimolienne. Terre Cimolienne. *The same.*

Cin de bois. *A knot, or knurre, in wood.*

Cinabre. *as* Cinnabre. *Synoper; Vermillion; or, a kind of Lybian Minerall, redder then Vermillion. Look* Cinnabre.

Cinabrin: m. ine: f. *Red, ruddie (as Vermillion.)*

Cincinatule: m. *One that continually frizles, or curles his haire; one whose head is frizled, or curled (by art;) any such effeminate, or spruce, youth.*

Cincture. *as* Ceincture. *A girdle.*

Cindre: f. *(The same.)*

Cindré: m. ée: f. *Girt; also, spotted; also, supported.*

Cindrer. *To gird; also, to spot; also, as* Cintrer.

Cinefaction: f. *A reducing into, a burning vnto, ashes.*

Cinge. *Looke* Singe.

Cinglant. *Sayling, cutting the sea.*

Cingler. *Looke* Singler.

Cinit: m. *The little bird called, a Siskin.*

Cinnabrisé: m. ée: f. *Mingled, or coloured, with Cynoper.*

Cinnabre: m. *Cynoper, Vermillion, Sanguinarie; is either naturall (a soft, red, and heauie stone found in Mines) or artificiall (the more common, and better coloured) made of calcinated Sulpher, and Quicksiluer.*

Cinnamé: m. ée: f. *Cinnamonized; sweetened with Cinnamon; or sweet as Cinnamon.*

Cinnamome: f. *Cinnamon: (Some learned men are of opinion, that the true Cinnamon of the Ancients (being a wood, and not, as ours, the barke of a tree) is hardlie to be found at this day; and that the rinde, or barke, which we commonly hold to be Cinnamon, is much inferior vnto it, and should rather be tearmed,* Cassia, *and* Canella.)

Cinq. *Fiue.*

Cinquaine: f. *The name of a certaine Vine, that thriues not in a moist soyle.*

Cinquante. *Fiftie.*

Cinquantenier: m. *A certaine Officer, or Magistrate in Paris, that somewhat resembles, in his authoritie, our Aldermans Deputie; also, a Captaine, or Commaunder, of fiftie men.*

Cinquantiéme. *The fiftieth.*

Cinquener. *To yeeld fiue for one.*

Cinquiéme. *The fifth, or fift.*

Cintre: m. *A Centrie, or Mould for an Arch; the frame of wood whereon it is built, and whereby it is vpheld in the building.*

Cintrer. *To mould an Arch; to build it on, or (in the building) to vphold it with, a Centrie, or frame of tymber.*

Cinturin. *Looke* Ceinturon.

Cion. *A great tempest, or whirlewind vpon the sea; also, as* Sion, *or* Scion.

Cipres: m. *The Cypresse tree. Looke* Cyprés.

Cipricini *(compounded of foure words.) Looke* Ci.

Cipsule: f. *as* Capsule.

Circée: f. *A kind of Nightshade, that beares manie small blacke flowers (not easily found now-a-daies.)*

Circombilivagination: f. *A circumbiliuigation, circular motion; going round, wheeling about.*

Circombilivaginer. *To turne, goe round, wheele about; and (in discourse) to vse many circumstances.*

Circoncir. *To circumcise.*

Circoncis: m. ise: f. *Circumcised.*

Circoncision. *Circumcision, the cutting of the fore-skin; also, the nation, or generation of the Iewes.*

La Circoncision. *New yeares day.*

Circonference: f. *A circumference, compassing, or bringing about.*

Circonflex. Accent circonflex. *Looke* Accent.

Circongirer. *To turne, twirle, wheele about.*

Circonjacent: m. ente: f. *Lying about; situate, or abording, on each side of.*

Circonlocution: f. *A circumlocution; a tedious paraphrase, or description; a going about the bush (in words.)*

Circonscript: m. te: f. *Circumscribed, limitted, bounded; appointed; restrained; made briefe, short, succinct; also, deceiued, beguiled, fetcht ouer; also, abolished, raced, put out.*

Circonscription: f. *A circumscription; limitation, measuring, bounding; restraint, or prescription of compasse; also, guile, deceit, cousenage.*

Circonscrire. *To circumscribe; to restraine, or hold within certaine limits; to limit, appoint, or measure out bounds vnto; also, to cheat, beguile, deceiue, fetch ouer.*

Circonspection: f. *Circumspection; heed, aduisement, prouidence, warinesse; a vigilant consideration, a diligent looking round about.*

Circonstance: f. *A circumstance.*

Circonstancié. *Circumstanced; furnished with circumstances; or, compassed, as with circumstances.*

Circonvenir. *To enuiron, or incompasse; and hence; to circumuent, fetch in, or ouer; to beguile, deceiue, cousin, intrap, compasse with great sleight.*

Circonvention: f. *Circumuention, deceit, cousenage; an intrapping, beguiling, wylie compassing, or fetching ouer.*

Circonvenu: m. uë: f. *Enuironed, incompassed, come about; also, circumuented, fetched in or ouer; deceiued, beguiled, cousened, intrapped.*

Circonvoisin: m. ine: f. *Neighbouring, neere, hard by,*

by, lying close vnto, neere adioyning to.

Circonvolution: f. *A circumuolution; a wrapping, or foulding; also, a rowling, or tumbling, about.*

Circuir. *To circuit; enuiron, incompasse, or goe about; also, to inwrap, infould, inclose.*

Circuit: m. *A circuit, compasse, going about; a round course, or race.*

Circuit: m. ite: f. *Enuironed, incompassed; gone about; also, inwrapped, infoulded, inclosed.*

Circuition: f. *A circuition; a circular course, or motion.*

Circuition de paroles. *A circumlocution, paraphrase, great circumstance of words; a going about the bush.*

Circulaire: com. *Round, circular, orbicular, compassing about, in a ring; belonging to a circle, round, ring.*

Cautere Circulaire. *See* Cautere.

Circulairement. *Roundly, orbicularly, circularly, with a compasse, in a circle.*

Circularité: f. *Circularitie, roundnesse, orbicularnesse.*

Circulateur: m. *A Ieaster, Iugler, Imposter; one that delights, or deceiues with fables, tricks, and sleights, the people gathered about him.*

Circulation: f. *A circulation; a subliming, or extracting of water, or oyle by a Lembicke &c; tearmed so, because the vapour, before it be resolued into either, seemes to goe round, or circle-wise.*

Circulatoire: com. *Circulatorie; circulating; subliming; extracting, or seruing for extraction; whence;* Vaisseau circulatoire. *A Lembicke, Stillitorie, &c.*

Circulé: m. ée: f. *Circulated; sublimed, extracted; (exactly) distilled.*

Circuler. *To circulate; sublime, extract, or distill (exactly.)*

Ou se circulent les humeurs. *Wherein the humors make many a circle, before they produce, or be resolued into, any water &c.*

Cire: f. *Wax; also, a combe of wax in the hiue.*

Cire d'Espaigne. *Hard-wax; or, as* Lacre.

Cire gommée. *Wax mingled with Rosin and Turpentine.*

Cire jaulne. *Yellow wax; is vsed onely in the Chauncenes of France.*

Cire minerale. Pissasphalte *is called so in some places.*

Cire verde. *Greene wax; wherewith the writs, and other dispatches of inferiour Courts; as also, all Charters, Perpetuities, and generall Pardons graunted by the King, are sealed.*

Droict de cire. *is eighteene pence* Tourn. *in euerie pound aboue twentie, giuen, or agreed vpon, for a woodsale; due vnto the King in regard of the lights which are (said to be) spent while the bargaine is in making.*

'A yeux de cire. *Tender; easily melting, or quickly shedding teares.*

Chauffer la cire. *To attend long for a promised good turne.*

Faire vn nez de cire à. *To plie, or applie a thing at pleasure; to giue it any forme that is for his turne, or serues his purposes.*

Ciré: m. ée: f. *Waxed; seared; dressed, couered, closed, or mingled with wax.*

Cirement: m. *A waxing; a searing; a dressing, closing, couering, or mingling, with wax.*

Cirer. *To wax; to seare; to dresse, couer, close, or mingle with wax.*

Cirette. *The name of a certaine Peare, that yeelds most excellent Perrie.*

Cireux: m. euse: f. *Waxie; of wax; full of wax.*

Cirier: m. *A Wax-chandler.*

Cirier: m. ere: f. *Waxie, of wax.*

Cirine: f. *as* Gyrine.

Ciroesne. *A Seare-cloth; or any plaister, or ointment whereof Wax, Rosin, or Gummes, and Wine are the principall Ingredients.*

Ciron: m. *A Hand-worme.*

Mais dont me vient ce ciron icy entre ces deux doigts? *But whence comes this worme betweene these two fingers? (A knauish question from as knauish an action; to put the fore finger of one hand betweene the first, and second finger of the other; vnder pretence, that a worme makes the place itch, but with a purpose to make hornes at the partie of whom the question is asked.)*

Cironnier. Main cironniere. *A hand that is full of, or troubled with, wormes.*

Cirop: m. *Sirrup.*

Cirque. *A place in Rome, wherein the people sate to behold Playes, Games, and publicke Exercises.*

Cirre: m. *A tuft, or locke of curled haire; also, the featherie tuffe, crest, or cop on the heads of some birds; also, the small staulke of some hearbs (as Withywind, &c;) intangled like a bush of haire; also, the hairie substance cleauing vnto oysters.*

Cirsotomie: f. *The cutting, or opening of the corrupt veines, called* Varices.

Cisaille: f. *The clipping of coyne presently after the stampe.*

Cisaillé: m. ée: f. *Clipped, or cut with sheeres, or sizars; also, whose flesh is nipped off with hot pincers.*

Cisailler. *To clip, or cut with sizars, or sheeres; also, to nip, or pull off the flesh with hot pincers.*

Cisailles: f. *Garden sheeres; a Gardeners clipping sheeres; any great sheeres.*

Cisé: m. ée: f. *Carued; wrought with a chisell, or grauing yron.*

Ciseau: m. *A Surgeons Launce, Launcet, or Instrument of Incision; also, a chisell, or grauing yron.*

Ciseaux: m. *Sizars, or (little) sheeres.*

Le drap, & les ciseaux luy sont delivrez: Prov. *The whole matter is put vnto him; all is at his owne disposition, or in his owne hand; he may now be his owne caruer; he may now both part and chuse.*

Giselé: m. ée: f. *Carued, or grauen with a chisell; also, clipped, or cut with sizars.*

Ciseler. *To carue, or graue with a chisell; also, to clip, or cut with sizars.*

Ciselet: m. *A little sizar, or chisell.*

Ciseleure: f. *Chisell-worke; or as* Cizelleure.

Cisellage: m. *A clipping with sheeres, or sizars.*

Ciste: m. *The plant called* Cistus, *and Hollie Rose.*

Cisteaux: m. *An Order of white Friers (instituted in the yeare* 1090) *who vnder their (vpmost) white habit weare a blacke one, and red shoes.*

Cisterne: f. *A Cesterne.*

Cisternin: m. ine: f. *Of, or belonging to, a Cesterne.*

Cisternon: m. *A little Cesterne.*

Cistophore: m. *An auncient coyne worth about two pence farthing.*

Cistre: m. *A kind of brazen timbrell.*

Cisure. *Looke* Scissure.

Citadelle: f. *A Citadell; a strong Fort, or Castle, that serues*

serues both to defend, and to curbe, a citie.
Citadin: m. *A Citizen, Burgesse, Burguer, freeman in a citie.*
Citation: f. *A Citation, Summons, warning to appeare; also, a citing, adiourning, summoning.*
Cité: f. *A Citie; a walled, and incorporate Towne, being the seat, and sea, of a Bishop, and hauing a Cathedrall Church within it.*
Cité: m. ée: f. *Cited, summoned, adiourned, warned, to appeare; also, alledged, or cited as a Text.*
Citer. *To cite, summon, adiourne, warne, serue with a writ, to appeare; also, to cite, or alledge, as a Text.*
Citouart. *as* Zedoare; *a certaine root verie like to Ginger.*
Citoyen: m. *A Citizen, Burguer, Burgesse, freeman of a Citie.*
Citoyennerie: f. *A Citizenship, the freedome of a Citie.*
Citre. *The worst kind of Pompion; blacke of colour, and continued in gardens, onely for the seed, which is medicinable; the rest is throwne vnto hogs.*
Citrin: m. ine: f. *Of a Citron, Citron-like, pale-yellow, as a Citron.*
Concombre citrin. *A Citrull, or Citrull Cowcumber.*
Couleur citrine. *A Citron colour, pale Orange colour; pale-yellow.*
Myrobalan citrin. *The yellow, or Citron, Myrobalan.*
Citrinité: f. *Pale-yellownesse; or, a pale yellow.*
Citron: m. *A Citron, Pome-Citron.*
Citronne: f. *Baulme, sweet Baulme (an hearbe.)*
Citronnelle: f. *A kind of small Baulme, of a faire greene colour, and verie good in a Sallet.*
Citronnier: m. *A Citron tree.*
Citronnier: m. ere: f. *Citron-like; of a Citron.*
Basilic citronnier. *Citron Basill, middle Basill.*
Citrouille: f. *A Citrull; a Citrull Cowcumber, or Turkish gourd; a kind of great Melon, in colour, and forme resembling a Citron.*
Citrulle. *The same.*
Civade: f. *The Shrimpe, or beard-fish; also, Oats, or Prouender for horses.*
Civadier: m. *The fourth part of a* Quarteron. ¶Langued.
Civadiere: f. *The sprit-sayle of a ship.*
Civé: m. *A kind of blacke sauce for a Hare. Looke* Sivé.
Cive: f. *A Scallion; or vnset Leeke.*
Civelle: f. *A Lamprill; the small, or fresh-water Lamprey.* ¶Lyonnois.
Civets. des c. *Slices of bread toasted, then soaked an houre or two in water and wine; then strained, and spice put to them; an excellent sauce; we may call them, sippets.*
Civette: f. *Ciuet; also, (the beast that breeds it) a Ciuet cat; also, a Chiue, little Scallion, or Chiboll.*
Civettien: m. enne: f. *Perfumed with, or smelling of, Ciuet.*
Civiere: f. *A hand-barrow; (to carrie mucke, &c, on) also, a Beere (to carrie a dead corps on.)*
Civiere à col. *A necke-barrow, or Beere-like shrine, whereon Images, and Relickes, are carried in Processions, &c.*
En cent ans civiere en cent ans banniere: Prov. *See* Banniere.
Civil: m. ile: f. *Ciuill, courteous, gentle, mannerlie, well-behaued; also, temperat, mild, quiet; also, towne-bred, or, burguerlike; also, politicke, lay, secular, ciuill.*
Cause civile. *A priuat cause; or, such a one, as is neither Ecclesiasticall, criminall, nor capitall; but concerns a mans estate.*
Fruicts civils. *Are such as are gathered, or taken by the course of right, and without any helpe of nature; as hire for houses, wages for offices, arrerages of rent, &c.*
Iour civil. *The ciuill day; continues from Sunne-rising to Sunne-set. Looke* Iour.
Lieutenant civil. *See* Lieutenant.
Nuict civile. *Begins when the day ends, from Sunne-set vnto Sunne-rising.*
Partie civile. *A priuat man; one that is lyable to any action; also, an ordinarie Suitor, or Client.*
Partie civile & formée, ou interessée. *He that followes a criminall action, only in respect of, or to get some amends for, a wrong done to himselfe.*
Requeste civile. *Seeke* Requeste.
Civilement. *Ciuilly, gently, courteously; in a good fashion, decent order, comelie manner; also, mildly, quietly, temperately; also, according to Order, Iustice, and Law.*
Civilisé: m. ée: f. *Ciuilized; made ciuile; framed, or trained vp, to ciuilitie.*
Civiliser. *Looke* Civilizer.
Civilité: f. *Ciuilitie, gentlenesse, humanitie, courtesie; also, modestie, mildnes; quietnes of disposition, and fashion.*
Civilizer. *To ciuilize, bring to ciuilitie, make ciuill; to tame, quiet, reclaime.*
Civilizer vn criminel. *To change his Indictment into an action; to turne a criminall, into a ciuill, cause.*
Civois: m. *A bed of Scallions; or of vnset Leekes.*
Civot: m. *A Scallion; or vnset Leeke.*
Cizaillé: m. ée: f. *Clipped, or cut, with sizzars.*
Cizailler. *To clip, or cut with sizzars, or sheeres.*
Cizailles: f. *as* Cisailles.
Cizelé: m. ée: f. *Carued, or grauen with chizels.*
Cizeler. *To fashion, carue, or graue with a chizell; also, to cut, or clip with sizzars.*
Cizellage: m. *as* Cisellage.
Cizelleure: f. *Chizell-worke; caruing, or ingrauerie with the Chizell.*
Clabaud: m. *A name for a hound; also, the barke, or barking, of a bawling curre.*
Clabauder. *To barke; bawle, raile at; spightfully to accuse, or speake against.*
Clabauderie: f. *A barking, bawling, rayling; an enuious accusing, a spightfull reproching.*
Claboffer. *To hoyse, or tosse vp and down; also, to bedash, or beray, with durt.*
Clac: m. *A clicket, or clapper; any thing that makes a clacking, or clattering noise; hence (most properly) the clacket that frights away birds from fruit-trees, &c.*
Clache: f. *A certaine Engine wherewith (small) birds are caught.*
Claguet: m. *The name of a faire, sappie, & sauorie apple.*
Claigner. *Looke* Cligner.
Claim: m. *A publicke demaund, or claime; a pretence of title vnto land, &c; also, a Declaration, or Bill of Complaint put, or preferred, into a Court.*
Clain: m. *as* Claim; *also, an Arrest, or seisure of a debtors goods, vpon an Execution; also, a fine of* xx d, *or of three* solz Tourn. *due vnto Iustice for the seisure of beasts damage-fesant; also, a penaltie (in some places, of* xx d. Tourn. *in others, of* xxx d. Parisis) *inflicted on the partie that yeelds by confession in Court before the suit come to contestation.*
Clair: m. *as* Clarté; *or, a cleere thing; whence;*
Clair de la Lune. *Moone-light, or Moone-shine.*
Clair d'un oeuf. *The white of an egge.*
Clair: m. ire: f. *Cleere, light, shining, bright. as* Cler.

Clair-coulant. *Cleere-gliding, cleere-streaming, running cleere.*
Clairement. *Cleerely, brightly; euidently, plainly.*
Clairet: m. ette: f. *Somewhat cleere, bright, or shining.*
Eau clairette. *A water (made of Aquauite, Cinnamon, Sugar, and old red Rose water) soueraigne against all the diseases of the wombe.*
Vin clairet. *Claret wine; (is commonly made of white and red grapes mingled, or growing, together.)*
Clairins: m. *A certaine Order of Cordeliers, or Gray Friers.*
Clairon: m. *A Clarion; a kind of small, strait-mouthed, and shrill-sounding Trumpet, vsed (commonly) as a Treble vnto the ordinarie one.*
'A pain, & oignon trompette, ne clairon: Prov. *Hard fare, poore dyet, course Acates require neither State in the seruing, nor Musicke in the eating; or, the sound of forraine Trumpets is but seldome heard in a poore, and barren State.*
Claironner. *To sound a Clarion; also, to squeake, squeale; speake shrilly, smally, or with an effeminate voice.*
Clamable: com. *Claimeable, challengeable.*
Clamant: m. *A claimer, a challenger; one that makes title vnto land, &c; also, a Creditor, that seizes his debtors goods vpon an Execution.*
Clamant: m. ante: f. *Calling, crying out; also, claiming, or challenging.*
Clame: f. *A fine leuied, in some places, vpon those that deferre the payment of their debts; also, the fine payed vnto Iustice, or a Lord hauing iurisdiction, for the seisure of beasts found Damage fesant; also, as* Clain.
Clamé: m. ée: f. *Claimed, challenged, demaunded; called, or cried out; spoken aloud, or with a high voice.*
Clamer. *To call, crie, speake aloud, or out; also, to claime; to make a claime to, or lay in a claime for; to challenge, demaund, pretend a title vnto; also, to arrest, or seize, his debtors goods.*
Clamer en garend, ou en garieur. *To demaund a thing by way of possession, or of propertie; or, to complaine, in Court, of the wrongs which haue beene done him those wayes.*
Clamer à Iustice. *To exhibit a claime, or demaund; or, to preferre a Bill of Complaint vnto a Court.*
Clamer son subiect de serve condition qui se veut advouër d'autre seigneur; c'est, le poursuivre.
Il le clama fils de putain. *He called, or cleaped, him whoreson.*
Se clamer en Cour suzeraine de Cour inferieure. *To addresse himselfe, for the more expedition, vnto a superior Court, though he were summoned by an inferiour.*
Clameur: f. *A clamour, crie, outcrie, exclamation, shout, roaring; also, a claime vnto, a challenge, or demaund of, a publicke suit for, a thing.*
Clameur d'Haro. *Looke* Haro.
Clameur pour le Seigneur Iusticier. *The fine that is due vnto him vpon the seisure of beasts found Damage fesant within his Iurisdiction.*
Forte clameur. *Looke* Fort.
Clamme: f. *A Pilgrims Cloke, Pelt, or Gabardine.*
Clamporte. *as* Cloporte.
Clanche: f. *The latch of a dore.*
Clandestin: m. ine: f. *Clandestine, close, priuie, secret, hidden.*
Clandestinement. *Priuily, secretly, closely, vnder hand, in huggar muggar.*
Clangueur: f. *A skreaking, shrillnesse, or shrill noise; a skriking, ringing, loud resounding.*
Clangueux: m. euse: f. *Shrill, skriking, skreaking, loudly squeaking, ringing, resounding.*
Clanponniere. *as* Clapponniere.
Clapier: m. *A Clapper of Conies; a heape of stones, &c, whereinto they retire themselues; or (as our clapper) a Court walled about, and full of neasts of boords, or stone, for tame Conies; also, a Rabbets neast: (In old time Baudie houses were also tearmed,* Clapiers.)
Clapiers d'vlcere. *The Sinus, bosomes, or angles of an Vlcer; the many crosse, or ouerthwart holes wherein it putrifies as it goes.*
Clapoir: m. *A botch in the Groyne, or yard; a Winchester Goose.*
Clapoire: f. *The same.*
Claponnice. *as* Clapponniere.
Claponnier: m. *The same.*
Clappetter. *To clap on with the hand.*
Clapponniere: f. *The buckle, pastle, or pasterne, bone of a beast.*
Claque-dent: m. *A lazie rogue, idle luske, slouthfull idlesbie; one that will rather starue with cold, and hunger, then worke to get heat, or meat.*
Claquer. *To clacke, to clap, to clatter; to crash; to crack; to creake.*
Claquer les dents. *To gnash the teeth; or, to chatter, or didder, like an Ape, thats afraid of blowes.*
Claquet. *The name of an Apple whereof excellent Cyder is made.*
Claquet de moulin. *The Clapper, or clacke, of a Millhopper.*
Claquetant: m. ante: f. *Clacking, clapping, clattering; chattering; crashing; cracking, creaking.*
Claquetement: m. *A clattering, clacking, crashing, chattering, creaking, clapping.*
Claqueter. *as* Claquer.
Claquetis: m. *A clattering, clacking, clapping; a crashing; a cracking; a creaking; a chattering.*
Claquette: f. *A Lazers Clicket, or Clapper.*
Claré: m. *as* Eau Clairette.
Claret. Vin claret. *Claret wine.*
Clarifié: m. ée: f. *Clarified, cleered, fined, purified.*
Clarifier. *To clarifie; cleere, fine, purifie.*
Clariné. vache clarinée d'Azur. *A Cow with Azur bels hanging about her necke; our Blasonners say no more but, the bels Azur.*
Clarté: f. *Cleerenesse, light, brightnesse, lustre, transparancie.*
Clas: m. *as* Glas; *a knell, or wofull noyse.*
Classe. *A ranke, order, or distribution of people according to their seuerall degrees; In Schooles (wherein this word is most vsed) a forme, or Lecture restrained vnto a certaine companie of Schollers, or Auditors; and hence;*
Escolier babillard prez le feu, & badin hors la classe: Pro.
Classique: com. *Classicall; formall, orderlie, in due, or fit ranke; also, approued, authenticall; chiefe, principall.*
Clavaire: m. *A kind of Receiuer, or Officer that lookes to the receit, of the Kings demesne.*
Claval. Cautre Claval. *See* Cautre.
Clavaller. *To settle, or strengthen, the yong shoots, or slips of a vine against the furie of strong winds.*
Clavandier: m. *A porter, or key-bearer; one to whom keyes are committed to be kept; also, the chaine whereon women vse to weare their keyes.*
Clavandiere: f. *A she porter, key-keeper, or key-bearer.*

Clavarins.

Clavarins. *An Order of blacke Friers, which weare two great paper keyes vpon their habits.*
Claudication: f. *A limping, halting, lamenesse.*
Claudition: f. *as* Claudication.
Claveau: m. *The Scab among Sheepe; also, the Haunse, or Lintell of a doore; also, a claspe, hooke, or buckle.*
Clavelade: f. *A Thornebacke.* ¶Langued.
Clavelé: m. ée: f. *Scabbed, or infected with the scab, as a sheepe; also, nayled, or fastened with nayles; also, rooted surely in.*
Herbe clavelée. *Paunsie, hearbe Trinitie, Heartsease.*
Raye clavelée. *The Rocke Ray; or, as* Raye bouclée. *Seeke* Raye.
Clavelée: f. *The scab among sheepe; also, the scabbinesse of a horses legs.*
Claveler. *To nayle, or fasten with nayles; to settle, or set, fast in.*
Clavellé: m. ée: f. *as* Clavelé.
Claveller. *See* Claveler.
Clavessins: m. *Claricords, or Claricols.*
Clavet: m. *as* Clavelée. *(In the first sence.)*
Clavette: f. *The Cannell bone, or Craw-bone; also, a Spring-pinne; the little peece of yron wherwith tradesmen keepe in the yron pinnes of their shop-windowes; also, the Capsquire, or Fore-locke of the carriage of a Canon; or (more properly, that which fastens it) the fore-locke key.*
Clavette du pied. *The heele, or hinder bone of the foot.*
Claveure: f. *A key-hole; or all that part of a locke wherein the key turnes, or playes; also, a chinke, or cranny.*
Plus rouillé que la claveure d' un vieil charnier. *More rustie then the key-hole of an old poudering tub.*
Le visage leur reluisoit comme la claveure d' un charnier. *Their faces glistened (with grease) like the locke, or key-hole, of a poudering tub.*
Clavicules: f. *The kannell bones, channell bones, neckebones, craw-bones; extending (on each side one) from the bottome of the throat vnto the top of the shoulder.*
Clavier: m. *A key-chaine; or chaine for keyes, or chaine whereat keyes are hanged.*
Clavier d'une espinette, &c. *The keyes of, or, a set of keyes for, a paire of Virginals.*
Claviere: f. *A key-keeper, or key-carrier; a woman that hath charge of all the keyes in a house.*
Clavin: m. *A little graple, or hooke like a claw.*
Claune. *as* Mare; *a Poole, or Pond of standing water.*
Clause: f. *A Clause, Period, conclusiue sentence, or conclusion.*
Claustier: m. ere: f. *Of, or belonging to, a Cloyster; liuing in a Monasterie, or Cloyster.*
Claustral. *as* Claustier.
Prieur claustral. *The Prior, or Head of a Frierie; an ordinarie Prior.*
Clausule: f. *A little clause; end, conclusion.*
Claye: f. *A hurdle, or lattice of (Ozier) twigs, &c; also, a (watled) gate, or yate, in a hedge.*
Clayer. *To wattle with rods, or with reeds, &c; to compasse, hedge or close in, make or shut vp, with watlings, hurdles, lattices, &c.*
Cléé: m. éee: f. *Watled, latticed, hurdled; incompassed, hedged or closed in, made or shut vp, with watlings, hurdles, lattices, &c.*

Clef: f. *A Key; also, a brace to hold beames together; also, a knot, or scutcheon in the middest of a vault, whereat (in Tymber-worke) the ends of the posts doe meet; and (in Masonrie) the course of Stone-worke ends; also, a Cliff in Musicke; also, the middle wedge of a boot-last.*
Les clefs. *as* Clavicules.
Clef d'arbaleste. *The Gaffle of a Crosse-bow.*
La Clef d'une fontaine. *The head of a Fountaine, or Conduit.*
La clef de la main. *The wrist.*
La clef d' une porte. *The Pendall, or key-stone of a gate; the stone which hangs downe somewhat below it fellowes iust in the middle of the Arch.*
Clef surpenduë. *The Scutcheon; the peece of wood, or stone that knits vp an Arch, or Vault, and hangs downe in the verie middle thereof; the key of an Arch deepelie carued.*
Le jeu des clefs. *A kind of Shuffle-boord play with keyes, a kniues-point being the marke.*
Donner la clef des champs à. *To dismisse, discharge, let goe, set at libertie, send out.*
Mettre les clefs sur la fosse. *A widow to refuse, and waiue, the goods, or her part in the goods, left by her indebted husband, by laying her keyes on his graue as soone as it is couered, and renouncing her said part, in the presence of a Notarie publicke.*
Prendre la clef des champs. *To get out, giue it selfe roome, take libertie, slip, by a priuat way, away.*
Cleigner. *as* Cligner. *To twinckle, or winke often.*
Clematide. *as* Clematite.
Clematite: f. *A third kind of the hearbe Hartwort, or Birtwort, called, climing Birthwort.*
Clemence: f. *Clemencie, mildnesse, meekenesse, mercifulnesse, benignitie, pitie, fauor.*
Clement. *Clement; gentle, mild, gracious, benigne, humane; meeke, mercifull, pitifull, easily-pardoning, soone-forgiuing.*
Clepsydre: f. *A Gardeners watering pot; also, an houre-glasse, or vessell which measureth houres by the running of water, or sand thereout; also, an Astronomicall instrument wherewith the measure of Starres is taken.*
Clepsydrie: f. *A proportionable, iust, or limitted running, or distilling, as of water out of a* Clepsydre, *or of sand in an houre-glasse.*
Cler: m. clere: f. *Cleere, bright, lightsome, transparent, pure-coloured; shining; also, perspicuous, plaine, apparant, euident, easie to be discerned.*
Laict cler. *Whey.*
Toile clere. *Lawne.*
Cler semé. *Rare, thin-set, growing not thicke, whereof there are, or grow, but verie few.*
Clerc: m. *A Clarke; a scholler, or learned person; hence; also, a Churchman (who should be learned;) also, a Clarke in an Office; a Lawyers Clarke; and generally, any Penneman.*
Clercs de la Chambre. *The Kings principal, or domesticall, Secretaries; (tearmed so in old time.)*
Clerc des fiefs. *The Kings, or any other lords, Atturney is called so; because he keepes a Register of the homages their vassals are to do, and of the duties they are to pay.*
Clerc solut. *A lay, or secular Churchman* (Qui n' a qu' une simple tonsure, & n' est lié a l' esglise) *as a Deacon, Prebend, Canon, &c.*
Clerc tonsuré. *A Priest, a Shaueling; one thats fully entred into Orders.*
Pas de Clerc. *A foolish tricke, impertinent act, fond part; any childish, or ignorant proceeding in matters of the world.*

Vin des Clercs. *Looke* Vin.

Clerc iusques aux dents. *Well red in a porridge-pot, an excellent Clarke in a Cookes shop.*

Iamais danseur ne fut bon clerc: Prov. *See* Danseur.

Il en parle comme vn clerc d' armes. *Hee speakes thereof ignorantly, simply, without proofe, or skill; onely by hearesay.*

On croit d' un fol bien souvent, qu' il soit Clerc pour ses vestemens: Prov. *Handsome, or decent apparrell makes fooles oft passe for wise men.*

Tout ce que le Clerc laboure folle femme deuore: Pro. *All that the scholler gaines his wench consumes.*

Clerceliere: f. *A kind of course ribban wherwith countrey wenches gird themselues; also, a string, or chayne, wherewith women hang their keyes to their girdles.*

Cleré. *A kind of red Hypocras.*

Clerement. *cleerely, brightly; apparantly, euidently.*

Cleres-voyes: f. *Lattices, or secret holes to spie out at; crosse-barred windows (of wood or yron) through which one may see, and not be seene.*

Clergé: m. *The Clergie.*

Clergez. *The Officers of Iustice (who either are, or should be learned) were called so in former times.*

Clergeau: m. *A pettie Clarke, vnder Clarke, or young Clarke.*

Clergeon: m. *as* Clergeau; *or, a Singing man, or Quirester, in a Queere.*

Clergesse: f. *A learned woman.*

Plume clergesse. *A learned penne.*

Clergie: f. *Learning, skill, science, Clarkeship.*

Il a des muids de clergie en la teste. (*So were they wont, in old time, to say of, a great learned man;*) *Hee hath a bushell of learning in his head.*

Mieux uaut plein poing de bonne vie qu' avoir plein muy de clergie: Prov. *Better a little honestie then a great deale of learning.*

Clerical. privilege clerical. *The priuiledge of the Clergie, of his Clergie, or of a Clarke.* *Looke* Clericature.

Clericalement. *Clarkely, Priest-like, Scholler-like.*

Clericature: f. *Clarkeship; or, the being a Clarke, or Priest, or in Orders.*

Privilege de Clericature. *The priuiledg of the Clergie; which is, to be tried before the Ordinarie, and not before any temporall Iudge.*

Alleguer sa clericature. *To alledge his Orders, and claime the priuiledge of his Clergie; or, to appeale from a Ciuile, or lay Iudge vnto his Ordinarie.*

Clerté: f. *as* Clarté.

Clesché. *as* Clissé.

Clicquettes: f. *Clickets; or flat bones, wherewith a prettie ratling noise is made. See* Cliquette.

Clide: f. *A woodden Engine of warre (now out of vse) which holding by a counterpoise, hurld out, when it was loosed, a great number of stones.*

Clie. *as* Claye; *a hurdle, or yate, in a hedge.*

Client: m. *A Clyent, or Suitor; a Noblemans Retainer, or Follower, the scope of whose attendance, or dutie is, to be protected.*

Clientelle: f. *Protection, countenance, defence, tuition, safegard; also, number, or store of clients.*

Clifoire: f. *A Plaisterers Tray, or Bosse.*

Cligné. *winked, or twinckled as with the eyes.*

Clignement des yeux: m. *A winking, or twinckling with the eyes.*

Clignemusset. *The childish play called Hodman blind, Harrie-racket, or, are you all hid.*

Cligner les yeux. *To winke, or twinckle with the eyes.*

Clignetter. *To twinckle, to winke often, and thicke.*

Clignottement: m. *An often winking, or twinckling with the eyes.*

Clignotter. *as* Clignetter.

Climactere: com. *Climatericall; whence;*

L' an climactere. *The Climatericall yeare; euerie seuenth, or ninth, or the 63 yeare of a mans life; all very dangerous, but the last, most.*

Climacteric de 63 ans. *The Climatericall, or dangerous, yeare of 63, at which age diuers worthie men haue died.*

Climat: m. *A Clyme, or Clymate; a diuision in the Skie, or Portion of the world, betweene South and North.*

Climatere. l'an climatere. *See* Climactere.

Climée: f. Cadmia, *Brasse-oare.*

Clin d'oeil: m. *The twinckling of an eye.*

Clincaille. *Chinkes, money, coyne.* (v.m.)

Cline-mucette: f. *The game called Hodman-blind; Harrie-racket; or, are you all hid.*

Clinique: com. *One that is bedred; or so sicke that he cannot rise.*

Clinquaille. *as* Clincaille.

Clinquallerie: f. *A chinking, clinking, ringing of much money; or of many pannes and skellets together; also, coyne, or (as we say) chinkes.*

Clinquant: m. *Thinne plate-lace of Gold, or Siluer.*

Clinquet. *as* Cliquet; *also, a certaine tricke in wrestling.*

Cliquaille. *as* Clincaille.

Cliquefoire. *A Squirt.*

Cliquer. *To clacke, clap, clatter, clicke it.*

Cliquet: m. *The ring, knocker, or hammer of a dore; also, a Lazers clicket, or clapper; also, a certaine Engine to catch fish withall.*

Cliqueter. *as* Cliquer; *or as* Cloquer.

Cliquetis: m. *as* Cliquettement.

Cliquette: f. *A clicket, or clapper; such as Lazers carrie about with them; also, a childs rattle, or clacke.*

Cliquettes. *as* Castagnettes.

Cliquettement: m. *A clicketting, clattering, clapping, clacking; chattering.*

Clisse: f. *A little wreath of wicker, to set vnder a dish on the Table; also, a wattle, or hurdle of willow, or ozier twigs.*

Treillis de clisse. *A Lattice, or Grate of wicker.*

Clissé: m. ée: f. *Made of wicker; plaited, or watled with ozier, or willow twigs.*

Clistere. *See* Clystere.

Clitie. Or de Clitie. *A Marigold.*

Clitoris: m. *A womans Priuities.*

Cliver. *To bow, leane, or hang outward, as the Cliffe, or steepe side of a hill; (an old word.)*

Cloaque: f. *A common Sinke, or Sewer in a towne.*

Cloche: f. *A Bell, or Clocke; to ring, or strike; also, the vpper part of a Lymbecke, wherein the vapours are gathered, and resolued into water; also, a little Bell-resembling vessell, wherein Peares are ordinarily stewed, or sodden.*

Cloches de S. Laurens. *Great blisters rising in the face, through heat.*

Herbe aux cloches. *Withywind, Bindweed, Hedgebels.*

Mettre la cloche au chat. *To set people together by the eares.*

C'est

C'est le son des cloches. *This is a matter that may be varied, or turned at pleasure.*

A conseil de fol cloche de bois: Prov. *Call fooles to counsell by a woodden bell.*

Cloche-man. Mouton cl. *A Bell-weather.*

Clochement: m. *A halting.*

Cloche-pied. à cloche-pied. *Haulting, limping, lamely.*

Clocher: m. *A Bell-founder.*

Clocher d'eglise. *as* Clochier.

Clocher. *To hault, or limpe; to be lame, or goe lamely, of a leg; also (in some places) to ring, or toll a Bell; to make a bell sound, or strike.*

Clocher devant les boiteux. *To applie himselfe vnto the (faultie) humors of others, with a purpose to indeere, or deceiue them; also, to speake Latine before Clarkes; or (more generally) to shew cunning, vse tricks, dissemble, or play the knaue any way, in presence of those that are as skilfull as himselfe; (In all which sences we also vse the same Prouerbiall phrase;) to hault before a criple.*

Clocher des deux costez. *To hault with, or on both sides; inconstantly to doubt, or be vncertain, whose part he shall take, what side he shall follow; or, to follow now the one, then the other side, without holding touch with, or doing good vnto, either.*

Ie sçay bien de quel pied il cloche. *I know his disease or defects well enough.*

Clocherie: f. *A ringing, or peale of Bells.*

Clochetier: m. *A Bell-founder.*

Clochette: f. *A little Bell; also, Withiewind, &c, as* Campanette.

Clochier: m. *A Steeple; also, a Parish, Borough, or village; and sometimes (in a large sence) a Bishopricke, or Diocesse.*

Cloisier. *as* Cloisonneur.

Cloisin: f. *A closure, or inclosure.*

Cloison: f. *Any thing that incloseth, as a hedge, pale, or rayles; and (most properly) a mud wall.*

Cloisonneux: m. *A maker of mud wals, or inclosures.*

Cloisonneux: m. euse: f. *Full of, or belonging to, mud wals, hedges, or inclosures.*

Cloistral: m. ale: f. *Of, or belonging to, an Abbey, or Cloister.*

Cloistre: m. *A Cloister; a round walke or inclosure (couered ouer head, and) enuironed with pillars; also, an Abbey, Priorie, Religious house; also, as* Colostre.

Clomassoles: f. *The defence which a horse makes with his nether lip, or gummes, against his Bitt.*

Clonisse: f. *The little, sharpe, and muddie cockle, tearmed, a Palour.*

Cloper. *as* Clocher.

Clopiner. *To limpe, or hault.* (v.m.)

Cloporte: m. *A Woodlouse, Cheslop, Kitchin-bole.*

Cloquer. *as* Clocher. *To limpe, hault, goe lamely.*

Se mocque qui cloque: Prov. *He mocks that worst may; some ieast at other mens defects, and yet are most defectiue.*

Clorre. *To close; inclose, hedge in, shut vp; also, to finish, accomplish, perfect, make an end of; also, to stop, to barre; to preuent.*

Clorre comptes. *To passe, conclude, or finish Accompts.*

Clorre le pas. Qui clost le pas. *That concludes, or giues a full resolution of, or end to, the controuersie; (said most properly of one, that leaping furthest, both ends the sport, and wins what he leapt for.)*

Clorre le pas à. *To interclude, barre, stop, set a blocke in the way of.*

En vain plante qui ne clost: Prov. *In vaine hee plants that hedges not.*

Clos: m. *A Close, or Field inclosed.*

Clos bruneau. *The tayle, arse, nock-androe.*

Clos: m. close: f. *Closed, inclosed; hedged in, shut vp; also, barred, stopped; forestalled, preuented; also, finished, fulfilled, perfected, accomplished.*

Clos, & muni de toutes parts. *Armed at all points; furnished to all purposes; prepared against all attempts.*

Estat clos. son estat est clos. *The offices, or places of his house are all bestowed.*

Ville close. *A Citie, or walled Towne.*

'A clos yeux. *Blindfould, hoodwinkt.*

Closcuau: m. *The Nestling, or Nest-cockle; the last-hatched bird in a neast.*

Closerie: f. *An Inclosure, or thing inclosed.*

Closier: m. *A hedger; an incloser.*

Closporte. *as* Cloporte.

Closser. *To clocke like a henne.*

Closser les grains. *Many stalkes, or eares to shoot vp, or come from one graine of seed.*

Clostier. *as* Claustier.

Closture: f. *An inclosure; an inclosement of, or inclosing with, hedges, pales, &c; also, a conclusion, closing, finishing, or shutting vp; as, of speech, of accompts, &c.*

Clot: m. Iouër au clot. *To play at Harry-racket, or Hide and find.*

Clou: m. *A Nayle; also, a corne (in a foot, or toe;) and hence, the Pinne (in the bottome of a Haukes foot.)*

Clou à bandes. *A streake nayle.*

Clou de caravelle. *A great nayle, at least a foot long; vsed in ships.*

Clou à crochet. *A Tentar hooke.*

Clou d'estoupe. *A speake, or sheathing nayle; vsed in ships.*

Clou de girofle. *A Cloue.*

Clou à hape. *A clowte Nayle.*

Clou de manguiere. *A scupper nayle; vsed in shipping.*

Clou à soufflet. *A tacke-nayle; or the small nayle wherewith bellowes are made vp, or mended.*

Ie n'en donneroye pas vn clou à soufflet. *I would not giue a pinne, a chip, a rush, for it.*

'A cloux de diamant. *Most fast, most sure, not to be stirred, impossible to be loosed.*

Compter les cloux. *See* Compter.

Riuer ses cloux à. Ie luy ay bien rivé ses cloux. *I haue giuen him his full payment; or, I haue fitted him with an vnanswerable replie; I haue puzled, or setled him with a sound answer.*

Vn clou sert à pousser l'autre: Pro. *One nayle serues to driue out another; one friend imployed to supplant the other.*

Cloüage: m. *A nayling.*

Cloucouquer. *To clocke; as a henne, that hath (or would haue) chickens.*

Clouë: f. *A blocke.*

Cloüé: m. ée: f. *Nayled; fastened, ioyned, set on with nayles.*

Raye cloüée. *The rocke Ray, or buckled Ray.*

Clouëment: m. *A nayling.*

Clouër. *To nayle; to fasten, ioyne, or set on, with nayles.*

Clouër à cloux de diamant. *See* Clou.

Clouestre: m. *A Cloyster in an Abbey, &c; or, as* Cloistre.

Clouët: m. *A little nayle; a tacke nayle.*
Cloueür: m. *A nayler.*
Cloueüre: f. *A nayling.*
Clouïr. *To open, and produce young ones, as egges that haue beene sitten on their full time.*
Clouïsse: f. *as* Pelarde. ¶Marseillos.
Clousser. *as* Closser.
Clousseuse: f. *A clocking henne, or henne that vses to clocke much.*
Cloutier: m. *A nayler, a nayle-smith; a seller or maker of nayles.*
Cloye. *as* Claye. *A hurdle,&c.*
Clucher. *as* Closser. *To clocke.*
Clye. *as* Claye; *a hurdle, or lattice of wicker,&c.*
Clypsedrie. *Looke* Clepsydre.
Clystere: m. *A glister.*
Ie luy apresteray vn clystere barbarin. *I will prouide for her bellie a plaister of warme guts.* ¶Rab.
Clysterisé: m. ée: f. *Clisterized; applied as, or, made into, a glister; conueyed by a glister vp into the guts.*
Clysteriser. *To applie a glister; to conuey by glister vp into the guts; also, to make, or put a thing into, a glister.*
Clytoris: m. *as* Clitoris.
Coäc: m. *The croaking, or crie of frogs.*
Coäcervation: f. *A coaceruation, or heaping together.*
Coädjuteur: m. *A coadiutor, helping fellow, or fellow helper.*
Coädunation: f. *A coadunation, gathering, assembling, vniting, ioyning together.*
Coägulation: f. *A coagulation, congealing, or curding; a turning vnto curd.*
Coäguler. *To coagulate; curd, or congeale into a curd; to ioyne together, or make to ioyne.*
Coäille: f. *Course wooll*; mot Berruyer.
Coäine. *as* Coenne.
Coälescer. *To close, ioyne, or grow together againe.*
Coärcté: m. ée: f. *Strained, pressed, or thrust hard together; restrained, or brought within a narrow compasse.*
Coärcter. *To straine, presse, or thrust hard together; to restraine, or bring within a narrow compasse.*
Coässer. *To croake, or crie as a toad, or frog.*
Coät: m. *The vnderling, starueling, or writling of a beast; the wrecking, or nest-cockle, of birds.*
Coäugmenté: m. ée: f. *Increased together; or, much increased.*
Coäxer. *as* Coasser.
Cobbir. *To bruise, or breake into peeces.* ¶Rab.
Cobeter vne cloche. *To toule a bell; or, to ring it not full out, but so, as it strikes onely the one side.*
Cobter. *as* Cobeter, *or* Copter.
Coc: m. *See* Coq.
Cocard: m. *A nice doult, quaint Goose, fond, or saucie cokes, proud, or forward Meacocke. See* Coquard.
Cocarde. bonnet à la cocarde. *A Spanish cap; or cap made after the old fashion. See* Coquarde.
Cocardeau: m. *A proud Asse, pert Gull, shitten Saucebox; one that hath better store of clothes on his backe, then of wit in his head.*
Coccognide. *The blacke Cameleon thistle.*
Coche: m. *A Coach.*
Coche: f. *A nocke, notch, nicke, snip, or neb; (and hence) also, the Nut-hole of a Crosse-bow; also, a young Sow, or Sow-pig; also, a fustilugs; a woman growne fat by ease, and lazinesse; also, a spell, or splint.*
Coché: m. ée: f. *Nocked, notched, nicked, snipped; furrowed.*
Front bien coché. *That is high on both sides of the foretop.*
Pillules cochées. *A certaine composition of Pills, which purge the head verie stronglie.*
Cochelin: m. *A kind of cake full of notches, and giuen in some parts of France (as about* Blois*) vnto children for New-yeares-gifts.*
Cochenille. *Cutchancale, wherewith Skarlet is dyed.*
Cochepierre. *A bird like a Bull-finch, that feeds most on the kernels of cherristones.*
Cocher: m. *A Coachman.*
Cocher: m. ere: f. *Of a Coach, or Coach-house; whence;* Porte cochere. *A Coach-house dore.*
Cocher. *To nicke, nocke, or make notches, as on a tally; (also, to haue to doe with a woman.* ¶Pic.)
Cochet: m. *A Cockerell, or cocke chicke; also, a shote, or shete, Pigge.*
Cochevis: m. *The copped Larke; the Larke that hath a little tuft standing on her head.*
Cochier: m. *A Coachman.*
Cochiere: f. *A Coach-woman; a woman that driues a Coach.*
Cochin: m. *A Pigge.*
Poisson, gorret, & cochin, vie en l'eau, & mort en vin. *Waterish Acates require much wine both for their dressing, and disgestion.*
Cochon: m. *A Pigge.*
Gras comme vn cochon. (*We say the same*) *as fat as a Pigge.*
Manger le cochon ensemble. *To complot, agree in a plot, ioyne in a conspiracie together; (belike in old time when conspirators met to conferre, and conclude, their principall dish was a Pigge.)*
Rappeler le cochon. *To repeat the words wherwith he began; to come to the matter againe.*
Cochonné: m. ée: f. *Pigged, farrowed.*
Cochonner. *To farrow, to pigge; to breed, or bring forth pigges, as a Sow; also, to cocker, cherish, nourish daintily, make a fedle of.*
Cochonnet: m. *A shote, or shete pigge, a prettie big pigge.*
Cochonniere: f. *A Sow; or Sow-pigge.*
Cocles. des c. *as* Coquelourdes.
Cocluchon. *as* Coqueluchon.
Cocodrille: m. *See* Crocodile; *a Crocodile.*
Cocque: f. *A Cockle.*
Cocque de Cyprés. *A Nut, or Clog, of the Cypres tree.*
Cocque d'oeuf. *An egge-shell.*
Cocqueter. *as* Coqueter.
Cocquillé: m. ée: f. *Shellie, shell-like; or, as* Coquillé.
Cocu: m. *A Cuckoe; also, a Gurnard, or Curre-fish; also, a Cuckold. (See* Coucou.)
Cocu cocuant. *A Cuckold-maker, a Graffe-horne.*
Cocu cocuë. *A Cuckold, or Wittall.*
Brayes de cocu. *Cowslips, pettie Mulleins, Palsieworts.*
Pain à cocu. *The smallest, and daintiest red Mushrome.*
Pain de cocu. *Cuckoe-bread, Alleluya, Stubworte, soure Trefoile, Wood-sorrell, Wood-sower.*
Il vaut mieux estre cocu que coquin: Pro. *See* Coquin.
Cocu: m. cocuë: f. *Cuckolded; made a Cuckold, or crooked.*
Mary cocu. *The hedge-Sparrow; called so, because she hatches, and feeds the Cuckoes young ones, esteeming them her owne.*
'A l'enfourner on fait les pains cocus: Pro. *Loaues get their crookednesse at the setting in. Looke* Pain.

Cocuäge : m. *A cuckoldship; the being a cuckold.*
Cocuant. *Cuckolding,cuckoldmaking,horne graffing.*
Cocuë : f. *Hemlocke,homlocke,hearbe bennet,kex.*
Cocuye. *See* Cucuye.
Cocytide. homme cocytide. *A lim of the diuell; a most fell,cruell,or hellish fellow.*
Codicilaire : com. *One that is elected vnto,or instituted into,a benefice,&c,by Codicile.*
Codicile : m. *A Codicile,scedule,bill annexed.*
Codicillaire. *as* Codicilaire.
Codignat : m. *Codiniack,or Marmalade of Quinces.*
Codignat de four. *Bread.*
Coeffe : f. *A quife, or coyfe; also, a night-cap; See* Coiffe.
Coeffé. *Coyfed; See* Coiffé.
Coeffer. *To coyfe, weare a coyfe, put on a coyfe; See* Coiffer.
Coeffure : f. *as* Coeffe.
Coegal : m. *A fellow, or match vnto, one thats in all points equall to another.*
Coeliaque : com. *as* Celiaque.
Artere coeliaque. *A maine braunch of the great Arterie, from which it descends vnto the Midriffe, and intralls.*
Coelibat. *Looke* Celibat.
Coeneux : m. euse : f. *Mirie,durtie, filthie.*
Coënne de lard : f. *The skinne of bacon; See* Coisne.
Coëpeller. *To chip wood.* (v.m.)
Coëque : m. *A coopartner,or cooparcener.*
Coërtion,ou Coërction. *A restraint,compulsion,constraining; a keeping in subiection.*
Coeste : m. *A verie thicke,and great gloue, vsed by the auncient Grecians in their Theater combats.*
Coeston. *The same.*
Coëternel : m. elle : f. *Coeternall.*
Coétivé : m. ée : f. *Fomented, cherished, kept warme.*
Coétivement : m. *A keeping warme, a cherishing, fomenting,or preseruing in naturall heat.*
Coétiver. *To foment,or keepe warme; to cherish, or preserue,in naturall heat.*
Coëval. ses coëvaux. *His equalls in age; those that be as old as he.*
Coeur : m. *A heart; also,the heart, mind, thought, affection; inward conceit,fancie, or opinion; also, courage,mettall, stomacke; also,the core of fruit; also, the Queere of a Church; also, the heart-resembling cherrie,called,the French,or Spanish,cherrie; also,the vpper, larger, and more sencible, orifice of the stomacke.*
Coeur d'hyuer: au fin coeur d'hyuer. *In the depth, or middest,of Winter.*
Enfant de coeur. *A Quirester,or singing boy.*
Herbe de coeur. *Heart-wort, or Heart-mint; The Picards call Sage, and Cowslip of Ierusalem, so.*
Par coeur. *By heart,by roat, readily, without booke, without missing.*
Mon coeur luy est,ou fait,mal. *I beare him a grudge, I like him not, I cannot abide him.*
Avoir le coeur. Il a le coeur assis en bonne part. *He is an honest, gallant, valiant, worthie, fellow.*
Il en aura le coeur net. *He will be fully satisfied in, resolued of the matter.*
Mettre corps,& coeur. *To labour,striue, indeuor by all the meanes he hath.*
Cela leur mit le coeur au ventre. *That cheered, heartened,encouraged them.*
Sentant son coeur. *Growing stout,recouering his stomacke; taking heart at grasse,or,feeling his heart come to him.*
Tenir son coeur. *To beare a grudge,owe a spight vnto; to carrie a spleene a long time against.*
Coeur content,& manteau sur l'espaule: Prov. *The heart content, and cloke throwne ouer the shoulder; (either because the contented man weares it so in iollitie; or because he cares not greatly how hee weares it.)*
Le coeur fait l' oeuvre; non pas les grand iours: Prov. *Not length of day, but strength of heart, rids worke.*
Le coeur ne veut douloir ce que l' oeil ne peut veoir: Prov. *What the eye sees not, the heart rues not.*
A coeur dolent l'oeil pleure : Prov. *Teares in the eyes,ruth in the heart.*
A povre coeur petit souhait : Prov. *Little things content low thoughts; or,an humble heart is humble in desires.*
Belle chere, & coeur arriere : Prov. *A faire looke, and false thoughts; or,a froward looke, and froward thoughts; one that speakes me faire, and wishes my throat were cut.*
Bon coeur ne peut mentir : Prov. *An honest heart cannot dissemble; Seeke* Mentir.
En petit ventre grand coeur: Prov. *A great heart in a little bodie; great courage in a small corps.*
Ioye triste,& coeur travaillé : Prov. *All ioy hath sad effects in troubled hearts.*
Quand les yeux voyent ce qu'ils ne veirent oncques, le coeur pense ce qu'il ne pensa oncques: Prov. *Vnwoonted obiects breed vnwoonted thoughts.*
Qui n'a coeur, ait jambes : Prov. *He that dares not trust to his hands had best trust to his heeles; or,he that dares not fight may do well to flie.*
Coeuret : m. *A little heart.*
Coeur-failli : m. *A lazie, slothfull, faint-hearted, white liuered, creature; a flincher; one that hath not the courage to end what he hath begun.*
Coferrumíner. *To mingle, ioyne, or solder, yron with other mettalls.*
Coffre : m. *A coffer, chest, hutch, arke; also, the bulke, or chest of the bodie.*
En coffre ouvert le juste peché: Prov. *Opportunitie makes,or warrants, a thiefe.*
Coffré : m. ée : f. *Put into a chest,or coffer; also, imprisoned,or layed vp.*
Coffrer. *To put into a chest,or coffer.*
Coffrer aulcun en prison. *To imprison; to cast, and keepe in prison; to lay vp close,or where he shall see no light.*
Coffret : m. *A casket,cabinet, forset; a little chest, or coffer.*
Coffrier : m. *A coffer-maker; also, a Cofferer vnto a Prince.*
Cofin : m. *A coffin; a great candle-case; or any such close, great,and round Vtensile of wicker.*
Cofin à roupies. *A womans maske.*
Cofinet : m. *A little coffin, basket, or box (of wicker, &c.)*
Cogitation : f. *A cogitation,thought,imagination, consideration,purpose,proiect.*
Cogiter. *To cogitate, thinke, muse, imagine, consider, contemplate, cast in the mind; studie on, aduise himselfe, deuise with himselfe; intend, purpose, determine, mind.*
Cognaciere : f. *A Quince tree.*
Cognation: f. *Cognation, affinitie, alliance, kindred, parentage.*

Cogneu : m. euë : f. *Knowne, kenned, discerned, perceiued, vnderstood; noted, notable, notorious, of note; acknowledged, owned, aduowed.*

Chose perduë est lors cogneuë : Prov. *The worth of things is knowne when they be lost.*

Cognil: m. *The bastard Tunnie fish; or, as* Coguoil.

Cognoissance : f. *Knowledge; acquaintance, familiaritie with; skill, cunning, experience in; a notice, or notion; an intelligence, vnderstanding, or apprehension of; also, a deed, or scedule of acknowledgement, or confession of a debt, &c; also, a badge, or cognisaunce.*

Cognoissant. *Knowing; vnderstanding; apprehending, perceiuing; also, wise, cunning, learned, expert, skilfull, well seene, in.*

Cognoistre. *To know; vnderstand; skill, wot well, or be assured, of; be fully acquainted with; to kenne, discerne, apprehend, perceiue; also, to confesse, acknowledge; aduow.*

Cognoistre d' vne cause. *To take notice of, deale in, or intermeddle with, a suit, or cause, depending in law.*

Qui ne te cognoistroit (bonne beste!) *If a man knew thee not thou wouldst make him beleeue thou wert a verie Saint; I know thee but too well.*

Se cognoistre en Medecine. *To haue insight, or prettie skill, in Physicke.*

L' herbe qu' on cognoist on la doit lier à son doigt : Prov. *(For it is most vnsafe to deale with vnknowne medicines.)*

La Maison fait cognoistre le Maistre : Prov. *By the house one may ghesse at the owner; by the fashion, or gouernement thereof, what his abilitie, and humor is.*

On cognoist le diable à ses griffes : Prov. *Looke* Diable.

Qui bien se cognoist peu se prise, qui peu se prise Dieu l'avise : Prov. *Who knowes himselfe himselfe despises, the selfe-despiser God aduises.*

Cognoscitive : f. *The facultie of knowing, vnderstanding, discerning; an apprehensiue propertie.*

Coguoil : m. *A fish like vnto a Mackerell, but greater, and thicker; or as* Cognil.

Coherence : f. *A coherence, or coherencie; a cleauing, or sticking of matters together; a hanging thereof one vpon another; a knitting, vniting, or fastening thereof one vnto the other.*

Cohertion : f. *as* Coërtion.

Cohibé: m. ée : f. *Restrained, stopped, repressed; curbed, held in, kept vnder.*

Cohiber. *To restraine, stop, let, represse; curbe, hold in, keepe short or vnder.*

Cohier: m. *The female oake; (which beares a longer and broader leafe, and a shorter and lesse nourishing acorne, than the male.*

Cohorte : f. *A cohort, or companie, band, or troupe, of souldiours.*

Cohourde f. *A goord.*

Cohüe : f. *A hall to plead in; a Sessions-house, or shirehall :* ¶Brett. & Norm.

Coi : m. *The crie, or grunting, of pigges, and young swine.*

Coi. *as* Coy; *Quiet, still.*

Coiaux: m. *Returned, or hip, rafters (in Building.)*

Coiche : f. *The feathering of an arrow.* (v.m.)

Coiffant. *Putting on a coife; or any other thing as a coyfe; also, besotting; or gulling, beguiling, deceiuing; (Looke* se Coiffer.

Coiffe: f. *A coife, cawle, or cap, for the head: also, the fat pannicle, or kell, wherein the bowels are lapped.*

Coiffe d'une tour. *The couering, or highest out-set windowes, of a tower.*

Coiffé : m. ée : f. *Coifed, attired with a coife; also, gulled, beguiled, abused; also, filled, or possessed; and, pestered, or besotted, with.*

Cailles coiffées. *Women.*

Il est né tout coiffé. *Borne rich, honourable, fortunate; borne with his mothers kercher about his head; wrapt in his mothers smocke, say we; also, hee is verie maidenlie, shamefac'de, beloe.*

Coiffer. *To coife, or put a coyfe vpon; also, to beguile, gull, cousen, deceiue.*

Se coiffer de folles opinions. *To intertaine, or put on fond opinions; to besot himselfe, or to fill, possesse, or pester his head, withall.*

Coignacier : m. *The great, or peare, Quince tree.*

Coignant: m. ante: f. *Wedging, fastening with a wedge, driuing, or knocking fast in.*

Coignasse : f. *A female Quince, or peare Quince; the greatest kind of Quince.*

Coignaufond. *Knocking, leacherie, Venerie :* ¶Rab.

Coigné: m. ée : f. *Wedged; driuen, or knocked in; stamped, coyned.*

Coigneau. *Priuet, or Primprint; called so at* Fontainebleau.

Coignée : f. *An hatchet, or axe.*

Ietter le manche apres la coignée. *To throw the helue after the hatchet; to loose courage in aduersitie; or after one losse to make wilfull shipwracke of all.*

Contre coignée serrure ne peut: Pro. *Weake locks cannot resist strong hatchets.*

Coigne-festu : m. *An idle fellow; one that spends his time and trauell to no purpose; or, one, that will neither do good himselfe, nor suffer others to do any.*

Coigner. *To wedge, to fasten with a wedge; to driue hard, or knocke fast in, as with a wedge; also, to stamp, or coine.*

Coigner festus. *To loose his time, or spend it to no purpose.*

Coigner ses larmes. *To suppresse, or hold in his teares by force.*

Coignet. *A litle wedge; also, a little cone, or corner.*

Coigniaux. *A kind of small, and bright-greene vermine, which sharke off, and cut in peeces, the tendrels, and grapes, of Vines.*

Coignier : m. *A Quince tree.*

Coignoir: m. *A wedging toole; a Wedger.*

Coin as Coing; *also, the cry, or grunting off pigs, and yong Swine; also, the spawne, row, or egs, of fish, Caterpillers; &c.*

Coin de beurre. *A cake, or dish (of the ordinarie fashion of our pound) of butter.*

Coin de mer. *A kind of Mullet fish.*

Se Coincher. *as,* se Conchier.

Coine. *as,* Coënne; *The skinne of Bakon; also, a thick filme, or skumme, such as is vsually on a standing, and stinking pudle.*

Coing : m. *A wedge; also, a quince; also, an angle, nooke, or corner; also, a coyne, or stamp, vpon a peece of coyne.*

Coing de beurre : *See* Coin.

Enter au coing. *To lodge a graffe in the clefted top of a stocke.*

Pour fendre le bois il fit des coings du bois mesme. *Looke* Bois.

Tous frappez à vn mesme coing. *All made in one mould,*

mould; all stamped with one figure; all birds of a feather.

`A dur, ou mauvais noeud mauvais coing: Prov. *Sayd of a swaggering, or litigious fellow, matched with one, in his owne kind, worse then himselfe.*

Fol est qui de son poing faict coing: Prov. *He is a foole that makes a wedge of his fist; as did strong Milo; who attempting to riue assunder a great tree which lay in a forest halfe clouen, and held open with wedges, they slipping downe it closed, and inclosed his hands so fast, that he could not pull them out, but quickly became a pray vnto wild beasts; whereupon this prouerb calls any man foole, that presumes too much on his owne strength, or knowes not the right vse of his owne things.)*

Meschante vie quiert le coing: Prov. *An euill-liuer would euer be lurking.*

Coingné: m. ée: f. *as* Coigné.

Coïnquination: f. *A coinquination, or coinquinating; a soyling, defiling, polluting; defaming.*

Coïnquiné: m. ée: f. *Coinquinated; soyled, polluted, defiled; also, defamed.*

Coïnquiner. *To coinquinate; pollute, soyle, defile; also, to defame.*

Coint: m. cointe: f. *Quant, compt, neat, fine, spruce, brisk, smirke, smug, daintie, trim, tricked vp.*

Coïntelligent. *Hauing intelligence, holding priuat correspondencie, with.*

Cointement. *Quaintly, comptly, finely, sprucely, neatly, trimly, daintily.*

Cointise: f. *Quaintnes, comptnes, neatnes, trimnes, finenes, sprucenes, daintines.*

Coipeau: m. *A chip.*

Vin de coipeau. *See* Vin.

Coiraux: m. *Fat oxen; such as haue bene fed both in the house, and field.*

Coisne. *as* Coënne. *The skinne of Bacon; and, th'outward hard rinde, or skinne, of any such thing.*

Coissin: m. *A cushion; also, a pillow.*

Coistre: f. *A tick for a bed.*

Coiti: &; Coitis: *as* Coitte; *or, the blue-streaked stuffe whereof tis made,*

Coitte: f. *The tick of a bed.*

Coitte-pointe: f. *A Quilt, or quilted couering, for a bed.*

Col: m. *The neck; a necke.*

Col du bras. *The wrist.*

Col de grue. *Cranes-bill, Storkes-bill, Hearons-bill, Pinkneedle; an hearb.*

Col d'un os. *The necke of a bone; the slenderest part thereof, hauing a broad, or bigge part next vnto it.*

Col d'oye. *The port, or vpset of some Bits, made round, and bowing like the neck of a goose.*

Col du pied. *The instup.*

Col rompu. *The neck-burst; a small halfe-rising in the midle of the mouth of some bits.*

Col d'une Vigne. *The stock of a Vine; or, as* Courson.

Tordre le col à. *To skorne disdaine, contemne, looke askew on.*

Colac: m. *The shadfish:* ¶Langued.

Colaphiser. *To box, or buffet.*

Colas. *A Deriuatiue, or diminutiue of* Nicolas; *whence;*

Dieu colas faillon. *By Saint* Nicholas; *or for Saint* Nicholas *sake;* ¶Lorrainois. Rab.

Colatoire du nez. *The spungie bone through which the sniuell passeth from the braine into the nosethrils.*

Colature: f. *An expression, or straining; also, a colature; the thing strained; or, a thinne liquor which hath passed through a strainer.*

Cole: m. *A stormie, or tempestuous gale of wind.*

Cole: f. *Anger, choller.*

Colere: f. *See* Cholere.

Colet. *as* Collet.

Coleté: m. ée: f. *Imbraced about the neck; also, wrastled, striuen, or strugled with.*

Coleter. *To imbrace about the necke; also, to wrastle, striue, or strugle with.*

Coleuvre. *as* Couleuvre; *An Adder.*

Coleuvrée. *as* Coulevré.

Coliart. *A kind of smooth, and straw-coloured Rayfish.*

Coliaux. *The name of a kind of Oliues.*

Colier. *See* Collier.

Colimbades. *Small pickled Oliues.*

Colimbales. *The same.*

Colin: m. *Collin; a proper name (and a deriuatiue of* Nicholas; *) also, a Sea-cob, or Gull; (or as* Collin.)

Colin tampon. *The Drumme-sound of the Suissers march.*

Grand colin. *A disgracefull tearme of the ranke of* Maraud, belistre, coquin, &c.

Gros colin. *Branne, or the great of the siftings of corne; also, dogs meat made of it.*

Coline. *as* Colline; *A little hill.*

Colique: f. *The Chollicke; a painfull windinesse in the stomacke, or entrails.*

Colique: com. *Of the Chollicke, belonging to the Chollicke.*

Coliqueux: m. euse: f. *Full of, or subiect vnto, the Chollicke.*

Colisée: m. *A Colossus, or Coliseum.*

Colitor. *The name of a certaine Vine.*

Collane: f. *A neck-lace.*

Collateral: m. ale: f. *Collaterall; not direct, on th'one side.*

Muscles collateraux. *Two muscles in the mouth, one bringing the tongue, the other drawing the Larinx, a-to-side.*

Vent collaterall. *A side wind, or quarter wind, at sea.*

Collateralité: f. *Collateralitie, or collateralnesse.*

Collateur: m. *A Patron; or, any officer who hath the bestowing of Benefices.*

Collation: f. *A comparing, or examining of one thing by another; also, a collation, rere-supper, or repast after supper; also, a collation, conferring, or gift of a Benefice.*

Collation de Moyne. *A Monks nuncheon; as much as another man eats at a large meale.*

Collationné: m. ée: f. *Compared with, or examined by, another; also, hauing made, or, intertained with, a collation; also, conferred, or bestowed (as a Benefice.)*

Collationner. *To examine a copie by the originall; to confer, or compare one writing, or thing, with another; also, to collation it, or make a rere-supper, to banquet, or take a repast (after supper;) also, to giue, confer, bestow a Benefice.*

Collaudation: f. *A mutuall commendation, praising, extolling.*

Collaudé: m. ée: f. *Collauded; praised, or commended with others.*

Collauder. *To collaud, prayse, extoll, commend, with others.*

Colle : f. *Anger, choller; also, as* Colline ; *or, as in* Colles.
'A chaude colle. *In anger, in choller, in hoat bloud, or while the bloud was vp.*
Colle : f. *Glue ; also, solder ; also, the vnprofitable corners of hides, and skinnes, cut off in the dressing.*
Colle de bouche. *Mouth glue, water glue ; (the best kind of glue.)*
Colle de cerf. *as* Forte ; *White, and cleere-coloured glue ; made of the skinnes of all kind of foure-footed beasts.*
Colle de farine. *(Stationers) past.*
Colle forte. *Ordinarie white glue ; as in* Colle de cerf.
Colle à or. *Borax, or greene earth; vsed in the souldering of gold.*
Colle à pierres. *Cement; made of ordinarie marble, Parian marble, and the strongest glue.*
Colle de poisson. *Mouth glue, water glue.*
Colle de taureau. *The strongest kind of glue, vsed by Carpenters, Ioyners, &c.*
Collé : m. ée : f. *Glued; soldered; pasted; fast ioyned, surely closed.*
Collectage : m. *A collecting, or gathering together.*
Collectanes : m. *A certaine Order of Franciscan, or Grey Friers.*
Collecte : f. *A collection, leuie, gathering.*
Collecteur : m. *A Collector, leuier, gatherer of.*
Sergent collecteur. *Looke* Sergent.
Collectif : m. iue : f. *Collectiue, gathering, or that gathereth.*
En nom collectif. *All together, one with another.*
Collection : f. *A collection, or gathering together.*
Collée : f. *A necke-imbracement, an imbracing about the necke ; a greeting, or welcome, expressed by such an imbracement; also, a dust, thumpe, or blow, in the neck; and hence ;*
Donner la collée. *To knight.*
College : m. *A Colledge.*
Collegue : m. *A Colleague, fellow, or copartener, in Office.*
Collement : m. *A gluing, or soldering together.*
Coller. *To glue ; solder ; past ; ioyne, or close vp, surely.*
Collerage : m. *Collerage ; a pecuniarie duetie exacted, in some places, for the collers worne by wine-drawing horses, or men.*
Collerette de femme. *A small necke-ruffe, neckercher, or neck-band, (worne by women.)*
Colles : f. *Crosse walls of stone, &c, in some vineyards ; Looke* Bancs.
Collet : m. *The throat, or forepart, of the necke ; also, the coller of a Jerkin &c ; the cape of a cloke ; the neckepeece of any garment ; also, a kind of ginne, or snarle, wherewith Conies are caught (most commonly by the necke.)*
Collet de chimise. *A shirt-band.*
Collet de femme. *A neckercher.*
Collet de marroquin. *A Spanish-leather Jerkin.*
Collet de mouton. *A necke of mutton.*
Vn collet à peignoir. *A large raile which women put about their neckes when they combé themselues.*
Mettre la main sur le collet à. *To stay, arrest, or seize on ; to take one prisoner.*
Colletages : m. *Taxes, aides, and subsidies leuied of the people.*
Colleter. *To imbrace about the necke , &c ; See* Coleter.
Colletier : m. *A Jerkin-maker.*
Colletin : m. *A Jerkin.*
Colleur : m. *A gluer.*
Colleure : f. *A gluing ; or soldering; a sure closing.*
Colleux : m. euse : f. *Glewie, full of glue , cleauing as glue.*
Collier : m. *A coller (or chaine) of gold , &c , for the necke ; also, a dog-coller ; horse-coller ; &c ; any coller.*
Colliers. *Earings, or clues; the strings wherewith the bottome of a sayle, or the bonnet, and the tacke, or sheat, are tied together.*
Vous estiez le chien au grand collier. *You were the onely noted man, th'onely kill-cow, th'onely terrible fellow ; (rustically.)*
Tirer au collier contre. *To contend, striue, wrestle hard with.*
Colligance : f. *A binding, tying, or knitting together.*
Colligé : m. ée : f. *Gathered, or brought together ; also, vnited, or assembled.*
Colligence. *as* Colligance ; *Or, a gathering, or bringing together.*
Colliger. *To gather, or bring together ; also, to vnite, or assemble in one.*
Collin : m. *A long beaked Riuer-fowle, of a beautifull grayish colour ; also, as* Colin.
Colline : f. *A little hill.*
Colliquatif : m. iue : f. *Subiect to the chollicke.*
Colliquation : f. *A colliquation ; a consumption of the radicall humor, or substance of the bodie ; also, a melting, resoluing, or dissoluing.*
Collique pasſion. *The Chollicke ; See* Colique.
Colliqueux : m. euse : f. *Sicke , or full , of the Chollicke.*
Collision : f. *A knocking, dashing, clapping, beating together.*
Collitigant : m. ante : f. *Wrangling, iangling, going to law together ; at suit one with another, litigiously handling one another.*
Collizée. *See* Colisée.
Collobe : m. *A kind of sleeuelesse vpper garment in fashion among the old Romans.*
Collocation. *An orderlie placing, setling, or disposing of things together.*
Colloir : m. Colloire : f. *A cullander, or strainer.*
Colloque : m. *A conference, communication ; consultation.*
Colloqué. *Set, setled, placed, disposed ; applied, bestowed.*
Colloquer. *To place together ; to settle in, or assigne to, one, and the same ranke ; to dispose, put, set, bestow, applie, fitly, equally, orderly.*
Colludant : m. *One that doth any thing by couin, or collusion ; a deceiuer, a double dealer.*
Colludant : m. ante : f. *Colluding, dealing by couin, or, doubly dealing.*
Colluder. *To collude ; to make shew of one thing, and do the contrarie ; to deale by couine, and collusion ; to betray his cause vnto an aduersarie ; to plead doubly, and further his aduersaries cause, thereby to deceiue a third person.*
Collusion : f. *Collusion, fraud, couine, deceit, guile, double dealing ; a shew of disagreement , or controuersie with one, thereby to deceiue another.*
Collyre : m. *A (liquid) medicine for the eyes ; or a medicine applied to the eyes in a liquid forme ; also, a kind of Samian earth, whereof, among other things, eye-medicines are made.*

Colobe: m. *A short, and sleeuelesse garment, or iacket, in fashion among the auncient Romanes; also, a furred hood, or tippet, worne by graduate Priests.*
Colocasie. *The hearbe Aaron, wake Robin, Calues-foot, Cuckoe-pint, Priests-pintle; also, the root of the Ægyptian beane.*
Colocinthe. *as* Coloquinte.
Colom: m. *The fist, or great gut* Colon, *wherein the Chollicke breedeth; also, a colume, or member of a sentence.*
Colom: m. *A Doue, Pigeon, Culuer.*
Grand colomb. *A Queest, or Stockdoue.*
Colombage: m. *Boord-worke on th'outside of walls, &c; or, the boording, or boords, betweene which mudde walls, &c, are made.*
Colombain: m. ine: f. *Doue-like; of the nature of Doues; of, or belonging to, Doues.*
Colombe: f. *A henne Pigeon, or, female Pigeon.*
Colombe de Tonnelier. *A toole of his, which resembles a plane turnd vpside-downe.*
Pied de colombe. *A kind of Cranes-bill, or Pinkeneedle called, Pigeons-foot, or Doues-foot.*
Colombeau: m. *A little yong Pigeon.*
Colombelle: f. *A Pigeon, or yong doue.*
Colombier: m. *A doue-cote.*
Cela chassera les pigeons du colombier. *That will driue away your (sillie) clients, or Customers; or that will force irresolute folke out of their hold.*
Colombin. *The hearbe Colombine; also, Colombine, or doue-colour; or, the stuffe whereof tis made.*
Colombine: f. *A whitish, and spungie stone, found in leaden mines; also, a delicate Italian peare, thats ripe in August.*
Colomne: f. *A columne, or piller.*
La colomne du nez. *The bridge of the nose; or the whole bone thereof.*
Colomneux: m. euse: f. *Full of columnes, full of pillers.*
Colonie: f. *A colonie; a countrey, or citie, which people are sent to inhabite; also, the people so sent, and setled; also, a Grange, Farme-house, or Farmers house.*
Colonnation: f. *A pillering, or making of pillers.*
Colonnel: *A Colonell, or Coronell; the Commaunder of of a Regiment.*
Colonnel general de l'Infanterie Francoise. *The Coronell Generall of the French foot; whose place was in old time conferred, at the beginning of a warre, on some valiant, and experienced Captaine (therefore tearmed* le grand Capitaine des gens de pied) *and againe taken from him as soone as th'armie was cassed; But it hath since beene made an office perpetuall, or ordinarie, and of the Crowne.*
Colophone. *The hearbe Scammonie; also, as* Resine Colophonienne.
Colophonien: m. enne: f. Resine Colophonienne. *Clarified, or hard Rozen; such as wee rub Violl stickes withall.*
Coloquinthe: f. *The wild, and flegme-purging Citrull* Coloquintida.
Coloration: f. *A colouring; a shadowing.*
Coloré: m. ée: f. *Coloured; shadowed.*
Tiltre coloré (en matiere de Benefices) est reputé celuy qui vient du vray, & ordinaire Collateur, duquel l'incapacité n'est cogneuë; & la possession prise en vertu d'iceluy est ditte colorée: ¶Code Henry.
Colossal: m. ale: f. *Huge, mightie, Colossus-like.*
Colosse: m. *A Colosse, or Colossus; a huge image, or statue.*

Colossien: m. enne: f. *Colossus-like; of, or belonging to, a Colossus; also, as* Colossal; *and hence;*
Fais colossien. *A most heauie, or mightie burthen.*
Colostration: f. *Colostration; or, the indisposition of infant-stomacks, by the sucking of beest.*
Colostre: m. *The first milke, tearmed beest, or beestings; accompted dangerous for some two, or three dayes, in which time it vsually is drawne out.*
Colot. Iean Colot; *The name of a certaine merie Artificer in* Troyes, *who ordinarily wore about him three kniues in one sheath, all not worth a good sheath; wherof the Prouerbe;*
Les cousteaux Iean Colot, l'un vaut l'autre. *Like to our; Neither barrell better herring.*
Colouvrine: f. *A Culuerin.*
Colporté. *Carried on the neckes, or shoulders of men.*
Colporter. *To carrie vpon the necke, or shoulders (as a coarse vnto buriall, &c.)*
Colporteur: m. *A paultrie Pedler; as* Bisouart.
Columb. *as* Colomb.
Columelle. *The vuula; or a spungious flesh resembling a cockes spurre, and hanging downe in the bottome of the roofe of the mouth; also, the swelling thereof.*
Colure: m. *An imperfect circle in the Spheare, wherof there be diuers (all imagined to meet in the Poles) but the two principall ones, are;*
Le colure des equinoxes. *Goes through the beginnings of* Aries, *and* Libra.
Le colure des solstices. *Goes through the beginnings of* Cancer, *and* Capricornus.
Colure: f. *The necke, or crest, of a horse.*
Colure de vignes. *as* Coulure.
Colymbades. *Oliues (as we haue them) preserued in pickle.*
Combat: m. *A combat, conflict, battell, bickering, fight; strife, debate, contention, extreame iarring.*
Combatant: m. *A combatant, combater, fighter; a champion, that is to fight a combat; or souldiour inrolled, and readie for the battell.*
Combatant; part. *Combating; fighting, bickering, battelling.*
Combateur. *as* Combatant; *A combater; &c.*
Combatre. *To combate, fight, bicker, battell; to conflict, skirmish, contend, scuffle with; also, to ouercome in combate.*
Combatre son ombre. *To fight with his owne shadow; to be angrie without cause, or, hee knowes not at what; also, to reuile, or slaunder the absent; also, to forge, or deuise things, & afterwards disgrace, or raile at them.*
Combatre contre la plume. *To striue in vaine.*
Qui combat avec armes d'argent est asseuré de vaincre: Prov. *Those that with siluer weapons fight are sure to ouercome.*
Qui se combat n'est pas mort: Prov. *He that doth fight's not dead.*
Combatu: m. uë: f. *Combated, fought, bickered, battelled; contended, striuen, conflicted, skirmished.*
Combe: f. *A narrow valley, or passage betweene two hills; wherein commonly theeues do lurke.*
Combiberon: m. *A fellow drunkard, or companion in drinking.*
Combien. *How; how much, how great, how many; &c.*
Combien que. *Although, albeit that, howsoeuer that.*
Non combien mais comment bien; *not how much, or how long, but how well.*

Com-

Combinage: m. *A combination, coupling; vniting, or ioyning of paires; or of seuerall things, together.*

Comble: m. *Fulnesse, aboundance, heaped measure; the chiefe point, whole summe, summarie, or accomplishment of; also, the roofe of a house, &c.*

De fonds en comble. *Fully, wholly, throughly; vtterly; from the top to the bottome.*

Comblé: m. ée: f. *Heaped full of, or filled vp with; also, fullfilled, accomplished; made, or closed vp; rooved, roofed.*

Comble: com. *Full to the top; or vp to the roofe.*

Combleau: m. *A great cable, vsed about the carriage of a peece of ordnance; wee call it, the breeching.*

Comblement: m. *A heaping, vp-filling, or filling vp to the top; a fulfilling, accomplishing; making, or closing, vp.*

Combler. *To fill, or heape, vp; also, to accomplish, fulfill; saciate; make, or close, vp.*

Celuy est bien mon Oncle qui le ventre me comble: Prov. *Hee's my best vncle, who fills my bellie most.*

Comblette: f. *The cleft, or diuision of a red Deeres foot.*

Combourgeois: m. *A fellow citizen.*

Combourgeoisie: f. *Fellow-bourgessship; a communitie of freedome betweene th'inhabitants of one citie; or betweene two cities, and their inhabitants.*

Combré: *in stead of* Cambré: *(in some editions of* Bartas.)

Combrecelle: f. *A tumbling tricke, or Sommer-sault, wherein the heeles are cast ouer the head; also, reciprocation of venerie.*

Combressell e. *The same.*

Combustible: com. *Combustible, soone fired, easie to be burned.*

Combustion: f. *A combustion, burning, or consuming with fire; also, a tumult; and hence;*

Entrer en combustion avec. *To make a stirre, to raise an vprore, to keepe an old coyle against.*

Comedie: f. *A Comedie; a Play, or Enterlude (that begins in dissention, or sorrow, and ends with agreement or meriment.)*

Comestible: com. *Comestible, eatable, fit to bee eaten.*

Comete: f. *A commet, or blazing starre.*

Comette: f. *as* Comete.

Cometteux: m. euse: f. *Like vnto a commet; of a commet; or full of commets.*

Comic. *as* Comique.

Comin: m. *The hearbe Cummine.*

Comique: com. *A Comedian, Player, Stage-Player.*

Comique: com. *Comicall; Comedie-like; of, or belonging to, a Comedie; intreated of in Comedies.*

Comite: m. *The Captaine, Gouernour, or Maister of a Gallie; or, an Officer that lookes to the sure chaining of the slaues; whom sometimes he incourages, but more commonly scourges, vnto their businesse; also, the Boteswaine of a ship.*

Command: m. *Commaund, power, authoritie; the absolute sway, rule, or disposition of a thing; also, a* Mandamus, *or an Iniunction for possession, &c; also, an inioyner, commaunder.*

Commande: f. *as* Commende; *Also, the maine, or maister cable of a ship, whereby it is moored fast vnto a key, &c; also, a thing left in trust with, or committed vnto the charge of, another.*

Droict de commande. *ij. d.* Parisis *taken yearely by some Lords of euerie one of their widowes (that holds by Villenage) in acknowledgement, and preseruation, of the right of their authoritie ouer them.*

Commandé: m. ée: f. *Commaunded, bidden; charged; appointed, prescribed, inioyned; also, ruled, gouerned, domineered ouer; also, recommended, or committed ouer vnto the charge, or care of.*

Commandement: m. *A charge, commaund, precept, rule, commaundement, prescription, appointment; also, a Proclamation,* Mandamus, *decree, or ordinance, passing from such as are in authoritie.*

Commander. *To commaund, bid, charge, appoint, prescribe, inioyne vnto; also, to rule, sway, gouerne, commaund; also, to recommend, or to commit ouer vnto the care of another.*

Commander à baguette. *To commaund absolutely, wholly, peremptorily.*

'A Dieu vous command. *God be with you; fare you well.*

Commanderesse: f. *A commaundresse, gouernesse, ruleresse; also, authoritie, rule, commaund.*

Commanderie: f. *A commaunderie, or commaundership; the place, or office of a Commaunder (of one of the Orders.)*

Commandeur: m. *A commaunder, bidder, appointer; prescriber of lawes vnto others; also, a Commaunder, Ruler, Gouernor, Maister, ouer others.*

Commandeurs de l'Ordre du S. Esprit. *Are ix. viz. Foure Cardinals, th'Amner, and foure other Prelates of note; who haue greater authoritie, and larger priuiledges, than the knights, or the rest of the brethren of that order.*

Comme: f. *See* Gomme.

Comme. *As, euen as, euen like as, much like vnto, as much as.*

Comme à cette heure. *About this time aday.*

Comme ainsi fust que. *It being so, or, admit it were so.*

Comme celà. *Thereabouts.*

Comme en serois ie si &c. *In what a case, in what a pickle, in what tearmes should I be? how should I doe it, what course should I take, what shift should I make, if, &c.*

Commedial: m. *A fine, or merie, discourse.*

Commemorable: com. *Commemorable, memorable, worthie to be mencioned, fit to be remembred.*

Commemoration: f. *A commemoration, mentioning, rehearsing, remembring, putting in mind of.*

Commemoré: m. ée: f. *Commemorated, mentioned, remembred; rehearsed, recorded.*

Commemorer. *To commemorate, remember, mention, rehearse; record; also, to aduertise, or put in mind of.*

Commencé: m. ée: f. *Commenced, begun, vndertaken, entred into.*

Commencement: m. *A beginning, a commencement, an ouerture, an entrance into.*

Commencement n'est pas fusée: Pro. *Things are not done as soone as begun; or, things are not therfore compassed because they are vndertaken.*

'A tout il y a commencement; ou; il y a commencement par tout: Prov. *Euerie thing hath a beginning.*

Sur petit commencement on fait grande fusée: Prov. *Of small beginnings are great matters raised.*

Vn fol fait tousiours le commencement: Prov. *The foole begins, but perfects not, a worke; when hee hath begun, he hath done.*

Commencer. *To commence, begin, take in hand, vndertake,*

take, enter into, make an ouerture vnto.
Tel cuide avoit fait qui commence: Prov. *Some thinke they haue done when they are to begin; or, when they haue but begun; or, some are new to begin, when they thinke they haue done, a businesse.*
Commendaces: f. *Funerall Orations; prayers made for the dead; verses made in praise of the dead.*
Commendataire: m. *A commendatarie; one that hath, or sues for, a* Commendum.
Commendataire: com. *Commendatarie; giuen in, enioyed, or enioying by,* Commendum.
Abbé commendataire. *A Secular Abbot; one that hath an Abbey in* Commendum, *and yet was neuer Monke, nor Priest.*
Commende: f. *A* Commendum; *or Benefice giuen in* Commendum.
Commendeneresse: f. *as* Commanderesse.
Commenial. (¶Rabelais l.4. chap. 44.) *A barbarous or ieasting repetition of the word* comme *going some two lines before, and vsed by Frier John.*
Commensal: m. *A companion at table; a soiourner, or dailie guest.*
Les commensaux de la maison du Roy. *Such officers as be in ordinarie, or haue* bouche *(which we call budge)* à Court.
Commensalité: f. *Commensalitie; a continuall feeding together at one table.*
Commensuration: f. *Commensuration; a ioynt measuring.*
Comment: m. *as* Commentaire.
Comment. *How, in what sort, after what fashion, by what meanes, for what reason, in what manner.*
Le comment a nom de sa femme. *His wiues how-should-I-call-it:* ¶Rab.
Commentaire: m. *A comment, commentarie, glosse, exposition.*
Commentateur: m. *A commentator, or commenter; a glosser, expositor, or expounder of a text.*
Commenté: m. ée: f. *Expounded, commented on.*
Commenter. *To comment, to write commentaries; to expound.*
Commerage: f. *Gossiping; the acquaintance, affinitie, or league that growes betweene women by christening a child together, or one for another.*
Commerce: m. *Commerce, intercourse of trafficke; familiaritie, or acquaintance gotten; correspondencie, or intelligence continued, betweene people, in dealing, or trading, together.*
Leurs offices tombent en commerce. *Their offices are saleable, vendible; set to sale; to be bought, and sold.*
Commere: f. *A she-gossip, or godmother; a gomme.*
Commere de fesses. *A bed-broaker, an arse-gossip; a gossip for all buttocke-matches, or, in all baudie meetings.*
Vin de commeres. *A sweet, and pleasant wine.*
Tout y va par compere, & commere. *All things are carried among them by fauour, and friendship; like good drunken gossips, they will do any thing one for another.*
Commerer. *To gossip it, to play the gossip.*
Commesurable: com. *Measurable together, or with one and the same measure.*
Commettre. *To commit, referre, giue ouer, assigne, or inioyne a charge, or businesse vnto; also, to appoint, or delegate vnto a charge, or businesse; also, to doe, commit, or perpetrate an offence.*
Commettre son fief. *To forfeit his inheritance.*
Se commettre à. *To commit, betake, or yeeld himselfe ouer vnto; to venture vpon.*
Commeu: m. euë: f. *Moued, or stirred much; troubled, disturbed; chafed; shaken.*
Commin: m. *Cummine (seed, or hearbe.)*
Commination: f. *A commination; an extreame, or vehement threatning.*
Comminatoire: com. *Comminatorie; threatfull, threatening much.*
Comminé: m. ée: f. *Threatned extreamely, menaced vehemently.*
Comminer. *To threaten extreamely, menace vehemently.*
Comminué: m. ée: f. *Brayed small; beaten, or broken, into small peeces; also, diminished, minished, lessened.*
Comminuer. *To bray small; to beat, or breake, into small peeces; also, to lessen, minish, diminish.*
Commis: m. *A committee; one thats appointed to examine, or decide, a matter; also, a Deputie in an office; also, a Commissioner; also, a Commissarie; also, a forfeiture.*
Commis: m. ise: f. *Assigned, appointed, delegated; also, referred, vnto; also, done, acted, committed, as an offence, &c; also, forfeited.*
Commise: f. *A forfeiture, or forfeiting.*
Droict de commise. *The right, or power a Landlord hath to confiscate, seise, or enter on, the land held by his vassall, or tenant, who disaduowes him, giues him the lye, or commits felonie.*
Commiseration: f. *Commiseration; compassion; a sencible apprehension, or pitie taken of other mens miseries.*
Commissaire: *A Commissioner; one that receiues his authoritie by Commission; hence, a Iustice, or Commissioner, of the peace; who is to inquire after faults, disorders, and trespasses committed; also, a Judge Delegate; also, a Judge, or Arbitrator appointed to examine, determine, or accord, a priuate controuersie; also, an Ouerseer, Sequestrator, or seller of goods, authorized thereto by the Magistrate; and one, that hath, by the same authoritie, the possession, and keeping of lands, that are seized by publike order, giuen him.*
Commissaires de l'artillerie. *Are a certaine number of Commissioners, or Commissaries, one whereof the Master of the Ordnance assignes to euerie Prouince of Gouernment for th'ouerseeing of th'Ordnance that is therein.*
Commissaires du Chastelet. *Are, in Paris, little other than our London Scauengers; for their principall office is to looke that the streets bee kept cleane, and well paued.*
Commissaires des fermes. *Certaine Officers, who looke that the farmes of the Aides be well passed, and the reuenue thereof duely paied.*
Commissaires des guerres. *Commissaries, or Muster-masters of armies: these must be Gentlemen, such as haue beene* Gens d'armes des ordonnances *(at the least) six yeares; and are commaunded onely by the Marshalls of France, or, in their absence, by the Kings Lieutenants generall.*
Commissaires des Monstres. *The same; or ordinarie Muster-masters.*
Commissaires des Vivres, & Munitions. *Generall Ouerseers, appointed, by Commission, to looke that the victualls prouided for armies, and garrisons, bee iustly distributed, and disposed of.*

Les grands commissaires des procez. *A select companie of the Presidents, and Counsellors (or assistants) of a Court, who ordinarily pronounce Iudgements, and make decrees.*

Les petis commissaires des procez. *Are others, who by th'appointment, and limitation of the Court, examine the proues, or contradictions, and dates of euidences, bookes, depositions, &c; and thereof making a report, proceed no further.*

Repaistre en commissaire. *To feed plentifully, or apace, at other mens tables, or charges.*

Traicté en commissaire. *That hath both fish and flesh set afore him; or, as we say, intertained like a Lord.*

Commission: f. *A commission, or delegation; a charge, Mandate, commaundement, or warrant, for th'exercising of iurisdiction, &c, giuen by letters patents, or vnder a publicke seale.*

Elle a tousiours quelque commission par la ville. *Said merily of a woman thats euer gadding abroad.*

Commissure: f. *A commissure, or seame in a boane, (as in the skull;) also, any neere closing, ioyning, or couching of things together.*

Commistion: f. *A commixtion; a mixing, or mingling of seuerall things together,*

Committimus: lettres de com. *Speciall commissions, directed, in the behalf of priuiledged persons, vnto their peculiar Judges.*

Commodat: m. *A loane, or lending.*

Commode: com. *Commodious; conuenient; proper, apt, meet, fit.*

Commodement. *Commodiously; conueniently; aptly, fitly, meetly; to the purpose, as one would haue it.*

Commoderation du corps. *A good disposition of the whole bodie; a corresp̄ondencie, or equall proportion, of good temper in euerie part, or member thereof.*

Commodité: f. *Commoditie, vtilitie, profit, benefit, thrift; also, aptnesse, fitnesse; conueniencie, ease, handsomenesse.*

Commoditer. *To thriue, gaine, grow rich, preuaile; benefit, or accommodate, himselfe.*

Commotion. *A commotion, tumult, stirre; vprore, hurly burly; a perturbation; trouble, disquietnesse.*

Commourans. *Dying together.*

Commourir. *To die together, or one for companie of another.*

Commouvoir. *To vex, trouble, disturbe; shake, moue, raise, or stirre vp; (also, to rise, or stirre) together against.*

Commué: m. ée: f. *Changed, altered; bartered, exchanged.*

Commuer. *To change, alter; barter, trucke, exchange one thing for another.*

Commun: m. *A people, the common people; a comminaltie; a corporation; also, a thing thats common, or enioyed in common; whence;*

Commun n'est pas vn: Pro. *Common things are no one mans things; or, that which is common belongs to no man.*

Ouvrage de commun ouvrage de nul: Prov. *All mens worke is no mans worke; or, that which is done for many is acknowledged by none.*

Qui sert commun nul ne le paye, & s'il defaut chascun l'abbaye: Prov. *The seruice done to a people no man rewards, the disseruices euery man railes at.*

Commun: m. une: f. *Common, publicke, vulgar, generall, that belongs to one as well as to another; also, much vsed.*

Chemin commun. *The high-way, road way.*

Chiens communs. *Hounds that will deale with any kind of game.*

Veine commune. *Looke* Veine.

De bien commun on ne fait pas souvent monceau: Prov. *Men seldome raise great heapes of publicke treasure.*

Communal: m. *A common, or great peece of vntilled land.*

Communauté: f. *The comminaltie, or common people; also, communitie, participation, fellowship, societie, fraternitie; good correspondencie, neere familiaritie one with another; also, a societie, brotherhood, corporation, or companie incorporate; also, a commoning, or holding in common with others.*

Commune. la com. *The common people, the vulgar, the rude and rascall multitude; also, a commons, common field, or towne field.*

Communes. *Companies of footmen leuied, and taken-out of villages.*

Communément. *Commonly, vsually, ordinarily, generally, publikely, in common, with common consent.*

Communicable: com. *Communicable; fit for, appliable vnto; also, conuersable, affable.*

Communicatif: m. iue: f. *Familiar, courteous, affable, easie to be spoken with; also, communicatiue, or whereof many are to haue part.*

Communication: f. *A communication, or conuersation; a talking, a consultation; also, a participation, imparting, or making common a thing with others.*

Communier. *To communicate, to receiue the Communion.*

Communion: f. *A Communion, fellowship, mutuall participation.*

Communiqué: m. ée: f. *Communicated, participated, imparted; also, conferred, talked, or communed, with.*

Communiquer. *To communicate, participate, impart, mix with, take, or giue part of; also, to conferre, talke, or commune with; to reueale a councell, or secret vnto.*

Commutatif: m. iue: f. *Commutatiue; bartering, trucking, exchanging one with, or for, another.*

Compacte: com. *Compacted; well set, knit, trust, pight, or ioyned together.*

Compacture: f. *The compacture, solide frame, substantiall ioyning of all the parts of a thing together.*

Compagn. *as* Compagnon: ¶Rab.

Compagnable: com. *Companable, friendlie, sociable, conuersable.*

Compagne: f. *A she mate, fellow, friend, companion.*

C'est vne bonne compagne. *she is a sociable wench, a good merrie lasse; (a phrase not taken altogether so ill as our good fellow would be.)*

Compagnie: f. *Companie, fellowship, societie; also, a crue, rout, assemblie, consort, or knot of; also, a companie, or band of souldiors.*

Compagnie Françoise. *Wenches (in the opinion of a wanton Priest.)*

Bestes de compagnie. *Yong wild swine which follow their dammes, in great troups, vntill they be about 18 moneths old, and then leaue them, and with them, this title.*

Compagnon: m. *A companion, associate fellow, mate, colleague, partner, or copartner; also, an accessarie in an offence.*

Compagnon d'armes. *A companion, or fellow in armes; (a tearme of more eminencie than,* Compagnon de guerre.)

Cōpagnon de guerre. *he that serues in the same action,*

on, armie, and armes, and vnder the same colours, with another.

Compagnon de mestier. *A Journeyman; an artificer that hath not set vp for himselfe.*

Petit compagnon. *An vpstart, meane companion; scoundrell, base fellow; a scuruie, saucie, or proud Groome.*

Demandez le à mon compagnon qui est aussi menteur que moy. *We say, aske my fellow whether I be a theefe or no.*

Compagnon bien parlant vaut en chemin chariot branslant: Prov. *(Neere to the Latine,* Comes facundus in via pro vehiculo est.)

Qui a compagnon a maistre: Prov. *Hee that is tied vnto companie is tired with controlements; (And therefore the way to be absolute is, to be alone.)*

Compagnonné: m. ée: f. *Accompanied, associated, consorted, fallen in companie, ioyned in fellowship, with.*

Compagnonner. *To accompanie, associate, consort, be familiar, ioyne in fellowship, walke together, goe cheeke by iowle, with.*

Compaignie: Compaignon: &c; *as* Compagnie, Compagnon; &c.

Compaing. *as* Compagnon: ¶Pic.

Companage: m. *Meat, acates, victualls; all kind of food except bread, and drinke.*

Comparagé: m. ée: f. *Compared, or paragoned with.*

Comparager. *To Paragon, or compare, with.*

Comparaison: f. *A comparison; a matching, or paragoning a likening, or conferring of things together.*

Comparé: m. ée: f. *Compared, paragoned, proportioned with; equalled, matched, conferred together; also, bought, or paied for, deerely.*

Comparence: f. *An apparance, an appearing.*

Comparent: m. *An appearer.*

Comparer: m. Le comparer du corps. *The price of a mans life; or, the buying of a thing with the losse therof.*

Comparer. *To compare, liken, confer together; to equall, paragon, proportion one with, or by, another; Also, to buy, or pay deerely for; and hence;*

Ie le te feray bien comparer. *I wil make thee smart, or pay soundly for it; I will cause thee to rue, bewaile, repent it.*

Comparition: f. *A comparition; an apparance, appearing, or representing of himselfe to open view.*

Comparoir. *To appeare; to present, or shew himselfe; also, to assist, or be present at.*

Comparoir vne faute. *To be punished, or pay deerly, for a fault.*

Comparoistre. *as* Comparoir.

Comparsonnier: m. *A fellow Officer, or fellow laborer.*

Comparti: m. ie: f. *Diuided, parted, put into equall parts.*

Compartiment: m. *A compartement; a square (table, or peece) in building (especially of stone) also, a bed, or border in a garden; also, a partition, or equall, and proportionable diuision.*

Compartir. *To diuide, part, or put, into equall peeces.*

Compartissant: m. *A copartner, or fellow-partner.*

Compartissant. *Diuiding, or parting with.*

Comparuit. *An act, order, or testimoniall, signifying the apparance of a partie.*

Comparution: f. *An apparance; or as* Comparition.

Compas: m. *A compasse; a circle, a round; also, a paire of compasses.*

Compassé. *Compassed, begirt, incircled; also, measured, by compasses.*

Compassement: m. *A compassing, incircling, turning round; also, a measuring by compasses.*

Compasser. *To compasse, incircle, begird; also, to turne round; also, to make a circle, or compasse; also, to measure, or square out by compasse, or compasses.*

Compassion: f. *Compassion, pitie, mercie.*

Compassionnaire: com. *Compassionarie, compassionate, hauing compassion of.*

Compassionner. *To take compassion, to haue pitie of.*

Compatibilité: f. *Compatibilitie; a concurrencie, accord, agreement together; a mutuall induring of, or bearing with, one another.*

Compatible: com. *Compatible, concurrable; which can abide, or agree together; or indure, or beare with, one another.*

Compatir. *To suffer, indure, abide, or beare with, one another; to agree, concurre, accord, together.*

Compatriote: m. *Ones countrey-man.*

Compensable: com. *Able to recompence, or make amends for.*

Compensation: f. *Satisfaction, recōpence, equal amends*

Compense: f. *as* Compensation.

Compensé: m. ée: f. *Recompensed, or satisfied (with a like measure, proportion, store, &c.)*

Compenser. *To satisfie, recompence, make amends vnto, with the like.*

Comperage: m. *A gossipship; a gossiping of, or between, men; th'affinitie, or friendship gotten by their christening of children.*

Compere: m. *A gossip.*

Compere d'oribus. *A superficiall friend, or cōpanion.*

Compere prestez moy vostre sac. *Words vsed in a certaine Xew-game.*

Tout y va par compere, & commere. *All things there do go by friendship.*

Compere de la Pouille couste & despouille: Pro. *Seeke* Pouille.

Entre deux comperes se perdit le fossoir: Pro. *Our neerest friends oft make vs the worst accounts; so may a cosen safely be tearmed a cousener.*

Qui de mastin fait son compere plus de baston ne doit porter: Prov. *He thats in league with a churle hath no need of a cudgell.*

Compermutant: m. *A changer, scoorser, barterer, interchanger.*

Compermutant: m. ante: f. *Changing, scoorsing, bartering, interchanging.*

Compermutation: f. *A change, exchange, interchange.*

Compermuté: m. ée: f. *Changed, exchanged, interchanged.*

Comperre. *as* Comparer; *To buy, or pay deerely for.*

Competemment. *Competently, conueniently, sufficiently, meetly well; a prettie deale, or time; also, aptly, fitly, agreeably.*

Competence: f. *Competencie; conueniencie, sufficiencie; aptnesse, fitnesse, agreeablenesse; also, a concurrencie, or competitorship; and hence;*

Venir en competence avec vn autre. *To striue or contend for, to make equall claime to, a thing, with another; to challenge, couet, or sue for, a thing as well as another; also, to paragon, or compare himself, or, to be laid in equall ballance with, another; to make, or hold, himselfe euery way as good as another.*

Competent. *Competent, sufficient, able, full, conuenient.*

Competer. *To be sufficient for, sutable with, agreeable vnto; also, to belong, or appertaine to; also, to demaund, or sue for the same thing that another doth.*

Competiteur : m. *A competitor, concurrent, fellow suitor, or seeker for.*

Compilation : f. *A compilation, or compiling; also a rapsodie; a booke, treatise, or collection, of sundrie matters, heaped together.*

Compilé : m. ée : f. *Compiled, heaped together.*

Compissant : m. ante : f. *Staying to pisse at euery post; bepissing euery place; all-to-bepissing.*

Compissé : m. ée : f. *Bepissed, all to bepissed.*

Compisser. *All to bepisse; to pisse euery where, or bepisse euerie place he comes in, euerie corner he comes neere.*

Compite : m. *A crosse way, or place where diuers waies doe meete; as, the corner of a street, &c.*

Complaignant : m. *A complainant, or complayner; properly, one that complaines, of an Offence committed, vnto a Magistrate, or court, of Iustice; referring to them the prosecution, and punishment thereof, and refusing to medle further in it.*

Complaignant : m. ante : f. *Complayning; playning, or finding himselfe aggrieued; or expressing his griefe.*

Complaindre. *To playne, complaine; bemone, bewaile, finde himselfe aggrieued, or expresse his griefe.*

Se Complaindre en matiere de saisine, & de nouvelleté. *To bring a writ of* Nouel disseisin *against.*

Complainte : f. *A plaint, complaint, moane, lamentation; also, an accusation, or bill of complaint.*

Complainte de Novelleté. *A Writ, or Action of* Nouel disseisin *(must be brought within a yeare of the disseisin.)*

Ramener la complainte sur les lieux. *To procure a Iudge to heare, examine, and determine a controuersie vpon the land in controuersie.*

Complaire. *To please, like, delight; serue, obserue, be obedient, or obsequious vnto; conforme, or apply himselfe to the humors of.*

Complaisance : f. *Delight, pleasure; fulnesse of, or fellowship in, ioy.*

Complaisant : m. ante : f. *Obsequious, obseruant, soothing, (and thereby) pleasing.*

Complant : m. *A vine plant; also, a place thats planted with yong vines; the nurserie of a vineyard; also, veriuice; also, as* Complanterie.

Tenir vignes à complans. *Which is, on condition to plant new, or preserue the old, vine-plants; or, to yeeld vnto the Lord a certaine portion of the fruits, and reuenue, of the vine-yard.*

Complanté : m. ée : f. *Planted, or stored with yong plants.*

Complanter. *To plant a vine-yard; to store it with vine-plants; to set new, or preserue old vine-plants; also, to lay out, or deliuer ouer, a Lords part, or share, in the fruits of a vine-yard let by him vnto parts, or halues; or to let a vine-yard in that manner.*

Complanterie : f. *A letting out of a vine-yard to halues, or for part of the fruit thereof; also, the part, or portion due vnto the Landlord by such a lease, or estate made.*

Complexion : f. *The complexion, making, temper, constitution of the bodie; also, the disposition, affection, humors, or inclination of the mind; also, as* Simploce.

Complexionné : m. ée : f. *Complexioned; made, framed, composed; of complexion, or constitution; disposed, affected, inclined.*

Corps bien complexionné. *Well fashioned, or tempered, well set together; of a good constitution, of an excellent composition.*

Mal complexionné. *Ill disposed, affected, inclined; of leud behauior, bad manners, and worse conditions.*

Complication : f. *A complication, or folding together.*

Complice : m. *A Complice, confederate, companion (in a leud Action.)*

Complicité : f. *A conspiracie, a bad confideracie.*

Complie : f. *The complyne; or, a part of the Popish Euensong.*

l'heure de complie : *Seeke,* Heure.

Compliqué : m. ée : f. *Foulded, enwrapped, intangled together.*

Complot : m. *A complot, conspiracie, couin, confederacie, packe, or compacting together.*

Comploté : m. ée : f. *Complotted, conspired, packed betweene, or among.*

Comploter. *To complot, conspire, combine or packe together.*

Comploteux : m. euse : f. *Full of, or addicted vnto, complots, or complotting.*

Componé. La bordure componée. *A border Gobonnie, in Blason.*

Comporté : m. ée : f. *Comported; indured, borne, suffered; behaued, maintained, sustained.*

Comportement : m. *Comportment, behauior, carriage, the bearing of himselfe.*

Comporter. *To indure, beare; suffer; also, to extend, or ly (in Surueying.)*

Se Comporter. *To carrie, beare, behaue; maintaine, or sustaine, himselfe.*

Composé : m. ée : f. *Composed, compounded, made, framed; disposed, ordered, digested; written, or done in verse; also, accorded, agreed, attoned, compounded, reconciled.*

Composer. *To compound, make, frame; dispose, order, digest; to write verses, compose, or poetize it; also, to accord, attone, reconcile aduersaries; or, to compound, finish, take vp, their differences, and hence;*

Composer auec. *To agree, take an order, make an end, fall to attonement, come to a composition, with.*

Composer son esprit contre les afflictions, &c; *To frame, enure, or settle, his mind to resist griefes, indure crosses, beare mischances.*

Composeur : m. *A composer, poet, writer, maker; a setter in Musicke.*

Compositeur : m. *as* Composeur; *also, a Printers Compositor, he that setteth the letters for the Presse; also, an Arbitrator, stickler, vmpier, frendlie compounder of differences.*

Composition : f. *A composition; making, framing; a confection, compositure; compounding; also, a worke, or booke, or the writing of a worke, or booke; also, an accord, composition, attonement, agreement; also, a* Quietus est, *or generall acquitance from the king to a Treasurer, &c.*

Compossesseur : m. *A compossessor; a ioint possessor; one that enioyes, or hath part in, a thing with another.*

Composte : f. *A condiment, or composition; a wet sucket, (wherein sweet wine was vsed in stead of sugar) also, a pickled, or winter Sallet of hearbes, fruits, or flowers, condited in vinegar, salt, sugar or sweet wine, and so keeping all the yeare long; any hearbes, fruit, or flowers in pickle; also pickle it selfe.*

Porter le bras en composte. *To carry th' arme in a Skarfe.*

Composté : m. ée : f. *Compounded; bedrugged; mingled, or made of condiments, or compound stuffe; also, pickled.*

Composter. *To compound, sophisticate, bedrug; to season with, or make of, condiments; also, to pickle.*

Comprehension: f. *A comprehension, containing; apprehension, vnderstanding of.*

Comprendre. *To comprehend, containe, comprise, compasse; to perceiue, vnderstand, apprehend, attaine vnto the knowledge of; to conceiue, to be capable of.*

Comprer. *as* Comparer; *To buy:* ❡Pic.

Compresse: f. *A boulster, pillow, or fould of linnen, to bind vp, or lay on, a wound.*

Comprimé: m. ée: f. *Pressed, squeezed, thrust, closed, or strained hard together.*

Comprimer. *To presse, to squeeze, to thrust, close, or straine, together.*

Comprimeur: m. *A presser, thruster, squeezer together.*

Comprins: m. inse: f. *Comprised, comprehended, contained within the compasse, or limits, of.*

Compromettre. *To compromit, or put vnto compromise.*

Compromis: m. *A compromise; a mutuall promise of aduersaries to referre their differences vnto arbitrement; or, a priuate power to end a controuersie, giuen by the mutuall consent of the parties in controuersie.*

Compromis: m. ise: f. *Compromitted, put vnto compromise.*

Compromissaire: m. *He vnto whom a controuersie is compromitted.*

Comptable: com. *Accountable, accountant, lyable vnto account.*

Comptant. *Counting, accounting, reckoning numbring.*

Argent comptant. *Readie money; Looke* Argent.

Bailler comptant. *To giue readie money; to pay presently, out of hand, or downe in hand.*

Compte: m. *An account, a reckoning; a computation, or calculation; a number; also, a respect had, regard made; of; also, the reason, or cause of a matter; also, a fib, gull, tale; an idle, or vnlikelie tale, historie, relation; (See* Conte.)

La chambre des comptes. *The Court of Accounts; the Exchequer, or Exchequer chamber.*

Homme de bon compte. *One that is true in all his dealings; a right honest man.*

Ligne de compte. *Seeke* Ligne.

Perle de compte. *A Paragon; a faire, great, Orientall Pearle.*

Roué de compte. *A notch-wheele (in a watch, or clocke.)*

Petis comptes. *Trifling words, ridiculous tearmes, toyes to mocke Apes withall.*

'A ton compte. *As thou tellest it; or, as thou thinkest, or makest account; according to thy reason.*

Hors de compte. Se voyant hors &c; *Seeing, that he had mist of his reckoning; or, that matters answered not his expectation.*

Abreger son compte. *To make the matter short.*

Avoir son compte. *To be merie, iollie, liuelie, lighthearted, all-a-hoight; Looke* Avoir.

C'est le compte. *This reckoning fals out right.*

Il est bien au compte de la douzaine. *He is a sorie fellow, sillie mate, simple companion.*

Servir dieu par compte. *That is, iust so many times a day, weeke, moneth, yeare, &c, and no more.*

Tenir compte. *To score, or keepe reckoning.*

Tenir compte de. *To prize, respect, esteeme, regard, make reckoning of.*

Trouver son compte. Ie trouve mō compte. *I haue reason for it; or, it appeares by my reckoning; I know it well ynough; I am certaine of it; my conceit of it falls out right.*

'A vieux comptes nouvelles disputes: Pro. *Old accounts breed new disputations (whereto, either their disorder, or the forgetfulnesse of those they concerne, makes them verie subiect.)*

Qui vit à compte il vit à honte: Prov. *Hee liues but shamefully that reckons all he spends; (yet is there verie little difference betweene a gallant that knowes not how, and a gull that cares not what, he spends.)*

Compté: m. ée: f. *Told, reckoned, numbred, counted, calculated, accounted.*

Comptement: m. *A counting, telling, reckoning, numbring, calculating, accounting.*

Compter. *To count, account, reckon, tell, number; to calculate, or cast, an account; also, to make, or giue vp, an account; also, to fib, fable, cog, talke vainely, chat idly, tell a foolish, fabulous, or vnlikelie, tale.*

Compter les ais, & souliveaux. *To picke strawes, to loose time, or spend it to small purpose.*

Compter les chevilles. *When one makes another wait a little too long at his doore before he open it, the Frenchmen say,* c'est luy faire compter les chevilles; viz. *To mocke, or amuse him to no purpose; and when they wil threaten to make one attend long for the thing he desires, they say,* Ie te feray compter des chevilles; *(I will make you coole your heeles before you haue it;) and hence, are most Courtiers tearmed,* grands compteurs de Chevilles.

Compter les cloux. *The same; or, to loose time; or consume it in idle feasting.*

Compter sans son hoste. *(We say the same) to reckon without his host; Looke* Hoste.

Qui compte sans son hoste, il faut qu'il compte deux fois: Prov. *Hee that reckons without his host must reckon twice; he that concludes, or determines of, businesse, without the priuitie, or presence of him whom it most concerns, is like ynough to heare of it, or be troubled with it, at least once more.*

Vne fois faut compter à l'hoste: Prov. *Our account must be made, our reckoning paid; (our liues examined, our vices censured) one time or other.*

Apres compter il faut boire: Prov. *Looke* Boire.

C'est vn marchant qui prend l' argent sans compter, ni peser. *One of Saint Nicholas Clerks; or an arrant theefe.*

Comptereau: m. *A booke of accounts; a bill of reckoning.*

Compteur: m. *A reckoner, counter, accounter; a caster of accounts; also, the Numerator; or figure that stands aboue the line, in an Arithmeticall fraction.*

Compteur de chevilles. *An ordinarie, or thred-bare Courtier; as in* Compter les chevilles.

Comptoir: m. *A Counter, or Table to cast accounts on.*

Comptoir de chemin. *A box, cabinet, or little coffer to carrie letters, or other writings in.*

Compulsé: m. ée: f. *Compelled, forced, constrained vnto.*

Compulser. *To compell, force, constraine vnto.*

Compulsoire: f. *A compelling, or compulsion; also, an instrument or meanes of compulsion; also, a commission inioyning a Register, Notarie, or Clerke, to deliuer the contracts, pleadings, acts, orders, or iudgements which a suiter hath need of.*

Componction: f. *Compunction, remorse; the pricke, or sting of conscience.*

Compurgateur: m. *A compurgator; one that by oath iustifies the (innocencie) report, or oath, of another.*

Computiste: m. *A computist, or computatist; a reckoner, calculator, or counter of.*

Comte: m. *A Count, an Earle. As soone as the auncient Frankes had woon* Gallia *from the Romanes, their kings appointed some of their principall followers, (by the names of* Comtes*) to be the Gouernours, and Judges of Prouinces; and others (by the same title) of good townes; giuing them withall the territories thereof, to be held of them as* Fiefs; *and so they became both Officers, and vassals; yet were they neither but at the will of their Soueraigne, or, at most, not longer than during their owne liues; But within a while they found means to make their* Fiefs *hereditarie; and afterwards procured their gouernments to bee annexed vnto their* Fiefs; *and at length (taking aduantage of the misfortunes, weakenesse, or facilitie of their Princes) incroached on the Soueraigntie of them both: (In all which time the Earles of Prouinces were no whit inferior vnto Dukes; hauing as large dominions as they, and Earles of townes vnder them as well as they; besides that, the Gouernours of diuers Prouinces (as Normandie, Britaine, and others) were as often called Earles, as Dukes.) Being at this height, and thereupon growing emulators, and sometimes th'enemies, of kings, they on the other side tooke a course, at first by the Parliament, (setled at Paris) to abridge part of the royalties; and afterwards by Escheats, Confiscations, or mariages, to reunite vnto the Crowne the whole Estates, of as many of them, (whether Earles, or Dukes) as yet acknowledged any dependancie on them by Homage, or otherwise; (The rest, either at first (as Lorraine, and Savoy) hauing vsurped an absolute Soueraigntie; or since by mischances (as Burgundie, and Flanders, by the imprisonment of Francis the first) being alienated from the Crowne;) And creating other Earles, haue graunted them only a iurisdiction, or soueraigntie (if so they will haue it) thats wholly controllable by the Parliaments, and subiect vnto themselues.*

Comte d'Estable. *Was in old time the title of the Maister of the Horse; and hence (doe some perswade themselues) was the name of* Connestable *deriued.*

Comte du Palais. *Was the title of the Lord High Steward of the Kings house; now tearmed,* Le Grand Maistre de France, & de la maison du Roy.

Comté: m. *A Countie, Shire; Earledome: (In France it is to haue foure Baronnies, and euerie Baronnie the estates of, at the least, tenne Gentlemen, belonging to it:* ¶Nicot. *But by an Edict, made in the yere* 1579, *and grounded on a decree of the Priuie Councell the tenth of March* 1578 *(though confirmed onely in the Parliament of Britaine) it was enacted, That an Earledome should consist of two Baronnies, and at the least three* Chastellenies *(which countervaile one Baronnie) or of one Baronnie, and six* Chastellenies; *all vnited together, and held, by one homage, of the King.)*

Con. *A womans &c.*

Conare: m. *A kernell (resembling a Pine-apple) that stickes to th'outside of the braine.*

Concassé: m. ée: f. *Squashed, or burst into peeces.*

Concasser. *To squash, dash, bruise, or burst in peeces.*

Concathenation: f. *A concathenation; chaining, or linking of things together.*

Concathenature. *The same.*

Concathené: m. ée: f. *Concathenated; chained, or linked together.*

Concathener. *To concathenate; to linke, or chaine, to tie, as with linkes, or chaines, together.*

Concavé: m. ée: f. *Hollowed, made concaue.*

Concavité: f. *A concauitie; hollow bowing, or boughtie hollownesse.*

La concavité des cieux. *The round firmament, or cope of heauen.*

Concedé: m. ée: f. *Granted, consented, or yeelded vnto.*

Conceder. *To grant, consent vnto; beleeue.*

Concentrer. *To ioyne in one center.*

Concentrique: com. *Hauing one, and the same center.*

Concept: m. *as* Conception.

Conceptacle: m. *A conceptacle; any hollow thing, which is apt to receiue, hold, or containe.*

Conception: f. *A conceit; also, sence, apprehension, iudgement, vnderstanding; also, the conception, or conceiuing, of women with child; whence;*

La conception nostre Dame. *The conception of our Ladie; a solemne holy-day kept by the Church of Rome on the eight of December.*

Concerner. *To concerne, touch, import; appertaine, or belong vnto.*

Concert de Musique. *A consort of Musicke.*

Concerté. *Consorted, accorded, agreed together.*

Concerter. *To consort, or agree, together.*

Concession. *A concession, grant, or granting; a leaue, permission, sufferance.*

Conceu: m. euë: f. *Conceiued; apprehended, gathered, vnderstood; also, conceiued, or a breeding in the wombe.*

Concevoir. *To conceiue, apprehend, vnderstand; also, a female to conceiue, or breed yong (bones) in her womb.*

Conchambrier: m. *A chamber-fellow, a comerade.*

Conche: f. *A kind of bason, or open vessell resembling a bason; as* Coquille; *also, as the Latine* Concha, *the shell of a muscle, cockle, &c; also, order, equipage, or furniture; whence;*

Estre bien en conche, ou en bonne conche. *To be well clothed, handsomely attired, in good fashion or order, in fit equipage or array.*

Conches. *certaine receptacles for sea-water (as in* Amezeau.)

Conchier. *To beshite, bedung, besquatter, beray.*

Conchilion: m. *Any shell-fish, or scaled fish, with whose bloud purple is died; but especially one (bearing scales) which yeelds a reddish-purple, or scarlet colour.*

Concierge: m. *A house-keeper; he that keepes a great mans house, or lookes to the stuffe that is therein; also, a Keeper, Goaler, Warder of a prison; also, a principall, rector, chiefe maister, or gouernor of a publique exercise, or schoole.*

Conciergerie: f. *The name of the common goale belonging to Paris; hence, also, a prison, or goale.*

Concile: m. *A Councell; an assemblie, Session, or sitting of councellors; also, a (generall) Councell (for Church matters.)*

Conciliabule. *A Conuenticle; a small, or priuate assemblie.*

Conciliateur: m. *A reconciler, peace-maker, procurer of fauour, and goodwill for, or betwixt others.*

Conciliation: f. *A conciliation, a reconcilement, or procuring of fauour; an attone-making; an agreement, reconciliation, vnion, league of friendship made among such as were foes.*

Conciliatrice: f. *A conciliatrix, reconciliatrix; a woman that reconciles those that were enemies.*

Concilié: m. ée: f. *Attoned, vnited, accorded, agreed, or made friends with; reconciled vnto.*

Concilier. *To attone, reconcile, accord, or make friends together;*

together; to ioyne, or knit in loue one with another.

Concilipete. *One that is going towards a generall counsell.*

Concion: f. *An assemblie, or congregation of people, called together; also, the Oration, or Speech deliuered and addressed, vnto them.*

Concis: m. ise: f. *Concise, briefe, short, succinct, compendious.*

Concitateur: m. *An incitor, incensor, vrger, prouoker, stirrer, or quickener vp vnto.*

Concitation: f. *A concitation; inciting, vrging, prouoking; a raising, rousing, stirring, or quickning, vp vnto.*

Concitatrice: f. *A concitatrix; incitresse, prouokeresse.*

Concité: m. ée: f. *Concited; incited, vrged, prouoked; raised, stirred, or quickened, vp vnto.*

Conciter. *To concite; incite, excite; vrge, pricke forward, prouoke; raise, quicken, or stirre, vp vnto.*

Concitoyen: m. *A fellow Citizen.*

Conclave: m. *A conclaue, or Closet; an inner parlour, or chamber; a secret, or priuate roome; and especially that (for it is seldome vsed but to expresse that) wherein the Cardinalls assemble about the election of a new Pope; also, the assemblie it selfe.*

Conclu: m. uë: f. *Concluded; decreed, determined, resolued on.*

'A ces fins conclu. *See* Fin.

Conclure. *To conclude; decree, determine, resolue vpon.*

Conclure in Barocco. *See* Barocco.

Conclure à la mort. *To giue sentence of death; to adiudge, or condemne vnto death; or, in an Argument, to conclude that the partie accused is worthie of death.*

Conclusion: f. *A conclusion; end, issue, close; resolution, determination; the Epilogue, or last part of.*

Prendre conclusions rigoureuses à l' encontre d' un criminel. *To vrge the Euidence hard against a prisoner; to lay sore vnto him; to put him to his neck-verse;* (C' est le Procureur du Roy, & la Partie civile qui prennent leurs conclusions: Celuy-la conclud à la peine, & reparation publique; cestuy-cy en reparation de son honneur (s'il y eschet) & en despés, dammages, & interests: ¶Code Henry.)

Concoction: f. *Concoction; good disgestion; a boyling, or seething (of meat in the stomack.)*

Concombre: m. *A Cowcumber.*

Concombre asinin. *as* Concombre sauvage.

Concombre citrin. *A Citrull, or citrull Cowcumber, a Pome Citrull.*

Concombre long. *The crooked, long, or Adders, Cowcumber.*

Concombre marin. *The round Pompion, or Melon.*

Concombre sauvage. *The wild Cowcumber, Spirting Cowcumber, Touch-me-not.*

Concombre Turquois. *A muske Melon; also, the Turkie Cowcumber, some what resembling a Pompion, and hauing a more solide, and firme pulpe then the ordinarie one.*

Concombriere: f. *A bed of Cowcumbers; a plot of ground wherein Cowcumbers grow.*

Concomitance: f. *Concomitancie; fellowship, or association with, companie together.*

Concordat: m. *An accord, agreement, concordancie pacification, peaceablenesse; also, an Act, or Article of agreement; and particulerly, the solemne Act, or booke of agreement, that passes betweene the Pope, and the French king touching the disposition of Benefices.*

Concorde: f. *Concord, accord, harmonie; peace, agreement, quietnesse; a composition.*

Concorder. *To accord, compound, pacifie, quiet, agree; also to liue in peace, and concord together.*

Concreé: m. eée: f. *Bred, composed, made, created together; also, congealed, compacted, gathered close together*

Concreér. *To breed, compose, make, or create together.*

Se concreér. *To be bred, composed, made, &c; also, to thicken, congeale, curd, or close together.*

Concret: m. *A coniunction, or conglutination; an intirenesse, or intire thing.*

Concret: m. ete: f. *Concrete; hardened, thickened, compacted, congealed, conioyned together.*

Concretion. *A compaction, conglutination, congealement, thickning, ioyning, curding, clottering, fastening together.*

Concubin: m. *A man vnlawfully kept, and vsed, by a woman.*

Concubinage: m. *Concubinage; the keeping of a whore for his owne filthie vse.*

Concubinaire. enfant concubinaire. *A bastard borne of a concubine; a whores sonne, the brood of a whore.*

Concubine: f. *A concubine, a leyman; a woman vsed ordinarily, as a wife.*

Conculcation: f. *A Conculcation, or treading vnder foot; a suppression, or extreame keeping vnder.*

Conculqué: m. ée: f. *Oppressed; trodden vnder foot.*

Conculquer. *To oppresse, or tread vnder foot; to bruise, or weare with often treading, or stamping on.*

Concupiscence: f. *Concupiscence, lust, feruent desire, greedie appetite vnto.*

Concupiscible. faculté concupiscible. *The vnreasonable, or sensuall part of the soule, which couets meats, drinkes, and all sorts of delights beyond measure.*

Concurrence: f. *A concurrence, or concurrencie; an agreement, of seuerall matters, or in circumstances (all comming to one point, or ayming at one thing;) a running, meeting, or ioyning, in course, together.*

Iusques à la concurrence de sa debte; *to the value, or quantitie of his debt; vntill it be fully satisfied, or run vp.*

Concurrent: m. *A concurrent, corriuall, competitor.*

Concurrent: m. ente: f. *Concurrent, concurring, agreeing with, ioyning or meeting in course, running together.*

Concusseur. *as* Concussionaire.

Concussion: f. *Concussion; publicke extortion, close rapine; an extorting of gifts by a false shew of authoritie, or imposition of crimes; any violent, and vniust procurement of bribes; also, a ioulting, or knocking one against another.*

Concussionaire: m. *A Concussionarie, or publicke extortioner; one that (counterfaiting an authoritie) extorts gifts from men by threatning to punish, or prosecute their offences; or any officer, or Magistrate, that will neither do right, nor giue good words vnlesse he be soundly bribed.*

Condamnation; & Condamnatoire. *as* Condemnation, *&* Condemnatoire.

Condamné; & Condamner. *See* Condemné, & Condemner.

Conde: m. *A butler; or, a yeoman of the Larder;* ¶Rab.

Condemnade. *A kind of Card-play, like vnto* Lansquenet. ¶Rab.

Condemnation: f. *A condemnation; a damning or condemning.*

Condemnation d'amende. *An amercing, or putting to a fine.*

Passer condemnation. *To giue ouer a suit, to yeeld vnto an agreement, to desist from brabling, in Law.*

Il passa condemnation de tout ce qu' ils desiroyent. *He graunted, or yeelded vnto, whatsoeuer they required.*

Condemnatoire: com. *Condemnatorie, condemning; amercing, fining.*

Condemné: m. ée: f. *Condemned, damned, ouerthrowne in Law; also, amerced, fined, put vnto his fine.*

Vn lieu condemné. *An vncouth, or vnaccessable place.*

Tel a bonne cause qui est condemné: Prov. *Hee thats i'the right oft times receiues the foile.*

Condemner. *To condemne, or damne; to ouerthrow in iudgement, ouercome by Law.*

Condemner à l'amende. *To amerce, fine, or put vnto his fine.*

Condensé: m. ée: f. *Thickened, made thicke, compacted, or closed together.*

Condense: com. *Condense; thicke, close together.*

Condenser. *To thicken, or make thicke; to gather, or flocke together.*

Condensité: f. *Condensitie, thicknesse, hardnesse, closenesse.*

Condescendre. *To condescend, vouchsafe, yeeld, graunt vnto.*

Condescendu: m. uë: f. *Condescended; vouchsafed; graunted, or yeelded vnto.*

Condignac. *as* Codignat; *Marmalade of Quinces.* ¶Rab.

Condigne: com. *Condigne, well-worthie.*

Condignement. *Condignely, worthily, honestly; as it behoueth.*

Condile. *as* Condyle.

Condisciple. *A schoole-fellow, or fellow disciple.*

Condition: f. *A condition, couenant; law, or bargaine conditionall; also, the propertie, nature, disposition, manner, one vseth, or is of; also, ones estate, fortune; place; birth; qualitie, (especially meane, or base.)*

Ie ne sçay pas les conditions du ieu. *I know not the lawes of the Game.*

Conditionaire: com. *Conditionarie, conditionall, vpon condition, vnder couenant, couenanting.*

Conditionnel. *as* Conditionaire.

Conditionnellement. *Conditionally, vpon, or vnder, a condition.*

Condol: m. *A ridge, or raising of earth.*

Condoloir. *See* Condouloir.

Condonné: m. ée: f. *Giuen freely, forgiuen, pardoned.*

Condonner. *Freely to giue; to pardon, or forgiue.*

Condore. *The name of a great, strong, and rauenous Indian bird.*

Condot: m. *as* Condol.

Condouloir. *To sorrow, or moane with, to sympathize with the griefe, or paine of.*

Conducteur: m. *A Conductor, Leader, Guide, Ringleader; also, a Captaine.*

Conductrice: f. *A Conductresse.*

Conduict: m. *A Conduit; also, a gutter, or trench of stone, &c, whereby the water, or course of a riuer is turned, and fetcht into, or by, any place.*

Conduicts de fleuves. *The heads of riuers.*

Conduicte: f. *A conduct, conduction, guiding, leading, bringing on; a trayning, or gouernment; also, a managing, or handling.*

Conduicte de l'esprit. *The inclination, motions, or sway of the mind.*

Conduire. *To conduct, lead, guide, bring on; gouerne, sway, rule, wholly dispose of; also, to handle, or manage.*

Conduire sourdement vne Orne. *Looke* Orne.

Conduiseur: m. *A Leader, Guider, Conductor.*

Condui-somne. *Sleepe-conducting, silent, quiet.*

Conduit: m. ite: f. *Conducted, led, guided, brought on; trained, gouerned; swayed, wholly disposed of.*

Conduit: m. *as* Conduict.

Conduite: f. *as* Conduicte.

Condyle: m. *The tuberiositie; out-swelling, roundnesse, or knots, of the thigh, knee, ankle, elbow, or knuckle-bones; also, a blow with the fist; a box, or cuffe.*

Condylome: m. *A swelling, or excrescence of flesh (like vnto little warts, or the stones of a raisin, or figge) in the fundament, or in a womans priuities.*

Cone: m. *A Cone; a Geometricall bodie; or any figure, that is broad, and round below, and sharpens towards the top.*

Conestable. *See* Connestable.

Conestablie: f. *A Constableship; also, a Captaineship, or gouernment held in Peerdome; also, a companie, band, or battalion of Souldiers.*

Confanon. *A Standard, or Banner, &c; as* Gonfanon.

Confanonier: m. *A Standard-bearer.*

Confanons. *The wild Poppie.*

Confection: f. *A confection, or composition; a mingling; a confecting, or comfet making.*

Confederation: f. *A confederation, or confederacie; the making of, or entring into, a league with others; also, a complot, or conspiracie.*

Confederez. *Confederate, in friendship, entred into a league, together; also, ioyning in a plot, or conspiracie.*

Conference: f. *A conference; also, a comparison.*

Conferer. *To conferre, commune, deuise, or talk, together;* (conferer ensemble;) *also, to contribute, or be at alike, and equall charge with another;* (conferer avec vn autre.)

Confermé: m. ée: f. *Confirmed, strengthened, fortified, setled; hardened; incouraged, assured; ratified, established; auouched, auerred for truth.*

Confermer. *To confirme, strengthen, fortifie, settle, harden; assure; establish, ratifie, make good; incourage, comfort; auouch, or auerre for truth.*

Confesse: f. *as* Confession.

Aller à la confesse. *To goe to shrift.*

Confessé: m. ée: f. *Confessed; acknowledged, yeelded vnto; discouered, reuealed, bewrayed; also, shriuen.*

Confesser. *To confesse, acknowledge, yeeld vnto; reueale, discouer, bewray.*

Se confesser au prestre. *To be shriuen.*

Confesseur: m. *A Confessor, or ghostlie father.*

Confession: f. *A confession, or acknowledgement; a reuealing, or bewraying, of a secret.*

Confession auriculaire. *Shriuing, auricular confession.*

Confessionnaire: com. *Confessionarie; belonging to, or treating of, auricular confession.*

Confessionnat: m. *An act of confession tending to absolution.*

Confez. *Confessed, shriuen.*

Confiance: f. *Confidence, trust, assurance, hardinesse.*

Confiant. *Trusting, hauing confidence in, building vpon.*

Confidant: m. *A friend to whom one trusts, in whom he hath confidence, on whose assistance he relyes; a second in a single combat, such a one as a man takes into the field with him.*

Confident. *as* Confidant.

Confidentiaire: com. *Trecherous, faith-breaking, trust-deceiuing.*

Confidentionnaire. *as* Confidentiaire.

Confier. *To trust, beleeue, haue confidence in; assure himselfe of; build, rely, or depend, vpon.*

Confiez de Cour. *as* Pairs de la Cour.

Configuration: f. *A likenesse, or resemblance, of figures.*

Confin: m. ine: f. *Neere, neighbor, confining, or adioyning, vnto; bounding, or bordering, vpon.*

Confinant: m. ante: f. *Confining, bounding, bordering, abbutting, adioyning, lying neere vnto; also, confining, banishing.*

Confiner. *To confine; to abbut, or bound vpon; to abboord, adioyne, lye neere vnto; also, to assigne limits, appoint marches, lay out bounds vnto; also, to confine, relegate, banish into a certaine, or limitted, place.*

Confire. *To preserue, confect, soake, or steepe in; also, to season, relish, or giue sauor vnto.*

Confirmatif: m. iue: f. *Confirmatiue, confirming; establishing, ratifying; assuring; auouching.*

Confirmation: f. *A confirmation, strengthening, setling, assurance; ratification, establishment; also, a hartning, or incouragement; also, an auouching, or auerrall of a thing for truth; also, confirmation, Bishopping, or (as the vulgar) Bisping.*

Droict de confirmation. *The fine, or fee due, by all Officers of the kingdome of France, vnto the King at his first comming to the Crowne, for confirming them, by his Letters Patents, in their places.*

Confirmé. *as* Confermé.

Confirmer. *See* Confermer.

Confis: m. *Any thing that hath beene soaked, or steeped; any pickled, or preserued thing.*

Confisc: m. *A confiscation, or thing confisqued.*

Confiscation: f. *A confiscation; a publick seisure; also, a forfeiture.*

Confiseur: m. *A Confector, Preseruer, or Confet-maker.*

Confisqué: m. ée: f. *Confiscated; seised to publicke, or vnto the Princes, vse; also, forfeited; lost by, or made subiect to, forfeiture.*

Confisquer. *To confiscate; to seise, as forfeited vnto the Princes, or common, Treasurie; also, to forfeit.*

Confissable: com. *Fit to be steeped, soaked, preserued, confected.*

Confisseur: m. *A Confector, Confet-maker; Preseruer.*

Confit: m. ite: f. *Steeped, confected; fully soaked, wholly imbrued with.*

Confit en amertume. *Whose heart is full of bitternesse; a most dolefull person, a most wofull man.*

Confit en malice. *A most vngracious fellow; one that hath gotten a full habit of wickednesse; one thats obdurate in, or giuen ouer to, roguerie; one that minds, or is made of, nought but villanie.*

Confiture: f. *A confecting, preseruing; steeping, soaking; saucing, seasoning; also, a confection, condiment, preserue; and hence;*

Confitures. *Confets, ionkets, all kind of sweet-meats; and, most properly, fruits, blossomes, leaues, stalkes, &c, of plants, preserued whole; Preserues.*

Conflagration: f. *A conflagration; a generall burning, or consuming with fire.*

Conflant: m. *A place whereat two riuers meet.*

Conflé: m. ée: f. *Blowne, or, puffed vp. See* Gonflé.

Conflict: m. *A conflict, skirmish, bickering, or battell.*

Confluant. *as* Conflant.

Confondre. *To confound; disorderly to mingle, or tumble together.*

Conformateur: m. *A conformer; a maker of things like one another, and fit altogether.*

Conformation: f. *A conforming; a framing, fashioning, or disposition of things to a likenes betweene themselues, and a fitnesse altogether.*

Conforme: com. *Conformable, conforme, agreeable vnto; agreeing, or of a like fashion, one to the other.*

Conformé: m. ée: f. *Conformed; made apt for, fitted with, fashioned like.*

Conformément. *Conformably, accordingly, thereafter.*

Conformer. *To conforme; fit with; fashion as; make apt for, like to, proportionable vnto; also (simply) to make, frame, fashion, proportion.*

Conformité: f. *Conformitie, conformeablenesse; a resemblance, likenesse, fitnesse, or befitting.*

Confort: m. *Comfort, solace, consolation; an incouragement, or cheering vp; an easing, or mitigating of griefe; the application of strength vnto weaknesse, thereby to inforce it.*

Confortatif: m. iue: f. *Comfortatiue; of power, or propertie, to comfort.*

Conforté: m. ée: f. *Comforted, eased, solaced; strengthened; supported.*

Conforte-main. *The strengthening, and confirmation of an inferior persons seisure by the superiors assistance; as when a Lord, hauing seised an inheritanse held of him, prayes in aide of the King (or a Mesne Lord of the Lord Paramount) and procures it, for the better assurance of his possession.*

Donner conforte-main. *To helpe, succour, aide, assist; to lend a helping hand vnto.*

Conforter. *To comfort, solace, recreate; to encourage, or cheere vp; also, to confirme, helpe, strengthen, reinforce.*

Comforter vne playe. *To corroborate a wound by fomentations, or other (externall) applications.*

Confoulant. *A certaine village hard by Paris; tearmed so, because two riuers (*Marne, *and* Seine*) meet at it.*

Confrairie: f. *A Fraternitie, Brotherhood, Fellowship, Societie; a Companie of one trade, or profession.*

Le pain benist de la confrairie. *Bobbes, thumpes, thwackes, blowes.*

Confreres: m. *Fellowes of one, and the same Companie, or Societie.*

Confrontation: f. *A confronting, or bringing face to face; also, a reading, or examining of the depositions of accusers in presence of the accused.*

Confronté: m. ée: f. *Confronted, brought face to face; examined, compared, conferred one by another; layed neere together.*

Confronter. *To confront, or bring face to face; to examine,*

mine, or compare, one by another; to conferre, or lay, seuerall things together.

Confronter tesmoins. *To confront witnesses; to bring accusers, or accusing witnesses, before the accused; and, to examine them, or to read and examine the euidence they haue giuen in, or depositions which they haue made, in his presence.*

Confus: m. use: f. *Confused, disordered; hudling, indistinct; also, confounded, troubled; abashed, amazed, dismayed, put or dasht out of countenance.*

Confusément. *Confusedly, vndistinctly, without order; one with another.*

Confusion: f. *A confusion, or disorder; a rude mingle-mangle, chaos, hurly-burly; a confounding; also, a thick Ruffe thats worne close before.*

Confuté: m. ée: f. *Confuted, conuinced, refelled, disproued, ouercome in arguing.*

Confuter. *To confute, conuince, refell, disproue, ouercome in arguing.*

Confuter vn tesmoing. *To disgrace, confound, puzle, blanke him; to put him out of countenance, or, driue him to a Non-plus.*

Congé: m. *Leaue, licence, permission; graunt of libertie, discharge, dismission; also, a pasport.*

Congé de Cour. *Looke* Renvoy.

Congé deffault. *A dismission vpon default*; (Se donne à l'appellant, qui a esté anticipé, contre l'anticipant defaillant; Quia fungitur vice rei, & actoris. ¶Ragueau.)

Congé de Mortesaison. *Looke* Mortesaison.

Congé simple. *A simple dismission, or discharge out of a Court*; (S'obtient par vn defendeur contre vn demandeur non comparant, ou à faute de repliquer: & par l'intimé contre l' appellant defaillant qui avoit relevé, & adsigné. ¶Ragueau.)

Il me donna congé de ma chambre. *He gaue vp my chamber.*

Congeable: com. *Dismisseable, licensable, dischargeable.*

Domaine congeable. *Which the possessor is to leaue when his Landlord pleases; a demayne held at will.*

Congedié: m. ée: f. *Dismissed, discharged, licenced, that hath leaue to be gone.*

Congedier. *To dismisse, discharge, licence, giue leaue vnto, permit to goe, suffer to depart.*

Congedier vne armée. *To break vp an armie.*

Congelation: f. *A congelation, congealing, freezing; also, the disease tearmed* Catalepsis, viz. *a suddain detention, or occupation of the bodie, and mind; the Patient continuing in the same forme, and holding the same posture, which he had when he was taken with it.*

Congelé: m. ée: f. *Congealed, frozen, closed, together.*

Congeler. *To congeale; to be frozen, or close together with freezing, &c.*

Congemination: f. *A congemination, doubling, often repeating; (whence) also, as* Epizeuxe.

Congeneré: m. ée: f. *Congenerated; begotten, or ingendred together.*

Congiaire: m. *A dole; a largesse, or liberall gift (of money, or victuals) vnto the people.*

Congie: m. *A vessell among the ancient Romanes containing some foure pints and a halfe, of Parisien measure; or very neere our gallon.*

Conglutination: f. *A conglutination; a ioyning, a knitting, a closing, or gluing together.*

Conglutiné: m. ée: f. *Conglutinated; glued, closed, or knit with.*

Conglutiner. *To conglutinate; ioyne, glue, close, knit with, or together.*

Congnoistre. *See* Cognoistre.

Congratulation: f. *A congratulation, or verball reioycing with one for his good fortune.*

Congratulé: m. ée: f. *Congratulated, reioyced with.*

Congratuler. *To congratulate; or, in words, to reioyce with another for his good fortune.*

Congre: m. *A Congar, or Cungar (fish.)*

Congreé: m. eée: f. *Congealed, thickened, curded, gathered close together, clottered; compact, made hard.*

Congréement: m. *A congealing, curding, thickening, growing, or clotting together.*

Se Congréer. *To congeale, thicken, curd, close; gather, compact together.*

Congregation: f. *A congregation; assemblie, or company of people gathered together in a publicke place.*

Congregé: m. ée. f. *Congregated, gathered, assembled together.*

Congréger. *To congregate, gather, assemble together.*

Il se congrége en pierre precieuse. *It growes, or congeales into, a precious stone.*

Congression: f. *Companie, congression with others; or, as* Congrez; *an assemblie, meeting, &c.*

Congrez: m. *A solemne assemblie, or meeting; also, an incounter, coaping, or scuffling together.*

Conjectural: m. ale: f. *Coniecturall; which may be gathered by ghesse, or scand at by coniecture.*

Conjecturalement. *Coniecturally, by ghesse, or coniecture, habnab, hittie-missie.*

Conjecturant: m. ante: f. *Coniecturing, ghessing at.*

Con. le lion par les ongles. *See* Lion.

Conjecture: f. *A coniecture, or gesse; a iudgement giuen, or conceit taken, on vncertain grounds, or at randome.*

Conjecturé: m. ée: f. *Coniectured, ghessed, imagined; deemed, diuined.*

Conjecturer. *To coniecture, ghesse, diuine; to iudge, or imagine by.*

Coniguer. *To scratch, or claw.*

Conillart. *A certaine very tender, and delicat peare.*

Conillier. *To play the coward, or lurke in corners; to seeke a hole to hide his head in; to sneake, or slinke from place to place, as a connie that boults from bush to bush.*

Conilliere: f. *A Conny-hole, or Conny-borow.*

Conioignant: m. ante: f. *Ioyning, vniting, combining, coupling with, or together.*

Conjoinct: m. cte: f. *Ioyned, conioyned, combined, coupled, vnited, knit, sure with.*

Conjoinctement. *Ioyntly, wholly, together, as well the one as the other.*

Conjoindre. *To conioyne, combine, couple, counite; to ioyne, associate; fasten, knit; marrie, make sure with, or together.*

Conjonctif: m. iue: f. *Coniunctiue; ioyning, coupling, combining, vniting with, or together.*

Membrane conjonctiue. *The white of the eye; or, the skin that couers it.*

Conjonction: f. *A coniunction; combination, coupling, or knitting together; also, the part of speech tearmed, a Coniunction.*

Conjouï. *Congratulated, or gladded with.*

Se Conjouïr. *To congratulate, or be glad with.*

Conjouïssement. *A congratulation, or reioycing with.*

Se Conjoyr. *as* Conjouïr.

Conjoyssement. *as* Conjouïssement.

Conise. *Flea-bane, or Flea-bane Mullet; (an hearbe.)*

Conjugal: m. ale: f. *Coniugall; belonging vnto man and wife, or vnto wedlocke; ioyned, or yoaked together, as man and wife in wedlocke.*

Os conjugal. *as* Os Iougal.

Conjuger. *To play the part of a husband; to know, or vse, his owne wife.*

Conjunction. *as* Conjonction.

Conjuncture: f. *A coniuncture; a ioyning together.*

Il venoit en vne fort mauvaise conjuncture. *Hee came when all things were cleane off the hindges, or quite out of ioint.*

Conjurateur: m. *A conspirator.*

Conjuration: f. *A conspiracie; complotment, priuat confederacie against; also, a coniuration, or coniuring.*

Conjure: f. *as* Conjuration; *also, a summoning, or calling of people together.*

Conjuré: m. ée: f. *Coniured; adiured; earnestly besought, or intreated; also, coniured, or exorcised; also, warned, summoned, or called together; also, conspired against.*

Conjurer. *To coniure; adiure; beseech earnestly, intreat vehemently; also, to coniure, or exorcise (a spirit;) also, to conspire; complot; ioyne in a priuat confederacie, against.*

Conjurer la Cour; ou ses hommes. *To call, or warne, a Court; to summon, or send for, his people together.*

Connaturel: m. elle: f. *Connaturall; naturall vnto all alike; also, agreeable to the nature of.*

Connestable: m. *A Constable; (In former times the maisters of the Kings Horse, and the captaines of certaine bands ingarisonned in frontier townes, and other forts of importance, were tearmed,* Connestables: *At this day the Constable of France is the principall officer of that Crowne, especially in warlike Expeditions, whereof, in his Princes absence, he is (or should be) the Generall; He also keepes the Kings Sword, and does him homage for it.)*

Connestablie: f. *A Constableship; the Office, or Place, of a Constable; also, a Captaineship, or Gouernment, held in Peerdome; also, a Squadron, Band, or Batallion, of souldiors.*

Connexé: m. ée: f. *Knit, ioyned, tyed, trussed together.*

Connexion. *A connexion; ioyning, knitting, tying, trussing together.*

Connexité: f. *as* Connexion.

Connil: m. *A Connie, a Rabbet.*

Connille: f. *A Doe Connie.*

Conniller. *See* Coniller.

Connilleur: m. *A coward; one that playes least in sight, or hides his head in a hole for feare of being seene.*

Connin: m. *as* Connil, *A Connie.*

Connin, & vilain avec la main: Prov. *A Connie dismembred with the hand, a knaue well pummelled with the fists, are much the sooner eaten, or amended.*

Conniniere: f. *A Connigrey, or warren of Connies.*

Connivé: m. ée: f. *Winked at; tollerated, suffered, borne with, seene and not seene (of purpose, or by consent.)*

Connivence: f. *A conniuence, or winking at; a sufferance, tolleration, permission; a seeing, and not seeing (by consent.)*

Conniver. *To winke at; suffer, tollerate, beare with; to see and not to see; to make as though he neither saw, nor knew ought of the matter.*

Connoissance: f. *Knowledge. See* Cognoissance.

Connoistre. *To know. See* Cognoistre.

Connon: m. *A long Dray, or Cart, hauing at the fore-end a Pulley for the drawing vp of loading.* ¶Pic.

Conoeïdal: m. ale: f. *Cone-like; broad, and round at the bottome, and sharpe at the top.*

Conopée: f. *A Canopie; a Tent, or Pauilion.*

Conquassé: m. ée: f. *Stamped, pounded; broken, split, quashed in pieces.*

Conquasser. *To powne, breake, or bruze; to stampe in a morter; to split, or quash in peeces; or, as* Concasser.

Conque: f. *Shell-fish; also, the shell it selfe; sometimes the pearle found in a shell-fish; also, a certaine measure for corne, of 58 pound weight.*

Conquerable: com. *Conquerable, vanquishable, subdueable, winneable.*

Conquerant: m. *A conqueror, or ouercommer; a subduer, a vanquisher.*

Conquereur. *as* Conquerant.

Conquerir. *To conquer, subdue, vanquish, ouercome; ouermaister, bring vnder obedience; also, to get, purchase, win, acquire (during mariage, or iointly with another.)*

Conquerre. *as* Conquerir.

Conquest: m. *An Estate, or Purchase compassed by a mans owne industrie, labour, or meanes; also, a thing got, or matter come by, wherein another is to haue a share; (therein differing from* Acquest.)

Conqueste: f. *A Conquest; the subduing of a forraine countrey; or, the inlarging of his owne dominions by the winning of other mens.*

Conquesté: m. ée: f. *Conquered, subdued; woon, gotten, purchased.*

Conquester. *as* Conquerir. *To subdue, conquer; win; get, purchase.*

Conquis: m. ise: f. *Conquered; subdued, vanquished, woon; ouermaistered, ouercome, wholly brought vnder; also, gotten, acquired, purchased (as in* Conquerir.)

Conroy: m. *Stuffe throughly tawed, or curried.*

Conroyé: m. ée: f. *Curried, tawed, or dressed, as leather; rough-hewed, chipped, squared, or fashioned as tymber; also, well wrought; well sadned, or setled, by working.*

Conroyement: m. *A currying, or dressing of leather; a chipping, or squaring of tymber.*

Conroyer. *To currie, tawe, or dresse, as leather; also, to chip, rough hew, or square, as tymber; and (metaphorically) to worke throughly; or, to sadden, or settle together by a through working.*

Conroyeur: m. *A Currier; a Leather dresser.*

Consacré: m. ée: f. *Consecrated, hallowed, dedicated, deuoted vnto.*

Consacrer. *To consecrate, hallow, dedicate, or deuote vnto.*

Consalme de mer. *The great horse-muskle.*

Consanguinité: f. *Consanguinitie, neerenesse in bloud, kindred by birth, or bloud.*

Consaul. *as* Conseil. *(an old word.)*

Consçachance: f. *A full knowledge, or notice of.*

Consçachant de. *Fully acquainted with, or priuie vnto; hauing notice, or knowledge enough of.*

Conscience: f. *Conscience; the testimonie of our owne knowledge, the witnesse of our owne thoughts; a remorse, or a remorsefull remembrance, of.*

Conscience à pont levis. *A very large conscience; the humor of such as dare commit, or will admit of, any villanie.*

Charger sa conscience. *To commit a wicked, or lewd act.*

Faire conscience de. *To sticke at, or make a scruple of.*

Qui veut la conscience monde, Il doit fuir le monde immonde: Prov. *Looke* Monde.

Conscientieusement. *Religiously, deuoutly, with a good conscience; curiously, scrupulously.*

Conscientieux: m. euse: f. *Conscientious; godlie, deuout, religious, of a good conscience, full of conscience; also, scrupulous, timerous, curious.*

Conscinomantie. *Diuination by a siue, and a paire of sheeres.* ¶Rab.

Consecutif: m. iue: f. *Consecutiue, or consequent; next or immediatly succeeding; ensuing necessarily, certainly following.*

Consecution: f. *A consequence, or consequent; an order, succession, following; a necessarie issue, or ensuing.*

Consecutivement. *Consequently.*

Conseigneur: m. *A fellow Lord; a Partner, Associate, equall in dominion, or seignorie.*

Conseil: m. *Counsell, aduise; a iudgement, or opinion demaunded, or giuen; also, a Court, Companie, Assemblie, or Association of Counsellors; The bodie of the Counsell; whence;*

Conseil des Affaires. *The Counsell of State; the Priuie Counsell; held ordinarily in the Kings closet, and most commonly a mornings, or at his getting vp; when the Packets of forraine Princes, Embassadours, and Gouernors of Prouinces be opened, and resolutions taken as well vpon them, as vpon other important, and State-affaires of the time; the ouerture, and dispatch whereof is committed ouer vnto the principall Secretaries, who euer attend his Maiestie in this Counsell, either alone, or with such Lords as he pleases extraordinarily to call vnto it.*

Conseil d'Estat. *An assemblie of Counsellors, wherein, when it concerns matters of warre, the Constable, when causes of Iustice, the Chancelor, the Presidents; and the Princes of the bloud, Peeres of France, Officers of the Crowne, Gouernours of Prouinces, chiefe Presidents of the Parliaments, and (by speciall fauour, or commission from the King) other great Personages, be assistants; yet none, with any obligation of ordinarie attendance, but a few of them (commonly of the long Robe) who haue pensions allowed them for it. This Counsell is thus tearmed when it is assembled about publicke, and important businesses; for vpon other occasions it is tearmed otherwise.*

Conseil estroit. *as* Conseil des Affaires.

Conseil des finances. *as* Conseil d'Estat; *when it is assembled about the ordering, or disposing of the Kings Reuenue.*

Conseil privé. *as* Conseil d'Estat; *but called thus when it is assembled about particular controuersies, or causes betweene partie and partie, and of some resemblance with those, which are determined at our Counsell Table.*

Conseil secret; & Conseil secret d'Estat; *as* Conseil des Affaires.

Le grand conseil. *A Court composed of foure Presidents (who are withall to be Maisters of Requests) and twentie Counsellors; which determine ordinarily of appeales from the Prouost of the Kings houshold; and extraordinarily of such causes as be referred vnto them by commission from* Le Conseil privé.

Le privé conseil. *as* Conseil privé.

Nos gens ne parlent pas en conseil, viz. *They gape so loud that all the house rings of them.*

A conseil de fol cloche de bois: Prov. *For woodcocks counsels wodden bells.*

Chose faicte conseil prins: Prov. *For things alreadie done the care's alreadie taken; matters once past it's bootlesse to talke of them; a businesse ended ends dispute about it.*

De chose perduë le conseil ne se remuë: Pro. *Aduise is idle when a thing is lost; or when things are lost why should we aske aduise?*

Il peche sagement qui fait folie par conseil: Prov. *Looke* Pecher.

La nuict donne conseil: Prov. *Night giues aduise; we say, take counsell of your pillow.*

Pour neant demande conseil qui ne le veut croire: Prov. *In vaine he counsell askes that will not trust in't.*

Conseiller: m. *as* Conseillier.

Conseiller. *To counsell, aduise, direct; persuade, admonish, warne.*

Se conseiller à. *To demaund counsell, take th'aduise, aske th'opinion, craue the direction, of.*

Se conseiller sur. *To examine, weigh, ponder; to aduise, deliberate, consult of.*

Conseillerie: f. *A Counsellorship; the place, or office of a Counsellor, or* Conseillier.

Conseillier: m. *A Counsellor; one that giues his aduise, or deliuers his opinion, vpon a doubt propounded, businesse discussed, or cause to be determined; hence, a priuie Counsellor vnto a Prince; a Senatour in a citie; and an Assistant in a Court of Iustice; also, (in Normand-French) an Aduocate, or Counsellor at Law.*

Conseillier de son oreille. *Said of a priuie Counsellor, whose aduise his Prince euer likes well, and loues to heare often; one that frames his wordes to fit the well-knowne humour of his Prince; one that, in respect thereof, is very gracious with him, or hath his eare.*

Consemblable: com. *Very like vnto, much resembling, matching with.*

Ses consemblables. *His fellowes, consorts, complices, companions.*

Consentant: m. ante: f. *Consenting, or partaking, with; accessarie, or agreeing, vnto; approouing, or allowing, of.*

Consentant du cas. *A consenter, accessarie, partaker.*

Consentement: m. *A consent; an agreement, or accord, vnto; an approbation, or allowance, of.*

Consentir. *To consent; accord, or agree, vnto; iumpe, or concurre, with; approue, or allow, of.*

Assez consent qui ne dit mot: Prov. *He consents enough that sayes nothing; (Many, who know not much more Latine, can say,* Qui tacet consentire videtur.)

Tel consent qui se repent: Prov. *Some yeelding (in hast) repent (at leisure;) or, some agreements prooue agreeuances.*

Consequemment. *Consequently; successiuely, by course, in order; thereafter.*

Consequence: f. *A consequence, consequent, (necessarie) sequele.*

Vne matiere de consequence. *A matter of importance, moment, or weight.*

Consequent: m. ente: f. *Consequent, following, successiue, succeeding, orderlie, well ranked, in consequence, fitly hanging together.*

Con-

Consequentieux: m. euse: f. *Most important, full of consequence.*

Consequutif: m. iue: f. *Consecutiue; or as* Consecutif.

Conserte: f. *A conference.*

Conserté: m. ée: f. *Ordained, made, stirred, or set, vp.*

Consertion: f. *A ioyning, coupling; interlacing, intermingling.*

Conservateur: m. *A Conseruator; Preseruer, Maintainer; Defendor, Protector; Sauer, or Sauior.*

Conservateur Apostolique. *The Popes Conseruator in Vniuersities; an Officer that both vpholds the priuiledges graunted, by the Church of Rome, thereto; and takes notice of all the Ecclesiasticall controuersies, and causes, therein.*

Conservateur des foires de Lyons. *A Magistrate, who hath iurisdiction ouer all manner of debtors, for commodities taken vp at any of the said Fayres.*

Conservateur Royal. *The Kings Conseruator in Vniuersities; an Officer that both maintaines the priuiledges graunted by the Crowne vnto them; and is their Iudge of all causes, and controuersies that be meerely ciuile, or lay. (In Paris the Prouost of the Citie alwaies holds this place.)*

Conservation: f. *A conseruation; keeping, maintaining; preseruation; defence, protection.*

Conservatoire: f. *Th' Office of a Conseruator; his Court, or the roome wherein he vseth to keepe it.*

Conservatrice: f. *A Conseruatrix; Preseruer esse; Protectrix, Defendere sse.*

Conserve: f. *Preseruation, gard, safe custodie, keeping; also, a Conserue, as of Roses, Violets, &c.*

Conserve de grain. *A caue, pit, or hole vnder ground, to keepe corne in.*

Navires de conserve. *Ships of a Fleet, or of one consort.*

Conservé: m. ée: f. *Conserued; kept, garded, maintained, preserued, saued; protected, defended, vpheld.*

Conserver. *To conserue; keepe, gard, maintaine, preserue, saue; defend, protect, vphold.*

Conserve-santé. *Holesome, or health-preseruing.*

Considerable: com. *Considerable; to be considered, aduised on, or thought of.*

Consideratif: m. *One that does things with consideration, and aduisement.*

Consideration: f. *Consideration; aduisement; also, discretion, circumspection, heedfulnesse, carefulnesse; also, an examination, or discussion of.*

Consideré: m. ée: f. *Considered, thought of, aduised on; examined, pondered, perpended, reuolued, weighed in the mind.*

Considereément. *Considerately, aduisedly, discreetly, circumspectly; with great consideration, vpon a good, or a safe, ground.*

Considerer. *To consider, aduise vpon, thinke of; examine; ponder, perpend, reuolue, or weigh in the mind.*

Consierge. *See* Concierge.

Consignation: f. *A consignation; presentation, exhibiting, deliuerie in hand, or into the hands of; also, the gaging, or laying downe of a stake, or pawne.*

Consignature: f. *A consignature; a full stamping, or absolute signature of.*

Consigné: m. ée: f. *Consigned; presented, exhibited, or deliuered in hand, or into the hands of; also, deliuered, or appointed ouer; also, deliuered, or layed downe, as a stake, pawne, or gage.*

Consigner. *To consigne; present, exhibite, or deliuer, in hand, or into the hands of; to deliuer, assigne, or appoint (absolutely) ouer; to deliuer, gage, or lay downe, as a pledge, pawne, or stake.*

Consilles. *Two conduits, or pipes in the throat.*

Consimilitude: f. *Consimilitude; likenesse, concurrence, equalitie, agreement together.*

Consin: m. *A Mite, or Weeuell.*

Consire: f. *The hearbe Comfrey, Consound, Asse eare, Knitbacke, Backwort.*

Consire moyenne. *Middle Consound, middle Comfrey, browne Bugle; also, the Daisie.*

La grande consire. *Great Comfrey, &c; as* Consire.

Petite consire. *The little wild Daisie, called otherwise, Bruisewort; also, the hearbe Prunell, Carpenters hearbe, Selfeheale, Hookeheale, Sicklewort.*

Consistence: f. *A consistence, or being; a residence, or setling.*

Consister. *To consist, be; rest, reside, abide; to settle, stand still, or at a stay.*

Consistoire: m. *A Consistorie; a Counsell house of, or Counsell held by, Prelats; a session, sitting, or assemblie of Ecclesiasticall persons.*

Consistorié: m. ée: f. *Censured, or determined of, in Consistorie.*

Consistorier. *To censure, or determine of, in Consistorie.*

Consolateur: m. *A consolator, solacer, comforter; also, a Corbell (in building;) or, as* Consolc de bastiment.

Consolation: f. *Consolation, comfort, solace.*

Consolde: f. *Comfrey, or Consound, Wall-wort, Asseeare.*

Consolc de bastiment: f. *A Corbell, or pendant of stone; a bracket, or cartridge, of timber.*

Consolé: m. ée: f. *Consolated, comforted, solaced.*

Consoler. *To comfort, solace; cherish, or cheere vp.*

Consolidation: f. *A consolidation, a strengthening, sound-making; a closing, or ioyning vp, as of a wound.*

Consolidé: m. ée: f. *Consolidated, made sound, healed, or closed vp.*

Consolider. *To consolidate, or make sound; to heale, or close vp, as a wound, or vlcer.*

Consommé: m. ée: f. *Consummated, accomplished, perfected, fulfilled, finished; summed vp.*

Consommé en Grammaire. *A perfect, or absolute Grammarian.*

Consommé en bonnes lettres. *A sound (and generall) Scholler.*

Consommer. *To consummate, accomplish, perfect, finish, fulfill; to make, or summe, vp.*

Consonance: f. *Consonance, accord, harmonie, concordance, agreement, good proportion.*

Consonant. *Consonant, accordant, harmonious, agreeing in sound, consorting with.*

Consone. *A Consonant.*

Consoner. *To accord, consort, agree, or sound, alike.*

Consors: m. *Consorts, mates, fellowes, complices, partakers, companions; also, neighbours, whose lands lye together.*

Consorte: f. ma Con. *My wife, yoake-mate, bedfellow.*

Consoulde: f. *The hearbe Comfrey, Consound, Asseeare, Knitbacke, Backwort.*

Consoulde moyenne. *Middle Consound, middle Comfrey, browne Bugle; also, the great white Daisie.*

Consoulde royale. *Larks heele, Larks spurre, Larks toe, Larks claw, Monks hood, Kings Consound.*

La grande Consoulde. *Comfrey Consound, great frey, &c, as* Consoulde.

La petite Consoulde. *The ordinarie little Daisie, and Bruisewort; or, as* Petite Consire.

Consourde. *as* Consoulde.

Conspection: f. *A conspection, seeing, beholding.*

Conspiration: f. *A conspiracie.*

Conspiré: m. ée: f. *Conspired; contriued, or complotted; entred into a conspiracie, with others.*

Conspirer. *To conspire; to enter into a conspiracie; to ioyne, or agree, in a plot, or opinion, with others.*

Constamment. *Constantly, stedfastly, firmely, stably, vnremoueably, perseueringly, euer alike, in one manner.*

Constance: f. *Constancie, stabilitie, stedfastnesse, firmenesse, vnremoueablenesse, perseuerance, strength of continuance.*

Constant. *Constant, stedfast, firme, stable; durable, sure, setled, vnremoueable, perseuering, euer the same.*

Conster. Il conste. *(as the Latin Impersonall* Constat) *it is cleere, plaine, certaine, euident, manifest, apparant; generally agreed on, out of all doubt, without any manner of controuersie.*

Constellation: f. *A constellation, or assemblie of starres together in one signe.*

Consternation: f. *Consternation, astonishment, dismay; a great, or stupifying, feare.*

Consterné: m. ée: f. *Astonished, dismayed, amazed, amated, deiected in courage, heart-fallen; afraid.*

Consterner. *To astonish, dismay, amaze; dull, deiect, amate; affray.*

Constipé: m. ée: f. *Constipated; costiue, or bound in bellie.*

Constitu: m. *An order, institution, decree, sentence, constitution, ordinance, act, statute; a matter throughly enacted, or determined.*

Constituant: m. *He that appointeth to his place, or setteth in his roome, some other.*

Constituant: m. ante: f. *Constituting, making, creating; ordaining; appointing, assigning vnto; establishing; setling, or confirming in.*

Constitué: m. ée: f. *Constituted, made, ordained, created; appointed vnto, established, setled, confirmed, in; also, concluded.*

Constitué prisonnier. *Taken prisoner; also, arrested, apprehended.*

Constitué sur vn'affaire. *Imployed as a Committee, or Commissioner, in a matter.*

Rente constituée. *A rent vpon morgage; or, a rent thats raised vpon, or procured by, money.*

Constituer. *To constitute, make, ordaine, create; appoint, or assigne vnto; also, to settle, establish; or, confirme, in.*

Constituer vne Rente sur. *To raise a rent vpon; or, to charge with a Rent.*

Constituëur: m. *A constitutor, maker, ordainer, appointer, establisher, enactor.*

Constitutif: m. iue: f. *Constitutiue; making, ordaining, enacting, appointing.*

Parties constitutives de l'homme. *The parts whereof he consists.*

Constitution: f. *A constitution, act, order, decree, determination, ordinance, appointment; also, the raysing of a Rent; also, the constitution, temper, or complexion of the bodie.*

Construction: f. *A construction; composition, building, framing; also, a construing, or exposition of words.*

Construict: m. icte: f. *Made, built, framed; also, construed, or expounded.*

Construire. *To build, make, frame, found; also, to construe, or expound, words.*

Constupration: f. *A constupration, rauishing, deflouring, defiling of a woman.*

Constuprer. *To constuprate, rauish, defloure, defile a woman.*

Consubstantial: m. ale: f. *Consubstantiall; of the same substance, or stuffe whereof another is made.*

Consubstantialité: f. *Consubstantialitie; the being of the substance whereof another is made.*

Consuivre. *See* Consuyvre.

Consul: m. *A Consull. (The old Romanes chose yearely two Consuls, to gouerne their citie, and command their Armies: In Paris,* Les Consuls *are fiue honest, and substantiall citizens, who determine all cases of debt (not exceeding* 500 l. Tour.) *betweene Marchant, and Marchant; Their authoritie continues but a yeare, and the vtmost punishment they can inflict is but imprisonment: In most Cities of Aquitaine the chiefe Gouernors are tearmed* Consuls; *the rest of the good townes in France haue such Consuls as Paris, by the names of,* Les Iuges, & Consuls des Marchands.)

Consulat: m. *A Consulship; the office, or place, of a Consul.*

Consultatif: m. iue: f. *Consultatiue; consulting.*

Qui a voix consultative. *Who (in a Court, or Counsell) propounds his opinion, deliuers his aduice, or giues his voice, as an Assistant; but neither concludes, nor determines, as Iudge.*

Consultation: f. *A consultation; a solemne deliberating, or discussing of; a deliberation, aduisement, or pawsing, on.*

Consulte. *as* Consultation.

Consulté. *Consulted, deliberated, pondered of.*

Consulter. *To giue, or take, aduise; to consult, or deliberate; ponder, or thinke of; rest, or pause on, the matter.*

Consulteur: m. *A consultor; a counsellor; an aduiser; a demaunder, or giuer, of aduise.*

Consumé: m. *A Coulis.*

Consumé: m. ée: f. *Consumed, wasted, spent out, worne away, brought vnto nothing.*

Consumer. *To wast, consume, spend out, weare away, destroy, bring vnto nothing.*

Consumption: f. *A consumption; destruction; consuming, wasting, wearing out; pining away.*

Consuyvre. *To ouertake, reach, attaine vnto; also, to get, obtaine, atchieue.*

Consyre: f. *See* Consire.

Contablerie: f. *A Constableship; the office of a Constable; or, place wherein his office is kept.*

Contact: m. *A mutuall touching, or carnall feeling, one of another.*

Contadin: m. *A countreyman, hind, swaine, clowne, boore, husbandman.*

Contagieux. *Contagious, infecting, pestilent.*

Contagion: f. *Contagion, infection, pestilent sicknesse.*

Contaminé: m. ée: f. *Defiled, polluted, contaminated; stained, violated.*

Contaminer. *To defile, pollute, contaminate; to staine, distaine, violate.*

Contant. *Telling, declaring, deliuering, reporting; also, counting, numbering, reckoning.*

Argent contant. *Sheere money, readie coyne.*

Argent contant porte medecine. *Looke* Argent.

Vous vous abusez contant. *You abuse your selfe openly, plainly, extreamely.*

Vous avez perdu tout contant. *You haue flatly, vtterly, absolutely, lost.*

Conte: m. *An Earle. See* Comte.

Conté: f. *An Earledome. See* Comté.

Conte: m. *A storie, relation, historie; tale, fib, fable. See* Compte.

Contes de la Cigogne. *Foolish, idle, vaine, fantasticall, stories; tales of a tub, or of a rosted horse.*

Contes de la quenouille. *Old wiues tales.*

Fin de conte. *To be briefe, to conclude, to come to an end; or, in the end of his tale.*

Ils en font leurs contes. *It is their common table talke; tis growne to be a publicke, or ordinarie ieast among them.*

Vn conte attire l'autre: Prov. *One tale drawes on another.*

De sot homme on n' en peut faire vn bon conte: Prov. *A sots whole life affoords not one good tale.*

Conte: m. *An account. See* Compte.

Ie sçay le conte de mon argent. *I know how much money I haue.*

Contemné: m. ée: f. *Contemned, despised, scorned, neglected, set at naught.*

Contemnement: m. *A contemning, despising, scorning, neglecting, setting at naught.*

Contemner. *To contemne, scorne, despise, neglect, make light of, set at nought.*

Contemneur. *A contemner, despiser, scorner; a disdainefull person; one that snuffes at euery thing, and likes nothing, or one that neglects, or disesteemes, another.*

Contemperé: m. ée: f. *Seasoned, mingled, tempered together.*

Contemperer. *To temper, season, qualifie, mingle one thing with another.*

Contemplateur. *A contemplator, great thinker, serious beholder of matters.*

Contemplatif: m. iue: f. *Contemplatiue, musing, thinking much, mind-beholding, meditating.*

Contemplatifs: m. *Certain Friers (of S. Marie Maudlins Order) who feed on all sorts of flesh, and weare blacke vpper habits, and white vnder ones.*

Contemplation: f. *Contemplation, deepe consideration, inward beholding of, profound musing on, a matter.*

Contemplé: m. ée: f. *Contemplated, deeply considered, or mused on.*

Contemplement: m. *A contemplating, deepe considering, profound musing; serious beholding of.*

Contempler. *To contemplate, muse, or meditate vpon; to behold seriously, to view with great earnestnesse, or affection.*

Contempleur. *as* Contemplateur.

Contemporain: m. aine: f. *Of a like time, equall age, one standing; that liues in the same time.*

Contempt: m. *Contempt, scorne, despight, neglect.*

Contemptible: com. *Contemptible, abiect, base; fit to be scorned, neglected, disdained, sleightly regarded.*

Contenance: f. *The countenance, looke, cheere, visage, fauor; gesture, posture, behauior, carriage; presence, or composition of the whole bodie; also, the fanne, or little skreene, which women hold before their faces, to preserue them from the scorching heat of a great fire; also, the small looking glasse which some Ladies haue vsually hanging at their girdles; also, one of their Snuffkins, or Muffes; (called so in times past when they vsed to play with it for feare of being out of countenance.)*

Contenancé: m. ée: f. *Countenanced, fauoured, graced.*

Maintien contenancé. *Gracefull audacitie, comelie boldnesse; a constant, and pleasing set, or garbe of the countenance.*

Contenancer. *To countenance, fauor, grace, maintaine, giue countenance vnto; also, to frame, or set the face handsomely; to giue it a gracefull and constant garbe.*

Contendre. *To striue, contend, brable, debate, wrangle, iarre, be at oddes, or variance, with.*

Contenir. *To containe, hold, or comprehend; also, to bridle, restraine, moderate; keepe in.*

Se contenir. *To refraine, forbeare, withhold from.*

Content. *Content, satisfied, pleased with what he hath; also, indifferent, which takes all things well.*

Coeur content & manteau sur l'espaule: Prov. *In an honest estate, how meane soeuer, there is great contentment to be found. See* Coeur.

Contenté: m. ée: f. *Contented, satisfied, satiated, fully pleased, throughly appeased.*

Contentement: m. *Satisfaction, contentment, full pleasure, or delight in; also, indifferencie.*

Faire contentement. *To doe one reason, or giue him satisfaction.*

Contenter. *To content, satisfie, satiate, fulfill the mind, or appetite; also, to please; quiet, pacifie.*

Se Contenter. *To liue at rest, be in peace, rest at ease; to quiet, please, content himselfe with.*

Assez a qui se contente: Prov. *We say, a contented mind is a great treasure; or, is worth all.*

Contentieusement. *Contentiously, litigiously, debatefully, with much wrangling.*

Contentieux: m. euse: f. *Contentious, debatefull, wrangling, litigious, full of controuersie.*

Contention: f. *Contention, strife, debate, variance, controuersie, quarrelling; brawling, iarring, brabling.*

Contentor. Droict de Registre, ou de con. *is* xl. s. Tour. *vpon euery Charter; The fee of the* Audienciers *of Chaunceries.*

Contenu: m. uë: f. *Contained, comprehended, held in.*

Contenuë: f. *Capacitie; or, a containing.*

Conter. *To tell, say, speake, report, deliuer, declare, expresse, relate, reckon vp.*

Tu m'en veux conter. *Thou art disposed to talke.*

Tu nous en contes bien. *Tis a wise tale you tell vs; or, such a tale pist a goose.*

Vn homme qui conte vingt & onze. *A coxcombe, noddypeake, ninnyhammer.*

Contereau. *as* Comptereau. *A bill of reckoning, &c.*

Conterolle: m. *as* Contreroolle.

Contesse: f. *A Countesse; the wife of an Earle.*

Contestablement. *By way of protestation.*

Contestation: f. *A contestation; a protestation, taking, or calling to witnesse; also, a contesting, striuing, debating, reasoning, brabling about a matter; also, a contestation against; a gainsaying, denying, or waging, of Law.*

Contestation de cause. *An opening, before a Iudge, the points contained in the Bill and Answer.*

Contestation en cause. *A Rule giuen by the Iudge vpon the said opening; or the waging of Law by the defendant, hauing made a default, or being put from his other helpes.*

Contestation feinte, *is but a flourish or shew of contestation, by reason, or vertue, of defaults.*

Contestation vraye. *A resolute, or peremptorie contestation made by both parties.*

Contesté: m. ée: f. *Contested; protested; called, or taken to witnesse; also, debated, reasoned, argued, brabled about; also, denied, gainsayed, contested against.*

Contester. *To contest; call, or take to witnesse, make an earnest protestation, or complaint vnto; also, to brable, argue, debate a matter with; also, to denie, gainesay, contest against.*

Contester la cause. *To open before a Iudge the chiefe points of the bill and answer.*

Conteur: m. *An idle talker, vaine speaker, ordinarie teller of old wiues tales; also, as* Compteur; *also, a Counsellor, or Atturney intertained for the pleading, or opening of a cause in Court.*

`A fol conteur sage escouteur: Prov. *A foolish talker had need to find a wise hearer; or, let him talke neuer so foolishly, they are wise enough that heare him.*

Contexte: m. *A context; a whole web, composition, worke; or, an interlacing, ioyning, or weauing together; also, the forme, or stile of a Proces, Booke, or Discourse.*

Par vn contexte. *Altogether; with one tenour, in one manner; without any interruption, or intermission.*

Contigu: m. uë: f. *Neere adioyning, fast by, close together, touching one another.*

Contigué: m. ée: f. *Ioyned; layed neere, or close vnto.*

Contin. Mon contin. *My countreyman.*

Continemment. *Continently, soberly, chastly; sparingly; with much temper, and moderation; abstemiously.*

Continence: f. *Continencie, sobrietie, forbearance of, abstinence from, pleasure.*

Continent. *Continent; sober, moderate; abstinent, abstemious, delights-forbearing.*

Continu: m. uë: f. *Continuall, perpetuall, day by day, without intermission, or interruption; intire, whole.*

Continu à faire quelque chose. *Diligent, laborious, euer at it, perseuering in it.*

Fiévre continuë. *A continuall feuer, whose fit neuer ceaseth till the disease, or diseased, end.*

Continuätion: f. *A continuation, or holding on without any stop, or intermission; a perseuerance.*

Continuë: f. *as* Continuätion.

`A la continuë l'eau cave la pierre: Prov. *At length, or in continuance of time, the water pierceth stone.*

Continué: m. ée: f. *Continued, held on; perseuered in; prolonged, drawne out in length, perpetuated.*

Continuël: m. ëlle: f. *Continuall, perpetuall, vnstinted, without intermission, daylie, that euer dureth.*

Continuëllement. *Continually, incessantly, without stop, or stint; perpetually, euerlastingly, for euer.*

Continuër. *To continue, last, hold out; proceed, perseuer, hold on; to perpetuate, prolong, draw out in length.*

Continuïté. *Continuation; a wholenesse; an intirenesse, or intire coniunction.*

Solution de continuïté. *The diuision of a whole part, or thing.*

Contoir: m. *A Closet, or Counting-house.*

Contorsion: f. *A contorsion; a wrything, wresting, drawing, or pulling awry.*

Contorsion de maschoire. *A disease whereby the lower iaw is drawne altogether awry.*

Contour: m. le contour d'une ville. *The compasse, or whole round of territorie, or ground, lying next vnto, and about, a towne.*

Contourements fievreux. *The turnings, tossings, and other vnquiet stirrings of those that haue an ague.*

Contournable: com. *Plyable; which may be turned any way.*

Contournant. *Turning, wheeling, winding about.*

Contournant la teste comme vn Singe qui avalle pillules. *Wheeling his head like a Mare ouer thistles.*

Contourné: m. ée: f. *Turned round, wheeled, or compassed about.*

Contournement: m. *A nimble turning, or winding.*

Contourner. *To round, turne round, wheele, compasse about.*

Contract: m. *A contract, bargaine, agreement; a coaping; treatie; couenant.*

Contractation: f. *A bargaining, contracting, couenanting with.*

Contracte: m. *as* Contract.

Contracté: m. ée: f. *Contracted, bargained, agreed; coaped, or couenanted with.*

Contracter. *To contract, bargain, agree; to coape, chaffer, couenant with.*

Contraction de nerfs: f. *The Crampe; a conuulsion, or shrinking of the sinewes.*

Contracture: f. *A contraction, straitening, gathering, or drawing vp narrower and narrower; a making smaller in one place then in another.*

Contradiction: f. *A contradiction, gainsaying, thwarting; a crosse word, or speech.*

Contrahant: m. ante: f. *Contracting, or making a contract.*

Contraignable: com. *Constrainable, compellable.*

Contraigneur. *A forcer, compeller, constrainer.*

Contrainct: m. cte: f. *Constrained, compelled, forced, thrust, or put, on against his will.*

Le bransle contrainct. *The shaking of the sheets.*

Contraincte: f. *Constraint, violence, compulsion.*

`A toute contraincte. *Most strictly, in all extremitie.*

Sans contraincte. *Freely, willingly, of his owne accord.*

Contrainctement. *Forcibly, violently, by compulsion, by constraint.*

Contraindre. *To constraine, compell, force, thrust forward, or against his will.*

Contraire: com. *Contrarie, aduerse; against, much disagreeing; also, directly oueragainst.*

Au contraire. *Contrariwise, on the other side, or part, much otherwise; also, oueragainst.*

Contrarié: m. ée: f. *Contraried, crossed, impugned, thwarted, resisted, withstood, or striuen against.*

Contrarier à. *To contrarie, crosse, thwart, impugne; resist, withstand, striue, or be against.*

Contrarieté: f. *Contrarietie; extreame difference, maine opposition, mightie disagreement.*

Contraste: m. *Withstanding, strife, contention, difference, repugnance.*

Contrasté: m. ée: f. *Withstood, striuen, contended against.*

Contraster. *To striue, withstand, contend against.*

Contravention. *as* Contrevention.

Contre. *(Substantiuely, as)* faire le contre. *To second, assist, helpe forward; and (in Musicke) to beare the burden; or sing the Plainesong whereon another descants. Looke* Faire.

Contre. *Against, contrarie to; much oppugnant, opposite, or in opposition, vnto; also, ouer-against, on the other side; also, towards; as,* Contre disner; contre la nuict; *and sometimes in composition; as in* Contre-bas, Contremont, &c.

Il estoit tout contre. *He was very neere, or hard by; also, he was right ouer against, them.*

Halener contre. *To blow vpon.*

Contr'-adveu: m. *An Answer, or Opposition to a Bill of Complaint for possession of moueables.*

Contreadveu. *See* Contr'-adveu.

Contre-advoué: m. ée: f. *Owned, or claymed by seuerall parts, one saying tis his, another that tis his.*

Contr'amour: m. *A holie, and honest loue; opposite vnto the lasciuious, & dissolute passion, which is commonly tearmed loue.*

Contr'animé: m. ée: f. *Animated, or incouraged, against.*

Contr'antidote: m. *A remedie, or poison against a preseruatiue; a counterantidote.*

Contr'applegement. *An Answer, or Opposition, to a Bill of Complaint for the possession of an immoueable.*

Contrebalance: f. *A counterbalance, or counterpeise.*

Contrebalancé: m. ée: f. *Counterbalanced, counterpeised.*

Contrebalancer. *To counterbalance, or counterpeise; to weigh against; or to esteeme by; to make of equall weight with.*

Contrebande. Marchandise de contrebande. *Marchandise that is forbidden (by Proclamation, &c.)*

Contrebarre: f. *A counterbarre; the long (outward) barre, wherewith some (two-leaued) dores and windowes, and the most shop-windowes, are shut in.*

Contrebarré: m. ée: f. *Counterbarred; barred, or shut in, on the outside; also (in Blason) counterbarrie.*

Contre-bas. *Downeward.*

Contre-base: f. *A counterbase; the lowest part of a Basis; or the part, or peece, whereon it stands.*

Contre-basse: f. *The Base part in Musicke.*

Contrebondi. *Rebounded, leaped backe or against.*

Contrebondir. *To rebound; leape backe, or against.*

Contreboutant. *as* Contrefort.

Contrebouté: m. ée: f. *Vnderpropped, borne vp, or borne against.*

Contrebouter. *To vnderprop, support, beare vp, or, beare against.*

Contrecarre: f. *A counterstrength, opposition, resistance, defence; (also, a reasoning, or arguing) against; also, comparison, or equalitie.*

Contrecarré: m. ée: f. *Set, or opposed against; also, compared, equalled, or layed in ballance with.*

Contrecarrer. *To resist, withstand, contrarie, set, or oppose himselfe against; also, to paragon, equall, compare, set in euen ballance with.*

Contrecedule: f. *The counterpane of a Scedule.*

Contrechange: m. *A counterchange; mutuall changing, or, crosse exchange.*

Contrechangé: m. ée: f. *Counterchanged, exchanged acrosse.*

Contrechanger. *To counterchange, or exchange acrosse one thing for another.*

Contrechanter. *To record in singing; to answer in the same note, or tune.*

Contrecharger. *To countercharge; to interchange burthens, or accusations.*

Contrechifre: m. *A countercypher; a note explanatorie of particular cyphers; or, as,* Le Chifre d'un Prince.

Contrechifrer. *To answere cyphers with cyphers; also, to expound cyphers; also, to requite priuat affection in a priuat fashion.*

Contrecoeur. *as* Contrecueur.

Contrecourbé: m. ée: f. *Bent fromward, or one from the other.*

Contrecourber. *To bend one from another, as wrestlers doe their backes.*

Contrecueur: m. *Loathing, irkesomenesse; also, the backe of a chimney.*

Cela me vient à contrecueur. *That goes against my stomacke; my thoughts loath, mind hates, heart abhorres, it.*

Contredict: m. *A contradiction, gainesaying; refutation, confutation; a crosse answer; a replication; a prouing of the contrarie.*

Contredict: m. icte: f. *Contradicted, gainesayed; thwarted, contraried in words; refelled, refuted, confuted.*

Contredigué: m. ée: f. *Fenced, or fortified with bankes and ditches against bankes and ditches.*

Contrediguer. *To fence, or fortifie with banks and ditches; or, to oppose, or set vp, banks against banks.*

Contredire. *To contradict, gainesay, thwart, crosse, contrarie in words; also, to refell, conuince, confute.*

Contredisant: m. ante: f. *Crossing, contradicting, thwarting, gainsaying; quarrelsome, contentious, contrarie, crosse.*

Contredise: f. *as* Contredite.

Contredite: f. *A contradiction, or crosse speech.*

Contrée: f. *A Countrey, Land, Region, Part, Coast, Quarter.*

Contr'effort: m. *A counter effort; or, effort vsed against force; a withstanding, striuing, resistance, indeuour against a strong, and stirring, aduersarie.*

Contr'elider. *To counterhit, counterstrike, counterdash, countersquize; to breake a stroke, or dash, &c, with a stroake, or dash &c.*

Contr'escarpe: f. *A counterscarfe, or countermure in a fortified towne.*

Contr'eschangé: m. ée: f. *Counterchanged.*

Contr'eschanger. *as* Contrechanger.

Contr'escript: m. *A reply vnto a former writing; a writing repugnant; a confutation, or treatise written against; also, a copie.*

Contr'escript: m. ipte: f. *Confuted, written against; also, copied, written out.*

Contr'escrire. *To confute, or write against; also, to copie, or write out.*

Contr'-essay: m. *A second essay, a further triall of.*

Contr'estang: m. *A Poole-damme; a backe-poole, or counter-pond; a great ditch, or hollow ground, whereinto the water of a Pond, thats to be fished, is let.*

Contr'ester. *To withstand, resist, contend with; to repugne.*

Contrefaict: m. icte: f. *Counterfeit, adulterate, fained, forged, false; also, deformed, disfigured, misshapen, ill fauoured; crooked, hulchbacked; or (as we say) a changeling.*

Contrefaire. *To counterfeit, imitate, resemble, faine.*

Contrefaire le loup en paille. *See* Loup.

Se contrefaire. *To dissemble, or disguise himselfe, to seeme other then he is.*

Contre-fenestre: f. *A woodden window (on the outside of a glasen one) a counter window, or outward window.*

Contrefente: f. *The bruise, or craze of a bone in another, or opposite, part to the place where the blow (that caused it) was giuen; this happens, especially, in the skull.*

Contreferme. *A counter-affirmation, or coûter-auouchment; an affirmation of that whereof another affirmes the contrarie.*

Contreferme: m. ée: f. *Counter-affirmed, counter-auouched; the contrarie whereof is affirmed, or auouched.*

Contrefermer. *To oppose an affirmation vnto an affirmation; to affirme the contrarie of that which another hath affirmed; a Law-tearme.*

Contrefeu: m. *An yron backe, or Plate for the backe, of a chimney.*

Contre-fil. à contre-fil. *Contrariwise, cleane kamme, or against the haire.*

Contrefinesse: f. *Counter-cunning, deceiuing of the deceiuer; the meeting with as craftie a knaue as himselfe.*

Contreflaté: m. ée: f. *Whose flatterie is requited, or answered with flatterie.*

Contreflater. *To returne one faire word, or flatterie for another; to flatter as fast as another.*

Contreflux: m. *An ebbe, or ebbing; the fall, or going out, of a Tide; or a checke, or stop, vnto a Tide.*

Contrefort. *(in Architecture) a Buttresse, prop, or shore-post; an vp-bearing arch, or pillar.*

Contrefortuner. *To arme against the iniuries of fortune; to make shift for one (howsoeuer the world goe.)*

Contrefrontail: m. *The brow-peece, or vpmost post, of a dore; a haunse, or breast summer.*

Contregage: m. *A counter-gage, or counter-pawne;* (Que aucuns seigneurs ont pretendu, pour pouvoir de leur auctorité faire prinses, quand on leur avoit fait tort. ¶Ragueau.)

Contre-garde: m. *An vnder Warden, or counter-warden.*

Contre-garde des monnoyes. *An Officer of the Mint; who takes notice, and keepes a reckoning, of the mettall that is deliuered in to be coyned; and afterward ouersees the working thereof, together with the Warden, whose place he executes, (as the other his) in absence.*

Contregardé: m. ée: f. *Kept, saued, preserued, made much of, looked well vnto.*

Contregarder. *To keepe, saue, preserue, conserue, looke well to, make much of.*

Se contregarder. *To reserue, spare, or forbeare himselfe; to take his ease.*

Contrehastier: m. *A Racke, to turne spits on.*

Contrehaulte: f. *as* Haultecontre.

Contr'imiter. *To resemble, imitate, counterfeit; or to imitate one that imitates him.*

Contr'invective: f. *A counter-inuectiue; an answer to an inuectiue.*

Contrejouëur: m. *A counter-player; an aduersarie, or opponent, in play.*

Contre-lettre: f. *A counter-letter, or counter-maund; a retractation of a letter by letter; and particularly, a priuat release, or acquittance, in discharge of a Bond passed; or a priuat discharge of a dutie, or seruice acknowledged, before a publicke Notarie.*

Contre-lettre secrette. *Notice giuen in writing from a buyer vnto a seller, of a priuat agreement made betweene them, contrarie to the tenor of the deed they haue passed before a Notarie; or, a priuat agreement made betweeee two that are contracted, without the knowledge, or consent of their kindred that were present at the contract.*

Contrelouër. *To returne praise with praise, or a good word for a good word; to commend one that hath commended him before; to scratch the backe of one who hath alreadie clawed his elbow.*

Contrelutté: m. ée: f. *Wrastled, striuen, contended against.*

Contrelutter. *To wrastle, striue, contend against.*

Contre-maistre: m. *The Maisters mate in a ship.*

Contremanche: f. *A false sleeue, halfe sleeue, or, drawer ouer a sleeue.*

Contremand: m. *A countermaund; a reuocation, or contradiction of a former commaund.*

Contremandé: m. ée: f. *Countermaunded; contradicted.*

Contremandement: m. *A countermaund, or countermaunding.*

Contremander. *To countermaund; to recall, or contradict, a former commaund.*

Contremarque: f. *A countermarke.*

Contremejane. *The second mizen, or after-mizen, of a ship.*

Contrementir. *To set one ly against another.*

Contremettre. *To oppose; obiect, lay, set, or wage against.*

Contremine: f. *A countermine; a mine digged, by defendants, within a fortresse, to meet with another made by the enemie, without it.*

Contreminé: m. ée: f. *Countermined.*

Contreminer. *To countermine.*

Contremont. *Vpward; also, vp; as,*

Contremont l'eau. *Vp the water, directly against the streame.*

Contremonté: m. ée: f. *Mounted, or got vp against.*

Contremonter. *To mount, or goe vp against.*

Contremunir. *To fortifie inner, or hinder parts, thereby to sustaine the outward, or forward, ones; also, to repaire suddainely suddaine ruines; as in a siege.*

Contreoffrir. *To change his offer; to offer otherwise then before; or, to make an offer contrarie to that he made before.*

Contreouvrier: m. *One that works against another.*

Contrepan: m. *A pledge, gage, or pawne, especially of an immoueable; (It is commonly the eight pennie of the worth of land, as it is rented) or as* Hypotheque.

Contrepané: m. ée: f. *Pledged, pawned, engaged.*

Contrepaner. *To pledge, pawne, engage an immoueable; also, as* Compenser.

Contrepant. *A gage; or counterpane; or as* Contrepan.

Contrepensé: m. ée: f. *Disliked, or distrusted after liking, or trust; thought otherwise of then before.*

Contrepenser. *To thinke otherwise then he hath done; to dislike a thing which he hath affected, or distrust those whom he hath relyed on.*

Contrepenseur: m. *A counterthinker; one that thinks otherwise then, or contrarie to, that he hath done; one that changes, or doubts of, the conceit, or assurance hee hath had of a thing.*

Contrepesant. *Counterpeising; counteruailing.*

Contrepesé. *Counterpeised.*

Contrepeser. *To counterpeise; counteruaile, weigh in equall ballance.*

Mal poise qui ne contrepoise: Prov. *He peiseth ill that counterpeiseth not; he vses not good lucke aright that thinkes not of, or prouides not for, ill lucke.*

Contrepeter. *To answer one cracke with another; also, to counterfeit, or play the counterfeit.*

Con-

Contrepicqué: m. ée: f. *Countergirded, counterpricked, counternipped.*

Contrepicquer. *To returne gird for gird; to giue a nip for a nip; or, one pricke for another.*

Contre-pied. *That which we call Counter in hunting; whence;*

Tenir contrepied à. *To set, or hold his foot against another mans, thereby to stop him from going any further; to crosse, or impeach all he may the designes, or enterprises of another.*

Contrepleige: m. *A Countersuretie; one thats bound to saue a suretie harmelesse.*

Contrepleigement: m. *A counterband; or, the securitie giuen to a suertie.*

Contrepleiger. *To saue a suretie harmelesse by counterband, &c; To giue him a countersuretie, or other securitie.*

Contreplié: m. ée: f. *Bent, bowed, or foulded backe; made straight thereby.*

Contreplier. *To bend, bow, or fould backe; to make, or set straight by such a bending, &c.*

Contrepoids. *as* Contrepois.

Contrepoil. à contrepoil. *Against the wooll, the wrong way, cleane contrarie, quite kamme.*

ça que ie t'espluche à contrepoil. *Seeke* Esplucher.

Contrepoinct: m. *The backe stitch, or quilting stitch; also, a quilt, counterpoint, (quilted) couering; also, a crossing, difference, opposition; also, a ground, or plainsong (in Musicke.)*

A contrepoinct; ou à contrepoincts. *By a quilting, with quilt stitch, or in a quilted fashion; also, backward and forward, interchangeably; now one way then another; also, crossely, thwartly, oppositely, contrarie-waies.*

Contrepoincte: f. *as* Contrepoinct.

Contrepoincté: m. ée: f. *Quilted, wrought with the backe stitch; also, interchanged, set backeward and forward; crossed, stood against, opposed, or in opposition with.*

I'ay la peau toute contrepoinctée de coups. *My skinne-coat hath receiued as many knockes as a quilt hath stitches.*

Contrepoincter. *To quilt, to worke the backe stitch, or worke with the backe stitch; also, to interchange, or set backeward and forward; also, to crosse, thwart, oppose vnto, stand opposite against, bee in opposition with.*

Contrepoinctier: m. *A Quilter, or quilt-maker.*

Contrepoint; & **Contrepointer**; *as* Contrepoincte; & Contrepoincter.

Contrepointerie: f. *The shop of a Quilter, or Counterpoint-maker.*

Contrepois: m. *Counterpois, equall weight; also, a ground, or plaine-song, in Musicke.*

Bailler contrepois. *To counterpoise, balast, make of euen or equall weight.*

Marcher à contrepois. *To walke formally, or by line and leuell; to proportion, or measure out his steps.*

Contrepoison: m. *A counterpoison, antidote, medicine, or preseruatiue against poison.*

Contreporteur: m. *as* Bisoüart *(So tearmed, because he carries his packe, or burthen before him.)*

Contrepotencé: m. ée: f. *Counterpotencie (a tearme of Blason.)*

Contrequarre. *as* Contrecarre.

Contrequerant: m. *A riuall, competitor, concurrent.*

Contrequictence: f. *A counter-acquittance.*

Contrerepliqué: m. ée: f. *Replied againe, or against.*

Contrerepliquer. *To replie againe, or against.*

Contrerolle: m. *A controlement, or contrarolement; the copie of a roll (of accounts &c;) a Paralell of the same qualitie and content, with th'originall; also, a controlling, or ouerseeing; and, th'Office of a Controller, or ouerseer; also, a Controller, or ouerseer.*

Contrerollé: m. ée: f. *Controlled, ouerseene, obserued; also, the copie whereof is taken, and kept.*

Contreroller. *To controll; obserue, ouersee, spie faults in; also, to take, and keepe a copie of a roll of accounts; to play the controller any way.*

Contrerolleur: m. *A Controller; obseruer, ouerseer; properly, an Officer, that takes notes, or keepes a roll, of another Officers accounts, thereby to discouer him if he do amisse.*

Contrerolleurs des Aides. *Controllers of th'*Aides, *looke that the* Esleus, *Assessors, Collectors, and Receiuors of Subsidies doe their duetie; of all the particulers whereof they must euerie yeare send a roll into the Chamber of Accounts.*

Contrerolleur de l' Audience de France. *The Controller of the Chancerie attendant on the kings person; vnto whom* les,

Contrerolleurs des Chanceleries *(whereof there is in euerie Court of Chauncerie one) send halfe-yearely a particular account of the reuenue of the Seale receiued in their seuerall places.*

Contrerolleurs du Domaine. *Controllers of the Kings Demaine; one established in euerie seat of ordinarie Receit for the Demaine; who is to assist at the said Receit; at the making of leases of farmes; and at the sales of wood, wine, corne, hay, fish, &c, got in the Kings lands; and is to take notice of all escheats, dueties, and rights of Seigneurie, due, or occurring thereby; and keepes a reckoning of all works, reparations, almes, costs of suit, and other charges, defrayed by th'ordinarie Receiuors: Of all which he makes a roll, and sends it vnto the Treasurers generall, who therby keepe in awe the said Receiuors.*

Contrerolleur general de l' Artillerie. *The Controller generall of th'Ordnance; next in place, and degree vnto the Lieutenant: he keepes a Register of all munition that comes into, or goes out of, the store; and Inuentories (deliuered vnto him by the Warden generall) of all that remaines in particular Fortresses, &c; and certifies them, with his controlement of them, euerie yeare, into th'Exchequer.*

Contrerolleur general du Domaine. *One established in euerie generalitie by Henry the third in the yeare 1581, and suppressed again by himselfe in the yere 1584.*

Contrerolleurs generaux des finances. *One in euerie generall Receit, who lookes that the kings money be payed ouer by the particular Receiuors (or farmers) vnto the generall one; to which end they are to bring vnto him the others acquitances, which if they omit, or slacke, he informes the Treasurers generall who the fault is in. The money being paied, he keepes one key of the chest wherein tis layed, and the Receiuor generall (in whose house it stands) another; this vntill, amounting vnto a round summe, they both together see it conueyed vnto th'Exchequer. Of all which, as also of euery sort of coyne so conueyed, and of the charge of leuying, and conueying it, he is to send a roll, or Inuentorie into the Chamber of Acccount.*

Contrerolleur general des guerres. *Tearmed also,* Secretaire, & Con. general des guerres. *The Controller generall of the warres; Looke* Secretaire.

Contrerolleurs des Mines. *Controllers of the mines; euery one whereof is bound to send, from yere to yere, one Roll, or controlement (containing the proportion of siluer, which hath beene deliuered by the Master of the mines vnto the masters of the mint, or otherwise drawn from, and fined within, the said Mines that yeare) vnto the Receiuers, or Treasurers within whose charge the Mines are; and another vnto the chiefe Maister of the Mint.*

Contrerolleurs prouinciaux, ou ordinaires, des guerres. *Prouinciall, ordinarie, or inferior Controllers of the warres; must, in the seuerall Prouinces assigned vnto them, be present at all Musters, and fifteene dayes after euerie one, send vnto the Controller generall a summarie thereof, containing, the iust number of the men that were mustered, and an account of the moneys paid, or laid out thereat.*

Conteroolle: & Contreroolleur; *as* Contrerolle, &c.

Contreruse: f. *A counter-sleight; a wile for a wile; one tricke in lieu of another.*

Contre-sanglot: m. *A Tab; the leather whereto a girth is fastened; a girth-leather.*

Contrescarpe. *A counterscarfe, or countermure.*

Contrescedule: m. *The counterpane of a Schedule.*

Contreschange: m. *A counterchange, interchange, crosse exchange.*

Contrechangé: m. ée: f. *Counterchanged.*

Contreseel: m. *A (little) seale put vnto a labell, &c, whereby diuers writings alreadie sealed are ioyned, or closed together; a counter-seale.*

Contreseeller. *To seale the labell, &c, whereby sealed writings are ioyned, or fastened together.*

Contresigné: m. ée: f. *Subsigned; signed after, or vnder, the signature of another.*

Contresigner. *To subsigne; to signe a letter, &c, or put his name, or set his marke vnto it, after, or vnder, another; (so doe the French Secretaries of State set their names vnto letters Patents, vnder the Kings.)*

Contresing: m. *A subsignature; a hand, name, or marke, set to a letter, &c, vnder another; a subscription made lower than th'other.*

Contresommer. *To reuoke, or countermaund, a Summons, or Citation.*

Contresonné: m. ée: f. *The contrarie whereof is sounded.*

Contresonner. *To sound the contrarie, or to the contrarie.*

Contre-soufflé: m. ée: f. *Counter-blowne, crosse-blown; blowne on both sides, or blowne vp two contrarie wayes.*

Contretaille: f. *The one part of a tallie, or score, alreadie marked, or notched; also, the Counter-tenor part, in Musicke, and he that sings, or beares, it.*

Contretaluër. *To opposse banke vnto banke, or causey against causey; to resist, or strengthen, as with a double banke, or causey.*

Contretemperament: m. *A crosse, or contrarie temper; whence;*

Faire vn contr. à la nature. *To alter nature.*

Contre-temps. *Ill, or false time; or, motions out of time.*

Contreteneur: m. *The Counter-tenor part in Musicke.*

Contretenir. *To hold, or hale, against; also, to challenge, quarell, debate for, pretend title vnto, a thing against another.*

Contretenon de potence. *A stop (in a watch, or clock.)*

Contretenu. *Held against, or on th'other side; also, claimed, challenged, quarelled for, pretended vnto.*

Contreteste. faire contreteste à; *To withstand, resist, make head against.*

Contretiré: m. ée: f. *Drawne against; also, drawne after the patterne of.*

Contretirer. *To tug, hale, pull; hurle, throw, fling, against; also, to draw after the patterne of.*

Contretrahison: f. *A counter-treason; treason against treason.*

Contretrancher. *To counter-trench, or fortifie against an enemie intrenched.*

Contretraversant: m. ante: f. *Counter-crossing, counter-trauersing.*

Contreval. *Downeward; also, downe.*

Contrevenant: m. ante: f. *Swaruing, transgressing, departing from; going, or doing against an agreement, promise, or bargaine; also, crossing, thwarting, contradicting; resisting.*

Contrevengé: m. ée: f. *Fully reuenged.*

Contrevenger. *To reuenge one blow, or iniurie, with another.*

Contrevenir. *To swarue, transgresse, decline, go, or depart from; to do contrarie to promise, or otherwise than was agreed; also, to crosse, thwart, contradict, resist, or be against.*

Contrevent: m. *A contrarie mind.*

Contreventer. *To hold against the wind:* ¶Rab.

Contrevention: f. *A swaruing from a promise, or contract; a going against ones word; also, a thwarting, contradiction; resistance.*

Contrevenu: m. uë: f. *Swarued, transgressed, gone from his word, or agreement; also, crossed, thwarted, resisted, opposed against.*

Contre-vitre. *A counter-window, outward-window, or fence for a glasse window.*

Contreuve. *A fib, leasing; tale of inuention; or matter inuented.*

Contribuable: com. *Contributable; fit, able, or accustomed, to contribute; liable, or subiect vnto contribution.*

Contribué. *Contributed.*

Contribuer. *To contribute, to giue, or disburse together, to make a common purse, to lay their moneyes together.*

Contributeur. *A contributer.*

Garend contributeur. *See* Garent.

Contribution: f. *A contribution; a ioynt gift of many; also, as* Desconfiture; *A distribution, or sharing of a debtors, or bankrupts goods among all his creditors.*

Contristé: m. ée: f. *Grieued, afflicted, made sorrowfull.*

Contrister. *To grieue, sadden, afflict, make sorrowfull.*

Contrit: m. ite: f. *Contrite, aggrieued, remorsefull, most penitent, or sorrowfull, for misdeeds.*

Contrition: f. *Contrition, remorse, repentance; heartie sorrow, inward lamenting for, a painefull apprehension, or memorie of, offences.*

Controle, & controolle. *as* Contrerolle.

Controngle: f. *The Deaw-claw, or water-claw of dogs, &c.*

Controversé: m. ée: f. *Litigious, in controuersie; full of strife, and controuersie; also, gainsaid, called in question, disputed against; made, or handled as, a controuersie.*

Controuerse: f. *Controuersie, variance, debate, strife, altercation.*

Con-

Controuvé: m. ée: f. *Fained, forged, inuented, deuised.*

Controuvement: m. *A faining, fibbing, lying; a matter inuented, meere imagination, forged stuffe.*

Controuver. *To faine, forge, deuise, inuent, imagine, out of his owne braine.*

Contr'ouverture. *A counter-opening;* See Contr'ouvrir.

Controuveur: m. *A fainer, forger, inuenter, deuiser, lyer.*

Contr'ouvrir. *To open counter, to make a reuoltion; to pierce, or open a thing (as a part of the bodie) either farre off, or oppositely against, the place th'ouerture is intended for.*

Contumace: f. *Stubbornnesse, obstinacie, wilfulnesse, peruersenesse; disobedience, contempt.*

Contumacer. *To deale stubbornely, be peruerse; follow his owne will; disobey, or rebell against his superiours; to make a contempt; also, to iudge, or proceed against, as disobedient, obstinate, rebellious; to punish or censure, a contempt.*

Contumax: m. ace: f. *Stubborne, sullen, refractarie, rebellious, contemptuous, disobedient; obstinate, stiffe-necked, headstrong, wilfull, headie, selfe-willed: (The French Lawyers make,* deux especes des contumax; *The first, such as after three seuerall, and publike, summons refuse to appeare; the second, those that appearing stand mute, and will not answer; A silence which imports a confession.)*

Contumelie: f. *Contumelie; reproach, an outrage in words; a spightfull reproofe, iniurious checke, scandalous or slanderous rebuke.*

Contumelieusement. *contumeliously, reproachfully, in despightfull tearmes.*

Contumelieux: m. euse: f. *Contumelious; reproachfull, despightfull, outragious or most iniurious, in words.*

Contundre. *To beat, knocke, thumpe, bruise, pound, or stampe in peeces.*

Contusion: f. *A knocking, thumping, bruising, beating, pounding, stamping.*

Contuteur: m. *A Joynt Tutor, or Gardein.*

Conu: m. uë: f. *Knowne, &c; as* Cogneu.

Convaincre. *To conuict, conuince, take tardie, prooue faultie; find in the manner.*

Convaincu: m. uë: f. *Conuicted, conuinced; taken tardie, proued faultie, found in the manner.*

Convalescence: f. *A recouerie of health, strength, and and vigor; a waxing strong againe.*

Convalidé: m. ée: f. *Recouered, restored vnto health, growne well againe.*

Cõvalider. *To recouer, to restore vnto health, or strength.*

Convassal: m. *A fellow vassall.*

Convenable: com. *Conuenient; apt, fit, meet for; agreeable, sutable, according vnto; proper, comelie, decent, beseeming, seemlie.*

Convenablement. *Conueniently; aptly, fitly, agreeably, sutably, properly, to the purpose; decently, seemingly; well.*

Convenance: f. *An accord, concordance, agreement, condition; couenanting; also, conueniencie, proportion, handsomenesse, agreeablenesse.*

Convenancé: m. ée: f. *Couenanted; agreed; promised, contracted vpon couenants.*

Convenancer. *To couenant, bargaine, contract, agree with, promise vnto, vpon couenants.*

Convenant: m. *A couenant, or agreement vpon couenant; a conditionall bargaine, or contract; a faithfull, and publicke, or solemne promise.*

Convenant: m. ante: f. *as* Convenable; *Also, agreeing, suiting with; befitting, beseeming.*

Convenir. *To assemble, meet, or come together; also, to befit, beseeme, sort well vnto; to be meet, proper, or conuenient for; also, to agree, consent, accord with; also, to couple, conclude, ioyne; come to the point.*

Convenir en justice. *To bring in suit, conuent before a Judge, enter an action against.*

Il me convient. *I must, I should, I haue need, tis necessarie for me; proper, or belonging to me.*

Convent: *A Couent, Cloister, or Abbey of Monkes, or Nunnes.*

Abbe & convent ce n'est qu'un; mais la bourse se garde en divers lieux: Prov. *An Abbot and Couent though but one bodie haue seuerall mindes, ends, or meanes.*

Pour vn Moine ne faut convent: Prov. *One onely Monke deserues not an Abbey; or, one Swallow makes not a Summer.*

Conventicule: m. *A conuenticle; a little, or priuate, (and, most commonly, vnlawfull, or ill-affected) assemblie.*

Convention: f. *A couenant, contract, bargaine, agreement; also, a suing, impleading, or conuenting before a Judge; and, hence;*

Cecy n'est pas de facile convention. *This is hard to be compassed by suit of law.*

Conventioné. *as* Conventionel.

Conventionel: m. elle: f. *Contracted, couenanted, agreed vpon; or passed by contract; done by agreement, vnder articles, or couenants.*

Interest conventionel. *Interest, or vse for the lone of money, &c; as in* Interest.

Propre conventionel. *Seeke* Propre.

Conventuël. prieuré conventuël. *A Priorie wherein there are Friers.*

Conventuëls: m. *An order of* Observantin *Friers; not altogether so strict as the ordinarie ones.*

Convenu: m. uë: f. *Assembled, met, or come, together; also, couenanted, promised; accorded, or agreed vnto; also, impleaded, sued, conuented or called, before a Judge.*

Convereau: m. *A fish that somewhat resembles, but is lesser than, th'*Alose.

Convers: vn con. *A conuertite; one that hath turned to the Faith; or is woon vnto a religious profession; or hath abandonned a loose to follow a godlie, a vicious to lead a vertuous, life.*

Conversation: f. *Conuersation, commerce, great acquaintance, familiaritie, association, with.*

Converse: f. *A Nunne (that formerly hath beene of loose behauiour, or hath, in her time, beene a good one.)*

Converser avec. *To conuerse, or be much conuersant, associate, or keepe much companie, with; to haunt, frequent, resort often vnto.*

Conversion: f. *A conuersion; alteration, change; a turning; reuolution, compasse, or course of things.*

Conversion Sainct Paul. *A Holy day kept by the Church of Rome the xxv. of Ianuarie.*

Converti: m. ie: f. *Conuerted, altered, changed, turned, transformed, translated.*

Convertir. *To conuert; alter, change, transforme, turne; translate.*

Convertissement: m. *A conuerting, turning, altering, changing.*

Convertoir. *Part of the head, or chapter of an Ionian pillar.*

Con-

Convexe: com. *Crooked, bowing, or bending downe on euerie side, as an Arch, &c.*
Convexion: f. *The crookednesse, or bending of a hollow thing turned downeward.*
Convi: m. *A banquet, feast, great supper, or dinner, whereto acquaintants, and friends are inuited.*
Convice: m. *A reproach, railing word, biting tearme, spightfull scoffe, despightfull gird, or glaunce, malicious taunt.*
Convié: m. ée: f. *Inuited, or bidden vnto a feast.*
Conviement. *An inuiting, or bidding vnto a feast.*
Convient. il con. que vous; *(Impersonally) you must, or should; it beseemes, or behooues you;* See Convenir.
Convier. *To inuite, or bid, vnto a feast, &c.*
Conviticux: m. euse: f. *Reuiling, reproachfull, rayling, maliciously taunting, despightfully girding at.*
Convocation. *A Conuocation; an assemblie, or calling together.*
Convoitable: com. *Couetable, fit to be coueted, or lusted after.*
Convoitant. *Coueting, desiring, longing for, lusting after.*
Convoité: m. ée: f. *Coueted, desired, affected, longed for, lusted after.*
Convoitement: m. *A coueting, desire, lust; a stomack, or appetite vnto.*
Convoiter. *To couet, desire, affect greedily, wish, or long for, thirst, or lust after.*
Qui tout convoite tout perd: Prov. *He that couets all looses all.*
Convoiteux: m. euse: f. *Couetous, greedie, desirous of, longing for, lusting after.*
Convoitise: f. *Couetousnesse, concupiscence; an earnest desire, a restlesse affection, greedie thirst, vnsatiable lust, after.*
Convoler en secondes nopces. *To marrie a second wife (in hast.)*
Convoqué: m. ée: f. *Called, assembled.*
Convoquer. *To call, or assemble many together.*
Convoy: m. *An accompanying; a following, waiting, or attending on (especially in mariage, and buriall matters;) also, a conuoy, or companie of souldiours, or ships, for the wasting, or safe-conducting of passengers.*
Convoyé: m. ée: f. *Conuoyed, accompanied; followed, waited, attended on.*
Convoyer. *To conuoy, or accompanie; to follow, wait, or attend on.*
Convulsion: f. *A conuulsion; a plucking vp, or shrinking, as, of the sinewes in a crampe; also, a pricking, or shooting ache.*
Conyle: f. *Great Cheruill, sweet Cheruill, mirrhe Cheruill.*
Conyse. *The hearbe Flea-bane, or Flea-wort; of three kinds.*
Conyse grande. *Great Flea-wort.*
Conyse moyenne. *Flea-bane Mullet.*
Conyse petite. *Dwarfe, or small Flea-bane.*
Coöperer. *To worke, effect, or labour, with.*
Cope gorgée, *in stead of,* Gorge coupée: ¶Rab.
Copeaux. *as* Coupeaux; *Chips.*
Copelle: f. *as* Coupelle; *A Test, or Coppell.*
Copellé: m. ée: f. *Tested; melted, or fined, as siluer, in a Test, or Coppell.*
Copené. face copenée; *A Fesse Gobonie, (a tearme of Blazon.)*
Copet: m. *as* Couperet.
Cophin: m. *A basket, skep, or small pannier of wicker;* See Cofin.
Copie: f. *The copie of a writing; also, store, plentie, abundance of.*
Copié. *Copied, written out; also, flowted.*
Copier. *To copie, or write out; also, to flowt, scoffe, deride, ride, mocke, gibe at; to play the knaue with in words, &c.*
Copiere. Herbe copiere. *as* Oeil de Cerf.
Copieusement. *Copiously, plenteously, abundantly, greatly, at large, in great measure.*
Copieux: m. *A well-spoken, or Courtlie person; (a word misused by clownes;) also, a flowting, or ieasting companion; whence;*
Les Copieux d'Angers. *(Th'Angeuins being held great flowters.)*
Copieux: m. euse: f. *Copious, abundant, plentifull; great large, full; well furnished, throughly prouided of.*
Copiosité: f. *Plentie, store, abundance, fulnesse, copiousnesse.*
Copiste: m. *A maker of Counterpanes, a writer out of copies.*
Coppe. *A measure; the halfe of a Burgonian Bushell.*
Coppé. *as* Coupé; *Cut.*
Coppeau. *as* Coupeau. *A chip.*
Copper. *To cut;* See Couper.
Coppeter. *To ring all-in, or the last peale.*
Coppier. *To rouse, and stretch out himselfe, as one that goes about an exercise, or to try a masterie; (an old word.)*
Coppon: m. *A pecke; or, the eight part of a Parisien bushell.*
Cops. *A certaine fish verie like vnto a Sturgeon.*
Copté: m. ée: f. *Tolled, or strucken only on the one side, as a Bell, &c.*
Copter. *To toll, or strike only on one side; as a bell, when it is not fully rung out.*
Copuland: m. *A coupling, or ioyning together; or as* Copulasse: ¶Rab.
Copulasse. *An exercise in Schooles; when schollers dispute, and he that hath done best is placed highest.*
Copule: f. *A coniunction, a ioyning, or coupling together.*
Coq: m. *A cocke;* (vn coq;) *also, the Dorce, or Saint Peters fish;* (le coq;) *also, Costmarie, Balsamine, Alecoast; also, (and the more properly) Dittanie, Dittander, Pepperwort* (du coq.)
Coq à l'asne. *A libell, pasquin, Satyre.*
Coq de bois. *A blacke, and rough-legd Moore-cocke, full twice as big as ours, and liuing altogether in the mountaines.*
Coq d'esglise. *A Weather-cocke.*
Coq d'Inde. *A Turkie; a Turkie-cocke.*
Creste au coq. *The hearbe Coxcombe, Pennie-grasse, yellow and white Rattle; also, the hearbe Clarie.*
Pied de coq. *Hedge Fumitorie, Hennes-foot; also, bastard Parsley; also, the hearbe Crow-foot, Kings-cob, Gold-cup, Gold-flower, Butter-flower (the single one; the double one being ordinarily called) double Crowfoot, or Batchelers buttons.*
Elle chante le coq. *Said when a henne crowes.*
Il n'y fera rien, non plus que le coq sur les oeufs. *(Whereon he cannot by any meanes be brought to sit.)*
On n'y a iamais ouy le coq chanter. *Said of an vnhaunted, and vnhabited place.*
Sauter du coq à l'asne. *To run, without order, out of one matter into another.*

Ia ne chante le coq qui viendra le iour: Pro. *Though the cocke neuer crow, day will come.*

Coqu: m. *A cuckow, or cuckold*; *See* Cocu.

Coquäge: m. *Cuckoldrie, the state of a cuckold.*

Coquar: m. *An egge; or egge shell; or, as,*

Coquard: m. *A proud gull, peart goose, quaint fop, saucie doult, malapert coxcombe, rash or forward cokes.*

Mieux vaut l' ombre d'un sage vieillard que les armes d'un ieune coquard: Prov. *The shadow of an aduised grandsire is better than the sword of an aduenturous goosecap.*

Coquard: m. Coquarde: f. *as* Coquart.

Coquarde. bonnet à la coquarde. *A Spanish cap, or fashion of bonnet vsed by the most substantiall men of yore; (Tearmed so (perhaps) because those that wore of them grew thereby the prouder, & presumed the more of themselues) also, any bonnet, or cap, worne proudly, or peartly on th'one side.*

Coquardeau: m. *A proud asse, bold goose, fond saucebox; one that hath more wealth than wit, or is much more forward than wise.*

Coquardise: f. *Fond pride, saucinesse, presumption, malapertneße; vnaduised peartnesse, iollitie, chearefulnesse, cocketnesse.*

Coquart: m. arde: f. *Foolishly proud, saucie, presumptuous, malapert; vndiscreetly peart, cocket, iollie, cheerfull; more bold than welcome, forward than wise.*

Coquasse: f. *A kettle, or chafer.*

Coquassier: m. *A seller of egge-shells; also, a maker, or seller of kettles, or chafers.*

Coquatris: m. *A Basiliske, or Cockatrice.*

Coque: f. *A cockle; also, a bump, or knob on the forehead; also, an egge-shell, &c.*

Coque de Levant. *The small medicinable shel called in shops,* Vnguis odoratus.

Nulle noix sans coque: Prov. *No nut without a shell.*

Coquefredouille: m. *A meacocke, milkesop, sneaksbie, worthlesse fellow.*

Coquelicon: m. *Cocke-crowing; the song of a cocke.*

Coquelicoq. *as* Coquelicon; *Also, the wild Poppie, Corne-rose, red Corne-rose.*

Coqueliné: m. ée: f. *Dandled, fedled, cockered, pampered, made a wanton of.*

Coquelinement: m. *A dandling, fedling, cockering.*

Coqueliner vn enfant. *To dandle, cocker, fedle, pamper, make a wanton of, a child.*

Coquelineux: m. euse: f. *Fantasticall, brainesicke, humorous, moodie, giddie, shittle-headed; whose head is full of crochets.*

Coquelourdes: f. *The Wind-flower; also, the bastard Wind-flower, Passe-flower, Pasque-flower, Flaw-flower; also, the flower called, Rose-campion.*

Coqueluche: f. *A hood; also, the Coqueluchoe, or new disease; which troubled the French about the yeares 1510, and 1557; and vs but a while agoe.*

Coqueluchon: m. *The Capuche, or hood of a cloke; also, a weather-hood.*

Coqueluchonné: m. ée: f. *That weares a hood, or a Spanish Capuche.*

Coquemare: f. *The disease called the Night-mare.*

Coquemart: m. *A brazen pot, or chafer, hauing a couer.*

Coqueplumet. *A proud cockescombe, a scarrecrow; a wag-feather; one that swaggers, or stalkes vp & down the streets, with a top like a fore-horse; or, one who, by th'authoritie of his high feather, presumes he may ouerrule, or put downe, a whole street.*

Coquer. *To play the cocke, to tread hennes like a cocke.*

Se coquer contre. *To knocke himselfe, or runne his head against.*

Coquerelles: f. *Red Night-shade, Alkakengie, Winter-cherries.*

Coqueret: m. *The name of a certaine red, and verie sweet apple, thats ripe about Allhallowtide.*

Coquerets. des co. *as* Coquerelles.

Des Coquerettes. *The same.*

Des Coquerez. *The same.*

Coques. des coques: f. *Cockles.*

Coquet: m. *A Cocke-boat; also, a weather-cocke.*

Coqueté. *Cackled, or chucked; also, strowted, or swaggered.*

Coqueter. *A cocke to call his hennes; or to chucke, as a cocke among hennes; also, to swagger, or strowt it, like a cocke on his owne dung-hill.*

Coquetier: m. *A seller of egges, or of egge-shels.*

Coquette: f. *A pratling, or proud gossip; a fisking, or fliperous minx; a cocket, or tatling houswife; a titifill, a flebergebit.*

Coquillade: f. *A certaine little, slender, scalesse, small mouthed, and grey-eyed sea-fish, liuing among rocks.*

Coquillage: m. *Shell-worke; worke made of, or trimd with, shells.*

Coquillant. *Making, or vaulting, like a shell.*

Coquillard. *as* Coquardeau; *Also, a small vessell wheron, in Paris, they serue reare egges vnto the table.*

Coquillard: m. arde: f. *Shellie, full of shells.*

Coquille: f. *The shell of a fish; of a snaile; of a nut; or of an egge; also, a boat-bason, or any open vessell thats fashioned like a bason, or Scallop-shell; also, a French-hood; also a measure containing fiue spoonefuls.*

Coquille de S.Iacques. *The Scallop fish; also, a Cockle.*

Coquille de S.Michel. *A Cockle.*

Coquille de Prestre. *The hearbe Chickeweed; or a kind thereof, held by* Dodoneus *to be the right Mouse-eare.*

Coquille sabottée. *The Yealke; a shell-fish called so, because it somewhat resembles a Top.*

Large coquille. *A Scallop.*

Bailler de coquilles. *A cousener, cheater, conie-catcher, impostor, mountebanke; Hence, also,*

Dresser vne coquille. *To deuise a gulling tricke; to inuent a cheating deuise; to lay a snare for a foole.*

A qui vendez vous vos coquilles? *followed by,* à ceux qui viennent de S. Michel? *Why should you thinke to cousen vs, that are as cunning as your selues? tis ill haulting before a criple.*

Coquillé: m. ée: f. *Set thicke with shells; also, made, or fashioned, like a shell.*

Pain coquillé. *A fashion of an hard-crusted loafe, somewhat like our Stillyard Bunne.*

Coquiller. *To vault, bow, or fashion, a thing like a shell; also, as* Recroquiller.

Coquilleux: m. euse: f. *Shellie, full of shells.*

Coquillier: m. ere: f. *Hauing a shell, or bearing a shell; of, or belonging to, a shell.*

Coquilliere: f. *A woman that (now) makes biggens, and caps; (but whose chiefest worke, in times past was the French-hood* Coquille.)

Coquillon: m. *A little shell; or hood; also, a fooles hood; or a hooded foole.*

Coquimbert qui gaigne pert. *A game at cards; like our loosing Lodam.*

Coquin: m. *A beggar, poore snake, needie wretch, tattered rogue, lousie vagabond that begs from doore to doore;*

doore; any base scoundrell, or scuruie fellow; also, as Egau.

C'est vn grand cas la fureur de deux coquins à vne porte. *A prouerbe meant, as well of th'ordinarie iarring, and thwartings that passe between two ambitious Competitors, as of the scoulding, or other scuruie sturre made by two hungrie, and enuious beggers at a mans doore,*

Il n'est vie que de coquins: Prov. *There's no life to the beggers; Looke* Vie.

Il vaut mieux estre coquu que coquin: Prov. *Better be a cuckold than a beggerlie knaue.*

Coquin: m. ine: f. *Beggerlie, needie; lousie; roguish, vagabond-like.*

Mouton coquin. *A Bell-weather.*

Pigeon coquin. *A tame Pigeon.*

Elle entrejetta la jambe coquine. *She interposed her wanton, lasciuious, or harlots, leg.*

Coquine: f. *A begger-woman; also, a cockney, simper-decockit, nice thing.*

Coquineau: m. *A scoundrell, base varlet, beggerlie rascall, beastlie fellow.*

Coquiner. *To beg, to craue like a begger; to play the rogue, or base rascall.*

Coquinerie: f. *Beggerie, begging; also, roguerie, knauerie, basenesse; or base humors; also, meats that are more toothsome than holesome; forced meats.*

Coquiol: f. *A degenerate Barlie, or weed, commonly, growing among Barlie, and called, Hauer-grasse.*

Coquu. *as* Cocu.

Cor: m. *A Hunters horne; a Bugle, or Hutchet; also, a corne in the foot; also, the hard, and hornie swelling in horses, tearmed, the Sit-fast.*

Cors. *The broches of a Deers head; all the pegs therof from the second, or third vpwards.*

Cor de mer. *The Sea-horne; a shell-fish that somewhat resembles a horne.*

A cor & à cry. *By Proclamation; also, by might and maine, with heaue and hoe; eagerly, vehemently, seriously.*

Corail: m. *Corrall; (growes in the sea, like a thicke shrub, and is then of a greenish colour; taken thence, it waxeth verie hard, and (after it hath been dressed) becomes red, and smooth; (There is also a white, a black, and a yellow, kind of Corrall.)*

Coralin: m. ine: f. *Corralin, of Corrall, like vnto Corrall.*

Coraline: f. *Sea-mosse, Corralline, or Corrall-mosse.*

Corapei. *A Princes cloth of Estate.*

Corbat pescheret. *A Cormorant:* ¶Dauph.

Corbature. *as* Courbature.

Corbau: m. *The Cabot fish; or, as* Corp.

Corbeau: m. *A Rauen; also, a Corbell (in Masonrie;) and, a bracket, or shouldering peece (in timber worke;) also, a certaine warlike instrument; also, the broyled bone of a leg, or shoulder, of mutton, hauing some flesh left about it.*

Corbeau d'eau. *A Cormorant.*

Corbeau de mer. *The same; or, the sea-Rauen.*

Corbeau du nuict. *The Night-Rauen.*

Corbeau pescheret. *A Cormorant.*

Repaistre les corbeaux. *To hang in chaines; or, to lie vnburied in the fields.*

Tromper vn corbeau à bouche beante. *To cousen a greedie fellow of a bit which he gapes after; or, as in* Tromper.

De mauvais corbeau mauvais oeuf: Pro. *Of an ill bird, an ill brood.*

La censure tourmente les pigeons laissant aller les corbeaux libres: Prov. *Censure torments Pigeons, and frees Rauens; and hence are Lawes compared vnto Cobwebs; little flies are caught in them, great ones breake through them.*

Corbeil. *The name of a towne that is not far from Paris; and hence the prouerbiall phrase;*

Prendre Paris pour Corbeil. *To take an apple for an oister; to mistake the matter quite and cleane.*

Corbeille: f. *A wicker basket, or maund; also, a dosser.*

Qui fait corbeille il fait panier: Pro. *He that makes a basket makes a pannier; he that can do one thing can do another.*

Corbeillée: f. *A basket-full of.*

Corbeilleux: m. euse: f. *Belonging to a basket or maund; also, full of baskets, &c.*

Corbeillon: m. *A little basket, pannier, or maund.*

Corbieu. *Gogs heart.*

Corbigeau: m. *A Cormorant, or Sea-Rauen.*

Corbillat: m. *A yong Rauen.*

Corbillon. *as* Corbeillon.

Corbin: m. *A (carrion, or carre) Crow.*

Bec de corbin. *A Pentioners halberd, or pollaxe; also a Chirurgions toole, called a Crowes-bill; See* Bec.

Os corbin. *A certaine hollow bone in the crupper of a Deere.*

Pied de corbin. *The hearbe Crow-foot, Kings-cob, Gold-cups, Gold-flower, Butter-flower.*

Corbiné: m. ée: f. *Stollen, filtched, purloined, lurched; also, polled, exacted, extorted; extreamely vsed.*

Corbiner. *To steale, filtch, purloine, lurch; also, to poll, extort, or exact more than is due.*

Corbinerie: f. *Stealing, filtching, lurching; also, polling, exaction, extortion.*

Corbinet: m. *The crooking of Rauens, or Crowes.*

Corbineur. *A filtcher, lurcher, poller, exacter.*

Corbineurs du Palais. *Lawyers, and Clerkes; which ordinarily fleece, lurch, poll, and spoile, poore suiters.*

Corcalihat: m. *The crie of Quailes.*

Corcesque: f. *A kind of broad-headed Iaueline, or dart.*

Corchiere: f. *The battlement of a wall; also, (in a gallie) as* Coursie.

Cordace. *A kind of countrey daunce:* ¶Rab.

Cordage: m. *Cordage, ropes; or stuffe to make ropes of.*

Cordaille de navire. *Tackling.*

Corde: f. *A cord, rope, halter; a twisted string, band, or line; also, as* Tendon.

Corde de bois. *A certaine measure, or quantitie, of wood (whether fagots, or billets) laid together; eight, or ten foot in length, about foure in height, and hauing at either end two stakes to hold it in.*

Corde du bras. *The greatest, and most notable, branch of the shoulder veine.*

Corde d'un Cordelier. *A grey Friers girdle; or, the knotted cord wherewith he girds himselfe.*

Cordes du iarret. *The ham-strings.*

Haut mal de la corde. *A hanging.*

Homme de sac & de corde. *One for whom the gallowes grone; Looke* Sac.

Avoir deux cordes à son arc. *To bee furnished with two helpes, to haue a double hope of successe, in his businesse; (we also vse the same phrase.)*

Bailler à vn la corde pour se pendre. *Cunningly to giue one an aduantage which if he vse will turne to his preiudice.*

Coucher sous corde. *In game, &c, to stake downe readie coine; from Tennis-players, that lay the money they play for vnder the line.*
Elle n'est si fine que la corde n'y apparoisse. *As cunning as shee thinkes her selfe, her tricks may be discerned: (a metaphor from cloth, whose thread may be seene.)*
Il est au bout de sa corde. *He is at the end of his meanes; he hath shewed his vtmost skill in the matter; he can do no more to it, say nought else of it, goe no further in it.*
Il y aura beau ieu si la corde ne rompt. *Wee shall haue good sport if the line breake not; s. if all things continue as they are, or hold, that are now, good.*
Pendant que la corde est au puis. *While the matter is hot; while there is opportunitie; while your hand is in.*
Plus couste la corde que le fardeau. *Said when the charges of law, or trafficke, &c, exceed the principall, or diminish ones stocke.*
'A grosse larron grosse corde: Prov. *A strong halter for a strong theefe.*
'A longue corde tire qui d' autruy mort desire: Prov. *Hee that longs for another mans death, hath a long (or a cold) suit of it; We say, he that waits for dead mens shoone shall goe long barefoot.*
Qui plus qu'il n'a vaillant despend il fait la corde à quoy se pend: Pro. *Who more than he is worth doth spend, he makes a rope his life to end.*
Cordé. *Corded; twisted as a cord; bound with cords; also, out of season; (a Metaphor from Lampreyes, which being out of season haue a hard string in their backes.)*
Cordeau: m. *A Carpenters chalked, or Oakered, line.*
Cordeau courant. *A Gardeners line; the line wherwith he measures out his plots, and beds.*
Cordeau volant. *The same.*
Cordée: f. *A string-full of; also, a ranke, row, list, file.*
Cordelé: m. ée: f. *Twisted, or made into cords.*
Cordeler. *To twist, or make roapes; or make into cords, ropes, &c.*
Cordelette: f. *A small cord; a twine, or packthread; a twisted lace, line, or string.*
Cordeleux: m. euse: f. *Cordie, cord-like; full of cords.*
Cordelier: m. *A Grey Frier (of the Order of S. Francis) a Cordelier; also, twist.*
Monnoye de Cordelier. *Thankes; or a Benedicitee; (for Grey Friers are to carrie no money about them.)*
Cordeliere: f. *A Grey Friers girdle (made of a peece of a rope full of equally-distant knots;) Hence, any knotted thread, or string; and the blacke, and knotted necke-lace (no better than a string) worne by some Gentlewomen; also, knotted cord-worke in Imbroderie, &c; also, a Nunne of Saint Francis his Order; also, a row, file, course, ranke of seuered, or seuerall things; and hence;*
Vne longue cordeliere de montaignes.
Cordelle: f. *as* Cordelette; *A little cord, or twisted string.*
Tirer en sa cordelle. *To win vnto his faction; allure, or draw, vnto his side.*
Corder. *To twist, or make ropes; also, to bind, or packe vp with ropes, or cords; also, to measure with ropes, or cords.*

Cette Lamproye se corde. *This Lamprey is out of season; (by hauing a hard string in her backe.)*
Cordeur de terres. *A Surueyor; or Measurer of lands.*
Cordial: m. ale: f. *Cordiall, heartie; sincere, vnfained; affectionate; also, heart-strengthening, heart-comforting.*
Les trois fleurs cordiales. *Roses, Bourage, and Buglosse.*
Cordiale: f. *The hearbe Motherwort, (good against the throbbing, or excessiue beating of the heart.)*
Cordialement. *Cordially, heartily; truly, faithfully, with the whole heart.*
Cordialeuse: m. ée: f. *Heartie, cordiall; full of heart, or heartinesse; also, heartened, cheered; well comforted, or encouraged.*
Cordialité: f. *Cordiallnesse, heartinesse, heartfulnesse.*
Cordiaque: com. *Cordiall, heart-comforting, mind-cheering.*
Cordier: m. *A Roper, a Cord-maker.*
Desmarche de cordier. *A stepping, or going, backwards.*
Cordillat d' Espagne. *A kind of twisted stuffe made of fine wooll.*
Cordilles. *The yong frie of Tunnie.*
Cordon: m. *A string, twine, twist; one of the twists of a rope, or corde; also, a wreath; and, thence, an out-standing wreath, or edge of stone (commonly distinguishing the seuerall stories) on th'outside of a building.*
Cordon de chapeau. *A (wreathed) hatband.*
Cordons d'une trompette. *The cordines, or strings of a Trumpet.*
Tel larron tel cordon: Prov. *Such theefe, such halter; a punishment befitting th'offence.*
Cordonné: m. ée: f. *Twisted, twined, plaited; wreathed; also, made as, or into, a cord.*
Cordonner. *To twine, twist, plait; wreath; also, to make as, or into, a cord.*
Cordouan: m. *Cordouan leather; (which is properly, a Goats skin tanned.)*
Cordouannerie: f. *Shoo-making, the trade of a Shoomaker; also, the part of a towne wherein Shoomakers worke; Shoomaker-row, Shoomaker-street.*
Cordouannier: m. *A Shoomaker; a Cordwainer.*
Cordouanniere: f. *The wife of a Shoomaker; or woman that is a Shoomaker.*
Cordueil: m. *Hearts-griefe, teene, anguish, heartie sorrow.*
Cordule: m. *A kind of verie small water-Newt, or Lizard, mistaken, and oft mis-used, in stead of the* Scinque.
Core: f. *The broad peece thats betweene the crosse-bars of the hilt of a sword.*
Corée de pourceau. *A swines gullet, or a hogs haslet.*
Corgeal: m. ale: f. *Choaking; of a choaking propertie, or qualitie.*
Coriace. *(The feminine of* Corias; *) as tough as a hide; as hard as leather.*
Corial: m. *A Singing-man, Quire-man, or Quirrester.*
Coriandre: m. *The hearbe, or seed Coriander.*
Corias: m. ace: f. *As tough as leather, as hard as a hide.*
Corions de souliers: m. *The latchets of shooes.*
Corlieu: m. *A Curlue.*
Corlis. *as* Corlieu.

Corman: m. *The greedie water-fowle tearmed a Cormorant; also, the Cabot fish.*
Corné. *A drinke, or wine made of the Sorbe apple; it surpasses in goodnesse Perrie, or Cider; and comes neerest, of any of those kinds, vnto white wine.*
Corme: f. *The Seruice, or Sorb-apple.*
Cormier: m. *The Seruice tree, Sorb-apple tree.*
Cormorant: m. *as* Corman.
Cornabon. *A musicall Cornet; or such a wreathed instrument:* ¶Rab.
Cornadiz d'Espaigne. *Base peeces of money, thirtie six of them being worth but one* Douzain.
Cornage: m. *Hornage; an yearely duetie of corne exacted by the Lord* Chastelain *of* Berri *(in the iurisdiction of* Bourges*) vpon euerie Oxe that labours in the Winter-corne-ground which is within his territorie.*
Cornaline: f. *The Cornix, or Cornaline; a flesh-coloured stone that is easie to bee grauen on, and therefore much vsed in signets.*
Cornalique: com. *Cuckoldlie, cuckold-like.*
Cornard: m. *A cuckold, or horned beast; one of the forked Order.*
Cornardise: f. *Cuckoldrie.*
Corne: f. *A horne; also, horne; also, the hoofe of a beasts foot; also, the Sit-fast; (a hard, or hornie swelling in the backe-part of a horse) also, a corner; limit, or bound.*
Corne boeuf. *The hearbe Fenegreeke.*
Corne de cerf. *Buckhorne Plantaine, Crowfoot Plantaine, Harts-horne, Sandwort, hearbe Iuie, or Eue.*
Cornes du front. *The swelling, or out-bearing, of the bone of the temples on either side of the forehead.*
Corne prendre. *To wax proud.*
Auoir du foin aux cornes. Il a du foin aux cor. *He is a fierce; proud; sturdie, surlie mate; a shrewd, curst, vnsociable campanion; a dangerous fellow to deale with.*
Bailler foin en corne. *To deceiue, cousen, gull, giue a gleeke, sell a bargaine.*
Baisser les cornes. *To humble himselfe, to let fall his crest; to yeeld, stoope, strike saile.*
Haulser, ou, leuer la corne. *To grow proud, wax hautie, become loftie, (or liuelie) begin to take state vpon him.*
Prendre vn boeuf par les cornes. *To vndertake, or performe, a dangerous act.*
Dieu donne biens, & boeuf, mais ce n'est pas par la corne: Prov. *Looke* Boeuf.
Corné. *Horned, hauing hornes.*
Corne-boeuf. *The hearbe Fenegrecke.*
Cornée de l'oeil. *The hornie Tunicle wherein the apple of the eye is placed; so called, because both in colour, and consistence, it resembles a thinne, and transparent, horne.*
Corneille: f. *A Crow; also, a Cornill berrie.*
Corneille emmantelée. *The Roiston Crow, or Winter Crow, whose backe, and bellie are of an ashie colour.*
Corneille sauvage. *The same.*
Pied de corneille. *Crowfoot Plantaine, Buckehorne Plantaine, Coronop Plantaine, Hearbie Iuie, Hartes-horne.*
Putain fait comme la corneille, plus se laue, & plus noire est elle: Prov. *A whoore is like a Crow; the more shee washes her the blacker shee is;* viz. *the more she excuses, the more she betraies, her selfe; or, in striuing to iustifie, she condemnes, her selfe.*
Cornelle. *as* Corneole.
Cornement des oreilles. *The glowing, or tingling of the eares.*
Cornemuse: f. *A Bagpipe; also, as* Cornuë; *the vessell, or Lymbecke whereby oyles are extracted from Gummes, wood, or mettals.*
Toutes ces choses procedent de la mesme cornemuse. *All these things come from one head, runne from one spring, haue one and the selfe-same originall.*
Cornemuseur: m. *A Bagpiper.*
Corneole: f. *Willow-hearbe, Loose-strife, Water-willow.*
Corne-pied. *Hoofed, horne-footed.*
Corner. *To sound a Cornet, to wind a Horne; also, to stinke, or smell mustily, as meat that hath taken wind.*
Cela cornoit prise. *That finished the chace, that made a full end of the matter.*
Les oreilles me cornent. *My eares glow, or tingle.*
Cornes. *as* Cornilles.
Cornet: m. *A Cornet, a Trumpe; a little Horne; also, a sea-Cut, or Cuttle-fish; or, as* Casseron, *about* Bayonne; *also, as,* Sifflet.
Cornet à bouquin. *A Musicall Cornet.*
Cornet à encre. *An Inkehorne.*
Cornet de papier. *The Cornet, or Coffin of paper, wherein a Grocer makes vp his retailed parcel of Spice &c.*
Corneté: m. ée: f. *Scarified, or cupped.*
Corneter. *To cup, or scarifie with horned cups.*
Corneteux: m. euse: f. *Vsed in cupping, or scarifying.*
Cornette: f. *A Bugle, Hutchet, or little Horne; also, a Doctors Tippet; also, a Cornet of horse; and, the Ensigne of a horse-companie; also, a fashion of Shadow, or Boonegrace, vsed in old time, and at this day, by some old women; also, the tuft, or tipping, of a Hawkes Hood.*
Les cornettes d'un arc. *The hornes, or hornie tips of a long Bow.*
La cornette basse. *An old-fashioned Shadow, or Boonegrace; (as in th'originall.)*
La cornette d'un chaperon. *The Cornet of a French-hood.*
Corneur: m. *A Horner; a winder of a Horne.*
Corniat: m. *The Juice, or Syrop of Cornill berries.*
Cornice: f. *The cornish, or brow of a piller, or wall.*
Corniche: f. *A kind of little Sea-cut, or Cuttle-fish; or, as* Cornichet; *also, the cornish, or brow of a wall, piller, or other peece of building.*
Cornichet: m. *The sleeue, or Calamarie (fish.)*
Cornichon: m. *A little Horne; also, a Deeres head while it is young, or but new put out; also, a play at Quoites, wherein a peece of horne is led, or layed for the marke; or a play at Bowles with a Mistresse (for commonly they play at Prickes) tearmed* Cornichon.
Cornier: m. *as* Cornillier; *Also, a Horner.*
Cornier: m. ere: f. *Belonging to, standing in, the corner; angular.*
Pieds corniers. *Looke* Pied.
Corniere: f. *A corner; also, a ske horner.*
Cornillat. *A little yong Crow, a nest Crow.*
Cornillé: m. ée: f. *Jurred, or butted with hornes.*
Corniller. *To iurre, or butt with the hornes.*

Cro-

Cornilles: f. *Cornill berries.*

Cornillier: m. *The long cherrie, wild cherrie, or Cornill tree;* Cornillier masle.

Cornillier femelle. *Hounds-tree, Dog-berrie tree, Prick-tymber tree; Gaten, or Gater, tree.*

Cornillier sauvage. *The same.*

Corniole: f. *Part of a Stags throat; or, as* Gargatte, *the Vuula; See* Gargatte.

Cornoaller: m. *The Cornill tree; as* Cornillier.

Cornoalles: f. *Cornill berries.*

Cornoiller. *as* Cornillier.

Cornoilles: f. *Cornill berries.*

Cornoüaille: f. *Cornewall; one of the shires of England; also, a part of Low Brittaine; whence;*

Chevalier de Cornoüaille. *A Cuckold, a horned beast, one of the forked, or cornuted, Order.*

Estaim de Cornoüaille. *Seeke* Estaim.

Voyager en Cornoüaille. *To weare the horne, to be one of the head men of his parish.*

Cornu: m. *A kind of Serpent; as* Serpent cornu.

Cornu: m. uë: f. *Hornie, horned; cornuted; hauing hornes; bearing, or wearing hornes; also, crooked, or boughtie, like a horne.*

Argument cornu. *A fantasticall, friuolous, impertinent, ill-made argum nt.*

Aspic cornu. *Looke* Aspic.

Astre cornu. *The Moone.*

Baston cornu. *A Battle-ax (of the old fashion.)*

Bonnet cornu. *A cornered, or square, cap.*

Pain cornu. *A loafe that is not round, but made with corners, or fashioned illfauouredly, and with vneuen sides.*

Perle cornuë. *A ragged pearle.*

Pois cornus. *A kind of flat, or square, peason; being either Sheepes Ciches, or* Dodoneus *his Cichelings, called also, flat peason.*

Serpent cornu. *A sand-coloured Serpent, which hath two, or (as* Iulius Solinus *reports) foure Snayle-like hornes on his head, and his hinder parts full of skales, which make him seeme to hisse as he goes; (his biting is almost incureable.)*

Bailler des plus cornuës. Il vous en baillera, &c. *He will tell you many a loud ly.*

Fust il plus Diable qu'il n'est cornu. *Were he more terrible indeed then he is in shew.*

Ie le rendray plus Diable qu'il n'est cornu. *I will put him in greater feare than he puts others.*

'A l'enfourner on fait les pains cornus: Prov. *A carelesse, erronious, or ignorant entrance into a busines disorders the whole course of it, and, in conclusion, mars it; of the same sence is;*

Qui mal enfourne tire les pains cornus: Prov. *He that begins vnseatly ends ill-fauoredly.*

Cornuaille. *as* Cornoüaille.

Cornuchet. *A little Cornet.*

Enter en cornuchet. *Looke* Enter.

Cornuë: f. *A kind of bending Limbecke (like a Bagpipe) of glasse, varnished, and leaded within; vsed for th'extracting of oyles out of hard and drie things, as wood, mettalls, &c; also, as* Malarmat, *a kind of Gurnet.*

Cornüette: f. *The small Pulse called Axe-seed, Axewort, Axfitch, and Hatchetfitch; also, horned wild Cummin.*

Corolaire: m. *A Corollaire; a surplusage, ouerplus, addition to, vantage aboue measure; also, a small gift, or largesse bestowed on the people at publicke feasts, and playes.*

Coronal: m. ale: f. *Coronall, Crowne-like; of, or belonging to, a Crowne.*

Artere coronale. *Seeke* Artere.

Commissure coronale. *The Coronall Suture, or seame, which compasses the forehead, or forepart of the scull, in forme of a halfe circle.*

Os coronal. *Seeke* Os.

Veine coronale. *A branch of the hollow veine, so tearmed, because it enuirons the heart in forme of a Crowne; there is also another of that name, a branch of the Spleene veine; as* Stomachique.

Coronne: f. *A Crowne, or Garland, &c; See* Couronne.

Corp: m. *A blackish sea-fish, whose head shineth almost like gold; some tearme it a Cabot.*

Corpaut. *A pot:* ¶Barrag.

Corporail: m. *The Corporall; the fine linnen wherein the Sacrament is put.*

Corporalier: m. *A Pix, or box for the foresaid linnen, or Sacrament.*

Corporance: f. *Corporature; the quantitie, fashion, or constitution of the bodie.*

Corporel: m. elle: f. *Corporall, bodilie, personall.*

Veine corporelle. *as* Mediane.

Corporellement. *Corporally, bodily, personally; in person; without Atturney, or Deputie.*

Corporence: f. *as* Corporance.

Corporu: m. uë: f. *Corpulent, big-bodied, grosse, fleshie, well fed, of a great stature.*

Corps: m. *A bodie, a corps; the whole bulk, or substance, of; also, a volume; also, a companie, or corporation; also, as* Vaisseau corpulent; *also, (in cloth, or stuffe) substance, tacke, stuffinesse.*

Le corps d'un arbre. *The stocke, or bodie of a tree.*

Vn corps de cuirasse. *A Corselet.*

Corps de garde. *A Court of gard, in a Campe, or Fort.*

Vn corps d'hostel. *The bodie, or heart of a house; that part wherein the chiefe roomes, and lodgings, are contriued.*

Le corps d'un navire. *The Hull of a Ship.*

Femme de corps. *A Villeinesse, or woman of a seruile condition.*

'A corps perdu. *Desperatly, furiously, headlong, without any care of his owne safetie.*

Droguer le corps. *To make an Apothecaries shop of his bellie.*

Excuser aucun par son corps. *To fight in another mans quarell; to defend another mans innocencie with the hazard of his owne bodie.*

Logez sous nostre corps. viz. *Vnder our roofe, or couert; at our charge, or allowance.*

Marcher en corps. *as* la Cour marche en corps; *All the Officers of the Court go along together.*

Mettre corps & coeur. *To labour tooth and naile, to indeuour by all meanes possible.*

Prendre au corps. *To arrest; or, take prisoner.*

Bon chausteau garde qui sçait son corps garder: Prov. *Looke* Chasteau.

Homme endormi corps enseveli: Prov. *There is no difference betweene a dead, and a sleepie, bodie; or, as good be dead outright, as aliue, and do nought.*

Quand les biens viennent les corps faillent: Prov. *Most mens liues are neere spent before they haue got any thing to spend.*

Corpset: m. *A little bodie; also, a paire of bodies, or, a womans bodies.*

Corpulence: f. *Corpulencie, grossenesse, fatnesse, bignesse of bodie.*

Corpulent : m. ente : f. *Corpulent, grosse, big-bodied, quarrie, fat.*
Vaisseau corpulent. *The bodie, or the lower part of a Limbecke; that which containes the stuffe which is to be distilled.*
Corratage : m. *Brokage; also, horse-scoorsing; also, cousenage; or, as* Courretage.
Corraterie : f. *A broking; also, horse-scoursing; also, cousening.*
Corratier : m. *A Broker; also, a horse-scoorser.*
Corraye : f. *as* Courroye; *A thong, or belt of leather.*
Correct : m. correcte : f. *Correct, congruous, perfect; good, pure, neat.*
Correctement. *Correctly, purely, neatly, with congruitie, without fault.*
Correcteur : m. *A reformer, correcter, controller, amender, fault-finder.*
Correcteur des comptes. *An Officer that examines and controlls, or passes, th'accounts of the Receiuors, vnder-Treasurers, & others the like accountants of the Exchequer; (there are foure of them belonging to the Chamber of Accounts.)*
Correction : f. *A correction, reformation, controlement.*
Corregiole : f. *as* Corrigiole.
Correlaire : m. *An addition, aduantage, surplusage, ouerplus of measure; or, as* Corolaire.
Correlatif : m. iue : f. *Correlatiue.*
Corrente. *A strait of the sea, as that of* Gibraltar, *of* Magellan, *&c; where commonly it runnes violently.*
Correspondance : f. *A correspondencie; a mutuall agreement, or answer; a resemblance, or equalitie of humors, affections, qualities, quantitie.*
Correspondant : m. *A suretie.*
Correspondant : m. ante : f. *Correspondent; answerable, or according vnto; equall, or agreeable with, in all points.*
Correspondre. *To correspond, hold correspondencie with; be correspondent vnto; to accord, consent, agree all together; to run one, and the same course together; or, to resemble, answer, equall; to be like, answerable, or equall, in all points.*
Corret : m. *An agnaile, or little corne, vpon a toe.*
Corriasse. *as* Coriace.
Corridor. *A curtaine, in fortification.*
Corrigé : m. ée : f. *Corrected, amended, reformed; improued; redressed, straightened.*
Corriger. *To correct, amend, reforme, redresse, better; straighten.*
Corrigiole : f. *Male Knot-grasse, Swines-grasse, Birds-tongue.*
Corrion : m. *A latchet, strap; little thong, or belt of leather.*
Corroboré : m. ée : f. *Corroborated, strengthened, fortified, confirmed.*
Corroborer. *To corroborate, strengthen, fortifie, confirme.*
Corrodé : m. ée : f. *Gnawen, worne, or fretted, away, about the sides.*
Corroder. *To gnaw, bite; weare, or fret away, about the sides, or edges.*
Corrompable : com. *Corrumpable, corruptible, peruertable, deprauable.*
Corromperesse : f. *A corruptresse, a woman that mars others.*
Corrompeur : m. *A corrupter; deprauer, defiler, misleader, peruerter.*
Corrompeur de filles. *A deflowrer of maids, a filthie leacher.*
Corompeuse : f. *She that mars, or misleads, others.*
Corrompre. *To corrupt, rot, putrifie taint; marre, spill, spoyle; depraue, infect, viciate; inuert, peruert, mislead; also, to bribe; suborne, or win, by gifts.*
Corrompu : m. *A dissolute youth, vnthriftie packe, riotous yonker, loose mate, notable wag, terrible wencher.*
Corrompu : m. uë : f. *Corrupted, tainted, putrified; marred, spoyled; infected, viciated; misled, peruerted; also, bribed; woon, seduced, or suborned, by bribes.*
Corrompu comme la fesse d'un Postillon. *Looke* Postillon.
Corrompure : f. *A corrupting, or corruption; also, wast, losse, or spoyle by corruption.*
Corrosé : m. ée : f. *Corroded; fretted, bitten, gnawen, worne or wasted about, or on th'edges, or sides.*
Corrosif : m. iue : f. *Corrosiue; biting, gnawing, or fretting away (on th'edges, or sides.)*
Corrosion : f. *A corrosion; a fretting, gnawing, or biting away (on th'edges, or sides.)*
Corrosivité : f. *as* Corrosion; *or corrosiuenesse.*
Corroye : f. *See* Courroye.
Corrude : f. *Stone Asparagus, mountaine Sperage.*
Corrugation : f. *A corrugation, a wrinkling, or furrowing of the skin; a frowning.*
Corruptelle : f. *A corruption, deprauation; falsification.*
Corruptement. *Corruptly; to the spoyle, marring, or putrifaction of.*
Corruptible : com. *Corruptible; subiect vnto corruption; easie to be corrupted.*
Corruption : f. *Corruption; putrifaction; also, a marring, deprauing, peruerting, vitiating; also, a fasifying.*
Corruptrice : f. *A corruptrix; a woman that marres, or misleads, others.*
Cors. *The Plurall of* Cor; *See* Cor.
A cors & à cri. *By Proclamation, or, with hue and crie; also, by might and maine, with heaue and hoe, earnestly, eagerly, vnhemently, seriously.*
Corsage : m. *The forme, habit, or constitution of the bodie.*
Gens de corsage. *Villeins; or such as hold their land by a slauish, and seruile tenure.*
Corsaire : m. *A courser; as* Coursier; *also, a pyrat.*
De corsaire à corsaire n'y pend que barriques rompues: Pro. *Nought is to be got of rouers but trash, or blowes.*
Corselet : m. *A verie little bodie.*
Corser. *To imbrace, take, or hold, by the bodie; to catch, take, or lay, hold of the bodie.*
Corsesque : f. *A kind of broad-headed Iauelin, Gleue, or Dart.*
Corset : m. *A little bodie; also, a paire of bodies (for a woman.)*
Corsu : m. uë : f. *Grosse, fleshie, corpulent, big-bodied.*
Corsyre. *A kind of hearbe.*
Cortine. *See* Courtine.
Corveable : com. *Liable, or subiect vnto base, and personall seruices; bound to performe, or of whom a Landlord may exact, certaine dayes workes in the yeare.*
Corvée : f. *A boone, or bound; a toilesome, and drudging dayes worke; lent vnto a friend; or (the more properly) due by a vassall, or tenant; and to be done, either (and most properly) in his owne person, or by*

by his cattell, plough, or teame, in the ground, or about the house, of his Lord, or Landlord; also, any seruice of duetie for which there is no recompence expected; and hence;

Faire corvée. *To do a thing with an ill will, as one that knowes he shall not be rewarded for his paines.*

Faire vne grande corvée. *See* Courvée.

Corybanter. *Madly to run vp and downe, playing on a Cymball, and wagging his head, like one of* Cybeles *Priests; also, to sleepe with open eyes.*

Corybantiant. *So running; or sleeping.*

Corymbe: m. *An Iuie berrie.*

Coryphée: m. *The first in a ranke, the best at a game, the chiefe of an Order; a President, Principall, or prime man; hence, the leader of a daunce; and, hee that in any manner of knowledge excells, or exceeds, all others.*

Coscossons: m. *Curdes; or as* Coscotons.

Coscoté: m. ée: f. *Spotted, or pounced.*

Coscotons: m. *Fresh cheese; or as* Coscossons.

Cosmographe: m. *A Cosmographer, or describer of the whole world.*

Cosmographie: f. *Cosmographie; or the description of the whole world.*

Cosmo-vague: m. *A wanderer, or traueller throughout the world.*

Cossats de febues, pois &c. *The huskes, or cods of beans &c.*

Cosse: f. *as* Gousse; *A huske; also, the iurring of two Rammes in their fight; also, the vpper part of the mast of a ship; also, as* Coste; *a rib.*

Cossé. *Butted, iurred.*

Cosser. *To but, or iurre, as fighting Rammes.*

Cossi: m. *The warbling note of a Swallow.*

Cosson: m. *A mite, or weeuell.*

Cossonnerie: f. *The market for Fowle, or Venison, in Paris.*

Cossot. *as* Cosson.

Cossu: m. ue: f. *Codded, husked, hulled.*

Cost: m. du cost. *Costmarie, Balsamine, Alecoast.*

Costal: m. ale: f. *Belonging to the sides, or the ribs.*

Costamer: m. *Costmarie, or Alecoast.*

Costau: m. *A little hill.*

Costaux de mõtaignes. *The sides, or skirts of mountaines.*

Costé: m. *The side (of any thing;) also, a partie, or faction; also, a coast, or quarter.*

Haut costé. *A Surloyne.*

De costé. *Sideling, sidewayes.*

Clocher des deux costez. *Looke* Clocher.

Couper des deux costez. *To play with both hands, bet on both sides, intertaine both parties with good, or hopefull, tearmes.*

Dormir sur les deux costez. *To barrell vp sleepe; Looke* Dormir.

Coste: m. *Th' Aromaticall, and medicinable root* Costus.

Coste: f. *A rib; also, the side of a man, &c; also, the stemme, or staulke of an hearb; also, a cloue of garlick, &c; also, a little hill, or descent of land; also, a coast, or land by the sea side; also, the tow of fine silke.*

Les costes. *The wedge-like peeces of wood wherwith the sides of a Boot-tree, or Boot-last are inlarged.*

Coste à coste. *Equally, in euen ranke, side by side, cheeke by iowle.*

Costeau. *as* Costau.

Costelette: f. (*The Diminutiue of* Coste) *a little rib, side, &c.*

Costelettes de porc. *The Sparribs.*

Costereauls. *A nickname giuen vnto certaine footmen, that serued the kings of England in their French warres; or as* Cotereaux; *or* Cottereaux.

Costié: m. ée: f. *Sided, on a side, of the one side; also, tainted, or (applied vnto fruit) bruised.*

Costier: m. ere: f. *Side, sideling; of, or on, a side.*

Costiere. à costiere. *Aside, sideling, sidewaies.*

Costin. huile costin. *An oyle made of* Costus *(a medicinable root) or, of the hearb, Alecoast.*

Coston: m. *The staulke of an hearbe; also, the Aromaticall root,* Costus; *(the best kind whereof, being white and light, comes from Arabia; the second, light and blacke, from the Indies; and the third, heauie & yellow, from* Suria.)

Coston bastard. *The root of Chirons Allheale.*

Costoyé: m. ée: f. *Accoasted, sided, abborded; coasted, or gone along by.*

Costoyer. *To accoast, side, abbord; to bee, or ly, by the side of; also, to coast along by, or goe by the coast of.*

Cotée: f. *A Coot, or Moore-henne.*

Coter. *To quote; See* Quoter.

Cotereaux. *as* Costereaux; *Or, a certaine crue of peasantlie outlawes, who, in old time, did much mischiefe vnto the Nobilitie, and Clergie.*

Coteret: m. *A fagot made of great stickes, or clouen wood; also, a kind of peasantlie weapon vsed in old time; also, a vessell containing 48 pintes of* Neuers *measure.*

Coterie: f. *Companie, societie, association of countrey people; or, as* Cotterie.

Cothurne: f. *A fashion of high-soled buskin vsed by the auncient Tragedians; also, a high, and loftie stile, as of a Tragedie.*

Cothurné: m. ée: f. *Shod with high pantofles, or, wearing high-soled buskins, as in a Tragedie.*

Cotice. *as* Cottice.

Cotignac: m. *Codinniack; Conserue, or Marmalade of Quinces.*

Cotile: ¶Rab. *as* Cotyle.

Cotillon: m. *A Petticoat.*

Cotine: m. *Venice Sumach, silken Sumach, red Sumach.*

Cotis: m. *The sparribs of a porke.*

Cotisation. *See* Cottisation.

Cotiser. *See* Cottiser.

Cotivet: m. *The vpper part of a hennes, or capons, necke.*

Cotollaire. *in stead of* Corolaire: ¶Rab.

Coton. *as* Coston.

Cotouere. *as* Cottoire.

Cotte: f. *A coat, or frocke; also, as* Quote; *also, a ticke for a bed.*

Cotte d'armes. *A Coat-armor; a long coat worne ouer armor.*

Cotte de femme. *A Kirtle.*

Cotte de mailles. *A shirt of maile.*

Ils tiennent cotte & ligne. *They haue both ends of the staffe, the law in their owne hands; or, the world at will.*

Femme sotte se cognoist à la cotte: Prov. *Looke* Femme.

Cotté: m. ée: f. *Coated; that hath gotten, or put on a coat; also, (of a hawke) full, or well mued; also, whose sides are vnderpropped, sustained, or underset.*

Cotte-maillé. *Armed with a coat of maile.*

Cotter. *(as* Accoter.) *To vnderset, sustaine, vnderprop, hold vp the side of.*

Cottereaux: m. *Takers, outlawes, freebooters, highway-robbers, peasant-fleecers, church-ransackers; (an old word; See* Cotereaux.)

Cotterie: f. *A base, ignoble, and seruile tenure, or tenement, not held in fee, and yeelding only rent, or if more, but* cens, *or* surcens *at most; as* Possession Roturiere, *or* de main-ferme.

Cottice: f. *A Cottice, or Battune; a third part lesse than a Bend, in Blazon.*

Cottier: m. ere: f. *as* Roturier; *Or, yeelding only rent, and* cens, *or* surcens, *and no better dueties, nor seruices; also, base, ignoble, seruile, not held in fee; or, held, or holding, by a seruile, base, and ignoble tenure; (for this word is euer opposed vnto* feudal, noble, *&* franc; *and, like enough, is an originall to our cottager.)*

Iuge Cottier. *Before whom a* Cottier *is, or ought to be, tried.*

Cottierement. *Ignobly, basely, Roturier-like, seruily, not in fee, onely for rent, or* cens, *or at most,* surcens.

Cottir. *To iurre, butt, rush, iustle, knocke heads together.*

Cottisation: f. *A Cottisation, assessement, or taxation.*

Cottisé: m. ée: f. *Taxed, assessed, rated at his part.*

Cottiser aucun. *To tax, assesse, rate, or set downe his part of paiment.*

Cottité: f. *A particular mans rate, part, or portion of an assessement, or imposition.*

Cottization; &, **Cottizer.** *as* Cottisation; & Cottiser.

Cottoire (de Perles.) *A chaine (of Pearle.*

Cotton: m. *Bumbasie, cotton.*

L' herbe à cotton. *as* Cottonniere.

Manne de cotton. *The worst kind of Manna, resembling flockes of bumbasie.*

Cottonné: m. ée: f. *Bumbasted, or stuffed with cotton.*

Cottonner. *To bumbast, or stuffe with cotton.*

Cottonner le moule du pourpoint. *To feed soundly, or excessiuely.*

Cottonneux. *Cottonnie; full of cotton; soft as cotton; ouergrowne with a white, soft, or cotton-like downe.*

Cottonniere: f. *The hearbe Chaffeweed, Cudwort, Cudweed, Cotton-weed, pettie Cotton.*

Cottouere. *as* Cottoire.

Coturniqué: m. ée: f. *Bebuskined, in buskins*: Rab.

Cotyle. *An ancient measure containing about 24 spoonfuls.*

Cotyledons: m. *The mouthes, or ends of the Menstruall veines, whereby the superfluous bloud of all the bodie falls into the wombe, & giues nourishment vnto the child there (if there be any.)*

Cou: f. *A whetstone.*

Couäné: m. ée: f. *All foamie, or froathie.*

Coüanne. *as* Couënne.

Coüard: m. *A coward, a dastard, a cow.*

Ia coüard n' aura belle amie: Prov. *Faint heart neuer woon faire Ladie.*

Mieux vaut coüard que trop hardi: Prov. *Tis better to be a coward than foole-hardie.*

Couard: m. arde: f. *Cowardlie, dastardlie, vnmanlie; timerous, fearfull, white-liuered, heartlesse, faint hearted.*

Plus couard qu'un Lievre. *More heartlesse than a Hare.*

Hardie langue couärde lance: Prov. *as in* Langue.

Coüardement. *Cowardly, dastardly, heartlesly, timerously, fearfully.*

Coüarder. *To be a coward, or play the coward.*

Coüardise: f. *Cowardise, dastardie, cowardlinesse, vnmanlinesse, faint-heartednesse, timerousnesse.*

Couät: m. *The vnderling, writling, starueling, or dwarfe, of any beast, or bird.*

Coubde: m. *as* Coude; *The Elbow.*

Coubdée. *as* Coudée.

Couble. chevaux de couble. *Paires, or couples of horses; coach-horses; draught-horses.*

Coubte. *The Elbow.*

Couchable: com. *Fit, easie, or possible to be lien on.*

Couchant. *Couchant, couching, lying; laying along.*

Couche: f. *A bedstead; also, a couch, or bed; also, a (square high) bed in a garden; also, a womans lying in (child-bed;) also, the Post, or most of a sute, at cards; also, a set, lay, or stake, at any game.*

Couches. *A childes clowts; also, receptacles, or ponds for sea-water (as in* Amezeau; *) also, a womans lying in.*

Vn lict à triple couche de plumes. *A bed stuffed with three course of feathers one aboue the other.*

Panneau de couche. *as* Sommier.

I'entends le pair & la couche. *I vnderstand the matter throughly.*

Prins au pair, & à la couche. *Beset, intangled, indaungered, ouertaken, at losse, in extremitie, on all hands.*

Couché: m. ée: f. *Couched, layed along, lying; also, couched, mentioned, or set downe in writing; also, staked, or set, at play.*

Couché à quatre pattes. *Prostrated, layed all along, or vpon all foure.*

Couché en estat. *Being made Officer*; qui n'est couché en l'estat: *Baulked, omitted, passed in election, and not chosen.*

Couché entre l' enclume & les marteaux. *Seated in the middest of dangers; or, inuironed on all sides, with dangerous mischiefes; pestered, perplexed, afflicted which way soeuer he turne him.*

Couchement: m. *A couching, lying, or laying downe.*

Couche-m'-icy. *The weed called Dodder.*

Couchenil: m. *Cuchannele.*

Coucher. *To couch, or ly (also, to lay) downe, or along; to goe (also, to get, bring, or haue) to bed; also, to mention, or set downe in writing; also, to plant, or set a root, or slip, flat along within the ground; also, to stake, at play.*

Coucher de belles. Ils en couchent de belles. *They write goodlie matters sure; tis sweet stuffe that they set downe; ironically.*

Coucher en chappon. *To go earely to bed.*

Coucher soubs corde. *To stake downe readie coine; See* Corde.

Coucher à l' enseigne de l' estoille. *To lye without doores all night.*

Coucher tout à bander & à racler. *To venture all on desperat tearmes, to set all on sixes and seuens.*

Se coucher abouchon. *To lie groueling, to sleepe on the face.*

Se despouiller avant que se coucher. *Said of him that in his life time giues his heires absolute possession of all he hath.*

Qui se couche avec les chiens se leue avec des puces: Prov. *From filthie companie what can one bring but filth?*

Couchette: f. *A little bed; a couch, or bed of ease.*

Mignon de couchette. *A Carpet-Knight, one that euer loues to be in womens chambers.*
Coucheur: m. *A coucher, staker; layer downe of; also, a Bedfellow.*
Couchille. *The tree that beares the graine Kermes, wherewith Skarlet is dyed; wee call it, the Skarlet Oake.*
Couchine. *The name of a certaine apple.*
Coucombre. *A Cowcumber. See* Concombre.
Coucon. *The little bottome, or clue of silke spunne by the silkeworme.*
Coucou: m. *A Cuckoe.*
(I'ay beau luy remonstrer;) ie ne fais non plus que le coucou aux cannes. *No wordes terrifie him, or preuaile with him.*
Coucourbe. *as* Coucourde.
Coucourde: f. *A round Gourd; also, a kind of large Stillitorie; or, as* Courge.
Coucourelle. *The name of a certaine Fig.*
Coude: m. *The elbow.*
Coude de la branche. *The elbow, or out-bearing of the branch of a Bit.*
Os du coude. *The vnder bone of the arme, from the elbow to the wrist.*
Il y a mis la main iusques au coude; &, il a entré en la paste iusques aux coudes. *He hath gone very farre in the matter; he is vp to the eares in it.*
Plier le coude. *To drinke hard, to ply the pot apace; or, to fall to chat seriously, to settle himselfe to talke; (for, such as doe so, commonly leane vpon their elbowes.)*
Poulser du coude. *Proudly to iustle, and shoulder euerie one that comes in his way.*
Coudé: m. ée: f. *Bowed, or crooked, or standing, elbowwise.*
Coudée: f. *A cubit; (extends from the elbow to the end of the middle finger; and is in ordinarie measure, a foot and a halfe.)*
Coudées franches. *Elbow-roome, free libertie.*
Coudée Geometrique. *Containeth six ordinarie cubits.*
Coudée royale. *is three fingers longer then the ordinarie one.*
Coudéer. *To iog, or ioult with the elbow.*
Coudepied. *The instup.*
Coudoyer. *as* Coudéer.
Coudraye: f. *See* Couldraye.
Coudre: m. *A Hasell; a small Nut tree; a Filberd tree; (for this word comprehendeth all those kinds of small Nut trees.)*
Coudre: f. *A small Nut, a Hasell Nut; and a Filberd; (for it comprehends them all.)*
Coudre franche. *A Filberd.*
Coudré: m. ée: f. *Tanned, steeped in a Tanfat.*
Coudre. *To sow; to stitch together.*
Coudre la peau de regnard à celle de lion. *To attempt that by craftie, which he cannot get by forcible, meanes.*
Ie ne sçay quelle piece coudre à cecy. *I know not what remedie to apply vnto this, nor what art to vse in the repaire of it.*
Coudrer. *To tanne; to steepe, or stiffen, in a Tanfat.*
Coudrier: m. *A small Nut tree, of what kind soeuer.*
Coudroir. *A Tanfat, or Tanpit.*
Couë: f. *as* Queuë; *a tayle.*
Coué: m. ée: f. *Tayled, hauing a tayle.*
Couënne de lard. *The skin of Bacon.*
Couët: m. *(The name of) a certaine little apple.*
Couëts. *Two ropes belonging to the mizen sayle of a ship.*
Couëtte: f. *A ticke (to ly, or sit on;) as* Coitte.
Coufler. *To swell, or be puffed vp.*
Cougourde: f. *A Bottle-Gourd; the round Gourd whereof Bottles are made.*
Cougourle. *The same.*
Couhourde. *The same.*
Couillage: m. *A Tribute payed in times past by Priests for Licences to keepe wenches.*
Couillards: m. *as* Clides; *or, certaine round, and ringed pieces of yron, which in old time they vsed to shoot out of ships.*
Couillatris. *Well hangd (betweene the legs.)*
Couille: f. *A mans yard; also (but lesse properly) a cod, ballocke, or testicle; also, a long, lanke, and lubberlie coward; a heartlesse, faint-hearted, or white-liuered slimme.*
Couille barbe. *A certaine little apple, which is red on the one side; and yeelds an excellent Cyder.*
Couille de belier. *A kind of ball made of a Rammes cod.*
Couille au chien. *as* Couillon de chien.
Couille à l'Euesque. *A kind of sallet hearbe.*
Couille au loup. *Wild Prickmadame, Wormegrasse, great Stonecrop.*
Les couilles luy pendent à faute de gibbeciere. *He hath taken too much of the lower sheet, or he is tame enough by this time: (Spoken of a young man, after hee hath beene married some two or three moneths.)*
Couille-barbe. *See* Couille.
Couilleu. *Stoned; or, that wants not his stones.*
Couillon: m. *A cod, stone, testicle, cullion.*
Couillon de bouc. *Goats stones, Goats cullions; (an hearbe.)*
Couillon de chien. *Dogs-stones, Dogs cullions, Gandergoose, Standlewort, Standergrasse, Ballock-grasse, Adders grasse, bastard Satyrion.*
Couillon de prestre. *Spindletree, Prickwood, Pricktymber.*
Couïnne. *as* Couënne. *The skin of Bacon.*
Couïonnade. *as* Coyonnade.
Coulac. *The Shad fish; (called so in Bourdeaux.)*
Coulagion: f. *The running of a sore, &c.*
Les Coulans d'un jardinier. *A Gardeners lines, wherewith he measures out his beds, and plots.*
Coulant: m. Le c. d'une Riviere. *The streame of a riuer.*
Vn coulant d'eau de mer. *An arme of the sea.*
Coulant: m. ante: f. *Gliding, slipping, flowing gently along.*
Vaine doucement coulante. *A sweet smooth veine in Poetrie, &c.*
Coulde. *as* Coude. *The elbow.*
Couldée. *as* Coudée; *also, a certaine crooked toole belonging to Masons.*
Couldier: m. *A dwarfe; one thats no higher then three horse-loaues, one thats but a shaftment high.*
Couldoye. à c. *Made with an out nooke like an elbow.*
Couldrasse: f. *A hedge toad, or land toad.*
Couldray: m. *as* Couldraye.
Couldraye: f. *A Wood, Groue, or Orchard, of Hasell, or of small Nut, trees; a Hasell wood, or Hasell groue.*
Couldre: m. *A Hasell tree, a small Nut tree, of what kind soeuer.*

Couldre: f. *A Hasell Nut, or small Nut, of what kind soeuer.*
Couldre franche. *A Filberd.*
Couldré. *as* Coudré.
Couldrer. *as* Coudrer.
Couldrier: m. *A Hasell, or small Nut tree, of what kind soeuer.*
Couldroir. *as* Coudroir.
Coulé: m. ée: f. *Runne, glid, gone, slipped gently along; slid, trilled, trickled downe; also, strained; also, leaked.*
Coulée: f. *as* Coulement.
Coulement: m. *A gentle running, easie passing, soft gliding, glib sliding, (as of water, &c) along; a trilling, or trickling downe; also, a leaking; also, a straining.*
Couler. *To slide, slip, runne quietly along; to goe glib away; to flow gently, glide easily by; to trill, trickle, or fall downe softly; also, to leake; also, to straine.*
Se couler. *To creepe through, or into; to crawle ouer.*
Le navire couloit à bas en pleine mer. *Went, or sunke, downe to the bottome.*
Cette pluye fait couler les raisins. *Makes them drop, or fall off.*
Coule-sang: m. *A certaine Viper, so called, because those that are bitten by her bleed to death.*
Coulet: m. *as* Collet.
Couletage. Droict de c. *A pennie, or halfe-pennie toll collected, & taken, of all wares, or marchandise bought and sold.*
Couleur: f. *A colour, hue; dye; staine; also, a pretext, pretence, cloake, shew, shadow, for a matter.*
Couleur bastarde. *A weake, pale, wan, decayed colour.*
Couleur de Cassidoine. *A mingled colour betweene purple, and white; a Mallow colour.*
Couleur chargée. *A deepe colour, in any kind.*
Couleur de ciel serein. *A bright skie colour.*
Couleur d'enfer. *as much as*, Noir-brun enfumé.
Couleur flamboyante. *A flame colour.*
Couleur de fleur de pescher. *A Peach colour.*
Couleur de gris violant. *A whitish purple, or the Mallow-flower colour.*
Couleur de jaulne paille. *Straw colour.*
Couleur incarnat. *A Carnation, or Damaske-Rose, colour.*
Couleur d'Inde. *A Painters browne Violet, made of the scumming of woad sodden with slaked lyme, or chalke, and mixed afterwards with a little* Amydon.
Couleur de Minime. *A huswiues darke gray, or light soote colour, wherein there is an eye of gray.*
Couleur paillarde. *The greene sicknesse; or, a pale, wan, bleake hue.*
Couleur pasle. *A vaded, or vnperfect colour, such as that of Box wood is.*
Couleur pers. *A Blue, or Watchet.*
Couleur perse. *Skie-colour, Azure colour, a Blunket, or light blue.*
Couleur de poil de souris. *A Mouse-dunne.*
Couleurs Rhetoriques. *Phrases, conceits, figures, flourishes of Rhetoricke; ornaments of speech.*
Couleur de Roses seiches. *The best darke Crimson, or Murrey.*
Couleur de Roy, *was in old time, Purple; but now is the bright Tawnie, which wee also tearme, Colour de Roy.*
Couleur Turquine. *A right blue, or Venice blue; the colour of the Turkie stone.*
Couleur de verd de mer. *A sea-greene.*
Haulte couleur. *A fierie red, or flame colour.*
Les pasles couleurs. *The greene sicknesse.*
Les riches couleurs. *The yellow Iaundise.*
Il en parle comme vn aveugle de couleurs. *Hee speakes he knowes not what, nor of what; Seeke* Aveugle.
Couleurée: f. *The weed Bryonie; or, as;*
Couleurée blanche. *Bryonie, white Bryonie, the white Vine, Tettar-berrie.*
Couleurée noire. *The wild Vine, blacke Bryonie, our Ladies Seale.*
Couleurée sauvage. *Wild Bryonie, or the wild blacke Bryonie.*
Coulevriner. *as* Couleuvriner.
Couleuvre: f. *An Adder.*
Couleuvré: m. ée: f. *Made after the fashion of an Adder.*
Couleuvreé. *Snakeweed, Oysterloit.*
Couleuvreau: m. *A yong Adder.*
Couleuvrin: m. ine: f. *Adder like, of an Adder.*
Couleuvrine: f. *A Culuerin; the peece of ordnance called so.*
Couleuvriner. *To squat, lurke, ly close, or flat along; also, to glide wrigling along.*
Coulier: m. *See* Collier.
Coulis: m. *A cullis, or broth of boiled meat strained; fit for a sicke, or weake bodie.*
Coulis: m. isse: f. *as* Coulant; *Gliding.*
Potage coulis. *as* Coulis.
Vent coulis. *The hurtfull, or vnwholesome wind, which blowes through a hole, creuise, or crannie.*
Coulisse: f. *A Portcullis; or any other doore, or thing, which, as a portcullis, falls, or slips, or is let, downe; also, a web in the eye.*
Coulisse d'un arbaleste. *The hollow furrow wherein the arrow lyes; we call it, the gutter, or chace (of a crosse-bow.)*
Coullebobes: f. *The hearbe Alkakengie, or, the fruit thereof; Winter-cherries.*
Coullon. *as* Coulon.
Couloir: m. *A cullander, or strainer.*
Couloir: m. ire: f. *Cullender-like, belonging to a cullander, straining through it, as a cullander.*
Os couloir du nez. *The head bone, or inner bone of the nose.*
Couloire: f. *as* Couloir. *A cullander.*
Coulomb: m. *A Doue, a Pigeon.*
Coulomb biset. *A Stocke-doue, Queest, Culuer.*
Coulombier: m. *A Doue-cote, a Pigeonhouse.*
Coulombin. *Doue colour. See* Colombin.
Coulomne: f. *as* Colomne; *a pillar.*
Coulon: m. *A Doue, Pigeon, or Culuer.*
Coulon ramier. *A Queest, Cowshot, Ringdoue, Stockdoue, Wood-culuer.*
Coulouëre. *as* Couloire; *also, a channell, gutter, or any such hollow, along which melted things are to runne, as Bell-mettall, from the furnace to the mould.*
Coulouöir: m. *A sliding blow.*
Coulouré: m. ée: f. *Coloured. See* Coloré.
Coulourer. *To colour; shadow; make pretences.*
Coulpable: com. *Culpable, guiltie, offending, faultie, blame-worthie.*
Coulpe: f. *A fault, offence, trespasse, misdeed, or ill deed.*
Batre sa coulpe. *To beat his breast for his faults.*

En

En dire sa coulpe. Le mesme.

Coulper. *To blame, tax, reproue, chide, reprehend, find fault with.*

Coulteau; &, Coultel. *as* Cousteau. *A knife.*

Coultre: m. *The Sexton of a Church; also, the Culter, or knife of a Plow.*

Coulture: f. *A great plowed field; a large close of tilled land; also, plowing, or tillage.*

Coulure: f. *A gentle running, slipping, or sliding along; trilling, or falling downe; creeping through, or into; gliding, or crawling ouer; also, a leaking; also, a straining.*

Coulure de Vignes. *A fault, or imperfection in Vines, the chiefe grapes falling, and the residue verie little; comes by much raine when they were young, or in knitting.*

Counil: m. *A Connie.*

Counille: f. *A Doe Connie, a female Rabbet.*

Counilleau: m. *A young Rabbet, little young Connie.*

Counin: m. *as* Counil. *See* Connin.

Coup: m. *A blow, stroake; knocke, rap, thumpe, cuffe, whirret; also, a hit, or touch; a Vennie, in fencing; also, a fling, or cast, as at Dice, &c; also, a Cuckold.*

Coup de bec. *A pecking, or pecke (of a birds beake;) also, a quip, taunt, cut, or bad word; also, a kisse.*

Coup d' essay. *A tryall-peece, or Maister-peece; Looke* Essay.

Coup d'estoc. *A thrust, foine, stab; also, a prick-cast.*

Coup de haut. *A downe-right blow; also, a quaffe, carousse, or sound draught.*

Coup de langue. *A checke, taunt, rebuke; also, a quip, cut, gird; slaunder, disgracefull nip, reprochfull touch; a tearme of imputation; and hence the Prouerbe;*

Vn coup de langue est plus dangereux qu' un coup de lance. *A word is (oft) more dangerous then a wound.*

Coup de mer. *A violent waue, a mightie sea; or, a blow giuen by a waue of the sea.*

Coup de rets. *The draught (of a Net.)*

Coup de taille. *A slash, cut, gash, wype.*

Coup orbe. *A bruise, crush, thumpe, dust, dry-blow.*

Coup-orbe. *Red pimples in the face.*

Coup perdu. *A Misse; also, a cast, or throw made at randome, and without any apparant hope, or likelyhood of hitting; whence;*

'A coup perdu. *Fruitlesly, in vaine, vnto no purpose; also, at randome; without any certaine aime, or hope of hitting; and,*

Prins à coup perdu. *Atchieued by chance, obtained by meere fortune, succeeding beyond expectation, gotten more by hap then by any manner of cunning.*

Le tiers coup de baston. *The knocke which in a Portsale (or Act which any other way) gaines a full, and absolute possession.*

Coup à coup. *Euer; euerie time; or, from time to time.*

Coup sur coup. *Often, eftsoones, now and anon, successiuely, one in the necke of another.*

'A coup; tout à coup; tout à vn coup; tout d'un coup. *Speedily, suddainly, at once, all at once, all together.*

'A tous coups. *Often, eftsoones; euery time, continually, at each blow.*

Au bon du coup. *When the matter is at best, or in best tearmes; or, when it is time to do a mans best in it.*

Le coup valoit bien la boule. *His good casting was worth all other aduantages; or, his good play was vnto him as great an aduantage, as leading vnto the other.*

Donner coup à. *To strike the onely stroake; to be of most auaile, to doe all in all, in.*

Donner vn coup de gaule par sous l' huis. *To supplant, or giue a priuie lift. See* Gaule.

Faire coup sur. *To strike home vnto, be of great consequence in, worke an important effect on.*

Faire vn coup de sa main. Il a fait &c. *He hath played a leud part.*

Faire vn mauvais coup. de peur qu'il ne feist quelque mauvais coup. *Least he should enter into some naughtie practise, or execute any villanous proiect.*

Faire selon la jambe le coup. *(as we say) to cut his coat according to his cloth.*

D'une pierre faire deux coups. *To kill two birds with one stone; to make a double vse, or profit, of his trauell.*

Gauchir au coup. *To auoid a blow by turning, or by wrinching, the bodie aside.*

Gauchir le coup. *To giue a winding blow, thrust indirectly, strike awry.*

Porter coup. *To hit home; to preuaile; to attaine to the purpose it was directed vnto.*

Porter coup à la foy. *To wrong, blemish, violate, infringe, breake, faith giuen.*

Prendre coup. cela a desja pris coup. *Hath alreadie receiued a fatall blow; or, is come vnto so ill a state, that the ruine thereof must of necessitie follow.*

Rompre le coup. *To beat, or put by a blow. Seeke* Rompre.

Suivre ses coups. *To prosecute, or second, with great earnestnesse, an enterprise begun.*

Tenir coup à la besongne. *To ply a matter; to follow it diligently, prosecute it seriously, hold hard vnto it.*

'A tout perdre n' y a qu' un coup perilleux: Prov. *One sound blow will serue to vndoe vs all.*

Chascun est sage apres le coup: Prov. *Looke* Sage.

En adventure gisent grands coups: Pro. *In doubtfull cases great blowes are bestowed.*

L'arbre ne tombe pas du premier coup: Pro. *The first blow fels not the tree; the first attempt, or effort, carries not a great matter.*

On ne fait pas à grand coups douce vielle: Prov. *Tis not the great (but the apt) stroake that makes the harmonie.*

Qui vise loing iamais ne rend son coup heureux: Prov. *The farre-off leueller shall neuer hit the white.*

Coupant: m. *A Spade; or such another earth-cutting instrument of Husbandrie.*

Les Coupans des costez des traces d' un sanglier. *The sharpe edges, or sides, of the foot of a wilde Bore.*

Coupant: m. ante: f. *Cutting; cleauing; hacking, hewing; launcing, slitting; caruing, intailing; lopping; mowing.*

Coupau: m. *A Cuckold; also, a greene Goose.*

Coupe: f. *A cut, or cutting; a gash, a slit, an incision; also, a cup, goblet, or mazer; also, the roofe of a house, made almost round; the cop of a house.*

Coupe de balance. *The scole of a Balance.*

Coupe de bois. *The cutting, felling, or lopping of wood; also, the season thats fittest to cut, or fell, it in; also, the soyle whereon the wood so cut, or felled, grew.*

Bois de coupe. *Wood thats betweene ten, and thirtie, yeares growth.*
Tel bois à la coupe rouge. *Such wood cuts red.*
Coupé: m. ée: f. *Cut; clouen, sliced; hacked, slashed, hewed; carued, grauen, intailed; slit, launced; pruined, lopped, felled, as a tree; mowed, as grasse.*
Croix coupée. *A crosse-humet;* Blazon.
Coupeau: m. *The cop, head, or top of a thing.*
Coupeau de bois. *A chip.*
Coupeau d'oignon. *The head, or peele of an Onyon.*
Coupeau de la teste. *The Crowne, or Noddle.*
Piquant coupeau. *A kind of pricklie thistle, tearmed thus about Paris.*
Coupe-aureille. *See* Coupe-oreille.
Coupe-bourse: m. *A Cut-purse.*
Hardi en coupe-bourse. *as bold as a Cut-purse.*
Coupelle: f. *A Coppell; the little Ashen pot, or vessell, wherein Goldsmiths melt, or fine their mettals.*
Argent de coupelle. *Siluer that hath beene tested, or tryed; fine siluer.*
Coupement: m. *A cutting, slicing, hewing, slashing; a cleauing, slitting; launcing, incision-making; also, a pruning, lopping, or felling of trees; a sheering of corne, mowing of grasse; also, a diuiding, sundering, seperating.*
Coupe-oreille: f. *A (fashion of) sharpe, and thin-bladed French knife, wherewith the eares of rogues, and pettie theeues are cut off.*
Coupe-queuë. Deux mots à coupe-queuë. *Two short, and soone-done words; two words, and there's an end; but two bare words, and no more.*
Couper. *To cut, slice, hacke, slash, hew; to cleaue, slit; launce, make an incision; also, to carue, graue, intayle; also, to prune, lop, or fell trees; mow corne, or grasse; also, to diuide, sunder, seperate.*
Se Couper. *To cut himselfe; also (in speaking) to trip.*
Couper broche à. *To preuent, cut off, cut short.*
Couper chemin à. *To stop, crosse, forestall, preuent, let from proceeding any further.*
Couper de deux costez. *To deale on both hands, to intertaine both sides with promise of his assistance.*
Couper l'herbe sous les pieds à. *To supplant, vndermine; marre the market of; set beside the cushion.*
Couper les ongles de prés à. *To curbe very short; to keepe very bare, or neere; to restraine, impouerish, yeeld hard, or scant allowance to; or withdraw most of his meanes, or allowance from.*
Couper la queuë à. *To desist, giue ouer, leaue off from; (and particularly) to breake off talke with.*
Couper la queuë au ieu. *To leaue playing with one whose money he hath woon; to giue ouer a winner.*
Couper le vin. *To leaue blowne drinke; or to drinke but part.*
Il a vn nez qui coupe. *He hath a most searching wit, a most piercing spirit.*
Se Couper soy mesme par ses defenses. *To speake against, in thinking to defend, himselfe.*
Il se coupe de son propre cousteau. *He wounds himselfe with his owne weapons; as does a learned Diuine that fals into heresie; an eloquent speaker, that wrests or peruerts the Law; a beautifull person that grows dissolute, or effeminate; a wealthie man that becomes either a miser, or an vnthrift, &c.*
Couperet: m. *A Butchers Knife, or Cleauer.*
Couperose: f. *Copres; also, extreame rednesse of the face, accompanied with many pimples, and rubies, especially about the nose.*
Couperosé: m. ée: f. *Mingled, seasoned, or dressed with Coperons; also, Crimson-faced, Copper-nosed, red, ruddie.*
Coupet: m. *The top, head, height, cop, crest, ridge, of.*
Coupet de cheveux. *A tuft, or topping, of haire.*
Coupeur: m. *A cutter, cleauer; hacker, hewer; caruer, intayler; launcer, slitter; mower; lopper, feller of trees; and most particularly, a reaper or cutter of grapes, in the time of Vintage.*
Coupeur de bourses. *A Cut-purse; whence;* Estonné comme vn coupeur de bourses pris sur le fait; *Amazed like a Cut-purse, taken in the manner.*
Coupeur de cuir. *A Cut-purse.*
Coupeure: f. *See* Coupure.
Coupeuse: f. *A woman that reapes, or cuts grapes in the time of Vintage.*
Coupeux: m. euse: f. *Cutting; or, full of cutting; or fit to cut.*
Dents coupeuses. *The fore-teeth.*
Coupier: m. *A cup-bearer; one that waiteth on his masters cup.*
Couple: f. *A couple; a paire; also, a paire of dogge-couples.*
En couple. *Coupled, by paires, two and two together.*
Couplé: m. ée: f. *Coupled; yoaked, vnited, ioyned; grapled, together.*
Coupler. *To couple, ioyne, yoake, vnite together; also, to coape, or graple together, as in fight.*
Couplet de chanson. *A Staffe, or Stanzo of a Poeme, or Song.*
Couplot de bois. *A woodden sole, or Nut for a Scrue; the foot of a Scrue, &c.*
Coupon: m. *A great Cup, or Bowle; also, a Tray of wood, &c; also, a cut of; or, a thicke and short slice, or peece cut from, a thing.*
Coupon de drap. *A shred of cloth.*
Coup-orbe. *Red pimples on the face.*
Couppe. *as* Coupe.
Couppe-bourse. *as* Coupebourse.
Couppelettes de gland. *Akorne cups.*
Couperet: m. *A Butchers Knife, or Cleauer.*
Couppier: m. *A cup-bearer; or one that waiteth on his masters cup.*
Couppon. *as* Coupon.
Coupure: f. *A cutting; slicing; cleeuing; launcing; lopping; sheering (&c. as in* Coupement;*) also, a cut (&c. as in* Coupe;*) and hence;*
Par coupures. *Peece-meale; by peeces; in slices; by shreds.*
Cour: f. *A Court of Law, or Iustice; any Session, or Assemblie of Iudges; or the place wherein they vse to assemble; also, the Court of a Prince; or of a priuat house. See* Court.
Cour des Aides. *A soueraigne Court, wherein all causes that concerne the Aides,* Tailles, *&c, are heard, and determined: (Some report, that King Iohn, others that Charles the fift, about the yere* 1380, *erected that which is at Paris; Charles the seuenth erected another at Montpelier,* Anno 1437. *There be others also, at Roan, and at Montferrant in Auvergne; and one at Bourdeaux, the which was first at Perigueux.)*
Cour feudale. *A Court Leet, or Baron; the Lords Court, whereto his vassales and tenants owe their suit, and seruice.*
Cour fonciere. *A Court Baron; or, Court of base iurisdiction.*

La Cour des monnoyes. *as*, La Chambre des monnoyes.
La Cour des Pairs. *A Court Leet, or Baron.*
La Cour de Parlement. *Looke* Parlement.
Cour personnelle. *See* Personnel.
Cours souverains. *The highest Courts, from which there is no appealing.*
Retraict de barre, ou de Cour. *See* Retraict.
De par la Cour. *By the opinion, consent, or sentence of the Iudges, in Court.*
En pleine Cour. *In the hearing of the whole Court; when all the Iudges and Officers thereof were present.*
Courage: m. *Courage; mettall, spirit, hart, stomacke; valour, stoutnesse, bouldnesse, hardinesse, forwardnesse; also, confidence, assurance, hopefulnesse; also, liuelinesse, alacritie, iolitie, cheerefulnesse; also, willingnesse; also, the mind, will, humor, fancie, affection, disposition.*
Courage de brebis. *(A merrie forme of incouraging, or cheering vp; wherein tis meant that,* Le nez en terre, *should follow) On with a sheepes heart.*
Dur courage. *A rude, stiffe, obdurate, inflexible, humor.*
Felon courage. *A fiercenesse, rigor, crueltie, an vntractable, or vnsociable disposition.*
Franc courage. *Opennesse, plainnesse, freeheartednesse;* de franc courage. *Cheerefully, freely, willingly, with a heart.*
Lasche courage. *Negligence, carelesnesse, faintnesse; slacknesse, weaknesse; abiection, lowlinesse.*
Petit courage. *Weaknesse, feeblenesse, pusillanimitie; slender wit, little spirit, poore mettall.*
De courage. *as* Courageusement.
Sans courage. *Dully, slackly, cowardly.*
Tu cognois mon courage. *Thou knowest my minde, thou art well acquainted with my humor.*
I'ay bon courage mais les jambes me faillent. *My heart is verie good, but my heeles* (viz. *my meanes) doe faile me.*
A grand danger grand courage: Prov. *Courage, when danger is, had need be great.*
Courageusement. *Couragiously, stoutly, valiantly, boldly, forwardly, hardily; confidently, with great assurednesse.*
Courageux: m. euse: f. *Couragious, valiant, hardie, bold, stout, manlie, aduenturous, forward; full of confidence, full of assurance, full of assurednesse.*
Couramment. *Swiftly, glibly, readily, without stop.*
Courance: f. *A flux, or laxatiuenesse in the bodie; the Squirt.*
Courans. *as* Coulans.
Courant: m. *A current, or swift course of waters; also, an vpper Mill-stone, called (also by our Millers) the runner.*
Courant. *Running, speeding, poasting; coursing, chasing.*
Cordeau courant. *See* Cordeau.
Queste courant. *Such an imposition as may be layed by a Lord on his tenants, when, and in what proportion he list.*
Rente courant. *A rent-secke, or charge; raised of, or bought with, money.*
Courante: f. *A Curranto.*
Courbassé: m. ée: f. *Hulch-backed, or crooke-shouldered.*
Cour-baston: m. *A truncheon, or short cudgell; also (in a ship) a crooked peece of tymber, tearmed a Knee, or Futtocke.*

Courbatu: m. uë: f. *Tyred, ouertoyled, worne out, growne crooked, with extreame labour; also, beaten till he stoope againe, or so much, that he is grown crooked withall; also, foundered.*
Courbature: f. *The foundering of a horse, or heating of his feet, by ouer-much trauell.*
Courbe: f. *A bought; also, a crooked, or bowing peece of tymber; and (more particularly) a compasse, or moulded, Rafter; also, the Curbes (in a horses hinder legs.)*
Courbes d'un navire. *The ribs of a ship; called by Mariners, the Futtocks, or Nauell tymbers.*
Courbes d'une voulte. *The arching of a Vault.*
Courbé: m. ée: f. *Crooked, bowed, plyed, vaulted, arched, bent arch-wise.*
Les bras courbez en anse. *With armes a-kemboll.*
Courbée: f. *as* Courvée. ¶Gasc.
Courbe-espine. *The name of a delicate Normand apple.*
Courbement: m. *A crooking, bowing; vaulting, arching; plying, or bending, arch-wise.*
Courber. *To crooke, bow; vault, arch; ply, or bend, arch-wise.*
Courbes: f. *The legs;* ¶Barrag; *also, the plurall vnto* Courbe.
Courbette: f. *A small crooked Rafter, or peece of Tymber; also, a curuet, or, the curuetting of a horse.*
Courbure: f. *as* Courbement; *or, a bought.*
Courcaillée de cailles. *The calling of Quayles.*
Courcie: f. *Part of a Galley tearmed, the Coursey.*
Courde: f. *A Gourd.*
Courdier: m. *A Gourd-plant.*
Courée de mouton: f. *A Sheepes Plucke; the intrailes, or inwards of a Mutton.*
Courement: m. *A running; poasting, coursing, passing on apace.*
Coureur: m. *A runner; a courser; a Poaster, a Poste; also, a roamer, or wanderer abroad; one whose shooes are made of running leather; one that neuer keepes at home, or where he should be; also, a courror, outrider, rank-rider; and hence;*
Coureurs. *Light horsemen, imployed in the ouerrunning, rauaging, or forraging, of an enemies countrey.*
Coureuse: f. *A gadding huswife; also, a common, publicke, notorious, whore.*
Courge: f. *The fruit called, a Gourd; also, a wide, and deepe Lymbecke, made somewhat Gourd-like; also (and the more properly) the wide bellie, or lower part of such a Lymbecke; also, a Stang, Pale-staffe, or Colestaffe, carried on the shoulder, and notched (for the hanging of a Pale &c) at both ends.*
Courge blanche. *The white Gourd, a very holesome fruit either boyled, fryed, or preserued.*
Courge d'hyver. *The ordinarie great round Pompion, or Gourd, hung vp in Kitchins for Winter prouision.*
Courge d'Inde. *as* Courge d'hyver; *so called, because the first seedes thereof came out of the Indies;* ¶Mathiolus; *(yet are there, besides this, three seuerall kinds of Indian Pompions; a small round one; a cornered one; and the Mushrome Pompion.* ¶Gerard.)
Courge longue. *The Snakes Gourd, or long Gourd.*
Courge marine. *The sea Gourd, whereof there be diuers kinds; (though* Gerard *haue none.)*
Courge sauvage. *The wild Gourd; some also call so the wild Citrull, or fleame-purging* Coloquintida.

Courge de Turquie. *The Turkie Gourd.*
Grande courge. *The great round Gourd.*
Petite courge. *The bottle Gourd, or lesse Gourd.*
Courier: m. *A Post,&c*; *as* Courrier.
Courin. *as* Cousin.
Courir. *To runne; post, gallop; make speed, hye apace, goe verie hastily, passe verie swiftly; runne on; proceed fast in; also, to ride a running horse, or (as in posting) runne on horseback; also, to hunt, course vp and down, follow hard, pursue hastily, giue hot chase vnto; also, to ouerrun, rauage, ransack, make hostile incursions vpon; also, to haue course, or be currant; to be in date, vse, request, or fashion.*
Courir les champs en pourpoint. *To play the Bedlam; to runne vp and downe like a mad man.*
Courir les choses legierement. *To runne, or passe ouer things verie sleightly; to take a snatch, and be gone; to giue onely a touch, and away.*
Courir danger. *To be in danger, or, in a doubtfull estate; to be as like to speed ill as well.*
Courir au deuant de. *To meet with.*
Courir l'esguillette. *To play the impudent, or importunate, whore; extreamly to lust, or maddingly to run, after a P.*
Courir fortune. *To be in danger of shipwracke; or, to abandon a ship, in a great storme, vnto the mercie and conduction of the wind and waues.*
Courir fortune auec; ou, courir la fortune de. *To imbarke himselfe, or take part, with another, in all his attempts, or hazards whatsoeuer.*
Courir la lance. *To tilt, or, to run at tilt.*
Courir la lance S. Crespin sur vn escabelle à trois pieds. *To play the Shoomaker.*
Courir vn livre; *To runne ouer a booke with the eye, noting onely the words, and neglecting the matter; or, to read a booke sleightly, and hastily ouer, without much respect had, or heed taken, either to the phrase, or matter.*
Courir vn office. *To ride post for the getting of an Office.*
Courir apres son ombre. *To spend his time idly, fondly, vainely; or, to loose time.*
Courir la poule. *To forrage, rauage, ransacke, spoyle, or make pillage of, euery thing that comes in his way; (Said of a disorderlie, and ill-gouerned, souldior, who in his march, or residence in a countrey, twitches vp euery poore mans henne that peepes out.)*
Courir comme vne rasle, viz. *Very swiftly.*
Courir les rues. *To play the Bedlam; to range, roame, or gad vp and downe, like a mad man.*
Courir sus à. *Furiously to inuade, assaile, or set vpon; also, to vsurpe, or incroach on, to interrupt, or intermeddle with, another mans profit, or imployment.*
Ce n'est pas tout de courir, Il faut partir à temps: Prov. *Tis not enough to pursue diligently, vnlesse we haue begun discreetly.*
Il ne faut iamais courir apres son esteuf: Prov. *One must neuer let go a thing, which he hath, and may hold, with a purpose to follow, or for any hope to recouer, it; Looke* Esteuf.
L'eau qui dort est pire que celle qui court: Prov. *Standing waters are much worse then running ones; sleepie dispositions of lesse worth (or more dangerous) then giddie ones.*
Courle: f. *as* Courge; *a Gourd.*
Courle sauvage. *Wild Nep, white Bryonie, the wild or white Vine; also, the wild flegme-purging Gourd,* Coloquintida.

Courlis: m. *A Curlue.*
Courmaran: m. *A Cormorant.*
Couronne: f. *A Crowne; the Diademe, or circlet wherwith Princes be crowned; also, a wreath, garland, or chaplet of flowers, &c, for the head; also, the coyne so called; also, the crowne, top, or beginning of a horses hoofe; the place, or part whereat it ioynes vnto the leg; also, a round, or a ring made by many persons that stand close, or hold hands, together; (In Architecture) also, the* Corona, *crowne, or member of greatest sayle, in a Cornish.*
Couronne de Clercs. *The crowne of a Shaueling, or, a Priests shauen crowne.*
Couronne Imperiale. *The Imperiall Crowne; (a goodlie flower.)*
Couronne de Prestre. *Dandelyon, Piss-a-bed; (an hearbe.)*
Lettre de couronne. *A cup; or as* Tasse. ¶Barrag.
Enter en petite couronne. *Seeke* Enter.
Femme bonne vaut vne couronne: Prov. *A vertuous dame is worth a Diadem.*
Couronné: m. ée: f. *Crowned.*
Couronnement: m. *A crowning; also, the outward mouth of the wombe, so tearmed by Midwiues.*
Couronner. *To crowne; to set a crowne, diadem, circlet, or garland vpon (the head.)*
Couronneure: f. *The broad-spread, and crowne-resembling, top of a Deeres head.*
Couroye, & Couroyer. *See* Courroye, *&* Conroyer.
Cour-pendu. Pomme de cour-pendu. *The short-start, or short-shanke; (an excellent apple.)*
Courquaillet: m. *A Quayle-pipe.*
Courracteur. *See* Courratier. ¶Rab.
Courrail: m. *as* Courreau.
Courratage: m. *Brokage; scoursing, horse-scoursing; See* Courretage.
Courraterie: f. *as* Courratage.
Courratier: m. *A Broker; one that sels other mens stuffe for them; also, a foot-post, messenger, or carrier.*
Courratier de chevaux. *A horse-courser.*
Courratiere: f. *A Brokeresse; or Brokers wife.*
Courre. *as* Courir; laisser courre; *to let slip, or, to hound a dog, at.*
Courreau d'une huisserie. *The bolt, or barre of a dore.*
Courretage: m. *Brokage; horse-scoursing; busie dealing or intermedling betweene partie and partie.*
Courretier: m. *as* Courratier.
Courrier: m. *A Post, or, a Poster; also, a horse-rider; also, a Broker.*
Courrier de mer. *A kind of very swift fish. Looke* Poste de Mer.
Courroucé: m. ée: f. *Angrie, offended, fuming, displeased, in a great chafe; also, vexed, grieued, afflicted; impatient, out of quiet.*
Bien courroucé de peu pleure: Prov. *He thats throughly angred hardly weepes.*
Il n'est pas aise qui est courroucé: Prov. *Hee's not at ease thats in a chafe.*
Courroucéement. *Angrily, chafingly; as one that is offended, or in a fume.*
Courroucer. *To anger; offend, moue, displease; vex, grieue, afflict, put out of quiet.*
Se courroucer. *To fret, fume, chafe, be angrie, take pet, or pepper, in the nose.*
Se courroucer contre ses morceaux. *To be angrie at his own morsels; rather to starue then chaw his own meat, rather to want then vse his owne meanes.*

Courrouceusement. *Wrathfully; most angrily.*
Courroux: m. *Anger; chafing, fuming; wrath, rage, indignation; displeasure, stomacke against; also, vexation, griefe, sorrow, affliction of mind; impatiencie.*
Courroye: f. *A thong, or belt of leather; a strong leatherne strap, or string; also, the latchet of a shooe.*
Alonger la courroye. *To delay, prolong, or draw out in length, a gainefull imployment; as many Lawyers do their clients causes, and some Generals the warres they commaund in.*
Avoir les deux bouts de la courroye. *To haue the Law (or the absolute disposition of a thing) in his owne hands.*
Il veut avoir les deux bouts de la courroye, & le milieu. *He is a hard, and sore dealer; he will neither do right, nor take wrong; or, no lesse will serue him then all; he will haue the verie extremitie of Law.*
Faire d'autruy cuir large courroye. *To spend liberally on another mans purse.*
On a fait de son dos courroye. *He hath been whipped extreamely.*
Mieux vaut avoir amy en voye qu'or, ny argent en courroye: Prov. *We say (with some little difference) better is a friend in Court then a pennie in the purse.*
Qui cuir voit tailler courroye en demande: Prov. *While a thing's whole it may be wholly kept.*
Courroyé: m. ée: f. *Curried; tawed, or dressed, as leather.*
Courroyement. *as* Conroyement *(in the first sence.)*
Courroyer. *as* Conroyer; *to curry; tew, or dresse, leather.*
Courroyeur: m. *A Currier (of leather.)*
Cours: m. *A course, race, running; also, the place wherein a race is runne; also, a continuall iourney, passage, traine, trace, motion forward; also, length, or tract of time; also, a stile, fashion, way, manner, or meanes of proceeding; also, a road, or expedition against an enemie at sea; (and hence, piracie, rouing, searobbing.)*
Cours du ciel. *The course of the Starres, Planets, or of the Regions wherein they are seated; also (among Gardeners) a certaine bad constellation, whereby the growth of hearbes is hindered.*
Vn Cours Civil, ou Cannon. *All the Volumes, or Bookes, of the Ciuill, or Cannon Law.*
Le cours des Loix, de Medecine, de Philosophie, &c; *the whole order, or proceeding of studie in those Arts, from the first and sleightest rudiments, to the last and deepest mysteries thereof.*
Cette marchandise n'a plus de cours. *Is cleane out of date, out of vse, out of request; no chapman will buy it, no tradesman can vtter it, there is no further dealing in it.*
Coursable. Monnoye coursable. *Currant money.*
Coursaire: m. *A Rouer, a Pyrate, a sea-theefe. See* Corsaire.
Course: f. *A course, a race; a course, running, speed; also, a road, or incursion into an enemies countrey; also, a small and light chariot, or waggon.*
Courserot: m. *A little Pyrate; also, a little Courser, or Horse of seruice.*
Coursey. *as* Courson.
Coursie: f. *Part of the Hatches of a Galley, tearmed the Coursey; or, the Gallerie-like space, on both sides whereof the seats of the slaues are placed.*
Coursier: m. *A Courser of Naples; also, a Tilting-horse, or horse for the Careere.*
Coursier: m. ere: f. *Belonging, or like, vnto a Courser; and hence;*
Mule coursiere. *Which in height & breadth resembles, or equalls, an ordinarie Courser.*
Coursiere: f. *The Grating, in a ship of warre; also, a compendious course, readie meane, short cut, speedie way.*
Coursif: m. iue: f. *Swift, speedie, fast, running.*
Lettres coursives. *Written by a quick, or swift hand; fast written.*
Courson: m. *A young vine-branch, or shoot, reserued, in the cutting of the vine, for store.*
Coursouër. *as* Escoursouër.
Court: f. *The Court of a Prince; the Estate, or State, of his house, and houshold; also, his houshold seruants, or followers; also, the assembly of Nobles a bout him; also, Courtship, the humors, or fashions of Court; and the courting, or wooing of a wench; also, the court, or yard, or, the court-yard, of a house; also, as* Cour.
Bouche à Court. *Budge-a-Court, diet allowed at Court.*
Eau beniste de Court. *Court holie-water; fawning, soothing, smoothing, flatterie, faire (but false) words.*
Faire la court à. *To court, wooe, fawne vpon, solicite, or sue vnto; collogue, or cog with.*
Sçavoir sa court. *To be a skilfull Courtier; to know well the fashion of intertainement, the phrases of complement, the humors and proceedings, vsed in Court.*
Tenir Court; ou, Tenir Court planiere. *A Prince to keepe open house; or to intertaine, and feast, all commers.*
La Court du Roy Petaud, ou chascun est maistre: Pro. *Looke* Petaud.
En la Court du Roy chascun est pour soy: Pro. *In Court men studie onely their owne fortunes.*
Court: m. courte: f. *Short, briefe, succinct, cutted, compendious; low; also, little, small.*
Courte boule. *Our round bowle.*
Courtes chausses. *Short hose; also, women.*
Court en paste. *Short, crummie, not holding, ill cleauing together.*
Robbe courte. Gens de robbe c. *Noblemen, Gentlemen, or Souldiers; or Officers, that be any of them.*
`A leur courte honte. *To their exceeding shame.*
Demeurer court. *To play at Mumbudget, or be at a Nonplus; not to haue a word to throw at a dog.*
C'estoit le plus court, & le plus aisé, de les renvoyer. *The best, or the neerest, and easiest course was, to send them backe.*
Il y alla tout court. *He went thither on a suddaine, or without any manner of staying.*
Pour le faire court. *In summe, or in few words; to conclude; to abridge the matter; not to hold you long.*
Tenir court. *To restraine, bridle, keepe vnder, tye vp short, hold vnto hard meat.*
Tourner court: I'apprédray bien à tourner court à celuy. *I will teach him to be more ductifull, readie, supple, pliable.*
Courtes folies sont les meilleures: Pro. *The shortest follies are the best.*
Courtault, ou Courtaut: m. *A Curtall.*
Courtaut de boutique. *A tradesmans prentise; a shop-keeping boy.*
Double courtaut. *A strong curtall; or, a horse of a middle size betweene th'ordinarie curtall, and horse of seruice.*
Courtaut: m. aude: f. *Curtall; being curtalled.*

Fouëtter quelqu'un en chien courtaut. *To whip one extreamely.*

Court-baston. *A truncheon, or short cudgell; See* Courbaston.

Court-d'aleaune. *The name of a certaine bitter sweet apple.*

Courte-pointe: f. *A Quilt, or quilted counterpoint.*

Courtes-fesses. *A Button-breech; one that is pin-buttockt; or hath but small or slender buttocks.*

Court-festu: m. *Drawing of cutts.*

Courtiban; *or* Courtibau. *A coat-armour, long cassock, or horsemans coat, worne by a Prince, or Commander in an armie.*

Courtier. *as* Courratier; *a Broker; Horse-scourser, Messenger.*

Courtil: m. *A backe-yard; or garden.*

Courtilliere: f. *A kind of Palmer, or yellowish, and many legd vermine, that abides almost euer in the ground, and is a great enemie to hearbes (especially Onions) whose roots she gnawes asunder.*

Courtinages: m. *Curtaines; hangings for beds, or windowes.*

Courtine: f. *A Curtaine; and (in fortification) the plainenesse of the wall betweene bulwarke and bulwarke.*

Sous la courtine. *Secretly, closely, priuately, vnderhand, in corners, in hugger-mugger.*

Courtineau: m. *A little Curtaine; also, the head-peece, or peece that hangs downe at the head, of a stuffebed.*

Courtisan: m. *A Courtier.*

Courtisane: f. *A Ladie, Gentlewoman, or waiting-woman of the Court; also (but lesse properly) a curtizan, professed strumpet, famous (or infamous) whore.*

Courtisanie: f. *Court-ship; courtlie behauiour, or humour.*

Courtisanne: f. *as* Courtisane.

Courtisanneau: m. *A young, little; paultrie, or scuruie, Courtier.*

Courtisanner. *To play the Courtier.*

Courtisé: m. ée: f. *Courted, sued vnto; intertained with respectiue complements; also, flattered, fawned on, cogged with.*

Courtiser. *To court, make court vnto; intertaine with all complements, or offices of respect, and obseruance; also, to flatter, sooth, fawne on, cog with.*

Courtois: m. ise: f. *Courteous, gentle, debonaire; ciuile; gratious, benigne, affable; tractable, faire-conditioned; complementall.*

Chambre courtoise. *An Aiax; or, as* Chambre aisée.

Lance courtoise. *A tilting-staffe; or, launce with a blunt, or buttoned, head.*

Qui fut François si fut courtois: Pro. *The French were euer full of courtesie.*

Courtoisement. *Courteously, gently, affably, benignely, ciuilly, gratiously.*

Courtoisie: f. *Courtesie, ciuilitie, affabilitie, gentlenesse, humanitie, debonaritie, benignitie, graciousnesse; also, a kindnesse, fauour, good office; whence;*

Courtoisie tardiue est discourtoisie: Pro. *A fauour long in comming proues disfauour.*

Courtoisie qui ne vient que d'un costé ne peut longuement durer: Prov. *Courtesies vnrequited continue not.*

Couru: m. uë: f. *Runne, coursed, hyed, speeded, posted, gallopped; also, hunted, chased, followed hard, hotly pursued; also, ouerrun, ransacked, rauaged.*

Fortune luy a couru sus. *Fortune hath assaulted, or afflicted him; a great misfortune is befallen him.*

Courvé. *as* Courbé.

Courvée: f. *A dayes worke, due by a Tenant vnto his Lord. See* Corvée.

Il a fait vne grande courvée. *He hath done a great dayes worke, he hath made a long dayes iourney; or, he hath dispatched the matter with verie much toyle.*

Courver. *To crooke, bow, bend, arch, vault.*

Cousant. *Sewing, or sowing.*

Couse: f. *A ieast, a toy, a sleight matter.*

Cousement: m. *A sewing; or, a seame.*

Cousin: m. *A cousin, or kinsman; also, a Gnat, or Midge.*

Au prester cousin, au rendre fils de putain: Prov. *Some, when they would borrow giue good wordes, but when they should repay, most bad ones.*

Cousinage: m. *Kindred, consanguinitie, cousinship.*

Cousiner. *To clayme kindred for aduantage, or particular ends; as he, who to saue charges in trauelling, goes from house to house, as cousin to the owner of euerie one.*

Cousinette. *The name of a certaine little red apple.*

Coussegail: m. *Messelin, corne mingled.* ¶Langued.

Cousser. *To butt, or iurre, as Rammes doe.*

Cousseur: m. *A butter, a iurrer.*

Coussi: m. *The name of a small (but excellent) blacke Grape.*

Coussin: m. *A cushion to sit on.*

Coussinet: m. *A cushinet, or little cushion; also, a stuffing, or boulstering vsed in womens garments, when one shoulder is higher then another, to make them seeme straight though they be not; also, a cushinet, or boulster of folded linnen, layed on the plaister of a wound.*

Coussinet de la fesse. *The fleshie tip, or muscle of the buttockes.*

Coussinet de la trompe. *The first bed, or couching of stones, on the right hand of the vault of the out-iuttying roome* Trompe.

Coussineux: m. euse: f. *Full of, or stored with, cushions; also, soft as a cushion; fit to vse as a cushion.*

Cousson: m. *The gusset of a shirt, or smocke; also, a Mite, or Weeuill.*

Coust: m. *Cost, charges, expence.*

Coustange: m. *as* Coust.

Coustangeux: m. euse: f. *Deere, costlie, chargeable.*

Coustau: m. *A little hill, or rising of ground; a Downe, or high ground.*

Coustau de montaigne. *The side, or skirt of a mountaine.*

Cousté. (*The Participle of* Couster;) *cost.*

Cousteau: m. *A knife, or whittle; also, a sword, or any such cutting weapon; also, the principall feather in a Hawkes wing, tearmed by our Faulkoners (in short-winged Hawkes) the Cut, or Cuttie.*

Cousteau marin, ou de mer. *The Pyrot, or Hagfish; a long and round shell-fish, of a bright, and shining colour; In some parts of France, the Sleeue-fish, and by some French Authors, the Sword-fish, are also called so.*

Cousteau des moissons. *Corne-Sedge, Corne-Flags, Corne-Gladen, the right Gladen.*

Cousteau à pied. *A Shoomakers round cutting-knife.*

Cousteau à rongner. *The knife wherewith Bookebinders cut the leaues of their bookes.*

Cousteau de tripiere. *A (fashion of) two-edged knife; and by Metaphor, one that playes Iacke on both sides.*

Manche

Manche de cousteau. *as* Cousteau marin *(in the first sence.)*
Pied de cousteau. *A Play at Shuffleboord with keyes, a knife being the marke.*
Au pain,& au cousteau avec. *Familiar, conuersant, a daylie companion, hayle fellow well met, with.*
Se couper de son propre cousteau. *To cut himselfe with his owne knife*; See Couper.
Iouër des cousteaux. *To fight, combat, bicker, battaile; to come to open warre; to lay lustily about him; also, to feed eagerly, bestirre himselfe at a Table, fall hotly to his victuals.*
Les cousteaux de Iehan Colot, l'un vaut l'autre: Prov. *See* Colot.
Dans vne gaine d'or vn cousteau de plomb: Pro. *A leaden sword in a golden sheath; a foule heart in a faire bodie.*
Peu peut bailler à son escuyer qui son cousteau leche: Prov. *Where the Maister pinches the seruants pine; or, he can spare others but little that hath but little for himselfe.*
Selon la gaine le cousteau: Prov. *An inside answerable vnto the outside.*
Selon le pain il faut le cousteau: Prov. *(Like our) the coat according to the cloth.*
Vn mesme cousteau me coupe le pain,& le doigt: Pro. *One knife both cuts me bread, and my finger; (said of any thing that one while helpes, and another while hurts.)*
Coustelet: m. *A little knife, or sword.*
Cousteleux. *Full of, or furnished with, kniues.*
Gaine cousteleuse. *A sheath which is neuer without kniues.*
Coustelier: m. *A Cutler, or maker of kniues.*
Coustellerie: f. *A Cutlers shop, or worke-house.*
Coustemens: m. *Costs, and charges.*
Couste-pointe: f. *A counterpoint, or double couerlet.*
Couster. *To cost, in price*; (Cecy me cousta cent livres; *I gaue a hundred pounds for this*; Telle chose ne me couste gueres. *I haue such a thing for little, or nothing.)*
Couste & vaille. *Whatsoeuer come of it, howsoeuer I come by it; at what price, or perill soeuer I buy it; or, I care not what I pay for it so it be good.*
Compere de la Pouille, couste, & despouille: Pro. *(Said of a dangerous companion) one that will both feed on you, and filch from you, and at length wholly fleece you*; See Pouille.
Cousteux: m. euse: f. *Costlie, chargeable, very deere.*
Coustier: m. ere: f. *Wide, aside, or of one side; also, as* Cottier.
Coustil. *as* Coutil; *a ticke for a bed.*
Coustilier. *as* Coustillier.
Coustillade. *See* Coutillade.
Coustille: f. *A kind of long Ponniard, vsed heretofore by Esquires.*
Coustillé: m. ée: f. *Oft strucken, or stabbed with a* Coustille.
Coustiller. *To strike, or stab, often with a* Coustille.
Coustilleur. *as* Coustillier.
Coustillier: m. *An Esquire of the bodie; an Armour-bearer vnto a Knight; the seruant of a man at Armes; also, a groome of a stable, a horse-keeper.*
Coustre. *as* Coultre.
Coustume: f. *Custome, vse, vre, vsage, wont, guise; habit, manner; continuall fashion, or order; also, an auncient Law, or Custome in a countrey; also, a Custome, Imposition, Tax, Toll; also, a customarie Rent, Seruice, or Tenure; also, the vse of, or freedome in, another mans woods, or grounds.*
La petite coustume. *is (in most places) a pennie for an Ox, Cow, Pipe of wine, or load of corne sold, and carried out of the Territorie belonging to a Lord Iusticer; for other lesse beasts, as Hogs, and Sheep, a halfepennie, or* Maille; *for a cart-load of moueables* iiij d. Tourn: *for a Horseload*, ij d; *for a mans burthen, a pennie.*
Droict de coustume. *is (in Normandie) the Toll thats payed for commodities vttered in the Market place; and by the custome of grand* Perche, *a pennie* Tourn: *due vnto the Lord (that hath low Iurisdiction) for euery foure-footed beast (not milch) that hath beene bred, bought, and deliuered, within his Territorie.*
Droict de grosse coustume. *Looke* Droict.
Prendre heritage en coustume. *That is on condition to pay yearely a certaine quantitie of Corne, or Hennes; which if they be vnpayed (hauing beene demaunded) three yeares together, the Landlord may reenter; as he may also, if the thing be aliened, or sold without his consent; or if the Tenant die without issue lawfully begotten.*
Gasteau, & mauvaise coustume se doivent rompre: Prov. *(For the one does no good, the other much hurt, if it be kept.)*
Le loup alla à Rome, & y laissa de son poil, mais rien de ses coustumes: Prov. *The Wolfe went vnto Rome, and there left part of his coat, but none of his ill conditions, behind him.*
Coustumerie: f. *A custome-taking, or custome-leuying; also, a Place, Passage, or Libertie, whereunto custome is due.*
Coustumier: m. *A customarie tenant, or tenant by custome; a Copie-holder*; See Coustumiers.
Coustumier: m. ere: f. *Customarie, vsuall, wonted, inueterate.*
Aides coustumiers. *as* Aides chevels. *Looke* Aides.
Bourse coustumiere. *A purchase of land made, or price giuen for a purchase, by a yeoman,* Roturier, *or ignoble person.*
Païs coustumier. *A countrey thats altogether gouerned by particular customes; (as most of the Prouinces in France be.)*
Quint coustumier. *The portion of younger brethren in the inheritance left by their father; which is (by the custome of diuers places) a fift part onely, diuided among them.*
Coustumierement. *Ordinarily, vsually, commonly, customarily; after, or according to, the ordinarie vse, and custome.*
Coustumiers. *Auncient, and experienced Lawyers, who are able to informe the Court what the Law, and locall customes are in any case.*
Cousture: f. *A Seame.*
Cousture incarnatiue. *Looke* Incarnatif.
Herbe sans cousture. *Adders tongue, Serpēts tongue.*
Desfait à plate cousture. *Vtterly defeated; ouerthrowne horse and man.*
Harenguer à plate cousture. *To make a rude, plaine, or homelie, Oration.*
De forte cousture dure deschirure: Pro. *A strong seame strongly rent asunder.*
Cousturier: m. *A Taylor, or Botcher; a Seamster; also, a little red worme, or fly, of the kind of Moathes.*
A ce drap cousturiers. *To this geare, to it, set to it my maisters; lets roundly about this businesse*; *Looke* Drap.

Cousturiere: f. *A Seamster; or woman botcher.*
Cousturiers: m. *Certaine long muscles in the outward part of the thigh, which they make plyable, to crosse one leg ouer the other.*
Cousu: m. uë: f. *Sewed, seamed, stitched, fastened together; also, pierced, gored, run through.*
Vn visage cousu. *A wrinkled, or a writhen visage, that lookes as if the skin thereof had beene gathered, or plaited with a needle.*
Ses finesses ne sont cousuës que de fil blanc. *His deuises are plaine, and apparant enough; euery one may see how subtilly he hath dealt.*
Cousyre: f. *Bugle, Comfrey, Wallwort.*
Coutau: m. *A hillocke, or little hill; a Downe, or high ground.*
Coute: f. *A seame; as in* Coutes.
Couteau. *A knife, &c. See* Cousteau.
Coutelas: m. *A Cuttelas, Courtelas, or short sword, for a man at armes.*
Coutelasse sur le visage: f. *A slash ouer the face with a Cuttelas.*
Coutelassé: m. ée: f. *Wounded, slashed, or stricken with a Cuttelas.*
Coutelasser. *To wound, slash, cut, or strike with a Cuttelas.*
Couteleu. *as* Cousteau de mer.
Coutes: f. *The seames; or distances that are betweene Planke and Planke (in a ship.)*
Coutil: m. *A Ticke, or Quilt stuffed with flocks, wooll, or feathers; a Mattresse, Wooll-bed, Flock-bed, Featherbed.*
Coutillades: f. *Hackes, gashes, wipes, cuts, wounds, giuen or made by edge-tooles.*
Couton: m. *A faggot-sticke; or, the thicke stalke of some Plants, as of Cabbage, &c.*
Coutonner. *To cudgell, thwacke, baste, belamme.*
Coutre: m. *as* Coteret *(in the first sence.)*
Coutre: f. *as* Coutil *(in the latter sence.)*
Coutrepointer. *(in stead of* Contrepoincter*) to quilt.*
Couture. *See* Coulture.
Couvade: f. *as* Couvée; *or, as* Couvement.
Faire la couvade. *To sit cowring, or skowking within dores; to lurke in the campe when Gallants are at the Battell; (any way) to play least in sight.*
Couvaison: f. *as* Couvement.
Couvé: m. ée: f. *Brooded, set on, couered or cowred ouer, cherished, or kept warme; hatched; bred, or brought to perfection, by being continually set on.*
Couvé de mauvaise pie. *Ill-bred, of an euill race, come of an euill kind.*
Couvecendre. *A lazie huswife; one that is euer hanging her nose ouer the fire.*
Couvée de poussins: f. *A brood, or hatching of chickens; as many as came of one sitting.*
Couveleque: f. *The lid of a pot, or cup.* (v. m.)
Couvement: m. *A brooding, sitting on, cowring ouer; a cherishing, or keeping warme; also, a hatching.*
Couvement de poussins. *A brooding, or hatching of chickens; or, a brood, &c; as* Couvée.
Couver. *To brood, sit on, or cowre ouer; to cherish, keepe warme; breed, or bring to perfection (by a continuall sitting ouer;) Hence also, to hatch.*
Couver vn mauvais oeuf. *To nourish an ill dessigne.*
Elle y peut bien pondre, mais elle n'y couvera pas. *She may perhaps be there for a day or two, but longer then that she stayes not.*
Iamais mauvaise poule ne le couva. *He is come of gentle kind, of a right noble straine; he hath no manner of ill breeding in him.*
Couvercle: m. *A Couer, or Lid.*
Couvercle digne du chauderon: Prov. *A Couer good enough for the Cauldron.*
Tel pot tel couvercle: Prov. *Such pot such pot-lid, like maister like man.*
Couveresse: f. *A sitting henne.*
Couvert: m. *A Couert; a wooddie plot, or countrey; a place full of bushes, and trees; also, the couering, or furniture of Table for the meale of a Prince, &c; also, a young Shad (called so in* Anjou.)
Nous sommes mal à couvert sous. *Wee are ill shadowed, or shrowded vnder.*
Couvert: m. erte: f. *Couered, vayled; closed; secret, hidden; buried; ouercast, ouershadowed; clowdie, or darkened, as a thing ouershadowed.*
Fief couvert. *An inheritance for which homage and fealtie is done, or hath beene duly offered, vpon change of the Tenant, or Tenure.*
Homme couvert. *A still, silent, or close fellow.*
Les rachapts, & arrerages de cens couverts. *An absolute possession, or prescription; a quiet enioying of land held by* Cens, *for thirtie yeares together.*
Les rachapts d'un fief couverts. *Happening, or fallen before the receit of homage and fealtie, or a discharge giuen by the lord to the vassall for them; and without any reseruation of them; so that he hath no way to get them but by Action.*
Vin couvert. *Red, blacke, or darke-coloured wine.*
Le feu plus couvert est le plus ardent: Prov. *The fire thats couered most burnes most; or, the more tis hidden the hoter it burnes.*
Couverte: f. *A Couerlet, or bed-couering.*
Tirer la couverte de son costé. *Looke* Tirer.
Couvertement. *Couertly, closely, secretly, obscurely, darkly, priuily, vnder hand.*
Couvertoir: m. *A tricke, or Engin wherewith water-fowle is caught.*
Couverture: f. *A couerture, or couering; an arraying, cloathing, cladding, attiring; also, apparrell, rayment, attire; also, a hiding, vayling, obscuring, ouer-shadowing; also, a couerlet, or couering for a bed.*
Couverture de maison. *The roofe of a house.*
Couverture de murailles. *The plaistering, dawbing, white-liming, pargetting, rough-casting; also, the coping, of walls.*
Couverture veluë. *An Irish Rug, Mantle, or Cadowe.*
Sous couverture de. *Vnder the pretext, shadow, or colour, of.*
Couvi. oeuf couvi. *An addle egge, or a rotten egge (that hath beene set on.)*
Couvine: f. Il en sçait bien toute la co. *Hee is well acquainted with their packing; he knows full well how the matter hath beene carried.*
Couvoir: m. *A hennes nest; the place where she sits her egges; also, the height, or top, of a bed in a garden.*
Couvoiter. *See* Convoiter.
Couvrailles: f. *Gossymeare; or, the white, and cobweb-like exhalations which flye abroad in hot Sunnie weather.*
Couvre-chef: m. *A Kerchiefe.*
Couvre-coeur. *The* Pericardium, *a thin skin, or membrane, wherewith the heart is couered.*
Couvrement: m. *A couering; concealing, hiding, obscuring; burying; vayling, ouercasting, ouershadowing.*

Couvre-

Couvre-ordure. *Gold; also, a womans Maske.*
Couvre-rive. *Banke-couering, shoare-surrounding.*
Couvrir. *To couer; vayle, cloake; hide, conceale, stop, or close vp; to hoodwinke, ouerspread, ouercast, ouershadow; also, to cloath, apparrell, attire all ouer; also, a dog (or such like beast) to lyne a bitch; (In which sence,* Aligner *is the word for Wolues; and* Saillir *for Horses, Bulls, and such other great beasts.)*
Couvrir le feu de son fivatier. *A Lord to seise, or make an entrie vpon, his tenants land for default of payment of the rents, rights, and seruices due vnto him; which, as it seemes, is done by raking out, or couering ouer, the fire found in the tenement.*
Couvrir la jouë à. *To giue a box on the eare vnto.*
Couvrir son mommon à. *To tickle a wench.*
Couvrir leur rastelier. *Seeke* Rastelier.
Se couvrir d'un sac mouillé. *To colour his bard, or ill dealing with idle, and insufficient pretences; to alledge for himselfe excuses, which rather condemne, then cleere, him.*
Couyol: m. *as* Coyon.
Coy: m. *A Sinke; or, as* Fosse coye.
Coy: m. coye: f. *Quiet, still, peaceable, calme, restfull, husht; See* Quoy.
Fosse coye. *A Priuie, Jakes, house of Office.*
Coyau: m. *A returned, or hip, Rafter.*
Coyed. *as* Cayer. ¶Pic.
Coyement. *Quietly, peaceably, stilly, calmely; soberly; patiently.*
Coymeaux: m. *A kind of Cherries.*
Coyon: m. *A coward, cullion, scowndrell, base fellow, faint-hearted companion.*
Coyonnade: f. *A cowardlie, or cullionlie tricke, a base, or dastardlie part.*
Coyonnerie: f. *Base roguerie, cowardise, cullionnerie.*
Coypellé: m. ée: f. *Chipped; also, thwyted, whitled, or cut as a sticke, &c.*
Coypeller. *To chip; also, to thwyte, or cut a sticke, &c.*
Coyraul. *See* Coiraux.
Coyté: f. *Quietnesse, calmenesse, peaceablenesse, gentlenesse; patience; sobernesse.*
Coytes: f. *Tackes; great Ropes vsed about the (maine) sayle of a ship.*
Coytis. *as* Coytes. *Ticke; or, the blew-rewed stuffe whereof Tickes for beds are made; also, a bed-Ticke.*
Coyts. *as* Coytes.
Crabbat: m. ate: f. *Comelie, proper, decent, handsome, gracious, of a sweet presence, pleasing to the eye.*
Crabron: m. *A Hornet.*
Crac: m. *A cracke, or thing that crackes.*
Crachard. *as* Crachat.
Crachat: m. *Spittle, or spit; also, a spitting.*
Craché: m. ée: f. *Spet, or spatled out; spattered, bespawled.*
C'estoit luy tout craché. *He resembled him in euerie part; he was as like him as if he had beene spit out of his mouth.*
Crache-en-ruelle. *A spawling, or spattering fellow.*
Crache-fil. *Thread-spinning (the Epithete of a Spider.)*
Crachement: m. *A spitting, spatling, spattering, spawling.*
Cracher. *To spit; spawle; spattle, bespatter.*
Cracher au bassin. *To pay downe readie coyne; to giue readie money; to come off with round fees; to bestow a reward in hand; also, to spit (as a man may doe with his mouth shut) into a fleshlie basen; also, to play a mad, fond, retchlesse, or carelesse, part.*
Cracher vn Iacobin. *Looke* Iacobin.
Cracheur: m. *A spitter, spawler, spatterer.*
Cracquer. *as* Craquer.
Crage: f. *as* Croye. *Chalke; (a rusticall word.)*
Craie: f. *as* Croye. *Chalke.*
Craies. *Wild Peares, choake Peares.*
Craignant. *Dreading, fearing; doubting, redoubting, standing in awe of.*
Craillement: m. *The croaking of a Rauen, or Toad.*
Crailler. *as* Croailler.
Craindre. *To dread, feare; doubt, redoubt; stand in awe of.*
Il ne craind ny les rez, ny les tondus. *He respects no man, feares no bodie, is awed by no creature liuing; Looke* Rez.
Craine: m. *The skull, or braine-pan of the head.*
Crainser. *To shrinke in, or together; (also, to crackle) as Parchement, &c, throwne into the fire.*
Craint: m. ainte: f. *Dreaded, feared; doubted, redoubted.*
Crainte: f. *Feare, dread; awe, doubt of, redoubting.*
Craintif: m. iue: f. *Fearefull, dreading, timerous; bashfull, cowardlie, dastardlie, faint-hearted, white-liuered.*
Craintivément. *Fearefully, timerously, with a faint heart.*
Craïon. *See* Crayon.
Cramaillere: f. *The pot-hanger, or pot-hookes.*
Cramas: m. *Stones torne from rockes by tempests, inundations, or the violent working of the sea.*
Cramoisi: m. *Crimson colour.*
Sot en cramoisi. *An Asse in graine.*
Cramoisi: m. ie: f. *Crimson, Crimson-coloured, of a Crimson hue.*
Crampe: f. *The Crampe.*
La crampe du pied d'un cheval. *A horses hoofe.*
Les gouttes crampes. *Convulsions; tensions, or stiffenesse of the muscles, caused by sharpe, and grosse vapors inclosed among the Membranes.*
Crampelle: f. *A Grampell, Grit, or Pungar-fish.*
Crampon: m. *A Cramp-yron; a hooke, or crampe of yron, &c.*
Crampon de cuir. *A loope, or tab, of leather.*
Les crampons d'un fer de cheval. *Caulkes; or, caulkings.*
Cramponné: m. ée: f. *Ioyned, or fastened with Cramp-yrons; also, tatched, hasped, hooked; looped; caulked.*
Cramponner. *To ioyne, or fasten together with Cramp-yrons; also, to tatch, haspe, hooke; loope; caulke.*
Cramponnet: m. *A little Cramp-yron; tacke, or loope.*
Crane: m. *The skull, braine-pan, or bone of the head.*
Cranequin: m. *The Gaffle of a Crosse-bow; or, as* Crennequin; *also, an Engin for batterie, vsed in old time.*
Cranequinier: m. *A Crosse-bow man (whether he serue on horseback, or on foot) or, as* Crennequinier; *also, an (inferior) Officer, that had, in old time, the conduction of warlike Engines.*
Crannequin. *as* Cranequin.
Crapaud: m. *A Toad.*
Crapaud de mer. *The sea-Toad; an ouglie, and vnholesome fish; or, the full-rowed bellie of the Dog-fish, &c.*
La danse des crapauds. *A State, or Gouernment wherein knaues, and fooles are supported.*
Il en estoit chargé comme vn crapaud de plumes. *He was little burthened, nothing troubled, withall.*

Crapaudaille: f. *A crue of ouglie knaues, of noysome Rogues: a packe of base, and beastlie Scowndrels.*
Crapaudeau: m. *A young, or little, Toad.*
Crapaudine: f. *The stone* Chelonitis, *or, the Toad-stone; also, the square peece of yron, &c, wherein the Piuot playes, or turnes, in the bottome of a Gate; some of our workmen call it, the sole.*
Crapaudon: m. *A young Toad.*
Crape: m. *The Crabfish tearmed, a Pungar.*
Crappaude: f. *The sea-Toad, or sea-Diuell; (an ouglie, and rauenous fish.)*
Crappe. *as* Crappaude.
Crapule: f. *Drunkennesse, or drunken surfetting; heauinesse of the head by excessiue drinking.*
Craquant: m. ante: f. *Cracking, creaking, crashing, clashing.*
Craquelin: m. *A Cracknell; made of the yolks of egges, water, and flower; and fashioned like a hollow trendle; hence also, a little light cap of that fashion.*
Craquement: m. *A cracking, creaking, clashing.*
Craquement des dents. *The crashing of the teeth.*
Craquer. *To cracke, to creake; to crash; to clash.*
Craquetant: m. ante: f. *Cracking, creaking; crashing often.*
Cerceau craquetant. *The ierting circle made by a Peacocke with his tayle, by a Turkie-cocke with his wings.*
Craqueter. *Often to cracke, creake, clash, crash.*
Craquetis: m. *An often creaking, clashing, cracking, crashing.*
Cras. *as* Croyé. *Chalke.* ¶Villageois.
Cras. *as* Chraies; *Choake-Peares.*
Crasse: f. *(Thick-growne) filth, or ordure; slouenrie, sluttishnesse, greasinesse, bawdinesse, nastinesse; loathsome array.*
Crasse de bronze. *The skumme of melted Brasse.*
Crasse de la teste. *Dandriff; the skales that fall from the head, &c, in combing, &c.*
Crasseusement. *Filthily, nastily, greasily, bawdily, slouenly, sluttishly.*
Crasseux: m. euse: f. *Filthie, greasie, bawdie, begreased, nastie, durtie, slouenlie, sluttish, full of vncleanenesse, full of ordure.*
Plus crasseux que la tasse d'un Meseau. *More loathsome then a Lazers dish.*
Crassi *A certaine Italian coyne worth about* j d. q.
Crassitie: f. *as* Crassitude.
Crassitude: f. *Thicknesse, fatnesse, grossenesse.*
Cravant: m. *The small Goose, or Goose-like fowle, tearmed, a Brigander.*
Cravanté: m. ée: f. *Oppressed, foyled, or spoyled with excessiue toyle, or stripes.*
Cravanter. *To oppresse, foyle, or spoyle with excessiue toyle, or stripes.*
Craye: f. *Chalke.*
Mal de craye. *The stone-Cray; a disease in Hawkes.*
Crayé: m. ée: f. *Chalked; marked, whited, scowred, or cleansed, with chalke.*
Crayement: m. *A chalking; a marking, dressing, scowring, or cleansing, with chalke.*
Crayer. *To chalke; to dresse, marke, white, scowre, or clense, with chalke.*
Crayon: m. *Dry painting; or, a painting in, or Picture of, dry colours; also, the Table whereon a Painter mingleth (such) colours; and the first draught, or lineaments of a picture, made with any of them; hence also, a patterne, or example.*
Crayonné: m. ée: f. *Painted, or drawne in dry colours; also, rudely drawne, as a Picture is at the first.*
Crayonner. *To paint, or draw in dry colours; also, to draw the first lines, or make the first draught, of a Picture.*
Creable. *as* Credible; *or,* Croyable.
Creac, ou Creal; *a Sturgeon.* ¶Langued.
Creac de Busc. *The Scate-fish.*
Creance: f. *Faith, beleefe; trust, affiance, confidence; also, credulitie, or credulousnesse; also, credit with Marchants, &c; also, a debt entrusted; also, dociblenesse; apprehension of, or obedience vnto, precepts; also, behauiour, fashion, carriage, good or ill manners; also, a taste, or essay taken of another mans meat; also, a Hawkes cryants.*
La creance d' un Embassadeur. *The effect, or substance of his Embassage, referred vnto his owne report.*
Lettres de creance. *Letters of trust, and credence; wherein the writer wills, that his messenger be credited in those things which he shall deliuer by word of mouth.*
Creancer. *To promise; to assure by his promise, to vndertake vpon his word* (v. m.) *also, to tast another mans meat, or drinke; to play the taster.*
Creancier: m. *A creditor, or truster.*
Creanciere: f. *A creditrix; the woman that trusteth.*
Createur: m. *A Creator; maker, framer; founder.*
Creation: f. *A creation, creating, framing, making.*
Creature: f. *A creature; a thing made of nothing.*
Il est creature d'un tel Seigneur. *He is the creature of, or hath beene onely aduaunced by, such a Lord; he hath made him all that he is; but for him he had beene of no wealth, no credit, no authoritie.*
Crecerelle: f. *A Rattle, or Clacke for children to play with; also, a Kestrell, Fleiagall, or Fuckwinde.*
Credence. *as* Creance.
Tesmoing de credence. *That deposes onely what he beleeues, or thinkes is true, without any absolute, or further, assuring of it.*
Credence d'argent. *Siluer plate; or, a cupboord of siluer plate.*
Credentier: m. *A cupboord-keeper; also, a Princes Taster, Essayer, Cup-bearer.*
Credible: com. *Credible, beleeuable; to be credited, or beleeued.*
Credit: m. *Credit; reputation, account, renowme; esteeme in, fauour with, good opinion of, the world; also, trust, beleefe, affiance, faith; also, loyaltie; also, as* Creance; *trust, or credit giuen; or, a debt entrusted.*
Batre à credit. *Looke* Batre.
Plaisir à credit. *A sleight pleasure.*
Perdre leurs ames à credit. *To hazard their soules on a shallow, or vpon no, ground.*
Servir Dieu à credit, & par procureur. *To serue God but sleightly, carelesly, or onely for a shew.*
Assez a qui bon credit a: Prov. *A good name is a sufficient treasure.*
Crediteur: m. *A creditor; one that beleeueth, or trusteth.*
Credos, qui fait credos charge son dos: *He that lendeth often looseth.*
Credule: com. *Credulous, trustfull; easie, or light, of beleefe.*
Credulité: f. *Credulitie, lightnesse of beleefe.*

Crée : f. *as* Croye.
Creé : m. creée : f. *Created, made, framed, formed; chosen, ordained, established; also, marked with chalke.*
Créer. *To create, make, forme, frame, giue the first being vnto; also, to chuse, ordaine, establish; also, as* Croyer; *to marke with chalke.*
Creiche : f. *A cratch, racke, Oxe-stall, or crib; also, a Bullace, or small plumme.*
Cremaillée. *as* Cremaillere.
Cremaillere : f. *A hooke to hang any thing on; especially a pot-hooke, or pot-hanger.*
Cremant. *Fearing, dreading.*
Cremasteres. *Two sinewes, or muskles, wherby the cods do hang:* ¶Rab.
Creme : f. *Creame.*
Cremeau. *as* Cresmeau.
Cremeu. *Fearefull, or full of dread.* (v.m.)
Cremeur : f. *Feare, dread; also, a creamie, or milkie disposition, or humor.*
Cremillée, & Cremillére. *as* Cremaillere.
Cremir. *To feare, to dread.*
Cren : m. *A breach, or snip in a knife, toole, &c; a notch in a score; a nocke in a bow, or arrow; also, the cleft, or clouen neb of a pen; also, the nicke of an Indenture; or iag about the edge of a leafe.*
Crene : f. *as* Cren.
Crené : m. ée : f. *Nicked, snipped, broken into; nocked, notched; iagged, indented.*
Creneau : m. *A nooke, or corner.*
Creneaux. *as* Carneaux; *the battlements of a wall.*
Crenelé : m. ée : f. *Imbattled; made into, or fashioned like, battlements; or, as* Crené.
Creneler. *To imbattle; to make into, or fashion like, battlements.*
Creneleure : f. *An imbattling; a making into, or like vnto, battlements.*
Crenequin. *as* Cranequin, *or* Crennequin.
Creneure : f. *A iagging, nicking, notching; indenting; or an imbattling, or making into square notches.*
Crenne. *as* Cren.
Crennequin. *as* Cranequin; *or (as some interpret it) a fashion of horsemans head-peece, resembling the Helmet.*
Crennequinier. *as* Cranequinier; *or, a Crossebow-man armed with a fashion of head-peece that resembles an Helmet.*
Crenquenier : m. *A Catchpole, Sergeant; or Officer, that can execute, or serue Executions.*
Crenure. *as* Creneure; *and as* Cren.
Crepature : f. *A bursting, cracking, riuing asunder.*
Crepelu. *as* Crespu.
Crepez, ou Crepets : m. *Fritters; also, Wafers.*
Crepillé : m. ée : f. *Frizled, curled.*
Crepiller. *To frizle, or curle.*
Crépine : f. *as* Crespine.
Crepir. *as* Crespir; *To parget.*
Crepissage : m. *Pargetting, rough-casting.*
Crepisseure. *as* Crespisseure.
Crepitation : f. *A creaking, crashing, crackling, ratling noyse.*
Creppe. *as* Crespe.
Crepuscule : m. *The twilight; (either in the euening, or morning.)*
Crepusculin : m. ine : f. *Betweene day and night, of the twilight.*
Crescent : m. *as* Croissant; *an halfe-Moone.*
Cresche. *as* Creiche; *a cratch, racke, or crib.*
Creseau : m. *Kersie.*
Creseul : m. *A Cruzet, or Cruible; a Goldsmithes melting pot.*
Cresme : m. *The Crisome, or oyle wherewith a Baptized child is annointed; (And because it is to be blessed, by a Bishop, before it be vsed, it signifies) also, a Dioces.*
Homme de bon cresme. *An open-hearted, good-natured, plaine-dealing, man.*
Cresme : f. *Creame.*
Cresmé : m. ée : f. *Fleeted, creamed, or, whose creame is scummed off; also, full of creame.*
Cresmeau : m. *The Crisome wherwith a child is annointed (in Popish Churches;) or (more properly) the cloth, or Christening cap, thats put on the head of the child as soone as it hath beene annointed.*
Cresnette : f. *A pen-knife; or, a sharpe, and small graffing knife.*
Crespe : m. *Cipres; also, Cobweb Lawne.*
Crespe de chaperon. *A Crepine; the Crepine of a French-hood (most commonly of Cobweb Lawne, or white Cipres.)*
Crespe : com. *Curled, frizled; crisped; also, crispe.*
Crespé : m. ée : f. *The same; also, crackled, creaked; crashed.*
Crespelet : m. ette : f. *Curled, frizled, crisped, a little.*
Crespelu. *as* Crespelet.
Crespelure : f. *A curling, frizling, ruffling.*
Crespément. *Crispingly; frizlingly, curlingly.*
Cresper. *To crackle, or creake, as new shooes, or drie stickes that are layed in the fire; also, to crash between the teeth (a thing thats crispe, or brittle;) also, to crisp, curle, frizle, ruffle, braid; also, to sleeke, make to shine, or glitter.*
Cresçpi : m. *Parget, rough-cast.*
Crespi : m. ie : f. *Pargetted, rough-cast; also, curled, or frizled.*
Femme crespie de couleurs. *Whose face is all-to-bedawbed, or plaistered ouer, with painting.*
Crespillé : m. ée : f. *Frizled, curled, crisped.*
Crespiller. *To frizle, to curle, to crispe.*
Crespillonné. *as* Crespu.
Crespillonner. *as* Crespiller.
Crespin : m. *A proper name for a man; and, the name of a certaine Saint, who is Patron to Shoomakers; whence;*
Apprenti de S. Crespin. *A Shoomaker.*
Lance de S. Crespin. *An Awle.*
Crespine : f. *The Crepine of a French-hood.*
Crespine de chevreau. *The call of a Kid.*
Crespine du ciel. *The skie, the coape of heauen.*
Crespinette : f. *A third kind of Knot-grasse, held (by some) to be Gerards Knawell, or Parsley peart.*
Crespir. *To parget, or rough-cast; also, to curle.*
Crespissement : m. *A pargetting, rough-casting; curling.*
Crespisseure : f. *A pargetting, rough-casting.*
Crespon : m. *A curled, or frizled locke.*
Crespu : m. uë : f. *Curled, frizled, ruffled, crisped; sleeked, shining.*
Cresserelle. *as* Crecerelle; *a Rattle, or Clacke for children; also, a Kestrell, Stanniell, Fleingall.*
Cressiné. *Crackled, or clattered; also, chattered.*
Cressiner. *To creake, or crackle, or clatter.*
Cressiner des dents. *To chatter; to say an Apes Paternoster.*
Cresson : m. *The hearbe tearmed Karres, or Cresses.*
Cresson alenois. *Kerse, garden Cresses, towne Karres, towne Cresses.*
Cresson d'eau. *as* Cresson de ruisseau.
Cresson de ruisseau. *Water Karres, water Cresses,*

ses, browne Cresses.
Petit cresson aquatique. *Little water Cresses, or Cuckow flowers.*
Cressonadiere: f. *A bed of Cresses, or place where they grow.*
Cressonniere: f. *The place, bed, or plot whereon Cresses grow; also, a woman that ordinarily sells Cresses.*
Creste: f. *A crest, cop, combe; also, a tuft, or little plume standing on the top of.*
La creste des cheveux. *The seame of the head, or parting of the haire in the middle of the head.*
Creste au coq, ou, de coq. *The hearbe Coxcombe, Penie-grasse, yellow and white Rattle; also, the hearbe Clarie.*
La creste d'un fer de cheval. *A welt about a horse-shooe.*
Creste à geline. *as* Creste au coq; *Coxcombe.*
Creste marine. *Sampier, sea Fennell, Crestmarine.*
Fourni d'entendement comme vn oison de creste. *As wise as a Woodcocke.*
Cresté: m. ée: f. *Crested, copped, adorned with a combe.*
Cresteaux: m. *The battlements of a wall, &c.*
Crestelé. murs crestelez. *Imbattled, hauing battlements.*
Crester. *Crested, combed; hauing a crest, or combe.*
Iamais tigneux n'aima le pigne, ny chapon crester geline: Prov. *The guiltie cannot abide reproofe, nor a weake man a woman.*
Crete. *as* Creste; *and hence;*
Crete marine. *as* Creste marine; *Sampier.*
Crete: com. *Gay, fine, gawdie, spruce, neat.*
Creteleé. tour creteleé d'argent. *Imbattled siluer.*
Cretisme. *Lying; falshood, or falsenesse, in words.*
Cretonart: m. *The drug tearmed Zedoarie, or Serapions Zedoarie.*
Cretons: m. *The crispie peeces, or mammockes, remaining of lard, that hath beene first shred, then boiled, and then strained through a cloth, &c.*
Creu: m. *Groweth; increase, &c; as* Cru.
Creu: m. euë: f. *Growne, waxen, increased; (The Participle of* Croistre;*) also, trusted, credited, beleeued; (of* Croire.*)*
Il veut estre creu. *He will stand to his owne opinion, none shall ouerrule him;* (Creu de;) *He will haue what he propounds, or appoints, to passe for currant; he will haue things to goe as he list himselfe.*
Crevacé: m. ée: f. *Riuen, cleft, chinked, chawned, chapped.*
Crevailles. Il nous invita à ses crevailles. *He inuited vs vnto his bursting; (spoken of a huge fat-guts)*
Crevasse: f. *A creuis, chinke, rift, cleft, chap, chawne.*
Crevasses d'un cheval. *Cratches, or Rats-tailes in a horses legs.*
Crevasses du fondement. *The Piles, or Emrods.*
Crevassé: m. ée: f. *as* Crevacé.
Crevasser. *To chop, chawne, chap, chinke, riue, or cleaue asunder.*
Creuë: f. *A groweth, accesse, rising; augmentation; increase, eeking; also, a fifteene; or any other increase of Subsidie.*
De creuë. *Ouer and besides, moreouer.*
Creve: m. ée: f. *Burst, broken, riuen asunder.*
Creve-coeur: m. *Hearts-sore, heart-breaking sorrow, extreame griefe of heart, anguish of spirit.*
A creve-coeur. *Sore against the will; or to despight, or breake, his heart withall.*
Crevellé. muraille crevellée. *See* Crenelé.

Creventrissime. *An ironicall allusion vnto* Reverendissime.
Crever. *To burst, or breake asunder; to chinke, riue, cleeue, or chawne.*
Crever les yeux à. *To put, plucke, or dig, out the eyes of.*
Crevette: f. *A Shrimpe, or Prawne.*
Petite crevette de riviere. *The Beard, or fresh-water Shrimpe.*
Creveure: f. *as* Crevasse; *a chinke, cleft, rift.*
Creusé: m. ée: f. *Hollowed, made hollow; vndermined, vnder-digged.*
Creusement: m. *A hollowing, or making hollow; an vndermining, a digging into, or vnder.*
Creuser. *To hollow, make hollow, dig into, or vnder; to vndermine.*
Creuset: m. *A Cruible, Cruzet, or Cruet; a little earthen pot, wherein Goldsmithes melt their siluer, &c.*
Creux: m. *A caue, hole, hollow place, or corner.*
Le creux de l'estomach. *The hole, or pit of the stomacke.*
Le creux des mains. *The palme, or middle of the palme, of the hands.*
Creux: m. creuse: f. *Hollow, deepe, caued, full of holes.*
Racine creuse. *The hearbe Holewort, or Hollowroot.*
Songer creux. *To muse deepely of a matter.*
Teste creuse. *A shallow braine.*
La viande creuse (asçavoir, les bestes à deux pieds) *Wenches, trulls, female raskalls.*
Creziou: m. *as* Creseul: ¶Rab.
Cri: m. *A crie, clamor, skrike; showt; an outcrie, lowd noyse, acclamation; also, a Proclamation.*
Le cri, & les Armes. *The name, title, qualitie; Armes, Deuice, or Scutcheon of a noble familie; belonging onely, or chiefely (at least) vnto the eldest heire (as he pretends.)*
A cor, & à cri. *See Cry.*
En bas cri. *Whisperingly; or, in a low, and still voyce.*
Criage: m. *The Cryers fee; also, a crying, or proclaiming of; also, a Criership; or, the Office, or place, of a publicke Crier.*
Criaillé. *Bawled, cried, squeaked out often and alowd; spoken earnestly, protested vehemently.*
Criaillement: m. *A bawling; as* Criaillerie.
Criailler. *To bawle, crie, or squeake out often, & alowd; to speake high and earnestly; to protest with great vehemencie.*
Criaillerie: f. *Lowd babling, or brawling; a clamorous vrging, or protestation.*
Criailleur: m. *A bawling fellow, clamorous person; a lowd and importunate speaker; one who with his high speaking deafes all that are about him.*
Criard: m. arde: f. *Clamorous, out-crying, full of noise; that does nothing but bawle, bray, and crie out.*
Criarde: f. *A scowld; an vnquiet woman of her tongue.*
Criblage: m. *A sifting.*
Crible: m. *A siue, or sifter; raunging siue.*
Criblé: m. ée: f. *Sifted, raunged.*
Cribler. *To sift, or to raunge.*
Cribleur: m. *A sifter.*
Cribleure; *or,* Criblure: f. *A sifting, or raunging of meale; also, siftings.*
Cribleux: m. euse: f. *Siue-like; full of holes as a siue; also, full of siues.*
Os cribleux. *The bone* Etmoïde, *whereof the top of the nose is made; so tearmed, because it is full of little holes*

holes like a siue.
Cricaille: f. *Chinkes, coine.*
Cride. *A publike Crier.*
Cridons: m. *Certaine thicke haires of a pinnes length, which vex, & paine children in their turning, as much as if they had so many thornes, in their backs.*
Crie: f. *A Proclamation, Crie, or outcrie; also, a Criers fee; also, a Crier.*
Crié: m. ée: f. *Cried, skreeked, showted, hallowed; exclaimed of, complained on; also, proclaimed.*
Criée: f. *Any Proclamation, crie, or outcrie; whence also, an outrope, or outcrie of goods (tearmed more commonly than properly, a Portsale, which is rather a present sale of fish in Hauens;) also, a crying, exclaiming, bawling, braying.*
Criées. *The publication of a future seisure, & sale of a mans goods, made by a Sergeant, or Crier, at the doore of his parish Church, on sundrie dayes, & sundrie times, before the seisure, or sale, be executed.*
Criement: m. *A crying, calling, showting; an exclaiming, railing, complaining, crying out against, a proclaiming; also, a wrangling, brabling, brawling.*
Crier. *To crie, skrecke; hallow, showt; bray, bawle; exclaime, complaine of, crie out vpon; also, to wrangle, brawle, brable, contend in words; also, to proclaime; to summon, signifie, denounce by proclamation.*
Crier harol. *To make hue & crie after; or to exclaime vpon, &c; Seeke* Harol.
Crier au lard sur. *To flowt, deride, scoffe at publickly; to disgrace with outcries, and acclamations.*
Crier au regnard l'un sur l'autre. *To reuile extreamely, raile on bitterly one another.*
On crie le loup plus grand qu'il n'est: Prov. *Report makes mischiefes greater than they be.*
La pire rouë du chariot est celle qui crie le plus fort: Prov. *The worst wheele of the wagon is that which creakes most; the most ignorant sot in assemblies talkes highest; and the veriest cow in a companie brags most.*
On plume l'oye sans la faire crier: Prov. *Looke* Oye.
Tandis que le chien crie le loup s'enfuit: Prov. *While the dog doth nought but barke, the wolfe hath leasure to escape.*
Tant crie on Noel qu'il vient: Prov. *We call so oft on Christmas, that at length it comes.*
Trop tard crie l'oiseau quand il est prins: Prov. *Too late cries the bird when shee is taken; too late comes repentance when we are sure of punishment; or we repent vs too late of wrongs done when wee are paying for them.*
Crierie: f. *A showt, exclamation, bawling, or crying out.*
Crieur: m. *A Crier; proclaimer; exclaimer.*
Crieurs de trespassez. *Certaine Bell-men, who attired in blacke, & bearing on either side of their gowns the Armes of one thats lately dead, go vp and downe the streets tinging their bells, and publishing his death, and the time, and place, of his buriall; at which they march before the coarse, attired, and tinging, as before: In Paris there be 24 of them; all which are neuer imployed except it be at the funerall of the King, or Queene; for at others (how great soeuer) there must be but 23 at the most.*
Crieurs de vin. *Wine-criers; those that publish throughout the neighbour streets the names, and dwelling places of such as haue wine to sell; together with the price tis held at, and goodnesse it is of; which to approue, they carrie some of it in a pot, and a siluer cup, to giue any man, that demaunds, a tast of it.*
Crignon: m. *A field Cricket, or Grassehopper.*
Crime: m. *A crime, fault, offence; imputation.*
Criminalité: f. *Criminalitie; a criminall action, case, or cause.*
Crimination: f. *A crimination, or accrimination; an accusing of, or charging with, a crime.*
Criminatoire: com. *Criminatorie, accusatorie; criminall, accusing.*
Criminel: m. *A malefactor, guiltie person, offendor; the defendant in a criminall action, or accusation; the prisoner at the barre; also, an accuser.*
Criminel: m. elle: f. *Criminall; guiltie, faultie, culpable; also, capitall, or, of life and death; whence;*
Iuge criminel. *The Judge that sits on life and death.*
Lieutenant criminel. *The same; See* Lieutenant.
Criminellement. *Criminally; culpably, faultily, guiltily; also, capitally.*
Crimineux: m. euse: f. *Faultfull, naughtie, lewd, wicked, subiect vnto accusation.*
Crin: m. *A haire; See* Crins.
Il n'est si petit crin qui ne porte son ombre: Prov. *The smallest haire hath it shadow; the least act a circumstance; the lowest word a sound.*
Crineux: m. euse: f. *Hairie, full of haire.*
Criniere: f. *A haire-cloth; also, a hood for a horse; also, a Crannet; armor for the necke, or mane, of a horse; also, haire; or a locke, or tuft of haire; whence;*
Criniere horrible. *An ouglie bush of haire.*
Verte criniere. *The haires of trees; viz. the boughes, or branches.*
Crinons des cheminées. *Crickets:* Pic.
Il a beaucoup de crinons en la teste. *His head is troubled, or full of crochets; he is much perplexed in his thoughts.*
Crinons en teste gastent la feste: Prov. *Looke* Teste.
Crins. les crins. *The haires; haire.*
Les crins d'un cheval, &c. *The mane of a horse, &c.*
Cripaulme. *as* Agripaulme; *The hearbe Motherwort.*
Criquemelette: f. *A crackling, rustling, ruffing, or buffing wench; one that bustles, or brushes the ground, as she goes.*
Criquement: m. *A creaking, crackling, ratling; bustling, rumbling, rustling.*
Criquer. *To creake, rattle, crackle; bustle, rumble, rustle.*
Criqueter. *as* Criquer; *Also, to knacke, or knap with the fingers.*
Criqueter des dents. *To gnash, or chatter with the teeth.*
Crise: f. *The Judgement of Physicke vpon the alteration of a disease; also, the conflict betweene nature, and the disease.*
Crissant. *Crackling, or creaking; or crashing.*
Crissement: m. *A creaking, as of a doore; a crashing, as of things broken; a whistling, as of the wind; any such lowd, or shrill noise.*
Cristal: m. *Crystall.*
Cristalin: m. ine: f. *Crystallie, crystall-like; white, and transparent, as crystall; of, or belonging to, crystall.*
Humeur cristalin. *The crystaline humour; seated in the middest of the eye, and of a round figure, somewhat flattened both before and behind; it is the first instrument of sight; and a glasse wherin the spirit examines, iudges*

Judges of, the formes represented vnto it.
Critiquer. *To play the Criticke; to controll, or correct what another hath done; also, to shew the signes of it selfe; or, to foreshew, by signes, what will succeed.*
La maladie critiquoit. *Came to a Crisis, or, altered on a criticall day.*
Critiqueur: m. *A Criticke; a Controller, or Corrector of other mens works, or doings.*
Croac: m. *The croaking of Rauens, Frogs, or Toads.*
Croäceux: m. euse: f. *Croaking, as a Rauen, &c.*
Croäillement: m. *The croaking of a Rauen, or Toad.*
Croäiller. *To croake like a Rauen, or Toad.*
Croäillerie: f. *The croaking of a Rauen, or Toad.*
Croäilleur: m. *A croaker.*
Croäilleur: m. eure. *as* Croäilleux.
Croäilleux: m. euse: f. *Often croaking, full of croaking, vsing much to croake.*
Croäquer. *To croake as a Rauen.*
Croässement. *as* Croäillement.
Croässer. *To croake like a Rauen, or Toad.*
Croässeur: m. *A croaker, a croaking Rauen, or Toad; one that cries like a Rauen, or croakes like a Toad.*
Croc: m. *A graple, or great hooke.*
Donner le croc en jambe à. *To ouerthrow, foile, ouerturne; supplant.*
Vn proces pendu au croc. *A suit put off, deferred, or hanging by the wall; the like is;*
Sac au croc. *A suit vndecided.*
Croce. *A Crosier, or Bishops staffe; also, a kind of game; See* Crosse.
Crocer. *as* Crosser; *To play at Cricket.*
Envoyer croçer. *To send packing; See* Crosser.
Crocette: f. *A vine-slip; a small twig, or shoot of a vine, springing from the stalke, and fit to be planted.*
Croceux. *as* Croäceux.
Croché: m. ée: f. *Crooked, hooked; as* Crochu.
Crochement des dents. *The crookednesse, or outward bending of the teeth, or tusks.*
Crochet: m. *A small hooke, or fish-hooke; also, a nut-hooke; or, a kind of hooke wherewith Mulberries bee gathered; also, a grubbing forke, or hooke-like instrument, wherewith the earth is digged, or turned vp; also, the double skrue-hooke whereat saddles be hung vp in Stables; also, the tush, tuske, or fang of a beast; also, a Quauer in Musicke; also, a place in, or part of, a market, wherein many things are confusedly sold together; also, a Romane Beame, or Stelleere; a beame of yron or wood full of nickes, or notches, along which a certaine peize of lead, &c, playing, and at length setling towards the one end, shewes the iust weight of a commoditie hanging by a hooke at the other end.*
Le crochet d'un crocheteur. *The forke, or crooked staffe, vsed by a (burthen-bearing) Porter.*
Clou à crochet. *A tenter hooke.*
'A crochets. *Cleauing one to another; by heaps, or hudling one among another.*
Donner le crochet à. *To trip, cast, ouerturne, ouerthrow.*
Il ne faut aller aux Meures sans crochet: Prov. *Mulberries must not be gathered without a hooke; nor harsh worke fingered with naked hands.*
Crocheté: m. ée: f. *Picked open with a hooke; also, hanged on a hooke.*
Crocheter. *To open, picke open, with a hooke, &c; also, to hang on a hooke.*
Crocheterie: f. *A picking of lockes.*
Crocheteur. *A Porter, or common burthen-bearer.*
Crocheteur de serrures. *A pick-locke, a filtcher, or filtching theefe.*
Il les fit crocheteurs. *He laid load on them.*
Crocheton. *A peece of siluer money, worth about iij s. ix. d.* sterl.
Crochu: m. *The Cormorant tearmed, a Sea-Drake.*
Crochu: m. uë: f. *Hooked, crooked, bowed downwards, or inwards.*
Avoir les maines crochuës. *Looke* Main.
Crochuë: f. *A Quauer in Musicke; whence;*
Il a des crochuës en teste. *(We say) his head is full of crochets.*
Crochuëment des dents. *The crookednesse, or bending out of the teeth, or tuskes.*
Crochure: f. *Crookednesse, hookednesse.*
Crociteur. *as* Crocheteur de serrures.
Crocodile: m. *A Crocodile.*
Le petit crocodile. *The small Crocodile tearmed* Scinque.
Crocodilée: f. *A medicine, made of some parts of a Crocodile, for the suffusions, and webs of eyes.*
Crocomagnie. *An ointment made of Saffron; also, the dregs of Saffron oyle.*
Crocqué. *as* Croqué.
Crocquer. *as* Croquer.
Crocquer la pie. *To wet the whistle, or weason, throughly; to drinke hard.*
Crocqueter. *as* Croqueter.
Crocute. *The Corcute; a monster begot of a Lyonesse by the Hyena.*
Croie. *as* Croye; *Chalke.*
Croier. *as* Croyer.
Croire. *To beleeue, or thinke assuredly; to trust, haue confidece in, giue credit vnto; also, to lend, put in trust with, commit into the hands of; also, as* Croyer; *and thence;*
Si vous ne le voulez croire, charbonnez-le. *If you will not (chalke, or) beleeue him, bleach him.*
Et pour le faire croire. *And to make it be beleeued.*
S'en faire croire. *To ouerrule, preuaile in, make himselfe sure of; absolutely, or at his owne pleasure to dispose of; also, to winne, gaine, or haue, credit by; &c; as in* Accroire.
Si m'en croyez. *If you credit, relie on, or will be ruled by, me.*
Ne croire à Dieu que sur bons gages, ou à bonnes enseignes. *To trust no man further than hee sees him; to beleeue no promise, nor protestation before the deed be done.*
Fol ne croit iusques à tant qu'il reçoit: Prov. *The foole beleeues not till he do receiue (the whole fruit of his owne hopes, or of other mens promises.)*
Pour neant demande conseil qui ne le veut croire: Prov. *In vaine he craues aduice that will not follow it.*
Qui femme croit, & asne meine, son corps ne sera ia sans peine: Pro. *He that trusts a woman, and leads an Asse, is neuer without one trouble or other.*
Crois: f. *as* Croix.
Croisade: f. *An expedition of Christians, assembled, out of diuers countries, (by preachings, and the Popes Bulls) against the Turkes, or other Infidels; tearmed so, because euerie one of them, when he vndertakes the iourney, accepts of, and weares on his cassocke, or coat armour, the badge of the Crosse.*
Croisades. *Crossings.*
Croisadeur: m. *A crosser; he that crosses, or sets, or makes the signe of the Crosse on himselfe, or others.*

Croisé: m.ée: f. *Crossed; layed acrosse, or ouerthwart; also, that hath taken on him the crosse, or vndertaken to fight against Infidels.*

Les bras croisez. *Idly, sloathfully, lazily; carelesly; also, mournefully, wofully, dolefully, with heauie cheere.*

Croix croisée. *A crosse crosset (in Blazon.)*

Paroles mal croisées. *Ill cooched, or set together.*

Croiseau: m. *A Stockdoue, Queest, Culuer.*

Croisée: f. *The crosse-barre of a window; also, a window so crosse-barred; also, the space that is betweene the shoulders on the top of the backe; and (generally) any crosse, or crosse-like proportion, or thing thats made crosse-wise, or set acrosse; also, the hearbe Crosewort Gentian; or a kind of small Gentian, that beares red flowers, and hath a white, long, and most bitter root, soueraigne against bellie-wormes, the plague, the stinging of Serpents, &c, and vlcered throat-wennes, or the Kings Euill.*

Les croisées d'un'espée. *The crosse-barres, or hilts, of a sword.*

Demy croisée. *A window that hath but one barre, from side to side.*

`A la croisée. *Crosse-wise, or ecrosse, or one ouerthwart another.*

Croiser. *To crosse; to signe, or marke with a crosse; to set crossewise; to lay ouerthwart, or one orecrosse another; also, to cut, or diuide in forme of a crosse-like* X; *also, to cancell, or crosse, a writing; also, (at Tennis) the ball to crosse, or to take a touch of the side-wall before it touch the wall at th'end.*

Se croiser. *To crosse himselfe, or make the signe of the crosse on himselfe; also, to take on him the crosse, or vndertake, with others, a holy iourney, or warre against miscreants, and Infidels.*

Croiset: m. *A Cruet, Cruible, or little earthen pot, such as Goldsmithes melt their gold in; also, a greene Frog.*

Croisette: f. *A little crosse; also, the hearbe Crossewort Gentian; or as* Croisée.

Croiseur: m. *One that sets, makes, or stampes a crosse on any thing.*

Croisi. *as* Croiseau.

Croisie: f. *A crosse, a crossing, a marking with a crosse.*

Croisillons. *The small crosse barres of a window.*

Croissance: f. *Groweth, increase, a growing, augmentation, eeking.*

Croissant: m. *The halfe-Moone; in Blazon, a Cressant.*

Le croissant du jour. *Is about nine a clocke in the morning.*

Ordre du Croissant. *Seeke* Ordre.

Croissant: m.ante: f. *Growing, increasing, waxing bigger and bigger.*

Croisset: m. *A greene Frog.*

Croissette. *as* Crocette.

Croissir. *To cracke, or crash, or crackle, as wood thats readie to breake.*

Croist: m. *A groweth, increase, thriuing.*

Bail de bestes à croist. *A lease made of beasts (with reseruation of their propertie) for part of whatsoeuer profit shall be made of them.*

Croistre. *To increase, grow, thriue, wax bigger, augment; swell, or rise in height, shoot vp; come on apace.*

Le nez luy croist. *Said of one that quietly swallowes, and disgests, a publicke affront, or disgrace, which hee might haue returned, reuenged, or preuented; we say of such a one, he will carrie coales; or, he is an Asse whom any man may ride.*

Mauvaise herbe croist tousiours: Prov. *An ill weed growes apace.*

Croisure: f. *A crosse, a crossing, the forme of a crosse; or, a making of the signe of a crosse, or forme of a crosse.*

La Croisure des espaules. *The breadth of, or space betweene, the shoulders; the top or part, of the backe, which is betweene the shoulders.*

Croix: f. *A crosse; also, the signe, badge, or forme, of the crosse.*

La croix du cerf. *The bone thats found in the heart of a Stag.*

La croix de par Dieu. *The Christs-crosse-row; or, the hornebooke wherein a child learnes it.*

Exaltation Saincte croix. *Holy-rood-day; (the foureteenth of September.)*

Invention Saincte croix. *Th'inuention of the Holy Crosse; a holy-day kept by the Church of Rome on the third of May; also, a shift, inuention, or deuice for the getting of money.*

Croizer. *See* Croiser.

Crolant. *as* Croulant; *whence;* Bois crolant d'un ladre. *A Lazers clacke, or clicket.*

Cronique. *See* Chronique.

Crope: f. *The top, or knap of a hill; See* Croupe.

Cropion: m. *The rumpe, or crupper; a little thing like a taile, or Cuckoes beak, composed of foure small bones, and hanging at th'end of the* Os Satré.

Le cropion du becquefigue. *The haunch, or flanke, of a Gnat-snapper.*

Le mal de cropion. *The Rumpe-euill, or Crupper-euill; a disease wherewith small (cage) birds are often troubled.*

Croppe: f. *as* Crope.

Croppiere. *as* Croupiere; *A Crupper.*

Bonnet à croppiere. *A square cap.*

Croqué: m.ée: f. *Creaked, cracked, crackled, crashed; also, eaten, or snatcht vp at a bit; swallowed, or let downe at a gulpe; dispatched on a sudden, in a trice.*

Croque-jarret *A Baker-legd fellow; one whose hammes are warpt, or, that goes in with the hammes.*

Croque-lardon: m. *A smell-feast, a lickorous fellow; a wastfull glutton, a greedie eater; and (most properly) one that pickes the lard out of meat, as it roasts.*

Croque-mouche: m. *A flie-catcher; an idle gaping hoidon.*

Croque-noisette. *A nut-cracker.*

Croque-notaire: m. *A Pregnotarie, or Pronotarie; a word deuised by* Rabelais *in derision of* Prothonotaire.

Croque-quenouille. *He whose wife beats him with a distaffe:* ¶Rab.

Croquer. *To croake, creake, cracke, crash, crackle, as a bone which a dog breakes; also, to eat, or chaw; to catch, or snatch at a bit; also, to gulpe, as a man that drinkes hastily.*

Croquer la pie. *Seeke* Pie.

Croqueter. *To eat lickorously, to picke out the daintiest morsells; to deuour, or feed greedily.*

Croqueterie: f. *Lickorous feeding, or, gourmandizing.*

Croqueteur: m. *An eatnell; a greedie, and lickorous feeder.*

Cros: m. *Deepe holes digged into the earth to preserue corne in.*

Crosilles: f. *The shells which Pilgrims weare about their hats.*

Croslé:

Croslé: m. ée: f. *Shaken, wagged, fast moued.*
Crosler. *To shake, wag, tremble; quauer, moue fast; quiuer, quake.*
Croslier: m. ere: f. *Shaking, wagging, quaking, trembling.*
Crosliere: f. *A quagmire, bog; or peece of loosse, and soft ground, that shakes vnder the feet.*
Crosse: f. *A Crosier, or Bishops staffe; also, a Cricket-staffe; or, the crooked staffe wherewith boyes play at Cricket.*
Donner la Mitre, & la crosse à. *To authorise, or beare out, by the priuiledge of a religious function; to couer with the specious cloake of Religion.*
Evesque d'or crosse de bois, crosse d'or Evesque de bois: Prov. *The lesse a Bishops staffe, the more his vertue, shines; pompe first corrupted Prelacie.*
Crosser. *To play at Cricket.*
Aller ou envoyer crosser. *To send one packing, to bid him goe shake his eares.*
Crossette: f. *A slip of a tree, or plant; See* Crocette.
Crossir. *as* Grincer.
Crostes. *as* Crottes.
Crot: m. *A hole, denne, caue, grot:* ¶Parisien.
Crotaphique: com. *Belonging, or neere vnto, the* Crotaphiques.
Artere crotaphique. *A great sinew neere vnto the temples.*
Crotaphiques. *The two muskles of the temples.*
Croté. *as* Crotté.
Crotenotaire. *as* Croquenotaire.
Crotes. *as* Crottes.
Crotesque: f. *Rude countrey painting, or caruing, wherein many things are confusedly represented; See* Grotesques.
Croton: m. *as* Crotton; *and (more particularly) the dungeon of a prison.*
Crotpescheret. *A kind of blacke Osprey:* ¶Bourg.
Crotte. *See* Crottes.
Crotté: m. ée: f. *Bedagled, bemired, berayed, with durt.*
Crotté en Archediacre. *Dagged vp to the hard heeles, extreamly bedurtied, all to be dabled; (Belike when this phrase came first in vse, Archdeacons trudged vp and downe on foot.)*
Crotter. *To dig, or make holes in the earth, or in old wals; also, to daggle, bedurtie, bemire.*
Crottes: f. *Durt, filth, mire; dagling stuffe; also, the dung, excrements, or ordure of Sheepe, Goats, Conies, Hares, &c.*
Crotton: m. *A deepe hole, a filthie dungeon.*
Croüacement. *as* Croüas.
Croüas: m. *The croaking, or crie of Rauens.*
Croüasser. *To croake or crie like a Rauen, or Crow.*
Croue d'un pressoüer. *as* Escroüe; *or the vppermost boord, and the hole thereof, whereinto the Vice-pinne enters.*
Crouillet: m. *The latch of a doore.*
Croulant: m. ante: f. *Shaking, wagging, mouing, trembling.*
Crouler. *as* Crosler; *to shake, wag, or quake.*
Croule-vniuers. *World-shogging, all-shaking.*
Croulier: m. ere: f. (prez crouliers. *Which tremble, or shake vnder one;) shaking, wagging, trembling, quagmire-like.*
Crouliere: f. *A quagmire; a trembling, or shaking peece of ground; as* Crosliere.
Croupant: m. ante: f. *Crooching, stooping, bowing downwards; also, long standing in one place; & hence;*
Eau croupante; *puddle water.*
Croupe. *as* Crope; *the top or knap of a hill; also, the rumpe, or crupper peece.*
La croupe du dos. *The ridge of the backe.*
Vn chien assis sur la croupe. *A dog sitting on his taile, or buttocks.*
Porter en croupe. *To carrie behind on horsebacke.*
Croupeton. vn lievre estant à croupeton. *That sits vpon her buttocks (as she doth often while she is at reliefe) and raises her selfe thereon, to listen at euerie wag of a feather.*
Croupi: m. ie: f. *as* Croupy.
Eau Croupie. *Standing water, which hath no course, as that of lakes, puddles, &c.*
Croupie. chasser à la croupie. *To find a Hare at reliefe, and then course her with Greyhounds.*
Croupiere de cheval. *A horse-crupper.*
Croupir. *To crooch, bow, stoope, grow or goe double; also, to rest, or grow idle; stand, or abide long in a place.*
Croupissant. eau croupissante. *A standing puddle, a dead water.*
Crouppe: f. *The top, or knap, of a hill.*
Croupy: m. ye: f. *Crooched, or crooching; inclined, crooked, stooping, bowing; also, resting, standing, being idle.*
Crousille: f. *The shell-fish, called a Scallop.*
Croussiller entre les dents. *To crash, or crackle betweene the teeth, as a nut shell, &c.*
Crouste: f. *A crust; a scab, or hard scurfe.*
Crouste de pastez valent bien pain: Pro. *Piecrust is alwayes worth a peece of bread; or may well serue in stead of bread.*
Crousteau: m. *A great crust; or great scab.*
Crousteau de cire. *A wax comb wherein bees make, or lay vp, their honie.*
Crousteleve. *Scuruie, bescabbed; full of the pocks.*
Crousteleveure: f. *Scuruinesse, scabbinesse, pockinesse.*
Crousteleux. *Crustie; as* Crousteux.
Croustelles; ou Croustellettes. *Little crusts, or scabs.*
Crouster. *To crust, or scab; to bring a crust, or scab vpon.*
Crousteux: m. euse: f. *Crustie, bescabbed; hard, and rugged, like a wall that is pargetted.*
Croustons: m. *Sharpe flintie stones.*
Croute: f. *A hole, grot, caue, denne.*
Crouteleve. *as* Crousteleve: ¶Rab.
Croyable: com. *Credible, beleeuable, to be trusted vnto, relyed on.*
Chose aisée croyable: Prov. *That which is easily done is soone beleeued.*
Croyablement. *credibly.*
Croyance: f. *Beliefe, beleeuing, credit giuen vnto.*
Croye: f. *Chalke.*
Croye pour nettoyer draps. *Fullers earth.*
Croye rouge. *Ruddle, red Lead, red Oaker.*
Croye teincte de pourpre. *Cheeke vernish, red painting.*
Croye verde. *as* Verd de terre.
Croyé: m. ée: f. *Chalked, marked, or whited with chalk.*
Croyer. *To chalke; to marke, or white, with chalke.*
Croyeux: m. euse: f. *Chalkie, full of chalke.*
Cru: m. *A groweth, growing; increase, or increasing.*
Armé à cru. *In compleat armour; or, all-ouer armed.*
Cela n'est pas de son cru. *That was none of his owne setting, or planting; that is none of his owne inuention, or doing.*

Cru: m. uë: f. *Crude, raw, vnripe, ouer-new; imperfect, vnprepared; also, vnsauorie.*
Cruauté: f. *Crueltie, inhumanitie, fiercenesse, tyrannie, rigour, bloudthirstinesse.*
Cruche: f. *An earthen pot, pitcher, or steane; also (in old French) a stable.*
Telle terre telle cruche: Pro. *Such stuffe, such work; such wit, such words; such affection, such actions; such discretion, such directions.*
Cruché: m. eé: f. *Hollow, or hollowed, as a pitcher; made like a pitcher.*
Crucher. (quasi le mesme que, jucher; *or*) *To crouch; also, to make hollow like a pitcher.*
Cruchеter. *as* Chucheter.
Cruchette. *A little pitcher.*
Crucial: m. ale: f. *Crosse-wise, crosse-like.*
Crucié: m. ée: f. *Tormented; vexed, grieued, afflicted.*
Crucier. *To torture, torment; vex, grieue, afflict.*
Crucifié: m. ée: f. *Crucified, nailed on the crosse.*
Crucifiement: m. *A crucifying, or nailing on the crosse.*
Crucifier. *To crucifie; to naile, or put to death on a crosse.*
Crucifix: m. *A Crucifix.*
Mangeur de crucifix. *An hypocrite.*
Crucifix: m. ixe: f. *Crucified, put to death on the crosse.*
Crucigeres: m. *Crosse-bearers; or, an Order of Fryers which weare crosses on their habits.*
Crud. *as* Cru. *Crude, raw, vnripe; vnprepared.*
Crudité: f. *Cruditie; rawnesse, vnripenesse; indigestion.*
Cruë. *as* Creuë.
Cruel: m. elle: f. *Cruell, fell, vngentle, fierce; tyrannous, rigorous, vnmercifull; bloudie, bloudthirstie, bloudie minded.*
Cruelisé: m. ée: f. *Vsed, or handled cruelly.*
Cruellement. *Cruelly, fiercely, bloudily, felly, rigorously, vnmercifully.*
Cruëment. *Rawly, barely, nakedly; also, rashly.*
Cruente. le flux cr. *The bloudie flix.*
Crujon: m. *Any round thing, as a mans skull, or braine panne.*
Cruon. *The skull, or braine panne; or, as* Crujon.
Crural: m. ale: f. *Of, or belonging to the thighes.*
Muscle crural. *as* Cuissier.
Veine crurale. *A branch of the descendent trunke of the hollow veine; diuided into foure branches.*
Crusol. *as* Cruzeul.
Cruzeul. *A Founders mould, wherinto the melted mettall is conueyed.*
Cry. *The motto, or deuice of an Embleme.*
Cry. à cor & a cry. *By proclamation; or, by hue and crie.*
Cryptoportique. *A secret walke, or vault vnder ground, or in some low place; a close low gallerie for coolenesse in Summer.*
Crysolite. *A pretious stone; as* Chrysolite.
Crystal: m. *Crystall.*
Crystalin. *as* Crystal.
Crystalin: m. ine: f. *Crystaline, of Crystall.*
Cubaseau: m. *The little Sea-nettle:* ¶Bourdelois.
Cube: m. *A Cube; or, figure of Geometrie, foure square like a Die.*
Cubebes: f. *Cubebs; an Aromaticall, and Indian fruit.*
Cubiculaire: m. *A Groome of the Chamber.*
Cubiculaire: com. *Cubicular; belonging to the bedchamber.*
Cubique: com. *Square, or made square.*
Cubital: m. ale: f. *Cubitall; of, or belonging to the Cubite.*
Artere cubitale. *Seeke* Artere.
Cucube. Herbe cuc. *Garden Nightshade.*
Cucurbite: f. *A gourd.*
Cucurbitin: m. ine: f. *Of, or belonging to, gourds.*
Cucuye. *An admirable bird in* Hispaniola *(no bigger than a thombe) hauing two eyes in her head, and two vnder her wings (which are double, a greater and smaller paire) so shining in the night (wherein only she flies) that fiue or six of them tied together, giue as much light as a torch.*
Cueillement: m. *A gathering, reaping, picking vp; a culling, collecting, choice, or chusing out.*
Cueiller: m. *An oare.*
Cueillette: f. *A collection, a reaping, or gathering together.*
Bonne cueillette. *Plentie of corne, and of all other fruits; a plentifull Autumne, or Haruest.*
Cueilleur: m. *A gatherer; a reaper; a picker, chuser, or culler.*
Mis en cuilleur de pommes. *Turned into the habit of an Applesquire.*
Cueilleure: f. *A gathering; reaping; picking, culling, or chusing out.*
Cueilli: m. ie: f. *Gathered, reaped, picked vp; chosen, culled, collected out.*
Cueillier. *The fowle tearmed a Shoueler; also, as* Cuillier, *a spoone; and hence the Prouerbe;*
Entre la bouche & la cueillier souvent advient grand destourbier. *Much may happen betweene the cup and the lip.*
Cueillir. *To gather; to reape; to picke vp; to cull, collect, or chuse out.*
Cuens. *An Earle, or Count.* (v.m.)
Cueur: m. *The heart;* See Coeur.
Cueurs. *The heart-resembling Cherries, called* French *Cherries, or Spanish Cherrie.*
Cueut: f. *A whetstone.*
Cueux de plomb. *A Sow of Lead.*
Cuferin: m. *A running at the Nose got by a Horse after an ouer-long course, or gallop, whereby the Veines of his Braine are opened so wide, that they are hardly, or not in a small time, closed againe.*
Cuict: m. icte: f. *Sodden; baked; concocted, digested, ripe ynough; fit to be eaten.*
Bois cuict. *Charcoale.*
Matiere cuicte. *(Sometimes vsed for)* Matiere fecale.
Miel cuict. *A kind of pancake made of, or seasoned with, honie.*
Teste mal cuict. *An vnstaied, or greene, head.*
Cuidance: f. *Thought, weening, imagination, supposition, presumption.*
Orgueilleuse semblance monstre folle cuidance: Prov. *Looke* Semblance.
Cuidant. *Thinking, weening, supposing, imagining, deeming; presuming.*
Cuidé. *Thought, weened, imagined, supposed, deemed; presumed.*
Cuider: m. *A thought, conceit, ghesse, weening, imagination, opinion, supposition, presumption.*
Cuider n'est pas iuste mesure: Prov. *Imagination is no iust measurer.*
Cuider. *To thinke, weene, deeme, imagine, suppose, presume, haue an opinion of, make a ghesse at.*

Cela cuide avenir à. *That had like to haue happened at.*

Cuidereau: m. *A Braggadochio; a pretie bardie fellow; one that thinks well of himselfe; one that is bold or so.*

Cuideur: m. *A thinker, weener, deemer, supposer; imaginer; presumer.*

Cuideur de vendenge. *One that is deceiued in that he thinketh; and, more particularly, one that farts in syrrope; or, meaning but to fart, mars all.*

Cuideurs sont en vendenge: Prov. *Vpon a merrie Haruest many ground fond hopes.*

Cuidrelles. *See* Cuydrelles.

Cuigner. *To wedge, or hold open with wedges.*

Cuignet: m. *A little corner; also, a little wedge.*

Cuilier: f. *A spoone; See* Cuillier.

Cuiliere: f. *A ladle.*

Cuillerée: f. *A spoone-full of.*

Cuillier: f. *A spoone.*

Cuillier de mer. *The Sea-spoone; a kind of long Cockle.*

Herbe aux cuilliers. *Spoonewort, Scuruie-grasse.*

De vieilles maisons bruslées il sçait tirer des cuilliers neufues. *(Said of a skilfull, & thriftie house-keeper;) he can extract new spoones from old burnt houses.*

Entre la bouche & la cuillier souvent advient grand destourbier: Pro. *Disturbance oft steps in twixt cup, and lip.*

Cuillier. boyau cuil. *The arse-gut; See* Boyau.

Cuin: m. *A wedge.*

Cuir: m. *The skin; also, a skin, fell, hide; also, leather.*

Coupeur de cuir. *A cut-purse.*

Le cuir luy tient. *He is clungd, or hide-bound.*

Faire d'autruy cuir large courroye. *To spend freely on another mans purse; to cut a large thong out of another mans leather.*

Il se iette sur tout cuir. *He deales with euery thing; all is fish that comes to his net, all good prise that comes in his way; hee greedily falls aboord on any trash, or trull.*

On s' est ioué de son cuir. *His skin hath beene plaid with, to his paine; (said of one that hath been throughly whipped.)*

Tremblant entre cuir & chair. *Trembling inwardly, extreamely, throughly, or (as wee say) at the the verie heart.*

Qui cuir voit tailler courroye en demande: Prov. *Hee that sees Leather cut requires a thong of it.*

Cuirace. *as* Cuirasse.

Cuirain: m. *Leatherne stuffe; prouision, or marchandise, of leather.*

Cuirasse: f. *A Cuirats; armour for the breast, and backe.*

Cuirassé: m. ée: f. *Armed with a Cuirats.*

Lievres cuirassez, ou morionnez. *Sillie, or cowardlie Artificers watching in armor; the ordinarie watchmen of good townes.*

Cuirasseux: m. euse: f. *Leatherie, of a hide; or, thicke and stiffe, as a hide.*

Cuirassier: m. ere: f. *Of, or belonging to, seruing for, a Cuirats.*

Cuirassine: f. *A sleight Cuirats for a light Horseman.*

Cuire. *To seeth, boyle; bake; disgest; make ripe, or readie; also, to itch, or smart.*

Cela me cuict. *That vexeth, fretteth, stingeth, or grieueth me.*

Trop grater cuict, trop parler nuit: Prov. *Too much scratching paines, too much talking plagues.*

Cuirie: f. *A leatherne Jerkin; (an old word.)*

Cuissant: m. ante: f. *Smarting, itching, netling, stinging.*

Cuisinal: m. ale: f. *Of, or belonging to, a Kitchin.*

Livre cuisinal. *A booke of Cookerie.*

Cuisine: f. *A Kitchin; (and sometimes) also, meat; whence;*

Leur cuisine ordinaire. *Their ordinarie diet, or proportion of victualls.*

Harpye de cuisine. *A rauenous, or most greedie deuourer; a beastlie feeder; one that eats extreamly much, and spoyles the rest which he cannot eat.*

Latin de cuisine. *Grosse Latine.*

Faire la cuisine. *To play the Cooke, to dresse meat.*

Se ruer tresbien en cuisine. *To fall eagarly to his victualls, to be a verie good trencher-man.*

Grasse cuisine maigre testament: Prov, *Great house-keepers leaue poore executors; The like is;*

De grasse cuisine povreté s'avoisine: Prov.

Mauvais chien ne veut iamais compagnon en cuisine: Prov. *A churle cannot endure a companion in his gainfull imploiments.*

Cuisinement: m. *A dressing of meat, a cooking, or playing of the Cooke.*

Cuisiner. *To cooke, play the Cooke, dresse meat as a Cooke.*

Cuisineux: m. euse: f. *Fit for Cookerie, belonging to the Kitchin.*

Cuisinier: m. *A Cooke.*

Cuisiniere: f. *A woman Cooke.*

Cuissal; or, Cuissaux. *Cuisses; Armour for the thighes.*

Cuisse: f. *The thigh.*

Vne cuisse d'ail. *A cloue of Garlicke.*

Cuissedame: f. *The name of a kind of peare.*

Cuisselette: f. *A litttle thigh.*

Cuisse-né. *Thigh-borne; (an Epithete of* Bacchus.)

Cuissette: f. *as* Cuisselette.

Cuissier. *Of, or belonging to, the thigh.*

Muscle cuissier. *One of the foure principall muscles whereby the thigh is bent, or stretched out.*

Cuissin: m. *A cushion.*

Cuissinet: m. *A little cushion.*

Cuissineux: m. euse: f. *Soft as a cushion; fit for a cushion; holding of the cushion; full of cushions.*

Cuisson: f. *A seething; also, a smarting; a stinging, as of Nettles.*

Cuissots: m. *Tasses; armour for the thighes.*

Cuit. *as* Cuict.

Cuite: f. *A seething; baking, batch; also, digestion.*

Cuivre: m. *Copper.*

Cuivreux: m. euse: f. *Full of Copper.*

Cul: m. *An arse, bumme, tayle, nockandroe, fundament.*

Cul d'asne. *as* Cubaseau. *The small Sea-nettle.*

Cul blanc. *The bird called a Whittaile.*

Cul de cheval. *A small, and ouglie fish, or excrescence of the Sea, resembling a mans bung-hole, and called, the red Nettle.*

Le Cul d'un 'esguille. *The eye of a needle.*

Cul d'un 'espingle. *The head of a pin.*

Cul de fosse. *A dungeon.*

Cul de four. *The bottome of an ouen.*

Cul de lampe. *See* Lampe.
Cul noüé. *The name of a certaine short-tailed Apple.*
Cul de poule. *A certaine hard, and eminent swelling on the Orifice, or edge of a Fistula; also, a bringing, or setting all the tops of the fingers close together.*
Cul sur pointe. *Topsie turuie, arsie-varsie, vpside-downe.*
Cul rouge. *The bird called a Specht, or Speght.*
Cul sur teste. *as* Cul sur pointe.
Au cul du sac. *At length; in th'end, or bottome; when all is done and gone.*
De cul & de teste. *Furiously, fiercely, on all hands, on euerie side, euerie way.*
Assis entre deux selles le cul à terre. *Betweene two stooles the breech goes to the ground.*
Grattant le cul au soleil. *Idlely, sloathfully, slouenly; as one that lies clawing his breech, or bleaking himselfe, in the Sunne.*
Il leur fit leuer le cul à Dreux. *He raisd their siege, or made them rise, from before* Dreux.
Iouër à pique en cul. *To thrust out the harlot, or driue out one naile with another.*
Vn Mangeur de culs de poules. *A nickname for a souldior.*
Mettre de cul. *To set on his arse; to ouercome, confound, ouerturne, ouerthrow.*
Torcher à autruy le cul de sa chemise. *To doe a man a pleasure, but (which he could haue done himselfe) only by his owne meanes; Looke* Chemise.
`A cul de foirard tousiours abonde merde: Prov. *A shitten taile hath euer store of ordure; a shitten fellow is stored with filthie humours, or scuruie followers.*
Il est mal caché à qui le cul paroist: Prov. *Hee's but ill hid that shewes his taile; he is but a shallow dissembler that suffers the world to take notice of his worst humors.*
Culace: f. *as* Culasse.
Culaçon. *The breech of a peece of Ordnance.*
Culant. *Setting on his taile, giuing an arse-posse vnto.*
Culasse: f. *The Counter (in the Poope) of a Ship; also, the breech of a Gunne; also, a foule-great, or full-growen arse, or breech; also, a lumpe of gold or siluer melted in a cruible, &c, and still retaining the forme of the bottome thereof.*
Qui ne chastie culot, ne chastie culasse: Prov. *He that corrects not youth, controuls not age; he that nips not vice in the bud, suffers it, a branch.*
Culassé: m. eé: f. *Foyled, ouerthrowne, set on the taile; that hath receiued an arse-posse, or fall on the arse.*
Culasseur: m. *One that foyles, or sets another on his taile.*
Culbute: f. *A tumbling; a turning, or tossing vpside downe; See* Culebute.
Faire la culbute. *To play the tumbler; or, to turne as a tumbler, top ouer taile.*
Culbuté: m. ée: f. *Tumbled, throwne topsie turuie; ouerturned, turned top ouer taile.*
Culbuter. *To tumble, throw topsie turuie, turne vpside downe; also, to ouerturne, set on the taile; tumble one vpon another.*
Culebute. bidet de culebute. *The sinewie instrument of mankind.*
Culeron: m. *The hinder part of the buttockes of a horse.*
Culetage: m. *Buttocke-stirring, taile-wagging, leacherie.*
Culeter. *To wag, or stirre the buttockes vp and downe; to moue the taile in a wanton time, or with the taile keep time vnto a wanton musicke.*
Culetis: m. *as* Culetage.
Culette: f. *as* Culaçon.
Culier: m. ere: f. *Of, or belonging to the taile, arse, or fundament.*
Boyau culier. *The arse-gut; See* Boyau.
Culiere: f. *A crupper for a horse.*
Culinaire: com. *Of, or belonging to, a kitchin.*
Cul-leve. Iouër à cul-leve. *To play at leuell-coyle.*
Cullot. *as* Culot; *Also, a cushion (made) to ride post on.*
Cullottes. *as* Culottes.
Culot: m. *A little arse, a small taile; (and by metaphor, a lad, or yong bodie;) also, as* Qulocul; *and, the lag, or last of a companie; also, as* Cullot.
Culot de bronze. *A hollow barre, or wedge of brasse.*
Culot de fondeur. *The mould wherein a Bell-founder, &c, casts his mettall.*
Marcher comme culots. *To come behind, or, in the rereward of the rest.*
Qui ne chastie culot ne chastie culasse: Prov. *Hee that corrects not small faults, will not controll great ones; or, he that corrects not a knaue while hee is young, will not bee able to controll him when hee is old.*
Culottes: f. *Armour for the hinder parts, or taile peece, of a horse; also, (a fashion of) close breeches.*
Culpe d'un artichaud. *(Perhaps mistaken for* Pulpe; *) The pulp, pith, or substance of an Artichocke.*
Cul-pelé: m. ée: f. *Bauld-arst, bare-taild, pild-breecht.*
Culrage. *as* Curage.
Culte: m. *Respect, worship, honour giuen, seruice done one.*
Cultellaire: com. *Of a knife, or knife-like.*
Cautere cultellaire. *See* Cautere.
Cultivage: m. *Tillage.*
Cultivant. *Tilling, husbanding, dressing, labouring.*
Cultivation: f. *A tilling, or tillage.*
Cultivé: m. ée: f. *Tilled, wrought, laboured, husbanded; improued by plowing, bettered by tillage.*
Cultivement: m. *A tilling, husbanding, labouring, plowing; culture, or improuing by culture.*
Cultiver. *To labour, till, plow; improue by culture, better by plowing.*
Cultiveur: m. *A husbandman; a labourer, or tiller of land.*
Culture: f. *Culture, tillage, husbandrie.*
Cumané. *Of the Sybill* Cumana: ¶Rab.
Cume de pressouër. *(Belike mistaken for* Cuve; *) the vat, or trough which receiues the liquor expressed.*
Cumin: m. *The hearbe, or seed, Cummin.*
Cumin sauvage. *Wild Cummin; whereof there are three kinds; the ordinarie, the codded, and the horned one.*
Cumulativement. *Largely, abundantly, by heaps.*
Cumulé: m. ée: f. *Heaped, accumulated, filled vp; gathered by heaps.*
Cumuler. *To heape, accumulate, fill vp; to augment, or gather together, by heaps.*
Cunctation: f. *Cunctation, tarriance, delay, abiding, lingering, prolonging of the time.*
Cuneiforme. *Wedge-resembling, wedge-like, of the fashion of a wedge.*
Os cuneiforme. *Seeke* Os.
Cuniculeux: m. euse: f. *Full of inward holes, or by-corners.*

Cunilage. *Sauorie, Winter Sauorie; also, wild, or bastard Marierome; (some also call Fleabane,* Cunilago.)
Cunöct. *A Kennet (apple.)*
Cupide: com. *Couetous, greedie, desirous of, lusting after.*
Cupidique. Embloquer à la Cupidique; autant que, besongner.
Cupidité: f. *Cupiditie; lust; couetousnesse; wanton affection, dishonest loue; vniust, or ill-seasoned, desiring.*
Cupule: f. *The little cup, or shell, of an Acorne.*
Curage: f. *The hearbe Water-pepper, Arse-smart, Killridge, or Culerage.*
Curage rouge. *Water Dragon, or Marsh Dragon.*
Curailles de maison: f. *The dust, filth, sweepings, or cleansing, of houses.*
Curatelle: f. *Wardship; the office of a Gardian, or Tutor; a surueying, an ouerseeing.*
Curateur: m. *A Gardian in Socage; a Tutor, an ouerseer; a Surueyor, &c.*
Curation: f. *A cure; curing, healing.*
Curé: m. *The Curate, or Parson of a Church; he that hath the spirituall charge of a Parish.*
Bourse de curé. *The hearb Toywort, Pickepurse, Cooseweed, Shepheards-pouch, or purse, poore-mans Parmacetie.*
Cure: f. *Care, heed, respect, regard; carke, thought, pensiuenesse; also, a Cure, or charge of Souls; a Parsonage, or Vicarage; also, a cure, healing, restoring to health; also, a Hawkes casting.*
Il est tout presché qui n'a cure de bien faire: Pro. *He that will not be saued needs no preaching; aduice preuailes not with such as are carelesse of their owne good.*
Curé: m. eé: f. *Cleansed, purged, purified, cleered, voided of ordure; picked, pruned; also, healed, cured, recouered.*
Cure-dent: m. *A tooth-picke.*
Curée: f. *A (dogs) reward; the hounds fees of, or part in, the game they haue killed.*
La curée d'un fossé. *The cleansing, or scowring of a ditch; the mud, slime, or durt thats taken out of it.*
Cure-oreille. *An eare-picker.*
Curer. *To cleanse, cleere, purifie, purge, void of ordure; picke, prune; also, to heale, recouer, cure; also, to cast, as a Hawke doth.*
Curestable: m. *A stable-cleanser; an Ostler, Horsekeeper, or Groome of a Stable.*
Curette: f. *A Chirurgions Proofe, or Probe; an instrument wherewith he sounds the bladder, & gathers together such grauell, congealed bloud, or other filth, as remaines in it, after a stone taken out; also, an eare-picker; also, a Plough-staffe, or Aker-staffe (wherwith the Culter is cleansed.)*
Cureures de maison. *as* Curailles.
Curial: m. ale: f. *Of the Court, belonging to a Court.*
Amende curiale. *Seeke* Amende.
Curialiste: m. *A Courtier.*
Curialité: f. *Formalitie, courtesie, or courtship.*
Curie: f. *A Tribe, or ward in a Citie.*
Curieusement. *Curiously, precisely, nicely, quaintly, daintily; doubtfully, scrupulously; carefully, heedfully, busily, too too diligently.*
Curieux: m. euse: f. *Curious; quaint, nice, daintie, precise; doubtfull, scrupulous, heedfull, busie; too too diligent; more carefull than needs.*
Curin: m. *A thinne, or small skin.*
Curiosité: f. *Curiositie, curiousnesse; daintinesse, nicenesse; affectation.*
Curoir: m. *as* Curette *(in the first sence.)*
Curtille: f. *A little many-legd vermine, that gnawes asunder the roots of plants.*
Curtin: m. *(The name of) a verie sweet, and long-lasting Apple.*
Cuscoamy. *as* Cuscouil: ¶Rab.
Cuscouil. *Well hanged, well stoned.*
Cuscute. *A kind of worme; also, the weed Dodder.*
Cusins: m. *Whurtle-berries, or Winberries.*
Cussonné: m. ée: f. *Worme-eaten.*
Custode: m. *A Gardian, Warden, keeper, ouerseer*
Custode (de lict.) *A Curtaine (for a bed.)*
Cutané: m. ée: f. *Skinnie, or, of the skin.*
Cuticulaire; peau cuticulaire. *Full of Pores, or of holes, for sweat to come out at.*
Cuve: f. *An open tub; a fat, or vat.*
'A fonds de cuve. *Largely, throughly, fully.*
Fossé fait à fonds de cuve. *Hauing a bottome like a fat, or, flat-bottomed, and downe-right sided.*
Goutte à goutte on emplit la cuve: Prov. *By drop after drop the the fat is filled; See* Goutte.
Cuvé: m. ée: f. *Put into, or seasoned in, a great vat, or tub.*
Cuveau: m. *A little fat, or tub.*
Cuvée: f. *A tub-full of.*
Cecy est d'un'autre cuvée. *This is of another vessell, of another edition; of another sort, of another fashion.*
Cuvelier: m. *A vat-maker, or tub-maker.*
Cuver. *To tunne, or put into a fat, or tub; to season, let worke, or stand in, a vat, or tub.*
Cuver son vin. *To disgest his liquor; to euacuate, or passe ouer, the fumes thereof by a good nap, or any other helpe.*
Cuvette: f. *A little fat, or tub.*
Cuvette de Venus. *The Teazell, or Fullers Thistle.*
Cuviel: m. *A bathing tub.*
Cuvier. *as* Cuviel; *Also, a Dying fat, or lead.*
Cuviere: f. *An open vessell, or cesterne to wash, or coole drinking pots in Summer; or as* Cuvier.
Cuyderolles. *as* Cuydrelles.
Cuydrelles: f. *Crow-flowers, wild Williams, marsh Gilliflowers, Cuckoe Gilliflowers.*
Cuyrassine. *See* Cuirassine.
Cuyvre: m. *Copper.*
Cuyvreux: m. euse: f. *Full of copper.*
Cy: f. *The name of a Saint; whence;*
Pain benist de la S. Cy. *Wine, good liquor, Nippitatie.*
Cy. *Here, in this place, hither, in this matter; Looke* Ci.
Cy devant. *Heretofore.*
Cyané: m. ée: f. *Azure, bright, blew of colour.*
Cyathe: m. *A small cup, or measure among th'auncient Romanes, containing about foure spoonefulls; and in weight an ounce, halfe a quarter, two charats, and fifteene graines of our weight; Looke* Ciathe.
Cyboïde. os Cyb. *A certaine bone in the instup.*
Cyclamine. *The hearbe Hogs-bread, Sowes-bread, Swines-bread; also, the wild vine, blacke Brionie, our Ladies Seale; also, Wood-Nightshade, Bittersweet.*
Cycle. *A round, or circle.*
Cyclopique. *Monstrous; one-eyed, halfe-blind; cruell, furious.*
Cycogne. *A Storke; Looke* Cicogne.
Cycogneau: m. *A yong Storke.*
Cyerce. *The Northerne wind:* ¶Rab.

Cygne: m. *A Swan*; *Looke* Cigne.
Cygnean: m.anne: f. *Like a Swan*; *of, or belonging to a Swan.*
Cygneur: m. *A Swan-keeper*; *(a word sometimes vsed in derision of* Seigneur.)
Cylindre: m. *A rowler*; *the woodden instrument wherwith clods are broken, and allies plained.*
Cymace: f. *A ledge, or outward member in Architecture, fashioned somewhat like a Roman* S, *and tearmed a Waue, or Ogee.*
Cymacion. *A small waue, or Ogee.*
Cymaise. *as* Cymace.
Cymas. *The same.*
Cymat. *A small waue, or Ogee (in building.)*
Cymbale: f. *A Cymball to play on.*
Iouër des cymbales. autant que paillarder: ¶Rab.
Cymie. *as* Cymace; *also, as* Cime.
Cymettes: f. *The shoots, or tender buds yeelded by the staulks of Coleworts, after the greater leaues haue beene cropped off.*
Cymier: m. *as* Cimier; *Also, a Crest, Cognisaunce, or deuice, borne on the top of an helmet.*
Cymitiere. *A Churchyard*; *Looke* Cimitiere.
Cynabre. *Cynoper*; *a kind of Vermilion*; *Looke* Cinnabre.
Cynamolge. *An Arabian bird, that vseth to sucke bitches.*
Cynanthropie. *A frenzie, which maketh a man haunt vnfrequented places, with a conceit, that hee is turned into a dog.*
Cynic: m. ique: f. *Dogged, cinicall, doggish, currish, churlish.*
Cyniphe. *A gnat, midge, or dog-flie.*
Cyniphé: m. ée: f. *Dogged.*
Cynocephale: m. *A Baboone.*
Cyntre. *Looke* Cintre.
Cyon: m. *A Whirlewind*; *or, the boisterous incounter of two strong winds (at Sea.)*
Cypere: m. *Cyperus, or Cypresse, Galingale, (a kind of reed.)*
Cyprés: m. *The Cyprus tree*; *or Cyprus wood.*
Cyprés de Candie. *The Candian Cyprus tree*; *(is lower, and smaller, and spreads it boughes in a rounder forme, than the ordinarie one.)*
Cyprés de Iardin. *Lauender Cotton*; *or, garden Cyprus.*
Cyprés sauvage. *Female Soothernwood.*
Le menu, ou petit Cyprés. *The same*; *or sweet Soothernwood.*
Droict de branche de Cyprés. *A duetie yeelded in old time by Englishmen arriuing at* Bourdeaux, *as a signe that they had beene there.*
Cypressier: m. ere: f. *Of, or belonging to, Cyprus.*
Cyprin: m. ine: f. *Of, or belonging to, th'Island Cyprus, or vnto Venus, the Patronesse thereof*; *whence*;
Torche cyprine. *The flame of loue.*
Cyre. *Looke* Sire.
Cyron: m. *A hand-worme*; *Looke* Ciron.
Cyronne. *A seare-cloth*; *&c*; *as* Ceroesne.
Cysimbre: m. *Water-Mint, fish-Mint, brooke-Mint, and horse-Mint.*
Cystepatique. Artere cys. *A braunch of the Arterie* Coeliaque; *which goes to the liuer, and gall.*
Cystique. veine cystique. *A certaine little veine issuing from the trunke of the Port veine, and thence mounting to the bladder of the gall*; *before it comes at which it is sometime single, and sometimes double*; *but there diuided into two branches.*

Cythariser. *To sing, or whizze as the wind.*
Cytise. *The shrubbie plant* Citisus, *shrub-Trefoyle, Herbarist, and Tetrifolie*; *some also call it, milke Trefoile*; *because it increases milke in the cattell that feed on it.*
Cyvade. *A Shrimpe, or Prawne.*

D

Dâ, *for* deà. *An Interiection, confirming the word whereto it is ioyned*; *as* ouy dâ, *yes verily*; non-dâ, *no in truth, or, no forsooth.*
Dabblée. *See* Dablée.
D abbordée. *At first, at first sight, at their arriuall, as soone as they touched*¶ *as soone as they came together.*
Dablée: f. *A crop of corne, &c*; *corne growing, or standing, on the ground*; *also, Haruest, or the reaping of corne, &c.*
Daces: f. *Tolles.*
Dacier: m. *A toll-gatherer.*
Dacque. *A certaine weed like vnto our Docke.*
Dacte: m. *A Date.*
Dactier. *The Palme, or Date tree.*
Dactier d' Inde. *Th'Indian Date tree.*
Dactilaire: com. *Of, or belonging to, a Date*; *also, Datelike.*
Cautere dactilaire. *See* Cautere.
Dactiliomantie: f. *Finger-Magicke.*
Dactyle: m. *The Date-grape, or Finger-grape*; *also, the hearbe Dogges-tooth*; *also, a kind of long shell-fish*; *also, a long precious stone found in Candia*; *also (in versifying) a foot of three sillables, whereof the first is long, the two other short.*
Dactylogie: f. *Finger-talke*; *speech made with the fingers.*
Dada. *A horse*; *(Childishly.)*
Dadée: f. *Childish toying, speech, or dalliance*; *whence*;
Souffrir à vn enfant toutes ses dadées. *To cocker, or cokes it*; *to make a feddle, or wanton of it.*
Dadvantage. *Moreouer*; *furthermore*; *ouer-and besides*; *also, better then*; *as,* il estoit monté d'advantage, *Hee was better mounted than the rest*; *(in which sence it must euer bee written with an Apostrophe.)*
Daemon: m. *A diuell, spirit, soule.*
Dagard: m. *A Brocket, Spitter*; *Pricket*; *a young male Deere that but begins to put forth a head.*
Dagasse: f. *A great dagger.*
Dagobert. *The name of a certaine ruddie, & very good peare.*
Dagorie: f. *The name of a faire yellow apple.*
Dagorne: f. *A decrepite, and toothlesse beldame.*
Dague: f. *A dagger*; *also, the head of the young Deere, called a Spitter, or Pricket.*
Dague & baston. *Large measure, heaped measure, measure with aduantage.*
Dague à roëlles. *A Scottish dagger*; *or Dudgeon haft dagger.*
Servante faicte à la dague. *A soothing wench, a colloguing queane.*
Daguenet: m. *A little (pocket) dagger.*
Daguer. *To stab with a dagger.*
Daguette: f. *A little dagger.*
Daignant. *Deigning, vouchsafing.*
Daigner. *To deigne, vouchsafe, thinke worthie of.*

Dail: m. *A sithe to mow with.*
Daille: f. *A kind of long shell-fish, thats couered, or armed with two shells.*
Daim: m. *A fallow Deere.*
Dain: m. *as* Daim.
Dain: m. Daine: f. *Daintie, fine, quaint, curious; (an old word.)*
Daincean. *as* Dainteau.
Daine: f. *The Sea-fish called, otherwise,* Maigre.
Daing: m. *as* Daine.
Dainteau: m. *A yong fallow Deere.*
Daintiers: m. *The Doucets, tenderings, or stones of a Deere.*
Dais, *or* Daiz. *A cloth of Estate, Canopie, or Heauen, that stands ouer the heads of Princes thrones; also, the whole State, or seat of Estate; also, the boords of a beds tester whereat the valances be hanged.*
Daissellé: m. ée: f. *Made of, or couered with, boords.*
Dalader. *A kind of fruitlesse, and barren Priuet.*
Daldre. *A Flemish coine worth about* iiij. s.
Dale. *as* Daldre; *Also, a slice.*
Dalle: m. *A sewer, or pit, whereinto the washings, dishwater, and other such ordure of houses, are conueyed.*
Dalle: f. *as* Dale; *also, as* Daille.
Daller: m. *The coine called, a Doller.*
Dalmatique: f. *(A fashion of) a long white gowne, or Vestment (spotted, or tufted all ouer with purple) at first broght vp by the Dalmatian, or Sclauonian Priests; also, a wide-sleeued Vestment, or Surplus worne, at this day, by Deacons during the celebration of solemne daies Masses.*
Dain. *Sir; (an addition, or title of respect, and honour, giuen, in courtesie, vnto a Gentleman, or Knight: This in old time; and yet the Gouernors of the Charterhouse Monks are stiled* Dams.*)*
Dam: m. *Dammage, losse, hinderance, harme.*
Damage. *as* Dam: ¶Pic. *Losse, dammage, hurt.*
Damaisine: f. *A Damascene, or Damsen plum.*
Damas: m. *Damaske.*
Eau de Damas. *Damaske, or sweet, water (distilled from all sorts of odoriferous hearbs.)*
Huile de Damas. *Oyle Damascene.*
Raisins de Damas. *The best sort of Raisins of the Sun.*
Rose de Damas. *The Damaske, or Muske Rose.*
Terebenthine de Damas. *Turpentine of Venice.*
Damasceure: f. *Damasking, or Damaske worke.*
Damasquin: m. ine: f. *Of Damaske, or, wrought like vnto Damaske.*
Rose Damasquine. *The white Muske Rose.*
Damasquinage: m. *Damaske worke.*
Damasquine: f. *Damasking, or Damaske worke.*
Damasquiné. *as* Damassé.
Damasquiner. *To Damaske, to worke Damaske work; to flourish, carue, or ingraue Damaske-wise.*
Damasquineure: f. *as* Damasceure.
Damassé: m. ée: f. *Damasked; of Damaske; wrought or flourished, like Damaske.*
Damasser. *as* Damasquiner.
Damastic: m. *A kind of varnish like vnto Damasking.*
Dame: f. *A Dame; a Mistresse; a Ladie; also, a Stepdame; also, a man at Tables, or Draughts; also, a Pie, Pianet, Magatepie. (In old time this word, signifying that which* Monsieur *or* Seigneur *doth now, was appropriated vnto men.)*
Dame du milieu. *A certaine thicke skin, or filme, which is broken when a virgine is made a woman.*
Belle Dame. *Seeke* Beau.
Mes Dames. *The title, and stile of the French kings daughters.*
Nostre Dame. *Our Ladie; the virgine Marie, the blessed virgine.*
L'assumption nostre Dame. *Our Ladie day in Haruest.*
Chardon de nostre Dame. *The white Thistle, milke Thistle, our Ladies Thistle.*
La conception nostre Dame. *The conception of our Ladie; the eighth of December, kept holyday by the Church of Rome.*
Les cinq doigts nostre Dame. *Fiue leaued grasse.*
Fillasse de nostre Dame. *The slender threads of Cobwebs.*
Herbe de nostre Dame. *The hearbe Clarie; so called in* Languedoc.
Laict de nostre Dame. *as* Chardon de nostre Dame.
Mente de nostre Dame. *Speare-mint, Baulme-mint, Browne-mint, Macrell-mint, our Ladies Mint, common Garden Mint.*
La Nativité de nostre Dame. *A solemne holy-day kept by the Church of Rome on the eighth of September.*
Poire de nostre Dame. *A verie good peare, called Maries Peare, or, our Ladies peare.*
La presentation nostre Dame. *The Presentation of our Ladie; a holy-day kept by the Church of Rome on the 21 of Nouember.*
Rose de nostre Dame. *Peonie, Pionie, Kings Bloome, Rose of the Mount; also, the shrub called Rose of Hierusalem, Rose of Jerico, our Ladies Rose, & heath Rose.*
Seau de nostre Dame. *Our Ladies Seale, black Brionie, wild Vine; (an hearbe.)*
La Visitation nostre Dame. *The Visitation of our Ladie; a holy-day kept by the Church of Rome, on the second of Iuly.*
Dame qui trop se mire peu file: Prov. *She that heeds her beautie much, tends her benefit but little; a proud, and a good, huswife are incompatible.*
En moissons Dames chambrieres sont: Pro. *While Haruest lasts, all fellowes.*
Pour l'amour du Chevalier baise la Dame l'Escuyer: Prov. *The Ladie kisses her man for his Masters sake (an excesse of her loue which verie well might be spared.)*
Quand la Messe fut chantée, si fut la Dame parée: Prov. *By that time Prayers were done her tiers were on.*
Vuides chambres font les Dames folles: Pro. *The roome once voided, farewell modestie.*
Damé: m. ée: f. *Made a Queene, as a Pawne at Chests; doubled at Draughts.*
Damer. *To make a Queene at Chests; to double a man, or make a king, at Draughts.*
Ie dameray ceste-cy. *I will requite, or second this tale; I will tell another vpon the necke of it; (a Metaphor from the making of a King, by doubling of a man, at draughts.)*
Dameret: m. *An effeminate fondling, or fond carpet Knight; one that spends his whole time in the intertaining, or courting, of women.*
Dames. *(The Plurall to* Dame; *also,) the play on the outside of a paire of Tables, called Draughts.*
Iouër aux dames rabbatuës. *To leacher it.*
Damier: m. *A Chesse-boord; or, paire of Tables.*
Damnable: com. *Damnable, condemnable; blameable, vnfit to be allowed.*
Damnation: f. *Damnation; a damning, a condemning.*
Damné: m. ée: f. *Damned, condemned, adiudged vnto death.*

Damner. *To damne, condemne, giue iudgement against, adiudge vnto death.*

Damoiseau. *as* Damoisel; *and as* Damoiselet; *also, a neat fellow, spruce yonker, effeminate youth.*

Damoisel: m. *A young gentleman professing Armes, and not yet knighted.*

Damoisel d'un tel lieu. *The Lord of such a place (an ancient forme of speech.)*

Damoiselet: m. ette: f. *Gentlewoman-like; or, waiting on a Gentlewoman.*

Teinct damoiselet. *An effeminate complexion; a face of hue more womanlie then manlike.*

Damoiselette: f. *A little Gentlewoman; a Gentlewoman of meane estate, or of low degree.*

Damoiselle: f. *A Gentlewoman; any one, vnder the degree of a Ladie, that weares, or may weare, a Veluet hood.*

Damoiselle d'attour. *The Gentlewoman, or waiting woman that vses to dresse, and make readie, her Ladie, or Mistresse.*

Mes damoiselles. *The title, and stile of the French Kings younger brothers daughters.*

Damp chevalier. *Thou sir Knight; or, as,* Dam.

Damyon. *The name of a certaine apple, that yeelds very cleere Cydar.*

Danché. *Indented; or (as in termes of blazon) dancy.*

Dandin: m. *A meacocke, noddie, ninnie; a hoydon, sot, lobcocke; one that knows not how to looke, and gapes at euery thing he knowes not.*

Dandiner. *To goe gaping ilfauoredly, looking vnsteaddily; to gape, and looke, like an Asse, Noddie, Ninnie.*

Dandrilles: f. *Hangars, Dantrils; Looke* Dendrille.

Danger: m. *Danger, perill, ieopardie, hazard.*

Les dangers des bois. *The amerciaments, and confiscations adiudged vnto the King by the Officers of woods, and forrests.*

Droict de tiers, & danger. *A third and tenth (as of xxx pound xiij) payed vnto the King out of the price of euery Woodsale made in the woods and forrests of his, or other lords demaynes (especially within* Normandie) *wherein he hath those rights.*

Fief de danger. *Looke* Fief.

Il y a danger que. *It is to be feared least.*

A grand danger grand courage: Prov. *Great courage is in greatest dangers tryed; or as in* Courage.

Il n'est danger que de vilain: ¶Pro. *A clowne (inraged) is most dangerous.*

Dangereusement. *Dangerously, perilously, with much ieopardie, with great hazard.*

Dangereux: m. euse: f. *Daungerous, perilous, ieopardous, full of hazard.*

Sergens dangereux. *Certaine Officers, that leuied, vnto the Kings vse,* les dangers des bois, & le droict de tiers & danger, *vntill the yeare 1563, when they were cassed by* Charles *the ninth.*

Dans. *as* Dedans. *In, within.*

Danse: f. *A daunce, or dauncing.*

La Danse des crapaux. *as in* Crapaud.

Danse du loup la queuë entre les jambes. *Lecherie.*

Danse Macabré. *Death; (a daunce wherein there is no respect of age, degree, worth, or dignitie.)*

Danse Trevisanne. *Lecherie.*

Elle sçait assez de la vieille danse. *She knowes well enough what belongs to the Game; she hath bin a backster, a twigger, a good one, in her time.*

De la panse vient la danse: Pro. *Men are the merriest when their bellies are fullest; or, when the bellie is full the breech would be figging; (for by this* Danse *is any lustfull, or sensuall, motion vnderstood.)*

Dansé. *Daunced; hopped, skipped.*

Dansement. *A dauncing; hopping, skipping; a motion directed by time, and harmonie.*

Danser: m. *To daunce; also, to hop, skip, or leape (for ioy.)*

Danser en bille. *To daunce very liuely.*

Danser la grue. *To hop, leape, skip, daunce often; or but vpon one leg.*

Il ne sçait sur quel pied danser. *Hee is at his wits end, he knowes not what in the earth to doe.*

Amour apprend les asnes à danser: Pro. *Loue makes the cokes turne courtier.*

Chascun n'est pas aise qui danse: Prov. *Euerie one is not merrie that daunces; of such a one wee say, his heart is not so light as his heeles.*

Danseresse: f. *A woman dauncer.*

Danserie: f. *A dauncing, &c; as* Dansement.

Danseur: m. *A dauncer, hopper, skipper.*

Iamais danseur ne fut bon clerc: Prov. *Neuer was dauncer good scholler.*

Danspied. *The hollow part of the sole of the foot.*

Dante. *A certaine hard-skind Indian beast, resembling a Mule.*

Daphnomantie. *Diuination by a Lawrell, or Bay tree.*

Dapifer. *The great Master, or Steward of the Kings house; (tearmed so in old time.)*

Darceau. *A certaine fish; as* Derceau.

Dard: m. *A Dart, a Iaueline, a Gleaue; also, a kind of ash-coloured serpent, which from high trees throweth it selfe at passengers; also, a Dace, or Darc fish.*

Dardanaire: m. *A Regrator, Ingrater, or Ingrosser; one that buyes, and hoords vp corne, or other prouision, with a purpose to sell it againe when tis growne deere.*

Dardanier. *as* Dardanaire.

Darde: f. *A play, wherein boyes hauing layed a heape of points vnder a stone, and made a circle about them, dart at them with a rod, and win as many as they driue out of that circle; (Our boyes laying their points in a heape of dust, and throwing at them with a stone, call that play of theirs, Dust-point.)*

Dardé: m. ée: f. *Darted; flung, hurled, cast, throwne, as a dart; also, hit, hurt, strucken, wounded with a dart.*

Darder. *To dart; to fling, hurle, cast, or throw a dart; also, to hit, wound, pierce, or hurt with a dart.*

Darderesse: f. *A woman that casteth a dart.*

Darde-tonnere. *Thunder-hurling, thunder-shooting.*

Dardeur: m. *A darter, or thrower of a dart.*

Dardiller. *To shake, or wauer, like a dart cast with violence.*

Dardoises fourmis. *Beasts among the* Dardes *(in the North part of* India) *coloured like cats, and as big as Egyptian wolues; they dig gold oare, as Moles earth, and keepe it carefully, till creeping, in extreame heat, into caues, they are cousened thereof by the countrey people.*

Dare. *A huge big bellie; also, Dole.*

Darioles: f. *Small pasties filled with flesh, hearbes, and spices, mingled, and minced together.*

Dariolette: f. *A bawd, or carrier of loue-messages.*

Darne: m. *A slice; a broad, and thin peece, or partition of.*

Dartre: f. *A Tettar, or Ring-worme.*

Das-

Dassez. *Fully, enough.*
Dataire: m. *A dater of writings; and (more particularly) the dater, or dispatcher of the Popes Bulls; an ordinarie Officer in the Court of Rome.*
Date: m. *Pisse, vrine, lant.*
Date de lettres: f. *The date of Letters, or Euidences.*
Mis en date. *Brought into date, or into reckoning; come in request.*
Mis en date de. *Set in the ranke, or number of.*
Daté: m. ée: f. *Dated, as a letter &c.*
Dater. *To date a writing; also to pisse.* ¶Normand.)
Datif: m. iue: f. *Datiue; giuing; of power to giue.*
Quint datif. *See* Quint.
Datil. *A Date.*
Dation: f. *A gift, or giuing.*
Datte. *as* Dacte. *A Date.*
Dattier: m. *The Palme, or Date tree.*
Davantage. *See* Dadvantage.
Davanture. *Peraduenture, by chance, perhaps.*
Daubé. *as* Dobé.
Dauber. *To beat, swindge, lamme, canuasse throughly.*
Davesnes. *Horse-plums.*
Daugier. Droict de tiers, & daugier. *Looke* Danger.
Davier de barbier. *The Pinser wherewith he drawes, or puls out, teeth.*
Davier d' un pelican: m. *A certaine instrument to picke a locke withall; an yron hooke, or crampiron for that purpose.*
Daulphin. *as* Dauphin. *A Dolphin.*
Daulphin de France. *The Dolphin, or eldest sonne of France; called so of* Daulphiné, *a Prouince giuen, or (as some report it) sold, in the yeare* 1349, *by* Humbert *Earle thereof to* Philippe de Valois; *partly on condition, that for euer the French Kings eldest sonne should hold it (during his fathers life) of the Empire.*
Davoines. *A kind of Plummes; or, as* Davesnes.
Dauphin: m. *The fish called, a Dolphin; Looke* Daulphin.
Fort comme vn dauphin en terre: Prov. *Most weake, most feeble, without force; (for a Dolphin dies as soone as he is out of the water.)*
Daurade: f. *The fish tearmed a Guilt-head; also, as* Dorée.
Daurée. *as* Dorée.
Dausse d'ail. *A cloue of Garlicke.*
Daussé: m. ée: f. *Cloued; diuided into seuerall parts, or cloues, as a head of Garlicke.*
Se Dausser. *To be diuided in seuerall parts, or cloues, like a head of Garlicke.*
Daymon. *Looke* Demon.
Day: m. *as* Ders.
Dé: m. *A Dye.*
Dé à couldre. *A thimble.*
Les dez luy disent fort bien. *The dice are verie fauourable to him; or, hee hath passing good lucke at dice.*
Le dé soit ietté. *Put the matter in hazard; set all on six and seuen; it can be but an ill cast; whatsoeuer it be let's venture on it.*
Les dez sont desia iettez. *The worst is past; or, the action is alreadie begun, the matter alreadie determined; we must now stand to it, or abide the brunt of it.*
Les dez ne me veulent. *The dice crosse me, or runne not as I would haue them.*
Sans flatter le dé. *Roundly, plainly, truly, without soothing, smoothing, or making things better then indeed they be.*
Les graces du Lombard sont trois dez sur table: Pro. *See* Lombard.
De. *Sometimes signifies, of, (the note of the Genitiue case) as,* Le chappeau de Iaques; le chaulme de l'avoine; *Sometimes (a Preposition) it signifies from; as,* Ie viens de Paris; *Sometimes, in, or at; as,* de mon temps, de ce temps là; *and sometimes, by; as,* Nul si beau don fut onques donné de prince; la sentence, ou iugement donné de nous, &c.
De. *Sometimes giues Nownes an Aduerbiall signification; as;* Il vit de reigle; Il court de vistesse, &c; *He liues regularly, runnes swiftly.*
D'icy à vn an. *Till this time tweluemonth; also, a yeare hence.*
De par Dieu soit. *In the name of God be it; God prosper it, or send it well to speed.*
De par luy bon Dieu. *In the name of God; or, for Gods sake.* ¶Lymosin.
De par moy; &, De par le Roy. *Looke* Par.
De partie à partie. *Betweene partie and partie.*
Deâ. *An Interiection, as,* Dâ; ouy deâ; *Yes truely, verily, without doubt; also, a tearme of expostulation; as,* deâ, qui vous mouvoit? *Why, or, good God, what reason had you? or, what a Gods name mooued you?*
Dealbatoire: com. *Whiting, whitening, making white.*
Deambulatif. *as* Ambulatif.
Deambulatoire: com. *Oft remouing, euer going, neuer resting; or, remooueable, or changeable from place to place.*
Iusticé deambulatoire. *Iustice administred in circuits.*
Debaccher. *To raue, rage, rayle, take on like a drunken man.*
Debagoulé: m. ée: f. *as* Desbagoulé; *also, mumbled, or muttered.*
Debagouler. *as* Desbagouler; *also, to mumble, or mutter.*
Debail: m. *A Gardien, Tutor, Gouernour; as the husband is (or should be) of his wife.* ¶Boullenois.
Debaquer. *as* Debaccher.
Debardeur: m. *A Lighter-man; a Porter that belongs to a Ship, or Lighter, for the vnlading thereof.*
Debarrassé: m. ée: f. *Disintangled, rid from.*
Debarrasser. *To loosen, disintangle, rid from.*
Debasté. *Vnsadled, rid of his pack-sadle, as an Asse after his worke done.*
On y va comme asnes debastez. *Looke* Asne.
Debaster. *To take off the Pack-saddle from an Asse, &c.*
Debat: m. *Strife, debate, variance, contention, difference, disagreement; iarring, altercation, dispute, controuersie, brabling, wrangling.*
Ronde table oste le debat: Pro. *The reason followes;* Chascun estant aupres du plat.
Debatable: com. *Disputeable, debateable, subiect to opposition.*
Debatement: m. *A debating; or, as* Debattement.
Debateur: m. *A debater, arguer, disputer, contender.*
Debatis: m. *The bating, or vnquiet fluttering of a Hauke.*

Debatre. *To debate, argue, discusse, examine, dispute of; to wrangle, cauill, iarre, brable; to striue, contend, bicker, differ about; in law to demurre vpon.*

Nous debatons de la chappe à l'Abbé. *We striue for that whereto neyther of vs hath right; or that we shall both go without; for that which belongs, or is due to another; or, we brable about had I wist; castles in the aire; mooneshine in the water. (The lesse properly.)*

Se Debatre, & demener. *To bestirre himselfe hard, or apace.*

Par trop debatre la verité se perd: Prov. *By too much arguing truth is lost.*

Debattement des flancs. *A panting in the flancke.*

Debatu: m. uë: f. *Debated, argued; disputed on; brabled about.*

Au temps que cela n' estoit debatu aux ieunes hommes; *When that was not refused, or denyed yong men; when there was no difficultie made of admitting yong men vnto it.*

Debauchement. *Looke,* Desbauchement.

Debaucher. *Looke* Baucher.

Debellé: m. ée: f. *Conquered, vanquished, subdued, ouercome in warre.*

Debeller. *To subdue, vanquish, ouercome by warre.*

Debendade: f. *A suddaine disbanding of a companie one from another; an vnbending; a violent loosing, or letting go, as of an arrow out of a bow.*

'A la debendade. *Confusedly; without order, or array; also, violently, or furiously.*

Debexiller. *To crush, or breake asunder, to beate vnto peeces.*

Debiffé. *Razed, or scraped out; also, ragged, tattered; rent in peeces, torne asunder; also, out of order, much out of tune; looking sorrily as one that is not well; also, farre spent, sore decayed, shrewdly shaken, as one that is but newly recouerd of a great sicknes; of whom, compared to that he hath bin may be sayd, he is as a letter almost scraped out, which hardly shews what it was.*

Debiffer. *To raze, or scrape out, as a letter; also, to rend, or teare in peeces.*

Se Debiffer. *To split, or fly asunder; as boords that riue, or cleaue in a ship, or other building, for want of due seasoning, or close ioyning together.*

Debile: com. *Debile, weake, feeble, faint, infirme.*

Au plus debile la chandelle en la main: ¶Pro. *He that worst may the candle holdeth; or, let him that is the weakest hold the candle.*

Debilitation. *A Debilitation, weakening, enfeebling, faintnesse; infirmitie, feeblenesse.*

Debilitation de veuë. *Shortnesse of sight, weaknes of the eyes.*

Debilité: f. *Debilitie, weakenesse, faintnesse, feeblenesse, infirmitie, imbecilitie, decay of strength.*

Debilité. *Debilitated, weakened, enfeebled.*

Debiliter. *To debilitate, weaken, enfeeble.*

Debiller. *To vnloose the rope of a boate fastened vnto the peece of wood which runs orecrosse the bammes of boate-haling horses.*

Debit: m. *as* Debite.

Debitage: m. *Retaylage.*

Debite: f. *A distribution, or sale of any thing by parcels; vtterance of commodities, in retaile, & vpon trust, or otherwise.*

Ces bleds n'ont aucune debite. *This corn is not saleable, will take no mony, yeelds no commodious returne.*

Debité: m. ée: f. *Distributed, vttered, retayled, passed away by parcels, vpon trust.*

Terres debitées. *Lands giuen by the Lord vnto a tenant to be held of him by rents, or seruices, or both.*

Debitement: m. *A distributing; a selling, vttering, passing away by retayle, or in parcels, and (most properly,) vpon trust.*

Debiter. *To distribute, or doe away things, one by one; to sell, or vtter by parcels, to passe away by retayle (and most properly, vpon trust;) also, to rid much worke, dispatch businesse a pace.*

Debiter vn arbre qui est abatu. *To peecemeale it, to cut it into manie seuerall peeces, or parcels.*

Debiteur. *A distributer; or seller by retayle; a retayler, vpon trust; also, as* Debteur.

Debitis. Lettres, ou mandement de debitis. *A generall, and peremptorie writ, graunted out of the Chauncerie, or by some of the chiefe Iustices, to compell a debtor, by the seisure, and sale of his goods, and imprisonment of his person (if he be bound, or subiect thereto) to satisfie his creditor, that procured it.*

Debitoribus. il est tout deb. tourné à gauche; *he is cleane spoyled, ouerthrowne horse and foot, vtterly vndone; or he dares not loooke his creditor in the face.*

Deblée. *as* Desblée.

Debleure: f. *Corne standing; or hanging by the roots.*

Deboire: m. *An after taste, ill smacke, or twang, which an vnsauorie thing leaues behind in the mouth.*

Deboité. *Looke* Desboité.

Debonnaire: com. *Debonnaire, courteous, affable; gentle, mild; of a sweet, or friendlie conuersation.*

Debonnaire Mire fait playe puante: Prov. *a tender-harted Surgeon makes a wound to stinke.*

Oiseau debonnaire de luy mesme se fait: Pro. *The gentle hauke (halfe) mannes herselfe.*

Debonnairement. *Debonnairely, courteously, affably; gently, mildly.*

Debonnaireté: f. *Debonnairitie, or debonnairnesse; courtesie, friendlines, affabilitie; gentlenesse, mildnesse, faire or sweet behauiour.*

Grand' debonnaireté a maintes hommes grevé: Prov. *Much courtesie hath ruined many.*

Debosquer. *To rush, or issue out of a wood; to rush, or arise from an Ambuscadoe (in a wood.)*

Deboucler. *as* Desboucler.

Debourrer. *See* Desbourrer.

Debout. *Vp, standing, vpright, boult-vpright.*

Bois debout. *The branch of a vine, that (when all the rest are cut off as superfluous) is left growing for the next yeares increase.*

Debouté: m. ée: f. *Debouted; put, or thrust from; driuen fro; depriued, or turned out, of; deposed; expelled, excluded; also, repulsed, reiected, vtterly refused; also, denyed, or dismissed with a sharpe, and short answer.*

Deboutement: m. *A deposing, putting or thrusting, from; a depriuing, or turning out, of; an expelling, or excluding; a repulse; an absolute refusall, or peremptorie denyall, of; a short and sharpe dismission; also weakenesse, imbecillitie, infirmitie.*

Debouter. *To deboute; to put, thrust, or driue from; to depose, depriue, or turne out, of; to expell, repulse, exclude, reiect; refuse absolutely, or peremptorily; also, to dismisse with a short, and sharpe answer; to send away with a flea in the eare.*

Deboutonne: m. ée: f. *Vnbuttoned; vnbraced,*

Manger à ventre deboutonné. *To eat while his skin will hold; or, till his bellie cracke againe.*

Deboutonner. *To vnbutton, to vndoe a button, to loose, or let slip, a button.*

Debradé: m. ée. f. *Vnarmed, or whose arme is burst asunder,*

sunder; without an arme, wanting an arme. ¶Rab.
Debraguetter: m. *An vntying of the codpeece.*
Elle ne vault pas le debraguetter. *She is but a homelie peece of stuffe; she is not worth the paines one should take with her.*
Debraguetter. *To vnty the codpeece.*
Debranchi: m. ie: f. *Lopped, vnbranched.*
Debranchir. *To lop a tree; to cut, or pull off the branches thereof.*
Debrigandé: m. ée: f. *Tattered, ragged, or stript naked, as one that hath past through the hands of needie theeues.*
Debris: m. *A wracke; a breaking, or splitting asunder, as of a ship against a rocke; also, any rupture, or breach.*
Debrisé: m. ée: f. *Burst, broken, split asunder; also, nimbly footed (in dauncing.)*
Debrisement: m. *as* Debris.
Debriser. *To breake, burst, or split asunder; also, to foot it nimbly in dauncing.*
Debriser la voix. *To diuide, or relish cunningly.*
Debrisure. *as* Debris.
Debrouillé: m. ée: f. *Disintangled, vnpestered.*
Debrouiller. *To vnpester, disintangle, rid from trouble.*
Debte: f. *A debt; a dutie, or thing due.*
Debtes actives. *Debts owing, or due, by others vnto vs.*
Debtes Hypothecaires. *Looke* Hypothecaire.
Debtes passives. *Debts which are owed, or due by vs vnto others.*
Debtes personnelles. *Personall debts; those that grow due vpon a bare promise; or appeare to be due by a Scedule, or Scroll.*
Ie t'en feray la debte bonne. *I will warrant it, vndertake for it, make it good.*
Il ne laisse dormir la debte sur le soleil. *He is an excellent quicke paymaster.*
Vieilles debtes duisent: Pro. *Looke* Duire.
Debteur: m. *A debtor.*
Debvoir: m. *Dutie, deuoire, indeuour; a seruice, good office, obligation; also, a Haukes reward, or part, of the game she hath taken.*
Debvoirs. *The act of submission, and acknowledgement of dutie, vnto a landlord, expressed by the tenants mouth, hands, and oath of fealtie.*
Debvoir des Delicts. *A bushell of Rye payed vnto the Lord of the Borough of* Pont Niusillac *(in Britain) by euerie householder of auncient tenure, that keepes Tillage within the Territorie thereof.*
Debvoir de Ligence; *Seeke* Ligence.
Debvoir de lignage. *A certaine toll exacted vpon euerie load of wood thats brought into* Rennes.
Debvoir de luets. *as* Debvoir des Delicts.
Debvoir de moulage. *The fee, or Toll thats due, for grinding, vnto the Miller, or Lord of the Mill.*
Debvoir de Pasques. *A Lambe at Easter, due vnto some Curates, by euerie one that keepes Sheepe within their Parishes.*
Francs debvoirs. Ce sont les charges que doivent les hommes de franche, & libre condition, pour vsage de bois, pour pascage, panage, ou autrement. ¶Ragueau.
Debvoir. *To owe; to be due; to be bound vnto.*
Ie luy doy cela de retour. *I am beholden to him, or, I am bound to requite him, for that.*
Le temps le debvoit. *The time gaue, required; allowed, or approoued, it.*

Ceux qui nous doibvent nous demandent: Pro. *Our debtors are as bold with vs as if they were our creditors; (applyable vnto those that hauing receiued great fauours, are not satisfied, but either impudently demand more, or vngratefully complaine they haue not had enough.)*
Fais ce que tu doys advienne ce que pourra: Pro. *Doe thou thy dutie, happen what hap may.*
Il sied mal à qui doibt de parler plus haut qu'il ne doibt: Prov. *It ill becomes him that owes to speake lowder then hee ought;* (viz: *to stand on prowd tearmes.)*
Il n'est pas quite qui doibt de reste: Pro. *He is not out of debt that is to pay ought.*
Va ou tu peux, meurs ou tu doys: Pro. *Goe whether thou canst, but dy where thou shouldst; yong men may trauell, but the old must rest at home.*
Debusquer. *as* Desbusquer.
Debuter. *as* Desbuter.
Deça. *On this side; from hence; hether.*
Decacheté: m. ée: f. *Vnsealed, as a letter &c.*
Decacheter vne lettre. *To vnseale a letter.*
Decade. *A Decade; the tearme, or number of tenne yeares, or moneths; also, a tenth, or, the number of tenne.*
Decadenasser. *To vndoe a padlocke; also, to resolue a Riddle.*
Decadence: f. *Decay, ruine; declining, falling away.*
Decal d'argent. *Want of alloy in siluer.*
Decaller. *To slacken, or grow soft; to become lesse firme, hard, or strong then before.*
Decalogue. *The tenne Commaundements.*
Decapité: m. ée: f. *Decapitated, beheaded.*
Decapiter. *To decapitate, or behead.*
Decaptivé: m. ée: f. *Vncaptiuated, deliuered from captiuitie.*
Decaptiver. *To vncaptiuate; free from captiuitie, set at libertie.*
Decartelé: m. ée: f. *Quartered.*
Decarteler. *To quarter.*
Decedé: m. ée: f. *Deceased, departed, dead.*
Deceder. *To dy, decease, depart this life.*
Decelé: m. ée: f. *Detected, discouered, disclosed, bewrayed.*
Decelement: m. *A detection, disclosing, discouering, bewraying.*
Deceler. *To discouer, detect, disclose, lay open, bewray.*
Deceleur: m. *A detecter, discloser, discouerer, bewrayer of.*
Decemment. *as* Decentement. *Decently, seemely, comelily.*
Decempedal: m. ale: f. *Of tenne foot, or tenne foot long, &c.*
Ombre decempedale. *The shadow of a Dyall falling vpon the point of tenne.*
Decence: f. *Decencie, seemelinesse, comelinesse, handsomenesse.*
Decent. *Decent, seemelie, handsome, comelie, gracefull, becomming, beseeming, befitting; meet, conuenient, apt, fit.*
Decentement. *Decently, comelily, handsomely, gracefully, beseemingly; aptly, fitly, conueniently.*
Deceptif: m. iue: f. *Deceptiue, deceitfull, deceiuing; wilie, craftie, full of subtiltie.*
Deception: f. *Deception, deceit, fallacie, craft, subtiltie, cousenage.*
Decerclé: m. ée: f. *Vncircled; squared as a circle; taken*

taken out of a circle.
Decercler. *To vncircle; square a circle; take out of a circle.*
Decerné: m. ée: f. *Decreed, sentenced, adiudged, ordered; determined, concluded; appointed by iudgement.*
Decerner. *To decree, determine, sentence, order, iudge; conclude, appoint, in Court.*
Deceu: m. euë: f. *Deceiued, beguiled, gulled, cousened, circumuented, ouer-raught; disappointed; betrayed.*
Il est tost deceu qui mal ne pense: Prov. *He that thinkes no hurt is soone deceiued; the harmelesse man is quickly ouer-raught.*
Decevable: com. *Deceiueable; deceitfull, apt to beguile, cousen, gull.*
Decevance: f. *as* Deception.
Decevant. *Deceiuing, beguiling, gulling, cousening.*
Deceveur: m. *A deceiuer, beguiler, guller, cousener, imposter, cheater, connycatcher.*
Decevoir. *To deceiue, beguile, gull, cousen, circumuent, ouer-reach; mocke; disappoint; betray.*
Decez: m. *A decease, or deceasing; death, or a departure out of this life.*
Dechalandé: m. ée: f. *Out of trade, without customers.*
Dechassé: m. ée: f. *Expelled, eiected, driuen, or chased away.*
Dechassement: m. *A driuing, expelling, or chasing away; an expulsion, eiection, abdication.*
Dechasser. *To chase, or driue away, from, or out of; to abdicate, expell, eiect, thrust out.*
Decheant: m. ante: f. *Falling away from; also, decaying, wasting, lessening, diminishing.*
Decheoir. *To fall away from; also, to minish, lessen; decay, wast, fall to want.*
Decheoir de claim; *To relinquish, or giue ouer, his clayme; or, to be nonsuited.*
Decheoir du droict de. *To loose, or forfeit his right in.*
Dechet: m. *A fall from former worth, or goodnesse; a decay, wast, lessening, minishing, in gold, siluer, wine, oyle, &c.*
Decheu: m. euë: f. *Fallen away (from;) minished, lessened; wasted, decayed; (Looke* Decheoir.*)*
Dechiffrer. *To decypher.*
Dechiqueté. *Looke* Deschiqueté.
Gelée dechiquetée. *Cut Dyamond-wise.*
Dechiqueter. *as* Deschiqueter.
Dechiré: m. ée: f. *Torne, rent, mangled, dismembred.*
Dechirer. *To rend, teare, mangle, dismember.*
Decidé: m. ée: f. *Decided, determined, compounded, ended; also, cut off, cut shorter.*
Decider. *To decide, determine, compound, bring a matter to end; also, to cut off, or cut shorter.*
Decidu: m. uë: f. *Falling, or fallen off; hanging, or falling downe.*
Decimable: com. *Tytheable.*
Decimal: m. ale: f. *Tything, or belonging to tythe; whence;*
Fruicts decimaux. *Tythe-fruits.*
Decime: f. *The tythe, or tenth of.*
Decimé: m. ée: f. *Tythed; payed as, or, put vnto, tythe.*
Armée decimée. *Whereof euerie tenth souldior is culled out, and put to death for an offence commited by them all.*
Decimer. *as* Disme*r. To pay, or take tythe.*
Decimestre. *Of tenne moneths.*
Decicif: m. iue: f. *Decisiue, deciding, determining; fit, or able, to end a controuersie.*
Decision: f. *A decision, determination, end of a controuersie.*
Decisoire: com. *Decisorie, deciding; fit, vsed, or able, to decide controuersies.*
Declamateur: m. *A declamor; also, an outcryer.*
Declamation: f. *A declamation; an Oration made of a fained subiect, or onely for exercise; also, a crying out aloud.*
Declamatoire: com. *Declamatorie, declayming.*
Declamer. *To declaime; to make Orations of fained subiects, or onely for exercise; also, to cry out aloud.*
Declarant. *Declaring, telling, relating, publishing, manifesting; signifying; expressing, explaning, expounding; denouncing.*
Declaration. *A declaration; a relation; an interpretation, explication, exposition; a shewing, signifying, denouncing; a suruey of land, or Inuentorie of goods, couched in writing.*
Declaré. *Declared, told, related; published, denounced, manifested; signified; expressed, explaned, expounded.*
Declarer. *To declare, tell, relate; signifie, testifie; denounce, publish, pronounce; open, cleere, manifest, expresse, expound, explane.*
Declaveté: m. ée: f. *Vnpegged, vnboulted, vnpinned.*
Declaveter. *To vnboult, vnpinne, vnpeg; loose from.*
Declin: m. *A fall, declining, descent, or bending downewards; also, an eschewing, waiuing, swaruing, winding, or bending from; also, a wayning, decaying, decreasing; or, as in* Declinement.
Declinatoire: f. *An exception taken against a Iudge, or to the Iurisdiction of a Court of Iustice; the disabling, or a refusall, of either of them, in a tryall.*
Declinatoire: com. *Disabling, excepting against, or refusing to be tryed by, a Judge, or Court of Iustice.*
Fin declinatoire. *Looke* Fin.
Declinant. *Declining, downe-falling; also, eschewing, wayuing, auoiding, bending from.*
Decliné. *Declined, bent, or fallen downewards; also, declined, eschewed, wayued, auoided, swarued, wound, or turned away from.*
Declinement. *as* Declin; le declinement du jour. *The later part of the day.*
Decliner. *To decline, bend, or fall downewards; also, to eschew, decline, bend from, wayue, auoid, swarue, turne away, passe by.*
Decliner la Iurisdiction. *To except against, or refuse to be tryed by, a Court, as of insufficient Iurisdiction.*
Decliquer. *To iert, clacke, or clatter out; rashly to blab, or bable; to let fly, let goe, rap out.*
Declive: com. *Steepe, deepe, hanging, or bending downward.*
Declos. *Disparked, wide open; See* Desclos.
Decoction: f. *A boyling, or seething; also, a decoction; or the liquor wherin things haue been sodden.*
Decognoistre. *as* Descognoistre; *To vnknow, or, not to know.*
Decoler. *as* Descoler; *To vnglue.*
Decollation. *A beheading.*

De-

Decollation Sainct Iean. *An holyday kept the 29 of August.*
Decombres: f. *Looke* Descombres.
Decompter. *See* Descompter.
Deconte. *A preposterous numbring, or reckoning backwards; Looke* Descompt.
Decoration: f. *A decoration, beautifying, bedecking, adorning, garnishing, trimming, gracing.*
Decoré: m. ée: f. *Decked, adorned, graced, trimmed, beautified.*
Decore: com. *Handsome, comelie, gracefull, seemelie, beautifull, with a good* Decorum.
Decorement. *as* Decoration.
Decorer. *To decorate, garnish, adorne, trimme, grace, beautifie, make gorgeous, set forth unto the eye.*
Decoucher. *See* Descoucher.
Decoulé: m. ée: f. *Flowed, runne, glid, or fallen (gently) downeward; slipped away; also, faded, wasted, consumed, come vnto nothing.*
Decoulement: m. *A flowing, running, or falling downward; a fading, consuming, melting away.*
Decouler. *To flow, runne, or fall (gently) downward; to glide, or slip away; to fade, consume, come vnto nothing.*
Decoulouré: m. ée: f. *Discoloured; pale, bleake, wan, lew.*
Decoulourement. *A stayning, discolouring, or loosing of colour.*
Decoulourer. *To staine, discolour, take away the colour of.*
Decoupé: m. ée: f. *Cut downe, cut off; pared, or cut away; slit, sliced.*
Decouper. *To cut downe, or cut off; to pare, or cut away; to slice; to slit.*
Decoupure: f. *A cutting, paring; slicing; slitting.*
Par decoupures. *Peecemeale, in slices, by slits.*
Decourir. *To runne downe; to hast, or hy apace; also, to purge downewards.*
Decouronné: m. ée: f. *Uncrowned; bereaued of a Crowne.*
Decouronner. *To vncrowne; or depriue of a Crowne.*
Decours: m. *A course, a streame, a running; a passing ouer; the time a man hath past through; the end of his course.*
Decours de la Lune. *The wayne, decrease, or later age of the Moone.*
Decouru: m. uë: f. *Runne downe; hasted, hyed; also, purged downewards.*
Decoustemens: m. *Costs, and charges.*
Decramponné: m. ée: f. *Unhooked, vnclasped, vndone.*
Decramponner. *To vnhooke, vnclaspe, vndoe.*
Decrassé: m. ée: f. *Looke* Descrassé.
Decrasser. *To cleanse, or rid from filth; Looke* Descrasser.
Decrepite: com. *Decrepite, verie old; whose candle is almost burnt out; that hath one foot alreadie in the graue.*
Decrepiteux: m. euse: f. *Full of agednesse, and aches.*
Decrepitude: f. *Extreame agednesse.*
Decret: m. *A Statute, Ordnance, or Decree; also, a Sentence, or Order passed in Court for the sale of a debtors goods, alreadie seised into the hands of Iustice.*
Decretales. *The Decretals; Bookes containing the Decrees of sundrie Popes.*
Decretaliarche: m. *An absolute Commaunder; one that commaunds by decrees; or, whose commaund is, and is obeyed as, a Decree.*
Decretant: m. *The creditor, at whose suit a debtors goods are decreed to be sold.*
Decretant. *Ordering, ordaining, decreeing.*
Decretation: f. *An Order passed in Court for the sale of a debtors goods; or, a proceeding thereby.*
Decreté: m. *The debtor whose goods, after a publicke seisure, are ordered to be sold.*
Decreté: m. ée: f. *Decreed, enacted, ordered, ordained, awarded, appointed.*
Decreter. *To order, ordaine, decree, enact, establish, award, appoint; also, to giue a iudgement, passe an order, in Court for the sale of a debtors goods.*
Decroire. *To vnbeleeue; or, not to beleeue; to distrust, or, thinke otherwise of then he hath done.*
Decroissant. *Decreasing, wayning, lessening.*
Decroistre. *To lessen, decrease, wayne; weare away.*
Decroter; Decrotoire. *See* Descroter, &c.
Decrustation: f. *A decrustation, or vncrusting; a paring away of the vppermost part, or outmost rind.*
Decrusté: m. ée: f. *Vncrusted; bared of crust, or whose crust is pared away.*
Decruster. *To vncrust; to pare off the vppermost part, barke, or crust of.*
Decuisant. *Boyling, or seething very much.*
Decuit: m. itte: f. *Vnsodden; made raw againe; also, boyled, or sodden, very much.*
Deculpé: m. ée: f. *Excused, purged, iustified, deliuered from imputation, discharged of blame.*
Deculper. *To excuse; purge; deliuer from imputation, or discharge of blame.*
Decumane. *Large, mightie, huge, as big as tenne.* Rab.
Porte Decumane. *The chiefest gate of the Romane campe.*
Decuple: com. *Tenne times as much.*
Decurie: f. *A band of tenne, Senatours, or Souldiors; (a diuision of much vse among the auncient Romanes.)*
Dedalé. *Intricate, perplexed; Dedalian, Mazelike.*
Dedaler. *To make a Maze, or Laberinth.*
Dedans. *Within, inwardly, in.*
Dedans ou dehors. *Fast, or loose (a Iuglers phrase.)*
Estre dedans. *To be drunken, to be in drinke.*
Dedans-terré. *Vpland, or inland.*
Dedens. *as* Dedans.
Dedicace: f. *A dedication, a consecration; a giuing for euer.*
Dedicasse, & Dedication. *as* Dedicace.
Dedié: m. ée: f. *Dedicated, deuoted, consecrated.*
Dedier. *To dedicate, deuote, or giue for euer.*
Dedoré: m. ée: f. *Vngilt.*
Dedorer. *To vngild.*
Deduction: f. *A deduction; diminution, abatement, withdrawing, deducting; also, a guiding.*
Deduire. *To deduct, abate, plucke backe; diminish part of a summe; to draw out, or withdraw; also, to handle, intreat, or discourse of.*
Se deduire. *To sport, or solace himselfe; to take pleasure, and delight in.*
Deduisant. *Deducting, abating; intreating, discoursing of.*
Deduit: m. *Delectation, sport, pastime, solace, pleasure, delight.*
Deduite: f. *A Deduction, Diminution, Abatement.*

Deesse:

Deesse: f. *A Goddesse.*

Defaillance: f. *A fayling, languor, faintnesse; defect, want, lacke, defection; also, a fainting.*

Defaillance de coeur. *A swonding; when all strength failes one by reason that the orifice of his stomacke is ill affected.*

Defaillancé. *Fainted, languished, out of heart, growne feeble, decayed, worne, or withered away.*

Defaillant. *Fayling, defectiue; fainting, pining, decaying; wanting, lacking, making a default.*

Defaille: f. *A default, defect, or fayling; a pining, languishing, or wearing away.*

Defaillement: m. *as* Defaille.

Defaillir. *To decay, languish, pine, faint, wax feeble, weare, or wither away; also, to want, lacke, faile; to be away, or wanting; to make a default.*

Defaitte: f. *A defeat, or ouerthrow; also, proportion, shape, shew, making (but outward;) also, any sleight vsed by a Hare for the auoiding of the dogs that pursue her.*

Il est de belle defaitte; *He is faire to look on, or faire in shew, but otherwise of little worth; also (simply) he is of a goodlie presence.*

Defalqué: m. *Defaulked, deduced, deducted, bated, abated, taken out of.*

Defalquer. *To defaulke, deduce, diminish, cut off, or take away part of; See* Deffalquer.

Defané: m. ée: f. *Vnwithered; recouered, restored to it former life, or freshnesse.*

Defardé: m. ée: f. *Vnpainted; whose painting is worne, wyped, or washed away.*

Defarder. *To vnpaint; to wash, take, or wype off, painting.*

Defaroucher. *as* Desfaroucher. *To make tame.*

Defaucillé: m. ée: f. *Put out of ioint.*

Defauciller. *To put out of ioint.*

Defaveur: f. *Disfauor; losse, or lacke of fauor.*

Default, ou defaut: m. *A default, fault, offence, defect; want of apparance before a Iudge; the default which dogs are sometimes at in hunting; any want, lack, penurie, scantnesse, or scarcenesse; a defection.*

Default d'homme. *Want, or omission, of due homage, and fealtie.*

Default simple, ou pur. *Looke* Simple.

Default. *(The third person of the present tense of* Defaillir.) Rien ne me default. *I want nothing.*

Defaux. *The ground, or pasture wherein a beast should not be; or, wherein it is a trespasser; or, as* Default.

Defectueux: m. euse: f. *Defectiue; wanting, lacking, fayling, maimed, full of defects.*

Defectuosité: f. *Lacke, want, defect, maymednesse.*

Defedation: f. *A fowling, soyling, filing, defiling, staying, spotting of.*

Defence. *as* Defense.

Defences. *Defences, flankes, casemats, and such like parts of fortification, prouided for the safegard of those that make good a Place beleaguered; also, the tuskes of a wild Bore.*

Defendant. *Defending, sauing, shielding, preseruing.*

Defendeur: m. *A defendor, or protector; also, a defendant; a partie challenged, accused, or sued.*

Defendo. *A play with bits of bread (ranked one by another) which the player counts with certaine words, and the last his words end on, he takes, whether it be little, or great.* ¶Rab.

Defendre. *To defend, saue, guard, ward, shield; preserue, maintaine; protect, patrocinate, sustaine; also, to forbid the doing of a thing.*

Harnois ne vaut rien qui ne defend: Prov. *The Armour is worth nothing that defends not.*

Defensable. *Defendable, defensible, which may be definded, guarded, or preserued.*

Defense: f. *A defence, a defending; a preseruation, safegard, protection; a fence, or fortification; also, an iniunction, prohibition, forbidding; also, a reply, answer, argument, or allegation vsed, or vrged in defence.*

Defenses. *as* Defences.

Se couper soy mesme par ses defenses. *To accuse, by meaning to excuse, himselfe.*

Defenseur. *as* Defendeur. *A defender, or defendant.*

Defensible. *as* Defensable.

Defensif: m. *A defensatiue; a medicine that keepes humors from comming vnto a sore, or place affected; or binders the inflamation thereof.*

Defensif: m. iue: f. *Defensiue, defending.*

Defensoire: com. *Defensorie, which defendeth, guardeth, or preserueth.*

Defequé: m. ée: f. *Cleansed, fined, purged, purified.*

Defequer. *To fine, purge, cleanse, purifie.*

Deferé: m. ée: f. *Charged, appeached, accused; also, admitted, allowed, accepted of; yeelded vnto.*

Deferer. *To charge, accuse, appeach.*

Deferer à vn appel. *To admit, allow, or accept of; to giue way vnto, an Appeale.*

Deferer à vne compaigne. *To yeeld, referre, or attribute much vnto, a companie.*

Defermer. *as* Desfermer. *To open; vnshut; loosse, vndoe.*

Deferrer. *See* Desferrer.

Deferrure: f. *An vnshooing, or casting of a shooe.*

Defeublé: m. ée: f. *Vnclasped; vnmuffled; open, discouered, vncouered, vnclothed.*

Defeubler. *To vnclaspe, vnbutton; vnmuffle; open, discouer, vncouer; put by, or cast off, the clothes that hide, or pester.*

Deffaicte. *as* Desfaicte.

Deffaire, & Deffait; *as* Desfaire, & Desfaict.

Deffalqué: m. ée: f. *Defaulked, deducted, bated, abated.*

Deffalquer. *To defaulke, deduct, bate, abate.*

Deffascher. *Looke* Desfascher.

Deffaveur: f. *Disfauor; want, or losse, of (accustomed) fauor.*

Deffault. *as* Default.

Deffavorisé: m. ée: f. *Disfauoured, out of fauour.*

Deffavoriser. *To disfauour, not to fauour, to withdraw his fauour from.*

Deffectueux de ses membres. *Maimed, lame, impotent, wanting his limmes, or the vse of them.*

Deffené. *Hay-fed; or, as* Affené; *inseamed with Hay.*

Mon estomac est bien à poinct deffené, & aggrené. *My stomacke is throughly furnished, hath drinke, and meat enough in it; (for seeing that* fené *signifies withered, or dryed, as Hay,* deffené *a Priuatiue may perhaps, for a need, be taken for wet, moistened, or fresh.)*

Deffensatrice: f. *A defendresse.*

Defferné: m. ée: f. *Opened; vnshut; vndone.*

Deffermer. *To open; to vnshut, or vndoe a thing shut.*

Defferré: m. ée: f. *Vnshooed, as a horse; also, the yron whereof is taken, or plucked off.*

Defferrer. *To vnshooe a horse, &c; and (more generally) to take, or plucke off, the yron from any thing.*

Se Defferrer l'un l' autre. *To ruine one another; See* Desferrer.
Deffiamment. *Mistrustfully, diffidently, distrustfully.*
Deffiance: f. *Distrust, diffidence, mistrust.*
Deffier. *To mistrust; (Looke* Desfier;) *also, to defeat; also, as* Defier.
Deffilé: m. ée: f. *Vntwisted, rauelled; also, disordered; Seeke* Desfilé.
Deffiler. *To vntwist, vnspinne, loosse, rauell; also, to put out of his ranke, or file; also, to take off a file.*
Deffileure: f. *An vntwisting, rauelling; disordering; displacing.*
Deffleurer. *To rase, scotch, or scratch; Looke* Desfleurer, *or* Defleurer.
Defformité. *as* Difformité.
Deffortune: m. *Misfortune, mischance.*
Deffortuné: m. ée: f. *Vnfortunate.*
Deffouir. *To dig vp, to vnearth, to take out of the earth.*
Deffrayer. *as* Defrayer.
Deffriché. *as* Defriché; *Grubd vp, &c.*
Deffroncer. *To vnfrounce, vnwrinckle, vncrumple.*
Deffrongner. *The same; and (as the same) to smooth the forehead, or leaue frowning.*
Deffroqué: m. ée: f. *Stripped, vnclothed.*
Deffuler. *as* Defeubler, *or* Desfuler.
Defi: m. *A challenge, defy, prouocation, defiance.*
Defiance: f. *A defying, or defiance.*
Defiché: m. ée: f. *Vnfixed, loossed, vnfastened.*
Deficher. *To loosse, vnfix, vnfasten.*
Defié. *Defyed, prouoked, or challenged to fight, or contend.*
Defiement: m. *A defying, or challenging to fight.*
Defier. *To defie, challenge, prouoke, or call vnto fight, or contention.*
Defiguré: m. ée: f. *Disfigured, deformed, misshapen, defaced; whose fashion is marred.*
Defigurement: m. *A disfiguring, disgracing, misshaping, defacing; a marring of the fashion of.*
Defigurer. *To disfigure, deforme, deface, disgrace; to spoyle the fashion, marre the figure of.*
Defilé: m. ée: f. *Rauelled.*
Se Defiler. *To rauell, as cloth, stuffe, silke, or linnen doth after it is cut.*
Defilocher. *as* Defiler. *To rauell.*
Defiloter. *The same.*
Definant. *Pining, wasting, consuming, wearing away; also, blasting, taking, suddainely benumming.*
Definé: m. ée: f. *Wasted, consumed, worne, fallen away; at an end, come to nothing; also, blasted, or taken.*
Definement: m. *A pining, wasting, consuming, wearing, or falling away.* (Le Definement du monde. *The later end of the world;) also, a blasting, taking, suddaine benumming, or putrefaction of a member.*
Definer. *To pine, consume, waste, weare away; also, to blast, or suddainely benumme (a member, &c.)*
Definir. *To define; conclude, determine, or discusse; precisely to expresse; fully to describe, exactly to declare.*
Definitif: m. iue: f. *Definitiue; which limitteth, expresseth, describeth, or determineth, fully; which makes a full end of.*
Definition: f. *A definition; exact description; precise limitation; short, and full declaration; a defining; apt, and iust expressing; true, and liuelie describing.*
Definitivement. *Definitiuely, determinately, expressely, precisely, fully.*
Deflamé: m. ée: f. *Whose flame is extinguished, or put out.*
Deflamer. *To quench, extinguish; put out, or take away, the flame of.*
Defleuré: m. ée: f. *Deflowred; distained; defiled, violated; whose floures be cropped, or shed.*
Defleurer. *To defloure; to defile; to crop the flower of; to distaine, violate, blemish; diminish the chiefest grace, and beautie of a thing.*
Se defleurer. *as* Defleurir.
Defleurir. *To shed, or let fall it flowers; hence, to loose the beautie, or grace, which erst it had; or, it former beautie to fade, faile, or fall away.*
Se Deflicher. *To plucke an arrow, or arrowes out of his (owne) bodie.*
Defloration. *A deflowring; the change from a flourishing colour to the contrarie.*
Se Deflorer. *as* Defleurir.
Defluer. *To flow, or to runne, as water, or a sore.*
Defluxion: f. *A Defluxion, Rhewme, Catarrhe.*
Defoncé. *as* Desfoncé. *Knockt out, as the head of a wine-vessell, &c.*
Deforcé: m. ée: f. *Dispossessed, disseised.*
Deforcer. *To disseise, dispossesse, violently take, forcibly plucke from.*
Deformation. *A deforming, disfiguring, defacing; disgracing.*
Deformé: m. ée: f. *Deformed, defaced, disfigured, made ouglie; disgraced.*
Deformer. *To deforme, disfigure, deface, make ouglie; disgrace.*
Defortifié: m. ée: f. *Vnfortified; rased.*
Defortifier. *To vnfortifie; to rase a fortification.*
Defoulé: m. ée: f. *Troden, trampled on; also, taunted, rebuked, reproched.*
Defoulement. *A treading, or trampling on; also, a taunting, rebuking, reproching.*
Defouler. *To tread, or trample on; also, to rebuke, reproch, taunt, or take vp.*
Defraudateur. *A defrauder, deceiuer, beguiler; lurcher.*
Defraudé: m. ée: f. *Defrauded, beguiled.*
Defraudement: m. *A defrauding, deceiuing, beguiling.*
Defrauder. *To defraud, beguile, cousen, deceiue, imbeasill, or take away the profit belonging to another.*
Defrayé: m. ée: f. *Defrayed; discharged; acquited.*
Defrayer. *To defray; to discharge; to furnish, or beare, all the charges of.*
Defrayeur: m. *A Cater, or Steward; one that in a iourney furnishes, and defrayes the prouision, and expence of the whole companie.*
Defreloqué: m. ée: f. *Torne, ragged, tattered; that hath not a whole clout on him.*
Defreloquer. *To teare into rags, make tatters of.*
Defrichage: m. *The shrubbing, or grubbing vp of yong wood, or bushes; any such preparation, or worke, fitting land for tillage.*
Defriché. *Grubd, rid of bushes, roots, &c, hindering the Plough; prepared, or first broken vp for tillage; made arable.*
Defrichement: m. *A grubbing, shrubbing, ridding the ground from bushes, and thereby to make it arable; a preparation, or breaking vp for tillage.*

Defricher. *To grub, shrub, rid a ground from rootes, bushes, thistles, &c; thereby to make it arable; to prepare, or breake vp land for tillage.*

Defrichis: m. *Grubbings; bushes, rootes, thistles, &c, pluckt out of the ground.*

Se Defriper. *To rub, or scrub with the shoulders, after the fashion of lowsie hedge-creepers.*

Defroissé: m. ée: f. *Crushed in peeces.*

Defroisser. *To crush in peeces.*

Defroque: f. *Spoyle, bootie, pillage, got by stripping of poore men.*

Defroqué: m. ée: f. *Stripped, vnclothed, despoyled, or depriued of garments.*

Defroquer. *To strip, vncloth, dispoyle, depriue of his habillements.*

Defroy: m. *A defraying; a bearing of other mens charges.*

Defueillé: m. ée: f. *Vnleaued; bared, or bereft of leaues.*

Defueiller. *To vnleaue, to plucke the leaues from, to depriue of leaues.*

Defunct. Vn defunct. *A deceased, or dead person; one that is departed this life.*

Defunctoirement. *By discent, or succession after the decease of another.*

Degaerie: f. *An vnder Bayliwicke; the Office, Authoritie, Precinct, or Circuit of a* Degan.

Degallicó. *Waxen poore, vndone, downe the weather.* Pic.

Degan: m. *A certaine inferiour Officer, or vnder Bayliffe, chosen euerie May day within the seuerall members, or Hamlets of the Iurisdiction of* La Solle; *(hee cannot arrest a Gentleman; and deales most in personall Actions.)*

Degasouiller. *To sing, or warble fast, and confusedly; as a troope of small birds met, and set downe in a tree, bush, or hedge, together.*

Degast: m. *Wast, losse, spoyle, rauage, ransacke, ruine, destruction.*

Degasté: m. ée: f. *Wasted, spoyled, ransacked, rauaged, ruined.*

Degastement: m. *A wasting, spoyling, rauaging, ransacking, destroying, deuastation.*

Degastement de maisons. *The rasing, or ruining of houses.*

Degaster. *To wast, spoyle, ransacke, rauage, deuast, destroy, ruine.*

Degasteur: m. *A waster, spoyler, ransacker, rauager, destroyer.*

Degel: m. *A thawe, or thawing weather.*

Degeler. *To thawe the ice; to resolue.*

Degeneré: m. ée: f. *Degenerated.*

Degenerer. *To degenerate, grow out of kind, be vnlike his auncestors.*

Deglouti: m. ie: f. *Deuoured, swallowed downe.*

Degloutir. *as* Engloutir. *To deuoure, or swallow vp.*

Deglution: f. *A deuouring, or swallowing downe; also, the passage, or descending of meat and drinke from the mouth into the stomacke.*

Degodalie. *Skittish, iadish.* ¶Rab.

Degoisé: m. ée: f. *Warbled, chirped.*

Degoisement: m. *The chirping, or warbling of birds.*

Se Degoiser. *To chirpe, or warble (as a singing bird.)*

Degondé: m. ée: f. *Lift off the hindges.*

Degonder. *To lift, or heaue off the hindges.*

Ils commencent à se degonder. *They begin to lash, or fly out; to reuell it, or play reakes; they begin verie much to disorder themselues.*

Degourt. *Blithe, iocond, lustie, frolicke.* ¶Rab.

Degoust. *as* Degout.

Degout: m. *A drop, or dropping.*

Le degout du rost. *The grauie, or fat that drops from meat as it rosts.*

Degouttant. *Dropping, distilling.*

Degoutté: m. ée: f. *Dropped, distilled.*

Degouttement. *A distilling, or dropping.*

Degoutter. *To drop; distill; fall downe by little and little.*

Degracié: m. ée: f. *Vnacceptable, (and therefore) vnsuccessiue; whence;*

Saison degraciée. *An ill, or vnluckie, season.*

Degradant. *Degrading; depriuing of office, degree, &c; also, spoyling, wasting, making hauocke of.*

Degradation: f. *A degradation; a degrading, or depriuing of office, estate, benefice, dignitie, or degree.*

Degradé: m. ée: f. *Degraded, depriued of his degree; also, wasted, spoyled; defaced.*

Degradement. *as* Degradation; *also, wast, spoyle, or hurt done, and committed in other mens houses, gardens, woods, &c.*

Degrader. *To degrade, or depriue of degree, office, estate, or dignitie; also, to spoyle, or wast; or make wast, and hauocke of.*

Degrader vne forest. *To hagge, or fell it all downe.*

Degraffer. *as* Desgrafer.

Degravé. *Vngrauelled, set afloat; also, taken out of, or, plucked from, the ground.*

Degraver. *To vngrauell, or set afloat a ship that stucke fast in the sand; also, to take out of the ground; also, to plucke vp by the roots.*

Degré: m. *A staire, step, greese; also, a degree, ranke, or place of honour; also, an occasion, meane, or way vnto a thing.*

Degrez tetradiques. *Looke* Tetradique.

De degré en degré. *By degrees, by leisure, by little and little; faire and softly; also, in order, one after another.*

Degresseur: m. *A skowrer of greasie things.*

Degrossi: m. ie: f. *Refined, ciuilized.*

Degrossir. *To refine; to ciuilize.*

Degroumelé: m. ée: f. *Resolued, vnclotted, vnclutered.*

Degroumeler. *To resolue, or vnclot a thing thats cluttered, congealed, or curded together.*

Deguener. *as* Desgainer. *To vnsheath, or draw out of the sheath.* ¶Rab.

Deguerpi: m. ie: f. *Quit, left, abandoned, forsaken, forgone, throwne away, yeelded vp, giuen ouer.*

Deguerpir. *To quit, leaue, abandon, forgoe, forsake, yeeld vp, giue ouer; to throw away, as wee doe things which we care not for, or will not keepe, in our houses.*

Deguerpissement: m. *A quitting, leauing, abandoning, forgoing, forsaking, giuing ouer, yeelding vp of a thing; a throwing out, or away.*

Deguerpisseur. *A quitter, leauer, forgoer, abandoner.*

Deguerpy: m. ie: f. *Seeke* Desguerpy.

Deguestré: m. ée: f. *whence;* Femme deguestrée. *A slut, or slattern; one thats vnhandsome in her clothes, or weares them most vnhandsomely.*

Degun. *Any one;* Gasc. ¶Rab.

Dehaché: m. ée: f. *Hacked, hewed, cut into small peeces; made into a hachey.*

Dehacher. *To hacke, or cut in small peeces; to make a hachey of.*

Dehait: m. itte: f. *Merrie, pleasant, iocond, blithe, lustie, frolicke.*
Dehaité. *as* Deshaité. *Ill at ease.*
Dehalé: m. ée: f. *Leane, meagar, skraggie, disfigured, ouglie, or illfauoured, by extreame leanenesse.*
Dehayté: m. ée: f. *Distasted, or loathed as meat; also, out of tune, ill at ease.*
Dehayter. *To distast, or loath meat; to be out of tune, ill at ease.*
Dehinch. *Away hence;* Allem. ¶Rab.
Dehonté: m. ée: f. *Shamelesse, impudent, brasen-faced.*
Dehors. *Without, abroad, out of, on the outside of.*
De dehors. *From abroad, from forraine places.*
Dedans, ou dehors. *Fast, or loose (a Iuglers tearme.)*
Par dehors. *Outward, without, on the outside.*
Dehotté: m. ée: f. *Drawne out of the mire.*
Dehotter. *To draw (as a fast-sticking coach &c) out of the mire.*
Dehousé: m. ée: f. *Dispatched, rid out of the way; also, vnbooted, or whose boots are pulled off.*
Dehoussé: m. ée: f. *Vnfootclothed; vncouered; also, vnrugged, or made low napped, as new cloth, with the Teazell.*
Deiect: m. iecte: f. *as* Deiecté.
Deiecté: m. ée: f. *Deiected, abased, brought low, cast downe; also, repelled, reiected, thrust from with contumelie or contempt.*
Deiectement: m. *A deiecting, abiecting, bringing low; also, a contemptible reiection, contumelious repulse.*
Deiecter. *To deiect, abiect, abase, abate, bring low, throw downe; also, to repell, reiect, shake off, thrust fro, put from with contumelie, or contempt.*
Se Dejecter. *To stand on tearmes; or, proudly to bestirre himselfe.* ¶Nicot.
Deïfication: f. *A deifying.*
Deïfié: m. ée: f. *Deified, made a god.*
Deïfier. *To deifie, to make a god of.*
Deillavier. *To starue, to bereaue of life.*
Dejoindre. *as* Desjoindre.
Deité: f. *The deitie, or godhead.*
Delà. *Beyond, ouer, on the further or other, side of.*
Par deça, & par delà. *On this side and that, on both sides, euerie way.*
Vingt escus, & par delà. *Twentie crownes and better; and more; and aboue.*
Delabré: m. ée: f. *Vnbraced, vnloosed, vntrussed; also, ragged, torne, tattered.*
Delacher. *as* Deslacher. *To loosse, discharge, let goe, let fly.*
Delai. *as* Delay.
Delaissé: m. ée: f. *Forsaken, abandoned, left or cast off; relinquished, or giuen ouer; also, forgotten, ouerslipped, neglected, or left out, when good was t'haue bene done; also, destitute, forlorne, or left alone; also, deuoid of, or left without.*
Toutes autres choses delaissées. *All other things layed apart, or set aside.*
Delaissement: m. *A forsaking, abandoning, leauing, or casting of; relinquishing, or giuing ouer; also, a forgetting, ouerslipping, neglecting, or leauing out; also, a depriuing of, or leauing without; also, a destituting, or leauing alone; or (passiuely, as in the two next phrases) a being destitute, or left alone.*
Delaissement d'amis. *The wretched, or succourlesse estate of one that hath not a friend left to helpe him.*
Delaissement d'enfans. *The forlorn, or pitifull estate of Orphans, left to looke vnto, or shift for, themselues.*
Delaissement de raison. *A defection, declining; reuolting, or swaruing, from reason.*
Delaisser. *To forsake, abandon, leaue, or cast of; relinquish, or giue ouer; to destitute, leaue alone, or without; also, to ouerslip, ouerpasse, neglect, or leaue out (when good may be done;) also, to swarue, reuolt, or decline, from.*
Delateur: m. *A Promooter, Informer, Complainer, Pickthanke, Tell-tale, or Tale-bearer; (properly such a one, as either in loue vnto Iustice and the State, or in hope of reward or gaine, prosecutes offendors, or publishes Concealements, at his owne charge.)*
Delation: f. *An Information; or bill of Complaint exhibited, and followed by an Informer; also, a priuate accusation, or tale framed against.*
Delavé: m. ée: f. *Washed away.*
Delay: m. *A delay; stay, lingering, protraction, tergiuersation, deferring, or driuing off; a pause, a space, an intermission; also (in Law) a day giuen, for apparance; or for the bringing in, or amending of, a Plea, &c; and hence;*
Delay peremptoire. *A peremptorie day; the last of delayes.*
Injure de delay. *A wrong so hainous, that a suddaine reuenge will not serue, but opportunitie must be waited for the quitting of it in a more cruell manner.*
Paroles de delay. *(Of the same sence; or) Reproches, or Slanders in the highest degree; as the tearme of Traytor, Murtherer, Church-robber; which to prooue, were enough to ruine, or for euer to disgrace, a man.*
Delayant. *Delaying, deferring; also, allaying, or macerating.*
Delayé: m. ée: f. *Delayed, deferred, suspended, prolonged, protracted; driuen, shifted, or put off; also, allayed, or softened, by steeping; also, made thin.*
Delayement: m. *A delaying, deferring, protracting, pawsing, suspending; also, a macerating, or allaying.*
Delayer. *To delay, deferre, procrastinate, protract, suspend, prolong; driue, put, or shift off from day to day; to pawse, linger, wiredraw it, or draw out in length; also, to macerate, allay, or soften, by steeping, &c; also, to make thin.*
Delayeur: m. *A delayer, deferrer, protractor, prolonger, lingerer, wiredrawer.*
Delectable: com. *Delectable, delightfull; pleasant, pleasing.*
Delectation: f. *Delectation, delight, pleasure, oblectatiõ.*
Delecter. *To delight, please, ioy; make sport, yeeld pleasure, giue contentment, vnto.*
Delegation: f. *A delegation; a chusing for, or appointment vnto, a charge, &c.*
Delegué: m. ée: f. *Delegated, appointed, assigned, or chosen, vnto a charge, &c.*
Deleguer. *To assigne, commit, or appoint vnto an office, charge, or commission; to chuse, or delegate vnto a businesse, or for a message.*
Les Deleguez. *The Delegates; Iudges appointed, or chosen to decide, and determine of certaine matters.*
Deleuce. *in stead of* d'ellend. *Of the colour of an Elk.* ¶Rab.
Delez. *Hard by.* (vieil mot.)
Deliberatif: m. iue: f. *Deliberatiue; determinatiue.*
Deliberation. *A deliberation, consultation, thinking, aduising; also, a determination vpon former aduisement.*
Deliberé: m. ée: f. *Deliberated, consulted, aduised of; also, determined, concluded, resolued on; also, resolute, couragious, readie, cheerfull, in the middest of dangers; hartie; merrie, iocond, of a pleasant humor.*

Deliberer. *To deliberate; aduise, consult, thinke what were best to be done; also, to purpose, resolue, determine.*

Delicat: m. ate: f. *Delicate; daintie; pleasing, prettie, delicious; tender, nice; effeminate, of a weake complexion.*

Vn ouvrage delicat. *An excellent, or prime, peece of worke.*

Delicatement. *Delicately, daintily; deliciously; pleasantly, sweetly; prettily, tenderly; nicely, wantonly, weakely, effeminately.*

Delicatesse: f. *Delicacie, daintinesse; tendernesse, nicenesse, wantonnesse, effeminacie; sensualitie.*

Delicateté: f. *The same.*

Delices: f. *Delights, dainties, pleasures, pleasant fantasies; sports, pastimes; prettie toyes.*

Delicieusement. *Deliciously, delightsomely, delicately, pleasantly.*

Delicieux: m. euse: f. *Delicious, delightsome, delicate, pleasant.*

Delict: m. *A fault, offence; misdeed, omission of dutie; a trespas; also, a rift, or cleft in a stone.*

Debvoir des delicts. *A bushell of Rye, payed vnto the Lord of the Borough of* Pont Niusillac *(in Britaine) by euery householder of auncient tenure that keepes a fire, and tillage within the Territorie thereof.*

Se Delicter. Cette pierre facilement se delicte. *This stone quickly riues, or easily cleaues asunder.*

Delié: m. ée: f. *Thin, slender, fine, small, sparing, scant.*

Deliément. *Thinly, smally, slenderly, finely, scantly.*

Delier. *To make thin, small, fine, slender; to lessen, extenuate, or minish.*

Delineation. *The delineation; first draught, or portraiture of a thing.*

Delineature. *The same; or, a delineature.*

Deliniment: m. *A smoothing, assuaging, appeasing, mitigation, qualification.*

Delinquant: m. *A delinquent, offendor, faultie, or guiltie person.*

Delinquer. *To offend, misdoe, commit a fault, faile in dutie.*

Deliot. *Sodden pot-hearbes.*

Deliré. *Doated; raued.*

Delire. *To chuse, cull, select, gather, picke out.*

Delirement: m. *A rauing, or doating.*

Delirer. *To doat, raue, do things against reason.*

Delitescence: f. *A lurking, or lying hidden.*

Delivrance: f. *A deliuerance, deliuerie, deliuering; a releasing, discharging; setting at libertie; also, as* Arrierefaix.

Delivre: f. *The seconds, or after-birth; the skin wherein a child is wrapped at it birth; (a Midwiues tearme.)*

Delivre de sa personne: com. *An actiue nimble wight; whose ioints are not tyed with points; one that can wield his limmes at pleasure.*

'A delivre. *Loosely, freely, at full scope, with good libertie.*

Delivré: m. ée: f. *Deliuered, freed, loosed, released; also, dispatched, rid from; also, deliuered, or yeelded ouer vnto.*

Delivrer: m. *To deliuer, free, loose, release; dispatch, rid from; also, to deliuer, giue, make, or yeeld ouer vnto.*

Delivreur. *A deliuerer, preseruer, loosser, a ridder from.*

Deloché: m. ée: f. *Vnioynted, or put out of ioynt.*

Delocher. *To loosen, disioynt, put out of ioynt.*

Deloisir. à deloisir. *At leisure, hauing little to doe.*

Deloüer. *as* Desloüer.

Deltoïde. Muscle d. *A certaine Muscle, which drawes the arme vpwards.*

Deluge: m. *A deluge, great floud, or inundation of waters.*

Bois de deluge. *Tymber a long time ouerwhelmed by waters; Looke* Bois.

Delugé. Eauës delugées. *Waters broken out of their bankes, or ouerflowing their bounds; surrounding waters.*

Delurer. *To picke.*

Demachoiré: m. ée: f. *Vniawed; whose iaw is rent, or cut from the cheeke.*

Demachoirer. *To vniaw; to cut, or teare a iaw from.*

Demacqué: m. ée: f. *Vnchawed; put, spit, or spued out of the mouth; also, loosed, or let goe.* ¶Pic.

Demacquer. *To vnchew; to put, or spit forth of the mouth; to tell, or spue out; also, to loosse, or let goe.* ¶Pic.

Demain. *To morrow; (Looke* Aujourd'huy.)

Quand mes amis me prient ie n' ay point de demain. *When my friends intreat me, I cannot delay thẽ, I cannot post them off to the next day.*

Chasque demain apporte son pain: Pro. *(So mercifully doth God prouide for his creatures.)*

Ia ne vienne demain qu'il n'apporte son pain: Pro. *Looke* Pain.

Tels sont huy qui demain ne verront pas: Prov. *Some are aliue to day, that will be dead to morrow.*

Demaine: m. *A Demaine, &c; as* Domaine.

Demainier: m. *An owner of a Demaine, or of lands &c. in Demaine.*

Demaisonné: m. ée: f. *Depriued, or turned out, of a house.*

Demaisonner. *To depriue, or turne out, of a house.*

Demanché: m. ée: f. *Vnhafted; bereft, or taken out of, it handle; See* Desmanché.

Demandant. *Asking, demaunding, questioning; requesting, beseeching, suing for.*

Demande: f. *A Demaund, or Question; also, a request; Suit, Action; Petition, Supplication; also, a Clayme.*

Beaucoup offrir à vn qui peu demande, c' est luy nier tout à plat sa demande: Prov. *Looke* Demander.

Demandé: m. ée: f. *Demaunded, asked, questioned; also, requested, required, sued for.*

Demander. *To demaund, aske, propound a question vnto; also, to desire, woe, craue, beg, request, require, make suit, or bring an Action, for.*

On luy demanda la chanson; *They intreated him to sing; (Spoken mockingly of one thats newly come out of prison, where hauing bene, as a bird in a cage, pent vp, he may, perhaps haue learnt to chaunt it.)*

Se demander en vn lieu. *To wish himselfe in a place.*

Assez demande qui se pleint: Pro. *He begs enough that playnes his wants.*

Assez demande qui bien sert: Pro. *Looke* Assez.

Chascun demande sa sorte: Pro. *Like will to like; a Iacke lookes for a Gill.*

Qui demande ce qu'il ne devroit, il oit ce qu'il ne vouldroit: Prov. *He that askes what he should not, heares what he would not.*

Beaucoup offrir à vn qui peu demande, c'est luy nier tout à plat sa demande: Pro. *An offer of more then is required, imports a flat denyall.*
Ceux qui nous doibvent nous demandent: Prov. *Looke* Debvoir.
Il est bien fol qui à fol sens demande: Prov. *He is a verie foole that lookes for wit from a foole.*
Il n'aura ia bon marché qui ne le demande: Pro. *Let no man thinke to haue, that asks not, things good cheape.*
Demanderesse: f. *A demaunderesse; a woman that is a Plaintife; or Petitioner.*
Demandeur. *A demaunder; asker, begger, requester; questioner; also, a demaundant, plaintife, complainant, petitioner.*
A bon demandeur bon refuseur: Prov. *Wee say, shamefull crauing must haue a shamefull nay.*
Demange-chair. *Flesh-tickling, setting an itch on the flesh.*
Demangement: m. *An itching, or itch.*
Se Demanger. *To itch.*
Demangerie. *An itch, an itching.*
Demangéson: f. *An itch, or itching.*
Demangéson de dents. *The painefull itch thats felt by children while their teeth are in breeding.*
Demangeure: f. *as* Demangéson.
Demantelé: m. ée: f. *Dismanteled.*
Demanteler vne ville. *To dismantle, or deface the wals of a towne.*
Demantellement: m. *A dismantelling.*
Demantibulé: m. ée: f. *Vniawed, or, whose iawes are dasht in peeces.* ¶Rab.
Demaquer. *as* Demacquer.
Demarche: f. *A gate, pace, going; the setting of one foot before the other; or (most properly) behind another; the trauersing of ground; also, ward, fence, or, the lying of the bodie in fencing; and generally, the setting, posture, or carriage of the bodie in any kind whatsoeuer.*
Demarche de bourse. *Looke* Bourse.
Demaré: m. ée: f. *Vnmoored, as a ship.*
Demarer. *To vnmoore; to loosen a ship thats moored, or ankored, and put out to sea.*
Demarrier. *To vnmarrie, diuorce, vnwed.*
Demence: f. *Madnesse.*
Demené: m. *A practise; or, as* Demenée.
Demené: m. ée: f. *Stirred, wagged, iogged, mooued to and fro, remooued often; tumbled, tossed, canuassed vp and downe; much handled, managed, or dealt in.*
Demené parmi tous les communs proverbes. *A common by-word; the subiect of common prouerbes; a subiect throughly, or ordinarily, played on.*
Le procés s'est ainsi demené iusques à icy. *The suit hath so bene carried, or followed, hetherto.*
Demenée: f. *A stirre, iog, wag, vnquiet motion, frequent remoue; a tumble, tosse, canuasse; or, as* Demenement; *also, a practise, plot, secret enterprise, or deuice.*
Demenement: m. *A stirring, iogging, wagging, mooving to and fro, remouing often; a tumbling, tossing, or canuassing vp and downe; a frequent handling, or serious following of.*
Demener, & se Demener. *To stirre much, mooue to and fro, remoue often; to wag or iog, tumble, or tosse, vp and downe; to sit fidging as if the itch were in his taile.*
Demener le dueil de. *To lament, or mourne for.*
Demener ioye. *To reioyce, make merrie, be glad.*
Demener marchandise. *To trade, or traffique; to turne ouer, or passe away, commodities.*
Demener vn procés. *To follow, pursue, or deale in, a suit.*
Se Dementer. *To complaine, make mone, bewayle himselfe.*
Se Dementer de. *To meddle with; to busie, or intangle, himselfe in.*
Dementi. *as* Desmenti.
Dementir. *Looke* Desmentir.
Se Dementir. *To fayle; proue nought or false; to bely, or derogate from, himselfe; to dissemble, or force, his owne nature, or humor.*
Demerite: m. *Desert, merite, deseruing; also (the contrarie) a duseruice, demerite, misdeed, ill carriage, ill deseruing; (In which sence it is most commonly vsed at this day.)*
Demesler. *See* Desmesler; *To disintangle.*
Demesler vn fuseau avec. *To haue to doe with in a matter; to performe a businesse iointly with.*
Demettre. *To dismisse, or let goe; See* Desmettre.
Demeurance: m. *A tarrying, staying, remaining, abiding, continuing, dwelling.*
Demeurant: m. *A residue, remnant, remainder, arrerage, relicke; the rest of.*
Au demeurant. *Moreouer; as touching, or for, the rest; also, in other matters.*
Tenez chaud le pied, & la teste, au demeurant vivez en beste: Pro. *The foot and head kept warme, no matter for the rest.*
Demeurant. (particip.) *Abiding, staying, tarrying, remaining, continuing, dwelling.*
Demeure: f. *An abode, stay, tarriance; delay; continuance; also, a seat, mansion, habitation, house, dwelling, lodging, place of abiding.*
Longue demeure faict changer amy: Prov. *Long absence changes loue; looses friends; alters affection.*
Demeuré: m. ée: f. *Left, remaining; behind; stayed, or continuing, behind.*
Il est demeuré entre deux selles à terre. *Betweene two stooles his tayle is come to ground.*
Demeurer. *To abide, remaine, tarrie, stay; linger, stand long on, continue, perseuere; to dwell, soiourne, inhabite, seat, settle, or plant himselfe in a place; Looke* Demourer.
Demeurer court. *To be graueld, plunged, put to silence, or to a Nonplus.*
Demeurer entre deux & as. *Looke* As.
Il ne demeure pas trop qui vient: Prov. *He tarries not too long that comes at length.*
De ce que fol pense souvent en demeure: Prov. *A foole comes often short of his intentions.*
Demi: m. Demie: f. *Halfe, demy.*
Demi-arpent: m. *The halfe Arpent; the French halfe aker; containes 50 Perches, and euery Perch 20 foot.*
Demi-boisseau: m. *A halfe Bushell.*
Demi-bosse. *as* Basse-taille.
Demi-ceinct: m. *A halfe-girdle; or, a fashion of womans girdle, whose forepart is of gold or siluer, and hinder of silke, &c.*
Demi-ceinctier. *A maker of such halfe-girdles.*
Demicinct, & Demicinctier. *as* Demiceinct, &c.
Demi-crochuë: f. *A semyquauer, in Musicke.*
Demi-dieu: m. *A demy god; one that is partly God, and partly man.*
Demi-espineux. Muscle dem. *One of the two muscles that extend the flanke.*
Demi-veuë. en dem. *That one can see but halfe thereof.*
Demi-frere: m. *A half-brother; a brother of one side only.*

Demi-

Demigraine. *as* Migraine *The Megrum.*

Demi-lict: m. *The halfe-bed; brotherhood, or sisterhood, on th' one side onely.*

Demi-membraneux: m. euse: f. *Halfe-skinnie.*

Demincé: m. ée: f. *Minced; cut small; shred.*

Demi-nerveux: m. euse: f. *Halfe-sinewie, halfe a sinew.*

Muscle demi-nerveux. *One of the foure muscles which bow the thigh.*

Demi-quart. *as* Demy-quart.

Demi-quarteron. *The halfe of a Quarteron; See* Quarteron.

Demiqueuë: f. *The name of a wine vessell much vsed in* Orleans, Anjou, *and* Maine; *it containes twentie seuen* Septiers, *and euerie* Septier *eight of their pintes.*

Demisaut: m. *A halfe-leape; also, the roape-leape, or some mens last-leape; whence;*

Faire le demisaut. *To leape short; stretch a rope; be hanged.*

Demi-seur: f. *A halfe-sister; a sister onely by father, or mother.*

Demi-sextier. *The quarter of a French pinte, & much about our halfe pinte; (a measure.)*

Demission: f. *An humbling, casting, or letting downe; also, a demise, letting, or demising; and hence;*

Demission de foy. *A reseruation of fealtie made by a vassall, in th' alienation, or letting out of his estate (in part, or in whole) vnto another.*

Demisphere: f. *An Hemisphere; or, halfe the compasse of the visible heauen.*

Demi-taille: f. *as* Demi Relief: figure de demi-taille. *A representation thats halfe carued, halfe imbossed.*

Demi-vent. vn d. *A side-wind, or halfe-wind.*

Democratie: f. *A Democratie; popular gouernment, rule, or authoritie.*

Democratique: com. *Mocking, geering, laughing (as old Democrates) at euerie thing; also, popular.*

Democratiquement. *Vulgarly, popularly, commonly; also, scoffingly.*

Demoli: m. ie: f. *Demolished; rased, ruined, subuerted, throwne, or pulled downe.*

Demolir. *To demolish, rase, ruine, subuert, ouerthrow, pull downe, a building.*

Demolition: f. *A demolishment; the ruine, subuersion, ouerthrow; rasing, ruining, beating, or pulling down, of buildings, &c.*

Demon: m. *A diuell, spirit, hobgoblin.*

Demonachation. *An abandoning, or depriuing, of Monkish profession.*

Demoniaque: com. *Possest with a spirit, or diuell.*

Demonique: com. *Diuellish, hellish.*

Demonstrance: f. *A demonstrance, or demonstration; a plaine declaration, euident shewing, apparant signification.*

Demonstrateur: m. *A demonstrator; one that euidently shewes, plainely declares, perspicuously deliuers things.*

Demonstratif: m. iue: f. *Demonstratiue; plainely shewing, euidently signifying.*

Demonstré: m. ée: f. *Demonstrated, shewed plainely, declared euidently, signified manifestly.*

Demonstrer. *To demonstrate, shew plainely, declare manifestly, deliuer perspicuously, point to (as it were) with the finger.*

Demordre. *as* Desmordre; *To forgoe, or giue ouer.*

Demoulé: m. ée: f. *Vnmoulded; whose mould is broken, forme spoiled, frame defaced.*

Demouler. *To vnmould; breake the mould, marre the forme, spoyle the frame, &c.*

Demourance. *as* Demeurance.

Demoure. *as* Demeure; *An abiding place, &c.*

Demourer. *To abide, stay, tarrie, &c; as* Demeurer.

Demourez. *Rub (at bowles.)*

Ne demourez pas. *Bee not short; (a Bowlers tearme.)*

Demoussé: m. ée: f. *Rid, or bared of mosse, from which the mosse hath beene pulled.*

Demousser. *To rid, or bare of mosse; to pull mosse from, plucke the mosse off.*

Demusser. *To vnhide, vnhoodwinke, vncouer the eyes.*

Demy. *Halfe, demie.*

Demy-arpent. *A quantitie of, or measure for, land, containing fiftie pearches, and euerie pearch twentie foot in length; Or, the halfe* Arpent *whatsoeuer.*

Demy-ceinct. *as* Demi-ceinct.

Demyon. *as* Demisextier: ¶Rab.

Demy-quart. *A kind of measure; See* Quart; *also, a peece of siluer money, worth the eighth part of a French Crowne, or* ix. d. sterl; *the halfe of a* Teston.

Demy-quarteron. *The halfe of a* Quarteron; *See* Quarteron.

Demy-taille. *as* Demi-taille.

Demy-teste. *An yron scull, or steele cap.*

Denaire. *The number of ten; or, a tenth.*

Dendrille: f. *The rag, or clout wherewith a leaking tub is stopped; also, a mans priuities; or that which hangs dangling betweene his legs.*

Deneanti: m. ie: f. *Abased, made worthlesse, vile, most base.*

Deneantir. *To abase; to make worthlesse, vile, most base.*

Deneantise: f. *Worthlesnesse, vilenesse, extreame basenesse.*

Denegation: f. *A denegation, denying, disaduowing, refusall, forsaking.*

Deneraux: m. *Patternes whereby coyne is to be made, or euerie peece weighed, before it be coyned.*

Denerée: f. *Ware, marchandise; as* Denrée.

Denerver. *To weaken; See* Desnerver.

Deni. *A Nay, deniall; refusall.*

Deniaiser. *To make, or become, wise by costlie experiences; to teach one wit by often cousening, or gulling of him.*

Denié: m. ée: f. *Denied; disaffirmed; inficiated.*

Deniement: m. *A deniall, denying, inficiation, disaffirming, saying nay vnto.*

Denier: m. *A pennie, a deneere; a small copper coyne valued at the tenth part of an English pennie; also, a pennie-weight; or 24 graines, in weight; also, the price of a thing.*

Deniers: (plural.) *Money, coyne, treasure; a summe, or stocke, of money.*

Deniers communs. *as* Deniers patrimoniaux; & Deniers d'octroy.

Denier à dieu. *An earnest pennie, or peece of siluer.*

Deniers d' Estat. *Looke* Estat.

Denier de Marc. *A pennie-weight; or, twentie foure graines.*

Deniers d' octroy. *The tolls, &c, which vpon speciall suit made by citizens, the Prince allowes them to leuie within their liberties; towards the repairing, and and vpholding of their walls, rampiers, gates, causeyes,*

seyes, bridges, &c.

Deniers patrimoniaux. *The common stocke, reuenue, or treasure of a towne; comming in by rent of lands, houses, stalls, and other commodities, or priuiledges, of a long time belonging to it.*

Denier de seruice. *Pennie rent; a quit, or chiefe rent; or, the reseruation of a single pennie in lieu of all other rents and seruices, (homage excepted.)*

Chambre aux deniers. *Looke* Chambre.

Droict du dixiesme denier. *The tenth pennie, or penniworth of all Mines, mineralls, mettalls, & other substances got within ground (in whatsoeuer part of France) due vnto the King; also, th' Admiralls tenth part, or share in all Shipwracks, prizes, conquests, &c, made at Sea.*

Droict de tiers denier. *The third pennie, or part of the price giuen for an inheritance* Roturier, *or* Bourdelier, *due, in some places, vnto the Land-lord*

Francs deniers. *Looke* Franc.

Au denier douze. *After twelue yeares purchace; & (in matters of interest) a pennie for a yeares loane of twelue pence, which comes to eight pounds and a noble in the hundred.*

Venir entre la bourse & les deniers. *To preuent, forestall, come betweene and home; a Law phrase; Looke* Venir.

Denier sur denier bastit la maison: Prov. *One pennie after another builds the house; by little and little great matters are effected, great workes finished.*

Deniers avancent les bediers: Prov. *Coine prefers Coxcombes.*

Apres besongne repos, & denier: Prov. *Ease, and wealth are the rewards of labour; or, when a man hath done his worke, he loues to rest, and lookes to be paid.*

Bonne la maille qui sauve le denier: Prov. *Well is the money spent that saues more than it selfe.*

Denier. *To denie, disaffirme, inficiate, say nay vnto.*

Denigré: m. ée: f. *Blackned, or smeared with blacke; also, defamed, blemished in reputation; also, vnnestled.*

Denigrer. *To blacken, or smeare with blacke; also, to defame, or blemish the reputation of; also, as* Denicher, *to vnnestle, or plucke out of his nest.*

Denis. *Dionisius, or Denis; a proper name for a man; and one of Bacchus his surnames.*

Denombrement: m. *A denumeration; a numbring, reckoning, or telling ouer; also, a list, roll, or catalogue of names; also, an Inuentorie of goods; also, a suruey of land, particularizing the quantitie, seat, rents, seruices, and tenure thereof.*

Denommé: m. ée: f. *Denominated, nominated, named.*

Les denommez en ceste charge. *The within-named, which are appointed to vndertake, or vndergoe this charge.*

Denommer. *To denominate, nominate, name; giue names, or titles vnto.*

Denoncé: m. ée: f. *Denounced; summoned; threatened; published; proclaimed; warned, aduertised; foreshewed, signified; also, accused, or appeached of; charged with, or blamed for; informed against.*

Denoncement: m. *A denouncing; a threatning; a signifying, declaring; warning, aduertising of; also, a publicke accusing of, charging with, or blaming for, a fault.*

Denoncer. *To denounce; threaten; summon; signifie, declare; warne; foreshew; publish, proclaime; also, publickly to accuse, appeach of; charge with, or blame for, an offence; to informe against.*

Denonciateur: m. *A denouncer; threatener; publisher, proclaimer; also, an Informer, or publicke accuser; as* Delateur.

Denonciation: f. *A denunciation; or threatning Summons; a publication, declaration; publicke threatening, sending of defiance.*

Denonciation faitte en Iustice. *An information, accusation, bill of complaint.*

Denoté: m. ée: f. *Denoted; shewed, signified.*

Denoter. *To denote; shew, signifie.*

Denouër, & Denoüé. *Looke* Desnouër, & Desnoüé.

Denrée: f. *Ware, stuffe, marchandise; any ordinarie chaffer that is retailed; also, a certaine measure, or proportion in buying and selling; as;*

Vne denrée d'herbes, &c. *A pennie-worth of hearbs &c.*

Dense: com. *Thicke, compact, hard closed together.*

Dent: f. *A tooth; or fang; tuske, or tush.*

Dents briseuses. *as* Dents canines.

Dents canines. *The tushes, or tuskes.*

Dent au chien. *Couch-grasse, Quitch-grasse, Dogges-grasse; also, (but lesse properly) Harts-horne Plantaine, or Crow-foot Plantaine; (Gerards* Dens caninus, *or Dogs-tooth is a kind of Satyrion.)*

Dent de chien. *Couch-grasse, Dogs-grasse; also, Dandelion, Priests-crowne; Pisseabed; also, a grudge, repining, ill meaning.*

Dents de chien. *The tushes.*

Les dents d'une herse. *Harrow-teeth.*

Dents incisiues. *The foure fore-teeth.*

Dents de laict. *Coults teeth, young teeth;* (il luy porta vn dent de laict; *he bore him a grudge, or spleene.*

Dents longues. qui a les dents bien longues. *That is throughly a hungred, or most sharpe set.*

Dent de lyon. *The hearbe Dandelyon, Pisseabed, Priests-crowne, Swines-snowt.*

Dents maschelieres. *Looke* Mascheliere.

Dents maschoires. *The cheeke teeth, or grinders.*

Dents molares. *The great Jaw-teeth, or eye-teeth; the grinders, or cheeke teeth, wherewith wee gently breake, and grind our meat.*

Dents oeillieres. *The vpper tushes, or eye-teeth.*

Dents riantes. *The fore-teeth; (because in laughing they are commonly seene.)*

Dents de sens & de sagesse. *The Jaw-teeth.*

Dents tranchantes. *as* Incisiues.

Arracher les dents en dormant à. *Looke* Dormant.

Mal aux dents. *The tooth-ache; also extreame hunger, or an hunger-starued estate; whence;* Qui a mal aux dents a mauvais parents: Prov.

Mauvaise dent. *as* Dent de chien.

Elle a les dents à maschecoulis, le haut defendant le bas. *She hath a thinne row of teeth, whose stench, and rottennesse driue men from her trench.*

Batre le tambour avec les dents. *To didder, or chatter, as an Ape that sayes his Paternoster.*

Cheoir à dents. *To fall groueling.*

Clerc iusques aux dents. *A good trencher scholler; an excellent Clerke in a Cookes shop.*

Faire de l'argent avec les dents. *To grow rich by eating little.*

Ne marcher que sur les dents. Ils ne marchent que sur &c. *They stirre not a foot but for good cheere; they are true parasites, trencher-friends, smell-feasts.*

Mettre vn pot &c à dents. *To turne it vpside-down, to whauve it with the mouth downewards.*

Mettre sur les dents. *To toyle out, or to ouertoyle; to take too much of; to spend or spoyle, by putting to too much.*
Monstrer la dent. *To girne, or grinne at; looke threateningly, or grimly on; fall into anger, grow into choller with.*
Parler à vn des grosses dents. *To checke, taunt, reproue, take vp, chide throughly, speake roughly to; to talke to one as if he would eat him.*
Prendre le frein aux dents. *To take the bit betweene his teeth; to resist authoritie, as a stubborne horse doth his rider; or, obstinately to follow his owne course, or go on with his owne proiect, whatsoeuer aduice, or command be giuen to the contrarie.*
Prendre la lune à belles dents. *To performe impossibilities.*
Rire à grosses dents. *To laugh onely from the teeth outward.*
Telle dent telle morsure: Prov. *Looke* Morsure.
En vne herse bien dentée n'y faut nulles dents: Prov. *A thing being once well done, what need additions?*
Tel a du pain lors qu'il n'a plus de dents: Prov. *Some haue great plentie when they can take no pleasure in't.*
Vin trouble ne brise dents: Pro. *Thicke wine breaks no teeth.*
Dentade: f. *A biting, or bit of the teeth; such a snatch, or pinch as a dog will sometimes giue on a sudden.*
Dentaire: f. *A kind of Sanicle; also, Toothwort, or clownes Lungwort.*
Dental: m. *as* Denté.
Dentateur: m. *A Tooth-drawer.*
Denté: m. *The ruddie, and spotted Sea-Breame, or Goldenie; called so for the tushes that appeare out of his mouth; whereas the other fishes of that kind, either haue none, or none so appearing.*
Denté: m. ée: f. *Toothed, furnished with teeth; hauing many teeth; also, indented, notched, iagged.*
En vne herse bien dentée n'y faut nulles dents: Prov. *Looke* Dent.
Dentée: f. *as* Dentade; *or, a gash made, or blow giuen, by the tush of an angrie boare, &c.*
Dentelé: m. *A kind of mischieuous Dog-fish, that doth much hurt with his teeth.*
Dentelé: m. ée: f. *Toothed, toothie; full of iags resembling little teeth.*
Rouët dentelé. *A cog-wheele.*
Dentelet: m. *A little tooth; (also, a repast, or meale:* ¶Barrag.)
Dentelez: m. *Foure muscles (two little, and two great ones) belonging to the breast.*
Denteliz: m. *Teeth; or, a tooth-like notching, or iagging, in Imagerie, &c.*
Dentelle: f. *Small edging (and indented) Bonelace, or Needleworke.*
Denteleure: f. *A tusking, or toothing, or tooth-like iagging, in Architecture.*
Denticules: m. *Tuskings, tooth-like iags, or caruing, on the chapters of pillers, or on any ledge, or edging.*
Dentier: m. *The part of an helmet that couers the teeth.*
Dentir. *To breed yong teeth.*
Denudation: f. *A denudation, or denuding; a laying, or leauing, bare.*
Denué: m. ée: f. *Denuded, bared; stript naked.*
Denuer. *To denude, bare, strip naked; leaue, or lay, bare.*
Denys: m. *as* Denis.

Deoppilatif: m. iue: f. *Deoppilatiue; opening, or vnstopping obstructions.*
Depaïsé: m. ée: f. *Driuen out of his countrey; also, growne courtlie, or, that hath left the countrey fashion.*
Depaïser. *To driue out of his countrey.*
Se depaïser. *To grow courtlie, make it fine, leaue the countrey fashion.*
Depaïser le bestial. *To change their soile, to send them out of the countrey they were bred in.*
Depaistre. *as* Despaistre.
De par. *From; by the commaundement, or authoritie of.*
De-par vous. *From you; on your part; in your name, roome, or place.*
Deparceler. *as* S'accorder. *To agree, or come to an agreement.*
Deparler. *To dispraise, blame, despise.* (v.m.)
Deparqué: m. ée: f. *Disparked, disinclosed, layed open; also, broken, or got out, of a Parke, or inclosure.*
Se Deparquer. *To breake out of a Parke, or inclosed place; also, to goe out, or away from.*
Depart: m. *A departure, or going from; also, the parting of mettalls; and hence;*
Eau de depart. *A kind of strong water, vsed in the parting of mettalls.*
Departement: m. *A parting, or departing; also, a diuiding; an alotting, parting, or appointing out vnto euerie one his part; and hence; a diuision, or partition of a countrey, as;*
Chaque Gouverneur est allé à son departement. *vnto the place of gouernment allotted vnto him.*
Departeur: m. *A diuider, parter, distributer.*
Departeur d'or, & d'argent. *One that parts mettalls, or seuers the one from another.*
Departi: m. ie: f. *Parted, gone, departed; also, diuided, distributed, disposed, sorted, or set into parts; also, refused, renounced, quitted, left, desisted from; also, parted, or seuered, as mettalls.*
Departie: f. *as* Depart; *A parting, or departure.*
Departiment: m. *A diuision, parting; squaring, or sorting out into seuerall parts, or for sundrie purposes.*
Departir. *To part, depart, or go from; also, to diuide, distribute, sort, or dispose into seuerall parts; also, to part, or seuer mettalls asunder.*
Se departir de, &c. *To refuse, quit, renounce; also, to leaue, or desist from.*
Departir vn procez. *When one Court is equally diuided, to require th'opinion of the Judges of another; that making vp one of two of the three, iudgement may bee thereon giuen.*
Departissement. *A parting, diuiding, distribution, partition; a sorting, or setting into parts; also, a leauing, departing, or going from.*
Depassionner. *To be angrie, or grow into choller.*
Depecé. *Dismembred;* Looke Despecé.
Depeinct: m. cte: f. *Purtrayed, painted, liuely drawn, or described.*
Depeindre. *To draw, paint, purtray; describe liuely.*
Ie vous depeindray de vos couleurs. *I will set you forth in your colours.*
Depellé: m. ée: f. *Pilled, skinned; blanched; flayed; pared.*
Depenaillé. *as* Despenaillé.
Dependance: f. *A dependancie; waiting, relying on; the hanging of one thing vpon another.*

Dependant. *Depending, relying, hanging, waiting on.*

Dependre. *To depend, relie, hang on; to rest, or consist in; also, to vnhang; or take downe from the gallowes.*

Dependre l' huis, ou fenestres de la maison. *Looke* Huis.

Dependu: m. uë: f. *Vnhanged; or, taken downe from the gallowes; also, (more generally) vnhung, or taken off that whereon it hung.*

Deperdition: f. *Vtter ruine, totall perdition.*

Deperi: m. ie: f. *Perished, quite lost.*

Deperir. *To perish; to be lost, to be ruined, or vtterly vndone.*

Deperissant: f. *Perishing.*

Depesche. *as* Despesche.

Depesché: m. ée: f. *Dispatched.*

Depescher. *To dispatch; Looke* Despescher.

Depescher quelqu'vn. *To talke freely of, to censure at pleasure, to rip vp a mans actions; also, to ieast at.*

Depestrer. *as* Despestrer; *To vnpester.*

Depié de fief. *A dismembring of an inheritance; an aliening part thereof.*

Depilatoire: m. *A depilatorie; any ointment, salue, water, &c, which takes away haire.*

Depilé: m. ée: f. *Bauld; bare, or bared of haire.*

Depiteux. *as* Despiteux.

Depitonné. *See* Despitonné.

Deplanter. *To displant, or vnplant; to vnset; to remoue.*

Deplastrer. *To vnplaister, to pull the plaister off; hence also, to bare, or discouer.*

Deplayé: m. ée: f. *Extreamely wounded, sore hurt.*

Deplayer. *To wound extreamely, hurt verie sore.*

Deplicer. *To vnplait, or vnfold; to vndoe the plaits, to open the foulds, of.*

Se Deplicer de. *To rid himselfe of; to vnfould himselfe out of; to disintangle himselfe.*

Deplorant. *Deploring, bewailing, lamenting.*

Deploré: m. ée: f. *Deplored, bemoaned, bewailed, lamented for; also, desperate, remedilesse, past helpe, out of hope; forsaken, or giuen ouer.*

Deplorer. *To deplore, bewaile, moane, bemoane, lament for.*

Deplumation: f. *A deplumation, pluming, vnfeathering; also, an inflamed, and hard thicknesse of th' eyelids, with losse of all their haire, which once gone, either cannot get through againe, or being got through, fasten not within them.*

Depoché: m. ée: f. *Vnpouched, vnpocketted.*

Depocher. *To vnpouch; to pull, or draw a thing, out of a pocket.*

Depopulé: m. ée: f. *Depopulated, vnpeopled; also, destroyed, wasted, rauaged.*

Depopuler. *To depopulate, vnpeople, or dispeople; also, to wast, rauage, ruine, destroy.*

Deport: m. *Disport, sport, pastime, recreation; pleasure; also, two of the three parts of a Wards reuenew, due vnto a Land-lord.*

Le deport des benefices. *The first fruits; or one yeres reuenue of vacant benefices (due vnto the Prince, Patron, or Prelate, as the custome, or case is.)*

Sans aucun deport. *Without any let, stop, or delay.*

Deporté: m. ée: f. *Saued, spared, exempted, excused from; borne with, forborne; left off, let alone, abstained from; also, disported, sported, played; also banished.*

Deportemens: m. *Deportments, demeanor.*

Deporter. *To beare, suffer, indure; also, to spare, or exempt from; also, to banish (into an Island, &c.)*

Se deporter. *To cease, forbeare, leaue off, giue ouer, pause on, quiet himselfe, hold his hand; also, to disport, play, recreate himselfe, passe away the time.*

Se deporter de. *To omit, let alone, let passe; abstaine, surcease, forbeare, from.*

Se deporter sur quelqu'un (d' vne chose.) *To relie, or beare himselfe altogether vpon one (in a matter;) to referre, or commit it, wholly vnto him.*

Deportet: m. *A sporting bable; a wenches &c.*

Deposé: m. ée: f. *Deposed, sworne vnto; also, deposed, or put from.*

Deposer. *To depose, to testifie by oath; also, to depose, depriue of, or put from.*

Depositaire: m. *Hee vnto whom a thing is layed in gage, or cõmitted for safer keeping; a Gardian, or feoffee, vpon trust.*

Deposité: m. ée: f. *Laied downe as a gage; committed vnto the trust, or keeping of.*

Depositer. *To lay downe as a gage; to infeoffe vpon trust, to commit vnto the keeping, or trust of.*

Deposition de tesmoignes. *The deposition, or testimonie of witnesses (written downe.)*

Depossedé: m. ée: f. *Dispossessed; depriued, or disseised of.*

Depossséder. *To dispossesse, depriue, disseise of.*

Depost: m. *A pledge, or gage; a thing left in, or committed vnto, another mans keeping.*

Depourprer. *To vnpurple, or make pale.*

Deppié. *Looke* Depié.

Depraver. *To depraue, marre, viciate, corrupt.*

Depredé: m. ée: f. *Rauaged, ransacked, robbed, made bootie of.*

Depreder. *To rauage, ransacke, rob, make spoyle, prey, or bootie of.*

Depressoir de la membrane. *An instrument wherewith, after trepaning, the membrane that couers the braine is held downe, thereby to know if there bee any thing left betweene it and the scull, to hurt, or annoy it.*

Depri: m. *as* Depry.

Depriant: m. *The purchaser that agrees with the Lord* Censuel *for his* Lods *and* Ventes, *or prays time for the paiment of them.*

Depriant. *Earnestly praying; humbly beseeching.*

Deprier. *To pray earnestly, request instantly; beseech humbly; also, as* Desprier; *also, a purchaser to agree before-hand with the Lord* Censuel *for his* Lods *and* Ventes; *or to shew him the contract of his purchase, and beseech him to forbeare for a while his censuall duties, that, if they be not paied in due time, he may incur the lesse danger.*

Deprimé: m. ée: f. *Depressed, abased, brought low, kept downe.*

Deprimer. *To depresse, abase, bring low; to keepe, hold, thrust, or weigh, downe.*

Depry: m. *An agreement made by a purchaser with the Lord* Censuel *for his* Lods *and* Ventes; *or rather, a signification of his purchase, and humble request, vnto him, that he will forbeare his duties; that, if they be not paid in due, or th' accustomed time, there may be the lesse aduantage taken against him.*

Deps: m. *A kind of royaltie, or Seigneuriall dutie.*

Depucelé: m. ée: f. *Depucelated, deflowred; Looke* Despucelé.

Depuceler. *To depucelate, or deflower a virgine; to take*

take her maidenhead.
Depucellé. *as* Depucelé.
Depuis. *Since, or sithence.*
Depuration: f. *A depuration; purging, purifying, or clarifying.*
Depuré. *Purged, cleered, purified, clarified.*
Depurer. *To purge, cleere, purifie, clarifie.*
Depurgatoire: com. *Depurgatorie; purging.*
Deputé: m. *A Deputie; (properly, one thats imployed by subiects vnto their Prince.)*
Deputé: m. ée: f. *Deputed, ordained, appointed, assigned.*
Deputer. *To depute, appoint, ordaine, assigne.*
Dequoy: m. *(Substantiuely) stuffe, substance, wherewithall.*
Dequoy. (Adverb.) *whereto, wherefore, to what end; as,* Dequoy me sert cela? *wherto doth that serue me? what vse haue I of that? or, what am I the better for it?*
Il y a bien dequoy. *There is good cause for it.*
Derbro: m. *A kind of small-mouthed, blew-backt, and white-bellied Sea-fish.*
Derceau. *A little Dace, or Dare-fish:* ¶Rab.
Derechef. *Againe, moreouer; once, or ouer, againe.*
Deregler. *Looke* Se Desreigler.
Dereté. *Disintangled, vnsnared, got out of the net.*
Deridé: m. ée: f. *Smoothed, vnwrinkled, planed, made plaine; also, loossened, slackened, vnstiffened.*
Derider. *To smooth, plane, or make plaine a thing that had wrinkles; or as in;*
Derider les cordes, les voiles; &c; *To loossen, vnstiffen, or slacken the tackling, sailes, &c.*
Deris: m. *A mocke, flout, gibe, derision.*
Derision: f. *Derision, mockerie, flouting, scoffing.*
Derivé: m. ée: f. *Deriued, or drawne from; also, drayned.*
Deriver. *To deriue; or draw from; also, to draine, or draw drie.*
Derme: m. *The (true) skin which couers the extreame parts of the bodie.*
Derne: m. *as* Darne; *A slice; a broad and thin peece, or partition of.*
Dernier: m. ere: f. *The last, hindmost; vttermost, farthest, or furthermost; also, the later, or second, in ranke, or place.*
Au dernier. *Finally, at the last cast.*
Maudissant le dernier. *Cursing the last; viz. striuing to run (away) with the formost.*
Le dernier le loup le mange: Prov. *The lag, (or laziest) of a flocke is preyed on.*
Le dernier venu est le mieux aimé: Prov. *He that came last is best beloued; the newest friend, &c, most trusted, best vsed.*
Les derniers venus ferment les portes: Prov. *The last commer shuts the doore; strikes vp the bargaine; ends the businesse.*
Les derniers venus sont les Maistres: Prov. *The last commers get the maisterie, ouerrule the rest, rule the roast.*
Vn iour iuge de l'autre, & le dernier iuge de tous: Prov. *One day rules another, but the last ouerrules all.*
Dernierain: m. aine: f. *Late, or lateward; verie backward; which is long in comming, or late before it bee ripe.*
Dernierement. *Lately, or, not long agoe.*
Deroché: m. ée: f. *Pulled, or fallen, from a rocke; Looke* Desroché.
Derogant. *Looke* Derogeant.
Derogation: f. *A derogation; a disabling, or disparaging of; a diminution; abrogation, or abolishment of part of.*
Derogatoire: m. *A derogatorie, or act of derogation, or of disparagement.*
Derogatoire: com. *Derogatorie; disparaging, derogating from; also, diminishing; abrogating, or abolishing part of.*
Derogé: m. ée: f. *Disparaged, or derogated from; disabled; also, abrogated, or abolished in part.*
Derogeant. *Derogating from; disparaging; disabling; impairing; abrogating, or abolishing part of.*
Deroger. *To derogate from; to disparage; to disable, or impaire; to abrogate a peece, abolish a part, of.*
Deroguer. *as* Deroger.
Derompement: m. *A breaking, or bursting in peeces; a riuing asunder.*
Derompement de maisons. *A rasing, ouerthrowing, pulling, or breaking downe of houses.*
Derompre. *To burst, or breake in peeces; to riue or teare asunder; to ouerthrow, rase, ruine, breake downe.*
Derompu: m. uë: f. *Burst, or broken, in peeces; riuen, or torne, asunder; full of breaches; broken downe.*
Deroute: f. *A rout, a defeature, or flight of men.*
Derrain. *as* Dernier. *The last:* ¶Pic.
Derrainier. *The same.*
Derrée. *as* Denrée; *Ware, &c.*
Derrenier. *See* Dernier.
Derrider. *To smooth, plane, vnwrinkle, stretch out.*
Derrider les voiles. *To loossen, or slacken the sayles; a Mariners phrase.*
Derriere. *(Substantiuely; as)* le derriere de. *The hinder part, backe part, or backeside of.*
Courir sur le derriere. *A horse to gallop all vpon his hinder parts.*
Derriere. *(An Aduerbe of Place;) Behind, backward, on the backe-side, or backe-part of.*
Au devant par derriere. *The wrong way to the wood; round about next way, and in at further doore; Looke* Devant.
Gaigner le devant par derriere. *See* Devant; *or* Gaigner.
Cheval qui porte derriere. *A double gelding, a horse that will carrie double.*
Ders: m. *A cloath of State, hanging full ouer, and falling low behind, a Soueraigne Princes chaire of Estate.*
Derselet: m. *A little square Canopie, or cloath of Estate.*
Dertre. *as* Dartre; *A tetter, or ring-worme.*
Des. *From, euen from, since.*
Des à present. *Forthwith, incontinently, from this verie time forword.*
Des que i'auray disné; *As soone as euer I haue dined.*
Desabillé: m. ée: f. *vncloathed, vndressed, vnarrayed.*
Desabiller: m. *A Ladies cushion-cloth.*
Desabiller. *To vncloath, vndresse, vnray, put off habilements.*
Desabusé: m. ée: f. *Disabused; vnblinded; deliuered of errors, rid from abuses.*
Desabuser. *To disabuse, to rid from abuses.*
Desaccointé: m. ée: f. *Disacquainted; growne out of acquaintance with; made strange vnto.*
Desaccointer. *To disacquaint; to breake, or dissolue the*

the acquaintance of; also, to renounce, or forgoe all acquaintance with.

Desaccommodé: m.ée: f. *Disaccommodated.*

Desaccommoder. *To disaccommodate.*

Desaccord: m. *A iarre, discord, vntuneablenesse; disagreement, contention, difference.*

Desaccordance: f. *A discordance, or disaccording; a squaring, iarring, differing, variance, disagreeing.*

Desaccordant. *Discordant; squaring, iarring, disagreeing, discrepant, repugnant vnto.*

Desaccordé. *Discordant, iarring, out of tune; also, disaccorded.*

Desaccorder. *To discord, or disaccord; to iarre, differ, disagree, dissent, square, be repugnant.*

Desaccostable: com. *Vnaccoastable, vnapproachable; vncompanable, vnsociable.*

Desaccouplé: m.ée: f. *Vncoupled; vnyoaked.*

Desaccoupler. *To vncouple; vnyoke; disioyne.*

Desaccoustumance: f. *A disuse, vnwontednesse, vnaccustomednesse; discontinuance; a leauing of a fashion, a forgoing of a custome.*

Desaccoustumé. *Disaccustomed, left off, disused, giuen ouer, worne out of vse, growne out of fashion.*

Desaccoustumer. *To disaccustome; disuse, bring out of vse; to discontinue the custome, forgoe the fashion of.*

Desaccroché: m. ée: f. *Vnhoked.*

Desaccrocher. *To vnhooke.*

Desacré: m.eé: f. *Vnhallowed, prophaned.*

Desacrer. *To prophane, to vnhallow.*

Disadjusté: m.ée: f. *Disadiusted; disapted; disordered; made vneuen, or vnsteaddie.*

Desadjuster. *To disadiust, vnsettle, disorder, disapt, make vneuen, or vnsteaddie.*

Desadmonesté: m.ée: f. *Disadmonished, or disswaded; warned from, or to the contrarie of.*

Desadmonester. *To disadmonish, or disswade.*

Desadvenant. *A portion of an inheritance left a vassall, but not sufficient for the homage due vnto the Lord.*

Desadventageusement. *Disaduantagiously.*

Desadventure: f. *Misfortune, misaduenture.*

Desadvest: m. *A Disseisin, dispossession, disaduesture, disinheriting.*

Desadvestir. *To disseise, disaduest, dispossesse, disinherite.*

Desadveu. *A disclaime, disaduowing, renouncing; also, a thing done at vnawares, or against the will.*

Desadvisé: m.ée: f. *Vnaduised, inconsiderate, foolish, rash.*

Desadvoüé: m.ée: f. *Disaduowed, disclaimed from.*

Desadvoüement: m. *A disaduowing, or disclaiming from.*

Desadvoüer. *To disaduow, disclaime, refuse, renounce.*

Desaffamé: m. ée: f. *Whose hunger is slaked, or satisfied.*

Desaffamer. *To slake, or satisfie the hunger of.*

Desaffleuré: m. ée: f. *Deflowred; or, whose flourishing is hindered.*

Desaffleurer. *To deflower, or vnflower; to plucke the flowers from; to hinder the flowring, or flourishing of.*

Desaffublé: m. ée: f. *Vnmuffled, vnhooded, vnhoodwinked.*

Desaffubler. *To vnmuffle, vnhood, vnhoodwinke; vncouer.*

Il se disaffubla. *He cast open his gowne, or cassocke, wherewith he had couered his face.*

Desagé: m.ée: f. *Vnder age, not of full age, not yet of yeares; also, decrepit, verie old, or so old, as hee hath need of tending.*

Desagencé: m. ée: f. *Disadapted, disadiusted, disordered.*

Desagencement: m. *A disadapting, disadiusting, disordering.*

Desagencer. *To disadapt, disadiust, disaccommodate, disproportion, disorder; to set out of frame, put out of fashion, bring out of the right, into a wrong place.*

Desagenouillé: m.ée: f. *Risen, or got vp from kneeling.*

Se Desagenouiller. *To arise, or get vp from kneeling.*

Desagrafé: m. ée: f. *Vnclasped, vngrapled, vnhasped.*

Desagrafer. *To vnclaspe, vngraple, vnhaspe.*

Desagreable: com. *Disagreeable, vnacceptable, vnpleasing.*

Desajancer. *as* Desagencer.

Desaigri: m.ie: f. *Sweetned; appeased.*

Desaigrir. *To sweeten, or vnsharpen, to allay the sowernesse of; also, to asswage, mitigate, pacifie, appease.*

Desaiguilleter. *To vntrusse, or vndoe points; also, to take the points from, or depriue of points.*

Desaimé: m. ée: f. *Vnloued; fallen into the dislike of.*

Desaimer. *To vnloue; desist from louing; loath what before was loued; fall into dislike, or disgust of.*

Desairer. *To vnayrie; or, spoyle, and destroy an ayrie of Hawkes &c.*

Desaise: f. *A Sicknesse, a disease, a being ill at ease.*

Desaisé: m. ée: f. *Diseased, sicke, out of temper, ill at ease.*

Desaisine. *Looke* Dessaisine.

Desalé: m.ée: f. *Taught wit by experience, purged of the foole, that hath seene the Lyons.*

Desalier. *as* Deslier; *To vnbind.*

Desallé. *as* Desalé.

Desalteré: m. ée: f. *Whose thirst is quenched, slaked, alayed.*

Desalterer. *To quench, allay, slake thirst.*

Desamassé: m.ée: f. *Vnheaped, vnpiled.*

Desamasser. *To vnheape, vnpile; pull downe a heape; consume things heaped.*

Desancré. *Weighed, as an anker; let goe, or loossed, as a hold.*

Desancrer. *To weigh anker, and be gone; also, to loosse ones hold.*

Desangé: m.ée: f. *Extirpated; the race whereof is destroyed.*

Desanger. *as* Desenger; *To extirpate, or destroy the race of.*

Desaniné: m.ée: f. *Depriued of spirit, or life.*

Desanimer. *To depriue of life, or spirit,*

Desantourat. *Deflowred, as a virgine that hath leachered:* ¶Langued.

Desapareillé: m. ée: f. *Disordered, ruffled, made vnreadie.*

Desapareiller. *To ruffle, disorder, make vnreadie, put out of tune, or trim.*

Desapareilleur: m. *An vndresser; a maker vnreadie; a disorderer.*

Desaparié: m.ée: f. *Vnmatched, vnpaired, vncoupled; whose match, mate, or companion is taken from him.*

Desaparier. *To vnmatch, vnpaire, vncouple; to diuide, sunder, or seperate mates, fellowes, couples.*
Desapetisſance: f. *A distast, or loathing of meats.*
Desapetisſé: m. ée: f. *Distasted, loathed, as meat.*
Desapetisſer. *To distast, marre the stomacke; take away the appetite; to breed a dislike, or loathing, of meats.*
Desapointé: m. ée: f. *Disappointed, frustrated; also, remoued, or put from an office, estate, or authoritie.*
Desapointer. *To diappoint, or frustrate; also, to remoue, or put from an office, or estate; to depriue, or bereaue of authoritie; also, to wry the leuell, put by the aime of.*
Desappetit: m. *Want of appetite; an ill, or no stomacke vnto a thing; a queasinesse, or disgust of stomacke.*
Desapprendre. *To vnlearne, or learne anew, or otherwise than before; also, to leaue a fashion vsed, or forget what hath beene learned.*
Desapresent. *Fom this verie instant;* See Des.
Desarboré: m. ée: f. *Let, or strucke downe; as the mast of a ship.*
Desarborer. *To let, or strike, downe the mast of a ship.*
Desarçonné: m. ée: f. *Dismounted, vnhorsed, cast out of the saddle.*
Desarçonner. *To vnhorse, dismount; throw ouer, set beside, cast out of the saddle.*
Desarester. *To take the bones out of fish.*
Desargenté: m. ée: f. *Vnsiluered, without siluer, cleane out of siluer.*
Desarmé. *Disarmed, depriued of armes.*
Desarmement: m. *A disarming, a depriuing of Armes.*
Desarmer. *To disarme; to depriue of armour; bereaue of weapons.*
Se desarmer. *To vnarme himselfe; to put off his arms, lay downe his weapons.*
Desarnaché: m. ée: f. *Vnharnessed; whose harnesse, or furniture is taken off.*
Desarnacher vn cheval. *To vnharnesse a horse, to take off his harnesse, or furniture.*
Desarrengé: m. ée: f. *Disordered, vnranked, disarrayed.*
Desarrengement: m. *An vnranking, disordering, disarraying.*
Desarrenger. *To vnranke, disorder, disarray.*
Desarresser. *To make fall a standing yard; to coole, or take downe the courage of.*
Desarroy: m. *Disorder, confusion, disarray; spoyle, hauocke, hurly-burly; also, a rout, ouerthrow, discomfiture, as of an armie.*
En desarroy. *Pel-mell, confusedly, out of array, cleane without order; also, in rout.*
Desarroyé: m. ée: f. *Disordered, disarrayed; put into rout; confounded, discomfited.*
Desarroyer. *To disorder, disarray, confound, marre the order, or fashion of; also, to discomfit, ouerthrow, or put to rout, an armie, &c.*
Desassemblé: m. ée: f. *Disassembled, disioyned, parted, diuided, seperated, disunited; dispersed, scattered.*
Desassembler. *To disassemble, disioyne, disunite, part, or take in peeces; to seperate, scatter, disperse, disassociate, dissipate.*
Ce qu' assemble pille pille desassemble tire tire: Prov. *That which prowling gathers prodigalitie scatters.*
Desasseuré: m. ée: f. *Disassured; put in feare, brought into doubt; made vnsetled, vncertaine, vnsteadie; made to stagger.*

Desassurer. *To disassure; to put in feare, or bring into doubt, one that was well resolued; to make vnsetled, vnassured, vnsteadie, what formerly was stayed.*
Desassiegé: m. ée: f. *Deliuered from siege.*
Desassieger. *To raise a siege; to deliuer from a siege.*
Desassocié: m. ée: f. *Disassociated; seperated, parted from the companie of.*
Desassocier. *To disassociate, breake companie, dissolue societie, seperate, or part, friends.*
Desastre: m. *A distaster, misfortune, calamitie, misaduenture, hard chance.*
Desastré: m. ée: f. *Disasterous, vnfortunate; vnhappie.*
Desatteler. *as* Desteler.
Desattisé: m. ée: f. *Quenched, slaked, put out, as a kindled firebrand.*
Desattiser. *To quench, put out, or slake a (kindled) fire, or firebrand.*
Desavancé: m. ée: f. *Hindered, impeached, kept back, driuen backeward.*
Desavancer. *To hinder, cast backward, keepe or driue backe; impeach the proceedings of.*
Desavantage: m. *Disaduantage, hinderance, dammage, losse.*
Desavantagé: m. ée: f. *Disaduantaged; incommodated, indammaged, hindered.*
Desavantager. *To disaduantage, hinder, displeasure, incommodate, indammage, impeach.*
Desaubé: m. ée: f. *Off the hinges, out of reparations; torne, ragged, tattered, all in peeces:* ¶Blesien.
Desaventureux: m. euse: f. *Vnhappie, vnfortunate.*
Desaugmenter. *To disaugment, wane, diminish, decrease, wast, grow lesse and lesse.*
Desavié: m. ée: f. *Starued; or, bereft of life.*
Desavier. *To bereaue of life; to starue, murder, kill.*
Desavoüé: m. ée: f. *Disaduowed, disallowed; renounced, disclaimed, refused.*
Desavouër. *To disaduow, disallow; refuse, renounce; disclaime.*
Desbagager. *To packe, or trusse vp his bag and bagage.*
Desbagoulé. crin desbagoulé. *Ruffled, staring, or disordered haire.*
Morceau desbagoulé. *A morsell chawed, and put out of the mouth againe.*
Desbagouler. *To ruffle, or disorder; also, to spue, or put out of the mouth a morsell halfe chawed.*
Desballé: m. ée: f. *Vnpacked; vntrussed.*
Desballer. *To vnpacke, or vntrusse; to vndoe a packe, or trusse.*
Desbandade: f. *A disbanding; a cassing of whole troups, or companies of souldiours; also, as* Debendade.
Desbandage: m. *A disbanding; an vnbending.*
Desbandé: m. ée: f. *Disbanded; vnbent; vnbound; loosse; carelesse; dispersed, scattered.*
Desbandée. à la desbandée. *Out of their ranks, out of order, out of array.*
Desbander. *To loossen, vnbind, vnbend; also, to casse, disband; scatter, disperse.*
Se desbander. *To disband; leaue his ranke; forsake his Companie, or Colours.*
Desbander l' arc ne guerist pas la playe: Prov. *The bowes vnbending heales no wound it made; the disusing of a mischieuous instrument is no amends for the hurt it hath done.*
Desbaraté: m. ée: f. *Disordered, out of order.*
Desbarbouillé: m. ée: f. *Cleansed, rid of spots.*

Desbarbouiller. *To cleanse, make cleane, vnspot, or cleere from spots.*

Desbardé: m. ée: f. *Vnladen, as a ship; disarmed, as a great horse; vnsadled, as an Asse.*

Desbarder. *To vnload a ship, or boat; to vnheape, vnburthen, disburthen; also, to vnbarbe, or disarme a horse of seruice; to vnsadle a Moyle, or Asse.*

Desbardeur: m. *A Lyter-man, or Lighter-man; a Porter that vses to vnload ships, or carrie wares out of ships &c.*

Desbarger. c'est, abbatre la terre du chevalier de costé, & d'autre qui peut cheoir sur les plantes de Vigne.

Desbarqué: m. ée: f. *Disimbarked, put a land, set on shore.*

Desbarquer. *To disimbarke, put a land, set on shore.*

Desbarré: m. ée: f. *Vnbarred, vnboulted.*

Desbarrer. *To vnbar, vnboult; open.*

Desbasté: m. ée: f. *Vnsadled; or, whose packesadle is taken off.*

Desbaster vn asne. *To vnsadle an Asse; to take off his packesadle.*

Desbasti: m. ie: f. *Pulled downe, as a building.*

Desbastiment: m. *A pulling downe of buildings.*

Desbastir. *To ruine, vnbuild, take downe, or pull downe a building.*

Desbastonné: m. ée: f. *Disarmed; depriued of weapons.*

Desbastonner. *To disarme, or depriue of weapons.*

Desbauche: f. *Incontinencie, dissolutenesse, lewdnesse, riot, vnrulinesse, disorder.*

Desbauché: m. ée: f. *Deboshed, lewd, incontinent, vngracious, dissolute, naught; vnthriftie, riotous, vnrulie, disordered; also, depraued, misled, ill-aduised, or led by ill aduice.*

Desbauchement: m. *A deboshement; a corrupting, marring, deprauing, viciating; seducing, misleading.*

Desbaucher. *To debosh; marre, corrupt, spoyle, viciate; seduce, mislead; make lewd, bring to disorder, draw from goodnesse.*

Il se desbauche. *He roames, digresses, flies out, goes from the purpose, runs altogether from the matter.*

Desbaudi: m. ie: f. *Made sad, or ashamed.*

Desbaudir. *To make sad, or ashamed; (old words.)*

Desbaugé: m. eé: f. *Vnsloughed; raised (as a wild swine) out of the durt wherein he lay wallowing.*

Desbauger vn sanglier. *To raise, or to rouse a wild boare from the place he lies, or wallows in; to vnslough him.*

Desbellé: m. ée: f. *Subdued, vanquished, ouercome by warre, &c.*

Desbeller. *To subdue, vanquish, ouercome, in warre.*

Desbaux: m. *A generall deboshement, disorder, dissolutenesse.*

Desbendade: f. *as* Debendade; *An vnbending.*

`A la desbendade. *Swiftly, violently, furiously, like an arrow out of a bow; also, disorderly.*

Desbender. *To vnbend, loossen; disband; vnbind.*

Desberger. *as* Desbarger.

Desbifé. *as* Debiffé.

Desbifement: m. *A rasing, or scraping out; also, decay, pining, languor, sorie looking, low taking, poore estate of bodie; also, a rending, or a riuing asunder.*

Desblaver. *To reape corne; to despoile, or vnfurnish of corne; to gather a crop of corne.*

Desblayé: m. *Disincumbred, vnpestered; cleere of, rid from.*

Desblayer. *To vnpester, disincumber, cleere; take away lets, remoue impediments.*

Desblée: f. *Hinderance, dammage, disaduantage by scarcitie; also, corne; or a crop of corne; also, a stacke, or halfe-thraue, of corne.*

Desbléer. *as* Desblayer.

Desbleure. la desb: ou les desbleures. *Hay, or stuble, whether it be made in cockes, or lie vnmade vp on the ground.*

Desbleyer. *as* Desblayer.

Desblouqué: m. ée: f. *Vnblocked; also, vnbuckled.*

Desblouquer. *To vnblocke, or open the (blockt-vp) passages of; also, to vnbuckle.*

Desböeté: m. ée: f. *Vnboxed, taken out of a box; put out of ioint.*

Desböeter. *To vnbox, or take out of a box; also, to put out of ioynt; (in which sence it is vsed most.)*

Desböeture. *A putting out of ioynt.*

Desboire: m. *Looke* Deboire.

Desboisté: m. ée: f. *Vnboxed; out of it right box; or, as* Desböeté.

Desboistement. *The being out of ioynt.*

Desboité. *as* Desboisté.

Desboiter. *To vnbox, vnioynt, take out of a box; put out of ioynt.*

Desbondé: m. ée: f. *Vnbunged, opened, vnstopped.*

Desbonder. *To vnbung, open, vnstop; to take out the bung, pull out the stople of.*

Se desbonder. *To gush, rush, or breake strongly, (as water thats let) out of a spowt, sluce, or bunghole.*

Desbondonner. *as* Desbonder.

Desbord: m. *as* Desbordement.

Desbordé: m. ée: f. *Ouerflowne or broken (as water) out of it bankes, or bounds; also, excessiue, profuse, disordered.*

Desbordement: m. *An ouerflowing, surrounding, or breaking out, as of waters; also, riot, excesse, disorder, superfluitie, profusion.*

Se Desborder. *To ouerflow, surround, runne ouer his bankes, breake out of his bounds; exceed rule, order, measure.*

Desborné: m. ée: f. *Vnbounded; whose bounds are laid open.*

Desbornement: m. *An vnbounding, or laying open of bounds.*

Desborner. *To vnbound, lay open the bounds; plucke vp, or pull downe the meeres of.*

Desbort. *as* Desbordement.

Desbossué: m. ée: f. *Vnbunched; smoothed, planed, plained, leuelled, fallen, made flat, or without bunches.*

Desbossuër. *To vnbunch, plane, leuell, make flat, plaine, without bunches, or bunching.*

Desbouché: m. ée: f. *Opened, vnstopped; also, disparked, disinclosed; also, vnmuffled, vnmasked, whose mouth is vncouered.*

Vn cheval desbouché. *Ill-mouthed, of an vnsetled mouth; also, not fitted by his bit.*

Desbouchement: m. *An vnstopping; a disparking, an opening of inclosures.*

Desboucher. *To vnstop, open, broach; to disparke, to breake downe hedges, or inclosures; also, to vnmuffle, vnmaske, vncouer the mouth.*

Desbouclé: m. ée: f. *Vnbuckled, loosse, vnfastened.*

Desboucler. *To vnbuckle, to open, to loose.*

Desboucler vne ville. *To raise a siege, or free it from those that had blocked it vp.*

Desbour-

Desbourbé : m. ée : f. *Drawne out of the mire.*
Desbourber. *To pull out of a slough, or muddie puddle; to draw out of the mire.*
Desbourgeonner. *To plucke, or nip off yong buds.*
Desbourrer. *To rid of* bourre; *Looke* Bourre.
Il commence à desbourrer. *Said of a stranger that begins to speake tollerable French; as also of one that hauing beene kept vnder, and thereby liued barely, begins a little to slie out, and liues in a better fashion than he did before.*
Desbours : m. *A disbursement of money.*
Desboursé : m. ée : f. *Disbursed, laid out of a purse.*
Desboursement : m. *A disbursing; or laying out of money.*
Desbouscher. *Looke* Desboucher.
Desboutonné. *Vnbuttonned; Looke* Deboutonné.
Desboutonnement : m. *An vnbuttonning.*
Desboutonner. *To vnbutton, or vndoe a button; See* Deboutonner.
Desbraguetter. *To vntie the codpeece point; Looke* Debraguetter.
Desbraillé : m. ée : f. *Vnbraced, vnbuttonned, all open afore.*
Desbrailler. *To vnbrace, or vnbutton himselfe.*
Desbranchi : m. ie : f. *Lopped, or topped; whose branches are cut, or pulled off.*
Desbranchir. *To top, or lop the boughes; to cut, or pluck off, the branches of a tree.*
Desbraquer. *To vnplant, or dismount artillerie; to wry, or disappoint the leuell thereof.*
Desbride : f. *An eare-wire; or, the wire that stayes the flaps, or head-peece, of a French-hood.*
Desbridé : m. ée : f. *Vnbridled.*
Desbrider. *To vnbridle.*
Desbrigandiner. *To depriue of a Brigandine; to rip, vndoe, take, pull, or cut, off a Brigandine.*
Desbris. *as* Debris.
Desbrisé : m. ée : f. *Riuen, clouen, torne, burst, or split asunder.*
Desbrisement. *A riuing, cleauing, bursting, or splitting asunder.*
Desbriser. se desbriser. *To riue, or cleaue asunder, as boords that gape; See* Debriser.
Desbrodequiné : m. ée : f. *Whose buskins are drawn, or pulled off.*
Desbrodequiner. *To vnbuskin; to plucke, or draw, off buskins.*
Desbrouillant. *Cleering; disintangling.*
Desbrouillé : m. ée : f. *Disintangled, vnpestered; cleered.*
Desbrouillement : m. *A disintangling; a cleering.*
Desbrouiller. *To disintangle; rid from incombrance, wind out of trouble; also, to cleere, manifest, lighten, expell the mist of.*
Desbuissonné : m. ée : f. *Roused, forced, or driuen from a couert, or thicket.*
Desbuissonner. *To rouse, raise, driue, or force, out of a couert, or thicket.*
Desbusqué : m. ée : f. *Parted, flit, gone roundly from; scudded away.*
Desbusquer. *To part, or depart, flit, stirre, goe roundly from, to scud away; to get him gone.*
Desbuté : m. ée : f. *Repelled, thrust backe; driuen or put from his marke; pretences, appointments.*
Desbuter. *To repell, thrust back, driue from his pretence, or place; to put from the marke he was, or aimed, at; to disappoint.*
Descaché : m. ée : f. *Discouered, vncouered, vnhidden, reuealed, opened, brought to light.*
Descacher. *To vncouer, disclose, open, reueale, discouer.*
Descacheté : m. ée : f. *Vnsealed, or, whose seal is burst ope.*
Descacheter lettres. *To vnseale, or breake open, letters.*
Descaillé : m. ée : f. *Vncurded, resolued.*
Se Descailler. *To resolue, vncurd, fall asunder.*
Descalengé : m. ée : f. *Vnarrested, vnapprehended,* non inuentus; *also, discharged; or redeliuered after a seisure.*
Descampé : m. ée : f. *Discamped.*
Descampement : m. *A discamping; a raising, or a remouing of; a departing from, the camp.*
Descamper. *To discamp; to raise, or to remoue a camp; to depart from the campe.*
Descapité : m. ée : f. *Decapitated, beheaded.*
Descapiter. *To decapitate, behead, strike off the head.*
Descapuchonné : m. ée : f. *Vnhooded, vncowled; vncouered, bare headed.*
Descapuchonner. *To vnhood, vncowle, vncouer.*
Desceinct : m. cte : f. *Vngirt, without a girdle.*
Desceindre. *To vngird, vnloosse, or vndoe a girdle.*
Se desceindre, & iecter sa ceincture à terre. *A ceremonie, by which (being done in Court) a debtor giues vnto his creditors the possession of his whole estate; A vassall also when he prepares himselfe to do his homage, or fealtie, must put off his girdle, and lay by the sword, or other weapon which he vsually weares.*
Desceler. *To discouer, disclose, detect, bewray.*
Descendant. les descendans de. *The progenie, or ofspring of.*
Descendant. *Descending; alighting; going downwards.*
Qui va en descendant. *Steepe, declining, enclined, bowing, bending, or hanging downewards.*
Descendement. *as* Descente; *Or, a descending, alighting; a going, falling, lighting downe; also, a casting, taking, laying downe.*
Descendre. *To descend, goe downe, come from, alight, light off, or downe; also, to cast, bring, take, or lay down; to fetch from a higher place vnto a lower.*
Descendu : m. uë : f. *Descended, deriued, come from; also, cast, brought, let, laied, taken downe; also, put ouer, as the meat a Hawke hath eaten.*
Descenduë : f. *A Discent, race, progenie, offspring, linage.*
Descenglé : m. ée : f. *Vngirded, or vngirthed.*
Descengler. *To vngird, or vngirth.*
Descensoire : com. *Descensiue, descending; of power, or propertie to descend.*
Descente : f. *A descent; fall; steepe side of a hill, &c; also, a descending, declining, or going downe.*
Desceptré : m. ée : f. *Deposed, vnkinged, depriued of a (royall, or kinglie) Scepter.*
Desceptrer. *To depose, or put from, to bereaue, or depriue of, a (kinglie) Scepter.*
Desceu. à mon desceu. *Vnwitting to me, without my knowledge.*
Deschainé : m. ée : f. *Vnchained; vnfettered; loossed, or deliuered from chaines; fetters; bondage.*
C'est vn diable deschainé. *He is a verie furie, an incarnate diuell; or limme of the diuell; a man would thinke that hell's broke loosse where he is.*
Deschainer. *To vnchaine; to loosse out of chaines; to deliuer from slauish captiuitie.*
Deschalandé : m. ée : f. *Out of trade, without custome, or customers.*
Deschalander. *To driue away customers; or depriue of custome.*
Deschambré : m. ée : f. *Seperated, scattered, parted, as chamber-fellowes; also, driuen, roused, or thrust out of*

of a lodging, or chamber.

Deschambrer. *To diuide, seperate, scatter, disperse, part a companie, that liued, or lay together in a chamber; also, to rouse, driue, or thrust out of a lodging, or chamber.*

Deschampé: m. ée: f. *Vnfoulded; also, broken out of a fould.*

Deschamper. *To vnfould; also, to breake out of a fould, like vnto sheepe.*

Deschant: m. *Descant (of Musicke;) also, a Palinodie, recantation, or contrarie song to the former.*

Deschanté: m. ée. f. *Descanted; also, recanted.*

Deschanter. *To Descant; also, to recant, or vnsay what one hath formerly deliuered.*

Deschaperonné: m. ée: f. *Vnhooded; capped; vncouered.*

Deschaperonner. *To vnhood; to cap; to pul off the hood, or couering of.*

Descharge: f. *A discharge; acquitance;* Quietus-est.

Les descharges. *Costs, and charges (in a suit.)*

Deschargé: m. ée: f. *Discharged, vnloaden, disburdened.*

Deschargé de chair. *A cleane timberd man, one that hath not too much flesh on his backe.*

Couleur deschargée en bleu. *Neere vnto a light blew, or of a light blew; light, (& so of other colours.)*

Deschargement: m. *A discharging, vnloading, easing, disburdening; a cleering, or acquiting.*

Deschargeoir: m. *A sluce, or water-passage of plankes bored full of holes, whereout the superfluous water of a Mill damme dischargeth it selfe.*

Descharger. *To discharge, disburden, exonerate, vnload; ease; also, to cleere or acquit of, rid or deliuer from, a charge; also, to purge, draine, euacuate, put out, or take away, superfluities.*

Se descharger sur vn autre. *To lay the blame which he hath deserued vpon another; to charge with the fault which he hath committed, another; to excuse himselfe by accusing another.*

Descharges. les descharges. *Costs and charges (in a suit.)*

Descharmé: m. ée: f. *Vncharmed, vnspelled.*

Descharmer. *To vncharme, vnspell; frustrate a charme, dissolue a spell.*

Descharné: m. ée: f. *Lanke, scraggie, fleshlesse, dogleane, fallen away, cleane starued, looking like a ghost, that hath nought but skinne and bone left on him.*

Descharner. *To take flesh from; to make leane.*

Descharner les os. *To teare, cut, loossen, or diuide, the flesh from the bones.*

Descharongné: m. ée: f. *Torne, rent, or plucked, as carrion, or flesh, asunder.*

Descharongnement. *A tearing, renting, or breaking of flesh into peeces.*

Descharongner. *To teare in peeces, to rent asunder flesh, or carrion.*

Descharper. *Looke* Descharpir.

Descharpi: m. ie: f. *Cleered, freed from, got rid of; Looke* Charpi.

Descharpir la trame d'un escarlate: c'est autant que deffiler. *Or, to take off the nap thereof, to make it thread-bare.*

Ie ne me puis descharpir de luy. *I cannot free my selfe from him; I cannot rid my hands, I cannot get cleere, of him.*

Deschaud, & Deschault. *Bare-foot, and bare-legged.*

Deschaussé. *as* Deschaud; *Also, vncouered, or opened, as a tree, at the root.*

Deschaussement: m. *An vnshooing.*

Deschaussement d'arbres. *An opening, or baring of trees at the root.*

Deschausser. *To vnshooe, to pull off shooes; also, to vnhose, or draw off hosen.*

Deschausser vn'arbre. *To open, or bare a tree at the root.*

Deschausser Bertrand. *To be whitled, cup-shotten, throughly drunken.*

Deschausser les dents. *To bare their bottomes; to cut, or diuide the gummes from about them.*

Deschaussoir: m. *A Fleame; the toole wherewith Barbers diuide the gum from the tooth which they would draw out.*

Deschaux. *as* Deschaud.

Descheance: f. *A decay, diminution, wast, consumption; ruine of.*

Descheoir. *as* Decheoir; *To minish, lessen, decay; fall away.*

Descherpilleur. *A notable robber, or freebooter; a famous pursetaker.*

Deschet: m. *as* Descheance; *or,* Dechet.

Descheu. *Fallen away &c; as* Dechu.

Deschevalé: m. ée: f. *Vnhorsed, cast, or tumbled from horsebacke.*

Deschevaler. *To vnhorse, to throw off horsback.*

Deschevancé: m. ée: f. *Robbed, despoiled, beggered.*

Deschevancer. *To rob, ransacke, begger, depriue, or despoile of wealth, or substance.*

Descheuauché: m. ée: f. *as* Deschevalé.

Deschevaucher vn homme. *To throw, or tumble a man from his horse.*

Deschevelé. vne femme toute deschevelée. *Discheueled, with all her haire disorderly falling about her eares.*

Descheveler. *To discheuell; to loosse, disorder, scatter; pull the haire about the eares.*

Descheveſtré: m. ée: f. *Vnhaltered; loossed, disintangled.*

Descheveſtrer. *To vnhalter, or take off the halter from; to vnfetter, vnpester, disintangle, vntie, vnloosse, vndoe, rid, wind out of.*

Deschiffré: m. ée: f. *Decyphered.*

Deschiffrer. *To decypher; expound, explane, explicate an obscure matter, or mysterie.*

Deschiffreur: m. *A decypherer; an expounder, vnfoulder, interpreter of cyphers; of mystical, or dark writings.*

Deschiqueté: m. ée: f. *Cut, slit, shred, jagged; pinked, or cut thicke, small, and neere together.*

Deschiquetement: m. *A cutting, slitting; a iagging, mangling, or shredding into little peeces; a pinking, or, small, and thicke cutting.*

Deschiqueter. *To pinke, or cut full of small holes; to iag, slit, mangle, slash, or shred into many small peeces or parcels.*

Deschiquoter. *as* Eschiquoter.

Deschirant. *Rending, tearing, dismembring, mangling.*

Deschiré. *Rent, torne, dismembred, mangled, plucked in peeces, rashed in two.*

Deschirement: m. *A tearing, renting, dismembring, mangling, plucking in peeces, rashing in two.*

Deschirer. *To teare, dismember, mangle, rend, or plucke in peeces; to riue asunder, to rash in two.*

Deschirure: f. *A teare, a rent, a violent rash, dismembring, riue; also, a tearing, rending, riuing.*

De forte cousture dure deschirure: Prov. *Strong seames by sturdie hands are torne asunder.*

Deschute:

Deſchute: f. *A lapſe or fall.*
Deſcigler. *Looke* Deſiller.
Deſcimenter. Cette Muraille ſe deſcimente. *This wall growes vnmortered, or hath worne out it morter.*
Deſciré; Deſcirer: &c; *as* Deſchiré; Deſchirer; &c.
Deſclaveté: m. ée: f. *Diſmounted, vnlocked, or taken, as a cannon from it carriage.*
Deſclaueter vn Canon. *To diſmount a cannon; (properly to vnlocke the carriage thereof.)*
Deſcliquer. *To let goe, let flye; rap out: See* Decliquer.
Deſclorre. *To diſparke, vncloſe; diſincloſe, pull downe hedges, or incloſures.*
Deſclos: m. oſe: f. *Diſparked, vncloſed, layed open, diſincloſed.*
Fleur deſcloſe. *A flower thats ſpred, full blowen, fully bloomed.*
Secret deſclos. *diſcloſed, reuealed, bewrayed,.*
Deſcloüé: m. ée: f. *Vnnayled, vncloyed.*
Deſclouër. *To vnnayle, or vncloy; to looſſe, pull off, drawe out, a nayle.*
Deſcoché: m. ée: f. *Shot, looſſed, or ſent, as an arrow out of a Bow.*
Deſcocher vne fleiche. *To ſhoote; looſſe, or ſend an arrow from a bow.*
Deſcoeffé: m. ée: f. *Vncoifed, vnhooded, whoſe head is diſarrayed, or vncouered.*
Deſcoeffer. *To vncoife; to diſarray, diſattire, vnhood, vncouer, the head.*
Deſcogneu: m. euë: f. *Vnknowne, not kowne, forgotten; alſo, diſaduowed, or denyed.*
Deſcognoiſſance: f. *A not knowing, or forgetting of; alſo, a diſaduowing, or denyall.*
Deſcognoiſtre. *To vnknow, or to not know, to forget what one hath knowne; alſo, to diſaduow, deny; take no notice of.*
Deſcoiffer. *To vncoiſe, or pull a coife off the head; or, as* Deſcoeffer.
Deſcolé: m. ée: f. *Vnglued.*
Deſcoler. *To vnglue, to looſſe, or plucke aſunder, things that are glued.*
Deſcollé: m. ée: f. *Decapitated, beheaded.*
Deſcoller. *To decapitate; behead, or cut the head off.*
Deſcoloré: m. ée: f. *Diſcoloured, or decayed in colour; that hath loſt colour; alſo, pale, bleake, wanne, lew.*
Se Deſcombatre de. *To rid his hands of, or deliuer himſelfe from.*
Deſcombré: m. ée: f. *Diſincombred; vnpeſtered; cleered of; rid, or freed from; alſo, warranted (in law.)*
Deſcombrement: m. *A diſincombring, or vnpeſtering; alſo, a warranting (in law.)*
Deſcombrer. *To diſincomber, or vnpeſter; to rid, free, deliuer from, cleere of, incombrances; alſo, to warrant (in law.)*
Deſcombres: f. *The ruines of decayed, the rubbiſh of downe-fallen, buildings; alſo, a cleering of a ground &c from them.*
Deſcompt: m. *An accompt giuen for things receaued; a backe-reckoning.*
Deſcompter. *To accompt (for the proffits of land &c receaued,) to accompt backe, or make a backe reckoning.*
Deſconfire. *To diſcomfit, vanquiſh, defeate; ruine.*
Deſconfiture: f. *A defeature, ouerthrow, diſcomfiture; alſo a diſtribution, or equall ſharing of a bankrupts goods among all his creditors, as farre as they will goe; whence;*
Payer par deſconfiture. *A debtor bankrupt, or decayed, to pay his creditors after ſome ſuch ſmall rate as xij pence in the pound.*
Deſconfiz. *Defeated, diſcomfited, vanquiſhed; ouerthrowne.*
Deſconfort: m. *Diſcomfort; ſadneſſe, penſiueneſſe, heauineſſe of hart; griefe, that will not admit, or cannot taſte, of comfort.*
Deſconforté: m. ée: f. *Diſcomforted, diſconſolated; moſt heauie, ſad, penſiue; much out of hart.*
Se Deſconforter. *To be diſcomforted; moſt heauie, ſad, penſiue; to be much out of hart.*
Deſconſeillé: m. ée: f. *Diſcounſelled, diſſuaded from, aduiſed to the contrarie of; alſo, vncounſelled, void of counſell, wanting aduiſe.*
Deſconſeiller. *To diſcounſell, diſſuade, dehort, aduiſe vnto the contrary.*
Deſconſeilleur. *A diſſuader, dehorter; a counſellor, or aduiſer, to the contrarie.*
Deſconſolé: m. ée: f. *Comfortleſſe, diſcomforted.*
Deſconſoler. *To diſcomfort, ſadden, grieue; to make or leaue deſolate.*
Deſcontenancé: m. ée: f. *Abaſhed, put out of countenance.*
Geſtes fols, & deſcontenancez. *Vncomelie, vngracefull, ill-fauored, geſtures.*
Deſconvenuë: f. *Griefe, ſorrow, trouble, diſcomfort; misfortune, inconuenience.*
Deſcordant. *Vntwiſting, vndoing, looſſing a cord, or ſtring.*
Deſcordelé. *Vntwiſted, vntwined.*
Deſcordeler. *To vntwiſt a cord, or ſtring.*
Deſcorder en chantant. *as* Deſaccorder. *To iarre.*
Deſcorder vne corde. *To vndoe, or vntwiſt, a cord.*
Deſcouché: m. ée: f. *Gotten vp, riſen out of bed; alſo, lyen from; alſo, diſlodged, or put from his lodging.*
Deſcoucher. *To ly from, alſo to diſlodge; to depriue of, or put beſide, his lodging.*
Se Deſcoucher. *To get vp, to riſe out of bed.*
Deſcoudre. *To vnſowe, vndoe ſtitches, rip or breake open ſtitched things.*
Deſcouler. *To ſlide, or ſlip away, to glide along; See* Decouler.
Deſcoulouré: m. ée: f. *Diſcoulored, diſtayned; growne pale, wanne, lewe; that hath loſt it colour, or hue.*
Deſcoulourement: m. *A diſcoulcring, or diſtayning; a looſing, or taking away, of coulcr.*
Deſcoulorer. *To diſcoulour, or diſtaine; to make pale, wanne, lew; to take away the hue of.*
Deſcoulpé: m. ée: f. *Diſcharged; cleered, purged, rid of an imputation, deliuered from blame.*
Deſcoulper. *To diſcharge, cleere, purge, rid of an imputation, free from blame.*
Deſcoupé. *Looke* Decoupé.
Deſcouple: m. *The vncoupling of houndes, or looſſing them after their game.*
Deſcouplé: m. ée: f. *Vncoupled.*
Deſcoupler. *To vncouple; to looſſe, or let goe, out of couples.*
Deſcourable: com. *Slipperie, flitting; eaſely eſcaping from the place it was put in.*
Deſcouragé: m. ée: f. *Diſcouraged, amated, made heartleſſe, in diſpaire, out of conceit with his own fortune, or valour.*
Deſcourager. *To diſcourage, vnharten, feare, frighten, apall, put into doubt, driue out of hart, bring out of conceit, with his owne fortune, or worth.*
Deſcouronné: m. ée: f. *Vncrowned, put frõ a crown.*

Descouronner. *To vncrowne; depriue of a crowne; dispossesse of a diadem.*
Descourtoisie: f. *Discourtesie, want of courtesie;* Looke Discourtoisie.
Descouseur: m. *A ripper, vnsower; vndooer of.*
Descousu: m. uë: f. *Ripped, vnsowed; vndone.*
Estre tout descousu (apres la colere.) *To be as calme as a (standing) clocke; to haue no mettall, spirit, vigor in him; to be as good as nobodie.*
Descousure: f. *A ripping, vnsowing, vndoing of.*
Descouvert: m. erte: f. *Discouered; vncouered; detected, disclosed; exposed vnto the worlds view; open, euident, manifest, apparant, without any cloke, pretext, or colour; also, descried, or discerned a farre off.*
A descouvert. *Manifestly, openly, euidently, apparantly, in the view of all men, abroad in the ayer, without doores.*
Il a descouvert le pasté. Looke Pasté.
Descouverte: f. *A discouerie, detection, disclosure, denudation; a descrying, discerning, perceiuing, or spying out of.*
Descouvrement: m. *A discouering, vncouering, detecting, disclosing; a descrying, discerning, or perceiuing a farre off.*
Descouvreur: m. *A discouerer; detector, discloser; a scout, an espiall.*
Descouvrir. *To discouer; to vncouer, vnhill, denude, lay naked, make bare; to disclose, detect, manifest, open, lay open, expose vnto the worlds view; also, to descrie, discerne, perceiue a farre off.*
Descouvrir la meiche. *To vent (and auoid) a deadlie mischiefe;* Looke Meiche.
Descouvrir Sainct Pierre pour couvrir Sainct Paul. *To rob, or borrow of, one, therewith to inrich, or pay, another.*
Descrassé: m. ée: f. *Cleansed, made cleane, cleered, of grease, or greasinesse; rid from filthie, or slouenlie ordure; the thicke-growne durt whereof is gotten out.*
Descrasser. *To cleanse, make cleane, wipe away greasie filth, get out thicke-growne durt, rid from slouenlie ordure.*
Descri. *as* Descrit.
Descrié: m. eé: f. *Cried downe, called in; as naughtie, or false, money; also, discredited, whose credit is broken, or crackt; openly defamed, in disgrace with the publicke.*
Descriement: m. *A crying downe, or calling in; also, an open discrediting, publicke disgracing, or disparaging.*
Descrier. *To crie downe, or call in, vncurrent, or naughtie coine; also, publickly to discredit, disparage, disgrace; to publish the faults, divulge the imperfections, blaze the wants, proclaime the defects, of.*
On le descrie comme la vieille monnoye. *He hath a verie bad report among the people; his credit is wholly crackt, fame blemished, reputation lost.*
Descript: m. ipte: f. *Described, set downe, or declared.*
Description: f. *A description.*
Descrire. *To describe; set downe, or declare.*
Descrit de monnoye: m. *The calling in of money.*
Descroché: m. ée: f. *Vnhooked, loossed, vndone.*
Ancre leuée, & descrochée. *Weighed, pulled vp.*
Descrocher. *To vnhooke, to vndoe, or loossen a hooke; to shake, or pull a thing off a hooke.*
Descrocheter. *as* Descrocher.

Descroire. *To discredit; or, to giue no credit vnto; not to beleeue.*
Descroisé: m. ée: f. *Vncrossed; set straight.*
Descroiser. *To vncrosse; to open, diuide, lay, or set straight a thing which stands acrosse.*
Descroissement: m. *A decreasing; minishing; lessening, waning.*
Descroistre. *To decrease, diminish, wane, wax lesse, weare away.*
Descroté: m. ée: f. *Rubbed off, scowred out, wiped away, as durt, &c.*
Descroter. *To rub off, scowre out, wipe away, dirt.*
Descroteur: m. *A rubber, or maker cleane of cloakes; also, one that rubs on, or runnes ouer, things.*
Descrotoire: f. *A rubbing-brush.*
Descroulé: m. ée: f. *Shaken asunder.*
Descrouler. *To shake asunder.*
Descroyant. *Distrusting, misbeleeuing, not beleeuing.*
Descuire. *To vnseeth; or leaue seething.*
Descuvé: m. ée: f. *Tunned, or taken out of a fat, or tub.*
Descuver. *To take out of a fat, or tub.*
Desdaignable: com. *Disdainable, contemptible, despiseable.*
Desdaigné: m. ée: f. *Disdained, scorned, contemned, despised.*
Desdaignement: m. *A disdaining, despising, scorning, contemning.*
Desdaigner. *To disdaine, despise, contemne, scorne, loath, not to vouchsafe; to make vile account of.*
Desdaigneur: m. *A disdainer, scorner, contemner, despiser.*
Desdaigneusement. *Disdainfully, scornfully, contemptibly; proudly, coily, squeamishly.*
Desdaigneux: m. euse: f. *Disdainfull, scornefull, coy, squeamish.*
Desdaing: m. *Disdaine, scorne, contempt; coinesse; proud squeamishnesse; hautinesse; despight; moodinesse.*
Desdainer. *To vnladie; to denie a Ladie her due title, or stile; to depriue her of the title, or stile of Ladie; also, to take a man at Tables, a Queene at Draughts.*
Desdetté: m. ée: f. *Rid out of debt, set cleere aboord.*
Desdetter. *To rid out of debt.*
Desdict: m. icte: f. *Vnsayed, recanted, reuoked; contradicted; forbidden.*
Desdié: m. ée: f. *Dedicated; giuen, or deuoted vnto; destined, purposed, reserued for.*
Desdiement: m. *A dedicating, deuoting; destining vnto; reseruing, or purposing for.*
Desdier. *To dedicate, giue, or deuote vnto; to destine, reserue, or purpose for.*
Se Desdire. *To vnsay, recant, retract, reuoke; forbid; contradict himselfe, go from his word.*
Desdommage. *as* Desdommagement.
Desdommagé: m. ée: f. *indemnified, saued harmelesse; discharged.*
Desdommagement: m. *An indemnitie, or indemnifying; a sauing harmelesse; an amends-making.*
Desdommager. *To indemnifie, saue harmelesse; discharge; make an amends vnto.*
Desdoré: m. ée: f. *vngilt; or whose gilding is worne off.*
Desdorer. *To vngild; to take the gold off.*
Desdormi. *Awaked; roused, raised from sleeping.*
Les mains desdormies. *Vnastonied, vnbenummed hands.*
Desdormir. *To awake, rouse, raise from sleepe; to quicken, vnbenumme, take away the drousinesse of.*

Desdormissement: m. *An awaking, rowsing, raising from sleepe; a quickening, or vnbenumming.*
Desdoublé: m. ée: f. *Vnlyned, whose lynings are taken out.*
Desdoubler. *To vnlyne, or take the lynings out of a garment.*
Desdouloir. *To leaue off sorrow, to surcease from mourning.*
Desduict: m. icte: f. *Discoursed, handled, intreated, dilated of.*
Desduire vn poinct. *To handle, intreat, dilate, or discourse of a point; See* Deduit.
Desduit: m. *Sport, pastime, recreation, delight.*
Desduite: f. *A Discourse; the handling of a matter; also, as* Deduite.
Desembarqué: m. ée: f. *Disimbarked.*
Desembarquement: m. *A disimbarking.*
Desembarquer. *To disimbarke, or vnload a ship; also, to land, or goe ashore out of a ship, &c.*
Desembarrassé: m. ée: f. *Disintangled, vnpestered.*
Desembarrasser. *To vnpester, disintangle; rid from intricatenesse, or troubles.*
Desembellir. *To disimbellish, disfigure, impaire the beautie of.*
Desembroché: m. ée: f. *Vnbroached, vnspitted.*
Desembrocher. *To vnbroach, vnspit; pull off the broach, or spit.*
Desembusché: m. ée: f. *Risen from an Ambuscadoe; gone, or gotten from among bushes.*
Desembuscher: m. *The place, or part of a Thicket, whereout wild beasts vse to goe into the Plaines.*
Se Desembuscher. *To rise from an Ambuscadoe; to rush vp from among bushes; to goe out of a thicket into plaine ground.*
Desemmuré: m. ée: f. *Dismmured; taken out of a wall wherein it was inclosed; also, vnwalled; or whose wals are taken downe.*
Desemmurer. *To take a thing out of a wall wherein it was inclosed; also, to vnwall, or take downe the walls of.*
Desempacqueté: m. ée: f. *Vnpacked; taken out of a packe, or packet.*
Desempacqueter. *To vnpacke, to vnloose a packe; to take out of a packe, or packet.*
Desemparable. *Partable, seuerable, seperable; depriueable; abandonable; disorderable.*
Desemparé: m. ée: f. *Disseised, depriued, dispossessed of; also, diuided, parted, seuered, seperated; also, left, quit, abandoned; also, disordered, vnsorted.*
Desemparement: m. *A disseising, depriuing, dispossessing; a disseisin; a leauing, quitting, abandoning; a loosing, or letting goe, the possession of; also, a seuering, parting, seperating; also, a disordering, or vnsorting of.*
Desemparer. *To disseise, depriue, dispossesse of; also, to seuer, diuide, part, put asunder; also, to disorder, or vnsort what lay in order; also, to leaue, quit, abandon.*
Se desemparer. *To loose, leaue, or let goe the possession of a thing; also, to be gone; to quit, or abandon a place.*
Desempartement. *A diuision, seperation; a diuiding, or departing from.*
Desempenné: m. ée: f. *Vnfeathered, whose feathers are pulled off.*
Desempenner. *To vnfeather; to pull the feathers off an arrow, &c.*
Desempesché: m. ée: f. *Disimpeached, cleered, disincombered.*
Desempescher. *To disimpeach, disincomber, cleere.*
Desempestré: m. ée: f. *Cleered, freed, vnpestered, disintangled.*
Desempestrer. *To vnpester, cleere, vntangle, free, deliuer from intricacie.*
Desempli: m. ie: f. *Emptied, or vnfilled.*
Desemplir. *To emptie, or vnfill; to lade, or shift, out of one thing into another.*
Desemplumé: m. ée: f. *Plumed; whose plumes are plucked, feathers pulled.*
Desemplumer. *To plume; to pull his plumes, to plucke his feathers off.*
Desemprisonné: m. ée: f. *Disimprisoned; freed, set at libertie, deliuered out of prison.*
Se Desemprisonner. *To free, or deliuer himselfe; to set himselfe at libertie, or get himselfe out of prison.*
Desenchainé: m. ée: f. *Vnchayned, or loosed from chaynes.*
Desenchainer. *To vnchayne, to loosse from chaynes.*
Desenchanté: m. ée: f. *Disinchaunted.*
Desenchanter. *To disinchaunt; to rid from charmes, or inchauntments.*
Desencloué: m. ée: f. *Vnnayled; vncloyed.*
Desenclouër. *To vnnayle; to vncloy; to take the nayles out of; also, to ease a horse that hath beene prickt in shooing.*
Desencordé. *Vncorded, vnstrung.*
Desencoulpé: m. ée: f. *Purged, or discharged from blame.*
Desencoulper. *To discharge from blame.*
Desendetté: m. ée: f. *Rid out of debt.*
Desendetter. *To bring out of debt.*
Desendormir. *as* Desdormir.
Desendormissement. *as* Desdormissement.
Desenduire. *To vndawbe; to bare; to pull the dawbing off; to discouer whats vnder a dawbing.*
Desenflé: m. ée: f. *Vnswelled; whose swelling is abated, or assuaged.*
Se Desenfler. *To vnswell; to assuage, fall, or wax lesse, after swelling.*
Desenforgé: m. ée: f. *Disinforged.*
Desenfourné: m. ée: f. *Drawne, or taken out of an Ouen.*
Desenfourner. *To draw, or take, out of an Ouen.*
Se Desenfrongner. *To looke cheerefully, to leaue frowning.*
Desengagé: m. ée: f. *Disingaged, redeemed.*
Desengager. *To disingage, vngage, redeeme.*
Desengeancé: m. ée: f. *The race whereof is extinguished.*
Desengeancer. *To ruine, or extinguish the race of.*
Desengé: m. ée: f. *Extirpated, or destroyed, as a noysome plant.*
Desenger. *To root vp, to plucke vp by the root; to destroy an euill impe, a noysome plant.*
Desengigné: m. ée: f. *Disinchanted, deliuered from inchauntments.*
Desengourdi: m. ie: f. *Vnbenummed, awaked, restored from sleepinesse, or clumpsinesse, to sence.*
Desengrossir. *A full-bellied women to miscarrie.*
Desenhorté: m. ée: f. *Dehorted, disswaded.*
Desenhorter. *To dehort, disswade, aduise to the contrarie of.*
Desenhorteur: m. *A dehorter, disswader.*
Desennuyance: f. *Pastime, sporting, driuing away of time, or of trouble.*
Desennuyé: m. ée: f. *Cheered vp, deliuered from heauinesse,*

heauinesse, irksomenesse, carke, or care.
Desennuyer. *To expell wearinesse, or tediousnesse; to driue away heauinesse, carke, or care.*
Desenrouillé: m. ée: f. *Skowred, furbushed, or cleansed from rust.*
Desenrouiller. *To skowre, furbush, or take the rust from.*
Desenroulé: m. ée: f. *Cassed, put from his wages, rased out of the roule, or list of; also, vnrouled, vnfoulded.*
Desenrouler. *To vnfold, or vnroule; as* Desrouler; *also, to casse, discharge, put out of the rowle, or list of.*
Desenseigner. *To vnteach, or teach otherwise then was taught before.*
Desenseveli: m. ie: f. *Vnburied, taken out of the graue.*
Desensevelir. *To vnburie, to take out of a graue.*
Desensorcelé: m. ée: f. *Vnbewitched, exorcised.*
Desensorceler. *To vnbewitch, exorcise, rid from sorcerie.*
Desentassé: m. ée: f. *Vnheaped; taken off a heape.*
Desentasser. *To vnheape, vnload; take off a heape, or load.*
Desenterré: m. ée: f. *Disinterred, vnburied.*
Desenterrer. *To vnburie, to take out of the earth againe.*
Desentortillé: m. ée: f. *Vntwisted, vnwrithen, vnwouen.*
Desentourner. *To turne, or wind off; to take from about.*
Desentraillé: m. ée: f. *Paunched, bowelled.*
Desentrailler. *To paunch, to bowell, or vnbowell; to draw.*
Desenvelopper. *as* Desveloper.
Desenyvré: m. ée: f. *Made, or become sober, (after drunkennesse.)*
Desenyvrer. *To rid from drunkennesse, to make sober againe.*
Desèqué. *as* Defequé.
Desert: m. *A Desart, a Wildernesse, a place vnfrequented, or abandoned of inhabitants.*
Desert. *as* Deserté.
Appel desert. *An appeale made before the time, or vnfitly, and out of time; or, an appeale neither begun, nor followed, as it ought to haue beene.*
Deserte: f. *Desert, merit;* Sans deserte. *Vndeseruedly.*
Deserté: m. ée: f. *Forsaken, desolate, desart, vnhabited, abandoned of all men.*
Deserter. *To make desart, to ruine a whole nation; of an inhabited place to make an vninhabited Wildernesse.*
Deserteur: m. *A forsaker, stragler, fugitiue; runneaway; one that abandoneth his friend, cause, or countrey.*
Desertion: f. *A leauing, abandoning, forsaking.*
Desertion d'appel. *An vnfit, vndue, or vntimelie appealing; an appeale vnseasonably begun, and vnorderly followed; also, a fayling in, or giuing ouer of, an appeale.*
Desertion de cause. *A Nonsuit, or letting fall of a Suit.*
Deservice. *Diseruice, a displeasure, ill office, bad turne.*
Deservi: m. ie: f. *Deserued, merited; earned.*
Deservir. *To deserue, to earne, to merite, (whether it be well or ill.)*
Deservir sus table. *To take away. See* Desservir.
Desesperable: com. *Despaireable, vnhopefull.*
Desesperade: f. *A kind of mournefull song.*
Iouër à la desesperade. *To set his whole rest, or set all on sixes, and seuens; to throw at all.*
Desesperance: f. *Desperatenesse, despaire.*
Desesperément. *Desperatly, hopelessely, in desperation, without any hope of helpe, or of successe.*
Desesperer. *To despaire; to be in despaire, or without hope.*
Desespoir: m. *Despaire, desperation.*
Desestimé: m. ée: f. *Disesteemed, neglected, set naught by.*
Desestimer. *To disesteeme, neglect, contemne, set naught by, make no reckoning of.*
Desestouffé: m. ée: f. *Vnstuffed, emptied, euacuated.*
Desestouffer. *To emptie, euacuate, vnstuffe.*
Desestourdi: m. ie: f. *Vnamased, recouered of, roused from, astonishment.*
Desestourdir. *To recouer of, or to rouse from, an astonishment.*
Desfacer. *as* Effacer.
Desfacher. *Looke* Desfascher.
Desfacilé: m. ée: f. *Put out of ioynt.* ¶Rab.
Desfaict: m. cte: f. *Vndone; broken; defeated, discomfited, ouercome; ruined, destroyed, ouerthrowne.*
Vn visage desfaict. *Growne very leane, pale, wan; or, decayed in feature, and colour.*
Desfaicte: f. *A defeat, or defeature; a discomfiture, or ouerthrow; also, a shift, excuse, euasion, auoidance; (Looke* Defaitte*) also, a riddance, dispatch, cleering the hands of, putting off.*
Il sçait ses desfaictes. *He is a very cunning Marchant, he will make shift for one.*
Desfaire. *To vndoe; breake; defeat, discomfit, ouercome; ruine, destroy, ouerthrow.*
Desfaire vn cerf. *To breake vp a red Deere.*
Se Desfaire de. *To rid, or deliuer himselfe from; to quit himselfe, to dispatch, or cleere his hands, of.*
Se desfaire soy mesme. *To murther, or make away, himselfe; to lay violent hands on himselfe.*
Assez faict qui s'en desfaict: Prov. *He does enough that rids himselfe of (a whore.)*
Desfait, & Desfaitte. *as* Desfaict, & Desfaicte.
Desfarouché: m. ée: f. *Reclaymed, made gentle, tamed.*
Desfaroucher. *To make gentle, to reclayme, or tame.*
Desfasché: m. ée: f. *Appeased, quieted, calmed; eased, comforted, lightened at the hart.*
Desfascher. *To appease, quiet; ease, comfort, lighten the hart; to take away loathing, or irksomenesse.*
Desfaveur. *Disfauor; want, or losse, of fauour.*
Desfavorisé: m. ée: f. *Disfauoured, out of fauour with.*
Desfavoriser. *To disfauor, not to fauour; to withdraw his fauor from, to banish from his fauour.*
Desfermé: m. ée: f. *Vnshut, layed open, disclosed; discouered.*
Desfermer. *To vnshut, lay open, disclose; discouer.*
Desferre: f. *An old suit of apparrell, cast clothes; also, as* Disferre; *also, an intangled, and vnprofitable businesse; also, a shift, or shifting.*
Ces gens sont de fascheuse desferre. *These are vnrulie, stubborne, obstinate, froward people; they are ill to be gouerned, hard to be pleased.*
Desferré. *Vnshod, or, hauing cast his shooes, as a horse; also,*

also, weakened, or depriued of his best helpes; of rich become poore.
Desferre-cheval. *The small pulse, or Hatchet Fetch, called Horse-shoe.*
Desferrer vn cheval. *To vnshooe a horse.*
Desferrer l'asne. *To ride the wild Mare.*
Se desferrer. *To contradict (and thereby betray) himselfe; also, to cast, or loose his shooes, as a horse.*
Desfi: m. *as* Defi; *a challenge, or hostile defiance.*
Desfiance: f. *A diffidence, or mistrust.*
Desfiant. *Distrusting; despairing in; mistrustfull; also, defying.*
Desfiché: m. ée: f. *Loossed, vnfixed, vnfastened.*
Desficher. *To loosse, vnfix, vnfasten, vnsettle.*
Desfiement: m. *A defying; also, a distrusting.*
Desfier. *To defy, to challenge vnto the combat.*
Se Desfier. *To distrust; or to dispaire.*
Se Desfier l' un de l' autre comme aveugles. *To mistrust, like two blind men, one another.*
Desfigurer. *See* Defigurer.
Desfilé: m. ée: f. *Vntwisted; vnwouen; rauelled; disordered.*
Soye desfilée. *Sleue silke.*
Desfiler. *To vntwist, vntwine, vnweaue, loosse, rauell; also, to vnranke, disorder; put off a file.*
Desfinancé: m. ée: f. *Depriued, vnfurnished, drayned, of treasure.*
Desflammé: m. ée: f. *Quenched, extinguished, put out, as a flame.*
Desflammer. *To quench, extinguish, put out the flame.*
Desfleurer. *To defloure; See* Defleurer.
Desfleuri: m. ie: f. *Whose flowers are cast, or shed.*
Desfleurir. *as* Defleurir.
Desfoncé: m. ée: f. *Knocked out, broken open, as the head of Caske.*
Desfoncer vn vaisseau. *To knocke out the head, or bottome of a vessell.*
Desfonser. *as* Desfoncer.
Desfortune: m. *Misfortune, misaduenture, mishap.*
Desfortuné: m. ée: f. *Vnluckie, vnhappie, vnfortunate.*
Desfouï: m. ie: f. *Digged out.*
Desfouïr. *To dig out.*
Desfrais. à frais & desfrais. *Defraying, or freeing of charges.*
Desfrayé: m. ée: f. *Defrayed, discharged, whose charges are borne.*
Desfrayer. *To defray, discharge, or beare the charges of.*
Desfriché. *as* Defriché.
Desfrichement. *as* Defrichement.
Desfricher. *To grub, shrub, rid the ground from rootes, bushes, &c; Looke* Defricher.
Desfroissé: m. ée: f. *Crushed in peeces.*
Desfroncé: m. ée: f. *Vnwrinckled, smoothed; cleered, or cheered vp.*
Desfroncer son visage. *To looke merrily; to cleere, vncloud, or vnwrinckle his visage, to shew a cheerefull countenance.*
Desfrongner. *as* Desfroncer, *or* Desenfrongner.
Desfroquer. *as* Defroquer.
Se Desfroquer. *To renounce, or abandon his Monkish habit, as* Luther *did.*
Desfroy: m. *A defraying, or bearing of charges.*
Desfuite: f. *An excuse, euasion, starting-hole, shift, cauil.*
Desfulé: m. ée: f. *Vncapped, vnmitred, vncouered, bare headed.*
Desfuler. Se Desfuler. *To put off his cap, hat, or miter; to be vncouered, or stand bare headed before.*
Desgagé: m. ée: f. *Vngaged, disingaged, redeemed.*
Desgagement. *An vngaging, disingaging; a redeeming, or fetching out of a gage.*
Desgager. *To vngage, disingage, redeeme; fetch out a gage, or pledge.*
Desgageur: m. *A disingager, or redeemer.*
Desgaine: f. *An vnsheathing, or drawing out, of a weapon.*
Il y marcha bien d'un' autre desgaine. *He proceeded in a farre quicker fashion; he went about it with another manner of resolution.*
Desgainé: m. ée: f. *Vnsheathed, drawne out of the sheath.*
Desgainée, & Desgainement. *as* Desgaine; *a drawing forth of the scabberd.*
Desgainer. *To vnsheath; to draw out of the scabberd, or sheath.*
Desgainnade: f. *An vnsheathing, or drawing of weapons; also, a bickering wherein edged tooles are vsed; also, a Purchase made, or Prize taken, by theeues, or pyrats.*
Desgarni: m. ie: f. *Disgarnished, vnfurnished of.*
Desgarnir. *To disgarnish, vnfurnish, depriue of, take away from.*
Desgarnir la terre. *A vassall to transport his moueables, or commodities out of his Lords territorie.*
Desgaroté: m. ée: f. *Vnbound, vnloossed, vnfettered, vntyed, deliuered from bands; also, torne, ragged, tattered; whence;*
Vn vallet desgaroté. *A Raggamuffian; and we say when the toes, or knees peepe out, they haue broken loosse, or broken prison.*
Desgasté: m. ée: f. *as* Degasté.
Desgaste-parcs. *Fould-rauaging, parke-wasting.*
Desgaster. *To wast, spoyle, make hauocke of, bring losse vnto.*
Desgelé: m. ée: f. *Thawed; melted, resolued.*
Se Desgeler. *To resolue, melt, thawe.*
Desgister vn lieure. *To put a Hare off her forme.*
Desglacé: m. eé: f. *Thawed; the ice whereof is melted.*
Desglacer. *To thawe, or take the yce of; to make warme.*
Desglouti: m. ie: f. *Gulped, or swallowed downe.*
Desgloutir. *To gulpe, or swallow downe.*
Desglué: m. ée: f. *Vnglued; loossed; seuered.*
Desgluer. *To vnglue, to loosse, to sunder, to seuer.*
Desgobillé: m. ée: f. *Spued, cast, vomited out; also, as* Desgozillé.
Desgobiller. *To spue, cast, or vomit.*
Desgofiller. *To rob.*
Desgonder. *Looke* Degonder.
Desgorgé: m. ée: f. *Disgorged, spued, vomited out; emptied, euacuated, voided; also, scowred, or cleansed from grease, &c by fulling.*
Desgorgement. *A disgorging, vomiting, spuing, casting; an emptying, euacuating.*
Le desgorgement d'un lac. *The mouth, or issue of a lake thats nourished by a Spring.*
Desgorger. *To disgorge, vomit, spue out, cast his gorge, vnburthen his stomacke; to void, euacuate, emptie; also, to scoure, or take out grease, &c by fulling.*
Desgouler. *To vomit, spue, cast, or put out of the throat.*
Desgourdi: m. ie: f. *Vnbenummed; suppled; made nim-*

nimble,gentle,pliant; also, dispatched, rid out of the way.

Desgourdir. *To vnbenumme; to quicken, reuiue, resolue a thing that is benummed,or stiffe with cold; also,to supple; to make,or wax nimble,gentle,plyant; also,to rid,or dispatch out of the way.*

Desgourmé: m. ée: f. *Vncurbed.*

Desgourmer vn cheval. *To vncurbe a horse.*

Desgoust: m. *as* Degout.

Desgousté. *Tastlesse,distastfull,without stomacke; nice, daintie; disdainefull, wayward, froward; loathing euerie thing, pleased with nothing; out of the humour with,hauing no mind vnto.*

Desgoustement: m. *A distasting, loathing, abhorring of meats; also, the strange lusting, or longing of women.*

Desgouster. *To distast,loath; dislike, abhorre; be out of humor with,haue no mind,nor maw vnto.*

Desgouziller. *To gulpe,or swill vp, to swallow downe.*

Desgozillé. *Whose throat is cut.*

Desgradé: m. ée: f. *Degraded, deposed, put from a place, or degree.*

Desgrader. *To degrade,or depose; to depriue of,or put from,a place, or degree.*

Desgrafé: m. ée: f. *Vnclasped, vngrapled, vnhooked, loossed from.*

Desgrafer. *To vngraple, vnclaspe, vnhooke; loosse, or sunder,things that are grapled.*

Desgraissé:m.ée:f. *Vnfattened,made leane; also,cleansed,purged,vngreased,rid of grease; also,rifled.*

Desgraisser. *To vnfatten; vngrease; rid of fat; purge from grease; make leane; or cleane; also,to rifle.*

Terre à desgraisser. *Fullers earth.*

Desgrapher. *as* Desgrafer.

Desgravir. *To fetch, or throw, downe a climbing thing.*

Desgressé; &, Desgresser. *as* Desgraissé, & Desgraisser.

Desgrossé: m. ée: f. *Lessened, subtilized,made small, fine,or lesse grosse; also,polished, refined, made handsome,brought into fashion.*

Desgrosser. *To lessen,vngreaten,subtilize, make small, fine,or lesse grosse;also,to polish,refine,make handsome, bring into fashion.*

Desgrossir. *as* Desgrosser.

Desguerpir. *Looke* Deguerpir.

Desguerpissement: m. *A quitting, leauing, abandoning,forgoing,giuing ouer of.*

Desguerpisseur: m. *as* Deguerpisseur.

Desguerpy: m. ie: f. *Quit, left, abandoned, forgone, yeelded vp,giuen ouer.*

Desguilleté: m. ée: f. *Vntrussed; or whose hose are depriued of their points.*

Desguilletter. *To vntrusse,vnty,or vndoe points; also, to take points from.*

Desguindé: m. ée: f. *Let downe, or let fall, from the height it was lift vp vnto.*

Desguinder. *To let downe, or let fall (a thing) from the height it was lift vp vnto.*

Desguisé: m. ée: f. *Disguised; dissembled, fained, counterfeited; adulterated, falsified, sophisticated.*

Desguisement: m. *A disguising; a dissembling, counterfeiting, faining; a falsifying, adulterating, sophisticating.*

Desguiser. *To disguise; to counterfeit, or set a false coat or glosse on; to alter, adulterate, falsifie, sophisticate.*

Se desguiser. *To faine,dissemble,counterfeit,be double, false, hollow-hearted; say one thing, and meane another.*

Desguiseure: f. *as* Deguisement.

Deshabillé: m. ée: f. *Disarrayed,vnclothed.*

Deshabiller. *To disarray,vncloth,make vnreadie; put, or take,off clothes.*

Deshabité. *Disinhabited,without inhabitants.*

Deshabiter. *To disinhabitate, or depriue of inhabitants.*

Deshaict: m. *Sadnesse, heauinesse, pensiuenesse; disquiet.*

Deshait. *as* Deshaict.

Deshaité: m. ée: f. *Sad,grieued,pensiue,heauie-hearted, depriued of ioy, deuoid of gladnesse; also, crasie, sicklie,vnhealthfull.*

Tu m'as deshaité. *Thou hast turned my ioy into sadnesse.*

Deshaitement: m. *Vnhealthfulnesse, infirmitie, sadnesse,pensiuenesse.*

Deshalé de famine. *Pined, withered, worne away through hunger; starued.*

Vn cheval deshalé. *Out of heart; haled, or tyred out.*

Deshanché: m.ée: f. *Whose hanches are broken, or put out of ioynt.*

Deshancher. *To breake,or put out of ioynt, the hips, or hanches.*

Deshanté: m. ée: f. *Disused,or not haunted as in former times; also, whose handle,or staffe is broken,or taken from it.*

Deshanter. *To forbeare his haunt; to leaue the companie of; also, to take from the head of a Speare &c the handle, or staffe thereto belonging.*

Desharnaché: m. ée: f. *Vnharnessed,vntrapped;vnfurnished,or whose furniture is taken off.*

Desharnacher. *To vnharnesse, or vntrap; to take off the furniture from a horse.*

Desheaulmé. *Bereaued of his helmet.*

Desheaulmer. *To take a helmet from the head.*

Desherance. *Want of heires; or,the inheritance of one that hath left no heire behind him; an Escheat for want of heires.*

Droict de des. *See* Droict.

Desheritance: f. *A disseisin.*

Desherité. *Disseised, disinherited,depriued of an inheritance.*

Desheritement: m. *A disinheriting,a disseising.*

Desheriter. *To disseise, disinherite, bereaue of an inheritance.*

Deshingandé: m. ée: f. *Lift,or throwne,off the hindges; out of frame,out of all order.*

Deshingander. *To lift,or throw,off the hindges; to put out of frame,bring out of all order.*

Deshonneste: com. *Dishonest, leud, bad; foule, impure, filthie,villanous; vnfitting,vnbeseeming, dishonourable.*

Deshonnestement. *Dishonestly, impurely, vilely, filthily, badly, leudly, naughtily, dishonourably, shamefully.*

Deshonnesteté. *Dishonestie, leudnesse, villanie,badnesse; filthinesse, impuritie; basenesse, vilenesse, vnseemelinesse.*

Deshonneur: f. *Dishonour, shame,reproach, infamie, disgrace,obloquie,discredit,ignominie.*

Deshonoration. *A dishonouring,discrediting,disgracing,defaming,traducing.*

Deshonoré: m. ée: f. *Dishonoured, discredited, disgraced,shamed,traduced,defamed.*

Deshonorement. *as* Deshonoration.
Deshonorer. *To dishonour, discredit, shame; defame, traduce, disgrace.*
Deshonté: m. ée: f. *Impudent, shamelesse, brasen-faced.*
Deshontément. *Impudently, shamefully, shamelesly.*
Deshousé. *Whose boots are pulled off.*
Deshouser. *To plucke off boots.*
Deshoussé: m. ée: f. *Whose footcloth is taken off.*
Deshousser vne mule. *To take off the footcloth from a Mule.*
Desia. *Alreadie.*
Des-ja. *So farre; or, thus farre.*
Desjanté: m. ée: f. *Vnstraked, as a wheele.*
Desjanter vne rouë. *To vnstrake a wheele, to pull the strakes from about it.*
Desiccatif: m. iue: f. *Desiccatiue; of power, or propertie to dry vp.*
Desiccation. *A drying vp.*
Desidence: f. *Idlenesse, nonresidencie.*
Desidieux: m. euse: f. *Idle, lazie, lither, slouthfull.*
Desjeuné: m. ée: f. *Whose fast is broken (in a morning.)*
Il a esté desjeuné de ce nouveau style. *He hath (to his cost) learnt what these new tearmes meane.*
Desjeuner. *See* Desjuner.
Designatif: m. iue: f. *Designatiue, denotatiue; appointing; shewing, declaring.*
Designé: m. ée: f. *Denoted, signified, shewed by signes, or tokens; also, designed, prescribed, appointed.*
Designer. *To denote, signifie, or shew by a marke, or token; also, to designe, prescribe, appoint; as,* Designer les limites de, &c.
Desinence: f. *A desinence, ending, closing; an end, or close.*
Desing: m. *A designe, purpose, proiect, priuat intention, or determination.*
Desinteressé: m. ée: f. *Discharged from; or, that hath forgone, or lost, all interest in.*
Desinteresser. *To discharge, or saue harmelesse; to rid from all interest in.*
Desjoinct: m. cte: f. *Disioyned; parted, seuered, seperated, sundered, diuided, disunited, vncoupled.*
Desjoindre. *To disioyne, disunite, part, vncouple, diuide, seperate, seuer, sunder.*
Desjoingnement: m. *A disioyning, disuniting, parting, seperation, diuision, seuering, sundering.*
Desioussé: m. ée: f. *Vnhusked.*
Desir: m. *Desire; a coueting of; a wish, wishing, or longing for; a fancie, affection, or appetite, vnto; a lusting after.*
Il commence bien à mourir qui abandonne son desir: Prov. *He that leaues to desire begins to dy.*
Desirable: com. *Desirable; fit, or worthie to be wished for.*
Desirant. *Desiring; coueting, affecting, wishing for, lusting after.*
Desiré: m. ée: f. *Desired, coueted, wished, or longed for; affected, fancied, lusted after.*
Pasques long temps desirées sont en vn iour tost passées: Pro. *(So that which was expected long is enioyed but little.)*
Desirer. *To desire; couet, wish, or long for; to fancie, affect; require; lust after.*
Desireux: m. euse: f. *Desirous, full of desire.*
Desisté: m. ée: f. *Desisted, ceased, forborne, left off, giuen ouer.*
Desistement: m. *A desisting, ceasing, forbearing, leauing off, giuing ouer.*
Desister. *To desist, cease, forbeare, leaue off, giue ouer.*
Desjuché: m. *Vnrousted; taken downe (as a bird) from the roust whereon it rested.*
Desjucher vn oyseau. *To vnroust, or take downe a bird from his roust, or pearch where he resteth.*
Desjuné: m. *as* Desjuner: m.
Desjuné: m. ée: f. *That hath broken his fast; Looke* Desjeuné.
Desjuner: m. *A breakfast, a mornings repast.*
Desjuner de chasseur. *A large breakfast, meale, repast.*
Desjuner. *To breake fast in the morning.*
Leuer matin n'est pas heur; mais desjuner est le plus seur: Prov. *There is more safetie in eating, then happinesse in rising, early a mornings.*
Deslabré: m. ée: f. *Torne, ragged, full of rags; also, all vnbraced, or loosely vntrussed.*
Deslabrer. *To teare, tatter, make ragged, or make rags of; also, to vnbrace.*
Deslacé: m. ée: f. *Vntyed, vnlaced, as a woman.*
Deslacer. *To vnlace; to vnty.*
Deslaché: m. ée: f. *Discharged; loossened; let goe, let fly.*
Deslacher. *To discharge, as a Gunne, or Crosse-bow; to let goe, let fly, let loosse.*
Deslaicté: m. ée: f. *Milked; also, weaned.*
Deslaicter. *To milke, or draw the milke from; also, to weane.*
Deslainé: m. ée: f. *Fleeced; whose wooll is pouled, or pulled off.*
Deslainer. *To fleece; poule, pill; despoyle of substance.*
Deslaitté. *as* Deslaicté.
Deslaitter. *To weane; to take from the damme, or nurse; or, as* Deslaicter.
Deslasché: m. ée: f. *Loossed, let fly.*
Deslascher. *To loosse, or let fly.*
Deslassé: m. ée: f. *Eased, refreshed, vnwearied.*
Deslasser. *To refresh; to ease after much trauell; to rid from wearinesse, or wearisome incumbrances.*
Deslaté: m. ée: f. *Vnlathed.*
Deslater. *To vnlath; to take, or pull, away lathes.*
Deslavé: m. ée: f. *Washed away.*
Deslavement. *A washing away; an inundation.*
Deslaver. *To wash away.*
Deslayé: m. ée: f. *Supled, softened, allayed; soaked, steeped.*
Deslayer. *To supple, soften, allay; soake, steepe.*
Desléement. *A softening, allaying, suppling; soaking, steeping.*
Desléer. *as* Deslayer.
Deslié: m. ée: f. *Vnbound, vnfettered, vndone, vntyed, at libertie, loosse, free.*
Deslier. *To vnloosse, vntye, vnbind, vndoe; to deliuer, to free, to rid from.*
On eust dit qu'il n'eust sceu deslier vne mousche. *One would haue thought that butter would not haue melted in his mouth.*
Desli-soing: m. *An Epithete of* Bacchus, *or Wine, which deliuers men from care, pensiuenesse, or thoughttaking.*
Deslogé: m. ée: f. *Dislodged; remoued, parted, or departed from an vsuall lodging.*
Deslogement: m. *A dislodging, remouing, shifting of an ordinarie lodging; a flitting, parting, or departure*

ture from an accustomed abode.
Desſlogement de vie. *A dying, deceasing, departing.*
Desſloger. *To dislodge, remoue; shift, flit, part, or depart from an accustomed lodging.*
Se desſloger. *The same.*
Faire desſloger de. *To vnnestle; to thrust, or driue, out of; to dispossesse, or disseise of.*
Desſloqueté: m. ée: f. *Ragged, torne, tattered.*
Desſloqueter. *To teare vnto rags, or tatters; to make clouts of.*
Desſloué: m. ée: f. *Dispraised; disallowed, reproued; also, loossened, or put out of it place.*
Desſlouër. *To dispraise, disallow, blame, reproove; also, to loossen, or put out of it place.*
Desſlouëure: f. *A loossing, mouing, or putting of a thing out of it right place.*
Desſloyal: m. ale: f. *Disloyall, vnfaithfull, trustlesse, trecherous, false, traiterous.*
Desſloyalement. *Disloyally, vnfaithfully, falsely, trecherously.*
Desloyauté: f. *Disloyaltie, trecherie, falsehood, faithlesnesse, vntruth, vnfaithfulnesse, infidelitie.*
Desſmaché: m. ée: f. *Vnchawed; also, blurted out.*
Desſmacher. *To vnchaw; also, to blurt out, by force, a secret, and concealed matter; or, as* Demacquer.
Desſmaçonné: m. ée: f. *Pulled downe, or taken asunder, as stone-worke.*
Desſmaçonner. *To vndoe, take asunder, pull downe, stone-worke.*
Desſmaillé: m. ée: f. *Vnmailed; vnlinked; vndone, cut in peeces, hacked vnto peeces, as a coat of maile.*
Desſmailler. *To vnlinke, vndoe, cut in peeces, or hacke to peeces, a coat of maile.*
Desſmailloté: m. ée: f. *Vnswathed, vnswadled.*
Desſmaillotement: m. *An vnswadling, or vnswathing.*
Desſmailloter. *To vnswadle, or vnswath; to loosse, or take, a child out of the swathing bands.*
Desſmaillure: f. *An vnmailing; an vndoing, tearing, or cutting, as of maile, in peeces.*
Desſmaintenant. *Presently, euen now; from henceforth.*
Desſmaisonné: m. ée: f. *Turned out of his house; thrust out of his owne dores; disseised, or dispossessed of his owne dwelling.*
Desſmaisonner. *To dispossesse, or disseise of his owne dwelling, to driue out of house and harbour; to turne out of his owne dores.*
Desſmanché: m. ée: f. *Loosse, disorderlie, vnhelued, off the hindges.*
Desſmanchement: m. *An vnhafting; a flying out of it haft, or helue; hence, any out-lashing, or vnrulie, disordinate, or disobedient, pranke.*
Desſmancher. *To vnhelue, or take off the helue, or haft from an axe, &c; also, to loossen, disorder, put out of frame; turne out of it right place.*
Desſmandibulé: m. ée: f. *Vniawed; whose iawes are burst, or put out of ioynt.*
Desſmandibuler. *To breake, or vnioynt the iawes of.*
Desſmantelé: m. ée: f. *Dismanteled.*
Desſmanteler. *as* Desſmanteller.
Desſmantellement: m. *A dismantling; razing, or beating downe the wals of a towne.*
Desſmanteller. *To take a mans cloake off his backe; also, to dismantle, raze, or beat downe the walls of a fortresse.*
Desſmarche: f. *A backe step; a stepping, or stirring backward; a setting of one foot behind the other; also, a stepping aside, a trauersing of ground; and (more generally, and most vsually) any pace, gate, or going; also, ward, fence, or the lying of the bodie in fencing; and the posture, or carriage thereof in any motion, or action whatsoeuer.*
Desſmarche de cordier. *A stepping, or going backward.*
Desſmarché: m. ée: f. *Stepped backe, remoued backward; that hath lost ground; thats gone, or put, from the place he held; thats recoyled, thats retired.*
Desſmarcher. *To step, or goe, backe; to plucke, twitch, or bring backe a step; to remoue a foot backward; to recoyle, retire, stirre from, giue backe, loose ground.*
Desſmarer. *To vnmoore; or, as* Demarer.
Desſmarié: m. ée: f. *Diuorced, vnmarried againe.*
Desſmarier. *To diuorce, vnwed, or vnmarrie.*
Desſmarquer. *To take away the marke from; or, to put from his marke.*
Desſmarrer. *as* Demarer.
Desſmasquer. *To vnmaske, discouer, pull, or take off his maske.*
Desſmelancolié: m. ée: f. *Vnmelancholized, rid of melancholie.*
Desſmelancolier. *To rid of melancholie, take away sadnesse; gladden, reuiue, cheere vp; comfort, solace.*
Desſmembré: m. ée: f. *Dismembred, peecemealed, rent, or torne from.*
Desſmembrement: m. *A tearing, dismembring, rending from, or in peeces.*
Desſmembrer. *To dismember, peecemeale; teare, mangle, cut, rend from, or in peeces; to make hauocke of.*
Desſmembrer son fief. *To sell, alien, passe away, or part with, a part thereof.*
Desſmenacer. *To vnthreaten, to reuoke a threat.*
Desſmenagé: m. ée: f. *Scattered as a familie, remooued as a houshold, broken vp as a house; also, transported, or shifted, as houshold-stuffe, from one lodging to another.*
Desſmenagement: m. *A dissoluing, or scattering of a familie, a breaking vp of house.*
Desſmenager. *To giue vp house, to dissolue, or scatter his familie, to remoue houshold; also, to transport houshold-stuffe out of one lodging into another.*
Desſmenter. *See* Dementer.
Desſmenti: m. *The Ly (giuen, or taken;) also, a little Stiletto, or sharpe-pointed dagger.*
Desſmenti: m. ie: f. *Digressed, or derogated from; proued naught, grown false; fayling in word, or of expectation; also, by whom, or to whom the Ly is giuen.*
En cette maison il n' y a rien de desſmenti. *This house is not a whit sunke, shrunke, or fallen into decay.*
Desſmentir. *To giue the Ly vnto; also, to fayle; digresse, or derogate from; proue naught, or false; doe contrarie to expectation.*
Se Desſmentir. *Looke* Se Dementir.
Vn bon arbre ne desſmentira poinct son fruict en sa saison. *A good tree will not deny it fruit, or will not fayle to yeeld it fruit, in due season.*
La maison desſment. *The house begins to faile, shrink, sinke, fall into decay.*
Desſmenture: f. *A fayling, decaying, shrinking, sinking.*
Desſmeslé: m. ée: f. *Loosed, opened, cleered, vnpestered, disintricated, disintangled; also, dealt in, handled, managed.*
Desſmeslement: m. *A loossing, opening, cleering, vnpestering, disintricating, disintangling; also, a handling, managing, dispatching of, dealing in, businesses.*

Desmesler. *To loosse, open, cleere, vnpester, disintricate, resolue, disintangle; also, to handle, manage; dispatch; and hence;*
Se desmesler de. *To determine, finish, dispatch; or, to rid his hands, get cleere of, vnwind himselfe out of.*
Vne chose à desmesler. *A matter to deale in, a course to meddle with, a thing to scuffle for.*
Desmesnager. *as* Desmenager.
Desmesuré: m. ée: f. *Huge, vnmeasurable, immense, infinite, exceeding great; enormous, excessiue, outragious, vnsatiable, vnreasonable; most vnrulie, vnbridled, lauish, disordered, immoderate.*
Desmesurément: m. *A hugenesse, immensenesse, vnmeasurablenesse, exceeding greatnesse; also, outragiousnesse, enormitie, vnsatiablenesse, vnreasonablenesse, extreame disorder, excessiue vnrulinesse.*
Desmesurement. *Hugely, immensly, vnmeasurably, exceeding greatly; outragiously, vnsatiably, excessiuely, most vnreasonably; the most out of square, out of rule, out of order that may be.*
Desmettre. *To displace, or put out of his right place, as a member out of ioynt; also, to dismisse, let goe, lay down; also, to depose.*
Se desmettre du bien qu'on nous a fait. *To return, send, or giue backe the good turne one hath done vs.*
Se desmettre d'un 'entreprise. *To abandon, leaue off, desist from, an enterprise.*
Se desmettre d'un'office. *To resigne, surrender, giue ouer, an office.*
Desmeu: m. euë: f. *Remoued, altered, put off; desisting from.*
Desmeublé: m. ée: f. *Disfurnished, or depriued of moueables.*
Desmeubler. *To vnfurnish, or depriue of moueables; to take away the houshold-stuffe from a place.*
Desmis: m ise: f. *Displaced, deposed; misplaced, put out of due place; also, dismissed, resigned, let goe, left off, giuen ouer; also, submitted, humbled, submissiue.*
Desmission: f. *A demission, deposition; a displacing, misplacing; a resignation; dismissing, forgoing.*
Desmission de foy. *An acknowledgement of tenure made by the tenant vnto his Land-lord; a submission, or humbling of himselfe.*
Desmoelé: m. eé: f. *Emptied, or depriued of marrow; weakened.*
Desmoeler. *To emptie, or depriue of marrow; hence, also, to weaken.*
Desmonté: m. ée: f. *Dismounted; taken, or lift off; cast, or throwne downe.*
Desmonter. *To dismount; to take, or cast, or lift, off; also, to discend, or goe downeward.*
Desmonter vn canon. *To dismount, or throw downe a Canon with counter-batterie; also, to take it off the carriages.*
Desmonter vn'espee. *To take it out of the hilts.*
Desmonter vn homme. *To vnhorse a man.*
Desmonter vne navire. *To disarme a ship, to despoile her of all her munition, and furniture.*
Desmorché. *Without powder in his touch-hole:* ¶Rab.
Desmordre. *To distast; to part from; to forgoe, giue ouer, loose, let go his hold.*
Desmouvoir. *To remoue, displace, driue backe, put from.*
Se desmouvoir de. *To decline, swarue, change, bee carried from.*
Desmuni: m. ie: f. *Vnfurnished, disgarnished, vnprouided, left bare of.*

Desmunir. *To vnfurnish, disgarnish, leaue bare, or vnprouided of.*
Desnaturé: m. ée: f. *Vnnaturall, churlish, vnkind, without naturall affection; also, weakened through the lessening, or losse of nature; also, vnnaturalized vpon his owne petition, or by renouncing publickly, and to that end, his naturall Prince, and countrey.*
Desnaturer. *To make vnnaturall; to weaken in nature; to renounce his naturall Prince, or Countrey, to th'end he may liue where, and vnder whom, he list.*
Desnervé: m. ée: f. *Bereaued of sinewes, or of strength.*
Desnerver. *To bereaue of sinewes, or strength; to weaken, enfeeble, debilitate.*
Desni: m. *A nay, denyall, denying.*
Desniaisé: m. ée: f. *That hath beene extreamely cheated, or gulled; also, purged of the foole, that hath seene the Lyons; made wise, taught wit, by costlie experience, or by many tricks put vpon him.*
Desniaiser. *To cousen, cheat, gull of; also, to purge of the foole; to make wise, or teach wit by often deceiuing, or putting many tricks vpon.*
Se Desniaiser; *or* Desniaiser *(without* se.*) To put off childishnesse, learne wit, gaine experience, by hauing beene often cheated, or much gulled.*
Desniaseur: m. *A cousener, guller, cheater, connycatcher; or, one that makes th' ignorant grow cunning by cousening them.*
Desniché: m. ée: f. *Vnneasted, or vnneastled; driuen, chased, or plucked out of a neast, hole, or hold.*
Desnicher. *To vnneastle; to driue, chase, or plucke out of a neast, hole, or hold.*
Desnigration: f. *A defaming, slaundering, discrediting; a blemishing, or blotting the good name of.*
Desnigré: m. ée: f. *Defamed, traduced, reproached, discredited, whose good name is foulely stained, or blemished.*
Desnigrement: m. *as* Desnigration.
Desnigrer. *To defame, traduce, reproach, discredit, blemish, or blot the good name of.*
Desnoüé: m. ée: f. *Loossed, dissolued, vnknit, vnbound; vnfolded, resolued; out of ioynt.*
Desnouëment: m. *An vntying, vnknitting, vnbinding (of knots;) a putting out of ioynt.*
Desnouër. *To vnknit, vnbind, vnty; dissolue, resolue; to explicate, manifest, vnfould.*
Se Desnouër quelque membre. *To loosse the bone thereof, or put it out of ioynt.*
Desnoüeure: f. *as* Desnouëment; *also, a part, or member of the bodie, thats out of ioynt.*
Desnué: m. ée: f. *Bared, stripped; bereaued, depriued; voided, or deuoid of; cleane without.*
Vn enfant desnué. *Bared of flesh, that hath nought but skin and bone left on it.*
Desnuër. *To bare, strip, turne naked, bereaue, depriue, or void of.*
Desobeïr. *To disobey, resist authoritie; be stubborne, restie, vnrulie.*
Desobeïssance: f. *Disobedience, stubbornnesse, headinesse, wilfulnesse, restinesse, vnrulinesse.*
Desobeïssant. *Disobedient; stubborne, vnrulie, restie, self-willed; sullen; hard, stif, vnpliant.*
Desobligé: m. ée: f. *Disobliged; discharged, from all obligation, or behouldingnesse.*
Desobliger. *To disoblige; to release, or discharge of a bond, to acquit of an obligation.*
Desolation: f. *Desolation, deuastation, extreame solitarinesse, or lonelinesse; vtter ruine, or destruction.*

Desolé: m. ée: f. *Desolate, deavelie, desart; made solitarie; abandoned of all comfort, or companie.*
Desolemént: m. *A desolating, extreame wasting, making desart, or solitarie; a ruining, vtter destroying.*
Desolément. *Desolately, solitarily; without solace, comfort, or companie.*
Desoler. *To desolate; make lonelie, solitarie, deavelie, or desart; to deuast, wast extreamely, ruine vtterly.*
Desoppilé: m. ée: f. *Vnstopped, set open.*
Desoppiler. *To vnstop, vnshut, or set open.*
Desordonnance: f. *Disarray, disorder, breach of order, confusion.*
Desordonné: m. ée: f. *Disorderlie, disordinate, vnrulie, disordered, outragious, vnbridled, out of all good compasse.*
Desordonnément. *Disorderly, disordinately, disorderedly, vnrulily, outragiously, without meane, without measure, without any manner of order.*
Desordre: m. *Disorder, confusion, vnrulinesse, licentiousnesse, excesse.*
Desoreres. *From henceforth.*
Desormais. *Yet; for all that; also, from henceforth.*
Desossé: m. ée: f. *Vnboned; whose bones are taken out.*
Desosser. *To take out, or away, the bones from; to depriue of bones.*
Desourat. *Deflowred before her time.* ¶Langued.
Desourdi: m. ie: f. *Vnwouen; vnwound; done, and vndone.*
Desourdir. *To vnweaue; vnwind; to doe, and vndoe, or vndoe what is alreadie done.*
Despaïsé: m. ée: f. *Banished, or driuen out of his naturall countrey; also, growne courtlie, or hauing left rude countrey fashions.*
Despaïsement: m. *The abandoning of, or driuing one out of, his naturall countrey; also, a leauing of rude countrey fashions.*
Despaïser. *To driue, or send out of his naturall country; See* Depaïser.
Despaistre. *To feed, graze, pasture.*
Despampé: m. ée: f. *Bared, as a Vine, of leaues.*
Despamper. *To vnleafe, bare of leaues, pull the leaues off a Vine &c.*
La vigne, ou la Rose, se despampe. *Sheeds her leaues, or leauie branches.*
Despamprer. *as* Despamper.
Despaqueté: m. ée: f. *Vnpacked; broken open as a packe, or packet.*
Despaqueter. *To vnpacke; to rifle, open, or breake vp a packet.*
Desparagé: m. ée: f. *Disparaged.*
Desparager. *To disparage; to offer vnto, or impose on, a man vnfit, or vnworthie conditions.*
Despartement. *as* Departement.
Despartir. *Looke* Departir.
Se despartir. *To be diuided; to part, or goe asunder.*
Desparty. *as* Departi.
Despecé: m. ée: f. *Dismembred, peecemealed, cut in peeces; pulled, plucked, rent, or torne asunder.*
Despecé à grands coups d'injures. *Extreamely reuiled, cruelly ratled, horribly railed on.*
Despecement: m. *A dismembring, peecemealing, or cutting in peeces; a pulling, breaking, rending, or tearing asunder.*
Despecer. *To dismember, peecemeale, cut in peeces, breake into parcels; pull, plucke, rend, or teare asunder.*
Despecer son fief. *as* Desmembrer son fief.
Despeinct: m. cte: f. *Vnpainted; whose painting is defaced, luster decayed, colours worne, or blotted, out; also, as* Depeinct.
Despeindre. *To vnpaint; to deface, blemish, raze, blot, or put out, things painted.*
Despeint. *as* Despeinct.
Despenaillé: m. ée: f. *Ragged, torne, tattered; full of clouts, rags, tatters.*
Despence: f. *A larder, storehouse, gardemanger; also, houshold wine; or, small wine mingled with water.*
Despencé: m. ée: f. *Dispended, expended, spent; bestowed, or disposed of.*
Despencer. *To dispend, spend, expend; bestow, dispose of.*
Despencerie: f. *A Spence, Larder, Storehouse, for victuals.*
Despendance: f. *A dependancie; a relying, or hanging on.*
Despendeur: m. *A spender, lauisher, spend-thrift, wast-good, riotous or prodigall fellow.*
Despendeux: m. euse: f. *Spendfull, wastfull, riotous, lauish, prodigall, expensiue.*
Despendre: m. *(Substantiuely) spending, expence; as in this Prouerbe:*
Au despendre gist le profit. *There's gaine made by (some) spending; or, (not much vnlike our) Euer spare and euer bare; Looke* Profit.
Despendre. *To dispend, spend, expend, disburse; bestow, imploy, lay out vpon; also, as* Dependre.
Despendre tout. *To wast, consume, or squander all away.*
Despendre trop. *To prodigalize it, lauish, or lash out.*
Autant despend chiche que large: Prov. *Looke* Chiche.
Prou despendre, & peu gaigner saccage le mesnager: Pro. *Lauish expence and little gaine put a house-keeper to much paine.*
Ce que chiche espargne large despend: Pro. *That which the wretch doth spare the waster spends.*
Qui bien gaigne, & bien despend, ne luy faut bourse à mettre argent: &, Qui plus despend qu'il ne pourchasse, il ne luy faut pas de besace: Pro. *He that spends all he gets, or, prodigall, wasts any more, needs not a purse with the rich (but may need a scrip with the poore.)*
Qui plus qu'il n'a vaillant despend, il fait la corde à quoy se pend: Pro. *He that spendeth aboue his abilitie, may at length hang himselfe with great agilitie.*
Trop tard se repend qui tout despend: Prov. *When all's consum'd repentance comes too late; or, repentance is neuer in season with one thats euer an vnthrift.*
Despendu: m. uë: f. *Dispended, spent, expended; bestowed, imployed, layed out vpon; also, prodigalized, lauished, lasht out; wasted, consumed, squandered away.*
Despens: m. *Expence, cost, charge; or, expences, disbursements, layings out, costs, and charges.*
Maison de despens. *Looke* Maison.
Despensaire: m. *as* Dispensaire.
Despense: f. *Charge, cost, expence; or, an expending, dispending, or laying out of money; also, as* Despence.
Despensé: m. ée: f. *Dispended, spent, expended; disposed of.*
Despenser. *To dispend, spend, expend; bestow, dispose of.*
Despensier: m. *A spender, waster, prodigall, spend-thrift, wast-good; also, a cater, or clarke of a Kitchin.*

Despensier: m. ere: f. *Spending, expensiue, spendfull, prodigall, vnthriftie, wastfull; excessiue in, lauish of, expence.*
Despensiere: f. *as* Despencerie; *also, a woman cater, keeper, or disposer of victuals.*
Desperché: m. ée: f. *Vnpearched; throwne, beaten, or fetched, off a pearch.*
Despercher. *To vnpearch; to throw, beat, or fetch, off a pearch.*
Desperonné: m. ée: f. *Without spurres.*
Desperonner. *To depriue of spurres.*
Despersuadé: m. ée: f. *Dissuaded.*
Despersuader. *To dissuade.*
Despesche: f. *A dispatch, hast, riddance; discharge.*
Despesché: m. ée: f. *Dispatched, hastened, rid, sent away quickly; also, deliuered, freed, discharged.*
Despescher. *To hasten, dispatch, rid, send away quickly; to take a speedie course with, make a speedie end of; also, to deliuer, free, discharge; Looke* Depescher.
Despescher au petit point. *To canuasse throughly, curry soundly, take vp for halting.*
Despessi: m. ie: f. *Vnthickened, or made thinne; also, clarified.*
Despessir. *To vnthicken, or make thinne; also, to clarifie.*
Despestré: m. ée: f. *Vnpestered, cleered, disintangled; vnwound, vnfoulded, rid out of.*
Despestrer. *To vnpester, disintangle; vnfould, vnwind, cleere, deliuer, rid out of.*
Despeuplé: m. ée: f. *Dispeopled, or vnpeopled, disinhabited.*
Despeupler. *To dispeople, or vnpeople; to disinhabite.*
Despié. *as* Depié.
Despieça. *Long agoe.*
Despiecé, Despiecement, & Despiecer; *Looke* Despecé, Despecement, *&* Despecer.
Despit: m. *Despight, spight, anger, spleene, stomacke, vexation.*
Il n'est si grand despit que de pauvre orgueilleux: Prov. *There's no despight to that of a proud beggar.*
Despitant. *Despighting, spighting; angring, vexing, chafing.*
Despité: m. ée: f. *Angrie, vexed, fuming, chafing, snuffing at; offended, moodie, much moued.*
Despiter. *To despight, spight, or doe a thing in spight of.*
Se despiter. *To be exceeding angrie; to fret, fume, chafe, stomacke extreamely; to take in great scorne, dudgeon, or snuffe.*
Despiteusement. *Despightfully, most angrily, moodily; maliciously; with great spleene, or spight.*
Despiteux: m. euse: f. *Testie, fumish, despightfull, stomackfull, exceeding angrie, or moodie; full of spleene, or spight.*
Despitonné: m. ée: f. *Wayward; coy, squeamish.*
Desplacé: m. ée: f. *Displaced, or put from his place.*
Desplacer. *To displace; to put from a place; also, to part, or depart from a place.*
Fol se doit nommer en face qui bien assis se desplace: Prov. *Looke* Fol.
Desplaire. *To displease, dislike, offend, anger, vex, grieue.*
Qu'il ne vous desplaise. *By your leaue, with your fauour, on good tearmes be it.*

Desplaisance: f. *Greefe, vnpleasantnesse, anguish, heauinesse; also, a displeasure, or ill turne; as* Desplaisir.
Desplaisant. *Displeasing, offensiue, troublesome, vnpleasant, irkesome.*
Estre desplaisant de. *To take in ill part, or, not to be well contented with.*
Desplaisir: m. *A displeasure, offence, bad office, ill turn; affront, wrong, iniurie; trouble; preiudice.*
Desplanché: m. ée: f. *Vnfloored, or, whose floore is taken vp.*
Desplancher. *To take, or pull vp the (boorded) floore of.*
Desplanté: m. ée: f. *Displanted, plucked vp by the root; vnplanted, vnset, remoued.*
Desplanter. *To displant, or plucke vp by the root; to vnplant, vnset, remoue.*
Desplié: m. ée: f. *Displayed, vnplaited, vnfoulded; manifested, made plaine, layed open, spread abroad.*
Despliement: m. *An vnfoulding; displaying, vnplaiting; plaining; manifesting; opening, discouering.*
Despliement des jambes. *The nimblenesse of the legges; or, a nimble bestirring, or gathering vp thereof.*
Desplier. *To display, vnplait, vnfould; manifest, make plaine, lay open, spread abroad.*
Desplier les jambes. *To runne lightly, nimbly to bestirre, or gather vp, his legges.*
Desplissé: m. ée: f. *Vnfoulded, vnplaited, vnwrinckled.*
Desplisser. *To vnfould, vnplait; vnwrinkle, vncrumple; smooth, plaine; Looke* Deplicer.
Desplissure: f. *An vnfoulding, vnplaiting, vnwrinckling, vncrumpling; a smoothing, plaining, making plaine.*
Desplorable: com. *Lamentable, deploreable; remedilesse, desperate, past all recouerie.*
Desploré. *See* Deploré.
Desployé: m. ée: f. *Displayed, opened, vnfoulded, spred abroad.*
'A voile desployée. *With might and maine; as fast, or as much, as one can.*
Desployer. *as* Desplier; *to vnfould, or lay open vnto view, as a Marchant his wares, or a pedler his packe, in a Market.*
Desplumation. *Looke* Deplumation.
Desplumé: m. ée: f. *Plumed, or bereft of feathers.*
Desplumer. *To plume, or depriue of feathers.*
Despluvié. Toicts despluviez, (C'est à dire, faicts en dos d'Asne.) *Looke vnder* Dos.
Despoché: m. ée: f. *Vnpouched, or, drawne out of a pouch.*
Despocher. *To vnpouch, draw out of a pouch, or pocket.*
Despoissé: m. ée: f. *Vnpitched.*
Despoisser. *To vnpitch, or get the pitch from.*
Despossedé: m. ée: f. *Dispossessed; put out of possession.*
Desposseder. *To dispossesse, to put out of possession.*
Despote: m. *A Despote; the chiefe, or soueraigne Lord of a Countrey.*
Despouille: f. *A bootie, prey, spoyle, pillage taken from enemies; also, the skin, fell, or hide of a beast; also, a Tiring-house in Tenis-Courts; the roome wherein such as intend to play may attire themselues for the purpose.*

La despouille d'arbres. *Their fruit, leaues, barke, boughes.*

Les despouilles de bastimens. *All kind of rubbish.*

Les despouilles de iardins. *Weedes; withered, or dead hearbes; refuse, or out-cast staulkes, leaues, &c.*

La despouille de terres. *Corne, hay; all kind of fruits comming in by Husbandrie; or of themselues yeelded by, or otherwise gotten within, grounds.*

La despouille de vignes. *Grapes.*

Despouillé: m. ée: f. *Stript, disarrayed, vnclothed; despoyled, depriued, vnfurnished of; robbed, pilled, polled; also, flayed, mued, vncoated.*

Despouille-autels. *Sacrilegious, altar-spoyling, church-despoyling.*

Despouillement. *A despoyling, taking off, or away; a stripping, disarraying; depriuing, or vnfurnishing of; a flaying; a muing, a casting of the skin, or coat.*

Despouiller. *To strip, vncloth, disarray; to despoyle, take away, vnfurnish, depriue, or bare of; to rob, pill, pole, spoyle; also, to flay, or take the skin off.*

Despouiller vn cerf; *to breake vp a Deere.*

Se Despouiller. *To vncloth himselfe; to mue himselfe; to cast his coat, or skin.*

Se despouiller avant que se coucher; *to make his heires, in his life time, absolute Maisters of all he hath.*

On ne peut despouiller vn homme nud: Prov. *Of a naked man who can haue clothes? Where there is nothing, the King looses his rights.*

Despoulser. *To expulse, or thrust out of.*

Despourpré: m. ée: f. *Whose (purple) hue is lost, altered, or decayed.*

Se Despourprer. *To loose it purple hue.*

Despourveu. *as* Desprouveu; *Vnprouided.*

Despravation. *A corrupting, deprauing, marring; a crooking, wrying, spoyling.*

Despravé: m. ée: f. *Depraued, marred, corrupted, spoyled.*

Despraver. *To depraue, corrupt, viciate, spoyle, marre; make crooked, wrest, wry to bad purposes.*

Desprendre. *To loosse from, to let his hold goe.*

Desprier. *To vnpray, disintreat; reuoke a suit, recall prayers, desire to the contrary.*

Despris: m. *Disesteeme, despisall, neglect, little regard, small respect, contempt, or disdaine of.*

Despris de Dieu. *Impietie, wickednesse, vngraciousnesse, extreame vngodlinesse.*

Desprisable: com. *Vile, base, despiseable, contemptible.*

Desprisé: m. ée: f. *Disesteemed, neglected, made light of, prised verie low; despised, disdained, contemned; also, dispraised, discommended, blamed, condemned.*

Desprisement: m. *A disesteeming, neglecting, low-prising; despising, disdaining, contemning; dispraising, blaming, condemning.*

Despriser. *To disesteeme, vilipend, neglect, make light of, set naught by, prize at a low rate; to despise, contemne, disdaine; also, to blame, condemne, dispraise, discommend.*

Despriseresse: f. *A disesteemeresse, despiseresse, or dispraiseresse of; a scornefull, or disdainefull, woman.*

Despriseur: m. *A disesteemer, neglecter, despiser, or dispraiser of.*

Desprisonné: m. ée: f. *Disimprisoned; deliuered from, got out of, prison; freed, set at libertie.*

Desprisonner. *To vnprison, or disimprison; to deliuer from, to get, or take, out of prison; to free; to set at libertie.*

Desprouveu: m. euë: f. *Vnprouided, vnfurnished; deuoid of, without.*

'A desprouveu. *At vnawares; without thinking of, or looking for; or, vnthought on, vnlooked for; napping, as Mosse tooke his Mare.*

Despucelé: m. ée: f. *Depucelated, deflowred, vnmaidened; depriued of, or that hath lost, her maidenhead.*

Espée despucelée. *That hath beene imbrued; that hath beene dipped in, or seasoned with, bloud; that hath drawne bloud.*

Despuceler. *To depucelate, deflowre, take the maidenhead of, depriue of her maidenhead.*

Despucellage: m. *Depucelage; a deflowring.*

Despucellement: m. *A depucelating, or deflowring; the taking of a maidenhead.*

Despumé: m. ée: f. *Scummed; clarified; whose foame, or froath is taken away.*

Despumer. *To clarifie; to scumme the foame, or froth, off.*

Desracher. *To plucke off, or teare away.* ¶Rab.

Desraciné: m. ée: f. *Rooted vp, or out; plucked vp by the roots.*

Desracinement: m. *A rooting out, a plucking vp by the root.*

Desraciner. *To deracinate, root out, or plucke vp by the root.*

Desraison: f. *Wrong, iniustice, vnreasonablenesse, want of reason.*

Desraisonnable: com. *Wrongfull, vniust, vnreasonable.*

Desraisonné: m. ée: f. *Without reason, bereft of reason.*

Desramé: m. ée: f. *Without boughes, or branches; whose boughes haue bene cut, and lopped off.*

Desramer. *To vnpearch, to plucke off, or pull downe from a bough; to rid, bare, or depriue of boughes.*

Desrangé: m. ée: f. *Disranked, disordered, disarrayed.*

Desranger. *To disranke, disarray, disorder; to thrust out of his ranke, put out of array; turne out of order.*

Desrayé: m. ée: f. *Disordered, out of order and array, out of his due place.*

Desreiglé: m. ée: f. *Vnrulie, disordered, outragious, vnbridled; vnmannerlie; immoderate, immodest; irregular, vnreasonable, vnmeasurable, out of frame.*

Desreiglement: m. *Vnrulinesse; disorder, outrage; immoderatenesse, immodestie, lauishneße, outlashing; irregularitie.*

Desreiglément. *Disorderedly, vnrulily, outragiously, immoderately, immodestly; out of square, beyond all meane, without all measure.*

Se Desreigler. *To be vnrulie, or vnreasonable; to disorder himselfe; to be out of order, out of all frame.*

Desrene: f. *A iustification, or proofe of the denyall of an act, or fact, wherewith a man is charged by his aduersarie.* ¶Norm.

Desrener. *To dereine; to iustifie, or make good, the denyall of an act, or fact.* ¶Norm.

Desreté: m. ée: f. *Vnsnared, freed, or deliuered out of a net.*

Desreter. *To vnsnare; free, rid, or deliuer out of a net.*
Desreumé: m. ée: f. *Whose rhewme is dried vp.*
Desreumer. *To dry vp the rhewme.*
Desridant. *Planing, smoothing; loossening, slackening.*
Desridé: m. ée: f. *Vnwrinkled, vnfolded; planed, smoothed; also, loossened, or slackened.*
Desridement: m. *A planing, vnwrinkling, vnfoulding.*
Desrider. *To vnfold, vnwrinkle, or take away wrinkles; to smooth, plane, or make plaine.*
Desrider les voiles, cordes, &c; *to loossen, or slacken the sayles, tackling, &c.*
Desrivé: m. ée: f. *Variuetted; also, ouerflowne, broken out of; or, ouerflowing, breaking ouer it bankes, or ordinarie channell.*
Desrivement. *An vnriuetting; also, an ouerflowing, breaking ouer, going out of it bankes, or ordinarie channell.*
Desriver. *To vnriuet; to loossen a nayle, or take out a pinne that is riuetted.*
Se desriver. *To ouerflow, breake ouer, goe out of it banks, or ordinarie channell.*
Desrobbant. *Stealing, filching, lurching, pilfering.*
Desrobbé: m. ée: f. *Stollen, filched, nimmed, lurched, pilfered; also, contriued.*
Enfant desrobbé; *that was begotten in Adulterie.*
Vn huis desrobbé. *A secret, or priuie dore.*
Desrobbée. à la desrobbée. *Priuily, secretly, by stealth, couertly, closely, vnder hand.*
Desrobbement: m. *Stealth; a stealing, filching, pilfering, nimming, lurching.*
Desrobber. *To steale, filch, pilfer, picke, nimme, purloine; slyly to lurch, priuily to take, secretly to withdraw, from.*
Desrobber la bosse à S. Roch; *Looke* Bosse.
Il est caut larron qui desrobbe à vn larron: Prov. *He is a cunning theefe that robs a theefe.*
Desrobbeur: m. *A theefe, stealer, filcher, pilferer, nimmer, purloyner.*
Desroché: m. ée: f. *Taken, or hewed out of a rocke; violently pulled, cast, beaten, throwne; also, fallen down, as the broken peeces of a rocke.*
Desrocher. *To beat, or hew out of a rocke; also, violently to pull, breake, throw downe; also, to fall downe, as the broken peeces of a rocke.*
Se desrocher d' un rivage. *Suddainely to put off from shore (as a ship that gets cleere off a rocke;) or, to part from the shore, as a ship from a rocke.*
Desroller. *To vnroule, to open a roule; or, as* Desrouler.
Desrompre. *as* Derompre.
Desrompu. *See* Derompu.
Desrondir. *To vnround, vnbow, vncompasse, bring out of roundnesse, or compasse.*
Desroqué: m. ée: f. *Ouerthrowne in wrastling.*
Desroquer. *To ouerthrow, as in wrastling.*
Desroté: m. ée: f. *Vntyed, vnbound.*
Desrougi: m. ie: f. *Growne pale, or decayed in rednesse.*
Desrougir. *To grow pale, to loose his rednesse.*
Desrouillé: m. ée: f. *Scoured, vnrusted, or, whose rust is got off, rustinesse taken away.*
Desrouiller. *To scoure, furbish, get out rust, fetch off rustinesse.*
Desroulé: m. ée: f. *Vnrouled, vnfoulded, layed open, displayed.*
Desrouler. *To vnroule, vnfould, lay open, display.*
Desroute: f. *A rout, breaking, discomfiture, putting to flight.*
Desrouté: m. ée: f. *Put, forced, or inticed out of the way; also, broken, discomfited, put into rout, vnto flight.*
Desroutéement. *Cleane awry, as one out of the way, as one thats put by, or driuen from, his way.*
Refuser tout desroutéement; *to refuse wholly, vtterly, altogether; or to put a demaunder, by an absolute denyall, cleane out of the way of renewing his request; or to breake his heart, or crush his hopes, by a resolute denyall.*
Desrouter. *To put by, driue from, intice out of, the way; also, to breake, discomfit, put into rout, or vnto flight.*
Desroy: m. *Disorder, disarray, vnrulinesse, confusion; or, as* Desarroy.
Desroyé. *as* Desarroyé.
Desroyer. *To disorder, disarray, driue out of order, put out of array; See* Desarroyer.
Desruer. *To goe amisse, or loose his way, in a towne; to mistake one street for another.*
Desrumé: m. ée: f. *Rid of the Rhewme, dryed vp as a Rhewme.*
Desrumer. *To rid, or dry vp, the Rhewme.*
Desruné: m. ée: f. *Disordered, disiusted, peruerted, vnfitly disioyned, ill-fauoredly taken asunder, or set together.*
Desruner. *To disorder, disiust, peruert, put out of fashion, or array, a thing which before was euerie way well fitted; ill-fauoredly to take asunder, or set together.*
Dessacré: m. ée: f. *Prophaned, vnhallowed, violated.*
Dessacrer. *To prophane, violate, vnhallow.*
Dessaisi: m. ie: f. *Disseised, dispossessed, depriued, bereaued, put out of.*
Dessaisine: f. *A disseisin, dispossession, depriuation, bereauement; a loossing, forgoing, or letting goe his hold of; in Law, most properly, a yeelding of possession; or the leaue giuen by the seller vnto the purchasor, to enter into the land sold.*
Se Dessaisir de. *To disseise, dispossesse, bereaue, depriue himselfe of; to forgoe, giue ouer, loosse, or let goe, his hold of.*
Dessaisonné: m. ée: f. *Vnkindlie, vnseasonable.*
Dessaler. *To vnsalt; make fresh; become fresh.*
Dessallé: m. ée: f. *That hath seene the Lyons; or, as* Desniaisé.
Dessanglé: m. ée: f. *Vngirt, or vngirthed.*
Dessangler. *To vngird; to loosse, or loossen, a girth.*
Dessarrier. *A woman to cast her child.*
Dessauvagé: m. ée: f. *Tamed, ciuilized, reclaymed, brought from wildnesse.*
Dessauvager. *To tame, reclaime, ciuilize, bring from wildnesse.*
Desseelé: m. ée: f. *Vnsealed.*
Desséeler. *To vnseale, take away the seale from, open a thing thats sealed.*
Desseigné: m. ée: f. *Designed, purposed, proiected.*
Desseigner. *To designe, purpose, proiect, lay a plot.*
Desseiller. *as* Desiller.
Desseing: m. *A designe, plot, proiect, purpose, determination; resolution.*
Dessellé: m. ée: f. *Vnsadled.*
Desseller. *To vnsadle.*

Dessemblé: m.ée: f. *Disassembled, disioyned, diuided, seperated.*
Dessembler. *To disassemble, disioyne, diuide, seperate.*
Dessenglé. *as* Dessanglé.
Dessengler. *To vngirth, or loossen the girthes of.*
Dessente. *The Gout proceeding from a rhewme.*
Desserpilleurs de passans. *Riflers, ransackers of passenger* ' *obbers by the high way.*
Desserre: f. *A suddaine loossing, opening, vnshutting; releasing, discharging, inlarging, or setting at large; a violent, or quicke letting goe.*
Desserré: m. ée: f. *Released, opened, vnshut, loossed, discharged, set at large.*
Desserrer. *To loosse, or set at large; to release, discharge, open, vnshut, vndoe.*
Dessert: m. *The last course, or seruice at table; of fruits, comfets, sweet meats, &c.*
Desserte: f. *as* Dessert; *or, the reuersion of a meale; also, merit, or deseruing.*
Desservice: f. *A disseruice, demerite, offence, ill office, misdeed.*
Desservir. *To doe one ill seruice, or bad offices.*
Desservir sus table. *To take away the table.*
Desserviteur: m. *A table-attendant, an ordinarie waiter.*
Desseveli: m. ie: f. *Disinterred, vnburied.*
Dessevelir. *To disinterre, vnburie, take vp, or out of the ground.*
Dessevré: m.ée: f. *Disseuered, parted, sundered.*
Dessevrer. *To disseuer, part, sunder.*
Dessiccatif. *as* Desiccatif. *Dessicatiue, or drying vp.*
Dessiegé: m. ée: f. *Freed from a siege.*
Dessieger. *To raise a siege, to free from siege.*
Dessillé: m. ée: f. *Vnseeled, vnhoodwinkt, whose eyes, or sight is opened.*
Dessiller. *To vnseele, vnhoodwinke; open the eyes of, restore vnto sight.*
Dessiner, *or rather* Deschirer. *To rend, or teare.* ¶Rab.
Dessing. *as* Desseing.
Dessoivé: m. ée: f. *Whose thirst is quenched.*
Se Dessoiver. *To quench the thirst.*
Dessolé: m. ée: f. *Vnsoled; the bottome of whose foot, or hoofe is pared quite away.*
Dessoler vn cheval. *To vnsole; to pare away, or wholly cut off, the bottome of a horses foot.*
Dessonger. *To breake off sleepe with a snort, or start; to awake out of a dreame, starting.*
Dessorcelé: m. ée: f. *Disinchanted, vnbewitched.*
Dessorceler. *To disinchant, vnbewitch, vnwitch.*
Dessoté: m. ée: f. *Vnbesotted; much quickened, or improued in vnderstanding.*
Dessoler. *To vnbesot; to quicken, refine, or cleere a dull vnderstanding.*
Dessoubs: m. *(Substantiuely)* le des. *The bottome, lowest, or vndermost part of.*
Dessoubs. adverb. *Vnder, beneath, below.*
S'en dessus dessoubs. *Vpside downe, topsie turuie, with the bottome vpwards.*
Dessoulde. En dessoulde. *Scattered, out of order, disarrayed, stragling.*
Dessouldé: m. ée: f. *Vnsoldered; vnloossed.*
Dessoulder. *To vnsolder, loosse, dissolue.*
Dessous. *as* Dessoubs.
Dessous-mis. Muscle des. *A muscle (in the inner part of the hand) whereby the fingers are bowed.*
Dessuëtude: f. *Disuse.*

Dessus: m. (substant.) le dessus de; *the Superficies, top, or vpper part of; also, the treble part, in Musicke.*
Le dessus d'un habit; *the outside of a garment (called so by taylors.*
Vn dessus de porte; *the haunse of a dore.*
Faire le dessus; *to sing the treble part; also, to play the Maister, ouerrule, dominiere ouer; and hence;*
L'homme fait la malencontre quand sa femme fait le dessus: Prov. *(Wherein there is a double meaning.)*
Dessus. (adverb.) *Aboue, ouer, vpon, aloft, on high.*
Dessus & dessoubs. *as* s'en dessus dessoubs; *in* Dessoubs.
Et bien, là dessus? *Well, what then? what of that? what came of that?*
Estre dessus; *to be on foot, or stand vp on his feet.*
Il est tout dessus; *he is vpon the head of it (a Bowlers phrase.)*
Leur estant tousiours dessus; *hauing alwaies the better of them, preuailing euer against them; also, being still vpon their Iacks.*
Estre au dessus du vent encontre; *to haue the wind, aduantage, or vpper hand of; to haue on the hip.*
Venir au dessus de; *to atchieue, compasse, obtaine, subdue, conquer, ouercome.*
Dessus-mis: m. ise: f. *Put ouer, set aboue.*
Destaché: m. ée: f. *Vntyed, loossed, vnbound; also, cleansed, or purged from spots.*
Destacher. *To vnty, loosse, vnbind; also, to take out, or purge from, spots.*
Destail. *as* Detail.
Destaillé: m. ée: f. *Cut, slit, gashed, hacked, nicked, notched; also, retayled.*
Destailler. *To cut, slit, gash, hacke; nicke, notch; also, to retayle, or passe away by parcels.*
Destaindre. *To staine, distaine, take away the colour of; or as* Desteindre.
Destampé: m. ée: f. *Vnpropped, whose tressles are taken from vnder it.*
Destamper. *To vnprop; to take the tressles from.*
Desteinct: m. cte: f. *Distained; pale, wan, bleake, illcoloured; whose dy is decayed, or colour lost.*
Desteindre. *To distaine; to dead, or take away, the colour of.*
Se desteindre. *To decay in colour, to loose it (liuelie) dy.*
Desteler les chevaux. *To vnloosse, vnteame, vnspang the draught horses.*
Destendre. *To vnbend, slacken, vnstretch, loosse, vndoe, or let downe.*
Destendre la Tapisserie. *To vnhang, or take downe Hangings.*
Destendu: m. uë: f. *Slackened, vnbent, vnstretched, loossed, vnhanged, let, or taken downe.*
Le temps est destendu. *The weather is opened, or begins to thaw.*
Destenture: f. *An vnbending, vnstretching, slackening, loossing, vnhanging, letting, or taking downe.*
Desterré: m. ée: f. *Digged, or taken, out of the ground.*
Desterrer. *To dig, or take out of the ground.*
Desthroné: m. ée: f. *Disthronized, deposed from a Throne.*
Desthroner. *To disthronize, or vnthrone; to depose from, or put out of, a Throne.*
Destiltre. *To vnweaue; or, as* Destitre.
Destin: m. *Destinie, fate; Gods prouidence, ordinance, purpose, or decree.*

Destination: f. *A destination, ordainement, appointment.*

Destiné: m. ée: f. *Destinated, ordained, appointed vnto, purposed for.*

Nul vent ne fait pour celuy qui n'a point de port destiné. *No helpe serues him that runnes vncertaine courses (or knowes not where to end them.)*

Destinée: f. *as* Destin.

Destiner. *To destinate, ordaine, appoint vnto; to purpose for.*

Destistre. *To vnweaue, vntwist, vnplait; loosse, dissolue, vndoe.*

Destituable: com. *Destituable; disappointable.*

Destitué: m. ée: f. *Destitute, vnfurnished, or disappointed of.*

Destituer. *To disappoint, abandon, forsake, faile at a pinch; to leaue destitute, or vnfurnished of.*

Destitution: f. *A destitution, or destituting; a leauing, failing, disappointing.*

Destitution de compagnie. *Lonelinesse, or solitarinesse, want of companie.*

Ils poursuyvirent la destitution d' aucuns Capitaines. *They sued to haue some Captaines cassed.*

Destombi: m. ie: f. *Vnclumpsed, vnbenummed, vnastonied; restored vnto warmth, sence, motion.*

Destombir. *To vnbenumme, vnclumpse, vnastonie; restore vnto warmth, sence, or motion.*

Destonnement: m. *A discord, or iarre, in sound; also, a changing of tune.*

Destonner. *To change, or alter, a tune; to take it higher, or lower.*

Destordement: m. *A wringing, writhing, wrinching, a crooking, bowing, bending awrie.*

Destordre. *To writh, wrie, crooke, wrinch, wring, bow, bend, wreath, turne out of the right way.*

Se destordre. *To stray, to erre, wander, decline from, or goe out of, the way.*

Destorse: f. *A writh, wrinch, wring; also, an errour; also, an erring, straying, or wandering out of the way; also, a by-way, side-way, or turning-way; also, misfortune, hinderance, incombrance.*

Destortillé: m. ée: f. *Opened, vnwrithen, vnwrapped, vnwound.*

Destortiller. *To vnwrith, vnwind, open, vnwrap.*

Destortoire. *as* Destournoire.

Destoupé. *Vnstopped, vnstoppelled.*

Destouper. *To vnstop, or pull the stopple out of.*

Destour: m. *A turning, by-way, crooked way; also, a blind corner betweene hills, or in a house, wherein men may hide themselues; also, a cunning shift, suttle euasion, craftie auoidance.*

Destourbé: m. ée: f. *Disturbed, troubled, impeached, hindered, interrupted, incombred.*

Destourbement: m. *A hindering, letting, stopping, impeaching.*

Destourber. *To disturbe, trouble, comber; let, hinder, interrupt; also, as* Destourner; *whence;*

Sans vous destourber gueres de vostre chemin. *without turning you much out of your way.*

Destourbeur: m. *A disturber, troubler; hinderer, letter, interrupter; a troublesome fellow, combersome ghest, prating, or busie companion.*

Destourbier: m. *A disturbance; comber, trouble, interruption, impediment, incombrance, let, hindrance.*

Entre la bouche, & la cuillier souvent advient grand destourbier: Prov. *Great lets oft thrust betweene the spoone and mouth; mischances happen when men thinke all sure.*

Destourné: m. ée: f. *Turned, declined, withdrawne, diuerted, alienated, disswaded, remoued, altered from; also, conueyed, filched, purloyned.*

Lieux destournez. *By-places, blind corners, vnhaunted roomes, deauelie habitations, solitarie lodgings, dwellings which stand out of all high-wayes.*

Destournement: m. *A turning, diuersion, diuerting; a withdrawing, disswasion, distraction; alienating, estranging, remouing from; also, a conueying, or pilfering away.*

Destournement de pieces de procez. *A cōcealing, or suppressing of bookes, or euidences.*

Destourner. *To turne, diuert, distract, auert, withdraw, disswade, remoue, alter, alienate, estrange from; also, to take away craftily, conuey away falsly, forestall with violence; to filtch, pilfer, conuert vnto his owne vse what was prouided for another.*

Se destourner de. *To forbeare the companie of; to withdraw his fauour, and loue from.*

Se destourner du chemin. *To erre, wander, swarue, goe astray, decline from the right way; or (as we say) goe by the way.*

Se destourner d'un dard. *To auoid, eschew, or bend from, a dart, by a nimble turning, or leaping aside.*

Destournoire: f. *A hunting-pole (wherewith combersome branches are turned aside by a wood-man passing through thickets.)*

Destourtoire. *as* Destournoire.

Destrabord. *Starboord; the right side of a ship.*

Destracqué: m. ée: f. *as* Destraqué.

Destracquer. *To put from a racke, or, to spoyle the rack, marre the pace, of; to put out of his racke, or pace; (Hence) also, to depraue, disorder, mislead, corrupt, seduce, or draw from honest courses; also, to slaunder, or detract from.*

Destracquer vn lievre. *To vntie the doubles of a Hare.*

Destrainct: m. cte: f. *Strained, pressed, wrung, vexed extreamely; also, straitened, restrained, abridged of libertie.*

Destraincte: f. *A narrow strait, or pinch; a hard, or extreame wring; also, a restraint of libertie.*

Destraincte d'amour. *The anguish, impatience, or extremitie of passion, in loue.*

Destraindre. *To straine, presse, wring, vexe extreamely; also, to straiten, restraine, or abridge of libertie.*

Destranché: m. ée: f. *Cut off, hewed from, hacked asunder, chopped in peeces.*

Destranchement: m. *A cutting off, hewing asunder, chopping in peeces.*

Destrancher. *To cut off, hew from, hacke asunder, mangle, or chop in peeces.*

Destrancher à coups de langue. *To reuile, reproach, rattle vp, raile on.*

Destrapé. *Beaten, or stamped with the feet; also, rid, or freed (as the feet) from intanglements.*

Destraper. *To beat, or stampe with the feet; also, to free, rid, or cleere the feet from the things intangling them.*

Destraqué: m. ée: f. *Put out of a racke, or pace; also, seduced, misled, corrupted, depraued, or drawne from honest courses; also, slaundered, or detracted from.*

Destraquer. *To spoyle the pace of, or put out of his pace; hence; to depraue, corrupt, mislead, seduce, or draw from honest courses; also, to slaunder, or detract from; Looke* Destracquer.

Destravé: m. ée: f. *Vnshackled, vngyued, vnfettered.*

Destraver. *To vnshackle, vngyue, vnfetter.*

Destrem-

Destrempé : m.ée : f. *Steeped, soaked, moistened, made fluide, liquid, or thinne; seasoned, or laied in water; softened, or allayed by watering.*
Destrempement : m. *A soaking, steeping; moistening, watering.*
Destremper. *To soake, steepe, moisten, water, season, or lay in water; soften, or allay, by laying in water; to make fluide, liquid, or thinne.*
Destrempis. *as* Destrempement.
Destrenché. *as* Destranché.
Destrencher. *as* Destrancher.
Destresse : f. *Distresse, perplexitie, anguish of mind, scarcitie in estate; a strait, narrow pinch, hard tearmes.*
Destrier : m. *A steed, a great horse, or horse of seruice; also, a kind of wafer.*
Destroict : m. *A strait; a narrow place, or passage; a narrow entrance into, or comming vnto, a way; a way between two hills; also, a narrow sea, or strait between two lands.*
Le destroict d'un Bailliage. *The iurisdiction, precincts, or liberties of a Bailiwicke.*
Destroict de la gorge. *The bottome of the mouth, or iawes, next aboue the* Larinx.
Destroit. *as* Destroict.
Destroquer. *To vntrucke; to alter, annihilate, or goe from, a change agreed on.*
Destrousse : f. *Spoyle, bootie, pillage, or baggage got from; a ransacking, or stripping of; a band made vpon, enemies; also, a hostile road, incursion, or inuasion wherin such bootie is got; also, a defeature, ouerthrow; beggering, or vndoing of people.*
Destroussé : m. ée : f. *Vntrussed, vntucked, vnpacked, vnloaden, vndone; also, robbed, ransacked, stripped, (& thereby) vndone.*
Destroussement : m. *An vntrussing, vnpacking, vnloading.*
Destroussement de gents. *A robbing, rifling, ransacking, (ruining) of people; a freebooting.*
Destroussément. tout destroussément. *Flatly, plainly; confidently, resolutely; or, quickly, speedily, hastily.*
Destrousser. *To vntrusse, vntucke; vnload, vnpacke, vndoe; also, to rob, rifle, strip, ransacke, despoile, all commers, or passengers; to freeboot, or boothale.*
Destrousseur de gens. *A robber, a ransacker of people by the high-way-side; one of S. Nicholas Clerkes; also, a freebooter, or boothaler.*
Destruction : f. *Destruction; an vtter subuersion, or deuastation; an absolute ruine, or ouerthrow of.*
Destruict : m. cte : f. *Destroyed: vtterly subuerted, or deuasted; absolutely ruined, or ouerthrowne.*
Destruire. *To destroy; ruine, subuert, ouerthrow; deuast, make desolate; rauage, or spoile, vtterly.*
Destruisant. *Destroying; vtterly subuerting, or deuasting; absolutely ruining, or ouerthrowing.*
Destruiseur : m. *A destroyer; a ruiner, subuerter, spoyler of euerie thing he deales with, or comes neere.*
Desvalizé : m. ée : f. *Rifled, stripped, robbed of all hee hath.*
Desvalizement : m. *A rifling, robbing, stripping.*
Desvalizer. *To rob, despoyle, rifle; strip out of all hee hath; to depriue of cloake-bag, bag and baggage.*
Desveiné : m. ée : f. *Bereft of all his veines, or bloud.*
Desveiner. *To bereaue, or depriue of all his veines; to sucke the bloud out of.*
Desvelopé : m. eé : f. *Vnwrapped, vnfoulden; opened, vndone; displaied, spread abroad; also, cleered.*
Desvelopement : m. *An vnwrapping, vnfoulding; vndoing, opening; manifesting, displaying, spreading open.*
Desveloper. *To vnwrap, vnfould; vndoe, open, shew forth, display, spread abroad; rid, vnpester, cleere.*
Desvely : m.ie : f. *Changed through sicknesse, or indisposition; whose face is so altered that a man can hardly know him.*
Desverdiat. *Deflowred, as a virgine that leachers:* ¶Langued.
Desverrouillé : m.ée : f. *Vnboulted.*
Desverouiller vn huis. *To vnboult, or vnsparre a doore.*
Desvesti : m. ie : f. *Deuested, vncloathed; disseised, dispossessed.*
Desvestir. *To vncloath, despoyle, depriue; disseise, dispossesse of.*
Se desvestir de. *To forgoe, leaue, giue ouer, passe away, dispossesse himselfe of.*
Desvidé : m. ée : f. *as* Devidé.
Desvider. *To wind thread &c, from blades into bottomes.*
Desvidoir : m. *A paire of blades, or yarnwindles.*
Desvié : m. ée : f. *Misled, put out of the way; also, dead, or deceased.*
Desvier. *To mislead, or put out of the way; also, to die, decease, or depart this life.*
Desvisagé : m. ée : f. *Deformed, disfigured; defaced; whose face is rent, or torne.*
Desvisager. *To deforme, disfigure, bereaue of feature; to deface.*
Desultoire. Chevaux desultoires. *Two horses (tied together) from the one whereof an actiue rider leapes vpon the other, in a full carecre; also, horses that bee led, and kept fresh for the vse of Souldiors, which in a fight haue tired those they serued on.*
Desumbré : m. ée : f. *Vnshaded, or depriued of the shadow.*
Desumbrer. *To vnshade, or depriue of shadow.*
Desuni : m. ie : f. *Disunited, disioyned, vncoupled, seuered, sundered.*
Desunion : f. *Disuniting, disunion, disiunction, seperation.*
Desunir. *To disunite, vncouple, disioyne, diuide, seperate, sunder.*
Desvoilé : m. ée : f. *Vnuayled, manifested, openly shewed.*
Desvoiler. *To vnuayle, discouer, manifest, take away the vayle from.*
Desvoyé : m. ée : f. *Misled, strayed; in an errour; brought out of the way.*
Chemin desvoyé. *An indirect, vnusuall, or vncertaine, way.*
Estomac desvoyé. *A loosse, weakened, or distempered, stomacke.*
Desvoyement : m. *An erring, wandering, straying one knowes not whither; a misleading.*
Desvoyement d'estomac. *Loosenesse, or weaknesse, of the stomacke.*
Desvoyement de riviere. *The turning of a riuer out of it vsuall course, or channell; also, a damme, or banke made for that purpose.*
Desvoyer. *To mislead, or bring out of the way.*
Se desvoyer. *To erre, stray, swarue, decline out of the way.*
Desusage : m. *Disusage, discontinuance.*
Desusitation. *A disusing, discontinuing, leauing off.*
Desusité : m. ée : f. *Disused, discontinued, left off, grown out of vse.*
Desusiter. *To disuse, discontinue, disaccustome, leaue off.*

Desyvré: m.ée: f. *Made sober againe.*
Desyvrer. *To make sober after drunkennesse.*
Det: m. *A dye to play with*; *See* Dé.
Detail: m. *A Peecemealing; a hewing, or cutting in peeces; (hence) also, retaile, small sale, or a selling by parcells, or in peeces.*
Detaillé: m. ée: f. *Peecemealed; cut into parcells, hewed in peeces (or, as* Destaillé;*) also, retailed, sold by retaile.*
Detailler. *To peecemeale, to cut into parcells, or peeces; (hence) also, to retaile, or sell by retaile.*
Detailleur. *A retailer, or tradesman that sells by retaile.*
Detalenté: m. ée: f. *Vnwilling, lustlesse, vndisposed, out of the humor, that hath no disposition vnto a thing.*
Detapper. *To vnbung, to open the bung-hole of:* ¶Blesien.)
Detendre. *See* Destendre.
Detenir. *To detaine, or withhold; also, to retaine, busie, occupie, stay, hold, continue in a place; also, to restraine, or keepe in.*
Detente d' arquebuse: f. *The Tent of a Caleeuer; the little peece of yron that keepes the Cocke vp.*
Detenteur: m. *A detainer; a wrongfull keeper of possession; a withholder of another mans right.*
Detention: f. *A detention; detaining, withhoulding; restraining.*
Detenu: m. uë: f. *Detained, withheld; restrained, kept in; busied, occupied.*
Detenuë: f. *as* Detention.
Detergent: m. ente: f. *Cleansing, scouring, rubbing away, wiping off.*
Deterioration: f. *An impairing, or making worse.*
Deterioré: m. ée: f. *Impaired, marred, spoiled; growne, or made, worse.*
Deteriorer. *To impaire, make worse, marre, spoyle, stroy.*
Determinance: f. *An order, decree, ordinance, sentence, determination; an ending, conclusion, determination of a matter alreadie debated.*
Determiné: m. ée: f. *Determined, resolued on, ended, concluded.*
Vn homme determiné. *A resolute, or couragious fellow; one that feares no dangers, dreads no colours.*
Determinément. *Resolutely, couragiously; also, with a full end, and conclusion of matters; determinately.*
Determiner. *To determine, conclude, resolue on, end, finish.*
Deterré: m. ée: f. *Digged, or taken out of the earth; also, disinherited, disseised, left landlesse.*
Deterrer. *To dig, or take out of the ground; also, to disinherit; depriue of, leaue without, land.*
Detersif: m. iue: f. *Detersiue; of a scouring, or cleansing qualitie.*
Detestable: com. *Detestable, execrable, abhominable, most odious, exceeding loathsome.*
Detestation: f. *A detestation, loathing, abhorring.*
Detesté: m. ée: f. *Detested, loathed, abhorred.*
Detester. *To detest, loath, abhorre, haue in abhomination.*
Dethroner, ou Dethrosner. *as* Desthroner.
Detiré: m. ée: f. *Racked, retched, or stretched out with violence; almost pulled in peeces.*
Detirer. *To racke, retch, or stretch out with violence; to pull almost in peeces.*
Detomber. *To vntombe, or take out of a tombe.*
Detordre. *To wrie, to writh, &c; See* Destordre.
Detouillé: m. ée: f. *Disincombred; also, disintangled, vnsnarled.*
Detouiller. *To disincomber, or vnpester; also, to vnsnarle, or disintangle; and hence;*
I'ay beaucoup à detouiller. *I haue much intricate, and shuffled, businesse to order.*
Detourbier. *as* Destourbier.
Detracter. *To detract from; to slaunder, backbite, depraue, dispraise, traduce, report ill of; disparage in speeches; raile on, reuile one, behind his backe.*
Detracteur: m. *A detractor; slaunderer, backbiter, deprauer; an ordinarie traducer, or disparager of others behind their backs; an ill-tongued, or foule-mouthed fellow.*
Detraction: f. *Detraction; slaunder, backbiting, deprauation, discrediting, misreport of, priuate disgracing, or disparaging; slaunderous speeches, reproachfull tearmes giuen of one behind his backe.*
Detrapper. *as* Destraper.
Detraqué: m. ée: f. *Out of the tract, iust path, right way; or, as* Destraqué.
Se Detraquer. *To put himselfe out of his path, or out of the way; Looke* Destraquer.
Detravé. le monde est tout detravé. *The world is cleane out of square, out of fashion, out of frame, out of order, off the hindges.*
Detrencher. *See* Destrancher.
Detresse: f. *Looke,* Destresse.
Detrichoüere: *as* Dextrochere; *also, the fould of leather wherewith yarne-winders preserue their fingers from skarres; also, the sharp Iron wherein the quill, or spindle of a wheele doeth twirle.*
Detriment: m. *Detriment, losse, domage, hurt, hinderance, decay.*
Detrimenteux: m. euse: f. *Hurtfull, dommageous; much hindering, full of losse, dammage, disaduantage.*
Detristé: m. ée: f. *Comforted, cheered vp; whose griefe is allayed, whose sorrow layed aside.*
Detrister. *To driue away sadnesse.*
Detrompé: m. ée: f. *Deliuered from error.*
Detromper. *To vndeceiue, to rid of error.*
Detroussément. *as* Destroussément.
Dette: f. *A debt; See* Debte.
Deturper. *To defile, file, fowle, soyle, make foule or ill-fauored.*
Deu: m. deuë: f. *Due, owed, or owing, ones owne; also, iust, fit, right, apt, seasonable, conuenient.*
Devallant. *Descending, alighting; bringing, or letting downe; tumbling, or throwing downe.*
Devallé: m. ée: f. *Brought, or let downe; tumbled, or throwne downeward; descended, alighted.*
Devallée: f. *A descent, or low ground; a fall in ground.*
Devallement: m. *A descent, an alighting; a sliding, or going downe; a bringing, or letting, a tumbling, or throwing, downeward.*
Devaller. *To bring, or let downe, to tumble, or throw downeward; also, to descend, alight; slide, or goe downe.*
Devancé: m. ée: f. *Outgone, exceeded, stripped, ouerrunne, preceded, got before.*
Devancer. *To strip, outgoe, ouerrunne, get, or goe before; to preuent; precede, forerunne.*
Devancier. nos Deuanciers. *Our auncestors, or predecessors, our forefathers.*
Devancier: m. ere: f. *Forerunning, preceding, more old, of greater antiquitie then; got, or gone before; outgoing, exceeding, that hath ouerrunne another.*

Devant: m. *(Substantiuely) as*; vn devant de robbe; *a kirtle; or, apron.*
Le devant d'un pourpoint &c. *The forebodie.*
Gaigner le devant par derriere. *To outstrip, or outgoe by wrong, priuate, or by-wayes; to crosse, or preuent a mans proiects by courses different from th'ordinarie, or his.*
Devant. *(of the verbe* Devoir;*)* laquelle chose devant estre. *Which thing since it must be.*
Devant. *Before, formerly.*
Par ci devant. *Heretofore, in former times.*
S'en*(or* Sens*)* devant derriere. *The wrong end forward; the inside outward; the cart before the horses; cleane kamme.*
Tout devant. *Right against, ouer against.*
Aller au devant. *To goe meet.*
Aller au devant par derriere. *To goe the wrong way to worke.*
Devant. (Interject.) *Vsed, as our, Auaunt, in the driuing away of a dog.*
Devanteau: m. *An apron.*
Devantel: &, Devantier. *The same.*
Devants: m. *Stands; or places wherein men stand with bowes, dogs, or otherwise, to shoot, hound, or looke, at a Deere, as he passes along.*
Deuës à vetando. *Priuiledges of forbidding (others to fish, or gather stickes, in his waters, or woods.)*
Deveiner. *as* Desveiner.
Developpé: m. ée: f. *Disinueloped, vnwrapped, vnfoulded.*
Developper. *To vnwrap, vnfould, display.*
Deüement. *Duely, rightly, fitly, as it should be.*
Devely. *Changed, or altered, so that a man cannot know him.*
Devenir. *To wax, to grow, to become.*
Que deviendra cest argent? *What will become of, what shall be done with, this money? how shall it be bestowed, how must it be disposed of?*
Que deviendray je? *What will befall me, what shall betide mee? how shall I shift, what shall I doe?*
Devenu: m. uë: f. *Become, waxen, or growne.*
Devergondé: m. ée: f. *Shamelesse; (a rusticall word.)*
Deverrouillé: m. ée: f. *Vnboulted, vnsparred.*
Deverrouiller. *To vnboult, or vnsparre a doore.*
Devers. *Towards.*
Devers Orient. *Towards the East; also, of the Easterne coast, or countries; as,* je suis fille d'un Roy devers Orient; *I am the daughter of an Easterne King.*
Ie viens de devers la riviere. *From, or fromwards the riuer come I.*
Devertaper. *To open, or vnbung:* ¶Orleannois.
Devest. *A disaduesture; or as* Dessaisine.
Devestir. *To put himselfe out of possession of; Looke* Desvestir.
Devestu: m. uë: f. *Disseised, put out of possession of.*
Devexité: f. *Deuexitie; a hollownesse, bowing, bending, hanging double, or downewards.*
Devidé: m. ée: f. *Wound from blades (or yarnewindles) into bottomes; also, reeled.*
Devideau: m. *A little paire of blades, or of yarnewindles.*
Devider. *To wind (as yarne &c) from blades &c into bottomes; also, to reele; whence;*
Pour devider la fusée il faut trouver le bout du fil: Prov. *To conceiue, dispose, or discourse of things rightly one must find out their beginnings.*
Devideresse: f. *A woman that winds yarne &c from the blades &c into bottomes; or from the spindle on a reele.*
Devidet. *as* Devideau.
Devidoir: m. *A paire of blades, or of yarne windles.*
Devidoire: f. *as* Devidoir.
Devier. *See* Desvier.
Devin: m. *A Diuiner, Soothsayer, Fortune-teller, ghesser at, foreteller of, things to come.*
Renvoyer quelqu'un au devin. cecy nous renvoit au devin. *We not know what this is, what it was, what to make, or thinke of it.*
Devinailles: f. *Diuinations, predictions, coniectures, ghesses.*
Devinaises: f. *as* Devinailles.
Devinance. *as* Devinement.
Deviné: m. ée: f. *Diuined, foretold, ghessed, coniectured.*
Devinement: m. *A diuining, soothsaying, foredeeming, coniecturing, ghessing, supposing, surmising what will follow.*
Deviner. *To Diuine, presage, soothsay it; to coniecture, ghesse, foredeeme, suppose, surmise, presume, what will follow.*
Il nous a mis à deviner. *He hath put vs to our plunges, or dumps; he hath driuen vs to our wits end, or to search euerie corner of our wits.*
Devineresse: f. *A Diuineresse, or Prophetesse; a woman that ghesses at, or foretells of, things to come.*
Devineur. *A Soothsayer; &c; as* Devin.
Devis: m. *Speech, talke, discourse, a conference, or communication; deuising, conferring, or talking together; also, a deuice, inuention; disposition, or appointment of.*
Devisagé: m. ée: f. *as* Desvisagé.
Devisager. *as* Desvisager.
Devise: f. *A deuice, posie; Embleme; conceit, coat, or Colizance borne, or giuen for some priuate respect; an inuention; also, a diuision; bound, meere, or marke diuiding land.*
Quelle devise y avoit il en cela? *What reason, or sence was there in that?*
Devisé: m. ée: f. *Discoursed, talked; inuented, deuised; ordered, disgested, disposed of.*
Deviser. *To commune, talke, discourse, conferre, deuise, chat, conuerse with; also, to deuise, or inuent; also, to order, disgest, or dispose of.*
Deument. *as* Deüement.
Devoir: m. *See* Debvoir.
Devolu: m. *A lapse; a thing deuolued, letten fall, or fallen into lapse; or as* Devolut.
Devolu: m. uë: f. *Deuolued; in lapse, fallen into lapse; or fallen from one to another; also, letten fall; and hence;*
Proces devolu. *An action, or suit surceased, nonsuited, abandonned, giuen ouer.*
Devolut: m. *as* Devolutaire; *also, a grant of, or presentment vnto, a Benefice, by lapse; also, as* Devolu.
Devolutaire: m. *A deuolutarie; one that obtaines the grant of a Benefice by a complaint, or pretence of insufficiencie, or intrusion in him that possesses it; also, hee whom the superior presents to one, fallen into lapse, for want of due presentment by the Patron, or Ordinarie.*
Devolutif: m. iue: f. *Deuolutiue; readie, or like, to deuolue.*
Devolution: f. *A deuolution, or falling into lapse.*
Devoré: m. ée: f. *Deuoured, rauined.*
Devorer. *To rauine, deuoure, inglut; eat greedily, swallow*

low whole, gulpe or let downe without chawing.

Devot: m. te: f. Deuout, holie, godlie, zealous, religious; also, scrupulous, or curious (religiously.)

Devotement. Deuoutly, holily, religiously, zealously; also, curiously, scrupulously, with feare of conscience.

Devotieusement. Most deuoutly.

Devotieux: m. euse: f. Full of deuotion.

Devotion: f. Deuotion, zeale, holinesse, conscience, godlinesse; a religious awe, reuerend feare, scruple, curiositie.

Hommage de devotion. Looke Hommage.

Devotionné: m. ée: f. Deuoted, affected vnto.

Devoüé: m. ée: f. Deuoted, vowed, or destined vnto; appointed, ordained, prouided for.

Devouëment: m. A vowing; or, deuoting vnto.

Devouer. To vow, deuote, or destine vnto; appoint, ordaine, or prouide for.

Devouté: m. ée: f. Vnvaulted, vnarched; vnbent; as a bow &c.

Devouter. To vnvault, or vnbend, as a bow in shooting it off.

Deusdet. as Masse d'armes.

Deuvet. as Duvet; Soft downe.

Deux. Two.

Les deux; ou tous deux. Both, or each of them.

Deux à deux. By two and two, from two to two, by couples, euerie two.

Deux fois. Twice.

Deux pour vn. A Snipe-knaue; so called, because two of them are worth but one Snipe.

Entre deux. Doubtfull, indifferent, in suspence, one knowes not whether; also, in the mid-way, or betweene both; also, readie, in mind, or about to do a thing; also, at his owne choice, as he lists himselfe.

Demeurer entre deux & as. Looke As.

Mettre en deux. To double (in foulding;) or to fould double.

Respondre entre deux & as. Cunningly to frame so doubtfull an answer betweene yea and no, that the demaunder knowes not what to make of it; (from a Die that stands edgling, and thereby yeelds an vncertaine chance.)

Deux chiens ne s'accordent point à vn os: Prov. Looke Accorder.

Deux hommes se rencontrent bien; mais iamais deux Montagnes: Prov. Two men may often meet, but mountaines neuer.

Deux loups mangent bien vne brebis: Prov. Two wolues can make good shift with one poore sheepe.

Deux orgueilleux ne peuvent estre portez sur vn asne: Prov. One simple Asse cannot beare two proud Asses.

Deux yeux voyent plus clair qu'un: Prov. Two eyes see better (two men know more) then one.

Qui bien tire deux en a: Prov. He that drawes well drawes twice; a good draught counteruailes a double draught.

Secret de deux secret de Dieu: Prov. Looke Dieu.

Deux-pour-vn. A Snipe-knaue.

Dexterité: f. Dexteritie, nimblenesse, quicknesse, readinesse, aptnesse; also, handsomenesse, comelinesse, gracefulnesse.

Dextre: com. vn homme dextre. An able, actiue, proper, handsome, well-behaued man; Seeke Adestre.

Dextre. à dextre; ou, à costé dextre. On the right hand, or side.

Dextrement. Nimbly, aptly, actiuely, properly, fitly, featly, handsomely, gracefully.

Dextrier. as Destrier; a Steed, or horse of seruice.

Dextrochere: m. The right arme (from th' elbow to the wrist) whereon there hangs a Maniple fringed at the bottome, and charged all ouer with Ermines.

Dez en Dez. Incontinently, by and by, forthwith; euer and anone.

Dia. The cry wherewith Carters make their horses turne on the left hand; also, a tearme set before medicinall Confections, or Electuaries, that were deuised by the Greekes.

Diabete: m. A continuall, and immoderate voiding of vrine, accompanied with extreame thirst.

Diable: m. A Diuell, a Fiend, an euill Spirit.

Diable deschainé. A diuell got loose; a Hell-hound, or Furie broken out of hell; a diuellish, horrible, or terrible fellow.

Diable de mer. A sea-Coot; or, sea-Cormorant; also, the ouglie wide-mouthed fish, called, the sea Frog, or sea Toad.

Diable en procez. A notable wrangler, or cauiller, a wonderfull plodding, stirring, or busie-headed companion.

Vn povre diable. A poore wretch, poore snake, ragged, needie, or beggerlie fellow.

Banquet de diables. Wherein there is no salt.

Mors à diable. Hearbe Auens, Bennet, or blessed (called so by some.)

Mors du diable. The hearbe Forebit, or Diuels bit.

Vallet du diable. C'est vn val: du d; il fait plus que l'on luy commande. Said of one thats too diligent, officious, or busie.

Voix de diable: Aile d' Ange, & voix de diable. The description, or stile, of a Peacocke.

Le diable y sera bien. There will be a foule coyle, horrible stirre, monstrous confusion, or garboyle.

'A ces diables: To it apace and spare not, sirs; forbeare it not as long as it will last.

Faire le diable de Vauvert. To keepe an old coyle, horrible bustling, terrible swaggering; to play monstrous reakes, or raks-iakes.

Faire d'un diable deux. To make a thing the worse by seeking to amend it; to commit two errors in striuing to salue one.

Fust il plus diable qu'il n'est cornu. Were he much more terrible then he seemes to be.

Ie le rendray plus diable qu'il n'est cornu; I will affright him more then he feares others.

Il n'est si diable qu'il est noir. He is not so lewd as he lookes, nor so bad as he is taken, for; he is nothing so offensiue, mischieuous, or dangerous as he seems to be.

Le diable n'est pas tousiours à vn huis: Prov. The diuell is not alwaies at one dore; he tempts, and attempts, men sundrie wayes.

Au prester Ange, au rendre diable: Pro. (Thus doe vngratefull men when they would borrow, flatter, when they must repay, ryle.)

De jeune Angelot vieux diable: Prov. We say, a young Saint an old diuell.

Et plus a le diable, & plus veut avoir: Prov. The more the diuell hath the more he would; (And herein, as in most points else, the greedie scrape-good humors him.)

Ire de Freres, ire de Diables: Prov. Looke, Ire.

La farine du diable s'en va moitié en son: Pro. Halfe of the diuels meale turnes vnto branne.

On cognoit le diable à ses griffes: Pro. The diuell is

is knowne by his clawes; a couetous heart discerned by catching hands.

Quand le François dort le diable le berse. *(A Prouerbe made by the Flemings out of patience with th'impatient, and restlesse humors of the French.)*

Qui a marastre il a le diable à l' atre: Prov. *Looke* Atre.

Diablerie: f. *Diuellishnesse; also, a diuellish crue, knot, or companie; also, a Play, or Shew of diuells; and hence;*

La diablerie à quatre personnages. *A great matter, or mischiefe; a mischieuous hap; also, a wonderous rumbling, terrible coile, horrible stirre.*

Diablesse: f. *A she diuell, or female diuell.*

Diableteau. *A little diuell, a yong diuell.*

Diableteau de coeur. *A lad-diuell, or nouice diuell (a prophane allusion to,* Enfant de coeur; *a Quirrester:)* ¶Rab.

Diableusement. *Most diuellishly.*

Diabolique: com. *Diabolicall, diuellish, feend-like.*

Diaboliquement. *Diabollically, diuellishly.*

Diacartami. *A purging composition, made of sundrie ingredients.*

Diacatholicon. *A composition so tearmed, because it purgeth all kind of humors.*

Diaciminon. *A composition made of Simples fit to dissolue windinesse in the stomacke.*

Diaconal: m. ale: f. *Diaconall; of, or belonging to, a Deacon.*

Diaconat: m. *as* Diaconie.

Diaconie: f. *A Deaconrie; the place of a Deacon.*

Diacre: m. *A Deacon.*

Diaculon. *A certaine mollifying plaister, tearmed otherwise,* Diachylon, *because it is made of iuices.*

Diademe: m. *A Diadem; a Crowne, or wreath for the head of a King; properly it signifies, a wreathed headband (with which the auncient Kings were contented, as thinking, that the Crowne belonged onely to the gods.)*

Diafane: com. *Cleere, bright, transparent, translucent, through-shining, through which one may see.*

Diagalange. *A confection, or salue made of Galingale.*

Diagonal: m. ale: f. *Diagonall; or extending from one corner to another.*

Diagonalement. *Diagonally; from corner to corner.*

Diagone: m. *A line that extends from one corner to another.*

Diagoné: m. ée: f. *as* Diagonal; *also, more high, or deepe, than broad.*

Diagredé. *A medicine, or ointment made of the Gumme* Diagredi.

Diagredi. *A strong-purging Gumme, which distilleth from the root of the hearbe Scammonie.*

Diagredié: m. ée: f. *Mixt with* Diagredium, *or Scammonie prepared.*

Diaire: m. *A Diarie, or Jornall; a relation of things done euerie day.*

Diaire: com. *Of a day, of one day, continuing for a day (and no longer.)*

Diale. *The diuell:* ¶Pic.

Dialecte: m. *A Dialect, or proprietie of language.*

Dialecticien. *A Logician.*

Dialectique: f. *Logicke, the Art of reason, or of reasoning.*

Dialectiquement. *Logically, by the art of Logicke; as a good Logician.*

Diallement. *Diuellishly, furiously, felly.*

Dialogisme: m. *A figure, or discourse, wherein one arguing with himselfe as if hee talked to another, both moues the question, and makes the answer.*

Dialogue: m. *A Dialogue; a discourse betweene two, or more.*

Dialthée. *An ointment, whose principall ingredient is the mucilage, or slime of* Althea, *or marsh Mallow.*

Diamant: m. *A Diamond; also, the Loadstone; (in stead of* Aymant.)

Cloué à clous de diamant. *Most fast, most sure.*

Diamantin: m. ine: f. *Of a Diamond, as hard as a Diamond.*

Diamargariton. *An Electuarie, so called by reason of the Pearles whereof tis made.*

Diambre. *A confection of Amber, and other heart-comforting simples.*

Diamerdis. *A confection of turds, pilgrims salue; also, a shitten fellow.*

Diametralement. *Oppositiuely, right euerthwart, cleane crosse, in opposition to, or one ouer against another.*

Diametraler à. *To correspond, or answer vnto diametrally; to stand right ouer against.*

Diametre: m. *A Diameter; a straight line, which passing through the middle, or center of a square, circle, or other figure, diuides it into two equall parts.*

Diammour. *The Diuell:* ¶Barrag.

Diamouron. *Syrop of Mulberries.*

Diamoschum. *A kind of cordiall powder.*

Diane. à la diane. *In the morning, at the breaking vp of the watch (a militarie tearme.)*

Bailler la diane. *To giue a cold pie, or mornings camisadoe; also, to surprise, or assault, by Moone-light.*

Sonner la Diane. *Trumpetters to sound in a morning to their Generall, and Captaines.*

Dianier: m. ere: f. *Consecrated to Diana; or, that hath vowed chastitie.*

Dianisum. *An Electuarie made of Anise seeds and other things good to breake wind.*

Diantre. *The diuell, the god of darkenesse:* ¶Norm. ¶Rab.

Diapason. *A Diapason, in Musicke; also, as* Iauge; *a gage to measure caske with.*

Diapente. *A powder, or composition, wherein there are fiue simples equally incorporated; Myrhe, Gentian, long Birthwort, Bay berries, and shauen or scraped Iuorie.*

Diaphane. *as* Diafane; *Transparent, translucent, cleere as Crystall.*

Diaphaner. *To cleere, brighten, make transparent.*

Diaphenicum. *A purging Electuarie made of the Dates called* Phenices.

Diaphoretique: com. *Dissoluing, or euaporating humors.*

Diphragmatique. veine diaph. *Looke* Veine.

Diaphragme. *The Midriffe; a long, and round muscle, whereby the vitall parts are seperated from the naturall, and, the heart & lights from the stomack, and nether bowels.*

Diapré: m. ée: f. *Diaperd, or diapred; diuersified with flourishes, or sundrie figures.*

Diaprer. *To diaper, flourish, diuersifie with flourishings.*

Diaprerie: f. *Flourishing in worke; or, flourisht worke.*

Diapreure: f. *A diapring, or flourishing in worke; as in Diapers.*

Diarrhée. *A laske, or flux without inflammation.*
Diarrhoëtique. *That hath such a laske.*
Diarrodon. *A kind of paine-abating syrrop.*
Diarthrose. *A knitting, or connexion of bones, that euidently moue together.*
Diasene. *as* Diasenné.
Diasenné. *A purging composition made of Sene, or Trifolie.*
Diaspertisant *(or rather)* Diaspermatisant. *Disseminating, or sowing of seed:* ¶Rab.
Diastolé. *The dilatation of the heart.*
Diatipose: f. *A double Description, or Figuring.*
Diatolique: com. *Continuall, without intermission:* ¶Rab.
Diaule: m. *A measure containing two furlongs.*
Dicastes: m. *The Judges of the auncient Thebans:* ¶Rab.
D'ici. *Looke* D'icy.
Dict: m. cte: f. *Sayed, spoken, deliuered, vttered, expressed, shewen, told, declared, signified, reported vnto.*
Dictam: m. *as* Dictame.
Dictame: m. *The hearbe Dittanie, Dittander, garden Ginger.*
Dictame bastard. *Bastard Dittanie; somewhat resembles the right one, but is neither sweet of smell, nor biting in tast; some also call* Fraxinella *so.*
Dictame blanc. Tragium, Fraxinella; *called also, bastard, or false Dittanie; and oft mistaken, and much vsed, by Apothecaries, for the right Dittanie, though, in forme, it be nothing like it:* (¶Mathiolus.)
Dictame de Candie. *Dittanie, &, Dittanie of* Candia, *the right Dittander.*
Dictamon. *as* Dictame.
Dictateur: m. *A Dictator; an Officer among the Romanes, who, for the time he ruled, had Soueraigne authoritie.*
Dictature: f. *The Dictatorship.*
Dicté: m. ée: f. *Dictated; indicted.*
Dicter. *To dictate, appoint, or tell another, what and how, he shall write.*
Diction: f. *A diction, speech, or saying.*
Diction: m. *A conceit, pithie sentence, prettie saying; an Apothegme; also, a finall arrest, sentence, iudgement, order, penned at large, and commonly subscribed by the Judge, and his assistants.*
D'icy. *From hence; from this place, or time.*
D'icy à quel temps? *How long? in what time? till when?*
Diesble, *for* Diable; *The diuell:* ¶Parisien.
Diése: f. *A sharpe, in Musicke.*
Diete: f. *Diet, or dailie fare; also, a Diet, Parliament, or assemblie of the States, & Princes of the Empire.*
Dietitique: com. *Of, or belonging to, diet; prescribing a diet.*
Dieu: m. *God.*
Dieux! *An Interiection of admiring; as we say, good God!*
Boeuf de dieu. *A Wren.*
La Croix de par dieu. *The Christs-crosse-row; or Horne-booke wherein a child learnes it.*
La feste dieu. *Whitsunday.*
Vne Iambe de dieu. *So doe the canting, and blasphemous rogues of France tearme a cankered, gangrened, or desperately-sore leg.*
Maison dieu. *A Spittle, or Hospitall.*
Paulme dieu. Palma Christi, *Satyrion royall.*
Vn pleust à dieu. *Looke* Plaire.
Dieu Colas. *By S. Nicholas, or for S. Nicholas sake:* ¶Lorrainois: ¶Rab.
`A dieu ne plaise. *God forbid, God shield, God sware-bot.*
De par dieu soit. *In the name of God be it; God prosper it, or send it well to speed.*
De par luy bon dieu. *In the name of God; or, for Gods sake:* ¶Lymosin: ¶Rab.
Et encor pour dieu soit, si. *And he may thanke God, or, hee is beholden to his aduersaries pietie, if.*
Ne croire à dieu que sur bons gages. *To trust no man, how rich soeuer hee bee, without good pawnes; to beleeue no man, how honest soeuer, without great proofes: (In which phrase though God bee mentioned, yet is not an impious, but a churlish, distrust meant by it.)*
Faire le doux dieu dessous vne pesle. Il fait &c. *He is very nice, quaint, precise, or curious in all his actoins; Looke* Pesle.
Oublier dieu parmi tous les Saincts. Il oublie, &c; *The neerer he is to the Church, the further he is from God.*
Dieu donne biens, & boeuf, mais ce n'est pas par la corne: Prov. *Looke* Boeuf.
Dieu donne le froid selon le drap: Prov. *God sends men cold according to their cloath*; viz. *afflictions according to their faith.*
Dieu sçait qui est bon pelerin: Prov. *God knowes the hearts of Pilgrims.*
`A pere à maistre, à dieu tout puissant, nul ne peut rendre l'equivolent: Prov. *No man can sufficiently requite his Father, Maister, Maker.*
`A toile ourdie dieu mande le fil: Prov. *God works begun enables vs to follow.*
En petite maison dieu a grand part: Prov. *In a little mansion God hath a great portion.*
En peu d'heure dieu labeure: Pro. *God quickly does what he will doe.*
Il ne perd rien qui ne perd dieu: Prov. *Hee looses nothing that keepes God his friend.*
Là ou dieu veut il pleut: Prov. *Looke* Plouvoir.
Pour devenir bien tost riche il faut tourner le dos à dieu: Prov. *The way to grow soone rich is, to forsake religion.*
Qui sert dieu il a bon maistre: Pro. *He that serues God, serues a good maister.*
Secret de deux secret de dieu: Prov. *Yet wee say, that, two can keepe counsell when one is away.*
Dieu-donné: m. *Theodore (a proper name for a man.)*
Dieu-gard: vn dieu-gard. *A salutation; or, a, God-saue-you.*
Dieutelet: m. *A little god.*
Dieux! Interject. *Looke* Dieu.
Diffamation: f. *A defamation; defaming, deprauing, discrediting, traducing, open disgracing in speeches.*
Diffamatoire: com. *Diffamatorie.*
Diffame: m. *Infamie, obloquie, reproach, discredit, ignominie, dishonour, disgrace, an ill report, an euill name, an imputation.*
Diffamé: m. ée: f. *Defamed, infamous, discredited, dishonoured, much and ill spoken of; whose good name is tainted, reputation blemished, credit lost.*

Diffamer. To defame, traduce, discredit, reproach, depraue, disgrace, dishonor.

Differanté: m. ée: f. Differed, or disagreed from; in debate, or at variance with; also, diuersified.

Differanter. To differ, or disagree from; to iarre, contend, debate, or be at variance with; also, as Differenter.

Differé: m. ée: f. Differed, protracted, delayed, lingered, driuen, put, or shifted off.

Differemment. Distinctly, seuerally, differently, with a difference.

Difference: f. A difference, diuersitie; vnlikelinesse; distinction; disagreeing; also, a certaine distance, or measure in Geometrie.

Differencié: m. ée: f. Distinguished, made different from.

Different: m. A difference, controuersie, suit, variance, disagreement, contention, strife, debate, ods; also, a different marke, or thing; or a marke whereby one thing is distinguished from another.

Different. Different; vnlike, diuers, differing, varying, disagreeing, seuerall, from; of another condition or qualitie, nature or kind.

Differenter. as Differanter; Also, to diuersifie, or varie.

Differer. To deferre, delay, driue, or put off; to protract, prolong, linger, procrastinate, shift off day after day.

Sans differer. Presently, at the verie instant, without staying one iot more, any whit longer.

Difficile: com. Difficile, difficult; hard, vneasie, troublesome, intricate, painefull, almost impossible.

Qui fait du difficile. Thats backeward, vnwilling; stubborne; squeamish, coy, nice; thats verie loath to meddle with, or to be drawne vnto, a thing; thats verie hard to bee intreated, or woon to vndertake a thing.

Difficilement. Difficultly, hardly, vneasily, troublesomely; scantly, scarcely; with great paine, with much adoe.

Difficulté: f. A difficultie; a great let, maine impediment, a trouble, a painefull or intricate enterprise.

Difficulté de digestion. Ill disgestion, rawnesse of the stomacke.

Difficulté d'haleine. Pursinesse; obstruction of the conduits of the lights.

Difficulté d'vriner. The Stranguric.

Difficulter. To difficultate, or difficilitate; to make difficult, or vneasie; to make it a hard matter; to make bones of.

Difficultueux. Verie hard, verie difficult, full of difficulties.

Diffinitivement. as Definitivement.

Difflation: f. A difflation, blowing, or breathing.

Difforme: com. Deformed, ouglie, ill-fauoured, vnseemelie, vncomelie, mishapen, formelesse, out of fashion.

Difformité: f. Deformitie,ouglinesse, vnseemelinesse, vncomelinesse, ill-fauourednesse; a blemish in fauour.

Diffus: m. use: f. Diffused, spred, scattered abroad; large, wide, extended; hanging loosse; also, spilt, powred out.

Diffusément. Diffusedly, scatteredly, disorderedly.

Digame. One that hath two wiues together; also, one that marieth after his first wiues death; one that hath had two wiues.

Digastrique. Hauing two bellies.

Muscle digastrique. A muscle issuing from the Processe called Mastoïde (sometimes from Stilloïde) the vse of it is, to draw the lower iaw downeward.

Digeré: m. ée: f. Disgested, concocted, digested, borne, abiden; also, disposed, sorted, ordered.

Digerer. To disgest, concoct; brooke, beare, digest, abide, away with; also, to sort, order, dispose.

Digerer bien vn conseil. Throughly to examine, weigh, thinke, or consider of, a counsell giuen.

Digestif: m. iue: f. Disgestiue, or procuring disgestion.

Digestion: f. Disgestion, concoction, digestion.

Digitale. The hearbe called Fox-gloues.

Digitale jaulne. Fox-gloues with the yellow flower, (is lesse, and lesse common then)

Digitale purpure. Purple Fox-gloues; called so of the colour of the flowers.

Digitation: f. The forme of the fingers of both hands ioyned together; or the manner of their so ioyning.

Digitte: m. A Diget, the Character which expresseth a figure in Arithmeticke; as an v, the figure of fiue; &c.

Digne: com. Worthie; condigne, deseruing; meet, fit for.

Dignement. Worthily, condignely, deseruedly, according to merit.

Dignité: f. Dignitie; promotion; honour; authoritie, superioritie; greatnesse of estate, or in office; great estimation, or worthinesse; Nobilitie, or noblenesse.

Fief de dignité. A Fief that hath a dignitie, or title of Nobilitie, annexed vnto it; Looke Fief.

Seigneurs de dignité. Are Dukes, Marquises, Earls, Princes, Vicounts, Barons, and Chattelains; Noble-men; or such Gentlemen as are Lords by inheritance, or birth.

Digonner. To dig, or pricke: ¶Norm.

Digression: f. A digression, or digressing; a going, straying, swaruing, aside, or from the matter; a changing of purpose, an altering of discourse.

Digue. A ditch, bound, or banke; a iettie, damme, or mount, raised vp for a defence against the incursions, or inundations of waters.

Dilaceration: f. A tearing, or rending asunder.

Dilaceré: m. ée: f. Dilacerated; rent, or torne in peeces.

Dilacerer. To dilacerate, rend, or teare in peeces.

Dilaié: m. ée: f. Delayed; or allayed.

Dilaïer. To delay; or, allay.

Dilapidé: m. ée: f. Dilapidated.

Dilapider. To dilapidate; ruine, or pull downe stone-buildings; also, to rid of, or purge from, stones.

Dilatable: com. Dilatable, inlargeable, extendable, widenable.

Dilatateur: m. A dilatator, inlarger, widener; extender.

Dilatation: f. A dilatation; a widening, inlarging, stretching out, spreading abroad.

Dilatatoire: m. A dilatatorie, or inlarger; an Instrument wherewith Chirurgions open those partes that by sickenesse, or other accident, are too much closed.

Dilaté: m. ée: f. Dilated, widened, inlarged, stretched out, spred abroad, made broad.

Dilater. To dilate, widen, inlarge, extend, stretch out, spread abroad, make broad.

Dilation: f. A deferring, delaying, prolonging, protraction.

Dilatoire: com. Dilatorie, delaying, deferring.

Dilayant.

Dilayant. *Delaying, deferring, protracting, prolonging.*
Dilayement: m. *as* Dilation.
Diligemment. *Diligently, sedulously, quickly, speedily; laboriously, studiously, carefully, industriously; intentiuely, vigilantly.*
Diligence: f. *Speed; sedulitie; diligence, quicknesse; much trauell, or studie; great instance; laborious industrie; earnest intention, about.*
Faire ses diligences. *To performe, or pay his dueties; meant of such as are to be performed before one can recouer land sold by his next kinsman, or forfeited by his owne default; also; in the first case, to enter his action for; or, to enter, and take possession of, the land so aliened.*
Diligence passe science: Prov. *Diligence exceedeth Science; painefulnesse of more merit then skilfulnesse.*
Diligent. *Diligent, sedulous, quicke, speedie; studious, laborious, painfull; vigilant, intentiue, carefull; earnest, or busie about a thing.*
Diligenté: m. ée: f. *Speeded, hastened; quickly prepared, soone prouided; forwarded apace.*
Diligenter. *To hasten, forward, giue speed vnto, set on apace.*
Se diligenter. *To be diligent, nimble, quicke; painful, earnest about; to make speed, or bestirre himselfe apace, in a businesse.*
Dille: f. *The Quill, or Fawcet of a Hogshead &c.*
Dillon: m. *A Quinsell, for a horse.*
Dilucide: com. *Cleere, bright, plaine, manifest, euident, easie to be discerned.*
Dilucidé: m. ée: f. *Dilucidated; cleered.*
Delucider. *To cleere, dilucidate; explaine, manifest, make plaine to be vnderstood.*
Dimenche: m. *Sunday; the Sabboth day.*
Dimenche de blanches. *Palmes-Sunday.*
Le Dimenche de pasques fleuries. *(The same.)*
Dimencheret. valet dimencheret. *A Holy-day seruant; one that waits but on good dayes.*
Dimension: f. *A dimension, or measuring.*
Diminué: m. ée: f. *Diminished, lessened, impaired, abated, extenuated; qualified.*
Diminuer. *To diminish, lessen, impaire, abate, extenuate; also, to qualifie; also, to diuide (in singing.)*
Diminution: f. *A diminution; appairing, lessening, impairing, diminishing, extenuation; abatement.*
Diminutions. *Diuision (in Musicke.)*
Dinanderie: f. *Broken ware, Copper ware, Tinkers worke; also, the place where such stuffe is sold; or made.*
Dinandier: m. *A Copper-Smith, or Brasier; a word (as the former) deriued from* Dinand, *a towne (standing on the riuer of* Meuse*) wherein copper kettles, &c, are made.*
Dinarchie: f. *The ioynt gouernement of two Princes.*
Dindan: m. *The ding-dong, or ringing out of bells.*
Dindar. *A Turkie-cocke; Seeke* Indar.
Diner. *A dinner; See* Disner.
Dintiers: m. *The cods, dowcets, or tenderings of a Deere.*
Diocese: m. *A Diocesse; the iurisdiction of a Bishop.*
Diole. *The diuell:* ¶Brett.
Diphthere. Peau Diphthere. *The skinne of th' Amalthean Goat, wherein Jupiter is fained to record humane occurrences:* ¶Rab.
Dipsade. *A Snake whose biting brings with it a mortall drinesse.*
Dipsode. *A thirstie fellow:* ¶Rab.
Diptam, ou Diptame. *Hearbe Dittanie, Garden Ginger; Looke* Dictame.
Dique: f. *as* Digue.
Dire: m. *A saying, tale, speech, talke, word.*
Du dire au faict y a grand traict: Prov. *Deeds and words dwell farre asunder: either because many things that are spoken are not intended to be done; or because few things will so quickly, or can so easily be done, as they are spoken.*
Dire. *To say, speake, talke, vtter, expresse, deliuer, tell, declare, shew, signifie, relate, report vnto; also, to bid, or commaund.*
En dire sa coulpe. *To beat, or thumpe his breast, as a repentant sinner, for his faults.*
Dire par jeu. *To ieast.*
Dire le mot. *To breake a ieast.*
Dire mille pouilles à. *To reuile, reproach, raile on, scould at.*
'A dire. Il y a autãt à dire, que du. *There is as much difference, as betweene.*
Trouver à dire. *To misse, lacke, need, want the things we had before.*
Ie ne trouve rien à dire en cela. *I find no fault with, I see no defect in, that.*
Ie ne dis pas. (Encore si elle estoit ieune, ie ne dis pas.) *I would neuer speake on't.*
Mal dire. fortune voulut mal dire à. *Would crosse, or become foe vnto.*
Ouy dire. par ouy dire. *By heare-say, by the report of others.*
Sans dire guare. *On a sudden, without warning, at vnawares.*
Que faut il tant dire? *What need so many words about the matter?*
Dis tu? *Indeed? It is euen so? (an angrie manner of speaking.)*
Que dis tu! *(In admiration) Is it possible? good God who would haue thought it! tis a wonder you tell me!*
Ie ne dis qui le dit? *I am nothing, who is any thing? (a Card-players phrase.)*
Les dez luy disent fort bien. *He casts verie well, or hath passing good lucke, at dice; the dice are exceeding fauourable vnto him; The like is;*
Fortune vous dit. *Fortune answers your expectation, or, is fauourable vnto you.*
La livre dit douze onces. *The pound containes, or consists of, 12 ounces.*
On dit. *The speech is, the report goes; tis said, or talked abroad.*
On me dit ton frere. *Men call, name, or tearme mee thy brother.*
Vous dites d'orgues. *You speake to the purpose, you say maruellous well; (Ironically.)*
Assez en dit qui apporte bonnes nouvelles: Prov. *He sayes ynough that sayes his newes are good; or, he that brings good newes loues to tell them often.*
Bien dire fait rire, bien faire fait taire: Prov. *Good words breed laughter, good deeds admiration.*
Entre faire & dire il y a grand à dire: Prov. *Betweene saying and doing there is great difference; (Looke before in* Dire, Substan.*)*
On doit dire du bien le bien: Prov. *Of things well done we ought to speake well.*
Tout ouïr, tout voir, & rien dire, merite en tout temps qu'on l' admire: Prov. *Heare and see all, but say nothing, so maiest thou still be admired.*

Tout vray n'est pas bon à dire : Prov. *Euerie trueth is not to be told.*

Direct : m. cte : f. *Direct, straight, right, iust, plaine; immedidiate, peculier.*

Seigneur direct. *A Land-lord; a direct, immediate, or next Lord.*

Directement. *Directly, rightly, straightly, iustly; immediately; plainely, without circumstances, to the purpose.*

Directer. *To direct, guide, lead, conduct; rule, order; straighten the course of; or keepe in a straight course; also, to acknowledge from whence a good commeth.*

Directeur : m. *A directer, leader, conducter, guide; ruler, gouernor, instructer.*

Direction : f. *A direction; guide, conduction; instruction.*

Directoire : com. *Directorie, directiue, directing.*

Direption : f. *A spoyling, robbing, ransacking; pulling, rending, tearing, or taking away by violence.*

Dirigé : m. ée : f. *Directed, guided, conducted, led; ordered, ruled, gouerned; addressed, leuelled, made right, kept straight.*

Diriger. *To direct, guide, lead, conduct; addresse, leuell, make right, keepe straight; rule, order, gouerne.*

Disceptateur : m. *An arguer, disputer, contender, debater; a pleader; also, a Dayes-man, arbitrator, or stickler.*

Disceptation : f. *A disceptation; disputation, contention, arguing, debating, reasoning about a matter; also, an arbitrement.*

Disceptatrice : f. *A woman that disputes, reasons, or debates, a matter; also, an arbitratrix.*

Discepté : m. ée : f. *Disputed, debated, reasoned, pleaded, argued; examined, arbitrated.*

Discepter. *To dispute, debate, reason, plead, argue a case; also, to arbitrate, or examine a controuersie betweene partie and partie.*

Discerné : m. ée : f. *Discerned, or distinguished; parted, seuered, sundered.*

Discerner. *To discerne, or distinguish one thing from another; also, to part, seperate, seuer, diuide asunder; to make, or put a difference betwene.*

Disciple : m. *A Scholler, a learner, a Pupill, a Disciple.*

Disciplinable : com. *Disciplinable; teachable, fit to learne.*

Disciplinaire : com. *Disciplinarie; belonging to discipline, full of instruction; correctiue, schooling.*

Discipline : f. *Discipline, learning, doctrine, instruction; an art, a science; also, correction, schooling, and penance; or a whip to doe penance, or giue punishment with.*

Discipliné : m. ée : f. *Disciplined, schooled, corrected; put vnto penance.*

Discipliner. *To discipline, schoole, correct, bring vnder coram; (and hence) also, to whip, or put vnto a sharpe penance.*

Discole : com. *Vnrulie, not obseruing orders, without gouernment.*

Dicommodation. *Dammage, hurt, inconuenience, hinderance, disease, displeasure.*

Discommodé : m. ée : f. *Discommodated, or incommodated; hurt, indammaged, hindered.*

Discommoder. *To discommodate, incommodate, hurt, hinder, bring dammage, breed inconueniences, vnto.*

Disconcerté : m. ée : f. *Disordered, confused; set awry.*

Discontinuation : f. *A discontinuation, or discontinuing; an intermission, surceasing, discontinuance, breaking off, giuing ouer, for a time.*

Discontinué : m. ée : f. *Discontinued, surceased, intermitted.*

Discontinuément. *Discontinuingly, intermissiuely, by stops, with interruptions.*

Discontinuer. *To discontinue, surcease, intermit, forbeare, put off for a time.*

Disconvenance : f. *A disagreeing with, a dissenting from; a being vnfit for, or vnlike vnto.*

Disconvenir. *To disagree, or be at ods with; to be vnfit for, or vnlike vnto; to dissent from.*

Discord : m. *Discord, iarring, repugnancie, disagreement; variance, debate, altercation, strife; dissention; contention.*

Discordamment. *Iarringly, repugnantly, disagreeingly, without any order, or harmonie.*

Discordant. *Discordāt, iarring, disagreeing, repugnant, contrarie; most harsh, most vntuneable.*

Discorder. *To disagree, differ, dissent from; to iarre, striue, be at discord with; to be repugnant, vnlike, or contrarie vnto.*

Discoste : com. *Distant, remote, farre, farre asunder, farre off.*

Se Discotter de. *To remoue, put from him, rid himselfe of, leaue aside, abandon, quit, forsake, forgoe.*

Discourir. *To discourse of; to relate, report, recite, rehearse; to particularize point after point; also, to peruse, examine, search into; suruey, discouer, runne ouer; and hence;*

Discourir plusieurs païs. *To passe, or trauell through, many lands.*

Discours : m. *A discourse, report, relation, rehearsall of a matter; also, a suruey, perusall, examination, pondering of things in the mind.*

Discourtois : m. ise : f. *Discourteous, vngentle, vnciuile, rude, harsh, without humanitie.*

Courtoisie tardiue est discourtoise : Prov. *A lateward courtesie is a discourtesie; fauours that are long a doing are loathsome, done.*

Discourtoisie : f. *A disfauour, discourtesie, vngentle tricke, vnciuile pranke, rude part.*

Discrasié : m. ée : f. *Pulled, haled; also, drie, drained, or wrung drie; of an ill complexion:* ¶Rab.

Discrepance : f. *A discrepancie, difference, repugnancie, disagreement.*

Discrepant : m. ante : f. *Discrepant, different, disagreeing from, repugnant vnto.*

Discret : m. ete : f. *Discreet, aduised; prudent, sage; prouident, heedfull, circumspect.*

Discretement. *Discreetly, aduisedly; prudently; prouidently, heedfully, circumspectly.*

Discretion : f. *Discretion, (true) discerning; a difference made, or a sencibleneſſe of difference had, betweene things; hence, iudgement, aduisednesse, knowledge; wit enough, to find out whats good, t'eschew what is bad, and to make the best vse of either; also, a wager, (but an vncertaine one; it being at the losers choice to pay what he things good.)*

Vivre à discretion. *To liue as he list, to pay for his board &c what he list.*

Discrucié : m. ée : f. *Excruciated, extreamely afflicted.*

Discrucier. *To excruciate, vexe, torment, afflict extreamely.*

Discussion : f. *A discussion, or strict examination, by parcells; a searching into, or sifting out of.*

Faire discussion sur les biens d' un debteur. *To prise, or examine the value of; a debtors goods, thereby to know how able he is to satisfie Creditors.*
Discuté: m. ée: f. *Discussed, debated, examined, diligently sought into, narrowly sifted out; also, prised, or praised, as a debtors goods.*
Discuter. *To discusse, examine, debate, search into, sift out; also, to value, or praise goods.*
Discuteur: m. *A discusser, examiner, debater; also, a valuer, or praiser of goods, to see what they are worth.*
Discution. *as* Discussion.
Diseaux de gerbes. *Sheafes of corne set tenne and tenne in a heape; halfe-thraues of tenne sheaues apeece; (tensheaued) stonks, or shocks of corne.*
Disenier: m. *A Counsellor, or Alderman of a Citie; also, a Captaine, or Commaunder ouer tenne souldiours; Looke* Dixenier.
Disentourner. *To vnturne, or turne off.*
Disert: m. erte: f. *Eloquent, well spoken, of good vtterance.*
Disertement. *Eloquently, elegantly, with choice words and good vtterance.*
Disetteux: m. euse: f. *Needie, wanting, in want, poore, beggarlie, penurious, vnfurnished of necessaries.*
Disette: f. *Want, scarcitie, beggarie, lacke, pouertie, necessitie, dearth, penurie, needinesse.*
Diseur: m. *A speaker, an arguer, a pleader, a prater.*
Diseur d'heures. *A Chaplaine; a sayer of prayers.*
Disferre: f. *An horse-shoe of two peeces ioyned together at the top with an yron pinne, and thereby straitened, or enlarged, to fit the foot, at pleasure.*
Disgrace: f. *A disgrace; an ill fortune, hard lucke; defeature, check-mate, mishap; also, vncomelinesse, vnseemelinesse, illfauorednesse; a deformitie, ill fashion, rude behauior, ougly manner.*
Disgratié: m. ée: f. *Vnhappie, vnluckie, disastrous, vnfortunate; also, vnseemelie, deformed, vnhandsome, vncomelie.*
Disgregé: m. ee: f. *Disgregated, dispersed, scattered, seuered, sundered.*
Disgreger. *To disgregate, disperse, scatter, seuer, sunder.*
Disjonctif: m. iue: f. *Disiunctiue, disioyning, disuniting, diuiding.*
Disjonction: f. *A disiunction, diuision, disunitement, parting, or putting asunder.*
Dislayer. *as* Delayer. *To deferre, delay, put off.*
Dislocation: f. *A dislocation, a displacing.*
Dislocation de membre. *A putting out of ioynt.*
Disloqué: m. ée: f. *Displaced; put out of ioynt.*
Disloquer. *To put out of ioynt; to remoue out of his due place; to displace.*
Disinages. *Tythings, or matters belonging to tythes.*
Disine: f. *A tythe, or tenth of.*
Disnes infeudées, ou infeodées. *Impropriations of tythes.*
Disine, & terrage à deux mains. *Looke* Main.
Veau de disine. *A notable sot, blockhead, lobcocke.*
Amasser la disine de l'ail. *To procure vnto himselfe a sound beating; (In* Poictou *they say of one that hath beene well cudgelled,* Il vouloit amasser la disine de l'ail. *Because the Poicteuins will not suffer Tythe-Garlicke to be payed.*
Disiné: m. ée: f. *Tythed, whereof tythe is taken.*
Disiner. *To tythe, or take the tenth of.*
Disinerie: f. *A tenth, tythe, or tything; the title, or possession of a tythe; a place whereout tythe is due.*
Disineur: m. *A tythe-gatherer; the owner of tythes, or he to whom tythe is due.*
Disinier. *A tyther; or, as* Disineur.
Disné. *Dined.*
Ou nous avous disné nous souperons: Prov. *Looke* Souper.
Disner: m. *A dinner; and (sometimes more generally) a meale.*
Disner d'Advocats. *A large meale; (eaten, not giuen.)*
Disner de chien. *Hounds fare, onely bread and water; or a meale wherein there is nothing drunke but water.*
Disner de mouche. *A poore pittance, a small bit, a little morsell, a Sparrowes dinner.*
Disner de semonce. *A feast, or solemn dinner, whereunto many guests are inuited aforehand.*
Contre disner appert vallet: Prov. *When meat is to be had my man appeares (sayes the ill-serued Maister.)*
Petit disner longuement attendu, n'est pas donné, mais cherement vendu: Pro. *Looke* Attendu.
Qui garde son disner il a mieux à souper: Prov. *He that keepes his dinner hath the better supper.*
Disner. *To dine.*
Mal soupe qui tout disne: Prov. *Hee suppes ill that dines all; after a gluttonous, and disordinat youth followes a needie, and hungrie age.*
Disparagement: m. *A disparagement; an vnfit, or vnworthie condition offered vnto, or imposed on, a man.* ¶Norm.
Disparer. ou, se Disparoir. *To vanish away, to withdraw himselfe, or slinke out of sight on a suddaine.*
Disparoissance: f. *A disappearing, or vanishing out of sight; a suddaine withdrawing, or slinking out of companie.*
Disparution: f. *A disparition; or, as* Disparoissance.
Dispathie: f. *An Antipathie, or naturall disagreement.*
Dispensaire: m. *A Dispensatorie, or Booke, that teacheth how to make all Phisicall compositions.*
Dispensateur: m. *A Dispenser; a Disposer of things.*
Dispensation: f. *A dispensation; a distribution, or disposing of things.*
Dispense: f. *as* Dispensation.
Dispensé: m. ée: f. *Dispensed with; released, or held excused; also, proportionably distributed, or disposed of.*
Dispenser. *To dispence with, to take leaue of; to release, or giue leaue vnto; also, proportionably to distribute, or dispose of.*
Dispersé: m. ée: f. *Dispersed, scattered, sundered farre.*
Dispersion: f. *A dispersing, scattering, dissipation.*
Dispos: m. ose: f. *Nimble, actiue, lustie, sound, well disposed in body.*
Disposé: m. ée: f. *Disposed, ordered, sorted, appointed, trimmed, set in frame, put in array.*
Disposer. *To dispose, raunge, order, trim, dresse, appoint, set in frame, put in array.*
Dispositeur: m. *A disposer, sorter, orderer, arraunger of.*

Dispositif: m. ive: f. Dispositiue, dispositorie, disposing.
Disposition: f. A disposing, ordering, sorting, arraying, ranging, ranking; also, an inclination, or disposition; a naturall humor, or affection vnto.
Disposte: com. as Dispos.
Dispostement. Nimbly, actiuely, lustily, soundly, with a good strength, with great agilitie.
Disproportion: f. A disproportion, an inequalitie.
Disproportionné: m. ée: f. Disproportioned, vnequall, ill agreeing.
Disputable: com. Disputable; which may be reasoned of, which will admit the debating.
Disputaillé: m. ée: f. Fondly disputed of, idly debated.
Disputailler. To dispute fondly, to debate a matter scuruily.
Disputation: f. A disputation; reasoning, talking, or debating of a matter pro & contra.
Dispute: f. A dispute, difference, debate, altercation.
'A vieux comptes nouvelles disputes: Prov. Old accompts breed new differences.
Grande dispute verité rebute: Prov. Looke Verité.
Disputé: m. ée: f. Disputed, debated; reasoned, argued, talked, or treated of on both sides.
Disputer. To dispute, reason, argue, talke, or treat of, pro & contra, to debate a matter in controuersie.
Disruption: f. A bursting, or breaking asunder.
Dissection: f. A dissection; a cleauing in peeces, a cutting off, or asunder.
Disseiché: m. ée: f. Dried vp.
Disseicher. To dry vp.
Dissiller. To vnseele, or open the eyes.
Dissemblable: com. Dissemblable, vnlike, diuers, different, vnresembling.
Dissemelé: m. eé: f. Vnsoled, or, whose soles are pulled off.
Dissemeler. To vnsole, or pull the soles off a shoe.
Dissentiment: m. Dissent, disagreement, disaccord, repugnancie in opinions.
Dissention: f. Dissention, strife, debate, variance; controuersie, iarring, discord.
Dissequé: m. ée: f. Cut in peeces, clouen asunder.
Dissequer. To cut in peeces; to open, or cleaue asunder.
Dissimilaire: com. Parties du corps dissimilaires. Such compound parts of the bodie as are of sundrie substances.
Dissimulateur: m. A dissembler, hypocrite, disguiser, double-dealer.
Dissimulation: f. Dissimulation, dissembling, disguising, hypocrisie, cloaking.
Dissimulatrice: f. A woman dissembler.
Dissimulé: m. ée: f. Dissembled; pretended, counterfeited.
Dissimulément. Dissemblingly, closely, couertly, vnder hand, as though he were not the man.
Dissimuler. To dissemble, counterfeit, play the hypocrite, pretend one thing and doe another.
Dissipateur. A dissipator, disperser, or scatterer abroad; an vnthrift, spendall, waster, consumer.
Dissipation: f. A dissipation, dispersing, scattering; a wasting, vnthriftinesse, prodigalitie, consuming.
Dissipé: m. ée: f. Dissipated, dispersed, scattered; wasted, rioted, consumed.
Dissipendre. as Despendre, or Dissiper.
Dissiper. To dissipate, scatter, disperse, dissolue, or send packing; to wast, consume, riot, bring vnto naught.
Dissociable: com. Vnsociable, vnaccompanable; sterne, rude, churlish, froward, vnfriendlie.
Dissociation. A dissociation; or diuiding of companie, a seperation of fellowship.
Dissocié: m. ée: f. Dissociated; seperated, or seuered from the rest.
Dissolu: m. uë: f. Dissolute, loosse, leud, retchlesse, vnrulie, disordered.
Dissoluëment. Dissolutely, loossely.
Dissolution: f. A dissoluing, abolishing; a dissolution, or loossing; also, disorder, excesse, retchlesnesse, loossenesse of conuersation.
Dissonant. Dissonant; discording, disagreeing, iarring, vntuneable, of different tune from, sounding vnlikely.
Dissouldre. To dissolue, vndoe, breake, ouerthrow.
Dissuadé: m. ée: f. Dissuaded, or dehorted from.
Dissuader. To dissuade, or dehort from.
Dissuasion: f. A dissuasion, dissuading, dehorting, aduising to the contrarie.
Dissuëtude: f. Disuse; the leauing of a custome, or vse.
Dissyllabe: com. Of two syllables.
Distance: f. A distance, or difference; a space betweene place and place.
Distant. Distant, different, diuers, farre off, farre remooued, farre asunder.
Distension: f. A distension, stretching, retching, racking, or strouting out.
Distension, & conuulsion de nerfs. The Crampe.
Distillable: com. Distillable; fit, or apt to be distilled.
Distillation: f. A distilling, trilling, or dropping downe.
Distillation d'humeurs. A Rhewme, or Catarrhe.
Distillé: m. ée: f. Distilled; trilled, dropped downe.
Distillement: m. as Distillation.
Distiller. To distill, trill, drop downe by little and little.
Distinct: m. cte: f. Distinguished, diuided, seperated, seuered, differing, alone; distinct, orderlie; marked, noted, pointed.
Distinctement. Distinctly, seuerally, asunder; pointed in order, plainely.
Distinction: f. A distinction, diuersitie, difference, a seperation; also, a note, point, or marke of difference.
Distingué: m. ée: f. Distinguished, diuided.
Distinguer. To distinguish, diuide; seperate, seuer; to discerne, or put a difference betweene; to sunder by different markes, notes, or colours.
Distique: m. A Distic; a couplet, or couple of verses.
Distract: m. Any distraction, or diuision of a Contract, Right, or Act.
Distraction: f. A distraction; a pulling, into diuers parts, or by diuers parties; a violent withdrawing, dissuading, or leading away, from.
Distraict: m. cte: f. Distracted, or distraught; plucked into diuers parts, pulled by diuers parties; violently withdrawne, dissuaded, or led away, from.
Distraict & tiré d'une part & d'autre. Wonderfully distraught, or distracted; in a thousand minds, most vnresolued which way to take; which part to chuse; what side to follow, or fall in with.

Distraire. *To distract, or distraught; to rend into seuerall peeces, or hale into seuerall wayes; to draw into sundrie parts, or driue into sundrie passions; violently, and diuersly to withdraw, dismember, or dissolue.*

Distrait. *as* Distraict.

Distrayant: m.ante: f. *Distracting; drawing into seuerall parts, driuing into sundrie passions; violently, and diuersly withdrawing, or dismembring.*

Distribué: m.ée: f. *Distributed, diuided, parted; dealt, bestowed; deliuered, allotted, appointed.*

Procez distribué. *Looke* Distribuer les procez.

Distribuer. *To distribute; to distinguish, diuide, sort; to deale, bestow, giue in sundrie parts; to allot, or appoint vnto euerie one his portion.*

Distribuer les procez. *To referre th'examination of causes vnto some iudicious* Conseillier, *that may report vnto the Court the true state thereof; also, to appoint causes their seuerall dayes of hearing.*

Distributeur: m. *A distributor, dealer, diuider; hee that appoints vnto others their seuerall portions in a thing bestowed.*

Distributif: m.iue: f. *Distributiue; dealing, diuiding, distributing.*

Distribution. *A distribution, dealing, parting, diuision; a sorting, or seuering; a doale; an allotting or appointing out vnto each his portion.*

Distribution des procez. *The sorting of causes vnto their seuerall dayes of hearing, and Courts to be heard in; or as in* Distribuer les procez.

District: m. *A district; the liberties, or precincts of a place; the territorie, or circuit of countrey, within which a Lord, or his Officers may iudge, compell, or call in question, the inhabitants.*

Distroict. *as* District.

Distroict de moulin. *as* Banlieuë de moulin.

Dit: m. *A saying, speech, tearme, word.*

Il ne faut pas enquerir d' ou soit le dit, mais qu'il soit bon: Prov. *Inquire not whence a speech came so it be good.*

Dit: m.ite: f. *as* Dict.

Ditateur: m. *An inricher.*

Dite: f. à sa dite. *At his becke, at his nod; after his will and pleasure.*

Ditellet: m. *A little worke, a Pamphlet, a small Treatise.*

Divague: com. *Straying, raunging, roguing about, roaming abroad, wandering vp and downe, whose shooes are made of running leather.*

Divagué. *Strayed, raunged, roamed; wandered about.*

Divaguer. *To stray, raunge, rogue about, roame abroad, runne vnsteadily from place to place, wander inconstantly vp and downe.*

Divers: m.erse: f. *Diuers, differing, vnlike, sundrie, repugnant; also, froward, vnquiet, waspish, diuerous, waiward, hard to please.*

Diversement. *Diuersly, seuerally, asunder, apart by it selfe; differently, in seuerall fashions, in sundrie manner.*

Diversifié: m.ée: f. *Diuersified, varied; made of diuers formes, fashions, colours.*

Diversifier. *To varie, diuersifie; decke with sundrie colours, worke in diuers fashions; interlace, or mingle sundrie formes together; to change, or alter often.*

Diversité: f. *A diuersitie; seueraltie; varietie; a difference, or vnlikenesse.*

Diverti: m.ie: f. *Diuerted, turned, altered, withdrawne, dissuaded, averted, kept, or driuen from.*

Divertir. *To diuert, auert, alter, withdraw, dissuade, keepe, or driue from.*

Divin: m.ine: f. *Diuine, godlie, heauenlie, most holie; participating of the Godhead; belonging to, or comming from, God.*

Huile divin. *Oyle extracted by distillation from tiles, or brickes which haue bene some time steeped in verie old oyle.*

Divinance: f. *A diuining, presaging, foretelling, ghessing, prophecying.*

Divination: f. *A diuination, presage, or coniecturall iudgement of things to come.*

Divinement. *Diuinely, godlily, heauenly, most holily.*

Diviner. *To diuine, presage, foretell; See* Deviner.

Divinité: f. *Diuinitie, Godhead.*

Divis. *as* Divisé; *Or, deuised; passed, or graunted by deuise.*

Dot, & mariage divis. *The dowrie, or portion giuen, or appointed out for, a daughter by her father, or mother.*

Doüaire divis. *The ioynture, or dower accorded, assigned, and laid out at the time of the contract.*

Divisé. *Diuided, parted, seperated, disioyned, sundered, distinguished.*

Doüaire divisé. *as* Doüaire devis.

Divisément. *Diuidedly, or diuisiuely; seperately, distinctly, seuerally.*

Diviser. *To diuide, part, sunder, distinguish, disioyne, seperate; sort into seuerall parcells, cut out into equall portions.*

Divisible: com. *Diuisible, diuidable.*

Division: f. *A diuision, partition, seperation, distribution, disposing of a thing into sundrie members, parcells, or portions.*

Divorce: m. *A diuorce; a seperation, sundering, parting of man and wife; the dissolution of mariage; also, trouble, crosses, ouerthwarting.*

Diuretique: com. *Which hath the power, or propertie to make one pisse.*

Diurne: com. *Diurnall, dailie, done by day, belonging to the day.*

Diuturne: com. *Long-lasting, of long continuance.*

Divulgateur. *A diuulger, publisher, proclaimer.*

Divulgué: m.ée: f. *Diuulged, published, proclaimed, talked, or knowne all the world ouer.*

Divulguer. *To diuulge, publish, make common, spread abroad in the world.*

Divulsion: f. *A diuulsion, or pulling vp; also, a cutting, section, or diuision.*

Dix. *Tenne.*

Dixain. *See* Dizain.

Dixaine: f. *A Ward in a Citie, comprehending ten parishes, Constableships, or Tribes; also, a halfe-thraue of corne consisting of ten sheaues.*

Dixenier. *An Officer, or Ouerseer, next in authoritie vnto the* Quartenier, *in a* Dixaine, *or Ward; & somewhat resembling our Aldermans Deputie; but that euery* Quartenier *hath diuers of these vnder him.*

Dixhuict. *Eighteene; also, a Lapwing, or Blacke-Plouer; (so tearmed because her ordinarie crie sounds not vnlike this word.)*

Dixhuitiesme. *The eighteenth.*

Dixiesme. *The tenth.*

Droict de dixiesme denier. *The tenth penie, or pennie-worth of all Mines, Minerals, Mettalls, and other*

other substances gotten within the ground, throughout France, due unto the King; also, the Admiralls share, or part (being a tenth) of all shipwrackes, prizes, conquests, &c, made at Sea.

Dixme; &, Dixmer. *as* Disme; &, Dismer.

Dixneuf. *Nineteene.*

Dixneufiesme. *The nineteenth.*

Dixsept. *Seuenteene.*

Dizain: m. *A tenth; also, a Dittie of tenne Stanzoes, or Stanzo of tenne verses; also, a paire of beades containing tenne peeces (or courses;) also, a (French) Pennie.*

Dizain: m. ine: f. *Of, or belonging to, tenne; tenne, or containing iust tenne.*

Dizaine: f. *A tenth; tenne whole parts; the number of tenne.*

Dizeaux. *as* Diseaux.

Döanne. *as* Doüane.

Dobbe: f. *A Tub.*

Dobé: m. ée: f. *Beaten, lammed, belthwacked.*

Dober. *To beat, swinge, lamme, belthwacke; to canuasse throughly.*

Docile: com. *Docible, teachable, tractable, apt to learne, quickly taught, easily instructed, soone conceiuing.*

Docilisé: m. ée: f. *Made docible, teachable; tractable.*

Dociliser. *To docilize, to make docible, tractable, teachable.*

Docilité: f. *Docilitie, aptnesse to learne, quicknesse of apprehension.*

Docte: com. *Learned, skillfull, cunning, throughly instructed.*

Doctement. *Learnedly, skilfully, cunningly, Clerkelike.*

Docteur: m. *A Doctor.*

Docteur de Quandoque. *A Dunsicall Doctor.*

Docteur en gaye science. *A Doctor of Rie; (In* Thoulouse *they sometimes vse to make a merrie companion proceed Doctor with this title:)* ¶Rab.

Doctoral: m. ale: f. *Doctorall; of, or belonging to, a Doctor.*

Doctorande: f. *The solemnitie, or time of proceeding Doctor in any Art; Doctors commencement.*

Doctorat: m. *A Doctorship; the degree of a Doctor.*

Doctorie: f. *The degree of a Doctor; a Doctorship.*

Doctrinable: com. *Docible, teachable, apt to learne, fit to be taught.*

Doctrinal. *The patterne of learning.*

Doctrine: f. *Learning, doctrine, schollership, science, Clerkeship; skill in, knowledge of, good letters.*

Doctrine du Palais: *Ciuilitie, curtesie, good maners, courtlie behauiour, fashion, carriage.*

Document: m. *A document, precept; instruction, admonition; experiment, example.*

Dodecaëdre. *A Geometricall bodie, or figure, of twelue faces.*

Dodechedron. *A twelue-conered proportion, or figure.*

Dodeliné: m. ée: f. *Rocked; also, fondly nodding, vnsteadily carried; also, dandled, lolled, lulled, fedled.*

Dodelinement: m. *A rocking; also, a foolish nodding, vnsteadie wagging (as of the head) vp and downe; also, a dandling, lolling, or lulling of.*

Dodeliner. *To rocke, or iog vp and downe; also, to dandle, to loll, or lull, to fedle, cocker, hug fondly, make a wanton of.*

Dodeliner de la teste. *To nod often, or wag the head much; to carrie the head vnsteadily, or like a boat in a storme.*

Dodelineur. *The rocker of a cradle; or as* Dodelineux.

Dodelineux: m. *A rocker; also, one that nods much, or wags his head verie often; also, a fond, fantasticall, or giddie-headed noddie; one whose head, and humours are most vnsteadie; also, a fawning, or flattering companion.*

Dodelineux: m. euse: f. *Much nodding, often wagging the head; also, toyish, fond, fantasticall, humorous, vnsteadie-headed, giddie-braind.*

Dodentral. *See* Dodrental.

Dodine: f. *A fond, or giddie wag of the head; or as* Dodelinement.

Canars à la dodine. *Serued in with (French) onion sauce.*

Dodiner. *To rocke; shake, shog, wag vp and downe; or, as* Dodeliner.

Dodineux. *as* Dodelineux.

Dodo. *A word wherewith Nurses rocke, or lull, their sucklings asleepe.*

Apres bu dodo: Prov. *After swink sleepe.*

Dodrental: m. ale: f. *Nine ounces heauie; nine inches, or a full span, long.*

Dodu: m. *A fat chops, or chuffe.*

Dodu: m. uë: f. *Fat, plump, chuffie, round-cheeked, fullbodied.*

Doët: m. *A brooke, or spring.*

Dogguin: m. *A filthie great old curre.*

Dogmatiser. *To teach strange doctrine; to breed a sect, or broach new opinions.*

Dogmatisme: m. *The teaching, or preaching of new doctrine, the producing of a new sect.*

Dogmatiste: m. *A forger of new sects, or opinions; one that makes, or would trie, conclusions.*

Dogue: m. *A Mastiffe, or great dog.*

Doigt: m. *A finger; also, a fingers breadth; or the sixteenth part of a foot, in measuring.*

Les cinq doigts nostre Dame. *Fiue-leaued grasse.*

Se donner du doigt dans l'oeil. se pensans signer se donnent du doigt dans l'oeil. *Thinking to crosse, they scratch, themselues: (appliable to ignorant, or heedlesse coxcombes.)*

Mettre le doigt dessus. Tu as mis le doigt dessus. *Thou hast hit it, or ghessed aright (from them that lay their hand on their smut.)*

Mettre le doigt entre le bois, & l'escorce. *To loue medling, to be of a busie humor; or sawcily to intermeddle with, or take too much notice of, the businesses that are, or differences that may be, betweene two neere friends; also, to breed quarrels, make debate, or set diuision, betweene them.*

I'en mettray le doigt au feu. *I am most assured of it; I dare answer for it, or pawne my head on it; I know it is most true.*

Monstrer au doigt. *To shew manifestly, point out euidently, lead one (as it were) by the hand vnto a thing.*

Mordre les doigts. *To chafe, or fret inwardly at a thing which is past helpe, or out of his power to alter.*

Servy au doigt, & à l'oeil. *Serued at a becke.*

Toucher du bout des doigts. *To runne lightly, or*

or sleightly ouer.; onely to glaunce at.

Les Alemanes ont l' esprit aux doigts: Pro. *The Germanes are excellent Artificers; or haue nimbler fingers then heads.*

L'herbe qu'on cognoist on la doit lier à son doigt. pro. *Looke*, Herbe.

Qui a besoing de feu le cerche avec le doigt: Pro. *Let him that needeth fire, take paines to find it.*

Qui remue les pierres ses doigts casse. Pro. *He that remoueth stones crusheth his fingers; harsh things are seldome stirred without harme.*

Vn mesme couteau me coupe le pain, & le doigt. Pro. (*Appliable vnto any thing that does both good and ill offices.*)

Doigtier: m. *A thimble or fingerstall; also, as* Digital.

Doil: m. *A pipestaffe; and, (lesse properly) any vessell, or caske of a (reasonable) big size.*

Doile: *The same; or, as* Douille.

Panneau de doile *A cant pane, or peece.*

Doille: *as* Douille.

Doire; *for* Douäire; *A dower, or dowrie.*

Doisil: m. *A faucet.*

Dol: m. *The name of a city in Burgondy.*

Fiebvre de Dol. *The french pockes.*

Dol. m. *Deceit, fraud, guile, craft, tromperie, trecherie, falshood, wilinesse.*

Dolé m. ee: f. *Squared, planed, hewed smooth, wrought, or made plaine with an ax, or addis.*

Doleance: f. *A wayling, lamentation, moaning complaining, waymenting.*

Dolent. *Sorrowfull, heauie, greeuing; painfull, aking, smarting; wretched, wailefull, miserable, wofull.*

Dolentement. *Mournefully, heauily, sorrowfully, wofully, grieuously, wailefully.*

Doler (du bois.) *To chip, to square, to plane, to hew smooth, to make plaine with an ax, or addis.*

Doleur: f. *Griefe, sorrow, anguish, woe, sadnesse, teene, heauinesse, ache, paine, smart, sorenesse; a throw, throbbing, wringing.*

Doleux: m. euse f. *Wilie, deceitfull, Subtill, guilefull, fraudulent; false, trecherous.*

Doliman *as* Dolyman.

Doloir. *To greeue, sorrow; moane; throb; to ake, warch, paine, smart.*

Bien escorche à qui ne deult: Pro. *No matter though they flayed be who feele no paine in flaying.*

Femme se plaind, femme se deult, femme est malade quand elle veut: Pro. *Looke* Femme.

Doloire: f. *A (Coopers) ax, or addis; also a Carpenters ax, or plaining hatchet.*

Doloüere. *as* Doloire.

Dolouretisement. *Dolourously; heauily, sorrowfully, wailefully, most wofully; also, grieuously, or till it ake gaine.*

Doloureux: m. euse: f. *Sorrowfull, dolorous, painefull, wofull; also, smarting, grieuing, payning, or putting to much paine.*

Parties douloureuses. *Tender, or which cannot indure to be touched.*

Dolousant. *Wayling, lamenting, waymenting, making moane.*

Dolouser. *To wayle, moane, lament, wayment, complaine.*

Dolyman: m. *A Turkish gowne, long coate, or vpper garment; collerlesse, and closed with long buttons downe to the girdlestead.*

Dom Iehan. *Sir Iohn, or, lord Iohn.*

Domaine: m. *A demaine; a mans patrimonie or Inheritance, proper and hereditarie possessions; those whereof he is the right or true Lord, possessor, and absolute owner; also, an absolute, and hereditarie propertie in, and possession of, land, &c; also, an honor; or a principall* Fief, *Mannor, or Mannorhouse; the place whereof inferior* Fiefs *are held, or vassalls hould.*

Domaine congeable; *See* Congeable.

Domaine de la Couronne. *The crowne land; Ancient demesne; or th'ancient Inheritance of the crowne; also, any land which hath remained in the Kings hands, and bene disposed of by his officers, for the space of ten yeares.*

Domaine forain; *Was at the first, in* Francis *the firsts time, an Imposition of* iiij. d. *in the pound vpon all kind of wares, and* v. s. Tour. *vpon euery* Queuë *of wine, sold: whereunto* Henry *the second ioyned two other Imposts,* Resve, & Haut passage, *& tooke for them all together* viij. d. *in the pound; but afterwards disunited them in effect (leuying their seuerall and vsuall rates,) and ioyned them onely in this name.*

Domaine de France. *as* Domaine de la Couronne, *And, as it, vnalienable; not by any especiall law, but by the generall custome of all Monarchies, interessed in the preseruation thereof, as of the chiefest dowrie which they bring to their princes at their comming to the crowne.*

Domaine immuable. Censives, *Chiefe rents, and all fundamentall rights, and seruices, which follow the land howsoeuer it descend, or be disposed of.*

Domaine muable. *A propertie in a thing whose value may be improoued, or impaired, according to the yearelie letting of it; (generally) such land as is, or may be ordinarily, and often leassed; and the rents thereof raised, or lessened vpon euerie lease.*

Domaine du Roy. *The kings demaine; the rents, reuenue, profits, & fruits of the crown lands; also, the benefit of casualties, and rights of Seigneurie, or of Iurisdiction thereunto belonging; also all manner of lands confiscated by, or forfeited vnto him; and such as he had in his owne right before he came to the crowne; and such as he purchased after.*

Domaine du Royaume. *as* Domaine de la Couronne.

De son domaine faire son Fief. *Looke* Fief.

De son Fief faire son domaine. c'est, reünir à sa Table, & raproprier à son domaine le Fief, ou Censif tenu de soy: ¶ Ragueau.

Domanial: m. ale f. *Of, or belonging to, a demayne, Mannor, or principall* Fief.

Exploict domanial. *A seisure made by a Lord of his tenants land, for his homage, rights, and seruices withheld from him.*

Domanier: m. *Th'owner of a demayne, or of land in demayne.*

Domanier: m. ere f. *as* Domanial.

Droict domanier. *The priuiledge a Lord Iusticer hath, to proceed, of his owne authoritie, by way of execution, without any written commission, in cases that concerne his ancient demaine, or th'accustomed rights thereof.*

Seigneur domanier. *The Lord of the soile of a Mannor; a chiefe Lord.*

Dome. *A Townehouse, Guildhall, Statehouse, Meetinghouse in a Citie (from that of Florence, which is called so;) also, as* Dosme.

Domestique: com. *Domesticall, housall, of our household: also, tame, familier, priuie.*

Domestiquement. *Domestically, tamely, familierly, priuately, at home, within doores.*

Do-

Domestiquer. *To tame, reclaime; ciuilize, make familier, gentle, tractable, housall.*

Domestiqué: m. ée. f. *Tamed, reclaymed, ciuilized, made familier, gentle, tractable, housall.*

Domicile: m. *An house, mansion; habitation, dwelling, place of aboade.*

Domicilié. homme domicilié en vn tel lieu. *Housed, or that hath a dwelling, in such a place; an inhabitant of.*

Domicilier: m. *A housekeeper.*

Se Domicilier. *To house himselfe; to goe to inhabit, or to keepe house.*

Dominant. *Gouerning, ruling, commaunding, bearing sway, hauing authoritie ouer.*

Fief suzerain, & dominant. *A mannor held in chief, or whereof diuers others hould.*

Seigneur dominant. *A Lord paramount, or chiefe Lord.*

Dominateur. *A maister, ruler, commaunder, gouerner.*

Domination: f. *Dominion, rule, power, authoritie, gouernment, soueraignty, sway ouer others.*

Dominatrice: f. *A gouernesse, commaunderesse, Mistresse, Ladie of.*

Dominé: m. ée: f. *Gouerned ruled, commanded, swayed, maistered, seigniorized, domineered ouer.*

Dominer. *To gouerne, rule, commaund, maister, domineere, to haue soueraigntie, beare sway ouer, a stroke among, others; to seigniorize it.*

Domineur. *as* Dominateur.

Dominical. la lettre dominicale. *The dominicall letter.*

L'oraison dominicale. *The Lords prayer, the Pater-ster.*

Domino: m. *A kind of hood, or habit for the head, worne by Cannons; (and hence) also, a fashion of vaile vsed by some women that mourne.*

Dominorié: m. ée. f. *Domineered ouer.*

Dominorier. *To domineere, to beare sway; as* Dominer.

Dominotier: m. *A maker of the hood called* Domino.

Dommage: m. *Dammage, losse, detriment, hinderance, incommoditie, discommoditie, hurt, harme, scath, displeasure; disaduantage; a mischiefe done, or ouer-heauie charge imposed.*

Mais dommage que, &c. *But it is strange, or tis a wonder, that, &c.*

Qui est loing du plat est prez de son dommage. Pro. *He that sits farre from the dish is neere his disaduantage.*

Dommageable: com. *Dammageable; hurtfull, harmefull, hindering, incommodious vnto.*

Dommageablement. *Hurtfully, with dammage, to ones harme, losse, and hinderance.*

Dommas: m. *A Cope-wearer; or, the Priest, or Cannon, who, by turne, is to weare a Cope for a weeke together.*

Dompté: m. ée. f. *Tamed, reclaimed, subdued.*

Dompter. *To tame, reclaime; daunt; &c; as* Donter.

Dompte-venin: m. *Celandine the greater, swallowes hearb, tetterworte, pileworte, figworte.*

Dompte-villain: m. *A good cudgell, or any thing wherby a Stubborne knaue is tamed, or awed.*

Dompture: f. *A taming, reclaiming; daunting; breaking, subduing.*

Ce que poulain prend en dompture il le maintient tant comme il dure: Pro: *Looke* Poulain.

Don: m. *A gift, graunt; offering, present; bribe; reward; also, as* Dom.

le don de mercy. *The gift wherein a woman is more mercifull then modest.*

Donaison: f. *A free gift, or deed of gift.*

Donat. *The name of a certaine Gramarian, read in some Schooles; whence;*

Les diables estoient encores à leur Donat. *The diuells were, as then, but breeching boyes, like Grammar Schoole boyes, but young in experience, but Nouices in the world.*

Donataire: m. *A donatarie, or donee.*

Donateur: m. *A donor: giuer, bestower.*

Donation: f. *A donation; a present, gift, or deed of gift; also, a giuing.*

Donation à cause de mort. *See,* Mort.

Donation entre vifs. *A perfect, and vnreuocable gift; an absolute deed of gift, (made, and executed in a mans life time.)*

Dondaine: f. *A certaine warlike engine (out of vse in these daies) whereout great round stones were shot; also, the burden of a song.*

Dondon: f. *A short, fat, and grosse woman; a small bundle of farts.*

Dongeon: m. *A Dungeon; a strong Tower, or platforme, in the middle of a Castle or fort, wherein the besieged make their last efforts (of defence) when the rest is forced.*

Donjon. *as* Dongeon.

Donné: m. ée. f. *Giuen, conferred, bestowed; presented; yeelded, or deliuered vp; also, dated.*

Vn donné à entendre. *A relation, speech, tale, narration.*

Il s'en est bien donné. *He hath tipled squarely.*

On luy a donné son sac, & ses quilles: *He is cassed, dismissed, or turned out of seruice.*

Chose bien donnée n'est iamais perduë: Pro: *He that giues discretly gaines directly.*

Donnée: f. *A dole, guift, or distribution, a donatiue.*

Donne-lardon: m. *A mocker, flouter, giber, ieaster; one that bestowes a liuery, or cast of his wit, vpon euery one he sees.*

Donnement: m. *A giuing, bestowing, conferring; presenting; yeelding, or deliuering vp.*

Donner. *To giue, bestow, conferre, minister; presēt, grant; offer; yeeld or deliuer vp.*

Donner des adots. *To lay lustily about him, to bestirre himselfe like a man.*

Donner barres à. *To stop, or stay the current of; to shut vp.*

Donner le bond à. *Looke,* Bond.

Donner carriere à. *To set a running, a gallopping, a gadding; also, to let goe, or giue scope vnto.*

se donner carriere. *To raunge, flie out; make a vagarie; to take some libertie, or a little swindge abroad; to recreate himselfe a little.*

Donner la carte blanche à: *To deliuer a man a blanke signed with his hand; hence, to offer to receiue, or vndergoe, any conditions he will tye him too, or exact of him.*

Donner les champs à. *To free, or set at libertie.*

Donner la clef des champs à. *To dismisse, let goe, send out.*

Donner la cognoissance de. *To bring acquainted with.*

Donner coup à: *To worke effect, or doe good in.*

Donner le croc en jambe à. *To foyle, supplant, ouerturne, ouerthrow.*

Don-

Donner dedans les. *To breake in vpon, rush among the thickest of, them.*
Donner à dos à. *To assaile, or set vpon, behind; Looke* Dos.
Donner dronos. *Looke* Dronos.
Donner le flanc à tout propos. *To yeeld vnto, or bee woon by, euerie word.*
Donner fond. *To cast anker.*
Donner es gauffriers. *To leacher.*
Donner iour à. *To grace, beautifie, decorate, giue light, or luster vnto.*
Donner jour à sa despence. *So to spend as the world may take most notice of his expences; Looke* Iour.
Donner main-levée de. *To restore, giue backe, yeeld vp, things taken, or seised.*
Donner mal de teste à. *To make iealous.*
Donner en mandement. *To commaund, bid, giue in charge; to will and commaund (the phrase of Princes in their Letters Patents.)*
Donner la mitre, & la crosse à. *To countenance, or authorize by the specious pretext of religious Ornaments.*
Donner la muse à. *To put into a dumpe; to make to studie, or pause about a matter.*
Donner des oeufs de Pasques à toutes restes: *Look* Pasque.
Donner ombrage à. *To make iealous, fill with suspition; giue an inkling of.*
Donner parole à. *Looke* Parole.
Donner pente à. *In wrastling, to offer play, or an aduantage, vnto his aduersarie.*
Donner pied à. *To set afoot, send abroad into the world; giue beginning to.*
Donner pied ferme à. *To ground, settle, assure the seat of, giue sure footing vnto.*
Donner du pied à. *To scorne, contemne, spurne.*
Donner le plein & le rond à. *To accomplish, or perfect.*
Donner à poinct nommé. *To hit point-blanke; to strike the marke he shoots at.*
Donner du rosmarin. *To giue a wooer his answer; or, a flat deniall.*
Donner vn mauvais sault. *To do a man a mischiefe; giue him a vild push; make him catch great harme.*
Donner vne lourde strette. *To ierke shrewdly, pinch extreamely; See* Strette.
Donner de la teste. *To butt, or iurre; to runne his head against.*
Il ne sçait ou donner de la teste. *Hee knowes not what to do, nor whither to betake him.*
Donner entre deux vertes vne meure. *To season matters, or iumble good and bad together.*
Donner d'vne. *To tell a lie; to giue a gudgeon, a lurch, a gleeke; a drie lift; to gull, or make a foole of.*
Donner vogue à. *To authorize; to giue sway, or scope vnto.*
Donner voile à tous vents. *To saile with all winds; weakely, to be persuaded by euerie one that speakes to him; inconstantly, to be swayed by euerie seuerall humor that moues him.*
Se donner du doigt dans l'oeil. qui se pensant signer se donnent du doigt &c. *Who (with their fingers) meaning to blesse, are like to blind, themselues: (applicable to Ninny-hammers.)*
Se donner de garde. *To beware, take heed, be circumspect, looke well about him.*
Se donner de bon temps. *To make much of himselfe, to liue merrily, or at ease; to passe away his time delightfully.*
Ie te le donne gaigné. *I grant it, I yeeld vnto thee, I giue thee place, I leaue thee the victorie.*
Ce qu'on donne luit, ce qu'on mange puit: Prov. *(a true difference betweene bountie and sensualitie.)*
Entre promettre, & donner doit on la fille marier: Prov. *Betweene promising, and giuing the maid ought to be maried; (or as vnder* Promettre.)
Fille qui donne s'abandonne. Pro. *Looke* Fille.
Promettre sans donner est fol recomforter: Prov. *Faire words make fooles faine.*
Qui tost donne deux fois donne: Prov. *Hee that giues quickly giues twice:* viz. *Doubles th'estimate of his gift.*
Qui tout me donne, tout me nie: Prov. *Hee that giues me all denies me all:* viz. *He that offers me all, meanes to giue me nothing.*
Tout est perdu ce qu'on donne à fol: Prov. *Whatsoeuer is giuen to fooles is lost: for either they are simple and cannot, or vngratefull and will not, requite it.*
Donneur: m. *A donor; a giuer, a bestower.*
Donq. *Then, therefore.*
Donques. *The same.*
Dont. *Whence, whereby, whereof, whereupon; and (in the beginning of questions) how comes it to passe.*
Dontable: com. *Tameable; reclaimeable, which may be ruled.*
Donté: m. ée: f. *Tamed, broken, reclaimed, ruled; daunted, subdued, ouercome, brought vnder.*
Dontement: m. *A taming, reclaiming, breaking; ouercomming, subduing.*
Donte-mer. *Sea-taming, waues-breaking, surges-calming.*
Donte-orgueil. *Pride-taming, stoutnesse-daunting, hautinesse-downe-pulling.*
Donter. *To tame, reclaime, breake; daunt; vanquish, ouercome, subdue, bring vnder.*
Donteresse: f. *She that tameth, or subdueth.*
Donteur. *A tamer, reclaimer, breaker, ruler; daunter, subduer, ouercommer.*
Donzelle: f. *An Eele-powt.*
Dorade: f. *The fish Guilthead, or Goldenie; also, as* Dorée.
Dorcade. *A Roe-Bucke.*
Doré: m. ée: f. *Gilt ouer; also, of gold; also, faire, beautifull, brightly shining.*
Brandon doré. *The Sunne.*
Il eschappa par la porte dorée. viz. *By mouey.*
Dorée: f. *The Dorce, or Saint Peters fish; also (though not so properly) the Goldfish, or Goldenie; also, a kind of delicate yellow Summer peare; the gold peare.*
Dorelle: f. *The pulse* Orobus, *bitter Vetch, or bitter Fitch.*
Dorelot: m. *A darling, dilling, sweet heart; wanton, fedle; also, as* Dorlot.
Dorelotté. *as* Dorlotté.
Doreloteur. *A cockerer, dandler, hugger; fawner, soother, flatterer of.*
Dorelotter. *as* Dorletter.
Dorer. *To gild, or doe ouer with gold.*
Dorerie: f. *Gilt worke; also, a gilding.*
Dores-en avant. *Henceforth, from hence forward; hereafter.*
Doreur. *A gilder.*
Doreur de la nuict. *A Gold-finder, a Jakes-farmer.*
Doreure: f. *A gilding; also, a Billement, or Jewell of two peeces.*

Doriphage:

Doriphage: m. *A Munch-present; a deuourer of bribes, an eater of gifts.*

Dorlot: m. *A iewell, or prettie trinket, as a Chaine, brooche, ring, aglet, button, billement, &c, wherewith a woman sets out her apparell, or decks herselfe;* ¶ Pic: *and hence, as* Dorelot.

Dorlotté: m. ée: *Decked, or set out with prettie trinkets; also, dandled, cockered, hugged, much made of; also, drowned in pleasure, vp to th'eares in delights; also, nice, quaint, mincing it, making it fine or goodlie.*

Dorlotter. *To furnish, decke, or set out with prettie trinkets; also, to cocker, dandle, hug, stroake, make much of; also, to mince it, make it fine, or goodlie; also, to tumble or wallow in fulnesse of delights.*

Dormailler. *To slumber.*

Dormant. *Sleeping;* En dormant; *in his sleepe, while he tooke his rest, as he slumbered.*

Eau dormante. *Standing water, such as is in pits, cesternes, &c.*

Fenestre à voirre dormant. *A close window of glasse without any casement; a standing window that is not to be opened, nor shut.*

`A qui l'on peut sans les resveiller arracher les dents en dormant. *Whose teeth one may plucke out without awaking them; (Appliable to such as be sluggish, dull, or sencelesse in extremitie.)*

Dormart: m. *A slug-a-bed, a drousie companion, a heauie-headed luske, one that euer sleepes as he goes, one of the seauen sleepers.*

Dormeveille: f. *A being betweene a sleep and awake; or a counterfeiting of sleepe.*

Dormeur: m. *A sleeper.*

Iamais dormeur ne fit bon guet, ni paresseux ne fit beau faict: Pro. *Looke* paresseux.

Dormilieuse, *as* Dormilleuse.

Dormille: f. *The sicknesse of silkewormes, during which they sleepe; also, a kind of small Lamprey.*

Dormilleuse. *The cramp fish, whose propertie is to benumme the hands of her taker.*

Dormilleux: m. *as* Dormillart.

Dormilleux: m. euse: f. *Heauie, sleepie, drousie, sluggish.*

Dormir: m. *A nap, a sleep; a sleeping.*

Vn dormir attrait l'autre: Pro: *The more a man sleepes, the more he may.*

Dormir. *To sleepe, rest; slumber, take a nap; also to slug it, or be negligent.*

Dormir en chien. *To sleep before dinner or fasting, in an open Sunne.*

Dormir sur les deux costez. *To barrell vp sleep; or, when one is wearie with sleeping on th'one side, to turn, and to it againe on th'other.*

Dormir la grasse matinée. *To lie in bed long a mornings.*

Dormir sur le jour. *To take a nap at dinner time, or presently after; to sleepe at noone dayes.*

Dormir son vin. *To sleepe vpon a drinking, or disgest his drink with sleeping.*

Ce sont des contes à dormir debout. *These are most idle, friuolous, or foolish tales.*

Il ne laisse dormir sa debte sur le Soleil. *He lets not the Sunne goe downe vpon his debt; he alwaies payes his debts before he goe to bed.*

Assez dort qui rien ne fait: Prov. *As good be fast asleep as idle awake.*

En seureté dort qui n'a que perdre: Pro. *He sleepes securely that hath nought to loose.*

Le lict est vne belle chose, qui n'y dort ony repose: Prov. *As in* Lict.

Qui a bruit de se lever matin peut dormir iusques à disner: Prov. *He that is thought an earlie man may sleepe till dinner time; he that is held an honest man may long abuse the world; common report gulles manie, who thinke no hurt when outwardly they see none.*

Tant dort le chat qu'il se resveille: Prov. *The slugging or sleepie Cat at length awakes.*

Regnard qui dort la matinée n'a pas la langue emplumée: Pro, *He cannot thriue that lies in bed a mornings.*

Dormitoire. *A sleep-procuring medecine.*

Dorque. *A kind of great and round earthen vessel;* ¶ Lang: *also a great fish thats enemy to the Whale.*

Dorsal: m. ale: f. *Of, or belonging to, the backe; whence;*

Cautere dorsal. *The backe-cauter; somewhat like a knife; or hauing a back like a knife, and searing onely on the other side.*

Dortoir: m. *A dorter, or lodging wherein manie sleepe together; also, a Churchyard.*

Dortuit. *Sleepie, drowsie.*

Dorure: f. *as* Doreure. *A gilding.*

Dos: m. *The backe; a back-part, or backside; also a ridge.*

Dos du nez. *The bridge of the nose.*

Nichil au dos. *Looke* Nichil.

`A dos d'Asne. *Ridgill-backed, high-ridged, or hauing a sharp ridge; high, or highest, in the middle; sharp, or sharpening, toward the top, or middle; resembling the backe of an asse.*

Donner à dos à. *To assaile, or set vpon behinde:* se donnerent eux mesmes à dos. *They tumbled for hast, one ouer another.*

Faire ensemble la beste à deux dos. *To leacher.*

On a fait de son dos courroye. *He hath bene whipped soundly, lashed horribly.*

Mal est caché à qui l'on void le dos. Prov: *He's but ill hid whose backe is seene.*

Qui faict credos charge son dos. Prov: *He that credits much carries much; or, he that giues much credit vndergoes a great charge.*

Dose. *A dose; the quantitie of potion, or medecine, which a Phisition appoints his patient shall take at once.*

Dosme: m. *A flat-round louer, or open roofe, to a steeple, bankettinghouse, piggeon-house &c somewhat resembling the bell of a great watch.*

Dosse d'ail *A cloue of garlicke.*

Dossé: m. ée: f. *Indorsed.*

Dosserasse: f. *A buttresse, or supporter to beare vp the great beame of a wall.*

Dossier: m. *A back-stay; any thing that easeth, or staieth the backe, or serues for it to leane on; as a rayle behind a forme; the back of a chaire, &c; also, the backe of a chimney.*

Vn dossier de pavillon. *The head of a Pauillion, or Canopie,; the peece that hangs down at the head thereof.*

Dossier de sable. *A shelfe, or banke of sand.*

Dossier: m. *Of, or belonging to, the backe; also, easing, bearing, or, staying the backe; also, growing on the back; and hence;*

Soye dossiere. *A hogs bristles.*

Dossiere: f. *The part of a draught horses harnesse which runnes ore-crosse his backe; we call it the ridgeband.*

Dost: m. *A dowrie; a maidens portion; goods or lands giuen*

giuen with a woman in mariage.
Dot. *as* Doſt.
Dotal: m. ale: f. *Dotall; giuen in dowrie; of, or belonging to, a dowrie.*
Dotateur: m. *An endower.*
Doté: m. ée: f. *Indued, or endowed with; hauing a portion in.*
Dotter. *To doate.*
Doüaire: m. *A dower, or ioynture for a woman after her husbands death; alſo her mariage good, or the portion ſhe hath, or brings, to her mariage.*
Doüaire plein &, entier. *A ioynture of, or thirds in, the whole land deſcended; which is eſpecially, when no other woman hath any dower out of it.*
Doüairiére: f. *A dowager; a widow endowed, or that hath a ioyntrue.*
Doüane. *The name of the Cuſtomehouſe at Lyons; hence alſo, any cuſtome, or impoſt; and particularly, two French Crownes taken by th'Officers of that houſe, for euerie peece of gold, or ſiluer (and ratably for all other kinds of ſtuffe, and marchandiſe) imported.*
Doüanne: f. *as* Doüane.
Doüannier: m. *An Officer of the Cuſtome-houſe.*
Doubé: m. ée: f. *Rigged, or trimmed vp, as a ſhip.*
Douber. *To rig, or trimme, a ſhip.*
Doublage. *as* Aides Chevels; *Called ſo in the Cuſtomes of* Aniou, *and* Maine; *Looke* Aides; *a reliefe is alſo called,* doublage; *becauſe a double, or two yeres, rent, or* Cens *is paid for it.*
Doublant. *Doubling, making double, or as much more.*
Double: m. *A double; double part; or double pace; twice as much; alſo, the copie of a writing; alſo, a peece of baſe coine worth two pence* Tourn.
Double d' Aouſt. *Looke* Aouſt.
Le double d'un cerf. *Deeres ſuet.*
Au double. *Doubly, with great vſurie, two-fold, vnto his great aduantage.*
Double: com. *Double; twice as big, as great againe; of as much weight, or worth againe.*
Double vaiſſeau. *A cauldron, or kettle, full of hot water; or, as* Bain de Marie.
Habillement double. *A garment thats lined, or furred cleane through, or double all ouer.*
Doublé: m. ée: f. *Doubled; made two-fold, or twice as much; increaſed verie much, or vnto as much more; alſo, bowed much, or made almoſt to meet at the ends; alſo, copied out as a writing; alſo, lined, as a garment; alſo, repeated, reiterated.*
Doubleau: m. *as* Hemicycle; *A halfe circle; alſo, a double quarter of timber.*
Doubleau. *Somewhat double, almoſt two-fold.*
Arcs doubleaux. *as* Branches d'Augiues.
Double-marcheur: m. *The little, ſpotted, and wormlike Serpent* Amphisbæna; *which hauing a head at both ends (an errour in auntient authors, in the opinion of* Mathiolus, *and* Grevinus) *can goe both wayes.*
Doublemént: m. *A doubling; a making two-fold, or twice as much; a riſing vnto as much more; alſo, the copying out of a writing; In a Portſale, a double outbidding, or double the price of the moſt that was at firſt bidden (which he that ariſes vnto, moſt commonly carries the thing.)*
Doublément. *Doubly, two wayes, in two ſorts, for two cauſes.*
Doubler. *To double; to make two-fold, or twice as much; to increaſe very much, or vnto as much more; alſo, to bow much, or make both ends meet; alſo, to copie out a writing; alſo, to line a garment; alſo, to reiterate.*
Doublet: m. *A Doublet; a Jewell, or ſtone of two peeces ioyned, or glued together.*
Doublet en caſe. *A corner-point taken with two men at Tables.*
Double-teſtu: m. *The worme-like Serpent* Amphisbæna; *double-headed, as auncient authors haue imagined; But no Serpent, ſayes* Mathiolus, *hath naturally two heads; Looke* Double-marcheur.
Double-vaiſſeau. *as* Bain de Marie.
Doublier: m. *A long, and large Table-cloth of Damask, Diaper, &c, hanging to the ground on both ſides of the boord, and laid double thereon; a Table-cloth for Princes, and great States.*
Doublure: f. *Lining for a garment.*
Fin contre fin n'eſt bon à faire de doublure: Pro. *Two craftie knaues being matcht, will neuer agree together.*
Doutable: com. *Doubtable; redoubtable; vncertaine, fit to be feared.*
Doubtance: f. *Doubt; ſuſpition; feare; vncertaintie.*
Doubtant. *Doubting; ſuſpecting; vncertainly thinking of; (and ſometimes) alſo, as much as hoping.*
Doubte: f. *A doubt; ſuſpect; feare, ſcruple; miſtruſt; ſuſpence; vncertaintie of, or ſtaggering in, opinion; alſo, a reuerent awe, or dread of.*
Sans doubte. *Queſtionleſſe, vndoubtedly, certainely, without faile, as ſure as can be.*
Amener, ou mettre, en doubte. *To call in queſtion, bring in controuerſie, make men doubtfull of.*
Tenir en doubte. *To delay, deferre, hold in ſuſpence.*
Doubté: m. ée: f. *Doubted; ſuſpected; miſtruſted; feared; awed.*
Doubtement: m. *A doubting, ſuſpecting; fearing.*
Doubter. *To doubt, ſuſpect, miſtruſt; bee vncertaine, make a queſtion, or ſcruple of; to ſtagger, ſtammer, wauer betweene hope and feare; to be in ſuſpence; alſo, to feare, awe, dread, redoubt; (ſometimes) alſo (as much as) to hope.*
Qui ne ſcait rien de rien ne doubte: Pro. *He that knowes nothing liues in feare of nothing.*
Doubteuſement. *Doubtfully, vncertainly; inconſtantly, waueringly; miſtruſtfully.*
Doubteux: m. euſe: f. *Doubtfull, vncertaine, in ſuſpence; alſo, variable, inconſtant, ſtaggering; alſo, ambiguous, perplexed, ſubiect to cauilling, or exception; whereof a queſtion may be made, a controuerſie raiſed, or diuers ſences gathered; alſo, fearefull, terrible, redoubtable.*
Douce (*The feminine of* Doux) la douce perſonne. *A ſweet fellow ſure; Ironically; See* Doux.
Douceaſtre: com. *Sweetiſh.*
Doucelet: m. ette: f. *Dulcet, prettie and ſweet, or, a little ſweet.*
Doucement. *Sweetly, deliciouſly; ſoftly, ſmoothly; mildly, graciouſly, courteouſly, louingly; eaſily, tractably.*
Douce-ente: f. *The name of a certaine thicke, ruddie, and ſappie apple.*
Doucereux: m. euſe: f. *Full of ſweetneſſe, delicious; moſt pleaſant; moſt courteous.*
Doucet: m. *A kind of ſea-fiſh like a Hedgehog; Looke* Douſin.
Doucet: m. ette: f. *Dulcet; prettie and ſweet; or, a little ſweet.*
Doucettement. *Sweetly; prettily; mildly, gently, eaſily.*
Douceur: f. *Sweetnes, delight, pleaſātnes, daintines; ſoftnes, ſmoothnes; meeknes, gētlenes, mildnes, tractablenes; kindnes,*

kindnesse, humanitie, courtesie; indulgencie, mercie, clemencie.

Douceur de chant. *The melodie, or harmonie of tuneable singing.*

Il faut avoir mauvaise beste par douceur: Pro. *(Some-what like to our, the rough Net is not the best catcher of Birds;) shreud beasts would be caught by sweet baites.*

Doucin. *as* Doussin.

Doucine. *as* Doulcine.

Dove: f. *A castle, ditch, or Towne-ditch (with water in it.)*

Doüé: m. ée: *Endued; endowed.*

Douëlle: f. *A Pipe-staffe; also, the strickle vsed in the measuring of Corne.*

Douen d'antan. *Hence ouer a yeare:* ¶Norm.

Douër. *To indue, endow, or giue a dowrie vnto.*

Douës: f. *as* Douves.

Douët: m. *A brooke, or spring.*

Douëtte. à longues douëttes. *In long rowes, files, ranks:* ¶Bret.

Dougé: m. ée: f. *Small, fine; little; slender, thinne.*

Douger. *To trip; as a horse that stumbleth not outright, (an old word.)*

Douille: f. *The socket of the head of a pike, iauelin, &c; also, the socket of a candlesticke; any socket; also, the barrell of an harguebuze, or pistoll.*

Douillet: m. ette: f. *Daintie, tender, delicate, soft, effeminate; a milke-sop; one that cannot beare a feather without breathing; also, quaint, curious, as nice as a Nunnes henne.*

Douillettement. *Daintily, tenderly, delicately, effeminately; also, quaintly, nicely, curiously.*

Douït: m. as Douët: *a brooke.*

Doulcin: m. *The fish cald, the sea Vrchin:* ¶Marseillois.

Doulcin rascaz. *A greater, and white, kind thereof; Looke* Doussin.

Doulcine. *as* Cymaise, *or* Cymace.

Douleur: f. *as* Doleur.

Doulouëre. *A planing ax, a coopers addis.*

Doulourеusement, Douloureux. *as* Doloureusement, & Doloureux.

Se Doulousant. *Pittifully complaining, in a lamentable taking, waimenting, most woe-begon.*

Se Doulouser. *To lament, wayle, complaine, wayment.*

Doulx: m. Doulce: f. *Looke,* Doux.

Dour: m. *A hands breadth; or the breadth of foure fingers; the fourth part of a Geometricall foot, in measuring.*

Dourdé: m. ée: f. *Knocked, mawled, thumped, rapped, beaten.*

Dourder. *To knocke, mawle, beat, thump, rap.*

Dourdier: m. *A luske, lowt, slouch.*

Dousil: m. *A spigot.*

Doussaine: f. *A certein musicall instrument.*

Doussé: m. ée: f. *Indorsed.*

Dousser. *To indorse, a paper, &c.*

Dousseresse. *as* Dosserasse.

Doussier: m. *An indorsement.*

Doussin. *The sea Vrchin; a fish thats eatable, though vnsauorie enough.*

Doussin rascas. *The greatest, and whitest kind thereof; not to be eaten.*

Doutance: f. *Looke* Doubtance.

Douve: f. *A castle-ditch (hauing water in it) also, a certeine hearbe, that kils the sheepe which eat of it.*

Douves. *A mortall disease bred in sheeps pluckes, or intrails, by th'eating of the hearbe aforesaid.*

Douves d'un tonneau, &c. *The head-peeces of a Tunne, &c.*

Douvelle: f. *A Cinter, or Centrie; the frame of wood whereby a vault, or arch is both in the making, and for a while after, held vp.*

Doux: m. douce: f. *Sweet; delicious, delightsome, daintie, pleasing; soft, pliant; smooth, tractable; gentle, mild, meeke; louelie; kind, courteous, louing.*

Doux de sel. *Fresh, vnsauorie, not throughly seasoned; also, of small standing, or experience.*

Doux à taster. *Smooth, soft, without any roughnesse; also, sweet, or without any manner of harshnesse.*

Eau douce. *Fresh water.* Medecin d'eau douce. *A yong, or vnexperienced Physitian.*

Estain doux. *The best kind of Tinne; gotten in our Cornewall.*

Pierre douce. *A certaine white stone, called, the Honie stone.*

Taille douce. *Sweet cutting; small ingrauerie, such as prints in copper are cut with.*

Tout doux. *Husht; quietly, stilly, calmely, without noise, or dinne.*

Faire les doux yeux. *To counterfeit ciuilitie, or modestie; to seeme coy; also, to make as though he slept, and saw nothing; or to be betweene sleeping and waking; also, to winke, or smile prettily with the eyes.*

Faire les doux yeux à. *To play at boe-peepe with; to winke lasciuiously, or wantonly at; also, to frame, or set th'eyes to looke alluringly, flatteringly, or pitifully at one, thereby to get somewhat of him.*

Filer doux. *To flatter, or speake faire.*

Douce parole n'escorche langue: Prov. *Wee say, good words breake no bones.*

Douce parole rompt grand'ire: Prov. *Gentle words appease the irefull.*

Douces promesses obligent les fols: Prov. *Faire promises oblige fools; or (as our) faire words make fools faine.*

De doux arbre douces pommes: Prov. *Such as the tree such is the fruit; sweet th'one, saurie th'other; (yet we say, that many a good cow hath but an euell calfe.)*

Doux-amer. *Bitter-sweet.*

Doux-auvesque. *The name of a sweet, and tender apple, as big as a middle Orange.*

Doux-balon. *A certaine round, great, greene, soft, and sweet apple.*

Doux-belheur. *A certaine great, sweet, round, and hard-skinned apple.*

Doux-glissant. *Glib, gently-gliding.*

Doux grave. viz. Doucement grave.

Doux de la Lande. *The name of a white sweet apple, that yeelds most excellent cyder.*

Doux-Martin. *A certaine white, long, and drie apple.*

Doux-veret. *The name of a white, long, and tender apple.*

Douzain: m. *A* Sous, *or French shilling; (whereof ten make but one of sterling money.)*

Douzaine: f. *A dozen.*

Il est bien au compte de la douzaine. *He is a sorrie fellow, a sillie companion; one thats neither able ynough to doe hurt, nor wise ynough to doe good; (for things that are sold by the dozen, (because not curiously heeded) are often sleightly made.)*

Douze. *Twelue; a dozen.*

Au denier douze. *Looke* Denier.

Douze-doigtier. *A small gut, or entrall, seated on the right side, & desceding oblikely towards the back-bone and*

and ending where the circumuolution of the guts begins.

Douzil: m. *A spigot.*

Douziesme. *The twelfth; also, an imposition of* 12.d. *in the pound vpon all wares sold; first raised by King Charls the fift.*

Droict de douziesme. *An yearelie rent of* 12.d. *due by euerie affranchised inhabitant of* Haynault, *vnto the Earle thereof, in acknowledgement of his former thraldome, & as a recompence of his now-got freedom.*

Doyen: m. *A Deane; the head of a Colledge, or Cathedrall Church.*

Doyenné: m. *A Deanerie; or Deaneship.*

Doygé: m. ée: f. *as* Dougé.

Doze de Venise. *The Duke of Venice.*

Drache: f. *The little staulke whereby a grape cleaues to the bunch.*

Drachme. *as* Drame; *A dram; the eighth part of an ounce.*

Dragacanth. *as* Dragagant.

Dragagant: m. *Gumme Dragagant, a gummie liquor which distills from the root of the Candian shrub, called Goats-beard.*

Dragée: f. *A kind of disgestiue powder, vsually prescribed vnto weake stomackes after meat; and hence, any ionkets, comfets, or sweet meats, serued in at the last course, (or otherwise) for stomacke-closers; also small haile shot, of lead, &c.*

Dragée aux chevaux. *Prouender of diuers sorts of pulse mingled together; or, as* Farrage; *also, the course graine called Bolymong, French-wheat, Blocke-wheat, or Bucke-wheat.*

Drageoir. *A comfet box, of siluer; also, the fat, or vessell that receiues new wine, falling by a narrow passage, from the presse.*

Drageon: m. *A vine branch, twig, or sprig.*

Drageon fourcheran. *A sprig that spurteth out betweene two branches, as from the middle of a forke.*

Drageon fruictier. *The branch that beareth the grape.*

Drageon pampier. *A vine branch, or twig that beareth no fruit, but onely leaues.*

Drageries: f. *Comfets, ionkets, sweet meats.*

Dragme: m. *A dramme; the eighth part of an ounce, or three scruples; also, a handfull of.*

Dragme sarmentine. *A cup of wine; See* Pilure.

Dragoir. *Looke* Drageoir.

Dragon: m. *A Dragon; also, the hearbe Dragonwort, or Dragons.*

Dragon marin. *The Viuer, or Quauiuer; a monstrous, and venomous fish.*

Sang de dragon. *Dragons-bloud; is not (as ignorant people imagine) the bloud of a Dragon crusht to death by an Elephant, but the Gumme of the Dragon tree opened, or bruised in the dog-daies; also, Bloudwort, red Patience, bloudie Patience, (an hearbe.)*

Dragonceau: m. *A yong, or little Dragon.*

Dragoncelle: f. *as* Dragontée.

Dragonné: m. ée: f. *Dragonie; whose hinder parts resemble a Dragon: (a word of Blazon.)*

Dragonneau: m. *A yong, or little Dragon; also, the ouerfulnesse of any great veine being bent, or stretched out.*

Dragontée: f. *The hearbe Dragons, or Dragonwort.*

Dragontée mineur. *Small Dragonwort.*

Draguinage. *So do they at Lyons tearme a kind of Gibridge, whereby prisoners vse to fetch drinking money from new-come guests.*

Dramant. *Miching, pinching, drawing out things scantly, vsing them so scarcely as if he were affraid, or loath, to touch them.*

Drame: m. *as* Dragme; *A dramme.*

Dramé: m. ée: f. *Miched, pinched, miserably vsed, scantly disposed of, strictly measured, or deliuered, out.*

Dramer. *To miche, pinch, dodge; to vse, dispose of, or deliuer out, things by a precise weight, or strict measure; or so scantly, so scarcely, as if the measurer were afraid to touch them, or loath to haue them touched.*

Drap: m. *Cloth; woollen cloth; broad cloth.*

Drap mortuaire. *A Hearse-cloth.*

Demy drap. *Cloth-rash.*

Estre des draps de. *To be towards; to be an attendant, or seruant of, to belong, or be a retainer, vnto.*

Le drap, & les ciseaux luy sont delivrez. *The matter is wholly referred vnto him; he hath the law in his owne hands.*

Le drap des deux est d'une mesme piece. *They are both of one kind of stuffe, mettall, humor; there went but a paire of sheeres betweene them.*

'A ce drap cousturiers. *To it whoresons; or, let vs go roundly to worke; also, there was old cutting, snipping, shredding, laying about them.*

Au bout de l'aulne faut le drap. *There is but iust measure, no more then will serue the turne; more were too much, lesse too little.*

Il veut avoir drap, & argent ensemble. *He is an extreame, or vniust dealer; he would haue mens ware without paying for it; or, he would haue both stuffe, and money; one thing contents him not, he would haue both.*

Dieu donne le froid selon le drap: Prov. *Looke* Froid.

Drapé. *as* Drappé.

Drapeau: m. *A (linnen) cloth, or clowt; also, an Ensigne, Standard, Banner, Colours.*

Drapeau d'un fusil. *Tinder.*

Drapeau de la Meleze. *A white, and leatherlike filme, or skinne (found neere to the pith of the bodies of old Larch trees) wherewith countrey people close wounds, and staunch bloud.*

Vieux drapeaux. *Old rags, clowts, clothes past wearing; trash, trumperie, odde ends; outcast friperie.*

Chevalier au drapeau quarré. *A Knight Banneret; so called, because his Colours in the field are to be of a square forme; as also, his Armes may be painted in a square field.*

Il est tout pasle, & mort comme vn drapeau. *Hee lookes like death; or as pale as a clowt.*

Drapelet. *A little linnen cloth, clowt; or Ensigne.*

Draper. *To make, or worke cloth; to dresse, or full cloth; to beat, or thicken, as cloth, in the fulling; also, to seise, or take another mans goods, &c, vnder a faire pretext; also, to mock, flowt, deride, ieast at; also, to eat, or champ apace.*

Draperie: f. *Draperie; cloath-selling, cloth-working; also, a flourishing with leaues, and flowers in wood, or stone, vsed especially on the heads of pillers, & tearmed by our workemen Draperie, or Cilerie.*

Drapier: m. *A Draper.*

Drapier drappant. *A Clothworker.*

Drappant. *Working, dressing, or fulling of cloth; thickning, or beating cloth in the fulling; also, mocking, flowting, deriding, ieasting at.*

Drappé: m. ée: f. *Dressed, wrought, fulled (as cloth;) beaten, or, thickned (by beating) as cloth is in the*

 filling;

fulling; also, derided, mocked, flouted; also, taken, or seised vnder a faire pretext.
Sarge drappée. *Milled Sey.*
Drappeau: m. *as* Drapeau.
Drappelet: m. *A little linnen cloth, rag, or clowt.*
Drapper. *as* Draper.
Drapperie: f. *Looke* Draperie.
Drappeux: m. euse: f. *Full of cloth, or fit to make cloth.*
Drappier. *as* Drapier.
Drappier: m. ere: f. *Of, or belonging to cloth; also, fit to make cloth.*
Drave: f. *Spanish, or Babylonian Cresses.*
Dravée: f. *All kind of pulse, as Beanes, pease, &c.*
Draule: m. *as* Drole; *A wag, or merrie grig.*
Daulerie: f. *Waggerie; also, the figure of a Maske, Satire, Monkie, or such like apish visages, and anticke resemblances, set on the top of a Scutcheon, or coat of Armes.*
Drege: f. *A kind of fish-net; forbidden to bee vsed, except for the catching of Oisters.*
Drelotter. *as* Dorlotter.
Dressé: m. ée: f. *Straightened, leuelled, euened, set right, made straight; also, raised, aduanced, erected; held, lifted, set, or taken vp; also, directed, instructed, trained vp; ordered; framed, made, fashioned; also, deuised, contriued, inuented; also, found of, as Deere by dogs; also, couered, as a table; dished vp, as meat for a meale.*
Dresser. *To straighten, set right, make straight, leuell, euen; also, to raise, aduance, erect; lift, set, hold, or take vp; also, to direct, instruct, order, gouerne, traine vp; to fashion; frame, build, make.*
Dresser vn cerf. *The dogs to find of a Deere.*
Dresser les cheveux. *To stroake vp the haire.*
Dresser vne coquille. *To set a trap for a Woodcocke; See* Coquille.
Dresser vne entreprise. *To plot, proiect, contriue an enterprise.*
Dresser des finesses. *To deuise sleights, or lay snares, for fooles.*
Dresser vn lict. *To make a bed.*
Dis au Cuisinier qu'il dresse. *Bid the Cooke dish vp his meat;* ou, au sommelier qu'il dresse; *or the Butler, that he couer.*
Se dresser. *To raise, to aduance himselfe; to stand boult-vp-right.*
Se dresser vn bon heur. *To procure vnto, or prouide for, himselfe a great fortune.*
Il se dresse vne guerre. *A warre is in preparing.*
Les cheveux luy dressent. *His haire stares, or stands annend.*
Se faire dresser quelque chose à quelqu'un. *To get him to set it straight, or to giue order for it.*
Dresseur: m. *A straightner, directer, leueller; setler; a raiser, erecter, framer, fashioner, orderer, instructer.*
Dresseur de compte. *An Accompt-caster.*
Dressiere: f. *A straight or outright path, or tract; a direct, or directiue, way.*
Dressoir: m. *A cupboord; a court-cupboord (without box, or drawer) onely to set plate on.*
Dressouïr: m. *A setting yron, or poating sticke, for ruffe bands; a standing thing.*
Dridiller. *To gingle, as a Hawkes bells.*
Drillant. *Twinkling, sparkling, glistering, like a starre, or good diamond.*
Driller. *To twinkle, or sparkle; to cast a glittering, or yeeld a glistening, light.*
Drilles: f. *Rags, tatters, beggerlie clowts.*
Drilleux: m. euse: f. *Tattered, ragged, in beggerlie aray.*
Dringuemorigue. *A nickname for a Dutchman.*
Marcher en dringuemorigue. *To staulk, or strout it like a swaggering huffesnuffe.*
Drogue: f. *A drug.*
Drogué: m. ée: f. *Bedrugged; mingled, purged, or seasoned with drugs.*
Boisson drogué. *A spiced cup; also, an impoisoned one.*
Drogueman: m. *An Interpreter.*
Droguement: m. *A drenching, bedrugging, or ministring of drugs.*
Droguer. *To drug, bedrug; season, purge, or mingle, with drugs.*
Droguer le corps. *To stuffe himselfe with drugs, to make an Apothecaries shop of his bellie.*
Droguerie: f. *The season of fishing for herrings, and other such fish, which is to be salted, and barrelled vp.*
Drogueries: f. *Drugs, druggeries, confections; also, trash.*
Droguet: m. *A kind of stuffe thats halfe silke, halfe wooll.*
Drogueur: m. *A druggist, or drug-seller.*
Droict: m. *The Law (Ciuile, Canon, or Common;) also, right, law, iustice, equitie, reason; also, a right or title vnto, an interest or propertie in, a thing; a mans due; that which either he hath, or should haue.*
Droict escrit. *(Is particularly) the Ciuile Law.*
'A bon droict. *Lawfully, worthily, vpon iust cause, with good reason. (See* Droict *Aduerb.)*
Ses menus droicts. *His vailes, fees, wages.*
Venir à ses droicts. *A Ward, or Pupill, comming vnto his yeares, to enter into the possessions that were left him.*
Venir, ou estre appellé, aux droicts du Roy. *To come, or be called into the Court of the Peeres of France, for the triall of his cause.*
Bon droict a bon mestier d'aide. *(A Prouerb taxing th'iniquitie, and iniustice of our times; wherein good right hath oftentimes need of great fauour.)*
Droict: m. *(also) A ductie, right, fee, prerogatiue, priuiledge, royaltie, power.*
Droict d'acquest; ou de nouvel acquest; ou de nouveaux aquests. *The fine due vnto the king vpon purchases made by Church-men, or in Mortmaine; and either to the king, or vnto other Lords, vpon purchases, made by th'ignoble, of* Fiefs, *or noble inheritances held of them; The rate of it is, one yeares profit in three; or otherwise, as their composition, or the custome is; (for this Rate is most proper vnto* Droict de nouvel acquest, *a personall right.)*
Droict d'acquit. *The right of Toll, or Custome, due by passengers vnto the Lord of the place wherein tis vsually taken, and payable if they be not free by birth (as the Noble) or by condition (as Church-men) or by Patent, or Charter (as some Officers, and Townesmen) In which cases they must, in a good fashion, acquaint him beforehand with their estates, or priuiledges.*
Droict d'advouërie. *Soueraigne patronage, or protection.*
Droict d'affeurage. *as* Droict d'afforage.
Droict d'afforage. *Two pots of wine, &c, due vpon the broaching of euerie vessell retailed; one to the Lord Feodall, his right for the standing thereof in his Mannor, & for his leaue (if he haue iurisdiction) to sel it; another vnto the magistrate, for allowance of the liquor, and for the rate which he sets on it.*

Droict d' aide. *Looke* Aide.

Droict d' aisnesse. *The right, and prerogatiue of an eldest heire; or, the portion due, by prime birth, vnto him; which is, in most places, the principall house, and garden with th'inclosure thereof; and if it haue no garden, the furlong of ground which lies next vnto it; or as much as a Capon can flie ouer from it: In the rest of the land he hath but an equall share with the younger: (But this is not generall.)*

Droict d'Aisneté, ou d'Aisneage; *The same.*

Droict d'Amende. *Power to fine a new purchaser for not acquainting the Lord of the Mannor, or soyle, with his bargaine, so soone, as by the custome of the place he was bound to doe.*

Droict d'Annate. *A yeares reuenew of a vacant rest Benefice; challenged heretofore in most Countries by the Pope; but taken from him by the* Pragmatique Sanction, *and some other Edicts, before Luthers time.*

Droict d'arrest de meubles. *Libertie, or power to argoods for a debt not acknowledged; a Priuiledge of diuers townes; and either giuen them by the Prince, or taken, and approued by custome.*

Droict d'Assize de six deniers. 6. d. Tour. *due vnto the Towneship of* Tournay *for euerie pottle of wine thats retailed within it.*

Droict d'Aubaine. *Eschcatage by strangers; the right of succession in the estates of all strangers, who die (in any part of France) without Naturalization, and French-borne issue; Looke* Aubaine.

Droict d'Aubenage. *The same.*

Droict d' Aurillage. *The profit of Bee-hiues; or a fee due, to a Lord, or to the King (as in* Provence) *vpon the profit thats made of euerie hiue, by the owner.*

Droict de bac. *The fare due vnto the Lord, or owner, of a Ferrie-boat.*

Droict de Bailliage. *Looke* Bailliage.

Droict de ban à vin. *An vnalienable Priuiledge, enioyed by many Gentlemen in* Touraine; *who for fortie daies together after vintage may forbid any other wine then their owne, to be sold within their Precincts.*

Droict de bannerie. *The Royaltie of hauing a common Mill, Ouen, Presse, &c, whereto the tenants of, and dwellers within, a Libertie, or Mannor are to resort.*

Droict de bannie. *The same; and the reuenew therof; or the power to take fees for the vse of such a Mill, Ouen, Presse, &c.*

Droict de banniere. *as* Droict de Bannerie.

Droict de blairie. *The power a Lord hath to fine any forreiners, who without his permission turne their cattel into the wastes, or* Vaines pastures, *belonging to his Mannors; as in* Blayrie.

Droict de bordage. *The drudgerie, or base seruices reserued by some Lords vpon the letting of their cottages, or small tenements; which cannot be sold, giuen, nor ingaged by the poore slaues that haue taken them.*

Droict de bornage. *Power to place meeres on, appoint limits vnto, lay out the bounds of, other mens lands.*

Droict de boucherie. *The Priuiledge of keeping a common slaughter house, whereat all the inhabitants of that Quarter are to haue their beasts killed; also, the fees belonging thereto; enioyed by such Lords as haue* Moyenne Iustice.

Droict de bourgeoisie. *Freedome; Looke* Bourgeoisie.

Droict de boutage. *A certaine dutie, or fee, exacted by the Lord of* Breci *(a member of* Bourges) *for the wine thats retailed within his iurisdiction.*

Droict de branche de Cypres. *A ductie paied, in old time, by English men arriuing at* Bourdeaux; *In signe, and as a token, that they had beene there.*

Droict de brassage. *The fee due, to the particular Maisters of the Mint, out of euerie sort of money thats coined; also, the fees of the workman, cutter, stamper, &c, (whom the Maisters are to pay,) Looke* Brassage.

Droict de brefs, ou briefs. *Looke* Bref.

Droict de bris. *The Admiraltie of a Sea-coast, which giues a man all wreckes, and shipwracks.*

Droict de buche; ou de busche. *The Officers of the wood-yards fees; or, the proportion of wood allowed, vnto euerie Office at Court; and vnto diuers Officers of th'Exchequer, ouer and besides their ordinarie wages.*

Droict de Carnalage. *A Priuiledge enioyed by the inhabitants of some places, to kill, and eat, or make profit of, such beasts as breake into their grounds; but this onely in some cases, and for a certaine number; which if they exceed they are answerable for all, as other men.*

Droict de meilleur Cattel. *Heriotage; the best chatell a tenant hath when he dies, due vnto his Landlord.*

Droict de Cauciage. *The power of imposing taxes on tenants, or of taking toll of passengers, towards the reparation, or maintenance of a common causey; (In some Lords of* Haynault.)

Droict de Cellerage. *Sellerage; a ductie, or fee paied vnto some Lords, at the laying of wines into sellers.*

Droict de Centiesme. *Looke* Centiesme.

Droict de Chambellage. *An Income; or the fine due by euerie new tenant (that comes in as heire by a direct succession) vnto the Lord of the Mannor whereof his land is held: the rate of it is, by the customes of* Mante, *a Crowne of the Sunne; by those of* Senlis, 20. s. Parisis; *as also, by those of* Vallois; *and those of* Noyon, *(wherby tis due at euerie change of tenant:) by those of* S. Quintins, *a peece of gold worth (at least) halfe a Crowne; by those of* S. Paul, 30. s. Paris. *by those of* Laon, *a peece of gold of what value the tenant will: In other places he paies more, or lesse, according to their customes: Also, a fee due vnto the chiefe Vsher of the Chamber of Accompts, by euerie one of the Kings tenants, when he does his homage.*

Droict de Chambellenage. *Is, by the customes of* Britaine, *a dutie of* 5. s. Tour. *paid by euerie vassall at the doing of his fealtie, vnto his Liege Lord.*

Droict de Chambrelage. *as* Droict de Chambellage; *Stiled so, in the customes of* Cambray; *and of* Haynault; *in which countrey the rate of it is*, 60. s.

Droict de Champagne. *The fees due vnto the Officers of th'Exchequer vpon the letting of the farms which belong to* Champagne: viz. 2. s. 6. d. sterl. *for such as are worth* 100. l. *or lesse; and* 4. s. *for those which exceed that rate.*

Droict de Champart. *Looke* Champart.

Droict de Chantellage. *Gauntellage; or, a certaine fee due vnto some Lords for the Gauntries whereon wine, thats any way to be sold, doth stand.*

Droict de Charrüage. *as* Droict de suitte de disme.

Droict de Chastellenie. *The Royalties belonging to a Castleship, or Castleward; Looke* Chastellenie.

Droict de chauffage. *Looke* Chauffage.

Droict de Chemage. *The passage-toll, or, through-toll, thats taken at* Sens.

Droict de Cheminage. *The same.*

Droict de Chevage. *An yearely duetie, fine, or fee, of* 12.d. Parisis, *paied, to the Kings vse, within* Vermandois *(and some other places) by euerie bastard, stranger, forreiner, and affranchised person, that is, or hath beene, married.*

Droict de Chevalerie. *The Priuiledge of Knighthood, or to bee made a Knight; Looke* Chevalerie.

Droict de Chevauchée. *Composition money, due (vpon agreement) by some towneships; thereby exempted, in the Kings iourneyes, and progresses, from prouiding of horses, and carts for his traine.*

Droict de chevelure. *The wearing of a locke, which in old time, none but a Prince of the bloud might weare.*

Droict des chiens. *That part of the game which belongs to the hounds for their reward.*

Droict de Cire. *Is* 18.d.Tour. *in euerie pound aboue twentie giuen, or agreed, for a wood-sale; due vnto the King, in regard of the lights, which are (imagined to be) spent, while the bargaine is in making.*

Droict de Collerage. *Collerage; a fee due for the collers worne by the horses, or men, which draw wine vp and downe.*

Droict de commande. *Is* 2.d. Parisis, *taken yearely, by some Lords, of euerie one of their widowes (that hold by Villenage) in acknowledgement, and preseruation of the right of their authoritie ouer them.*

Droict de commis. *The right, or power some Landlords haue, to confiscate, seise, or enter on the inheritances of such their tenants, or vassalls, as disaduow them, giue them the lye, or commit felonie.*

Droict de commise. *The same.*

Droict de confirmation. *The fine due by all Officers of the kingdome of France vnto the King, at his first comming to the Crowne, for establishing them by his letters Patents, in their places.*

Droict de contentor. *See* Contentor.

Droict de Cornage. *Hornage; or a quantitie of corne, taken yearely by the Lord Chastellain of* Berri *(a member of* Bourges*) for euerie Oxe, or horned beast that workes at the plough in the Winter-corne grounds which be within his iurisdiction.*

Droict de Couletage. *See* Couletage.

Droict de Coustome. *Is (in Normandie) the custome, or toll, due vpon the sale of wares in Markets; In* Grand Perche; *it is a penie* Tour. *payable vnto Lords that haue base Iurisdiction, for euerie beast that giues no milke, and was bred, bought, and deliuered within their territories; This vnder a penaltie of* 2.s. 6.d. *for euerie one thats not so paid for.*

Droict de grosse coustome. *A toll, or impost of* 48.s. 10.d. Tour. *vpon euerie eighteene* Muids *of Salt passing along by* Chartres; *due vnto, and equally diuided betweene, the King, and the Bishop of that citie.*

Droict de petite coustome. *See* La petite coustome, *in,* Coustome.

Droict de desherance. *Escheatage; power to seise, and conuert vnto his owne vse, an inheritance whose owner dies intestate, and without heire; belongs to the King, Lord high Iusticer, or Land-lord.*

Droict de directe, ou fondalité. *The Seigneuriall rights, or dueties annexed vnto the soile, or belonging to the Lord thereof.*

Droict du dixiesme denier. *The tenth penie, or penniworth, of all mines, mettalls, minerall, and other (extraordinarie) substances got within ground, throughout all France, due vnto the King; also, th' Admiralls tenth part, or share in all shipwracks, prizes, conquests, &c, made at sea.*

Droict de tiers denier. *The third pennie, or part of the price giuen for an inheritance* Roturier, *or* Bourdelier, *due, in some places, vnto the Land-lord.*

Droict de dixiesme. *Looke* Dixiesme.

Droict domainer. *The Priuiledge a Lord Iusticer hath, to right himselfe by execution, without any former proceeding, in cases that concerne his auncient demaine, or the customarie duties thereto belonging.*

Droict de doublage. *Looke* Doublage.

Droict de douziesme. *An yearely rent of* 12. d. *due by euerie affranchised inhabitant of* Henault *vnto the Earle thereof, in acknowledgement of his former thraldome, and in thankefulnesse for his new-got freedome.*

Droict de folle enchere. *The right of confiscating money paied beforehand for an Office, which after the bargaine made the chapman would refuse, as too deere.*

Droict d'Entrage. *Entrage; a fee due for th' entrance of marchandise into the Hauens, and walled townes of the kingdome; also, an Income payable to a Lessor at th' entrie of the Lessee.*

Droict d'Entrée. *Looke* Entrée; *Also, halfe a crown due to euerie Treasurer, and Generall of the Finances (besides their ordinarie wages) for residence, euery day they meet, and sit in their Courts, about the Kings businesse.*

Droict d'escas. *The tenth pennie of the value of moneables which are left by a freeman vnto a forreiner within* Seclin, *and* Bassée sous Lisle; *due vnto the common Treasurie of those townes.*

Droict d'eschats, & Tavernes. *A certaine Imposition vpon wines that are sold by retaile, & in Tauernes; (from which all Priests beneficed within* Bourdeaux *are exempted, for as much as grew in their owne grounds, glebe, or Prebendaries.)*

Droict d'Escheance. *Escheatage.*

Droict d' Eschevinage. *Power to incorporate a towne.*

Droict d' Esslongne. *A duetie, or fine, paiable (in Brittaine) by the heire, or successor of a deceased tenant vnto the Lord, vnder whose* Censiue *he held, and enioyed land at the time of his death: And thus is, a pennie* Parisis, *or two, or twelue; or more or lesse, according to the annuall value of the land, and according to the custome, seuerall, in seuerall places.*

Droict d'Establage. *That which in our law is called* Stallage; *or a fee taken by Lords, of Marchants, for permitting them to open, & sell their wares in their Faires, and Markets; also, Stablage, or, that which is paied for the standing of a horse in a stable.*

Droict d'Estallage. *Stallage.*

Droict d'Estallonnage. *The Royaltie, or Priuiledge of assigning, and assizing of publicke weights, and measures.*

Droict d'Estellage. *Stallage.*

Droict de faultrage; ou fautrage. *A certaine vnalienable fee, due vpon each head of cattell that runnes in the common medowes, or pastures of a Mannor; In lieu whereof a heardsman is maintained, to keepe the ground in good order, & to looke that the beasts at first put in be not after changed.*

Droict de ferrage. *A priuiledge whereby some speciall officers, and followers of Court claime to haue their horses*

horses shod at the Kings charge; also, a certein fee due to the Cutters of the mint.

Droict de festage. *An yerelie dutie payable vnto certein lords for euery ridge, roofe, or housetop within their dominion; also, the feasts that are due by some Prelats vnto their Chapters.*

Droict de festin. *The same (in the later part.)*

Droict de feurmariage; *as,* Droict de formariage.

Droict de foire, & marchez: *The royaltie, or priuiledge, of houlding a faire, or keeping markets, within a mans owne territorie (originally of the Kings grant.)*

Droicts de fondalité. *The rights, or royalties which are annexed vnto the soile, & belong euer vnto the lord thereof.*

Droict de forage. *A certein fee, or part, out of wines that are sould, belonging to the lords of the Iurisdiction, or place wherein they are sould: by the custome of* Amiens, *and of* Beauquesne, *it is two pots on euery single vessell, or bottome thats retayled; and belongs to the lord high, meane, or low Iusticer: by the customes of* Teroanne, *it is also two pots vpon euery vessel thats sould in grosse, and belongs to the Bishop: In* Beauvois, *there in* xx. d. *for euery vessell sould in grosse, and* xvj. d. *for euery one retailed in the town, paied vnto the Bishop of that Sea: And by the customes of* Ponthieu *a Lord of a soile, that hath but low Iurisdiction, may take two pots of euery barred vessell thats broched vpon his soyle, or within the limits of his authoritie; In other places, otherwise.*

Droict de forban. *The royaltie, or power, of banishing an offendor out of his territories.*

Droict de formariage. *The halfe, or third, or (as the custome is) other part of a villens substance, due vnto his landlord, or the lord of the Iurisdiction wherein he liues, if he marrie a woman thats free, or a forreiner; & this, although he haue leaue to do it, for otherwise he looses sixtie shillings more: In old time bastards, and strangers, who maried out of their owne condition, were subiect vnto this penalty; Now those in most places, and these in some, are priuiledged.*

Droict de foüage. *Chimney-pence; or, an yearelie tax leuied in old time by some supreame Lords vpon euery chimney, or fire, kept within their territories: In Charles the fifts time it was foure pound* Tour. *and s[illegible] tooke foure bushels of Oats; others bread; and others other things: the Blacke Prince would haue exacted a* franc *of euery fire kept in* Aquitaine; *which bred him great mischiefe (sayes a Frenchman:) Since those times the* Tailles *haue succeeded this taxation in most places.*

Droict de francs-fiefs. *Looke,* Francs-fiefs.

Droict de fournage. *The fee thats due for baking in a common Ouen; also, the fine paied by vassals or tenants, bound to resort vnto their lords, for a licence to vse their owne.*

Droict de fresange. *One hog, or more, due vnto the master of the waters and forrests of* Aubigny *(and elsewhere) by the farmer of the mastage, and browsage thereof.*

Droict de Gabelle de sel; *Th'impost, or gabell of salt; See,* Gabelle.

Droict de Gabelle de vins. *Th'impost of wines, due to the duke of* Buillon.

Droict de gambage. *Foure bottles of beere vpon euerie brewing, due vnto diuers Lords within the county of* Boullenois.

Droict de Gants. *A paire of gloues, or in lieu thereof, money (more or lesse according to the custome) due by a purchaser, as a conclusion of all his first seruices, vnto the Lord* Censuel, *or of the soyle; Seek,* Droict de ventes & gants.

Droict de garde. *Soueraigne patronage, or protection.*

Droict de garde noble. *The wardship of gentlemens lands held in Capite, or by knights seruice, due by the customes of Normandie, vnto the king, or lords, of whom they are held.*

Droict de giste. *Power to lie at the house of a tenant, vassall, or subiect in passing along by it; due to the king onely, not to the Queene; (though some dukes, and earles haue had it at the abbayes, & monasteries within their territories;) now the great Bishops, and Abbots, by an yearelie allowance in money, haue got themselues dispensed withall.*

Droict de garene. *Free warren; or, a liberty to hunt all ouer the grounds of his subiects, or vassals.*

Droict de Grarie. *The Kings fee out of euerie sale of wood made in his subiects forrests; due vnto him for the Iustice done, and good order kept, within them, by his officers; thereby also, he challenges a part, or property in part, of the demaine, and reuenues thereof.*

Droict de greffe: *Sixtie three shillings nine pence* Tour. *due to the king vpon a sale of wood, in Normandie, and elsewhere.*

Droict de gruerie: *The browsage, or pawnage of some woods; belongs to the lords that haue high Iurisdiction ouer their owners; or, as* Droict de grurie.

Droict de grurie. *Consists in the fines and amerciaments leuied, & in the confiscation of trespassing beasts, within forests; and belongs vnto the King. See* Grurie.

Droict de guerre: *Feud; or the libertie which one subiect had, in old time, to make warre vpon another whom he had first defied.*

Droict de guet. *Castle-gard, or Castle-ward; whereunto the vassals of diuers lords, that haue Castles, are bound (in time, or expectation, of war) by their tenures; yet are they not bound to doe this seruice at any other place then the Castle whereof they hould; nor to doe it there at, if it be very ruinous, vntill it be repaired: also, the watch which a vassall, inhabiting a frontire, or sea coast, is tied to keepe, ordinarily, once a moneth; in lieu, or default, whereof he paies his lord* v. s. Tour. *a time; or an yearelie quantitie of corne, or number of hens, &c, as the custome of the place is, or as they can agree.*

Droict d' hallage. *Hallage; the toll due to a lord by those, that sell wares in the common halls of townes, wherein the king hath licensed him to keep faires, or markets.*

Droict d' harenc. *A certein number of herrings, heretofore due euery lent vnto th' officers of the Chamber of accompts; who at this day haue, in lieu thereof, an yerelie allowance in money.*

Droict d' Haubert. *A certeine priuiledge whereof there are many parts, the most of high Iurisdiction, enioyed by diuers lords of Normandie.*

Droict d' Haultban. *An yearelie tax of* vj. s. Parisis, *leuied, for the king of euery baker, and some other Artificers, within Paris.*

Droict d' Herbage. *Herbage; or the liberty some haue to graze their cattell in other mens woods.*

Droict d' herbage mort. *A penny, or halfe-penny (as the custome is) payed by a poore Cottager, or copieholder vnto the Lord that hath high, or meane Iurisdiction ouer him, for euery sheep he hath, if he haue not aboue tenne, or (as in some places) twentie.*

Droict

Droict d'herbage vif. *If he haue more then tenne, or twentie, then he giues euerie tenth sheepe; which is chosen by the Lord, or his Officers. These dueties are leuied at Midsummer, and grow due from Christmas Eue.*

Droict d'hommes. *The Kings Prerogatiue, and power of his officers, to moderate, or diminish th'excessiue taxes laied, by mesne Lords, in the iurisdiction of* Tours, *vpon their villeines, whom otherwise they might tax at pleasure.*

Droict d'hostelage. *The rate Marchant-strangers are at, in some parts of France, for their warehouses; and which, if they hold them, but a night, they pay, if a whole yeare, they doe but pay; also, as* Pains d'hostelage; *in* Hostelage.

Droict de Iallage. *One, two, or three pintes (as the custome is) of wine, taken by a Lord vpon euerie* Poinson *retailed within his iurisdiction.*

Droict d'Indemnité. *Looke* Indemnité.

Droict d'Inquant. *Fiue in the hundreth, due to the King in some parts of* Provence.

Droict d'Intestat. *A priuiledge which the next of bloud hath (in some places) to enter on the possessions left by his intestate kinsman.*

Droict d'Investison. *The right of Inuesture of Prelates, &c, due vnto the Prince.*

Droict d'Issuë. *The custome due for the transportation, or exportatio of marchandise, &c, out of the land; also, the rights, fine, or seruices due vnto a mesne Lord vpon his tenants alienation, or leauing of his tenement vnto another.*

Droict de Iurée. *A duetie, or fine leuied yearely by th'old Earles of* Champagne, *vpon all their subiects, and vassalls;* viz. 6. d. *in the pound for mouables, and* 2. d. *for euerie pounds worth of immoueables; yet might the richest be quit for* 4. s. sterl. *yearely; others not vnder* 12. d. *At this day the King, and other Lords of Iurisdiction take this duetie, in some places, of their Burgesses, or freemen.*

Droict de Levage. *An Imposition of three bushells, and three quarters, or* 15. s. Tour. *vpon euerie boatfull of salt transported: In some parts of France (as within* Anjou, *and* le Maine) *tis also, a pennie for a beefe, pipe of wine, load of corne, &c, and a halfe-pennie for a sheepe, hog &c, due vnto a Lord of Iurisdiction, if they haue bene within his libertie eight dayes together before their sale, or transportation.*

Droict de Liage. *Hoopage; or a fee due vnto some Lords vpon euerie hooped vessell of wine which their vassalls haue, or sell.*

Droict de ligne esteinte. *Escheatage; the right which a Lord hath in the land of his tenant, dying without heires of his bodie, or bloud.*

Droict de litige. *The right of presentation to a Benefice, by a Lord, while his vassalls are at suit for it; was the Dukes of Normandie, now tis the Kings; some hold it to be rather a receiuing of the fruits, & profits therof, while the suit lasts.*

Droict de loges. *A certaine annuall fee due vnto some Lords for the lodgings their vassalls haue within their castles, in time of warre.*

Droict de logies. *An yearelie tax of* 16. s. 6. d. sterl. *leuied vnto the Kings vse vpon euerie Prouostship within the Countie of* Poictou; *ouer and besides the rent at which, or price for which, it is farmed; and* 18. d. *for the Officers of the Chamber of Accompts.*

Droict de logues. *A certain fee due, to th'vnder Butler of th'Abbey of* Deots *in* Berri, *out of the tithes belonging to that Abbey.*

Droict de lots. *Certaine dueties paied by a purchaser vnto the Lord* Censuel, *who in receiuing them giues him possission of the land he hath bought; (They be commonly as much as the* Ventes, *and goe together.)*

Droict de maille d'or. *A golden halfe-penie due. vnto the Duke of* Nevers, *by the Prior of* S. Privé, *for the Faire he keepes in that place.*

Droict de Mainbournie. *Soueraigne patronage, or protection.*

Droict de Maire, & Communauté. *The priuiledge of hauing, being, or belonging to, a Corporation.*

Droict de Mancé de sel. *A certain quantitie of salt, vpon euerie horse-load thereof entring into* Bourges, *and of euerie one that sells any within* Bourges; *taken by th'Abbot, and Couent of* S. Sulpice; *Looke* Mancé.

Droict de Manteaux. *Is* 20. s. sterl. *a yeare; and belongs both to euerie Secretarie of the house, and Crown of France, that takes wages, and vnto those Counsellors of Parliament, which are of, or for, the Church.*

Droict de Marc. *The Prouost of the Mints fee vpon euerie Marke, or halfe pound of gold, siluer, or* Billon *thats coined; Looke* Marc.

Droict de Marchage. *The Common of pasture which the inhabitants of one Iurisdiction, Parish, Village, or Mannor, haue ouer all the grounds belonging to another.*

Droict de Marché. *The royaltie of hauing, or keeping a Market within his territorie; belongs to a Lord Chattelain; and sometimes is conferred by the King on meaner Lords of Iurisdiction.*

Droict de Marciage. *Is, euerie third yeare, all the profit of naturall fruits, as hay &c, and the halfe of all others, as wine, corne, &c, due, within* Bourbonnois, *vnto a Landlord, in lieu of his whole rent; tis also due, as a fine, vpon euerie change of Lord and tenant.*

Droict de Marque. *Power to arrest the bodie, and seise the goods, of another; graunted by the King, and, in old time, giuen by the Parliament, against a stranger, or forreiner.*

Droict de Mesurage. *Th'appointing, or proportioning of measures in a territorie; belongs to the Lord thereof; also, toll-corne, and toll-salt; a dishfull vpon euery* Septier *of either.*

Droict de Minage. *The toll due vnto some Lords, vpon euerie* Mine *of corne thats measured within their Iurisdictions.*

Droict de Moisson. *A certaine quantitie of corne due yearely, vnto the King, out of the towne, and Iurisdiction of* Bourges.

Droict de Monneage. *An Aid, or Subsidie of* 12. d. *paid, each third yere, by euerie housholder within Normandie, vnto the Duke, or (as now) the King, on condition, that the money of the countrey be not altered: from this, are all Church-Officers; beneficed men; Gentlemen; widowes that haue not aboue* 2. s. *yearelie reuenewe, or* 4. s. *in goods (besides their apparell, and household-stuffe) and diuers others, by their Charters, exempted.*

Droict de Montenage. *Toll paied vnto certaine Lords by those that buy, and sell beasts, or other marchandise within their territories.*

Droict de Monteuvage. *The same (false Printed.)*

Droict de Morte-main. *The right a Lord hath to the estate of villeine dying without heire of his bodie, and no tenant in Common with any other of his owne condition.*

Droict de Mortuage. *A mortuarie; due to a Parson at the death of one of his parishioners; Looke,* Droict de Neufme.

Droict de Moulage. *Multure; the fee, or toll, for grinding, due unto the Miller, or Lord of the Mill; is (by the customes of Britaine) the sixteenth part of the Corne that is to be ground.*

Droict de Moulture; ou de Moulure; *the same.*

Droict de Moutonnage: *as,* Droict de Montenage.

Droict de Neufiesme. *A ninth part of th' yearelie profits of some benefices in Britaine, demanded by the Pope.*

Droict de Neufme. *A ninth of a third part of a deceased persons moueables, due to the Parson for his Mortuarie.*

Droict de Nommer aux Euesches,& Abbayes du Royaulme: *Belongs to the king.*

Droict de nopsages. *The fee due to a Parson for a mariage.*

Droict d' obliages. *The fine due vnto a Lord by his tenant who hath omitted, or forgotten to pay his rent, or yearelie duties at his day.*

Droict d' obole. *A halfepennie in the pound due to the King vpon all Obligations of money lent, and contracts of sale, exceeding* xv. li. Tourn.

Droict d' ostizes. *A certein number of hennes due euerie yeare vnto Lords from their tenants, in lieu of their Chimney-pence, or as a rent for their houses.*

Droict de oublie. *A* Douzain, *or* Sol *in the mouth of a Capon, payed, in some places, as a rent.*

Droict de padventage. *The right of common of pasture in one, or more parishes.*

Droict du paillé. *The priuiledge of the Pall, or of wearing a Pall, due onely to some Bishops.*

Droict de pain de paniere. *A great white-loafe due yerelie by the tenants of Saint* Gondon sur Loire *(besides their* Cens*) vnto their Lord.*

Droict de parée. *A correspondencie held betweene some neighbouring Lords, for the pursuing of one anothers villeins into their seuerall territories; thereby to take from them the pretence, they would otherwise haue, of being affranchised by being got out of their lords dominions.*

Droict de pariage. *A perpetual association, or correspondencie of Iurisdiction, agreed vpon betweene a spirituall, and a temporall Lord; also, the right of common of pasture in one anothers grounds.*

Droict de parnage. *Pawnage; or, (more generally,) the profit made, or mony receiued by the lord of a forrest for th' agistment, laying, or feeding of swine with the maste, or of Cattell with the herbage, thereof.*

Droict de patronnage. *The patronage, or aduowson of a benefice either when a man, that giues land to the Church, reserues the seigneurie thereof; or when the founder of a Church conditions, that he and his heires shall haue power to nominate, and present vnto the Bishop a person capable of the benefice, whensoeuer tis vacant.*

Droict de peage. *A through-toll or passage-toll.*

Droict de pescherie. *A right of fishing, or libertie to fish, in waters from which all others be restrayned.*

Droict de plassage: *A fee due, in some places, by Marchants and ware-sellers, for the shewing, and selling of their commodities in the market place, or publike streetes, and for the roomes wherein they shew, and sell them; therein like our stallage.*

Droict de poisage. *Poisage; or, a fee due in some places, vnto the king, for the weighing of wares in the Market-hall, or Towne-house.*

Droict de police. *Looke,* Police.

Droict de pontenage. *Pontage; passage-toll at a bridge, or, toll due for Marchandize passed ouer a bridge.*

Droict de porte. *A certein dutie paied by the Schollers of Paris, at their admission into colledges.*

Droict de preage. *A priuiledge enioyed by some lords, to put, at certein times, and with sufficient gard, their horses, and kine into their vassals meadowes; for which they are, at all times bound to find one that shall keepe, and looke vnto them.*

Droict de prelation. *The priuiledge of being preferred before others in a purchase.*

Droict de premice. *A sheafe of corne, or* ij. s. Tour. *and a lamb, if there be ten or more; if fewer a pennie for euery lamb, due vnto Parsons.*

Droict de premices. *The first fruits of Ecclesiasticall liuings.*

Droict de presence. *Halfe a Crowne due vnto euerie Treasurer, & generall of the* Finances *(besides their ordinarie wages) for residence; or, euery day they meet and sit about the kings businesse.*

Droict de Preuosté: *The priuiledge of hauing a Prouost vnder him to keepe his Courts, and leuie his tolles, rights, fines, &c; (belongs vnto a Lord Baron, or Chattelain that haue Iurisdiction;) also, a passage toll.*

Droict de quart denier du prix, ou de l'estimation. *The fourth pennie, or part, of the worth of an Inheritance* Cottier, *due vnto Landlords vpon any alienation thereof.*

Droict de quatrieme. *The fourth pot of, or pennie taken for, Wine, Cyder, and other ordinarie drinke retailed; due in some places vnto the king; & first graunted, for wine, vnto Charles the fift at a parliament helde in Paris.*

Droict de quenaise. *The right of Escheatage, whereby an Inheritance* Roturier *falles into the Lords hands, if his tenant leaue no lawfull issue of his bodie behind him:* ¶ Bretton.

Droict de quint. *The fift part of the price of land sould; belongs to the Lord of the soile vpon the sale thereof, and is paied sometimes by the seller, in some places by the buyer, and in some equally by both.*

Droict de Regale: *Seeke,* Regale.

Droict de Registration. est deu pour insinuer en Iustice vn transport d'heritage, de cens, ou rente: ou pour l'approbation d'une saisine. ¶ Regueau.

Droict de Registre. *A foure-pennie dutie paied by a tenant* Cottier *vnto his Landlord, when he puts him in possession of his tenement.*

Droict de Registre, ou Contentor. *A certein fee due vnto th' audienciers of Chanceries; (*viz. iiij. s. *sterling vpon euery Charter.)*

Droict de Relevoison. *A yeares rent in some cases, in others* vj. d. *for each pennie of yearelie* Cens, *payed by tenants* Censiers *vnto their Lord when they first enter into their tenements:* Looke, Relevoison.

Droict de Relief. *Reliefe; a fine due to the Lord of a Mannor, vpon the change of a tenant which houlds of him in fee: by the customes of* Amiens *it is* 60. s. Parisis *for euerie Noble fee held by a full homage, and* x. li. Paris. *for euerie one held in Peeredome: by the customes of* Peronne, *the yeres reuenue after the change,*

or

or the third part of the Reuenue of the three yeares next before it, at the Lords choice: By the customes of Valançai, S. Aignan, *and* Selles, xij. d. *for euerie pennie of yearelie* Cens: *And by the customes of Paris, and (almost) all other places, the Lord may chuse whether he will take a yeares Reuenue, or a whole Summe at once offered vnto him by the Tenant.*

Droict de Relods. xx d. Tour. *payable by a purchaser vnto the Landlord vpon euerie pound due to him for the* Lods *and* Ventes.

Droict de Rendage de chascun ouvrage; *containes both the Kings Right of* Seigneuriage, *and the Master of the Mints* Brassage.

Droict de Represailles, ou Repressailles. *Libertie, or Power to take, in time of warre, a stranger prisoner, and to keepe him, vntill he haue repayed vnto his Taker the ransome he payed formerly, or satisfied him for goods taken from him by one of his countreymen; Looke* Repressailles.

Droict de Requart. *A Quarter of a Quarter of the price, or worth of an Inheritance* Cottier, *due vnto the Landlord vpon the alienation thereof; (abolished by some late Customes.)*

Droict de Requint. *A fift pennie of the fift pennie of the price, or value of an Inheritance* feodal, *due in all alienations vnto the Lord* feodal; *but abolished, by the customes of some places, as the* Requart.

Droict de Ressort. *Looke* Ressort.

Droict de Resue. *An auncient Tax, or Imposition of* iiij d. *in the pound for Marchandise, and* x s. Tour. *for euerie Pipe of wine, brought into, or sent out of, the kingdome.*

Droict de Retenuë. *A Priuiledge of some Landlords; who may redeeme, within fortie dayes, the lands which their tenants haue sold, paying for them vnto the purchaser, ouer and besides his lawfull costs and charges, as much as he gaue.*

Droict de Retiers; *as* Droict de Reventes.

Droict de Reventes. *A fine due, besides the* Lods *and* Ventes, *vnto the Lord* Censuel, *by a Purchaser, who buying an Inheritance thats charged with* Cens, *doth vndertake to acquit the seller from the payment of* Lods.

Droict de Reventons. *The same.*

Droict de Reversion. *The right of Reuersion; power to take backe, and reunite vnto the demaine of the Crowne, such lands as haue beene diuided from it by Dowers, younger brothers Portions, &c; as also to seize on Duchies, & Earldomes that fall among daughters.*

Droict de Rivage. *Shorage, or Boatage; the Custome, or Toll for wine, or other wares, put vpon, or brought from, the water, by boats.*

Droict de Robbes de Pasques. *Gownes at Easter, due vnto the Officers of the chamber of Accompts.*

Droict de Rodage. *A certaine Toll exacted by some countrey Lords vpon euerie Wayne that passes (through the high way) by their Seigniories, whether it be loaden or no; for if it be, they will also be payed for the Load.*

Droict de Roses. *A certaine quantitie of Roses, or a fee in lieu of them, belonging to the Officers of the chamber of Accompts.*

Droict de Roüage. *Wheelage; a certaine Toll, or Imposition vpon wine sould in grosse, and carried away in Carts; leuied, before a wheele thereof bee suffered to turne: In some places, a Lord* Terrageur *hath also, as a wheelage, a sheafe vpon euerie load of his tenants corne, towards the carrying of his* Terrage *vnto his Barne, whereto by couenant, or custome they are bound to lead it.*

Droicts Royaux. *The Royall Prerogatiue, or Priuiledges; such as be the Protection of Vniuersities, and Cathedrall Churches (whose Officers, Members, Ministers, Seruants, and Vassals are not to bee tried before any other Iudges then the Kings) Exemption from Excommunication, both for himselfe, and his Officers (by reason of their Offices;) Power to prohibit the publication, and execution of Admonitions, Interdictions, or Suspensions denounced against the Prelates, or Officers of his Kingdome; Absolute, and onely power, to forgiue offences committed against the Publicke; to recall the Banished, release the Gallyslaue, and free other mens Villaines; to giue Protections, generall Passeports, and Safeconducts; to punish Traitors, Rebels, and Coyners; to giue Letters of Mart, and Reprisall; of Nobilitation, Legitimation, and full restitution; to raise new Customes, and Taxes; graunt Faires, and Markets; found Vniuersities; erect Corporations, and new Offices; make all kind of Knights; to enter into Warre, Peace, League, or Truce with an enemie; to create of a Chastellenie, a Baronie, or Countie; and of this a Marquisdome, or Duchie; to acknowledge no Superiour in temporall matters, no subiection vnto the Lawes Imperiall; generally, to exercise, and execute, all Soueraigne, and Monarchall Jurisdiction.*

Droict de saintre; *belongs vnto some Lords; who may thereby eat, with (onely) their cattell, all the wast, vntilled, stuble, or bushie grounds that be within their Manors.*

Droict de saisine. *The money due vnto the Lo.* Censuel, *and of the Soyle, by a Purchaser of an Jnheritance* Censuel, *when he is inseisined, and put into possession thereof; (by the customes of Paris it is* xij d. Parisis.)

Droict de salage. *A certaine quantitie of Salt due vnto the Abbot of* Bourgmoien *within* Blois, *vpon euerie boat that carries any into the hauen, or vnder the bridges, of that Towne.*

Droict de Salin. *as* Gabelle de Sel.

Droict de Salvage. *A tenth part of goods which were like to perish by shipwracke, due vnto him that saues them.*

Droict de Saunelage; *the same.* ¶Breton.

Droict de Sauvelage; *the same.*

Droict de Seel. *The Priuiledge of hauing a Seale, wherewith his vassals are to stampe all their contracts.*

Droict de Segorage. *A certaine dutie, or fee, belonging to the Lord of the Isle* Savari *within the Bayliwike of* Touraine.

Droict de Segreage; *the same.*

Droict de Seigneuriage. *Whereby defectiue coyne is forfeited vnto the Crowne; also, the right of coynage, or fee for coyning, due vnto the King; the first is, the profit he makes, in generall, by the defect of the coyne which he authorises; the second is (most commonly)* 65 s. Tour. *vpon euerie* Marc *of gold;* iiij s. vj d. *vpon a* Marc *of siluer; and* xx d. *vpon euerie* Marc *of* Billon, *or courser mettall, coyned.*

Droicts Seigneuriaux. *Rents, Seruices, Wardships, Escheats, and all other Rights due, or Profits accruing, vnto a Lord out of the land thats held of him; Looke* Seigneurial.

Droict de Sepulture. *A Parsons dutie, or fee, for the buriall of one of his Parishioners.*

Droict de sixiesme; &, du sixiesme denier; *Looke* Sixiesme.

Droicts de Souveraineté. *Looke* Souveraineté.
Droict de Stellage. *Toll-corne, and Toll-salt; a dishfull vpon euerie Septier of either sold within* Buillon, *due vnto the Duke thereof.*
Droict de Stippes, & nobis. *is, in some parts of Normandie, a pennie* Tour. *in other places* iij d, *vpon euerie pound made of the farmes of the Kings* Domaine muable, *due to the Officers of the Court of Accompts.*
Droict de suitte de bestes. *The power one hath, who lets a beast out to halues, or hire, to challenge and seize it, being sold, or passed away, without his knowledge, by him he let it vnto.*
Droict de suitte de disme. *A right, whereby a Lord of tythe-grounds which haue kept, and wintered cattell, whose owners worke with them in the tythe grounds of another Lord, may lawfully take halfe of those tythes, when they are to be gathered; (The maintaining of this vnreasonable Right breedes many suites and quarrels; and therefore it might, without wrong to the Publicke, be spared; sayes* Ragueau.)
Droict de suitte de gens; *as;*
Droict de suitte de personnes serves. *The power some Lords haue to compell their villaines, or others that hold land of them by villenage, to reside, and keepe a continuall fire, on their tenements; from this Right (which extends vnto their goods, or persons) all the Inhabitants of the Kings Townes within* Berry, *are exempted.*
Droict de suriect. *Power to adde vnto the last price thats offered in a Portsale, or Outrope.*
Droict de Tabellionnage. *The Priuiledge of a Lord Chattelain, or high Iusticier to make, and keepe vnder him a Notarie for the ingrossing of all deedes, and contracts passed within his Iurisdiction; Looke* Tabellionnage.
Droict de Taille. *The right of Subsidie, Tax, or Tallage; belongs as well vnto diuers Lords, by the customes of their Manors, as vnto the King; also, the Prerogatiue, or power to raise new taxes (onely in the King.)*
Droict de Terceau. *A certaine dutie taken by a Lord at the Fatt, or other vessell of his vassals wine; and to be payed vnto himselfe, or his Officer, before the wine be drawne, or else the vassall forfeits sixtie* sols Tour.
Droict de Terrage. *Field-Rent; Countrey-toll; Seeke* Terrage.
Droict de Thonnieu. *as* Droict de Tonlieu.
Droict de Tiers & danger. *A third, and a tenth part, of the price for which wood is sold in the woods, and forrests belonging to the Kings Demaine (especially within Normandie) due vnto him; Looke* Danger.
Droict de Tiers denier. *The third pennie of the price giuen for the purchase of an Inheritance* Roturier, *or* Bourdelier, *due, in some places, vnto the Landlord.*
Droict de Tirage. *Draggage; or a toll, or fee for draggage (of salt, or wine) due vnto some Lords.*
Droict de Tonlieu. *Toll due to the Lord of a Faire, or Market, for all kind of Marchandise, and Cattell, bought and sold: (By the customes of* Boulenois *it is* iiij d. *from the Buyer, and as much from the Seller, of a Horse, Ox, or Cow; a pennie for a Sheepe, or Goat; and* ij d. *for a Hog, equally payable, as the former, betweene the Buyer and Seller, before Sunne set.)*
Droict de Tonnelieu; &, de Toulieu; *the same.*
Droict de Traicte, *is* ij d. Tour. *leuied for the King of euerie cartload of Marchandise transported out of the Territorie of* Mehun; *Looke* Traicte.
Droict de Traicte de bleds. *An Imposition of* vij s. *sterl. vpon euerie Tunne of wheat (and rateably of all other kinds of graine) transported out of the Realme.*
Droict de Traicte foraine; *Looke* Forain.
Droict de Trainage, *as* Droict de suitte de disme.
Droict de Travers. *Crosse-toll; passage-toll; or, through-toll.*
Droict de Treu. *The Toll, or Custome due vnto Lords for Salt, or Marchandise, carried through their dominions; and generally, any Toll.*
Droict de Treu accoustumé. *A Priuiledge of the Lords high Iusticers in the Countie of Burgundie; where if a beast be taken, or killed in any one of their dominions, it must be brought, and giuen vnto him, or to some one of his Officers for him, whosoeuer the hunter be, or from whence soeuer the game was chased.*
Droict de treziesme. *The thirteenth pennie, or part, of the money for which land is sold, payable vnto the Lord, of whom tis held in fee by the Seller (vnlesse there be a couenant to the contrarie;) also, the thirteenth sheafe of a crop, due vnto a Lord that hath field-Rent, or countrey-toll.*
Droict du treziesme denier; *the same (in the first part.)*
Droict de treziesme de Vin. *The thirteenth pot, or pennie of the price of wine retayled; due, in some places, vnto the Lord of the Soyle, or of the Iurisdiction.*
Droict de Trousse. *A certaine number of Geese, or dutie payed in Geese, within the Iurisdiction of* Crosses *neere vnto* Bourges.
Droict de Truage. *as,* Droict de Treu.
Droict de Venditions. *The Toll which Lords of Markets, and Faires take for the sale of wares, and marchandise therein.*
Droict des Veneurs. *The Huntsmens, or Hunters, part of the Deere, or other game.*
Droict de venterolles. *A certaine fine due to a Landlord by the Purchaser that vndertakes to discharge the seller of all fines: By the Customes of* Lagni *(within the Iurisdiction of* Meaux) *it is* xx d. *in euerie pound which he giues; by those of* Senlis, *the sixteenth part of the* Droict de ventes; *by those of* Amiens, *the thirteenth pennie of the* Treziesme; *and by those of* Doulens, *the sixt of the* Sixiesme: *By those of* Clermont *it is called* Reventes; *and by those of* Arthois *it is as* Droict de Requint.
Droict de ventes. *is (most commonly) the twelfth part of the price of land* Censuel, *due to the Lord of whom it is held; and payable, in some places, by the Purchaser, in others by the Seller, and in others betweene them both: (The French Lawes and Customes often ioyne, with this, another dutie called* Lods, *or* Lots; *which is euer as much as this; both together swallowing vp a sixt part of that which is giuen for the purchase.)*
Droict de ventes, & Gants. *A twelfth part (as before) and* xv d. *(by the customes of* Tours) *or* x d. *(by the customes of* Lodunois) *for a paire of gloues.*
Droict de ventes, & honneurs. *The sixt, or other part (as the custome is) due onely by the Purchaser.*
Droict de ventes & issuës. *is also a sixt part, or* iij s. iiij d. *in the pound; (whereof, as if it were* Lods *and* Ventes, *there is but halfe meant for* Ventes.)
Droict de Verre. *A certaine number of drinking glasses, diuided, in old time, among the Officers of the chamber of Accompts, but at this day allowed them in money.*
Droict de Vertemoulte. *A certaine dutie, or fine payable vnto Lords in Normandie, by their tenants that inne*

inne their corne out of their Manors.

Droict de vest. *Power to make Liuerie and Seisin vnto a Purchaser, belongs in a few places to the seller, in many to the Lord* Censier, *or* Foncier; *also, the fine, or fee due to a Lord for Liuerie and Seisin made by him.*

Droict de veuës. *Authoritie to make windowes in other mens houses, for the commoditie and aduantage of a neighbour; or to damme vp such as hinder, or annoy a neighbour.*

Droict de Veufve. *Looke* Veufve.

Droict de viager. *An estate for life in; or libertie to enioy a thing during his life.*

Droict de vignages. *A certaine toll, or fee, taken by Lords of Marchants, or Drouers, &c, which with their commodities, or cattell passe by their territories.*

Droict de ville close. *Libertie, or power to inclose a Towne with walls, or fortifie it with Rampiers, procured from the Prince.*

Droict de Vin, ou de Vins. *A fine of iij s. vpon euerie alienation of an Inheritance* Censuel *exceeding* xx s, *due, besides* Lods *and* Ventes, *vnto the Couent of* Faresmontier, *by the inhabitants of* Iouy *(in the Iurisdiction of* Meaux.)

Droict de mettre prix au Vin. *A Priuiledge which a Lord, high or meane Iusticer, hath ouer all those that retayle Wine, or sell it by the pot, within his Iurisdiction; also, the fee thereto belonging; which is, a loafe of bread, and a lot of the Wine, deliuered vnto his Officers as a tast of it.*

Droict de Vins & stippes. 45 s. Tour. *vpon euerie Sale of wood within the Dominions of the Duke of* Buillon, *payable vnto the officers of the forrest out of which the sale is made.*

Droict de Vins & ventes. *A Iallée full of Wine, due to a Lord* Censuel *vpon the sale of land held of him, ouer and besides the twelfth part of the price for the* Ventes, *and payable by the Purchaser.*

Droict de Vinade. *The vse, and worke of two yoake of Oxen, or of a Cart, all Vintage time, due vnto the Lords of some Places, from their vassals and tenants.*

Droict de Vinage. *Twelue pence, due to the Officers of the Court of* Aides, *vpon a pound comming in for Wine (onely in some cases;) Also, the portion of Wine due out of a Vineyard vnto a Lord* Censier, *in lieu of his* Censive, *and to bee allowed him at the head of the Vatt, before the tenant can (lawfully) draw any Wine out of it; At* Angiers, *and in other places, this dutie is turned into a pecuniarie, and yerelie* Cens.

Droict de Vinenote. *as* Droict de Vivelotte.

Droict de Vingtiesme. *The twentieth part of Wine thats made, and Corne thats gotten, euerie yeare, payed in* Dauphiné, *and elsewhere, towards the building, fortifying, and reparation of the wals of Towns, Holds, and Castles.*

Droict de Vivelotte. *The Dower, or thirds due to the widow of a* Cottier, *or tenant of* Mainferme.

Droict de Vivenotte. *The same.*

Droict d'extreme Vnction. *The fee due to the Priest for that ceremonie.*

Droict de Voirie. *The right of Iustice; or power to exercise Iurisdiction as a* Voyer; *Looke* Voyer.

Droict de Voüade. *The labour of two Oxen, or vse of a small Cart, due certaine dayes in Summer by tenants (that hold by Villenage, or* Mortaille) *vnto their Landlords for the turning vp of their Vineyards.*

Droict de Vouerie. *Meane Iurisdiction; or, as* Droict de Voirie.

Droict: m. cte: f. *Right, streight, direct; leuell, euen; iust, lawfull, reasonable; sincere; vpright.*

Intestin, ou boyau droict. *The streight gut, or arsegut.*

Muscle droict. *The name of one of the foure principall muscles in the thigh.*

Pied droict. *The Iaume, or Iaumbe of a dore, chimney, window, &c.*

`A droict fil. *Directly forward, right forth, streight on.*

Mal droict. *Vnapt, vnwieldie; vnhandsome, vncomelie in euerie thing he does.*

Droict. *(Adverbially) as,* Droict en ce lieu, *iust here, in this verie place, or, precisely in this place.*

`A droict. *as,* `A droict fil.

Parler à droict. *To speake distinctly, or to the purpose.*

Tenez cest homme à droict. *Deale iustly with this man; vse him indifferently, or well.*

`A droict, ou à tort. *By hooke, or crooke; by right or by wrong; one way or another.*

Au droict d'entre eux. *Right ouer against them.*

Tout droict. *Right forth, streight on, directly forward.*

Droictement. *Streightly, directly, rightly; iustly, vprightly, rightfully.*

Droictement à l'heure. *Iust at the time, at the very houre appointed.*

Droicture: f. *Right, reason, iustice, directnesse, impartialitie, vprightnesse; also, a Right, or due, or, the rights and duties belonging to a Landlord, &c; also, a full, or iust possession of land.*

Droicture de Patronnage. *Patronnage, or the Right of Presentation to a Benefice.*

Relever droicture. *as* Droicturer.

Qui d' honneur n' a cure honte est sa droicture: Prov. *Hee that for honour doth not care, disgrace besmeares him, shame's his share.*

Droicturé: m. ée. f. *That hath payed his Reliefe, and all other the rights, or duties of Tenancie.*

Droicturer. *A new tenant, or vassall to doe his Lord all right, and pay him all the rights, belonging to him.*

Droicturier: m. ere: f. *Iust, rightfull, sincere, vnpartiall, intire, incorrupt, vpright; also, seuere, strict, according to the letter of the Law; also, direct, or next.*

Droicturier Seigneur. *A mans true, right, or lawfull Lord.*

Seigneur droicturier. *as* Seigneur feudal.

Droicturierement. *Iustly, rightfully, incorruptly, vprightly, vnpartially; strictly, seuerely.*

Droisser. *as* Dresser. *To direct; erect; instruct.*

Droit, & Droiturier. *See* Droict, *&* Droicturier.

Droitier. *Right-handed; also, as* Droicturier.

Drolatique: com. *Waggish, knauish, full of rye, pleasant, merrie, sportfull.*

Drole: m. *A good fellow, boone companion, merrie grig, pleasant wag; one that cares not which end goes forward, or how the world goes.*

Droler. *To play the wag; to passe away the time, as a good fellow, merrily, or carelesly; also, to beat soundly.*

Drolerie: f. *Rye, waggerie, good roguerie; a merrie pranke, a pleasant, and knauish part; good-fellowship; See* Draulerie.

Dromant: m. *A Drumbler, Carauell, or such like small, and swift vessell, vsed by Pyrats.*

Dromedaire: m. *A Dromedarie, or great beast of burthen, like a Camell; verie swift & hardie in trauell, and of little charge to him that vseth him.*

Dromille: f. *A little fish caught (all Summer long, but seldome during Winter) in the riuers about Lions.*

Dromon. *as* Dromant.

Dronine: f. *A spade.*

Dronos. donner dronos. *Knockes, thumpes, raps, thwacks.* ¶Rab.

Dropace. *A depilatorie; an oyntment, or medicine to take away haire.* ¶Rab.

Dru: m. druë: f. *Thicke, close together, full of, many one by another; copious, plenteous.*

Oiseau dru. *A full-fledg'd bird, a young bird readie to fly.*

Druëment. *Thickly, many together, close one by another, plenteously, copiously.*

Druge: f. *as* Truffe; *a daintie, round, and russet root, thats all inclosed within, but not on any part fastened vnto, the ground; by the bulking out whereof tis found.*

Drugé: m. ée: f. *Wet, throughly moistened.*

Drugeon: m. *A little branch, twig, or sprig.*

Drugeonnement. *A bearing, or putting forth of small branches, or twigs.*

Drugeonner. *To beare, or put forth many small branches, or twigs.*

Drugeonneux. *Twiggie, spriggie, full of small branches.*

Druger. Voilà que druge bien. *(Spoken of a sound shower) thus wets throughly.*

Druguement. *A Trucheman, or Interpretor.* (v.m.)

Drusse: f. *as* Drylle.

Dryinade. *as* Chelydre.

Drylle: f. *The Mastie, or Akorne of the (female) Oake.*

Du. *is sometimes (as an Article) set before Masculine words, which begin with a Consonant, and signifie the kinds, or* species *of things; as,* du pain, du vin, &c; *(then of little, or no signification:) Sometimes it serues as a note of the Genitiue Case, vnto Nownes of the nature aforesaid; and then signifies, of them; as,* Le fruict du iardin: *Sometimes it does the Office of a Preposition; and then signifies, in the; as,* Si i'eusse du commencement faict cela; du temps du Roy Henry, &c; *or, from the; as,* Il vient du iardin; du milieu d'eux; *or, by the; as,* Il a esté batu du Maistre.

Du moins. *At the least.*

Du tout. *Throughly, vtterly, altogether.*

Dubitation: f. *Doubtfulnesse, vncertainetie, suspence, or suspition.*

Duc: m. *A Duke. (When the French Kings had chased the Romanes out of* Gallia, *and found some of the Prouinces thereof gouerned, vnder the Emperours, by certaine martiall Commaunders tearmed* Duces, *they, who altered but few of the auncient fashions of the countrey, bestowed the same Title (a little curtalled* à la Françoise*) on such of their own principall captaines as they placed in the roomes of the others: At which time Dukes were but Officers, and Vassalls; and their Functions, and* Fiefs *reuocable at the Princes pleasure, or determined with their liues; howsoeuer afterwards, they vsurped, first, the Inheritance of, and then a Soueraignetie ouer, them both: Looke the word* Comte; *wherein whatsoeuer is said of the ancient, or moderne estate of (Prouinciall) Earles agrees with that of Dukes; with this onely difference, that, commonly, the Title of Duke was conferred on the more warlike, and* Comte *on the more ciuill, followers of Princes; whereupon it is coniectured, that when both a Duke, and an Earle haue beene in one Towne, the one gouerned the Souldiors, the other the People.)*

Duc: m. *(is also) the great Owle tearmed, a Horne-owle, or Horne-coot; of three kinds.*

Grand duc. *The great Horne-coot; is bigger then a Goose, and keepes alwayes in forrests, and desert places.*

Moyen duc. *is somewhat lesse then the former: Both of them be hairie-legd, and rough-footed; and haue tufts of feathers, on either side of their heads, bearing out like hornes; and now and then breath out horrible skrikes.*

Petit duc. *The small Horne-owle, or Horne-coot; shaped like, but somewhat lesse then,* le Moyen duc.

Poudre de duc. *The name of a most comfortable pouder, made of Aromaticall drugs, and spices.*

Ducal: m. ale: f. *Ducall, Duke-like; of, or belonging, to a Duke.*

Ducat: m. *A Dukedome, or Duchie.*

Ducat: m. *The coyne, tearmed a Ducket; worth* vj s. viij d.

Ducat d'Aragon; de Bolongne; de Castille; d'Espaigne à deux testes *(the duckat thats currant among vs)* de Florence; de Gennes; d'Hongrie; de Portugal; de Portugal à la longue croix; de Portugal à la petite croix; de Portugal à la palme, de Sicile, de Valence, de Venize; *All forraine coynes; of whose value (often changed by the French Kings) no certaine interpretation can be giuen, other then that they hold a rate much about* v, *or* vj s. *sterl. the peece.*

Ducat Henry. *A coyne of Gold worth* vj d. *sterl. more then the ordinarie Crowne of the Sunne.*

Ducaton. *A small duckat, or halfe duckat.*

Duché: m. *A Dukedome, a Duchie.*

Ducteur. *as* Conducteur; *a guide, leader, &c.*

Ductile: com. *Easie to be hammered, or beaten into thin plates.*

Dudepuis. *Since, sithence, from that time.*

Dueil: m. *Dole, griefe, sorrow, heauinesse; mourning, wayling, moaning, lamentation; also, mourning weeds, or mourning attire; as,* Il porte le dueil; *also, a mourner, or mourners, following a course to the graue; as,* voila le dueil, *or,* le dueil passe; *also, a* duello, *single combat, or fight betweene two.*

Apres tout dueil boit on bien: Prov. *Drinke after dole goes merrily downe; or, they tiple now as much as erst they teend.*

Assez boit qui a dueil: Pro. *Sorrow is dry, say we; or, as in* Boire.

Bon est le dueil qui apres aide: Prov. *That mourning's well bestowed that helpes the mourner.*

Chacune vieille son dueil plaind: Pro. *See* Plaindre.

De petit enfant petit dueil: Pro. *The death of little ones is not much bemoand.*

Duelle: f. *The third part of an ounce.*

Duire. *To vse, accustome, enure; fashion, traine vp, frame; lead, induce, bring, vnto.*

Cela me duit. *That is good, or maketh, for me; that is helpefull, auaileable, or commodious, vnto me; in which sence they say;* Vieilles debtes duisent: Prov. asçavoir; *helpe the creditor, (but hurt the debtor.)*

Duisable: com. *Conuenient, fit, for ones turne; auaileable, profitable, whereof good vse, or great benefit, may be made.*

Duisant. *Apt, meet, conuenient, fitting; handsome, seemelie, becomming.*

Duisible. *as* Duisable.
Duisson : f. *An accustoming, vsing, enuring; fashioning, training, framing, making fit, or apt for.*
Duit : m. duite : f. *Accustomed, vsed, enured; framed, fashioned, trained vp vnto; also, fitting, auaileable, helpefull, conuenient, good for, to the purpose.*
Duiter. *To frame vnto vse, to make fit for his purpose.*
Dumetté : m. ée : f. *Downie; of downe; soft as, full of, stuffed with, downe.*
Dun. *An old French word, signifying a hill, or rocke; (and therefore the townes whose names end in it haue, commonly, a rockie accesse, or seat.)*
Dune : f. *A waue, or surge of the sea; also, a Downe; a sandie banke, or hill neere the sea; called so, (at first by the Flemmings) because it resists the violence of those waues; and vsed, most commonly, in the plurall number,* Dunes.
Duner. *To plaine, as a horse, that neither halteth outright, nor setteth his foot hard on the ground.*
Dunes. *Looke* Dune.
Dunette : f. *A Thrush; also, a little downe, or sandie hill.*
Dunne : f. *as* Dune.
Duodene : m. *as* Douze-doigtier.
Dupe : f. *A whoope, or hooper; a bird that hath on her head a great crest, or tuft of feathers, and loues ordure so well, that she euer nestles in it.*
Duplication : f. *as* Duplique.
Duplique : f. *A reioynder; or, the second answer of a defendant.*
Duppe. *as* Dupe.
Dupliquer. *To double; also, to reioyne, or answere the second time.*
Duquel. *Of whom, from whom, whereof.*
Dur : m. dure : f. *Hard; stiffe, solide; also, rough, harsh, rude; also, sturdie, fierce, cruell, difficile, rigorous, inflexible, vnmercifull; also, dull, grosse, heauie, sottish, or slow of apprehension; and hence;*
Dur à l'esperon. *Dull, sluggish, heauie-mettled, that will not be moued, nor stirred vp by any instigation.*
Dure mere de la teste. *The outward skinne of the braines.*
Dure taye. *as* Dure mere.
Ouïr dur. *To be thicke of hearing.*
Tunique dure. *One of the thin skins of the eye, the which it enuirons; it comes from the* dure mere, *and couers also the Opticke sinew.*
Durable : com. *Durable, lasting, of long continuance.*
Duracines. *The Peaches, Plummes, Cherries, &c, whose pulpe cleaues fast vnto their stones; also, such as are of a hard, or firme pulpe, and thereby long-lasting.*
Duraines. *as* Duracines.
Durant. (Particip.) *During, lasting, continuing; induring, brooking, suffering.*
Durant (Conjunct.) ces iours-là. *During that age, in those dayes.*
Durant que. *Whiles that, whilome that, vntill that.*
Trois mois durant. *Three moneths together.*
Durci : m. ie : f. *Hardened, stiffened.*
Durcir. *To harden, stiffen; wax hard, become stiffe, grow solide.*
Dure : f. Coucher sur la dure (terre, *is vnderstood) to ly on the bare earth.*
Duré. *Dured, indured, lasted, continued, remained; brooked, suffered, sustained.*
Durée : f. *A during, a lasting, a continuance.*
Longue durée. *Euerlastingnesse, perpetualnesse, long lasting.*
Dureines. *as* Duracines.
Durement. *Hardly; streightly, stiffely; harshly, roughly, rudely; cruelly, fiercely, rigorously; also, greatly, mainly, extreamely, exceeding much; as,* Il est durement haï des Seigneurs.
Durer. *To dure, last, continue, indure, abide, remaine, persist; also, to sustaine, brooke, suffer.*
Homme à qui on ne peut durer. *A froward, wayward, sullen, harsh, rude, soure, vnsociable fellow.*
Ils ont bien besoing que ie leur dure. *My liues continuance imports them verie much; it stands them much vpon to haue me long among them.*
Endurer faut pour durer : Pro. *To dure we must indure.*
Tousiours ne dure orage ne guerre : Pro. *Extremities last not alwayes.*
Duresse : f. *Hardnesse, soliditie, stiffenesse.*
Duret : m. ette : f. *Somewhat hard; stiffe, solide; rough, harsh; difficile, inflexible; sturdie, rude, fierce.*
Dureté : f. as Duresse; *also, roughnesse, harshnesse, rudenesse; asperitie, rigor.*
Dure-teste : f. *A kind of spotted, and hard-headed Spider.*
Durillon : m. *A hard knot, or knurre in a peece of timber, or stone, which dulls the workemans tooles; also, a corne, or hard skin in the feet, or hands; also, a hard sparkle, or graine in some Saphires, &c, hindering the cutting thereof.*
Duvet : m. *Downe, soft feathers.*
Duvet du linge. *Lint.*
Duvetté : m. ée : f. *Downie, soft as downe; full of, or filled with, downe.*
Duyere : f. *A Conny-hole.*
Dy, ay, & hory ho. *The Cry of Carters.*
Dyafané, & Dyaphané. *Transparent; See* Diafané.
Dynandrie. *as* Dinanderie; *brasen ware, &c.*
Dynarchie. *The ioynt rule of two princes.*
Dyscole : com. *Wayward, froward, hard to rule, ill to intreat; out of all order.*
Dyscrasié. *Looke* Discrasié.
Dysenterie : f. *The bloudie flix.*
Dysenterique : com. *Troubled with, or sicke of, the bloudie flix.*
Dysopie. *Vicious, or excessiue shamefastnesse.*
Dysurie : f. *Difficultie of voiding vrine, and paine withall when it voides, by the sharpenesse thereof, and the inflammation, or exulceration of the necke of the Bladder.*

E

EAge : m. *Age; Seeke* Aage.
Eagé. *Old, aged, of such an age, of so manie yeares.*
Eale. *A blackish (Ethyopian) beast, that hath cheekes like a Boare, a tayle like an Elephant, and two long hornes, which he extends, or drawes inward, at pleasure.* ¶Rab.
Eard : m. *The blacke Poplar tree.*
Eau : f. *Water; also, the Element of water; also, the yellowish sweat which euaporeth continually from the*

the skinne of an infant (and lyes betweene the coife, or biggin, called Amnios, *and the bodie) while it is in the wombe.*

Les Eaux. *Windgalls in a horses legs.*

Eau d'Ange. *A kind of excellent sweet compound water.*

Eau ardant. *Aquauite.*

Eau beniste de cave. *Good wine, or strong beere.*

Eau beniste de Cour. *Court holie water; complemēts, faire words, flattering speeches, glosing, soothing, palpable cogging.*

Eau de bouchet. *A compound water, which with Coriander water makes a kind of Hypocras.*

Eau clairette. *A water (made of Aquauite, Cinnamon, Sugar, and old red Rose water) excellent against all the diseases of the Matrix.*

Eau endormie. *Seeke* Endormi.

Eau ferrée. *Wherein a gad of hot steele hath beene quenched.*

Eau Gringoriane. *Holie-water.* ¶Rab.

Eau de laict. *Clarified whay.*

Eau de nafe, ou de naphe. *Orange-flower water.*

Eau de vie. *Aquauite.*

Eau vifve. *A spring; a running water.*

Beuveur d'eau. *Looke* Beuveur.

Fil d'eau. à fil d' eau. *With the streame.*

Fleur d'eau. *The water Lillie, water Rose, yellow or white Nenuphar.*

'A fleur d eau. *Close by the water, betweene wind and water.*

Medecin d'eau douce. *A yong, raw, or vnexperienced Phisition; (we say, a fresh water souldior.)*

Pierre d' eau de mer. *A kind of white, and glittering Gemme; as* Oeil de Chat.

Verseur d'eau. *The celestiall signe,* Aquarius.

De belle eau. Perle de belle eau. *Of a faire luster, or water.*

De bonne eau. *Of a good rellish, or tast, hauing a good smacke with it.*

De delà l'eau. Gens de delà l'eau. *Simple fellowes, witlesse companions, ignorant creatures.*

Affleurir l'eau. *To skimme the water; or, goe close by it, as doth a ships lee-side in a strong side-wind.*

Amener l'eau au moulin. *To draw in gaine, to bring in crownes, to furnish with customers, or commodities.*

Avoir de l'eau vers les garces. *To haue sap, and moisture enough for his lecherie.*

Batre l'eau. *To loose his labour, to spend his time in vaine.*

Batre les eaux. *A Deere to take soyle.*

Batre leur eau. *To disgest, or shake down their drinke, as a horse thats ridden two or three miles after watering.*

Estre en eau. *To sweat; (we say also) to be all on a water;* Estre en l'eau. *To be in, or vpon the water; (so that the Article makes the difference.)*

Faire eau. *To leake; also, to water, or take in fresh water, for the prouision of a ship.*

Laisser de l'eau en son moulin. *To leaue himselfe euer somewhat to doe.*

Mener à la bonne eau. *To steale (as) a horse, (whereto this Phrase is chiefely applyed.)*

Mettre de l'eau dedans leur vin. *To temper, coole, qualifie, tame them; to take them a hole lower.*

Nager en grand' eau. *To haunt, frequent, or abide in places, wherein most honour, gaine, roome, and companie may be gotten; Looke* Nager.

Nager entre deux eaux. *To be in danger on all sides; to saile betweene* Scilla *and* Charybdis; *also, to hold on a middle course betweene two extreames; also, to play on both hands, or apply himselfe vnto the time, whatsoeuer; Looke* Nager.

Paistry d'eau froide. *White-liuered, dull, fearefull, without spirit, without mettall.*

Pescher en eau trouble. *To seeke for gaine by other mens losses, or brables; or, to make a benefit of publicke tumults, or calamities.*

Piler l'eau en vn mortier. *To loose time, or spend it verie fondly.*

Tenir le bec en l'eau: Pro. *To hold in suspence; to put off with dalliances, or delayes.*

Il n'a pas tenu le bec en l' eau. *Hee hath plyed the wine-pot, and is become tipsie; hee is throughly drunke (but not with water.)*

Tirer de l'eau en son moulin. *To draw all dealings into his owne hands; to seeke only his own profit, without respecting the interest of others.*

Tomber de l'eau. *To pisse, leake, make water.*

Cela luy fit venir l'eau en la bouche. *That made his teeth water;* viz. *put him into an extreame longing.*

L'eau qui dort est pire que celle qui court: Pro. *So is a sleepie humor worse then a giddie.*

Eau & pain c'est la viande du chien: Prov. *Bread, and water is diet for dogs.*

En petite eau souvent on trouve grand bieure: Pro. *A great beauer is often found in a little brooke.*

Fol est qui se fie en eau endormie: Pro. *Looke* Endormi.

Il fait beau pescher en eau large: Prov. *There is no fishing to the sea, say we.*

Il n'a pas soif qui de l'eau ne boit: Prov. *Hee's not athirst that will not water drinke.*

Il n'est nager qu' en grand' eau: Prov. *The biggest waters are the best to swimme in.*

Il n'y a pire eau que la quoye: Prov. *The stillest waters (and humors) are euer the worst.*

Eauë. *as* Eau.

Eauïer: m. *A gutter, channell, sinke, sewer for the voiding of foule water.*

Eaulice: f. *The hearbe Helicampanie, Scabwort, Horseheale.*

Eaurolle: f. *as* Aerolle; *a wheale, or blister.*

Eauvier. *as* Esvier.

Ebaucher. *To rough-hew; as* Esbaucher.

Ebe. *An ebbe; or the ebbing of water.*

Tout ce que vient d' Ebe s'en retournera de flot: Prov. *The Tyde will fetch away what th' ebbe brings in.*

Ebene: m. *The blacke wood called Heben, or Ibonie.*

Ebesté: m. eé: f. *Made, or growne bestiall, beastlie, blockish.*

Eborgner. *To depriue of one eye.*

Ebouiller. *Seeke* Esbouillir.

Ebouller. *as* Esbouler; *to throw, or tumble downe.*

Eboulu. *Seeke* Esboulu.

Ebreché: m. ée: f. *That hath lost diuers teeth; or, in whose mouth the losse of teeth hath made diuers breaches.*

Ebrieté: f. *Drunkennesse.*

Ebriosité: f. *Continuall drunkennesse.*

Ebulition. *as* Ebullition.

Ebullition: f. *An ebullition, boyling, seething, or bubling vp; a rising vp in bubles.*

Eburnin: m. ine: f. *Of, or belonging to Iuorie.*

Ecaille: f. *as* Escaille.

Ecaillé: m. ée: f. *Scaled, or shaled.*

Ecailler. *To scale, or shale; to pull the scales off, to rid of shales.*
Ecamoter. *To change, disguise, or alter; Seeke* Escamoter.
Ecarboté: m. ée: f. *Stirred, or scattered, as the fire; also, bruised, or crushed, as an apple.*
Ecarboter le feu. *To stirre vp, or scatter, the fire.*
Ecarboter vne pomme. *To bruize, or crush an apple.*
Ecardan. *Nice, daintie, queasie-stomacked; whence;* Ie suis plus ecar. à boire qu' à manger; *any sluttishnesse is more loathsome to my stomacke in drinke then in meat.*
Ecclesiaste: m. *A Preacher.*
Ecclise. *as* Eglise. *The Church.*
Eccliſſe. *as* Escliſſe.
Ecclisser. *as* Esclisser.
Ecentrique: com. *Without center, out of the center; also, without measure, whereof no measure can be taken.*
Fol ecentrique. *An vnrulie, or irregular coxcombe; one that can be held within no compasse.*
Ecervelé. *as* Escervelé. *Brainelesse, harebraind.*
Echaudé: m. ée: f. *Scalded; Looke* Eschaudé.
S'Echauder. *To be scalded; to grow too hot, or be put into ouermuch heat.*
Echelette. *Seeke* Eschelette.
Echelle: f. *A ladder.*
Echelon: m. *The step of a ladder.*
Echevelé. *Discheueled. as* Deschevelé.
Echevement: m. *as* Eschevement.
Echidne: f. *A Viper, or Hydra; any kind of Serpent.*
Echine. *as* Eschine.
Eclat, & Eclater; *Seeke* Esclat, *&* Esclater.
Eclipse: f. *An Eclipse; a lessening, diminution, defect of.*
Eclipsé: m. ée: f. *Eclipsed; lessened, impaired.*
Eclipsement: m. *An eclipsing, lessening, diminishing, impairing.*
Eclipser. *To disappeare, to vanish out of sight (in part;) also, to eclipse, lessen, diminish, impaire.*
Ecliptique. *The Eclipticke line, or way of the Sunne; so tearmed, because Eclipses happen, when the Moone is either in coniunction, or opposition, vnder this line.*
Ecliptique: com. *Belonging to an Eclipse.*
Eclisse. *Looke* Esclisse.
Ecloy: m. *Lant, pisse, vrine.* ¶Pic.
Ecluse. *as* Escluse.
Eclyptique. *as* Ecliptique.
Ecolleté. *as* Escouleté.
Econome, & Economie. *as* Oeconome, *&* Oeconomie.
Ecosse. *as* Escosse; *a cod, huske &c.*
Ecoüé: m. ée: f. *Curtall, curtalled, without a tayle.*
Ecouër. *To curtall, or cut off the taile; Seeke* Escouër.
Ecphrase: f. *A plaine declaration, or exposition.*
Ecraser. *as* Escraser.
Ecreté: m. ée: f. *Topped, vncrested; whose top, or crest is taken off.*
Ecrioches: f. *Crutches (at* Tours.)
Ecstase: f. *An extasie, swooning, traunce; astonishment; a dampe, or dumpe; a great amazement.*
Ecstatique. *In an Extasie; Seeke* Extatique.
Ectique: com. *In a consumption; or, sick of an Hecticke feuer; The word properly signifieth, habituall; (as any thing is, that by continuance is turned vnto nature) & thence is a feuer called Hecticke, when it hath possessed all parts of the bodie, without any alteration in it selfe.*

Eculée: f. *A dishfull.*
Ecume: f. *Looke* Escume.
Edent. il tomba edent. *He fell groueling, on his face, on his teeth.*
Edenté: m. ée: f. *as* Edent; *also, toothlesse, whose teeth are dasht, or fallen, out of his mouth.*
Edenter. *To make toothlesse; to bereaue of teeth; to draw, or strike, out the teeth of.*
Edenter la morsure de. *To disappoint, or make vaine the biting of.*
Edenter vn pot, ou autre vaisseau. *To ouerturne a pot, or set it on the ground with the mouth downeward.*
Edict: m. *A Statute, Edict. Ordinance.*
La Chambre de l'Edict. *as,* Chambre mipartie.
Edificateur: m. *An edifier; builder; maker, framer.*
Edification: f. *An edification, building, erecting, framing, making.*
Edifice: m. *An Edifice, building, or house readie built; also, the frame of a building; also, the art, or worke of building.*
Edifié: m. ée: f. *Edified, builded, framed, erected, founded; also, bred, come, or brought, vp of.*
Edifier. *To edifie, build; frame, erect, found, make vp (any thing, but especially) a house.*
Tell'herbe s'edifie de. *is set, or planted by; is bred, or comes, vp of.*
Education: f. *Nurture, education, bringing vp.*
Eduction: f. *An eduction, leading, drawing out, bringing forth.*
Efaisté: m. ée: f. *Topped, or whose top is cut off, or taken downe.*
Efaister. *To top, or cut the top of, a plant; to take downe the top of.*
Efemeridiaire. fievre ef. *An ague that continues but one day.*
Effable: com. *Speakeable; which may be vttered, or specified in words.*
Effacé: m. ée: f. *Defaced, effaced, razed, blotted out.*
Effacement: m. *An effacing, defacing, razing, blotting out.*
Effacer. *To efface, deface, raze, blot, rub out, wipe away; to abolish.*
Effaré: m. ée: f. *Skared, amazed, astonied; wilde, or ghastlie of looke; also, disturbed, moued; altered, distempered, or put into passion.*
Effarer. *To skare, amaze, terrifie, appall; moue, perturbe, distemper, put into passion.*
Effaroucher. *To mad, make wood, skittish, wild, fierce, cruell; to exasperate; also, to fright, skare, feare away.*
Qui veut prendre vn oiseau, qu'il ne l'effarouche: Prov. *Let not him anger, that would take, a bird.*
Effassure: f. *A defacement, raze; blot, blurre; a dash, or stroke through a thing written, or painted.*
Effect: m. *An effect, or worke; the issue, or successe of a thing; a working, bringing to passe, making to be.*
Homme de peu d'effect. *A weake, and witlesse fellow; one that can do little, thats scarse worth taking vp; one in whom there is no manner of worth.*
Qui n'a point d'effect. *Vain, void, succeslesse; that is come to no proofe, whereby one is much disappointed.*
Effectrice: f. *An effectrix; she that causeth, procureth, or bringeth to passe.*
Effectué: m. ée: f. *Effectuated, effected; executed.*
Effectuër. *To effectuate, effect, execute, performe, dispatch, bring to passe.*

Ef-

Effectueux. *Effectuall; to the purpose; also, effecting, working, doing, causing, procuring, dispatching.*
Effemination: f. *An effemination, or effeminacie; a womanizing, weakning, wantonizing; a making womanish, weake, wanton.*
Effeminé: m. ée: f. *Effeminate, womanish, womanlike, heartlesse, weake, tender, delicate; that hath no hardinesse, that can endure no hardnesse.*
Homme effeminé. *A weakling, milksop, sensuall and refined goose, puling or faint-hearted cokes.*
Effeminement. *Effeminately, womanishly; weakely, tenderly, delicately.*
Effeminer. *To effeminate, weaken, make daintie, tender, nice, quaint, womanish.*
Efferé. *Wild, skittish, giddie, wood; also, proud.*
Effiancé: m. ée: f. *Affianced, betrothed.*
Efficace: f. *Efficacie, force, effectualnesse, vertue, strength, ablenesse.*
Efficacement. *Forcibly, effectually, strongly, throughly, pithily, with efficacie, to purpose.*
Efficacieusement. *Most effectually, very forcibly, with much strength, to great purpose.*
Efficacieux: m. euse: f. *Most effectuall, forcible, strong, of much power, of great efficacie.*
Efficient. *Efficient, causing, effecting, accomplishing, making, wholly procuring, onely finishing.*
Effigial: m. ale: f. *Representing, resembling; also, belonging to an image, or shape.*
Effigie: f. *An image, picture, figure, counterfeit, resemblance, representation of a shape, or feature.*
Pendu en effigie. *Hangd in picture; if an offendor, whose fault deserues hanging, escape, yet is he, by the Customes of France, adiudged to the gallowes, and his picture hanged thereon; A signe, that whensoeuer he is taken, he shall be trussed vp in person.*
Effigié: m. ée: f. *Drawne, figured, pourtrayed, counterfeited, resembled, represented.*
Effigier. *To figure, draw, picture, pourtray, counterfeit, expresse the forme, represent the shape, make a true resemblance of, (by painting, caruing, or otherwise.)*
Effilé: m. ée: f. *Rauelled, unwound, loossened; also, weakened, or loose-hangled.*
Effiler. *To rauell, vnwind, loosse; loosen; also, to weaken, or loosen the ioynts.*
Efflanché. (Cheval efflanché.) *Swayed in the backe.*
Efflanqué: m. ée: f. *as* Esflanqué.
Effleurant. *Deflowring; also, skimming ouer, grazing along vpon.*
Effleuré: m. ée: f. *Deflowred, or depriued of flowers; also, skummed, gone lightly ouer, grazed along on; also, razed a little; whose beautie, or best peeces are gone.*
Effleurer. *To deflowre; or, depriue of flowers; also, to skum, or take onely the top of; to graze along, as a bullet on the side of a wall; to goe lightly ouer, as a stone on the water; also, to picke out sleightly the best, and most gracefull peeces of a thing.*
Efflorescence: f. *The outward face, or superficies, the vpmost rinde, pilling, or skinne, of any thing; whence;*
Efflorescence du cuir. *The superficiall, and outmost thin skin of the bodie; that which riseth in blisters after a burning, & the skalie substance pilled from scabdryed hands, &c.*
Effoncé: m. ée: f. *Whose bottome is beaten out.*
Effoncer. *To driue, or beat out the head, or bottome of a vessell, &c; to bulge.*
Effondément. *Profusely, extreamely, exceedingly, without measure.*
Effondré: m. ée: f. *Paunched, bowelled, or drawne; burst open; strucke through; also, as* Enfondré.
Chemin effondré. *A way full of holes, or myrie sloughes; a verie deepe, and durtie way.*
Effondrer. *To bowell, paunch, draw the guts, or garbage out of.*
Effondrer vn cheval. *To strike, or thrust a horse through the bellie.*
Effondrer vn huis, ou vn vaisseau. *To burst open a dore, to knocke, or beat, out the bottome of a vessell.*
Effondrille. *The groũd, bottome, lees, or dregs of liquor.*
Efforcé: m. ée: f. *Indeuored, labored, trauelled in with vtmost force, striuen in with might and maine.*
Efforcement: m. *Indeuor, &c; as* Effort. (v. mot.)
Efforcément. *Earnestly, vehemẽtly, with all his might, with great indeuour, with tooth and nayle.*
S'Efforcer. *To indeuor, labor, inforce himselfe; to striue with might and maine; to vse his vtmost strength, apply all his vigour, imploy his whole power.*
Efforcillons. *A certaine disease, or distemperature, in a Haukes tongue.*
Effort: m. *An effort; indeuor; labour, trauell, painestaking; a striuing for a matter with whole force, power, meanes.*
Effort de gens de guerre. *A violent assault, a furious onset, or attempt.*
Faire effort à. *To offer violence, or do opẽ wrong vnto.*
Ils font leur effort. *They doe what lyes in them; they doe their best, or worst; they do performe their vtmost; or, they are at their height of strength.*
Effray. *as* Effroy.
Effrayable: com. *Fearefull, dreadfull, terrible, hideous, horrible.*
Effrayablement. *In a fearefull, and terrible manner.*
Effrayant: m. ante: f. *Hideous, fearefull, horride, gastlie, frighting, horrible; also, affrighting, skaring, fraying.*
Effraye: f. *A Scricheowle, or Lychefowle; an vnluckie night-bird, which in shape, colour, and bignes resembles a Cuckoe.*
Effrayé: m. ée: f. *Affrighted, frayed, skared, feared; amazed, appalled, daunted, dismayed.*
Effrayement. *Dreadfully, terribly, after a fearefull sort, in a horrible manner.*
Effrayer. *To affright, fray, skare, feare; also, to daunt, appall, amaze, dismay.*
Effreinte: f. *A default of hounds.*
Effrenation: f. *Vnrulinesse, vnbridled headinesse, immoderate libertie, headlong rashnesse.*
Effrené: m. ée: f. *Vnbridled, rash, headie, dissolute, vnrulie, disordered, without gouernment.*
Effrenément. *Rashly, headily, dissolutely, disorderedly.*
Effrener. *To vnbridle; set at large, turn loose, giue head vnto, leaue wholly to his owne swindge, direction, or gouernment.*
Effrité: m. ée: f. *Frighted, agast, afraid.*
Effriter. *To affright, skare, affray.*
Effroidi: m. ie: f. *Cooled.*
Effroidir. *To coole.*
Effrondille. *The lees, dregs, or grounds of wine, &c.*
Effronté: m. ée: f. *Shamelesse, impudent, ouer-bold, brasen-faced, whõ nothing can dash out of cõtenance; also, one that hath a great, and large forhead.*
Effronté en putain. *as impudent as a whore.*
Effrontement: m. *Impudencie, malapertnesse, vnshamefastnesse, shamelesnesse.*
Effrontément. *Impudently, shamelessely, vnshamefastly, without blushing, with a brasen face.*

Effronterie. *as* Effrontemént; *also, an impudent, or shamelesse part.*

Effroué: m. ée: f. *Crummed, crumbled, broken verie small.*

Effrouër. *To crum, crumble, breake very small.*

Effroy: m. *A fright, feare, dread, affright, terror, astonishment, amazement.*

Effroyable. *as* Effrayable.

Effroyablement. *Fearefully, dreadfully, terribly, hideously.*

Effroyant. *Hideous, ghastfull, terrible, horrible, dreadfull, fearefull, affrighting.*

Effroyé: *as* Effrayé.

Effroyer. *To fray, skare, feare, affright; also, to daunt, amaze, astonish, appall, dismay.*

Effruicté: m. ée: f. *Whose fruit is cropped, gotten, or gathered.*

Effruicter. *To take, or gather the fruit of.*

Effucillé. *Vnleaued; stripped, or bared of leaues.*

Effueillement: m. *An vnleauing; a cutting, or pulling off superfluous leaues from plants.*

Effueiller. *To vnleafe; to cut, plucke, or nip off superfluous leaues; to strip, or bare of leaues.*

Effueilleur: m. *A pruner of trees; a puller of leaues from trees.*

Effusément. *Profusely, extreamely, out of measure.*

Effusion: f. *An effusion, shedding, spilling, pouring out.*

Efielé: m. ée: f. *Mild, calme, vnmoued, without spleene, or gall.*

Egal: m. ale: f. *Equall, semblable, euen, well matched, alike.*

Egalement. *as* Egualement.

Egale-nuicts. *Nights-equalling; or night and day matching.*

Cercle egale-nuicts. *The Equator, or Equinoctiall circle.*

Egaler. *To equall, euen, leuell, match.*

Egalizement. *as* Egualizement.

Egalizer. *Looke* Egualizer.

Egaronné: m. ée: f. *Trodden, as a shooe, downe at the heeles.*

Egaronner vn soulier. *To tread a shooe downe at the heeles.*

Egasé: m. ée: f. *Set on edge, as a tooth.*

Egau: m. *The lesse kind of the bastard Mackerell; or a yong one.* ¶Marseillois.

Egelfin: m. *The Haddocke; as* Egrefin.

Egener le labeur. *To run through their worke; to dispatch, or to rid away worke apace. (A Ploughmans terme.)*

Egestion: f. *A voiding, euacuation, casting out of excrements, and ordure.*

Egipanes. *Satyres; or beasts like men, but footed as goats.* ¶Rab.

Egiptiaque. L'onguent Eg. *A certaine salue, or ointment, of a cleansing facultie, and good to preuent mortification.*

Eglise: f. *A Church; or Congregation of Christians.*

Coq d'Eglise. *A Weathercocke.*

Gens d'Eglise. *Churchmen, Priests, &c.*

Pres de l'Eglise est souvent loing de Dieu. Prov. *The neerer to the Church, the further from God; (say we.)*

Egosse: f. *A cod, huske, or hull, of pulse, &c.*

s'Egouffrer. *as* s'Engouffrer; *or, to ingulfe it selfe.*

Egousser. *To shale a cod, pill: Seeke* Esgousser.

Egout. *as* Esgout.

Egozillé: m. ée: f. *Whose throat is cut; also, vomited, or spued out.*

Egoziller. *To cut the throat of; also, to vomit, or spue out.*

Egratigné: m. ée: f. *Scratched, scraped, rent, or torne with the nailes.*

Egratigner. *To scratch, to scrape, to rend, or teare, with the nayles.*

Egratigneure: f. *A scraping, or scratching; also, a scratch, or little skarre.*

Egrefin: m. *A kind of Haddocke.*

Egrege: com. *Excellent, notable, singular, principall, passing good, of chiefe marke, of speciall woorth, one of the choisest.*

Egremé: m. ée: f. *Vncreamed; fleeted, or skummed, as milke.*

Egrette. *as* Aigrette; *A foule that resembles a Heron.*

Egrugé: m. ée: f. *Crummed, crumbled, broken into small peeces.*

Egruger. *To crum, crumble, breake into small peeces.*

Egrumer. *To vncluster, or plucke from the cluster.*

Egrun: m. *Any thing that angers, or exasperats, a disease, or sore.*

Egual: m. ale: f. *Equall, euen, leuell; semblable, well matched, of a like estate, nature, age, condition, qualitie.*

Egualé: m. ée: f. *Equalled, matched, leuelled, euened, made like; resembled, compared vnto.*

Egualement. *Euenly, equally, alike, semblably; in euen parts, in equall portions, indifferently, as much the one as the other.*

Egualer. *To equall, match; euen, leuell; make like, resemble, compare.*

Egualizé: m. ée: f. *Equalled, matched, or made euen with.*

Egualizement: m. *An equalling, leuelling, matching, resembling, making euen, or alike.*

Egualizer. *To match, equall, euen, leuell; make one thing like another.*

Eguillat: m. *A kind of Dog-fish, that hath two long and stiffe prickles on his backe.*

Eguillon: m. *A pricke, or sting; Looke,* Esguillon.

Eguillonner. *To pricke, sting, prouoke, incense: Looke,* Esguillonner.

Eguiser. *To whet, or sharpen; Seeke* Esguiser.

Egyptelle. *A kind of white stone, or minerall, that hath blacke and red veins, or streakes.*

Egyptiac: m. *An excellent (though sharpe) ointment, or salue to preuent, or correct the putrifaction, and mortification of wounds, and sores.*

Ehancé. *as* Ehanché.

Ehanché: m. ée: f. *Whose hip, or hanche, is bruized, or out of ioint.*

Ehancher. *To bruize the hanch, or put it out of ioint; also, to leaue hanchlesse, or cut off a hanch.*

Ejaculation: f. *An eiaculation; a violent casting, flinging, hurling forth; spurting, ierting, spouting out.*

Ejaculatoire: com. *Eiaculatorie; of propertie, or power to cast, spout, or spurt forth; and hence;*

Vaisseaux ejaculatoires. *Certaine assistant, & actiue parts in the worke of generation.*

Ejaculatrice. vertu eja. *Darting, shooting, spouting, spurting, casting from afar.*

Ejarté: m. ée: f. *Houghed, cut off by the hammes.*

Ejarter. *To hough, or cut off at the hammes.*

Eine: f. *The groine, or grine; the part thats next about our priuities.*

Ela. *The highest note of the Gamuth.*

Nous sommes au dessus d'Ela, hors toute la Gamme. *We are cleane off the hinges, or out of all good compasse; also, we are in very great extremitie.*

Elaboratoire : m. *An Elaboratorie, or workehouse.*
Elaboré. *as* Elabouré.
Elabouration : f. *Elaboration; diligent labour, paines-taking; a perfect, or skilfull working.*
Elabouré : m. ée : f. *Elaborated; cunningly wrought, exactly done; laboured painfully, trauelled throughly in.*
Elabourer. *To elaborate; labour painfully, trauell throughly; to worke exactly, doe a thing fully, and finely.*
Elambiqué. *as* Alambiqué; *Distilled.*
Elambiquer. *as* Alambiquer; *To distill, or extract by Lymbecke.*
Elan. *A certaine wild beast; as* Ellend.
Elancé : m. ée : f. *Launced, cut, pierced, or pricked with a launcet.*
Elancement : m. *A cutting, launcing, piercing, pricking with a launcet; also, as* Eslancement.
Elancer. *To launce, cut, pricke, pierce with a launcet; also, to hurt, paine, pinch as a stitch doth; Seeke* Eslancer.
Elangoré : m. ée : f. *Langourous, languishing, deiected, crest-fallen.*
Elargir. *Looke* Eslargir.
Elariné de pleurs. *That can weepe no more; whose eyes are wholly drained with much weeping.*
Elatine : f. *The hearbe called Speedwell, or Fluellin the female.*
Elation : f. *Loftinesse, hautinesse.*
Elebore. *Seeke* Ellebore.
Electeur : m. *An Elector, a chuser.*
Electif : m. iue : f. *Electiue, subiect vnto choice; gotten, or passing, by election.*
Election : f. *An election, or choice, a chusing, culling, or picking out; also, the Prouince, or circuit of an* Eleu, *or generall assessor of Subsidies.*
Electorat : m. *An Electorship; a chusing, or electing; or the right, or power of election, such as the seuen Electors of the Empire haue.*
Electre : m. *Amber whereof beads, and bracelets are made; also, a mixture of gold, copper, and a fift part of siluer.*
Electuaire : m. *An Electuarie; a medicinable composition made of choice drugs, and of substance betweene a syrrope and a conserue, but more enclining to this then to that.*
Elegamment. *Elegantly, eloquently; neatly, comptly, quaintly, finely, politely, trimly, minion-like.*
Elegance : f. *Elegancie, eloquence, daintie speech, neat words, choice of tearmes; also, comptnesse, quaintnesse, neatnesse, trimnesse, delicacie, finesse.*
Elegant. *Elegant, eloquent, fine-spoken, choice in words, neat in tearmes; also, compt, quaint, spruce, trimme, daintie, delicate, polite.*
Elegiaque. *Elegiacall, belonging to an Elegie; lamenting, mournefull.*
Elegie : f. *An Elegie; a mournefull verse, Poeme, Song, or Dittie.*
Element : m. *An element; as water, earth, fire, or aire; also, a rudiment, or first principle of Art; the ground, foundation, or beginning of any thing.*
Elementaire. *Elementall; belonging to elements, rudiments, principles.*
Elemi. *A kind of Gumme, or Rosen (as some will haue it, because it melts before the fire) which is an excellent healer, and closer of head-wounds.*
Elemny. *as* Elemi.
Elenchie. vnion elenchie. *A pendant pearle of the fashion of an egge.*
Eleomeli. *A sweet, and fat liquor that issues from the old trunks of certaine trees in Syria.*
Elephangines. *Certaine pills (by Physitians tearmed so, or* de aromatibus) *good to strengthen the stomacke, and to helpe digestion.*
Elephant : m. *An Elephant.*
Elephant de mer. *A kind of great Lobster.*
Elephanteau : m. *A yong Elephant.*
Elephantin. *Elephantine; of, or belonging to, an Elephant.*
Elephantique. *Leaprous, infected with a leaprosie.*
Eleu. *A generall Assessor of the Kings Aides, and Subsidies in euery particular Circuit, Prouince, or Diocesse; Looke* Esleu.
Elevation : f. *An eleuation, lifting, heauing, holding, raising, or rearing vp; Looke* Eslevation.
Elevatoire : m. *An Eleuatorie; th'instrument wherewith Chirurgions lift vp the broken, and sunke-in parts of the scull; and draw out bullets, or haile-shot thats entred but a little way into the flesh, or bones.*
Eleveur : m. *A raiser, or lifter vp.*
Elice. *The signe in heauen called Charles waine, or* Vrsa major.
Elicie. *A fierie vapour drawne from the clouds:* Rab.
Elider. *To quash, dash, breake, split, or hit against; to pound, or stampe; to squeeze, or presse; to strike, or dash, out; also, to strangle, throttle, stifle.*
S'Elider de. *To rise, or burst, vp out of.*
Elider la production de la partie adverse. *Priuily to conuey, or purloine from an aduersarie his chiefest euidence, or proofes; thereby to weaken his cause.*
Eligible : com. *Eligible; to be elected; fit, or like, to be chosen.*
Eliminé : m. ée : f. *Thrust, cast, hurled, or put out of doores; also, divulged, or published.*
Eliminer. *To thrust, cast, hurle, or put out of doore; also, to divulge, or publish abroad.*
Elingue. *A sling:* ¶Nom.
Elire. *as* Eslire; *To chuse.*
Eliser la monnoye. *To pare, clip, or cut, money round about the hemme.*
Elixe. *Quintessence; or the Philosophers stone; as* Elixir.
Elixir. *Quintessence; or, the Philosophers stone; or one of the names thereof; some take it for the chymicall powder of Production; (the word originally signifies force, or strength.)*
Elle. *(The feminine of* il, *or* luy) *she.*
Ellebore blanc. *White Hellebore, Lingwort, Neesewort.*
Ellebore bastard. *The hearb Oxe-eye; also, the black bastard Hellebore.*
Ellebore noir. *Blacke Hellebore; whereof Gerard describes foure kinds; the true blacke Hellebore; the bastard, or wild blacke Hellebore; great Oxe-heele, or great wild blacke Hellebore; and the ordinarie Oxe-heele, Beares-foot, Setterwort; the two last are also called Lowsie-grasse, and Lowse-worts.*
Elleborine : f. *Wild white Ellebore.*
Ellée. bailler les ellées à vn cheval. *To giue a horse the head; to gallop with bridle laid on his necke.*
Ellend : m. *Th'Elke; a most fearefull, melancholike, strong, swift, short-neckt, and sharp-hooued, wild beast; much troubled with the falling sicknesse, and (by reason of the extraordinarie length of his vpper lip) euer going backward as he grazeth; (some report, that his forelegs are ioyntlesse, and his flesh good venison; but* Vigenere *(vpon*

(vpon Cæsar) denies th'one, and Gesner. dislikes th'other.)

Elocher. *To loosen, or make loosse;* Looke Eslocher.

Elocquer. *To shake off; (a word properly vsed of things that are firmely ioyned together.)*

Eloise: f. *A lightning; also, (metaphorically) a little space of time.*

Elope. *as* Elopien; *Also, a kind of Sea-fish whose finnes are turned towards her head; shee liues in the deepe Pamphilian sea; when she is taken, (which is but seldome) the fishers crowne themselues with garlands, and bring her to shore with ioyfull applauses, & sound of pipes, hoping they shall haue good lucke for a long time after.*

Elopien. *A kind of harmelesse Serpent.*

Eloquence: f. *Eloquence; gracefull speaking, sweet vtterance; tearmes choicely sorted, readily deliuered.*

Eloquent. *Eloquent, well-spoken, of a sweet deliuerie; whose words are choice, vtterance gracefull, speech most plausible.*

Elourdé: m. ée: f. *Dulled, amazed, astonished.*

Elourder. *To dull; dall, amaze, astonish.*

Eloyse. *as* Eloise.

Elucidation. *An elucidation; a cleere manifestation, or exposition; an outward shining.*

Elucidé: m. ée: f. *Cleered, manifested, made bright, euident, apparant; expressed, expounded.*

Elucider. *To cleere, manifest, make bright, or perspicuous; to expound, or expresse; also, to shine outward.*

Elue. *The wild Pine tree.*

Emaceration: f. *An emaceration; leanenesse, or falling away in flesh; or, as* Emaciation.

Emaciation: f. *A pulling downe, or making leane; a falling away in flesh.*

Emacie: f. *Leannesse.*

Emacié: m. ée: f. *Made, or growne, leane.*

Email: m. *Amell, or Enamell.*

Emaillé: m. ée: f. *Enamelled.*

Emailler. *To enamell.*

Emaillure: f. *An enamelling, or worke enamelled.*

Emanation: f. *An issuing, or comming forth; also, a publication of.*

Emancipé: m. ée: f. *Affranchised, made free, set at libertie; also, alienated, made away, put ouer to another.*

Emanciper. *To affranchise, dismisse, make free, set at libertie; also, to alienate, passe away, make ouer an interest, or possession.*

Emané: m. ée: f. *Proceeded, issued, flowed, or come out from; also, published, diuulged, spred abroad.*

Emaner. *To proceed, issue, flow, or come out from; also, to publish, diuulgue, spread abroad.*

Emant: m. *The Adamant, or Loadstone.*

Emantellement. *A mantle; also, a bemantling, or couering, as with a mantle.*

Emanuër. *as* Emanciper; *Or, to manumit.*

Emargé: m. ée: f. *Noted, or quoted in the Margent.*

Ematite: f. *The Bloud-stone.*

Embabillé. vn courtisan bien em. *Well-spoken; that hath tongue at will, or that wants no* Babil.

Embabionné. *as* Embabouïné.

Embabouïné: m. ée: f. *Gulled, deceiued, besotted, made a child of, brought into a fooles Paradise.*

Embabouïner. *To deceiue, gull, ride, bring into a fools Paradise; to giue sucke vnto; to vse like a child.*

S'Embabouïner. *To besot, or deceiue himselfe; to bring himselfe into a fooles Paradise; also, to be medling with matters he hath little skill in; or foolishly to wind himselfe into a businesse which he is not able to get well out of.*

S'Embadurnoser. *To annoint himselfe.*

Embagué: m. ée: f. *Beiewelled; furnished, inriched, bedecked, with Jewels.*

Embaguer. *To furnish, inrich, or decke with Jewels.*

Embaillonné: m. ée: f. *Gagged, begagged.*

Embaillonner. *To gag, begag.*

Embaler, &c. *as* Emballer, &c.

Emballage: m. *The packing vp of ware, or marchandise.*

Emballé: m. ée: f. *Packed vp, made vp in packes.*

Emballer. *To packe vp, to make vp in packes.*

Emballer quelqu'un d'un trousseau. *To play one a fine tricke; to serue one a prettie touch.*

Emballeur: m. *A packer vp of wares.*

Embaras, &c; *as* Embarras, &c.

Embarbouillé: m. ée: f. *Berayed, besmeared, bemired, bespotted, begrimed.*

Embarbouiller. *To beray, besmeare, bespot, begrime.*

Embarqué: m. ée: f. *Imbarked, imbargued, shipped, put or got a shipboord.*

Embarquement: m. *An imbarking, taking ship, going a shipboord, putting into a ship; also, an imbarguing.*

Embarquer. *To imbarke, ship, get or put on shipboord; also, to imbargue; to furnish, or imploy shipping.*

S'embarquer. *To take ship, or go on shipboord.*

S'embarquer en vn entreprise. *To vndertake, enter into, or ingage himselfe in, an action; to make one.*

S'embarquer sans biscuit. *To vndertake an enterprise without helpes to begin, or meanes to follow, it.*

Embarras: m. *A pesterment, intricacie, perplexitie, confusion, garboile, trouble.*

Embarassé: m. ée: f. *Pestered, intricated, intangled, perplexed, troubled.*

Embarassement. *as* Embarras; *Or, a pestering, intangling, intricating, perplexing, troubling.*

Embarasser. *To intricate, pester, intangle, perplex, confound, comber, trouble.*

Embarasseur: m. *An intricator, pesterer, comberer.*

Embarré. Heaume embarré. *Sore bruised, beaten in, or fastened to, the head with blowes.*

Embarrer. *To rayle, or set barres on; also, to crush, bruise, ding, or beat inward.*

Embarrer son espée en vn Arbre. *To fasten his sword in a tree.*

Embarrure: f. *A bruising, dinging, or beating inward.*

Embas. *Below, or beneath.*

Trape d'embas. *Looke* Trape.

Vent d'embas. *The Westerne wind.*

Embaser. *To giue a Basis, or bottome vnto; also, to ground, make a Basis, haue a bottome; end at the Basis, or bottome.*

Embasmé: m. ée: f. *Imbalmed; annointed, or dressed with Baulme.*

Embasmer. *To imbaulme; to dresse, or annoint all ouer with Baulme.*

Embassade: f. *An embassage, or message; also, an Embassador accompanied with his ordinarie traine; as,* Voila l'embassade de tel Royaume.

Embassadeur: m. *An Embassadour; a (publicke) messenger.*

Embassement. *Looke* Soubassement.

Embasté: m. ée: f. *Sadled with a packesaddle; also, seised,*

seised, or put into possession of.

Embaster. *To saddle with a packesaddle; also, to put into possession of (land, &c.)*

Embastonné: m. ée: f. *Armed with, or prouided of, weapons; also, cudgelled.*

Embastonner. *To arme, or furnish with weapons; also, to cudgell; belabour, bethwacke with cudgels.*

Embatage: m. *The laying of streakes about the wheele of a Carroche &c.*

Embatonner. *as* Embastonner.

Embatre. *To arriue, rush, or come in vpon suddenly.*

Embatre les bandages de rouës. *To nayle, or fasten the streakes vnto wheels.*

Ie m' embati sur luy. *I fell vpon him by chance, I met with him on a sudden, I light on him ere I was aware.*

Il luy embatit l' espée iusques au foye. *Hee thrust him into the liuer.*

Embattage. *as* Embatage.

Embattes. *The Easterlie winds which ordinarily raign about the Dog-days.*

Embatu: m. uë: f. *Arriued, rushed, thrust, cast, or come in vpon on a sudden; lighted, or slipt into, fallen vpon, ere he was aware.*

Embauché: m. ée: f. *Imployed, vsed, occupied, bestowed in, or put vnto, worke.*

Embaucher. *To imploy, occupie, vse in businesse, put vnto worke.*

Embaveté, ou Embavieté: m. ée: f. *Imbibbed; that, as a child, hath a bib, or mocket put before his breast, to keepe him from driueling thereon.*

Embavieté de machoueres. *Whose broken Jawes hanging downe, serued him, in stead of a bib, to slaver on.*

Embaumé: m. ée: f. *Imbaulmed; annointed, or preserued with Baulme.*

Embaumement: m. *An imbaulming.*

Embaumer. *To imbaulme; to dresse, annoint, or preserue with Baulme.*

Embecqué. *That hath his lesson; instructed beforehand.*

L' oiseau gazouille selon qu'il est embecqué: Prov. *A man speaks euen as his hopes do moue, or passions vrge him; It may be also applied to a Lawyer, who according to the fee he hath receiued, pleads for his Client, better or worse.*

Embecquer. *as* Emboucher; *To giue one his lesson beforehand.*

Embelli: m. ie: f. *Imbellished, beautified; garnished, bedecked, adorned, set out.*

Embellir. *To imbellish, beautifie; garnish, adorne, bedecke; trimme vp, set out vnto the eye.*

Embellissage: m. *An imbellishing, beautifying; decking, adorning, garnishing.*

Embellissement. *as* Embellissage; *Or, an imbellishment.*

Embellissement de maison. *A pleasant tuft, or groue of trees, growing neere, or about, a house; tearmed so in Law.*

Emberni: m. ie: f. *Couered with, or clad in, rug.*

Embernir. *To couer with, or clad in, rug.*

Embesongné: m. ée: f. *Busied, imployed, occupied, set on worke.*

Embesongnement: m. *A businesse, or busie worke; also, an imploying, or busying.*

Embesongner. *To busie, imploy, occupie, set on worke.*

Embeurré: m. ée: f. *Buttered, dressed, or annoynted with butter.*

Embeurrer. *To butter, or bebutter; to dresse, or annoint all ouer with butter.*

Embezars. *Aumes ace on the dice:* ¶Rab.

Emblavé: m. ée: f. *Sowen, as a field, with corne; also, whose corne is put vp a prettie height aboue ground.*

Emblavence de bled. *Corne sprung, or put vp, a prettie height aboue ground; or, the springing, or putting vp of corne.*

Emblaver. *To sow the ground with corne.*

Emblaveures. *Corne; whether growing, or in sheaues.*

Emblayement. *A trouble, comber, pesterment.*

Emblé: m. ée: f. *Stollen, filched, pilfered, purloined, imbezeled.*

Ie me suis emblé de la troupe. *I slunke out of the companie.*

Emble-coeur. *Alluring, winning, heart-stealing.*

Emblée. à l'emblée. *Priuily, closely, by stealth, with two fingers and a reach.*

D'emblée. *Subtily, craftily, vnderhand, at vnawares.*

Emblemature: f. *An emblemizing, or making of Emblemes.*

Embleme: m. *An Embleme; a Picture, and short Posie, expressing some particular conceit.*

Embler. *To steale, filch, lurch, pilfer, nimme, purloyne, imbezel, conuey away.*

Emblesne: m. *A Cataplasme, or Poultis.*

Embleures. *Corne standing, or hanging by the roots.*

Emblic. *A kind of round Mirabolan, wherewith th' Indians, for want of other things, tanne their leather, and make inke and blacking; neuer putting it, as we doe, (and as they all other Mirabolans) vnto Physicall vses.*

Emblocquer à la Cupidique; autant que, besongner.

Embobeliné: m. ée: f. *Botched, or patched vp; also, deceiued, gulled, beguiled; whose eyes are bleared.*

Embobeliner. *To botch, or patch vp; also, to deceiue, gull, beguile, bleare the eyes of.*

Emboëtture: f. *An imboxing, or putting in a box; as* Emboiture.

Emboire. *To imbue, moisten, bedeaw; also, to soke, or drinke vp.*

Emboistement. *as* Emboitement.

Emboister. *To imbox; inclose, insert, fasten, put, or shut vp, as within a box; also, to ioyne, or close together.*

S'Emboister. *To enter, or be included, as a lesse thing within a greater, or one thing within another.*

Emboisture: f. *as* Emboiture; *Also, the ring, or plate of yron, &c, that keepes the box of a wheele from wearing.*

Emboité: m. ée: f. *Imboxed; inserted, inclosed, entered, or put within a bigger, or other thing; also, ioyned, bound, or fastened together.*

Emboitement: m. *An imboxing, or inclosing within a bigger, or other, thing; any such fastening, ioyning, or closing.*

Emboiter. *as* Emboister.

Emboiture: f. *An imboxing; inclosing, entering, or insertion, (as of one bone into the hollow end of another) any such colligation, closing, ioyning, or fastening of things together; also, the ioynt, part, bone, or thing so inclosed, or closed; also, as* Emboisture.

Embolismal: m. ale: f. *Added, as a day vnto a yere; or increased, as the yeare, by so many dayes.*

Embolisme: m. *An addition; as of a day (or more) vnto a yeare.*

Embon-

Embonpoint: m. *Fullnesse, plumpnesse, healthfull estate, good liking, sound disposition, of the bodie.*
Vn embonpoint de nourrice. *A fat, or foggie constitution of a woman.*
Embosqué: m.ée: f. *Wooded; set with wood; shrowded in a wood.*
Embosquer vne terre. *To plant, or set wood in it; to turne it into a wood.*
S'embosquer. *To shrowd himselfe in a wood; to get a wood on his backe, to take into a wood.*
Embosser. *To swell, or arise in bunches, bulches, knobs; to grow knottie, or knurrie.*
Embottelé: m.ée: f. *Imbottelled; made, or packt vp in bundles, or bottles.*
Embotteler. *To make vp in bundles, or bottles.*
Embouché: m.ée: f. *Mouthed; put into the mouth of; instructed, suborned, made, prepared, lessonned, beforehand; also, bitted; furnished, or fitted with a Bit; also, entered into; also, straitned, or narrowing (as a riuer from the mouth vpwards.)*
Bas embouché. *Whose mouth stands low.*
Fourreau de cuir embouché de velours. *Whose mouth, or top is tipped with veluet.*
Homme mal embouché. *A detractor, slaunderer, backbiter; a foule-mouthed fellow; one that hath bene ill taught, lessonned, instructed.*
Embouchement: m. *A mouthing, or putting into the mouth of; a subornation, or fore-instruction; a lesson giuen, or conned beforehand; also, the bitting, or bridling of a horse.*
Emboucher. *To mouth, or put into the mouth of; hence, to suborne; instruct, prepare, or make, beforehand; to giue one his lesson aforehand; also, to bit a horse; to furnish, or fit him with a Bit.*
S'emboucher. *To enter into; also, to straiten, or grow narrow, as a riuer from the mouth vpwards.*
Emboucher d' vn mensonge. *To put a lie into the mouth of, to teach to lie; also, to face downe, or flap in the mouth, with an (apparant) lie.*
Il m' emboucha de l' argent qu'il me presta. *Hee vpbraided me, or cast me in the teeth, with the money he lent me.*
Emboucher en la mer. *To fall, or enter into the sea, (as a riuer;) also, to runne, or enter, farre into the sea (as the streame of a violent, or swift riuer.)*
Embouscheure: f. *as* Embouchement; *Also, a mouth, or open passage; an entrie, or ouerture.*
Embouscheure d' vn cheval. *The barres, or part of his nether iaw, whereon the Bit resteth; also, a Bit, or, the mouth of a Bit.*
Cheval de mauvaise embouscheure. *An ill, or vicious, mouthed horse.*
Embouscheure de farines. *A putting of the best meale in the mouth, or at the top, of a sacke; (a cousening tricke among Meale-men.)*
Embouscheure de Montagne. *A gullet, strait passage, or narrow entrie, at the foot of a mountaine.*
Embouscheure d' vne Riviere. *The mouth of a riuer; the place whereat it runs, or empties it selfe, into the Sea.*
Embouchoir: m. *A Boot-last, or Boot-tree; also, a horn to drench a horse with; or, as* Embouchouër.
Embouchonné: m.ée: f. *Stopt with a stopple; also, hauing a bush (as a Tauerne, or Alehouse) hanging before it.*
Embouchouër: m. *A horne to drench a horse with; (generally) any thing that serues to conuey another thing into a mouth.*

Embouchure: f. *as* Embouscheure.
Embouclé: m.ée: f. *Buckled, clasped.*
Emboucler. *To buckle, fasten, claspe together.*
Emboüé: m. ée: f. *Bemired, bedurtied, berayed with mud, bespatled with ordure.*
Embouër. *To bemire, bedurt, beray, bedash with mud, bespatle with ordure.*
Embouqueté: m.ée: f. *Beset, or bedecked, with nosegayes.*
Embourbé: m. ée: f. *Bemudded; berayed with, laied or stucke fast in, mud; also, made or growne muddie; ouergrowne with mud.*
Embourbement: m. *A bemudding; a beraying with, or sticking fast in, mud.*
Embourber. *To bemud; to beray with, or lay fast in, mud.*
S'embourber. *To sticke fast in, or be berayed with, mud; also, to corrupt, wax thicke, or turne into mud, as a standing water that wants a spring to feed it.*
Embourbeure: f. *as* Embourbement.
Embourré: m.ée: f. *Stuffed, bumbasted, or puffed vp with flockes, &c.*
Embourrement: m. *A stuffing, or bumbasting with flockes, haire, &c; also, a cushion, boulster, &c, so stuffed.*
Embourrer. *To stuffe, bumbast, or puffe vp with flockes, haire, &c; to make strout out.*
Embourreur: m. *A stuffer, bumbaster, or puffer vp of things with flockes, haire, &c.*
Embourse: m. ée: f. *Pursed, imbursed; put into, or laied vp in, a purse.*
Embourser. *To purse vp, to imburse; to put into, or lay vp in, a purse.*
Embouscher en la mer. *To runne, or fall into the sea;* *Seeke* Emboucher.
Embousé: m. ée: f. *Bedunged; berayed with Cowes ordure.*
Embouté: m. ée: f. *Plated, stiffened; or, as* Embouti; *imbossed.*
Marteau embouté d' argent. *Tipped, or trimmed at the end, with siluer.*
Embouti: m. ie: f. *Extended, retched, stretched out; also, puffed, or drawne out with puffes; also, raised, imbossed; or boultled; raised into, wrought with boultles.*
Emboutir. *To retch, extend, stretch out; also, to raise, or imbosse; also, to draw out with puffes; also, to stitch with packthread; whence;*
Esguille à emboutir. *A pack-needle.*
Emboutissement: m. *An extending, retching, stretching out; also, a raising, or imbossing; also, a puffe, or a drawing out with puffes.*
Emboutissemens de soye. *Silke thrummes.*
Emboutoir. *as* Boutoir.
Embouzé. *as* Embousé.
Emboysture. *as* Emboiture.
Embrabile: com. *Broad headed.* (vieil mot.)
Embraceler. *To furnish, or bedecke with bracelets.*
Embrase. *as* Braise. *(Barbarously.)*
Embrasé. *Fired, inflamed, set on, consumed with, a light fire; also, skued, or chamfretted.*
Embrasement: m. *A consuming with fire, a burning to ashes, or coles; also, a kindling, inflaming, firing, setting on fire; also, as* Embrasure.
Embraser. *To burne vnto coales, or askes, to consume with fire; also, to kindle, inflame, fire, set on a light fire; also, to skue, or chamfret off the Iaumbes of a a doore, or window.*
Embrassade: f. *An imbracement; a clipping, hugging, colling, imbracing in the armes.*

Embrassant. *Imbracing, hugging, foulding in the armes.*
Embrassé: m. ée: f. *Imbraced, clipped, colled, hugged; held, taken, or infolded in; put, or buckled vnto, the arme; also, comprehended.*
Embrassée: f. *An arme-full, or fadome.*
Embrasselé: m. ée: f. *Bebraceletted, hauing a bracelet on; furnished, or bedecked, with a bracelet.*
Embrassement. *as* Embrassade.
Embrasser. *To imbrace, coll, hug, clip, imbrace, or infold in the armes; to intreat kindly, intertaine louingly.*
Embrasser son escu. *To put his shield vpon his arme; to buckle his shield vnto his arme.*
Trop embrasser, & peu estraigner. *To meddle with more businesse then he can wield; to haue too many yrons in the fire; to loose all by coueting all.*
Embrasse-tout. *Huge, immense, all-imbracing, all-comprehending.*
Embrasure: f. *as* Embrasement; *Also, the skuing, splaying, or chamfretting of a doore, or window.*
Embrazé. *as* Embrasé.
Embrené: m. ée: f. *Berayed, beshitten.*
Embrener. *To beray, or beshite.*
Embretelé. lié, ou ceinct avec bretelles; *Looke* Bretelles.
Embreuvé: m. ée: f. *Moistened, soaked in, softened with, liquor; also, died, indued, imbued.*
Embreuver. *To moisten, bedeaw, soake in, soften with, liquor; also, to die, indue, imbue; as* Abbreuver.
Embridé: m. ée: f. *Bridled; restrained, held backe, tamed, kept in.*
Embrider. *To bridle; restraine, hold backe, tame, keepe in.*
Embrion. *as* Embryon.
Embrocation: f. *An embrochation; a fomenting, besprinkling, or gentle bathing of the head, or any other part, with a liquor falling from aloft vpon it in the maner of raine.*
Embroché: m. ée: f. *Spitted, broached, put vpon a spit, or broach.*
Embrocher. *To spit, broach, put vpon a spit, or broach.*
Embrocheure: f. *A spitting, or broaching.*
Embronché: m. ée: f. *Astonied, amazed, dizzied with a blow; whose head hangs downe, or totters vp and downe, after a blow receiued; also, hudwinked; also, as* Renfrongné.
Embroncher. *To bow, or hold downe the necke, and head; as one that is stonied with a rap on the sconce; also, to hide the face, or eyes with hands, a cloth, or any such matter.*
Embroqué: m. ée: f. *Gently bathed, wet, or bedeawed with moist things; as in* Embrocation.
Embroquer. *Gently to bath, wet, besprinkle, or bedeaw with moist things; as in* Embrocation.
Embroué: m. ée: f. *bedurtied, soiled, defiled.*
Embrouillasser. *as* Embrouiller.
Embrouillé: m. ée: f. *Intricated, incombred; confounded; intangled, pestered.*
Embrouillement. *A pestering, intangling, incombring, intricatenesse, confusion, ambiguitie.*
Embrouiller. *To pester, intangle, incomber, intricate; confound.*
Embrouilleur: m. *A confounder, intricater, incombrer, pesterer of.*
s'Embruer. *To indeuor himselfe; also, to imbrue, or bedable himselfe with.*
Embrunché: m. ée: f. *Wainscotted, seeled; also, as* Renfrongné.
Embruncher. *To wainscot, or seele with wainscot.*

Embruni: m. ie: f. *Darkened, obscured, made browne, or blackish; growne browne, darke, or blacke.*
Embrunir. *To darken, obscure, make browne or blackish; also, to grow darke, or blacke.*
Embryon. *The infant in the mothers wombe before it hath got perfect shape; or, the seed thats receiued into the wombe before the infant bee fashioned; any rude masse, or lumpe of flesh.*
Embu: m. uë: f. *Imbued, imbrued, wet, moistened, indued; drunke with; died, or stained with.*
Embuche, & Embucher. *as* Embusche, & Embuscher.
Embufflé: m. ée: f. *Deceiued, cousened, gulled, besotted, led (as a Busle) by the nose.*
Embuffler. *To deceiue, cousen, gull, besot; lead (as a Busle) by the nose.*
Emburelucoqué: m. ée: f. *Turmoiled, blundered, or pestered, as the braine about a troublesome businesse.*
Emburelucoquer l' esprit de. *To trouble, blunder, or or pester the mind with, to beat the braines about:* Rab.
Embuscade: f. *An Ambuscadoe, or ambush; a way-laying, or lying in wait for.*
Embusche: f. *as* Embuscade.
Embusché. *Layed in ambush; belaying, way-laying.*
Embuscher. *To belay, to lay in ambuscadoe for; to waylay; also, to take a wood; or get into a thicket, for shelter.*
S'embuscher. *To lie in wait, or ambush for; or as* Embuscher.
s'Embusquer. *as* s'Embuscher.
Embut. *A funnell; also, a pipe to sucke with.*
Emedullé: m. ée: f. *Vnmarrowed, whereout the marrow is taken; depriued of marrow.*
Emeduller. *To vnmarrow, draw the marrow out of, depriue of marrow.*
Emembré: m. ée: f. *Diuided, dismembred, disioyned, disioynted.*
Emendateur: m. *Amender, amender, reformer, corrector, ruler.*
Emendation: f. *An amending, mending, reformation, correction.*
Emendatrice: f. *She that correcteth, amendeth, reformeth, redresseth; a correcteresse, reformeresse.*
Emende: f. *as* Amende.
Emendé: m. ée: f. *Mended, amended, reformed, corrected.*
Emender. *To mend, amend, reforme, redresse, better; improue; correct.*
Emeril: m. *The blacke hard minerall substance, or stone, called an Emerod; wherewith yron-workes are furbished and precious stones and glasse, cut.*
Emerillon: m. *A Merlin, or Marlin.*
Emerillonné: m. ée: f. *Watched narrowly, looked to neerely; obserued, or prosecuted with a quicke (& cruell) eye.*
Emerillonner. *To watch narrowly, looke too neerely; to obserue with a quicke (and cruell) eye.*
Emerillonner à feu & à sang. *To prosecute with fire and sword.*
Emeute: f. *A stirre, commotion, rebellion, vprore.*
Emeute des chiens. *as* Meute.
Emicicle: m. *An Hemicycle, or halfe circle.*
Emier. *as* Esmier.
Emine: f. *A measure that containes three* Posons; *and comes to, in weight (about seuen and a halfe of our moderne ounces; I call them moderne, because th'auntient*

ent Hemina *was ten ounces.*

Eminemment. *Eminently, apparantly.*

Eminence: f. *Eminencie, excellencie, apparantnesse, surpassing of others; also, a rising vp aboue, or bearing out beyond, others.*

Eminent. *Eminent, apparant, bearing outwards, high, or loftie in sight; excelling, surpassing, ouerpeering, others.*

Emissaire: m. *A sluce, or floudgate to let water out of a riuer, or pond.*

Emissole. *A smooth-skind, and toothlesse, kind of Dogfish.*

Emmaigri: m. ie: f. *Made leane, starued, pined.*

Emmaigrir. *To make leane, to starue, to pine.*

S'emmaigrir. *To grow leane, wast in flesh, fall away.*

Emmaigrissant. *Making leane.*

Emmailloté: m. ée: f. *Swadled, swathed.*

Emmaillotement: m. *A swadling, or a wrapping in swathe-bands.*

Emmailloter. *To swadle, to swathe, to wrap in swathebands.*

Emmaisonné: m. ée: f. *Housed, furnished with a house.*

Emmaisonner. *To house; to put into, or furnish with a house.*

Emmaistrisé. *Made, or passed Master, that hath taken the degree of a Maister; that is growne as cunning in an Art as any Master.*

Emmaladi: m. ie: f. *Made, or growne, sicke.*

Emmaladir. *To make sicke.*

Emmalicé: m. ée: f. *Full of rancor, or malice; enraged with spight, verie despightfull.*

Emmalissant. *Maliciously raging, or growing malicious.*

Emmanché: m. ée: f. *Helued; set into a haft, or handle.*

Lasche emmanché. *Lazie, idle, slothfull, weake, feeble, loosse ioynted, faint-hearted.*

Emmancher. *To helue; to set a haft, or handle on; (and hence) also, to set in order, bring into fashion, make as it should be.*

Emmancheure: f. *A heluing; a setting on of a haft, or handle; also, the vpper part, or setting on, of a sleeue.*

Emmanchoir: m. *The hole, or eye of a hatchet, &c, whereinto the handle is put.*

Emmanné: m. ée: f. *Full of, or bedeawed with, Manna.*

Emmanoté: m. ée: f. *Manacled, handfast.*

Emmanoter. *To manacle; to handfast, or tie the hands together.*

Emmantelé: m. ée: f. *Becloked; couered with, wrapped as in, a cloke; Seeke* Emmentelé.

Emmaroté: m. ée: f. *Wearing a Scepter; or, a fooles bable.*

Emmarré: m. ée: f. *Cast into the Sea; also, as* Amarré.

Emmarrer. *To cast into the bottome of the sea; also, as* Amarrer.

Emmartelé: m. ée: f. *Put into a iealousie; possessed, or perplexed with a restlesse passion.*

Emmarteler. *To put into a iealousie, possesse with loue; besot, or perplexe with any restlesse passion.*

Emmati: m. ie: f. *Mated, amated; decayed; quailed, allayed, abated in vigor; mortified; faded, vpon withering.*

Emmatir. *To mate, or amate; to quaile, abate, or allay some part of the vigor of; also, to mortifie, make fade, wither, decay.*

Emmassé: m. ée: f. *Piled, heaped, gathered together.*

Emmatrelé. *Hoarse; troubled with a pose, or stuffed with cold:* ¶Pic.

Emmatriculé: m. ée: f. *Matriculated.*

Emmatriculer. *To matriculate; to sweare of an Vniversitie, to incorporate, or confirme, by oath, in a Societie.*

Emmayé: m. ée: f. *Decked, hung, or strewed with May flowers &c.*

Emmayer. *To decke, hang, strew, or furnish with greene hearbes, boughes, or May flowers.*

Emmeché: m. ée: f. *Furnished with match, or candleweeke; also, snuffed.*

Emmecher. *To furnish with a match, or candleweeke; also, to snuffe.*

Emmelie. *A quiet kind of daunce, as the Pauin, Measure, &c:* ¶Rab.

Emmelioré: m. ée: f. *Bettered, improued, amended.*

Emmeliorer. *To better, improue, amend.*

Emmené: m. ée: f. *as* Amené.

Emmener. *To bring, or lead vnto; to fetch in, or to; Looke* Amener.

Emmener par force. *To hale, pull, dragge, force to come away with him.*

Emmener vne chose à son proffit. *To make profitable vse of a thing; to deriue, conuey, or draw a thing vnto his owne benefit.*

Emmenoté. *as* Emmanoté. *Manacled.*

Emmentelé. *as* Emmantelé; *Wrapped in a cloke, couered, as with a cloke; bemantled, becloked.*

Beuf emmentelé de noir. *A blacke, or blackish Oxe; a blacke-bodied Oxe.*

Corneille emmentelée. *The Winter-crow, whose backe, and bellie are of a darke ash-colour; we call her a Royston Crow.*

Emmenteler. *To couer with, to wrap in, a cloke, or mantle; to cloke, mantle, bemantle.*

Emmenuisé: m. ée: f. *Small, or made small; peecemealed, in little peeces, or parcels.*

Emmenuiser. *To make small, to peecemeale, to reduce into little parcels, or peeces.*

Emmerdé: m. ée: f. *Beturded; berayed with ordure.*

Emmerder. *To beturd, or beray with ordure.*

s'Emmesler. *To meddle, to deale much; to busie, pester, intangle himselfe with.*

Emmesnager. *To set a house, or houshold in good order; to play the good husband.*

Emmeublé: m. ée: f. *Furnished with mouables.*

Emmeublement. *Furniture; or, a furnishing with mouables.*

Emmeubler sa maison. *To furnish his house with stuffe, prouision, mouables.*

Emmeurer. *as* Emmurer.

Emmi. *Through, or in the middest of.*

Courrir emmi les rues. *To runne along, or about, the streets.*

Emmiellé: m. ée: f. *Honied, made of honie, seasoned, or sweetened with honie; sweet as honie; also, inticed, inueagled, allured, tolled, or drawne on by sweet meanes.*

Emmiellement: m. *An allurement, inticement, pleasant inducement, sweet prouocation; also, a dressing, seasoning, sweetening, annointing with honie.*

Emmieller. *To behonie; to sweeten; dresse, annoint, mingle,*

mingle, or season with honie; also, to allure, inueagle, intice, winne, draw, or toll on; pacifie, or appease, with sweet meanes.
Emmielleure, or Emmiellure: f. *Sweetnesse, bonied-nesse; or, as* Emmiellement.
Emminer. *To put into a mine.*
Emmitouflé: m. ée: f. *Muffled, hooded, hudled, or hidden within furres, or furred clothes.*
s'Emmitoufler. *To muffle, hood, hide, shrowd, lap, or keep himselfe warme in furres, or furred clothes.*
Emmitré: m. ée: f. *Bemitered; crowned, or hooded with a Myter.*
Emmitrer. *To bemyter; to crowne, or hood with a Myter.*
Emmoeller. *Seeke* Esmoeller.
Emmoncelé: m. ée: f. *Heaped, piled, compacted; gathered, packed, or made vp together.*
Emmonceler. *To pile, compact, packe; assemble, gather, or make vp into a heape; to heape together; Looke* Amonceler.
Emmont. *as* Amont; *Vpward.*
Emmorionné: m. ée: f. *Couered, or armed, with a Murrion, or Headpeece.*
Emmorisque: com. *Moorish, Mauritanian, Moore-like; that sounds, or sauors, of the Moore.*
Emmortaisé: m. ée: f. *Mortaised; ioyned, or closed by mortaise.*
Emmortaiser. *To mortaise; to ioyne, or close by mortaise.*
Emmouflé: m. ée: f. *Couered, or kept warme, as the hand, with a mittaine; also, bemuffled, wrapped, or lapped close within (warme) clothes.*
Emmoufler. *To put on his mittaines; to couer, or keepe warme his hands with mittaines; also, to bemuffle, hide, wrap, or lap vp his whole bodie within (warme) clothes.*
Emmuré: m. ée: f. *Immured; walled about, inclosed with, or within a wall; flanked, or defended by walls.*
Emmurer. *To immure, or wall about; to close vp into a wall, or betweene two walls; to flanke, or defend with walls.*
Emmuselé: m. ée: f. *Muffled.*
Emmuseler. *To muffle.*
Emmusqué: m. ée: f. *Bemusked, perfumed with musk.*
Emmusquer. *To bemuske, or perfume with muske.*
Emolli: m. ie: f. *Mollified, softened.*
Emollient. *Softening, mollifying, asswaging.*
Emollir. *To soften, mollifie; make gentle, or pliant.*
Emologation: f. *An admission, allowance, approuement, or approbation of; a consent, or assent vnto.*
Emologué: m. ée: f. *Admitted, allowed, accepted, approued of, assented, or consented, vnto.*
Emologuer. *To admit, intertaine, accept, approue, allow of; to consent, or assent, vnto.*
Emolument: m. *Emolument, profit, commoditie, benefit, gaine.*
Emonctoire: m. *An Emunctorie; a kernellie place of the bodie, that serues for the voyding of such humors as be superfluous in, or offensiue vnto, a principall, or noble part; such be vnder th'eaues for the braines, th'arme-pits for the heart, and the groine or share for the liuer; also, a snuffer.*
Emondé. *as* Esmondé. *Cleansed, cleered, purged.*
Orge emondée. *Naked Barlie; whose huske falls of it selfe from the graine, as soone as it is ripe.*
Emonder. *To cleanse, &c; Looke* Esmonder.
Emorcer. *as* Amorcer. *To baite, inueagle, beguile.*
Emorcher. *To put powder into the touch-hole of a peece.*
Emotté: m. ée: f. *Whose clods be broken.*
Emotter. *To breake clods, or turues on the ground.*
Emoucé: m. ée: f. *Dulled, blunted.*
Emoucer. *To dull, blunt; breake, or spoyle the edge of.*
Emouchail: m. *A flie-flap.*
Emoucher. *Seeke* Esmoucher.
Emouchon: m. *A holy-water sprinkle.*
Emoussé: m. ée: f. *Rid, or bared, of mosse.*
Emousser. *To rid, or bare, of mosse.*
Emouvant. *Mouing, stirring vp.*
Empacqué: m. ée: f. Il s'est empacqué. *He is most wilfull, obstinate, or obstinately sullen; from the sheepe* Pacos *(whereon th'Indians, in stead, or for want, of horses, carrie their marchandise) which being angred, lie downe with their burthens, and will not rise for any blowes, vntill their mood be fully past, and disgested.*
Empacté: m. ée: f. *Heaped, compacted, or packed vp close together; also, crusted, or hard baked.*
Empacter. *To heape, compact, or pack vp close together; also, to crust, or bake hard.*
Empaillé: m. ée: f. *Bestrawed; filled, made, furnished, with straw.*
Empaindre. *Violently to assaile, or set vpon; to strike, or hit with violence.*
Empaint: m. te: f. *Violently assailed, shocked, set on; hard pressed; furiously hit, or strucken.*
Empaint en mer. *Entred farre into the sea; a great way in the sea.*
Empainte: f. *A violent shocke, impression, assailing, or setting on.*
Empalé: m. ée: f. *Impaled, or spitted on a stake.*
Empaler. *To impale; to spit on a stake; to thrust a stake in at the fundament, and out at the mouth; (a manner of death inflicted on offendors by the Turks.)*
Empaletoqué: m. ée: f. *Muffled, or lapt vp about the chinne, as with a Cassocke, or Gaberdine.*
Empalin: m. *as* Empan; *Or, a little spanne.*
Empalmé: m. ée: f. *Strucken with the paulme of the hand; hit full, or taken right (as a Ball) with an open hand.*
Empalmer. *To strike (or box) with the paulme of the hand; to hit full, or take right, a Ball, &c, with an open hand; to giue a sound whirret, or full blow therewith.*
Empampré: m. ée: f. *Decked with Vine braunches.*
Empan: m. *A spanne.*
Empanaché. *Beplumed, feathered; decked, adorned, stucke, or set out with feathers, or plumes of feathers; wearing, or hauing, a plume; and hence;*
Armet bien empanaché. *Whose crest is beautified with a goodlie plume.*
Empanage. *as* Appennage.
Empaneré. *Put into panniers, or wicker baskets.*
Empanarer. *To put into panniers, or wicker baskets.*
Empanné. *as* Empenné. *Feathered.*
Empantouflé: m. ée: f. *Impantofled, or wearing pantofles.*
Livre empantoflé. *A Booke with a thicke couer.*
Empaqueté: m. ée: f. *Made vp in, or into, a packet, bundle, or fardle.*
Empaqueter. *To packe vp, to make vp in, or into, a packet, bundle, or fardle.*

Empaqueteur : m. *A packer vp of.*
Emparagé. *That hath his due part, or portion.*
Fille emparagée suffisamment, ou deuëment. *Fitly matched, equally maried; no way disparaged by her match.*
Emparché : m. ée : f. *Impounded; put into a pound.*
Emparé : m. ée : f. *Seised, caught hold of, laid hands on; got into his possession, or got possession of.*
Emparement. *A seising, or laying hands on; a catching hold, or taking possession of.*
Emparence : f. *Defence.*
Emparenter. *To ioyne in kindred, to make one of kinne to another.*
Emparer. *To seise, or lay hands on; to catch hold, or take possession of; also, to assemble, or gather forces together for the performance of one push, or brunt.*
Emparfumé : m. ée : f. *Perfumed, sweetned with odors.*
Emparfumer. *To perfume, or sweeten with odors.*
Emparlé. homme bien emparlé. *An eloquent, or welspoken man.*
Emparle-silence. *A dumbe shew, or speaking by signes.*
Emparlier. *A Counsellor, Barrester, Pleader, imparler.* (vieil mot.)
Empas : m. *Shackles, fetters, or pasternes for vnrulie, or vnbroken horses.*
Empasté : m. ée : f. *Crusted, or baked hard; kneaded, put, or made into past; impasted.*
Empastelé : m. ée : f. *Crammed (as pullein) with rolls of past.*
Empasteler. *To cramme pullein with rolls of past.*
Empastement : m. *Past; or, a pasting, or bedawbing with dough; or, a making of dough into past.*
Empaster. *To knead, or make into dough, or past; to past; to bedawbe with dough, or past.*
Empatement. *as* Empiettement.
Empatenostré : m. ée : f. *Full of, loaden with (Paternosters, or) Beads; hypocriticall, superstitious; that hath a paire of Beads, or is neuer without a paire of Beads, hanging at his girdle.*
Empatronné. *Seised on; made Lord, or Maister of.*
s'Empatronner de. *To seise on, to make himselfe the Lord, and Maister, to take on himselfe the Seigniorie, and commaund of.*
Empatté. *as* Espaté.
Empattement. *as* Espatement.
Empaulmé : m. ée : f. *Impaulmed; fully griped, seised, or taken into the hands.*
Empaulmer. *To impaulme; to gripe, seise, lay full hand on; to take into his hand; also, as* Empalmer.
Empavoisé : m. ée : f. *Defended, shielded, couered, or shrowded vnder a Targuet, or Targuet-fence.*
s'Empavoiser. *To defend, shield, or couer themselues, as with Targuets.*
Empayser. *To grow natural to, or inward with; to thriue, or prosper, in, as one of, a countrey.*
Empeau : m. *An Impe to graffe.*
Empeigne : f. *The barre-pinnes of a peece of caske.*
Empeigné : m. ée : f. *Fastened within the teeth of a combe; also, scratched with a combe; (*¶Rab. *as* Empiegé; *insnared;) also, pinned, as the barre of a peece of caske.*
Empeigner. *To combe; to pricke, rub, scratch, dresse, currie, as with a combe.*
Empeigner le bout d' vne douve. *To pinne the bar of a peece of caske.*
Empeinte. de cett' empeinte. *At this push, at this shocke; at this verie instant; Seeke* Empainte.

Empennaché. *as* Empanaché.
Empenné : m. ée : f. *Feathered, as an arrow.*
Empenner. *To feather, as an arrow.*
Empennon : m. *The feather of an arrow.*
Empereur : m. *An Emperour; also, the Sword-fish.*
Emperier : m. ere : f. *Imperiall; belonging, or like, vnto an Emperour.*
Grandeur emperiere. *The highest greatnes, or greatest dignitie, a most supreame authoritie.*
Emperiere : f. *An Empresse.*
Emperlé : m. ée : f. *Impearled, bepearled; inriched, adorned, or set thicke with pearle.*
Emperler. *To impearle, or bepearle; to inrich, decke, or set thicke, with pearle.*
Emperruqué : m. ée : f. *Imperiwigged, that weares a Periwig, or Gregorian.*
Empesché : m. ée : f. *Impeached; let, hindered; pestered, incombered; also, busie, busied, occupied, imployed; also, seised, entred vpon, or taken into his owne hands; also, withstood, or kept backe; also, shut, or dammed vp.*
Empesché de sa personne. *Vnweldie, heauie-bodied, pursie, grosse.*
Poictrine empeschée. *Stopped; obstructed, or troubled with obstructions; and (more particularly) as in* Poictrine.
Faire l' empesché. *To be (or seeme) verie busie, to bestirre himselfe hard, in a matter; also, as in;*
Vous faictes bien de l' empesché. *You make as though.*
Empesche-maison : m. *A trouble-house; a lazie, vnprofitable, or combersome guest; one thats good for nothing, or fit for no imployment, in a house.*
Empeschement : m. *An impeachment; a let, stop, hinderance, impediment, obstacle; disturbance, comber, trouble; difficultie; businesse; also, a withstanding; also, a shutting, or damming vp.*
Empeschement de fief. *A seising, or seisure of, an entrie made vpon, a fief.*
Empeschement de personne. *Vnweldinesse of bodie.*
Empescher. *To hinder, let, barre, stop; impeach; pester, trouble, disturbe, incomber; busie, toyle, hold occupied, keepe imployed; also, to withstand, or keepe backe; also, to shut, or damme vp.*
Il ne peut empescher le fief mouvant de luy. *Hee cannot seise on, or take into his possession, the &c.*
Qui peut, & n' empesche, peche : Prov. *He sinnes, that may, and will not, hinder euill.*
Empesé : m. ée : f. *Starched; also, hauing a wherle, or ioyned to a wherle (as a spindle hath, or is.)*
Empeser. *To starch.*
Empesté : m. ée : f. *Infected, or visited with the plague; also, plaguie, pestilent, pestiferous.*
Empester. *To infect, or visit with the plague; to set the plague on, giue the plague vnto.*
Empestre : f. *A pesterment, incombrance, intricacie, trouble, intanglement.*
Empestré : m. ée : f. *Impestered, intricated, intangled, incombred.*
Empestrement : m. *A pestering, intricating, intangling, troubling, incombring.*
Empestrer. *To pester, intricate, intangle, trouble, incomber.*
Empetuosité : f. *Looke* Impetuosité.
Emphase : f. *An Emphasis; a strong or vigorous pronunciation of a word; an expresse or earnest signification*

fication of an act; a significant force in either.
Emphastique: com. *Emphasticall; spoken, or done with an Emphasis; (hence) also, vigorous, forcible, earnest, expresse.*
Emphatiquement. *Emphatically, effectually.*
Emphyteose: f. *The making of a thing better then it was when it was receiued; land improued in goodnes, or, an estate vpon condition to improue it; an improuement.*
Emphyteosien. *A Farmer, or one that taketh land, or other commodities, on condition, to better, and improue them.*
Emphyteote. *as* Emphyteosien.
Emphyteuse. *as* Emphyteose.
Emphyteutique. *Whence;*
Seigneur emphyteutique. *That raises, or improues, his rents.*
Empiece. *Not of a great while.*
Empiegé: m. ée: f. *Ensnared; taken, or intangled in a snare.*
Empieme. *as* Empyeme.
Empienne de soulier. *Th'vpper leather of a shooe.*
Empierré: m. ée: f. *Turned into stone.*
Coeur empierré. *An obdurate, hard, stonie, or flintie heart.*
Empierrement: m. *A turning into stone.*
Empierrer. *To turne, or transforme, into stone.*
Empieté. *Pawed, pounced, clawed, talented; that hath pounces, &c; also, seised, held, griped in clawes, or clouches; also, vsurped; also, intangled, or fettered by the feet.*
Empietement. *A seising, griping, holding, as in clawes, clouches; &c; an vsurpation of another mans right; Looke* Empiettement.
Empietement d' vne montaigne. *The foot, or bottome of a hill.*
Empieter. *To seise, gripe, hold within the pawes, clawes, pounces, talents, clouches; to set forward the foot therby to catch at a thing; also, to vsurpe another mans right.*
s'Empieter. *To fetter, ensnare, intangle himselfe by the feet.*
Empietté. *as* Empieté.
Empiettement. *as* Empietement; *Also, the foot, or bottome of; and hence;*
Empiettement de colomne. *The Basis, or foot of a pillar.*
Empieture: f. *The footing, or bottome of a thing; the part whereby it stands on, or is setled into, another thing.*
Empillé: m. ée: f. *Piled, heaped on.*
Empillier: m. ere: f. *Bepillered; set on pillers; made with pillers.*
Empiné: m. ée: f. *Turned into a Pine tree.*
Empirance: f. *An impairing, or impairement; the wast, losse, or decay of a thing by vse, or wearing; also, the proportion of allay, or imbasement, in coines of gold, or siluer; which is, in peeces of gold of 23 Carats finenesse, a foure and twentieth part of siluer, & copper, or of either; and in peeces of siluer of* 11. d. *finenesse, a twelft part of copper.*
Empire: m. *An Empire, or Emperie; also, empire; Imperiall dominion, Seignorie, Soueraigntie; preheminence; iurisdiction, rule, gouernment; the highest dignitie, the greatest sway, the most supreame power, most absolute authoritie.*
Empire. à l' empire. *Impairing, decaying, waxing worse and worse, mending as sowre Ale in the Summer; Look* Monde.

Empiré: m. ée: f. *Impaired, wasted, decayed, growne worse for the wearing; imbased.*
Empirement: m. *as* Empirance; *Or, a growing worse and worse.*
Empirer. *To impaire, imbase, or make worse; also, to wast, weare, decay in goodnesse, grow worse and worse, or worse for the wearing.*
Il ne l' empire en rien. *He is euen as good as be.*
Femme mauvaise qui n' empire, encore n'est elle pas la pire: Prov. *A bad woman that paires not is not the worst of women.*
Empireume: m. *A marke of fire, scorching, or burning; a remainder of warmth, or heat; a sparkle, or small fire.*
Empirique: com. *An Empiricke; a Physition which without regard either of the cause of a disease, or of the constitution of the patient, applies those medicines whereof he hath had experience in others, worke they how they will.*
Empistolé. *Armed with a Pistoll.*
Empistoler. *To arme, or furnish, with Pistolls.*
Emplacé: m. ée: f. *Placed, planted, seated, setled.*
Emplacement d' vne ville. *The seat of a towne.*
Emplacer. *To settle, seat, place, plant.*
Emplage: m. *A filling.*
Au feur l' emplage. *Looke* Furemplage.
Emplaidé: m. ée: f. *Impleaded, sued.*
Emplaider. *To sue, to implead, to bring an action against.*
Emplastration: f. *A plaistering, or dawbing; a laying of plaister; also, an emplastration; a grafting by inoculation without a Scutcheon; and, in Physicke, th'applying of a salue, or plaister.*
Emplastre: m. *A plaister.*
Emplastré: m. ée: f. *Plaistered, beplaistered; couered with a plaister.*
Emplastrer. *To plaister, or beplaister; to couer with a plaister.*
Emplastreure: f. *A plaistering, or beplaistering; also, a plaister.*
Emplastreux: m. euse: f. *Full of plaisters; also, belonging to, or seruing for, a plaister.*
Emplatement: m. *A flatting; a laying flat vnto; a making broad, or flat; also, a flat, or broad, part of.*
Emplette. *as* Emploicte.
Empli: m. ie: f. *Filled, replenished; complete; top-full, vp to the necke, mouth, or brinke.*
Emplier. *as* Employer.
Emplir. *To fill, replenish; gorge; make, or stuffe vp to the top.*
Emplir vne femelle. *To serue, bag, make her great, fill her panniers, giue her her paiment, get her with yong.*
Achever d' emplir. *To performe, finish, fulfill, accomplish, make complete.*
Emploi: m. *Vse, or imployment of a thing; as* Employ.
Emploicte: f. *as* Employ; *Also, businesse, occupying, trafficke, trade, commerse; also, a bargaine made, purchase bought; or, a thing whereon money hath beene, or may be, well imployed; also, vtterance of commodities.*
Femme qui est encores de bonne emploicte. *That is yet of a tollerable age, that hath yet some good stuffe in her; with whom, as yet, prettie sport might bee made.*
Marchandise d' emploicte. *Ware that sells well, that vtters quickly, that goes away apace; marchandable ware.*

Emploicter. *To traffique, trade; bargaine, chaffer for; bestow, or imploy money in.*
Emploite. *as* Emploicte.
Emplomber. *To lead; couer with lead; set in lead.*
Emplotonné: m. ée: f. *Wound vpon a clue, made into a bottome, conglomerated.*
Emplotonner. *To wind vpon clues, to make into bottomes, or, to make bottomes of; to conglomerate.*
Employ: m. *Imployment, vse, dailie occupation of, necessarie businesse for, a thing.*
Employé: m. ée: f. *Imployed, applied, vsed, busied, occupied; bestowed, conferred, dispended, layed out.*
Employement: m. *An imploying, applying, vsing, occupying; a bestowing, dispending, distribution, laying out.*
Employer. *To imploy, applie; vse, occupie, busie; confer, bestow, dispend, distribute, lay out.*
s'Employer. *To indeuor, labour, be earnest vpon, to set himselfe about; to giue, applie, or addict himselfe vnto.*
Emplumassé: m. ée: f. *Beplumed; decked, adorned, garnished, set out with, stucke full of, plumes, or plums of feathers.*
Emplumé: m. ée: f. *Feathered, befeathered; set, stuck, adorned, garnished with feathers.*
Regnard qui dort la Matinée n'a pas la langue emplumée: Prov. *The sleepie Fox hath seldome feathered breakefasts.*
Emplumer. *To feather, befeather; sticke, set, garnish, or dresse with feathers.*
Emply. *as* Employ.
Empoché: m. ée: f. *Impoaked, impouched.*
Empocher. *To impouch, to put into a pouch, or budget; to bag, poake, or pocket vp.*
Empoigné: m. ée: f. *Seised, griped, caught, got into the fist, layed hold of.*
Empoigner. *To seise, gripe, catch, lay hands on, attach, take, lay hold of.*
Empoignure: f. *A handle; or the part whereof hold is taken.*
Empoinctant. *Pointing on; making a point for, giuing a point vnto.*
Empoincter. *as* Empointer.
Empoint. bien empoint de faire &c. *About, readie, or likelie, to doe &c.*
Mal-empoint. *Vnhandsome, vntrimmed, foule, sluttish, in ill plight, out of array.*
Empointer. *To point on; make a point for, giue or set, a point vnto.*
Empointer les doigts sur le luth. *To finger a Lute; also, handsomely to set, couch, or place, the fingers ends thereon.*
Empois: m. *Starch.*
Empoisonné: m. ée: f. *Poisoned, impoisoned; venomed.*
Empoisonnement: m. *A poisoning, impoisoning; venoming.*
Empoisonner. *To poison, impoison; venome.*
Empoisonneresse: f. *A poisonneresse, a woman that impoisons.*
Empoisonneur: m. *A poisoner, impoisoner.*
Empoisonneuse: f. *as* Empoisonneresse.
Empoissé: m. ée: f. *Pitched, bepitched; couered, or dressed with pitch; also, starched.*
Empoisser. *To bepitch; to dresse, or couer with pitch; also, to starch.*
Empoissonné: m. ée: f. *Filled, serued, furnished, with fish.*
Empoissonnement. *A storing of a pond, &c, with fish.*
Empoissonner. *To furnish or fill, to serue or store, with fish.*
Empor: m. *A Mart towne; a place wherein an vniuersall Faire is kept.*
Emporté: m. ée: f. *Carried, borne, taken, conueyed away; also, woon, gained, gone away with.*
Il a emporté à la chandelle. *He hath (out-sit all commers) out bid all customers; he hath gotten it, by bidding the most for it.*
Emportement: m. *A carrying, bearing, taking, or conueying away.*
Emporte-piece. *See* Cautere.
Emporter. *To carrie, beare, conuey, or take away; to win, gaine, get, or goe away with; also, as* Importer; *also, to bring, or beare vnto.*
Emporter la balance, ou le poids. *To beare downe the ballance; to ouerweigh, or weigh more then.*
Autant en emporte le vent. *So much breath is lost; (vsed, when one, hauing spoken to such as heare, or heed, him not, will signifie, that he hath lost his labour.)*
Il se laisse emporter du vent. *Hee runnes on freely without stopping; also, he is inconstant, fitting, variable, vnsteadie, light; or suffers himselfe to be swayed altogether by his owne giddie humors.*
Le ventre emporte la teste: Prov. *Said of Apostataes, who in hope of ease and preferment abandon a knowne truth; said also of those, who aboue all things respect their bellies; or by an excessiue diet ruine, or dull, their vnderstandings.*
Empoudré: m. ée: f. *Bedusted, or powdered; filled, or defiled, with dust.*
Empouldrer. *To bedust; to fill, or defile, with dust.*
Empoule: f. *A little wheale, blister, push, water-powke; a rising of the skin, such as comes after netling, &c; also, a small bubble on the water.*
Empoulé: m. ée: f. *Blistered, pimpled, or vneuenly puft vp in many places, as the skin after netling; bubblie; or raised, or rising, in bubbles, as water in a great showre of raine.*
Empoulément. *Swellingly, bubblingly, puffe-like, or push-like.*
Empoulure: f. *A blistered part of the bodie; a place full of wheales, powkes, pushes.*
Empouppant. *Being, or blowing, as wind in the poope of a ship.*
Empouppé. *Hit in the poope; driuen, or blown forward by a wind in the poope.*
Empoupper. *To hit the poope; to be, or blow, as wind in the poope of a ship; to driue, set, or beare forward, as a full wind doth a ship.*
Vn vent empouppe mon navire. *My ship goes with a full, or forc, wind.*
Empourpré. *Impurpled; clothed, or decked with purple.*
Vn traict empourpré de sang. *Died, distained, imbrued with bloud.*
Empourprer. *To cloth, adorne, or enrich with purple.*
Empraignant. *Printing, imprinting, pressing in.*
Emprainte: f. *as* Empreinte.
Empré. *Medowie, turned into a medow, growne a medow, and fit to beare hay.*
Empréer. *To make a medow of; to turne pasture, or corne-grounds, into medowes; to turne medow.*
Empreignée. *With child, conceiued; bagd.*
Empreinct. *The Palsie, wherein any one of the sides looseth both sence, and motion.*
Empreinct. *as* Empreint.
Empreincte: f. *A stampe, a print; as* Empreinte.

Empreincte. *Bagd, full, with yong, that hath taken.*

Empreindre. *To print, stampe, set, presse, or thrust hard in; also, to assaile, or set on with violence.*

Empreint: m. te: f. *Printed, stamped, pressed, thrust hard in; also, violently assailed, furiously set on.*

Empreinte: f. *A stampe, a print, impression, hard setting in; a violent assault, a furious and forcible onset.*

Emprendre. *as* Entreprendre; *To vndertake.*

Empres. *Hard-by, neere-hand, close adioyning.* (v.m.)

Empressé: m. ée: f. *Pressed, squeezed, thrust, crowded, or strained together.*

Fort empressé. *Verie busie, forward, sawcily intruding into matters; hard layed to, or put extreamely to his shifts, to his plunges.*

Empresser. *To presse, squeeze, thrust, crowd, or straine together.*

Empreut. *One; the first word of reckoning, or numbring; or, as we say,* Imprimis.

Empris. *as* Entrepris; *Vndertaken.*

Emprise. *as* Entreprise.

Emprisonné: m. ée: f. *Imprisoned, layed by the heeles.*

Emprisonnement: m. *An imprisonment, a shutting vp, a full restraint of libertie.*

Emprisonner. *To imprison, to cast in prison, to lay by the heeles, to shut vp.*

Emprunelé: m. ée: f. *Belonging to the apple of the eye.*

Emprunt: m. *A borrowing.*

Mis à l' emprunt. *Charged with a priuie Seale.*

Emprunté: m. ée: f. *Borrowed.*

Il n' est pas emprunté en son discours. *His speech is naturall, or his owne; hee is beholden to no bodie for it.*

Emprunter. *To borrow.*

Emprunter le nom d' autruy. *To vse, or abuse another mans name in a matter.*

Il ne choisit pas qui emprunte: Prov. *Borrowers (we say beggers) are no chusers.*

Emption: f. *A purchasing, a buying.*

Empuanti: m. ie: f. *Bestunke, filled or defiled with stench, perfumed or annoyed with ill sauors.*

Empuantir. *To bestinke; to fill with stinke, annoy with loathsome smells, perfume with filthie odors.*

s'Empuantir. *To wax vnsauorie, to beginne to smell.*

Empunaisi: m. ie: f. *as* Empuanti.

Empunaisir. *as* Empuantir.

Emputé: m. ée: f. *Appeached, accused, complayned of.*

Emputement: m. *An imputation, aspersion; accusation, or bill of complaint.*

Emputer. *To appeach, accuse, complaine of; to lay an imputation, cast an aspersion, on.*

Emputeur: m. *A secret accuser; a pickthanke, telltale, complainer, apeacher, informer.*

Empyeme: m. *An inward collection of corrupt matter in any part of the bodie, but especially betweene the breast, and lungs.*

Empyré. ciel empyré. *Th' Imperiall, or highest heauen; the mansion, and dwelling place of God, and his elect.*

Empyreume: m. *A drie, and accidentall heat, or fierie qualitie; or, as* Empireume.

Emunctoire. *Looke* Emonctoire: ¶Rab.

Emulateur: m. *An emulator, imitator, or enuier of another; a competitor, concurrent, or corriuall.*

Emulation. *Emulation, counterfeiting, imitation with desire to excell; also, enuie.*

Emulgeant. *Milking; Looke* Emulgent.

Emulgence: f. *A milking, or stroaking.*

Emulgent. veine emulgente. *One of the two maine branches of the hollow veine; which goes to the reines, and there is diuided into diuers others; some call it the pumping veine.*

Emulsion: f. *An emulsion; any kind of seed &c, brayed in water, and then strained to the consistence of an Almond milke; also, any kind of creame, or milkie humor.*

Emut. *as* Esmeut.

Emutissement: m. *The muting, or droppings of birds.*

Emyne. *A kind of measure; as* Emine.

En. *(Relating to a thing meant, or mentioned before, signifies) thereof; as,* Il m' a faict tort, il s'en repentira; *also, any, or none, thereof; whence;* vous parlez d' argent, en avez vous? ie n'en ay point.

En avoir; *whence;* En as tu? *Hast thou that I asked for? hast thou the thing I inquired after? also, as in;* I' en aura. *(blowes being vnderstood) I shall be well beaten; my skin-coat will be soundly curried.*

I' en ay bien avallé: &; Ie m' en suis bien donné. *I haue taken in my liquor freely.*

I' en ay trop. *(at Bowles, &c;) I am too hard throwen.*

Il y en a en ce monde à qui ne chault. *There be some in this world that care not.*

En estre; *whence;* En voulez vous estre? *Will you make one?*

C'en est faict. *(The businesse is) alreadie dispatched, or finished; (the man is) vtterly vndone, or but a dead man.*

Cela n'en est pas. *(at game) That is no play.*

I' en suis ainsi. *I am in this taking; such is my case, it is euen so with me.*

Qu'en est il? *What of that?*

Que vous en est il? *What is that vnto you?*

Nous en venons tout maintenant. *We come from it, or from doing it, but euen now.*

En. *(Relating to a place before mentioned, signifies) thither; as;* Il va en France; vous en allez vous? *also, thence, or from thence; as,* Ie viens du temple, en venez vous aussi?

En. *Set before Verbes of motion (as in the last example) without reference vnto a place certaine, or specified before, hath little, or no signification; as in,* Ie m' en vay; en quel lieu m' en fuiray-ie?

En. *A Preposition; hath diuers significations; as in, into; at, on, or vpon.*

En amont. *Vpward;* en bas; *Beneath, below, downward.*

En apres. *Afterward.*

En ce disant. *The while, or whilest he said this.*

En outre. *Moreouer, furthermore.*

En pour. *(Vulgarly) in lieu, in stead.*

En tout advenement. *Whatsoeuer happen; howsoeuer it be.*

En vision d' esprit. *By a vision.*

Adopter en filz. *To adopt, or chuse one for his sonne.*

C'est fait en homme, en beste. *This is done like a man, like a beast.*

Enaigri: m. ie: f. *Sharpened; exasperated; angered; made, or growne worse and worse.*

Enaigrir. *To make, or grow sharpe; to anger, exasperate, make a matter the worse.*

s'Enaigrir. *To grow worse and worse.*

Enameré: m. ée: f. *Made bitter.*

Enamerer. *To make bitter.*

Enamouré de. *Enamoured of, in loue with.*

s'Enamourer de. *To grow enamoured of, to fall in loue with.*
s'Enarbrer. *A horse to rise so high that he is like to fall backward.*
Enarché: m. ée: f. *Arched; couered with an arch.*
Enarcher. *To arch, or couer with an arch.*
Enarmes: f. *The handles of a shield, or targuet.*
Enarthrose: f. *A full, and perfect vnion, or vniting of bones, the head of the one being wholly receiued, and shrowded, within the hollow end of the other.*
Enasé. *Noselesse; Looke* Esnasé.
Enaser. *To cut off the nose; to depriue of a nose.*
Enaspri: m. ie: f. *Sharpened, made eager, exasperated.*
Enasprir. *To sharpen, make eager, exasperate, hurt with sharpenesse.*
Encacqué: m. ée: f. *Incagged; put into a cag.*
Encacquer. *To put into a little barrell, or cag.*
Encadené: m. ée: f. *Chained, tied in, or with, a chaine.*
Encadener. *To chaine, or tie in a chaine.*
Encagé: m. ée: f. *Incaged, imprisoned.*
Encager. *To incage; to shut within a cage; to imprison.*
s'Encaillouïr. *To become hard, or flintie, or, as hard as flint.*
Encaissé: m. ée: f. *Put into a case, or chest.*
Encaisser. *To put into a case, or chest.*
Encaloché: m. ée: f. *That wears high wooden shooes.*
Encaly: m. ie: f. *Hardened, or kernelled, as the skinne of a mechanicall, and toyling hand.*
Encant: m. vendre à l' en. *To sell by Portsale, or Outrope; Seeke* Incant.
En vn encant tiens la bouche coye: (Prov.) vid. *Be not hastie to ouerbid another.*
Encapé: m. ée: f. *Cloked, hooded; couered with a hood, or cloke.*
Encapeliné. *Wearing a little, flat, narrow-brimd hat; or, armed with a scull of yron.*
Encapeluchonné: m. ée: f. *Wearing a Cowle, as a Monke; incapuched, wearing a Capuche.*
Encaper. *To hood, or cloke; to furnish, or couer with a hood, or cloke.*
Encapitonner. *To hood, or couer the head.*
Encapuchonné. *as* Encapeluchonné; *Or, hooded.*
Encapuchonner. *To incapuche; to hood with a Capuche, &c.*
Encarené: m. ée: f. *Carried-in; or layed on the side, (as a ship.)*
Encarener vne nef. *To carrie-in a ship, to lay her on her side.*
Encarné: m. ée: f. *Incarnated; made fleshie, or fat.*
Encarner. *To incarnate, fatten, or make fleshie.*
Encarré. nef encarrée. *Grauelled; or, as* Encarené.
Encarrer. *To leuell at; or, as* Acarer.
Encassé: m. ée: f. *Cased, inchested; made vp in, put vp into, a case, or chest.*
Encasser. *To case, or inchest; to make vp in, or put vp into, a case, or chest.*
Encastellé: m. ée: f. *Incastellated, or narrow-heeled, (as a horse.)*
s'Encasteller. *To grow incastellated, or narrow-heeled.*
Encastelure: f. *A being incastellated, or growing narrow heeled; a vicious, or painfull narrownesse in a horses heele.*
Encastillement: m. *as* Enchassement; *An inchacement.*

Encavé: m. ée: f. *Hollowed, or made hollow; also, lodged in, let downe, or laied into, a Sellar; also, frequenting, or dwelling in, Sellars, &c.*
Encaver. *To hollow, to make hollow.*
Encaver les nids des poules. *To make places in walls for hennes to lay, or sit, in.*
Encaver les vins. *To lay, or let downe, wines into a Sellar.*
Encaveur: m. *A hollower, or maker of things hollow.*
Encaveure: f. *An hollowing, or making hollow; also, a concauitie, or hollownesse.*
Encaunché: m. ée: f. *Pestered, intangled (and thereby) stucke fast, or hindered from going on:* ¶Orleannois.
Encauste: m. *Enamell, or varnish; any such flourishing, wrought with fire.*
Encaustique. *Enamelled, varnished; wrought with fire.*
Enceinct: m. cte: f. *Girded, enuironned, compassed.*
Vne femme enceincte. *A woman great with child.*
Enceincte: f. les enceinctes d' vne esglise. *A close; or, the wall or circuit of, or the pillers set round about, the close of a Cathedrall, or great Church; also, as* Enceinte.
Enceindre. *To gird, compasse, enuiron, inclose, hemme in, set about with.*
Enceint. *as* Enceinct.
Enceinte: f. *as* Enceincte; *Also, the walke of a Deere, the place of his ordinarie haunt, or passage.*
Encellé. *as* Ensellé.
Encens: m. *Incense; Frankincense.*
Encens Amomite. *A kind of whitish Incense, which in handling becommeth soft like Masticke.*
Encens d' Arabie. *Arabian Incense; the second, or next in goodnesse, vnto the male.*
Encens blanc. *White Frankincense.*
Encens d' Inde. *Indian Incense; of a faint, and withered red colour, is made round by art; (And this is held to be, our ordinarie Frankincense.)*
Encens masle. *Male Incense; the whitest, and best kind of all others; of it selfe round; and, broken, fattie within.*
Herbe d' Encens. *Wormewood.*
Manne d' Encens. *Looke* Manne.
Encensé: m. ée: f. *Censed; perfumed with Incense.*
Encensement: m. *A censing; a perfuming with Incense.*
Encenser. *To cense, or perfume with Frankincense.*
Encensier: m. *A starre in heauen; called the Altar, or Censer; placed vnder the sting of the Scorpion.*
Encensier: m. ere: f. *Censing, perfuming.*
Herbe encensiere. *Fleabane, Coniza, Fleabane Mullet.*
Encensoir: m. *A Censor; a censing, or perfuming pan.*
Souffler à l' encensoir. *To drinke hard; to plie the pot; (for they that vse to blow the Censor, becomming drie, steale often to the wine-pot prouided for the Communion; and there sucke vp as much wine, as before they let out wind.)*
Encentrer. *(Sometimes vsed for* Entrer*) to graffe.*
Encepé: m. ée: f. *Set in the stockes; also, loaden with yrons.*
Enceper. *To set in the stockes; also, to clap yrons on the legs of.*
Encercelé: m. ée: f. *Incircled, encompassed; bound about with hoopes, as a wine vessell, &c.*
Encerclé: m. ée: f. *Incircled, encompassed; hooped, bound about.*

Encercler. *To incircle, or incompasse; also, to hoope, or bind about.*
Encernant. *Enuironing, incompassing; incircling, hooping in, or about.*
Encerné: m. ée: f. *Enuironed, incompassed; incircled, hooped in, or about.*
Enchafouiné: m. ée: f. *Out of tune, out of temper, scuruie, as one that, through cold, hurkles like a cat, or is know not how.*
Enchagriné: m. ée: f. *Made melancholike, filled with melancholie; grieued, vexed, afflicted.*
Enchagriner. *To vex, afflict, make melancholicke, fill with carefulnesse.*
Enchainé: m. ée: f. *Enchayned, chayned; bound or tyed in, decked or inriched with, chaynes.*
Enchainement: m. *A chayning; a binding in, or bedecking with, chaynes.*
Enchainer. *To enchayne, to chayne; to bind, or ty in chaines; to decke, or inrich with chaynes.*
Enchainure: f. *A chayning; a chayne; chaynage; also, as* Enchesneure.
Enchalassé: m. ée: f. *Propped, vnderset, held vp, as a vine, by poles, &c.*
Enchalasser vne vigne. *To prop, or vnderset a vine.*
Enchambré: m. ée: f. *Inchambred; lodged as in a chamber; also, mortaised, enclosed within.*
Enchampre: f. *A chizell; a cutting, caruing, or grauing toole.*
Enchancré: m. ée: f. *Cankered, festered, growne to a canker.*
Enchancrer. *To canker, or fester, as an old sore.*
Enchanté: m. ée: f. *Charmed, inchaunted; bewitched.*
Enchante-coeur. *Heart-charming, heart-inchaunting.*
Enchantelé: m. ée: f. *Supported, vnderset, borne or propped vp by stakes, as a vine, &c.*
Enchanteler. *To support; beare, stay, or prop, vp with stakes, as vines.*
Enchanteler du bois. *To pile vp wood.*
Enchantement: m. *An inchaunting, or charming.*
Enchanter. *To charme, inchaunt, bewitch; bleare the eyes, deceiue the vnderstanding.*
Enchanteries. *Charmings, inchauntments; deceits, delusions, iugling trickes, subtill conueyances, sleights of legerdemain.*
Enchanteusement. *Charmingly, inchauntingly.*
Enchapelé: m. ée: f. *Crowned, or decked with garlands; also, hatted, or couered, as with a hat.*
Enchapeler. *To decke, or crowne with chaplets, or garlands; also, to hat, or set a hat on the head.*
Enchapement d' une cheminée. *The head, or broad top, of a chimney.*
Enchaperonné: m. ée: f. *Hooded, or attired with a French-hood.*
Enchaperonnement: m. *A hooding; also, the outiutting, or ouer-hanging of the eaues, or bottome of a Roofe.*
Enchaperonner. *To hood; or couer the head with a (French) hood.*
Enchappé. *Wearing a coape; attired in a coape.*
Enchappeler. *as* Enchapeler.
Encharacteré: m. ée: f. *Incharactered, written, or printed in characters.*
Encharacterer. *To incharacter, to write, or print, in characters.*
Encharbouté: m. ée: f. *Confused, or crumpled; ruffled on knots, as haire that hath beene long vncombed.*
Enchardonné: m. ée: f. *Weeded, rid, of thistles.*
Enchardonner. *To weed out thistles.*
Enchargé: m. ée: f. *Bid, commaunded, charged, inioyned; giuen in charge; also, cloyed, or ouer-charged.*
Encharger. *To bid, commaund, inioyne, charge, giue in charge to doe a thing.*
Encharger l' estomac. *To surfet; to cloy, or ouercharge the stomacke with too much meat.*
Femme qui encharge. *That growes big on't; who burnishes, or whose bellie increases.*
Encharné: m. ée: f. *Incarnated, fleshed; whereon flesh is bred, or made grow.*
Encharné au coeur. *Rooted, or fleshed, in the heart.*
Encharnelé: m. ée: f. *Propped, vnderset, vpheld, as a vine.*
Encharneler vne vigne. *To prop, or vnderset a vine.*
Encharner. *To incarnate, flesh, breed flesh on, make the flesh grow; A tearme of Chirurgerie.*
Enchassé: m. ée: f. *Enchaced, set into; also, driuen, or hunted away.*
Enchassement: m. *An enchacing, or enchacement; also, a driuing, or hunting away.*
Enchasser. *as* Chasser; *to driue, or hunt away.* ¶Pic.
Enchasser en or &c; *to enchace, or set, in gold, &c.*
Enchasseure: f. *An enchacement; an enchacing, or setting in; and particularly, the stocke of a band, or cuffes.*
Enchassillé de menuiserie. *Compassed, bound, held in, by a frame, or band of wainscot; set in a wainscot frame.*
Presse enchassillée. *A Printers Presse with a Tympan.*
Enchassiller. *To set in; to enclose, compasse, bind, hold, in with a woodden frame.*
Enchassure. *Looke* Enchasseure.
Enchatonner. *as* Enchasser; *to enchace.*
Enchaucié: m. ée: f. *Chaced, pursued; (An old word.)*
Enchaulmé: m. ée: f. *Thatched, or couered with straw.*
Enchaulmer. *To thatch, or couer with straw.*
Enchausseure: f. *A shooing; also, the measure of a foot, taken to make a shooe by.*
Enche. *as* Anche.
Encheinure. *as* Enchainure.
Encheminer. *as* Acheminer; *to set in the way.*
Enchemisé: m. ée: f. *Couered, or clothed with, put into, a shirt, or smocke.*
Enchenard: m. *Part of a womans, &c.*
Enchepé: m. ée: f. *Set in the stockes.*
Encheper. *To set in the stockes; also, to clap shackles, or boults on the legs of.*
Enchere: f. *A bidding, or out-bidding; the making or offering, the raising or enhauncing, of a price; any Portsale, Outrope, or bargaining, wherein he that bids most for a thing is to carrie it.*
Folle enchere. *is, when one hath bid too much for a thing, and then would go from his bargaine, but cannot; whence;* Droict de folle enchere; *See* Droict.
Il en payera la folle enchere. *He shall smart for it; he shall deerely abuy his being so busie, lustie, foole-hardie.*
Mettre enchere sur. *To outbid; or, bid money for what another is about to buy.*
Mettre à l' enchere. *To raise, or enhaunce the price of; to make deere; to set, or hold, at a very high rate; to*

to let goe vnto him that will bid most.

Encheri: m. ie: f. *Raised, or enhaunced (also, risen) in price; made, held, or growne, deere; also, let goe, or passed ouer vnto such as haue bid most; also, endeered, or deerely cherished.*

Elle ne faisoit de l'encherie. *She played not the cut-throat; she set not the dice on her customers; she held not her ware very deere.*

Encherie: f. *The Preparatiue vnto Melting, or Extraction; the first part of Alchimie.*

Encherinent: m. *An ouerprising; a raising, or enhauncing of a price; a rising in price, a growing very deere; also, an out-bidding; also, an endeering, or deere cherishing.*

Encherir. *To raise, or enhaunce the price of; to ouerprise, or make too deere; also, to rise in price, or grow deere; also, to out-bid, or bid more then another; also, to let a thing go vnto out-bidders; also, to endeere, or cherish deerely.*

Encherisseur: m. *A high-bidder, or out-bidder of others; a raiser or enhauncer of the price of things, in an Outrope, or Portsale.*

Encherner. *as* Encharner. *To flesh.*

Encherre. *as* Encherir.

Enchesneure: f. *A chayne, or chayning; also, a rew, course, or succession of things linked together.*

Enchet: m. *A falling, or dropping; as of water, or of mettall that melteth.*

Enchevallé: m. eé: f. *Set, or lapped, as one foot ouer another.*

Enchevaller. *A horse to set, or lap, one foot ouer another.*

Encheveſtré: m. ée: f. *Haltered; tyed, or fettered in a halter, or horse-coller; insnarled, intangled, as a horse with his owne coller; also, inueagled; insnared.*

Encheveſtrement. *A haltering, or fettering; a being intangled with his owne halter, or coller; also, an inueagling.*

Encheveſtrer. *To halter, fetter, tye in a halter, put in a coller; to insnarle, intangle, as a horse with his owne coller; also, to inueagle; or any way, to insnare.*

Encheveſtrure: f. *A haltering, or tying in a horse-coller; a fettering, insnarling, intangling.*

Encheveſtrure de cheminée. *The Mantle-tree of a chimney.*

Encheux. *as* Ançois; (vieil mot.)

Enchiffré: m. ée: f. *Cyphred; expressed, or set downe, in cyphers.*

Enchiffrené: m. ée: f. *Whose nose is stopt with a cold, or a rhewme; that hath the murrhe, or poze.*

Enchiffrer. *To cypher.*

Enciré: m. ée: f. *Waxed, waxie; mingled, couered, or seared with; made, compounded, or full of, wax.*

Encirer. *To wax; to couer, or doe ouer with wax; to make, or compound of wax.*

Encis: m. *The murthering of a great-bellied woman, or of the infant within her bellie.*

Encisé: m. ée: f. *Cut vp, or into.*

Enciser. *To cut vp, or into; to make an incision.*

Enclave: f. *A mortaise, or inlocking; an entrie into, or within, another thing; a lying one within another; also, a march, bound, or limit of Territorie, or Iurisdiction; a Precinct, or Libertie.*

Les enclaves d'une Province. *The marches, bounds, or limits thereof (especially such as ly intermingled with those of another Prouince.)*

Enclavé: m. ée: f. *Inlocked, cocketed, mortaised, closed, or entered into, or within, another; layed, or lying within another; also, within the marches, or limits of.*

Enclavement: m. *An inlocking, or mortaising; a closing, or shutting; also, an entring within another; a laying, or lying, one within another.*

Enclavemens. *as* Enclaves.

Enclaver. *To close, mortaise, locke, set, or shut one thing within another; also, to enter into another; to lay, or ly, as peeces of seuerall mens land, one within th' other.*

Enclaveure: f. *as* Enclavement; *or, a mortaise, or mortaised closure.*

Enclin: m. *An inclination, disposition, addiction, naturall affection, instinct, or humor vnto.*

Enclin: m. ine: f. *Inclined, bent, prone, giuen, addicted, or disposed, vnto.*

Encliné: m. ée: f. *Inclined, declined; bent, bowed, crouching, or stooping downeward; humbled, readie, or likelie, to fall.*

Encliner. *To incline, decline; bend, bow, looke, stoope downeward; to decay; to begin, or be readie, to fall; to hang to the ground-ward.*

S'encliner. *To crouche, ducke, lout, make low courtesies; to humble himselfe before another.*

Enclorre. *To include, inclose, compasse, hedge, imparke, infould; shut in, or vp; also, to comprehend, containe, or comprise.*

Enclos: m. *An inclosure, or inclosing.*

Enclos: m. se: f. *Inclosed, enuironed, shut vp, kept in, on euerie side; imparked, infoulded, compassed, hedged in on all parts; also, contained, comprehended, comprised.*

Encloſtré: m. ée: f. *Incloistered, shut vp within a cloister.*

Encloſtrer. *To incloister, to shut vp within a cloister.*

Encloſture: f. *An inclosure, or inclosing; a close, or place hedged in.*

Enclotir. *To earth; to driue a Fox, or Conny into an earth, or berrie.*

Enclouſcher. *To prompt, or tell one what he shall say; (an old word.)*

Encloüé: m. ée: f. *Nayled; fastened, pricked, cloyed with a nayle.*

Ie m'y suis encloüé. *I am ingaged therein to my great hurt, or disaduantage.*

Enclouër. *To nayle, to driue in a nayle; to fasten with a nayle.*

Enclouër artillerie. *To cloy a peece of Ordnance; to driue a nayle, or yron pinne, into the touch-hole thereof.*

Enclouër vn cheval. *To pricke a horses foot in the shooing.*

Enclouëure: f. *A pricke in a horses foot.*

Il y a bien de l'enclouëure. *There is somwhat amisse, or some notable flaw in the matter.*

Il se doubta bien de l'enclouëure. *Hee mistrusted, that all was not well, that there was some mischieuous plot in working.*

Encloyer. *To cloy, choake, or stop vp.*

Enclume: f. *An Anuyle; also, a little bone seated within the eare, and seruing, together with other parts, as a principall Instrument to distinguish the sounds brought vnto it.*

Couché entre l'enclume, & les marteaux. *Lodged betweene two extreame dangers, or difficulties; perplexed, or afflicted which way soeuer he turne him.*

'A l'enclume le marteau: Prov. *A quarrelling, mutinous, or litigious fellow should be matched with one thats*

thats worse then himselfe; or, a hard heart needs hammering.
'A dure enclume marteau de plume: Pro. *By gentlenesse, and patience we surmount all difficulties: So doe skilfull Engineers oppose bags of wooll, and walls of soft earth, vnto the furie of the Cannon.*
Enclumeau: m. *A little Anuile.*
Encoche: f. *A nocke, or notch; as* Coche.
Encoché: m. ée: f. *Nocked, or notched, as an arrow; also, fastened, tyed fast, moored, as a cable, or a ship with cables.*
Encocher vne fleiche. *To nocke an arrow; to put the nocke thereof into the bow-string.*
Encocher les gumenes. *To fasten, or ty them fast, to moore a ship with them.*
Encochure: f. *A nocking, notching, snipping, nicking; also, a nocke, notch, or nicke; also, a fastening, or mooring.*
Encoeur. *as* Encueur.
Encoffré: m. ée: f. *Incoffred; layed, or put, vp in a coffer.*
Encoffrer. *To inclose, lay, or put vp, in a chest, or coffer, &c.*
Encoigné: m. ée: f. *Made corner-wise; thrust into a corner; also, wedged, or fastened in with wedges.*
Encoigneure: f. *A cone, or corner; also, a corner-peece, or part, of.*
Encoigneure de chemin. *A short, or narrow turning of a way; a strait corner whereinto one winds before he be aware.*
Encoleure: f. *The neck-peece; or, a neck-like peece of any thing; also, the part wherein one member, or peece is ioyned vnto another; and, such a ioyning; (whence) also, the setting on of the head, necke, or crest, &c; also, the countenance, gesture, or behauior of a man; the reyne of a horse, or, the posture, or carriage of his crest; also, a barre, necke, or narrow peece, of land lying betweene two seas.*
Encoleure du bras. *The wrist, or part of the arme thats next vnto it.*
Encoleure du pied d' un arbre. *The bottome of the stocke, bodie, or trunke; the setting on of the foot, or of the root, thereof; the necke of the foot.*
Encollé: m. ée: f. *Necked; hauing a faire, stiffe, and big necke; also, put about the necke of.*
Long encollé. *Necked like a Crane.*
Encoller. *To put about the necke.*
Encollure: f. *as* Encoleure.
Encoloré: m. ée: f. *Full of colours, much coloured, coloured all ouer, all in colours.*
Encombre: f. *as* Encombrier; *also, the rubbish, or ruines of falling, or decayed buildings.*
Encombré. *Troubled, pestered, incombred; disquieted.*
Mariage encombré. *Looke* Encombrer; *or,* Mariage.
Encombrement: m. *An incombring, pestering, molesting, troubling; an annoyance; or, as* Encombrier.
Encombrer. *To comber, incomber, perplex, pester; hinder, trouble, giue much businesse vnto; to afflict, vex, annoy; disquiet, molest; put vnto great labour, toyle, trouble.*
Encombrer le mariage de sa femme. *A husband to alien his wiues land, whether it be with, or without, her consent; See Mariage.*
Encombrier: m. *A comber, incombrance, pesterment; hinderance; trouble; molestation, affliction, vexation, annoyance; mischiefe; misfortune.*
Encomiastique: com. *Praising, commending, extolling to the skies.*
Encommencé: m. ée: f. *Begun, commenced, vndertaken, gone about, or in hand with.*
Encommencement. *A beginning; an vndertaking, or taking in hand.*
Encommencer. *To commence, begin, goe about, fall in hand with.*
Encommenceur: m. *A commencer, beginner, vndertaker.*
Enconché: m. ée: f. *Trimmed, drest, arrayed;* Nous voilà bien enconchez; *we are fairely drest, we are euen well handled.*
Encontenancé: m. ée: f. *Bold, audacious; well behaued; of a setled countenauce; seldome, or neuer out of countenance; that hath put a good face on the matter.*
Encontenancer. *To gesture it; to set a face on; to put on a gesture, or behauior.*
Encontre: f. *(a Substantiue) An encounter, a meeting; an encountring, or shocke of enemies; also, hap, lucke, chaunce, fortune.*
Encontre. *(a Preposition) Towards; against, oppositely; right against, oueragainst, iust on the other side.*
Aller encontre quelqu'un, ou luy aller à l'encontre. *To goe meet one.*
Encontré: m. ée: f. *Incountred, or met with; lighted, or happened, on.*
Encontrer. *To incounter, or meet with; to light, or happen on.*
Enconvenancé: m. ée: f. *Couenanted, conditioned; contracted, indented with.*
Enconvenancer. *To couenant, condition, indent, or contract with; to promise vnto.*
Encoqueluché: m. ée: f. *Sicke of the Coqueluchoe, or new disease; also, hooded.*
Encoqueluchonné. *Hooded; wearing a hood, or Spanish Capuche.*
Encoquillé. Poisson en. *Shell-fish.*
Encorbellement. *as* Corbeau; *or, a shouldering, or supporting, by Corbels, or Brackets.*
Encordé: m. ée: f. *Becorded, bound with cords.*
Encordelé: m. ée: f. *Corded, strung, or stringed; fastened, or made vp with cords, or strings; also, caught, fettered, intangled, or insnared therewith.*
Encordeler. *To string, or becord; to bind, fasten, packe, or make vp; to catch, fetter, intangle, or insnare, with strings, or little cords.*
Encorder. *To cord, becord, string; to bind, fasten, or make vp; to fetter, intangle, or insnare, with cords.*
Encordonné: m. ée: f. *Twisted of many strings; twyned, plaited.*
Encordonner. *To twist, plait, or twyne of many strings.*
Encore. *Yet, as yet, euen yet.*
Encore lors. *Euen then, euen to that time.*
Encore pas. *Not yet, or, not that, neither.*
Encore de present. *Euen now, as yet, vntill this very time.*
Encore que. *Albeit that, though that.*
Mais encores. *But for all that.*
Encoremes. *The signes of Vrine; especially those that swim on the top thereof.*
Encornal: m. *The Hounds of a Maste.*
Encorné: m. ée: f. *Horned; trimmed, nocked, or tipped with horne; also, put into a horne, or cornet; also, put into the nocke of; also, wearing, or hauing hornes.*

Encorner. *To haft, nocke, tip, or trim, with hornes; also, as* Encorneter; *also, to put into the horned nocke of.*

Encorneté: m. ée: f. *Incornetted; put into a horne; wrapped vp, as spice, &c, in a cornet, or coffin.*

Encorneter. *To put into a horne; also, to wrap vp in a cornet, or Grocers Coffin, spice, &c.*

Encornure: f. *A hafting, tipping, or trimming with horne; also, the hornes, or horned head, of a beast.*

Encorny. Lieu encorny. *A place thats hard (and smooth) as horne; or, as* Pelouse.

Encoronné: m. ée: f. *Crowned.*

Encoronner. *To crowne; to decke, or adorne with a crowne.*

Encotonné: m. ée: f. *Bumbasted, or stuffed with cotton.*

Encotonner. *To bumbast, to stuffe with cotton.*

Encotonner de barbe le menton. *To furnish the chin with soft, and tender haire; to make it bud, shoot, or put out abundantly.*

Encoüardé: m. ée: f. *Made cowardlie, bereaued of courage.*

Encoüarder. *To make a coward, bereaue of courage.*

Encoüardi: m. ie: f. *Growne cowardlie, become dastardlie, faint-hearted, white-liuered.*

Encoüardir. *To wax a coward, proue a dastard, become faint-hearted, grow white-liuered.*

Encouleure. *as* Encoleure.

Encoulpé: m. ée: f. *Accused, or blamed for.*

Encoulper. *To appeach, accuse, blame for, lay the fault, cast the imputation, of a matter on.*

Encoulpeur: m. *An accuser, appeacher, promooter, informer.*

Encoultré: m. ée: f. *Furnished with a culter.*

Encoultrer. *To furnish (a Plough) with a culter.*

Encouragé: m. ée: f. *Incouraged, heartened, imboldened.*

Encouragement: m. *A heartening, imboldening, incouraging, incouragement.*

Encourager. *To hearten, imbolden, incourage; to put mettall into, giue stomacke vnto.*

Encourement. *A punishment, or penaltie incurred.*

Encourir. *To incurre; to runne, or fall into; to get, or procure vnto himselfe; to vndergoe a danger, disgrace, penaltie, &c.*

Encourrayé: m. ée: f. *Bound, or furnished with leatherne thongs.*

Encourrayer. *To bind, or furnish, with leatherne thongs.*

Encourtiné: m. ée: f. *Becurtained; ouer which a curtaine is drawne; couered or hanged with, shadowed by, hidden behind, a curtaine.*

Encourtiner. *To becurtaine; to draw a curtaine ouer; to couer or hang with, to shadow by, to hide behind, a curtaine.*

Encouru: m. uë: f. *Incurred, runne into.*

Encoutelassé: m. ée: f. *Armed with a short sword, or cuttleas.*

Encoutelasser. *To furnish, or arme with a curtleax, or cuttleas.*

Encrassé: m. ée: f. *Bedawbed, begrymed, begreased by slouenlynesse; growne thicke with filth, and ordure.*

Encrasser. *To begryme, begrease, beray, bedawbe with slouenlie filth, or ordure.*

Encre: m. *Inke; also, blacking.*

Encrené: m. ée: f. *Nicked, notched, indented on; or, as* Encroüé; *whence;*

Besicles encrenées sur le nez. *Lodged, or ledged, on both sides of the nose.*

Encresmé. *Creamie, creamed; full of creame, made of creame.*

Encresmer. *To fill, or furnish with creame.*

Encreté: f. *Bitternesse; also, inkinesse, or blacknesse.*

Encreusé: m. ée: f. *Hollowed; also, hoorded, or layed vp in holes, or hollow places.*

Encreuser. *To hollow; also, to hoord, or lay vp, in holes, or hollow places.*

Encrier: m. *An Inke-maker.*

Encrier: m. ere: f. *Inkie; of, or belonging to, Inke.*

Encrou. *as* Escrou.

Encroüé: m. ée: f. *Lodged, as a cudgell in a tree; hanging on, or ledged in.* ¶Norm.

Encrouër. *To lodge, as a cudgell in a tree; to hang on, or ledge in.*

Encrousté: m. ée: f. *Pargetted, rough-cast; becrusted, or whereon a scab is set.*

Encroustement: m. *A pargetting, rough-casting, a setting of a crust, a bringing of a scab on.*

Encrouster. *To parget, rough-cast; make crustie, bring a scab on.*

Encruché: m. ée: f. *Put into an earthen pot; also, as* Encroüé.

Encrucher. *To put into an earthen pot.*

Encrudi: m. ie: f. *Made, or become, raw.*

Encrudir. *To make, or become, raw.*

Encueur: m. *The Stithie; (a disease of horses, and cattell.)*

Encuict: m. cte: f. *Raw, vndisgested, not yet concocted, not fully boyled, not throughly baked; also, hardened through heat.*

Encuirassé: m. ée: f. *Hardened, growne hard, thicke, rough, or harsh; also, bound hard.*

Vn linge encuirassé. *A linnen cloth growne stiffe with nastinesse, and ordure.*

Encuirasser. *To harden, thicken, make rough, harsh, thicke, or stiffe (with ordure, &c.) as leather; also, to bind hard.*

Enculé: m. ée: f. *Set, or setled vpon the tayle; nether, or lower part; possed downe; also, planted, or stucke downe with the bottome turned vp, or doubled; set a-slope, or with an imbowed bottome.*

Encusé: m. ée: f. *Accused, appeached; detected, bewrayed.*

Encusement: m. *A detection, disclosing, bewraying; appeaching, accusing.*

Encuser. *To appeach, accuse, informe against; bewray, detect, disclose.*

Encuseur: m. *A detecter, discloser, appeacher, accuser, betrayer, bewrayer.*

Encuvé: m. ée: f. *Put into a fatt, or tub.*

Encuver. *To put into a fatt, or tub.*

Encyclopedie: f. *The perfection of all knowledge, and liberall sciences; an art that comprehends all others; or, learning that comprehends all Arts.*

Encyliglotte. *The tongue-string.*

Encyrer. *as* Inciser.

Enda. *In faith, in deed, in sooth, in truth, trust me, on my word.*

Endaims. *Looke* Andaims.

Endamoisellé. *Effeminated, growne womanish; attired in gentlewomans apparrell.*

Endare; & endare; *and he went his way.*

Endazé: m. ée: f. *Earnest, or hastie in a matter.*

Endebté: m. ée: f. *Indebted, in debt, brought into debt.*

Endebtement: m. *A debt; or being indebted; a bringing into debt.*
Endebter. *To bring into debt.*
s'Endebter. *To be indebted; to owe.*
Endelechie: f. *Assiduitie, continualnesse, perennitie, perpetualnesse, or, perpetuall motion; as,* Entelechie.
Endemené: m. ée: f. *Wanton, liuelie, stirring, waggish, lasciuious, that loues to be fisking, fidging, or frigging.*
Endementiers. *In the meane while, in the meane time, space, or season; (an old word.)*
Endenté: m. ée: f. *Indented, snipt on the edges, notcht in the sides.*
Endenter. *To indent, snip, notch, iag on the edges; also, to set, or make teeth in.*
Endernier. *The last, or, the later end.*
Endesvé: m. ée: f. *Mad, furious, raging; earnest, vehement, full of ardor.*
Endesver. *To rage, be mad after, or most hot vpon, a thing; to long for vehemently, lust for exceedingly, desire most feruently, affect most immoderately.*
Endetter. *as* Endebter.
Endiablé: m. ée: f. *Possessed with a diuell; full of diuellishnesse; diuellish, horrible; damned, hellish.*
Endiabler. *To possesse with a diuell, to fill with diuellishnesse.*
Endiamenté: m. ée: f. *Set with Dyamonds.*
Endicté: m. ée: f. *Indicted, accused, informed, complained of.*
Endictement: m. *An indictment, accusation, information, or bill of Complaint.*
Endicter. *To indict, accuse, appeach; informe against; complaine vpon, charge with an offence.*
Endicteur. *An indicter, accuser, informer.*
Endimanché: m. ée: f. *Attired for high-dayes, or, that hath his hollyday face on.*
Endité: m. ée: f. *as* Endicté; *also, demonstrated, manifested, shewed, or pointed at, with a finger.*
Enditement. *as* Endictement.
Enditer. *as* Endicter; *also, to demonstrate, manifest, bewray, declare, shew, or point at with a finger.*
Endive: f. *The hearbe Endiue.*
Endive crespe. *Curled Endiue.*
Endive grande. *Great garden Endiue.*
Endive petite. *The lesse Endiue, bitter garden Endiue.*
Endive sauvage. *Wild Endiue (whose stalke is full of a milkie iuice.)*
Endizeler les gerbes. *To stonke, or shocke vp sheaues of corne; to set, or make them vp in (tenne-sheaued) halfe-thraues.*
Endoctrinable: com. *Docible, teacheable, instructable.*
Endoctriné: m. ée: f. *Taught, instructed; nurtured, trayned vp, in learning, &c.*
Endoctrinement: m. *Instruction, teaching, nurture, a trayning vp in learning, &c.*
Endoctriner. *To teach, instruct; nurture; to traine, or bring, vp in the knowledge of Learning, or Arts.*
Endoille. *as* Andouille.
Endommagé: m. ée: f. *Indommaged, incommodated, hindered.*
Endommagement: m. *A losse, dammage, indommagement, or indommaging.*
Endommager. *To indommage, incommodate, hinder; bring, or breed losse vnto.*
Endoré: m. ée: f. *Gilt all ouer; beset, inriched, adorned with gold.*
Endorer. *To gild all ouer; to beset, inrich, adorne with gold.*
Endormant. *The Serpent* Cenchris, *whose stinging breeds rottennesse, and a continuall sleeping.*
Endormi: m. ie: f. *Sleepie, drowsie, heauie, lazie, sluggish, euer asleepe, that sleepes as he goes; also, asleepe, husht, quiet, calme, appeased, at ease, at rest.*
Eau endormie. *A calme, still, or standing water.*
Fol est qui se fie en eau endormie: Prov. *Men of a still, sad, sleepie, melancholicke disposition are not to be relyed on; for either they can doe little, or that which they doe is full of trecherie, and dissimulation.*
Membres endormis. *Astonied, benummed, asleepe.*
Endormi comme vn Envent. *Looke* Envent.
Homme endormi corps enseueli: Pro. *There is as much vse of a dead corse, as of a drowsie creature; or, a drowsie bodie is little better then a dead.*
Endormie: f. *The hearbe Henbane; or Poppie.*
Endormir. *To lay, or lull asleepe; to cast into a sleepe; to calme, quiet, appease, bring to rest; also, to astonish, or benumme.*
Endormir sur l'une & l'autre aureille. *To giue much ease vnto, bestow all wished contentments on; to bring a-bed (say we.)*
Endormir vn trompe. *To set a Top.*
s'Endormir. *To fall asleepe; to be fast, or sound asleepe; to giue himselfe to sleeping.*
s' Endormir sur les iniures. *To be vnsencible of wrongs; dully to foreslow, or cowardly to delay, the reuenge thereof.*
s'Endormir sur le mestier. *See* Mestier.
s'endormir sur le rosty. *To sleepe vpon the offer of a great aduantage, faire opportunitie; or lazily to neglect, or foreslow the acceptance of them.*
s' endormir en sentinelle. *To sleepe when he hath most cause to watch; to laze it when he hath most need to looke about him.*
Endormissement: m. *Sleepinesse, drowsinesse, or sluggishnesse; also, a bringing, laying, or lulling asleepe.*
Endormisson de membres. *Numnesse, vnsencibleneße, benumming, astonishment, or stupiditie of the Members.*
Endos. *as* Endossement.
Endosé. *That hath his share, or portion of; whose part is limitted, or prescribed vnto him.*
Endossé: m. ée: f. *Indorsed; put vpon the backe; also, backed, or hauing a backe; whence;*
Vn banc endossé. *A Bench, a Forme, hauing a backe, or stay for the backe; also, the Bench thats next, or ioyning to, a wall.*
Espée bien endossée. *A sword thats well, or strongly backt.*
Endossement: m. *An indorsing, or indorsement; also, a putting on the back; also, a backing, or setting a backe vnto.*
Endosser. *To indorse; also, to backe, or put a backe vnto; also, to put on the backe; whence;*
Endosser vn harnois. *To arme himselfe; to put on his harnesse; to get an Armor on his backe.*
Endosseure: f. *The backe, or backe-part of any thing; also, an indorsement.*
Endoüairé: m. ée: f. *Endowed; indued with.*
Endoüairer. *To endow, to indue with.*
Endouille: f. *as* Andouille. *A linke; a chitterling.*

Endouiller: m. *The Browankler, or lowest branch of a Deeres head.*
Endoulouri: m. ie: f. *Grieued, pained.*
Endoubté: m. ée: f. *Vncertaine, staggering, doubtfull, in doubt.*
Endroict: m. *The Superficies, face, or side of a thing; also, a Coast, Quarter, Place, or Part; and hence;*
En cet endroict. *Hereabouts.*
Robbe à deux endroicts. *A gowne thats made alike on both sides, or is as good on the one side as the other.*
Chascun en son endroict. *Euerie one in his qualitie, state, place, ranke; euerie one to his power; as much as lyes in euerie one.*
Nager à l'endroict. *To swim on the bellie.*
Nul endroict sans son envers: Prov. *No outside without an inside.*
Endroict: m. cte: f. *Direct; and hence;*
Parjure endroict. *A plaine oath-breaker, or palpable faith-breaker; a most false man. (An old phrase.)*
Endroict. (Prepos.) *By; neere, or nigh to; about; round about; also, with, towards, in respect of.*
Endroict moy. *For my part, as for me.*
Endroit. *as* Endroict.
Endüe. vne femme bien endüe en la saincte Escriture; *a woman thats skilfull, or well seene, in the Scripture.*
Enduict: m. *Looke* Enduit.
Enduict: m. icte: f. *Dawbed, plaistered; also, annointed, bismeared, rubbed ouer with; also, as* Enduit.
Enduire. *To plaister, dawbe; annoynt, bismeare; doe, rub, or couer, ouer with; also, to indue, or disgest, as a hawke doth her meat.*
Enduisement: m. *A plaistering, dawbing; annoynting, bismearing; doing, rubbing, or couering ouer with.*
Enduiseur: m. *A plaisterer, dawber, annoynter, smearer.*
Enduisson: f. *as* Enduisement; *or,* Enduit.
Enduit: m. *Plaister; also, a bed, or lay of plaister; also, a plaistering, or couering ouer, as with plaister; also, a dawbing, annoynting, smearing, or bismearing.*
Enduit: m. te: f. *Plaistered &c; as* Enduict; *also, induced, or disgested, as meat by a hawke.*
Enduite: f. *as* Enduit; *a plaistering; also, a bed, or lay of plaister.*
Endurable: com. *Indurable, bearcable, tollerable, sufferable.*
Endurant. *Induring, patient, suffering, abiding, bearing with.*
Endurci: m. ie: f. *Hardened, indurated, confirmed, obdurated.*
Endurcir. *To indurate, harden, obdurate, confirme.*
s'Endurcir. *To wax hard, grow stiffe, abide long, sustaine with constancie; beare off with head and shoulders.*
Enduré: m. ée: f. *Dured, lasted, continued; borne, indured, sustained, suffered, abidden, tollerated, vndergone.*
Endurement: m. *A during, lasting, long continuance; an induring, suffering, tolleration, bearing, standing to it, abiding by it.*
Endurer. *To dure, last, continue long; also, (& most properly) to indure, tollerate, suffer, beare, sustaine, abide, vndergoe.*
Endurer de quelqu'vn. *To vse one respectfully, or tenderly; to deale with him kindly, intreat him fauourably, beare with much at his hands.*
Endurer faut pour durer: Prov. *Such as will dure must indure.*
L'on endure tout fors que trop d'aise: Prov. *Looke* Aise.
Le papier endure tout: Prov. *as, foule blurres, false reckonings, all kind of hard, or ill words.*
Enduvetter. *To bedowne; to fill, or stuffe, with downe.*
Eneaüé. *Watered; seasoned with, turned into water.*
Eneauër. *To turne into water; to mingle, or season with water.*
Enenda. *In faith, in truth, in sooth, trust me, on my word, in verie deed.*
Energie: f. *Energie, effectuall operation, force, efficacie.*
Enervation. *An eneruation, weakening, enfeebling; also, the synewie seperation of the Muscles.*
Enervé. *Eneruated, weakened, enfeebled; also, feeble, weake, tender, effeminate, without force, without pith, without vigor.*
Enerver. *To eneruate, weaken, debilitate, enfeeble; to bereaue of force, of pith, of vigor.*
Enfagotté: m. ée: f. *Put into a fagot; made vp in the forme of a fagot.*
Enfagotter. *To put into a fagot; or, make vp in the forme of a fagot.*
Enfaissé: m. ée: f. *Made vp into a bundle, or trusse.*
Enfaisser. *To packe, or trusse vp; to make into a packe, bundle, trusse.*
Enfaistau: m. *A Ridge-tyle, Creast-tyle, Roofe-tyle.*
Enfaisté: m. ée: f. *Roofed; or, as* Enfesté; *in* Maison Enfestée.
Enfaisture: f. *A ridge, or a ridging; or the frame of a ridge, roofe, or house-top.*
Pieces d'enfaisture. *Sparres, rafters, ridge-peeces of timber.*
Enfance: f. *Infancie, childhood.*
Enfanchonnets. *Nephewes; or, the children of our children.*
Enfançon: m. *A little infant; a babie, or sucking child.*
Enfangé: m. ée: f. *Bedurtied, bemyred, bemudded.*
Enfangement. *A bedurtying, bemyring, bemudding.*
Enfanger. *To bedurtie, bemud, bemyre; to spatle, beray, or durtie all ouer with myre.*
Enfanson. *as* Enfançon.
Enfant: m. *An infant; a child.*
Enfant de choeur. *A Quirrester.*
Enfant de choeur de la messe de minuict. *A rakehellie night-walker.*
Enfans de famille. *Yonkers of account, youthes of good houses, children of rich parents (yet aliue.)*
Enfant de France. *The sonne of a King of France.*
Enfant de la mate. *A ruffin, hackster, swash-buckler, swaggerer, mad shauer; also, a cut-purse.*
Enfans perdus. Perdus, *in warre; (ordinarily) gentlemen of companies, reserued for, and exposed vnto, all desperate seruices.*
Enfans rouges. *Children brought vp in a certaine Hospitall at Paris, & attired in red, (as ours of Christs-church in blew.)*
Enfant sans soucy. *An vnthrift, spend-good, carelesse companion; also, a Jugler; Buffoone, or Tumbler.*
Enfans de la terre. *Licentious, dissolute, sensuall persons; those that are wholly swayed by their voluptuous,*

or intemperate, humors; those that make earth their heauen, or haue their heauen on earth.
Enfans trouvez. *The name of a Parisien Hospitall, wherein children, found by chance, are nourished.*
Bons enfans. *The name of the most auncient Colledge in the Vniuersitie of Paris.*
Vn fait d'enfant. *A trifling, simple, boyish, or childish part.*
Enfans deviennent grands gens: Pro. *Children, in time, grow men; or (as we say) boyes will be men one day.*
Enfans sont richesses de pauvres gens: Prov. *Children are poore mens riches: (In other Countries, whose people are industrious, they may perhaps be so; but in ours, for the most part, store of children make poore men plaine beggers.)*
Ce que l'enfant oit au fouyer, est tost conu iusques au Monstier: Pro. *What children heare at home soone flyes abroad.*
De petit enfant petit dueil: Pro. *A little mourning serues for little children.*
Il faut laisser son enfant morveux plustost que luy arracher le nez: Prov. *Better a snottie child then a noselesse.*
Qui voit enfant, il voit neant: Pro. *He that sees an infant, sees nothing (belike because it alters so quickly.)*
Soleil qui luisarne au matin, femme qui parle Latin, & enfant nourry de vin, ne viennent point à bonne fin: Pro.
Enfantant. *Bringing forth a child.*
Enfanté: m. ée: f. *Bred, brought forth, or, brought to bed of a child.*
Enfantement: m. *A bringing to bed, a birth, or bringing forth of children; the time of a womans trauell.*
Enfanter. *To bring forth a child, to be deliuered, as a woman, of child.*
Enfantiere. Femme en. *A child-bearing woman, or woman that lyes in child-bed.*
Enfantil: m. ile: f. *Childish, boyish, trifling, simple, fond.*
Enfantilement. *Childishly, fondly, boy-like.*
Enfantillage: m. *Childishnesse, boyishnesse, childish humors.*
Enfantiller. *To play the child, or play as children doe; to trifle, to toy it.*
Enfantin. *as* Enfantil.
Enfantinément. *Childishly, boyishly, infant-like.*
Enfardelé: m. ée: f. *Packed, or made vp into a fardle, or bundle.*
Enfardeler. *To packe; to make vp into a fardle, or bundle.*
Enfariné: m. ée: f. *Bemealed; whited, or strewed, ouer with meale.*
Bien enfariné. *Flush, mellow, cupshotten, that hath his headgeere soundly; (a metaphor taken from flower cast on meat, that it cleaue not to the Gridiron, & so burne; for here his drinke is as flower to keepe his liuer from burning his meat.)*
Enfariner. *To bemeale; to white, or strew ouer with meale.*
Qui entre dans vn moulin il convient de necessité qu'il s'enfarine: Pro. *He that goes into a Mill must needs be bemealed; he that touches pitch must needs be defiled.*
Enfeconder. *To fertilize; to make fruitfull, or fertile.*
Enfelonni: m. ie: f. *Become fierce, waxt curst, growne cruell.*
s'Enfelonnir. *To become fierce, wax curst, grow cruell.*
s'Enfelonissant. *Becomming fierce, waxing curst, growing cruell.*
Enfer: m. *Hell.*
Couleur d'enfer. *A darke, and smoakie browne.*
Ou rendre, ou prendre, ou mort d'enfer attendre: Prov. *The theefe that restores not, or is not punished, in this life, hath cause to expect damnation in the next.*
Enferger. *To shackle, or fetter.*
Enferges: f. *Shackles, fetters, yrons for the legs.*
Enfermé: m. ée: f. *Shut, kept, locked vp close; vnder locke and key; also, inclosed, hedged, or hemmed in.*
Enferme: com. *Infirme, weake, feeble, vnable; crasie, broken, sickish.*
Enfermement: m. *A shutting, locking, or keeping vp; an inclosing, hedging, or hemming in.*
Enfermer. *To shut, locke, or keepe close vp; to inclose, hedge, or hemme in.*
Enfermerie: f. *An Hospitall, or Spittle for sicke, or maimed people; also, a Cloister, or Fryerie.*
Enfermier: m. *An ouerseer of the sicke in Hospitals; also, the Porter of a Fryerie.*
Enferré: m. ée: f. *Shackled, layed in yrons, chained vp; also, pierced, or thrust into, with an yron blade; as;*
Il s'est enferré. *He hath run, or fallen, vpon his owne sword; he hath run himselfe quite through.*
Enferrer. *To shackle, chaine vp, or lay in yrons; also, to strike, runne, pierce, or thrust into, with a sword, &c.*
Les Enfers. *Hell; Seeke* Enfer.
Enfestau: m. *A Roofe-tyle, or, a Ridge-tyle.*
Enfesté: m. ée: f. *Kept holyday; or, solemnized with a holyday; also, roofed; whence;*
Maison enfestée. *Whose roofe is furnished, or tyled.*
Enfester. *To keepe holyday; to solemnize with a holyday; to make holyday for the sake, or make a holyday in remembrance, of.*
Enfester vn edifice. *To tyle a house, or, to finish the roofe thereof by tyling it.*
Enfueillé: m. ée: f. *Couered with, or hidden among, leaues.*
s'Enfueiller. *To couer himselfe with, or hide himselfe among, leaues.*
Enfiellé: m. ée: f. *Made bitter as gall; filled, or mingled, with gall.*
Enfieller. *To make bitter; to fill, or mingle, with gall.*
Enfieri: m. ie: f. *Growne proud, loftie, statelie.*
s'Enfierir. *To wax proud, grow statelie, become loftie, take much vpon him.*
Enfievré: m. ée: f. *Driuen, put, or cast into an ague.*
Enfievrer. *To put, or cast into an ague; to driue into a feauer.*
Enfilé: m. ée: f. *Threaded as a needle; also, put on a thread, as pearle, &c; also, intangled, insnared, caught fast.*
Enfiler. *To thread; also, to intangle, or insnare; also, to stab, or pierce into.*
Enfiler la venelle. *To runne away.*
Il en cuida bien enfiler son aiguille. *He thought to haue gotten much by the bargaine, he meant to feather his neast well by it.*
Enfinceux: m. euse: f. *Wanton, lascinious, petulant; or, as* Endemené.
Enfistulé: m. ée: f. *Infistulated; that hath gotten a Fistula.*
Enflambant. *Inflaming, firing, or, setting on a light fire.*
Enflambé: m. ée: f. *Inflamed; inkindled, set on a light fire.*
Amende enflambée. *Looke* Amende.

Enflambement: m. *An inflaming, firing; incensing, inkindling; an inflammation.*
Enflamber. *To inflame, fire, set on a light fire; blister with heat; incense, inkindle; fill with ardor.*
s'enflamber de courroux. *To fume, chafe, wax as hot as a toast.*
Enflammant. *Inflaming, inkindling, firing, or setting on a light fire.*
Enflammé: m. ée: f. *as* Enflambé.
Enflé: m. ée: f. *Swollen; risen; puffed vp, strouted out.*
Enfle-boeuf: m. *The long-legd Beetle, or Ox-fly.*
Enflecheures: f. *The ratlings; the cordie steps whereby Mariners climbe vp to the top of a Mast.*
Enflemént: m. *A swelling; rising; raising; puffing vp, strouting out.*
Enflément. *Swellingly; puffingly, stroutingly.*
Enfler. *To swell, raise, blow, or puffe vp; also, as;*
s'enfler. *To swell, rise, wax big, strout out.*
Enflescher. *To pierce, or shoot into with arrowes.*
Enfleure: f. *A swelling, rising, inflation, puffing vp, strouting out.*
Enfleurer. *as* Enfleurir.
Enfleurir. *To beflower; to spread, strew, set, or decke, with flowers.*
Enfleuronner. *as* Enfleurir.
Enflure: f. *as* Enfleure.
Enfoiri: m. ie: f. *Berayed, besquattered, beshitten.*
Enfoirir. *To besquirt, besquatter, beray, beshite.*
Enfolastré: m. ée: f. *Foolishly enamoured, or doating on, fondly in loue with.*
Enfoncé: m. ée: f. *Sunke deepe, gone farre, into; fallen into the bottome of; as* Enfonsé.
Enfoncement: m. *A sinking; a bulging; a driuing, or dinging farre in; a beating, or forcing downe; a breaking, going, or working deepe into; also, a ding, dint; hole, bottome, hollow.*
Enfoncer. *as* Enfonser.
Enfondrant. *Sinking, drowning, ouerwhelming (as in a puddle, or mire;) also, yeelding, as a soft thing to the force, or violence of a hard.*
Enfondré: m. ée: f. *Sunke, drowned, ouerwhelmed, plunged into the bottome of (a puddle, or mire;) also, extreamely dinted, or beaten farre in.*
Enfondrer. *To sinke; drowne, ouerwhelme, plunge into the bottome (of a puddle, slough, or myre.)*
Enfondrer vn chemin. *To weare, or make great holes in, a way; to make a deepe way.*
Enfondrer vn harnois. *To make a great dint in an armour.*
Enfondu: m. uë: f. *Mucke-wet, wringing-wet.*
Enfonsé: m. ée: f. *Sunke, gone deepe; driuen, forced, or fallen, downe into the bottome of; bulged; beaten farre in; broken open; wrought deepe into.*
Il a enfonsé la matiere. *He hath thrust himselfe very farre, he hath runne himselfe ouer head and eares, into the matter.*
Enfonser. *To driue, or force downe to the bottome; to beat deepe, or thrust farre, into; to bulge.*
s'enfonser. *To sinke, or goe deepe; to fall downe into the bottome; to ouerwhelme himselfe; to run ouer head and eares into.*
Enfonser vn arc. *To bend a bowe very hard; or, to draw a bowe as farre as it will bend.*
Enfonser vn huis. *To beat in, or breake open, a dore.*
Enfonser vn lict. *To boord the bottome of a bed.*
Enfonser de la marchandise en de tonneaux. *To packe vp wares into Dryfats, or Tunnes.*
Enfonser le poignet. *To grease in the fist, to corrupt with gifts or bribes; also, to gaine, or grow rich, by such corruption.*
Enfonsure: f. *A beating or dinging, a sinking or thrusting, farre in; or, as* Enfoncement.
L'enfonsure d'un chalit. *The boorded bottome of a Bedstead.*
L' enfonsure du test d'une noix. *The bottome of a Nutshell.*
Enforcé: m. ée: f. *Strengthned, confirmed, giuen force vnto; or whereunto force is giuen.*
s'Enforcer. Alors s'enforça la feste. *Then did the feast increase.*
Enforci: m. ie: f. *Inforced, confirmed, strengthened.*
Enforcir. *To inforce, confirme, strengthen; add power, apply force, giue strength, vnto.*
s'enforcir. *To grow strong, become lustie, wax couragious, or vigorous; take heart, recouer his force, picke vp his crummes.*
Enformé: m. ée: f. *Formed, fashioned.*
Enformer. *To forme, fashion, add shape, or making vnto.*
Enforti: m. ie: f. *Strengthned; fastened; inforced, fortified; also, thickned (as cloth is by fulling.)*
Enfoüé: m. ée: f. *Conuerted, or turned, into fire.*
Enfoüer. *To conuert into fire, to turne to fire.*
Enfouï: m. *Digged in; buried, interred.*
Enfouïr. *To dig in; to burie, interre, hide, or lay, in the ground.*
Enfouïssement: m. *A digging; an interring, a burying, or hiding in the ground.*
Enfourché: m. ée: f. *Forked, made forkewise.*
Enfourchir. *To beforke; also, to bestride.*
Enfourchure: m. *as* Fourcheure.
Enfourné: m. ée: f. *Put into, or shut vp in, an ouen; also, begun, set on worke, taken in hand.*
Enfournement: m. *A putting into, or shutting vp in, an ouen; a setting in; also, the beginning, or first part, of a matter.*
Enfourner. *To put or set, place or shut vp, in an ouen; also, to begin, set in hand, or on worke.*
s'Enfourner en. *To vndertake, enter into, imbarke himselfe in.*
Il est aussi sage qu'oncques puis n'enfournasmes nous. *He is euen as wise as he was at first; a coxcomb he was, and a cokes he is.*
'A l'enfourner on faict les pains cornus. Pro. *A businesse is soonest marde while it is abeginning; or, at the setting in is most hurt done; for then are faults most easily committed, and (a little ouerslipt) hardly amended; of a like sence is;*
Qui mal enfourne tire les pains cornus, Pro. *He that begins (a matter) vntowardly, ends (it) ilfauoredly.*
Enfouy. *Digged in; buried, interred; layed, put, or hid, in the ground.*
Enfouyr. *as* Enfouïr.
Enfractueux: m. euse: f. *Intricate, mazelike, inuolued, perplexed; that hath many turnings, and windings.*
Enfractuosité: f. *A manifold winding, turning, inuolution, intricacie, compasse.*
Enfrainct: m. cte: f. *Infringed, violated, broken.*
Enfraindre. *To infringe, violate; breake in peeces.*
Enfrangé: m. ée: f. *Befringed; edged with fringe.*
Enfranger. *To befringe; to edge, or set, with fringe.*

Enfriché: m. ée: f. *Growne wild, ouergrowne with shrubs, or weeds; for want of tillage &c.*
s'Enfricher. *To grow wild, or be ouergrown with shrubs, or weeds, as land for want of tillage &c.*
Enfroiduré. Ie suis enfroiduré. *I haue gotten a cold, I haue taken cold.*
s'Enfroidurer. *To take cold, to get a cold.*
Enfroqué: m. ée: f. *Attired in, or couered with, a Monks hood, or Cowle; and hence;*
Cerveaux enfroquez. *Monkes, Friers, &c.*
Enfroquer. *To attire in, or couer with, a Cowle; & hence, to make, or institute a Monke, &c.*
Enfruité: m. ée: f. *Stored, filled, or garnished, with fruit.*
Enfruiter. *To store, fill, or garnish, with fruit.*
Enfueillé: m. ée: f. *Leaued, stucke or set, stored or furnished, with leaues.*
Enfueiller. *To beleafe; to stick or set, store or furnish, with leaues.*
s'Enfueiller. *To hide, or shrowd himselfe among leaues.*
s'Enfuir. *To fly, take his heeles, run away, get packing as fast as he can, shew a faire paire of heeles.*
s'enfuir en cachette. *To giue the slip, flinch away priuily, slinke out of companie.*
Le vin s'enfuit par dessus. *The wine spils, or runnes ouer, at the top of.*
Qui s'enfuit on l' ensuit: Prov. *Men follow those that fly.*
Enfumé: m. *as* Canthare. *A duskie sea-fish, that liues vpon slyme, and ordure.*
Enfumé: m. ée: f. *Smoaked, or besmoaked; perfumed or smathered, with smoake; hanged or dried, in the smoake; also, smoakie; and, of a smoakie-browne, or duskie-russet, colour; smoakie-coloured.*
Enfumement: m. *A smoaking, or besmoaking; a perfuming with smoake, or hanging in the smoake.*
Enfumer. *To smoke, or besmoake; to smother or perfume, with smoake; to hang or dry, in the smoake.*
Enfurié: m. ée: f. *Inraged, inflamed with furie, stark mad.*
Enfusté: m. ée: f. *Inpiped, or incasked; ioyned or fastened vnto, entered or put into, the staues, or side-boords, of Cask.*
Engage: m. *A pledge, pawne, gage, ingagement.*
Engagé: m. ée: f. *Ingaged, impledged, pawned.*
Engagement: m. *A pawning, ingaging, impledging, laying to pawne.*
Engager. *To pawne, impledge, ingage, to lay to pawne, or to pledge.*
Engageur: m. *A pledger, ingager, pawner.*
Engageure: f. *as* Engagement.
Engaigne: f. *A wyle, deceit, sleight, craft, fraude.*
Engaigné. *as* Engigné. ¶Pic: *also, egged vrged, prouoked.*
Engaigner. *To cosen, gull, deceiue; also, to charme, or inchaunt; also, to eg, incite, set on, prouoke.*
Engain: m. *Anger, choller;* ¶Pic: *also, a deceit, wile, sleight, cosening tricke.*
Engainé: m. ée: f. *Sheathed; put into a sheath.*
Engainer. *To sheath, to put vp into the sheath.*
Engane-pastre. *The little bird called, a water-wagtayle.*
Enganer. *To deceiue; and (more particularly) a nurse to conceale her being with child; wherby she defrauds her charge of due nourishment.* ¶Langued.
Enganté: m. ée: f. *Beglouéd.*
Mitaines engantées. *Mittaines like gloues.*
Engarber. *as* Encontenancer *(but with more boldnesse, and brauerie;) also, to couer.*
Engardé: m. ée: f. *Kept, withheld, letted, hindered, stopped, stayed from; prohibited, forbidden, stinted, repressed, restrayned.*
Engarder. *To withhold, keep from; let, stop, hinder, stay; prohibite, forbid, stint, restrayne.*
Engarder la hardiesse de. *To bridle the saucinesse, curb the boldnesse, keepe downe the stomack, of.*
Engastrimyte. *That speaks out of the bellie, as one that is possessed, seemes to doe.*
Engastrimythes. *(The same) crooked-backt-men are so termed because, commonly, their voice is hollow.*
Engaunché. *as* Encaunché.
Enge *as* Engeance.
Engé: m. ée: f. *Stored, furnished, filled with th'increase, or kind of; also, growen, increased, spred farre abroad.*
De poules, & de pauvreté on en est bien tost engé. Pro: *Chickens and pouertie come on a pace.*
Engeance: f. *A breed, race, brood; the seed, or off-spring of.*
Engeancement. *A breeding, increasing, continuing the race of.*
Engeancer. *To breed, grow; increase in growth.*
Engelé: m. ée: f. *Frozen, congealed.*
Engeler. *To freeze, congeale, set an ice on.*
Engeleure: f. *A chilblane; or, the bloud-shot which cold settles, and congeales, vpon the fingers.*
Engendré: m. ée: f. *Ingendred, procreated, begotten, bred; made, caused, procured, begun.*
Engendrement: m. *An ingendring, procreating, begetting, breeding; a causing, making, procuring, beginning.*
Engendrer. *To ingender, procreate, beget, breed; cause, make, procure, begin.*
Engendreur: m. *An ingenderer, begetter, breeder; a maker, procurer, beginner of.*
Engendreure: *or* Engendrure: f. *A procreation; or as,* Engendrement.
Engeolé. *as* Enjaûlé; *also incaged, or ingaoled.*
Engeoler. *To attract, intice, allure, winne, inueagle, besot, inthrall (by faire and deceitfull words;) also, to incage, or ingaole; to put in a cage, to lay in gaole.*
Enger. *To produce, or make to grow; to store, furnish, or fill with th'increase, or kind of; also, to grow, increase, extend, or spred it selfe abroad.*
Engerbé: m. ée: f. *Bound vp together in a sheafe, as Corne.*
Engerber. *To sheafe, or bind vp (as corne) in a sheafe.*
Engeronné: m. ée: f. *Dandled on, or hugged in, the lap.*
Engeronner. *To dandle vpon the lap, as a nurse, or mother, her child.*
Engigné: m. ée: f. *Charmed, bewitched, inchaunted; also, cousened, beguiled, gulled.*
Engigner. *To charme, bewitch, inchaunt; also, to cousen, gull, deceiue, beguile.*
Engigneur: m. *A deceiuer, beguiler, cousener; also, an Inchaunter.*
Engin: m. *An engin, toole, instrument; also vnderstanding, policie, reach of wit; also, suttletie, fraud, craft, wilinesse, deceit.*
Vn homme sans mal engin. *A sincere, vpright, plane-dealing man.*
Mieux vaut engin que force. Pro: *Better be wise then strong.*
Enginé: m. ée: f. *Bewitched, incharmed, inchaunted, cousened, gulled, beguyled.*
Enginer. *as* Engigner.

Enginier: m. *An Enginer; a maker of Engins.*
Engiponné: m. ée: f. *Clothed, muffled, or lapped vp in a coat, or short cassocke; also, ragged, or, in rags.*
Englacé: m. ée: f. *Growne cold as ice.*
s'Englacer. *To wax as cold as ice.*
Englantine. *An Eglantine; Seeke* Anglantine.
Engle: f. *as* Angle; *a corner.*
Englentier. *A Sweet-brier tree.*
Engler. *To shut vp in a corner; Seeke* Angler.
Englet. *Seeke* Anglet.
Englobé: m. ée: f. *Inglobed; comprehended, or contained within the circumference of.*
Englober. *To inglobe; to comprehend, or containe within the circumference of.*
Englobure: f. *An inglobing; also, a globe-like circumference, or compasse.*
Englouti: m. ie: f. *Inglutted, ingulfed, greedily deuoured, swallowed vp.*
Engloutir. *To deuour, inglut, ingulfe, swallow vp.*
Englué: m. ée: f. *Belymed; caught, or dressed, with birdlyme.*
Engluer. *To lyme, to dresse, or catch, with birdlyme.*
Englume. *as* Enclume; *an Anuile.*
Engolfé: m. ée: f. *Ingulphed, swallowed vp in a gulfe.*
Engolfer. *To ingulfe.*
Engoncé: m. ée: f. *Pinn'd in by, or set fast in; straitned, wanting libertie, not able to stirre for; (a Metaphor from dores, which turne not well vpon their hindges.)*
Engorgé: m. ée: f. *Ingorged, rauened, deuoured, swilled vp, swallowed downe; also, choaked.*
Engorgement: m. *A glutting, rauening, deuouring, ingorging; a swallowing vp, as of a riuer by the sea; also, a choaking, or stopping the throat of; also, a giuing of a full gorge vnto.*
Engorger. *To rauen, ingorge, deuoure, glut, swill vp, swallow downe.*
Engorger le cours d'un moulin. *To choake, or stop vp, a mill with too much water.*
Engorger vn oyseau. *To giue a Hawke a full gorge.*
Engorgeur: m. *A rauener, glutton, gulch, ingorger; one that, to eat the faster, swallowes downe his meat whole.*
Engorgeux: m. euse: f. *Ingorging, rauenous, greedie, deuouring, swilling vp, swallowing downe.*
Engoüé: m. ée: f. *Choaked, stifled, strangled with too great a morsell.*
Engoüer. *as* Anoüer; *or (altogether) to choake, or stifle.*
Engouffrer. *To ingulfe.*
s'engouffrer. *A little thing violently to fall into, and vtterly be lost in (or deuoured by) a greater; as a brooke when it meets with a Riuer, or a Riuer when it comes to the sea; to sinke downe, or deepe, as into a gulfe.*
Le vent s'engouffre, & s'entonne en ce lieu là. *The wind whirles, and whizzes terribly; or hath a great strength, and makes a great noise, in that hollow place.*
Engouler. *To put into, or send downe, the throat; to deuoure, to ingorge.*
Engouleur. *A rauener; as* Engorgeur.
Engoulphé: m. ée: f. *Ingulfed; entred into, or swallowed by, a gulfe.*
Engourdi: m. ie: f. *Benummed, nummed, astonied, stupified, senceless, asleepe.*
Esprit engourdi. *A dull, and blockish wit; a wit thats deuoid of inuention.*
Engourdir. *To numme, benumme, stupifie, make sencelesse, astonish; also, to be, or grow numme, stonied, sencelesse.*
Engourdissement: m. *A benumming, or numnesse; an astonying, or sencelesnesse, a stupiditie, or dullnesse; a sleeping of any limbe, or member.*
Engourmelé: m. ée: f. *Curded, or curdled thicke.*
Sang engourmelé. *Clotted bloud.*
Engourmeler. *To curd, or curdle much; also, to thicken, or clot, as bloud when it growes cold.*
Engousté: m. ée: f. *Put in tast, brought vnto a stomacke; also, inchased, inclosed, or set into.*
Engrais de terre: m. *The manuring, or dunging of land, whereby it growes the fatter, and fitter for any vse.*
Engrais de volaille. *The franking, or fattening of fowle.*
Beufs d'engrais. *Fat Oxen, Beeues alreadie fed.*
Tenir son ventre à l'engrais. *To feed, franke, or fatten himselfe.*
Engraissant. *Fattening, franking, feeding.*
Engraissé: m. ée: f. *Fed, fattened, franked; crammed; also, marled, or manured.*
Engraissement: m. *A franking, fattening, feeding, batling; a putting, or growing into flesh, and fatnesse.*
Engraisser. *To feed, franke, fatten; to put, or bring, into flesh, and fatnesse.*
Engraisser vn champ. *To marle, manure, or dung a field; to battle it, or make it fertile.*
Le temps s'engraisse. *The weather growes thicke.*
Engraississant. *as* Engraissant.
Engraiz: m. *Looke* Engrais.
Engrand. Tu es bien engrand de trotter. *Thou wouldst faine be packing; thou longest much to be gadding, thou hast a moneths mind to be gone.*
Engrangé: m. ée: f. *Inned, or put into a barne, as corne &c.*
Engrangement: m. *An inning of corne &c; a putting, or shutting vp in a barne.*
Engranger. *To inne corne &c; to put, or shut, vp in a barne.*
Engravé: m. ée: f. *Ingrauen, carued, intailed.*
Engraver. *To ingraue, cut, carue, intaile.*
Engraveur: m. *A caruer, cutter, ingrauer, intailer.*
Engraveure: f. *An intailing, cutting, ingrauing; ingrauerie; also, a figure ingraued.*
s'Engreger. *To grow worse, become sorer, wax more painefull, grieuous, or troublesome.*
Engreigné. Porc engreigné. *A measeld Hog.*
Engrené: m. ée: f. *Ingrained; filled, or furnished with Seed, or Corne.*
Engrener. *To ingraine; to fill, or furnish with seed, corne, or graine.*
Engreslé: m. ée: f. *Ingrayled, or inuecked (a tearme of Blason.)*
Engreslure: f. *An ingrayling, or inuecking; a kind of small indenting, or iagging, in a coat of Armes.*
Engressement: m. *as* Engraissement.
Engriner. *To biggen, increase, grow greater.*
Engroigné: m. ée: f. *Sullen, powting, lowring, grunting, frowning.*
Engroin: m. *Sullennesse, powting; lowring, frowning; malice, despightfulnesse.*
Engroissi: m. ie: f. *Greatned; made, or growne big.*
Engrommelé. *Clotted, cluttered, curded thicke; gathered into knobs, or knots.*
Engrossi: m. ie: f. *Greatned, increased, inlarged, well thriuen, batled apace; growne large, become grosse, waxt great, made big.*

Engrossir vne femme. *To greaten, make great, or grosse; to get with child.*
s'Engrossir. *To thriue, increase, become grosse, grow large, wax big; to fatten, or battle apace.*
Engrossissement. *A growing, increasing; thriuing;* (de femelles) *a bagging; a being great with child, or big with young.*
Engroüé: m. ée: f. *Stopped, cloyed, or choaked vp, as the course of a water-mill, by weedes, &c; or as* Angoüé.
Pie engroüée. *A Wariangle; or a small Woodpecker, white and blacke of colour, and but halfe as big as the ordinarie greene one; called thus about* Tours.
Enguigné: m. ée: f. *Deceiued, cousened, gulled, beguiled.*
Enguigner. *To deceiue, cousen, gull, beguile.*
Enguipponné. *as* Engiponné.
Enguirlandé: m. ée: f. *Adorned, or crowned, with a garland; wearing a garland.*
Enguirlander. *To adorne, or crowne, with a garland.*
Engyronner. *To inuiron, incompasse; as* Enuironner.
Engys. *as* Aupres. ¶Rab.
Enhaillonné: m. ée: f. *Tattered, ragged, full of clouts, or of patches; wearing torne, or patched clothes.*
Enhaïr. *To hate, loath, detest.*
Enhanné. *Toyled hard, laboured extreamely, wrought vnto sweating, toyled vnto sighing.*
Enhanner. *To toyle hard, labour extreamely, or vehemently; worke till he sweat, or sigh withall.*
Enhanté: m. ée: f. *Hauing a staffe, or handle put vnto it.*
Enhanter vne pique. *To put the staffe into the head of a Pike.*
Enhardi: m. ie: f. *Heartened, animated, imboldened, incouraged; growne bold, hardie, confident.*
Ie me suis enhardi, de. *I presumed, or was so bold as.*
Enhardir. *To hearten, imbolden, animate, incourage; make hardie, giue heart vnto, put mettall into.*
s'enhardir. *To wax hardie, get heart, grow confident; also, to presume, or venture on.*
Enharnaché: m. ée: f. *Harneised; furnished, fully trapped.*
Enharnachement: m. *The harneis, or furniture; also, a harneising, of a horse.*
Enharnacher vn cheval. *To harneis a horse; to put on all his furniture.*
Enharnichement. *as* Enharnachement.
Enhasté: m. ée: f. *Spitted, put vpon a spit.*
Enhaster. *To spit, to put on the spit.*
Enhault. *Aloft, aboue;* d'enhaut. *From aboue.*
Enhazé: m. ée: f. *Very busie, keene, or eager at worke; full of imployments, that hath many yrons in the fire, or much to doe.* ¶Parisien.
Il est tout enhazé à plouvoir. *It is set to raine.*
Enherbé: m. ée: f. *Charmed, bewitched, or impoysoned, with hearbes.*
Enherbement: m. *A bewitching, or impoysoning, with hearbes.*
Enherber. *To charme, bewitch, or poyson, with hearbes.*
Enheriter aucun. *To make one his heire.*
Enheudé: m. ée: f. *Fettered, or tethered.*
Enheuder. *To fetter, tether, fasten the legs, or fasten by the leg.* ¶Brett.
Enhorner. *To tip, or nocke with horne.*
Enhort: m. *An exhortation, persuasion, request; incitement, incouragement.*
Enhorté: m. ée: f. *Exhorted, required; persuaded, aduised; incited, animated, incouraged, vnto.*
Enhortement. *as* Enhort; *also, an exhorting, requiring; persuading, aduising; inciting, incouraging vnto.*
Enhorter. *To exhort, require, desire; moue, persuade, aduise; incite, incourage, animate; stirre, or cheere vp, vnto.*
Enhorteur: m. *An exhorter, persuader; mouer, aduiser; inciter, incourager, cheerer vp, vnto.*
Enhotté: m. ée: f. *Stucke fast (as a coach, &c) in the mire.*
Enhui. *To day, this day.*
Enhuilé: m. ée: f. *Oyled; annoynted, mingled, or seasoned, with oyle.*
Enhuiler. *To oyle; to dresse, annoynt, season, mingle, bismeare, with oyle.*
Enhuiler vn homme qui meurt. *To minister the Sacrament of extreame Vnction.*
Enhydrer. *To breed many mischiefes by the cutting off of one; or many mischiefes to breed by &c.*
Enhydride. *An Adder, or water-Snake.* ¶Rab.
Enjablé: m. ée: f. *Whose Crowes are made; or, whose head is fitted for the Crowes.*
Enjabler. *To rigell a peece of caske; or, to make the Crowes; also, to make the head fit for the Crowes.*
s'Enjalouser. *To grow iealous.*
Enjambé: m. ée: f. *Strid ouer; also, incroached on.*
Enjambée: f. *A stride; or, as much ground as one can stride ouer.*
Enjambement: m. *An incroaching vpon, or, striding ouer.*
Enjamber. *To stride ouer; also, to incroach vpon; and hence;*
Enjamber sur les marches d'autruy. *To vsurpe, intrude vpon, or meddle with another mans right.*
Enjambeure: f. *as* Enjambée; *a stride.*
Enjambure. *The same.*
Enjavelé: m. ée: f. *Made, or bound vp, as corne, into Iauels.*
Enjaveler. *To make vp corne into Iauels, or Gauels.*
Enjaveleur: m. *A maker, or binder, vp of corne into Iauels.*
Enjaveliner. *To arme, or strike, with a Iaueline.*
Enjaulé: m. ée: f. *Attracted, inticed, allured, inueagled, besotted, inthralled by faire, (but deceitfull) words.*
Enjauler. *To intice, attract, allure, besot, inueagle, winne, inthrall by faire, (and deceitfull) tearmes; to cog extreamely with.*
Enjauleur: m. *A beguiler, inueagler; guller, a foisting companion, cogging marchant, cousening mate; one that by faire speech deceiues them he deales with.*
Enjauleuse: f. *An inticing huswife.*
s'Enjaunir. *To wax yellow.*
Enjeoller. *as* Enjauler, *or* Engeoler.
En-jeu. vn en. *A stake at play.*
Enig. *With.* ¶Alleman. ¶Rab.
Enigmatique: com. *Enigmaticall; obscure, mysticall, hard to be vnderstood.*
Enigme: m. *A riddle; a darke question, an obscure, and mysticall demaund.*
Enjobeliné: m. ée: f. *Besotted, gulled, abused, brought into a fooles Paradise.*
Enjobeliner. *To deceiue, besot, bring into a fooles Paradise; to gull, to abuse.*
Enjoinct: m. cte: f. *Inioyned, commaunded, appointed to be done.*
Enjoincté: m. ée: f. Bas enjoincté. *Low ioynted.*
Enjoindre. *To inioyne, ordaine, appoint, or commaund a thing to be done.*

Enjoler. *as* Enjauler. *To deceiue, or besot with faire words.*
Enjolivement: m. *Neatnesse, finenesse, comelinesse, handsomenesse, gallantnesse, curiositie (in attire.)*
Enjoliver. *To decke, adorne, pranke, trim; to make neat, fine, gallant, handsome.*
Enjoliveure: f. *A decking, pranking, trimming; attiring; also, an attire.*
Enjolleur: m. *as* Enjauleur.
Enjonché: m. ée: f. *Strewed, bedecked, or set out, with greene rushes, fresh hearbes, or prettie flowers.*
Enjoncher. *To strew, imbellish, or deck; as with greene rushes, prettie flowers, fresh hearbes.*
Enjoüé: m. ée: f. *Chuffie, full-cheeked, swolne-cheeked; also, lecherous, lasciuious, wanton; blithe, iocond, frolicke.*
Enjoyaller. *To beiewell; to decke, furnish, inrich, with iewels.*
Enjuvencé: m. ée: f. *Made young, or youthfull.*
Enjuvencer. *To make youthfull, young, lustie, frolicke.*
Enixe: com. *Earnest, indeuoring, labouring hard.*
Enlacé: m. ée: f. *Snarled, intangled, insnared.*
Enlacer. *To snarle, intangle, insnare.*
Enlaidi: m. ie: f. *Growne foule, ouglie, illfauored, filthie, sluttish, disfigured, out of fauour.*
Enlaidir. *To make foule, ouglie, illfauored; to disfigure, defile, distaine.*
Enlaidissant. *Disfiguring, defiling, making foule.*
Enlaidissement: m. *A disfiguring, or defiling; a making foule, ouglie, loathsome to the eye.*
Enlanguagé. Bien en. *An eloquent, or well spoken man.*
Enlassé: m. ée: f. *Hard-knit, strait-bound; also, insnarled, intangled.*
Enlassement: m. *A strait knitting, or binding; also, an intangling, insnarling, insnaring.*
Enlevé. *Swollen; lifted, raised vp; also, conueyed, or caried away.*
Imagette enlevée. *A small imbossed image.*
Enlevement: m. *A lifting, raising, or heauing vp; also, a conueying, or carrying away.*
Enlever. *To lift, heaue, raise vp; also, to take, conuey, or carrie away (by force &c.)*
Enleveure: f. *as* Enlevement; *a swelling, rising, puffing, raising vp of.*
Enleveure d'un os. *An extraordinarie, and vnnaturall swelling of a bone in any part thereof.*
Enlié: m. eé: f. *Bound, or knit vp together.*
Enlier. *To bind, or knit vp together.*
Enlignagé. Bien en. *Of a good kinred, very well allyed, of a great house.*
Enlissé: m. ée: f. *Smoothed, slecked.*
Enlisseure: f. *A smoothing, or sleeking;* Seeke Parer.
Enlourdi: m. ie: f. *Growne dull, sottish, lumpish, beanie-headed, lob-like.*
Enluminé: m. ée: f. *Cleered, brightened, inlightened, illuminated; sleeked, burnished; also, limned.*
Visage enluminé. *The flusht, or fierie countenance of one that hath taken, or vses to take, a pot too much.*
Enluminer. *To illuminate, inlighten, cleere, brighten, illustrate; also to sleeke, or burnish; also, to limne.*
Enlumineur de livres. *A burnisher of bookes; (we call one that coloureth, or painteth vpon Paper, or Parchement, an Alluminer.)*
Enlumineure: f. *A burnishing, or sleeking; also, a limning.*
Ennasin. *Belonging to the nose.*
Ennassé: m. ée: f. *Intrapped, inclosed, imprisoned, or caught, as fish in a weele.*
s'Ennasser. *To be inthralled, imprisoned, intrapped, inclosed, or caught, as fish in a weele, (which is easily entred, but hardly got out of.)*
Ennazé: m. ée: f. *Put on the nose.*
Ennazer. *To put on the nose.*
Enneigé. *Full of snow.*
Ennelé. Iambes ennelées. *Baker-legs.*
Ennemi: m. *An enemie, a foe, an aduersarie.*
Il n'est nuls petis ennemis: Pro. *No enemie can be tearmed little: the least enemie is too great for him that loueth peace.*
Qui passe vn iour d'hyuer; il passe vn de ses ennemis mortels: Pro. *Looke* Passer.
Ennemie: f. *A shee-foe.*
Ennicroché: m. ée: f. *Hooked, intangled, inwrapped, or wrought one within another.* ¶Rab.
Enniellé. *Blasted, as corne, &c.*
s'Enniellér. *Corne, vines, or fruits, to be blasted.*
Ennobli: m. ie: f. *Ennobled, nobilitated, made noble, made a gentleman (most properly meant of one that hath bought his Gentrie of the French King, who makes many such Gentlemen when he wants money.)*
Ennoblir. *To ennoble, nobilitate, make noble.*
Ennoblissement: m. *An ennobling, nobilitating, making noble, or of gentle bloud.*
Ennoirci: m. ie: f. *Blacked, growne blacke, made blacke.*
Ennoircir. *To blacke; to make blacke; also, to wax blacke.*
Ennombré: m. ée: f. *Enumerated, numbred out; told, or counted ouer.*
Ennombrer. *To enumerate, or number out; to tell, or count ouer.*
Ennossé. *Almost choaked with a bone;* Seeke Enossé.
Ennoüé: m. ée: f. *Tyed vp, or on a knot.*
Ennoüer. *To make a knot, or ty on a knot.*
Ennoye: f. *A certaine venemous worme, which going both wayes, and hauing (as a ground-worme) her head, and tayle of one bignesse, is said to haue two heads.*
Ennuagé: m. ée: f. *Ouerclouded, ouershadowed with a cloud.*
Ennuager. *To ouercloud; or ouershadow, as with a cloud.*
s'Ennuër. *To wax cloudie, as the skie before ill weather.*
Ennuicté: m. ée: f. *Benighted; turned into night.*
Ennuicter. *To benight, make night, turne into night;* Looke Anuicter.
Ennuicti: m. ie: f. *Benighted.*
Ennuy: m. *Annoy; vexation, trouble, disquiet, molestation; sorrow, griefe, anguish; wearisomenesse, tediousnesse, irkesomenesse; importunitie; a loathing, or sacietie, of; a discontentment, or offence, at.*
Ennuyé: m. ée: f. *Annoyed; vexed, disquieted, molested, grieued, afflicted; wearied, loathed, ouer-much importuned; offended at, or discontented with.*
Ennuyer. *To annoy; vex, trouble, disquiet, molest; discontent, grieue, afflict, offend; wearie, loath, irke, distast; importune ouer-much.*
Ennuyeux: m. euse: f. *Troublesome, displeasing, offensiue; grieuous; loathsome, wearisome, tedious, irksome; distastfull; most importunate.*
Les mauvais Musiciens ne sont iamais ennuyeux à eux mesmes. *Harsh voices neuer are vnpleasing to themselues; or, men seldome grow wearie of their owne iarring.*
Enny. *as* Ennoye.

Enom-

Enombragé : m. ée : f. *Ouershadowed; or as* Enombré.
Enombrager. *To shadow, couer, cloke, hide, cast a mist ouer.*
Enombré. *Shadowed, ouershadowed; couered, or hidden, with, or vnder, the shadow of.*
Enombrer. *as* Enombrager.
Enoncé : m. ée : f. *Signified, declared, denounced, published, pronounced.*
Enoncer. *as* Annoncer.
Enondé : m. ée : f. *Waued; wrought, floating, or shining, like waues.*
Enordi : m. ie : f. *Defiled, polluted, berayed.*
Enordir. *To defile, pollute, beray himselfe.*
Enorgueilli : m. ie : f. *Made loftie, become proud.*
Enorgueillir. *To make loftie, or proud; to puffe, or swell vp the mind; to giue, or bring presumption vnto.*
Enorme : com. *Huge, excessiue, vnmeasurable, enormous; exceeding great; disordered, immoderate; hainous, most wicked.*
Enormément. *Enormously, hainously, vnmeasurably, excessiuely, without measure, much amisse, farre out of square.*
Enormissime. *Most enormous, or hainous; most wicked, most excessiue.*
Enormité : f. *An enormitie, hainousnesse; great iniquitie, or wickednesse; extreame want of measure, moderation, order.*
Enortié : m. ée : f. *Netled, benetled; stung, pricked, rubbed ouer, with nettles.*
Enortier. *To nettle, or benettle; to sting, pricke, rub ouer, with nettles.*
Enossé. *Choaked with a bone; also, hauing a bone in his throat; also, hauing a bone taken out of his throat; also, rooted, or setled in the bones.*
Enoyselé : m. ée : f. *Fed with, or fleshed vpon, birds, as a Hawke.*
Enperruqué. *Looke* Emperruqué.
Enquaissé : m. ée : f. *Inchested; put, or packed vp, into a chest.*
Enquaisser. *To inchest; to put into, or pack vp in, a chest, or case.*
Enquant. *as* Inquant.
Enquantellé. baston bien enquantellé de fer. *A staffe well piked, or well grained, with yron.*
Enquenouiller de filace. *To draw a distaffe.*
Enquerir. *To inquire, aske, demaund, make search, or inquisition after.*
Il ne faut pas enquerir d'ou soit l'homme, le vin, & le dit; mais qu'il soit bon. *Looke* Homme, Vin, &, Dit.
Enquerquenner. *To yoke swine.*
Enquerre. *as* Enquerir.
Enqueste : f. *An Inquest, Inquisition, search, inquirie, examination, or questioning with; also, the testimonie, or deposition of witnesses.*
Enqueste d'establissement. *A request, or a writ, for the establishing of a possession.*
Les chambres des enquestes. *Looke* Chambre.
s'Enquester. *To search, examine, inquire, question, aske, make inquisition after.*
Enquesteur : m. *A searcher, examiner, demaunder, questioner, inquisitor; a Iuror.*
Enracinable : com. *Rootable, fit to take root.*
Enraciné : m. ée : f. *Rooted, grounded, or setled in.*
Enracinement : m. *A rooting, or taking root.*
Enraciner. *To settle, to root in a thing; to inracinate; also, to root, or take root.*
Enragé : m. ée : f. *Enraged, raging, madde, wood, franticke, furious, outragious, besides himselfe, out of his little wits.*
Chien enragé ne peut longuement vivre : Prov. *A madde Dogge liues not, violent humors last not, long.*
Vn fol vn enragé : Prov. *Once a foole euer madde; or there's little difference betweene a foole & a madde man.*
Vilain affamé, demy enragé : Prov. *Barre a clowne of his victualls, you halfe madde him.*
Enragemént : m. *Rage, inraging; madnesse, furie, frenzie; felnesse; outragiousnesse.*
Enragémènt. *Ragingly, madly, woodly, franticklу, furiously, outragiously, Bedlam-like.*
Enrager. *To rage; raue, storme, play the Bedlam, fare like a madde-man, be starke madde.*
Enrailler. *as* Esrailler; *To stare.*
Enramé : m. ée : f. *Stucke, or set thicke with boughes; also, pearched, mounted, or got vpon a bough.*
Enramement : m. *A laying, or spreading of boughes; a pearching, leaping, skipping, mounting, or climbing on boughes.*
Enramer. *To lay, sticke, or spread boughes.*
s'Enramer. *To pearch, or take a stand in a bough; to leape, mount, or climbe vpon boughes.*
Enranci : m. ie : f. *Growne mustie, fustie, restie.*
Enrancir. *To grow mustie, fustie, restie.*
Enraqué : m. ée : f. *Bemired, or sticking in the mire:* ¶Pic.
Enrassé. *as* Enragé. *Starke madde:* ¶Rab.
Enrayé : m. ée : f. *Stayed, or held backe, as a wheele by a Trigger.*
Enrayer vne roue. *To stay, or hold a wheele backe with a Trigger.*
Enrayoir : m. *The wheele-gate, or beame, that stoppeth the course of a water-mill; also, a Trigger, the staffe thats put before a cart-wheele, to keepe it from ouerthrowing, or ouer-hastie going.*
Enregistrable : com. *Fit to be registred, or enrolled.*
Enregistré : m. ée : f. *Registred, enrolled.*
Enregistrement : m. *A registring, or enrolling.*
Enregistrer. *To register, to inroll.*
Enrencé : m. ée : f. *Growne mustie, fustie, restie.*
Enrethé : m. ée : f. *Caught, intangled, insnared, inwrapped, in a net.*
Enrether. *To catch, intangle, insnare, inwrap, in a net.*
Enrheumé : m. ée : f. *Troubled with the rhewme, pose, or murre.*
Enrichi : m. ie : f. *Inriched, made wealthie.*
Il n'est orgueil que de povre enrichi : Prov. *No man's so surlie as th'inriched begger.*
Vilain enrichi ne connoit parent, ni ami : Prov. *Looke* Vilain.
Enrichir. *To inrich, to make wealthie.*
Enrichir vn conte. *To amplifie, enlarge, adde vnto, it.*
Qui s'acquite s'enrichit : Prov. *Looke* Acquiter.
Enrichisseure : f. *An inrichment; an inriching.*
Enrimé : m. ée : f. *as* Enrheumé.
Enrimer. *To get the rhewme, the murre, the pose.* (v.m.)
Enroché : m. ée : f. *Made rockie, turned into a rocke.*
Enrocher. *To make rockie, to turne into a rocke.*
Enrocheur. tonnelier enrocheur. *as* Encaveur.
Enroidi : m. ie : f. *Growne stiffe; become obstinate.*

s'Enroidir. *To grow stiffe; to become obstinate.*
Enrolié: m. ée: f. *Inrolled, registred; mustered, among others.*
Enrollement. *An inrolling.*
Enroiler. *To enroll, to register; to muster, enter, or put names, &c, into a booke, or bill.*
Enrollement: m. *as* Enrollement.
Enrotulé: m. ée: f. *Inrolled; set downe in a roll.*
Enrotuler. *To inroll, to couch, or passe in a roll among others.*
Enroüé: m. ée: f. *Hoarse, whizzing, or wheazing, of a broken sound.*
Enrouëment: m. *Hoarsenesse, wheazing.*
Enroüément. *Hoarsly, or as one that wheazes.*
s'Enrouër. *To grow hoarse, to get the Murre, or Pose; to wheaze, to yeeld a broken, and vnpleasing sound.*
Enrouëure: f. *as* Enrouëment.
Enrouillé: m. ée: f. *Rustie, rusted, cankered.*
s'Enrouiller. *To rust, to canker.*
Enrouilleure. f. *Rust, canker, rustinesse of mettalls.*
Enroulé. *Seeke* Enrollé.
Enrouler. *as* Enroller.
Enroullir les yeux. *To roll the eyes; to stare, gaze, or looke about him amazedly, or madly.*
Enroupié. *Snottie, besniueled, dropping at the nose.*
Enrousé. *as* Arrousé.
Enrouser. *To water, to bedeaw; as* Arrouser.
Enruché: m. ée: f. *Inhiued, put into hiues, abiding in a hiue.*
Enrucher. *To inhiue, or put into a hiue.*
s'Enruisseler. *To runne out in, or to diuide it selfe into, little streames, brookes, channels.*
Ens. *In, within, inward.*
Faire venir les deniers du Roy ens. *To gather, and send vp the Kings money into th'Exchequer.*
Ensablé: m. ée: f. *Filled, strawed, or couered with sand; also, runne, or split, as a ship, on the sands.*
Ensabler. *To fill, couer, or strow with sand; also, to split, or runne on the sands, as a ship.*
Ensablonner. *To besprinkle, strow, or fill with grauell, or great sand.*
Ensaché: m. ée: f. *Insachelled, impoaked, put vp into a bag, sachell, or poake.*
Ensacher. *To poake vp; to put into a bagge, sacke, or poake.*
Ensafrané: m. ée: f. *Besaffroned; mingled or seasoned, stained or coloured, with Saffron.*
Ensafranner. *To mingle, season, dresse, or furnish; to die, staine, colour, or paint ouer, with saffron.*
Ensagi: m. ie: f. *Growne sage, made wise.*
Ensagir. *To grow sage, or wise; to wax aduised.*
Ensaisiné: m. ée: f. *Fully seised; put into absolute possession of.*
Ensaisinement: m. *An inseisining; a deliuerie of, or putting into, possession.*
Ensaisiner. *To giue seisin, or a seisure; to put into full possession of.*
Ensalli: m. ie: f. *Defiled, fouled, polluted; made nastie, growne filthie.*
Ensallir. *To defile, foule, pollute; infect; corrupt; make nastie, beastlie, filthie.*
Ensallissement: m. *A filing, defiling, polluting; infecting corrupting.*
Ensanglanté: m. ée: f. *Bebloudied; imbrued with, died, in bloud.*
Ensanglanter. *To bebloudie, to make bloudie; to die in bloud; to imbrue, or besprinkle with gore.*
Ensaqué: m. ée: f. *Put into a sacke, or wallet.*
Ensaquer. *To put vp into a sacke, or wallet.*
Ensavonné: m. ée: f. *Besoaped; washed, or done ouer, with soape.*
Ensavonner. *To besoape; to wash or lather in, to annoint or bismeare with, sope.*
Ensceptré: m. ée: f. *Wearing, or bearing, a Scepter; possessed of a Scepter.*
Enscophionné: m. ée: f. *Coifed, wearing a cawle, or coife.*
Enseigne: m. *An Ensigne, Auntient, Standard-bearer; He that, in warre, carries the Colours of a Companie of foot.*
Enseigne: f. *A signe, token, marke, note, badge, argument, or presumption of a thing; a print, trace, or tract to find it out by; also, an Ensigne, Standard, or Banner; the Colours vnder which a Band, or Companie of footmen serue; also, the Band, or Companie it selfe; also, a Signe hung out at a doore; also, a Jewell (giuen.)*
'A bonnes enseignes. *Truely, throughly, for a certaine, in good earnest, not onely in shew.*
'A fausses enseignes. *Fainedly, falsly, counterfeitly, by forged markes, or tokens; onely for a colour.*
Coucher à l' enseigne de l' estoille. *To lie without doores all night.*
Enseigné: m. ée: f. *Taught, instructed, lessoned; ordered, fashioned, trained vp; directed, shewed, pointed out vnto.*
Enseignement: m. *A teaching, instruction, document, precept, institution, doctrine; lesson, or example set; a discipling, ordering, fashioning, directing, or trayning vp.*
Les Enseignements d' vn procez. *Instructions, Bookes, Euidences, Instruments, Authorities.*
Enseigner. *To teach, to instruct; to giue precepts, to set lessons to; to direct, shew, marke, point, or trace out vnto; also, to fashion, or traine vp.*
Enseigneur: m. *A Teacher, or Instructer; and, (more particularly,) the Vsher of a Free-schoole; also, the first finger, pointing finger, or fore-finger.*
Enseigneurié. *Inseignorized, made Lord, or owner of.*
Ensel. *Sword-like, of a sword.*
Cautere ensel. *See* Cautere.
Ensellé: m. ée: f. *Saddle-backt; also, sadled.*
Enseller vn cheval. *To saddle a horse; (a word seldome vsed.)*
Ensemble. *Also, likewise; with, withall, ioyntly, together, one with another, one in companie of another; also, one against th'other.*
Nous sommes bien ensemble. *We are good friends; or well met; also (angerly) I care as little as you.*
Ensemblement. *Together, one with another, ioyntly; all, or both at once; as well th'one as th'other.*
Ensemencé: m. ée: f. *Sowed, seeded; furnished with seed.*
Ensemencement: m. *A sowing, seeding, or furnishing with seed.*
Ensemencer. *To sow; to set, or furnish with seed.*
Ensement. *Likewise; as* Semblablement. (v. m.)
Ensencement. *as* Encensement.
Ensepvelir. *Seeke* Ensevelir.
Ensepulturé: m. ée: f. *Buried, intombed, laied in a Sepulchre.*
Ensepulturer. *To lay in a Tombe, or Sepulchre.*
Ensepenté. *Full of Serpents, couered with Serpents.*
Enserré: m. ée: f. *Closed, inclosed, locked, or shut, fast vp; kept close, held hard in; straitned, restrained, sore pressed, neere pinched.*
Enserrement: m. *A closing, or shutting fast vp; a keeping, or*

or hold close in.
Enserrer. *To close, inclose, locke, or shut, fast vp; keepe close, hold hard in; straiten, restraine, presse verie sore, pinch verie neere.*
Enseveli: m. ie: f. *Buried, intombed, interred, layed in graue.*
Homme endormi corps enseveli: Prov. *Looke* Endormi.
Ensevelir. *To burie, interre, intombe, lay in a graue; also, to wrap vp a dead coarse in a winding-sheet.*
Ensoigne. *An Essoine; a lawfull excuse for an absent, or, good cause of discharge for an impotent, person.*
Ensoigner. *To Essoine; to excuse an absent, or discharge an impotent, person:* ¶Wallon.
Ensoing; & Ensoingne. *as* Ensoigne.
Ensoitte. *A Shooe-makers taching-end; or hogs bristle.*
Ensoitter. *To dresse, or furnish with hogs bristles.*
Ensongnie, & Ensonie. *as* Ensoigne.
Ensorcelé: m. ée: f. *Charmed, inchaunted, bewitched, forspoken.*
Ensorcelement: m. *A bewitching, inchaunting, charming, forspeaking.*
Ensorceler. *To charme, inchaunt, bewitch, forspeake, forelooke, eye-bite.*
Ensorcelerie: f. *Witchcrie, Sorcerie, forspeaking, eye-biting.*
Ensorceleur: m. *A Witch, Charmer, Inchaunter, Sorcerer.*
Ensoufflé: m. ée: f. *Blowen, gently puffed, or breathed; also, breathing, gently puffing, or blowing.*
Ensoulfré: m. ée: f. *Insulphured; mingled, perfumed, or dressed, with Sulpher.*
Ensoulfrer. *To insulpher; to dresse, mingle, fill, or perfume, with brimstone.*
Ensouple: m. *A Weauers Yarne-beame.*
Ensoupleau: m. *A Weauers Cloth-beame.*
Enstocatte. *A field enclosed with pikes, and appointed for a single combat, by permission of the Prince, or of his Lieutenant Generall.*
Ensuairé: m. ée: f. *Wound vp, as a coarse in a sheet.*
Ensuairer. *To wind a coarse in a sheet; also, to wipe with, or lap in, a handkercher; &c.*
Ensuble de tisseran. *A Weauers beame; that wherewith he makes his threads to close together; or, as* Ensouple.
Ensuccré: m. ée: f. *Sugarie, besugared; sweetned, or seasoned, with sugar.*
Vne ensuccrée. *A nice, coy, quaint wench; one that euer minces it, euer makes it goodlie.*
Ensuccrer. *To besugar; to sweeten, or season with sugar.*
Ensué: m. ée: f. *Sowed vp.*
Ensuer: *To sow vp; or, as* Ensuerer.
Ensuerer. *To wind a coarse in a sheet, &c; as* Ensuairer.
Ensuyvant. *Following, succeeding, next after.*
Ensuyvi: m. ie: f. *Followed, pursued, runne after; or come next vnto; also, imitated, or emulated.*
Ensuyvre. *To follow, pursue, runne, or chase after; also, to imitate, or emulate.*
S' ensuyvre. *To insue, succeed, follow, come immediately after, or vpon.*
Qui s' enfuit on l' ensuit: Prov. *Such as flie are followed.*
Entablature: f. *An Intablature; or, as* Entablement.
Entablé: m. ée: f. *Boorded, planked; seeled.*
Entablement: m. *A boording, or planking; a ioyning, or closing of boords; a couering, or seeling with boords; also, seeling, wainscot, boord-worke; any thing made (onely) of boords; or a close lay, course, or frame of boords vpon, or ouer, a thing; also, as* Vireson.
Entablement d' vn pilier. *The (square) foot, or Base of a piller.*
Entaché: m. ée: f. *Spotted, stained, soyled; polluted, corrupted, tainted; touched with, or guiltie of, an offence.*
Entacher. *To spot; staine, defile, taint, infect; pollute, corrupt.*
Entacher vne besongne. *To vndertake, or take vpon him &c.*
Entacheure: f. *A spot; also, a spotting; also, a stayning; tainting, or taint; a vicious marke.*
Entail: m. *A mortaise, or incutting.*
Entaillé: m. ée: f. *Intailed, carued, grauen, cut.*
Entailler. *To intaile, graue, carue, cut in.*
Entailleur: m. *A caruer, grauer, cutter, intailer.*
Entailleure: f. *A caruing, grauing, incutting, intailing; also, a cut, gash, or garse.*
Entalenté: m. ée: f. *Much desiring, affecting, or longing after, hauing a great mind, or appetite vnto.*
Mal entalenté envers. *Ill affected towards, spighting, bearing a grudge vnto.*
Entalenter. *To breed a longing, imprint a desire in; beget an affection, giue a great appetite, vnto.*
Entamé: m. ée: f. *Cut, opened, or broken, vp; (alreadie) begun, or tasted of; also, exulcerated, wounded, hurt; violated; marde, spoyled.*
Entamer. *To cut, open, or breake vp; to begin vnto; to tast, or take an essay of; also, to violate, marre, spoyle, wound, hurt.*
Entamer l' honnesteté. *To disgrace, depraue, or detract from; to hurt the good name of.*
Entamer le pas. *To begin; to lead the daunce, or breake the yce, vnto; to make an ouerture vnto.*
Entamer le peau. *To exulcerate, breake, or cut, the skinne.*
Entameure: f. *A cutting, opening, breaking vp; a beginning, or ouerture; an assay taken of; also, an exulcerating, hurting, wounding; violating, marring.*
Entant que. *Seeing that, in as much, or forasmuch, as.*
Entant qu' en moy est. *With all my meanes, as far as I can, as much as lieth in me.*
Entassé: m. ée: f. *Heaped, packed, piled, laied vp together, or one vpon th' other.*
Entassement: m. *A heaping, piling, packing, laying vp together, or one vpon another.*
Entasser. *To heape, packe, pile, lay vp together, or one vpon another; to exaggerate, gather in heapes, add heape vnto heape.*
Entasseur: m. *A heaper, or piler vp of.*
Ente: f. *A graffe.*
Enté: m. ée: f. *Graffed; ingraffed; fixed, fastened, or setled, in.*
Entelechie: f. *Absolute perfection, or efficacie; perfect motion, or essence; force mouing of it selfe; also, as* Endelechie.
Entellectual: m. ale: f. *Intellectuall, belonging to the vnderstanding.*
Entement: m. *A graffing; a fastening, or setling in.*
Entendement: m. *Vnderstanding, apprehension, conceit; iudgement; intelligence; naturall knowledge.*
Mettre son entendement à. *To giue his mind to, set his wit on; addict, or applie himselfe vnto; to intend, or attend, with diligence.*

Entendeur: m. *An vnderstander, concciuer, apprehender.*

Entendible: com. *Concciuable, intelligible, vnderstandable, plaine, euident.*

Entendiblement. *Plainely, perspicuously, intelligibly; so as it may be vnderstood with ease; also learnedly, sencibly, vnderstandingly, with good iudgement.*

Entendoire. *as* Entendement.

Entendre. *To vnderstand, conceiue, apprehend, perceiue, iudge of; also, to learne, or heare; to haue notice, get intelligence, come by the knowledge of.*

Entendre à. *To studie, mind, heed, care for, looke to; addict, apply, or giue, himselfe vnto.*

Il entend le numero. *He is throughly acquainted with the matter.*

Il n' en entend que le haut Alleman. *He vnderstands not a iot, hee is vtterly ignorant, of it.*

I' en feray comme ie l'entendray. *I wil doe as I see cause.*

Tu l' entens mal. *You are much mistaken, you take your marks amisse, you make a wrong interpretation of the matter.*

S' entendre avec. *To practise vnder-hand, haue secret intelligence, be in league and friendship, hould priuate correspondencie, with.*

Qui mal entend mal respond. Pro: *He that vnderstands wrong answers awry.*

Entends-tu. *Looke* Enten-tu.

Entend-trois. *An equiuocation of doubtfull, or double meaning.*

Il fait de l' entend-trois. *He answers (of purpose from the purpose,) as though he vnderstood not the question; or, he seemes to listen to somewhat else; or, makes as if he had three to answere at once, and therefore cannot satisfie euery one.*

Entendu: m. uë: f. *Vnderstood, conceiued, apprehended, perceiued; also, wise, cunning, wittie, skilfull, expert, knowne, well seene or experienced, in.*

Entendu que. *Seing, or considering that; now that, in as much as.*

Entenne: f. *A sayle-yard.*

Entente: f. *Intention, purpose, meaning; mind, fancie, will, affection; diligence, indeauour; also, as* Entendement.

Respondre à deux ententes. *To answer equiuocally, doubly, ambiguously, doubtfully.*

Ententif: m. iue: f. *Busie, earnest, intentiue, studious, diligent, vehemently set or bent vpon, firmely resolued, constantly disposed vnto.*

Ententivement. *Intentiuely, busily, earnestly; attentiuely, carefully, heedfully.*

Enten-tu: m. *Wit, conceit, vnderstanding, apprehension.*

'A bon enten-tu il ne fault qu' un demy mot: Prov. *A good wit needs but one word to informe it; or, a wise man pickes whole sence from halfe a word.*

Entenu. ie vous suis fort entenu. *I am very much beoulden to you.*

Enteprinse. *as* Entreprinse; *An enterprise.*

Enter. *To graffe; also, to fasten, settle, or fix, in.*

Enter en Canon. *To lodge a short graffe (cut off with some more barke at the foote then needes to couer it,) within the tender barke of a shoote, or branch, thats little bigger then the graffe it selfe.*

Enter au Coin. *To graffe within a cleft made in the top of a Stock; (the ordinarie fashion.)*

Enter en cornuchet; *as*, Enter en Canon.

Enter en petite couronne. *To graffe betweene the barke and the tree; much after the fashion of*, Enter en Canon; *but with this difference, that the graffe must be lodged within the thick bark of a well-grown tree.*

Enter en escusson. *Looke*, Escusson.

Enter en fente. *To graffe within a cleft made in the top of a Stock; (our ordinarie fashion.)*

Enter en flusteau. *as*, Enter en Canon.

Enter à la hanede. *as*, Enter en perche.

Enter un oeillet. *To fasten a bud with clay in the bark of a tree.*

Enter en perche. *To graffe in a willow pole; take a good big branch of willow, or of any other soft wood; pearce it with a wimble vnto the pith in (seuerall places at least halfe a foot asunder; put into each hole a graffe, well closed at the foot (to keepe out water) then lay your pole along in the earth, and couer it ouer, leauing onely some two inches of each graffe to peere, & spread, aboue ground: of the substance of this pole (which quickly takes roote) they being nourished, within three or foure yeares grow prettie trees; then is it taken vp, & with a saw parted among them, to serue to root them in the next ground they are set in.*

Enter en poupeé. *To lodge a graffe within a cleft made in the top of a Stocke.*

Enter en tuyau: *as*, Enter en Canon.

Enteriné: m. ée: f. *Admitted, allowed, approued of; confirmed, consented vnto; absolutely passed, wholly granted, and thereupon fully executed, obtained, or accomplished.*

Enterinement: m. *An absolute admitting, allowing, approuing, letting passe; a full graunt, or confirmation, followed by th' effect, or execution thereof; for it also imports (more then a bare approbation) an accomplishment; or, at least, a decree for it.*

Enteriner. *To admit, approue, allow of; to let passe; yeeld consent, or giue confirmation, vnto, and thereupon to effect, execute, accomplish; or iudge, and pronounce fit to be effected, executed, accomplished.*

Enterrage: m. *as* Enterrement.

Enterré: m. ée: f. *Interred, buried, layed in a graue; hid in the earth, put into the ground, couered ouer with mould.*

Auiourd'uy en terre demain enterré: Pro: *Looke*, Terre.

Enterrement: m. *An interring, burying, buriall; also, a graue, sepulcher, or place of buriall.*

Enterrer. *To interre, burie, lay in a graue; to hide in the earth, couer ouer with mould, put into the ground.*

Enterreur: m. *An Interrer, or burier.*

Entesté: m. ée: f. *Buzzed into th' eares, put into the head of; made heauie headed; also, put on the head, or, whereinto the head is put.*

Entester. *To trouble, or make heauie, the head; to breed, or bring, the headach; also, to put (an opinion, or conceit) into the head; also, to put the head into, or put a thing on the head.*

Entesteure: f. *A troubling, or making of the head very heauie; a breeding, or bringing, of the headach; also, a putting of the head into; or putting vpon the head; a hooding; also, a hole to put the head through.*

Enteur: m. *A graffer.*

Enteure: f. *A graffing.*

Enteyser son arc iusques à l' oreille. *To drawe his bowe vp to his eare.* v. m.

Enthroné: m. ée: f. *Inthronized, placed in a throne.*

Enthroner. *To inthronize, or set in a throne.*

Enthusiasme: m. *A rauishment of the spirit; diuine motion, or inspiration; poeticall furie.*

Enthyrsé: m. ée: f. *Decked, stucke thicke, wrapped about, with Ivie.*

Entiché: m. ée: f. *Tainted; faultie, vnsound, corrupt, corrupted, polluted; or, as* Entaché; *spotted, &c.*

Entier: m. *A graffing, or graffed stocke; also, a plot, or nurserie of graffed, or graffing stockes.*

Entier: m. ere: f. *Intire, whole, solide, sound; full; inuiolate; vnbroken; strong, firme, steadfast; assured, faithfull; also, vpright, sincere, honest, vnpartiall, iust; also, fast, constant, stiffe, obstinate in his opinion, whom nothing can remoue, no reasons disswade, from a conceit once taken.*

Cheval entier. *A stone-horse; also, a horse that turns vnwillingly, or is not pliant to his turne.*

Entiercé: m. ée: f. *Sequestred, into a third hand:* ¶Orleannois.

Entiercement: m. *A sequestration, sequestring, or putting into a third hand.*

Entiercer. *To sequester, or put into a third hand.*

Entierement. *Intirely, wholly, fully, soundly, throughly, altogether; strongly, firmely, steadfastly, faithfully; vprightly, iustly, sincerely, honestly, vncorruptly.*

Entiereté: f. *Entirenesse, wholenesse, soliditie, soundnesse; also, honestie, integritie, sinceritie, vprightnesse; also, constancie, or obstinacie, in an opinion.*

Entimbraillé. *That beares a deuice on the top, or flourish hanging from the top, of his helmet.*

Entimbré. *as* Entimbraillé.

Entiquer. *To cleaue, or sticke fast like a Ticke.*

Entoilé: m. ée: f. *Made of, or furnished with, linnen, or canuas; also, intangled, or caught, in toyles.*

Entoiler. *To make of linnen, to furnish, or garnish with, linnen cloth, or canuas; also, to intangle, or catch in toyles; or, to compasse, or hemme in with toiles.*

Entoisé: m. ée: f. *Bent, as a bow; lift vp, as a sword readie to execute, or strike.*

Entoiser vn arc. *To bend a bow.*

Entoiser vne espée. *To lift vp a sword with an intention to strike.*

Entombé: m. ée: f. *Intombed, laied in a Sepulchre.*

Entomber. *To intombe, interre, lay in a Sepulchre.*

Entombi: m. ie: f. *Stonied, benummed, clumpse, asleepe.*

Entommeure. *as* Entoumeure; *or, as* Entonnoir.

Enton. *A little graffe.*

Entonnage: m. *Tunnage, tunning.*

Entonnelé. *Tunned, put into caske.*

Entonnelement: m. *A tunning; or putting of liquor into caske.*

Entonneler. *To tunne (by a funnell.)*

Entonné: m. ée: f. *Singing, sounding, resounding; also, sung, tuned, or sounded; also, tunned, or put into a vessell with a funnell.*

Entonnement. *A sounding, or singing; also, a tuning, or giuing of a tune.*

Entonner. *as* Entonneler; *Also, to tune, sing, chaunt it; sound, resound; and most properly, to begin, or giue a tune, in singing &c.*

Entonnoir: m. *A funnell, or tunning-dish.*

Entonnoir matrical. *An instrument vsed for th' infusion of medicines into the matrix; it may be also vnderstood of a P.*

Entorce: f. *A wrinch, wring, straine, gird, griping; also, crookednesse; also, a shrewd turne, sore part, or aggrieuance; an ouerthwarting.*

Entorce: com. *Wrie, crooked; and hence;* Iambe entorce.

Entorceure. *as* Entorseure; *And, more peculierly, a wrinch in the backe-bone which turnes, and wries the ioynts thereof, and makes it of the forme of a Roman* S.

Entorné. *Rounded, or incircled by; compassed about with.*

Entors: m. *A wrinch, wring, straine.*

Entorse: f. *as* Entorce.

Entorsé: m. ée: f. *Wrinched; wrung, strained, wried, by-straying; wrested, griped; vexed, grieued, extreamely.*

Entorser. *To wrinch; to wring; to straine, or wrie by straining; to wrest, gripe; vex, aggrieue, extreamely.*

Entorseure: f. *A wrinch, wresting, wrying; Looke* Entorceure.

Entortillé. *Writhed, writhen, wrigled; wound, twirld, twined about.*

Intestin entortillé. *The third small gut, seated in the lower part of the Nauell; it is verie red, and makes many turnes, which extend vnto th'* Os sacrum: *In it the Chylus waxing thicker beginneth to rest.*

Entortillement: m. *A writhing, or winding about a thing; a turning into a rundle, or circle; a twining, twisting, curling, twirling.*

Entortiller. *To turne, writhe, wreath, or wind about; to plie, or fould into a round, rundle, or circle; to twine, twirle, twist, curle, round.*

Entortillonné; & Entortillonner. *as* Entortillé, & Entortiller.

Entouillé: m. ée: f. *(Signifies most properly, berayed, or defiled; but the more commonly) pestered, incombered, hindered; snarled, intangled, confounded, without head or foot.*

Entouillement: m. *A filthie pestering, incombrance, impeachment, hinderance; confusion; intanglement.*

Entouiller. *(Is most properly, to beray, defile, make foule: but most commonly vsed for) to pester, incomber; insnarle, insnare, intangle; (and thereby) to confound, or hinder.*

Entoumeure: f. *A gobbet, a great bit, or cut of meat, &c; or as* Entonnoir.

Entour: m. *A round, circle, rundle, compasse.*

Les entours d' vn ville. *The liberties, or territorie belonging to a towne; the compasse of ground, or circuit of countrey, thats next vnto, or about, it.*

Entour. *About, round about; on all sides, on each hand, of.*

Tout à l' entour. *In all places, countries, or quarters thereabouts.*

Entouré: m. ée: f. *Compassed, rounded, enuironed; inwrapped, inclosed, or hemmed in, on all sides; also, betowred; furnished, or beautified with towers, or turrets.*

Damoiselle entourée. *Masked:* ¶Rab.

Entourellé: m. ée: f. *Betowred; bedeckt, or begirt, with turrets.*

Entourement: m. *A compassing, enuironing, rounding, incircling, inclosing on all sides.*

Entourement d' eaux. *A surrounding of waters.*

Entourer. *To compasse, enuiron, goe about, round, surround; inclose, infould, hemme in on euerie side; also, to furnish, or beautifie with towers.*

Entoureure: f. *Looke* Entourure; & Entourement.

Entourné: m. ée: f. *Rounded, inuironed, incircled, or compassed by; also, turned, or wound on; put, or wound about.*

En-

Entourner. *To turne, wind, or put about; also, to compasse, inclose, inuiron, hemme in, or about.*
s'Entourner. *To goe round, or turne into a round forme; to twirle, or wheele about.*
Entournoy. m. *as* Entonnoir; *A funnell.*
Entournure: f. *A round, a circle, a rundle.*
Entourtillant. *Wreathing; rowling about with.*
Entourtillé. *as* Entortillé.
Entourtillon. *A wreath, twirle, rowle.*
Entourtillure: f. *A wreathing, twirling, twining, rowling about with; also, as* Entortillon.
Entourure: f. *A compasse, a compassing; any thing that compasseth, and incloseth another; a goe-about.*
Entracassé: m. ée: f. *Halfe-broken.*
Entract: m. *The greenish salue called* Trait.
Entrage: m. *as* Entrée; *A fee, or custome due at th'entering of marchandize into a place; also, a fine, or income payed for a lease.*
Entrailles: f. *The intrals, intestines, inwards, bowels, guts.*
Entrainé: m. ée: f. *Drawen, haled, or pulled away; trayned, or trayled, along.*
Entrainer. *To hale, draw, or pull away; to traine, drag, or trayle, along.*
Entrait: m. *A short peece of timber indented within another peece, thereby to hold it the faster.*
Entrange. *as* Entrage.
Entrant. *Entering; beginning; going into.*
Caresme entrant. *Shrouetide, or Shrouetewsday.*
Vn homme entrant. *A bould or audacious fellow; one that (without inuiting) thrusts into any company.*
Entrape: m. *A pesterment, comber, trouble, incombrance; any thing that catches, hinders, or intricats, a man as he goes.*
Entrapé: m. ée: f. *Combered, pestered, troubled; intricated, intrapped; caught, or confined, within a trap.*
Entraper. *To pester, comber, trouble, take vp too much roome; also, to intricate, or as* Entraver; *also to intrap.*
Entraver. *To shackle, or fetter, the legs.*
Entraverser. *To run, goe, or bind, orecrosse; to ouerthwart.*
Entraves: f. *Shackles, fetters; pasterns for the legs of vnrulie horses.*
Entravestissement: m. *An interuesting, or interuesture; a mutuall possession, or ioint possessing of.*
Entravestissement de sang. *Is betweene such as are ioyned by mariage; where the suruiuor hath all, or the most part of that which was iointly possessed.*
Entraveur: m. *A fetterer, or shackler.*
Entré: m. ée: f. *Entered, gone into; also, begun in.*
Vn visage entré. *A hollow, iaw-fallen, sunke-in, countenance.*
Entre. *Betweene, amongst, in, among, together, one with another.*
Entre deux. *Doubtfull, indifferent, in suspence, at his owne choice whether yea or no; also, readie, or about.*
Entre deux & as; *Looke,* Deux.
Droict d'entr'eux. *Right ouer against them.*
s'Entr'accointer. *To become acquainted, or grow familiar, together.*
s'Entr'accoller. *To embrace, coll, or clip one another; to catch hould each by others neck.*
s'Entr'accompaigner. *To keepe companie, hould societie, conuerse together; to trauell both one way.*
s'Entr'accrocher. *To claspe, graple, hooke, or close together; to lay fast hold one of another.*
s'Entr'accuser. *To accuse, or appeach one another.*
s'Entr'advertir. *To hould intelligence together, to haue intelligence one with another.*
s'Entr'affoler. *To hurt, wound, fell one another.*
s'Entr'aguiser. *To sharpen each th'other.*
s'Entr'aider. *To giue mutuall assistance one to the other.*
s'Entr'aimans. *Mutuall friends, equally affecting each other; betweene whom no loue is lost.*
s'Entr'appeler. *To call one another.*
s'Entr'approcher. *To approach one another, to draw neere together.*
Entr'arraché: m. ée: f. *Plucked vp heere & there, rooted out from betweene.*
Entr'arracher. *To pluck vp here and there, to roote out from betweene.*
s'Entr'assener des espées. *To strike, or hit one another with their swords.*
Entr'attacher. *To ty, fasten, clasp, knit together, or one within another.*
Entr'attachez: m. ées: f. *Tyed, fastened, clasped, knit together, or one within another.*
Entr'avoir. *To haue, or possesse, one another; Looke* Fol.
Entrebaail: m. *A cleft, rift, chinck, chap; halfe-gape, or yawne; halfe opening, small ouerture, or diuision in the midle of a thing.*
Entrebaaillé: m. ée: f. *Halfe gaping; halfe, or yawning-open, chinked, chopped, riuen, clouen, ill ioyned, or couched together.*
Entrebaailler. *Halfe, or in the middle, to gape, yawne; cleeue, riue, open; or set open.*
Entrebailler. *as,* Entrebaailler.
s'Entrebaiser. *To interchange kisses; to kisse one another.*
Entrebasti: m. ie: f. *Built betwixt.*
Entrebastir. *To build betwixt, to ioyne one building to another.*
s'Entrebatre. *To fight, to fall together by the eares; or scuffle one with another.*
Entrebatu. ils se sont entrebatus. *They haue pummeld, or cudgelled, one another; they haue fought, or beene by th'eares, together.*
Entrebayement: m. *A halfe-gaping, or halfe-opening; a chinke, chap, cleft, rift betweene, or in the middle of a thing.*
Entrebecqueter. *To pecke at one another.*
Entrebeu: m. euë: f. *Halfe drunke, almost whift, whose cap is neerehand set.*
s'Entreblesser. *To hurt, or wound, each other.*
Entreboyau: m. *A thicke, and fat skin, that fastens the bowels to the backe, and each of them to th'other.*
s'Entrebrecher. *To breake, or make breaches into, one another.*
Entrebrisé: m. ée: f. *Halfe broken, broken betweene, or in the middest; (hence) also, distinct, distinguished; also, vneeuen, as a thing that is halfe burst.*
s'Entrebrouiller. *To intangle, or trouble, one another.*
Entrebruire. *To make a rumbling, or humming noise, to keepe a iarring, rumor, or murmure among others.*
s'Entrebrusler. *To burne each other.*
Entrebruslez: m. ées: f. *Burned by both parties, or both sides; mutually burned.*
s'Entrecaresser. *To cherish, welcome, vse kindly, one another; to bestow mutuall complements, to interchange kindnesses.*
Entrecassé: m. ée: f. *Halfe broken, almost broken, neyther*

ther fullie whole, nor broken.

Entrecasser. *Halfe, or almost to breake.*

s'Entrecasser les dents. *To bruise the teeth by gnashing them hard one against another.*

s'Entreceder. *To yeeld, or giue place one to th'other.*

s'Entreceler. *To hide, or conceale one another.*

Entre-cep. *The distance betweene stocke and stocke.*

s'Entrecercher. *To search for each other.*

Entrecesse. sans en. *Without intermission, intermedium, rest, pause; or ceasing.*

s'Entrechamailler. *Armed men to hacke, or slash one another, or each other.*

Entrechangé: m. ée: f. *Interchanged.*

s'Entrechanger. *To interchange; or, halfe to alter, almost to change; and hence;*

La veuë m' entrechange. *My sight diminisheth, mine eyes grow dimme.*

s'Entrecharger. *To charge one another.*

Entrechasse: f. *A crosse caper.*

Entrechaucher. *To tread vpon, to trample amongst.*

s'Entrecherir. *as* s'Entrecaresser.

Entrecheris: m. ies: f. *Mutually cherished, made much of one by th'other.*

Entrechevaucher. *To ride betwixt, or among.*

Entrechoc: m. *An intershocke; a mutuall, or interchangeable, rushing one vpon another.*

s'Entrechoisir. *To cull, picke, chuse out, one another.*

s'Entrechoquer. *Two armies, or enemies violently to cope one with, rush one against, or presse one vpon, another; to interchange, or come together with, a furious shocke.*

Entrecler: m. ere: f. *A little cleere, somewhat bright or light, or betweene darke and light, as in a twylight.*

Entrecognoistre. *To discerne from others, to know one among many others.*

s'Entrecognoistre. *To know one another, or haue acquaintance together.*

Entrecogneu: m. euë: f. *Knowne among others, discerned from others.*

Entrecolomne. *The space, or place betweene pillers.*

Entrecolomnement. *A leauing of space between piller and piller.*

s'Entrecommuniquer. *To communicate one with another.*

s'Entreconvier. *To lathe, bid, inuite, one another.*

s'Entrecosser. *To iurre, or butt together, as Rammes.*

s'Entrecoudoyer. *To iustle, or elbow, one another; to giue one another the elbow.*

Entrecoulé: m. ée: f. *Glid, slid, runne in betweene, or among.*

Entrecouler. *To glide, slide, runne betweene, or among.*

Entrecoupé: m. ée: f. *Cut betweene, halfe cut; cut off in the middest; interrupted.*

Entrecouper. *To cut betweene, or in the middest; halfe to cut; also, to prune, cut off, or picke out, vnnecessarie sprigs from among the fruitfull braunches; also, to interrupt.*

Entrecoupeuse: f. *An intercutting; an halfe cutting; an interruption, a cutting off in the middest.*

Entrecourir. *To runne on both sides, ioyntly to runne.*

s'Entrecourir. *To incounter; to runne one vpon another.*

s'Entrecraindre. *To stand in feare one of another.*

Entrecroisé: m. ée: f. *Thwarted, intercrossed, wrought, or marked ouercrosse.*

Entrecroisement: m. *A thwarting, or intercrossing, or lying one ore crosse another.*

s'Entrecroiser. *To intercrosse; to thwart, intangle, or lie ore crosse one another.*

Entrecroisure: f. *A double crosse, or intercrossing.*

Entrecueilli: m. ie: f. *Picked betweene, gathered from among.*

Entrecuellir. *To picke, or gather betweene, or from among.*

Entrecuisses. *The cods of a wild Boare.*

s'Entredebvoir. *To owe each vnto other.*

s'Entredefendre. *To defend one another.*

s'Entredemander des nouvelles. *To aske one of another how the world goes.*

Entredent. *The space that is betweene two teeth.*

s'Entredepecer. *To pull one another in peeces.*

s'Entredeschirer. *To teare each other asunder.*

s'Entredesfaire. *To vndoe, or defeat, one another.*

Entredeu: m. euë: f. *Due interchangeably, betweene man and man, or from one to another.*

Entredeux: m. *A distance, a space, partition, vacant place, or time betweene, or in the middest of; an intermedium, or interual; any thing that parts, or diuides, other things.*

Il fut entredeux de le tuer. *He was about to kill him; or in doubt whether to kill him or no.*

Vn livre relié avec du papier blanc entredeux. *A booke bound with a leafe of cleane, between each leafe of printed, paper.*

s'Entrediffamer. *To defame, disgrace, discredit one another.*

s'Entredire iniures. *To raile at, or to reuile, one another.*

s'Entredisants. *Telling one another, saying one to the other.*

Entre-discerner. *To discerne, or know one from the other; to make a difference betweene themselues.*

s'Entredommager. *To wrong, or hinder each th'other.*

Entredonné: m. ée: f. *Interchanged, exchanged, giuen one for another.*

s'Entredonner. *To interchange, exchange, giue each to the other;* s'entredonner courage. *To hearten, or encourage one another.*

Entredormir. *To slumber; to lie betweene sleeping, and waking.*

Entredoubté: m. ée: f. *Staggered at, somewhat doubted of, or whereof one is partly in suspence.*

Entredoubter. *To stagger at, somewhat to doubt of; to be in suspence.*

Entrée: f. *An entrie, passage, entrance, allie, way, or path leading vnto a place; a gate, a doore, or threshold of a house; an accesse; a meane to come vnto a thing; an entring, or going in; a beginning, or ouerture; the first blow giuen, stone laid, yce broken; also, custome, or impost, for marchandise brought into a place; also, the income paid by a purchaser vnto his new Land-lord; also, a present, or gratuitie bestowed on a Prince, &c, at his first entrie into a place.*

L'entrée de table. *The first course; or, the meat thats first serued vp, at table.*

Entrée de vin és villes closes. *An imposition of* v.s. Tour. *vpon euerie Muid of wine brought into a walled towne, or into the suburbes thereof, to be sold; first raised by* Charles *the* ix. *and since enhaunced by* Henrie *the third vnto* xx.s. Tournois.

Amende de tost entrée. *Looke* Amende.

Droict d'entrée. *as* Droict de presence.

La souris qui n' a qu' vne entrée est incontinent happée: Prov. *The mouse that hath but one hole is soon caught;*

caught; the man that hath but one helpe's soone overthrowne.

s'Entr'embrasser. *To imbrace, or hug one another in their armes.*

s'Entr'empoigner. *To claspe (as wrastlers) one another by the wrists, or armes.*

s'Entr'encourageants. *Incouraging one another.*

s'Entr'encourager. *To hearten, or incourage, one another.*

s'Entr'entendre. *Underhand to serue one anothers purposes, to hold secret intelligence one with another.*

Entr'esclos: m. ose: f. *Halfe hatched.*

Entr'escrire. *To interline, or write betweene.*

Entr'escrit: m. ite: f. *Interlined, written betweene.*

s'Entr'essayer à la. *To trie one another at.*

Entrefaicte. sur ces entrefaictes. *In the meane while, hereupon, while these things were a doing.*

s'Entrefaire grande feste. *To make verie much one of another; to congratulate with great ioy their good haps together.*

s'Entrefascher. *To be angrie, or fall out, one with th'other; to brable, or brawle together.*

Entrefendre. *To diuide, cut betweene, cleeue in two, part in halues; also, halfe to cut, almost to cleeue.*

Entrefendu: m. uë: f. *Halfe clouen, almost diuided; also, clouen in two, parted in halues.*

Entreferir. *To interchange some blowes; to strike, or hit, at once, one another; also, to interfeere, as a horse.*

Entrefessier: m. *The space betweene the buttocks.*

Entrefesson: m. *The space betweene the priuities, and the fundament; or as* Entrefessier.

Entrefileures de drap. *The space betweene thread and thread.*

s'Entreflatter. *To sooth each other, to smooth one with another.*

s'Entrefondre. *as* s'Enfonser; *To runne, or sinke ouer head and eares into; or, to sinke deepe into the filthie, or dreggie bottome of.*

Entrefossé: m. *The distance, or space that is betweene pit and pit, or betweene ditch and ditch.*

s'Entrefouetter. *To whip each other.*

Entrefouïr. *To dig betweene.*

Entrefouler. *To tread among, to trample in the middest, or thickest of.*

s'Entrefrapper. *To strike, or smite, each other.*

Entrefrizé: m. ée: f. *Frizled, or curled, one within another.*

Entrefrizer. *To curle, frizle, ruffle (the haire, &c.)*

s'Entrefroisser. *To clap, clash, knocke, breake, bruise, one against another; to crash one another in peeces.*

Entrefroissez: m. ées: f. *Clapped, knocked, broken, cracked, one against another.*

s'Entrefrotter. *To rub one against another; to interfeere; also, to beat, bethwacke, or thumpe, each other soundly.*

Entrefrotture: f. *A rubbing one against another; a horses interfeering.*

s'Entregaller. *To rub, scratch, or claw, one another.*

Entregent: m. *Ciuilitie, courtesie, complement, good carriage; a bold, and comelie fashion of behauiour.*

Qui sçait bien son entregent. *as* Entregenté.

Entregenté: m. ée: f. *Well behaued; that knowes good fashions (and vses them) that becomes whatsoeuer he does.*

s'Entregenter. Il se sçavoit en: en toutes compagnies. *Hee knew well how to carrie himselfe in all companies.*

Entreget. *as* Entreject.

s'Entregratter. *To scratch, claw, scrub, each other.*

s'Entregronder. *To whurre, yarre, grumble, one at another; whence;*

Pendant que les chiens s'engrondent le loup devore la brebis: Prov. *Looke* Chien, *or* Brebis.

s'Entreguerroyer. *To make warres one vpon another.*

s'Entrehaïr. *To hate one another.*

s'Entrehanter. *To conuerse much together.*

s'Entrehapper. *To catch hold one of another.*

s'Entreharceler. *To vexe, harrie, trouble, tug, one another.*

Entreheurt: m. *An interchocke; or, as* Entreheurtement.

Entreheurtement: m. *A scuffling, iustling, iustling, butting, bickering, together; a knocking, one against th'other.*

s'Entreheurter. *To iustle, butt, or iurre, one another; to scuffle, or bustle, together.*

Entreheurtis. *as* Entreheurtement.

s'Entrehucher. *To call, whoop, or whistle, one to, or for, another.*

Entrejamber. *To crosse legs.*

Entreiant: m. *as* Entregent.

Entreject: m. *An interposition; a casting, or putting betweene; a word cast, or speech giuen, forth by way of motion, or otherwise.*

Entrejectant. *Interlacing, interposing, thrusting, or casting, betweene.*

Entrejecté: m. ée: f. *Interposed, intermingled; cast, or thrust betweene, or among.*

Entrejecter. *To interpose, interlace, intermingle; cast, thrust, or forcibly put in, betweene or among.*

Entreillizé: m. ée: f. *Intergrated, thick lattised, crossebarred.*

Entrejoindre. *To couple, or ioyne, together.*

s'Entrejoindre. *To clip, coll, imbrace, each other.*

s'Entrejouër. *To play, or sport, one with another.*

Entrelacement. *as* Entrelassement.

Entrelaissé. *Deferred, intermitted, put or left off a while, discontinued for a time.*

Entrelaisser. *To intermit, leaue, deferre, discontinue, slacken, put off for a time.*

Entrelardé: m. ée: f. *Interlarded; fat, and leane together.*

Entrelardement: m. *An interlarding; a mingling of different things, as fat and leane, great and small, together.*

Entrelarder. *To interlard; to mingle different things together.*

Entrelas: m. *A knot hard to be loosed, an intricate businesse, a worke much intangled; also, as* Entrelassement.

Entrelassé: m. ée: f. *Interlaced, intermingled; foulded, plaited, intangled, one within another; set, put, thrust in, betweene or among; interposed.*

Enterlassement: m. *An interlacing, intermingling, interposing; a plaiting, wrapping, foulding, or intangling one within another; a setting, putting, or thrusting, in, betweene, or among.*

Entrelasser. *To interlace, intermingle, interlard; fould, plait, twine, or intangle one within another; to set, put, or thrust in, betweene or among.*

s'Entrelasser. *To wearie, or tire out, one another.*

Entrelasseure. *as* Entrelassement.

Toicts ornez d'enterlasseures. *Roofes decked with interlaced frets.*

Entrelassis: m. *An interlacing, plaiting, interweauing.*

Entrelié: m. ée: f. *Tyed together; bound betweene.*

Entrelier. *To tie together; to bind betweene.*

Entreligne: f. *An interline, or interlining.*

Entreligné: m. ée: f. *Interlined.*

Entreligner. *To interline (a writing.)*

Entrelire. *To read together.*

s'Entrelouër. *To commend one another.*

Entreluicter. *To wrastle one with another.*

Entreluire. *To appeare, shine, or be seene among, betweene, or in the middest of; also, to giue a glimpse, or shine by halfe.*

Entrelunaires. Iours en. *The dayes, or space, wherein neither the old, nor new Moone is seene.*

Entremander. *To send betweene partie and partie.*

s'Entremanger. *To eat vp, or vndoe, each other.*

Entrement: m. *An entring, or going in; a beginning, an entrance.*

Entremeslé: m. ée: f. *Interlaced, intermixed, intermingled; set, inserted, mingled among.*

Entremesler. *To intermingle, interlace, intermix; to shuffle vp one with another; to insert, or set among.*

s'Entremesler de. *To Intermeddle with; to imbark, or put, himselfe into.*

Entremets: m. *Certaine choice dishes serued in between the courses at a feast, or banquet.*

Entremetteur: m. *A stickler, mediator, dayes-man; an intermedler, or dealer in other mens causes, or controuersies.*

Entremettre la besongne. *To intermit, slacken, deferre, discontinue, delay, put, or leaue it off for a time.*

s'Entremettre de. *To meddle, or deale with; to thrust himselfe into.*

s'Entremeurir. *To wax, or be, halfe ripe.*

s'Entremignarder. *To dandle, cocker, or flatter, one another.*

Entremise: f. *A meanes, or mediation; an intermedling, or brokage; a dealing betweene partie and partie; any medling in, or managing of, (other mens) businesses.*

s'Entremocquer. *To interchange mocks, gibes, quips, scoffs, flouts; to ride, or deride, one another.*

s'Entremordre. *To bite one another.*

s'Entremouiller. *To wet, bedeaw, besprinkle, moisten, each other.*

Entremoyen: m. *A distance, intermedium, meane, or meane while.*

s'Entrempescher. *To disturbe, or hinder one another.*

Entre mutiner. *To put into a mutinie; to set together by th'eares.*

Entremuye de moulin. *The mill hopper.*

Entremy. par en. *Amongst, or in the middest of.*

Entrenaistre. *To spring vp, arise, be borne, betweene, or among.*

s'Entrenavrer. *To wound each other.*

Entrenavrez. *Wounded, each by th'other.*

Entrenoüé: m. ée: f. *Interlaced, intangled; tied, or knotted betweene; also, swumme betweene, or among.*

Entrenouër. *To swimme betweene, or among; also, to intangle, or tie knots betweene.*

s'Entrenuire. *To hurt, endammage; hinder, pester, one another.*

s'Entr'injurier. *To reuile, or abuse, one another.*

s'Entr'obliger. *To bind, oblige, or make beholden themselues, one to the other; to enter into mutuall bonds.*

Entr'obligez. *Bound, obliged, beholden, the one to the other.*

s'Entr'occir. *To kill each other.*

Entr'oeil: m. *The space betweene the eyes.*

Entr'oublié: m. ée: f. *Forgotten in the meane while; slipt out of memorie since that time.*

Entr'oublier. *To forget in the meane while, or since then.*

s'Entr'oublier. *To forget each other.*

Entr'ouï: m. ie: f. *Heard scatteringly, by halues, or but here and there a word.*

Entr'ouïr. *To heare by halues; to heare here and there a word; to heare vnto his thinking; or to thinke hee heares.*

Entr'ouvert: m. erte: f. *Chopped, chawned, clouen, gaping; halfe, or almost open; neither fully shut, nor open; whence;*

Les yeux cachez à doigts entr'ouverts. *Couered with stradling, and halfe-open, fingers; rather hidden in shew then hindered of their sight; or so hidden by them that the hider may with ease looke through them.*

Entr'ouvrir. *Halfe to open, to make way through; also, to lay (halfe) open vnto.*

s'Entr'ouvrir. *Halfe, or almost to open, to gape, cleaue, goe asunder of it selfe.*

s'Entrepardonner. *To forgiue one another.*

Entreparlement. *An interrupting, a speaking in a mans cast.*

Entreparler. *To interrupt one that speakes; to speake in his tale, to hinder his speech, with demaunds.*

Entrepas: m. *A fast walke, a racke; a racking, or great pace of some horses, that cannot amble, and must not trot.*

Entrepend: m. *Part of a womans &c.*

s'Entrepicquer. *To pricke, nip, taunt, quip, cut, each other.*

s'Entrepigner. *To combe, or claw one another; to pluck one another by the beards; to goe together by the ears.*

Entreplanter. *To plant, or set betweene.*

Entreplié: m. ée: f. *Interfoulded, or foulded between.*

Entreplier. *To fould betweene, to interfould.*

s'Entrepoindre. *To pricke, sting, nettle; gird, gall, or vex, one another.*

Entrepos: m. *An interposition; or, thing thats put, in an equall distance betweene others; also, a setting, putting, laying.*

Entreposer. *Seeke* Interposer.

Entreposition. *as* Interposition.

s'Entrepoulser. *To thrust out the barlot; to thrust, or push one another.*

s'Entrepoussans. *Thrusting, or crowding one another.*

Entreprenant. *Enterprising, attempting; bold, hardie, couragious, forward, aduenturous; that cares as little for his flesh as another.*

Entreprendre. *To enterprise, attempt, vndertake, or take in hand; assume, or take vpon him; to venter vpon, enter into, goe in hand with; also, to vsurpe, or incroach vpon.*

s'Entreprendre. *To congeale, curdle, thicken; knit, or ioyne together.*

s'Entreprendre par les mains. *To shake hands, to ioyne hands together.*

Entrepreneur. *An enterpriser, attempter, vndertaker; also, a Broker, Pettifogger, or intermedler in other mens contrueries.*

Marchand entrepreneur. *A Marchant venturer.*

Entrepressé. *Closed, crowded, thrust, pressed in, or, one betweene another.*

Entrepresser. *To stop, close, or presse in, or one betwixt another.*

s'Entrepresser. *To presse, crowd, or thrust hard one another.*

s'Entreprester. *To lend one to another.*

Entreprins: m. se: f. *Vndertaken, attempted, enterprised.*

Entreprins de ses membres. *Taken, benummed, or blasted.*

Entreprinse: f. *An enterprise, action, attempt, aduenture; also, an vndertaking, or taking in hand; also, an vsurpation, or incroachment vpon.*

Homme d' entreprinse. *A man thats fit for great imployments.*

s'Entrepromettre vne chose. *To promise a thing one vnto another.*

s'Entreprouver. *To proue, trie, assay one another.*

s'Entrequerir. *To seeke each other.*

Entrer: m. *An entrie, or going into; an accesse vnto.*

Entrer de fief servi. *Looke* Servi.

Entrer. *To enter, goe, or step in; to haue accesse vnto; to begin to put himselfe into.*

Entrer en bettes. *To fall a tipling, or quaffing; or to grow tipsie by tipling.*

Entrer en combustion avec. *To fall to deadlie feud with; to raise a great tumult against.*

Entrer par la fenestre. *See* Fenestre.

Entrer en la haute game. *To stretch, or busie, his wits.*

Entrer en quartier. *To begin his waiting; to get into fauour, credit, authoritie, dealings; to come in request.*

Entreraclé: m. ée: f. *Scraped about; filed, or polished betweene.*

Entreracler. *To scrape about; to file, or polish betweene.*

s'Entreregarder. *To behold, or looke on each the other.*

s'Entreregretter. *To deplore, or bemoane each other; passionately to wish for one another.*

s'Entrerencontrer. *To meet one another, or together.*

Entrerompant. *Interrupting, stopping.*

Entrerompre. *To interrupt, stop, confound, breake off in the mids.*

Entrerougir. *To blush a little, to looke somewhat red.*

Entreroulé: m. ée: f. *Rowled betweene; or now and then.*

Entrerouler. *To rowle betweene.*

s'Entreruer des pierres. *To pelt one another with stones; to throw stones one at another.*

s'Entresaisir bras à bras. *To seize one another by the armes.*

s'Entresaluër. *To salute each other.*

Entrescieures: f. *Intersawings; frequent (but distant) cuts, or entries, made by a saw, &c.*

s'Entresecourir. *To assist, releeue, or succour, one another.*

s'Entresembler. *To resemble one another.*

Entresemé: m. ée: f. *Set, sowed, inserted, interlaced betweene.*

Entresemer. *To set, sow, insert, interlace betweene, or here and there one.*

Entreserré: m. ée: f. *Stopped, shut, or closed in, or betweene.*

Entreserrer. *To stop, shut, or close in, or betweene.*

Entresolive. *A space, or quarter betweene two rafters.*

s'Entresouffrir. *To endure, abide, or brooke each other.*

s'Entresouvenir de. *To remember one another of; also, halfe to remember.*

Entrespace. *An intermedium, or space betweene.*

s'Entr'espier. *To spie, or prie into one anothers doings.*

s'Entresuir. *as* s'Entresuyvre.

s'Entresurprendre. *To surprise, or take napping one, another.*

Entresuytte: f. *A continuation, or immediate succeeding one of the other; a close, or neere following one of another.*

s'Entresuyvre. *To follow (close, or neere) one another; to succeed immediately, or in the necke one of the other.*

Entretaché: m. ée: f. *Spotted (and spatled) here and there.*

Entretaillé: m. ée: f. *Cut betweene, or in the middest; cut here and there; cut by peeces, and with pauses; cut at seuerall times; also, interfeered.*

Entretaillement: m. *A cutting betweene, or in the middest; a cutting here and there; a cutting by peeces (with pauses, or at seuerall times;) also, an interfeering; and hence, a tripping, or contrarietie, in speech.*

Entretailler. *To cut betweene, or in the middest of; to cut here and there; to cut (an entire thing) by peeces, and with pauses, or at seuerall times.*

s'Entretailler. *To cut, or hacke one another; also, to interfeere; to hit, (and in hitting to hurt, or bedurt) one leg with th'other; also, to trip, or contrarie, himselfe in his owne speech.*

Entretailleure: f. *as* Entretaillement; *Or, a cut here and there.*

s'Entretaster. *To tast, feele, essay, sound, handle, or grope, another.*

Entretemps: m. *An intermedium, or meane while.*

Entretenement: m. *A coherencie, or hanging of things together; an vninterrupted continuation of matters; an intertaining; also, a pension, wages, intertainment.*

Entretenement de voix sans respirer. *The holding of a note.*

Entretenir. *Mutually to hold, or keepe; (both sides) to intertaine, or continue in a course agreed on; also, (without reciprocation) to obserue, or keepe inuiolably; also, to intertaine, defray, sustaine, maintaine; also, to intertaine, or hold in talke; to chat or conuerse with; to vse affably, courteously, kindly; also, to intertaine, or accept of, an offer; also, to hold, keepe, retaine, together.*

Ie ne fais point les bresches, mais ie les entretiens fort bien. *(The speech of an aged leacher.)*

s'Entretenir. *To cleaue, hold, or hang close together.*

s'Entretenir de. *To nourish, intertaine, or sustaine himselfe with.*

Ils s'entretiennent comme font les gruës. *Said of such as obstinately follow a sect, or fashion.*

Qui veut entretenir son ami n' ait nuls affaires avec luy: Prov. *He that loues to continue a friend must haue but little to doe with him.*

Entretenu: m. uë: f. *Intertained; held, kept, obserued; also, defrayed, sustained, maintained; also, held in talke, or chat, complemented with, courteously vsed; also, accepted of; also, retained, or held together.*

Entretien: m. *Intertainement, maintenance, meanes, nourishment; also, complement, complementing, or intertaining of one another with courteous speeches.*
Entretisseure: f. *The woofe of cloth.*
Entretissu: m. uë: f. *Wouen, or wrought betweene, as gold plate in tinsell; interlaced.*
Entretistre. *To interlace, or weaue betweene.*
Entretoise. *A crosse quarter, or ouerthwart rafter, of timber.*
Entretortillé: m. ée: f. *Interlaced, much intangled, or twined.*
Entretortiller. *To interlace; to twine, or intangle much.*
Entretouchement: m. *A touching, sticking, cleauing, or hanging of things closely together; also, a continuation.*
s'Entretoucher. *To touch one another; to abut, neighbour, or be neere one to the other.*
Entretouillé: m. ée: f. *Intangled, fubbled, confounded; pestered, incombered.*
Entretouiller. *To mingle, intangle, confound, fubble vp things together; to pester, to incomber.*
s'Entrouver. *To find each other.*
s'Entretuër. *To kill one another.*
Entreveché: m. ée: f. *Intangled, insnarled, fettered, intricated.*
Entrevecher. *To intangle, insnarle, fetter, intricate.*
Entreveillé. *Halfe awake, or betweene sleeping and waking.*
Entreveiller. *To be waking now and then; or to lie betweene sleeping and waking.*
Entrevenir. *To come in on a sudden; to happen, or befall at vnawares; to be present among others; also, to mediate, or come betwixt.*
Tels Seigneurs entreviennent au traité. *Such Lords are contained, or comprised, within the treatie.*
Entrevenu: m. uë: f. *Come, happened, befallen, in the meane while, or on a sudden.*
Entrever. *To vnderstand:* ¶Barrag.
Entreverdir. *To be greenish; or to be greene among other colours.*
Entreverdoyer. *The same.*
s'Entreverser. *To ouerturne, or ouerthrow one another.*
Entrevesché: m. ée: f. *Pestered, intangled, insnarled, intricated.*
Entrevescher. *To snarle, or intangle one within another; or as* Entrevecher.
Entrevisé: m. ée: f. *Viewed, or visited, now and then.*
Entreviser. *To view, or visit now and then.*
Entrevisité: m. ée: f. *Seene, or visited now and then.*
Entrevisiter. *To goe to see, or visit sometimes.*
Entrevoir. *Scarcely to see, to haue but a glimpse of.*
s'Entrevoir. *To behold, or visit, one another.*
Entrevomi: m. ie: f. *Vomited, spued, or cast out now and then, or among other things.*
Entrevomir. *To cast, or vomit out among other things; to parbreake sometimes, or by fits.*
Entroupelé. *Trouped, or flocked together; assembled, or gathered, by troups.*
Entroupeler. *To troupe, heape, or flocke together; to gather in companies; to assemble.*
Entrouper. *as* Entroupeler.
Entuilé: m. ée: f. *Tiled; couered with tiles.*
Entuiler. *To tile; to couer with tiles.*
Enture: f. *as* Entement; *A graffing.*
Envahi: m. ie: f. *Inuaded, assailed, assaulted, set on.*
Vne volonté de fuïr les avoit premier envahie. *They had from the beginning resolued to flie; or, feare had at first possest their minds, and put them into a humor of flying.*
Envahie: f. *An assault, an onset, an inuasion.*
Envahir. *To inuade, assaile, assault, or set vpon; also, to seise, apprehend, or lay hold on; (as in th'example vnder* Envahi.)
Envain. *A kind of Serpent; as* Envent.
Envaisselé: m. ée: f. *Inuesselled, put into a vessell.*
Vn bel esprit envaisselé. *A good pot wit.*
Envasé: m. ée: f. *Inuesselled, put into a vessell.*
Envaser. *To put into a vessell.*
Envasquiné: m. ée: f. *In a long, Spanish, or old-fashioned, Vardingale.*
Enucleation. *An enucleation, or vnkernelling; an explanation, full interpretation, absolute exposition, plaine manifestation of.*
Envelope: f. *Any thing that serues to wrap another in; a couer; a sarplier; a wrapper; a peece of wast paper for that purpose.*
Envelopé. m. ée: f. *Inueloped; wrapped, infoulded, inclosed, inuolued; also, pestered, intangled, perplexed, incombred.*
Envelopement: m. *An inueloping, wrapping, infoulding; intanglement, implication, incombrance.*
Envelopément. *Obscurely, intricately; combersomely, by wrapping, or inuolution.*
Enveloper. *To wrap, infould, inuolue, implicate, inclose; also, to pester, intangle, insnare, perplexe, incomber.*
Envelopoir: m. *as* Envelope.
Enveloppe, & Envelopper; & Enveloppoir. *as* Envelope, Enveloper, &c.
Enveloute: m. ée: f. *Of Veluet, or cloathed with Veluet.*
Envenimé: m. ée: f. *Inuenomed; impoisoned.*
Envenimer. *To inuenome; also, to poison th'outside of.*
Envent: m. *A short blind Serpent, which is thought to sleepe all Winter; whence;*
Endormy comme vn envent. *An extreame slug.*
Envergongné: m. ée: f. *Much ashamed, far out of countenance.*
Envermé: m. ée: f. *Filled with, or growne full of, wormes.*
Envermer. *To fill with, or grow full of, wormes.*
Enverré: m. ée: f. *Displeased with, incensed against:* ¶Norm.
Envers: *(A Substantiue)* m. *Th'inside, or wrong side of a thing;* l'envers du drap.
Mettre à l'envers. *To ouerthrow, turne vpside-down, tumble, or cast topsie turuie.*
Nager à l'envers. *To swim on his backe.*
Tourner à l'envers. *To turne the inside, or wrongside, outward.*
Nul endroict sans son envers: Prov. *No commoditie without a discommoditie.*
Envers. *(A Preposition, signifies) towards, neere to, about; also, in the presence, or in respect, of; also, against.*
Enversé: m. ée: f. *Inuerted; turned vpside-downeward, or th'inside outward; also, turned in and out.*
Enverser. *To inuert; to turne vpside-downeward, or the inside outward; also, to turne in and out.*

Envi. *as* Envy; *With an ill will.*

Envictailler. *To victuall; to furnish with, or prouide of, victualls.*

Envictuailler. *The same.*

Envié: m. *The spot, or marke which a child hath on some part of his bodie, representing the thing his mother longed for, or was afrighted with, when hee was in her bellie.*

Envie: f. *Enuie, spight, grudge, repining; griefe, displeasure at the prosperitie, or good parts of another; a malicious emulation; also, a desire, or lust vnto, a longing after; whence;*

Vous auriez bien envie de me faire peur. *Belike you would faine make me afraid.*

Envieux meurent, mais envie ne mourra iamais: Prov. *Th'enuious die, but enuie liueth alwaies.*

Il n'est envie que de moine: Prov. *Looke* Moine.

Envié: m. ée: f. *Enuied, spighted, maligned; repined at.*

Envieillir. *To wax old, grow in yeares; become stale; beginne to decay; to quaile, faile, draw towards his end.*

Envieillissement: m. *A waxing decrepite, a growing into age, a stepping into yeares; a quailing, failing, decaying, becomming old, or stale.*

Envier. *To enuie; to maligne, spight, grudge, repine at the worth, or good fortune of others; also, to desire earnestly, to long for.*

Envier (au ieu.) *To vie.*

Envieusement. *Enuiously, spightfully, maliciously.*

Envieux: m. *A Slow-worme, or Blind-worme.*

Envieux: m. euse: f. *Enuious, malignant, repining, despightfull, spighting at another mans worth, or fortune.*

Femme envieuse. *A woman that longeth.*

Envieux meurent, mais envie ne mourra iamais: Prov. *Though enuious people die, yet enuie shall liue euer.*

Envinaigré: m. ée: f. *Seasoned with vinegar.*

Envinaigrer. *To season, or sharpen, with vinegar.*

Enviné: m. ée: f. *Stored, furnished, or seasoned, with wine.*

Envirollé. *Whose top, end, or tip is bound about with a ring, or hoope of yron, &c.*

Environ: m. les environs d'vne ville. *The compasse of ground, or circuit of countrey, next about it.*

Environ. *About; thereabouts; nigh vnto.*

Et mon homme environ. *And my marchant to worke, fell close to it, went roundly about it.*

Tout à l'environ. *All thereabouts, round about, on each side, on euerie part.*

I'ay assez à faire environ les mains. *I haue my hands full of businesse; I haue as much to doe as I can turne me to.*

Environné. *Inuironed, compassed, begirt, inclosed, hedged, or hemd in on euerie side.*

Environnement: m. *An incompassing, inuironing, inclosing round about.*

Environner. *To inuiron, incompasse, begird, inclose, hedge or hemme in, on all sides.*

Envis. bien envis. *Vnwillingly, loathly; repiningly.*

Toutesfois est faict ce qu' envis ont fait. *Looke* Faict.

Envisagé: m. ée: f. *Set with the visage or face towards, opposite in the forepart vnto.*

Envisager. *To set the face or visage towards, to looke towards or against; the forepart of a thing to be in opposition with another.*

Envitaillement: *A victualling; a prouiding of, or furnishing with, victualls.*

Envitailler. *as* Envictailler.

Envis. *Vies at play:* ¶Rab.

Enule-campane. *The hearbe called Helicampanie, Scabwort, and Horse-heale.*

Enumeration: f. *An enumeration, reckoning, numbring, rehearsall.*

Enunciation. *An enunciation, signification, declaration; a denouncing; also, a maxime, or proposition.*

Envoisiné: m. ée: f. *Beneighboured; compassed with, neere vnto, hard by, neighbours.*

Envolé: m. ée: f. *Fled away, passed hastily or swiftly, gone suddenly; escaped, got packing, departed.*

s'Envoler. *To flie away; to escape, depart, get packing; hie away speedily, hast away quickly, passe away suddenly.*

Envoulté. qui a l' esguillette nouée. *Charmed in his chiefe member.*

Envouté: m. ée: f. *Vaulted, arched; bowed, or bending, downwards like a vault.*

Envoutement. *as* Desgoustement; *A distasting.* (v.m.)

Envoy. *A message, or sending; also, th'Enuoy, or conclusion of a Ballet, or Sonnet; in a short stanzo by it selfe, and seruing, oftentimes, as a dedication of the whole.*

Envoyé: m. *A speciall messenger sent by a Prince vnto his Embassador in a forreine countrey.*

Le sainct Envoyé. *The holie Apostle.*

Envoye: f. *Looke* Ennoye.

Envoyé: m. ée: f. *Sent; delegated; addressed or directed, vnto; also, cast or thrust, out.*

Envoyer. *To send; to delegate; addresse or direct, vnto; also, to cast or thrust, out.*

Envoyer au grat. *To send agrazing; a Maister to put away his man; (and, perhaps from this phrase came our contemptuous, Goe scrape.)*

Ie le vous envoyeray par le borgne. *I will send it you by Iohn Long the Carrier.*

Qui envoye chetif à la mer il n'en rapporte ne poisson ne sel: Prov. *See* Poisson.

Qui fol envoye fol attend: Prov. *He that sends a foole, staies (either) for (or as) a foole.*

Envoyriner. *To glase a window.*

Envoyseure: f. *Mockerie; an old word.*

Envy. *Vnwillingly, repiningly, grudgingly, loathly, against the will, much against the humor of.*

A l' envy l' vn de l' autre. *One to despight the other; or in emulation one of the other.*

Enyvré: m. ée: f. *Drunke, drunken; made, or become drunke; in drinke, mellow, tipled, foxed, ouerseene.*

Enyvrer. *To make drunke; to fox.*

s'Enyvrer. *To be drunke, or in drinke; to be mellow, tipled, flusht, ouerseene.*

Il s'enyvre de sa propre bouteille. *Hee is drunke by his owne bottle; (said of one thats too farre in loue with a good part of his owne, or abuses it vnto his ruine.)*

Le Tavernier s'enyvre de sa Taverne: Prov. *Of the same, or like, sence.*

Eolipyles: f. *Hollow brasen bowles, (or balls) which being filled with water, and set by the fire vntill they bee throughly heated, yeeld forth of the narrow holes (whereof they haue many) strong puffes of wind, and continue them vntill all the water be euaporated.*

Epacte. *An addition; (in Almanacks) the Epact.*

Epaigneul. *as* Espaigneul.

Epalouïr. *To melt, or swelter with extreame heat.*
Epanalepse: f. *The repetition of a word, whereby a sentence or verse is ended, at the beginning of the next; also, a repetition after a long Parenthesis; the figure of Resumption.*
Epanode. *A seuerall rehearsall of two things which at first were spoken of ioyntly; or (more generally) any returne, regression, renouation, repetition.*
Epanons d'un dard. *The feathers of a dart.*
Epanter. *as* Espouvanter; *to dismay.*
Epatique. *The hearbe Trinitie, or noble Agrimonie.*
Epaular: m. *An Orke; a great sea-fish mortall enemie vnto the Whall.*
Epe. *in stead of,* Et puis; *a rusticall word.*
Epeiche: f. *A Speight; the red-tayled Woodpecker, or Highaw.*
Epelan: m. *A Smelt.*
Epelé: m. *Spealt, or spealed.*
Epeler. *To speale.*
Eperge: f. *A Brush.*
Eperlan: m. *A Smelt.*
Ephebe: m. *A mariageable youth or stripling; one thats fouretecne and vpwards.*
Ephectique: com. *One that after long studie, & search, is more doubtfull then he was at first.*
Ephemere. *The hearbe Liricumfancie, or May-Lillies; also, an ague of but one dayes continuance.*
L'Ephemere Colchique. *The wild Medow Saffron with the dark-red roots.*
Ephemerique. Fievre eph. *That lasts but a day.*
Ephimeris. *A Iournall, or daylie Register of things done.*
Epicaie: f. *Equitie, mitigation of the rigour of the Law.*
Epicaïzer. *To iudge according to equitie, to mitigate the rigor of the Law.*
Epiche: f. *A Speight; the red-tayled Wood-pecker, or Highaw.*
Epicycle. *A lesser circle, whose centre is within the circumference of a greater; hence, a lesser circle that comprehends, and carries about with it, a Planet, it selfe being carried about by a greater; the Seat of a Planet, or Storie wherein it is fixed.*
Epiderme. *The most outward thinne skinne of the bodie.*
Epidimial. Maladie Epidimiale. *as* Epidimie.
Epidimie. *An vniuersall sicknesse, or generall infection; a most catching, or contagious disease.*
Epidimique: com. *Infectious, contagious, pestilent; or, vniuersall, generall, growne common, very much dispersed, among the people.*
Epiecé: m. ée: f. *Diuided, peecemealed, rent in peeces.*
Epiecer. *To peecemeale, diuide, rend asunder, pull in peeces.*
Epigastre: m. *All the outward part of the bellie from the bulke to the priuities.*
Epigastrique. *Belonging thereto.*
Artere Epigastrique. *Looke* Artere.
Veine Epigastrique. *A branch of the Iliack, or flanke veine; there are two of them; an outward, and an inward one, both which at length are ioyned with the* Mammales.
Epiglottide. *The couer, weesell, or flap of the throat.*
Epigrammatique: com. *Epigrammaticall, or Epigramlike.*
Epigrammatiste. *An Epigrammatist, a writer of Epigrams.*
Epigramme: m. *An Epigram; a Couplet, Stanzo, or shor Poeme, wittily taxing a particular person, or fault; also, a title, inscription, or superscription.*
Epigrer. *as* Escacher, & Fouler. *(at* Tours.)
Epilemie. *A song of the superscription of a thing.* ¶Rab.
Epilence. *A kind of falling euill in a Hawke.*
Epilepsie. *The falling sicknesse, or foule euill.*
Epileptique. *That hath the falling sicknesse.*
Epilogue: m. *An Epilogue; the conclusion, knitting vp, or finall end, of a Play, &c.*
Epilogué: m. ée: f. *Concluded, ended, finished, knit vp.*
Epiloguer. *To conclude, or knit vp; to make a conclusion, epilogue, or finall end of.*
Epinarde. *A little fish; as* Espinoche.
Epinete. *as* Espinette; *a paire of Virginals.*
Epinices. *Feasts, verses, or songs of triumph after a victorie.* ¶Rab.
Epinoche. *as* Espinoche.
Epinyctide: f. *A wheale, or push that rises on the skinne by night.*
Epiphanie: f. *The Epiphanie, or Twelfth day in Christmas.*
Epiphore: f. *The Rhewmaticke moistnesse, waterinesse, or dropping of the eyes; also, violence, impression, vehemencie.*
Epiphyse: f. *An addition, or appendix to a bone, obtaining a peculiar circumscription within, and annexation to, it, though otherwise it be no true part of it.*
Epiploïque. Veine epiploïque. *See* Veine.
Episcopal: m. ale: f. *Episcopall; of, or belonging to, a Bishop.*
Episcopaux: m. *The followers, fauorites, or fauorers, of Bishops.*
Episemasie: f. *A note, or designation; a signification of the mind by the countenance, or gesture:* Rabelais *vses it (as if it were* Episemanomie) *for a popular shout, or acclamation.*
Epistemon. *A Teacher.* ¶Rab.
Epistre: f. *An Epistle, a letter missiue.*
Epistrophe. *The ending of two verses with one word; (a figure.)*
Epistyle: m. *as* Architrave; *also, a little piller set vpon a greater.*
Epitaphe: m. *An Epitaph; a funerall poeme, or inscription.*
Epitasse d'une tragedie. *The busiest part of a Tragedie.*
Epithalme. *A wedding Song, or Poeme; verses made, or a song sung, at a wedding, in commendation of the parties married.*
Epitheme: m. *A liquid medicine, applyed vnto an outward part of the bodie, by a peece of thinne linnen, or cotton dipped in it; thereby to supple the place, or coole and comfort the inward (heart, stomacke, or liuer) thats vnder it.*
Epithemé: m. ée: f. *Bathed, moistened, wet, bedeawed.*
Epithemer. *To bath, moisten, wet, bedeaw.*
Epithimer. *as* Epithemer.
Epithin: m. *The weed Dodder; especially that kind thereof, which growes twyning about the branches of Time.*
Epitoge: m. *A long Cloke, or Cassocke, worne loose ouer other apparrell; also, a Graduats hood.*
Epitome: m. *An Epitomie, Abridgement, Breuiarie.*

Epizeuxe. *A figure, whereby a word, or more, hauing no other betweene them, are doubled in one sence.*
Epodes. *A kind of Lyricke verses; the first whereof is longer then the second.*
Epotique. *Drunken, swilling.* ¶Rab.
Eprenas. *The bloudie flix, and bellie ache, that come by the vlceration, or excoriation of the bowels.* ¶Dauph.
Eptasyllabe: com. *Of seuen syllables.*
Epulotique. *Skinne-breeding.*
Epuré: m. ée: f. *Cleansed, purified, clarified; also, dryed by running, drayned of liquor by wringing.*
Epurer. *as* Espurer.
Equable: com. *Euen, equall, of one sort, all alike.*
Equalisé: m. ée: f. *Equalled, matched, made euen; resembled, compared.*
Equaliser. *To equall, match, make euen; resemble, compare.*
Equalité: f. *Equalitie, euennesse, matchablenesse; resemblance; indifferencie; comparison.*
Equalizer. *as* Equaliser.
Equanimité: f. *Indifferencie, moderation, quietnesse of mind; a humor that takes all things well.*
Equarri: m. ie: f. *Measured, or squared out, by a Squire.*
Equarrir. *To measure, or square out, by a Squire.*
Equarrissement: m. *A measuring, or squaring out, by a Squire.*
Equateur: m. *The Equator, or Equinoctiall Circle; one of the six chiefe Circles imagined to be in the Firmament; thus called, because tis equally distant from the two Poles; and because when the Sunne is in it the day, and night are of equall length.*
Equerre. *as* Esquierre.
Equestre: com. *Of, or belonging to, Horsemen, Knights, or Gentlemen.*
Equibiens. *The Halses; or two holes in the prow of a ship, through which the Anchor-cables passe.*
Equidiametral: m. ale: f. *Equidiametrall.*
Equidistamment. *Of equall distance asunder.*
Equidistance: f. *An equall space, an euen distance, asunder.*
Equidistant. *Equally distant one from the other.*
Equierre. *as* Esquierre.
Equilance: f. *The hole or hollow, wherein the tongue of a balance playeth.*
Equilibre: m. *Equalitie of weight.*
Equilibré: m. ée: f. *Weighed in equall balances.*
Equilibrer. *To poise, or weigh, in equall balance.*
Equinancie: f. *The Squinsie, or Squinancie; an impostumous swelling about the necke.*
Equinocce: m. *The Equinoctiall; or equall length of day and night; It falls out in the Spring about the eleuenth of March; in Autumne, about the sixteenth of September.*
Equipage: m. *Equipage, furniture, good armour, fit attire; store of necessaries; full order, sufficient array.*
Equipage d'un navire. *(Most properly) her Marriners, and Souldiors.*
Equiparable. *Fit to be compared, or equalled vnto.*
Equiparaison: f. *Likenesse, resemblance, matching, equalitie; comparison.*
Equiparé: m. ée: f. *Matched, equalled; resembled, likened; compared; altogether as well done.*
Equiparer. *To compare, liken; match, make equall; to doe as well as another.*
Equippé: m. ée: f. *Equipped; armed, attired, stored with, prouided of, all necessarie furniture, prepared for an exploit, set in good order, sufficient array, full equipage.*
Equiper. *To equip, arme, attire, store with, prouide of, necessarie furniture; to prepare, make readie, set in array, enable, by full prouision, for an action, seruice, or exploit.*
Equipolence: f. *Equipolencie, equalitie in value.*
Equipolent: m. *Composition money; or, as* Equivalent.
'A l'equipolent. *Accordingly, of a like value, proportionably, by euen portions, for his proportion or part.*
Equipolent. *Equiualent, of equall worth, of a like value, as good as the other.*
Equipoler. *To be of like, or equall value; to counteruaile the worth of; also, to make equall in value with.*
Equipollé: m. ée: f. *Counteruailed, equalled in value with.*
Equipoller. *as* Equipoler.
Equippage: m. *Equipage, furniture; &c; as,* Equipage.
Equippé: m. ée: f. *as* Equipé.
Equippée: f. *Equipage; or, a being in, or putting into, array, order, equipage; also, a suddaine, and fantasticall prank, or out-iert; a youthfull flying out of the way; and hence also, a digression.*
Les equippées d'un lievre. *Her running an end, an outright course.*
Equitable: com. *Equitable; iust, euen, equall, sincere; vpright.*
Equitation: f. *A riding on horsebacke.*
Equité: f. *Equitie, equalitie; euennesse; vprightnesse; mitigation of rigor; moderation of humour; mildnesse, clemencie, mercifulnesse.*
Equivalent: m. *Equall value; like for the like, one thing for another; or, the worth of a thing in exchange; hence; composition money; or, an yearelie composition, yeelded vnto the King by most of the commons, in lieu, and for th' abolishment, of an ancient Toll of xij d in the pound, leuied vpon all small wares, victuals, and other prouision, retayled by countrey people in their ordinarie Markets:* The Auvergnois, Limosins, Perigordins, *& the inhabitants of some other countries thereabouts, do also pay a composition to be exempted from the* Gabelle de sel, *and others the like Impositions; All, to auoid the exactions, and hard dealing of the collectors, and farmers of them; for otherwise, this composition is as beneficiall to the Prince, and chargeable to the Subiect, as those Tols, and Taxes were.*
Rendre l'equivalent. *To acquit, requite; returne like for the like, or, one good turne for another; whence;* 'A pere, à Maistre, à Dieu tout-puissant, nul ne peut rendre l'equivalent: Prov.
Equivalent. (Adject.) *Equiualent; of a like worth, or equall value; as good as another.*
Equivoque: f. *An equiuocation; a double, or diuers sence in one word, &c.*
Nous sommes en equivoque. *You meane one thing, and I another; or we mistake, or misconceiue, one another.*
Equivoqué: m. ée: f. *Equiuocated; doubtfully spoken, doubly meant.*
Ie me suis equivoqué. *I mistooke one word for another.*
Equivoquer. *To equiuocate, or vse words of diuers significations; to speake doubtfully, or with a double meaning.*
Erable. *The small Maple, or common Maple tree.*

Grand

Grand erable. *The great Maple (erroniously) called the Sycomore tree.*
Eraige: m. *An ayrie of Hawkes; or, as* Herage; *whence;* En est il encore de l'eraige? *What? is there yet more left of the kind of them?*
Eraigne. *as* Eraige. ¶Rab.
Eraillé. *as* Esraillé.
Erailler. *Seeke* Esrailler.
Erain. *as* Airain. *Brasse.*
Eramme: m. *A fine, or amerciament set on a parties head for want of due apparance.*
Eraser. *Looke* Escraser.
Erater. *To vnmilt, or take the milt out of.*
Erbergé: m. ée: f. *Lodged, harbowred.*
Erberger. *To lodge, to harbor.*
Erchat. *as* Archat. *Yellow wire made of Latten, or Copper.*
Erculisse: f. *Liccorice.*
Erectif: m. iue: f. *Erectiue; raising, aduancing, lifting vp, making to stand, setting bolt vpright.*
Eremodicié: m. ée: f. *Forsaken, desert, solitarie, forlorne.*
Cause eremodiciée. *A matter thats giuen ouer for desperate.*
Ereole: m. *A small weight of two graines.*
Ergalie: f. *The framing, and disposition of vessels, and furnaces for Extractions, &c.*
Ergastule: m. *A Prison, or House of Correction (as our Bridewell) for dissolute, and idle persons.*
Ergate: m. *A Windlesse, Windbeame, or Draw-beame; also, a Racke for a Crosse-bow.*
Ergot: m. *The spurre of a Cocke; the deaw-claw of a dog; the heele, or tallon of a Hog.*
Estre sur ses ergots. *To be verie statelie, loftie, surlie; to stand on tearmes, or on his Pantofles.*
Plein d'ergots. *(as if it were,* Ergo*) full of conclusions; quiddities, cauilling.*
Fendre l'ergot. *To runne away.*
Ergoté: m. ée: f. *Spurred, or hauing spurres; deaw-clawed; armed, or furnished with spurres, or deaw-clawes.*
Ergoter. *To rise on his toes, or stand vpon his tip-toes; also, to wrangle, debate, cauill, contend.*
Ergoteure: f. *as* Ergoture.
Ergotique: com. *Sophisticall, cauilling, full of conclusions, or quiddities.*
Ergotisme: m. *Arguing, cauilling, sophistrie, quiddities.*
Ergotiste: m. *A wrangling arguer, a cauilling sophister.*
Ergoture: f. *as* Ergot; *also, an arming, or furnishing, with spurres, or deaw-clawes; also, as* Ergotisme.
Erigé: m. ée: f. *Erected, raised, aduaunced, lift or set vp; also, created.*
Eriger. *To raise, erect, aduaunce, lift, or set vp.*
Eriger en Duc, ou Conte. *To create a Duke, or Earle.*
Erigoteures. *The spurres of a Cocke; the deaw-clawes of a dog, &c; Seeke* Ergoture.
Ermaire. *as* Armaire.
Erme. Terres ermes. *That ly wast, desart, and vntilled.*
Ermine. *The (bate-spot) Ermeline; also, the skin, or furre thereof; Ermines.*
Erminé: m. ée: f. *Furred with Ermines; poudered Ermines.*
Erminer. *To furre with Ermines.*
Erminette. *A little planing Ax.*
Ermitage: m. *An Hermitage.*
Ermite: m. *An Hermite; one that liueth alone in a desart.*

Erné: m. ée: f. *as* Esrené.
Erner. *To breake, or bruise, the reynes; to crush, or weaken, the backe.*
Erodé: m. ée: f. *Gnawne off, or about; eaten into.*
Eroder. *To gnaw off, or about; to eat into; also, to driue from field to field, from hill to hill.*
Erogene. *A certaine loue-procuring hearbe.*
Eron. *as* Heron. *A Herneshawe.*
Erosion. *A gnawing, or eating into.*
Erraillé: m. ée: f. *Spred wide open, set farre asunder.*
Oeil erraillé. *A staring eye.*
Errailler. *To spread wide open, set farre asunder; (and hence) also, to stare with the eyes; to shale with the feet; to straddle with the legs, or thighes.*
Erramme. *A fine, or amerciament set on a plaintifs, or defendants head, for not appearing.*
Errainment. *Quickly, presently, out of hand; nimbly, readily; also, at randome.*
Ferir errainment. *To strike among the thickest, one knowes not whom.*
Errandonner. *To fly away at randome, or he cares not which way, so he may be gone; (an old word.)*
Errant. *Errant, wandering, vncertaine, rouing, roaming, straying, vagabond, stragling.*
Erraté: m. ée: f. *Vnmilted; (& thereby) nimble, or light.*
Errater. *To take out a mans milt, thereby to make him the nimbler.*
Erratique. *as* Errant.
Fiebvres erratiques. *Agues whose fits hold no certain time of returne.*
Erre: f. *A way, path; course, or pace.*
Erres. *In the (plurall) number; as* Erre; *also, the view, or footing of a Deere.*
Erre de chasserie. *All the furniture, prouision, and equipage of hunting; as dogs, &c; and hence;*
Prendre erre de chasserie. *To prepare, or get, himselfe to hunting; to begin to hunt.*
Erre de la mer. *The floating, or wauing of the sea; the course of tydes.*
Grand erre. *Swiftly, fastly, speedily, quickly, hastily, with noteable diligence, with great celeritie; whence;*
Aller grand erre, ou, à grand erre, ou grand erres. *To speed, make hast, hy apace, goe very fast.*
Limier de hautes erres, & bonnes. *A fleet, or speedie hound.*
Poursuyvre ses erres. *To pursue his first argument; or, to continue the subiect he began with.*
Reprendre ses erres. *To returne vnto the way, or subiect from which he was diuerted; to come to his way, or matter againe.*
Erré: m. ée: f. *Erred, strayed, wandered, roued, roamed; mistaken, missed, fayled; offended, transgressed.*
Errement. *as* Arrement; *also, a path, step, tract, or way.*
Errementer. C'est (au stil du païs de Normandie) prendre expedition, & proceder en la cause avec sa partie adverse. ¶Ragueau.
Errer. *To erre; stray; wander; misse, fayle, mistake; also, to transgresse, offend, be faultie.*
Qui ne parle n'erre: Prov. *He that speaks not, erres not (in speech.)*
Erres. de erres. *Much, or verie much; (an old word.)*
Erreur: f. *An error, ouersight, ouerslip, mistaking; an ignorance, or false opinion; a wandering, or straying out of the right way; also, a misse, fault, offence, transgression; In Law, an Error (not as ours, in proces or pleading, but) in an Arrest, or Iudgement; and that two wayes;*

Erreur de Droict. *Error in Law; is when a Iudge hath giuen sentence directly against Law; See* Proposition d'erreur.

Erreur de faict. *Error in fact; is when he hath decreed against the Prooues made, or Euidence giuen in.*

Proposition d'erreur. *A writ of Error; is procured out of the highest Chauncerie; oftenest, when Errors in fact are complained of; for it is not easily beleeued, that the Judges, who can make Lawes, can erre in Law.*

Errhine. *A tent-like medicine applyed vnto, or put into, the nose, to purge it, or the braine; as also, to stop bleeding; prouoke sneezing; or to procure childbirth.*

Erroné: m. ée: f. *Erronious, fraught with errors; false.*

Erronnée: f. *The hearbe Centorie, Earth-gall, Feuerwort.*

Erronnéement. *Erroniously, falsely.*

Ers. les Ers d'un cheval. *as,* Les Ars, *or* Harts.

Ers. des Ers. *The Pulse called Cich,* Orobus, *bitter Vetch, or bitter Fitch; It commonly beares a white flower, and therefore some doe tearme it,* Ers blancs.

Ers de Crete, ou de Candie; *Candian* Orobus; *lesse in the cod, and seed then the ordinarie one.*

Ers roux. *The great wild Tare, Cichling, Pease euerlasting.*

Ers sauvage. *Wild* Orobus *(growes of it selfe among corne, and is oft mistaken for the wild Fitch.)*

Erte: f. *A place that stands high, or is somewhat high to be looked at; a steepe, or craggie ascent; a watch-tower.*

Estre à l'erte. *To obserue, or watch (from a high place) to lye in wait for; to haue a nimble, or carefull eye; to be circumspect, vigilant, warie, readie for all aduantages; to looke most heedfully about him.*

Tirer vn ennemy à l'erte. *To draw out an enemie into the field, or to fight.*

Erubescence: f. *Blushing, shamefastnesse.*

Eruce: f. *The hearbe Rocket; also, the Canker-worme.*

Erucé: m. ée: f. *Nibled finely, licked vp daintily.*

Erucer. *To nible finely, to licke vp daintily.*

Eructation: f. *A belching, or breaking of wind.*

Erudition: f. *Erudition, learning, teaching, doctrine.*

Erugineux: m. euse: f. *Of the colour of Verdigreece; rustie, cankred, or corrupted.*

Eruité. *as* Eviré. *Weakened.* ¶Rab.

Erysimon. Dioscorides *called so, banke Cresses, or winter Cresses:* Theophrastus, *and* Galen, *two hearbes of one kind; the one called* Miagrum, *or gold of pleasure; the other* Cameline, *or Treacle Wormeseed.*

Erysipele. *A painefull, and hot swelling, or impostumation, the matter whereof being verie thinne, and cleere, makes it looke almost as though it shined; some call it, the holie fire.*

Es. *(Of the Verbe,* Estre) tu es. *Thou art.*

Es. *(A Preposition, euer set before wordes of the plurall number, as,* en, *before those of the Singular.) In the, at the; into, or vnto the.*

Es vous; *for* voicy; *behold; (an old word.)*

Esbaaillé: m. ée: f. *Clouen, riuen, gaping wide, set open, or wide asunder.*

Esbahi: m. ie: f. *Abashed, astonished, amazed, appalled.*

A l'Esbahi. *Bashfully, amazedly, with great admiration, with much astonishment.*

s'Esbahir. *To wonder, maruell, be astonied, wax amazed, at.*

Faire esbahir. *To appall, affright, astonish, put out of countenance.*

Esbahissement: m. *A wondering, maruelling, admiration; appallment, astonishment.*

Esbahy. *as* Esbahi.

Esbailleure: f. *A gaping, or opennesse.*

Esbalançon. *A horses disordered leape out of time, and measure.*

Esbannoy: m. &, Esbannoye: f. *as* Esbanoy.

Esbanoie: f. *Pastime, sport, recreation.*

Esbanoy: m. *Pastime, sport, recreation.*

Esbanoye: f. *The same.*

s'Esbanoyer. *To sport, play, recreate himselfe.*

Esbarbé: m. ée: f. *Made beardlesse; barbed, shauen, sheered; pruined, cut, or cropped off; also, smoothed.*

Esbarbement: m. *A barbing, shauing, sheering, clipping; a cutting, pruining, or cropping, off; also, a smoothing.*

Esbarber. *To cut, shaue, clip, sheere off, haire, shag, a nap, &c; also, to cut, picke, pruine, or crop off, small sprigs, &c; also, to smooth (a rugged thing.)*

Esbarber vn livre. *To cut off, or pare away, the edges, or corners, of the leaues of a booke.*

Esbarluër. *as* Esberluër.

Esbasé: m. ée: f. *Loosse, or shaken at; loossed, or slipt from; driuen, or fled out of, it* Basis, *ground, or foundation.*

Esbaser. *To loosse, or make loosse, at the bottome; to dig vp, or take away, the foundation of; to shake from, or driue out of, it base, ground, or foundation.*

s'Esbaser. *To slip from, or fly out of it* Basis, *ground, foundation.*

Esbat: m. *Sport, pastime, play, recreation; delight, pleasure, dalliance, ieasting.*

Esbatement: m. *A sporting, playing, dallying, ieasting, recreation.*

s'Esbatre. *To sport, play, dally, ieast, passe away the time in mirth, and recreation.*

Esbauché: m. ée: f. *Rough-hewed, rudely begun, squared, framed, or cut grossely out of the whole peece.*

Esbauché (en peincture.) *Tricked.*

Esbauchement: m. *A rough-hewing; a grosse framing, squaring, or cutting out of a whole peece; a rude beginning; also, a tricking.*

Esbaucher. *To rough-hew; grossely to frame, forme, square, or cut out of the whole peece; to begin rudely, any peece of worke; also, to pruine a tree; and, in painting, to tricke.*

Esbaudi: m. ie: f. *Glad, merrie, cheerefull; heartened, exhilerated, cheered.*

Esbaudir. *To glad, reioyce, exhilerate, make merrie, hearten, cheere vp; also, to rowse, awake, or stirre vp from sleepe.*

Esberge: m. *A house, lodging, or harbour; also, an Inne.*

Esbergé: m. ée: f. *Lodged, harboured, housed, soiourned, or abood in.*

Esbergement: m. *A house, lodging, harbour, station, place of stay, abode, retreat.*

Esberger. *To lodge, harbour, house; to stay, abide, or soiourne in.*

Esberger en soy vne faute. *To commit, or be guiltie of, a fault; also, to take a fault vpon himselfe.*

Esberlué: m. ée: f. *Dazled, dimmed, made purblind.*

Esberluër. *To dazle, or dimme the eyes; to make them purblind.*

Esblaré: m.ée: f. *Gastlie, or pale of countenance; bleake, wan, as one that is affrighted, or hath had a feauer.*
Esbloui. *Dazeled; dimme-sighted; or whose sight is darkened.*
Esblouïr les yeux. *To dazle, dimme, cast a mist before the eyes; to make them glimmer.*
Esblouïssant. *Dimming, dazling, casting a mist before.*
Esblouïssement: m. *A dazeling, dimnesse, obscuritie.*
Esblouïsson: f. *as* Esblouïssement; *or, a mist cast before the eyes.*
Esblouïsson de la teste. *Giddinesse of the braine.*
Esboché: m. ée: f. *Rough-hewed, squared out, begun rudely; cut grossely out of a grosse peece; Looke* Esbauché.
Esbocher. *To rough-hew, square out in great; begin rudely; cut grossely out of the whole peece; Looke* Esbaucher.
Esboire. *To soake in, to drinke vp.*
Esboitement: m. *A lamenesse; or laming.*
Esborgné: m. ée: f. *Depriued of an eye.*
Esborgner. *To put out an eye, to depriue of one eye.*
Esbouffer. *To burst out into a laughter; also, as* Esboufler.
s'esbouffer à parler. *To buffe, or burst out in speech.*
Esbouflé: m. ée: f. *Spurted, spouted, or blowne (as moisture) vpon.*
Esboufler. *To spurt, spout, or blow moisture vpon.*
Esbouilli: m. ie: f. *Throughly boyled; ouerboyled; lessened, or decayed, in boyling; almost dryed vp with boyling.*
Esbouillir. *To boyle throughly; to boyle to the diminution of the liquor thats in boyling; to ouerboyle, or boyle almost dry; also, to worke, as new beere, &c.*
Esbouilluë: f. *Stuffe ouerboyled; burnt, or decayed in boyling.*
Esboulé: m. ée: f. *Ruinous, decaying; tumbled downe, fallen, or broken off; mouldred away of it selfe.*
Terres esboulées. *Decayed, or tyred out, by ouermuch tillage.*
Esboulement: m. *The ruine, decay, falling away, or tumbling downe, of a thing.*
Esbouler. *To rowle, or tumble downe; to fall, or burst off; to moulder away of it selfe; as earth, stone, &c, in the hanging sides of an old, or ill made, wall, banke, &c, thereby going to decay.*
Esbouli. *as* Esbouilli.
Esboulu. *as* Esboulé; *or, boyled out, or away.*
Esbourgeonné: m. ée: f. *Pruined, picked.*
Esbourgeonnement. *as* Esbourjonnement.
Esbourgeonner la vigne. *To pruine, shred, or nip off, the superfluous, and needlesse buds, or sprigs of a vine.*
Esbourgeonneur: m. *A pruiner, picker, or nipper off, of Vine buds.*
Esbourjonnage. *as* Esbourjonnement.
Esbourjonnement: m. *A cutting off, or plucking away of, superfluous buds, or sprigs from Vines; a pruining, or shredding of their small branches.*
Esbourjonner. *as* Esbourgeonner.
Esbourjonneur: m. *A pruiner of Vines.*
Esbourré: m. ée: f. *Cleansed, winnowed, purged, taken out of it huske.*
Esbourrer. *To winnow, vnhuske, vnshale; to rid, purge, cleanse from chaffe, haire, huskes, flocks, downe, &c; also, to rinch, or wash (a cloath &c) lightly, or sleightly.*

Esbouy, *for* Esbloui. *Dazeled.* ¶Rab.
Esbraillé: m. ée: f. *Vnbraced, vnbuttonned, vntrussed, loosely dressed; also, with his puddings about his heeles.*
Esbranche: f. *as* Esbranchement.
Esbranché: m. ée: f. *Lopped; bared, or depriued, of branches.*
Esbranchement: m. *A lopping; a baring, or depriuing, of branches.*
Esbrancher. *To lop, or cut off boughes; to bare, or depriue, of branches.*
Esbrandi: m. ie: f. *Imbrandished; cast violently, or furiously vpon.*
Quand le feu est esbrandi en plusieurs maisons. *When fire hath violently seized on, or flashes into, many houses.*
Esbranlé, Esbranlement, & Esbranler; *as,* Esbranslé, Esbranslement, & Esbransler.
Esbranslé: m. ée: f. *Shaken, iogged, shogged; brandished; stirred, moued; made to quake; wauer, stagger; incline, or decline.*
La partie est bien esbranslée pour luy. *is farre spent, or neere hand lost.*
Esbranslement: m. *A shaking, iogging, shogging; mouing, stirring; brandishing; wagging.*
Esbransler. *To shake, shog, iog; brandish; moue, wag, stirre vp and downe; to make tremble, quake, wauer, totter, stagger; incline, or decline; and hence;*
Esbransler quelqu'un de son opinion. *To remoue one from, or make him alter, his opinion.*
s'Esbransler de son devoir. *To swarue from his dutie; to transgresse.*
Esbransle-rocher. *Rocke-shaking; (an Epithete for a blustering wind.)*
Esbreché: m. ée: f. *Broken, or whereinto a breach is made.*
Esbrecher. *To breake, or make a breach into.*
Esbrillade: f. *A iert, ierke, or correction, giuen a horse with the bit, or bridle.*
Esbroüé: m. ée: f. *Hard-rubbed (in the washing;) also, snurted, or snuftered.*
Esbrouëment: m. *A rubbing hard, as in the washing of a nastie cloth; also, a snurting, or snuftering with the nose.*
Esbrouër. *To rub hard, or together; as in the washing of a foule, or hard thing.*
Esbrouër des narines. *To snurt, or snufter.*
Esbrouëure: f. *as* Esbrouëment.
Esbruché: m. ée: f. *Scattered, dispersed, sowed abroad.*
Esbrucher. *To scatter, disperse, or sow abroad.*
Esbu: m. uë: f. *Soaked in, drunke vp.*
Esbucheter. *To gather, or picke vp, stickes.*
Esburré: m. ée: f. *Vnbuttered; or, from which butter hath beene taken.*
Laict esburré. *Butter-milke, churnd milke.*
Esburrer. *To take butter from; to make butter-milke of.*
Escabeau: m. *A stoole.*
Escabelle: f. *A little, or low stoole.*
Escabreux: m. euse: f. *Rough, rugged.*
Escache: f. *The Bitt called, a Scatch.*
Escaché: m. ée: f. *Squashed; beaten, battered, or crushed flat; pressed, thrust, knocked, squeezed hard together.*
Escachement: m. *A squashing; a beating, battering, or crushing, flat; a pressing, thrusting, knocking, squeesing hard, or close, together.*

Es-

Escacher. *To squash; beat, batter, or crush, flat; to thrust, presse, knocke, squeeze, hard or close together.*

Escacheur: m. *A squasher; a beater, or crusher of things flat; a thruster, presser, or squeezer of things, hard or close together.*

Escachure: f. *A squashing; beating, or crushing, flat; a thrusting, pressing, or squeezing, hard or close together; also, a squash, crush, knocke, or squeeze, (whereby a thing is flatted, or beaten close together.)*

Escadre: f. *as* Esquadre. *A squadron; or square batallion.*

Escadres isnelles. *Swift, and light companies, as of birds, &c.*

Escadron: m. *as* Esquadron; *a squadron of Souldiors.*

Escaffette: f. *A kind of great, and long muskle-shell (resembling a little Skiffe, or Trey) wherewith the women of Picardie skumme their milke.*

Escaffignon: m. *A Socke; also, a Pumpe; or, a close, and single-soled shoe of thin leather.*

Escaigne de fil, ou de soye: f. *A skaine of thread, &c.*

Escaille: f. *The skale of a fish, &c; any skale, broken shell, or shale; also, as* Coucon; *also, the crust, or vpper laying, of a Pauement.*

Escailles. *(also) peeces of wood wherewith ioynts, or crannies left betweene stones, in building, are filled vp; also, the little skalie plats whereby an Armour is made plyant vnto the bodie.*

Escaille d'acier, de bronze, d'erain, de fer, &c; *the Offalls of Steele, &c; the skales that fly from them whē they are hammered; (very medicinable; especially those, that fall from the vnwrought brasse, or copper; whereof nayles are forged.)*

Alun d'escaille. *Seeke* Alun.

Angelot à la grosse escaille. *An old Angell: and (metaphorically) one that hath in him more stuffe and worth, then forme or fashion.*

Bois d'escaille. *The heart of Wood; (called so by Joyners.)*

Pourpoint d'escaille. *A plated Corselet made scale-fashion.*

Tel cuide avoir des oeufs au feu qui n' y a que les escailles: Pro. *Some weene they haue egges, that haue but shels, i'the fire.*

Escaillé: m. ée: f. *Skaled, skalie, hauing skales, or shales.*

Mur escaillé. *A wall full of cracks, or chinks.*

Escaillement: m. *A skaling; pilling, shaling of.*

Escailler. *To skale, or pull the skales of; also, to beat, bethwacke, belabor the skin-coat of.*

Escailler sa ieunesse. *To spend, passe; consume, or wast, his youth in dissolute, riotous, or licentious courses.*

Escailler des noix. *To pill, or shale Walnuts.*

Escailleur: m. *A skaler; piller, shaler of.*

Escailleure: f. *A skaling, &c, as* Escaillement.

Escailleures de pierres. *Shards, or spalls; small peeces broken, or hewed, from stones.*

Escailleux: m. euse: f. *Skalie; full of skales, or shales.*

Escaillon: m. *A horses tush, or tuske.*

Les Escaillons du palais. *(Signifie also) the skales, or skale-like diuisions, in the roofe, or palate of the mouth of a horse.*

Escalade: f. *A scalado; a skaling; the taking, or surprisall, of a place, by skaling.*

Escaladé: m. ée: f. *Skaled; taken, surprised, or entred into, by scalado.*

Escalarder des noix. *To shale Nuts.* ¶Norm.

Escalbotté: m. ée: f. *Pilled, vnhusked.*

Escalbotter. *To pill; as Pease doe in boyling; to vnhuske, or loossen the huske of.*

Escalé: m. ée: f. *as* Escaillé.

Escalier: m. *A winding stayre.*

Escalle. *Looke* Scalle.

Escallé: m. ée: f. *Skaled; taken, surprised, or entred into (as a Towne) by scalado; also, gone into diuers parts, and ports; also, as* Escaillé.

Escaller. *To skale; to take, surprise, or enter into, by scalado; also, to goe into diuers parts, and Ports; also, as* Escailler.

Escallier: m. *as* Escalier.

Escalonnier: m. ere: f. (Dents escalonnieres. *A horses tuskes, or tushes.)*

Escalque: m. *An Vsher, or Sewer.*

Escalventré: m. ée: f. *Whose guts are squashed out, or bellie burst, by treading on it.*

Escalventrer. *To tread out the guts; to burst the bellie with trampling on it.*

Escamme. *as* Escamne.

Escamne: m. *A Bench, Forme, or Seat; also, a step to get vp vnto a higher thing by.* ¶Pic.

Escamoté: m. ée: f. *Disguised, changed, sophisticated.*

Escamoter. *To change, disguise, alter, sophisticate, foist in ill wares.*

Escampe: f. *A scaping, flitting, shifting, flying away; a speedie dislodging, quicke retyring.*

Escampé. *Scaped, flit, fled, auoided, recoyled, dislodged, runne away.*

s'Escamper. *To scape, flit, fly, auoid, recoile, retire; to runne away, or dislodge quickly out of a place.*

Escandal: m. *A Mariners sounding Plummet.*

Escandillé: m. ée: f. *Scantled; made according to the patterne or scantling of.*

Escanné: m. ée: f. *Stifled, throtled, strangled.*

Escantuole: f. *The Pumpe of a ship; or, as* Escandal. ¶Rab.

Escapade: f. *An escape, or escaping; and (more particularly) a licentious, rebellious, or disordered motion, in a horse; and (sometimes) the disordered, or licentious flying out of a man.*

Escaper. *as* Eschapper.

Escapolin: m. *A remnant, or parcell, of a peece of stuffe.*

Escappe. *A small square-edged circle, or fillet in a piller, &c; also, the bodie of a piller.*

Escarade: f. *The opening of the nether part of the branch of a horses Bitt.*

Escaras. *as* Eschalas. ¶Pic.

Escarbelotte: f. *A small Beetle.*

Escarbillat: m. ate: f. *Quicke, lustie, liuelie, frolicke, spiritfull, stirring, that will stand on no ground; also, fantasticall, humorous, giddie, haire-braind.*

Escarbot: m. *The blacke Flie called, a Beetle.*

Escarbot cornu. *as* Cerf volant.

Escarboté: m. ée: f. *Stirred vp, as the fire.*

Escarboter le feu. *To stirre vp the fire.*

Escarbotte: f. *as* Escarbot.

Escarboucle: m. *The precious stone tearmed, a Carbuncle.*

Escarboucle: f. *The pestilent botch, or sore, tearmed a Carbuncle.*

Escarbouillé: m. ée: f. *Crushed, squeezed, battered, burst in peeces.*

Escarbouiller. *To crush, squeeze, batter, burst in peeces.*

Escarbouiller la cervelle. *To braine.*
Escardé: m. ée: f. *Carded.*
Escarder. *To card, as wooll.*
Escardes. *Cardes for wooll, &c.*
Escardeur: m. *A carder.*
Escardeure: f. *A carding.*
Escare: m. *A certein fish which (against the custome of all others) chewes his meate.*
Escare: f. *A skarre, or scab, or as* Escharé.
Escargot. *A snayle.*
Escargot de mer. *A whelke; also, a winckle, or periwinkle; (the first, the greatest; th'others, lesse kinds, thereof.)*
Escarlate: f. *Scarlet; also, the Scarlet apple.*
Escarlatin: m. ine: f. *Of skarlet, or of a skarlet hue.*
Rose escarlatine. *A Damaske rose.*
Escarlatte. *as* Escarlate.
Escarmouchant. *Bickering, skirmishing.*
Escarmouche: f. *A skirmish, bickering, brablement; a small fight, or fray.*
Escarmouché. *Bickered, skirmished; brabled.*
Il s'est bien escarmouché. *He hath talked throughly; he hath wrangled, or bestirred himselfe exceedingly in the matter.*
Escarmoucher. *To skirmish, bicker, brable; to bestirre himselfe like a horse that driues away flyes with his tayle.*
Escarmoucheur: m. *A bickerer, skirmisher; brabler.*
Escarotique. *Skarre-breeding; skab-bringing.*
Escarouflé: m. ée: f. *Scratched, torne, rent.*
Escaroufler. *To scratch; to teare, to rend.*
Escarpe: f. *A scarfe, or little wall without the mayne rampire of a fort.*
Escarpé: m. ée: f. *Vaulted; also, cut steepe downe; and hence;*
Fossé escarpé en plomb. *A dike made plum downe.*
Escarper. *To cut smooth, and steepe.*
Escarpins: m. *Pumpes; light, or single-soled shooes; also, a kind of torture.*
Escarpoulette: f. *A kind of swing (wherein a man sits as he swings.)*
Escarque. *as* Escalque: ¶Rab.
Escarquiller. *as* Esquarquiller; *to set wide open.*
Escarrabillade: com. *as* Escarbillat.
Escarre: f. *A Skarre, or hard scab vpon a wound; Looke* Eschare.
Escarure: f. *A womans square.*
Escart: m. *A discarding; a departing, or putting aside, and out of the way; also, a place of solitarie retirall.*
'A l'escart. *Apart, aside, out of the way; asunder, one from another.*
Escarté: m. ée: f. *Scattreed, dispersed; disparcled; discarded; throwne abroad.*
Escartelé. *Quartered; cut into quarters.*
Femme bien escartelée. *A woman big set, of thicke limmes, and large quarters.*
Escarteler. *To quarter; to slaughter, butcher, cut in quarters.*
Escartellé. *as*, Escartelé, *Quartered.*
Escarter. *To scatter, dissipate, disparcle; also, to discard; to set, or lay apart; also, to sheed, squatter, throw about, or abroad.*
s'Escarter. *To goe aside, get out of companie, slip out of the way.*
Escas. *The tenth penie of the value of moueables, wherein a forreiner succeeds a freeman, due vnto the townes of* Seclin, & Bassée sous Lille, *by their particular customes and charters.*
Escassable. Meubles escassables. *Moueables subiect vnto* Escas.
Escavessade: f. *A shake, iert, or blow, with the cord of a Caueson.*
Escéer. *To cut, or slyve; also, to pill.*
Escelles: f. *The arme-holes.*
Escerné: m. ée: f. *Vnkernelled, whose kernell is taken or cut out; also, opened, scraped, or scarified round about.*
Escerner. *To vnkernell; to take, or cut a thing cleane out of the round place wherein it was; also, to open, scrape, or scarifie a thing round about, or on euerie part or side of it.*
Escervelé: m. ée: f. *Braine-sicke, haire-braind, wild-braind, cocke-braind; headie, giddie, humorous; also, brained; whose braines are knocked, or dasht out; also, braineless, or depriued of braines.*
Esceveler. *To braine, to knocke, or dash out the braines of; also, to take the braines out of.*
Escervellement: m. *A braining.*
Eschabouillé: m. ée: f. *Scorched, ouerheated.*
Eschafaudage: m. *A scaffolding; a building or setting vp of, a presenting or shewing out on, scaffolds; also, a scaffold, or scaffold-like Stage, &c.*
Eschafaudé: m. ée: f. *Made into a scaffold; also, presented on a scaffold; or, caried from scaffold to scaffold, for a shew, or to his greater disgrace; also, set on the Pillorie.*
Eschafauder. *To build scaffolds; to present on a scaffold; to set on the pillorie; also, to deuise, inuent, plot, or practise villanie.*
Eschafaudis: m. *A scaffold.*
Eschafaulder. *as* Eschafauder.
Eschafaut: m. *A Scaffold, or high Stage; also, a Pillorie.*
Eschaffaudage: m. *as* Eschafaudage.
Eschalas: m. *A Pole, prop, stake, or stay, whereby a Vine, or any other weake-branched, vp-creeping, or high-growing Plant is held, and helped, vp.*
L'eschalas fait tomber la Vigne: Pro. *Looke* Vigne.
Eschalassé: m. ée: f. *Propped, sustained, vnderset with a pole, or stake.*
Eschalasseau: m. *A short, or small pole, prop, or stake.*
Eschalassement: m. *The propping, sustaining, or vndersetting of Vines, &c.*
Eschalasser. *To prop, sustaine, vnderset, or stay vp a Vine, Hop-plant, &c.*
Eschalassier: m. ere: f. *Of or belonging to, furnishing or bearing store of, poles, props, &c, for Vines, &c.*
Eschalier: m. *A winding staire; whence;*
Aussi tost prest qu'un chien auroit sauté vn eschalier. *Readie after a while; or as soone readie as one, that does all things with deliberation, can be; (for whether a dog leape vp or downe such a staire, he commonly takes him leisure; Looke* Sauté.)
Eschallat: m. *as* Eschalas.
Eschalle: f. *A little ringing, or tinging Bell.*
Eschallier. *as* Eschalier.
Eschallon: m. *A kind of great ladder for a high loft, &c.*
Eschalon. *as* Eschellon.
Eschalote. *as* Eschalotte.
Eschalotte: f. *A Ciue, or Chiue; (In which sence, the Plurall,* des eschalottes, *is most vsed) also, a bruised stalke of Hempe.*
Se mettre en rang d'oignon & ne valoir vn eschalotte. *To vsurpe a place, or imployment, whereof he is no way worthie.*

Eschambouillure: f. *as* Eschaubouillure; *a push.*
Eschampé: m. ée: f. *Flowne out, runne, or gotten loosse; got abroad, at libertie, or at randome.*
s'Eschamper. *To fly out, to take libertie; to runne loosse, freely, licentiously, or at randome.*
Eschampre. *as* Enchampre.
Eschancré: m. ée: f. *Infected with, or eaten into, by a Canker, or cankered sore; also, cut or made hollow, and into a halfe-round; semi-circled, halfe-rounded; also, neere pared, or nipped off; also, notched.*
Souliers eschancrez. *Voided, or cut with an opening, in the sides.*
Eschancrer. *To eat, as a Canker, into; also, to cut or make hollow, and halfe-round; also, to pare very neere, nip off too too neere; also, to notch.*
Eschancrure: f. *A halfe-round; or a halfe-round notch, dint, or hole cut, made, or eaten; also, an eating into; a cutting, or making hollow, and halfe-round; a notching; a neere paring, or nipping off.*
Eschandille: m. *as* Eschantillon.
Eschandillé: m. ée: f. *Scantled; or, as* Eschantillé.
Eschandillon. *as* Eschantillon.
Eschandole: f. *A short boord, or shingle, such as, in some places, houses are couered withall; also, a Thatchers Beater, or Combe and Beater.*
Eschange: f. *An exchange, trucking, barter, scoorsing.*
Eschangé: m. ée: f. *Exchanged, interchanged, chopped, scoorsed, bartered, trucked.*
Eschanger. *To exchange, interchange, trucke, chop, scoorse, barter, change one for another.*
Eschanson: m. *A cup-bearer, or cup-taster vnto a great person.*
Eschansonne: f. *A woman cup-bearer.*
Eschansonner. *To play the cup-bearer; and, to tast, or take an assay of another mans cup.*
Eschansonnerie: f. *The Office of a cup-bearer, or cup-taster.*
Eschanteler. *To breake into cantles; or, to cut off the corners, or edges of.*
Eschantillé: m. ée: f. *Curtalled, abridged; broken, or cut into corners, or cantles.*
Eschantillon. *A small cantle, or corner-peece; also, a scantling, sample, patterne, proofe of any sort of Marchandise.*
Vn petit eschantillon de ieunesse. *A tricke of youth.*
Eschantillonner. *To breake off a small cantle, or corner peece; also, to cut, or take off a sample, proofe, patterne, or scantling.*
Eschapeler. *as* Chapeler. *To chip.*
Eschappatoire: m. *An euasion, starting hole, by-corner, meane to escape by, chinke to creepe out at; a shift, or excuse; also, an exception against.*
Eschappé: m. ée: f. *Escaped, euaded; shifted, slipt, or got safe away; deliuered, freed, rid, or discharged from; also, dissolute, licentious.*
La pierre est eschappée. *Looke* Pierre.
Il n'est pas eschappé qui traine son lien: Pro. *He is not freed that trayles his shackles after him; or, due punishment euer comes at length, although sometimes it be deferred a while.*
Eschappée: f. *A scape, escape, slip; shift, euasion.*
Eschapper. *To escape, fly, euade, auoid, shift away; to scape, come, or passe through, safely; to free himselfe, or get rid, from; to slip, creepe, or wind out of.*
Eschaque: f. *Scurfe, scales, or dandriffe in the head, or beard.*

Eschar. *as* Eschars.
Escharalle: f. *A dead, and stinking flesh, which breeds about wounds made with shot, or otherwise much brused.*
Escharas. *as* Eschalas.
Escharaveau. *as* Charaveau.
Escharbot. *as* Escarbot; *a Beetle; also, a Saligot, Caltrop, water Nut.*
Escharboter. *as* Escarboter. ¶Rab.
Escharcement. *Scarcely, scantly, barely, hardly, miserably, needily; sauingly, neerely, niggishly, niggardly, pinchingly, pennyfather-like.*
Escharceté: f. *Scarcitie, scantnes, barenesse; pinching, neerenesse, miserie; also, basenesse, or want of due alloy, in coyne.*
Escharcette: f. *as* Escharceté *(in the last sence.)*
Escharde: f. *A splint, or splinter; a sharp, & short stumpe, of clouen wood, or flying from wood in the cleauing; also, a little, leane, or skraggie girle, that lookes as if shee were starued.*
Eschardonner. *To weed, or plucke vp, thistles; to cleere a ground, or garden, of thistles.*
Eschardonneur: m. *A weeder of thistles.*
Eschardonneuse: f. *A woman that weeds, or plucks vp, thistles.*
Eschare: f. *A skarre, or hard scab vpon a sore, hurt, wound; also, the crust which ariseth vpon an actuall, or potentiall cauterie.*
Escharfaud, ou, Escharfaut. *as* Eschaffault. *A scaffold.*
Escharfaudé. *as* Eschaffaudé.
Eschargotté: m. ée: f. *Pruined, as a tree; picked round about.*
Eschargotter. *To pruine a tree; to picke any thing round about.*
Escharné: m. ée: f. *Fleshlesse; pulplesse, pithlesse; depriued of flesh; pulp, or pith.*
Escharotique: com. *Which breeds, or brings a scab, or skarre vpon a wound, sore, vlcer, &c.*
Escharpe: f. *A Scarfe; a Baudricke; also, a rap, or wipe ouer the shoulder with a sword.*
Escharpes de cordage. *The ropes which strengthen, and settle the iaumbes, or cheekes of Cranes, or the like Engins.*
L'escharpe d'un pelerin. *The scrip, wallet, or pouch wherein he carries his meat.*
Escharpeux: m. euse: f. *Scarfie; scarfe-like; flaunting it with many scarfes about him.*
Escharre: f. *as* Eschare.
Eschars: m. arse: f. *Scarce, needie, scantie; sauing, sparing, hard, niggard, pinching, niggish, couetous, neere, strait-handed.*
Eschars plaidoyeur hardi perdeur: Pro. *A niggardlie pleader is an euill speeder.*
Escharsement. *Seeke* Escharcement.
Escharseté: f. *Scantnesse, or scarcitie; also, defect, or want of weight, in coyne.*
Eschat. Droict des eschats, & Tavernes. *A certaine dutie, or imposition vpon wine sold by retayle, & in Tauernes; from which all Priests beneficed within* Bourdeaux *are exempted, for as much as grew in their own grounds, glebe, or Prebendaries.*
Eschasses: f. *Stilts, or scatches to goe on.*
Mieux vaut vn pied que deux eschasses: Pro. *Better is one foot then two stilts.*
Eschasseur. *One that goes vpon stilts, or scatches.*
Eschassier. *as* Eschasseur.
Eschaubouillant. *Scalding hot; or so hot, that it blisters where it touches.*

Eschaubouillé: m. ée: f. *Full of hot blaines, pushes, wheales; beblistered; or, hauing the Shingles.*
Eschaubouillure: f. *A hot push, blaine, blister; or, a kind of inflammation, which brings with it vneuennesse, and ruggednesse to the skinne, with many little buds, or blisters that fret it; Some call it the Shingles, some the running worme; others, wild fire.*
Eschauboulé, & Eschauboulure. *as* Eschaubouillé, & Eschaubouillure.
Eschaubourré: m. ée: f. *Troubled, moued, in an agonie; (a word vsed about* Tours.)
Eschaudé: m. *A kind of Wigg, or Symnell, fashioned somewhat like a Hart; a three-cornered Symnell.*
Eschaudé: m. ée: f. *Scalded with, bathed in, hot liquor.*
Chat eschaudé craint l' eau froide: &, Chien eschaudé craint l'eau froide: Prov. *Looke* Chat, *or* Chien.
Eschauder. *To scald, or cast hot liquor vpon.*
Eschaudet. *as* Eschaudé.
Eschaudure: f. *A scalding.*
Eschaufaison: f. *A heating, chafing, warming, making hot; also, a heat; or, a disease that comes of immoderate heat.*
Eschaufant. *Chafing, heating, warming.*
Eschaufé: m. ée: f. *Chafed, warmed, heated, set in a heat; also, hot, feruent, ardent; vehement, eager, earnest, in a matter.*
Eschaufement: m. *as* Eschauffement.
Eschaufer. *as* Eschauffer.
Eschaufeture: f. *A chafing, warming, heating; or, as* Eschaufaison.
Eschauffadasse: f. *A burnt whore.* ¶Langued.
Eschauffader. *as* Eschafauder.
Eschauffaison: f. *as* Eschaufaison.
Eschauffé: m. ée: f. *as* Eschaufé.
Eschauffement: m. *A chafing, warming, beating, setting in a heat.*
Eschauffer. *To chafe, warme, heat, make hot, set in a heat.*
Il s'eschauffe en son harnois. *Said of one that growes in choler, or into passion, for the satisfying of some disordinate humor.*
Bonne beste s'eschauffe en mangeant: Prov. *A good beast eates till he sweat againe; or, eates that he sweat withall; we say, good at meat good at worke.*
Eschaufferette: f. *A little Chafing-dish.*
Eschauffette: f. *A Chafing-dish.*
Eschauffeture: f. *as* Eschaufeture.
Eschaufure: f. *A chafing, or fretting by heat.*
Eschauguette: f. *A Sentrie, Watch-tower, Beacon.*
Eschauguetté: m. ée: f. *Watched in a Beacon, or high Tower; beheld from high, or a farre off.*
Eschauguetter. *To watch at a Beacon, or in a high tower; to espy, behold, see from high, farre about, or a farre off; to stand Sentinell.*
Eschauguetteur: m. *A Sentinell, or Watchman in a high Tower, or at a Beacon; hence, any Spy, Scout, Espyall.*
Eschays. Aller eschays. *To shale, stradle, goe crooked, or wide betweene the feet, or legs.*
Escheable: com. *Escheatable.*
Escheance: f. *An Escheatage, or escheating; also, an Escheat (for want of heires.)*
Eschec: m. *A Checke at Chesse-play.*
Des eschecs. *The Chesse-men.*
Eschec & mat. *Checke-mate at Chests; and (metaphorically) a remedilesse disaster, miserie, or misfortune.*
Donner eschec & mat à. *To subdue, conquer, ouercome; surmount, surpasse; win, or get the better, of; also, to ruine, or ouerthrow, the fortunes of.*
Eschef: m. *A fall, wasting, or diminution.*
Escheler. *as* Escheller.
Eschelette: m. *A Skelton, or Anotamie.*
Eschelette: f. *The bird called a Wall-pecker; also, the little stalke of a Grape; also, as* Eschellette.
Eschellage: m. *as* Eschellement.
Eschelle: f. *A Ladder, or Skale; (also, a squadron of souldiors; in old French.)*
Eschelle altimetre. *Part of an Astrolabe.*
Mis à l'eschelle. *Set on, or fastened vnto, a ladder with a Miter, or Paper, about his head; hence (also) publikely disgraced, put vnto open shame (any way.)*
Se voyant au pied du mur sans eschelle. *See* Mur.
Eschellé: m. ée: f. *Skaled, or climbed vp on; also, publikely disgraced (by standing in open Market on a ladder.)*
Eschellement: m. *A skaling, or climbing vp vnto, a getting vp on, by a ladder.*
Escheller. *To climbe; to skale, or get vp vnto, by a ladder; also, publikely to disgrace, or put vnto open shame, an Offendor, by setting him, in open Market, on a Ladder with a Miter, or Paper about his head.*
Escheller vne grandeur. *To aspire vnto a dignitie, to mount vnto greatnesse.*
Eschellette: f. *A little ladder, or skale; a small step, or greece; also, a little hand-bell, such as Cryers vse.*
Eschelleur: m. *A climber by, or skaler with, a ladder.*
Eschellon d' eschelle. *The round, or step, of a ladder.*
Tondre à eschellons. *To clip vneuenly; to notch, or make steps in the haire.*
Eschelon. *as* Eschellon.
Eschemeau: m. *The bed of a Vine; the ridge wherein it stands.*
Eschemer. *To swarme, or breed young, as Bees.*
Eschenal: m. *A gutter, or channell.*
Eschenillé: m. ée: f. *Rid from Caterpillers.*
Escheniller. *To rid of Caterpillers.*
Escheoir. *To happen, chance, betide, fall out, befall; to fall, or come vnto.*
Escheoir en foy, ou main tierce; *Looke* Tiers.
Il n'eschet point à vn homme de bien de mentir. *An honest man cannot ly; or, is verie seldome knowne to ly.*
A vn bon chien n'escheut oncques vn bon os: Pro. *A good dog neuer lighted on good bone; an honest person rarely comes to preferment; the verier knaue the better lucke, say we.*
Eschequé: m. ée: f. *Checkered; or (as Blasoners) checkie.*
Escheque-mat: m. *A check-mate at Chests.*
Eschequier: m. *A Checker, or Chesse-boord.*
Escherpillerie: f. *Robbing on the high way, pursetaking, violent stripping, or despoyling of a passenger.*
Escherui. *The Skirret root.*
Eschet: m. *An Escheat, or thing fallen to.*
Escheu: m. euë: f. *Befallen, happened, chaunced; fallen, or come vnto.*
Il y avoit deux jours escheus. *Two dayes were come and gone.*
Eschevé: m. ée: f. *Eschewed, shunned, auoided, bent or bowed from.*
Escheveau: m. *A skaine, or loope of thred, or silke.*
Desmesler vn escheveau. *To wind himselfe out of an intricate businesse, or danger.*

Eschevelé: m. ée: f. *Dischceuled, ruffled; whose haire fals loosse, or in disorder, about the eares; (a word most proper, and most vsed, in the feminine;) also, bared (as of haire;) made bare, or bald.*

Eschevement: m. *A shunning, eschewing, auoiding, bending from.*

Eschever. *To shun, eschew, auoid, bend from.*

Eschevin: m. *The Sherife of a Towne; or, an Officer who (representing the Roman* Ædilis) *lookes that the Market be duly furnisht, and well serued; the houses fitly ranked, and well built; the streets euen paued, or cleane kept: And where a Towne hath, by any Priuiledge, the disposall of it owne* Police, *the* Eschevins *(for there be euer more then one) dispose of it; and (howsoeuer) they be in authoritie next vnto the Mayor, (or, as in Paris, to the* Provost des Marchands) *and, in the Townes that haue no Mayors, the principall Magistrats.*

Eschevinage: m. *The Sherifeship of a Towne; the Office, or Authoritie of a Sherife, or* Eschevin; *also, a Sherifes Court, or, the Iurisdiction thereof; also, a Corporation; or the Incorporation of a Towne; and hence;*

Droict d'eschevinage. *Looke* Droict.

Eschevissement. *as* Eschevement.

Escheute: f. *as* Eschoëtte. *An Escheat, &c.*

Eschez. *Looke* Eschec.

Eschif: m. iue: f. *Rauenous, or greedie at meat; (a Hunters tearme.)*

Eschiffeur. *A Cutter, or Pinker.*

Eschifflé: m. ée: f. *Split, riuen.*

Eschiffler vne branche d'arbre. *To split, riue, or halfebreake off, a branch.*

Eschimeau. *as* Eschemeau.

Eschinal: m. *The head of a Sinke, couered with a Grate.*

Eschine: f. *The Chyne, backe bone, ridge of the backe; also, (in a Pillar) a round boultell cut with egges.*

Longue eschine. *A slimme, lunges, luske; long-backt, or ill-shaped, loobie.*

Eschiné: m. ée: f. *Chyned, broken-backed.*

Eschinée (de Porc.) *A chyne (of Porke.)*

Eschiner. *To chyne; to diuide, or breake, the backe of.*

Eschineux: m. euse: f. *Of a great, and strong backe.*

Eschinon: m. *The chyne, or vpper part of the backe betweene the shoulders.*

Eschiquetté. *Checkie; (a tearme of Blason.)*

Eschiquier: m. *The Exchequer; (in Normandie) is an Assemblie of high Iusticers, wherein the Decrees, Orders, Commissions, and Iniunctions awarded by Baylifes, Vicounts, and inferior Iusticers, may be censured, and amended; (This Assemblie was extraordinarie, and held at vncertaine and vnset times, vntill that* Lewis *the twelfth made it ordinarie, and of it, (as it still continues) a Soueraign Court;) also, a Chess-boord; also, Checker-worke.*

Planter à l'eschiquier. *To plant trees Checker-wise; to set them in equall distance one from the other; or, so to set them, as which way soeuer one lookes betweene them, he sees direct Alleyes, and Rowes, in equall distance one from the other.*

Eschiquoté: m. ée: f. *Rid, as a tree, of vnprofitable shoots, or siences.*

Eschiquoter. *To cut off, or take away vnprofitable shoots, or siences from trees.*

Eschoëtte: f. *An Escheat; land that falls to a man by Accident; Succession, or Discent; also, (more generally) any Succession.*

Eschoir. *as* Escheoir; *To befall, happen; fall vnto.*

Eschoite: f. *An Escheat; land fallen, &c; as in* Eschoëtte.

Eschoitter. *To succeed, or follow in the roome of another.* ¶Bourbon.

Escholage. *as* Escolage.

Escholastre. *as* Escolastre.

Eschole. *as* Escole.

Eschope: f. *A little, and (most commonly) low shop; such a one as one of our meaner Seamsters, or Pedlers hath.*

Eschoppe. *as* Eschope.

Faire essay à l'eschoppe. *To lay a small, and thinne peece of siluer, &c, vpon a hot burning coale, thereby to try the value, and alloy of it; (a Goldsmithes phrase.)*

Eschoué: m. ée: f. *That hath escaped after a shipwracke; also, runne a land, fast on ground, as a ship.*

Eschouër. *To run, or touch vpon a banke, shelfe, or shore, and there make shipwracke.*

Esciemment. *Wittingly, of set purpose.*

Escient. à bon escient. *In deed, in earnest, in good faith, in good sadnesse, from the heart.*

`A son escient. *With his consent, or knowledge; wittingly, willingly, or for the nonce.*

De tel escient. *In such sober sadnesse, in so good sooth.*

Escimé: m. ée: f. *Topped, whose top, or head is cut off.*

Escimer. *To top; to cut off the tops, or heads off.*

Esclaboché: m. ée: f. *Bespotted, bespatled, besprinckled with water, or durt.*

Esclabocher. *To besprinckle, bespattle, bespot with water, or durt.*

Esclaboter. *as* Esclabocher. ¶Pic.

Esclaffer. *To buff, or burst, out into a laughter.*

Esclair: m. *Lightning; a leame, or flash of lightning; a suddaine blase, or flash of light.*

Esclairci: m. ie: f. *Cleered, discouered; explaned, displayed; fined, clarified.*

Esclaircir. *as* Esclercir.

Esclaircissement. *as* Esclercissement.

Esclaire: f. *The hearbe Celandine, Swallowort, Tetterwort; (*La grande Esclaire.)

Petite Esclaire. *Little Celandine, Pilewort, Figwort.*

Esclairé: m. ée: f. *Lightned; lighted; also, watched, obserued.*

Edifices bien esclairez. *Lightsome, or well-windowed, houses.*

Esclairer. *To shine, glisten, glister; to lighten, to flash out; to appeare, or manifest it selfe; to giue light vnto; also, to watch, or obserue; to spy, or pry into.*

Pourveu que ie voye esclairer, ce sera fait; *If I may see the gold glister, or some chinks stirring, it shall be done.*

Esclaire-tout. *All-seeing, all-lighting; all-obseruing.*

Esclaireur: m. *An obseruer, or ouerseer of others; also, an assistant vnto a plaintife, or accuser, for his benefit, and to preuent the corruption, or collusion, which otherwise might be vsed in the handling of his suit.*

Esclame: com. *Gaunt, lanke, small bellied.*

Esclamme: f. *A long, and thicke riding cloake to beare off the raine; a Pilgrims cloake or mantle; a cloake for a traueller.*

Esclanche de mouton. *A leg of Mutton (cut large with the whole bone at it.)*
Esclandre: m. *A slaunder; a defamation, detraction, vniust imputation; also, a slaughter; also, a mishap, danger; tumult, vprore; mischiefe.*
'A grand pecheur esclandre: Prov. *Great sinners euer come to shame.*
Esclandreux. *Scandalous, slaunderous, or slaunder-breeding.*
Esclandrir. *To slaunder, defame, dishonour, depraue, detract from.*
Esclappe: f. *Grossenesse, corpulencie, fatnesse.*
Esclat: m. *A Shiuer, splinter, or little peece of wood broken off with violence; also, a small, and thin Lath, or Shingle.*
Esclat de lumiere. *A glimpse, or suddaine flash of light.*
Esclat de tonnerre. *A clap, or crack, of thunder.*
Diamond de bon esclat. *A diamond that shines very faire, or sparkles much in the eye; a dyamond of a good luster, or water.*
Par esclats. *Peece-meale, in sheeuers, into a thousand peeces.*
Esclatant: m. ante: f. *Splitting, crashing, cracking; ringing; bright-shining, glistering, glittering, flashing, brandishing; hauing a fresh, or faire glosse.*
Oraison esclatante. *An earnest, vehement, or pearcing, speech.*
Esclate. *A kind of disease among children.*
Esclaté: m. ée: f. *Burst, split, crashed, shiuered into splinters; also sparkled, glittered, glistered, flashed out.*
Esclater. *To shine, sparkle, glisten, glitter; to flash out; also; to haue a fresh or faire glosse.*
s'esclater. *To split, burst, crash, breake, shiuer into splinters, or peeces.*
Esclature. *A splitting; shiuering in peeces, a bursting into shiuers, or splinters; also, a glistening, sparkling, glittering; flashing.*
Esclau. *as* Esclave. *A slaue.*
Esclavage: m. *Slauerie, bondmanship; villenage.*
Esclave: m. *A slaue, bondman, bondslaue, bought seruant.*
Esclaver. *To enthrall, make slauish, bring vnto slauerie or bondage.*
Esclavine: f. *as* Esclamme; *or a sea-gowne; or a course, high-collered, and short-sleeued gowne, reaching downe to the mid leg, and vsed most by sea-men, and Saylors.*
Esclayer. *To vnhurdle, vnwattle; vnbarre; to breake open, pull away, or make way through, hurdles &c.*
Escleche. *A dismembring; or seperation; also, a part, or peece dismembred, or seperated from.*
Escleché: m. ée: f. *Dismembred; rent, or torne from; in parcels, diuided, seperated from.*
Escler.. *Seeke* Esclair.
Esclerci: m. ie: f. *Cleered; explaned, manifested, illustrated; fined, clarified; growne thin, light, faire.*
Esclercir. *To cleere; illustrate, manifest, explane, display; also, to fine, clarifie, make cleere.*
s'Esclercir. *To wax thin in substance; to grow few, or small in number; light, or faire in colour; to cleere vp.*
Esclercissement: m. *A cleering, manifestation, explanation, illustrating of matters; also, a fining, or clarifying.*
Esclere, ou Esclerre. *as* Esclaire. *The hearbe Selandine.*

Esclerement. *Cleerely, brightly; plainly, manifestly.*
Esclesche: f. *as* Escleche.
Esclichoir: m. *A Squirt, or Siringe.*
Esclische. *as* Escleche. ¶Wallon.
Esclisché: m. ée: f. *Dismembred, diuided, peece-mealed, parted.*
Esclischement: m. *A dismembring, parting, diuiding of an entire thing.*
Esclisse: f. *Any (small) Hurdle, or any Vtensill of watled Ozier, or Wicker, &c; hence; a Cheese-fat, or Chesfoord thereof; and, the Rundle, or Circlet put vnder a dish at Table; a wicker bottome for a dish; also, a twig, or sticke of Ozier, or Wicker; and hence;*
Esclisses. *Splents, bound about a broken leg, &c; also, the sides of a Violl, or Fiddle.*
Esclissé: m. ée: f. *Squirted; spurted, spatled, or spouted from (or as from) a Squirt; also, watled; wouen of, or made vp with, Ozier or Wicker twigs, &c; also, splented; bound vp in, or kept straight by, splents.*
Fromage esclissé. *Formed in the Cheese-fat; or, that hath still on it the print of the Chesfoord.*
Esclisser. *To squirt; to spurt, spatle, or spout from (or as from) a Squirt; also, to watle, or make vp with Ozier or Wicker twigs, &c; also, to splent; to bind vp in splents, or keepe straight by splenting.*
Esclissoire. *A Squirt.*
Esclistre. *as* Fouldre.
Esclop: m. *A Patten, or woodden shooe.* ¶Tholosain.
Esclopé: m. ée: f. *Maymed, limping, lame.*
Escloppé. *The same.*
Escloppér. *To maime, to lame.*
Esclorre. *To hatch; also, to disclose, produce, bring forth.*
Esclorre la bouche. *To open the mouth.*
Esclos: m. se: f. *Hatched; disclosed; opened.*
Esclot: m. *as* Esclop; *also, a Reed, or Cane, to sucke with; also, a Rest in Musicke; also, a Galley-slaue.*
Esclotouëre. *A Clap Net.*
Esclou: m. *The print of a horses foot.*
Escloy: m. *Pisse, lant, vrine, lee, stale.* ¶Pic.
Escluine. *as* Esclamme.
Esclusant. *Stopping, as by a Sluice; or, as* Excluant.
Escluse: f. *A Sluice, Floud-gate, or Water-gate; also, a Mill-damme; also, any Damme, Cesterne, or great Vessell, whereby the water that comes from a Spring is receiued, and kept for vse; also, a passage betweene hils, or at the foot of a hill, which by a high, and betowred gate seperates the marches, or territories of one countrey from another.*
Escodilles: f. *The bulbes, or bulbed roots, of Daffodils, or Daffadowndillies.*
Escoffier: m. *A Shoomaker.*
Escoffraye: f. *A Shoomakers Stall, or the boord whereon he works.*
Escoffret: m. *as* Escoffraye; *or, a little one.*
Escofion: m. *A Coyfe, or Cawle.*
Escofraye. *as* Escoffraye.
Escogrifte: m. *A Luske, a great Slouch, Clusterfist, foule Clunch.* ¶Orleannois.
Escoinson: m. *A Scunche; the backe part of the iaumbe of a window.*
Escolage: m. *Schoole-hire; a stipend, or money, giuen for the teaching, or tutoring of a Scholler.*
Escolastre: m. *The Rector, chiefe Maister, Superintendent, or Ouerseer, of a Schoole; also, an vnlearned, or meane Scholler; one that is but halfe a Scholler.*

Escolastrerie: f. *A Rectorship or gouernment of, a Superintendencie ouer, a Schoole; also, meane Schollership.*
Escole: f. *A Schoole; or Colledge, wherein any Art is taught.*
Chemin de l'escole. *The longest way.*
Faire l'escole buissonniere. *To play the truant.*
Table vaut escole notable: Prov. *Table talke is an excellent Schoolemaster.*
Escolier: m. *A Scholler, Learner; Pupill, Student.*
Il en parle comme vn escolier d'armes. *He speakes thereof ignorantly, improperly, or from the purpose.*
Escolier babillard prez le feu, & badin hors la classe: Pro. *(Meant onely of a meere Scholler; as our) A Master of Art is not worth a fart vnlesse he be in the Schooles.*
Escolleté: m. ée: f. *Vncollered; whose coller is taken off, or pulled away.*
Escolleter. *To vncoller; to diuide, plucke, or take away the coller from a garment.*
Escolté. Soulier escolté. *Looke* Escouleté.
Escome. *The blade (or broad end) of an Oare.*
Escomé. Peis escomé. *The Spit-fish, or Sea Pike, so tearmed at* Marseille.
Esconduire. *To deny, or say nay vnto; to refuse, or reiect the request of.*
Esconduit: m. ite: f. *Denyed; whose request is refused.*
Esconjuré: m. ée: f. *Driuen, or gotten, away by intreatie, or coniuring.*
Esconjurer. *To driue away by intreatie, or coniuring.*
Esconsé: m. ée: f. *Hidden, couered, concealed; set, as the Sunne.* ¶Pic.
Esconsement. *as* Absconsement; *a concealing.* ¶Pic.
Esconsement de soleil. *The setting of the Sunne.*
Esconser. *as* Absconser; *To hide, conceale, couer.* ¶Pic.
Escopetade. *The shot of a Harguebuze, or small Peece.*
Escopetin. *as* Squiopetin.
Escopette: f. *A Petronell, Carbine, long Pistoll, short Harguebuze; any such small Gun that goes off by a fire-lock.*
Escopetterie: f. *Gun-shot; a voley of shot.*
Escorce: f. *The rinde, or barke of a tree; the outward skin, or pilling of fruit.*
Mettre le doigt entre le bois & l'escorce. *Busily to intermeddle with, or take much notice of, the differences, or vnkindnesses that are betwixt neere friends.*
Escorcé: m. ée: f. *Barked, pilled, vnrinded; blanched; pared.*
Escorcée: f. *as* Escorcement; *also, the pilled, or vnrinded part of a Plant.*
Escorcement: m. *A barking, pilling, vnrinding; blanching; paring.*
Escorcer. *To barke, or vnbarke; to pill, pare, blanch, vnrind.*
Escorcesque: m. *as* Corcesque.
Escorceur. *A barker of trees.*
Escorché: m. ée: f. *Flayed; vnskinned; excoriated.*
Escorche-cul. à escorche-cul. *To the flaying of the buttocks; or (as in,* Tirer à es.*) With bare arse kissing, or dragd along on, the ground.*
Escorchement: m. *A flaying, or pulling the skin off; also, an excoriation; and hence;*
Escorchement des boyaux. *The bloudie flix.*
Escorcher. *To flay, or plucke off the skin; also, to excoriate.*
Escorcher les anguilles par la queuë. *To goe the wrong way to worke.*
Escorcher le Latin. *To inkhornize it, or vse inkhorne tearmes.*
Escorcher le Règnard. *To spue, cast, vomit; (from the subiect to the effect; for the flaying of so stinking a beast is like enough to make them spue that feele it; Looke* Regnard.)
Assez escorche qui tient le pied: Pro. *The Assistant is as guiltie as the Actor; the Accessarie as the Principall; he does mischiefe enough that helpes to doe mischiefe.*
Bien escorche à qui ne deult: Prov. *Sencelesse people may well enough be flayed; or, tis good fleecing of them that haue so much, as they misse not what is gone.*
`A la preuve l'on escorche l'Asne: Pro. *(Applyable vnto such things as cannot be tryed without danger.)*
Beau parler n'escorche langue: Prov. *Faire words flay not the tongue; teare no skin, breake no bones.*
Escorcherie: f. *A flaying house; the place wherein slaughtered beasts are vsually flayed.*
Escorcheter. *To flay; to pill the rind off, or pull the skin from.*
Escorcheur: m. *A flayer; also, an Outlaw, or Freebooter.*
Escorchouër: m. *A flaying of beasts.*
Escorchure: f. *A flaying, or pulling the skin off; a gauling, or peeldnesse of any part of the bodie.*
Escorçu: m. uë: f. *Barkie, hauing a barke.*
Escore: com. *Plumpe, or straight down, in depth; whence;*
La mer est escore en ceste coste. *The sea is very deepe, or, the channell is on this coast.*
Escores. *The stocks whereon a ship stands in the docke.*
Escorgée: f. *A thong, or belt (of leather;) also, a stripe, or lash with a leatherne thong.*
Escorne: f. *Shame, disgrace, contempt, scorne.*
Escorné: m. ée: f. *Vnhorned, without hornes, that hath lost his hornes; hence (also) melancholicke, out of heart, out of countenance, ashamed to shew himselfe, as a Deere is, when he hath cast his head; also, vncornered; whose corners are broken, or cut off; and hence; defaced, ruined; scorned, disgraced.*
Arbre escorné. *A tree whose branches are lopt off.*
Dez escornez. *Ground Dice, blunt-cornered Dice.*
Escornement: m. *An vnhorning, or depriuing of hornes; a disgracing; defacing; baring or bereauing of ornaments.*
Escorner. *To vnhorne, dishorne, or depriue of hornes; to cut, pull, or take from one a thing which is (or he thinkes is) an ornament, and grace vnto him; to breake off the corners of a square thing; to lop, or shred off the boughes of Trees; to ruine, deface, disgrace any thing.*
Se laisser escorner. *To suffer himselfe to be ridden, made a foole, vsed like a Gull.*
Escornicher. *In stead of* Escorner, *or* Escorcher. ¶Rab.
Escornifé: m. ée: f. *Vncornered; whose corners haue beene eaten, or broken off.*
Escornifler. *To knap, eat, or breake off the corners of; also, to smell a feast, or eat hard, at a feast (which another man payes for;) also, to pick a thanke, or carry tales for victuals; or, (vnder pretence of ieasting, or tale-carrying) to procure himselfe accesse vnto feasts, or other mens tables.*
Escornif lerie: f. *Feast-smelling; fast eating at (other mens) feasts; also, base Parasitisme, ieasting, or tale-carrying, for victuals.*

Escornifleur: m. *A base pickthanke, or parasite; greedie feeder, or smell-feast; one that carries tales, ieasts, or newes from house to house, thereby to get victualls.*
Escornizer. *as* Escorner.
Escort: m. orte: f. *Discreet, warie, heedie, aduised, circumspect; obseruant; that knowes well how to carrie himselfe, in any businesse wherin he meddles, or companie wherewith he meets.*
Escorte: f. *A guide; conuoy; safeconduct; a direction, or safegard for the way.*
Escosse: f. *The huske, hull, or cod of a beane, pease, &c.*
Escossé: m. ée: f. *Vnhusked, shaled, hulled.*
Escosser. *To vnhuske, shale, hull.*
Escossois: m. oise: f. *Scottish, of Scotland.*
Magot Escossois. *A Coot, or Moorehenne,*
Escot: m. *A shot; also, a yong shute of a tree; also, a splinter, thorne, or stumpe of a thorne offensiue to the barefooted.*
Disner à escot. *A dinner at an ordinarie; or, whereat euerie guest payes his part, or, share and share like.*
Faisons l' escot. *Words vsed by the Capuchines when they shake their robes ouer the imbers, to auoid their vermine, and to consume by the aire of the fire the matter whereof they breed.*
Parler par escot. *To speake by turnes, to heare one another speake.*
Payer l' escot pour autruy. *To pay, or be punished for other men.*
Il a prins, ou fait cela, soubs l' escot. *He hath taken, &c, that in secret, vnder-hand, by stealth, in hugger mugger.*
Il s' a beau taire de l' escot qui ne paye rien: Prov. *He may wel ynough conceale the shot that payes no part of it.*
Escotté: m. ée: f. *That is within a shot, or hath paied a shot.*
Escotter. *Euery one to pay his shot, or to contribute somewhat towards it, &c.*
Escoüade: f. *The traine, or followers of a Captaine, or Leader; also, the companie of souldiors whereof a Corporall hath the leading; a squadron.*
Escoüarde. *as* Escoüade; vn cap d' es. *A Corporall.*
Escoube: f. *A brush; also, a maukin for an ouen:* ¶Langued.
Escoudé: m. ée: f. *Depriued of his support, of the stay whereon he leaned, of the meanes whereon he relied.*
Escoüé: m. ée: f. *Curtalled; whose taile is lost, or cut off; also, wagged, or shaken vp and downe.*
Escouër. *To curtall, or cut off the taile; also, to wag, or shake a thing vp and downe.*
Escouëtte: f. *A Plaisterers whiting brush.*
Escouëttes. *Sheates; Looke* Escoutes.
Escoufle: f. *A Kite, Puttocke, or Glead.*
Escouillé: m. ée: f. *Gelt, libd, vnstoned; bereaued, or maimed of his stones.*
Escouillé de Sybille. *One of Sybells (gelt) Priests.*
Escouillement: m. *A gelding, libbing, bereauing of stones.*
Escouiller. *To geld, lib, vnstone, cut away the stones of, bereaue of stones; also, to maime, or make impotent, by striking on the cods, or stones.*
Escouillon: m. *A wispe, or dishclowt; a maukin, or drag, to cleanse, or sweepe an ouen.*
Escouillure: f. *A gelding, or libbing; a cutting away of the cullions.*
Escouisson. *as* Escoinson.
Escoulable: com. *Drainable; consumeable; easie to be dried, or decayed; soone slipping, or gliding by.*
La memorie de le homme est escoulable. *Quickly past, easily rased, soone gone.*
Escoulant: m. *as* Escoulement; *Or, a draine; or strainer; also, a sloping part, or place, downe which a thing easily glides, or is apt to runne.*
Escoulant. *Drayning, or drying vp; gliding, or slipping by.*
Escoulé: m. ée: f. *Drained; also, strained; also, derived from one to another; also, slid, slipt, passed, runne, fled smoothly, glibly, quietly along, or away; also, consumed, wasted, pined away by little and little.*
Iour escoulé. *A day ouerslipt, ouerpast, or gone, almost before it was thought of.*
Escoulement: m. *A draining, or drying vp; also, a straining; also, a consuming, wasting, or pining away, as of the bodie.*
Escoulement d' eau. *A gliding, sliding, slipping, smooth running, glib falling, gentle passing along, of water.*
Escouler. *To draine, or drie vp; also, to deriue from one to another; also, to straine through.*
S' escouler. *To glide, slip, slide, runne quietly, passe couertly, along; to fall downe glibly, flie smoothly away; also, to wast, pine, decay, consume.*
Escouleté. souliers escouletez. *Welted; also, cut, or open on th' instup, and tied with a lachet passing ouer it.*
Escouleure: f. *A strainer.*
Escoullement. *as* Escoulement.
Escouller. *as* Escouler.
Escoupellé: m. ée: f. *Topped, or whose top is cut off.*
Escoupeller. *To top, or cut off the top of a tree.* (v.m.)
Escoupette. *as* Escopette; *A Petronell, or long Pistoll.*
Escourgée: f. *A thong, latchet; scourge, or whip.*
Escourgeon: m. *Amelcorne, Starch-corne; a kind of base and degenerate wheat, which being ground yeelds verie white (but verie light, and little nourishing) meale.*
Escourre. *To thrash, or seuer corne from the chaffe; also, to beat, or shake, as dustie clothes, &c.*
Escoursouër: m. *The dale of a (ships) pumpe, whereby the water is passed out.*
Escourté: m. ée: f. *Curtalled, shortened, cut, or chopped off.*
Escourter. *To curtall, shorten; cut, or chop off.*
Escousse: f. *A shaking, swagging, swinging, shogging, iogging; also, a swag, swing, or violent sway; also, as* Rescousse.
Escousse. *(The feminine of* Escoux.*)*
Escoutant. *Hearing, hearkening, listening vnto.*
Il ne seroit nuls mesdisans s' il n' estoit des escoutans: Prov. *None would reuile if none would heare.*
Escoute: m. *A spie, eaue-dropper, prying companion; also, a scout, scout-watch, or Sentinell; the discouerer, or forerunner, of an armie.*
Croupir aux escoutes de gros morceaux. *Looke* Morceau.
Estre aux escoutes. *To listen, hearken, watch, or spie, whats done abroad; to eaue-drop, to prie into mens actions, or courses; priuately to obserue their lookes, or ordinarie speeches.*
Escouté: m. ée: f. *Hearkened, listened, giuen eare vnto.*
Escoutement: m. *A hearkening, or listening; a hearing with attention.*
Escouter. *To hearken, heare, listen, giue eare, yeeld attention vnto; to heed the speech, obserue the words of.*

Escoutes. *The Sheates; the double ropes which serue to fasten the maine saile behind.*

Escouteur. *An hearer, hearkener, listener, eaues-dropper.*

'A fol conteur sage escouteur: Prov. *While fooles doe speake wise men had need to heare.*

Escoutilles: f. *The scutles, or hatches of a ship; th'ouertures, or trap doores, whereat things are let downe into the hold.*

Escoutillon: m. *A scuttle.*

Escoux: m. Escousse: f. *Shaken, iogged, swinged, swagged.*

Paille escousse. *Wherein no corne is left.*

Escouvelle: f. *A brush; as* Escouëtte.

Escouvillon. *as* Escouillon.

Escouvillonner. *To spunge a peece; to cleanse her before and after she is discharged.*

Escrageant. *Crushing, or squeezing out.*

Escragé: m. ée: f. *Crushed, or squeezed out.*

Escrager. *To crush, or squeeze out of.*

Esraigne. *A little houell, made of poles set round with their ends meeting at the top, and couered with turues, sods, and dung, so thicke, that no weather can pierce it.*

Escrain: m. *A Casket, or small Cabinet; a little Ring-box, or Iewell-box; also, the till of a chest.*

Escran: m. *A skreene to set betweene and the fire; also, the tester of a bed.*

Faire escran contre le vent. *To turne his nose into the wind, to set his nose against the wind; or, to stand betweene one and the wind.*

Escrasé: m. ée: f. *Squasht downe, beaten flat, crushed in peeces with much pressing, or hard leaning on.*

Escrasement: m. *A crushing flat, or squashing downe.*

Escraser. *To squash downe, beat flat, crush in peeces with much pressing, or hard leaning on.*

Escraseur: m. *A crusher; squasher, or beater of things flat by hard pressing of them.*

s'Escravanter. *To burst, or split himselfe.*

Escriere. Pie es. *The rauenous bird called, a Shrike, Nimmurder, Wariangle:* ¶Savoyard.

Escrazé. *Looke* Escrase.

Escrein: m. *A skreene.*

Escremé: m. ée: f. *Vncreamed, flected, as milke.*

Escremer. *To fleet, or take away the creame from milke.*

Escresmer. *The same.*

Escreté: m. ée: f. *Vnchaulked; or depriued of chaulkie whitenesse.*

Escrevé: m. ée: f. *Riuen, clouen, burst, or split, asunder.*

Escrever. l' es. du iour, ou de la nuict. *The dawning of the day; the twilight.*

s'Escrever. *To riue, cleaue, burst, or split, asunder.*

Escrevisse: f. *A Creuice, or Crayfish; (By some Authors, but not so properly, the Crab-fish is also tearmed so.)*

Escrevisse de fumier. *The great, & venomous black Beetle.*

Escrevisse de mer. *A Lobster; or, (more properly) a Sea-Creuice.*

Pas d' escrevisse. *A backe-step, a going backward.*

Pierres d' escrevisse. *Looke* Pierre.

Plus lunatique qu' vn' escrevisse. *More lunaticke then a Creuice.*

Escrevisser. *To goe backeward.*

Escrevisses. *The ioynted plates, or part, of a Cuirats, resembling the backe of a Creuice.*

Escri: m. *An outcrie, or acclamation.*

Escrié: m. ée: f. *Exclaimed, cried out.*

Escriement. *as* Escri; *Or, An exclaiming, or crying out.*

Escrier aucun. *To exclaime, crie out on, call vpon one.*

s'Escrier. *To exclaime, crie out, make an outcrie; to rore, bray, or yell.*

Escrime: f. *Fencing, the Art of fencing.*

Escrimer. *To fence, or play at fence; also, to lay hard about him.*

Escrimerie: f. *as* Escrime.

Escrimeur: m. *A Fencer, a Maister of Fence.*

Escrin. *as* Escrain; *A Casket.*

Escriner. *To barbe; to powle, or plucke off the haire.*

Escrinier: m. *A Ioyner; and (more particularly) a Casket-maker, Cabinet-maker.*

Escript: m. *A writing; a manuscript, scrowle, scedule, thing written; an Indenture, or peece of euidence.*

Bailler par escript. *To publish, declare, offer, exhibit, put forth, set out, in writing.*

Mettre par escript. *To couch, digest, record, set downe in, commit vnto, writing.*

Escript: m. te: f. *Written; described or decyphered, published or declared, couched or set downe, in writing.*

Droict escript. *The Ciuile Law.*

Escripteau: m. *A note, or bill of ones hand; an inscription, title; short memorandum, libell, certificate; a declaration, or description of a thing, in writing.*

Escriptoire: f. *A Penner.*

Escripture: f. *Writ, Scripture, writing; a stile, or manner of writing; the making, or writing of bookes; an inscription, or title; a deed, writing, or euidence.*

Scavoir moult d' escripture. *To be learned, or skilfull in, or well acquainted with, most bookes.*

Escrire. *To write; scribble, scribe it; to indite, decipher, pourtray, display, couch, or set downe, in writing; to make a booke, or worke.*

Escrire nicement. *Looke* Nicement.

'A mal exploicter bien escrire. *Appliable when a man by a faire tale, or wel-couched words, indeuors to extenuate the guilt of his faults, or of his errors in proceeding.*

En la peau de brebis ce que tu veux y escris: Prov. *One may write what hee will in a sheepes skin.*

Escrit: m. ite: f. *Written; Looke* Escript.

Escriteau: m. *as* Escripteau.

Escriture: f. *as* Escripture.

Escrivaillé: m. ée: f. *Scribled, scuruily penned, bauldly written.*

Escrivaillerie: f. *Scribling, bauld writing.*

Escrivailleur: m. *A scribler, bauld writer, paultrie penman.*

Escrivain: m. *A Notarie, Scribe, Scriuener.*

Escrivainerie: f. *Scriuenership; the Art, or Act, of a Scriuener.*

Escrivisse. *as* Escrevisse.

Escrober. *To shog, or iog, as a cart in an vneuen way.*

Escroë. *as* Escrouë.

Escrotter. *To gnaw, or bite with the teeth.*

Escrou: m. *A Goalers booke, &c; as in* Escrouë.

Escrouë: m. *A scrue; the hole, or hollow thing wherein the vice of a presse, &c, doth turne; also, a scrowle; also, the booke wherein a Goaler sets downe, and registers the names, and surnames of his prisoners, and the day, moneth, and yeare of their entrance, and dismission; also, a Suruey of the ground held by a Cottier, or Copiholder, deliuered vnto his Landlord; also, a roll containing the particulars of the Courts expence in acates, &c, digested, and signed euerie day by the Steward,*

Steward, and Comptroller of the houshold, and deliuered ouer vnto the Treasurer; also, the Breuiate of a case, or cause, in controuersie; also, the warrant thats deliuered by a generall Assessor vnto inferior Collectors, for the leuying of a Subsidie, tax, or imposition.

Escruoëlle: f. *A little Shrimp-resembling worme, or vermine in puddles, and some springs.*

Escrouëllé: m. ée: f. *Troubled with the Kings euill.*

Ame escrouëllée. *An infected, traiterous, or depraued spirit.*

Les Escrouëlles. *The Kings euill.*

Herbe des escrouëlles. *Little Celandine, Pilewort, Figwort.*

Escroulé: m. ée: f. *Shaken, tottered, shogged.*

Escroulement. *A shaking, shogging, tottering.*

Escrouler. *To shake, totter, shog.*

Escroupionné: m. ée: f. *Rumplesse; whose crupper is broken.*

Escrousté: m. ée: f. *Chipped; vncrusted; vnscabbed.*

Escroustement: m. *An vncrusting; or vnscabbing.*

Escrouster. *To chip; vncrust; vnscab; to pare the crust off, pull or pill the scab from.*

Escrouter. *To vncrust; to chip, or pull the crust off.*

Escru. drap escru. *Raw, new, fresh, vndressed, vntrimmed cloth; euen as it comes from the weauer.*

Escruë. *as* Accreuë.

Escu: m. *A crowne in money; also, a shield, or targuet; also, a Scutcheon (of Armes; and sometimes th'Armes themselues) or coat of Armes.*

Escu couronne. *Is lesse in value, by a* Sous, *then the* Escu Sol.

Escus à l'estoille Pousiniere. *Looke* Estoille.

Escu du Palais. *A counter.*

L'escu du soc. *Th'eare of the plow-share.*

Escu sol. *A Crowne of the Sunne; (the best kind of Crowne that is now made) hath a little starre on th'one side.*

Escu vieil. *An old Crowne; is worth* vij. s. ij. d. sterl.

Il n'a escu ny targe. *The diuell may freely daunce in his purse; there is not a crosse to fright him, or blesse th'owner, withall.*

Il fait de son teston vn escu. *He thriues well, gaines much, increases mightily in estate.*

Escudes. *as* Escudettes.

Escudettes. *The hearbe Hipwort, Venus-nauell, Pennywort, Pennie-grasse.*

Escueil: m. *A rocke; also, a rockie place.*

Escuelle: f. *A dish.*

Escuelle à oreillons. *A porrenger.*

Grande escuelle. *A platter, or charger.*

Petite escuelle. *A saucer; or small dish.*

Les affaires domestiques y vont par escuelles. *All things are squandered, rioted, or disorderly wasted, in that house; the like is;*

Tout y va par escuelles. *There is cheere in bowles; there is no sparing, pinching, nor sauing of anything; and;*

Mettre tout par escuelles. *(As we say) to throw the house out at windowes.*

Qui s'attend à l'escuelle d'autruy il disne souuent bien tard: Prov. *Tis long before hee bee serued that waits for another mans leauings.*

Escuellée: f. *A dish full of.*

Escuelles. *Hipwort, Wall-penniewort, Ladies-nauell; (an hearbe.)*

Escuellette: f. *A little dish.*

Escueuil: m. *A kind of Oake whose acornes are good to bee eaten; some hold it to be, the barren Scarlet Oake.*

Escuier. *as* Escuyer; *An Esquier, &c.*

Escuirie: f. *as* Escuyrie.

Escuisant. *Smarting, itching, netling, stinging.*

Escuissé: m. ée: f. *Hipped; or, whose hip, or thigh is put out of ioynt.*

Escuisser. *To hip; to put the hip, or thigh out of ioynt.*

Esculé: m. ée: f. *Whose taile is burst; heele troden downe.*

Esculée: f. *A dish full of.*

Esculer. *To burst the taile of.*

Esculer vne aiguille. *To breake a needles eye.*

Esculer ses souliers. *To tread his shooes downe at the heeles.*

Escume: f. *Scumme, drosse, foame, froth.*

Escume de Mareschal. *The refuse, or drosse of yron; smithie dust.*

Escume de plomb. *Lead-foame, comes by cleere water cast vpon hot lead, presently after it hath beene melted.*

Escume de sel. *Looke* Sel.

Escumé: m. ée: f. *Scummed, or skimmed; refined, clarified; cleansed in th'outward parts; also, scowred, as the sea by a pyrat &c.*

Escumement: m. *A foaming; also, a scumming, or skimming; also, a raunging, rouing; also, a scowring of the seas.*

Escumer. *To foame, or yeeld a frothie slauer; to gather vnto a froth, or scumme; also, to skimme, or clarifie, liquor; to refine, or take off the (outward) filth from; also, to raunge, roue, deale at randome; whence;*

Escumer la mer. *To scowre, as a fleet of warlike ships, the sea; to play the pyrat, to vse piracie.*

Escumeur: m. *(Is properly) a scummer, or skimmer of liquor; also (lesse properly, but more commonly) a pirate, or a rouer at sea.*

Escumeux: m. euse: f. *Foamie, frothie, filthie.*

Escumier: m. ere: f. *Of foame, or froth; wherupon some Poets tearme Venus,* fille escumiere, *because shee is fained to haue beene bred of the sea-foame.*

Escumoir: m. *A scummer.*

Escumoire: f. *The same.*

Escurage: m. *A scowring; cleansing; feying.*

Escuré: m. ée: f. *Scowred; cleansed; feyed.*

Escurer. *To scowre; fey, rinse, cleanse, or make cleane:* ¶Rab.

Escureur. *as* Escurieu; *A Squirrell; also, a scowrer, cleanser; feyer.*

Escurie: f. *as* Escuyrie.

Escurieu: m. *A squirell.*

Escurs. *The little sallade hearb called, Ciues, or Chiues.*

Escusson: m. *A Scutcheon; a small targuet, or shield; also, the knop in the middle of a timber-vault where the ends of the courbed poasts doe meete; also the bud of a tree, cut off with part of the barke, in forme of an ordinarie scutcheon, and hence.*

Enter en escusson. *To lodge that bud in the bark of a tree by an incision made thereinto of the forme of a T, or by any other hole apt to receaue it; the clefts, and breaches therof being afterwards closed vp with wax, or clay.*

Escussonnable: com. *Fit to be so graffed.*

Escussonné: m. ée: f. *Defended, or couered with a scutcheon, or shield.*

Escussonner. *as* Enter en escusson; *also, to defend, or couer with a scutcheon, or shield.*

Escuyer:

Escuyer : m. *An Esquire, or Squire; also, he that beares an Errant knights launce & shield; also, an Vsher, or Sewer; also, the false bud of a Vine; also, a yong male deere which, ordinarily, keeps an old one company; also, a kind of yellow, and hard-rinded Peare.*

Escuyer de Cuisine. *The clarke of a kitchin.*

Escuyer d'Escuyrie. *A querrie, in a Princes Stable; the gentleman of a lords horse.*

Escuyer trenchant. *A caruer, or squire of the mouth; also a Taster; (for he that carues to a Prince, euer tasts of what he carues, before his master touch it.)*

Le grand Escuyer de France. *The master of the horse; who besides his authoritie ouer all th'Officers of the kings stables, hath also (which here belongs to the Earle marshall) Iurisdiction ouer heralds, and pursiuants; In old time the great master, or steward of the Kings house, was also called thus.*

Peu peut bailler à son Escuyer qui son cousteau lesche: Prov. *He that hath but little for himselfe hath not much for his man.*

Pour l'amour du Chevalier baise la Dame l'escuyer: Pro. *(Wherein his worship is, often, but little beholden to her Ladieship.)*

Escuyere : f. *A woman-esquire; a Gentlewoman that attends on a knight as his Esquire.*

Escuyrie : f. *The stable of a Prince, or nobleman; also, a Querry-ship; or the ducties, or offices belonging thereto; also (in old authors) a Squires place; or, the dignitie, title, or estate of an Esquire.*

Esdenter. *as* Edenter.

Esfarouché : m. ée : f. *Frighted, scared, frightened, feared away; also, tamed, reclaimed, made gentle, inward, or tractable.*

Esfaroucher. *To fright, scare, frighten, affray, feare away; also, to tame, winne, reclaime, make gentle, tractable, inward.*

Esfilé. *as* Effilé.

Esflanqué : m. ée : f. *Swayed in the backe; also, leane, meager, gaunt, thinne-flanked, or shrunke in the flanke, that hath no bellie at all.*

Esflanqué en cheval de postillon. *As lanke as a post-horse.*

Esflanquer. *To sway in the backe; or, to make leane, meager, gaunt, thinne-flanked, small-bellied.*

Esflorer. *To depriue of flower, or of flowers; Looke* Effleurer.

Esfoiré : m. ée : f. *Bedunged, bemired, berayed.*

Esfrontément. *as* Effrontément; *Impudently.*

Esgail : m. *A fine morning-frost, that shines like glasse.*

Esgal. *as* Egual; *Equall, euen, leuell.*

Les Ondes sont à l'esgal. *Plaine, smooth, calme.*

Esgaler. *as* Egualer.

Esgallé : m. ée : f. *Equalled, matched, euened, leuelled.*

Esgallement. *Equally, euenly, alike, matchably.*

Esgaller. *To equall, match; leuell, euen.*

Esgard : m. *Respect, heed, regard, obseruation; aduisement, consideration; reckoning, account; also, a report made, or account giuen, of.*

Esgards. sont gens expers, & cognoisants à faire visitations, & rapports: ¶ Ragueau.

Esgaré. il s'est esgaré de, &c. *He is wandered or straied, he swarues or digresses, from; he is out of the way.*

Esgaré de bouche. *(Of a horse) not subiect to the bit, vnstayed, in all things disobedient.*

Mais il ne fut pas pourtant esgaré. *Yet was he not abashed, or put downe; he had not yet lost himselfe; he knew, for all that, well ynough where he was.*

Esgarement : m. *A straying, wandering; swaruing, digressing from; also, a scattering, dispersing, mislaying.*

Esgarement en la veuë. *A staring, gastlinesse, amazednesse of looke; or, an vncertaine fashion of gazing vp and downe.*

Esgarer. *To scatter, disperse, mislay.*

s'Esgarer. *To erre, wander, stray, roue, to flie out, swarue, or digresse from, to runne out of the high way.*

Esgargaté de crier. *Whose throat is almost burst, or welnigh riuen, with crying.*

Esgaronné : m. ée : f. *Trodden downe, as a shooe at the heele.*

Esgaronner vn soulier. *To tread a shooe downe at the heele.*

Esgarouillé. yeux esgarouillez. *Wide-staring, or gloring, eyes.*

s'Esgaudir. *To reioyce; to be iocond, merrie, glad; to be full of glee.*

s'Esgayer. *To sport, make merrie, be gamesome; to skip, leape, or play, as duckes, or fish, in the water.*

Esgeré : m. ée : f. *Ploughed, or broken vp, as land for fallowes.*

Esgerer. *To plough, or breake vp land for fallowes.*

Esglantier : m. *The Eglantine, sweet Brier, Hep-tree, wild Rose-tree.*

Esglantier odorant. *The sweet Brier.*

Esglise : f. *as* Eglise; *A Church.*

Esgommé : m. ée : f. *Vngummed, whose gumme is taken away.*

Esgommer. *To vngumme; to take away the gumme from.*

Esgorgé : m. ée : f. *Whose throat is cut.*

Esgorgement. *The cutting of a throat; also, a whirlepoole, or swallowing abisme, or gulfe.*

Esgorger. *To cut the throat of.*

Esgorgeté : m. ée : f. *Whose throat is cut; also, bareneckt; bare, or open breasted; or wearing a verie low, or no, coller to his shirt, doublet, ierkin, &c.*

Esgorgeter. *as* Esgorger; *Also, to goe bare-neckt, openbrested; or to fould downe the coller of a garment, thereby to bare, or discouer the necke, or bosome.*

Esgosillé : m. ée : f. *Whose throat is cut.*

Esgosillement : m. *A throat-cutting.*

Esgosiller. *To cut the throat of.*

Esgosse : f. *A cod, huske, hulling.*

Esgoüé : m. ée : f. *Cloyed, saded, ouer full, or full vnto sacietie.*

Esgouër. *To be cloyed, saded, ouer full; to eat vnto sacietie.*

Esgousser. *To vnhuske; to pill, or shale husked fruits.*

Esgoust : m. *as* Esgout.

Esgout : m. *A drop, or dropping, as of water from a house eaues; also, a little sinke, channell, or gutter to void filth by.*

Pluye de Fevrier vaut esgout de fumier: Pro. *Look* Fumier.

Esgouté : m. ée : f. *Drained, dried, soaked of moisture, by little and little.*

Esgoutement : m. *A draining by dropping.*

Esgouter. *To draine, or make drie by little and little; to leaue neuer a drop in.*

Goutte à goutte la mer s'esgoute: Prov. *The sea by a continuall draining will grow drie.*

Esgouteur : m. *A drainer, soaker, drier vp by drops.*

Esgoutille : f. *A little hole, or gullet, through which water can doe little more then drop.*

Esgoutoir : m. *A draine, channell, sinke, or low gutter in a dairie, kitchen, &c.*

Esgrailler. *To shale, or straddle with the feet, or legs.*

Esgrai-

Esgrainer. *as* Esgrener.
Esgraphé: m.ée: f. *Loossed, pulled asunder, pulled away from; or as* Desgrafé.
Esgrapher. *To loosse, pull asunder, or pull away from; or as* Desgrafer.
Esgraphigner. *as* Esgratigner.
Esgratigné: m.ée: f. *Scratched, scraped, rent, or torne with the nailes.*
Esgratignement: m. *A scratching, scraping, tearing with the nailes.*
Esgratigner. *To scrape, scratch, rend, or teare with the nailes.*
Esgratigneur: m. *A scraper, or scratcher.*
Esgratigneure: f. *as* Esgratignement; *Also, a scratch, rend, or teare, with the nailes.*
Esgrené: m. ee: f. *Fruitlesse, barren, sterile, without corne; also, vngrained, vnseeded; depriued, as an husk of it seed, an eare of it corne, or graine.*
Esgrener. *To shake corne out of it eare; pease, or beanes out of their husks; to depriue, or make barren of corne; to vnseed, or take the seed out of.*
Esgrette. *as* Aigrette.
Esgrugé: m.ée: f. *Grated small; also, crumbled, crummed, or broken into small peeces.*
Esgrugeoir: m. *The little round grater of lattin, thats kept in a case of the same, and vsed most for the Nutmeg.*
Esgruger. *To grate small; also, to crumble, or breake vnto crummes.*
Esgrumé: m.ée: f. *Vnclustered; vncluttered; shaken, or taken, from it cluster.*
Esgrumelé. *as* Esgrumé.
Esgrumeler. *To vncluster, or vnclutter; to shake, or take asunder things that hang loosse together.*
Esgrumer. *To pluck grapes from their cluster.*
Esgruné: m. ée: f. *Crummed, crumbled, broken small.*
Esgruner. *To crumme, crumble, breake small.*
Esgual. *as* Egual.
Esgualation. *An equalling, matching, leuelling, making like.*
Esgualé, &, Esgualer. *Seeke* Egualé, &, Egualer.
Esgue: f. *A leane, ill-fauoured, carrion mare.*
Esgueré. la bouche esguerée. *Seeke* Esgaré.
Esguerer. *as* Esgarer.
Esgueulé: m.ée: f. *Gorged; whose throat is cut, or mouth burst.*
Esgueuler. *To gorge; to cut the throat, or burst the mouth of.*
s'Esgueuler de crier. *To split his mouth by vehement exclaiming.*
Esguiere: f. *An Ewer, a Lauer.*
Esguille: f. *A needle; also, a small fish called, a Hornebeake, Snacot-fish, Ganc-fish, Piper-fish; Looke* Aiguille.
Esguillé: m. ée: f. *Of a needle, full of needles; wrought with the needle; pricked with needles.*
Esguillée: f. *A needlefull of; also, a pricke, or stitch with a needle.*
Esguilleter. *To trusse the points.*
Esguillette: f. *A point.*
Esguillettes d'armes. *Looke* Aiguillettes.
Esguillette de chien. *A course leatherne point.*
Esguillettes de souliers. *The straps.*
Esguillette nouée. *The charming of a mans codpeece point so, as he shall not be able to vse his owne wife, or woman (though he may vse any other;) Hence;* avoir l'esguillette nouée, *signifies, to want erection: (This impotencie is supposed to come by the force of certaine words vttered by the Charmer, while he ties a knot on the parties codpeece-point.)*
Courir l'esguillette. *To be madde after a P. to run vp and downe after her leacherie, like a salt bitch; to play the common whoore; (In old time common wenches were enioyned to weare a point on one of their shoulders, thereby to distinguish them from those that professed honestie.)*
Esguillier: m. *A needle-maker.*
Esguillon: m. *A pricke, a goad, a sting, a spurre; a prouocation; any thing that incenseth, stirreth, or vrgeth forward; also, an inward griefe, pinch, or biting hurt.*
Esguillons. *Little stakes headed with yron, and stuck into the ground, for the galling of horsemen.*
De petit esguillon poinct on bien grande asnesse: Prov. *A little goad can pricke a great she Asse.*
Qui contre esguillon recule, deux fois se poind: Prov. *Seeke* Reculer.
Tel asne tel esguillon: Prov. *Looke* Asne.
Esguillonné: m. ée f. *Pricked, stung; pinched; vexed; vrged, incensed, prouoked forward.*
Esguillonnement: m. *A pricking, stinging; pinching; vrging, incensing, forward.*
Esguillonner. *To pricke, sting; pinch; vex; vrge, egge; force, prouoke, incite, instigate, forward.*
Esguillonneur: m. *A pricker, stinger; vrger, incenser, prouoker, instigater.*
Esguillonneuse: f. *She that moueth, incenseth, vrgeth, pricketh forward.*
Esguisé: m. ée: f. *Whetted, sharpened, whereon a good edge is set.*
Esguiser. *To whet, sharpen, set an edge on.*
Esguiseur: m. *A sharpener, or whetter of blades.*
Eshanché: m.ée: f. *Whose hip, or hanch is out of ioynt.*
Eshancher. *To put a hanch, or hip out of ioynt.*
Eshancheure: f. *A putting of the hip, or hanch out of ioynt.*
Esherbé: m. ée: f. *Weeded.*
Esherbement: m. *A weeding; a ridding of weeds, a plucking vp of grasse, or weeds,*
Esherber. *To weed; rid of weeds; plucke vp the grasse, or weeds.*
Eshonté: m. ée: f. *Shamelesse, impudent, brasen-faced, ouer-bold, whom nothing can put out of countenance.*
Os eshonté. *The forehead bone, so called by some.*
Eshontement: m. *Shamelesnesse, impudencie, vnshamefastnesse, gracelesnesse.*
Eshontément. *Shamelesly, impudently.*
s'Eshonter. *To be shamelesse, impudēt, ouer-bold; to haue a brasen face; to blush at nothing; to be past grace.*
Esjetté: m.ée: f. *Eiected, ierted, or squirted vp; cast out, launched forth.*
s'Esjetter. *To iert, or squirt vp; to eiect, cast out, or launch forth, it selfe.*
Esjeuné: m. ée: f. *Kept fasting, starued.*
Esjeuner. *To keepe fasting, to starue.*
s'Esjouir. *To reioyce, make merrie; be glad, blithe, iocond, pleasant, frolicke, full of glee.*
Esjouissance: f. *Ioy, mirth, glee, reioycing, gladnesse.*
s'Esjouissant. *Gladsome, frolicke, iocond, reioycing.*
s'Esjourner. *To linger, tarrie long, take his leasure, vse delayes; Looke* Sejourner.
Eslagué: m. ée: f. *Pruned, rid, or cleansed of vnprofitable shutes, boughes, or branches.*
Eslaguer. *To crop, and cut off vnprofitable, hurtfull, or vnhandsome branches from trees.*
Eslaguoir: m. *Th'instrument wherewith such branches are cut off.*

Eslaguisant. *Pruning; cropping, or plucking off vnprofitable branches.*
Eslaïnde. *An engine wherewith great stones are lifted vp.*
Eslançant. *Violently launching, shooting, hurling, throwing, thrusting, pushing forward; stretching out.*
s'Eslançant. *Furiously leaping, running, setting, or flying vpon.*
Eslancé: m. ée: f. *(Violently, or with an out-stretched bodie) leaped, girded, skipped, launched; put, pushed, thrust on, or forward; throwne, cast, hurled, flung, darted, shot out, or from; also, stretched vp, or out; also, gaunt, lanke, long, thinne or leane bodied; scrag-like, right like a Gangrell.*
Eslancement: m. *A violent leaping, launching, skipping; putting, pushing, thrusting on, vp, out, or forward; hurling, throwing, darting, shooting out, or from; a retching, or stretching out of the bodie in any of those actions; also, as* Elancement; *also, a stitch, or pricking in the bodie, caused by an Imposthume, Pluresie, &c.*
Eslancement de l'esprit. *An vnquietnesse; a disquieting, or stirring vp of passions; an out-ierting of the spirit, a sudden motion of the mind, or transportation of thoughts.*
Eslancer. *(Violently, or with an out-stretcht bodie) to thrust, put, push, vp, forward, on, or vpon; also (and in the same manner) to hurle, throw, cast, fling, dart, shoot out, or from; also, to stretch out, as the bodie, in any of these actions; also, as* Elancer.
Eslancer vn cerf. *To rowse a Stag.*
Eslancer vn cheval. *Suddenly to thrust a horse forward, with the spurre, &c.*
s'Eslancer. *Violently, or suddenly to leape, skip, iert, gird, launch forward.*
s'Eslancer sur vn ennemy. *To make furiously towards him, set fiercely vpon him; leape, or flie, at his face.*
Eslangouré. *as* Eslangoré.
Eslangui: m. ie: f. *Languished, in languishment, or fallen into languishment.*
Eslans: m. *A stretching out, or ierting vp, or thrusting forward, of the bodie prepared vnto a violent action, or motion, as leaping, hurling, darting, &c; hence also, any liuelie, violent, or sudden motion, be it leap, skip, iert, thrust, or stretch; also, the wild, and disordered pressing forward of a doing horse.*
Eslargi: m. ie: f. *Dilated, widened, inlarged, greatened, increased; also, freed, inlarged, released, set at libertie; also, giuen largely, dealt frankly, bestowed bountifully.*
Eslargir. *To dilate, inlarge, widen, greaten, increase; also, to free, set at large, giue libertie, or scope vnto; also, to giue largely, bestow frankly, deale bountifully.*
s'Eslarger en la mer. *To get sea-roome, or goe roomeward to sea; to get, put, or make out into the maine.*
Eslargissant. *Dilating, inlarging, widening, increasing; also, freeing, setting at large, or at libertie; also, giuing, dealing, bestowing largely, frankly, bountifully.*
Eslargissement: m. *An inlarging, dilating, widening; also, a freeing; a giuing of scope vnto, or setting at libertie; also, a large, or liberall giuing, dealing, bestowing.*
Eslargissement de la prunelle. *An imperfection in the eye; when the grapie Membrane being greater then it was, or should be, confounds all obiects, and makes them seeme farre bigger then they be.*
Defaillir au jour de son eslargissement. *To make default on the day of his apparance (whereto he was bound.)*
Eslavé: m. ée: f. *Moistened, bedeawed, washed ouer; weshie, deawie; washed away.*
Eslaver. *To moisten, bedeaw, wash ouer; wash away.*
Eslay: m. *A Careere, or course on horsebacke; (an old word.)*
Esle. *as* Aile.
Eslection: f. *An election, choice, or chusing; also, an Election; the seat, or circuit of an* Esleu; *a Towne, or Diuision (whereof there be diuers in each Generalitie) within which a certaine number of* Esleus *doe exercise their iurisdiction.*
Esleus: m. *Generall Assessors of Subsidies, &c; or Magistrates, who, when any Aide, Subsidie, or Imposition is to bee leuied, rate, at a certaine summe, euerie Parish, and Village of the Election, or Diuision wherein they reside; and accordingly send their warrants vnto the particular Officers, or chiefe inhabitants thereof, for the present gathering of what they haue rated: They also take notice of the raising, and maintenance of publicke bankes, and causeyes; and of collections of money for the walling, or fortification of Townes; and (as Iudges) of all actions (whether ciuile, or criminall) that concerne, or come of, any of these matters. At first, when the Aides were not leuied but in time of warre, nor then without consent of the people, they chose two Assessors in euerie Towneship, and from that choyce gaue them this name, which they held no longer then during the leuie: But after that they grew ordinarie, and to be imposed at the pleasure of the Prince, the* Esleus *changing their Maisters, became his officers, & officers during their liues; yet receiue they still their wages of the people, & sometimes large* Espices *to boot: Since then they haue increased both in number, and authoritie, so much, that they are now become verie burdensome vnto the whole countrey.]*
Esleu: m. euë: f. *Elected, chosen, culled, picked out.*
Eslevable: com. *Fit to be eleuated, raised, aduanced; reared bred, brought vp.*
Eslevation: f. *An eleuation; or as* Eslevement; *also, a rebellion, commotion, or vprising of people.*
Eslevé: m. ée: f. *Eleuated, raised, lifted, heuen vp; aduanced, extolled, promoted; also, risen, swollen, puffed vp, strouted out; bolt vpright; also, high, loftie, hautie, stout; also, heaped, or piled on; also, reared, bred, brought vp.*
Eslevement: m. *A lifting, raising, heauing vp; aduancing, extolling, promoting; also, a mounting, rising, swelling, puffing vp, strouting out; also, a rearing, breeding, or bringing vp.*
Eslever. *To eleuate, lift, raise, heaue vp, aduance on high; extoll, promote; also, to heape, lay, pile, or put one thing vpon another; also, to reare, breed, or bring vp.*
s'Eslever. *To rise, mount, swell, puffe vp, strout out; to grow loftie, hautie, high-minded, proud, presumptuous.*
Esleveur: m. *A raiser, lifter, mounter, heauer vp; an aduancer; a piler vp; a rearer, breeder, bringer vp of.*
Esleveur. *Eleuating, lifting, raising vp; and hence;* Muscle esleveur. *Looke* Muscle.
Esleveure: f. *A raising; or, a rearing; also, a rising, or swelling*

swelling vp in height; an imbossing, or outstrouting; also, an imbossement, or bunch; a thing risen, swollen, or puffed vp.
Esligible: com. *Eligible; worthie, fit, or like, to be elected; in election.*
Eslingé: m. ée: f. *Slender, lanke.*
Eslire. *To choose, elect, cull, pick out.*
Eslite: f. *A choice, election, picking out.*
Gens d'eslite; mots d'eslite. *Choice people, quaint termes; men, or words, of the better sort.*
Esloché: m. ée: f. *Shaken, wagged, iogged; loossed in the ioynt.*
Eslochement: m. *A Shaking or loossening, as of a ioint.*
Eslocher. *To shake, wag, iog, wauer; to loose in the ioynt.*
Esloigné; ou Esloingné: m. ée: f. *Remooued, sent, set, put, banished, or driuen, farre away.*
Faire la part au plus esloigné. *To yeald but a small part, allot a poore share, vnto.*
Esloignement, ou esloingnement. *A remoouing, or conueying away; a banishing from; a putting, or setting farre of.*
Esloigner; ou esloingner. *To remooue, banish, driue, set, put, farre away; to keepe aloofe, to send a great away from.*
S'esloigner de. *To leaue, abandon, forsake; to depart, or get him farre from.*
Eslourdement: m. *A dulling, or dulnesse; an astonishing, amazing; a dizzines, an amazement.*
Eslourdir. *To dull, blunt, make heauie, sottish, lumpish; also, to astonish, dizze, amaze.*
S'eslourdir. *To wax dull, grow sottish, proue heauie headed; also, to be amazed, astonied, dizzed.*
Esluder. *To deceiue, mock, scoffe at; to dallie with; to auoid, or shift off with words.*
Esmail: m. *Ammell, or enammell; (is made of glasse, and mettals, or* Chaulx metalique; *for which Looke* Chaulx.)
Esmail de Venise. *A kind of blacke enammell made at* Venice.
Esmaillé: m. ée: f. *Enammelled.*
Esmailler. *To enammell.*
Esmailleur: m. *An enammeller.*
Esmaillure: f. *An enammelling.*
Esmané: *as* Emané.
Esmaner. *Seeke* Emaner.
Esmarmelé: m. ée: f. *Crushed, croosed, or burst in peeces.*
Esmarmeler. *To crush, croose, or burst in peeces.*
Esmay *as* Esmoy. *Thought, care, carke.*
s'Esmayer. *To be sad, pensiue, astonyed, carefull; to take thought.*
Esme: m. *An ayme, or leuell taken; also, a purpose, intention, determination.*
Esmenuisé: m. ée: f. *Made small, broken or beaten into little peeces.*
Esmenuiser. *To breake, or beate into small peeces; to make small; or, as* Esmier.
Esmer. *To ayme, or leuell at; to make an offer to strike, &c; also, to purpose, determine, intend.*
Esmeraude: f. *An emerauld.*
Esmerauldin: m. ine: f. *Like an emerald, belonging to an emerauld.*
Esmeril: m. *An Emrod, or Emerill stone.*
Esmerillon: m. *The hawk termed a marlin; also, a small peece of Ordnance, about the size of a Robinet.*
Ioyeux comme un esmerillon. *As merrie as a marlin.*

Esmerillonnant. *Watching narrowly; obseruing with a quick eye.*
Esmerillonné: m. ée: f. *Liuelie, quicke, sprightfull; or as* Emerillonné.
Esmerillonner. *Looke* Emerillonner.
Esmerveillable: com. *Maruelous, admirable, miraculous, wonderfull, much to be wondered at.*
Esmerveillé. *Maruelled, wondered.*
Esmerveillement: m. *A marvelling, wondering; admiration, admiring; a gazing at.*
Esmerveiller. *To make to wonder, admire, or maruell at; to breed astonishment, or admiration in.*
S'esmerveiller. *To wonder, maruell, admire; also, to looke, or gaze at with astonishment.*
Esmery: m. *An Emrod, or Emerill stone; vsed by Iuellers, Lapidaries, Glasiors, &c.*
Esmesché: m. ée: f. *Snuffed.*
Esmescher. *To snuffe a light.*
Esmeu: m. euë: f. *Moued, or stirred vp; excited, incited, incouraged, prouoked, set on; pricked, put, vrged, or egged, forward; also, wagged or shaken vp & down.*
Esmeut: m. *The mute, or dropping of a bird.*
Esmeute: f. *A tumult, stirre, vprore, commotion, insurrection, or rising of people; a broyle, riot, sedition, hurly-burly, old coyle; also, a priuate motion, or suddain instinct vnto a thing.*
Esmeute de chiens. *A kennell of hounds that be much of a size, and color: See* Meute.
Esmeuti. *Muted, dropped; purged.*
Esmeutir. *To mute, or drop, as birds doe; hence, also, to purge any way.*
Esmiable: com. *Crummable, crumblable.*
Esmié m. ée: f. *Crummed, crumbled; mouldred; broken into small peeces,*
Esmier. *To crum, crumble, breake into small peeces.*
S'esmier. *To fall into small peeces; to moulder away.*
Esmiettement: m. *A crumming, crumbling, breaking into small peeces.*
Esmieure: f. *A crumming, crumbling; mouldering.*
Esminage: m. *A measure in some parts of Burgundie, conteyning about halfe a bushell.*
Esminal: m. *Another measure; being the halfe of the* Bichot.
Espinotte: f. *A measure of about ij Burgonian bushels.*
Esmoëllé: m. ée: f. *Without marrow; bereaued of pith; depriued of marrow.*
Esmoëller. *To depriue of marrow; to pick marrow out of bones, pith out of trees; to bereaue of strength.*
Esmoignonné: m. ée: f. *Stumped, cut off at the stump; made a stump of.*
Esmoignonner. *To stump; to cut off at the stump; or make a stump of.*
Esmonctoires. *Looke* Emonctoire.
Esmonde real. *Osmond royall, male fearne.*
Esmondé: m. ée: f. *Cleansed, purged, cleered, made cleane, picked; pruned; weeded (by hand.)*
Esmondement: m. *A cleansing, purging, cleering; or making cleane; a picking; pruning; weeding (by hand.)*
Esmonder. *To cleanse, purge, cleere, make cleane; to pick (as Corne;) to prune (as trees;) also, to weed (by hand) or pull vp weeds (with the hands.)*
Esmondeur: m. *A cleanser, purger, cleerer, maker cleane; a picker (of Corne); a pruner (of trees) a weeder by hand.*
Esmont. *as* Esmeut. *(An old word.)*
Esmorche: f. *Touch-powder; also, a tickling; also, the ordure that cleaues to an vnwiped, or ill-wiped arse.*

Esmorcellé: m.ée: f. *Peecemealed; beaten, or pulled, into small peeces.*
Esmorceller. *To peecemeale; to beat in peeces, or break into small morcells.*
Esmotelé: m. ée: f. *whose clods are broken; also, consumed, or eaten.*
Esmoteler. *as* Esmotter; *Also, to eat, or consume.*
Esmotion: f. *An emotion, commotion, sudden, or turbulent stirring; an agitation of the spirit, violent motion of the thoughts, vehement inclination of the mind.*
Esmotter. *To breake the clods of a plowed land.*
Esmoucé: m.ée: f. *Dulled, blunted.*
Esmoucer. *To dull, blunt, or take away the edge of.*
Esmouchail: m. *as* Esmouchoir.
Esmouché: m. ée: f. *Rid of flies.*
Esmouche-lourdaut. *A cheater, guller, conicatcher, foisting companion; a craftie flattering knaue; a deceiuer of simple, or sottish people.*
Esmoucher. *To rid of, or driue away, flies.*
Esmoucheté. *Flie-blowne; also, pinked, or set with little tufts.*
Esmouchette: f. *The round tuft, or head of hearbes, wherein their seed is contained.*
Des Esmouchettes. *A paire of snuffers.*
Esmouchoir: m. *A flie-flap; or fan to driue away flies.*
Esmoüellé. *as* Esmoëlle.
Esmoulage: m. *A grinding, whetting, sharpening of.*
Esmouldre. *To grinde, whet, make sharpe.*
Esmoulendier: m. *A sheere-grinder.*
Esmouleur: m. *A grinder, whetter, sharpner of blades.*
Esmoulu: m.uë: f. *Whetted, sharpened, ground, that hath an edge set on it.*
'A fer esmoulu. *Violently, vehemently, throughly, in full earnest, to the proofe, without boording, with all extremitie.*
Gentilhomme frais esmoulu. *A gentleman newly forged; a gentleman of the first head.*
Esmoulure: f. *A grinding, whetting, sharpening, a giuing of an edge vnto.*
Esmoussé: m.ée: f. *Rid, or bared of mosse.*
Esmousser. *To rid of mosse, to plucke the mosse from.*
Esmouvement: m. *A mouing, or stirring vp; an exciting, inciting, vrging, prouoking vnto; also, a tossing, agitation; exercise; wagging, or shaking vp & downe.*
Esmouveur: m. *A mouer, or stirrer vp; an exciter, inciter, incourager, prouoker, setter on; a picker, putter, egger, or vrger forward.*
Esmouvoir. *To moue, or stirre vp; to agitate; excite, incite, incourage, prouoke, set on; to pricke, put, vrge, or egge, forward; also, to wag, or shake vp and downe.*
Esmoy: m. *Carke, care, thought, sorrow, heauinesse, pensiuenesse.*
s'Esmoyer de. *Earnestly to aske, or enquire, of.*
Esmundé: m. ée: f. *Rid or cleered of, cleansed or purged from, dead, broken, withered boughes, &c.*
Esmundement. *as* Esmondement; *A pruning.*
Esmunder. *To cleanse; to prune; Seeke* Esmonder.
Esmutir. *as* Esmeutir; *To mute, or mowt.*
Esmutissement. *as* Esmeut; *A muting.*
Esmyne. *A kind of measure; as* Emine.
Esnasé: m.ée: f. *Noselesse; made noselesse; whose nose is cut off, or pulled away.*
Ie me suis esnasé contre. *I haue dasht, or almost burst, my nose against.*
Esnaser. *To make noselesse; to cut, or pull off, the nose.*
Esnervé: m. ée: f. *Weakened, enfeebled, made sinewlesse, depriued of sinewes.*
Esnerver. *To weaken, infeeble, make sinewlesse, depriue of sinewes, bereaue of strength.*
Esor. Oyseaux esors. *Wild, vnmade, or ill-mand hawks; apt, when they are a-wing, to take a toy, or to flie their countrey.*
Espace: f. *A space, or distance; a respite, pause, intermedium.*
Espade: f. *A broad short sword.*
Espadon: m. *A short two-handed sword.*
Espagneul: m. *A Spaniell.*
Espagnol: m. *A Spaniard; also, a Spaniell.*
Le feu des Espagnols. *A hot scorching Sunne.*
Vn Espagnol sans Iesuite est vne perdris sans orange: Prov. *A Spaniard without a Jesuite is (wee may say) cheese without mustard.*
Espagnol: m. ole: f. *Spanish, of Spaine.*
Espée Espagnole. *A Rapier, or Tucke.*
Espagnolade: f. *A Spanish tricke, blow, bob.*
Espagnole. 'A l'Espagnole. *After the Spanish maner, fashion, humor.*
Payer à l'Espagnole. *To giue knockes in stead of coine; or to rifle such as he should requite; (a phrase deuised by some Dutchman.)*
Espagnolé: m. ée: f. *Spaniolized; made Spanish, or Spaniard-like.*
Corps bien Espagnolé. *A bodie made slender.*
Espagnolette: f. *A Band-supporter of wire in workes done ouer with silke.*
Espagnoliser. *To play the Spaniard; to speake, or doe like a Spaniard.*
Espagnotter. *To wooe, to court; as* Muguetter.
Espaillier. *Looke* Espallier.
Espais. *Thicke; Seeke* Espez.
Espaississant. *Thickening.*
Espaix: m. *Thicknesse, closenesse, densitie, grossenesse.*
Espalé: m. ée: f. *Scattered, cast, or spred abroad, with a shouell.*
Espaler. *To scatter, cast, or spread, abroad with a shouell.*
Espalier: m. *He that rowes with the first oare in a gallie; also, as* Espallier.
Espaller. *as* Espaler.
Espallier: m. *An hedge-row of sundrie fruit trees set close together, their boughes interlaced one within another, and held in with stakes, railes, or pales; also, a buttresse, shore-post, or shouldering peece (in Architecture.)*
Espalmé: m. ée: f. *Caulked, or pitched ouer, as a ship.*
Espaime: m. *The crampe.*
Espamé: m. ée: f. *Infeebled, weakened, made leane, as with fasting; also, troubled with a crampe, or conuulsion, fallen into a swoond.*
Espamer. *To infeeble, weaken, make leane, as with fasting; also, as* Espausmer.
Espampé. roses espampées. *Which be fully blowne.*
Espampré: m. ée: f. *Pruned, as a vine, of superfluous shoots, &c.*
Espamprement: m. *The pruning of a vine.*
Espamprer la vigne. *To prune a vine; to plucke, or cut, away the superfluous shoots thereof.*
Espan: m. *A span.*
Espanché: m. ée: f. *Squattered, spilled, shed, or powred out in hast, or disorder.*
Espanchement: m. *A disordered, or hastie squattering, spilling, sheeding, or powring out.*
Espancher. *To squatter, spill, sheed, or powre out disorderedly, or in hast.*
Espancher de l'eau. *To spill water; also, to pisse.*
Espandable: com. *Which may be shed, spilled, powred out.*

Espande-

Espandement : m. *A sheeding, spilling, powring out; a spreading, dilating, extending.*
Espandre. *To sheed, spill, powre out; to spread, cast, or scatter abroad in great abundance.*
s'espandre. *To spread, run abroad; ouerflow, dilate, increase; extend it selfe.*
Espandu : m. uë : f. *Shed, spilled, powred out; spred, cast, or scattered abroad; dilated, largely extended.*
Espani : m. ie : f. *Blowen; spred abroad; stretched, displayed.*
Espanir. *To blow, or spread, as a blooming Rose, or any other flower, in the height of it flourishing; also, to display, stretch, or spread out.*
Espanité. *as* Espavité.
Espanouï : m. ie : f. *Blowen, displayed, spred out.*
Espanouïr. *as* Espanir.
Espanouïssement : m. *A blowing, or blooming of flowers; a spreading, or displaying.*
Espapilloté : m. ée : f. *Bespangled; bespatled, bespotted.*
Espapilloter. *To bespangle; bespot, bespatle.*
Esparcet : m. *A kind of thicke grasse, or pulse in* Dauphiné, *the hay whereof is very good for cattell, and the seed for pulleyn; tis newly sowen euery fourth yeare.*
Esparcete. *as* Parietaire. *Pellitorie of the wall.*
Esparcetiere : f. *A plot, or close thats sowed with* Esparcet.
Espardement : m. *A scattering, sprinkling, dispersing, dissipation.*
Espardre. *To scatter, disperse, spread abroad, to dissipate, dissolue, break into many peeces, to cast heere and there.*
Esparer. *To fling, or yerke out with the heeles, as a horse in a high manage.*
Le ciel commence s'esparer. *The skie begins to breake; or to scatter, or throw asunder the cloudes that ouercast it.*
Esparges. *Sparagus.*
Espargnant. *Hard, neere, warie, thriftie, scantie, sauing, frugall, sparing, niggardlie, somewhat miserable.*
Espargne : f. *Thrift, frugalitie, sauing, sparing, warinesse, neerenesse, parcimonie, good husbandrie; also, a strait, compendious, or scantie course of proceeding; also, the Treasurie or Exchequer of a Prince; also, ground reserued, by particular men, onely for pasture.*
Taillé d' espargne. *Cut with sparing worke; the incutting being filled with enamell, and the work set out, or appearing among it, in gold, &c.*
Espargné : m. ée : f. *Spared, saued, husbanded; reserued; forgiuen, forborne; also, contriued, cut, or made out of.*
Espargner. *To spare, saue, husband; forgiue, forbeare, or beare with; also, to contriue, make, or cut, out of.*
Sans espargner ne Roy ny Roc. *Without mercie, or respect of persons; with as little fauour to one as to another; indifferently, or alike seuerely to all.*
Bons mots n' espargnent nul : Prov. *See* Mot.
Ce que chiche espargne, large despend : Pro. *That which a niggard saues his heire consumes; or that which one spares another spends.*
Marchandise n' espargne nuls : Prov. *Ware will deceiue any bodie, spares no bodie.*
Qui bien gaigne, & bien espargne devient tantost riche : Prov. *He that gets and saues, much, grows quickly rich.*
Espargoutte : f. *The hearbe Feuerfew, Fedderfew, White-wort, Mother-wort.*
Petite espargoutte. *Starwort, Sharewort, Cudwort.*

Esparpillé : m. ée : f. *Scattered, dispersed, disparkled; also, toused, disordered, disheuelled, as a womans haire; also, spred, wide opened, set farre asunder.*
Esparpillement : m. *A scattering, dispersing, disparkling of many things asunder; a disordering, disheueling, or vntoward tousing of things; also, a spreading, wide opening, setting farre asunder.*
Esparpiller. *To scatter, disperse, disparkle asunder; also, to set wide open, or far asunder; also, to disheuell, disorder, touse, as a womans haire.*
Esparpiller son beurre. *To spread his butter.*
Esparre. *The barre of yron thats nailed on a doore, and turnes at th' end on the hindge.*
Espars. *Scattered, dispersed, dissipated, dismembred, rent, or broken into many parcels, cast here and there.*
Esparsément. *Scatteringly, disorderedly, vncertainly, here and there, all abroad, not one neere to another.*
Espartant. *Scattering, dispersing, diuiding, far-sundering.*
Espartillé : m. ée : f. *Disparkled; or dispersed; infused by small parcells; diuided by partitions.*
Espartir. *To scatter, disperse, part, diuide, set asunder.*
Esparvain : m. *A spauen in the leg of a horse, or beast.*
Esparvier : m. *A Sparhawke, or Sparrow-hawke; and (more generally) a short-wingd hawke; also, a great Sweepe-net for fishing.*
Esparvier de Montagu. *A lowse.*
Herbe d' esparvier. *as* Cichorée iaulne.
Mieux vault mestier qu' esparvier. *Better is a good occupation then hawking; or, better it is to follow a trade then a Hawke.*
On ne peut faire d' hibou esparvier : Prov. *He thats a clowne by nature, cannot be gentilized by nurture; The like is;*
On ne peut d' vn Pigeon faire vn vif esparvier : Prov.
Espase : f. *A sword:* ¶Langued.
Peis espase. *Looke* Spase.
Espaté : m. ée : f. *Broad-footed, flat-footed; well vnderlayed; well spred, or of a good breadth, at the bottom; well grounded, fixed, setled, at the foot.*
Espatement : m. *The (broad) foot, or footing; the groundworke, or foundation, of.*
s' Espater. *To be broad-footed, or wel vnderlaid; to spread, haue some compasse, beare a good breadth, at the bottome; and (thereby) to be well grounded, fixed, setled.*
Espatté. *as* Espaté.
Espattement. *as* Espatement.
Espatule : f. *A (Chirurgions, or Apothecaries) little slice.*
Espave. *A waife, or stray; a chattell, or beast vnowned; any thing whose originall, or owner, is not knowne; (hence) also, a stranger borne in a farre countrey.*
Espave & effreinte des chiens. *A foule default of dogs, hauing vtterly lost both sight, and sent, of the game which they hunted.*
Espave : com. *Maisterlesse; without author, or owner; also, forreine, farre-borne; of vnknowne birth, or beginning.*
Mots espaves. *Strange, new-forged, vnaccustomed, words.*
Espavent : m. *A Spauen in a horse.*
Espavité : f. *The right a Soueraigne Lord hath to the lands, or goods of strangers, dying within his dominions; or the being a stranger; as* Espave.
Espaulart : m. *A Sea-monster, enemie to Whales; as* Orque.
Espaule : f. *A shoulder.*

Par dessus l' espaule. Ouer the shoulder, or the wrong way; and hence; Riche, ou vertueux, par dessus l' espaule; (signifies) a verie begger, or, an arrant knaue.

Baisser les espaules. To yeeld; or vndergoe.

Faire espaule à. To helpe, assist, second, back, support.

Hausser l' espaule. To lift vp the shoulders; (a gesture gotten from th' Italians, and much vsed when wee refuse to doe a thing which we are afraid, or loath, to meddle with; and imports as much, as if wee should say, you shall pardon me sir; &c.)

Porter à deux espaules. (In a faction) to shift often from side to side; to adhere sometimes vnto th'one, sometimes to th'other; or, to be neither constant, nor verie behouefull, to either.

Porter sur les espaules. To carrie a burthen on his shoulders; also, to grow wearie of, or find himselfe ouercharged with.

Pousser le temps à l' espaule. To delay, or driue off, the time; to spend, or passe away his dayes idly, but so so; or, euen as he may.

Prester espaule à. To helpe to beare, to lend a helping hand vnto.

Ie me recommande à leurs espaules. Woe to their shoulders; or, their shoulders are like to pay for it; or, their shoulders are sure of a whipping.

Sentir son espaule de mouton. To smell verie rank, verie strong, verie rammish.

Tenir espaule à. as Faire espaule.

Tirer l' espaule. To shrinke in the shoulders, as one that likes not what he sees, or heares.

Les belles robbes pleurent sur des espaules indignes: Prov. Good clothes weepe on vnworthie shoulders.

Espaulé: m. ée: f. Whose shoulder is burst, or out of ioynt.

Vne beste espaulée. Crackt stuffe, broken ware; a wench that hath had a clap.

Espaulée: f. par espaulées. By fits, by shoues, by diuers shoulderings; now and then; with many pauses betweene.

Espaulement: m. A bursting, or vnioynting of the shoulder.

Espauler. To burst a shoulder; to put a shoulder out of ioynt; also, to shoulder; to support with, or beare on, the shoulders.

Espauletée. as Espaulée; whence;

Reprendre, ou refaire vne muraille par espauletées. To repaire a wall by parcells, without taking any of it downe.

Espaulette: f. A little shoulder; also, the wing of a gowne, doublet; &c; also, a buttresse, shore-post, or shouldering peece.

Maçonnerie à espaulettes. Vneuen worke in walls, &c, built vp by fits, and peeces, and by those intermissions, left higher in one part then in another; or, shouldering, bearing, or standing out in one place more then in another.

Espaulier. Belonging to, supporting or seruing for, the shoulder.

Veine espauliere. See Veine.

Espauliere: f. A shoulder peece; the peece of armour, or apparell that serues for the shoulder; also, a buttresse, shore-peece, or shouldering peece to support, or strengthen a wall.

Espaulu: m. uë: f. Broad-shouldered.

Espaulure: f. as Espaulement.

Espausiner. To fall in a swoone. (v.m.)

Espausmure: f. A swoonding, or falling into a trance.

Espautré: m. ée: f. Pelted, pauted, beaten, threshed.

Espautrer. To paut, pelt, thrash, beat, crush, bruise.

Espe. (at Blois) as Empan (in other places.)

Espeaultre. Spelt, or spelt-corne.

Espece: f. A kind, or sort of.

Especial. par especial. Especially, particularly, peculiarly.

Espectative. estre à l' espectative. To stand waiting, looking, attending, expecting for.

Espée: f. A Sword; Rapier; Tucke; a Glaiue, Cuttelasse, Faucheon, Hanger; Blade; also, a certaine round staffe, that lies betweene the vpper boords of a Vinepresse, and the mother, or substance of the grapes; (sometimes) also, valour; and, a valiant man; (c'est vn' des meilleures espées de la France.)

Espée d' armes. as Espée de Chevalier; or, Estoc d' armes.

Espée blanche. Looke Blanc.

Espée des bleds. Corne sedge, corne flags, corne gladen.

Espée de Chevalier. A sharpe, and broad sword, of a reasonable length, and plaine-hilted, hauing but onely one crosse-barre.

Espée Espagnole. A Rapier, or Tucke.

Espée Hunisque. A kind of Scimiter.

Espée de mer. The Sword-fish.

Espée misericorde. Looke Misericorde.

Espée des moissons. Corne sedge, corne gladen.

Espée rabatuë. A foile.

Espée Romaine. Certaine twined, and retorted haires on a horse; resembling, and by some called, a feather.

Pled de l' espée. High iurisdiction; authoritie to punish, or pursue, offendors with the sword.

Sergent de l' espée. Looke Sergent.

Hardi comme vne espée. As bold, or hardie as a sword (which is oft more bold then welcome.)

Iouër de l'espée à deux Iambes. To shew a faire paire of heeles; to runne away.

S'en iouër de l' espée à deux mains, To doe what he list withall; See Iouër.

Espelé: m. ée: f. Spealed, spelled; pilled, flayed.

Espelement: m. A spelling, or spealing of words; a ioyning of letters, or of sillables together.

Espeler. To spell, to speale; to ioyne letters, or sillables together; to make of letters sillables, of sillables words; also, to flea, pill, or pull the skinne, or rind off.

Espeller. as Espeler; (Especially in the last signification.)

Espeluche: f. Plush.

Espendre. Looke Espandre.

Espenaillé: m. ée: f. Torne, ragged, all to tatters.

Espeoir. Seeke Espoir.

Esperable: com. Hopeable, fit to be hoped for; hopefull.

Esperance: f. Hope, trust, confidence, affiance.

En esperance d' avoir mieux tant vit le loup, qu'il devient vieux: Prov. The Wolfe growes old by hoping still for better; or, while the Wolfe hopes for better hee growes old.

Esperdu: m. uë: f. Forlorne, lost, firegone, farre-gone, in a desperate or miserable taking; also, dismaied, astonished, appalled, amazed, abashed.

Esperdument. Desperately, forlornely; dismayedly, amazedly; vtterly, extreamely, without measure.

Esperé: m. ée: f. Hoped for, trusted after.

Esperer. To hope, trust, haue affiance, repose confidence, in.

Esperit. *Seeke* Esprit.
Esperlan: m. *A Smelt.*
Esperlucat: m. *A locke, or bush of curled haire.* (v.m.) *also, a neat, spruce, pleasant, and liuelie companion; a feat, or deft youth.*
Esperon: m. *A spurre; also, a kind of fortification called, a Spurre; also, the stemme, nose, or beake-head of a gallie.*
La Iournée des esperons. *Looke* Iournée.
Os de l' esperon. *The lesse bone of the leg.*
'A esperons pareils. *With both spurres at once, and in the same part, of each side of a horse.*
Arrondir les esperons. *Looke* Arrondir.
Chausser les esperons à. *To course, or pursue amaine, to giue hard chace vnto; to make one runne, or scud away as fire were at his taile; also, to hasten, or make forward, in.*
Dur à l' esperon. *Dull, sluggish, heauie-mettalled; that will not be moued, or put forward by any instigation.*
'A morceau restif esperon de vin: Prov. *(A cup of sacke agrees with a cold stomacke;) a restiue morsell needs a spurre of wine.*
Tout cheval a besoing d' esperon: Prov. *All men haue need of some correction.*
Le vilain ne sçait qu' esperons valent: Prov. *Full little knowes the clowne what spurres can doe; base people know not, or cannot vse, braue helpes.*
Esperonnade: f. *A spurring; a iert, or pricke, with a spurre.*
Esperonné: m. ée: f. *Spurred; also, bespurred, hauing spurres on his heeles.*
Fol est qui est esperonné, & à cheval dit, hay: Pro. *Looke* Hay.
Esperonnement: m. *A spurring; a pricking forward; an inciting, or vrging onward.*
Esperonner. *To spurre; pricke forward; incite, or vrge, onward.*
s'Esperonner. *To put on his owne spurres; also, to pricke himselfe on.*
Esperonnier: m. *A Spurrier; also, a Bit-maker.*
Esperonnier: m. ere: f. *Belonging to a spurre; or to the lesse bone of the leg.*
Muscle esperonnier. *A double muscle; one of the fiue whereby we stretch out the first part of our feet.*
Esperruqué: m. ée: f. *That weares long lockes, or curled haire.*
Espervain: m. *A splint in a horses leg.*
Espervier. *Looke* Esparvier.
Espessement. *Thickly, spissely, close together.*
Espesseur: f. *Thicknesse, densitie, spissenesse, closenesse; massiuenesse, bignesse, grossenesse.*
Espessi: m. ie: f. *Thickened; compacted, closed hard together, ingrossed, made big.*
Espessir. *To thicken; ingrosse, increase, make big; to compact, or close hard together.*
Espessissement: m. *A thickning; an ingrossing, or making big; a compacting, or closing hard together.*
Espessisseure: f. *as* Espesseur.
Espeuré: m. ée: f. *Frightened, affrighted, affrayed, made fearefull.*
Espeurer. *To frighten, affright, make fearefull, affray.*
Espez.: m. esse: f. *Thicke; massiue, grosse, big; close, neere, hard compact together.*
Espi de bled. *An eare of corne.*
Espi d' eau. *Pond-weed, Water-spike; (an hearbe.)*
Espi de lard. *Seeke* Espis.
Tuiles couchées en façon d' espi. *Laied edgelong, or edge to edge.*
Espiant. *Spying, prying, watching, marking, obseruing narrowly; dogging, way-laying, lying for.*
Espice: f. *Spice; also, the Spice-apple (whereof excellent Cyder is made.)*
Espices. *Spices, or Spice; also, the fees that be taken by the (French) Judges, and their assistants, for Bookes perused, Consultations had, and sentence giuen, in a cause; (from the auncient manner of gratefull suitors; who, hauing preuailed, were woont to present the Judges, or the Reporters, of their causes, with Comfets, or other Jonkets; which gratuitie they afterwards turned into money, and by degrees haue suffered it to become a dutie, and (as it is at this day) the onely, or best, reuenew belonging to Judiciall places.)*
L' on perd l' appareil d' vne poule, à faute d' acheter pour vn liard d' espices: Prov. *Some to spare a pennie loose the vse of that which cost them a pound.*
Espicé: m. ée: f. *Spiced; seasoned, or sweetened with spice.*
Telle cause est espicée. *The fees due to the Judges, &c, vpon such a cause bee taxed, rated, or set downe.*
Espicenaire: com. *Of both sexes, male and female.*
Espicer. *To bespice; to season, or sweeten with spice; also, to taxe, rate, or set downe the Judges fees, or* Espices, *in a cause.*
Espicerie: f. *A Spicerie; also, Spices.*
Es petis sacs sont les fines espiceries: Prov. *The finest Spices are in little bags.*
Espiceur: m. *A taker, or taxer, of fees.*
Espicier: m. *A Grocer, a seller of Spices, a Drug-seller.*
Espie: f. *A spie, scowt, espiall; priuie marker, obseruer, dogger of people; eaue-dropper, prying companion.*
Espies. *Ambushes, way-layings; malicious obseruing, treacherous dogging, of people.*
Espié: m. ée: f. *Resembling an eare of corne; also, eared; growne to an eare; (as* le bled est espié;*) also, spied, watched, way layed, narrowly obserued.*
Lard espié. *Seeke* Lard.
Espiecé: m. ée: f. *Peecemealed; cut, broken, or torne in peeces.*
Espiecer. *To diuide, peecemeale; cut, breake, or teare in peeces.*
Espiement: m. *A spying, scowting, prying, watching, marking, narrow obseruing; a lying in ambush, or in wait for.*
Espier. *To spie, watch, marke, prie into; obserue narrowly; to dog, lie for, way-lay; also, to eare, or shoot out in an eare, as a blade of corne.*
Espierré: m. ée: f. *Vnstoned; rid from, cleered of, stones.*
Espierrement. *A picking stones off land, a ridding from stones.*
Espierrer. *To vnstone; to rid from stones; to picke stones from.*
Espierreur: m. *A stone-picker, stone-gatherer.*
Espieu: m. *A Boare-speare; a hunting staffe, or Jauelin; also, a Partisan, or Captaines leading-staffe.*
Espieur: m. *A spier, marker, obseruer; also, a scowt, or watchman.*
Espieur des chemins. *A taker, purse taker, theefe on the high-way, one of Robinhoods followers, one of S. Nicholas Clerkes.*
Espij d' eau. *as* Espi d' eau.
Espinal: m. *A thornie groue, plot, or place.*

Espinarde. *as* Espinoche; *A Sticklebacke.*
Espinars. des espinars: m. *Spinage, or Spinach.*
Espinar femelle. *A barren kind thereof, which bears no seed at all.*
Espinaye: f. *A thornie plot, bramble-bush, place full of briers.*
Espince: f. *A pinching, nipping, or pricking; also, as* Pince.
Espincettes. des es: f. *A paire of Pincers.*
Espine: f. *A thorne, bramble, brier; a pricke, sting, or prickle; also, a quill, or faucet for a wine-vessell; also, a kind of Caltrop vsed in warre for the galling of horses feet, &c.*
Espine Arabique. *Th'Arabian thorne, or thistle; a kind of white thistle.*
Espine blanche. *Milke thistle; white thistle, our Ladies thistle; also, the white thorne, or hawthorne.*
Blanche espine. *The Carline thistle.*
Espine benoiste. *The Barberrie-tree.*
Espine de bouc. *Goats thorne; whose roots yeeld Gumme Dragagant.*
Espine du dos. *The backe-bone.*
Espine noire. *The blacke thorne.*
Espine vinette. *as* Espine benoiste.
Qui seme des chardons, recueille des espines: Prov. *He that sowes thistles gathers thornes.*
Qui veut aller les pieds nuds ne doit semer des espines: Prov. *He that will bare-foot goe, must sow no thornes.*
Trop achette le miel qui sur espines le leche: Prov. *Too deere's the sweet thats bought with much affliction.*
Espiné: m. ée: f. *Pricked, as with a thorne.*
Du filet espiné. *Thread thats whitened, or whited.*
Espinée: f. *The chine, or backe-bone of a porke.*
Espinelle: f. *A kind of Rubie.*
Espiner. *To pricke, as a thorne.*
s'Espiner. *To pricke; also, to intangle himselfe, as among briers, and thornes.*
Espineses. des es. *Splents in a horses legs.*
Espinette: f. *A paire of Virginalls.*
Espinette organisée. *A Virginall and wind Instrument ioyned together; a set of Pipes added to a Virginall.*
Espineux: m. euse: f. *Thornie, brierie, full of brambles; also, belonging to the backe-bone; and hence;*
Muscle espineux. *A certaine muscle which helpes to stretch out the necke.*
Espingarderie. *The Harguebuzerie; or, a troupe of Harguebuziers.* v.m. *(Looke* Espringalle*)*: ¶Rab.
Espingardier. *An Harguebuzier, or small shot.*
Espingardine: f. *A small (and old fashioned) Chamber, (Peece.)*
Espingle: f. *A pinne.*
Il tira son espingle du jeu. *He slipt his necke out of the coller.*
Espinglé: m. ée: f. *Pinned; fastened, or furnished with pinnes.*
Espingler. *To pinne; to fasten, or furnish with pinnes.*
Espingleur: m. *A Pinner, or Pinne-maker.*
Espinglier. *as* Espingleur; *Also, a Pinpillow, or cushinet to sticke pinnes on; also, a pincase, or thing to put pinnes in.*
Espinglon: m. *A little pinne.*
Espinguer. *To spring, or leape sprightly.* (v.m.)
Espinoche: f. *A Sharpling, Shafling, stickling, Bankstickle, or Sticklebacke.*
Espinon: m. *A little thorne; hence also, the tongue, or thong of a buckle.*
Espinoye: m. *A thicket, groue, or ground full of thornes; a thornie plot.*
Espinoye: f. *The same.*
Espinse. *as* Pinse.
Espion: m. *A spie, scowt, espiall; a priuie obseruer of, or prier into, mens behauiour; a malicious dogger, watcher, way-layer of others; also, a swift Barke sent out to sea, for discouerie; also, the little Sea-shrimp, or Beard.*
Espionné: m. ée: f. *Spied, pried into; obserued, watched, way-laied.*
Espionnement: m. *A spying, or prying into; an obseruing, or watching of.*
Espionner. *To spie, or prie into; to watch priuily, obserue narrowly; to dog, staulke, way-lay.*
Espionneur: m. *as* Espion *(In the first sence.)*
Espis. *The two vtmost, and fattest, peeces of a side of Porke, diuided (after the Parisien fashion) into three parts, the legs being first cut off for gammons.*
Esplan: m. *A Smelt.*
Esplanade: f. *A planing, leuelling, euening of wayes, by grubbing vp of trees, and remouing all other incumbrances out of them.*
Esplanadé: m. ée: f. *Leuelled, planed, layed euen; disincumbred.*
Esplanader. *To leuell, plane, lay euen; remoue impediments, deliuer from incumbrances.*
Esplanaderaye. *A plaine way, or strand.*
Esplané: m. ée: f. *Made plaine; leuelled, layed euen with the ground; also, explained, or expounded.*
Esplaner. *To make plaine; to leuell, or lay euen, with the ground; also, to explaine, declare, manifest, expound.*
Espleuré: m. ée: f. *Full of, all-to beblubbered with, teares; whose eyes are, by excessiue weeping, drained of moisture.*
Espleurer. *To waile bitterly, and beyond measure; to weepe the eyes drie.*
Esplingue. *as* Espingle; *A pinne:* ¶Norm.
Esplinguette: f. *A small pinne:* ¶Norm. *Also, a priming yron; that wherewith the touch-hole of a peece is vsually cleansed.*
Esploucher. *as* Esplucher.
Esplouré: m. ée: f. *Beblubbered with teares; Looke* Espleuré.
Esplourer. *as* Espleurer.
Esployé: m. ée: f. *Displayed; and hence;*
Aigle esployée. *A spred Eagle.*
Espluché: m. ée: f. *Picked, or culled, as pease, &c; also, plucked, or teised, as flowers, wooll, &c; (hence) also, throughly sifted, or searched into, examined narrowly, perused diligently.*
Espluchement: m. *A picking, or culling; a plucking, or teising; also, a through sifting, full searching, diligent examining of.*
Esplucher. *To picke, or cull, as pease, &c; to plucke, or teyse, as Roses, Wooll, &c; also, to sift throughly, search narrowly, examine fully, peruse diligently.*
ça que ie t'espluche à contrepoil. *Come hither and let me claw, or scratch, thee for thy labour.*
Qui trop espluche les choses n'a pas vne vie asseurée: Prov. *He liues vnsafely that lookes too neerely to matters.*
Esplucheur: m. *A picker, plucker, teyser; a curious, or diligent sifter, or searcher into.*

Esplu-

Esplucheures: f. *The pickings, or cullings; the pluckings, or teysings of.*
Esplugebant. *A kind of riuer-fowle.*
Esplumé: m. ée: f. *Plucked, vnplumed, without feathers; bereaued, or bared, of feathers.*
Espluquer. *as* Esplucher. ¶Pic.
Espluyé: m. ée: f. *Sprinkled, spatled, or spattered vpon.*
Espluyer. *To sprinkle, spattle, spatter, or cast vpon.*
Espoictriné, &c. *Looke* Espoitriné.
Espoinçonner. *as* Espoindre.
Espoinct: m. cte: f. *Pricked, spurred; incited, prouoked, violently moued, vehemently stirred.*
Espoincté: m. ée: f. *Vnpointed, blunted; whose point is dulled, broken, or cut off.*
Espoincter. *To vnpoint, or blunt; to dull, breake, or cut off the point of.*
Espoindre. *To prick, spurre; prouoke, vrge, incite; stirre vehemently, moue extreamely.*
Espointement: m. *An vnpointing; a blunting; a breaking the point of.*
Espointement de questions. *A pacifying of quarrels, a quieting of altercations; also, a resolution of questions.*
Espointer. *as* Espoincter.
Espoir: m. *Hope, trust, confidence, affiance.*
Espois d'un cerf. *The top of a red Deeres head; of a fallow, the Spellers.*
Espois. *as* Espez; *thicke.*
Espoissir. *To thicken; Seeke* Espessir.
Espoitriné: m. ée: f. *Open breasted; whose bosome lyes open to view.*
Espoitronnement: m. *A discouering of the bosome, a going open breasted.*
Esponce d'heritage: f. *A quitting, abandoning, forgoing, giuing ouer an estate in land.*
Esponcé: m. ée: f. *Quit, left, abandoned, forgone, giuen ouer.*
Esponcer. *To quit, leaue, abandon, forsake, forgoe, giue ouer.*
Esponcion. *as* Esponce.
Esponge: f. *A Spunge.*
Esponges d'asperge. *The clottered root of garden Sparagus.*
Esponge d'eau douce. *A certaine hearbe, that flotes on riuers, and is called, Spunge of the riuer.*
Esponges femelles. *Those which haue the fewest, and least holes.*
Esponge de riviere. *Spunge of the riuer; an hearbe.*
Pierre d'esponge. *Looke* Pierre.
Porter l'esponge; ou, passer l'esponge, sur. *To deface, or blot out.*
Espongette: f. *A little Spunge.*
Espongette du Rosier sauvage. *A Brier-ball, or canker-Rose ball; the round, and spungie excrescence, which cleaues to the branch of a wild Rose, brier-Rose, or Hep tree.*
Espongieux: m. euse: f. *Spungie; full of Spunges; light, or full of holes, like a Spunge.*
Esporle: f. *A vassals acknowledgement of the seruices, and duties which he owes vnto his Lord.*
Esporler. *A vassall to acknowledge the duties and seruices he owes, to his Lord.*
Esporte: f. *A handbasket.*
Espoudré: m. ée: f. *Dusted; cleered from, cleansed of, dust.*
Espoudrer. *To dust; to beat, or wipe the dust from; to cleanse, or cleere from dust.*

Espoventable: com. *Dreadfull, frightfull, fearefull; horrible, gastfull, horride; monstrous, terrible; able to scare, or amaze any man.*
Espoventablement. *Dreadfully, frightfully, fearefully; terribly, horribly, ghastfully, with great amazement.*
Espoventail: m. *A Bug-beare, or Scar-crow; a man of clouts to feare birds with.*
Espoventaire. *The same.*
Espoventant. *Frighting, flighting, skaring, terrifying, amazing with dread, filling with horror.*
Espovente: f. *Dread, fright, great feare; terror, horror, ghastlinesse; astonishment, consternation, amazement.*
Ils ont prins l'espovente. *They are mightily skared; they haue taken a terrible allarum; they are afraid of euerie feather that wags, or shadow that appeares; or, they scud away as fast, and as fearefully, as if fire were at their tayles.*
Espoventé: m. ée: f. *Frighted, frayed, monstrously afrayed, skared, terrified; appalled by dread, amazed by terror, filled with horror.*
Espoventement: m. *as* Espovente; *or, a frighting, fraying, skaring, terrifying.*
Espoventer. *To fright, flight, fray, terrifie, feare exceedingly; amaze, appall, astonish by feare; fill with horror or terror, or with horrible or terrible apprehensions.*
Espouillé: m. ée: f. *Lowsed, rid of lice.*
Espouiller. *To lowse, kill lice, rid of lice.*
Espouilleresse: f. *A woman that picketh, or killeth, lice.*
Espousailles: f. *An Espousalls, or Bridall; a wedding, or mariage.*
Espouse: f. *A Spowse; a Wife.*
Espouse du soleil. *The Marygould; so called by some.*
Espousé: m. ée: f. *Espoused, wedded, married.*
Espousée: f. *A Spouse, an Espoused.*
Espouser. *To espouse, wed, marrie; also, to defend, imbrace, vndertake, intertaine as his owne, take wholly vpon him; whence;* Espouser la querelle d'aucun.
Espouser la gruë. *See* Gruë.
Espouser vne rouë. *To be broken vpon a wheele.*
Espousse. *as* Pousse; *a disease in a horse.*
Espoussété: m. ée: f. *Brushed; dusted; wiped downe.*
Espoussetter. *To brush; dust, wipe the dust off.*
Espoussette: f. *A brush; also, a duster, or dusting cloth for a horse; and hence;*
Donner des espoussettes, (que ie ne die des estrivieres) à. *Lightly to touch, (if not to tax.)*
Espouventable, &c. *Looke* Espoventable, &c.
Espoux: m. *A Spouse, Bridegroome, new married man; one that is married, wedded, espoused.*
Espoys. *The vttermost, or vppermost branches of a Deeres head; Looke* Espois.
Espraintes. *The dung of an Otter, or other such vermine.*
Espreinctes. *as* Espraintes.
Espreindre. *To presse, wring, straine, squeese out, thrust together.*
Espreint: m. te: f. *Pressed, wrung, strained, squeesed out, thrust hard together.*
Espreinte: f. *A pressing, straining, wringing, thrusting together; a squeesing out; also, a great desire to goe to the stoole.*
Espreintes. *as* Espraintes.

Espremaſon: f. *The bloudie flix, accompanied with a painefull wringing of the bowels.* ¶Gaſc.
S'Esprendre. *To take, ſeiſe, catch hold; alſo, to fire, to kindle.*
Espreu. Tout à espreu. *Expreſſely, of ſet purpoſe, for the nonce.*
Esprevains. *A Splint, or Spauin in a horſes leg.*
Esprevier: m. *A Sparhauke; alſo, any kind of ſhort-winged Hauke.*
Espreuve: f. *A proofe, tryall, experiment, eſſay, attempt.*
Mettre en eſpreuve. *To put vnto tryall, or to the touch; to aduenture, hazard, ſee what will happen, try what may be done.*
Espringalle: f. *An auncient Engin of warre, whereout stones, peeces of yron, and great arrowes were ſhot at the walls of a beleaguered Towne, and the defendors thereof; (now out of vſe.)*
Espringaller. *To leape, ſpring, bound, ſpurt; (an old word.)*
Espringarde. *as* Eſpringalle.
Espris: m. iſe: f. *Taken, ſurpriſed, ſeiſed; alſo, inflamed, kindled, wholly poſſeſſed with.*
Esprit: m. *The Spirit, Soule; Heart; breath, heat; mind, thought; opinion; wit, conceit; alſo, life, courage, mettall, ſtomacke, viuacitie, liuelineſſe, or ſmartneſſe of humor; alſo, affection, fancie, diſpoſition, inclination; alſo, a ghoſt, or ſpirit.*
Voicy vn'eſtoffe qui n'a que l'eſprit. *(Merrily) this ſtuffe is but ſleight, or hath no ſubstance in it.*
Les Alemans ont l' esprit aux doigts: Prov. *The Germans wit reſts in their fingers; viz. they are better Artſans then Artiſts, better at handy-crafts then at head-craft.*
Espronnade. *as* Eſperonnade.
Esprouvé: m. ée: f. *Proued, tryed; approued, experimented; attempted, hazarded, aſſayed; ſearched, ſounded.*
Esprouver. *To proue, try; attempt, aſſay; ſound, looke, or search into.*
Esprouvette: f. *A probe; a little inſtrument wherewith wounds, and vlcers are ſearched.*
Espucer. *To flea; to rid of fleas; to kill fleas.*
Espucé: m. ée: f. *Fleaed, rid of fleas.*
Espuceter. *as* Eſpucer.
Espuiſé: m. ée: f. *Drayned; exhauſted, emptied, drawne dry (as a Well of water;) alſo, drawne out (as water out of a Well;) alſo, withered; waſted, conſumed; (as a ſubſtance whoſe moiſture is ſpent.)*
Espuiſement: m. *A drayning; exhauſting, emptying, drawing out, or drawing dry.*
Espuiſer. *To drayne; exhauſt, emptie; draw dry (as a Well of water;) alſo, to draw out (as water out of a Well;) alſo, to waſt, conſume, ſoake, or ſucke vp the moiſture of.*
Espuiſeur: m. *A drayner; exhauſter, emptier of moiſture; alſo, a drawer of water out of a Well.*
Espuiſoir: m. *Any thing that ſerues to drayne, exhauſt, or emptie another thing of moiſture; and hence, the hollow ſhouell wherewith Watermen lade their leakie Boats.*
Espulcer. *as* Eſpucer.
Espuration: f. *A running, as of a ſore; alſo, a cleanſing, or clarifying; alſo, a ſtrayning, or ſqueeſing of liquor from.*
Espuré: m. ée: f. *Cleanſed, purified, clarified; alſo, drayned, or growne dry. as a ſore that ranne; alſo, ſtrayned, wrung, or ſqueeſed out.*
Espurer. *To runne, as a broken ſore; alſo, to run, or drop, dry; alſo, to ſtraine, wring, or ſqueeſe liquor out of; alſo, to cleanſe, purifie, clarifie.*
Espurge: f. *Garden Spurge, whereof there are two kinds, a greater, and a leſſe.*
Espurgé: m. ée: f. *Purged out; cleanſed, cleered, rid of; alſo, pruined.*
Espurger. *To purge, cleere, cleanſe, rid of; alſo, to pruine, or picke off the noyſome knobs, or buds of trees.*
Espy. *as* Eſpi; *alſo, as* Eſpée Romaine.
Eſquadre: f. *A ſquadron (of footmen;) Looke* Eſcadre.
Eſquadron: m. *A Squadron; a troope of ſouldiors ranged into a ſquare bodie, or batallion. (This word is moſt commonly meant onely of horſemen,* (Bataillon *of footmen) and ſometimes both of horſe, and foot.)*
Eſquaille: f. *as* Eſcaille; *a ſcale, or ſhale.*
Eſquailler. *To pill, ſhale, or ſcale.*
Eſqualié: m. ée: f. *Leuelled, plained, ſmoothed, made euen.*
Eſqualier. *To leuell, plaine, ſmooth, make euen.*
Eſqualle. *as* Eſcaille.
Eſqualler. *as* Eſquailler.
Eſquarcelle: f. *A leatherne pouch.*
Eſquarquillé. *Put, ſpred, wide open; ſet, ſeuered, farre aſunder; ſtradled.*
Eſquarquillement: m. *A ſpreading, or ſetting wide aſunder; a ſtradling.*
Eſquarquiller. *To ſpread, ſet, or open, wide; to put farre aſunder.*
Eſquarquiller les jambes. *To ſtradle, ſtride, ſet the legs wide open.*
Eſquarquiller les yeux. *To ſtare; to looke big on it.*
Eſquarre: f. *A ſquare, or ſquareneſſe.*
Eſquarré: m. ée: f. *Square, or ſquared.*
Eſquarrir. *To ſquare; make ſquare; hew, or cut ſquare.*
Eſquarriſſeur. *A ſquarer of ſtones, or timber.*
Eſquarriſſure: f. *Squareneſſe; or, a ſquaring.*
Eſquarrure: f. *The ſame.*
Eſquartelé: m. ée: f. *Quartered; diſmembred.*
Eſquartelement: m. *A quartering; a diſmembring; Looke* Eſquartellement.
Eſquarteler. *To quarter; diſmember; cut or hew, into quarters; rent or teare, in peeces.*
Eſquarteleure: f. *as* Eſquartellement.
Eſquartellement: m. *A quartering, diſmembring, tearing, or hewing in peeces; alſo, the caſt or caſting, proportion or compoſition, of members or quarters.*
Eſquarter. *as* Eſcarter; *to ſcatter &c; alſo, to emptie quart-pots.*
Eſquené: m. ée: f. *Broken-backed, or ſwayed in the backe.*
Eſquener. *To breake the backe of, to ſway in the backe.*
Eſqueüé: m. ée: f. *Curtall, curtalled; vntayled, without tayle, depriued of a tayle.*
Eſqueuilles: f. *Dregs, ouen-ſweepings; excrements, offalls.*
Eſqueuillon. *A Spunge, or Scourer for a peece of Ordnance; or, as* Eſcouillon.
Eſqueuré: m. ée: f. *Out of heart; leane, poore, pulled downe, fallen away extreamely.*
Eſquiavine: f. *A long, and violent correction, or beating, of a ſtubborne, and vntoward Iade.*
Eſquiche. *The firſt rude, or ſleight draught of a Modell, or platforme, for a building.*
Eſquiché: m. ée: f. *Imboſſed; rudely done, or ſleightly drawne.*

Esquicher. *To imbosse; to make a rude, or sleight, or the first, draught of a Modell, or Platforme.*

Esquierre: f. *A Rule, or Squire; an Instrument vsed by Masons, Carpenters, Joyners, &c; also, an Instrument wherewith Surueyors measure land.*

Vn trait d'esquierre. *A perpendicular line, or measure; tearmed so by workemen.*

'A l'esquierre. *Iustly, directly, euenly, straightly; by line and leuell, to a haire.*

Aux esquierres des Cloches, & Eglises. *Iust ouer against the Steeples, and Churches; or, as farre as the Steeples, and Churches.*

Esquiers. *as* Esquierres.

Esquif: m. *A Skiffe, or little boat; also, the bone* Scaphoïde; *called so, because it somewhat resembles a small Skiffe.*

Esquifon: m. *A little Skiffe, a verie small boat.*

Esquignon: m. *A fescue;* ¶Pic.

Esquignonné: m. ée: f. *Cut, or broken off, as a lumpe, cantle, or crustie heele from a loafe of bread; also, cut, or broken into lumpes, luncheons, or cantles.*

Esquignonner. *To cut, or breake off a lumpe, cantle, crustie heele, or peece from a loafe of bread; also, to cut, or breake into lumpes, luncheons, or cantles.*

Esquille: f. *A little scale, or splint of a broken bone, &c.*

Esquilleux: m. euse: f. *Splintie, scalie, full of little splints, or scales.*

Esquinance: f. *The Squincie, or Squinancie; (a disease.)*

Esquine. Bois d'esquine. *The knottie, and medicinall root of a certaine Indian Bull-rush.*

Esquiper. *as* Equiper.

Esquirener. *To breake the backe.* ¶Gasc. ¶Rab.

Esquivé: m. ée: f. *Shunned, eschewed, auoided; also, scorned, reiected, despised; also, shifted away; slipped aside.*

Esquiver. *To shun, auoid, eschew; to scorne, reiect, despise; to shift away; to slinke, or slip aside.*

Esquoüé. *as* Escoüé.

Esraciné: m. ée: f. *Rooted vp, or plucked vp by the root.*

Esraciner. *To root vp; or, plucke vp by the root.*

Esrafflade: f. *A scratch, or scratching.*

Esrafflé: m. ée: f. *Scraped, scratched.*

Esraffler. *To scrape, or scratch.*

Esraillé: m. ée: f. *Spred, or set wide open; staring; shaling, stradling, or stradled; also, frayed.*

Oeil esraillé. *An eye whose lower lid (by a cicatrice, or other accident) is reuersed, leauing that part of the white altogether vncouered.*

Esraillement: m. *A spreading abroad, or setting wide open; a staring; stradling, shaling; fraying.*

Esrailler. *To spread, or set wide open; hence, to stare; stradle, shale; also, to fray, as in starching.*

Esrené: m. ée: f. *Feeble, weake, broken-reinde, loose-backt; vnfit for Venerie, vtterly disabled (that way.)*

Esrener. *To weaken, infeeble, breake, or crush the reines.*

Essaim: m. *as* Essain.

Essaimer. *To swarme, as Bees.*

Essain: m. *A Swarme (of Bees.)*

Essais de fourrage. *Scatterings, or leauings, of fodder.*

Essangé: m. ée: f. *Wet, as linnen before it be layed in the bucking tub.*

Essanger. *To wet linnen, before it be layed in the bucking tub.*

Essardé: m. ée: f. *Dry, thirstie, lacking moisture; burnt vp.*

Soif essardée. *An extreame thirst, a thirst which can hardly be quenched.*

Essargoter. *as* Essarter.

Essart: m. *A glade in a wood; also, a peece of vntilled ground.*

Essarté: m. ée: f. *Gladed; made into a glade; or, wherein glades are made; also, lopped off, as the boughes of a tree; or bared, as a tree of boughes; also, grubd vp, as bushes, &c, or, cleered, as a ground of bushes, &c.*

Essartement: m. *A glading; lopping; grubbing vp of, or cleering of a ground from, shrubs, &c.*

Essarter. *To glade, or make glades in a wood; also, to lop off the boughes of a tree, or bare, as a tree, of boughes; also, to grub vp, or cleere a ground of, bushes, shrubs, thornes, &c.*

Essaur: m. *as* Essor.

Essay: m. *An essay, proofe, tryall, experiment; an offer, attempt; a tast, or touch of a thing to know it by; also, the tast, or Essay taken of a Princes meat, or drinke; also, the vessell whereout, or peece whereof, it is taken.*

Essay de bled. *A tryall, or proofe of Corne; a course taken to know how much it weighes, and how much flower, meale, and branne it yeelds, when it is ground, in respect of that which it weighed, and was, before.*

Coup d' essay. *The Maister-peece of a young workeman, or of one thats but newly come out of his yeares; a beginning, entrance, onset, attempt; a flourish, or preamble, whereby a tast of a thing is giuen, or taken.*

Essayant. *Essaying; trying, prouing, tasting, attempting; feeling before hand.*

Essayé: m. ée: f. *Essayed, tried, proued, attempted; tasted, felt before hand.*

Essayer. *To essay; try, proue, tast, attempt; take a tast, make a tryall of; to feele before hand.*

Essayer à prendre. *To catch, reach, leape at; offer to take.*

Essayerie: f. *A trying-house.*

Essayeur: m. *An essayer; tryer, prouer; attempter; one that tasts, or takes an assay; and particularly, an Officer in the Mint, who touches euerie kind of new coyne before it be deliuered out.*

Esse. *The letter S; also, the forme of an S in any workmanship.*

Esseau: m. *A Coopers chipping ax.*

Essedaires. *A kind of warriors in old time, who marched in waggons, but fought on foot, and hard layed to, retyred againe to their waggons.*

Esseillé: m. ée: f. *Wasted, consumed.* ¶Pic.

Esseiller. *To wast, or consume.* ¶Pic.

Essein. *as* Essain; *a swarme.*

Esseiner. *To swarme (as Bees.)*

Essemé: m. ée: f. *Inseamed; vnfattened; cleansed from, purged of, grossenesse or grosse humors; also, swarmed.*

Essemement: m. *An inseaming, vnfattening; cleansing; also, a swarming.*

Essemer. *To inseame; vnfatten; cleanse from, or purge of, grossenesse or grosse humors; also, to swarme.*

Essence: f. *An essence, or being; the nature, or subsistence of things.*

Essencié. *as* Essentié.

Essencier. *To bring vnto the same nature, or being, that another is of; to make, or become both of one nature, and essence; essentially to mingle with, or be ioyned vnto.*

Essende: f. *A Shingle (of wood.)*

Essentié: m. ée: f. *Made, or become, of one essence with; essen-*

essentially ioyned, or linked vnto.
Essentiel: m. elle: f. *Essentiall, reall, naturall, materiall; effectuall; forcible, powerfull.*
Essentier. *as* Essencier.
Esseppé: m. ée: f. *Stocked, or whose stocke is cut.*
Essepper. *To stocke, or cut the stocke of.*
Essette de Tonnelier. *A Coopers Chipping-ax, or Addis.*
Esseulé: m. ée: f. *Abandoned, forsaken, left all alone.*
Esseuoüere. *A common Sinke, or Sewer.*
Essieu: m. *An axletree.*
Essil: m. *A Shingle, or thin boord of wood, such as we couer houses with.*
Essiller. *To lauish, or spend wastfully.*
Essilliere: f. *The clout thats layed betweene the legs of an infant.*
Essimé: m. ée: f. *Made leane, drawne dry, pulled downe, brought low.*
Essimé comme vn harang soret. *as leane as a rake, or a red Herring.*
Essimer. *To vnfatten, or take away superfluous fat; to pull downe, make leane, bring low.*
S'essimer avec les femmes. *To keepe much with women; to drayne, soake, or draw himselfe dry in their companie.*
Essoin. *as* Essein; *a swarme of Bees.*
Essoine. *as* Exoine; *also, want of abilitie in Souldiors to defend, or besiege, a place.*
Essoinner. *To swarme, as Bees.*
Essois: m. *Axletrees of Carts &c.*
Essongne. Droict d'essongne. *Looke* Droict.
Essonnier. *To essoine; to excuse, or discharge an absent, or impotent person, &c; as* Essoyner, *or* Exonier.
Essor: m. *Drought, dry weather; drynesse, lacke of moisture; also, a withering, decaying, or comming to nought, by excessiue drought, or drynesse; also, as* Essort.
L'essor du iour. *The heat, or hot, and drying time, of the day.*
Aller à l' essor. *To goe weather him; also, a Hawke to fly downe the wind, or goe out.*
Mettre à l'essor. *To drayne, soake, draw dry; to wast, consume, bring to decay by drought; also, to lay out, a drying, or in the heat of the day; or to expose vnto the ayre; to weather.*
Essorbé: m. ée: f. *Supped vp.*
Essorber. *To sup vp.*
Essoré: m. ée: f. *Dryed, drayned, soaked, or drawne dry; withered, or consumed by drought; also, weathered, ayred; layed out in the ayre, exposed vnto all weathers; also, mounted or soared vp; also, flowne downe the wind; fled, or carried away by the wind; gone out; also, vented, breathed, issued, or passed, out into the ayre.*
Esparvier essoré. *A sore Sparhawke.*
Lieu essoré. *An open place, a Sunnie brow, or banke.*
Essoreillé: m. ée: f. *Earelesse, without eares, that hath lost his eares; Looke* Essorillé.
Essoreiller. *To make earelesse, cut off eares, depriue of eares.*
Essorer. *To dry; drayne, draw dry; soake; to marre, make wither or decay by ouermuch drought; also, to ayre, or weather; to expose vnto, or lay out in, the weather; also, to mount or soare vp; also (being mounted) to fly downe the wind; fly his countrey; fly away, or goe out; also, to vent, breath, issue or passe, out into the ayre.*

S'essorer. *To weather himselfe, or dry himselfe in the weather; also, to mount, or soare vp, &c; as in* Essorer; *also, to keepe himselfe dry; to shade or shrowd himselfe from wetting; to shun approaching, or threatned, stormes.*
Essorillé. *as* Essoreillé; *whence;*
Cette coiffe est trop essorillée. *The eares of this coife are too short, or too little.*
Essort: m. *as* Essor; *also, a soaring, mounting, eleuation, high-rising; also, a vent, issue, passage, hole to breath or breake out at.*
Essourdé. *as* Essourdi.
Essourder. *To deafen, to make deafe.*
Essourdi: m. ie: f. *Growne deafe, made deafe, stonedeafe.*
Essourdir. *as* Essourder.
Essoyné: m. ée: f. *Weakened, disabled of bodie, made impotent by stripes, blowes, wounds, &c; hence also, essoyned, whose absence is excused by reason of his impotencie.*
Essoyner. *To weaken, enfeeble, disable, make impotent by stripes, blowes, wounds, &c; also, to essoine, or excuse; Looke* Exonier.
Essuccé: m. ée: f. *Soaked, drayned, drawne dry, without sap, without moisture.*
Essucer. *To drinke, soake, or sucke vp; to drayne, to draw dry.*
Essué. *as* Essuit.
Essueil: m. *The threshold of a dore.*
Essuiau: m. *A dish-clowt.*
Essuiau de bois. *Billet-wood fastened together with young Polls, and so conueyed downe riuers.*
Essuier. *To wipe, cleanse, make cleane; dry vp.*
Essuit: m. ite: f. *Wiped, cleansed, made cleane; dryed vp.*
Essuler. *To exile, to banish.*
Essuyé: m. ée: f. *Wiped; cleansed, or made cleane on the outside; also, dryed, or dry; also, tallowed, or annointed with tallow.*
Essuye-main: m. *A Hand-towell; or cloth to wipe the hands on.*
Essuyer. *To wipe; to cleanse, or make cleane (also, to dry) the outside of; also, to tallow, or annoynt with tallow.*
Est: m. l'Est. *The East; or, the East wind.*
Establage: m. *Stabling for horses; also, a fee due for their standing in an Inne, &c; also, as* Estallage; *stallage.*
Estable: f. *A Stable; an Osterie, or Ostellerie; also, a sheepe-house, or fould.*
Estable à bœufs, &c; *an Ox-stall, or Ox-house.*
Estable à oyes. *A penne, or coope for Geese.*
Estable à pourceaux. *An hogge-stie, a swines-stie.*
De grosse table à l'estable: Prov. *He that in housekeeping spends more then he's able, may fall to horsekeeping, and dy in a stable.*
Establement. *Stabling, or standing for horses.*
Establer. *To stable; to put into, or set vp in, a stable.*
Establi: m. *A stall.*
Establi: m. ie: f. *Established; setled, assured, fixed, confirmed, made fast; enacted, ordained, surely appointed.*
Establie: f. *The stall of a Taylor, &c; also, as* Establissement; *and hence;*
Brief d'establie. *A Writ, or Iniunction for the setling, or establishment of a Possession.*
Establier: m. *as* Establie; *a stall.*
Establies: f. *Companies, squadrons, or battallions of soul-*

souldiors; tearmed so in old time, because they were appointed together vnto certaine places, or standings; which they were to hold, or make good.

Establir. *To establish; to settle, fix, confirme, assure, make steafast, set fast; to enact, institute, ordaine, appoint surely.*

Establissement: m. *An establishment, or stablishing; a setling, assuring, fixing, confirming; also, an instituting, enacting, ordaining, appointing; in law, the setling of a possession; and hence;*

Enqueste d'establissement. *Looke* Enqueste.

Establisseur: m. *An establisher; setler, fixer; confirmer, enacter.*

Estacade: f. *A Lists; or place rayled in for a combat.*

Estacher. *To fasten, to tye; Seeke* Attacher.

Estacquer. *To marke for his owne; to set his marke vpon.*

Estaffier: m. *A Lackey, or foot-boy, that runnes by the stirrup; a footman, or seruingman that waites afoot, while his Master rides; also, an armed Sergeant attending on an Officer of Iustice.*

Estaffier S.Martin. *The deuill.* ¶Rab.

Estaffilade: f. *A stripe, ierke, or lash with a whip, or strap of leather; also, a slash ouer the face.*

Estage: m. *A storie, stage, loft, or height of a house; also, a lodging, dwelling, house, or place of abiding; also, lastage, or the balast of a ship.*

L'estage de rez de chaussée. *The floore, or lowest roome of a house.*

Droict d'estage. *A fee, or custome exacted for the harbouring of forraine corne within the ports, or hauens of some townes in France.*

Estager: m. *A vassall, subiect, inhabitant; one that hath a house, or dwelling vnder one Lord, or other; a tenant, and dweller within such or such a Libertie, or Mannor.*

Estagier: m. *as* Estager.

Estagné: m. ée: f. *Guelt, or lopped, as a tree.*

Estagner. *To gueld trees, to lop, or cut off their branches.*

Estagues. *Two ropes (fastened to the middle of the maine yard) which passing through the* Encornal, *serue to hoise vp the sayle; we call them, Tyes.*

Estaie: f. *as* Estaye.

Estaier. *Looke* Estayer.

Estail: m. *as* Estal; *a stall.*

Il leur tient estail. *He holds them tacke, or play.*

Estaillé. (Barbet estaillé.) *Handsomely clipt, or shorne; so cut, as he lookes like a Lyon.*

Estailleures de pierres. *Shards, or peeces that fly from stones in the hewing, or squaring of them.*

Estaillier: m. *A stall-man; or the foreman of a shop; he that lookes to the stall, and there exposes his ware to shew, and sale.*

Estails: m. *Tyes; the strings, or ropes of sayles.* ¶Rab.

Estaim: m. *Tynne.*

Estaim de Cornoüaille. *as* Estain doux.

Estaim doux. *The best kind of Tynne; gotten in Cornwall.*

Estaim de glace. *Another kind, vsed in the timing of the backsides of Looking-glasses, and for the dust of houre-glasses; being of a substance most thinne, small, euen, dry, and little subiect to giuing by anie change of weather.*

Estaim sonnant. *Pewter.*

Estaimmé: m. ée: f. *Tinned; leaded.*

Estaimmer. *To tinne; to lead; to couer, glaze, or doe ouer with Tynne, &c.*

Estain. *as* Estaim; *also, fine woollen (or linnen) yarne, thread, or woofe.*

Bouc d'estain. *The great-bearded, and long-horned wild goat, Ibex.*

Estainct: m. cte: f. *Extinguished, quenched, put out; spent, lost, abolished, vtterly perished; consumed, come to nought.*

'A la chandelle estaincte. *Looke* Chandelle.

Estaingnier: m. *A Pewterer, a Tinner.*

Estainier: m. ere: f. *Of Tynne, or Pewter; belonging vnto Tynne, or Pewter.*

Estal: m. *The stall of a shop, or booth; any thing whereon wares are layed, and shewed to be sold.*

Estalé: m. ée: f. *Displayed, opened, set, layed abroad, spred wide; exposed vnto view, as ware, on a stall.*

Estaler. *To display, vnfould, shew, spread wide, lay open wares on stalls; to expose vnto the view of all passengers, commers, customers; to place, or set vpon a stall.*

Estalier: m. *as* Estaillier.

Estallage: m. *Stallage.*

Estallé. *as* Estalé; *or set, or placed, as a commoditie, on a stall.*

Estallement: m. *The stall of a shop; also, the laying out of wares vpon a stall; a displaying; an exposing vnto publike view.*

Estaller. *as* Estaler.

Estallier. *as* Estaillier.

Estallon: m. *The iust quantitie, scantling, patterne, or size, of measures appointed by authoritie, and commonly hung vp in some publike place of a towne; Looke* Estalon.

Estallonnage. *as* Estallonnement; *also, a fee due for that assizing; or the power, or priuiledge, to assize publike weights, and measures.*

Estallonné: m. ée: f. *(Of a measure) assized; reduced vnto the iust proportion of the common size, and stamped with the publike marke; Looke* Estalonné.

Estallonnement: m. *The assizing of measures.*

Estallonner. *as* Estalonner.

Estalon. *as* Estallon; *also, a Stalion for Mares; also, a stale (as a Larke, &c) wherewith Fowlers traine sillie birds vnto their destruction; also, as* Baliveau, *a Stander in a wood; also, a short, and thicke peg, or peece of timber, whereby two sparres are fastened byas-wise together.*

Estalonage. *as* Estallonnage.

Estaloner. *as* Estalonner.

Estalonné: m. ée: f. *as* Estallonné; *also, couered, as a Mare, with a horse; and hence;*

Iument estalonnée. *A Mare which hath taken the horse.*

Estalonner. *To assize measures; to adiust weights; to giue them their iust scantling, their due size; also, to make a horse a Stalion; or to turne him among Mares; also, to play the Stalion, or couer Mares.*

Estalonner vn soulier. *To tread a shooe downe at the heeles.*

Estambor: m. *A peece of wood in a ship, that extends from the Keele to the top of the Poupe, and bends together with it; we call it, the Sterne post.*

Estambres. *The two thicke peeces of wood that enuiron the hole through which a Mast passes the Decke, or Hatches; we call them Partnours.*

Estamé: m. *Worsted; or, as* Estamet.

Estamé: m. ée: f. *Tynned; or, done ouer with tynne; glazed, made smooth, and sleeke, as an earthen vessell.*

Esta-

Estamet: m. Cloth-rash.
Estameure: f. A tynning.
Estamier: m. A Tynner, Tynne-man; Pewterer.
Estamine: f. The stuffe Tamine; also, a strayner, searce, boulter, or boulting cloth; (so called, because made (commonly) of a thinne kind thereof.)
Passer par l'estamine. To straine; to bring vnto the touch; to put vnto proofe, or tryall; to passe the pikes.
Estaminé: m. ée: f. Strayned, searced, boulted; passed through a strayner, searce, boulter; also, tryed, or throughly examined.
Estaminer. To strayne, searce, boult; to passe through a searce; also, to try, or examine the worth of.
Estamineux. Which vseth a strayner, searce, or boulter; also, fit to make a strayner of.
Estampe: f. A stampe, impression, presse, print, printing; also, as Console.
Estampé: m. ée: f. Supported, or vnderpropped, with tresles.
Estampeau: m. A tresse.
Estamper. To support, or vnderprop with tresses.
Estamperche: f. A great vpright beame, in building; a principall post.
Estancer. as Estançonner; to stay; to prop.
Estanceure: f. A supporting, or vnderpropping.
Estanche. A stanching; and hence;
Pierre d'estanche. The bloud-stone.
Estanché: m. ée: f. Stanched; slaked, quenched, quailed; stopped, stayed.
Estanchement: m. A stanching; a quayling; slaking; stopping, staying.
Estancher. To stanch; stop, or stay (an issue of bloud, &c) to quayle; slake, or quench hunger, thirst, &c.)
Estancheur: m. A stancher; stopper (of an issue of bloud, &c) quailer, slaker, quencher (of hunger, thirst, &c.)
Estançonner. Looke Estansonner.
Estandart: m. A Standart; a kind of Ensigne for horsemen, vsed in old time; also, the measure, or scantling for measure, which we also call the Standard.
Estang: m. A great pond, poole, or standing water.
Estanson: m. A prop, stay; tresse; a forked peece of wood wherewith a Vine, &c, is vnderset.
Estansonné: m. ée: f. Vnderset, vpheld, propped or stayed vp.
Estansonner. To prop, stay vp, vnderset, vphold.
Estansonner le mensonge d'un roseau. To support a ly with a reed; to maintaine an vntruth with sleight or friuolous arguments.
Estant. Being; subsisting; resting; also, standing vpon his feet, bolt vpright; whence;
En son estant. Standing, bolt vpright, vpon his feet.
Navire bien estant. A ship that is tight, sound, whole, and without leake.
Estanterol. Part of a ship verie neere vnto the poupe. ☛Rab.
Estape: f. A Staple; a Mart, or generall Market; a publike Store-house in a sea-towne, or towne of trafficke, wherein Marchants strangers lodge their wine, oyle, corne, or other commodities which they meane to vent; also, a certain Place, or Towne, whereto the countrey is inioyned to bring in victuals for the prouision of a (marching) Armie, or Troopes; also, the pecuniarie contribution allowed by those townes, or persons that bring in none; (In both which sences this word is most vsed plurally:) also, as Estanson.
Vivre par estapes. To liue on the pennie; to haue no more then he payes for, no manner of prouision other then he buyes (for souldiors, in their marches, either do, or should, pay for all the victuals they take of the countrey people.)
Estaphe: f. A Stirrup (for a saddle.)
Estaphilagrie: f. Staues-aker, Lowse-wort; (an hearbe.)
Estappe. as Estape.
Estaques. Oliue plants, or Suckers.
Estarnuër. as Esternuër; to sneeze.
Estase. as Extase.
Estasques. The Suckers, or scions that spring vp at the feet of Oliue trees.
Estat: m. The estate; case; nature, substance, being; fashion, propertie, condition, qualitie of things; also, the estate, meanes, wealth, fortunes; trade, calling; office, dignitie; ranke, degree, which a man hath, or is of; also, the state, head, issue, knot, principall point of a matter in controuersie; also, the state, or pompe of great persons, appearing by the richnesse of their apparrell, or multitude of their followers; (Tel porte grand estat;) also, the speciall note and marke taken, respect had, or account made, of such great ones; whence; Personnage de grand estat.
L'estat, & bon d'estat d'un Compte. The Remainder, or ouerplus due by, or in the hands of, an Accomptant, after all charges deducted, and allowed him.
L'estat d'un Decret. A particular Catalogue, or Suruey of the quantitie, and scite of each parcell of land thats seised by publike order.
L'estat d'un finance; l'estat de la recepte; bailler par estat ce qu'a esté receu, ou frayé &c; A Collection, Booke, or Bill of Receits, and Disbursements; any List, Roll, Register, Summarie, or Suruey of such like matters.
L'estat d'une Maison. A certaine, and setled order of the gouernment, seruice and expence of a (great) mans house; also, the List, Catalogue, Register, or Check-roll, containing the names, rankes, and functions of all the officers, and seruants therein.
Estat en matiere de Regale. is that, which in the cases of other Benefices, and Ecclesiasticall functions, is tearmed, Recreance; Looke Recreance.
L'estat du Roy; as in, l'estat d'une maison.
L'estat d'un Royaulme. The State; or the state of a Kingdome; the disposition, managing, policie, conduct of, the order, course, proceedings held in, State-affaires.
Les estats; &, les gens des trois estats. The whole bodie of a Realme, or Prouince, consisting of three seuerall Members, Estates, or Orders; the Clergie, Nobility, and Comminaltie.
Les estats (generaux.) A Parliament; or generall Assemblie of the aforesaid Orders, in a Kingdome, &c.
Les estats particuliers. A Prouinciall Sessions, or Assemblie, for consultation.
Deniers d'estat. An estimate made, by the Treasurers of France, in the beginning of a yeare, of all the summes which are to be leuied, and receiued that yeare.
Lettres d'estat. A Writ, or Iniunction for the stay of a suit, for a time, in cases, when either the Counsell of one of the parties is otherwise busied, or the partie himselfe imployed in seruice of the State (as an Embassador &c) and cannot attend, or be present, in Court.
Non-valoirs d'estat. Such summes as (whatsoeuer account

count the Treasurers made of them in the beginning) are not by the end of the yeare got in, though the Collectors, and Receiuers did their vtmost.

Plus-valeurs d'estat. *The summes which by the end of the yeare are payed in, ouer and besides all these, that are mentioned in the aforesaid Estimate (in* Deniers d'estat.)

Restats d'estat. *The summes due, at the yeres end, and after accounts giuen vp, vnto the Receiuers generall, and particular, by the Treasurers of France.*

Couché en estat. *Made Officer; intertained into seruice, or pay.*

Qui n'est couché en l'estat. *Ouerslipt, left out, forgotten, not chosen.*

Faire estat de. *To purpose, or make account to; also, to vse, or make a practise of.*

Faire l'estat de. *Looke* Faire.

Faire son estat. *To doe his dutie, play his part, execute his office, exercise his authoritie.*

Mettre estat en la cause. *To stop, or stay the proceedings in a cause.*

Tenir en estat. *To keepe in order; hold in awe.*

Tout estat, & rien au plat: Prov. *All pompe, no hospitalitie; the bellie is starued by the backe.*

Tout estat est viande aux vers: Prov. *Euerie creature is wormes meat.*

Estau: m. *as* Estal; *also, a hollow place vnder the root of a tree, that stands by a water side; also, the yron instrument wherewith Smithes hold fast their worke in the forging thereof.*

Demeurer estau. *To stand still.*

Estaudeau: m. *as* Hestoudeau.

Estaudi: m. ie: f. *Sheltered, or shrowded, as vnder a scaffold, or stall.*

Estaudir. *To shrowd, or shelter himselfe, as vnder a scaffold, or stall.*

Estaudy: m. *A scaffold, in building; also, a stall before a shop; also, a certaine defence of boords, vsed in approches, or at the entring of a breach.*

Estay: m. *A rope fastened to the top of the maine Mast, and holding it steadie when the maine sayle is hoised vp; we call it, the Stay.*

Estaye: f. *A prop, stay, supporter, shore, buttresse.*

Estayé: m. ée: f. *Propped, supported, shored, underset.*

Estayement: m. *A shoring, propping, supporting, vndersetting.*

Estayer. *To prop, shore, stay, vnderset, support.*

Esté: m. *Summer.*

Esté S. Martin. *The later part of Autumne.*

Cela ne faict ny hyver, ny esté. *is neither fish, nor flesh; doe: neither good nor harme; (and therefore may be spared.)*

En hyver par tout pleut; en esté là ou dieu veut: Prov. *In Winter it raines all ouer, in Summer but some where.*

Esté. *Beene, subsisted; remained, stood.*

Il y a esté trois iours. *He hath stayed three dayes about it.*

Tout a esté à autruy, & sera à autruy: Prov. *Looke* Autruy.

Esteignement: m. *A quenching, slaking, extinguishing, extinguishment.*

Esteigneur: m. *A quencher, slaker, extinguisher.*

Esteinct. *as* Estainct; *quenched, extinguished.*

Esteindement. *as* Esteignement.

Esteindible: com. *Extinguishable, quenchable.*

Esteindre. *To extinguish; to quench, to slake, or put out; to abolish, or bring vnto nothing.*

Cela est plus propre à estendre, qu'à esteindre, le mal. *That is more apt to extend, then to extinguish, the mischiefe.*

Esteinte: f. *An extinguishment, or extinguishing.*

Gambadans à esteinte de chandelle; viz. *vntill the candle burnt, or went, out.*

Estel. *as* Estal; *a stall.*

Estelé: m. ée: f. *Starrie, set with starres; hauing (as a horse) a starre in the forhead.*

Raye estelée. *Looke* Raye.

Esteler. *To bestarre, to set thicke with starres.*

Esteler les chevaux; *Looke* Atteler.

Estelin. *as* Estellin; *a weight of eight and twentie graines.*

Estellage: m. *Stallage; also, as* Attelage.

Estelle: f. *A rod, or sticke; also, a little starre; and the rowell of a spurre; (barbarously.)*

Esteller. *as* Estaler.

Estellin: m. *A Goldsmithes weight, containing eight and twentie graines, or the twentieth part of an ounce.*

Estellon. *as* Estallon; *a size, or patterne for measures, or proportions; also, a patterne of Marchandise, such as shop-keepers lay forth vpon their stals; also, a Stallion.*

Estelloner. *as* Estalonner.

Estelon. *as* Estalon; *also, a crosse-beame, or binding peece of timber.*

Estenché, Estencher. *Looke* Estanché, Estancher.

Estendant. *Extending, retching, stretching out.*

Estendart: m. *An Ensigne, or Standart; Looke* Estandart.

Estendement: m. *An extending; retching, or stretching out; a pulling or spreading forth; a lengthening; widening, inlarging; also, a planing, vnfoulding; displaying, setting, or shewing, abroad.*

Estendre. *To extend; retch or stretch, forth; pull or spread out; lengthen, widen, inlarge; vnfold, plane, display, set or shew abroad.*

Estendre la loy. *To wrest, or straine the Law; to make large expositions, or vse farre-fetcht interpretations, thereof.*

S'estendre. *To extend, or stretch out it selfe; also, to increase, propagate, or multiply exceedingly.*

Estendu: m. uë: f. *Extended; retched or stretched forth; pulled or spred out; lengthened, widened, inlarged; vnfoulded, planed, displayed, set or shewed abroad; also, increased, or multiplyed, or dispersed mightily.*

Tout plat estendu. *Layed all along, or at full length; lying as flat as a flooke.*

Estenduë: f. *Extent, extension; an out-stretched proportion; length; wideneße, largeneße, greatneße, dilatation, spaciousneße.*

L'estenduë du ciel. *The out-stretcht cope, or scope of heauen; all the space that is betweene heauen, and earth.*

Estendure: f. *An extension, or extending.*

Ester. *To stand; indure, abide by it, continue in, sticke vnto.*

Ester à vne chose convenuë. *To keepe touch; hold tacke, stand to a bargaine.*

Ester à droict. *To referre himselfe vnto the Law.*

Ester en iugement. *To sue; to commence, or defend a suit; to stand to his tryall; or to referre his cause vnto ordinarie tryall; also, to appeare, as a partie, in Court.*

Esterdre le bestiail. *To litter cattell.*

Esterlin. *as* Estellin; *or, a pennie sterling; our pennie.*

Esterni: m. ie: f. *Strowed, spred, displayed, throwne abroad, layed along.*
Esternir. *To strow, spread, throw, lay abroad, or along; to display.*
Esternissement: m. *A strowing, spreading, displaying; laying abroad or along.*
Esternuement: m. *A neezing, or sneezing.*
Esternuer. *To neeze, or sneeze.*
Herbe à esternuer. *Sneesingwort, or Sneesewort of Austria, wild Pellitorie of Spaine.*
Esteſté. *Looke* Eteſté.
Esteſter. *Looke* Eteſter.
Esteuf: m. *A Tennisball.*
Courir apres son esteuf. *Foolishly to pursue a thing, which he had, and might haue held, in his hands; also, (as foolishly) to rely on, strayne himselfe for, or follow after, incertainties.*
Se donner l'esteuf l'un à l'autre. *To assist, or serue one anothers turne.*
Il se mit encores apres son esteuf. *He betooke himselfe vnto his first enterprise; or, to that he had most in his head; or (as before) he obstinately followed that againe, which himselfe let goe.*
Il releva cet esteuf. *He apprehended this occasion, he seised on, or made vse of, this aduantage.*
Se renvoyer l'esteuf l'un à l'autre; *Looke* Renvoyer.
Esteule: f. *Straw, or stuble growing.*
Nouvelles esteules. *New stuble, or stuble ground; so tearmed for the three next dayes after the sheaues are bound vp.*
Estienne. *Stephen (a mans proper name.)*
Invention Sainct Estienne. *An holyday kept by the Church of Rome, the third of August.*
Miches de S. Estienne. *Stones.*
Estier: m. *Looke* Septier.
Estimable: com. *Esteemeable, valuable, priseable.*
Estimateur: m. *An estimator, valuer, prizer, esteemer of things.*
Estimation: f. *An estimation, prizing, valuing; a consideration had, or iudgement giuen, of.*
Estime: f. *An estimate, estimation, price, value, esteeme, valuation; an account, regard, reckoning made of; the reputation, or credit giuen to; the opinion had of.*
Estimé: m. ée: f. *Esteemed; thought, supposed; held, reputed; prised, valued; respected, regarded; held deere, set much by, made account of; iudged; weighed, considered.*
Estimer. *To esteeme; thinke, deeme, trowe, suppose, repute, hold; weigh, consider; iudge; prise, value; regard, respect, hold deere, set by, make much account of.*
Estincelle: f. *A sparke, or sparkle of fire; a twinckle; a flash.*
Estincellé: m. ée: f. *Sparkled, sparked, twinkled; also, powdered, or set with sparkles.*
Estincellement: m. *A sparkling, a twinkling.*
Estinceller. *To sparke, to sparkle, as fire; to twinkle, as a starre, or Dyamond; to sprinkle as wine; to powder, or set thicke with sparkles.*
Estincellette: f. *A little sparkle, a small twinkling.*
Estiomene. *S. Anthonies fire (a painefull swelling full of heat, and rednesse.)*
Estiomené: m. ée: f. *Inflamed, or infected with S. Anthonies fire.*
Estiomener. *To cut off the member so inflamed, or infected.*
Estire: m. *The yron toole wherewith a Currier draynes the skins he receiues from the Tanpit; some call it, a Sleeker.*

Estiré: m. ée: f. *Strained, stretched, wrested, retched; set on the tenter hookes.*
Estirement: m. *A stretching, or retching; a straining, or setting on the tenter hookes.*
Estirer. *To retch, or straine aboue compasse; to wrest, or stretch, to set on the tenter hookes.*
Estival: m. ale: f. *Of Summer, belonging vnto Summer.*
Estivalet: m. *A Buskin, or Summer boot.*
Estive: f. *The loading, or lading of a ship; also, the Hold wherein most of that lading is contained.*
Estivé: m. ée: f. *Loaden, or laden (as a ship.)*
Estiveler. *as* Etiveler.
Estiver. *To Summer, to passe the Summer in; to rest in Summer.*
Estivet: m. *A little Summer, halfe a Summer, another Summer.*
L'estivet de S. Martin. *The later end of Autumne.*
Estoc: m. *The stocke, trunke, or bodie of a tree; also, the principall stocke or stemme, direct and chiefe line, of a Familie, Kinred, or Pettigree; also, the race, kind, or sort of other things; also, a Rapier, or tucke; also, a thrust; also, a Vice.*
Estoc d'armes. *A kind of strong, sharpe, and short horsemans sword, broad at the handle (where it hath but one barre for defence) and narrowing to the pointwards.*
Coup d'estoc. *A thrust, foine, stockado, stab; also, a prick-cast.*
D'estoc. *Thrusting, foining; stabbing.*
D'estoc & de taille. *Both with the point and the edge; also, both wayes, in both kinds; or, by all kind of means, molestations, mischiefes.*
Se tenir à l'estoc sans s'amuser aux branches. *To adhere vnto the principall, without respect of dependants.*
Estocage: m. *A linage, or the chiefe stemme of a linage.* ¶Wallon.
Estoccade: f. *A stoccado; stab, foine, thrust.*
Estoccader. *To giue the stoccado; to stab, foine at, pricke deepe into, thrust through.*
Estoccage: m. iiij d *vpon the sale of an inheritance, due (in some places) vnto the Landlord, and to be payed him, in lieu of a Reliefe, the same day it is sold.*
Estocquer. *as* Estoccader; *or, as* Estoquer.
Estoeuf. *as* Esteuf.
Estoeuvier: m. ere: f. *Of, or belonging to, a Tennisball.*
Estoffe: f. *Stuffe; matter, substance; ware, chaffer; also, the qualitie, ranke; abilitie, or worth of a man.*
Chevaliers de bonne estoffe. *Knights well armed, and well managing their Armes.*
Estoffé: m. ée: f. *Stuffed; made with stuffe; stored, or furnished with necessaries; also, carued, grauen, intayled.*
Estoffer. *To stuffe; to make with stuffe; to furnish, or store with all necessaries; also, to carue, graue, intayle.*
Estofferie: f. *The art of ingrauing.*
Estoffeur: m. *A cutter, grauer, caruer, intailer.*
Estoillé: m. *The Lizard Stellio, whose necke is full of starre-like spots.*
Estoille: f. *A starre; a planet; also, the hearb Sharewort, Starre-wort, Cudwort.*
Estoille de mer. *An excrement of the sea, called the Fiue-foot, or Starre-fish.*
Estoille polaire. *The North starre. See* Polaire.
Estoille Poussiniere. *The seuen starres; called by some, the Henne and her Chickens.*
Escus à l'estoille Poussiniere. *Counters (for there are no such Crownes.)*

Herbe de l'estoille. *Buck horne, Crowfoot Plantaine, Harts-horne Plaintaine, Sandwort, hearbe Iuie, or hearbe Eue.*

Ordre de l'estoille. *An Order of Knighthood, institu-ted by* Iohn *King of France in the yeare* 1351; *aban-doned long agoe by the Nobilitie, because it grew too common; and retained at this day onely by the ordina-rie watchmen of Paris.*

Pierre d'estoilles. *A kind of Orange-coloured Car-buncle, wherein (setting it betweene and the light) ma-ny golden, sparkling, and starre-like drops may be dis-cerned.*

La belle estoille. *The name of a Village that lyes in the high way betweene* S.Denis *and* Pontoise.

'A l'enseigne de l'estoille. (Coucher à l'en. *To lye without dores all night) vnder the Canopie of the faire heauens.*

On les fait croire que les estoilles sont des papil-lottes. *They are made beleeue that starres be (no bet-ter then) spangles;* viz. *They are extreamely gulled, or abused.*

'A midi estoille ne luit: Prov. *At mid day no starre shines; Looke* Midi.

Estoillé: m. ée: f. *Starrie, full of starres; poudered, or set thicke, with starres.*

Estoilée: f. *The hearbe Lyons foot, Ladies mantle, great Sanicle.*

Estoiller. *To set with starres.*

Estoilleux: m. euse: f. *Starrie, full of starres, set thicke with starres.*

Estoillins: m. *An Order of Friers, that weare starres on the breasts of their gownes.*

Estoitlette: f. *A kind of rich furre.*

Estole: f. *A stole, (for the necke of a Priest.)*

Estomach: m. *The Stomacke; the gorge; also, the bulke, bosome, or breast (being the seat of the stomacke;) also, a stomacke, lust, appetite vnto, desire of, meat.*

Vn estomach de perdrix. *The wing, and brawne; the breast (the best) peece.*

Les viandes nouvelles font rebondir l'estomach: Prov. *Looke* Rebondir.

Estomaqué: m. ée: f. *Angrie at, in a rage against.*

s'Estomaquer à l'encontre de. *To be angrie with, to take the pet, or pepper in the nose, at.*

Estomisseur. Vn vieil estomisseur de sacre. *An old bangling, or buzzing Saker.*

Estommi: m. ie: f. *Stonnied, benummed, dulled, made senceless.*

Estonné: m. ée: f. *Daunted, astonished, amazed, ap-palled, agast; abashed.*

Estonnez comme canes. *Dismayed like so manie Ducks.*

Estonné comme vn coupeur de bourses. *Confoun-ded like a Cutpurse (taken in the manner.)*

Estonné comme vn fondeur de cloches. *Much out of countenance, as a Bell-founder (whose worke miscar-ries.)*

Estonnement: m. *An astonishment, astonishing, or ston-nying; a sleepinesse, numnesse, or benumming; a sence-lesnesse; dulnesse, amazednesse; dulling, amazing.*

Estonner. *To astonish, amaze, daunt, appall; abash, put out of countenance; make agast; also, to stonnie, be-numme, or dull the sences of.*

Tout ce que tonne ne nous estonne point: Prov. *All that does thunder does not blunder vs.*

Estophe. *as* Estoffe.

Estoquant. *Thrusting, foyning, stabbing, pricking, giuing the Stockado vnto; also, reuiling, rayling at.*

Estoqué: m. ée: f. *Thrust, foyned, pricked, stabbed into; also, reproched, reuiled, rayled at.*

Estoquer. *To thrust, or foyne at; pricke, or stab into; also, to reproch, reuile, rayle at, scold with.*

Estorce: f. *A straine, wring, wrinch; also, a bad part; hard measure offred; an vnhappie turne played.*

Estorcir. *as* Estordre.

Estordant. *Wringing, wrinching, wresting, writhing.*

Estordre. *To wring, wrinch, wrest, writhe; extort vio-lently, take wrongfully; pull out of, or from betweene, the fingers of another.*

Estoré: m. ée: f. *Built, made, erected, edified; also, fur-nished, stored, garnished with, prouided of.*

Tenir à Cour feste haute, & estorée. *To keepe at Court a plentifull, or bountifull feast.*

Estorer. *To build, make, edifie, erect, raise, reare; also, to store, garnish, or furnish.*

Estorse: f. *as* Estorce.

Estorsement: m. *A wringing, wresting, wrinching, writhing; extorting, violent pulling out of the hands of another.*

Estouble: f. *Stuble, or straw growing.*

Estoubles. *Stuble ground.*

Estoudeau. *as* Hestoudeau.

Vn ieune estoudeau superbe. *A proud princox boy.*

Estouffé: m. ée: f. *Stifled, suffocated, smothered.*

Estouffement: m. *A stifling, smothering, choaking, suf-focating, stopping of the breath.*

Estouffer. *To stifle, smother, choake, whirken, suffocate, stop the breath.*

Estouillon: m. *A fanne to gather wind withall.*

Estoupade: f. *A stoppage, or stopping.*

Estoupade des reins. *A certaine kernell neere about the reines.*

Estoupe: f. *Towe, heards; Ockam.*

Clou d'estoupe. *A Speeke, or sheathing nayle, vsed in shipping.*

Souffler aux estoupes. *To (helpe to) continue, or in-crease, a trouble, or troublesome businesse; to keepe the wheele agate.*

Il a tissu lin avec estoupe. *He hath mingled, or ium-bled good, and bad together.*

Estoupé: m. ée: f. *Stopped, closed, shut, made vp.*

Estoupement: m. *A stopping, or shutting vp.*

Estouper. *To stop, to close; to shut, or make vp.*

Estoupeux: m. euse: f. *Heardie, flaxie, full of towe.*

Estoupillon: m. *A stopple, or thing that stoppeth.*

Estouppade: f. *as* Estoupade; *or, a tent, or stopple, (of towe, &c.)*

Estour: m. *A fight, combat, conflict, scuffling, shocke, in-counter; also, the assault of a towne, or fortresse.*

Estourbillon: m. *A whirlewind.*

Estourdi: m. ie: f. *Dulled, amazed, astonished, dizzie-headed, or whose head seems very much troubled; (hence) also, heedlesse, inconsiderate, vnaduised, witlesse, vncir-cumspect, rash, retchlesse, or carelesse; and sottish, bloc-kish, lumpish, lusk-like, without life, mettall, spirit; also, malled, felled, or knocked downe.*

Estourdi de baston, ou de bateau. *Extreamely be-nummed, or amazed; most vnfit, or vnreadie, for a sud-dain imployment; or, at his wits end when he is suddain-ly put to any thing; also, in a desperate, or pitifull taking.*

'A l'estourdi. *Amazedly; heedlesly, vnheedfully, wit-lesly, inconsiderately, carelesly, rashly, at randome; as one that minds not the worke he is about, or knowes not what he does; also, dully, sottishly, blockishly, heauily, drowsily, dreamingly.*

De bouc estourdi. *Rashly, turbulently, with a hurrie.*

Plus eſtourdi que le premier ſon de Matines; *Looke* Matines.

Eſtourdie: f. *as* Eſtourdiſſement.

'A l'eſtourdie. *as*, à l'eſtourdi.

Eſtourdir. *To aſtoniſh, amaze, dull, trouble the braines, depriue of wit, and heed; make giddie, or dizzie in the head; alſo, to mall, or knocke downe.*

Eſtourdir ſes morceaux. *To chaw his meat ill, or ſwallow it downe without chawing (hauing rouled it once about his mouth;) we ſay, to make bricke walls.*

Eſtourdiſſement: m. *A dulling, amazing, aſtoniſhing, depriuing of ſence, wit, heed; alſo, an amazedneſſe, aſtoniſhment, ſencelesneſſe, dizzineſſe, or the ſwimming of the head; alſo, heedleſneſſe, inconſideration, vnaduiſedneſſe, raſhneſſe, retchleſneſſe, careleſneſſe; and ſottiſhneſſe, dulneſſe, blockiſhneſſe; alſo, a malling, felling, or knocking downe.*

Eſtourgeon: m. *A Sturgeon; the fiſh Sturgeon.*

Eſtourneau: m. *A Stare, or Starling.*

Eſtrace: f. *Raw ſilke thats ſo ruffled or tangled, as it cannot be wound, and therefore they are faine to card, and afterwards to ſpin, it.*

Eſtrade: f. *A ſtreet; a way, a high way.*

Batteurs d'eſtrade. *The Scouts, Forragers, or Forerunners of an Armie; alſo, Purſe-takers, Boot-halers, or S. Nicholas clarkes.*

Eſtradiot: m. *A light-horſe, an Albanian horſeman; a Carbine.*

Eſtradiote. Chevaucher à l'Eſtradiote. *To ride long, or with long ſtirrups.*

Eſtragon: m. *The hearbe Tarragon.*

Eſtraigné: m. ée: f. *Wrung, or griped within the fiſt.*

Eſtraigner. *To wring, or gripe with the fiſt.*

Trop embraſſer, & peu eſtraigner. *To haue too many yrons in the fire at once; to deale in ſo many trades (or matters) that he can thriue by none.*

Eſtrain: m. *Straw; litter, fodder of ſtraw, or ſtuble.*

De grand train ſur l'eſtrain: Prov. *From (keeping) a great traine into the ſtraw; viz. vnto beggerie.*

Eſtrainéte: f. *as* Eſtreinte.

Eſtraindre. *To ſtrayne, wring hard, bind faſt, thruſt vp cloſe together; Looke* Eſtreindre.

Eſtraines. *as* Eſtreines.

Eſtrainte: f. *as* Eſtreinte; *alſo, a kind of cloſe buckle, or claſpe (moſt commonly of ſiluer) vſed in the faſtnings of clokes, hatbands, womens girdles, &c, and much more cloſe, and comelie then the ordinarie buckle, or claſpe.*

Eſtraires. *as* Eſtrayeres; *or as* Eſpaves.

Eſtraïure: f. *An Eſcheat, or Perquiſite; an Eſcheating.*

Eſtramaçon: m. *A downe-right blow; gaſh, or cut; alſo, a cuff, bang, rap.*

Eſtrancher. *as* Trancher; *to cut.*

Eſtrangé: m. ée: f. *Eſtranged, alienated, altered, ſeperated from; growne ſtrange, or out of knowledge, and acquaintance.*

Eſtrange: com. *Strange, vncouth, vnuſuall; forraine, alien, outlandiſh; vnaccuſtomed, vnacquainted; alſo, harſh, rude, od (in condition, or conſtitution.)*

Eſtrangement: m. *An eſtranging, or alienating himſelfe from others; a ſhunning of companie; a quitting of all vſuall faſhions.*

Eſtrangément. *Strangely, vnuſually, wonderfully; out of ordinarie courſe, in an vncouth manner.*

Eſtranger: m. *as* Eſtrangier.

Eſtranger. *To eſtrange, alienate; alter, diuide, ſeperate, withdraw from.*

S'eſtranger de. *To ſhun, auoid; leaue the haunt of; withdraw his mind, diſuſe himſelfe, from.*

Eſtrangeté: f. *Strangeneſſe, vnwontedneſſe, vncouthneſſe; alſo, a ſtrange act, or accident; a rare, or wonderfull matter; (In which ſence tis moſt vſed in the Plurall number;) alſo, rudeneſſe, harſhneſſe, frowardneſſe, peruerſeneſſe.*

Eſtrangier: m. *A ſtranger, alien, forreiner, an outlander, or outlandiſh man; alſo, a ſtrange bodie, that is neither a dweller with, nor of kinne vnto, vs; one with whom we haue no familiaritie, or hold no correſpondencie.*

Eſtranglé: m. ée: f. *Strangled, ſtifled, choaked, throtled, whirkned, ſmoothered.*

Eſtrangle-leopard: m. *Libbards bane, Crayfiſh wolues-bane; (an hearbe.)*

Eſtrangle-loup. *Wolues-bane, Wolfe-wort; (a moſt pernicious hearbe.)*

Eſtranglement: m. *A ſtrangling, ſtifling, throtling, whirkning, choaking.*

Eſtrangler. *To ſtrangle, choake, throtle, ſtifle, whirken, ſmother.*

Eſtranguillon. Poire d'es. *A choake peare.*

Pomme d'eſtranguillon. *A Crab, or Wilding.*

Eſtranguillons: m. *The Strangles; a diſeaſe (in horſes, &c.)*

Eſtrapade: f. *The puniſhment called, the Strappado.*

Eſtrapaſſé: m. ée: f. *Harried, ouer-toyled, oppreſſed with labour, whereof too much is taken.*

Eſtrapaſſer. *To harrie, ouer-toyle, oppreſſe with labour, take too much of.*

Eſtraper. *To mow, or cut downe ſtuble.*

Eſtrapoire. *as* Eſtrappoire.

Eſtrappade. *as* Eſtrapade.

Eſtrappé: m. ée: f. *Mowed, or cut downe, as ſtuble.*

Eſtrapper. *To mow, or cut downe, ſtuble.*

Eſtrappoire: f. *A kind of little, and long-handled Sickle, wherewith ſtuble is cut downe.*

Eſtraſſe. *as* Eſtrace.

Eſtraſſier: m. *One that cards, or ſpinnes ruffled ſilke.*

Eſtrave: f. *The ſtemme, or ſtemme-poſt of a ſhip.*

Eſtravé: m. ée: f. *Vnſhackled; freed from ſhackles.*

Eſtraver. *To vnſhackle; to free, or deliuer from ſhackles.*

Eſtrayer: m. ere: f. *as* Eſpave: com.

Eſtrayeres: f. *Eſcheats; the goods of ſtrangers dead without French-borne iſſue; and of baſtards, dead inteſtate, or without iſſue.*

Eſtre: m. *A ſubſtance, or ſubſiſtence; an eſſence, being; ſtate; alſo, the ſtocke, ſtemme, or direct line of a Pettigree, kindred, or familie.*

Les Eſtres d'une maiſon. *The inward conueyances, priuate windings or turnings within, entries into, iſſues out of, a houſe.*

Se maintenir touſiours en meſme eſtre. *To hold at one ſtay, continue in one eſtate, keepe ſtill his former ſtate, be alwayes the man he was, or the ſame man.*

Eſtre. *To be, ſubſiſt; remaine, abide, ſtand, reſt.*

Eſtre à cheval. *To ride, or ſit a horſe, or on horſebacke; alſo, to deale vpon aduantage; alſo, to ſtand on loftie, or high tearmes, as one that knowes he hath the aduantage.*

Eſtre apres quelqu' un. *To ly at, or be earneſt with, one to doe any thing.*

Eſtre deſſus. *To ſtand; Looke* Deſſus.

Eſtre en eau. *To ſweat; or, as we ſay, to be all on a water.*

Eſtre en l'eau. *To be in, or vpon, the water.*

Estre entre deux fers. *Looke* Fer.

Estre de garde. *To continue long in good plight; to keepe well; beare his age well.*

Estre du guet. *To be taken napping; also, to be gulled, or to swallow a gudgeon.*

Estre à la grosse haleine. *To gape, or gaspe for breath; to be almost cleane out of breath.*

Estre à l'herte. *Looke* Erte.

Estre du lard: tout y estoit du lard. *All went on wheeles there; there was no hoe with them, they were so lustie.*

Estre en son lourdant. *To sell Sowce; to be sicke of the Mumpes; to be troubled with the sullens.*

Estre malade. *A woman to haue her flowers.*

Estre de Rhodais. *The same.*

Estre à soy. *To be his owne Maister, or Man; to be at his owne commaund; to haue the absolute gouernment of himselfe; also, to find himselfe; whence;* Faulcon qui est à soy; *a wild, or hagard Hawke; a Hawke that preyes for her selfe.*

Estre sur. Femme qui n'est point sur les hommes. *That is verie chast, or continent; that is not eager of the Man; that cares not verie much for a man; Hence also;* Estre sur le Vin. *To loue Wine; also, to haue the right smacke of, or a right tast for, Wine.*

Fust qu'aucun raccontast. *Whether one tell of.*

En estre. En voulez vous estre? *Will you make one? (at play, &c.)*

Et en suis là. *And I am of the same opinion.*

I'en suis ainsi. *Such is my case, it is euen so with me.*

Qu' en est il? *What of that?* Que vous en est il? *What is that to you?*

Y estre. Il y est. *(at Tennis;) the Ball is in the hazard;* &, Il y estoit. *It had beene there but that I saued it.*

Vous y estes. *You are in the right; you haue hit it; you haue said as truly, done as fitly, as is possible; also, you stirre not, or cannot stirre; you sticke fast, or are set fast, therein.*

Vous n' y estes pas *(at Bowles;) you are, or haue throwne, wide.*

Vous n'y estes de rien. *You haue nothing to do in the matter.*

Ce m'est Dieu. *So helpe me God (corruptly.)*

Quand ce fut à faire cecy, ou cela. *When it comes to the doing of this, or of that.*

Qui n'y est n'y a sa part: Prov. *He that comes not, shares not, among them.*

Tout à esté à autruy, & sera à autruy: Pro. *All came from, and will goe to, others.*

Estreci: m. ie: f. *Streitned; pinched, shrunke in, plucked neere together; contracted, abridged, made or drawne short, brought into a narrow compasse.*

Estrecir. *To streiten, pinch, draw, or shrinke in, plucke neere together; to contract, abridge, make short, bring into a narrow compasse.*

Estrecissement: m. *A streitning, pinching, shrinking in; a contracting, abridging, drawing neere, bringing narrow, together.*

Estrecisson: f. *A streitnesse, or streit; a shrinke, pinch, contraction, abridgement.*

Estrecissure: f. *as* Estrecissement.

Estrée: f. *A house; an abiding, or place of abode.*

Estreignement: m. *A straining, wringing, squeezing, fast-griping, hard-holding, sore-pressing; close thrusting vp together.*

Estreiller. *as* Estriller.

Estreinct: m. cte: f. *Strayned, wrung, squeezed, gripped fast; also, streitned, pinched, shrunke vp, restrained; bound hard, kept fast in; also, strait, strict, or close.*

Estreindre. *To wring, straine, squeeze; to straiten, restraine, presse hard, thrust vp close together.*

Estreindre les fesses. *To twindge in the buttockes, as one thats hard set, and must not yet goe to it.*

Et plus gele et plus estreinct: Pro. *The more it freezes the harder it growes.*

Estreine: f. *A New-yeares gift, or Present; also, a Handsell.*

En bonne estreine. *In good time, a Gods name, luckily may it be.*

A bon iour bonne estreine: Prov. *On so holie a day happie successe betide vs (Sometimes tis also applyed (Ironically, and in a contrarie sence) vnto one, that on a great day commits any grieuous offence) he hath hanselled the day fairely; or, faire betide him for his goodlie act on so godlie a day.*

Estreiné: m. ée: f. *Handselled; that hath the handsell or first vse of; also, beaten, swindged, cudgelled, or corrected.*

Estreint: m. te: f. *as* Estreinct.

Estreinte: f. *A strayning, &c; as* Estreignement; *also, a straine, gird, wring, narrow, or sore pinch; also, a kind of siluer girdle, for women; or, as* Estrainte.

Estreintif: m. *A restringent and binding medicine, or plaister.*

Estrelures. *as* Estrayers; *also, escheatings.*

Estrelin: m. *An Easterling; one of the East parts, or of the Hanse-townes, of Germanie; also, a drunken huff-snuff, swaggerer, swash-buckler.*

Estrelin: m. ine: f. *(whence;)* Livre Estrelin. *A pound sterling.*

Estrene: f. *as* Estreine.

Estrené: m. ée: f. *Handselled; or, that hath had a New-yeares gift; also, cudgelled, swindged, corrected.*

Estrener. *To handsell, or bestow a New-yeares gift on; also, to beat, swindge, cudgell, correct.*

Estrette: f. *A gird, pinch, nip, wrench, yerke, wring; also, a violent onset on an enemie; also, a kind of punishment.*

Estrez. *A Crosse of Gueules, (in Heraldrie.)*

Estribort. *The Starboord; or, the right side of a ship.*

Estricqué: m. ée: f. *Pranked, decked, neat, fine, spruce, trickt vp.*

Estricquoyes. *Iron Pinsers.* (v.m.)

Estrié. *A kind of bread, or paste, of fine flower kneaded with water, white wine, the yolkes of egges, salt, and sugar.*

Estrié. Vn homme bien estrié. *Soaked, drayned, drawne dry, by wenching.*

Estrief: m. *One of the three little bones that be seated far within the eare, and serue as instruments of hearing.*

Estrier: m. *A stirrup.*

Alonger les estriers. *To lengthen his (lasciuious) delight; or draw it out, and make it continue, as long as he can.*

Estrier. *To drayne, or draw dry; to soake, or draw liquor, sap, iuice, &c, from.*

Estrieu. *as* Estrier.

Estrif: m. *Strife, debate, contention discord; brabling, altercation.*

Estrille: f. *A horse-combe, or curry-combe.*

Vn manche d'estrille. *A Dwarfe; the diminutiue of a man.*

Estrillé: m. ée: f. *Curried; also, bangd, thwacked, beaten, belaboured; also, thin, slender, gaunt, lanke.*

Estriller. *To currie (a horse;) to rub ouer with a curry-combe;*

combe; also, to lamme, cudgell, bang, thwacke, belabor, beat.
Cheval roigneux n'a cure qu' on l' estrille: Prov. *The scabbed horse cares not for currying.*
Tel estrille fauveau qui puis le mord: Prov. *The vngratefull iade bites him that does him good.*
Estrilloir: m. *That which is wrapped about thread, in winding, to keep the fingers from being cut therewith.* ¶ Orleannois.
Estrindore. *A kind of Brittish daunce.* ¶ Rab.
Estripé: m. ée: f. *Vntriped, vnbowelled, with his guts, or bowels about his heeles.*
Estriqué: m. ée: *Pulled on, as a boot, &c; also, as* Estricqué.
Estriquer. *To pull on boots, or boot-hose; also, to force a wild beast out of his denne, or out of his thickets, into the plaine.*
S'estriquer. *To pranke, tricke, decke, or trimme vp himselfe.*
Estriver. *To put foot into the stirrup; as,* Il estrive trop; *he puts his foot too farre into the stirrup; also, to striue, debate, varie, contend, brawle, or brable with.*
Estriveur: m. *A scolder, brawler, brabler, contentious person.*
Estriveux: m. euse: f. *Contentious, litigious, brabling, vnquiet, brawling, full of debate, euer wrangling with one or other.*
Estriviere: f. *A stirrup leather.*
Bailler les estrivieres. *To beat, or lash, with a stirrup leather.*
En disant cela il donne des expoussettes (que ie ne die des estrivieres) à l'autre; *in saying that, he somewhat touches (perhaps he taxes) or, he lugs (if he lash not) the other.*
Estroicissement: m. *A contraction, straitning, narrowing, restraining.*
Estroict: m. *A strait of land betweene two hills, or of the sea betweene two lands; and (more generally) any strait, narrow place, or plot.*
Mettre à l'estroict. *To driue to a narrow strait, or to an extremitie; to put vnto the pinch, or to his plunges.*
Ranger à l'estroict. *The same; or, as;*
Tenir à l'estroict. *To restraine, keepe short, hold vnto hard meat, or conditions.*
Estroict: m. ete: f. *Strait, narrow, close; contracted, restrained; also, strict, hard, pinching; rigorous, austere, seuere.*
Large de bouche, & estroict de Ceincture; *liberall of tongue, but sparing in purse.*
Voila vn cheval qui est estroict, viz. *Thats narrow before.* ¶ Parisien.
Estroictement. *Straitly, narrowly, closely; strictly, hardly; austerely, seuerely.*
Estroisseur: f. *Straitnesse, narrownesse, contraction.*
Estroissi: m. ie: f. *as* Estreci.
Estroissir. *To straiten, pinch, restraine, contract, make narrow or close; hemme in.*
Estroit. *as* Estroict.
Estron: m. *A turd.*
Estronçonné: m. ée: f. *Trunked, or cut off by the trunk.*
Estronçonner. *To trunke, to cut off by the trunke.*
Estropiat. *Lame, criple, maymed, halting, wanting some principall member.*
Estropié. *Lamed, maymed; made criple.*
Estropié de caboche, ou de ceruelle; *frantick, witlesse, braine-sicke, braine-crackt.*
Estropier. *To mayme, lame, becriple, or make a criple.*
Estrouble. *as* Estouble. *Stuble.*
Estrousse: f. *An absolute sale, and deliuerie of a thing vnto him that offers the most for it.*
Estroussé: m. ée: f. *Vnpacked, vntrussed; also, sold outright, and deliuered to him that offers most.*
Estrousser. *To vntrusse, vnpacke; vnty, or vndo a trusse, or packe; also, to sell, and deliuer a thing vnto him that offers, or giues, most for it.*
Estude: f. *A Studie; a priuate Cabinet or Closet to studie in; also, studie; diligent search, musing, meditation, beating of the braine about matters of learning; and (more generally) a care, diligence, labour, indeuour to compasse any matter; also, an affection, fancie, humor, desire, appetite, good will, great mind, vnto.*
Estudiant: m. *A Student, a Scholler, one that followes his booke.*
Estudie: f. *as* Estude.
Estudié: m. ée: f. *Studied; mused, meditated on, seriously thought of; also, indeuoured, laboured, diligently plied; also, affected, fancied.*
Estudier. *To studie, muse, meditate; beat the braines about; indeuour, labour, cast how to get; vse diligence in, bend the mind vnto, bestow great care vpon; also, to affect, or fancie in the heart.*
Esturgeon: m. *A Sturgeon fish.*
Pescher des Esturgeons en l'air. *Seeke* Pescher.
Estuve: f. *A Stoue; Hot-house, hot-bath.*
Estuvé: m. ée: f. *Soaked, bathed, stued, washed in warme liquor.*
Estuvée. Vne carpe à l'estuvée. *A stued Carpe.*
Estuvement: m. *A soaking, bathing, stuing.*
Estuver. *To stue; soake, bathe; also, to warme.*
S'estuver. *To sweat in a Hot-house; to wash himselfe in hot waters.*
Quand vous avez si longuement demeuré à vous estuver, & crié à gorge rompuë. *When you haue stayed so long soaking in the raine, &c.*
Estuves: f. *Stewes; also, Stoues, or Hot-houses.*
Estuvier: m. ere: f. *Of, or belonging to, a Stewes, or Hot-house.*
Estuy: m. *A sheath, case, or box to put things in; and (more particularly) a case of little instruments, as sizzars, bodkin, pen-knife, &c, now commonly tearmed, an Ettwee.*
Estuy d'escriptoire. *A Pennar.*
L'Estuy des grains. *The huske, pill, hull, or hulling of corne.*
L'Estuy d'un'Image. *A Tabernacle, Case, or Couering for an Image.*
Estuyé: m. ée: f. *Sheathed, cased; couered with, put into, shut vp in, a sheath, or case.*
Estuyer. *To sheath, case; couer with, put into, shut vp in, a sheath, or case.*
Estyrolle: f. *The loosenesse, and pilling, or clefts, of the skin about the root of the nayles.*
Esvachir. *To flag; to slacken, or grow loosse, and ratch, or stretch by loosenesse.*
Esvaluer. *To value; rate, prize, estimate.*
Esvanide: com. *Feeble, weake, faint, of no force; withered, fruitlesse, decayed, without vigor, stale, past the best.*
Esvanoui: m. ie: f. *Vanished; slipt out of sight, gone on a sudden; also, swooned, or in a trance.*
s'Esvanouir. *To vanish; to slip out of sight, be gone on a sudden; also, to swoone, or fall into a traunce.*
Esvanouissement: m. *A swooning; also, a vanishing out of sight.*
Esvanouy. *Vanished; swooned, fallen into a traunce.*

Esvasé. *as* Evasé.
Esvaiement: m. *Spaciousnesse, widenesse; an open and broad concauitie.*
Esvaser. *as* Esbaser; *and as* Evaser.
Esvasure: f. *An opening wide; a gaping; widening, or setting wide open; also, a hollowing, or inward sloaping.*
Esveillé: m. ée: f. *Awaked, rowsed, raised out of sleepe; also, quicke, vigilant, watchfull, heedie, warie, carefull, industrious, diligent, wittie, readie to take hold of any aduantage.*
Esveillé & non esveillé. *Betweene sleeping and waking.*
Plus esveillé qu'vn chat qu'on fouëtte. *More nimble, or obseruant then a cat with a whip at her breech.*
Esveiller. *To waken, awake, rowse, raise from sleepe; also, to excite, or stirre vp.*
Esveiller le chat qui dort. *To awake the sleeping Lyon (say we;) Looke* Chat.
Esveilleur: m. *An awaker, or waker; a rowser, a raiser from sleepe.*
Esvent: m. *The vent of a wine vessell.*
Vin qui sent l'esvent. *Wine that hath taken wind, or vnto which too much vent hath beene giuen.*
Esventail: m. *as* Esventoir.
Esventé. vn esventé. *A giddie, humorous, fantasticall, harebraind, rash, vndiscreet, light-headed fellow; one whose words are but wind; hence also, a boaster, braggard, swaggerer.*
Esventé: m. ée: f. *winded, tainted, mard with wind, that hath taken wind; windie; stale, out of season, past the best; also, discouered, vented, found out; published, spred abroad; also, fanned, winnowed; aired, as with a fanne; cooled; or breathed with wind.*
Esventelles. *The sailes of a wind-mill.*
Esventement: m. *A fanning, or winnowing; a giuing aire, or wind vnto; also, a venting; or taking, or giuing, of wind; also, a publishing, or discouering.*
Esventer. *To fann, or winnow; also, to puffe, blow, breath giue, or yeeld wind; also, to descrie, discouer, vent, or find out; also, to divulge, publish, or spread abroad.*
s'Esventer. *To take vent, or wind.*
Esventeur: m. *A fanner, or winnower of corne; also, a venter, or vent-giuer.*
Esventilé: m. ée: f. *Fanned, winnowed; blowne, breathed on; whereunto wind is giuen.*
Esventiler. *To fanne, winnow, blow, breath on; giue wind vnto.*
Esventoir: m. *A fanne; flip-flap, flie-flap, or flabell, to gather wind, giue aire, or driue away flies.*
Esventoire: f. *as* Esventoir.
Esventoise: f. *A vent in caske, &c.*
Esveré: m. ée: f. *wormed, as a dog, &c.*
Esverer. *To worme a dog, &c.*
Esveux: m. euse: f. *waterish, full of water.*
Esvier: m. *A sinke, or channell to void water by.*
Esvisagé: m. ée: f. *Plucked by, or scratched on, the face.*
Esvisager. *To pull by, or scratch on, the face.*
Esule: f. *The hearbe* Esula, *Diuells-milke, Quacksaluers Turbith, Quacksaluers Spurge: (Apothecaries giue euery kind of Tithymal, or Spurge, the name of* Esula: ¶ Mathiolus.
Esule ronde. *Pettie Spurge.*
Esvolé: m. ée: f. *Shamelesse, impudent, brasen-faced, ouer-bold; also, light, inconstant, haire-braind, shittle-headed, shallow, that can keepe no counsell.*
Faulcon esvolé. *A hawke that hath flown away from some one or other; a taken-vp hawke.*
Esvolement. *Rashly, ouer-boldly; shamelesly, impudently; lightly, inconstantly; on a sleight occasion.*
Esurial: m. ale: f. *Fasting, meat-forbearing.*
Et. *And, likewise, also, aswell, both.*
Et puis. *well then; what though; what of that; suppose, or, put the case it be so; Looke* Puis.
Eternel: m. elle: f. *Eternall, euerlasting, immortall, continuall, perpetuall, most durable, ay-during, without end.*
Eternellement. *Eternally, immortally, euerlastingly, continually, perpetually, for euer, euermore, alwayes.*
Eterni: m. ie: f. *Throwne or strucke downe, layed flat along.*
Eternité: f. *Eternitie, immortalitie, euerlastingnesse, endlesse continuance.*
Eternizé: m. ée: f. *Eternized, immortallized, perpetuated.*
Eternizer. *To eternize, perpetuate, immortalize.*
Etesies. *Th'Easterlie winds which commonly blow in the Dog-dayes.*
Etesté: m. ée: f. *Headlesse; headed; topped, lopped.*
Etestement: m. *A heading; topping, or lopping of trees.*
Etester. *To make headlesse; to top, lop, or cut off all the branches of a tree.*
Etheré: m. ée: f. *Airie, of aire.*
Ethologie: f. *A morall; an Enterlude of a morall subiect, or wherein mens manners are acted, and expressed.*
Etique: com. *In a consumption, meager, languishing.*
Etiquet. *A little note, breuiate, bill, or ticket; especially such a one, as is stucke vp on the gate of a Court, signifying the seisure, &c; of an inheritance by order of iustice.*
Etiqueté. *Noted, titled, intitled; also, lodged by billet.*
Etiqueter. *To note, marke, or tittle a booke, bag, or bill, on the outside, the better to remember, or conceiue on a sudden, the subiect of it; also, to lodge by ticket, or billet, as Harbingers doe.*
Etiqueter les tesmoings. *To deliuer vnto a Judge, Examiner, or Commissioner a breuiate, containing the witnesses names, and the points whereon they are to be examined.*
Etiquetier: m. *A Harbinger.*
Etiquette: f. *A ticket fastened within the mouth of a Lawyers booke-bag, and containing the titles of the bookes, and the names of them to whom they belong; any inscription, superscription, title, note, or marke set on th'outside of a thing, thereby to find it out the sooner; also, a token, billet, or ticket, deliuered for the benefit, or aduantage of him that receiues it.*
Besongner à l'etiquette. *To worke close, hard, continually; or, to worke taske-worke.*
Etirement. *Looke* Estirement.
Etiveler. *To whistle, or whoope, as a hunter.*
Etmoïde Os Et. *The bone whereof the top of the nose is made.*
Etrichoir: m. *That which, in winding of thread, is (to saue the fingers) wrapped, or put about it:* ¶ Parisien.
Ettiquet; &, Ettiqueter. *as* Etiquet; &, Etiqueter.
Ettaie; &, Ettaier. *Seeke* Estaye; &, Estayer.
Etymologie: f. *Th'Etimologie; or true exposition of words.*
Etymologizer. *To etimologize; to interpret, or expound words truely.*
Evacuatif: m. iue: f. *Euacuatiue; purgatiue.*

Evacuation : f. *An euacuation, voiding, emptying, purging.*
Evacué : m. ée : f. *Euacuated, voided, emptied; purged.*
Evacuer. *To euacuate, emptie, void; purge.*
Evadé : m. ée : f. *Euaded, escaped; slipped, passed, or got, away without hurt.*
Evader. *To escape, euade, make an euasion, giue the slip, get away safely, passe without danger.*
Evagation : f. *A wandering, rouing, straying abroad; an vncertaine course of iourneying.*
Evaguer. *To wander, stray, roue, trauell vncertainly.*
Evaluation : f. *An eualuation, estimation, rating, prizing, valuing.*
Evalué : m. ée : f. *Valued, prized, esteemed, rated at.*
Evaluer. *To rate, prize, esteeme, value, set a prise on, consider of the worth of.*
Evangile : m. *The Gospell; good newes.*
Evangelique : com. *Euangelicall; of the Gospell, belonging to the Gospell.*
Evangelisé : m. ée : f. *Preached, as the Gospell.*
Evangeliser. *To preach the Gospell.*
Evangeliser vn procez. c'est verifier la production, ou le rapport d'iceluy, sur les pieces, & productions des parties : ¶Ragueau.
Evangeliste : m. *An Euangelist; a reporter, or bringer of good newes.*
Les Evangelistes d'vn procez. *Are two Counsellors, appointed by the Court as assistants vnto the reporter of a Proces:* (Le Conseiller qui verifie le rapport d'vn proces, sur les pieces, & productions des parties; Et le Maistre des Comptes, qui tient les acquits du comptable, lors que l'Auditeur rapporte au Bureau, sont appellez Evangelistes: ¶Ragueau.)
Evanide. *as* Esvanide.
Evaporail : m. *A hole, pipe, or place, to breath out at.*
Evaporation : f. *An euaporation, breathing, steaming.*
Evaporé : m. ée : f. *Euaporated, breathed out.*
Evaporer. *To euaporate; breath, or steame out.*
Evaré : m. ée : f. *Frightned, affrighted, scared.*
Evarer. *To frighten, scare, make afraid.*
Evasé : m. ée : f. *Wide open, wide spred, gaping wide.*
Evasement : m. *A wide opening, or wide spreading; also, the wide, open, and hollow circumference, or concauitie of a thing.*
Evaser. *To widen; to open wide; to gape, or set, wide open; also, as* Esbaser.
Eucharistie : f. *The Eucharist; the Sacrament of the bodie and bloud of Christ.*
Eucharistique : com. *Belonging to the Eucharist.*
Iour Eucharistique. *A Communion day.*
Eudemon. *Ones good Angell :* ¶Rab.
Evé. *The shrubbie hearb called, Wallwort, Danewort, and Dwarfe-Alder :* ¶Langued.
Euë : f. *Water.*
Eué : m. ée : f. *Watered, moistened, or mingled with water.*
Evendiqué : m. ée : f. *Claimed, or challenged; or recouered by claime, or challenge.*
Evendiquer. *To claime, or challenge; to recouer by claime, or challenge.*
Evenement : m. *An euent, successe, end, issue of a matter; also, aduenture, hope, chance, fortune, hazard; whence;*
A tout evenement. *Whatsoeuer come of it; howsoeuer it happen, what chance soeuer may follow.*

Event : m. *as* Esvent; *A vent.*
Poulce & event. *A thummes breadth giuen betweene euerie ell in the measuring of cloth.*
Eventation. *A venting; also, the opening of a veine.*
Eventé : m. ée : f. *as* Esventé.
Eventer. *as* Esventer.
Eventré : m. ée : f. *Drawne, paunched, bowelled.*
Eventrer. *To draw, paunch, bowell; to pull the guts, or garbadge out of.*
Euër. *To water; to moisten, or mingle with water.*
Everdumé : m. ée : f. *Whose freshnesse, or fresh tast (and sharpenesse) is decayed; also, drained of iuyce.*
Everdumer. *To wring, or squeeze the greene iuyce out of hearbs; to depriue of greenenesse, freshnesse, or sharpnesse.*
Evergongné : m. ée : f. *Shamelesse, impudent, immodest.*
Everseur : m. *A subuerter, ouerturner, ouerthrower.*
Eversion : f. *An euersion, subuerting, ouerthrow, ruine, ouerturning.*
Everti : m. ie : f. *Euerted, subuerted, ouerturned, ruined, ouerthrowne.*
Evertir. *To euert, subuert, ruine, ouerturne, or turne vpside-downe.*
Evertisseur. *as* Everseur.
Evertuement. *Lustily, effectually, with whole power, or vttermost indeuor.*
s'Evertuer. *To labour, striue, indeuor, trauell; inforce himselfe, vse his vtmost strength, in.*
Evesché : f. *A Bishopricke.*
Evesque : m. *A Bishop; A Prelate.*
Evesque des champs. *One that is hangd in chaines.*
Les Trois Evesques. *The name of a Parisian Colledge (built by three Bishops) wherein the kings Lectures be, at this day, read.*
Debatre de la chappe à l'Evesque. *Two to brabble about a thing that belongs to a third.*
Devenir d'Evesque Aumosnier. *To become of a Prelate a priuate man; to fall from a high, to a low, estate; (Many say rather,* d'Evesque devenir Musnier; *for which, Looke* Musnier.)
Evesque d'or crosse de bois, crosse d'or Evesque de bois : Prov. *as in* Crosse.
Evesté. *Marred, spoiled, ruined, vndone; (a word most vsed in ieast; and by the inhabitants of* Blois.)
Eueux : m. euse : f. *Waterish, waterie, full of water.*
Euf. *as* Oeuf.
Eviction : f. *An euiction, conuincement, or conuicting.*
Evidemment. *Euidently, plainely, cleerely, apparently, perspicuously, that all the world may see it.*
Evidence : f. *An euidence; a manifestation; cleerenesse, plainnesse, opennesse, perspicuitie; apparentnesse.*
Evident. *Euident, perspicuous, cleere, apparent; manifest, plaine, open.*
Evier : m. *Seeke* Esvier.
Eviere : f. *An Ewer, or Lauer.*
Evieux : m. euse : f. *Waterish, waterie, full of water.*
Terre evieuse. *Sobbie earth, soyle full of springs.*
Evig. *Without :* ¶Aleman. ¶Rab.
Evincé : m. ée : f. *Euinced, euicted, conuinced, conuicted; ouercome by, ouerthrowne in, law.*
Evincer. *To euince, or euict; conuince, or conuict; ouercome by, ouerthrow in, law.*
Eviré : m. ée : f. *Weakened, enfeebled, without strength, without force, without vigor.*
Eviscéré : m. ée : f. *Drawne, bowelled, paunched.*
Eviscerer. *To bowell, paunch; draw out the bowells, or guts of.*

Evitation. *as* Evitement.
Evité: m. ée: f. *Auoyded, eschewed, shunned, shrunk from.*
Evitement: m. *An eschewing, voiding, auoiding, shunning.*
Eviter. *To auoid, eschew, shun, shrinke from.*
Euloge: m. *A praise, or benediction; also, a report made, or testimoniall giuen, of ones praise, or dispraise; also, an Epitaph, or superscription on a tombe; also, a Testament, or last will.*
Evneuque: m. *An Eunuch; a gelded man.*
Evocation: f. *An euocation; a withdrawing, pulling, or calling backe; a calling out, or forth; also, a calling before one by authoritie; a transferring, or remouing of causes vnto a higher Court by commaund of the Judges thereof; a calling from one to another.*
Evohe. *The crie of madde men; or th'ordinarie acclamation of Bacchus his madde Priests:* ¶Rab.
Evonyme. *Spindle-tree, Pricke-timber tree.*
Evoqué: m. ée: f. *Called out, forth, backe, or away; withdrawne, transferred, remoued; called from one to another; also, assembled, or called together; also, summoned, or cited before.*
Toute la force de la ville y fut evoquée. *All the troupes in the towne were drawne together into that quarter.*
Evoquer. *To call out, forth, or away; to withdraw, remoue, transferre, call from one to another; also, to assemble, or call together; also, to call, commaund, or summon to come before a Judge, &c.*
Eupatoire: m. *The hearbe called Agrimonie, and Liuerwort; Looke* Aigremoine.
Eupatoire bastard. *Bastard Agrimonie, water Agrimonie, water Hempe.*
Euphorbe: m. *The poisonous gummie Thistle* Euphorbium; *also, the caustícke, and congealed sap, teare, or iuyce thereof, sold ordinarily in Apotheries shops by the name of,* Euphorbium.
Euphraise: f. *Eye-bright.*
Euphrosine. *Buglosse; also, as* Euphraise.
Eur; &, Eureux. *Looke* Heur; &, Heureux.
Eustagues: f. *Ropes in a ship called, the Ties.*
Evulsion: f. *An evulsion; a pulling vp; a drawing out; also, as (or mistaken, in* Maison Rustique, *for)* Emulsion.
Euvre. *as* Oeuvre; *A worke.*
Exacerbation: f. *An exasperating.*
Exacerbé: m. ée: f. *Exasperated.*
s'Exacerber. *To be exasperated, or verie angrie; to grow into great choller.*
Exacté: m. ée: f. *Exacted; extorted; extreamely dealt withall.*
Exactement. *Exactly, perfectly, fully well.*
Exacter. *To exact, extort, take th'vtmost of, deale extreamly with, take violently from.*
Exacteur. *An exacter, extortioner, hard dealer, mercilesse collector; seuere corrector; one that takes, or looks for, the vtmost, or extremitie of a debt, or dutie.*
Exaction: f. *Exaction, hard dealing, a taking th'vtmost or extremitie of a debt, or dutie.*
Exaggeration: f. *An exaggeration, or heaping together; also, an aggrauating, or adding of wrong vnto wrong.*
Exaggeré: m. ée: f. *Exaggerated; aggrauated; increased, amplified.*
Exaggerer. *To exaggerate, aggrauate, lay on load; adde heape vnto heape, or heape one on another; to augment, amplifie, increase.*
Exagitation: f. *An exagitation, stirring, tossing, hurrying, turmoiling, vexing, shaking vp.*
Exagité: m. ée: f. *Exagitated; vexed, disquieted, troubled; tossed, canuassed, hurried, turmoiled, shaken vp; also, debated, or discussed throughly.*
Exagiter. *To exagitate; vex, trouble, turmoile, disquiet; canuasse, tosse, hurrie, shake vp; also, to debate, or discusse throughly.*
Exagone: com. *Six-cornered.*
Exaltation: f. *An exaltation, or exalting; an extolling, high-raising, renowming.*
Exaltation saincte Croix. *Holy-Rood day.*
Exalté: m. ée: f. *Exalted, high-raised, extolled, lift vp on high; magnified, renowmed, glorified, exceedingly commended.*
Exalter. *To exalt, extoll, raise high; renowme, glorifie, magnifie; commend exceedingly, lift vp vnto the skies.*
Exalumineux. perles exalumineuses. *Bright, shining, orient Pearles.*
Examen: m. *as* Examination.
Examen à futur. *A preexamination of witnesses, by Commission, before a suit be begun, or before the vsuall time, when it is begun, vpon doubt of their death, or absence, when they are sicklie, aged, or in imployment that necessarily will require their presence elsewhere.*
Examinateur. *An examiner, an inquisitor.*
Examination: f. *An examination, inquisition; search, inquirie after; discussion of.*
Examiné: m. ée: f. *Examined; searched into, inquired after; discussed, pondered.*
Examiner. *To examine; or minister interrogatories vnto; to search into, inquire after; discusse; weigh, ponder, thinke of.*
Exangue: com. *Bloudlesse; timerous, fearefull; pale, wanne.*
Exanthemes. *The small pocks; also, wheals, or pushes on the skinne.*
Exarcat: m. *The chiefe place of dignitie vnder the Emperour; the Lieutenancie of the Empire.*
Exarche. *A Vice-Emperour, or Lieutenant of the Empire.*
Exasperation: f. *An exasperation; prouocation, vrging, exasperating, vexing, bringing out of quiet.*
Exasperé: m. ée: f. *Exasperated; made rough, sharpe, harsh, angrie; aggrauated, incensed, prouoked, vrged vnto curstnesse, stirred vnto choller.*
Exasperer. *To exasperate; make sharpe, harsh, rough, or angrie; to aggrauate, prouoke, vex; incite vnto crueltie, vrge vnto curstnesse, whet vnto choller.*
Exaulcé: m. ée: f. *Exalted, extolled; also, heard perfectly, and to purpose.*
Exaulcement: m. *An exalting, extolling, magnifying; also, a perfect, and effectuall hearing.*
Exaulcer. *To exalt, magnifie, extoll, praise highly; also, to heare perfectly, and effectually; to lend a gentle eare vnto.*
Exauthoration. *A degradation, or disauthorizing.*
Exauthoré: m. ée: f. *Exauthorized, vnauthorized; put from, depriued of, authoritie.*
Exauthorer. *To exauthorize, or vnauthorize; to dispossesse of, or degrade from, authoritie.*
Excalfactif: m. iue: f. *Excalfactiue; heating, chafing, warming.*
Excandescence: *An inclination, or promptnesse vnto anger; an anger soone taken, soone come and gone.*
Excavation: f. *An excauation; a hollowing, a making hollow.*
Excedé: m. ée: f. *Exceeded, passed, gone beyond.*
Exceder. *To exceed, passe, go beyond.*
Excellement. *Excellently, exceedingly, notably, in the high-*

highest degree, passing well, most worthily.

Excellence: f. *Excellencie, exceeding worth, prime worthinesse, principall goodnesse.*

Excellent. *Excellent; excelling in worth, exceeding in goodnesse, passing in value, surpassing in worthinesse.*

Exceller. *To excell; to surmount in worth, exced in worthinesse, passe in value, surpasse in goodnesse, all others.*

Excentriqué: m. ée: f. *Disclosed, laied open, brought forth, drawne out of.*

Excentriquer. *To disclose, lay open, bring forth, draw out of.*

Excepté: m. ée: f. *Excepted, reserued, forepriсed; restrained, limited; seperated from; also, besides, or, ouer and besides.*

Excepter. *To except, foreprize, reserue, take out of; restraine, limit; seperate, or diuide from.*

Exception: f. *An exception, reseruation, foreprisall, restraint, or clause that restraineth a generaltie; also (in Law) a stop, or stay vnto an Action; a Barre pleaded, or put in, by a defendant.*

Excessif: m. iue: f. *Excessiue, exceeding, vnmeasurable, immoderate, extreame; riotous, lauish, outlashing.*

Excessiuement. *Excessiuely, immoderately, extreamely, too much, aboue measure.*

Excessiueté: f. *Excessiuenesse; extremitie, immoderatenesse, vnmeasurablenesse.*

Excez: m. *Superfluitie, excesse, outlashing, intemperancie, riot, lauishing.*

Excez de main non garnie. *A thump, or blow giuen by a weaponlesse hand.*

Exciper. *as* Excepter; *Or, to put in an exception, or clause of assurance; to giue, or take securitie, or warrantise; to take bond, or be bound, for.*

Excision: f. *A wasting, destroying, razing, breaking downe.*

Excitatif: m. iue: f. *Exciting; rowsing, raising vp.*

Excitation. *An excitation, exciting, awaking; a rowsing, raising, or stirring vp.*

Excité: m. ée: f. *Excited, raised, rowsed, stirred vp.*

Exciter. *To excite, incite, stirre vp, raise, rowse; incourage vnto.*

Exclamation: f. *An exclamation, an outcrie, or crying out.*

Exclamé. *Exclaimed.*

Exclamer. *To exclaime, crie vnto, make an outcrie, to call alowd.*

Excluant. *Excluding, shutting out; reiecting.*

Exclure. *To exclude, shut out; reiect, refuse.*

Exclus: m. use: f. *Excluded, put or shut out.*

Excluse. *A sluce, or pond head.*

Exclusiuement. *Exclusiuely; debarring, or out-shutting, all others; also, outwardly, or, out of the compasse of; also, definitiuely, or without hope of appeale.*

Exclusiuement à tous autres. *Absolutely his owne; wherein none else haue, or are to haue, ought to doe.*

Excogité: m. ée: f. *Excogitated; seriously thought, earnestly considered of; inuented, or found out by an earnest thinking; exactly, or studiously deuised.*

Excogiter. *To excogitate; seriously to thinke, earnestly to consider, intentiuely to studie of; also, to inuent by serious thinking, deuise after an exact consideration, find out with earnest studie.*

Excolé: m. ée: f. *Garnished, decked, furnished, trimmed vp.*

Excommange. *An Excommunication.*

Excommunié: m. ée: f. *Excommunicated.*

Excommuniement: m. *as* Excommange; *Or, an excommunicating.*

Excommunier. *To excommunicate.*

Excoriation. *An excoriation, a flaying; or fretting the skinne off.*

Excorié: m. ée: f. *Excoriated, flayed; fretted, as the skinne.*

Excorier. *To excoriate, flay; plucke, strip, or fret the skin off.*

Excortiquer. *as* Escorcer; *To flay, pill, or pull off the rind from.*

Excremens: m. *Excrements; or, the purging of any part of the bodie; (hence) also, dregs, ordure, filth, or filthie euacuations.*

Excrementeux: m. euse: f. *Dreggie, filthie, full of excrements.*

Excrescence. *An excrescence; a superfluous, or vnnaturall growing out of a thing, as of a wart, wen, &c.*

Excretion: f. *The purging, or voiding of the superfluities, and excrements of the bodie.*

Excroissance: f. *An excrescence; a swelling, or shooting out beyond the parts about it; as in a bunch, knob, bulch, wheale, &c.*

Excrucié: m. ée: f. *Excruciated; tormented; extreamly vexed, or afflicted.*

Excrucier. *To excruciate; torment, vex, grieue, afflict extreamely.*

Excusable: com. *Excusable; that may be excused, thats worthie of excuse.*

Excusation: f. *An excusing, or excuse-making; some satisfaction giuen, or iustification alledged.*

Excuse: f. *An excuse; a colourable or tollerable answer, shift, helpe, auoidance, purgation, or satisfaction; and, in Law, an Essoine.*

Elle a perdu son excuse. *Said of a wanton widow, which gotten with child now wants a husband to father it on; or awed by that want, is afraid to eat her fill of the dish that she most affects.*

Excusé: m. ée: f. *Excused; essoined; tollerably answered, indifferently cleered, prettily well auoided.*

Excuser. *To excuse; colour; essoine; to answer tollerably, auoid prettily, shift off indifferently well, an obiection, charge, or imputation.*

Ie ne me puis excuser de la mort, si. *I cannot escape death, if.*

Tel s'excuse qui s'accuse: Prov. *Some when they meane to excuse, accuse, themselues.*

Excuseur: m. *An excuser, an essoiner.*

Execrable: com. *Execrable, accursed, abhominable, detestable.*

Execration: f. *An execration, cursing, horrible banning, or blasphemie, a wishing at the diuell.*

Execré. *as* Execrable; *Also, execrated, cursed, banned, abhorred.*

Execrer. *To execrate, curse, banne, abhorre, detest, wish at the diuell.*

Executé: m. ée: f. *Executed, acted, accomplished; put to death; distrained, or seised for a debt, &c.*

Executer. *To execute, performe, effect, act, accomplish, finish; to execute, or put to death; to distraine; seize, or leuie, for debt, &c.*

Le mort execute le vif. *The heire, &c, of a creditor may put an Obligor in execution; but not his heire; for all personall Executions end with the Obligor.*

Executeur. *An Executor, effecter, performer, accomplisher of what he hath in charge; also, the Executor of a Testament; also, an Executioner, or Hangman.*

Sergent executeur. *That distraines, or seizes a debtors goods, &c, in the behalfe of the creditor.*

Execu-

Execution : f. *An execution, act, performance; th'accomplishing, or doing of a thing giuen in charge; also, an Execution vpon a Iudgement, or for debt, &c.*
Executoire : m. *A writ of Execution; or, authoritie giuen by commission, to distrain, or seize a suitors goods, for costs of suit awarded; or for the fees due vnto the Court, or vnto his Counsell, &c.*
Executoire : com. *Executorie, executing, or importing an Execution.*
Exemplaire : m. *A patterne, sample, or sampler; an example, president, or precedent, for others to follow, or to take heed by; also, the copie, or counterpane of a writing.*
Exemplairement. *Exemplarily; for others to follow, or to take example by.*
Exemple : m. *An example, sample, patterne, or president to follow; a copie, or counterpane of a writing; one thing alledged to proue, or inforce, another that resembles it.*
Exempt : m. pte : f. *Exempt; freed, discharged, priuiledged; also, void of, without part in.*
Exempté : m. ée : f. *Exempted; priuiledged, freed from, discharged of.*
Exempter. *To exempt, free, discharge; acquit, release, from; to priuiledge.*
Exemptible : com. *Exemptible; looſſe, free, quit, priuiledged; that may be remoued with ease.*
Exemption : f. *Exemption; freedome, immunitie, priuiledge, franchise, discharge, from.*
Exenteré : m. ée : f. *Drawn, paunched, bowelled, whose intralls are taken out.*
Exenterer. *To bowell, paunch, draw, pull out the intralls of.*
Exequant. *Finishing, performing, executing; also, prosecuting, pursuing; also, expressing, declaring.*
Exeques. *Funeralls, or funerall solemnities.*
Exercé : m. ée : f. *Exercised, vsed, practised; executed; managed, medled with.*
Exercer. *To vse, practise, exercise; to execute; handle, manage; to meddle with.*
s'Exercer. *To practise; to enure himselfe.*
Exerceur : m. *An exerciser, a practiser.*
Exercice : m. *Exercise; enurement, vse, practise; action, execution.*
Estre en exercice. *To wait; (as in alternatiue Offices, wherein attendance is to be giuen by turnes, or onely for a time.)*
s'Exercitant. *Exercising, vsing, practising, enuring himselfe.*
Exercitation. *An exercising, vsing, practising, enuring.*
Exercité : m. ée : f. *Exercised, vsed, practised; enured, stiled, much occupied, of good experience in.*
Exercite : m. *An hoast, or armie of men.*
Exercité : m. ée : f. *Exercised, practised in, vsed or enured vnto.*
s'Exerciter. *To exercise, practise, vse, enure himselfe, meddle or deale with, verie much.*
Exfoliatif. trepane exfoliatif. *That goes no further then the superficies of the skull.*
Exfoliation d'os. *An opening, or taking vp of th'onely superficies of a bone.*
Exhalaison : f. *as* Exhalation.
Exhalation : f. *An exhalation, fume, dampe, vapour arising from the earth.*
Exhalé : m. ée : f. *Exhaled, breathed forth, puffed out.*
Exhaler. *To exhale, breath forth, cast vp, puffe out, a fume, or vapour.*
Exhaulsé : m. ée : f. *Exalted, raised, mounted, aduanced.*
Exhaulser. *To exalt, mount, raise, aduance.*
Exherbé : m. ée : f. *Cleane weeded, grasleſſe, bared of grasse.*
Exherber. *To plucke vp, or weed out, hearbes, grasse, weedes.*
Exheredation : f. *A disinheriting.*
Exheredé : m. ée : f. *Disinherited.*
Exhereder. *To disherite, or disinherite, to depriue of the rights of inheritance.*
Exhibé : m. ée : f. *Exhibited; presented, offered, giuen; publickly shewed, or set forth.*
Exhiber. *To exhibit, offer, present; giue, deliuer; also, to shew, or set forth publickly; or as* Exiber.
Exhibition : f. *A presenting, offering, exhibiting; a gift, an exhibition; a shew, or setting forth.*
Exhilaré : m. ée : f. *Exhilerated, gladded, reioyced.*
Exhilarer. *To exhilerate, glad, reioyce, make frolick.*
Exhorter. *as* Enhorter.
Exibé : m. ée : f. *Exhibited, presented, shewed, or layed out vnto view; also, offered, ministred, brought in.*
Exiber. *To exhibit, shew, present, lay out vnto view; also, to offer, minister, bestow, bring in, things necessarie.*
Exigence : f. *Exigence, necessitie, extremitie.*
Selon l'exigence du cas. *According to the need of the businesse, euen as the case requireth.*
Exiguer. *To redeliuer, or giue vp a beast kept vnto halues; or to part the profit that hath bene made, or increase that hath come, thereof.*
Exil : m. *An exile, banishment, relegation.*
Exilé : m. ée : f. *Exiled, banished, relegated.*
Exile : com. *Exile, slender, thinne, fine, small; worthlesse, of little value.*
Exilement : m. *A banishing, an exilement.*
Exilement de païs. *The dispeopling of a countrey.*
Exiler. *To exile, to banish; or, as* Exuler.
Exiler vn pays. *To destroy, depopulate, make desolate, a countrey.*
Eximé : m. ée : f. *Leane, drained, drawne drie; also, exempted, freed, discharged from.*
Eximer. *To exempt, free, discharge, deliuer from; also, as* Esimer.
Exinané : m. ée : f. *Emptied, euacuated.*
Exinanition : f. *An emptinesse, an euacuation.*
Existimé. *as* Estimé.
Exitial : m. ale : f. *Banefull, deadlie, destruction-bringing.*
Exiture : f. *An egresse, issue, departing, or going forth; also, a ripe impostume.*
Exoine : m. *An Essoine; or excuse; a discharge of, or telleration for, absence, vpon a lawfull cause alledged; a delay in Court, vpō an Atturneys oath, or affirmation, that one of the parties is sicke, or not able to trauell; also, as* Exoniateur.
Exoiné : m. ée : f. *Essoined; excused, or borne with (although absent, or not appearing) by reason of sicknesse, or some other lawfull impediment, alledged, or deposed, by another.*
Exoineur : m. *An Essoiner; or, as* Exoniateur.
Exoinié : m. ée : f. *as* Exoiné.
Exolution : f. *A faintnesse, or loosenesse in all parts of the bodie.*
Exoniateur : m. *An Essoiner; an Atturney, &c, who sufficiently excuses th'absence of another, by swearing, or affirming, that he is sicke, or not able to appeare.*
Exonié : m. ée : f. *Essoined; or excused; as* Exoiné; *or, as*

as Essoyné; *also, saued harmelesse.*
Exonier. *To essoine; to excuse one from appearing in Court, or going to the warres, by oath, that he is impotent, insufficient, sicke, or otherwise necessarily imployed; also, to saue harmelesse;* Looke Essoyner.
Exorable: com. *Exorable; fit, or easie, to be intreated.*
Exorbitant. *Exorbitant; monstrous, irregular, enormous, exceeding great.*
Exorcisme: m. *An exorcisme, or exorcising, a coniuring, an adiuring.*
Exorciste: m. *An Exorcist; or, Coniurer.*
Exorde: m. *An exordium, beginning, entrance, vnto.*
Exostose. *A swelling of the bones.*
Exotique: com. *Strange, forreine, outlandish:* ¶Rab.
Expatriation: f. *A banishment, absence, or being, out of his owne countrey.*
Expatrié: m. ée: f. *From home, banished, absent from, or out of, his owne countrey.*
Expectatif: m. iue: f. *Expectatiue, expecting.*
Expectation: f. *An expectation, attending, longing, looking for.*
Expectative. *as* Expectation. son Expectative.
Benefices conferez en expectative. *In reuersion, or expectance; or, which must be waited for.*
Expedié: m. ée: f. *Dispatched, performed, finished, expedited, rid out of the way.*
Oeuvre expedié. *Such a setting of pillers, &c, against a wall, as makes them, afarre off, seeme part of it, although, indeed, they touch it not.*
Expedient: m. *A helpe, fit meanes, deuice, tricke, shift, euasion, to auoid a mischiefe, or compasse any matter; & (particularly) a proposition, course, or meanes of agreement, to preuent further suit, or charge in suit.*
Expedient. *Expedient, fit, behoouefull; needfull, necessarie.*
Expedier. *To expedite, atchieue, dispatch, performe, goe through with, hasten to an end, rid out of the way.*
Expeditif: m. iue: f. *Quicke, speedie, expeditiue, prompt, readie, ridding, dispatching, soone atchieuing.*
Expedition: f. *Expedition, riddance, dispatch of; also, an expedition, voyage, Action, warlike enterprise.*
Prendre expedition. *Looke* Prendre.
La chose sera de longue expedition. *Will be long a doing.*
Experience: f. *Experience; cunning, skill, knowledge, wisedome, gotten by much practise, and many trialls.*
Experiment: m. *A triall, proofe, experiment.*
Experimenté. *Tried, proued, experimented; also, as* Expert; *of good experience.*
Experimenter. *To experiment, prooue, assay, trie; attempt.*
Expert. *Expert, skilfull, cunning, well seene, much experienced in things.*
Expertise: f. *Expertnesse, cunning, skilfulnesse.*
Expiation: f. *An expiation, purgation, satisfaction.*
Expiatoire: com. *Purging, satisfying, sacrificing for.*
Expié: m. ée: f. *Expiated; purged by sacrifice, &c.*
Expier. *To expiate; to purge, or cleanse by sacrifice; to make amends, or satisfaction for.*
Expilé: m. ée: f. *Pilled, fleeced, robbed, extorted vpon.*
Expiré: m. ée: f. *Expired; breathed out, passed, or vanished, as a breath; dead, perished; determined, ended, finished.*
Expirer. *To expire; to die, perish, breath out his last; to passe away, as a breath, or vapor; to determine, end, finish.*
Explanade: f. *A plaine passage, euen path, easie way.*
Explanadé: m. ée: f. *Plained, planed, leuelled.*
Explanader. *To plaine, plane, leuell.*
Explaner. *To expound, expresse, explaine, make plaine; declare, manifest.*
Explaudé. *Publickly exploded; disgraced, or driuen away with hissing, or clapping of the hands.*
Explauder. *as* Exploder.
Expletif: m. iue: f. *Filling, making vp; fullfilling, perfecting.*
Expletivement. *Fillingly, compleatly, perfectly.*
Explication: f. *An explication, vnfolding, explanation, exposition, interpretation.*
Expliqué: m. ée: f. *Explicated, vnfolded, explained, interpreted, expounded.*
Expliquer. *To explicate, vnfold, explaine, interpret, expound.*
Expliqueur: m. *An explicator, vnfolder, explainer, interpreter, expounder.*
Exploder. *To explode; publickly to disgrace, or driue out, by hissing, or clapping of hands.*
Exploict: m. *An exploit; act, action, deed, worke, execution, dispatch, atchieuement, matter performed; also, an adiournement, or Citation; also, an Execution of, or vpon, a Judgement; and a seisure by vertue thereof; also, the possession, vse, holding, or enioying, of a thing.*
Exploict de Cour: C'est vne expedition de cause par defaut, ou congé, ou Congé defaut, selon la qualité d' icelle, au profit de celuy qui compare à l' audience, contre le defaillant.
Exploict libellé. *See* Libellé.
Exploict de Sergent. *The warrant which hee hath for, also, the report, or returne he makes of, an Adiournment, Arrest, Execution, or seisure of person or goods, ordered by the Court.*
Les derniers exploicts, & actes de possession. *Looke* Acte.
Exploictable: com. *Seisable; liable vnto an Execution, or to seisure; also, as* Exploitable.
Exploictation de biens. *An Execution against goods; or a seisure of them by the King, a Court, or Landlord.*
Exploicté: m. ée: f. *Dispatched, exploicted, acted, executed, done, performed; also, seised, or taken by Execution; entred vpon, by a Lord; also, possessed, vsed, enioyed.*
C'est bien exploicté à toy. *You take great care of, or make great hast in, the matter sure; (Ironically.)*
Exploicter. *To exploict; performe, dispatch; act, execute, atchieue; also, to seise; enter vpon; put in execution; also, to hold, enioy, possesse, vse.*
Exploicter chemin. *To make hast, goe fast, rid way apace.*
Exploicter le fief à pure perte. *Looke* Perte.
Exploicter le vassal. *A Lord to enter on, and take the fruits of, his vassalls land.*
'A mal exploicter bien escrit: Pro. *A faire pretence for a foule act; good words after euill deeds.*
Exploicteur: m. *An acter, atchieuer, executer, performer, dispatcher, doer of an exploit; also, as* Sergent exploicteur.
Exploicteur. *Acting, performing, executing; seruing an Execution vpon.*
Sergent exploicteur. *Th'ordinarie Sergeant, or Messenger of a Court, for Seisures, Executions, &c.*
Exploit. *Seeke* Exploict.
Exploitable: com. *Exploitable, dispatchable, riddable, readie to be performed, easie to be done; also, as* Exploictable.
Exploiter. *as* Exploicter.

Explorateur: m. *An explorator, espiall, scowt, priuie searcher.*
Exploration: f. *An exploration, search, or tryall by search.*
Exploré: m. ée: f. *Searched, or proued by search; looked farre into.*
Explorer. *To explore, spie, search or looke farre, into; to proue, or trie, by searching.*
Expoliateur: m. *A spoyler, robber, bereauer, or depriuer.*
Expolié: m. ée: f. *Dispoyled, robbed, bereaued, or depriued of.*
Expolier. *To spoyle, dispoyle, rob, depriue, bereaue, of.*
Expoly: m. ye: f. *Polished, smoothed, sleeked, burnished; cleanlie, neat, fine, trimme, polite.*
Exponce. *as* Esponce. *A lawfull quitting, leauing, or forsaking of the possession of land, &c.*
Exponction. *as* Exponce.
Exposé: m. ée: f. *Exposed, set out, put or layed open to; a faire marke for; also, expounded, interpreted, explained.*
Enfant exposé. *An outcast, or vnknowne child, that hath beene left in the fields, or at some doore.*
Exposer. *To expose, lay out, put or set open to; also, to expound, interpret, explaine.*
Exposeur: m. *An exposer; an expounder, interpreter, explainer.*
Exposition: f. *An exposition, interpretation, explanation.*
Expres: m. esse: f. *Expresse, speciall; of purpose; direct; manifest.*
Par expres; & tout expres. *Expresly, specially, purposely; namely, chiefely; directly; seriously.*
Expressement. *as* Par expres.
Expression: f. *An expression; pressing, straining, wringing, thrusting, squeezing hard together.*
Les expressions. *A great motion and desire, but little or no power, to purge downewards.*
Exprimé: m. ée: f. *Expressed, shewed, declared, vttered, pronounced, signified; expounded, or translated.*
Estoit il assez exprimé de paroles? *Could more haue beene said to that purpose? were there not words ynow spent in the matter?*
Exprimer. *To expresse, declare, shew, signifie; vtter, pronounce; also, to expound, or translate.*
Exprobation: f. *An exprobation; vpbraiding, reproaching, twitting in the teeth; laying in the dish of.*
Exproprié: m. ée: f. *Expropriated; put from the proprietie of, depriued of all proprietie in.*
Expugnable: com. *Expugnable, pregnable, which may be forced, or won by force.*
Expugnateur: m. *An expugner, forcer, subduer, ouerthrower of townes, &c.*
Expugnation: f. *An expugnation, forcing, subduing, ouerthrowing of townes by violence.*
Expugné: m. ée: f. *Expugned, forced, won by assault, ouercome with violence.*
Expugner. *To expugne; force, breake open, or into by violence; win by assault; vanquish, conquer, ouercome.*
Expulsé: m. ée: f. *Expulsed, expelled; thrust, or chaced out, by force.*
Expulser. *To expulse, expell; driue, chace, or thrust out.*
Expulseur: m. *An expulser, an expeller.*
Expulsion. *An expulsion, or expelling; a forcible putting, or driuing forth.*
Exquis: m. ise: f. *Exquisite, exact, excellent, perfect; curious, daintie, choice, picked.*
Exquisement. *Exquisitely, exactly, excellently, perfectly, throughly; choicely; daintily, curiously.*
Exsiccatif: m. iue: f. *Exsiccatiue; of a drying propertie.*
Exsiccation: f. *A drinesse, or drying vp of.*
Extase: f. *An extasie; or trance; a rauishment, or transportation of the spirit, by passion, &c.*
Extatique: com. *In a trance, in a swoone, in an extasie; in an extreame passion.*
Extenseur: m. *An extender, drawer, stretcher out at length.*
Extensible. *Extensible; which may be extended, or drawne out in length.*
Extension. *An extension, or extending; a wresting, wiredrawing, drawing, or stretching out; also, a kind of crampe;* (extension des nerfs.)
Extension de la loy. *A wresting, strayning, large exposition, or far-fetcht interpretation, of the Law.*
Les trois extensions. *The three measures; length, breadth, and depth.*
Extention. *as* Extension.
Extenuation: f. *An extenuation, or extenuating; a lessening, impairing, diminution.*
Extenué: m. ée: f. *Extenuated; made slender, or thin; lessened, impaired, much wasted, or decayed; fallen away, growne leane, pulled downe; looking verie thin on it.*
Extenuer. *To extenuate; make slender, or thin; to lessen, diminish, impaire; wast or decay much; pull downe, make leane.*
Exterieur: m. eure: f. *Exterior, outward.*
Exterieureté: f. *Exterioritie, outwardnesse; the superficies, outside, or vpper part.*
Exteriorité: f. *as* Exterieureté.
Exterminant. *Exterminating.*
Exterminateur: m. *An exterminator, banisher; destroyer.*
Extermination: f. *An extermination, or exterminating; a casting, or driuing forth; a ruining, or destroying (thereby.)*
Exterminé: m. ée: f. *Exterminated; driuen forth, cast out, chaced away; & ruined, vndone, destroyed (therby.)*
Exterminer. *To exterminate, cast out, chace forth, driue away; to ruine, vndoe, destroy (by banishment.)*
Extinction: f. *An extinction, extinguishment, extinguishing; an vtter stinting, or putting out; an abolishing.*
Extipiscine: f. *Diuination, or southsaying by th'inspection of the intralls of beasts:* ¶Rab.
Extirpation: f. *An extirpation, rooting out, or plucking vp by the roots.*
Extirpé: m. ée: f. *Extirpated, rooted out.*
Extirper. *To extirpate; root out, or plucke vp by the root.*
Extiture: f. *An apparance, a shew, or standing forth.*
Extorqué: m. ée: f. *Extorted; wrested from.*
Extorquer. *To extort, exact, wrest from by force, take away by violence.*
Extorqueur: m. *An extorter, exacter, violent dealer.*
Extorsion: f. *Extortion, exaction; a violent wringing, or wresting of things from others.*
Extraction: f. *An extraction, issue, deriuall, originall, drawing from.*
De noble extraction. *Verie well discended, or bred; come of a noble stocke, a great house, a worthie straine.*
Extraict: m. ecte: f. *Extracted, drawne, deriued, issuing or comming from; also, taken from by force.*
Extraict: m. *An extract, breuiate, abridgement, sum-*

summarie collection, or draught out of; also, the right of succession in the goods of intestate bastards.

Extraire: m. *as* Extraict; *or, as* Estrayere.

Extraire. *To draw, write, or copie out; to abridge, reduce into a briefe, or make a short collection of, the principall points in a matter.*

Extrait: m. *as* Extraict.

Extrajudiciaire: com. *Extraiudiciall; done out of Court.*

Extraïures. *as* Estrayeres.

Extraneïser. *To chace, driue, or banish into a forreine countrey*: ¶Rab.

Extraordinaire: com. *Extraordinarie, vnwoonted, vnusuall, out of custome, against the common, fashion.*

Offices extraordinaires, s'entendent ceux des finances, Aides, tailles, & des greniers à sel, à la difference de ceux de la Iustice ordinaire, & du Domaine: ¶Code Henry.

Vn procez extraordinaire. *A criminall action, or suit.*

Extraordinairement. *Extraordinarily; vnwoontedly, vnusually, out of common order.*

Extravagance: f. *An extrauagancie; an idle digression; a giddie, vnsteadie, fantasticall action.*

Extravagant. *Extrauagant; idle, astray, out of the way.*

Extravagation: f. *as* Extravagance; *Or, an extrauagation, or extrauagating; an idle digressing, vaine raunging, fantasticall gadding out of the way.*

Extravagué: m. ée: f. *Extrauagated, idly digressed, vainely raunged, gone, in a humor, out of the way; also, extrauagant, wandering, digressing.*

Extravaguer. *To extrauagate; roame, raunge, wander, erre in a humour, digresse from the purpose, or matter; stray, or gad, fantastically out of the way.*

Extrayeur de procez. *A Reporter, or Abridger, of Cases; a breuiate-maker.*

Extreme: com. *Extreame; worst, furthest from a meane, or from goodnesse; exceeding ill; also, the last, or vttermost.*

Extremement. *Extreamely, in extreames; most badly, most violently; beyond measure, without order.*

Extremité: f. *The extremitie; end, or top; hemme, skirt, edge, brinke, brimme, or border; th'vtmost peece, last part, furthest point, of a thing; also, an extremitie; vice, or violence.*

Extrinseque: com, *Extrinsecall; outward, from without, on the outside.*

Extrinsequement. *Extrinsecally, outwardly.*

Extumescence: f. *An extumescence; a swelling, a rising vp.*

Exture. *as* Exciture.

Exuberance: f. *Exuberancie; swelling, abundance, great plentie, or fruitfulnesse, exceeding store, of.*

Exuberant. *Exuberant; plenteous, abundant, swelling with store of fruit.*

Exuberer. *To abound, be plentifull, swell with store of fruit, beare in great abundance.*

Exulceration: f. *An exulceration; an eating into, or a rasing of, the skin, or flesh, by a fretting humor.*

Exulceratoire: com. *Exulceratorie; exulcerating; skinne-breaking, blister-raising, making sore, eating into the flesh.*

Exulceré: m. ée: f. *Exulcerated; galled, fretted, or eaten into, as the skinne, or flesh; also, exasperated, filled with rancor.*

Exulcerer. *To exulcerate; or make vlcerous; to gall, fret, breake, or eat into, the skinne, or flesh; also, to vex, exasperate, corrupt, or fill with rancor.*

Exuler. *as* Exiler; *Or, to be banished; or, to liue in exile.*

Exultation: f. *Exultation, great glee, much gladnesse, triumphing, leaping for ioy.*

Exuperance: f. *Passing store, great abundance; as* Exuberance.

Exustion: f. *An exustion; parching, or burning.*

F

FAbagine: f. *Iudas tree; the kind of tree whereon (tis thought) he hanged himselfe.*

Fabal. le fa: de febues. *The chaffe, hulls, or shalings of beanes; the cleansing of beanes.*

Fable: f. *A fable, fib, lie, leasing, false tale, vnlikelie thing reported; also, a Comedie, or Enterlude.*

Fabloyer. *To tell tales, talke idly, prate foolishly; to fable, to fib it.*

Fabre: f. *A forge; a smithie.*

Fabregue: f. *An odoriferous garden hearbe, which put, and kept in a vessell full of water thriues exceedingly.*

Fabric: m. *as* Fabrice.

Fabricateur: m. *A Fabricator, framer, builder, maker, forger; inuenter, deuiser.*

Fabrication: f. *A fabrication; framing, building, making, forging.*

Fabricque; &, Fabricquer. *as* Fabrique, &c.

Fabrice: f. *The fabricke; reparation, or maintenance of a Parish Church; also, the state, or estate of the Parish it selfe.*

Fabricier: m. *A Churchwarden; or an Officer, that lookes to the fabricke, reparation, or maintenance of a Parish Church; the chiefe Officer of a Parish, and he that in publicke meetings represents it.*

Fabril: m. ile: f. *Fabrile; of stone, or timber; of, or belonging to the craft of a Smith, Mason, or Carpenter.*

Fabrique: f. *A fabricke; a worke; frame, or building; also, the Art of making, framing, or building; also, the fabricke, facture, framing, or forging of things.*

Fabrique d'vn' Esglise. *The fabricke, raparation, or maintenance of a Church; also, the reuenew, or affairs thereof; also, th'Officers that haue the same in charge.*

Fabriqué: m. ée: f. *Fabricated, framed; built, forged, made; plotted, inuented, contriued, deuised.*

Fabriquer. *To fabricate; frame; build, make, forge; fashion, forme; plot, inuent, contriue, deuise.*

Fabriqueur. *as* Fabricier.

Fabuleux: m. euse: f. *Lying, fained, fabulous, full of fables.*

Fabuliste: m. *A fabler, a fibber, an ordinarie teller of fibs, or fables.*

Fabulosité: f. *Fabulousnesse; th'inuention of lyes, tales, fables, or fained reports.*

Façade: f. *The forefront, forepart, outside, or representation of the outside, of a house.*

Maison qui a belle façade. *A faire, goodlie, seemelie, statelie house, or front of a house.*

Façadé. Maison façadé. *Whose forefront, or outside is pourtrayed; also, of a goodlie forme, faire outside, beautifull front.*

Face: f. *A face; visage; looke, cheere, countenance; also, the forme, figure, proportion, shew, representation, resemblance; (also, the) superficies, vpper side, outward part, or side of; also, a Fesse, in Blazon.*

Face d'Abbé. *A red, or illumined face; a fierie facies.*
La face de l'architrave. *The face of a (pillers) Architraue; a large fillet, or bend, that commonly, makes a fift part thereof.*
De prime face. *At the first; at first sight; as soone as euer I saw him.*
Facé. *Fessed, or barred; a tearme of Herauldrie.*
Facecie. *as* Facetie.
Facendes: f. *Businesse, doings, affaires, dealings in matters, trafficking, and plotting one with another.*
Facet: m. *A Primmer, or Grammer for a yong scholler.*
Facetie: f. *Wittie mirth, a merrie conceit, a prettie incounter in speech.*
Facetieusement. *Merrily, conceitedly, wittily, pleasantly.*
Facetieux: m. euse: f. *Facetious; merrily conceited, wittily pleasant.*
Faciate: f. *A forepart, or forefront.*
Faciendaire: m. *An Agent, or Negociator; one thats imployed in a businesse, or made th'instrument of effecting it, for another.*
Faciendes: f. *Looke* Facendes.
Facile: com. *Easie; facile, ceth, prone; gentle, gracious, tractable, pliable, soone pleased, quickly intreated.*
Plus facile recompense. *A recõpence sooner come by.*
Facilement. *Easily, with good facilitie, with little stirre, with small trouble, with no great adoe; also, lightly, quickly, readily; gently, pliably, tractably.*
Facilité: f. *Facilitie, easinesse; procliuitie, pliablenesse, aptnesse, promptnesse, readinesse; lenitie, courtesie, gentlenesse, good nature.*
Facilité: m. ée: f. *Facilitated, made easie.*
Faciliter. *To facilitate, or make easie.*
Façon: f. *The fashion; forme; outward frame, or shape; a making, proportion, workemanship; manner, behauior, order; custome, guise, wont.*
Les façons de la femme en la vigne. *A womans worke in a vineyard, (is twofold; the binding of the plants, or yong shutes vnto their poles; and the ridding them of their superfluous, or noisome sprigs.)*
Les façons des terres labourables. *As many seuerall breakings, or turnings vp, as the seed that is to be lodged in them requires.*
Les façons de la vigne. *Are foure;* la taille; le hoüage; le binage; & le terçage; *(For which looke in their seuerall places.)*
C'est vn homme qui a ses façons. *The man is a little humorous, or fantasticall.*
Il a toutes ses façons. *He is fully prouided of, throughly furnished with, all things he hath need of; he hath all that he should haue; he hath his full due; also;*
Il luy a baillé toutes ses façons. *He hath coursed him soundly, hamperd him throughly, paied him home; he forbore him not, he dallied not with him; he gaue him his due.*
Le liure est de sa façon. *Is right of his phrase, or stile.*
Il trouva façon de faire cela. *He found a meanes to doe that.*
Facond: m. de: f. *Eloquent, well spoken, of a gracefull vtterance, of a sweet deliuerie.*
Faconde: f. *Eloquence, readie vtterance, gracefull speaking, sweet deliuerie.*
Facondement. *Eloquently.*
Façonné: m. ée: f. *Fashioned, formed, figured, proportioned, shaped, made, framed; also, mannered, behaued.*
Façonnement: m. *A fashioning; forming, figuring, proportioning, shaping; outward making, or framing.*

Façonner. *To fashion; forme, figure, proportion, shape, make, or frame (th'outside of;) also, to accommodate, adapt, or make fit for.*
Se façonner à. *To applie, or conforme himselfe, vnto.*
Façonnier: m. *A Cloth-worker.*
Facque: m. *as* Faquin.
Facque: f. *A little pocket, or pouch.*
Facteur: m. *A factor; an Agent; a dealer for another.*
Aujourd'uy facteur demain fracteur: Prov. *To day a Banker, to morrow a bankrupt.*
Facteure: f. *Facture, workemanship.*
Factieux. *Factious, seditious, troublesome, contentious.*
Faction: f. *A faction, or sect; a side, or partie, diuided, or dissenting, from others; also, a mutinous companie, turbulent crue, seditious troupe; also, an enterprise, action, or matter in action.*
Factionnaire: com. *Factious, mutinous, turbulent, seditious, much giuen to sects, or siding.*
Factiste: m. *A maker, a Play maker, a Poet that writes Comedies, &c.*
Factorerie: f. *as* Facturerie.
Facture: f. *The facture, workemanship, framing, making of a thing; also, a factorship; or, the dutie, and charge of a factor.*
Lettres de facture. *Bills of lading.*
Facturerie: *A Factorie; a house for factors to trade, and abide in.*
Faculté: f. *Facultie; leaue, licence; aptnesse, readinesse; power, abilitie; occasion, force, opportunitie.*
Facultez. *Wealth, substance, riches, possessions, goods.*
Fadas. *as* Fat; *Sottish, foolish.*
Fade: com. *Vnsauorie, tastlesse, wallowish, waterish; weake, faint; witlesse.*
Fadement. *Vnsauorily, tastlesly; also, weakely, faintly; foolishly.*
Fadese: f. *Tastlesnesse, want of sauor, wallowishnesse, weaknesse, waterishnesse in tast.*
Fadeses. *Follies, toyes, trifles, fopperies, fooleries, gulleries.*
Fadeseries. *as* Fadeses.
Fadeur: f. *as* Fadese.
Fadoche. *The name of a certaine peare.*
Fadrin: m. *The Maisters mate in a ship; in a gallie, the Officer that rules the slaues.*
Fafelu: m. uë: f. *Puffed vp; fat cheeked; a chops.*
Faffelu: m. uë: f. *as* Fafelu.
Fafiloches: f. *Rauellings of linnen, or cloth.*
Fagot: m. *A fagot; a bundle of stickes.*
Les tripes du fagot. *The smallest stickes of the fagot.*
Fagotage: m. *A heaping together, a trussing vp in bundles; fagot-making.*
Fagoté: m. ée: f. *Made into fagots; tied, or trussed vp in bundles, or fagots; huddled, or clapped vp together.*
Fagoter. *To make fagots; to tie, or trusse vp in bundles or fagots; to huddle, or clap vp together.*
Fagoteur: m. *A fagot-maker.*
Fagoteur de tabus. *A contentious person:* ¶Rab.
Fagouë: f. *A certaine kernell vnder the kannell bone (in men slender, thicke in beasts) also, the fag-peece, or kernellie part, next vnto the necke, of a Boare.*
Fagoule: f. *A Grit, grampell, pungar;* ¶Marseil.
Faguenat: m. *A filthie rammish smell.*
Fagule: f. *The Crab-fish tearmed, a Pungar.*
Faict: m. *A fact, act, action, worke; deed; a feat, pranke, part; performance, atchieuement, exploit; also, an allegation, proposition, argument, or article, in pleading.*

Le faict fort. *The full price of the farme of moneyes; or the full rate of seigneuriage (agreed to vpon the farming thereof) yeelded vnto the King by the Master of the Mint, whether he have made any money, or no.*
Les faicts nouveaux. *Looke* Nouveau.
Faict à faict que ie l' escris. *As fast as I writ it.*
'A faict, &, de faict. *Seriously, throughly, roundly, in good earnest, vnto purpose, indeed.*
De faict aduisé, ou de faict à pense. *Aduisedly, wittingly, willingly, of purpose, to his knowledge, with his full consent.*
Tout à faict. *Throughly, wholly, alltogether.*
Par voye de faict. *By force, or violence.*
Il fait bien son petit faict. *He manageth discreetly his meane estate; or, by his diligence he improues, by his forecast he increases, the little he hath.*
Faire son propre faict de. *Looke* Faire.
Du dire au faict y a grand traict: Prov. *There is great difference betweene words, and deeds; we haue an old, and triuiall rime somewhat to this purpose; Saying, and doing end both with a letter; saying is good, but doing is better.*
Faict: m. faicte: f. *Done, acted, made, wrought, forged, composed, framed; fashioned; performed, exploited; atchieued, compassed; finished, accomplished.*
Faict au hola. *Dutifull, obsequious, readie, comming at a becke, running at one call.*
Faict à i'en veux. chaperon faict &c. *A bold, swaggering, and lasciuious queane.*
Faict à la vieille mode. *Seeke* Vieil.
C' est faict de moy. *I am vtterly ruined, ouerthrown, vndone.*
C' en est faict. *The matter is alreadie passed, dispatched, finished, at an end.*
Cinq mille de nombre faict. *Full fiue thousand.*
Ie suis faict tout au rebours de vous. *I am of a contrarie humor, or opinion; I thinke, or iudge otherwise then you.*
C' est vn papelard tout faict. *He is a ranke dissembler, a notable counterfeit, a verie hypocrite.*
Son proces est faict. *He is alreadie conuicted, and condemned.*
Teste bien faicte. *A well-bred spirit; a learned, and discreet headpeece.*
Cela vault faict; *or,* la chose vault faicte. *The matter is welnigh dispatched, or, as good as done.*
Bien faict n'est iamais perdu: Prov. *One seldome looses by a good deeds doing.*
Toutesfois est faict ce qu' enuis ont faict: Prov. *Though gainst their wills they did it, yet tis done.*
Faictis: m. isse: f. *Made according to, framed after the likenesse, forged vnto the resemblance, of, another; also, neat, feat, comelie, handsome, proper, well made, well featured, well set together.*
Faictissement. *Neatly, handsomely, featly, trimly, fitly, gayly, exactly, quaintly, with much comelinesse.*
Faicture: f. *as* Facture.
Faillance: f. *A defection, failing; decaying.*
Faille: f. *The (round and out-bearing) vaile worne by Nunnes, and widowes of the better sort; also, a faile, misse, fault, or default; and hence;*
Sans faille. *Certainly, assuredly, without doubt; also, without missing of a iot, of a bit, of a haire, &c.*
Failli: m. ie: f. *Failed; slipped, erred, missed, mistaken; offended, gone astray, done amisse; also, imperfect, wãting; fainting; decayed, extreamly weakned; also, deceiued, or disappointed; also, ended, surceased, left off; also, broken, or, out at heeles as a bankrupt.*
'A iour failli. *At darke night, whẽ day was euen done.*
Encore n' a pas failli qui a à ruer: Pro. *He hath not mist that hath one throw to cast; or, he hath not yet mist that hath once to throw.*
Faillir. *To faile; slip, slide; erre, misse; mistake, misunderstand; offend, goe astray, doe amisse; also, to omit; lacke, want; also, to quaile, decay, fade; faint, or tire; also, to deceiue, or disappoint; also, to surcease, leaue, end.*
Faillir par le bec. *To want words; or, to faile for want of words.*
Faillir de promesse. *To breake promise, to go from his word.*
Faillir au style. *To commit an errour in pleading, or in his plea.*
Il faillit à. *He was welnigh, or verie neere; he had like to haue.*
Il faillit belle. *He had a faire scape.*
Il n' est si bon qui ne faille: Prov. *The best men haue their faults, the honestest their errors.*
Les plus sages faillent souvent en beau chemin: Prov. *The skilfullest are often deceiued in ordinarie matters.*
Faillite: f. *A failing, as of corne, &c, in an vnseasonable yeare; a deceiuing, disappointing; decaying wasting; fainting.*
Faire faillite. *To breake, or fall bankrupt.*
Faire faillite à. *To cousen, deceiue, disappoint; breake his word with; frustrate th' expectation of.*
Payer ses creanciers en faillites. *To pay his creditors in papers.*
Faillon. (Dieu Colas faillon.) *as* Compagnon. ¶Lorrain. ¶Rab.
Faim: f. *Hunger; a great appetite, or exceeding stomacke, vnto meat; and hence, an exceeding desire of, or great longing after, any thing; also, dearth, famine, extreame want of victualls.*
Manger avec vne faim de biscuit. *Looke* Biscuit.
La faim chasse le loup hors du bois: Prov. *Hunger driues the wolfe out of the wood.*
'A la faim il n'y a point de mauvais pain: Prov. *To him thats hungrie any bread seemes good; we say, hungrie dogs loue durtie puddings.*
Fainct: m. cte: f. *Fained, deuised, forged, adulterated, counterfeited, supposed; false, dissembled, seeming other then it is; Looke* Feinct.
Oeuvres fainctes. *Things in Masonrie so ioyned vnto a wall, that the halfe, or part of them beares out, the rest being fastened, or supposed to be, within it.*
Faindre. *To faine, forge, dissemble; See* Feindre.
Faine: m. *A Beech-tree.*
Faine: f. *Beech-mast, or Buck-mast; the fruit of the Beech-tree.*
Faineance: f. *as* Faineantise.
Faineant: m. *An idle, drowsie, lither, slothfull luske; a heartlesse loytrer, a lazie fellow; one thats without wit, without vertue, without spirit; a droane, a dullard, a house-doue; also, a lewd companion, loose fellow.*
Faineantise: f. *Idlenes, lazines, loitring, slothfulnes, lithernes; drowsines; faintheartednes, heartlesnes; dulnes.*
Fainin: m. *A kind of coyne.*
Faintement. *Falsly, faintly, fainedly, fabulously, counterfeitly, with much dissembling.*
Faintise: f. *Dissembling, hypocrisie, faining, cogging, counterfeiting, forging, foisting; a false pretence, or colour.*
Faire. *To do, act, exploit, performe, effect, commit, worke; to cause, make, forme, forge, compose, frame, giue a being, or fashion vnto; also, to counterfeit, resemble, imitate; also, to be; as* Faire chaud, froid, beu temps; &c.

Faire les affres à. *To fright, scare, affright, affray.*
Faire aiguade. *To water, or take fresh water into ships.*
Faire ambezatz. *To cast aumes-ace;* *Looke* Ambezatz.
Faire armes. *To fight; also, to fight valiantly.*
Faire l'asne. *To play th'Asse; and particularly in a kind of card-play, to loose a double stake, by loosing a game which he vndertooke to win.*
Faire la babaye; ou, la babou. *Scoffingly to gape, or make a mouth at.*
Faire la banniere. Il fait la ban: *Said of a theeuish Tailor, who in cutting out a garment makes ouer-large shreds.*
Faire barbe. *To assemble together in troups; as bees do, before, or about, the doors of their hiues, when they purpose to seeke out a new lodging; a phrase in vse among the countrey people of* Languedoc.
Faire la barbe à vn. *To barbe one; also, to withstand, beard, or braue him to his teeth.*
Faire barbe de foarre à. *To contemne, scorne; cousen, delude; abuse.*
Faire barriere à. *To stop; raile, or hemme in; also, to backe; shrowd, or shield.*
Faire de tout bois fleches. *To make vse of any thing that comes in his way.*
Il ne sçait plus de quel bois faire fleches. *He knows no longer what to doe, nor whither to betake him.*
Faire bon pour. *To answer, vndertake, or giue his word for; also, to play the game of.*
Faire vn faux bond. *Looke* Bond.
Faire la bouche à. *To instruct one, or giue him his lesson, beforehand.*
Faire la petite bouche. *To mince, or simper it; to make it goodly; to stand on nice tearmes; Looke* Bouche.
Faire bourre voler. *To play at tẽnis; or, as in* Bourre.
Faire vn bringue à. *To drinke vnto.*
Faire la buée. *To lay, or wash, a bucke.*
Faire la cavalcade. *To course vp and downe on horsebacke.*
Faire de cent sous quatre. *To bring a noble to ninepence; to consume a great summe quickly.*
Faire vne chambre. *To dresse vp a chamber.*
Faire vne charruë de Regnards. *To spend the time in most trifling imployments.*
Faire les cheveux à. *To powle, barbe, trim.*
Faire ses choux gras de. *Greatly to inrich, or improue his estate by.*
Faire le contre. *To second, or helpe forward; or as in Musicke, to beare a burden, or sing the plain song wheron another descants; also, at a card-play to hold, or vndertake, the game, as well as another.*
Faire corvée. *To doe a thing vnwillingly; or onely of duetie, without any hope of recompence.*
Faire d' autruy cuir large courroye. *To cut a wide sleeue out of anothers cloth; to spend freely on another mans purse.*
Faire la cuisine. *To dresse meat, as a Cooke in a Kitchin; or to dresse vp a Kitchin.*
Faire la culbute. *To play the tumbler, to flie top ouer taile.*
Faire le demy sault. *To caper on a paire of gallowes.*
Faire le dessus. *To domineere, to signorize it; also, to hold, or sing a treble part.*
Faire d' vn Diable deux. *To make an ill thing worse by striuing to amend it.*
Faire le Diable de vauvert. *To play reaks; to keep an old coile, a horrible stirre; to make a hurlyburly.*
Faire ses diligences. *Looke* Diligence.

Faire la dormeveille. *To counterfeit sleepe, to make as though he were asleepe.*
Faire eau. *To leake; also, to take in fresh water.*
Faire de l' entend-trois. *To answer from the purpose, as though he vnderstood not, or as one that will not vnderstand, what was demaunded.*
Faire envers (quelqu'vn.) *To deale with, to be a meanes vnto.*
Faire l' escole buissonniere. *To play the truant; to lurke among bushes when he should be at his booke.*
Faire l' escroue d' vn prisonnier. *To write his name in the Goalers booke.*
Faire espaule à. *To helpe, assist, backe, support, second, giue succour vnto.*
Faire estat de. *To purpose, or make account; also, to vse, or make a practise of.*
Faire l' estat de. *To execute, or enioy th'Office, or place of another.*
Faire l' estat de sa maison. *To settle, or set downe an order in; to looke into, or take a view of, the estate of his familie.*
Faire son estat. *To do his dutie; to execute, or exercise his Office; to performe whats fit for one of his calling, or place.*
Faire le faict, & le desfaict. *To doe and vndoe; to weaue Penelopes web.*
Faire son propre faict de. *To manage a businesse as well, or take as great care of it, as if it were his owne.*
Faire faillite. *To breake, or fall bankrupt.*
Faire faillite à. *To deceiue, disappoint, faile, breake with; also, to offend, or trespas against.*
Faire faire. *To cause, procure, or force to be done;*
faire faire ses cheveux. *To get himselfe powled.*
Faire faucée. *To pierce, breake through, runne in vpon, runne through.*
Faire faute à. *To faile, or forsake.*
Faire ferme. *To stand fast; or, to make a stand; also, to stop, or make to stand.*
Faire feste à. *Looke* Feste.
Faire feste de. *To reioyce at, or ioy in; also, to brag, boast, be proud, make much, of.*
Faire fin. *To finish, conclude, end; also, to thriue, cheeue, prosper.*
Faire le fin. *To make it daintie, seeme strange where he would be bold, refuse a thing he would be inuited to take.*
Faire finance. *To giue money for an Office; also, to gather a stocke of money.*
Faire folie. *To play the wanton, tread her shooe awry.*
Faire force. *To indeuor, striue, inforce himselfe.*
Faire force de. *Looke* Force.
Faire les forces. *A horse to hold his mouth open, and often turne his chaps from one side to another.*
Faire foy de. *To giue credit vnto.*
Faire vne frasque à. *To gull, cousen, coniecatch, put a tricke vpon.*
Faire fredon sur fredon. *To vse many nice, or curious tricks one vpon the necke of another.*
Faire la fringue. *To iet, brag, spruce it, wantonnize it.*
Faire les fruicts siens. *Looke* Fruict.
Faire gambades à la terre. *To hang on a gallowes; or in chaines.*
Faire gille. *To flie, escape, giue the slip.*
Faire glane. *To gleane after reapers. Looke* Glane.
Faire gloire. *To take pride in.*
Faire du grobis. *To grow proud, or take a surlie state vpon him.*
Faire le groin. *To powt, lowre, gruntle, or grow sullen.*

Faire vne grosse grauité. *To be surlie, or take much state vpon him.*
Faire de guedon guedon. *To make it goodlie, seeme loath; or, say nay and take it, as maides (that would be no maids) doe; See* Guedon.
Faire le guet. *To watch, to keepe watch.*
Faire le guet à Montfaucon. *To be hanged.*
Faire le guet au temps. *To obserue narrowly the change of seasons, course of the starres, reuolutions of the skies; to affect, or studie for, weather-wisedome; also, to let slip no aduantage that the time offers, or affoords.*
Faire gros hahay. *To make a huge stirre, or mightie slaughter.*
Faire halte. *To stop, stay, make a stand.*
Faire haut le bois. *To drinke for the heauens; also, soldiers, aduancing their pikes, to stop, or make a stand.*
Faire du herr. *To play the maister; to take more vpon him then he should doe; Looke* Herr.
Faire le hola. *To stop, stay, bid stand.*
Faire hon de la teste. *To seeme loath, or shew himselfe vnwilling, to do a thing.*
Faire iambes de vin. *To drinke hard when he is readie to take a iourney.*
Faire selon la jambe le coup; *as;*
Faire selon la jambe le pied. *To cut his coat according to his cloth; or, to doe things proportionably.*
Faire la jambette. *A horse to goe, or manage, on three legs, and gracefully hold vp the fourth.*
Faire iarret. *See* Iarret.
Faire le ject. *In a storme to cast ouerboord the loding of a ship.*
Faire ioug à. *To yeeld, or submit himselfe vnto.*
Faire jour. *Day to breake, or appeare; Looke* Iour.
Faire jour à. *To make way vnto.*
Faire jour en. *To passe, or pierce through & through.*
Faire du lard. *To liue idly, fare daintily, grow fat with ease, pleasure, and good cheere.*
Faire largesse. *Princes to throw money among the people; See* Largesse.
Faire largue. *To make roome, giue place, leaue space enough.*
Faire la lexiue. *To wash the bucke.*
Faire littiere de. *To scorne, contemne, abase, tread, or pull vnder foot; to abuse, violate, prophane.*
Faire lignade. *To take firewood into a ship.*
Faire le lime sourde. *To make as though hee heard not, or cared not, what were spoken.*
Faire de liperquam. *To shew his authoritie to be absolute, to take verie much vpon him.*
Faire le logis à. *To prouide, prepare, or take vp, a lodging, for.*
Faire le long. *See* Long.
Faire longue. Il ne la fera longue en ce monde. *He is no man of this world, hee cannot liue any long time.*
Faire le loup à la carriere. *See* Loup.
Faire le loup plus grand qu'il n'est. *To report, or imagine, a mischiefe greater then it is.*
Faire la lype. *To powt, sell sowce, hang the lip.*
Faire la maille bonne de. *To warrant, make good, answer, or vndertake for.*
Faire main basse. *To put all vnto the sword.*
Faire main forte à. *To ioyne strongly with.*
Faire main mise. *To seise vpon; See* Main mise.
Faire sa main. *To inrich himselfe, or feather his neast by prises taken, purchases gotten.*
Faire d'une main l'autre. *To applie one thing vnto diuers vses; or after the vse of it one way to imploy it another.*
Faire mal de: (mon coeur luy fait mal. Ils me veulent faire mal de vous.) *To fall out with; to hate, loath, detest, wish ill vnto; Looke* Mal.
Faire vn marc. *Looke* Marc.
Faire le mauvais. *To cracke, brag, swagger, keepe a stinking sturre.*
Faire mine. *To seeme, or make a shew of.*
Faire des mines. *Looke* Mine.
Faire la mine. *To lowt, or lowre vpon.*
Faire les mines. *To act it, or play on a stage.*
Faire bonne mine. *Looke* Mine.
Faire bonne mine, & mauvais ieu. *To set a good face on a bad matter.*
Faire le mitou. *To dissemble, play the hypocrite; to looke humbly, poorely, simply, sowrely on it.*
Faire la morgue. *To looke sadly, grauely, seuerely, austerely.*
Faire mort. On le faisoit mort. *They gaue him out for dead.*
Faire la mouë aux harengieres. *To be set on the pillorie.*
Faire vn nez de Cire à. *Looke* Nez, *or* Cire.
Faire la nique. *To mocke, by nodding of the head, or lifting vp of the chin; or, to bid a fig for &c; as in* Nique.
Faire sa nuict. *(When a man sells vp his houshold-stuffe, they say (in some parts of France)* Il fait sa nuict.
Faire de ses oeufs poules. *To count his chickens before they be hatched.*
Faire l'oreille sourde. *To giue no eare, nor heed vnto, to be deafe of that eare.*
Faire leurs orges. *To speed exceeding well; to make a good market, or their mouthes vp to the full.*
Faire de tel pain soupes. *Looke* Soupe.
Faire le Palais. *To plead, or argue at the Barre.*
Faire du pall-allant. *To staulke, or strout it; to march with a statelie gate.*
Faire la part au plus esloingné; ou, au plus ieune. *To part and chuse; or to allot one but a small part, but a poore share out of.*
Faire vn faux pas. *To slip, misse his footing; erre, mistake.*
Faire les Pasques. *To receiue the Sacrament.*
Faire la patrouille. *To be driuen to linger, and spend his time idly, as one thats forced to watch.*
Faire vn peigne. *To flie, auoid, giue the slip.*
Faire vn pertuis dedans vn trou. *To be idle, or busie about nothing.*
Faire le pet à. *To bid a fart for.*
Faire vn pet. *To let a fart.*
Faire le petit. *To humble himselfe; or vse many courtesies; also, to pretend great insufficiencie; or take verie little vpon him.*
Faire le petit pain. *To liue necrely, to play the nigard.*
Faire ses petits. *To whelpe, kittle, kindle, farrow, &c; breed little ones, bring forth yong ones.*
Faire le pied de veau. *To make an vntowardlie, or clownish leg; or, to vse a foolish lifting vp of the leg in dauncing, &c.*
Faire pieds neufs. *To cast his hoofes, as a horse; to be deliuered of child, as a woman.*
Faire de pierres pain. *To make vse of any thing; to turne to his aduantage, or applie vnto his purpose, any matter whatsoeuer.*
Faire la pirouëtte. *To whirle, or turne often about.*
Faire du plait. *To talke, babble, or prattle much; to keepe*

keepe an old coyle, a filthie stirre, a scuruie adoe with his tongue.
Faire planche à. *Looke* Planche.
Faire de son poing vn maillet. *To make hard shift, or to be ignorant of the right vse of things; or, sottishly to put himselfe, or his vnto ouer-rude vses.*
Faire la poule. *To play the coward.*
Faire pourquoy, & ne fera pourquoy; *and there shall be no cause why.* ¶Rab.
Faire le precedent. *To sit first, or to come first vnto a sitting.*
Faire le prestre Martin. *To answer himselfe; to play both Priest, and Clarke.*
Faire le procez à. *To indite, or arraigne.*
Faire le quant à moy. *To be well conceited of himselfe; also, to seeme daintie, or stand on nice, and curious tearmes.*
Faire quartier neuf, ou faux quartier. *A horses hoofe to riue, or cleaue from the top to the bottome.*
Faire quartier à part. *See* Quartier.
Faire la queuë. *To drag, or come behind the rest; also, to play the coward, or be in the rereward when blowes are a dealing.*
Faire quinaut. *To pose, or driue to a Nonplus.*
Faire la quine à. *Scoffingly to point at with the finger.*
Faire quinquenelle. *To fall bankrupt; to breake.*
Faire race. *To get children; also, to breed, or begin a race of horses, dogs, &c.*
Faire sa rafe. *To get many purchases, to take many prises, and thereby feather his neast, or fatten his purse.*
Faire vne raffle. *To sweepe, or snatch vp all that is before him;* See Raffle.
Faire rage. *To be very briefe, or very busie; to worke wonders, to keepe a great coyle, a stinking stirre.*
Faire de son Raminagrobis. *To counterfeit grauitie; See* Raminagrobis.
Faire le Regnard. *To slinke away, to slip aside, when a danger approches, or any likelihood of being taken in the manner; also, to play the truant.*
Faire de renvois. *Looke* Renvoy.
Faire sa reste à. *To speake roundly vnto, handle rudely, deale roughly with.*
Faire le Roland. *To swagger; Looke* Roland.
Faire la ronde. *To walke, or goe the round.*
Faire la rouë. *To turne, or wheele about; See* Rouë.
Faire à quelqu'un son roulet. *To prompt, or appoint one what he shall speake.*
Faire le saut. *To breake, or turne bankrupt; also, to leape, or be turned off a ladder; also, as* Franchir le saut; *in* Franchir.
Faire le saut de la carpe. *To turne ouer topsie turuie.*
Faire scalle. *To land, set foot on land; also, to ascend, mount, or goe vp vnto.*
Faire Séession. *To breake, to fall bankrupt.*
Faire le senaud. *To play the knaue; also, to miche it, or a rich man to make shew of pouertie.*
Faire la sentinelle. *To stand Sentinell.*
Faire serment. *To take his oath.*
Faire la serpente. *To wriggle, writhe, wind in and out.*
Faire soleil. Il fait soleil. *The Sunne shines; in which sence this Verbe is not so neerely ioyned to* Lune; *for they say not,* Il fait Lune; *but,* Il fait cler de Lune.
Faire stoques. *Looke* Stoques.
Faire le sucré. *To frig, to wriggle; to commit* Diogenes *his sinne.*
Faire la succrée. *To mince it, or make it goodlie.*
Faire son temps. *To lead his life, to passe his time,* Il a fait son temps; *he is growne old, or out of date.*
Faire tenir vne chose à. *To send, or conuey a thing.*
Faire de la terre le fossé. *To dispose of his owne at his owne pleasure; Looke* Fossé.
Faire teste à. *To resist, or withstand.*
Faire tin; *Looke* Tin.
Faire le tour du labyrinthe. *To returne, after much turning, into the way he first tooke; or to deale with a perplexed, intricate, and endlesse businesse.*
Faire tout sous soy. *(a child) to beray himselfe.*
Faire trembler le lard au charnier. *To swagger extreamely, threaten horribly, to vse big, or bugs words; (Ironically.)* ¶Rab.
Faire vn trou à la nuict; *Looke* Trou.
Faire la veille. *To watch, keepe watch; listen, or looke about him while others are asleepe.*
Faire bon ventre. *To loossen, or soften the bellie, to make soluble.*
Faire versure. *To make shift in the world; or as in* Versure.
Faire visage de bois à. *To shut the dore against; to exclude, or shut without dore.*
Faire le voiage de Baviere. *To get, or trauell for, the Pox.*
Faire voile. *To set sayle, to make out to sea.*
Faire voile en Levant. *To sayle Eastward; to be stolne, or pilfered away.*
Faire voile à tout vent. *Inconstantly to follow all fashions, adhere to euerie faction, professe any religion thats in vse, authoritie, or sway.*
Faire les yeux. *To winke, or twinkle with the eyes.*
Faire les doux yeux. *To make it goodlie, counterfeit ciuilitie or modestie, seeme coy; also, to winke, or smile pretily with the eyes; also, to be betweene sleeping and waking, or seeme to sleepe and see nothing.*
Faire les doux yeux à. *To play at boe-peepe; or to winke lasciuiously, to looke flatteringly, or pitifully, at one, thereby to get somewhat.*
Se faire; *whence,* Se faire tous les iours en meilleur poinct. *To battle, or to grow fatter and fairer euerie day then other.*
Se faire honneur. *To win, or gaine honour; to procure to himselfe great honour.*
Se faire tenir. *To be lustie, play the gallant, take vpon him, doe whatsoeuer he list.*
S'en faire accroire. *Looke* Accroire.
S'en faire fort. *To depend, rely, build, or be bold, on; to make sure account, or full reckoning, of.*
Se laisser faire au clerc. *To let the Clarke take his pleasure of her, or doe with her what he will.*
A que faire? *To what purpose, to what end?*
Aussi ne feray ie. *So will I not, or no more I will.*
Ce fais mon. *So I doe indeed, or, so I doe, so I doe.*
Cela ne fait rien. *It boots, or auailes, not; it makes no matter.*
Cela se faisoit au temps iadis. *That was the old fashion; or, thats at this day cleane out of fashion.*
Ie n'ay que faire à luy. *I haue no businesse, no traffick, no commerce, with him.*
Ie n'en ay que faire. *It touches, or concernes, not me; I weigh it not, I care not for it.*
Il fait bien son petit faict. *Looke* Faict.
Il me fait mal de luy. *I am sorrie for him.*
Il ne s'en fait que mocquer. *He doth but mocke them.*
Les faisoit moult bon voir. *They were very well worth*

worth looking on, it was a passing goodlie sight to behold them.

Le diable vous en feroit bien mal trouver. *The diuel were in't if you should not be well withall; or, you must needs be well withall I trow.*

Mon autre mari ne me faisoit pas ainsi. *My other husband vsed me otherwise.*

Se peut il faire? *is it possible? can it be?*

Avoir fort à faire à. *To be extreamely pestered with, or busied about.*

Bailler fort à faire à. *To imploy much, taske hard, lay many businesses vpon, put vnto toyle enough.*

Estre à tout faire. *To be for all purposes, be fit for all vses, be readie for any thing he is put vnto.*

Fais ce que tu dois, advienne ce que pourra: Pro. *Doe thou thy dutie happen what hap may.*

Il fait assez qui fait faire: Pro. *He doeth hurt, or good enough, that makes it to be done.*

Mal fait qui ne parfait: Pro. *Ill does he that all does not; discontinuance of worke dishonours the workeman.*

Tel fait la faulte qu'un autre boit: Prov. *One doth the scathe, and another hath the scorne.*

Tel fait le mieux qu'il peut qui ne fait chose qui vaille: Prov. *Some doe their best, and yet doe nothing well; or, some though they doe their best doe nothing well.*

Assez dort qui rien ne fait: Prov. *As good one sleepe as be idle and doe nothing.*

Bien dire fait rire, bien faire fait taire: Pro. *Good words breed laughter, good deeds admiration.*

De ce que tu pourras faire iamais n'attens autruy: Pro. *For that which thou canst doe thy selfe rely not on another.*

Entre dire & faire il y a grand adire: Prov. *Betweene saying and doing there is great difference.*

Il faut acheter Maison faicte, & femme à faire: Pro. *Looke* Femme.

Il ne sçait rien qui ne veut bien faire: Pro. *He nothing knowes that will not do his dutie; or, vaine is the skill thats without vertue.*

La fin fait tout: Prov. *The end proues all; or, is all in all.*

Qui bien fera bien trouvera: Prov. *Well thriues he that does well; or he that does well cheeues well.*

Fais: m. *A bundle, fardle, packe, bunch of; also, any heauie load, charge, burthen.*

Faisable: com. *Feasible, doeable, effectable, makeable, which may be performed, acted, or done.*

Faisan: m. *A Phesant.*

Faisan bruyant. *The great blacke Moore-cocke; or, as* Coq de bois.

Faisances. *as* Corvées. ¶Norm.

Faisandé: m. ée: f. *Mortified, made tender, and (thereby) as daintie as a Phesant.*

Faisander. *To mortifie fowle, &c; to make it tender, by hanging it vp, or (otherwise) keeping it some while after it is killed.*

Faisanne: f. *A Phesant-henne.*

Faisanneau: m. *A Phesant-poot, a yong Phesant.*

Faisannier: m. *A keeper, or breeder of Phesants.*

Faisant. *as* Faisan.

Faisant. *Acting, doing, exploiting, effecting; making, causing, forging, framing, &c.*

Faisceau: m. *A little bundle, or fardle; a packet; a small bunch, or sheaue; a handfull of.*

Faiseur: m. *A doer, actor, performer; maker, causer, forger, framer, worker, composer.*

Faiseur d'oeuvre blanche. *as* Taillandier.

Grands vanteurs petis faiseurs: Prov. *Great promisers weake performers.*

Faisible: com. *Feasible, makeable, effectable, doeable.*

Faisseau. *as* Faisceau.

Faissellè: f. *A Chesford, or Cheesefat, of wicker; or of earth, pierced in the bottome to let out the whay when the cheese receiues it forme.*

Faisser. *as* Enfaisser.

Faissine: f. *A bundle, or faggot.*

Faist. *as* Faiste.

Faiste: m. *The top, height, ridge, roofe of; also, the better end of a peece of cloth.*

Par le fin faiste. *Strictly, straitly, vnto the vtmost, to a haire.*

Faistiere. *A ridge-tyle, Creast-tile, Roofe-tile.*

Fait. *See* Faict.

Faitard: m. de: f. *Sluggish, drowsie, lazie, slothfull, idle, negligent; also, cowardlie, faint-hearted; slow, dull, by lazinesse.*

Faitardement. *Slothfully, drowsily, lazily, sluggishly; also, faint-heartedly.*

Faitardise: f. *Sloth, sluggishnesse, idlenesse, drowsinesse, lazinesse, negligence; also, dulnes, or faint-heartednesse (bred thereby.)*

Faitifs. *as* Faictis.

Faitis. *The same.*

Faitissé. *as* Faictis.

Faitneantise: f. *Idlenesse, lazinesse; faint-heartednesse, heartlesnesse.*

Faix: m. *A packe, load, or burden; a weightie charge.*

Pierres de faix. *Great, or weightie stones.*

Plier sur le faix. *To shrinke vnder his burden; to find or acknowledge, the charge layed on him too heauie for him.*

Cela a prins son faix. *That thing is setled, sunke in as farre, pressed downe as much, as it will be.*

A haute montée le faix encombre: Prov. *To a high climber a burden is combersome.*

Faizander. *To dresse a Pullet, or Capon like a Phesant; or, as* Faisander.

Fal: m. *A player, or playing ring, in a Bitt.*

Falaize: f. *A banke, downe, or hill by the sea side; also, fine sand gotten by a water side.*

Faldes: f. *A paire of Bases to ride with.*

Fallace: f. *A fallacie; guile, deceit, wile, tromperie, a craftie tricke, cheating sleight, cousening deuice.*

Fallacieux: m. euse: f. *Full of fallacies; false, craftie, wylie, deceitfull, cousening, cheating, beguiling; counterfeiting; vncertaine.*

Falleré: m. ée: f. *Barded, trapped; decked, tricked vp.*

Fallevuches: f. *The sparkles, or fierie and small flakes, that arise from furnaces wherein mettals are melted.*

Falloir. *A Verbe Impersonall; or vsed onely in the third Person.*

Il fault, or, il faut. *It ought, it must, it shall, it needs, it behoues, it is expedient.*

C'est un faire le fault. *Tis a matter of necessitie; it must needs be so; there is no remedie; there is no gainsaying of it, no striuing against it.*

Il s'en fault. *It misses, wants, lacks.*

Il ne s'en fallut gueres que luy. *He fayled but little of; he had well-nigh; he was verie neere, verie like to haue, &c.*

Il te fault trop de choses. *Thou art too nice, daintie, curious; nothing pleases thee; or, enough contents thee not.*

Tant s'en faut que luy. *So farre is it from him, so vn-*

vnlikelie is it that he.

Quand argent faut tout faut: Prov. *When money is missing all's amisse.*

Fallope. *as* Farlouse. *The Chit, the Meddow Larke, or Heath Larke.*

Fallot. *as* Falot.

Fallu. *Fayled, wanted, lacked, missed.*

Il ne s en est rien fallu que. *He had well-nigh, he was verie neere, or like to haue; he fayled but little of, &c.*

Faloise. *as* Falaize; *especially in the later sence.*

Faloppe: f. *The Chit, Meddow Larke, or Heath-Larke.*

Falot: m. *A Cresset light (such as they vse in Play-houses) made of ropes wreathed, pitched, and put into small, and ope cages of yron; also, a craftie, subtill, wilie mate; also, the hearbe Cats tayle.*

Vn gentil falot. *A trimme mate, sweet youth, fine fellow indeed; a good companion sure; (Ironically, or with an Ironicall allusion to our word, fellow.)*

Falotement. *Good-fellow-like.*

Falotier: m. ere: f. *Seruing for, or belonging to, a Cresset, &c.*

Falouidin. *See* Falourdin. ¶Rab.

Falouque: f. *A Barge, or a kind of Barge-like boat, that hath some fiue or six oares on a side.*

Falourde: f. *A great faggot; or, a bundle of sticks thats bigger, and heauier then an ordinarie faggot.*

Falourdin: m. *A luske, lowt, lurden, a lubberlie slouen, heauie sot, lumpish hoydon.*

Falouze: f. Elaphoboscum, Gratia Dei, *Harts fodder, or Harts ey; held by some Authors to be the wild Parsenip, and by others, wild or bastard Dittany; Howsoeuer, they say that if a Hart stung by a Serpent eat of it, he is presently cured.*

Falsifiable: com. *Falsifiable; which may be falsified, adulterated; forged, sophisticated.*

Falsification: f. *A falsification, or falsifying; a forging, adulterating, sophisticating.*

Falsifié: m. ée: f. *Falsified, adulterated, sophisticated; forged, foisted in; altered, depraued.*

Falsifié de col, ou de queuë. *A horse whose necke, or traine is vnsteadie.*

Falsifier. *To falsifie; sophisticate, adulterate, forge, counterfeit, or marre with counterfeiting; to alter; to depraue, or spoyle, by altering.*

Falvise: m. *A kind of Serpent; as* Cenchre.

Fame: f. *Fame, credit, report, reputation, renowme.*

Famé. Personnage bien famé. *A man of good credit, of honest reputation, that hath a good report among his neighbors.*

Fameilleusement. *Greedily, hungrily, as if he were starued.*

Fameilleux: m. euse: f. *Hungrie, starued, pined, kept long fasting.*

Famelic, ou famelique. *as* Fameilleux. *Pinched with hunger.*

Fameux: m. euse: f. *Famous, renowmed, notable, of much credit, of great reputation.*

Famfreluches. *as* Fanfreluches.

Familiarement. *Familiarly, friendly, boldly and plainly, priuately; homely, ordinarily.*

Familiarizer aucun. *To grow familiar, wax acquainted, become bold, with any one; to vse friendly, priuatly, boldly, familiarly.*

Se familiarizer d'aucun. *The same.*

Familiarité: f. *Familiaritie; neere acquaintance, custome, friendship; homelie or ordinarie vsage of, priuate conuersation with.*

Familier: m. ere: f. *Familiar, friendlie, well acquainted, much conuersant, with; also, tame, inward, housall; vsuall, homelie, ordinarie.*

Famille: f. *A familie, or household; a kindred, flocke, house, linage, generation of.*

Enfans ou fils de famille. *Youthes of good houses, rich young men, (whose parents are liuing.)*

La famille d' Archimbaud plus y en a & pis vaut: Prov. *A knot of naughtie packes; a state, or familie swarming with leud, and dissolute companions; a disordered, corrupted, vicious Familie, or State.*

Famine: f. *Famine, dearth, a generall hunger.*

Famuse: m. *as* Cenchre.

Fan: m. *A Fawne, or Hind-calfe; the young one of any such beast; as also, of an Elephant.*

Fanal: m. *The Lanterne of a ship, or galley; also, a huge lanterne, standing on the top of a tower, and seruing to guide ships, by night, vnto, or into, a Hauen.*

Fanatique: com. *Mad, franticke, in a frenzie, besides himselfe, out of his little wits; also, rauished, or inspired with a Propheticall furie.*

Fandesteuf. *as* Faudeteul. (vieil mot.)

Fané: m. ée: f. *Vaded, withered; putrified, corrupted; or, as* Fené.

Fanegue: f. *A certaine measure that containes about as much as the (French) bushell.*

se Faner. *To fade, wither, wax dead; or, as* se Fener.

Fanessant. *Withering, fading; rotting, corrupting.*

Fanfare: f. *A sounding of Trumpets, or a comming into the Lists with sound of Trumpets, at a publike Iusts; hence (also) any publike brauado, or flourish; any loud-resounding brag, or ostentation.*

Fanfarer. *To sound, or resound, as Trumpets; to challenge, or braue one another with sound of Trumpets; to brag, vaunt; make a great flourish, or brauado.*

Fanfaronnades: f. *Resoundings of Trumpets; gallant, brauing, or bragging acclamations.*

Fanfrelucher. *To swyue, to leacher; also, to trifle it.*

Fanfreluches: f. *Loose threds, or hanging shreds in rags, and torne clothes; any such trash, excrement, riffraffe; or, as* Finfreluches.

Fanfreluches antidotées. *Vanities, fopperies, fooleries, fond tricks.*

Fangas: m. *A heape of mud, or durt; See* Fangeat.

Fange: f. *Mud, mire, durt, filth.*

Fangeas. *as* Fangeat.

Fangeat: m. *A durtie, or muddie slough on the high way.*

Fangeux: m. euse: f. *Durtie, muddie, mirie, filthie, bedashed, bemired, bedabled.*

se Fanir. *as* se Faner; *to wither; to corrupt.*

Fanné: f. *as* Faine; *Beech-mast.*

Fanner. *as* Faonner.

Fanon: m. *as* Fanal; *also, the deaw-clap of an Ox, &c; also, a Fannell, or Maniple; a scarfe-like ornament worn in the left arme of a sacrificing Priest; also, an Ensigne, or Banner; also (in Blason) any large bracelet, that hangs downe (in fashion of the aforesaid Maniple) from the arme.*

Fantasiant. *Fancying, imagining; fayning.*

Fantasie: f. *The fancie, or fantasie; opinion, humor, imagination, conceit, affection, iudgement; the mind of a bodie; also, a vision, representation, or image of things conceiued in the mind; also, the Musicall lesson, tearmed a Fancie.*

Il a pris subitement vne fantasie. *He hath taken a toy.*

Fantasié: m. ée: f. *Fancied, imagined, fained; made, or painted fantastically; also, affected.*

Fantasier. *To imagine, deuise, conceiue, inuent; cast about, thinke of, reuolue in mind; represent by imagination; also, to fancie, or affect.*

Fantasme. *as* Fantosme.

Fantasque. *as* Fantastique.

Fantasquement. *Fantastically, humorously, conceitedly, skittishly, giddily.*

Fantassin: m. *A footman in warres.*

Fantassin: m. ine: f. *Of, or belonging to, a footman; and hence;*

Forces fantassines. *Footmen, or a power of footmen.*

Fantastique: com. *Fantasticall, humorous, new-fangled, giddie, skittish; inuentiue, conceited.*

Fantastiquer. *To conceiue, imagine, deuise, cast about, represent in the imagination; also, to affect fantastically; to fill with, or feed on, idle fancies.*

Fantastiqueries: f. *Fantasticall tricks, humorous toyes; idle thoughts, vaine imaginations.*

Fantosme: m. *A spirit, ghost, bug, hobgoblin; vision, apparition; false imagination; hence also, a skarrecrow.*

Fantosmeries: f. *Strange fancies, extrauagant conceits idle visions, odde imaginations, castles in the ayre.*

Fanuise. *as* Cenchre; *and should be* Falvise, *or* Famuse.

Faon. *as* Fan: m. *A Fawne.*

Faonné. *Fawned.*

Faonnemént: m. *A fawning.*

Faonner. *A Doe to fawne, or bring forth yong.*

Faque: f. *A pocket, or poutch; a satchell, or sacke.*

Faquin: m. *A Porter, or Packe-bearer; any base-conditioned fellow.*

Comme vn faquin porte faix ainsi vn baston la paix: Pro. *Looke* Baston.

Faquinage: m. *Portage; the fee, or furniture, belonging to a Porter.*

Far: m. *A high Tower, or Beacon at the mouth of a Hauen, wherein continuall lights are kept anights for the direction of sea-faring people; a Lanterne on a Watchtower by the sea side.*

Farain. Pain farain. *A kind of great, and verie yellow houshold bread, of the better sort.*

Faras: m. *A great confused heape; also, a mixture of sundrie graines together, called Bolymong.*

Farasse: f. *A Cresset; also, the coursest of Hempe, Swingle foot herds, course towe.*

Farce: f. *A (fond and dissolute) Play, Comedie, or Enterlude; also, the Iyg at the end of an Enterlude, wherein some pretie knauerie is acted; also, a Pudding, Haggas, Liuering; any stuffing, in meats.*

C'est vne vraye farce. *Tis a meere ieast, a very mockerie.*

Il ioue sa farce. *He playes his prankes; he acts his part.*

Farcer; ou, se farcer de. *To mocke, deride, flout, or gibe at.*

Farcereau: m. *A maker of Playes; a deuiser of ieasts; an inuentor of lyes.*

Farcerie: f. *A playing, ieasting; an acting, or making, of Playes, Ieasts, Enterludes; a counterfeiting.*

Farcesque: com. *Counterfeit, Player-like.*

Farceur: m. *A Comedian, or Stage-player; a common ieaster, or counterfeiter of mens gestures.*

Farci: m. *A Haggas-pudding.*

Farci: m. ie: f. *Stuffed, franked, fed, filled vp.*

Tout farci d'escus. *That hath store of crownes; a great monyed man.*

Farciere: f. *One of the three skins which enwrap an infant in the wombe.*

Farcin: m. *Scurfe; a leaprosie proceeding of melancholie, choller, or fleagme exceedingly adust, and filling the skin with blacke wan spots, and dry parched scales; also, the farcie in a horse.*

Farcineux: m. euse: f. *Leaprous, scuruie, bescabbed.*

Farcir. *To stuffe, cramme, fill vp; to franke, to feed.*

Farcisseure: f. *A stuffing, cramming, filling vp.*

Fard: m. *Fard; painting (properly, Ceruse, or white Lead) also, any coloured, or adulterate beautie; a deceit, pretence, falsehood, cousenage, blearing of the eyes.*

Fardé: m. ée: f. *Farded; coloured, painted, of an adulterate luster; whose beautie is disguised, or borrowed.*

Fardeau: m. *A fardle, burthen, trusse, packe, bundle.*

Donner le fardeau selon le chameau. *Looke* Chameau.

Plus couste la corde que le fardeau. *The suit counteruailes not the charge one hath beene at about it.*

En grand fardeau n'est pas l'acquest: Prov. *Greatnesse makes not a burthen gainefull; or the gaine rests not in the greatnesse of a burthen; tis not the great, but the good burthen one thriues by.*

Petit fardeau poise à la longue: Prov. *We say, light burthen farre heauie.*

`A vn chascun son fardeau poise: Prov. *Euerie one finds his owne burthen heauie enough.*

Fardeler. *To trusse, or packe vp; to reduce, or make into fardles, burthens, bundles.*

Fardelet: m. *A fardlet; a little fardle.*

Fardement: m. *A painting, a colouring with fard; a beautifying with borrowed, or false colours; a pranking, or setting out of things, the sooner to sell, or the better to shew, them.*

Farder. *To paint, colour, disguise, tricke vp, set out, with false beauties; to polish with a borrowed luster; to vse pretences; to deceiue the eares, or bleare the eyes with faire, but counterfeit, matters.*

De toute femme qui se farde donne toy soigneusement garde: Pro. *Take heed of any woman that doth paint.*

Fardeur: m. *A painter, colourer, disguiser, counterfeiter; a tricker vp, or setter out, of a thing with borrowed, or false ornaments.*

Fardeur de chevaux. *A Horse-courser.*

Fare. *as* Far.

Farfadet: m. *A little spirit, yong hobgoblin.*

Farfanterie. *Looke* Forfanterie.

Farfelu: m. uë: f. *Druggellie, short and thicke, as thicke as long; or, as* Fafelu.

Farfonte. *A Wrenne.*

Farfouillé: m. ée: f. *Towsed, ruffled, berumpled by rifling; disorderly searched, or disordered by searching into.*

Farfouiller. *To ruffle, towse, crumple, berumple with rifling; to search disorderedly, or vntowardly; or, to disorder by an vntoward search; also, to dabble, or paddle in the water, fomble in the durt, rake in the mire.*

Fariboles: f. *Trifles, nifles, flim-flams, why-whawes, idle discourses, fond tatling, tales of a tub, or of a roasted horse.*

Farigoulier. *as* Fregolier. *The Lote tree.*

Farine: f. *Meale, or flower.*

La farine de Febvrier. *Snow.*

Farine folle. *Meale-dust, or Mill-dust; the meale that flyes vp and downe a Mill.*
Farine volante. *as* Farine folle.
Badin sans farine. *An arrant Doult, noble Asse, notable Cokes, egregious Cocks-combe.*
Paistry de folle farine. *Compounded of light, or sleight stuffe; a vaine-headed, or idle-humored woodcocke; one that hath no manner of substance in him.*
Pour recueillir farine il verse l'huile. *(Of an vndiscreet husband, who to saue a pennie looses a pound.)*
Vanner sa farine au vent. *To squander away his reuenue in vaine, and idle humors.*
La farine du diable va moitié en vent ou au son: Pro. *Little good comes of that the diuell hath, or doth; or, ill gotten goods come to little good.*
Sasse bonne farine sans trompe ny buccine: Prov. *Fare well, and hold thy peace.*
Farineux: m. euse: f. *Mealie, beflowred, bemealed; made white, or done ouer with meale; also, dry, as meale.*
Lepre farineuse. *The white Leprosie.*
Farline: f. *An Irish Rug.*
Farlouse. *The little Medow Larke, or Heath Larke.*
Farne. *A kind of Oake.*
Faron: m. *The weeke of a Linke, or Torche.*
Farouche: com. *Wild, sauage, vntamed, fierce, vntractable, fell, cruell, froward shrewd, curst.*
Farouchеté: m. ée: f. *Made wild, sauage, vntractable, cruell, shrewd, froward, curst.*
Farrage: m. *A mixture of sundrie graines, and seeds gathered from the winnowings of corne (as also, diuers sorts of course graine, and pulse mingled) and sowed pell-mell together for Winter forrage, or fodder.*
Farragiere: f. *A plot, or peece of ground sowed with the winnowings of corne; or with course corne, and pulse mingled all together.*
Farre. *as* Foarre.
Fasché: m. ée: f. *Displeased, angred, offended; vexed, grieued, molested, disquieted, annoyed; troubled, importuned, wearied, cloyed, brought vnto a loathing of.*
Fascher. *To anger, displease, offend; vex, grieue, irke, disquiet; annoy, trouble, molest; importune, wearie, toyle, harrie, cloy, bring to a loathing of.*
Fascherie: f. *Offence, vexation; anger, displeasure; annoyance, trouble, disquiet, care, griefe; importunitie; irksomenesse, wearinesse, loathsomenesse, or a loathing of.*
Fascheusement. *Offensiuely, troublesomely, tediously, harshly, most vnpleasingly, painefully; angrily, frowardly.*
Fascheux: m. euse: f. *Offensiue, troublesome, tedious, importunate, irksome, loathsome; harsh, grieuous, painfull, most vnpleasing; also, angrie, froward, vnquiet, peeuish, ouerthwart, crosse, aduerse.*
Fascheux à ferrer. *Stubborne, surlie, obstinate, headie, vnrulie, selfe-willed.*
Temps fascheux. *An ill, hard, ill fauored, or vnfortunate season.*
Faire le fascheux. *To make it daintie; to stand on strict, nice, or curious tearmes.*
Fascinateur: m. *A Charmer, Sorcerer, Inchaunter.*
Fascination: f. *A charme, or Inchauntment; a bewitching, ey-biting, forspeaking.*
Fascine: f. *as* Fassine.
Fasciné: m. ée: f. *Charmed, bewitched, ey-bitten, forspoken: disfigured, or transformed by Inchauntments.*
Fasciner. *To charme, bewitch, ey-bite, forspeake; to disfigure, or transforme by Inchauntments.*

Faseoles: m. *Fasels, long Peason, Kidney Beanes, Sperage Beanes, French Beanes, Romane Beanes, Garden Smilax;* Looke Phaseoles.
Fasqué: m. ée: f. *Loaden.*
Fassade. *The forefront, forepart, or outside of a house.*
Fasse: f. *as* Nasse; *a Weele, or a Bow-net.*
Fassine: f. *A faggot, bauin, kidd, or bundle of sticks.*
Faste: m. *Pride, scorne, contempt, disdaine, loftinesse, haughtinesse, arrogancie, surquedrie.*
Fastide: com. *Tedious, loathsome, irksome, vnpleasing.*
Fastidiosité: f. *A loathing, or abhorring, as of meats, by an ill disposed stomacke.*
Fastueux: m. euse: f. *Proud, loftie, scornefull, disdainfull, arrogant, high-minded.*
Fat. *Foolish, foppish;* vn fat; *a sot, an ideot, a ninnie, a noddie, an asse, a gull.*
Fatal: m. ale: f. *Fatall, destined; appointed by, belonging to, destinie; also, ineuitable, vnauoidable.*
Fatalement. *Fatally, by destinie.*
Fatalité: f. *Fatalitie, or fatalnesse; also, vnauoidablenes, as of a thing appointed by destinie.*
Fatalizer. *To destinate, appoint, or designe vnto an ineuitable issue.*
Fatidic: m. ique: f. *Presaging, prophecying, fore-telling.*
Fatidique: com. *A Prophet, presager, fore-teller of things to come.*
Fatidiquement. *Prophetically, presagingly.*
Fatigable: com. *Wearying, tyring; troubling; or, which may be wearied, tyred; troubled.*
Fatigation: f. *A wearying, tyring, cloying, troubling; also, as* Fatigue.
Fatigue: f. *Wearinesse, tediousnesse; trauaile, trouble, vexation; labour, toyle, ouer-much paines.*
Fatiguer. *To wearie, tyre, trouble, cloy, ouer-toyle; to giue no rest vnto.*
Fatiste: m. *A maker, or a Poet that makes Playes.*
Fatraille. *Trash, trumperie, things of no value.*
Fatras: m. *A confused heape, or bundle of trash, toyes, trifles, vaine and idle things, fooleries, fopperies.*
Vn fatras de clefs. *A bunch of keyes.* ¶Rab.
Il sçait tout le fatras. *All the packe; all that roguerie, or roguish plot is he acquainted with.*
Fatrassé: m. ée: f. *Patched, botched, ill fauoredly set on; confusedly heaped, foolishly put together; also, trifling, vaine, idle; made, or consisting of, trash.*
Fatrassier. *Trifling, paltrie, vaine; also, confused, bungling, budled or fumbled together botcher-like.*
Fatrer. *To botch, patch, or bungle vp a thing, like an vnskilfull workman.*
Fatrin. *as* Fatraille.
Fatrouiller. *To trifle, toy, foole it, play the fop; inuent, or busie himselfe about, idle and friuolous vanities; also, as* Fatrer; *to botch.*
Fatrouilleur: m. *A trifler, dallier, vaine fellow; also, a botcher, patcher, bungler.*
Fatuité: f. *Foolishnesse, doltishnesse, blockishnesse, dulnesse, ideotisme, sottishnesse.*
Fau: m. *A Beech tree.*
Favade: f. *Beane straw, or a Beane stalke.*
Faval: m. *The chaffe, shalings, hullings, offals, or cleansing of Beanes.*
Favas: m. *as* Faval; *also, a Beane close; also, (but lesse properly) Beane straw.*
Fau-bourgs. *Looke* Faux-bourgs.
Fauce-foy: m. *A faith-breaker, a trecherous companion.*

Fauceol. *A little Sythe.*
Faucer. *To stand, as a crooked blade; See* Faulser.
Fauchage: m. *A mowing; or the hire of a mower.*
Fauche. *A reaping; mowing; haruest.*
Fauché. *Mowed, cut close by the ground, or cleane away.*
Il a fauché, & fené. *He hath made a cleane house, or shop; he hath left himselfe nothing in them; all is gone, spent, consumed, lost.*
Fauchement: m. *A mowing.*
Faucher. *To mow; to cut close by the ground; to sweepe, or cut cleane away; also, to dispatch, or rid businesse apace; and hence (of a Clarke.)*
Il fauche bien. *He writes verie swiftly.*
Faucher l'herbe sous les pieds à. *To supplant; also, to preuent.*
Faucheson: f. *A mowing; or, season good to mowe in.*
Fauchet. *A Sythe, or toole to mowe with.*
Faucheur: m. *A mower.*
Fauchon: m. *A Fauchion, Curtleax, or Hangar.*
Faucille: m. *as* Focille; *and (in a horse) the bought, or pestle of the thigh.*
Faucille: f. *A Sickle.*
Ie ne mettray la faucille en sa moisson. *I will not meddle with his matters, deale in his profession, incroach vpon his interest, looke into his dealings; I will not procure to my selfe any gaine, assume to my selfe a reward, thats due vnto his labor.*
Faucillon. *A little sickle.*
Bois à faucillon. *Brush wood, small wood.*
Faucon. *See* Faulcon.
Fauconniere: f. *A Faulkoners bag, or powch.*
Faudesteul, & Faudeteul. *as* Fauldetueil.
Faudiere: f. *The Pouldron, or skirt-peece of an Armour.*
Faudrinier: m. *as* Fourdrinier.
Faverots: m. *A kind of small Beanes; or, as* Faverottes.
Faverottes: f. *Earth-nuts, Kipper nuts, Earth-chestnuts.*
Faveur: f. *Fauor, grace, good opinion; kindnesse, loue, good-will; support, maintenance, protection; also, a fauor bestowed, and worne for the giuers sake.*
Faviere: f. *A Beane-field, land, or plot.*
Faulce. *as* Faulx; *a Sythe.*
Faulcé. *as* Faussé.
Faulcon: m. *A Faulcon; and (generally) any long-winged Hawke, or Hawke thats made vnto the Lure.*
Faulcon gentil. *A Faulcon gentle; the best, and boldest kind of Faulcon; somewhat lesse, but much better, then the* Pelerin.
Faulcon gerfaut. *A Gerfaulcon.*
Faulcon lanier. *A Lanner, or a Lanneret.*
Faulcon de mer. *A kind of small-mouthed Mullet that hath long finnes like wings.*
Faulcon nocturne. *The night-Faulcon; a kind of Scrichowle.*
Faulcon pelerin. *Looke* Pelerin.
Faulcon sacre. *A Saker.*
Faulcon Tunicien. *A Barbarie Faulcon.*
Bec de faulcon. *A kind of Pollax, borne sometimes for state by the Peeres of France, and ordinarily by the French Kings Pentioners.*
Faulconneau: m. *The peece of Ordnance called, a Faulcon; also, a young, or little Faulcon.*
Faulconnerie: f. *Faulconrie; Hawke-manning; or, the art of keeping Hawkes.*
Faulconnier: m. *A Faulkoner.*
Faulconniere: f. *A hawking bag.*
Faulde: f. *as* Giron. ¶Langued.
Fauldetueil: m. *A low, large, and easie foulding chaire, hauing both a backe and elbowes.*
Fauldiere: f. *as* Faudiere.
Fauls: m. *Looke* Faux.
Fauls: m. faulse: f. *False, counterfeit, vntrue, lying, deceiuing, vnfaithfull, trecherous; double, hollow-harted, halting with friends.*
Fauls adveu. *The vassals challenging, or acknowledging of a wrong Iusticer, or Landlord.*
Fauls germe. *A Moone-calfe. Looke* Germe.
Fauls pas. *Looke* Pas.
Fauls rompu. Vn f. *A subtill fellow, one that hath bin much beaten to the world.*
Fauls visage. *A Visard, or Maske.*
Queuë faulse. *An vnsteadie, much whisking, or often wagling, traine of a horse.*
Faulsaire: m. *A forger of Writings, a falsifier of Euidences; one that counterfeits another mans hand with a false intent; also, a trecherous violater of his faith; Look* Faux.
Faulsé. *as* Faussé; *pierced, &c; also, forged, falsified, counterfeited; also, standing, or made crooked, as a sword by a fall, &c.*
Faulse-braye: f. *A false braye (in fortification;) Looke* Braye.
Faulsée: f. *A breach (as in a wall, &c;) also, a transpiercing, violent piercing; striking, or charging, through and through.*
Faulse-foy. Vn f. *A faith-breaker.*
Faulsement. *Falsely, vntruly, deceitfully, counterfeitly.*
Faulser. *To falsifie, forge, counterfeit; to deale vntruly in; also, as* Faucer.
Faulser compagnie. *To forsake, or abandon the companie which one hath sworne, vndertaken, or promised to keepe; also, to part, or breake companie, to leaue anie companie.*
Faulser vn escu, ou vn haubert. *To pierce, to strike, or to runne, through a shield, &c; to make a breach into it.*
Faulser les gonds. *To force, or breake asunder, the hindges.*
Faulser vne troupe. *To charge through, and through a troupe.*
Faulset: m. *A fayning, in song; also, a discord.*
Chanter en faulset. *To faine; also, to sing louder and louder, or to rise from note to note, in singing.*
Voix en faulset. *Looke* Voix.
Faulset: m. *A faucet; See* Fausset.
Faulseté: f. *Falshood, vntruth, lying, trecherie.*
Faulseteux: m. euse: f. *Most false; fraught with vntruths, full of lyes.*
Fault. Il fault. *It ought, it behooues, &c; Looke* Falloir.
Faulte: f. *A fault; a sinne, vice, delict, offence, trespasse, transgression; also, an error, slip, misse, fayle, default, omission; also, want, lacke, need, pouertie, penurie, scarcitie of; also, a baulke vntilled betweene two furrowes.*
Faulte d'homme. *Looke* Homme.
Sans faulte. *Pure, innocent, perfect, spotlesse, blamelesse, faultles; also, assuredly, certainly, without doubt, without fayling, not to misse.*
Faire faulte à. *To fayle, disappoint, or shrinke from.*
Tirer à faulte. *To misse what he shot at; and so,* Voler à faulte. *To misse his flight, or what he flew at.*

Qui a fait la faulte si la boive: Pro. *Let him that did the wrong incurre the penaltie.*

Tel fait la faulte qu' un autre boit: Prov. *Th' one playes the pranke, and th' other payes for't.*

Faultif: m. iue: f. *Faultie, offending, misdoing, fayling, subiect, or apt to doe amisse.*

Faultrage. *as* Preage.

Faulveret. *A little bird like a Reed-Sparrow, which buildeth her neast among Beanes; or, as* Fauvette.

Faulx: m. *as* Faux.

Faulx: f. *A Sythe (to mowe with.)*

La faulx paye les prez: Prov. *The keene Sythe giueth Meades their due.*

Faulx: m. faulse: f. *as* Fauls.

Faulx-bourgs: m. *The suburbes of a towne; Looke* Faux-bourgs.

Favorable: com. *Fauourable, gracious, propitious; kind, friendlie, louing.*

Favorablement. *Fauourably, propitiously, kindly, graciously, louingly.*

Favori: m. *A fauourite, or minion; one thats in fauour.*

Favori: m. ie: f. *Fauoured, graced, countenanced; kindly vsed.*

Favorisant. *Fauouring, gracing, affecting, cherishing.*

Favorisé: m. ée: f. *Fauoured, graced, countenanced; affected, loued, cherished.*

Favoriser. *To fauour, grace, countenance; affect, loue, cherish.*

Favoriseur: m. *A fauourer, supporter; furtherer.*

Favorit. *as* Favori.

Favorite: f. *A Princes Mistresse; a Sweet-heart, or she-fauourite.*

Favot de febves: m. *A Beane-stacke; also, as* Faval.

Fauperdrieux: m. *A Hawke somewhat lesse then a Kite, yet higher; her beake, and tallons not so crooked as those of other Hawkes; her legs small, and yellow; her traine, and tip of wings, blacke; the top of her head, and bottome of her throat, of a reddish white; the rest of a darke tawnie colour.*

Fauquet: m. *A shaling wry-legd fellow.* ¶Pic.

Fausonnerie: f. *A forging, or falsifying of Euidences; a false counterfeiting of another mans hand.*

Fausaire. *as* Faulsaire; *or, an Impostor.*

Faussé. *Pierced, runne, thrust through; also, violently burst, broken, diuided; Looke* Faulsé.

Faussée: f. *as* Faulsée.

Fausser. *as* Faulser.

Fausset: m. *A faucet, for a Hogs-head, &c.*

Par le petit fausset. *Niggardly, sparingly, scantly, in small measure.*

Fausterne. *The hearbe called, round Birthwort.*

Faut. Il faut; *it ought, it must, &c; See* Falloir.

Faute. *A fault, offence; want of; See* Faulte.

Fauteur: m. *A fautor, fauourer; furtherer, helper; supporter, protector; a partaker, a companion.*

Fautier. *as* Faultif; *faultie, blame-worthie.*

Fautrage. Droict de f. *Looke* Droict.

Fauve: com. *Fallow, deepe-yellow, Lyon-tawnie, light-dunne.*

Bestes fauves: *(A generall word for) all kind of Deere, wild Goats, and such like beasts.*

Fauveau: m. *A dunne horse; also, a Puffin, or Fork-fish.*

Tel estrille fauveau que puis le mord: Prov. *Some make but bad returne of a good turne; or, th' vngratefull vse those worst that haue beene best vnto them.*

Fauveau. *Yellowish, darke yellow, dunne, somewhat fallow.*

Fauvette: f. *A yellowish bird somewhat lesse then the Nightingale, whereunto she resembles both in singing, and shape; some call her, a Linget.*

Fauvette rousse. *A certaine ruddie bird, which is no bigger then the end of a mans finger.*

Faux: m. *A Beech-tree; also, falsehood, falsenesse, or a falsifying; Hence, the Crime tearmed among Lawyers;*

Le Faux. *Which is the falsifying of Writs, Instruments, or Euidences; and the bearing of false witnesse; and the coyning of false money; and the wilfull vsing of false weights, or measures.*

Faux à Connils. *A Clapper, or imperfect Warren of Conies.*

Faux du corps. *The Wast, or Middle.*

Le faux d'un harnois. *The part thereof thats next vnto the* Tasses; *called so, because it is the weakest, or made the sleightest.*

Peine de faux. *Was, in auncient Rome, confiscation of goods, if the offendor were a freeman; and death, if a seruant, or slaue, by the Law* Cornelia: *But the Lawes of France, making no such difference, inflict Death, on all that forge Contracts, or beare false witnesse (in a Court of Iustice;) or falsifie the Kings Chauncerie Letters, and Seales; and vpon all Exchequer men, that haue falsified Accompts, Rolls, Acquittances, or Discharges, &c.*

S' inscrire en faux. *is, to vndertake, that an Euidence, &c, is false; or, to vndertake, in a Court of Iustice, to proue it false, or falsified; also, to accuse of, or charge with, falsehood, or falsenesse, any thing.*

Maintenir de faux. *To challenge, or except against, a Deed; to offer to proue it false, or forged;* (Celuy qui veut Maintenir de faux somme la partie que produit la piece, de declarer s' il s' en veut aider; & apres sa declaration de s' en aider, se fait l' inscription en faux contre la minute originale, laquelle l' accusé doit faire representer, & mettre au greffe.)

Faux: f. *as* Faulx; *a Sythe.*

Faux: m. fausse: f. *False; Looke* Fauls.

Faux. à faux. *(Aduerbially) amisse, not rightly; to no purpose, vainely; and hence;*

Ce coup tomba à faux. *This blow was lost; or, hit not the intended place, but was defended, auoided, or put by.*

Faux-bond. *A false trick, a faithlesse part, a trecherous pranke; a deceitfull, or cousening, action.*

Elle a fait vn faux-bond. *She hath played false, or trod her shooe awry.*

Faux-bourdon. *The drone of a Bagpipe.*

Faux-bourgs: m. *The suburbes of a Towne; whence;*

Iardin aux faux-bourgs vaut cent solz au rebours: Prov. *A Garden in the suburbes is worth a hundred pound backwards; (which diuers of our fond citizens haue to their cost found true.)*

Faux-feu. *A fayling, missing, or not taking of effect; a deceiuing, or disappointing; also, a shrewd turne, or ill office, done vnder hand.*

Fauxmarcher. *To step, or goe awry; to set the foot ill in going; also, to slip, or stumble, by such going.*

Faux-marchure: f. *A wrinch, or strayne in a bone, or ioynt of the foote, &c, got by a slip, or wry step.*

Fauxoiseau: m. *as* Fauperdrieux; *or (more generally) any rauenous bird which hath not the name of a Hawke.*

Faux-pas. *A false, or hollow peece of ground that sinkes vnder the feet in going; also, a slip, or misse in footing; a slipping, an error, a mistaking.*

Fauxperdriau. *as* Fauperdrieux.

Fayant: m. *A Beech tree.*

Fayerie: f. *as* Féerie; *or, a fancie, imagination, illusion, or vision of Fairies.*

Fayfort: m. *A warranting of the goodnesse, and sufficiencie of sale-ware; or, as* Le faict fort.

Faymidroict. *Base, or low iurisdiction; called so by the Customes of* Solle.

Fays. *as* Fais. ¶Langued.

Faysse: f. *A swath-band for a child.* ¶Langued.

Faziols: m. *Fasels, long Peason, Kidney Beanes, French Beanes, Romane Beanes.*

Fé: f. *as* Foy; *faith (an old word,)* par la fé Dieu; *(now turned by the countrey people into,* Par la feste Dieu) *by the faith I owe to God.*

Fé Dieu *(an Interiection of admiring;)* si telle chose advint onc; *Oh God man, or, Gods me, such a thing was neuer.*

Feable. *as* Feal. *Honest, trustie, faithfull; also, worthie of account, of reputation.*

Onction feable. *The pruining, or annointing which a Hawke giues her feathers, by the moisture she sucks from her Crupper.*

Feablement. *as* Fealement. *Honestly, loyally.*

Feage: m. *Fee simple; or, an inheritance, or house held in fee simple.*

Feal: m. ale: f. *Faithfull, trustie, loyall, true, honest.*

Fealement. *Faithfully, trustily, loyally, honestly.*

Feaulté: f. *Fealtie; fidelitie, faithfulnesse, loyaltie, trustinesse.*

Feauté. *The same.*

Febé: m. *A double secret, or secret storie; a thing hidden; (Originally, this is the word thats spoken, or, as a question demaunded, in the Cake-choice of King and Queene at the later end of Christmas, by him that would haue a peece of the Cake.)*

Feble. *as* Foible. *Feeble, weake.*

Febricitant. *Sicke of an ague.*

Febrifique: com. *Ague-breeding; full of the feauer; aguish, apt for feauers.*

Febril: m. ile: f. *Feauerie; of a feauer; aguish, belonging to an ague.*

Febve: f. *A Beane.*

Febve Egyptiaque. *The Beane of Egipt; a water plant that beares a Rose-coloured flower, and a verie great leafe; (the fruit, or Beane, and the root thereof (tearmed by some,* Colocasia) *are medicinable, and no ill meat;) also, the fruit of the Lote tree.*

Febve espesse. *Orpine, Liblong, or Liuelong; (an hearbe.)*

Febves frittes. *The Note, or Character ff in the Ciuile Law, signifying* Digesta; *(tearmed so by yong Students.)*

Febve de mer. *A kind of hard, ruddie, and writhen shell-fish.*

Febves peintes. *French Beanes, or Beanes of Rome; as* Febves de Rome.

Febve Pontique. *as* Febve Egyptiaque.

Febve de porc. *The weed Henbane; so called in former times.*

Febves de Rome. *Kidney Beanes, Sperage Beanes, French Beanes, Phasels, or long Peason.*

Febve sauvage. *The wild Beane-plant, whose flowers be of a bright Crimson colour, and whose pease-like pulse is most vnsauorie.*

Bailleur de febves à my-croist. *A cousener, cheater, imposter, deceiuer, conycatcher.*

Comme vne febve en la gueule d'un Lion. *We say, like a Beane in a Monkes hood.*

Trouver la febve au gasteau. *To find what one looks for, to meet with a thing for his purpose.*

Quand les febves sont flories les sots commencent leurs folies: Prov. *When Beanes doe flower youth enters into follie.*

Febveux: m. euse. f. *Beanie, full of Beanes, yeelding Beanes.*

Febvre: m. *A Black-smith.*

En forgeant on devient febvre: Prov. *Continuall practise begets cunning.*

Febrier: m. *as* Fevrier.

Fecal: m. ale: f. *Durtie, dreggie, vnsetled, vnfined.*

La matiere fecale. *Dung, or excrements.*

Fece: f. *Lees, dregs, grounds; any thicke substance setled in the bottome of liquor.*

Fecond: m. de: f. *Abundant, ranke, full, fertile, fruitfull, plentifull.*

Fecondement. *Fully, fertilly, fruitfully, abundantly.*

Feconder. *To make fertile, fruitfull; ranke, abundant.*

Fecondité: f. *Fruitfulnesse, fertilitie, store, fulnesse, plentie, abundance of fruits.*

Fecot: m. *The yongling of an Ewe (or of any other such beast) newly come out of her bellie.*

Fecture. *as* Facture; *the finishing, or making vp of.*

Feculent: m. te: f. *Thicke, muddie, dreggie.*

Fée: f. *A Fairie.*

Feé: m. eée: f. *Fatall, appointed, destined; also, taken, bewitched, or forespoken; also, charmed, inchaunted.*

Féerie. Par féerie. *Fatally, by destinie, by appointment of the Fairies.*

Fein: m. *Hay. See* Foin.

Feinct: m. cte: f. *Fained, forged, supposed, &c; as* Fainct.

Feincte: f. *A small, or yong Shad; the riuer Pilchard.*

Feindre. *To faine, dissemble, forge, cog, foist, counterfeit, pretend, play the hypocrite, make false resemblances, or offers; also, to imagine, suppose, deuise.*

Il feignoit à marcher. *He hung an arse, dragd behind, came but slowly forward, or on.*

Se feindre. *To make shew of one thing, and doe another; to suffer of purpose his aduersarie to preuaile against him; to disable himselfe more then he needs; to proceed coldly in a matter; to come slowly forward; to drag behind; any way to forbeare, or doe lesse then he can doe.*

Se feindre au train de derriere. *A beast to fauour his hinder parts; or, to halt behind.*

Sans se feindre. *Diligently, seriously, carefully, indeed, in very good earnest, throughly, home.*

Feine: f. *Beech Maste; also, a kind of apple, the cyder whereof is of long continuance.*

Feinte: f. *An Apparition, or Phantasme; also, a dumbe shew; also, one that represents, or acts it; also, a Sharp, in Musicke.*

Feintement. *as* Faintement; *faintly; fainingly.*

Feintise: f. *Dissembling, faining, cogging, &c; See* Faintise.

Feletin: m. *Flannen; or, a stuffe like Flannen, whereof hangings are (sometimes) made.*

Felice: com. *Happie, luckie, blissefull, prosperous; fauourable; also, good, fat, fertile, fruitfull, abundant in increase.*

Felicité: f. *Felicitie, happinesse, blisse, prosperitie, great lucke, exceeding good fortune.*
Feliciter. *To make prosperous, happie, luckie.*
Feliciter avec vn de. *To reioyce, or congratulate with one for.*
Felin: m. *A certaine weight; (among Goldsmiths, seuen graines, among Lapidaries, two carrats) also, the stuffe, or thin woollen cloth, called Wadnall.*
Felle. *A kind of fish-net, forbidden to be vsed.*
Felle: com. *Fell, spightfull, disdainefull, cruell, fierce, furious, vntractable, outragious.*
Fellé: m. ée: f. *Crazed, cracked, flawed, a little riuen, or broken.*
Felleure: f. *as* Fellure.
Felleux: m. euse: f. *Full of bitternesse.*
Fellin. *as* Felin.
Fellon. *as* Felon.
Fellonie. *Looke* Felonnie.
Fellure: f. *A small craze, cracke, or flaw (in a Jewell, Glasse, Pot, &c) no bigger then a haire.*
Felon: m. *A sicknesse of the stomacke, tearmed, the chollericke passion; or, a flux (accompanied with vomiting) that proceeds of choller.*
Felon: m. ne: f. *Fell; fellonious; furious, despightfull, cruell, curst, pitilesse, harsh, rough, froward, vntractable, outragious.*
Regard felon. *A grimme, sterne, terrible, frowning, lowring, soure, mischieuous looke.*
Amour vainc tout fors que le cœur felon: Prov. *Loue conquers any thing but a fellonious heart.*
Felongne: f. *Selandine the greater, Swallowes hearb, Swallow-wort, Tettar-wort.*
Felonie: f. *as* Felonnie.
Felonnement. *Felly; fellaniously; furiously, despightfully, cruelly, curstly, harshly, frowardly; grimly, sternely, sourely; outragiously.*
Felonnie: f. *Fellnesse, curstnesse, despightfulnesse, ire, anger; vntractablenesse, crueltie, vnmercifulnesse, outragiousnesse; also, disobedience; trecherie, treason; any such hainous falsehood, or offence, committed by a vassall against his Lord, or by a subiect against his Soueraigne, whereby he looses, or is worthie to loose, his estate.*
Felouque: f. *as* Falouque.
Felure: f. *A flaw, craze, or small cracke.*
Femelin: m. ine: f. *Womanish, effeminate; weake, tender, delicate.*
Femelle: f. *The female, or shee of man, or beast.*
Femelles. *The rings which beare vp the Rudder of a ship; we call them, Gudgeons.*
Femelle. *Female; of the female sex, or kind.*
Femellette: f. *A little female creature.*
Femier: m. *A Baylife, or ouerseer of the Husbandrie, in a Gentlemans house.*
Feminin: m. ine: f. *Feminine; or, as* Femelin; *effeminate.*
Femme: f. *A woman; a wife; a female.*
Femme de chambre. *A chamber-maid.*
Femme de corps. *A Villenesse, or woman of a seruile condition.*
Pomme de belle femme. *The name of a certaine beautifull, delicate, and iuicie, apple.*
Folettes femmes. *The hearbe Orage, or Orache.*
Sage femme. *A Midwife.*
En femme. *Effeminately, womanishly, woman-like, nicely, tenderly, daintily; weakely; faintly, fearefully.*
Femme, argent, & vin, ont leur bien, & leur venin: Prov. *A woman, coyne, and wine haue good, and bad things in them.*
Femme de bien vaut vn grand bien: Prov. *An honest woman is worth much.*
Femme bonne qui a mauvais mari a bien souvent le cœur marri: Prov. *The good wife of a wilfull man hath many a wofull day; The like is;*
Femme qui a mari mauvais a peu souvent le cœur en paix.
Femme bonne vaut vne couronne: Prov. *A vertuous dame is worth a Diademe.*
Femme fiere en toute saison veut estre maistre de sa maison: Pro. *The proud shroe scornes to be a subiect.*
Femme lecheresse ne fera ia porée espaisse: Prov. *Looke* Porée.
Femme mauvaise qui n' empire encore n' est elle pas la pire: Prov. *An ill wife that growes not worse is not of wiues the worst.*
Femme trop piteuse faict sa famille teigneuse: Pro. *The ouer gentle huswife marres her houshold.*
Femme se plaind, femme se deult, femme est malade quand elle veut: Pro. *Women lament, weepe, sicken, when they list.*
Femme prudente, & sage est l' ornement de son mesnage: Prov. *Looke* Prudent.
Femme qui envis file porte chemise vile: Pro. *Beggerie, and nastinesse are the fruits of ill huswiuerie, and lazinesse.*
Femme qui ses levres mord, & qui son alleure tord, se mesle du mestier ord, ou fait à soy mesme tort: Pro. *The wife that bites her lips and treads askue, is to her husband, or her selfe, vntrue.*
Femme qui perd sa honte est sans estime, & conte: Pro. *A woman that hath lost her shame, hath lost respect, esteeme, good name.*
Femme rit quand elle peut, & pleure quand elle veut: Pro. *A woman laughes when she can, and weepes when she will.*
Femme safre, & yvrongnesse, de son corps n' est pas maistresse: Pro. *Looke* Yvrongnesse.
Femme sage, & de façon de peu remplit sa maison: Pro. *The wise, and well-behaued woman fils her house with little; or, a woman wise, and prouident by thrift doth stocke her tenement.*
Femme sotte se cognoist à la cotte: Prov. *The foolish woman's by her weeds discerned; the womans garment shewes how fond she is.*
De femme volage, & friande, En tout temps bon heur nous defende: Pro. *From women light, and lickorous, good fortune still deliuer vs.*
De toute femme qui se farde, donne toy soigneusement garde: Prov. *Let no womans painting breed thy stomacks fainting.*
Qui femme a noise a: Prov. *Looke* Noise.
Qui femme croit, & Asne meine son corps ne sera ia sans peine: Prov. *(Belike because the one is (somtime) false, as the other is euer foolish.)*
Toutes les femmes se resemblent: Pro. *All women are (in good, or bad) alike.*
A peine cognoist on la femme, & le Melon: Prov. *(The meaning is, vntill they be broken, or cut vp; and, the outside is often the best part of them.)*
'A qui Dieu veut aider sa femme luy meurt: Prov. *The wife of him whom God will helpe soone dyes.*
Aux Receveurs les honneurs, & aux femmes leurs douleurs: Prov. *Receiuers get preferment, foolish women paine; or (as truly for the matter) womens paine brings them honour, Receiuers honour breedes their paine.*

Beauté de femme fascheux resveille-matin: Prov. *Looke* Resveille-matin.
C'est folie de se prendre aux femmes, & aux bestes: Prov. *Hee's mad that quarrels (with women, or beasts.)*
Ce n'est rien, c' est vne femme qui se noye: Prov. *Tis no great matter though a woman drowne her selfe.*
Chascun cuide avoir la meilleure femme: Pro. *Euerie Ape thinkes her puppie the fairest.*
Deux pots au feu signifient feste, & deux femmes font la tempeste: Prov. *Two pots well fild are signes of a feast; two women ill-wild of a storme.*
Il faut acheter maison faicte, & femme à faire: Pro. *(For by building is many a man vndone; and with a widow (if she list) any man shall haue ynough to doe.)*
Il ne se faut fier ni à femme, ni au giron: Pro. *Looke* Giron.
Il n'est si bon que femme n'assotte: Prov. *The best man may b'asotted on a woman.*
Les hommes donnent aux femmes ce qu' ils n'ont pas, & ne peuvent avoir: Pro. viz. *Milke.*
Par trop trotter la poule, & la femme se perdent facilement: Prov. *A gadding henne, and houswife are soone lost.*
Qui perd sa femme, & cinq sols c'est grand dommage de l'argent: Pro. *He that looses his wife, and six pence hath some losse by the money.*
Soleil qui luisarne au matin, femme qui parle Latin, & Enfant nourry de Vin, ne viennent point à bonne fin: Prov. *A learned woman seldome proues a good one.*
Tout ce que Clerc laboure folle femme devore: Prov. *All that the Clarke toyles for his Punke deuoures.*
Vn homme de paille vaut vne femme d'or: Prov. *A man of straw is worth a woman of gold (for rude, or violent purposes will some say.)*
Femmelette: f. *A pretie little wife, or woman.*
Femmette. *A little wife, low woman.*
Femois: m. *A certaine (forbidden) fish-catching Net, or Engine.*
Fenaison: f. *Hay time, Hay-haruest; the season wherein Hay is gotten.*
Fenasse: f. *as* Sainct-foin.
Fenault: m. *A Hay-loft, or Hay-house.*
Fendant: m. *A slash, gash, wype, great cut, or downe-right blow; also, a cutter, backster, swaggerer, swashbuckler.*
'A poincte, & à fendant. *Both thrusting, and striking; in all extremitie; by all meanes, euerie way.*
Fendant. *Cleauing, slitting, chapping, chopping, riuing asunder.*
Geler à pierres fendant. *To freeze extreamely.*
Fendasse: f. *A cleft, rift, chop, choane.*
Fendement: m. *A cleauing, chopping, chapping, diuiding, riuing, or cutting asunder.*
Fendeur: m. *A cleauer, slitter; a riuer; a diuider.*
Fendeur de naseaux. *A cutter, swaggerer, swashbuckler.*
Fendillé: m. ée: f. *Clouen, riuen, chapped, opened in, or broken into, small rifts, or chinks.*
Fendiller. *To cleaue, riue; chap, choane, open, or breake, in small chinks, or rifts.*
Fendre. *To cleaue, slit; riue; diuide, or cut, asunder.*
Se fendre. *To cleaue, riue, gape, chap, chinke, or choane; to open, breake, or goe, asunder of it selfe.*
Fendre l'ergot. *To run his countrey; or, to run away.*
Fendre à noyau. *To take the essay of a Deere.*
Fendre les pieds à. *To runne away from.* Il luy faudroit fendre les pieds, & l'envoyer paistre, comme vne pecore. *(Applyable to an vnmannerlie logarhead) he should be turned to the hogs-trough; or, sent a grazing; he is fitter to feed with beasts then with men.*
Fendre le vent. *as* Fendre l'ergot.
Fendu: m. *The slit, or clouen side of a thing.*
Fendu: m. uë: f. *Cleft, slit, riuen, clouen, diuided, cut asunder; opened, or open; gaping, chappie, full of cranies, full of choanes.*
Levre fenduë. *A Hares mouth; See* Levre.
Oignon fendu. *A Scallion.*
Radis fendu. *The cleft Raddish, double Raddish, many-rooted Raddish.*
Bien fendu de gueule. *Wide-mouthed, sparrow-mouthed, mouthed vp to the eares.*
Fené: m. ée: f. *Withered; also, weathered; made as, or into, Hay.*
Il a fauché & fené. *He hath consumed, or lost all; or, he is at his height, at his best; he hath got all he is like to get.*
Fener. *To make Hay, or make into Hay.*
Se fener. *To fade, wither, wax deadish; to decay.*
Fenerateur: m. *An Vsurer.*
Feneration: f. *Vsurie, or the practise thereof.*
Feneratoire: com. *Vsurious.*
Fenestrage: m. *Windowes; or, the fashion, seat, cast, placing, or contriuement thereof.*
Fenestre: f. *A window.*
Fenestre bastarde. *A false window; or fashion of sloping window (as in some shops) yeelding a false light.*
Fenestre dormante; ou à voirre dormant. *A Dorre window, or close window of glasse, &c.*
Fenestre Flamende *A fiue-cornered window of timber-worke, bearing out, in the vpper parts, from the roofe of a house, &c; and setled, in the bottome, vpon the height of the house wall.*
Pain de fenestre. *Houshold bread, wheaten bread; bread made of vnboulted corne.*
Entrer par la fenestre. *To come vnto by indirect courses, to enter the wrong way; (whence belike we say that a bastard came in at the window.)*
S'ils ne veulent passer par là qu'ils passent par la fenestre. *If they will not take that course, let them doe worse (or amisse) and spare not.*
Fenestré: m. ée: f. *Windowed, hauing windowes, open, pierced.*
Fenestrelle: f. *A little window.*
Fenestrier: m. ere: f. *Belonging to a window; also, placed in, or looking out at, a window; whence;*
Fille fenestriere, & trotiere rarement bonne mesnagere: Prov. *Seldome proues gazer, or gadder a good houswife.*
Feneur: m. *A hay-maker.*
Feneux: m. euse: f. *Hayie, full of hay.*
Fenicte. *A little Shad-fish.*
Fenier: m. *as* Fenil.
Fenil: m. *A hay-loft, hay-mowe, hay-house; a Reeke, or Stacke of hay; also, the Racke wherein hay is put.*
Fenné. *Withered, faded.*
Fenoil: m. *as* Fenouil. *Fennell.*
Fenons: m. *Rowles made of sticks about a finger thick, first wrapped in hay, or straw, then within a peece of linnen, and applyed vnto broken thighes, or legs, about the splints, and bands, to settle them, and keepe them in order; outward splints.*

Fenouil: m. *The hearbe Fennell; also, the seed thereof.*

Fenouil de Barbarie. *Fennell giant, great Fennell, Barbarie Fennell.*

Fenouil doux. *Sweet Fennell (in all respects bigger then the ordinarie one, and therfore distinguished from it.)*

Fenouil marin. *Rocke Sampire, Crestmarin.*

Fenouil de porceau. *Sow-fennell, Hogs-fennell, Horestrange, Horestrong, Sulpherwort, Brimstonewort.*

Fenouil Romain. *The hearbe Annise, or Anniseed.*

Fenouil sauvage. *Wild Fennell, horse Fennell, great Fennell.*

Fente: f. *A cleft, rift, slifter, chinke, slit, cranie, chap, choane.*

Fente en poil. *A cleft in a bone, as small as any haire.*

Fenugrec: m. *The hearbe, or seed, Fenigreeke.*

Feodal: m. ale: f. *Feodall; of, or belonging to, a* Fief; *also, held (by homage and fealtie) as a* Fief; *also, possessing diuers* fiefs; *Looke* Feudal.

Seigneur feodal. *A Lord Paramont, or chiefe Lord; one of whose* fief *diuers other* fiefs *are held, by homage and fealtie.*

Cela nous appartient par forfaiture du Seigneur feodal. *We haue no possibilitie of right vnto that.*

Feodalité: f. *The estate of a Feodall, or chiefe Lord; the possession of, or Seigniorie ouer, diuers* fiefs; *feudalitie, or feodalitie; also, a tenure in* fief; *or, by homage and fealtie.*

Feodé: m. ée: f. *Infeoffed; giuen vnto in* fief; *also, held in* fief, *or in fee.*

Sergent feodé. *Looke* Sergent.

Fer: m. *Iron; also, the head of a Pike, Launce, Arrow, &c; also, the tag of a Point.*

Fers. *Shackles, fetters, boults, irons; also, horseshooes.*

Fer d'archail. *Iron wire.*

Fer blanc. *White Lattin.*

Fer de cheval. Vn fer de cheval. *A horse-shooe;* Le fer de cheval. *A kind of Axseed, or small Pulse, called Horse-shooe.*

Fer de guerre. *The steelie, and sharpe head of a Pike, Launce, or horsemans staffe.*

Fer maillé. Fenestre à fer maillé. *An Iron-grated window, whose barres are not (or ought not to be) aboue foure ynches asunder.*

Fer de Moulin. *A Mill-ring, or Mill-rind; called by Heralds, an Inkmolyne.*

Fer à ravaler. *A Tanner, or Leather-dressers shauing knife, beame knife, or working knife.*

Fer de richard. *as* Fil d' archal; *or, great Iron wire.*

Fer de rochet. *A Burre; or, the blunt, or dulled head of a tilting staffe.*

Vieux fers. *Old Iron; old, or broken things of Iron; also, old rags; any ouer-worne trash.*

'A fer esmoulu. *Extreamely; or, in good earnest; Looke* Esmoulu.

Entre deux fers. *In equall ballance; of a like, or iust weight, of the same substance, qualitie, proportion, goodnesse.*

Elle n'a eu fer à Pied. *She is vntainted, pure, vndefiled, she hath not yet beene manned; she hath not yet beene broken vp.*

Batre le fer. *To play at blunt, or at foyles.*

On frotte tant le fer qu'a la fin il s'eschauffe: Pro. *Cold Iron by much rubbing will grow hot; Applyable vnto a dull spirit, which by much vrging enters into choller.*

Fere: f. *A wild beast.*

Fercules: m. *The things whereon Images, or Pageants are carried; also, Beeres for dead men.*

Fereluche. *as* Freluche; *a moat, &c.*

Feri: m. ie: f. *Hit, strucken; wounded, hurt.*

Feriage. *as* Feage.

Ferial: m. ale: f. *Of, or belonging to, a holyday; idle, resting, vacant, vnoccupied; also, iocond, merrie, pleasant; also, ridiculous.*

Vn ferial beuveur. *A square drinker, a faithfull drunkard; one that will take his liquor soundly.*

Feriat: m. *A vacation time; an idle, or play day.*

Feries: f. *Holydaies, festiuall daies, resting daies, idle times, Wakes, Vacations, or vacant seasons; properly such holydaies as Monday and Tuesday in Easter weeke, &c.*

Ferin: m. ine: f. *Wild, sauage, beastlie, cruell.*

Ferir. *To hit, strike; wound, hurt.*

Mal ioue qui fiert la ioue: Prov. *He makes but ill sport whose play tends to hurt.*

Fermage: m. *Farmage; the profit made of, reuenue comming in by, a farme.*

Fermail: m. *The claspe of a booke, &c.*

Fermaille: f. *A small buckle, or claspe.*

Fenestre à fermaille. *A window that shuts with a haspe; or (in stead of,* à fer maillé) *as in* Fer.

Fermaillé: m. ée: f. *Buckled; hasped; clasped; also, garnished, or set thicke with small buckles.*

Fermailler: m. *A Buckle-maker, or Claspe-maker.*

Fermailler. *To buckle, haspe, claspe; also, to set, or garnish with small buckles.*

Fermaillet: m. *A Carkanet, or border of gold, &c, such as Gentlewomen weare about their heads, or hoods; also, an inchaunted image, collar, or chayne, worne about the necke, as a preseruatiue against poyson, witchcraft, wounds, &c; also, a small buckle, or claspe.*

Fermance: m. *A certaine officer within the iurisdiction of* La Solle.

Fermant: m. *A buckle, haspe, or claspe; also, a shutter; any thing that (surely) binds, fastens, closes.*

Fermant. *Shutting, stopping vp, closing, sealing, locking, fastening, making vp.*

Fermative: f. *An affirmation, asseueration, or protestation of right vnto a thing in controuersie, made before a Iudge, by him that pretends it.*

Ferme: f. *A Farme, or Lease; a thing farmed; a Toll, Rent, Mannor, or Demesne in farme; also, the farming thereof, or an estate therein by farme, or lease; also, a farme, or farme-house in the countrey; also, as* Fermative.

Les fermes du Roy. *Those parts of his Reuenue, or Demesne, which may be let out.*

Ferme: com. *Firme, stable, sure, fast, steadie, setled, certaine, assured; constant, stedfast; also, decreed, ratified, confirmed, established.*

Faire ferme. *To stand still; to make a stop, or stand; also, to stop, cause to stop, make to stand* (faire ferme à.)

Fermé: m. ée: f. *Closed, shut, fastened, locked, sealed vp; inclosed, kept in; made vp.*

Ferme, Adverb. (*as* Fermement;) *and hence;* Ferme à ferme *(in Horsemanship) anie Aire done in a little roome, and a iust time.*

Fort & ferme. *Verie hard, verie much, amaine, stiffely; extreamely, excessiuely, exceedingly; fiercely, violently, vehemently; assuredly, confidently.*

Fermeille: f. *as* Fermaille.
Ferneillet: m. *as* Fermaillet.
Fermemént: m. *A closing, shutting, fastening, locking, sealing, making vp.*
Ferméinent. *Firmely, fastly, surely, steadily; soundly; certainely, assuredly; constantly, stedfastly.*
Fermentation: f. *A fastening, setling, assuring; also, a fermentation; a raysing, as of paste with leauen, a leauening; also, a working, as of ale or beere; also, an infusion, or infusing; a setting, or letting stand, diuers simples together, in the Sunne, ouer a furnace, or among horse dung, vntill they be fully incorporated, or their substances throughly mingled.*
Fermenté: m. ée: f. *Setled, fastened, assured; wrought; raised, as beere, or bread; also, infused, steeped.*
Fermenter. *To settle, fasten, assure, make firme; also, to worke, as ale or beere; also, to infuse; or ly steeping; as in* Fermentation.
Fermenter la paste. *To leauen it; or, to make it rise, as leauen doth.*
Fermer. *To shut, stop, close, locke, seale, fasten, or make vp; also, (a demaundant, and defendant) to affirme, or protest before a Judge, holding their hands within his, that they haue good right vnto the thing they sue for.*
Fermesse: f. *as* Fermeté.
Fermeté: f. *Stabilitie, steadinesse, firmenesse; constancie, stedfastnesse; certainetie, surenesse, assurednesse; also, a fortresse, or place of strength.*
Fermeture: f. *A closing, shutting, fastening, locking vp, or in; also, the end of a place (for where it is shut vp, it endeth;) also, the claspes of a booke.*
Fermeur: m. *A shutter, closer, fastener, locker, stopper, maker vp of.*
Fermeure: f. *as* Fermement.
Fermier: m. *A Farmer; a Lessee; also, a chiefe Hind, or Husbandman; a Baylife, or Ouerseer of another mans Husbandrie.*
Fermier du Revendage du Roy. *Looke* Revendage.
Fermier: m. ere: f. *Farming; taking to, or enioying by, farme.*
Prevost fermier. *A certaine Officer, who had all publike fines and amerciaments, and was (before Charles the eights time) Iudge of all causes, and controuersies raised by reason of his Office.*
Sergent fermier. *That hath farmed his place (which by Law he should not doe.)*
Fermoirs: m. *The claspes of a booke; or, as* Fremoirs.
Fernel: m. *A certaine beame in the prow of a ship.*
Feroce: com. *Cruell, fierce, curst, vntractable; hardhearted, sterne, rigorous, austere.*
Ferocité: f. *Fiercenesse, crueltie, vntractablenesse; rigor, austeritie, sternenesse.*
Feronnier: m. *An Iron-monger.*
Ferrage: m. *The shooing of horses; also, any worke of, or working in, Iron.*
Droict de ferrage. *Looke* Droict.
Ferraille: f. *(Old) Iron worke; Iron implements, Iron tooles.*
Ferrailles. *Old Iron.*
Cette ferraille de moines. *These old, rustie, out-cast Monkes.*
Ferrailleries: f. *Iron worke, implements, or tooles.*
Ferran: m. *as* Aguillade.
Ferrandier: m. *A dresser of Hempe.*
Ferrant. *Shooing a horse, &c; whence;*
Mareschal ferrant. *A farrier.*
Ferrasse: f. *The smooth, and long-taylde Skate called, the Eorke-fish; also, the coursest of Hempe, Swinglefoot herds, course Towe.*
Ferrat. *Shod (as a horse with Iron.)*
Barbe rase pied ferrat: Pro. *Looke* Barbe.
Ferré: m. ée: f. *Shod (as a horse with Iron;) also, couered, headed, tipped, or bound about, with Iron; also, hard, obdurate, stiffe; stubborne, obstinate.*
Ferré à glace. *Frosted, or shod with frost-nayles; hence also, steadie-footed, sure of foot, seldome slipping, neuer fayling, or falling.*
Gosier ferré à glace. *A paued mouth; See* Gosier.
Eau ferrée. *Wherein a peece of hot Iron, or Steele hath beene quenched.*
Mangeur de charrettes ferrées. *A terrible bufffnuffe, scarre-crow, braggadochio.*
Il n'y a cheval si bien ferré qui ne glisse: Prov. *The wisest erre; the best offend; he that hath surest footing sometime falls.*
Ferrement: m. *An Instrument, or toole of Iron.*
Ferrements de la Messe. *The ornaments, implements, or instruments, belonging to the Masse.*
Ferrementiporte. *A wandering Priest that euer carries about with him those ornaments, or implements; also, a carrier of tooles, or heads of speares, or blades of weapons.*
Ferrer. *To shooe a horse, &c; also, to couer, head, or bind about, with Iron.*
Ferrer vne ceincture. *To set buckles vnto a girdle.*
Ferrer les cigales. *To spend the time in trifling; to vndertake a foolish businesse; to loose time altogether.*
Ferrer la mule à. *To bring in an extraordinarie, or false reckoning vnto; any way to play the close theefe with.*
Ferrer les oyes. *as,* Ferrer les cigales.
Il est fort difficile à ferrer. *He is verie stubborne, selfewillie, vnrulie, froward; hee will hardly be tamed, hee will carrie no coales.*
Ferret: m. *The tag of a point.*
Ferreur: m. *A flax-combe, or hatchell (of Iron.)*
Ferreux: m. euse: f. *Of Iron, as hard as Iron.*
Ferriere: f. *A kind of big Dutch Leatherne bottle; also, a place to keepe Iron in; also, a powch to put horsenayles in; or, a great case, or powch of leather (closed, as a Portemantue, with chaine, and locke) wherein tooles for the shooing of horses are kept, and carried; also, a kind of Adamant.*
Ferronnerie: f. *An Iron mill, or forge; also, an Ironmongers shop.*
Ferronnier: m. *An Ironmonger; one that sels vnwrought Iron in Barres &c.*
Ferruginosité: f. *Rust of Iron.*
Ferrumination: f. *A soldering, cimenting, fastening together, properly, in matters of Iron.*
Ferrure: f. *The shooing of horses; or, as* Ferrement; *also, Iron worke.*
Fers. *Looke* Fer.
Fertile: com. *Fertile, fruitfull, abundant, full, ranke, batle, store-bringing, much-yeelding.*
Fertilement. *Fertilly, fruitfully, abundantly, rankely, plenteously.*
Fertilité: f. *Fertilitie, fruitfulnesse, ranknesse, fullnesse, fatnesse; plentie, store, abundance.*
Fertilizé: m. ée: f. *Fertilized, made fertile, or fruitfull.*
Fertilizer. *To make fruitfull, fertile, ranke, abundant; also, to increase, grow fertile, fruitfull, &c.*

Feru: m. **uë**: f. *Strucke, hurt, hit, wounded, beaten, knockt.*
Mal feru. *A malander in the bought of a horses knee.*
Nerf feru. *In a man; the disease of frenzie or madnesse; in a horse; a sinew sprung in his knee, or other ioynt.*
Ferve. par ferve. *According to, after the rate of:* ¶Bourbonnois.
Fervement. *Feruently, hotly, ardently, earnestly, eagerly, fiercely, vehemently.*
Fervent: m. **ente**: f. *Feruent, hot, ardent, scaulding, scorching, burning; chafed; eager, angrie, fierce; vehement, earnest.*
Fervesti; &, **Fervestu.** *(Old words) clad in, or armed with, yron.*
Ferveur: f. *Feruor, feruencie; heat, burning, ardor, anger, violence; hastinesse; vehemence, eagernesse, earnestnesse.*
Ferulacé. *Round; also, of the kind of th'hearbe Ferula.*
Ferule: f. *A Ferula, or Paulmer vsed in Schooles for correction; also, the hearbe Ferula, Sagapene, Fennell Giant; also, a reed, or cane.*
Ferules. *Splents for broken legs, armes, fingers, &c.*
Ferun: m. *Ranknesse, rammishnesse; extreame, or strong vnsauorinesse.*
Ferure: f. *A stroke, hit, striking, hitting.*
Feslé. *Crazed; as* Fellé.
Fesse: f. *A buttocke; a haunch; a breech, or one side of the breech.*
La fesse tonduë. *Bare-breecht; that hath not a rag to couer his taile withall.*
Commere de fesses. *A gossip for the buttockes, an arse gossip, a gossipping bawd.*
Corrumpu comme la fesse d' vn Postillon. *Seeke* Postillon.
N' y aller que d' vne fesse. *To go slackly, or vnwillingly to worke; to worke by halues.*
Il cerche trop bas la Charité qui fouille prés des fesses: Prov. *Tis an vntoward charitie thats groped for neere to the buttocks.*
Fessé: m. **ée**: f. *Breeched, scutched, jerked; whipt, or beaten on the buttocks.*
Fesseau. *as* Faisceau.
Fesse-breviaire: m. *A Priest that quickly whips ouer, or mumbles vp, his Breuiarie; any one that sayes ouer his ordinarie prayers too fast.*
Fesse-cul. *A Pedanticall whip-arse.*
Fessée: f. *A scutch on the breech, a lash on the buttocks, a ierke on the posteriorums.*
Fesse-matthieu. *An Vsurer; a Banker; a Returner, or letter out of money, vpon interest, or by exchange.*
Fesse pain. *A great eater of bread.*
Fesse pinte. *A tipler, bibber, quaffer, can-killer, potwhipper, faithfull drunkard.*
Fesser. *To breech, beat, whip, scourge, on the buttockes.*
Fesses: f. *The buttockes, the breech, the bumme; Looke* Fesse.
Fesse-tonduë. *A bawdie companion, a notable whipster; or, a knauish Epithite for a smell-smocke; Looke* Fesse; *(for it hath also another sence.)*
Fesseur. *A whipper, scourger, breecher.*
Fessier: m. **ere**: f. *Belonging to the breech, or buttocks.*
Muscles fessiers. *Three muscles in the breech, a great, middle, and little one; all which doe serue to stretch out the thigh.*
Fessiffier. *To worke, doe, or play with the buttockes; to leacher it.*
Fessu: m. **uë**: f. *Fat-bumd, well-breeched, great buttockt.*

Fest. *as* Faiste; *whence;*
Gibet à fest. *A gibet that hath a topping, or chaplet made ouer it.*
Festage. *An yearely duetie paid vnto certaine Lords for euerie roofe, ridge, or house-top within their iurisdiction, or Seigneurie; also, a feasting, or feasts due by certaine Prelates vnto their Chapters.*
Festard: m. **arde**: f. *Sluggish, drowsie, lazie; dull, slow; faint-hearted.*
Festardise: f. *Sloth, sluggishnesse, drowsinesse; also, dulnesse, slownesse; cowardise, faint-heartednesse; (bred by sloth.)*
Feste: m. *The ridge, or top of a house; Looke* Faiste.
Feste: f. *A feast; a holy-day; a festiuall day; (Looke* Fe.)
Feste à baston. *A publicke feast, wherat all the companies of an incorporate Towne goe in (a kind of) Procession.*
La feste Dieu. *Corpus Christi day.*
La feste des festes. *Palme-Sunday.*
La feste des morts *All-soules day.*
La guerre est la feste des morts: Prov. *Warre is the dead mans holy day.*
Festes au palais. *Such holy-dayes as are not Hall-dayes.*
La feste des rameaux. *Palmes-Sunday.*
La feste des Rois. *The Epiphanie, or Twelfth-day in Christmas.*
La feste du Sacré. *The Coronation day; or, the feast of the dedication of a Parish Church, &c.*
La feste de tous Saincts. *All-Saints, All-hallowmasse, All-hallow day.*
La paix est la feste de tous Saincts: Prov. *Peace is the holie mans holy-day.*
Les festes du village. *Wakes; Ales; Plough-mens feasts, or holy-dayes.*
La petite feste dieu. *Th'Octaues of, or, some eight dayes after, Corpus Christi day.*
Chanter devant la feste. *To triumph before the victorie.*
Estre bien avant de feste. *To liue merrily, or in iollitie.*
Faire feste à. *To flatter, smooth, fawne on, make fayre weather vnto.*
Faire feste de. *To ioy in, reioyce at, be glad of; to brag, boast, be proud, make much, of.*
Apres la feste & le Ieu, les pois au feu: Prov. *After feasting and iollitie, sobrietie.*
Apres la feste on grate la teste: Prov. (viz: *After a feast made.)*
Crinons en teste gastent la feste: Prov. *One humorous, or discontented guest marres a whole feast.*
Deux pots au feu signifient la feste, & deux femmes font la tempeste: Prov. *Two pots oth'fire a feast, two women a storme, portend.*
Le fol reste apres la feste: Prov. *The foole doth rest after a feast; or (more properly) after a feast once made a foole for euer.*
Les grillons gastent la feste: Prov. *See* Grillons.
Il n'est pas tousiours feste: Prov. *Feasts last not alwayes; or, we must not alwayes thinke to feast it; euerie day is not Sunday (say we.)*
Festé: m. **ée**: f. *Festiuall, kept holie; feasted.*
Fester. *To feast it; keepe holy-day, make a vacation.*
Festide. *as* Fascherie.
Festier. *as* Festoyer.
Festiere: f. *A ridge-tile; or (being turned) a gutter-tile; See* Faistiere.

Festin. *A feast, or banquet.*
Droict de festin. *Looke* Festage.
Il a esté au festin de Martin baston. *He hath had a triall in Stafford Court, or hath receiued Iacke Drums intertainment.*
Festination: f. *Festination, speed, hast, quicke proceeding.*
Festivant. *A feaster, or feast-maker.*
Feston: m. *A garland, bundle, or border of fruits, and flowers; especially in grauen, or imbossed works; also, a nosegay.*
Festondienne. *(as much as)* Par la feste de dieu; *Corruptly; or by one that dares not sweare out.*
Festoyant: m. *A feaster, or he that feasts.*
Festoyant: m. ante: f. *Feasting, banquetting; cherishing, making verie much of.*
Festoyement. *A feasting, banquetting; a cherishing, or kind intertaining of.*
Festoyer. *To feast, banquet, intertaine with feasts, and banquets; to cherish, vse kindly, make much of; also, to celebrate an holy-day.*
Festu: m. *A feskue; a straw, rush, little staulke, or sticke, vsed for a feskue.*
Foible comme vn festu. *As weake as a rush; or (as we say) water.*
Coigner festus. *To spend the time verie foolishly; or to loose it altogether.*
Ie n'en donneroye pas vn festu. *I value it not of a rush; I would not giue a straw for it.*
Rompre le festu avec. *To fall out, or at oddes with a friend.*
Profit sans vertu ne vaut vn festu: Prov. *Dishonest gaine's not worth a chip; or, no scoundrell to th' vnhonest rich man.*
Festuser. *See* Fetuser.
Fetardise: f. *Sloth; cowardise; as* Festardise.
Feteur: f. *Stinch, filthinesse, ill smell, or sauor.*
Fetide: com. *Stinking, filthie, ill-smelling.*
Fetisse. liqueurs fetisses. *Made, or compounded liquors.*
Feton. *as* Feston; *Also, the frush, or middle of the sole of a horses foot.*
Fetusé: m. ée: f. *Touched, or wiped ouer with a feskue; also, tickled by such a touching.*
Fetuser. *To touch, or wipe ouer with a feskue; also, to tickle by touching with a feskue.*
Feu: m. *Fire; also, as* Foüage; *(also, a house, or familie; in old French;) also, light.*
Le feu. *A kind of light, (neere a foot long) made of old clouts steeped in tallow, & writhen like a torch; wherwith Fowlers catch Duckes, Teales, Pochards, &c, in the night; also, a scab, tetter, or scurfe among cattle.*
Feu S. Anthoine. *Saint Anthonies fire; a swelling (full of heat and rednesse) that beginnes of a blister; and growes to a scab, or sore, like a tetter; and in the end mortifies the part (especially the bone) it hath seised on.*
Feu ardent. *(as* Coulevrée blanche.) *White Brionie, wild Nep, Tetter-berrie; The Wallons (sayes Gerard) call Garden Nightshade,* Feu ardent.
Feu de behourdis. *A bone-fire.* (v. m.)
Le feu des Espagnols. *A hot, scorching, or shining Sunne.*
Feu Gregeois. *Wild-fire; or the best kind therof; such as will burne within the water, &c.*
Feu d'Helene. *as* Feu S. Herme.
Feu S. Herme. *Saint Helens, or S. Hermes fire; a Meteor that often appeares at sea; Looke* Furole.
Feu S. Marcel; ou, feu Martial; *as* Feu S. Anthonie.
Feus missiles. *Squibs; or, any fireworkes throwne to a mischieuous end.*
Feu Persien. *An inflamed, and painfull imposthumation, the bloud or matter whereof being very thin, makes it looke almost as if it shined: some call it, the holie fire; the Grecians,* Erysipelas.
Feu de riqueraque. le mau fin feu de riqueraque. *Wild-fire; or as* Feu Persien.
Les feus du Roy. *An yearely reuenew of* ij. s. Parisis *paid vnto the King by th' inhabitants of diuers villages in the Prouostship of* Laon, *thereby exempted from certaine Appeales.*
Feu Sacré. *Looke* Sacré; *or, as* Feu Persien.
Feu sauvage. *The shingles, running-worme, or wild fire.*
Feu volage. *A ring-worme, or tetter.*
Pierre à feu. *A flint-stone; also, the Marcasite, or fire-stone.*
Attiser le feu avec l'espée. *To prouoke an angrie, or angred person.*
Avoir le feu à la teste. *To be hot, hastie, cholericke; fierce, furious; also, to be forward, hazardous, aduentureus.*
Avoir les pieds au feu. Il semble qu'il ait les pieds au feu. *Said of one that in a restlesse humor, will not settle, or cannot sit still, any where.*
Iecter le feu par la gorge. *To spit fire; to be in a great furie, fume, chafe; or, to keepe a terrible swaggering, a horrible stirre.*
Ie n'iroye pas du banc au feu. *I would not step ouer the doore, I would not moue one foot, for it.*
I'en mettray le doigt au feu. *I dare answer for, I may presume on, I am assured of, it.*
Verser de l'huyle sur le feu. *To adde fuell to the fire, say we (better acquainted with wood then with oyle) to furnish a violent passion, or humor with matter to work on.*
Vivre à pot, & à feu avec. *See* Pot.
Le feu est bon en tout temps: Prov. *(Belike it should be,* le bon feu; *for fire sometimes does mischiefe too much.)*
Le feu est demie vie de l'homme: Pro. *(And worth his whole life vnto him; for without it either he cannot liue, or shall doe verie little.)*
Le feu plus couvert est le plus ardant: Prov. *The more that fire's kept downe the more it burns; suppressed heat workes vehemently.*
Il n'est feu que de gros bois: Pro. *Great wood makes the best fire.*
Amour de putain feu d'estoupe: Prov. *(Th' exposition is)* qui luit fort, & dure peu.
En petite cheminée fait on bien grand feu: Prov. *Men sometimes make great fires in little chimneyes (to their cost.)*
Qui a affaire de feu le doit cercher: &, Qui a besoing de feu le cerche avec le doigt: Prov. *He that wants necessaries must take any paines for them.*
Tortuë busche fait droict feu: Prov. *The crooked log makes a straight fire.*
Verde busche fait chaud feu: Prov. *Looke* Busche.
Feu: m. feuë: f. *Dead, deceased, departed.*
Feu mon pere. *My late father.*
Feüaige: m. *as* Foüage.
Feuchere. *as* Feuchiere.
Feuchiere: f. *Fearne, brakes.*
Feuchiere aquatique. *Water Fearne, Osmund, Osmund*

mund royall, Osmund the Waterman, S. Christophers hearbe.
Feuchiere des chesnes. *Oake-fearne, pettie fearne, mosse-fearne, pild Osmund.*
Feuchiere femelle. *She fearne, female fearne, common fearne, brakes.*
Feuchiere masle. *Male fearne, great fearne.*
Feudal: m. ale: f. *Of, or belonging to, a* Fief, *Mannor, Fee, or Fee simple; also, held in* fief, *or in fee; also, holding diuers* Fiefs.
Cour feudale. *A Court Leet, or Baron; the Lords Court, whereto his vassalls, and tenants owe suit and seruice.*
Homme feudal. *(Signifies both) a Lord that hath tenants holding of him; and (the more commonly) a vassall, or tenant.*
Retraict feudal. *The power of redemption which a Landlord hath by the priuiledge of his Seigneurie.*
Seigneur feudal. *A Lord Paramount, or chiefe Lord.*
Fief de condition feudale. *A Fee simple; or, an absolute, and hereditarie* fief; *(for some fiefs descend not.)*
Feudalité: f. *as* Feodalité; *Especially in the last sence.*
Feudataire: com. *Owing fealtie, holding by fealtie; also, held by fealtie, or, held of another.*
Feve. *as* Febue; *A beane.*
Feverondes: f. *The eaues, or casings of a house.*
Feugiere. *Fearne.*
Feugiere de chesnes. *The hearbe Oake-fearne, pettie fearne, pild Osmund.*
Feuille; &, Feuillée. *See* Fueille; &, Fueillée.
Feuillure. *Seeke* Fueillure.
Feultre: m. *Felt; a felt, a peece of felt; Looke* Feutre.
Feultré: m. ée: f. *Made of felt; couered with, or, as with, felt.*
Feultrer. *To make of, couer with, felt.*
Feulu. *as* Fueillu.
Feur: m. *The cost and charge a husbandman is at in the tilling, & reaping of his ground; also, as* Foire; *a Faire; also, a rate, or price set on a thing; and hence;*
'A feur de. *According to, after the rate or proportion of.*
Au feur l'emplage. *The same.*
Si boute tel feur telle vente. *Looke* Bouter.
Fevre: m. *A Blacksmith; Looke* Febvre.
Fevrier: m. *(The Moneth) Februarie.*
La farine de Fevrier. *Snow.*
Fevrier le court pire de tous: Pro. *Because it is commonly the foulest; and thereupon wee call it, Filldike.*
Aujourd'huy Fevrier demain Chandelier: Prov. *Looke* Chandelier.
Pluye de Fevrier vaut esgout de fumier: Prov. *We say, Aprill showres bring in May flowers.*
Toute Chatte a son Fevrier: Prov. *Euerie dog hath his day (say we) or (more properly) euerie woman hath her wanton fit.*
Feurmariage. *as* Formariage: ¶Bourgognois.
Feurolles. *Night-fires; Looke* Furole.
Feurre. *as* Foarre; *Straw.*
Vn Seigneur de feurre combat bien vn vassal d'acier; *Looke* Seigneur.
Feurs. *The Plurall vnto* Feur; *onely in the two first sences.*
Feustre. *as* Feultre; *Or the thicke, hairen, and felt-like stuffe, vsed by Sadlers for stuffing, or in stiffenings.*

Feutraict. *A man drawne out of his countrey, bounds, or borders; also, wine, corne, or such commodities taken thence.*
Feutre: m. *Felt; also, a filter; a peece of felt, or thicke woollen cloth to distill, or straine things through.*
Feutré: m. ée: f. *Wrought thicke, as felt; also, stuffed, or stiffened, with felt.*
Feutré d'herbe. *Set thicke, or ouergrowne, with grasse.*
Feyturage: m. *A charme, or inchauntment.*
Fez. *as* Faix; *A burden.*
Fi. *(An Interiection;)* et fi fi va t'en d'icy; *Fie vpon thee, get thee hence, I cannot abide thee; Looke* Fy.
Maistre fi fi. *A Gold-finder, Dung-farmer, cleanser of iakes, feyer of priuies.*
Fiable: com. *as* Feable; *Trustie; or credulous, that easily trusteth.*
Fiacre. *The name of a Saint.*
Fic, &, Fil S. Fiacre. *Looke* Fic, &, Fil.
Mal S. Fiacre. *A kind of scab, or great wart in the fundament; or in a womans priuities.*
Fiançailles: f. *A publicke betrothing of a couple before their full mariage; (and sometimes) also, mariage it selfe; whence;*
Fiançailles chevauchent en selle, & repentailles en croupe: Prov. *Repentance sits full close (or dwells next doore) to mariage.*
Fiance: f. *Trust, credit, affiance, assurance, confidence.*
'A ma fiance. *Vpon my word.*
Fiancé: m. ée: f. *Affianced, betrothed, handfast, promised, sure vnto.*
Fiancé à la corde. *Condemmed, or destined, vnto the gallowes; for whom the gallowes grone.*
Fiancer. *To affiance, betroth, promise, make fast, assure, vnto.*
Fiansailles: f. *A publicke betrothing of man and woman before full mariage; Looke* Fiançailles.
se Fiant. *Trusting, beleeuing, hoping on, or in; intrusting vnto, committing to the trust of.*
Fiat: m. *Trust, assurance, affiance.*
Fibres: f. *The small strings, or haire-like threads of roots; also, the fibers, threads, or strings of muscles, & veines; in Lincolne-shire they are tearmed Cheyres.*
Fibreux: m. euse: f. *Fibrous; full of haire-like threads, or strings.*
Fic: m. *A certaine scab, or hard, round, and red sore, in the fundament, called also,* Fic S. Fiacre.
Ficelle: f. *Packthread.*
Fiche: f. *A Gardeners dible, or setting yron.*
Par ma fiche. *By my fey.*
Planter à la fiche. *See* Planter.
Fiché: m. ée: f. *Fixed, fastened, setled; thrust, planted, set farre in, firme, steadie, sure, sticking fast in; also, decreed, established, resolued on.*
Croix fichée. *A crosse Fitchet (in Herauldrie.)*
Fichemént: m. *A fixing, fastening, setting, setling.*
Fichément. *Fixedly; setledly.*
Fiche pain. *The vermine called an Eare-wig; some also call so the Wood-louse.*
Ficher. *To fix, fasten, settle; to driue, sticke, set, thrust, plant fast, or farre in.*
Fichet. arbre de fichet. *A tree that is come of a twig, or tender scion planted.*
Ficheur: m. *A fixer, fastener, setler, or setter in.*
Ficheure: f. *A fixing, fastening, driuing, sticking, planting, setting, thrusting farre in.*
Fichu: m. ue: f. *as* Saugreru; *Or absurd.*
Ficotte. par ma ficotte. *A diminutiue of,* ma foy, *or* ma

ma fique; *as we say, by my feckins.*
Ficte. *A little Shad-fish.*
Fictil: m. ile: f. *Earthen, or, made of earth.*
Fiction: f. *A fiction, inuention, lie, fib, cog; a thing imagined, fained, or foisted in.*
Dire sans fiction. *To speake sincerely, confesse plainly, professe from the heart.*
Fidei-commis: m. *A Feoffement in trust.*
Fideiusseur: m. *A suretie, pledge, caution.*
Fidele: com. *Faithfull, trustie, loyall, true, sure of his word, or to his side; also, religious.*
Fidelement. *Faithfully, loyally, trustily; vnfainedly, truely, surely; religiously.*
Fidelité: f. *Fidelitie, faithfulnesse, loyaltie, trustinesse; truth, sinceritie, vnfainednesse.*
Serment de fidelité. *Th'oath of fidelitie made by all Prelates vnto the King, at their inuesture, in acknowledgement of his Soueraignetie, and of th'obedience, and fidelitie which they owe him; This, although they hold no fiefs in right of their Prelacies; for if they doe, they also doe both homage, and fealtie for them.*
Fidelium. *The last prayer thats said for the dead.*
Il passe plusieurs choses par vn fidelium. *He huddles, or shuffles vp many things vnder one; he sleightly dispatches, runnes, or goes ouer the matters committed vnto him.*
Fidicule: f. *The Harpe of heauen; a companie of starres which resemble a Harpe.*
Fiduciale. *Part of an Astrolabe turning round about the border, or edge thereof; th'Index, or hand of an Astrolabe.*
Fié: m. ée: f. *Trusted, beleeued, hoped on or in; also, intrusted, trusted with, committed vnto the trust of.*
Fiebvre: f. *A feauer;* Looke Fievre.
Fiebvrette: f. *A sleight ague.*
Fiebvreux: m. euse: f. *Full or sicke of, subiect vnto, a feauer; also, feauer-breeding, ague-bringing.*
Fied. *as* Fief: ¶Bourgognois.
Fief: m. *A Fief; a (Knights) fee; a Mannor, or inheritance held by homage, and fealtie; and giuen at the first, in trust, and vpon promise of assistance, or seruice in the warres: (A learned Frenchman defines it,* L'heritage tenu à foy & hommage, baillé à aucun pour la fiance qu'on a cuë en luy: *Another;* La terre concedée à cause de confiance, ou foy promise par le preneur d'icelle, d'assister son Seigneur en guerre: *which both together make good my definition:) Also, a tenure, or estate in* fief, *or in fee. This word was first heard of after the conquest of* Gallia *by the* Francs *(or auncient French men) when their Soueraigne Princes, reseruing some land for their owne Demaines, distributed the rest (by whole countries, or large territories) among their Captaines, and principall followers, on condition, that they should hold of them, and aid them in their warres; In which distribution respect was also had of, and prouision made for, th'inferiour French souldiours (whereof the more, or fewer those Captaines had vnder them, the greater, or lesse were their portions) whereupon the Captaines, hauing (as formerly their Princes) reserued somewhat for their particular demaines, they diuided the best part of the rest among them, to be held of themselues by the same tenure, and on the same condition, that they held the whole of the King: (Hence came th'*Arriere fiefs:) *Th'other part they shared among the naturall inhabitants of the countrey, on much baser conditions (expressed in the word* Cens:) *In those times all* Fiefs *were determined by the death of the feoffees, and reuocable at the will of the feoffor: But not long after they became (as the most of them are now) patrimoniall, or hereditarie.*
Fief abregé. *A* fief *abridged, restrained, or not noble; a* fief *that wants, and is not capable of, iurisdiction; a tenure in* Censiue; *or in Socage.*
Fief ample. *A full, or whole* fief, *or Knights fee; for which the Lord of whom tis held hath the tenants best horse (or if he had none 60.s.*Tour.) *and part of his armor, for a Heriot.*
Fief de Basoche. *Looke* Basoche.
Fief boursal. *The* fief, *or portion of a* fief, *that belongs to a younger brother.*
Fief en chef; &, fief chevel. *A Noble* fief; *an inheritance held in* Capite, *and hauing iurisdiction.*
Fief de condition feudale. *An absolute fee simple, or hereditarie* fief; *(for some* fiefs *descend not; say the Feudists.)*
Fief de danger. *Such a* fief *as is forfeited vnto the Lord of whom tis held, if it be entred into by the tenant (vnder any title other then of lineall discent) before homage and fealtie done, or at the least, offered.*
Fief de dignité. *A Noble* fief; *such a one as hath some title of dignitie (as a Countie, Vicountie, Baronnie, or or Chastellenie) annexed vnto it; a* fief *that dignifieth (a gentleman; for a* Roturier, *vnlesse he haue it by lineall discent from his grandfather, or be withall ennobled by the King, receiues no manner of dignitie by it.)*
Fief dominant. *A* fief, *or Mannor belonging to a Lo. Paramount; a* fief *held in chiefe, and whereof many others hold.*
Fief d'Hauber, ou d'Haubert. *Any* fief, *or inheritance, whose owner is bound to serue in the Kings wars with an Haubergeon, or coat of maile; (whereto one addes, a horse, a sword, a shield, and an helmet.)*
Fief liege, ou lige, ou tenu en plein lige; *as* Fief ample; *Held directly, and without mesne, of the Crowne.*
Fief mort. *An inheritance that yeelds the Lord no manner of profit other then a bare rent; and therefore may bee tearmed, a* Fief sec.
Fief noble. *A Noble* fief, *or Manor; the marks whereof be, Antiquitie, Iurisdiction,* Censiue, *a dependancie of diuers inferiour* fiefs; *and (onely in some places) a faire house with ditches, or a mote round about it; but the most certaine marke of it (for the King may at any time erect a Noble* fief; *and the Iurisdiction, a thing seuerall, may be diuided from it) is, that it be held either of the Crowne, or of some other* fief *thats held immediately thereof.*
Fief ouvert. *Is when no vassall, or tenant presents himselfe to do the seruices, and pay the rights which be due vnto the Lord thereof; or when by the change of the tenant (by death, or otherwise) the Lord wants those rights, and seruices.*
Fief Patrimonial. *See* Patrimonial.
Fief en Regale. *A Noble* fief, *held immediately, and in* Capite *of the King; or, as* Fief de Dignité.
Fief restrainct. *as* Fief abregé.
Fief de revenuë. *A fee; a rent charge, or annuitie in fee, out of land.*
Fief rural. *Is (by the Customes of* Nevers) *a* fief *that wants Iurisdiction, a moted house, and all other such markes of Nobilitie, and antiquitie.*
Fief servant. *A mesne, or inferiour* fief; *a* fief *that holds of a* fief Dominant.
Fief vif. *In opposition to* Fief mort; *that yeelds the Lord no more profit then a bare rent.*

Francs fiefs. *Free, or affranchising* fiefs; *or as in* Franc.
Menu fief. *An inferior* fief, *of small value, and altogether without iurisdiction; opposed vnto;*
Plein fief. *A full, or whole* fief; *an intire Knights fee; of iurisdiction, and good worth.*
Clerc des fiefs. *Looke* Clerc.
Entrer de fief servi. *The homage, &c, due by a vassall at his first entrie, done well-ynough by another; as by th'eldest brother for the yonger, by a husband for his wife, &c; and thereby the Lords entrie preuented.*
Hommes de fief. *Freeholders; or Lords of (inferior)* fiefs, *bound to assist the* Bailli *of the Iurisdiction in the Courts he keepes, and answerable, or finable, for all wrongfull iudgements giuen therein.*
Sergent du fief. *Looke* Sergent.
De son domaine faire son fief. *A vassall to alien part of his* fief, *and thereof create a new tenure, or cause it to be held of him by a mesne tenure.*
De son fief faire son domaine. *To reunite vnto his demaine a* fief *that held of him.*
Exploicter le fief à pure perte. *To make a full, or absolute seisure of the inheritance forfeited vnto him.*
Relever vn fief. *Seeke* Relever.
Tenir fief. *To enioy an inheritance feodall; to be seised of land in his demesne as of fee.*
Tenir en fief. *To be seised of a right, or priuiledge, in fee, or in the qualitie of a* fief.
Qui fief nie fief perd. *He that denies his tenure, forfeits his estate.*
Fieffal: m. ale: f. *Feoffall; of a* fief; *in fee, held in fee; Looke* Iurisdiction.
Fieffe: f. *as* Fief: ¶Norm.
Fieffé: m. ée: f. *Infeoffed; giuen, or granted in fee; held as a* fief, *or in fee.*
Domaine fieffé (ou non fieffé.) *A Noble inheritance held by homage and fealtie; (or an vnnoble one for which no homage is due:)* ¶Norm.
Goutteux fieffez. *A fit Epithite; for the gowt, most commonly, descends, which way soeuer the land goes.*
Heritiers fieffez. *Whom the Lord puts in possession; or to whom he makes liuery and seisin, of th'inheritance belonging to them.*
Sergent fieffé. *Looke* Sergent.
Fiefter. *To infeoffe; to grant, passe, alien, a* fief, *or an inheritance in fee.*
Fiefferme. *A fee farme.*
Fieffvé; &, Fiefvé. *as* Fieffé.
Fiefvement: m. *A feoffement, or an infeoffing.*
Fiel: m. *Gall; or, the Gall.*
Fiel de terre. *The hearb Earthgall, Feuerwort, small Centorie, common Centorie, Centorie the lesse.*
Pierre de fiel. *Seeke* Pierre.
Fieller. *To make bitter.*
Fielleux: m. euse: f. *As bitter as gall; full of bitternesse, or of gall.*
Fiens: m. *Dung, ordure; mucke, manure.*
Fiens de chien, & marc d'argent seront tout vn au iour de Iugement: Prov. *All will be one at the later day, say we.*
Fiente: f. *Dung, turd, filth, ordure, excrements of man, or beast; especially of vermine, as Foxes, Badgers, &c.*
Fienté: m. ée: f. *Dunged; fed or filled, couered or compassed, manured or mingled, with dung; also, shitten, or beshit.*
Fienter. *To dung, shite, scumber; also, to fill, feed, couer, compasse, mingle, or manure, with dung.*
Fienteux: m. euse: f. *Full of dung, turds, ordure.*
Fientifié: m. ée: f. *Beshitten, berayed, beturded.*
Fier: m. ere: f. *(of one sillable) Proud, arrogant, insolent, scornefull, disdainfull, high-minded; also, fierce, eager, bloudie, cruell, sauage, vnmercifull, inhumane; also, bold, stout, confident, couragious, audacious.*
Il en est fier comme vn asne d'vn bast neuf. *He is as proud of it as an Asse of a new packesaddle (which if he were not an Asse he wou'd not be proud of.)*
Femme fiere en toute saison, veut estre maistre de sa maison: Prov. *Looke* Femme.
se Fier. *(of two sillables) To trust, or intrust vnto; to beleeue or haue affiance, to put his hope or confidence, in.*
De qui ie me fie dieu me garde: Pro. *God preserue me from him whom I trust.*
Fierement. *Proudly, insolently, hautily, arrogantly; fiercely, cruelly, sauagely, inhumanely, vnmercifully; also, boldly, stoutly, audaciously.*
Fieret: m. ette: f. *Somewhat loftie; a little fierce.*
Fiereté: f. *Pride, insolencie, statelinesse, arrogancie, surlinesse, disdaine, scornefulnesse; crueltie, fiercenesse, inhumanitie; also, boldnesse, audacitie, stoutnesse, mettall, spirit.*
Fierettement. *Somewhat hautily, insolently, arrogantly; a little fiercely, sauagely, cruelly.*
Fier-humble. *Stoutly-humble; a stout heart humbled.*
Fiert. *A Verb Impersonall;* Cecy fiert à. *This is like vnto, or, agrees well with.*
Fierté. *as* Fiereté.
Fierte: f. *A shrine, or coffin wherein the bones of Saints are inclosed.*
Fieul. *as* Filz; *A sonne:* ¶Pic.
Fievre: f. *An ague, a feauer.*
Fievre ardente. *A burning feauer.*
Fievres blanches. *The agues wherwith maidens that haue the greene sicknesse are troubled; and hence;*
Il a les fievres blanches. *Either he is in loue, or sicke of wantonnesse.*
Fievre continuë. *See* Continu.
Fievre de Dol. *The French pockes.*
Fievre intermittente. *Any ague that comes and goes by fits.*
Fievre de veau. (qui tremble quand il est saoul.) *Trembling after meat; sicknesse vpon surfetting.*
De fievre en chaud mal. *From ill to worse, out of the frying-pan into the fire.*
Tes fortes fievres. *A pestilence take thee, a plague choake thee.*
Fifre: m. *A Fife; a Flute, or little pipe accorded with a Drumme, or Taber.*
Figé: m. ée: f. *Fixed, setled, fastened; compacted, closed together.*
Laict figé. *Milke thickened, or curded, as with the runnet.*
Sang figé. *Bloud clotted, or cluttered together, as when it is cold.*
Figement: m. *A fixing, fastening, closing; (and hence) also, a thickning, curding, or curdling.*
Figer. *To fix, fasten, setle, close, or compact together.*
Se figer. *To thicken, curd, clutter, curdle, coagulate.*
Figon: m. *A louer, or ordinarie eater, of figs.*
Figue: f. *A fig; also, the disease in a horses hoofe, called, the fig.*
Figue de Caresme. *A drie fig, a Lenten fig.*
Figue folle. *The fruit of th'outlandish Siccamore, or Mulberrie-fig tree; it resembles the wild fig, but is, withall, the sweeter of the two, and without seeds: It* ri-

ripens not (especially if the tree be ouerladen) vntill it be scraped with an yron hooke: Also, a fig date; or any fig that opens of it selfe, and discouers it seeds, as it growes.

Figues primerouges. *The first figs that come vpon the tree; starueling-figs.*

Figue royalle. *A Date.*

Ces figues sont trop hautes. *These dainties are aboue our reach; they cost too much, they grow too deere.*

Il n' est ny figue ny raisin. *He is neither fish nor flesh; hot nor cold; there is nothing in him.*

Moitié figues moitié raisins. *Betweene ieast and earnest; or, halfe th'one halfe th'other.*

Figueraye: f. *An Orchard of fig trees.*

Figuerie: f. *as* Figuiére.

Figuier: m. *A fig tree.*

Figuiére: f. *A fig-yard; an Orchard of fig trees.*

Figuratif: m. iue: f. *Figuratiue, spoken by a figure.*

Figure: f. *A figure, shape, image, forme: fauor, likenesse; resemblance, representation, counterfeit; fashion, making of; also, a figure, or flourish of Rhetoricke.*

Figure accordée. *An exact suruey of land in controuersie, drawne by the consent of both parties.*

Veuë figure. *A description, of a place by the eye; or of a place which is present, and in th'eye.*

Figuré: m. ée: f. *Figured, fashioned, delineated, painted, represented, purtrayed; also, figuratiue, in figures, by a figure.*

Velours figuré. *Looke* Velours.

Figurement: m. *A figuring, shaping, forming, delineating, representing, pourtraying.*

Figurer. *To figure, paint, picture, draw, delineate, pourtray, represent; to forme, shape, fashion; imagine, conceiue.*

Figurine: f. *A prettie little image, picture, counterfeit, figure.*

Fil: m. *Thread; also, a thread, line, or string; also, a streak, small dash, or stroke; also, a file, rank, order, course, row, ray; also, an infection, or imperfection in trees, whereby their barkes come to be gnawen, and eaten into.*

Fil d' archal. *(Great) yellow wire, made of copper, or latten.*

Fil de caret. *Packthread.*

Fil d' eau. à fil d' eau. *With the streame.*

Fil d' entendement. *Sharpnesse of wit, nimblenesse of apprehension, quicknesse of conceit.*

Fil d' vn espée. *The edge of a sword; Looke* Passer.

Fil d' Espinay. *A kind of loosse-twisted, and (somewhat) course thread; made at* Espinay, *a towne in* Artois.

Fil. S. Fiacre. *A great wart, hard swelling, or excrescence of flesh.*

Fil de Florence. *A fine, & hard-twisted thread, made in* Florence.

Fil d' or traict. *The smallest gold wire.*

Fil perlé. *Looke* Perlé.

De fil en aiguille. *From point to point, from one end to the other, all wholly ouer.*

De droict fil. *Directly on, straight forward, with the thread, as euen as a thread.*

Donner de droict fil. *To hit iust; to passe right on.*

Tout d' vn fil. *Wholly, altogether, without stop, or intermission.*

Bailler le fil. *To cog, foist, sooth, flatter, smooth, deceiue, gull, gloze with.*

Bailler le fil à. *To set an edge on.*

Cousu de fil blanc. *Manifest, euident, apparent.*

Fourni de fil & d' aiguille. *Furnished with necessaries, readie for all essayes.*

`A toile ourdie dieu mande le fil: Prov. *The worke thats well begunne God helpes to end; or, beginne thy worke, and God will helpe to end it. (Some expound it more prophanely.)*

Filace: f. *Fine flexe, dressed flaxe, flaxe made readie for the distaffe; Looke* Fillasse.

Filacier: m. ere: f. *Fit, readie, or easie to be spunne.*

Filamens: m. *Filaments; little strings, threads, or hairs, in veines, plants, roots &c; the beard of a root.*

Filamenteux: m. euse: f. *Full of those strings, &c.*

Filandier. *A man that spinnes.*

Filandiere: f. *A Spinster; a Flaxe-woman; also, a kind of small boat.*

Filandré: m. ée: f. *Streaked with, or full of, small threads, fibers; filanders.*

Filandrerie: f. *Spinstrie, spinning.*

Filandres: f. *The felanders; small wormes that breed in bruised, surfeited, or foule-fed, hawkes; also, nets to catch wild beasts with.*

Filant. *Twisting, or spinning.*

Filant les moustaches. *Twirling, twining, or often stroking, his mustachoes.*

Filat: m. *Congar; so tearmed about* Marseilles.

Filé: m. *A net to catch wild beasts, or fishes with; a toile, hay, drag-net, &c; also, a snare, snarle, ginne.*

File: f. *A file, ranke, direct, and euen row of.*

`A la file. *One after another, one by one, in due course, all on a row.*

Filé: m. ée: f. *Twisted, spunne, drawne out; made into thread.*

Filée: f. *The Eagle tearmed, a Bone-breaker.*

File-habits. *Clothes-spinning.*

Filer. *To twist, spin, draw out threads; also, to linger, delay; prolong, extend in length; also (among Mariners) to loosen, vndoe, and make vp.*

Filer doux. *To speak smooth, flatter, or giue faire words; also, to heare much and say little.*

Filer gros. Ils filent bien gros. *They worke rudely, deale grosly, proceed sottishly.*

Filer prim. *To runne thinne, or by little and little.*

Filer de la soye. *To take a purse; to rob by the highway side.*

Faire filer quelque chose. *To draw a thing out in length, to make it goe a great way.*

Au temps passé Berthe filoit: Prov. *In old time the greatest women were the greatest huswiues; Looke* Berthe.

Dame qui trop se mire peu file: Prov. *Seeke* Dame.

Femme qui enuis file porte chemise vile: Pro. *Beggerie, and sluttishnesse are the fruits of ill huswiferie, and of lazinesse.*

Fileret. *as* Filleret.

Filerie: f. *A spinning; or, spinstrie; also, a friendly meeting betweene the young men, and maids of a countrey towne; where they play at many sorts of (actiue) games, while these both spinne, and looke on.*

Filet: m. *A little thread, string, or twist; also, as* Filé; *also, the fillet of a beast; also, a horses watering bit.*

Filet carré. *A small square part, or member of a piller; &c; a square fillet.*

Filet d' huyle. *A small drop, or threading of oyle.*

Les Filets d' vn mords. *as* Bracelets.

Avoir le filet. *To be tongue-tied.*

Fretaillé de filets. *Looke* Fretaillé.

Filette: f. *Yarne.*

Fileul: m. *A Godsonne.*

Fileure: f. *Thread spunne; or, the spinning thereof.*

Fil-gros. *Shoomakers thread.*

Filiastre: m. *A sonne in law, step-sonne, sonne by a former marriage.*

Filiation: f. *The being a sonne; the estate of a sonne.*

Filiére: f. *A cryance; or a long thread tyed to the lunes of an Hagard, or young Hawke, when she is taught to come vnto the fist, or lure; also, a net; also, a ranke, file, row; also, a Lyon-peece, or Ridge-peece, of timber; a side-wauer.*

Filipende. *as* Filipendule.

Filipendule: f. *Filipendula, Dropwort, red Saxifrage.*

Fillains: m. *The tackling of a ship; small tackle.*

Fillandrerie. *See* Filandrerie.

Fillasse: f. *as* Filace.

La fillasse de nostre Dame. *The small, and slender strings of a Cobweb.*

Fillastre: m. *A sonne in law, or step-sonne.*

Fille: f. *A daughter; also, a maid; girle, modder, lasse, wench.*

Fille de France. *A daughter of France, the French Kings daughter.*

Fille de ioye. *A whore, punke, harlot, queane, strumpet, cockatrice, common hackney, pleasant sinner.*

Filles penitentes. *as* Filles Repenties.

Fille perduë. *A desperate filth, gracelesse flurt; or, as* Fille de ioye.

Filles repenties. *An Order of Nunnes, which haue beene profest whores; Conuertists.*

Belle fille. *A step-daughter; daughter by a former marriage, daughter in law.*

Les sept filles de la Preuosté de Paris. *Seuen Bayliwikes, or Towne-ships, which belong, and are subiect, vnto the Chastelet of Paris;* viz. Poissy, S. Germain en Laye, Tornan & Torcy en Brie, Corbeil, Monlehery, & Gonnesse en France.

D'une fille deux gendres. *A seuerall commoditie, or hire, drawne from seuerall parts, or parties, for the vse of one thing.*

Se fier en vne fille? Allez vous y frotter. *Looke* Frotter.

Fille aimant silence est douée de grand science: Pro. *The loue of silence in a maid's great science.*

Fille brunette est de nature gaye, & nette: Prov. *The nut-browne lasse for mirth and neatnesse doth surpasse.*

Fille fenestriere, & trotiere rarement bonne mesnagere: Pro. *A gazing, and gadding maid seld proues good houswife.*

Fille honneste, & moriginée, est assez riche, & bien dotée: Pro. *An honest maid of mannerlie behauiour, hath wealth ynough for any man to haue her.*

Fille oiseuse rarement vertuëuse: Prov. *An idle maid is rarelie vertuous; or, a maid that does nought learnes to doe naught.*

Fille oisive à mal pensive: Pro. *The sloathfull maid still thinks of sinne; a maiden sit-still thinks on ill.*

Fille qui donne s'abandonne: Pro. *A maid that giues is easily gotten.*

Fille qui prend elle se rend: Pro. *A maid that takes (much) is as good as taken.*

Fille trop veuë, Robbe trop vestuë, n'est pas chere tenuë: Prov. *A maid oft seene, gowne too oft worne, are disesteem'd, and held in scorne.*

Mauvaise fille se mocque de sa mere: Prov. *So does the filthie bird beray her neast.*

Les sottes filles à marier sont fascheux troupeaux à garder: Prov. *Wenches fond of mariage are troublesome cattell to keepe.*

Quand la fille pese vn auque on luy peut mettre la cauque: Prov. *See* Cauque.

Autant se prise beau varlet que belle fille: Prov. *A faire lad thinkes himselfe good ynough for any lasse, or thinkes as well of himselfe as any lasse; a Jack's at all times worthie of a Gill.*

Entre promettre, & donner se doit la fille marier: Pro. *See* Promettre.

La Goutte en la hanche la fille en la pance: Prov. *The Gout in the hanch, a girle in the panch;* viz: *If a woman feele often paine in her backe, flanke, hips, legs, & knuckles, tis a signe that she is withchild of a girle.*

Mere piteuse fait sa fille roigneuse: Prov. *A gentle mother breeds a scuruie daughter.*

Fille-femme. *A crackt peece, one that hath got a clap; one that goes for a maid, (but is none.)*

Filleret: m. ette: f. *Maidenlie, white-liuered, effeminate.*

Fillerie. *as* Filerie.

Fillet. *A watering bit for a horse; or, as* Filet.

Fillette: f. *A girle, yong maid, little wench; also, a firkin, barriquet, small wine vessell.*

Fillette de Bourgongne. *The halfe of a* Muid; *holds nine* Stiers, *and the* Stier *eight (French) pintes.*

Filleul: m. *A god-sonne.*

Filleule: f. *A god-daughter.*

Filliastre. *as* Fillastre.

Filliere. *as* Filiere.

Filloche: f. *A little thread.*

Fillol: m. *as* Filleul; *A god-sonne.*

Fillole: f. *A buddie knob in a vine, like a wart.*

Fillot: m. *A god-sonne.*

Filoire: f. *A spinster.*

Filon. *A veine of mettall in a mine.*

Filoselle: f. *Ferret-silke, or flurt-silke; and the stuffe Filozella, being all, or the better halfe, of ferret-silke.*

Fils: m. *A sonne; a boy; a man-child.*

Fils de putain. *A whoore-sonne; a bastard; Looke* Putain.

Beau fils. *A step sonne; or sonne by a former mariage.*

'A pere amasseur fils gaspilleur: Prov. *See* Pere.

Filtration: f. *A straining, distilling, or passing of simples, &c, through a felt.*

Filtré: m. ée: f. *Strained, distilled, or passed, through a felt.*

Filtrer. *To straine, distill, or passe, through a felt.*

Fimport: m. *A forme of, or, course in, Law, binding a plaintife to fetch in, & make ioyne in suit with him, all such as can pretend any right, interest, or portion in the thing which he meanes to recouer: (By the customes of Britaine.)*

Fimporter. *A plaintife to fetch in, and make ioyne in suit with him, all such, as pretend any right, interest, or portion in the thing he meanes to sue for.*

Fin: m. le fin de l'essay de monnoye. *The remainder, ouerplus, or surplusage thereof.*

Fin: f. *A fine, end, issue, conclusion, successe; also, a finishing, ceasing, ending; also, a seame, or veine, in a quarrey of stone; also, a barre, exclusion, refusall, or exception, vrged, or pleaded in issue; & sometimes th'issue it selfe.*

Fins de non proceder. *Are no better then dilatorie pleas; as an exception, against the iurisdiction of the Court, or by reason of the qualitie of the person vnfit to be impleaded therein, &c.*

Fins de non recevoir. *Looke* Recevoir.

Fin de terre. *A Promontorie in Britaine, so tearmed, because it is one of th'ends of France.*

Bonne fin. faire bonne fin. *To thriue, cheeue, increase, or prosper well.*

Faucon de bonne fin. *A well-liking, or well-prouing hawke.*

`A toutes fins. *Of force, of necessitie, howsoeuer wee come by it, by hooke, or crooke, by any meanes whatsoeuer.*

La fin fait tout: Prov. *The end does all in all.*

`A la fin sçaura on qui a mangé le lard: Prov. *The theefe will be at length discouered (howsoeuer he conceale, or, how cunningly soeuer he carrie, himselfe.)*

Telle vie telle fin: Prov. *Such as his life such was his end.*

Fin: m. fine: f. *Wittie, craftie, subtile, cunning, wilie, fraudulent, cautelous, beguiling; also, fine, small, prettie, curious; perfect, exact, pure, exceeding good, of the verie best; also, most, very vtmost.*

Anguille fine. *The female Eele; called so in Languedoc.*

Fin à dorer. *A notable imposter, cheater, cousener, coniecatcher.*

Fin comme vne mouche. *As craftie as a fox; and;* Vne fine mouche. *A subtile fox, or peece of flesh.*

Le mau fin feu de riqueraque; *Looke* Feu.

Du fin fond. *Out of th'vtmost depth, or bottome, from the verie middest of.*

Par le fin faiste. *Strictly, straitly, exactly, by line and leuell, to a haire, or to th'vtmost, in all extremitie.*

Pour le fin moins. *At the least.*

Chargé de la plus fine. *Thats paied soundly, powdered throughly, that hath his load of the most delicate pockes; also, as in* Chargé.

Faire le fin. *To be squeamish, make it daintie, seeme strange, refuse an offer (cunningly, and with a hope to be the more inuited.)*

Mais à fin contre fin. *But craft met with cunning, or, two craftie knaues were therein verie well met.*

Fin contre fin n'est bon à faire de doubleure: Pro. *Craft in both parties hinders all attonement.*

Fin. Adverb. *and hence.*

Fin à tel jour. *Vntill such a day; and;* fin que; *vntill that, whilest that.*

Fin de conte. *Finally, to conclude, to be briefe, to make short, to make hast.*

Fin de propos, il disoit, que. *The last he said was, or in the end he said, that; or (as in* Fin de Conte*) to make an end; he said, that.*

Pour le fin moins. *At the least.*

Tout fin *Euen now, straight; hard by; also, wholly.*

Tout fin à Noel. *Verie neere to Christmas, when it was almost christmas.*

Tout fin mere nu. *All discouered, starke-bellie naked; as naked as my naile.*

Finablement. *as* Finalement.

Finage: m. *All the small cordage in a ship; tackling.*

Finages: m. *Th'vtmost limits or liberties, the furthest bounds or borders, of a countrey, or citie.*

Finaison. Quand argent faut finaison nulle. *No bargaine, or satisfaction, without money.*

Final: m. ale: f. *Finall, finishing, last, concluding, vtmost; also, subiect vnto a conclusion, or end; and hence;*

Creature finale. *A mortall creature; a creature that must end one time or other (his dayes.)*

Fin finale. *The last end of all; a peremptorie conclusion, or issue.*

Finalement. *Finally; at length, at the last; in summe, in conclusion, in the end.*

Finance: *or;* Finances: f. *Wealth, substance, riches, goods; also, a Princes reuenew, or treasure. (The French word* Thresor *signifies (most properly) the Kings demaine, which consists of ordinarie reuenewes; but* Finance *(more generall) comprehends both the demaine, and all extraordinarie leuies; as th'Aides, taxes, impositions, &c.)*

Perte de finance. *Losse of publicke treasure by a robberie, &c; the ruine, or decay of a priuate estate by excessiue, or needlesse vsurie.*

Prendre à perte de finance. *Looke* Prendre.

Faire finance. *To giue money for an Office; also, to make, or gather, a stocke of money.*

Financé: m. ée: f. *That hath yeelded some treasure, or a reuenew (to the king;) or (more generally) disbursed.*

Financer. *To yeeld a reuenew, or treasure to the king, &c; also (more generally) to disburse; to giue, or pay money for.*

Financier: m. *A financer, or Exchequer-man; a Receiuer, vnder-Treasurer, or Teller, in th'Exchequer.*

Fine de poules: f. *Hennes dung, or ordure.*

Finé: m. ée: f. *Ended, finished, determined, concluded, accomplished; come to an issue.*

Finemént: m. *An end, issue, conclusion, expiration; or, an ending, determining, finishing of.*

Finément. *Subtilly, craftily, slily, wilily, cunningly; hence, also, industriously; prouidently, discreetly, warily, cautelously; & guilefully, deceitfully, fraudulently, or, with a fraudulent intent.*

Finer. *as* Finir; *To end; also, to obtaine, get, recouer; ouerrule, commaund, preuaile with; also, to furnish, or affoord; also, as* Affiner; *to trie, cleanse, fine.*

Ie ne me puis finer d'argent. *I cannot come by any money.*

Homme de qui on fine aisément. *A gentle, or tractable fellow; one thats easily won, or soone preuailed with.*

Finerot. chemin fin. *A way that is about 18 foot broad:* ¶Bourgong.

Finesse: f. *Craft, subtiltie, guile, deceit, policie, cunning, fraud. sleight, slinesse, wilinesse.*

Finesses de verre. *Shallow trickes; such as are easily lookt into; or seene thorow.*

Finet: m. finette: f. *A pettie craftie slaue; a slie rogue, a wilie mate, a subtile companion.*

Finfreluches: f. *Shales, or scales, or scalie excrements; as dandriffe, &c; or, as* Fanfreluches.

Fingard: m. de: f. *Lazie, lither, idle, slothfull, sluggish, dull, retchlesse, carelesse, negligent.*

Fini: m. finie: *Finished, ended, concluded, determined, accomplished; also, prescribed, limited, stinted; compassed, comprehended.*

Finir. *To end, conclude, finish, determine, accomplish; also, to define; prescribe, limit, stint; comprehend, compasse.*

Finissant. *Ending, determining, defining, limiting.*

Le cercle finissant. *The Horizon; Looke* Cercle.

Finiteur: m. *The circumference of a piller, from the top to the bottome thereof.*

Finoinct. *A kind of peare; good raw, or roasted.*

Fins: m. *The marches, borders, frontiers, vtmost ends, or limits of a countrey.*

Fiole: f. *A violl of glasse, &c.*

Fiquatelle: f. *A womans priuities.*

Fique. par ma fique. *By my fickins.*

Fiquer. *as* Ficher; *To fasten:* ¶Pic.

Firmament: m. *The skie, welkin, firmament.*

Firme: com. *Firme, strong, stable; See* Ferme.

Firmeté: f. *Strength, firmenesse; Looke* Fermeté.

Fiscal: m. ale: f. *Fiscall; belonging, or comming to the publick purse, treasure; Treasurie, or Exchequer.*

Pro.

Procureur fiscal. *A Lord high Iusticers ordinarie Atturney, who pleads, and prosecutes within his circuit, all causes wherein either the publicke, or his Lords inheritance, or both, be interressed.*
Fiscalins: m. *Children, or freed men maintained, or nourished in the Kings house, or vpon his land.*
Fiscelle: f. *Packthread.*
Fiscellette: f. *Small packthread.*
Fiselle: m. ée: f. *Fuzellie; or, bendie counterbendie; a tearme of Blazon.*
Fisq: m. *as* Fisque.
Fisque: m. *The publicke purse; the publicke reuenew, or Treasure; a Treasurie, or Exchequer.*
Fissaigne. *A certaine tumbling tricke.*
Fissau. *A Fitch, or Fulmart.*
Fissaye: f. *A quicke, and violent daunce much vsed by the French.*
Fisselle. *as* Fiscelle; *Packthread.*
Fissure: f. *A cleft, rift, chinke, chop.*
Fissuré: m. ée: f. *Cleft, riuen, chinked.*
Fist. il fist. *He did;* See Faire.
Fisticin: m. ine: f. *Of Pistachoes, or fisticke nuts.*
Fistique. *The Pistachoe, or fisticke nut.*
Fiston: m. *A little sonne, or boy.*
Fistonneau. *(The diminutiue of* Fiston) *a verie little sonne, or boy.*
Fistule: f. *A pipe, or flute; a tap, or fancet; also, the running sore called an Issue, or Fistula.*
Fistuleux: m. euse: f. *Full of Fistulaes; or of holes, like a spunge.*
Fivatier: m. *A vassall, copieholder, or customarie tenant, properly, the vassall, or tenant of a Lord* Cavier.
Fivele: f. *A buckle:* ¶ Langued.
Fixe: com. *Fixed, setled, fastened, sure, steadie, vnmouable.*
Fizain: m. *Spindle-tree, pricke-timber.*
Fizellé. *as* Fisellé.
Flabellation. *A fanning, airing, or giuing of wind vnto.*
Flabellé: m. ée: f. *Fanned, aired, blowne on, that hath wind giuen to it.*
Flac: m. *A flat, flap, flampe, or clap giuen by a thing that is violently thrown against a wall, or vnto the ground; and the report, or sound made by hands, &c, strucke, or hit, one against the other.*
Mettre à la flac. *To emptie a purse (of the sound an emptie purse makes) also, as* Flacquer; *or, suddainely (and with a hurrie) to ruine, cast downe, ouerthrow.*
De grand vilain grand flac: Prov. *He that liues villanously falls violently; or, the fall of a great rogue makes a great report.*
Flaccide: com. *Weake, flaggie, limber, flagging, hanging loosse; faded, withered.*
Flaccon. *as* Flascon.
Flacconner. *To plie the pot; to quaffe, or tipple hard.*
Flache: com. *Weake, limber, flaggie; lolling, drooping, hanging downe the head; withered, faded; faint, effeminate.*
Flacon. *as* Flascon; *A (great) leatherne bottle.*
Flacquer. *To make a thing to flap, flamp, or clap, by casting it violently against a wall, or to the ground.*
Il la vous flacca là. *He squasht, flat, or squat her downe there; he gaue her an arsepoße; he made her buttockes ring with the fall he gaue her; there he clapt her, and so left her.*
Flafla. *as* Flagorneur; *A blab.*
Flagellation: f. *A whipping, scourging, lashing, ierking.*
Flagellé: m. ée: f. *Whipped, lashed, ierked, scourged.*
Flageller. *To whip, scourge, lash, ierke.*
Flageol. *as* Flageolet.
Flageoler. *To pipe, or play on a whistle.*
Flageoler en l'oreille. *To flatter; to whisper.*
Flageolet: m. *A pipe, whistle, flute; also, as* Flageollet.
Flageoleur: m. *A piper, a whistler; also, a cousener, cheater, coniecatcher, notable deceiuer.*
Flageollet: m. *Iris, flag, or Flowerdeluce.*
Flagorner. *To blab, tattle, tell tales, report idle newes; also, priuately to appeach, disgrace, detract from others, thereby to please the hearers.*
Flagorneur: m. *A blab, tell-tale, tatler, tale-carrier; also, a pickthanke, priuate detractor, secret accusor; one that by such base Offices hopes to win fauour.*
Flagrance d'vn delict. *Plaine apparencie, or palpablenesse, of an offence; the crying of a sinne.*
Flagrant: m. ante: f. *Flagrant, ardent, burning, flaming; earnest, feruent.*
Prendre au faict flagrant. *To take at it, or in the manner; to apprehend vpon the deed doing, or presently after.*
Flaine: f. *A ticke for a bed.*
Flair: m. *Sent, smell.*
Flairé: m. ée: f. *Sented, smelled, vented, winded; also, perfumed.*
Flairement: m. *A senting, smelling, sauoring, venting, winding.*
Flairer. *To sent, smell, vent, wind; also, to perfume, cast a smell, yeeld a sauor, breath out a sent.*
On flaire cela. *There is great doubt, or suspition had thereof; or, men begin to discouer it, vent it, find it, out.*
Flaireur: m. *A senter, smeller, venter.*
Flaironné: m. ée: f. *Sented, smelt, vented.*
Flaironner. *To sent, smell, vent; sucke vp his breath at his nosethrills often together.*
Flaistri: m. ie: f. *Marked, branded, burnt, as a rogue, in some apparent member, with an hot yron; also, publickly defamed, openly disgraced, knowne for a knaue.*
Flaistrir. *To burne in the hand, or eare, to brand in the forehead, to marke for a rogue, with an hot yron; also, to defame publickly, disgrace openly; blemish the reputation of, lay a foule imputation on; also, as* Flestrir.
Flaistrissure: f. *A disgracefull brand, or marke; an open blemish; also, a fading, or withering.*
Flaitrir. *as* Flaistrir.
Flaman: m. *A certaine reddish, long-bild, and long-legd, Sea-fowle; of the bignesse of a Stork, or somewhat bigger, and indifferent good meat.*
Flambant. *as* Flaman.
Flambant. *Flaming, shining, glistering, yeelding a bright luster.*
Flambart. *as* Furole; *S. Hermes fire; also, the hearbe Water-torch, or Cats taile.*
Flambe: f. *A flame, a great blaze of fire; also, the blew Flowerdeluce (called otherwise) Garden flags; also, as* Spase.
Flambe bastarde. *Sedge, Gladen, Glader, Swordgrasse, Water-flag, yellow Flag, Lauers, Leuers.*
Flambe blanche. *The white Flowerdeluce; also, the Flowerdeluce of* Florence, *of whose Aromaticall root our Orice powder is made.*
Flambe de riviere. *Water-flag, water Flowerdeluce; or, as* Flambe bastarde.

Flambé. *Flamed, blazed, glistered; also, basted with flaming, or hot scaulding lead.*

Flambeau: m. *Is (generally) a light; or any thing that yeelds a flame, and is carried, in the darke, for light; and (particularly,) a linke, or torch of wax, hauing neither any rosen in it, nor wodden handle vnto it; and, the great wax candle, thats vsed, for state, in the houses of great men.*

Il porta le flambeau en ces secrets. *He divulged, or discouered, he led men to the knowledge of, these secrets.*

Flambelot: m. *A small torch, linke, or light.*

Flamber. *To flame, to blaze; to shine, glister, yeeld a great luster, giue much light; also, to bast (meat) with flaming, or hot scaulding lard.*

Flamberge: f. *A sword*: ¶Barrag.

Flambillon. *A small flame, light, or linke.*

Flambo. *A kind of long, slender, & flame-coloured sea-fish*: ¶Langued.

Flamboyant. *Flaming, blazing, shining, radiant.*

Couleur flamboyante. *A flame-colour.*

Flamboyantement. *Flamingly, shiningly, radiantly, most brightly.*

Flamboyer. *To flame, shine, blaze, giue much light.*

Flamend: m. de: f. *Of Flaunders, Flemish, belonging to a Fleming.*

Fenestre Flamende. *Looke* Fenestre.

Flamiche: f. *(In Paris, and thereabouts they call so) a kind of better bread then ordinarie, reserued for the Maisters, and Mistresses own mouthes; as also, a cake made of butter, cheese, flower, and yolkes of egges; after baking glazed ouer with sugar, and rosewater.*

Flamman. *as* Flaman.

Flamme: f. *A flame, or great blaze.*

Des flammes. *The greater kind of those round muscles, or cockles which the Latines tearme* Chamæ, *and which, being eaten, inflame the mouth like pepper; the lesse, & lesse-inflaming ones are tearmed,* flammettes.

Flammeche. *as* Flammesche.

Flammerolles: f. *Fire-Drakes; strange representations of fire, appearing, sometimes in the skie; or, as* Furoles.

Flammesche: f. *A sparke, or sparkle.*

Flammette: f. *A little flame; also, the hearbe Crowfoot; also, a kind of Launcet, pointed like a broad arrow head, wherewith Chirurgians vse to open a veine.*

Des flammettes. *Look* des flammes, *vnder* flamme.

Flammie: f. *Th'Office, or dignitie of a (Pagan) Archpriest; a Flaminship.*

Flamme-vome: com. *Flame-vomiting.*

Flammuche. *as* Flamiche.

Flammule: f. *The hearbe called vpright Clamberer, or vpright Virgines-bower; also, the hearbe called, Spear-wort, or Speare-Crowfoot.*

Flanc: m. *The flanke, or side; also, a flanker (in fortification;) also, a coping, planchet, or plate of mettall readie to be stamped on, or coyned.*

Mal de flancs. *A continuall stitch in the side; or, a Pleuresie.*

Aller du flanc. *To pant.*

Batre les flancs. *To pant hard.*

Donner le flanc à tous propos. *To yeeld vnto, or be won by, euerie word.*

Tirer des flancs. *A horse to strike (often) at his owne flanke.*

Il a tourné en mes flancs. *I bore him; I carried him in my bellie.*

Flançais. *A draught-horses drawing traces; those that run along his sides.*

Flancars: m. *Side Langes; Armour for the flankes, or sides of a barbed horse.*

Flanchere: f. *A flanker, side peece, or flanking peece of timber, in building.*

Flannet: m. *A doucet, or little custard.*

Flanquers: m. *as* Flançais; *also, as* Flancars.

Flanqué: m. ée: f. *Flanked, strengthened with flanks; fenced, defended; accoasted.*

Flanquer. *To flanke, strengthen with flankes; accoast, runne along by the side of; to defend, support, or fence; to be at ones elbow for a helpe at need.*

Flans: m. *Flawnes, Custards, Egge-pies; also, round planchets, or plates of mettall; See* Flanc.

Flaons: m. *Round planchets, or plates of mettall, readie to be stamped, or coyned.*

Flaque: com. *Weake, feeble, faint, flaggie; See* Flache.

Flasche. *as* Flache.

Flascon: m. *A (great) leathern bottle.*

Terre loing de soy n'apporte que flascons, & bouteilles: Prov. *Ground that lies farre off yeelds nought but pots, and bottles.*

Flasconner. *as* Flacconner.

Flasque. *as* Flascon; *Also, a flaske, or box for powder; also, the carriage of a peece of ordnance; the frame whereon it lyes.*

Flasquet: m. *A little flaske.*

Flassade: f. *The couering of a bed; also, the daintiest kind of Ray, or smooth Thornebacke.*

Flastereau: m. *A kind of flat* Naveau.

Flastrer. *To marke, burne, or brand with an hot yron.*

Flastri: m. ie: f. *Marked, burnt, or branded with an hot yron.*

Flastrir. *as* Flastrer; *or, as* Flaistrir.

Flatant. *Flattering, fawning on, colloguing with, clawing, smoothing, stroaking.*

Flatard: m. de: f. *The same.*

Flaté: m. ée: f. *Flatered; soothed, smoothed, stroaked, fawned on, glozed with.*

Flatelet: m. *A Hallibut (fish.)*

Flatement: m. *A flattering; soothing, smoothing; fawning on, colloguing or glozing with.*

Flatement aux chevaux. *A stroaking of them with the hand; also, the popping, or smacking vsed by riders.*

Flater. *To flatter; sooth, smooth, fawne on, gloze or collogue with, vse faire words, giue (ouer) good tearms vnto; also, to claw, stroke, clap gently.*

Sans flater le dé. *Plainely, Sincerely, roundly, without making the matter better then it is.*

Qui flate il grate: Prov. *He that flatters, thriues.*

Flatereau: m. *Halfe a flatterer, one that somewhat flatters.*

Flateresse: f. *A flattering, or cogging wench.*

Flaterie: f. *Flatterie, fawning, glozing, adulation, assentation, soothing, smoothing, cogging, foisting.*

Flateur: m. *A flatterer, glozer, fawner, soother, foister, smoother; a claw-backe, Sycophant, pickthanke.*

Flateuse. *as* Flateresse.

Flateusement. *Glozingly, fawningly, flatteringly.*

Flatré: m. ée: f. *Branded in the forehead, bored through the eare, marked for a knaue.*

Flatrer. *To brand, burne, or marke with an hot yron; See* Flaistrir.

Flatri. *as* Flatré.

Flatrissement: m. *A branding in the forehead, a burning through the eare; an open marke of disgrace; a publicke defamation.*

Flatti: m. ie: f. *Flatted; beaten, or made flat.*

Flattir. *To flat; to beat, or make flat.*
Flatueux: m. euse: f. *Flatulent, windie, full of windie humors.*
Flatulent. *as* Flatueux.
Flatuosité: f. *Flatulencie, windinesse, fulnesse of wind.*
Flavelle: f. *Trifling.* (v. m.)
Flayau: m. *A flaile to thresh with.*
Fleau: m. *as* Flayau; *Also, the beame of a great Balance; also, the tendrell, or tender shute of a vine, whereby it catcheth hold on what is next vnto it; It is also much vsed, by metaphor, for a scourge, plague, or iudgement of God.*
Les Fleaux des poissons. *The finnes of fishes.*
Les Fleaux des rameaux des arbres. *The small tops, or twigs, of branches.*
Fleble: *as* Foible.
Fleche: f. *A shaft, an arrow; also, a peece of wood in the beakehead of a ship; the sprit sayle whereof it serues to hold in.*
Fleche d'vn arbre. *The trunke, or bodie of a tree.*
Fleche de lard. *A flich of bacon.*
Faire de tout bois fleches. *Looke* Bois.
Il ne sçait plus de quel bois faire fleches. *He knows no longer what wood to make arrowes of,* viz: *what stuffe to make vse of, what helps to relie on, what friends to recourse to.*
Flecheurs. *Benders, pliers, bowers; and (more particularly) the muscles that serue to bow the ioynts of the fingers.*
Flechi: m. ie: f. *Bent, bowed, plied; moued, turned; gone, awrie, or on th'one side.*
Flechir. *To bend, bow, plie; to moue; turne, goe, awrie, or on th'one side.*
Facile à flechir. *Gentle, pliant, flexible, tractable, turnable; tender; inconstant; mouable; soone bent, easily bowed.*
Flechissant. *Yeelding, plying, bending, bowing vnto.*
Flechissement: m. *A bowing, bending, plying.*
Flechissure: f. *A bought, or crookednesse; also, a bending, crooking, bowing.*
Flection. *as* Flechissement.
Flegart. *A common place, or, way:* ¶Pic.
Flegmatique: com. *Flegmaticke; full of fleame; breeding fleame; subiect vnto fleame.*
Flegme: m. *Fleame.*
Flegmon: m. *A hot, and red swelling, or inflamation of bloud, called by Physitians a Flegman.*
Fleiche. *as* Fleche.
Fleschade: f. *A wound, or pricke of an arrow.*
Flesche. *as* Fleche; *Also, a kind of water grasse.*
Fleschier: m. *An Archer.*
Fleschissant. *as* Flechissant.
Flestri. *as* Flatré; *Also, faded, withered; quailed, decaied.*
Flestrir. *as* Flatrer; *Also, to fade, wither; flag, droope; decay, or drie vp; to quaile, faile, or fall away.*
Laisser flestrir pour graine. *To let run to seed; See* Graine.
Flestrisseure: f. *A withering, fading, quailing, decaying; a failing, drooping, flagginesse, falling away; also, as* Flaistrissure.
Fletan. *as* Flettan.
Fletelet. *A Hallibut, or holy-but fish.*
Flettan. *The greatest kind of Sole-fish.*
Flette. *A lyter; a small barke; also, a Flounder.*
Fleve: com. *as* Foible.
Fleumatique: com. *Flegmatick, subiect vnto flegme.*
Fleume. *as* Flegme.
Fleur: f. *A flower; bloome, blossome; a catkin, or blowing.*
Fleurs. *A womans monethlie flux, or flowers.*
Fleur d'aage. *The prime, or most flourishing time, of ones age.*
Fleur d'amour. *Flower-gentle, Flower-amour.*
Fleurs blanches. *The Whites; (a disease well knowne among women.)*
Fleur des Chardons. *Thistle-downe.*
Fleurs cordiales. les trois fleurs cordiales. *The three cordiall flowers; Roses, Buglosse, and Bourrage flowers.*
La fleur du cuir. *The graine, or vpper part of leather.*
Fleur d'eau. *The water Lillie, water Rose, yellow, or white Nenuphar.*
Fleur d'erain. *Little red, and shining graines, that fall from the smoake arising of cleere water cast vpon melted, liquid, and red-hot brasse; (of great vse in Physick, and Chirurgerie.)*
Fleur de farine. *Flower, or the finest meale; also, meal-dust, or mill dust.*
Fleur d'huyle. *as* Mere goutte.
Fleur S. Iaques. *Ragwort, Staggerwort, Stauerwort, S. Iames-wort.*
Fleur à jaulnir. *Dyers weed, greening weed, woodwaxen, base broome.*
La Fleur de mouton. *The best of the rack; & the ribs of the breast which be not vnder the shoulder.*
Fleur de la pierre Assienne. *The saltish mold, or hoare, that growes on that stone; an excellent preseruer of the things which are seasoned withall.*
Fleur de sel. *as in* Sel.
Fleur du vin. *The mother of wine; the white, or mouldie spots that float on the top of old wine.*
Choux fleurs. *Collie-florie, Cypres Coleworts.*
Couleur de fleur de Pescher. *A Peach colour.*
La noble fleur. *Flower-gentle, Veluet flower, Flower amour, Flower valure.*
'A fleur. Blanchir de la toile à fleur. *To bleach, or whiten linnen.*
'A fleur d'eau. *Close by the water, betweene wind and water.*
'A fleur de terre. *Close vnto, euen with, hard at, the ground.*
La fleur n'est que cendre. *The best is but trash; the fairest no better then a dead flourish.*
Fleurage: m. *Flourinesse; a heape, or abound ance of flowers.*
Fleurant le plan de la terre. *as* à Fleur de terre.
Fleurant comme le calemard d'vn retraict. *Smelling, or casting a sent, like the funnell of an Aiax.*
Fleurdelisé. *Branded, or marked for a rogue, with the print of a Flowerdeluce, between his shoulders, &c.*
Fleurdelisé d'or. *Set, inriched, flourished, beautified, with golden Flowerdeluces.*
Fleurdeliser. *To set a Flowerdeluce betweene the shoulders with a hot yron (the marke of a rogue;) also, to flourish, beautifie, sticke, set thicke, with Flowerdeluces.*
Fleurée: f. *The froath, foame, or vpmost flowerie scumme of a thing that boiles.*
Fleuret. *Course silke; floret silke.*
Mesler la soye avec le fleuret. *To mingle good and bad, fine and course, deere and cheape, together.*
Fleuretant. *Sleightly running, lightly passing ouer; onely touching in the passing by; also, venting, or winding.*
Fleureter. *Sleightly to run, lightly to passe ouer; onely to touch a thing in going by it (metaphorically from the little Bees nimble skipping from flower to flower as she feeds;) also, as* Fleuretter.

Fleuretis de paroles. *Fine tearmes to small purpose; an idle flourish of words.*
Fleurette: f. *A little flower, small bloome, or blossome.*
Fleuretté. *Fleurettie (a tearme of Blazon;) also, vented, or winded.*
Fleuretter. *To vent, or wind; also, to sneake, or eaue-drop it; also, as* Fleureter.
Fleureux: m. euse: f. *Flowerie; stored with choice of flowers; also, fragrant, odoriferous, sweet-smelling.*
Fleuri: m. ie: f. *Flourishing, flowred, blossomed.*
Choux fleuris. *Collie-florie; Cypres cole.*
Pasques fleuries. *Palme-Sunday.*
Vieillesse fleurie. *White, or gray-headed.*
Fleurin: m. *as* Florin; *Or, a Low-Countrey coyne worth about* ij.s.sterl.
Fleurir. *To blossome, bloome, flower, bring or beare, flowers; also, to prosper, excell, flourish, be renowmed, come into credit, haue much reputation in the world.*
Fleurissant. *Blooming, blossoming, flourishing, bearing many flowers; also, prosperous, renowmed, had in estimation.*
Fleuron: m. *A Fleuron, or Fleuret; a small flower, little blossome, young blowme.*
Fleuronné: m. ée: f. *Flourishing; decked, or set thicke, with yong flowers, blossomes, bloomes.*
Croix fleuronnée. *A crosse botonic; (in Blazon.)*
Fleuronner. *To bloome, to blow; to beginne to blossome.*
Fleurtis: m. *A flourish, or flourishing.*
Fleurtis des oysillons. *The warbling of little birds.*
Fleury. *as* Fleuri.
Fleute: f. *A flute; a pipe.*
Le fleute d'vn Alambic. *The beake, or nose of a Limbecke.*
Fleute d'Aleman. *A Lamprey; called so in some places by reason of the little holes which she hath in th'vpper part of her bodie.*
Il y a de l'ordure dans leurs fleutes. *All goes not wel with them; somewhat is amisse among them.*
Ils ont accordé leurs fleutes. *They are agreed vpon the matter.*
Ce qui est venu par la fleute s'en retourne avec le Tabourin: Prov. *What the pipe hath gathered the Taber scattereth; goods ill gotten are commonly ill spent.*
Robin se souvient tousjours de sa fleute: Prov. *Looke* Robin.
Fleuter. *To play on the flute.*
Fleuteur: m. *A Fluter, a Piper.*
Fleuteuse: f. *A Fluteresse; a woman that playes on a flute.*
Fleutrer. *See* Flatrer.
Fleuve: m. *A floud, streame, riuer.*
Le fleuve passé le Sainct oublié: Prov. *The danger once past our vowes are ill paid.*
Flexible: com. *Pliant, flexible; tractable; soone bent, quickly bowed, easily won or changed; good to be dealt with, fit to be wrought on.*
Flexir. *To bend, bow, plie; turne, wind about.*
Flexueux: m. euse: f. *Intricate, crooking or crooked, full of cranklings, that hath many turnings, winding in and out.*
Flexuosité: f. *Flexuositie; a most crooked, or manifold turning; an intricate, or often winding in and out.*
Flez. *A Flounder.*
Flic: m. *A iert, or ierke; a twang, a dash, a flat, or flamp; also, an arrow, or shaft.*
Fliche de larde: f. *A flich, or side, of bacon.*
Flin: m. *A thunder-stone; a kind of stone wherwith Cutlers furbush their blades; or as* Esmeril.
Flion. *A kind of tender, and daintie shell-fish, not much vnlike a Cockle, but that the shell thereof is somewhat whiter, and much smoother.*
Flique de lard. *as* Fliche: ¶Pic.
Flis: m. *A flight-shaft.*
Flisquant: m. ante: f. *Whisking, ierting, twanging.*
Flo: m. *The high-water marke, at sea; Looke* Flot.
A flo. *Floating, or swimming vpon the sea.*
Choses du flo. *Flotsens, or flotzams; goods that lie floating, or swimming on the top of the water.*
Floc de laine. *A locke, or flocke of wooll.*
Floc de Moine. *as* Froc.
Floccard: m. *A fashion of head-attire put on by the betrothed maidens of* Lyons, *and left off when they haue beene maried a twelue-month.*
Floche. *Looke* Flosche.
Flocon. *as* Floc.
Flocquars: m. *Tassels, puffes, or tufts, as of Sarcenet thats drawne out of, or cut vnder, another stuffe.*
Flocquer. *To puffe out, as Sarcenet in a breech cut after the Swisse fashion; to hang forth loosse, to sit bagging, flagging, or ofrumpled, as an ouer-wide garment.*
Flocquoir: m. *A squirt.*
Floflotant. *Flowing, floating, surging; sounding like waues, or billowes.*
Floflotement. *A floating, or surging; a bubling, or tempestuous noise.*
Flofloter. *To float, surge, or waue vp and downe; also, to make a surging, bubling, or tempestuous noise.*
Flon. *as* Felon; *Also, a white-meat made of milke, egs, butter, and meale; or, as;*
Flondelaict: m. *A certaine baked-meat that somewhat resembles our flawne.*
Floquer. *See* Flocquer.
Floquet. gentil floquet. *A sweet youth, spruce companion; minion, milk-sop:* ¶Rab.
Floquets de poil. *Flockes, or lockes of haire.*
Florable. *The herb Cheese-runnell, or Cheese-renning, our Ladies Bedstraw, pettie Mugwet, Maides-haire.*
Floraux. Ieux Floraux. *A certaine wittie, & pleasant contention among French Rimers, or Poets; a siluer Eglantine being the reward, or prize, for the best doer, and a Marigold for the second.*
Florée: f. *The blew scumme of woad boyling in the Dyers lead; which fleeted off, and dried vnto powder, serues Painters, and Silke-Dyers for diuers vses.*
Florencé. croix florencée. *A crosse flurt; (in Blazon.)*
Floret: m. *A foile; or sword with the edge rebated.*
Flori: m. ie: f. *Bloomed, blossomed, flourishing, in the flower; whence;*
Quand les febues sont flories, les sots cõmencent leurs folies: Prov. *Looke* Febue.
Floride: com. *Liuelie, fresh, lustie, flourishing.*
Florin: m. *A Florin, or Franc; an ancient coine of gold in France, worth* ij.s.sterl: *not currant at this day; (though* Languedoc, *and the countries adioyning retaine the name still, in a peece thats worth* 18.d.sterl.)
Florin de Metz. *Is worth* iij.s.sterl.
Florin au traict. *Wants somewhat of* iij. s. (29.s. Tour.)
Florin de Vic. *Goes for* 33.s.Tourn.
Qui a Florin, latin, roussin, par tout il trouve chemin: Prov. *(Wherein, by* florin, *store of coyne is vnderstood.)*
Flosche: com. *Flaggie, weake, soft; as a bonelesse lump of flesh.*
Soye flosche. *Sleaue silke.*

Flot: m. *A waue, surge, floud; or, the wauing, floating, or flowing of any water; also, a tyde, or the tyde; or, as* Flo; *the high-water marke at sea.*
Le flot de Mars. *The great Spring-tydes which come in about the Equinoctiall, or thirteenth, of March.*
Le flot de Septembre. *The like tydes, comming in about the Autumne Equinoctiall.*
'A flot griffe graffe. *Floating, surging, swimming aloft on the waues.*
Tout ce que vient d' Ebe s' en retournera de flot: Prov. *What's got by one hand will be lost by another.*
Flotage: m. *A floating, surging, swimming on the top of.*
Le premier flotage d'un Navire. *The launching of a new ship.*
Flotelant. *as* Floflotant.
Floter. *as* Flotter.
Floton: m. *A tuft, locke, or puffe of.*
Flottage. *as* Flotage.
Flottant. *Floating, flowing, surging, wauing, as water; also, sayling, or swimming on the water.*
Flotte: f. *A Brewers Cooler; also, a fleet of ships.*
Flotte de gens. *A crue, rout, a troupe, flocke, a companie, multitude, streame, of people.*
Flotte de marrein. *A raft, or float-boat of timber ioyned together, and sent downe a riuer.*
Flotté: m. ée: f. *Floating; set aflote; also, shaken, tossed, moued; carried vp and downe by, or on, the waues.*
Bois flotté. *Looke* Bois.
Flottement: m. *A floating, swimming, wauing.*
Flotter. *To flote; bouer, swimme aloft on the water; to boyle, flow, surge, rise in waues, or billowes.*
Floüet: m. ette: f. *Weake, washie, tender, delicate, nice.* ¶Norm.
Vne main floüette. *A soft, or daintie hand.*
Floüin: m. *A Barke of some fortie, or fiftie tunne; higher decked then a Galley, and lower then an ordinarie Barke; and going both with sayles, and oares (without bankes) and fitted both for fight, and burthen; we may call it a Ry-boat, or a Ry-man (for the fashion of it came from Ry, sayes* Nicot.)
Flour. *as* Fleur; *a blossome, or flower.*
Flouré: m. ée: f. *Flowrie (in Blason.)*
Flourir. *See* Fleurir.
Fluction: f. *An issue, flux, flowing.*
Fluctuation. *A surging, floating, swimming; a doubting, wauering, vncertainetie, inconstancie.*
Fluctuer. *To float, surge, waue vp and downe, as the water; to be tossed, turmoyled, disquieted; also, to wauer, doubt, hold an vncertaine course, haue an vncertaine estate, be at no certainetie, behaue himselfe inconstantly.*
Fluer. *To flow, runne, slip, slide, glide, or passe along, as water.*
Flueürs de femme. *A womans monthlie flowers.*
Fluïde: com. *Flowing, running, washie, flashie, moist, waterish; thinne, feeble, weake, as water; also, glib, currant, smoothly running along.*
Fluïdement. *Flowingly, running; moistly, waterishly; thinnely; weakely; also, currantly, glibly, smoothly along.*
Fluïdité: f. *A flowing, moistnesse, washinesse, waterishnesse; thinnesse; flashinesse; weakenesse.*
Flusteau. *A little Flute, or Pipe; Seeke* Enter.
Fluste-bergiere. *An hearbe, which some hold to be water Plantane.*

Flute. *as* Fleute; *also, a certaine peece of small Artillerie.*
Fluter, & Fluteur. *See* Fleuter & Fleuteur.
Fluviatile: com. *Of a riuer, streame, or water; belonging to, or bred in, a riuer, streame, or water.*
Flux: m. *A flowing, running, streaming, or rushing out; a current (or tide) of water; also, a flux, flix, laske, loossenesse; a (thinne, or liquid) issue; also, a flush, at Cardes.*
Cela est encores en flux. *That is as yet in action, or vpon th'increase.*
Passe sans flux. *Passe, I am not flush; also, let-goe, no matter, or not a pinne matter.*
Fluxible: com. *Fluxible, fluide, or flitting.*
Fluxil: m. ile: f. *Fluxie, fluent, flowing, flitting, running.*
Fluxion: f. *A fluxion; a running, flowing, or floating of waters; also, a flux, flix, or issue.*
Foarre: m. *Straw; also, litter, or fodder.*
Foarreux: m. euse: f. *Full of, well furnished with, straw.*
Focile: m. *The arme from the elbow to the wrist; the leg, or shanke from the knee to the ankle; each consisting of two bones.*
Focile grand. *Th'vpper of those two bones, being the longer, and greater.*
Focile mineur; ou, petit focile. *The vndermost, and lesse of them.*
Fodine: f. *A quarrey, or mine; a place or pit whereout any thing is digged.*
Foetide. *as* Fetide. *Stinking.*
Foeu. *Seeke* Feu; *A fire.*
Fogat. *A kind of engine to catch fish with.*
Fogner. *To grumble; powt, lowre.*
Fogon d' vne navire. *as* Fougon.
Foiblage de poids. *Want of weight, scant weight.*
Foible: com. *Feeble, weake, strengthlesse, faint, forcelesse.*
Foible comme vn festu. *We say, as weake as water.*
Le fort portant le foible. *One with another, good and bad together, some better to make amends for the worse.*
Qui a le ressort foible. *That wants erection.*
Foiblement. *Feebly, weakely, faintly; without strength, without force, without vigor.*
Foiblesse: f. *Feeblenesse, weaknesse, want of strength; faintnesse, infirmitie; a fainting, or falling into a qualm; also, want of due weight, or, scant weight, in coine.*
Foiblesse de coeur. *Dastardie, faint-heartednes, cowardise, want of courage.*
Foie. *as* Foye.
Foignasse: f. *Medicke fodder, Spanish Trifolie, Snaile Clauer.*
Foigne: f. *A long staffe that hath at th'one end a square casting-net; vsed most by sea-fishermen.*
Foigner. *To powt, lowre, grumble, murmure, or be offended, at; also, as* Feindre; *and hence;*
Ils ne se foignoyent de gueres. *They dissembled, or forbore, but a little.*
Foin: m. *Hay; also, a great white Moath, or night-flie, that somewhat resembles a Beetle.*
Foin d' arriere saisin. *Fog, late Math, lateward Hay.*
Foin de Bourgongne. *Spanish Trifolie, Medick fodder, Snaile Clauer.*
Foin dur. *Hard Hay, S. Peters wort, square or great S. Iohns grasse.*
Foin Grec. *(The hearbe, or seed) Fenigreeke.*

Sain foin, ou sainct foin. *Spanish Trifolie, Medicke fodder, Snayle Clauer.*

Bailleur de foin à la mule. *A Cheater, Cousener, Conycatcher.*

Chapitreur de foin. *A skarre-crow; one that seemes better then he is, or assumes more then he should.*

Bailler foin en corne. *To deceiue, gull, cousen, sell a bargaine, giue a gudgeon.*

Bailler de l' avoine pour du foin. *To loose by an exchange, to giue cake for bread.*

Botté de foin. *Rusticke, rusticall, clownish, Boore-like, rude; also, ignorant, simple, sillie.*

Il y a du foin, il n'y a que les bestes qui s'y amusent. *Your hopes are verie meane, or vaine; the thing you gape for's most vnworthie of you.*

Se remplir de foin, ou de paille. *To stop his guts with, to glut himselfe on, any thing; (from a horse, that wanting Hay falls to his Litter.)*

Tirer du foin aux chiens. *To spue, cast, vomit (after a surfet.)*

Tourner les truyes au foin. *To answer from the matter, to speake from the purpose.*

Foin en corne: Prov. *A good warning, or marke, for the auoiding of a dangerous person; a thing worne to giue notice that the wearer is not to be safely accoasted; (from the auncient Romanes, who vsed to ty a wispe of Hay about the one horne of a shrewd, or curst Beast;) and hence;*

Il a du foin aux cornes. *He is a dangerous beast; a fierce, proud, sturdie, surlie, vnsociable, fellow.*

De mauvais payeurs foin, ou paille: Prov. *For a desperate debt take any satisfaction, of an ill paymaister any thing.*

Foine. *as* Fouinne. *A Foyne, or Polecat.*

Foine. *A Pigeon-house, that hath one entrie on the top, without other hole, or window for light, or ayre; also, as* Faine; *Beech-Mast.*

Foinil: m. *A Hay-stacke, Hay-reeke, Hay-mow; Hay-loft, Hay-house.*

Foirard: m. *A shitten fellow; also, a kind of white Vine, or grape of no great worth; so tearmed, of the propertie it hath to loosen the bellie.*

`A cul de foirard tousiours abonde merde: Prov. *A filthie tale seld wanteth filthie Auditors.*

Foire: f. *A Faire; a Mart; a generall Market.*

Il s'est bien trouvé de la foire. *He hath made a good match, or market; he hath sped very well; (Applyable vnto one that hath gotten a good wife.)*

On ne s'en va pas des foires comme du marché; *Looke* Marché.

Foire: f. *Squirt, thinne dung; a laske.*

Faire barbe de foire à. *To disgrace, violate, wrong extreamely, abuse egregiously.*

`A saincte Foire chandelle de merde: Prov. *A gift agreeable to her nature, or humor; fit (and filthie) Lettuce for her (stinking) lips.*

Foirelle: f. *French Mercurie, garden Mercurie.*

Foirer. *To squirt, to shite thinne, as in a laske; also, to besquirt, or beray with squirting.*

Foiret: m. *as* Foret.

Foireux: m. euse: f. *All to beshitten, or berayed with squirting; also, hauing the squirt, troubled with a lask, loose behind.*

Foirolle: f. *as* Foirelle.

Fois: m. Le fois du corps. *The waste, or middle.*

Fois: f. *A time, turne, course, bout; (A word that hath euer another before it.)*

L'autre fois. *Th' other time;* Les autres fois, *th'other times;* & Autre fois *(an Aduerbe, and most vsed as one word;) heretofore, in times past; while-eare; sometimes, at another time.*

Quelque fois. *Sometimes, one time or another.*

Toutes fois. *Neuerthelesse, notwithstanding.*

Toutes fois & quantes. *Euerie time and tide; as often as.*

Vne fois; *once:* deux fois; *twice:* trois fois; *thrice:* quatre fois; *foure times; (and so forward, reckoning by so many times.)*

De fois à autre. *Estsoones, now and then, euer and anon; one time after another.*

Par fois. *Sometimes, or by times, now and then.*

Foison: f. *Store, plentie, abundance, great fullnesse, enough.*

`A foison. *Copiously, plentifully, abundantly.*

Foisonnant. *Abounding with, hauing plentie of.*

Foisonner. *To abound; be full, haue plentie of.*

Foisonneux: m. euse: f. *Plentifull, abundant, full of, well stored with.*

Foite-cul: m. *A Pedant; a whip-arse.*

Foiter. *as* Fouëtter.

Fol: m. *A foole; asse, goose, calfe, dotterell, woodcocke; noddie, cokes, goosecap, coxcombe, dizard, peagoose, ninnie, naturall, ideot, wisakers; also, a Bishop, at Chesse; also, a kind of great Canarie bird, so called, because she neuer linnes wagging her head.*

Il en est plus assotté qu' un fol de sa marotte. *He dotes more on it then a foole on's bable (which, we say, hee'le not giue for the Tower of London.)*

Fol est qui se coupe de son propre cousteau: Pro. *He is an asse that hurts himself with his own helps; or, abuses his owne good parts to his owne destruction.*

Fol est qui s'enyvre de sa propre bouteille: Prov. *Of the same sence; or, he is an asse thats besotted on his owne good parts.*

Fol est qui est esperonné, & à cheval dit hai: Prov. *He is an asse that hauing sufficient, doth vse insufficient helpes.*

Fol est qui est à table, & n'ose manger: Prov. *He is an asse that hauing wealth enough dares not vse it; or being where tis to be had, dares not put for it.*

Fol est qui iette à ses pieds ce qu' il tient en ses mains: Prov. *He is an asse that throwes at his heeles what hee holds in his hands; viz. that neglects his own (whatsoeuer.)*

Fol est qui perd la chair pour les os: Prov. *He is an asse that looses flesh for bones; viz. that leaues important, to follow paultrie, matters.*

Fol est qui de son poing fait coing: Prov. *He is an asse that presumes too much on his owne strength, or knowes not the right vse of his owne things.*

Fol & avoir ne se peuvent entr' avoir: Pro. *A foole and wealth cannot possesse each other.*

Fol qui beaucoup desire choisit, & prend le pire: Prov. *The greedie foole that all would purse, by hastie choise lights on the worse.*

Fol se doit nommer en face qui bien assis se desplace: Prov. *He should be call'd a foole to his face, that being well doth quit his place.*

Fol quiert iusques au crever ce qui ne se peut trouver: Pro. *(Meant especially of the Alchymist.)*

Fols sont sages quand ils se taisent: Prov. *Fooles are wise vntill they speake.*

Le fol est sot quant & quant, mais tout sot n' est pas fol: Prov. *All fooles be sots, but all sots be not fooles.*

Le fol reste apres la feste: Prov. *Looke* Feste.

Vn

Vn fol advise bien vn sage: Prov. *A foole may sometimes giue a wise man counsaile.*
Vn fol cerche son malheur: Prov. *A foole doth seeke his owne mishap; the curious searcher finds himselfe vnfortunate.*
Vn fol vn enragé: Prov. *Once a foole, euer a mad man; or, he that hath played the foole once, will, ere he leaue, play the mad man.*
Vn fol fait tousiours le commencement: Pro. *The foole begins, but neuer ends, a businesse.*
'A fol avantureux n'est mestier d' avoir sens: Prov. *An enterprizing foole needs little wit.*
'A fol ne faut point de sonnette: Prov. *(So quickly his words, and gesture tell you what he is.)*
Au fol la marotte: Prov. *We say also, Giue the foole his bable; or, whats a foole without a bable?*
Il est bien fol qui cuide tousiours vivre: Prov. *He is a verie asse that thinkes he shall liue euer.*
Il est bien fol qui à fol sens demande: Prov. *Hee's a true asse that lookes for wit in an asse.*
Il est bien fol qui s'oublie: Prov. *He is a right foole that forgets himselfe.*
De ce que fol pense souvent en demeure: Prov. *A foole oft finds himselfe short of his reckonings.*
Mettez fol à par soy il pensera: Prov. *Leaue a foole alone, and he will bethinke himselfe (what he hath to doe.)*
Qui fol envoye fol attend: Pro. *Seeke* Envoyer.
Qui fol va à Rome fol en retourne: Prov. *Let no foole hope to become wise by trauelling (at least, we vse to say of some of our giddie Trauellers) he is come home as verie a foole as he went.*
Quoy que fol tarde, iour ne tarde: Prov. *While fooles doe pause the day is spent; time stayes not the fooles leisure.*
Si le fol n'alloit au marché on ne vendroit pas la mauvaise denrée: Prov. *If fooles went not to Market ill wares would be kept.*
Si le fol ne folie il perd sa saison: Prov. *A foole that would seeme wise is most vnseasonable; or, the foole is most fittie when he is least foolish.*
Si tous les fols portoient marotte, on ne sçait pas de quel bois on se chaufferoit: Prov. *If all fooles bables bore, wood would be verie deere.*
'A barbe de fol on apprend à raire: Prov. *By shauing a foole one learnes to shaue.*
'A barbe de fol hardi rasoir: Prov. *The razor may boldly graze on a fooles beard.*
'A barbe de fol le rasoir est mol: Prov. *A foole brookes any disgrace; A foole's not sensible of any wrong.*
'A conseil de fol cloche de bois: Prov. *When loggarheads consult logs serue for bells.*
En larmes de fol ne se doit on fier: Pro. *The teares of a foole are not to be trusted.*
Belle promesse fol lie: Prov. *Secke* Promesse.
Bonne iournée fait qui de fol se delivre: Prov. *He does a good dayes worke that gets cleere of a foole.*
Douces promesses obligent les fols: Pro. *Faire promises oblige th' improuident.*
En defaut de sage monte vn fol en chaire: Prov. *Looke* Sage.
Grand besoing a de fol qui de soy mesme le fait: Prov. *He needs a foole too much that will needes play the foole.*
On croit d' un fol bien souvent qu' il soit Clerc, pour ses vestemens: Pro. *Graue clothes make dunces often seeme great Clarkes.*

Promettre sans donner est fol reconforter: Prov. *Fruitlesse promises appease none but fooles.*
Qui commet affaire à vn fol s'appreste à le suyvre: Prov. *(Least hee wish hee had gone about it himselfe; also) he that imployes a foole may follow him for companie; for wise men vse to imploy wise men.*
Tout est perdu ce qu'on donne à fol: Pro. *All that is giuen to a foole is cast away; (whereupon some Critick will perhaps conclude, that all the labour bestowed on this word hath been misbestowed.)*
Fol: m. folle: f. *Foolish, fond, simple, witlesse, foppish, idle, vaine.*
Farine folle. *Meale-dust, or Mill-dust.*
Paistri de folle farine. *A sleight, vaine, or idle fellow.*
Figue folle. *A Fig-date; also, a Sicamore fig; the fruit of the outlandish Sicamore, or Mulberrie Figtree.*
Paille folle de bled. *The vpmost thinne rind, or outside, of straw.*
De fol Iuge breve sentence: Pro. *A foole soone giues his verdict.*
Vuides chambres font les Dames folles: Pro. *Looke* Chambre.
Folastre: com. *Wanton, lasciuious, toying, fond, effeminate.*
Folastremént: m. *Wantonnesse, ribaldrie, lasciuious toying, effeminacie, foolish daliance.*
Folastrément. *Wantonly, fondly, lasciuiously, effeminately.*
Folastrer. *To play the wanton, leacher it, vse lasciuious tricks.*
Folastrerie: f. *A fashion of taking Woodcockes; also, as* Folastremént.
Folatre, Folatrément. *as* Folastre, Folastrément.
Folatrer. *as* Folastrer.
Folatreries: f. *Fond trickes, lasciuious prankes, wanton fashions, effeminate actions.*
Folatrie: f. *Wantonnesse, fopperie, foolerie.*
Folement. *Fondly, simply, foppishly, witlesly, foolishly, vnaduisedly, rashly.*
Folet: m. *A prettie foole, a little fop, a yong coxe, none of the wisest.*
Folet: m. ette: f. *Somewhat fond, prettie and foppish, a little foolish, or, young and foolish.*
Esprit folet. *An Hobgoblin, Robin-goodfellow.*
Poil folet. *A young mossie beard; also, the first downe of young birds.*
Foleton. *as* Folet.
Folie: f. *Follie, simplicitie, foolishnesse, fondnesse, vnaduisednesse, foppishnesse, indiscretion, ideotisme; also, a kind of spiced bread.*
Folie aux garçons. *Lecherie; and hence;*
Faire folie. *A woman to play false, enter a man more then she ought, or tread her shooe awry.*
Folie faire, & folie recognoistre, sont deux pairs de folie: Prov. *Hee's doubly fond that iustifies his fondnesse.*
C'est folie de se prendre aux femmes, & aux bestes: Prov. *Mad is the man that brables with women, and beasts.*
Courtes folies sont les meilleures: Prov. *Short follies are the best; or, the best of a fond act is the shortnesse of it; or, follies the lesse while they last the more they are to be borne with.*
En amour est folie, & sens: Pro. *In loue there is both wit, and witaldrie.*
Il peche sagement qui fait folie par conseil: Prov. *He wisely failes whom counsell makes to faile; or, faults done b' aduise are most excusable.*

Qui le bien void, & le mal prend, fait folie en bon escient: Prov. *He that sees what's good, and takes what's bad, is guiltie of wilfull ideotisme.*

Folier. *To play the foole, doe like an asse, behaue himselfe like an ideot.*

Il n'est si sage qui ne folie aucunes fois: Prov. *The wisest man is foolish now and then.*

Si le fol ne folie il perd sa saison: Prov. *A foole is most absurd when he playes not the foole.*

Follasses: f. *The hearbe Beets.*

Follastrerie: f. *as* Folastrerie.

Follet; *or*, Esprit follet. *An Hobgoblin, Robin-good-fellow, Bugbeare.*

Follettes. *Orage, Atriplex, golden hearbe.*

Follicule: m. *A little bag, powch, or sacke; also, a huske, hull, peele, or skin inclosing seed.*

Follier. *as* Folier.

Folliner. *To play the wanton, to vse lasciuious tricks.*

Fomentation: f. *A fomentation, or fomenting; a comforting, cherishing, easing, asswaging; a thing applyed in a bladder, spunge, &c, (if it be moist) or within a bag, or quilt (if it be dry) either to cherish, comfort, or ease the part it is layed on, or to make way, by opening the pores, for ointments, or plaisters to be layed on it.*

Fomenté: m. ée: f. *Fomented; cherished, comforted, refreshed, eased.*

Fomenter. *To foment; cherish, comfort, refresh, ease, or asswage the paine of; as in* Fomentation.

Foncé: m. ée: f. *Furnished, well grounded, whose ground is strewed, or stored with; also, headed, that (as a peece of caske, &c) hath a head, or bottome set into it.*

Fonceau: m. *A little bottome, hole, hollow, or deepe place.*

Fonceau d'un Canon. *The big, or broad end of a Canon bitt.*

Foncer. *To head a peece of Caske; to set a bottome, or head into any such vessell.*

Foncier: m. ere: f. *Fundamentall; or, of the soyle, for the soyle, belonging to the soyle.*

Cour fonciere. *A Court Baron; or, Court of base Jurisdiction.*

Iustice fonciere. *Low Iurisdiction, or a kind thereof, exercised by the Lords of* Fiefs, *for the recouerie of their rights from their vassalls; and often too farre strained, and therefore disallowed, and forbidden, by the Customes of diuers Prouinces.*

Rente fonciere. *A Rent-seruice, Rent-charge, or Feefarme-rent; an accession vnto* Cens; *or, a second charge imposed on land vpon the second graunt thereof, called thus, because the soyle is euer after lyable vnto it.*

Seigneur foncier. *The (direct) Lord of a* Fief; *the Lord of the Soyle.*

Serfs fonciers. *Such as hauing beene conquered by the auncient French, receiued lands of them, on the Condition of doing them any seruice; these were by no means permitted to change the habitation they first betooke them to.*

Fond: m. *A bottome, floore, ground, foundation, deepe, or depth; also, land, soyle, mould; a plot, or peece of ground;* (vn fond.) *also, the drawing out of a (cut) garment; also, the head of Caske, or of any hollow vessell; also, a Marchants stocke, whether it be money, or money worth.*

Fond de terre. *So was the Tax, or Aide (which in the yeare 1412 should haue beene imposed on euerie Arpent) called.*

Vn bon fond de deniers. *A good round summe of money, gathered before hand for the bearing out of, or going through with, an action; and hence;*

Il n'a point de fond. *He is not within, or not in the leather, or hath it not in the leather; he wants wherewithall; he hath made no prouision, or but small prouision of money.*

'A fonds de cuve. *Throughly, fully, largely, home.*

Fossé faict à fonds de cuve. *Broad, and flat-bottomde.*

De fond en comble. *See* Comble; *or*, Fons.

'A fin fond de. *From the verie middest; out of the depth, or bottome of.*

'A plein fond. *Large, deepe, side, full enough.*

Donner fond. *To cast anker; or, to let fall an Anker.*

Labourer en fond. *To plow verie deepe.*

Mettre à fonds. *To sinke (a ship) &c.*

Au matin les monts, au soir les fonds: Pro. *Looke* Mont.

Il est plus aisé se tirer de la rive que du fond: Pro. *It is more easie to leaue a businesse in the beginning, then in the middest of it; or, a man may better desist when he hath but entered, then when he is farre engaged.*

Fond de cire: f. *The melting of wax.*

Fondalité: f. *Fundalitie; right of, or interest in, the soyle; the title or estate of the Lord of a soyle.*

Fondamental: m. ale: f. *Fundamentall; belonging to a foundation, or ground-worke.*

Pierre fondamentale. *The principall stone, the chiefe strength of a foundation.*

Fondamment. *as* Fondéement.

Fondant. *Founding, or grounding; also, melting, resoluing; consuming, wasting away; also, sinking, falling, or comming downe on a suddaine.*

Fondateur. *A founder, maker, creator, builder, first inuentor, chiefe deuiser, principall author of.*

Fondation. *A foundation, or ground-worke; the first building, or erection of.*

Fonde: f. *A sling, to cast stones with.*

Fondé: m. ée: f. *Founded, grounded; built; erected, established; resting in, consisting of.*

Fondé par dessoubs. *Vnderset, vnderlayed, or layed vnder.*

Ie suis fondé en equité. *The right is on my side; I stand on iust, and honest tearmes; my cause I am sure is good.*

Nous y sommes aussi bien fondez l'un que l'autre: *Our causes are much of one goodnesse, or much after one; we haue both reason alike.*

Fondéement. Pleurer fondéement. *To weepe extreamely, to resolue, or melt, into teares.*

Fondegue: f. *A Marchants ware-house, or store-house.*

Fondelfe. *A kind of Engine for batterie; vsed in old time.*

Fondement: m. *A foundation, ground, ground-worke; a principall stay, chiefe meanes; good beginning, or way; also, a melting, resoluing; wasting, consuming away; also, the fundament.*

Il faisoit grand fondement de. *He relyed, or built verie much vpon.*

Rien ne peut estre grand qui n'a bon fondement: Prov. *Nothing that wants a good ground can be great.*

Fonder. *To found, ground, lay the foundation of, make a beginning to; to build, settle, rest, or stay vpon.*

Fon-

Fonderie: f. *Bell-founding, the trade of melting, or of casting things in mettall.*
Fondeur: m. *A melter, or trier of mettals; a founder.*
Estonnez comme fondeurs de cloches (quand la fonte n'a pas bien pris) *extreamly amazed, appalled, abashed, out of countenance.*
Fondier: m. *A slinger; one that throws stones out of a sling.*
Fondileures: f. *Chops, rifts, choanes, in a womans ouer-full breasts.*
Fondrailles: f. *The grounds, lees, or dregs of liquor.*
Fondre. *To melt, or cast, as mettals, &c; to resolue, as snow before a hot Sunne; also, to powre, or shead abroad; also, to sinke; fall, or goe downe; and hence;*
Fondre d'enhaut. *To stoope; to fall downe plump, to come downe amaync, as an eager, and high-flying hawk do's vpon her prey.*
Fondre à terre. *The same; or to stoope, as a hawke; to drop as a partridge.*
Se Fondre. *to melt, wast, resolue, consume away; to sink downe on a suddaine.*
Fondreau. *as* Fondrillon.
Fondrée: f. *as* Fondrilles.
Fondriere: f. *A bog, or quagmire; also, a great bottome, or large, and deep valley; also, as;*
Fondrilles: f. *The grounds, dregs, lees, or thick-growne bottome of liquor that hath stood any time; the settlings of liquor.*
Fondrillon: m. *A bottom to wind silke, thread, or yarne on; also, a knot tangled in thread.*
Fondroyer. *To hangdowne to the ground; to hang low, or towards the ground; to hang so low that it touches the ground.*
Fonds: *Looke* Fond; *also, a font; looke* Fons.
Fondu: m. uë: f. *Melted, resolued; cast as mettall, founded, as a thing of mettall; consumed, worne, wasted vnto nothing.*
Bastiment fondu. *Sunke, or fallen, downe.*
Poix fonduë. *Tarre.*
Fondure: f. *A founding, melting, or casting of mettals; &c.*
Fonge: m. *A Mushrome, or toadsstoole.*
Fongeux: m. euse: f. *Spungie; light, or full of holes, as a spunge.*
Fongnement: m. *A frowning, powting, louting, louring; also, a discontented grombling.*
Fongner. *To frowne, powt, lowt, loure, glow, sell sowce, also, to gromble.*
Fons. *Looke* Fond.
De fons en comble. *From the very foundation; or, from the top to the bottome; wholly, throughly, fully.*
Fons: m. *A font to baptise children.*
Lever vn enfant des fons. *To be a childs witnesse, or Godfather, at the font.*
Tenir vn enfant sur le fons. *To Christen a child; to name the childe; as,* Lever.
Font. *as* Fontaine; *and hence;*
Au matin vers les monts, au soir vers les fonts: Prov. *Looke* Mont.
Fontaigner: m. ere: f. *Of, or belonging to, a fountaine; or, as* Fontenier.
Fontaine: f. *A fountaine; spring, source; well; also, a Cocke, or spout in a fountaine; and, the quill, or faucet of a wine-vessell.*
La fontaine de meschanceté. *The head, root, originall source, principall cause, of wickednesse.*
Fontaine de la teste. *The mould of the head.*
Endurer la soif aupres d'une fontaine. *To starue in a Cookes shop, we say.*
'A petite fontaine boit on à son aise: Pro. *Looke,* Boire.
Qui n'a laine boive à la fontaine: Pro. *Let him that hath no wooll (viz. no wealth) drink water.*
Fontaineux. *Full of springs, or fountaines.*
Fontainier. *as* Fontaigner.
Fontanel: m. elle: f. veine fontanelle. *The principall veine in the thigh of a horse, &c.*
Fontanelle f. *A running sore; or, an issue made for a griefe or sore; as* Cabrol.
Fonte: f. *A melting, founding, or casting of mettalls.*
Torche de fonte. *A kind of great linke, all of wax; Looke* Torche.
Fontenelle. *A little spring, a small fountaine; also, as* Fontanelle; *an issue.*
Fontenelle de la teste. *The vpper part of the head forward.*
Fontenette. *as* Fontenelle; *a little fountaine.*
Fontenier: m. *A fountaine-maker; a digger of wells, a searcher for springs; a conduit-maker, a conueyer of water from springs to conduits.*
Fontenil: m. *A small fountaine.*
Fontenille: f. *The same.*
For: m. *A Court, or common place for pleading; as,* Le For l'Evesque. *The bishops Court:* ¶Parisien.
For. *(In Composition) signifies, out or without; as in* Forclos, *&c, and sometimes also, badly or ill; as in* Forconseiller, &c.
Foradjour. *as* Adiour.
Forage. droict de fo. *Foure pots of wine vpon euery peece thats sould by retayle, due vnto the lord of the Iurisdiction wherein tis sold; In some places it is also, two pots vpon euery peece thats sould in grosse; Looke* Droict.
Forain: m. ine: f. *Forreine, strange, alien, outlandish.*
Chemin forain (de Boullenois) *Is to be fiftene foot broat.*
Domaine forain. *An ancient imposition of iiij d.* Tour. *in the pound, vpon marchandice, &c; or, as* Refuë.
Imposition foraine. *An imposition of xij d.* Tour. *in the pound vpon marchandice, and commodities imported, or brought into the Realme (onely within Paris there is but vi d. taken.)*
Prevost forain. *Seeke* Prevost.
Traite foraine. *Is as* Imposition foraine; *but leuyed vpon commodities transported, or carryed out of the Realme.*
Foraines: f. *The Customes, or Tolls that are leuyed in faires, and markets.*
Forans. *A certaine receptacle for Sea-water (whereof salt is made) conueyed into it out of others by a trunk, or pipe of wood.*
Forban. *as,* Ban; *or an exclusion.*
Forbanni: m. ie: f. *Expelled, bannished, cast forth, driuen out.*
Forbannir. *To banish, reiect, expell, cast forth, driue out.*
Forbannissement: m. *A bannishment, expulsion, exclusion, out-casting, forth-driuing.*
Forbatu: m. uë: f. *Canuased, or beaten throughly; swinged out of doores.*
Forbe: f. *as* Fourbe. *A cunning, and coosening tricke.*
Forbeu: m. euë: f. *Mellow, fine, cup-taken, pot-shotten, whose fudling or barley Cap is on.*
Cheval forbeu. *A horse that hath drunke being too hot, and is thereby foundered.*
Se Forboire. *To surfet with drinking, to be somewhat ouer-*

ouerseene, or too blame; to take a dram too much; to drinke vntil he stare againe; also, to founder, as a horse, by drinking when he is verie hot.

Forbours. *as* Faulxbourgs. *Suburbes.*

Forçable. *Forceable, compellable.*

Forçat: m. *A galley-slaue; also, a game at draughts, wherein one must take his aduersarie when he may, or else he himselfe is taken.*

Force: f. *Force, might, strength, power, abilitie, vigour, vehemencie; vertue, effect, operation, energie, efficacie, powerfull working; violence, constraint, compulsion, rauishment; (also, store, plentie, aboundance, many of; whence,* Force escus; force arbres.)

Force forcée. *Of force, of necessitie, will he nill he, in spight of his teeth.*

A force. *With great might, with much indeauor; whence,* Couru à force. *Hardly, eagarly, or extreamly, pursued.*

La force luy en est demeurée. *He hath got the victorie; the vpper hand, the better end of the staffe, in the matter.*

Ce que luy sera force. *Which he shall be faine, or forced, to doe.*

Faire force. *To indeauor, labour, striue, inforce, himselfe.*

Ie ne fais point force de cela. *I care not for, I force not of, I am not mooued by, that thing.*

Mieux vaut engin que force: Pro. *Better be wise then strong.*

Forcé: m. ée: f. *Forced, compelled, constrayned; also, rauished, as a woman; also, burst open, broke through; also, hard layed too; brought vnto a narrow strait, hard pinch, ill passe.*

Force forcée. *Of necessitie; Looke* Force.

Forcement: m. *A forcing; a compelling, or constrayning; also, a bursting open, or breaking through.*

Forcenant. Chien forcenant. *A dog thats eagar in chace, hot after his game, and will stand long.*

Forcené: m. ée: f. *Mad, wood, franticke; raging, furious, out of his wits.*

Forcenement: m. *Madnesse, raging, furie, woodnesse, frenzie.*

Forcener. *To be mad, franticke, furious.*

Forcenerie. *as* Forcenement.

Forcer. *To force, compell, vrge, constraine; also, to violate, force, or rauish (as a woman;) also, to breake open (as a dore;) also, to lay hard vnto, or bring into extremitie (as dogs doe a deere after a long chace;) also, to ouercome, subdue, force, passe through by force;* (forcer les gardes d'une porte.)

Forcer de la laine. *To pick, or tease wooll:* v.m.

Forces: f. *A paire of sheeres.*

Faire les forces. *A horse to hold his mouth open, and turne his chaps often from one side to the other.*

Forcette: f. *A cizar, a small paire of sheeres.*

Forceur: m. *A forcer, compeller, vrger, constrainer; a violent subduer, conqueror, ouercommer.*

Forchasser, come vn arc. *To cast, or shoot awrie, as a bow, that is stronger on one side then of another.*

Forcheminé. *Wandered, gone out of the way.*

Forcheminer. *To wander, stragle, take a wrong course, goe out of the way.*

Forchette. *Looke* Fourchette.

Forclorre. *To exclude, reiect, expel, shut out; to dismisse from, or, not admit vnto.*

Forclos: m. ose: f. *Excluded, reiected, expelled, shut out; dismissed, or debarred from.*

Forclusion: f. *An exclusion, or shutting out; a dismissing; or debarring from.*

Forcommand: m. *A putting out of possession, or a voiding of possession, by order, or commaund of a Court.*

Forcommandé: m. ée: f. *Voided, outed, or put out, of possession.*

Forconseillé: m. ée: f. *Ill aduised, counselled amisse.*

Forconseiller. *To giue ill counsell.*

Forconte: m. *A misreckoning, or miscounting.*

Forconté: m. ée: f. *Misreckoned, counted amisse.*

Forconter. *To misreckon, or count amisse.*

Fore: f. *as* For; *a Court.*

Foré: m. ée: f. *Bored, pierced; wherein holes are made.*

Forer. *To bore, pierce, make holes in.*

Fores. De fores. *Without, forth of.*

Forest: m. *Looke* Foret.

Forest: f. *A Forest; a great, (and priuiledged) wood, or wooddie wildernesse; Some (Frenchmen) haue generally interpreted it (from the Latine words* foris, & sta) *a Place whereto the accesse, and entrie is forbidden, by the owner, vnto others; and hence, it seemes, that priuiledged fishings, or large waters (wherein none but the Lords thereof could fish) were also tearmed,* Forests.

Forestain: m. ine: f. *Wooddie, wild, forrest-like.*

Forestier: m. *A forrester, or foster; a Keeper of, or in, a forrest; a Raunger, Woodman, or Wood-warden; an Officer that lookes to the Kings woods, or forrests; (In old time the Gouernours of Flanders (for the French) were tearmed* Forestiers;) *also, a forrainer, alien, stranger.*

Forestier: m. ere: f. *Woodie, forrest-like; of or belonging to, a forrest; wild, sauage; also, forraine.*

Sergent forestier. *Looke* Sergent.

Foret: m. *A Gimblet, or Piercer.*

Forfaict: m. *A crime, sinne, fault, misdeed, offence, trespasse, transgression.*

Forfaict: m. cte: f. *Offended, sinned, misdone, trespassed; also, offending, sinning, misdoing.*

Forfaicture. *as* Forfaict; *a transgression; also, a forfeiture, or confiscation.*

Cela nous appartient par forfaicture du seigneur feodal. *Thereto we haue no possibilitie of right.*

Forfaire. *To sinne, offend, commit a fault, misdoe, transgresse, trespasse against; also, to forfeit.*

Si truye forfaict les pourceaux le souffrent: Pro. *Pigs fare the worse for harmes done by the Sow.*

Forfaiture. *as* Forfaicture.

Forfait. *as* Forfaict.

Forfan: m. *A knaue, rogue, rascall, rakehell, varlet, villaine, vagabond, base fellow, filthie slaue, naughtie packe, leud companion.*

Forfanter. *To play the rogue; to marre all he meddles with.*

Forfanterie: f. *Roguerie, knauerie, villanie; also, a crue of rakehellie scowndrells.*

Forgagé: m. ée: f. *Redeemed, had from pawne.*

Forgager. *To redeeme, or fetch out, a pawne, &c.*

Forgas: m. *A seisure, or sale of goods, vpon execution.* ¶Norm.

Temps de forgas. *Certaine dayes after the open sale of goods in execution, giuen vnto the executee to proue the execution wrongfull, and recouer them with costs; or to satisfie his creditor; or to haue his goods againe for the money which was bid for them; which time if he neglect, they are gone for euer.* ¶Norm.

Forge à fer. *A Smithes Forge.*

Gens de bonne forge. *People of good credit, much worth, great honestie; or of an honest disposition.*
Forgé: m. ée: f. *Forged, made, framed; formed, fashioned.*
Forgeant. *Forging, framing; working at the Anuyle.*
En forgeant on devient febvre: Pro. *Looke* Febvre.
Forgement: m. *A forging, making, framing; also, a horses euer-reaching.*
Forger. *To forge, make, frame, compose; hammer, deuise, coyne, inuent; also, a horse to ouer-reach, or cut his fore-feet with his hinder.*
Forgeron: m. *A Forger, or Forge-man; a Smith.*
Forgetture: f. *Looke* Forjecture.
Forgeur: m. *A forger, maker, framer, composer, coyner, inuentor, deuiser.*
Forhu. *A whoo-whup; or, the call, hooting, or whooping of huntsmen at the death of their chace.*
Forhuer. *To whoope, shout, hoot, hollow; crie whoo-whup.*
Foriboles. *as* Fariboles. ¶Rab.
Forject: m. *A iutting, or leaning out, or ouer; a rellish, or out-footing.*
Forjecture: f. *The coping, or water table of a wall; a rellish, or footing out of a wall, or from a foundation.*
Forjet. *as* Forject.
Forjetter. *To iut, rellish, cope, leane out, hang ouer; also, as* Forchasser.
Forjetture. *as* Forjecture.
Forissir de raison. *To transgresse, or exceed the limits of reason.*
Forissu: m. uë: f. *Sprung, or issued out of.*
Forjugé: m. ée: f. *Wrongfully iudged; also, dispossessed, or outed by a Iudgement.*
Forjugement: m. *A wrongfull iudging, or vniust condemning of; also, a disinheriting, depriuing, dispossessing of; also, an outing vpon a Judgement.*
Forjuger. *To iudge, or condemne, wrongfully; also, to disinherite, depriue, dispossesse of; also, to out by Iudgement.*
Forjuger l'absent. *as*, Forjurer l'absent.
Forjur: m. *A quitting, release, discharge of; or, as* Forjurement.
Forjurement: m. *A quitting, forsaking, abandoning, abiuring, renouncing; also, a selling, or aliening; also, a discharging.*
Forjurer. *To quit, forsake, abandon, renounce, abiure, giue ouer; to release vnto; also, to sell, alien, passe away.*
Forjurer l'absent. *To barre, and amerce, by decree, an absent, and wilfull defendant, or, a defendant that will not appeare.*
Forjurer les facteurs. *To quit, excuse, discharge, or leaue prosecuting of, the committers, actors, or malefactors.*
Forlignant. *Degenerating, growing out of kind.*
Forligné. *Degenerated, growne out of kind.*
Forlignement: m. *A degenerating.*
Forligner. *To degenerate, or grow out of kind; to differ in conditions from his auncestors; also, a villaine, bastard, or stranger, to match with a free, true-bred, home-borne woman; to marrie out of his ranke, or condition; also, land to descend collaterally, or goe out of one line into another.*
Forliner. *as* Forligner.
Forlonge. *Verie farre off; (a tearme of Hunting.)*
Les chiens chassent de forlonge. *The dogs are farre behind the Deere, Hare, &c.*
Les chiens resentent de forlonge. *The dogs find of the Deere, though he be farre off, or before, them.*

Forlongé: m. ée: f. *Gone farre before, left farre behind.*
Forlonger. *To goe farre before, leaue farre behind.*
Formage. *See* Fourmage.
Formagerie. *as* Fourmagerie.
Formaillet: m. *An inchaunted Image, or representation of some creature, worne about the necke, to preserue the wearer from danger; See* Fermaillet.
Formalité: f. *Formalitie, quaintnesse, precisenesse in outward matters; also, the strict forme of proceeding, or pleading, in law.*
Perdre son procez par vne formalité. *To loose his suit, by an error committed, or clause mistaken, in his declaration, &c.*
se Formalizer. *To take in dudgeon; to be discontented with, or oppose himselfe against.*
Se formalizer pour aucun. *To vndertake ones quarrell openly; to imbarke himselfe into a quarrell for another.*
Formarcher. *as* Faux-marcher.
Formariage: m. *Marriage against Law, or Custome; also, mariage out of ranke, or condition.*
Amende, ou droict de formariage. *Is the halfe, or third, or (as the custome is) other part of whatsoeuer a villaine is worth, forfeited to his Landlord, or Lord of the Iurisdiction wherein he liues, by marrying a woman thats free, or of a forraine Iurisdiction; this, although he haue got leaue to doe it; whereas if he doe it without leaue, he looses 60 s more; In former times bastards, and strangers, who married other then bastards, or strangers, were subiect to this penaltie; Now those in most places, and these in some, are wholly exempted from it.*
Formarié. *Married out of his ranke, degree, or condition; or to a woman of a forraine Iurisdiction.*
Formarier. *To marrie out of his ranke, degree, or condition; or to a woman of a forraine Iurisdiction.*
Formation. *A forming, framing, fashioning.*
Forme: m. *A kind of Faulcon, or long-wingd Hawke.*
Forme: f. *A forme, fashion; manner, method; a mould, patterne, draught, frame, representation, tipe, character; shape, resemblance, fauor, figure of; also, a cheesefat, or chesford; also, a long Bench, or Forme to sit on; also, a Shoomakers last; also, a Hares forme.*
En forme. *Formally, handsomly, orderly, as it should be.*
En forme de. *Resembling, or like vnto.*
'A telle forme tel soulier: Prov. *(Of a thing fitted, or fitly suited.)*
Formé: m. ée: f. *Formed, shaped, fashioned; drawne, pictured, printed, figured; framed.*
Heretique formé. *A full, resolute, arrant, hereticke.*
Partie formée. *An accuser in, or follower of, a criminall action (in respect of his particular interest;) Looke* Formel.
Formel: m. elle: f. *Formall, plaine, open, flat, expresse, exact; absolute, proper, according to Art; earnest, vehement, violent, resolute, stiffe, obstinate.*
Contradiction formelle. *Which appeares, or is expressed, in the case, and cause.*
Ennemy formel. *A professed, open, or vtter enemie.*
Garent formel. *See* Garent.
Partage reel, & formel. *A partition fully executed; a reall, or actuall partition.*
Partie formelle. *A Complainant, or Accuser in a criminall action; as in* Partie formée; *(This accuser offers to ly in prison with him he accuses, vntill he haue made good his accusation; but is seldome taken at his word.)*
Formelier: m. *A Last-maker.*
Formelizé: m. ée: f. *Formed, whereunto forme is giuen.*
Formelizer. *To forme; to giue, or adde forme vnto.*

Formellement. *Flatly, plainely, directly, expressely, openly, wholly, vtterly, without exception; stiffely, earnestly, vehemently, resolutely; exactly, precisely; also, quickly, speedily, forthwith, immediatly, without delay.*

Formené: m. ée: f. *Disquieted, vexed, afflicted, molested, harried, tormented.*

Formener. *To vex, disquiet, afflict, molest, harrie, torment, giue much trouble vnto.*

Forment: m. & formentée: f. *Furmentie, Wheat; See* Froument & Froumentée.

Forment. *Almost (as in,* forment guery;) *also, exceedingly, greatly, mightily, verie much;* (forment malade.)

Formentin: m. ine: f. *Of Wheat.*

Vne pilure formentine. *A loafe, or lunchion of white bread.*

Former. *To forme, fashion, shape; make, frame, order, dispose, institute; figure, draw, picture, deuise, represent.*

Former le procez à. *To draw an Indictment against.*

Formerets: m. *The small branches of a vault, in the ends, or inside thereof.*

Formi: m. *An Ant, a Pismeare; Looke* Fourmi.

Formiant. Poulx for. *The pulse that beats verie fast, but verie weakely; (a signe of approching death.)*

Formidable: com. *Fearefull, dreadfull, terrible.*

Formie: f. *as* Formi.

Formiere: f. *An Ants hill, or neast of Pismeares.*

Formiliere. *as* Formiere; *also, a kind of wart in the fundament, somewhat resembling a Mulberrie.*

Formillement: m. *The prickling smart of Ringwormes, or Warts, like the stinging of Ants.*

Formilles. *as* Herpes.

Formillon. *A small blacke Spider like an Ant, and spotted on the backe with little starre-like specks.*

Formion: m. *A small Ant, or Pismeare.*

Formoret: m. *A kind of strong Lye whereof Soape is made.*

Formort. *as* Formorture.

Formorture: f. *An Escheat falling to, or succession falling on, a man, by the death of another.*

Formosité: f. *Beautie, comelinesse, well-fauourednesse, sweet feature.*

Formoture. *as* Formorture.

Formulaire: m. *The stile, fashion, or manner of proceeding in the Law; a President for the drawing of a Deed, Patent, Pleading, &c; also, a womans thing.*

Practicien qui entend bien son formulaire. *A cunning pleader.*

Formule: f. *A stile in writing; a certaine rule, order, manner, fashion of proceeding, or pleading, in Law.*

Fornage. *See* Fournage.

Fornaise. *as* Fournaise; *a furnace.*

Fornicateur: m. *A fornicator, wencher, smell-smocke, mutton-munger, whore-hunter.*

Fornication: f. *Fornication; lecherie committed by an vnmarried couple.*

Forniquer. *To play the fornicator; to leacher it, vnmarried, with an vnmarried person.*

Forpaiser. *To wander farre out of his countrey; also, a wild beast to abandon the Couert (wherein he vseth to lodge) and flye, or take, into the Champion.*

Forparler. *To mispeake, or speake ill.*

se Forpasser d'un pas. *To go a step further then he needs, or should.*

Forpie: f. *The mouth, or middle of an opened paire of sheeres.*

Forrage. *as* Forage.

Forregardant. *Out-looking, or awry-looking.*

Fors. *Except, vnlesse, but onely, without it be; also, without doores, or abroad; also, out, right out, all out.*

Forsage. *Ouer-weight in money; when a peece is heauier then it should be.*

Forsaire: m. *A Gally-slaue.*

Forsené. *as* Forcené.

Fort: m. *A Fort, Hold, Fortresse; also, a standing, or setled Campe, defended and girt about with ditches, rampiers, or pallisadoes, and little Bastions; also, the hearbe Wormewood (so tearmed of the strong smell which it hath.)*

Le fort d'un affaire. *The chiefest point in, hardest part of, a businesse.*

Le fort d'une boule. *The drawing part, or byas of a Bowle.*

Le fort d'un cerf. *The hold of a Stag; the thicket, or couert wherein he lyes, or whereto he flyes.*

Les forts des forests. *Thickets, or the thickest parts of forrests.*

Le fort d'un lievre. *The couert of a Hare.*

Fort: m. forte: f. *Strong; tough, massiue; hardie, sturdie, lustie, able-bodied; mightie, forcible, powerfull, effectuall; able to beare a great shocke, assault, or brunt.*

Forte clameur. *A fine of* ij s. vj d. Tour. *due to the King within the Chastellenie of* Montereau *(vpon euerie personall action) for the first summons, or seruing of the Writ, although the parties agree, and the cause proceed no further; If it doe, and come to a hearing,* vij s. vj d. *must be payed; both, by the partie that first yeelds, or is foyled.*

Forte monnoye, solz forts. *Good money, money of the best sort, or most value; (for* 25 solz forts *are worth* 40 solz Tour.) *A word peculiar to the Sol, and vsed when the reckoning and rates of money were grounded thereon.*

Vn bois fort. *A thicke wood.*

Le faict fort. *See* Faict

Terroir fort. *A hard, or hungrie soyle.*

Fort en bride. *Stubborne, stout, vnrulie, head-strong.*

Fort comme vn Dauphin en terre. *Most weake, most feeble, of no force at all.*

Le fort portant le foible. *Good and bad together, one with another.*

Tes fortes fievres. *A plague choake thee, a pestilence take thee.*

Cecy n'est pas fort à faire. *There is no great difficultie in this; it is not hard to doe.*

Ie me fais fort de cela. *I take that matter vpon me; I am assured of it; I presume, rely, or build on it; I dare vndertake that it will beare me out.*

Faire main forte à. *Looke* Faire.

Fort est qui abbat, & plus fort qui se releve: Prov. *He that recouers a foyle is stronger then he that gaue it.*

Qui attend il a fort temps: Prov. viz. *Thinkes his time verie long.*

Fort. (Adverb.) *Verie, most, verie much, mainely, exceedingly, excessiuely, extreamely, vehemently.*

Fort & Ferme. *Looke* Ferme.

Au fort aller. *At most, at worst, if the worst come to the worst.*

Fortelet: m. ette: f. *A little strong, pretie and forcible, or pretie and strong to his age.*

For-

Fortement. *Strongly; forcibly, mightily, powerfully, ably; effectually; toughly, hardily; extreamely; mainly, verie much.*
Forteresse: f. *A Fortresse, or Hold.*
Fortet. *as* Fortelet. *Pretie and strong.*
Fortifiable: com. *Fortifiable; which may be fortified.*
Fortification: f. *Fortification; the Art, or worke, of fortifying.*
Fortifié: m. ée: f. *Fortified; strengthened, corroborated; inforced, enabled, confirmed; hardened, setled, assured.*
Fortifiement: m. *A fortifying, strengthening, inforcing, enabling.*
Fortifier. *To fortifie, strengthen, corroborate; enable, inforce, confirme; harden, settle, assure.*
Fortiltrer. *A Deere to shun the place wherein dogs are layed for him.*
Fortraction: f. *A lurching, purloyning; withdrawing.*
Fortraire. *To lurch, purloyne; withdraw from.*
Fortrait: m. aite: f. *Lurched, purloyned; withdrawne.*
Fortuit: m. ite: f. *Casuall, accidentall, at aduenture, happening by chance.*
Cas fortuit. *An offence committed by chance-medley.*
Fortuitement. *Casually, by chance, at aduenture, by hap hazard; more by hap then any cunning.*
Fortunable: com. *Disastrous, vnfortunate.* (v.m.)
Fortunal. *as* Fortune; *also, a great, and suddaine tempest at sea.*
Fortune: f. *Fortune; also, hap, chaunce, luck, lot, hazard, aduenture; also, destinie, fatall necessitie.*
Courir fortune. *To be in great danger; to incurre a great hazard (whether of shipwracke, or any other mischiefe;) to be neere, or next dore, to a shipwracke.*
Suyvre la fortune. *To follow, or adhere vnto, the stronger side.*
Fortune aide à celuy qui se veut aider: Pro. *Fortune aides him that loues to aid himselfe; fortune helps on the forward.*
Fortune n' espargne ny serviteur ny Maistre, elle donne & reprend, tel est son estre: Prov. *Fortune spares no man, keepes no couenants, obserues no condition.*
Fortune ne vient seule: Prov. *Ill lucke comes not alone; or, one ill lucke followes in the necke of another.*
Les biens de fortune passent comme la Lune: Pro. *Fortunes blessings flit like the Moone; or hardly continue the age of a Moone.*
Contre fortune nul ne peut: Prov. *No man can withstand his destinie; or, be against a chance.*
Assez fait qui fortune passe, & plus encor qui putain chasse: Prov. *He does much that ill fortune misses, but he does more that quits a whore.*
Aux yeux la Lune bonne fortune: Pro. *See* Lune.
Mieux vaut vne once de fortune qu' une livre de sagesse: Prov. *Better is an ounce of good fortune then a pound of good forecast.*
Fortuné: m. ée: f. *Fortunate, happie, luckie; also, made fortunate, blessed with good hap.*
Fortunément. *Fortunately, happily, luckily, successiuely, prosperously.*
Fortuner. *To make fortunate, blesse with good hap, giue good successe vnto.*
Forvoyer. *To erre, to goe astray; See* Fourvoyer.
Fossailli: m. ie: f. *Ditched in, trenched about; or, that hath a pit made into it.*
Fossaillir. *To ditch in; to make a pit, or ditch.*
Fossat: m. *as* Fossé, *or* Fosse. ¶Langued.

Fossé: m. *A long hole, or pit made into the ground; hence, a dike, ditch, or trench about a towne, fort, camp, close, or house; Looke* Fosse.
Cul de fossé. *A dungeon, or deepe hole in a prison for haynous malefactors.*
Entre la haye & le fossé. *Betweene barke and tree; on narrow tearmes; at a strait pinch; when one hath but little shift to make for himselfe; when he must either breake through the hedge, and be scratched; or, wade through the ditch, and be wet.*
Faire de la terre le fossé. *To dispose of his owne at his owne pleasure; or, to make reasonable good shift with that he hath; or, by charging to discharge, by hurting to helpe, himselfe.*
De terre d' autruy remplir son fossé. *To make vp his mouth, or stuffe his purse full, with another mans money.*
Fosse: f. *Any pit, or hole; but most commonly that, which is round (for* Fossé *is more properly a long one,) and made into, and appearing aboue, the ground (for a caue, denne, or hollow, whose greater part is hidden vnder ground, is more fitly tearmed,* Caverne, &c.) *hence, a Graue; a Mote, or Pond for fish; and sometimes (though seldome) a ditch, trench, or deepe channell.*
Fosse coye. *A priuie, iakes, house of office.*
Fosse à poissons. *A little fish pond, or stue for fish.*
Il est sur le bord de la fosse. *He hath alreadie one foot in the graue.*
Mettre les clefs sur la fosse. *A widow to renounce the administration of her husbands goods.*
Vn aveugle meine l'autre en la fosse: Prov. *Looke* Aveugle.
Fosselu: m. uë: f. *Dimpled; that hath a little pit, or hole in the middest of it.*
Fossette: f. *A little pit; small hole; narrow ditch, or trench; also, a dimple on the cheeke, or chin; also, the hollownesse that is betweene the shoulder blades.*
Fossette de l'oeil. *The eye-pit.*
Fossette de la teste. *The nape of the necke.*
Iouër à la fossette. *To play at cherrie-pit (with nuts.)*
Fossetterie: f. *Pockinesse, or the being full of pock-holes.*
Fossetteux: m. euse: f. *Full of little pits, pockars, or pock-holes.*
Fossile. Grand f. *The bigger of the two bones in the leg.*
Petit fossile. *The lesse. Looke* Focile.
Fossile: com. *Which is, or may be, digged.*
Fossoir: m. *as* Hoyau.
Entre deux comperes se perdit le fossoir: Prov. *Betweene two stooles the tayle goes to the ground; or, as vnder* Compere.
Fossourer. *as* Fossoyer.
Fossoyant. *Digging, ditching, trenching.*
Fossoye: f. *A certaine garment vsed in old time.*
Fossoyé: m. ée: f. *Digged; ditched, trenched about.*
Fossoyement: m. *A digging; a ditching, trenching, pit-making.*
Fossoyer. *To dig; to ditch, or trench about; to make a pit.*
Fossoyeur: m. *A digger, or ditcher; also, a graue-maker.*
Fossoyeure: f. *A digging; a ditching, a pit-making.*
Foterle. *Sarasins Birthwort, or Hartwort.*
Foterne. *as* Foterle.
Fotu: m. *A fomentation, or medicine, applyed to warme, or comfort, a diseased part.*
Fou: m. *A Beech tree.*
Fou. (Buvez fou; venez fou; *drinke, or come, out) corruptly vsed for* Fors.
Foüace: f. *A thicke cake hastily baked, on a hot harth, by hot imbers layed on it, and burning coales ouer them;*

a round Bunne; also, a great Kid, Bauen, or faggot of small sticks; Looke Fougasse.

Manger sa foüace sans pain. To eat dry bread for want of other victuals.

Foüacier: m. One that makes, or sells, Foüaces.

Foüage. Any yearelie tax, or dutie, leuied in old time by supreame Lords vpon euerie chymney, or house-fire kept within their dominions; In Charles the fifths time it was 4 livres Tourn: since that time, in most places, the Tailles haue beene introduced in lieu thereof.

Foüaille. The reward which hunters giue their dogs at the death of a wild Swyne.

Foüailler: m. The singing, or dressing of a wild Swyne.

Foüant: m. A Muske-cat; or, as Fouïnne.

Fouarre. as Foarre.

Foüasse: f. A Bunne, or Cake hastily baked; Looke Foüace.

Foüassier. A Cake-maker; as Foüacier.

Foucque: f. A Coote, or fenne-Ducke.

Foudre. as Fouldre.

Foudroyant. Thunder-striking; darting thunderbolts; violently beating, impetuously bearing downe (as thunder, and lightning) whatsoeuer it lights on.

Foudroyer. as Fouldroyer.

Foüées: f. The smallest sort of Bauens, Kids.

Fouere: f. la fo. The Squirt.

Foüet: m. A whip, scourge, rod.

Vn foüet sans corde. A Sergeants Mace wherewith he arresteth.

Vie foüet, & au vent. Auant, get you packing, be gone (a speech wherein foüet is vsed as if one called for a whip to driue the partie spoken to away.)

Il n'a pas le foüet pour mener cette trompe. He is not sufficient for so bouncing a wench.

Foüettable: com. Worthie to be whipped.

Foüettade: f. A lashing, whipping, scourging.

Foüetté: m. ée: f. Whipped, lashed, scourged, ierked, swindged.

Foüettement: m. A whipping, lashing, scourging, breeching.

Foüetter. To scourge, whip, lash, yerke, or ierke, swindge, breech.

Foüetteur: m. A whipper, scourger, breecher, swindger, ierker, lasher.

Foüetteux: m. euse: f. Fit to be whipped, ierked, scourged.

Foufoulet; whence, Iouër au foufoulet. To play the whore.

Fougade: f. A Mine; an vp-blowing fire-worke, or wild fire; also, as Fougue.

Fougasse: f. A (thicke) cake baked on a hot harth, with hot embers layed on it, and burning coales ouer them; Looke Foüace.

Ie vous rendray pain (ou paste) pour fougasse. You shall haue of me one for another, or as good euerie whit as you bring.

Fouge: f. The rooting of wild Swyne among Fearne, &c.

Fouger. To root, as a Swyne; to stirre vp ordure.

Fougeraye. A Fearnie plot of ground.

Fougiere: f. Fearne brakes; Looke Feuchiere.

Fougon d'une navire. The Cooke-roome of a ship.

Fougoux: m. ouse: f. Soone heated, easily angred; readie, prompt vnto, suddainely falling into, furie; also, proceeding, or carrying himselfe, in his anger, or heat, without either feare, or wit.

Fougue: f. Inclination, or aptnesse, vnto suddaine anger, or furie; also, a desperate, and suddaine effort, or effect of furie, or of any such turbulent, and impetuous passion.

Foui: m. ie: f. Digged, or delued into; mined, or whereinto holes are made.

Fouïer: m. Looke Fouyer.

Fouïer. as Fouiller.

Fouigner. To whyne; powt, lowre, hang the lip, sell Sowce.

Fouillard: m. A leauie bough, or branch. ¶Norm.

Fouillé: m. ée: f. Groped, searched, felt, rifled; also, rooted, or digged (with the nose) for.

Fouillement: m. A groping, feeling, searching, rifling; also, a rooting, or digging (with the nose) for.

Fouille-merde. A Beetle (fly.)

Fouiller. To grope, search, feele (all ouer;) to rifle; also, to root, or dig (with the nose) for.

C'est trop bas cercher la charité de fouiller prez des fesses: Prov. He lookes too low for charitie that lookes so low as the buttocks.

Fouilleur: m. A groper, searcher, feeler; a rifler; a rooter; a digger (with the nose) for.

Fouilleur de Taupes. A Mole-catcher.

Fouillouse: f. A bag, scrip, or powch. ¶Barrag.

Fouïne: f. as Fouïnne; also, a kind of instrument in ships like an Eele-speare, to strike fish with; also, as Faine; Beech-mast.

Fouïnne: f. The Foyne, wood-Martin, or Beech-Martin.

Fouïr. To dig, delue, mine, make holes in the ground.

Fouïr aux taupes. To turne vp the heeles; goe feed wormes, make a dy.

Fouïssement: m. A digging, or deluing.

Fouïsseur: m. A digger, deluer; ditcher; labourer.

Fouïsseure: f. as Fouïssement.

Foulage: m. as Foulement.

Foulcre. A Coote, moore-Henne, fenne-Ducke.

Fouldre: f. A thunderbolt.

Fouldroyant. Thundering and lightning; darting thunderbolts; Looke Foudroyant.

Fouldroyé: m. ée: f. Thunder-stricken, blasted with lightning, and thunder; also, violently beaten, or borne downe.

Fouldroyement: m. A thunder-striking; a darting of thunderbolts; a blasting with lightning, or (inlightned) thunderbolts.

Fouldroyer. To cast, or dart thunderbolts; to strike, burne, or blast with lightning, or (inlightned) thunderbolts; Hence also, to beat, or beare downe with great violence all that comes in his way.

Foule: f. A crowd, presse, or throng of people; also, a fulling Mill.

'A la foule. Thrusting, thronging, hudling, or shoouing hard, one vpon the necke of another.

Foulé: m. ée: f. Troden, stamped, or trampled on; bruised, or crushed by the feet, &c; also, thronged, or thrust together; also, foyled, oppressed, ouercharged; weighed downe; grieued, vexed, afflicted, harried.

L'hoste est tousiours le plus foulé: Prov. The guest (or Host) is alwayes charged most.

Foulée: f. The Slot of a Stag, the Fuse of a Bucke (the view, or footing of either) vpon hard ground, grasse, leaues, or dust; wee call it (most properly) his fiyling.

Foulement: m. A treading, trampling, or stamping on; a bruising, or crushing with the feet, &c; also, a foyling, oppressing, surcharging, ouercharging, extreame wronging.

Fouler. To tread, stampe, or trample on; to bruise, or crush, by stamping; hurt, or obtuse, by treading on; to thrust

thrust, or weigh downe; to leane exceeding hard against; to presse, oppresse, foyle, ouercharge, extreamely.
Fouler l' honneur de; *To disgrace, or scandalize; to reproach, or vse opprobriously.*
Le cheval se foule. *The horse is surbated, or heated of his feet.*
Foulerie: f. *as* Foulement; *also, as* Fouloire.
Fouleur: m. *A treader (of grapes, &c;) a stamper, or trampler on.*
Fouleure: f. *A straine, or wrinch, in a ioynt.*
Fouleures. *as* Foulées.
Fouliere. *as* Foulerie.
Foulis. *as* Foulement.
Foullage. *Fullage; money payed for the thickening of cloth at a fulling Mill.*
Foullé: m. ée: f. *Fulled as cloth in a Mill; also, as* Foulé.
Fouller. *To full, or thicken cloth in a Mill.*
Foulleure. *as* Fouleure.
Foullon. *as* Foulon.
Foullonné: m. ée: f. *Thickened, or fulled.*
Foullonner. *To full, or thicken cloth in a Mill.*
Foullouaire. *as* Fouloire. ¶Rab.
Fouloire. *The round trough, wherein the wheele of a presse, often turning, or the treader, often stamping, crushes the stuffe that is in it.*
Foulon: m. *A fuller, or thickener of clothes; also, a fulling Mill; also, the great, and stinking Droane, or dorre-Bee.*
Chardon à foulon. *The Teazle, or Fullers thistle.*
Herbe à foulon. *Fullers hearbe, Sopeweed, Sopewort, Bruisewort.*
Foulque. *A Coote, moore-Henne, or fenne-Ducke.*
Foulure: f. *A treading, stamping, or trampling on; as* Foulement.
Foulz. *Certain peeces of Venison cut out from betweene the necke, and the essay of a Deere; that part of the side which is next to the necke.*
Foupi: m. ie: f. *Crumpled, rumpled, crushed, trampled on, or crushed by trampling on.*
Foupier: m. *as* Fripier.
Foupir. *To rumple, or crumple; to crush, or marre the fashion of, by sitting, or treading on.*
Fouquer. *To finger, lay hold on, get into his fingers.* ¶Tour.
Fouquet. *The proper name of a man; also, a certaine game like ours, wherein one, setting a staffe against his nose, runnes tilting at a candle.*
Petit Fouquet. *A leacherous, effeminate, licorous tayled fellow; a smell-smocke, wencher, muttonmonger.*
Et puis adieu Fouquet. *And then we may euen goe hang our selues; or bid farewell to all goodfellowship.*
Four: m. *An Ouen; also, a Furnace; also, a great peece of timber in the prowe of a Ship, called, the Hooke.*
Four balet. *A Maukin.*
Four à ban, ou bannal, ou bannier. *A common Ouen for the tenants, or inhabitants of the Iurisdiction wherein it stands.*
Béer contre vn four. *To halt before a criple.*
Ce n'est pas pour luy que le four chauffe. *Tis not for him that this prouision is made; this is no meat for his mouth; no grasse for his mowing.*
Il ne peut estre ensemble au four, & au moulin. *He cannot follow two businesses together; he cannot be here and there too.*
Mettre le pain en vn four froid. *Looke* Pain.
Ils luy mettoyent vn pain au four. *They raught him a bone to gnaw on; or, they made him haue somewhat to doe.*
Il a monté dessus le four. *He is at his full growth.*
Il en porta la paste au four. *He bore the burthen of it; in whomsoeuer the fault was, the punishment fell onely on him.*
Le four appelle le moulin bruslé: Prov. *The micher tearmes the coward couetous; (and may be applyed to anie, that checks another for a fault whereof onely himselfe is guiltie.)*
C'est au four, & au moulin, ou l'on sçait des nouvelles: Pro. *For while the bread bakes, and the corne grinds, people haue some leisure to tell how the world goes.*
En four chaud ne croist herbe: Prov. *Hot Ouens breed no hearbes.*
Quand vn four est bien chaud la gueule s' en ressent: Prov. *Out of the abundance of the heart the mouth speaketh.*
Prodigue, & grand beuveur de vin, n' a du sien ne four, ne moulin: Prov. *The swilling prodigall soone wasts, and sells, both Mill, and Ouen, and each good thing else.*
Fourbe: f. *A fib, ieast, fitton, gudgeon, mockerie, gullerie; a wyle, guile, deceit, imposture; a cosening, cheating, conycatching tale, or tricke.*
Fourbi: m. ie: f. *Furbished, polished, burnished.*
Fourbir. *To furbish, polish, burnish, make bright.*
Fourbisseur: m. *An Armorer; a Cutler; or, most properly, a furbisher, scowrer, burnisher, polisher.*
Teste à teste comme deux fourbisseurs. *(Which commonly worke with their heads close together.)*
Fourbisseure: f. *A furbishing, scowring; polishing, burnishing.*
Fourbouilly. *Boyled, or stued meat with broth, or pottage.*
Fourbure: f. *The foundering of a horse.*
Fourc: m. *A Forke; or any thing which, forke-like, makes a sharpe angle; also, a forkednesse.*
Le fourc d'un arbre. *The twist of a tree; (Looke* Fourcheure.)
Le fourc d'un chemin. *The angle, or corner of a way that parts in two; and the same partition, or the wayes that come thereof.*
Le fourc des doigts. *The part that lyes betweene the setting on of euerie two of the fingers; or the parting thereof.*
Le fourc des ruës. *That part of streets whereat they are parted in two.*
Fourcelle: f. *The breast blade, or heart-blade; also, the channell bone, or craw-bone; Looke* Fourchette.
Fourchage: m. *A branch of a linage, familie, or kindred; any branch, member, or side of a stock diuided.*
Fourché: m. *A forke, or forkednesse; also, the forked, or double broched, top of a Deeres head.*
Fourché: m. ée: f. *Forked, diuided in two, set, or made forke-wise; also, hanged.*
Fourche: f. *A Forke, Pitch-forke, or Prong; also, a gibbet, or paire of gallowes; whence;*
Fourche patibulaire. *(An appurtenant, or marke of high Iurisdiction) standing on two pillars, it belongs to a* Seigneur haut Iusticier; *on 3, to a Lo. Chattelain; on 4, to a Baron; & on 6, to an Earle: (And yet by the customes of* Blois *the* Moyen Iusticier *may haue that with 2 pillars; and by the Customes of* Auxerre, *those that stand on 3 or 4, belong to high Iusticers; and elsewhere those that stand on 4. belōg only to Lo. Chattelains; but these proportiōs are nothing so proper, nor so general, as the former.)*

Fourche à trois pointes. *A Trout-speare, or Eele-speare.*
Coups de fourche baillez par quelques femmes à leurs maris; *Hornes like forked tines.*
Panser vn cheval à la fourche. *To dresse a horse but sleightly; or, to giue him blowes in stead of currying.*
Passer soubs la fourche. *To yeeld his necke to the yoake; abandon his freedome; submit himselfe vnto thraldome.*
Traicter à la fourche. *To swaddle, bast, lamme, swindge well fauoredly; to vse hardly, intertaine rudely, deale roughly with.*
Fourché: m. ée: f. *as* Fourchu.
Fourche-fiere: f. *A long Staffe, or Quarter staffe, hauing at the one end a forke, and at the other a Pike.*
Fourche-fiere à trois pointes. *A Trowt-speare, or Eele-speare.*
Fourchelle. *A little forke; or, as* Fourchette.
Fourchément. *Forkedly; also, crookedly.*
Fourcheon. *A forket; the tooth, or graine of a forke.*
Fourcher. *To forke; to cleaue, or diuide in two; also, to stay, or make a stand, as a Muskettier does when he sets downe his rest; also, to be hanged.*
Ce chemin fourche, ou se fourche. *This way parts in two.*
La langue luy fourche. *He stuts; or trips with his tongue.*
Fourcheran. Drageon fourcheran. *The (Vine) sprig that shoots out betweene two branches.*
Fourchette: f. *A forket, or small forke; also, the breast-blade, or heart-blade; (the forked, or triangular gristle which cleaues to the bottome of the breast-bone;) also, the putting of the neck-ioynts out of ioynt; also, a horses Fete-lock; also, a Musket-rest.*
Fourchette d' enhaut, ou superieure. *The craw-bone, canell-bone, neck-bone, throat-bone.*
Fourcheu. *as* Fourchu.
Fourcheure: f. *A forkinesse, or forkednesse; a fork-like diuision, or cleauing; also, that part of the bodie from whence the thighes doe part; (I thinke we call it the Twist.)*
Fourcheure d'un arbre. *The twist of a tree; the top of the bodie, where it begins to be diuided by the maine branches.*
Fourchier: m. *A cord vntwisted in the middest, and (a stone being put thereinto) vsed as a sling.*
Fourchier à trois dents. *(A triple-toothed forke) a Trout-speare, or Eele-speare.*
Fourchon. *as* Fourcheon.
Fourchon du raisin. *The staulke of a cluster of grapes.*
Fourchu: m. uë: f. *Forked; diuided, or clouen in two.*
L'Arbre fourchu. *A standing on the hands with outstretcht legs.*
Pied fourchu. Bestes à pied fourchu. *Halfe-hoofed, or clouen-footed beasts; as Neate, Sheepe, Swyne, &c.*
L'Impost du pied fourchu. *The toll that is payed in Fayres, or Markets, vpon the sale of any of those kind of cattell.*
Fourchument. *Forkedly, forke-like.*
Fourchure: f. *The part of a mans bodie, whence his thighes part; Looke* Fourcheure.
Fourdrines: f. *Sloes;* ¶Pic. *also, wild, or mountaine, Plummes.*
Fourdrinier. *The blacke thorne that beareth Sloes; also, the wild, or mountaine, Plumme tree.*
Fourgangnement: m. *A recouering of, or a reentring into, land, for non-payment of Rent.* ¶Wallon.
Fourgangner. *To recouer, or to reenter into land, for non-payment of Rent.* ¶Wallon.
Fourgon: m. *An Ouen-forke, (tearmed in Lincolnshire, a Fruggin) wherewith fuell is both put into an Ouen, and stirred when it is (on fire) in it.*
'A telle paelle tel fourgon: Prov. *One filthie knaue matcht with another.*
La paelle se mocque du fourgon: Prov. *The Peele derides the Ouen-forke; one slouen, or neighbor another.*
Fourgonner. *To put fuell into an Ouen; also, (and the more properly) to tosse, or stirre it (being on fire) in the Ouen, with a Fruggin.*
Que fourgonnes tu la? *What a stirre, what a rumbling, what a puddering, keepest thou there?*
Fourgonneur: m. *An Ouen-tender, or Ouen-stirrer; one that lookes to an Ouen, with a Fruggin, or forke, in his hand.*
Fourmage: m. *Cheese.*
Fourmage de Bans. *A cheese made of Goats milke, or as the Angelot.*
Fourmage de Betune. *A kind of cheese made of Sheepes milke.*
Fourmage de Loüans. *A kind of hard cheese, made at a village of that name.*
Fourmage est bon quand il y en a peu: Prov. *The lesse cheese the better; or, cheese is good when a miserable hand giues it; according whereunto they say also,* Tout fourmage est bien sain qui vient de chiche main.
Fourmage de taupe, & pain d'Argus: Pro. *Heauie cheese, and light bread (are, commonly, the best.)*
Nul ne pele son fourmage qui n'y ait honte, ou dommage: Prov. *No man pares his cheese without shame, or losse.*
Qui a fourmage pour tous mets, il le doit couper bien espez: Prov. *He must not scant his cheese that hath nought else to feed on.*
Fourmageon: m. *A little cheese.*
Fourmagere: f. *A cheese-presse.*
Fourmagerie: f. *Cheese ware, a commoditie of cheese; also, a cheese-house, or cheese-dairie; a roome, or place, wherein cheese is vsually made.*
Fourmageur: m. *A cheese-seller, Cheesemonger, marchant of cheese.*
Fourmageux: m. euse: f. *Cheesie, full of cheese, belonging vnto cheese.*
Fourmagier: m. *A cheese-monger; also, a great eater of cheese.*
Fourmagiere. *as* Fourmagere.
Fourman. Vn grand pain fourman. *A great wheaten, or white loafe; (so great, that the mouth of an ordinarie Ouen is filled withall.)*
Fourne. *A kind of net for water fowle.*
Fourment. *Wheat; See* Froment.
Fourmentée: f. *Furmentie; boyled wheat.*
Fourmenter. *To yeeld, or bring forth, wheat.*
Fourmentier: m. ere: f. *Wheat-yeelding, wheatie, of wheat.*
Fourmi: m. *An Ant, Pismire, Emmot.*
Fourmi d'Inde; ou, Dardoise fourmi. *Looke* Dardoise.
Ventre de fourmi. *A swag-bellie.*
Plus ioyeux que fourmis en grain. *More frolicke then Ants in a heape of corne.*
Souffler les fourmis dans leurs fourmillieres. *To blow Ants into their holes. Looke* Fourmilliere.

Fourmiant. frappement fourmiant. *Such a soft, and gentle stroake as is giuen by the touch, or feet, of a creeping Ant.*
Fourmier. *as* Fourmiller.
Fourmiere: f. *An Ants hole, or neast; a hillock, or banke full of Ants; also, a disease of hawkes, making the hornie part of their beakes to pill.*
Fourmiller. *To abound, or swarme in great troupes, as Ants in their neasts, or caues; also, to paine, or pricke, as the stinging of Pismeares.*
Fourmilliere: f. *An Ants hole, or neast; a hillocke, or banke full of Ants.*
Vne fourmilliere de gens. *A great number, a huge troupe, of people crowding together like Ants.*
Souffler les fourmis dans leurs fourmillieres. *To blow Ants into their holes; to striue against the streame, or draw on himselfe a mischiefe by striuing to expell it; (for the more one labours, by blowing, to get them in, the more he prouokes them, and makes them to come out.)*
Fourmion: m. *A little Ant, small Pismeare.*
Fournage: m. *The fee taken by a Lord of his vassalls, and teaants, bound to bake in his common ouen; or for a permission to vse their owne; also, as* Foüage.
Fournaillé: m. ée: f. *Baked (in an ouen.)*
Fournailler. *To bake (in an ouen.)*
Fournaise: f. *A furnace.*
Fournaiser: m. ere: f. *Belonging to a furnace.*
Fourneau. *A little ouen.*
Fournée de pain; *A batch, or ouen full of bread.*
Prendre vn pain sur la fournée. *To get a snatch at his wench before she be maryed.*
Fourni: m. *A bakehouse.*
Fourni: m. ie: f. *Furnished, fraught, appointed, prouided of, supplied with; in a compleate fashion, with full equipage.*
Lance fournie. *Seeke* Lance.
Fournier: m. *A baker; or one that keepes, or gouernes a common ouen.*
Fourniere: f. *A woman-baker, or she that keepes a common ouen.*
Fournil: m. *A bake-house.*
Fournillé: m. ée: f. *Baked (in an ouen, or bake-house.)*
Fourniller: m. ere: f. *Much in a bake-house; haunting the bake-house.*
Fourniller. *To bake (in an ouen, or bake-house.)*
Fourniment: m. *Full fraught, prouision, furniture; perfection; that which compleats, or makes vp a thing; also, a furnishing, or fraughting.*
Le fourniment d' vne Pistole. *A case for a Pistoll.*
Le fourniment des reins. *The muscles of the backe, about the kidneyes.*
Fournir. *To furnish, fraught, supplie, minister, find, prouide of, accommodate with.*
Fournir à vn appointment. *To performe, fulfill, or accomplish the conditions of an agreement.*
Fournir la complainćte. *Looke* Resaisir.
Autrement on n'en fournira pas. *Otherwise one shall not get him, one shall haue no helpe, or vse of him.*
Fournissement: m. *A furnishing, or furnishment; a fraughting, supplying, fiting with, prouiding of, things necessarie; (In Law,* C'est le sequestre de la chose contentieuse en matiere possessoire, & de complainte, & le restablissement des fruićts, qui doit estre faićt es mains du Commissaire: ¶Ragueau.)
Fournisseur: m. *a furnisher, fraughter, prouider, supplier.*
Fourniture: f. *Furniture, fraught, prouision; a full measure, or supplie of necessarie implements, or equipage.*
Fournoyé: m. ée: f. *Baked (in an ouen.)*
Fournoyer. *To bake (in an ouen.)*
Fourquat: m. *A kind of plough vsed in* Languedoc.
Fourque. *as* Fourche; *A forke; a paire of gallowes.*
Fourquier: m. *A Brewers stirrer.*
Fourrage: m. *Forrage for horses; also, fodder for cattell.*
Fourrage des corbeaux. *A false knaue, a filthie lewd fellow, crowes-meat, one for whom the gallowes grones.*
Fourragé: m. ée: f. *Foddered; forraged, rauaged, forrayed.*
Fourragement. *A foddering; forraging, rauaging, forraying.*
Fourrager. le four. *as* Fourragement.
Fourrager. *To fodder; also, to forrage, prey, forray, goe a forraging; to ransacke, rauage, boot-hale it.*
Fourrageur: m. *A fodderer; a forrager, a purueyor of vićtuall for horses, and cattle; also, a boot-haler.*
Fourré: m. *A kind of fish-net stretched out with hoopes in the forme of a whale-bone sleeue.*
Fourré: m. ée: f. *Furred; also, entred, thrust, or put far in; sheathed, cased; lodged within.*
Coups fourrez. *Interchanged blowes.*
Paix fourrée. *A counterfeit peace; a peace made with a purpose to be broken.*
Fourreau. *A sheath; a scabbard.*
Le fourreau d' vne beste. *The thicke skin wherein the yard, or pizzle of a beast is sheathed.*
Le fourreau d' vne halebarde, harquebouse, pistole; &c. *A case for a halbeard, harguebuse, pistoll, &c.*
N' admirons le fourreau pour mespriser la lame. *Let not a faire outside make th' inside lesse esteemed of.*
Fourrelier: m. *A scabberd maker.*
Fourrer. *To put, thrust, or throw into, to lodge in or hide within, a hole or hollow thing; Hence; to case; and to sheath; also, to furre; also, as* Fourrager.
Se fourrer en. *To enter boldly, thrust freely, pierce far into; also, to ingage, or intangle himselfe in.*
Se fourrer es biens d'autruy. *To intrude vpon the gouernment of other mens goods; to dispose of them vnbidden, or whether th' owners will or no.*
S'y fourrer iusques aux oreilles. *To plunge himselfe vp to th' eares in.*
Fourrer vn gasteau. *To butter a cake.*
Fourrer la main à. *To bribe, to grease the fist of.*
Fourreur: m. *A Furrier; a Skinner; also, a Forrager.*
Fourreure: f. *See* Fourrure.
Fourrie: f. *Pillage, forrage; rauaging, boot-haling, ransacking.*
Fourier: m. *An Harbinger.*
Le fourrier de la Lune a marqué le logis. *Appliable to a woman that hath her flowers.*
Fourriere: f. *A caue, or close seller, to lay wine, or oyle in.*
Fourrons. *An opprobrious name, or nickname, giuen by the* Tholosains *vnto the Sergeants, or attendants, of the Captaine of the watch.*
Fourrure: f. *Furre, furring, skins to furre with.*
Fourser. *To spawne, as carpes in a pond.*
Fourvoyé: m. ée: f. *Strayed, erred, swarued, gone out of the way; that hath missed, or mistaken the way.*
Fourvoyement: m. *A straying, erring, wandring, going out of the way.*
Fourvoyer. *To misse, or mistake the way; to erre in, swarue from; roue, wander, stray, or goe, out of, the way.*
Ce nous sera fort ioyeux, & si ne te fourvoyeras de

de rien. *This will be a great pleasure to vs, and no hinderance vnto you, or no whit out of your way.*

Il ne se fourvoit point qui à bon hostel va: Prov. *He goes not out of his way that goes to a good Inne.*

Qui trop se haste en cheminant, en beau chemin se fourvoye souvent: Prov. *He that makes too much hast oft wanders in plaine way.*

Foußer. *as* Fouïr; *To dig; &(more particularly) to dig, or turne vp, a vineyard, somewhat before the vines begin to bud.*

Foussette. *as* Fossette.

Fousteau. *as* Fouteau.

Fouteau: m. *A Beech tree.*

Foutoir: m. *A (battering) Ramme; also, a rammer; or, a rammer head for a peece of Ordnance.*

Fouton: m. *A Snite; so called, because she wags her taile verie much.*

Foutouër: m. *The warlike Engine called a Ramme, wherewith, in old time, walls were battered; Looke* Foutoir.

Foutre. *To leacher.*

Foutu. vn foutu. *A scowndrell; a fellow of small accompt.*

Foutu: m. uë: f. *(The Participle of* Foutre.*)*

Fouyasse. *as* Fouace: ¶Bourbon.

Fouyer: m. *The harth (of a chymney.)*

Le Fouyer d'une arquebuse. *The fire-pan, or touchpan of an Harguebuse.*

Fouyer de Galere. *The Cooke-roome in a galley.*

Ce que l'enfant oit au fouyer est bien tost cogneu iusques au Monstier: Pro. *Little pitchers haue wide eares (wee say; and it seemes by this prouerbe that) little children haue long tongues.*

Fouynne. *as* Fouïnne.

Fouzil. *as* Fusil.

Foy: m. Le foy du corps. *The middle, or wast.*

Foy: f. *Faith, trust, confidence, assurance, beliefe in; credit giuen; also, loyaltie, faithfulnesse, trustinesse; also, fealtie; also, fee simple; also, a ring closed with a hand in hand.*

Demission de foy. *Looke* Demission.

Homme de foy. *A vassall, tenant, subiect, that owes, or holds by, fealtie.*

Possesseur de bonne foy. *He that possesses a thing vpon a title which he knowes, and is, good.*

Possesseur de mauvaise foy. *Is he, that either by force detaines another mans goods, or vses them, knowing that they belong to another.*

En bonne foy? *Is it possible? is there any such matter? can it be so?*

En bonne foy. *(without interrogation) In good earnest, in good sooth, in good sadnesse.*

Il y va à la bonne foy. *He goes roundly, plainly, simply, sincerely, to worke.*

Il y va aussi à la bonne foy que le loup qui mangea la chevre. *(Said of a great deceiuer.)*

Faire foy de. *To beleeue, trust, giue credit vnto.*

Mis sous sa foy. *Left to his owne discretion, or gouernment; giuen ouer to himselfe.*

Tomber, ou venir en foy tierce. *An inheritance to fall into a third hand, or come vnto the hands of a third heire; Looke* Tiers.

Foy de Granes: Prov. *Treacherie, or treason.*

Nul n'a trop pour soy de sens, d'argent, de foy: Prov. *No man hath for himselfe too much wit, faith, or pelfe.*

Foye: m. *The liuer.*

Foye marin. *The sea Liuer; a kind of Breame-like fish, that is but seldome seene; also, a stinking excrescence resembling a sodden liuer, and cleauing, in the bottome of the sea, vnto the weed* Alge.

Iamais homme ne mange foye que le sien non ait ioye: Prov. *The liuer of the liuer-eater, is comforted and much the better.*

Foyer. *as* Fouyer.

Foyes: f. *The slot of a Stag, the view of a Bucke, the footing of either.*

Foyne. *as* Faine; *Beech mast:* ¶Bourbonnois.

Foynne. *as* Fouïnne; *A Foine, or Polecat.*

Frac. On ne trouve chez luy ni fric ni frac. *There's nothing to be had, or gotten, at his house.*

Fracas: m. *Violent breaches; extreame bruises; wracks, destruction; hauocke, hurlyburly.*

Fracassé: m. ée: f. *Broken, crashed; extreamly crushed; wracked; battered; ruined, made hauocke of.*

Fracasser. *To crash; to breake, batter, bruise, or crush, extreamely; to wracke, destroy, ruine, make hauocke of.*

Fracasseur: m. *A crasher, violent breaker, batterer; or crusher.*

Fracein: m. *as* Vlcere ambulatif.

Fracteur: m. *A breaker; also, a bankrupt; and hence the prouerbe;*

Aujourd'uy facteur demain fracteur.

Fraction: f. *A fraction, or fracture; a breaking, bursting; rending, tearing in peeces.*

Fracture: f. *A fracture, breach, or bursting.*

Fracture faicte en raifort. *Looke* Raifort.

Fracturé: m. ée: f. *Burst, broken.*

Fragate: f. *A Frigate.*

Fragile: com. *Fraile; brittle, soone burst, easily broken, weake; mortall.*

Fragilité: f. *Frailtie, fragilitie, brittlenesse; weakenesse.*

Fragment: m. *A fragment; a peece, or parcell, of a broken thing; a gobbet, or shard.*

Fragrant. *Fragrant, odoriferous.*

En fragrant delict. *While th'offence is fresh in memorie; or, presently after the committing thereof.*

Fraiche. *The feminine of* Frais; *Looke* Frais; *or* Frez.

Fraile: com. *Fraile, brittle, weake, easily broken.*

Fraille. *as* Fraile.

Fraillé: m. ée: f. *Crumbled in peeces, broken into small crumlockes, or mammocks.*

Frailler. *To crumble in peeces, to breake into small crumlockes (brittle things.)*

Frain: m. *A bit; the part of a bridle which is in the horses mouth.*

Prendre le frain aux dents. *To be verie earnest; or, to goe forward notwithstanding any commaund, or aduice, to the contrarie.*

Ronger son frain. *To bite of the bit.*

A vieille nul frain doré: Pro. *Said in derision of an old woman, that hath newly, trimd vp, or sleeked ouer, her selfe.*

Fraire. *To surfet; to fill full; also, to swell, rise, or increase, as a womans dugs, when the menstruall bloud begins to dilate the veines of the matrix.*

Frairie: f. *A Frierie; a brotherhood.*

Frais. *as* Fraiz.

Frais. le fr. (d'vn homme.) *The fresh, new, or late steps, tract, or footing of a man.*

Frais: m. Fraische: f. *Coole; fresh; young, new, lustie; vnfoiled; vntoiled; also, fresh, or, without salt; Looke* Frez.

Fraischement. *Freshly; See* Frefchement.

Fraischeur: f. *Coolenesse; freshnesse; newneße; lustinesse.*
Fraise: f. *A strawberrie; also, a ruffe; also, a calues chaldern.*
Fraisé: m. ée: f. (*Looke* Frezé;) pain fraisé. *A Panadoe of the crummes of stale Manchet, steeped some while in two or three changes of water, and then boiled in a pipkin with butter, or in chickin or capon broth, & often stirred with a spoone vntill it be readie.*
Fraisier: m. *A strawberrie-plant; or, the hearb that beareth strawberries.*
Fraislé: m. ée: f. *Broken, burst (into many small peeces.)*
Fraisle: com. *as* Fraile; *Fraile.*
Frailler. *To breake, to burst (into many small peeces.)*
Fraisllure: f. *Brittlenesse, frailtie.*
Fraisllusement. *Brittlely, weakely; of a fraile strength; in a fraile manner.*
Fraisne: m. *An Ash tree.*
Fraiz: m. *Costs, expences, charges.*
Peindre à fraiz. *To paint with water-colours on a greene, or new-mortered, wall.*
Fraiz: m. Fraische: f. *Looke* Frais; *or,* Frez.
Fraize: f. *as* Fraise.
Fraizé. febves fraizées. *Pilled, or shaled, beanes.*
Fralaté: m. ée: f. *Racked, or drawne off the Lees; also, powred out of one veßell into another, as wine.*
Fralatement: m. *A racking of wine; a drawing it off the lees; or shifting it out of one vessell into another.*
Fralater. *To racke wine, to draw it off the lees; to shift, or powre it out of one vessell into another.*
Framboise: f. *A Raspis, hindberrie, framboiseberrie; also, a pleasing smell or sauor in wine, or fruites; and hence;*
Ce vin sent sa framboise. *This wine smells delicately.*
Framboisier: m. *A Raspis bush; the plant, or shrub, that beareth Raspises.*
Franc: m. *A franke, or stie to feed, and fatten hogs in.*
Franc. *A peece of money worth, in old time, but one* Sol Tournois; *now it goes for twentie; which amount vnto* ij.s. sterl.
FrancBourdelois. *Is but* 15. Solz Tourn. 18. d. sterl.
Franc à cheval. *An old peece of gold worth betweene* vj. *and* vij.s. *now it goes, as th'ordinarie* Franc, *but for* ij.s. sterl.
Franc à pied. *Another worth about foure, or fiue shillings sterling.*
Franc: m. Franche: f. *Franke, free; at libertie; subiect vnto no man; exempt from subsidies, dueties, or seruices; also, franke, liberall, bountifull; courteous, gracious; also, valiant, hardie, forward, bold, couragious; also, plaine, round, open-hearted; sincere, honest; without any fault, or ill qualitie; also, tame, naturall, kindlie, seasonable, well tempered, of the right stampe.*
Franc aleu. *Free tenure; or, a free tenant; Seeke* Alleud.
Franc archer. *One trained bow-man in euerie Parish, well armed, and readie vpon summons, and at a rate certaine, to march; in regard whereof he is exempted from all taxes, and subsidies.*
Franc argent. *as* Francs deniers.
Francs Bourgeois. *Free Burgesses; which pay no yerelie fines for their freedome, nor so many amerciaments of Courts as others; although they yeeld some other contributions, and seruices, vnto their Lords.*
Francs deniers en vente de fief, &c. *A sellers freeing, or discharging of the purchaser from those fines which he were otherwise to pay, at his entrie, vnto the Landlord.*
Francs devoirs. *Looke* Debvoir.
Franc fief. *A free, or affranchising, fief; as all* Fiefs *be (and therefore one sayes, that* Franc *is a generall, and perpetuall Epithite vnto a* Fief;) *whereof, at first, none were capable but* les Francs (*a people of the Germane* Franconia) *who conquered* Gallia; *nor ought any to hold them at this day, but such as are noble, freeborne, and exempted from subsidies; yet if a villeine get one of them it makes him a free-man, though not a Gentleman; but he cannot hold it without his Lords permission, and a licence from the King; and hence;*
Droict de francs fiefs. *The fine thats due vnto the King vpon the purchase of a fief by a Burguer (of an vnpriuiledged towne; for Paris, and some others are priuiledged)* Roturier, *Villeine, or other ignoble person: (this was certaine, viz: six yeres value if the land were held of the King, and three yeares, if of another Lord; but now it is whatsoeuer th'Officers of th'Exchequer will set downe;) also, the power of enabling them to purchase fiefs; a point of Soueraigntie peculiar to the King.*
Imposition de francs fiefs. *The same (in the first part.)*
Franc homme. *A vassall, or tenant that owes fealtie.*
Franche salaison. *as* Franc-salé.
Francs Taulpins. *Trained men; souldiers leuied in villages, or made of husbandmen.*
Franche verité. *An inquirie of disorders committed within a Jurisdiction, or Mannor (by especiall order, & authoritie from the Lo. thereof) before any actuall complaint, or apprehension of offenders be made; a priuie Sessions.*
Cave franche. *A fat well seasoned, or fit to receiue new wine.*
Pierre franche. *The (soft white) free stone.*
Repeuë franche. *A meale come freely by, or which costs th'eater nothing.*
Rose franche. *A red Rose.*
Sergent franc. *An Officer which some vassalls may keepe to looke vnto their woods, and to seise, and detaine such beasts, as are found Dammage fesant within them.*
Terre franche. *Mould, pure soyle, soyle of it selfe; a soyle without sand, grauell, stones, or* tuph.
Franc au collier; franc au traict. *That drawes, or labours hard; that does, falls to, goes through with, his businesse lustily, roundly, willingly, freely.*
A la franche Marguerite. *In the plainest fashion, after the homeliest maner.*
Refuser tout à franc. *To refuse absolutely, denie resolutely, vtterly, altogether; and to depriue himselfe, by such a refusall, of all power, or means of acceptance, or yeelding afterwards.*
Franc de Carreau. *A certaine play with a peece of money at a square crossed:* ¶Rab.
Francarchers: m. *Archers, or trained bow-men, that serue on foot; exempt from Subsidies, because bound to march, on a sudden, and at a certaine monethlie rate, whensoeuer they be commaunded.*
Franc-a-tripe *One that feeds on free-cost; or, a tall trencher-man, glutton, bellie-god; one thats bountifull to his guts, free to his paunch; one that loues his bellie well.*
Franc-estu: m. *The Garden Globe; an excellent apple.*

France.

France. *(The kingdome of) France.*
De France. *An honourable addition, bestowed onely on the French Kings children(as* Enfant de France;*) or on th'immediate Officers of the Crowne (whence,* Connestable de France; Chancelier de France; Admiral de France,&c.)
Franc-fief. *Looke* Franc.
Franc-gontier. *A good rich Yeoman, substantiall yonker, wealthie chuffe.*
Franche-mariette. *The name of a great, and tender apple, spotted with red on th'one side.*
Franchement. *Frankly, freely; liberally, bountifully; sincerely; plainely, roundly, boldly, without halting, with an open heart.*
Franchemulle d'vn mouton. *A sheepes call, or kell.*
Franchi: m. ie: f. *Freed, quit, vnthralled, set at libertie, deliuered; redeemed, discharged; also, leaped, or iumped, on, or ouer.*
Le coup est franchi. *Ouerthrowne, out-gone.*
Franchir. *To quit, free, deliuer, vnthrall; redeeme, discharge; also, to leape, iumpe, or bound, on, or ouer; hence;*
Franchir le Rubicon. *Looke* Rubicon.
Franchir le sault. *To out-leape, exceed, goe beyond (ordinarie, or fit limits;) and particularly, to grow prophane, to make a ieast, or (at least) haue no care, of religion.*
Franchise: f. *Franchise, freenesse, libertie, freedome, exemption; also, good breeding, free birth, tamenesse, seasonablenesse, kindlinesse, right kind; also, a Sanctuarie, Franchise, Libertie, Priuiledged place; also, the discharge of a debt.*
Francier. *To speake fine, and eloquent French; (Ironically.)*
Francisque: f. *A kind of axe; as* Ancon; *or a fashion of sword vsed by the auncient French.*
François: m. *Francis (a proper name.)*
Mal S. Francois. *Want of money.*
François: m. oise: f. *French, of France.*
Compagnie Françoise. *A wench (among wanton Church-men.)*
Vins François. *Wines that are gotten below the bridge of* Sens, *and in the countries on either side of the riuers of* Marne, Seine, *and* Oise.
A la Françoise. *After the French fashion; rashly; retchlesly, carelesly, leauing all at randome.*
Iamais François ne furent veus recreus de bien faire: Prov. *Frenchmen were neuer seene wearie of well-doing.*
Quand le François dort le Diable le berse. *A Prouerbe deuised by the Flemings in taxation of the restlesse humor of the French.*
Qui fut François si fut courtois: Pro. *If he a French man were, courteous he was.*
Françoise: f. *as* Francisque; *Also, the name Frances (for a woman.)*
Francolin: m. *A delicate red-legged fowle, of two kinds; one somewhat resembles our Godwit, and feeds altogether on fish; another (more like to a Partridge) liues among hills, and high grounds, and is the rarer, & deerer, and (perhaps) the daintier of the two; In some parts of Naples they are bigger bodied then Hennes, and haue verie long bills, necks, and feet.*
Francolin de mer. *A kind of small, and smooth-skinned Tunnie, held verie daintie, and much esteemed of by the inhabitants of Creet, and Candie, neere whereunto it is most commonly taken.*
Il est muet comme vn francolin pris. *He vses very few words, or fewer then he was wont; (for this fowle being at libertie sings (after her fashion) but in a cage is silent.)*
Francoly. *as* Francolin: ¶Rab.
Francoule; *or,* Francourle. *as* Francolin; *or (as some imagine) our Moore-game, or Grouse:* ¶Rab.
Francquiesme. *A certaine free tenure, or Mannor, differing from a* Fief, *and conferring on such as hold by it, or owe it, many priuiledges.*
Franc-salé. *A priuiledge of selling, and buying of salt (for priuate vse) without paying any custome for it; enioyed by th'inhabitants of* Auvergne, Rhetelois, *and the countries adioyning.*
Francsoreau. *The name of a certaine peare.*
Franctopin: m. *A clowne, carle, churle, chuffe, clusterfist, hind, boore; or as* Franc taulpin.
Frange: f. *Fringe.*
Frangé: m. ée: f. *Fringed; edged with fringe; also, wrimpled; notched, snipt, or iagd on the edges.*
Fustaine frangée. *Course tufted fustian; the course fustian-like stuffe, thats tufted in fringe-like rowes.*
Franger. *To fringe; to edge, or set with fringe; also, to crumple; wrimple, iag, or snip on th'edges.*
Frangible: com. *Frangible, breakable.*
Frapart. *as* Frappart.
Frappart: m. *A knocker, striker, beater.*
Frappart: m. arde: f. *Knocking, rapping, striking, beating.*
Frere frappart. *A lustie, strong, tough Frier; a good boxer, a sound knocker; a notable striker, a bellie-bumper.*
Frappé: m. ée: f. *Strucke, knockt, rapt, hit; wounded; also, blasted, as with lightning.*
Cela est frappé à la porte d'vn trespassé. *All that is labour lost, done to no purpose, spoken to deafe eares, or shewed vnto blind eyes.*
Tous frappez à vn mesme coing. *All of one opinion, fashion, or faction.*
Frappement: m. *A striking, knocking, rapping, hitting, smiting, dashing; clapping; also, a blasting.*
Frapper. *To knocke, rap, clap, thumpe, hit; bat, strike, smite; also, to dash; also, to blast; Looke* Batre.
Frapper coup sur. *To giue a blow vnto.*
Frapper dedans. *Violently to rush, enter, or break in vpon.*
Frapper d'estoc. *To foyne, thrust, or giue a thrust vnto.*
Frapper d'estoc & de taille. *To strike euerie way, in all fashions, on all hands; to lay about him like a madman.*
Frapper en paulme. *Looke* Paulme.
Frapper des pieds contre terre. *To stampe with the feet.*
Frapper à route. *To roose a Deere with a linehound.*
Tel cuide frapper qui tue: Prov. *Some kill those whom they would but strike.*
Tel se cuide bien garder qui se frappe sur le nez: Prov. *Some thinking to defend, offend, themselues.*
Tousiours ne frappe l'on pas ce à quoy l'on vise: Prov. *One alwayes hits not what he aimes at.*
Frapperie: f. *Knocking-stuffe; or, as* Frappement; *a knocking, rapping; &c.*
Frappe-teste. *A certaine Spider whose sting is neere, or in, her head.*
Frappeur: m. *A rapper, knocker, clapper, hitter, thumper; striker, smiter, boxer.*
Frarachage. *as* Faresche.

Frarachaux: m. *Coheires, coparceners, partners in an inheritance, or succession.*

Frarager. *as* Frarescher. (v.m.)

Fraresche: f. *Partition of lands among brethren, neere kinsmen, or coheires.*

Frarescher. *To part land, or a succession, as brethren, or coheirs.*

Frarescheur: m. *A partner, a coparcener, or coheire.*

Frareuseté: f. *The custome, course, or title of Partition among brethren, coparceners, or coheirs:* ¶Wallon.

Frareux: m. euse: f. *Parted, or partable among coparceners; also, belonging to a coparcener:* ¶Wallon.

Frarieparage: m. *Fraternitie, brotherhood.* (v.m.)

Frasque: f. *A gull, gullerie, mockerie; also, an odde trick, strange pranke, idle part.*

Frater. *A Frier; (a word vsed most commonly in mockage.)*

Fraternel: m. elle: f. *Fraternall, brotherlie, belonging to a brother.*

Fraternellement. *Fraternally; brotherly.*

Fraterniser. *To fraternize; concurre with; be neere vnto; agree as brothers.*

Fraternité: f. *Fraternitie, brotherhood.*

Fratesque: com. *Frier-like; of, or belonging to a Frier; also, hypocriticall; superstitious.*

Fratre: m. *A Frier; a brother; a confederate.*

Fratricide: m. *A murtherer of his owne brother.*

Fratrisseau: m. *A nouice; a yong, and vnexperienced Frier.*

Fraudateur. *as* Fraudeur.

Fraudation: f. *A defrauding, deceiuing, beguiling.*

Fraude: f. *Fraud, guile, deceit, cousenage, gullerie, couin, cheating, trumperie.*

Fraudé: m. ée: f. *Defrauded, deceiued, beguiled, cousened, cheated, circumuented, disappointed.*

Frauder. *To deceiue, defraud, beguile, circumuent, fetch ouer, cousen, cheat, gull, disappoint.*

Fraudeur: m. *A defrauder, cousener, deceiuer, cheater, beguiler.*

Fraudulemment. *as* Fraudulentement; *and the better French (sayes* Nicot.)

Fraudulent. *Fraudulent, craftie, deceitfull, cousening, cheating, wilie, cunning.*

Fraudulentement. *Fraudulently, deceitfully, craftily, guilefully, cunningly.*

Frauduler. *To deceiue; as* Frauder

Frauduleusement. *as* Fraudulentement; *or, full craftily, most deceitfully.*

Frauduleux: m. *A deceiuer, cheater, cousener, craftie mate, wilie packe, ouerreaching companion.*

Frauduleux: m. euse: f. *Most craftie, fraudulent, guilefull, deceitfull.*

Fraux: m. *Commons; or common, publicke, and void grounds, wayes, places; or, as* Fros.

Frax. *A kind of rauenous fish (or as* Lamie*) called thus about* Bayonne.

Fraxinelle: f. *Bastard Dittanie, false Dittander.*

Fray: m. *A Frier; also, the spawne of fish; whence;*
Quand la grenouille n'est plus en fray. *When the frog is emptie, or without spawne; or, when shee hath done breeding.*

Frayable. chemin frayable. *An vsuall, beaten, or well-troden, way.*

Frayé: m. ée: f. *Hit sideling, grated vpon, raked along on; also, rubbed; and rased, fretted, much worne by much rubbing; also, defrayed; also, burnished.*
Chemin frayé. *A way much vsed, or trod on; a beaten way.*

Frayement. *A hitting sideling, a grating vpon, a raking along on; a rubbing, fretting, rasing, wearing of things by often hitting one against another; a burnishing.*

Frayer. *To hit sideling; to grate vpon; to rake along on; also, to rub; and to rase, or fret by often rubbing; also, to burnish (as a Deere his head) by rubbing; also, to weare, beat downe, make plaine, smooth, or euen by much vsing, or treading on; also, to spawne, as fishes, &c; also, to defray, or beare the charges of.*

Frayeur: f. *Feare, dread, fright, affrighting, terror, scaring, horror.*

Frayeure: f. *as* Frayement.

Frayeux: m. euse: f. *Fearefull, dreadfull, terrible, horrible.*

Frayoire. *The racke-staffe, or nog of a mill; the little peece of wood which rubbing against the hopper makes the corne fall from it.*

Frayouër: m. *A Deeres burnishing of his head.*

Fredaine: f. *A gudgeon, mockerie, wile, gullerie; a deceitfull part, a roguish pranke, a knauish or cousening deuice.*

Fredinfredailler. *To leacher:* ¶Rab.

Fredon: m. *A Semie-quauer, or Semie-semie-quauer, in Musicke; and hence, Diuision; and a warbling, shaking, or quauering.*
Faire fredon sur fredon. *To heape curiositie vpon curiositie, to adde one nice point vnto another, or vse many together.*

Fredonner. *To shake, diuide, warble, quauer in singing, or playing on an instrument.*

Fredonneux: m. euse: f. *Full of Semie-semie-quauers; or of quauering, shaking, warbling; diuiding much.*

Fredonnisé. *Shaked, quauered, warbled, diuided.*

Fredonniser. *as* Fredonner.

Fregate: f. *A Frigate; a swift Pinnace.*

Fregolier. *The Lote tree, or Nettle tree.*

Freguereul. *The little fish called, a Mennow.*

Frein. *See* Frain.

Frelan: m. *A rough, and prickled shrub, called, Butchers-Broome, Kneeholme, and Petigree; also, a Butchers Broome, or a rough brush, made thereof.*

Frelaté. vin frelaté. *That is shifted out of old into new vessells; or drawne off the lees, and kept in bottles; we say, racked.*

Frelatement: m. *A racking of wine; or as* Fralatement.

Frelater. *To racke, or draw wine from the lees, and put it into a new vessell; Seeke* Fralater.

Frelateur: m. *A racker of wine.*

Frelaut. *A good fellow:* ¶Rab.

Frelon: m. *A Hornet; also, a Dorre, or Drone-bee; (See* Freslon*) also, as* Frelan.

Freloque: f. *A tatter that hangs downe trailing from a garment, &c.*

Frelore: com. *Vndone, forlorne, lost, cast away:* ¶Rab.

Frelot. *as* Frelaut.

Freluche: f. *A moat; a small straw, or lint.*

Freluquet: m. *A French halfe-pennie; also, a spruce dwarfe, or prettie dapper fellow.*

Frelus. *as* Frelore; *or, Ouerthrowne horse and foot.*

Fremiller. *as* Fourmiller.

Fremir. *To quake, tremble, shiuer, shake; be exceedingly moued, either with anger, or feare.*

Fremoirs: m. *The claspes of a booke; also, a Joyners straight Chizells.*

Frenaisie: f. *Frenzie, rauing, lunacie.*

Frenatique: com. *Franticke, rauing, lunaticke; besides him-*

himselfe,out of his little wit.
Frenouiller. *To fidder,to rake,to pudder in:* ¶Blesien.
Frequence: f. *Frequencie; a great haunt,meeting, resort, companie,assemblie of.*
Frequentation: f. *A frequentation, frequenting, haunting, resorting, often assembling, thicke setting together.*
Frequenté: m. ée: f. *Frequented, haunted, much visited, often resorted vnto.*
Frequenter. *To frequent, haunt, vse much, visit often, resort many times vnto.*
Frerage. *as* Fraresche; *or, A partition made betweene brothers, coheires.*
Frere: m. *A brother; also, a Frier.*
Frere d'armes. *A brother in Armes; (a title thats vsed betweene Prince and Prince, or where th'one is a Prince; whereas ordinarie Knights tearme themselues onely,* Compagnons d'armes.)
Freres de la Cour. *Fellow vassalls, or tenants holding of their Lord in one manner, or by one kind of tenure, and hauing equall authoritie in his Courts.*
Frere de laict. *A foster brother; the sonne of a mans Nurse.*
Freres des Lombards. *(as* Harpies;) *Moles, or Moone-calues; tearmed so because they are often ingendered with a liuing child; and if without, yet being bred in the same wombe, and nourished with the same milk, they may in scorne bee called brothers of the perfect children; See* Lombard.
Freres vterins. *Harpies, monsters, monstrous children; Moles, or Moone-calues; by the same reason.*
Le frere veut bien que sa soeur ait, mais que rien du sien n'y ait: Prov. *The brother would haue his sister rich, any way, but at his charges.*
Ire de freres ire de Diables: Prov. *Brothers anger diuellish anger.*
Il n'y a terme qui passe par delà celuy de frere: Prov. *Calls he me brother? how can he call me more? no friendlie tearme exceeds the tearme of brother.*
Frere-lay. *A seruant, or houshold Officer in an Abbey, or Couent.*
Frerer. *To swell; also, to itch; Looke* Fraire.
Frerescheur. *as* Frarescheur; *A coparcener.*
Frereux. Cousin frereux. *A Cousen-germaine by the brothers side; my fathers brothers sonne.*
Frerie: f. *A Frierie.*
Frerot: m. *A shauing, or shifting, fellow.*
Fres: m. *Charge, cost; expence.*
Fres: m. Fresche: f. *as* Frais; *Fresh, new; coole; or as* Frez.
Fresange. *One hog, or more, due vnto the Maister of the waters, and forrests of* Aubigny *(and elsewhere) by the farmers of the Mastage, and brousage thereof.*
Fresaye: f. *A Scrich-owle.*
Frescades: f. *Refreshments, or things-refreshing; as (in Summer-time) light garments, coole aire, cold places; bowres, or shades, ouerspred with greene boughes.*
Freschedent: m. *A glutton, rauenor, greedie fellow, good trencher-man; one that eats as if he had beene hunger-starued.*
Freschement. *Newly, lately, freshly, euen now, but a small while agoe; also, coolely.*
Frescheur: f. *Freshnesse; coolenesse.*
Freschin. *A certaine bitter-sweet apple; also, ranknesse; or, the smell, or sent of vermine, as* Foxes, Polecats, *&c.*
Vn freschin de salive. *Sweetnesse, or freshnesse, of spittle.*
Fresillon. *Priuit, Primprint.*
Fresle: com. *Fraile, weake, feeble, brittle, soone broken.*
Freslé: m. ée: f. *Furled; vndone, or slackened, & made vp.*
Fresler. *To furle; to slacken, or vndoe, and make vp.*
Freslon: m. *A Hornet; also (but lesse properly) a Dorre, or Drone Bee; also, the shrub called Pettigree, Butchers Broome, Kneeholme, and Kneehuluer.*
Irriter les freslons. *To prouoke angrie persons.*
Les abeilles ne deviement point freslons: Prov. *Looke* Abeille.
Freslonné: m. ée: f. *Bitten, or stung with Hornets.*
Fresnaye: f. *A groue, or wood of Ash trees.*
Fresne: m. *An Ash tree.*
Fresne champestre. *The field Ash, great Ash, common Ash.*
Fresne de montaigne. *The wild Ash, Whicken tree, Quicken tree, Quicke-beame tree.*
Fresne petit. *Bastard, or false, Dittanie.*
Fresne sauvage. *as* Fresne de montaigne; *The Whicken tree, &c.*
Fresnier: m. ere: f. *Of Ash, Ashen, belonging to an Ash.*
Fresnin: m. ine: f. *as* Fresnier.
Fresnoy: m. *A groue, tuft, or wood of Ash trees.*
Fresquades. *Looke* Frescades.
Fressurades: f. *Complements of outward courtesie in matters of intertainment, or salutation; as, the bowing of the knee, or a stooping to touch one anothers knees; also, trifling, fondnesse, toying, idle gestures, actions to no purpose; also, a horses lifting vp of his legs.*
Fressure, ou Fresure. *The inwards, or intraills; as* Fres. de mouton. *A sheepes plucke.*
Fressure de pourceau. *A hogs haslet.*
Fret: m. *The fraught, or fraight of a ship; also, the hire thats payed for a ship, or for the fraught thereof.*
Fretail de perles. *Refuse, or ragged Pearles, Pearles of small value.*
Fretaillé: m. ée: f. *Cut, hackt, notcht, iagged.*
Chemise fretaillée de filets. *A shirt, or smocke wrought in frets about the skirts.*
Frete. *A Verrill; th'yron band, or hoope that keeps a wooden toole from riuing.*
Freté: m. ée: f. *Hired, fraughted, and furnished, as a ship.*
Fretel. *A kind of whistle which the Sowgelders of France vsually carrie out them.*
Freter. *To hire a ship of burden; & to fraught, or load her, hired.*
Freteure: f. *A fraughting, loading, or furnishing of a (hired) ship.*
Fretille: f. *Straw:* ¶Barrag.
Fretillant. *Lasciuious, wanton, lustfull, ticklish, wrigling, frigging, itching; busie, mouing, wagging; nimble, stirring; standing on thornes, longing to be at it.*
Fretillard: m. arde: f. *The same; or, as* Fretilleur.
Fretiller. *To moue, wag, stirre often, stand on no ground; to wriggle, frig, tickle, itch, lust to be at it.*
Fretilleur: m. *A lasciuious, wanton, ticklish, lustfull companion; also, a busie bodie, a restlesse fop, one that often stirres, or figs vp and downe, as if he had an itch on his breech.*
Fretillon: m. *A little nimble dwarfe, or hop-on-my thombe; a Iacke of the Clocke-house; a little busie-bodie, medler, Iacke-stickler; one that hath an oare in euerie mans Boat, or his hand in euerie mans dish.*
Fretin: m. *Furniture, fraught, prouision; also, the size, largenesse, or goodnesse of Cod, or Greene-fish; (a tearme*

tearme in that sence applied vnto that onely fish;) also the frie of any fish.

Le menu fretin. *The least size, and worst sort, of Cod; of people, the meanest commoners, rascall vulgar, base rout.*

Fretinfretailler. *as* Fredinfredailler.

Fretrots. *A Sect of Religious men, and women (which wore a secret Crowne on their heads) incestuous, as the Adamites, by night, and suppressed in the yeare* 1310.

Fretté. *Frettie; a tearme of Blason.*

Frettin: m. *as* Fretin.

Freux: m. *A Rooke, or white-billed Crow.*

Frez: m. *as* Frescheur; *Coolenesse.*

Frez: m. Fresche: f. *New, fresh, recent, raw, greene; sound, lustie, newly come, lately done; also, coole; also, fresh, or without salt.*

Bouche fresche. *A lickorous, or hungrie palate; one whose stomacke is alwayes readie, whose appetite euer awake; also, as in;*

Tant vous avez la bouche fresche. *What fine tearms you vse; what goodlie words you come out with; (Ironically.)*

Gueule fresche. *One that hath a notable good stomacke.*

Frezaye. *A Scrich-owle.*

Freze: f. *A calues chalderne; also, a ruffe.*

Entrer en freze. *Silke-worms to begin to mount vpon the boughes layed for them (In which mounting they spinne their silke.)*

Frezé: m. ée: f. *Set, as a ruffe; or, (more properly) ruffled, or set rufflingly, after the manner of the (thicke) French ruffe;*

Febves frezées. *Pilled, or shaled beanes.*

Frezillon: m. *Priuet, Primprint.*

Friable: com. *Bruiseable, easie to be broken.*

Friand. vn fr. *A sweet-lips, picke-morsell, curious feeder, lickorous companion, daintie-mouthed fellow; an eatnell, slap-sauce, lick-dish.*

Friand: m. de: f. *Saucie, lickorous, daintie-mouthed, sweet-toothed; also, delicate, of a pleasing smacke, tast-inticing, delicious in tast.*

Navire friand à la voile. *A ship that sayles exceeding well; an excellent sayler.*

Trebuchet friand. *An alluring trap, sweet poison, pleasing bait.*

De femme volage, & friande en tout temps bon heur nous defende: Prov. *Looke* Femme.

Friandeau: m. *A sweet-lips; Looke* Friand.

Friandement. *Saucily, lickorously; sweetly, deliciously.*

Friander. *To feed daintily, tast curiously, eat lickorously, picke the best morsells out of meat; to loue, or to liue on, sweet and daintie acates.*

Friandise: f. *Daintinesse, or lickorousnesse of tast; a curious choice, or chusing of meats; also, delicious fare, and hence;*

Friandises. *Dainties, Jonkets, sweet meats, curious acates.*

Qui a le nez tourné à la friandise. *Said of a light housewife; (belike from the affinitie thats betweene a lickorous tongue, and a leacherous taile.)*

Fribours: m. *A kind of counterfeit* Doubles; *(The Huguenots haue also beene tearmed so by such as accounted them counterfeit stuffe:)* ¶Poictevin.

Fric. On ne trouve chez luy ny frac ny fric. *There is no prouision to be got, no intertainment to be had, at his house.*

Fricandeaux: m. *Short, skinlesse, and daintie puddings, or Quelkchoses, made of good flesh and hearbes chopped together, then rolled vp into the forme of Liuerings, &c, and so boyled.*

Fricassé: m. ée: f. *Fried; also, spent, or squandered away.*

Fricassée: f. *Any meat fried in a panne; also, a kind of charge for a Morter, or murdering peece, of stones, bullets, nailes, and peeces of old yron closed together with grease, and gunpowder.*

Fricasser. *To frie; also, to spend, or squander all away.*

Friche. en friche. *Wild, vntilled, sauage, desert, neglected, vnhusbanded, vnmanured.*

Bois en friche. *Wood newly lopt, or cut, and let stand vntill it be growne vp againe.*

Terre delaissée en friche. *Land vntilled; or once tilled, and afterwards neglected; whereby it becomes ouergrowne with shrubs, and weeds.*

Friction: f. *A friction, or frication; a frigging; rubbing, chafing.*

Frid. *as* Frit.

Fries: f. *The view, or footing of a Deere.*

Friez. terres laissées en friez. *Looke* Friche.

Frigaler. *To feed curiously, daintily, lickorously; to picke (onely) the best morsells out of a peece of meat.*

Frigalet: m. *A lickorous, or daintie-mouthed youth; a slap-sauce, picke-morsell, sweet-lips.*

Frigalleries: f. *Dainties; lickorous morsells, lushious acates.*

Frigoule: f. *The hearbe Time:* ¶Langued.

Friller. *To shiuer, chatter, or didder for cold.*

Frilleux: m. euse: f. *Chill, cold of nature.*

Frimas; ou Frimats: m. *A rime, or thicke mist, which in Winter most commonly falls, and leaues behind it a whitish, or frothie hoare.*

Avalleurs de frimats. *Cousening knaues, idle companions, loytering rogues; also, a nickname for Judges; who vsing to rise, and goe abroad early, swallow a great deale of mist in their dayes.*

Frime. Il n'en fit point de frime. *He shewed no passion, he seemed not to be moued, at it.*

Frime. bled frime. *Cow-wheat, Ox-wheat, Black-wheat, Horse-flower.*

Fringant. *Gay, spruce, compt, gallant, fine.*

Fringoter. *To quauer, to diuide in singing; also, as* Fringotter.

Fringoteries: f. *Frets; cranklings, wrigled flourishings, in caruing, &c.*

Fringotter. *To fret; or worke frets in gold, siluer, &c.*

Fringue. faire la fringue. *To frig, or wantonnize it, &c; as* Fringuer.

Fringuer. *To iet, or braue it; to be fine, spruce, trimme, neat; also, to minionize, or wantonize it; and (more particularly) to leacher, or lasciuiously to frig with the taile, in leachering.*

Fringuereau: m. *A ietter, spruce minion, gay fellow, compt youth; also, a licentious, or lasciuious person.*

Fringuerie: f. *A ietting, sprucenesse, trimnesse; also, leacherie, taile-frigging, sensuall wantonnesse.*

Frinson. *as* Pinson.

Friolé: m. ée: f. *Consumed; rauined, deuoured (cracklingly, or with a noise, as stubble by the fire.)*

Frioler. *To consume, rauine, deuour, (cracklingly, or with a noise, as fire does stubble) also, to braue it.*

Friolet. *A lickorous boy; or as* Vn-friand.

Frioller. *as* Frioler.

Fripaillé: m. ée: f. *Foiled, or torne, with wearing, and handling; ragged, or full of iags.*

Fripé: m. ée: f. *as* Frippé.
Vestments fripez. *Old clothes new trimd, and exposed vnto sale; Brokers ware; friperie.*
Friperie: f. *A friperie; Brokers shop, street of Brokers, or of Fripiers.*
Fripe-sauce: m. *A snap-sauce, licke-dish, lickorous fellow:* ¶Rab.
Fripier: m. *A Fripier, or Broker; a mender, or trimmer vp of old garments, and a seller of them so mended.*
Fripiére: f. *A woman that sells, or trimmes vp, old garments.*
Fripon: m. *A rag, or tattered clowt; also, an vnworthie fellow; one that vseth, or is giuen to, base trickes, and shifts; or, one that hath no inclination to any goodnesse; whence;*
Fripon de College. *A wag, a rakehell; or one that loues to be gadding abroad when he should be at his booke.*
Frippé: m. ée: f. *Rubbed much; also, worne vnto rags (by much rubbing;) also, beatē, banged, belammed; spoiled, robbed; roughly handled; also, as vnder* Fripe.
Frippe-lippe: m. *A lickorous slaue, a saucie companion:* ¶Rab.
Fripper. *To rub vp and downe; to weare vnto rags (by often rubbing;) also, to beat, bang, belamme, belabour; vse roughly, deale hardly with; rob, despoyle.*
Frippon. *as* Fripon.
Fripponnerie: f. *A base shift, or shifting tricke.*
Friquandeaux. *as* Fricandeaux.
Friquenelles: f. *Slender, and small chitterlings, or links;* (¶Rab.) *also, a rascall companie, or a roguish crue of base, and rude bisonians; ignorant clownes, scoundrels, shagrags.*
Friquet: m. *A little slice, or scummer, to turne fish in a frying-pan; also, a sticke of Lickorice; also, a kind of sparrow that keepes altogether about Wallnut trees.*
Friquette: f. *A lingell, small sklice, little scummer; also, a prettie, nimble, gay, iollie, blithe, lasse.*
Frire. *To frie.*
Il n'y a que frire. *There is nothing to be had, no good to be done; we haue not wherewithall.*
Il n'y a plus que frire. *All is consumed, wasted, spent, gone.*
Il ne luy chaut d' avoir paesle puis qu'il n'y a plus que frire. *He cares not for that which he cannot vse; or, he esteemes not of a thing longer then he hath vse for it.*
Friscades. *as* Frescades; *Fresh aire, coole places, &c.*
Frise. drap de frise. *Frise.*
Frisé: m. ée: f. *Curled, frizled, braided, crisped, ruffled; See* Frizé.
Friser. *as* Frizer; *Also, to cut a stroake, at Tennis.*
Friseure: f. *A frizling, curling, crisping, ruffling; also, as* Frizure.
Frison: m. *A Dutch tankerd; also, a man, or horse, of Frizeland.*
Frisotté: m. ée: f. *Crisped, curled, ruffled in many knots.*
Frisquaire: com. *as* Frisque.
Frisque: com. *Friske, liuelie, iollie, blithe; briske, fine, spruce, gay.*
Frissement d'un traict. *The whizzing sound of a flying arrow.*
Frisson. *A shiuering, quaking, diddering, through cold, or feare; a trembling, an horror.*
Frissonnant. *Shiuering, shrugging, diddering, shuddering.*
Frissonner. *To tremble, quake, shrug, shiuer, didder, shudder, earne, through cold, or feare.*
Frissure: f. *as* Frizure.
Frisure: f. *A light hurt; rase, or scratch; also, as* Friseure.
Frit: m. *A bending, or leaning inwards; (a Masons tearme.)*
Frit: m. ite: f. *Fried, also, wasted, spent, consumed.*
Resine frite. *Drie clarified Rosen.*
Sa part est frite de. *He may roast all his part thereof vpon his finger, or put it into his eye, and neither hurt finger, nor eye.*
Friteau: m. *A Fritter; also, as* Fritou.
Fritou: m. *A kind of shell-fish of a spannes length, and somewhat like a Mullet.*
Friture: f. *A frying.*
Frivole: com. *Friuolous, vaine, sleight, idle, trifling, of no value.*
Frivolement. *Friuolously, vainely, triflingly, to no purpose.*
Frivuscule: m. *A toy, trifle, nifle, friuolous matter.*
Frizailles: f. *Frises, or, peeces of frise.*
Frize: f. *The cloth called Frise; also (in Architecture) the broad and flat band, or member, thats next below the Cornish, or betweene it and th'Architraue; called also by our workemen, the Frize.*
Frizé: m. ée: f. *Frizled, curled, crisped, braided, ruffled; also, razed or grazed along on; touched lightly, passed sleightly ouer; onely, or but a little, scratched.*
Frizer. *To frizle; crispe; curle (as water blowne on by a gentle wind) ruffle, braid; also, to touch lightly, or passe ouer sleightly, th'vpmost part of; to raze, or graze along on; to scratch a little.*
Frizer la queuë. *To leacher; or, to wriggle the tayle (in leachering.)*
Frizer les carreaux. *To strike a ball vnder the line (at Tennis.)*
Frizons: m. *Frizled, or raised worke of gold or siluer wire, &c; also, stone pots printed.*
Frizoté: m. ée: f. *Frizled, curled, braided.*
Frizoter. *To frizle, curle, braid, ruffle.*
Frizure: f. *A frizling, &c; as in* Friseure; *also, the raised worke which is vpon cloth of gold, or Tissue; bodkin worke.*
Froc: m. *as* Frou.
Froc de moine. *A Monkes Cowle; or Hood.*
Ietter le froc aux orties. *A Monke to abandon his Order, and profession; (and hence) also, to Apostatise it.*
Frocs. *Common, or void grounds, waies, places; or as* Fros.
Frodiere. *A coole place; also, a deepe caue neere vnto* Bezançon, *in which there is great store of yce all Summer.*
Frodille. *as* Aphrodille.
Froid: m. *Cold, cooth; coldnesse, chilnesse.*
Avoir froid. *To be acold.*
Avoir froid aux pieds. *To be in ill tearmes, or ill at ease (in estate, or mind) to haue no list (or cause) to laugh, or to be merrie; also, to be iealous.*
Batre à froid. *(A metaphor from Smithes) to proceed slowly, or, goe but slackely to worke; to worke a thing out with extreame toyle; or to bestow much toile & get but little forward; and hence, also, to labour in vaine; also, as* Bransler la pique.
Dieu donne le froid selon le drap: Prov. *God sends his cooth according to their cloth; viz: such afflictions as he knowes them able to beare.*
Froid: m. de: f. *Cold, acold, breame, chill, coole, Winter-like;*

ter-like; also, slacke, slow, remisse, backward in proceeding; also, feareful, faint, weake, impuissant, that cannot performe nuptiall rites.

Avoir les pieds froids. *as* Avoir froid aux pieds; *Looke* Froid.

Dieu t'en doint vne froide ioye. *God send thee much ill lucke with, or but small ioy of, it.*

Froidelet: m. ette: f. *Chillie, coldish.*

Froidelettement. *Chilly, coldishly.*

Froidement. *Coldly, chilly; slackly, remisly; weakely, faintly.*

Froidilleux. *Chill; See* Frilleux. (v. m.)

Froidure: f. *Coldnesse; Winter-weather.*

Froidureux: m. euse: f. *Verie chill, verie cold.*

Froilon: m. *as* Freslon; *A Hornet.*

Froissé: m. ée: f. *Crashed, burst, or broken, in peeces; also, crushed, quashed, bruised; also, dashed, knocked, or clattered together.*

Froissement: m. *A crashing, bursting, or breaking in peeces; also, a crushing, quashing, bruising; also, a dashing, knocking, or clattering together.*

Froisser. *To crash, burst, or breake in peeces; also, to crush, quash, bruise; also, to dash, knocke, or clatter together.*

Froisser la iachere. *as* Iascherer: ¶Norm.

Froissis: m. *as* Froissement; *or, A rushing, clattering, crashing, iustling, bustling, knocking of armed bodies one against another; also, fallow ground, plowed lands.*

Le froissis des causes. *The conflict, or contradictions of aduerse allegations, or pleadings.*

Froissure: f. *as* Froissement; *or, A crash, or breach.*

Fromage. *as* Fourmage; *Cheese.*

Froment: m. *Wheat; also (any kind of) bread-corne; See* Froument.

Fromentée: f. *Furmentie, or, sodden wheat.*

Fromentin: m. ine: f. *Of, or belonging to, wheat.*

Pilure fromentine. *A white loafe; See* Pilure.

Froncé: m. ée: f. *Gathered, plaited, folded; wrinkled, crumpled, frumpled.*

Froncer. *as* Fronser.

Fronceure: f. *as* Fronsure.

Froncis: m. *A plait, fold, gathering; a wrinkle, or crumple; or as* Fronsure.

Le froncis du sourcil. *The knitting of th'eyebrowes.*

Froncle: m. *The hot, and hard bumpe, or swelling, tearmed, a Fellon, or vncome.*

Fronde. *A sling, or engine wherewith stones are cast; also, a (greene, or leauie) branch, or bough.*

Frondé: m. ée: f. *Cast, hurled, or flung from a sling.*

Frondelée: f. *The cast or shot of, (also) a rap or blow from, a sling.*

D'vne mesme frondelée. *At once; at one iert, or assay, with one stone.*

Frondelet: m. *A baked-meat somewhat resembling a Flawne.*

Fronder. *To cast, hurle, or throwe out of a sling.*

Frondillon. *read* Fondrillon; *A bottome to wind silke, thread, yarne, &c, on:* ¶Rab.

Frondoyer. *To branch; to yeeld, or bring forth leaues, or leaued branches.*

Fronsé. *as* Froncé.

Fronser. *To gather; plait, fold, wrinkle, crumple, frumple.*

Fronser la bouche. *To twinge the mouth in, or draw the mouth close together.*

Fronser le front. *To frowne, or knit the browes.*

Fronsure: f. *A gathering, wrinkling, frumpling; frowning.*

Front: m. *The forhead; the brow; the front, or forepart of a thing.*

Baisser le front. *To humble, or submit himselfe; to bow downe the head in signe of humilitie, or of submission.*

Eschauffer le front à. *To nettle, warme, chafe, set in a heat, put in an anger.*

Qui a le front rompu. *as* Effronté; *or, An impudent fellow.*

Frontal: m. *A frontlet; or forhead-band; also, a medicine applied to the forhead to prouoke sleepe, or ease paine.*

Le frontal. *The torture of tying a cord about the forhead, & wresting it vntill the eyes be readie to start out.*

Frontal: m. ale: f. *Of the forhead; belonging to the forhead.*

Apparence frontal. *An open face, cleere countenance, vnwrinkled forhead.*

Os frontal. *The forhead bone.*

Veine frontale, ou du front. *Looke* Veine.

Fronteau: m. *A fillet, frontlet; forhead-cloth; also, the the forepart of a cart, or tumbrell.*

Fronteau d'vne porte. *The haunse of a doore.*

Fronteau volant. *The sight, or viser of an helmet.*

Frontiere: f. *The frontire, marches, or border of a countrey.*

Frontiere d'vne bride. *The frontstall, or headstall of a bridle.*

Frontiger. *To front, or accoast; also, to rest, or dwell on the frontiers of.*

Frontispice: m. *The frontispice, or forefront, of a house, &c.*

Frontoyant. *Fronting, affronting, neere vnto a front.*

Frontoyer. *To front, affront, be neere vnto a front.*

Froqueur: m. *A mender of highwayes:* ¶Pic.

Fros: m. *Flouds, riuers, meares, ponds, springs; all kind of common waters; or, as* Frocs: ¶Pic.

Frotis: m. *A common place, or void ground in a towne; (an old word.)*

Frotte: f. *as* Frete.

Frotté: m. ée: f. *Rubbed, fretted, chafed; also, bathed; also, lambd, thwackt, basted, beaten.*

Frotte-botte. *A base drudge; boot-rubber, maker of boots cleane.*

Frottée: f. *as* Frottement.

Frottement: m. *A chafing, rubbing, fretting; a lamming, thwacking, swindging.*

Frotter. *To rub, to chafe; to fret, or grate against; also, to bathe; also, to cudgell, thwack, bast, or knock soundly.*

Se frotter le cul au panicaut. *To doe vaine, or idle things; to spend the time in trifles; or in lazie, and vnprofitable exercises.*

Frotter leur lard ensemble. *To coape, grapple, close, or scuffle together; also, to leacher it.*

Frotter à quelqu'vn son lard. *To bethwacke one soundly.*

Il ne s'y fait pas bon frotter. *It is not good medling with it; the matter is somewhat too hot for our handling; (of which sence is;)*

Ne t'y frotte pas. *(said by way of aduise vnto one that meanes to quarell with a man of more strength, and better meanes, then himselfe) meddle not with him.*

Se fier en vne fille? Allez vous y frotter. *Trust a maid? not I; you may if you will: Or (because* Frotter *hath, in this phrase, a double signification) thus; Rely on a maid? not I; you may lie on her if you will.*

On frotte tant le fer qu' à la fin il s' eschauffe: Pro. *Cold humors may at length be vrged vnto choller.*
Frottis: m. *as* Frottement.
Frottoir: m. *A rubbing, or friction; also, a rubber, a rubbing cloth.*
Frou. *A publick, and common place, free for euerie man to resort vnto, or make vse of; hence, a wast ground, highway, &c;* ¶Pic.
Frouelle. *An agnell, pinne, or warnell in the toe.*
Frouër. *To crumme, crumble, breake small.*
Froument: m. *Wheat; also, any kind of bread-corne.*
Froument quoüé. *A soft, hairie, earie, or spikie flower, shaped like a Foxes taile, and therefore called Foxtaile.*
Quiers tu meilleur pain que de froument? Prov. *(A taxation of ouer-much curiositie, or daintinesse) would you haue better bread then's made of wheat.*
Frumenté. *A kind of sweete, and pleasing white grape.*
Froumentée: f. *Furmentie; wheat boyled, pottage of of wheat; or, as* Frumentée.
Froumenteux: m. euse: f. *Wheatie; full of, or abounding with, wheat.*
Froyé: m. ée: f. *Rubbed, grated vpon; fretted, rased, much worne by much rubbing; or, as* Frayé.
Froyement: m. *A rubbing; or often hitting against; See* Frayement.
Froyer: m. *A rubber; also, a raspe.*
Froyer. *To rub; fret, rase, grate vpon; hit, or smite often one against another; See* Frayer.
Fructifier. *To fructifie; to increase, or abound with fruit; to beare fruit.*
Jamais grain ne fructifie si premier ne se mortifie: Prov. *See* Grain.
Fructueux: m. euse: f. *Fruitfull, copious, plentifull; commodious.*
Fructuosité: f. *Fruitfulnesse; plentie, store, aboundance of, fruit.*
Fructure: f. *The fructure, vse, fruition, possession, or enioyment of.*
Frugal: m. ale: f. *Frugall, thriftie, sparing, prouident, neere, temperate in expence.*
Frugalement. *Frugally, thriftily, sparingly, sauingly.*
Frugalité: f. *Frugalitie, thriftinesse, good husbandrie, sparing, sauing, moderate or small expence.*
Fruict: m. *Fruit (of the earth; trees; plants; females; our actions;) returne, or increase, of profit made, in time, out of the things one hath, or doth; or, as in;*
Fruicts. *All the reuenew, or commoditie raised out of a thing (whether it bee mouable, or immouable) or receiued by the occasion, or meanes thereof.*
Fruicts civils. *Looke* Civil.
Fruicts naturels. *Are such as come onely by the nature of a thing; or both by nature, and culture; as pears, apples, hay, corne, &c.*
Faire les fruicts siens. *To applie vnto his owne vse, or t'enioy in his owne right, the profits of land forfeited vnto him.*
Fruictier: m. *A Fruiterer, fruit-seller, Costermunger; also, an Orchard, or ground wherein fruit growes.*
Fruictier: m. ere: f. *Fruit-bearing, yeelding fruit; also, full of, stored with, abounding in, fruit.*
Fruictiere: f. *A Fruit-wife; or woman that selleth fruits.*
Fruïr. *To enioy, hold, haue; take the profit, keepe the possession, make a continuall vse, of.*
Fruitage: m. *Fruitage, fruits.*
Fruiterie: f. *A Fruiterie; or place to keepe Fruit in.*
Fruition: f. *Fruition, enioying; vse, or possession of a thing.*
Frumentau. *The wild Mulberie; (a low shrub.)*
Frumenteau. *A kind of white vine.*
Frumentée: f. *Furmentie; or wheat steeped in water, then pilled, or skinned; then dried in the Sunne; then ground a verie little, as oatmeale, and reserued for pottage, Panadoes, &c.*
Frumentelle. *A certaine peare good to be dried; and dried, continuing longer then any other.*
Frustration. *A frustration, defrauding, deceiuing, disappointing, beguiling of an expectation.*
Frustratoire: com. *Frustratorie; frustrating, disappointing, deceiuing; also, void, vaine, idle, frustrate, of no force, to no purpose.*
Frustratoirement. *Voidly, in vaine, with no effect, vnto no purpose.*
Frustré: m. ée: f. *Disappointed, frustrated; put by; deceiued, beguiled.*
Frustrer. *To disappoint, frustrate, put by, make loose; deceiue, defraud, beguile the expectation, or hopes of.*
Fryez: m. *The view, or footing of a Deere.*
Fuchiere. *as* Feuchiere.
Fueillade: f. *A greene arbor, or bower; a shadie place vnder trees; also, the shadow of leaues, or of leauie trees.*
Fueillage: m. *Branched worke, in Painting, or in Tapistrie.*
Le mensonge est mal à couvert sous ce fueillage. *A lie is but ill countenanced by such pretexts; these colours are not sufficient to couer an vntruth.*
Fueillame: m. *A bunch of leaues.*
Fueillants: m. *An Order of begging Friers that weare habits of a brownish colour.*
Fueillar: m. *A greene, or leauie braunch, or bough of a tree; also, a close theefe, pilferer, night-robber.*
Fueille: f. *A leafe (of an hearbe, or tree) also; a sheet, or leafe, of paper; also, a flaw in yron-worke; also, the foyle of pretious stones, or looking glasses; and hence; a grace, beautie, or glosse giuen vnto; a colour, pretence, or excuse made for, a matter.*
Fueille d' vn espée. *The blade of a sword.*
Fueille d' Inde. *An Aromaticall leafe, that (as some hold) swimmes on pooles, and ditches without any apparent root; yet Gerard sayes, it is the leafe of a great tree, which growes in* Arabia, *and* Can baia, *farre from any water, and calls it* Tamalapatra, Tembul, *and* Malabathrum.
Fueille de poulmon. *A lobe of the lungs; whence;*
Il ne sçait de quelle fueille de poulmon respirer. *He knowes not what to doe, whether to betake him, how to behaue himselfe; he is euen readie to goe hang himselfe.*
Fueilles de scie. *The teeth of a saw; in Blazon, a fesse indented.*
Vin de deux fueilles. *Wine thats two yeares old.*
Bourse liée avec fueilles de porreaux. *Thats readie, or easie, to be opened.*
Porter des fueilles au bois. *To present gifts to the rich, or bestow things on those that haue alreadie as much as they can vse.*

Les mauldissons sont fueilles qui les seme les recueille : Prov. *Those that curse often shall accursed be.*

Qui a peur des fueilles ne doit aller au bois : Pro. *(like our) let him that feares the wagging of feathers keepe from among wildfowle.*

Qui se garre dessous la fueille deux fois se mouille: Prov. *Hee's doubly wet that shrowds him vnder trees.*

Telle racine telle fueille : Prov. *We say; such as the tree such is the fruit.*

Fueillée : f. *as* Fueillade ; *An arbor, or bower, framed of leauie plants, or branches ; a greene arbor.*

Fueiller. *To leafe, or leaue; to beare, or bring forth leaues; to wax greene with leaues.*

Fueillet : m. *A leafe (of a booke.)*

Fueilleté : m. ée : f. *Leaued; also, looked, or turned ouer, as the leaues of a booke; seriously perused, throughly examined, studied hard, read much vpon.*

Gasteau fueilleté. *A cake of puffe-past.*

Fueilleter. *To turne, or looke ouer, the leaues of a booke; to peruse, examine, studie hard, read much on, bookes.*

Fueillette : f. *A wine vessell, or measure containing about eleuen and a halfe of our gallons.*

Fueillette d' Avignon. *Is somewhat bigger then the demie* Sestier *of Paris.*

Fueilletter. *as* Fueilleter.

Fueilleux : m. euse : f. *Leauie, full of leaues.*

Fueillir. *as* Fueiller.

Fueillu : m. *A kind of round, red, and verie sweet apple.*

Fueillu marin. *Sea-weed, Sea-mosse, Lungwort, Oister-greene ; a broad-leaued hearbe.*

Fueillu : m. uë : f. *Leauie, full of leaues.*

Vent fueillu. *A Westerlie wind.*

Fueillure : f. *Leauinesse; also, leaues ; also, leafe-worke, or a leauie flourishing.*

Fugitif: m. iue : f. *Fugitiue; gadding, flitting, run-away, runagate, quickly gone, of no continuance, of no sure abiding, of no certaine stay; inconstant, giddie, fickle; (also) full of euasions.*

Fugue : f. *A chace, or report of Musicke, like two, or more parts in one.*

Fuir. *To flie, escape, runne fast, scoure, scud, or slip away; to shew a faire paire of heeles; also, to shunne, auoid, eschew, refuse to deale with; also, to flinch, dally, delay, excuse, put or shift off, vse euasions.*

Remede contre la peste par art, fuir tost, & loing, retourner tard : Prov. *According to the Latine,* Citò, longè, tardè.

Fuirolles. *Fire-drakes; or, as* Furoles.

Fuite : f. *A flight, escape, slip, running away; a shunning, auoyding; euasion, shift, excuse, delay.*

Sans estre poursuyvi le meschant prend la fuite: Prov. *Selfe-guilt (if nothing else) makes sinners flie.*

Fuitif. *as* Fugitif.

Fulci : m. ie : f. *Supported, vnderset, vpheld, vnderpropped, sustained; fortified.*

Fulcir. *To vnderset, vnderprop, support, sustaine, vphold, stay, fortifie.*

Fuligine : f. *Soot, sootinesse; smoakinesse.*

Fuligineux: m. euse: f. *Sootie, blacke; smoakie.*

Fulmination : f. *A thunder-striking.*

Fulminatoire: com. *Fulminatorie; thundering, lightening; destroying, terrible.*

Fulminer. *To thunder, lighten, strike with thunder, blast with lightening; to storme, rage, take on like a Diuell.*

Fumage : m. *A dunging, manuring, fatning with dung.*

Fumat : m. *Ray, or Scate-fish :* ¶Langued.

Fumé : m. ée : f. *Dunged, manured, fattened with dung; also, fumed, smoaked; euaporated; besmoaked; hung, or dried in the smoake.*

Fumeau : m. *A brand, or smoaking sticke.*

Fumée: f. *Smoake; a fume, reeke, steame; a vapor, an exhalation.*

Fumée des Peintres. *Painters soot, or bleach; got in glasse-houses, and vsed also by Chirurgians.*

Fumeés : f. *The dung, or excrements of Deere, called by woodmen, fewmets, or fewmishing.*

Fumées en plateaux. *Flat gratching, or fewmishing.*

Fumelle. *See* Femelle.

Fumement: m. *A dunging or manuring of th'earth; also, a smoaking, fuming, reeking; a bloating, besmoaking, or hanging in the smoake.*

Fumer. *To smoake, reeke; fume; euaporate; bloat, besmoake, hang, or drie in the smoake; also, to dung, manure, fatten with dung.*

Fumeron. *A little dung-hill, a small heape of dung.*

Fume-terre : f. *The hearbe Fumitorie.*

Fumeusement. *Smoakily, fumingly, reekingly.*

Fumeux : m. euse : f. *Smoakie, fumie, reeking; also, hot, fumish, cholericke.*

Fumier : m. *A mexen, dung-hill, heape of dung.*

Relevé du fumier. *Raised from a dung-hill; of a late Clowne become a lame Gentleman.*

Chien sur son fumier est hardi : Prov. *We say the same of a Cocke.*

Pluye de Fevrier vaut esgout de fumier: Prov. *We say, Aprill showers bring in May flowers.*

Fumier. *Of dung; as* Estable fumiere; *a stable full of dung.*

Fumieres : f. *as* Fumées.

Fumigation : f. *Fumigation; a smoaking, or perfuming with smoake.*

Funain. mettre vn navire en funain. *To moore a ship, or tie her vnder a lee shore.*

Funambule: m. *A Tumbler that walketh, & doth tricks, vpon a rope.*

Function : f. *A function; a charge, or office exercised, or executed.*

Fundigue. *A ware-house, or store-house.*

Fundique. *as* Fundigue.

Funebre : com. *Funerall; mourning, deadlie, or dolefull; done at, or belonging vnto, funeralls.*

Honneurs funebres. *Looke* Honneur.

Funebrement. *Mourningly, dolefully; in manner, or after the fashion, of a funerall.*

Funerailles : f. *Funeralls, burialls.*

Funeste: com. *Mournfull; deadlie, mortall; vnluckie; lamentable; abbominable, detestable.*

Funge : m. *A mushrome, or toad-stoole.*

Fungosité: f. *Spunginesse; hollownes, thinnesse, lightnesse.*

Fungueux : m. euse : f. *Hollow, spungie; thinne, light; mushrome-like; full of mushromes.*

Fur. au fur de. *Proportionably, according to, after the rate of.*

Furain. *Looke* Funain.

Furas. *in stead of* Fatras : ¶Rab.

Furculaire. Os furculaires. *The points of the forepart of the shoulders meeting a little below the necke.*

Furemplage. au furemplage de. *Proportionably, according to, after the rate of.*

Furet : m. *A ferret.*

Fureté : m. ée : f. *Ferreted; searched, hunted, boulted out; narrowly pried, neerely spied into.*

Fureter. *To ferret; search, hunt, boult out; prie, looke, spie narrowly into euerie corner of.*
Fureteur: m. *A ferreter, searcher; prier, spier.*
Fureur: f. *Furie, rage, madnesse; fiercenesse, outragiousnesse; extreame wrath, anger, impatiencie.*
Furfuré: m. ée: f. *Brannie, scalie like branne.*
Furfures. *Dandriffe; the scurfe, or scales, which fall from the head in combing.*
Furgon. *See* Fourgon.
Furial: m. ale: f. *Raging, furious, furie-like; horrible, outragious.*
Furibond: m. de: f. *Wood, madde, raging, furious.*
Furie: f. *Furie, madnesse, frenzie, woodnesse.*
Furies. *The Furies of hell.*
Furieusement. *Furiously, madly, ragingly, woodly, wrathfully, bedlam-like.*
Furieux: m. euse: f. *Furious, raging, most impatient, franticke, madde, wood, brainsicke, outragious.*
Furiole. *See* Furole.
Furlucqué: m. ée: f. *Searched, ferreted, hunted out.*
Furole: f. *A little blaze of fire appearing by night on the tops of souldiers launces, or at sea on the sayle-yards, where it whirles, and leapes in a moment from one place to another; some Mariners call it S. Hermes fire; if it come double tis held a signe of good luck, if single, otherwise.*
Furt: m. *A robbing, theft, stealth, filching, purloining, pilfering.*
Furtif: m. iue: f. *Filching, theeuish, felonious; also, nimbd, pilfered, imbezelled, stollen, conueyed away.*
Furtivement. *Theeuishly, feloniously, filchingly, by stealth; priuily, closely, underhand; at vnawares.*
Furuncule: m. *A felon, or whitlaw.*
Fusain. *Spindle-tree, Prick-wood, Pricke-timber.*
Fusé: m. ée: f. *Dissolued, melted; spred, scattered.*
Chaux fusée. *Slaked, or sleckt lime.*
Fuseau: m. *A spindle; or spoole; also, as* Fusée; *also, a sticke to set Acornes with; also, (in cases of succession) the feminine line.*
Fuseau des champs. *Wild bastard Saffron.*
Demesler vn fuseau. *To handle, manage, deale in; or, to debate; vnpester, dispatch, rid away, a businesse.*
Ie sçay bien avec lequel i'ay à demesler ce fuseau. *I know well ynough whom I haue to doe with in this businesse.*
Le fuseau doit suyvre le gorreau: Prov. *While the husband labours abroad the wife must not idle it at home; or, a wife is to follow her husband in what course of his fortune soeuer.*
Fusée: f. *A spoole-full, or spindle-full, of thread, yarne, &c; also, a squib; also, as* Fuzée.
Fusée avec ses pesons; *as* Astragale; *because commonly the worke on it resembles many spooles and werbles threaded, or ioyned together.*
Cela meslera nos fusées. *That will iumble, confound, or make alike, our imployments, causes, occasions.*
Recherchons le bout de nostre fusée. *Let vs return vnto our matter.*
Il en sçait toute la fusée. *He is acquainted with the whole matter, he knowes it all from the one end to the other.*
Commencement n'est pas fusée: Prov. *He hath not done, that hath begunne, a businesse.*
Sur petit commencement on fait grande fusée: Pro. *Great mischiefes often haue but small beginnings.*
Pour devider la fusée il faut trouver le bout du fil: Prov. *Looke* Devider.

Fuselé: m. ée: f. *Spunne vpon a spindle, or spoole; also, made like a spindle, or spoole.*
Fuselier: m. *A spindle-maker, a maker of spooles.*
Fusible: com. *Fusible; meltable, which may be melted.*
Fusier. *as* Fusain; *Spindle-tree.*
Fusil: m. *A fire-steele for a tinder-box; also, the steele wherewith a Butcher whets his kniues.*
Pierre à fusil. *A flint-stone.*
Fusiller. *as* Fureter. *To search, or ferret euerie corner of.*
Fusque: com. *Duskie, browne, darke, swart, tawnie, of a Moores hew.*
Fust: m. *Any staffe, stake, stocke, stumpe, trunke, or log (thats headlesse; or, vnderstood without it head;) hence, the staffe of a speare; the steale of a dart, or iauelin; also, the frame, or carriage of a peece of Ordnance; also, the great beame of a wine-presse; also, fustines.*
Fust de selle. *The tree of a saddle.*
Aulner fust à fust. *To giue hard, strait, or scant measure, where ell is laid close vnto ell.*
Livrement de fust, & terre. *A forme of Liuerie and seisin vsed in some parts of France.*
Mettre le doigt entre le fust, & l'escorce. *Busily to meddle with, or take notice of, the differences which are betweene priuate, or neere friends.*
Fustaille: f. *Caske; vessells for wine.*
Fustaillier: m. *A Cooper, or Caske-maker.*
Fustaine: f. *Fustian.*
Fustaine frangée. *Tufted fustian in fringelike rewes; therein differing from* Fustaine houpée; *which is tufted all ouer.*
Fustaine à grain d'orge. *Bustian.*
Fustaine houpée, ou mouschetée. *Tufted fustian; a course fustian-like stuffe thats tufted all ouer.*
Fustainier: m. ere: f. *Of fustian, belonging vnto fustian.*
Fustaye. *A wood, or forrest of high trees; and hence;* Bois de haute fustaye. *Great trees, high trees; properly such, as haue not been cut, nor lopt of (at the least) 30 yeares, or as some affirme of 100 yeares; for no lesse time serues to make of a Copse,* vn Bois de haute, ou bonne fustaye.
Vne chose de haute fustaye. *A gallant, statelie, loftie, worthie, notable, thing.*
Fuste: f. *A foist; a light gallie that hath about 16, or 18 oares on a side, & two rowers to an oare; also, caske; any vessell, or peece, for wine; as a Pipe, Hogshead, &c.*
Fuste de selle. *The tree of a saddle.*
Fusté: m. ée: f. *Fustie; tasting of the caske, smelling of the vessell, wherein it hath beene kept; also, stocked, branchlesse, without boughes, as a tree; also, rifled, ransacked, vnfurnished by violence of all it had, or held.*
Fustée: f. Bois de fustée. *Branchlesse wood; naked, or powled trees.*
Fuster. *To stocke a tree; to cut off, or bare it of, it branches; also, to rauage, ransacke, rifle, carrie away by violence all thats in a place.*
Fusterne: f. *Th'vpper part of a Firre tree, full of ioynts, or knots.*
Fustier. *Any Artificer that works in wood; as a Carpenter, Joyner, &c.*
Fustigation: f. *A whipping, scourging, breeching; also, a lamming, thwacking, basting with a cudgell.*
Fustiger. *as* Fustiguer.
Fustigué: m. ée: f. *Whipped, lashed, scourged, breeched; also, cudgelled, lammed, curried, basted, bethwacked.*
Fustiguer. *To whip, scourge, lash, breech; also, to cudgell, belabour, currie, lamme.*

Fu-

Futile: com. *Light, vaine, vnprofitable, foolish.*
Futur: m. ure: f. *Future, succeeding, hereafter, to come.*
Examen à futur; *Looke* Examen.
Fuy: m. ye: f. *Fled, escaped, gone, euaded, slipt aside, runne away.*
Tous les prisonniers s' en sont fuys de sa bourse. *All the prisoners are got out of his purse; viz. he is purse pennilesse, or he hath not a pennie left him.*
Fuyant. *Flying, escaping, euading, got away; shunning, auoiding, eschewing; excusing, delaying; loathing, loth to deale with; also, momentarie, of small continuance, quickly past, soone gone.*
Fuyard: m. *A kind of Stock-doue.*
Fuyard: m. *A coward, a flyer, a runne-away; also, a shunner of companie; also, a halter, flincher, delayer, shifter, one that draweth backe when a matter comes to an vpshot, or to the pinch, and point of tryall.*
Fuyard: m. de: f. *Momentarie, soone gone, flitting, running, passing away; also, cowardly flying, running away for feare; whence;*
Fuyard en lievre. *Scudding away like a Hare (with dogs at her heeles;) or gone vpon the first, or least, apprehension of danger.*
Fuye: f. *A Pigeon-house; also, a flight of Pigeons.*
Fuyeur: m. *A flyer, coward, runneaway; runner; flincher.*
Fuzain: m. *Spindle tree, Prick-wood, Pricke-timber.*
Fuzé: m. ée: f. *as* Fusé.
Fuzée: f. *as* Fusée; *also, the barrell, or the axletree of a Crane.*
Fuzelier: m. *A Spindle-maker.*
Fuzil. *as* Fusil.
Fy. *as* Foy; *Faith;* ¶Pic. Par ma fy. *By my fecke.*
Fy. (Interiect.) *Fy, away, fy away, fy fy, out vpon it.*
Maistre fy fy. *A Dung-farmer, Gould-finder, feyer of Priuies.*
Fy d' avoir qui n'a ioye, & d' amours sans monnoye: Pro. *Fy vpon meanes without mirth, and a mistresse without money.*
Fy de ieunesse, & de beauté desgarnie d'humilité: Prov. *Fy vpon youth, and beautie deuoid of humilitie.*
Fy de manteau quand il fait beau: Pro. *Fy vpon a cloake in faire weather.*
Fy de plaisirs, d'estats, & d'or, qui de vertu n'a le thresor: Prov. *Out vpon honor, wealth, and pleasure, which of vertue want the treasure.*
Fy de science, & d' art, qui en raison n' a part: Prov. *Fy on Knowledge, and on Art, which in reasõ haue no part.*

G

Gaban: m. *A cloake of Felt, for raynie weather; a Gabardine.*
Gabaonite: m. *A maker of such Cloakes, or Gabardines.*
Gabarre: f. *A Lighter; the boat whereby ships are loaden, and vnloaden.*
Gabarrier: m. *A Lighter-man.*
Gabellage: m. *A customing; an imposing, or paying of custome.*
Gabelle: f. *(Any kind of) impost, imposition, or custome; especially that which is payed vnto the King vpon sale of salt; and hence;*
Gabelle de sel. *The Impost of salt; first begun by Philip the Long, who took for it a* Double (ij d Tour:) *vpon the pound; after whõ* Philip de Valois *doubled that; and* Charles *the seuenth raised it vnto* vj d, *which was doubled by* Lewis *the eleuenth; since whose time it hath been altered, from so much vpon the pound, vnto a rate vpon euerie* Muid; *as vncertaine as the former (being sometimes 30 pound, sometimes 44 poũd, and sometimes 45 pound) and rising, or falling, at the will and pleasure of the Prince.*
Gabelle de Tonnieu. *A certaine Impost taken by the Duke of* Buillon *vpon euerie Tunne, and Hogshead of Wine transported, or sold by Great.*
Gabellé: m. ée: f. *Customed for; on which an Impost is layed.*
Gabeller. *To pay custome for; also, to impose a custome, lay an Impost, on.*
Gabellier: m. *A leuier, or gatherer of, Impost.*
Gabeloux: m. *A scoffing knaue, gibing marchant; cogging companion.*
Gaber. *To mocke, flout, ride; cog with; to gull, cheat, cosen, fetch ouer.*
Gaberies: f. *Mockes, flouts; tales, fibs, foists, gleekes, gudgeons, gulleries.*
Gabes. *as* Gaberies.
Gabet: m. *A white leaper; so called about* Bourdeaux.
Gabeur: m. *A mocker, flouter; cogger, foister; cheater, cousener; seller of bargaines.*
Gabgregeux: m. *Rogues, varlets, rascals, scowndrels, base fellowes.*
Gabian. *as* Gavian.
Gabie: f. *The vpper part of a Mast whereto the shrouds are fastened; the head of the Mast.*
Gabinet: m. *A Cabinet.*
Gabion: m. *A gabion; a defence for Canoniers, made of great baskets filled with earth.*
Gabionnade: f. *A ranke, or defence, of gabions.*
Gabionné: m. ée: f. *Gabioned; fenced, or fortified with gabions.*
Gabionner. *To defend, or fortifie with gabions; to make a defence of gabions.*
Gabors: m. *The Ribbes, or Knees of a Ship.*
Gabot: m. *A white leaper; as* Caquot; *also a red fish, or Gurnard; also, as* Gavot.
Gaboux: m. ouse: f. *Full of flouts, mocks, ieasts, derision, scoffes.*
Gache. *as* Gasche.
Gacher. *as* Gascher; *also, to feed, or surfet on.*
Gachis: m. *A dashing, or flashing of water; also, the stroake of an Oare, or noise which it makes in rowing.*
Gades: f. *Red Goosberries, beyond-sea Gooseberries, bastard Currans, common Ribes.*
Gadille. *as* Gadrille.
Gadiller. *To padle; iog, or stirre vp and downe.*
Gadoüard: m. *A Gould-finder, Iakes-farmer, feyer of Priuies; also, a Scauinger.*
Gadouë: f. *Durt, filth; dung, ordure.*
La charrette de la gadouë. *A common Dung-cart; or Scauingers Carre.*
Gadriers. *as* Gades. *Red Gooseberries.*
Gadrille: f. *The little bird called a Robin-red-breast.*
Gadriller. *(A wench) to raump, or play the rig.*
Gadrouillette: f. *A minx, gigle, flirt, callet, Gixie; (a fained word, applyable to any such cattell.)*
Gaffe: f. *An Iron hooke wherewith sea-men pull great fishes into their ships.*

Gagate: f. *The blacke stone called, Iet.*

Gage: m. *A gage, pawne, pledge; also, a wager; and, a stake at play; also, a guerdon, reward, or salarie; also, a distresse, or moueable taken for a distresse.*

Gages. Plural. *Wages, hire, stipend, intertainement; also, goods taken by a Sergeant vpon an Execution.*

Gage de bataille, ou de combat. *A gage, or pledge (and most commonly, a gloue, or gantelet) throwne down by one that offers, or vndertakes, to fight with another.*

Amende de gage. *Looke* Amende.

Clameur de gage pleige. C'est vne Action proprietaire, & possessoire ensemble; quand aucun se doute qu' autre face entreprise sur saisine possessoire, ou droicture à luy appartenant.

Gagé: m. ée: f. *Gaged, pledged, pawned; also, taken to pledge, or in pawne; also, betted, or layed, as a wager; also, waged, as battell; also, distrained, or taken, as a distresse.*

Gagement: m. *A gaging, pawning, impledging; also, a betting, or laying; also, a waging of battell; also, a distraining, or taking as a distresse; also, the obligation, assurance, or pawne of an obliged debtors goods.*

Gage-mort: m. *as* Mortgage; *also, the pawne, or fee giuen for the deliuerie of beasts found Damage-fesant.*

Gager: m. *as* Gaiger.

Gager. *To gage, or ingage, to pledge, or lay to pawne; also, to take in pawne; also, to bet, or lay a wager; also, to wage battell; also, to distraine, take a distresse, or take as a distresse.*

Gager l'amende. *To discharge, or pay the amercement.*

Gager personnes en son domaine. *To arrest their bodies, or seize vpon, as a pawne, somewhat about them.*

Gager le rachapt. *To pay, or offer to pay it downe.*

Gagerie: f. *A distraining; a distresse; or, as* Gagement.

Gagerie de rachapt. *as in* Gager.

Simple gagerie. *A distraining, without carrying away the distresse.*

Gages. *A kind of artificiall stone (made of Bitumen) the smoake whereof driues away Serpents; (Looke vnder* Gage.)

Gageure: f. *A wager; also, a reall and actuall offer.*

Gagier: m. *An hireling, or stipendarie; one that hath, or taketh, wages.*

Gagnole: f. *A little, long, small-eyed, and lesse-mouthed fish, couered, in stead of scales, with a hard, and crustie skin; Some hold it to be a kind of Hornebeake.*

Gagrille: f. *The Robin-red-breast.*

Gahets. *A generation of poore, irreligious, and verie laborious leapers, in Gascoigne.*

Gai. *as* Gay; *Merrie, iocond, buxome, blithe.*

Gaian: m. *A fish (and by* Gesners *description, the ninth kind of the fish* Turdus) *not much vnlike a Pearch, and of colour in some parts yellow, in others, greene; onely it hath a white line running along from the gylls to the tayle; Some also call so, the fish* Auriol.

Gaiderope. *The vnsauorie, or ill-tasting oyster, tearmed in Latin,* Spondylus.

Gaige-plege. *A kind of Iurisdiction, or Court, in Normandie, wherein the parties must bind themselues by pawnes, or sureties, to continue, or make good, their suites.*

Gaiger: m. *A Church-warden, or ouerseer of a particular Churches businesses.*

Gaignable: com. *Gettable, winnable, gaineable; to be got; auaileable, commodious, profitable.*

Terres gaignables. *Rich, or fruitfull ground; arable grounds that yeeld much, or are of great, increase.*

Gaignage: m. *The crop, or fruits of tilled, or planted grounds; the gaine, reuenue, profit, or increase thereof; also, a Ground, Coast, or Countrey, wherein there growes plentie of corne, and hearbes; a fruitfull Plot, or Place; also, a Farme (so tearmed by the inhabitants of* Champaigne;) *also, a kind of graine.*

Gaignages. *(Hunters tearme so) all kind of corne-grounds, and gardens, wherein there grow no trees.)*

Bon gaignage fait bon potage: Prov. *Fruitfull crops yeeld fattening sops; or, good hearbes good pottage yeeld.*

Gaignaux. Prez gaignaux. *Fertile medowes, which yeeld a double crop, or may be twice mowed.*

Gaigne: f. *Gaine, profit, increase, commings in; or, as* Gaignage *in the first sence.*

Gaigne coustumiere. *The part, or portion of goods whereunto, by custome, the suruiuor of a married couple succeeds.*

Gaigné: m. ée: f. *Gained, woon, procured, gotten.*

Ie te le donne gaigné. *I graunt it, I yeeld it thee; I confesse thy action; I giue thee the bucklers.*

Il a bien gaigné la mort. *He hath well deserued to dye.*

Sans l'avoir gaigné. *Without cause, without desert.*

Gaigneau. Pré gaigneau. *as* Gaignau. ¶Poictevin.

Gaigne-denier. *A Porter; or, a day-Labourer; who, in old time, tooke for his dayes worke but a* Denier; *(but then it was of siluer, and worth vj d sterl.)*

Gaigne-iournée. *A Labourer by the day.*

Gaigne-pain. *as* Gaigne-denier; *(and hence,* Vn bon gaigne-pain. *A painefull Labourer; a thriftie, and prouident workeman;) also, the trade, art, exercise, occupation, or meanes, whereby one gets his liuing; and thence will the French souldior tearme, oft times his Sword, and sometimes his Harguebuse,* Son Gaigne-pain.

Gaigner. *To gaine, get, win; procure, purchase, obtaine; to profit, or thriue by; to atchieue, attaine; reach, or come vnto; also, to ouercome, conquer, win; also, to merit, or deserue.*

Gaigner son avoine. *Looke* Avoine.

Gaigner les champs. *To runne away.*

Gaigner chemin. *To make hast, rid way apace.*

Gaigner le devant par derriere. *To outstrip, ouerrun, or get before, one by a contrarie course; or, to preuent the designes of another by policies contrarie to his.*

Gaigner les gigoteaux; *To betake him to his heeles; to fly as fast as his legs will carry him.*

Gaigner le hault. *To runne his countrey; to fly as if fire were at his tayle.*

Gaigner le hault bout. *To win the spurres, to carry away the best prize; also, to take the highest place at a table.*

Gaigner païs. *To steale on, to rid way.*

Gaigner peine &c. pour gaigner peine & papier ie le fais brief. *To saue labor, and spare paper I write the lesse.*

Gaigner au pied. *To run away.*

Gaigner le temps. *To dispatch; to rid away time apace.*

Gaigner leur vie à reculons. *To liue by going backward; viz. by rope-making.* ¶Rab.

Gaigner le tour du roule. *See* Roule.

Assez gaigne qui malheur perd : Prov. *He gets ynough that misses an ill turne.*
Iamais ne gaigne qui plaide à son seigneur; (ou qui procede à son Maistre:) Pro. *No man euer throue by suing his Lord or Maister; (for either God blesses not so vndutifull a strife, or successe followes not in so vnequall a match.)*
Marchand qui ne gaigne perd : Pro. *The marchant looses when he gaines not; and yet;*
Il n'est pas marchand qui tousiours gaigne : Prov. *He trades not cunningly that alwaies gayneth.*
Qui bien gaigne, & bien despéd ne luy faut bourse à mettre argent: Pro. *Looke* Despendre.
Qui bien gaigne, & bien espargne devient tantost riche: Prov. *He that gets well, and spares wisely, soone growes rich.*
Tel change qui ne gaigne pas: Prov. *Some change for the worse.*
Gaignerie: f. *A tilled ground; also, tillage, or tilling; also, the profit thats made of tillage, or of the beasts that be vsed therein.*
Gaigneur: m. *A gainer, getter, winner, obtainer; one that thriues by, or makes a profit of, his trafficke, labor, industrie.*
Mon gaigneur. *My Hind, Husbandman, Ploughman; one that labours, and by his labour gets, for me; one that labours to make me liue, or gaine.*
Hardi gaigneur hardi mangeur: Pro. *A sore toyler, a sound trencherman; they that worke hard eat hard.*
Mieux vaut bon gardeur que bon gaigneur: Pro. *See* Gardeur.
Gaillard: m. *The round house, or hinder castle, of a ship.*
Gaillard: m. arde: f. *Lustie, liuelie; frolicke, buxome, cheerefull, blithe, iocond, pleasant, gamesome; braue, gallant; valiant; well disposed, in good tune; also, rash, or somewhat vndiscreet, by too much iollitie.*
Galop gaillard. *See* Galop.
Il a le cerveau vn peu gaillard. *He is a little humorous, toyish, fantasticall, new-fangled, light-headed.*
Ouvrier gaillard cele son art: Prov. *The industrious workman prostitutes not his Art.*
Gaillardement. *Liuely, lustily; cheerefully, pleasantly; gallantly, like a gallant.*
Gaillardet: m. *See* Guaillardet.
Gaillardeté: f. *Lustinesse, liuelinesse; cheerefulnesse, pleasantnesse, iocondnesse, glee; gallantrie, brauerie; also, rashnesse, follie, indiscretion; or an act rashly, foolishly, or vndiscreetly done, by the headinesse, iollitie, or too much forwardnesse, of youth.*
Gaillardise: f. *as* Gaillardeté; *(and the better, and more vsuall word.)*
Gaille. Perdrix gaille. *The French Partridge; a kind of great browne Partridge, that hath a red beake, and red legs.*
Gaimaux. Prex gaimaux. *as* Gaignaux. ¶Lodunois.
Gain: m. *Gaine, profit, lucre, aduantage, gettings, increase, commoditie, commings in.*
Gain de cause. *A victorie, or speeding in a suit.*
Le petit gain emplit la bourse: Prov. *Many a little makes a mickle; or, light gaines make heauie purses.*
Gaine: f. *A sheath, or scabberd.*
Dans vne gaine d'or vn cousteau de plomb: Prov. *A leaden sword in a golden sheath; a godlesse heart in a goodlie bodie.*
Selon la gaine le cousteau: Pro. *Like sheath like knife.*
Gaineaux. Prez gaineaux. *as* Gaignaux.
Gainette: f. *A little sheath, or scabberd.*
Gaing: m. *as* Gain.
Gaings. *The fruits growing on, or comming of, tilled grounds; or the profit comming in by sowing of grounds.*
Gains. *as* Gaings; *and comprehends all kinds of graine, pulse, and such like fruits* (tenants encore par les racines. ¶Nicot.)
Gaïofle d'un moulin, *for* Gayole; *See* Gayole.
Gaïole. *as* Gayole: f. *A Cage.* ¶Pic.
Gaïoler. *To pratle, tatle, chatter, like a bird in a Cage.*
Gaïon. *A Jay.*
Gajure: f. *A wager.*
Gajure de rachapt; *See* Gagerie.
Gaiz *(for* Guez.) *Foords, or shallow places.*
Gal: m. *A Cocke; also, a Dorce, or Gold-fish.* ¶Langued.
Gals escouillez. *Capons; Eunuches.* ¶Rab.
Galactite. Pierre galactite. *See* Pierre.
Galaffre: m. *A rauenous feeder, greedie deuourer, glutton, gulch, cormorant.*
Galaffrerie: f. *Gourmandizing; rauenous, or greedie feeding.*
Galange. *as* Galangue.
Galangue: f. *Sweet Ciperus, English Galingale; or the Aromaticall root thereof.*
Galaxie: f. *The Milkie way in the Firmament.*
Galbanon. *Galbanum; a gumme, or liquor issuing out of the Syrian* Ferula, *or Fennell giant.*
Galbe. *A Wenne; also, garbe, comelinesse, gracefullnesse; also, the bellie, or forepart, of a doublet.*
Galbé: m. ée: f. Bien galbé. *Comelie, gracefull, well-behaued, hauing a good garbe.*
Galbuge. *See* Garbouil, *or* Grabuge.
Gale. *A Gall-nut, or Oake-apple; seruing both for dying, and making of inke.*
Galeace: f. *A Galeasse.*
Gale-bon-temps. *A merrie grig, a good fellow, good drunkard, pot-companion.*
Galée: f. *The top, or scuttle, of a galley.*
Gale-fesson. *A scratcht-bum, or scabd-arse.*
Galefreté: m. ée: f. *Rigged, or trimmed vp, as a ship.*
Galefreter. *as* Calfeutrer; *To trimme, to rig vp a ship.*
Galefretier: m. *A rigger, trimmer, mender of ships; also, as* Galefrotier.
Galefrotier: m. *An idle vagabond; a poore scabbie knaue.*
Galemar: m. *A Pennar.*
Galemment. *Gallantly, brauely, goodlily, nobly, worthily.*
Galeote. *A kind of Lizard, thats an enemie vnto all serpents.* ¶Rab.
Galerand: m. *The Fowle tearmed a Bittor.* ¶Brett.
Galere. *A Galley; See* Gallere.
Galerie. *as* Gallerie; *a Gallerie.*
Galerien: m. *A Galley-slaue; a Souldior, or Marriner in a Galley.*
Galerien: m. enne: f. *Of, or belonging to, a Galley; haunting, or frequenting the Gallyes.*
Galerite: f. *The (Medow) Larke.*
Galerne: f. *A North-west wind.*
Galerneux: m. euse: f. *North-westerlie.*
Galetage: m. *Garrets; Galleries; also, Garret-worke.*
Galetas: m. *A Garret.*
Galette: f. *A broad thin cake; also, a little itch, or scab.*

Galier: m. *A Iade, or dull horse.*
Galiffre: m. *A greedie feeder, a rauenous eater.*
Galiffré: m. ée: f. *Greedily fed on, rauenously eaten.*
Galiffrer. *To deuoure, eat greedily, feed rauenously.*
Galimachuë. *as* Massuë; *a club.* ¶Pic.
Galimassuë: f. *A club.*
Galimatias. Iargon de Gal. *Gibbrish, Fustian language, Pedlers French.*
Galingal. *The Aromaticall root of the rush called Cypresse, and English Galingale.*
Galin-Galois, ou Galin-galon. *A merrie scabd whoreson.*
Galion: m. *A Gallion, or great ship of warre; See* Gallion.
Galiot: m. *A Pirate, a Rouer; one that robs, or scoures the seas with a Galliot; also, a Rower in a Galley, or Galliot, whether he be a slaue, or doe it voluntarily; also, the hearbe Auens, Bennet, or Blessed.*
Galiote: f. *A Galliot; a small Galley, or Galley-like vessell, hauing twentie Oares on a side, and two or three Rowers to an Oare; much vsed by Turkish, and Moorish, Rouers.*
Gallangue: f. *as* Galangue; *also, the sea-Toad.*
Gallant homme. *A gallant, goodlie; noble, worthie, vertuous; also, a subtill, wise, craftie, cunning, wylie, fellow.*
Gallanterie: f. *Gallantnesse, worthinesse, brauerie, stoutnesse, frankenesse of humour; also, a knauish pranke.*
Gallantise: f. *Gallantnesse, noblenesse, brauerie; also, a gallant, and merrie pranke; a pleasant, and noble, or open-hearted humor.*
Galle. Noix galle. *The fruit called a Gall; also, an Oake-apple.*
Galle: f. *A galling, fretting, itching of the skin; a dry scab, or scurfe.*
Galle S. Main. *The wild scab.*
L'Amour, la tousse, & la galle ne se peuuent celer: Prov. *Loue, scabs, and coughing will not bee concealed.*
Gallé: m. ée: f. *Rubbed, scrubbed, scraped, scratched; also, intertained with varietie of sport, game, or glee.*
Gallée. *as* Gallere; *a Galley.*
Gallemar. *A Pennar.*
Galler. *To gall, fret, itch; also, to rub, scrape, scrub, claw, scratch where it itcheth; also, to be verie iocond, or full of glee; to intertaine with varietie of sport, game, or glee.*
Galler le bon temps. *To make merrie, to passe the time pleasantly, to play the good fellow.*
Gallerand: m. *A Bittor.* ¶Breton.
Gallere: f. *A Galley; also, an Inkborne.*
Vogue la gallere. *Let the world wag, slide, goe how it will; let goe a Gods name; not a pinne matter whether we sinke or swimme.*
Gallerie: f. *A Gallerie, or long roome to walke in; also, mirth, glee, pleasantnesse, good sport.*
Galleriens: m. *Galley-slaues.*
Galles: f. *The plurall of* Galle.
Gallet: m. *The shoulder peece, or point; the binder (and vpper) part of the necke; in a horse, the Withers.*
Gallette: f. *A kind of wreathed cake.*
Galleverdine: f. *A Gabbardine; a long Coat, or Cassock of course, and (for the most part) motley, or partie-coloured, stuffe.*
Galleux: m. euse: f. *Scabbie, scurvie, mangie, itchie.*
Gallicelle: f. *as* Biaut, *or* Sequenie.
Gallico. Prendre au gal: ou de gal: *To surprize; take napping, or vnprouided; (A Picuerdiall phrase, that seemes to haue beene deuised either in commendation of the liuelinesse, and quicknesse of the French, whereby they are able to surprize others; or, as a taxation of their negligence, and carelesnesse, which make them apt to be surprized by others.)*
Gallie: f. *Garbe, or gracefulnesse.*
Gallien: m. *A Galley slaue.*
Gallier: m. *A scuruie fellow, shifting companion; or, as* Galier. ¶Rab.
Gallimart: m. *A Pennar, a case for pennes.*
Galline: f. *A Gurnard; so called about* Marseillis.
Gallion: m. *A Gallion, an Armada, a great ship of warre; also, the hearbe Cheese-runnell.*
Galliot: m. *The hearbe Auens, hearbe Bennet, hearbe Blessed.*
Galloches: m. *Schollers in Vniuersities, admitted of no Colledge, but lying in the Towne, and being at libertie to resort vnto what (publike) Readers, or Lectures they please; tearmed thus, because, in passing the streets, they commonly weare* Galloches.
Galloches: f. *High woodden Pattens, or Clogs, &c; as in* Galoche.
Gallochier: m. *A Messenger, or Foot-post; one that goeth to and fro on errands; Looke* Galochier.
Gallon: m. *Brawne, or hardnesse of the flesh, or skinne; also, as* Galon.
Les gallons des cheveux. *Hard curled locks.*
Gallonné: m. ée: f. *Stroaked, cherished; gently rubbed, or clawed; also, edged, laced, or tyed with galloone lace.*
Gallonner. *To stroake, cherish, claw, or clap on the back; to smooth; to rub gently; also, to edge, or lace with galloone.*
Gallop. *as* Galop.
Galloper. *See* Galoper.
Gallopins: m. *Vnder Cookes, or Scullions in Monasteries.*
Galoche: m. *as* Galochier.
Galoche: f. *A woodden Shooe, or Patten, made all of a peece, without any latchet, or ty of leather, and worne by the poore clowne in Winter.*
Galocher. *To behaue himselfe rudely, vnciuilly, rustically; to play the clowne; also, to trot, or wander vndiscreetly vp and downe.*
Galochier: m. *A maker of* Galoches, *or woodden shooes.*
Galochier: m. ere: f. *Base, meane, poore; also, clownish, rude, vnciuill, rusticall, without manners; as those are that, ordinarily, weare those woodden shooes.*
Galoise: f. *A scuruie trull, scabbie queane, mangie punk, filthie whore.*
Galon: m. *Galloone lace.*
Galonné: m. ée: f. *as* Gallonné; *and hence;*
Tresses galonnées. *Lockes plaited, or tyed vp with galloone lace.*
Galonner. *as* Gallonner; *and, to plait, bind, or ty vp with lace.*
Galop: m. *A (horses) gallop; or galloping.*
Galop gaillard. *The Gallop Galliard; or, a Passasalto; or, one pace, and a leape.*
Aller le grand galop. *To runne in hast, to fly apace; to passe a full carriere.*
Galopade: f. *A galloping.*
Galopé. *Galloped; also, coursed, chased; curried, vsed somewhat roughly, taken vp roundly.*
Galoper. *To gallop; also, to course, currie, vse rudely, take*

take vp for halting; giue chase vnto.
Galopins. *as* Gallopins.
Galvardine: f. *A Gabardine.*
Galvol: m. *A Shittlecocke.*
Gambade: f. *A gamboll, yew-game, tumbling tricke.*
La gambade du rocher. *The rocke gamboll; the being throwne headlong from a rocke.*
Faire gambades à la terre. *To hang, or hang in chaynes.*
Payer en gambades. *To runne away when he should pay.*
Les vieilles gens qui font gambades, à la mort sonnent des aubades: Prov. *Old peoples frisking doth presage their ending.*
Gambader. *To turne heeles ouer head, make many gambols, fetch many friskes, shew tumbling trickes.*
Gambadeur: m. *A tumbler, a maker of gambols.*
Gambage. Droict de g. *A fee, or dutie of foure pottles vpon euerie brewing, payed vnto diuers Lords within the Countie of* Boullenois.
Gambayer. *To wag the legs in sitting, as children vse to doe.*
Gambe. *as* Iambe; *a leg, or shanke.* ¶Pic.
Le plus en gambe. *The best footman, the swiftest runner, the quickest goer, the lightest of his legs.*
Gambeson: f. *A fashion of long horsemans coat; See* Gobisson.
Gambi: m. ie: f. *Bent, crooked, bowed.*
Gambier. *To wag the legs in sitting, as children vse to doe.* ¶Pic: *also, to walke, or goe.*
Gambiller. *as* Gambier.
Gambir. *To bow, crooke, bend.*
Gambre: m. *The sea-Creuisse.*
Game: f. *Gamvt (in Musicke.)*
Fol à la haulte game. *An arrant foole, notable coxe, true dunce; an Asse in graine.*
Entrer en la haulte game. *To busie, or pester his braines with many matters; to enter into deepe, and serious meditations; to stretch his wits.*
Nous sommes hors toute la Game. *We are out of all good compasse; or, quite off the bindges.*
Gamelle: f. *A woodden bowle.*
Gammare: m. *A Lobster, or sea-Creuisse.*
Gamme: f. *A chime; also, as* Game.
Sonner la gamme. *A chime to sound at certaine houres.*
Gan. *as* Gant; *a Gloue.*
Ganabin. *The Northerne wind.* ¶Rab.
Gances: f. *Loopes (of twist, lace, &c.)*
Ganché: m. ée: f. *Let fall (as in a strappado) on sharpe stakes pointed with yron, and thereon languishing vntill he dye.*
Gandalin: m. *A bawd, or carrier of loue-messages.*
Gandole. *as* Gondole; *a Gondola.*
Ganglion. *A waterie impostumation in the throat.*
Gangrene: f. *A Gangrene; the rotting, or mortifying of a member.*
Gangrené: m. ée: f. *Rotted, putrified, mortified, become senceless, fallen into a Gangrene.*
Gangules: f. *Kernels, or wartles in the throat.*
Ganif: m. *A pen-knife.*
Ganivet: m. *A little pen-knife.*
Ganivetier: m. *A pen-knife-maker.*
Ganse: f. *A loope (of lace, &c.)*
Gant: m. *A Gloue.*
Gans de nostre Dame. *The hearbe called Fox gloues, London buttons; and, our Ladies gloues; (a name which is also giuen vnto the male* Coniza, *or great Fleabane.)*
Gans d'ocaigne. *Dogs leather gloues oyled in the inside to keepe the hands moist, and coole.*
Droict de gans; &, ventes & gans. *A paire of gloues, or in lieu thereof money (more, or lesse, as is the custome of seuerall places) due, and payed as an Income by a purchaser vnto the Lord* Censuel, *or of the soyle.*
Gante. *as* Iante. ¶Pic.
Gantelée: f. *The hearbe called Fox-gloues, our Ladies gloues; (which name (also) the male* Coniza, *or great Fleawort hath) and London buttons.*
Gantelet: m. *A gantlet, or arming gloue.*
Hausser le gantelet. *A Marchant to put into his Booke, or Bill, that which was neuer taken vp; to ouerreach with false reckonings.*
Plier le gantelet. *To yeeld, stoope, submit himselfe; to confesse himselfe ouercome.*
Gantes. *as* Iantes; *the felles of a Cart-wheele.* ¶Pic.
Gantier: m. *A Glouer.*
Ganymedes. *The name of a Troian boy, whom* Iupiter *so loued (say the Poets) as he tooke him vp to heauen, and made him his cup-bearer; hence, any boy thats loued for carnall abuse; an Ingle.*
Gaquiere. *as* Iachere; *Land which lyeth lay; a fallow field, sowne euerie other yeare.* ¶Pic.
Gar. Vn regard à gar. *A squint looke; the cast of a skenning eye.*
Garagnon: m. *A Stallion.*
Garance: f. *The hearbe Madder; with whose root Dyers make cloth Orange tawnie; or, for a need, red; and ioyning it with woad, blacke.*
Garance sauvage. *Wild Madder; (Some also call so the hearb Woodroofe, or Woodrowell.)*
Garancé: m. ée: f. *Dyed with Madder.*
Garand. *See* Garant, *or* Garent.
Garans de palenc. *Two slender cords tyed to the bottome of the great pullie of a mast, and passing from that, through diuers others.*
Garant: m. *A vouchee; warrant; warranter of the thing he hath passed vnto another; a supporter, defender, maintainer, protector; also, an author, in a report; See* Garent.
Se bouter à garant. *To take Sanctuarie; to fly into a safe, or strong place for refuge.*
Tenir fort à garant. *To hold off; (a sea tearme.)*
Garantage: m. *A warranting, or warrantie.*
Garanti: m. ie: f. *Warranted, protected, saued harmelesse.*
Garrantie: f. *Garrantie, warrantie, or warrantise; protection, maintenance, defence, supportation.*
Recours de garrantie. *See* Recours.
Garantir. *To warrant; or passe by warrantie; to saue harmelesse; to protect, support, defend, keepe safe from danger.*
Garavelle: f. *The name of a delicate Peare, thats ripe in August.*
Garbe: f. *A garbe, comelinesse, handsomenesse, gracefulnesse, good fashion.*
Garber. *To spruce it; to adorne, decke, set forth, make fine, comelie, neat, gracefull.*
Garbin: m. *A Southwest wind.*
Garbot: m. *A kind of fish about Orleans.*
Garbouil: m. *A garboyle, hurlyburly, great stirre, monstrous rambling, horrible rumbling.*
Garburge: f. *as* Garbouil.
Garçe: f. *A wench, lasse, girle; also, (and as wee often meane by the first) a Punke, or Whore.*
Avoir de l'eau vers les garces. *To haue sap, and moisture enough to satisfie his priuate lecherie withall.*

Amour de garçe & saut de chien ne dure si l' on ne dit,tien: Pro. *Looke* Amour.

Garchote: f. *A water fowle, somewhat lesse then, but otherwise resembling, a Mallard.*

Garçon. *A boy, lad; youth, stripling; See* Garson.

Folie aux garçons. *Leacherie, whoredome, incontinencie, lasciuiousnesse.*

C'est vn mauuais garçon. *He is a shrewd (or tall) fellow; one that will throughly both lay, and looke, about him.*

Garçonné: m. ée: f. *Leachered withall; swyued, ridden by boyes.*

Garçonner. *To play the boy; also, to leacher; to defile a woman, deflowre a maid; play the lasciuious boy with.*

Garçonniere: f. *A leacherous, or lasciuious queane.*

Gardant. *Garding, warding, keeping, preseruing, reseruing for himselfe, or others.*

Garde: m. *A Guardian, Warden, Keeper; any Officer vnto whose keeping a thing is entrusted; hence;*

Garde de bois. *The Warden of, or a Keeper in, a Wood, or Forrest.*

Garde des Coffres. *The (keeper of the) Priuie Purse; or, as* Thresorier des menus.

Garde general de l'Artillerie. *The Warden generall, or chiefe Warden, of the Artillerie; keepes a reckoning of all the peeces of Ordnance that be within the realme; to which end he takes particular Inuentories from all Commaunders of Fortresses, &c, containing the number, size, and qualitie thereof, and informes himselfe by them of all their store, and wants: He also visites the places themselues, to see whether the Peeces bee well kept, and safely bestowed: After all which, he deliuers ouer the said Inuentories vnto the Controller generall, who hauing registred, redeliuers, them. This Officer hath a Deputie resident in euerie one of the tenne generall Gouernments of France.*

Garde de Iustice. *A royall Prouost, or Iudge, that keepes either the Kings (inferior) Courts, or the Courts of a Lord Iusticer; and is inferior, in all respects, vnto a* Bailli.

Garde des Livres de la Chambre des Comptes. *The keeper of all the Records of that Court.*

Garde d'un Malade. *A Keeper; one that lookes to a sicke bodie.*

Garde des Monnoyes. *The Warden of the Mint; an Officer, who is to be present at all finings, allayings, and prouings of Mettall; and ouersees both the deliuerie thereof to the workemen, and them in their working; to which end he weighes, and viewes euerie peece, and forces them, at their owne charge, to new-make the light, and misshapen ones, or censures them otherwise as he thinkes good: The Money being full made, he deliuers it vnto the Maisters; to whõ, though in place he be inferior, yet may he at any time call them to an accoũt, for as much as they haue receiued from him.*

Gardes des Portes. *Wardens of the out-Ports; Officers, that looke there be no prohibited commodities transported, or imported; They also receiue of Marchants the Bills that containe all the parcels they haue bought, and the acquittances of duties payed, within land; and onely they, and the Searchers, may arrest the bodies, or goods of such, as, to deceiue the King of his custome, or to transport forbidden commodities, would slip out of the Realme by oblique Passages, odd Creekes, decayed Ports, or any by-wayes.*

Garde de la Prevosté. *A rurall Prouost; or, as* Garde de Iustice.

Garde des Salines. *The Warden of the (Kings) Saltpits; an Officer that deliuers out the salt vnto Marchants, and, together with the Clarke thereof, keepes a Register of the quantitie deliuered, of their names to whom it is deliuered, and of the places whereunto it is carried.*

Garde des seaux. *The keeper of the Seale; one in euerie Chancerie established in the seuen (inferior) Parliamentall, and in the Presidiall, townes; whither when any of the Maisters of Requests are come in circuit, he is bound to bring, and deliuer vp vnto them the Seale, whereof at all other times he hath the absolute charge, and keeping.*

Garde du seel Royal. *The Commissioner, who in the sicknesse, absence, or suspension of the Lord Chancelour is appointed to seale, and passe Letters Patents, &c; or he, that hath the keeping of the ordinarie (royall) seale of contracts, or of iudiciall dispatches: For the vse of which Seale there is no fee taken of the Secretaries, nor of the Lord high Chamberlaine of France (who keepes the Kings Priuie Signet while he attends) nor of some other Officers of the Crowne.*

Garde: f. *Gard, ward, custodie; safe, or long keeping; the reseruing, or preseruing of a thing for priuate vse; also, the Guard of a Prince; (and hence) the charge of, or looking vnto, a thing; and, heed, care, obseruation, vigilancie, aduisement; also, defence, maintenance, protection, safetie; also, the Wardship of an infant, or heire; (wherein* Garde *is most commonly meant of direct,* Bail *of collaterall, kinsmen; or of an againe-married mother, or grandmother.)*

Les gardes d'un canon. *The branches of a Canonbit.*

La garde d'un'espée. *The hilt of a sword.*

Les gardes d'un sanglier. *The deaw-clawes, or hinder-clawes of a wild Bore.*

Garde faicte. *Is, when beasts that are kept in other mens grounds make spoyle, or doe hurt by the craft, or fault of their keepers.*

Garde gardienne. *A Priuiledge of the Schollers and Officers of Vniuersities, and of the Priests, Prelats, and Possessors of some Churches, Abbeyes, Colledges, Hospitals, &c; and of the Officers of the Crowne, and Kings house, not to be impleaded before other then their peculiar Iudges.*

Garde liges. *Seeke* Lige.

Denier de garde. *A certaine summe, or small piece of money, payable, by old Leases, in stead of Rent, those yeares wherein the ground lay fallow, and could not be eared.*

Droict de garde noble. *See* Droict.

Poire de garde. *A Warden, or a winter Peare.*

Prevost de garde; ou, en garde. *An vnder Iudge to a* Bailli; *or, the Deputie of a Prouost, or vnder-Prouost.*

Il n'a garde de s'y laisser aller. *He hath no mind, list, maw, stomacke, humor, to goe thither.*

Il n'a garde de s'en vanter. *I beleeue he will not brag thereof in hast; or, he is not verie hastie, forward, willing, to brag thereof.*

Se donner de garde. *as* Prendre Garde.

Estre de garde. *To keepe, or continue long, vntainted; to beare age verie well.*

Faire la garde. *To make fast; (a phrase vsed by reelers, or winders of yarne.)*

Prendre garde. *To heed; looke well, haue an eye, vnto; beware, take heed; preuent by fore-sight, prouide that a thing doe not happen.*

La mauvaise garde paist souvent le loup: Prov. *Ill watch doth fatten the Wolfe; or, the sleepie shepheard fattens the hungrie wolfe.*

Gardé: m. ée: f. *Warded, garded, kept; preserued, saued; shielded, defended, protected, maintained; watched, heeded, marked, obserued, regarded, looked vnto.*

Garde-bras. *A Vambrace; Armour for an arme.*

Garde-corps: m. *A Yeoman of the Gard; an Halberdier, or Sergeant, that gards, or attends on, the person of a Prince, Commaunder, or publicke Officer.*

Garde-fol: m. *as* Garde-serre.

Garde-fols; &, Garde-foux. *Rayles, stayes, or sleight walls on th'outsides of a bridge, high walke, Terrace, or open Gallerie.*

Garde-fort. *as in* Garde-fols.

Garde-main. *A strong gloue for a Mason, or Stone-cutter to worke with.*

Gardemaneur. *A creditor, or any other placed by order of Law in a debtors house; the which he may keepe vntill he be satisfied, or haue securitie for satisfaction.*

Gardemanger. *An Ambrie, Gardemanger, cupboord to keepe meat in.*

Garde-nappe: f. *A wreath, ring, or circlet of wicker, &c; set vnder a dish at meale times, to saue the Table-cloth from soyling.*

Garde-notes. Notaire garde-notes. *Looke* Notaire.

Garde-poing: m. *A Vamplate.*

Garde-porte: f. *A peece of Tapistrie hung before an open dore; a dore-peece.*

Garder. *To keepe; ward, gard; saue, preserue; shield; protect, maintaine, defend; watch, heed, marke, obserue, regard, or looke vnto.*

Se garder de. *To refraine, forbeare, abstaine from; to hold off, beare backe, restraine himselfe.*

Garder le change. *A hound to keepe vnto his first game without chaunging; to runne, or hunt, his owne.*

Garder vne fille à graine; *To let a maid runne to seed; to keepe her long without a husband; See* Graine.

Garder la lune des loups. *Foolishly to care for that which cannot doe amisse.*

Dieu gard la Lune des loups. *See* Loup.

Dieu gard de mal qui voit bien & ne oit goutte. *For my part I conceiue no iot of it; or, care not for it if I conceiued it; or, will not beleeue it though I know it to be so.*

Il la luy garda bonne. *He owed him a good turne; or, (the contrarie) he bore him a grudge for it, a long time after.*

Sainct Anthoine te gardera. *Thou art, or wilt proue, but a Hog, or a Sow.*

'A qui est l'asne si le garde. *Let him that owes the Asse looke to him; (a Prouerb applyable vnto any thing thats in danger of straying.)*

Bon chasteau garde qui sçait son corps garder: Prov. *A good fort saues he that can saue his bodie.*

De qui ie me fie dieu me garde: Pro. *(For, in trust is Treason, say we.)*

Il ne se garde pas bien qui ne se garde tousiours: Prov. *He lookes not, that still lookes not, to himselfe; or, he gards not well, himselfe, that alwayes gards not.*

Qui garde son disner, il a mieux à souper: Pro. *He that keepes his dinner hath the more to sup withall; youth preserued breeds an able old-age.*

Qui n'a qu'un oeil bien le garde: Prov. *He that hath but one eye had need make much of it, had best looke well to it.*

Tel se cuide bien garder qui se frappe sur le nez: Prov. *Looke* Frapper.

Garderobbe: f. *A Wardrobe; also, a house of Office; also, a cloth, or cloake worne, or cast ouer a garment, to keepe it from dust, raine, &c; also, the hearbe Sothernwood.*

Garde-serre. *The rest of the locke of a Harguebuse.*

Gardeur: m. *A Keeper, Warder, Warden, Gardien, Ouerseer, looker vnto.*

Gardeur de bestiail. *A Pastor, Heardsman, Neatheard.*

Mieux vaut bon gardeur que bon gaigneur: Prov. *(A degree beyond the Latine,* Non minor est virtus quam quærere parta tueri.)

Gardien: m. *A Warden, Keeper, Gardien; a Sequestree; one vnto whose keeping a thing is committed.*

Gardien de biens. *A Sequestree, or keeper of the goods of an indebted, or condemned person, seised by order of Law.*

Gardien d'un enfant mineur. *A Gardien; one that hath the wardship, or tuition of a child vnder age.*

Gardien: m. enne: f. *Keeping, warding, garding; obseruing, ouerseeing, looking vnto.*

Garde gardienne. *See* Garde.

Pere gardien. *The chiefe Ouerseer, Controller, or Visitor of a Frierie.*

De pere gardien filz garde-rien: Prov. *A retchlesse sonne of a wretched father.*

Gardin. *as* Iardin; *a Garden.* ¶Pic.

Gardon: m. *A certaine fresh-water fish that resembles the Cheuin; onely his head is lesse, and bodie broader; Some hold it to be the fresh-water Mullet; others (more probably, though* Gesner *say otherwise) the Roche, or a kind thereof.*

Plus sain qu'un gardon. *More liuelie, and healthfull then a* Gardon *(then which, there is not any fish more healthfull, nor more liuelie.)*

Ils iettent les gardons pour tirer des brochets. *They reiect small, to obtaine great, matters.*

Gardouche. *A Store-house, or Garner.*

Gardoüer: m. *A little Pond, or Stue, to keepe fish in.*

Gare. Intonation de gare & serre. *The sounding of Drumme, or Trumpet, whereby souldiors are warned to stand close, and looke vnto themselues.*

Gare le heurt. *(The voice of them that driue horned-beasts) warre hornes.*

Sans dire gare. *On the suddaine, at vnawares; before any word sent, or warning giuen.*

Garé. Terre garée. *Old fallow ground.*

Garence. *as* Garance; *Madder.*

Garenciere: f. *A Field, or Plot of ground, sowed with Madder; a Madder-yard, or Madder-ground.*

Garendie. *as* Garentie; *Warrantie.*

Garene. *as* Carine; *and, as* Garenne.

Garené. *as* Garenné.

Garrenne: f. *A Warren of Connies, &c; also, a (certaine, or limitted) fishing in a riuer.*

Garenné: m. ée: f. *Warrenned; made into a Warren; inclosed; priuiledged, restrained from common vse; made priuat, or belonging to a priuat person, as a warren &c.*

Garrenneux: m. euse: f. *Haunting, or louing, or liuing in, Warrens.*

Garennier: m. *A Warrenner.*

Garent: m. *A Warranter, Protector, Defendor; securer, vndertaker for; a seller with warrantie; a Vouchee; also, Warrantie.*

Garent absolut. *One that undertakes a suit for another, wholly ridding, and discharging him of it; (This warrantie is proper unto reall actions.)*

Garent contributeur. *One that undertakes but part of a suit for another; whom he leaues to follow the rest at his owne charge.*

Garent formel. *as* Garent absolut.

Garent simple. *One that is vouched to assist, and ioyne with the vouchor in the proues, and defences needfull in a personall action.*

Qui tire à garent & garent n'ha, sa cause perduë il a. (Cela estoit de la vieille pratique; & n'a plus de lieu; *The rigour thereof being qualified.)*

Garentage: m. *Warrantie, warrantize, warrantage.*

Garenti: m. ie: f. *Warranted, secured, undertaken for, borne out, saued harmelesse.*

Garentie: f. *Warrantie, securitie; protection, defence.*

Garentigionné. Instrument ga. *An authenticall Instrument, made by a Notarie publicke, and signifying, that execution is readie to come out against a confessing, and almost condemned, debtor; By the customes of* Bayonne *tis also a kind of inrolled Bond, whereby both a mans bodie is subiect vnto arrest, and his goods to execution.*

Garentir. *To warrant, make good, undertake for, sell, or passe with warrantie; to secure, saue harmelesse, defend, protect, beare out.*

Garentissement: m. *A warranting, undertaking for, making good; a securing, sauing harmelesse, protecting, defending.*

Garentisseur: m. *A warranter, &c; as* Garent.

Garenty: m. *One that is warranted.*

Garer. *To ware, beware, take heed of; to shun, eschew, auoid by slipping aside; See* Gare.

Garet. *See* Gueret.

Gargameile: f. *The throat.*

Garganton: m. *A great glutton, or belly-god, one that wasts his substance on good cheere.*

Gargantua. *Great throat.* ¶Rab.

Gargareon: m. *The forepart of the throat.*

Gargarization. *as* Gargarizement.

Gargarizé. *Gargled, gargarized.*

Gargarizement: m. *A gargling, or gargarizing; a gargarisme.*

Gargarizer. *To gargle, to gargalize.*

Gargassane: f. *The Wind-pipe.*

Gargate: f. *as* Gargassane; *or, the throat-pipe.* ¶Pic.

Gargatte: f. *The Vuula; a little peece of spongious flesh resembling a Cocks spurre, and hanging downe in the roofe of the mouth, neere the passage into the nosethrils.*

Gargouille: f. *The weesle, or weason of the throat; also, the mouth of a Spowt, representing a Serpent, or the Anticke face of some other ouglie creature; also, a gutter that receiues, and voids the raine falling on diuers roofes, or houses; also, a bubble, or puffe, made by wind on the water; also, the ioynt of a flat hindge; or, such a ioynt as is in the flat hindge of a window, or small dore.*

Gargouillé. *Gargled, gargarized; also, ratled in the throat.*

Gargouillement: m. *A gargling, or gargarizing; also, a ratling in the throat.*

Gargouiller. *To gargle, or gargarize; also, to ratle in the throat.*

Gargouillis: m. *A gargling, or gargling noyse.*

Gargouïle. *as* Gargouille.

Garguesques: f. *A fashion of strait venetians without codpeeces.*

Garguette. *as* Gargatte.

Garguille: m. *(A nickname for) an odd, mad, or foolish companion; such a one as we (somewhat contemptuously, or to his derogation) stile, a certaine fellow.*

Garguillon: m. *The Pipe, or throat-pipe, whereby meat passeth into the stomacke, or craw of birds.*

Garieur: m. *A warrantor.* ¶Gasc.

Garignon: m. *A buckle-bone; whence,* Iouër aux garignons. *To play at Cockall.*

Garigues. *as* Guarigues.

Gariment: m. *Garrantie, or warrantie.* ¶Gasc.

Tenir en gariment. *To hold part of a fief otherwise then by succession, and upon couenant, to pay, or yeeld for it some dutie which is noble, and no way* roturier.

Garine: f. *The shrub Cistus, or Hollie-rose.*

Garingal. *as* Galingal.

Garinnon. *See* Garignon.

Gariofilé. Aromatique gar. *A certaine composition (wherein there are Cloues) good for the passions of the heart.*

Gariollér. *To whistle, chirpe, or warble, as birds.*

Gariophyllate. *Hearbe Auens, Bennet, or Blessed.*

Gariot: m. *The wind-pipe of a horse, or other beast.*

Garipot: m. *The wild Pine, or Pitch tree.*

Garite: f. *A place of refuge, and of safe retyrall in a rowt, disaster, or danger; the recourse of such as are discomfited; (hence) also, the dungeon of a fortresse, whither the beleaguered souldiors make their last retire, and flight; also, a by-way, or path that leads one aside, and out of the high way; also, a Sentrie, or little lodge for a Sentinell, built on high.*

Prendre la garite. *To fly, slip o'th' to-side, run away.*

Garlande. *as* Ghirlande; *a Garland; and hence;*

Garlande d'argent; *Is due in some parts of Auvergne vnto a widow by the heire of her deceased husband, and ought to be of the value of their nuptiall bed.*

Garnache: f. *A frocke for a Carter.*

Garlet: m. *A little Plaice.*

Garnement: m. *Prouision, furniture, or munition layed in for the maintenance, or defence of a Place; also, a rakehell, slip string, rascall, naughtie-packe, lewd vnthrift, gracelesse patch, vngracious wretch, one for whō the gallowes groane; (In which sence it is vsed either (Ironically) alone, or with the Adiectiue* Mauvais; *as;)*

En mauvais garnement. *Lewdly, naughtily, wickedly, vnthriftily, vngraciously, roguishly, villanously.*

Garni: m. ie: f. *Garnished; prouided, stored, supplyed, furnished, full of; decked, trimmed, adorned, beautified, set out with; perfected, throughly wrought.*

Poing garni. *An armed fist; a hand that holds a stone, or weapon, to strike withall.*

Garniment. *as* Garnement.

Garnir. *To garnish; prouide, store, supply, furnish, accommodate, fill with; decke, adorne, trimme, beautifie, set forth with.*

Garnir vne accusation. *To accuse throughly, to bring in much euidence, many witnesses against.*

Garnir à caution. *To prouide, or bring in sureties, or a sufficient pawne for the securitie of a debt, &c.*

Garnir la main. *To take a thing to pawn, or morgage; also, to seize, or distraine, vpon an execution, for debt; or (more properly) an arrested debtor to pay down what he owes, or to giue saleable goods, to the value of the debt, for the securitie thereof.*

Garnis. *A kind of engine to catch fish with.*

Garnison: f. *Store of furniture; prouision, munition, preparation; also, the garrison of a towne; also, a garrison towne.*

Garnison de main. *A taking to pawne, or in mortgage; also, a seising, or distraining vpon an execution, or otherwise, for debt, for arrerages of rent &c; or (more properly) present payment of a debt; or saleable goods deliuered by the arrested debtor, for the securitie thereof.*

Le magistrat envoya le demandeur en garnison en la maison du defendeur. *Put him in possession, or sent him to take possession, of the defendants house.*

Garnissement: m. *A garnishment, or garnishing; a furnishing, storing, supplying; a decking, trimming, adorning, setting forth, with; also, a taking to pawne, or in mortgage; also, the giuing of assurance, or securitie for a debt, &c.*

Garniture: f. *Garniture, garnishment, furniture; prouision, munition, store, necessarie implements; also, a ruffe-band; also, any kind of ornament, or attire.*

Garniture de doigts. *A gloue; ring; finger-stall; thimble, and such like.*

Garniture d'esperon. *A spurre-leather.*

Garniture d'un pourpoint. *The facing; (also) the quilt of a doublet.*

Garon: m. *Pickle of fish; or, the liquor wherein salt fish hath beene resolued, or long soaked; also, the little Anchoua-like fish,* Garum, *whereof (being heated in a dish, with oyle or butter, and thereby melted) the best kind of that liquor is made.*

Garot. *as* Garrot.

Garou. *Wild, sauage, hideous, cruell.*

Garoüage. Aller en garoüage. *(A married man) to goe a caterwawling, or steale abroad by night a wenching.*

Garoupe: f. *The shrub called, Spurge Oliue, and widow wayle.* ¶Prouençal.

Garous. *(A Syncope of the words,* Gardez-vous, *or* Garez-vous; *take heed, turne aside, looke to your selues;) See* Loup-garou.

Garoute: f. *A Carrot root.*

Garrau. *as* Garrot.

Garrer vn bateau. *To hale, or pull a boat ashoare, or vnder a shed; (there to trimme her;) also, to moore, or tye her vnto a key, or vnder a lee shore.*

Se garrer dessous. *To skowke; shadow, shrowd, or put himselfe, vnder; whence;*

Qui se garre dessous la fueille deux fois se mouille: Prov.

Garrigues. *as* Guarrigues.

Garrobe. *The Carob-beane-cod; See* Carrobe.

Garrobier: m. *The Plant that beares Carobs.*

Garrot: m. *A boult for a Crossebow; also, the Wythers of a horse, &c; also, a wring, or pinch in the Wythers; also, the Cudgell wherewith a Carrier, &c, winds vp, and straines hard, the cord he binds his packe withall.*

Garroté: m. ée: f. *Strained, or wound vp, as a pack-cord with a cudgell; also, hard tyed, or bound with cords.*

Garrotement: m. *The straining, or winding vp of a cord with a cudgell; also, a binding, or tying hard with cords.*

Garroter. *To straine, wring, or wind vp a pack-cord with a cudgell, &c; also, to bind fast in, tye hard with, cords, &c.*

Garruité: f. *Garrulitie, prating, pratling, tatling, chattering, cackling, busie talking, much babling, ouermuch chat.*

Gars: m. *A lad, boy, stripling, youth, yonker; wag.*

Aller à gars. *To hunt after lads; (a wench) to goe a caterwawling.*

Garscher. *To chap, as the hands, or lips doe in a sharpe wind.* (v.m.)

Garse: f. *A wench, lasse, girle; and (as we commonly vse the first) a punke, or whore; See* Garce.

Garsette: f. *A yong lasse, little wench; pretie whore.*

Garson: m. *A lad, boy, youth, stripling; See* Garçon.

Faire le garson. *To play the sot; vse apish, or childish, tricks.*

Garson-fillette. *An Hermaphrodite.*

Garsonnaille: f. *A crue of lads, a troupe of boyes.*

Garsonner. *To play the boy, or vse boyish tricks.*

Garsonner la femme d' autruy. *To lye with another mans wife.*

Garsonnet: m. *A little boy.*

Garsote: f. *The water-fowle called, a Teale.*

Garsouiller la femme d'autruy. *as* Garsonner.

Garuche: f. *A torturing wheele, vpon which the accused hauing heauie bolts, or yrons on his legs, is hoysed on high, vntill he confesse.*

Garvences: f. *Fitches; Chichlings.*

Garum: m. *Pickle of salt fish; or liquor wherein it hath beene resolued, or long soaked; See* Garon.

Garzignole: f. *The name of a delicate Peare thats ripe in August.*

Gasche: f. *An Oare, or Scull to row with; also, a staple for a locke; (also, a cake.* ¶Norm.)

Gaschement: m. *A rowing; also, a flashing, dashing, or plashing, as of water in rowing; also, a making of morter; or, a mingling and beating of lime, or clay with water, as in the making of morter.*

Gascher. *To row, or pull at an Oare; also, to dash, plash, flash (as water in rowing;) also, to make plaister, or morter; to beat lyme, clay, or sand and water together (as in the making of morter.)*

Gascher du gros. *To shite; also, to spue; to purge vpwards, or downewards.*

Gascher du poisson (salé.) *To water it, to cast water on it; or lay it in water.*

Gaschettes pour tenir les doigts fermes. *Splints for broken, or crooked, fingers.*

Gascheur: m. *A Rower; also, a flasher, or dasher of water.*

Gascheux: m. euse: f. *Flashie, plashie, washie, dashing, bespatling.*

Gaschis d'eau: m. *A dashing, plashing, or flashing of water, in rowing; See* Gachis.

Gascon: m. *A Gascon; one of Gascoigne; also, the Mackerell (fish.)*

Gasconner. *To steale, filch, pilfer.*

Gason: m. *A greene sodd, a sodd of grassie earth; also, a banke made of, or hill couered with, greene sodds; any fine grassie, or mossie, banke.*

Gasouillement: m. *A warbling, whistling, or whizzing noyse.*

Gasouiller. *as* Gazouiller.

Gasouilleur: m. *A warbler, chirper, whistler, or whizzer.*

Gaspillé: m. ée: f. *Wasted, lauished; carelesly, prodigally.*

Gaspiller. *To squander, wast, lash out, lauish away needlesly, carelesly, prodigally.*

Gaspilleur: m. *A spend-all, wast-good, vnthrift, lauisher, squanderer, prodigall and carelesse waster; whence;*

A pere amasseur fils gaspilleur: Prov. *A wastfull sonne succeeds a wretched father.*

Gasse: f. *The weed called, Darnell, Ray, and Ivray.*

Gast: m. *Wast, spoyle, &c; or, as* Gastement.

Gastadour: m. *A Pioner.*

Gasté: m. ée: f. *Marred, spild, spoyled; rotten, viciate, corrupted, wasted, cõsumed; ruined, defaced, ouerthrowne, destroyed, vndone; soyled, defiled, stained, peruerted; besotted.*

Gasteau: m. *A (great) Cake.*
Le gasteau ne cuict pas pour luy. *The cake's not baken for him; his part is like to be least in it; he is not like to licke his lips after it; (applyable vnto any thing that's in hand for another then him that lookes for it.)*
Il a sa part au gasteau. *He hath a hand in the practise; a part in the fruit, or punishment, thereof.*
Partir le gasteau. *To assigne vnto euerie conspirator the part he is to act, or share he is to haue, in a Practise.*
Trouver la febve au gasteau. *To meet with the thing he lookes for, to light on that which will serue his turne.*
Gasteau, & mauvaise coustume se doivent rompre: Prov. *A (good) cake, and an ill custome should be broken.*
Gaste-bois: m. *An vnskilfull Carpenter.*
Gastelet: m. *A little cake; also (the name of) an excellent Cyder-apple.*
Gastelier: m. *A seller, or maker of cakes.*
Gastement: m. *A marring, spoyling, spilling; a wasting, consuming, corrupting; a soyling, defiling, distaining; a ruining, defacing, destroying.*
Gaste-museau: m. *A little round lumpe, or bunne, made of fine meale, oyle, and raisins; a Lenten loafe.*
Gaste-pavé: m. *A gadder, wanderer, earth-planet, pauement-beater, street-wearer, way-wearier; one that does nought but trot vp and downe the towne.*
Gaster: m. *The bellie.* ¶Rab.
Gaster. *A woman to cast her child.*
Gaster. *To wast, marre, spill, spoyle; viciate, corrupt, inuert, peruert, seduce, depraue; infect; violate; soyle, defile, distaine; consume, ruine, vndoe, deface, destroy, turne vpside-downe.*
Vous ne sçauriez rien gaster. *You can do no harme; (a Bowlers phrase.)*
Gasteresse: f. *A woman that marreth; wasteth; destroyeth.*
Gaste-santé. *Vnholesome, infectiue, health-spoyling.*
Gasteur: m. *A marrer, spoyler; waster, consumer; soyler, defiler; seducer, peruerter; defacer, destroyer.*
Gastier. *An Officer appointed by Justice, at the nomination, and request of the inhabitants of a place, to gard and watch the fruits of their Grounds, & Vineyards, and to keepe them from being imbezeled, or spoyled by men, or beasts.*
Gastine: f. *A Wast, a Desart; a Rocke, or sandie Ground; also, a Close, or Pasture inclosed, and enioyed in common; a Commons belonging to particular men, and the particular Commons of a Towneship, or Parish; also, a kind of earth found in Mynes of Iron, and helping to melt it; also, the name of a Crosse in Paris, planted where once the house of one who bore that name (and was burnt for Religion) stood.*
Gastis: m. *Wast, spoyle, or a trespasse done in grounds by (a strangers) beasts.*
Gastrepiploique. Veine gas. *The third branch of the trunke of the Porte veine, issuing side-wayes out of the right side thereof, and spreading abroad in the bottome of the ventricle.*
Gastrimythe: m. *A belly-god.*
Gastrique. *The second branch of the trunke of the Portveine.*
Gastrolatre. *A belly-god; one that makes a god of his bellie.* ¶Rab.
Gastromantie: f. *Diuination by the bellie.*
Gastroraphie: f. *The stitching vp of a rent, or diuided, bellie.*
Gastrotomie: f. *The section, or cutting vp of the bellie.*
Gate. *as* Iatte; *A bowle, or mazer.* ¶Pic.
Gathe: f. *A little Shad-fish.* ¶Bourdel.
Gatte: f. *The top of the maine Mast.* ¶Norm.
Gattouiller. *as* Chatouiller; *To tickle.*
Gau. *as* Geau.
Gavache: m. *A countrey clowne, or clusterfist; and hence, any scowndrell, or base companion.*
Gavache: com. *Lennow, flaggie, limber; also, licentious, dissolute, sensuall, gluttonish; also, clownish.*
Gavar: m. arre: f. *Shaling, splay-footed, or baker-legd; (at* Tours.)
Gaubison. *as* Gobisson.
Gauché: m. *A blow with the left hand.*
Gauche: com. *Left, left-handed; being on the left hand; belonging to the left side; wrong, sinister, awry.*
Pied gauche. *A splay foot.*
Planté sur le pied gauche. *Looke* Planté.
Gauché: m. ée: f. *Wrong, wryed, crooked, awry.*
Gaucher. *as* Gauchier; *and, as* Gauche.
Gauchi: m. ie: f. *Wryed; bent, or turned awry, or from the right side; also, auoided by turning awry.*
Gauchier: m. ere: f. *Left-handed, key-fisted.*
Gauchir. *To wry; to turne, bend, wrythe from the right, or any way aside; also, to shun, or auoid by turning awry; and hence;*
Gauchir au coup. *To eschew a blow by winding, turning, bending, or wrinching of the bodie.*
Gauchir le coup. *To giue a winding blow, to thrust, or strike indirectly; to ayme at one place, and strike another.*
Gaudé. *See* Gaudez.
Gaude: f. *The stalke of a certaine plant, wherewith Dyers make their clothes yellow, and afterwards (adding Woad) greene; we may call it, Dyers weed, or greening weed; also, a small shower of raine.*
Gaudebillaux: m. *The fat tripes of stall-fed Oxen.*
Gaudées: f. *Babling prayers; or, as* Gaudez.
Gaudence. *An Estate in an Inheritance, let from nine to nine yeares, and so forward for euer.*
Gauderon. *as* Goderon.
Gauderonné. *as* Coderonné.
Gauderonner. *To trimme, decke, or pranke vp a thing; See* Goderonner.
Gaudez: m. *Prayers (whereof the Papists haue diuers) beginning with a* Gaudete.
Gaudi: m. ie: f. *Scoffed, flowted, played on, ieasted at.*
Gaudine: f. *A pleasant lasse, a gamesome wench.*
Gaudinette. *The diminutiue of* Gaudine.
Gaudipise: f. *A codpeece.* ¶Rab.
Gaudipisé: m. ée: f. *Codpeeced; or, wearing a codpeece.*
Gaudir. *To be frolicke, liuelie, iollie, pleasant, merrie; gybe, ieast; play the good fellow, make good cheere.*
Se gaudir de. *To flowt, scoffe, ieast at, be pleasant with.*
Gaudissant. *Flowting, gybing; ieasting, being merrie with.*
Gaudisserie: f. *A ieasting, flowting; merriment.*
Gaudisseur: m. *A ieaster, flowter, gyber; a pleasant-headed fellow; also, a glutton, pot-hunter, Ale-house-haunter, (drunken) good fellow.*
Gave: f. *The gorge, or craw of a bird, whereinto her meat is at first receiued, after shee hath swallowed it.*
Gaveau: m. *A Hole, Stue, or little Pit to keepe fish in.*

Gavellé. (Ceux qui font le sel l'appellent gabellé, ou gavellé, quand il est essuyé. ¶Ragueau.)

Gavereau: m. *A kind of sea-fowle that ducketh verie much.*

Gauffre. *as* Gaffre.

Gauffré: m. ée: f. *Printed (as a garment;) also, set with puffes.*

Gauffrer. *To print (a garment;) also, (but lesse properly) to decke, or set out, with puffes.*

Gauffreure: f. *The printing of a garment &c; also, (but lesse properly) a decking, or setting out with puffes.*

Gauffrier: m. *A Waferers Iron, or Print; a Wafer-mould, or Wafer-print.*

Donner es gauffriers. *To leacher, to firke.*

Gauge. *as* Iauge.

Gaugo. à gaugo. *See* Gogo.

Gavian: m. *A Mew, or sea-Mew.*

Gavier: m. *The throat.*

Gavion: m. *The gullet, or throat-boll.*

Gaulde. *as* Gaude.

Gaule: f. *A pole, big rod; long staffe, or pearch.*

Gaule de gibiere. *A hawking Pole.*

Donner vn coup de gaule par sous l'huis; *To lurch secretly, or giue a priuie lift vnto; to do a shrewd turne, or bad office, vnder hand.*

En Normandie l'on vendange avec la gaule: Pro. *The Grapes of Normandie (viz. Apples, and Peares) are gathered (or beaten downe) with poles.*

Gaulé: m. ée: f. *Beaten with a cudgell; beaten downe with a pole; also, robbed, or despoyled of.*

Gaulée: f. *A beating, or dinging downe (as of fruit, &c) with poles; and hence; a cudgelling, basting, thwacking, lamming; also, the decaying, or hurting of trees by an excessiue, or vnseasonable beating downe of their fruit.*

Gauler. *To ding, beat, or fetch downe with poles; and thence, to cudgell, thwacke, bast, belamme; also, to rob, rifle, or despoyle of.*

Gauleur: m. *An vnlearned, or countrey Surueyor, that measures land onely by the Pole.*

Gaulge. *as* Iauge; *A gage for caske.*

Gaulger. *as* Iauger.

Gaulgeur: m. *A gager of wine vessels.*

Gaulois: m. ise: f. *Of France, French, a Frenchman.*

Gaultier: m. *A mad whorson, mad wag, rakehell, good-fellow; also, a noddie, ninnie, goosecap, coxcombe, ideot; and, as* Garguille.

Gaultiere: f. *A whore, punke, drab, queane, gill, flirt, strumpet, cockatrice, mad wench, common hackney, good one.*

Gavot: m. *A little sharpe-toothed, scalelesse, liuelie, and slipperie sea-fish, that at first sight resembles a gudgeon, or the little sea-dragon; he lyes much vnder stones, and among rockes; where he is taken (at an ebbing water) sometimes to the takers paine; for if he looke not verie well to him, he will nip him by the fingers.*

Gavote: f. *A (kind of) Brawle, daunced, commonly, by one alone.*

Gaupe: f. *A waspe.* ¶Norm. *also, as* Gaultiere; *and hence;*

C'est vne laide gaupe. *She is a filthie ouglie whore; or (as we say) a foule Scawpe.*

Gauque: f. *as* Cauque; *a tent for a wound.*

Gaurrier. *as* Gorrier; *Arrogant, proud, huffing.*

Gausse d'ail. *A cloue of Garlicke.*

Gaussé. *Mocked, flowted, scoffed, gybed, ieasted at, ridden, derided.*

Gausser. *as* Gosser; *To mocke, flowt, scoffe, gybe, ieast at, ride, or deride.*

Gausseur: m. *A mocker, flowter, gyber, scoffer, ieaster, derider.*

Gautier. Toile Gautier; *A kind of Seare-cloth; or, Linnen, dipped in a melted Salue.*

Gautte: f. *A Shad-fish; called so about* Bayonne.

Gay. *as* Geay: m. *Also, a Iay; and sometimes (but lesse properly) a Cornish Chough, or Iacke Daw.*

Gay; *whence,* Hur le gay. *Drunken, cup-shotten, soundly whitled, throughly tipled.*

Gay: m. gaye: f. *Merrie, frolicke, blithe, iollie, cheerefull, iocond, pleasant, gladsome, buxome, light-hearted; lustie, liuelie; also, willing, heartie; resolute; quicke, readie, prompt, in action; also, light, or bright, of colour.*

Perdrix gaye. *as* Gaille.

Gayable: com. *Wadeable, which may be waded ouer.*

Gayac: m. *Gwacum,* Lignum vitę, *Pockewood.*

Gaye: f. *Iet.*

Gayé: m. ée: f. *Waded ouer.*

Gayement. *Merrily, gladly, ioyfully, iocondly, blithely, pleasantly; cheerefully, lustily, willingly, with a heart, with a good will.*

Gayer: m. *A Foord, or wadeable passage ouer a riuer.*

Gayer. *To wade.*

Gayet: m. *Iet.*

Gayeté: f. *Mirth, glee, liuelinesse, cheerefulnesse, ioyfulnesse, alacritie, gladnesse; readinesse, willingnesse, heartinesse.*

Gayetier: m. *One that makes all manner of small toyes in Iet; also, one that carries people ouer a foord on his shoulders.*

Gaymau. Pré gay. *as in* Prez guimaux.

Gayole. *A cage; also, a prison.* ¶Pic.

Gayole d' un moulin. *The trundle; or, a paire of trundleheads.*

Gayoler. *as* Gaïoler.

Gayon. *A kind of small fish.*

Gayvé: m. ée: f. *Wayued; left, forsaken, abandoned, relinquished, quitted.*

Gayver. *To wayue; to leaue, abandon, relinquish, quit, forsake.*

Gayves. Choses gayves. *Weifes; things forsaken, miscarried, or lost; which, not being iustly claymed in a yere and a day, may be lawfully retained by the finder, or by the Lord of the Mannor wherein they were found.*

Gazaille: f. *A Commons, or common field, wherein the inhabitants of seuerall parishes haue distinct parts.*

Gaze: f. *Cushion Canuas; the thinne Canuas that serues women for a ground vnto their Cushions, or Purse-worke, &c; also, (the sleight stuffe) Tiffanie; also, a Mantle, Fall, Scarfe, or long peece thereof; also, wealth, substance, riches, goods; and, a Princes Treasurie.*

Gazeau. *as* Gazon.

Gazel. *as* Gazelle.

Gazelle. *A kind of wild Goat.*

Gazette. *A certaine Venetian coyne scarce worth our farthing; also, a Bill of Newes; or, a short Relation of the generall occurrences of the Time, forged most commonly at Venice, and thence dispersed, euery month, into most parts of Christendome.*

Gazon: m. *A greene sodd, or turfe of earth; also, rich, and fat land; See* Gason.

Gazonné: m. ée: f. *Couered with greene sodd.*

Gazouil. *as* Gazouillis.

Gazouillard: m. arde: f. *Singing, chirping, or warbling, as a bird; that makes a whistling, or whizzing noise.*

Gazouiller. *To sing, whistle, chirpe, as many birds together; also, to warble, as a young bird when it first begins, or learnes, to sing; also, to make, or yeeld a whistling, or whizzing sound.*
L'oiseau gazouille selon qu'il est embecqué: Pro. *Looke* Embecqué.
Gazouilleux. *as* Gazouillard.
Gazouillis: m. *A singing, chirping, warbling, whistling, whizzing; the confused voice, or song of many birds, &c, together.*
Gazouillis de fontaine. *The trickling fall of water from the cocke, or spout, of a Fountaine.*
Gé: m. *Yeast.*
Geais: m. Du g. *Iet.*
Gealloye: f. *A measure containing about twelue of our quarts.*
Geant: m. *A Giant; a man of a huge stature, or size.*
Celuy qui est sur les espaules du geant voit plus loing que celuy qui le porte: Prov. *We, hauing the aid of our auncestors knowledge, vnderstand somewhat more then they did.*
Geante: f. *A Giantesse; a woman Giant.*
Geanterie: f. *Giantrie; the generation, race, kind, or brood, of Giants.*
Geantin: m. *A young, or little Giant.*
Geantin: m. ine: f. *Gianthe, Giant-like, huge-bodied, big made.*
Geantiser. *To Giantize; to make as big as a Giant; also, to play the Giant.*
Geau: m. *A Cocke.*
Geay: m. *Iet; also, as* Gay.
Geɛt: m. *A cast, or throw, as at dice; also, the draught of a Fish net; also, a Marriners sounding lead; also, a gard, or welt; also, a full set of Counters.*
Les geɛts d'un oyseau. *A Hawkes Iesses.*
Geɛtons: m. *Counters.*
Gede. *A washing Bowle.*
Gehainer. *To grone, or grunt.*
Gehenne: f. *A racke, or torture; a place, or instrument of racking, and retching torments.*
Gehenné: m. ée: f. *Racked; retched, or stretched vpon a racke; tortured, tormented.*
Gehenner. *To racke, torture, torment; to retch, or stretch vpon the racke.*
Gehenneux: m. euse: f. *Full of racking.*
Gehi: m. ie: f. *Racked, tortured; or wrung out by extreame torture.*
Gehine: f. *as* Gehenne.
Gehir. *To racke; to wring out a confession by extreame torture.* (v.m.)
Geindre. *To grone; mourne, lament, complaine (as the oppressed) grieuously; also, to crooe, crooke, or mourne as a Doue.*
Geine: f. *as* Gehenne.
Geiné: m. ée: f. *Racked; retched, or stretched vpon the racke; tortured, tormented in racking; also, extorted by torture.*
Geiner. *To racke, torture, torment; to retch, or stretch vpon the racke; to extort confessions by torture.*
Geisses: f. *A kind of flat, or square Pease, resembling somewhat the Chichling.* ¶Langued.
Gel. *as* Gelée.
Gelais. Arbaleste à gelais; *a Stone-bow.*
Gelamine: f. *A kind of minerall earth.*
Gelasin: m. *A wimple in the face, or, a dimple in the cheeke of one that laugheth.*
Gelatine: f. *An excellent white-broth made of the fish* Maigre.

Gelé: m. ée: f. *Frozen; congealed, thickened, or stiffened with extreame cold.*
Gouttes gelées. *Isicles.*
Avoir le bec gelé. *To be tongue-tyed.*
Il est gelé de ne rien faire. *He is euen starued with idlenesse.*
Gelée: f. *A frost; also, gellie.*
Geleniabin. *Honey mixt with Roses.* ¶Arab. ¶Rab.
Gelement: m. *A freezing, or congealing, by cold.*
Geler. *To freeze; to thicken, or congeale with cold.*
Et plus gele, & plus estrainɛt: Prov. *The more the earth freezes the closer it growes.*
Geleur: m. *A freezer.*
Geline: f. *A Henne.*
Geline d'Aphrique. *A Guinnie, or Barbarie Henne.*
Geline de bois. *as* Gelinote de bois.
Creste à geline. *The hearb Coxcombe, Tennie-grasse, yellow and white ratle.*
La journée d'une geline. *An egge.*
Laiɛt de geline. *See* Laiɛt.
Pied de geline. *Hennes-foot, Hennes-Claw, hedge or yellow Fumentorie; also, a trench, ditch, or pit vnder ground, whereby marshes, and ouer-moist corne-lands are drayned; it is fed by many branches, filled with stones (through which the moisture hath sufficient passage) and couered all ouer with earth.*
Geline qui poind, & ne pond: Prov. *A barren shrew.*
La geline pond par le bec: Prov. *A Henne layes as she is fed.*
En Aoust les gelines sont sourdes: Prov. *In August Hennes are deafe.*
Iamais grasse geline n'aima chapon: Pro. *A wanton wife neuer loued a defectiue husband.*
Iamais chapon crester n'aima geline: Prov. *See* Crester.
Noire geline pond blanc œuf: Prov. *A black Henne may breed a white Chicke; a black woman a beautifull child.*
Pour grasse que soit la geline elle a mestier de sa voisine: Prov. *How rich, or powerfull soeuer a man be, he may haue need of his neighbors.*
Qui naist de geline il aime a grater: Prov. *Cat after kind good Mouse-hunt.*
Gelinette: f. *A little Henne.*
Gelinette d'eau. *A Coote.*
Gelinette sauvage; *as* Gelinote; *or, as* Francolin *(in the last sence.)*
Gelineux: m. euse: f. *Of, or belonging to, Hennes.*
Gelinier: m. *A Henne-house, or Henne roost.*
Gelinote: f. *as* Gelinote de bois.
Gelinote de bois. *The pied, or peckled Pheasant, or wood Henne; somewhat rounder bodied, and much daintier meat, then an ordinarie Henne.*
Gelinote de Numidie. *The Guinnie Henne.*
Gelure: f. *Ice, frost; also, a freezing.*
Gembette. *as* Iambette. ¶Rab.
Geme. *Tarre; or Pitch.*
Gemeau: m. *A twinne.*
Gemeaux. *Two muscles of equall bignesse, the one outward, the other inward, which springing from the root of the thighes* Condyles, *and meeting in the middle of the leg, make one big gristle, that ends on the heele; their office is, to turne the thigh a-round inwards.*
Gemelier: m. ere: f. *Double, or twinne-like.*
Arteres gemelieres. *Looke* Artere.
Gemelle: f. *A she twinne.*

Geminé: m. ée: f. *Iterated, doubled, redoubled.*
Geminer. *To double, iterate, redouble.*
Gemir. *To grone; sigh, sob, mourne, complaine grieuously, as those which are opprest, or ouercharged.*
Gemissable: com. *Most lamentable, fit to be groned for, or sighed at.*
Gemissement: m. *A groning; sighing, wailing, sobbing, mourning, heauie lamentation.*
Gemme: f. *A gemme, a iewell, a pretious stone; also, pitch.*
Gemmé. couleur gemmée. *A pearle, or peacocke colour.*
Gemmeux: m. euse: f. *Pretious, rich, full of gemmes, iewells, pretious stones.*
Genaux: m. *casters of Natiuities.*
Gencive: f. *A gumme.*
Souliers à double gencive. *Double soled, or two-soled, shooes.*
Gendarme: m. *A man of Armes; a horseman armed at all points; one that serues in compleat armor, and on a great horse.*
Gensdarmes des Ordonnances. *The ordinarie men of Armes of France; first reduced by Charles the seuenth (in the yeare 1444) into certaine Companies, & vnder particular Orders; Part whereof be; that the* Gendarme *must be, at the yongest, betweene 20 and 21 yeares old; and must haue beene, at least, one yeare, an* Archer *(which no man should bee but a Gentleman borne, and bred; or one that hath beene a Captaine, Lieutenant, Ensigne, or Sergeant Maior of a foot-Companie six yeares:) He must also keepe three horses; two for seruice, and one for his baggage; In regard whereof, &c, he hath* 400. l. Tourn. *of ordinarie, and yerelie, intertainment; (These* Gensdarmes *were at first only* 1500; *but since they haue bin increased vnto* 100 *Companies.*
se Gendarmer. *To strout, or square it like a mã of arms; to put the better leg before; also, to tricke, set out, or stirre vp, himselfe; to prepare himselfe for a scuffling; to arme himselfe with all his helps, against a warre.*
Gendarmerie: f. *The Gendarmerie, men of Armes, or compleat horsemen, of an armie; a troupe of great horse.*
Gendre: m. *A sonne in law; (by the mariage of a daughter.)*
D'une fille deux gendres: Prov. *Two friends gotten by one good office performed, or fauour done; a seuerall gaine drawne from sundrie men by the venting, or vse, of one thing.*
Tel est le gendre comme le soleil d'hyver: Prov. viz: *That does but a little good, and that but a little while.*
Gendresse: f. *A daughter in law (by the mariage of a sonne.)*
Genealogie: f. *A Genealogie; Pedegree.*
General: m. *A Generall, or chiefe Commaunder, of an Armie; or of an Order of Friers, &c.*
Les Generaux des Aides. *Were at first foure Commissioners deputed for the leuying of th'* Aides *throughout all the kingdome; to which end each of them had assigned him certaine generall Prouinces, whose particular Townes, Diocesses, and Diuisions he rated at such summes as he thought they could beare: At length by reason of the warres they were made ordinarie Officers; and haue since increased much in number, and somewhat in authoritie; being Assistants, and next in degree, vnto* les Presidens de la Cour des Aides; *whereof they are stiled ordinarily,* Conseillers generaux, *or* Generaux Conseillers.
Les Generaux des finances. *The Treasurers, or disposers of the publicke treasure; or as* Thresoriers de France.
Les Generaux des Monnoyes. *Are Counsellors assistant vnto the Presidents of the Court of Moneyes, & th'ordinarie riders of circuit for that Court; In which seruice halfe of them (by halfe-yerelie turnes) are still abroad, (licensing, and swearing of Goldsmithes, and giuing them authoritie to fine their* Laveures; *visiting, and searching the houses of money-changers; and prouiding, in generall, that th' Orders of that Court be duely obserued, and the breakers thereof quickly reformed, or informed against) whilest th'other halfe attend, and sit in, the Court, without any vacation, from before eight vnto ten of the clocke in the forenoone, and from three to fiue in the afternoone. These are also tearmed* Conseillers generaux de la Cour des Monnoyes.
Les Generaux provinciaux, & subsidiaires, des Monnoyes. *Whereof there is one belonging to euery one of the seuen (inferiour) Parliaments, within the precincts whereof he rides his circuit, with authoritie like vnto the* Generaux *that be sent from the Court of Moneyes, vnlesse they meet; for then he giues them place, and does nothing before he haue acquainted them withall.*
Les quatre Generaux. *The foure high Treasurers of France; or may be also meant of the* Generaux des Aides, *who in their first institution were but foure.*
General: m. ale: f. *Generall, vniuersall; common, or kindlie, vnto all.*
Conseillers generaux de la Cour des Aides; &, de la Cour des Monnoyes; *as* Les generaux des Aides; & des Monnoyes.
Les Thresoriers generaux. *Tearmed otherwise,* Les Thresoriers de France; *whereof there is a number certaine in euerie Generaltie; Looke* Thresorier.
La Generale: f. *An Admirall gallie, or ship.*
Generalement. *Generally, vniuersally, all-comprehending, altogether.*
Generalité: f. *Generalitie, generalnesse, vniuersalitie; also, a Generaltie; a place of generall receit of the* Finances; *whereof there be at this day,* 21; viz: Paris, Rouen, Caen, Nantes, Tours, Bourges, Poictiers, Agen, Tholouse, Montpellier, Aix, Grenoble, Lyon, Dijon, Chaalons, Amiens, Orleans, Lymoges, Soissons, *and* Moulin; *each hauing it peculiar limits, and Officers.*
Generateur: m. *An ingenderer, begetter, father, progenitor; creator.*
Generatif: m. iue: f. *Generatiue; ingendring; of an ingendering facultie, or breeding power.*
Generation: f. *A generation, linage, brood, kind; also, an ingendring, begetting, breeding.*
Generatrice. humeur gen. *Which breedeth, or ingendereth.*
Generé: m. ée: f. *Ingendered, begotten, bred, brought forth; made, created, forged, framed.*
Generer. *To beget, or ingender, as the male; to breed, or bring forth, as the female; to make, forge, create, frame.*
Genereux: m. euse: f. *Generous; noble, gentle, worthie, gallant; of a braue humor, of an excellent race, of the right stampe, of a good kind; also, valiant, couragious, hardie, stout.*
Plaids genereux. *Sessions; Assises:* ¶Valenciennois.
Vin genereux. *Strong, lustie, mightie wine.*

Generosité: f. *Generositie; gentilitie, gentrie; generousnesse, nobleneßse, great worthinesse; brauerie of disposition, gallantnesse of humor; courage, valour, stoutnesse.*

Genesie: f. *Generation, natiuitie; also, a kind of hearb of sundrie colours.*

Geneſt: m. *Broome; (especially that kind thereof which is called, Bastard Spanish Broome.)*

Geneſt d'Afrique. *as* Geneſt d' Espaigne; *Spanish Broome.*

Geneſt d' Espaigne. *Spanish Broome; (some also tearme* Gaude *so, because they resemble one another.)*

Geneſt espineux. *Furres, Whinnes, Gorse, Thorne-broome.*

Petit geneſt. *Sweet Broome, Heath, or Ling.*

Geneſtay: m. *A Broome close.*

Geneſte: f. *Ordinarie Broome, or the Broome whereof Beesomes are made; also, a kind of garden hearbe resembling Beets.*

Geneſteux: m. euse: f. *Full of Broome.*

Geneſtier: m. ere: f. *Of Broome, belonging to Broome.*

Geneſtriere: f. *A ground, or countrey full of Broome, or Iuniper.*

Genet: m. *A kind of bit with a round port; a bit for a Genet; a Genet-bit.*

Genethliaque. *Birth, natiuitie.*

Genethliatique. *A Caster, or Calculator, of Natiuities.*

Genette: f. *A Genet, or Spanish horse; also, a bit for a Genet; also, a kind of Weesell, blacke-spotted, and bred in Spaine.*

Vne housse à la genette. *A verie short foot-cloth.*

Ordre de la genette. *Seeke* Ordre.

Chevaucher à la genette. *To ride with verie short stirrups.*

Genevre: m. *Iuniper.*

Genevrier: m. *A shrub, or plant of Iuniper.*

Genevrier rouge. *Cedar Iuniper; the crimzon, or pricklie Cedar.*

Gengive: f. *as* Gencive; *A Gumme.*

Genial: m. ale: f. *Geniall; belonging to lucke, or chance; or to a mans nature, disposition, inclination.*

Genie. la g. *Ones good, or bad angell; also, his nature, instinct, inclination, originall disposition.*

Geniculiere. *The hearbe Salomons seale,* Scala cœli, *White-root, or White-wort.*

Genillette. *A Henne:* ¶Savoyard.

Genin: m. *A Wittall.*

Genisse: f. *A heyfer.*

Mener la genisse au taureau. *To play the Baud, sell a Virginitie, prostitute a maid.*

Genital. *Genitall, fit for breed, apt to beget, seruing to ingender.*

Genitif: m. *The Genitiue case.*

Genitif: m. iue: f. *Naturall, ingendering, of an ingendering facultie.*

Genitoires: m. *The genitories, or genitalls; the priuie parts, the instruments of generation.*

Geniture: f. *A race, linage, progenie, generation; also, a birth; an ingendering, breeding, begetting.*

Genne: f. *as* Gehenne.

Genner. *as* Gehenner.

Genoillet: m. *The hearbe called White-root, or White-wort, Salomons seale, and* Scala cœli.

Genoilliere: f. *as* Genoillet.

Genouil: m. *A knee; also, a certaine peece of crooked wood in the poope of a ship.*

Rompre l' anguille au genouil. *To attempt impossibilities; to labour in vaine.*

Genouillé: m. ée: f. *Knottie; kneed; full of ioynts, as the staulke of some hearbes.*

Genouillée: f. *Kneed grasse; also, as* Geniculiere; *Some also call the hearbe Stitchwort so, because it is full of ioynts.*

Genouillere: f. *Salomons seale,* Scala cœli, *White-root, White-wort.*

Genouilleres: f. *Pullie-peeces (Armour) for the knees.*

Genouillet: m. *A little knee; also, a knot, or ioynt in the staulke of an hearbe, or of corne; also, as* Genoillet.

Genre: m. *Kind; a kind of.*

Gens: m. *Men, people, folke; nations, inhabitants of a countrey; also, the ordinarie attendants, or followers of a great man.*

Gens d' armes. *Compleat horsemen, men of Armes; Looke* Gensdarmes.

Gens de comptes. *The Officers, or Ouerseers of the Chamber of Accompts.*

Gens de corps, ou de corsage. *Villeines; or such as hold by a seruile tenure.*

Gens d' eglise. *The Ministerie, Clergie, Church-men; Prelates, Priests, Friers, &c.*

Gens de Iustice. *Counsellors, Judges, Justicers, Magistrates, Officers of Justice.*

Gens de main morte. *as* Gens de poeste.

Gens de mestier. *Artificers, or handicrafts-men.*

Gens d'Ordonnance. *Trained horsmen; or, as* Gensdarmes des Ordonnances.

Gens perdus. *Desperate people; also, souldiors exposed vnto the greatest hazards; the forlorne hope.*

Gens de pied. *Footmen; or th' Infanterie of an Armie.*

Gens de poeste, poste, ou pote. *Yeomen,* Roturiers, *ignoble vassalls, or tenants; vnnoble persons.*

Gens de robbe longue. *Lawyers; also, all others, whose ciuile professiō enioyns them, ordinarily, to weare long gownes.*

Les gens du Roy. *The Kings Counsell learned.*

Gens de sac & de licol. *Rascalls, rakehells, rogues, vagabonds, loytering scoundrells; also, begging Friers.*

Gens de suitte. *Villeines; Looke* Suitte.

Gens de voirie. *Scauingers, Dung-farmers, Gold-finders.*

Gens de bien sont tousiours gracieux: Prov. *Good men are euer gracious, affable, courteous.*

`A gens de bien on ne pert rien: Prov. *One seldome looses by dealing with, or dwelling neere, honest men.*

De gens de bien vient tout bien: Prov. *From good men comes all goodnesse.*

Les gens de bien font tousjours bien, ont tousjours bien, & sont tousjours bien: Prov.

Il y a gens & gens: Prov. *There are of all sorts, good and bad; there is much choice of, great difference in, men; one should not expect (that cannot deserue) as much as another.*

Tant de gens tant de guises: Prov. *As many different natures as nations; as many seuerall fashions as folke.*

Gens-d'-armes. *Looke* Gendarme.

Gensemy: m. *The little sweet flower Jasmine, Celsomine, or Gesse.*

Gent: f. *A nation, people; flocke, race, kind, linage, familie, kindred; Looke* Gens.

Gent: m. gente: f. *Neat, spruce, fine, compt, prettie, picked,*

picked, well arrayed, featly suited, quaintly dressed, handsomely attired; also, gentle, pliant, soft, easie.

Le gent corps. *Auncientl signified one of a small stature; and may yet be applied to a prettie dapper man, or (if a woman) to a pretie soule.*

Gente: f. *as* Iante.

Gentement. *Neatly, sprucely, finely, comptly, prettily, featly, quaintly, handsomly; also, gently, easily, softly, gingerly.*

Gentiane: f. *Gentian, Bitterwort, Fellwort, Baldmoine, or Baldmonie.*

Gentiane grande. *Great Gentian; beares a yellow flower.*

Gentiane moindre. *Crossewort Gentian; bearing a blew flower.*

Gentiane petite. *Little Crossewort Gentian; beares a small red flower.*

Gentienne. *as* Gentiane.

Gentifame: f. *A Gentlewoman.*

Gentil: m. ile: f. *Gentle, tame, tractable, mild; affable, courteous, gracious; kind, louing; pliant, soft, supple, tender; smooth; also, comelie, sightlie; prettie, quaint, neat, fine; well-fashioned, well-behaued; goodlie, faire; gallant, noble; delightsome, pleasant; also, Gentile, Pagan, Heathenish; (When* Gallia *was conquered by the* Francs, *or ancient French, the Gaules, who were at that time Christians, tearmed the Côquerors, by reason of their Heathenish Religion,* Gentils, *or* Gentils-hommes.)

Gentil bois. *Wild Line, wild Flax.*

Bois gentil. *Spurge-Flax, German Oliue Spurge, Mezereon, Dwarfe Bay.*

Ouvrier gentil à l'hospital: Prov. *The fine workeman dies in an Hospitall; (whether his pride, idlenesse, or ill-husbandrie seldome failes to send him;) Looke* Ouvrier.

Gentilesse: f. *Gentrie, Gentilitie, Nobilitie.*

Gentilesses. *Prettie conceits, deuises, knacks, feats, trickes.*

Gentilhomme: m. *A Gentleman; also, a certain hollow engine (set thick on th'outside with pikes, and charged with powder and shot) which discharged, scatters it selfe, to the ruine of those it lights on; Looke* Gentil.

Gentilhomme servant. *A waiter, or attendant on the King, at meale-times.*

Gentilhomme de ville. *A Gentleman of the first head, an vpstart Gentleman.*

Il iure comme vn Gentilhomme. *He sweares after a thousand pound a yeare.*

Gentilhommeau: m. *A small, or single-soled, Gentleman; a Gentleman of low degree.*

Gentiliser. *To gentilize it, liue as the Heathen, play the Pagan.*

Gentilisme: m. *Paganisme, Heathenishnesse.*

Gentilité: f. *The same.*

Gentillastre: m. *A meane Gentleman; a new Gentleman, one that is scarce a Gentleman; one that passes, or affects to goe, for a Gentleman, though he be none.*

Gentillastreté: f. *Poore gentrie, meane gentrie; vsurped, or new gentrie.*

Gentillement. *Gently, louingly, kindly, graciously; softly, smoothly, tenderly; neatly, quaintly, handsomely; nobly, gallantly.*

Gentils. les Gentils. *The Gentiles, Pagans, Heathen people.*

Gentiment. *as* Gentement; *or as* Gentillement.

Gentre. *Looke* Iantre.

Genuflexion: f. *A bowing, or bending, of the knee.*

Geoffroy. *Geffrey; a proper name.*

Geographie: f. *The description of the earth; Geographie.*

Geographique: com. *Geographicall, earth-describing.*

Geolage: m. *A Goalership; or the being in Goale; also, the fee thats due to a Goaler at th'entrie, and departure of a prisoner.*

Geole: f. *A Goale, or Prison; also, a cage, or coope for birds; also, the pinne, or circle in the middle of a white, or marke, at shooting.*

Geoliage. *as* Geolage.

Geolier: m. *A Goaler; a Keeper.*

Geoliere: f. *A Goalers wife, a woman Goaler.*

Geollage. *as* Geolage.

Geolle, & Geollier. *Looke* Geole, & Geolier.

Geomantie: f. *Diuination by points, and circles made on the earth:* ¶Rab.

Geometrie. *Geometrie; the measuring, or proportioning of figures.*

Geometrien: m. *A Geometrician; a professor of, or Maister in, Geometrie.*

Geometrique. *Geometricall; of, or belonging to, Geometrie.*

Pied Geometrique. *The Geometricall foot; is foure hand-breadthes, or sixteene fingers-breadthes.*

Geraffe. *as* Giraffe.

Geratien. *A kind of blackish stone.*

Gerbe de blé. *A sheafe of corne.*

Faire gerbe de foarre à dieu. *To mocke, scorne, abuse, delude, defraud God of his right; or (in matters of Religion, and conscience, where bountie is required) to play the micher; In the Iewes law it was held a great impietie in any man to giue the Leuites chaffe, or straw, in stead of corne; thence came this Prouerbe, wherein many, abusiuely, vse* Barbe, *in stead of* Gerbe.

Gerbé: m. ée: f. *Bound vp (as corne) into sheaues; also, ranged, ranked, or placed in order one vpon another.*

Gerbée: f. *A shocke, halfe-thraue, or heape of sheaues; also, a bundle of straw.*

Gerber des javelles. *To bind corne of swath into sheaues; to sheafe vp corne.*

Gerber des tonneaux. *To raunge, or set wine vessels one vpon another.*

Gerbier: m. *A stacke, or halfe-thraue, of corne; also, a great Garner to keepe salt in.*

Gerbiere: f. *A recke, or stacke, of corne.*

Gercé: m. ée: f. *Chapped, riuen, cleft, chawned, with cold.*

Gercer. *To cleeue, riue, cut in many places, and by small clefts; to chinke, chap, chawne (as the North wind does) the face, hands, &c.*

Gerceure. *as* Iarsure; *or* Gersure.

Gere: f. *The Hebrew halfepennie, somewhat more then our pennie, 40 of them going to the ounce.*

Geré: m. ée: f. *Done, wrought, executed, managed, handled; also, carried, brought, or borne.*

Gerer. *To doe, make, worke, exercise, execute, manage, handle; also, to carrie, or beare.*

Gerfault: m. *A Gerfaulcon; the greatest of Hawks; called also,* Faulcon gerfaut.

Germain. *(A proper name for a man) German.*

Germain: m. ine: f. *Germaine; come of the same stock, bred of the same kind; neere of kinne, of all-one race.*

Germaine. *The name of an Apple, that yeeldes verie cleere, and pleasant cyder.*

Germandrée: f. *Germaunder, English treacle (an hearbe.)*

Germandrée aquatique, ou d'eau. *Water Germander, Scordion. Garlicke Germander.*

Germandrée bastarde. *Bastard, or wild Germander.*

Germe des arbres, herbes, &c: m. *A yong shute, sprout, bud, sprig, or twig of trees, &c.*

Germe des aulx, oignons, &c. *The middle staulkes which are betweene the blades, and roots of Garlicke, Onions, &c.*

Germe d'vn oeuf. *The sperme of an egge; the little string which is on either side of the yolke of a raw, or a reare, egge.*

Fauls germe. *A Mooncalfe; a hard swelling, or shapelesse peece of flesh in the wombe, which makes women beleeue they are with child when they are not.*

Germe. *A fashion of open boat, or barke without hatches, vsed in the Leuant Seas for the transportation of marchandise, and passengers.*

Germé: m. ée: f. *Budded, burgeonned, sprouted, sprung out, put forth.*

Germement: m. *A sprouting, budding, burgeonning, putting forth, shuting out, of trees, &c.*

Germer. *To sprout, bud, burgeon, spring, put forth, shute out, yong sprigs, buds, tenderells, &c.*

Germeux: m. euse: f. *Sprouting, budding, burgeonning; also, full of yong sprigs, or buds; also, full of seed.*

Germination: f. *A sprouting, &c; as* Germinement.

Geron. *Looke* Giron.

Gerre: f. *The small, or white Cackerell fish; or as* Picarel.

Gerse: f. *A Woodlouse; or Ladicow.*

Gersé: m. ée: f. *Looke* Gercé.

Gersure: f. *A cleft, rist, chinke, chap, chawne; also, the neb of a pinne.*

Gesante. vne ges. *A woman that lieth in.*

Gesier. *as* Iesier. *The guiserne of a bird.*

Gesine: f. *A lying in child-bed; a lying in.*

Bras à la poictrine, jambe en gesine: Prov. *Keepe a sore arme to thy bosome, a sore leg in thy bed.*

Gesir. *To lie; to lie downe, along, or long by it; to lie in child-bed, or in the straw, as a woman; also, to consist, or rest in; also, to remaine, or abide.*

Gesir aupres. *To lie neere vnto, to bound, abutt, or border vpon.*

Nous sçavons ou gist le lievre. *Seeke* Lievre.

Ma vie eust ieu en cela. *My life had lien therein, or depended thereon.*

Tant gratte la cheure que mal gist: Prov. *One often speeds the worse for being too curious, or desirous of speeding well; Looke* Cheure.

Tout ce que gist en peril n'est pas perdu: Prov. *All is not lost that is in danger.*

Gesne. *as* Gehenne; *Racking, torture.*

Gesse: f. *A common sinke, or sewer; a gutter for the voiding of ordure:* ¶Bretton.

Gesses. *A kind of pease; as* Geisses.

Gestation: f. *A bearing, or carrying.*

Geste: m. *Gesture, fashion, behauiour, carriage, demeanor; also, a making of signes, or countenances; a motion, or stirring of any part of the bodie.*

Gestion: f. *An action; or, an acting, doing, exploiting.*

Gesver. *as* Guesver.

Get: m. *A casting, or throwing out; also, a set of counters; also (the blacke hard earth, or minerall, called) Jet.*

Getisse. terre getisse. *Such as is throwne out of a house, &c.*

Gets. *Looke* Gects.

Gettéen: m. enne: f. *Of Jet; blacke as Jet.*

Getter. *as* Iecter; *To cast, &c.*

Gettonner. *To bud, sprout, or shute out.*

Gettons: m. *Counters.*

Gettons des arbres. *Buds; Looke* Iectons.

Geve: f. *A cage, coope, or open basket, to keepe chickens, &c. in.*

Geural: m. *A Certificate, Passeport, or Safeconduct for a traueller.*

Geure. *as* Giure.

Ghirlande. *A garland.*

Giaret: m. *A small bright-coloured sea-fish, not much vnlike to, but that it is somewhat lesse (and yet bigger scaled) then, the Cackarell:* ¶Marseillois.

Gibbar. *A kind of slender, and long-nosed Whale, that hath a bulch backe, and a pipe on his forhead, out of which he spouts water with great violence.*

Gibbasse: f. *A pouch, or budget; also, a great bunch, or bulch-like swelling.*

Gibbe: f. *A bunch, or swelling; a bulch; any thing that stands poking out.*

Gibbecier: m. *A pouch-maker.*

Gibbeciere: f. *A pouch, bag, poake, budget.*

Gibbet: m. *A gibbet, gallow-tree, paire of gallowes; (In France all Gentlemen that haue* Haute Iustice, *haue also (or may haue) gibbets (for th'executing of malefactors) within their territories, though (ordinarily) with some difference in making, or fashion, according to their difference in estate, or dignitie; for the gibbet of the (simple) high* Iusticier *hath but two pillers; the Lord Chattelaines, three; the Barons, foure; the Earls, six; and the Dukes, eight; And yet these differences are more precise then generall; for all customes agree not in them.)*

Que gibbet veut dire cecy? *What a mischiefe meane you by this?*

Il est plus malheureux que le bois dont on fait le gibbet. *He is a most vnfortunate man.*

Au gibbet le repentir vient trop tard: Prov. *Too late he repents that repents at the gallowes.*

Les beaux hommes au gibbet: Pro. *Faire men come often to foule ends; the properer the men the worse their lucke.*

Gibbeux: m. euse: f. *Hulch, bunched, much swelling, imbossed.*

Gibbeyer. *as* Gibboyer.

Gibbier: m. *Game (of any kind thats hunted, or hawked at; but most properly, the later) fowle; whence;*

Gaule de gibbier. *A hawking powle.*

Cecy n'est pas de vostre gibbier. *This is not your trade, not your profession; this is no subiect for you to speake, no course for you to deale, in; you are here out of your proper element.*

Chacun à son gibbier. *Euerie one to that hee is fit for, to that he hath skill in.*

Estre en beau gibbier. *To be faire and fat; to like exceeding well.*

Gibbosité: f. *The being bulch-backt; swelling, bunchinesse.*

Gibboyer. *To hawke; hunt; fowle, or shoot at fowle.*

Gibboyeur: m. *A Fowler, or Gunner; one that ordinarily shoots at fowle.*

Gibet. *as* Gibbet.

Gibets. *Little packets of grapes wrapt vp in fig leaues, whereby they are preserued fresh two yeres together.*

Gibier. *Looke* Gibbier.
Giblet: m. *A gimlet, or piercer.*
Gibolée: f. *A swift, great, and sudden showre of raine.*
Giboulée. *as* Gibolée.
Gieroglіphique: com. *Gieroglіphicall; of, or belonging to, Gieroglіphickes.*
Giez. *as* Gects; *A hawkes gests.*
Gifflard: m. arde: f. *Chuffie, full-cheekt; swollen, or puft vp, in the face, and throat.*
Giffle: f. *A cheeke, or chap; or (most properly) the bag on either side of the chap, wherein meat is hidden, or held.*
Gigandal: m. ale: f. *Huge, monstrous big, Giant-like.*
Gigantal. *The same.*
Gigantin: m. ine: f. *Huge, big-bodied, of an extraordinarie stature, Giant-like.*
Gigantomachie: f. *The warres of the Giants against the gods.*
Gigot (de mouton.) *A leg (of mutton) cut large with the whole bone at it, and so roasted; some also, call so a loyne from which the chine is taken.*
Gigoteau: m. *A knuckle; or, the bonie end of the leg.*
Gaigner les gigoteaux. *To betake him to his legs, to shew his heeles, to runne away.*
Gigotte. chausses à la gigotte. *Looke* Chausses.
Gile. *as* Gille.
Gille. faire gille. *To flie, giue the slip; runne away; And hence will some in choller say;* Avant gille; *Out, be packing, be gone.*
Gilles. *(A proper name) Giles.*
Mal de S. Gilles. *A kind of Canker, or Fistula.*
Pomme de S. Gilles. *A certaine greene sweet apple.*
Vis S. Gilles. *A fashion of winding staires, vaulted vnder the steps.*
Faire Gilles. *as* Faire gille.
Gimbelet: m. *A gimlet, or piercer.*
Gimbreter. *To play the wanton, to doe lasciuiously, to leacher it.*
Gimbreteux: m. euse: f. *Leacherous, wanton, lasciuious.*
Gimpier: m. *A maker of Crepines for hoods.*
Gindre. *See* Geindre.
Gingembre: m. *Ginger.*
Gingembre blanc. *White Ginger.*
Gingembre de iardin. *The hearbe Dittanie, or Dittander; some also call so, the plant that bears Guinnie Pepper.*
Gingembré: m. ée: f. *Begingered; seasoned, or strewed with Ginger.*
Gingioule: f. *A longish, and yellow fruit of a reasonable good tast, but inferiour to the Lotebеrrie, for which it hath beene mistaken by some Authors.*
Gingioulier: m. *The narrow-leaued tree that beares the* Gingioule.
Ginglyme: m. *A mutuall receiuing, or lodging of one bone within another.*
Ginguets: m. *Sower wines; a tearme first giuen them in the yeare 1555, which being extraordinarily cold, and moist, the grapes could not possibly ripen.*
Ginguette: f. *Small, poore, or sower wine; called so about* Tours.
Gippon: m. *A (short) Cassocke; also, a rag, clowt, or tatter throwne vp and downe.*
Cottonner le moule du gippon. *To eat much; to balast the bellie, stuffe the guts; to feed soundly, or excessiuely.*
Gips: m. *Morter, Plaister, Parget.*

Giraffe: f. *A certaine spotted, and long-necked beast, (gotten (as tis thought) by a Cammell on a female Panther) whose fore-legs are much longer then her hinder; both which shee moues, as shee goes (in their seuerall turnes) together.*
Girandin: m. *A certaine Snyte-like bird, that vses to wind, or wheele about, in rising.*
Girasole: f. *A Girasole; or precious stone, of the kind of Opalls, that yeelds an eye-like luster, which way soeuer you turne it, vnlesse it be towards the Sunne; for then it casts forth beames like the Sunne.*
Giraudette: f. *The name of an Apple.*
Girbe: f. *The Cawle, or Kell, wherein the bowels be wrapped.*
Giré: m. ée: f. *Veered, or turned with the wind; twirled, whirled, or twyned about.*
Girelle: f. *A little sharpe-nosed rocke-fish in the Italian seas, that bites fishers, and swimmers, like a flea.*
Girer. *To veere, or turne with the wind, to twerle, whirle, or wheele about.*
Girets: m. *Armour for the thighes of horses.*
Giroflade. *as* Girofleé: ¶Langued.
Giroflade de mer. *A certaine Gillouer-like excrescence growing on rockes.*
Girofle. cloux de girofle. *Cloues.*
Giroflé: m. ée: f. *Set, stucke, sweetened, or seasoned with Cloues.*
Girofleat. *Made of Cloues, or of Gilloflowers.*
Giroflée: f. *A Gilloflower; and, most properly, the Cloue Gilloflower.*
Giroflée jaulne. *The Winter, or wall Gilloflower.*
Giroflée de Inde. *A kind of Tansie that bears a flower like a Gilloflower; or, as* Oeillet d'Inde; *the French Marigold, Affrican Gilloflower, or Gingioline flower.*
Girole: f. *The Skirwort, or Skirret-root.*
Giromantie: m. *Diuination by circles:* ¶Rab.
Giron: m. *The lap, or bosome.*
Tender le giron en la Iustice. *A defendant to appeare, and confesse the Action.*
Il ne se faut fier ni à femme, ny au giron: Prov. *(For neither of them keepes verie surely the things entrusted vnto them.)*
Gironnée: f. *A lapfull, or bosomefull of.*
Gironomique: com. *Circular:* ¶Rab.
Girouët: m. *as* Girouëtte.
Girouëtte: f. *A fane, or weather-flag; also, (but nothing so properly) a weathercocke.*
Girouëtté: m. ée: f. *Furnished with a fane, or weathercocke; also, inconstant, variable, turned by euerie wind, as a fane.*
Girousle. *as* Girofle.
Giroule. *as* Girole; *A Skerret root.*
Gisant: m. *The lowest of the three railes of a Cart, &c.*
Le gisant d' vn moulin. *The Bed, Bedder, or vndermill-stone.*
Gisant: m. ante: f. *Lying, layed along.*
Gisante: f. *A woman that lies in.*
Gisié: m. *The giserne of birds.*
Giste: m. *A bed, couch, lodging, place to lie on, or to rest in.*
Giste d' vn lievre. *The forme of a hare.*
Droict de giste. *Looke vnder* Droict.
Tost attrapée est la souris qui n'a pour giste qu' vn pertuis: Prov. *Looke* Souris.
Giste de boeuf: f. *A rand of beefe; a long, and fleshie peece, cut out from betweene the flanke, and buttocke.*
Gith. *Hearbe githen, Bishops wort, Saint Katherines flower,* Nigella Romana.

Gith sauvage. *Wild Githen, wild Nigella.*
Gitte : f. *A sprig ; or putting out, in a branch.*
Giver. *as* Girer.
Givereau : m. *A pide, or black and white water-fowle, somewhat lesse then a ducke.*
Giure : m. *A white, or hoare frost vpon trees after great, and long freezing.*
Glace : f. *Ice ; also, the glasse of a looking-glasse.*
Alun de glace. *Roche Allum ; so tearmed because at first it is melted, and made into great flakes, like yce.*
Estaim de glace. *Looke* Estaim.
Ferré à glace. *Shod with frost-nayles (whence) also, steadie-footed, sure of foot, seldome slipping, failing, or falling.*
Gosier ferré à glace. *An hardened or senceleſſe palate, a paued mouth.*
Glacé : m. ée : f. *Frozen, congealed, hardened, turned into, couered ouer with, yce ; also, benummed, or grown senceleſſe by extremitie of cold ; also, flesh-basted, as the lining of a cloke, &c ; also, inserted, or foisted, as a word, line, chapter, &c, into a booke.*
Glacer. *To freeze ; harden, congeale, turne into yce ; to couer, or ouercast with yce ; also, to benumme, beclumpse, make senceleſſe, by extreame cold ; also, to flesh-bast ; or stitch downe the lyning of a garment thereby to keepe it from sagging.*
Glacer vn mot. *To insert, put ; thrust, or foist, a word into a writing.*
Glacial : m. ale : f. *Ycie, ouergrowne with yce, euer frozen, or congealed by extreame cold ; also, extreamely cold.*
Glacis : m. *A place made slipperie by wet lately fallen, and frozen on ; also, a sloaping banke or causey ; also, a sloaping, sloapeneſſe, gentle bending downewards ; and hence ;*
En glacis. *Sloaping, asloape, gently inclining, declining by little and little.*
Glaçoir : m. *A Iakes, or Priuie.*
Glaçons : m. *Isicles, or flakes of yce ; also, flawes in stones resembling flakes of yce.*
Gladiateur : m. *A Fencer, or Maister of Fence.*
Gladiation : f. *Fencing.*
Glagou : *as* Glayeul ; *or, Sedge ; also, a dot, or collop of flegme spet out.*
Glaieul. *as* Glayeul.
Glainage : m. *A gleaning.*
Glainé : m. ée : f. *Gleaned.*
Glainer. *as* Glaner ; *To gleane.*
Glaineur : m. *A Gleaner.*
Glaire : f. *Grauell ; sand, and small pible stones ; or, sand mingled with stones ; also, a whitish, and slimie soyle.*
La glaire d' vn oeuf. *The white of an egge.*
Glaireux : m. euse : f. *Slimie ; also, grauellie, full of grauell.*
Terre glaireuse (*in* Maison Rustique.) *as* Terre glaize.
Glais. *as* Glayeul ; *Corne-flag, Corne-sedge, Corne-gladen.*
Glaitel. *as* Glais.
Glaive : m. *A Gleaue, or Sword ; also, a Launce, or horsemans staffe.*
Glaize. terre glaize. *A moist, and slimie white soyle.*
Glammet : m. *A Mew, or Sea-mew.*
Gland : m. *An Acorne ; Mast of Oakes, or other trees.*
Gland de Iupiter. *A Chesnut.*
Gland de mer. *A kind of Muscle, or shell-fish, that somewhat resembles an Acorne.*
Gland onguentaire. *The Aromaticall nut, or fruit, whereof the Perfumers oyle of Benne is made.*
Attendre le gland qui tombe. *To liue in expectation of profit, or preferment (at Court, &c.)*
Glandage : m. *Mast ; also, Mastage ; the season of turning hogs into the woods ; the feeding of hogs, by Mast, in woods ; th' Agistment, or laying of swine into mastie woods.*
Glandagé : m. ée : f. *Fed, or nourished (as hogs) with mast.*
Glandager les porceaux. *To feed, or nourish hogs with Mast ; to agist, or lay, swine in mastie woods.*
Glandaux. *The name of a kind of Oliues.*
Glande : f. *A kernell ; a fleshie substance filled with pores, and growing betweene the flesh and skin.*
Glande pituitaire. *A certaine kernell in the head, which receiues the excrements contained in the Tunnell thereof.*
Glandée. bonne glandée. *Good store of Mast, a good yeare for Acornes.*
Glandéer. *To get, or gather Mast.*
Glandeux : m. euse : f. *Mastie, full of Mast, well stored with Acornes.*
Glandier : m. ere : f. *Of, or belonging to Mast ; also, as* Glandeux.
Glands : m. *Pellets, Bullets.*
Glandulaire : com. *Kernellie ; of a kernell, like a kernell, in kernells.*
Glandule : f. *A little kernell.*
Glandule carniforme. *A great, fleshie, and soft kernell, consisting of many small ones, & placed vnder the ventricle, to keepe it from touching the back, which otherwise would hurt it ; we call it (especially in edible beasts) the Sweet-bread.*
Glanduleux : m. euse : f. *Kernellie, full of fleshie kernells.*
Glane : f. *A gleaning ; also, the corne thats gleaned, or left for the gleaner.*
Il y a assez de champ pour faire glane. *There is stuffe ynough to worke on, meanes enow to profit by.*
Glané : m. ée : f. *Gleaned.*
Glanement. *A gleaning ; as* Glaneure.
Glaner. *To gleane ; to picke vp eares of corne after reapers.*
Qui glane il ne fait pas ce qu' il veut : Prov. *Somewhat like our, Beggers must be no chusers.*
Glaneur : m. *A gleaner.*
Glaneure : f. *A gleaning, or gathering vp of looſſe eares of corne, left by reapers ; a leasing of corne.*
Glangion ; m. *A little Sea-cut, or Cuttle-fish.*
Glap : m. *The barking of a dog.*
Glappier. *as* Clapier.
Glappir. *To barke like a dog, to yealpe ; yawle, bawle.*
Glappissement. *A barking, or yealping ; a bawling, or yawling.*
Glappisseur : m. *A barker, yealper ; bawler, yawler.*
Glas : m. *Noise, crying, bawling ; also, yce ; also, a knell for the dead.*
Glas. Bled glas. *Blought Wheat.*
Terre glase. *Fat earth.*
Glason. *as* Glazon ; *A clod, sod, or turfe of earth.*
Glasonneux : m. euse : f. *Cloddie, soddie, turfie ; full of clods, of sods, of turues.*
Glassé : m. ée : f. *Seeke* Glacé.
Glasser. *as* Glacer.
Glassis : m. *A strong penthouse vpon the walls, or the rampire, of a fortresse ; also, a sloaping causey, damme, or banke, neere the water ; See* Glacis.

Glasson. *as* Glaçon.
Glassouër: m. *A Jakes, or Priuie.*
Glastre: m. *Ouse, or mud of the sea.*
Glatir. *To barke; yawle, bawle.*
Glatissant. *Barking; yawling, bawling.*
Glatissement: m. *A barking, or bawling.*
Glatisseur: m. *A barker; bawler, yawler.*
Glatteron: m. *The Burre Docke, Clote Burre, great Burre.*
Glattir, Glattissement, Glattisseur. *as* Glatir, &c.
Glaumet: m. *A Sea-cob, or Sea-gull.*
Glavoir: m. *A braying, yelling, skreaking, bawling, out-crying:* (¶Blesien.)
Glay. *as* Glas; *A noise:* ¶Pic. *also, as* Glaye.
Glaye: f. *The blew Lillie, or Flowerdeluce.*
Glayeul: m. *Corne-flag, Corne-sedge, Corne-gladen, right Gladen, Glader, Sword-grasse.*
Glayeul bastard. *Sedge, wild flags, water flags, yellow wild Ireos, bastard Flowerdeluce, water Flowerdeluce, Lauers, or Leuers.*
Glayeul jaulne. *The same.*
Glayeul de maraiz. *as* Glayeul bastard.
Glayeul puant. *Stinking Gladen, Spurge-wort, wild Ireos.*
Glayeul de riviere. *Sedge, Water-flags, Sword-grasse, Gladen, Glader, wild Flags; yellow, bastard, or water, Flowerdeluce, Lauers, and Leuers.*
Glayeul sauvage. *as* Glayeul puant.
Glaz. *as* Glace: ¶Rab.
Glazeux: m. euse: f. *Cloddie, turfie; clammie, fat, clayish.*
Glebe. *Glebe; land belonging to a Parsonage:* ¶Norm.
Glene. *A small hollownesse in a bone; and (most properly) the outward concauitie of the shoulder-blades.*
Gleneur: m. eure: f. *Gleaning, or gathering after.*
Glenoïde. *as* Glene.
Gleteron. *as* Glatteron; *The Clote Burre.*
Glette: f. *The froth of an egge; also, the gellie of any thing that congealeth; also, the flegme, or filth, which a hawke throwes out at her beake, after her casting.*
Gletteux: m. euse: f. *Slimie, frothie, flegmie, filthie.*
Glic. jouer au glic. *To leacher; to play at fast and loosse.*
Gliceau. *A bottome of thread.* (v.m.)
Glimpe. *A light made of the staulke, or stemme of an hearbe dried, and afterward greased ouer.*
Glincer. *as* Glisser; *To glide, or slide.* (v.m.)
Glire. *read* Dire, *or*, luy dire: ¶Rab.
Gliron: m. *A Dormouse.*
Gras comme glirons. *We say, fat as pigs, or hogs, &c.*
Glischer. *as* Glisser: ¶*Pic.*
Glissade: f. *A slip, or slipping; a gliding, sliding; stealing or creeping along; also, glibnesse.*
Glissant. *Slipping; gliding, sliding; stealing, wrigling, or creeping along; also, slipperie; or, whereof no certaine hold can be taken.*
Glissé: m. ée: f. *Slipped; slid; crept, or stollen along.*
Glisseau: m. *A bottome of thread.*
Glissement: m. *A slipping, &c;* *as* Glissade.
Glisser. *To slip; to slide, or glide; creepe, wriggle, or steale along; to be slipperie; to runne glib; to trickle downe by little and little.*
Il n'y a cheval si bien ferré qui ne glisse: Prov. *The best shod horse doth slip sometimes.*
Mieux vault glisser du pied que de la langue: Pro. *Better the foot slip then the tongue trip.*
Glisse-tousjours. *Euer gliding, still wrigling, alwayes mouing.*
Glissoire: f. *A slipperie place.*

Glix: m. *A Dormouse:* ¶Rab.
Globe: m. *A Globe; a round bowle, or ball.*
Globeux: m. euse: f. *Globie; round like a globe; of, or belonging to, a globe; full of globes.*
Globuleux. *as* Globeux.
Gloc. *The clocking of a henne:* ¶Langued.
Gloë. *A clouen peece of wood:* ¶Norm.
Gloire: f. *Glorie, fame, reputation, renowme, a great name, or generall commendation; the consent of good men in the praise of.*
Faire gloire. *To take a pride.*
Gloire vaine assez fleurit, porte fueille, & point de fruit: Prov. *Vaineglorie brings forth nought but flowers, and leaues; or, vaineglorie hauing blossomd, perisheth.*
Gloriation. *A glorying, boasting, vaunting, bragging, cracking.*
Gloriette: f. *Small glorie, little praise, not much commendation; also, a little roome in the top of a tower; also, a little banquetting house in a garden.*
Glorieuse: f. *A kind of Scate-fish that hath a head like a Toad, and a venimous pricke in her taile; called so, because of her slow, and (seeming) stateli e, manner of swimming.*
Glorieusement. *Gloriously, renowmedly, with great reputation; also, proudly, vainely, boastingly, vaineglori ously.*
Glorieuseté: f. *Pride, boasting, vaineglorie, cracking, vaunting, selfe-loue, selfe-liking.*
Glorieux: m. euse: f. *Glorious, famous, renowmed, notable, excellent, exceedingly esteemed, much praised, much praise-worthie, highly commended, of great reputation; also, proud, vaunting, boasting, vaineglorious, cracking, bragging; selfe-conceited, selfe-louing.*
Glorifié: m. ée: f. *Glorified; magnified, renowmed.*
Glorifier. *To glorifie; to bring vnto glorie; to renowme.*
se Glorifier. *To vaunt, cracke, brag, boast of his owne acts; to commend, or magnifie, himselfe.*
Glorin. *A kind of Scate, called, the Forke-fish.*
Glose: f. *A glosse; comment, or exposition.*
Glosé: m. ée: f. *Glossed; expounded, commented on.*
Glosier. *A kind of white Vine, verie fruitfull.*
Glossateur: m. *A Glosser, an Interpreter; one that writes a Glosse, or Comment vpon a text.*
Glossement: m. *The clucking, or clocking of a brood Henne.*
Glosser. *To clucke, or clocke, as a Henne.*
Glouglouter. *To guggle; to sound like a narrow-mouthed pot, or strait-neckt bottle, when it is emptied.*
Gloussant. poule gloussante. *A clucking Henne.*
Glout: m. gloute: f. *Gluttonous, greedie, deuouring, rauenous.*
Gloutement. *Gluttonously, rauenously, greedily.*
Glouteron: m. *The Clote, Burre Docke, or great Burre.*
Petit glouteron. *The Louse Burre, Ditch Burre, lesse Burre Docke.*
Glouton: m. *A glutton, deuourer, cormorant, rauiner; greedie-gut, bellie-god, great eater; also, a knaue, rascall, filthie fellow.*
Chair de mouton manger de glouton: Prov. *See* Mouton.
Glouton: m. onne: f. *Gluttonous, greedie, rauinous.*
Gloutonnaire: com. *Gluttonous, greedie, deuouring, gormandizing.*
Gloutonnie. *Gluttonie, a rauining, deuouring, or great eating, a gormandizing, or greedie feeding.*
Gloux. *Gluttonous, greedie, deuouring:* ¶Rab.
Glu de foarre: m. *A bundle of straw.*

Glu: f. *Glew; or(more properly)birdlime.*
Glu de Damas. *Birdlime of Damascus; is made of the Sebesten, or Assyrian Plumme.*
Gluant: m. te: f. *Glewish, glewie, clammie; glewing, cleauing, sticking to, like birdlime, whatsoeuer it toucheth.*
Gluaux: m. *Lime-twigs.*
Gluber. *To flay, or pill.*
Gluc. ergo gluc. *(A word vsed by the Schollers of Paris, in derision of an absurd conclusion;) Well concluded Roger; wisely brother James.*
Glué: m. ée: f. *Limed; caught with, or intangled by, birdlime; also, glewed.*
Gluement: m. *A glewing; a fast-ioyning, sure-closing; a liming, a catching with, or intangling in, birdlime.*
Gluer. *To lime; to glew; to ioyne, or close verie fast, as with birdlime, or glew; to catch with, or intangle in, birdlime.*
Glueur: m. *A glewer.*
Glueur: f. *Glewinesse, clamminesse.*
Glueux: m. *Glewie, full of glew; also, as* Gluant.
Gluits: m. *Long, and whole straw.*
Gluön: m. *A lime-twig.*
Glutinosité: f. *Glutinositie, glewinesse, clamminesse.*
Gluy. *as* Gluïts; *Straw.*
Glyphonoire: m. *as* Clifoire; *A Plaisterers bosse:* ¶Rab.
Goache. perdrix g. *The gray Partridge.*
Goalon. *A slouen; one that weares his clothes vnhandsomely, or puts them on carelesly; so tearmed about* Blois.
Gob. l'avalla tout de gob. *At one gulpe, or, as one gobbet, he swallowed it.*
Gobeau: m. *A bit, gobbet, or morsell; also, a violl, or strait-mouthed vessell(of glasse;) also, a Maser, or great Goblet.*
Gobelet: m. *A Goblet, Bole, or wide-mouthed cup to drinke in; also, the flower Crowfoot, Gold-knap, Yellow Craw.*
Le gobelet du gland. *The head, shell, or cup of an Acorne.*
Le gobelet d'vne Rose. *The bud of a Rose when it is almost full-blowne; or(more properly)the fiue-leaued Cup, or buske thereof; called, by some, the fiue brothers of the Rose.*
Le retraict du Gobelet. *The Butterie, or Winesellar.*
Gobelets. des gobelets. *Crowfoot, Gold-knap, yellow Craw, Butter-flower.*
Gobelin: m. *A Goblin, Hob-goblin, Robin-good-fellow, Bug.*
Gobelin. face gobeline. *A crimzon face; the visage of a plie-pot.*
Gobeliner. *To play the Goblin; to rumble, or make a horrible noise, like a Goblin.*
Gobe-mouche. *as* Moineau de haye.
Gobequinaut: m. *A greedie feeder, a rauenous, and ouglie deuourer; one that makes bricke-walls of his chaps, or hastily swallowes whole, and vnchawed gobbets.*
Gober. *To rauine, deuoure; feed greedily, swallow great morsells, let downe whole gobbets.*
Gobe quinault. *Sup her vp tis cold ynough, downe with it whoresonne.*
Goberge: f. *A kind of Haddocke, or Cod-fish.*
Goberger. *To cast, vomit, spue.*
Gobier. chant gobier. *Plaine, homelie, ordinarie, without Art.*
Gobisson: m. *A fashion of long, and quilted horsemans cassocke, or coat, vsed in old time.*
Gocourt. *as* Court; *Short:* ¶Rab. (v.m.)
Godal: m. *A tit, a iade:* ¶Norm.
Godde. vne lasche godde. *A sloathfull hylding.*
Goddon: m. *A filthie glutton, or swiller; one that hath a vile wide swallow.*
Gode. *as* Godde.
Godeau: m. *A Gardeners setting yron.*
En godeau. *Right downward; (a Gardeners tearme.)*
Godeluré: m. ée: f. *Fumbled, crumpled, ruffled.*
Godelureau: m. *A gull, fop, asse, coxcombe; a proud woodcocke.*
Godemare. *The disease called, the Night-mare; also, a sound made, or word cast out, at a feast, whereby the guests are warned to forbeare eating for a certain time; (This* Godemare *was a King of* Bourgongne, *so redoubted by the French, that th'onely sound of his name astonied them, & made them desist from that they were in hand with: yet was he at length surprised by* Clotaire *in* Autun, *and the terrour of his name turned into a ieast.)*
Godemiche: f. *A Dildoe.*
Goderon: m. *The set of a (single) ruffe, after the Spanish (or plaine) fashion; also, the setting thereof; also, a ruffe so set; also, as* Godran; *also, a fashion of imbossement vsed by Goldsmithes, &c, and tearmed knurling.*
Goderon de beau langage. *affectation in speech, the trimming of the tongue, with quaint phrases, choyce tearmes, &c.*
`A goderons. *Wrought with knurles.*
Goderonné: m. ée: f. *Set, as a ruffe; pitched, or tighted, as a ship; also, knurled, wrought or set with knurles.*
Oeufs goderonnez. *Whose white, and yolke are beaten together with a little veriuice.*
Goderonner. *To set, a ruffe; to pitch or tight a ship; to worke, or set with knurles.*
Godet: m. *An earthen Bole; a stone Cup, or Jug.*
Godichon. mon godichon. *My pillocke.*
Godillon: m. *A girle:* ¶Poictevin.
Godin: m. ine: f. *Neat, fine, trimme, spruce, comelie, proper, handsome.*
Godinet: m. ette: f. *Prettie, dapper, feat, peart, indifferently handsome.*
Godinette: f. *A prettie peart lasse; a louing, or louelie girle.*
Godiveaux. *See* Goudiveaux.
Godran: m. *Ship-pitch; or, the Pitch (and Tarre) wherwith ships are tighted, or trimmed.*
Godron. *See* Goderon.
Godronné: m. ée: f. *as* Goderonné.
Godronner vne fraise. *To set a ruffe.*
Goerin. *as* Gorret.
Goés. *The name of a kind of Grapes.*
Goëtie: f. *The Blacke Art, diuellish Magicke, or Witchcraft.*
Goffe: com. *Dull, sottish, doltish, lumpish, blockish, heauie headed, grosse-witted, sodden-brained.*
Goffre: f. *A wafer; also a honnie combe; also a kinde of scurfe, like to the ordinarie one, but that the humor it yeelds is more like, in colour, to honie.*
Gogaille. *(A cheerefull, or cheering word, much like our) frolick.*
Gogayer. *as* Goguer.

Gogo. à gogo. *With full contentment, or his bellie full.*

Gogue: f. *A sheepes paunch; and thence, a baggas made of good hearbs, chopt lard, spices, egges, and cheese; the which incorporated, and moistened with the warme bloud of the (new-killed) beast, are put into her paunch, and sodden with other meat.*

Gogues. *Jollitie, glee, ioyfulnesse, lightheartednesse; and hence;*

Estre en ses gogues. *To be frolick, lustie, liuelie, wanton, gamesome; all-a-hoight, in a pleasant humor, in a veine of mirth, or in a merrie mood.*

Goguelu: m. uë: f. *Proud, cocket, scornefull, braggard, vaineglorious; that takes more state vpon him then becomes him.*

Goguelureau. *A proud coxcombe; one thats of no worth at all, how well soeuer he thinke of himselfe.*

Goguenarder. *To buffonize it; breake ieasts, tell merrie tales.*

Goguenelle: f. *A fained title, or tearme, for a wench; like our Gixie, Callet, Minx, &c.*

se Goguer. *To be most frolicke, liuelie, blithe, cranke, merrie; to take his pleasure, sport at ease, make good cheere, set cocke-a-hoope, throw the house out at windowes; enioy all wished delights, or affected contentments.*

Goguette. *A small sheepes baggas; (made, as before, in* Gogue; *) also, a kind of blackish, and short-tailed Cherrie.*

Auoir vne femme en ses goguettes. *To haue his full pleasure of a woman.*

Estre en ses goguettes. *as* Estre en ses gogues; *or to be set vpon the merrie pinne.*

Gohée: f. *A welcome, ioyfull salutation, or heartie intertainment at meeting:* ¶Norm.

Goiart: m. *A long hedging bill, or hooke; a Welsh hooke.*

Goibier: m. ere: f. *Baker-legd; also, splay-footed, shailing, ill-fauouredly treading.*

Goie: f. *A little hand-bill, hedging hooke, or hedging knife.*

Goiffon: m. *A Gudgeon:* ¶Lionnois.

Goilant: m. *A certaine white Sea-fowle as big as a Pigeon, which when tempests approach flies vp vnto fresh waters.*

Goildronneur. *A pitcher, trimmer, or tighter of ships.*

Goimpre. *as* Goinfre.

Goinfre: m. *A wag, slipstring, knauish lad; a merrie conceited whoresonne, a notable good fellow, an excellent companion.*

Goiran. *as* Bondrée; *A kind of short-winged Eagle, that liues altogether on fish.*

Goitre: f. *A Wenne; a swelling, bunch, or lumpe of flesh vnder the throat; verie common among those which dwell about the Alpes, because they vse to drinke much cold, and vnwholesome water.*

Goitreux: m. euse: f. *Full of Wennes; or hauing a Wen vnder the throat.*

Goitrons: m. *Waddles, or wattles; the two little, and long excrescences, which hang, teat-like, at either side of the throat of some hogs; also, the wennie bags that breed vnder the throats of the most inhabitants of the Alpes, by reason of their continuall drinking of water.*

Goiveau. Il fait goi. *It is deawie; (a rusticall word.)*

Golette de maille. *as* Holette.

Golfe: m. *A gulfe, whirlepoole, or bottomelesse pit; also, a bosome, or gulfe of the sea betweene two Capes, or high lands.*

Gomar: m. le gom. d'vn Boulengier, ou Pastissier. *A kneading table; the boord whereon they worke their bread, or make their pies.*

Gomene. *as* Gumene.

Gomir. *To vomit, cast, spue.* (v m.)

Gomissement: m. *A vomiting, casting, spuing.*

Gomme: m. *Gumme.*

Gomme Arabic. *Gumme Arabicke; comes from the shrub* Acacia, *the Ægyptian thorne.*

Gomme Elemmy. *Seeke* Elemy.

Gommé: m. ée: f. *Gummed; stiffened, thickened, mixed, or seasoned with Gumme.*

Cire gommée. *Wax mingled with Rozen, and Turpentine.*

Gommement: m. *A gumming; a thickening, or stiffening, with Gumme.*

Gommene: f. *See* Gumene.

Gommer. *To gumme; to stiffen, thicken, season, or anoint, with Gumme.*

Gommeux: m. euse: f. *Gummie, full of Gumme, stiffe by gumming, thicke with Gumme.*

Gomorrhean: m. *A Sodomite, a Buggerer.*

Gomphose. *A fastening of one bone within another, as of a nayle, or wedge into a peece of wood; so are the teeth set into the Jaw bone.*

Gonagre. *The Gowt in the knees.*

Gondole: f. *A Gundola, or Venetian wherrie.*

Sa teste se berse en gondole. *His head totters like a boat in a storme.*

Gondolier: m. *A Venetian Wherrie-man.*

Gonds d'vne porte. *The hookes, or hindges of a doore.*

Sortir les gonds. *To grow impatient, fall into extreames, flie out, forget his duetie; proceed with too much violence, or vehemencie.*

Gonesse. *A Village neere vnto Paris, wherein excellent bread is made; and hence;* Pain de Gonesse.

Gonfalonnier. *as* Gonfanonnier.

Gonfanier: m. *An Ensigne, or Standerd-bearer.*

Gonfanon: m. *A little square Flag, or Penon at the end of a Launce; or (more particularly) an old fashioned Banner, or square Standard, borne on the top of a Launce; such as, euen to this day, is vsed in the warres mades by the Pope; and hence;*

Le gonfanon de l'Eglise. *The Generall of the Churches forces (before whom such a Standard is carried.*

Gonfanonnier: m. *A chiefe Standard bearer.*

Gonin. Maistre Gonin. *A notable Jugler, nimble or actiue Tumbler, one thats perfectly seene in trickes or cleanlie conueyances, (and thence) also, a subtile whoresonne, wilie or slie mate, a Maister in craft, or his crafts Master.*

Gonnelle: f. *A whole Petticote; the bodies, and skirts being ioyned together.*

Gonomphe. *A kind of box:* ¶Rab.

Gonorrhée: f. *The running of the reines.*

Gont-fanon. *The royall Standard; (so tearmed in old time) or as* Gonfanon.

Gontier. franc gontier. *A rich Chuffe, good Yeoman, wealthie whoresonne; a substantiall fellow.*

Gorbion: m. *as* Euphorbe.

Gorde. *as* Corde; *A rope.*

Gorgaillet: m. *A Quaile-pipe.*

Gorge: f. *The throat, or gullet, (most properly) the bottome of the mouth; or, the most deepe, and inward part thereof; in a woman, the outward, and vpper part of the breast, betweene the necke and pappes; also, the gorge, or craw of birds; and, a meale, or gorgefull giuen vnto birds (especially Hawkes)*

Gorge droicte. *in Architecture; as* Nasselle.

Gorge renversée. *A gullet reuerst, or an Ogee.*

Gorge-rouge. *A Robin-red-breast.*

Ietter le feu par la gorge. *To fume, chafe, take on extreamely, play terrible reakes.*

Passer le pied sur la gorge à. *Looke* Passer.

Rendre sa gorge. *To cast, vomit, spue.*

Rire soubs gorge. *To laugh in his sleeue.*

Tenir le pied sur la gorge à vn. *To haue one at his mercie, his throat vnder his feet; his necke vnder his girdle.*

Voler sur la gorge. *To exercise, or labour hard, on a full stomacke.*

Gorgé: m. ée: f. *Gorged, crammed, filled with.*

Gorgée de vin. *A gulpe, or swallow; as much wine as one lets downe his throat at once.*

Gorgément. *Vp to the throat.*

Gorger. s'en gorger de viandes. *To gormandize it, or full-gorge himselfe, to eat vntill his bellie cracke.*

Gorgerette: f. *A Gorget, Mocket, Bib, or breastcloth.*

Gorgerin: m. *A Gorget of maile; also, a Carkanet (worne ouerthwart the breast) also, the necke-peece, or coller, of a garment; and somtimes the necke, or throat it selfe; and hence;*

Il est bien vuidé du gorgerin. *He hath a goodlie wide throat, or swallow.*

Gorgerin. *(in Architecture) is a small round member, accompanied with a square one, in the foot, or bottome of the Chapter of a Piller, &c; a small Boultell (with a fillet vnder it) in the Chapter of a Piller, &c.*

Gorgerin: m. ine: f. *Of, or belonging to, the throat.*

Escrouelles gorgerines. *The Kings euill (in the throat.)*

Gorge-rouge. *A Robin-red-breast.*

Gorgette. *A prettie little throat, or mouth.*

Gorgias: m. *as* Gorgerette; *A Gorget.*

Gorgias: m. ase: f. *Gorgeous, gaudie, flaunting, braue, gallant, gay, fine, trimme; quaintly clothed, richly attired, sumptuously apparelled; also, glorying, delighting, or pleased, in brauerie; also, feeding, or balling with mirth.*

Gorgiasement. *Gorgeously, gaudily, gayly, gallantly.*

se Gorgiaser. *To flaunt, braue, or gallantize it; to cut it out of the whole peece; also, to be proud of, or please himselfe in, the brauerie of his apparell.*

Gorgiaseté: f. *Brauerie, gallantnesse, finenesse, trimnesse, gorgeousnesse, gaudinesse.*

Gorme: f. *The thicke humor which young horses void at their narrells, or by the ouerture made vnder their throat; some call it the Strangles.*

Gormette. *as* Gourmette.

Gorre: f. *A Sow; (also, the French Pockes;* ¶Norm.*) also, brauerie, gallantnesse, gorgeousnesse, pompe, magnificence, sumptuousnesse.*

Femmes à la grande gorre. *Huffing or flaunting wenches; costlie or statelie dames.*

Gorreau: m. *as* Gorret; *Also, the thread, or quantitie, of flax, &c, thats drawne, at once, from a distaffe, in spinning.*

Gorrerie: f. *Gallanterie, brauerie, sumptuousnesse in apparell, statelinesse of gesture; also, pride, vaunting, vaineglorie.*

Gorret: m. *A little Sheat, or Barrow-pig.*

Poisson, gorret, & cochin, vie en l'eau & mort en vin: Prov. *(Such flegmaticke meates requiring much wine to be drunke with them.)*

Gorrette: f. *A cap; also, a iustle, iurre; thumpe, or thwacke.*

Gorrier: m. ere: f. *as* Gorgias; *or (more then it) gallant both in apparell, carriage, and gesture; also, proud, braggard, vaunting, vaineglorious.*

Gorrierement. *Brauely, gaudily, gallantly; proudly, vaingloriously.*

Gorron: m.: *A Sheat, or little yong hog.*

Gort: f. *A weare in a running water; or, as* Gourt.

Gosaran. *A necklace, carkanet, border; an ornament for the bosome, or necke.*

Goscoté. *See* Coscoté.

Gosier: m. *The throat; and (most properly) that part of it which makes the head of the Larinx.*

Le mal de gosier. *The Squinancie, or Squinzie:*

Gossampine: f. *The Bumbast, or Cotton-bush; the plant that beares Cotton, or Bumbast.*

Gosse: f. *as* Gousse; *Also, a scoffe, gibe, flowt.*

Gosse d'aulx. *A cloue of Garlicke:*

Gossé: m. ée: f. *Mocked, flowted, scoffed at; boorded with.*

Gosser. *To gibe; deride, mocke, flowt, scoffe at; boord, or ieast with.*

Gosserie: f. *Mockerie, scoffing, flowting, gibing.*

Gosseur: m. *A scoffer, mocker, flowter, giber, ieaster.*

Gotereux. *as* Goitreux.

Gothique: com. *Gothlike; rude, cruell, barbarous.*

Goton: m. *in stead of* Groton; *A little grot.*

Goualon. *as* Goalon.

Gouasche. *A kind of Partridge; as* Goasche.

Goubeau. *as* Gobeau.

Goubelet. *as* Gobelet; *Also, a kind of little round pie resembling our Chuet.*

Goubelettes: f. *Little vessells of tinne made like goblets, but without feet; vsed by Juglers, & Inchaunters.*

Gouber: m. *An aunders-meat, or afternoones repast.*

Goude: f. *A Marigold.*

Goudeau. *as* Godeau.

Planter au goudeau. *as* Planter à la barre; *See* Barre.

Goud-fallot. *A boone companion, a good fellow:* ¶Rab.

Goudiveau: m. *A kind of open Pie, made of minced veale, butter, hearbs, and spice, baked together, and afterwards hard yolks of egs put on the top of it; also, a figure in caruing, like that pie; or, a long painted Ouall.*

Goudronné: m. ée: f. *Set (stiffe) as a ruffe; also, pitched, or tighted, as a ship; See* Goderonné.

Goudronner. *To set a ruffe; also, to pitch, trimme, or tight a ship: See* Goderonner.

Goueastre: m. *as* Goitreux; *That hath a wen, bunch, or swelling, vnder his throat.*

Gouest. *The name of a fruitfull vine, whose wood is of a tawnie colour.*

Gouët: m. *A kind of little short knife, wherewith in France the boyes cracke nuts, and pill greene wallnuts; a little cut-purse knife.*

Gouët. faulcon gouët; *whose feathers are ill marked, mailed, or coloured; we call such a one, a dropt Hawke.*

Gouffre: m. *A gulfe; whirlepoole, deepe hole, or vnmeasurable depth (of waters) that swallowes vp whatsoeuer approaches, or comes into, it.*

Vn gouffre d'argent. *A most vnsatiable swallow-wealth, wast-coyne, spend-good.*
Gouffreux: m. euse: f. *Gulfie, full of gulfes; infinitely deepe; (vnsatiably) deuouring, or swallowing vp whatsoeuer approaches, or comes into, it.*
Gouge. *as* Vouge; *Also a Ioyners Googe; also, a Souldiors Pug, or Punke; a Whore that followes the Camp; also, the Hammer wherewith trees are marked in the King Forrests.*
Gouhourde: f. *A Gourd.*
Goujar. *A Gudgeon.*
Goujar de mer. *The Sand-eele, or Sea-Gudgeon.*
Goujat: m. *A Souldiors boy.*
Goujataille: f. *A troupe of Souldiors boyes; a crue of crackropes, a knot of slipstrings.*
Goujate: f. *A Souldiors wench; as* Gouge.
Goujaterie: f. la g. *Souldiors boyes, or the young rakehells that follow a Campe.*
Gouillarder; &, Gouillardise. *as* Goularder; &, Goulardise: ¶Savoyard.
Gouillart. *as* Goulard; *A glutton, or greedie-gut.*
Gouinfre: m. *A mad-cap, merrie grig, pleasant knaue, conceited whoresonne.*
Goujon: m. *A Gudgeon-fish; also, the pinne which the truckle of a pullie runneth on; also, the Gudgeon of the Spindle of a wheele; any Gudgeon.*
Govions: m. *Shackles, or fetters, for prisoners.*
Gouïr. *as* Iouïr. *To enioy:* ¶Pic.
Gouju: m. uë: f. *Full-cheeked, plump-faced, chuffie, or puft vp in the face.*
Goulard: m. *A rauenor, deuourer, swallower, gully-gut, greedie feeder.*
Goulard: m. arde: f. *Rauenous, greedie, deuouring, that hath a great swallow.*
Goulardé: m. ée: f. *Eaten greedily, deuoured hastily, gulped, or goggled downe.*
Goularder. *To eat greedily, feed hastily, deuoure extreamely; to rauine, goggle, glut vp, swallow downe, huge morsells, or mouthfulls.*
Goulardise: f. *A rauening, deuouring, hastie or greedie feeding.*
Gouldron. *as* Goultran; *also, as* Gouderon.
Gouldronné: m. ée: f. *Pitched, or tighted, as a ship; or, as* Gouderonné.
Gouldronner. *as* Gouderonner.
Goulée: f. *A throatfull, or mouthfull of &c.*
Elle n'en peut finer sinon à la goulée. *She can get but a snatch and away; there is no lying for her at rack and manger; See* Goullée.
Gouléeur. *as* Arpenteur; *or, as* Gauleur; *A Surueyor of land, that measures onely by the Pole.*
Goulet: m. *A gullet; the end of a Conduit pipe whereat it dischargeth it selfe; also, the mouth, or necke of a Violl, Bottle, or other long, and narrow-neckt Vessell; also, the hole, or earth of a Fox, or Badger; also, a narrow brooke, or deepe gutter of water.*
Goulet de cheminée. *The funnell, or tunnell of a chimney.*
Goulet de fenestre. *A narrow loopehole, or long Crannie, in the wall of a Prison, &c, such a one (especially) as hath a round, or is widest, in the middle.*
Goulette de vin. *A gulpe, mouthfull, or small quantitie of wine.*
Goulfe. *See* Golfe.
Goulfi: m. ie: f. *Swollen, or puft vp; full, plumpe, fat, well-fed.*
Goulfre. *as* Gouffre.
Goullardise. *as* Goulardise; *Also, ribaldrie; licentious, or dissolute tattle.*
Goullée. à la g. *Priuily, secretly, by stealth; or, as in* Goulée.
Goulot: m. *The pipe of a sinke, or gutter.*
Goultran: m. *Ship-pitch.*
Goulu: m. uë: f. *Gluttonous, greedie, rauenous, deuouring, vnsatiate, swallowing vp.*
Gouluëment. *Greedily, gluttonously, rauenously, like a gully-gut.*
Gouphon: m. *The hindge of a doore, window, &c;* ¶Langued.
Goupil: m. *A Fox.* (v.m.)
'A goupil endormy rien ne tombe en la gueule: Prov. *He that knowes what's fit to be done, and vses to sleepe when it should be done, liues a beast, and dies a begger.*
Goupille: f. *The yron pinne that goes through the ioynt of a hindge, or haspe of a claspe.*
Goupillon. *as* Guepillon; *An holie-water sprinkle; also, the brush of bristles wherewith glasses, &c, be rinched; also, as* Toupillon; *a stopple; also, a yong, or little Fox; whence;*
Faire le goupillon. *To play the Truant.*
Gourat. *for* Goujat.
Gourd: m. *as* Gourt; *or, A whirlepoole; or deepe (and long) hole in a riuer, or other water; also, as* Gourgue.
Gourd: m. de: f. *Numme, astonied, asleepe, stiffe, sencelesse, benummed, as the hands with much cold; also, drousie, slow, dull, heauie, lumpish.*
Gourd-foulement: m. *A crushing, or bruising; a mortifying, by violent handling.*
Gourdi. *Numme, benummed, astonied, stonnied (by coldnesse.)*
se Gourdir. *To be numme, sencelesse, astonied, stonnied, (by the extremitie of cold.)*
Gouret. *as* Gorret; *A Sheat, or Barrow big.*
Gourfoulé: m. ée: f. *Crushed, bruised; mortified, by violent handling, &c.*
Gourfoulement. *as* Gourd-foulement.
Gourfouler. *To crush, or bruise; to mortifie, by a violent handling, &c.*
Gourgias. *as* Gorgias; *Also, proud, loftie, statelie, standing on his pantofles:* ¶Rab.
Gourgue de moulin: f. *The Conduit of a water-mill; the water-course, or ditch, that is directly vnder the wheele.*
Gournade: f. *A cuffe on the mouth, a pash on the nose.*
Gourmand: m. *A glutton, gormand, bellie-god, greedie-gut; a great eater, monstrous feeder, gully-gut.*
Gourmandant. *Gluttonizing, or gormandizing; also, proudly brauing, taunting, misusing.*
Gourmander. *To rauine, deuoure, glut, gormandize, or gluttonize it; swill vp, swallow downe greedily; also, proudly to domineere, insult, or crow ouer; insolently to taunt, checke, take vp; imperiously to curbe; misuse, abuse.*
Gourmanderesse. *A gluttonnesse.*
Gourmandeur: m. *A glutton; (a word whereby* Rabelais *meanes, and describes, a Cannon of a Cathedrall Church.)*
Gourmandise: f. *Gluttonie, gormandizing; deuouring, rauining; excessiue eating, immoderate feeding.*

Gourmandise tue plus de gens qu'espée en guerre trenchant: Prov. *More are killed by surfeting then by the sword.*

Gourme: f. *The Strangles; the thicke humor which young horses void at their narells; also, foame, or a foamie slime.*

Gourmé: m. ée: f. *Curbed; also, cuffed on the mouth, pashed on the nose, or face; also, purged from slime, or foame.*

Gourmer. *To curbe (a horse;) also, to knocke, buffet, pommell, cuffe, pash on the mouth, or face.*

Se gourmer. *To void his slime, to purge his foame.*

Gourmet: m. *A Wine-cunner; a Wine-marchants Broker; one whom he trusts with the watching, and imployes in the venting, of his new-come commodities.*

Gourmeter. *To curbe.*

Gourmette: f. *A curbe.*

Tenir en gourmette. *To curbe, or keepe in awe.*

Gourmetté: m. ée: f. *Curbed.*

Gourmetter. *To curbe.*

Gournauld: m. *A Gurnard fish.*

Gournay. *The name of a towne in Normandie.*

Vous avez passé sur le pont de Gournay. *You are without care, shame, or feare; you dare doe any obscene thing openly.*

Gourneau. *A Gurnard.*

Gourré. *Beguiled, cheated, cousened, conie-caught:* ¶Barr.

Gourrier. *as* Gourgias; *or, as* Gorrier.

Gourt: m. *A violent streame, or gulfe of waters; or, a whirlepoole, or deepe hole in a water.*

Gousse: f. *The huske, swad, cod, hull of beanes, pease, &c.*

Gousse d' aulx. *A head of Garlicke.*

Goussé: m. ée: f. *Deuoured, rauined, eaten; stuffed with eating.*

Goussepillé: m. ée: f. *Shaken, or tugged, as a Cat by a Dog; also, vnhusked, shaled, vncased, stripped.*

Goussepiller. *To shake, or tug, as a Dog doth a Cat, &c; also, (and most properly) to vnshale, or take pulse out of the swads; and hence, to strip, or vncase.*

Gousser. *To eat, rauine, deuoure; to stuffe, or fill with meat.*

Gousset: m. *A Gusset; the peece of Armour, or of a shirt, whereby the armehole is couered; also, a Bracket in Joyners worke.*

Goussu: m. uë: f. *Coddie, hullie, huskie, swaddie.*

Goust: m. *The tast; also, a smacke, or sauor; also, a good conceit, or liking, vpon the first essay, of a thing; also, a little skill, insight, or experience in a matter; also, as* Esgoust; *or th'end of a gutter whence the raine falls, in drops, from a house.*

En cela est le goust de la noix. *Looke* Noix.

Gousté: m. ée: f. *Tasted; sauored, smacked; essayed; touched vpon; felt, or conceiued a little; disgested indifferently; admitted of; wherein some insight, or experience is had.*

Gouster: m. *A nunchion, drinking, aunders-meat, afternoones-collation, mouthes-recreation.*

Gouster. *To tast, or take an essay of; to tast, sauor; touch vpon; feele, or conceiue a little; also, to admit of, disgest indifferently, take a liking to, begin to affect, or fancie; also, to haue some experience, a little insight, meane knowledge, in.*

Goute: f. *as* Goutte.

Gouté: m. ée: f. *Gowtie, or troubled with the gowt.*

Goutran: m. *Ship-pitch; or Pitch wherewith ships are tighted.*

Goutte: f. *A drop of water, &c; also, a little, a iot, a whit, a verie small deale.*

La mere goutte. *Vnpressed wine, or oyle; that which of it selfe, and without pressing, comes from the grapes or Oliues, as soone as they are settled in the Presse-trough.*

Goutte à goutte. *By little and little, by degrees, drop after drop, or, one drop after another; and hence;*

Goutte à goutte on emplit la Cuve: &, goutte à goutte la mer s'esgoutte: Prov.

Boire la goutte sur l' ongle. *To leaue emptie bowls, make cleane cups; drinke vp all but so much as will stand on the drinkers nayle.*

Ie n'y voy ny grain ny goutte. *I see it not a whit, I discerne it not a iot; I perceiue, or conceiue it not at all.*

Dieu garde mal qui voit bien, & n'oit goutte. *For my part, I am loath to conceiue it, though I see it, well ynough.*

Il est bien povre qu' ne voit goutte: Prov. *Hee's verie poore that wants his eye-sight.*

Goutte: f. *The Gowt.*

Goutte crampe ou, crappe. *The Crampe; or, a Conuulsion.*

Goutte de lin. *The weed called Dodder; See* Lin.

Goutte maurequine. *as* Goutte serene.

Goutte nouée. *The Gowt in any of the ioynts.*

Goutte serene. *Blindnesse, or extreame dimnesse of sight, caused by the obturation of the Opticke Sinewes.*

Goutte Sciatique. *The Sciatica; a pain, ache, or stitch in the hippes.*

La goutte en la hanche, la fille en la pance: Pro. *Looke* Fille.

`A la goutte le medecin ne voit goutte: Prov. *(As they find (by the little helpe they find) that haue it, and take Physick for it.)*

Goutteron: m. *A Violl, or Cruet wherein Oyle, or Vinegar is serued to the table; also, a small Ewer, or Lauer; also, a little drop.*

Goutte-rose. *An extreame rednesse of the face; pimpled, and set thicke with rubies, or fierie speckles.*

Goutteux: m. euse: f. *Gowtie, full of the Gowt.*

Gouttiere: f. *A gutter; a channell.*

Gouttieres. *The little furrowes that runne along the head, or hornes of a red Deere.*

Bonnets à quatre gouttieres. *Foure-cornered, or square, caps.*

Gouttreuse. *A certain white, long-beaked, and tonglesse bird, that hath a great red pouch hanging from her neather beake to her breast; otherwise (in bignesse, and shape) somewhat resembling a Swanne.*

Gouvernail: m. *The rudder, or sterne of a ship.*

Gouvernal. *The same.*

Gouvernant. *Gouerning, ruling, swaying, maistering; ordering, ouerseeing; tempering, moderating.*

Gouvernante: f. *A Gouernesse, a Commaundresse.*

Gouverné: m. ée: f. *Gouerned, ruled, cōmanded, swaied, maistered; ordered, ouerseene; tempered, moderated; also, intertained with talke, held with discourse.*

Gouvernement. *The rule, gouernment, command, absolute sway of; a power, empire, dominion, regiment, authoritie, seigneurie ouer; also, a gouerning, ruling, commanding, maistering; full order in, totall conduction, whole dierction of.*

Le faict, & gouvernement d'une republique. *The policie, or course of proceeding in State-matters; the managing of publicke businesse in a countrey.*

Gouverner. *To gouerne, rule, commaund, maister, sway; ouersee; to seignorize, or haue authoritie, ouer; also, to guide, order, direct, conduct, looke vnto, haue the charge of; also, to temper, moderate, restraine; also, to intertaine with discourse.*

Qui gouverne bien la bouche. *That is a temperate feeder.*

Qui gouverne bien son cas. *One that lookes well to his businesse.*

Ie le gouvernay teste à teste environ vne bonne heure. *I conuersed with him hand to hand; I held him chat, or in discourse, I intertained him with talke, an houre together.*

Celuy gouverne bien mal le miel qui n'en taste: Prov. *Hee's but an ill cooke that licks not his owne fingers; Looke* Miel.

Gouverneresse: f. *as* Gouvernante.

Gouverneur: m. *A Ruler, Gouernour, Commaunder, Ouerseer.*

Gouvert. *as* Gouvernement.

Gouytrouz. *as* Goitrons; *Swines wadles.* ¶Rab.

Goy: m. *A little hand-bill, Vine-hooke, or Vine-knife.*

Goyart. *A long hedging bill, or Welsh hooke.*

Goye: f. *Ioy.* ¶Pic. *also, as* Goy.

Goyelle: f. *A kind of Cheese-cake; as* Talmouse. ¶Pic.

Goyon. *A Gudgeon.*

Gozal: m. *A sitting Pigeon.* ¶Rab.

Grabat: m. *A poore mans bed; a course Mattresse, a Straw-bed; also, a Couche.*

Grabeau: m. *A garbelling of spices, &c; (hence) also, a curious examination, neere sifting of, precise search into, matters.*

Grabellé: m. ée: f. *Garbelled; also, neerely examined, precisely sifted, narrowly looked, curiously searched, into.*

Grabeller. *To garbell spices &c; (and hence) also, to examine precisely, sift neerely, looke narrowly, search curiously, into.*

Grabué. *An Ironicall allusion to* Gradué; *a Graduate.*

Grabuge: f. *A great coyle, stirre, garboyle, turmoyle, hurlyburly.*

Grabuger. *To keepe a foule coyle; to make a great stirre, or monstrous hurlyburly.*

Grace: f. *Grace, fauour, good will, good liking, good opinion; credit, reckoning, reputation; also, beautie, seemelinesse, comelinesse, handsomenesse; a Decorum; a grace in, or becomming of; also, vertue, honestie, integritie; a good disposition, an inclination vnto goodnesse; also, a pardon, forgiuenesse, remission; dispensation; (In old time the Licence procured by Gentlemen for* Roturiers *to buy their* Fiefs, *(when they wanted money to follow the warres) was also tearmed* Grace.)

Graces (Plurall.) *Thanks.*

Grace de Sainct Canart. *The bestowing of a thing which the bestower cannot keepe; or, a fauour done because one cannot doe withall.*

Grace de Sainct Paul. *A certaine little stone thats good against the biting, and stinging of venomous beasts (as the Coseners say that would sell it.)*

Bonne grace. *as* Bonne-grace; *also, a Snufkin, or Muffe.*

Lettres de grace. *Are, generally, such as proceed from the meere grace, liberalitie, bountie, or goodnesse of the Prince; and which he may refuse without violation of common right, or of the Lawes; as Pardons, Remissions, Gifts, Graunts, Dispensations, Priuiledges, Patents of Offices, Warrants for money, &c; more particularly, a Pardon for Murther, Manslaughter, or of a person condemned for an offence, which the Law, of it selfe, cannot dispence with; (in which sence, this word* grace *is also generall, both to Remission, and Pardon, sayth* Rageau; *though another make it a* species *vnto Remission;) And this Pardon is to be procured from the King himselfe, and in the highest Court of Chancerie.*

Moines de grace. *An Order of white Monkes, which weare on their breasts a great red Crosse.*

Avec grace. *Gracefully, decently, pleasingly, plausibly, with a good fashion, in comelie sort, after a handsome manner.*

De grace. *Of courtesie, I pray you heartily, I beseech you sir.*

Pour grace. *The same.*

N'aurois-ie bonne grace de? *Would it not become me well to?*

Graces: f. *The three Graces;* viz. Aglaia, Thalia, *and* Euphrosine, *reputed the daughters of* Iupiter *and* Venus, *and adored as Goddesses, by the auncient Painims; whence;*

Il a besoing de sacrifier aux Graces. *He is a harsh, vnpleasant, rough-hewed, currish, or churlish, fellow.*

Grachinoier. *as* Grafigner.

Gracieusement. *as* Gratieusement.

Gracieuseté: f. *Graciousnesse, fauourablenesse; affabilitie, courtesie; humanitie, benignitie, gentlenesse; also, as* Gratuité.

Gracieux: m. euse: f. *Gracious; gentle, affable, courteous, benigne, plausible, debonaire; See* Gratieux.

Gracieux seigneur. *A skalelesse fish, of a long forme, euer cleauing vnto Rockes, and so daintie, and seldome found, that countrey people hold him a fit present for their Landlords.*

Gradation: f. *A Gradation, step, degree, stayre.*

Grade: f. *A degree, state, or dignitie; aduancement vnto greatnesse; a step, stayre, greese.*

Gradé: m. ée: f. *Graduate, or hauing taken a degree.*

Gradot: m. *A Gurnard.*

Gradué. *A Graduate; one that hath taken a degree in an Vniuersitie.*

Gradué: m. ée: f. *Graduated, hauing taken a degree.*

Homme non gradué. *(Opposed vnto,* Homme marié) *a single, or vnmarried man.*

Graduel. *A Masse-booke, or part of the Masse, inuented by Pope* Celestine *in the yeare* 430.

Graduellement. *Gradually, by degrees, orderly, step after step, from hand to hand.*

Grafigner. *To scratch, or scrape; to rend, or teare vp with the nayles.*

Graffe. Griffe graffe. *By hooke or by crooke, scamblingly, catch that catch may, any way.*

Graffions. *In old time the Lieutenants of Earles were, now a kind of the best sweet Cherries are, called so.*

Graier: m. *The Officer that gathers the Kings right of* Grarie *in woods, and forrests.*

Graigneur. *as* Greigneur; *Greater.* ¶Norm.

Graillant. *as* Grailleux.

Graillat: m. *A Rooke, or white-bild Crow.*

Graille: f. *The same.*

Graille: com. *as* Gresle; *Slender.*

Grailler. *To winde a Horne hollowly; to blurre a Trumpet; to speake hoarsely, or with a broken voice; to sing harshly,*

harshly, vntuneably; to croake, or cry like a Rooke.

Grailleux: m. euse: f. *Speaking hoarsely, sounding hollowly, or harshly; blurring; ratling in the throat; croaking like a Rooke.*

Grain: m. *Graine, corne; seed; also, a graine, or bitt of salt, sand, &c; a Moat; (and hence, a little, iot, whit;) also, the kernell, or little stone of a Grape, or other Berrie; also, a Grape; also, a Barlie-corne, or the fourth part of an ynch, in measures; also, a graine, or the foure and twentieth part of a pennie-weight; (also, a whirlewind, or storme of wind, at sea.* ¶Norm.)

Grain bernage. *The peculiar corne of one countrey; or corne that grew on a mans owne land, or in his owne soyle; also, Messelin; or, Wheat, Rie, and Barlie mingled together.*

Grains de ladrige. *Spots of leaprosie; mezild spots.*

Grain de sel. *A graine of salt*; Vn gros grain de sel. *A great ball, or stone, of salt.*

Grain de Turquie. *Turkie corne, Turkie wheat, Indian wheat, Mays.*

Grain sur bord. *Scant, or hard-stricken measure of corne, salt, &c.*

'A grain d'orge. *In a triangular forme.*

Ie n'en ay grain, ne goutte; &, Ie n'y voy ny grain, ny goutte. *I neither haue a iot, nor see a drop, of it.*

Il y a plus de paille que de grain. *There is more trash then good stuffe to be had.*

Ioyeux comme fourmis en grain. *As merrie as an Ant on a Corne-heape.*

Iamais grain ne fructifie si premier ne se mortifie: Prov. *Seed neuer comes to fructifie vntill it first haue mortified.*

Nul grain sans paille: Prov. *No corne without straw (or chaffe;) good and bad are commonly together.*

Tel grain tel pain: Prov. *Looke* Pain.

Vin de grain est plus doux que n'est pas Vin de presse: Prov. *The first Wine is better then the second expression; good offices willingly done are of much more worth then such as be extorted.*

Vn sac percé ne peut tenir le grain: Prov. *A sacke thats full of holes can hold no corne.*

Grainant. *Seeding, running to seed.*

Graine: f. *The seed of hearbes, &c; also, graine, wherewith cloth is dyed in graine; Scarlet dye, Scarlet in graine; whence;*

Graine d'escarlate. *as in* Chermes.

Graine de Paradis; *Graines of Paradise; or, the spice which we call, Graines.*

Graine de perroquet. *Wild Saffron, bastard Saffron, mocke Saffron, Saffron dort.*

Graine des vers. *as* Mort aux vers.

Laisser vne fille flestrir pour graine. *To keepe a maid long without a husband; of such a one may be sayd, she is let runne to seed, as well as of hearbes vngathered, for that onely purpose*; Garder vne fille à graine, ou grenie, *hath the same meaning.*

Grainé: m. ée: f. *Seeded, runne vnto seed.*

Grainer. *To seed; or, to runne vnto seed.*

Temps de grainer. *The season of laying Swine; the time wherein they are driuen into forrests, and woods, for Mastage, and other feeding.*

Grairie. *as* Grarie.

Grais: m. *A kind of Potters clay, or earth, fit to make vessels of; also, a hard, and sparkling-browne free stone; as* Grez; *also, the name of a certaine vine that hath a verie big stocke.*

Graisle: com. *as* Gresle.

Graisleté. *as* Gresleté.

Graissayer. *To lispe.*

Graisse: f. *Fat, seame, grease.*

De haute graisse. *Full, plumpe, goodlie, fat, well-fed, in good liking.*

Il n'y a pas grande graisse. *There is not much good to be done, wealth to be had, profit to be gotten, gaine to be made.*

Graissé: m. ée: f. *Greased, annointed, or smeared with fat.*

se Graisse-fondre. *To swelt, swelter, founder.*

Graissement. *Fatly, grossely, greasily.*

Graisser. *To grease; to annoynt, or smeare with fat.*

Graisset: m. *The little (venomous) greene frog, or toad.*

Graisseure: f. *Fattinesse, greasinesse, greasing.*

Graisseux: m. euse: f. *Fattie, greasie, full of grease.*

Graissier: m. *One that loues fat things; also, a Grasier, or fattener of cattell.*

Graissin: m. *Fat mould, or dung to manure ground with.*

Graller. *To parch, as Pease, Nuts, &c.* ¶Blesien.

Grame, ou Gramen. *Couch-grasse, Quitch-grasse, Dogs-grasse; also, any kind of grasse; and hence;*

Grame de Manne. *Manna-grasse, Deaw-grasse, (whose seed the Hollanders eat, as we doe Oatmeale.)*

Grame de Parnasse. *Pernassus grasse, white Liuerwort.*

Grame piquant. *Pricking, or sharpe Dogs-grasse.*

Grainigne. *Couch-grasse, Quitch-grasse, Dogs-grasse.*

Grammaire: f. *Grammer; the Art of Grammer.*

Grammairien: m. *A Grammarian; a Professor of Grammer.*

Grammatical: m. ale: f. *Grammaticall; of, or belonging vnto, Grammer.*

Gramment. *as* Grandement; *Greatly.* (v.m.)

N'a pas gramment. *It is not long agoe.*

Gramouse: f. *A dish made of slices of cold meat fryed with Hogs seame, and serued vp in sauce of beaten eggs, and veriuice boyled, a while, in a little of the broth wherein the meat was sodden.*

Grampé: m. ée: f. *Taken with the Crampe; or, not able to stirre, as one that hath the Crampe.*

Grampelle: f. *The sea-Crab tearmed, a Grampell, Grit, and Pungar.*

Granche: f. *as* Grange; *also, the Carkasse of a fowle.*

Grand: m. Le grand des biens, ou de la terre; *the whole (masse of) substance, or inheritance, thats to be parted among Coheires.* ¶Breton.

Grand: m. grande: f. *Great; big, large; huge; mightie; substantiall; also, high, loftie, statelie.*

Le grand bras. *The whole arme and hand together.*

Grands iours. *A generall, and extraordinarie Sessions called by Commission, or Letters Patents, from the King, (most commonly) after a warre, ciuile broyle, or Insurrection, whereby the course of Law, and proceedings of Iustice haue beene impeached; Looke* Iour.

Grand d'oye. *Good store, a great deale, abundance, numbers of.*

La grande piece. *Looke* Piece.

Le grand vendredi. *Good Friday.*

On a veu d'aussi grand vent venter; *We haue heard as big words as these without trembling; or, little ynough hath beene seene to come of as great words; a Mountaine hath beene brought to bed of a Mouse ere now.*

Grand bandon fait grand larron: Prov. *Great libertie makes great theeues.*

Grand bien ne vient pas en peu d'heure: Pro. *Rome*

Rome was not built on a day.

Grand debonnaireté a maintes hommes greué: Prov. *Many haue ru'd their great courtesie.*

Grande moisson l'obeissant recueille: Prov. *Great is the gaine of those that are obedient.*

Le grand bœuf apprend à labourer au petit: Prov. *The old Ox learnes the young to draw.*

Les grands bœufs ne font pas les grandes iournées: Prov. *The greatest Ox rids not most worke.*

Le plus grand est le premier poutry: Prov. *The greatest is the soonest rotten.*

'A grand cheval grand gué: Prov. *A tall horse can make shift with a deepe foord; or, what needes a tall horse for a shallow foord?*

'A grand danger grand courage: Prov. *Great dangers are by courage great orecome; or, much danger needs much courage.*

'A grand homme grand verre: Prov. *A little glasse befits not a great gulch.*

'A grand pecheur esclandre: Prov. *Great shame is the great sinners meed.*

'A grand pescheur eschappe anguille: Pro. *An Eele escapes from th' expert Angler.*

Aux grands est deu grand honneur: Prov. *Great reuerence is due vnto great persons.*

Aux grands honneurs grands envieux: Prov. *Enuie the companion of honour.*

De grande maladie vient on bien en grande santé: Prov. *Sound health comes after sore diseases.*

De grand peché grand pardon: Prov. *A gracious pardon for a foule offence.*

De grand train sur l'estrain: Prov. *Looke* Estrain.

De grands vanteurs petis faiseurs: Prov. *Great braggers little doers.*

De grand vilain grand flac: Prov. *A great offendor merits a great fall; or, a noysome knaue deserues a noysome knocke; or;*

De grand vilain lourde cheute. *A great offendor hath a grieuous fall.*

En grand fardeau n'est pas l'acquest: Prov. *Hee gaines not most that carries most; not weight but worth, not greatnesse but goodnesse, makes a burthen gainefull.*

En grande pauvreté n'y a pas grande loyauté: Prov. *Those that are verie poore are not verie loyall.*

Il n'est si grand iour qui ne vienne à vespre: Prov. *The longest dayes haue euenings; (all earthlie things an end.)*

De petit esguillon poind on bien grande asnesse: Pro. *A little goad sets on the great shee Asse.*

Douce parole rompt grand'ire: Pro. *A gentle answer quayles fell anger.*

Du petit vient on au grand: Prov. *From little men come to great; viz. from a meane estate vnto much wealth; from errors to wilfull disorders; from veniall to mortall offences,&c.*

En adventure gisent grands coups: Prov. *While things are doubtfull great things may be done.*

En petit buisson trouve on grand lievre: Prov. *A little groue may harbor a great Hare.*

En petite cheminée fait on bien grand feu: Prov. *A little chimney can hold a great fire.*

En petite maison Dieu a grand part: Prov. *Looke* Maison.

En petite teste gist grand sens: Prov. *In a little head great wit.*

Enfans deviennent grands gens: Prov. *(Wee say) boyes will be men one day.*

Il faut hasarder vn petit poisson pour prendre vn grand: Prov. *We must aduenture a pennie to gaine a pound.*

Il n'est nager qu'en grand eau: Prov. *(We say) there is no fishing to the sea.*

Le cœur fait l'œuvre, non pas les grands iours: Prov. *Not long dayes, but strong hearts, dispatch a worke.*

Les petis ruisseaux font les grandes rivieres: Pro. *Narrow brookes make nauigable riuers.*

Mort n'espargne ny petit ny grand: Prov. *Looke* Mort.

On ne fait pas à grands coups douce vieille: Pro. *Hard stroakes yeeld but harsh Musicke.*

Petit homme abat bien grand chesne: Pro. *A low man can fell a tall Oake.*

Petite pluye abat grand vent: Prov. *(So sayd a mad fellow, who, lying in bed, bepist his farting wiues backe.)*

Grand. *In stead of* Grandement; *whence;*

Fenestre, ou Porte toute grand ouverte. *Wide open.*

Grandelet: m. ette: f. *Somewhat great, pretie and big.*

Grandement: m. *Greatly, bigly, largely; hugely, mightily; exceedingly, extreamely; earnestly, vehemently; verie much.*

Grandesse: f. *as* Grandeur.

Grandet. *as* Grandelet; *Biggish, greatish.*

Grandeur: f. *Greatnesse, bignesse, largenesse; hugenesse; mightinesse; fullnesse, amplenesse; highnesse, loftinesse, statelinesse.*

Grandeur de lieu. *Spaciousnesse, capacitie, widenesse.*

Grandissime: com. *Huge, mightie, excessiue, exceeding great.*

Grands-iours. *Looke* Iour.

Grand-ville. *The name of a soure apple.*

Granes. Foy de Granes: Pro. *Treacherie, treason, vnfaithfulnesse, disloyaltie.*

Grange: f. *A Barne, for corne; also, a Grange.*

La grange est prés des bateurs. *Said of a Nunnerie thats seated neere a Priorie.*

Grangeage: m. *Corne; or fruits layd vp in barnes; also, a fee payed for Corne-roome in a Barne.*

Passer grangeage d'un champ. *To lease out a cornefield, or the crop thereof.*

Grangée: f. *A Graunge, or countrey houshold.*

Grangée de bled. *A Barne-full, or aboundance; a large heape, or huge quantitie, of corne.*

Granger: m. *A Farmer; a Barne-keeper.*

Granger: m. ere: f. *Of, or belonging to, a Barne.*

Grangeux: m. euse: f. *Of a Barne, full of Barnes.*

Grangier: m. *as* Granger.

Grangiere: f. *A Farmers wife; or, a woman that keeps a Barne.*

Grangousier. *Great swallow, mightie throat.* ¶Rab.

Granit oriental. *An orientall Garnet; a stone verie neere as good, and well-coloured, as the Rubie.*

Granulé: m. ée: f. *Reduced into seed, or graine.*

Granuler. *To reduce into seed, or graine.*

Granuleux: m. euse: f. *Grainie, seedie; also, in graines, or little seed-like peeces.*

Graphide: f. *A description, or delineation.* ¶Rab.

Graphigné: m. ée: f. *Scraped, scratched, or clawed.*

Graphigner. *To scratch, to scrape, to claw.*

Grapillon. *See* Grappillon.

Grapir. *To creepe, crawle, or climbe vp (hardly, and with some paine.)*
Grappage: m. *Cluster-gathering, Grape-gathering, Vintage, Wine-haruest.*
Grappe: f. *A bunch, or cluster, of grapes.*
Grappe de mer. *A thing in the sea couered as it were with the flowers of a Vine; otherwise of a rude, and ouglie shape.*
Il sembloit mordre à la grappe. *He spake so heartily, so earnestly, so hotly, that he seemed to act what he vttered.*
Grappelle: f. *The Lowse-burre, Ditch-burre, lesse Burre docke.*
Grapper. *To gleane after grape-gatherers.*
Grappes: f. *The Scratches (in horses legs.)*
Grappetant. *Gleaning after grape-gatherers.*
Grappetté. *Gleaned, or gathered (as grapes.)*
Grappeuse: f. *A grape-gleaneresse; a woman that gleanes after grape-gatherers.*
Grappil: m. *The graple of a ship.*
Grappillage: m. *Grape-gleaning.*
Grappiller. *To gleane after grape-gatherers.*
Grappilleur: m. *A grape-gleaner.*
Grappillon: m. *A little cluster of grapes.*
Grappin: m. *as* Grappil.
Grappu: m. uë: f. *Grapie, clusterie, full of clusters of grapes.*
Grarie: f. *The Kings right, part, or fee, in euerie sale of wood made in the forrests of his subiects, due vnto him by reason of the Iustice done, and good order kept, within them, by his Officers; he doth also challenge thereby a part in the propertie of the soyle, demaine, fruits, and reuenue thereof; (for generally,* la grarie *is a Right that one hath in the propertie, and soyle of another mans woods, and forrests; whereby he lookes for a part of the price when they are sold, and of the fruits, &c, when they are gathered.)*
Gras: m. Vn gras. *A broad, or bawdie, tale.*
Le gras de la iambe. *The calfe of the leg.*
Gras: m. grasse: f. *Fat, greasie, well-fed; grosse, quarrie; pursie; also, fertile, much-yeelding, fruitfull.*
Le gras boyau. *The Inch-pinne, or Jane-pinne; See* Boyau.
Le gras double. *The fat tripe; or, that part of the paunch which yeelds the fattest, and thickest tripes.*
Causes grasses. *Bawdie suits, immodest actions.*
Pain gras. *Thats doughie, or not baked ynough.*
Parler gras. *A lisping; or not pronouncing of R.*
Paroles grasses. *Ribauldrie, lasciuious speeches.*
Son gras. *Bran that hath some meale among it (whereby it feeles smooth, full, or fattie;) Some call it Pollard.*
Vin gras. *Fat, oylie, or greasie, wine.*
Gras comme vn cochon. *as fat as a Pig.*
Gras comme vn gliron. *as fat as a Dormouse.*
Gras comme vn moine, ou comme vn pourceau; *as fat as a Frier, &c.*
Dormir la grasse matinée. *To ly long in bed; or, sleepe all the morning long; (for, morning sleepe is thought to fatten such as vse it.)*
Il en fait ses choux gras. *He gaines well, gets much, thriues apace, &c.*
Grasselet: m. ette: f. *Fattish, fattie, somewhat fat, in pretie good liking.*
Grassesse: f. *Fatnesse, greasinesse; grossenesse.*
Grasset. *as* Grasselet.
Grassette: f. *The hearbe Orpine, Liblong, or Liue-long.*
Grasseur: f. *Fatnesse; grossenesse, fleshinesse.*
Grassier. *To lispe.* (v.m.)
Grassure. *as* Grasseur.
Grat: m. *Pasture, feeding, grazing for cattell; also, a scraping, scratching, or clawing.*
Envoyer au grat. *To send a grazing; a maister to turne away his seruant.*
Gratant. *Scratching, scraping, clawing, rubbing, scrubbing.*
Gratant le cul au soleil. *Idly, slouthfully, lazily, like a lowsie begger.*
Grate: com. *Gratefull, acceptable, pleasing vnto.*
Graté: m. ée: f. *Scratched, scraped, clawed, scrubbed.*
Grate-cul: m. *A Hep; the fruit of the wild Brier, &c.*
La Rose en fin devient vn grate-cul: Prov. *The Rose at length becomes a Hep.*
Grateleux: m. euse: f. *Scabbie, itchie, scuruie.*
Gratelle: f. *Itch; or scurfe.*
Gratement: m. *A scratching, scraping, clawing, scrubbing; also, an itching, which makes one scratch.*
Grater. *To scratch, to scrape, to scrub, claw, rub.*
Grater païs. *To flye, take his heeles, trust to his legs, runne away.*
Tant grate la Chevre que mal gist. *(A Prouerbe applyable to such as cannot be quiet when they are well.)*
Trop grater cuit trop parler nuit: Prov. *Too much scratching hurts the skin, too much talking the whole bodie.*
Apres la feste on grate la teste: Prov. *Repentance begins where feasting ends.*
Qui flate il grate: Prov. *Great flatterers are great scrape-goods.*
Qui naist de geline il aime à grater: Prov. *He thats borne of a Henne loues to be scraping.*
Qui suit les poules apprend à grater la terre: Pro. *Henne-followers turne earth-scrapers; wee quickly learne the bent of those we much frequent.*
Grateron: m. *The small Burre called Goose-share, Goose-grasse, Loue-man, Cleaner, and Clauer.*
Gratia Dei. Elaphoboscum, *or Harts fodder, held by some Authors to be a kind of wild Parsenip, and by others the wild, or bastard Dittanie; wee call other hearbes; viz. Hedge Hyssope; and blue Cranes-bill, or Crowfoot Cranes-bill; and Dwarfe, or low* Cistus, Gratia Dei.
Gratieusement. *Graciously, courteously, affably, respectiuely; benignely, gently, fauourably.*
Gratieuseté: f. *Graciousnesse, fauourablenesse; affabilitie, courtesie, respectiuenesse; humanitie, benignitie, gentlenesse.*
Gratieux: m. euse: f. *Gracious, courteous, affable, respectiue, debonaire; gentle, benigne, fauourable; full of humanitie; also, in good grace, or in great fauour, with; See* Gracieux.
Gens de bien sont tousiours gratieux: Prov. *Honest people are euer full of respect.*
Gratification: f. *A gratification, or gratifying; the doing of a pleasure in lieu of a pleasure done.*
Gratifié: m. ée: f. *Gratified; honestly recompenced, thankfully requited.*
Gratifier. *To gratifie; requite, recompence; conferre a benefit on, doe a pleasure vnto (in thankfulnesse.)*
Gratigné: m. ée: f. *Scratched, scraped, clawed.*
Gratigner. *To scratch, claw, scrape.*
Gratin: m. *The remnant of childrens pap, left in, or sticking to, the bottome of the skellet wherein it was boyled.*

Gratiole: f. *The hearb called Hedge-hyssope, and* Gratia Dei.
Gratitude: f. *Thankefulnesse, gratefulnesse.*
Graton de porc. *Of the fat that houlds th'entrals, being melted, there remaines a fleshie part, which cut in peeces, is thus tearmed (at Paris.)*
Grattement. See Gratement.
Gratter. *as* Grater.
Grattoir: m. *A bread-grater, or great grater.*
Gratture: f. *A scratch, a scrape; a scratching, or scraping.*
Gratuit. don gratuit *A free gift.*
Gratuité: f. *A gratuitie, or free gift.*
Gratuitement. *Freely; of meere good-will; without hope of recompence, or of returne.*
Grauade: f. *A reproach, taxation, or hard tearme; also, any hard measure.*
Gravage de la mer. *The sands, the sea shore.*
Gravaigne. *The wild goose tearmed a Barnacle.*
Gravan. *The name of a small sea-fish; as* Belonne.
Gravant. *Grauing, caruing, cutting; also, creeping, climbing, or scrambling vp a thing.*
Grave: f. *Sand, or grauell; also, the pulse Ax-fitch, hatchet-fitch, ax-seed, ax-wort.*
Grave: com. *Graue; statelie, solemne; seuere, austere; stayed, setled, cōstant; sage, discreet, aduised; sad, important, heauie; greeuous.*
Gravé: m. ée: f. *Graued, carued, cut; pearced, or entered into.*
Gravée: f. *A shaking.* ¶Norm.
Grauelé. cendres gravelées. *Ashes made of wine-lees burned.*
Gravelée. *Tartar; old lees of wine.*
Gravelleux: m. euse: f. *Grauellie, full of the stone.*
Gravelle: f. *Small grauell, or sand; such as is in springs, or streames; also, the stone.*
Gravelleon: m. *The stone.*
Gravement. *Grauely; solemnly; seuerely, austerely; setledly, constantly, stayedly; sagely, discreetly, aduisedly; sadly, heauily.*
Graventer. *as* Greuanter.
Graveolence: f. *An euill smell, smacke, or sauour.*
Graver. *To graue, cut, carue; pierce, or enter into.*
Graveur: m. *A grauer, caruer, cutter.*
Graveure: f. *A grauing, caruing, cutting; piercing.*
Graui: m. ie: f. *Climbed, scaled, crawled, scrambled, crept vp, or vpon.*
Gravier: m. *Grauell; sand mixed with small stones.*
Gravir. *To climbe, scale, crawle, scramble, creepe, vp or vpon, by little and little.*
Gravissant. *Climbing, scaling, creeping vpward.*
Gravité: f. *Grauitie; state, authoritie, solemnitie; seueritie, austeritie; stayednesse; a sage and setled fashion of behauior, and carriage; also, importance, heauinesse; greeuousnesse.*
Faire vne grosse gravité. *To walke like an Alderman; be surlie, take a great deale of state vpon him.*
Gravoir: m. *A heape of grauell.*
Gravois: m. *Grauell.*
Gravonner. *To proke, or dig, with the fingers, into the ground; (hence) also, to search out.*
Gravouer. *as* Gravier.
Graux: m. *Sluces, or open passages, made of purpose to let the Sea into ponds, or low places.*
Graye: f. *The Rooke, or white-bild Crow; also, the Cornish Chough; See* Grole.
Grayerie. *See* Grarie.
Gré: m. *Will, willingnesse; allowance, liking; accord, consent; affection; hart, mind; wish, desire, humor; also thanks, thankfulnesse, gratefulnesse, or a gratefull and good acceptation.*
A gré. *Willingly, freely, without constraint, of himselfe, of his owne free will, with his whole consent; also, with good successe, after a mans wish, vnto his liking.*
A mon gré. *Willingly, by my good will; after my mind, according to my fancie or humor, euen as I would haue it.*
En gré. *Gratefully, thankfully, acceptably, in good part.*
Tout de gré. *Wittingly, willingly, of set purpose.*
Porter gré à quelqu'un de. *To take thankfully at the hands of, to acknowledge himselfe behoulden to, one for.*
Ie vous en sçay bon gré. *I like you well, or giue you hartie thanks, for it.*
Bon gré mal gré va le Prestre au Sené: Prov. *Needes must he goe whom the Diuell (necessitie) driueth.*
Greal. sang greal; *Looke* Sangreal. ¶Rab.
Greau. *A dish, or dish-full of.* ¶Bourg.
Grebe. *as* Griaibe.
Grebonde: f. *A seruice at Tennice, wherein the ball runnes not along on the house, but bounds on the side thereof.*
Grec: m. *A Greeke, or Grecian, one of Greece; also, a booke vsed in Popish Churches.*
Il est Grec. *He is a most craftie, or subtill Courtier.*
Grec: m. Grecque: f. *Greeke, Greekish, Grecian; of, or belonging to, Greece.*
Beauté Grecque. *A foggie plumpnesse, or fatnesse of bodie; (for the Grecians hould the fat bodie the fairest.)*
Foing Grec. *The hearbe, or seed, fenegreeke.*
Ortie Grecque. *The Roman, or male, Nettle.*
Vent Grec'evant. *A Northeast wind.*
Relier vn livre à la Grecque. *To make the backe thereof plaine.*
Grecanizant. *Grecanizing, or Grecianizing it; speaking Greeke; imitating a Grecian.*
Grecizer. *To Grecianize it; to play the Grecian; or to speake Greeke.*
Grecques: f. *Gregs, Gallogaskins, wide venitians.*
Grecs: m. *A wild bores vpper tushes.*
Gredillé m. ée: f. *Frizled, curled, crisped; also, puckered, or crumpled, by heat, &c; also, flattered, or soothed.*
Gredillеr. *To frizle, curle, or crispe the haire, &c, with a hot Iron; also, to crumple, or pucker with heat; also, to sooth, flatter, or feed with good words.*
Grée: f. *An agreement, accord, attonement.* ¶Bret.
Greé m. ée: f. *Agreed vnto; allowed of.*
Gréer. *To agree, or giue consent, vnto; to approue, allow; accept, admit, of.*
Gref. *See* Grief.
Greffe: m. *Th'Office of a Pregnotarie, Secondarie, or chiefe Clerke to a Court; a Registrie; a Clerkes Office.*
Droict de greffe. 63: s. 9: d. Tour. *due, in diuers places, vnto the king vpon euery sale of wood.*
Greffe: f. *A graffe; a slip, or yong shoot fit to be graffed.*
Greffe de Monsieur. *The name of a certaine great sweet apple.*
Greffé: m. ée: f. *Graffed, ingraffed.*
Greffer. *To graffe; or ingraffe.*

Greffier: m. *A Register, Pregnotarie, or principall clerke to a Court; a Secondarie in an Office, or Court; a clerke of Assise, or of Inrollments.*
Greffiere: f. *A Notaresse, Registresse; a she Clerke, a Registers, or Clerkes, wife.*
Greffiers: m. *A kind of white hounds; as* Bauds.
Gregeois: m. oise: f. *Grecian, Greekish, of Greece.*
Feu gregeois. *Looke* Feu.
Gregual: m. *A Northeast wind.*
Gregues: f. *Wide Slops, Gregs, Gallogascoines, Venitians; great Gascon, or Spanish, hose.*
Greguesque. *as* Gregeois.
Greguesques: f. *Slops, Gregs, Gallogascoines, Venitians.*
Greigneur. *Great; also, greater, larger, bigger; elder.*
Greinselle: f. *A Goosebberrie.*
Grelace: f. *Great Hayle.*
Grelle. *as* Gresle. *Hayle.*
Grelot. Trembler le grelot. *as* Grelotter.
Grelotter. *To shake, tremble, didder, quake for cold; to say an Apes Pater-noster.*
Grelurette. *as* Gurluret.
Gremeaux de sang. *Clots of congealed bloud.*
Gremeler. *as* Grommeler.
Gremil: m. *The hearb Gromill, Grummell, or Graymill, Peare-plant, Lichewall.*
Grenade: f. *A Pomegranet; also, a ball of wild-fire, made like a Pomegranet.*
Grenadier: m. *A Pomegranet tree.*
Grenadille: f. *A Pomegranet blossome; also, a little Pomegranet.*
Grenage: m. *Graine, corne, seed; or the growth, or increase thereof.*
Grenaille: f. *Graine, or seed; also, the gold, siluer, &c, taken out of water, whereinto it had beene throwne red hot out of the Cruible; so tearmed, because it is commonly in graines.*
Grenaille de bronze. *The skalie dust, or substance lying on brasse, &c, after it hath beene melted; and falling from it of it selfe, or with a little blowing.*
Grenat: m. *The precious stone called a Granat, or Garnet; also, a Carbuncle of a Pomegranet colour.*
Grenat rouge. *A kind of botch, or pockie sore.*
Grenatier: m. *The little border ingrauen about a seale; so tearmed, because tis like a row of Pomegranet kernels.*
Grenatine: f. *A small Granat, or Garnet; also, marble spotted red, whether naturally or artificially.*
Grene: f. *as* Graine.
Grené: m. ée: f. *Seeded; eared.*
Marbre grené. *Sparkled, or spotted marble.*
Grenée. Pouldre de grosse grenée. *Great graine powder fit for the Canon.*
Grener. *To seed, as hearbes; to eare, as corne.*
Greneterie: f. *The place, or Office, wherein the Controllers of the Kings Garners reside.*
Grenetiers: m. *Ouerseers, Keepers, or Controllers, of the Kings salt-Garners.*
Grenie. Garder vne fille à grenie. *See* Graine.
Grenier: m. *A Garner; a Corne-loft; a roome to keepe salt, or corne, in.*
Grenier à coups de poing. *A knaue; one that often deserues to be pommelled.*
Grenier à morpions. *A filthie lowsie fellow, or one thats full of Crab-lice.*
Monter au grenier sans chandelle. *To light in a turd.*

Grenil. *as* Gremil. *Hearbe Grummell, &c.*
Grenouillant. *Swilling, quaffing; bibbing, sipping; also, croaking, like a Frog.*
Grenouille: f. *A Frog, a Paddocke.*
Grenouille pescheresse. *The sea-Frog, sea-diuell, sea-toad.*
Grenouiller. *Continually to bib, tiple, sip, swill in drinke; to spend his whole time in potting; also, to croake, or cry like a Frog.*
Grenouillere: f. *A froggie place; as* Grenouilliere.
Grenouillette: f. *A little Frog.*
Grenouillette: f. *Crowfoot, Kings Kob, gold Cups, gold Knops, butter Flower.*
Grenouillette aquatique. *Water Crowfoot, marsh Crowfoot.*
Grenouillette de bois. *Wood Crowfoot, sweet Crowfoot.*
Grenouillette dorée. *Gold-Crap, golden Crowfoot, gold-haire Crowfoot, yellow Craw.*
Grenouillette herissonnée. *White Crowfoot, or Vrchin Crowfoot.*
Grenouillette petite. *White Crowfoot; or, as* Grenouillette de bois.
Grenouilliere: f. *A froggie place.*
Grenouillon: m. *A little Frog.*
Grenu: m. uë: f. *Grained; full of graine, of seed, of graines.*
Gres. *as* Grez.
Gresil: m. *Hayle, drizling; also, reeme, or the white frost that hangs on trees.*
Gresillé. *Drizled on; couered, or hoare, with reeme.*
Gresiller. *To hayle, drizle, sleet; reeme to fall; also, as* Greziller.
Gresillon: m. *A Cricket.*
Gresillonné. *Whitish, or hoarie, as grasse with frost, &c.*
Gresillonner. *To creake, or chirpe like a Cricket.*
Gresle: f. *Hayle.*
Gresle: com. *Thin, small, slender; lanke; little, pretie; diminished; also, shrill, or squeaking.*
Greslé: m. ée: f. *Hayled on; also, pockie, or that hath the pocks.*
Greslement. *Thinly, smally, slenderly; lankely; prettily; also, shrilly, or squeakingly.*
Gresler. *To hayle.*
Gresler sur le persil. *To dominiere ouer a weake aduersarie; to shew himselfe bold, and stout against one thats not able to resist him.*
Greslet: m. ette: f. *Little, prettie, deft, smallish.*
Gresleté: f. *Smallnesse, littlenesse, exilitie, slendernesse, thinnesse.*
Gresleux: m. euse: f. *Haylie, full of hayle, subiect vnto hayle; stormie.*
Greslier: m. ere: f. *Haylie; of, or belonging to, hayle.*
Chapeau greslier. *A hat for the hayle, or to be worne while it hayles.*
Gresse. *as* Graisse; *Fat; grease.*
Gresser. *as* Graisser.
Gressier: m. *A lisper, one that lispeth.*
Gressier: m. ere: f. *Fattie, greasie.*
Gretiller. *To crackle; See* Greziller.
Grettes de lin: f. *The hards, or towe of flax.*
Grevable: com. *Grieuous, painefull; also, likelie to burst.*
Grevance: f. *A grieuance, or aggrieuance.*
Grevant. *Grieuing, aggrieuing, vexing, oppressing.*
Grevanté: m. ée: f. *Grieued, aggrieued, vexed, oppressed.*
Grevanter. *To grieue, aggrieue, molest, vex, oppresse.*

Greve: f. *The place of Execution, in Paris.*
Ange de Greve. *A Porter, or burthen-bearer; also, one that hangs on a Gibbet.*
Faict Cardinal en Greve. *One thats beheaded at the* Greve.
Greve: f. *Sand, or Grauell; and, a sandie Strand, or Shore; also, the shanke, shinne, or (fore-part of the) leg.*
La greve des cheveux (&, les cheveux departis en greve.) *The shedding, or shading of the haire; the parting thereof on the forehead (after the old fashion.)*
Grevé: m. ée: f. *Grieued, aggrieued, pained; vexed, hurt; molested, annoyed; wronged, oppressed, ouercharged, ouerburthened; also, burst, or whose bowels are fallen into his cods.*
Grevelure. *The mayle of a Hawke.*
Grever. *To grieue, aggrieue, paine, vex, hurt; afflict, annoy, trouble, disquiet, molest; wrong, iniure, ouercharge, ouerburthen, oppresse; also, to dig into, or make hollow, with the nayles.*
Greves: f. *Bootes; also, greaues, or armour for the legs.*
Greveure: f. *An inward rupture, or bursting (of the lower part of the bellie) or an extraordinarie swelling of the cods, by the bowels falling into them; a bursting, or being burst.*
Grevolable: com. *Deseruing the Rope; for whom the Gallowes groane.*
Greux. Les greux: m. *The nayles.* ¶Pic.
Grez: m. *A greetie, browne-gray, shining, hard, and long-lasting free-stone, good to paue with; and (small-broken) to scowre brasen, or pewter vessell; See* Grais.
Grezillé. *Wrigled; crumpled; crackled; curled, frizled, twirled.*
Greziller. *To wrigle, or stirre as a liue fish on a hot grid-iron; to crumple together, as leather, or parchment in the fire; also, to crackle, as a shell in fire, or salted flesh on coales; also, to curle, twirle, frizle haire &c.*
Grezillons. *Hawkes bells; also, as* Grillons; *also, little gobbets of fat, or salt meat broyled; also, crumplings, or twirles, as of haire curled.*
Griache *as* Griesche. ¶Rab.
Griaibe. *A Sea-Mew.* ¶Savoyard.
Griais: m. *A kind of daintie red-legd Partridge; or, as* Perdrix griesche.
Griais. *Gray; or, of the colour of a Starling.*
Griblettes: f. *Collops.*
Gribouiller. *To rumble, or croake (as the guts doe through windinesse.)*
Gribouillis: m. *The rumbling, croaking, or stirring of the guts; also, a fained name for a diuell.*
Gribouri: m. *A Goblin, Robingoodfellow, walking spirit that rumbles in houses a nights.*
Grief: m. *An aggreuance, wrong, iniurie; oppression; vexation, molestation, trouble.*
Bailler griefs en plaidoirie. *An Appealant to alledge the wrongs, and points of iniustice, done vnto him by the sentence, from which he hath appealed.*
Grief: m. ieve: f. *Grieuous, offensiue; noysome, troublesome; heauie, wrongfull, obnoxious.*
Griesche: com. *Gray; or peckled as a Stare; also, sharp, or prickling; whence;*
Ortie griesche. *The male, Romane, or Greeke nettle; (a stranger in England;) some also call so the small, red, stinging, nettle.*
Perdrix griesche. *The ordinarie, or gray, Partridge.*
Pie griesche. *The Wariangle; (a rauenous bird.)*
Grieux: m. *A villaine, theefe, rascall.* (v.m.)
Grifes. *See* Griffes.
Griffade: f. *A clawing; a scratch, or gripe with the clawes; a ranche, or clinch with a beasts paw.*
Griffe: m. *A kind of big Tumbler, or dog thats bodied (but not deepe-hung) like the Talbot.*
Griffe: f. *A Claw, nayle, tallon.*
Griffe graffe. *By hooke or by crooke, squimble squamble, scamblingly, catch that catch may.*
On cognoist le Diable à ses griffes: Prov. *The diuell is knowne by his clawes.*
Griffé: m. ée: f. *Clawed, or hauing clawes; also, griped, or grasped with clawes.*
Griffer. *To gripe, graspe, seize, catch, lay hold on with clawes, &c; also, to seize, or catch at violently, greedily, and wrongfully.*
Griffon: m. *A Gripe, or Griffon.*
Pied de griffon. *A Griffons foot; an instrument (made like the foot of a Griffon) wherewith Surgeons draw moles, or the parts of a dead child, out of womens wombes; also, as* Pommelaye, *or* Pomelée.
Griffonner. *To write fast, and ill; to scrible, to scrall it.*
Griffu: m. üe: f. *Hauing great clawes, or sharpe tallons.*
Grigne: com. *Wrinkled.*
Grigner. *To grinne.*
Grignette. Perdrix g. *The ordinarie Partridge.*
Grigneur. *Greater, huger, larger, mightier.*
Grignon de pain. *A crustie peece of bread, or corner of a loafe.*
Grignoté: m. ée: f. *Gnawed, knapled, or nibled away.*
Grignoter. *To mumble, or eat, like a Conny, or Squirrell; also, to gnaw, knaple, or nible away.*
Gril: m. *A Gridiron.*
Grillant. *Broyling on a Gridiron; also, grating vp; also, gliding, sliding, glib-running, trickling, along.*
Grille: f. *An Iron grate.*
Grille de bois. *An Engine made of stickes, or peeces of wood, bound together, and applyed vnto the very necke of a beast, thereby to force it vnto straitnesse.*
Les grilles d'une fenestre. *The grating, or barres of a window.*
Grillé: m. ée: f. *Broyled on a Gridiron; hence, also, parched, withered, or dryed vp with extreame heat; also, glid, or slipped along; also, grated, or close barred vp.*
Grillement: m. *A broyling on a Gridiron; also, a parching with extreame heat; also, a gliding, or sliding along; also, a grating, or shutting vp with grates.*
Griller. *To broyle on a Gridiron; also, to scorch, parch, or dry vp with extreame heat; also, to grate; set a grate before, shut vp with grates; also, to glide, slip, slide, steale, trickle, runne, glib along; also, as* Grisser; *also, to sit rumpled, or in plaits, as a garment thats too side-wasted; also, to ruffle, or snarle, as ouertwisted thread.*
Grillet: m. *A Hawkes bell; also, as* Grillon.
Grilletier: m. *A Cricket-catcher; also, a maker of Hawkes bells.*

Grilletté: m. ée: f. *Furnished with bells, as a Hawke.*
Grilleux: m. euse: f. *Gratie; full of grates; made like a grate.*
Grillon des champs; *a Grashopper*; de cheminée; *a Cricket.*
Il a beaucoup de grillons en la teste. *He is in his dumpes; his head is much troubled, full of crochets, or of Proclamations.*
Les grillons gastent la feste: Prov. *Loud bablers are euer offensiue at feasts; a Prouerbe taxing Buffoones, and Sycophants, who with their idle chat are troublesome to all that heare them.*
Grillons. *A kind of manacles, or torment for the fingers.*
Grillot: m. *(The name of) a certaine apple thats ripe about August.*
Grillotier: m. *A Gridiron-maker; also, a maker of Rattles, Curralls with Bells, and such like toyes for children.* ¶Rab.
Grillottement: m. *A ringing, rickling, ratling, or crackling; also, a shogging, or iogging.*
Grillotter. *To ring, rickle, ratle, crackle; also, to shog, or iog.*
Grimace: f. *A crabd looke; a face, wry mouth, ill-fauoured countenance made; a mowing, or Apes face.*
Grimacer. *To make a face, or a wry mouth; to mowe.*
Grimacier: m. *A caruer, or maker of such Monkeyes, or Antickes, as in sumptuous buildings seeme to support great arches, pillars, beames.*
Grimasseur: m. *A maker of mouthes, or faces.*
Grimau, ou Grimaud. *as* Grimauld.
Grimaude: f. *A kind of Owle; as* Cheveche.
Grimauderie: f. *A schoole, or crue of Petties, or of meane Grammer schollers.*
Grimauld: m. *A grim-faced fellow; a crabbed, wayward, froward, vnpleasing person; also, as* Grimaude; *also, a Grammar-schoole boy.*
Grimbetilolletée. *as* Besongnée. ¶Rab.
Grimelet: m. *as* Grimouche; *or, a smatterer in matters of learning.*
Grimoire. *A booke of coniuring, or exorcising, much in vse among Popish Priests.*
Mots de la Grimoire. *Coniurations, Exorcismes; coniuring, or exorcising tearmes.*
Grimouche: m. *A paltrie Pedant, meane Grammarian.*
Grimpement: m. *A climbing, crawling, creeping, ramping, running, vpwards.*
Grimpe-mur. *A climbe-wall, one that scrambles vp a wall.*
Grimper. *To climbe, crawle, creepe, scramble, vp; to rampe, or runne vpwards, as plants that are set against a wall.*
Grimpereau: m. *The little climbing, and restlesse bird called, a Wood-pecker.*
Grimpeur: m. *A climber; a crawler, creeper, scrambler, vpwards.*
Grimpreau. *as* Grimpereau.
Grimpure: f. *as* Grimpement.
Grincé: m. ée: f. *Gnashed, or crashed together.*
Grincement: m. *A gnashing, grinding, or grating of the teeth together.*
Grincer les dents. *To gnash, grind, grate, or crash the teeth together for anger.*
Grinceur: m. *An angrie gnasher of the teeth.*
Grinches. *as* Guisnes noires; *A kind of blacke sweet Cherries.*
Grimeur. *for,* Plus grand; *Greater.* (v.m.)
Gringalet: m. *A merrie grig, pleasant rogue, sportfull knaue, conceited whoreson.*
Gringette. *See* Grignette.
Gringoriane. Eau Gringoriane. *Holy-water; tearmed so, because first inuented by a Pope* Gregorie.
Gringotement: m. *A quauering, or shaking with the voice.*
Gringoter. *To warble, quauer, shake with the voice.*
Gringotis: m. *A quauering, warbling, diuision.*
Gringuenaudes: f. *The filth which, after purging, sticks to the tayle.*
Gringuenotant. *warbling, quauering, shaking of the voice.*
Gringuenoter. *as* Gringoter.
Gringuenoteur: m. *A warbler, shaker, quauerer; one that in singing vseth to diuide much.*
Gringuenotis: m. *as* Gringotis.
Grinon. *as* Grillon; *A Cricket.*
Grinson: m. *A Spinke, Sheldaple, Chaffinch.*
Grinsser. *as* Grincer; *also, to crackle, or clash.*
Grio: m. *New Barlie steeped in water, then dryed by a fire, and then fryed, and kept for (phisicall) vses.*
Griote: f. *A kind of tart, or soure Cherrie.*
Griote seiche. *as* Grio.
Grioter. *To gather those Cherries.*
Grioteux: m. euse: f. *Grauellie; also, light.*
Griotier: m. *A soure Cherrie-tree.*
Griotier à roses. *A certaine great tree that resembles the double-flowred Cherrie tree.*
Griotte: f. *Grauell; also, the meale, or floure of parched, or fryed Barlie; or, as* Grio.
Grip: m. *Rapine, violence; or, a violent catching, forcible taking, of other mens things.*
Allons au Cap de grip. *Let's abroad for a prize, or purchace; (a phrase of Pirates, when they would to sea.)*
Gripauline. *The hearbe Motherwort.*
Griphe. *as* Griffe.
Gripher. *as* Griffer.
Gripp'argent: m. *A Gripe-money, or Catch-coyne; a greedie, or couetous Judge, Magistrate, Officer, Lawyer.*
Grippé: m. grippée: f. *Seised, grasped, caught at greedily, griped, or taken violently.*
Grippement: m. *A griping, seizing, grasping.*
Grippeminaud. *A griping, catching, greedie, couetous, cruell fellow.*
Grippeminer. *To gripe, graspe, seise greedily, cruelly, couetously.*
Gripper. *To seise, gripe, graspe; clinch, catch, or snatch, at; lay violent hold, or couetous hands, on.*
Pouldre à gripper. *Any lasciuious, or lust-begetting, Powder.*
Grippets: m. *The rumples of an ouer-long, or ill-made garment; also, the rufflings, or snarles of ouer-twisted thread.*
Grippeur: m. *A griper; catcher, snatcher, greedie taker, violent seizer of other mens goods.*
Gris: m. *A kind of Weesell, or little beast of a bluish colour; also, grayenesse, or the colour gray; a gray.*
Gris de Minime. *See* Minime.
Gris pommelé. *A daple gray.*

Gris violant. *Mallow-flower colour.*
Gris: m. ise: f. *Gray, light-russet, grizle, ash-coloured, hoarie, whitish.*
Nihil gris. *Looke* Nihil.
Perdrix grise. *The ordinarie gray Partridge.*
Le pied gris. *The Hob, Clowne, Boore, Hind; so called, of his euer-dustie, or durtie shooes.*
Grisard: m. *A Badger, Boason, Brocke, or Gray; also, a sea-Cob, or sea-Gull.*
Grisastre: com. *Grayish, hoarie, whitish.*
Griser. *To grow gray-haired, to wax hoare-headed.*
Grisle. *as* Grille.
Grislement: m. *A crackling noyse, as of meat in the broyling.*
Grison. Pierre de grison. *A kind of free stone, which is but soft when it is taken out of the Quarrey, but afterward growes verie hard.*
Grison: m. onne: f. *Gray with age; whitish, hoarie, grizle; oldish, or somewhat old; and hence;*
Oyson verd bon, grison guerebon: Pro.
Grisonné: m. ée: f. *Growne gray, hoarie, whitish.*
Grisonnement: m. *Graynesse, hoarinesse, whitishnesse; a growing whitish.*
Grisonner. *as* Griser.
Grisonneure: f. *Graynesse, hoarinesse, whitishnesse; or, the growing hoarie, &c.*
Grisser. *To crackle, or (like a shoe) to creake.*
Elles grissoient d'ardeur de le voir. *They longed extreamely to see it; or, their desires were on fire vntill they saw it.*
Grive: f. *The great Thrush called a Fieldfare, or Feldifare; also, the Throstle.*
Grive sisalle. *Looke* Sisalle.
Grivelé: m. ée: f. *Peckled, speckled; meneld, mayled, (blacke and white, or dunne and white.)*
Grivelée: f. *A Bill, Scroll, or Scedule; (because it is blacke, and white.)*
Grivelement: m. *Pecklednesse; or, a speckled colour; especially such a one as is composed of black and white, or dunne and white.*
Griveleure: f. *A pecklednesse, or specklednesse.*
Grivette. *A Throstle, or Mauis.*
Grivolé: m. ée: f. *Peckled, speckled, meneld, black and white, like the bellie of a Snayle.*
Grivolement. *See* Grivelement.
Grivoler. *To peckle, or speckle; to spot with diuers colours; or (most properly) with black and white, or dunne and white.*
Grivolure: f. *as* Griveleure.
Grizonner. *as* Griser.
Gro-bec: m. *A certaine ash-coloured, and great-headed bird, somewhat lesse then a Thrush.*
Grobianisme. *Grobianisme, slouenlinesse; vnmannerlie parts, or precepts.*
Grobis. Faire du grobis. *To be prowd, or surlie; to take much state vpon him.*
Groée: f. *A great quantitie, or number of stirring, or stirred things; whence;*
A la groée. *The boyish scrambling for nuts, &c, cast on the ground; a Musse.*
Groigner. *To nuzle, or to root, with the snowt.*
Groignon. *A kind of Peach.*
Groin de porceau. *The snowt, or nose of a Hog.*
Le groin de lievre. *A Hares mouth; often counterfeited by wantons, with lippes thrust out together.*
Groin de Porc. *The head, or vpper part of the shoulder-blade, so tearmed by Anatomists; also, the hearbe Dandelion, Priests Crowne, Pisse-abed.*
Faire le groin. *To powt, lowre, frowne, be sullen, or surlie; to hang the lip, or sell sowce.*
Rengourmer le groin à. *To cuffe soundly; or, to pash on the mouth.*
Groiselier: m. *A Gooseberrie shrub.*
Groiselles. *Gooseberries; Thorn-berries; Fea-berries.*
Groiselles noires. *Blacke Gooseberries, blacke Ribes; an ill-tasting kind of the beyond-sea Gooseberrie.*
Groiselles d'outre mer. *as* Groiselles rouges.
Groiselles rouges. *Red Gooseberries, beyond-sea Gooseberries, Garden Currans, bastard Currans.*
Groisellettes trans-marins. *as* Groiselles rouges.
Groisse: f. *as* Grossesse.
Groisselet. *as* Groiselier; *the Gooseberrie Shrub.*
Groizil: m. *Broken Glasse.*
Grole: f. *A Rooke, or white-billed Crow; also, a Cornish Chough; or, the red-billd Rooke.*
Grolle: f. *The round circle in the white, at Butts;* ¶Poict.
Grollé: m. ée: f. *Parched, or carled, as Pease, Beanes, &c.*
Grollier: m. *A Cobler.*
Grollier. Noyer grollier. *A Wallnut-tree thats so young, or little, as it may yet be shaken.* ¶Rab.
Gromé: m. ée: f. *Buffetted, cuffed.*
Grommelement: m. *A grumbling, muttering, murmuring.*
Grommeler. *To grumble, repine, murmure, mutter betweene the teeth.*
Grommeleur: m. *A grumbler, mutterer, murmurer.*
Grommeleux: m. euse: f. *Grumbling, muttering, murmuring; also, rugged, rough, curdie, clottie, cluttering, clusterie.*
Bruit grommeleux. *A confused, buzzing, humming, or deepe noyse.*
Grommellement: m. *A grumbling, muttering, murmuring.*
Grommé: m. ée: f. *Buffetted, cuffed.*
Grommer. *To buffet, or cuffe.*
Gronau: m. *A Gurnard.* ¶Langued.
Groncer. *To roare, as the sea in a storme.*
Grondeller. *To rumble; or, to roare, as a tempestuous water that beats against rockes, or roots growing to the bankes thereof.*
Grondement: m. *as* Gronderie.
Gronder. *To whurle, whurre, yarre, like a dog that is angrie; also, to grunt, groane, grumble (with threatning) against a commaundement.*
Gronderie: f. *A grunting, grumbling; whurling, yarring.*
Grondeur: m. *A grunter, or grumbler; a whurrer, or yarrer.*
Grondin. *A Hog.* ¶Barrag.
Grondir. *as* Grondeller.
Grongnard: m. arde: f. *Grunting; also, powting, or frowning.*
Grongnement: m. *A grunting.*
Grongner. *To grunt, like a Hog.*
Gros: m. *Greatnesse, bignesse; or, the great, summe, or grosse of; also, an imposition vpon Wine, sold by great.*
Le gros d'un affaire. *The most difficult, and most important, part of a businesse.*
Le gros d'une armée. *The Batallion which hath*

the most and best men in it; or, the thickest, and greatest troope in the Grosse, or bodie, of an armie.
Le gros de la gorge. *The throat-boll; the Dew-lap.*
Le gros d'une herbe. *The stemme, or stalke of an hearbe.*
Le gros d'une ville. *The most rich, eminent, and able persons in a towne.*
Vendre en gros. *To sell by great; to vent, or vtter his commodities by whole-sale.*
Gros: m. *The coyne called, a Groat; also, a Dramme, or the eight part of an ounce, of Gold, or Siluer; of other wares, the 32 part of an ounce; or, the 256 part of a pound.*
Gros de Iacques Cœur. *An old coyne of fine siluer, weighing three deniers, and first deuised at* Bourges, *by one of that name, in the yeare* 1448.
Gros de Lorraine. *A coyne worth* ij s. viij d. Tour.
Gros de Mets. *Is of the same value.*
Gros de Neesle. *Is worth* iij d *sterl.*
Gros de Naples. *Silke Grogeran.*
Gros: m. grosse: f. *Grosse, great, big, thicke; also, beauie, sad, weightie; also, dull, blunt, rude, sottish, blockish.*
Grosse haleine. à grosse haleine. *Blowing hard, or with full breath.*
Estre à la grosse haleine. *To gaspe, or gape for breath; to be almost out of breath.*
Les grosses maisons de la ville. *The richest houses; or, the most powerfull, and most eminent families, in the Towne.*
Gros mal. *The falling sicknesse; or, foule euill.*
Gros voyers. *Such as haue meane, or middle Iurisdiction.*
Grosse teste. Il a vne grosse teste. *He is a verie blockhead, grouthead, ioulthead.*
Il n'a pas la teste si grosse. *He is not so wise, or not so well seene in matters; he is not of so deepe a reach, of so great an vnderstanding.*
Amende grosse. *A fine, or amerciament of* vj s. *sterl. or vpwards.*
Gros comme le bras. *As big as an arme; as sure as a club.*
Filer gros. *Looke* Filer.
Regarder d'un gros oeil. *To frowne, looke big, or sowre on; to cast a surlie eye at.*
Gros-bec. *An ash-coloured, and great-headed bird, somewhat lesse then a Thrush.*
Gros-doux. *A kind of faire, great, and sweet apple.*
Groselier: m. *A Gooseberrie shrub.*
Groselier rouge. *The shrub that beares the red Gooseberrie, beyond-sea Gooseberrie, red Corinthes, or bastard Corants.*
Groselles. *as* Groiselles. *Gooseberries.*
Gros-grain. *The stuffe Grogeran.*
Groslé: m. ée: f. *Tottered, rocked, shaken.*
Febves groslées. *as* Groulées.
Grosler. *To rocke, totter, or shake, as a weake building in wind; also, as* Graller.
Groslier. *See* Grollier.
Gros-menil. *The name of a certaine hard, and rough-skind Peare.*
Gros-oeil. *The name of an excellent apple for Cyder.*
Grosse: f. *A Grosse, or twelue dozen; also, as* Grossesse de femme; *also, the ingrossement of an Instrument, Pleading, Euidence, &c; or an Instrument &c ingrossed.*
Grosselles. *as* Groiselles.
Grossement. *Grossely, rudely; heauily, sadly, bluntly, blockishly.*
Grosser. *To rattle in the throat.*
Grosserie: f. *Great worke, things wrought by great; also, rudenesse, grossenesse; also, Grosserie; wares vttered, or the vttering of wares, by whole-sale.*
Grossesse de femme. *A womans grossenesse, greatnesse, or being great with child.*
Grosseur: f. *Grossenesse, bignesse, thicknesse, greatnesse, fullnesse.*
Grossier: m. *A Grocer; or, as* Marchant grossier.
Grossier: m. ere: f. *Grosse, rude, vnpolished; blockish, dull, clownish, lumpish.*
Marchant grossier. *That sells onely by Great, or vtters his commodities by whole-sale.*
Noix grossiere. *A Wallnut.*
Grossierement. *as* Grossement.
Grossir. *To grow big, to wax fat, thicke, or grosse.*
Grossissement: m. *Thick-making; or, a growing big, fat, grosse.*
Grossoyé: m. ée: f. *Ingrossed; written faire, or in great and faire letters.*
Grossoyer. *To ingrosse; to write faire, or in great and faire letters.*
Grote: f. *A coole roome vnder-ground for the Summer; or, as* Grotte.
Grotesque. *as* Grotte.
Grotesquer. *To lurke in caues, dennes, and obscure places.*
Grotesques: f. *Pictures wherein (as please the Painter) all kind of odde things are represented without anie peculiar sence, or meaning, but onely to feed the eye.*
Groton: m. *A little grot, cauerne, or hole; also, as* Croton.
Grotte: f. *A grot, caue, denne, cauerne, hole, (vnder the ground.)*
Groüée. La groüée des fruicts; *That fruit which falls in the night; wind-falls, night-falls, or night-wind-falls.*
Groueteux. *as* Grouetteux.
Grouette: f. *Grauell; or, a grauellie soyle.*
Grouetteux: m. euse: f. *Grauellie; stonie.*
Grougnaut: m. *A Gurnard.* ¶Langued.
Grougouler. *To rumble, or croake, like the guts.*
Grouiller. *To moue, stirre, scrall; to make shew, or giue signes, of life by stirring; to spring, as a child in his mothers wombe; also, to rumble, as those that in a house remoue heauie things; also, to swarme, abound, or breake out confusedly in great numbers.*
Grouillier: m. *as* Grollier.
Grouillis: m. *A stirring heape of wormes, or other vermine; also, the springing of a child in the wombe.*
Groulard. *The bird called, a Bunting.*
Groulé. Febves groulées. *Parched, or carled, Beanes.*
Grouller. *as* Grouiller.
Groumeler. *To murmure, grumble, mutter.*
Grouppade: f. *A certaine loftie manage, which must be beaten with a liuelie, and setled measure; the turne being more wide, and the horses hinder parts more raised, then in an ordinarie curuet.*
se Groyer. *To boast, vaunt, cracke of his deeds.*
Gruage. Coustume de gruage. *The custome, order, or manner, of surueying, measuring, rating, and deliuering, of wood sold in forrests, &c.*
Gruan: m. *Oatmeale.*
Gruant: m. *Oatmeale, Groates.*

Gruau. *Course meale,or,the great of corne; also,a young Crane; also,as* Grio; *also,a Shittlecocke.*
Gruaux d'avoine. *Oatmeale,Groates.*
Gruë: f. *A Crane; also, the Engine so called; also, a sot, asse,goosecap,boydon,lobcocke.*
Gruë franche. *Free lading and vnlading at a wharfe; (a Priuiledge due vnto some Marchants.)*
Bec de gruë. *as* Col de gruë; *also, a Cranes bill (or Pinsers fashioned like a Cranes bill) wherewith Surgeons pull bullets,and arrow-heads out of wounded bodies.*
Col de gruë. *The hearbe Cranes-bill, Herons-bill, Storkes-bill,Pinke-needle; also,the hearbe Doues-foot; also, the hearbe Robert; (The later two being seuerall kinds of the first.)*
Teste de gruë. *as* Col de gruë.
Danser la gruë. *To hop; or daunce vpon (onely) one leg.*
S'entretenir comme font les gruës. *Obstinatly to follow together one sect, side, or faction.*
Gruë: com. *Simple, sillie; sottish,foolish; and hence;*
Le monde n'est plus gruë. *The world growes wise adayes.*
Gruërie. *as* Grurie; *also, the walke of a* Gruyer.
Droict de gruërie, & garenne. *A royaltie belonging vnto some Lords Iusticers, who haue thereby the hunting, brousage, and pawnage of their subiects, or vassalls,woods.*
Grugeoir: m. *A small Grater; as* Esgrugeoir.
Grugeons. *The smallest,or most writhen fruit on a tree; Writlings.* ¶Norm.
Gruger. *To grudge, repine, mutter* (v. m.) *also, to crumble, or breake into small peeces; or,as* Esgruger.
Gruier: m. *as* Gruyer; *Part of whose Office is,the keeping of the Hammer wherewith the wood, and timber thats felled for sale,or for the vse of Commoners,in Forrests,is marked.*
Gruierie. *as* Grurie.
Gruiner. *To gruntle,or grunt like a Hog.*
Gruir. *To crunkle,or creake,like a Crane.*
Gruitie. *as* Grurie.
Grum. *as* Grain. ¶Langued.
Grume: m. *A knot,bunch,cluster; clutter; also,a twinckling,or sparkling,as of a Dyamond.*
Grumeau de sang: m. *A clot, or clutter of congealed bloud.*
Grumelement: m. *A grunting,as of Hogs.*
Grumeler. *as* Grommeler.
Grumeleux: m. euse: f. *Clottie, cluttering, clusterie.*
Bois grumeleux. *Rough,knottie,rugged wood.*
Grumer. *To shite grapes; or,to void a dung that shewes the dunguer to haue eaten grapes;(a word applyed most vnto wild Swine.)*
Grumeux. *as* Grumeleux.
Gruo. *Barley flower dryed by the fire,&c; as* Grio.
Gruolleux: m.euse: f. *Grauellie, stonie.*
Gruotte. *as* Griotte.
Grupé: m. ée: f. *Grasped, seised, griped.*
Grupement: m. *A grasping,or griping; a seisure.*
Gruper. *To seise,gripe,graspe.*
Ie le vous gruperay au truc. *See* Truc.
Gruppade: f. *A violent gripe, seisure, graspe, catching, snatching at.*
Grurie: f. *Is a right of Iurisdiction (most properly) in the woods,and forrests that belong to another man;and consists of the notice taken of,and of the amerciaments and confiscations raised by, the offences committed therein. This right belongs wholly to the King in all the woods that be inclosed within his forrests; by reason whereof, the amerciaments and confiscations are euer adiudged vnto him,and the restitutions and dammages vnto the Proprietaries: (And yet if another haue so great a proportion of woods inclosed within, or ioyning vnto, the Kings forrests, that he must of necessitie keepe Officers to looke vnto them,and haue withall (by Prescription,or Charter) this right,or a Iurisdiction, within them, he may exercise it by his Officers, without the impeachment of the Kings;) also, the Office, or the walke,of a* Gruyer.
Grurie du charbon. *Such a like Iurisdiction ouer the makers of Charcoale; as also,a propertie in part thereof, belonging to the King, in whose woods soeuer they be made.*
Grus: m. *Gruell; or water wherein any corne is boyled; Corne-broth; and hence;*
Grus de froment. *Furmentie.*
Grus d'orge. *as* Orgemondé.
Gruser. *To grieue,or to repine,at.*
Grusler des pois. *To parch Pease.*
Gruyau: m. *Oat-meale; or the course meale of any other corne; the great of corne.*
Gruyer: m. *A principall forrester; a chiefe Warden, or Verderer; a maister Sergeant in a forrest; for this name is generall, and proper vnto all these seuerall officers; who in the title, and right thereof, belonging to the King, haue authoritie,to cause his Ordinances to be kept,& to punish the breakers thereof (as well within other Lords woods,as within his) either by setting amerciaments on their heads, or by confiscating of their cattell (the whole benefit whereof is, in most places,adiudged vnto him) yet if the fact committed (in his forrests) require a greater penaltie then* 60 s.Tourn. *they must referre it ouer to the censure of the maisters of the Forrests; also,as in* Gruier.
Gruyer: m. ere: f. *Of a Crane;also,made(as a Hawke) onely for the Crane.*
Gruyerie,& Gruyrie. *as* Grurie.
Gruyo sec. *as* Grio.
Gryllon: m. *A Cricket,or Grasse-hopper.*
Gryotte. *as* Griotte.
Grypaume: f. *The hearbe Motherwort.*
Gryper. *See* Griper.
Grys. *as* Gris.
Guaillardet: m. *A Streamer, Pennon, or Pendant, in Ships,&c.*
Guainier: m. *The tree called, Iudas-tree; (belike because he hanged himselfe on one of that kind.)*
Guaire. *as* Guere; *Little.*
Guaive. Choses guaives. *Waifes, or strayes; or, things quitted, abandoned, forsaken, left at randome.*
Gualebaut: m. *A hoyse-cup,or tosse-pot.*
Guaranion. *A kind of horse; (an old word.)*
Guarantir. *as* Garantir; *To warrant.*
Guarbances: f. *Fitches,Vetches.*
Guarde-manger. *See* Garde-manger.
Guardon. *as* Gardon.
Guare guare. *War,war; take heed,take heed.*
Sans dire guare. *On a suddaine,at vnawares, before any warning giuen,without bidding beware.*
Guarent. *See* Garent.
Guari: m. ie: f. *Healed, whole, cured, recouered, of a disease.*
Guarigues. *Plaine champian fields.* ¶Rab.

Guarir. *To heale, cure, mend, recouer, make whole, restore vnto health.*

Bon est le medicin qui se sçait guarir: Prov. *He is a good Phisition that can heale himselfe.*

Guarison: f. *Health; curing, healing; recouerie, amendment.*

Qui veut la guarison du Mire, il luy convient tout son mal dire: Prov. *He that would cured be must all his ill confesse.*

Guarissable: com. *Healeable, cureable, recouerable.*

Guarite: f. *as* Garite.

Guarrot. *See* Garrot.

Guastaliens. *An Order of religious people, consisting both of men and women, and instituted the yeare* 1537 *by the Countesse of* Guastala, *a Mantuan Ladie.*

Guastier: m. *One that is hired to tend other mens grounds; or, as* Gastier.

Guatte: f. *The small, or young Shad, the riuer Pilchard.* ¶Bayonnois.

Guault. *The name of an apple, that yeelds very pleasant, and cleere Cyder.*

Guayac. Guacum, Lignum vitæ, *Pockewood.*

Guayer. *as* Guéer.

Guaynier. *as* Guainier.

Guayre. *as* Guere. ¶Provençal.

Gué: m. *A Foord; a shallow part of a riuer, where it may be waded ouer.*

`A grand cheval grand gué: Prov. *A great horse a great Foord must haue.*

Gueable: com. *Wadeable; fit, likelie, or easie, to be waded ouer.*

Guedde, ou Guede: f. *as* Guesde; *(Course) Woad.*

Guedé: m. ée: f. *Stuffed, strouting, crammed full of, or filled vp with, meat and drinke.*

Guedon. Faire de guedon guedon. *To mince, or simper it; to be nice, quaint, scrupulous of receiuing what inwardly is longed for; to say nay and take it, as men say maids doe; whence;*

Et apres guedon. *(Of women which do a thing after they haue made it strange a while;) and afterwards they fell to it with a better stomacke then they had refused it.*

Guedouar. *as* Gadouard.

Guedoufle: f. *A small oyle-pot, or bottle (most commonly) couered with leather; a small Burrachoe.*

Guedouille: f. *as* Guedoufle.

Guedousse de vinaigre; *(Corruptly for* Guedoufle.) *A small vineger bottle.*

Guéé: m. éee: f. *Waded ouer; also, rinced.*

Guéer. *To wade.*

Guéer vn cheval. *To wash, or water a horse in a riuer.*

Guéer du linge. *To rince linnen.*

Guelphe: com. *Of the Guelphian faction (in Italie;) also, factious, or seditious.*

Guementé: m. ée: f. *Asked, or inquired after; also, lamented, or complained of.*

se **Guementer.** *To aske, or inquire after; or, as* Se Guermenter.

Guenaud: m. *A begger; also, a digger of graues.*

Guenchir. *To start, shrinke, or wrench aside, thereby to auoid a comming blow.* (v.m.)

Gueneau: m. *The throtle, or throat-boll.* ¶Blesien.

Guenille: f. *A rag; or old, and tattered clowt.*

Guenipe: f. *as* Guenille.

Guenon: f. *A Monkie; also, an Ape; whence;*

Guenon de mer. *as* Singe de mer.

Guenonnée: f. *A most beastlie wench; one that hath beene ridden by a Monkie.*

Guenot: m. *A Shepheards Familiar; a Spirit, or Hobgoblin, which (as some of those ignorant Swaynes imagine) preserues, and defends from wolues, and theeues, the sheepe of him he belongs to.* ¶Blesien.

Guenupe: f. *A little Monkie, or Marmouset.*

Guepillon. *A holie-water-sprinkle.*

Guepillonneux: m. euse: f. *Sprinkling, bedewing, casting water vpon.*

Guerb. *Common of pasture for a mans beasts throughout all his neighbours grounds; (In some parts of Brittanie.)*

Temps de guerb. *Is from mid September to the middle of Februarie.*

Guerdon: m. *Guerdon, recompence, meed, remuneration, reward; also, as* Gardon.

Guerdonné: m. ée: f. *Guerdoned, rewarded.*

Guerdonnement. *A guerdoning, recompencing, remunerating, rewarding.*

Guerdonner. *To guerdon, remunerate, recompence, reward.*

Guere. *But little, small, scant, scarce, rare; but a while, not long, but a little, not much.*

Guere souvent. *Rarely, seldome, not often, not many times.*

Il ne s'en fault guere. *There wants not much; there scarce wants any; tis like, or verie neere.*

Gueres. *as* Guere; *and hence;*

Il n'y a gueres. *It was but lately; it is not long agoe.*

Quand il n'est gueres de Lune. *When it is but yong Moone.*

Gueret: m. *Fallow, or fallow ground; land well manured, laboured, tilled; fitted, and prepared for seed, &c; also, mould, or soyle; also, mud, or filth.*

Gueret vieux. Terres de g. *Ground which hath lyen fallow a whole yeare at least.*

Guereté: m. ée: f. *Layed, or made fallow; manured; laboured; fitted for seed, &c.*

Guereter. *To lay, or make land fallow; to eare, manure, till; to labour, or prepare for seed, &c.*

Guerguesses: f. *Wide Slops, or Gallogaskins, great Gascon, or Spanish hose.*

Gueri: m. ie: f. *Healed, cured.*

Guerir. *as* Guarir; *To heale; to cure.*

Guerir aulcun de tous ses maulx; *To kill one.*

Guerison. *See* Guarison.

Guerissable: com. *Healeable, cureable.*

Guerisseur: m. *A healer, or curer.*

Guerite: f. *as* Garite; *or, a place of retreat, or hiding hole (whereof diuers were wont to be made) in thicke Rampiers, for the preseruation of those that, in a surprize, had the lucke, or leisure, to get into them; also, a Sentrie, or Watch-tower.*

Guerité. Murs gueritez. *Rampiers furnished with such defences, or places of retreat; or Sentries.*

Guerle: f. *A Siue made of a skin dryed, and pierced full of holes.*

Guerle: com. *Squint-eyed, or gogle-eyed.*

Guerler. *To sift (through a* Guerle.)

Guerluset. *(Somewhat like our Shagrag;) a by-word for a beggerlie souldior.*

se **Guermenter.** *To lament, mourne, complaine, groane; also, to fret, afflict, or vex himselfe; also, to aske, or enquire after; (an old, and rusticke word.)*

Guernette: f. *A Prawne*: ¶Parisien.
Guernier. *See* Grenier.
Guerpi: m. ie: f. *Left, quit, forsaken, abandoned, relinquished, giuen ouer; also, crept, crawled, gone forward by little and little.*
Guerpie: f. *as* Guerpine; *Also, a creeping, crawling, mouing forward by little and little.*
La guerpie. (*In some ancient customes doth signifie*) *a widow.*
Guerpine: f. *A quitting, leauing, abandoning, relinquishing, forgoing, forsaking.*
Guerpir. *To quit, leaue, abandon, relinquish, forgoe, forsake; yeeld, or giue ouer; also (in a contrarie sence) to seise, get, lay hold on, take possession of; also, to creepe, crawle, moue, or goe forward by little and little.*
Guerpison: f. *as* Guerpine.
Guerre: f. *Warre; warfare; discord, strife, contention, debate.*
Guerre guerroyable. *Open, or mortall, warre.*
Bonne guerre. *Faire play; or, the keeping of Quarter; a taking, and ransoming, of prisoners in warre.*
Droict de guerre. *See* Droict.
Fer de guerre. *The sharpe head of a horsemans staffe.*
Tour de vieille guerre. *A notable sleight, plot, shift; an excellent stratagem.*
Sentir la vieille guerre. *To be of the old stampe, cut, fashion, or humor.*
La guerre est la feste des morts: Prov. *Warre is deathes holy-day.*
Argent faict guerre: Prov. *Money makes warre: viz: incites men to vndertake, and enables them to vndergoe, it.*
Homme mort ne fait guerre: Prov. *A dead man deales no blowes.*
Mieux vaut en paix vn oeuf qu' en guerre vn boeuf: &, Mieux vaut seruitude en paix que seigneurie en guerre: Prov. *Looke* Paix.
Nulle terre sans guerre: Prov. *No land without warre; he that hath land is seldome out of law; The like is;*
Qui a terre, si, a guerre: Prov. *He that hath soyle hath suits.*
Tousjours ne dure orage ne guerre: Prov. *Nor storme, nor sturre, continues euer.*
Guerrier: m. *A Warrier, a Martiall man.*
Guerrier: m. ere: f. *Warlike, Martiall, valiant, or forward in warre; also, contentious, brabling, litigious.*
Guerrier. *To warre, make warre vpon, fight, or contend against.*
Guerrite. *A kind of defence in a rampier; See* Guerite.
Guerroyable: com. *Warrable; fit to be warred on; See* Guerre.
Guerroyant. *Warring, fighting, contentious.*
Guerroyé: m. ée: f. *Warred or contended against, brabled or brawled with.*
Guerroyement: m. *Warre, warfare, or warfaring.*
Guerroyer. *To warre; fight, or contend against; brabble with; make warre vpon.*
Guerroyeur: m. *A Martialist, or Warrior; also, a fraymaker, swaggerer, contentious person.*
Guery: m. ye: f. *Healed, cured.*
Guesde: f. *Woad, or Wade; both hearbe, and stuffe thats made of the leaues thereof; Many of the French Dyers call the courser sort of the stuffe* Guesde, *and the finer* Pastel; *most writers confound them; we call the hearbe Garden or tame Woad, therein to make it differ from;*
Guesde sauvage. *Wild Woad; which growes of it selfe in grounds wherein th'other hath beene sowne; and differs not much from it but in staulke, wherein this is the tenderer, browner, and smaller of the two.*
Guesdé: m. ée: f. *Woaded; died with Woad.*
Guespe: f. *A Waspe.*
Guespée: f. *A neast, or swarme of Waspes.*
Guespier: m. *A Woodwall, Wood-pecker, Eat-bee (a little bird;) also, a kind of Spider that somewhat resembles a Waspe.*
Guespiere: f. *A Waspes neast.*
Guespilleur: m. *as* Gaspilleur; *A squanderer.*
Guespillonné: m. ée: f. *Besprinkled, bedewed with a sprinkle.*
Guespillonner. *To besprinkle, or bedew, as with a holy-water sprinkle.*
Guespine: f. *A waspish dame; or (as our Cockney of London) a nickname for a woman of* Orleans.
Guest. harang guest. *A shotten, or leane herring.*
Guestré: m. ée: f. *Hauing startups on.*
Guestres: f. *Startups; high shooes, or gamashes, for countrey folkes.*
Guesvé: m. ée: f. *Waiued; refused, abandoned, giuen ouer.*
Guesve. Seigneur guesve. *A Landlord vnto whom surrender is made of the ground held of him.*
Choses guesves. *Waifes, strayes, or things left, quitted, abandoned.*
Guesvement: m. *A wayving, a refusing; also, a resignation, or surrender of land.*
Guesver. *To waiue, refuse, abandon, giue ouer; also, to surrender, giue backe, resigne, redeliuer.*
Guesveux: m. euse: f. *Plashie, flashie; also, beplashed.*
Guet: m. *Watch, ward, watch and ward; also, heed, obseruation, carefull spying, diligent looking about; also, the Watch, or companie appointed to watch.*
Guet à pens; ou, à pensé; ou, appens; ou, appensé. *An ambush prepared, or laid with a purpose to intrap, deceiue, or despoyle the partie watched for; also, the act done, or offence committed, by the meanes of such an ambush; and hence;*
De guet à pensée. *Wittingly, willingly, aduisedly, deliberately, of set purpose; and, with a malicious intent, or a resolution to doe mischiefe.*
Archers du guet. *Looke* Archer.
Chevalier du guet. *The Captaine of the ordinarie watch of Paris.*
Droict du guet. *A Prerogatiue some Lords (inhabitants of the borders of the sea coast) haue ouer their tenants, euerie one of whom they may compell to watch the coast one day in a moneth (whether there be occasion or no) or to pay for each default 5 s.* Tourn. *which are often changed into a certaine quantitie of corne, hennes, &c, according to the custome of the place, or the composition made with them; also, Castle gard, or Castle-ward; See* Droict.
Accoustré pour aller au guet. *Throughly tipled, soundly whitled, that hath seene the diuell.*
Aller de guet à ses affaires. *To goe slowly, lazily, drousily, sleepily about his businesse.*
Estre du guet. *as* Avoir la cassade; me voila bien du guet. *I am now plainely cousened, beguiled, ouerraught; I am come to a faire passe, I am finely drest indeed.*
Faire le guet à Montfaucon. *To be hanged (we may say at Tiburne;* Montfaucon *being a hill (neere Paris) whereon the common Gibbet stands.)*
Faire le guet au temps. *To obserue narrowly the course;*

course; and reuolutions of times, and seasons; Looke Faire.

Tenir le guet. *To watch and ward.*

Bon guet chasse malaventure: Prov. *Good heed preuents misfortunes,(or expells them.)*

Guettable. *Watchable; subiect vnto watching, and warding.*

Guettant. *Watching, warding; prying, spying; heeding, marking, obseruing; dogging, staulking after.*

En guettant, & espiant. *Craftily, falsly; on aduantage, at vnawares.*

Guette: f. *A watchman, warder; spie, espiall; a scoutwatch; also, a Sentinell, or watch-tower in a castle, or fortresse.*

Guetté: m. ée: f. *Watched, warded; also, pried, or spied into; narrowly obserued, maliciously dogged.*

Guettement: m. *A watching, warding; prying; heeding, obseruing; dogging, lying in wait for.*

Guetter. *To watch, ward, watch and ward; spie, prie, looke about; marke, heed, note, obserue narrowly; dog, staulke after, lye in wait for.*

Guetteur: m. *A watcher, warder; spie, espiall; prier, busie obseruer of.*

Guetteur de chemins. *A way-layer, a robber on the highway, a purse-taker, one of Saint Nicholas Clerkes.*

Gueu. *as* Queux; *A Cooke.*

Gueüant. *Begging in the highway; or, like a rogue any way.*

Guever. *See* Guesver.

Gueüer. *as* Gueuser.

Gueüesse: f. *as* Gueuse; *A woman begger.*

Gueule: f. *The mouth; also, (and most properly) the throat, gullet, pipe, or passage, wherby meat is sent from the mouth downe to the stomacke; also, the stomacke it selfe; or the mouth, or Orifice thereof.*

Gueule droitte. *(In Architecture) as* Nasselle.

Gueule renversée. *as* Cyme.

Harnois de gueule. *Meat, victualls, mouth-armour, throat-harnesse.*

Marchandise de gueule. *Victualls, Kitchen ware.*

Mot de gueule. *A ieast, or merrie word.*

Tonneau à gueule bée. *A Tunne whose head is beaten out; or, thats open at the one end.*

Bien fendu de gueule. *Well mouth-clouen, that hath a goodlie wide mouth.*

Au chat cendreux jamais ne tombe rien en gueule: &, à regnard endormi rien ne chet en la gueule: Prov. *Sluggish, or idle people neuer get any thing to purpose; we say, of idlenesse comes no goodnesse.*

Au chat lescheur bat on souvent la gueule: Prov. *Looke* Chat.

Gueules. *Gules; red, or sanguine, in Blazon.*

Gueullard: m. *The muzzle, or mouth of a beast; also, a wide-mouthed fellow; also, an imbosse (like the head of a Lyon) vpon auncient buskins.*

Gueulle: f. *See* Gueule.

Gueus: m. *A begger; an idle rogue, a louzie tattered vagabond.*

Gueusant. *as* Gueüant.

Gueuse: f. *A woman begger, a she rogue, a great, lazie, and louzie queane; a Doxie, or Mort; also, a great lump of melted yron, rude, and vnfashioned, euen as it comes from the furnace.*

Gueuser. *To beg on the highway, like a rogue.*

Gueuserie: f. *Beggarie; a canting, or begging.*

Guey: m. *as* Gué; *A foord.*

Gueuze. *as* Gueuse.

Gui: m. *See* Guy.

Guichet: m. *A wicket; or hatch of a doore.*

Madame du guichet *(A nickname for a Midwife.)*

Guichetier: m. *He that keepeth the wicket of a prison.*

Guidage. *A Passport, or Writ of safeconduct.*

Guide: f. *A guide, leader, conductor, director; also, a certain little sea-fish that continually swimmes before the Whale; also, a kind of disease, or sore, in a horses withers.*

Guidé: m. ée: f. *Guided, conducted, directed.*

Guideau: m. *A kind of fish-net.*

Guider. *To guide, lead, direct, conduct; set, or keepe, in the way.*

Guideymant. *The needle of a sea-compasse.*

Guidon: m. *A Standard, Ensigne, or Banner, vnder which a troupe of men of Armes doe serue; also, he that beares it.*

Guieor. *as* Guide; *An old word.*

Guier. *as* Guider; *To guide.* (v.m.)

Guieres. *as* Guere.

Guiges: f. *The handles of a Targuet, or Shield.*

Guignade: f. *as* Guignement.

Guignement: m. *A winking, or aiming at a thing with one eye.*

Guigne-queuë. *The little bird called, a Wagtaile, or Dish-washer.*

Guigner. *To winke, or aime at with one eye; to leuell at a thing, winking; also, to blinke; to winke and looke askew.*

Guigneur: m. *A winker; an aimer with one eye, as a Gunner taking his leuell; also, a blinker.*

Guignons de roches. *The corners, or edges of rockes.*

Guigneron. *A Gold-finder, a Dung-farmer.*

Guilée: f. *A great shower of raine.*

Guilhedin: m. *A gelding.*

Guillardet. *as* Gaillard: ¶Rab.

Guillaume. *(A name;) William; also, a nickname for a gull, dolt, fop, foole.*

Guillaume baillez moy la lance. *A play (or punishment) wherein one thats hudwinkt rides on anothers backe, and calling thus, hath a shitten staffe raught him.*

Guille: f. *The quill, or faucet of a wine vessell; also, the keele of a ship; also, guile, craft, deceit.*

Guille de beurre. *A peece of butter made of the fashion of a finger.*

Guillé: m. ée: f. *Beguiled.*

Guillebardeau: m. *A toole, or instrument.*

Guillée. *as* Guilée.

Guillemine: f. *A certaine Edict against some exorbitant priuiledges of the Church; deuised, and published by* Guillaume Pojet, *a Chauncellor of Fraunce.*

Guillemins: m. *An Order of Hermites, instituted by* Guillaume, *Duke of* Guienne, *and Earle of* Poictou; *Seeke* Les Blancs Manteaux, *in* Manteau.

Guillemot: m. *A certain three-towed fowle, that somewhat resembles a Plouer.*

Guillenard: m. *Part of a womans &c.*

Guiller. *To cousen, beguile, deceiue.* (v.m.)

Guilleret: m. ette: f. *Merrie, frolicke, pleasant, liuelie; also, red about the gills, as one that is cup-shotten, or hath drunke somewhat hard.*

Guillerie de passereaux: f. *The chirping of Sparrowes.*

Guillery: m. *as* Guillerie.

Guillochis: m. *A kind of flourishing in Masonrie, or Carpentrie.*

Guilloquet. *Part of a womans &c.*

Guillot:

Guillot : m. *A proper name for a man ; and hence ;*
Guillot le Songeur. *A dreaming fellow, a dull sleepi loggar-head.*
Logé chez Guillot le Songeur. *Put into a dump, muse, dreame, driuen into a studie.*
Guilmin : m. *A noddie, ninnie, coxe, ideot.*
Guilon : f. *A rigge ; a wanton, or wandering, girle.*
Guilverdons : m. *Great gobbets of liquid meats, as of oysters, &c.*
Guimauves : f. *Marsh Mallowes, moorish Mallowes, white Mallowes.*
Guimauves sauvages. *The wild Mallowes called, Veruine Mallowes, cut Mallowes, & Simons Mallowes.*
Guimaux. prez guimaux. *Fertill medowes, which are mowed twice a yeare.* ¶Rab.
Guimpe, *or* Guimphe : f. *as* Guimple.
Guimpier : m. *A maker of Crepines.*
Guimple : f. *The Crepine of a French-hood.*
Guinche : f. *A sword, or hatchell for a flax-wife.*
Guincher. *To wrigle, writhe, wrinch a toeside.*
Guindage : m. *A hoising, or lifting vp ; or an engine to lift vp things with.*
Guindal : m. *An engine to lift vp stones, or timber with.*
Guindé : m. ée : f. *Lift, or hoysed vp.*
Guinder. *To hoyse, or lift vp on high.*
Guinder les cieux. *To bow downe the heauens.*
Se Guinder. *To bound, skip, or leap vp ; also, to knit, or gather himselfe together.*
Guinderesse. la g. de la misaine. *The mizen halliards ; the rope whereby the mizen sayle is hoysed vp.*
Guindol. *See* Guindal.
Guindoles. *as* Guindoules.
Guindoules : f. *The fruit called, Iuiubes.*
Guindre : f. *A reele, or wheele to winde silke on.*
Guines. *See* Guisnes.
Guinguois. de guinguois. *Slouenly, vneuenly, vnhandsomely, awry ; also, huffingly, swaggeringly, aswash.*
Guinson. *as* Pinson.
Guipilon. *An holiewater sprinkle.*
Guipure : f. *A grosse black thread (couered, or whipt about with silke) whereof corded hat-bands be made.*
Guipures d'or. *Goulden (and wreathed) Aglets, or Tags.*
Guirlande : f. *A garland.*
Guirlandé : m. ée : f. *Begarlanded ; wearing a Garland ; bedecked, or set out, with Garlands.*
Guisarme : f. *A kind of (offensiue) long-handled, and long-headed, weapon ; or (as the Spanish* Visarma*) a staffe, that hath within it two long pikes, which with a shoot, or thrust forward, come forth.*
Guise : f. *Guise ; manner, fashion, custome, vsage ; humor.*
Chascun a sa guise : Pro. *Euery one as he likes.*
Tant de villes tant de guises : Pro. *In euery towne he seuerall customes, or fashions.*
Guisnes : f. *A kind of little, sweet, and long cherries ; tearmed so, because at first they came out of* Guyenne*; also, any kind of Cherries.*
Guisner : m. *A sweet-cherrie tree.*
Guiterne ; *or* Guiterre : f. *A Gitterne.*
Gulpe : f. *A wound, or bloud-wipe ; (in Blazon, a golp ; and must be purple.)*
Gulpine : f. *A quitting, leauing, abandoning, forsaking, waiuing, giuing ouer an estate in land.*
Gulpir. *as* Guerpir. *To quit, leaue, waiue.*
Gumenes : f. *The tackling of a ship.*
Guoguette. *as* Gogue.
Le coeur luy dit guoguette. *He is exceeding merrie, liuelie, iocond, frolicke ; his hart leaps for ioy.*
Guorre : f. *as* Gorre ; *A sow.* ¶Rab.
Guoy : m. *A little hand-bill, vsed for the cutting, and pruining of Vines.*
Gurleret. *A nickname, or by-word for a beggarlie souldier.*
Gurpir. *To quit, forgoe, leaue, abandon.*
Gurpison. : f. *A quitting, forgoing, leauing, abandoning.*
Guses. *The ball of the eye ; so tearmed in blazon ; and must euer be sanguine.*
Gutale, ou Guttale. *Ale, good Ale.*
Guttural : m. ale : f. *Gutturall ; belonging to the throat.*
Guy : m. *Misseltoe, or Misseldine.*
Guy de Flandres. *A kind of morter wherewith fretworke is made.*
Guyberges. *as* Guymberges.
Guybourc. *The name of a certaine greene, and sweet apple.*
Guymauves. *as* Guimauves.
Guymberges. *Flourisht worke in seeling, or vaulting.*
Guynettes : f. *Yong Guinnie hennes.*
Guynnes. *as,* Guisnes.
Guypierre. *as* Guipure.
Guypure. *as.* Guipure.
Guyron. *That which we call Geronne, in blasing of Armes.*
Guysarme. *as* Guisarme.
Guysarmier. *One that serues with a* Guisarme.
Guyvre : f. *A snake, an adder.*
Gy : m. *Plaister, morter ; looke* Gyp.
Gymnaste. *Exercised ; or, nimble at exercise.* ¶Rab.
Gynecocratie : f. *Feminine rule, or authoritie, the gouernment of a woman.*
Gyngois. à gyngois. *as,* de Guinguois.
Gynocratie : f. *The Gouernment of a woman.*
Gyp, *or* Gyps. *Morter, plaister ; or, a kind of white stone whereof plaister is made.*
Gypsé : m. ée : f. *Like morter, or plaister ; also, mortered, or plaistered.*
Gyraffe : *as* Giraffe.
Gyrine : f. *The frog tearmed, a Tadpole.*
Gyroflée : f. *A gilloflower. See* Giroflée.
Gyroles : f. *Skirret roots.*
Gyron. *as* Guyron *(a tearme of blasonrie.)*
Gyrouët : m. *A fane ; or weathercocke ; See* Girouëtte.
Gyrouëtte : f. *as* Gyrouët.
Gyrouëtteux : m. euse : f. *Flitting, wauering, inconstant, giddie, vnsteddie, as a fane, or weathercock.*

H

HA. *(The third person of the Present tense of the verb* Avoir*)* Il ha : *He hath.*
Ha. *An Interiection, sometimes denoting a wish ; as* ha s'il m' estoit permis ! *sometimes griefe ; as,* ha, quelle fascherie ! *Ah, or alas, what a trouble ! sometimes threatning, or anger ; as,* ha meschant tu es mort. *Ha villaine thou art dead.*
Ha ha. *An Interiection of feare, or of wonder (vpon the seeing, or finding of a thing on a suddain) A ha ; also, of laughter (then acompanied with* hé*) as,* ha ha hé.
Haaler. *as* Hasler.

Habarre: f. *A Lyter; See* Gabarre.
Habatre. *as* Abbatre.
Habeliné: m.ée: f. *Distempered; or, (as some haue vnderstood it) all-to-bepissed:* ¶Rab.
Habile: com. *Able; strong, lustie, powerfull, hardie; quicke, nimble, actiue, readie, cunning, expert; sufficient; fit for, handsome in, apt vnto, any thing he vndertakes, or is put vnto.*
Habilement. *Ably; strongly, lustily, hardily; nimbly, quickly, readily; aptly, fitly, with good decorum; cunningly, expertly; sufficiently.*
Habileté: f. *Ablenesse, abilitie; strength, lustinesse; quicknesse, lightnesse, actiuitie, nimblenesse; aptnesse, readinesse, handsomenesse, dexteritie; cunning; sufficiencie.*
Il ne tient ia qu' à vne habileté de main. *There needs no more but one right blow; one blow well set on would serue the turne.*
Habilité. *as* Habileté.
Habilité: m.ée: f. *Enabled; fitted; confirmed; auowed, allowed of.*
Habiliter. *To enable; confirme, giue strength, or power vnto; to apt, or make fit for; to auow, or allow of.*
Habiliter vn mineur. *To enable an infant to sue, or answer in law, by appointing him a Gardian who may doe it for him.*
Habiliter vn proces. C'est quand les parties droissent leurs procedures, pieces, & productions avec inventaire, pour en mettre les sacs par devers le Iuge, pour avoir droict, & iugement: ¶Ragueau.
Habillage de poullailles. *The dressing thereof; as the pluming, drawing, &c.*
Habillé: m.ée: f. *Dressed, clothed, arrayed, attired, apparelled; furnished; decked, adorned.*
Habillé comme vn brusleur de maisons. *In tattered, or desperate, array.*
Habillement: m. *Apparell, clothing, array, attire; a sute of apparell; also, a garment, rayment, vestment, or vesture; also, armour, or harnesse; and hence;*
Habillement de teste. *An helmet, or headpeece.*
Habiller. *To cloth, dresse, apparell, array, attire; to furnish; also, to decke, trimme, adorne.*
Habit: m. *A garment, raiment, vestiment, or vesture; apparell, or a sute of apparell; also, an habit; a fashion setled, a vse or custome gotten.*
Il n'est pas si fol qu'il en porte l' habit. *He is not so fond as he seemes, or makes shew for.*
L' habit ne fait pas le moine: Prov. *Tis not the habit (but the heart) that makes a man religious.*
Habitable: com. *Inhabitable; which may be dwelt in.*
Habitacle: m. *An habitacle, or habitation; a dwelling, or abiding place.*
Habitant: m. *An inhabitant, or inhabitor; a dweller, or abider in a place.*
Habitant. *Inhabiting, dwelling, abiding in.*
Habitation: f. *An habitation, or inhabitation, a dwelling, or place of abiding.*
Habité. *Dwelt, inhabited, lodged, remained, aboad.*
Habiter. *To dwell, inhabit, lodge, reside, remaine, wone, abide, or liue in a place.*
Habitual: m. ale: f. *Habituall; customarie, continuall; also, wholly possessing.*
Habituation: f. *An habit, vse, or custome; a manner gotten, fashion setled, forme taken.*
Habitude: f. *Custome, vse, acquaintance, familiaritie with.*
L'habitude de corps. *The estate, plight, liking, or disposition of the bodie.*
Avoir habitude avec. *To conuerse, or commerce; to meddle, deale, or haue much to doe, with.*
Habitué: m. *A houshold seruant, or attendant; one that dwells with, and weares the Liuerie of, him he belongs to.*
Habitué: m. ée: f. *Vsed, enured, accustomed, framed, or made, vnto; setled, well practised, that hath got an habit, in; also, well shaped, well liking, of good constitution of bodie.*
Habituer. *To vse, accustome, enure, make, or frame, vnto; to settle, practise, breed an habit, in.*
Hable: m. *A Port, or Hauen.*
Habler. *To speake; whence;*
Quand Marthe file, & Ambrose hable, leur cas est triste, & pitoyable: Prov. *When wiues doe spinne, and husbands babble, their case is hard, and lamentable.*
Hableur: m. *A talkatiue person, a man full of words.*
Habordean: m. *The fish Haberdine.*
Habrizer. *To get into the shade, or shrowd himselfe vnder a couert; also, to sleepe.*
Hache: f. *An axe; also, a crooked peece of land somewhat resembling the bowed beake of an axe; also, the hearbe Smallage; (for which looke* Ache*) also, a Torch.*
Hache d'armes. *A Battle-axe, or Mase of Armes.*
Hache royalle. *The Affodill, or Asphodill flower; especially (the small kind thereof called) the Speare for a King.*
Haché: m. ée: f. *Hacked, shred, sliced, chopped, cut, or hewed in peeces; also, hatched, as the hilt of a sword.*
Hachement: m. *A hacking, shredding, slicing; hewing, or cutting in peeces.*
Par hachemens. *In peecemeale, slices, or shreds; as a hachee; or, as small as meat in a hachee, or flesh to the pot.*
Hacher. *To hacke, shread, slice; hew, chop, cut in peeces (as with an axe;) also, to cut the aire, as a bird that flies apace; also, to hatch a hilt.*
Hachereau: m. *A little axe; an Addis.*
Hachette: f. *A hatchet, or small axe.*
Hachis: m. *A hachey, or hachée; a sliced gallimaufrey, or minced meat.*
Hacquebute: f. *An Haquebut, or Harguebuze.*
Hacquebuter. *To shoot in, or with, an Harguebuze.*
Hacquet: m. *as* Haquet; *Also, a little Cesterne, or open vessell, for the rinsing of glasses, or cooling of wine in Summer.*
Hacquetier. *as* Haquetier.
Hadea. *(An Interiection of perceiuing, or surprising) ha are you there?*
Hadot: m. *A salt Haddocke.*
Hadou. *as* Hadot.
Haffres: f. *Fright, astonishment; Looke* Affres.
Haffreux. *as* Affreux.
Hagard: m.arde: f. *Hagard, wild, strange; froward, contrarie, crosse; vnsociable, vncompanable, incompatible.*
Faulcon hagard. *A Hagard; a Faulcon that preyed for her selfe long before she was taken.*
Hagiographe: com. *Written holily, or sacredly.*
Haglé: m. ée: f. *Mailed; speckled as the coat of a hawke.*
Haglure: f. *The maile (or specklednesse) of the coat of a hawke.*
Hahay. faire gros hahay. *To make a great stirre, or mightie slaughter.*
Haï: m. Haie: f. *Hated, loathed; detested, abhorred.*

Il est povre qui est de Dieu haï: Prov. *Poore is the man whom God abhorres.*

Qui de ses subiects est haï n'est pas Seigneur de son païs: Prov. *The Prince thats hated, is not Lord, of his countrey.*

Hai. *An Interiection, of encouragement, as,* hai avant; *On afore there hoe; also, of complayning, as,* hai hai hai vous me blessez; *Alas, fie, out, you hurt me; Looke* Hay.

Haias: m. *A kind of Beech tree.*

Haict. *Seeke* Hait.

Haie: f. *A hedge; Looke* Haye.

Hailler: m. *A great thicke bush, or bushie place; a thornie plot, ground full of briers, thicket of brambles.*

Haillier. *as* Hailler.

Haillon: m. *A clowt, a tatter, a rag; also, an old, torne, or tattered garment.*

O les beaux haillons. *(So say they in some parts of France, when they see a man most richly attired.)*

Haillonné: m. ée: f. *Cut into rags, or tatters; whereof clowts are made.*

Discours haillonnez. *Ragged, or patched discourses.*

Haillonner. *To cut into rags, or tatters; to clowt, or make clowts of.*

Haillonneux: m. euse: f. *Ragged, torne, tattered; full of clowts, patches; rags, or tatters.*

Haim: m. *A (fishing) hooke.*

Haine: f. *Hate, hatred; loathing, detestation; malice, rancor, a grudge, ill-will.*

Haine de Prince signifie mort d'homme: Prov. *A Princes hate imports the death of man.*

Nul bien sans haine: Prov. *No happinesse without hatred.*

Haines. les haines: f. *The hips; or, as* l'Eine.

Haineur: m. *A hater, loather, detester, abhorrer.*

Haineuseté: f. *Hatefulnesse, odiousnesse; or an extreame detestation of.*

Haineux: m. euse: f. *Full of hate; hating, loathing, detesting extreamely; also, hatefull, detestable, most odious.*

Haïr. *To hate; loath, detest, abhorre, spight, malice, repine at, beare ill-will vnto.*

Oncques n'ayma bien qui pour si peu haït: Prov. *He neuer soundly loued that hateth for a toy.*

Haire: m. *A leane, or ill-fauoured curtall; a carrion iade; (hence) also, a wretched or miserable fellow; a poore snake.*

Haire: f. *A Sackcloth; a sleeuelesse shirt, &c, made of rugged haire, and worne (as a penance, or flesh-tamer;) also, a Temmes, Boulter, or Strainer; also, a shrewd, or villanous pranke; and hence;*

Bailler la haire. *(Seeke* Bailler; *)* &;

Faire mille haires à. *To vexe, trouble, disquiet, molest extreamely.*

Haireux: m. euse: f. *Rough, rugged, harsh, like Sackecloth.*

Hairon: *A heron, herne, herneshaw.*

Hairon marin. *The Sword-fish.*

Haironneau: m. *A yong heron.*

Haironnier. m. ere: f. *Of, or belonging to a heron; also, heron-like; hence, long, tall; slender; leane, starueling, meager; lanke.*

Faulcon haironnier. *A herner, a faulcon made onely to the heron.*

Haironniere: f. *A herons neast, or ayrie; a herneshaw, or shaw of wood, wherein herons breed.*

Haïssable: com. *Hatable; fit, or worthie to be hated.*

Haistre: m. *A Beech tree.*

Hait: m. *Liuelinesse, lustinesse; gladnesse, cheerefulnesse; willingnesse; readinesse.*

Cela est bien à mon hait. *That fits my humor, pleases my fancie; sorts to my wish, iumpes with my desires.*

Haité: m. ée: f. *Liuelie, lustie, sound, blithe, buxome; cheerefull, dispose.*

Haiter. *To like well of, or be well pleased with; also, to cheere vp.*

Haitié. *as* Haité.

Haitoudeau: m. *Looke* Hestoudeau.

Hal: m. *An ashie coloured Scate-fish, whose skinne is powdered all ouer with browne spots:* ¶Norm.

Halachie: f. *A Shad-fish:* (¶Marseillois.)

Halainé: m. ée: f. *as* Halené.

Halbrené: m. ée: f. *Beshitten, ill berayed; also, sad of looke, or, all out of heart; as a man discontented, or tired, or hurt; Looke* Hallebrené.

Faulcon halbrené. *A Faulcon thats ragged, or broken-feathered.*

Halcion vocal. *The Nightingale of the riuer.*

Hale: m. *Sunne-burning, or th'extreame heat of the Sunne.*

Hale: f. *An open Market house, or hall, standing on pillers; (as that vnder which meale is sold in Newgate Market; or that of the Wooll Staple in Westminster;) also, a common hall, or Towne-house.*

Les hales. *Such a Market house, hall, or shambles, wherein flesh, and other victualls are sold.*

Halé: m. ée: f. *Sunne-burnt; as* Haslé; *also, veered, as a cable; also, hounded, or set, as a dog at.*

Halebant. *as* Albrent.

Halebarde: f. *An halbert; also, a kind of copper good to make Ordnance of.*

Halebardier: m. *An halberdeere; one that serues, or fights, altogether with an halberd.*

Halebran: m. *A Teale; also, as* Albrent *(in the two former significations thereof.)*

Halebreda: com. *A great, vnweldie, long, misshapen, ill-fauoured, or ill-fashioned, man, or woman; a luske, a slouch; a sosse.*

Halebrent. *as* Halebran.

Halecret: m. *A Corslet.*

Halecreté. *Armed with a Corslet.*

Haleine: f. *Ones breath, or wind; breathing.*

A la grosse haleine. *See* Gros.

Pousser à toute haleine. *To thrust with all his force, to labour tooth and naile.*

Haleineux: m. euse: f. *Long winded, full of breath.*

Halené: m. ée: f. *Breathed on; winded, vented; searched, or smelt out; whose nature is discouered, whose humor's found out.*

Halené de la flatterie. *Fed with the breath, or sucking vp th'aire, of flatterie.*

Halenée: f. *A breathing, venting, winding, exhaling; also, a breath, exhalation, wind.*

Halenement: m. *A breathing, or blowing on; a venting, winding; a smelling, or searching out.*

Halener. *To breath, or blow vpon; also, to vent, snooke, wind; smell, or search out; and (by metaphor) to discouer th'inclination, or find the humour, of.*

Haler. *To Sunne-burne, or scorch in the Sunne; to bleak, or make swart, a thing, by displaying it in a hot Sunne; also, to hound, or set, a dog at.*

Haler vn chable. *To veere a cable; to let it out, or let it runne out, at full length, or as farre as is needfull.*

Haletant. *Pursie, short winded, panting, breathing fast.*

Haletement: m. *A (painfull, or fast) panting; a thicke breathing, or letting in and out of the breath; also, a breathing, exhaling, euaporating, or venting out.*

Haleter. *To pant, or blow apace; to breath fast, or draw the breath verie thicke, and painfully, as one thats readie to die; also, to breath, exhale, euaporate, or vent out.*

Haleter apres les beautez d' vne femme. *Extreamly to long for, or lust after, them; (a metaphor from the manner of a dogs wooing.)*

Haliboron. *as* Aliboron.

Haligornes: f. *Trash; old or outcast stuffe.*

Halime: m. *A kind of sea Purslane much eaten in Sallades.*

Haliter. *as* Haleter; *Also, to excite, or stirre vp.*

Halitre: m. *as* Hasle.

Hallage. droict d' hallage. *Hallage; the toll thats due to the Lord of a Faire, or Market, for such commodities as are vented in the* Hale *of the place.*

Halle. *as* Hale: f.

Halle. *(An Interiection, of cheering, or setting on of a dog;) ha boy, now now.*

Hallebatté. ¶Rab. *as* Hallebotté.

Halleboter. *To gleane after grape-gatherers; (hence) also, to rake, or gather together.*

Hallebotté: m. ée: f. *Flaggie, or ill-filled, like the;*

Hallebottes: f. *The prettie-big, and bladder-like tops, or flowers, of a certaine weed, containing some two or three little red seeds apeece.*

Hallebrené: m. ée: f. *Sad, crest-fallen, heauie-looking, drooping; off the hindges, cleane out of heart (as a mooting ducke; or a ragged hawke;) also, beshitten, bedunged, grieuously beraied.*

Hallebrent. *as* Albrent.

Hallecret. *as* Halecret.

Hallefessier: m. *A scoundrell; a base, contemptible, or scuruie fellow; (This word is often applied vnto, and (as some thinke) was deuised for, the flattering attendant, or prying instrument, of a tyrant.)*

Hallené. *as* Halené.

Hallener. *as* Halener.

Haller. *To hallow, or incourage dogs with hallowing; also, to hound, or set them at.*

Halleron: m. *Part of a womans &c.*

Halles. les Halles. *as* les Hales.

Halleter. *Seeke* Haleter.

Hallier. *as* Hailler.

Halmyrach: m. *An Admirall.*

Halot: m. *as* Bruine; *A hot, and blasting mist.*

Halte. faire halte. *To stop, stay, make a stand.*

Hambour: m. *A kind of barrelet, or firkin.*

Hambourg. *as* Hambour.

Hamé: m. ée: f. *Hooked, furnished with a hooke.*

Hameau: m. *A hamlet; a small village.*

Hamech. Confection h. *A purging composition; tearmed thus by the deuisor thereof.*

Hameçon: m. *A little fish-hooke.*

Hameçonné: m. ée: f. *Behooked; full of, or furnished with, fish-hookes.*

Hameçonner. *To behooke, to furnish with fish-hookes.*

Hamesson. *as* Hameçon.

Hamessonné. *as* Hameçonné.

Hamet: m. *A small fish-hooke.*

Hampe: f. *The breast, brisket, or essay of a Deere.*

Hampe d' halebarde. *as* Hante.

Han. *The groane, or forced, and sigh-like voyce, wherwith woodcleauers, &c. keepe time to their stroakes.*

I'ay chanté à son han. *I haue spoken with him:* ¶Barragouin.

Hanap: m. *A drinking cup, or goblet.*

Hanche: f. *The haunch, or hip; also, as* Anche.

La goutte en la hanche la fille en la pance: Prov. *The gowt in the haunch, a girle in the paunch (of a great bellied woman.)*

Hancher. *To gnaspe, or snatch at with the teeth.* (vieil mot.)

Hanchois: m. *A Pilchard (fish.)*

Hanchu: m. uë: f. *Big haunched, well bumme-growne, great hipt.*

Handon: m. *A kind of Dragon, whose biting is not venomous.*

Hanebane: f. *(The weed) Henbane.*

Hanebane iaulne. *Yellow henbane, English Tobacco.*

Hanede. *whence,* Enter à la hanede. *as* Enter en perche; *(vnder the word* Enter.)

Hanegue: f. *A corne measure, containing about six Parisian bushells.*

Haneton: m. *A Locust, or huge flie, which hath six tawnie, and solide legs; and foure wings; two (the vpper, and larger) tawnie of colour, and somewhat thicke; the other two yellowish, and verie slender: Now the naturall stupiditie of these flies, or their violent and rash manner of flying; and their ingendering (like silkewormes) backward, and taile to taile; or their holding each by others taile (as they lie in holes, and hollow trees, all Winter long) haue produced the prouerbs following.*

Estourdi comme vn Haneton. *As dull, or heedlesse, as an* Haneton.

Parentage d' hanetons. *Lecherous alliance; kindred intertained vpon a lustfull proiect, or with a wanton purpose: (Tis also applied vnto such, as (like the Princes of the house of Austria) match, for the most part, in their owne families.)*

Hannicroches. *as* Hannicrochemens.

Hannebane. *as* Hanebane.

Hannicrochemens: m. *Subtilties, intanglements, cauills, troublesome vexations.*

Hanni. *Neighed like a horse.*

Hannir. *To neigh.*

Elles ne hannissoient à autre avoine. *They longed for no other thing; their minds ran on, their teeth watered at, nought else.*

Hannissement: m. *The neighing of a horse.*

Hannon: m. *A Cockle, tearmed so at Roan.*

Hanse: f. *The* Hanse; *a companie, societie, or corporation (for so it signifies in the booke of the Ordonnances of Paris, and in some other old books) of Marchants; Or (as a Ciuilian interprets it) a certaine societie of Marchants combined together for the good vsage, and safe passage, of Marchandises; also, an association with, or the freedome of, the* Hanse; *also, the fee, or fine, which is paid for that freedome.*

Hanse Teuthonique. *An association with the Marchants of the* Hanse; *or, a participation with, or communication of, the priuiledges granted (any time these 300 yeares) by soueraigne Princes vnto the Germane Marchants, trafficking vnto London in England,* Bruges *in Flanders,* Berges *in Norway, &* Nonogred *in Russia.*

Hansé: m. ée: f. *Free of the* Hanse; *or sworne of the companie of* Hanse *Marchants; whence also, sworn, & made free, of any Companie, or Corporation.*

Hanser.

Hanser. *To make free of the* Hanse; *or of any ciuile companie, or corporation.*
Hante: f. *The staffe, or shaft of a Iauelin, Halberd, &c.*
Hanté: m. ée: f. *Haunted, frequented, much resorted vnto.*
 Chemin fort hanté. *A way verie much vsed, a full-beaten way.*
Hantement: m. *A haunting, frequenting, or frequent resorting vnto; also, as* Hantise.
Hanter. *To haunt, frequent, resort vnto; to be familier with; to conuerse, or commerce with.*
Hantise: f. *An ordinarie haunt, or haunting; frequentation; commerce, conuersation; familiaritie, or great acquaintance, with; much resort vnto.*
Hape. *as* Happe.
Happe: f. *A claspe, or, the hooke of a claspe; or a hooke to claspe with; also, the clowt, or band of yron thats nayled vpon th'arme, or end of an Axletree, and keeps it from being worne by th'often turning of the* Naue *(of a wheele.)*
 Clou à happe. *A clowt-nayle.*
Happé: m. ée: f. *Caught, happed, snatched, or grasped at.*
Happée: f. *A catch, a graspe, a snatch.*
 Saisine d' happée. *A violent seisure of, or entrie into, another mans land; a forcible entrie, or disseisin.*
Happelopin: m. *A catch-bit, sycophant, smell-feast.*
Happelourde: f. *A thing that makes a faire shew, but is of no worth at all; hence, a counterfeit Iewell; and a fellow in whom there is nothing good but an outside; also, an arrant, and (almost) apparent lie; a gull, fib, foist; a faire tale fit onely to catch fooles; also, a grosse part in behauiour.*
Happement: m. *A catching.*
Happer. *To hap, or catch; to snatch, or graspe at.*
Happe-soupe. *A spoone.*
Haquebute: f. *An Haquebut, or Arquebuse; a Caliuer.*
Haquebutier: m. *An Arquebusier, or small shot.*
Haquenée: com. *An ambling Horse, Gelding, or Mare.*
Haquet: m. *A Dray; or low, and open Cart, such as London Brewers vse.*
Haquetier: m. *A Dray-man.*
Har: f. *A with of greene stickes; the band of a fagot.*
 Sur paine de la har. *Vpon your life, vpon paine of the haulter; (Malefactors in old time were, and at this day in some barbarous countries are, hanged with withes.)*
Harang: m. *A Herring; Looke* Harenc.
Harangeson: f. *Herring-season.*
Harangiere: f. *A Herring-wife; also, as* Harengue.
Haranguant: m. *as* Harangueur.
Haranguant. *Pleading vnto, discoursing before.*
Harangue: f. *An Oration, Pleading, Declaration; set speech, long tale.*
Harangué: m. ée: f. *Pleaded before, preached vnto, held with a long discourse.*
Haranguer. *To make an Oration; to hold with a long discourse; to plead before, to preach, or speak long, vnto.*
Harangueur: m. *An Orator, or Oration-maker; a Pleader; a Preacher.*
Haranier: m. ere: f. *Of, belonging or like vnto, a Herring.*
Haransor. *as* Harencsor. *A red Herring.*
Haras: m. *A Race; horses, and mares kept onely for breed.*
Harassé: m. ée: f. *Tired, or toyled out; weakened with ouertoyling; harried, molested, hurried; vexed, importuned, troubled, turmoiled, tormented.*
Harasser. *To tire, or toyle out; to spend or weaken, wearie or weare out, by ouertoyling, or taking too much of; also, to vex, disquiet, importune, harrie, hurrie, turmoile, torment.*
Harassier: m. *The owner, or ouerseer of a Race.*
Haraud: m. *The forme of a Hare; also, a certaine crie vsed in Normandie; Looke* Haro.
Haraudé: m. ée: f. *Openly reuiled, reproached, rayled at, exclaimed against, cried out vpon.*
Harauder. *To reuile, reproach, raile at, or scould with, openly; to exclaime against, or crie out vpon.*
Harault. *as* Haraud, *or* Haro; *(and hence;)*
 Le monde luy crie harault. *The world exclaimes, cries out, or bids fie, vpon him.*
Harce. *Looke* Herce.
Harcelé: m. ée: f. *Vexed, harried, hurried, turmoiled, much troubled, or annoyed; and prouoked, incensed, or vrged (withall.)*
Harceler. *To vexe, harrie, turmoyle, hurrie; trouble, molest, or disquiet, much; also, to prouoke, incense, or vrge (therewith;) also, to haggle, hucke, hedge, or paulter long in the buying of a commoditie.*
Harceleur: m. *A firebrand, make-bate, stirre-suit; a brabling, litigious, or contentious fellow.*
Harcelle: f. *A little with.*
Hard. *as* Har.
Hardage. *as* Hardes.
Harde: f. *A heard, flocke, or troupe of wild beasts; also, an egge laied with a soft skin, or filme (about it) in stead of a shell; a soft-sheld egge; a wind egge; also, a hoord.*
 Hardes. *(The Plurall of* Harde; *also) furniture, stuffe, implements, baggage, necessarie chaffer.*
Hardé: m. ée: f. *Loaden with stuffe, or necessarie baggage; also, trucked, bartered, exchanged.*
Hardeau: m. *A little with, or fagot-band; also, a yong lad, or boy; also, a clownish fellow that thinkes verie well of himselfe.*
Hardelle: f. *A little with, or fagot-band; also, a troupe, or heard of beasts; (and) a rout, or crue of men; also, a girle, yong maid, lasse, or mother.*
Hardiment: m. *Hardinesse, boldnesse, audacitie, stoutnesse; (an old word.)*
Harder. *To trucke, barter, scorse, exchange.*
Hardes. *Looke* Harde.
Hardeux: m. euse: f. *Full of, or loaden with, stuffe, or baggage.*
Hardi: m. ie: f. *Hardie, daring, stout, bold, confident, aduenturous; valiant, couragious.*
 Hardi en couppe-bourse. *As confident, or impudent, as a cut-purse.*
 Hardi comme vne espée. *Looke* Espée.
 Hardi gaigneur hardi mangeur: Prov. *Good at meat good at worke, say we.*
 Hardie langue coüarde lance: Pro. *A hardie speech a heartlesse speare.*
 Mieux vaut coüard que trop hardi: Prov. *Better no heart then too much hardinesse.*
Hardiement. *as* Hardiment.
Hardiesse: f. *Hardinesse, boldnesse, audacitie, stomack, stoutnesse, mettall; courage; confidence in, or assurance of, his owne force, abilitie, valour.*
Hardillon: m. *The thong of a buckle.*
Hardiment. *Hardily, boldly, stoutly; aduenturously;* con-

confidently; couragiously.

Hardiment parle teste saine: Prov. *Looke* Sain.

Hardiment heurte à la porte qui bonne nouvelle apporte: Pro. *He that brings good news boldly knocks at doore.*

Hardoüer: m. *A resorting, or, a repaire, vnto.*

Hardré. Oeuf hardré. *A wind egge, or soft-sheld egge.*

Hare-levrier. *Hoo hoo, loo loo, now now, hoe dogs.*

Harelle: f. *A troupe, heard, flocke; also, a popular commotion; (for so was once tearmed one begun, at Roan, by the oppressed people.)*

Harenc: m. *A Herring.*

Harenc de mar. *A great, fat, & full-rowed Herring.*

Harenc de la nuict. *A red Herring.*

Harenc saur, ou sauret; & sor, ou soret. *A red Herring.*

Esimé comme vn harenc soret. *As leane as a rake; as lanke as a shotten Herring.*

Droict d'harenc. *A certaine number of Herrings, heretofore due, euerie Lent, vnto the Treasurors, and Officers of the Chamber of Accompts, but at this day allowed them in money.*

La caque (ou la poche) sent tousiours l'harenc: Prov. *The poke still of the Herring smells; Our nature will, doe what we can, subsist.*

Harengade: f. *A fish that resembles a little shad, called so at* Marseillis.

Harengerie: f. *A Herring celler, shop, or market; the place wherein Herrings are kept, shewed, or sold; also, a selling of Herring, or the Herring sellers trade.*

Harengeson: f. *The season of Herring fishing; the time when Herrings are in season; Herring season.*

Harengiere: f. *A Herring-wife; a woman that cries, or sells Herrings.*

Faire la moüe aux harengieres. *To stand on the Pillorie.*

Harer vn chien. *To hound a dog at, or set a dog on, a beast, &c; also, to incourage him by some voyce, or by clapping on the backe, when he is set on.*

Harfleur. *Signifies as much as*, le Contreflus de la mer.

Hargas. faulcon hargas. *A Sore Faulcon.*

Hargneux. *Peeuish, wrangling, diuerous, ouerthwart, crosse, waiward, froward; ill to please, euer complayning, neuer quiet; hence also, verie litigious; also, as* Hergneux.

Chien hargneux a tousiours les oreilles deschirées: Prov. *A brabling curre is neuer without torne eares.*

Haricot: m. *Mutton sod with little turneps, some wine, and tosts of bread crumbled among; tis also made otherwise, of small peeces of mutton first a little sodden, then fried in seam, with sliced onions, and lastly boiled in beefe broath with Parsley, Isop, and Sage: And in another fashion, of liuers boyled in a pipkin with sliced onions and lard, veriuice, red wine, and vineger, and serued vp with tosts, small spices, and (sometimes) chopped hearbs.*

Haridelle: f. *A poore tit, or leane ill-fauoured iade.*

Harié: m. ée: f. *Harried, vexed, molested, importuned, toiled, turmoiled.*

Harier. *To harrie, hurrie, vex, trouble, disturbe, disquiet, molest, importune, annoy; toyle, turmoyle.*

Harigot. *A kind of Jigge.*

Harle: f. *A kind of Sheldrake.*

Harlou. *in stead of* Hare-loup. *A word wherewith dogs that hunt, or assaile, a Wolfe, are cheered, and incouraged.*

Harmene. *A barbarous name for, a little Basiliske.*

Harmonie: f. *Harmonie, melodie, tunablenesse, a sweet consent of sounds; also, a coniunction of bones by a single line which fits them one to th'other (and so are the bones of the nose conioyned.*

Harmonieux: m. euse: f. *Harmonious, musicall, melodious, tunably sounding, sweetly resounding.*

Harmonique: com. *as* Harmonieux.

Harnaché: m. ée: f. *Harnessed, as a horse.*

Harnachement: m. *The harnesse of a horse.*

Harnachemens. *as* Harnas.

Harnacher vn cheval. *To harnesse, or make readie, a horse; to put on his furniture.*

Harnacheur: m. *A harnesser of a horse; a Groome of a stable; also, a bungling Armourer, or Harnesse-maker.*

Harnas de cheval. *A horses harnesse, or furniture.*

Vn harnas de Mouton. *The head, and plucke of a sheepe.*

Harnas de roture. *A plough.*

Harnois: m. *Armour, harnesse; also, a teame, cart, or carriage, &c; also, as* Harnas.

Harnois de gueule. *Meat, victualls, acates, mouth-armor, bellie-furniture.*

Harnois noirs. *Reisters, Rutters, Pistoliers on horsebacke.*

Il s'eschauffe en son harnois. *He heats himselfe in his armor; said of one that grows in choller, or falls into passion, for the satisfaction of some other intemperate humor.*

Harnois ne vaut rien qui ne se defend: Prov. *Defend thy selfe or else all armor's vaine.*

Haro. ou Harol. Crier Haro sur. *To crie out vpon, or make huy and crie after; (vsed in Normandie by such as are outraged, or in some high degree wronged; therby seeming to implore th'aid of their Duke* Rol, *who is reported to haue beene a most iust Prince;) In which case those that are within the hearing therof must pursue the malefactor, or else they pay a fine.*

Clameur de Haro, ou Haro crié. *A claime, or protestation of such as are in possession of land which others goe about to put them from; it must be made before a Sergeant, or two witnesses, and then is a sufficient warrant for the holding of the possession.*

Haroder. *as* Harauder.

Harondelle: f. *A Swallow; Seeke* Arondelle.

A la nouvelle venuë des harondelles. *(A description of the Springs approach.)*

Harou. *as* Haro.

Harpade: f. *A catching, or snatching at, a griping, or seizing on, with the clawes.*

Harpail: m. *A troupe, flocke, heard, crue, rout.*

Harpaille. *Seeke* Herpaille.

Harpailleur: m. *A keeper, or ouerseer of Deere; also, as* Arpailleur.

Harpanter. *To suruey, or measure land.*

Harpaut. *The name of a shepheards dog.*

Harpe: f. *A Harpe; also, the iaumbe, or side of a doore.*

L'harpe d'vn chien. *A dogs claw, or paw.*

Il mania tresbien ses harpes. *He stirred his fingers verie nimbly.*

Harpechorde: f. *An Arpsicord, or Harpsicord; a Dulcimer.*

Harpens: m. *A kind of night-bird:* ¶Dauphinois.

Harper. *To harpe, or play on a Harpe.*

Se harper l'vn à l'autre. *To grapple, graspe, haspe, claspe, imbrace, cope, close, together; to scuffle, or fall together by th'eares.*

Harpes. *in stead of* Hardes: ¶Rab.

Harpeur: m. *A Harper; one that playes on the Harpe.*
Harpi: m.ie: f. *Greedie, deuouring; catching, snatching, grasping at.*
Harpie: f. *A Harpie; Looke* Harpye.
Harpon: m. *A crampiron wherewith Masons fasten stones together.*
Harpoy: m. *Poison; (an old word.)*
Harpye: f. *An Harpie; one of those monstrous, and rauenous birds which Poets faine to haue had womens faces, hands armed with talons, and bellies full of an ordure wherwith they infected all the meat they touched; and hereof are the monstrous brood (Moles, or Moonecalues) of some women so tearmed.*
Harpye de cuisine. *A most rauenous, and filthie deuourer.*
Harquebousade: f. *The shot of an Arquebuse.*
Harqueboúse; &, Harqueboúsé. *as* Harquebuse; &, Harquebusé.
Harquebusade: f. *as* Harquebousade.
Harquebuse: f. *An Arquebuse, or Caliuer; Looke* Arquebuse.
Harquebuse de chasse. *A fowling peece.*
Harquebusé: m.ée: f. *Shot, or shot at with, slaine with the shot of, an Arquebuse.*
Harquebuser. *To shoot, or shoot at with, to kill with the shot of, an Arquebuse.*
Harquebusier: m. *An Arquebusier, or small shot.*
Harquebutier. *The same.*
Harry. (*A Carterlie voice of exciting*) Hay ree.
Harry bourriquet. *Rudely, clownishly, confusedly; or braying out in a lowd, and harsh accent, such as the French Millers vse in the driuing of their Asses; Looke* Bourriquet.
Hars. *as* Har.
Harse: f. *A Harrow.*
Harselle: f. *A little with.*
Harseller. *as* Harceler.
Harsement: m. *A harrowing; also, a stiffe, or vpward standing.*
Harser. *To harrow; also, to stand vp streight, or stiffe.*
Harseur: m. *A harrower.*
Hart: f. *A with; also, a haulter; Looke* Har.
Les harts. *The shoulder veine, or necke veine of a horse, whereat most commonly he is let bloud; or as* les Ars.
Hasard: m. *Hazard, aduenture, ieopard, fortune, chance.*
Hasardé: m.ée: f. *Hazarded, aduentured, ieoparded, committed vnto fortune, or chance.*
Hasarder. *To hazard, aduenture, ieopard, set on sixes and seuens, committed vnto fortune and chance.*
Il faut hasarder vn petit poisson pour prendre vn grand. *A little, for a great gaine must be hazarded.*
Hasardeur: m. *A hazarder, venturer, ieoparder, aduenturer.*
Hasardeusement. *Hazardously, aduenturously, hab nab, hittie missie, on sixes and seuens.*
Hasardeux: m.euse: f. *Hazardous, venturous, aduenturous.*
Haschehsach. *A fained voyce of coughing, in* Rabelais.
Hascher. *as* Hacher: ¶Rab.
Hase: f. *An old female Conie, or Hare.*
Haseau: m. *A Breame of a middle size.*
Hasle: m. *Sunne-burning; or th'extreame, and scorching heat of a Summer Sunne.*
Haslé: m. ée: f. *Sunne-burnt; scorched in the Sunne.*
Hasler. *To Sun-burne, or scorch in the Sunne; to bleake, or make swart a thing by displaying it in a hot Sunne; also, to bound, set a dog, or turne a dog loose, at.*
Haste: m. *A spit, or broach.*
Armes d'haste. *Looke* Armes.
Haste: f. *Hast, speed, swiftnesse, quicknesse, posting suddennesse.*
Haste ne vient seule: Prov. *Hast neuer comes alone;* viz: *hath euer some trouble or other t'accompanie it.*
Hasté: m.ée: f. *Hasted, speeded, quickly got, come, or done; set on apace; also, hastie, or speedie; also, requiring hast.*
Hastelé: m. ée: f. *Bound vp with small splints.*
Hastelettes: f. *Little splints, wherwith Faulconers bind vp their hawkes broken legs.*
Hasteleux: m. euse: f. *Hastie, full of hast, quicke, speedie, nimble, swiftly mouing.*
Hastemenuë: f. *A hogs haslet.*
Haster. *To hasten, accelerate, speed, quicken, set forward apace; also, to hedge, or inclose with a hedge.*
S'haster. *To hast, make hast, goe fast, moue quickly, run speedily, hie apace.*
Qui trop se haste en cheminant en beau chemin se fourvoye souvent: Prov. *The more hast the worse speed; they that make too much hast mistake the fairest way.*
Hastereau: m. *The throat-peece, or forepart of the neck, of a hog (belike frõ the Wallons, by whom a mans throat, or necke is thus tearmed;) also, one liuer or more of a calfe, &c, wrapped vp (whole, or sliced, and seasoned with good hearbes, and spices) in the call of the beast, and afterwards roasted, or fried, and serued vp hot with Oranges, or in some good sauce: (This dish, as also another (if not more) dressed in another fashion, is called* Hastereaux.)
Hasterel: m. *as* Hastereau; *or, A hogs haslet.*
Hasteur: m. *A hedger, or hedge-maker.*
Hastif: m. *Hastie, sudden, rash, quicke, speedie, forward, soone-comming, hying apace.*
Poires, ou pommes hastives. *Hastings; such as are soonest ripe.*
Hastilles: f. *Th'inwards of a beast; as a hogs haslet, calues gather, sheepes plucke, &c.*
Hastiveau: m. *An hastie, rash, inconsiderate, harebraind Asse; also, a hasting apple, or peare; and hence;*
Roses d'hastiveau. *Verie forward Roses.*
Hastivel. *as* Hastiveau; *or, A soone-ripe apple called, the S. Johns apple.*
Hastivement. *Hastily, headlong, suddenly, rashly; quickly, swiftly, speedily, forwardly; apace, in a moment, on a sudden, out of hand.*
Hastiveté: f. *Hastinesse; rashnesse; acceleration, speedinesse, swiftnesse, quickenesse; post-hast-making.*
Hatelier. *as* Attelier.
Hattereau. *Looke* Hastereau.
Hau. *An Interiection of calling; Haw, heare ye me, hoe there.*
Haubans: m. *as* Aubans; *The shrowds of a ship.*
Haubelon: m. *Hops.*
Haubereau. *as* Hobreau.
Haubergeon: m. (*The Diminutiue of* Haubert;) *a little coat of maile; or, only sleeues, and gorget of maile.*
Haubergeon de femmes. *The roll wherewith they beare vp their gownes about their hips.*
Maille à maille on fait les haubergeons: Prov. *Linke after linke the coat is made at length; peece after peece things come to full perfection.*
Haubergeonnier: m. *A maker of coats of maile.*
Haubert: m. *A coat of maile; also, as* Haulbert; *a high, or chiefe Lord.*

Droict d' haubert. *A certaine priuiledge enioyed by diuers Norman Lords; it consists of many parts, and the most of them of high Iurisdiction.*

Fief d' haubert. *An inheritance (held immediately, and in* Capite *of the King) whose owner is bound to serue, on horsebacke, in compleat armor, & with a coat of mayle, shield, sword, and helmet, in the warres.*

Have: com. *as* Havé; *and hence,* yeux haves. *Full-drained, hollow, sad, or sunke-in eyes.*

Havé: m. ée: f. *Soaked, withered, wasted; also, dreadfull, disfigured, wild-looking, ghastlie, ghost-like.*

Havée: f. *A gripe, or handfull; also, a bootie, or prey; also, a toll exacted by the executioner of some towns vpon small wares, and fruit sold on Market dayes.*

Havement. *Greedily, rauinously, couetously.*

Haver. *as* Happer; *or, To hooke, or grapple with a hooke.*

Haveron. *as* Aveneron; *Wild Oats.*

Havet: m. *A little hooke; also, a boat-hooke, or pole hauing a hooke at th'end; also, a little dandiprat, short hop-on-my-thombe.*

Havi: m. ie: f. *Parched, scorched, withered, burnt vp, as grasse by a hot Sunne.*

Havi de froid. *Stiffe, clumpse, benummed.*

Havir. *To scorch, parch, wither, burne or drie vp, as a hot Sunne doth grasse, &c.*

Haulbert: m. *A high, or chiefe Lord; Looke* Haubert.

Haulche: f. *A raising, or out-bidding, in an Outrope, or Outcry.* ¶Wallon.

Haulcher. *To raise, or out-bid, in an Outrope, or Outcry.* ¶Wallon.

Haulchié: m. ée: f. *Raised, out-bid:* ¶Wallon.

Haulchier. *as* Haulcher.

Haulsage: m. *as* Hausſage; *Also, pride, arrogancie, surquedrie, powerfull oppression.*

Haulsaire: com. *Loftie, statelie, proud, arrogant, high-minded (by a presumption of abilitie, or power.)*

Haulse: f. *The vnderlaying of a shooe, or peece of leather that vnderlayes it.*

Haulsé: m. ée: f. *Hoysed, &c; as* Haussé.

Haulse-bec: m. *A lifting vp of the chinne in scorne, or mockerie; also, a blow, or chocke vnder the chinne.*

Haulse-col: m. *A Gorget; or, Armour for the necke.*

Haulse-menton: m. *A crutch-like prop of wood, seruing to beare vp the head of one thats fallen into extreame weakenesse; also, a lowd lye, proud foist, false or vaine brag.*

Haulse-pied. *A net, or engine wherewith Wolues, Badgers, Foxes, &c, are caught.*

Haulser. *Looke* Hausser.

Haulserée: f. *The drawing, or haling of Barges, or great Boats vp a riuer by the force of men ashore.*

Haulserie: f. *A hoysing, raising, aduancing, heauing vp, setting aloft; also, loftinesse, hautinesse.*

Hault. *Looke* Haut.

Haultain: m. aine: f. *Hautie, loftie, statelie, proud, high-minded, surlie, disdainfull, arrogant.*

Faulcon haultain. *A high-flying hawke.*

Vent haultain. *The South wind.*

Faire le haultain. *To be high in th'instup, stand on his pantofles, take state vpon him; also, to be extreamely in choller.*

Haultainement. *Hautily, loftily, proudly, arrogantly, disdainfully.*

Haultaineté: f. *Hautinesse, loftinesse, statelinesse, pride, arrogancie, disdainfulnesse.*

Haultban. Droict d' haultban. *The summe of 6* solz Parisis *leuied yearely to the Kings vse of euerie Baker (and of some other Artificers) within the towne of Paris.*

Haultbaniers. *Such Artificers as are subiect to the* Haultban.

Haultbert. *as* Haubert.

Haultbois: m. *A Hobois, or Hoboy.*

Haulte-contre: com. *The Countertenor part in singing; also, (a Countertenor) he that beares it.*

Haulte-lisse. Tapisserie de haulte-lisse. *Large, and rich Tapistrie.*

Haultement. *as* Hautement.

Haultesse: f. *Height, hautinesse; highnesse, excellencie, sublimitie.*

Haulteur. *as* Hauteur.

Haultmuré: m. ée: f. *High-walled; compassed, or flanked with high walls; also, tall and foule, slim, slangam, luskish, loobie-like.*

Vn plat de souppes haultmurées. *A dish of browes whose soppes are heaped roofewise one vpon another.*

Hault-murer. *To compasse, fortifie, or flanke with high rampiers.*

Haumelotte: f. *An Omelet, or Pancake of egges.*

Havoir. *Seeke* Avoir.

Havre: m. *A Hauen, Port, Harbor for shipping.*

Havre: com. *Grim, fell, horride, ghastlie.*

Haussage: m. *A hoysing, raising, heauing vp, lifting high; also, as* Haulsage.

Haussaire: com. *as* Haulsaire.

Haussant. *Hoising, raising, heauing vp.*

Hausse: f. *A scoope to lade, or fetch vp water.*

Iouër à la hausse qui baisse. *To play at titter totter, or at totter-arse; to ride the wild-mare.*

Haussé: m. ée: f. *Hoised, raised, aduanced, eleuated, houen vp, lifted high, set aloft.*

Hausse-bec: m. *A disdainfull casting vp of the head, or lifting vp of the chinne.*

Hausse-col. *as* Haulse-col.

Hausse-cul: m. *A French Vardingale; or (more properly) the kind of roll vsed by such women, as weare (or are to weare) no Vardingales.*

Hausse-plie: f. *A Vardingale (tearmed so by citizens wiues.)*

Hausse-plié: m. ée: f. *Furnished with a Vardingale.*

Hausse-queuë: f. *The yellow Water-wagtaile.*

Elle s'en va à hausse-queuë. *See* Queuë.

Hausser. *To hoise, raise, eleuate, heaue vp, lift high; set aloft, aduance.*

Hausser l'espaule. *To lift vp the shoulders; to vse the Italian shrug; an argument of vnwillingnesse, or feare to doe; or of a forced, and silent contentment of, or consent vnto, what is done.*

Hausser le gantelet. *To ouerreach with false reckonings; a shopkeeper to put more in his booke then the chapman had of him.*

Hausser les moustaches. Ce seroit pour luy bien hausser les moustaches. *That would set him on the hoight.*

Hausser le rastelier à. *See* Rastelier.

Hausser vn soulier. *To vnderlay a shooe.*

Hausser le temps. *To spend or passe away the time in quaffing, swilling, carousing.*

Iouër à la hausse qui baisse. *Looke* Hausse.

Haut. (Substant.) *A high place; whence;* Gaigner le haut. *To run his countrey, to flie away;* S'en aller en haut. *The same.*

Sur le haut de son age. *Being well in yeares, well stept into yeares.*

Haut: m. haute: f. *High, tall; hautie, loftie; great, noble, honorable; chiefe, eminent, excellent; sumptuous, magnificent, most glorious; also, deepe, secret, profound; weightie, of importance; also, lewd.*
Haut costé. *A Surloine.*
Haute cour. *The Court of a King, or great Lord.*
Hautes erres. Limier d'hautes erres. *A fleet hound.*
Haute fustaye. Bois d' h: f. *Looke* Fustaye.
Haute heure. *Late, or farre on the day (from morning to noone.)*
Haute game. *See* Game.
Haut homme. *A great, eminent, most noble, right honourable personage.*
Haute Iustice. *High iurisdiction; Looke* Iustice.
Haute lice. *as in* Haute-lice.
Haute luicte. de h. l. *Violently, forcibly, with extremitie, by maine strength.*
La Haute main. *(Sometimes) the vpper hand.*
Haut mal. *The falling sicknesse.*
Le haut mal de la corde. *Hanging.*
Haute mer, en h. m. *In the wide, or deepe seas, farre in the sea.*
Haut nez. Chien d' h. n. *A well-sented, or cold-nosed dog.*
Haut parage. *Looke* Haut-parage.
Haut passage. *An imposition of seuen pence in the pound, vpon woolls, clothes, linnens, canuasses, &c.*
La haute piece. *A Poldron; or the vpper part therof.*
Chambre haute. *A dining chamber.*
Iour haut. *High adayes, late, farre on the day.*
Matiere haute. *Weightie, important, mysticall, excellent stuffe.*
Haut d' aureilles. *Deafe, or thicke of hearing.*
Haut à la main. *Proud, surlie, statelie; a striker, one with whom there is but a word and a blow.*
Tenir la bride haute à. *To awe, restraine, keepe short, hold in.*
Haut. (Adverb.) *Highly, aboue, aloft, on high; also, lowdly, or alowd.*
Haut & bas la cheminée. *The crie of Chimney-sweepers.*
Haut le pied. s'en aller h. le p. *To runne away apace, or, as fast as his feet can carrie him.*
Faire haut le bois. *(Pikemen) to make a stand; also, to quaffe, tipple, carouse for the heauens.*
Faulcon trop haut assis. *Whose staulkes, or legs are too long.*
Taillables haut & bas. *Taxable at the will and pleasure of the Lord.*
Qui plus haut monte qu'il ne doit de plus haut chet qu'il ne vouldroit: Prov. *He that climbes higher then he should, falls lower then he would.*
Hautaignes: f. *Vines which (as hops) embrace, & creep vp on, long poles.*
Hautain. *Seeke* Haultain.
Hautainement, &, Hautaineté. *as* Haultainement; &, Haultaineté.
Haut-bert. *A high, or chiefe Lord.*
Haut-costé. *A Surloyne.*
Haut-d'-ais. *A cloth of Estate.*
Haute: m. *A Docke to mend, or build ships in.*
Haute. vn' h. de manche. *The wing of a sleeue.*
Haute-contre: com. *The Countertenor part, in singing, &c; also (a Countertenor, or) he which bears that part.*
Haute-lice. Tapisserie de haute-lice, ou hautes lisses. *Tapistrie of rich stuffe, or high price; the best, and largest kind of Tapistrie.*
Haute-lissier: m. *A maker of (rich, and large) Tapistrie.*
Hautement. *Highly, tally; hautily, loftily; greatly; nobly, honourably, eminently, excellently; sumptuously, magnificently; deeply, profoundly; weightily, importantly.*
Hautesse: f. *Looke* Haultesse.
Hauteur: f. *Height, length, tallnesse; eminence, altitude, eleuation; also, depth, or deepnesse.*
Haut-gourdier: m. *A desperate bankrupt; one that hauing but little to loose, cares for himselfe but a little.*
Hautin: m. *The Sea-pike, or Spit-fish.*
Hautins. *as* Autins.
Haut-licier: m. *as* Hautelissier.
Haut-mal: m. *The falling sicknesse.*
Haut-parage. *The highest Peeredome; a title, or tenure whereby the Peeres, & Princes of the bloud, of France, hold their land; or (more generally) a tenure in* Capite; *for (as that tenure) it moues wholly, and directly of the Crowne.*
Haut-passage. *Looke* Haut.
Hauvens: m. *Penthouses of cloth hung before shop-windowes.*
Hay: m. Haye: f. *Hated, &c; as* Haî.
Hay. *An Interiection of forwarding, or of incouragement; Looke* Hai.
Fol est qui est esperonné & à cheval dit hay: Prov. *The asse hauing spurres on, cries On to his horse; or he is an asse, who furnished with sound meanes, makes vse of sleight ones.*
Haye: f. *A hedge; a fence of shrubs, thornes, &c.*
Haye vive. *A quick-set hedge.*
Anguille de haye. *The blackest hedge or dunghill Adder; not verie venomous.*
Mords à haye. *A Scatche.*
Combatre, ou marcher, en haye. s. *By files.*
Pendre entre la haye, & le bled: &, entre la haye, & le fossé. *To surprise, take vnawares, or set vpon on a sudden.*
Qui fait haye souvent dit haye: Prov. *Looke* Haye *Interiect.*
Hayé: m. ée: f. *Hedged; inclosed with a hedge.*
Haye. *(An Interiection of complayning, or crying out for paine) Oh, alas, out alas.*
Qui fait haye souvent dit haye: Prov. *He that makes hedges often prickes his fingers.*
Hayer. *To hedge; also, to hate.*
Hayeson: f. *Hedge-making; also, hedging time, or, the season to make hedges in.*
Hayeur: m. *A hater, loather, detester.*
Hayneux. *as* Haineux.
Hayon. *as* Tente.
Hayreux: m. euse: f. *Leane, scraggie; poore; miserable, wretched, forlorne; also, as* Haireux.
Hayt. de bon hayt. *Willingly, freely, heartily, cheerfully.*
Hazard; &, Hazarder. *Looke* Hasard; &, Hasarder.
Haze. *as* Hase.
Pomme d Haze. *The name of a certaine long yellow apple.*
Hé. *An Interiection of calling.* Vien ça hé. *Come hither hoe.*
Heaulme: m. *An helmet; the headpeece of a man of Armes; also, the Helmet cherrie, Heart-cherrie, French cherrie; Looke* Heaume.
Heaulme doré, & ouvert. *A gilt, and open helmet; which on the top of a coat of Armes denotes, that the bearer is either a Vicount, Baron, or Chattelain; (Look for more touching this in* Ouvert.)
Heaulmerie: f. *An Armorers shop, or warehouse; also, the name of a street in Paris, wherein many Armorers dwell.*

Heaulmier : m. *An Armorer, or Helmet-maker; also, the Heart-cherrie tree.*
Heaulmiere : f. *The Rudder-port of a ship.*
Heaume: m. *An helmet, the headpeece of a man of arms; also, the helme, or rudder of a ship; also, the Heart-cherrie, French cherrie, Spanish cherrie; Looke* Heaulme.
Heaumé. *Wearing a helmet, armed with an helmet.*
Heaumer. *To put on an helmet, to arme his head with an helmet.*
Hebbe de la mer. *Th'ebbe, or ebbing of the sea.*
Hebene : m. *Heben, or Ebonie; the blacke, and hard wood of a certaine tree growing in Æthyopia, and the East Indies.*
Hebené : m. ée : f. *Blacke, Heben-like; made of Ebonie.*
Sourcils hebenez. *Blacke, dismall, frowning, lowring browes.*
Hebenin : m. ine : f. *Of, or belonging to, Ebonie.*
Heberge : f. *A house, lodging, harbour.*
Hebergé : m. ée : f. *Housed, lodged, harboured.*
Hebergement : m. *as* Heberge.
Heberger. *To lodge, harbor, dwel, abide in; also, to lodge, harbour, house, giue house-roome, lend a dwelling vnto.*
Hebeté : m. ée : f. *Dull, sottish, witlesse, blockish, blunt, slow, sencelesse, heauie headed; also, dulled, blunted; made blockish.*
Hebeter. *To dull, blunt, sot, make blockish.*
Hebraïsme : m. *Hebrewisme; the speech, fashion, or disposition of the Hebrewes.*
Hebrieu : m. *An Hebrew, or Jew; also, the Hebrew, or language of the Hebrewes.*
Il entend l'Hebrieu. *He is drunke, or (as we say) learned: (from th' Analogie of the Latine word* Ebrius.)
Hecatombe. *A Sacrifice wherein an hundred beasts were killed.*
Hectique : com. *Sicke of an Hectick, or continuall Feauer; (hence) also, meager, leane, dried vp, in a Consumption.*
Hederiforme : com. *Fashioned like Ivie.*
Veine hederiforme. *A certaine veine which passes downe along by the sides of the wombe.*
Hedre. *as* Hestre; *A Beech tree.*
Hedret. *Looke* Haidroict.
Hee. *(An Interiection of lamenting) Ay me.*
Hei. *as* Hé.
Helaine : m. *Elecampane, Scabwort, Horseheale.*
Helas. *Alas, wellaway, welladay.*
Helenites. *An Order of White Friers, that weare a yellow crosse on their breasts.*
Heleoseline : m. *Smallage.*
Helepolle. *A great woodden engine wherewith, in old time, the tops of rampiers were battered.*
Helesie : f. *A many-coloured garden hearb, in proportion somewhat like Beets.*
Heliotrope : m. *The hearbe Turnesole, Ruds, Wartwort; also, a precious stone which, as a burning glasse, receiueth, and retorteth the Sunne-beames.*
Helixine. *Barren, or creeping Ivie.*
Helvenaque. *The name of a kind of grape.*
Hematide. Pierre Hematide. *The Bloudstone.*
Hemicraine : m. *The Megrum, or headache by fits.*
Hemicranique : com. *Troubled with, or subiect vnto, the Megrum.*
Hemicycle : m. *An Hemicicle, or halfe circle.*
Hemine : f. *as* Emine.
Hemiolie. *So much, and halfe so much againe; (an Arithmeticall proportion.)*
Hemiplexie : f. *A dead Palsie, in halfe of the bodie.*

Hemisphere : m. *An hemisphere; halfe the compasse of the visible heauen.*
Hemistique : com. *A halfe verse.*
Hemitrité. la fiebvre hemitritée. *An Ague compounded of a continuall Tertian, and an intermittent Quotidian.*
Hemorrhagie : f. *An abundant flux of bloud.*
Hemorrhoïdal : m. ale : f. Veine hemorrhoïdale. *A small branch of the spleene veine comming to the fundament; also, a certaine veine in the necke of a womans wombe; (Looke* Veine.)
Hemorrhoïde : f. *An issue of bloud by the veines of the fundament.*
Hemorrhuës : f. *The same, called ordinarily, the Emrods, or Piles.*
Hemy. *(An Interiection of lamenting) Ay me, alas for me.*
Hen heu hasch. *Fained words, wherewith* Rabelais *expresseth a coughing.*
Hen hen. *Oh hò:* ¶Rab.
Hennir. *To neigh, or whinnie like a horse; Looke* Hannir.
Hennissement : m. *The neighing, or whinnying of a horse.*
Henouars : m. *Salt-Porters, carriers of salt, whereof onely 24 be allowed, within Paris, to carrie it from the Salt-wharfe vnto the Garners, & Warehouses of Marchants.*
Henricus. *A golden Crowne worth about two French Crownes.*
Henry : m. *(A proper name) Henrie, Harrie; also, a coine of gold worth about 6 s.sterl.*
Bon Henry. *Roman Sorrell, round Sorrell,* Tours *Sorrell; also, the hearbe which we call, Good Henrie, and All-good.*
Double Henry. *Is worth about* 14 s.sterl.
Ducat Henry. *Is ordinarily worth more by 6* d.sterl. *then the Crowne of the Sunne.*
Heouse. *Holly, or the Holme tree.*
Hepathique : f. *The mosse called Liuerwort, and stone Liuerwort; also, the hearbe golden Trestyle, noble Liuerwort, three-leaued Liuerwort, noble Agrimonie, hearbe Trinitie.*
Hepatique : f. *The same.*
Hepatique : com. *Hepaticall; of, or belonging to, the liuer; also, Liuer-helping; comforting a whole, or curing a diseased, liuer.*
Aloës hepatique. *The middle (in goodnesse) of the three sorts of Aloes.*
Heptaphon. (¶Rab.) *Seuen-fold.*
Heptomagene : m. *The seuenth male.*
Herage : m. *An ayrie of hawkes; and hence, a brood, kind; flocke, linage.*
Herauder. *To blaze; publickly to denounce, manifest, or commend.*
Herault : m. *An Herauld; a King of Armes.*
Heraut. *as* Herault.
Herbage : m. *Herbage, Pasture; or that which is payed for the herbage, or pasture of cattell; also, Common of pasture in other mens woods, or grounds.*
Herbage mort. *Is a penie, or halfepenie* Tourn. *paied by euery poore Cottager, or customarie tenant vnto the Lord that hath high, or meane Jurisdiction ouer him, for euerie sheepe he hath, if he haue not aboue ten, or (as in some places) twentie.*
Herbage vif. *Is euerie tenth sheepe (where the tenant hath more then ten, or twentie) chosen by the Lord, or his Officer: These Rights grow due from Christmas eue to Midsummer, and then are leuied.*

Franc herbage. *Free herbage; is when the tenants sheepe goe in grounds held by a free, or noble tenure; for then the Lord hath neither* Mort, *nor* Vif herbage *for them.*

Herbageux: m. euse: f. *Grassie, hearbie; full of grasse, fraught with hearbes.*

Herbaut. *The name of a merrie Diuell, or Hobgoblin, that appeared most commonly on horsebacke.* ¶Rab.

Herbaux. *Certaine duties, or charges, whereto some inheritances are, by the customes of* Poictou, *lyable.*

Herbe: f. *An hearbe; weed; plant, wort; also, grasse.*

Herbe d'Aloes. *Hearbe Aloe, sea Houseleeke, sea Aigreene.*

Herbe de l' Ambassadeur. *Nicotian, or French Tobacco.*

Herbe d'arondelles. *Celandine, Swallow-wort, Tettarwort.*

Herbe aux aulx. *Sauce alone, Jacke of the hedge.*

Herbe de l'aune. *Helicampane, Scabwort, Horseheale.*

Herbe de Saincte Barbe. *Winter Cresses, Saint Barbaraes hearbe.*

Herbe de benjoin. *Laserwort, Magydare.*

Herbe beurreuse. *Cudweed, Chaffweed, Cottonweed.*

Herbe aux cailles. *Plantaine, Waybred.*

Herbe au cerf. *Harts fodder, wild Parsenip,* Gratia Dei.

Herbe au chancre. Heliotropium, *Tornesole, Wartwort.*

Herbe chandeliere. *Colewort, or Cabbage hearb; also, Mullein, Higtaper, Torches; or, Candle-weeke Mullein (a kind thereof.)*

Herbe chaperonniere. *Wild Larkes-heele, or Monkshood, with the Purple flower.*

Herbe au charpentier. *Prunell, Hooke-heale, Selfeheale, Sickle-wort, Carpenters hearbe; Some also call Browne Bugle so; others (the more properly) Ribwort, Lambes tongue, small Plantaine; and others call Millfoyle, or Yarrow,* Herbe à charpentier, *because tis good for wounds, and cuts.*

Herbe au chat ou de chat. *Nep, Nip, Cats-mint.*

Herbe aux chats. *The same; also, as* Ortie puante.

Herbe aux chevres. *Shrub Trefoile, milke Trefoile, Citisus bush.*

Herbe à chien. *The Burre called Dogs Burre; also, the dogs Cole.*

Herbe de Christ. *Christs hearbe; or, as* Ellebore noir; *so tearmed, because it flourisheth about Christmas.*

Herbe du cigne. *Looke* Cigne.

Herbe clavelée. *Paunsie, Harts-ease, cull me to you, loue or liue in idlenesse, two faces vnder a hood.*

Herbe aux cloches. *Withywind, Bindweed, Hedgebells.*

Herbe de cœur. *Hartwort, or Hartmint; (The Piccard calls spotted Comfrey, Sage of Ierusalem, or Cowslip of Ierusalem, thus.)*

Herbe copiere. *A kind of wild Parsenip thats not ill meat.*

Herbe à coqu. *The Cowslip, or Paigle.*

Herbe à cotton. *Cudwort, Chaffweed, Cudweed, Cotton-weed, pettie Cotton.*

Herbe sans cousture. *Adders tongue, Serpents tongue.*

Herbe cucube. *Garden Nightshade.*

Herbe aux cuilliers. *Spoonewort, Scuruie-grasse.*

Herbe d'Encens. *Wormewood.*

Herbe Encensiere. *The same; or, Fleabane, Flea-bane Mullet.*

Herbe d'Escarlate. *The Skarlet Oke, or Skarlet Holme-Oke.*

Herbe des Escrouëlles. *Little Celandine, Pilewort, Figwort.*

Herbe d'Espaigne. *Spinage.*

Herbe d'Esparvier. *The Haukeweed called yellow Cichorie.*

L'Herbe à esternuër. *Sneesingwort, wild Pellitorie of Spaine.*

Herbe de l'estoille. *Crowfoot Plaintain, Harts-horne Plantaine, Buckhorne, hearbe Iuie, hearbe Eue.*

Herbe forte. *Sarracens Consound, Comfrey, or Woundwort.*

Herbe à foulon. *Fullers hearbe, Sopewort, Mockegillouers, Bruisewort.*

Herbe à vne fueille. *The hearbe called One blade, or One-leafe.*

Herbe de S. Iacques. *S. Iames his wort, or flower; countrey people call it Staggerwort, Stauerwort, and Ragwort.*

Herbe à iaulnir. *Dyers weed, welde, yellow weed; also, base Broome, Wood-waxen, Greene-weed, or Greening weed.*

Herbe de S. Iean. *Thin-leaued Mugwort; some also call Clarie so.*

Herbe impie. *Hearbe impious, wicked Cottonweed, Chaffweed, or Cudweed.*

Herbe de S. Innocent. *Centinodie, male Knot-grasse, Birds tongue, Swines grasse.*

Herbe Iudaïque. *Jewes hearbe, Tetrabit, Glidewort (a kind of Balme.)*

Herbe aux ladres. *Speedwell, Ground-heele, Paules Betonie, male Fluellin.*

Herbe à laict. *Spurge, Tithimal, Milke-weed, Wolues milke.*

Herbe au laict. *The same; also, Milke-wort, sea Milkewort, sea Trifolie, blacke Saltwort.*

Herbe aux langues. *Tongue-wort, Tongue-blade, Pagan tongue, Double Tongue, Horse tongue, Lawrell of Alexandria.*

Herbe Laurageoise. *Woad.*

Herbe à limaçon. *Medicke Fother, Snayle Clauer.*

Herbe au loup. *See* Loup.

Herbe à cent maladies. *Monnie-wort, hearbe twopence, two-pennie grasse.*

Herbe de Saincte Marie. *Our Ladies Mint, Speare-Mint, common garden Mint; also, Costmarie, and Alecost; by some also the hearbe Crowfoot, or yellow Camomill; by others, Hogs-bread, Swines-bread, or Sowbread, is called so.*

Herbe marine. *Sea grasse, or weed of the sea; Slanke, Wrake, Lauer.*

Herbe à masses. *Water torch, Cats tayle, reed Mace, marsh Beetle or Pestle, Dutch Downe.*

Herbe à tous maux. *as* Nicotiane.

Herbe militaire à millefueilles. *Knights Millfoyle, Souldiors Yarrow, yellow or little Yarrow, yellow Knighten Yarrow.*

Herbe aux mites. *Purple, or Mothe, Mullein.*

Herbe Mithridate. *Scordium, water Germaunder (so called of King* Mithridates, *the first finder thereof.)*

Herbe moniale. *Wild Larkes-heele, purple Monkes flower.*

Herbe au moyneau. *as* Morgeline.

Herbe nervis. *(or more properly,* Neris.) *Rose-bay, Rose-tree, Oleander.*

Herbe de nostre Dame. *as* Orvale ; *so called in* Languedoc.

Herbe nouée. *Centinodie, Knot-grasse, Birds-tongue, Swines grasse.*

Herbe de la nuict. *An hearbe, or Arbor plant, whose flower, shut vp all day, opens onely anights.*

Herbe du papier. *The Egyptian great rush* Papyrus, *whereof the first paper was made.*

Herbe de paralysie. *The Cowslip, or Ox-slip, tearmed otherwise Palsie-wort, and pettie Mullein.*

Herbe aux pattes. *Fole-foot, Colts-foot, Horse-foot, Hall-foot.*

Herbe aux perles. *Perle-plant, Lich-wall, Grommill, Gremill.*

Herbe de S.Pierre. *Sampire, Crestmarin.*

Herbe à piment. *as* Piment.

Herbe aux pouilleux. *Lice-bane, Staues-aker, Louse-wort, Louse-powder.*

Herbe aux poulmons. *Sage or Cowslip of Jerusalem, Sage of Bethlem, spotted Comfrey, Lungwort ; also, the mosse called Lungwort, or Oister-greene.*

Herbe aux poulx. *as* Herbe aux pouilleux.

Herbe poyvrée. *Dittander, Dittanie, Pepperwort.*

Herbe du grand Prieur. *Tobacco, or the hearbe Nicotian.*

Herbe puante. *A fourth kind of small Flea-bane Coniza; of a strong smell, or stinking sauor.*

Herbe à pulces. *Fleawort ; also, Fleabane, or Fleabane Mullet ; (The seedes of that are like, the smell of this is death, to fleas.)*

Herbe à punaises. *Fleabane, Coniza, Fleabane Mullet.*

Herbe Robert. *Hearbe Robert ; a kind of Storkes Bill.*

Herbe de S.Roch. *Coniza, Fleabane.*

Herbe de la Roine mere. *French Tobacco.*

Herbe saincte. *Nicotian, Tobacco.*

Herbe Sardonique. *Crowfoot of the fallow field, or Crowfoot of Illiria.*

Herbe Savonniere. *Sopewort, Sopeweed, Struthie, Bruisewort, mocke Gillouer ; also, wild Rose Campion, Crow-sope.*

Herbe sauvage. *A weed, or Wilding.*

Herbe aux scorpions. *Scorpion wort, Scorpion grasse, Caterpillers.*

Herbe aux serpens. *Snakes Buglosse, Vipers Buglosse, Vipers hearbe, wild Buglosse the lesser.*

Herbe de S. Simeon. *Simeons Mallow, Verueine Mallow, cut Mallow.*

Herbe solaire. *The Marigold.*

Herbe au soleil. *A verie great, round, flat, and faire yellow flower, which turnes with the Sunne, and euer lookes towards it ; the stalke it groweth (single) on, dryed (though verie great, and betweene twelue and fifteene foot long) is verie light ; being little other then so much pith wrapped vp in a solide, and woodie rinde, which makes it strong, and fit to serue for a Prop.*

Herbe du soleil. *The Marigold ; also,* Heliotropium, *Turnesole, Wartwort.*

Herbe du tac. *Lungwort, wood Liuerwort ; (a kind of Mosse.)*

Herbe aux tainctuiers. *Madder.*

Herbe terrestre. *A third kind of* Sideritis, *or Ironwort ; an hearbe thus called, because it growes close to the ground.*

Herbe aux tigneux. *The butter Burre.*

Herbe tore. *Broad-leaued* Aconitum, *Wolues bane, Wolfewort.*

Herbe de la Trinité. *Hearb Trinitie, Paunsie, Harts-ease, two faces vnder a hood ; also, Harefoot, or Harefoot Trefoyle.*

Herbe qui tue les brebis. *Moneywort, hearbe two-pennie, two-pennie grasse.*

Herbe de tunicis. *Frothie or spatling Poppie, white Ben ; also, the hearbe Sweet Williams.*

Herbe au Turc ; &, Herbe du grand Turc. *Rupturewort, Burstwort.*

Herbe veluë. *as* Herbe à cotton.

Herbe du vent. *The wind flower.*

Herbe vermineuse. *Purple or Mothe Mullein.*

Herbe aux Viperes. *Wild Buglosse the lesser, Snakes Buglosse, Vipers Buglosse, Vipers hearbe.*

Les bonnes herbes. *as* Herbettes.

Arracher les bonnes herbes, & planter les mauvaises. *To supplant vertue, and support vice ; or, to plucke vp vertue to set vp vice.*

Couper l'herbe sous les pieds à. *To supplant.*

Manger son bled en herbe. *To turne his cattell into his corne ; to spend (the value of) his reuenue before it come in.*

Mettre toutes les herbes de la S. Iean. *To imploy all his skill on, or meanes in ; (Diuers imagine, that the hearbes, which are to be kept for the whole yeares store, are better, gathered on Midsummer day, then on any other ; and therefore be Markets extraordinarily furnished, on that day, with all sorts of new-gathered hearbes.)*

Reduict à l'herbe. *Brought to extreame want, in great necessitie, full of pouertie.*

L'herbe qu'on cognoist on la doit lier à son doigt : Prov. *Those, or that, which a man knowes best, he must vse most.*

En four chaud ne croist herbe : Prov. *Grasse growes not in hot Ouens.*

Il faut que l' herbe soit bien courte quand on ne trouve que repaistre : Prov. *Commons must needs be short where no meat's to be come by.*

Mauvaise herbe croist tousiours : Prov. *An ill weed growes apace.*

Herbé : m. ée : f. *Fed with grasse ; layed on the grasse ; turned into grasse.*

Herbeillé : m. ée : f. *Fed on, or with, grasse.*

Herbeiller. *To feed on, or with, grasse.*

Herbelette : f. *A small hearbe ; or small grasse.*

Herber. *To graze, or feed on grasse ; to lay on the grasse ; to turne into, or out to, grasse.*

Herbergage : m. *A lodging, or dwelling.*

Herberge : f. *A house, harbour, lodging.*

Herbergé : m. ée : f. *Inhabited, or dwelt on.*

Herbergement : m. *A lodging, tenement, or house lyen in ; also, a lodging, harbouring, dwelling.*

Herberger. *To harbour, lodge, or dwell in a house.*

Herbergerement : m. *An harbour ; house, tenement, lodging, dwelling.*

Herbergerie : f. *The same.*

Herberie : f. *Hearbes ; increase, prouision, or store, of hearbes ; also, a birds weason, or wind-pipe ; a beasts gullet, or throat-bole.*

Herbette : f. *Small grasse ; or, a small hearbe.*

Herbettes. *Lettuce, Burrage, Purslane, Sorrell, and such like holesome hearbes ; tearmed so by the vulgar.*

Herbeux : m. euse : f. *Grassie, hearbie ; full of grasse, or of hearbes.*

Herbier: m. *An Herball; also, an Herballist; also, a Gardener, or Hearb-seller.*
Herbiere: f. *An Hearb-wife; also, the weason, or wind-pipe of a bird; and, the throat-boll, throat-pipe, or gullet of a beast.*
Herbis: m. *Grassie, or well-growne, Pastures.*
Herbiste: com. *An Herbist, or Herballist; one that vnderstands the nature, and temper of hearbes.*
Herboriser. *To gather hearbes; to be much among them; or, to obserue, examine, or studie their seuerall natures; to play the Herballist.*
Herboriste: m. *as* Herbiste.
Herbregé: m. ée: f. *Commonly dwelt on, vsually lodged, or lyen in.*
Herbregement: m. *as* Herbergement.
Herbreger. *To dwell on; commonly to lodge, or ly in.*
Herbregerie: f. *A lodging, or dwelling; a tenement to lodge, or house to dwell in.*
Herbu: m. uë: f. *Grassie, hearbie.*
Herce: f. *A Harrow; also, a kind of Port-cullis, thats stucke (as a Harrow) full of sharpe, strong, and out-standing (Iron) pinnes.*
Herces. *Pikes, or sharpe Iron pinnes vpon gates.*
En vne herce bien dentée n'y faut nulles dents: Prov. *A thing well done needs no addition.*
Herceler. *Seeke* Harceler.
Hercement: m. *A harrowing.*
Hercer. *To harrow; also, to ioult, or iustle one thing against another.*
Herceur: m. *A harrower; he that leads, and guides the harrow horses.*
Herceure: f. *A harrowing.*
Hercher. *as* Hercer. ¶Norm.
Herculiane, & Pierre Herculienne. *A Loadstone.*
Herdertifler. *The great, or maister Deuill.* ¶Rab.
Herdre. *To cleaue, or sticke fast vnto; (an old word.)*
Here. *as* Haire.
Hereditable: com. *Hereditable, inheritable.*
Hereditaire: com. *Hereditarie, successiue; comming by inheritance, belonging to an inheritance.*
Heredital. *The same; or, as* Herital.
Quint hereditał. *See* Quint.
Heredité: f. *An heritage, inheritance, patrimonie.*
Heresiarche, ou Heresiarque; *an arch-hereticke.*
Heresie: f. *Heresie; obstinate, or wicked error.*
Heresié: m. ée: f. *Growne hereticall, turn'd Hereticke, grounded in heresie; as obstinate, or impious, as an Hereticke.*
Hereste de poisson. *as* Areste.
Heretique: com. *An Hereticke.*
Hergne: f. *Bursting; or a rupture within the cods; also, waywardnesse, peeuishnesse, frowardnesse; also, a starueling or ill-thriuing tree, a stockt tree; also, a sucker that springs vp from the root of a tree.*
Hergneux. *Burst; also, froward; Looke* Hargneux.
Herigoté: m. ée: f. *Dew-clawed; hauing spurres, or dew-clawes.*
Herigotes: f. *Dew-clawes; also, spurres.*
Herigoteure: f. *The hauing of dew-clawes, or spurres.*
Heripé. *as* Herupé.
Heriper. *as* Heruper.
Herissé: m. ée: f. *Set, staring, or standing vp, like bristles, or the haire of an affrighted creature; horride; rough, rugged.*
Herissement: m. *A setting vp of the bristles; a staring, or horride standing vp, as of bristles; also, as* Herissonnement.
Herisser. *To set vp his bristles; to make his haire to stare.*
Se **Herisser.** *His haire to stare; also, to shiuer, or yearne, through feare.*
Herisson: m. *An Vrchin, a Hedgehog.*
Herisson de mer. *The sea Vrchin; a fish whose outside somewhat resembles the land-Vrchin.*
Parez l'herisson il semblera Baron: Prov. *Good clothes hide much deformitie; or, a clowne well cloathed seemes a Gentleman.*
Herissonné. *as* Herissé.
Herissonnement: m. *A suddaine quiuering, shiuering, or yearning, by the sence, or apprehension of an abhorred thing.*
se **Herissonner.** *as* s'Herisser.
Heritable: com. *Inheritable; also, held in fee simple, or for euer.*
Heritablement. *Inheritably, in fee simple, for euer.*
Heritableté: f. *An Inheritance; the soyle inherited.* ¶Wallon.
Heritage: m. *An Inheritance, Heritage, Patrimonie.*
Rentes à heritage. *Looke* Rente.
Mettre les mains à l'heritage. *To fall on his hands to the ground.*
De ieune Advocat heritage perdu: Prov. *The land is lost which a young Lawyer pleads for.*
Vie n'est pas seur heritage: Prov. *Life (though it be free-hold) is no inheritance (no sure hold;) or, life's no inheritance to build on.*
Herital: m. ale: f. *Of inheritance; also, inherited, or held in fee.*
Heritance. *as* Heritage; *(an old word.)*
Herité: m. *An Inheritance, or heritage.*
Herité: m. ée: f. *Inherited; gotten, or come vnto, by discent.*
Il est herité en ces marches; *he hath gotten land, or an estate of inheritance, in these Quarters.*
Heritel: m. elle: f. *Inheritable; or, of inheritance.*
Heriter. *To inherite; to get, or come vnto by inheritance, or discent; also, to get land of inheritance, or an estate of inheritance in land.*
Heritier: m. *An heire, or inheritor.*
Heritier conventionnel. *An adopted heire by reason of marriage; as a sonne, or daughter in law made by the father one of his heires, either in lieu of one of his other children, or as one among the rest.*
Heritier simple. *An heire by discent.*
Heritier: m. ere: f. *Of, or belonging to, an heire, inheritor, or inheritance.*
Herle. *as* Harle.
Hermaire. *as* Armaire.
Hermandrée. *Looke* Germandrée.
Herme: m. Hermes; *The name of a Saint.*
Feu S. Herme. *A firie meteor appearing on the tops of ship-masts at sea; Looke* Furole.
Herme: com. *as* Ferme. ¶Gasc. *also, desert, wast, vntilled; solitarie, vnhaunted, vnfrequented.*
Hermile. *A little round member in Architecture, tearmed otherwise* Astragale.
Herminer. *To furre with Ermines.*
Herminette: f. *A little planing Axe.*
Hermitage: m. *An Hermitage.*
Hermite: m. *An Hermit.*
Hermite marin. *as* Branchuë; *A kind of small red Crayfish.*
Bernard l'Hermite. *The same.*
Le Regnard est devenu hermite: Prov. *The Fox doth preach (beware your Geese.)*
Hermitresse: f. *An Hermitresse; a woman Hermite.*

Hermodacte. *Hermodactill, Dogs bane, wild Bulbe, Meade or Medow Saffron, the sonne before the father.*
Hermole: f. *Burstwort, Rupturewort.*
Herné: m. **ée**: f. *Burst; hauing a rupture about the Priuities.*
Herniaire: f. *as* Hermole.
Hernie. *Bursting; or, a rupture within the cods.*
Heroë: m. *A Worthie; a Demygod; one whom his valor hath deified, or immortalized.*
Heroïne: f. *A Ladie of admirable beautie, or of most excellent parts; a most worthie Ladie.*
Heroique: com. *Heroicall; most worthie, noble, gallant, high-minded, or valiant.*
Heron: m. *A Heron. Looke* Hairon.
Herouët. *(The name of) a certaine great, yellow, and soft apple.*
Herpail: m. *A troope, heard, flocke, a crue, a rowt.*
Herpaille: f. *A knot, or crue of beggarlie, and roguish vagabonds, that liue by pilfering, or vpon the spoile.*
Herpailleur: m. *A seller of old trinkets of Iron, &c.*
Herpé: m. **ée**: f. *Grasped, snatched, caught at greedily; griped, hooked, violently seised; also, Harpe-like, shaped or fashioned like a Harpe; out-breasted, and well voided or lanke in the Groine, like a well-made Greyhound.*
Herpelu. *A Stiuer, or French shilling.* ¶Barrag.
Herper. *To graspe, snatch, catch, clinch greedily; to gripe, hooke, seize violently, lay violent hands on.*
Herper contre terre. *To creepe, or crawle.*
Herpes: f. *The Shingles, Running worme, or wild fire.*
Herr. *Maister, or Sir.* ¶Aleman.
Vous faictes du herr. *(A rusticall taxation of a sawcie yong man, or seruant;) you are verie cockit, or lustie; you take too much vpon you.*
Herre: m. *A rogue, beggar, vagabond.*
Herry: m. *The fundament, or arse-gut.*
Hers. *(An Interiection of calling) hoe, here ho.*
Herse: f. *A harrow; also, a kind of Portcullis; Looke* Herce.
Herselé. *Seeke* Harcelé.
Hersement: m. *A harrowing.*
Herser. *To harrow; also, to vex, turmoyle, disquiet, hurrie, torment.*
Herseur: m. *A harrower; also, a vexer, or tormentor of.*
Hersoir. *Yesternight.*
Herte. Estre à l'herte. *Looke* Erte.
Hertringue. *I drinke to you (in Dutch.)* ¶Rab.
Herupé: m. **ée**: f. *Whose haire stares, or stands an end; also, bristlie, prickled, rough, horride; also, towsed, discheuelled, disordered.*
Heruper. *To discheuell, towse, or disorder the haire; to make it stare, or stand illfauoredly.*
S'Heruper. *To set vp the bristles, as one that growes into choller; also, his haire to stare; or, as* Se Herisser.
Heruppé. *as* Herupé.
Hesitation: f. *Hesitation, doubtfulnesse, vncertainetie; stammering, staggering.*
Hesité. *Doubted, stucke at; stammered, staggered (in opinion.)*
Hesiter. *To doubt, feare, sticke, stammer, stagger (in opinion.)*
Hespalier: m. *A Sayler, or Marriner.*
Hesperie. *The West Tower.* ¶Rab.
Hestoudeau. *A Cockerell, or great Cocke chicke; also, a Caponet; and in some few places (wherein any sort of yong, big, or well-grown pullein is termed thus) a Pullet.*
Hestre: m. *A Beech tree.*
Hestreau: m. *A yong, or little, Beech tree.*
Hetaudeau. *as* Hestoudeau.
Heteroclite: com. *Irregular, extraordinarie, not declined as other Nownes.*
Resolu comme Pihourt en ses heteroclites. *Looke* Resolu.
Hetique: com. *as* Hectique.
Heù: m. *A (Dutch) Hoy; also, a Lighter.*
Heu hasch. *Fained words for a Cough.* ¶Rab.
Heudri: m. **ie**: f. *Mustie, corrupted, putrified; stained, or spotted, as vn-ayred linnen.*
Heudrir. *To must, corrupt, putrifie; to spoyle, or marre by ill keeping, or want of ayring.*
Heulet: m. *A Hoult, or little Isle cut out of the land of purpose to be ouerflowed euerie tyde by the sea; that of the froth thereof (then left behind, and gathered after) salt may be made.*
Heullant. *Yelling, howling.*
Heur: m. *Hap, lucke, fortune, chaunce.*
Le bon heur tost se passe qui n'en a soing: Prov. *Good fortune quickly slips from such as heed it not.*
Heure: f. *An houre; also, time, season, space; also, the clocke.*
Heures. *A Prayer booke for certaine houres; Looke after* Heurelival.
L'heure de complie. *Compline-time; Euening-song tide, the edge of the euening.*
Heures equinoctiales. *The 24 equal parts, or houres, whereof a naturall day consists.*
Heures d'horologes. *The same; or, equall, or euen houres (such as clockes make) one iust as long as the other; ordinarie houres.*
Heures inesgales. *The 12 vnequall parts of the artificers day; which lasts (all the yeare long) from the rising to the setting, of the Sunne.*
Heures des Planettes. *as* Heures inesgales; *Vnequall houres; such as are sometimes longer, sometimes shorter then, and sometimes like vnto, the ordinarie houres.*
Haute heure. *Farre on the day; (the season from about eight in the morning vntill noone.)*
'A l'heure. *At that houre, at that instant, than, in the time of.*
'A l'heure que. *When, whilest that.*
'A la bonne heure. *Happily, luckily, fortunately, in good time, in a good houre.*
De bonne heure. *In good time; also, early, betimes.*
Pour l'heure. *Than, at that instant, for that present.*
Sur l'heure. *as* Pour l'heure.
Tout à cette heure. *Now, euen now, incontinently, forthwith, presently, at this verie instant, by and by.*
L'heure a sonné. *It hath strucke eleuen; (a Lawyers phrase.)*
Toutes heures ne sont pas meures: Prov. *All times are not in season for all things.*
Il n'est qu'une mauvaise heure au jour: Pro. *There is but one ill (or vnluckie) houre in the day.*
Heuré: m. **ée**: f. *Set, or appointed an houre; limitted, stinted, or tasked by the houre.*
Bien heuré. *as* Heureux.
Heurelival. *The name of a soure apple, fit to make Cyder.*
Heures: f. *A Latine booke of prayers, appropriated vnto certaine houres in the morning, and then said of dutie by Shauelings, and in deuotion by others.*
Heureté: f. *Happinesse, blessednesse, blissefullnesse, prospe-*

prosperitie, felicitie, fortunatenesse.
Heureusement. *Happily, blessedly, blissefully, fortunately, prosperously.*
Heureuseté: f. *as* Heureté.
Heureux: m. euse: f. *Happie, blessed, blissefull, prosperous, luckie, fortunate.*
Il est bien heureux qui se mesle de ses affaires: Prov. *He is verie happie that followes his owne businesse; (then is the dullard that cannot, the sluggard that will not, and the vnfree that must not, doe it, verie vnhappie.)*
Heurlement: m. *A howling, or yelling.*
Heurler. *To howle; Seeke* Hurler.
Heurlerie: f. *as* Heurlement.
Heurt: m. *A shocke; push, or dash; a violent meeting, or conflict, scuffling, or incounter; a knocke, or knocking together of; also, a peece of high ground; also, the top, or vpper part of a mountaine.*
Tout à heurt. *Headie, all-ahead.*
Bastir en heurt. *To build high; or on the vpper part, or side, of a hill.*
Gare le heurt. *See* Gare.
Ils ont eu tant de heurts. *They haue beene so much afflicted; they haue receiued so many ioults; so many mischiefes haue assaulted them.*
Heurtade: f. *A shocke, knocke, iurre, ioult, push, dash.*
Heurtant. *Shocking, pushing, knocking, iurring, ioulting; violently meeting.*
Heurté: f. *as* Heureté.
Heurte, à toute heurte. *Still, euer, euerie foot, now and then.*
Heurté: m. ée: f. *Knocked, pushed, ioulted, iurred, violently hit against.*
Heurtement: m. *A knocking, ioulting, pushing, dashing, striking, iurring, violent hitting against.*
Heurter. *To knocke, push, iurre, ioult, strike, dash, or hit violently against.*
Heurter des pieds. *To stampe, or applaud by often stamping.*
Se Heurter à vne pierre. *To stumble at a stone.*
Heurter la teste contre l'huis. *To runne his head against the doore; to take wax off the doore with his head.*
Hardiment heurte à la porte qui bonne nouvelle apporte: Prov. *He that brings good newes boldly knocks at doore.*
Heurtes: f. *Small Azure balls; tearmed (in Heraldric) hurts on men, and tongue-moles on women.*
Heurtis: m. *as* Heurtement.
Heuse. *Looke* House.
Heusse: f. *The Linch pinne, whereby the arme of th'axletree is kept within the naue of a Cartwheele &c.*
Heyron: m. *as* Hairon; *also, a sea-Mew.* ¶Savoyard.
Hiacinthe. *Looke* Hyacinthe.
Hiacinthin: m. ine: f. *Light-blue; Purple, Violet; of the colour of a Iacinth (flower.)*
Hibernal: m. ale: f. *Winterie; of, or belonging to, the winter.*
Hibou: m. *An Owle; the ordinarie great Owle.*
Hibou cornu. *as* Moyen duc. *See* Duc.
On ne peut faire de hibou esparvier: Prov. *One cannot make a Hawke of an Owle.*
Hideur: f. *Dread, horror, quaking, feare, (or the cause thereof) a thing horrible, and fearefull to behold; also, ghastlinesse, terriblenesse, ouglinesse, hideousnesse.*
Hideusement. *Hideously, ghastly, grimly, horribly, terribly, fearefully.*
Hideux: m. euse: f. *Hideous, grimme, dreadfull, ghastlie, terrible, horrible.*
Hie: f. *A Rammer, or Pauiers beetle; also, a Commaunder, or water-Pile Sledge, wherewith great stakes are driuen downe into the ground.*
Hié: m. ée: f. *Rammed in, driuen, or beaten downe.*
Hieble: m. *Wallwort, dwarfe Elderne, Danewort.*
Hiement: m. *A ramming; a driuing downe of stones, or piles into the ground.*
Hier. *To ramme; to beat, or driue downe stones, or piles into the ground; also, to beat flat, or sadden (as a floore) with beating.*
Hier. *Yesterday.*
Devant hier. *Two dayes agoe.*
Hier vachier huy chevalier: Prov. *Looke* Vachier.
Hieracite. Pierre h. *A kind of Bloud-stone, or stone that staunchetb bloud.*
Hierarchie: f. *An Hierarchie; a sacred Principalitie, a holie Gouernment.*
Hiere picre. *A certaine yellow, and verie bitter composition in powder.*
Hierobotane: f. *Veruine, Junoes teares, holie hearbe, Mercuries moist bloud.*
Hierre: m. *Ivie; Seeke* Lierre.
Hierre terrestre. *Ground Iuie, Alehoofe, Cats foot, Gill-creep-by-the-ground.*
Hileux: m. euse: f. *Blacke-tayled, or blacke on the tayle, as a Beane is.*
Hillots: m. *Fellowes;* ¶Gasc. ¶Rab.
Hinard: m. arde: f. *Wry-neckt, wry-headed.*
Hinnellement. *Seeke* Isnellement.
Hipate: f. *A sixt; or the proportion of six, in Musicke.*
Hipocras: m. *(The compound wine called)* Hipocras.
Hipocras d'eau. *Metheglin; wine, or drinke made of honey and water.*
Hipogriphe: m. *Looke* Hypogriphe.
Hipothecaire. *Seeke* Hypothecaire.
Hipothequé: m. ée: f. *Ingaged, morgaged, layed to pawne.*
Hipothequer. *To pawne, ingage, or morgage (immouables.)*
Hippiatrie: f. *Horse-phisicke.*
Hippocras. *as* Hipocras.
Hippoglosse: m. *Horse-tongue, Double-tongue, Tongue-blade.*
Hippopotame: m. *A water-horse (liuing in the riuer Nilus) that hath feet like an Ox, backe and mane like a Horse, tuskes like a Bore, and a winged tayle.*
Hirable. *as* Giraffe.
Hiraudie: f. *A paltrie garment (In old French.)*
Hircin: m. ine: f. *Goat-like; of a Goat.*
Branche hircine. *Brank-Vrsin, Beares-claw, Beares-breech.*
Hire: f. *A Rammer, or Beater.*
Hireté. *as* Heredité; *(an old word.)*
Hirondelle, *or* Hirundelle; *A Swallow; Seeke* Arondelle.
Hirondelle de mer. *as in* Arondelle; *also, the small ash-coloured Mew, which, after the departure of the ordinarie sea-Mew, flyes alone, and in flying fishes along Riuers.*
Hirondelle de rivage. *A sea Swallow; a little bird that builds in the banks of riuers.*
Hisnel. *Seeke* Isnel.
Hisope: f. *(The hearbe)* Hisope.
Histoire: f. *A Historie, Storie, Chronicle, Relation.*

Historial: m. ale: f. *Historicall; of, or belonging to, a Historie.*

Historié: m. ée: f. *Flourished, wrought, or beautified, with storie-worke; also, contained in Histories.*

Historien: m. *A Historiographer, Chronicler, Storie-writer.*

Historier. *To write, or compile Histories; also, to flourish, or beautifie Wainscot, or Tapistrie with Histories, or Storie-worke.*

Histrion: m. *A Comedian, Enterluder, Stage-player.*

Histrionique: com. *Player-like; fit for, or belonging to, a Stage-player.*

Hiulque: com. *Gaping as the earth in drought; full of chaps, or chinkes; ill couched, ioyned, or set together.*

Ho: m. *A Grosse, or great troupe of Caualleric; many troupes of horsemen together.*

Hobain. *as* Aubain.

Hobeine. *as* Aubaine.

Hober. *To stirre, moue, remoue from place to place; (a rustie, and rusticall word.)*

Hobere: m. *as* Aubere.

Hoberger. *To fly; or, to saue himselfe by flying.*

Hobille: f. *A Ierkin, Iacket, or Coat.* ¶Pic.

Hobin: m. *A Hobbie; a little ambling (and shorne-maned) horse.*

Aller le hobin. *To amble, or pace, like a Hobbie.*

Hobineux: m. euse: f. *Hobbie-like; or belonging to a Hobbie.*

Hobreau: m. *(The Hawke tearmed) a Hobbie; also, a mungrell, or halfe-gentleman; one whose father, or mother were of meane parentage.*

Hoc: m. *as* Croc; *also, as* Ho.

Hoche: f. *A nicke, or notch, on a Tallie, &c.*

Hochebos. *A kind of Boat (an old word.)*

Hochebride: m. *A retchlesse rakehell, a desperate or carelesse companion.*

Hochecüe. *as* Hoche-queuë.

Hochement: m. *A shaking, wagging, iogging, iobbing, nodding.*

Hochepli: m. *A Vardingale.*

Hochepot: m. *A hotch-pot, or Gallimaufrey; a confused mingle-mangle of diuers things iumbled, or put together.*

Hoche-prunier. *A Plum-tree shaker; a mans yard.*

Hoche-queuë: f. *A water Wagtayle.*

Hocher. *To shake, wag, iog; nob; nod.*

Hocher du nez. *Disdainefully to snuffe at.*

Hocher de la teste. *To nod, or cast vp the head; as one that would seeme to refuse a thing offered, or deny a thing spoken.*

Hochet de petis enfans. *A Rattle, or Clacke wherewith children play.*

Hocquet, & Hocqueter. *as* Hoquet, & Hoqueter.

Hocqueteur: m. *A Basket-carrier.* (v.m.)

Hocqueton: m. *A (sleeuelesse, and short) Iacket, Coat, Cassock, or Ierkin (at Court) a Coat for one of the Gard; Looke* Hoqueton.

Hocton. *as* Hocqueton; *and hence;*

Qui a le loup pour compaignon porte le chien sous l'hocton: Pro. *Let him thats yoakt with a knaue be armd with a cudgell.*

Hodé: f. *Toyle, tiring, wearisomenesse.*

Hodé: m. ée: f. *Wearied, tired, ouer-toyled.*

Hoder. *To wearie, tire, ouer-toyle.*

Hoe. *An Interiection of wondering; as* Hoho; *also, reprehension; whence,* vous estez bien hardi, hoe; *also, of forbidding to touch a thing; as when they say,* Allons hoe.

Hogner. *as* Hoigner.

Hoguiné: m. ée: f. *Vexed, molested, annoyed, infested, offended.*

Hoguinement: m. *A vexing, molesting, annoying, infesting, offending.*

Hoguiner. *To vex, trouble, disquiet, annoy, molest, infest, offend.*

Hoguines: f. *The peeces of Armour which couer the armes, thighes, and legs.*

Hoho. *(An Interiection of wondering) what hoe! is it possible!*

Hoigne: f. *A grumbling, muttering, murmuring, repining; whyning; (The Normand Towne* Valoignes *hath beene surnamed* La Hoigne, *because the inhabitants thereof are by nature verie litigious.)*

Hoigner. *To grumble, mutter, murmure; to repine; also, to whyne as a child, or dog.*

Hoir: m. *An heire, or inheritor; (In some French lawes (wherein the Appennages of the Sonnes of France are treated of) an heire male, and in some auncient Farmes and Leases, a direct heire, is vnderstood by this word.)*

Hoir de quenouille. *An inheritrix, heire female, daughter and heire.*

Hoirie: f. *An heritage, inheritance; heiredome; inheriting.*

Holà. *(An Interiection) hoe there, enough, soft soft, no more of that if you loue me; also, heare you me, or come hither.*

Faict au hola. *Dutifull, obseruant, readie, at a becke, at call.*

Faire le hola. *To stop, stay, interrupt, bid stand; also, to part a fray.*

Holette de maille. *A shirt of Mayle.*

Holocauste: m. *A sacrifice killed, and layed whole on the Altar.*

Holos. *for* Helas. ¶Rab.

Holosteon. *Hairie small Plantaine, flouring sea Plantaine; also, mountaine Plantaine; also, the hearbe called Stitchwort, or All-bonie.*

Holothurie: f. *A certaine thing found in the sea, yet neither Plant, Fish, nor fit to be eaten.*

Holotte: f. *A Madge-howlet, or little Owle.*

Hom. *as* Homme; *a man.* (vieil mot.)

Homage. *Looke* Hommage.

Homar: m. *A sea-Creuice, or small Lobster.*

Grand homar. *The great, or ordinarie, Lobster.*

Homelette. *as* Aumelette; *an Omelet, or Pancake of egges.*

Homenage. *as* Hommage. ¶Bearnois.

Homenas. *A good sillie cokes.* ¶Rab.

Homicide: m. *Manslaughter, or murther; also, an homicide, man-killer, murtherer.*

Homicidé: m. ée: f. *Killed, slaine, murthered.*

Homicider. *To slay, kill, murther (a man.)*

Homicidere: com. *An homicide, man-killer, murtherer.*

Hommace: f. *A* Virago; *a manlie, or stout woman.*

Hommage: m. *Homage.*

Hommage de bouche, & des mains. *Is done by a vassall with head vncouered, hands ioyned, and a kisse receiued; and bindes him to fight for his Lord onely in defence of the land whereof hee holds.*

Hommage de deuotion. *Which is giuen to the Church in Frankalmoine, and carries with it neither fief, Iurisdiction, nor any other dutie.*

Hom-

Hommage lige. *Is done by the vassall vngirt, and bare-headed, with ioyned hands layed on the Euangelists, and a kisse receiued in the taking of his oath; and binds him to become an enemie to all his Lords enemies, and to follow him all his life time against all men (except the King.)*
Hommage plein. *Full, or absolute homage; or, as* Hommage lige. *(And yet some Customes make them differ; Seeke* Lige.)
Hommage simple. *as* Hommage de bouche, & des mains.
Hommagé: m. ée: f. *Held by homage; for which homage is due, or done.*
Hommager. *To owe, or doe homage vnto; also, to reuerence.*
Hommasse: f. *as* Hommace.
Homme: m. *A Man; also, a tenant, &c; (Looke the next marginall word.)*
Homme de bras. *An Artificer, or Handicrafts man; one that gets his liuing by the labour of his hands.*
Homme de Capeline. *A resolute, or valiant fellow.*
Homme de peine. *A laborious, or painefull fellow; an extreame toyler, or traueller; also, as* Homme de bras.
Homme de bon cresme. *A plaine, honest, sincere, open-hearted companion.*
Il le despecha comme vn homme de son païs. *He vsed him rudely, or contemptibly; he handled him like a clowne as he is; he baffled, or abused him.*
Homme assailli à demy vaincu: Prov. *He thats assaulted is halfe ouercome.*
Homme chiche iamais riche: Prov. *Looke* Riche.
Homme endormi corps enseveli: Prov. *A sleeping, is no better then a dead, man.*
Homme matineux sain, alaigre, & soigneux: Pro. *Looke* Matineux.
Homme mort ne fait guerre: &, Homme mort ne mord point: Prov. *A dead man fights not; we say; A dead dog bites not.*
Homme mutin, brusque Roussin, flascon de vin prennent tost fin: Prov. *A factious asse, free horse, good cup of wine, are quickly spent.*
Homme rusé tard abusé: Prov. *Looke* Rusé.
Homme seul est viande aux loups: Prov. *The lone man is Wolues meat.*
Homme à deux visages n'agrée en villes, ny villages: Prov. *Looke* Visage.
Les hommes donnent aux femmes ce qu'ils n'ont pas, & ne peuvent avoir: Prov. viz. *Milke.*
Les hommes se rencontrent, & non pas les montagnes: Prov. *Not hills, but men, doe vse to meet.*
Vn homme de paille vaut vne femme d'or: Prov. *Looke* Femme
Estre homme de bien c'est mestier iuré, il ne l'est pas qui veut: Prov. *Euerie one cannot be honest that would (for some by ignorance, and others by necessitie, are, or must be, knaues.)*
Celuy est homme de bien qui est homme de biens: Prov. *He is a righteous, that is a rich, man (sayes the worldling.)*
'A grand homme grand verre: Prov. *Looke* Verre.
De meschant homme bon Roy: Prov. *A froward man becomes a good King.*
Autant chemine vn homme en vn iour comme vn limaçon en cent ans: Pro. *Seeke* Limaçon.
Bon poete mauvais homme: Prov. *A good Poet an euill person.*
Il ne faut pas enquerir d'ou soit l'homme mais qu'il soit bon: Prov. *No matter whence one comes so he be good.*
Le bœuf par la corne, & l'homme par la parole: Prov. *An Ox (is bound) by the horne, a man by his word.*
Tant travaille, & tracasse l'homme qu'il se rompt, ou somme. *Looke* Travailler.
Tant vaut l'homme tant vaut sa terre: Prov. *A man is prised by his land; See* Terre.
Vne science requiert tout son homme: Prov. *One Art requires a whole man; a man that will be perfect in an Art must follow nothing else.*
Homme: m. *A Tenant, Liegeman, Vassall, Subiect.*
Homme de corps. *A villaine, or one that holds by a seruile tenure.*
Hommes de la Cour du seigneur. *Such as owe suite and seruice to his Court.*
Homme feudal. *Is, in some Customes, the title of a Lord; but in the most, of a vassall.*
Homme de fief. *A Vassall, or Tenant in freehold; and sometimes the Lord of a* Fief.
Hommes de la loy (de Gand.) *The Magistrats (of Gaunt.)*
Homme sans moyen. *That holds immediatly (and by homage) of the Crowne.*
Homme de paix. *A vassall that ought to be at peace with his Lord; or ought (by the vertue of his homage) to keepe the peace made by his Lord; or one that hath sworne friendship, and fellowship with a greater then himselfe.*
Homme de plejure. *A vassall that is, or may be, a Bayle, Pledge, or Suretie for his Lord.*
Hommes proffitables. *Of whom the Lord makes profit, or from whom he hath his reuenue.*
Homme de service. *That holds his land by fealtie, and certaine manuall, or meane seruices.*
Homme de servitude. *A villaine; or one that holds by a seruile tenure.*
Homme vivant, mourant, & confiscant. *A Vicar, Substitute, or Deputie for a Church, Colledge, or Comminaltie; at whose death the Lords of their fiefs are to haue such rights as would haue beene due out of them at the death of a temporall, or single, tenant.*
Droict d'hommes. *A Priuiledge which the Kings Officers haue, in some places, to qualifie, and lessen the excessiue taxes imposed by Lords on their Tenants, whom otherwise they might tax at their pleasure.*
Faute, ou defaut d'homme. *Want, or omission of due homage, fealtie, or seruices; whereby the Landlord is enabled to seize into his hands the fief out of which they be due.*
Hommeau: m. *A dwarfe, dandiprat, little man, low fellow.*
Hommelet, & Hommenet. *as* Hommeau; *or, a verie little man.*
Hommesse: f. *A* Virago; *a manlie, or stout woman.*
Hommet. *as* Hommeau.
Homocentricalement. *In one Center.*
Homogené: m. ée: f. *Of one kind.* ¶Rab.
Homologation: f. *An admission, allowance, approuement, or approbation of; a consent vnto.*
Homologué: m. ée: f. *Admitted, accepted, allowed, approued of; assented, or consented vnto.*
Homologuer. *To admit, accept, allow, approue of; to assent, or consent vnto.*

Homonceau: m. *A pettie, or paultrie, fellow.*
Homonyme: f. *An equiuocation, or word of diuers significations.*
Homonyme: com. *Equiuocall.*
Homonymie: f. *An equiuocation; or, a double, or different sence in one word.*
Homs. *as* Homme; *a man.* (vieil mot.)
Hon hon. (*An Interiection expressing wonder, or a fearefull apprehension of approaching mischiefe;*) *aha, aha.*
Faire hon de la teste. *To seeme loath; Seeke* Faire.
Hondelée de foing. *A load of Hay.*
Hondrespondre: m. *A drunken, or swaggering Dutchman.* ¶Rab.
Hongner. *as* Hoigner.
Hongre: m. *An Hungarian; also, a guelded man, or horse; an Eunuch, a Guelding.*
Honneste: com. *Honest, good, vertuous; iust, vpright, sincere; also, gentle, ciuill, courteous; also, worthie, noble, honorable, of good reputation; also, comelie, seemelie, handsome, well befitting.*
Honnestement. *Honestly, vertuously, sincerely, vprightly; gently, ciuilly, courteously; worthily, nobly, with good credit; handsomely, decently, in a good fashion.*
Honnesteté: f. *Honestie, vertue, goodnesse, integritie, truth, sinceritie; iustnesse, vprightnesse; humanitie, courtesie, ciuilitie, gentlenesse; worth, or worthinesse; freedome of nature, open-heartednesse, a noble disposition; decencie, a Decorum.*
Honneur: f. *Honour; renowme, reputation, credit, praise, glorie, fame, great account, high reckoning, much estimation; worship, reuerence; dignitie, promotion; also, an Honour; or, an honourable estate, inheritance, or title, bestowed by a Prince, or great Lord.*
Honneurs funebres. *Funerall solemnities, rites, or rights.*
Le morceau d'honneur. *The last bit of a dish of meat; Looke* Morceau.
Vefve d'honneur. *Honours widow; a woman that had a good report, but now hath lost it.*
Ventes, & honneurs. *Looke* Vente.
Pressé de son honneur. *Hard set, sore layed to, that must needs goe to it, that must of necessitie purge, or vntrusse; (a mannerlie phrase.)*
'A tous seigneurs tous honneurs: Pro. *Giue to all Lords all th' honours due vnto them.*
Qui d'honneur n'a cure honte est sa droicture: Prov. *Shame falls on him that cares not for (true) honour; or, he that his credit doth not weigh, reproch attends him, sham's his pay.*
Qui n'a honte il n'aura ja honneur: Prov. *Hee that wants shame shall neuer much credit winne.*
Honni: m. ie: f. *Reproached, shamed, disgraced, dishonoured, defamed; cursed, reuiled, outraged, in words; (also, spotted, blemished, fouled, polluted, defiled.* ¶Pic.)
Honnir. *To reproach, disgrace, dishonour, defame, shame; reuile, curse, or outrage, in words; (also, to spot, blemish, pollute, foule, file, defile.* ¶Pic.)
Honnorance. *as* Honoraire.
Honorable: com. *Honourable, noble; worthie, famous, renowmed; reuerend, worshipfull; great, high, statelie, magnificent, sumptuous.*
Amende honorable. *Seeke* Amende.
Honorablement. *Honorably, nobly; worthily, famously, renowmedly; reuerently, worshipfully; stately, magnificently, sumptuously; in a high degree, after a gallant manner.*
Honoraire: m. *An honourable Present giuen to a Prince, Embassador, or great Officer at his first entrie; also, a fee due, by custome, or for aduice giuen, paines taken, or seruice done; hence, also, a Donatiue bestowed on Souldiors.*
Honoraire: com. *Honourable; or worthie of honour.*
Chevaliers honoraires. *Such as are Knights by the priuiledge of their birth, and not in the right of any Order; (as all Noblemen, from the Duke to the Chattelain, are.)*
Honorance: m. *as* Honoraire; (*especially in the last sence.*)
Honoré: m. ée: f. *Honoured; reuerenced, renowmed, praised, prised; much respected, greatly esteemed, highly accompted of.*
Honorer. *To honour; renowme; reuerence; praise exceedingly, prise highly, respect verie much.*
Honorifique: com. *Honourable, honour-breeding, noble, worthie, worshipfull.*
Honouars: m. *Looke* Henouars.
Honte: f. *Shame; shamefullnesse, or shamefastnesse; also, discredit, infamie, ignominie, imputation, disgrace.*
'A leur courte honte. *With much disgrace vnto them, to their exceeding shame.*
Dire honte. *To infame, defame, reuile, reproach, dishonour, cry shame on, or out vpon.*
Femme qui perd sa honte est sans estime, & conte: Prov. *Looke* Femme.
Il ne va pas du tout à honte qui de demie voye retourne: Prov. *He that turnes backe (hauing beene halfe way) goes not at all for shame.*
Qui a honte de manger a honte de vivre: Prov. *He that's ashamed to eat's ashamed to liue.*
Qui n'a honte il n'aura ja honneur: Prov. *Looke* Honneur.
Qui d'honneur n'a cure honte est sa droicture: Prov. *His meed is shame that weighes not his good name.*
Qui vit à compte vit à honte: Prov. *He basely liues that reckons all hee spends; (yet is there small difference betweene him that knowes not what he spends, and him that spends he knowes not what.)*
Tel cuide vanger sa honte qui l'accroist: Prov. *Some thinking to reuenge, renue, their shame.*
Vieil peché fait nouvelle honte: Prov. *Old sinne inflicts new shame.*
Honteux: m. euse: f. *Shamefast, bashfull, helo, modest, backward, fearefull; also, shamefull, infamous, ignominious, dishonourable, reproachfull, dishonest; also, belonging, or seated neere, to the priuie parts; whence;*
Artere, or veine honteuse. *Looke* Artere, & Veine.
La partie honteuse. *The groine, or part whereon the* Pubes *groweth.*
Honteux comme vne truye qui emporte vn levain. *As shamefast as a Sow that slaps vp a Sillibub.*
se **Hontir.** *as,* se Hontoyer.
se **Hontoyer.** *To be ashamed of; to blush, or be bashfull, at; to hang downe the head for shame.*
Hopelande: f. *as* Houpelande.
Hopperie: f. *A whooping, or showting.*
Hoquet: m. *The hickocke, or yexing.*

Ho-

Hoqueter. *To yex, or clocke; to haue the Hickup, or Hickocke.*
Hoqueton: m. *A (fashion of) short Coat, Cassocke, or Iacket, without sleeues, and most in fashion among the countrey people.*
Hoqueton argenté. *A Coat for one of the Kings Gard.*
Hoqueton de guerre. *A Souldiors Cassocke, a Horsemans coat-armour.*
Hoqueton orfavrisé. *as* Hoqueton argenté.
Horaprime. *as* Oraprime.
Horcentric, ou Horcentrique. *Out of the Center, cleane without the compasse of; (Mathematicians apply this word to the Sunne, when the Center thereof, being at the full height of his Epicycle, is furthest from the centre of the earth.)*
Horche. à horche. *Looke* à Ourse.
Hord. *as* Heurt.
Hordeat: m. *Barlie water; drinke made of Barlie.*
Hordoux. *Slouenlie, greasie, nastie, filthie.*
Hore. de là en hore. *From that time to this.*
Horée: f. *A great shower of raine.*
Horepole: f. *A Whirlepoole (fish.)*
Horion: m. *A dust, cuffe, rap, knocke, thumpe; also, a luncheon, or big peece.*
Horizon: m. *A Horizon; so much of the Firmament as wee can behold; or, a circle diuiding the Firmaments halfe-Sphere, which we see, from that halfe which we see not.*
Horloge: m. *A Clocke, or Dyall.*
Horloge d'eau. *A* Clepsydra, *or water Dyall; a vessell out of which water runnes continually, and in a certaine proportion for euerie houre.*
Horloge à sablon. *An Houre-glasse.*
Horloge au soleil. *A Sunne-dyall.*
Horloge des villageois. *The Marigold; (so tearmed because it sheweth them, by the changes of turning towards the Sunne, how the day passeth.)*
Il n' est horloge plus iuste que le ventre: Pro. *The bellie is the best, or truest Clocke.*
Horloger: m. *as* Horlogeur.
Horlogeur: m. *A Clock-maker, or Dyall-maker.*
Hormale. *as* Orvale.
Hormin: m. *Clarie; or (as* Mathiolus *affirmes) so mistaken by diuers Herballists; (for Clarie beares a Carnation flower (sayes he) or a whitish one (sayes* Gerard) *and* Horminium *a purple one; besides, the seed of Clarie is round, that of* Horminium *long; notwithstanding which differences, it may well ynough passe for a kind of Clarie.)*
Hormis. *Sauing, excepting, besides, onely, but, otherwise then.*
Horo. *I see him; (a Hunters tearme, or voice, whereby he signifies that he hath the sight of the beast in chase.)*
Horologeur. *as* Horlogeur.
Horologier. *The same.*
Horoscope: m. *The Horoscope, or Ascendant of a natiuitie; a diligent obseruation of the iust time wherein one was borne; also, the part of the firmament which riseth euerie houre from the East.*
Horreau: m. *A Mackerell.* ¶Marseillois.
Horreur: f. *Horror, loathing, detestation, abhorring; also, dread, or feare.*
Horrible: com. *Horrible; terrible; detestable, execrable, abhominable; hideous, most ouglie.*
Horriblement. *Horribly; terribly; hideously; execrably, abhominably.*
Horribler. *To make horrible, or most ouglie.*
Horribleté. *Horriblenesse; terriblenesse; hideousnesse.*
Horripilation: f. *A suddaine quaking, yerning, shuddering, shiuering, or quiuering; also, a growing rough with haire.*
Horripiration: f. *Smart; or, a suddaine quaking, &c; as* Horripilation.
Hors. *Out of, without.*
Hors d'icy. *Hence.*
Du costé hors le montoir. *On the wrong, or the other, side of the horse.*
Du tetin en hors. *From his verie infancie, euer since he sucked.*
Horsmis. *Looke* Hormis.
Hortailles: f. *All kind of Gardening Utensiles; or, as* Hottailles.
Hortatif: m. iue: f. *Hortatiue, exhorting.*
Hortie. *as* Ortie; *a Netle.*
Hortolages: m. *Hearbes, fruits, roots, Garden stuffe; things growing in Orchards, or Gardens.*
Hortolan: m. *A delicate bird (of the bignesse of a Larke) that hath a reddish beake and thighes; a necke, and breast streaked with yellow and greene; a Scarlet bellie spotted with Ash colour, and the feathers of his wings and tayle in some parts blacke, in some red, in some ash-coloured.*
Hory ho, hay & ho. *(The ordinarie harsh accent, or voice, of Carters.)*
Hoscher. *as* Hocher; *also, to swyne.*
Hoseaux. *Looke* Houseaux.
Hospillé, & Hospiller. *Seeke* Houspillé, & Houspiller.
Hospitable: com. *Hospitable; also, inhabitable, or fit to dwell in.*
Hospital: m. *An Hospitall, a Spittle.*
Aller à l'hospital. Ie m'en vay à l'h. *My fortunes are in the wane, or at a verie low ebbe; I may goe whether I will for any thing I haue.*
Envoyer à l'hospital. *To begger, vndoe, turne (in a poore pickle) out of doores.*
L'Ouvrier gentil à l'hospital: Prov. *Seeke* Ouvrier.
Hospitaler. *To receiue into, (and) to relieue within, an Hospitall.*
Hospitalier: m. *The Maister of an Hospitall; also, a Knight of the religious Order of the Hospitall.*
Hospitalier: m. ere: f. *Verie hospitable, vsing hospitalitie, that keepeth a good house.*
Hospitalité: f. *Hospitalitie, good house-keeping.*
Hosquet. *as* Hoquet.
Host: m. *An Host, or Armie; and (more particularly) a Troope, Squadron, or Batallion of Souldiors ranked, not in file, but close together; a Squadron, or Batallion trooping, or in troopes.*
Host banni. *as* Ban & Arriereban.
Hostage: m. *An Hostage, Pawne, Suretie, Pledge; (A terme of payment being expired, the Debtor must deliuer Hostages; to wit, three, or foure, who goe to an Inne, and there continue (hauing both wages, and their charges allowed them by him) vntill he haue taken order.)*
Hostager: m. ere: f. *Giuen in hostage, layed in pawne, left in pledge for.*
Hostarde: f. *A Bustard.*
Hostau. as Hostel. ¶Langued.
Hoste: m. *An Hoste, Inne-keeper, Inne-holder; also, a guest; also, a tenant, or vassall.*

Compter sans son hoste. *To reckon without his host; to make himselfe sure of things which are wholly at the disposition of others.*

Qui compte sans son hoste il faut qu' il compte deux fois: Prov. *Twice must he reckon without his host who reckons.*

Vne fois faut compter à l'hoste: Prov. *Our reckoning must be made one time or other.*

L'hoste & le poisson, passé trois iours, puent: Prov. *A guest and fish after three dayes are fustie.*

L'hoste est tousiours le plus foulé: Pro. *(Applyable to Gossipping feasts;) The intertainer's alwaies troubled most.*

Tel hoste tel hostel: Pro. *Like host like house.*

De meschant hoste bon reconduiseur: Pro. *A needie host (or guest) is a friendlie guide.*

Il se peut bien seoir sans contredit qui se met là ou son hoste luy dit: Prov. *Hee that sits where his host him bids, may lawfully keepe his place.*

Le sanglier n'est qu'un hoste: Prov. *Because hee raunges continually from wood to wood, from forrest to forrest.*

Mestier n'avons d'hoste à chere marrie: Prov. *A soure-fac't host (or guest) may well enough be spared.*

Hostel: m. *An Hostell, House, Lodging; Hall, Place, Palace; (This word is commonly a marke of Greatnesse; as* L'Hostel de Bourbon; L'Hostel de ville, &c; *other inferior Houses being tearmed* Maisons, *and* Logis.)

Hostel Dieu. *A Spitle, or Hospitall.*

Hostel de ville. *A Guild-hall, common Hall, Towne-house.*

Vn corps d'hostel. *See* Corps.

Maistre d' hostel. *A Steward, or Clarke of the Kitchin.*

`A l'hostel priser, & au marché vendre: Prov. *Prise goods at home, but sell them in the market.*

C' est l' hostel du Roy Petaud ou chascun est Maistre: Prov. *Applyable to a disordered household, wherein euerie one commaunds, and does, what he list.*

Il ne se fourvoit point qui à bon hostel va: Prov. *He goes not out of his way that goes to a good house.*

La belle chere amende beaucoup l' hostel: Prov. *Good cheere makes good amends for a bad house; or, a bad house by good cheere is much amended.*

Qui tost vient à son hostel mieux luy en est à son souper: Prov. *He fares the better that comes earlie home.*

Tel hoste tel hostel: Prov. *The host, and the house are (commonly) alike.*

Hostelage: m. *Hospitalitie; also, a bed, or nights-lodging (for a guest.)*

Droict d'hostelage. *Looke* Droict.

Pains d'hostelage. *A certaine dutie payed (within the Seigniorie of* Dunois) *by vassalls vnto their Lords, in regard of the houses wherein they dwell.*

Hostelé: m. ée: f. *Lodged.*

Hosteler. *To lodge; to giue, lend, or hire out lodging vnto; also, to lodge, or take a lodging, in.*

Hostelerie: f. *An Inne; an Hosterie; a victualling house, wherein meat and lodging may be had for money.*

Hostelier: m. *An Host, Inne-keeper, Inne-holder.*

Ris d'hostelier: Prov. *A ieering, or fained laughter; a dissembling cheerefulnesse; mirth onely from the teeth outward.*

Hostellage. *Looke* Hostelage.

Hosteller. *To lodge; giue, or affoord lodging vnto; also, to take, or haue a lodging in.*

Hostesse: f. *An Hostesse.*

Belle hostesse c'est vn mal pour la bourse: Prov. *A faire hostesse is a foule pick-purse; or, the beautie of an Hostesse is the purses bane.*

Hostie: f. *A sacrifice, or thing sacrificed.*

Hostiere. Gueux d'hostiere. *Such as beg from doore to doore.*

Hostierie: f. *An Hospitall; also, an Hosterie, or little Inne.*

Hostigement de fief. *A declaration in open Court, to whom a fief belongs after the decease of him that held it last; or for the securitie of a debt.*

Hostigié. Heritage hostigié. *Whose true owner is named in Court; as in* Hostigement.

Hostile: com. *Hostile, hatefull, enemie-like, belonging to an enemie.*

Hostilement. *Hostilely, hatefully, deadly, mortally, with deadlie feud.*

Hostilité: f. *Hostilitie, feud, enmitie, deadlie hatred, mortall hate.*

Hostise: f. *as* Ostize.

Hot. *Looke* Host.

Hottailles: f. *(All kind of) Baskets, Dossers, &c.*

Hotte: f. *A Scuttle, Dosser, Basket to carrie on the backe; (The right* Hotte *is wide at the top, and narrow at the bottome;) See* Buttet.

Hotte de cheminée. *The first part of the funnell of a chimney, reaching from the Mantletree to the middle thereof.*

Mors à hotte. *A flat Cannon; or, a Scatch bit.*

Hottée: f. *A Scuttle-full of.*

Hotter. *To beare a Scuttle, to carrie a Dosser, on the backe.*

Hottereau: m. *A Scuttle; a small (wide-mouthed, and narrow-bottomd) basket.*

Hotteur: m. *A Basket-carrier, or Scuttle-carrier; one that carries a Dosser on his backe.*

Hottier. *as* Hotteur.

Hotton: m. *The staulke of an eare of corne.*

Hottons. *Broken peeces of eares, or of corne, and other superfluities, diuided by the winnower from the cleane, and whole corne, and reserued for Pullein.*

Hou hou hou. *Hootings, or whoopings; voices wherewith Swine are scared, or infamous old women disgraced.*

Hoüage: m. *A digging, or turning vp of the ground; an opening at the root, with a* Houë.

Hoüaller. *To yawle, wawle, or cry out aloud.* ¶ Blesien.

Hoüay. *How now.* ¶ Parisien.

Houbelande. *as* Houpelande.

Houbelon: m. *Hop, or Hops.*

Houbiller vne vache. *To milke a Cow.*

Houcle. *A Surgeons Instrument, wherewith the mouth of a wound is stitched, and drawne together.*

Houë: f. *An Instrument of Husbandrie, which hath a crooked handle, or helue of wood, some two foot long, and a broad, and in-bending head of Iron.*

Houë fourchuë. *A grubbing ax; or forked pickax, whose double tongue bends inward as the head of the ordinarie* Houë, *and is vsed for stonie ground, whereinto the other cannot well enter.*

Houë platte. *A dible, or setting sticke.*

La petite houë. *The fee belonging to the Millers, and Bakers that grind, and make bread of, prouant corne;*

corne; viz. *to those, a cupfull vpon euerie bushell; to these, all the branne.*

Houé: m. ée: f. *Digged vp, into, or about; turned, or broken vp, as the earth; opened at the root as a tree with a* Houë.

Houëau. *as* Hoyau.

Houëment: m. *A digging vp, into, or about; a turning, or breaking vp of the earth; an opening at the root with a* Houë.

Hoüer. *To dig vp, into, or about; to breake, or turne vp ground; to open a plant at the root, with a* Houë.

Hoüet: m. *A Tentar hooke.*

Hoüeur: m. *A digger; or, one that workes with a* Houë.

Houille: f. *Sedge, or Fenne-grasse; also, a kind of Minerall (in the countrey of* Liege) *that makes verie good fires.*

Houische. *(An Interiection wherby silence is imposed) husht, whist, ist, not a word for your life.*

Houlette de berger. *A Sheepe-hooke, or Shepheards Crooke.*

Houlette de connil. *A Rabbits neast.*

Houlle. *The waues, or the rolling of the waues, of the sea.* ¶Rab.

Houpe: f. *as* Houppe.

Houpé: m. ée: f. *Tufted, or tassellled; set, or trimmed with tufts, tassels, or pretie lockes; also, whooped at, or vnto.*

Fustaine houpée. *Looke* Fustaine.

Houpelande: f. *A Shepheards Cloke, Pelt, or Gabardine; (hence) also, a short gowne, or long cloke with sleeues.*

Houpelu: m. uë: f. *Lockie, tassellie, tufted; or, as* Houpé *(in the first sence.)*

Houper. *To tuft; to trimme with tassels, or pretie locks; also, to whoope vnto, or call a farre off.*

Houpier d'un Arbre: m. *The tuft, thicke top, or topping of a tree.*

Houplande. *as* Houpelande.

Houppe: f. *A tuft, or topping; a tassell, or pretie locke.*

Houppelande. *as* Houpelande.

Houppier. *as* Houpier.

Houquet: m. *The Hickock.*

Hourd: m. *A Scaffold.* ¶Pic. *also, as* Heurt; *and hence;*

Ou est meu le hourd. *Where blowes are walking, thumpes giuen, thwackes dealt; or where there is such rude bustling together.*

Hourdage: m. *A fashion of walling, or couering for walls, of reeds wrought like hurdles, and dawbed ouer with loame, or clay.*

Hourde. *as* Harde *(in the first sence.)*

Hourdé: m. ée: f. *Loaded, burthened; also, couered with hurdles, or with reed wrought hurdle-wise, and dawbed ouer with loame.*

Hourder. *To charge, burthen, load; also, to couer with hurdles, or with reed wrought hurdle-wise, and dawbed ouer with loame, or clay.*

Hourdis. *as* Hourd; *also, burdles, or reeds wrought like hurdles, and couered ouer with loame.*

Hourque: f. *A Hulke, or huge Fly-boat.*

Hourt: m. *A boisterous incounter, a violent conflict, or shocke; Looke* Heurt.

Hourvaris. *The doublings of a pursued Hare, or Deere.*

Hous. *as* Houx.

House: f. *A drawer, or course stocking worne ouer a finer, by countrey people.*

Housé: m. ée: f. *That hath drawers on; (hence) also, booted.*

Tel est housé qui n'est pas prest: Pro. *Sayd of one thats furnished many wayes, and yet wants his principall helpe.*

Houseau: m. *A course drawer worne ouer a Stocking in stead of a Boot.*

Il a laissé les houseaux. *He hath got him to (his last) bed; he is euen as good as gone; he is no better then a dead man.*

Housée: f. *as* Houseau; *also, an Hipocras-bag, or hose to straine Hipocras through; also, a shower of raine.*

se Houser. *To pull on drawers, to draw on bootes.*

'A l' an soixante & douze, temps est que l'on se house: Prov. *At 72 we had need to thinke of our last deed.*

Housleau: m. *The Hollie, Huluer, or Holme tree.*

Houspaillier: m. *A Horse-keeper; a Groome of, or Lad in, a Stable.*

Houspillé: m. ée: f. *Tugged, towsed, lugged, hurried; ruffled, disordered; torne, ragged, tattered.*

Houspillée. *as* Houssepillée.

Houspillement: m. *A violent pulling, dragging, lugging, tugging, towsing; tearing of ones garments, or of one by the garments.*

se Houspiller l' un l' autre. *To tug, lug, hurrie, teare one another; to shake, or towse, as one dog doth another.*

Housse: f. *A short mantle of course cloth (and all of a peece) worne in ill weather by countrey women, about their head and shoulders; also, a foot-cloth for a horse; also, a Couerlet, or Counter-point for a bed (in which sence it is most vsed among Leapers, or in Spitles for Leapers.)*

Houssé: m. ée: f. *Couered with a foot-cloth, as a horse; with a Blanket, as a Bed; or with a short, and course Mantle, as a countrey woman; also, swept, or made cleane, as a chimney, or the seeling, &c, of a dustie house.*

Houssée de pluye. *A shower of raine.*

Houssepaillée: f. *A sluttish dragle-tayle, whose gowne euer sticks full of straw.*

Houssepailler. *as* Houspiller.

Houssepailleur. *as* Hespalier; *or* Houspaillier. ¶Rab.

Houssepillée: f. *A ragged slut, a tattered huswife; one whose gowne hath neuer a whole peece about it.*

Houssepillement. *as* Houspillement.

Housser. *To sweepe, or make cleane a chimney, or the vpper parts of a dustie roome, with a long beesome; also, to couer with a foot-cloth, or put a foot-cloth on.*

Housser vn arbre. *To shake a tree.*

Housseur: m. *A sweeper; or one that sweepes with a* Houssoir.

Housseuse: f. *A woman that sweepes, dustes, or makes cleane, a house with a* Houssoir.

Houssine: f. *A Switch, or Whisker; (most properly) a riding rod of Hollie; a Hollie wand; a crop of Hollie.*

Houssiner. *To swindge with a Switch; to bang, or beat with a Hollie-rod.*

Houssineux: m. euse: f. *Full of Hollie-wands, or Switches.*

Houssoir: m. *A brush, or beesome of Butchers broome; and (more generally) any broome tyed to the end of a long staffe, or pole, for the sweeping of chimneyes, or the vpper parts of dustie roomes.*

Housson: m. *Kneehull, Kneehuluer, Kneeholme, Pettigreé, Butchers Broome.*
Houssouer. *as* Houssoir.
Houssu: m. uë: f. *Hairie, high-haired, rugged with haire.*
Crins houssus. *Thicke lockes, or tufts of haire.*
Mouton houssu. *A sheepe well woolled, or of great burthen.*
Houssure de laine: f. *A fleece, or great locke of wooll.*
Houtarde: f. *A Bustard.*
Houtin. *as* Autin.
Houx: m. *The Hollie, Holme, or Huluer tree.*
Petit houx. *Kneeholme, Kneehuluer, Pettigree, Butchers Broome.*
Houzé. *Looke* Housé.
se Houzer. *Looke* se Houser.
Hoyau: m. *The French Mattocke; or an Instrument of Husbandrie, hauing a strait and strong helue of wood some two foot long, and an yron head some foot and a halfe long, and about three ynches broad.*
Hoyé: m. ée: f. *Crushed, tired, ouertoyled; also, lame, or impotent, by nature.*
Hu: m. *as* Huée.
Hua: m. *A kind of black Kyte (rare, if at all, in England) whose tayle is not forked.*
Huan. *as* Hua.
Huant, ou chat huant. *The rough-legd Owle; or, as in* Chat-huant.
Huant. *Hooting, showting, crying out, making hue and cry.*
Huard: m. *A Buzzard-like Eagle that preyes altogether vpon Coots, and wild-Ducks.*
Huau: m. *as* Hua.
Huaume: m. *The helme of a Ship.*
Hubi: m. ie: f. *Liuelie, sprightfull; also, well batled, well amended in flesh, &c.*
Hubir. *To rayse, make thriue, cause to grow, by holesome dyet, and other good vsage.*
Il s'en faut hubir le mieux qu' on pourra. *We must make as good shift with it as we can.*
Hubit: m. *A bristling, or setting vp of the bristles.*
Huchant. *Calling for; whooping, or hallowing vnto.*
Huchant en paume. *Whistling for, or calling vnto by whistling in the fist.*
Huche: f. *A Hutch, or Binne; a kneading Trough, or Tub; also, a Mill-hopper.*
Huché: m. ée: f. *Whooped, called, or hallowed vnto.*
Huchement: m. *A whooping, or hallowing for, a calling vnto.*
Hucher. *To whoope, or hallow for; to call vnto.*
Huchet: m. *A Hutchet, Bugle, or small Horne; such a one as Post-boyes vse.*
Hué: m. ée: f. *Hooted, or showted after; exclaimed, or cryed out vpon; followed with hue and cry.*
Huée: f. *A showting, or hooting; an exclamation, outcry, or hue and cry, of many voices together.*
Huer. *To hoot, shout, exclaime, cry out, make hue and cry.*
Huerie: f. *A hooting, showting, acclamation, crying, outcry.*
Huet. *A proper name; also, a Nick-name; and hence;*
Ie consens estre appellé Huet. *Then call me Cut and spare not.*
Huetant. *as* Huant.

Huette: f. *An Howlet, or the little Horne-Owle; as* Hulotte.
Huge. *as* Huche.
Hugrement. *Brauely, gallantly.* ¶Rab.
Huguenots: m. *Huguenots, Caluinists, Reformists; those of the Religion in France; (at first tearmed thus of a Gate in* Tours *called* Hugon, *neere vnto which they assembled when they stirred first; or of the beginning of their first Protestation,* Huc nos venimus.)
Huguenot: m. otte: f. Gent Huguenotte. *as* Huguenots.
Huguenotterie: f. *Huguenotisme, Caluinisme.*
Huguenottique: com. *Huguenot-like; of, or belonging to, a Huguenot.*
Hui. (Adverb.) *To day, this day; Looke* Huy.
Hui mais. *as* Meshuy.
Huict. *Eight.*
Huictaine: f. *An eighth; the number of eight; also, (a proportion of) eight dayes; whence;*
A huictaine. *Eight dayes hence, or within eight dayes.*
Huictante. *Eightie, fourescore.*
Huictiesme: m. *An eighth part; and (more particularly) the eighth pennie of the price of retayled Wine, Cyder, and other such drinkes, payed vnto the King by the retayler thereof; (This Impost was begun in, and hath continued since, the raigne of* Charles *the sixt,* Anno Dom. 1382.)
Huictiesme: com. *The eighth.*
Huile: com. *Oyle.*
Huile de Maguelet. *Oyle of the Arabian Cherrie Macalet.*
Huile Omphacin. *Oyle thats made of greene, or vnripe Oliues.*
Huile d'onction. *The oyle vsed in Popish Baptisme, and Extreame Vnction.*
Huile de pierre. *A soft, and sulphurous mould or earth, which is easily inflamed by any fire thats neere it, and once fired will not be quenched, especially not by water, which cast vpon it, makes it burne the more vehemently; Looke* Naphte.
Huile sacrée. *Oyle of Amber; called so of it admirable, and secret vertues.*
Huile sainct. *Holie Oyle; the Oyle wherewith children in baptizing, and others in dying, are among Papists annointed.*
Huile Saincte, ou de Sapience. *Looke* Sapience.
Huile sambacin. *Oyle of Jelsomin flowers; good against cold diseases.*
Huile sambucin. *Oyle of Elders.*
Huile Sicyonien. *Is made of Oyle Omphacin twice boiled with a lesse quantitie of cleere water in a widemouthed Copper vessell.*
Huile de vie. *Oyle of Vitrioll, called so of it excellent propertie.*
Huile Virginal. *Virgins Oyle; the Oyle that comes from the Oliue of it selfe, and without pressing.*
Huile de Zambach. *as* Huile Sambacin.
Pour recueillir farine il verse l' huile. *To gaine a small commoditie he wilfully looses a great one; Or (because there is no such difference betweene Meale, and Oyle) to gaine one thing he looses another.*
Tirer de l'huile d'un mur. *To draw Oyle out of a wall (an impossibilitie.)*
Verser de l'huile sur le feu. *To poure Oyle vpon fire; to feed any violent passion.*

Qui mesure l' huile il s'en oingt les mains: Prov. *He that measures oyle besmeares his fingers.*

Huilé: m. ée: f. *Oyled; annointed, or seasoned with oyle; also, as* Huillé.

Huilement: m. *An oyling; a seasoning, annointing, or besmearing, with oyle.*

Huilerie: f. *An oyle-celler, oyle-shop, oyle-house; a roome to keepe oyle in.*

Huileux: m. euse: f. *Oylie, full of oyle.*

Huille. *as* Huile; *Oyle.*

Huillé: m. ée: f. *as* Huilé; *Also, stained with oyle, or stained for euer, as a garment thats spotted with oyle.*

Huis: m. *A doore.*

Huis de derriere. *A back-doore:* Iustices qui n'ont point de huis de der: *High, and Soueraigne Courts, from which there is no appealing.*

Huis verd. *A peece of Tapistrie, or of Darnix hanging before a doore.*

`A huis clos. *Priuily, secretly, in hugger mugger.*

`A huis ouvert. *Openly, plainely, fully, wholly, in open Court.*

Dependre l' huis de la maison. *To heaue, or throw, the doore off the hindges, in signe of a seisure of the house for non-payment of the rent, &c.*

Donner vn coup de gaule par sous l' huis. *To supplant, or giue a priuate lift vnto.*

Le diable n'est pas tousiours à vn huis: Prov. *The diuell is not euer at one doore.*

Tant de povres ne sont pas bons à vn huis: Prov. *So many beggers at one doore, so many suitors for one thing, are not good, or, are not like to speed.*

Huisserie: f. *Th'Office of an Vsher, Messenger, or doore-keeper in a Court; also, dooreship; th'appurtenances, or furniture, of a doore; stuffe for a doore.*

Huisseries. *The iaumbes, lintells, and groundsils of doores.*

Huisset: m. *A wicket, or little doore.*

Huissier: m. *An Vsher, or doore-keeper of a Court, or of a chamber in Court; also, a Messenger, or Apparitor.*

Huissiere: f. *A woman doore-keeper.*

Huit. *as* Huict; *Eight.*

Huitiesme. *as* Huictiesme.

Huitre: f. *An Oyster.*

Les huitres d' vne poule. *The two daintie morsells on the sides of the bottome of a Hennes backe-bone.*

Huitriere: f. *A bed of Oysters; the place wherein Oysters are got, fished, or found.*

Huleu: m. *The name of a Stewes in Paris.*

Hullement: m. *A howling, or yelling.*

Huller. *To howle, or yell.*

Hulotte: f. *A Madge-howlet; or a small kind of hairie-legd, and rough-footed Owle, which hath sticking out on either side of her head a little tuft of feathers.*

Hum hum. *A coughing accent, or voyce.*

Humable: com. *Suppable.*

Humaige: m. *as* Humée. (v.m.)

Humain: m. ine: f. *Gentle, courteous, friendlie, ciuile, mild, affable, tractable; also, humane, manlike; of, or belonging to, a man.*

Humainement. *Gently, courteously, mildly, affably, tractably, friendly, ciuilely, humanely.*

Humanité: f. *Humanitie, courtesie, ciuilitie, gentlenesse, mildnesse, affabilitie, tractablenesse; also, humanitie, or mans nature, humane condition, or state.*

Humanthin. *as* Bernadet.

Humble: f. *A kind of Trout, or Trout-like fish; Looke* Vmble.

Humble: com. *Humble, submisse, lowlie; creeping, ducking, croocking; also, poore, simple, base, low; deiected, abiect.*

Humble-fier. *Meeke and mild well dealt with, stout and forward being abused.*

Humblement. *Humbly, submisly, lowly, alow; with creeping, and crooching; with great reuerence; also, basely, poorely, simply.*

Humblesse: f. *as* Humilité.

Humé: m. ée: f. *Supped, sipped, or sucked vp; fetched, or drawne in with the breath.*

Il m'a humé le sang. *He hath handled me cruelly, or put me downe extreamely, by the bitternesse of his ieasts.*

Humectation: f. *An humectation, moistening, wetting.*

Humecté: m. ée: f. *Moistened.*

Humecter. *To moisten.*

Humée: f. *as* Humet; *or, A broath for a sicke man.*

Humement: m. *A supping, sipping, or sucking vp; drawing or fetching in with the breath; also, a bibbing, swilling, bowsing.*

Humer. *To sup, sip, or sucke vp; also, to fetch, or draw in, as the breath, or with the breath; also, to bib, swill, quaffe, bowse.*

Humer la parole. *Foolishly to sup, or sucke vp, his owne words; to speake abruptly, or vndistinctly; scarce to be able to speake, or not to speake of a long time, through feare, abashment, or amazement.*

Humer la parole à. *To tongue-tie, or depriue of speech, by a sudden amazing, or scaring.*

Humer la sang à. *Looke* Humé.

Humeraire: com. *Of, or belonging to the shoulder.*

Humeral: m. ale: f. *Humerall; or, as* Humeraire.

Veine humerale. *Seeke* Veine.

Humerie: f. *A supping, sipping; sucking vp; also, a bibbing, swilling, bowsing.*

Hume-sang. *The hearbe Burnet.*

Humet: m. *A broath, pottage, cawdle; any liquid, and supping meat; also, a sup thereof.*

Humetter. *To sup, sip, or bib; also, to wet, or moisten.*

Hume-vesne. *A sucke-fist; one that layes his nose on his next fellowes bumme.*

Humeur: m. *A supper vp of.*

Humeur: f. *Humor, moisture, sap, iuice, wet, liquor.*

Humeux: m. *A sucke-pinte, or swill-pot; a notable drunkard.*

Humide: com. *Humide, moist, wet, waterish, iuicie, sappie, full of liquor.*

Humidité: f. *Humiditie, moisture, sappinesse, iuycinesse, wetnesse, waterishnesse.*

Humier: m. *Th'Occupant of a thing whereof another is th'owner; one that reapes the profit of, though he haue no propertie in, a thing.*

Humiere: f. *as* Humerie; *Also, th'occupancie of another mans land, &c.*

Humilié: m. ée: f. *Humbled, brought low, cast downe, pulled vnder, taken a hole lower.*

Humiliez: m. *The Humilists; Gray Friers of the Order of S. Bennet.*

Humilité: f. *Humilitie, humblenesse, lowlinesse, abiection, submission, meekenesse, gentlenesse.*

Humoire. *A close bit, or bit without any libertie for a horse.*

Humoral: m. ale: f. *Humorall; of humors; moist, iuycie, sappie.*

Fiebvre humorale. *An Ague bred of the abundance, or*

or corruption of humors in the bodie.

Flux de ventre humoral. *A lask, or loosenesse without inflamation.*

Vertu substantifique, & humorale. *Any strong, or substantiall liquor, as mans seed, &c.*

Hune: f. *The scuttle of the mast of a ship.*

Hunisque. Espée Hunisque. *A kind of Scimiter vsed in old time.*

Hupe: f. *A little woollen thread, or tuft in the top of a cap; also, the crest, or cop on the head of a bird; also, the Whoope or dunghill Cocke (a bird that nestles in mans ordure.)*

Hupé: m.ée: f. *Copped, crested, high-crowned; (hence) also, tall of stature; also, proud, cocket, loftie, statelie, that beares himselfe high, that thinkes well of himselfe.*

Pigeons hupez. *Copped, or crested Pigeons, called about London, Turne-pats.*

Hupée: f. *as* Huquée.

s'Huper. *To raise, or set vp his crest against; to become proud, loftie, statelie.*

Huppe. *as* Hupe.

Huppé. *as* Hupé.

Huque: f. *A Huke, or Dutch Mantle, or Dutch womans Mantle.*

Huquée: f. Il n'y a qu' vne huquée. *(Much like our Northerne Weebit;) you haue but a little (sayes the clowne, when you haue a great) way thither.*

Hur le gay. *Soundly whitled, throughly tipled, that hath seene the diuell.*

Huraut: m. *A great, or full-growne wild boare; a boare thats (at the least) three yeares old.*

Hurbec. *as* Liset; *The worme called a Vine-fretter, or diuells goldring.*

Hure: f. *The head of a Beare, Wolfe, wild Boare, or any other sauage, and dangerous beast; (hence) also, a staring, horride, vnkembd, or ill-kept, pate of haire.*

Hure à hure. *Face to face; or as in* Huze.

Huré: m.ée: f. *Staring, rude, vnkembd, bristlie, horride like a wild Boares head.*

Hurebais. *Vine-fretters, the diuells gold-rings.*

Hurgon: m. *Blits, red Beets.*

Hurlé. *Yelled, howled.*

Hurlement: m. *A howling, or yelling.*

Hurler. *To howle, to yell.*

Hurler avec les loups. *To howle when others yell; to follow the fashion how rude, or vile, soeuer it be.*

Hurque: f. *A hulke.*

Hurt. *as* Heurt.

Hurte-bise. *One that scuffles with, or kickes against, the Northerne wind:* ¶Rab.

Hurteller. *To trample on with the feet.*

Hurter. *as* Heurter.

Hurtis: m. *Shockes, knockes, or knockings, dashes, hits.*

Hus. du hus. *The Elder tree.*

Husche. *Looke* Huche.

Husciame: m. *Henbane.*

Hussite: m. *A Bohemian coyne; so tearmed in memorie of Iohn Hus, the Bohemian Protestants first (burnt) Martyr.*

Hussité: m. ée: f. *Turned Protestant.*

Hustaudeau: m. *A cockerell, or big cocke chicke; also, a Caponet; also, as in* Hestaudeau.

Hutaudeau. *as* Hustaudeau.

Hute: f. *A cote, or cottage; Looke* Hutte.

Huter. *To build, or set vp; (also) to lodge, or lurke in, a cote, or cottage.*

Hutin: m. *A brabling, brawling, scoulding, chiding, clamor, acclamation; mutinie, contention; disquiet, vexation, trouble, annoyance.*

Hutin: m.ine: f. *Brabling, clamorous, mutinous, contentious, vnquiet.*

Hutinement: m. *as* Hutin.

Hutiner. *To chide, reuile, reproach, brabble with, brawle on, scould at; also, to vex, trouble, disquiet, harrie, annoy.*

Hutineux: m.euse: f. *Clamorous, contentious, mutinous, full of brabling, verie troublesome.*

Hutte: f. *A cote, or cottage; also, the cloth or bush behind which men hide themselues in staulking for the Wolfe.*

Venir de la maison aux huttes. *To fall from wealth to beggerie, from something to little or nothing.*

Hutudeau. *as* Hustaudeau.

Huvelot. Haut huvelot. *Vp-heaped, well heaped on:* ¶Norm.

Huy. (Adverb.) *To day, this day; also, the voice wherewith Carters turne their horses on the right hand.*

D' huy. *as* D'icy: ¶Rab.

Hier vachier huy chevalier: Prov. *Hee's now a Knight who last day was but a clowne.*

Tels sont huy qui demain ne verront pas: Prov. *Some that are blithe to day to morrow will be blind.*

Huyé: m. ée: f. *Hooted at, showted after; exclaimed on, cried out vpon, followed with huy and crie.*

Huyer. *To hoot at, showt after, exclaime on, crie out vpon, follow with hue and crie.*

Huyle: f. *Oyle; Seeke* Huile.

Huylé: m.ée: f. *Oyled; seasoned, annoynted, bismeared, or spotted with oyle.*

Huyler. *To oyle; to season, annoint, bismeare, or spot with oyle.*

Huys: m. *A doore; Looke* Huis.

Huyssier. *as* Huissier.

Huystres: f. *Oysters; Looke* Huitres.

Huze à huze. *Side by side, checke by iowle; face to face, right ouer against.*

Hyacinthe: m. *The blew, or purple Iacint, or Hyacinth flower; we call it also, Crow-toes.*

Hyacinthe Oriental. *The Orientall blew Jacint (a beautifull flower.)*

Hyades: f. *The fiue (or seuen) rainie starres which be in the head of the Signe Taurus.*

Hyascyame: m. *Henbane.*

Hybleanne: f. *The Bee (so tearmed because she feedes much on the dwarfe Elderne.)*

Hydrargire. *Quicke siluer, liquid siluer.*

Hydraulique. voix hy. *The sound of (running) waters; or Musicke made thereby.*

Hydre: f. *An Hyder; a water Adder.*

Hydrie: f. *A water pot, or bucket to draw water with.*

Hydrocele: f. *The being burst; or the falling downe of humors into one of the stones.*

Hydrographie: f. *A Sea-card.*

Hydromantie: f. *Diuination by the obseruation of water, or by spirits appearing in it.*

Hydromel: m. *Metheglin; or drinke made of water and honie sodden together.*

Hydrophobie: f. *An extreame feare of water, and of euerie kind of liquor; (caused by melancholie, or by the biting of a mad dog.)*

Hydropique: com. *Sicke of, or subiect vnto, the dropsie.*

Hydropisie: f. *The dropsie.*

Hye: f. *as* Hie.

Hyeble: m. *Dwarfe Elderne, Danewort, Wallwort, Woodwort.*

Hyer. *as* Hier.
Hyere: f. *A powder compounded of Aloes, and other (bitter) simples.*
Hyeuse. *as* Yeuse.
Hygienique: f. *Health-preseruing Physicke.*
Hymenean: m. anne: f. *Of, or belonging to, a wedding, or marriage.*
Hymenée: f. *A wedding, or marriage; also, a wedding song, or song of ioy at a wedding; also, a certaine filme, or thicke skinne, which is broken when a maid is made a woman.*
Hymne: m. *A hymne; a song of praise.*
Chanter l' hymne du Cigne. *To sing, or speake, his last.*
Hynaire: m. *A Saker passenger.*
Hyoïde. Os hyoïde. *The forked bone which is at the root of the tongue.*
Hypate: f. *as* Hipate.
Hypenemien: m. enne: f. *Windie, barren, fruitlesse, like the egges layed by an vntroden henne:* ¶Rab.
Hyperbole: f. *An Hiperbole; an excesse in depressing, or aduancing.*
Hyperbolic: m. ique: f. *Hyperbolicall, excessiue, vnlikelie, passing all credit, beyond the limits of truth, without the scope of beliefe.*
Hyperdulie: f. *The highest worship, worship that belongs onely to God.*
Hypernepheliste: m. *A contemplator of high matters among the clowds.*
Hypocauste: m. *A stew, stoue, or hot-house.*
Hypochondres: m. *The flankes, or soft parts vnder the short ribs.*
Hypochondres de tous les diables. *By the bellie, and bowells of all the diuells.*
Hypochondriaque: com. *In, or of, the Hypochondres; also, troubled with a windie melancholie in those parts.*
Hypociste. *Th'excressence that shoots vp from the root of the shrub* Cistus, *or Hollierose; also, the medicinable iuyce extracted from it, and hardened by druggists.*
Hypocras. *as* Hipocras.
Hypocriser. *To dissemble, or counterfeit goodnesse, to set a good face on a bad mind, to play the hypocrite.*
Hypocrisie: f. *Hypocrisie, dissembling, counterfeit goodnesse, famed holinesse.*
Hypocrite: m. *An hypocrite, a dissembler, a counterfeit companion.*
Oeil d' hypocrite. *An often-twinkling eye.*
Hypocritement. *Hypocritically, dissembler-like.*
Hypogastre: m. *The lower part of the bellie, from the nauell to the* Pubes, *or haire of the priuities.*
Hypogastrique: com. *Of, or belonging to, the* Hypogastrium.
Veine hypogastrique. *Looke* Veine.
Hypogée: m. *A vault, celler, or such like vnder-ground roome, arched ouer head.*
Hypogriphe: com. (*A monster*) *halfe horse halfe Griffon.*
Hypopie: f. *Bealing, or matter growing, or gathering in a crushed eye; also, a bone vnder the eye.*
Hyposarque: f. *A kind of dropsie, or swelling of the bodie, bred of the fulnesse of cold, and flegmaticke, humors.*
Hypostase: f. *A substance; also, a residence in vrine flitting towards the bottome thereof.*
Hypothadée. *Giuen, or deuoted, vnto, God.*
Hypothecaire. Debtes hypothecaires; sont celles qui sont deuës par Obligation emportant hypotheque generale, ou speciale, ou par iugement, ou acte engendrant hypotheque; comme est la dation de tutele.
Hypotheque: f. *An ingagement, morgage, or pawning (of an immouable.)*
Hypothequé; &, Hypothequer. *as* Hipothequé; &, Hipothequer.
Hyppodrome: m. *A course, or running place for horses; also, a place wherein horses are broken, rid, managed, or made.*
Hyrundelle. *Seeke* Arondelle.
Hyrundinier: m. ere: f. *Of, or belonging to, a Swallow.*
Hysgin: m. *A light red, or bright bay; or a kind of purple staine made by the black-berrie.*
Hysser. *To hoyse vp; (A Mariners tearme.)*
Hyssope: f. *Hisop.*
Hysterique. Affection hysterique. *The suffocation of the matrix.*
Hyver: m. *The Winter.*
Cela ne faict ny hyver, ny esté. *That is little to the purpose, makes little to the matter, does neither good nor harme.*
En hyver par tout pleut, en esté là ou Dieu veut: Prov. *Looke* Plouvoir.
Si l' hyver estoit outre la mer, si viendra il à S. Nicolas parler: Prov. *Were Winter beyond sea, yet would it haue a saying to S. Nicholas; (whose feast is on the sixt of December.)*
`A la S. Pierre l' hyver s' en va ou il reserre: Prov. *Looke* Reserrer.
Qui passe vn iour d' hyver il passe vn de ses ennemis mortels: Prov. *One of his mortall foes h'auoides that auoides a Winters day.*
Hyvernal: m ale: f. *Winterie, Winterlie, Winter-like; of the Winter.*
Hyverné: m. ée: f. *Wintered.*
Hyvernée: f. *The Winter season.*
Hyverner. *To winter; also, to dig, or dresse a vineyard in Winter, or immediately after the Vintage.*

I

IA. *(An Aduerbe of time) nigh, welnigh, welneere, almost, lacking but a little; also, neuer; also, a Particle whereby a Negatiue is inforced; as,* Il ne viendra ja; *he will not come at all.*
Ia soit que. *Though, although, notwithstanding, albeit that.*
Iables: m. *The Croes of a peece of caske; the furrow, or hollow (at either end of the pipe-staues) whereinto the head-peeces be enchased.*
Iabler. *To make the Croes of Caske;* viz: *a furrow or hollow (at th' ends of the pipe-staues) whereinto the head-peeces may be enchased.*
Iabol: m. *A truckle, or pullie.*
Iabot: m. *The craw, crop, or gorge of a bird.*
Iacée: f. *Hearbe Trinitie, Hearts-ease.*
Iacent: m. ente: f. *Lying.*
Iachere: f. *Fallowes, fallow ground, lay-land, plowed lands; also, any earth that lyes idle.*
Iacinthe: m. *The pretious stone, called a Jacint; also, as* Hyacinthe.
Couleur de Iacinthe. *Purple, blew, or violet; the colour of an Hyacinth flower.*
Iacobin: m. *A Jacobin, or white Frier.*
Cracher vn Iacobin. *To spit out a collop, or dol of flegme.*

Iaçoit que. *Looke* Ia.
Iacot: m. *A proper name for a man, and a Diminutiue of* Iacques.
Iacotin: m. *Another, the Diminutiue of* Iacot.
Iacqué: m. ée: f. *Jacked, or, thats armed with a iack; Looke* Iaque.
Iacquelet: m. *A Jacke of the Clocke-house; or, the little man that strikes the quarters in a Clocke.*
Iacquemard: m. *A coat, or shirt of maile; also, a great statue of wood, against which, in old time, young souldiors practised to fight.*
Iacquemin. *as* Iaquelin.
Iacques: m. *Iames, Iacob.*
Iacques bons homs. *The substantiall men of the Parish.*
Iacques du four. *The name of a verie delicate, and tender peare.*
Fleur de S. Iacques. *Staggerwort, Stauerwort, Ragwort, Saint Iames his hearbe, Saint Iames his flower.*
Herbe de S. Iacques. *The same.*
Iacquet: m. *A Parasite, claw-backe, beggerlie tale-carrier; a smell-feast, or trencher-friend; Looke* Iaquet.
Iacquette: f. *Looke* Iaquette.
Iactance: f. *A bragging, boasting, vaunting, cracking, proud ostentation.*
Iactateur: m. *A boaster, vaunter, cracker, bragger, braggard, braggadochio.*
Iactation: f. *as* Iactance; *Also, a swinging, tossing, shaking vp and downe.*
Iacter. *To brag, vaunt, boast, cracke; also, to swing, tosse, tumble, or shake vp and downe.*
Iacture: f. *Losse, dammage, decay, much hurt, great hinderance; a casting away, as of a ships lading in a tempest.*
Iadeau: m. *A bowle, or mazer.*
Iadis. (Adverb.) *Of old, in times past, before time, formerly, heretofore.*
Iaet: m. *Iet, or Ieat.*
Iagayette: f. *A kind of short speare hauing a bone handle, and to be throwne, as a dart, on horsebacke.*
Iagleur. *See* Glayeul.
Iaguette: f. *A Pie, Pie-annat, Megatapie.*
Iaiant. *Looke* Geant.
Iaibeau: m. *A little pit, or hole full of water to keepe fish in.*
Iaiet: m. *Jeat.*
Ialaye: f. *A wine measure, or vessell for wine, &c, containing twelue (French) Pintes; also, a See, or Tub.*
Ialet. *See* Iallet.
Iallage: m. *as* Forage; *Also, a Ialaye-full of wine, &c.*
Iallay. *as* Ialaye.
Ialle: f. *A chilblaine, or a redswelling that comes of cold;* (Blesien;) *also, as* Ialaye.
Iallée. *as* Ialaye; *Also, a Soe-full, or Tub-full.*
Iallet: m. *A little casting bowle.*
Iallet embrasé. *A fire-ball.*
Arc à iallet. *A stone-bow.*
Ialli: m. *Spurted out, sprowted vp.*
Iallir. *To spurt out, sprowt vp, spin vpward, as water forced out of a spout.*
Iallissement: m. *A spurting, sprowting, spouting, or spinning vp (of water.)*
Ialousement. *Iealously, suspitiously, zealously.*
Ialousie: f. *Iealousie, suspition, mistrust; also, a lattice window, or grate to looke through; also, the flower called, Flower gentle.*
Ialoux: m. ouse: f. *Iealous; mistrustfull, suspitious.*
Ialoux comme vn Tigre. *Looke* Tigre.
Iamais. vn iamais. *A verie long time, a mightie while, an euer lasting age.*
Iamais. (Adverb.) *Neuer.*
`A iamais. *Eternally, euerlastingly, for euer;* `A grand iamais: &, `A tout iamais. *For euer and a day, for euer and euer.*
Iambages: f. *The iaumbes, or side-posts of a doore, &c.*
Iambe: f. *The leg, or shanke (extending from the knee to the ankle;) also, (in Architecture) a Corbell, or peere; and, the iaumbe, or sidepost of a doore, &c.*
Iambe de Dieu. *Looke* Dieu.
Iambe de pourceau. *A pestle of porke; a gammon.*
La grande iambe. *The whole thigh, leg, and foot; so tearmed by Anatomists.*
Os de la iambe. *Is properly, the bigger bone of the leg; the shin-bone.*
Iambe deça iambe delà. *Stradling, with wide-open legs.*
Donner le croc en iambe à. *To giue a fall, or foile vnto; to supplant, ruine, ouerthrow.*
Faire iambes de vin. *To drinke hard before a iourney.*
Iecter le chat aux iambes. *Looke* Chat.
Iouër de l'espée à deux iambes. *To make the most vse he can of his legs; or, to weld them as nimbly as a Fencer a two-hand sword; to runne away.*
La queuë entre les iambes. *Much ashamed, or out of countenanace, as one thats taken in the manner; also, fouly disgraced or shamed, with shame ynough.*
Selon la iambe le coup: selon la iambe le pied: &, selon la iambe la seignée: Prov. *Ratably, proportionably, with effort answerable to force, according to the measure of his meanes.*
Danse du loup la queuë entre les iambes: Prov. *Lecherie.*
Ils ont du coeur, mais les iambes leur faillent. *They haue more stomacke then strength, more courage then meanes.*
Qui n'a coeur ait iambes: Prov. *Let him that hath not a heart haue heeles; or let him that dares not vse his hands bestirre his heeles.*
Iambette: f. *A little leg, or shanke.*
Donner la iambette. *To giue a trip, or foile.*
Faire la iambette. *A horse to goe on three legs, and gracefully to shift, and hold vp, the fourth.*
Iambier: m. ere: f. *Of, or belonging to, the leg.*
Iambier. *as* Gambier.
Iambiere: f. *A greaue, leg-harnesse, or, armor for a leg; also, a leg, leg-peece, or part of the bodie about the leg.*
Iambon: m. *A gammon.*
Iambonnier: m. *A begger (also, a seller) of bacon, or of gammons of bacon.*
Iamboyer. *To iet, or, wantonly to goe in and out with the legs; also, to crosse the legs often in dauncing.*
Iamme: f. *Pearle.*
Ian. *as* Iean; *Iohn; also, a cuckold.*
Ian le blanc. *A Hen-harme, or white Kite; also, the consecrated bread, or bodie of Christ in the Popish Eucharists; (tearmed so by the Caluinists.)*
Ian gipon. *A gull, sot, ninnie, fop, cokes.*
Iancer vn cheval. *To stirre a horse in the stable till hee sweat withall; or (as our) to iaunt; (an old word.)*
Iane: f. *A certaine vessell, or measure, for vineger, &c.*
Ianequin. *(A Diminutiue of* Ian; *) Ienkin, or Iacke.*
Ianet. *Iacke.*
Ian-femme. *An Hermaphrodite; one that is both man and*

and woman; alſo, an effeminate meacocke, faint-hearted milkeſop.
Iangler. *To iangle, prattle, tattle ſaucily, or ſcuruily.*
Ianglerie: f. *Iangling, ſaucie pratling, ſcuruie tatling, ſcurrile ieaſting.*
Iangleur: m. *A iangler, ſaucie pratler, ſcuruie tatler, ſcurrile ieaſter.*
Iannet d'eau. *Nenuphar, Water Lillie, water Roſe.*
Iannette: f. *Iug, Iinnie; (a womans name.)*
Iannin: m. *A wittall; one that knowes, and bears with, or winkes at, his wiues diſhoneſtie.*
Ianniſſaires: m. *Ianizaries; the Turkes principall footmen, and of his Gard.*
Iannot: m. *(A Diminutiue of* Ian) *Ienkin, or Iacke.*
Ianot. *as* Iannot.
Ians-femme. *Looke* Ian-femme.
Ianſpillhommes. *Gentlemen:* ¶Rab.
Iantes: f. *The fellowes of a wheele; the peeces (of wood) whereof the ring, or the rime conſiſts.*
Ianvier: m. *Ianuarie.*
Iappé. *Barked; yawled, bayed, bawled.*
Iappement: m. *A barking; yawling, baying; bawling.*
Iapper. *To barke, or bay like a dog; to yawle, to bawle.*
Chien qui iappe ne mord pas: Prov. *The dog that barkes much bites but little.*
Vn vieil chien iamais ne iappe en vain: Prov. *An old dog neuer barkes in vaine; the warning, or aduiſe of an old man is euer to ſome purpoſe.*
Iapperie: f. *Looke* Iappement.
Iappeur: m. *A barker, bayer; yawler, bawler.*
Iaque: m. *Iames; alſo, a Iacke, or coat of maile; and thence, a Iacke for the bodie of an Iriſh greyhound, &c, made commonly of a wild Boares tanned skinne, and put on him when hee is to coape with that violent beaſt.*
Iaquelin: m. & Iaqueline: f. *Diminutiues of* Iaques.
Iaquelot: m. & Iaquelotte: f. *Other Diminutiues of the name* Iaques.
Iaquemin; &, Iaquemine, *Others.*
Iaquerie de Beauvoiſin. *(The name of) an inſurrection of the people, incenſed againſt all gentlemen, in king Iohns time; ſuppreſſed by Charles the Wiſe, and the king of Nauarre, while Iohn was in England.*
Iaques: m. *Iames; Looke* Iacques.
Iaquet: m. *A Pilgrim to S. Iames of* Compoſtella; *alſo, a Paraſite, ſycophant, clawbacke, pickthanke, flattering ſmell-feaſt.*
Marche cela Iaquet. *Looke* Marcher.
Tu dis vray Iaquet. *True Roger, ſay we, and vſe it (as the French that) in ſcorne, and to the diſgrace, of a lyer.*
Iaquette: f. *(A proper name for a woman; alſo) a Pieannat, or Megatapie; alſo, a filthie dungeon, or loathſome hole in a priſon; alſo, a iacket, or ſhort and ſleeueleſſe countrey-coat, hauing plaine, or (the more properly) gathered, skirts.*
Tourner ſa iaquette. *Looke* Tourner.
Iaquetter. *To prattle, babble, tattle; or to claw, flatter, fawne on; to play the* Iaquet.
Iaquiers: m. *The Rebells before mentioned (in* Iaquerie) *tearmed ſo, becauſe they wore a faſhion of Iackets vſed by the ſouldiors of thoſe times.*
Iar: m. *A Gander.*
Pied de iar. *The hearbe Gooſe-foot, or wild Orage.*
En iar. *A caterwawling, or bitch-hunting.*
Iarbe. *Looke* Gerbe.
Iarcé: m. ée: f. *Cleft, rift, chapt, chinked, chawned.*
ſe Iarcer. *To cleaue, riue, chap, chawne (as the hands in cold weather.)*
Iarceure: f. *Looke* Iarſure.
Iard. *as* Iar; *Alſo, the firſt great receptacle, or pond of ſalt water whereof ſalt is made.*
Iardeau: m. *A codded weed that windes about corne, and intangles it.*
Iardereau. *as* Iardeau.
Iardin: m. *A Garden.*
C'eſt vne pierre iettée en ſon iardin. *This bone is caſt at him to gnaw on; in this taxation he is meant though he be not mentioned.*
Cette pierre tomboit en ſon iardin. *This matter much concerned, or came neere, him; turned to his preiudice, touched his freehold.*
Iardin aux faux-bourgs vaut cent ſolz au rebours: Prov. *Looke* Faux-bourgs.
Iardinage: m. *as* Iardinement; *Alſo, a Garden.*
Iardiné: m. ée: f. *Gardened; made into, or wrought as, a Garden.*
Iardinement: m. *A gardening; a working in, or a keeping of, a Garden.*
Iardiner. *To make a Garden, keepe a Garden, worke, or labour, in Gardens.*
Iardiner les oyſeaux ſur des billots. *To weather Hawkes, or ſet them out a weathering, vpon blockes in Gardens, &c.*
Iardinet: m. *A ſmall Garden.*
Iardinier: m. *A Gardener.*
Iare. *A iarre.*
Iargeot. *Looke* Iargot.
Iargon: m. *Gibridge, fuſtian language, Pedlers French; a barbarous iangling.*
Iargonnement: m. *as* Iargon; *or, A ſpeaking fuſtian.*
Iargonner. *To ſpeake fuſtian, or gibridge; to iangle, chatter, babble, confuſedly.*
Iargonneur: m. *A chatterer, gibridgemunger, counterfeit rogue that ſpeakes fuſtian, or a language, which either himſelfe, or his hearers vnderſtand not.*
Iargonnois: m. *Fuſtian, gibridge, pedlers French.*
Iargot: m. *A kind of courſe garment worne by countrey people.*
Iargouiller. *To warble, chirpe, or chatter.*
Iargueul: m. *The weaſon, or windpipe of birds, whereout they warble.*
Iargnage: m. *A ſwaggering; or a ſwaggerer.*
Iarnat: m. *A ruffian, ſwaggerer, ſwaſhbuckler, blaſphemous or foule-mouthed huffeſnuffe.*
Iarnigoi: m. *The ſame; or, a nickname for a ſwaggering, and ſwearing ſouldior, &c; from;*
Iarnigoy. *as much as,* Ie renie Dieu; *(an old, and ruſticall blaſphemie.)*
Iarre: m. *The name of a codded, and corne-intangling, weed.*
Iarret: m. *The hamme, or hough.*
L'oeuvre fait iarret. *Crookes, bends, or giues, inward.*
Roidir le jarret. *To ſtretch out the hammes, as one that feeles the pangs of death; to make a die.*
Iarretade: f. *A houghing, a ſlaſh ouer the hammes.*
Iarretier: m. ere: f. *Baker-legd, that goes in at the knees.*
Cheval iarretier. *An enterfeering horſe.*
Iarrons d'vne roue. *The fellowes of a wheele.*
Iarrouſſes: f. *A kind of tares, or ſmall vetches.*
Iarrus. *Wake-robin, Starchwort, Rampe, Aaron, Calues-foot,*

foot, Cuckoe Pint.
Iarryc: m. *The Oke tree:* ¶Perigordin.
Iars. *A Gander;* *Looke* Iar.
Iarser. *Looke* Iarcer.
Iarsure: f. *A cleft, rift, slifter, chinke, chap, chawne; hence, the neb of a pen; also, a cleauing, riuing, chapping, chawning.*
se Iarter. *To garter himselfe; to tie his garters.*
Iartier: m. *A garter.*
Iartier: m.ere: f. *Of, belonging to, or seruing for, a garter; gartering.*
Veine iartiere. *The garter veine, or hamme veine; the fourth branch of the thigh veine descending vnto the bought of the hamme, where it gets this name.*
Iartiere: f. *A garter.*
Iasard: m. *A prater, pratler, babler, tatler, chatterer, iangler, idle talker.*
Iasarde: f. *A prating gossip, a pratling housewife; a tittle tattle; a wench whose tongue neuer lies.*
Iasement: m. *as* Iaserie.
Iaser. *To prate, prattle, babble, tattle, chatter, iangle, talk verie idly.*
Iaseran: m. *A flagon chaine; also, a bracelet, or neckelace of that chain fashion; also, a coat, or shirt of great, and close-wouen maile; also, the hoope of a shackle.*
Iasereau. *as* Iasard.
Iaserie: f. *A prating, pratling, babling, iangling; tittle tattle, garrulitie, idle chat.*
Iaseur. *as* Iasard.
Iasinin: m. *Jasmin, Jessemine, Jelsomine, Jesse; (an arbor plant.)*
Vnguent Iasmin. *An oyntment made (not of Ielsomine flowers, as many imagine, but) of white Violets.*
Iaspe: m. *A Iasper stone.*
Iaspé: m. ée: f. *Of Iasper; coloured like, or made to resemble, the Iasper stone.*
Iasper. *To paint (or by painting to make looke) like a Iasper; to counterfeit the Iasper stone.*
Iate: f. *A Bowle, a Mazer.*
Iatte: f. *The same; or, a measure about* Tholose *containing neere a Parisian pinte.*
Iau: m. *A Cocke; also, a Barbell; or as* Dorée, *a Dorce, fish.*
Iavar: m. *as* Iavard.
Iavard: m. *A swelling in the hollow of the pasterne of a horse.*
Iavarre: m. *as* Iavard.
Iavelé: m. ée: f. *Swathed, or made into sheaues.*
Iaveler. *To swathe, or gauel corn; to make it into sheaues, or gauells.*
Iaveleur: m. *A swather, or binder vp of corne into gavells.*
Iavelier: m. *A corne-pike, or pitchforke, wherewith sheaues of corne be loaden, and vnloaded.*
Iaveliere: f. *The same.*
Iavelin: m. *as* Iaveline.
Iavelin de barde. *A barbed horsemans Iavelin.*
Iaveline: f. *A Iavelin; a weapon of a size betweene the Pike, and Partisan.*
Iavelinier: m. *One that beareth, vseth, or serueth with, a Iavelin.*
Iavelle: f. *A gavell, or sheafe of corne; also, a bauen, or bundle of drie stickes.*
Iavelot: m. *A Gleaue, Dart, or small Iavelin.*
Iavelotier: m. *A Darter; one that beares, vses, or throwes, a small Iavelin, or Dart.*
Iauge: f. *A Gage; the instrument wherewith caske is measured; also, an yron Leauer; also, the soyle of ground; whence,* Labourer à iauge. *To plough deep, or as deep as there is any soyle.*
Iaugé: m. ée: f. *Gaged, or measured as caske, &c.*
Iaugeage: m. *The gaging, or measuring of caske, &c.*
Iauger. *To gage, or measure a peece of caske, &c.*
Iaugeur: m. *A gager, or measurer of caske, &c.*
Iavioler. *To gabble, prate, or prattle.*
Iavioleur: m. *A gabbler, prater, pratler.*
Iaule: f. *A cage; a prison; or, a place enuironed with an yron grate, or woodden lattice, for th'inclosing, or safekeeping, of a thing.*
Iaulge. Iaulger. &, Iaulgeur. *as* Iauge. Iauger. &, Iaugeur.
Iaulnastre: com. *Yellowish.*
Iaulne: m. *Yellow colour.*
Iaulne d'eau. *The yellow water Lillie, or water Rose.*
Le jaulne d'vn oeuf. *The yolke of an egge.*
Iaulne paille. *Straw colour.*
Iaulne: com. *Yellow.*
Bec jaulne. *Looke* Bejaune.
Terre jaulne. *Gold.*
Iaulnement. *Yellowly; of a yellow hew.*
Iaulnet d'eau. *The yellow water Lillie, or water Rose.*
Iaulnet: m. ette: f. *Yellowish, a little yellow.*
Iaulnette: f. *Hardway, S. Peters wort, square S. Iohns grasse, great S. Iohns wort.*
Iaulni: m. ie: f. *Growne yellow.*
Iaulnir. *To make yellow.*
Herbe à jaulnir. *Looke* Herbe.
Iaulnisse: f. *The Iaundice; also, the Yellowes.*
Iaulnissure: f. *A yellownesse; also, a yellowing, or making yellow.*
Iay: m. *as* Gay; *A Iay; also, the Shrinke, or Wariangle (called so by some.)*
Iayon: m. *The Iay.*
Iazer. *Looke* Iaser.
Iazeran. *as* Iaseran; *Flagon chaine.*
Iazerane. à la jaz. *Of a flagon-chaine fashion.*
Ibice: m. *Th'Ibix; a swift, and long-horned-wild Goat, or beast like a Goat, liuing among the snowie tops of the Alpes, and other cold mountaines.*
Iceluy: m. Icelle: f. *He; she; the same man, or woman.*
Ichneumon: m. *The Indian, or (more properly) the Ægyptian Rat, Pharoes Mouse; a mortall enemie, as to the Crocodile, so to all Serpents, and therefore vsually tamed, and made housall, by the people of Ægypt.*
Ichoreux: m. euse: f. *Whayish, waterish.*
Ichthyomantie: f. *Diuination by fish:* ¶Rab.
Ichthyophagie: f. *Fish-eating.*
Ici (Adverb.) *Here; in this place.*
D'ici. *Hence, from hence.*
D'ici pres. *Hard by, neere at hand.*
Icosaedre. *One of the fiue regular bodies in Geometrie; consists of twentie equiangle triangles.*
Icosimité. *See* Lychnocosimité: ¶Rab.
Ictere: m. *The yellow Iaundice.*
Icterique: com. *Sicke of, or troubled with, the yellow Iaundice.*
Ictide. Belette Ictide. *Seeke* Belette.
Icy. *as* Ici.
Ideal: m. ale: f. *Ideall; imaginarie, conceiued in th'imagination; onely in fancie.*
Identité: f. *Identitie, likenesse, the being almost the very same.*
Ides: f. *The Ides of a Moneth; the eight day after the Nones.*

Idiome: m. *An Idiom, or proper forme of speech.*
Idiot: m. *An ideot, or naturall foole; a sot, fop, doult, ninnie, sillie cokes; also, an idle, or vnprofitable person; one that hath no charge, no function in a Commonwealth.*
Idiotisme: m. *Ideotisme, naturall follie, simplicitie, sottishnesse; also, proprietie in a language.*
Idoine: com. *Apt, meet, fit, proper; conuenient, sufficient; commodious; durable, substantiall, sound.*
Idoineté: f. *Aptnesse, fitnesse, meetnesse, conueniencie, sufficiencie.*
Idolatre: m. *An Idolater, a worshipper of Idols.*
Idolatrer. *To Idolatrize it, to worship Idols.*
Idolatrie: f. *Idolatrie; the worship, or worshipping of Idols.*
Idumois. fruict Idumois. *Dates (for they grow in* Idumea.)
Ie. *(A Pronowne) I: sometimes vsed by the vulgar Parisians in stead of* Nous; *as* Ie sommes; *We are.*
I'en veux. *Looke* I'-en-veux.
Iean: m. *John; also, a double game at Ticktacke.*
Decollation S. Iean. *The feast of the beheading of S. Iohn; a holy-day (in some places) kept the 29 of August.*
Herbe de S. Iean. *Thin-leaued Mugwort; also, Clarie.*
Mal, ou Maladie, de S. Iean. *The falling sicknesse.*
La Natiuité de S. Iean. *Midsummer day.*
Pomme de S. Iean. *as* Hastivel.
Ie me faisois appeller Maistre Iean en cela. *I was old excellent, I was held verie good, at that.*
Mettre toutes les herbes de la S. Iean. *To imploy all his skill, or meanes on; (This day being by many imagined most fit for the gathering of such hearbes as are to be vsed the rest of the yeare;* Looke *Herbe.)*
Ie an. *(An Interiection)* ie le vous nie. *By your fauor sir, I denie it flatly.*
Iean-Almy. *The name of a sweet apple that yeelds excellent cyder.*
Iecoraire: com. *Of, or belonging to, the liuer.*
Veine iecoraire. *The liuer veine; Looke* Veine.
Iect: m. *A counter to cast withall; also, a hemme of a garment.*
Le premier iect. *The first, rude, or fast-penned draught of a writing.*
Faire le iect. *To throw the lading of a ship ouerboord.*
Iecté: m. ée: f. *Cast, throwne, hurled, flung, darted; violently sent forth; put, or pushed out.*
Terre iectée. *Looke* Iectice.
Le dé soit iecté. *Set all on six and seuen; come on't what will let's hazard it.*
Meschante parole iectée va par tout à la volée: Prov. *A bad word blurted out (soone) roaueth all abroad.*
Iectée: f. *A cast, hurle, throw, fling; Looke* Iettée.
Iectement: m. *A casting, hurling, throwing, flinging; darting; putting, or pushing forth.*
Iecter. *To cast, hurle, throw, fling; dart, or send out violently; put, or push, forth.*
Iecter l'ancre sacrée. *To implore the diuine assistance; to imploy, or essay his last helpes, his chiefest meanes.*
Iecter la barre. *To lie.*
Iecter la boursette. *Looke* Boursette.
Iecter sa ceincture à terre. *A debtor vngirt, and bare-headed, to giue vp, or yeeld ouer, in open Court, his whole estate vnto his creditors, by throwing his girdle to the ground.*
Iecter le chat aux iambes. *Looke* Chat.
Iecter le feu par la gorge. *To spit fire like a diuell, or Dragon; to rage, or be mad with anger; to be in a horrible chafe.*
Iecter fleurs. *To bloome, or blossome, fruits; to yeeld, or bring forth, fruit.*
Iecter les gens à païs. *To set the men on land, to put them ashore.*
Iecter son lard aux chiens. *To be lauish, prodigall, wastfull; to spend his meanes vnworthily, or vntowardly; to cast his money away.*
Iecter le manche apres la coignée. *To throw the helue after the hatchet; after one losse to aduenture for another.*
Iecter la pierre & cacher le bras. *Looke* Pierre.
Iecter vne pierre à coup perdu. Ie ne iecte cette pierre &c. *I speake not thus in vaine, I am sure I hit it now.*
Iecter vne pierre au iardin de. *Looke* Iardin.
Iecter à ses pieds ce qu'il tenoit es mains. *Foolishly to leaue the certaine for th'vncertaine.*
Iecter la plume au vent. *To grow carelesse, to abandon himselfe vnto the blind direction of fortune; to let the world wag, or goe as it will; See* Vent.
Iecter sa teste. *A Deere to mue his head.*
Iecter son vent. *To breath his last; to giue vp the ghost.*
Il iectera aux autres la pouldre aux yeux. *He will outgoe all his competitors, outstrip all his concurrents; the victorie will sure enough be his; Looke* Pouldre.
Il se laisse iecter de la pousiere aux yeux. *He suffers dust to be throwne in his eyes; viz: He is willingly blinded, besotted, or hindered.*
Il se iecte sur tout cuir. *Any thing serues his turne, any sauce his stomacke, any meat his mouth; so hungrie a dog will feed on durtie puddings.*
Iecteur: m. *A caster, hurler, thrower, flinger, darter.*
Iectice. Terre iectice. *Earth newly cast vp out of a ditch, or furrow.*
Iectigation des espaules. *A wagging, or shrugging of the shoulders.*
Iectisse. *as* Iectice.
Iecton: m. *A shute, sience, twig, sprig; also, a swarme of Bees.*
Iecton à iecton. *Shute by shute, from twig to twig, one sience after another.*
Iectonner. *To shute, sprig, bred siences, put forth twigs.*
Iehan. *as* Iean.
Iehanne: f. *Joane (a womans name.)*
Iehannette: f. *Jug, or Jinnie.*
Ienice: f. *A Heyfer, or young Cow.*
Ienin. Cocu ienin. *An arrant cuckold.*
I'-en-veux. à la i'. *Lasciuiously; as one that will haue a licke at it.*
Iens: m. *An hearbe like Rosemarie, much vsed in the cleansing of gold oare.*
Iercer. *as* Iarcer.
Ieré: m. ée: f. *Brought, carried, borne; or, as* Geré.
Iervir. *Whence;* Ie me iervi tant à prendre cette medecine. *I had so much adoe to take &c.*
Iesier: m. *The giserne of birds.*
Iessemin. *as* Iasmin.
Iesuitains: m. *An Order of White Friers, which weare hoods on their heads like women, & shaue their beards continually.*

Iesuite: m. *A Iesuite; a Priest of the societie of Iesus.*
Vn Espagnol sans Iesuite est vn Perdrix sans Orange. *A Spaniard without a Iesuite is (like) a Partridge without an Orange.*
Iet: m. *Ieat.*
Iette: f. *The same.*
Ietté: m. ée: f. *Cast, throwne; Looke* Iecté.
Iettée: f. *A cast, hurle, throw, fling; also, a iettie, or iuttie; a bearing out, or leaning ouer, in buildings; also, the banke of a ditch, or th'earth cast out of it when it is made; which commonly is a marke of propertie to the owner of the land whereon it lyeth.*
Ietter. *as* Iecter.
Iettien: m. enne: f. *Made of Iet.*
Iettonner. *See* Iectonner.
Ieu: m. *A play, sport, game, pastime, recreation; also, play, sport, &c, mirth, ieast; also, a lesson on the Lute, &c; also, the alley wherein they play, at* Paille-maille; *also, the vpper end of a Tennis court (next to the house) or so much of it as is comprised within the streake of chaulke, &c, drawne ouerthwart the court.*
Ieux Floraux. *A wittie contention (among Rimers, or Poets) wherein the price for the best doer is an Eglantine, for the second a Marigold, of siluer.*
Ieux de Princes. *Are such as please them that play them.*
Vn ieu de violles. *A set, or chest of Violls.*
`A ieu couvert. *Secretly, priuately, couertly, vnder hand, in hugger mugger.*
Le ieu ne vaut pas la chandelle. *The businesse will not quit cost; it is not worth the money thats spent, or paines thats taken, about it.*
`A beau ieu bel argent, & `A beau ieu beau retour. *Square play, roundly, throughly, in good earnest; as good as is brought; one good, or bad turne for another.*
Il y aura beau ieu si la corde ne rompt. *We shall haue sport ynough if the time, or our intelligence, faile vs not.*
Il y a plus de mine que de ieu. *Looke* Mine.
Faire bonne mine, & mauvais ieu. *To beare a great misfortune in a cheerefull fashion; to looke merrily, or set a good face on't, how much soeuer he be troubled.*
Iouër le gros ieu: &, Iouër ses ieux. *Looke* Iouër.
Mettre en ieu. *To produce, to bring or shew forth; also, to stake, in play.*
Pour ne monstrer son ieu. *For feare of discouering his enterprise, or publishing his designes.*
Trier son espingle du ieu. *To slip his necke out of the coller; to flinch, or withdraw his stake, when he likes not the course of the play.*
`A vray dire perd on le ieu: Prov. *By speaking truth men (often) loose their game.*
Apres la feste & le ieu les pois au feu: Prov. *Those that will make good shift, must after play vse thrift.*
Il n'est ieu qu' a ioueurs: Prov. *There's no good play but among Gamesters; or the best playing is with them that vnderstand what they play.*
Il fait bon laisser le ieu quand il est beau: Prov. *Tis good leauing at play when it is at the fairest; or, tis good to leaue (when one hath got) at play.*
Les paroles font le ieu: Prov. *Words bind the gamester; make the game.*
Ieudy: m. *Thursday.*
Ieudy absolut. *Maundie Thursday, Sheere Thursday.*
Ieun: m. *A fast, or fasting.*
Ieunastre: com. *Youthlie, somewhat young.*
Ieunastrer. *To youth it; or play a young part; or behaue himselfe like a young man.*
Ieune: f. *as* Ieun.

Ieune: com. *Yong; youthlie, youthfull; tender; lustie.*
Faire la part au plus jeune. *Looke* Part.
Ieune en sa croissance a vn loup en la panse: Pro. *A youth in growing hath a Wolfe in his guts; viz. eats rauenously, greedily, or verie much.*
Amour se nourrit de ieune chair: Prov. *Yong flesh is a great nourishment to loue.*
Ieunement. *Yongly, youthfully, youth-like.*
Ieuner. *To fast; to abstaine from food.*
Assez ieune qui povrement vit: Prov. *He that liues poorely fasts sufficiently.*
Ieunesse: f. *Youth, yong age; also, youthes, yong people; also, a youthfull pranke, a tricke of youth.*
Appellez vous cela ieu de ieunesse? par Dieu ieu n'est ce. *(An equiuocation) If that be play I know not whats called paine*: ¶Rab.
Ieunesse oiseuse vieillesse disetteuse: Prov. *An idle youth a needie age.*
Fy de ieunesse, & de beauté desgarnie d'humilité: Prov. *Looke* Fy.
Si ieunesse sçavoit, & vieillesse pouvoit, iamais povreté n'auroit: Prov. *If youth knew what to doe, and age could doe what it knowes, no man would euer be poore.*
Ieunet: m. ette: f. *Somewhat young, or verie young; prettie and tender.*
Petite brebiette tousiours semble ieunette: Prov. *The little Ewe seemes alwayes young.*
Ieuneur: m. *A faster.*
Ieuneux: m. euse: f. *Much fasting, abstemious, meat-forbearing.*
Ieuse. *The barren Scarlet Oke, Holme Oke, French Oke.*
If: m. *An Yew, or Yew tree.*
If barbu. *So does th'Author of* l'Hippiatrique *(most ignorantly) tearme th'Italian* Tasso barbasso, *which is no kind of Yew (though* Tasso *be the Yew tree) but the hearbe Mulleyn, Hig-taper, Longwort.*
Ignave: com. *Lazie, lither, sloathfull, sluggish; also, cowardlie, without spirit, mettall, vertue, or force.*
Igné: m. ée: f. *Burning, fierie; also, fired, burned.*
Ignise: f. *A burning, or firing*: ¶Norm.
Ignition: f. *A burning, firing, or firinesse; the being red-hot, as gold is before it melt.*
Ignominie: f. *Ignominie, infamie, obloquie, dishonour, discredit, reproach.*
Ignominieusement. *Ignominiously, infamously.*
Ignominieux: m. euse: f. *Ignominious, infamous, dishonourable, shamefull, disgracefull, reproachfull.*
Ignoramment. *Ignorantly, vnskilfully, vnlearnedly, simply, vnwittingly, vnknowingly.*
Ignorance: f. *Ignorance, vnskilfulnesse, want of learning, lacke of knowledge.*
Ignorant. *Ignorant; vnlearned, vnskilfull, simple, wanting the knowledge of.*
Tout meschant est ignorant: Prov.
Ignoré: m. ée: f. *Ignored, not knowne.*
Ignorer. *To ignore, or be ignorant of, to want skill, not to know.*
Iky. *for* Icy; *Here*: ¶Pic.
Il: m. elle: f. *He, the same; also, it.*
Ila. Adverb. *as* Illec.
Iles: m. *The flankes; or the sides of the lower part of the bellie (so tearmed by Anatomists.)*
Os des Iles. *Looke* Os.
Iliade de maux: f. *As many mischiefes as befell the Troians, at the siege, and destruction of their Citie.*
Iliaque: com. *Of, or belonging to,* les Iles.

Iliaque paſsion. *Th'Iliacke paſsion: a painfull wringing in th'vpper ſmall guts obſtructed, or full of wind, or troubled with ſharpe humors.*

Artere, ou veines Iliaques. *Looke* Artere, ou Veine.

Ilias: f. vne Ilias de maux. *as* Iliade.

Ilicine. *Looke* Chelydre.

Illation: f. *An illation, inference, concluſion; a reaſon, or allegation that inforceth.*

Illec. (Adverb.) *There, thither, that way, on that ſide; to, or in, that place.*

D'illec. *thence; from that way, ſide, or place.*

Illegalité: f. *Illegalitie, lawleſneſſe, diſorder, vnrulineſſe.*

Illegitime: com. *Illegitimate; vnlawfully, or baſe, born.*

Illegitimement. *Illegitimately.*

Illeteré: m. ée: f. *Illiterate, vnlearned, ignorant.*

Illicite: com. *Illicitous, vnlawfull.*

Illicitement. *Illicitouſly, vnlawfully.*

Illimité: m. ée: f. *Boundleſſe, vnlimited.*

Illiné: m. ée: f. *Softly annointed, gently rubbed on.*

Illiner. *To annoint ſoftly, gently to rub on.*

Illiquide: com. *Obſcure, doubtfull; or, which is not euident or cleere.*

Illudé: m. eé: f. *Deluded, illuded, mocked; flowted, ſcorned.*

Illuder. *To illude, delude, mocke, flowt, ſcorne.*

Illuminateur: m. *An illuminator, inlightner; illuſtrator.*

Illumination: f. *An illumination, inlightning, illuſtration; an opening of the eyes.*

Illuminé: m. ée: f. *Illumined, illuſtrated, inlightened, brightened; cleared, beautified.*

Illuminer. *To illuminate, brighten, inlighten, giue light vnto; to beautifie, cleere, illuſtrate.*

Illuſion: f. *An illuſion; fantaſie, falſe viſion; a mockerie, or gullerie; an impoſture, or tricke of forgerie, put vpon dull, or dazeled eyes.*

Illuſoire: com. *Illuſorie, illuding; alſo, vaine, idle, to no purpoſe at all.*

Illuſtrateur: m. *An illuſtrator; a brightner, cleerer; beautifier; dignifier.*

Illuſtration: f. *An illuſtration; explanation, euidence; a brightning, or beautifying.*

Illuſtre: com. *Illuſtrious, excellent, famous, renowmed, honourable, moſt worthie; alſo, cleere, bright, lightſome, ſhining.*

Illuſtré: m. ée: f. *Illuſtrated; explained, made euident, cleered, brightened; alſo, dignified, honoured.*

Illuſtrer. *To illuſtrate; explaine, cleere, brighten, make euident; alſo, to dignifie, make famous, bring honor vnto.*

Illuvion. *as* Alluvion; *Alſo, filthineſſe, naſtineſſe, vncleanneſſe.*

Ilz: m. *The Yew tree:* ¶Norm.

Image: f. *An image, figure, counterfeit, reſemblance, repreſentation of; alſo, a Iewell, or Brooch to weare in the hat.*

Imagé: m. ée: f. *as* Imager: m. eré: f.

Imager: m. *as* Imagier.

Imager: m. ere: f. *Of, or belonging to, images; adorned, or furniſhed with, images.*

Imagette: f. *A little Image.*

Imagier: m. *An Image-maker, a caruer of Images.*

Imaginaire: com. *Imaginarie, fained, onely in conceit, in name onely, done for a faſhion, all in ſhew.*

Imaginatif: m. iue: f. *Imaginatiue, inuentiue; alſo, conceited, full of new deuiſes.*

Imagination: f. *Imagination, fancie, conceit, thought; a ſurmiſe, or ſurmiſing.*

Imaginative: f. *as* Imagination.

Imaginé: m. ée: f. *Imagined, thought, conceited, ſurmiſed.*

Imaginer. *To imagine, thinke, deuiſe, conceiue, ſurmiſe.*

Imbecille: com. *Weake, feeble, ſtrengthleſſe, faint, forceleſſe.*

Imbecillement. *Weakly, feebly, faintly, forceleſly.*

Imberbe: com. *Beardleſſe, without a beard.*

Imbibé: m. ée: f. *Imbued; moiſtened, bedewed; ſoaked, or drunke in.*

Imbleſſable: com. *Vnhurtable, vnwoundable.*

Imbriago: m. *A (moſt venomous) kind of the Sea-hare; alſo, the beardleſſe Sea-barbell, or Sore Mullet.*

Imbrocation. *as* Embrocation.

Imbu: m. uë: f. *Imbrued, died, diſtained; indued, taught, inſtructed; full of.*

Imbuvable: com. *Vndrinkable, vnfit to be drunke of.*

Imitable: com. *Imitable, followable.*

Imitateur: m. *An imitator; counterfeiter, follower of.*

Imitatif: m. iue: f. *Imitatiue, imitating, done by imitation.*

Imitation: f. *Imitation, counterfeiting, following.*

Imitatrice: f. *An imitatrix.*

Imité: m. ée: f. *Imitated, counterfeited, followed.*

Imiter. *To imitate, counterfeit, follow th'example of.*

Immaculé: m. ée: f. *Immaculate, vnſpotted, without blemiſh, cleane, pure, neat.*

Immangeable: com. *Vneatable, vnfit to be fed on.*

Immanité: f. *Immanitie; inhumanitie, crueltie, felneſſe; outragiouſneſſe; hugeneſſe, exceſſiue greatneſſe.*

Immarceſſible: com. *Incorruptible, vnuadeable, vnwitherable.*

Immariable: com. *Vnmarriable, paſt marriage.*

Immateriel: m. elle: f. *Immateriall; without matter, ſtuffe, or ſubſtance; impalpable, vntouchable.*

Immatriculé: m. ée: f. *Matriculated; inrolled, regiſtred, or entred into.*

Immatriculer. *To matriculate; to inroll, regiſter, enter into.*

Immediat: m. ate: f. *Immediate, next vnto; preſently ſucceeding, ſoone following.*

Immediatement. *Immediately; without interpoſition, or meſne; alſo, preſently, without pauſing, as faſt as may be, by and by.*

Immedicable: com. *Immedicable, vncurable; not to be healed, or helped.*

Immemorial: m. ale: f. *Without the compaſſe, reach, or ſcope of memorie.*

Poſſeſsion immemoriale. *Poſſeſsion held by preſcription, or time out of mind.*

Immenſe: com. *Immenſe, infinite, huge, exceſsiue, vnmeaſurable, proportion-exceeding, paſsing great.*

Immenſité: f. *Immenſitie; vnmeaſurableneſſe, hugeneſſe, infiniteneſſe, boundleſſe largeneſſe, paſsing greatneſſe.*

Immeuble: m. *An immouable, or thing vnmouable; as land, rent, &c.*

Immeuble: com. *Immouable, vnmouable.*

Immiſcé: m. *Intermedled with, dealt farre in.*

s'Immiſcer. *To intermeddle with, to deale farre in.*

Immiſericorde: f. *Vnmercifulneſſe, want of mercie, inhumanitie, crueltie.*

Immiſericordieuſement. *Vnmercifully.*

Immiſericordieux: m. euſe: f. *Vnmercifull.*

Immixte: com. *Simple, vnmixt, without mixture.*

Immobiliaire: com. *Vnmouable, immouable.*

Immobile: com. *Immouable, firme, ſetled, aſſured, ſteadfaſt, not to be ſtirred.*

Immobilement. *Immouably, firmly, ſteadfaſtly, aſſuredly.*

Immobilité : f. *Steadfastnesse, firmenesse, assurednesse, vnmoueablenesse.*
Immoderé : m.ée : f. *Immoderate; excessiue, intemperate, outlashing, disordinate, outragious.*
Immoderément. *Immoderately; excessiuely, intemperately, disorderedly, disordinately, outragiously.*
Immodeste : com. *Immodest; wanton, vnchast, lascinious; malapert, saucie, vnmanerlie.*
Immodestement. *Immodestly; wantonly, shamelesly; malapertly, saucily.*
Immodestie : f. *Immodestie; wantonnesse; malapertnesse.*
Immolateur : *A Sacrifice-offerer.*
Immolation : f. *An immolation, sacrifice, offering.*
Immolé : m.ée : f. *Immolated, sacrificed, offered.*
Immoler. *To offer, to sacrifice, to offer sacrifice.*
Immonde : com. *Vncleane, smeared, berayed, polluted, foule, filthie, nastie, sluttish.*
Qui veut la conscience monde, il doit fuïr le monde immonde : Prov. *Looke* Monde.
Immondice : f. *Filth, vncleannesse, nastinesse, pollution, sluttishnesse, ordure.*
Immondicité : f. *Vncleanenesse, filthinesse.*
Immortalisation : f. *An immortalization, an immortalizing.*
Immortalisé : m. ée : f. *Immortalized, eternized.*
Immortaliser. *To immortalize, eternize, make immortall.*
Immortalité : f. *Immortalitie, eternitie, euerlastingnesse; fame ay-during; a perpetuall memorie, life, renowme, name.*
Immortel : m.elle : f. *Immortall, eternall, euerlasting, euer-liuing, neuer ending, ay-during.*
Immortellement. *Immortally, eternally, euerlastingly, perpetually, for euer and euer.*
Immuable : com. *Vnchangeable, steadfast, firme, setled, constant, resolute.*
Immuablement. *Vnchangeably, steadfastly, constantly; resolutely.*
Immune : com. *Exempt, free, priuiledged, discharged from.*
Immunité : f. *Immunitie, freedome, exemption, libertie, priuiledge, franchise.*
Immutable. *as* Immuable.
Impact : m.acte : f. *Hard fastened; Looke* Empacté.
Impacter. *as* Empacter.
Impalpable : com. *Impalpable, vnfeelable.*
Impar. *Odde, vneuen, vnequall, vnlike.*
Impartir. *To impart, or communicate with; to make partaker of.*
Impassibilité : f. *Impassibilitie, vnsenciblenesse, vnpassionatenesse; also, impatience.*
Impassible : com. *Impassible, senceless e, vnpassionate, vnperturbed; also, impatient, which cannot suffer, or will not beare with.*
Impatiémment. *Impatiently, too passionately; furiously, violently, vehemently.*
Impatience : f. *Impatience, too much passionatenesse; violence, furie.*
Impatient. *Impatient, ouer passionate; too hot, violent, vehement; that cannot beare, that will not indure.*
Impatronisation : f. *An impatronization; th'absolute Maisterie, Seigneurie, or possession of.*
Impatronisé : m.ée : f. *Impatronized, maistered.*
s'Impatroniser de. *To maister, conquer, get absolute possession of, lay sure hold on, take as his owne.*
Impendent. *Impendent, hanging ouer, or vnto; neere approaching, neere at hand, hard by.*
Impenetrable : com. *Impenetrable, vnpierceable.*
Impenses : f. *Costs, charges, expences.*
Imperatif : m. *Th'Imperatiue mood in Grammar.*
Imperatif : m.iue : f. *Imperatiue, imperious, cōmanding.*
Imperatoire : f. *Maisterwort, false Pellitorie of Spaine.*
Imperceptible : com. *Imperceptible, vnperceiuable.*
Imperceptiblement. *Vnperceiuably.*
Imperer. *To rule, sway, command, seigneurize, domineere, haue absolute authoritie ouer.*
Imperfaict : m. ête : f. *Imperfect, vncompleat, lame, vnfinished, insufficient.*
Imperfection : f. *Imperfection; lamenesse, insufficiencie, weakenesse.*
Imperforation : f. *A closing, or shutting vp for want of boring, or piercing.*
Imperial : m.ale : f. *Imperiall, Emperor-like.*
Couronne imperiale. *Th'Imperiall Lillie, or Crowne Imperiall; a great, beautifull (but stinking) flower.*
Imperiale : f. *The name of an hearbe (mistaken by some moderne Herbarists for Smyrnium, or Candie Alexanders) that hath many excellent vertues; also, a kind of bit for a horse; also, a field-bed.*
Imperiale de Flanders. *A certaine coine worth about* 8 s. sterl.
Impericon. *S. Johns wort.*
Imperieusement. *Imperiously, Lordly, proudly, loftily, Soueraigne-like.*
Imperieux : m.euse : f. *Imperious, Lordlie, statelie, loftie, commanding, proud.*
Imperiosité : f. *Statelinesse, Lordlinesse; austeritie, seueritie; Imperiousnesse.*
Imperissable : com. *Vnperishable, which cannot miscarrie.*
Imperissible. *The same.*
Imperit. *Vnskilfull, vnlearned; vnexpert, vnexperienced; rude, simple, ignorant, easily deceiued.*
Imperitement. *Vnskilfully, vnlearnedly; vnexpertly, ignorantly, nouice-like.*
Impersonnel : m.elle : f. *Impersonall, that hath no persons.*
Impersonnellement. *Impersonally, without persons.*
Imperspirable : com. *Not to be breathed into, not to be pierced with aire.*
Impertinemment *Impertinently, vnproperly, vnfitly, to little or no purpose.*
Impertinence : f. *Impertinencie, vnfitnesse, vnpropernesse; a thing thats to no purpose.*
Impertinent. *Impertinent, vnfit, vnproper; cleane from the matter.*
Impetigine : f. *A ringworme, tetter, drie itching scab.*
Impetrable : com. *Impetrable, obtainable vpon request.*
Impetrans de letters Royaulx. *Patentees; or such as haue got the Kings letters Patents.*
Impetration : f. *An obtaining by suit, procuring by intreatie, compassing by request.*
Impetré : m. ée : f. *Obtained by suit, procured by intreatie, compassed by request.*
Impetrer. *To get by prayer, obtaine by suit, compasse by intreatie, procure by request.*
Impetueusement. *Impetuously, boisterously, violently, with a vehement swing, or forcible sway.*
Impetueux : m.euse : f. *Impetuous, boisterous, vehement, violent, raging, furious, most forcible, sweeping away whatsoeuer is before it.*
Impetuosité : f. *Impetuositie, boisterousnesse, great violence, raging force, ouer-bearing furie.*
Impie : com. *Impious, wicked, vngodlie, gracelesse, vngracious, irreligious, regarding neither God nor man.*

Impiement. Impiously, vngodlily, gracelesly, vngraciously, without respect of God, or of man.
Impieté: f. Impietie, vngodlinesse, vnrighteousnesse, gracelesnesse, villanie, wickednesse, a vile part, an irreligious pranke.
Impiteux: m. euse: f. Pitilesse, incompassionate, bloudie, sauage, cruell, void of humanitie, without mercie.
Impitoyable: com. as Impiteux.
Implacable: com. Implacable, vnpleasable, vnappeasable.
Implantation: f. An implantation, or implanting; a setting, or fixing into.
Implanter. To implant, to fix, or set into.
Implication: f. An implication, infolding, intangling, inuolution, incombrance.
Implicité: f. An implicitie, intanglement, incombrance, obscure inuolution.
Impliqué: m. ée: f. Infolded, inuolued, enwrapped; intangled, incombered, pestered.
Impliquer. To infold, inuolue, enwrap; intangle, pester, incomber, bring into the briers.
Implorateur: m. An implorer, beseecher, crauer, begger, humble and earnest intreater.
Imploration: f. An imploring, crauing, begging, beseeching; an earnest, humble, or lamentable intreating.
Imploré: m. ée: f. Implored, besought, begged, craued; humbly, earnestly, or lamentably intreated.
Implorer. To implore, beseech, craue, beg of; lamentably to request, to intreat with teares.
Imployable: com. Inflexible, vnbowable, indurate, obstinate.
Impoli: m. ie: f. Vnpollished, rude, out of trimme.
Impollu: m. uë: f. Vnpolluted, vntainted, vndefiled, without blemish, or staine.
Importable: com. Intollerable, vnsupportable, not to be borne.
Importamment. Importantly, weightily, forcibly.
Importance: f. Importance, force, weight, momẽt, value.
Important. Important, weightie, forcible, of great consequence.
Importer. cela importe moult. That imports much, thats of great consequence.
Importueux: m. euse: f. Without port, hauen, or harbor.
Importun: m. une: f. Importunate, vrgent, earnest with; troublesome, vnmanerlie, vnreasonable.
Importunément. Importunately, vrgently, earnestly; troublesomely, vnmanerly, too much; also, vnfitly, to no purpose.
Importunité: f. Importunitie, vrgencie, earnestnesse, much suing, often intreatie, great solicitation.
Imposé: m. ée: f. Imposed, put to, laid on; inioyned; also, taxed, charged with, exacted from; also, accused of.
Imposer. To impose; to put vnto, or lay vpon; to inioyne; to tax, charge with, exact from.
Imposer à aucun quelque cas. To accuse of a crime; to cast, or lay an imputation on.
Imposition: f. An impost, or imposition; a tax, exaction, charge laid on; also, an accusation, or imputation; an imposing, or laying on; (whence, Imposition de mains.)
Imposition de francs fiefs. An imposition, or fine imposed by way of licence, to enable a Roturier, or Yeoman, to hold a purchased fief; The rate of it hath been certaine, viz: six yeres value, if the land were held immediately of the King; and three yeares value, if it was held by a mesne tenure; but now it is vncertaine, and set downe by the Officers of th'Exchequer.
Imposition foraine. Is 12 d. (within Paris but 6 d.) in the pound vpon all kind of cattell, corne, victualls, and wares imported, or exported; (but where this imposition is paid, subsidie is spared.)
Imposition de nouveaux acquests. The fine which Churchmen pay to the king for purchases of land in Mortmaine; Looke Acquest.
Impossibilité: f. An impossibilitie.
Impossibiliter. To make impossible.
Impossible: com. Impossible, which cannot be done.
Impost: m. An impost, custome, imposition.
Impost de francs fiefs. Looke Imposition.
Impost du pied fourchu. The toll thats leuied vpon each head of cattell sold in Markets, and Faires.
Impost de sa personne. Vnweldie, vnfit to trauell, vnable to take paines.
Imposte: m. The springer of an arched gate, the moulding that beares th'arch.
Imposteur: m. An imposter, cousener, deceiuer, beguiler; a iugler, a mountebanke, a cheating Quacksaluer.
Imposture: f. Imposture, guile, deceit, falshood, cousening, iugling; a tricke of legierdemain; also, slaundering, or a slaunder.
Impotence: f. Impotencie, disabilitie, infirmitie, weaknesse, debilitie, feeblenesse.
Impotent. Impotent, vnable, power-wanting, infirme, lame, feeble, weake.
Impourveu. Seeke Improuveu.
Imprecation: f. An imprecation, curse, banning.
Impreciable: com. Vnprisable, vnualuable.
Impregnation: f. A bagging, or getting with young; a fillin, a conceiuing.
Impremedité: m. ée: f. Vnpremeditated, suddain, vnthought of before.
Imprenable: com. Impregnable, vnexpugnable, which will not be forced.
Imprescriptible: com. Without the compasse of prescription; which by no length of time can be aliened, or lost.
Imprestance: f. Prest, or imprest money, receiued, and to be imployed for another.
Imprevoyance: f. Improuidence.
Imprimé: m. vn im. A printed worke (a word vsed when one will not vouchsafe it the name of a booke.)
Imprimé: m. ée: f. Printed, imprinted; stamped, sealed.
Imprimer. To print, imprint, make an impression; to stampe, seale; set, or thrust, hard in.
Imprimerie: f. A print, impression; seale, stampe; also, a printing; also, a Printing house.
Imprimeur: m. A Printer.
Improbable: com. Improbable, vnprouable.
Impropere: m. An exprobration, vpbraiding, or twitting in the teeth; a reproach, or imputation; also, a nickname, or disgracefull title.
Improperer. To exprobrate, vpbraid, reproach, lay in the dish; cast, or twit in the teeth; also, to nickname, or miscall.
Impropre: com. Vnproper, vnapt, vnfit, no feat; vnnaturall, inconuenient.
Improprement. Improperly, vnaptly, vnfitly, vnfeatly; inconueniently.
Improviste. A l'im. as A l'improuveu.
Improuveu: m. euë: f. Vnprouided for, vnlooked for, vnheeded, vnthought vpon.
A l'improuveu. Suddenly, at vnawares, before it was thought of, or looked for.
Imprudemment. Imprudently, incircumspectly, improuidently, vnaduisedly; ignorantly, vnwittingly.

Imprudence: f. *Imprudencie, improuidence, incircumspection, inconsideration, vnaduisednesse; ignorance.*
Imprudent. *Imprudent, improuident, inconsiderate, vncircumspect, vnaduised, ignorant.*
Impudemment. *Impudently, shamelesly, malapertly, ouer-boldly, with a brasen face.*
Impudence: f. *Impudence, shamelesnesse, vnshamefac'dnesse, malapertnesse, ouer-boldnesse.*
Impudent. *Impudent, shamelesse, vnshamefac'd, brasen faced, malapert, saucie, ouer-bold.*
Impudicité: f. *Wantonnesse, vnchastnesse, incontinence, filthinesse, obscenitie, vncleannesse of life.*
Impudique: com. *Lasciuious, wanton, vnchast, obscene, shamelesse, incontinent, vncleane.*
Impudiquement. *Vnchastly, lasciuiously, wantonly, obscenely, shamelesly, incontinently, vncleanely.*
Impugnance: f. *A resistance; or as* Impugnation.
Impugnateur: m. *An impugner, withstander, fighter against.*
Impugnation: f. *An impugning, withstanding, resisting, fighting, or stirring against.*
Impugné: m. ée: f. *Impugned; stirred, or fought against, resisted, withstood.*
Impugner. *To impugne, fight, or stirre against; resist, withstand.*
Impuissamment. *Impotently, vnpowerfully.*
Impuissant. *Impotent, vnpowerful, infirme, abilitie-wanting.*
Impulsé: m. ée: f. *Vrged, pushed, or thrust vpon; forced, constrained, prouoked vnto.*
Impulser. *To push, thrust, or vrge vpon; to force, constraine, prouoke vnto.*
Impulseur: m. *A pusher, or thruster vpon; an vrger, prouoker, inciter, solicitor, instigator.*
Impulsif: m. iue: f. *Impulsiue; pushing, or thrusting vpon; vrging, stirring, inciting, prouoking, vnto.*
Impulsion: f. *An impulsion; pushing, or thrusting vpon; an vrging, incitement, prouocation, earnest solicitation.*
Impuni: m. ie: f. *Vnpunished, quit, freed.*
Impuniment. *Quit, scot-free, without punishment.*
Impunité: f. *Impunitie; freedome from, or without, punishment.*
Impur: m. ure: f. *Impure, foule, sluttish, vncleane, filthie, naughtie, vile, dishonest, obscene.*
Impurement. *Impurely, foulely, filthily, vncleanely, naughtily, dishonestly, obscenely.*
Impureté: f. *Impuritie, filthinesse, pollution, vncleanenesse, dishonestie, naughtinesse, obscenitie; loathsomnesse.*
Impurité: f. *as* Impureté.
Imputation: f. *An imputation; reproach, blame, or fault laid to the charge of.*
Imputé: m. ée: f. *Imputed, attributed, ascribed vnto; laid vnto the charge of.*
Imputer. *To impute, ascribe, or attribute vnto; also, to accuse, or charge with; to lay an imputation on.*
Imputeur: m. *An imputor; a putter of things vpon, an attributer of things vnto, others.*
Inabordable: com. *Vnaboordable, vnaccoastable, vnapproachable, not to be arriued vnto.*
Inaccessible: com. *Inaccessible; which cannot be come vnto.*
Inaccoustumé: m. ée: f. *Vnaccustomed, strange.*
Inacostable: com. *Vnaccoastable, vncompanable, sauage, austere, vnsociable.*
Inactionable: com. *Vnsuable; not to be touched, or troubled by any suit.*
Inadmissible: com. *Vnadmittable, vnreceiuable, vnacceptable, vnallowable.*
Inadvertamment. *Incircumspectly, inconsiderately, vnaduisedly, negligently, vnwarily.*
Inadvertence: f. *Inconsideration, vnwarinesse, improuidence, vnaduisednesse.*
Inaguerri: m. ie: f. *Growne, or become warlike; made skilfull in warfaring, trained vp to the warres.*
Inalienable: com. *Vnalienable; which cannot be sold, or passed away.*
Inamendable: com. *Vnamendable, incurable, vnrecouerable, past reformation, beyond all helpe.*
Inamollissable: com. *Obdurate, most hard, which cannot be softened, or will not be tender.*
Inanimé: m. ée: f. *Soulelesse, without a soule.*
Inanité: f. *Emptinesse, inanitie, vacuitie, voidnesse.*
Inanition: f. *as* Inanité; *or, An emptying.*
Inapercevance: f. *Dulnesse, blockishnesse, sottishnesse.*
Inarcature du col. *The bowing, or bought of the necke.*
Inassociable: com. *Vnsociable, vnaccompanable, hagard, sauage, froward, austere.*
Ination. *Looke* Inanité.
Inaudite: com. *Vnheard of, neuer heard before.*
Inauguré: m. eé: f. *Inaugurized, consecrated, dedicated.*
Incagant. *Becacking, beraying; disgracing.*
Incaguer. *To becacke, or beray; also, to defame, or disgrace.*
Incant. *as* Encant; *An outrope, or outcrie of goods.*
Incapable: com. *Vncapable; vnable to receiue, or conceiue.*
Incapacité: f. *Incapacitie, vncapablenesse; vnabilitie of receiuing, or conceiuing.*
Incaquer. *as* Incaguer.
Incarnadin: m. *A carnation; or more properly, a deep, rich, or bright, carnation; (This word hath often th'addition of,* d'Espagne.)
Incarnadin: m. ine: f. *Carnation; of a deepe, rich, or bright carnation.*
Incarnat: m. ate: f. *Carnation; & more particularly, light, or pale carnation; flesh-coloured, or of the colour of our damaske Rose.*
Incarnatif: m. iue: f. *Flesh-bringing, flesh-breeding.*
Cousture incarnative. *The stitching, or sowing vp of wounds, &c, by Chirurgians.*
Incarnation: f. *An incarnation, or assuming of flesh; also, carnation colour.*
Incarné: m. ée: f. *Incarnate, made flesh, brought into flesh.*
Diable incarné. *A diuell in the shape of a man; an incarnate, or verie diuell.*
Incarner. *To incarnate, or make fleshie; to bring into, or fill vp with, flesh.*
Incastré: m. ée: f. *Incastelled; strongly inclosed, or lodged, as in a castle.*
Incendiaire: com. *An Incendiarie, firebrand, setter of houses on fire.*
Incendie: m. *A burning, firing, setting on fire.*
Incentriquer. *To incenter, or place within a Center.*
Inceratif: m. iue: f. *Inceratiue, waxing; cleauing, or sticking vnto.*
Inceré. *Looke* Inseré.
Incertain: m. *An incertaintie.*
Incertain: m. aine: f. *Vncertaine, doubtfull, vnsure; wauering; vnknowne.*
Incertainement. *Vncertainly, vnsurely, doubtfully.*
Incertaineté: f. *Vncertaintie, vnsurenesse; wauering; doubtfulnesse.*
Incertitude: f. *Incertaintie, suspence, wauering, staggering, doubtfulnesse.*

In-

Inceſſamment. *Inceſſantly, continually, without any manner of intermiſſion.*
Inceſſible: com. *Vnceaſſable, vnendable, vndeterminable.*
Inceſſion: f. *A pace, gate, or going; alſo, a hot-bath for the lower parts of the belly.*
Inceſte: m. *Inceſt; carnall copulation with one thats neere of kinne.*
Inceſtueux: m. euſe: f. *Inceſtuous; full of, begotten in, polluted with, inceſt.*
Incidemment. *Incidently; by chaunce, by occaſion, by the way, vpon the by.*
Incident: m. *An incident, circumſtance, or by-matter; a thing which comes indirectly into a fact, or queſtion; or (being not properly of the ſubſtance thereof) ariſes from it collaterally, or ſide-wiſe; in Law, a ſmall controuerſie ſpringing from, or depending on, the maine ſuite (or as originally;) alſo, a chaunce, accident, caſualtie; alſo, a ſhift, ſleight, euaſion, excuſe.*
Par incident. *Vpon occaſion; by meere chance.*
Incineration: f. *A reducing, or burning vnto aſhes.*
Incirconcis. *Vncircumciſed.*
Incis: m. *A rocke, or hard ground; cut to giue paſſage vnto a Spring; (a Law-tearme)*
Inciſé: m. ée: f. *Cut into; ſlit, launced; grauen, intayled.*
Inciſer. *To cut into, to make an inciſion; to launce, open, ſlit; alſo, to carue, graue, intayle.*
Inciſif: m. iue: f. *Cutting, launcing, opening, inciſion-making.*
Inciſion: f. *An inciſion, or in-cutting; a launcing, opening; intayling.*
Inciſoires: m. *The foure fore-teeth, wherewith we bite, or cut, our meat.*
Incitant: m. (Subſtant.) *as* Incitateur.
Incitant. (Particip.) *Inciting, vrging, ſtirring vp.*
Incitateur: m. *An inciter, or ſtirrer vp; a prouoker, egger, vrger.*
Incitation: f. *An incitation, inſtigation, prouocation; a ſtirring vp; an incenſing, egging, vrging; incouraging.*
Incité: m. ée: f. *Incited, inſtigated, or ſtirred vp; vrged, egged, incenſed, prouoked; incouraged.*
Incitement: m. *An inciting, or incitement.*
Inciter. *To incite, inſtigate, or ſtirre vp; to egg, vrge, prouoke; incenſe; incourage.*
Incivil: m. ile: f. *Vnciuill; barbarous; vncourteous; ill-nurtured, rude, vnmannerlie, clowniſh, churliſh.*
Incivilement. *Vnciuilly; barbarouſly; diſcourteouſly; rudely, vnmannerly, clowniſhly, churliſhly.*
Incivilité: f. *Inciuilitie; barbarouſneſſe; ruſticitie, rudeneſſe, clowniſhneſſe, churliſhneſſe, vnmannerlineſſe; alſo, want of a ciuill cauſe, or ſubiect.*
Inclemence: f. *Inclemencie; rigor, ſharpeneſſe, auſteritie, ſeueritie; fellneſſe, mercileſueſſe, want of pitie.*
Inclement. *Vnclement; rigorous, auſtere, ſterne, ſharpe, ſeuere, pitileſſe, mercileſſe.*
Inclinant. *Inclining; bending, or leaning towards; diſpoſed, affected, addicted vnto.*
Inclination: f. *An inclination; a bending, leaning, or bowing, towards; a humor, diſpoſition, or affection, vnto.*
Incliné: m. ée: f. *Inclined; bent vnto.*
Incliner. *To incline; bend, bow, leane, towards; to haue a humor or diſpoſition, to beare good will, or carrie an affection, vnto.*
Inclite: com *Excellent; renowmed, famous, glorious.*
Incluſivement. *Incluſiuely; comprehenſiuely, as cõtained within; alſo, abſolutely, vtterly, indefinitely.*
Incogneu: m. euë: f. *Vnknowne, vnkend, vncouth, ſtrange; ignoble, obſcure.*
Incolumité: f. *Incolumitie, ſafetie, healthfullneſſe.*
Incombuſtible: com. *Incombuſtible, not to be burnt.*
Incommendable: com. *Diſcommendable.*
Incommenſurable: com. *Vnmeaſurable.*
Incommeſurable: com. *The ſame; or, not to be meaſured by one, and the ſame meaſure.*
Incommode: com. *Incommodious; vngainefull, vnprofitable; dommageous, hurtfull, noiſome, hindering; alſo, vnfit, vneuen, vnſeemelie, vnſeaſonable.*
Incommodément. *Incommodiouſly, vngainefully, vnprofitably; noiſomely, hurtfully, vnto ones hinderance; alſo, vnfitly, vnſeaſonably; vnhandſomely, illfauouredly.*
Incommoder. *To incommodate, hinder, trouble, impeach, diſturbe, diſeaſe; breed harme, bring loſſe, vnto.*
Incommodité: f. *Incommoditie, hinderance, trouble, diſturbance; dammage, diſpleaſure, loſſe, hurt; inconueniencie; vnaptneſſe, vnfitneſſe, vnſeaſonableneſſe.*
Incommuable: com. *Immutable, vnalterable, vnchangeable.*
Incommune: com. *Vncommon; or, not common.*
Incommunicable: com. *Vncommunicable, inconuerſible, vncompanable; harſh, churliſh, froward.*
Incommutable. *as* Incommuable.
Incomparable: com. *Incomparable, matchleſſe, without peere.*
Incompatibilité: f. *Incompatibilitie, iarring, diſagreement.*
Incompatible: com. *Incompatible, iarring, diſagreeing, not induring one another.*
Incompetence: f. *Incompetencie; vnſufficiencie, vnfitneſſe.*
Incompetent *Incompetent; vnfit; vnſufficient.*
Incomprehenſibilité: f. *Incomprehenſibleneſſe, vnconceiueableneſſe, innumerableneſſe.*
Incomprehenſible: com. *Incomprehenſible, vnconceiueable, vaſt, infinite.*
Incongelable: com. *Vncongealeable, not to be congealed.*
Incongruë: com. *Incongruous, vnagreeing; abſurd, ill-fauoured, vnfit, againſt forme, againſt rule.*
Incongruité: f. *Incongruitie; vnfitneſſe, illfauouredneſſe; abſurditie, irregularitie.*
Inconſiderant. *as* Inconſideré.
Inconſideration: f. *Inconſideration, indiſcretion, vnaduiſedneſſe, raſhneſſe.*
Inconſideré: m. ée: f. *Inconſiderate, vnaduiſed, vnregardfull, raſh, indiſcreet.*
Inconſidereément. *Inconſiderately, vnaduiſedly, vndiſcreetly, raſhly, vnregardfully.*
Inconſolable: com. *Inconſolable, vncomfortable; not to be comforted.*
Inconſolablement. *Vncomfortably, in a deſperate taking, moſt wofully.*
Inconſtamment. *Inconſtantly, vnſtedfaſtly, mutably, waueringly.*
Inconſtance: f. *Inconſtancie, vnſtedfaſtneſſe, fickleneſſe, lightneſſe, wauering, mutabilitie, changeableneſſe.*
Inconſtant. *Inconſtant, vnſtedfaſt, fickle, flitting, light, wauering, mutable, changeable.*
Inconſumptible: com. *Vnconſumeable, euerlaſting, aye-during.*
Incontaminé: m. ée: f. *Vncontaminated, vnpolluted, vnſpotted.*

Incontestable: com. *Not to be contested, or stood on.*
Incontinemment. *Incontinently, vnchastly; disorderedly, vnstayedly, immoderately, without any gouernment of himselfe.*
Incontinence: f. *Incontinence, immoderation; an vnbridled appetite vnto the satisfaction of lust, or lustfull affections.*
Incontinent. *Incontinent, immoderate, vnchast, of an vnbridled appetite, loosse of life.*
Incontinent. (Adverb.) *Incontinently, instantly, immediatly, presently, suddainely, forthwith, out of hand, as soone as may be.*
Inconvenable: com. *Inconuenient, improper, vnfitting, misbecomming.*
Inconvenance: f. *A misbecomming, vnhandsomenesse, vnfitnesse, vnseemelinesse, vnbeseeming.*
Inconvenient: m. *An inconuenience, or vnfit thing; also, a misfortune, mischiefe, mishap.*
Inconvenient. *as* Inconvenable.
Incornifistibuler. *To plod, or dunce vpon; to beat the braines about.*
Incorporant. *Incorporating; ioyning in one bodie.*
Incorporé: m. ée: f. *Incorporated, imbodied with; reduced vnto, or ioyned in, one bodie.*
Incorporel: m. elle: f. *Vncorporall, bodilesse, without a bodie.*
Incorporer. *To incorporate; to make one, or of one bodie; to ioyne wholly together.*
Incorrect: m. cte: f. *Incorrect, faultie, corrupt.*
Incorrectement. *Incorrectly, faultily, corruptly.*
Incorrection: f. *A fault, error, thing not corrected.*
Incorrigible: com. *Incorrigible, vnreformable, vnamendable.*
Incorrompable: com. *Vncorruptable; not to be corrupted, seduced, or woon, by gifts &c.*
Incorruptible: com. *Incorruptible, euerlasting, eternall.*
Incoulpable: com. *Inculpable, vnreproueable, perfect, faultlesse, blamelesse.*
Incrasser. *To incrassate, thicken, or make thicke.*
Incredible: com. *Incredible, vnbeleeuable.*
Incrediblement. *Incredibly, past beliefe.*
Incredule: com. *Incredulous; vnbeleeuing, or hard of beliefe.*
Incredulité: f. *Incredulitie, vnbelieuing, lacke of beliefe.*
Increpation: f. *An increpation, chiding, reproofe, rebuke.*
Increpé: m. ée: f. *Chidden, taunted, rebuked, reproued, blamed; accused.*
Increper. *To taunt, rebuke, chide, blame; reproue; accuse.*
Incroyable: com. *Incredible.*
Incroyablement. *Incredibly.*
Incrustation: f. *A pargetting, rough-casting; a crustinesse, ruggednesse, thicke scabbednesse.*
Incrusté: m. ée: f. *Growne to a scab, or crustinesse; pargetted, rough-cast.*
Incruster. *To set a scab, or crust on; to make rugged, and thicke, as a crust; (and hence) to parget, or rough-cast.*
Incuisable: com. *Vnfit, or vnpossible, to be sodden.*
Inculcation: f. *An inculcation; a frequent repetition.*
Inculpé: m. ée: f. *Blamed, or accused for, charged with, faultie of; also, blamelesse, innocent, perfect, vnreproueable.*
Inculqué: m. ée: f. *Inculcated; forcibly thrust, pressed, or beaten into; also, often repeated, vrged often.*
Inculquer. *To inculcate; to thrust, presse, or beat forcibly into; also, to repeat, or vrge one thing verie often.*
Incurable: com. *Incurable, vnhealeable, in a desperate estate.*
Incurie: f. *Carelesnesse, retchlesnesse, negligence, improuidence.*
Incurieusement. *Vncuriously, plainely, after a homelie manner.*
Incuriosité: f. *Plainenesse, vnaffectation, bluntnesse.*
Incurrir. *To incurre; Looke* Encourir.
Incursion: f. *An incursion, inrode, forray, inuasion.*
Indagateur: m. *A diligent searcher.*
Indague: com. *Dishonest, vnworthie, filthie, base, vile.*
Indalgos. *A Gentleman.* ¶Rab.
Indamnisé: m. ée: f. *Indemnified, saued harmelesse.*
Indamniser. *To indemnifie, discharge, or saue harmelesse.*
Indannisser. *as* Indamniser.
Indar: m. *A Turkie Cocke.*
Indé: m. *Indico; light Blue, Blunket, Azure.*
Inde: f. *India, the Indies.*
D'Inde. *A Turkie Henne.*
Coq d'Inde. *A Turkie Cocke.*
Fourmi d'Inde. *The Indian Ant; a beast thats as big as a Wolfe.*
Fueille d'Inde. *Looke* Fueille.
Indecemment. *Vndecently, vnhandsomely, vncomelily; vnfitly, inconueniently.*
Indecent. *Vndecent, vnseemelie, vncomelie; vnfit, inconuenient, vnmeet.*
Indecentement. *as* Indecemment.
Indecis: m. ise: f. *Vndecided, vndetermined, not cleered, remaining yet in the decke.*
Indecision: f. *An vndecision; a doubtfull, vndetermined, or vnclecred state of things.*
Indecisions. *Are, in an Accompt,* les parties qui ne sont iugées, & decidées definitivement.
Indecrotable: com. *Alwaies durtie, euer dagled; or, so durtie as it will neuer be made cleane.*
Indefatigable: com. *Indefatigable, vnweariable, vntirable, not to be toyled out.*
Indegene: com. *Home-bred; borne, or growing within the same Territorie.*
Indelebile: com. *Indelible, vneffaceable, vnrazeable; that cannot be put, that will neuer weare, out.*
Indeleble. *as* Indelebile.
Indemné: m. ée: f. *as* Indemnisé.
Deniers indemnez. *About which no cost is bestowed, no paines imployed, which come in cleere to the purse.*
Indemne: com. *Harmelesse, cleered of all domage, exempt from hurt, or harme.*
Indemnisé: m. ée: f. *Indemnized, or indamnified; saued harmelesse; exempted, or freed from harme.*
Indemniser. *To indemnize, or indamnifie; to saue harmlesse; to exempt, or free, from harme.*
Indemnité: f. *Indemnitie; an auoiding of dammage, escape from hurt, exemption from harme.*
Droict, ou profit d'Indemnité. *The fine due vnto Landlords for Inheritance purchased by, or bestowed on, Churchmen: In some places it is the fift pennie of the purchase, or fift part of the value of the thing; in others, three yeares profit; in others, both that, and the sixt pennie, or part: Also, the fine due vnto the Lord of the soyle, wherein a villaine, that purchases his free-*

freedome of the King, resides; *also, as* Droict de Formariage.

Indeterminé: m. ée: f. *Vndetermined, vndecided.*

Indeu: m. euë: f. *Vndue*; *wrongfull, vniust*; *vnfit, vnmeet, vntimelie, vnseasonable.*

Indevidable: com. *Vnwindable, vnreelable.*

Indevot: m. ote: f. *Coldly deuoted, little affected vnto.*

Indevotion: f. *Lacke of deuotion, want of affection*; *cold respect, carelesse regard, of.*

Indication: f. *The Marke whereby a Surgeon is directed vnto the remedie that will best fit his Patient*; *also, a commending, or prizing of sale wares.*

Indice: m. *An Index, hand*; *marke, signe, token*; *plaine argument, great presumption, euident signification.*

Indicible: com. *Vnspeakable, vnexpresseable by words.*

Indiciblement. *Vnspeakably, vnexpresseably.*

Indict: m. cte: f. *Denounced, commaunded, appointed, imposed by authoritie.*

Indicte: m. *An indiction, imposition, denouncement, commaund, appointment.*

Indiction: f. *A tearme of 5, 10, or 15 yeares, vsed by the auncient Romanes in their numbring of yeares*; *also, an imposition, tax, or tallage.*

Indien: m. enne: f. *Jndian*; *of the Jndies.*

Sel Indien. *Sugar*; *Looke* Sel.

Indifferemment. *Indifferently, meanely, tollerably, so so*; *also, agreeably, without any difference.*

Indifferent. *Jndifferent, equall, tollerable, in a meane, betweene both*; *also, agreeing, or not differing.*

Indigence: f. *Indigence, lacke, penurie, needinesse, pouertie, want, necessitie.*

Indigent. *Indigent, needie, penurious, necessitous, lacking, in want.*

Indigeste: com. *Vndigestiue*; *that disgesteth not*; *also, indigested, vnorderlie, ill-disposed.*

Indigestible: com. *Vndisgestible*; *which cannot, or will not, be disgested.*

Indigestion: f. *Indisgestion, want of disgestion*; *rudenesse.*

Indignation: f. *Indignation, wrath, furie, chafing, fuming.*

Indigné: m. ée: f. *Wroth, wrathfull, fuming, much offended, in choler.*

Indigne: com. *Vnworthie, vndeseruing, of no merit, vile, base.*

Indignement. *Vnworthily, vndeseruingly, basely, vilely, without merit.*

Indigner. *To anger, chafe, driue into wrath, put into a fume*; *also, to malice.*

Indigneté: f. *Indignitie, disgrace*; *an affront*; *vnworthie vsage of.*

Indiguer. *as* Indiquer.

Indiligent. *Vndiligent, negligent, retchlesse, carelesse.*

Indiquer. *To shew, signifie, betoken, demonstrate, declare*; *also, to detect, bewray, disclose.*

Indire. *To publish, denounce, declare, bid, summon, proclaime.*

Indirect: m. cte: f. *Jndirect, not right, sinister, crooked, oblique, awry*; *also, crosse, trauers, ouerthwart, sidelong.*

Indirectement. *Indirectly, not rightly, crookedly, awry*; *wrongfully, by vnfit meanes.*

Indiscret. *Vndiscreet, inconsiderate, vnaduised, rash, haire-braind, headie, fond, witlesse.*

Indiscretement. *Vndiscreetly, inconsiderately, vnaduisedly, fondly, rashly, headily.*

Indiscretion: f. *Jndiscretion, inconsideration, vnaduisednesse, fondnesse, rashnesse, headinesse.*

Indisert. *Vneloquent*; *rude, or harsh, in discourse.*

Indisertement. *Vneloquently*; *rudely, grossely, harshly (in speech &c.)*

Indispos: m. ose: f. *as* Indisposé.

Indisposé: m. ée: f. *Sicklie, crazie, vnhealthfull, ill-disposed, ill at ease*; *also, disorderlie, ill-couched, ill-sorted*; *ill-fauoured.*

Indisposition: f. *Sicklinesse, crazinesse, vnhealthfullnesse, distemperature, indisposition of bodie.*

L'indisposition du temps. *Vntemperatenesse, or vnseasonablenesse, of weather.*

Indissolu: m. uë: f. *Vndissolued.*

Indissoluble: com. *Indissoluble, inseperable, vndissolueable.*

Indissolublement. *Indissolubly, inseperably, vndissolueably.*

Indistinct: m. cte: f. *Indistinct, vndistinguished, vndiuided, confused, budled.*

Indistinctement. *Indistinctly, confusedly, budling, on heapes.*

Indition: f. *A numbring or shewing of time, or of yeares*; *also, a marke, signe, token, or notice of.*

Individu: m. *An* Individuum, *or bodie inseperable*; *a Moat.*

Individu: m. uë: f. *Vndiuideable, inseperable.*

Individuité: f. *Indiuiduitie, inseperablenesse.*

Indivinable: com. *Vndiuinable, most obscure, not to be ghessed at.*

Indivis. Par indivis. *By Moats or* Individuums, *by parts or members vndiuidable.*

Indivisible: com. *Indiuisible, vndiuidable, inseperable, vnpartable.*

Indivisiblement. *Indiuisibly, vndiuidably, inseperably, vnpartably.*

Indocile: com. *Indocible, vnteachable, dull, blockish, dunsicall, heauie-headed, grosse-witted, vnapt to learne, vnfit to be taught.*

Indocte: com. *Vnlearned, vnskilfull, ignorant.*

Indoctement. *Vnlearnedly, ignorantly.*

Indoleance: f. *No apprehension of griefe, no feeling of sorrow*; *vnsenciblenesse of, or want of sence in, paine.*

Indomptable: com. *Vntameable.*

Indompté: m. ée: f. *Vntamed, vnbroken*; *vnrulie, wild, hagard, outragious.*

Indon. d'Indon. *A Turkie bird, Turkie chicke, young Turkie.*

Indubitable: com. *Vndoubtable, vndoubted, assured, certaine.*

Indubitablement. *Vndoubtedly, assuredly, certainly, without all question.*

Indubitamment. *as* Indubitablement.

Induce: f. *A truce, or cessation from warre (or from proceeding in a suit) for a certaine time agreed on by both parties*; *also, a Vacation, or the season wherein a Court sits not.*

Induction: f. *An induction, entrie, or leading into*; *also, an inducement, allurement, or persuasion, vnto*; *also, a forme of argument from particulars to vniuersalls.*

Induction d'une loy. *The application of a Law*; *or, the comparing it with some other*; *also, a collection made of, or conclusion drawne from, it.*

Induëment. *Vnduely, vniustly, vnmeetly, vnfitly, by sinister courses, wrongfull proceedings, vnworthie meanes.*

Induict: m. cte: f. *Induced, led, brought in*; *moued, persuaded, allured.*

Induire. *To induce, lead, bring in, or vnto; to moue, perswade, allure.*
Induire le cas d'une loy à vne autre. *To lay, or apply Law vnto Law; to conferre one Law with another.*
Induit. *as* Induict.
Indulgemment. *Indulgently, too mercifully.*
Indulgence: f. *Indulgence, tender-heartednesse; (ouermuch) mercie, or gentlenesse; too mild intreatie, or vsage; too much libertie giuen; hence, a Pardon from the Pope.*
Indulgent. *Indulgent; cockering, tender-hearted; ouergentle, or tractable; too much libertie-graunting, too mercifull, too mild.*
Indulgentieux: m. euse: f. *Full of indulgence.*
Indult: m. *A Pardon of Indulgence; the Popes Bull, or Licence, forgiuing or dispensing with sinnes, remitting or permitting offences.*
Indult. (Adject.) *Yong, not* adultus, *not yet of age.*
Indultaire: com. *One that hath an Indulgence, or Pardon, from the Pope.*
Industrie: f. *Industrie; diligence, vigilancie; actiue carefullnesse; indeauour; aptnesse vnto, readinesse in, any thing.*
s' Induſtrier. *To labour, indeauour, bestirre himselfe; make himselfe readie in, or apt for, an imployment.*
Induſtrieusement. *Industriously; diligently, vigilantly, heedfully; laboriously.*
Induſtrieux: m. euse: f. *Industrious; diligent, vigilant; indeauouring; laborious, painefull, heedie, readie.*
Ine. *as* Vne, *One*; ¶Poictevin.
Inécroulable. *as* Inescroulable.
Ineffable: com. *Ineffable, vnspeakeable, vnutterable; which no tongue can tell, no speech deliuer, no tearmes expresse.*
Ineffaçable: com. *Vneffaceable, vndefaceable; which no time nor violence can weare out.*
Ineffaceable. *The same.*
Inefficace: com. *Vneffectuall, forcelesse, vaine, idle, weake.*
Ineffroyable: com. *Not to be frighted, scarred, appalled.*
Inegalement. *as* Inegualement.
Inegal: m. ale: f. *Vnequall, vneuen; different, ill-matching, vnlike.*
Inegualement. *Vnequally, vneuenly; vnlikely, on different tearmes.*
Inegualité. *as* Inequalité.
Ineloquent. *Vneloquent, without eloquence.*
Inenarrable: com. *Wonderfull, vnspeakeable; vnexpressable by any tongue, or tearmes.*
Inepte: com. *Inept, vnapt; vnseasonable; fond, idle, vaine.*
Ineptement. *Ineptly, vnaptly; fondly, vainely, idly, childishly; vnseasonably.*
Ineptie: f. *Vnaptnesse, vnseasonablenesse; fondnesse, trifling, vainnesse, fopperie, childishnesse.*
Ineptitude. *as* Ineptie.
Inequalité: f. *Inequalitie, vneuennesse; disproportion, odds, difference, vnlikenesse.*
Inescroulable: com. *Vnshakeable, immoueable, steadie, not to be stirred.*
Inesperé: m. ée: f. *Vnhoped; vnexpected, vnlooked for.*
Inesperément. *Beyond all hope, or expectation; on a suddaine, at vnawares.*
Inespuisable: com. *Vndraynable; which cannot be dryed vp, or laden dry.*

Inevitable: com. *Ineuitable, vnauoidable; which no prouidence can put by.*
Inevitablement. *Ineuitably, vnauoidably.*
Inexcroulable: com. *as* Inescroulable.
Inexcusable: com. *Vnexcusable.*
Inexcusablement. *Vnexcusably.*
Inexecuté: m. ée: f. *Vnexecuted, vnperformed, vndone.*
Inexorable: com. *Inexorable, vnintreatable; churlish, obdurate.*
Inexplicable: com. *Inexplicable, vnfouldable, inextricable, vnexpressable, vndisplayable, vnexpoundable.*
Inexpugnable: com. *Vnexpugnable, impregnable; not to be forced, not to be battered.*
Inexterminable: com. *Vnexterminable; vnbanishable, not to be cast out; not to be destroyed.*
Inextinguible: com. *Vnextinguible, vnquenchable.*
Inextricable: com. *Inextricable, inexplicable, whereof one cannot be rid.*
Infaict: m. cte: f. *Infected; impoysoned; corrupted.*
Infaicté: m. ée: f. *as* Infaict.
Infaicter. *To infect; impoison; corrupt.*
Infaire. *as* Infaicter.
Infallibilité: f. *Infallibilitie, or infalliblenesse; certaintie, assurance.*
Infallible: com. *Infallible, certaine, assured.*
Infalliblement. *Infallibly, without faile.*
Infamé: m. ée: f. *Infamed, defamed, discredited, shamed.*
Infame: com. *Infamous, ignominious, opprobrious, disgracefull, reproachfull; also, defamed, detected, tainted, shamed, verie ill spoken of.*
Infamément. *Infamously, ignominiously, opprobriously, reproachfully, disgracefully.*
Infamer. *To infame, defame, shame, traduce, discredit, reproach, disgrace; to speake badly, report vilely, of.*
Infameté: f. *A disgrace, discredit, imputation, infamous report.*
Infamie: f. *Infamie, obloquie, ignominie, dishonour, disgrace, discredit, reproach; detection; a defamation; an imputation.*
Infante. L'In. *The Title of a daughter of Spaine.*
Infanterie: f. *The Infanterie, or footmen of an Armie.*
Infanticide: com. *Child-murthering, infant-killing.*
Infantile: com. *as* Infantin.
Infantin: m. ine: f. *Infantine, childish; yong, tender.*
Infatigable: com. *as* Indefatigable.
Infatué: m. ée: f. *Gulled, besotted, made foolish.*
Infatuer. *To gull, besot, make foolish.*
Infauste: com. *Vnfortunate, vnluckie, vnhappie, dismall, ominous, dire.*
Infecond: m. de: f. *Vnfertill, vnfruitfull.*
Infecondité: f. *Infecunditie, vnfertillnesse, vnfruitfullnesse.*
Infect: m. cte: f. *Infect, infected, infectious.*
Infecté: m. ée: f. *Infected; poisoned; depraued, corrupted.*
Infecter. *To infect; poison; depraue, corrupt.*
Infection: f. *Infection, contagion.*
Infectionner. *as* Infecter; *or, to fill with infection.*
Infecundité. *Looke* Infecondité.
Infeodation: f. *An infeoffing.*
Infeodé: m. ée: f. *Infeoffed; seised in fee; also, graunted, aliened, or setled, in fee.*
Dismes infeodées; *impropriations of tythes.*
Rente infeodée. *A Rent-charge; a rent wherewith land is charged for euer.*
Inferé: m. ée: f. *Inferred, implyed, concluded vpon things*

things put, or gathered, together; signified, shewed, alledged, giuen to vnderstand.
Inferer. *To inferre, imply, conclude vpon things put, or gathered, together; to signifie, shew, alledge, giue to vnderstand.*
Inferieur: m. re: f. *Inferior; lower, nether; vnderling; more base, of smaller value, of lesse meanes.*
Infertile: com. *Infertill, vnfruitfull.*
Infertilité: f. *Infertilitie, vnfruitfullnesse.*
Infestation: f. *Infestation, molestation, annoyance, noysomnesse; also, a rauaging, wasting, spoyling.*
Infesté: m. ée: f. *Infested, annoyed, molested; rauaged.*
Infester. *To infest, annoy, molest; rauage, wast, or vex with frequent, and violent incursions.*
Infeudation: f. *An infeoffing.*
Infeudé: m. ée: f. *as* Infeodé.
Infeuder. *To infeoffe; to passe, or graunt in fee; also, to put, or admit, into the possession of an Inheritance.*
Infiable: com. *Trustlesse, vntrustie, faithlesse.*
Infibulation: f. *A buttoning, buckling, or clasping together; also, the ringing of the priuie parts.*
Inficiation: f. *An inficiation, disaffirmation, denyall.*
Infidele: com. *Infidell; faithlesse, vnfaithfull, false, disloyall, trecherous.*
Infidelité: f. *Infidelitie, faithlesnesse, vnfaithfullnesse, disloyaltie, trecherie.*
Infiguré: m. ée: f. *Infigured, figured; marked, or noted, with a figure.*
Infini: m. ie: f. *Infinite, endlesse; innumerable; vnmeasurable.*
Infiniement. *Infinitely, endlessly.*
Infinité: f. *Infiniteneße, endlesnesse; innumerablenesse, vnmeasurablenesse.*
Infinitude: f. *as* Infinité.
Infirmatif: m. iue: f. *Infirmatiue; weakening, infeebling; disannulling, disallowing.*
Infirmer. *To weaken, infeeble; dissolue; confute; disannull, disallow.*
Infirmité. f. *Infirmitie, weakenesse, feeblenesse; crazinesse; also, maladie, sicknesse.*
Inflammable: com. *Inflamable, burneable.*
Inflammation: f. *An inflamation, firing, burning; a blistering heat; a kindling, an incensing.*
Inflation: f. *An inflation; a windie swelling, or puffing vp.*
Inflechissable: com. *as* Inflexible.
Inflexible: com. *Inflexible, vnbowable, vntractable, vnrelentable, hard-hearted.*
Inflictif: m. iue: f. *Inflictiue, inflicting; or, of propertie to inflict.*
Influence: f. *A flowing in; (and particularly) an influence, or influent course, of the Planets; their vertue infused into, or their course working on, inferior creatures.*
Influer. *To flow, runne, enter, or sinke, into.*
Infoliature. *Boscage, or leafe-worke, in caruing &c.*
Infondre. *To infuse; to fill in; to put, or powre, into; also, to steepe.*
Inforçable: com. *Vnforcible, vnexpugnable, impregnable.*
Informateur: m. *An Informer, Promooter; searcher, inquirer, inquisitor.*
Information: f. *An information; instruction; search, quest, inquisition, enquest; examination.*
Informé: m. ée: f. *Informed; instructed in; examined, searched, or inquired after; also, informed against; also, vnformed, vnmade, vnfashioned.*
Informe: com. *Informe, shapelesse, ill-fauoured, fashionlesse; ouglie, rude.*
Informer. *To informe, instruct, giue notice of; also, as;*
S'Informer. *To search, inquire, examine, get information of, make inquisition after.*
Infortiat: m. *One of the three Volumes of the* Pandects.
Infortune: f. *Misfortune, misaduenture, mishap, mischance, calamitie; a disaster.*
Infortuné: m. ée: f. *Vnfortunate, vnhappie, vnluckie, successelesse, disastrous.*
Infortunément. *Vnfortunately, vnhappily, vnluckily, successlesly, disasterously.*
Infracteur: m. *An infringer, violater, breaker of.*
Infraction: f. *as* Infracture.
Infracture: f. *An infracture, infringement, violation, breach.*
Infrangible: com. *Infrangible, vnbreakable; inuincible.*
Infrasqué: m. ée: f. *Intricated, pestered, intangled.*
Infrasquer. *To intricate, pester, intangle; also, to feed with vaine hopes, to fet in or fetch ouer.*
Infrequence: f. *Vnfrequencie, solitarinesse, a small assemblie.*
Infrequent. *Vnfrequent, seldome haunting, little resorting to, much absent from; also, vnfrequented.*
Infructueusement. *Fruitlesly, vnfruitfully.*
Infructueux: m. euse: f. *Fruitlesse, vnfruitfull, barren, sterill, vnprofitable.*
Infus: m. use: f. *Infused, filled in, powred into, or vpon; also, steeped.*
Infuser. *To infuse, fill in, powre vpon; also, to steepe.*
Infusion: f. *An infusion; powring, or filling in; and (in Phisicke) a conueyance of some liquid medicine into the bodie by Clister, or other instrument; also, a steeping of drugs, &c, in a conuenient liquor; also, the liquor wherein they haue beene so steeped.*
Ingambé: m. ée: f. *Light-legd, nimble-heeled, fast-running, swift of foot.*
Ingargouillat: m. *The crosse point (in dauncing.)*
Ingenier. *To bend his wits vnto, or beat his braines about, the deuising of a thing.*
Ingenieur: m. *An Enginer, Engine-maker; Fortifier.*
Ingenieusement. *Ingeniously, wittily, with good inuention.*
Ingenieux: m. *as* Ingenieur.
Ingenieux: m. euse: f. *Ingenious, wittie, inuentiue, sharpe-witted, nimble-headed.*
Ingeniosité: f. *Ingeniositie, ingeniousnesse, quicknesse of inuention, dexteritie of wit.*
Ingenuë: com. *Ingenuous, open-hearted, free, liberall, nobly affected.*
Ingenuement. *Ingenuously; frankly, freely, liberally, with an open heart, and hand.*
Ingenuité: f. *Ingenuitie, ingenuousnesse; noblenesse, franknesse, gallantnesse of humor; an open, honest, franke, or liberall disposition.*
Ingeré: m. ée: f. *Thrust in, put on; vndertaken, or taken vpon; intruded, insinuated; put forth.*
s'Ingerer. *To thrust in, put on, offer or put forth, himselfe (vndesired) to intrude, insinuate himselfe into, take vpon him, a matter.*
Inglorieux: m. euse: f. *Inglorious; base, obscure, vnknowne, of no reputation, glorie, renowme.*
Ingrat: m. ate: f. *Vngratefull, thanklesse, vnthankfull, vnmindfull of benefits receiued.*
Ingratitude: f. *Ingratitude, vngratefulnesse, vnthankfulnesse.*
Ingravé: m. ée: f. *Ingrauen, intayled.*

In-

Ingraver. To ingraue, or intaile.

Ingredient: m. An Ingredient; a beginning, or entrance; also (in Phisicke) a simple put into a compound medicine, or vsed, among others, in the making thereof.

Inguerdonné: m. ée: f. Vnguerdoned, vnrecompenced.

Inguerissable: com. Incurable, vnhealable.

Inguine: m. The gryne, or groine.

Ingurgité: m. ée. f. Ingulfed; swill'd, or swallowed in; greedily deuoured.

Ingurgiter. To ingulfe; to swill, or swallow in; also, to rauine, or deuoure greedily.

Inhabile: com. Vnable, vnsufficient; weake; vnfit, vnmeet for; vnweldie, vneasie, vnhandsome; idle; sottish.

Inhabilement. Vnably, vnsufficiently; weakely; vnweldily, vneasily, vnhandsomely; vnaptly, vnfitly; sottishly.

Inhabilitation: f. A disabling.

Inhabilité: f. Disabilitie, insufficiencie, weakenesse; vnfitnesse, vnaptnesse, vnweldinesse; sottishnesse, want of braines.

Inhabilité: m. ée: f. Disabled, made vnable.

Inhabilitement: m. A disabling.

Inhabiliter. To disable; to make vnable.

Inhabitable: com. Vnhabitable; desert, sauage; which cannot be abid in, or dwelt on; also, inhabitable.

Inhabité: m. ée: f. Vnhabited; also, inhabited.

Inhabiter. To inhabit, reside, or dwell on.

Inhabitué: m. ée: f. Vnaccustomed, vnenured vnto; disused from.

Inherence: f. An inherence; a cleauing, sticking, ioyning close in, or vnto.

Inhibé: m. ée: f. Inhibited, forbidden; hindered, withheld.

Inhiber. To inhibit, forbid; stay, stop, or withhold.

Inhibition: f. An inhibition, forbidding; countermaund, stop, withholding.

Inhonneste: com. Dishonest, vnhonest, naughtie, lewd.

Inhonnestement. Dishonestly, vnhonestly, naughtily, lewdly.

Inhospitable: com. Vnhospitable, harbourlesse; churlish; no lodger of passengers, no intertainer of strangers, no housekeeper.

Inhumain: m. aine: f. Inhumane, vngentle, discourteous, vnciuill; beastlie, cruell, rude; barbarous.

Inhumainement. Inhumanely, vngently, discourteously, vnciuilly; beastly, cruelly, rudely, barbarously.

Inhumanité: f. Inhumanitie, vngentlenesse, inciuilitie, beastlinesse, crueltie, rudenesse, barbarousnesse.

Inhumation: f. A burying, an interring.

Inhumé: m. ée: f. Buried, interred, put into the ground.

Inhumer. To burie, interre, lay in a graue, put into the ground.

Inian. By S. Iohn (a childish Oath;) ¶Rab.

Inidoine: com. Vnapt, vnmeet, vnfit, improper, inconuenient, insufficient, incommodious.

Injectement. as Injection.

Injection: f. An iniection; a casting in, or vpon; also (in Phisicke) a squirting, or conueying of a liquid medicine, by Siringe, &c, into some part of the bodie, or into a hollow and fistulous vlcer.

Inimaginable: com. Vnimaginable, vnconceiueable, incomprehensible.

Inimitable: com. Vnimitable; incomparable; which cannot be followed.

Inimitié: f. Enmitie, hostilitie, hatred, fiud, strife, discord, variance.

Injonction: f. An Iniunction, or forbidding; a commaund importing an absolution, inhibition, or stay of proceeding.

Inique: com. Vnequall, vnindifferent, partiall, wrong, vniust; vnreasonable; vnrighteous, naughtie, wicked, impious.

Iniquement. Vnequally, vniustly, wrongfully, partially; vnreasonably, without cause; vnrighteously, wickedly, impiously.

Iniquité: f. Iniquitie; inequalitie, iniustice, wrong, partialitie; vnreasonablenesse; vnrighteousnesse, naughtinesse, impietie, wickednesse.

Initié: m. ée: f. Initiated, entered into, begun in; admitted of.

Initier. To initiate, enter into, begin in; giue the first instruction, lay a ground or foundation for; giue orders vnto; licence, or admit of, a societie.

Injure: f. Iniurie, wrong, misusage, an abuse, or affront offered; a trespasse, displeasure, offence, despight, or outrage done.

Injurié: m. ée: f. Iniured, wronged, misused, abused; outraged; miscalled, reproached, reuiled, rayled on.

Injurier To wrong, iniure, misuse, abuse; hurt, offend; outrage; miscall, reproach, reuile, rayle on.

Injurieur: m. An iniurer, a wronger.

Injurieusement. Iniuriously, wrongfully, offensiuely; outragiously, spightfully, reproachfully, contumeliously.

Injurieux: m. euse: f. Iniurious; wrongfull, abusiue, offensiue; outragious; despightfull; contumelious, reproachfull.

Injurieux en tripiere. Foule-mouthed like a Tripe-wife.

Injuste: com. Vniust, partiall, vnequall, iniurious, wrongfull, vnreasonable.

Injustement. Vniustly, partially, vnequally, iniuriously, wrongfully, vnreasonably.

Injustice: f. Iniustice, partialitie, wrong, hard measure.

Innavigable: com. Innauigable; that cannot be sayled in.

Inné: m. ée: f. Innate; borne, or bred in.

Innocemment. Innocently, guiltlesly, faultlesly, harmelesly, sillily, without any offence.

Innocence: f. Innocencie, guiltlesnesse, vnguiltinesse, harmelesnesse, integritie, sillinesse.

Innocence porte sa defense: Pro. Innocence beares it owne defence.

Innocent Innocent, Ninnie (a proper name for a man) whence;

Herbe de S. Innocent. Centinodie, Bloudwort, male Knot-grasse, Birds-tongue, Swines-grasse.

Innocent. Innocent, faultlesse, guiltlesse, harmelesse, without offence.

Le iour des innocents. Childermas day in Christmas.

Parchemin innocent. Parchment made of an abortiue skinne.

Donner les Innocens. as Innocenter.

Innocenter. To breech, whip, lash, (on Childermas, or Innocents, day; when the Papists of France haue a merrie custome, to ierke all such as they can find in bed, or others whose breech they may otherwise easily come at.)

Innombrable: com. Innumerable, vnnumerable.

Innomme. Contract innomme. An equall exchange of

of money, and land giuen onely for land.
Innovateur: m. *An innouator; a bringer in of new customes, &c.*
Innovation: f. *Innouation; alteration, change of old, for new, fashions.*
Innové: m. ée: f. *Innouated; altered from old vnto new.*
Innover. *To innouate; alter, change; bring vp new customes, bring in vnwonted fashions.*
Innumerable: com. *Innumerable, vnnumberable.*
Innumerablement. *Innumerably, vnnumberably.*
Innumerableté: f. *Innumerablenesse.*
Inobedience: f. *Disobedience, lacke of obedience.*
Inobedient. *Disobedient, vnobedient, wanting obedience.*
Inoffencible: com. *Inoffencible, not to be hurt.*
Inofficieux: m. euse: f. *Vnofficious, vnobseruant, vnseruiceable, vnrespectfull, vnkind.*
Inofficiosité: f. *Vnofficiousnesse, vnrespectiuenesse, or want of due respect; whence,* Querelle d'inoff. *A suit commenced by Orphans, &c, whose parents haue, by their Wills, giuen from them all they had, or giuen them lesse then by custome, and the right of their birth, was due vnto them; as where a man bequeathes all, or the most part of, his estate vnto his children by a second venter, neglecting those he had by a former wife, though they be as toward, and well-deseruing, as the others.*
Inondation: f. *An inundation, deluge, ouerflowing, surrounding.*
Inondé: m. ée: f. *Ouerflowne, surrounded, ouerwhelmed with water.*
Inonder. *To ouerflow; ouerwhelme, surround.*
Inopie: f. *Lacke, need, want, scarcitie, penurie, pouertie.*
Inopiné: m. ée: f. *Vnthought of, suddaine, vnawares.*
Inopinement. *On a suddaine, at vnawares, sooner then was thought, ere it was looked for.*
Inquant: m. *The place wherein things are sold by Outrope, or Outcry.*
Droict d'inquant. *Fiue in the hundred due vnto the King (vpon things sold by Outrope) in some parts of* Provence.
Inquanter. *To sell, or passe away at an Outcry.*
Inquietation: f. *A disquieting, disturbing, diseasing, vexing, molesting, troubling.*
Inquieté: m. ée: f. *Disquieted, diseased; vexed, annoyed, molested; disturbed, troubled; also, busie, restlesse, troublesome.*
Inquietement. *Vnquietly, restlesly, troublesomely.*
Inquieter. *To disquiet, disease, trouble, disturbe, vex, molest, annoy; giue small ease, or little rest vnto.*
Inquieteur: m. *A disquieter, troubler, disturber, annoyer, vexer, molester.*
Inquietude: f. *Disquiet, vnquietnesse, trouble, molestation, vnrest, carke, disease.*
Inquilin: m. *A Tenant; Lodger; Inmate; he that takes, or dwells in, a house (or part of a house) wherein neither he, nor his auncestors were borne.*
Inquisiteur: m. *An Inquisitor, strict searcher, seuere examiner; one of the Holie house, or Spanish Inquisition.*
Inquisition: f. *An inquisition; diligent search, or inquirie, strict examination.*
Inracinable: com. *Which cannot be rooted, which will not take root.*
Insail: m. *The Rudder, or Sterne of a Ship.* ¶Rab.
Insalubre: com. *Vnhealthfull, vnholesome; infectiue, corrupt, noysome.*
Insalubrité: f. *Vnhealthfullnesse, vnholesomenesse; corruption, infection.*
Insatiabilité: f. *Insatietie, vnsatiablenesse.*
Insatiable: com. *Insatiate, vnsatiable, vnfillable; rauenous, gluttonous, that neuer hath enough.*
Insatiablement. *Insatiately, vnsatiably.*
Insatiableté: f. *Insatietie, vnsatiablenesse; greedinesse, gluttonie, rauenousnesse.*
Insceu. à l'insceu de luy. *Vnwittingly to him; wherewith he was neuer made acquainted.*
Insciemment. *Vnwittingly, ignorantly, vnskilfully, vnknowingly, for want of knowledge.*
Inscience: f. *Vnskilfullnesse, ignorance, want of knowledge.*
Inscophié. *Looke* Inscrophié.
Inscript: m. ipte: f. *Inscribed, intituled, written on; graued, pourtrayed, printed in.*
Inscription: f. *An inscription, superscription, title, note, marke (written, or ingrauen.)*
Inscription en faux. *A challenge of, or exception against, the truth of an Euidence; a testimonie, or vndertaking to proue it false, entred in Court.*
Inscrire. *To inscribe, intitle, title, write in, or vpon; also, to graue, print, or pourtray vpon.*
S'Inscrire à faux, ou en faux, contre; *To enter a challenge against; or, as in* Faux.
Inscrit. *as* Inscript.
Inscrophié. Cheueux inscrophiez. *Haire turned vp after the neatest manner.* ¶Rab.
Inscrutable: com. *Inscrutable, vnsearchable; bottomelesse; misticall; not to be sounded; no way to be sought out.*
Insculpé: m. ée: f. *Insculped, ingraued, intayled.*
Insculper. *To insculpe, ingraue, intayle.*
Insectable: com. *Not to be cut; not to be diuided.*
Insecte: m. *An Insect; a small fleshlesse, and bloudlesse vermine, diuided (in some sort) betweene the head, bodie, and bellie, as an Ant, Fly, Bee, &c; vnder which, the Earthworme, Caterpiller, &c, be also comprehended.*
Insectible: com. *Insectible; or, as* Insectable.
Insensé: m. ée: f. *Mad, wood, raging, furious; vnreasonable, witlesse.*
Insensible: com *Insensible, sencelesse, vnfeeling; also, vnpalpable, vnfeelable.*
Insensibilité: f. *Sencelesnesse, vnsencibleneße.*
Inseperable: m. com. *Inseperable, vndiuidable.*
Inseperablement. *Inseperably.*
Inseré: m. ée: f. *Inserted; ingraffed; set, put, entred, or brought in; added, or ioyned vnto; mixed, or mingled with.*
Inserer. *To insert; ingraffe; set, put, enter, or bring in; add, or ioyne vnto; mix, or mingle with.*
Insidiation: f. *Guile, trecherie, deceitfullnesse; a lying in wait for; a laying of snares, a practising of wyles, to deceiue withall.*
Insidieux: m. euse: f. *Deceitfull, trecherous, insnaring, intrapping, lying in wait for.*
Insigne: m. *as* Enseigne.
Insigne: com. *Notable, notorious; famous, renowmed; apparant, goodlie, of marke.*
Insimulé: m. ée: f. *Accused of, charged with.*
Insinuation: f. *An insinuation; also, a registring, or entring into a Register booke.*
Insinué: m. ée: f. *Insinuated; crept, wound, or stolne into; gently, or closely incroached vpon; also, entred into a Register, or Office booke.*

Insinuer. *To enter; to register; or, to enter into a Register, or Office-booke; or (as a French Lawyer describes it)* publier, & notifier par Acte par devant le Iuge; qui ordonne en estre faict Registre.

S' Insinuer en. *To insinuate; creepe, wind, steale, conuey, himselfe into; gently to intrude, closely to incroach vpon.*

Insipide: com. *Vnsauorie, smacklesse, wallowish, without relish; also, weake of iudgement, or in discourse, fond, vndiscreet.*

Insipidité: f. *Insipiditie, wallowishnesse, vnsauourinesse, dullnesse in tast, want of smacke; also, fondnesse, indiscretion, weakenesse of iudgement, or in discourse.*

Insipience: f. *Dotage, indiscretion, sottishnesse, ideotisme, ignorance.*

Insipient. *Sottish, doting, witlesse, vndiscreet, foolish, ignorant.*

Insister. *To insist on; to vrge hard, stand much vpon, a matter; to labour, sollicite, pursue eagerly, be earnest with, or vpon; also, to rest, persist, abide fast, continue firmely.*

Insociable: com. *Vnsociable, vncompanable, inconuersible, incompatible.*

Insolation: f. *A sunning; a setting, or laying open, in the Sunne.*

Insolemment. *Insolently, malapertly, sawcily, presumptuously, arrogantly.*

Insolence: f. *Insolencie, sawcinesse, malapertnesse, presumption, arrogance.*

Insolent: m. te: f. *Insolent, malapert, sawcie, presumptuous, arrogant.*

Insolide: com. *Vnsolide, vnsound; loose, weake, feeble.*

Les Obligations du defunct sont insolides contre tous les heritiers; viz. *All the heires are not lyable vnto them; (yet may the Creditor addresse himselfe vnto any one of them.)*

Insolidement. *Vnsoundly, vnsolidely, weakely, feebly; also, throughly, wholly, for the whole.*

Insolite: com. *Strange, vnused, vnaccustomed, vnwont.*

Insolu: m. uë: f. *Vnpayed, vndischarged, vndefrayed.*

Insolvable: com. *Vnpayable, vnlikelie to be payed; also, vnapt, or vnable to pay.*

Insoluble: com. *Insoluble, indissoluble, vndissoluable.*

Inspecteur: m. *An inspector, ouerseer, controller; one that narrowly obserues, or pries into, mens behauior.*

Inspection: f. *An inspection; speculation; ouerseeing; prying, or looking into; viewing, or looking on.*

Insperé: m. ée: f. *Vnhoped for; vnlooked after.*

Insperément. *as* Inesperément.

Insperse: m. ee: f. *Inspersed; sprinckled, or cast vpon.*

Inspiration: f. *An inspiration, or inspiring; a blowing, or breathing into; an instinct.*

Inspiré: m. ée: f. *Inspired; moued; blowne, or breathed into.*

Inspirer. *To inspire; breath into; moue.*

Instabilité: f. *Instabilitie, vnsteadinesse, vnstedfastnesse; fickleneße, inconstancie, wauering, variablenesse.*

Instable: com. *Vnstable, vnsteadie, tottering, shittle, vnstedfast; flitting, wauering, fickle, skittish, inconstant.*

Instablement. *Vnstably, vnsteadily, totteringly, vnsetledly, vnstedfastly.*

Installation: f. *An installation, or installing; the setling of an Officer.*

Installé: m. ée: f. *Installed; setled, established, placed surely in.*

Installer. *To install; to settle, establish, place surely in.*

Instamment. *Instantly; earnestly, vrgently, importunately; diligently, inceßantly.*

Instance: f. *Instance, earnestnesse, vrgencie, importunitie, continuall diligence; also (in Law) a cause, or point in a cause, contested.*

En premiere instance. *At first, of the first ranke, in chiefe, or in the first degree, before all others.*

Faire instance sur. *To vrge vehemently, to stand much vpon.*

Faire l'instance. C'est, debatre la chose.

Instant: m. *An instant, point, moment.*

Instauration: f. *An instauration; restoring, renewing, repairing, reedifying.*

Instauré: m. ée: f. *Restored, renewed, repaired, reedified.*

Instaurer. *To restore, renew, reforme; reedifie, repaire.*

Instigateur: m. *An instigator; stirrer, incitor, vrger, egger on, prouoker, pricker forward; In Law,* Se prend generalement, & pour celuy qui seulemét se plaind sans se rendre partie; & pour celuy qui instruict l' accusation, donnant des preuves, & poursuyvant l' instruction du procez.

Instigation: f. *An instigation, stirring, inciting, vrging; a pricke, spurre, prouocation, strong motion vnto.*

Instigué: m. ée: f. *Instigated, incited, vrged.*

Instiguer. *To instigate, incite, stirre, vrge, egg, spurre on, pricke forward.*

Instillation: f. *An instillation; a gentle infusion; a letting, or falling, in drop by drop; a putting, or powring in by little and little.*

Instiller. *To drop, trill, drizle; gently to inforce; to let, or fall, in drop by drop; to put in, or powre on by little and little.*

Instinct: m. *An instinct, or inclination; an inward stirring, motion, or persuasion; an inspiration.*

Institué: m. ée: f. *Instituted, enacted, ordained, established, appointed, brought in, set vp.*

Instituer. *To institute, enact, ordaine, decree, establish, appoint; bring in, begin, set vp.*

Institutaire. *(A Title of the Emperour* Iustinian, *who writ the Institutes of the Ciuill Law.)*

Institute: m. Iustinians *Booke of Institutes.*

Institution: f. *An Institution; Precept; Ordinance, Decree, Statute, Establishment; an ordaining, appointing, setting vp, or bringing in.*

Instruction: f. *An instruction, direction, document, precept; caueat; memoriall, remembrance; also, instruction, teaching, tutoring, ordering.*

Instructive: f. *as* Instruction.

Instruer. *as* Instruire.

Instruict: m. cte: f. *Instructed, taught, tutored; directed; forewarned; furnished, well appointed; also, suborned.*

Vn procez instruict. *A Cause made readie for hearing.*

Instruire. *To teach, tutor, instruct; forewarne, direct; fashion, traine vp; furnish with matter; prompt, suborne.*

Instruire vn procez. *To furnish it, or make it fit, for a Hearing.*
Instruisable: com. *Instructable, teachable, docible.*
Instrument: m. *An Instrument; Implement, Engine, Toole; also, a Deed, Euidence, Conueyance; an Information, or Instruction, in writing; also, a meane, aid, helpe, direction in a matter.*
Instrumental: m. ale: f. *Instrumentall, vsed as an Instrument, applyed as a meanes.*
Instrumenter. *To draw, and ingrosse an Instrument, Conueyance, Euidence.*
Instrumentier: m. *A certaine Vine-deuouring vermine, so called, because it makes the Vine leafe (wherein it vsually wraps it selfe) looke like to a rowle of Parchement.*
Insuave: com. *Vnsweet, vnpleasant.*
Insubstantiel: m. elle: f. *Vnsubstantiall; light, idle, vaine.*
Insuffisamment. *Insufficiently.*
Insuffisance: f. *Insufficiencie, disabilitie, weakenesse, vnfitnesse.*
Insuffisant. *Insufficient, vnable; weake, vnfit.*
Insulain: m. *An Ilander, or Iland-man.*
Insulaire: com. *Insular, Iland-like; of, or belonging to, an Iland.*
Insult: m. *An assault, affront, brauado, open wrong.*
Insulter. *To insult, crow, vaunt, or triumph ouer; to wrong, reproach, affront; contemne; also, to rebound, reioice at, leape for ioy.*
Insuperable: com. *Insuperable, vnvanquishable, inuincible.*
Insupportable: com. *Vnsupportable, intollerable, not to be borne.*
Insurger. *To rise vp against, or oppose himselfe vnto; also, to trauell earnestly, mainely to inforce himselfe.*
Insurmontable: com. *Vnsurmountable, vnexceedable, vnsurpassable, vnvanquishable.*
Insuyvre. *To pursue, or follow hard vpon.*
Intarissable: com. *Not to be withered, or dryed vp.*
Integralité: f. *Integralitie, wholenesse.*
Integré: m. ée: f. *Integrated, perfected, made whole.*
Integrité: f. *Integritie, soundnesse; honestie, sinceritie, innocencie, vprightnesse.*
Intellect: m. *The intellect; the vertue, or facultie, of vnderstanding; also, vnderstanding, apprehension, capacitie; iudgement, knowledge, discretion.*
Intellectuel: m. elle: f. *Intellectuall, apprehensiue, vnderstanding.*
Intelligence: f. *Vnderstanding, apprehension, capacitie, conceit, sence, discretion, iudgement; also, intelligence; priuate notice of occurrences giuen, or gotten, (by) priuate intercourse, or correspondencie held with.*
Cela est de son intelligence. *Is done by his priuate appointment, or direction.*
Intelligencier: m. *An Intelligencer; an intelligence-giuer; a Spy.*
Intelligent. *Vnderstanding, apprehensiue, of good capacitie.*
Intelligible: com. *Intelligible, plaine, perspicuous, easie to be vnderstood.*
Intelligiblement. *Intelligibly, perspicuously, vnderstandingly.*
Intemperance: f. *Intemperance, immoderation, vnstayednesse, vnbridlednesse, vnrulinesse, outragiousnesse.*
Intemperance de l'air. *Vnseasonablenesse of the ayre, or weather.*
Intemperature: f. *Intemperature, or distemperature of the bodie; vnseasonablenesse, or foulenesse of weather.*
Intemperé: m. ée: f. *Intemperate, immoderate, vnstayed, vnbridled, vnorderlie, disordinate, outragious, vnrulie.*
Intemperément. *Intemperately, immoderately, vnstayedly, vnorderedly, disordinately, outragiously, vnrulily.*
Intempestif: m. iue: f. *Intempestiue, vntimelie, abortiue, vnseasonable; also, disordered, vnreasonable; also, vnluckie, or ill-presaging.*
Intempestivement. *Intempestiuely, vnseasonably, abortiuely; vnreasonably; out of course; also, vnluckily.*
Intendance: f. *An ouersight; a gouernment, or charge ouer.*
Intendants des finances. *The (foure) Ouerseers, or Controllers of the Exchequer; at first brought in by King* Francis *the first:* (Ont superintendance sur le Thresorier de l'espargne; des parties casuelles; de l'ordinaire & extraordinaire des guerres; de l'artillerie; de la marine; des officiers domestics; & autres qui ne sont sous la charge des Thresoriers de France, sur lesquels aussi ils ont intendance, & peuvent reformer leurs estats par estimation. ¶Rageau.)
Intendit: m. *A principall allegation, proofe, or deposition; writings, or bookes, wherein the chiefe, or maine points of a suit are contained.*
Intenté: m. ée: f. *Attempted, tryed, essayed, proued; also, intended, meant, purposed; also, commenced, begun, brought, or moued, as a suit.*
Intenter. *To attempt, proue, essay, trie; also, to intend, meane, purpose; also, to commence, begin, moue, bring, or set on foot (a suit.)*
Intenteur: m. *An intender; an attempter; also, the beginner of a suit.*
Intention: f. *An intention, intent, purpose, drift, meaning, will, mind.*
Interbasté: m. ée: f. *Interbasted; basted, or quilted betweene.*
Intercalaire: com. *Interlaced; put, or set betweene.*
Iour intercalaire. *The odd day of a Leape yeare, which falleth euerie fourth yeare.*
Intercalation: f. *An interlacing; a setting, or putting of an odd thing betweene euen ones.*
Intercaler. *To interlace; to put, or set (as the odd day of a Leape yeare) betweene.*
Interceder pour. *To intercede, mediate, intreat, sue, solicite; also, to vndertake, or giue his word, for.*
Intercepter. *To intercept, forestall, take vp, or make stay of, by the way.*
Intercesseur: m. *An intercessor, mediator, intreater, suitor, or suretie, for another.*
Intercession: f. *Intercession, mediation, intreatie, or suit for another.*
Interclaire: com. *as* Intercalaire.
Intercostal: m. ale: f. *Betweene the ribs.*
Veine intercostale. *A branch of the hollow veine, which feeds the spaces betweene the three highest ribs.*
Interdict: m. *An interdiction, prohibition, iniunction; also (in Law) a determination, or order in Court, for the possession of a thing in controuersie.*

Interdict: m. cte: f. *Interdicted, prohibited, inhibited, forbidden, inioyned to the contrarie.*
Interdiction: f. *An interdiction, prohibition, inhibition, iniunction, forbidding.*
Interdire. *To interdict, probibit, forbid, inioyne, or giue charge to the contrarie.*
Interessé: m. ée: f. *Interessed, or touched in; dishonoured, hurt, or hindered by; wronged, grieued, pained.*
Interessé de sa personne. *Of a weake, faint, crazie, or sicklie bodie.*
La partie civile, & interessée. *Looke* Partie.
Interest: m. *An interest in, a right or title vnto, a thing; also, interest, or vse for money, &c, lent; also, losse, dammage, hurt; hinderance, wrong, sustained in reputation, or estate; or (as a French Lawyer describes it) the losse one hath vndergone, or proff he hath failed of, by the default of another; and hereof he makes two kinds; viz.*
L'Interest conventionnel. Celuy qui est promis par convention, & contract fait entre les parties, ou vient de la nature du contract, & est appellé vsure au Droict Romain.
Interest iudiciaire: Qui vient de l'office du Iuge, ou est adiugé par iceluy. *This is double; viz.* celuy qui procede de la nature de la cause; (& vient des poursuittes temeraires, fuites, calomnies, ou tergiversations de la partie adverse; qui ont esté cause de faire à celuy qui a obtenu plusieurs frais vains, & inutiles, lesquels ne viennent en taxe de despens:) Et celuy qui prent origine de la chose mesme qui est controuersée, & à esté souffert à cause d'icelle; comme execution, emprisonnement, trouble, spoliation, refus de tradition de la chose, &c; *Hence,* Les dommages, & interests.
Ie y ay grand interest. *It neerely concernes, or touches me.*
Il n'y a pas grand interest en cela. *It greatly boots not, it is not a pinne matter.*
Interject: m. *An interposition; a speech put in, a word cast betweene.*
Interjecter. *To interiect, or interpose; to cast, put, set, betweene, or among; to bring in, or foist into the middle of; Looke* Interjetter.
Interjection: f. *An Interiection (in Grammar,) also, an interposition; or, the allegation of some matter, or vsing of some tricke, in the middle of a cause, thereby to crosse, or alter it.*
Interjetter. *as* Interjecter.
Interjetter vn appel. *To appeale, not in respect of the whole cause, but for some small, or by point thereof.*
Interieur: m. eure: f. *Interior, inward, priuate, neere vnto.*
Interieurement. *Inwardly, priuatly, within.*
Interiné *as* Enteriné.
Interiner. *Looke* Enteriner.
Interlocation: f. *An interlocation, interplacing, interposition.*
Interlocution: f. *An interlocution, interposition, or interruption of speech; also, as* Sentence interlocutoire.
Interlocutoire: com. *A stay, prolonging, or deferring of (sentence in) a cause in respect of some reasons alledged.*
Interlocutoire: com. *Interlocutorie; interrupting, speech interposing; casting in a word that giues a stop to, or breeds delay in, a cause.*
Sentence interlocutoire. *An opinion, or sentence of Court, which fully ends not the cause, but determines of some circumstance thereof; Or (as in the Customes of* Nivernois) Qui ne fait fin au procez, mais reigle les parties à faire quelque chose pour parvenir à cette fin.
Interloquer. *To interpose some speech, or speake in another mans tale; also, to delay a cause by some new allegation; or, to stay the whole, for a while, by ending onely some part thereof.*
Interlunaire: m. *The season betweene the going out of the old, and comming in of the new, Moone.*
Intermediat. *In the middle, or intermedium; that is betweene two; that lyeth, or happeneth, betweene both.*
Intermettre. *To intermit, or put betweene; also, to slacken, discontinue, giue ouer, ceasse, leaue, or put off for a time.*
Interminant. *Boundlesse, borderlesse, vncertaine; also, as* Intermittant.
Interminé: m. ée: f. *Vnbounded, boundlesse, infinite, endlesse, vndeterminable.*
Interminer. *To prescribe.*
Intermis: m. ise: f. *Intermitted, discontinued, pawsed on, left off for a season, let passe for a while.*
Intermission: f. *An intermission, discontinuance, pawse; a ceasing, or breaking off for a season; a leauing, or letting passe for a while.*
Intermittant. *Intermittant, intermitting, discontinuing, pawsing, or ceasing for a time; comming and going (as an ague) by fits.*
Interne: com. *Internall, inward.*
Internecion: f. *An vniuersall slaughter, a generall killing.*
Internément. *Internally, inwardly, within.*
Interossel: m. elle: f. *Betweene bones.*
Interpellateur: m. *An interrupter, disturber, troubler, incomberer; also, a suitor, or intercessor.*
Interpellation: f. *An interruption, disturbance; let, incombrance; also, a summons; request, suit, intercession.*
Interpellé: m. ée: f. *Interrupted, let, hindered, incombered; also, summoned, or called vpon; also, required, or moued vnto, by intercession; also, intermissiue, or, that comes (as an ague) by fits.*
Interpeller. *To interrupt, let, hinder, trouble, incomber; also, to summon, or call vpon; also, to require, or moue vnto, by intercession.*
Interpolation: f. *A polishing, scowring, furbishing, new dressing of things.*
Interposé: m. ée: f. *Interposed; set in, put betweene; intermingled, or intermedled.*
Personnes interposées. *Sticklers betweene partie and partie, Arbitrators, Mediators, Daysmen.*
Interposement. *as* Interposition.
Interposer. *To interpose; to put, or set betweene; to interlace, intermeddle, intermingle; also, to intermit, pawse, delay, driue off.*
Interposer son iugement de. *To giue his iudgement, vtter his opinion, passe his allowance of.*
Interposition: f. *An interposition, or putting betweene; an interlacing, or intermingling; also, an intermedling in, or stickling of, controuersies; also, an intermission, pawsing, delaying, letting passe, breaking off, for a time; also, an approbation, or allowance giuen.*
Interposition de temps. *A pawse, respit, intermedium, interim.*

Interpretateur: m. *An interpretor, expositor.*
Interpretation: f. *An Interpretation, Comment, Exposition; Translation.*
Interprete: m. *An interpretor, trucheman, expounder, translator.*
Interpreté: m. ée: f. *Interpreted, expounded.*
Interpreter. *To interpret, expound; translate, shew the meaning, tell the signification, of.*
Interpreter à mal. *To take in bad part, to conceiue ill, or iudge hardly, of; also, as;*
Mal interpreter. *To mistake, misconster; mistrust, misdeeme.*
Interregne: m. *An interraigne, or* Interregnum; *the space, or gouernment betweene the death, or deposition of one Prince, and the entrance, or election of another.*
Interrogant: m. *The Interrogatiue point, made thus ?*
Interrogant. *Demaunding, asking.*
Interrogat: m. *A questioning, demaunding, examining.*
Interrogateur. *A questioner, demaunder, examiner.*
Interrogation: f. *An interrogation, question, demaund, examination.*
Interrogatoire: f. *An interrogatorie; a question ministred vnto an examinant.*
Interrogué: m. ée: f. *Interrogated, questioned, demaunded, examined vpon interrogatories.*
Interroguer. *To interrogate, question, demaund of, examine vpon interrogatories.*
Interrompre. *To interrupt, stop, disturbe, or breake off in the middest.*
Interroy: m. *A Regent, or Protector, that gouernes a State from the death, or deposition of one Prince, to the entrance, or election of another.*
Interruption: f. *An interruption, let, stop, disturbance, discontinuance; In Law,* C'est vn acte qui entrecoupe le cours de la prescription, & ne souffre le temps prefini se continuer, & parfaire.
Intersigne: m. *A signe, or token of.*
Intervalle: m. *An Interual,* Intermedium, *respit, pawse, or space betweene; also, the flesh-daies between Christmas and Ashwednesday.*
Sans intervalle. *Continually, incessantly.*
Intervallé: m. ée: f. *Respited, put in distances, done by pawses.*
Intervenir. *To interpose himselfe, to come in the Interim, to preuent, or come betweene.*
Intervenir l'arrest. *To preuent, or stay sentence in a cause.*
Intervention: f. *An interuention, or comming between; an interposition, a preuention.*
Intervenu: m. uë: f. *Interposed, preuented, come betweene.*
Interversion: f. *A wrongfull turning, or conueighing away of; a purloyning, deceiuing, beguiling; also, an ouerthrowing, or turning vpside downe.*
Interverti: m. ie: f. *Interuerted; conueyed, or turned the wrong way; hence also, purloined; and beguiled, or deceiued; also, ouerturned.*
Intervertir. *To interuert; conuey, or turne the wrong way; (hence) to purloine; beguile, deceiue; also, to ouerthrow, ouerturne, or turne vpside downe.*
Intestat. *Intestate, that dies without a Will.*
Droict d'intestat. *A Priuiledge which the next of kinne vnto one that dyes intestate hath, to seize on all he left behind him.*
Intestin: m. *An intestine, inward, intrall, gut, bowell.*
Intestin affamé. *The hungrie gut; one of the three small guts that lye toward the right side of the vpper part of the nauell; euer kept emptie by the Mesenterick veines which passe from it vnto the Liuer.*
Intestin borgne. *The blind gut; Looke* Borgne.
Intestin cuillier. *as* Boyau culier.
Intestin douzedoigtier. *A small gut, or intrall seated on the right side; and which, descending obliquely towards the back-bone, ends where the circumuolution of the rest of the Guts begins.*
Intestin droict. *The straight gut, or arse-gut.*
Intestin entortillé. *The wreathed gut; one of the three small guts which lye towards the left side vnder the nauell; tis verie ruddie, and makes many windings which extend vnto the* Os sacrum.
Intestins tenuës. *The small guts wherein the meat passeth out of the stomacke.*
Intestin: m. ine: f. *Intestine, inward, priuie, hidden; despightfull, rancorous, deadlie.*
Intestinal: m. ale: f. *Of, or belonging to, the Intestines.*
Veine intestinale. *Seeke* Veine.
Intheriner. *as* Enteriner.
Inthimé. *Looke* Intimé.
Inthronization: f. *An inthronization, or inthroning.*
Inthronizé: m. ée: f. *Inthronized; placed in a throne.*
Inthronizer. *To inthronize; to place in a royall throne.*
Intimant. *An Appeallant; or, one that cites his aduersarie vpon an Appeale.*
Intimation: f. *An intimation, signification, denunciation, shewing, letting to wit, or giuing to know; also, an Adiournement, Citation, or Summons of a partie in an Appeale, and in cases wherein the Judge proceeds of course to right the plaintife though the defendant appeare not.*
Intimé: m. L'in. *An Appeallee; the defendant in an Appeale.*
Intime: com. *(Most) inward, secret, heartie, especiall, deere, intirely affected.*
Intimé: m. ée: f. *Intimated; signified, shewed, notified, denounced; also, adiourned, cited, summoned, warned to appeare (in an Appeale.)*
Officier intimé. *An Officer chosen by the King, and confirmed by Parliament.*
La partie intimée. *as* L'Intimé.
Intimément. *Inwardly, secretly, heartily, deerely, intirely; effectually, especially.*
Intimer. *To intimate, signifie, shew; denounce, proclaime; set on broach; also, to adiourne, cite, summon, bring an Action against; (especially in cases wherein a Iudge proceeds of course to right the plaintife, though the defendant appeare not.)*
Intimer le Seigneur. *A Tenant to sue an Appeale against his Lord, for denying to right him in his Court.*
Intimidation: f. *A fearing, skaring, affrighting, terrifying.*
Intimidé: m. ée: f. *Feared, skared, terrified, affrighted.*
Intimider. *To feare, skare, terrifie, affright.*
Intirable: com. *Not to be drawne, or pulled out.*
Intitulation: f. *An intitulation, or intituling; a denomination, a description.*
Intitulé: m. ée: f. *Intitled, or intituled.*
Intituler. *To intitle; denominate; describe.*

Intolerable: com. *Intollerable, insupportable, vnsufferable.*
Intolerablement. *Intollerably, vnsufferably.*
Intolerance: f. *Impatiencie.*
Intonation: f. *A lowd noise, tune, sound; a rumbling, or thundering.*
Intonation de gare & serre. *See* Gare.
Intouchable: com. *Vntoucheable.*
Intractable: com. *Intractable, harsh, vngentle, hard; wild, hagard, vnrulie, outragious; vnsociable, inconuersible, vncompanable.*
Intrade: f. *Reuenue, rent, profit comming in.*
Intraictable: com. *as* Intractable.
Intrans: m. *Senior Sophisters; such as prepare themselues to commence Batchelers.*
s'Intregenter. *Looke* s'Entregenter.
Intrication: f. *An intrication, or intricating; an intangling, insnaring, pestering, fettering; Laborinth, Maze; inwrapping, inuolution.*
Intrinqué: m. ée: f. *Intricated, intangled, incombered, perplexed, in a Laborinth.*
Intrinquément. *as* Intriquément.
Intrinquer. *as* Intriquer.
Intrinseque: com. *Intrinsecall, inward, secret, familiar.*
Intrinsequement. *Intrinsecally, inwardly, on the inside; verie familiarly.*
Intrique: f. *An intricacie, Laborinth, Maze, pesterment, incombrance, perplexitie, difficultie.*
Intriqué. *as* Intrinqué.
Intriquément. *Intricately, perplexedly, intangledly; darkly; difficultly.*
Intriquer. *To intricate, perplex, pester; insnare, inuolue, intangle; incomber.*
Introduction: f. *An introduction; a leading, or bringing in, or vnto; a way, entrance, beginning to; an institution.*
Introduire. *To introduce; lead, or bring in; to inuent, begin, broach, bring vp; also, to enter, instruct, or trayne vp in.*
Introduit: m. ite: f. *Introduced, brought in, begun, broached, brought vp; entred, or trayned in.*
Introite: m. *An entrance, entrie, beginning, or going into.*
Intronisation: f. *An inthronization, or inthronizing.*
Intronisé: m. ée: f. *Inthronized, placed in a throne.*
Introniser. *as* Inthroniser.
Intrus: m. use: f. *Intruded, thrust into.*
Intrusion: f. *An intrusion; a wrongfull intruding, or thrusting into the possession of a vacant thing.*
Intruz: m. *An intruder; an vsurper of the possession of a vacant thing.*
Intuitif: m. iue: f. *Intuitiue; which is, or may be seene into.*
Intumescence: f. *A swelling, puffing, vprising.*
Invadé: m. ée: f. *Inuaded.*
Invader. *To inuade, assaile, assault, enter, or set vpon in a forcible, or hostile manner.*
Invaincu: m. uë: f. *Vnvanquished, vnouercome; as yet in heart, or on foot.*
Invalide: com. *Impotent, infirme, vnable, strengthlesse, forcelesse, feeble, worthlesse.*
Invalider. *To weaken, debilitate, infeeble, make forcelesse, impaire the strength, debase the worth, disgrace the vertue of; also, to infringe, dissolue, confute.*
Invariable: com. *Vnvariable, immutable, vnchangeable; alwaies of one hue, euer in one humor.*
Invasible: com. *Inuasible, inuadible.*
Invasion: f. *An inuasion; an hostile assault, or incursion.*
Invective: f. *An Inuectiue; a rayling, biting, opprobrious discourse, or speech.*
Invectiver. *To inueigh, reuile, rayle vpon.*
Inventaire: m. *An Inuentorie; List, Roll; Memoriall, Record, Register of many seuerall things; In Law,* contient vne brieve description des pieces que la partie produit.
Inventé: m. ée: f. *Inuented, found out; contriued, deuised; fained, imagined, surmised.*
Inventer. *To inuent; to find, or spy out; to deuise, forge; contriue; imagine, faine, surmise.*
Inventeresse: f. *An inuentresse, or inuentrix.*
Inventeur: m. *An inuenter, contriuer, deuiser, finder out; an author, framer, forger; fainer, surmiser.*
Inventif: m. iue: f. *Inuentiue, wittie, plotting, full of tricks, fraught with deuises.*
Invention: f. *An inuention; a finding out, or thing found out; a deuise, forgerie, conceit; also, a tricke, shift; surmise, imagination.*
Invention Saincte Croix. *The Inuention of the holie Crosse; a solomne holyday celebrated by the Church of Rome on the third of May; also, a shift, or deuise to get money.*
Invention Saincte Estienne. *Another holyday kept the third of August.*
Inventorié: m. ée: f. *Inuentoried; digested into, or couched in, an Inuentorie.*
Inventorier. *To inuentorie; to take an Inuentorie of; to digest into an Inuentorie.*
Inventorizer. *as* Inventorier.
Inventrice. *as* Inventeresse.
Invers: m. erse: f. *Inuerted, misplaced, peruerted, wrested to a contrarie sence, vttered one for another; turned in and out, inside outward, vpside downe.*
Investi: m. ie: f. *Inuested; inrobed, indowed; also, inwrapped.*
Investir. *To inuest; inrobe, install, indow, put into possession of; also, to inwrap; also, to ioyne (a word of Horsemanship.)*
Investison: f. *An inuesting, or inuesture; an inrobing, installing, indowing, instituting, putting into possession.*
Investiture: f. *An inuestiture, or inuesture; an institution, installment, indowment.*
Inveteré: m. ée: f. *Inueterate, old, auncient, of long vse, rooted by custome, setled by continuance.*
s'Inveterer. *To inueterate, grow old; become rooted, or come to a habite, by custome.*
Invigilance: f. *Inuigilancie, sleepinesse, drowsinesse, lazinesse, lacke of waking.*
Invincible: com. *Inuincible, vnvanquishable, vnsubduable, vnconquerable.*
Inviolable: com. *Inuiolable; most firme; not to be corrupted, infringed, or broken.*
Inviolablement. *Inuiolably; faithfully.*
Inviolableté: f. *Inuiolablenesse.*
Inviolé: m. ée: f. *Inuiolate; sound, pure, vncorrupted, vnhurt; vnbroken, firme, constant, faithfull, true.*
Invitation: f. *An inuitation, or inuiting; a bidding, or desiring; an allurement, or inticement vnto.*
Invité: m. ée: f. *Inuited, bidden; desired, intreated; allured, inticed vnto.*
Invitement. *as* Invitation.
Inviter. *To inuite, bid; desire, intreat; allure, intice, vnto.*
Invocation: f. *An inuocation, or calling vpon.*

Mots

Mots d' invocation. *Coniuring tearmes.*
Involontaire: com. *Inuoluntarie; against the will of.*
Involucre: m. *A couer, cloke, or thing that serues to hide.*
Involver. *To inuolue, enwrap, infould; intricate, insnarle, intangle.*
Involution: f. *An inuolution, enwrapping, infoulding; insnarling, intricating, intangling.*
Involution de procez. *A iumbling, or confounding of a suit, in sort, that one knowes not what to make of it, or is further from ending it then he was when he began.*
Invoqué: m.ée: f. *Inuoked, called vpon.*
Invoquer. *To inuoke, or call vpon; to require, or intreat helpe of.*
Invoqueur: m. *An inuoker.*
Inusité: m.ée: f. *Vnused, vnwonted, vnusuall; disused, disaccustomed, discontinued, left off.*
Inutile: com. *Vnprofitable, vngainfull, incommodious, vnseruiceable; of no worth, for no vse, to no purpose.*
Il n'est iamais inutile. *He is alwayes well imployed, he is neuer idle.*
Inutilement. *Vnprofitably, incommodiously, vnseruiceably.*
Inutilité: f. *Inutilitie, vnprofitablenesse, disprofit, vnseruiceablenesse.*
Invulnerable: com. *Invulnerable, vnwoundable.*
Io. *as* Moy: ¶Poictevin: ¶Rab.
Ioannes. c'est vn Ioannes. *He is a Pedant, or poore Schoolemaister.*
Ioannitiques. *An Order of Monks that weare red habits, and the representation of a Chalice on their breasts.*
Iobelin: m. *A sot, gull, doult, asse, cokes; also, as* Gobelin.
Iocondale. *A Daller; a peece of money worth about 3 s.sterl.*
Iocquer. *To stop, or stand still, as a horse, or cart, in the way.*
Iodelle: f. *A Sea-coot.*
Ioeudi. *Thursday; Looke* Ieudy.
Ioffu: m.uë: f. *Chuffie, fat-cheeked, swelled or puft vp in the face.*
Ioiaulier. *Seeke* Ioyaulier.
Ioignant. (Partic.) *Ioyning, coupling, yoaking, putting together.*
Ioignant. (Adverb.) *Neere vnto, hard by, close adioyning, almost touching, bordering vpon.*
Ioinct: m. *A ioynt, ioyning, closure; seame.*
Ioinct: m.cte: f. *Ioyned; coupled, yoaked, grapled, put, couched, or closed together; knit, associated, or combined with; also, raught, fetcht vp, ouertaken.*
Ioinct que. *(A Coniunction) furthermore, adde moreouer, as also that.*
Ioincte: f. *as* Iointe.
Ioincture: f. *A ioynt of the bodie, a knot in trees; also, a ioyning, coupling, yoaking, closing, or couching together.*
Ioindre. *To ioyne, couple, yoake; knit, close, couch; associate, or combine together; to set neere, or bring hard, vnto; also, to reach, or ouertake; also, to buckle, grapple, or cope, as enemies, &c, together.*
Iointe: f. *A ioynt; closure; ioyning; seame.*
Iointée: f. *A ioynt, or double handfull of; as much as can be held within both hands together; In some countries of England it is called a yeaspen, in others a goppen-ful of.*

Ioletrin: m. *A youngster, or young gallant.*
Ioli: m. iolie: f. *Jollie; gay, trim, fine, gallant, neat, handsome, feat, well-fashioned, minion, compt, polite; also, liuelie, merrie, buxome, iocond.*
Iolice: f. *A kind of soft, and tender stone which in frostie weather falls vnto dust.*
Iolíement. *Jollily, gayly, trimly, finely, gallantly; neatly, featly; merrily, buxomely.*
Iolier. *as* Geolier; *A Goaler.*
Ioliet: m. ette: f. *Neat, fine, tricke, feat, spruce, nice, prettie, and handsome.*
Iolieté: f. *Jollitie, iollinesse; gainesse, trimnesse, finenesse, gallantnesse; neatnesse, handsomenesse, prettinesse, comelinesse; liuelinesse, iocondnesse, mirth, buxomnesse.*
Iolíveté. *as* Ioliett.
Iombarbe: f. *Houseleeke, Sengreene; Looke* Ioubarbe.
Ionc: m. *A rush, or bulrush.*
Ionc agu. *Our common hard rush, or sharpe rush.*
Ionc à cabas. *The pole-rush, mat-rush, fraile-rush, pannier-rush, bull-rush, great water rush.*
Ionc marin. *The sea-rush, or sea-rush grasse.*
Ionc marisc, ou de marez. *The marish rush, smooth rush, candle rush.*
Ionc odorant. *The sweet rush, Camells meat, Camells hay, Squinant.*
Ionc à racines odoriferantes. *Cypresse, English or Spanish Galingale.*
Ioncade: f. *A certaine spoone-meat made of creame, Rose-water, and Sugar.*
Ionché: m.ée: f. *Strewed with, wrought of, rushes; couered, or spread ouer, as with rushes; also, gulled, cogged with, deceiued, ieasted, or toyed with.*
Ionchée: f. *A bundle of rushes; also, a greene banke to sit on, or way to goe in, strewed with flowers, hearbes, grasse, or greene rushes; also, the rushes so strewed; also, a greene cheese, or fresh cheese made of milke thats curdled without any runnet, and serued in a fraile of greene rushes; also, a handfull of small Iuorie prickes wherewith maidens vse to play.*
Ionchement. *A strewing with, or making of, rushes; also, a gulling, deceiuing, beguiling.*
Ioncher. *To strew; to spread, or couer (as) with rushes; to worke, or make, of rushes; also, to gull; cog, or foist with; lie vnto, deceiue, giue gudgeons, beare in hand with vntruthes; also, to dallie, ieast, or toy with.*
Ioncheur: m. *A strewer (as) with rushes; a worker, or plaiter of things with rushes; also, a lyer, cogger, foister, deceiuer; or, a dissembler, imposter, abuser of people with false tales, or shewes.*
Ionchu: m.uë: f. *Rushie, full of rushes.*
Iong. *as* Ionc.
Iongler. *To iuggle; also, to play the Poet.*
Iongleries: f. *Jugling trickes, feats of legierdemaine; also, old Poeticall inuentions.*
Iongleur: m. *A Jugler:* ¶Pic. *also, a Rimer, or Poet.*
Ionne. *Young; Looke* Ieune *(an old word.)*
Ioquetter. *To leacher; or, to line, as a dog doth a bitch.*
Iorroise: f. *A horse-plumme.*
Iosmin: m. *The shrub Iasmin, Ielsomin, Iesse.*
Iota. *A iot, point, or pricke:* ¶Rab.
Iotte: f. *(The hearbe) Beet, or Beets.*
Iotteux: m.euse: f. *Claggie, clammie, cleauing.*
Iou: m. *as* Ioug.
Iou. *as* Moy; *Me:* ¶Gasc.
Et iou mot. *For my part I will be whist, or not speake one word.*
Ioüant. *Playing; gaming, sporting, dallying, ieasting, passing*

passing away the time.
En se ioüant. *In sport, game, ieast, boording, merrily.*
Ioüarre : m. *An old rimer, ballade-maker; or maker of Enterludes for children, and countrey folke to act.*
Ioüart : m. *A Windgall in the leg of a horse.*
Ioubarbe : f. *Houseleeke, Sengreene, Aygreene, Bullocks eye, Iupiters beard.*
Ioubarbe arborée. *Tree Housleeke.*
Ioubarbe femelle. *as* Ioubarbe à petites fueilles.
Ioubarbe à petites fueilles. *The female small Sengreene (with the pale-white flower) called wild Prickmadame, great Stone-crop, and Worme-grasse.*
Ioubarbe marine. *Sea Housleek, Sea Aygreen, hearb Aloes.*
Ioubarbe masle. *Prickmadame, or Sengreene the lesser, with the yellow flower.*
Ioubarbe sauvage. *Mouse-grasse, wild Prickmadame.*
Ioubarbe des vignes. *Orpine, Liblong, Liuelong.*
Grande Ioubarbe. *Great Sengreen, great Housleek, Iupiters beard.*
Petite Ioubarbe. *The male Prickmadame, or Sengreene the lesser; also, Mousetaile, Pricket, Stonehore, little Stonecrop, Wall-pepper, Countrey-pepper, Iacke of the Butterie.*
Iouc : m. *as* Iuc; *A henne-roost.*
Ioucher. *as* Ioncher; *To cog, to foist, &c; also, as* Iucher; *to roost, or pearch; whence;*
Qui avec mal plaisant se couche, souvent sur luy le vent se iouche : Prov.
Ioudarde : f. *A Sea-coot.*
Ioue : f. *The cheeke, the iowle.*
Bailler par les iouës de. *Looke* Bailler.
Il luy en bailla parmy les iouës. *He gaue him a sound box on th'eare.*
S'en batre les iouës. *To repent throughly, or afflict himselfe extreamely for.*
Il s'en est donné par les iouës. *He pulled, or snatched it violently vnto him.*
Mal iouë qui fiert la iouë: Prov. *He ieasts but ill that hurts him whom he ieasts with.*
Ioué : m. ée : f. *Played; gamed, sported, dallied.*
On s'est ioué de son cuir. *Hee hath beene soundly whipped.*
Iouée : f. *The whole cheeke extending from the eyebrow to the chinne; also, a box, cuffe, whirrit, buffet on the cheeke, or eare.*
Ioueigneur : m. *A younger brother :* ¶Breton.
Iouëlle : f. *A yoake.*
Iouëlles. *Arched, or yoaked vines; vines so vnderpropped, or fashioned that one may goe vnder the middle of them.*
Iouër. *To play, game, sport; dallie, ieast; recreate, or solace himselfe, passe away the time; also, to act, represent, or counterfeit (as a Comedian) the gestures of another.*
Iouër à l'amour. *One to hold vp his fingers, and another, turned from him, to ghesse how many he holds vp.*
Iouër à bander & à racler contre. *To deale in all extremitie against.*
Iouër à boule veuë. *Looke* Boule.
Iouër à boutehors. *To thrust out the harlot; (a game in some vse among Courtiers, and Competitors.)*
Iouër des cousteaux. *To fight; also, to eat hard, or bestirre himselfe apace, at a table.*
Iouër des cymbales & manequins. *To lecher:* ¶Rab.
Iouër d'espée. *To fence, or play at fence.*
En Iouër de l'espée à deux mains. *To doe what he list withall; also, to haue his hands full of; or to imploy both hands in.*
Iouër le gros ieu. *To play great game, to be at the fairest; to throw away all at a cast, to venture a whole rest at once.*
Iouër ses ieux. *To doe his feats, or play his prankes; also, to play reakes, or keepe a terrible coile.*
Iouër son jeu. Il ne iouë pas aujourd'huy son jeu. *He is cleane out of play.*
Iouëz vostre jeu. *Play an aime cast (at bowles.)*
Iouër de la navette. *To play fast and loose; or, a wench to enter a man into her Tables.*
Iouër des Orgues. autant que paillarder.
Iouër au rabat. *To make an abatement.*
Iouër du rebec. *Stubbornely to resist, withstand, or contradict.*
Iouër à la ronfle. *To snore; See* Ronfle.
Iouër son roolle, ou roule. *To play his part throughly, to lay about him lustily.*
Iouër le roule, ou roulet de. *To act, or counterfeit the gestures of.*
Iouër au Roy despouillé. *To leape ouer where the hedge is lowest; to pull a fleece from a declining state; to helpe him forward thats readie to fall.*
Iouër du serrecropiere. *To leacher :* ¶Rab.
Iouër vne trousse. *To giue a gudgeon; or, to serue a slie, or slipperie tricke.*
Iouër de la veze. *To play on the bagpipe; also, to fizzle.*
Il iouë de moy à la pelotte. *He handles me at his own pleasure; he tosses, or vses me he cares not how.*
Se iouër a. *To mocke, deride, frumpe, ieast with.*
Il veut se iouër à elle. *He would be doing with her, he would faine haue a flirt at her.*
Ne te iouë pas à luy; ne t'y iouë pas. *(Said, by way of admonition, vnto one that intends to quarrell with a man of greater strength, or meanes then himselfe) meddle not with him.*
Il ne se faut pas iouër au boeuf : Pro. *An Oxe is not to be dallied with.*
Mal iouë qui fiert la iouë : Prov. *He that will ieast must doe it gently.*
Iouëresse : f. *A woman-gamester, player, sporter.*
Iouët. *A shittlecocke.*
Iouëts. *Toyes; little sports, apish plaies, prettie or childish pastimes.*
Iouëté : f. *for* Ieunesse; *(an old word.)*
Iouëur: m. *A player, gamester; dallier, sporter.*
Iouëur d'espée. *A Fencer.*
Iouëur de farces. *A Comedian, Stage-player, or common Player.*
Iouëur de Moralitez. *An Enterlude-player; also, a Buffoone, or professed Ieaster.*
Iouëur de passe passe. *A Iugler.*
Il n'est ieu qu'à iouëurs: Prov. *There is no playing with any that cannot play.*
Iouffflu : m. uë: f. *Chuffie, fat cheeked, swolne, or puft vp in the face.*
Ioug : m. *A yoake; also, the head of a Lute, Violl, &c; also, the crosse-beame of a balance; also, as* Iouc; *a henroost.*
Faire ioug. *To yeeld, obey, submit himselfe.*
Faire faire ioug. *To tame, subdue, bring vnder, to reduce vnto obedience.*
Iougal. l'os iougal. *Th'end, or outward part of the cheeke bone towards the eare.*

Iougler.

Iougler. *as* Iongler.
Iougleur. *as* Iongleur.
Ioui: m. ie: f. *Enioyed, vsed, possessed, had.*
Iovial: m. ale: f. *Iouiall, sanguine, borne vnder the Planet Iupiter.*
Iovien: m. *A Iouialist; one thats naturally, and by complexion, pleasant, or sanguine.*
Iouigleur. *Seeke* Iongleur.
Iouir. *To enioy; possesse, hold, occupie, vse; to take the profit, receiue the fruit, haue the fruition of.*
Iouissance: f. *An enioying; possessing, occupying, holding; fruition, whole fruite, full vse, absolute possession of.*
Iouncher. *as* Ioncher; *(an old word.)*
Iour: m. *A day; also, light, or day-light; also, the shadow, or luster thats giuen vnto a picture by a skilfull workeman; also, a Court, or pleading place.*
Iour artificiel. *Th'artificiall, or tradesmans day; continues from the rising, to the setting, of the Sunne.*
Iours de cessation. *A vacation.*
Iour civil. *The ciuile day; continues (as* Iour naturel*) 24 houres, but differs in the beginning, by the different vse, or constitutions of seuerall nations; whereof some (as the Chaldeans, and Persians) begin it from Sunne-rising; others (as the Iewes, Athenians, auntient Ægyptians, and moderne Italians) from Sunne-set; others (as th'Vmbrians) from noone; and others (as th'auntient Romanes, and at this day, the French, Spaniards, Germanes, and the most part of the people of our world) from midnight.*
Iour de la Chandeleur. *Candlemas day.*
Iour egal. *Th'Equinoctiall, or Equator; the day that is as long as the night.*
Iour d'vne fenestre. *The hole, or whole compasse of a window, whereby the light comes in.*
Iour de loy. *A Hall day, Court day, Law day.*
Iour de morts. *All-soules day.*
Iour naturel. *The naturall day; consists of 24 houres.*
Iour de pain perdu. *Shroue-tewsday.*
Iour de Palais. *as* Iour de loy.
Iour des Roys. *Th'Epiphanie, or Twelfth day in Christmas.*
Iour de la Saincte croix. *Crouchmesse day.*
Iour du Sainct Sacrement. *Corpus Christi day.*
Iour servant. *Looke* Servant.
Iour du toile. *A day of pleading, a Court day.*
Les trois iours de tenebres. *The three dayes next before Easter.*
Iour haut, ou haut iour. *High adayes, at broad day-light, farre on the day.*
Iour de ma vie. *Neuer, not so long as I liue.*
Les bons iours. *The holy-daies of Christmas, or of any other good time.*
Les Grands iours. *An extraordinarie Sessions, called by vertue of the Kings Commission, or Letters Patents directed vnto certaine Iudges of the Parliament (within the precincts whereof it is to be held) and appointing them, what place they shall sit in, how long they shall sit it; what causes they shall deale in, and how farre they shall proceed in them: The Peeres of France haue also their* Grands iours, *which they hold once, or twice a yeare, for the execution of their highest Iurisdiction, and for the hearing of Appeales from their owne inferiour Courts.*
Vis à iour. *Looke* Vis.
'A iour. *Transparent; or so made, so cut, &c, as one may see through it in diuers places.*
Au iour la iournée. *Poorely, barely, needily, no more then from hand to mouth.*
Au demy iour. *Halfe shadowed, halfe appearing.*
De iour. *In the day time.*
Pour à tous les iours. *For the workie dayes, or to be vsed euerie day.*
Bacchus estant sorti par le iour de Iupiter; viz: *Out of the slit he made in his thigh for Bacchus to lie in.*
Bailleur de beaux iours. *A cogging, glozing, or fawning companion; one that vses many faire (but effectlesse) words.*
Bailleur de bons iours. *The same; or, an ordinarie street-saluter.*
Donner iour à. *To grace, beautifie, giue light, or luster vnto.*
Donner iour à sa despence. *To labour to get his expences a reputation; or, so to manage them as the world may take most notice of them.*
Faire iour. *Day to breake, or to appeare; (hence,* Compere ie dors, il ne fait pas encore iour. *I am not for you good neighbour;) also, to make a hole, or open a passage, for light to come in at.*
Faire iour à. *To make way, or open a passage, for another.*
Faire iour en. *To open; to passe, or pierce through and through.*
Pierres qui ne portent point de iour. *Stones that be not transparent.*
Trouver son iour. *To die.*
Vn iour iuge de l'autre, & le dernier iuge de tous: Prov. *One day another, and the last all, iudges.*
'A bon iour bonne estreine: Prov. *Looke* Estreine.
'A bon iour bon oeuvre: Prov. *The better day the better deed; Looke* Oeuvre.
Ce qui se faict de nuict paroit de iour: Prov. *The workes of darkenesse are at length discouered.*
Ia ne chante le coq si viendra le iour: Prov. *Though the cocke neuer crow day will appeare.*
Il n'est si grand iour que ne vienne vespre: Prov. *The longest day will haue a dawning.*
Il n'est qu'vne mauvaise heure au iour: Prov. *There is but one ill (or vnluckie) houre in the day.*
Il suffit au iour de sa misere: Prov. *One miserie is ynough at once.*
Le coeur fait l'oeuvre, non pas les grands iours: Prov. *as in* Oeuvre.
Longues paroles font les iours courts: Prov. *Long words make short dayes; a long discourse makes time to steale away.*
Nul soir sans iour: Prov. *Looke* Soir.
On revient sage des iours: Prov. *In time fooles get experience.*
Nous achetons tout fors le iour, & la nuict: Prov. *All things are vendible saue day and night.*
Quoy que fol tarde iour ne tarde: Prov. *Time stayeth not on fools; or, though the foole stay, time staies not.*
Iournal: m. *as* Iournau; *also, as* Livre, ou Papier Iournal.
Iournal: m. ale: f. *Iournall; daily; done in, or belonging to, the day.*
Livre, ou papier iournal. *A Iournall, Diarie, day-booke, Register kept of dailie occurrences.*
Iournalier: m. *A Iourney-man; one that workes by the day; also, a certaine poisonous hearbe, which being eaten of, kills within a day.*
Iournalier: m. ere: f. *Dailie, quotidian; ordinarie, continuall; also, vncertaine; to day one way, to morrow*

row another; whence;

Vn homme iournalier. *An inconstant or fickle headed; also, a carelesse or improuident, fellow; one that is onely for the present.*

Iournau: m. *A quantitie of land not much differen from th'* Arpent; *and in some countries (as in* Champaigne) *the verie same: Or, as much land as a yoake of Oxen can plough vp in one day; (which is of clayland about an Acre, and of sandie ground about an Acre and a halfe.)*

Iournau Bourdelois, ou de la ville de Bourdeaux. *(Wherin notwithstanding it is but little knowne, and lesse vsed) containes in breadth 112 foot, in length 224 but these feet (tearmed thereabouts,* pieds de terre) *are by an eighth part in three quarters longer then ordinarie ones.*

Iournau de Bourgogne (en terre, ou Vigne.) *Containes 360 Pearches, or Poles.*

Iournau de Bretaigne. *Is 20 Cords long, and foure broad, of 24 foot to the Cord.*

Iournau Engoumoisin. (*The true* Iugerum *of th'antient Latines) is 120 foot broad, & 240 long; or (which comes to the same proportion) 20 fadomes broad, and 40 long.*

Iournau de Xainctongne. *Containes 100 squares, or yron chaines, each of eighteene linkes, and euerie linke a foot in length.*

Iournée: f. *A day, or whole day; also, a day of battell, or the battell it selfe; also, a dayes worke, or labour; a dayes iourney, or trauell.*

Iournée blanche. *A holy-day, or play-day; called so by some countrey people.*

Iournée des Esperons. *The battell of Spurres, woon, in the yeare 1513, by the English vpon the French, possessed with a sudden feare, and preferring one paire of heeles before two paire of hands.*

La iournée d'vne geline. *An egge.*

Iournée servante. *Looke* Servant.

Au iour la iournée. *Onely from hand to mouth.*

Il a tousiours sa iournée faitte. *He is a loggerhead, or dull fellow.*

Bonne iournée fait qui de fol se delivre: Prov. *He does a good dayes worke that rids his hands of a foole.*

Les grands boeufs ne font pas le grandes iournées: Prov. *Looke* Boeuf.

Iournellement. *Daily, day by day, euerie day.*

Iourneu: m. *A quantitie of land (in the Seigneurie of* Conty *in* Clermont) *containing 100 roods, of 24 foot to the rood.*

Iournieur: m. *A dailie worke.* (v.m.)

Iouste: f. *A Iust; a Iusting, or Tilting; also, a fight, or battell.*

Iouste. (Adverb.) *Neere to, nigh adioyning, hard by, towards, beside.*

Iouster. *To Iust, Tilt, or Turney; to runne one against another; also, to fight, or bicker; as;*

Faire iouster les coqs. *To set the Cockes together by the eares.*

Iousteux: m. euse: f. *Iusting, full of Iusting, that loues to Iust.*

Iouvence. *as* Ieunesse. *Youth.*

Iouvenceau: m. *A youth, stripling, lad, springall, yong man.*

Argent frais & nouveau ruine le iouvenceau: Prov. *Looke* Argent.

Iouvencel. *as* Iouvenceau.

Iouxte. *as* Iouste (Adverb.) *Also, according to.*

Iouy. *as* Iouï.

Ioyallier: m. *A Jeweller; A Marchant, or maker of Jewells.*

Ioyau: m. *A Jewell.*

Ioyaulerie: f. *Jewelling; the trade, or mysterie of Jewelling.*

Ioyaulier: m. *A Ieweller.*

Ioye: f. *Ioy, mirth, glee, gladnesse, reioycing, iocondnesse; comfort, pleasure, delight, lightnesse of heart.*

Ioye de papillon. *Short ioy, momentarie gladnesse.*

Fille de ioye. *A punke, or pleasant sinner.*

Ioye au coeur fait beau teint: Prov. *Looke* Teint.

Ioye triste coeur travaillé: Prov. *Sad mirth denotes a troubled mind.*

Ioyeusement *Ioyfully, merrily, gladly, blithely, iocondly, cheerefully.*

Ioyeuseté: f. *Ioyfulnesse, cheerefulnesse, iollitie, iocondnesse.*

Ioyeux: m. euse: f. *Ioyfull, ioyous, glad, merrie, iocond, blithe, buxome, frolicke, iollie, cheerefull, pleasant, gamesome.*

Ioyeux comme vn esmerillon. *We may say, as crank as a Cocke Sparrow.*

Plus ioyeux que rats en paille, ou fourmis en grain. *More iocond then Rats among chaffe, or Ants among corne.*

Ioyeuse, & riche vie pere, & mere oublie: Prov. *Looke* Vie.

Ique. Les Maux terminez en ique font au medecin la nique: Prov. *Looke* Nique.

Ira. (*The third person of the Future Tense of the Verbe* Aller; *whence;*) Il n'en ira pas ainsi. *The matter shall not be carried in that manner.*

Iracond: m. de: f. *Angrie, teastie, cholericke, waspish, fumish, pettish, quickly moued, soone displeased.*

Iraigne. *in stead of* Araigne. Mot villageois.

Irascible: com. *Cholericke, soone angred, subiect vnto anger.*

Ire: f. *Ire, anger, choler, chafing, fuming, pettishnesse; wrath, rage, moodinesse, indignation.*

Ire de freres ire de Diables: Prov. *Brothers furie, diuelish follie.*

Douce parole rompt grand ire: Prov. *Great anger is by gentle teartmes asswaged.*

Iré: m. ée: f. *Angred, chafed, vexed, put into choler.*

Ireusement. *Irefully, wrathfully, stomackefully.*

Ireux: m. euse: f. *Irefull, wrathfull, stomackefull, moodie, fumish, cholericke, soone moued, quickly vexed, easily distempered.*

Irin: m. ine: f. *Of* Ireos.

Iris: f. *The rainbow; also, a Flowerdeluce.*

Iris de Florence. *The Flowerdeluce of Florence, whose root yeelds our Orice powder.*

Pierre d'Iris. *Some call so, th'Opall, because it resembles a rainbow; others, a stone thats of the kind, and colour, of the Girosole, but much harder then th'ordinarie one.*

Irrachetable: com. *Vnredeemable; not to be bought, had, or got againe, at any price.*

Irradiation: f. *An irradiation; an inlightning, or casting of beames; a shining vpon.*

Irraisonnable: com. *Vnreasonable, outragious, beastlie, brutish.*

Irrecevable: com. *Vnreceiuable, vnintertainable, not to be welcommed vnto.*

Irreconciliable: com. *Irreconcilable, vnreconcilable; most contrarie, at extreame oddes.*

Irrecuperable: com. *Vnrecouerable, vnrepairable, wholly*

wholly lost, fully gone.
Irrefragable : com. *Irrefragable, vnbreakable, inuiolable, vnreuocable.*
Irregularité : f. *Irregularitie, vnrulinesse, disorder, outlashing.*
Irregulier : m. ere : f. *Irregular, vnrulie, without rule, disorderlie, dissolute, lawlesse.*
Irregulierement. *Irregularly, vnorderly, lawlesly, without rule.*
Irreligieuseté : f. *Irreligion, want of religion; Atheisme, vngodlinesse.*
Irreligieux : m. euse : f. *Irreligious, without religion.*
Irremarquable : com. *Vnremarkable, not to be marked, no way to be noted.*
Irremeable : com. *Vnreturnable, or, from which one cannot goe backe.*
Irremediable : com. *Remedilesse, redreslesse, recurelesse, irrecuperable, vnrecouerable.*
Irremediablement. *Remedilesly, vnremediably.*
Irremissible : com. *Vnremittable, irremissible, vnpardonable.*
Irremissiblement. *Vnremittably, irremissibly.*
Irremittent. *Vnintermissiue, continuall, without any pausing.*
Irreparable : com. *Irreparable, vnrepairable, vnrestorable, vnrecouerable.*
Irreparablement. *Irreparably, vnrestorably, vnrecouerably.*
Irrepassable : com. *Vnrepassable, ouer which no returne can be made.*
Irreprehensible : com. *Irreprehensible, blamelesse, vnreprouable.*
Irreprehensiblement. *Irreprehensibly, blamelesly, vnreprouably.*
Irreprochable : com. *Vnreproachable; not subiect vnto imputation; pure, sincere.*
Irreprovable : com. *Vnreprouable, faultlesse, vnblamable.*
Irrequiet. *Restlesse, vnquiet, actiue, busie, turbulent, euer stirring.*
Irrespectueux : m. euse : f. *Vnrespectiue, inofficious, rude.*
Irreveillable : com. *Vnwakable, in a dead sleepe.*
Irreveland. *Vnreuealable, not to be reuealed.*
Irreveremment. *Vnreuerently, rudely.*
Irreverence : f. *Irreuerence, want of reuerence, vnmanerlinesse, vnrespectfulnesse.*
Irreverent. *Vnreuerent, vnrespectfull, vnmanerlie, rude, proud.*
Irrevocable : com. *Irreuocable, vnrecallable.*
Irrevocablement. *Irreuocably, vnrecallably.*
Irrision : f. *Irrision, mocking, flowting, scoffing at; a deriding, or laughing to scorne.*
Irritation : f. *An irritation, or stirring vp; an incensing, vrging, or mouing vnto anger; a prouocation; an appetite.*
Irrité : m. ée : f. *Stirred, incensed, vrged, nettled, prouoked, angred.*
Irriter. *To irrite, stirre, vrge, nettle, incense, prouoke, moue vnto anger, put into choler.*
Irriter les freslons. *To prouoke an angrie person.*
Irrogé : m. ée : f. *Imposed, inioyned; laied, or set vpon.*
Irruption : f. *An irruption; a forcible entrie; a violent bursting, or breaking into.*
Isars : m. *The wild Goats of whose skinnes our Shamois leather is made:* ¶Langued.
Ischie : f. *The Sciatica, or Hip-gowt:* ¶Rab.
Ischine : f. *The backe-bone.*
Ischion : m. *The huckle-bone, or hip-bone.*
Isciatique : com. *Troubled with the Sciatica; pained in the hips.*
Islaye : f. *A willow, or withie groue; a boult, or plot wherein Oziers, or twig-withies grow; also, a great bundle, multitude, or quantitie of Ozier twigs.*
Isle : f. *An Isle, or Island; also, a house that stands by it selfe in the middle of a street.*
Os des Isles. *Looke* Os.
Islette : f. *A little Island.*
Isleux : m. euse : f. *Islandie; full of, or belonging to, Islands.*
Islois : m. *An Islander; one that dwells in an Isle.*
Isnel : m. elle : f. *Quicke, light, fleet, swift, nimble, actiue, liuelie, speedie, readie.*
Isnellement. *Fleetly, swiftly, lightly, quickly, nimbly, actiuely, liuelily, readily.*
Isope : f. *(The hearbe) Isop, or Hisop.*
Isopleure. *A triangle, or other figure, whereof all the sides be equall.*
Issant. l' issant d' vn tombereau. *as* Timon.
Issant. *Going, flowing, or issuing, forth.*
Issir. *To issue; to goe, or depart out; to flow forth.*
Issu : m. uë : f. *Issued; flowen, sprung, proceeded from; come, risen, bred, or borne, of.*
Issuë : f. *The issue, end, successe, euent, or proofe of matters; also, the toll, or custome paied for marchandise exported.*
Les issuës d' vne beste. *The head, and intralls of a beast.*
Droict d' issuë. *The same; also, the fine thats due vnto a landlord vpon the sale, or alienation of his tenants estate; or as in;*
Ventes & issuës. *Issues; or,* iij s. iiij d. *vpon euerie pound thats taken for land sold by a tenant.*
Istau. *as* Tel; *Such a one:* ¶Poictevin.
Iste-miste. Parler en iste-miste. *To speake nicely, sprucely, quaintly, finically; to simper, or affect it, in speech.*
Isthme : m. *An Istmus; a necke, or narrow peece of land between two Seas; also, the bridge, or middle part of the nose.*
Istiomené. *as* Estiomené : ¶Rab.
Italianizer. *To Italianize it; to speake Italian, play the Italian, doe like an Italian.*
Italienniser. *The same.*
Item. vn item. *A parcell; a small peece, or summe.*
Iteratif : m. iue : f. *Iteratiue, repeating, redoubling, reinforcing.*
Iteration : f. *An iteration, repetition, renewment, reinforcement, redoubling, estsoones-doing.*
Iterato. C'est vne seconde Commission, ou decret de la cour de Parlement, par lequel il est mandé de mettre à execution ce qui avoit esté ordonné, nonobstant le susan; ou pour passer outre à l' execution d' vn executoire de despens, nonobstant opposition, ou appellation, pour avoir esté taxez en la presence de la partie condamnée: Comme aussi en finance l' on vse de lettres d' Iterato, & nouveau mandement : ¶Ragueau.
Iterer. *To iterate, reiterate, repeat, redouble, doe estsoons or againe.*
Ithiobole : m. *A swallower of bits, or morsels:* ¶Rab.
Ithyphalle : m. *A standing vp:* ¶Rab.
Itineraire : m. *An Itinerarie, or directorie for the way; a Booke, ar paper wherein the length, and course of highwayes be delineated.*

Iubé: m. *as* Iuppe; *Also, a high place made for singers, or other Musitians, ouer stages, &c.*
Faire venir a iubé. *To compell vnto reason.*
Iube: f. *The (thicke) mane of a horse, &c.*
Prendre vn lion par les Iubes. *as in* Lion.
Iubé: m. ée: f. *Thick-maned, like a horse, &c.*
Iubilation: f. *Iubilation, exultation, great ioy, much gladnesse.*
Iubilé: m. *A Jubilie; a yeare of releasing, libertie, reioycing.*
Iucheoir: m. *A roost, or pearch for pulleine to rest on.*
se **Iucher**. *To roost, or pearch (in a roost) as pulleine doe; Looke* Ioucher.
Iucondale: f. *A Daller; a coyne worth about* 3 s. sterl.
Iudaïque: com. *Iudaicall, Iewish, of Iurie.*
Herbe Iudaïque. *Iewes hearbe, Tetrahit, Glidewort.*
Pierre Iudaïque. *A faire white stone fashioned like an Acorne, & compassed with many lines in equall distance asunder.*
Iudaïser. *To Judaise it, play the Jew, liue after the maner of the Iewes.*
Iudas: m. *Iudas.*
Aureille de Iudas. (*The Mushrome called*) *a Iewes eare.*
Bran de Iudas. *Freckles, or freckled pimples in the face.*
Iudicature: f. *Iudicature, Iustice, Iudgement; hence;* Office de Iudicature. *A Iudges place.*
Iudiciaire: com. *Iudging, imperious; belonging to a Iudge, or Iudgement; also, iudiciarie, iudiciall, done in Court.*
Appellation iudiciaire. celle qu'on interjecte des sentences, appointemens, & actes qui se donnent, les choses estans conduictes en Iugement; & se fait tant de vive voix, que par escript.
Faveur iudiciaire. *The fauour done by a Iudge vnto a suitor.*
Interest iudiciaire. *Looke* Interest.
Iudiciairement. *Iudiciarily, iudicially.*
Iudiciel: m. elle: f. *Iudiciall.*
Iudiciellement. *Iudicially; according to the law, by due course of law.*
Iudicieusement. *Iudiciously, wisely, vnderstandingly.*
Iudicieux: m. euse: f. *Iudicious, wise, much vnderstanding, or of great vnderstanding.*
Ive: f. (*The hearbe*) *Ive.*
Ive arthritique. *Field Cypres, hearbe Ive, ground-Pine, Forget-me-not.*
Ive muscate. *The same.*
Ive musquée. *The same; also, Pellamountaine, white Poley.*
Iuene. *Looke* Ieune.
Iuge: m. *A Iudge, Iustice; Commissarie; a righter of causes, a decider of quarells, an ender of controuersies.*
Iuges es finances. *Certaine Officers who examine, and controll the Kings expences, and th'accounts of the Receiuors, &c.*
Iuges & Consuls des marchands. *as in* Consul.
Iuge dessous l'orme. *The Iudge of a village, or of the Courts of an infiriour Gentleman; so tearmed because he commonly sits to heare causes vnder some Elme &c that growes in the highway before the Gentlemans gate.*
Iuge pendanée. *as* Iuge dessous l'orme; *and called so because he is not to sit on a Tribunall, or high seat, but on some bench, or banke neere to the ground.*
Iuges de la porte. *In S. Lewis his time three of the Maisters of Requests were so tearmed, because they sat all the day long within the bars of the Court gate, there to receiue petitions; which if they contained ordinarie stuffe, they dispatched presently, but if they were extraordinarie, or concerned the State, they acquainted the King withall.*
Iuge à quo. *From whom* (*or* ad quem, *to whom*) *a partie appeales.*
Iuge veher. *Looke* Veher.
Il en aura la taux du Iuge. *He will be soundly payed, or throughly plagued, for it.*
Nos Iuges n'ont Dieu devant les yeux, ny ses Saincts. *An equiuocall ieast; for, in many Courts of France, God and the Saints are pictured in the roofes, and commonly iust ouer the Iudges heads.*
De fol iuge breve sentence: Prov. *A fooles boult is soone shot.*
Iuge: f. *A staulke, or branch.*
Iugé: m. ée: f. *Iudged, adiudged, doomed, sentenced, decreed; determined, ordered; awarded.*
Iugement: m. *A iudgement, sentence, doome, decree; determination, order, award; the finall decision of a controuersie; also, aduice, conceit, opinion; also, capacitie, discretion, vnderstanding, insight into matters.*
Fiens de chien, & marc d'argent seront tout vn au iour de iugement: Prov. *All will be one at the later day* (*say we.*)
Iugeolle: f. *as* Iugioline.
Iuger. *To iudge, doome, sentence, decree; determine, decide, order, award, censure; also, to deeme, thinke, imagine, conceiue, esteeme; discerne, apprehend.*
Vn iour iuge de l'autre, & le dernier iuge de tous: Pro. *This day of the last, the last of all, doth iudge:* Finis coronat opus.
Iugere: m. *A (Romane) furlong; 240 foot long, and 120 broad.*
Iugerie: f. *A Court, or seat of Iustice; also, the iurisdiction, liberties, territorie, or precincts of a towne.*
Iugioline: f. *Th'Indian oylie pulse, or white graine* Sesamum; *also, the plant that beares it.*
Iuglande. noix iuglande. *A Wallnut.*
Iugulaire: com. *Of, or belonging to, the throat.*
Veines iugulaires. *Looke* Veine.
Iuif: m. *A Iew.*
Iuifve: f. *A Iewesse.*
Iuifverie: f. *The Iewrie, or the part of a towne thats inhabited by Iewes; also, Iewdeisme; the religion, or sect of the Iewes.*
Iuillet: m. (*The moneth*) *Julie.*
Iuillet rosat. *A syrop made with Rose-water and Sugar.*
Iujubes: f. *The fruit, or plumme called Iuiubes.*
Iule: f. *A small worme that resembles the many-legd* Scolopendra, *or Palmer; also, an Italian coyne worth about* 6 d. sterl.
Iulep: m. *A Iulep, or Iuleb; a drinke made either of distilled waters and syrops mixed together; or of a decoction sweetned with honie or sugar, or else mingled with syrops; and ministred commonly as a preparatiue to open the passage of the inward parts, and to fit the humors for a purgation.*
Iumeau. *as* Gemeau; *A twin; also, a yong, or little mare.*
Iumelet: m. *A yong, or little twin.*
Iumelle. *A female twin, or sister twin; also (in Blason) a Barre* Gemeau.
Iumelles. *The cheekes, or side-beames of a presse.*
Iument: f. *A mare; also, water (in old French.)*

La grande iument Margot qui se bride par la queuë. *A Ship, or Gallie*; *See* Margot.
Iamais coup de iument ne fit mal à cheval: Prov. *A womans blow nere hurt the man she loued.*
Iune, & Iuner. *as* Ieune, & Ieuner.
Iunjubier: m. *A Iuiube tree, or plant.*
Iunonique. *Belonging to Iuno.* Oestre Iunonique. *Looke* Oestre.
Iuoil: m. *A white, and transparent fish, that is no bigger then a mans finger.*
Ivoire: m. *Ivorie, Elephants tooth.*
Ivoirin: m. ine: f. *Of Ivorie, like Ivorie.*
Iupin. *Iupiter.*
Iupinesque: com. *High, Soueraigne, Iouiall, Iupiter-like.*
Iupiter: m. *The God, or Planet Iupiter*; *also, tinne*; *so tearmed by Alchymists.*
Iupon. *as* Gippon; *A short Cassocke.*
Iuppe: f. *A shepheards pelt, frocke, or gaberdine*; *such a course long iacket as our Porters weare ouer the rest of their garments*; *(hence) also, a cassocke, long coat, loose ierkin.*
Iupper. *To whoot, showt, crie out alowd*; *(an old word.)*
Iurande: f. *An oath, deposition, swearing.*
Iuratoire: com. *Swearing, or, to be sworne.*
Iurats de Bourdeaux. *Are as the* Eschevins, *or Sherifes in other Cities.*
Iuraye. *as* Yvraye.
Iuré: m. ée: f. *Sworne, deposed, that hath taken an oath.*
Iurez. *Sworne Maisters in any Science, Trade, or facultie.*
Taille iurée. *Which is leuied, and paied without assesment, or any examination of the subiects abilitie.*
C'est mestier iuré il n'en est pas qui veut: Prov. *Looke* Mestier.
Iurée: f. *A Iurie*; *or rather a certaine companie of substantiall persons summoned, and sworne to giue in euidence betweene partie and partie.*
Les Bourgeois de Iurée. *Sworne Burgesses, or freemen.*
Droict de Iurée. *An yearelie dutie payed in old time vnto the Earles of* Champaigne *by all their subiects*; viz. vj. d. *in the pound vpon all their mouables*; *and* ij.d. *in the pound for all their immouables*; *yet might any of them be quit for* iiij.s. sterl. *a yeare. At this day the King, and other Lords of Iurisdiction receiue, in some places, the like from their Burgesses, or freemen.*
Taille & iurée. *as* Taille iurée.
Iurement: m. *An oath, deposition, swearing*; *the taking of an oath*; *a rapping out of an oath.*
Iurer. *To sweare, depose, take an oath, rap out an oath.*
Iurer és mains d'autruy. *(The old fashion of swearing) Looke* Main.
Il iure comme vn Abbé; chartier; gentilhomme; prelat. *Like a Tinker, say we.*
Ivreson: f. *(Th'act of) drunkennesse.*
Iureur: m. *A swearer, or deposer*; *one that takes an oath, or often raps out oathes*; *also, a Iuror, or witnesse deposed, whether to vtter the truth, or his knowledge.*
Iuridiciant: m. *A Iudge, or Magistrate*; *one that executes iustice, or deliuers the law.*
Iuridicié: m. *A partie, suitor, client*; *one that hath (or would haue) iustice done him*; *one that is in law.*
Iuridique: com. *Of, or belonging to, the law*; *also, actionable, suable, or which may be put in suit*; *also, iust, orderlie, iudiciall.*
Iuridiquement. *Iudicially, orderly, iustly, lawfully, according to law.*
Iurisconsulte: m. *A Lawyer.*
Iurisdiction: f. *Iurisdiction*; *authoritie, or power to administer iustice, and execute lawes*; (En droict la Iurisdiction ne signifie que la nue Iustice sans commandement: ¶Loyseau.)
Iurisdiction fieffale. *The Iurisdictiō a Landlord hath ouer his Tenants*; *or the priuiledge he hath to heare and determine the suites commenced against them, and all other complaints, or controuersies touching his, or their tenures.*
Basse Iurisdiction. *Looke* Basse Iustice.
Iurisprudence: f. *The skill, or knowledge of lawes*; *also, the stile, or forme of the law.*
Iuriste: m. *A Lawyer*; *also, a great swearer.*
Iuron: m. *An oath.*
Iuroye: f. *Darnell, Ray, Iueray.*
Ius: m. *Iuyce, liquor, sap, moisture*; *pottage, broath.*
Ius. Adverb. *Downe, or to the ground*; *whence*;
Ruer ius. *To ouerthrow.*
Mettre ius la saye. *To put off, or lay by, his coat.*
Iuscle: f. *The little Seafish tearmed a Cackerell.*
Iusier: m. *The giserne of a bird.*
Iusques. *Till, vntill, vnto.*
Iusques à ie ne dis mot; c'est, iusques au cul, ou au con.
Iusques à vous autres. *Euen you your selues.*
Iusquiame: m. *The weed Hogsbane, or Henbane.*
Iusquiame blanc. *White Henbane*; *called so of it white flower, and seed.*
Iusquiame iaulne. *Yellow Henbane, English Tobacco.*
Iusquiame noir. *Blacke Henbane*; *hath great and soft staulkes, broad and downie leaues, and bell-flowers yellowish in the top, and browne toward the bottome.*
Iussion: f. *A commaundement, appointment, expresse order set downe, expresse charge giuen.*
Iust: m. *as* Ius; *Iuice.*
Iuste: com. *Iust*; *equall, indifferent, impartiall, incorrupt, rightfull, vpright, sincere, lawfull, reasonable*; *due, right, euen, iumpe, leuell, straight*; *full, perfect*; *euen as it should be.*
Iustement. *Iustly, equally, indifferently, impartially, vprightly*; *lawfully*; *duely, euenly, straightly*; *fully, perfectly.*
Iustesse: f. *Iustnesse, iumpnesse, euennesse, true time, due measure, good proportion.*
Iustice: f. *Iustice, law, rightnesse, vprightnesse, indifferencie, impartialitie*; *also, a paire of Gallowes, or place (or instrument) of execution*; *also, Iurisdiction*; *(for which looke the next marginall word*; *) also, a Court of Iustice, or Iurisdiction.*
Iustice commutative. *Equalitie in exchange.*
Iustice corrective. *Penall iustice, punishment of offenders.*
Iustice criminelle. *That part of the law which deals with matters of life and death.*
Iustice distributive. *Equall distribution, dealing, or dole*; *the giuing vnto euerie one his owne.*
Iustice harmonique. *Harmonious, and iust proportion.*

Iustice de serment. *Triall of a cause by an oath ministred vnto one of the parties (an auntient forme of proceeding.)*

Appeller, ou mettre en Iustice. *To goe to law with; to sue, or commence a suit, against.*

Iustice: f. *Jurisdiction; power to administer iustice, authoritie to execute lawes, or to keep a Court for either; Of three principall kinds, High, Meane or middle, & Base or low; (although the word* Iustice *simply, and by it selfe imports onely the last;) also, the precinct, libertie, or territorie, wherein a Lord may exercise any of those kinds; also, the Court of such a Lord.*

Iustice censuelle, ou censiere. *An action, or suit, for* Censuel *rights; or, power to determine of controuersies that concerne his* Cens: *(A kind of* Iustice fonciere.)

Iustice domaniale. *as* Iustice fonciere.

Iustice pour ses droicts, & debites. *Jurisdiction vsurped by diuers Lords (of ample* Censiues, *and of many vassalls) for the righting of themselues in the recouerie of duties withheld from them.*

Iustice fonciere *(The second branch of* la Basse Iustice) *Exercised by the* Bas Iusticier *ouer his vassalls, and Tenants (at least) for the preseruation, and recouerie of his Seigneuriall dueties; (Diuers customes (as those of* Meaux, Valois, Xanctonge, S. Paul, *and the priuat ones of* Paris) *haue vtterly reiected, and forbidden this kind of base Jurisdiction; Others (as those of* Anjou, Touraine, le Mayne, *and* Lodunois) *confound it with the first branch.)*

Iustice manuelle. Quand le Seigneur, pour avoir payement des arrerages de sa rente, ou charge, prent de sa main namps sur l' heritage en la presence du Sergent, auquel il les delivre pour les discuter.

Iustice patibulaire à deux piliers. *Belongs vnto a Lord High* Iusticier; *Looke* Pilier.

Iustice à sang. *So doe the Customes of* Anjou, Touraine, *and* le Mayne, *tearme* La Moyenne Iustice; *giuing the Lord thereof power to iudge, and execute theeues, and men-killers; and to that end allowing him to set vp a paire of gallowes.*

Iustice du sang, & du Larron. *Power to take notice of blowes, and bloud-wipes (bestowed in hot bloud) and of theeueries which be not capitall; conferred on the Lord of* la Moyenne Iustice, *by the customes of Picardie, and Flanders.*

Iustice vicomtiere. la Moyenne Iustice; *tearmed so in all the customes of* la Gaule Belgique.

La basse Iustice. *Base, or low Iurisdiction; of two principall kinds;* viz: *Personall; which taketh notice of all personall Actions (not exceeding the value of 60 s. or not subiect to a greater amerciament then 7 s. 6 d.* Tourn.) *and reall, or* fonciere; *for which loooke* Iustice fonciere, *and for more touching this kind of Iurisdiction, in,* le Bas Iusticier.

La haute Iustice. *High Jurisdiction; authoritie to iudge, and determine all criminall, or capitall matters (except high treasons) and all ciuile Actions, or controuersies, except in Royall cases, and such as concerne Gentlemen, and the highwayes; wherewith no Lord, in the onely right of* haute Iustice, *is to meddle; Seeke* le haut Iusticier.

Acte de haute Iustice. *The condemnation of a malefactor, whether vnto death, or to indure some other corporall punishment.*

Executeur de haute Iustice. *An Executioner, or Hangman.*

La moyenne Iustice. *Meane, or middle Jurisdiction; authoritie to determine all ciuile controuersies (except the before excepted in* la haute Iustice; *) and to proceed against some kind of malefactors, (as in* le Moyen Iusticier.)

Iusticement: m. *Th' effect, or execution of Iustice, or of Iurisdiction.*

Iusticiable: com. *Iusticiable; vnder Iurisdiction, subiect vnto suit, or lawes; that is to doe his suit vnto the Court of another.*

Iusticiaire: com. *Of, or belonging vnto, Iustice, or Iurisdiction.*

Iusticier: m. *A Justice, or Justicer; a Gentleman that hath (as almost euerie Gentleman of meanes in France hath) High, Meane, or Low Jurisdiction, within a certaine Precinct; or within his owne (or another mans) Territories: All* Iusticiers *(though otherwise there be oddes ynough in their Priuiledges) must keepe Clerks; and Seales for Sentences, but not for Contracts, if they haue not* Droict de Tabellionné, ou Notariat *which onely some few high* Iusticiers *haue:) They may also haue to the number of six Sergeants, and Goalers for the keeping of their prisons.*

Le bas Iusticier; ou, le Seigneur bas Iusticier. *One that hath base Jurisdiction (within a certaine Precinct) ouer his owne, or another mans, tenants; takes notice of reall, or personall Actions not exceeding the value of 60 s; or wherein a greater amerciament, or fine then 7 s. 6 d.* Tour. *lies not: With trespasses a few Customes (as the reformed ones of* Paris, *and* Meleun) *allow him to deale, so they deserue not a greater fine then that; but the most restraine him to personall matters, and those especially that concerne his own rights; (with which onely the* Bas Iusticiers *of old time vsed to meddle; howsoeuer, their Iudges not content withall, haue in processe of time incroached on causes bred in villages betweene partie and partie, touching scisures, boundaries, deliuerie of possession, harme done by trespassing beasts, and other sleight and pettie differences, that require a speedie, and locall decision; for all which they are to keepe but foure Courts in a yeare:) Criminall persons taken in the manner he must apprehend, and may keepe them in his prison foure and twentie houres; but not longer, nor can he proceed further against them: Vpon euerie* Confiscation, Escheat, *or* Bien Vacant *that falls within his Libertie hee may take 7 s. 6 d.* Tourn. *but they are so few, and that so little, as many* Iusticiers *neglect it.*

Le haut Iusticier; ou, le Seigneur haut Iusticier. *A Lord of high Iurisdiction; iudges, and determines all ciuile, and criminall causes (except, as in* la haute Iustice) *happening within his Libertie, or Precinct; To which end hee keepes a Iudge, or* Garde de Iustice, *at this time stiled higher (* son Bailly, & Lieutenant, *) who must bee learned, and a Graduate (for a Iudge thats no Graduate is not, in France, held worthie to pronounce the sentence of death in an ordinarie Iurisdiction:) And because of his owne businesses determinable (if they concerne the rights of his Iurisdiction, or Seigneurie) in his owne Court, he also keepes a* Procureur fiscal, *by the name, and mouth of whom he pleads, euen as the King doth in higher Courts by his. He may hunt freely in fit seasons, ouer all the vninclosed groundes of his Liberties: Hee may fine his (offending) vassalls at his pleasure; and once in his time cause them all sweare, to acknowledge* *no other Iurisdiction then his; to preserue, by all possible meanes, the priuiledges thereof; and to informe him of any that shall offer to incroach vpon them: He leuies to his owne vse all fines, and confiscations (except for high treason) all Escheats (except bastards, & strangers goods) and all* Biens Vacans *(except some kind of wreckes) accruing within his Precincts: In Normandie he cannot keepe malefactors in his prison aboue 24 houres; after which (if he haue not the whilest condemned them) he must send them vnto the next Supreame Lord; In other Prouinces he may keepe them longer, and euerie where punish, according to the customes of the countrey, all sorts of them (euen to Sorcerers, Blasphemers, & Idolaters;) Only he refers ouer to the kings officers, and Courts, all such as commit, or be charged with, high treason.*

Le Moyen Iusticier. *The Lord of meane, or middle Iurisdiction; takes notice of all ciuile causes as well as the* Haut Iusticier *(except in th'ordering of the seperation of goods betweene married folkes; th'interdiction of vnthrifts;* & les Decrets; *wherein he comes as far short of him, as he goes beyond the* Bas Iusticier en le seellé, confection d' inventaire, emancipation, dation de tuteurs & curateurs, *wherewith the* Bas Iusticier *is not to deale:) But what criminall causes hee may take notice of is not agreed on by the customes of France; for some of them, as those of* Paris, Nivernois, *and others, assigne him none but such as are not finable aboue* 60 s. *(th'vtmost he can impose in any cause;) Others giue him power ouer Batteries, Bloudwipes, and sleight felonies; Others ouer Manslaughters, and capitall felonies: But others (the neerest vnto the Common Law of France) permit him to iudge no offendors but such as are to escape with life, & limme; And therfore his Iudge needs not be a Graduate: Nor hath he (as the* Haut Iusticier*) a* Procureur fiscal *(though he haue an Officer of almost the sa... nature, tearmed* Procureur d'Office*) because he hath no* fisque, *but onely an allowance of* 60 s. Tour. *o..t of euerie Confiscation, Escheat, or* Bien vacant, *thats leuied, or gotten, in his Precinct.*

Iusticier. *To iudge, gouerne, sway, haue iurisdiction ouer; chastise, correct, punish; execute the acts, or appointments of Iustice.*

Iusticier pour son fief. c'est, faire les saisies.

Iustificatif: m. iue: f. *Iustificatiue, iustifying, righting; making euen, or iust with.*

Iustification: f. *A iustification, purgation, cleering of.*

Iustifié: m. ée: f. *Iustified, purged, cleered,; also, made iust, euen, or equall with.*

Iustifier. *To iustifie, purge, cleere, excuse; also, to make iust, euen, or leuell with.*

Iusvert: m. *Greene-sauce.*

Iuveignerie: f. *Youngership; the condition, estate, or title of a younger brother:* ¶Breton.

Iuveigneur: m. *A younger brother.*

Iuveigneurie; ou, Iuveigneurerie. *as* Iuveignerie.

Iuvenile: com. *Young, youthfull, youthlie, childish.*

Iuvenilement. *Younglie, childishly, youthfully, youthlike.*

K

KAlendrier: m. *A Kalender, an Almanacke.*

Son Kalendrier est rubriché. *Her Kalender is full of Rubrickes; (saied of a woman that hath her Tearmes.)*

Kali. *(The hearbe) Glassewort, Saltwort, Crab-grasse, Frog-grasse.*

Karabe. *The best yellow Amber; Bead Amber, Bracelet Amber.* (Mot Arabique.)

Karat. *as* Carat.

Karesine. *as* Caresme.

Karobbe; ou, Karoble; *A Carob seed; also, the twentie fourth part of a grain (one of the least weights thats vsed by Goldsmithes.)*

Kebule. *The biggest kind of the Mirabolan plumme; long, and somewhat like a Peare, or small Leymon, in shape.*

Kebus. *as* Kebules.

Kedusudure: m. *The land Adder.* (Mot Barbare.)

Keratoïde. Tunique Keratoïde. *(as* Cornée;) *The hornie Tunicle of the eye.*

Kermes. *Scarlet berries, Scarlet graines; the seed of the Scarlet Oake.*

Kesudure. ¶Rab. *read* Kedusudure.

Kitre. *as* Pois liquide; *Tarre.*

Kyriele; ou, Kyrielles. *A multitude, or great number; also, a mightie coile, or noise.*

Kyst: m. *A membrane; little skin, or bladder, within the bodie, containing superfluous humors.*

L

LA. *An Article of the Feminine Gender (as in)* La maison; *the house; also, a Feminine Relatiue; (whence)* Ne la voyez vous pas? *See you not it, or her?)*

La faire longue. *To liue, abide, or stay, long.*

Là. *(An Aduerbe of place) There, thither, yonder, in that place; (also, of exhorting, or incouraging)* Là, ou lalà; *now now, goe to goe to; on there; againe there.*

Là bas. *Beneath, below; downe, downewards.*

I'en suis là. *I am of that mind, or humor.*

Que diriez vous là. *What would you say in that case?*

Ils ne passeront iamais par là. *They will neuer play that part, hold that course, yeeld vnto those conditions.*

Labdane: m. *Labdanum; a fat, clammie, transparent, & sweet-smelling Gumme, or liquor, gathered from off the leaues of the little shrub called* Cistus Ledon; *also, the sweet oyle thats made thereof.*

Labeche: f. *A South-west wind.*

Labeur: m. *Labour, trauell, toyle, paines; worke, exercise; contention, diligence, indeuour.*

Labeurer. *Sometimes vsed for* Labourer; *whence;*

En peu d'heure Dieu labeure: Prov. *God workes his will in a small while.*

Labie: f. *A lip.*

Labier: m. ere: f. *Of, or belonging to, a lip.*

Veine labiere. *The lip-veine; Seeke* Veine.

Labile: com. *Slipperie, vnstable, fleeting, subiect vnto falling.*

Laboration: f. *A labouring, working, trauelling, moyling, toiling.*

Labordean: m. *A Habera...*

Laborieusement. *Laboriously, painfully, toilesomely; diligently, industriously.*

Laborieux: m. euse: f. *Laborious, painefull, toylesome, difficult; industrious, diligent.*

Labour: m. *Tilth, tillage, husbandrie, labouring, ploughing, or breaking vp of the ground.*

Labourable: com. *Labourable, workable, fit to be wrought on; also, nauigable.*
Labourage: m. *as* Labour.
Labouré: m. ée: f. *Laboured; wrought, trauelled, toiled; striuen, contended, indeuoured, in; also, tilled, aired, ploughed, husbanded.*
Labourer. *To labour, trauell, worke, toyle, moile, drudge, take pains; to striue, contend, indeuour, be diligent, in.*
Labourer la terre. *To till, aire, plough, breake vp, husband the ground;* Labourer à bled la terre; *to sow it.*
Le grand boeuf apprend à labourer au petit: Pro. *The great Oxe learnes the little one to worke.*
Tout ce que le Clerc laboure folle femme devore: Prov. *All that the Clerke can scrape his trull consumes.*
Labouret: m. *Shepheards purse, Shepheards pouch, Toiwort, Caseweed, Pickepurse, poore-mans Parmacetie.*
Laboureur: m. *A labourer, worker, toyler; a Hind, ploughman, husbandman, labouring man; also, as* Courtilliere.
Laboureur de nature. *A mans yard.*
Piece de laboureur salé. *A peece of powdered beefe.*
Labrusque: m. *The wild (grape-bearing) vine.*
Labyrinthe: m. *A laborinth, maze; intricate matter.*
Faire le tour du labyrinthe. *To labour hard and be neuer a whit the neerer; also, to fall againe, after much adoe, into the matter he first handled.*
Labyrinthé: m. ée: f. *Made as a laborinth, framed like a maze; intricated; full of vnknowne crookes, creeks, turnings, windings.*
Labyrinther. *To make (or make like) a laborinth, or maze; to intricate; also, to wind, compasse, or turne many times in and out; to be full of many vnknowne crookes, or creekes.*
Labyrintheux: m. euse: f. *Most intricate; full of turnings, crookes, windings.*
Lac: m. *A lake; a great poole, or meere; also, a ginne, or snare; as in* Laqs.
Lacé: m. ée: f. *Laced; bound, or tied with a lace; also, snarled, or insnaring.*
Lacement: m. *A lacing; also, an insnaring; or a setting of snares for.*
Lacer. *To lace; to bind, or tie vp with a lace; also, to insnare; or to set ginnes, or snares for.*
Laceration: f. *A laceration, tearing, rending, dismembring, mangling.*
Laceré m. ée: f. *Lacerated, torne, rent, mangled, dismembred, peecemealed.*
Lacerer. *To lacerate, rend, peecemeale, teare, mangle, dismember.*
Laceron: m. *The Sow-thistle, Hares-thistle, Hares Colewort.*
Lacert: m. *A Lizard; also, the Viuer, or lesse Sea-dragon; tearmed so because it somewhat resembles a Dragon.*
Lacerte. *A fleshie muscle; tearmed so because it hath (as a Lezard) a long taile.*
Lacet: m. *The lace of a peticoat, a womans lace, or lacing; also, a snare, or ginne.*
Lachrymal: m. ale: f. *Weeping, bewailing; teare-like, dropping, moist:* ¶Rab.
Laconiquement. *Strictly, or sparingly (in life;) shortly, or pithily (in speech.)*

Laconiser. *To liue strictly, or sparingly; to speake briefely, or pithily.*
Lacquay. *as* Laquay.
Lacque: f. *Sanguine; rose or rubie, colour; (The true* Lacca *is an Armenian Gumme vsed in the dying of Crimsons, and afterwards (growne artificiall) imployed by Painters.)*
Lacre: m. *A confection, or stuffe, made of rosin, brimstone, and white wax mingled, and melted together; which growne cold is as hard as a stone, and cleaues inseperably vnto the thing thats closed with it; Our best hard wax is a kind of it.*
Lactifiant: m. ante: f. *as* Lactifique.
Lactifique: com. *Milk-breeding, milk-making, milkyeelding.*
Lacunaire: m. *The maine beame of a house being somewhat arched; also, an arched seeling, or floore of boords.*
Lacune: f. *A puddle, pit, or ditch of standing water; also, a fenne, marsh, or waterish ground.*
Lacustre: com. *Lakie, belonging to a lake.*
Ladane: m. *The sweet Gumme* Ladanum; *comes of a fat dew, or liquor, gathered from the leaues of the shrub* Cistus Ledon.
Ladre: com. *Leaprous, lazerous; mezeld, scuruie.*
Herbe aux ladres. *Fluellin, Speed-well, Groundheele, Paules Betonie.*
Riche comme vn ladre. *Seeke* Riche.
Celuy est bien ladre, il ne sent point quand on luy pique la chair. *Appliable to a dullard, or a coward; one thats vnsencible and cannot, or fearefull and will not, feele the wrongs done to him.*
Ladrerie: f. *A Spittle for leapers, a place wherein they abide; also, leaprosie, scuruinesse, meazeldnesse.*
Ladrige: f. *Leaprosie, leaprousnesse, meazeldnesse, scuruinesse.*
Ladronnerie: f. *A denne of theeues.*
Lagagne. *Corne-rose, red Poppie:* ¶Langued.
Lai: m. *Breadth of cloth, &c; Seeke* Lé, & Lais.
Lai: m. Laie: f. *Lay, secular; of the Laytie, none of the Clergie; temporall, vulgar.*
Frere lai. *A seruant in an Abbey, or Couent.*
Laict: m. *Milke.*
Laict aigre. *Whay; also, a sillibub, or merribowke.*
Laict caillé. *Curds, curded milke, fresh cheese.*
Laict clair. *Whay.*
Laict esburré. *Butter-milke.*
Laict de nostre Dame. *The white Thistle.*
Le laict nouveau. *Beest, or Beestings.*
Laict Tabian. *A milke thats verie healthfull for such as are in a consumption; of* Tabia, *a place in Italie, the aire whereof is said to haue the same vertue.*
Laict Virginal. *A milke compounded of the froth, or spume of gold steeped in vineger, and salt, infused in waters of Plantaine, Nightshade, and Roses.*
Dent le laict. *A coults tooth, or young tooth; also, a priuie grudge.*
Eau de laict. *Clarified whay; also, water of milke or drawne by stillitorie from milke.*
Frere de laict. *A foster brother.*
Herbe à laict. *Spurge, Milke-weed, Wolues-milke.*
Herbe au laict. *Sea Milke-wort, blacke Saltwort.*
Petit laict. *Whay.*
Mouches en laict. *A plaine matter, cleere case, euident demonstration.*
Son espée a bien du laict. *His sleeping sword (like a seldome-drawne vdder) hath surely store of milke in't.*

Il a tetté de bon laict. *He hath beene well bred; there is much worth, or a great deale of good stuffe, in him.*

Yvre de laict caillé. *Tipled, or distempered by a small matter; whose weake braines are ouerturned by any weake liquor.*

Vache de loing a laict assez: Prov. *A forreine commoditie cannot be defectiue; we esteeme that most that comes furthest.*

Vin sur laict c'est souhait, laict sur vin c'est venin: Prov. *Wash thy milke off thy liuer, (say we.)*

Laictages: m. *White meates, milke meat.*

Laictance: m. *The fat, or foame of lime, or chaulke, resembling milke, and therefore thus tearmed; also, as* Laicte.

Laicte: f. *The milt, or soft roe, of fishes.*

Laicté: m. ée: f. *Milkie.*

Laictée: f. *A litter of whelpes.*

Laictence. *as* Laictance.

Laicterie: f. *A Dairie, or milke-house.*

Laicteron: m. *The Sow-thistle.*

Laicteron aspre. *The pricklie Sow-thistle.*

Laicteron blanc. *The white-flowered Sow-thistle.*

Laicteron lissé. *Hares Lettuce; the smooth (or ordinarie) Sow-thistle.*

Laicteron noir. *The wild, and pricklie Sowthistle.*

Laictier: m. ere: f. *Milkie, full of milke, milke-yeelding, made of milke.*

L'herbe laictiere. *Tythimal, Spurge, Milke-reed, Wolues-milke.*

Vache laictiere. *A milch Cow.*

Laictifique: com. *Milke-making, milke-yeelding.*

Laictuë: f. *Lettuce.*

Laictuë aigre. *The bitter wild Endiue, or narrow-leaued Endiue.*

Laictuë capusse. *Cabbadge Lettuce.*

Laictuë de chevres. *Lambes Lettuce, Corne sallade.*

Laictuë crespe, ou crespuë. *Crisped, curled, wrinkled, or crumpled Lettuce.*

Laictuë pommée. *Cabbadge Lettuce, loafed Lettuce, headed Lettuce.*

Laictuë Romaine. *The greatest kind of Cabbadge Lettuce.*

Laictuë ronde. *Loafed, or headed Lettuce, that grows close by the ground.*

Laictuë sauvage. *Wild Lettuce, greene Endiue; also, the hearbe Hawkeweed; also, the bitter wild Endiue, or narrow-leaued Endiue.*

Laid: m. Laide: f. *Foule, deformed, mishapen, disfigured, ill-fauoured, ouglie, vncomelie; filthie; loathsome; vile.*

Laid comme vn marpaut. *See* Marpaut.

Laide vilenie. *as* Laidange.

Laidange: m. *Reproach, reuiling, railing, defamation; iniurious, opprobrious, or outragious language; a hainous imputation:* (dequoy celuy qui a iniurié vn autre à tort se doit desdire en iustice, en se prenant par le bout du nez: ¶Ragueau.)

Laidanger. *To reuile, reproach, defame, discredite, raile on, outrage in words.*

Laidangeux: m. euse: f. *Reproachfull, reuiling, opprobrious, defamatorie, slaunderous, contumelious.*

Laidement. *Foully, deformedly, mishapenly, ouglily, ill-fauouredly; loathsomely.*

Laideron: m. onne: f. *Somewhat ouglie, prettie and foule.*

Laideur: f. *Foulnesse, deformitie, ill-fauourednesse, ouglinesse; filthinesse, vilenesse, loathsomenesse.*

Laidoyer. *as* Laidanger.

Laie: f. *Wood-ground, by measure, or quantitie of* Arpens.

Laïer. c'est marquer les lais en vn bois taillis avant la couppe d'iceluy, pour les y laisser.

Laiete: f. *as* Layette.

Laignié: f. *Wood:* ¶Pic.

Laignier: m. *A wood-yard, or wood-pile.*

Laigs: m. *Legacies; things bequeathed by will.*

Laine: f. *Wooll.*

Laine de bois. *Cotton, bombast, or bombace.*

Laine sourge. *New-shorne, vnwashed, or greazie wooll.*

Laine avec le suin. *The same.*

Mouton à la grande laine. *Seeke* Mouton.

Batre la laine. *To lecher, to haire-beat it.*

Demander de la laine à vn Asne. *To aske a thing of them which haue it not.*

Tirer la laine. *(In spinning of wooll) to draw the thread out; also, to twitch a cloake off a mans backe, and runne away with it.*

A mol Pasteur le loup chie laine: Prov. *A gentle shepheard makes the Wolfe shite wooll.*

L'vn a le bruit l'autre lave la laine: Prov. *Th'one gets the credit th'other takes the paines.*

Qui n'a laine boiue à la fontaine: Prov. *Let him that hath no wooll drinke at the well.*

Laine-facture: f. *Spinning, carding, working of woll; Cloathing; or the labour, or trade, of Clothiers.*

Laineux: m. euse: f. *Woollie; full of wooll.*

Marcher avec les pieds laineux. *To goe softly, tread gingerly.*

Lairre: m. *as* Larron; *A thiefe.* (v.m.)

Lais: m. *Trees, or bushes, left as markes in a copse-wood; or, as* Layes *(in the later sence.)*

Laisard: m. *A Lizard; a Newt, an Aske; See* Lezard.

Laisarde: f. *as* Laisard, *or* Lezard.

Laisardin: m. *Lizard-like; of, or belonging to, a Lizard.*

Laische. *as* Lesche.

Laise: f. *The breadth of a peece of cloth, stuffe, ground, &c.*

Laisse: f. *as* Lesse; *Also, a lease of hounds, &c.*

Laissé: m. ée: f. *Left, relinquished, layed apart, put off, giuen ouer, abandoned, forsaken, omitted, forgone; See* Laisser.

Il a laissé ses houseaux. *He hath tipped vp the heels; or is readie to doe it.*

Laisser. *To leaue, relinquish, lay apart, set aside, put off, let alone, forgoe, let goe, forsake, abandon, giue ouer, omit.*

Laisser les botes. *Looke* Botes.

Laisser courre. *To hound, or let slip, a Dog at Deere.*

Laisser dire. cela se laisse dire. *That is commonly spoken;* Ie me suis laissé dire cela. *I was told that.*

Laisser de l'eau en son moulin. *To reserue vnto himselfe some worke, or somewhat to doe.*

Laisser le ieu quand il est beau. *To giue ouer a game at the fairest; (Appliable either to a temperate, or an irresolute, humor.)*

Laisser la lancette dans la veine. *Seeke* Veine.

Laisser le monstier ou il est. *Not to change, or alter an auntient custome (especially of the Church.)*

Laisser le moule du pourpoint. *Seeke* Moule.

On ne doit pas laisser bonne terre pour mauvais Seigneur: Prov. *Rich land must not be left for a rigorous Landlord; nor a good countrey quit because tis gouerned by a bad Prince.*

Laisses: m. *The lesses (or dung) of a wild Boare, Wolfe, or Beare.*

Laist: f. *as* Lé; *or* Lez.

Laitage: m. *as* Laittage.

Laite: f. *The milt, or soft roe of a fish.*

Laitisse. *A kind of whitish grey furre.*

Laiton: m. *Lattin (mettall.)*

Laittage: m. *The ballast of a ship.*

Laitterie: f. *as* Laicterie.

Laive: f. *A kind of tile.*

Laiz: m. *A Legacie; also, the increase that a riuer yeelds to a Lord (by an Island, or Hoult growing within it;) also, rews of shrubs, or bushes marked out in a Copse, or Vnderwood.*

Laize: f. *as* Laise; *Breadth.*

Laize de cuir. *A scourge, or thong of leather.*

'A la grande laize. *Amply, fully, or in full measure; also, at th'old rent.*

Lamaneur: m. *The Pilot of a ship.*

Lambdoïde. Commissure Lamb. *A certaine ioynt, or seame in the hinder part of the scull.*

Lambeau: m. *A shread, rag, or small peece of stuffe, or of a garment readie to fall from, or holding but little to, the whole; also, a Labell.*

Lambeaux. *Rags, or shreads; also, the ragged haire, or ragged (old) coat of a Deere.*

Lambeaux de feu. *Streakes, or flakes of fire.*

Mis par lambeaux. *Rent, or torne in peeces; ouerthrowne, ruined, spoiled.*

Cela ne se trouve point es lambeaux des Iurisconsultes. *There is no law for that opinion; or, the ragged, and beggerlie interpreters of the law haue no such thing among them.*

Lambel: m. *A Labell of three points; or a File with three Labells pendant; (The mark of an eldest sonne, in Blazon.)*

Lambeliner. *To gull, deceiue, delude, besot, bring into a fooles Paradice.*

Lambin: m. *The great partie-coloured, and stinging Bumble, or Humble-bee; also, a great cokes, doult, hoydon, lout, loobie, foolish lubber.*

Lambiqué: m. ée: f. *Distilled by Limbeck.*

Lambiquer. *To distill by a Limbeck.*

Lambourde: f. *A Summer-tree, full of mortaises for th'ends of Ioysts to lie in.*

Lambrequin: m. *The point of a Labell, or Labell of a File, in Blazon.*

se Lambriquer le cerveau. *To beat, puzzle, or toyle the head about.*

Lambris: m. *Wainscot, seeling; also, a frettized, or embowed seeling.*

Lambrissage: m. *A wainscotting, or seeling; also, an embowing, or frettizing in wainscot.*

Lambrissé: m. ée: f. *Seeled, wainscotted; fretted, embowed.*

Lambrissement. *as* Lambrissage.

Lambrisser. *To wainscot, seele; fret, embow.*

Lambruche. *as* Lambrunche.

Lambrun: m. *Wainscot, seeling.*

Lambrunche: f. *The wild grape-bearing vine.*

Lambrunchement: m. *Wainscot, or, a wainscotting.*

Lambrusque. *as* Lambrunche.

Lame: f. *A thinne plate of any mettall; (hence) also, a blade; also, a tombe, or tombe-stone; also, a great surge, or waue of the sea, after a tempest; also, the reed, or slay of a Weauers loome.*

N'admirons le fourreau pour mespriser la lame. *let not an outside be admired to the neglect of th'inside.*

Lamen: m. *as* Lamentation.

Lamentable: com. *Lamentable, wailefull, monefull, dolefull, wofull, drierie, pitifull.*

Lamentation: f. *A lamentation, wailing, bewailing, waymenting, moaning; a pitifull complaint.*

Lamenter. *To lament, wayment, waile, weepe, complaine pitifully, make moane.*

Lames: f. *(The Plurall of* Lame; *also) th'earthie dregs, or drosse of mettall after the first washing thereof.*

Lamibaudichon. *A tale of a tub, or of a roasted horse; also, a word vsed among boyes in a play (much like our Fox) wherein he to whom tis vsed must runne, and the rest indeuor to catch him.*

Lamie: f. *A Breake-net; the greatest, and most rauenous kind of Dog-fish.*

Lamine: f. *A thinne plate of mettall; a sword blade; a shingle, or slate; a thinne planke, or boord; also, a brason tombe, or tombe-plate; also, a Corslet made all of rib-like ioynts to moue with, or be the more pliant vnto, the bodie.*

Lampas: m. *The Lampasse (or swelling) in a horses mouth.*

Lampassé de gueules. *Langued, or, whose tongue is red; (a tearme of Blazon.)*

Lampast. *as* Lampas.

Lampe: f. *A Lampe; also, the sharpe-pointed Docke; (whence;)*

Lampe de marais. *The water Docke, water Sorrell, horse Sorrell.*

Cul de lampe. *The bottome of an out-iutting roome, fashioned like the foot of a Lampe.*

De main en main vous est la lampe baillée. *At length your turne is come; your course is now to speake, &c.*

Lampereau: m. *The name of a black vine which yeelds very good wine.*

Lamperon: m. *A little Lampe.*

Lampeux: m. euse: f. *Full of Lampes; of, or belonging to, a Lampe.*

Lampier: m. *A candlesticke, or branch, for a Lampe.*

Lampiride: f. *A Gloe-worme, or Glow-bird that shines by night.*

Lamponner. *as* Lanterner.

Lamponnier: m. *A vaine goose, a fond or idle companion.*

Lampourde: f. *The Cloat, or great Burre:* ¶Langued.

Lamprillon: m. *A Lamprill, or little Lamprey.*

Lamproye: f. *A Lamprey.*

Lamproyon: m. *A Lamprill, or small Lamprey.*

Lampsane: f. *as* Lampsans.

Lampsans: m. *Docke-cresses; (a wild pot-hearbe.)*

Lampugos. *A kind of Lobsters, which in cold weather hide themselues in hollow places, and cannot be taken.*

Lampugue: f. *A kind of delicate small-mouthed fish (in the Italian, or Adriaticke sea) which hath prickles both on her backe and bellie, and in stead of each rib seuen small bones:* ¶Marseillois.

Lanage: m. *Wollage; the trade of wooll, or gaine thats made thereof.*

Lanc: m. *A stroke in swimming; also, a space, pause, interval, intermedium.*

Lançade: f. *A launch, hurle, throw, fling, darting.*

Lance: f. *A Launce; a (horse-mans) speare, or staffe; also (the horseman that beares it,) a Lanceere, or man of Armes;*

Armes; also, the Masculine line in a Pedegree.

Lance à boëte. *A lance with a burre, or blunt head; a tilting staffe.*

Lance à bout d'or. *A mans yard.*

Lance de carriere. *A staffe to run at the Ring with.*

Lance courtoise. *as* Lance à boëte.

Lance de S.Crespin. *A Shoomakers nawle.*

Lance fournie. *A man of Armes furnished at all points; viz. with fiue great horses; two for himselfe; one for his Armour-bearer; and two for two Archers to serue on; (besides two others of lesse value for his prouision, and baggage.)*

Courir la lance. *To tilt, or to runne at tilt.*

Hà la bonne lance; &, o la hardie lance. *(Phrases commonly vsed in reproach, and to the disgrace, of a Coward.)*

Hardie langue couarde lance: Pro. *Couragious language a cowardlie lance.*

Lancé: m. ée: f. *Throwne, hurled, flung, darted; also, pierced, pricked, or thrust through; also, rowsed, or thrust vp, as a Deere; also, thinne, lanke, meagar, leane, starueling.*

Lancelée: f. *Ribwort Plantaine, Lambes-tongue.*

Lanceman: m. *A Compatriote, or Countreyman; (a word which the Frenchman borrowes of the Dutch to mocke him withall.)*

Lancement: m. *The same; also, a throwing, hurling, flinging, darting; also, a rowsing, or thrusting vp of a Deere.*

Lanceole, & Lanceolette. *as* Lancelée.

Lance-pessade: m. *A Lancepesado; the meanest officer in a foot-companie.*

Lancer. *(Violently) to throw, fling, hurle, dart; also, to pricke, pierce, hit, or strike, as with the point of a lance; also, to rowse, or thrust vp, a Deere.*

Se Lancer dedans. *To runne headlong, or cast himselfe hastily, into.*

Se Lancer sur. *To runne fiercely, rush furiously, giue a violent, or hot charge, vpon.*

Lanceron: m. *A Ieg, or Iacke; a Pickerell thats about a foot long.*

Lancette: f. *A Surgeons Launcet; also, a little lance.*

Laisser la lancette dans la veine. *Seeke* Veine.

Lanceur: m. *A hurler, darter, thrower.*

Lanci: m. *The Squinancie; also, a kind of stitch, or paine like a stitch.*

Lancier: m. *A Lance, Lanceere, Speareman; a horseman that serues with a Lance; also, as* Lanciere.

Lanciere: f. C' est vn sommier mis à vn cheminée passant à travers le mur mitoyen d'un voisin; *also, as* Abbée.

Lancinant. *Pricking, striking, or thrusting through; also, rending, or tearing with the teeth; also, wasting, or consuming.*

Lanciner. *To pricke, strike, open, or thrust into (as with the point of a lance;) also, to rend, or teare with the teeth; also, to wast, or consume.*

Lancy. *as* Lanci.

Lande: f. *A Land, or Laund; a wild, vntilled, shrubbie, or bushie Plaine.*

Landgrave: m. *A Lantgraue; the Earle of a Prouince.*

Landie: f. *The deaw-lap in a womans Priuities (as in* Landies;) *whence;*

Landie deschiquetée. *An ouglie nickname for an ouerridden Hackney (or Harlot.)*

Landier: m. *An Andiron.*

Landies: f. *The two Pterigones, or great wings within the lips of a womans Priuities.*

Landits. *as* Lendits.

Landore: m. *A rude clowne, gazing hoydon, staring lowt; also, a leaden fellow, poore sneakesbie, man of dowgh.* ¶Normand.

Landrivel: m. *The Lanterne of a Ship.*

Landyer. *To cloy, wearie, trouble, be tedious vnto.*

Laneret: m. *The Hawke so called.*

Lanfrelucher. *To lecher.* ¶Rab.

Langage: m. *Language, talke, speech; discourse; also, a Language, or Tongue.*

C'est vn langage du temps des hauts bonnets. *This is an old wiues tale; or a fashion of speech cleane out of fashion.*

Langager: m. *as* Langageur, *or* Langagier.

Langager. *To chat, pratle, bable, tattle, vse many words.*

Langageur: m. *A prater, pratler, tattler, babler.*

Langagier: m. ere: f. *Prating, babling, tattling, full of tongue.*

Langart. *as* Languard.

Langayer. *To reason, discourse, hold chat with; also, to worme, or search the root of the tongue of a Hog, &c.*

Langayerie: f. *The worming of Hogs, &c.*

Langayeur: m. *A great talker; also, an Officer that searches the tongues of Market-Hogs, thereby to discerne whether they be sound or no.*

Lange: m. *A kind of sea-bird, which diuing into the bellie of a Whall, feeds on his heart.*

Langeots: m. *Little Swath-bands, or clouts of wooll for little children.*

Langes: m. *Woollen Swath-bands, or clouts for little children.*

Langoureusement. *Languishingly, faintingly, droopingly, as one thats wholly decayed.*

Langoureux: m. euse: f. *Languishing, drooping, pining, faint, failing in strength, drayned of (naturall) moisture, depriued of vigor.*

Langouste: f. *A Locust, or Grashopper; also, a kind of Lobster that hath vndiuided cleyes, a long beake (or beard) and prickles on her backe.*

Langoustin: m. *A great (or the greatest) Prawne.* ¶Langued.

Langoyer. *To languish, or pine away.*

Langrole: f. *The Newte, Aske, or small Lizard that haunteth old, and ill-kept houses.* ¶Langued.

Langroust: m. *The sea-Creuice; or, as* Langouste.

Language. *as* Langage.

Languagier. *as* Langagier, *or* Languard.

Languard: m. *A blab, long-tongue, prating companion.*

Languarde: f. *A babling gossip, tattling houswife, chatting dame; a tittle-tattle, or twattle-basket; a wench whose tongue neuer lyes.*

Languayeur. *as* Langayeur.

Langue: f. *A Tongue (the instrument of speech;) also, a Language, Tongue, Speech; a phrase, or forme of speech; also, a particular Nation, or People vsing a peculiar speech; whence,* Ceux de la langue de France, d'Angleterre, d'Espagne; *the French, English, or Spanish Nation; also, the hearbe Adders tongue.*

Langue de bœuf. *Lang de beuf, Ox-tongue, rough or small Buglosse; also, a kind of weapon vsed in old time.*

Langue de bouc. *Wild Buglosse, wall Buglosse, Vipers Buglosse, Vipers hearbe.*

Langue de cerf. *Harts-tongue, stone Harts-tongue; mistaken, in many shops, for* Scolopendria, *Spleenwort, or stone-Fearne.*

Langue de chien. *Dogs tongue, Hounds tongue, Hounds pisse.*

Langue marine. *A kind of long, and narrow Sole, or daintie fish like a Sole.*

Langue de mer. *A narrow Promontorie, or peece of land running into the sea, and resembling a tongue thrust out of the mouth.*

Langue d'oyseau. *An Ashen Key, or Kite-key; the fruit of the Ash.*

Langue passerine. *as* Langue d'oyseau.

Langue de Serpent. *Adders-tongue, Serpents-tongue (an hearbe;) also, a certaine tongue-resembling precious stone, (as some hold) not bred on the earth, but in heauen, whence it falls in the wane of the Moone; also, the venomous tongue of a Detractor; also, the long, narrow, and Saw-like Snowt of a West Indian sea-fish.*

Langue de tripiere. *That scolds like an Oyster-wife, or butterwhore.*

Herbe aux langues. *Tongwort, Tong-blade, Double-tongue, Horse-tongue, Laurell of* Alexandria.

Avoir la langue en la bouche, non en la bourse. *Sayd of a Babler, or Blab, whose tongue-strings are quickly vnloossed.*

Avoir la langue bien pendue. *To haue an eloquent, and glib tongue in his head.*

Bailler du plat de la langue. *To sooth, smooth, flatter, gloze, collogue with.*

Prendre langue. *To learne newes, or get intelligence, abroad; to take prisoners thereby to examine what an enemie intends.*

Prendre langue entre eux. *To conferre, or debate a matter, together.*

Tirer la langue sur. *To scorne, flowt, mocke, deride.*

Hardie langue coüarde lance: Pro. *Those that brag most, execute least.*

Longue langue courte main: Prov. *Those that promise most performe least.*

Qui langue a à Rome va: Prov. *He that knowes what, and when, to speake, may trauell any whither.*

Beau parler n'escorche langue: Prov. *Good words cost nothing (say we.)*

Mieux vaut glisser du pied que de la langue: Pro. *Better may a foot slip then the tongue trip.*

Langué: m. ée: f. *Langued (a tearme of Blason.)*

Languette: f. *A little tongue; also, the weesell, or couer of the throat; also, the point, or tongue of a Leauer; also, the tryall, or cocke of a ballance.*

Languette de hault-bois. *The little pipe, tongue, or tenon, which is in the mouth of a Hoe-boy, &c.*

Langueur: f. *Langor, languishment, pining, drooping; faintnesse, feeblenesse; wearisomenesse; want of mettall, decay of spirit, losse of vigor; a consumption; also, idlenesse, lithernesse.*

Langui: m. ie: f. *Languished, pined, decayed, fainted, drooped.*

Langui de soif. *Halfe dead for thirst.*

Languir. *To languish, pine, decay, wast away; to droope, faint, hang downe the head; also, to linger, idle it, be lither.*

Languissant. *Languishing.*

Languissant d'amour. *Farre spent with, or gone in, loue.*

Languisson. *as* Langueur.

Lanice: com. *Of, or belonging to, Wooll; See* Lanisse.

Lanier: m. *A Lanner.*

Laniere: f. *A long, and narrow band, or thong, of leather; also, a leatherne string to hang keyes at.*

Lanieres. *Hawkes Lunes.*

A courte chausse longue laniere: Prov. *To short hose long points, and wide trussing; or (which is of harder disgestion;) let one mans store supply anothers wants.*

Lanifice: m. *Wooll-worke; or working with wooll; spinning, carding, clothworking.*

Lanifique: com. *Wooll-breeding.*

Lanisse: com. *Of, or belonging to, Wooll.*

Bourre lanisse. *Flocks of Wooll; also, the knottie, or vneuen swellings that be in some threads of ill-spunne Wooll.*

Lanoy. *as* Lanier. ¶Savoyard.

Lansquenet. *A Lanceknight, or Germane footman; also, the name of a game at Cards.*

Lanstringue. *Drinke countreyman; (a Dutch word.)* ¶Rab.

Lantagine: f. *A kind of Laurell, or Bay tree, whose leafe yeelds no manner of smell.*

Lantane: f. *The wayfaring tree.*

Lante. *A kind of Spider.*

Lantenaires: f. *Laniers; called so, when of themselues they come into France out of Northerne Countries; in which passage the cold and salt ayre of the sea commonly defaces the beautie of their feathers.*

Lanterne: f. *A Lanterne; also, the scutcheon, or closure of a Tymber vault, where the ends of the branches thereof doe meet.*

Lanterne de mer. *A fish which some hold to be the Rochet; others the* Milan Marin; *others, as* Arondelle de mer.

Lanterne à pagnons. *A paire of trundles, or trundle heads; that which is turned about by the cog wheele of a Mill.*

Lanterne sourde. *A close yron Lanterne, or theeues Lanterne.*

Croire que vessies sont lanternes. *To mistake verie grossely, to be of a most foolish beleefe.*

Lanterné: m. ée: f. *Puzled, confounded, troubled, much perplexed, distempered; miserable, wretched, in a pitifull taking, in a wofull or ill plight; also, abused, buggared.*

Lanterner. *To cog, foist, fib; dally, or play the foole with; also, to trouble, or be tedious vnto; also, to loyter; also, to buggar, or be buggared; also, to quaffe, reuell, feast it all night long, or many nights together.*

Lanterner la cervelle. *To puzle, confound, or intoxicate the braine; to fill the head with idle proclamations.*

Lanternerie: f. *Cogging, foisting; vanitie, foolerie; loytering, night-walking, night-reuells.*

Lanternerie de cervelle. *Trouble, or intoxication of the braine.*

Lanternier: m. *A Lanterne-carrier; also, a cogger, foister, dallying, or witlesse youngster, idle, or vaine companion; also, a night-walker; one that, when others are in bed, reuells abroad, or bankets at home.*

Lanugineux: m. euse: f. *Cottonie, downie; mossie; soft as cotton, or wooll; also, couered with soft, and short haire, downe, or wooll.*

Lanuleux: m. euse: f. *Woollie, downie, tender, soft, as plyant as any wooll.*

Lanzon: m. *A Pike, or Pickerell.*

Lapace: m. *The ordinarie, or sharpe-pointed Docke.*

Lapas: m. *Patience, Monks Rhewbarb.*

Lapas aigu. *The sharpe-pointed Docke.*

Lapereau: m. *A young Rabbet.*

Lapes. *Fierie eiaculations in the ayre.* ¶Rab.

Lapidaire: m. *A Lapidarie, or Ieweller.*
Lapidation: f. *A stoning; a battering, or killing with stones.*
Lapidé: m. ée: f. *Stoned; beaten, battered, or killed with stones.*
Lapidement: m. *A stoning.*
Vn lapidement de gresle. *A violent pattering of hailestones.*
Lapider. *To stone; to throw stones at; to batter, knocke, or kill with stones; also, to raine stones.*
Lapideur: m. *A stoner.*
Lapifidié: m. ée: f. *as* Lapifié.
Lapifié: m. ée: f. *Made or become stonie, turned into a stone.*
se Lapifier. *To be made stonie, become stone, be turned into a stone.*
Lapin: m. *A Rabbet.*
Il a memoire de lapin. *He hath a verie bad memorie; or forgets, by too much hast, wherefore he makes hast.*
Lappe: f. *A Burre (of what kind soeuer.)*
Lappe grande. *The Burre Docke, Clote burre, great Burre.*
Lappement: m. *A lapping, or licking vp.*
Lapper. *To lap, or licke vp.*
Lappeur: m. *A lapper, or licker vp of.*
Lapreau: m. *A young Rabbet.*
Laps: m. *A slip, slide, fall, faile.*
Par laps de temps. *In a space; with tract, or by course of time.*
Laqs: m. *A snare, ginne, or grinne.*
Laqs courant. *A noose, grinne, snitle, running knot.*
Laquais: m. *as* Laquay.
Laquay: m. *A Lackey, Footboy, Footman.*
Laquay de mer. *A kind of verie swift fish.*
Laque *as* Lacque.
Laquefenée. Membre viril.
Laquelle chose. *Which, the which, that, the very same, thing.*
Lar: f. *A mans chiefe house; (the right, or inheritance of his eldest sonne;)* ¶Bayonnois.
Larcin. *Theft; whence;*
Les larrons s' entrebatent, & les larcins se descouvrent: Prov. *When theeues fall out true men come to their owne.*
Lard: m. *Lard: fat Bakon, the fat of Bakon, or of Porke; also, a Flitch of Bakon; also, the tree of a saddle.*
Lard espié. *The lard of the two vtmost, and fattest peeces of a Flitch of Bakon diuided into three parts, the Legs or Gammons hauing beene formerly cut off.*
Il y a du lard en luy. *There is much substance, or great subtilitie, in him.*
Crier au lard sur. *Publikely to flowt, scoffe at, mocke, disgrace, deride.*
Tout y estoit du lard. *All was set a hoight, the world ran all on wheeles, there.*
Faire du lard. *To liue idly, fare deliciously, fatten with pleasure, and ease.*
Frotter leur lard ensemble; *Looke* Frotter.
Frotter à quelqu'un son lard. *To cudgell him soundly, to thwacke or belabor him throughly.*
Iecter son lard aux chiens. *To spend his substance wastfully, or vnworthily; to squander all away.*
Il a mangé le lard. *He is most guiltie, or he onely is guiltie, of that theft.*
Faire trembler le lard au charnier. *To skare, with his terrible swaggering, euerie peece of lard that beares him.*
A la fin sçaura on qui a mangé le lard: Prov. *A theefe, how cunning soeuer, will at the length be discouered.*
Qui a mangé le lard ronge l'os: Prov. *Let him that hath eaten the Bakon picke the bones.*
Lardasse: f. *A sticke, thrust, great pricke.*
Lardé: m. ée: f. *Larded; interlarded; stucke, seasoned, or drest with lard; also, nipped, quipped, taunted; also, pricked, or pierced into, as with a larding pricke.*
Larder. *To lard; to sticke, season, or dresse with lard; also, to pricke, or pierce, as with a larding pricke; also, to cut, quip, nip, taunt, breake a ieast on.*
Lardier: m. *A tub to keepe Lard, or Bakon in; also, a boord to lay it, salted, on; also, a beastlie, or slouenlie (fat) fellow.*
Lardier: m. ere: f. *Of, or belonging to, Lard.*
Lardoire: f. *A larding sticke, or pricke.*
Lardon: m. *The little slice or peece of Lard, wherewith meat is stucke; also, a flowt, cut, gird, nip, ieast broken on.*
Lardonnement: m. *A quipping, cutting, girding, flowting.*
Lardonner. *To quip, nip, cut, flowt, gird, breake a ieast vpon.*
Lardonneur: m. *A quipper, girder, flowter.*
Larege: f. *The Larch, or Larinx tree.*
Lareze. *The same.*
Resine de Lareze. *(Our ordinarie) Turpentine.*
Larfondement: m. *The disease wherein one voids his fat, or grease in his excrements.*
Larfondu: m. uë: f. *That voids his fat, or grease in his excrements.*
Large: m. (Substant.) *Roome, scope, space, width, or widenesse.*
Mettre au large. *To release, discharge, vnloose, vndoe, vnty; to open, widen, giue roome, or scope vnto.*
Large: com. (Adject.) *Large, wide, broad, spacious, roomthie; ample, great, big; open; abundant; bounteous, liberall.*
Large de bouche, & estroit de ceincture. *That promises much, but parts with little; or, that promises much more then he willingly parts with.*
Autant despend chiche que large: Prov. *The miser matches the vnthrift in expence; (the one often wasting as much by allowing too scant, as the other by giuing too large, a proportion;) it may also be interpreted thus; The liberall doth spend his pelfe, the pennyfather wasts himselfe.*
Largement. *Largely, widely, broadly, fully, amply, greatly; abundantly, plentifully; bountifully.*
Largesse: f. *Bountie, liberalitie; also, a largesse, or handfulls of money cast among the people; also, a donatiue bestowed on souldiors.*
Larget: m. ette: f. *Somewhat large, reasonable wide.*
Largeur: f. *Largenesse, breadth, widenesse, latitude, spaciousnesse; greatnesse, amplenesse, bignesse.*
Largiteur: m. *A liberall giuer, bestower, or spender on.*
Largue: f. *Roome, scope, spaciousnesse, width, widenesse.*
Faire largue. *To giue roome, make place, leaue space enough.*
Prendre la largue en haute mer. *To put out into the maine.*
Tenir la largue. *To keepe abroad, in the wide fields, or in the open high way.*
Larigau. *The head of the windpipe, or throat, consisting of three little gristles; the instrument of receiuing, and letting out, breath; also, a Flute or Pipe is called so by the*

the clownes in some parts of France.

Boire à tire larigau. *To drinke till his throat cracke withall.*

Laringe. *The root of the tongue; or, as* Larigau.

Laringuau. *The same.*

Larix: f. *The Larch, or Larinx tree.*

Larme: f. *A teare; also, a gumme-drop, the fat moisture that distills from diuers trees; and hence;*

La larme du sapin. *A cleere, and well-tasting liquid Rosin, that issues from betweene the barke, and inner rinde of a young Firre tree; In our shops it is commonly (but erroniously) tearmed Venice Turpentine, sayes* Mathiolus.

Larmes. *Beads made of the seeds of a certaine plant.*

En larmes de fol ne se doit on fier: Prov. *A fooles teares are not to be trusted.*

Ce que Maistre donne, & vallet pleure ce sont larmes perdues: Prov. *In vaine doe groomes deplore their maisters bountie.*

Larmelette: f. *A small teare.*

Larmette. *as* Larmelette.

Larmeux: m. euse: f. *All-beblubbered, full of teares.*

Larmier: m. *The eaue of a house; the brow, or coping of a wall, seruing to keepe, or cast off the raine; also, a loope-hole, or small hole in a wall to giue light; also, the eye-veine, or veine thats next to the eye of a horse.*

Larmot: m. *A kind of Lizard.*

Larmoyable: com. *Bewaylable, lamentable, wofull, worthie of teares.*

Larmoyement: m. *A weeping, bewayling, lamenting, shedding of teares.*

Larmoyer. *To weepe, wayle, whine, lament, shed teares, distill drops of moisture.*

Larmoyeux. *as* Larmeux.

Larmuse: f. *A little earth-Newte, or Aske.* ¶Dauphinois.

Larnesse. *as* Larronnesse; *a she theefe.*

Larre de chats: m. *Caterwawling.* (vieil mot.)

Larrecin: m. *Larcenie, theft, robberie, felonie, theeuerie, stealth, pilfering, filching, purloyning.*

Larreciner. *as* Larronner.

Larrecineusement. *Theeuishly, pilferingly, feloniously, with a felonious intent.*

Larrecineux: m. euse: f. *Felonious, theeuish, filching, pilfering, nimming, imbeazling.*

Larris: m. *Vnhusbanded land, vntilled ground.*

Larron: m. *A felon, theefe, robber, purloyner, stealer, imbeazeler, pilferer, filcher, nimmer.*

Larron d'eau. *A issue in a Conduit head for the voiding of superfluous water.*

Larron d'une plume. *The pith of a quill; the feather, or light stuffe that is within it.*

Pas de larron. *A gingerlie tread, soft gate, fearefull stepping, doubtfull pace.*

Les larrons s' entrebatent, & les larcins se descouvrent: Pro. *Theeues brabling helpes true men vnto their owne.*

D'un larron priué on ne se peut garder: Pro. *There is no ward for a familiar theefe.*

Tel larron tel cordon: Prov. *See* Cordon.

'A gros larron grosse corde: Prov. *A strong theefe deserues (or needs) a strong halter.*

Les gros larrons ont tousiours les manches pleins de baillons: Prov. *Great theeues haue euer store of gags* (viz. *of gifts) about them.*

Les gros larrons pendent les petits; &, les gros larrons meinent pendre les petits: Prov. *Applyable to such as being themselues guiltie of great faults, condemne, or punish, little ones in others.*

Abandon fait larron: Prov. *Things left at randon cause true men turne theeues.*

Il est cault larron qui desrobbe à vn larron: Prov. *He is a cunning theefe that robs a theefe.*

Il semble à vn larron que chascun luy resemble: Prov. *A theefe imagines euerie one bids, stand.*

Ou Marchand, ou larron: Prov. *Either a marchant or a theefe; a speech verie ordinarie in the mouthes of Shop-keepers, who thereby pretend, that not comming to their wares so easily, they cannot sell them so cheape, as theeues doe.*

Larronceau: m. *A pilferer, filcher, little theefe.*

Larronneau: m. *The same.*

Larronner. *To steale, imbeazell, purloyne, filch, nimme, pilfer, play the theefe.*

Larronnerie: f. *Theeuing, stealing, pilfering, filching, purloyning.*

Larronnesse: f. *A she theefe.*

Larronneux: m. euse: f. *Felonious, theeuish, full of theeuerie.*

Larronniere: f. *A denne of theeues, the retreat of theeues, theeues hauen, a place of resort for theeues.*

Larval: m. ale: f. *Haggish, grislie, ghastlie, ghost-like, dreadfull, wan, pale.*

Larve: m. *A Hag, Spirit, Goblin, Night-ghost; also, a leane, pale, meagar, withered scrag; one that looks like death, or like a ghost.*

Larynx. *as* Larigau.

Las: m. *as* Laqs; *a snare.*

Las: m. Lasse: f. *Wearie, tyred, harried, ouertoyled, or faint with toyling.*

Lasanon: m. *The panne of a Close-stoole.* ¶Rab.

Lasanophore: m. *The groome of the Close-stoole.*

Lasché. *A fish that somewhat resembles a little Shad; (caught, and called so, about* Montpelier.)

Lasche: f. *(The vermine called) a Ticke, or Sheepe-louse.*

Lasche: com. *Slacke, loose, wide, flagging; weake, faint, vnlustie, languishing, remisse, lither, slow; cold, cowardlie, faint-hearted, vnmanlie, effeminate; lewd, vnworthie, base, trecherous.*

Cousture à lasche. *An open seame.*

Oreilles lasches. *Slowching, or hanging eares.*

Lasché: m. ée: f. *Loossed, tyed; vnbent; released, free, deliuered.*

Laschée: f. *A loossing, slackening, widening, vnbending; remitting, releasing, freeing, letting goe.*

Laschement. *Slackly, loosely, flaggingly; remissely, weakly, vnlustily; slowly, litherly, negligently; coldly, faintly, effeminately; wickedly, lewdly; vnworthily.*

Lascher. *To slacken, wyden, loosse, vnbend, let out; free, release, remit, forgoe, let goe.*

Lascher la bride à. *To vse more gently, giue more libertie vnto.*

Lascheté: f. *Slacknesse, dullnesse, remissnesse; faintnesse, weakenesse, vnlustinesse; negligence, idlenesse, lithernesse; cowardise, vnmanlinesse, faintheartednesse; trecherie, lewdnesse, vnworthinesse; also, an absurd, sottish, or sencelesse part.*

Lasdaller: m. *A tyred Jade; also, a dreaming, or lazie draw-latch; also, a kind of bird.*

Lasnier. *as* Lanier.

Lassé: m. ée: f. *as* Las; *Wearied; also, snarled or insnared; also, laced; bound, or closed vp with laces.*

Lasser. *To wearie, toyle, tyre; also, to lace; to bind, or close vp with a lace; also, to set ginnes, or grinnes for birds; (& hece) also, to snarle, or insnare; also, a dog to lyne a bitch.*

On

On se lasse de bien chanter: Prov. *The best contentments breed sacietie.*
Lasseron. *as* Laicteron.
Lasset: m. *A snare, ginne, grinne; also, the lace of a womans Petticoat.*
Lasseté: f. *Wearinesse, vnlustinesse, fatigation, faintnesse.*
Lassiere: f. *A kind of net, or toyle for wild beasts.*
Lassis. Coitfure de lassis. *A Networke Coyfe.*
Lassitude. *as* Lasseté.
Lassus, ou Lasus. *Aboue, aboue yonder, there aboue; also, vpward.*
Latage: m. *A lathing; lath-worke; a couering, or closing, with lathes.*
Late: f. *A lath; also, a certaine fine due vpon claymes, or contestations within* Provence.
Latent. *Hidden, lurking, close, priuie, secret, vnknowne.*
Latentement. *Hiddenly, lurkingly, closely, priuily, secretly.*
Later. *To lath, to set on lathes.*
Laterne: f. *The scutcheon, or knob, in the middle of a Timber-vault.*
Laticlave: m. *A kind of Cassocke worne by the auncient Romans.*
Latiers: m. *Those which in* Provence *exact the fine before mentioned in* Late.
Latin: m. *Latin; the Latin language.*
Parler Latin. *To speake Latin; also, a fashion of speech vsed among prisoners, thereby to draw some drinking money from new-come guests.*
Femme qui parle Latin: Pro. *Seeke* Femme.
Il est bon Latin. *He is a good Latinist, he writes, or speakes, good Latin.*
Il y perdit son Latin. *He was there grauelled, plunged, or at a Non-plus; he knew not what to make of, or what to say vnto, it.*
Qui a florin, roussin, Latin, par tout il trouve le chemin: Pro. *He that can spend, and speake well, and hath a good horse vnder him, needs not goe out of his way.*
Latin: m. Latine: f. *Latine of countrey, or in speech; of, or belonging to, the Latine language.*
Marchandise Latine. *Excellent good stuffe; or, the best, or most vtterable commodities, tearmed so by Marchants.*
Voile Latine. *A mizen, or smacke sayle.*
Latinément. *In Latine; after the manner of the Latines.*
Latinier: m. *A Trucheman, or Interpretor.* (v.m.)
Latinisateur: m. *as* Latiniseur.
Latiniser. *To make Latine, turne into Latine, write or speake Latine; also, to inkhornize it.*
Latiniseur: m. *One that writes, or speakes Latine; also, an inkhorniser; one that vses inkhorne tearmes.*
Faire du Latiniseur. *A dunce, or ignorant fellow to counterfeit Schollership.*
Latinogotisé: m. ée: f. *Barbarous, Gibridge; mixed of Latine and the Gothes language.*
Laritation: f. *A hiding, lurking, lying hid; a playing least in sight.*
Latité: m. ée: f. *Hidden, concealed.*
Latiter. *To lurke, lye hid, play least in sight.*
Latitude: f. *Latitude, breadth, largenesse, widenesse, broadnesse.*
Latomie: f. *A Quarrie of stones.*
Latonien. Flambeaux Latoniens. *The Sunne and Moone* (Latonaes *children.*)
Latre. *A Churchyard.*
Latrie: f. *The seruice, or worship due vnto God.*
Latrine: f. *A Priuie, Jakes, House of Office; also, the sinke of a priuate house.*
Latrineux: m. euse: f. *Jakes-like, of a Jakes, full of Jakes, filthie, stinking, full of ordure.*
Latte: f. *as* Late; *a Lath; also, a Land-measure (as* Perche) *in some places longer then in others whence;*
Latte de Barbezieux. *is but nine foot,* Latte de Montignac Charante, *eleuen foot, long.*
Iustice sous latte. C'est sous le couvert de la maison du seigneur seulement.
Latteron. *See* Laicteron.
Lavace d'eaux. *An inundation, surrounding, rauage, or great flood, of waters (by the fall of much raine.)*
Lavacier: m. ere: f. *Washing away violently, rauaging, or sweeping before it (as a swift current) all it meetes with.*
Lavage: m. *A water-poole, or plash; a peece of land surrounded, or drowned vp, by water; also, a washing.*
Lavages. *as* Lavailles.
Lavage de chaux. *Whiting, or white-lime, wherewith walls, &c, are white-washed.*
Lavailles: f. *Swillings, Hogs-wash, washings for Swine.*
Lavanche de glace, & de neige. *A great heape of Snow tumbling from the top to the bottome of a Hill, and ouerthrowing whatsoeuer lyes in it way.*
Lavande: f. *Lauender, Spike.*
Lavande femelle. *White-flowred Lauender Spike.*
Lavande masle. *The common, or blew flowred Lauender Spike.*
Lavande Romaine. *Roman Lauender.*
Lavandiere: f. *A Laundresse, or washing woman; also, a Wagtayle, or Water-wagtayle.*
Lavaret: m. *A whitish Trout, or Shad-like fish, bred in the Lakes of* Savoy, *and* Dauphiné.
Lavaron: m. *Another small fish; as* Cabasson.
Lavasse. *as* Lavace.
Lavatoire: m. *A Lauatorie; a place, or vessell, to wash in.*
Laubaut. *as* Clabaut; *a great yelling Curre.*
Laude. *The toll thats payed for wares retayled in certaine Faires, and Markets within the dominion of* Berry; *(and elsewhere.)*
Lavé: m. ée: f. *Washed; rinsed; clensed (with water;) bathed.*
Main lavée moins levée: Pro. *See* Main.
A main lavée Dieu mande la repeuë: Prov. *God sends his blessings to cleane hands, and hearts.*
En vaisseau mal lavé ne peut on vin garder: Prov. *Wine will not keepe in an vncleane vessell.*
Lavedan: m. *An yron-gray Iennet; or a horse bred on* Lavedan, *one of the Pyrenean Mountaines whereon the best horses of France are bred: These horses (sayes a French Cosmographer) are more nimble, and more strong then Spanish Jennets; but the Mountaine is not large, and therefore there be not many of them.*
Lave-main: m. *An Ewer, or Lauer.*
Lavement: m. *A washing, rinsing, bathing, clensing (in water.)*
Laver. *To wash, rinse, bathe, clense (with water.)*
Terre à laver. *Fullers earth.*
Laver vne brique. *To loose labor, or to labor in vaine.*
Laver les mains de. *as in* Main.
Laver le nez à. *as,*
Laver la teste à. *To chide, reproue, checke, taunt bitterly; to take vp for halting; to vse hardly, handle rudely, deale extreamely with.*

Se laver d'une faute. *To purge, cleere, acquit himselfe of an imputation.*

L'un a le bruit l'autre lave la laine. *The one does what the other's said to doe*; (Sic vos non vobis.)

Pour laver ses mains on n' en vend pas sa terre: Prov. *Neuer did cleanlinesse any man vndoe.*

Vne main lave l'autre: Prov. *One serues anothers turne.*

Laveur: m. *A washer.*

Laveure: f. *The water wherewith a thing hath beene washed; also, a washing.*

Laveure de miel. *Liquor wherein Honie hath beene purified, or sodden.*

Laveure des Orfebvres. *The washing of Goldsmiths sweepes; viz. the stuffe which they find in the furnace after a melting, and among the dust of their shops after sweeping; all which they put into a vessell, and washing it, picke that which is good out of it.*

Lavoir: m. *A poole, or pond, whereat buckes, &c, be commonly washed; a washing place, a washing poole or pond; also (in some places) the peece of wood (some three foot long, or high) whereon a washing bason, supported by three or foure brackets, doth stand.*

Laurageois: m. ise: f. *Of* Lauraguez; *a part of* Languedoc.

Herbe Laurageoise. *Wood; so called, because it growes abundantly in* Lauraguez.

Lauraye: f. *A groue, or plot, of Laurell trees.*

Laurens. *Laurence.*

Cloches de Sainct Laurens. *Great blisters in the face.*

Laureole: f. *Lowrie, Lauriell, Spurge Laurell, little Laurell.*

Laureole masle. *Male Lauriell; hath only one stemme set verie thicke with leaues; but in all other parts resembles ordinarie Lowrie.*

Laurier: m. *A Laurell, or Bay tree.*

Laurier Alexandrin. *Laurell of Alexandria, tongue-Laurell, Tongue-blade, Horse-tongue, Double-tongue.*

Lauriere: f. *A plot, or groue of Bay-trees.*

Laurin: m. ine: f. *Of Bayes; set, or stucke with Bayes.*

Lauserne: f. *Shrub Trefoile, Milke Trefoile, Citisus Bush.*

Lauserte. *The same.*

Laxatif: m. iue: f. *Laxatiue, loose, soluble.*

Laxif: m. iue: f. *Laxatiue.*

Laxité: f. *Laxatiueneße.*

Lay: m. *A Lay, Song, Roundelay; also, as* Lé; *the breadth of cloth, &c; also, a dolefull complaint, passionate lamenting, pitifull wayling; Seeke* Lays.

Lay: m. laye: f. *Lay, secular, temporall.*

Causes de lay à lay. *Cases meerely temporall.*

Frere lay. *A seruant in an Abbey, or Couent.*

Laye: f. *A (wild) Sow that hath young ones.*

Layes. *The lesses (or dung) of a wild Bore; also, ranks of bushes, or of Copsewood, left as marks to limit how much of the rest is to be felled, and sold at once.*

Layé: m. ée: f. Bois layez. *Marked how farre to be felled, how much to be sold; or that hath rewes of Copsewood left growing to the same purpose.*

Layer vn bois. *To leaue markes (or trees, &c, as markes) in a Wood, for the felling, and sale thereof.*

Layette: f. *A Till, or Drawer; also, a Box with Tills, or Drawers.*

Layn. *Sober, modest, of a soft, or still disposition; (an old word.)*

Lays: m. *Trees, or rankes of trees, left in Copses; as in* Layes.

Lazaret: m. *A Lazaret, or Spittle for Lazers.*

Lazanon: m. *Seeke* Lasanon.

Lazur: m. *The Lazull, or Azure stone.*

Lé: m. *Breadth; also, the list of Cloth, or Stuffe.*

De deux lez. *On both sides.* Vn drap de deux lez. *A peece of broad cloth.*

D'un lé & d'autre. *On both sides.*

Du long, & du lé. *Euerie way.*

Le. *(A masculine Relatiue, or Article;) the, the said, the same.*

Lé: m. lée: f. *Broad, wide, large; Hence,* Sainct Pierre en sente lée; *S. Peters in the broad way*; ¶Orleannois.

Leal: m. ale: f. *Loyall, true, trustie, faithfull, honest.*

Leans. (Adverb.) *Within there, in that place.*

Leauté: f. *Loyaltie, faithfullnesse, trustinesse.*

Lebeche. *as* Leveche.

Lebre. *as* Lievre.

Leconomantie: f. *Diuination by water in a Bason.* ¶Rab.

Lechard. *as* Leschard.

Lechedoigt. à lech. *Daintily, sparingly, by degrees, peece-meale, by parcels, by little and little.*

Lechefrite: f. *A Dripping-panne.*

Lechement: m. *A licking, or lapping vp.*

Lecher. *To licke, lap, slap vp.*

Peu peut bailler à son escuyer qui son cousteau leche: Prov. *He that pinches himselfe must pine another.*

Qui va il leche, qui repose il seiche: Prov. *Looke* Seicher.

Lechercan: m. *A slap-sauce, lick-dish, lickorous companion.*

Lecheresse: f. *A lickerous, or sawcie woman.*

Femme lecheresse ne fera ia porée espaisse: Prov. *The lickerous houswife seldome makes thicke pottage.*

Lecheur: m. *A licker, or lapper vp of*; *See* Lescheur.

Leçon: f. *A Lesson; Lecture, Document, Instruction, Precept.*

Lecteur: m. *A reader.*

Lecteur publique. *A Profeßor, or publicke Reader, in an Vniuersitie &c.*

Lectrin: m. *as* Letrin.

Lecture: f. *A Lecture; a Reading.*

Ledanger. *as* Laidanger.

Lede. *as* Ledon.

Ledoires: f. *Reproches, reuilings, defamatorie tearmes.*

Ledomier: m. *The Lote, or Nettle tree.*

Ledon: m. *The shrub* Cistus Ledon, *from the leaues whereof* Ladanum *is gathered.*

Ledoyer. *as* Laidanger.

Lée: f. *A wild Sow.*

Legal: m. ale: f. *Legall, lawfull; of the Law; tryable by Law.*

Domicile legal. *The house thats enioyed by reason of an Estate, Benefice, or Office.*

Legalité: f. *Lawfullnesse, lawfull gouernment.*

Legart: m. *A Newte, or Lizard.*

Legat: m. *A Legat; the Popes Embaßadour; also, a Legacie.*

Legataire: com. *A Legatarie; the partie to whom a thing is bequeathed.*

Legater. *To bequeath, or giue by Will.*

Legation: f. *An Embassage, or Legateship.*

Legement: m. *A Lighter for Salt-barks; a boat whereinto a Salt-barke (thats heauie laden, and to passe into shallow waters) discharges part of it burthen.*

Legende: f. *A Legend, a Writing; also, the words that be about the edge of a peece of coyne.*

Legendier: m. *The golden Legend; a booke of the liues of the Saints.*
Leger,& **Legerement**. *as* Legier & Legierement.
Legereſſe: f. *Lightneſſe, nimbleneſſe, agilitie, ſwiftneſse, quickneſſe, ſpeedineſſe, liuelineſse.*
Legible: com. *Legible, readable.*
Legier: m. ere: f. *Light, ſwift, ſpeedie, fleet; quicke, nimble, actiue, readie, liuelie; fickle, inconſtant, humorous, vnſteadie, flitting, ſhittle, wauering; alſo, light, ſleight, ſpungie, of ſmall weight.*
Beſtes **legieres**. *The red and fallow Deere, the wild Goat, and the Roe.*
Legier à la main. *See* Main.
Legierement. *Lightly, fleetly, ſwiftly; nimbly, quickly, readily; vnſteadily, flittingly, inconſtantly; alſo, negligently, ſleightly, to no purpoſe.*
Legiereté: f. *Lightneſſe, fleetneſse, ſwiftneſſe; nimbleneſſe, quickneſſe, agilitie, liuelineſse; alſo, leuitie, wauering, inconſtancie, fickleneſſe; vainneſse, want of grauitie; ſleightneſſe.*
Legion: f. *A (Romane) Legion; a Band, or Squadron of 6830 ſouldiors; whereof 730 were horſemen, and 6100 footmen.*
Legionnaire: com. *Legionarie; of, or belonging to, a (Romane) Legion.*
Legiſlateur: m. *A Law-maker.*
Legitimation: f. *A legitimation, or legitimating; a making lawfull.*
Lettres de **legitimation**. *Letters of legitimation, are procured of the King by baſtards, that they may be capable of ſucceſſions, and lawfully diſpoſe of their owne as well as other men.*
Legitime: f. *A portion, or childs part; a younger brothers portion, or part in the inheritance left by his father; alſo, the portion of inheritance which a father may giue away from his ſonne; his owne free land.*
Mettre ſa **legitime** au vent. *To make (an vnthriftie) ſale of his portion; to ſquander away his childes part.*
Legitime: com. *Legitimate, lawfull, orderlie, iuſt, right; rightly borne, truly begot.*
Legitimement. *Legitimately, rightly, lawfully, according to the law.*
Leguer. *To bequeath, to leaue by Will.*
Legumage: m. *Pulſe; as Beanes, Peaſe, &c; any corne, &c, thats reaped, or gathered, by pulling.*
Legume: m. *as* Legumage.
Legumineux: m. euſe: f. *Of, or belonging to, pulſe.*
Legz: m. *A Legacie; a thing bequeathed, or giuen by Will.*
Leiche. *as* Leſſe.
Leicher. *Secke* Lecher.
Lende: f. *A nit, or chit; alſo, as* Lande; *alſo, a kind of Scate fiſh.*
Lendemain. *The morrow, day following, next day after.*
Au **Lendemain**. *Vntill to morrow.*
Lendeux: m. euſe: f. *Nittie, full of nits.*
Lendit: m. *A great Faire kept (in a field neere to S.* Denis) *from the ſecond Wedneſday of Iune vnto Midſummer Eue; whence;*
Lendits. *Gate-money, fairings, or yearelie preſents beſtowed by the ſchollers of Vniuerſities (eſpecially thoſe of Paris) on their Tutors.*
Lendole: f. *The flying fiſh.*
Lengaïer, & **Lengaïeur**. *See* Langayer, & Langayeur.
Leniment: m. *An aſſwaging, appeaſing, tempering, mitigation, qualification; a comforting, eaſing, refreſhing.*
Lenir. *To lenifie, ſlake, ſwage, temper, mitigate, ſweeten, ſmooth, qualifie, pacifie, appeaſe, comfort, refreſh, eaſe.*
Lenitif: m. *A Lenitiue; mitigation; refreſhment; an ache-aſſwaging medicine, greefe-appeaſing plaiſter.*
Lenklat: m. *A kind of Dogfiſh.*
Lent: m. **Lente**: f. *Slacke, ſlow, leiſurelie, lingering, backward, remiſſe; lazie, drowſie, dull, heauie, none of the haſtings; alſo, gentle, ſoft, facile, meeke, patient.*
Lente. *as* Lentille.
Lentement. *Slowly, leiſurely; ſlackly, lingeringly, backwardly, remiſsly, negligently; faire and ſoftly, not too faſt, by little and little, without haſt.*
Lenteur: f. *Slackneſſe, lingering, ſlowneſſe; remiſneſſe; eaſe, negligence, litherneſſe; alſo, clammineſſe, ſlymineſse, gluineſſe.*
Lenteux. m. euſe: f. *Nittie, full of nits.*
Lentice. *as* Lentiſque.
Lenticulaire: m. *An inſtrument wherewith Surgeons plane, and cut away, the broken bones of a wounded skull.*
Lentillade: f. *The ſpotted and long-noſed Scate, or Thorneback.* ¶Langued.
Lentillat: m. *The ſpotted dog-fiſh called by our fiſhermen, the Dunne-hound, or Dunne-cow.*
Lentille: f. *The Lintle, or Lentill (a ſmall pulſe;) alſo, the weight of a Lentill; or, a ſmall weight whereof three make but two graines.*
Lentilles. *Round ſpeckes, red pimples; wanne, ſmall, and Lentill-reſembling freckles, on the face, or hands.*
Lentilles d' eau. *as* Lentilles de marais.
Lentilles de marais, ou de mer. *Duckes-meat, fenne-Lentills, water Lentills, Graines.*
Lentillé: m. ée: f. *Freckled, ſormpeckled, pimpled.*
Lentilleux: m. euſe: f. *Frecklie; full of red pimples, or ſpots.*
Lentiſce. *as* Lentiſque.
Lentiſcine: f. *Maſticke.*
Lentiſque: m. *The Lentiske, or Maſticke tree.*
Lentitude: f. *as* Lenteur.
Leonceau: m. *A Lyons whelpe, or young Lyon.*
Leonin: m. ine: f. *Lyonlike; of, or belonging to, a Lyon.*
Leontin. *as* Leonceau.
Leopard: m. *A Leopard, or Libbard; a beaſt ingendred betweene a Lyon, and a Panther.*
Leopard de mer. *The Cod, or Greenefiſh.*
Leopardé. Lion **Leop**. *Libbard-like.*
Leporin: m. ine: f. *Of, or belonging to, a Hare.*
Leppe: f. *Sea-graſſe, Sea-weed, Reets.*
Lepre: f. *A leaproſie.*
Lepre farineuſe. *A white ſcurſe, or leaproſie.*
Lepreſerie: f. *Leaprouſneſſe; ſcurſe, ſcabbineſſe.*
Lepreux: m. euſe: f. *Leaprous; ſcuruie, or ſcabbed all ouer the bodie.*
Leproſerie: f. *A Spittle for the leaprous.*
Lequel: m. elle: f. *Which, the which.*
Lequel des deux *Whether, the whether, which ſoeuer, which of the two ſoeuer.*
Lequeſat: m. *A kind of ſauce for Woodcockes.*
Lerelot: m. *The foot, or downe of a countrey-maidens ſong.*
Lermier. *as* Larmier.
Lerot: m. *A Dormouſe; alſo, the great, and pild-eared Nut-mouſe, Haſell-mouſe, or Filbeard-mouſe; called ſo, becauſe he liueth onely on nuts.*
Lerre: m. *A theefe.*
Leſard: m. *A Lizard; See* Lezard.

Leſchard: m. *A lickorous, or ſweet-mouthed ſlapſawce; alſo, a micher, or miſerable niggard; one that continually licks vp, or lookes after, pelfe.*
Leſche: f. *A long ſlice, or ſhiue of bread, &c; alſo, as* Leſſe.
Leſche de mer. *A ſlymie worme, thicke as a finger, and a foot long; digged by fiſhermen (who vſe it for a bait) out of the ſand, wherein, vnleſſe it be quickly taken vp, it quickly hides it ſelfe againe.*
Leſchedoigt. *See* Lechedoigt.
Leſcher. *as* Lecher.
Leſcherie: f. *Sawcineſſe, lickorouſneſſe, much licking.*
Leſcheur: m. *A licker; a lickorous companion.*
Leſcheur. (Adject.) *Often licking; lickorous.*
Au chat leſcheur bat on ſouvent la gueule: Prov. *The lickorous cat comes vnto many a pat.*
Leſcive. *as* Lexive.
Leſciver. *To bucke clothes; to waſh, rince, or ſcoure with lye.*
Leſe-maieſté: f. *High treaſon.*
Leſer. *To hurt, wound, annoy, offend.*
Leſer la maieſté. *To commit high treaſon.*
Leſion: f. *Hurt, wounding, harme, offence, annoyance.*
Leſſe: f. *A Leaſh, to hold a dog &c in; a bridle, or falſe reine to hold a horſe by; any ſuch long ſtring.*
Leſſes. *as* Laiſſes.
Ie la voudrois pluſtoſt chevaucher que mener en leſſe. (*A knauiſh phraſe in* Rab.) *I had rather ride her then lead her.*
Leſſive. *as* Lexive.
Leſt. *as* Leſtage.
Leſtage: m. *The balaſt of a ſhip.*
Leſtager. *To balaſt a ſhip.*
Leſte. *as* Leſtage.
Leſté: m. ée: f. *Balaſted; alſo (but not ſo properly) full fraught, or loaden (as a ſhip.)*
Leſte: com. *Quicke, nimble, actiue, ſprightfull, diſpoſe, readie, liuelie; apt, or able for imployments; alſo, neat, comelie, handſome, quaint, or curious in attire.*
Leſtement. *Quickly, nimbly, actiuely, with great agilitie; liuely, merrily; alſo, neatly, quaintly, curiouſly.*
Leſter. *To balaſt; alſo, (but not ſo properly) to load, or full-fraught, a ſhip.*
Letabonde: com. *Iocond, frolicke, buxome, all-aboight, as merrie as may be.*
Letargie. *as* Lethargie.
Lethal: m. ale: f. *Deadlie, mortall; peſtiferous.*
Lethargie: f. *A Lethargie; a drowſie, and forgetfull ſickneſſe, called by ſome, the drowſie euill.*
Lethargique: com. *Sicke of a Lethargie, or of the drowſie ill; (and hence) alſo, dull, heauie, ſleepie, forgetfull.*
Lethe: m. *Death; mortalitie; obliuion.*
Lethean: m. anne: f. *Deadlie, mortall, peſtilent, death-inflicting.*
Letice: f. *A beaſt of a whitiſh gray colour.*
Letiere. *Seeke* Lictiere.
Leton: m. *Latten (mettall.)*
Letrin: m. *A (Pulpit, or) Deske in a Church.*
Lettager. *as* Leſtager.
Lettre: f. *A letter, or character of the Croſſe row; alſo, a Letter, Epiſtle, or Miſſiue; alſo, a Patent, Graunt, Commaund, Writ, or Decree paſſing from a Prince, or out of a Court of Iuſtice; (In which ſence it is altogether vſed in the Plurall.)*
Lettres d'acquieſcement. *A Letter of Atturney from a client to his counſell for the ſurceaſing, or compounding of the ſuit.*
Lettres de baillie. *Writs of Execution; or an execution againſt the goods of.*
Lettres de cargaiſon. *Bills of lading.*
Lettres de committimus. *A Commiſſion.*
Lettres d'eſtat. *Looke* Eſtat.
Lettres de pas, ou de paſſe. *A Paſſe, or Paſport; a Licence for the paſſage, trauell, or tranſportation of.*
Les bonnes lettres. *Learning.*
Au pied de la lettre. *Literally, ſtrictly, preciſely, according to the true ſence of the place.*
Ce me ſont lettres cloſes. *Theſe things are miſteries, or ſecrets vnto me.*
Prendre lettres. *Is (at a certaine Card-play) to craue leaue to giue ouer a game which he vndertooke to win.*
Teſmoing paſſe lettre: Prov. *The depoſition of a preſent witneſſe is a more effectuall euidence then a bare proofe out of any writing.*
Lettré: m. ée: f. *Lettered, learned; skilfull in, or furniſhed with, good letters.*
Lettriſé. Vers lettriſez. *Which runne vpon the letter; or all whoſe words begin with one and the ſame letter.*
Lettron: m. *Gumme Cichorie, ruſh Cichorie; or, as* Laicteron; *the Sow-thiſtle.*
Letuge: m. *The leakage of a ſhip.*
Leu: m. *as* Lieu; *a place; and hence;*
Sans feu ne leu. *Without houſe or harbor.*
Leu: m. leuë: f. *Red, peruſed.*
Levage. Droict de Levage. *Looke* Droict.
Levaille: f. *An vpſitting, vpriſing, or getting vp.*
Levain: m. *Leauen (for bread.)*
Honteux comme vne truye qui emporte vn levain. *Seeke* Honteux.
Levandiere: f. *A Midwiſe.*
Levant: m. *The Leuant, the Eaſt; the Eaſt wind, or countrey.*
Coque de Levant. *The ſmall medecinable ſhell, tearmed in ſhops,* Vnguis Odoratus.
Vent Grec Levant. *A Southeaſt wind.*
Faire voile en Levant. *To ſayle Eaſtward; to be ſtolne, filched, or purloyned away.*
Levant. *Raiſing, rearing; riſing, ariſing; leuying; leauening.*
Tombant levant. *Well or ill, hittie miſſie; here or there, one way or other; (Aduerbially.)*
Leuce. de Leuce. ¶Rab. *in ſtead of,* d'Ellend; *Seeke* Ellend.
Leucophlegmatie: f. *A flegmaticke dropſie; or, as* Hypoſarque.
Leucophlegmatique: com. *Sicke of, or troubled with (ſuch) a flegmaticke dropſie.*
Leud: m. *as* Leude.
Leude: m. *A vaſſall, tenant, liegeman.* (v.m.)
Leudes francs. *Gentlemen profeſſing Arms, or Souldierie; and holding their lands of others, but paying no tax, or impoſition, to any.*
Leudes ſerfs. *Villaines, peaſants, husbandmen; ſubiect to all impoſitions.*
Leve: m. *A tricke, at Cards.*
Leve: f. *A Mallet (hollowed like a ſalt-ſeller at both ends) wherewith the bowle is rayſed, and caſt through the* Paſſe, *at* Palemaille.
Levé: m. ée: f. *Lifted, raiſed, reared, heaued, hoiſted, eleuated, aduanced; alſo, leauened; alſo, leuied; alſo, riſen, ariſen, got, or growne vp.*

Arreſt

Arrest levé. *A sentence published, or exemplified.*
La main luy est levée. *His goods, which were seised, are deliuered backe vnto him.*
Au pied levé. Poursuyvre au pied levé. *To pursue hard, neere, foot hot, close at the heeles.*
Prendre au pied levé. *To take at aduantage, or at the worst; to surprise on a suddaine, or before prouision made.*
Respondre à pied levé. *To answer suddainely, or extempore.*
La teste levée. *Boldly, confidently, with head lift vp; or holding vp the head, as one that hath gotten the better of his aduersarie.*
Leveche: f. *A South-west wind.*
Levée: f. *A banke, or causey raised for the keeping in of a Riuer, or water; also, a leuie, or leuying of money, souldiors, &c; a gathering, or getting in of the profits, or fruits of land; also, a raysing, hoysing, aduancing; and, a rising, as of the Sunne.*
Vne levée de bouclier. *Much adoe about nothing; a great shew, or much doings, to little purpose; mightie preparations for a meane exploit; a notable coyle, or stirre, when it needs not.*
Levement: m. *A raysing, rearing, hoysing, aduancing, lifting, or setting vp; also, a leuie, or leuying; also, a leauening.*
Lever. *To lift, rayse, reare, eleuate, aduance, hoyse, heaue, or set vp; also, to leuie, collect, gather; also, to leauen.*
Se Lever. *To rise, arise, get, or grow vp.*
Lever vn arrest. *To publish a sentence, or decree.*
Lever boutique. *To set vp shop.*
Se Lever au Conseil. *To goe sit in Counsell.*
Lever le cul. Il leur fit lever le cul à. *He raised them, or their siege, from.*
Lever vn enfant des fons. *To christen, or be witnesse to, a child at the Font.*
Lever des estoffes. *To buy, or take vp, stuffes.*
Lever la main. *To take vp a tricke at Cards.*
Lever la main à quelqu'un. *To restore vnto him the goods taken from him by order, or authoritie.*
Lever en sa main. *To take into his hands, or possession; to seize vpon, in his owne right.*
Lever le masque à. *To vnmaske; lay open, discouer.*
Lever le menton à. *To hearten, harden, imbolden, incourage, assure.*
Lever le nez. *To take courage, or heart at grasse, to plucke vp the heart.*
Lever de sentinelle. *To relieue a Sentinell, to put one in his roome; hence also, to dislodge.*
Lever la table. *To take away.*
Lever matin n' est pas heur, mais desjuner est le plus seur: Prov. *Looke* Matin.
Il a beau se lever tard qui a le bruit de se lever matin: Prov. *He may well enough rise late thats thought to rise early; The like is;*
Qui a bruit de se lever matin peut dormir iusques à soir: Prov. *He thats well thought of, may play the knaue long before he be suspected, or detected a knaue; (so many men that are not as they seeme to be, beguile those, who seeing no hurt suspect none.)*
Levesche. *as* Leveche; *also, common Louage, Lombardie Louage; also, the hearbe Alexanders.*
Levesse. *as* Levesche.
Leveton: m. *Yeast, or Barme.*
Leveur: m. *A rayser, lifter, aduancer, hoyser, or heauer vp of; also, a leuier, collector, gatherer; also, a leauener.*

Leveure de biere: f. *Yeast.*
Levier: m. *A Leauer; an Iron crow, or woodden barre to lift vp things with.*
Leville: f. *Darnell; or, Tares.*
Levis: m. isse: f. *Foulding, or to be foulded vp; whence;* Table Levisse, &c.
Levistic: m. *Louage; or, as* Livesche.
Leur. *Their;* C'est leur maison; *also, theirs; as,* C'est le leur; *and, their owne, or their own meanes; whence,* Ils n'ont moyen de le faire du leur; *also, them; as in,* Il leur a dict.
Levrault: m. *A Leueret, or young Hare; also, a Romane beame, or stelleere; See* Crochet.
Il y a levrault au croc. *There is some good prey to be caught, stuffe to be found, thing to be had.*
Levre: f. *A Lip; (also, an Otter.* ¶Savoyard.)
Levre fenduë. *A Hare-lip, or Hare-mouth.*
Attaindre du bout des levres. *To touch daintily, or but sleightly.*
Bailler mornifle sur les levres. *To giue a cuffe on the mouth, a thumpe on the lips.*
Bailler mornifle sur les levres du Roy. *To coyne false money, to make false coyne.*
Femme qui ses levres mord, &c; *Looke* Femme.
Levresque: com. *Greyhound like; of, or belonging to, a Greyhound.*
Levrete: f. *as* Levrette.
Levreté: m. ée: f. *Kindled, as a young Leueret.*
Levretée. *A Hare-lipt, or blabber-lipt wench; also, a wench that hath beene buggared by a Greyhound.*
Levreteau: m. *A Leueret; a young, or little Hare.*
Levreter. *To kindle young Hares; or, a Hare to kindle.*
Levreton: m. *A Greyhound-whelpe, a young Greyhound.*
Levrette: f. *A Greyhound bitch; also, a most lasciuious and incontinent wench, a common hackney, a bitch-fox; also, a little tender lip.*
Levrier: m. *A Greyhound.*.
Levrier d'attache. *An Irish Greyhound, a great Greyhound.*
Pain de levrier. *A Chesse-loafe; bread made of the coursest of corne.*
Souppes de levrier. *Brewesse made of course browne bread, moistned with the last, and worst fat of the beefe-pot.*
Ha levrier. *(A voice of incouragement, or excitation;) hoo, now now, hoe dog, hoe well done dog; also (a voice of incensing such as be readie to fall together by the eares.) Now lads, to it boyes, cuffe or cudgell one another and spare not.*
Elle pense que de toute taille bon levrier. *She is so indifferent, or generall in the intertainment of seruants, that (so they be young and lustie) she cares not of what proportion, or stature they be. Looke* Taille.
Il n' est chasse que de vieux lievriers: Prov. *Old hounds doe hunt the surest; old Greyhounds bite the sorest.*
Oncques mastin n'aima levrier: Prov. *Neuer did clowne affect a Gentleman; nor a rude peasant a ciuill president.*
Levriere: f. *A Greyhound bitch.*
Levron: m. *A young, or little, Greyhound; also, a young wanton fellow that (as a young Greyhound) minds nothing but pleasure.*
Leurre: f. *A (Faulkoners) Lure.*
Oyseaux, ou faulcons de leurre. *Are, properly, seuen,* Le Faulcon gentil, Pelerin, Tartaire, Gerfault, Sacre, Lasnier, & le Tunicien.

Leurré: m. ée: f. *Lured; manned, or made vnto the lure; also, allured; also, better trayned then he was, or taught more wit then he formerly had; whence;*
Il n'a pas encores esté leurré. *(Said of a grosse, rude, ignorant, and vnexperienced fellow.)*

Leurrer. *To lure; to manne, or make vnto the lure; also, as* Desniaiser; *also, to allure, inueagle, intice.*

Lexive: f. *Lye (wherewith linnen is cleansed;) also, a bucke of (linnen) clothes.*

Lexiveux: m. euse: f. *Full of lye; or, as* Lexivier.

Lexivier: m. ere: f. *Of, or belonging to, lye; fit for lye.*

Lexivieux: m. euse: f. *as* Lexiveux.

Leyau: m. *A wound of the breadth, and depth of an ynch.* ¶Gasc.

Leyde: f. *A certaine tax, or imposition vpon Wine, and other commodities.*

Leyette. *as* Layette.

Lez: m. *An edge, brimme, or side; also, the list of cloth, &c; also, the breadth of any stuffe; also, a measure (especially for fish) not much different from our Last; whence;*
Le lez d'harenc. *Containes about twelue Barrells.*
Le lez d'harenc sor. *Containes tenne thousand red Herrings.*
Le lez de maquereau, ou moruë. *as* Le lez d'harenc.
Le lez d'un navire. *The ballasse; also (lesse properly) the fraight, or burthen, of a ship.*
Le lez de Saumon. *A measure of Salmon containing two* Hambours.

Lez. *Nigh, towards, hard by, neere to.*

Lezard: m. *A Lizard; Newte, Aske; also, a kind of small Dag.*
Lezard Chalcidique. *A spotted Lizard which is very venomous, and yet, taken in drinke, healeth the hurt he did.*
Lezard de mer. *A kind of Mackerell.*
Lezard verd. *The great, and harmelesse greene Lizard called in Italie (where he is most found, and best knowne)* Ramarro; *See* Lisarde.
Bec de Lezard. *A Lizards beake; an Instrument, or paire of tongs, wherewith Surgeons draw bullets, or bone-splents out of the bodie.*
Sel de Lezard. *Looke* Sel.

Lezard: m. arde: f. *Of, or belonging to, a Lizard.*
Plume Lezarde. *A biting, slanderous, or defamatorie penne.*

Liace. *as* Liasse.

Liage: m. *A binding, tying; fastening, knitting, vniting; haltering, fettering; souldering; combining together.*
Droict de liage. *Hoopage; or, a fee due to some Lords for the hooping of euery wine-vessell their vassals haue.*

Liairre. *as* Lierre.

Liais: m. *A verie hard free stone whereof staire-steps, and tombe-stones be commonly made.*

Liaison: f. *A band; connexion, colligation; knot, obligation; fastening, tying, or closing hard together; also, a locking, or binding in wrastling.*

Liants: m. *The bands of lead that fasten the panes of a window to the barres.*

Liard: m. *A brazen coyne worth three* deniers, *or the fourth part of a* sol.

Liarder. *To beg, or get poorely, slowly, or by the pennie.*

Liarre. *Iuie; See* Lierre.

Liasse: f. *A bundle, or handfull of.*
Liasse d'oignons. *A rope of Onions.*

Libament: m. *A sacrifice; a thing offered, or tasted of in the offering.*

Libanomantie: f. *Diuination by incense, or frankincense.*

Libanot, ou Libanotis. *Hearbe Frankincense, Rosemarie Frankincense, Libanotis Rosemaric, Hart-root.*

Libation: f. *A sacrifice, or thing offered; a tasting in sacrifice.*

Libellance. Le Clerc, & libell. du Baillage; C'est, le greffier.

Libelle: f. *A Libell, or defamatorie booke, &c; also, a Writ, Citation, or Processe, containing the substance of the suit; or (more properly) the originall declaration vpon any Action; also, a Bill, Certificate; Request, or Supplication, in writing.*

Libellé: m. ée: f. *Declared vpon.*
Adjournement libellé. Qui contient la demande du Demandeur, & les moyens d'icelle, afin que le defendant sçache s'il doit plaider, ou ceder; & s'il delibere plaider qu'il vienne instruict, au iour de l'assignation, pour defendre.
Commission libellée. C'est, narrative.
Exploict libellé. Qui contient le faict de l'exploict; ou les moyens de la demande, & conclusion du demandeur.
Mandement libellé de l'espargne; par lequel est declaré le nom de celuy auquel le Receveur general doit payer la somme, pour la bailler, & delivrer à vn tel, en l'acquit du Roy, à telle chose, pour tel employ, à tel effect. ¶Ragueau.

Libeller. *To declare vpon an Action of Trespas, Debt, Couenant, &c; as vnder* Libellé.

Liberal: m. ale: f. *Liberall, bountifull, franke, open-handed, free-hearted; beneficiall, gracious, helping, propitious, good vnto.*

Liberalement. *Liberally, frankly, freely, bountifully; beneficially, with an open hand, in full measure, in abundant manner.*

Liberalité: f. *Liberalitie, bountie, franknesse, largesse, beneficence; abundant and free giuing.*

Liberation: f. *A freeing, discharging, releasse, remitment of.*

Liberté: f. *Libertie, freedome; full scope, good leaue, ample or free choice; an vncontroulable condition; also, opennesse, plainnesse, boldnesse in speech or action.*

Libertinage: m. *Libertinage, Epicurisme, sensualitie, licentiousnesse, dissolutenesse.*

Libidineux: m. euse: f. *Libidinous, lasciuious, luxurious, lustfull, incontinent, lecherous.*

Libidinosité: f. *Lustfullnesse, luxurie, lasciuiousnesse, lecherousnesse, incontinencie, fleshlinesse.*

Libraire: m. *A Booke-seller, a Stationer.*

Librairie: f. *A Librarie; a studie, or shop, full of bookes.*

Libre: com. *Free, frank, at libertie, quit; open; vnbound, vnbounded, vnlimited, vnrestrained; exempted from, not subiect vnto; bold; vncontroulable.*

Librement. *Freely, frankly, vnboundedly; at pleasure, with full libertie, without controule; willingly, without constraint; boldly, without feare.*

Libure: f. *A little Isle (cut out of the land) whereon Bay salt is gathered after euerie tyde.*

Liburnique: f. *A verie light, and swift ship, or foist, vsed by the auncient Pyrats.*

Licaleil: m. *A Lampe;* ¶Limosin. ¶Rab.

Licanthrope: com. *Troubled with the frenzie, or melancholie tearmed* Lycanthropie.

Lice: f. *A Lists, or Tilt-yard; also, a bitch; also, a whore (See* Lyce;) *also, the woofe, or thread of the shittle, in weauing; also, a certaine round peece of wood in the fore-castle of a ship.*

Lice de charpenterie. *A frame, or double, and close-wrought rayle, or barre of timber; such as the foundations of water-worke piles, &c, are compassed with.*

De haute lice. *Of rich worke, much worth; high stile, excellent stuffe; hence,* Tapisserie de haute lice. *The best kind of Tapistrie.*

Fuir la lice. *To shun, or quit the field; to refuse, or abandon, the fight; (any way) to flinch.*

Lice: com. *Smooth, sleeke; See* Lissé.

Licence: f. *Licence, leaue, libertie; permission, sufferance.*

Licencié: m. *A Licenciate; a Batcheler of Diuinitie; one that hath his Grace for a Doctorship; In Law, one that hath leaue to plead for clyents; an vtter Barrister.*

Licencié sous la cheminée. *One that doth his acts in* Tenebris; *one that steales a Degree, or gets it without desert.*

Licencié: m. ée: f. *Dismissed, discharged.*

Licencier. *To dismisse, discharge, giue leaue, graunt licence vnto.*

Licencieusement. *Licentiously, freely, with full sufferance.*

Licharder. *To licke daintily, feed quaintly, pick vp morsels curiously.*

Liche. *A kind of the fish Glaucus.*

Liche-casse. *A lick-box, a sweet-lips.* ¶Rab.

Liche-doigt: m. *One that lickes his fingers one after the other; also, one that does things leisurely, or by peeces; whence;*

'A liche-doigt. *Peecemeale, by patches or parcels, by degrees, one after another; also, daintily, or sparingly.*

Liche-frite: f. *A Dripping-panne.*

Lichement: m. *A licking; lapping, or slapping vp.*

Lichene: f. *A Ring-worme, or Tettar.*

Licher. *To licke; lap; slap vp.*

Licherie: f. *A licking, sawcinesse, lickerousnesse.*

Licheron: m. *A sawcie companion.*

Licheur: m. *A licker, lapper, or slapper vp of; a lickerous, or sawcie companion.*

Licisque. *A dog ingendred betweene a wolfe, and a dog.*

Licisque orgoose. *A sault bitch.*

Licitation: f. *A proffering, or setting to sale, vnto him that will giue most; also, a prizing, or cheapening.*

Licitation & decret. *Fine and recouerie.*

Licite: com. *Lawfull; allowable.*

Licol: m. *A rope, halter; horse-collar; Looke* Cheuestre.

Gens de sac, & de licol. *Rogues, vagabonds; also, begging Friers.*

Licorne: f. *An Vnicorne; also, Vnicornes horne.*

Lict: m. *A bed, couch, pallet; also, a course, ranke, bed, or laire of stone, &c, in building.*

Lict brisé. *Mariage broken, a maried couple parted.*

Lict d'un cerf. *The lodge of a Deere.*

Lict de Iustice. *A Iudiciall Seat, or Throne of Iustice; the Kings Seat in a Court, or in Parliament.*

Lict de matlas. *A Matteresse, or Flock-bed.*

Lict de parement. *The bed wherein a woman lyes in; also, a Sparuer; Looke* Parement.

Licts de parlement. *Quilts stuffed with Chestnut leaues; tearmed so in mockage, because being stirred, or stirred on, they make a brabling, or confused noise.*

Lict d'une Riviere. *The channell of a Riuer.*

Lict verd. *A couch, or bed of ease to sit, or loll on in the day time.*

En lict de chien n'y a point d'oingture: Prov. *The kennell of a dog's without sweet ointments.*

Le Lict est vne belle chose, qui n'y dort on y repose: Pro. *A well-made bed's a good, and friendlie neast, for though one sleepe not on't, he takes his rest.*

Lictée. *Seeke* Littée.

Lictiere: f. *A Litter, or Horse-litter; also, litter for horses, &c; also, old dung, or manure.*

Batre la lictiere. *A horse to stay or continue in, or not to stirre out of, the stable.*

Faire lictiere de. *To violate, prophane, abuse; despise, contemne, make vile account, or base vse of; tread vnder foot.*

Mettre à la lictiere. *To ruine, ouerthrow, pull downe, put vnto most vile or base offices, tread vnder foot.*

Lide: f. *A kind of woodden, and warlike Engine vsed in old time.*

Lie: f. *The lees, dregs, grounds, thicke substance that settles in the bottome of liquor.*

Tirer vn traict sus la lie. *To broach a vessell below, or towards the bottome; to leacher it, or get a licke at.*

Lie: com. *Cheerefull, pleasant, buxome.*

Dire vne chose de chere lie. *To say a thing with a merrie countenance, cheerie visage, looke full of glee.*

Faire chere lie. *To be iocond, merrie, frolicke; to make great sport, or good cheere.*

Lié: m. ée: f. *Tyed, bound; fastened, fettered; obliged; annexed, or knit vnto; combined, or vnited with; holding, or hanging together.*

Potage lié. *Broth, or pottage thickened with the yolkes of egges, or crummes of white bread.*

Lié avec fueilles de pourreaux. *Weakely bound God wot; readie, or easie, to be loossed.*

Ou la Chevre est liée faut qu'elle broute: Pro. *The Goat must brouze where she is bound; where a man is setled let him seeke to liue.*

Liege: m. *Corke.*

Liege. Fief liege, *as* Fief ample; *Seeke* Ample.

Liegé: m. ée: f. *Corked; stopped, or vnderlayed with Corke; whence;*

Soulier liegé. *A Corke shooe.*

Lieger. *To corke; to stop, raise, or vnderlay, with Corke.*

Liement: m. *A binding, tying, fastening, fettering, knitting, annexing vnto; a combining, or vniting with; an vnion, or adherence; a closing, gluing, souldering; a holding, or hanging together.*

Liément. *Merrily, blithely, iocondly, buxomely, gladsomely, with much glee.*

Lien: m. *A band, or tye; a line, cord, string; any thing that fasteneth, or fettereth; as a thong, rope, gyue, manacle, shackle, &c; also, a ligament, or ligature; also, the loope of a dart.*

Iustice patibulaire à deux piliers, & liens par dedans & par dehors. *A Gibbet standing on two pillars; a paire of Gallowes, bound both within and without; belongs vnto, or may be kept by, a Lo. high* Iusticier.

Sainct Pierre aux liens. *Lammas day; or the first of August.*

Ce n'est que trainer son lien. *He does but diuert, for a while, the plagues which will fall vpon him; or, goe whether he will, make what shift he can, he carries his payment with him; hence the Prouerbe;* Il n'est pas eschappé qui traine son lien.

'A meschant chien court lien; &, à petit chien petit lien; &, à rude chien dur lien: Prov. *Looke* Chien.

Rien ne vaut poulain s'il ne rompt son lien: Pro. *The colt that's halter breakes not mettall wants.*

Liens. *as* Leans.

Lienteric. Flux lienteric. *as* Lienteric.
Lienterie: f. *A flux wherein meat is voided (raw, and vndigested) presently after the eating thereof.*
Lienterieux: m. euse: f. *Troubled with, or sicke of, that flux.*
Lienterique: com. *The same.*
Liepard: m. *A Libbard, or Leopard.*
Lier: m. *The allay of coyne.*
Lier. *To tye, bind, fasten, knit; halter, fetter; soulder, vnite, combine; oblige, or make beholden to.*
On lie bien le sac avant qu' il soit plein: Prov. *A sacke before't be full is easily bound vp; there's hope of compassing one that's in want.*
Il ne faut pas lier les Asnes avec les chevaux: Pro. *We must not mingle bad and good together.*
Liernes: f. *Slits, Enterlasses, or Entertoises of Timber.*
Lierre: m. *Iuie.*
Lierre arboré. *Tree Iuie, wall Iuie; the great, or climing Iuie.*
Lierre blanc. *The white Iuie, or female great Iuie, bearing a white berrie.*
Lierre clavelé. *as* Petit Lierre.
Lierre Helix. *Barren, or creeping Iuie.*
Lierre noir. *The ordinarie climing, or black-berried Iuie.*
Lierre piquant. *Rough Bindweed.*
Lierre terrestre. *Ground Iuie, Alehoose, Gill creepe by ground, Tunehoofe, Catsfoot.*
Lierre trainant. *as* Lierre terrestre; *or creeping, and barren Iuie.*
Petit Lierre. *Small Iuie, ground Iuie, creeping or barren Iuie*
Liesse: f. *Glee, mirth, gladnesse, ioyfullneße, cheerefullnesse, lightneße of heart.*
Liet. *as* Liais.
Liet: m. ette: f. *Glad, blithe, merrie, iocond, frolicke, pleasant, buxome, cheerefull.*
Liette: f. *A till, or drawer; also, a casket, or small coffer full of tills, or drawers.*
Lieu: m. *A place; roome; seat, ranke; stead; also, a qualitie, calling, degree, state; also, credit, esteeme, reckoning, account; also, a house, or dwelling place; and hence;*
Lieu chevels. *A Mannor-house.* ¶Norm.
Chef lieu. *A Lords chiefe House, Place, or Mannor; (and, in the customes of* Mons, *and* Valenciennes *each of those Townes is tearmed* Chef lieu.)
Au lieu, & en lieu de. *In lieu, in stead, in the roome of.*
En temps, & lieu. *Fitly, conueniently, seasonably, then when it should be.*
Sur le lieu. *There; in that verie place; also, presently, incontinently, forthwith, before he stirred one foot thence.*
Il n'a feu ne lieu. *He hath nor house nor harbour; he hath not a hole to hide his head in.*
S'il y a lieu de s'arrester à son dire. *If there be cause to stand on his report, if there be reason to build vpon his tale, if we may safely beleeue him.*
Bonne parole bon lieu tient, & Meschantes paroles ont meschant lieu: Pro. *Seeke* Parole.
Lieve: f. *as* Leve.
Lieuë: f. *A League; two miles.*
La Lieuë de Bourgongne; *Containes* 50 *Portées. Looke* Portée.
Les grandes lieuës, comme celles d' Allemaigne; *containe verie neere foure of our miles.*
Les moyennes lieuës, comme celles de Dauphiné, ou de Languedoc; *are about three of our miles.*
Les petites lieuës, comme celles d'Italie; *are little other then our miles.*
Lievement. *as* Levée.
Lieur: m. *A binder, tyer, fastener, knitter, halterer, fetterer; soulderer; vniter of.*
Lieure: f. *as* Liement; *or, as* Liaison.
Lievre: f. *A Hare.*
Lievres cuirassez, ou morionnez. *So doe some Authors tearme poore Artisans that watch.*
Lievre marin. *The sea Hare; an ouglie, and venomous fish, whose left side nothing resembles the right.*
Bec de lievre. *A Hares lip, or mouth; the vpper lip cleft in the middle vp to the nose.*
Memoire de lievre. *Extreame forgetfullneße.*
Oeil de lievre. *An eye whose lids keepe open in sleeping; also, one whose vpper lid (by conuulsion, or otherwise) is reuerted, and thereby hindered from couering the white.*
Oreille de lievre. *Seeke* Oreille.
Palais au lievre. *The smooth Sow-thistle; or the milke Thistle called, Hares Lettuce.*
Pied de lievre. *Hares-foot, Harefoot Trefoile, base Trefoile, rough Clauer.*
Plus coüard qu'un lievre. *More heartlesse then a Hare (then which no beast hath leße heart.)*
Fuyard en lievre. *That runnes when he should resist; or (more properly) that runnes because he cannot resist.*
Le lievre est mis au rouët. *Looke* Rouët.
Ie sçay bien ou gist le lievre. *I know well which is the verie point, or knot of the matter.* Voila ou gist le lievre *(to the same purpose.)*
Il fait accroire que les lievres pondent, & font des œufs. *(Applyable to one that is an extreame prater, and a monstrous lyer to boot;) He would make vs beleeue that Hares lay egges.*
Les chiens vous mangeront le lievre. *That which you haue gaped, or hunted for will be had, or got, from you.*
Prendre le lievre au tabourin. *To performe impossibilities; whence the Prouerbe.*
L'on ne prend le lievre au son de tambour. *Applyable to such, as striue to be obeyed by force; or thinke by lowd, and great words to ouermaister euerie bodie; or presume they can surprise a place whose inhabitants had notice of their comming: And is as much as to tell them, they labour in vaine; for Hares are not to be caught by drumming.*
Bon est le lievre dont la peau couste cent sous: Pro. *The Hare whose skin costs deere is worth the hauing: we say of a thing bought at a high rate, it had need be daintie it cost him so deere; or, it is a Hare dressed with Venison, or Deere, sauce.*
En petit buisson trouve on grand lievre: Prov. *A little bush may hold a great Hare; a little bodie a great heart.*
Pas à pas le bœuf prend le lievre: Pro. *By little and little an Ox may catch a Hare; The like is;*
Vne vache prend bien vn lievre: Prov. *Patient perseuerance wins ground of hastie vehemence; so may a slow-paced Cow oretake the nimble Hare.*
Lieutenant: m. *A Lieutenant, Deputie, Substitute, Vicegerent; also, an vnder Iudge, or the deputie of a* Bailli, *or of a Lo. high* Iusticiers *Iudge; whence;*
Lieutenant civil. *A Iudge of ordinarie controuersies betweene partie and partie.*

Lieutenant criminel. (Son office est de s'informer des crimes, & faire le procez aux criminels, par interrogatoires, recolemens, & confrontations; & en apres les iuger: cognoist des delicts non punis par le Iuge du lieu: cognoist de remissions, rappels de ban, & pardons: peut faire armer le peuple: ne doit assister au iugement des procez civils:) *There be two sorts of them*; viz. de robbe longue, & de robbe courte, *somewhat inferiour to th'others, as being receiued, and instituted by them.*

On n'y peut mettre Lieutenant. *This must be done in person, or cannot be done by Atturney.*

Lieutrin. *as* Letrin.

Lieux: m. euse: f. *Full of lees, dregs, or grounds; thick in the bottome after standing.*

Lifrelofre: m. *A buffe snuffe, swag-bellie, puffe-bag; (a word coined in derision of the Germanes, and Swissers.)*

Ligament: m. *A ligament, or ligature; a tie, band, or string; especially, th'insencible string thats seated either within, or neere vnto, a ioynt, and is tearmed by our Anatomists, a Ligament.*

Ligamenteux: m. euse: f. *Full of ligaments, strings, ligatures.*

Ligature: f. *A ligature, tie, band; also, a binding, tying, fastening.*

Lige: m. *Allegiance, or liegemanship; whence;*

Fiefs tenus à plein lige. Fiefs *held by full homage, or allegiance.*

Lige: com. *Liege, leall, or loyall; subiect, vassall; naturall, ones owne.*

Garde lige. *The gard, or defence of a Lord, or of his castle or principall house, due from the vassall (sufficiently, and for certaine dayes armed) when there is need, or when he is required thereto.*

Hommage lige. *Seeke* Hommage; *Where though (in* Hommage plein*) it be saied, that it, and* Lige *be all one (because the customes of most places confound them) yet by some* Plein *is held more absolute then* Lige.

Prince lige. *A liege Lord; the Prince to whom one is by birth, and fortune subiect.*

Seigneur lige. *The same; also, a direct, immediate, or next Lord.*

Tenuë lige. *as* Tenuë à ligence.

Ligeaulté: f. *Loyaltie, or the fidelitie due by a subiect vnto his naturall Prince.*

Ligement. *Loyally, by allegiance; also, directly, immediately, next vnto.*

Ligence: f. *Liegemanship, allegiance, faith, loyaltie.*

Devoir de ligence. *The garding of a Lords castle, or house, due by his vassall (armed, and on horsebacke) certaine dayes, and nights in the yeare; or when he is required thereto; or otherwise, as the custome of the place, or qualitie of his Tenure binds him.*

Tenuë à ligence. *A Tenure in chiefe; a direct, or immediate Tenure (subiect vnto the* Devoir *aforesaid.)*

Ligier. *as* Leger.

Lignade: f. *Wooddage; prouision of wood.*

Faire lignade. *A ship to take in, or to furnish a ship with, fuell, or fire-wood.*

Lignage: m. *A linage, progenie, stocke, race, kindred, familie, parentage; also, wooddage; and hence;*

Devoir de lignage. *A certaine toll taken for euerie load of wood thats brought into* Rennes *in Britaine.*

Lignager: m. *A direct kinsman; See* Linagier.

Lignagier: m. ere: f. *Directly akinne, of neere kindred; of the same stocke, line, house, race, familie; belonging to that linage.*

Retraict lignagier. *Seeke* Retraict.

Ligne: f. *A line; any streake, small draught, or lineament; also, a thread, or long string; a verse, or line in writing; a stocke, or branch in a pedegree, a degree of kindred; also, the third part of a barlie corne, or the twelfth part of an inch in measuring (and the last, and least of that kind of measure.)*

Ligne blanche. *The lower part of the bellie whereat the muscles thereof doe meet; the white line, the vmbelicall veine.*

Ligne de compte. *The line made (in an accompt) from the subiect to the summe; also, a ranke, or file of counters in casting.*

Mettre en ligne de compte. *To reckon, esteeme, account, allow of; to register in the Kalender of account; to remember, or mention in discourse, as a thing of some importance.*

Ligne estainte. *as* Droict de Desherance.

Ligne feincte. *A supposed line in Geometrie; vsed often as a Demetient, when a line is supposed to runne from one point (without latitude, or thicknesse) to another.*

Ligne de perles. *A thread of pearle.*

Bois de ligne. *Timber squared out by line and leuell; wrought timber; also, an angle-rod.*

Cotte & ligne. *(which should rather be,* costé & ligne;) *Signifies peculiar kindred; or a particular branch of a familie, or kindred; and so when a man giues his wife a thing,* à cotte & ligne, *he meanes it absolutely vnto her, and her owne kinsfolke.*

Tenir cotte & ligne. *To haue the law in his owne hands, to doe what he list.*

Biens meubles ne tiennent costé ne ligne; asçavoir, ne suivent estoc, costé, ny ligne.

Tirer hors ligne. *To summe vp; from the custome of Auditors, &c, who set the summe of euerie parcell at th'end, or outside of the subiect.*

Lignear: m. are: f. *Linear, by line, in a direct course, or line; also, belonging to a line.*

Lignée: f. *as* Lignage.

Ligner. *To line, as a dog (or dog-Wolfe) a bitch.*

Ligneraye: f. *A line-yard, or flax-yard.*

Ligneul: m. *Shoomakers thread; or, a tatching end.*

Ligneux: m. euse: f. *Wooddie, full of wood; also, full of lines, or small and long threads.*

Lignier: m. *A pile of wood.*

Lignoul. *as* Ligneul.

Ligombeau: m. *A sea Creuice, or little Lobster.*

Ligoter. *To prune a vine; to take from about it the stones, clods, or hearbes that hinder the budding thereof.*

Ligue: f. *A league, or confederacie; a complot, or combination of sides, or parties which haue beene diuided; an agreement made, or alliance contracted; also, mutuall intercourse of kindnesses; also, an excellent Soulder, eight parts whereof be fine gold, three siluer, and three copper.*

Ligué: m. ée: f. *Leagued, in league with; confederate, combined, allied with.*

se Liguer l'vn à l'autre. *To make a league, to cõtract alliance, to enter into confederacie one with another.*

Ligule: f. *A little tongue, lingell, tenon; a spoone, slice, or small ladle, vsed by Apothecaries; also, a small (Romane) measure containing about a spoonefull; and in weight three drammes, and a scruple.*

Ligumbault. *as* Ligombeau.

Ligustic: m. *The hearbe Louage.*

Lilac. *as* Ben (*of two sillables.*)
Limace: f. *A Snaile (most properly, the dew Snaile, or Snaile without a shell;) also, as* Volute; *any thing that winds, or turnes like a Snaile-shell, &c.*
Limaceux: m. euse: f. *Snailie, Snaile-like; full of Snailes; also, as*;
Limacial: m. ale: f. *Of a Snaile, resembling a Snaile; winding, twirling, or turning about like the shell of a Snaile.*
Limaçon: m. *A Snaile (and most properly that which hath a shell.)*
Limaçon de mer. *A Winkle, or Periwinkle.*
Petit Limaçon de mer. *as* Nerite.
Herbe à Limaçon. *Medicke fodder, Snaile Claver.*
Pierre de Limaçon. *The Snaile stone; found in the heads of some (dew) Snailes; tis white, somewhat transparent, and rugged; it seemes hard, and yet, being pressed betweene the teeth, breaks as small as sand: the vulgar hold it good for a Tertian, or Quartan Ague.*
Treffle au limaçon. *as* Herbe à limaçon.
Faire le limaçon. *To wind, twirle, or turne round about; souldiers to doe the ring, or to cast themselues into a ring.*
Autant chemine vn homme en vn iour comme vn limaçon en cent ans: Prov. *A quicke workeman dispatches as much in one day as a slowbacke in twentie.*
Contre la nuict s'arment les limaçons: Pro. *Snails arme themselues (put out their hornes) towards night.*
Limaçonner. *To twirle, turne, or wind about, like the shell of a Snaile, or as souldiers that cast themselues into a ring.*
Limaille: f. *File-dust, pinne-dust.*
Limailles: f. *as* Legumages; *Pulse.*
Limaire. *A young Tunnie.*
Limande: f. *A Burt, or Bret-fish; also, a broad Pipe-staffe, or boord, prepared, fashioned, and fit, for caske; also, a short cudgell.*
Limas. *as* Limaçon.
Limasse: f. *as* Limace.
Limasse à eau. *The little water Snaile.*
Limasson. *as* Limaçon.
Limature: f. *A filing; also file-dust.*
Limbe de bouteille. *The mouth, or brinke of a bottle.*
Limbes. *A low, and vnsauorie roome in prisons; also, the Purgatorie of vnbaptized children.*
Lime: f. *A file; also, as* Limaçon.
Limes. *A wild Boares nether tusks, or tushes.*
Lime sourde. *A soft, or smooth file, which makes no noise when tis vsed; also, a dreaming, slie, malicious knaue; or, as in*;
Faire la lime sourde. *To giue no eare vnto; or, to seeme as if he either heard not, or cared not to heare.*
Limé: m. ée: f. *Filed; smoothed, polished; scraped, or shauen vnto a sleeknesse, or euennesse; also, licked; also, gleeked, or looked askew at.*
Limer. *To file; smooth, polish; to scrape, or shaue a thing till it be sleeke, or euen; also, to licke, as a Hare doth her young ones; also, to gleeke, or looke askew at.*
Limes; &, Lime-sourde. *as in* Lime.
Limestre. *The cloth whereof hoods be made is called* Drap de limestre; *and from hence those that weare them be in contempt called* Limestres.
Limeur: m. *A filer.*
Limeure: f. *File-dust; also, a filing.*
Limier: m. *A Bloud-hound, or Lime-hound.*
Limignon d' vne chandelle. *The wieke of a candle.*
Liminaire: com. *Set before th'entrie, or at the beginning of; dedicatorie; forerunning.*
Limitateur: m. *A limiter, bounder, stinter, prescriber.*
Limitation: f. *A limitation, restriction, restraint, prescription, modification.*
Limite: f. *A limit, bound, stint; border, frontire; prescription; a condition, course, or compasse appointed one.*
Limité: m. ée: f. *Limited, bounded, stinted, restrained, prescribed a certaine course, or compasse.*
Limiter. *To limit, bound, stint; prescribe a condition, appoint a course, restraine within a compasse.*
Limiteur: m. *A limiter, bounder, stinter.*
Limitrophe: com. *Bordering vpon, adioyning or lying neere vnto.*
Limoine: f. *Pyrola, Winter-greene, Winter Beets, wild Beets.*
Limon: m. *Slime; or thicke, and slimie durt, mud, mire, puddle, dregs; also, a slimie soile; also, a Lemmon; also, the Thill of a waine, wagon, &c; In which sence (because a Thill consists of two beames) it is most vsed in the Plurall number.*
Limonier. Cerfs limoniers. *Stags painted, as Thill-horses, with carts at their heeles.*
Cheval limonier. *A Thill-horse, or Cop-horse; he that goes next to the waine, &c.*
Limonne. *as* Poncille.
Limonneux: m. euse: f. *Slimie; muddie, boggie, durtie, mirie, puddle, filthie, full of ordure.*
Limpide: com. *Cleere, bright, sheene, glazie, transparent.*
Limure. *File-dust; also, a filing.*
Lin: m. *Line, flax; flaxen or hempen yarne; linnen cloth.*
Lin sauuage. *Flax-weed, wild flax, tode-flax, Flainewort.*
Lin vif. *A kind of Indian line, or linnen, which the fire purifies, but consumes not.*
Goutte, ou podagre, de lin. *The weed Dodder; (and flax it selfe is said to haue the gowt, when one staulke twines about another as it growes.)*
Il a meslé le lin avec la chanure; &;
Il a tissu lin avec estouppe. *He hath mingled flax with toe; he hath iumbled good and bad together.*
Linage: m. *Linage, kindred; See* Lignage.
Linagier: m. *A direct, or neere kinsman.*
Linagier sur linagier n'a point de retenuë. *One kinsman cannot recouer the land that hath bin bought by another.*
Linagier: m. ere: f. *as* Lignagier; *Neere akinne, &c.*
Linaire. *Flax-weed, Flainewort, wild flax, tode-flax.*
Linarole: f. *The name of a delicate Italian peare which is ripe in August.*
Linceul: m. *A sheet (for a bed.)*
Le plus riche n'emporte qu'un linceul: Prov. *The richest carries but one sheet t' his graue.*
se **Linder** par terre. *To creepe, or crawle along the ground.*
Line. *as* Ligne.
Lineament: m. *A lineament, or feature, of the face, or of any other part.*
Lineature: f. *A lineature, or feature.*
Lineature des mains. *The lines, or streakes of the hands, wheron Palmisters, and Fortune-tellers ground their coniectures.*

Linée: f. *A stocke, linage, parentage.*
Linement. *as* Liniment.
Linge: m. *Linnen, flaxen; also, a peece of linnen cloth.*
Linge: com. *Lanke, thinne, meager, scraggie, leane.*
Lingere. *as* Lingiere.
Lingerie: f. *The making, or selling of linnen cloth; also, linnen, linnen stuffe, things made of linnen.*
Lingiere: f. *A Seamster; a woman that makes, or sells linnen, or linnen ware.*
Lingot: m. *An ingot, lumpe, or masse of mettall.*
Lingotiere: f. *The mould wherein ingots are framed, or cast.*
Linir: m. *A Flax-man; a seller of flax.*
Liniere: f. *A Flax-wife.*
Liniment: m. *A liniment, or thinne ointment; also, a smearing, annointing, gentle dawbing, soft rubbing on.*
Linier. *To smeare, annoint, rub softly, or gently on.*
Linitif: m. iue: f. *Mitigating, refreshing, paine-asswaging, ache-quailing; mollifying, suppling.*
Linition: f. *A smearing, annointing, gentle rubbing.*
Linomple: f. *A fine, thinne, or open-waled linnen, much vsed in Picardie (where it is made) for womens kerchers, and Church-mens surplesses.*
Linon: m. *as* Linomple; *Some also tearme Lawne so.*
Linostolie: f. *A cutting of the haire.*
Linotte: f. *A Linnet.*
Il a vne teste de linotte. *He hath but a light, or giddie head of his owne.*
Linsueil: m. *A sheet; See* Linceul.
Linteau: m. *The lintell, or headpeece, ouer a doore.*
Lintheau. *as* Linteau.
Lion: m. *A Lyon; also, the (Zodiacall) Signe Leo; also, a peece of coyne worth about 6 s. sterl.*
Lion de mer. *The sea Lion; resembles both in shape, and bignesse, the land one; also, a kind of great Lobster.*
Dent de lion. *Dandelion, Priestes crowne, Swines snowt, Pissabed.*
Pas de lion. *as* Pied de lion.
Patte de lion. *Lyons claw, Setterwort, Settergrasse, bastard blacke Ellebore; also, as;*
Pied de lion. *Lyons foot, Lyons paw, great Sanicle, our Ladies mantle, (some also tearme Lyons leafe, and Lyons Turnep,* pes Leoninus.*)*
Sault du lion. *A certaine tumbling tricke vpon a stoole, or little bench.*
Vin de lion. *Terrible strong wine; such as makes the drinker, fell, and furious.*
Batre le chien devant le lion. *See* Batre.
Conjecturant le lion par les ongles. *Ghessing at the Lyon by his clawes; at the humor of the man by his courses; Looke* Ongle.
Coudre la peau du regnard à celle du lion. *To attempt that by sleight which hee could not obtaine by might.*
Prendre le lion par les iubes. *To performe a difficult or dangerous act.*
Il n'y eut iamais bon marché de peaux de lions: Prov. *A Lyons skinne was neuer bought good cheape; the valiant euer sold their skinnes full deere.*
Lionceau: m. *A Lyons whelpe, or young Lyon.*
Lionin: m. ine: f. *Lyonish, Lyon-like, of a Lyon.*
Lionne: f. *A Lyonesse.*
Lionneau: m. *as* Lionceau.
Lionneux: m. euse: f. *Full of Lyons.*
Lionnier: m. *A keeper of Lyons.*
Lionnin. *as* Lionin; *Also, of a Lion-tawnie colour.*

Liperquam. faire de liper. *To shew his authoritie, to let the world see his power; to beare himselfe as one that can doe all in all; to take exceeding much vpon him: This word is (corruptly) vsed in stead of,* luy per quem *(all things are done.)*
Lipie. *See* Lippie.
Lipothymie: f. *A swoonding wherein the patient seems dead.*
Lippaire: m. *Lip-salue.*
Lippe: f. *A lip; (See* Lype*) also, as* Lippie; *or* Lippitude.
Lippée: f. *A big bit, a good morsell, a mouthfull; also, a meale, or bellifull of meat.*
Mouche de lippée. *A lickorous, or saucie companion.*
Il avoit sa lippée du butin. *Hee had a share in the bootie.*
Il flatte pour la lippée. *He collogues with one, of purpose to get a meale by him.*
Lippie: f. *The rednesse, or sorenesse of a bleare eye.*
Lippion. *Part of a womans &c.*
Lippitude: f. *Blearednesse, or bleare-eyednesse; a running of the eyes accompanied with paine, and rednesse.*
Lippu: m. uë: f. *Thicke-lipped, great-lipt; also, powting, or hanging the lip, as a child thats readie to crie.*
Liquabilité: f. *Aptnesse to melt, or to become liquid.*
Liquation: f. *A melting.*
Liquefié: m. ée: f. *Dissolued, melted, made liquid; clarified.*
Liquerice: f. *Lickorice.*
Liqueur: f. *Liquor, humor, moisture, sap, iuyce, water.*
Liqueur Septembrine. *Wine (because tis made in September.)*
Liquidation: f. *An euidence, cleering, manifestation; also, a discussing, or examination.*
Liquide: com. *Liquid, moist, wet; thinne, pure, cleere; manifest, euident, pregnant, apparent; certaine.*
Debte liquide. *A cleere, sure, sound debt.*
Liquidé: m. ée: f. *Cleered, manifested, made euident, pregnant, certaine, apparent; also, discussed, examined; also, made liquid, moist; thinne, pure.*
Liquider. *To cleere, manifest, make pregnant, certaine, apparent; also, to examine, or discusse; also, to make liquid, moist, or thinne.*
Liquider les despens d'vn procez. *To cleere, or to correct, them; a Judge to set downe which shall be allowed, and which not; (This phrase is applied especially, to th'examination of ordinarie, and well-knowne, charges; such as be the due fees of Counsellors, Atturneyes, Officers, Clerkes, &c.)*
Lire: f. *The musicall Instrument Lyra.*
Lire. *To read.*
Autant vaut celuy qui chasse & rien ne prend, comme celuy qui lit & rien n'entend: Prov. *Hee that hunts, and catches nought, is much like him that reads, and conceiues nought.*
Lire-liron. *The burthen of a song.*
Liripipié. *Hooded, as a Graduate.*
Liripipion: m. *A Graduates hood.*
Liripipionné. *as* Liripipié; *Also, mellow, cupshotten; or, faithfull to the pot, and therefore bearing the red-faced liuerie thereof.*
Liron: m. *A Dormouse.*
Liron de pain. *A little gobbet, luncheon, or cantle of bread.*
Lis: m. *A Lillie.*
Lis blanc. *Th'ordinarie white garden Lillie.*
Lis celeste. *The blew Lillie.*

Lis d'estang. *Water Lillie, water Rose, the yellow and white Nenuphar.*

Lis iaulne. *Liriconfancie, yellow Lillie.*

Lis de mer. *The white sea Daffadill, or white sea Onion.*

Lis sauvage. *Wild Lillie, mountaine Lillie; also, Liriconfancie, or the yellow Lillie.*

Lis de vent. *A gust, or flaw of wind; also, an opposition of two contrarie winds; or as* Rumb.

Aller au lis de vent. *To goe close by the wind, saile with a scant wind, lay tacke aboord.*

Lisable: com. *Legible, readable.*

Lisard: m. *as* Lisarde; *or* Lezard.

Lisarde: f. *A Lizard; Newt, Aske; (See* Lezard;*) also, a woman that reads much.*

Lisarde verde. *The great, greene, and harmelesse Lizard* Ramarro; *a friend vnto men, on whom she loues to gaze, and whom sleeping she vses to gard from the treacherous assaults of Serpents.*

Liser. *To list, or border a garment; also, to coast along by a countrey.*

Liseron: m. *Withiwind, Bindweed, Ropeweed, Hedge-bells.*

Liseron aspre. *Rough Bindweed.*

Liseron grand. *as* Grand liset.

Liset: m. *The Vine-fretter, or diuells Goldring; (a worme;) also, as* Liseron; *Withiwind; and hence;*

Liset petit. *Small Withiwind, or Bindweed; also, the blacke purging Bindweed.*

Liset picquant. *Rough Bindweed.*

Grand liset. *The great, smooth, white Bindweed, Ropeweed, Withiwind, Hedge-bells.*

Lisible: com. *Legible, readable.*

Lisiére: f. *The list of cloth, or of stuffe; th'edge, or hemme of a garment; also, th'end, or th'extreame outward part of any thing; and hence, a frontire, march, border, vtmost bound, or coast of a countrey.*

Lisiereux: m. euse: f. *Prescribing the limits, appointing or setting out the bounds, of seuerall countries.*

Lisisque. *as* Licisque.

Lissant. *Sleeking, glazing, polishing.*

Lissant de gueulles. *Scaled Gules; (a tearme of Blazon.)*

Lisse. *as* Lice; *Also, one of the ropes wherwith the main-yard of a ship is hoised vp; also, a rowler of massiue glasse wherewith Curriers doe sleeke, and glosse their leather.*

Lissé: m. ée: f. *Sleeked, glossed, glazed, polished; smooth, slipperie, glib.*

Lisser. *To sleeke, to glosse, to glaze, to polish, to smooth, to make slipperie.*

Lisseron: m. *Th'hearbe Peruinkle, or Periwinkle.*

Lissure: f. *A sleeking, glasing, polishing, setting a glosse on, smoothing.*

Liste: f. *A list, roll, checkroll, or catalogue of names, &c; also, a list, or seluedge; also, a small square out-iutting brow, or member of a piller; also, as* Littre.

Listeau: m. *A little list; roll, catalogue; seluedge.*

Litarge. *as* Litharge.

Literaire: com. *Of, or belonging to, letters, or learning.*

Literal: m. ale: f. *Learned, literall, well seene in liberall Artes.*

Literature: f. *Literature, learning.*

Literon: f. *as* Litron.

Litharge: m. *Litargie, white lead; lead mixed with the drosse of siluer and brasse.*

Litharge d' argent. *Siluer foame, or the spume of tried siluer; or rather, the lead wherein siluer oare hath beene melted (that it might be purged, and cleered from the lead, or copper that was in it) which being done by a gentle fire giues it a siluer hew, and thereby this name.*

Litharge d'or. *Gold sceame; the best kind of Litargie; comes of lead wherein siluer hath beene melted by a quick, and great fire, giuing it a golden luster, & thereby this name.*

Litharge de plomb. *as* Plombagine; *also, as* Escume de plomb.

Lithiase: f. *The stone in the bladder.*

Lithomantie: f. *Diuination by the casting of pible stones.*

Lithortipon. *for* Lithontripton; *Stone-dissoluing, or stone-breaking:* ¶Rab.

Liticontester. *To protest in a suit; viz. to deliuer, or lay open before a Judge the chiefe points of the declaration, and answer.*

Litiere: f. *A horselitter; also, litter for cattell; also, old dung, or manure; See* Lictiere.

Litige. *Suit, controuersie, difference, variance, contention, strife, debate: In law,* s'entend proprement quand y a Action intentée par adjournement, pour la chose contentieuse, & de qua controversia est.

Litiger. *To striue, wrangle, contend, maintaine a suit against; to be at variance, hold debate, goe to law with.*

Litigieux: m. euse: f. *Litigious, debatefull, contentious; in suit; or subiect vnto suit.*

Litiscontestation: f. *The deliuerie, or laying open of the chiefest points of a case,* pro & contra, *before a Judge; done after the declaration, and answer bee put in.*

Litispendence: f. *The hanging of a suit; or the triall, disceptation, or decision thereof.*

Litorne: f. *A Wing-thrush; or the red spotted Thrush, that seldome, or neuer, appeares in Summer.*

Litre. *as* Littre.

Litron: m. *A measure (most commonly) of wood, containing somewhat more then our pinte, and vsed by the Retailers of Salt, Pulse, Millet, Rapeseed, &c.*

Littée: f. *The litter of a Bitch, Lyonesse, &c; also, a bed, or cake of leaues, hay, grasse, &c, to lay, or packe vp things in.*

Litteron. *as* Litron.

Littre: f. *A funerall girdle; the blacke wherewith the vpper part of a Church is compassed, at the funerall of a great person.*

Littron. *as* Litron.

Lituë: m. *A certaine crooked staffe vsed by the Roman Augures; also, a Crosier, or Bishops staffe.*

Liture: f. *A dash, rase, or streake through a word with a penne; also, a dashing, rasing, striking out, a blotting, or blurring with a pen.*

Livane: f. *The (bird) Pellicane.*

Liveau. *Seeke* Niveau.

Livel. d'un livel. *Leuell.*

Livesche. *Lombardie Louage; also, Alexanders.*

Livide: com. *Wan, lew, bleake, pale, of a leaden, earthie, or dead, colour.*

Lividité: f. *Liuiditie, lewnesse, wannesse, bleakenesse, palenesse, blewishnesse; the colour appearing vpon a stroake, blacke and blew; a dead, earthie, leaden hew.*

Livoy: m. *A small vine-hooke, or vine-knife.*

Livraison: f. *A liuerie, or deliuerie; also, a court-dish; a dish furnished from a plentifull table with some part of all the meat thats on it.*

Livre: m. *A booke; a composition, or worke, in writing.*

Vn livre à personnages. *A Dialogue.*
Il veut tousiours tenir le livre. *He talkes continually, no bodie can get a word for him, he will suffer no bodie to speake.*
Livre: f. *A pound weight.*
La livre d' Anvers. *The ordinarie pound, containing 16 ounces.*
La livre des Apothecaries. *Containing (in many places) but 12 ounces, which we call Troy weight, and was th' auntient Romane weight: (Our Apothecaries vse the sixteene-ounce pound.)*
La livre d' Espaigne. *Containes 14 ounces.*
La livre des Espiciers, Grossiers, &c. *Containes but 12 ounces; (whereas our Grocers pound containeth 16.)*
La livre de Florence, & de Gennes. *Is 12 ounces.*
La livre de grosserie. *Containes 24 ounces.*
La livre de Lyon. *Is 15 ounces.*
La livre marchande. *Containes in some places 14, in others 18, but in the most 16, ounces; which be diuided into 32 halfe ounces, they into 64* Sezains, *those into 128* Treseaux, *they into 256* Gros, *and they into 512* Demi gros.
La livre des Marescbaux. *The Farriers pound; containes 12 ounces, diuided into 90 drammes, they into 270 scruples, and they into 540* Oboles, *or halfe pence.*
La livre Medecinale. *The Physitians pound; contains also 12 ounces; but they be diuided into 96 drammes, they into 288 scruples, those into 576* Oboles, *they into 1728* Siliques, *and they into 6912 graines.*
La livre de Milan, ou de la Soye. *Is but 12 ounces.*
La livre du gros poids. *Consists of 26 ounces.*
La livre du petit poids. *Is but 12 ounces.*
La livre Royale. *The Kings pound,* Aver du poids *pound, most ordinarie pound, containeth 16 ounces.*
Reduicts de livres en quarterons. *(Somewhat like our) brought from a noble to nine-pence.*
Livre: f. *A pound in money.*
Livre Barrois. *Is worth but* 14 s. Tournois, *one short of* 18 d. sterl.
Livre Bourdelois. *Is but* 12 Solz *and a halfe; or the halfe of the Parisian pound.*
Livre Mansais. *Is* 4 s. sterl. *or double the worth of the* Tournois.
Livre Parisis. *Is worth* 20 s. *of Paris, or* 25 s. Tourn. *which come to* 2 s. 6 d. sterl.
Livre Tournois. *The pound* Tournois; *the most ordinarie French pound; amounts but to* 2 s. sterl.
Livré: m. ée: f. *Deliuered, giuen, or distributed vnto.*
Livrée: f. *A deliuerie of a thing thats giuen; and (but lesse properly) the thing so giuen; hence, a Liuerie; Ones cloth, colours, or deuice in colours worn by his seruants, or others.*
La Livrée des Chanoines. *Their liuerie, or corrodie; their stipend, exhibition, dailie allowance in victualls, or money.*
Livrement: m. *A liuerie, or deliuerie; and hence;*
Livrement de fust, & terre. *Liuerie, and seisin.*
Livrer. *To giue; to deliuer, or distribute vnto; to bestow, or conferre on; to passe, or yeeld ouer; to put into the hands of.*
Livresque: com. *Bookish; of, or belonging to, a booke.*
Livret: m. *A Pamphlet, or little booke.*
Lixive. *as* Lexive.
Lizant. *Bordering; setting a list or border on; also, coasting along by the borders of.*
Lize: com. *Glib, smooth, sleeke:* ¶Rab.
Lizeron: m. *Withiwind, Bindweed, Hedge-bells.*
Lizet. *as* Liset.
Lizette: f. *A little grayish vermine (which gnawes, and does much hurt vnto the young buds of grafts) held to work the same effects in the yard that the* Cantharides *doe.*
Liziere: f. *as* Lisiere.
Lizieux: m. *Woollen clothes made at a Normand towne so called.*
Loage. *Seeke* Loüage.
Lobe: m. *The lap, or lowest part of the eare; also, a lobe, or lappet of the liuer, &c; also, as* Loupe; *(also, a lie, fib, ieast, gullerie, mockerie; In old French.)*
Lobeau: m. *A little lobe, lap, or lappie peece of.*
Lober. *To gull, cousen, deceiue, beguile.*
Local: m. ale: f. *Locall; belonging to, or contained in, a place.*
Localement: m. *Locally, in a place.*
Locar. bled locar. *A kind of wall Barlie, called S. Peters corne.*
Locataire: com. *A Lessee, or hirer of a house, or lodging; also, a hireling, one which is, or may be hired; also, as* Locateur.
Locateur: m. *A letter, or hirer out of.*
Locatif. *A tenant, inmate, soiourner; one that hireth a lodging or two to lie in.*
Location: f. *A hiring, or letting out of; also, a placing; a setting, or bestowing, in a place.*
Loch: m. *A Loche, or Loboche; a liquid confection, or soft medecine, thats not to be swallowed, but held in the mouth vntill it haue melted, and so past by degrees downe the throat; See* Lohoc.
Loche: f. *The Loach, a small fish; also, the dew-snayle, or snayle without a shell.*
Loche franche. *Is somewhat lesse, and daintier then th' ordinarie Loach, which is commonly tearmed;*
Loche grasse; *and liues much in the mud.*
Loche de mer. *A little fish bred of, but neuer so big as, the sea Gudgeon; some call it a sea Groundling.*
Locher. *To shog, shake, shocke, wag, make a noise like a thing thats loosse.*
Lochette: f. *A Groundling, or small-bearded Loach.*
Locquet. *as* Loquet.
Locule: m. *A little bag, pouch, or purse.*
Locupleter. *To inrich, or make wealthie.*
Locution: f. *A locution, saying, speech, manner of speaking.*
Lodier: m. *A quilt, or quilted counterpoint for a bed.*
Lodes. *as* Lods: ¶Breton.
Lods. *Fines of Alienation due to a Lord vpon the purchase of a* Censuel *inheritance held of him; Seeke* Ventes; *or,* Droict de ventes.
Loe: f. *A quantitie of fish taken, as a custome, by some few Normand Lords, of euerie fisher-boat that comes into, and moores within, their hauens, creekes or harbors; especially if the boat belong vnto any of their tenants, or any inhabitant of their territories.*
Loere: f. *as* Plongeon de Riviere.
Lof. *Seeke* Loo.
Loge. vn loge qui peut. *A lodging at randome, a lodging where one can get it, or a scambling for lodgings; from souldiers incamping, or entring of a towne, when commonly euerie one takes the first lodging hee lights on.*
Loge: f. *A lodge, cote, shed, or small house; a cabine in a ship; a booth in a Market, or Faire &c.*
Droict de loges. *Looke* Droict.
Il n'est pas mercier qui ne sçait faire sa loge: Pro. *He*

He is not worthie to vse a trade that cannot, with his owne hands, fit all things vnto it.

Logé: m. ée: f. *Lodged, housed, harboured; lying, soiourning at, abiding in, a place.*

I'en suis logé là. *I am of that mind, or humor.*

Nos gens en sont bien là logéz. *Are of a right mind in that, are in the right for that.*

Logeable: com. *Lodgeable, harbourable, intertainable in a house.*

Vne maison fort logeable. *A house of great receipt.*

Loger. *To lodge, lie, soiourne, harbour, dwell, abide for a time; to host, Inne, or lie in an Inne; also, to lodge, intertaine, giue house-roome, affoord a lodging, vnto.*

Vous me logez chez Guillot le songeur. *Looke* Songeur.

Se loger sur le blesme. *To looke, or wax, pale on't.*

En mauvais voisinage se loge on: Prov. *Seeke* Voisinage.

Logette: f. *A little lodge, cote, roome; booth; cabane, lodging.*

Les logettes és cosses des febues. *The holes, or dimples, wherein husked beanes are lodged.*

Logie. Droict de logies. *Looke* Droict.

Logique. *Logicke; the Art of reasoning; the way to reason.*

Pont aux asnes de Logique. *The conuersion of propositions; also, Looke* Asne.

Logis: m. *A lodging, house, dwelling.*

Le logis des gens de pied, ou l'on n'a point la peine de fermer les portes. *A prison.*

Logisme: m. *The due, and iudicious vnderstanding of a thing, formerly considered, and esteemed of, according to reason.*

Logistique: f. *Th'Art of counting, the practise of Arithmeticke; or, that part thereof which containes Addition, Substraction, Multiplication, and Diuision.*

Lohoc. *A Loch, or Lohoch; an Electuarie, or medicine more liquid then an Electuarie, appropriated to the lungs and windpipe; and to be licked, and let downe the throat by leasure.*

Loi. *as* Loy.

Loïel; &, Loïauté. *as* Loyal; &, Loyaulté.

Loiderer. *To defame, reproach, reuile, raile on.*

Loier: m. *as* Loyer.

Loinceau. *Seeke* Loinseau.

Loing. *Farre, much, a great way off.*

Demander de loing. *To aske a farre off, or propound a farre-fetched question, as one that would know a thing without seeming to desire it.*

Il ne regarde plus loing que le bout de son nez. *He is a dull, carelesse, idle, improuident fellow.*

Pas à pas on va bien loing: Prov. *Faire and softly goeth farre.*

Petite chose de loing poise: Prov. *A little, or light thing farre carried proues heauie.*

Loingnet: m. ette: f. *Somewhat long, or farre; little off.*

Loingnettement. *Somewhat long, or farre off; a little way off.*

Loingtain: m. aine: f. *Forreine, remote, much remoued, farre distant, farre off, a long way to, or from.*

Loingtaineté: f. *Farnesse, remotenesse, much distance from, great space betweene.*

Loinseau de fil. *A clue, or bottome of thread.*

Loir: m. *A Dormouse.*

Loisible: com. *Lawfull, allowable.*

Loisir: m. *Leasure; ease, rest; vacation, small doings, little to doe.*

De loisir. *At leasure, without imployment, out of worke, not troubled with much businesse.*

Tout à loisir. *Leasurely, faire and softly, not too fast, by degrees; idly, litherly, slowly.*

Loist. *(A Verbe Impersonall;)* il me loist. *I may, I am allowed, it is lawfull for me.*

Lombaire: com. *as* Lumbaire.

Lombales: f. *The parts which be on each side of the nauell.*

Lombard: m. *The name of a fertill vine; also, a Lombard; one of Lombardie.*

Le boucon des Lombards. *An impoisoned bit (for the Lombards are said to be great impoisoners.)*

Freres des Lombards. *Moles, Moonecalues, monstrous birthes; tearmed so, because the women of Lombardie by much feeding on hearbes, fruites, and other crudities, bring forth sometimes those monsters in stead of children; Looke* Frere.

Patience de Lombard. *Patience perforce, a forced or vnwilling patience.*

Les graces du Lombard sont trois dez sur table: Prov. *For so much as the Lombard affected vnto that meager, and vnworthie sport, as (by his good will) hee falls to it as soone as his meat is out of his mouth.*

Lombard: m. arde: f. *Lombard, of Lombardie.*

Lettres Lombardes. *Letters Patents whereby the Lombards, and other Italians are licensed to trade, or put out money to vse, in France.*

Manche Lombarde. *A flocke-sleeue; or fashion of halfe sleeue, whose vpper part is raised, and full of plaits, or gathers.*

Poule Lombarde. *A great Henne, or Henne of the Game.*

Lombardie: f. *Lombardie; the hithermost part of Italie.*

Secours de Lombardie. *Succour thats too long in comming; or so long, that its vnseasonable when it comes.*

Lombe: m. *The loyne, flanke, or haunch; the leg, or knuckle.*

Lombris: m. *A ground worme.*

L'on. *Many, some, they; as in,* l'on dit; *Some people report, the world is of opinion, men say.*

Lonce: f. *The Ounce, a rauenous beast.*

Lonche. *as* Louche; ¶Normand.

Long: m. *The name of an apple whereof excellent cyder is made; also, length; also, a long, or tedious person.*

Au long aller. *At the length, in th'end, in continuance, or processe of time.*

Tout au long de l'aulne. *Throughly, soundly, to some purpose, from one end of the thing to another.*

En bailler tout au long à. *To gull, beguile, delude, come ouer finely.*

Faire le long. *To linger, delay, protract, prolong, driue off the time; to be loath, to goe doubtfully, or drowsily to worke.*

Long: m. Longue: f. *Long; tall, slimme; extended, out-stretched; continuall, tedious, wearisome; also, great, large, much.*

Long bois. *A Pike, or Speare.*

Longue eschine. *A luske, slimme, long-backe, or slowbacke; a tall, ill-fauoured, loosse-hangled loobie; a gangrell, a slangam.*

Vaisseau long. *A Gallie, Foist, or Brigantine; See* Vaisseau.

'A la longue. *At length, in tract or continuance of time, yet at the last, after much adoc.*

Aller long. *To shite ouer nine hedges; to haue the squirt, or a laske.*

Avoir les dents bien longues. *To haue a terrible appetite, or extreame stomacke, to be continually, or cruelly, sharpe set.*

La faire longue. Il ne la fera longue en ce monde. *He cannot liue any time, hee will not be long aliue.*

Longues paroles font les iours courts: Prov. *Long discourses make short dayes.*

Longale: f. *A loyne.*

Longard: m. *A delayer, lingerer, protracter, prolonger.*

Longe: f. *The loyne; or flanke; (some name so the fleshie part of the necke, backe, and reines, cut along the back; others, more commonly, the peece that extends from the kidney to the end of the rumpe; and others call both these parts together,* la longe;) *also, a hawkes lune, or leash; and hence, any long string, or line of leather, &c.*

Longeastre: com. *Longish, or somewhat long.*

Long-encollé: m. ée: f. *Long-necked, necked like a Crane.*

Longiere: f. *A long narrow towell.*

Longis: m. *A lungis; a slimme, slow-backe, dreaming luske, drowsie gangrill; a tall and dull slangam, that hath no making to his height, nor wit to his making; also, one that being sent on an errand is long in returning.*

Longitude: f. *Longitude, length, longnesse, extension, continuance.*

Longue: f. *The loyne; See* Longe.

Longuement. *Longly, tediously, at length, long time, lastingly, of much continuance, a great while.*

Longuement proceder est à l' advocat vendenger: Prov. *Long pleading is the Lawyers haruest.*

Longuerie. *as* Longueur.

Long-uestu. *as* Obole de Gueldres.

Longuet: m. uette: f. *Longish, or somewhat long.*

Quarré longuet. *A square that is more long then broad.*

Longueur: f. *Length, longnesse; extension, tallnesse, height.*

Lonze: f. *A match to keepe fire with.*

Loo. *The loofe of a ship.*

Bouter de loo. *To goe by a wind, to sayle neere the wind, to lay tacke aboord.*

Looh; ou, Loot. *as* Loch.

Lopin: m. *A peece, gobbit, luncheon, lumpe, cantle, nuncheon, big morsell, or parcell of.*

Lopin de laine. *A locke of wooll.*

Qui suit les lopins. *A parasite, smell-feast, trencher friend.*

Qui bons lopins mange bons lopins le suivent: Prov. *Prouision followes them that loue to fare well.*

Lopiné: m. ée: f. *Cut into gobbits, parted into cantles, diuided into lumps.*

Lopiner. *To cut into gobbits, part into cantles, diuide into lumps; also, to munch, or nuncheon it, to eat greedily in a corner.*

Lopinet: m. *A bit, mammocke, small gobbit, little peece, or parcell of.*

Loppe. *as* Lopin; *or, A lumpe of mettall rugged and vnwrought, as it comes out of the mine; also, the drosse of any mettall.*

Loquacité: f. *Loquacitie, talkatiuenesse, prating, pratling, babling.*

Loque: f. *A rag, or tatter:* ¶Pic.

Loquence: f. *Speech, talking.*

Loquet d' vne huis. *The latch, or snecket of a doore.*

Loqueteux: m. euse: f. *Ragged, tattered; poore, needie, beggerlie in array:* ¶Pic.

Loquette: f. *A little rag, or tatter.*

Lordault. *as* Lourdault.

Lorderie: f. *Seeke* Lourderie.

Lorgnant. *Leering, looking askaunce, or askew at.*

Lorgne. tique, toque, lorgne. *(Words expressing a liberall, and free dole of blowes) thwicke thwacke; also, here and there, at randome, without discretion.*

Torche lorgne. *The same.*

Lorgner. *(Sowerly) to leere, looke askaunce, or askew, at; also, to knocke, or thumpe soundly, to lay vpon.*

Loricard: m. *A luske, lowt, lorell, slow-backe; an vnhandsome, or misshapen fellow.*

Loricarder. *To luske, lowt, or lubber it; to loyter about like a maisterlesse man.*

Lorion: m. *The bird called a Witwall, Yellow-peake, Hickway.*

Loriot. *as* Lorion.

Lormerie: f. *Small yron-Worke, as nayles, spurres, &c; or, a Spurriers trade.*

Lormier: m. *A worker in small yron, a maker of small yron trinkets, as nayles, spurres, &c: a word most vsed for a Spurrier; who is also tearmed* Lormier sellier, *because hee may retaile Sadlers ware as well as spurres.*

Lorry. *An auntient towne within the Jurisdiction of* Orleans.

Il est de le Lorry ou le batu paye l' amende. *He gets the blowes, and yet payes for the bloudwipe.*

Lors. *Then, whilome, the whilest that, in that time, in that season;* Lors que cela se fit; *then when that thing was done.*

Lors de l'enfantement. *At the time of childbirth, or when she lay in.*

Los: m. *Laud, praise, commendation; &c as* Loz; *also, willingnesse, consent, agreement, good will.*

Tel a bon los qui l'a à tort; tel l'a mauvais qui n'en peut mais: Prov. *Some are vniustly praisd, some blam'd vnworthily.*

Losenge: f. *A Losenge; the forme, or a thing of the forme, of an ordinarie quarrell of glasse, &c; as in* Lozenge.

Losengier: m. *A flatterer, cogger, foister, picke-thanke, prater; cousoner; guller, beguiler, deceiuer.*

Lossec: m. *The sinke, or well, of the pumpe of a ship.*

Lot: m. *A lot, portion, part, share, allowance; also, a pot, or vessell containing (about) our pottle.*

Lote: f. *The Lote, or Nettle tree; also, a fish; whence;*

Lote d' eau douce. *Th' Eele powt; or a little muddie fish thats headed, skinned, and finned like an Eele.*

Lote de mer. *A small-scaled fish, that hath one wattle in the end of her lower chap, and two on her vpper lip; otherwise resembling in some parts a Cod, in others the Lamprey, but tasting more like that then this; and seldome caught, or seene on our coast.*

Loti. *as* Loty.

Lotie: f. *A diuision, partition, sharing.*

Lotir. *To cast lots for; also, to diuide, part, apportion, share.*

Lotizé: m. ée: f. *Diuided, parted, apportioned, shared.*

Lots. *Fines of alienation; Seeke* Lods.

Lotte: f. *A Powt, or Eele powt; See* Lote.

Lottir. *as* Lotir.
Loty: m. ye: f. *Diuided by lots; parted, apportioned, shared.*
Loüable: com. *Laudable, commendable, praise-worthie, approuable.*
La chair loüable. *Holesome, sound, or good flesh;* Et, vne selle loüable; vrine loüable. *A good, or hopefull stoole, &c; such as promises, or is a signe of, health.*
Loüablement. *Laudably, commendably, praise-worthily.*
Loüade. *as* Laude.
Loüage: m. *A hire, hiring, farming, letting out; also, the rent, or hire for things let out.*
A chapt passe loüage. *One may lawfully dispossesse a hirer of the thing he hath purchased.*
Loüager, & Loüagier: m. *A hirer, farmer, lessee; a lodger, inmate, soiourner.*
Loüange: f. *Laud, praise, commendation; glorie, fame, credit, renowme, reputation.*
Loüanger. *To laud, praise, commend, extoll, renowme.*
Loüangier: m. *A praiser, lauder, commender.*
Loubet. *Seeke* May-loubet.
Loubine: f. *The sea-fish, called a Base.*
Louche: f. *A little ladle, or great spoone:* ¶Pic.
Louche: com. *as* Lousche.
Loucher. *To lade, emptie, or take vp with a ladle, or great spoone.*
Louchet: m. *A spade, or spade-like instrument, halfe headed with yron.*
Les louchets d' vne bale. *The corners of a packe.*
Loudier: m. *as* Lodier; *A Counterpoint, or Quilt; also, a smell smocke, haire-beater, leacherous knaue.*
Loudiere: f. vne grosse loudiere. *A filthie lasciuious queane, a common hackney, or hedge-whore.*
Vne vieille loudiere. *A beldame, old trot, ouer-ridden iade.*
Loüé: m. ée: f. *Lauded, praised, commended, extolled; also, hired, rented, farmed; letten, or taken, vpon rent.*
Louer. *as* Loir; *A Dormouse.*
Louër. *To laud, praise, commend, extoll, report or speake well of; also, to hire, farme, rent; let, or take, vpon rent.*
Louëresse: f. *A praiseresse, commenderesse.*
Louëur: m. *A lauder, praiser, commender, extoller.*
Lougarou. *Seeke* Loup-garou.
Loup: m. *A Wolfe; also, a Base (fish;) also, a kind of flie; also, the flie-deuouring spider; also, a malignant, and remedilesse Vlcer, or Cranker, in the legs, which in th'end it wholly consumes; also, a rauenous, greedie, cruell, vniust, fell, harsh companion.*
Loup marin. *A certaine Wolfe-like beast, which (sayes* Belon*) liues altogether of fish, vpon our sea-shore.*
Couille au loup. *Wild Prickmadame, great Stonecrop, Worme-grasse.*
Danse du loup (la queuë entre les jambes.) *Lecherie.*
Herbe au loup. *Wolues-bane, wolfe-wort (a kind of* Aconitum.)
Oeil de loup. *An eye of an vncertaine blackish colour; a duskie, or darke eye; also, a leering eye.*
Patte de loup. *The Thessalian loue-prouoking hearbe Catanance.*
Pied de loup. *Wolues-foot, wolues-claw, club-mosse (a mossie plant.)*
Ris de loup. *The name of a certaine peare.*

Vesse du loup. *A fusse-ball, puck-fusse, wolues-thistle, puffe-fiste, bull fist.*
Entre chien & loup. *At twie-light, or cocke-shoottime; in th'edge, or shutting vp of an euening; also, (of a mans sufficiencie) indifferently, ordinarily, so so.*
Personne ne luy demanda es tu chien, es tu loup. *No man respected him, no bodie tooke heed, or notice of him.*
Contrefaire le loup en paille. *To eaue-drop it; or, to lie scowking, and leering in a corner, or between sleeping and waking in bed, and vnderstand, but take no notice, what persons doe passe, or what things bee done, round about him.*
Faire le loup à la carriere. *Of the same sence.*
Faire le loup plus grand qu'il n'est. *To make, or imagine a mischiefe, or daunger to bee greater then it is.*
Garder la lune des loups. *Foolishly to care for that which cannot doe amisse, or looke to that which will not goe astray.*
Dieu gard la lune des loups. *God keepe the Moone from wolues; an ironicall answer vnto those braggadochioes, which threaten farre greater plagues then they are able to inflict (or promise greater matters then they can effect.)*
Hurler avec les loups. *To play the rude companion in rude companie.*
Marcher en pas de loup. *To tread like a theefe, priuately, subtilly, gingerly, faire and softly.*
Prendre vn loup par la queuë. *To performe a hard, or hazardous exploit.*
Regarder en loup. *Sowerly to leere, or looke askew at.*
Tenir le loup par les oreilles. *To bee in danger, or hard set, on euerie side (for if you hold him he bites you by the fingers; if you let him goe, he will goe neere to deuoure you.)*
Voir le loup. *Some say of one whose voyce is growne hoarse on a sudden;* Il a veu le loup; *Others,* le loup l'a veu: *from a vulgar opinion, that if a wolfe get sight of a man before he see him, he will astonish him, and make him so hoarse (by the force of his eyes, and vigour of his breath) that he shall hardly bee able to speake.*
Deux loups mangent bien vne brebis: Prov. *Two knaues with ease deuoure (or deceiue) one sillie foole.*
Le loup alla à Rome, & y laissa de son poil mais rien de ses coustumes: Prov. *The wolfe went to Rome, and left some of his coat, but none of his conditions, behind him.*
Le loup emporte le veau du povre: Prov. *Vnsaciate crueltie preyes most vpon the poore.*
Le loup mourra en sa peau qui ne l'escorchera vif: Prov. *A knaue will die in a knaues skinne, if hee formerly loose it not.*
Le loup sçait bien que male beste pense: Prov. *One lewd fellow is well acquainted with the purposes, or sleights of another.*
Vn loup ne devore iamais vn autre loup: Prov. *Those that are like doe seldome disagree; one knaue will euer beare with another.*
`A mauvais chien ne peut on monstrer le loup: Prov. *A bad dog hates to looke vpon a wolfe.*
`A mol pasteur le loup chie laine: Prov. *A gentle shepheard stuffes the wolfe with wooll.*
A petite achoison le loup prend le mouton: Prov. *When*

When Tyrants will oppresse th'innocent, a sleight pretext is made sufficient.

Au chair de loup sauce de chien: Prov. *Wolues flesh must be eaten with dogs sauce.*

Bien a crié le loup qui sa proye rescoult: Prov. *He followed the Wolfe to purpose that recouers his prey.*

Brebis contées mange bien le loup: Prov. *The Wolfe eats counted (and vncounted) sheepe; All's one to him that loues to haue his will.*

C'est vne bonne prise que d'vn ieune loup: Prov. *He hunts full well that catches a young Wolfe; bad plants would be plucked vp while they be young.*

Depuis que la brebis est vieille le loup la mange bien: Prov. *The hungrie feed well on tough, and drie meats.*

En esperance d'avoir mieux tant vit le loup qu'il devient vieux: Prov. *The Wolfe growes old by hoping still for better; or, the Wolfe, the whilest he hopes for better, is growne old.*

En fin les loups tuent le chien qui tue les loups: Prov. *The Wolues at length kill dogs that killed Wolues.*

En la peau ou le loup est luy convient mourir: Prov. *The Wolfe must die in his owne skinne; or, the skinne a Wolfe hath preyed, let him perish, in.*

Homme seul est viande aux loups: Prov. *The solitarie man becomes Wolues meat.*

Ieune en sa croissance a vn loup en la panse: Pro. *Young springalls haue Woluish, or great appetites.*

Il fait mauvais aller au bois quand les loups se mangent l'un l'autre: Prov. *It is not good to goe to the wood when Wolues deuoure one another.*

Il ne faut estre loup, ny en affubler la peau: Prov. *One must neither be, nor seeme, naught.*

Le dernier le loup le mange: Prov. *Delay breeds danger; lags come to the lash.*

La faim chasse les loups hors du bois: Prov. *Hunger makes men forgoe their safest holds.*

La mauvaise garde paist souvent le loup: Prov. *A Wolfe ill lookt to oftentimes growes fat.*

Mauvaise est la saison quand vn loup mange l'autre: Prov. *Hard is the time when Wolues doe feed on Wolues; or, tis a hard time when one Wolfe eats another.*

On crié tousiours le loup plus grand qu'il n'est: Prov. *Report makes dangers greater then they be.*

Peu à peu le loup mange l'oye: Prov. *Looke* Oye.

Qui a le loup pour compagnon porte le chien sous l'hocton: Prov. *He that hath a Wolfe to his mate had need of a dog to his man.*

Qui parle du loup on en voit la queuë: Prov. *Appliable (as* Lupus in fabula*) when one thats spoken of as absent suddenly appeares.*

Qui se fait brebis le loup le mange: Prov. *He that makes himselfe a sheepe will be vsed as a sheepe.*

Tandis que le chien chie le loup s'en va: &; Tandis que le chien crie le loup s'en fuit: Prov. *Whilest men attend vnnecessarie, they loose necessarie, aduantages.*

Tandis que les chiens s'entregrondent le loup devore la brebis: Prov. *While the dogs iarre the Wolfe deuours the sheepe.*

Tandis que le loup muse la brebis entre au bois: Prov. *Whilest the wicked consult th'innocent escape them; (Hereby also is meant, that opportunitie may be neglected, or aduantages lost, by tedious consultations.)*

Loup-araigne. *Any kind of Spider that hunts, or watches for, flies.*

Loupasson: m. *A small, or young Base; a little sea Wolfe.*

Loup-cervier: m. *A kind of white Wolfe, or beast ingendred betweene a Hind and a Wolfe, whose skinne is much esteemed by great men; yet some (not beleeuing that those beasts will, or can mingle) imagine it rather to bee the spotted Linx, or Ounce; or a kind thereof.*

Loup-chat: m. *The (rauenous, and spotted) Linx, or Ounce; or (as Gesner thinkes) the Hyena.*

Loupe: f. *A flegmaticke lumpe, wenne, bunch, or swelling of flesh vnder the throat, bellie, &c; also, a little one on the wrist, foot, or other ioynt, gotten by a blow whereby a sinew being wrested rises, and growes hard; also, a Weauers cloth-beame; that about which his web rowles as he weaues it.*

Loupeux: m. euse: f. *Full of wennes, or troubled with a wenne.*

Loup-garou: m. *A mankind Wolfe; such a one as once being flesht on men, and children will rather starue then feed on any thing else; also, one that, possessed with an extreame, and strange melancholie, beleeues he is turned Wolfe, and as a Wolfe behaues himselfe; also, a Hobgoblin, Hob-thrush, Robin-good-fellow; also, a night-walker, or flie-light; one thats neuer seene but by Owle-light; also, a suttle fellow, slie companion, wilie fox, craftie knaue.*

Loupie: f. *as* Loupe.

Louppe: f. *as* Loupe; *And, in a horse, the water Farcie.*

Lourche: f. *The game called Lurche; or, a Lurch in game.*

Il demeura lourche. *He was left in the lurch.*

Lourd: m. lourde: f. *Dull, sottish, blockish; clumpse, numme, heauie mettalled; rude, lumpish, lowtish, clownish, lob-like; vnhandsome, vnciuile, vnmannerlie.*

'A paroles lourdes sourdes oreilles: Prov. *Looke* Oreilles.

Lourdaut: m. *as* Lourderie; *and hence;*

Il est en son lourdaut. *He is in a surlie mood, or churlish humor; he is sicke of the mumps, or sullens; he sells sowce.*

Lourdaut: m. *A sot, dunce, dullard, grotnoll, iobernoll, blockhead; a lowt, lob, luske, boore, clowne, churle, clusterfist; a proud, ignorant, and vnmannerlie swaine.*

Lourdement. *Sottishly, dully, bluntly, blockishly, heauily; rudely, grossely, clownishly, churlishly; vnciuilely, vnhandsomely, vnmannerly.*

Bien lourdement chargé de debtes. *Farre indebted, ouer head and eares in debt.*

Lourderie: f. *Sottishnesse, blockishnesse; lumpishnesse, clownishnesse; surlinesse, churlishnesse; inciuilitie, rudenesse, vnmannerlinesse.*

Lourdin: m. ine: f. *Lourdaine; blunt, somewhat blockish; a little clownish, lumpish, rude; smelling of the churle, or lobcocke.*

Lourdinet. *as* Lourdin.

Lourdise: f. *as* Lourderie.

Lourdois. en son lourdois. *Bluntly, grossely, rudely; after his rude, clownish, homelie, or slouenlie manner.*

Loure: f. *A bagpipe:* ¶Poictevin.

Lourette: f. *A small bagpipe.*

Lourpidon: f. *The name of an old witch, or hag in Amadis;*

madis; hence, any such decrepite, and diuelish creature.

Lousche: com. *Skenning, squinting, looking askew; also, dull sighted, or wanting sight; purblind, or halfe-blind.*

Perle lousche. *A foule pearle.*

Vin lousche. *Thicke, or vnsetled, wine.*

Louschement: m. *A squinting, or looking askew.*

Louscher. *To squint, sken, or looke askew.*

Louschet. *as* Louchet.

Lousse. *as* Louche.

Loutre: f. *An Otter.*

Loutrier: m. *An Otter-hunter, or Otter-catcher.*

Louve: f. *A she Wolfe; also, a whore.*

Louve de fer. *A Rammes head; or, the (pinser-like) hooke of a Crane, &c.*

Louveau: m. *A young Wolfe.*

Louvet: m. *A little Wolfe, or young Wolfe.*

Louvetier: m. *A Wolfe-catcher; an Officer appointed in euerie forrest, and payed for the taking, or killing of Wolues (by euerie inhabitant within two miles compasse of the place wherein he takes, or kills them) after the rate of* ij.d. Tourn. *for a dog Wolfe, and* iiij.d. *for a bitch.*

Louveton: m. *A little young Wolfe.*

Louvette: f. *A ticke, or tike.*

Louvich: m. iche: f. *Greedie, rauenous, deuouring, swallowing downe whole morsells for hast.*

Louvichement. *Wolfe-like, rauenously, greedily, deuouringly.*

Louvier: m. *as* Louvetier.

Louvier: m. ere: f. *Woluie, Wolfe-like; of, or belonging to, a Wolfe.*

Melancholie louviere. *A frenzie which makes the patient shun all companie, vpon a conceit that he is turned Wolfe.*

Louviere: f. *A Woluerin; a gowne, or garment furred, or lined through with Wolues skinnes; also, a countrey full of Wolues; also, the denne, hole, or haunt of a Wolfe.*

Louvin: m. ine: f. *Woluie, Wolfe-like, of a Wolfe.*

Patte louvine. *The yellow, or blacke Wolues-banes; most poisonous hearbes, and little differing but in the colour of their flowers.*

Loy: f. *Law, the Law; Iustice, th'authoritie, course or proceeding, of Iustice; a Iudgement in, a triall by, Law; also, a Law, Statute, Ordinance, Rule or Decree that bindes; also, Jurisdiction, power, authoritie; free choyce, libertie; also, the vse, or custome of a place; also, an ordinarie or customarie fine, or amerciament of Law; also, the allay, temper, or mixture of coyne; the mettall, or matter whereof tis made.*

Loy de bataille. *A triall by combate.*

Loy de credence. *A proceeding by witnesses, who depose that they beleeue (not that they know;) like our, As this Deponent verily beleeues, &c.*

Loix des lieux. *(In the customes of* Artoys*) the Iudges of the places; or as in* Gens de loy.

Loy oultrée, ou outre. c'est, Different determiné par enqueste, ou par brief.

Loy simple; &, simple loy. *A summarie, or quicke proceeding in Law without Inquest, or Battell.*

Gens, ou hommes de loy. *(In diuers old Bookes, and Walloon customs) the Sherifes (who commonly were the Iudges) of townes.*

Iours de loy. *Law-dayes, Court-dayes, Hall-dayes.*

Prisonniers estans en loy. *In the hands of Iustice.*

Villes de loy. *Which haue their peculiar lawes, and customes; and wherein there is a seat of Iustice, and Officers of Iurisdiction.*

Faire les loix à l'heure de midy, en l'assize. c'est faire sa demande en iustice pour avoir droict & iugement: ¶Ragueau.

Passer par la loy. *To wage, or make his law; to sweare in Court that he hath duely paied the rent, or* Cens *demaunded of him.*

Venir à la loy. *To be admitted vnto such an oath.*

De meschante vie les bonnes loix sont venuës: Prov. *Bad liues haue bred good lawes.*

Que veut le Roy ce veut la loy: Prov. *What the King likes the Law allowes of; or, lawes are expounded as the King thinks good.*

Loyal: m. ale: f. *Loyall, faithfull; trustie, sure vnto; also, lawfull, iust, allowable, reasonable.*

Loyaulx Aides. *Looke* Aide.

Monnoye loyale. *Current money.*

Loyalement. *Loyally, faithfully, trustily; also, lawfully, iustly, rightfully.*

Loyaulment. *as* Loyalement.

Loyaulté: f. *Loyaltie, faithfulnesse, trustinesse; truth, and constancie in promises; honestie, or sinceritie in all manner of proceedings; iustnesse, vprightnesse; lawfulnesse; also, the strickle vsed in the measuring of corne.*

En grande pauvreté n'y a grande loyaulté: Prov. *Where pouertie is, loyaltie is not great.*

Loyer: m. *Hire giuen for a house, or countrey farme; or vnto seruants, or workefolkes; hence, a stipend, salarie, wages; also, a reward, guerdon, recompence, remuneration.*

Qui bon maistre sert bon loyer en attend: Prov. *A franke Lords Pages, looke for good wages.*

Loyette: f. *A Marlin.*

Loz: m. *Laud, praise, commendation; credit, fame, glorie, renowme, reputation; See* Los.

Lozange, & Lozanger. *as* Lozenge, & Lozenger.

Lozenge: f. *A Lozenge; a little square cake of preserued hearbes, flowers, &c; also, a quarrell of a glasse-window; any thing of that forme; also, guile, deceit, fraud, cousenage.*

Lozengé: m. ée: f. *Lozenged, Lozenge-like; also, mocked, gulled, beguiled.*

Lozenger. *To cousen, deceiue, beguile, gull.*

Lu. *Light; whence;*

Il n'y a ne feu ne lu. *(Of a darke, cold, or vncomfortable place;) there's neither fire, nor light to be had.*

Luberdine: f. *An old maid.*

Luberne: f. *The female Libbard; a Panther.*

Lubin: m. *A Base, or Sea-Wolfe; also, a nickname for a Monke, or Frier; whence,* Frere Lubin; *the true name of a certaine Monke, who loued a neighbors house better then his owne Couent.*

Lubine. *as* Lubin *(in the first sence:)* ¶Bourdelois.

Lubre: com. *Lubricke, filthie, scurrile.*

Lubricité: f. *Lubricitie, slipperinesse, vncertaintie; lecherie, wantonnesse, incontinencie.*

Lubrifier. *To lubrifie, or make slipperie.*

Lubrique: com. *Lubricke; slipperie; deceitfull, vncertaine; stirring, fast-mouing; lecherous, incontinent, wanton, lasciuious.*

Lubriquement. *Slipperily; vncertainely, loossely, deceitfully; stirringly; incontinently, lasciuiously, lecherously.*

Luc: m. *A Lute.*

Luc renversé. *is as much as* Cul.

Lucarne: f. *A garret window, or window in the roofe of a house,&c.*
Lucarné: m. ée: f. *Hauing windowes in the roofe.*
Luce: f. (*A womans name*) Luce; *and the name of a virgine-Saint registred in Kalenders on the* 13 *of December; Hence the Prouerbe;*)
`A la Sainte Luce du sault d'une puce; c'est à dire, le jour croist. (*Or not so much; for that is held the shortest day of the yeare.*)
Lucel, & Lucet. *A young Pike, a Pickerell.*
Lucheran: m. *A Scrich-owle.*
Luchet. *A spade; or as* Louchet: ¶Langued.
Lucifugue: f. *A kind of Beetle, or light-hating flie.*
Lucide: com. *Cleere, shining, bright, light.*
Lucratif: m. iue: f. *Lucratiue, commodious, gaine-bringing, whereof great profit is made.*
Lucrative: f. *Lucre, gaine, profit, commoditie, commings in; also, the profession of the Law (because it brings in store of Crownes.)*
Lucs. *as* Lus.
Luctation: f. *A wrastling, strugling, striuing with.*
Lucte. *as* Luicte.
Lucté: m. ée: f. *Wrastled, strugled, striuen with.*
Ludicre: com. *Light, childish, toyish, mocking, sportfull, gamesome.*
Ludificatoire: com. *Mocking, deceiuing, beguiling.*
Lueil: m. *Ray, Darnell.*
Luet. Devoir de luets. *A bushell of Rie due by euerie tenant, and housholder that keepes a fire, and tillage within a Parish in Britanie.*
Luette: f. *The Palate, or Vuula; a little peece of spungious flesh in the root of the roofe of the mouth.*
Luettes. *Little bundles of peeces of Iuorie cast loosse vpon a table; the play is to take vp one without shaking the rest, or else the taker looseth.*
Lueur: f. *Light, brightnesse, cleerenesse, luster, splendor, glittering, irradiation, glistering, a casting forth of beames.*
Luëux: m. euse: f. *Light, bright, splendent, shining, glittering, glistering.*
Lugubre: com. *Dolefull, mourning, mournefull, sorrowfull, wayling, funerall.*
Luicte: f. *Wrastling; th'exercise of wrastling; also, a strugling, or strife with.*
Vn tour de luicte en procez. *A cunning tricke, trip, or passage in pleading, which will goe neere to ouerthrow th'aduerse partie.*
Il l'emporta de haute luicte. *He carried it cleere, he bore it away by maine force; he imployed his vtmost strength in the compassing of it.*
Au fort bras la luicte: Prov. *See* Bras.
Luictement. m. *A wrastling, or strugling with.*
Luicter. *To wrastle, to struggle, or striue with.*
Luicter contre les ombres. *To wrastle with shadowes; to be angrie without cause, or purpose; also, to reuile the absent; also, to deuise things and afterwards raile at them.*
L'abbatu veut tousjours luicter: Prov. *No foile can quell an obstinacie.*
Luire. *To shine, glitter, glister; to cleere, be bright, giue light, yeeld a radiant luster.*
Ce qu'on donne luit, ce qu'on mange puit: Prov. *What we giue shines, what we eat smells.*
Luisans: m. *Sparkles, or fierie and starre-resembling Meteors, in the middle region of the aire.*
Luisant. *Shining, cleere, bright, beamie, lusterous, radiant, glittering, glistering.*
Luisantement. *Brightly, radiantly, shiningly, glisteningly, glitteringly.*
Luisarner. *To glow, glisten, glimmer.*
Luiton: m. *A Goblin, Bug, Robin-good-fellow, merrie diuell, that vses to mocke, and deceiue, sillie people.*
Luiton de mer. *A Triton, or Sea-man; a fish that resembles a man.*
Lumbaire: com. *Of, or belonging to, the flanke, or loyne.*
Arteres lumbaires. *Branches of the great Arterie distributed all ouer the loynes, and giuing life to the marrow of the backe.*
Muscle lumbaire. *One of the two muscles which bow the thighes.*
Veine lumbaire. *See* Veine.
Lumbrique. *A ground worme:* ¶Rab.
Lumer. *To shine; to giue light, to yeeld or cast a light.*
La chandelle lume mal. *Burnes dimly, or burnes but ill.*
Lumiere: f. *Light; brightnesse, cleerenesse, a shining; also, a light, candle, or lampe.*
La lumiere d'une haquebute, &c. *The touch-hole of an Harquebuse, &c.*
Mettre en lumiere. *To publish, divulge, set forth, send abroad into the world.*
Privé de la lumiere. *Depriued both of light, and life.*
Qui n'est point venu en lumiere. *Abstruse, obscure, vnknowne, that is not yet come abroad.*
`A l'oeil malade la lumiere nuit: Prov. *Light hurts diseased eyes; or, a sicke eye is offended with the light.*
Lumignon: m. *The weeke or cotton of a candle; the match of a lampe.*
Lumillette: f. *The hearbe Eye-bright.*
Luminaire: m. *A light, a candle, a lampe, &c; also, a Booke of the composition of Physicall receits.*
Luminette: f. *as* Lumillette.
Lumineux: m. euse: f. *Shining, glistering, most bright, full of cleerenesse, yeelding a great light.*
Luminier: m. *A Vesterer, or Vesterie-keeper; hee that hath the charge of the lights, and ornaments of a Church; also, an Agent, Atturney, or Solicitor for a whole Towneship.*
Luminon. *as* Lumignon.
Lunaire: f. *Lunarie, Moonewort.*
Lunaire majeur; ou grande lunaire. *Great Moonewort, Pennie-flower, Money-flower, Pricksongwort, Honestie, Sattin, white Sattin; (Alchymists call water Fearne* Lunaria major.)
Lunaire mineur; ou petite lunaire. *Small Lunarie, small Moonewort.*
Lunaire: com. *Lunarie; of, or belonging to, the Moone.*
Cicle lunaire. *The Golden number; Looke* Cicle.
Lunaison: f. *A Moneth, a Moone, or the season continuing a whole Moone; also, the shining of the Moone.*
Lunatique: com. *Lunaticke, in a Lunacie, franticke, wood, no wiser then he should be.*
Lundi: m. *Monday.*
Lune: f. *The Moone; one of the seuen Planets; also, siluer (called so by Alchymists;) also, the Molebut-fish.*
Lune de mer. *The Molebut; also, a kind of ash-coloured Starre-fish of a hard, and shellie substance.*

La bonne Lune. *The later end of September, and beginning of October; the best time to sow Winter-corne in, and therefore so tearmed by good husbands.*
Abbayer contre la lune. *Seeke* Abbayer.
Avoir vn quartier de la lune en la teste. *To bee halfe franticke, or haue a spice of Lunacie; The like is;*
Il y a de la lune. *He is a foolish, humorous, harebraind, giddie-headed fellow.*
Coucher à l' enseigne de la lune. *To lie without doores all night.*
Garder la lune des loups. *To wast indeuors vpon subiects that need them not; or spend time in watching of that which of it selfe is safe ynough.*
Dieu gard la lune des loups. *An ironicall answer vnto a bragging foole, that threatens to kill them whom he cannot hurt.*
Le fourrier de la lune a marqué le logis. *Said of a woman that hath her flowers.*
Prendre la lune aux dents. *To doe impossible matters.*
Tenir de la lune. *To be inconstant, fickle, mutable, giddie, vnsetled, wauering.*
Les biens de fortune passent comme la lune: Pro. *What fortune giues vs for a boone, is quickly wasted like the Moone.*
Luné: m. ée: f. *Round, compasse, rounded, or bowed like a halfe-Moone.*
Luner. *To round, bow, compasse; and hence;*
Luner vn arc. *To bend a bow.*
Lunette: f. *The merrie-thought; the forked craw-bone of a bird, which we vse, in sport, to put on our noses.*
Lunettes: f. *Spectacles.*
Il n'y a pas bien assis ses lunettes. *He hath not obserued the matter so neerely, he hath not looked into it so narrowly, as he might, or should, haue done.*
Lupasson. *as* Loupasson.
Lupege: f. *The whoope, or dung-hill Cocke.*
Lupin: m. *The pulse Lupines; also, the Base, or Sea-Wolfe.*
Lupoge. *as* Lupege.
Lurré: m. ée: f. *Lured; inticed, allured.*
Lus: m. *A Pike (fish.)*
Lus marin. *A Cod, or Cod-fish; some also call the Haddocke so.*
Luserne: f. *A Gloe-worme; also, as* Luzerne.
Lustre: m. *A luster, or glosse; a shining, or glistening; a gracefull bright colour; also, a terme of foure yeares, or fiftie moneths; also, a Censorian ouersight ouer Citizens estates, and behauiour.*
Donner lustre à. *To grace, beautifie, illustrate, adorne; sleeke, burnish, brighten; set a glosse on, giue a luster vnto.*
Lustrer. *To looke round about, view, or suruey on each side, behold euerie way; to weigh diligently, examine throughly, seriously consider of, prie narrowly into; also, to purge, or cleanse by sacrifice; also, as* Donner lustre.
Lustreux: m. euse: f. *Lusterous, radiant, shining, glistening, glistering, glittering.*
Lustrueux. *as* Lustreux.
Lut: m. *A Lute; also, clay, mould, loame, durt; also, a kind of barke, or boat.*
Luté: m. ée: f. *Dawbed, closed, or done ouer, with clay; also, bemired, bedawbed, berayed, bismeared.*
Luter. *To dawbe, or clay; to close, or doe ouer with loame, or clay; also, to bedawbe, defile, bemire, bismeare, beray.*
Luth: m. *A Lute.*
Lutin: m. *A Goblin, Robin-good-fellow, Hob-thrush; a spirit which playes reakes in mens houses anights.*
Lutiner. *To play the Goblin, or night-spirit; to keepe a foule rumbling, or terrible racket vp and downe a house in the night.*
Lutiz: m. *Clay, loame; durt.*
Lutre. *as* Loutre.
Lutrin: m. *A deske in a Church.*
Luxation: f. *A luxation, loossenesse, or loossening; a being out of ioynt.*
Luxe: m. *Excesse, riot, superfluitie.*
Luxer. *To loose, or put out of ioynt; also, to be cut of ioynt, or out of due place.*
Luxure: f. *Luxurie, sensualitie, concupiscence, fleshlinesse; any superfluitie, or excesse in carnall delights.*
Luxurieux: m. euse: f. *Luxurious, voluptuous, fleshlie, lustfull, sensuall; excessiue, riotous.*
Luy. *He, him, the same man.*
Luyton. *as* Luiton, *or* Lutin.
Luz: m. Lus.
Luzerne: f. *as* Luserne.; *Also, Medicke fodder, Spanish Trefoyle, horned Clauer, snaile Clauer.*
Luzerner. *To glow, glisten, or glimmer.* (v. m.)
Luzerniere: f. *A close, field, or plot sowed with Medicke fodder.*
Ly. *a* Le: ¶Gascon.
Lyarre: m. *Iuie; Seeke* Lierre.
Lyesse. *as* Liesse.
Lycanthropie: f. *A frenzie, or melancholie, which causeth the patient (who thinkes he is turned Wolfe) to flie all companie, and hide himselfe in dennes, and corners.*
Lyce: f. *A bitch, &c; as in* Lice.
Vne fausse lyce. *A lewd queane, false trull, vngracious whoore, wicked harlot.*
Lychnobien: m. *The weeke of a candle; or one who in stead of the day vseth the night, doing all his businesse by candle-light:* ¶Rab.
Lychnocosomité. *The chiefe flight, or lanterne of the world.*
Lychnon: m. *A light, candle, or linke; also, the wieke of a candle, or match of a lampe; also, a lanterne:* ¶Rab.
Lycopse. *A kind of the (red-rooted) hearbe Orchanet.*
Lycopthalmie: f. *A pretious stone of fiue sundrie colours:* ¶Rab.
Lye. *as* Lie.
Lyerre. *Iuie; Seeke* Lierre.
Lymitrophe: com. *Bordering vpon, adioyning, or lying neere vnto.*
Lymon. *as* Limon.
Lymphatique: com. *Allayed, or mixed with water; also, madde, furious, bestraught; giddie, fantasticall.*
Lyncée: f. *A Linx; a Wolfe-resembling beast thats full of spots.*
Yeux de Lincée. *Sharpe, quicke, piercing eyes.*
Lyncurie: f. *A pretious stone bred of the congealed vrine of a Linx, and preseruing the eyes from charmes.*
Lynges *as* Liens; *Bands, &c:* ¶Rab.
Lyon. *Seeke* Lion.
Lyonceau: m. *A Lyons whelpe, or young Lyon.*
Lype. *as* Lippe; *A lip.*
Faire la lype. *To powt, lowt, lowre, hang the lip, as a child thats sullen, or about to crie.*
Lypothomie: f. *A kind of deadlie swoning.*
Lyre: f. *A Lyra, or Harpe.*

Lyripipié,& Lyripipion. *as* Liripipié,& Liripipion.
Lyrique: com. *Lyricke; of a Harpe; sung to the Harpe; playing on a Harpe.*
Lys. *as* Lis.
Lysarde. *Seeke* Lisarde.
Lysimachie: f. *Willow-hearbe, Loose-strife, Water-willow.*
Lysimachie rouge. *The red, or codded Willow-hearbe.*
Lysteau. *as* Listeau.
Lyturgie, ou Lyturgue: f. *A Liturgie, or forme of Seruice vsed in Churches.*

M

MA. *The feminine of* Mon; *My.*
Madia. *Seeke* Madia. ¶Rab.
Macabré. Danse Macabré. *Death.*
Macaleb. *The bastard Corall, or Pomander, Priuet, of whose sweet, and shining blacke berries, chaynes and bracelets be made.*
Macalep,& Macalet. *as* Macaleb.
Macar: m. *A mate, match, marrow, fellow.*
Macareau: m. *A Mackerell fish.*
Macaronique: m. *A Macaronick; a confused heape, or huddle of many seuerall things.*
Macarons: m. *Macarons; little Fritter like Bunnes, or thicke Losenges compounded of Sugar, Almonds, Rose-water, and Muske, pounded together, and baked with a gentle fire; also, the Italian* Macaroni; *lumps, or gobbets of boyled paste serued vp in butter, and strewed ouer with spice and grated cheese.*
Macault: m. *A scrip, or wallet; also, a chest filled with precious stuffe, and hidden, or boorded vp, in a secret corner.*
Macé: m. *(A proper name for a man) Mathew.*
Ie suis Prestre Macé. *An equiuocall allusion to* Maistre passé. *A sworne maister, or freeman of a Trade.*
Mace. Iuge Mace. *as* Iuge Mage *(in* Mage.*)*
Macée: f. *Mat, or Macie; (a proper name for a woman.)*
Macer: m. *Is not Mace (as many imagine) but a reddish, aromaticall, and astringent rinde of a certaine Jndian root.*
Maceration: f. *A maceration, macerating, making leane; a mortifying, weakening, or taming of the bodie by abstinence, &c; also, a soaking, or steeping in liquor.*
Maceré: m. ée: f. *Macerated, made leane; weakened, mortified, brought low, tamed, subdued; also, allayed, soaked, or steeped in water.*
Macerer. *To macerate, or make leane; to mortifie, weaken, bring downe, punish or pull vnder the bodie; to suppresse, or subdue the lusts thereof by abstinence, or hard fare; also, to allay, soake, or steepe in liquor.*
Maceris. *as* Macer.
Maceron: m. *The hearb Candie Alexanders, or through-bored Parsely.*
Maceronne: f. *as* Maceron.
Mache: f. *Water-torch, Cats-tayle, Marsh pestill, Douch downe; (an hearbe.)*
Machecoulis. *Looke* Maschecoulis.
Machefer. *The drosse of Jron.*
Mache-foin. *A nick-name for such a Iudge, or Lawyer as takes of clients the hay his horses feed on; or, as* Maschefouyn.

Machelier: m. ere: f. *Of, or belonging to, a iaw.*
Dents Machelieres. *The cheeke-teeth, or grinders.*
Macher. *as* Mascher.
Mache-rave. *A Turnep-eater: An Epithete for a Lymosin (who feeds much on Turneps.)*
Mache-rivet. *A Cobler, or Shoomaker.*
Macheron. *as* Maceron.
Maches: f. *The mashes, or holes of a net between thread and thread.*
Machette: f. *The Owle, or Madge-howlet; as in* Cheveche.
Macheure: f. *A blacke smutch, or smeare; also, a crush, or bruise, which leaues a blacke, or blew spot after it.*
Macheure de fer. *The drosse of Jron.*
Macheuré: m. ée: f. *Smeared, smutched, begrymed; also, made blacke and blew by a crush, &c.*
Machiavelisme: m. *Machiauellisme; subtill policie, cunning roguerie.*
Machiavelizer. *To Machiauelize it; to practise Machiauellisme.*
Machicoulé: m. ée: f. *Fortified with* Maschecoulis.
Machicoulis. *Looke* Maschecoulis.
Machinateur: m. *A machinator, framer, contriuer, deuiser (especially of bad things.)*
Machination: f. *A machination, frame, contriuement; a subtill plot, or conspiracie; a craftie inuention, shifting stratageme, circumuenting tricke.*
Machine: f. *A frame, engine, toole, instrument, inuention, deuice.*
Machiné: m. ée: f. *Framed, contriued, deuised; plotted, conspired; practised against.*
Machiner. *To machinate, frame; contriue, deuise; to practise, plot, conspire against.*
Machoirier: m. *A horned, and great-iawed Snake.*
Machonner. *To chaw slowly, or gently; to mumble.*
Machoter. *To champe, or chaw slowly, or without any great effect.*
Machoüeres: f. *The iawes.*
Machurer. *To blacke, smeare, smutch, begryme, or disfigure with blacking.*
Le chauderon machure la poisle. *One knaue disgraces, or, one neighbour detracts from another.*
Macis: m. *The spice called Mace.*
Macle: f. *The Mash of a net; also (in* Blason*) a Mascle, or short Lozenge, hauing a square hole in the middest.*
Macle: com. *Raw.* ¶Rab.
Macles: f. *Pot-hangers; the Jrons whereupon pots are hung.*
Maçon. *as* Masson.
Maçonné: m. ée: f. *Wrought by Masons; built of stone; hewed, squared, layed, as stones by a Mason.*
Maçonner. *To play the Mason, to build with, or of stone; to hew, square, worke, lay stones, as a Mason; to worke Masons worke.*
Maçonnerie. *Seeke* Massonnerie.
Macque. *A Lozenge, or Net-mash.*
Macquereau. *as* Maquereau.
Macquignon. *Looke* Maquignon.
Macreau: m. *A Mackerell fish; Looke* Maquereau.
Macreon: m. *An old, or long-liued, man.* ¶Rab.
Macrobe. *Of old life; of long continuance, or that hath had a long time, in this life.* ¶Rab.
Macroule: f. *A sea-Coot, or Scottish Moore-henne.*
Maculatures: f. *Blotting, or wast, papers.*
Macule: f. *A spot, blot; speck, speckle; staine, blemish.*
Maculer. *To spot, blot; speck, speckle, bespatter; besmeare, taine, blemish, beray.*
Madame: f. *Madame. (The title, or stile of a Ladie.)*

Madame du guichet. *The Ladie of the Wicket; (a by-word for a Midwife.)*
Monsieur vaut bien Madame: Pro. *Look* Monsieur.
Madamoiselle: f. *(The title, or stile of a Gentlewoman;) Mistresse.*
Madamoiselle d'un'aulne de velours. *A mechanicall, or vpstart Gentlewoman; the proud wife of a shopkeeper that will needs be a Gentlewoman.*
Madamoiselle de la boutique. *(Of the same ranke, and ambition.)*
Madamoiselle de cinquante pour cent. *The same; or may be applyed to the loftie-humored wife of an extorting Vsurer.*
Madant. *Wet, moist; flowing; also, drunken with.*
Madefier. *To wet, moisten, liquifie.*
Madia. *In good sooth; as true as I liue; or (in stead of* Ce m'ait Dieu) *so God helpe me.*
Madia nò. *No forsooth, or, in sooth sir no; you shall be so good as to pardon me.*
Madiene, ou Madienne. *A cholericke old wiues oath importing as much as,* Mon Dieu, *or,* par mon Dieu.
Madier: m. *Tymber.*
Madoure: m. *A dull, or senceleße loggarhead.*
Madre: f. *A thicke-streaked graine in wood.*
Madré: m. ée: f. *(Of wood) whose graine is full of crooked, and speckled streakes; (of a man) subtill, craftie, shifting, full of fetches; whence;*
Ie suis plus Madré en ces affaires. *I am better experienced in these businesses.*
Madrer. *The graines of wood to be full of crooked, and speckled streakes, or veines.*
Madreure. *as* Madrure.
Madrier: m. *A planke, or peece of timber, whose graine is full of crooked, and speckled streakes.*
Madrure: f. *as* Madre, *or* Madrier; *also, a speckled, or diuersified streaking; whence,* Madrures; *Speckled streakes in the graine of cut wood; or the menild coat of some Hawkes.*
Maeut. *A maker of sallads, or May-sawces.* ¶Rab.
Mafé, *or* Mafi. *Much vsed in stead of,* Par ma foy.
Magagnat. *Maymed, &c, as* Mehaigné. ¶Langued.
Magaigne. *as* Mehaing. ¶Langued; *or, as the Italian* Magagna *(whence it comes) defect, imperfection, want, fault, corruption, putrifaction.*
Magault. *as* Macault.
Magazin: m. *A Magasin, publike storehouse, or warehouse.*
Magdaleon: m. *A Langate, a rowler.*
Magdaleon d'entract. *A salue spred vpon leather, or linnen, and hard rowled vp.*
Mage. *Chiefe, or principall; whence,* Iuge Mage. *A chiefe Iustice.*
Place Mage. *The chiefest, or most frequented place, as the Marketstead, in a Towne.*
Magicien: m. *A Magician, or Negromancer; one that practises the blacke Art; a Coniurer.*
Magie: f. *Magicke, Negromancie; Coniuring, the blacke Art.*
Magique: com. *Magicall; coniuring; of, or belonging to, the blacke Art.*
Magistere: m. *Maistership, authoritie, sway, cheefe rule; also, maisterie, a maisters part, or maisterpeece.*
Magistral: m. ale: f. *Magistrall; of a maister, or magistrate; done by a magistrate, or maister; also, maisterlike; artificiall, skilfull, cunning.*
Magistralement. *Maister-like, expertly, artificially, cunningly.*
Magistrat: m. *A Magistrate; Ruler, Gouernour, Iudge, or principall Officer in the Commonwealth.*
Magistrature: f. *Magistracie; gouernment, sway, rule, authoritie; the bearing of office in the Commonwealth.*
Magistronostralement. *Dunsically.* ¶Rab.
Magna gna. *Marry gip sir; true Roger.* ¶Rab.
Magnan: m. *A boore, clowne, hinde, yeoman, countrey fellow.*
Magnanime: com. *Magnanimous, generous, of a great mind; stout-hearted, gallant-humored, of a loftie spirit, of a noble stomacke.*
Magnanimement. *Magnanimiously, generously, gallantly, valiantly.*
Magnanimité: f. *Magnanimitie, generositie, greatnesse of mind; gallantnesse of humor, noblenesse of spirit, stoutneße of heart.*
Magniaux: m. *Silkewormes.* ¶Langued.
Magnie: f. *A meynie, companie, number of people.* ¶Bourg.
Magnificat: m. *The Magnificat; (part of the Euensong; whence;)*
Chanter Magnificat à matines. *To doe things disorderly, or vse a thing vnseasonably.*
Magnificence: f. *Magnificence; statelinesse, gorgeousnesse, sumptuousneße; high atchieuement, great performance; noble prouision.*
Magnifié: m. ée: f. *Magnified; highly commended, mightily praised, much honoured.*
Magnifier. *To magnifie; exalt, extoll; commend highly, praise mightily, honour much.*
Magnifique: com. *Magnificent, of high atchieuement, acting great matters, performing worthie acts; haughtie, loftie, statelie, sumptuous, maiesticall, solemne, graue.*
Magnifiquement. *Magnificently, magnifico-like; worthily, honourably, haughtily, sumptuously; solemnely, with a maiestie, with much grauitie, with great state.*
Magnigoules: m. *Wide-mouthed knaues.* ¶Norm.
Magny Magna. *Twitle twatle; or, as in* Magna.
Magot: m. *A Baboone, or Ape, thats faced like a dog; also, the (Scottish) Coote, or Moore-henne.*
Maguelet. *as* Macaleb.
Mahaleb. *as* Macaleb.
Maheustre: m. *A swaggerer, swash-buckler, desperate or careleße yonker.*
Mahonne: f. *A kind of great ship somewhat resembling the galliasse.*
Mahutte: f. *The pinion of a (birds) wing.*
Mai. *as* May.
Maict: f. *A hutch, kneading trough; salting tub.*
Maidin: m. *A Turkish coyne worth about a pennie.*
Maie: f. *The greatest kind of Sea-Crab; round, long-legd, and verie rough-shelled; some call her, a Frill.*
Maïens: m. *Timelie Hay; called so because tis commonly gotten in May.*
Majesté: f. *Maiestie; royaltie, soueraignetie, princelinesse, high dignitie, highest authoritie; a kinglie presence or prerogatiue; a most honourable grauitie; also (in Painting) such a radiant circle, or shadow, as is made about the head of a Saint.*
Majesteux: m. euse: f. *Maiesticall, kinglie, princelie, imperious, royall, soueraigne, supreame; of great grauitie, full of maiestie.*
Majeul de rouë: m. *The naue of a wheele.*
Maieur: m. *The Mayor of a Towne; or, as* Maire; *also, the* Major, *or first proposition of a Syllogisme; also,*

also, one that is of full yeares.
Nos maieurs. *Our auncestors, or forefathers.*
Le maieur d'un mestier. *Th maister of a Companie of artificers.*
Majeur. *as* La majeur partie; *the more; the greater part, or side.*
Maignan. *as* Magnan. ¶Rab.
Maigne: com. *Great; as,* Charles le maigne.
Maignen: m. *A Copper-smith, or Kettle-maker.*
Maigre: m. *A great, and skalie fish, hauing a wattle on his chinne; two holes on the top of his beake, neere his eyes; and two stones within his head, of some vertue (as is supposed) against the cholicke: The French doe tearme him thus, not because he is leane, but because by the whitenesse of his flesh he seemes so; howsoeuer, and howsoeuer he be dressed, he is reasonable good meat.*
Maigre: com. *Meagar, leane, scraggie, fleshlesse; thin, slender, gaunt, lanke; hungrie, barren; poore.*
Maigre chere. *Cold, or heartlesse intertainment.*
Maigre mine. *Small countenance, a respectlesse looke, or scarce a good looke.*
Maigre propos. *Dry, barren, faint, shallow, or carelesse discourse; talke whereby the hearer can profit but little.*
Iour maigre. *A fish, or fasting, day.*
Maigre en cuisse d'heron; &,
Maigres comme pies. *As leane as Rakes (we say.)*
Maigrelet: m. ette: f. *Somewhat meagar, thin, slender, somewhat leane.*
Maigrement. *Meagarly, leanely, scraggily; thinly, lankly, slenderly; hungrily; barrenly; dryly; poorely.*
Maigret. *as* Maigrelet.
Maigreté: f. *Meagarnesse, leannesse; thinnesse, lankenesse; hungrinesse, barrennesse; drynesse; pooreenesse.*
Maigue: m. *Whey.*
Mail: m. *A Mall, Mallet, or Beetle; also, as* Marne.
Maille: f. *A (French) halfepennie; the halfe of a pennie (in weight, or money;) also, looke the next marginall word.*
La maille Billeron. *A toll taken of euerie one that sells wares at certaine Fayres.*
Maille de Lorraine. *A coyne worth about* iij s. Tour.
Droict de maille d'or. *Looke* Droict.
Faire la maille bonne de. *To warrant, undertake or answer for, make good.*
Bonne la maille qui sauve le denier: Prov. *Well is the halfe-pennie (spent) that saues a pennie.*
Maille: f. *Mayle, or a linke of mayle (whereof coats of mayle be made;) also, a Hauther; or, any little ring of mettall resembling a linke of mayle; also, a mash of a net, the square hole that is between thread and thread; also, a web in the eye.*
Maille de boucle. *The loope of a buckle; (through which the latchet passes.)*
Maille à maille on fait les haubergeons: Pro. *Looke* Haubergeon.
Maillé: m. ée: f. *Armed with a coat of mayle, or priuie coat; also, marled, as ground.*
Perdrix maillée. *A maylde, menild, or spotted Partridge.*
Mailler. *To arme, or furnish with a coat of mayle; also, to marle a peece of ground.*
Maillerie: f. *A marle-pit, or marlie soyle; the place wherein marle is gotten.*
Maillet: m. *A mallet, or hammer; also, a battleax; also, as* Encueur.
Faire de son poing vn maillet. *To make hard shift; or be ignorant of the right vse of things.*
Pescher au maillet. *Foolishly to talke much, or make a great bruit, of a proiect, thereby discouering, and disappointing it.*
Mailleron: m. *A small twig, or shoot springing from the staulke of a Vine, &c; a young branch fit to be planted.*
Maillettes: f. *Small mashes, or links of mayle.*
Maillol: m. *as* Mailleton.
Maillon: m. *The knot a Gardener makes in binding, with willow-twigs, the stakes, and vine-branches of an arbour together.*
Mailloque: f. *as* Tierce; *or the* 24 *part of a* Seconde; *and the least weight that Jewellers, and Goldsmithes vse.*
Maillot: m. *A swadling clout, or swathe-band; (sometimes) also, a cradle; also, as* Mailleton.
Maillotant. *Powning, bruizing, beating, or breaking with a mallet.*
Mailloter. *To powne, beat, bruize, or breake with a mallet.*
Maillotins: m. *A factious multitude, which, in old time, did much mischiefe in, and about, Paris; whence;*
Maillotonnerie: f. *Any factious crue, seditious companie, tumultuous rising of people.*
Main: m. *The name of a Saint; whence;*
Mal S. Main. *The wild scab.*
Main. Pour Matin. *The morning; whence,* Demain.
Main: f. *A hand; also, the forefoot of a horse; also, the graple of a ship; also, the yron hooke that holds the bucket of a Well; also, a certaine three-fold hooke vsed by Wine-pressers; also, a quire of paper; also (in Law) publicke authoritie, or power.*
Main basse. *A bad hand, ill chance, course lucke, hard bargaine; whence;*
Faire main basse, & mener les mains basses. *To put all vnto the sword.*
Main burnie. *Ward, gard, custodie, &c; as* Mainbournie.
Main ferme. *A steadie hand; also, as* Main-ferme.
Les mains du foye. *Certaine branches of the portveine, which conuey the iuice of concocted meat vnto the liuer.*
Main garnie. *An armed hand; viz.* that holds a *stone, or weapon to strike withall; (Hence,* Excez de main non garnie; *a blow giuen with the (onely) hand; a cuffe, or dust with the fist;) also, as in,* Garnir la main.
Main de Iustice. *The hand of Iustice; viz. the authoritie, iurisdiction, or power thereof in any kind of execution, or seisure; also, an yuorie hand in the top of a Rod; (a marke of Royaltie, or Soueraignetie, as well as the Scepter, Crowne, or Sword.)*
Main levée. *A discharge, release, deliuerie from suit; also, a restoring, or giuing backe of things which were seised by order; a putting one in possession of a thing become by accident, or order, cleerely his.*
Main mise. *Seisure of the person or of possessions, by the Magistrate, or a Lord, vnto whom they are by law, or in right, or by the omission of duties, and due seruices, escheated, or forfeited.*
Main morte. *is much like the Mortmaine of our Law; also, villenage, or a seruile tenure.*
Gens de main morte condition. *Looke* Mainmorte.
Main pleine. *Sufficient goods taken, or land ynough seised, vpon an execution.*
Main souveraine. *Authoritie royall; the Kings pre-*

prerogatiue, or power.
Se faire recevoir par main souveraine. *Looke* Recevoir.
La bouche & les mains. *Homage, and fealtie; or, the ceremonies vsed in the doing thereof; for which looke* Hommage.
La derniere main. *The last touch, worke, or act, which giues a thing it full perfection.*
Disme, & terrage à deux mains. *A Lords taking of two sheaues vpon his tenants twelue;* viz. *one for his tythe, another for his* Terrage.
Garnison de main. *See* Garnison.
La grande main. *The whole arme and hand together.*
'A main. *Readie, neere, at hand.*
'A main armée. *By force of armes.*
'A main forte. *By maine force, or great power; with might and maine.*
'A main sauve. *Safely, securely, without any manner of losse, dammage, or danger.*
'A la main. *Nimbly, readily, actiuely, at hand (quoth pick-purse.)*
Haut à la main. *Proud, statelie, surlie, sullen, stubborne, a striker, like ynough to lay about him.*
Homme à la main, & Homme de main. *A man of execution or valour; a man of his hands.*
Leger à la main. *(Of a horse) light borne.*
'A pleine main. Vne bouche à pleine main. *A horses mouth which is neither too hard, nor too sensible, and thereby giues a full rest vnto the hand.*
De longue main. *Of old, long since, of great continuance, a great while agoe.*
Tout d'une main. *Hard after, all together, all vnder one.*
Les mains derriere le dos; &, les mains penduës à leur ceincture. *In an idle, or carelesse fashion.*
Avoir les mains crochuës. *To be a light-fingered, or lime-fingered filcher; euerie finger of his hand to be as good as a lime-twig.*
Avoir les mains longues. *To haue long hands, or large iurisdiction: applyable to Princes, whose power stretches verie farre.*
Avoir les mains nettes. *To be honest, sincere, vncorruptable, vpright.*
Avoir la main seure. *To be steadie handed (as he that would be a good workman must be;) also, to be honest, loyall, trustie, faithfull, true in his reckonings, iust in all his doings.*
Bailler la main. *To reach a hand; also, a wife to giue her consent, before a Notarie, vnto the sale, or morgage of her inheritance.*
Changer de main. *To shift out of one hand into another; also, to change the Lord, or Possessor; as land is said to doe vpon sales, gifts, exchanges, death &c.*
Faire main forte à. *To ioyne strongly with.*
Faire la main. *To make a hand, or make vp his mouth; to get a rich purchase, or great stake; to gaine much; to win all.*
Faire, & lever la main. *To take vp the tricke (at Cards.)*
Faire d'une main l'autre. *To patch vp one thing with another; to supply the defects of the one with the excesse of the other.*
Fourrer la main à. *To grease the fist with a bribe, &c.*
Garnir la main. *To take a thing to pawne, or in morgage; also, to seize, or distraine; or (more properly) an arrested debtor to pay the debt presently, or deliuer valuable goods for the securitie, or in cōsideration, thereof.*
Iouër des mains. *To fight.*
Iurer es mains d'autruy. *To sweare vnto, or (any way) to take an oath; for the old fashion was, that he which tooke an oath held his hands within his that receiued it.*
Laver les mains de. *To purge, cleere, iustifie, or excuse himselfe of.*
Mener les mains. *To bestirre the fingers; (and particularly) to deale blowes, fall to handie strokes, lay hard about him.*
Mener les mains basses. *To put vnto the sword.*
Mettre la main au baston. *See* Baston.
Mettre la main sur le collet de. *To arrest, or take prisoner.*
Mettre la main iusques au coude, Il y a mis la m. *He hath stept verie farre into; he hath deepely ingaged himselfe in; he hath sounded the depth of, the matter.*
Mettre la main à l'heritage. *To fall to the ground vpon his hands.*
Mettre la main à la paste. *To assist, helpe, further, set forward.*
Mettre la main à la verge. *Looke* Verge.
Partir de la main. *To part from the hand; suddainely, or hastily to passe, or start, forward.*
Prendre la main. *A Notarie to take the consent, and receiue the oath, of parties that agree to passe a contract.*
Se seigner de toutes mains. *To be horribly afraid, or grieuously distressed; or, all-to-be-crosse themselues in a time of affright, or extremitie.*
Tendre les mains. *To aske for mercie.*
Tenir la main à quelque affaire. *To haue a hand in, be medling with, heed or looke vnto, a matter.*
Tenir la main à vn en quelque affaire. *To further, fauor, helpe, or assist one in a matter.*
Tenir la main pour l'un & pour l'autre. *To be a newter, or equally affected to both sides; also, to vndertake both for the one and the other.*
Tenir sous main. *To keepe in secret, in priuate, in a corner, in hugger-mugger.*
Tirer à la main. *A horse to presse vpon the hand, or striue to get forward, or to goe faster then his rider would haue him.*
Tomber en main tierce. *Looke* Tiers.
Toucher en la main de. *To shake hands with, or take by the hand, in signe of friendship.*
Il toucha la main entre leurs mains. *He layed his hands betweene theirs, or gaue them his hand that he would be theirs.*
Venir aux mains. *To come to handie blowes; to buckle, graple, cope, or fight together.*
Venir es mains de. *To be at the mercie, fall into the laps, come into the power, or vnder the iurisdiction, of.*
Main lavée moins levée: Prov. *The more good parts one hath the lesse he should boast of them.*
'A main lavée Dieu mande la repeuë: Prov. *God sends th' vpright all necessarie food.*
Vne main lave l'autre: Prov. *One hand washes the other; applyable to such as giue vpon assurance, or hope, to be giuen vnto; or vnto such as any way serue one anothers turne.*
Pour laver ses mains on n'en vend pas sa terre: Prov. *A cleane-washt hand makes no man sell his land.*
De mains vuides prieres vaines: Pro. *Emptie hands (bad Orators) make intreatie proue idle.*
Connin, & vilain avec la main: Pro. *See* Connin.

Main-

Main-bonne. *as* Main-bournie.

Main-bournie: f. *Ward, gard; gouernment, administration, ouersight of; charge, power, authoritie ouer; also, the patronage, defence, or protection of a Soueraigne.*

Main-de-gourre. *A Hogs-foot; or, one thats handed like a Sow.* ¶Rab.

Main-ferme: f. *Farme, or fee-farme; a title in, or the possession of, an inheritance (either for a time certaine, or for euer) lyable vnto rent.*

Main-ferme: com. *Held in farme, or fee-farme*; Tous Heritages, & biens immeubles qui ne sont fief, sont communement appellez, reputez, & tenus heritages mainfermes. Coust. de Cambray tit. 2. ar. 2.

Main-mettre. *To manumit, or dismisse; to affranchise a villaine.*

Main-mis: m. *An affranchised person; one that is freed from seruitude, or slauerie.*

Main-mortable: com. *Holding, or held by villenage, or by a seruile tenure; whence;*

Main-mortable envers son seigneur. *Slauishly subiect vnto the impositions his Lord is pleased to lay on him while he liues; and at his death not able to bequeath, or giue away vj d without his permission.*

Heritages main-mortables. *Which are charged, at the Lords pleasure, with taxes; and of custome with an yearelie proportion of flesh, bread, or corne, payable vnto him; and which come cleere into his hands, if the tenant thereof dye without lawfull heires of his bodie.*

Main-morte: f. *Mortmaine; also, villenage; or, a seruile, and slauish tenure.*

Gens de main-morte. *Be Church-men; Abbots, Monks, Fryers; Deanes, Prebends, Canons; brothers of an Hospitall; freemen of a corporate Towne, or Trade; the fellowes, or members of all Corporations; also, villaines, or seruile tenants.*

Mainotte: f. *A small hand, or childs hand.*

Main-pleine. Looke Main.

Mainsine. *A bundle of grapes; or some six or seuen bunches tyed vp together; as* Moissine.

Mainsné: m. *A younger brother.*

Maint: m. te: f. *Many, a number, store of.*

Maintes fois. *Often, eftsoones, or at sundrie times.*

Maintenance: f. *Maintenance; protection, support, countenance, assistance.*

Maintenant. *Now, presently, at this instant, in this verie moment.*

Pour maintenant. *For this time; for this once.*

Maintenir. *To maintaine, vphold, support, protect, countenance, defend, backe, beare out; stand in, or vnto.*

Maintenir de faux. *To affirme, and offer, or set himselfe, to proue, that an euidence produced by his aduersarie is forged;* Looke Faux.

Maintenu: m. uë: f. *Maintained, vpheld, supported, defended; stood in, or vnto; countenanced, backed, or borne out.*

Maintenuë: f. *A maintenance, maintaining, vpholding, defense, countenance, assistance.*

La pleine maintenuë. *The full possession of a thing; or, a possession adiudged, and giuen after the full tryall of a suit, vnto him that hath most right.*

Maintien: m. *Gesture, behauior, demeanour, carriage.*

Main tourner, à m. *In the turning of a hand, instantly, suddainely.*

Majorité: f. *Maioritie; full age.*

Maire: m. *A Mayor; the highest Officer or Magistrate of an incorporate Towne; also, the Judge, or Steward of a Lord* Iusticiers *Courts.*

Maire de Chastel. *as* Merc.

Maire du Palais. *Was, in old time, the principall Officer of the Crowne, and Steward of the Kings house; since, he hath beene called* Seneschal de France; *now, the Constable, and Great Maister of France diuide his authoritie betweene them.*

Le Maire du village. *The Judge thereof.*

Maire laine. *The full-grown fleece, or well-combd wooll of a sheepe.*

Mairerie: f. *A Maiordome; the office, or place of a Mayor; also, his iurisdiction, or the precincts thereof.*

Mairgue: f. *as* Maigue; *Whay.* ¶Auvergnois.

Mairie: f. *A Maiordome, or Maiorship; the office, or place of a Maior, or of a village-Maior; also (in some old bookes, and customes) base, or low iurisdiction.*

Mais. (Adverb.) *But; also, more, any more; (whence,*

Mais de; *aboue, or more then;) also, rather.*

Mais que. *But what; also, when that, so that.*

Plus mais. Ie ne puis plus mais soustenir. *I can beare no longer, or not a whit more.*

'A tousiours mais. *Eternally, euerlastingly, for euer and euer.*

Ie n'en peux mais. *It's not my fault, it's no way long of me, I cannot doe withall.*

Mais-huy. *Not this day, or not as long as this day lasteth.*

Maisné: m. *A younger brother.*

Maisne. Argent baillé à maisne. *Let out to vse for the benefit of younger brethren, being infants, or orphans.*

Maisneaux. *as* Meneaux.

Maisneté: f. *Youngership, or younger brotherhood; the estate, or title of a younger brother.*

Maison: f. *A house, or mansion; also, a race, or familie.*

La maisons de Monsieur Boyau. *Whose foreparts be slated, and backe-parts thatched.*

Maisons au ciel. *Circles drawne from the one pole to the other, to seperate the twelue signes of the Zodiake, and diuiding the whole Sphere into twelue equall parts.*

Maison de despens. *A Roome, or Side (of extraordinarie expence) in Prisons, wherein a condemned debtor, that will not pay, is to be kept.*

Maison Dieu. *An Hospitall, or Spittle, for the poore.*

Maison de la Paix. *A Court of Iudgement or Iustice; a iudiciall Court.*

Toile de maison. *(Course) Huswiues cloth.*

De vieilles maisons bruslées il sçait tirer des cuilliers neufves. *He can picke new spoones out of old houses; (Applyable to a neere, and cunning house-keeper.)*

La maison fait cognoistre le maistre: Prov. *The house discouers the owner; or, looke into a house, you discerne the owner.*

En bonne maison l'on a tost apresté: Prov. *In a good house all things are quickly readie.*

En petite maison Dieu a grand part: Prov. *God hath a great share in a small house.*

'A l'entrée de la ville est le commencement des maisons: Prov. *The buildings begin at the townegate; One may ghesse at a mans whole speech by his Proeme; and by his first course what will be his whole proceeding.*

Achete paix, & maison faitte: Prov. *Buy peace, and*

and a house (alreadie) made; like whereunto is;
Il faut acheter maison faitte, & femme à faire: Pro. *Purchase a house readie made, but let thy wife bee of thine owne making.*
Chascun est maistre en sa maison: Prov. *Euery one is (or should be) master within his owne doores.*
Qui fait nopces, & maison, met le sien en abandon: Prov. *Much building, and often bridalls make bare pastures, and naked side-walls.*
Qui veut tenir nette maison il n'y faut prestre, ny pigeon: Prov *He that loues to haue a neat house must keepe neither Priest, nor Pigeon in it.*
Moisonage: m. *Timber-trees cut downe for the building of a house.*
Maisonnages: m. *Houses, housing; lodgings, dwellings.*
Maisonné: m. ée: f. *Housed, furnished, or stored with houses.*
Maisonnée: f. *A housefull, household, familie.*
Maisonner. *To build houses; to furnish, or store with houses.*
Maisonnette: f. *A little house; a lodging, a cote, a crib, a cottage.*
Maisonnier: m. ere: f. *Keeping a house: also, belonging to, or seruing for, a house.*
Maistraille. *The maine sayle (of a ship.)*
Maistral: m. *The North-west wind.* ¶ Rab.
Maistre: m. *A Master; Gouernour, Commaunder, President, Principall, chiefe Ruler; a Teacher, Instructor; Ouerseer; also, an Owner, Proprietarie, Professor; also, one that hath (or should haue) sufficient skill in the facultie which he professes; whence,* Maistre es arts, &c; *also, a title of honour (such as it is) belonging to all Artificers, and Tradesmen; whence,* Maistre Pierre, Maistre Iehan, &c; *which we giue not so generally, but qualifie the meaner sort of them (especially in countrey townes) with the title of Goodman (too good for many.)*
Les deux Maistres. *The two principall ropes of a Fishers Draw-net.*
Maistre des basses œuvres. *A Iakes-farmer, or Goldfinder.*
Maistres de la chambre aux deniers. *The principall officers of the Exchequer, called so in old time.*
Maistre des comptes. *Looke in* Chambre des Comptes.
Maistre des eaux, & forests. *The Lord chiefe Iustice, or Iustice in Eire, of the Kings Forrests, &c.*
Maistre des hautes œuvres. *A hangman.*
Maistre d'hostel. *The steward of a (great) household.*
Maistres du Parlement. *So were the* Conseillers du Parlement *called in old time.*
Maistre phy phy. *A Jakes-feyer (who hath often occasion enough to say* phy.)
Maistre des Ports. *An Officer that ouersees the leuying of the* Imposition foraine, Resue, & Haut passage.
Maistres rationnaux. *Certaine officers which haue the letting of the Kings farmes.*
Maistre des Requestes. *The Masters of Requests; Looke* Requeste.
Le Grand Maistre. *The Great Master of France; the Lord Steward of the Kings houshold; heretofore stiled,* Le Compte du Palais; &, le Seneschal de France.
Le grand Maistre des Arbalestiers. *The Master of the Crossebow-men; an officer in date vntill the comming vp of Gunnes, and holding the same ranke, and authoritie that, at this day, belongs to.*
Le grand Maistre de l'Artillerie. *The Master of the Ordnance.*
Vn second Maistre. *The Vsher of a Schoole.*
Servir son maistre. *To purge, vntrusse, goe to the stoole.*
'A pere; à maistre, & à Dieu tout puissant, nul ne peut rendre l'equivalent: Prov. *Looke* Dieu.
Ce que maistre donne, & valet pleure, ce sont larmes perduës: Prov. *The groome that wayles his masters gifts may well enough spare his teares.*
Chascun est maistre en sa maison: Prov. *Euery one rules in his owne house.*
De grand maistre hardi valet: Prov. *Said of a seruant, that bearing himselfe on his masters greatnesse, is more bold, and confident then otherwise he would be.*
En pont, en planche, & en riviere, valet devant, Maistre derriere: Prov. *In places of danger, or disaster, the seruant must precede his master.*
Fortune n'espargne ny serviteur ny maistre: Prov. *Looke* Fortune.
Iamais ne gaigne qui precede à son maistre: Prov. *He neuer gaines that stands in suit with's master.*
Il est plus d'ouvriers, que de maistres: Prov. *There be more workmen then skilfull workmen.*
Il se peut bien seoir à table quand le maistre luy commande: Prov. *Hee needs not wait thats bid sit downe by his master.*
La maison fait cognoistre le maistre: Prov. *Wee say, the seluidge makes shew of the cloth.*
L'oeil du maistre engraisse le cheval: Prov. *A horse is fattened by his masters eye.*
Les derniers venus sont les maistres: Prov. *Those that come last (oft) get the masterie.*
Nouveau apprenti n'est pas maistre: Prov. *A nouice (or new-come Prentice) is no master; viz. must neither looke for the respect, nor haue looked from him the skill of, a master.*
Qui a compagnon a maistre: Prov. *He that hath a mate hath a master.*
Qui bon maistre sert bon loyer en attend: Prov. *Hee that waites on a good master waites for a good turne.*
Qui sert Dieu il a bon maistre: Prov. *The seruant of God hath a good master.*
Qui sert le Roy il a bon maistre: Prov. *No seruice to the King.*
Tel maistre tel valet: Prov. *Like master like man.*
Maistre: com. *(Adiectiuely) chiefe, principall; whence;* Vn maistre cable, ou chable. *A sheat-cable.*
Le maistre doigt. *The middle finger.*
Maistre-garde: m. *A chiefe warden, or Master-warden in a forrest.*
Maistrement. *as* Magistralement; *(an old word.)*
Maistre-pied: m. *The stocke, or principall arme of a Plant.*
Maistre-sergent: m. *A Master-Sergeant, or chiefe Sergeant; an officer in forrests.*
Maistre-sergenterie: f. *The office, or walke of a Master-Sergeant, in forrests.*
Maistresse: f. *A mistresse, dame, commaundresse.*
La maistresse Esglise. *A Cathedrall Church, the mistresse Church, or chiefe Church in a Town (wherin this word, as well as* Maistre *before, is vsed Adiectiuely.)*
Maistrier. *as* Maistriser.
Maistrise: f. *Maisterie, seigniorie, commaund, authoritie,*

ritie,dominion,rule,sway; also,cunning,skill,artificiallnesse,expert or excellent workmanship;also,a Maistership; the office,or place of a Master; whence;

La grand maistrise. The office of le grand maistre; (for whom,looke vnder Maistre.)

Il y a eu de la maistrise à faire cela. The matter hath beene cunningly,or workmanly handled.

Maistriser. To master, gouerne,rule, sway; to bridle,order,containe,or keepe within compasse.

Maistroqueux. A master Cooke. ¶ Rab.

Majuscule: com. Somewhat greater,a little bigger;of good stature,of a reasonable age.

Maiz:m. Maïs,Turkie corne,Turkie wheat;(the graine whereof the Indians make the most of their bread.)

Mal:m. An euill,mischiefe;hurt,harme,domage,wrong, displeasure,annoyance; also, a griefe, paine; sicknesse, disease.

Mal de S.Acaire. as Acariastreté.

Mal aigre. A kind of wormes that breed in the gorge of a Hawke.

Mal d'Alcide. Hercules euill; the foule, or falling euill.

Mal d'amarry. The suffocation of the Matrix.

Mal de S.Apollonie. The toothache.

Mal de S.Avertin. Dizzinesse; or any disease of the head.

Mal caduc. The falling sicknesse.

Mal chaud, ou chaud mal. A continuall(or violent) burning ague; (whence the Prouerbe, De fievre en chaud mal. Out of the frying-panne into the fire.)

Mal de S.Claire. Red eyes; or,a painefull rednesse of the eyes.

Mal des comices. The falling sicknesse.

Mal de corne. The sitt-fast; a hornie swelling on the backe of a horse.

Mal de craye. The stone-cray; a Hawkes disease.

Mal de cropion. The rumpe-euill; a disease wherewith all birds (especially such as be kept in cages) are sometimes troubled.

Mal aux dents. The toothache; also,extreame hunger, or famishment by reason thereof; Looke Dent.

Mal feru. A Malander in the bought of a horses knee.

Mal S.Fiacre. An inflamed scab,or great wart in the fundament,the which it makes to swell.

Mal de flancs. A Pleurisie; or,as vnder Flanc.

Mal S.Francois. want of money, or, not a crosse in the purse (for those of his order must carrie no money about them.)

Mal de S.Genou. The Gowt.

Mal de S.Gilles. A Fistula, or Canker.

Mal de gosier. The Squinancie,or Squinzie.

Mal de S.Iean. The falling sicknesse.

Mal de Mahumet. The falling sicknesse (whereunto Mahomet was very subiect.)

Mal de S.Mammard. Sorenesse,or chaps,in the breasts of women.

Mal de S.Mathurin. Frenzie,madnesse.

Mal de S.Medard. Looke Medard.

Mal de S. Mein. The wild scab, or manginesse; a kind of (most itching) leaprosie, bred of a salt phlegme.

Mal mort. A running scab,or thicke morphew, which couering all ouer the vlcers that bee vnder it, seemes wholly dead: Some Northerne people call it, the Rigruffe (in beasts.)

Mal de Naples. The French Pocks; or, the Neapolitane disease, first gotten by the French (of the Spaniards) at the siege of Naples, Anno Dom. 1528.

Mal du pantois. Difficultie of breathing; See Pantois.

Mal du pion. A sicknesse that comes by excessiue drinking.

Mal de pippe. Drunkennesse.

Mal de S.Quentin. The Cough.

Mal de S.Raphine. The wild Scab.

Mal de S.Roch. Scurfe, or scabbinesse; an itching manginesse.

Mal sacrée. The Kings euill.

Mal de S.Sebastien. The Plague,or pestilence.

Mal subtil. The Ptiscke, or consumption of the lungs.

Mal de terre. The falling sicknesse.

Mal de teste. The head-ache; (and sometimes) also; iealousie.

Mal de S.Valentin. The falling sicknesse.

Mal de ventre. The wormes;or belly-ache; a painfull griping, or fretting in the guts.

Mal de ver. The farcie in a horse.

Mal S.Vitus. A pleasant disease,wherein the patient leapes, daunces, and laughes all the while his fit is on him.

Chaud mal. as before in Mal chaud.

Gros mal. The falling sicknesse; the foule euill.

Haut mal. The same.

Le haut mal de la corde. Hanging;a twitching vp in a rope.

Mal dessus mal n'est pas santé: Prov. Ill vpon ill is no health.

De mal est venu l'agneau, & à mal retourne la peau: Prov. From ill came the Lambe, and to ill goes it skinne; goods euill gotten are commonly ill spent.

A peine endure mal qui ne l'a appris: Pro. Hardly can he brooke miserie that neuer any bore.

Il est tost deceu qui mal ne pense: Prov. Hee that thinkes no harme is soone beguiled.

Tel se plaind qui n'a point de mal: Prov. Some though they feele no harme vnquiet are.

Mal: m. ale: f. Ill, bad, naughtie, lewd; scuruie; mischieuous, hurtfull, harmefull, shrewd; vnseemely, vncomely, vndecent; sicke, diseased, crazie, pained, sore, ill at ease.

La male bosse. A pestilent byle, or bunch; a plaguesore.

Mal. (Adverb.) Ill, euilly, badly, naughtily, mischieuously; hardly, vneasily; vnhandsomely, ill-fauouredly, scuruily.

Que bien que mal. Indifferently, so so; also, hittie missie, one way or other.

Ie fus bien mal de mon pere. I had my fathers anger, I got his displeasure, I was hardly vsed, ill intreated, by him.

Il me fait mal de luy. I am very sorrie for him.

Ils me veulent faire mal de vous. They would haue me fall out with you.

Mon cœur luy est, ou fait mal. I beare him a grudge, my heart cannot abide him.

Mal batu longuement pleure; &, Autant pleure mal batu que bien batu: Prov. Looke Batu.

Mal fait qui ne parfait: Prov. He does ill that does not all; the end crownes the worke.

Mal ioue qui fiert la ioue: Prov. Looke Ioue.

Mal pense qui ne repense: Prov. Better not thinke at all then not to weigh the thoughts.

Mal poise qui ne contrepoise: Pro. *He weighes but ill that weighes not one with another.*

Mal sert qui ne parsert: Prov. *He serues but ill that throughly serues not.*

Mal soupe qui tout disne: Pro. *Of a young spender comes an old beggar; of a riotous youth a ruinous age.*

Qui mal entend, mal respond: Prov. *He that vnderstands ill answers vnfitly.*

Qui bien void, & mal prend fait folie en bon escient: Prov. *He that discernes well, and chuses ill, is a true coxcombe.*

Malabatre: m. Malabathrum; *an aromaticall Indian leafe, which (as* Plinie *and* Dioscorides *imagined) swimmes on pooles and ditches, without any apparent root; but our* Gerard *(of another opinion) sayes it is the leafe of a great tree growing in Arabia, and Cambaya, farre from the water side.*

Malace: f. *A storme, tempest, or ill weather, at sea.*

Malade: com. *Sicke, diseased, crazie, out of temper, ill at ease.*

Elle est malade. *Said of a woman that hath her flowers.*

A l'œil malade la lumiere nuit: Pro. *Looke* Oeil.

La mort n'a point d'ami, le malade n'a qu'un demy: Prov. *The dead man hath no friends, the sicke no true ones.*

Point ne faut demander à malade s'il veut santé: Prov. *An answer for those busie bodies, that cast many doubts, and make many questions, in cases alreadie resolued on.*

Maladerie: f. *An Hospitall, or Spittle for the diseased; also, the sicke-mans ward in any Hospitall.*

Maladie: f. *A maladie, sicknesse, disease.*

Maladie de S. Iean. *The falling sicknesse.*

Maladie S. Main. *Mangines, an itching leprosie; the wild Scab.*

Maladie de S. Mathurin. *Frenzie, extreame follie, madnesse.*

Les maladies viennent a cheval, & s'en retournent à pied: Pro. *Diseases come a horsebacke, and returne on foot.*

De grande maladie vient on bien en grande santé: Prov. *From a long sicknesse a lasting health.*

Tard medicine est apprestée à maladie enracinée: Prov. *Sicknesse once rooted, all Phisicke comes too late.*

Maladif: m. iue: f. *Sicklie, crazie, queasie, distempered, ill disposed of bodie, subiect vnto sicknesse, apt to take diseases.*

Maladré: m. ée: f. *Infected with a scurfe, or leaprosie.* Rab.

Mal-adroict: m. cte: f. *Vnwieldie, aukward, vnwheeme; vnapt, improper, vnfit; vnseemelie, vnhandsome, vncomelie, without any manner of grace, decorum, or decencie.*

Maladvis: m. *Misaduise, vnaduisednesse, indiscretion, inconsideration, rashnesse.*

Maladvisé: m. ée: f. *Ill aduised, vnaduised, vnwise, improuident, heedlesse, inconsiderate, vndiscreet.*

Malaginer. *To mingle, or incorporate seuerall things (especially mettalls) together.*

Malagine: m. *A mollifying plaister for scabs, and hard impostumes.*

Mal-aigre. *A kind of wormes that breed in a Hawkes gorge.*

Malaisance: f. *Vneasinesse, hardnesse, difficultie, trouble.*

Malaise: f. *Disease, paine, trouble, disquiet.*

Malaisé: m. ée: f. *Vneasie, troublesome, difficult, hard.*

Malaisé a desmesler. *Intricate, perplexed, much intangled.*

Malaisé de sa personne. *Vnwieldie.*

Malaisement. *Vneasily, difficultly, hardly, not lightly, with much paine, with great adoe.*

Malaiser. *To disease, trouble, disquiet, perplex.*

Malandres: m. *The Malanders; (a horses disease.)*

Malandrin: m. *A cassed souldior without pay, or imployment.*

Malarmat: m. *A kind of rough-skaled Gurnard, which being aliue is red, but dying, of another colour.*

Malart: m. *A Mallard, or wild Drake.*

Mal-avenant. *Vncomelie, ill fitting, vnhandsome, ill suiting, vnseemelie; rude, vnciuile, vnmannerlie, ill behaued.*

Malaventure: f. *Misaduenture, misfortune, disaster, mishap, mischance.*

Bon guet chasse malaventure: Prov. *Hee that would euer be well must euer looke well about him.*

Malavisé. *Looke* Maladvisé.

Malaxé: m. ée: f. *Mixed, blent, and beaten together; also, kneaded, handled, or wrought with the hands, vntill it be soft.*

Malaxer. *To blend, and beat together, as egges; also, to soften, work, or knead vnto a softnesse, to handle a thing vntill it be soft.*

Mal-basti: m. *An ill fauoured, or vnfashioned fellow; one that hath neither manners, nor good making.*

Mal-cindré: m. ée: f. *Ill supported, weakely vnderpropped (by a weake, or ill-made Centrie.)*

Malcontent. *The name of a game at Cards.*

Malcontent. *Malecontent, moodie, discontent, melancholicke, angrie, displeased.*

Mal-contentement: m. *Malecontentednesse, discontentment, grudging, vnwillingnesse.*

Malcus: m. *A Fauchion, Hangar, Wood-knife.*

Male: f. *A Male, or great Budget.*

Sans cela il estoit troussé en male. *Without that he had beene trussed, or twitcht vp.*

Male: com. *as* Masle.

Maleable. *as* Malleable.

Male-bosse: f. *A pestilent byle, or botch; a plague-sore.*

Maledicence: f. *Detraction, reuiling, ill speech, hard censure, opprobrious words.*

Malediction: f. *A malediction, curse, banning, imprecation, execration.*

Malefaçon: f. *An absurditie, illfauorednesse, ill manner.*

Malefaçons des procez. *Faults committed in pleading.*

Malefice: m. *A mischiefe; offence, great fault, naughtie deed, ill act, lewd part, bad pranke; also, a charme (whereby hurt is done;) mischieuous witcherie.*

Maleficié: m. ée: f. *Deformed, disfigured, maymed, weakened, disabled, defectiue, by nature, enchauntment, or other accident; vnable to performe nuptiall rites.*

Male-grace. *Looke* Malgrace.

Maleir. *as* Mauldire; *(an old word.)*

Malement. *Ill, badly, lewdly, naughtily, mischieuously, shrewdly, sorely, hardly, hurtfully.*

Malencontre: m. *Mischance, misfortune, mishap, misaduenture, calamitie, disaster, bad successe.*

Malencontreux: m. euse: f. *Vnfortunate, successlesse, dismall, ominous, ill lucke bringing.*

Malendre: f. *The Malanders (of horses.)*

Malendurant. *Tichie, impatient.*
Malengin: m. *Fraud, guile, craft, subtiltie, deceit, cousenage, trumperie, cautele, treacherie, circumuention, double-dealing, ill-meaning.*
Malengineux: m. euse: f. *Deceitfull, fraudulent, cousening, ouer-reaching, false, double, trecherous.*
Malengroin: m. *Sullennesse, powting, surlynesse, a soure looke.*
Mal-enthalenté: m. ée: f. *Maliciously affected, ill-minded.*
Maleole. *as* Malleole.
Malesuade: f. *Hunger (because it persuades but ill.)*
Malesüade: f. *A sweating paine, or sicknesse.*
Maletoste: f. *An extraordinarie tax, or subsidie leuied the yeare* 1296 *by* Philip le bel; viz. *(at first) the value of the hundreth, (and afterwards) of the fiftieth part of all, either lay-mens, or clergie-mens, goods; hence also, any imposition, exaction, taxation.*
Maletote. *The same; or, as* Maltote.
Maletoulte. *as* Maletoste; *(called so, because held as* Mal tollue.*)*
Maletoultier: m. *A collector of taxes, or subsidies; a toll-gatherer.*
Malette: f. *A little male; a budget, or scrip.*
Malette de bergier. *A Shepheards scrip; also, the hearbe Shepheards purse, pouch, or scrip; called otherwise Toywort, Caseweed, Pickpurse, and poore mans Parmacetie.*
Malfaict: m. *A misdeed, fault, offence, trespasse, transgression, abuse, bad act, lewd tricke, foule part, naughtie pranke.*
Malfaicteur: m. *A malefactor, offendor, transgressor, trespasser, guiltie person.*
Malfaisant. *Lewd, wicked, offending, faultie, naughtie, culpable; shrewd, mischieuous, harmefull, hurtfull.*
Mal-feable: com. *Weake, or in whom there's no good trusting.*
Malgisant. *A maisterlesse man; or, such a one as hauing no home to take vnto, is often sped with a very bad lodging; also, a fellow of ill behauior, or lewd conuersation; a naughtie-packe.*
Malgrace: f. *Disfauor, displeasure, bad acceptance, ill opinion; anger, blame, or hate incurred.*
Malhabile: com. *Vnable, vnwieldie, vnapt, vnfit, sleight, weake, disabled, without vigor.*
Malhardi: m. ie: f. *Dastardlie, cowardlie, faint-hearted, white-liuered, vnmanlie, fearefull, timerous.*
Malheur: m. *Mishap, misfortune, mischance, aduersitie, disaster, calamitie, miserie.*
Malheur ne dure pas tousiours: Pro. *Ill lucke doth not alwayes last.*
Malheur ne vient iamais seul: Prov. *Mischances neuer come single; one misfortune succeeds in the necke of another.*
'A quelque chose malheur est bon: Prov. *Tis an ill wind that blowes no man to good.*
Pour neant recule qui malheur attend: Prov. *In vaine he giues backe that lookes for ill lucke.*
Vn fol cerche son malheur: Prov. *The foole by prying finds himselfe vnhappie; or, The prying foole meets with his owne mishap.*
Malheure. à la mal. *Vnluckily, vnhappily, vnfortunately, disasterously, in an euill houre.*
Malheurer. *To mischieue, afflict, make vnhappie, inflict miseries, lay calamities, on.*
Malheureté: f. *as* Malheur.
Malheureusement. *Vnhappily, vnluckily, vnfortunately, sinisterly, disasterously, miserably.*
Malheureux: m. euse: f. *Vnhappie, vnluckie, sinister, crosse, vnfortunate, vnprosperous, disastrous, miserable, wretched.*
Plus malheureux que le bois dont on fait le gibet. *More vnhappie then the wood of a Gibbet.*
Malheustre: f. *The pinion of a birds wing.*
Malice: f. *Guile, deceit, cousenage, trumperie, treacherie, knauerie, falsehood, shifting; malice, mischieuousnesse, ill meaning; a bad fetch, wicked sleight, lewd deuice.*
Homme ne connoit mieux la malice que l'Abbé qui a esté moine: Pro. *No man is better seene in knauerie then an Abbot that hath beene a Monke.*
Malicieusement. *Deceitfully, craftily, guilefully, falsely, treacherously; maliciously, despightfully, mischieuously, knauishly, with an ill meaning, with a bad intent.*
Malicieux: m. euse: f. *Deceitfull, craftie, cousening, false, treacherous; despightfull, malicious; knauish, mischieuous.*
Malier: m. *A Male-horse, Trunke-horse, or Sumpter-horse; he that carries the Cloake-bag.*
Maligne: f. *A Spring-tyde; called so by the Salters of* Xaintonge.
Maligne. *The feminine of* Maling.
Malignement. *Malignantly, maliciously; lewdly, wickedly, naughtily, shrewdly, knauishly, mischieuously; of set (and with a bad) purpose.*
Malignité: f. *Malignitie; malice prepensed, purposed villanie; mischiefe intended vnto; ill-will, grudge, despight; wickednesse, lewdnesse, naughtinesse, knauishnesse.*
Maling: m. maligne: f. *Malignant, ill-willie, grudge-bearing, despightfull, malicious; knauish, hurtfull, shrewd, villanous; naughtie, lewd, vicious, delighting in mischiefe.*
Malingre. Pomme de mal. *A sowrish apple, tearmed, the Maligar apple.*
Malingre: com. *Sore, scabbie, ouglie, loathsome.*
Malivole: com. *Maleuolent, maleuolous, ill-willie, malicious, despightfull, churlish, dogged, currish, repining at, ill minded vnto, fraught with rancour, full of hatred.*
Malleable: com. *Mallable, tractable, hammerable, plyant to the hammer, which may be wrought or beaten with the hammer.*
Malleation: f. *A hammering.*
Mallece. Molossus; *the dregs, or coursest, of Sugar.*
Mallement. *Greatly, much, mightily, a vile or filthie deale.*
Malleole: f. *The ankle, or ankle-bone; also, a veine that runnes along vpon the ankle.*
Malletier: m. ere: f. *Bearing, or belonging to, a male, budget, or wallet.*
Mallette. *as* Malette.
Malmené. *as* Maumené. *Misused, &c.*
Malobatre: m. *as* Malabatre.
Malot: m. *A little Boare.* ¶ Norm.
Malotru: m. uë: f. *Forlorne, wretched, wofull, miserable.*
Vn povre malotru. *A poore snake.*
Malpatient de. *Impatient of.*
Mal-plaisant. *Vnpleasing, vnacceptable, rude, lumpish, vnmannerlie, without grace, without fashion.*
Mal-sain: m. aine: f. *Vnholesome; sicklie, crazie, vnhealthie.*
Malseance: f. *Vncomelinesse, vnseemelinesse, vnhandsomenesse, illfauorednesse.*
Mal-talent: m. *Despight; ill will; anger gotten, disfauor incurred.*

Maltassé: m. ée: f. *Indigested, ill-piled, ill-fauouredly made vp, vnorderly hudled or iumbled together.*
Maltaulte. *as* Maletoste.
Maltaultier: m. *A Collector of the Subsidie, a Toll-gatherer.*
Maltote. *as* Maletoste; *or as*;
Mal-toute: f. *An exaction, imposition, toll; a new, or extraordinarie taxation.*
Maltraictement: m. *Hard dealing, bad intertainment, rudenesse, harshnesse, inciuilitie, crueltie.*
Malvaisie: f. *The wine Malmesie.*
Malubec: m. *The falling sicknesse; tearmed so in some parts of* Languedoc.
Malvedi: m. *A small Spanish coyne, six whereof are scarcely worth an English pennie.*
Mal-versation: f. *Misdemeanor, misbehauior, ill conuersation, lewd carriage.*
Malverser en son office. *To behaue himselfe ill in his office.*
Mal-vestu: m. uë: f. *Ill-clothed; ragged, or bare, in array.*
Les mal-vestus devers le vent: Prov. (*Like our*) *the weakest to the wall; those that worst may are euer put to the worst.*
Malvoisie: f. *Malmesie.*
Malvoisin: m. ine: f. *Of Malmesie.*
Malusité: m. ée: f. *Ill-fashioned, ill-mannered; rude, that hath not beene in much good companie; also, raw, vnexperienced, ignorant, a nouice.*
Malvueillance: f. *Malice, ill-will; hatred; pleasure taken in the misfortunes of another.*
Malvueillant. *Maleuolent, malignant, malicious; that beareth a grudge, or oweth ill will, vnto; that ioyeth in the miseries of another.*
Mamaluc: m. *A Mamaluke, or light-horseman (in the Syrian, and Arabian tongues;) The Mamalukes were an order of valiant horsemen in the last Empire of Egypt.*
Mamaye: f. *A great Indian Peach whereof a kind of Marmalade is made.*
Mambour, & Mambourg: m. *A Captaine; also, the Gouernour of a Prouince; also, the Gardian of an infant, protector of a widow, &c.*
Mambournie: f. *as* Main-bournie.
Mameluë. *See* Mammeluë.
M'amie: f. *My friend, loue, deere.*
Ma belle m'amie. *My prettie Pug (so fooles, hugging their bables, tearme them.)*
Par saincte m'amie. *In stead of,* Par saincte Marie. ¶Rab.
Mamillaire: com. *Of, or belonging to the breasts, paps, or dugs.*
Additions mamillaires. *That part of the braine which lyes next to the nose, and where the sence of smelling begins.*
Procez mamillaires. *Looke* Procés.
Mammal: m. ale: f. *Belonging to the breasts, or paps.*
Veine mammale. *Seeke* Veine.
Mammam. (*The voice of infants*) *Mam.*
Mammeaux: m. *A kind of Panick.*
Mammelette: f. *A little dug, breast, vdder.*
Mammeleux: m. euse: f. *Of, or belonging to, the dugs; also, hauing great dugs.*
Mammelle: f. *A dug, breast, pap; vdder.*
Mammellement. *Duggishly, breast-fashion, pap-like.* ¶Rab.
Mammelon: m. *The niple, or teat of a dug.*
Mammelons. *Be certaine little, red, hard, vlcerie, and teat like swellings, which breake out of the skin of the head, and yeeld a whayish, or waterish humor.*
Mammelu. *as* Mammeleux.
Mammeluch. *as* Mamaluc.
Mammeluë: f. *A fooles bable; so tearmed, because ordinarily it is made to resemble a laughing, and fat woman.*
Mammeron. *as* Mammelon.
Mammillaire. *Seeke* Mamillaire.
Mammuque: f. *A winglesse bird, of an vnknowne beginning, and after death not corrupting; she hath feet a hand long, & so light a bodie, so long feathers, that she is continually carried in the ayre, whereon she feeds; some call her the bird of Paradice, but erroniously; for that hath wings, and differs in other parts from this.*
Manable: com. *Habitable; which may be inhabited, or dwelt in.*
Manance: f. *A dwelling, abiding, inhabiting in.*
Manant: m. *A dweller, abider, inhabiter, or inhabitant; properly such a one as dwells where he was borne; also, a boore, clowne, hinde, husbandman, countrey fellow.*
Manat: m. *A monstrous Indian fish that resembles an Oxe, and hath a flat backe, and a verie thicke skin.*
Manbourg. *as* Mambour.
Mancelles: f. *Great Iron rings whereby the thill-horse &c, is fastened vnto a cart.*
Manche: m. *The haft, helue, or handle of a toole; also, the necke of a musicall Instrument; also, a mans toole.*
Le manche d'une charruë. *A Plough-tayle, or handle; the Plough-hale.*
Le manche d'un espieu. *The staffe of a Bore-speare.*
Vn manche d'estrille. *A dwarfe, elfe, dandiprat, low scrub.*
Manche de rasoir. Vn nez faict à manche de raisoir. *A Hawke-nose.*
Bransler au manche. *To shake in the helue, to be vnsetled in heart.*
Iecter le manche apres la coignée. *To increase a misfortune by desperate carelesnesse; vpon the losse of some to forgoe all.*
De l'arbre d'un pressoir le manche d'un Cernoir: Prov. Looke Cernoir.
Manche: f. *A sleeue; also, a long narrow bag (such as Hypocras is made in;) also, a flat, and large furnace, made somewhat like an Ouen, and vsed for the melting of mettall new come out of the Mine; also, a sleeuenet, a narrow and long fish-net; also, a sleeue-like narrowing of the sea betweene two lands; whence;*
La manche d' Angleterre. *Saint Georges channell.*
Manche de cousteau. *The Pitot; a long, and round shell-fish.*
Manche Lombarde. *Seeke* Lombard.
La manche de la parece. *The Bellfrey.* ¶Poictevin.
Manches de deux paroisses. *Sleeues of two parishes; viz. whereof the vpper part is of one stuffe, and the nether of another.*
C'est bien vn autre paire de manches. *This is another manner of matter.*
C'estoit du temps qu' on se mouchoit encor à la manche. *It was in the dayes of simplicitie, or ignorance; it was at a time when people either knew not, or cared not for good manners.*
Ils luy torchent le nez de sa manche. *They wipe his nose with his owne sleeue; they doe him a pleasure, but tis with the helpe of his owne meanes.*

Manché: m. **ée**: f. *Hafted, belued.*
Manchereau: m. *A little haft, or handle.*
Les manchereaux d' la charruë. *The plough-handles, or plough-hales.*
Mancheron: m. *A bracelet, or bracer; also, a halfe-sleeue, or wrist-sleeue; a sleeue that couers the arme from the elbow to the wrist.*
Mancherons de robbes. *The hanging halfe-sleeues of some fashioned gownes.*
Manchette: f. *A cuffe, or hand-ruffe.*
Manchon: m. *as* Mancheron; *also, a Snuffkin; also, a scarfe, bracelet, or other such like fauour worne vpon the sleeue, or arme in publike shewes, and assemblies.*
Manchon d'hermines. *A Maniple charged, or powdered, with Ermines.*
Manchot: m. **otte**: f. *Lame, that hath but one hand, that wanteth a limme.*
Manciper. *To dispossesse himselfe, to deliuer the possession, or make liuerie and seisin, of; to sell, passe away, giue vp.*
Mand. *as* Mandement. *An old word.*
Mandat: m. *A Mandate, or* Mandamus *for the preferment of one to a Benefice.*
Mandataire: m. *A Mandatarie; one that comes to a Benefice by a* Mandamus.
Mande. *as* Manne; *a Maund.* ¶Pic.
Mandé: m. **ée**: f. *Commaunded; sent, or called for; bid come; directed; appointed, charged.*
Mandegloire: f. *Mandrake; See* Mandragore.
Mandement: m. *A sending, or calling for; also, a charge, bidding, or commaundement; a Mandate,* Mandamus, *Commission, Warrant, Appointment.*
Mander. *To bid, or command; to call by commandement; to send, send for, send word of; to charge, or appoint.*
'A rien mander il ne faut point de messager; *(a flowting answer for such as say,* Me voulez vous rien mander.)
'A main lavée Dieu mande la repeuë: Prov. *The heauens powre downe their blessings on th' vpright.*
'A toile ordie Dieu mande le fil: Prov. *God furthers their indeauors that take paines.*
Mandibules: f. *The iawes.*
Mandication: f. *as* Manducation.
Mandil: m. *A Mandilian, or loose Cassocke.*
Mandille: f. *as* Mandil.
Mandole: f. *A Cackarell (fish.)*
Mandore: f. *A Kitt, small Gitterne, or instrument resembling a small Gitterne.*
Mandosiane: f. *A broad (and old-fashioned) short-sword.*
Mandoussiane. *The same.*
Mandragore: f. *Mandrake, Mandrage, Mandragon; whereof there be two kinds.*
Mandragore femelle. *The female, or blacke Mandrake, beares a darke greene leafe, and a long apple; but is otherwise like vnto;*
Mandragore masle. *Male Mandrake, white Mandrake, which beareth a round apple.*
Mandre: f. *The Cell of a Monke, or Hermit; also, a bouell, or shedd; a stall, or foddering place, for beasts, in the fields.*
Mandregloire. *as* Mandragore.
Manducation: f. *An eating, or chawing, a grinding, or champing with the teeth.*
Manducité: f. *Great eating.* ¶Rab.
Manée: f. *A small vessell, or measure, whereof* 96 *make but one* Minot.
Droict de manée de sel. *That measure-full vpon euerie horse-load of salt brought into* Bourges, *and of euerie one that sells any salt in* Bourges; *due to the Abbot, and Couent of* S. Sulpice.
Manege: m. *The manage, or managing of a horse.*
Manequin: m. *A little, open, wide-mouthed, and narrow bottomd Panier, or Maund, vsed for the carrying both of victualls, and of earth; also, a Puppet; (See* Mannequin;) *also, a rude instrument of Musicke; whence;*
Iouër des cymbales, & manequins. *To leacher.*
Iouër des manequins à basses marches. *The same.*
Manequinage: m. *Anticke ingrauerie, or caruing, in Wainscot, or Stone-worke.*
Manette: f. *A small hand; also, a manacle, or hand-fetter.*
Maneuvre. *as* Manouvrier.
Manganese: f. *A certaine minerall which being melted with glasse, amends the colour thereof; there is also good blue, or or blacke enamell made of it.*
Mangé: m. **ée**: f. *Eaten, fed on.*
Il a mangé le lard. *He onely is guiltie of the theft, or cousenage.*
'A la fin sçaura on qui a mangé le lard. *The theefe will at length be discouered.*
Qui a mangé le lard ronge l'os. *He that hath eaten the sweet shall tast of the soure: or, let him that hath gotten the best goe away with the worst.*
C'est trop mangé d'un pain en vn lieu. *Wee haue stayed too long in a place, or stood too much on one matter.*
Il a mangé de la biche blanche. *Looke* Biche.
Il a mangé les pigeonneaux. *Said of one whose voice being hoarse, hath some resemblance with their cry.*
Il a mangé de la vache enragée. *Looke* Manger.
Mangeaille: f. *Meat, food, sustenance, victualls.*
Mangeaille pour les pourceaux. *Swillings, washings, draffe, Hogs-wash.*
Il luy a baillé logis pour mangeaille. *He hath assigned him a house to eat, or to dresse & spend his meat, in.*
Mangeant. *Eating, feeding, falling to his victualls.*
En mangeant l'appetit se perd: Prov. *Eating and drinking will take away any mans stomacke.*
En mangeant l'appetit vient: Pro. *(Sometimes) the more one eats the more he may.*
Bonne beste s'eschauffe en mangeant: Prov. *A good beast heates it selfe while it eates; viz. eates hard, feeds heartily.*
Mangeatif: m. **iue**: f. *Eatable; which may be, or is fit to be, eaten.*
Mangemerde: f. *The name of a fish thats otherwise called,* Saupe.
Mangeoire: f. *A manger; also, the gullet, or swallow.*
Manger: m. *Meat, food, sustenance, belly-timber, victualls, eating stuffe.*
Chair de mouton manger de glouton; Prov. *Looke* Mouton.
Manger. *To eat, feed, take sustenance or nourishment, fall to his victualls.*
Il mange bien. *He is a daintie feeder, or, he keepes good meat in his house.*
Manger son avoine en son sac. *as in* Avoine; *or, as* Manger son pain en son sac.
Manger son bled en herbe. *To wast his reuenue before it come in.*
Manger le cochon ensemble. *To complot, conspire, ioyne in a practise, conclude an enterprise, together: (Belike from some notable meeting of conspirators, whereat Pigs-flesh was their best, or onely fare.)*

Manger les doigts: Vous en mangeriez vos doigts à force de lecher.) *You would licke your lips after them.*

Manger avec vne faim de biscuit. *To rauine, or eat verie greedily.*

Manger à vn grain de sel. *To eat a man at a mouthfull (the cracke of a braggadochio;) also, to eat his meat hastily, or greedily, without staying for any sawce, or seasoning, other then a corne of salt will yeeld him.*

Manger son pain blanc le premier. *To spend his best abilities (in estate, or bodie) on his youth, and leaue naught but wants, and weakenesse for old age.*

Manger son pain en son sac. *To snudge it, or munchion alone in a corner; to conceale, obscure, or spend priuately his goods, good things, or parts, that others may haue no part of them with them.*

Manger des pois verds au veau. *Looke* Veau.

Manger de la vache enragée. Il a mangé de la, &c. *He is reduced vnto a great necessitie, or extremitie; he is in a miserable taking; also, he hath endured much hardnesse, or (as we say) drunke of many waters.*

Donner à manger au chien, & au chat. *To maintaine hospitalitie, to keepe a plentifull house.*

Il est à table, & n'ose manger; (*Applyable to a miserable spare-good.*)

Il sçait plus que son pain manger. *He is no child, no nouice, no babe; he knowes more wayes to the wood then one.*

A qui chapon mange chapon luy vient: Pro. *Spend and God will send.*

Aller & parler peut on, boire ensemble & manger non: Prov. *Such as desire to continue a friend, must not feed on him; or, tis better to visit a friend sometimes then to dwell with him euer.*

Brebis contées mange bien le loup: Pro. *See* Loup.

Ce qu'on donne luit, ce qu'on mange puit: Prov. *Th' effects of bountie shine, of eating smell.*

Il fait mauvais aller au bois quand les loups se mangent l'un l'autre: Prov. *See* Loup.

Il ne faut pas manger des Cerises avec les grands seigneurs: Prov. *Meane men are not to eat cherries (viz. are not to be verie familiar) with great Lords; least the stones of the best flye faster at their eyes then (their portion) the worst into their mouthes. (Much alike whereunto, is;)*

Il ne faut pas manger des prunes avec son Seigneur: Prov.

Les gros poissons mangent les menus: Pro. *Poore men are (easily) supplanted by the rich, the weake by the strong, the meane by the mightie.*

Mauvaise est la saison quand vn loup mange l' autre: Prov. *See* Loup.

On se saoule bien de manger tartes: Prov. *A man may take too much of a good thing.*

Peu à peu le loup mange l'oye: Prov. *By little and little the Wolfe eates vp the Goose.*

Qui mange l'oye du Roy il en chie la plume cent ans apres: Prov. *Looke* Oye.

Qui a honte de manger a honte de vivre: Pro. *He thats ashamed to eat is ashamed to liue.*

Qui avec son seigneur mange poires il ne choisist pas des meilleures: Pro. *He that eates Peares with his Lord either cannot, or should not, pick such as he likes.*

Qui se fait brebis le loup le mange: Prov. *He that makes himselfe simple shall be sillily vsed.*

Vn seigneur de paille mange vn vassal d'acier: Pro. *A Lord of straw deuoures a vassall of steele.*

Mangerie: f. *Gluttonie, rauening, deuouring, hastie or greedie feeding; also, a roome, or house to eat in.*

Faire mangerie avec. *To eat, or keepe house with.*

Mangeson: f. *An itch.*

Mange-sujet. *A fit Epithite for a Tyrant.*

Mangeves: f. *Maste, Akornes; any thing that wild Swine vsually feed on.*

Mangeur: m. *An eater, feeder, glutton, rauener.*

Mangeur de charrettes ferrées. *A notable kill-cow, monstrous huff-snuff, terrible swaggerer; one that will kill all he meets, and eat all he kills.*

Mangeur de crucifix. *A notorious hypocrite; one who to seeme the more holie, is euer kissing of a Crucifix.*

Hardi gaigneur hardi mangeur: Prov. *The better one falls to his meat, the better he followes his worke.*

Mangeure: f. *The feeding of wild Bores, &c.*

Mangeurs. Qui estoient (jadis) ordonnez, & envoyez en garnison pour contraindre vn obligé au payement de son deu, ou vn condamné à souffrir l' execution d' un Arest, ou d'un mandement; & iusques à ce l'on vivoit en sa maison, & en ses biens, à ses despens. ¶Ragueau.

Mangonel: m. *as* Mangonneau.

Mangonisme: m. *The craft of pampering, trimming, or setting out of saleable things.*

Mangonne: f. *A Brokers wife, or brokerlie woman.*

Mangonneau: m. *An old-fashioned Sling, or Engine, whereout stones, old yron, and great arrowes were violently darted.*

Mangonner. *To pamper, trimme, sleeke, or set out vnto the eye sale things; also, to mangle, or disfigure by mangling.*

Mangouri: m. *A base Turkish coyne, whereof sixteene doe little more then counteruayle our pennie.*

Manguiere: f. *A great-headed, and short-stalked nayle vsed about ships.*

Maniable: com. *Tractable, wieldable, handleable, handsome, tollerable, passable.*

Maniacle. *as* Maniaque.

Maniance: f. *A managing, handling, wielding.*

Maniaque: com. *Mad, franticke, raging, furious, outragious, braine-sicke, bedlam-like.*

Morelle maniaque. Seeke Morelle.

Manicles. *Manacles, hand-fetters, or gyues.*

Manicordion: m. *An (old-fashioned) Claricord.*

Manie: f. *Madnesse, furie, rage (by too great abundance of good bloud intoxicating the head.)*

Manié: m. ée: f. *Handled, handed, wielded, managed, often touched, or vsed.*

Manié de fortune. *Afflicted, or persecuted by fortune, fallen into miserie, come to decay.*

Maniement: m. *A handling, managing, wielding, vsing, (often) touching.*

Maniement de sa personne. *The carriage of his person.*

Manier. *To handle, hand, manage, wield, vse, touch.*

Manier en bisse. *Looke* Bisse.

Manier tresbien ses harpes. *To stirre his fingers verie nimbly, or, to play a clenlie tricke of legerdemain.*

Maniere: f. *A manner, fashion, forme, kind, sort; a custome, vse, wont, guise; a course, order, stile; condition.*

Par maniere de dire. *As it were, as one should say.*

Manieur: m. *A handler, manager, wielder, vser, toucher of.*

Manieur de sable. *A Moulder, or caster of Medalls, or prints in sand.*

Manifacture: f. *Manifacture, workemanship, handie-worke.*

Manifacturé: m. ée: f. *Wrought, or done with the hands.*

Manifacturer. *To worke, or frame with the hands.*

Manifeste: m. *A manifestation, or declaration; also, as* la partie honteuse; *vnder* Honteux.

Manifeste: com. *Manifest, apparent, euident, notorious, open, knowne, publicke, plaine, cleere, vndoubted, certaine.*

Manifesté: m. ée: f. *Manifested, made apparent, published, divulged, discouered, detected, reuealed, bewrayed.*

Manifestement. *Manifestly, apparently, openly, cuidently, publickly, vndoubtedly, certainly.*

Manifester. *To manifest; publish, declare, detect, reueale, bewray, discouer, make plaine, cleere, open, apparent.*

Manigance: f. *An ill-set countenance, an vnsetled fashion, an vnstaied or vnseemelie behauiour; also, couert dealing, priuate shuffling, secret practising or packing in a matter.*

Manigotter. *To handle, or finger much; busily to trim, dresse, or fold vp with the hands, as children doe their babies.*

Maniguet: m. *The spice called Graines, or graines of Paradise.*

Maniguette: f. *as* Maniguet.

Manille: f. *The handle of a pot, &c.*

Maniller: m. *A bracelet maker; also, one that in Popish Churches gathers for a poore Preacher.*

Manjore. *A manger.*

Maniot: m. *A certain root which, boiled, is good meat, but raw, poison.*

Manipule: m. *A gripe, fistfull, handfull of; a bundle, a bottle; also, a wrist-band; or, as* Manipulon.

Manipulon: m. *A Maniple, or Fannell; a scarfe-like ornament worne about the left wrist of a sacrificing Priest.*

Manivelle: f. *An instrument that goes with a vice, hauing at it end a hooke, whereby disioynted bones are set in their former places; also, the handle whereby a grindlestone, &c, is turned; and hence;*

Manivelles. *The braces wherby a windlesse, or windbeame is turned.*

Manne: f. *A maund, flasket, open basket, or pannier hauing handles; also, a veine of earth, or sand, which giueth some hope of gold to be found; also, Manna, or the deaw of heauen, gathered in hot countries from plants, and trees wherein it congeales, and reserued as a gentle purger of choler; whence;*

Manne de Calabre. *Calabrian Manna; the best, and most lasting Manna; the graines wherof be small, heauie, white, cleere, transparent, and verie sweet.*

Manne de Cotton. *Great graines of Manna resembling lockes of wooll, or bumbast; the worse kind of Leuant Manna, and the worst of all others.*

Manne d' Encens. *Graine, crummes, or mammockes of Incense falling from it while it is in loading.*

Manne de fueilles. *The best kind of Calabrian Manna, gathered from off the leaues of hearbes, and trees.*

Manne de Levant. *Leuant Manna; a second (generall) kind of Manna, inferiour in goodnesse to the Calabrian.*

Mannequin: m. *A little, open, wide-mouthed, and narrow-bottomed maund, flasket, or pannier; also, a little basket, leape-head, or weele, made of bullrushes, and vsed by fishermen; also, a Puppet, or Anticke; Looke* Manequin.

Mannequinage. *as* Manequinage.

Manneux: m. euse: f. *Belonging to a maund, resembling a maund.*

Manoir: m. *A Mansion, Mannor, or Mannor-house; the scite of a Mannor; a place, or chiefe dwelling place; also, a roome in a house.*

Manople: f. *A kind of long Gauntlet; or as* Manipulon.

Manotte: f. *A little hand, a childs hand.*

Manottes. *Manacles, hand-fetters, gyues.*

Manouvrer. *To hold, occupie, possesse; (an old Normand word.)*

Manouvrier: m. *A mechanicall workeman, or labourer, an artificer, or handicrafts-man.*

Manque: f. *Defect, lacke, want.*

Manque: com. *Defectiue, lacking, wanting; maimed, lame; declining, in the wane; also, lesse; whence;* Va-de manque. *Goe lesse, at Primero.*

Manquement: m. *Want, lacke, defect, need; or a wanting, lacking; declining, waning.*

Manquer. *To want, lacke, need, faile of, be defectiue.*

Manquer à sa parole. *To breake his word.*

Manquerot. *A maimed, or lame creature; one that wants some of his limmes.*

Mansais. Deniers, & solz mansais. *Be double the worth of* Deniers, *and* solz Tournois.

Mansart: m. *A Culuer, Cooshot, Ringdoue:* ¶ Pic.

Manselies. *as* Mancelles.

Mansionnier: m. *A dweller, inhabitant, abider; one that hath a mansion in a place.*

Mansuet: m. ete: f. *Gentle, courteous, meeke, mild, humble; tame, tractable.*

Mansuetement. *Gently, meekely, mildly, courteously, tractably.*

Mansuetude: f. *Gentlenesse, meekenesse, courtesie, mildnesse, tractablenesse, humilitie; tamenesse.*

Mante: f. *A mantle; also, as* Menthe.

Mante veluë. *A rug, rough mantle, Irish mantle.*

Manteau: m. *A cloke; also, the mantle-tree of a chimney.*

Le manteau d' vn cheval. *His haire, or coat.*

Les blancs manteaux. *An antient Order of begging Friers, for whom S. Lewis built a house, or Couent in Paris; afterwards giuen by Philip the Faire vnto the* Guillemins *(an Order of Hermits instituted by* Guillaume *Duke of* Guienne, *and Earle of* Poictou) *who yet retaine it, and with it this title.*

Droict de manteaux. *Cloke-money; Looke* Droict.

Pendre son manteau à foible cheville. *To require aduise of a foole, or almes of a begger; vainely to relie on weake helpes, or settle his resolution on a tottering foundation.*

Coeur content, & manteau sur l'espaule: Pro. *See* Coeur; *ou*, Content.

Fy de manteau quand il faict beau: Prov. *A cloke is but a comber in faire weather.*

Mantel: m. *as* Manteau.

Mantelé: m. ée: f. *Cloked; couered with a cloke; shielded, or shadowed vnder a mantelet.*

Manteler. *To cloke; to couer with a cloke; to defend, shroud, or shield, as vnder a mantelet.*

Mantelet: m. *A little mantle; also, a mouable penthouse, or shed of boords, vnder which souldiers approaching a rampire are shrowded, and defended from whatsoeuer is throwne downe by the besieged.*

Manteline : f. *A mantle, sleight robe, or cloke, worne loosse about the shoulders; also, a Friers weed, or habit.*

Manthe. *as* Mantre veluë.

Manticore : f. *A rauenous, and mankind Indian beast, that hath a face like a man, a bodie like a Lyon, and three rankes of verie sharpe teeth.*

Mantil : m. *A table-cloth.*

Mantin : m. *A kind of Prawne.*

Mantonel : m. *The catch of a doore.*

Mantonniere : f. *A chocke, or bob vnder the chinne; also, the chinne-peece of an helmet; also, a chinne-cloth, or the little peece of fine linnen wherewith a masked Ladie couers her chinne.*

Habillement de teste à mantonniere. *A caske, or an helmet hauing a chinne-peece.*

Manuel : m. *A Manuell; a portable (prayer) booke.*

Manuel : m. elle : f. *Manuell, handie, of the hand, wrought or done with the hands.*

Argent manuel. *Present money, readie coyne.*

Iustice manuelle. *That rights it selfe; Looke* Iustice.

Seing manuel. *Ones hand subscribed, marke or signe put to.*

Manuellement. bailler m. *To giue in hand, pay readie money, deliuer presently.*

Manufacture : f. *as* Manifacture.

Manumission : f. *A manumission, or dismissing; a freeing, infranchising, setting at libertie, deliuering from bondage.*

Manutenteur : m. *A maintainer, vpholder, protector, countenancer.*

Manutention : f. *as* Maintenance.

Mappemonde : f. *A map of the world.*

Mappule : f. *A little peece of Lawne wherewith the (Sacramentall) Pix is couered.*

Maquereau : m. *A Mackerell (fish;) also, a (man) bawd.*

Maquereaux. *Red scorches, or spots on the legs of such as vse to sit neere the fire.*

Maquereau bastard. *The bastard Mackerell; somewhat lesse, and lesse good, then the right one.*

Maquerelage : m. *The practise, or trade, of bawderie.*

Maquerelle : f. *A (woman) bawd; the solicitrix of lecherie.*

Maquerelleux : m. euse : f. *Full of bawderie, vsing the trade of bawderie, belonging to the bawdie art.*

Maquignon : m. *A Hucster, Broker, Horse-scourser, cousening Marchant.*

Maquignonnage : m. *Deceitfull brokage, bargaining for, or selling of, things; hence, also, the trade of horsscoursing.*

Maquignonner. *To play the Broker, or Horse-scourser, to deale deceitfully in bargaines; also, to play the bawd.*

Mar : m. harenc de mar. *A great, faire, fat, and full-rowed Herring.*

Marabais. *A kind of base coyne.*

Maraine : f. *A Godmother.*

Marais : m. *A marsh, or fenne; Looke* Marets.

Maramedi. *as* Maravedi.

Maran : m. *An Infidell, miscreant, Apostata, Renegado; a Christian circumcised, or Iew turned Christian; Looke* Marrane.

Marant. *as* Mareant.

Marasine : m. *A consumption in the highest degree; an extreame, or totall consumption; an exsiccation, or drying vp of the whole bodie.*

Marasmé : m. ée : f. *Wholly consumed, wasted, withered, exhausted, or drained of moisture.*

Marastre : f. *A stepdame, or stepmother.*

Qui a marastre a le Diable en l' atre : Prov. *He that hath a stepdame hath a Diuell to his dame.*

Marastresque. *Stepmother-like.*

Maraud : m. *A rogue, begger, vagabond; a varlet, rascall, scoundrell, base knaue.*

Maraudaille : f. *A packe of lowsie rogues, a crue of beggerly vagabonds; also, rascallitie, scoundrellisme.*

Maraude : f. *A begger-woman, great lazie queane, roguish hedge-whore, Tinkers-bitch.*

Marauder. *To beg, to play the rogue, or idle vagabond.*

Maraudise : f. *Beggerie, roguerie, idle knauerie, base vagabondrie.*

Maravedi : m. *A little Spanish coyne, whereof 34 make but the Royall, or* vj.d.sterl.

Marbre : m. *Marble.*

Marbre gentil. *The hard white marble, whereof statues, or images be commonly made.*

Marbre grené. *See* Grené.

Marbre Parien. *A marble of a whitish colour, which indures all weathers, and being polished hath a resemblance of flesh.*

Marbre serpentin. *A spotted marble, the ground whereof is darke greene, the spots light.*

Marbre Thebaïque. *Whereof there be two kinds; one of a grayish ground spotted with two or three sundrie colours; another blacke, and beautified with golden drops.*

Le marbre de soy n'a que faire de peinture : Prov. *A beautifull thing needs no luster, an excellent thing no commendation.*

Marbré : m. ée : f. *Marbled, of marble, with marble, like vnto marble.*

Pierre marbrée. *Any hard, or grained stone, which, as marble, may be smoothed, or polished.*

Marbreux : m. *Full of, or abounding with, marble.*

Marbrier : m. *A marble-cutter, one that worketh in marble.*

Marbriere : f. *A quarrey of marble.*

Marbrin : m. ine : f. *Of marble, resembling marble.*

Marc : m. *Marke (a mans name;) also, the mother, grounds, dregs, lees, bottome, or setlings of liquor; also, the grosse, or thicke substance that remains of things which haue beene squeezed, or strained; also, ground manured, or dunged for the next yeares tillage; (Looke the next marginall word.)*

Marc des raisins. *The mother of the grapes; the husks, hullings, or skins of grapes after the last pressing.*

Faire vn marc. *To put grapes into the presse; to make, or make readie, a pressing of grapes.*

Marc : m. *A Marke; halfe a pound, or eight ounces of gold, siluer, or Billon.*

Marc d' argent. *Is esteemed at* 10 l. Parisis *by the customes of* Melun; *and is due vnto a Lord for the right of Reliefe, and* Rachapt, *ouer and besides a yeares reuenew, if the land be valued at aboue* 20 l. Parisis.

Droict de Marc. *A Sol vpon euerie* Marc *of gold;* iij.d. *vpon euerie* Marc *of siluer; and* j.d. *vpon euerie* Marc *of Billon perfectly coyned, is the Prouost of the Mints fee, besides his ordinarie intertainment.*

Chargé a poids de marc. *Soundly charged, throughly loaden; (appliable to one that hath taken in his liquor freely.)*

Fiens de chien, & marc d' argent seront tout vn au iour de iugement : Prov. *See* Iugement.

Mar-

Marcanet: m. *A kind of riuer fowle.*
Marcasite. *as* Marcasite.
Marcassin: m. *A young wild boare; a shoot, or grice; also, a kind of minerall; whence;*
Marcassin iaulne. *Red vitrioll; or as* Marcasite.
Marcassite: f. *The Marcassite, or fire-stone; a minerall that smells like brimstone; and is of two kinds; the yellow, shining as gold; and the white (the purer, and better of the two) like siluer.*
Marcesche. *March corne, Summer Barlie, Summer corne.*
Marcez: m. *March corne, Summer corne, such as is sowed about March; as Barlie, Oats, &c.*
Marcgrave: m. *A Marquis.*
Marchage. Droict de marchage. *Looke vnder* Droict.
Marchal. *as* Mareschal.
Marchand: m. *A Marchant; a trader, a trafficker; also, an occupier, or tradesman; any shop-keeper that retailes, or sells wares of the better sort, as silkes, good clothes, or stuffes; whence;*
Marchand de soye. *A Silkeman.*
Souper de marchand *A large, or great supper.*
Vn marchand qui prend l' argent sans compter, ne peser. *A theefe.*
Se faire marchand de poisson la vieille de Pasques. *To enter into a profession when there is no vse of it; to doe any thing vnseasonably, or too late.*
Marchand qui ne gaigne perd: Prov. *The Marchant that gaines not looses; and yet;*
Il n'est pas marchand qui tousiours gaigne: Prov. *He trades not well that alwayes is a gainer.*
Marchand qui perd ne peut rire: Prov. *A Marchant loosing cannot laugh.*
Aujourd'huy marchant demain meschant: Prov. *To day a Trader to morrow a Traytor.*
Ou marchand ou larron: Prov. *Either a trader, or a stealer; See* Larron.
Bonne marchandise trouve tousiours son marchand: Prov. *Good chaffer cannot want a chapman.*
Marchand: m. ande: f. *Of, or belonging to, a Marchant, or Market; well traded, much vsed, verie common.*
Livre marchande. *See* Livre.
Papier marchand *Browne, or blotting, paper.*
Place marchande. *The market place, or place of ordinarie bargaining, and paiments; any free place where men may meet on euen tearmes; whither any man that lists may come; or where a man, while he lists, may stay.*
Poids marchand. *Looke* Poids.
Marchandé: m. ée: f. *Cheapened, bought and sold, bargained, coped, or agreed for; also, houered, or stood aloofe from; braued, affronted, or dealt with afarre off; also, delayed, or trifled out, as the time, for an aduantage, or through feare.*
Marchandement. *As a Marchant, Marchant-like.*
Marchander. *To trafficke, trade, play the Marchant, buy and sell; to cheapen, bargaine, cope, or agree for; also, to delay, or trifle out the time; also, to houer or stand aloofe from; to braue, or deale with, afarre off (before a closing) either circumspectly and for aduantage, or cowardly and in feare.*
Marchander la peine d' aucun. *To hire one to doe his worke.*
Ils marchandent à se tourner. *They be readie, or about, to turne.*
Sans marchander. *Presently, instantly, readily, out of hand, without any paultring, haggling, or standing on the matter.*
Marchandise: f. *Marchandise, commodities, ware, chaffer, stuffe; also, trading, trafficking, bargaining, occupying, buying and selling, mechanicall commerce, or negociation.*
Marchandise de gueule. *Victualls.*
Marchandise Latine. *The best ware, or choicest stuffe, called so by Marchants.*
Demener marchandise. *To trade, or tumble ouer commodities.*
Marchandise n'espargne nuls: Prov. *The Marchants ware bids men beware, for he will gaine by his father; or, Marchandise holds no friendship, yeelds no fauour, hath no consideration but of gaine.*
Marchandise qui plaist est à demy venduë: Prov. *Please the eye, and picke the purse; or, content the eye, your bargaine is halfe made.*
Bonne marchandise trouve tousiours son Marchand: Prov. *Good ware is euer furnished with chapmen; or, finds euer store of customers.*
On n'a jamais bon marché de mauvaise marchandise: Prov. *One can neuer haue ill ware cheap ynough; or, his bargaine is not cheape that hath ill ware for his money.*
Marchant. *as* Marchand.
Marchant. *Marching, stepping, treading, going, walking, pacing, footing it.*
Marché: m. *A Market; Marketstead, or Market place; also, a bargaine, or match.*
Bon marché; & grand marché. *Good cheape, dog cheape, a low rate, a reasonable price; whence;*
Bon marché tire l'argent de la bourse: Prov. *No pickepurse to a cheape commoditie.*
Il n' aura ia bon marché qui ne le demande: Prov. *Those that require not, haue not, things good cheape.*
On n'a jamais bon marché de mauvaise marchandise: Prov. *For naughtie ware no price is low ynough.*
Le vin du marché. *Looke* Vin.
`A l' hostel priser, & au marché vendre: Prov. *Value at home, but sell in the market.*
On ne s'en va pas des foires comme du marché: *The case is not alike; for at Faires they pay toll, in Markets none.*
Si le fol n'alloit au marché on ne vendroit pas la mauvaise denrée: Prov. *If fooles went not to Markets bad wares would not be sold; (So fooles are sometimes good for something.)*
Marche: f. *A region, coast, or quarter; also, a march, frontire, or border of a countrey; also, a greece, the step of a staire; also, a step, the footing or print of a foot; also, a march, or marching of souldiers; also, a Virginall, or Organ, key; also, the finger-boord of a Violl.*
Basses marches. *Pedalls; the low keyes of some Organs to be touched with the feet; whence;*
Iouër des manequins à basses marches. *To leacher; and;*
Tenir des basses marches. *To hold of the smocke, or, his wife to be his master.*
Doubles marches. *Rests, or breathing steps; the broad steps of a halfe-pace staire.*
Enjamber sur les marches d'autruy. *To vsurpe, incroach on, or meddle with, another mans right.*
Marché: m. ée: f. *Marched, walked, paced, stepped, troden, gone; proceeded in, or on.*
Marchement: m. *A marching, walking, pacing, stepping, treading, proceeding.*

Marche-pied: m. *A foot-stoole; also, a step, low stoole or bench, that helpes one to get vpon a higher thing.*

'A marche-pied. *A fashion of fishing, wherin one goes stamping in the water, and carries before him (or another for him) a halfe bow-net.*

Marcher: m. *A pace, gate, walke, tread, stepping, going, footing.*

Marcher. *To march, goe, pace, walke, tread, step, foot it; to proceed; also, as* Marchiser.

Marche cela Iaquet. *Tread out you flattering rogue; a phrase vsed in contempt of a base obseruant parasite, who serues for nothing but to applaud euerie doting speech, and to tread out euerie dot of spit, his fond patron deliuers.*

Marcher en pas de loup. *To tread, or goe, like a theefe, cunningly, couertly, gingerly, faire and softly.*

Marcher de pied en terre. Il ne marche de &c. *He is rapt, or rauisht with pride, or ioy; he knowes not the ground he goes on.*

Marcher à quatre pattes. *To creepe on all foure like a beast.*

Cela marche à quatre rouës. *That goes very roundly forward.*

Marchette: f. *A little step, a small footing.*

Marchettes. *Small Organ keyes.*

Marchir. *as* Marchiser.

Marchis: m. *A thicke trace, or tract of men, or beasts; frequencie of steps, many footings together; also, a path beaten out by often patting, or treading.*

Marchiser. *To border, adioyne, or lie so neere together that one touch another; to abutt, or bound one on another.*

Marchons: m. *Stillings for wine vessells to stand on.*

Marchure: f. *A marching, walking, pacing, treading, stepping, footing, proceeding.*

Marciage. Droict de mar. *Looke vnder* Droict.

Marcier. *To receiue the rent, or fine,* Marciage.

Marcoter. *as* Marquotter.

Marcotte. *as* Marquotte.

Marcou: m. *An old male cat, a gib cat.*

Mardecathene. *Looke* Mat de cathene, *in* Cathene.

Mardelle d' vne puits. *The brinke, or brimme of a well; or, more properly, the round, and high border of wood, or stone, that compasses, beautifies, and keeps whole, the top of that brinke, or brimme.*

Mardi. *Tewsday.*

Mardi gras. *Shroue-tewsday.*

Cela sent son mardi gras. *That is a most licentious act; or (in matters of discourse) that is a most broad speech; (from the libertie taken by many, that day, to tax men, and talke at their pleasure.)*

Mare: f. *A standing poole, or water neere a house fit for the watering of cattell, and other vses of husbandrie; also, a little fish-pond.*

Maré: m. ée: f. *Moored; fastened with cables, held fast by ankers, as a ship in a harbor, &c.*

Mareant. *Mooring.*

Marée: f. *Sea-fish; also, salt water; also, the tide, or flowing of the sea; also, a sea, or billow, or the rolling of a billow; also, a wind that blowes from sea.*

Sentir la marée. *To looke like a whore (Venus the Goddesse of good-fellowship was bred of the sea-foame.)*

Maréer. *as* Marer.

Marelle: f. *A square in a chesse-boord, or on the backside of a paire of Tables; also, a Churchwardenship; and the place wherein Churchwardens &c, meet.*

Marenge: f. *Our (ordinarie) blew Titmouse.*

Marer. *To moore, or be moored; to lie fastened with cables, or hold fast by ankers, within a harbor, or neere to a shore.*

Marescage: m. *A great marsh, fenne, or moore; a fennie, or moorish place, ground, or countrey.*

Marescageux: m. euse: f. *Fennie, moorish, marshlike.*

Mareschal: m. *A Marshall of a kingdome, or of a camp, (an honourable place;) also, a Black-smith; also, a Farrier, Horseleech, or Horse-smith; also, a Harbinger; and hence;*

Mareschal du corps du Roy. *The Kings chiefe Harbinger.*

Mareschaux de France. *The Lord Marshalls of France; (whereof, in Francis the firsts time, there were but two, now there be ten) who hauing their seuerall Prouinces assigned them by the King, vide circuits into them, to be present at all generall musters; to see how militarie discipline is obserued in garrisons; to view the fortifications, and reparations of frontire townes; the munition, and victualls of Arsenalls, and store-houses; and lastly, to prouide for the punishment, and suppression of all vagrant, idle, and lewd rogues:* Ils doiuent se rendre aux armées les premiers en bon equipage; Et sont sous le Connestable *(sayes* Ragueau) *Vnder whom as they commaund all Dukes, Earls, Barons, Captains, and* Gensdarmes; *so may they neither giue battell, make proclamation, nor muster any men, without his commandement (sayes a good English Author.)*

Mareschal: m. ale: f *Of or belonging to, made or done by, a Smith, or Farrier.*

Main mareschale. *A Smithes hand; a fist that works in a Smithie.*

Mareschaucée: f. *A Marshallship; the place of a Marshall; also, the Marshall-sey, or Marshals Court.*

Mareschaucées: f. *Timber, or stuffe to build withall.*

Mareschaussée, & mareschaussées. *as* Mareschaucée, & Mareschaucées.

Marets: m. *A Meere, Fenne, (small) Marsh.*

Il s'est sauvé par les marets. *Said of one that hath, with shame ynough, cleered himselfe of a dishonor, difficultie, or danger wherein he was ingaged.*

Marez. *as* Marets.

Marfil: m. *Iuorie; or, the Elephants tooth vnwrought.*

Margaigne. *as* Mortgage.

Margaignon: m. *A male Eele.* ¶ Langued.

Margaire. *A Sauoyan bird of sundrie colours.*

Margariton: m. *Pearle; or the powder thereof.*

Margasin. *as* Magazin.

Marge: f. *The margent of a booke; also, any edge, brinke, or brimme.*

Marge du dos. *The inner margent; the space left white betweene the letters, and binding of a booke.*

Margelle. *as* Mardelle.

Marger. *To make a margent; brinke, edge, or brimme.*

Margne. *as* Marne.

Margot. *(for Marguerite; or, a rusticall diminutiue thereof;) Meg, or Peg.*

Tieu tieu margot. *Come beast come; a call for a Cow, vsed by countrey wenches.*

La grande iument margot qui se bride par la queuë. *A Ship, or Galley; also, a certaine engine vsed by false coyners.*

Margotte. *as* Marquotte.

Margotté: m. ée: f. *Dressed, or made to yeeld store of suckers.*

Margotter. *Looke* Marquotter.
Margouiller. *To gnaw; to mumble with the teeth, in stead of kissing to bite.*
Margoute: f. *as* Marquotte.
Margueillier: m. *A Churchwarden.*
Marguerite: f. *Margaret (a womans name;) also, a (Margarite) pearle; also, a Daisie.*
Marguerite blanche. *The great white Daisie, called Maudlinwort.*
Marguerite des prez. *Th'ordinarie, little, white, and wild Daisie, called (otherwise) Bruisewort.*
'A la franche Marguerite. *After the plainest fashion, in a homelie manner, euen as one thinkes.*
Marguillerie: f. *A Churchwardenship.*
Marguillier: m. *A Churchwarden.*
Marguy: m. *A Fauchion, Curtelax, Hanger.* (v.m.)
Mari: m. *A husband.*
Mari cocu. *An Hedge-sparrow, Dikesmowler, Dunnecke; See* Cocu.
Femme bonne qui a mauvais mari, a bien souvent le coeur marri: Prov. *The good wife of an ill husband hath often a sorrowfull heart of her owne.*
Mariable: com. *Mariable, weddable, mariageable.*
Mariage: m. *Mariage, matrimonie, wedding, wedlock; also, the mariage good, or portion which a man hath with his wife; also, a game at cards resembling (somewhat) our Saint.*
Aide de mariage. *Looke* Aides chevels.
Bref de mariage encombré. *Which a woman may bring within the yeare and day after her husbands decease, for the recouerie of her goods, and possessions aliened, by him or any other without her consent, or by her selfe without his permission, and authoritie.*
Mariaulet: m. *A man of no account, esteeme, or credit; one thats not worthie of beliefe; an insufficient witnesse, whether it be because of his yong age, or small honestie; or, as* Mariolet.
Marie: f. *Marie.*
Bain de Marie. *Maries bath; a cauldron, or kettle full of hot water.*
Herbe de S. Marie. *Looke* Herbe.
Seau de S. Marie. *Maries Seale, our Ladies seale, blacke Brionie, the wild Vine.*
Violettes de Marie. *Marians Violets, Couentrie bells, Couentrie Rapes (of the qualities, kind, and (almost) the forme, of Canterburie bells.)*
Marié: m. ée: f. *Maried, wedded, espoused.*
La mariée. *A Bride, a Spouse.*
Aujourd'uy marié demain marri: Prov. *To day wifefull, to morrow wofull.*
Mariée: f. *The caule, or kell of a beast.*
Mariement: m. *A marying, wedding, espousing.*
Marier. *To marie, wed, bestow in mariage, giue in wedlocke, ioyne in matrimonie.*
Se marier. *To marie, wed, espouse, enter into wedlocke.*
Marier la cave, & le puits. *To mingle wine and water together.*
Mariets: f. *Mariets, Marians Violets, Couentrie bells.*
Marieur: m. *A matcher, a marier, a maker of mariages.*
Marille: f. *A Register, or Matricular booke.*
Marin: m. *Marine; of the sea; neere to the sea; borne or bred in the sea.*
Herbe marine. *Slanke, Wrake, Lauer, Sea-grasse, weed of the sea.*
Paille marine. *Looke* Sagnie.
Vent marin. *A Southerlie wind.*

Marine: f. la mar. *The sea; or things of the sea; as a tide, &c.*
Grand homme de marine. *An excellent Mariner, or Saylor; a great Sea-man.*
Marine noire. *The name of a grape.*
Mariné: m. ée: f. Poisson mariné. *That tasts much of salt water, or of the pannier; also, dressed, or handled like sea-fish.*
Marinesque. 'A la mar. *Mariner-like; after the fashion of Mariners.*
Marinesques: f. *Long Mariners slops, breeches, hose.*
Marinette f: *The Load-stone; (an old word.)*
Marinier: m. *A Mariner, Saylor, Ship-man, Skipper, Seaman; also, as* Nautil.
Il n'est si bon marinier qui ne perisse: Prov. *The skilfullest Mariners feed Haddockes.*
Marinier: m. *Of, or belonging to, a Mariner.*
Pierre mariniere. *The Adamant, or Magnes stone.*
Marin-onfroy. *The name of an apple, which is round on th'one side, and flat on th'other.*
Marjolaine. f. *Marierome, sweet Marierome, fine Marierome, Marierome gentle.*
Marjolaine d'Angleterre. *Time (called so by many;) also, wild Origan, wild Marierome, English wild Marierome, groue Marierome.*
Marjolaine bastarde. *Bastard Marierome, Organie, Spanish Organie.*
Marjolaine de Curé. *Male Knot-grasse, Birdstongue, Swines-grasse.*
Marjolaine gentile. *Marierome gentle, fine Marierome, sweet Marierome.*
Marjolaine sauvage. *as* Marjolaine d'Angleterre.
La grande Marjolaine. *The great sweet Marierome; called thus (belike) to make a difference betweene it, and th'ordinarie* Marjolaine, *which is lesse, and sweeter then it.*
Petite Marjolaine. *Marierome gentle, fine Marierome, sweet Marierome.*
Primme Marjolaine. *Fine Marierome, sweet Marierome; also, Time.*
Mariolement: m. *Bawderie, lasciuiousnesse, a wanton, or lustfull tricke, as the groping of a wench, &c.*
Mariolet: m. *A leacher, wencher, wanton youth, lasciuious yonker; or as* Mariaulet.
Marioles: f. *The waddles, and stones of a Cocke; (wanton meat.)*
Marion: f. *Marian (a proper name for a woman.)*
Robin a trouvé Marion. *Iacke hath met with Gill; a filthie knaue with a fulsome queane.*
Marionnette: f. *Little Marian, or Mal; also, a kind of small German Ducket of base gold; also, a Puppet.*
Marisque: f. *A great vnsauorie fig, that ripening, opens on the sides, and discouers it seeds.*
Marital: m. ale: f. *Belonging to a mariage, or wedlocke (especially on the husbands side.)*
Maritime: com. *Maritime; neere the sea, bordering on the sea, of the sea side or coast; of, or belonging to, the sea.*
Marlane salé. *A dried Whiting.*
Marliere: f. *A marle-pit.*
Marlotte: f. *A fashion of light gowne, or mantle for the Summer.*
Marmaille: f. *Young rascalls or scoundrells, rakehells or slipstrings; the frie of the vulgar; a troupe of lewd, idle, or vnprofitable hoberdiboyes.*
Marmaride. Pierre mar. *A kind of verie hard gray marble.*
Marmaux. Arbres mar. *Hedge-trees, wild trees:* ¶Bourbonnois.

Mar-

Marme rayée. *A kind of sundrie-coloured sea-fish.*
Marme. *for* mon arme,*or*, mon ame: ¶Langued.
Marmentau. Bois marin. *A faire great wood,or beautifull tuft of high trees.*
Marmes. *A rusticall oath; as in* Marme.
Marmite: f. *A great pot,kettle, boyler,or boyling lead; especially such a one as is vsed for the boyling of beefe in the kitchins of Abbeyes.*
Marmiteux: m. euse: f. *Wretched, poore, miserable, heartlesse,that lookes pitifully on it.*
Marmiton: m. *A Scullion,or kitchin boy; also,a greasie,or slouenlie knaue; and,a saucie, malapert, or knauish fellow; also,a pettie,or young schoole-boy.*
Marmitonnage: m. *Scullionrie,or th'Office of a Scullion; also,nastinesse,greasinesse,slouenlinesse.*
Marmitonne: f. *A Kitchin-stuffe wench, or Kitchin wench; a filthie greasie queane.*
Marmitonner. *To play the saucie rogue, the malapert rascall,to vse knauish or saucie tricks; also,to tend the beefe-pot like a Kitchin-boy.*
Marmo. *as* Denté.
Marmonné: m.ée:f. *Mumbled,muttered,vttered betweene the teeth.*
Marmonner. *as* Marmoter.
Marmontaine. *as* Marmotaine.
Marmor: m. *The Goldenie, or a kind thereof; as* Denté.
Marmorat: m. *Morter, wherein, among other things, little peeces of the best marble are put.*
Marmoset: m. *as* Marmouset; *Also,a lewd flatterer, or vicious fellow; especially the base flatterer of a Prince,who to feed his maisters humor, applauds, and and imitates,his foulest vices.*
Marmot: m. *A Marmoset,or little Monkie; also,as;*
Marmotaine: f. *Th'Alpine Mouse, or mountaine Rat; broad-backed,great-eyed,and short-eared; as big,but not so high,as a Conie; her haire is, as a Badgers, long, and of diuers colours; her voyce verie small,and shrill; her taile but short; her clawes so sharpe, as with them she quickly digs her a hole into the hardest earth.*
Marmotan. *as* Marmotaine.
Marmote. *as* Marmotaine; *also, as* Marmotte; *also, the riuer Lote; a little muddie fish, headed, skinned, and finned, like an Eele.*
Marmoter. *To mumble,mutter,murmure; to speake,or vtter a thing,betweene the teeth.*
Marmoterie: f. *A muttering,or mumbling of words betweene the teeth.*
Marmotonné: m.ée: f. *Made to grumble, or, that yeelds a grumbling sound.*
Marmotonner. *To grumble, mutter, or murmure; to rumble,or make a rumbling noise.*
Marmotte: f. *A she Marmoset,or she Monkie.*
Marmotter. *as* Marmoter.
Marmouselle: f. *A little puppie,or pug to play with.*
Marmouserie: f. *Frenzie,doating, rauing, foolish melancholie; (An old word.)*
Marmouset: m. *The cocke of a cesterne, or fountaine, made like a womans dug; any Anticke Image, from whose teats water trilleth; any Puppet,or Anticke; any such foolish, or odde representation; also, the Minion, fauorite, or flatterer of a Prince; as in* Marmoset.
Marne: f. *Marle; a hard, and (most commonly) white earth, which in frostie weather fall's to dust, and fattens the ground it is laied on.*
Marné: m. ée: f. *Marled; fattened, or manured with (a whitish)marle.*
Marner. *To marle, or manure (with a white hard marle.)*
Marneux: m. euse: f. *Full of (white)marle.*
Marniere: f. *A marle-pit.*
Marochemin: m. *Horehound; or, as* Marrubin.
Marolle. *The name of a village,wherein a virgine of fifteene is hard to be found; whence;* Pucelle de marolle; *Seeke* Pucelle.
Maronne: f. *Whitewort, Fedderfew, Feuerfew; some also call sweet Mariereme so.*
Maronnier: m. *Looke* Marinier.
Maronnites: m. *A sect of poore Christians (in some parts of Turkie) that weare great belts, or girdles of leather.*
Marotte: f. *A (Princes) Scepter; also,a fooles bable(because made commonly like a Scepter.)*
Il en est plus assotté qu'un fol de sa marotte. *Hee doats more on it then a foole does on his bable.*
Il luy en fit porter la marotte. *He made him the authour,or commaunder of.*
Au fol la marotte: Prov. *The foole would haue a bable.*
Fol est qui sa marotte ne cognoist, & ne la maine comme il doit: Prov. *He is an asse that knowes not, and cannot rule, his owne(familie,or affections.)*
Si tous les fols portoient marotte, on ne sçait pas de quel bois on se chaufferoit: Prov. *If all that fooles are bables wore, of wood we should haue but small store.*
Marouque: f. *The tough, and hard thorne, or shrubbie tree, called* Paliurus, *Ram of Lybia, and Christs thorne; because (as it is imagined) hee was crowned withall.*
Maroute: f. *Bastard Camomill, false Camomill.*
Marpaut: m. *An ill-fauoured scrub, a little ouglie,or swartie wretch; also, a lickorous, or saucie fellow; one that catches at whatsoeuer dainties comes in his way.*
Marquable: com. *Markable, notable, of marke, of note.*
Marquasin: m. *A young wild boare.*
Marque: f. *A marke, signe, token; badge; print, stamp; spot; note,annotation; also,a distresse,arrest,or seisure of bodie, or goods; also, as* Merque; *also, a Marquisdome.*
Droict de marque. *Looke* Droict.
Faux marque. *A tearme by Wood-men bestowed on the head of a deere,which hath more rights,or branches on th'one side then on th'other.*
Homme de marque. *A renowmed,or notable person; a man of marke,or note.*
Marqué: m. ée: f. *Marked, noted, signed, spotted, printed; bearing the badge,or stampe of; also, heeded, obserued,regarded.*
Bien marqué. *Good, honest, vertuous, well inclined.*
Mal marqué. *Lewd, naughtie, vicious, badly giuen.*
Marquer. *To marke, note; signe, spot, set a print, or stampe on; to heed,regard,obserue, take especiall notice of.*
Cela ne marque rien. *(Of a counter,&c) that stands for nothing.*
Marquet: m. *A small Venetian coyne worth about* iiij.d. Tourn.
Marquetage. *as* Marqueterie.
Marqueté: m.ée: f. *Spotted; diuersified, or couered with sundrie-coloured spots; also,inlayed; wrought all ouer*

with small peeces of sundrie colours.

Marqueté d'estoilles. *Starrie, set thicke with stars.*

Marqueter. *To inlay; to diuersifie, flourish, or worke all ouer with small peeces of sundrie colours; also, to spot; to beautifie, or couer with sundrie-coloured speckes.*

Marqueterie: f. *Inlaying, or inlayed worke of sundrie colours.*

Marquette. *as* Marquet.

Marqueture: f. *A marking, spotting, or bespotting; also, as* Marqueterie; *also, a marke, or spot.*

Marquis: m. *A Marquesse; was in old time the Gouernour of a frontire, or frontire towne, and (as th'auncient Duke, and Earle) but an Officer either for life, or onely during the Princes pleasure: Then was he inferiour to th'Earle of a Prouince, but superiour to the Earle of an inland towne; And therefore, now that all those great Earledomes be annexed to the Crowne, his place is, without question, before any Earles.*

Elle a son marquis. *Saied of a woman that hath her flowers.*

Marquisat: m. *A Marquisate, Marquiship, or Marquisdome.*

Marquise: f. *A Marchionesse.*

Marquisotte. Barbe faitte à la marquisotte. *Cut after the Turkish fashion, all being shauen away but the mustachoes.*

Marquote. *as* Marquette.

Marquotte: f. *A Sucker, or young plant, that spurts vp from the root of a vine, &c, or is of it selfe rooted.*

Marquotter. *To prune, or dresse a vine so, as it may yeeld store of* Marquottes, *or Suckers.*

Marrabais. *as* Marrane.

Marrabaise. Bonnet à la mar. *A flat cap.*

Marrain. *as* Marrein.

Marraine: f. *A Godmother.*

Marran. *as* Marrane; *And most properly, the Christian circumcised, or turned Jew.*

Marrane: m. *A Renegado, or Apostata; a peruerted, or circumcised Christian; a Christian turned Turke, or Jew; also, a conuerted, or baptized Moore, Turke, or Iew; one that turnes Christian for feare rather then of deuotion; also, a Iewish, cruell, hard-hearted, or hollow-hearted fellow.*

Marranisé: m. ée: f. *Marranized, renegaded; turned Turke, growne miscreant, made a Iew; also, conuerted from a Iew to a (false, or false-hearted) Christian.*

Marrant. *Digging, working, or fetching vp weeds, with a (French) mattocke.*

Marrassau: m. *A kind of short sword or axe, for an Executioner.*

Marre: f. *A (French) Mattocke; also, the Saligot, water Calthrop, water Nut.*

Marré: m. ée: f. *Digged, wrought, opened, broken vp; fetched, or cut vp, with a (French) mattocke.*

Marreau: m. *The token of lead, &c, giuen for a remembrance, in Churches, to such as meane to receiue the Communion; and in Tauernes, &c, to such as cannot otherwise change money.*

Marrein: m. *Timber for building, or boords; hence also, Clapboord for caske; also, the beame of a Bucke; the branch of a Stag.*

Pour neant va au bois qui marrein ne cognoist: Prov. *In vaine goes he to the wood that hath no skill in wood; or, In vaine doth any man in forrests poake, that takes a dotard for a timber-oake.*

Marrer. *To dig, labour, worke, open or breake vp; (also, to cut, or fetch vp weeds) with a (French) mattocke.*

Marri: m. ie: f. *Sorie, sad, pensiue, aggrieued, afflicted, discontented, vexed at; repining, repentant; malecontent; angrie, fretting, chafing, displeased, offended, out of patience, in a fume.*

Anjourd'huy marié demain marri: Prov. *Maried to day, marred to morrow; to day wedded, to morrow wretched.*

Femme bonne qui a mauvais mari a bien souvent le coeur marri: Prov. *Looke* Mari.

Marrine: f. *A Godmother.*

se Marrir. *To grieue, or sorrow for, take heauily, be sad, or vexed at; to repine, repent, afflict himselfe about; also, to fret, fume, chafe, be discontented, angrie, displeased, out of all patience.*

Marrisson: f. *Griefe, sorrow, sadnesse, pensiuenesse, anguish, heauinesse; repentance; enuie, repining; discontent, melancholie, malecontentment; anger, indignation, impatience, fretting, chafing, fuming, vexation of mind.*

Marrobe: m. *The hearbe Horehound; Looke* Marrubin.

Marroche: f. *A mattocke, or instrument like a mattocke.*

Marrochon: m. *A little (French) mattocke.*

Marron: m. *The (domesticall, tilled, or) great Chesnut.*

Marronnier: m. *The great Chestnut tree.*

Marrons: m. *They which in great snowes make the way passable.*

Marroquin: m. *Spanish leather (made of Goats skins) or Goats leather not tanned, but dressed with Galls.*

Marroquin: m. ine: f. *Spanish, or Goats leather.*

Marrouchouïn. *as* Marrubin.

Marroufle. vn gros m. *A big cat; also, an ouglie luske, or clusterfist; also, a rich churle, or fat chuffe.*

Marrube: m. *as* Marrubin.

Marrubin: m. *Horehound.*

Marrubin blanc. *White Horehound.*

Marrubin d'eau. *Marsh Horehound, water Horehound.*

Marrubin noir. *Blacke, or stinking Horehound, black Archangell.*

Marrubin puant. *as* Marrubin noir.

Marrubin sauvage. *Wild, or yellow, Horehound.*

Marry. *Seeke* Marri.

Mars: m. *(The moneth) March; also, (the Planet) Mars; also, yron (called so by Alchymists;) also, course graine; or as;*

Les Mars. *March corne, or corne sowne about March.*

Le flot de Mars. *Looke* Flot.

Montaigne de Mars. *The fleshie part of the hand betweene the thumbe, and little finger; or the muscles whereof it consists.*

Violette de Mars. *Th'ordinarie blew Violet.*

Prendre Marthe pour Mars. *To take his markes amisse.*

Quand il tonne en Mars, nous pouvons dire helas: Prov. *(So euill a signe is that monethes thunder held.)*

Marsaul: m. *The cane Withie, or cane Willow.*

Marsés. bled Marsés. *Looke* Bled.

Marsois. &, bled Marsois. *March corne.*

Marson: m. *A shoat; a hog thats a yeare, or, vnder a yeare, old.*

Marsouin: m. *A Porpose, or Sea-hog; also, the fat, or bacon-like, fish thereof.*

Marsupie: f. *A purse, or pouch.*

Martagon: m. *The mountaine, or many-flowred, Lillie.*

Martagon de Constantinople. *The Lillie of Constantinople, the Bysantine Lillie.*
Marte: f. *The beast called a Martin.*
Martes sebellines, & soubellines, ou soublines. *Sables.*
Marteau: m. *A hammer; also, a sledge, or mallet; and (among Woodmen) a hammer that hath a stampe on the one side, wherewith the Surueyors, and Verderers of the Kings woods and forrests, marke the trees which are to bee felled, and sold; also, the hearbe Reedmace, Water-torch, or Cats-taile; also, a certaine little bone seated farre within the eare; also, the Stithie (a beasts disease.)*
Marteau de mer. *The huge, ouglie, vnluckie, staring, and wide-mouthed, Mullet-fish.*
'A Preuve de marteau. *Sound, currant, good, right stuffe.*
Couché entre l'enclume & les marteaux. *Seated in the middest of extremities, or in a dangerous strait; imbarked into vnauoydable mischiefs, or miseries.*
'A l'enclume le marteau: Prov. *(Said when a contentious, or litigious swaggerer meets, or is matched, with a worse then himselfe.)*
'A dure enclume marteau de plume: Prov. *By patience we quaile, or quell all harsh attempts: and now adayes we see bags of wooll, and walls of soft earth opposed to the furie of the Cannon.*
Martel: m. *Jealousie, suspition; throbbing, or panting, vpon passion; a buzze in the head, a flie in the eare.*
Martelage: m. *A malling, or hammering; a beating, working, or marking with a hammer.*
Martelé: m.ée: f. *Hammered, malled; beaten, wrought, or marked with a hammer; also, spotted, or speckled.*
Marteler. *To hammer, mall; beat, worke, or marke with a hammer; also, to spot, or speckle.*
Les dents luy marteloyent de froid. *His teeth chattered through co'd.*
Martelerie: f. *A hammering, or hammer worke.*
Martelet: m. *A little hammer; also, a Martlet, or Martin.*
Marteleur: m. *A hammerer; one that worketh with a hammer.*
Marteline: f. *A small hewing picke, or pauing picke; a Masons hammer, or picke.*
Martellé. *as* Martelé.
Martellement: m. *A hammering, or malling; a beating, working, or marking with a hammer.*
Marteller, *Seeke* Marteler.
Martengalle: f. *A kind of daunce, as common in* Provence, *as the* Bransle *in other parts of France.*
Marthe: f. *Martha (a womans name.)*
Prendre Mars pour Marthe. *(In things of some resemblance) to mistake one for another.*
Martial: m.ale: f. *Martiall, warlicke, valorous; borne vnder the Planet, or being of the humor, of Mars.*
Martin: m. *Martin (a mans name.)*
La S. Martin. *Martilmas; or the feast of S. Martin the Bishop, in Winter.*
Estaffier de S. Martin. *The diuell.*
Esté de S Martin. *The later end of Autumne.*
Oiseau de S. Martin. *The Ring-taile, or Hen-harme.*
Faire le prestre Martin. *To play both the Priest and the Clerke; to propound a question, and make himselfe an answer.*
A la S Martin lon boit le bon vin: Prov. *At Martilmas wine is fit to be drunke.*
Plus d'vn Asne à la foire a nom Martin: Prov. *If one will not another will; there be more wayes to the wood then one; or, as vnder* Asne.
Pour vn poil Martin perdit son asne: &, pour vn poinct Martin perdit son asne: Prov. *Looke* Asne.
Martin: m. *as* Marte; *A Martin.*
Prendre martin pour regnard. *(In alike things) to mistake one for another.*
Martiner. *To quaffe, swill, guzzle (from S. Martins day, when commonly the French people begin to drinke new wine.)*
Martinet: m. *A Martlet, or Martin (bird;) also, a water-mill for any yron forge; also, a little wooden candlesticke hauing on th'one side a handle, and on th'other a hooke (most in vse among Tauerners;) also, a kind of great hammer vsed in the breaking open of doores; also, a Student, or Scholler, that lodges in the towne, and resorts vnto Lectures, and Disputations in Colledges; also, the game called Cat and Trap; also, a Saints bell, or Antham bell.*
Martinet pescheur. *A Kings fisher.*
Grand Martinet. *The great blacke Martin.*
Martingale: f. *A Martingale for a horse.*
'A la martingale. *Absurdly, foolishly, vntowardly, grossely, rudely, in the homeliest manner.*
Martre. *as* Marte; *A Martin; also, a game played with buckle-bones, and a little ball.*
Martroy: m. *A place of execution, or punishment:* (¶Orleannois.)
Martyr: m. *A Martyre; one that suffers death for the truth.*
Martyre: m. *Martyrdome, death suffered for the truth; extreame paine, affliction, torment.*
Martyrément. *Martyre-like.*
Martyrer. *To martyr; torment, afflict extreamely, put vnto mightie paine.*
Martyriser. *To martyrize, to martyr.*
Martyrologie: f. *A Martyrologie; a Relation, Historie, or Booke of Martyrs.*
Mary. *as* Mari.
Marzol: m. *as* Escourgeon; *Called so, as it seemes, because it is most commonly sowne in March:* ¶Piedmontois.
Marzolin: m. *A kind of delicate Italian cheese made of sheeps milke not curdled with runnet, but with Artichock flowers.*
Mas de navire. *The mast of a ship.*
Mas de terre. *On Oxe-gang, plow-land, or hide of land, containing about 20 acres; (and hauing a house belonging to it.)*
Mascarade: f. *A Maske, or Mummerie.*
Mascarer. *To blot, soyle, blurre, sullie, disfigure.*
Mascaret d'eaux. *A huge, and sudden rauage, or inundatio of waters;* (L'on appelle mascaret vne grande montaigne d'eau qui se fait en la Riviere de Dordonne, vers les contrées de Libourne; Au temps d'esté, es saisons les plus paisibles, & tout en vn moment elle se forme, & fait vne course quelquesfois bien longue le long de l'eau, & quelquesfois plus courte, renversant les bateaux.)
Mascaut. *as* Macault.
Mascelles: f. *The Jawes.*
Maschaut: m. *A bag of money; or as* Macault.
Masché: m. *Chewed meat, such as Nurses giue vnto their children.*
Masché: m.ée: f. *Chawed, chewed, chammed, chemped.*
Il luy faut bailler la chose toute maschée. *(Said of one thats either vnable, or too lazie, to manage a difficult businesse; & therefore) it must be chawed, or tewed, vnto his hands.*

Maschecoulis : m. *The stones at the foot of a Parapet (especially ouer a gate) resembling a grate, through which offensiue things are throwne vpon Pioners, and other assailants; whence;*
Elle a les dents à maschecoulis le haut defendant le bas. *She hath a thin row of teeth, whose rottennesse, and stench driue men from her trench.*
Masche-crouste : m. *A gnaw-crust, hungrie companion, snatch-crust.*
Maschefer. *as* Machefer.
Maschefouyn : m. *A chuffe, boore, lobcocke, lozell; one thats fitter to feed with cattell, then to conuerse with men.*
Maschefrain : m. *A bridle-champer; a Lawyer (from his Mule, which attending while her master is in Court, hath leasure ynough to champe on the bridle.)*
Maschelier : m. ere : f. *Belonging to a Jaw, or chap.*
Les dents maschelieres. *The cheeke-teeth, Jaw-teeth, grinders.*
Maschement : m. *A chawing, chewing; champing; an eating, a gnawing with the teeth.*
Mascher. *To chaw, or chew; to champe; to eat, grind, or worke with the teeth.*
Mascher en belin. *To mumble like an old toothlesse beldame.*
Avaller gros, & mascher dru. *To leap ouer a block, and stumble at a straw.*
Mascherivet. *as* Macherivet.
Mascheur : m. *A chawer, chewer; champer; eater.*
Mascheur. *Chawing, chewing; champing; eating; whence;*
Muscle mascheur. *as* Masseter.
Mascheure. *as* Macheure.
Maschiller. *To nibble, or chaw prettily.*
Maschoire : f. *A Chap, or Jaw.*
Maschurer. *as* Machurer.
Masclon : m. *The Cholicke of the stomacke.*
Masculeyté : f. *Manhood, or the male kind.*
Masculin : m. ine : f. *Masculine, of the Masculine gender; male, manlie, virile.*
Masle : m. *A male, or he creature.*
Masles. *The pintles of a sterne; the yron pinnes that enter into the rings, or gudgeons thereof.*
Masle. Adject. *Male, masculine, virile.*
Masle-femelle : com. *An Hermaphrodite, or one that is both man and woman.*
Maspeton : m. *Laserwort, Madigare (an hearb.)*
Masquarade. *as* Mascarade.
Masquarizé : m. ée : f. *Masked, in a maske, hauing a maske, or visor on.*
Masque : m. *A maske; a visor.*
Masque de Caresme entrant. *The picture of Shroue tewsday; a guts, gulch, gorbellie, fat chuffe, or chops.*
Lever le masque à. *To vnmaske; to publish, or lay open a thing which was closely couered, or carried.*
Masqué : m. ée : f. *Masked, disguised, wearing a visor.*
Masquerade : f. *A Maske, or Mummerie.*
Masquerie. *as* Masquerade.
Masqueure : f. *A masking, mumming, disguising.*
Masquin. de masquin. *in stead of* Damasquin: ¶Rab.
Masquine : f. *The representation of a Lyons head, &c, vpon the elbow, or knee of some old-fashioned garmēts.*
Massacre : m. *A massacre, a generall slaughter, or murther.*
Massacre d'vn cerf. *The fall, death, or dismembring of a Stag; also, his head, or hornes violently pulled off when he is dead.*
Massacré : m. ée : f. *Massacred, slaughtered, murthered.*
Massacrer. *To massacre, slaughter, murther.*
Massacreur : m. *A massacrer, slaughterer, murtherer.*
Masse : f. *A masse, lumpe; heape, loafe; round peece of any thing; an ingot, or wedge of mettall; also, a club.*
Masse d'armes. *A Battle-axe.*
Masse de chair. *The muscle which possesseth, & filleth vp all the hollow bought of the sole of the foot; (called so by moderne Anatomists.)*
Masse d'eau. *as* L'herbe à masses.
L'herbe à masses. *Water-toarch, Cats-taile, March-beetle, March-pestill, Reed-mace, Dowch-downe.*
Sergent à masse. *Looke* Sergent.
Masserotte : f. *A Wood-cleauers beetle; also, the head, or but-end of a club, or beetle.*
Masseter. *One of the muscles whereby the nether Jaw is drawne vpwards.*
Massicor : m. *A yellow colour made of lead; or, as;*
Massicot : m. *Oaker made of Ceruse, or white lead.*
Massier : m. *A Mace-bearer, a Sergeant of the Mace.*
Massif : m. iue : f. *Massiue, solide, sound, firme, close, hard, strong, vnbroken, not hollow, well knit, hard-packt, together.*
Massir. *To make massiue, solide, hard, sound; to compact; to beat close, ramme hard in.*
Massitere : m. *A kneader of bread, or of past:* ¶Rab.
Massiveté : f. *Massiuenesse, soliditie, soundnesse.*
Masson : m. *A Mason; also, a kind of Mullet-fish.*
Pet de masson. *A fart in syrop; the fart that brings durt after it.*
'A propos truelle, bon iour masson. *Looke* Propos.
Il n'est pas masson qui pierres refuse: Prov. *The cunning Mason workes with any stone.*
Massonné : m. ée : f. *Built of stone; hewed, squared, wrought, or layed, as a stone by a Mason; also, (in Blazon) purfled.*
Massonner. *To build of stone; to make, or frame stone-buildings; to hew, square, fashion, lay stones; to worke Masons worke.*
Massonnerie : f. *Masonrie, Masons worke, the Masons trade; stone-worke, or building; the hewing, squaring, fitting, fashioning, laying, or iust placing, of stones in building.*
Massonnier : m. ere : f. *Of, belonging to, seruing for, a Mason, or Masons worke.*
Massoret : m. *A Spirit, Ghost, Hobgoblin.*
Massorets. *Such Jewes as corrected the false-written words of Scripture, not blotting them out (for of that they made a scruple) but noting them with a little O, and setting downe their corrections in the margent.*
Massuë : f. *A club; also, the name of a great sweet apple.*
Mast : m. *The mast of a ship.*
Master vn navire. *To furnish a ship with masts.*
Masterel : m. *A small mast; or any mast but the maine one.*
Mastic : m. *Masticke; (a sweet Gumme.)*
Mastic Achantique. *A Gumme which growes on the top of the Calthorp, or Starre-thistle.*

Maſtic de Candie. *Yellow, and bitter Maſticke.*

Maſtic de Chio. *White Maſticke, better then the former.*

Maſtic d'Egypte. *Blacke Maſtick; more drying, and and leſſe binding then the reſt.*

Maſtication: f. *A maſtication, chawing, or chewing betweene the teeth.*

Maſticatoire: m. *A Maſticatorie; a medecine for the rhewme chawed, or held betweene the teeth.*

Maſticatoire: com. *Maſticatorie, chewing, champing.*

Muſcles maſticatoires. *The muſcles from which the Jawes receiue their chawing motion.*

Maſtich. *as* Maſtic.

Maſtiché: m. ée: f. *Mingled, or cloſed with Maſtick; wherein there is Maſticke.*

Maſticine: f. *Manna in graines, Manna of the Leuant; ſo tearmed becauſe it reſembles Maſticke.*

Maſtin: m. *A Maſtiue, or Ban-dog; a great (countrey) curre; alſo, a rude, filthie, curriſh, or cruell fellow.*

Oncques maſtin n'aima levrier: Prov. *See* Levrier.

Qui de maſtin fait ſon compere plus de baſton ne doit porter: Pro. *He that will conuerſe with clowns, muſt paſſe by rudeneſſe without frownes.*

Maſtine: f. *A Maſtiue, or Curre-bitch; alſo, a fell queane.*

Maſtiné: m. ée: f. *Lined by a Maſtiue, or great curre; alſo, rudely handled, filthily vſed, curriſhly dealt with.*

Maſtiner. *To line, as a bitch with a Maſtiſe, or great curre; alſo, to vſe filthily, handle rudely, deale curriſhly or cruelly with.*

Maſtiquer. *as* Maſticher; *Alſo, to infuſe, or put Maſticke, Roſen, &c, vpon a thing before it be ſoldered; alſo, to ioyne, or cloſe with Maſticke, &c.*

Maſtoïde. Apophyſes maſtoïdes. *Proceſſes of bones deſcending from the ſides of the head behind the eares.*

Cavité maſtoïde. *A hollow part of the head wherein are certaine little caues, or winding hollowes, which receiue, and yeeld backe reuerberation of ſounds.*

Muſcle maſtoïde. *A muſcle that bends, and bowes downe, the head.*

Maſturbation: f. *Filthie frigging.*

Maſure: f. *An old decayed houſe, or wall; the ruines of a building.*

Maſure de terre. *A quantitie of ground containing about foure Oxe-gangs.*

Mat: m. *A foole, fop, gull; mad-paſh, harebraind ninnie; alſo, a mate at cheſſe-play.*

Eſchec & mat. *Check-mate; alſo, an vnauoydable diſaſter, a remedileſſe miſchiefe, or miſchance.*

Mat. *Deaded, mated, amated, quelled, ſubdued, ouercome; alſo, as* Flaccide.

Or mat. *Vnpolliſhed gold.*

Matachin: m. *The Matachin daunce; alſo, thoſe that daunce it.*

Matagaſſe: f. *A ſhrike, ninmurder, wariangle:* ¶Savoyard.

Matagot: m. *A kind of Ape; alſo, an hypocrite:* ¶Rab.

Mataſſin. *as* Matachin.

Mataſſiner des mains. *To moue, knacke, or waggle the fingers, like a Jugler, Player, Jeaſter, &c.*

Mate: f. *A number of ſprigs growing together vpon an hearbe; alſo, as* Matte; *whence;*

Enfans de la mate. *Ruffianlie cutters; Cheaters, Cutpurſes, &c.*

Matelas: m. *as* Materas; *Alſo, a kind of Violl, or Bottle.*

Matelot: m. *A Saylor, Shipman, Boatman, Waterman.*

Matelotage: m. *The hire of a ſhip, or boat, and of the Saylors, or Watermen thereto belonging; the fraight, or fare due for the vſe of a ſhip, or boat.*

Mateologie: f. *Vaine inquirie, or ouer-curious ſearch into high matters, and myſteries.*

Mateologien: m. *A vaine, or ouer-curious ſearcher into high matters.*

Mateotechne. *Vaine knowledge, crooked Art:* ¶Rab.

Mater. *To mate, or giue a mate vnto; to dead, amate, quell, ſubdue, ouercome.*

Materas: m. *A Mattereſſe, or Quilt to lie on; alſo, a quarrell (or arrow) for a croſſebow; alſo, as* Herbe à Maſſes.

Materas deſempenné. *A quarrell without feathers, or an vnfeathered quarrell; alſo, a light-braind, giddie-humord, ſhittle-headed fellow.*

Matereau. *as* Matz; *or as* Maſterel.

Materiaux: m. *Any kind of rubbidge, or ſtuffe.*

Materiel: m. elle: f. *Materiall; ſtuffie, ſubſtantiall, well growne, well fed; alſo, dull, groſſe, earthie, or earthlie.*

Materien. *as* Marrein. *An old word.*

Maternel: m. elle: f. *Maternall, motherlie, of a mother, on the mothers ſide.*

Maternellement. *Motherly, like a mother; tenderly, kindly, carefully.*

Maternité: f. *Maternitie, motherhood, the being a mother.*

Matetoultier. *Looke* Maletoultier.

Mathelin. *as* Mathurin.

Mathelineux: m. euſe: f. *Franticke, wild, wood, halfe mad.*

Mathematicien: m. *A Mathematician; a profeſſor or practiſer, of the Mathematikes; alſo, a caſter of Natiuities.*

Mathematique: com. *Mathematicall, belonging to the Mathematicks.*

Mathematiques: f. *The Mathematicks; (comprehend foure of the liberall Sciences;* viz.) *Arithmeticke, Geometrie, Muſicke, and Aſtronomie or Aſtrologie.*

Matheothecne. *Crooked Art, vaine knowledge:* ¶Rab.

Mathurin: m. *The name of a Saint in* Gaſtinois, *held to be the Phyſitian, or Patron of mad fooles; alſo, a* Mathurin *Frier; (of th'Order of the Trinitie.)*

Maladie de S. Mathurin. *Frenzie, extreame follie, madneſſe.*

Saillie de S. Mathurin. *A fooliſh tricke, fond prank, mad part.*

Mené à S. Mathurin. *Gulled, groſſely beguiled, ouerraught, made a foole.*

Matiere: f. *Matter; ſtuffe, ſubſtance; a matter, a thing; an argument, or ſubiect to write, or diſcourſe of; a buſineſſe, or affaire; a cauſe, caſe, or Action in Law.*

Matiere fecale. *Dung, excrement, ordure.*

Matin: m. *The morning; the breake of day, beginning of the day.*

Des le fin matin. *Verie earlie, as ſoone as one can ſee.*

Au matin les monts, au ſoir les fonds, &c. *Looke* Mont.

Les paroles du ſoir ne reſemblent pas à celles du matin: Prov. *He that giues thee a good morrow, may yet before night procure thy ſorrow.*

Le rouge ſoir, & blanc matin font resjouïr le pelerin: Prov. *The euening red, and morning gray preſage a faire ſucceeding day.*

Qui

Qui a bon voisin a bon matin : Prov. *He that hath a good neighbour hath a good morrow; viz. good words next his heart a mornings; or, as in* Avoir.

Tel au matin rit qui au soir pleure : Prov. *Some begin the day with laughter, and end it with teares.*

Matin. *(Aduerbially.) Early, betimes in the morning; whence;*

Lever matin n'est pas heur, mais desieuner est le plus seur : Prov. *There is lesse happinesse in earlie rising then safetie in eating after one is risen.*

Il a beau se lever tard qui a le bruit de se lever matin: &; Qui a bruit de se lever matin peut dormir iusques à disner : Prov. *Seeke* Lever.

Matinal : m. ale : f. *Earlie.*

Matine : f. *as* Mastine.

Matinée : f. *A forenoone, or morning-tide, a whole morning, the season of a morning; also, a mornings worke, or taske.*

Regnard qui dort la matinée n'a pas la langue emplumée: Prov. *The Fox that sleepes a mornings meets with no feathered breakfasts.*

Matines : f. *Matines, Morning Prayer.*

Matines Parisiennes. *The massacre of Paris; which began about midnight.*

Chanter Magnificat à Matines. *To sing* Magnificat *at Matins; to peruert th'order of things, or doe things out of order.*

Plus estourdi que le premier coup de Matines. *More drowsie, and amazed, then a Frier at the first toll of the morne-sacring bell.*

Le Retour de Matines : Prov. *A mischiefe done in the darke, or at vnawares; (from the customes of Friers, who commonly make choyce of that obscure season, for the surprising, and thumping of their hated companions; which hath bred another Prouerbe; viz.* Il n'y a rien tant à craindre que le retour de matines.)

Matineux : m. euse : f. *Earlie, soone rising, vp betimes.*

Homme matineux sain, alaigre, & soigneux : Pro. *An earlie man is buxome healthfull, carefull.*

Matinier : m. ere : f. *Of, or belonging to, the morning; also, Easterlie, of or towards the East; and hence;*

L' Inde matiniere. *The East India.*

Matlas. *as* Materas.

Matlassé: m. ée : f. *Of Materesses, or Quilts.*

Matois : m. *A vaine companion, worthlesse person; or as* Mattois.

Il entend le matois. *He vnderstands the whole traine, or plot.*

Matou : m. *A cat, a pusse.*

Matoüard : m. *The same.*

Matrac : m. *A straight, long, narrow-necked, and great, wide, round-bellied bottle, or violl, of strong, and thick glasse.*

Matrasser. *To mall, beat, or hew, downe; to bruise, or breake asunder.*

Matraz : m. *A glasse bottle, or violl; or as* Matrac; *also, as* Materas.

Matricaire : f. *Fedderfew, Feuerfew, Motherwort, Whitewort.*

Matricaire. Veine mat. *Looke* Veine.

Matrical : m. ale : f. *Belonging to, or seruing for, the Matrix.*

Entonnoir matrical. *Seeke* Entonnoir.

Matricave. *Fedderfew, &c; as* Matricaire.

Matrice : f. *The matrix, mother, or wombe of a woman; also, a certaine veine that runnes along the flank neere the reines; also, as* Matricule; *also, a money-makers, or letter-founders, Matrice; the mould or forme for the eyes of their markes, or letters.*

Matricide: com. *Mother-killing.*

Matricile : com. *Of, or belonging to, the matrix.*

Matricule : f. *A list, roll, catalogue, register of names; a matricular booke.*

Matrimonie : m. *Matrimonie, mariage, wedlocke.*

Matrimonial : m. ale : f. *Matrimoniall; of, or belonging to, matrimonie.*

Heritages matrimoniaux. *Which come by the mother.*

Matronal : m. ale : f. *Matronall, matron-like, modest, motherlie, graue.*

Matrone : f. *A Matron, a discreet, or sage dame; a sober, modest, graue, motherlie woman.*

Matrones. *Damaske or Dames Violets, Queenes Gilloflowers, Rogues Gilloflowers, close Sciences.*

Mattarruys : m. *A mad, rash, harebraind asse; one that throws whats next him at any one that moues him.*

Matte: f. *Was heretofore (in Paris) a raskallie place, whereat common Gamesters, Cheaters, Conicatchers, and Cutpurses vsually met. Thence,* Enfans, ou supposts de la Matte; *Such well-giuen youthes.*

Matté : m. ée : f. *Mated, amated, quelled, subdued, puld vnder, taken lower; tired, wearied.*

Mattelé : m. ée : f. *Clotted, knottie, curdled, or curdlike.*

Matter. *To quell, mate, amate; subdue, pull vnder, take lower; to giue a mate vnto.*

Mattes : f. *Curds, or curdles.*

Matti : m. ie : f. *Depriued of moisture and verdure, dried vp; whence, hearbes dried vpon a hot shouell, tile, or in a still, are said to be,* matties.

Mattois : m. *A Setter, Cutpurse; Cheater, Conicatcher; a subtill, or craftie fellow; also, as* Matois.

Mattonné. Ciel mattonné. *A curdled skie; or, a skie full of small curdled clowds.*

Mattraz. *as* Materaz.

Maturatif : m. iue : f. *Maturatiue, ripening, suppuring.*

Maturation : f. *A maturation, ripening; suppuring, growing to a head, mattering, resoluing into matter.*

Maturer. *To ripen, mellow, wax full, grow mature; also, to matter, to suppure.*

Maturin. *Looke* Mathurin.

Maturité : f. *Maturitie, ripenesse, mellownesse, fullnesse; perfection of growth, and bignesse.*

Matutinel : m. elle : f. *Of the morning; also, timelie, or earlie in the morning.*

Matz : m. *The mast of a ship.*

Mau : m. *An euill, mischiefe, dammage, annoyance; paine, griefe, sicknesse.*

Mau de pipe. *Drunkennesse; or as in* Pipe.

Mau de terre. *The falling sickenesse.*

Mau. (*for* Mal Adject.) *Bad, ill, naughtie; whence;*

'A mau chat mau rat : Prov. *Two knaues well met.*

Maubert. Place mau. *The Marketstead, and place of execution, for th'Vniuersitie of Paris.*

Cela sent sa Place Maubert. *Thats clownish, rude, verie homelie.*

Maubrenage. vne femme qui demeure à m. *A stinking, or nastie dragglet aile.*

Maucoeureux : m. euse : f. *Queasie-stomacked.*

Mauconduict : m. cte : f. *Ill guided, badly gouerned.*

Maudire. *Looke* Mauldire.

Maudisné: m. ée: f. *Ill dined, that hath had but a course dinner.*

Maud ssant. *Cursing, banning, blaspheming.*

Maudiſſon: f. *A curſe*; *Looke* Mauldiſſon.
Maudite: f. *A kind of ſandie-coloured vermine, like a Viper.*
Maudolé: m. ée: f. *Miſhapen, ill framed, ill-fauoured, luskiſh, without proportion.*
Mauduict: m. cte: f. *Vnmannerlie, clowniſh, ill-behaued, ill brought vp, vnciuile, rude.*
Mauffait: m. *A Goblin, Bug, Diuell, Spirit.* } *old words.*
Mauffe: f. *A Bug, Fairie, ſhe Spirit.* } *old words.*
Maufle: f. *A wretch*; *or as* Mauffe.
Maugiſant. *Ill bedded, ill lodged, lying ill fauouredly*; *or as* Malgiſant.
Maugratieuſement. *Haſtily, rudely, vnpleaſantly, improperly, vnpleaſingly.*
Maugratieux: m. euſe: f. *Vnpleaſing, rude, harſh, vnhandſome, vncomelie, vnſeemelie, without grace, without garbe.*
Maugré. *Looke* Maulgré.
Maugréement: m. *A curſing, banning, blaſpheming.*
Maugréer. *To curſe, banne, blaſpheme, reuile extreamly, raile on deſpightfully.*
Maujoin: m. *Th'Arabian Gumme called Beninne.*
Maujoinct: m. cte: f. *Looſe, gaping, ill ioyned, ill couched, badly ſet together.*
Maujoine. Barbier de mau. *A Barber of a womans &c.*
Maulavé: m. ée: f. *Ill waſhed*; *ſlubbered, naskie, naſtie, foule.*
Mauldict: m. cte: f. *Execrable, accurſed*; *moſt vnhappie*; *alſo, curſed, banned, execrated.*
Mauldire. *To curſe, banne, execrate, werrie, betake to the diuell*; *alſo, to blaſpheme.*
Mauldiſſon: f. *A malediction, curſe, banning, execration*; *a blaſphemie.*
Les mauldiſſons ſont fucilles qui les ſeme les recueille: Pro. *Curſes proue choke-peares vnto thoſe that plant them.*
Maulgré eux. *Mauger their teeth, in ſpight of their hearts, againſt their wills, whether they will or no.*
Mauloubet: m. *The Wolfe (a diſeaſe.)*
Maulubec: m. *as* Malubec; *or, as* Mauloubet.
Maulve: f. *The hearbe Mallow*; *alſo, a Sea-mew, or Sea-gull.*
Maulve blanche. *The white Mallow*; *or as* Guimauve.
Maulve cultivée. *Garden Mallowes, Hockes, Holyhockes.*
Maulve grande. *The great Mallow, or tree Mallow.*
Maulve de Iardin. *as* Maulve cultivée.
Maulve ſauvage. *The field Mallow, wild Mallow*; *our ordinarie Mallow.*
Maulve terreſtre. *Blacke Brionie*; *or an hearb that hath blacke berries, and is much vſed by Curriers.*
Maulx. *Miſchiefes*; *Looke* Mal.
Maumarié: m. ée: f. *Badly matched, ill maried,*
Maumené: m. ée: f. *Miſuſed*; *ſorely handled, extreamly perſecuted*; *purſued neere, hard laied to.*
Maunet: m. ette: f. *Vncleane, vncleanlie, ſullied, ſluttiſh, filthie, naſtie, ſlouenlie.*
Mavortien: m. enne: f. *Martiall.*
Maupiteux: m. euſe: f. *Pitileſſe, vnmercifull, mercileſſe, cruell, hard-hearted, rigorous.*
Mauplaiſamment. *Vnpleaſantly, vnpleaſingly, harſhly*; *vnhandſomely.*
Mauplaiſance: f. *Vnpleaſantneſſe, vnpleaſingneſſe, harſhneſſe, lumpiſhneſſe*; *vnhandſomeneſſe.*
Mauplaiſant. *Vnpleaſant, vnpleaſing, lumpiſh*; *vnhandſome, harſh.*

Maupreſt. *Vnreadie, vnprepared, vnprouided.*
Maurelle. *as* Morelle.
Maurequine. Goutte maurequine. *as* Goutte ſerene; *See* Goutte.
Mauſade: com. *Harſh, vnſauerie, lowtiſh, vnciuile, vnmannerlie, rude, vnproper, vnapt, vnſeaſonable.*
Mauſadement. *Harſhly, vnſauorily, vnproperly, vnaptly, vnſeaſonably, lowtiſhly, vnciuilly, rudely, vnmannerly.*
Mauſadeté: f. *Harſhneſſe, vnſauorineſſe, or want of ſauor*; *vnaptneſſe, vnhandſomeneſſe, vnſeaſonableneſſe*; *lacke of ciuilitie, rudeneſſe.*
Mausoigneux: m. euſe: f. *Careleſſe, retchleſſe, negligent.*
Mauſolée: m. *The ſtatelie ſepulchre of a great Prince, or Potentate.*
Mauſoupé: m. ée: f. *Ill ſupped, that hath had but a bad ſupper.*
Mauſſane: *The Wayfaring tree.*
Mauvais: m. aiſe: f. *Naughtie, bad, lewd, ill*; *ſhrewd, miſchieuous, hurtfull, vnhappie, knauiſh, curſt, churliſh, croſſe, froward, ſtubborne, obſtinate, ouerthwart*; *malicious*; *depraued, corrupt, mard.*
Mauvais garçon. *A ſhrewd lad*; *alſo, a ſhrewd, or tall fellow.*
Mauvais oeil. *Ivie Chickweed, Morgeline, Henbit.*
Mauvaiſe tigne. *A malignant ſcurfe bred in the head.*
Faire mauvais. *To depraue, marre, viciate, peruert, corrupt.*
Faire le mauvais. *To ſwagger*; *to boaſt, cracke, brag of his owne valour.*
Sentir mauvais. *To ſtinke, or ſmell ill, to be ſomewhat to blame.*
Mauvais chien ne trouve ou mordre: Prov. *The curriſh dog in fight not bold ſeekes where to ſnatch, not where to hold.*
Mauvaiſe fille ſe mocque de ſa mere: Prov. *A wicked daughter flowts her (witleſſe) mother.*
Mauvaiſe herbe croiſt touſiours: Prov. *An ill weed thriues apace.*
Le mauvais emporte le bon. *Where th'one of a maried couple is free, and th'other a villeine, their children ſhall be villeines, by the cuſtomes of* Nevers, *and* Bourbonnois.
Il faut avoir mauvaiſe beſte par douceur: Prov. *Looke* Avoir.
Il n'eſt qu' vne mauvaiſe heure au iour: Prov. *One day hath in it but one luckleſſe houre.*
On n'a jamais bon marché de mauvaiſe marchandiſe: Prov. *Bad ware is neuer cheape ynough.*
Mauvaiſement. *Badly, lewdly, naughtily, wickedly, vily, filthily*; *miſchieuouſly, hurtfully, ſhrewdly*; *frowardly, ſtubbornely, churliſhly.*
Mauvaiſtié: f. *Naughtineſſe, badneſſe, wickedneſſe, lewdneſſe, knauerie, miſchieuouſneſſe, ſhrewdneſſe, curſtneſſe, hurtfulneſſe*; *maliciouſneſſe*; *peruerſitie, ouerthwartneſſe, obſtinacie, ſtubbornneſſe.*
Mauve. *as* Maulve.
Mauvis: f. *A Mauis*; *a Throſtle, or Thruſh.*
Max. *as* Mas.
Maxillaire: com. *Of, or belonging to, the iaw-bone.*
Dents maxillaires. *The grinders, or cheeke teeth.*
Os maxillaires. *The bones into which th'vpper teeth are ſet*; *in men but two (diſcernable) in beaſts foure, two bigger and two leſſe.*
Maxime: m. *A maxime, principle, firme propoſition.*
May: m. *(The moneth of) May*; *alſo, a May-pole*; *whence*;

'A bon bluteur may propice: Pro. *Somewhat as stiffe as a maypole does well with him that boults in a fleshlie tub.*

Il ne sçait que c'est de vendre vin qui n' attend de May la fin: Prov. *Belike because he cannot before that time guesse what will be the next yeares Vintage.*

May: f. *A kneading trough, or tub; also, a stacke, or pile of wood, &c.*

Maye: f. *A kneading trough; a hutch, or binne; also, a halfe-thraue, or heape of corne (in the sheafe.)*

Mayenche: f. *A Titmouse.* ¶Savoyard.

Mayeres: f. *The branches of Poplers, and Willowes, fit to make rayles, props, or stayes for Vines.*

May-loubet. *The disease which wee call the Wolfe.* ¶Langued.

May-mis: m. ise: f. *Maimed.*

Mayrastre: f. *A stepmother.* ¶Langued.

Mays: m. *Maïs, Turkie corne, Turkie wheat.*

Maz: m. *A small countrey tenement; or, as* Mas; *also, the maste of a ship.*

Me. *Me, or to me; a Pronowne (of the Datiue, or Accusatiue Case) which euer goes before a Verbe, whereas* Moy *comes after.*

Means: m. *Void, and emptie places betweene beds in gardens, reserued for speciall hearbes; such are the spaces left for Cardoons betweene rowes of Onyons.*

Meat: m. *A way, or open passage; a hole, or pore in the bodie.*

Meat Cholagogue. *Looke* Cholagogue.

Mecanique: com. *Mechanicall, belonging to an handicraft; base, meane, ordinarie, vile.*

Mecaniquerie: f. *Mechanicallnesse; basenesse of humor.*

Mecaniqueté: f. *The same.*

Mecer. *for* Menacer; *to threaten.* ¶Rab.

Mechanique. *as* Mecanique.

Mechanizé: m. ée: f. *Mechanicalized; made, or growne base, vile, ordinarie, meane.*

Meche: f. *as* Meiche.

Mecheron: m. *A little match, or candle-weeke; also, a sparkle.*

Mechine: f. *A maid-seruant, a chamber-maid.*

Mechoir. *as* Meschoir.

Mect: f. *A kneading trough, or tub; Looke* Met.

Medaille: f. *A medall; an auncient and flat iewell, ouch, or bruche; or, a peece of auncient coyne, or plate, wherein the figure of some notable person is cast, or cut.*

Medaillé: m. ée: f. *Furnished, or set, with medalls.*

Medaillon: m. *A little medall, ouch, or bruche.*

Medalle. *as* Medaille.

Medamothi. *Of no place.* ¶Rab.

Medard. *The name of a sanctified Bishop of* Noyon, *and* Tournay, *in the yeare 524; by whose prayers (sayes* Gregoire de Tours) *diuers prisoners haue beene deliuered from captiuitie; whence;*

Mal S. Medard. *(May be) captiuitie, or imprisonment.*

Mede. *A precious stone that yeelds a Saffron-like sweat, and a tast like wine.*

Medecin: m. *A Phisition, a Leech.*

Medecin d'eau douce. *An vnskilfull, or vnexperienced Phisition, a duncicall dog-leach; one that hath not trauelled farre for the (little) skill he hath: (*Asclepiades, *a better Orator then Phisition (as* Plinie *reports) was the first that allowed a Patient to drinke cold water; and thereupon caused himselfe to be tearmed, The fresh-water Phisition.)*

Apres la mort le medecin: Prov. *After meat mustard; when steed is stolne shut the stable doore.*

Bon est le medecin qui se sçait guarir: Pro. *He is a right Phisition that can cure himselfe.*

De nouveau medecin cimitiere bossu: Pro. *A new Phisition makes a Churchyard swell.*

Vn piteux medecin fait vne playe mortelle: Prov. *A pitifull Surgeon spoileth a sore.*

Ieune barbier vieil medecin: Prov. *Looke* Barbier.

Les maux terminez en ique (comme Hydropique, Hectique, Paralytique, &c) font au medecin la nique: Prov. *Because they be hardly cured.*

Medecin: m. ine: f. *Phisicall, medicinall; belonging to Phisicke, or to a Phisition.*

Doigt medecin. *The ring finger, that which is next vnto the little one.*

Medecinable: com. *Medicinable, healable, curable.*

Medecinal: m. ale: f. *Medicinall, seruing for a medicine, curing, healing.*

Medecine: f. *A medicine, or phisicke; the art of Phisicke; healing, or curing; a remedie for diseases; also, a she Phisition.*

Contre la mort n'y a point de medecine: Pro. *No Phisicke can preuaile 'gainst death.*

Contre peché est vertu medecine: Prov. *Vertue is a salue for sinne.*

Tard medecine est apprestée a maladie enracinée: Prov. *Grounded diseases are incurable.*

Medeciné: m. ée: f. *Medecined, cured, healed.*

Medeciner. *To medicine, cure, heale, salue, leach; to apply a remedie; to practise, or minister Phisicke.*

Mediane: m. *as* Mesentere.

Mediane: f. *The blacke, or middle veine; the inward branch of the shoulder veine, discending downe the arme vnto the hand, and there dispersing it selfe among the fingers.*

Mediastine: m. *A partition made in the bodie by certaine thin skins which diuide the whole breast, from the throat to the midriffe, into two hollow bosomes.*

Mediateur: m. *A mediator, intercessor, meane or means for; also, an arbitrator.*

Mediation: f. *Mediation, intercession, suite, or meanes made for; also, an arbitrating, or compounding of (other mens) controuersies.*

Mediatrice: f. *A mediatrix, arbitratrix.*

Medicament: m. *A medicament, salue, medicine.*

Medicamenter. *To salue, cure, heale, apply a medicine, lay a plaister vnto.*

Medicamenteux: m. euse: f. *A curing, saluing, healing.*

Medication: f. *as* Medicinement.

Medicinement: m. *A curing, saluing, healing.*

Medier. *To diuide into halues; also, as* Moyenner.

Medieu, ou medieus. *So God helpe me, or, by the faith of my bodie.*

Medimne: m. *A corne-measure, containing almost two of our bushels.*

Medin: m. *An Egyptian coyne of siluer, worth about xx d Parisis.*

Mediocre: com. *Meane; moderate, indifferent, reasonable, competent, neither too big nor too little.*

Mediocrement. *Meanely, moderately, indifferently, competently, reasonably, measurably, meetly well.*

Mediocrer. *To qualifie, temper, moderate, add a meane vnto.*

Mediocrité: f. *Mediocritie; a meane, measure, competencie, indifferencie; temper, moderation, qualification.*

Medique: f. *Medick fodder, Spanish Trefoile, Snaile Clauer.*
Medisson. *Looke* Mesdisson.
Meditation: f. *A meditation, or meditating; a deepe consideration, carefull examination, studious casting, or deuising of things in the mind.*
Mediter. *To meditate, studie, muse on; to thinke seriously, resolue studiously, consider deepely, deuise carefully, ponder diligently.*
Mediterranée: f. *The Mediterranean, or mid-earth sea.*
Medon: m. *The drinke Mede, or Bragot.*
Medullaire: com. *Marrowie, of marrow.*
Medulle: f. *Marrow; pith.*
Spinale medulle. *Seeke* Spinal.
Medulleux: m. euse: f. *Marrowie, pithie, strong; full of marrow.*
Meffaict: m. *A fault, offence, trespasse, misdeed; a wrong, abuse, displeasure, bad part, shrewd turne.*
Meffaict: m. cte: f. *Misdone, trespassed, offended.*
Meffaire. *To trespasse, offend, misdoe against; to wrong, abuse, deale treacherously, play false with.*
Meffiance: f. *Distrust, mistrust, suspition, iealousie.*
Meffier. Se meffier de *To distrust, mistrust, haue in iealousie, put small confidence in.*
Megalopsychie: f. *Magnanimitie; or, as* Magnanimité.
Megicier. *as* Megissier.
Megis: m. *Tawings; the offalls, or peeces cut from skinnes in tawing; or the liquor wherein they are, or haue beene tawed.*
Megisserie: f. *The tawing, or dressing of (thinne) skinnes for Gloues, Purses, &c.*
Megissier: m. *A tawer, or tawyer; a Fell-monger, a Leather-dresser.*
Megiste. *Verie great.* ¶Rab.
Megle: m. *A kind of forked Pick-ax, or Grubbing-ax.*
Megre: f. *Looke* Maigre: f.
Megrelin: m. *A leane scrag, lanke staruel ing.*
Megue. *as* Maigue.
Mehaigné: m. ée: f. *Lamed, maymed; growne impotent, much weakened by extreame hurts receiued, care taken, or toyle indured.*
Mehaigner. *To mayme, or make lame with blowes; to weaken, bruize, or founder by extreame care, stripes, or toyle.*
Mehaing: m. *A mayme; or, an extreame weakenesse, impotencie, or abatement of strength, in the bodie, by hurts receiued, care taken, or toyle indured.*
Il n'est cheval qui n'ait son mehaing: Prov. *No horse without some bruize; no man without one fault or other.*
Mejane: f. *A mizzen sayle; also, a Guilt-head, or Goldennie of a middle size.*
Meiche: f. *The weeke (or snuffe) of a candle; the match of a lampe; also, Match for a Harquebuse, &c; also, a tent (for a wound) vniforme, or all of a bignesse, and therein differing from* Tente, *which is bigger at one end then at the other.*
Descouvrir la meiche. *as in* Descouvrir. *(from birds, or wild beasts, which venting a match, doe quickly get them gone.)*
Meicheron: m. *A little match, weeke, or snuffe; also, a sparkle.*
Meignie: f. *A meynie, or houshold; See* Mesgnie.
Meillauque: f. *Turkie Millet, great blacke Millet.*
Meilleur: m. eure: f. *Better, worthier, honester; also, the best, or chiefest; as,* Le meilleur de tous autres; &, la meilleure chose qu'ils ont, &c.
Il a eu du meilleur. *He hath gotten the victorie.*
Courtes folies sont les meilleures: Prov. *The shortest follies are the best; (and thereof may the next Prouerbe be vnderstood;)*
Le plus bref est le meilleur: Prov. *The shorter the better.*
Qui avec son seigneur mange poires il ne choisit pas des meilleures: Prov. *Looke* Manger.
Meilleurer. *To improue, better; make better.*
Mein: m. *A proper name for a man; and particularly, the name of a Saint, who is held the Patron of the Scuruie; and hence;*
Mal de sainct Mein. *The wild scab, mange, or scuruie.*
Meix. *as* Mex.
Melancholie: f. *Melancholie, blacke choler; sadnesse, pensiuenesse, heauinesse, thoughtfullnesse, care-taking; solitarinesse, retyrednesse.*
Melancholie artificielle. *Oyle of Vitrioll, or Coperas; tearmed so by some Phisitions, because being spilled on the ground, it boyles of it selfe, like the Melancholie called,* Atra bilis.
Melancholie louviere. *Seeke* Louvier.
Elle fait plusieurs petites melancholies à son amy. *She playes him many wanton trickes, or puts him into many prettie extasies.*
Melancholier. Se melan. *To be melancholicke, sad, pensiue, heauie; to sorrow, grieue, take thought.*
Melancholique: com. *Melancholicke, sad, pensiue, heauie, thoughtfull; retyred; sullen; full of blacke choler.*
Melandrin: m. *A sea-fish, that (his blackish colour excepted) resembles the Pearch.*
Melanterie: f. *A caustick e minerall (of the colour of Sulphure) found in Brasse mines.*
Melegette. *The spice called Graines, or Graines of Paradice.*
Melese: f. *The Larch, or Turpentine tree; and (as* Meleze) *the gumme, or teare issuing from it.*
Melet: m. *A small, great-eyed, and little-mouthed seafish, otherwise much resembling (though not so daintie as) the Anchoua, whereof some hold it to be a kind; or, as;*
Melette: f. *A verie small, soft, and fat sea-fish, bred of raine, and water, and called the Smie, or sea-Groundlin.*
Meleze: f. *The gumme, or teare of the Larch tree; also, the tree it selfe; whence;*
Resine de meleze. *The Turpentine thats ordinarily sold by Apothecaries.*
Meliceride: f. *An impostume, or sore, whose humor resembleth honie.*
Melichore. *A winged Scorpion that hath two stings; also, a precious stone thats white on the one side, and of a honie colour on the other.*
Melicrat: m. *Metheglin, or Mede; drinke made of water, and honie sodden together.*
Melilot: m. *Melilot, Plaister Clauer, Harts Clauer.*
Melilot d'Italie. *Italian Clauer.*
Melilot de montaigne. *Herborist, or Tetrifolie; tearmed (Northward) Hader, or Hather.*
Franc melilot. *The same; or milke-Trefoile, shrub Trefoile.*
Melin: m. *Bastard yellow, straw colour, a colour betweene white and yellow.*
Melioration: f. *An improuement, a bettering; a making, or growing, better; and in Law, as* Reparation Vtile;

Vtile; *for which looke* Reparation.
Meliorer. *To improue, better, mend, amend.*
Melisse: f. *The hearbe called Balme, or Bawme.*
Melisse Constantinopolitaine. *Molucca Balme; a rough Plant, whose flowers grow within cups or bells.*
Melisse Moldavique. *Moldauian, or Turkie Balme; a most sweet and goodlie Plant.*
Melisse sauvage. *Wild Balme, or Bawme.*
Melitite. Pierre mel. *Looke* Pierre.
Melle. *as* Pomme Appie; *also, a Medlar.*
Mellifier. *To make of honie.*
Melliflue: com. *Mellifluous, most sweet, honie-sweet, out of which honie floweth.*
Mellindres: f. *Delicate little pies made of Indian wheat, and sugar.*
Melline: f. *A Filberd.*
Melliturgie: f. *The making of honie; Bees-worke.*
Melodie: f. *Melodie, harmonie, a tunable sound, or singing; a musicall, or sweet Ayer.*
Melodieusement. *Melodiously, harmoniously, musically, tunably.*
Melodieux: m. euse: f. *Melodious, musicall, harmonious, tunable, eare-delighting, full of concords.*
Melon: m. *A Melon, or Million.*
A peine connoist on la femme, & le melon: Prov. *Seeke* Femme.
Melonniere: f. *A Garden, Ground, or Bed, of Melons.*
Melopepon: m. *A Melon-Pumpion; a certaine fruit that participates both of the Melon and Pumpion.*
Melte: f. *The circuit of a Judge, or Sergeant; the territorie wherein they exercise their iurisdiction.* ¶Wallon.
Melun. *The name of a good towne standing neere to the Riuer of* Seine.
Anguilles de Melun. *Seeke* Anguilles.
Melze. *as* Meleze.
Memarchure: f. *Surbating of the feet (of cattell.)*
Membrane: f. *A membrane; the vpmost thinne skinne of any thing; also, a skinne of Parchment; also, the pill, or pilling betweene the barke, and tree.*
Membrane Allantoïde. *The middle of the three coats wherein an infant lyes wrapped in the wombe.*
Membrane Amphiblistroïde. *One of the foure principall membranes of the eye; is fashioned like a net; conueyes the light vnto the Christaline humor; and returnes all formes vnto the Optick sinew, whence it carries them vnto the braine, which iudges of them.*
Membrane Aragnoïde. *The spiderie membrane; issues from* la pie mere, *and incloses the fore-part of the Christaline humor; it serues (as the foyle in a Looking-glasse) to vnite, and retaine formes in the eye.*
Membrane blanche. *as* Membrane Conjonctive.
Membrane Blepharoïde. *A small membrane, wherby the waterie humor of the eye is distinguished from the glassie one.*
Membrane Conjonctive. *The white of the eye; or the fourth principall membrane (that couers all ouer the white) of the eye.*
Membrane cornée. *The hornie membrane; another of the foure, which resembles both in colour, and consistence, a thinne peece of horne; it springs from* la dure Mere, *and containes, by it hardnesse, all the humors together, but serues especially as a glasse, or spectacle vnto the Christaline.*
Membrane piliforme. *One of the two small membranes of the eye (* Aragnoïde *the other;) issues from the* Vvée; *incloses the fore-part of the glassie humour, where it prepares, and whitens the bloud brought vnto it by many small veines, and arteries, for the nourishment of the Christaline humor.*
Membrane Pleuretique. *A large, and two-fold membrane, through whose doubles passe all the sinewes, veines, and arteries, which are betweene the ribs, the inside whereof (as also of the breast, or bulke) it wholly couers.*
Membrane Raisiniere. *as* Membrane Vvée.
Membrane Retiforme. *as* Membrane Amphiblistroïde.
Membrane Vitrée. *as* Membrane Piliforme.
Membrane Vvée. *The grapie membrane; one of the foure principall ones; (tearmed so, because it resembles the skinne of a blacke Grape) comes from* la pie mere, *and incloses the eye on all parts, the ball excepted, where it is full of holes; it serues to comfort the Christaline humor by the diuersitie of the colours of it inward part; to keepe it from being hurt by the hornie tunicle; and to hold, and vnite, by it outward blacknesse, the spirits which otherwise would be dispersed.*
Membraneux: m. euse: f. *Filmie, full of membranes.*
Muscle membraneux. *as* Peaucier; *also, another which drawes the leg outwards.*
Membre: m. *A member, a limme; a part of the bodie, or of any other thing.*
Membres des compagnies de gendarmerie. *Places of note, or of commaund, in those companies.*
Membres d' esperon. *The gimmewes, or ioints of a Spurre.*
Vn membre de veau, de mouton, &c. *A ioynt of Veale, Mutton, &c.*
Membré: m. ée: f. *Membred (in Blason.)*
Membret d' esperon. *The gimmew, or ioint of a Spurre.*
Membreure. *as* Membrure.
Membru: m. uë: f. *Big-membred, big-limmed, strong, well-set.*
Membrure de bois. *A clouen boord, a shingle.*
Membrures de pierre de taille. *Such peeces of free stone as runne through a wall, and appeare on either side thereof.*
Memelon. *as* Mammelon.
Memener. *To misuse, molest, oppresse; (an old word.)*
Meminges. *as* Meninges.
Meniithé: m. *The bitter, and stinking iuice of an hearb that growes neere vnto* Hierapolis *in* Suria, *and is called* Glaucium, *which* Gerard *holds to be the redhorned Poppie.*
Memoire: f. *Memorie, remembrance, mindfullnesse; thought had, or mention made, of things absent, or past; also, a memorandum; a Bill, or note of remembrance; and hence;*
Memoires. *Notes of, writings for, remembrance; and a charge, or instructions giuen in writing; also, Histories, Chronicles, Commentaries, Records.*
Il a memoire de lapin, ou lievre. *He hath a verie bad memorie; or forgets in running what he runnes for.*
Memorable: com. *Memorable, remembrable, worthie of memorie, or of remembrance.*
Memorablement. *Memorably.*
Memoratif: m. iue: f. *Memoratiue, mindfull, often remembring.*
Memorial: m. *A memoriall, record, register; a booke of remembrances, a note, marke, or token for remembrance.*
Memoriallement. *Memorably.*
Memorieux: m. euse: f. *Full of memorie, or of a good memorie.*

Menaçant. *Menacing, threatening.*
Menace: f. *A menace, a threat.*
Menacé: m. ée: f. *Menaced, threatened.*
Menacement: m. *A menacing, a threatening.*
Menacer. *To menace, to threaten.*
Il ne le menace pas de poires molles. *Tis no small matter, no sleight mischiefe, wherewith he threatens him.*
Tel menace qui est batu: Prov. *Some threaten that are beaten.*
Tel menace qui a grand peur: Prov. *Looke* Peur.
Menaceur: m. *A menacer, a threatner.*
De grand menaceur peu de faict: Prov. *Great menacers, little men-hackers.*
Menaceux: m. euse: f. *Menacing, threatfull.*
Menage: m. *A bringing, leading, conducting; handling, manage, carriage.*
Menandé. *Surely, out of question, without doubt; (a Gossiplie oath, or asseueration.)*
Mendé. *as* Menandé.
Mendeux: m. euse: f. *Erronious, faultie, naughtie, lewd, false.*
Suture mendeuse. *The seame whereby the bone of the temples is ioyned with the scull.*
Mendiant: m. *A beggar.*
Mendiant: m. ante: f. *Begging.*
Mendicité: f. *Mendicitie, beggarie, beggarlinesse.*
Mendience: f. *A begging.*
Mendier. *To beg, to craue an almes, to goe from doore to doore.*
Mendole: f. *A Cackarell fish.*
Mene: f. *as* Mendole.
Mené: m. ée: f. *Led, brought; guided, conducted, directed; managed; moued, induced, persuaded; also, ouerraught, subdued, fetcht in.*
Mené à S.Mathurin. *Gulled, made a foole of.*
Mal mené. *Ill handled, abused, hardly vsed; sore layed to; wearied, tyred, iaw-fallen; imbossed, or almost spêt, as a Deere by hard pursuit.*
Meneau de fenestre. *The transome, or crosse-barre of a window.*
Menée: f. *A plot, conspiracie, practise; priuate faction; a shift, subtiltie, deuise; a businesse carried closely; also, the direct, or outright course of a flying Deere.*
La menée du Sergent. C'est quand le Sergent va sur les lieux du fief, & meine tesmoins pour l' aider en son exploict.
Vn faiseur de menées. *A Polypragmon, medler, common barrater, busie bodie.*
Mener. *To bring, lead; guide, conduct, direct; also, to manage, or handle; also, to moue, induce, toll on, persuade; also, to subdue, ouer-reach, fetch in.*
Mener l'asne. *To be laughed at, or little accounted of, by all men.*
Mener batant deuant eux. *To driue, or chase before them with blowes; and in fight, to pursue hard, or giue hard chase vnto.*
Mener à dy ay & hory ho. *To put vnto carting, or cart-driuing; to bring vnto drudgerie.*
Mener à la bonne eau. *To steale (a horse, &c.)*
Mener la genisse au Taureau. *To play the bawd.*
Mener la loy. *To proceed in a suite; or, to follow the Law.*
Mener les mains. *To lay about him; deale blowes, fall to handie-stroakes.*
Mener les mains basses. *To make a generall slaughter, to put all to the sword.*
Mener au Tabourinet. *Looke* Tabourinet.
Mener le train de. *To follow the businesse of.*
Mener vne trompe. *To driue a top; Looke* Trompe.
Cela ne me meine pas. *I am not ruled, nor swayed by that; I neither heed, nor respect it; it preuailes nothing with me.*
Il y a vn mois que la lavandiere nous meine. *The Laundresse hath put vs off this month.*
Qui femme croit, & Asne meine, son corps ne sera ia sans peine: Prov. *He that beleeues a woman, and leads an Asse, hath brought his bodie (and mind) t'an euill passe.*
Les Oisons menent paistre les Oyes: Prov. *Looke* Oison.
Menestranderie: f. *A companie of Minstrells.*
Menestrandier: m. *A Minstrell, or Fidler.*
Menestrel. *The same.* (v.m.)
Menestrier: m. *The same; also, as* Gaian.
Menier. *as* Propre; *(an old word.)*
Meniguette. *Looke* Maniguette.
Meninges. *Two skinnes, or filmes which enwrap the braine.*
Mennetot. *The name of a sweet apple.*
Menon: m. *A guelded Goat.*
Menone. *A Minstrell.* ¶Poictevin.
Menotes: f. *Manacles, hand-fetters.*
Mensale: f. *The Table-line in the hand; (a tearme of Palmistrie.)*
Mensionnier. *as* Mansionnier.
Mensonge: m. *A lye, fib, leasing, vntruth; a tale, ieast, mockerie, fable, false report.*
Les songes sont mensonges: Pro. *There is no truth in dreames.*
Mensonger: m. ere: f. *Lying, false, vntrue, fained, forged, fabulous; amisse.*
Mensonger. *To lye, fib, foist, fable, cog, faine; to forge, report, or deliuer, an vntruth.*
Mensongerement. *Lyingly, fabulously, falsely, vntruly.*
Menstrual: m. ale: f. *Menstruall, or menstruous; belonging, or like, vnto a womans flowers.*
Menstrue: m. *A womans flowers; her monthlie disease, or tearmes.*
Mensurable: com. *Measurable.*
Mental: m. ale: f. *Mentall, thoughtsome, belonging to the mind, (onely) in the mind.*
Mentastre: m. *Calamint, mountaine Mint.*
Mente: f. *The hearbe Mint, or Mints.*
Mente aiguë. *Speare-Mint, garden Mint, browne Mint, Mackerell Mint, our Ladies mint.*
Mente aquatique. *Fish Mint, water Mint, brooke Mint.*
Mente chevaline. *Horse Mint, wild Mints; water Mint.*
Mente crespuë. *Curled Mint, red garden Mints.*
Mente de nostre Dame. *as* Mente Romaine.
Mente Grecque. *The same.*
Mente Romaine. *Speare-Mint, balme-Mint, Mackerell Mint, garden Mint, browne Mint, our Ladies Mint.*
Mente Sarrasine. *The same.*
Mente sauvage. *Horse Mint, wild Mints; also, water Mint.*
Mentereau: m. *A fabler, fibber, prettie lyer.*
Menterie: f. *A lying, cogging, foisting, fabling, fibbing; also, a lye.*
Menteur: m. *A lyer, fibber, foister, fabler, cogger, leasing-mungar, false limmer.*
Homme plaideur menteur: Prov. *See* Plaideur.

Menteusement. *Most vntruly, verie falsely.*
Menteux: m. euse: f. *Full of lyes, fraught with leasings, fables, vntruthes.*
Menthastre: m. *Calamint, mountaine Mint.*
Menthe. *Looke* Mente.
Menti: m. ie: f. *Lyed, fained, foisted, fabled.*
Mentibules: f. *The iawes.*
Mention: f. *Mention; remembrance; a nomination, or naming of; talke had, speech passed, of.*
Mentionné: m. ée: f. *Mentioned; nominated, named, remembred; somewhat spoken, or talked of; touched in discourse.*
Mentionner. *To mention; remember; nominate, name; speake or talke of; touch in discourse.*
Mentir. *To lye, fib, fable, cog, foist, faine, forge vntruths, coyne leasings, tell a lye; also, to doe any thing contrarie to it selfe; whence;*
Bon cœur ne peut mentir: Prov. *An honest heart cannot vtter (or be the author of) an vntruth; and;*
Le bon sang ne peut mentir. *A noble nature will not yeeld vnto base conditions; or cannot, when occasion is offered, conceale it selfe.*
Mentir comme vn arracheur de dents. *To lye like a tooth-drawer; (we say that Barbers haue all the newes in a countrey; and they that tell much newes tell many a lye.)*
On ne doit point mentir en Vin: Pro. *Wine telleth truth, and should not be belyed.*
Menton: m. *The chinne.*
Lever le menton à. *To harden, assure, hearten, imbolden, incourage.*
Rabaisser le menton à. *To humble, deiect, bring low, plucke downe.*
Tenir le menton à. *To succour, fauor, support, maintaine, vphold.*
Celuy peut hardiment nager à qui l'on soustient le menton: Pro. *He must needs swimme that is held vp by the chinne (say we.)*
La vertu ne fut iamais à menton blanc: Pro. *Vertue neuer grew old; the vigor thereof did neuer decay.*
Mentonnier: m. ere: f. *Of, or belonging to, the chinne.*
Mentule: f. *A mans yard.* ¶Rab.
Menu. Le menu. *The prettie dishes, or fine meates at Table; also, the head, feet, and paunch of a sheepe.*
Menu: m. uë: f. *Little, small, fine, thinne, slender, subtill, exile.*
Menus droicts. *All vailes, or fees belonging to an officer; and particularly, the head, feet, skin, and intralls of a slaughtered beast, or all such parts as a Cooke, or yeoman of the slaughter-house, reserues for himselfe.*
Menus panais. *The white Mallow, marsh Mallow, moorish Mallow.*
Menues pensées. *Paunsies, Harts-ease, loue or liue in idlenesse; also, idle, priuate, or prettie thoughts.*
Le menu peuple. *The vulgar; the rude multitude; the meaner sort; the rascall, or common people.*
Menus poetastres. *Common, paultrie, triuiall, ignorant, Poets.*
Menus propos. *Short speeches, prettie sayings, pleasant conferences; also, idle chat.*
Menu ver, ou verk. *The furre Mineuer; also, the beast that beares it.*
Par le menu. *By parcells, by peeces, by retayle, peecemeale.*
Menuailles: f. *Small ware, small trash, small offalls; a great sort of little peeces, trinkets, or trifles.*
Menuëment. *Smally, slenderly, thinly, by little parcels, or peeces.*
Menuet: m. *The name of a sweet apple, that yeelds excellent Cyder.*
Menuet: m. ette: f. *Smallish, little, prettie, fine, thinne.*
Menuëté: f. *Smallnesse, littlenesse, exilitie, slendernesse, finenesse, thinnesse.*
Menuïsailles: f. *Small trash, slender toyes, little trifles, or offalls; also, as* Menus droicts; *or, the head, feet, and paunch of an edible creature.*
Menuïse: f. *Small fish of diuers sorts; or, the small fry of fish cast into a Pond, &c, for the storing thereof; also, a kind of net wherewith such fish may be caught; also, any small trash, guts, or garbage; and the gobbets, or parings of fish cut, and cast away by Fishmongers; also, a small Gudgeon, or fish bred of the spawne, but neuer growing to the bignesse, of a Gudgeon.*
Menuïsement: m. *A minishing, extenuating, making small; a crumbling, or breaking verie small.*
Menuïser. *To minish, extenuate, impaire verie much, make verie small; to crumble; to grind, breake, or cut small.*
Menuiserie: f. *Seeling, wainscotting, Ioyners worke; also, any small worke.*
Menuïseté: f. *Smallnesse, littlenesse, thinnesse, finenesse, exilitie, slendernesse.*
Menuisier: m. *A Ioyner.*
Menuisier: m. ere: f. *Of, or belonging to, a Joyner, or to Joyners worke.*
Menusaillerie: f. *Small stuffe.*
Menuville: f. *as* Manivelle (*in the last sence.*)
Meon: m. *Mew, Spignell, Baldimonie, Bearewort.*
Mequine. *as* Mechine. ¶Pic.
Mer: f. *The Sea; the Mayne; also, the hollownesse, or channell of a Wine-presse; the round concauitie wherein the grapes are pressed.*
Mer d'amont. *The Adriaticke sea; the sea wherein Venice doth stand.*
Mer d'aval. *The Tyrrhenian, or Tuscane sea.*
Mer majour. *The Euxine sea; the sea which diuides* Europe *from* Asia.
Mer de procez. *An infinite, or endlesse suit.*
Diable de mer. *A sea-Coot, or Cormorant.*
La grande mer. *The first Bull of Priuiledges graunted (by* Paulus tertius) *vnto the Jesuits.*
Verd de mer. *Sea-greene colour.*
Entre deux mers: *Is vnderstood of the countrey that lyes betweene the two large Gascon Riuers* Dordonne, *and* Garonne.
Mesler la mer, & le ciel. *To make a horrible confusion.*
Singler en haute mer. *To sayle in the Mayne; to haue stuffe enough to worke on, or the world at will.*
Tenir la mer. *To commaund at, or be maister of, the sea.*
Tenir à la mer. *To worke, or sayle against the tyde.*
Celuy qui se met sur la mer ou il est fol, ou il est pouvre, ou il a envie de mourir: Prov. *He that vnto the sea commits his bodie, is either poore, or desp'rat, or a noddie.*
Goutte à goutte la mer s'esgoute: Prov. *Looke* Esgouter.
Les Rivieres retournent en la mer: Prov. *(Said when Princes doe squeeze out of their spungie Officers the moisture which they haue purloyned from them.)*
Qui envoye chetif à la mer il n'en rapporte ne poisson, ne sel: Prov. *A man either looses, or gets naught, by sending an vnfit messenger.*
Qui est sur la mer ne fait pas des vents ce qu'il veut:

veut: Prov. *Winds are not subiect vnto those that sayle.*

Qui veut apprendre à prier aille souvent sur la mer: Prov. *He that will learne to pray let him goe oft to sea.*

Merane. *for* Mejane. ¶Rab.

Meratre: f. *A stepmother.*

Merc de Chastel; du Gibet; de la Iustice. *The seat, place, or marke of the house of a Lord* Chastelain, *and of (his) Gibbet, or Gallowes, which be signes of high Iurisdiction.*

Mercadant: m. *A poore marchant, paltrie tradesman; one that deales but for small, or sleight ware.*

Mercadence: f. *Small trafficke.*

Mercader: m. *A Marchant, or Tradesman.*

Mercandeau: m. *A paltrie marchant; poore bargainer, sorrie chafferer, beggarlie chapman.*

Mercandier: m. *as* Mercandeau.

Mercantil: m. ile: f. *Marchantlie, marchant-like.*

Mercenaire: com. *Mercenarie, hireling, or hired; that takes hire, wages, or bribes.*

Mercerie: f. *Small ware, chaffer.*

Mercerot: m. *A Pedler, a paltrie Haberdasher.*

Merci: f. *Mercie; also, pitie, compassion; tender-heartednesse; also, pardon, remission, forgiuenesse; also, a benefit, or fauour; also, thankes giuen for a benefit.*

Relief à merci. *The reuenue of one, or (as in some places) of euerie third yeare, yeelded for a* Relief.

Merci: m. ie: f. *Thanked; as in* Dieu merci. *God be thanked.*

Merci-dieu vilain. *Gods mercie villaine; or though I say it, you rogue (an angrie womans oath.)*

Mercier: m. *A good Pedler, or meane Haberdasher of small wares; a tradesman that retayles all manner of small ware, and hath no better then a shed, or boothe for his shop.*

Roy des merciers. *Looke* Roy.

Tuer vn mercier pour vn peigne. *To punish light faults with heauie penalties; or, to take a great reuenge of a small wrong.*

Chascun mercier prise ses aiguilles, & son panier: Prov. *To euerie one his owne seemes faire.*

'A chasque mercier son pannier: Pro. *Let each man his owne burthen beare.*

Il n'est pas mercier qui ne sçait faire sa loge: Prov. *The Pedlers gaine will be but small that cannot reare himselfe a stall.*

Petit mercier petit pannier: Prov. *The little Pedler a little packe doth serue.*

Mercier. *(Of three syllables) to thanke, or giue thanks.*

Mercredi. *Wednesday.*

Mercuire: f. *as* Mercuriale.

Mercure: m. *The God Mercurie; Planet Mercurie; drug Mercurie; also, Quick-siluer.*

Il a du mercure à la teste. *He is fantasticall, humorous, new-fangled, giddie-headed; also, he is verie craftie.*

Mercurial: m. ale: f. *Of Mercurie; made of Mercurie; borne vnder the Planet Mercurie; hence, humorous, fantasticall, new-fangled; also, prating, talkatiue, long-tongued; also, craftie, subtill, deceitfull, theeuish.*

Mercuriale: f. *Mercvrie, French Mercurie; an hearb whereof there be three kinds; a male, female, and;*

Mercuriale sauvage. *Wild Mercurie, dogs Mercurie, dogs Cawle.*

Mercuriales: f. *After-noone Sittings, appointed to be held on Wednesdayes, at first euerie fifteene dayes, or, at least, once a month; afterwards (by an Edict of* Charles *the ninth, in the yeare* 1566) *once euerie three months, in all Townes of Parliament; and at length (by an Edict of* H. 3. Anno 1579) *in all Presidiall Townes, and but once in six months: The Judges in them be certaine select Presidents of the Place, who are to examine, and censure the faults committed by th' Officers of th' ordinarie Courts held there (or elsewhere within that Jurisdiction) and during the continuance of that businesse must intend no other.*

Mercurializer. *To mercurialize it; to be humorous, fantasticall, new-fangled; also, to prattle, bable, talke ouermuch.*

Mercy. *Looke* Merci.

Merdaille: f. *A crue of shitten knaues, of filthie scowndrells, of stinking fellowes.*

Merde: f. *Mans dung, turd, excrements, ordure.*

Merde de fer. *The drosse of Iron.*

Merde oye. *A Goose-turd greene.*

Robbe d'argent brodée de merde. *An excellent Text ill expounded, or commented on; (for which cause* Rabelais *calls so* Iustinians *Institutes.)*

'A cul de foirard tousiours abonde merde: Prov. *There wants no turd at shitten fellowes tayles.*

Le Porc a tout bon en soy fors que la merde: Prov. *Looke* Porc.

Merdé. *In stead of,* Mort Dieu.

Merdefer. *The drosse of Jron.*

Merdefin: m. *A Phisition; tearmed so in derision.*

Merdeux: m. euse: f. *Beshitten, berayed, all-to-beturded, full of ordure.*

Merdigues. *Mother of God; (a rusticall oath.)*

Merdré. *as* Merdé. ¶Rab.

Merdugues. *Mother of God; (a rusticall oath, or Interiection.)*

Mere: f. *A mother; also, the wombe, or Matrix of a woman; also, the earth of a Fox, or hole of a Badger; also, a great salting-tub for Hogs-flesh; also, a great pit, or trench, whereinto the superfluous moisture of waterie ground is conueyed by small cuts, or ditches; also, the anterior, and inner side, or face, of an Astrolabe.*

Mere des cailles. *A Rayle; or, a brooke-Owsell.*

Mere d'une fontaine. *The head of a Fountaine, or Conduit, walled about with, or couered with a vault of, stone.*

Mere grand. *A grandmother, a grandam.*

Dure mere de la teste. *The double skin that couereth th' outside of the braine, and keepeth it from being hurt, or touched by the skull.*

Pie mere. *A thin, and cleere skin, or filme, next to the braine, the which it inwraps on all sides, and nourishes by vessels receiued from other parts.*

C'est le ventre ma mere. *I will come no more there, I will doe no more so.*

Il s'en va prendre la mere au nid. *Said of one that steales (in ieast) towards another, with a purpose to doe him some vnhappie tricke: Said also of a nice, and precise hypocrite.*

Mere piteuse fait sa fille roigneuse: Prov. *A tender mother breeds a scabbie daughter.*

La mere du timide ne sçait que c'est de pleurer: Prov. *The cowards dam knowes not what weeping meanes.*

Mauvaise fille se mocque de sa mere: Prov. *Looke* Mauvais.

Mere: com. *Meere, vnmixed, sole, right, pure, plaine, without art, of it selfe.*

Mere goutte. *Vnpressed wine, or oyle; such as of it selfe, distills from the grapes, or oliues, immediatly after they be layed in the presse.*
Bateau mere. *A great salt-boat, or barke; or, the chiefest, or greatest of a fleet.*
Sentine mere. *A little salt-boat, or barke.*
Tout fin mere nud. *Naked vp, or euen, to the bellie.*
Mereau: m. *A Counter (to cast withall;) also, a Token (receiued at Church by one that meanes to communicate.)*
Meregrand. *Looke* Mere.
Merelles. Le Ieu des merelles. *The boyish game called Merills, or fiue-pennie Morris; played here most commonly with stones, but in France with pawnes, or men made of purpose, and tearmed* Merelles.
Mere-perle. *Mother of pearle.*
Merge: m. *A name for diuers water fowle, that vse to ducke much; as the Puffin, Cormorant, Didapper, &c.*
Meriane: f. *Noone-rest, sleeping adayes, or at mid-day.* ¶Norm.
Merianer. *To rest, or sleepe at noone-tide.*
Meridian. *as* Meridien.
Meridien: m. *The Meridian; a circle which passing through both the Poles, and through our Zenith (wheresoeuer) diuides the Sphere into two equall parts; th'one Orientall, th'other Occidentall.*
Meridien: m. enne: f. *Meridian; South, or Southerlie; of, or belonging to, the Meridian, mid-day, or noone.*
Meridional: m. ale: f. *Meridionall, Southerlie, of the South, on the South side; belonging to noone-tide.*
Cercle meridional. *as* Meridien; *called so, because whensoeuer, and wheresoeuer the Sunne comes into it it is noone.*
Merin: m. *A Sergeant, common Bayliffe, or such like rurall Officer in the Customes of* La Bourt.
Merise: f. *A small bitter Cherrie.*
Merisier: m. *The small and bitter Cherrie-tree.*
Merite: m. *Merite; desert; an act worthie of recompence.*
Les merites d'un procez. *The Pleadings of a cause; the Bill, Answer, Reply, and Reioinder; the titles alledged, proofes produced, or matter contained, therein.*
Merité: m. ée: f. *Merited, deserued, earned.*
Meritément. *Meritoriously, deseruedly, worthily, with good cause.*
Meriter. *To merit, to deserue.*
Meritoire: com. *Meritorious, well deseruing, worthie of reward.*
Meritoirement. *Meritoriously, deseruedly, worthily.*
Merlan: m. *A Whiting, a Merling.*
Merlan salé. *A dryed Whiting; the fish which we call (of it hardnesse) Buckhorne.*
Merlanc. *as* Merlan.
Merle: m. *A Mearle, Owsell, Blackbird.*
Merle bleu. *A small Owsell, that vsually builds among Rocks, and feeds on wormes, fruits, and seeds.*
Merle de Bresil. *A kind of Mearle of a liuelie red colour.*
Merle au collier. *A kind of Thrush that hath a whitish ring about her necke.*
Merle de mer. *The Cooke-fish, or sea-Tench; a duskie, and daintie fish, that resembles a Perch.*
Merle noir. *The Blackbird, or ordinarie Owsell.*
Grand merle. *A Goat-sucker; a mountaine bird, somewhat bigger then an Owsell, and lesse then a Cuckoe.*
Ie vous donneray vn merle blanc. *I will performe impossibilities, or bestow on you a most rare gift.*

Merle: f. *as* Mesle; *a Medlar.*
Merlet: m. *A battlement (of a wall.)*
Merlette: f. *A Martlet, in Blason.*
Merlier: m. *A Medlar tree.*
Merlus, ou Merluz: m. *A Mellwell, or Keeling, a kind of small Cod whereof Stockfish is made.*
Chausses à queuë de merlus. *Looke* Chausse.
Mermelade: f. *Marmalade.*
Merque. *as* Marque.
Merque de bois. *A rowe, tuft, or groue of trees neere to a house.*
Merques: f. *Be, in a paire of beads, the biggest, or least.*
Merrain, & Merrien. *as* Marrein.
Mers. Batture faicte au dessus des mers. *Vpon the head, or face.*
Merveillable: com. *Maruellous, admirable.*
Merveille: f. *A maruell, wonder; miracle; a monstrous thing, strange accident, admirable matter.*
`A merveilles. *Maruellously, miraculously, wonderfully, admirably, strangely.*
Pois de merveilles. *The blacke Winter Cherrie, Indian Hart, or Hart-pease.*
Merveille; ou, Pomme de mer. *The Balsam, or Balme apple; (an hearbe.)*
Merveille femelle. *The female Balsam apple; beares a purple flower, and differs from the male in all things but the fruit; which (though like vnto) is somewhat lesse then his.*
Merveille masle. *The male Balsame, or Balme apple, (tearmed particularly the apple of Ierusalem) beares a faint-yellow, or straw-coloured flower.*
Merveilleusement. *Maruellously, miraculously, wonderfully, strangely.*
Merveilleux: m. euse: f. *Maruellous, miraculous, wonderfull, admirable, strange.*
Mery: m. *The gullet, weason, or pipe, whereby meat passeth downe into the stomacke.*
Més: m. *A messe, or seruice of meat; a course of dishes at table.*
Belle chere vault bien vn més: Prov. *A cheerefull looke fills vp halfe-emptie dishes.*
Qui a fourmage pour tous més il le doit couper bien espez: Prov. *He that hath nought but Cheese at noone and night, must banish the Phisitions pennyweight.*
Mes. *The Plurall of* Mon; *as,* Mes livres, habits, &c.
Mes. *for* Plus, *as* Oncques mes. *Neuer more.*
Mes, *in Composition, is as much as* Mal, *peruerting and turning to ill the sence of the words it precedeth; as in* Mesaise, Mesfaire, &c; *Or as our Compounds, Vn, and Mis, which we vse vnto the same purpose.*
Mesadvenance: f. *Vncomelinesse, misbecomming.*
Mesadvenir à. *To mishappen, to succeed ill vnto.*
Mesadventure: f. *Misaduenture, mischance, misfortune, mishap.*
Mesadvenuë: f. *as* Mesadventure.
Mesaise: f. *Disease, trouble, molestation, calamitie, miserie, affliction.*
Mesange: f. *A Titmouse, or Tittling.*
Mesange bleuë. *Our ordinarie Titmouse.*
Mesange hupée. *A copped small Titmouse, that hath a blacke head spotted with white, a light-browne bodie, white breast, and ash-coloured thighes.*
Mesange à la longue queuë. *The lōg-tayled Titmouse; liues, for the most part, among hills, and in high places.*
Mesange nonnette. *The little Titmouse called a Nunne, because she seemes to weare (as a Nunne doth) a fillet about her head.*

Mesaraïques. Veine mes. *Looke* Veine.
Mesarriver. *To misarriue, to happen, or come vnfortunately vnto.*
`A qui il mesarrive on luy mesfaict: Prov. *(So apt are men to wrong th' vnfortunate.)*
Meschamment. *Wickedly, impiously, vngraciously, naughtily, filthily, most impurely, scuruily, roguishly, knauishly, villanously; curstly, frowardly, mischieuously; paltrily, coursely.*
Meschance: f. *A mischiefe, or mischance.*
Meschanceté: f. *Wickednesse, impietie, vngraciousnesse, knauerie, naughtinesse, villanie, vilenesse; a bad act, lewd pranke, filthie part, sinfull deed.*
Meschant. *Wicked, impious, vngracious, naughtie, bad, lewd, villanous, roguish; vile, filthie, scuruie, most impure; also, paltrie, course, vnworthie; also, curst, mischieuous, harsh, froward.*
Meschant ouvrier ia ne trouvera bons outils: Pro. *A bungler seldome fits him with good tooles.*
Meschantes paroles ont meschant lieu: Pro. *Bad words doe find but bad acceptance.*
Meschante parole iectée va par tout à la volée: Prov. *A bad word cast, soone roues, abroad.*
De meschant homme bon Roy: Pro. *The froward, or vntractable man proues a good King.*
De meschant hoste bon reconduiseur: Pro. *A needie host (or ghest) a notable guide.*
Tout meschant est ignorant: Prov. *All naughtie men are ignorant.*
Aujourd'uy marchant demain meschant: Pro. *To day a Marchant, to morrow a miscreant.*
Bon bastard, c'est avanture, mais meschant c' est de nature: Prov. *Bastards by chance are good, by nature bad.*
Sans estre poursuivy le meschant prend la fuite: Prov. *The sinner flyes before he be pursued; selfe-guilt, though nought else, makes a sinner fly.*
Mesche. *as* Meiche.
Mescheif: m. *Mischiefe.*
Mescheniere: f. *Candle-wecke Mullein.*
Mescheoir à. *To mishappen, succeed ill, fall out vnluckily for.*
`A qui meschet on luy mesoffre: Prov. *Those whom necessitie, or misfortune forces to sell, are neuer offered the full worth of things.*
Aux bons meschet il: Pro. *The best men (commonly) haue the worst fortune; whereupon we say, The honester man the worse his lucke.*
Il n'est pas en seurté à qui ne mescheust oncques: Prov. *He stands not surely that did neuer slip.*
Meschine: f. *A wench, maid seruant, miskin fro.*
Meschinon: f. *A girle; a little, or young maid seruant.*
Mescle: f. *Maslin; Wheat and Rye mingled.* ¶Langued.
Mescogneu. Il ne s'est point mescogneu. *He acknowledged, forgot not, was mindfull, or not ignorant, of.*
Mescognoissance: f. *Vnacknowledgement, ingratitude, vnthankfullnesse, churlishnesse; ignorance.*
Mescognoissant. *Vnacknowledging, ignorant; vngratefull, vnrespectiue, vnthankfull.*
Mescognoistre. *To mistake; ignore; forget; neglect.*
Mescompte: m. *A misreckoning, or wrong accompt; a mistaking; fayling, or erring, in accompt.*
Mesconseiller. *To miscounsell, misaduise, peruert, seduce.*
Mesconte: m. *as* Mescompte.
Mesconté: m. ée: f. *Misreckoned, miscompted.*

Mescontentement: m. *Discontentment, offence, ill satisfaction.*
Mescontenter. *To displease, discontent, offend, giue ill satisfaction to.*
Se mescontenter de. *To take the pet, or pepper in the nose, at; to be ill satisfied with; no way to like, or allow of.*
Mesconter. *To miscount, misreckon; fayle, or erre, in reckoning.*
Mescreable: com. *Vnbeleeuable, suspectable, not to be credited, vnfit to be trusted.*
Mescreance: f. *Miscreancie, misbeleefe, a wrong beleefe.*
Mescreant. *Miscreant, misbeleeuing; faithlesse; incredulous, mistrustfull.*
Mescreu. *as* Mescru.
Mescroire. *To mistrust, suspect, haue little beleefe, put small confidence, in; also, to play the miscreant, or beleeue amisse.*
Mescru: m. uë: f. *Mistrusted, suspected, not credited, no way beleeued.*
Mes-dames. *The title, or stile of the French Kings daughters.*
Mes-damoiselles. *The title, or stile of the French Kings brothers daughters.*
Mesdire. *To depraue, reproach, reuile; rayle on, detract from, speake ill of.*
Mesdisance. *as* Mesdisson.
Mesdisant. *Reproachfull, detractiue, obloquious, opprobrious, rayling, reuiling.*
Il ne seroit nuls mesdisans s'il n'estoit des escoutans: Pro. *There would be none to rayle if none would heare.*
Mesdisson: f. *Reproach, obloquie, detraction, obtrectation, opprobrious speech; reuiling, deprauing, rayling on.*
Mesdonner. *To misgiue, or bestow amisse.*
Mese: f. *An eighth, or proportion of eight, in Musicke; also, as* Mere *(wantonly.)*
Meseau: m. *A meselled, scuruie, leaporous, lazarous person.*
Plus crasseux que la tasse d'un meseau. *See* Crasseux.
Mesel. *as* Meseau.
Meselerie: f. *Meseldnesse, leaprosie, scuruinesse.*
Meseleux: m. euse: f. *Meseld, leaporous, full of the Scuruie.*
Meselle: f. *A leaporous, or scuruie woman.*
Mesellerie: f. *as* Meselerie.
Meselleux. *as* Meseleux.
Mesentere: m. *The* Mesenterium, *or the middle of the bowells; or, the fat, thicke, or double skinnes that fasten them to the backe, and each vnto other.*
Mesenterique: com. *Of, or belonging to, the* Mesenterium.
Arteres mesenteriques. *Are two; an vpper, which distributes it selfe among the small guts; and, an vnder one, which goes vnto the lower part of the* Mesenteriũ.
Veines mesenteriques. *Looke* Veine.
Mesescrire. *To write ill, or amisse, of; to write against.*
Mes-estimer. *To missesteeme, or disesteeme.*
Mesfaire. *To wrong, abuse, misdoe vnto.*
`A qui il mesarrive on luy mesfait: Pro. *Men (lightly) vse him ill that hath ill lucke.*
Mesfiance: f. *Distrust, mistrust.*
Mesgarde: f. *Heedlesnesse, retchlesnesse, improuidence, ouersight, carelesnesse, lacke of good-take-heed.*
Mesgnie: f. *A meynie, familie, houshold; or houshold seruants; Looke* Mesnie.

Mesgue: f. *Whay.*
Mesguis. *as* Megis.
Meshaigne: com. *Peeuish, wayward, froward, ill to please; (the humor of most lame persons.)*
Meshain. *as* Mehaing.
Meshingandé: m. ée: f. *(Almost) off the hindges; loose in euerie ioint.*
Meshuy. *Not to day, not this day, not till to morrow; (a word applyed most properly to the whole later part of the day.)*
Meslange: f. *A mixture, medley, mesh; mingling; hotchpot, gallymaufrey; a composition, or collection of many seuerall things.*
Meslangé: m. ée: f. *Mixed, mingled, melled, blent; iumbled, shuffled, hudled together.*
Meslanger. *To mingle, mix, blend; mash, mell; iumble, shuffle; make a confused medley, huddle things together.*
Meslangeur: m. *A mingler, mixer, blender; iumbler, shuffler, huddler of things together.*
Mesle: f. *A Medlar.* ¶Pic.
Auec le temps, & la paille lon meure les mesles: Prov. *Time and affliction supple harshest natures.*
Meslé: m. ée: f. *Mingled, mixed, put among; melled; medled, intermedled; shuffled, huddled, or iumbled, with.*
Cheveux meslez. *Tangled locks; also, gray haires; whence;*
Vn homme meslé. *One thats full of gray haires; also, a generall scholler, one that hath a smattering of all Arts.*
Pesle meslé. *Pell-mell, confusedly.*
Meslée: f. *A mixture, or medley; a blending, mingling, melling; also, a fight, fray, conflict, combat, bickering, battell.*
Meslément. *Mixtly, confusedly, in a huddle, as a hotchpot, one with another.*
Mesler. *To mingle, mix, blend, mash, mell; to huddle, shuffle, iumble; confound.*
Se mesler de. *To meddle, intermeddle, deale with, haue a hand in.*
Se mesler du mestier. *Looke* Mestier.
Cela meslera nos fusées. *That will vnite our causes, or make them alike.*
Il est bien heureux qui se mesle de ses affaires: Prov. *Happie is he that followes his owne businesse; Looke* Heureux.
Qui se mesle d' autruy mestier il trait sa vache en vn panier: Prov. *Looke* Mestier.
Mesleure: f. *A medley, mixture; mingling; medling.*
Meslié. *as* Meslé. ¶Vandosmois.
Meslier: m. *A Medlar tree; also (the name of) a fruitfull white Vine, whose leafe is almost round; whence;*
Le meslier commun. *The most fruitfull kind thereof.*
Le franc meslier. *Another, which beares the best fruit.*
Le gros meslier. *Hath the greatest stocke, and yeelds the greatest grape.*
Mesliers: m. *The plurall to* Meslier; *also, Vines of seuerall kinds, and colours growing together.*
Meslinge, & Meslingé. *as* Meslange, & Meslangé.
Meslinger. *as* Meslanger.
Meslouër. *To dispraise, discommend, detract from.*
Mesmarché: m. ée: f. *Trodden, or gone awry.*
Mesmarcher. *To tread, or goe awry, to set the steps amisse.*
Mesmarchure: f. *A wry step, or treading; an ill posture, or setting of the foot in treading; also, a wrinch, or straine got in a bone, or ioint by such treading.*
Mesme: com. *Same, the same, selfe, the selfe-same, the verie same.*
'A mesme terre. *On the verie ground.*
Estre à mesmes de quelque chose. *To haue a thing in his power, or choice.*
I'estois à mesme de ce faire. *I was euen readie, or about, to doe this.*
I'ay faict de mesme vous. *I haue done iust as you.*
Vous n'estes pas à vous mesme. *Your wits runne a wooll-gathering; or, you are not well in your wits.*
Les Bourgeois (de ce païs) boivent de bon Vin, & leurs serviteurs de Mesme: *An ordinarie Prouerb in* Maine; *from the equiuocation betweene this* mesme, *and* Mesme *the name of a Riuer in* Le Perche.
Mesmement. *Namely, especially, chiefely, principally.*
Mesmes. *The plurall to* Mesme; *also, as* Mesmement.
Mesmeté: f. *Selfenesse, it selfe, it owne essence, or being.*
Mesnage: m. *Houshold-stuffe, businesse, or people; a houshold, familie, or meynie.*
Poisson de mesnage. *as* Belenne.
'A profit de mesnage. *Soundly, throughly, with a witnesse, without ieasting or dalliance, to some purpose.*
Faire mauvais mesnage ensemble. *To agree illfauoredly together.*
Remuer mesnage contre. *To rise vp, or make an insurrection against; and hence;*
Remueur de mesnage. *An vnquiet, seditious, turbulent, or troublesome fellow.*
Tout vient à point qui tient mesnage: Prov. *All's fish that comes to the householders net.*
Mesnagé: m. ée: f. *Husbanded, thriftily vsed.*
Mesnageable: com. *Husbandable.*
Mesnagement: m. *Good husbandrie, thriftinesse, frugalitie, warinesse, prouidence; also, a husbanding, or thriftie disposall, of things.*
Mesnager: m. *as* Mesnagier; *whence the Prouerbe;*
Prou despendre, & peu gaigner saccage le mesnager.
Mesnager. *To husband, to vse thriftily, gouerne discreetly, make the best or most of a thing.*
Mesnagerément. *Frugally, thriftily, prouidently, like a good husband.*
Mesnagerie: f. *Husbandrie, or huswiferie; and the vse, or practise thereof.*
Mesnagier: m. *An husband, an householder.*
Vn bon mesnagier. *A thriftie, warie, frugall, prouident fellow, one that lookes verie well to his own profit.*
Vn mauvais mesnagier. *An vnthrift, scape-thrift, squāder-good, spēd-all, riotous, dissolute, carelesse yōker.*
Mesnagiere: f. *A houswife, or huswifelie woman.*
Mesnie: f. *A meynie, familie, houshold, houshold companie, or seruants.*
De nouveau Seigneur nouvelle mesnie: Pro. *New Lords new Lawes.*
De tel Seigneur telle mesnie: Pro. *Like maister like meynie.*
Mesoffrir. *To vnderbid; to offer lesse for a thing then tis worth; also, to wrong, misuse, abuse.*
A qui meschet on luy mesoffre: Pro. *Look* Mescheoir.
Mesolabe: m. *An halfe Astrolabe; an Instrument vsed for the finding out of one, or many proportionall lines.*
Mesoüan, ou mesouën. *Henceforward, frō henceforth.*
Mesparler. *To speak ill, or amisse of; to depraue, dispraise, misterme, detract from.*
Mespartement: m. *A misparting; an vnhonest, vnfit, or vnseemelie diuision.*
Mespert: m. *An halfe-part; or a keeping of a thing for halfe the profit comming of it.*

Mesple: f. *A Medlar, or Open-arse.*
Mesplier: m. *A Medlar tree.*
Mesplier sauvage. *The Hollie, Huluer, Holme tree.*
Mesprendre. *To erre, mistake; transgresse, offend.*
Mespris: m. *Despisall, disestimation, contempt, loathing, neglect, carelesse regard of.*
Mesprisant. *Contemning, despising, disesteeming, neglecting, heedlesse of.*
Mesprisé: m. ée: f. *Despised, disesteemed, contemned, neglected, not heeded, nought set by.*
Mesprisement: m. *A contemning, disesteeming, despising, disdaining, neglecting.*
Mespriser. *To disesteeme, contemne, disdaine, despise, neglect, make light of, set nought by.*
Mespriseresse: f. *A coy, squeamish, or scornefull dame.*
Mespriseur: m. *A disesteemer, contemner, disdainer, despiser; one that neglects, or makes light accompt of, things.*
Mesprison: f. *Misprision, error; offence; a thing done, or taken, amisse.*
Mesquin: m. *A wretch, caitife, sillie groome, poore swaine.*
Mesrien, & Mesrin. *as* Marrein.
Messadge, & Messadgerie. *as* Message, & Messagerie.
Message: m. *A message, errand, embassage; also, a messenger, or embassador.*
Mesager. *as* Messagier.
Messagere: f. *A she-messenger.*
Messagerie: f. *A messengership; the estate, office, or function of a messenger.*
Messagier: m. *A Messenger; Pursuiuant; Poste; Apostle.*
Messagier solennel. *An embassador.*
Ne fais pas d'un fol ton messagier: Pro. *Send not a foole on thine errand, make not a foole thy messenger.*
Messe: f. *The Masse, a Masse.*
Messe de chasseur. *A short, or soone-said Masse.*
La messe Martingault. *An Allarum, or Curfue bell, so tearmed by the inhabitants of* Touraine.
Enfans de choeur de la messe de minuict. *Quirresters of midnights Masse; night-walking rakehells, or such as haunt those nightlie Rites, not for any deuotion, but onely to rob, abuse, or play the knaues with, others.*
Quand la messe fut chantée, si fut la Dame parée: Prov. *When prayers were ended, Madame ends her pranking.*
Messeamment. *Vnseemely, ill-suitingly, vnhandsomely, ill-fauoredly, with small decorum, or comelinesse.*
Messeance: f. *A misbecomming, vnsutablenesse, vnfitnesse, vnseemelinesse, ill-fauorednesse.*
Messeant. *Ill-sitting, ill-suiting, misbecomming, vnbeseeming; vnhandsome, vndecent, vncomelie; vnworthie of.*
Messel: m. *A Masse-booke.*
Messer: m. *as* Maistre; *a Maister; whence;*
La Case monstre le messer: Prov. *The house the owner shewes.*
Messeresque. Generosité messeresque. *Italian generousnesse; or, the generositie of Italian gentlemen.*
Messied. *(A verbe Impersonall)* Cela messied à. *Misbecomes, ill becomes, or becomes not; is vnseemelie, vnhandsome, vnfit for, vnworthie of.*
Messier: m. *A keeper, or ouerseer of a Vineyard.*
Messiffiant. *Massing, saying or singing Masse.*
Messiffier. *To sing, or say Masse.*
Messilier: m. Sergent messilier. *An officer that lookes vnto Vineyards, and other fruit-bearing grounds.*
Mession: f. La Mession. *The Vacation (among Lawyers, and Schollers) during Vintage; for it begins the seuenth of September, and ends about the eleuenth of October.* ¶Norm.
Messire. *Sir; (The title of a Knight; of a Marchant; and of a countrey Curate.)*
Messottier: m. *A massing Priest; or a nickname for him.*
Mestaier. *as* Mestayer.
Mestairie: f. *A great Farme.*
Mestais. *as* Mestayer.
Mestayer: m. *A Farmer; a Husbandman, or Ploughman; especially such a one, as by contract, is to yeeld halfe the profits, or increase of his land vnto him of whom he holds it; or such a one, as takes or sowes another mans land to the halues.*
Mestier: m. *A Trade, Occupation, Misterie, Handicraft; also, need, lacke, necessitie, want, occasion for the vse, of a thing; also, a Weauers Frame, or Loome; also, the wort of Ale, or Beere; also, a kind of wafer, which is not altogether so thicke as the* Gauffre.
Mestiers. *A certaine Game wherein all trades are counterfeited by signes.*
Le mestier de la guerre. *The Art of Warre.*
Le mestier ord. *Lecherie, or bawderie;* Looke Femme.
S'endormir sur le mestier. *Lastly to foreslow, faint in, or giue ouer, a businesse, when it is at the height, or halfe done.*
Se mesler du mestier. Femmes qui se meslent du mestier. *That deale in the trade you wot of; that trade with their tayles.*
Mourir de faim prés le mestier. *To starue in a Cookes shop.*
C'est mestier iuré, il n'en est pas qui veut: Prov. *(Vnderstood of honestie.)*
Mieux vault mestier qu'esparvier: Prov. *Looke* Esparvier.
Qui sçait mestier il est renté: Pro. *The industrious tradesmans rents come in apace; or, he that hath a good trade hath a goodlie reuenue.*
Qui se mesle d'autruy mestier il trait sa vache en vn panier: Prov. *As good milke a Cow into a Siue, as deale in an vnknowne Trade.*
Mestif: m. *A Mongrell.*
Les mestis. *Such as are of a meane estate, or condition.*
Mestif: m. iue: f. *Mongrell; halfe the one halfe the other; whence;*
Vn chien mestif. *A Mongrell; vnderstood, by the French, especially of a Dog thats bred betweene a Mastiue or great Curre, and a Greyhound.*
Mestivailles: f. *Haruest feasts.*
Mestivales. *The same.*
Mestivé: m. ée: f. *Reaped, as Corne in Haruest.*
Mestiver. *To reape, to make Haruest.*
Mestives: f. *Haruest; Corne thats ripe, or readie to be reaped, or alreadie reaped, in Haruest.*
Mestivier: m. *A Reaper, a Haruest man.*
Mestoyant. *Middle, betweene both.*
Mesvenir. *as* Mesdvenir.
Mesurage: m. *Measurage; a measuring.*
Droict de mesurage. *The appointing, or proportioning of Measures, or the setting downe of their Assise, within a Territorie, belongs to none vnder the degree of a Lord* Chastellain; *for the authoritie of the* Haut Iusticier *extends no further then to a bare examination of their iustnesse; also, Toll-Corne, and Toll-Salt.*
Mesurant. *Measuring, meating.*

Mesure mesurante. *The vessell, or instrument wherewith a thing is measured.*

Mesure: f. *A measure; scantling, rule, square, proportion, size; an instrument, or vessell of measuring; also, modulation, or time, in Musicke; also, a measure, meane, moderation, temperature; also, a particular Corne-measure containing about a bushell and a halfe. For land there be foure kinds of* Mesures *in France; one consisting of 22 foot to the Perch, and 100 Perches (in square) to the Arpent; The second (more common then that) of 20 foot to the Perch, and 100 Perches to the Arpent; The third (least in vse) of 19 foot and a third to the Perch, and 100 Perches to the Arpent; The last (and most vsuall one) of 18 foot to the Perch, and (as in the rest) 100 Perches to the Arpent.*

Mesure d'un moulin. *A Mill-hopper.*

Mesure de Roy. *Looke* Roy.

Appetissement de mesure. *A certaine Impost vpon Wine retayled within* Tours, Mehun sur Eure, Vierzon, *and some other Townes; leuied towards the reparation of their walls, gates, bridges, causeyes, pauements, &c.*

La petite mesure. *The same.*

'A mesure que. *As, euen as, still as, euer as; by how much, or looke how much that.*

Oultre mesure. *Profusely, excessiuely, vnmeasurably, extreamely.*

Cuider n'est pas iuste mesure: Prov. *Coniecture is no iust measure; the iust conclude not by imagination; He often wrongs both himselfe and others, who makes a certain estimate, or giues a finall iudgement, vpon the first, or outward apparance of things.*

Mesuré: m. ée: f. *Measured, meated, proportioned, ruled, squared out; valued, rated; weighed, examined; moderated, tempered.*

Mesure mesurée. *The size, or quantitie of that which is measured.*

Mesurement: m. *A measuring, a meating.*

Mesurer. *To measure, meat, proportion, rule; square out; examine, weigh; rate, value, esteeme; temper, qualifie, moderate.*

Mesurer les sauts des puces. *To loose time, or spend it most idly, fondly, vainely.*

Qui mesure l'huile il s'en oingt les mains: Prov. *Looke* Huile.

Mesureur: m. *A measurer, meater, surueyor.*

Mes-usage: m. *Misusage, bad vsage, ill handling.*

Met: m. *Sometimes vsed (by the Parisians) in stead of* Maistre.

Met: f. *A kneading trough, or tub; also, a binne to keepe bread in; also, the trough, gutter, or furrow of a Winepresse; that whereinto the Wine falleth.*

Metacarpe: m. *The vpper part of the hand from the wrist to the knuckles, or the root, of the fingers.*

Metagraboulizé: m. ée: f. *Puzzled in, dunced vpon.*

Metagraboulizer. *To dunce vpon, to puzzle, or (too much) beat the braines about.*

Metail: m. *Meslin, or Maslin; Wheat and Rye mingled, sowed, and vsed together.*

Metairie: f. *A Farme, Tenement, Countrey house.*

Metais: m. *A Farmer, or Husbandman; for he holds not by rent, &c; but onely tills, and orders the Farme as seruant vnto the owner.*

Metaise: f. *Such a Farmers wife.*

Metal: m. *Mettall, mettle.*

Metalepse: f. *A figure whereby a word is put from it proper signification.*

Metalier: m. ere: f. *Of, or belonging to, mettall; full of, or abounding with, mettall.*

Metalisé: m. ée: f. *Made mettall, reduced into mettall.*

Metallier: m. *A mettall-man; one that deales in mettalls.*

Metallurgie: f. *A search, or searching for mettall in the bowells of the earth.*

Metamorphose: f. *A Metamorphosis; a transformation of shape.*

Metamorphoser. *To transforme; to alter, or change the shape of.*

Metaphore: f. *A Metaphor; the translation, or change of a word out of it proper, into another, sence.*

Metaphoriquement. *Metaphorically, by translation, figuratiuely.*

Metaphrene: m. *That part of the backe which is ouer-against the heart.*

Metaposcopie: f. *A mans phisiognomie.*

Metayer: m. *A Farmor, or Husbandman; properly one that takes grounds to the halues; or binds himselfe, by contract, to answer vnto him, of whom he holds them, halfe, or a great part, of the profits thereof.*

Metayere: f. *(Such) a Farmers wife, or woman Farmer.*

Metayerie: f. *A Farme; also, the reuenues thereof.*

Metayse. *as* Metaise; *and as* Metayerie.

Mete: f. *A limit, bound; end.*

Meteil. *as* Metail; *also, typhe wheat, bearded wheat, flat wheat, Roman wheat.*

Metelle. Noix metelle. *The thorne apple, or thornie apple of* Peru; *an Indian nut, or fruit, which being eaten off, causeth an extreame numnesse, heauinesse, or drowsinesse.*

Metempsicose: f. *The transmigration, or passage of the soule from one bodie to another;* (Pithagoras *error.*)

Meteore: m. *A meteor; an imperfect mixture bred in the ayre.*

Meteorologie: f. *A discourse of Meteors.*

Methelle. Noix methelle. *as* Metelle.

Methode: f. *A methode; a short, readie, and orderlie course for the teaching, learning, or doing of a thing.*

Methodique: com. *Methodicall, orderlie.*

Methridat: m. *Methridate; a strong Treacle, or Preseruatiue deuised at first by the Pontian King,* Mithridates.

Metiz: m. *Mongrells; or, as* Metis.

Metope: f. *A Metope; a square space between Trigliphes in a Dorick frize.*

Metopomantie: f. *Diuination by the face.* ¶Rab.

Metoyant. *Diuiding into halues, parting in two; also, equally belonging to, or depending on, two; whence;*

Mur metoyant. *A partition wall.*

Metre: m. *Meeter.*

Metrifié: m. ée: f. *Made into meeter, put into verse.*

Mets: m. *as* Més; *a messe, course, or seruice of meat; also, a house, or tenement; and hence;*

Chef mets. *The principall Mannor-house of a succession, or familie.* ¶Norm.

Mettable: com. *Passable, allowable, of good sufficiencie, of currant value.*

Mettant. *Putting, setting, placing; pitching, planting; grounding, situating; bringing, sending.*

Mette: f. *(The drinke) Meade.*

Metteur; & encherisseur de fermes. *A chapman for Farmes; one that bids readily, or roundly for a Farme which is to be let.*

Mettre: m. *A Corne-measure in some parts of* Burgundie, *containing the halfe of a* Bichot; *or two & a halfe of that countrey bushels.*

Mettre. *To put, set, lay; place, pitch, plant, situate, ground; thrust into; also, to bring, reduce, or send.*

Se mettre à. *To addresse, addict, or deuote himselfe; to fall vnto, or goe in hand with.*

Mettre aux ambles. *To bring a man into a faire traine or forwardnesse, of speaking or doing a thing, before he know how he was drawne vnto it.*

Mettre en avant. *To produce, publish, diuulge, broach, or bring vp; to mention, alledge, exhibit, preferre, propound.*

Mettre quelqu'un en avant. *To forward, aduance, promote.*

Mettre en barbe à. *To oppose against, or confront with.*

Mettre bas; *whence,* La lice a mis bas. *The bitch hath whelped.*

Mettre au bas. *To depose, debase, deiect.*

Mettre à la besace. *To beggar, impouerish, ruine, vndoe.*

Mettre à blanc. *To strip, ransacke; rifle, or depriue of all he hath; to turne into his shirt.*

Mettre haut le blanc à la butte. *To rate exceeding highly.*

Mettre la bride sur le col à. *Seeke* Bride.

Mettre sur le bureau. *To fall in talke of, to bring vpon the stage; also, to bring (a suit) vnto a publike hearing.*

Mettre la campane au chat. *To set at odds, or variance, to cause a difference, breed a quarrell betweene.*

Mettre aux champs. *Looke* Champ.

Se mettre aux champs. *To braue it, or put the better leg before; also, to roaue, roame, or fly out.*

Mettre au chandelier. *To vse; intertaine, accept of.*

Mettre les clefs sur la fosse. *See* Clef.

Mettre au contraire. *To oppose, or obiect against.*

Mettre corps, & cœur. *To labour tooth and nayle.*

Mettre de cul. *To ouerturne, ouerthrow; confound; ouercome, vndoe.*

Mettre sur les dents. *To bring vpon his knees; or, as in* Dent.

Mettre par dessus. *To cast, or heape vpon; to couer with; to lay ouer.*

Mettre au devant. *To oppose, or obiect against; also, as* Mettre en avant.

Mettre en deux. *(Of a Cloth, Couerlet, &c) to double.*

Mettre le doigt entre le bois & l'escorce. *To be medling in, or verie busie with, matters which belong vnto neere friends; also, to set them at odds.*

Mettre de l'eau dedans le vin à. *To temper, coole, tame, or take a hole lower.* Il mit de l'eau dedans leur vin. *He gaue them water to coole their pottage with.*

Mettre par escrit. *To couch, digest, set downe in, commit vnto, writing; to record.*

Mettre tout par escuelles. *To make all split;*

Mettre à l' essor. *To weather; soake, draine; Looke* Essor.

Mettre estat en la cause. *To stop, or stay the proceedings of the cause.*

Se mettre apres son esteuf. *Looke* Esteuf.

Mettre la faucille en la moisson d'autruy. *To thrust his fingers into the dish, his oare into the boat, that belongs vnto another.*

Mettre à la flac. *To squat, flat, squash, clap, or posse downe; to giue a violent, or terrible fall vnto; hence, vtterly to ruine, or vndoe on a suddaine; also, to emptie a purse; (of the flapping sound of an emptie purse.)*

Mettre à fonds. *To sinke a Ship, &c.*

Mettre en ieu: *To produce, exhibit, shew forth; also, to stake at play.*

Mettre au large. *To display, spread open, extend, inlarge.*

Mettre sa legitime au vent. *Seeke* Legitime.

Mettre à la litiere. *To turne vnto base vses, or tread vnder foot.*

Mettre la main au baston, ou à la verge. *To part from, or dispossesse himselfe of, an Inheritance, by deliuering, in his Landlords presence, a rod, or little sticke to the partie to whom he passes it.*

Mettre la main sur le collet de. *To arrest, or seize on, to take prisoner.*

Mettre la main iusques au coude. *Looke* Main.

Mettre la main à l'heritage. *To fall downe vpon the hands.*

Mettre la main à la paste. *To yeeld a helping hand vnto.*

Mettre la main à la verge. *Looke* Verge.

Mettre ad metam non loqui. *To driue to a nonplus, to put vnto silence.*

Mettre à neant. *To raze, abrogate, antiquate, auoid, make void.*

Mettre au net. *To clense, polish, trimme, smooth, make neat; also, to cleere, expound, explane; also, to write a thing faire.*

Se mettre à l'ombre des bouchons. *To get him into a Tauerne, to take sanctuarie in a Tap-house.*

Mettre in pace. *To burie; (a Frierlie phrase.)*

Mettre la paille au devant de. *To hinder, stop, interrupt, lay a blocke in the way of.*

Mettre vn pain au four à. *To doe a pleasure (and sometimes, a displeasure) vnto.*

Mettre en panne. *Looke* Panne.

Mettre peine. *To labour, indeauour, trauell, toyle, bestow much care, or great paines vpon.*

Mettre à plein pied; &, sur le plein pied. *Looke* Pied.

Mettre sous pieds. *To forgiue, and forget.*

Mettre toutes pierres en œuvre. *To make vse of any thing; to vse all the meanes, or imploy all the friends, he can make.*

Mettre à la pile. *Seeke* Pile.

Mettre sa plume au vent. *To grow desperate, carelesse, retchlesse.*

Mettre à point. *To garnish, decke, tricke vp, set out; to dresse, make readie, furnish with all the implements belonging to it.*

Mettre au pouls failli. *Seeke* Pouls.

Mettre à raison. *To reduce into, or compell vnto, order; Looke* Raison.

Mettre sur les rangs. *To propound, mention, set on foot, fall in talke, begin a discourse of; also, to flowt, mocke, deride, or ieast at.*

Mettre au rouët. *To plunge, grauell, confound. Looke* Rouët.

Mettre le sien. Il sçait bien ou il met le sien. *He is a verie warie fellow.*

Mettre sus à; ou, mettre à sus. *To accuse of, impute vnto, or charge with, a matter.*

Mettre en sa table. *Looke* Table.

Mettre à terre. *To set ashore; also, to hale, or draw ashore.*

Mettre en terre. *To burie, or interre; to couer with, or put into, the earth.*

Mettre par terre. *To ruine, ouerthrow, pull downe.*

Mettre en teste à. *To induce, perswade, put into the head, beat into the braines of; also, to confront with, or oppose against.*

On luy mettra la teste aux pieds. *He must be behea-ded, they will haue his head.*

Mettre en train. *To introduce, exhibit; make an o-uerture, set forward, breake the yce, or shew the way, vnto.*

Mettre en vente. *To expose vnto sale.*

Mais si ie m'y mets. *But if I fall in hand with it, if I vndertake it, if I set to it.*

Mettez fol à par soy, il pensera: Prov. *Leaue a foole to himselfe, and he will thinke, or (perhaps) make an end of the matter.*

Mets raison en toy, ou elle s'y mettra: Prov. *Hear-ken to reason, or she will be heard; Let reasons rudder steere thy prow, least thou make wrecke on woes enow.*

Metz: m. *A messuage, tenement, or plow-land:* ¶Wal-lon.

Meu: m. meuë: f. *Moued; stirred; remoued; iogged, wagged; troubled; also, induced, inclined, persuaded.*

Ou est meu le hourd. *Where the scuffling is begun; where blows begin to walk, thumps to be giuē, thwacks to be dealt.*

Meuble: m. *A mouable, or thing mouable; also, houshold stuffe, implements, or furniture.*

Les meubles suivent la personne. *Looke* Personne.

Meuble: com. *Mouable, mouing.*

Terre meuble. *Soft, and short earth (made so by of-ten stirring.)*

Meublé: m. ée: f. *Furnished with mouables, (well) sto-red with houshold stuffe.*

Meubler. *To furnish with mouables, to store with house-hold stuffe.*

Meuf: m. *The Mood of a Verbe.*

Meuglé: m. ée: f. *Lowed, bellowed.*

Meuglement: m. *A lowing, or bellowing.*

Meugler. *To low, to bellow.*

Meule: f. *A mill-stone; also, a grindlestone; also, the cab-badge of a Deeres head; also, a stacke, troden cocke, or great cocke, of hay.*

Meulette: f. *A little Mill-stone, or grindlestone.*

Meulier: m. ere: f. *Grinding; or belonging to a mill-stone, or grindlestone.*

Dents meulieres. *The cheeke-teeth, or grinders.*

Meulon de foin. *A cocke of hay.*

Meulonner. *To make vp hay into cocks, or stacks.*

Meulot: m. *A little cocke of hay.*

Meur. *Looke* Mur.

Meur: m. meure: f. *Ripe, mature, mellow; also, dis-creet, considerate, aduised, setled, stayed.*

Il en aura des plus meures du panier. *He shall bee throughly payed, soundly handled, roundly dealt with.*

Donner entre deux vertes vne meure. *To season matters, to iumble good and bad together.*

Toutes heures ne sont pas meures: Pro. *All houres are not successiue, or seasonable.*

Meure: f. *A Mulberrie.*

Meure de ronce. *The blacke-berrie, or bramble-ber-rie.*

Il ne faut aller aux meures sans crochet: Prov. *We must not goe about a businesse without helpes to facili-tate, and meanes to effect, it.*

Meurement. *Ripely, maturely; discreetly, aduisedly.*

Meureté: f. *Maturitie, ripenesse.*

Meuri: m. *Ripened, growne ripe.*

Meurier: m. *A mulberrie tree; of two principall kinds, a white, and a blacke one.*

Meurier blanc. *The white Mulberrie, is of 3 kinds; one bearing a white, another a red, and the third (and best) a blacke, berrie.*

Meuriere: f. *A ground, or groue of Mulberrie trees.*

Meurir. *To ripen, to make ripe.*

Meurisson: f. *A ripening; a making, or growing ripe.*

Meurler. *To low, to bellow.*

Meurlon: m. *The name of a certaine white vine, or grape.*

Meurole de pommes. *A hoord of apples.*

Meuron: m. *A blacke, or bramble-berrie.*

Meurs: m. *Manners, conditions, qualities, fashions, cus-tomes, behauiour, carriage.*

Meurte: m. *The Mirtle-tree, or shrub; (sweet-leaued, and euer full of leaues.)*

Meurte blanc. *The white Mirtle; hath smooth light-greene leaues, and beares white berries.*

Meurte de Brabant. *The sweet shrub Gaule, or sweet Willow; the Dutch Mirtle tree.*

Meurte estrange. *The strange, or forreine Mirtle; fuller of leaues (and those broader pointed) then the ordinarie one.*

Meurte des forests. *A certaine hearbe whose tender sprigs being sodden are verie good meat; it beares a white flower, and resembles Oake-fearne.*

Meurte noir. *Th'ordinarie Mirtle; or, any kind of Mirtle that beares a black berrie, and leaues of a dar-ker greene then the white.*

Meurte sauvage. *The wild Mirtle tree, or Mirtle shrub; also, Butchers Broome, Pettigree, Knee-holme.*

Meurte de Tarente. *Noble Mirtle; the least, most common, best, and best knowne of all the rest.*

Oiseau de meurte. *A Mirtle Thrush.*

Meurtre: m. *Murther, Homicide.*

Meurtri: m. ie: f. *Murthered; also, crushed, bruised, wan, lew, or bleake with beating, beaten blacke and blew.*

Meurtrier: m. *A murtherer, homicide, cut-throat, blou-die fellow.*

Meurtrier: m. ere: f. *Murthering, murtherous.*

Meurtriere: f. *A murthering peece.*

Meutrieres. *Holes (in that part of a rampire that hangs ouer the gate) whereat the assailed let fall stones on the heads of their too neere approaching aduer-saries.*

Meurtrierement. *Murtherously, cruelly, cut-throat-like.*

Meurtrir. *To murther, kill, slay, massacre; also, to bruise, or crush.*

Meurtrissure: f. *A crushing, or bruising of the flesh; al-so, the wan marke, or print of a stroake.*

Meusnier. *A Miller; Seeke* Munier; *or* Musnier.

Meusnier: m. ere: f. *Of, or belonging to, a Mill, or Miller.*

Meusniere: f. *A Millers wife, or woman Miller.*

Meute: f. *A kennell, or crie, of hounds.*

Bailler la meute, & route à vn cerf. *To follow him with a full crie.*

Mex: m. *A plow-land, and tenement thereto belonging; See* Mas.

Meyans. *as* Means.

Meynne: f. *Dung, durt, filthie, ordure.*

Mezarin: m. *A Physician:* ¶Rab.

Meze: f. *An vntilled wast, or champian, wherein many seuerall mens cattell runne:* ¶Auvergnois.

Mezeau. *as* Meseau.

Mezelle: f. *A kind of brasse, or copper, good to make ordnance of.*

Mezellerie: f. *Mezeldnesse, leaprosie.*

Mezenge. *Looke* Mesange.

Me-

Mezereon: m. *Dutch Mezereon, German Oliue Spurge, Dwarfe Bay tree: (a small shrub.)*
Mial. *for* Miel. *Honie*: ¶Norm.
Miaulement: m. *A mewling, or mewing.*
Miauler. *To mewle, or mew, like a cat.*
Miauleur: m. *A mewler, or mewer.*
Miauleux: m. euse: f. *Mewling, or mewing.*
Miault: m. *A mewing, or counterfeit voyce of wayling.*
Mibaudichon. faire le mib. *To doe a thing foolishly, or ill-fauouredly; vnhandsomely to goe about it.*
Mibrutal: m. ale: f. *Sauage, vnciuile, barbarous, halfe beast-like; almost as rude as a beast.*
Micacollier: m. *The Lote, or Nettle tree.*
Miche: f. *A certaine worme that feedeth on Bees; also, a fine Manchet, or, particularly, that kind of Manchet which is otherwise tearmed,* Pain de chapitre: *The countrey people of France call so also, a loafe of boulted bread, or Tems bread.*
Miches du Convent militaire. *Bullets, or stones.*
Miches de S. Estienne. *Stones.*
Michel: m. *Michael.*
L' Ordre de S. Michel. *Seeke* Ordre.
Michelot: m. *A Pilgrim to S. Michaels Mount.*
Michemis: m. *A Turkish fruict that somewhat resembles the Apricocke.*
Michette: f. *A small Manchet.*
Michon: m. *A sot, blocke, dunce, doult, a iobbernoll, dullard, loggerhead.*
Miclette: f. *(The name of) a most excellent composition that stops all kinds of fluxes, and dries vp the superfluous moisture of the bodie.*
Micocoules: f. *Lote berries (be round, and hang by long staulkes like Cherries.)*
Micocoulier: m. *The Lote, or Nettle, tree.*
Micocoulier d' Afrique. *Th' African Lote, or Nettle, tree; of whose blacke wood excellent Flutes are made.*
Micourber. *To bend, or bow himselfe a prettie deale; almost, or halfe to double.*
Micraine. *as* Migraine.
Microcosme: m. *A little world.*
Microist. *Looke* My-croist.
Mideloret. *(Coyned in derision of our) My Lord.*
Midenier: m. *Halfe a pennie, or halfe a fine.*
Mideronner. *To sleepe in th' afternoone*: ¶Norm.
Midi: m. *Midday, noone; also, the South.*
Poids de Midi. *One of the Pyrhenian mountaines, tearmed so, because the Sunne lyes euer on it about noone.*
Vent de Midi. *The Southerne wind.*
Cercher Midi ou il n'est qu' onze heures. *To looke for a thing before it be readie to come; to picke a quarell without cause, or find a fault where there is none; also, to seeke for his owne hurt, or striue to procure his owne harme.*
'A midi estoille ne luit: Prov. *Euerie thing hath it season; and, he that looks for night at noone-dayes may well be tearmed mad, or blind.*
Midy. *as* Midi.
Mie de pain. *The crumme, or pith of bread.*
Mie. (Adverb.) *Not, not at all, no wayes, by no maner of meanes.*
Mie en piece. *Not of a long time, not of a great while.*
Miel: m. *Honie; also, sweetnesse.*
Miel anacardin. *A venomous, and exulcerating oyle found betweene the kernell, and outward rind of the fruit* Anacardium.
Miel cuict. *A kind of sweet meat, or pancake made of, or seasoned with, honie.*
Miel Heracléen. *Heraclian honie; cleeres the skin, and takes away the blacke spots that come by crushes, or bruises; but in lieu thereof, makes them sneeze that smell at it, and mad that eat of it.*
Miel vierge. *Virgins honie, the honie which of it selfe, and without pressing, distills from the combe.*
Celuy gouverne bien mal le miel qui n'en taste, & ses doigts n'en leche: Prov. *We say, he is an ill Cooke that lickes not his owne fingers; One may say, he is vnwise, who in the managing of publicke businesse addes not somewhat vnto his priuate.*
Qui n'a argent en bourse, ait du moins du miel en bouche: Prov. *He that hath not meanes to pay, at least must frame his mouth to pray.*
Trop achepte le miel qui sur espines le leche: Pro. *He buyes honie too deere that lickes it off thornes.*
Vn'Abeille morte ne fait plus de miel: Prov. *A dead thing is good for nothing.*
Mielleusement. *Honie-like, sweetly, deliciously, lushiously.*
Mielleux: m. euse: f. *Sweet, lushious, delicious.*
Miellier: m. ere: f. *Of, or belonging to, honie, full of honie, bearing honie.*
Mielsaude. *Metheglin; or honie sodden, & therby made into drinke.*
Mien: m. enne: f. *Mine.*
Il est des miens. *He is one of my seruants, people, followers; he is of my traine.*
Mies mies. *The crie of new-borne children*: ¶Rab.
Mi-esté: f. *Midsummer.*
Mi-estoupement: m. *An halfe-stopping.*
Miesure: com. *as* Miesureux.
Miesuresse: f. *Incontinencie, wantonnesse, leacherie, lasciuiousnesse, lustfulnesse.*
Miesureux: m. euse: f. *Incontinent, lasciuious, wanton, leacherous, lustfull, that loues to be figging.*
Miettes: f. *Crummes, scraps, small fragments, or mammockes of bread, &c.*
Mieulx. *Looke* Mieux.
Müiere: com. *Malapert, outragious, euer doing one mischiefe, or other; or as* Miesureux.
Mieüresse: f. *A fancie queane, a bold, impudent, or vnchast housewife.*
Mieux. *Better; also, best.*
Au mieux aller (ou faire, ou venir.) *Fall out what can; let the best come to the best.*
'A qui mieux mieux. *The best take it, or, striuing who shall doe best.*
I'aimeroye mieux. *I had rather, I would leuer.*
Migeotté: m. ée: f. *Well ripened, fully ripe*: ¶Norm.
Migeotter. *To ripen fully*: ¶Norm.
Mignard: m. arde: f. *Migniard, prettie, quaint, neat, feat; wanton; daintie, delicate.*
Mignard en paroles. *Faire-spoken, smooth-tongued, gently languaged; plausible in speech.*
Mignardé: m. ée: f. *Dandled, fedled, cockered, much cherished, made a wanton.*
Mignardelet: m. ette: f. *Prettie, daintie, feat, peart.*
Mignardement. *Prettily, quaintly, neatly, finely, featly, daintily, wantonly; gently, smoothly, plausibly.*
Mignarder. *To lull, feddle, dandle, cherish, wantonnize, make much, or make a wanton, of.*
Mignardeur: m. *A luller, dandler, cherisher; a soother, smoother, flatterer.*
Mignardise: f. *Quaintnesse, neatnesse, daintinesse, delicacie, wantonnesse; smooth or faire speech, kind vsage.*

Mignardiser. *as* Mignarder.
Mignie : m. *A troupe, companie, or meinie; also, as* Meignie.
Mignon : m. *A minion, fauorite, wanton, dilling, darling.*
Mignon : m. onne : f. *Minion, daintie, neat, spruce, compt, fine, elegant, polite; also, pleasing, gentle, kind.*
Argent mignon. *Readie money.*
Dain mignon. *A tame Deere.*
Mignonne. sa mignonne. *His sweeting, or sweet-hart, his prettie minion, his louelie delight.*
Mignonnement. *Minionly, minion-like.*
Mignonnet : m. *A prettie, or young minion; a minikin.*
Mignonneté : f. *Minionisme, quaintnesse, trimnesse, delicacie, spruceneße, featnesse, finesse.*
Mignonnette. *as* Mignonne.
Mignot : m. *A wanton, feddle, fauourite; a dilling, dandling, darling.*
Mignotement : m. *as* Mignotise.
Mignotement. *Tenderly, nicely; fauorably, kindly, gently, cherishingly.*
Mignoter. *To dandle, feddle, cocker, cherish, handle gently, intertaine kindly, vse tenderly, make a wanton of.*
Mignotise : f. *A dandling, fedling, cockering, cherishing, gentle handling, tender vsage; also, wantonnesse; tamenesse, gentlenesse.*
Mignotises. *Prettie dainties, or trinkets; fine toyes; affected delights.*
Migraine : f. *The Megrim, or head-ach; also, a Pomegranet; also, the great Sea-vrchin; also, Scarlet, or Purple in graine.*
Migraine de feu. *A sticke, or brand of fire; also, a ball of wildfire.*
Migration : f. *A migration, a remouing, or shifting of places.*
Migrelin : m. *A small thinne scrag, or tender starueling.*
Migrer. *To remoue, to flit, or shift from one place to another.*
Mi-jour : m. *Midday, Noone.*
Mil : m. *(The graine) Mill, Millet, Hirse; Looke* Millet.
Mil Sarrasin. *French-wheat, Bucke-wheat, Bolymong.*
Milace : f. *A kind of the Holme, or Scarlet, Oake.*
Milacié : m. ée : f. *Mill-eating, millet-fed; a nickename for the Gascon, whose bread is, for the most part, made of Millet.*
Milaire : m. *A mile; also, as* Cenchrite.
Milan : m. *A Kite, Puttocke, Glead; also (the name of) a delicate peare.*
Milan marin. *A Gilden-pole, or kind of Gurnard, that shines in the night, and before change of weather flies (or seemes to flie) a little aboue the water.*
Milan Royal. *Th'ordinarie Kite, or Glead.*
Pied de Milan. *The hearbe Kites-foot.*
Milandre. *A little Dog-fish thats mortall enemie to mankind.*
Miliart. *Looke* Milliart.
Miliasse : f. *Thousands, or, a huge number of; (deriued, by the vulgar, from* vne Ilias.)
Milice : f. *Warlike discipline, warfare.*
La celestielle milice. *The hoast of heauen.*
Milieu : m. *The middest, middle, or center of.*
Dame du milieu. *Seeke* Dame.
Militaire : com. *Militarie, martiall, warlicke, souldierlike.*
Herbe militaire à millefueilles. *Knights Milfoile, souldiers Yarrow.*
Militer. *To warre, goe a warfaring, be in warres, practise the feats of warre; to souldierize it.*
Mille. *A thousand.*
Millefeuil : m. *as* Millefueille.
Millefueille : f. *Milfoile, nose-bleed Yarrow, common Yarrow.*
Millefueille aquatique. *Water Yarrow; also, water Sengreene, water Housleeke, Knights Pondwort, wading Pondweed, fresh-water souldier.*
Millefueille grande. *Great Yarrow (differs from the ordinarie one in onely bigneße.)*
Millefueille iaulne. *Knights Milfoile, souldiers Yarrow, yellow knighten Yarrow, yellow or little Yarrow.*
Millefueille petite. *The same.*
Millegraine : f. *Oake of Jerusalem, Oake of Paradice; (an hearbe.)*
Millene : f. vne mil. d'années. *A thousand of yeares.*
Millepertuis : m. *S. Iohns wort, S. Iohns grasse.*
Millepieds : m. *The worme, or vermine, called a Palmer.*
Milleraie : f. *A peece of ground sowed with Millet; a Millet-ground.*
Milleret : m. *A Middle Ray, the halfe of a Milleray; a peece of gold worth almost 7 s. sterl.*
Millerine : f. *The straw, or stubble of Millet.*
Millesoudiers : m. *Old maimed souldiers; such as haue a thousand* sous *(or 5 l. sterl.) of yearely pension.*
Millet : m. *Millet, Mill, Hirse.*
Millet d'Inde. *Mais, Turkie corne, Turkie wheat.*
Millet noir. *Blacke Millet; and, as* Millet de Turquie.
Millet Sarrasin. *French-wheat, Bucke-wheat, Bolymong.*
Millet de Turquie. *Turkie Hirse, Turkie Mill, blacke Millet.*
Percer vn grain de Millet d'vn tarriere. *To performe impossibilities.*
Milliart : m. *A thousand millions of millions.*
Millier : m. vn millier. *A thousand; a proportion, or number, of a thousand.*
Millier : m. ere : f. *Of, or belonging to, a thousand.*
Milliesme. la milliesme partie. *The thousandth part.*
Milliet : m. *A serpent of a greenish colour.*
Million : m. *A million; ten hundred thousand.*
Millon : m. *A kind of flint, or hard stone.*
Milloque : f. *Furmentie, or pottage, made of Millet: a Rab.*
Milods : m. *Halfe-fines due in cases of collaterall succession vnto* Censuel *inheritance (as in* Lodunois*) or in cases of Donation (as in* Dauphine.)
Milort : m. *My Lord; or as* Monseigneur *(a word borrowed of, and imployed on, vs.)*
Milrai : m. *A Milleray; a coyne of gold worth betweene 13 and 14 shillings* sterl.
Milret. *as* Milleret.
Mime : m. *A vice, foole, iester, scoffer, dauncer, in a Play; also, a foolish, wanton, shamelesse, ridiculous Poeme, part, or Play; also, a graue, and sententious Poeme.*
Mi-more : com. *Swartie, blackish, halfe-Moore.*
Minage : m. *A measuring of corne by the* Mine; *whence;*
Droict de minage. *A fee due vnto some Lords vpon euerie* Mine *of corne thats measured within their territorie.*
Minatere : m. *A Miner, mine-man, mine-digger.*

Minau : m. *A corne measure ; as* Mine.
Minauderies: f. *Foolish trickes, apish pranks, mumpings, mowings.*
Mince : com. *Thinne, fine, slender, little, small.*
Mincé : m. ée : f. *Minced, cut verie small.*
Mince-fueille : f. *Featherfew, fedderfew, feauerfew, Whitewort, called also, Motherwort, because tis good against the disease of the Mother (yet is not this the right Motherwort.)*
Mince-fueilles. *Thinne leaued, or hauing thinne leaues; whence* ; Armoise mince-fueilles. *Thinne-leaued Mugwort.*
Mincelet : m. ette : f. *Somewhat thin, verie fine, small, slender.*
Mincément. *Thinly, slenderly, smally.*
Mincer. *To mince ; to shred, or cut into small peeces.*
Mincetė : f. *Thinnesse, exilitie, slendernesse, littlenesse, smallnesse.*
Minchon : m. *A sot, blockhead, loggerhead.*
Mine : f. (*The halfe of a* Sextier, *and 24 part of a* Muid) *A measure for graine, &c, containing somewhat lesse then two of our (London) Bushells ; (if, as* Nicot *saith, it weighes but* 110 *pounds : But* Vigenere *vpon Liuie affirmes, that the* Mine *of wheat weighes about* 120 *pounds ; marrie in Rie, sayes he, it comes but to* 110 ;) *also, a Mine, or caue digged vnder ground ; also, a mine, or veine of mettall, &c.*
Mine de Clermont (pour le bled.) *Is the* 12 *part of a* Muid ; *or iust as big againe as th'ordinarie one.*
Mine de Paris. *as th'ordinarie* Mine.
Mine de plomb. *An Orenge tawnie minerall vsed by Painters.*
Plomb de mine. *Blacke lead.*
Mine de terre en la Chastellenie de Bulles. *Containes* 50 Verges *of* 24 *foot to the* Verge.
Mine de terre en Clermont. *Containes* 60 Verges *of* 22 *foot to the* Verge.
Mine de terre en la Seigneurie de Remy. *Containes* 80 Verges, *at* 22 *foot and the third part of a foot to the* Verge.
Mine : f. *The countenance, looke, cheere, visage ; the gesture, or posture of the face ; also, fauor, phisnomie, feature, outward face, or shew.*
Faire mine. *To seeme, or make a shew of ; whence* ;
Ce ne sont que mines.
Faire mines. *To make faces.*
Faire des mines. *The same ; also, to make an adoe, or shew of loathnesse to be drawne to a thing.*
Faire la mine. *To lowt, or lowre vpon.*
Faire les mines. *To make (strange) faces ; also, to act, or play on a stage.*
Faire bonne mine. *To excuse, colour, beare out a matter handsomely ; to set a good face on't, to make a good shew.*
Faire bonne mine, & mauvais ieu. *To set a good face on a bad matter ; to beare out crosses with a cheerefull countenance ; to affront miseries with a shew of mirth.*
Il y a plus de mine que de ieu. *There is more shew then substance, more ceremonie then soliditie, in it.*
Miné : m. ée : f. *Mined, vndermined, supplanted ; also, worne, or fretted away.*
Miner. *To mine, or vndermine ; to supplant ; weare, consume, or fret away.*
Mineral : m. *A minerall ; a thing found growing in Mines ; (hence) also, mettall.*
Mineur : m. *An infant ; one that's in minoritie, or vnder age ; also, a Miner, mine-deuisor, mine-maker ; also, as* Miniere ; *whence* ;
Qui n'a mineur n'a honneur : Prov. *He that wants money wants honour.*
Mineur : f. *The minor proposition of a syllogisme.*
Mineure : f. *as* Miniere.
Mineux : m. euse : f. *Outward, seeming, apparent ; belonging to, or consisting in, the countenance, or gesture of the face ; also, squeamish, quaint, coy, that minces it exceedingly ; also, mining, or vndermining ; also, full of mines.*
Mingant : m. *A broth thats thickened with the meale of pounded roots.*
Mingrelet : m. ette : f. *Thinne, gaunt, lanke, slender, leane, scraggie, meager.*
Miniere : f. *A mine of mettalls, or mineralls.*
Minime : m. *A name of Friers instituted by* François de Paule ; *a man renowmed for holinesse of life during the raigne of Lewis th'eleuenth ; who sent for him into France, in a hope, that by his meanes his life should bee prolonged.*
Couleur de minimes. *A light soot colour, hauing an eye of gray in it.*
Gris de minime. *The same.*
Minime (blanche.) *A Minume, in Musicke.*
Minime noire. *A Crochet.*
Minime : com. *The least, or smallest.*
Minion : m. *Synople, red lead, Vermillion ; Painters red made of burned Ceruse.*
Ministre : m. *A Minister, Seruant ; Officer ; Deputie ; Assistant ; Instrument.*
Ministres du Roy. *His Agents ; those that negociate, or deale, for him.*
Ministré : m. ée : f. *Ministred, serued ; assisted ; offered, yeelded, affoorded vnto.*
Ministreau : m. *A little Minister, small Officer, Assistant, or Seruant.*
Ministrer. *To minister, assist, serue vnto ; also, to offer, or affoord vnto.*
Ministresse : f. *A Ministresse ; a woman that assists, or serues vnto.*
Minois : m. *A sower face, harsh visage, crabbed countenance ; a craftie, or discontented looke.*
Minon : m. *A little kitling ; or such a tearme for a cat as is our Pusse ; whence* ;
Il entend le chat sans dire minon. *He apprehends the mans meaning before he speake vnto him.*
Minons : m. *Cat-tailes, or Catkins ; the long aglet-like buds of nut-trees.*
Minoratif. Medecine minorative. *Gentle Physicke, Physicke that workes easily, or is of gentle effect.*
Minorité : f. *Minoritie, vnder-age.*
Minot : m. *The halfe of a Mine ; three French Bushells ; Looke* Mine.
Minot d'avoine, de sel, & de legumes. *Containes 4 French Bushells.*
Minot de bled. (*Th'ordinarie* Minot) *containes three* Boisseaux.
Minot de noix, & d'oignons. *Containes foure* Boisseaux, *and a halfe, of stricken measure.*
Minu : m. *The particular suruey, or description which a purchaser is bound to deliuer vnto the Lord of whom his purchase is held.*
Minué : m. ée : f. *Diminished, minished.*
Minuer. *To minish, diminish, lessen, impaire, abate.*
Minuict : f. *Midnight.*
Minute : m. *A mite ; the smallest of weights.*
Minute : f. *The (first) draught of an Euidence, or Pleading ; a scroll, or scedule.*

Minuté: m.ée: f. *Minished, impaired, made little; abated; disabled; also, drawne, or whereof a draught is made (in writing;) also, deuised, cast, or concluded on, as the first proiect of a designe.*

Minuter. *To minish, diminish, impaire, lessen, or make little; to disable, or abate; also, to draw, or make a draught of, an Instrument in writing; and hence also, to deuise, cast, or lay the first proiect of a designe.*

Minuter ses papiers de raisons. *To cast, make vp, reduce to a head, his (stragling) accounts.*

Mioche: f. *A crumme, scrap, small fragment, or mammocke of.*

Mioler. *To mew, or crie like a cat.*

Mi-panché: m.ée: f. *Halfe bowed, halfe declining, halfe hanging, downewards.*

Miparti: m. ie: f. *Parted in the middest, or into (equall) halues.*

La Chambre mipartie. *Looke* Chambre.

Mipartir. *To part in the middest, or into halues; to diuide into two equall parts.*

Mipotence. en m. *Made, or fashioned, like a halfe gibbet; crooked, or bent into the forme of th'vpper part of a gibbet; as a tenter-hooke, &c.*

Mique. *A kind of hastie pudding.*

Miquelot: m. *A Pilgrim to S. Michaells Mount; also, a poore, pettie, vagabond Pedler, that with a spritstaffe crosses from place to place, to vtter small trifles, which he carries along with him in boxes.*

Mirabolan: m. *A Mirabolan plumme; Looke* Myrabolan.

Mirach: m. *Th'outward lower part of the bellie, couering all th'intraills:* ¶Arabesque: ¶Rab.

Miracle: m. *A miracle; a maruellous, or monstrous thing.*

Il n'est miracle que de vieux saincts: Prov. *We doe not credit reports, or miracles of a fresh date; Antiquitie is reuerend, and of awfull authoritie.*

Miracleur: m. *A doer of miracles.*

Miraclifique: com. *Wonder-working.*

Miraculeusement. *Miraculously, wonderfully.*

Miraculeux: m.euse: f. *Miraculous, wonderfull, maruelous, monstrous, beyond nature, past common vnderstanding.*

Miraillet: m. *A Thornebacke which hath on either of her sides, or finnes, a great eye-like spot; (a hard, and vnwholesome fish.)*

Miraillier: m. *A looking-glasse-maker.*

Miraillier: m. *Of a looking glasse.*

Miraine: f. *Oake of Jerusalem, Oake of Paradise:* ¶Savoyard.

Miramomelin: m. *A Lord ouer Lords; an Arabian word vsed in some old French Authors.*

Mire: m. *A Physitian, Leech, Chirurgian.*

Il n'a plus besoing de mire. *He hath no longer need, he hath no further vse, of a Physitian; viz. he is dead.*

Debonnaire mire fait playe puante: Prov. *A gentle Chirurgian makes a stinking sore.*

Qui veut la guarison du mire il luy convient tout son mal dire: Prov. *He that lookes to be cur'd must all his ill discouer.*

Mire: f. *The leuell, or little button at th'end, of a Peece; also, the tuske of a wild Boare.*

Miré: m.ée: f. *Aimed, leuelled at; looked, viewed, beheld through; watched, pried into, neerely obserued; also, long-tusked, full-tushed, as a full-growne Boare.*

Mirecoton: m. *The delicate yellow Peach, called a Melicotonie.*

Mirelicoton. *as* Mirecoton.

Mirelifique: com. *Exceeding wonderfull, passing admirable, horribly excellent (a word of ironicall commendation, or amplification.)*

Mirelifiques: f. *Toyes, bables; trickes to mocke Apes, or amaze infants with.*

Mirer. *To aime, or leuell at; to looke, view, regard, obserue, prie into, behold through, or throughly.*

Se mirer. *To looke in a glasse; to looke on, or into, himselfe; also, to take notice of, or example by.*

Dieu le vous mire. *God restore it you, or reward you for it.*

Dame qui trop se mire peu file: Pro. *She that looks too much at her selfe lookes too little to her selfe.*

Qui bien se mire bien se void; Qui bien se void bien se cognoist; Qui bien se cognoist peu se prise; Qui peu se prise Dieu l'avise: Prov.

Mires d' vn sanglier. *His tuskes, or tushes.*

Miriade: f. *A Miriade; ten thousand.*

Mirifique: com. *Strangely wrought, maruellously acted, admirably done.*

Mirlirot. *as* Melilot: ¶Parisien.

Mirloret: m. *A neat, spruce, quaint, compt fellow.*

Miroaillier: m. *A looking-glasse maker.*

Miroir: m. *A Myrror, a looking glasse; also, an instrument wherewith Chirurgians dilate the parts which be naturally hollow (as the mouth, fundament, &c,) when they haue occasion to looke into the bottome, or depth, of them.*

Miroir d' Asne. *A white transparent stone, (or congealed humor of the earth) vsed in old time in stead of glasse, (farre better then which) it indures th'extremities of heat and frosts, without breaking.*

Miroir de nostre Dame. *as* Miroir d'Asne.

Le bay à miroir. *A dapled bay.*

Pierre à miroir. *A light, white, and transparent stone, easily cleft into thinne flakes, and vsed by th'Arabians (among whom it growes) in stead of glasse; a nights it represents the Moone, and euer increases, or decreases, as the Moone doth.*

Il n'y a meilleur miroir que le vieil ami: Prov. *An old friend an excellent looking-glasse.*

Miroitier: m. *A looking-glasse maker.*

Mirond: m. de: f. *Semicirculer, halfe round.*

Mirouaillier. *as* Miroaillier.

Mirouaillier: m. ere: f. *Often looking, euer prying, into a glasse.*

Mirouer. *as* Miroir.

Mirtil. *A Mirtill berrie; also, a Salamander, or deafe worme.*

Mis: m.ise: f. *Put, set, layed; placed, pitched, planted, situated, grounded; thrust into; also, brought, reduced, sent.*

Mis en cueilleur de pommes. *Tucked vp like an apple-gatherer, dressed like an apple-squire; in base, poore, or beggerlie array.*

Mis à la pile, ou, au verjus. *Trounst, courst.*

Misaille: f. *A lay, a wager.*

Misaine: f. *The foresaile of a ship.*

Misanthrope: m. *A hater of mens companie:* ¶Rab.

Mise: f. *Expence, disbursement, money layed out, or the laying out of money; also, a chapter, or title of expences in an accompt; also, a price offered, or laied downe; also, the currantnesse, or goodnesse of coyne.*

Mise de faict. *A iudiciall putting into possession, for the preseruation of the true owners right.*

Folle mise. *So much as one hath bidden more then another, or former, chapman; which he is bound to pay if th'other refuse the thing in bargaine.*

Gens de mise. *Persons of worth, sort, qualitie.*
Mis-en-avant. mon m. *My subiect, my matter, the thing which I haue propounded, or set on foot.*
Miserable: com. *Miserable, wretched, vnfortunate; piteous, wofull, ruthfull, distressefull; disasterous.*
Miserablement. *Miserably, wretchedly, wofully, ruthfully, distreßefully; disasterously.*
Misere: f. *Miserie, wretchednesse, distreße; aduersitie, calamitie; wofulneße, or a wofull case; also, a poore drinke made of the water wherewith bee-hiues haue beene washed.*
Il suffit au jour de sa misere: Pro. *One affliction suffices for one day.*
Miserere. *The name (and beginning) of one of the seuen (penitentiall) Psalmes.*
Miserere mei. *A voiding of th'excrements vpwards; comes of th'obstruction of the small guts, and is verie painefull, the patient imagining that his guts are pulled out, and broken.*
Tu auras miserere iusques à vitulos. *Thou shalt be soundly whipped.*
Misericorde: f. *Mercie, pitie, compassion, ruth, tendernesse.*
Espée misericorde. *A waued sword.*
Misericordieusement. *Mercifully, compassionately, pitifully.*
Misericordieux: m. euse: f. *Mercifull, pitifull; compassionate.*
Misque: m. *Mosse.*
Missal: m. ale: f. *Of, or belonging to, the Masse.*
Pain missal. *A kind of wafer made only of flower, and a little salt.*
Missel: m. *A Masse-booke.*
Missile. feu missile. *A squib, or other fire-worke throwne.*
Mission: f. *as* Mise; *Expence, disbursement, charge:* ¶Bourgongnon.
Missive: f. *A letter missiue; a letter sent.*
Missotage: m. *Masserie, Masse-trinkets, Masse-stuffe; things belonging to the Masse.*
Missotier: m. ere: f. *Masse-monging, Masse-making; of the Masse.*
Mistagogue: m. *A teacher, or interpreter of mysteries, and ceremonies; also, a keeper of the Churches Reliques.*
Miste: com. *Neat, spruce, compt, quaint, picked, minion, trickesie, fine, gay.*
Mistement. *Neatly, sprucely, comptly, quaintly, finely, gaily, minion-like.*
Mistigouri. *My pillicocke, my prettie rogue:* ¶Norm.
Mistion: f. *A mixture, mash, medley, melling, blending; a confounding; a sophistication.*
Mistionné: m. ée: f. *Mixed, mingled, melled, blent; sophisticated by mixture.*
Mistionnement: m. *A mixing, mingling, melling, blending, medley-making; sophisticating.*
Mistionner. *To mix, mingle, mash, mell, blend or temper with, make a medley of; to falsifie, adulterate, sophisticate, by mixture.*
Mistoudin: m. *A neat fellow, a spruce companion.*
Mistrouille: f. *A foule great slut, a filthie draggletaile:* ¶Norm.
Misy: m. *A caustick drug, or minerall of a golden colour, and luster; found growing in little peeces, about, or aboue, naturall Chalcitis; whereunto it is like in vertue, and operation, though in temperature it be the more subtile of the two.*
Mitaille: f. *Great (or the grossest) file-dust.*
Mitaines: f. *Mittaines, Winter-gloues.*
Ils ne se laissent prédre sans mitaines. *They will not be taken without mittains; viz. much preparation, or adoe.*
Mitan: m. *The middest, or middle of:* ¶Norm.
Mitanier: m. ere: f. *Middle, of the middest.*
Mitaut. la Region du m. *The middle Region of the aire.*
Mite: f. *A Mite, the smallest of coynes; also, the little worme, called a Mite.*
Herbe aux mites. *Moth-Mullein.*
Mithologie: f. *Mithologie; an expounding, or moralizing, of fables.*
Mithologiquement. *Mithologikely; by a morall exposition of fables.*
Mithre: f. *Looke* Mitre.
Mithridat: m. *Mithridatum; Looke* Methridat.
Mitifier. *To soften; digest, concoct.*
Mitigatif: m. iue: f. *Mitigatiue, lenitiue, appeasiue.*
Mitigation: f. *A mitigation, qualification, allaying, tempering, asswaging, appeasing.*
Mitigué: m. ée: f. *Mitigated, qualified, moderated, allayed, asswaged, appeased.*
Mitiguer. *To mitigate, qualifie, temper, moderate, ease, asswage, allay, appease.*
Mi-tirer. *To draw out the halfe of.*
Mitis. *Nice, curious, precise; hypocriticall.*
Miton: m. *(The small worme, or vermine called) a Mite.*
Mitou: m. *A great cat.*
Faire le mitou. *To dissemble, or play the hypocrite; to put on a lowlie, meeke, humble, or afflicted countenance; to looke poorely, or pitifully on it.*
Mitoüard: m. *A cat; also, an hypocrite:* ¶Rab.
Mitouflé: m. ée: f. *Furred like a cat, or with cats skins; hidden in, wrapped, or lapped about with furres, or cat-furred garments.*
Mitouïn: m. *An hypocrite; a dissembler vnder the protection of a meeke, and lowlie countenance.*
Mitoyen. *as* Moitoyen.
Mitraille: f. *Broken brasse, or copper; or lumpes consisting of diuers mettalls, which haue beene mingled, and melted together.*
Mitrant. *Hooding, or crowning, with a miter.*
Mitre: f. *A Bishops miter; also, the hole (or cap) of a mans yard.*
Donner la mitre, & la crosse à. *To set a specious glosse of Religion on; or to authorize (an ill thing) by a goodlie shew of deuotion.*
Mitré: m. ée: f. *Mitred; hooded with a miter, wearing a miter; set on a pillorie, or scaffold, with a miter of paper on his head.*
Mitrement: m. *A mitring; a hooding, crowning, or couering of the head with a miter; for ornament, or in disgrace.*
Mitrer. *To hood, crowne, or couer the head with a miter, of rich stuffe for ornament (as at the consecration of a Bishop;) or of paper in disgrace.*
Mixtion. *as* Mistion.
Mixtionné, & Mixtionner. *as* Mistionné, & Mistionner.
Mizone: f. *The name of a delicate Italian peare thats ripe in August.*
Mnadies. *Barbarously for* Bona dies. *God-denne to you:* ¶Rab.
Mobile: com. *Mouable, which may be remoued.*
Mobiliaire: com. *as* Mobile.
Mobilité: f. *Mouableneße; a wagging, fitting, wauering,*

uering, inconstancie, ficklenesse.

Mocayart : m. *The stuffe Moccadoe ; or a kind thereof.*

Mocqué : m. ée : f. *Mocked, flowted, frumped, scoffed, ieasted at ; gulled, gudgeoned ; also, disappointed, frustrated.*

se Mocquer. *To mock, flowt, frump, scoffe, deride, ieast at, laugh to scorne ; to gull, gudgeon ; frustrate, make a foole of, disappoint.*

Vous vous mocquez du ieu. *You doe but dallie.*

Se mocque qui cloque: Pro. *he mocks that least may ; the greatest mockers haue cōmonly most imperfections.*

Mauvaise fille se mocque de sa mere: Prov. *The ill-bred daughter mocks her sillie mother.*

La paelle se mocque du fourgon : Pro. *One friend, or kinsman mocks another ; he that might well be flowted flowts his neighbor.*

Mocquereau : m. *A mocking child, or, a little mocker.*

Mocquerie : f. *A mock, flowt, frumpe, scoffe, gibe, ieast ; gull, gudgeon, derision ; a mockerie, tale of a tub, ridiculous discourse, foppish thing ; also, a mocking, flowting, scoffing, frumping.*

Mocqueur : m. *A mocker, flowter, frumper, scoffer, giber, derider.*

Mode : m. *as* Meuf ; *A Mood.*

Mode : f. *Manner, sort, fashion, guise, vse, custome ; way, meanes.*

'A la trotte qui mode. *Setting the cart before the horse.*

Modeler. *To modell, forme, fashion, plot, cast in a mould.*

Modelle : f. *A modell, patterne, mould, plot, forme, frame.*

Modelon. *as* Modillon.

Moderateur : m. *A moderator, gouernor, director, guider.*

Moderation : f. *A moderation, meane, temper, gouernement ; a good disposition, due proportion, right measure.*

Moderatrice : f. *A moderatrix.*

Moderé : m. ée : f. *Moderate, quiet, rulie, temperate, orderlie, patient ; also, moderated, allayed, tempered ; whose edge is somewhat taken off, or heart taken downe ; also, sloped, or cut aslope.*

Moderément. *Moderately, temperately, quietly, orderly, patiently, with reason, in good rule.*

Moderer. *To moderate, qualifie, temper, quiet, order, gouerne, rule, refraine, hold in, vse with measure, set a meane on ; abate th'edge, allay the heat of ; also, to slope, or cut aslope.*

Moderne : com. *Moderne, new, of this age, of these times, in our time.*

Modeste : com. *Modest, sober, ciuile, bashfull, shamefac'd, humble, maidenlie, mannerlie.*

Modestement. *Modestly, soberly, chastly, ciuilly.*

Modesteté : f. *as* Modestie.

Modestie : f. *Modestie, moderation, sobernesse, temperance, humilitie, bashfulnesse, maidenlinesse.*

Modicité : f. *Modicitie, moderatenesse, meanenesse, littlenesse.*

Modie : m. *An ancient Roman measure containing somewhat lesse then our pecke, and halfe.*

Modifiable : com. *Modifiable, qualifiable.*

Modification : f. *A modification, qualification, limitation, exception.*

Modifié : m. ée : f. *Modified, moderated, qualified, limited.*

Modifier. *To modifie, moderate, qualifie, limit.*

Modillon : m. *A cartridge, or cartoose, a foulding bracket, or corbell.*

Modulation : f. *Modulation, harmonie, musicall proportion, pleasant tuning.*

Module : m. *A modell, or module ; that wherby a whole worke is measured, proportioned, or squared ; also, the measure, bignesse, or quantitie of a thing ; also, a certaine measure in conduits, or conueyances of water ; also, modulation, melodie, or measure, in Musicke.*

Modurre. *as* Madoure : ¶Rab.

Moë. *as* Mouë.

Moëlle : f. *The marrow of bones ; the pith of plants ; also, as* Meule ; *a milstone.*

Moëlle de pain. *The pith of bread.*

Moëlleux : m. euse : f. *Marrowie, pithie, full of strength, or strong sap.*

Moëllon. *as* Moilon.

Moëtte. *A Sea-mew.*

Les Moëttes. *Forerunners, forериders, foretellers of ones comming.*

Moëtte blanche. *Th'ordinarie white Mew, or Sea-mew.*

Moëtte cendrée. *Th' (ordinarie) ash-coloured Sea-mew.*

La petite Moëtte. *The small ash-coloured Mew, tearmed otherwise* Hirondelle de mer.

Moeurs. *Manners ; Looke* Meurs.

Moge : f. *A measure containing about six bushells.*

Moïau. *as* Moyeu.

Moien, & Moienner. *Looke* Moyen, & Moyenner.

Moieu. *as* Moyeu.

Moignon : m. *A stump, or, the blunt end of a thing.*

Moignon des ailes. *The stumpes, or pinions of the wings.*

Moignon du bras. *The brawne, or brawnie part of th'arme.*

Gros moignons de chair. *Great lumps, or gobbets of masshe flesh.*

Moil : m. *A sea Barbell, or sore Mullet.*

Moile : f. *An arch, damme, or bay of planks, whereby the force of water is broken.*

Moileux. *Looke* Moëlleux.

Moillonneux : m. euse : f. *Full of rubbish, made of ruble ; also, full of the soft stone* Moilon.

Moilon : m. *Rubbish, ruble, shards, ragged stones, peeces of stone hewed, or broken off ; such as walls are built, or parget made, of ; also, the soft vpper crust of a quarrey of free stone ; or a kind of soft, or tender stone, that lyeth some 10, or 12 foot thick aboue the hardest free stone, in the quarreyes about Paris.*

Moilonneux. *as* Moillonneux.

Moindre : com. *Lesse, lesser, inferiour to ; also, the least, smallest, lowmost.*

Moine : m. *A Monke ; also, a casting top ; also, the little Titmouse ; also, as* Alballan.

Moines de la Charité. *An Order of Monkes, who by their statutes are bound to visit the sicke, and burie the dead.*

Moines de Grace. *An Order of white Monkes, who weare great white crosses on their bosomes.*

Collation de Moine. *A Monkes nunchion, a large collatiō ; as much as another man eats at a good meale.*

Teste de Moine. *A blunt, and round-nosed Porpose ; also, the hearbe Dandelion.*

Avoir le moine. *To be cousened, gleekt, poopt, bobbed, crossed ; to haue ill lucke.*

Bailler le moine. *To crampe, also, to bring ill lucke vnto.*

Bailler le moine par le col. *To hang, or twitch vp.*

'A la fin le regnard sera moine : Prov. *At length the Fox turnes Monke ; (viz. when hee can play the knaue no longer.)*

Homme ne cognoist mieux la malice que l' Abbé qui a esté moine: Prov. *There is no knaue to the Abbot that hath beene a Monke; or no man knowes how to play the knaue better then he.*

Il n'est envie que de moine: Prov. *No enuie like a Monkes.*

L'habit ne fait pas le moine: Pro. *The Cowle makes not the Monke; euerie one is not a souldier that weares armor; nor euerie one a scholler thats clad in blacke.*

Pour vn moine ne faut Convent: Prov. *For one Monke needs no Monasterie.*

Moineau: m. *A Sparrow; also, a Nouice; a young, or little Monke; also, a Rauelin in fortification; also, a certaine little peece of Ordnance.*

Moineau de bois. *The little Brambling, or mountaine Spinke.*

Moineau de haye. *Is not that which wee call the Hedge-sparrow, but a little bird that liues altogether on flies.*

Moineau de noyer. *as* Friquet.

Moineau à la soulsie. *The ring-Sparrow; a small bird that hath a yellow ring about it necke, and builds in the trunke of a tree; (Germanie hath many, England but few, of them.)*

Herbe au Moineau. *Iuie Chickweed, Henbit.*

Passereaux, & Moineaux sont de faux oyseaux. *A Prouerbe taxing the lasciuious conuersation of Cloister-Sparrowes.*

Moiner. *To breed Monks, to play the Monke:* ¶Rab.

Moinerie: f. *Monkerie, Monachisme, the state or profession of a Monke.*

Moinichon: m. *A little paultrie Monke.*

Moins. *Lesse, least.*

Moins deux tiers. *Lacking two third parts.*

Vn moins de cent. *An hundred wanting one.*

Au moins. A tout le moins. Tout au moins. *At least, yet at the least, neuerthelesse, notwithstanding, howsoeuer.*

Le moins de mon plus. *The most I can, the least I should.*

Ils portoient alors ie ne sçay quoy de moins. *They wore at that time some od thing or other of lesse value.*

Pour vn denier ny moins. *The losse, or expence of one pennie will make me neuer a whit the poorer.*

Moinsné. *as* Mainsné.

Mois: m. *A month, or moneth.*

Les mois des femmes. *Womens monthlie flowers.*

Mois blanches. *A kind thereof tearmed by our women, the Whites.*

Mois mort. *The season that is immediately before, or after, Christmas.*

Moise: f. *Full length, or growth in fish; also, a halfe-beame of timber.*

Moisi: m. ie: f. *Mouldie, hoarie, vinowed; also, mustie, or fustie, by mouldinesse.*

se Moisir. *To wax mouldie, hoarie, vinowed; also, to grow mustie, fustie; to get a white coat, and a ranke smell.*

Moisissure: f. *Mouldinesse, hoarinesse, vinowednesse; mustinesse, fustinesse.*

Moison: m. *The full length of a peece of cloth (which in old time was woont to be at the least 20 elles;) also, the rent of a farme, or tenement, paied in corne, or other things in kind.*

Vne truite de moison. *A Full-growne Trowt.*

Moissine: f. *A great bunch, or bundle of bunches of grapes; (an Ouerseers fee in vintage-time;) also, a little knot of bunches, or clusters, tied together with long staulkes, and hanged vp to be kept long.*

Moisson: m. *A Sparrow; also, a kind of small Parrat, called by th'Indians* Tovis.

Moisson: f. *Haruest; reaping time.*

Moissons. *Haruest; or haruest fruit; the corne reaped in haruest.*

La moisson des avoines, orges, & legumages. *Begins (in France) about the 16 of Julie.*

La moisson des froments. *About the 27 of Julie.*

La moisson des seigles. *Begins about the 27 of June.*

La moisson d' vne vache. *The milking of a cow, or as much as she giues at a milking.*

Droict de moisson. *An yearelie rent, or duetie of corne paid vnto the King out of the towne, and iurisdiction of* Bourges.

Espée des moissons. *Looke* Espée.

Ie ne mettray la faucille en sa moisson. *I will not meddle with, or incroach vpon, his gettings.*

En moissons Dames chambrieres sont: Prov. *See* Dames.

Grande moisson l'obeissant recueille: Pro. *Great is the haruest that th'obedient gathers.*

Telle semence telle moisson: Prov. *Ill seed, ill weed; or, such as the seed such is the crop.*

Moissonné: m. ée: f. *Reaped, gotten, as corn in haruest.*

Moissonner. *To reape, to make or get in, haruest; to work haruest worke.*

Avec le temps lon moissonne: Pro. *Looke* Temps.

Moissonneur: m. *A reaper, a haruest man.*

Moissonnier: m. ere: f. *Of, or belonging to, haruest.*

Chevreau moissonnier. *A fat Kid.*

Faucille moissonniere. *A reaping sickle.*

Oison moissonnier. *A stubble goose.*

Moissons. *Looke* Moisson.

Moite: com. *Moist, liquid, humide, wet, sweatie, giuing as stones in rainie weather.*

Moiteau. *as* Motte; *or, as* Motteau.

Moiteur: f. *Moisture, moistnesse, humiditie, wetnesse, waterishnesse.*

Moitié: f. *An halfe, or halfe part.*

Moitié figues moitié raisins. *Betweene ieast and earnest.*

Moiton: m. *The halfe of a* Bichot; *two bushells and a halfe; and, in some places, three:* ¶Bourguignon.

Moitoyen: m. *Any whole thing that is enioyed in common, or by vndiuided or vndiuisible halues.*

Moitoyen: m. enne: f. *Seuering, or parting in the middest seuerall possessions; also, enioyed in common, or by vndiuided or vndiuisible halues; whence;*

Mur moitoyen. *A partitiõ wall, whereof th'one halfe or side belongs to one, & th'other to another; also, a wall wherin many haue parts according to the scope of their tenements, or state of their tenures.*

Moitoyennerie: f. *Th'enioying of a thing by many in common; or by equall parts or vndiuided halues.*

Moitoyrie: f. *as* Metairie; *(An old word.)*

Mol: m. *Softnes; the soft, or softer part of a thing; whence;*

Le mol de la jambe. *The calfe of the leg.*

Le mol de l'oreille. *The lug, or list of th'eare.*

Mol: m. molle: f. *Soft; supple, tender, lithe, limber, pliant; easie, gentle, yeelding; mild, effeminate, remisse; daintie, delicate.*

B. mol. B. *flat, in Musicke.*

De B. carré en B. mol. *Inconstantly, or suddainely, from one matter into another.*

Mol en putain de bordeau. *As tender as a Priestes leyman (say we.)*

Molaine: f. *as* Moulaine.

Molard. poire de m. *A verie tender, & delicate peare.*

Molares. les dents mol. *The cheeke-teeth, or grinders.*
Mole: m. *A Peere; a banke, or causey on the sea-side neere vnto a Rode, or Hauen.*
Mole: f. *A Timpanie, or Moone-calfe; a shapelesse lump of flesh, or hard swelling, in the wombe, that makes a woman seeme with child; also, as* Molebout; *also, as* Tenche de mer.
Molé: m. ée: f. *Moulded; cast in, or framed by, a mould.*
Molebout: m. *A kind of great sea-lumpe.*
Moleste: com. *Troublesome, offensiue, irksome, grieuous, combersome, tedious, loathsome, painfull, burdensome, vnpleasing, noisome vnto.*
Molesté: m. ée: f. *Molested, troubled, offended, combered, vexed, annoyed, infested, afflicted; vrged, importuned.*
Molestément. *Troublesomely, offensiuely, combersomely, noisomely, to the wrong, or vexation of.*
Molester. *To molest, annoy, trouble, comber, vex, disquiet, offend, paine, infest, afflict; to vrge, presse, importune too much; be burdensome vnto, lye hard, and heauie vpon.*
Molesteur: m. *A molester, troubler, vexer, disquieter, annoyer.*
Molestie: f. *Molestation, trouble, annoyance; vexation, disquiet, affliction, offence, displeasure, irksomenesse, loathsomenesse, tediousnesse, too much importunitie, or businesse.*
Molet. *Seeke* Mollet.
Molette d'esperon. *The rowell of a spurre.*
Molibdene. *as* Plombagine; *Also, the hearbe Leadwort.*
Moliere: f. *A bog, or quagmire.*
Moliere; *whence,* Pierre de moliere. *A grindstone, or grindlestone.*
Molin. *as* Moulin.
Moliner. *To worke, or thicken in a mill.*
Molinet. *as* Moulinet; *Also, the roll wherein the whip of a Rudders tiller goes.*
Chascun n'a pas son molinet: Prov. viz. Chascun ne dort en lict mol, & net.
Molinier: m. *A Miller.*
Molition: f. *Indeauor, practise, attempt, enterprising, vndertaking.*
Mollart. *as* Molard.
Mollasse: com. *Quaggie, swagging, not firme, foggie, filthily soft, loathsomely supple, vnpleasantly pliant; quagmire-like.*
Molle. *(The name of) an Indian tree, of whose tender branches a kind of wine is made.*
Mollement. *Softly, supplely, tenderly; easily, gently, mildly; yeeldingly, remisly, effeminately.*
Mollesse: f. *Softnesse, supplenesse, tendernesse; limbernesse, pliantnesse; easinesse, gentlenesse, mildnesse, remisnesse, tractablenesse; wantonnesse, delicacie; faintnesse, effeminacie, cowardise; also, the monstrous appetite of some maids, and women, vnto paper, ashes, coales, and such other harsh, and vnsauorie acates.*
Mollet: m. *The fleshie part of the hand betweene the thumbe, and middle finger; also, the tip, lug, or soft part of the eare; also, the calfe of the leg; also, a muddie place in a riuer.*
Mollet: m. ette: f. *Somewhat soft, supple, tender; limber; tractable, remisse; delicate, effeminate.*
Pain mollet. *A verie light, crustie, and sauorie white bread, full of eyes, leauen, and salt.*
Molleté. *as* Mollesse.
Mollette: f. *A Mullet; a nipper, a pinser; also, the ramhead of a fearne, or windlesse; also, the rowell of a spurre.*
Mollette à brayer couleurs. *A Muller; the little flat-bottomed stone wherewith a Painter grindes his colours.*
Chaire de bois à mollette. *A folding chaire of wood.*
Mollice: f. *as* Mollesse.
Mollification: f. *A mollification, mollifying, softening, suppling.*
Mollifié: m. ée: f. *Mollified, softened, suppled.*
Mollifier. *To mollifie, soften, supple; smooth, make plyant, gentle, tender.*
Mollifieur: m. *A mollifier, softener, suppler; smoother, appeaser.*
Mollinets: m. *The Jewells at th'end of bodkins; also, rings hauing pearles hanging at them.*
Mollir. *To soften, mollifie; smooth; to make gentle, tender, pliant; to loossen, slacken, relax; also, to make wanton, effeminate, faint.*
Molu. *Seeke* Moulu.
Molosse: m. *A foot of three long syllables, in versifying.*
Moluë: f. *Cod, or Greene-fish; Looke* Moruë.
Molure. *Seeke* Moulure.
Molurien. *(The name of) a certaine harmelesse serpent.*
Molybdoide: f. *Is held of some, to be, the minerall, and leaden-coloured, Calamine; of others (more properly) the oare of lead, or lead-stone vntried.*
Mome: m. *A Momus, find-fault, carping fellow.*
Moment: m. *A moment, a minute, a iot of time; also, moment, importance, weight, value, validitie, consequence; the vertue, force, or strength of.*
Momentaine: com. *Momentarie, transitorie, of little durance, of small continuance.*
Momental: m. ale: f. *Forcible, weightie, important, of moment; also, as* Momentaine.
Momentané: m. ée: f. *as* Momentaine.
Momerie: f. *Momerie, momisme, carping, fault-finding.*
Mommerie: f. *A Mummerie, a Mumming.*
Mommeur: m. *A Mummer; one that goes a mumming.*
Mommon. *as* Mommeur; *Also, a troupe, or companie of Mummers; also, a visard, or maske; also, a set, by a Mummer, at dice.*
Il luy couvra son mommon. Il la besongna.
Mon: m. *The giserne of a bird.*
Mon: m. ma: f. *My.*
Mon. *(A Coniunction)* Asçavoir mon si. *Whether; This in Demaunds onely; for otherwise tis vsed as an inforcement of an affirmation; whence;* C'est mon; *yes forsooth, truely, certainly, doubtlesse, indeed.*
Monacal: m. ale: f. *Monacall, Monasticall, monklie, belonging to a Monke.*
Monacalement. *Monastically, Monke-like.*
Monade: f. *An vnitie, or singlenesse; an one.*
Monaquat: m. *Monkerie, Monkship, Monkisme, Monachisme; the ductie, or state of a Monke.*
Monarchie: f. *A Monarchie; a kingdome; the gouernment of one absolute Prince.*
Monarchique: com. *Monarchall; belonging to a Monarchie, or Monarch.*
Monarque: com. *A Monarch; an absolute Prince.*
Monastere: m. *A Monasterie, Cloister, Abbey, Couent.*
Monastique: com. *Monasticall, Monklie, Monkish.*
Moncaiart: m. *Silke Moccadoe; or, a kind thereof.*
Monceau: m. *A heape, a masse, a pile.*
Monceau de foin. *A cocke, reeke, or stacke of hay.*
Petit monceau de terre. *A barrow, hillocke, little hill.*

Se retirer en vn monceau. *To gather himselfe vp into a lumpe, or heape.*
Auarice fait petit monceau: Prov. *Looke* Auarice.
De bien commun on ne fait pas souuent monceau: Pro. *Of common goods men seldome gather heaps.*
Monceler. *To heape, or pile vp.*
Moncelet: m. *A little heape, masse, pile.*
Moncet. *as* Moineau; *A Sparrow.*
Mondain: m. *A worldling; one thats throughly acquainted with, or giues himselfe wholly to, worldlie businesses.*
Mondain: m. aine: f. *Mundane, worldlie, secular; prophane; dissolute, sensuall, fleshlie, epicurious.*
Mondaniser. *To world it, or, to play the worldling.*
Mondanité: f. *Worldlinesse; vanitie; sensualitie, fleshlinesse.*
Monde: m. *The world, the vniuers; all visible things vnder the cope of heauen; also, a (world, or) great number of people, great store of companie.*
Le monde va tousiours à l'empire: Pro. *The world growes euerie day worse and worse.*
Qui veut la conscience monde, il doit fuir le monde immonde: Prov. *He that affects a cleane conscience, must auoid vncleane copesmates.*
Monde: com. *Cleane, neat; pure, cleere, sincere.*
Qui veut la conscience monde, &c. *as before.*
Mondé: m. ée: f. *Cleansed, made cleane; also, pruned; picked, pilled; whence;*
Orge mondé. *Looke* Orge.
Monder vn arbre. *as* Esmonder.
Mondificatif: m. iue: f. *Mundificatiue, mundifying; cleansing, purging, purifying.*
Mondification. *A mundification, mundifying, cleansing, purging, purifying.*
Mondifié: m. ée: f. *Mundified, cleansed, purged, purified.*
Mondifier. *To mundifie, cleanse, purifie, purge, wipe, make cleane.*
Mondinet: m. *A neat, spruce, compt fellow.*
Monettes: f. *Warning, or admonishing women:* ¶Rab.
Monfaucon. *The great gallowes of Paris; (standing on 16 stone pillers;) whence;*
Banderolle à l' aduenir de Monfaucon. *One for whom the gallowes grones; one that deserueth, or is like to come to, the gallowes.*
Monial: m. ale: f. *Of, or belonging to, a Monke.*
Herbe moniale. *Wild Larks-heele, Monks-hood with the purple flower.*
Moniale: f. *A Nunne.*
Monilles: m. *Necklaces, Tablets, Brouches, or Ouches; any such Ornaments for the necke.*
Monine. *as* Monnine.
Moniteur: m. *A monitor, admonisher, warner; a Summoner, an Apparitor.*
Monition: f. *A monition, admonition, monishment; an aduertisement, information, warning, summons.*
Monitoire: m. *A monitorie, or admonition; the censure, or sentence of a Bishop in an Ecclesiasticall Court.*
Monitoire: com. *Monitorie, monishing, admonishing, aduertising, warning.*
Monitorial: m. ale: f. *Monitorial, monitorie, admonishing*
Monne: f. *A Monkie, or Pug.*
Monneage: m. *An Aid, or Subsidie of 12 d. paid vnto the Duke of Normandie, each third yere, by euery housholder (except Church officers, beneficed men, Gentlemen, poore widows, & some other priuiledged persons) to th'end that the coine of the countrey might not be altered.*
Monnier: m. *The Cheuin, or Chub-fish.*
Monnine: f. *A Marmoset, or little Monkie.*
Monnoyage: m. *The making, or coyning of money; also, the fees due vnto money-makers.*
Monnoye: f. *Money, coyne, chinks.*
Monnoyes. (*as in,* le faict des mon. les Generaux des mon. le Maistre des mon. &c.) *The Mint.*
Monnoye de Basoche. *Counters, or Palace Crowns; any such trash currant among Pages, & yong Clerkes.*
Monnoye de belistres. *Lice.*
Monnoye blāche. *Brasse or copper coine siluerd ouer.*
Monnoye de cordelier. *Thankes, or a Benedicite; wherwith gray Friers, who are to carrie no money about them, vse to pay their shots.*
Monnoye noire. *Seeke* Noir.
Monnoye de Roy. *French money of gold, or siluer; so called in old time.*
Monnoye de Singe. *Moes, mumps, mouthes; also, friskes, leaps, gambolls.*
Descrié comme la vieille monnoye. *Stale, out of vse, out of date; also, of bad report, that hath but an ill name, in the world.*
Payer toutes personnes en mesme monnoye. *To vse, or answer, all alike.*
Resembler la monnoye rongnée. *To be illiterate, or vnlearned;* Estre sans lettres.
'A pauures gens menuë monnoye: Prov. *Small money suffices, or fits, the poore.*
Monnoyé: m. ée: f. *Coined, or made into mony.*
Monnoyement: m. *A coyning, or money-making.*
Monnoyer: m. *A Coyner, or money-maker.*
Monnoyer. *To coine, make monye, or make into money.*
Monnoyeur: m. *A Coyner, Moneyer, money-maker.*
Monochordiser des doigts. *To quauer with the fingers, to wag or play with them, as if he touched a Manicordion.*
Monocle: com. *One eyed; hauing but one eye.*
Monocule. *as* Monocle.
Monogaine: m. *One that neuer had but one wife.*
Monologue: m. *One that loues to heare himselfe talke; or talkes verie much about a verie little.*
Monomachie: f. *A Monomachie, or single combat.*
Monon: m. *A certaine little green-leaued shrub, which beares a red fruit resembling a small cherrie, but not to be eaten.*
Monope: m. *A Peonian beast, that is as big as a Bull, and neerely pursued squirts out a sharpe, and fierie ordure, deadlie to such as it lights on.*
Monopole: f. *A Monopolie; a priuat conspiracie, factious combination, vniust cōfederation; hence also, the sale of a marchātable cōmoditie challenged by one, or few; th'ingrossing therof into one, or few mens hands, by Patent from the Prince, or packing with others.*
Monopolé: m. ée: f. *Monopoled, or monopolized; combined, conspired; ingrossed, as a commoditie, into one, or a few mens hands.*
Monopoler. *To conspire, or combine together; to molopolize it, or make a monopolie; One, or a few to ingrosse, and challenge the sale of, a commoditie, which many (if they had their due) should vtter.*
Monopolier: m. *A monopoler, or monopolizer; an ingrosser of sale commodities, by Patent from the Prince, or packing with others.*
Monosyllabe: com. *Of one sillable.*
Monouc. *An Eunuch:* ¶Turquesque.
Monseigneur. *My Lord; (a title cōferred on such great men as be in degree, or authoritie, farre aboue vs.)*
Monsieur. *Sir, or Maister; (a title fit for an equall, or such a one, as is not much superior to him that bestowes it.)*

Monsieur, de trois au boisseau: &, de trois à vne espée. *A thread-bare, single-soled, course-spunne, gentleman.*

Monsieur sans queuë. *A Cheater; also, a Maister without further addition; a gentleman without Arms, or Attendance; one thats troubled with no more gentrie then he needs.*

Monsieur vaut bien Madame: Prov. *A Lord deserues (or is worth) a Ladie at all times.*

Aujourd'huy monsieur demain Mouscheur: Pro. *To day a Maister, to morrow Maisterlesse.*

Monstier: m. *A Monasterie; also, a Minster, or Cathedrall Church; (and sometimes) also, any Parish Church.*

Laisser le monstier ou il est. *Not to alter an auncient custome; or, to leaue the determining of Church matters vnto Church-men.*

Ce que l'enfant oit au fouyer est tost connu iusques au monstier: Pro. *The Parish quickly knowes what infants heare in priuate.*

Monstre: m. *A monster; a deformed creature; a thing thats fashioned, or bred contrarie to nature.*

Monstre: f. *A patterne, scantling, proofe, example, essay; also, a muster, view, shew, or sight; the countenance, representation, or outward apparence of a thing; a demonstration; also, a watch, or little clocke that strikes not; also, the glassie box that stands on the stalls of Goldsmithes, Cutlers, &c; and generally, any thing that shewes, or points at, another thing; whence;*

La monstre d'vn horologe. *The hand of a clocke.*

La monstre d'vn maquignon de chevaux. *The place wherein a horse-scourser shews his commodities.*

Monstré: m. ée: f. *Shewed, represented; discouered, bewrayed; pointed at; signified, expressed, declared.*

Monstrée. *as* Monstre; *A view, shew, sight, muster of.*

Monstrement: m. *A shewing, representing, pointing at; a demonstrating, expressing, declaring.*

Monstrer. *To shew; represent; expresse, point at; manifest, signifie, demonstrate, declare; disclose, discouer, bewray, reueale.*

Se monstrer. *To appeare, stand out, present or put forth himselfe; also, to shew, or proue himselfe.*

Monstrer la dent. *To girne; to grow into choler.*

Monstrer le mouchoir blanc à. *Looke* Mouchoir.

Monstrer les talons; ou le cul. *To shew a faire paire of heeles; to runne away.*

Monstreur: m. *A shewer, a demonstrator.*

Monstrüeusement. *Monstrously; misshapenly, most deformedly, or defectiuely; against the course of nature.*

Monstrüeux: m. euse: f. *Monstrous; misshapen; defectiue, exorbitant, vnnaturall, or most contrary to nature.*

Mont: m. *A mount, hill, mountaine.*

Les monts. *(Without addition) are commonly vnderstood to be the Alpes; High mountaines which diuide Italie, and France.*

Mont Iovie. *A rising vnder (th'inside of) one of the fingers.*

Mont de pieté. *A publicke stocke, or purse maintained for the reliefe, assistance, and furtherance of young Tradesmen.*

Du mont à val. *From the top to the bottome.*

En mont. *Vpwards, aboue, on high.*

Par monts & par vaux. *In euerie coast, in euerie place, euerie where, all the world through.*

Promettre monts, & merveilles; ou, monts & vaux. *To promise wonders, or golden worlds; (as some doe that either will not, or cannot, performe any thing.)*

Au matin les monts, au soir les fonds: Pro. *So some men quickely fall from high full low.*

Au matin vers les monts, au soir vers les fonts: Pro. *A mornings walk vp th'hill, in th'euening downwards.*

Mont. *in stead of* Moult. *Much.*

C'est mont. *Looke* Mon.

Montable: com. *Mountable, ascendable, climable.*

Montagne. *as* Montaigne.

Montagner. faulcon mont. *as* Montain, *or* Montagon.

Montagon: m. *A kind of hardie faulcō, hard to be kept.*

Montagu. *The name of a beggerlie Colledge in Paris, founded in the yeare of Grace 1314.*

Esparvier de Montagu. *A lowse.*

Montaignard: m. *A mountainer, or mountaine man.*

Montaigne: f. *A mountaine, a great hill.*

Montaigne de Mars. *The fleshie part of the hand betweene the thumbe, and middle finger; or the muscles whereof it is made; (a tearme of Anatomie.)*

Les hommes se rencontrent, & non pas les montaignes: Prov. *Men meet often, mountaines neuer.*

se Montaigner. *To looke big on't; highly to exalt, or lift vp, himselfe.*

Montaignette: f. *A little mountaine.*

Montaigneux: m. euse: f. *Mountainous, mountainie, Full of mountaines.*

Montaignois: m. oise: f. *Of or belonging to, residing or dwelling in mountaines.*

Montaignolle: f. *as* Montaignette.

Montain: m. *A kind of short, strong, and excellent (but ill to be kept) Faulcon, that vseth to looke much on her feet; also, the little bird, called a Brambling.*

Montanage. *as* Montenage.

Montance. à la mon. de cent. *Arising, or amounting to aboue an hundred.*

Montant: m. *A Mountan; an vpright beame, or post in building; also, a boat that goes vp a riuer, or against the streame; also, as* Col rompu, *or a small rising in the middle of the mouth of a bit; also, an vpright blow, or thrust; also, th'ascent, or rising of a thing; or a thing, or any part thereof, considered in it ascent.*

Les montants d'vn lict. *The bed-posts.*

Le montant du pied. *Th'instep.*

Montant. *Mounting, ascending, rising, getting vp on; also, increasing, or growing deere; also, ouerbidding another.*

Monté: m. ée: f. *Mounted, ascended, risen, got vp, got vpon.*

Bien, ou mal monté. *Well, or ill mounted; viz. well, or ill horsed.*

Guiterre bien, ou mal monté. *Well, or ill strung.*

Monté iusques au nid de la pie. *At the height of his fortunes; as high as his meanes, or worth, can raise him.*

Il n'est pas asseuré qui trop haut est monté: Pro. *He sits not fast whose seat is raisd too high.*

Montée: f. *An ascent, rising, mounting, or climbing vp; also, the rising part of a horses bit.*

La montée d'vn bastiment. *Th'upper part of a building; or, a representation, or modell thereof, called the vpright plot of a building.*

'A haute montée le faix encombre: Prov. *He that climbes high feels euerie small weight heauie.*

Apres grande montée grande vallée: Prov. *After toyle rest, after paine ease.*

Apres grande vallée rude montée: Prov. *The contrarie.*

Montelet: m. *A little mountaine.*

Montenage: m. *Toll paied vnto certaine Lords by such as buy, and sell beasts, & other marchandise within their territories.*

Monter. *To mount, ascend, rise, climbe, to goe or get vp vnto; to leape as the male vpon the female; also, to increase, or grow deere; also, to ouerbid another; also, to shew in quantitie; to amount vnto; to raise, aduance, lift vp.*

Monte monte. *Words whereby yong Sparrowes are taught to climbe the lather.*

Monter vn arbaleste. *To set a crossebow in the stock.*

Monter sur l'asne, faire cession des biens. *Looke* Asne.

Monter sur ses grands chevaulx. *To speake high, stand vpon high tearmes.*

Monter au greiner sans chãdelle. *To light in a turd.*

Monter vne monstre. *To wind vp a watch.*

Monter à la navire. *To get a shipboord, to take ship.*

Qui plus haut monte qu'il ne doit de plus haut chet qu'il ne voudroit: Prov. *He that climbes higher then he should falls lower then he would.*

Monte-vin: m. *A strait-mouthed vessell of glasse, which if you fill with wine, and another of the same fashion with water, and then set this vpon that, the wine will straight mount through the water to the top of the one vessell, and the water descend through the wine to the bottome of th'other, without mixture of either with the other.*

Monticule: f. *A hillocke, a small hill.*

Montigené: m. ée: f. *Borne, or bred on the mountains.*

Mont joye: m. *The title of the chiefe Herauld in France.*

Mont joye: f. *A barrow; a little hill, or heape of stones, layed in, or neere a highway, for the better discerning thereof; or in remembrance of some notable act performed, or accident befallen, in that place; also, a goale to run at; also (metaphorically) any heape.*

Montoir. *as* Montouër; *or the side whereon we get on.*

Se ranger au montoir. *Metaphorically from a horse to a wench, that suffers a man to get on; or settles her selfe to giue him the easier getting on.*

Montouër: m. *A mounting blocke; or as* Montoir.

Montroüage. *as* Montenage.

Montueux. *as* Montaigneux.

Monture: f. *A horse to ride on, a saddle horse.*

Monument: m. *A monument; sepulchre, tombe; record, memoriall, remembrance of.*

Moquer. *Looke* Mocquer.

Moquettes: f. *Mockes, frumps, flowts, gudgeons.*

Moral: m. ale: f. *Morall, belonging vnto ciuilitie, or manners.*

Moralement. *Morally, in a morall sence, or fashion; also, doubly, or with a meaning different from his words.*

Moralisé: m. ée: f. *Moralized, morally expounded.*

Moraliser. *To morallize, to expound morally, to giue a morall sence vnto; also, to act a Morall, or Enterlude of manners.*

Moraliseur: m. *A moralizer, an expounder of moralities; an Ethicke Lectorer, or Philosopher.*

Moralité: f. *Moralitie; a morall sence, or subiect; also, a Morall, an Enterlude or Play of manners.*

Morbifique: com. *Vnwholesome, infectious, diseases-breeding, sicknesse-bringing.*

Morbilles: f. *The small pockes.*

Morceau: m. *A morsell; bit, mouthfull; also, a gobbet, fragment, broken peece of, or peece broken off from.*

Morceau d' Adam. *The head of the wind-pipe, or throat, consisting of three little gristles.*

Se courroucer contre ses morceaux. *as vnder* Courroucer.

Croupir aux escoutes de gras morceaux. *To lye in wait for wealthie Offices, fat benefices, &c.*

Cela leur fait tailler les morceaux plus menus. *That makes them liue the more sparingly, or pinch it the more.*

`A morceau restif esperon de vin: Prov. *Put on a restiue bit with spurres of wine.*

Au serviteur le morceau d' honneur: Pro. *The last morsell in the dish is the seruants fee (some holding it but a rude part to leaue a dish emptie.)*

Morcel: m. *as* Morceau *(in old French.)*

Morcelaire. Collation morcelaire. *A short collation, a bit and away.*

Morcelé: m. ée: f. *Nibled, eaten by bits, bitten by little and little.*

Morceler. *To bite small morsells, nibble, mince it, eat by little and little,*

Morcelet: m. *A bit, small mammocke, or morsell.*

Morche: f. *Food, victualls, cheere, batling.*

Morcillant: m. ante: f. *Peecemealing, diuiding into morsells, or small peeces; also, knapping, or nibling; biting fast and sleightly.*

Vn oeil morcillant. *A greedie, or hungrie eye; such a one as expresses a great appetite to be at it.*

Morcillé: m. ée: f. *Peecemealed; diuided into small morsells, or peeces; also, nibled; bitten fast and sleightly.*

Morciller. *To peecemeale; to diuide into small morsells, or peeces; also, to nibble, or knapple; to bite verie fast and verie sleightly, like a rabbit that mumbles a hard thing which her teeth cannot pierce.*

Mordacité: f. *Mordacitie, eager detraction, sharpe taunting, biting speech, bitter tearmes.*

Mordant: m. *A kind of great, blacke, and slow Spider.*

Mordant: m. ante: f. *Biting.*

Bestes mordantes. *The Wolfe, Boare, Otter, Fox, &c.*

En mordant. *Holding fast, biting hard.*

Mordeur: m. *A biter.*

Mordicant. *Nipping, pinching, biting.*

Mordication: f. *A nipping, pinching, biting.*

Mordienne. *Gogs deathlings; a foolish oath in* Rab.

Mordillé: m. ée: f. *Nibled, gnawed; fretted, snipped off.*

Mordiller. *To nibble, gnaw, fret, snip off.*

Mordiquer. *To bite, pinch, nip.*

Mordre. *To bite, or set the teeth in; to gnaw, brouse, champe, nibble; to pinch, nip, snip, or snap with the teeth; also, to sting; also, to smell (whence,* le mord; *there your nose;) also, to conceiue, apprehend, vnderstand.*

Mordre au baston. pour le faire mordre, &c. *To make him the more eager.*

Mordre les doigts. *To fret, or chafe inwardly at a thing past helpe.*

Mordre à la grappe: Il sembloit mordre à la grappe. *He spoke so heartily that he seemed to doe what he deliuered.*

Mordre l' oreille à. *as much as,* flatter, ou caresser mignonnement; *wherin the biting of th'eare is, with some, an vsuall Action.*

Mordre en riant. *To quip, or taunt by way, or with a shew, of ieast; to shew a man a goood countenance to his face, and cut his throat behind his backe.*

Il n'y pouvoit rien mordre. *He could not skill of it, he knew not what to make of it; twas past his reach, out of his course, out of his element.*

Vous avez bien envie de mordre sur mon language. *You would faine take hold of, you hope for some aduantage by, my words.*

Chien qui abbaye ne mord pas: Pro. *Many words few,*

few, or no blowes; they seldome strike home that threaten, or talke, much.

Homme mort mord iusques, & par delà la mort: Prov. *The bloud of the innocent cryes vnto God for vengeance, pursuing vnto, and stinging after, death the conscience of a murtherer: Howsoeuer some may flatter themselues with;*

Homme mort ne mord pas: Prov. *A dead man, (or as we say, a dead dog) bites not.*

Mauvais chien ne trouve ou mordre: Pro. *The curst curre knowes not where to set his teeth.*

On ne sçait qui mord ne qui rue: Prov. *A man knowes not what may fall out.*

Tel estrille fauveau qui puis le mord: Prov. *Looke* Fauveau.

Tel rid qui mord: Prov. *Some laugh that bite, some ieast that gall; or as before in,* Mordre en riant.

Mords: m. *A Bitt for a horse.*

Mords. *Bitten; gnawne, champed; nibled; nipped, or pinched with the teeth; stung.*

More: m. *A Moore, Morian, Blackamore.*

Petit more. *The name of an excellent Ordinarie in Paris.*

Teste de more. *Looke* Teste.

Il a esté pris comme le more. *His cunning is discouered; or he hath cousened himselfe in thinking to cousen others; he is caught in the snare he layed for another.* (Francis Sforce *the last absolute Duke of* Milain *(surnamed the Moore, because of his swart complexion, and the most craftie Prince of his time) hauing receiued a great ouerthrow, put on the apparrell of a Swisser, and thought so to haue liued, for a while, hidden among the Regiments of that Nation; but they within a while discouering, deliuered him vnto the French King, in whose prisons he ended his dayes.)*

Moreau. Cheval moreau. *A blacke horse.*

Morée: f. *A kind of murrey, or darke-red colour.*

Morel. *as* Moreau.

Morelle: f. *The hearbe Morell, pettie Morell, garden Nightshade.*

Morelle furieuse, ou maniaque. *Mad, raging, or furious Nightshade.*

Morelle marine. *A kind of sleeping Nightshade which growes in rockie places neere vnto the sea.*

Morelle mortelle. *Dwale, Deaths hearbe, deadlie Nightshade, great Nightshade.*

Morelle somnifique. *Sleepie Nightshade; or, as* Morelle mortelle.

Morelles: f. *Morell Cherries; late-ripe Cherries, dryed for Winter prouision.*

Morene: f. *as* Hemorrhoïde; *the Emrods, or Piles.*

Morengue. *The name of a kind of Oliue.*

Moresque: f. *A Mooresse, a shee Moore, a blacke woman.*

Moresque: com. *Moorish, Moore-like, of the Moores.*

Fueillage, & Ouvrage, moresque. *Moreske worke; a rude, or anticke painting, or caruing, wherein the feet and tayles of beasts, &c, are intermingled with, or made to resemble, a kind of wild leaues, &c.*

Moresse: f. *A Mooresse, a woman Moore, a blacke woman.*

Moret: m. *A kind of Lye whereof Sope is made; also, as* Morée.

Morets. Des morets. *winne-berries, hurtle-berries.*

Morse: f. *A feasting, or making of good cheere.*

Morsée: f. *as* Morphée.

Morsiaille: f. *Greedie eating, illfauoured or hastie deuouring; also, bad or dead wine, such as is no better then droppings.*

Morsiailler. *To feed greedily, eat or drinke hastily, and writhe the mouth illfauouredly in chawing, or swallowing.*

Morsiailleries: f. *Food or victualls greedily, and illfauouredly taken in.*

Morsil: m. *Iuorie, Elephants teeth.*

Le morsil d'un cousteau. *The edge-side of a new, and vnground knife.*

Morsondement: m. *as* Morsondure.

se Morsondre. *To take cold, catch cold, get a cold.*

Se morsondre sur. *To stand long, or dwell much vpon.*

Morsondu: m. uë: f. *That hath taken, or caught cold; that hath got a cold.*

Morsondure: f. *A cold; or a taking of cold.*

Morganegibe. *A matrimoniall gift; or, such a title as our frankmariage.*

Morgeline: f. *Iuie Chickweed, Henne-bit; also, the small, or fine Chickweed; also, Pimpernell; whence;*

Morgeline femelle. *Blew Pimpernell.*

Morgeline masle. *Red Pimpernell.*

Morgoy, *for* Mort Dieu; *(a rusticall oath.)*

Morgue: f. *A sad, or sadned looke; a solemne, or seuere countenance; a soure face; an austere posture, or sett of the visage; the mumping aspect of one that would seeme grauer then he is; Also (in the* Chastelet *of Paris) a certaine Chaire, wherein a new-come prisoner is set, and must continue some houres, without stirring either head or hand, that the Keepers ordinarie seruants may the better take notice of his face, and fauour.*

'A le voir tenir si bonne morgue. *Seeing him keepe his countenance so well, or set so good a face on the matter.*

Morguer. *To looke sourely on, or make a soure face at; to braue or outface with a soure, solemne, or stout countenance.*

Qui morgue le ciel, & fait gambades à la terre. *that hangs on a gibbet.*

Morguesoupe. à la m. *Whilest they were eating their browesse, or fat pottage.*

Morgueur: m. *A maker of strange mouthes, or soure faces.*

Morgueux. *The same; or one that illfauouredly writhes his face to a shew of grauitie.*

Morhouc: m. *A Porpose, or sea Hog.* ¶Breton.

Moribonde: com. *Dying; or vpon the point of dying; readie to dye.*

Morienne: com. *Dying a naturall death; or, not killed, but dead of it selfe.*

Morigené: m. ée: f. Bien mor. *Mannerlie, well mannered, well behaued, of good carriage, well fashioned, well brought vp.*

Morille: f. *The smallest, and daintiest kind of red Mushrome.*

Pinse morille. *The game called, Hinch pinch, and laugh not.*

Morillon: m. *A shell-Drake; or broad-beaked water-fowle, whose head and neckes vpper part is of a ruddie, or Chestnut colour, the lower part of his necke, back and tayle being black, and the rest of his back and his wings Mouse-coloured; also, the name of a blacke grape that yeelds verie good Wine.*

Morin. Vent morin. *The South wind.*

Morion: m. *A Murrian, or Head-peece.*

Morionné. *Armed, or couered with a Murrian.*

Lievres morionnez. *(Sillie Artificers, or cowardlie Trades-men, turned watchmen) the ordinarie watch-*

watchmen of good Townes.

Soldats morionnez. *Footmen.*

Morique. *for* Morisque. ¶Rab.

Morir. *Looke* Mourir.

Morisque: f. *A Morris (or Moorish) daunce; also, the mizzen sayle of a Ship.*

Morme. *The ruddie, and spotted sea-Breame, or Goldennie.*

Mormyre. *as* Morme.

Morne: com. *Sad, heauie, lumpish, lowting; pensiue, agreeued, in a melancholie mood, all in dumpes; also, dull, stupide, sottish, senceleße, blockish.*

Lance morne. *A launce with a blunt head; a tilting-staffe.*

Temps morne. *Blacke, duskie, clowdie, gloomie, lowring weather.*

Morné: m. ée: f. *Dulled, blunted, vnpointed; also, tipped, headed, or pointed with.*

Esperons mornez. *Spurres with blunt rowells.*

Mornement. *Sadly, pensiuely; moodily, lumpishly; dully, sottishly; clowdily, lowringly.*

Morner. *To blunt, or dull the point of a weapon.*

Mornifle: f. *A daintie round Italian fruit, growing like a Toadstoole; also, a tricke at Cards; also, a cuffe, or pash on the lips.*

Bailler mornifle sur les levres du Roy. *To coyne false money.*

Moroche: f. *The smallest, coursest, and dryest kind of Indian Wheat.*

Moromantie: f. *Foolish diuination.*

Moron. *as* Mouron.

Morosité: f. *Morositie, frowardnesse, waywardnesse, croßnesse, ouerthwartnesse.*

Morosophe: com. *Foolish-wise.*

Morphée: f. *The Morphew.*

Morphie: f. *Iuorie.*

Morpiaille. *as* Morfiaille. ¶Rab.

Morpion: m. *A Crablowse.*

Grenier à morpions. *A Harbour, or Garner for Crablice; a filthie, nastie, sluttish, or lowsie queane.*

Morquacassé: m. ée: f. *All-bruised, or out of ioint.* ¶Rab.

Morrail de mulet: m. *A kind of muzzle tyed about his nose, and hauing hanged at it a great poake full of Hay, or Oats for him to feed on as he goes.*

Morrailles. *as* Mourrailles.

Morre: f. *A powch-mouth; a mouth garded with great, out-standing, or slowching lips; (or, as* Mourre.)

Morrion. *as* Morion.

Morrude: f. *A Gurnard, or Curre-fish.*

Mors: m. *A bitt, or biting; also, as* Mords.

Mors à diable. *(So doe some call) the hearbe Auens, Bennet, or Blessed.*

Mors du diable. *Fore-bit, or Deuils-bit; (an hearbe.)*

Morsaul. *as* Marsaul.

Morsillant, & Morsiller, *as* Morcillant, & Morciller.

Morsilleure: f. *A peece-mealing; a breaking, or diuiding into many small peeces.*

Morsure: f. *A biting; a champing, gnawing, or nibling; a pinching, or nipping with the teeth; also, a stinging; also, a bit; a morsell, or mouthfull taken with the teeth.*

Morsure du diable. *as* Mors du diable.

En maigre poil a morsure: Pro. *A bald head yeelds a lowse a full bit; disarmed of protection, soone harmed by oppression.*

Telle dent telle morsure: Prov. *A sharpe tooth a smart wound; such as the tooth, such is the bit.*

Mort: f. *Death; bane; a decease, or departure out of this life.*

Mort aux bœufs. *Ox-bane; an hearbe whereof if an Ox eat, he dies forthwith of the Squinzie.*

Mort aux chiens. *Dogs-bane; also, meadow, or wild, Saffron.*

Mort d'enfer damnation. *Looke* Enfer.

Mort aux oisons. *Henbane; also, Hemlocks.*

Mort aux rats. *The confection tearmed Ratsbane.*

Mort Roland. *Thirst.* ¶Rab.

Mort aux vers. *The hearbe called Wormeseed, sea Wormewood, and Wormeseed wort.*

Donation à cause de mort. *A Deed of gift, in the nature of a Legacie, or Will, reuocable during the giuers life.*

`A mort à mort. *Kill, Kill; the cry of bloudie souldiors pursuing their fearefull enemies vnto death.*

La mort l'attend à deux pas prés. *Death is hard by him, or readie to seize on him.*

Il est bon à aller querir la mort. *He is a dreaming, lingering, or sluggish messenger.*

La mort n'espargne ny petit ny grand: Pro. *Death baulkes no creature, spares nor small nor great.*

La mort n'a point d'ami, le malade n'a qu'un demy: Prov. *Death hath no friend, the sicke man but an halfe one.*

Apres la mort le medecin: Pro. *After death drugs; the mischiefe past, a remedie.*

Bonne la mort qui nous donne la vie: Prov. *Good is the death which brings vs vnto life; Gods fauour's great not to repriue such as end well, and die to liue.*

Contre la mort n'y a point d'appel: Prov. *From death there's no appealing.*

Contre la mort n'y a point de medecine: Pro. *No medicine against death; no remedie for death.*

`A longue corde tire qui d'autruy la mort desire: Prov. *See* Corde.

Haine de Prince signifie mort d'homme: Prov. *He whom a Prince hates is as good as dead.*

Homme mort mord iusques, & par delà la mort: Pro. *Looke* Mordre.

Le pourpre au soc mort d'egal poix balance: Prov. *Death matches the poore clowne with purple Gallants.*

Mort: m. morte: f. *Dead, deceassed, departed; also, killed, murthered, slaine, made away.*

Mort bois; &, Bois mort. *Looke* Bois.

Mort herbage; ou, Herbage mort. *Looke* Herbage.

Mortes œuvres. *The sides, or outside of a ship from the wales vpward.*

Morte saison. *The time wherein Herrings, and such like fish, being out of season, are not, or should not be, caught.*

Le iour des morts. *All-soules day.*

Mal mort. *See* Mal.

La service des morts. *Dirges, Trentalls, Prayers, Vowes, or Sacrifices for the dead.*

Se faire mort d'un fief. *A father, &c, to passe ouer in his life time a fief, vnto his heire apparant.*

Le mort execute le Vif. *Looke* Executer.

Le mort saisit le vif, son heritier plus proche, & habile à luy succeder par coustume generale de Frãce: ce qui a lieu en plusieurs païs tant en ligne collaterale que directe, & tant par testament que ab intestat: Tellement que la iustice n'est pas saisie de la succession pour la delivrer à l'heritier. ¶Ragueau.

Homme mort mord iusques, & par delà la mort: &,Homme mort ne mord point: Pro. *Looke* Mordre.

Homme mort ne fait guerre: Prov. *Dead men are quiet; the dead man makes no warre.*

La guerre est la feste des morts: Pro. *Warre is the dead mans holyday.*

Qui se combat n'est pas mort: Prov. *A man's not dead as long as he doth fight: (Indeed there's oftentimes more life then honestie in a contention.)*

Mortaillable: com. *Subiect vnto his Lords Taxations, or vnto Mortmaine; or, as* Main-mortable.

Mortaillablement. *By, or in, Mortmaine; also, seruilly, slauishly, by villenage.*

Mortaille: f. *The Taxation, or Tax whereto a villain is subiect, either in his life time, or after his deceasse; at the (reasonable) will of his Lord, or by custome, or as he hath compounded with him.*

Mortailler. *A Lord to tax his villaines, or seruile Tenants.*

Mortaise: f. *A mortaise in a peece of timber.*

Mortalité: f. *Mortalitie, frailtie, subiection vnto death; also, a mortalitie, plague, murrein, rot.*

Mortau. *as* Mortel *(rustically.)*

Mortel: m. elle: f. *Mortall, humane, fraile, subiect vnto death; also, mortall, deadlie, bane-giuing, death-bringing, end-procuring.*

Mortellement. *Mortally, deadly, capitally, vnto the death, or vnto death.*

Morte-main: f. *as* Main-morte; *Mortmaine; also, the succession of, or estate left by, illegitimated bastards, vnnaturalized strangers, and vnaffranchized villaines.*

Mortement. *Deadly, as one thats dead; also, weakely, faintly, without force, like one that is halfe dead.*

Morte-payes: m. *Dead-payes; Souldiors in ordinarie pay, for the gard of a Fortresse, or frontier Towne, during their liues. In France they be exempted from the* Taille.

Morte-saison. *The season wherein Herrings, or other sea-fish are not fit to be caught.*

Congé de morte-saison. *A Licence to fish in that vnseasonable season.*

Mort-gage, & Mort-gaige: m. *Morgage, or Mortgage.*

Mortier: m. *A Morter (to bray things in;) also, the short, and wide-mouthed peece of Ordnance called a Morter; also, Morter (vsed by Dawbers, &c;) also, a fashion of Cap (with brimmes turned vp) worne by the Lord Chauncelor, and Presidents of soueraigne Courts on high dayes; also, a kind of small chamber-lampe.*

Mortier de Sagesse. *An excellent Morter, made (by some) of the whites of egges, a little Mastick, and Beane flower.*

Le mortier sent tousiours les aulx: Prov. *A bad impression made by nature, or an ill habit got by custome, leaue euer some tacke of themselues behind them.*

Mortifere: com. *Mortiferous, death-bringing, bane-giuing; deadlie, pestilent.*

Mortification: f. *Mortification; a mortifying; a quelling, taming, or punishing of the flesh; a deading of the appetite, a killing of lust.*

Mortifié: m. ée: f. *Mortified; made tender.*

Mortifier. *To mortifie; to dead the appetite, quell, tame, or punish the flesh; also, to mortifie, or make tender, flesh thats to be eaten.*

Iamais grain ne fructifie si premier ne se mortifie: Pro. *Seed yeelds no fruit before it haue been mortified.*

Mortifieur: m. *A mortifier.*

Mortmain. *Looke* Main-morte.

Mort-né: m. ée: f. *Borne dead, still-borne.*

Mortuage: m. *A Mortuarie; that which is due, or giuen, to a Parson out of a dead mans goods.*

Mortuaille. *as* Mortuaire.

Mortuaire: m. *A funerall, or buriall; also, a hearse-cloth, or funerall cloth.*

Banquet de mortuaire. *A funerall dinner, banquet, or feast.*

Mortuaire: com. *Belonging to a funerall, or to a Mortuarie.*

Cloche mortuaire. *A passing-bell; or, the bell that rings to a buriall.*

Drap mortuaire. *A hearse-cloth.*

Propos mortuaire. *Talke of death, funeralls, or burialls.*

Morvat: m. *A dot of sniuell, or of snot.*

Morve: m. *Snot, sniuell.*

Moruë: f. *The Cod, or Greenefish; (a lesse, and dull-eyed kind whereof is called by some, the Morhwell.)*

Moruë parée. *Haberdine.*

Moruë verte. *Greenefish.*

Oeil de moruë. *A great, out-strouting, and dull-sighted eye.*

Tripe de moruë. *Looke* Tripe.

Morveau: m. *Snot, sniuell.*

Le morveau de limaçons. *The slyme of snayles.*

Morvenic: m. *The rough Cedar of* Licia. ¶Provençal.

Morver. *To sniuell, be snottie, let snot fall.*

Morves. Les m. de petit point. *A kind of frenzie in a horse, which during it neither knowes any that haue tended him, nor heares any that come neere him.*

Morveux: m. euse: f. *Snottie, sniuellie; slymie.*

Il faut laisser son enfant morveux plustost que luy arracher le nez: Pro. *Better a snottie nose then none.*

Moruyer. Poissonnier mor. *A Fishmonger that sells nothing but Cod, or Greenefish.*

Mosaïque: f. *Worke of small in-layed peeces; Mosaicall worke.*

Moscaire. Os m. *as* Os sacré.

Moscellin: m. ine: f. *Of, or belonging to, Muske.*

Moschardins: m. *Small pellets, or graines of a delicate Paste, made of Gumme* Dragagant, *Rose-water, fine Sugar, Dragons bloud, and Muske.*

Mose: f. *A patterne, as of one Herring in a barrell, shewing the goodnesse of the rest; or, as* Moison.

Mosle. *as* Mole.

Moslé. Bois moslé. *See* Bois.

Mosler. *To frame by mould, to cast in a mould.*

Mosleur. *as* Mouleur.

Mosquée: f. *A Temple, or Church among the Turkes.*

Mosquets. *as* Mosquettes.

Mosquette. *as* Mosquée; *or a little Turkish Church; also, a Musket (Peece.)*

Mosquettes. *Little iewells, earings, &c.*

Mot: m. *A Motto, a word; a speech; also, the note winded by a huntsman on his horne; also, a quip, cut, nip, frumpe, scoffe, ieast.*

Mot de gueule. *A wanton or waggish ieast, an obscene or lasciuious conceit.*

Mot de rencontre. *A wittie conceit; or, as in* Rencontre.

Dire le mot. *To breake a ieast.*

Trencher le mot. *To speake briefely, and to the purpose;*

pose; also, to giue a quicke, and short answer.

A bon entend tu ne faut qu'un demy mot: Prov. *A good wit's well inform'd by halfe a Word.*

Bons mots n'espargent nuls: Prov. *Good words (or fit ieasts) pay home.*

En vne chanson n'y a qu'un bon mot: Pro. *There's but one good word in a song.*

Motacille: f. *A Wagtayle, or water-Wagtayle.*

Moté. *as* Motet.

Mote. *as* Motte.

Motelle: f. *A Powte, or Eele-powte.*

Motet: m. *A verse in Musicke, or of a Song; a Posie; a short Lay.*

Moteur: m. *A mouer, stirrer; persuader, prouoker; a motioner.*

Mothe. *A little earthen fortresse, or strong house, built on a hill; or, as in* Motte.

Motif: m. *A motiue; a mouing reason, argument, or cause; an incitement, inducement, or prouocation vnto a thing; also, the mouer, or author of an act.*

Motoire: com. *Mouing; that lends, yeelds, or affoords motion vnto.*

Motrice: f. *Mouing, stirring, inciting, inducing, persuading, prouoking vnto.*

Motté: m. *as* Motet.

Motte: f. *A clod, lumpe, round sodd, or turfe of earth; also, a little hill, or high place; a fit seat for a fort, or strong house; (hence) also, such a fort, or house (of earth;) also, the gryne, or Pubes; also, a Butt to shoot at.*

Motté: m. ée: f. *Set, or (vsually) sitting, on a clod, or sodd.*

Motteau: m. *as* Mottelet; *also, a clot of congealed moisture.*

Mottelet: m. *A little clod, lumpe, sodd, or turfe of earth.*

Mottelette: f. *as* Mottelet.

Motteux: m. euse: f. *Cloddie, turfie, soddie.*

Mouaïllon: m. *as* Moilon.

Moüaner. *To mawle, yawle, or cry like a little child.*

Moüard: m. arde: f. *Mumping, mowing, making mouthes.*

Moucade: f. *The Stuffe Moccadoe.*

Moucadou: m. *A hand-kerchiefe.* ¶Poictevin.

Mouce. *as* Mousse; *blunt.*

Moucet: m. *A Sparrow.*

Moucet petit. *A kind of small hedge-Sparrow, which feeds altogether on flyes.*

Mouchard: m. *A spy, pike-thanke, eaue-dropper, promooter; also, a craftie, or subtill fellow.*

Moucharder. *To spy, watch, obserue, or pry into other mens dealings; to eaue-drop it, or play the easing-dropper.*

Mouche: m. *A Ship-boy; or, a Saylor.*

Mouché. *A Vine-branch that runnes out in length, and is vnderpropped.*

Mouche: f. *A Fly; Looke* Mousche.

Mouché: m. ée: f. *Snyted, wiped; snuffed; mocked; curtalled.*

Mouchement: m. *A snyting, or wiping of the nose; a snuffing of a candle; a mocking; a curtalling.*

Moucher. *To snyte, blow, wipe, or make cleane the nose; also, to snuffe a candle; also, to frumpe, mocke, scoffe, deride.*

Moucher la queuë d'un cheval. *To curtall a horse.*

Les estoilles se mouchent. *The starres doe shoot, or fall.*

Il ne se mouche pas du pied. *He begins not at the wrong end, he does not things out of order, I warrant you; he is a subtill, craftie, or warie fellow.*

Du temps auquel on se mouchoit encor à la manche. *In a rude, simple, vnmannerlie, or ignorant age.*

Moucheron: m. *A little Fly; a Gnat; also, the little blacke patch thats glued by Masticke, &c, on the faces of many; also, the snuffe, or weeke of a candle.*

Avoir des moucherons en teste. *To be humorous, moodie, giddie-headed; or, to haue many proclamations or crotchets in the head.*

Autant chie vn bœuf que mille moucherons: Pro. *As much is shitten by one Oxe as by a thousand Gnats; (Some by this Prouerbe meane, that sparing should be onely in great matters.)*

Mouchet: m. *A Musket; the tassell of a Sparhawke; also, a little singing bird that resembles the* Friquet; *also, an eare of some kinds of corne, as of Millet, &c; also, the Cats-tayle, or Aglet that hangs on Nut-trees; also, any manner of flap.*

Mouchet petit. *as* Moucet petit.

Moucheter. *Looke* Mouscheter.

Mouchettes: f. *A paire of snuffers; also, a kind of flourishing among Caruers, &c.*

Moucheur: m. *A snyter, wiper, snuffer.*

Mouchoir: m. *A hand-kerchiefe.*

Monstrer le mouchoir blanc à. *To make an offer of submission; or (after a sound beating) to sue vnto for peace.*

Mouchon: m. *A little Fly; also, the snuffe of a candle; whence;*

Il gaste vne chandelle pour trouver vn petit mouchon. *He looses much to recouer a little.*

Moucle. f. *as* Moule; *a Muskle.*

Moudure. *as* Mousture.

Mouë: f. *A moe, or mouth; an (ill-fauoured) extension, or thrusting out, of the lips.*

Faire la mouë aux harengieres. *To stand on the Pillorie; (we say of one thats hang'd, he makes a wry mouth.)*

Oncques vieil Singe ne fit belle mouë: Prov. *An old-bred clowne was neuer mannerlie.*

Mouée: f. Mouée de gens. *A crowde, or thick troope, of people.*

Mouelle. *as* Moelle.

Mouette, & Mouettes; *as* Moette, & Moettes.

Mouffle: f. *A Winter Mittaine; also, as* Moufle; *also, the vaulted couer, or lid of a Goldsmithes Crurible.*

On ne prend pas tels chats sans mouffles. *Such places, or people are not to be woon without scratching, scuffling, strugling.*

Moufflet: m. ette: f. Hanches moufflettes. *Plumpe, or full hips.*

Moufle: f. *A truckle for a Pullie; also, as* Mouffle.

Mougnon. *See* Moignon.

Mouillé: m. ée: f. *Wet, moistened, soaked, or steeped in liquor.*

Se couvrir d'un sac mouillé. *Foolishly to thinke he couers his hard dealing with his idle pretexts; or, obstinately to stand on proofes, or alledge excuses, which rather conuince, then cleare, him.*

Mouillement: m. *A wetting, or moistening; a soaking, or steeping in moisture.*

Mouiller. *To wet, moisten, soake, or steepe in moisture.*

Mouiller l'ancre. *To cast ankor.*

Qui se garre dessous la fueille deux fois se mouille: Pro. *Seeke* Fueille.

Mouille-vent: m. *A tipler, quaffer, bibber; one that often wets his wind-pipe.* ¶Rab.

Mouilleure: f. *A wetting, or moistening; wetnesse, moisture.*
Mouilloir: m. *A certaine little vessell wherein Spinsters moisten their fingers.*
Mouillure. *as* Mouilleure.
Mouisson: f. *A Cowes milking.*
Moulage: m. *Grist, or a grinding; also,* Multure, *the fee, or toll thats due for grinding.*
Moulaine: f. *Mullein, Woll-blade, Long-wort, Haresbeard, Hig-taper, Torches.*
Moulaine blanche. *White Mullein, or white-flowred Mullein.*
Mouldeur: m. *A grinder.*
Mouldre. *To grind; also, to pownd, or stampe into peeces.*
Qui ne peut mouldre à vn moulin aille à l'autre: Prov. *Let him that cannot fadge in one course fall to another.*
Qui premier arrive au moulin le premier doit mouldre: Pro. *The first commer is to be serued first.*
Mouldure: f. *Multure, grist, grinding; also, a pownding, or stamping into peeces.*
Moule: m. *A mould (wherein a thing is cast, formed, or forged;) also, a high shore, or strand by the sea side; or, as* Mole, *a Peere, &c.*
Le moule à chaperon, ou du chaperon. *The head (of a woman.)*
Le moule du gippon. *The bulke, bellie, or bodie; whence,* Cotonner, ou doubler le moule du gippon. *To feed excessiuely; or, as in* Gippon.
Le moule du pourpoint; *The bulke, or vpper part of the bodie; whence,* Il y laissa le moule du pourpoint; *He was killed, or left his carkasse, there.*
Bois de moule. *Billets, or logs, of a certaine size; or which haue beene assized by the* Mouleur.
Chandelles de moule. *Candles made in moulds; (great) Christmas candles.*
Moule de bois. *A Wood-stacke, or pile of wood.*
Moule: f. *A Muskle (fish.)*
Moulé: m. ée: f. *Moulded; cast, or framed in a mould.*
Mouler. *To mould, or cast in a mould; to frame, or forge by mould; also, to appoint a mould for, prescribe a size vnto.*
Mouler vn visage. *To take the fashion or print of a face by couering it with plaister, &c.*
Il m'en a faict mouler. *He hath put me to a good deale of paines by it.*
Moulerie: f. *A moulding; a forging by mould, a casting in a mould.*
Moulette. *as* Molette.
Mouleur: m. *A moulder; a caster, forger, or framer of things in Moulds; also, as* Moulleur; *also, an assiser of wood (whether for building, or firing) an officer that lookes it be sufficient both in size, quantitie, and qualitie.*
Moulhe. Ma moulhe. *My wife.* ¶Gasc.
Moulin: m. *A Mill.*
Moulin à bras. *A Querne, or Hand-mill.*
Amener l'eau au moulin. *To bring water to the Mill;* viz. *fees, or crownes to the purse.*
Laisser de l'eau en son moulin. *Seeke* Eau.
Tirer l'eau en son moulin. *To procure his owne gaine without any respect of others iust interest.*
C'est la maistresse roué qui tourne le moulin. *This is a principall point, or doth all in all, in the matter.*
Il nous reste quelque autre moulin à tourner. *There is yet somewhat else for vs to doe.*
Assez va au moulin qui son asne y envoye: Pro. *He that sends another, is as farre engaged as if he went himselfe.*
C'est au four, & au moulin ou l'on sçait des nouvelles: Prov. *An Ouen, and Mill are nurseries of newes.*
Chascun ira au moulin avec son propre sac: Prov. *Euerie one shall beare his owne burthen, or answere for himselfe.*
Le four appelle le moulin brușlé: Prov. *The guiltie accuses the innocent.*
On ne peut estre ensemble au four, & au moulin: Prov. *One cannot be in two places, or follow two businesses, at once.*
Prodigue, & grand beuveur de vin, n'a du sien ne four, ne moulin: Pro. *The quaffing wast-good quickly rids his hands of royalties, possessions, goods, and lands.*
Qui ie sois Officier au moins d'un moulin: Prov. *Looke* Officier.
Qui entre dans vn moulin il convient de necessité qu'il s'enfarine: Prov. *He that goes into a Mill cannot auoid bemealing.*
Qui mieux aime autruy que soy au moulin il meurt de soif: Pro. *He that hurts himselfe to helpe others, will dye of thirst at the Mill-tayle.*
Qui ne peut mouldre à vn moulin aille à l'autre: Prov. *What one will not (or, if one will not) another will.*
Qui premier arrive au moulin le premier doit mouldre: Prov. *First come first serued.*
Raison est au moulin: Pro. *(Belike because Grist is taken in, and deliuered out, by measure.)*
Sous ombre d'asne entre chien au moulin: Prov. *Seeke* Asne, *or* Chien.
Mouliner. *as* Mouldre.
Moulinet: m. *A little Mill; also, a Morisdauncers Gamboll; also, a round feather on any part of a horse; also, a Fencer-like round flourish with a two-hand sword.*
Moulinet à aesle. *as* Ventail.
Moulinet à bras (pour monter arbalestes) *A Rack for a Crosse-bow.*
Moulinet à brassieres. *The barrell of a Windlesse, or Fearne.*
Moulinier: m. *A Miller, a Millner.*
Moulle. *as* Moule.
Moulleur: m. *A Grinder; also, as* Mouleur.
Moullon. *as* Moulon.
Moulon: m. *A dry wall made with lyme, or morter; also, a heape, or masse, of any such thing.*
Moulon d'eau. *A great billow of water.*
Moulon de foin. *A stacke, or great cocke of Hay.*
Mouloter. *To seeke, or hunt after field-Mice.*
Moult. *Much, greatly, passing, exceedingly.*
Moulture: f. *Multure; a grist, or grinding; the corne ground; also, the toll, or fee thats due for grinding; Looke* Mousture.
Bled moulture. *Moulture Corne, or Messlin; Wheat, Rye, and Barlie mingled together.*
Moulu: m. uë: f. *Ground; pownded, or broken into small peeces.*
Or, & argent moulu. Asçavoir; destrempé, & meslé avec vif argent, ou quelque liqueur, pour dorer.
I'ay le corps tout moulu. *My bodie is all broken, lamed, or maymed.*
Mouluë. *as* Moluë.

Mou-

Moulure: f. *A moulding; also, a mould; also, a moulding, an edge, or member standing out from a peece of timber, seeling, or stone-worke, and distinguished from the rest by a line on either side of it.*
Droict de moulure. *Seeke* Droict.
Mounier: m. *as* Musnier; *also, the bird called a Kingsfisher; also, the little, long-tayled, and black-headed Titmouse.*
Mourable: com. *Mortall; readie, or likelie, to dye; subiect, or neere, vnto death.*
Mourant. *Dying, deceasing; decaying, perishing.*
Homme vivant mourant. *Looke* Homme.
On s'advise tard en mourant: Prov. *Too late one takes aduise when he must leaue the world.*
Mourene: f. *A Lamprey; or, as* Murene.
Mourin: m. *The Corne-deuouring vermine, called a Weeuell.*
Mourir. *To dye, decease, depart this life; to perish; to decay.*
Tu me fais mourir. *Thou vexest, or troublest me exceedingly.*
Mourir sur les coffres. *To dye following the Court, or neuer to leaue the Court; (where poore wayters, and suitors vsually sit, and rest themselues on their Patrons Trunkes, and Coffers.)*
Mourir de faim pres le mestier. *To worke fast, and thriue but slowly; or, to starue in an abundant place, or Age.*
Aussi tost meurt veau comme vache (& le hardi comme le lasche;) Pro. *As soone dyes the yong as the old (the coward as the bold.)*
C'est trop aimer quand on en meurt: Pro. *He loues too much that dyes for loue.*
En la peau ou le loup est luy convient mourir: Pro. *See* Loup.
Le loup mourra en sa peau qui ne l'escorchera vif: Pro. *A knaue will sleepe in a knaues skin, vntill he either loose it, or his life.*
Envieux meurent, mais envie ne mourra iamais: Pro. *The enuious are mortall, but enuie eternall.*
Envis meurt qui appris ne l'a: Pro. *He that hath not well learnt, is loath, to dye.*
Il commence bien à mourir qui abandonne son desir: Prov. *Who quits what he desires, begins to dye in earnest.*
L'un meurt dont l'autre vit: Pro. *That whereof one dyes, another liues; that which is beneficiall to one, is banefull to another.*
Qui bien veut mourir bien vive: Prov. *He that would dye well must liue well; an honest life ends in a peacefull death.*
Qui mieux aime autruy que soy au moulin il meurt de soif: Pro. *Looke* Moulin.
Va ou tu peux, meurs ou tu dois: Pro. *Goe whether thou canst, but dye where thou shouldest; goe any whether so thou dye at home.*
Mourlon: m. *The name of a fertile Vine.*
Mouron. *as* Mourron.
Mourrailles: f. *Barnacles for a horses nose.*
Mourre: m. *The face, or part of the face about the mouth (most properly) of beasts; the muzzle, or chuffe.*
Mourre: f. *The play of loue; wherein one, turning his face from another, guesses how many fingers he holds vp.*
Mourrin. *A Mite, or Weeuell.*
Mourron: m. *The hearbe called Pimpernell; Some also tearme Chickweed so, because of the resemblance that is betweene some kinds of Chickweed, and Pimpernell.*
Mourron bastard. *Bastard Chickweed (whereof* Gerard *describeth foure kinds.)*
Mourron blanc. *Ordinarie Chickweed.*
Mourron bleu. *Blue Pimpernell, female Pimpernell.*
Mourron femelle. *as* Mourron bleu.
Mourron masle. *Male Pimpernell; the colour of whose flower is betweene a red, and a purple, and in some places fully red; and therefore it is also called,*
Mourron rouge. *Red Pimpernell.*
Mourron quarré. *So doe some (who expresse Chickweed by* Mourron) *tearme Pimpernell.*
Mourron sauvage. *as* Mourron violet.
Mourron violet. *Purple Snap-dragon, or Calues-snowt is called so (but somewhat improperly; for Snapdragon resembles no manner of Pimpernell;) Some also call great Henne-bit thus.*
Petit mourron. *as* Mourron quarré.
Mourru: m. uë: f. *Chuffie, broad, out-standing, like the face of a Lyon, muzzle of an Oxe, &c.*
Mourrues: f. *The Piles, or Emrods in the fundament; also, the Mumpes, or mourning of the Chyne.*
Mouruë: f. *The Mumpes; and (in a horse, &c) the mourning of the Chyne.*
Mousce. *as* Mousse.
Mouschard. *as* Mouchard.
Mousche: f. *A Fly; also, the play called Musse; also, a Spy, Eaue-dropper, Informer, Promooter.*
Mousche à chien. *A Ticke, or Tyke.*
Mousche de lippée. *A lickorous, or sawcie companion.*
Mousche de mer. *Th'ordinarie small Muskle.* ¶ Langued.
Mousche à miel. *A Bee, the small honie Bee.*
Mousches en laict. *A cleere proofe, manifest thing, a plaine and palpable matter.*
Abbreuvoir à mousches. *A wound, or bloud-wipe.*
L'Aube des mousches. *Some three or foure houres after Sunne-rise.*
Chasseur de mousches. *A kill-Fly, kill-Cow, braggadochio, vaine fellow; whence;*
Chasser apres les mousches. *To spend the time most idly, or vainely.*
Maistre mousche. *(The name of a cunning Jugler; hence also) a craftie fellow, subtill companion, slye mate.*
Teste de mousche. *An imperfection in the eye, which makes the membrane* Vvée *peere out through the hornie tunicle, in the forme, and of the quantitie, of a Flyes head.*
Quelle mousche l'a piqué? *What is the matter that so nettles him? what suddaine humor is there come vpon him?*
On eust dit qu'il n'eust sceu deslier vne mousche. *One would haue thought he had beene verie simple.*
Les mousches vont tousiours aux chevaux maigres: Pro. *Hungrie flyes are boldest with leane horses; purloining officers with thred-bare peasants.*
Mouschebout: m. *The spotted Cod whereof Haberdine is made.*
Mouscher. *To spy, pry, sneake into corners, thrust his nose into euerie thing.*
Mouscheron: m. *A Mushrome, or Toad-stoole; also, a little Fly; a Gnat; also, an vpstart Gentleman; also, as* Moucheron.
Mouschet. *as* Mouchet.
Mouscheté: m. ée: f. *Spotted; powdered with many spots of sundrie, or the same, colours (especially blacke;) also,*

also, pinked, or cut vpon with small cuts.
Fustaine mouschetée. *Looke* Fustaine.
Taffetas mouscheté. *Tuftaffata, or tufted Taffata.*
Mouscheter. *To spot; to powder, or diuersifie with many spots of sundrie, or the same, colours (especially blacke;) also, to pinke, or cut with small cuts; also, to tuft, or set thicke with little tufts; also, to twinkle, or sparkle, as a starre.*
Mouschetiere: f. *A Fly-flap; also, the end of a beasts tayle.*
Mouscheture: f. *A spottednesse, or spotting; also, a pinking, or tufting; also, little, and thicke spots; pinkes, or tufts, vpon a thing.*
Mouscheur: m. *A Fly-Catcher; (or, a nickname bestowed by the Italians, &c, on the French* Monsieur.)
Aujourd'uy Monsieur demain mouscheur: Prov. *To day a maister, to morrow a micher.*
Mouschon: m. *A little Fly.*
Mousque: m. *A nickname, or name of contempt, for an ordinarie boy; whence,* Venez ça mousque; *Come hither you rascall; or come hither wag (for it implies only an extenuation without iniurie;) also, a man that hath lost his eares; in which sence it is also vsed Adiectiuely; as in* Chien mousque. *A curtall, and earelesse curre; a dog that hath lost both his eares, and his tayle.*
Mousquet: m. *A Musket (Hawke, or Peece.)*
Mousquetaire: m. *A Musketteere; a souldior that serues with a Musket.*
Mousse: m. *A Skipper; or, a Ship-boy.*
Mousse: f. *Mosse; also, the mossie downe that growes vpon Quinces, Peaches, &c.*
Mousse marine. *Sea-Mosse, Corall-Mosse, Coralline.*
Mousse marine à larges fueilles. *Slanke, Wrake, Lauer; also, Oyster-greene, sea Lungwort.*
Mousse terrestre, ou de terre. *Common ground-Mosse; also, Club-Mosse, Wolfe-claw-Mosse, Wolues foot.*
La mousse luy est creuë au gosier. *His mouth is all Mosse-begrowne, his chaps haue long beene idle, he hath fasted long.*
Iamais tu ne cueilleras mousse. *Thou wilt neuer grow rich; from the Prouerbe;*
Pierre qui se remue n'accueille point de mousse: Pro. *The rolling stone gathers no Mosse.*
Mousse: com. *Dull, blunt; edgelesse, or pointlesse.*
Moussé: m. ée: f. *Dulled, blunted, made edgelesse, or pointlesse.*
Mousseau: m. *A little round heape, or ball, of Mosse.*
Mousselu: m. uë: f. *Mossie.*
Mousseron. *as* Mouscheron.
Mousseux: m. euse: f. *Mossie, full of Mosse.*
Mousson: f. *A Cowes milke, or milking; as much as she yeelds at a milking, or meale.*
Moussu. *as* Mousseux.
Moust: m. *Must; Wine vnrefined; new, or sweet Wine; also, the wort of Ale, or Beere.*
Moustache: m. *A mustachoe, or the Mustachoes.*
Ce seroit pour luy bien hausser les moustaches. *This would make him raise his hope, or thoughts, to a verie high pitch.*
Moustaché: m. ée: f. *Hauing a mustachoe, or long haire, on the vpper lip.*
Moustarde: f. *Mustard.*
Moustarde blanche. *White Senuie, white Mustard, garden Mustard.*
Moustarde noire. *Common Senuie, field Senuie, field Mustard.*
Moustarde sauvage. *Treacle Mustard, wild Mustard, wild Sene.*
Baveux comme vn pot à moustarde. *As frothie as a Mustard-pot; foaming at the mouth like a Bore (say we.)*
Les Enfans en vont à la moustarde. *It is so contemptible, or common, that Mustard-pots are stopt withall.*
Amuser quelqu'un à la moustarde. *To hold him busied about trifles (from such as trouble themselues, and others in controlling sleight expences (as, it is not possible that I should haue spent so much in sawce &c) and in the meane while passe ouer great matters.)*
Moustarde apres disner: Prov. *After meat mustard; helpe when danger, supply when want, hath left vs.*
Moustardier: m. *A Mustard-pot; also, a maker, or seller, of Mustard.*
Moustardier: m. ere: f. *Of, or affecting, Mustard.*
Moustele: f. *The little beast called, a Weesell.*
Moustoile. *as* Moustele.
Mousture: f. *as* Moulture; *Multure; grist, grinding; and the toll thats due for grinding; also, the meale that falls, as it grinds, into the bag, or Mill-chest.*
Prendre d'un sac deux moustures. *To take double fees.*
Mout. *as* Moult.
Moutardier: m. *The great, blacke, and scriching Martin, or Swallow.*
Moute: f. *Multure, grist, grinding.*
Mouton: m. *A Mutton, a Weather; also, Mutton; also, the battering Engine called a Ramme; also, a wild (Indian) Peacock; also, an ignorant, sillie, or plain-dealing fellow; one thats easily ouerraught, gulled, or beguiled.*
Mouton à la grande laine. *A Sheepe well-woolled, or of great burthen; also, a coyne of gold stamped on the one side with a Sheepe, on the other with a crosse* Fleury, *hauing at each angle a Flower de Luce; (John Duke of* Berry *first caused it to be made about the yeare 1371.)*
Pain mouton. *Small white loaues (with outsides stuck full of graines of wheat) for children.*
Sault du mouton. *Looke* Sault.
'A nos moutons. *To our matter againe.*
Cercher cinq pieds en vn mouton. *To expect more from a thing then it can yeeld.*
C'est vn mouton de Berry, il est marqué sur le nez. *He hath gotten a rap ouer the nose; (whereon the Shepheards of* Berry *marke their Sheepe.)*
Sentir son espaule de mouton. *To smell very ranke, or rammish.*
'A petite achoison le loup prend le mouton: Pro. *See* Loup.
Chair de mouton manger de glouton: Pro. *Flesh of a Mutton is food for a glutton; (or was held so in old time, when Beefe and Bacon were your onely dainties.)*
Moutonnage: m. *Toll payed vnto certaine Lords by those that buy and sell beasts, or other marchandize, within their Territories.*
Moutonnaille: f. *Sheepe, Weathers.*
Moutonnée: f. *A tractable, fond, or sillie wench.*
Moutonnier: m. *A Shepheard, or keeper of Sheepe.*
Moutonnier: m. ere: f. *Of Mutton; belonging to a Mutton, or Weather.*
Mouvance de fief. *A holding of, depending on, a doing of suit and seruice vnto, another, or a higher, fief.*
Mouvement: m. *A mouing, stirring; motion, agitation, course; agilitie; moueablenesse; an inclination, disposition, free will.*

Mouvement de terre. *An Earthquake.*

Mouveur: m. *A mouer, or stirrer; a stirring, busie, or troublesome fellow.*

Mouvoir. *To moue, stirre; iog, wag; to remoue; also, to induce, allure, intice, persuade, incline, prouoke, incite; also, as* Releuer, *to hold land of; also, to breake vp land for fallow.*

Mouvoir la Camerine. *To stirre a stinking puddle; to bring a troublesome, or filthie businesse on the Stage.*

Moux. *The plurall of* Mol.

Moy: m. *Me, I; my selfe, I my selfe.*

Il fait bien le quant à moy. *He brags, or braues it exceedingly; he will not take it as he hath done.*

Moyau: m. *The middle, or center of; and (in a wheele) as* Moyeu.

Au moyau de. *In the verie bowels of.*

Moyen: m. *A meane; course, way; manner, sort, forme, fashion, order; occasion, reason; indeauour; also, a moderation, or measure; also, a meanes, mediator; moderator; arbitrator; also, as* Vireson; *also, the greatest peece of the bottome of a Hogshead, &c.*

Moyen de fenestre. *The crosse-barre of a window.*

Homme sans moyen. *That holds of the King in chiefe, or by an immediate homage.*

Moyen: m. enne: f. *Meane, indifferent, moderate, measurable, competent, reasonable.*

Iustice moyenne. *Looke* Iustice.

Muscle moyen. *A muskle (in the hand) that serues to moue the thumbe towards the fingers.*

Moyennant. *Working, being the meane of, or a meanes for.*

Moyennant que. *So that, if so be that.*

Moyenné: m. ée: f. *Wrought by meanes; also, rich, well to liue, or that hath meanes to liue.*

Moyennement. *Meanely, moderately, measurably, reasonably, indifferently, competently.*

Moyenner. *To worke, effect, or compasse (by meanes;) to be the meanes of, or a meanes for.*

Moyenneté: f. *Meanenesse, indifferencie, competencie.*

Moyenneur: m. *A meanes, mediator; stickler, arbitrator, moderator betweene partie and partie.*

Moyeu: m. *The yolke of an egge; also, the naue, or stocke of a wheele.*

Moylon. *Seeke* Moilon.

Moyne. *as* Moine.

Moyneau. *Looke* Moineau.

Moynerie: f. *Monkerie; the state, or profession of a Monk.*

Moynesse: f. *A Nunne.*

Moynoton: m. *A little Monke; also, the lesse, or little Titmouse.*

Moyse: m. *Holie Moyses; whose ordinarie counterfeit hauing on either side of the head an eminence, or luster arising somewhat in the forme of a horne, hath imbouldened a prophane Author to stile Cuckolds,* Parents de Moyse.

Moyson. *Size, bignesse, quantitie, full length.*

Moyton. *as* Moiton.

Muable: com. *Mutable, changeable, variable, vnstedfast, vnsteadie, wauering, fickle, inconstant, vnstable.*

Domaine muable. *See* Domaine.

Muableté: f. *Mutablenesse, changeablenesse, variablenesse, ficklenesse, wauering, inconstancie, vnstablenesse.*

Muance: f. *Change, alteration; and particularly, a variation, or change of notes in singing; viz. when in going either aboue, or below the six Notes* (Vt, re, mi, fa, sol, la) *one of them is changed in the middle to gaine ground, and to knit the gradation; as if in stead of* Vt, re, mi, fa, sol, la, *in ascending, one should sing* Vt, re, mi, fa, re, mi, fa, sol, &c.

Mucagineux: m. euse: f. *Slymie.*

Mucer. *as* Musser. *To hide.* ¶Rab.

Muche: f. *A hiding hole.* ¶Norm.

Mucilage: m. *Slyme; or, a slymie liquor drawne from seeds, roots, &c; and thence, a clammie sap, glewie iuice, cleauing moisture.*

Mucosité: f. *Slyminesse; or filthie, and hoare moisture, as of slyme, snot, sniuell, &c; or the filthinesse thereof.*

Mucqueux: m. euse: f. *Slymie; snottie, sniuellie; (and hence) also, mustie, or fustie.*

Mucydan. *Slymie; mouldie, hoarie, all the yere lōg.* ¶Rab

Mue: f. *A change, or changing; (hence) any casting of the coat, or skin, as the muing of a Hawke; also, the age, or yeare of the age, of an Intermure, or white Hawke; also, a Hawkes Mue; and, a Mue, or Coope wherein fowle is fattened.*

La mue d'un cerf. *The casting of his head; also, his head, or hornes being cast.*

La mue d'une femme. *A womans muing; an elderlie womans wrinkled skin growne smooth, and sleeke, by the helpe of corrosiue drugs.*

Mué: m. ée: f. *Changed, altered, transformed, metamorphosed; also, mued, renued; cast, as the coat, or skin.*

Muel: m. *A Masons Plumb-rule.*

Muement: m. *A changing, altering, transforming; a turning, or casting of the coat; a muing.*

Muer. *To chāge, alter, trāsforme, trāsfigure, disguise, translate, shift, varie; to mue, to cast the head, coat, or skin.*

Muere: com. *Dampish.*

Muerier. *as* Meurier.

Muet: m. *A dumbe man.*

Muet: m. ette: f. *Dumbe, speechlesse, tongue-lesse; still silent, husht; mute; Looke* Mut.

Muet comme vn Francolin pris. *Looke* Francolin.

Plus muet qu'un poisson. *More dumbe then a fish.*

Muette: f. *The Chamber, or Lodge of a Lieutenant, or cheefe Raunger, of a Forrest; also, a Hares neast, the forme, or place, wherein she kindles.*

Mufle: m. *The snowt, or muzzle.*

Mugault. *as* Macault.

Muge: m. *(The sea-fish called) a Mullet.*

Muge volant. *A kind of small-mouthed Mullet, that hath long finnes like wings.*

Amour de muge: Pro. *Faithfull, and most affectionat loue of a wife; (the female Mullet chusing rather to be caught by fishers then to abandon her Make.)*

Mugereul: m. *A kind of Mullet.* ¶Narbonnois.

Mugir. *To low, or bellow, like an Ox, &c.*

Mugissement: m. *A lowing, or bellowing.*

Muglement. *as* Mugissement.

Mugler. *To low, or bellow.*

Mugot: m. *A hoord, or secret heape of treasure.*

Mugotté: m. ée: f. *Hoorded; also, ripened, as fruit in straw*

Mugotter. *To hoord; also, to ripen, as fruit in straw.*

Muguet: m. *Woodrow, Woodroofe, Woodrowell; also (and the more properly) as,*

Grand muguet. *The May-blossome, May-Lillie, Liricumfancie, Lillyconually.*

Petit muguet. *Pettie Muguet, Cheesewort, Cudwort, Cheese-running, Maids haire, our Ladies Bedstraw; also, the hearbe Harrewort, or Sharrewort.*

Muguet: m. Vn m. *A fond woer, or courter of wenches; an effeminate yongster, a spruce Carpet-knight; also, a curiously-dressed babie of clowts.*

Mugueté: m. ée: f. *Courted, woed, sued vnto, whereunto loue is made.*

Mugueter. *To court, woe, make loue, or be suitor vnto a woman* (Le plus ordinairement à mauvaise fin;) *also, to sneake in and out, or goe smelling (as it were) about a thing which he seekes to enioy; whence;*
Mugueter vne ville. *To attempt by all priuat meanes the surprisall, or taking in, of a Towne.*
Muguette: f. *A Nutmeg.*
Muguette de mouton. *The nut of a leg of Mutton.*
Mugueté, & Muguetter. *as* Mugueté, & Mugueter.
Muguot. *as* Mugot.
Muid: m. *A great Vessell, or Measure.*
Muid de bled (mesure de Paris;) *containes twelue* Septiers;(*the* Septier *two* Mines, *the* Mine *six* Boisseaux; *the* Boisseau *foure* Quarts) *which come to about fiue Quarters, a Combe, and a Bushell of London measure.*
Muid de charbon. *Containes 16* Mines (*which come to about 30 of our Bushels.*)
Muid de terre. C'est autant que 12 Arpens, ou Septiers.
Muid de Vin. *Containes (aboue the lees)* 36 Septiers *of eight (Parisian)* Pintes *to the* Septier; (*Three of them are to make a Tunne, say the Customes of* Clermont.)
Muid de Clergie. *Store of Clarkship, a bushell of cunning, abundance of learning.*
Muifle: f. *A kind of Sardinian Sheepe, whose wooll is hairie like a Goats.*
Muifleron. *as* Muifle.
Mular: m. *A kind of great Whall.* ¶Langued.
Mulard: m. *One that hath kibie heeles.*
Mulasse: m. *The sea-monster called, a Whirlepoole.* ¶Marseillois.
Mulataille: f. *Mules; the generation, race, or kind of Mules; also, a troope, or companie of Mules.*
Mulcté: m. ée: f. *Fined, amerced, punished by the purse.*
Mulctoire: com. *Finable, worthie to be fined; also, fining, amercing.*
Mule: f. *A Mule; also, a kibe; Looke Mules.*
Franche mule d'un bœuf. *The purse, bag, or skinne wherein the stones of an Ox, &c, be contained.*
C'est vne mule. *She is a barren Jade; (for Mules neuer beare young ones.)*
Fantastique comme vne vieille mule. *As humorous, and skittish as an old Mule.*
Opiniastre comme vne mule. *As headie, stubborne, or moodie, as a Mule.*
Aller sur mule. Il va sur mule aussi bien que le Pape. *(An equiuocation, applyable to one that hath kibed heeles.)*
Bailler du foin à la mule. *To cheat, gull, cousen, ouerreach, conycatch.*
Brider la mule à. *To daunce attendance on; or to drudge, or doe base offices for.*
Brider la mule aux despens d'autruy. *To doe his businesse, or furnish himselfe with necessaries, at another mans charge.*
Ferrer la mule à. *Seeke* Ferrer.
Il luy fit tenir la mule. *He ouerruled, ouercrowed, ouermastered him; he was euerie way too good for him; also, he made him daunce attendance, or stay long, for him.*
De bonne mule mauuaise beste. *A prouerbe taxing the giddie and skittish nature of that beast.*
A vieille mule frein doré: Pro. *Said in derision of an old woman, that paints and prankes her selfe.*
Qui ne s'avanture n'a cheval, ni mule: Prov. *we say, nothing aduenture nothing haue.*
Qui trop s' avanture perd cheval, & mule: Prov. *Venture too farre you loose all; (So the difference is, that the one wants but what he had not; the other looses what he had.)*
Mules: f. *Mules; also, kibes; also, moyles, pantofles, high slippers.*
Mulet: m. *A Moyle, Mulet, or great Mule; a beast much vsed in France for the carriage of Sumpters, &c; also, a bastard; also, the Mullet fish.*
Tour de mulet. *A iadish tricke.*
Ferrer le mulet. *as* Ferrer la Mule.
Le mulet garde longuement vn coup de pied à son Maistre: Prov. *The Moyle will one time or other lend his keeper a rap.*
Muletaille. *as* Mulataille.
Muletier: m. *A Mulletor, Moyle-keeper, Moyle-driuer.*
Mulette: f. *A little Mule; a small kibe; also, the pannell, or bellie of a Hawke; also, the maw of a Calfe; which being dressed is called the Renet-bag, Jreness-bag, or Cheslop-bag.*
Muliebre: com. *Womanlie, of a woman; womanish, effeminate.*
Muliebrement. *Womanly, woman-like; effeminately, womanishly.*
Mulin: m. *A narrow heele, and high coffin; such as all Mules haue.*
Mulin: m. ine: f. *Of, or belonging to, a Mule.*
Mullon d'eau. *See* Moulon.
Mullot. *as* Mulot.
Mulon de foin. *A hay-rick, hay-stack, or great hay-cock.*
Mulot: m. *A field Mouse.*
Muloter. *To hunt for, or feed on, field-Mice; or to turne vp their neasts, or teare open their holes for the Corne and Akornes which they haue hid in them.*
Muloteur. *Hunting for, or feeding on, field-Mice; or turning vp their neasts, or tearing ope their holes, for the Corne, and Akornes which are hidden in them.*
Mulotier. Sanglier mulotier. *as* Muloteur.
Multation: f. *A fining, amercing, punishing by the purse.*
Multe: f. *A fine, amerciament, penaltie, purse-punishment.*
Multer. *To fine, amerce, lay a penaltie on, punish by the purse.*
Multicuple: m. *A manifoldnesse, great multiplication.*
Multicuple: com. *Manifold; abounding in multiplication, or of diuers multiplication.*
Multipliable: com. *Multipliable, increaseable.*
Multipliant: m. *The multiplier; the figure whereby another figure is multiplied.*
Multipliant. *Multiplying, increasing.*
Multiplicable: com. *Multiplicable, multipliable.*
Multiplication: f. *Multiplication; augmentation, increase, great store, accesse.*
Multiplié: m. *The Multiplicand; the figure which is multiplied.*
Multiplié: m. ée: f. *Multiplied; increased, augmented (in number;) propagated.*
Multipliement: m. *A multiplying; a propagating; an augmenting, or increasing (in number.)*
Multiplier. *To multiplie; to augment, or increase in number; to propagate, store, grow many.*
Multiplieur: m. *A multiplyer; propagator, storer.*
Multitude: f. *A multitude, a many; a great number, companie, or store, of.*
Multre. *The skinne wherein the Calfe lyes in a Hindes belly.*

Muner: m. *The little Wagtayle, or water-Wagtayle.*
Mumie: f. *Mummie; mans flesh imbalmed; or rather the stuffe wherewith it hath beene long imbalmed (whether it be Pissasphalte, or Mirrhe, Saffron, Aloes, and Balme incorporated together.)*
Munde: com. *as* Monde.
Mundé: m. ée: f. *as* Mondé.
Mundificatif: m. iue: f. *Mundificatiue, mundifying; cleansing, purging, purifying.*
Mundifier. *Looke* Mondifier.
Muni: m. ie: f. *Munited, armed, fenced, fortified; prepared; stored or furnished with, fully prouided of, all kind of necessaries.*
Municipal: m. ale: f. *Municipall; proper, or peculiar vnto one onely Citie; belonging to the freemen of one Citie, or to the right of freedome in a Citie.*
Municipial. *as* Municipal.
Munier: m. *A Miller, or Millner; also, a Pollard, or Cheuin (fish.) In some parts of France (but not so generally) the Bull-head, or Millers thumbe is also called* Munier; *Seeke* Musnier.
Munificence: f. *Munificence, bountie, liberalitie, largesse.*
Muniment: m. *A muniting, strengthening, fortifying; also, as* Munition.
Munimens. *Iustifications of allegations, in law.*
Munir. *To munite, arme, fortifie, strengthen, furnish or store with, prouide of all sorts of necessaries.*
Munition: f. *Munition, store, furniture, preparation, prouision; prouant, or victuals for an armie.*
Munitionnaire: com. *Storing or furnishing with, prouiding of, munition, or victuals; also, belonging thereto.*
Munitionner. *To store; to prouide of, or furnish with, munition; to victuall before hand.*
Muque. *The nape of the necke.*
Muqueux: m. euse: f. *as* Mucqueux.
Mur: m. *A wall; a rampier.*
Ils tireront de l'huile d'un mur. *They will draw oyle out of a wall; they will doe more then any bodie else can doe; (Ironically, of Chimicall Extractors.)*
Se voyant au pied du mur sans eschelle. *Seeing himselfe neere to that he would haue without means to get vnto, or power to enioy, it.*
Muraille: f. *A rampier, a wall.*
Ce motte soit comme vne muraille d'airain. *Assure thy selfe this word will be performed; thou maiest rest, or build, thou maiest lay thy life, vpon it.*
Muraillé: m. ée: f. *Walled, rampired.*
Muraillier: m. ere: f. *Of walls; affecting walls, cleauing vnto walls, as Iuie.*
Mural: m. ale: f. *Murall; of, or belonging to, a wall.*
Couronne murale. *A Crowne, or Garland bestowed on the souldior that first gets vp on the rampier of an assaulted towne.*
Muré: m. ée: f. *Walled, rampired; also, inclosed, or shut vp betweene two walls.*
Vn plat de souppes haut murées. *A dish of vp-heaped, or high-roofed, browes.*
Murene: f. *A finne-lesse, and tongue-lesse fish, of a dunne colour powdered (especially in the female one) with yellow spots; other wayes resembling an Eele, or Congar, but that her bodie is, considering her length, somewhat thicker then theirs, and her mouth full of long, and sharpe teeth.*
Murer. *To wall, to rampire; to furnish, or compasse with walls; to strengthen, or fortifie with rampiers; also, to inclose, or shut vp betweene two walls.*
Mureraie: f. *A Groue of Mulberrie trees.*

Muret: m. *The purple shell-fish; also, a Bench (made against an out-wall) to sit on.*
Murette de poisson. *Fish-broth, or sawce wherein fish hath beene throughly boyled; also, the pickle wherein tis kept; Some also call the liuer, and long fat gut of a Pike,* La murette.
Murgé: m. *A heape of stones which haue beene picked vp out of a Vineyard, or Garden, in the dressing thereof.*
Murler. *To low, to bellow.*
Murmurantement. *Murmuringly, mutteringly, gruntingly, with a humming, in a buzzing, sound.*
Murmurateur: m. *A murmurer.*
Murmuration: f. *as* Murmurement.
Murmure: m. *A murmure, or murmuring; a repining; a muttering, or discontented mumbling; a grudging, grumbling, or grunting; also, a humming, or buzzing noyse.*
Murmuré: m. ée: f. *Murmured.*
Murmurement: m. *A murmuring; a grudging, or grumbling; a discontented muttering; also, a humming, or buzzing; a rumbling, or croaking.*
Murmurer. *To murmure, mutter, grumble; grunt; to grudge, repine at, or gainesay betweene the teeth; also, to buzze, or humme like a Beetle, &c; also, to rumble, or croake, as the guts doe.*
Muron: m. *A Salamander.* ¶Norm.
Murte: m. *The Mirtle shrub; Looke* Myrte.
Murtrir. *as* Meurtrir.
Musaïque. *See* Mosaïque.
Musangere: f. *A Titmouse.*
Musaphis: m. *Doctors, Prophets, or great Diuines, among the Turkes.*
Musaraigne. *A shrew Mouse.*
Musard: m. *A muser, dreamer, or dreaming fellow; one whom a little thing amuses, one that stands gazing at euerie thing; also, a pawser, lingerer, deferrer, delayer; one thats long about a businesse; a man of no dispatch.*
Musard: m. arde: f. *Musing, dreaming, amused at, gazing or pawsing on, euerie thing; lingering, prolonging, delaying; of no dispatch.*
Mort musarde. *Thats long a comming.*
Musardie: f. *A muse, dumpe, studie, dreaming; a pawse, delay, lingering.*
Musc: m. *Muske.*
Muscade: f. *A Nutmeg.*
Muscadeau. Vin muscadeau. *as* Muscadel.
Muscadel: m. *The Wine Muscadell, or Muscadine.*
Muscadelle: f. *A Muske-rose.*
Pomme muscadelle. *A Muske apple.*
Muscadet: m. *as* Muscadel; *also, a Cyder, which (made of a verie small, and sweet apple) resembles Muscadine in colour, tast, and smell; also, the Muscadine Raisin.*
Muscagineux. *Looke* Mucagineux.
Muscardins. *as* Moschardins.
Muscat: m. ate: f. *Muskie, of Muske, sweet as Muske, sweetned or seasoned with Muske, that hath Muske in it.*
Cerise muscate. *The Muske (a delicate) Cherrie.*
Raisin muscat. *The Muscadine Grape, or Muscadine Raisin.*
Rose muscate. *The Muske-rose.*
Muscatelin: m. ine: f. *as* Muscat.
Muscateline: f. *The Muske Peare; the smallest, sweetest, and soonest ripe of all other Peares.*
Muscellin: m. ine: f. *Muskie, of Muske, full of Muske, sweetned, or seasoned with Muske, hauing Muske in it.*

Huile muscelline. *Muske oyle; an oyle extracted from Muske, and other aromatick Simples; also, oyle of Ben; oyle drawne from the Nut, or fruit called Ben.*
Muschebout. *as* Mouschebout.
Muscle: m. *The great sea Muskle, or horse Muskle; also, a (fleshie) Muskle; the instrument of voluntarie motion, compounded of sinewes, veines, arteries, tennons, and flesh, and hauing a skin peculiar to it selfe.*
Muscositez: f. *Slymie, or snottie humors.*
Muscule. Veine musc. *See* Veine.
Musculeux: m. euse: f. *Brawnie, fleshie, musculous, full of Muskles.*
Veine musculeuse. *Looke* Veine.
Musculosité: f. *A musculous, or fleshie substance; a brawnie stiffnesse, hardnesse, or fullnesse of flesh.*
Muse: f. *One of the nine Muses; also, a Muse, Poeticall conceit, Vaine, Poeme, or Song; also, as* Musardie; *also, Adams Appletree; also, as* Toffe.
Donner la muse à. *To amuse, or put into dumpes; to driue into a browne studie; to make a man pawse, or studie, on the matter.*
Faire sa muse. *A male Deere to lift vp his muzzle after he hath smelt at the females nature.*
Museau: m. *The muzzle, snowt, or nose of a beast.*
Museleux: m. euse: f. *Muzzelling, tying vp the muzzle, closing the nose, or snowt.*
Muselier: m. ere: f. *as* Museleux.
Museliere: f. *A muzzle; also, the nose-band of a bridle; also, the prouender-bag that (vsually) hangs at a Mules nose as he trauels; also, a Barnacle for an vnrulie horses nose.*
Musequin: m. *A little dogs prettie snowt; also, an effeminate, or perfumed Courtier, that makes loue to euerie wench he accompanies; also, a place to muse in, or gaze out at, as an open window, &c.*
Muser. *To muse, dreame, studie, bethinke himselfe of; to pawse, or linger about a matter.*
Il muse quelque part. *He stayes somewhere, or other.*
Faire muser. *To amuse, put into a dumpe, driue into a studie; to deferre, delay, driue off, make stay his leisure, or daunce attendance on him.*
Tandis que le loup muse la brebis entre au bois: Pro. *While the Wolfe muses the Sheepe escapes; or, as in* Loup.
Tel cuide aimer qui muse: Pro. *Some meane to loue who doe but loose their labour; or, some think they loue, and yet but loose their labor.*
Muserolle: f. *A Musroll for a horse.*
Muset. *as* Musette *(in the later sence.)*
Musette: f. *A little Bag-pipe; or (more properly) as* Vielle; *also, the Shrew-mouse.*
Musicalement. *Musically, melodiously, harmoniously.*
Musicien: m. *A Musician; a professor of Musicke.*
Les mauvais musiciens ne sont iamais ennuyeux à eux mesmes: Pro. *Few men grow wearie of their owne absurdities; few men distast their owne harsh imperfections.*
Musien: m. enne: f. *Affecting the Muses.*
Musimone. *A beast thats bodied like a Sheepe, and coated like a Goat.* ¶Rab.
Musique: f. *Musicke, melodie, harmonie.*
Vn Asne n'entend rien en musique: Pro. *An Asse hath little skill in harmonie.*
Musnier: m. *A Miller; also, a Pollard, or Cheuin; also, a Millers thumbe.*
D'Evesque devenir musnier. *To become of rich poore, of noble base, of venerable miserable; to fall from a high estate to a low one; (The originall was,* Devenir d'Evesque Aumosnier; *but Time (and perhaps Reason) hath changed* Aumosnier *into* Musnier.)
Musnier: m. ere: f. *Of, or belonging to, a Miller.*
Pulces musnieres des Hostels-Dieu de Paris. *Lice.*
Musquardin. *as* Muscardin.
Musquat: m. *Muscadine; or, a kind of strong, and headie Wine.*
Musquat: m. ate: f. *as* Muscat.
Musqué: m. ée: f. *Musked, bemusked; muskie, of Muske; sweet as Muske.*
Aiguille musquée. *(The musked) Pinkneedle, or shepheards Bodkin.*
Musquer. *To bemuske, to perfume with Muske.*
Musqueté: m. ée: f. *as* Musqué.
Musquette: f. *as* Mosquette; *also, a certaine yellow, and hard-rinded Peare.*
Musqueux: m. euse: f. *Full of Muske; also, as* Mucqueux.
Mussale: f. *A kind of shell-fish that somewhat resembles a Muskle.*
Musse: f. *A secret corner, priuie hoord, hiding hole; an odd nooke to lay a thing out of the way in.*
Mussé: m. ée: f. *Hidden, concealed, kept close, conueyed out of the way; also, lurking, skowking, squat, layed close.*
Musser. *To hide, conceale, keepe close, lay out of the way; also, to lurke, skowke, or squat in a corner.*
Mussette: f. *A little hole, corner, or hoord to hide things in.*
Mustelle: f. *A Powte, or Eele-powte.*
Mut: m. *as* Mussette.
Mut. *as* Muet; *Dumbe; whence;*
Chiens muts. *A kind of white hounds, which neuer call on a change; also, lyne-hounds; tearmed otherwise,* Limiers de mut.
Mutation: f. *A mutation, change, alteration; changing; exchanging; also, a shadowing with colours of a different kind; Looke* Nuage.
Mute. *Looke* Meute.
Mutilation: f. *A mutilation, mayming; diminution; the cutting of a principall member from the bodie.*
Mutilé: m. ée: f. *Mutilated, lamed, maymed; also, defectiue, imperfect, wanting a principall member.*
Mutiler. *To mutilate, mayme, lame; to make imperfect, or defectiue; to cut off, diminish, or take away a part of.*
Mutin: m. ine: f. *Mutinous, tumultuous, turbulent, vnquiet, stirring, seditious, factious.*
Homme mutin, brusque Roussin, flascon de Vin, prennent tost fin: Pro. *Looke* Homme.
Mutinateur: m. *A mutiner; a raiser of broyles, beginner of stirres, breeder of tumults; a fire-brand of sedition.*
Mutination: f. *A mutining; or, as* Mutinerie.
Mutinement: m. *A mutining, a factious repining, a turbulent stirring.*
Mutiner. *To mutine; factiously to repine at, seditiously to stirre, or be the author of a stirre, against a superior.*
Mutinerie: f. *A mutinie; tumult, sedition, insurrection, vprore; a stirre, trouble, businesse, ruffling, hurlyburly.*
Mutir. *To mute, as a Hawke.*
Mutuël: m. elle: f. *Mutuall, reciprocall, interchangeable.*
Mutuëllement. *Mutually, reciprocally, interchangeably, on equall tearmes, or one for another.*
Mutules: m. *Brackets, Corbells, or shouldering peeces; also, (& the most properly) Compartiments (in Building.)*
Muy. *as* Muid.

Muyage. Bailler terre a muyages. *To let ground for a certaine number of* Muyds *of Corne, to be payed in lieu of Rent.*

Myagre. *A great, thicke, and greenish Snake, or Serpent, that haunts houses to hunt Mice; and is therefore (and because she is not verie venomous) not much feared, nor often hurt, by such as know her.*

Mycacoulier: m. *The Lote, or Nettle tree.*

My-chemin. à my-chemin. *Halfe-way, in the mid-way.*

My-cornu: m. uë: f. *Halfe-horned.*

My-croist: m. *Halfe-increase; or halfe the profit thats made, halfe of that which comes, of a thing; whence;*

Bail de bestes à my-croist. *A letting out of cattell to the halues.*

Bailleur de febves à my-croist. *A cousener, cheater, conycatcher, guller.*

Myere: m. *A Phisition, Leach, or Surgeon; whence;*

Apres le cerf la biere, apres le sanglier le myere: Pro. *(So dangerous are those beasts, when they be angry, vnto such as they can reach.)*

My-forchu: m. uë: f. *Halfe-forked.*

Mygale. *A shrew Mouse.*

Mygrene. *as* Migraine.

My-iour. *Mid-day, noone-dayes.* ¶Rab.

Mylord. *See* Milort.

Myne. *as* Mine.

Mynsser. *Looke* Mincer.

Myope. *A kind of dull-eyed Serpent, which hath feet though they be but little ones.*

Myrabolan. *as* Myrobalan.

Myre: m. *The male Lampurne, or Lamprey; also, as* Mire; *a Leech, &c.*

Myrepsique. Balan myrepsique. *The aromaticall, and oylie Nut, or Akorne, called Ben.*

Myrique: f. *The shrub Tamariske.*

Myrmecique. Escadrons myrmeciques. *Ants.*

Myrobalan: m. *An East-Indian Plumme called, the Myrobalan Plumme, whereof there be diuers kinds distinguished by seuerall names (as* Bellerics, Chebules, Emblics, &c.)

Myrobalan citrin. *The yellow, or Citron Myrobalan; whose tree is leaued like the Seruise tree.*

Myrrhe: f. *Mirrhe, or Myrre; a sweet Gumme whereof we haue but little, now a dayes, true, or vnsophisticated.*

Myrrhe blanche. *White Myrrhe, the best kind of Myrre.*

Myrrhe Boetique. *Comes from the cut root of a certaine Boetian tree (at this day vnknowne.)*

Myrrhe Stacte. *The best kind of Myrrhe; which (as* Plinie *thinkes) issues from the tree of it selfe; but is indeed the iuyce, or gummie liquor of the fattest Myrre, strained while it is new, and otherwise tearmed,* Storax liquide.

Myrte: m. *The Mirtle tree, or shrub; Looke* Meurte.

Myrtil: m. *A Mirtle berrie; also, the lesse kind of Myrtle, called Noble Myrtle.*

Myrtilles: f. *Mirtle berries.*

Myrtin: m. ine: f. *Of, or belonging to, the Mirtle tree, or shrub.*

Huile myrtin. *Mirtle oyle; oyle extracted from Mirtle leaues.*

Mysanthrope. *as* Misanthrope.

Mysoyé: m. ée: f. *Made halfe of silke.*

Mystagogue. *as* Mistagogue.

Mystaudique: com. *Seeming mysticall; that makes a great shew of sacred matter, and yet in truth is nothing.*

Mystaudiquement. *Mystically or sacredly in shew, shallowly or prophanely in effect.*

Myste: m. *A Priest.* ¶Rab.

Mystere: m. *Misterie; a religious secret, hidden rite, obscure and high point of Religion.*

Sans autre mystere. *Without other ceremonie, without more adoe.*

Mysterieux: m. *Misterious, full of misterie, verie misticall.*

Mystique: com. *Misticall, secret, sacred.*

Mystiquement. *Mistically, secretly, sacredly.*

Mythologe: m. *An expounder of fables.*

Mythologie: f. *An exposition, or moralizing of fables.*

Mythologiser. *To expound, or moralize, a fable.*

My-vouté: m. ée: f. *Halfe vaulted, halfe arched.*

N

NAbot: m. *An ill-fauoured dwarfe, elfe, twattle.*

Nabote: f. *A woman dwarfe.*

Nabotte: f. *The same.*

Nacelle: f. *A Skiffe, Cock-boat, Wherrie, small long boat; hence also, a Boat-bowle, or a cup fashioned like a Boat.*

Nacle. *as* Nacre.

Nacqueter. *as* Naqueter.

Nacre: f. *A Naker; a great, and long shell-fish, the outside of whose shell is rugged, and browne of colour, the inside smooth, and of a shining hue; the forme (broad at the one end, and narrow at the other) somewhat like a Smithes bellowes; (it is but seldome, or neuer found on our coast.)*

Nacre de perles. *Mother of Pearle; the beautifull shell of another fish, wherein the best, and most Pearles be found.*

Nadaïr. *The Point which is directly opposite vnto the Zenith, iust vnder our feet.*

Nadel: m. *A Slow-worme, or Blind-worme.*

Nadelle: f. *A Smy, or sea-Groundlin.*

Nafe. *See* Naphe.

Nagé: m. ée: f. *Swumme, floated on.*

Nageant. *Swimming, floating.*

Le mal an entre en nageant: Prov. *The vnseasonable yeare begins with raine.*

Nagement: m. *A swimming, a floating.*

Nageoir: m. *A swimming place, a water fit to swim in.*

Nageoire: m. *The finne of a fish; also, a round-set attire of fine, and well-starched Lawne or Cambricke, worne (for the most part) by widow-gentlewomen, betweene their haire (which it ouer-peeres) and their hoods.*

Nager: m. *as* Nagement; *a swimming; whence;*

Il n'est nager qu'en grand eau: Prov. *There is no swimming to the sea.*

Nager. *To swimme; also, to float.*

Nager en grand'eau. *To swimme in a spacious water; to practise in a soueraigne Court, studie in a famous Vniuersitie, traffique in a great Citie; generally to frequent, or negotiate in, places of most honor, most companie, or where a man may haue most scope.*

Nager entre deux eaux. *To diue, or swimme vnder the water; also, to stand on doubtfull, indifferent, or vncertaine tearmes; to play on both hands, hold with both sides, apply himselfe vnto the time; also, to chuse, or proceed in, a course betweene two extreames; also, to be in danger, or in an ill case, whatsoeuer fall out, howsoeuer matters goe.*

Celuy peut hardiment nager à qui l'on soustient le menton: Prov. *A fauourite of the time, or of authoritie, may boldly swimme where another would sinke.*

Il ne faut apprendre aux poissons à nager: Prov. *We must not teach a fish to swimme; a scholler to read, a maister to worke, &c.*
Nageur: m. *A swimmer.*
Les bons nageurs sont à la fin noyez: Prov. *Good swimmers at the length feed Haddocks.*
Nageure: f. *A swimming; a floating.*
Nagueres; ou, n'agueres. *Not long since, now of late, e. e-while, euen now.*
Nai: f. *as* Nef; *A ship.*
Naif: m. naifve: f. *Liuelie, quicke; naturall, kindlie, right, proper, true, no way counterfeit.*
L'humeur naifve. *The radicall humor.*
Naifvement. *Liuely, naturally, properly, rightly, truely, in it owne kind.*
Naifver. *To represent in liuelie colours, to present in it owne kind; to describe rightly, or properly; to make seeme quicke, or it selfe.*
Naifveté: f. *Liuelinesse, quicknesse, kindlinesse, proprietie, naturalnesse.*
Nain: m. *A dwarfe, or dandiprat, an elfe, or twattle; one thats no higher then three horse-loaues.*
Naine: f. *A she dwarfe, or woman dwarfe.*
Naintre, & Naintresse. *as* Nain, & Naine.
Naisé: m. ée: f. *Steeped, or soaked (as hempe) in water.*
Naiser. *To steepe, or soake (hempe) in water.*
Naissance: f. *Birth; a beginning, springing, rising, first appearing; also, ones auncient inheritance.*
Naissant. son propre naissant. *His auncient inheritance; land whereto he was borne, or comes by descent.*
Naissant conventionnel. *Money giuen, by a father, or mother, to be imployed on a purchase for their child; or, the land purchased with such money.*
Naissant: m. ante: f. *Beginning, springing, rising, first appearing, or comming into the world.*
Heritage naissant. *The land whereto one was borne; land that comes by lineall descent.*
Naistre. *To be borne, bred, or ingendred, of; to rise, proceed, grow, spring, take beginning, from; to be produced, or brought forth, by.*
Naizer. *as* Naiser.
Nambot: m. *A dwarfe; elfe, little starueling; a dandiprat, or low dapperling.*
Namps: m. *Mouables; chattells that moue, or may bee remoued; also, distresses.*
Morts namps. *Goods, houshold-stuffe, any dead mouables, or chaffer which may be remoued.*
Vifs namps. *Cattell, beasts, foule, fish; any goods that liue, or moue of themselues.*
Nampt: m. *A distresse; a beast, or mouable distrained; also, a beast seized for Trespasse, or Damage fesant; also, a seisure, or distraining; (in which sence our common Lawyers vse* Naam.*)*
Obligation par nampt. *A bond, and pawne to boot.*
Namptir, & Namptissement. *as* Nantir, & Nantissement.
Nancelle: f. *as* Nasselle.
Nani; ou, Nanin. *No, not so, by no meanes.*
Nanti: m. ie: f. *Gotten, seised on; possessed of; also, deliuered into the possession, or hands of; also, affected vnto; fastened, or tied on; appointed, or pointed out, for; Or, to whom a thing is affected; on whom it is fastened; for whom it is appointed, by Order, or in ordinarie course, of iustice.*
Crediteur nanti de gage. *That hath a pawne for his better securitie.*
Rente nantie. Dont le contract a esté exhibé au Seigneur, ou à ses Officers, pour acquerir droict reel, & hypotheque.
Sergent nanti de deniers. *Into whose hands the money, made by the sale of land, or goods in execution, is put.*
Nantilles: f. *Freckles.*
Nantir. *To consigne, lay downe, deliuer into the hands of; to giue a seisin, or possession of; to tye fast; affect, appoint, or point out, one thing for th'indemnitie, or assurance, of another.*
Se nantir de. *To seize on, to get the possession of.*
Nantissement: m. *A consignation, deliuerie, laying downe of; a yeelding of seisin, a giuing of possession, vnto; also, a publicke, or legall affectation, fastening, appointing, or pointing out of one thing for the securitie, or indemnitie of another; also, a seisure, seising, or getting the possession of.*
Nantissement de l'execution. sont les gages prins par Execution sur vn debteur.
Napel: m. *Helmet-flower, great Monkes-hood; (a venomous hearbe.)*
Naphe. Eau de naphe. *Orange-flower water.*
Naphte: f. *(Held to be liquid, or soft, Bitumen, or the strayning thereof, is in truth) a soft, & sulphurous earth, or mould, which is easily inflamed by any fire thats neere it, and once fired will not be quenched, especially not by water.*
Napleux: m. euse: f. *Pockie, full of the (French) pockes.*
Napolier: m. *The Burre docke, Clote Burre, great Burre.*
Napoller. *as* Napolier.
Nappe: f. *A table-cloth.*
Naquaire. *A lowd instrument of Musicke, somewhat resembling a Hoboy.*
Naque. *as* Nacre.
Naque mouche: m. *A Flie-catcher; a gaping hoydon, an idle gull.*
Naquer. *To gnaw, or bite often and with a harsh sound, as a dog doth when hee gnawes his itching ballockes; whence,* ce chien naque le cul; *(which is also an equiuocation to,* n'a que le cul.*)*
Naquet: m. *The boy that serues, or stops the ball after the first bound, to make a better chace, at Tennis; a Court-keeper, or Tennis Court-keepers boy.*
Naqueter. *To serue (or stop) a ball at Tennis; also, to wait at a great mans doore; (and thence) also, to obserue duetifully, attend on obsequiously*
Naqueter les dents. *To chatter the teeth.*
Naqueter de la queuë. *To wag the taile.*
Narcaphthe: f. *An Aromaticall Indian wood, called by some, red Stirax.*
Narcisse: m. *Narcissus, Primrose peerelesse; the Daffodill, Daffodillie, or Daffodowndillie.*
Narcisse Constantinopolitain. *The double-flowred Daffodill of Constantinople; also, the white sea Daffodill, or white sea Onion.*
Narcotique: com. *Stupefactiue, benumming, depriuing of sence.*
Nard: m. *Spike, or Spikenard; (an hearbe.)*
Nard bastard. *Lauender Spike.*
Nard Celtique. *French Spikenard, mountaine Spikenard.*
Nard Gaulois. *The same; or a bastard kind thereof, which we also call French Spikenard.*
Nard Indois. *Indian Spikenard.*
Nard d'Italie. *Lauender Spike; especially the common,*

mon, or blew-flowred one.
Nard de Lentice. *as* Oignon d'Inde.
Nard de montaigne. *Mountaine Spikenard.*
Nard rustique. *Wild Spikenard; Valerian, Caponstaile, Setwall; also, hearbe Auens, Bennet, or Blessed; also, Haslewort, Fole-foot, Asarabacca; (for euerie one of these hearbes is called by the Latines,* Nardus rustica.)
Nard sauvage. *as* Nard rustique; *But especially, Setwall; which is called in Latine as well* Nardus sylvestris, *as* Nardus rustica.
Nard Syriaque. *Syrian Spikenard, Indian Spikenard.*
Nardin: m. ine: f. *Of Nard, or Spikenard; whence;*
Huile nardin. *Spike oyle.*
Nareau: m. *A narrell, or nosethrill.*
Nargues. *Tush; blurt, pish, fie, it cannot be so.*
Naricard: m. *A bottle-nosed hoydon, a great-nosed goose; or (generally) one that hath nose ynough to spare for his neighbours, or (as we say in ieast) one that hath no-nose.*
Nariller. *as* Naziller; *(especially in the later sence.)*
Narilles: f. *(A Hawkes) narrells, or nosethrills.*
Narine: f. *The nosethrill.*
Narquin. *as* Narquois.
Narquois: m. *A Cousener, Imposter, counterfeit Rogue; most properly, one of those cheating and filching vagabonds, that call themselues Ægyptians, or Bohemians; also, the gibbridge, or barbarous language, vsed among them.*
Narrateur: m. *A Narrator, relater, declarer, teller, shewer of.*
Narratif: m. le nar. de lettres. *The subiect, or contents, of letters.*
Narratif: m. iue: f. *Narratiue, declaratiue, declaratorie; reporting, relating, expressing.*
Narration: f. *A narration, declaration, relation, tale, discourse, report.*
Narré: m. *as* Narration.
Narré: m. ée: f. *Told, said, declared, related, reported, expressed, signified, shewen.*
Narrement: m. *A telling, declaring, reporting, relating, expressing, shewing, saying.*
Narrer. *To tell, declare, speake, vtter, say, relate, report, expresse, discourse.*
Narreur. *as* Narrateur.
Nasal: m. ale: f. *Of, or belonging to, the nose.*
Veine nasale. *Seeke* Veine.
Nasarde: f. *A fillip; rap, or flirt, on the nose; also, a frumpe, mocke, ieast, flowt.*
Nasardé: m. ée: f. *Filliped, or flirted, on the nose; also, derided, frumped.*
Nasarder. *To fillip; to rap, or flirt, on the nose; also, to frumpe, or breake a ieast on; play with the nose of; also, to speake in the nose; whence;*
Cette corde nasarde. *This string iarreth.*
Naseaux: m. *The nosethrills, or narrells.*
Fendeurs de naseaux. *Swaggerers, cutters.*
Nasitort: m. *Nose-smart, garden Cresse, towne Kars, towne Cresses.*
Nasitort sauvage. *Iberis, wild Cresses; Sciatica Cresses.*
Nasomonite: f. *A certaine bloud-red stone streaked with many blacke veines.*
Nasquir. *To be borne, brought forth, or bred of; to spring, rise, haue a beginning.*
Nasse: f. *A (wicker) Leape, or Weele, for fish; also, a bundle of reeds, or bullrushes, &c, which boyes, that learne to swimme, lay vnder them.*
Nassel: m. *The chinne-band of an helmet.*
Nasselette: f. *A small skiffe, scull, or cocke-boat.*
Nasselier: m. ere: f. *Of, or belonging to, a skiffe, cockeboat, or long boat.*
Nasselle: f. *A skiffe, wherrie, or cock-boat; a small boat (of what forme soeuer;) also, a boat-bowle, or cup; also, a hollow in a piller, &c, called, a Casemate.*
Nasserie. *as* Nassiere.
Nassidure: f. *Any swelling, or tumor in the bodie, at it first rising, and before the kind thereof can be discerned:* ¶Langued.
Nassiere: f. *A Leape, Weele, or Weare to catch fish in.*
Naste: f. *A kind of Pole-reed, or Cane; also, as* Naphte.
Natal: m. le nat. de. *The birth-day of.*
Natal: m. ale: f. *Natall, natiue; naturall; of, or belonging to, a natiuitie, or birth.*
Natoire: m. *A place to swimme in.*
Natice. *as* Nerite.
Natif: m. iue: f. *Natiue, originall, borne or bred in, descended of.*
Nation: f. *A nation, a people.*
National: m. ale: f. *Nationall, of a nation.*
Concile national. *Which is held by the Diuines of one onely nation.*
Nationnaires. mes nat. *My countrey-men; those of my nation.*
Nativité: f. *Natiuitie, birth.*
La nativité de nostre Dame. *The feast of the Natiuitie of our Ladie, kept solemnly, in many parts of Christendome, on the* 8 *day of September.*
Natreté: f. *Knauerie, roguerie, gullerie, cheating, wilinesse, cousenage.*
Natte: f. *A mat.*
Natté: m. ée: f. *Matted.*
Natter. *To mat, make mats; furnish, hang, or couer, with mats.*
Nattier: m. *A Matter; or maker of mats.*
Nattier: m. ere: f. *Of mats, seruing to make mats.*
Naturaliste: m. *A Naturalist, or naturall Philosopher.*
Naturalité: f. *Naturalitie, naturalization.*
Naturalizé: m. ée: f. *Naturalized, made a naturall subiect.*
Naturalizer. *To naturalize; to make a naturall subiect, or admit into the number of his naturall subiects.*
Nature: f. *Nature; essence, being; also, an (in-bred) condition, humor, qualitie, disposition, inclination, propertie; manner, fashion.*
Nature faict chien tracer: Prov. *Looke* Tracer.
Nourriture passe nature: Prov. *Nurture passeth nature, good bringing vp any breeding.*
Naturel: m. *Nature, or naturall disposition, in-bred condition, qualitie, propertie; also, a Naturalist, or naturall Philosopher.*
Naturel: m. elle: f. *Naturall; of, or according to nature; kindlie, right.*
Fruicts naturels. *Fruits naturall; such as a thing yeelds either of it selfe, and in it owne nature, or by the helpe of industrie, or industrious culture.*
Iour naturel. *Seeke* Iour.
Quint naturel. *The portion of younger brethren in th'inheritance left by their father;* viz. *a fift part thereof, which is diuided among them: (But this in some places onely; See* Quint.)
Naturellement. *Naturally, by nature, kindly, rightly, according to it owne propertie.*
Nau. (Naufs *Plurall) as* Navire; *A ship.*

Nau. (Nauts *Plurall.) A gutter on the top, or side of a house.*
Navage. *as* Naufrage.
Naval: m.ale: f. *Navall; of or belonging to ships, or a nauie of ships.*
Naucelle. *as* Naſſelle.
Naucheux: m.euse: f. *Queaſie-stomacked; readie, or apt to vomit.*
Naudin: m. *A noddie, ninnie, gooſecap, coxcombe:* ¶Norm.
Nave. *as* Navire; *A ſhip.*
Naveau: m. *The Navew gentle, French Navew, long Rape (a ſauorie root.)*
Naveaux. *Vſed ſometimes in equiuocation of* Nezveaux; *naturall calues, fooles bred, aſſes by birth.*
Naveau blanc de Iardin. *Th'ordinarie Rape, or Turnep.*
Naveau rond. *A Turnep.*
Naveau ſauvage. *Rampions.*
Navée: f. vne Navée de. *A ſhip full of.*
Navet: m. *The ſmall Navew gentle, the leaſt (and daintieſt) kind of the French Navew.*
Gros navet. *The great, and bitter root of white Brionie; or the hearbe it ſelfe.*
Nauette: f. *Rape-ſeed; alſo, as* Naveau; *alſo, a Weavers ſhittle.*
Iouër de la navette. *Looke* Iouër.
Nauf: m. *A ſhip.*
Naufrage: m. *Shipwracke.*
Naufrageux: m. euſe: f. *Wracking, ſhipwrack-bringing.*
Naviculaire. Os na. *The ſecond bone of th'inſtup, ſo tearmed becauſe faſhioned like a boat.*
Navigable: com. *Nauigable, ſailable, paſſable by ſhipping.*
Navigage: m. *as* Navigation; *Alſo, a Nauie, or Fleet.*
Navigation: f. *Nauigation, ſayling.*
Navigé: m.ée: f. *Nauigated, ſailed.*
Naviger. *To nauigate, or ſaile.*
Navire: com. *A ſhip; a barke, ſaile, or veſſell for the ſea; alſo, a Nauie, or Fleet of ſhips; alſo, the hollow, or ball of the hand.*
Naulage: m. *Fraught, or fare; the money paied for paſſage in a ſhip.*
Naulager. *To pay his fraught, paſſage, fare.*
Naule. *as* Naulage.
Nauleage. *The ſame; whence;* Barques de nauleage; *Wafters, or paſſage barkes.*
Naumachie: f. *A fight at ſea.*
Navré: m.ée: f. *Wounded, hurt; afflicted, vexed; nipped ſorely, wrung extreamely.*
Navrer. *To wound, hurt; bruiſe, wring ſore, nip cruelly, pinch extreamely; vex, afflict.*
Navreur: m. *A wounder, or hurter.*
Navreur de gens. *A cheating ſhifter, common borrower, couſener of all he deales with.*
Navrure: f. *A wound, hurt, bloudwipe, ſore nip, ſhrewd pinch, cruell blow; alſo, a wounding, or hurting.*
Nauſeatif: m.iue: f. *Loathſome, againſt the ſtomacke, that makes one readie to ſpue.*
Nauſée: f. *A will, or offer, to vomit, but no vomit; a diſpoſition, without power, to ſpue; alſo, a loathing, or abhorring, of meats, &c.*
Nauſiclete: m. *The Maiſter, or owner of a ſhip:* ¶Rab.
Naut: m. *as* Nau; *A gutter.*
Nautil. *as* Nautile.
Nautile. *The ſhellie Pourcountrell, made ſomewhat like a round, and open boat, and ſwimming euer (except in time of danger) with her bellie, or th'inſide of her ſhell, vpwards.*
Nautonnier: m. *A Shipman, Saylor, Mariner.*
Naux. feſtes naux. *for* feſtes de Noel: ¶Poict.
Nayer en l'eau. *as* Noyer.
Nayf. *Seeke* Naïf.
Nazal: m. *The noſe-peece of a helmet; the part thereof which couereth the noſe.*
Nazard: m. *A kind of harſh, or iarring wind-inſtrument.*
Nazard: m. arde: f. *Iarring.*
Nazardant. *Fillipping, or flirting on the noſe; alſo, frumping; breaking ieaſts vpon; alſo, iarring.*
Nazarde. *as* Naſarde; *Alſo, a kind of peare.*
Nazarder. *Seeke* Naſarder.
Nazdecapre. *Goodman Goats-noſe:* ¶Rab.
Naze: f. *A noſe:* ¶Gaſc.
Nazeaux. *Looke* Naſeaux.
Naziller. *To root with the noſe; alſo, to thruſt his noſe into euerie companie.*
Nazilleux: m. euſe: f. *Well noſed; or, hauing a goodlie noſe.*
Né: m.née: f. *Borne; bred; riſen, deſcended, proceeding from; growne, iſſuing, or come out of.*
Teſte de cerf bien née. *A Stags head that hath all it rights.*
Né tout coiffé. *A verie rich, or a verie baſhfull, man.*
Né à tout le poil (le Diable l'a chié en volant.) *A luſtie cutter, worthie gallant, braue man (Ironically.)*
Ne. (Adverb.) *Not.*
Qu'il ne ſoit ainſi, voicy la raiſon. *as the Latine* Quin ita ſit: viz. *That it is ſo: (Held more elegant then without* ne, *which to make negatiue the word* pas *muſt be added after* ſoit.)
Ne. (Conjunct.) *Nor, neither.*
Neance: f. *A deniall, denying, or gainſaying; a Trauers in law.*
Neant. *Nothing, nought; (a word euer ſet downe in the beginning, or end of an account which is not allowed.)*
Choſe de neant. *A trifle, nifle, toy; a friuolous, vnſeaſonable, or ſleight matter.*
Mettre à neant. *To abrogate, antiquate, aboliſh, auoid, make void; alſo, to ruine, ſubuert, raſe, deface, ouerthrow.*
Tourner à neant. *The ſame.*
Pour neant demande conſeil qui ne le veut croire: Prov. *In vaine th'incredulous counſell asketh.*
Pour neant recule qui malheur attend: Prov. *They that ill lucke attend giue backe vnto no end.*
Pour neant va au bois qui marrein ne cognoiſt: Prov. *To no purpoſe goes he, who knowes not wood, vnto the wood.*
Qui voit enfant il voit neant: Prov. *Man (ſayes the Pſalmiſt) being weighed vpon the balance, is lighter then nothing it ſelfe; what then can a child be but the nought of nothing?*
Neantiſe: f. *Trifling, idleneſſe, baſeneſſe, cowardiſe, vnworthineſſe.*
Neant-moins. *Neuertheleſſe, notwithſtanding; and yet.*
Neant-prix. *A verie low rate, a verie ſmall price.*
Neble: f. *A (little) clowd; a miſt, a fog.*
Nebuleux: m. euſe f. *Clowdie; miſtie, foggie.*
Nebulon: m. *A knaue, raſcall, villaine, varlet, paultrie companion, ſcoundrell, ſcuruie fellow.*
Neceſſaire: com. *Neceſſarie, needfull; vrgent; vneuitable, vnauoidable.*

Ne-

Necessairement. *Necessarily, needs, of necessitie, of force.*

Necessitaire: com. *Needie, necessitous; or, as* Necessaire.

Necessité: f. *Necessitie, need; a hard strait, narrow pinch, great pressure, vrgent occasion.*

Les necessités de nature. *Th'easing, or purging of the bodie; such things as must needs be done.*

Chemise de necessité. *A charmed shirt which (as some imagine) preserues men in battailes, and eases women in their trauell; so tearmed, because tis not to bee vsed but in times of extreame necessitie.*

Necessité est la moitié de raison: Prov. *We say that necessitie hath no law.*

Necessité fait trotter les vieilles: Pro. *Need makes th'old wife trot (say we.)*

Necessité rend magnanime le coüard, & le pusillanime: Prov. *Necessitie addes mettall to the meacocke; makes the coward grow couragious.*

Tel a necessité qui ne s'en vante pas: Prov. *Some are in greater want then they will vaunt of.*

Necessité: m.ée: f. *Vrged, pressed, inforced, compelled, by necessitie.*

Necessiter. *To necessitate; to vrge, presse, constraine, compell, force by necessitie.*

Necessiteux: m. euse: f. *Necessitous, needie, poore, indigent, beggerlie, in want.*

Nectar: m. *Nectar; the drinke of the Gods.*

Nectar: m.are: f. *Of Nectar; most sweet as Nectar.*

Nectarin: m.ine: f. *Nectarine, of Nectar, diuinely sweet, as Nectar.*

Necyomance: f. *Diuination by conference with dead bodies raised.*

Neésle. Gros de neésle. *A peece of coyne thats worth about* iij.d.sterl.

Nef: f. *A ship; a sayle, a vessell for the sea; also, the bodie of a Church.*

Neffle: f. *A Medler, or Open-arse.*

Nefflier: m. *A Medler tree.*

Negatif: m. *Negatiue, inficiatiue, denying, saying nay.*

Negation: f. *A negation, deniall, inficiation, denying, nay.*

Negative: f. *A negatiue; deniall, nay.*

Negatoire: com. *Negatorie, inficiatorie, negatiue, denying.*

Negligemment. *Negligently, retchlessely, carelesly, heedlesly; idlely, sloathfully, sleepily.*

Tout est fait negligemment là ou l' vn a l' autre s'attend: Prov. *While one another trusts the worke is left vndone; (and so between two stooles the taile goes to the ground.)*

Negligence: f. *Negligence; retchlesnesse, carelesneße, heedlesnesse; neglect; sloath, lazinesse, lithernesse, sleepinesse, drowsinesse.*

Negligent. *Negligent; retchlesse, carelesse; slacke, remisse; lazie, lither, idle, sloathfull; drowsie, sleepie.*

Negliger. *To neglect, despise, regard lightly, passe ouer sleightly, make small account of, set little by; also, to be negligent, retchlesse, carelesse; heedlesse; to slug it, to looke ill vnto.*

Negoce: m. *A businesse, affaire; charge, imployment; occupying, trafficke, dealing; labour, trouble, comber.*

Negociateur: m. *A Negociator; trader, dealer; factor, Agent, Solicitor; follower, or manager of businesses.*

Negociation: f. *Negociation, imployment, handling of affaires, managing of busineßes; trafficke, dealing.*

Negocié: m.ée: f. *Negociated; handled, managed; traded, or dealt in; solicited, followed.*

Negocier. *To negociate; manage businesses, handle affaires, follow causes; deale, trafficke, trade in matters.*

Negocieux: m.euse: f. *Busie, occupied, euer in action, euer dealing, much imployed, full of businesse.*

Negotiation; &c. *as* Negociation; &c.

Negre: com. *A Negro, a Moore.*

Negrier: m. *A certaine wild vine that yeelds a blacke grape.*

Negriez. *as* Negrier; *Also, the blacke grapes thereof.*

Negroeil. *as* Nigroil.

Neige: f. *Snow.*

Neiges d' antan. *Things past, forgotten, or out of date long agoe.*

Neige en rosmarin. *The besprinkling of a Rosemarie branch with salt, or froathie creame.*

Questions de neige. *Foolish questions, idle, and friuolous demaunds.*

Il a pissé en beaucoup de neiges: Prov. *Hee hath outliued many a bitter Winter.*

Neiger. *To snow.*

Neigeux: m. euse: f. *Snowie, full of snow.*

Neigre: com. *Duskie, swart, blackish, of the colour of a Negro.*

Nele: f. *Cockle (growing among corne.)*

Nelle. *Seeke* Neésle.

Neller. *To varnish, enamell, or glaze with the stuffe* Nelleure.

Nelleure: f. *An enamell, varnish, or glazing, one part whereof is of fine siluer, two of copper, and three of lead; also, a varnishing, or enamelling withall.*

Nemorale: f. *The wood Tortoise.*

Nendea. *No indeed-law, marrie no forsooth; (a womans oath, or negatiue.)*

Nenuphard. *as* Nenuphar.

Nenuphar: m. *Nenuphar; the Water Lillie, or water Rose.*

Nenuphar blanc. *The white water Lillie.*

Nenuphar iaulne. *The yellow water Lillie, yellow water Rose.*

Nepheu. *Looke* Neveu.

Nephretique passion. *Paine in the reines, by grauell, or the stone.*

Nephritide. *The same; also, the stone, or grauell setled in the reines.*

Nephrocartaticon. *(in stead of* Nephrocatarticon*) Physicke that purgeth the reines:* ¶Rab.

Neptunales: f. *Neptunes feasts, or holy-dayes.*

Neptune: f. *Neptune; the God of the sea.*

Neptunien: m.enne: f. *Of the seas nature, of the sea.*

Neptunois: m.oise: f. *as* Neptunien.

Neraut: m. *A certaine vine whose wood and grapes are verie blacke: it is lesse hurt by frosts then any other, and yeelds a verie deepe-red wine.*

Nerée. *(The name of a God of the sea; hence also) the sea.*

Neret. le sol neret. *Is about a quarter lesse then the* Tournois, *or, one part in six, more then halfe the Parisian; for* 60 s. nerets *are worth* 36 s. *of Paris.*

Nerf: m. *A Synnow; (and thence, might, strength, force, power;) also, any band of yron wherewith a prisoner is fettered.*

Les nerfs. *The knuckles that sticke out on the backe of a booke.*

Nerf caverneux. *A mans yard.*

Nerf de cerf. *A Stags pizzle.*

Nerf feru. *(Is in a man) frenzie, or madnesse; (in a horse) a sinew sprung in the knee, or some other ioynt of the leg.*

Nerion. *The shrub Oleander, Rose tree, Rose Lawrell, Rose bay tree.*
Nerite: f. *A certaine little, round, and smooth shell-fish, or sea-snaile, verie like the Periwinkle.*
Nerme. *Nothing.*
Nerprun. *Buck-thorne, way-thorne, Rhein-berries, Laxatiue Ramme.*
Nerquois. *Looke* Narquois.
Nerte: f. *The Mirtle shrub.*
Oiseau de nerte. *The Mirtle Thrush; called so because she feeds much on Mirtle berries.*
Nerver. *To tye with sinewes.*
Nerveures: f. *Strong, or sinewie bands; hence also, as* Nervins; *also, welts; also, carued streakes in wood, or stone.*
Nerveusement. *Strongly, stifly, forcibly.*
Nerveux: m. euse: f. *Sinewie, full of sinewes; also, strong, stiffe, pithie, forcible.*
Nervins: m. *Bolt-ropes; the cords wherewith a saile is hemmed.*
Les nervins des bonnettes. *The latchets wherewith bonnets be fastened to a sayle.*
Nervosité: f. *Neruositie, sinewie strength, fulnesse of sinewes.*
Nervu: m. uë: f. *as* Nerveux.
Nes. *Looke* Nez.
Nesple: f. *A Medler, or Open-arse.*
Nesplier: m. *A Medler tree.*
Nesquin: m. *A base fellow; or as* Mesquin.
Nessum. *as* Nessun; *(an old word.)*
Nessun. *No one, no bodie, not any.*
Net: m. nette: f. *Neat, cleane, pure, cleere; spotlesse, vnspotted; polished, smooth; briske, smug; faire.*
Bien au net. *Exactly, perfectly; also, verie neatly.*
Cela est au net. *That is fairely written.*
Mettre au net. *To cleanse, make neat, smooth or trim vp; also, to cleere, expound, expresse, explaine.*
Avoir le coeur net de. *To be fully resolued of, or satisfied in.*
Netieures. *Looke* Nettieures.
Netre dene. *for* Nostre dame.
Nettelet: m. ette: f. *Prettie and neat; minion, briske, smug, tricksie, smirke.*
Nettement. *Neatly, cleanely, purely, cleerely; smoothly, smug.*
Netteté: f. *Neatnesse, cleannesse, cleanlinesse, cleerenesse; puritie, sinceritie, integritie, perfect honestie.*
Nettier. *as* Nettoyer.
Nettieures: f. *The sweepings of a house; any cleansings.*
Nettissoir: m. *A combe-brush.*
Nettoyable: com. *Cleansible, or cleansable.*
Nettoyé: m. ée: f. *Cleansed, wiped, scowred, purged, cleered, smoothed, swept.*
Nettoyer. *To cleanse; wipe, sweepe, scowre, purge; rub the durt, get the filth off; to cleere; smooth, make euen, or plaine.*
Nettoyer au balay. *To sweepe; to make cleane worke, leaue nought behind, carrie all away.*
Nettoyeures. *as* Nettieures.
Neuchu: m. uë: f. *Knottie, knobbie, rough, vneuen.*
Neud: m. *A knot; a knob, or hard bunch; a ioynt in staulkes; a knurre, or knurle in trees; also, the chiefe point, head, summe, or clause of a matter; the principall band, or hindge whereon it rests, or hangs.*
Les neuds des doigts. *The knuckles.*
Neud de la gorge. *as* Larigau.
'A dur, ou mauvais neud mauvais coing: Pro. *Said when a quarelling, troublesome, or litigious fellow hath met with his match.*
Neve: m. *A mole, freckle, or other the like natural mark, or blemish on the bodie.*
Neuëment. *Simply, absolutely; immediately, forthwith.*
Neveu: m. *A nephew; the sonne of a brother, or sister.*
Neuf: m. neufve: f. *New, fresh; vncouth, strange, vnknowne, vnused, vnheard of, before.*
Il est bien neuf. *He is a verie nouice; he is verie ignorant, vnexpert, raw; he hath but small experience in the world.*
Faire pieds neufs. *A woman to be deliuered of a child; a horse to cast his hoones.*
Neuf. *Nine (in number.)*
Neufain: m. ine: f. *Of nine; for nine dayes.*
Neufaine: f. *A ninth; a proportion, or the number, of nine; also, a terme, or the space, of nine dayes; also, a vow of nine dayes, or for the performance of a thing nine dayes together; also, prayers made for a dead bodie the ninth day after his decease.*
Neufiesme. *The ninth.*
Droict de neufiesme. *A ninth part of the cleere yerelie value of most of the Benefices in Britaine, exacted by the Pope.*
Neufiesmement. *Ninthly.*
Neufme. *as* Neume.
Neufvaine. *as* Neufaine; *whence;*
La saincte neufvaine. *The nine Muses.*
Neume: m. *A sound, song, or close of song after an Antham; or the long holding of the last note of an Antham, &c; vsed much in the Quires of Cathedrall Churches.*
Neutralité: f. *Neutralitie; indifferencie; the being on neither side.*
Neutralizer. se neut. *To stand newter; to take neither part, helpe neither side; when two are at oddes to giue them the looking on.*
Neutre: com. *Newter, taking neither part, helping neither side; also, of the Newter Gender.*
Corps neutre. *which is neither ill nor whole, sick nor sound.*
Neuvaine. *See* Neufaine.
Nez: m. *The nose; also, sence, or smelling; also, wit, or vnderstanding; also, disgrace, or shame.*
Nez d'as de treuffle. *A nose like an ace of the clubs; a broad flat nose.*
Nez de cire. *A nose of wax; a thing that may bee brought vnto any forme, wrought into any fashion, turned or changed any way.*
Nez coupé. *Saint Anthonies nut, Bladder nut, wild Pistachoes.*
Nez qui coupe. *A notable spirit, searching wit, piercing apprehension, sharpe vnderstanding.*
Haut nez. Chien de haut nez. *A dog of a deepe nose, or good sent; also, a dog that hath wide narrells.*
'A nez frotté de vinaigre. *Looke* Vinaigre.
Le nez luy croist. *Said of one that hath quietly swallowed, and basely disgested a publicke affront, or disgrace.*
Le nez aussi plat comme vne Andouille. *A nose as flat as a Flooke (say we;) Looke* Andouille.
Le nez faict à manche de rasoir. *A high-raisd, or hawke, nose.*
Le nez tourné à la friandise. *Saied of a lickorous, or leacherous wench; or one thats not so good as she should be.*

Avantagé en nez. *That hath a forward, or full-grown nose.*
Avoir du nez. s'il a du nez. *If he haue any wit, conceit, or iudgement.*
Cela n'a point de nez. *Is done foolishly, vnhandsomely, without any manner of garb; hath neither decorum without, nor sauor within, it.*
Bailler sur le nez du Roy. *To coyne false money.*
Donner de la porte sur le nez à. *To exclude, shut or keepe out; or, to shut the doore against.*
Fermer l' huis au nez à. *The same.*
Laver le nez à. *To schoole, censure, chide, reprehend, rattle soundly, reproue bitterly.*
Lever le nez. *To hold vp the head, pluck vp the heart, grow cheerefull, wax couragious.*
Marqué sur le nez. C'est vn Mouton de Berry, il est marqué sur le nez; *Looke* Mouton.
Mettre le nez par tout. *To thrust his nose into euerie corner; busily to search into, or meddle with, euerie thing.*
Se prendre au nez. *To acknowledge a fault, or find himselfe in th'errour, wherewith another is charged; whence;*
C'est à luy à s'en prendre au nez. *He may well ynough assume that imputation; tis for him to applie that censure to himselfe; also, tis long of himselfe, he may euen thanke himselfe for it.*
Se prendre au bout du nez. *Looke* Prendre.
Pris du nez. *That hath the murre, whose nose is stopped or stuffed with cold.*
Refaire son nez. *To picke, or gather, vp his crummes againe.*
Ne regarder plus loing que le bout de son nez. *To be negligent, carelesse, improuident, without any manner of forecast.*
Il se retira avec vn pied de nez. *He slunke away, or got him backe, with shame ynough: (sometimes* pied *is left out, but expressed with the hand; and then they say;* Il se retira avec autant de nez.)
Saigner du nez. *A mans heart to faint, or faile him; Looke* Saigner.
Il se tint fort par le nez de ce refus. *He remembred this refusall with a desire of reuenge, although at first he forbore to take notice of it.*
Ils luy torchent le nez de sa manche. *They wipe his nose with his owne sleeue, his taile with his owne shirt; they allow him meat, or meanes, out of his owne money.*
Tordre le nez à. *To wrest, bend, or plie a thing to his owne purpose.*
Viedazer le nez à. *To trouble, vex, molest; baffle, abuse.*
Il faut laisser son enfant morveux plustost que luy arracher le nez: Prov. *Better an inconuenience then a mischiefe; let the Henne liue although she haue the pip.*
Ni. vn ni *A no, nay, negatiue, deniall, refusall.*
Ni. *Neither; Seeke* Ny.
Niais: m. *A neastling; a young bird taken out of a neast; hence, a youngling, nouice, cunnie, ninnie, fop, noddie, cockney, dotterell, peagoose; a simple, witlesse, and vnexperienced gull; also, as* Niez.
La place des niais à la table. *Th'vpper end (where the wealthiest, or women, are placed.)*
Niaiser. *Looke* Niezer.
Niaiserie: f. *Simplicitie, sillinesse, childishnesse, want of experience, dotterelisme, fopperie, fondnesse; also, a sillie part.*
Niance. *as* Neance.
Niant: m. *A denier.*
Niant: m. ante: f. *Denying.*
Niard. faulcon niard. *A Nias Faulcon.*
Nice: com. *Lither, lazie, sloathfull, idle; faint, slacke; dull, simple.*
Action nice. *An Action vpon a bare promise, without article, or couenant.*
Promesse nice. *A single, or bare promise, without couenant, pawne, suretie, or obligation.*
Nicement. *Lazily, litherly, sloathfully; faintly, slackly, slowly; dully; simply, barely, singly.*
Niceté. *Sloath, lithernesse, lazinesse, idlenesse; slacknesse, slownesse; simplicitie, or simplenesse.*
Nicette. pucelle nicette. *A slow, dull, simple, foolish, or nice girle.*
Niche: f. *A Niche; a hollow seat, or standing for a statue, or image, made into a wall.*
Nichée. *as* Niée.
Nicher. *To neastle, build or make a neast in.*
Nicheul: m. *A neast-egge; th'egge thats alwayes left in a Hennes neast.*
Nichil-au-dos. *A doublet whose back is of courser stuffe then the forepart; and hence, any thing that makes an outward shew of goodnesse, or worth, which inwardly it wanteth, or commeth short of.*
Nichilodo. *The same.*
Nicolas: m. *Nicholas; a proper name for a man; and particularly the name of a Saint (Patron of the Russians, &c;) whose feast is the sixt day of December; hence;*
Si l' hyver estoit outre la mer si viendra il a S. Nicolas parler: Prov.
Nicotiane: f. *Nicotian, Tobacco; (first sent into France by* Nicot *(the maker of the great French Dictionarie) in the yeare* 1560, *when he was Embassador Leger in Portugall.)*
Petite Nicotiane. *Nicotian, yellow Henbane, English Tobacco; or, as* Petum femelle.
Nicquet: m. *A Burgonian (base) coyne, whereof three are worth* 5 d. Tournois.
Nid: m. *A neast.*
Nid d' oiseau. *Goose-neast, Birds-neast, an hearbe.*
Nid de la Pie. Monté iusques au nid de la Pie. *At his full height; as high, or as great, as euer he can be.*
Nids de Tirans. *Cittadells, and Castells; tearmed so by the common people awed by them.*
Il s'en va prendre la mere au nid. *Looke* Mere.
Nid tissu oiseau envolé: Prov. *We loose an opportunitie while we spend time in preparations.*
'A tous oiseaux leurs nids sont beaux: Prov. *Euerie bird likes his owne neast; euerie man thinkes well of, or is in loue with, his owne house, &c.*
Tel oiseau tel nid: Prov. *A house like th'inhabitant; such bird such neast.*
Nideur: f. *The stench, or fulsome sauor of things broiled, or burnt.*
Nidoreux: m. euse f. *Smelling or sauoring of (also, fulsome as the smell of) broiled, or burnt things.*
Nidorulent. *as* Nidoreux.
Nié: m. ée: f. *Denied, said nay vnto, disaduowed.*
Nieblé. *as* Niellé: ¶Rab.
Niece: f. *A neece; the daughter of a brother, or sister.*
Nieds. *as* Niez, *or* Niais.
Niée de poussins. *A brood of chickins.*
Nielle: f. *Blasting, or mildew, whereby corne, &c, is withered, or burnt vp; also, the hearbe Nigella, Gith, Bishops-wort, Sweet-sauor, S. Katherines flower.*

Nielle bastarde. *Cockle, field Nigella, bastard Nigella.*
Nielle blanche. *White Nigella, white Gith.*
Nielle des bleds. *as* Nielle bastarde.
Nielle Citrine. *The garden Nigella, whose seed is of a pale yellow, or Citron colour.*
Nielle de Damas. *Damaske Nigella.*
Nielle domestique. *Garden Nigella.*
Nielle jaulne. *as* Nielle Citrine.
Nielle noire. *Blacke Nigella; (a stranger in England as well as the white one; at least our Gerard mentions neither of them.)*
Nielle odorante. *Ordinarie Gith, or Nigella.*
Nielle Romaine. *The same; called also by our Herbalists,* Nigella Romana.
Nielle sauvage. *Wild Nigella, field Nigella.*
Niellé: m. ée: f. *Mildewed, blasted.*
Niement: m. *A denying, disaduowing; or gainsaying.*
Niepce: f. *as* Niece.
Nier. *To denie, disaduow; say nay, gainsay.*
Qui tout me donne tout me nie: Prov. *Hee that grants me all, giues me nothing, I aske.*
Niespe. *An Aspen tree.*
Nieu. *as* Nid; *A neast; whence;*
Oeuf nieu. *A neast egge; th'egge which is continually left in a Hennes neast.*
Nieur: m. *A denier.*
Nieuses. les n. de la maison. *The sweepings of the house.*
Niez. *as* Niais; *Also, a Nias hawke; also, an airie of hawkes.*
Niezer. *To deale simply, or sillily; to carrie himselfe like a nouice, or ignorant noddie.*
Niezeté: f. *Simplicitie, sillinesse, childishnesse, ignorance, rudenesse.*
Nifler. *To snifter, or snuffe vp sniuell; to draw it vp by drawing in the wind.*
Nigaud: m. *A fop, nidget, ideot; a doult, lobcock, vaine, trifling, or loytering fellow.*
Nigaude: f. *A sillie, fond, idle, trifling wench.*
Nigauder. *as* Niger.
Nigauderies: f. *Fopperies, fooleries, fond, idle, trifling prankes.*
Nigauld. *as* Nigaud.
Nigelle: f. *Gith, Nigella, Bishops-root, S. Katherines flower; Looke* Nielle.
Niger. *To trifle; to play the fop, or nidget.*
Nigeries: f. *Nidgeries, fopperies, fooleries, trifles, nifles, friuolous bables.*
Nigeur: m. *A nidget, fop, trifler.*
Nigeuse: f. *A fond, or idle wench.*
Nigroil: m. *The sea Breame.*
Nigromance: f. *Nigromancie, coniuring, the blacke Art.*
Nigromancien: m. *A Nigromancer, or Coniurer; one that practises the blacke Art.*
Nihil. *as* Neant.
Mettre nihil en. *To disannull, annihilate, rase, blot, or strike out.*
Nihil gris. *A dust, or soot, which mounting vp with the smoake of furnaces wherin copper, &c, is melted, stickes to the roofe of the house; tis called* Gris *vntill it come to it full perfection; for then it is white, and tearmed* Nihil blanc.
Nihilité: f. *Nullitie; the being nothing, or of no value.*
Nille: f. *The turning peg of a* Vielle; *also, the ware-band of a mill-stone.*
Nimbot: m. *A dwarfe, dandiprat, little skip-iacke, low dapperling, three-halfepenie horse-loafe.*
Nipes: f. *Trash, rags, nifles, trifles, things of a very small value.*

Niphleset. Membre viril: ¶Rab.
Nique. faire la nique. *To mocke by nodding, or lifting vp of the chinne; or more properly, to threaten or defie, by putting the thumbe naile into the mouth, and with a ierke (from th'vpper teeth) make it to knacke.*
Les maux terminez en ique font au medecin la nique: Prov. *Such be* Hydropique, Hectique, Paralitique, Apoplectique, Lethargique, &c, *because they are hardly, or neuer, cured.*
Niquet. *as* Nique; *Also, a knicke, tlicke, snap with the teeth, or fingers; a trifle, nifle, bable, matter of small value; also, as* Nicquet.
Niqueter. Il n'y a que niqueter. *There is no cause of, or place for, mockerie; there is no fault to be found.*
Nisi. soubs peine nisi. *Vnder the paine of curse, or excommunication.*
Nissole: f. *A whitish Dog-fish, which is indifferent good meat, or at least, the best of Dog-fishes.*
Nitouche. faire de la saincte nitouche. *To play the hypocrite, or make an innocent shew; to seeme not to thinke of, or not to care for, a most affected thing.*
Nitre: m. *Niter; a (Salt-resembling) substance of colour light-ruddie, or white, and full of holes like a spunge; (diuers late writers ignorantly mistake it for Salt-peeter.)*
Nitre d' Afrique. *A kind of light, and brittle Niter of a purple colour.*
Sel Nitre. *Salt-peeter candied, or fined like white Sugar-Candie.*
Nitreux: m. euse: f. *Of Niter, full of Niter, salt, or brackish, as Niter.*
Nitriere: f. *The place wherein Niter is found, or gotten.*
Nitrosité: f. *Nitrositie; the saltnesse, brackishnesse, or sharpe tast of Niter.*
Niveau: m. *A Masons, or Carpenters Leuell, or Triangle; th'instrument whereby he is guided in the laying of his floores, &c; also, a Mariners sounding plummet; also, a Periwinkle (fish.)*
A niveau. *Leuell, euen-floored.*
Au niveau de. *Euen, or leuell with; directly along with; vpon the same ground, or floore.*
Nivelé: m. ée: f. *Leuelled; measured, squared, or laid euen by a leuell; also, sounded with a plummet.*
Niveler. *To leuell; to measure, square, or lay euen by a leuell; also, to sound with a plummet,*
Niveleur: m. *A Leueller; one that measures, or layes euen, things by a leuell.*
Nivellement: m. *A leuelling; also, a sounding.*
Niveter. *To be idle, or lazie; also, to fidge, or be fidling here and there to no manner of purpose.*
Noble: m. *A Noble, in money.*
Vn Noble Edouard. *An Edward Noble; an old English coyne of gold, worth about* 15 s. sterl.
Noble à la Rose. *A Rose-noble.*
Noble: com. *Noble, of a Gentlemanlie race, of gentle bloud; also, noble, gentle, generous of humor; worthie, gallant; excellent, famous.*
Les Nobles. *Gentlemen (of what ranke, or qualitie soeuer) are stiled thus by the French, without any such distinction (betweene Noble, and Gentle) as we make.*
La Noble fleur. *Flower gentle, Flower amour, Flower valure.*
Les parties Nobles du corps. *The braine, heart, liuer, and those parts of the bodie which feed, or depend on, them.*
Les vilains s' entretiennent, les Nobles s' embrassent:

braſſent: Prov. *Clownes intertaine one another coldly, Gentlemen courteouſly.*

Noblement. *Nobly, generouſly, Gentleman-like; worthily, gallantly, couragiouſly, freely.*

Terre tenuë noblement. *Land held by Knights ſeruice, or ſome other Gentlemanlie tenure.*

Nobleſſe: f. *Nobilitie, gentrie, generouſneſſe, gentlemanlineſſe; alſo, a noble inheritance, or houſe.*

La nobleſſe (d'vn Royaulme.) *The Gentrie, or Gentlemen (of a Kingdome) what ranke ſoeuer they hold, or what title ſoeuer they haue.*

Noc. Con, *Turned backward (as our Tnuc) to be the leſſe offenſiue to chaſt eares.*

Nocher: m. *A Pilot, or Steeres-man; the Mariner that directs, or gouerns, the courſe of a ſhip.*

Le vent, la tempeſte, & l'orage, monſtrent du nocher le courage: Prov. *The wind and tempeſt being outragious, trie whether the Pilot be couragious.*

Nocturne: com. *Nightlie, by night, in the night time.*

Nodeux: m. euſe: f. *Knottie, knobbie, full of knurres, ioynts, or hard bunches.*

Nodoſité: f. *Knottineſſe, knobbineſſe.*

Noë. *as* Noue.

Noel: m. *Chriſtmas; the feaſt of the Natiuitie of our Sauiour; alſo, a Chriſtmas Caroll;* See Nouël.

'A Noel au perron, à Paſques au tiſon: Prov. *At Chriſtmas in the Sunne, at Eaſter by the fire (you muſt warme you.)*

Tant crie on Noel qu'il vient: Prov. *So long is Chriſtmas cried that at length it comes;* Looke Venir.

Noër. *To ſwimme; or to gird, or iert, forward in ſwimming; (an old word.)*

Noeud. *as* Neud.

Noeuf *as* Neuf.

Noialliere: f. *A Pepinnerie, or part of an Orchard, wherin the kernells, or ſtones of ſeuerall fruits are ſet, or ſowed for increaſe.*

Noïau. *as* Noyau.

Noïé: m. ée: f. *Drowned; whirkened, ouerwhelmed, as with water.*

Noïer. *as* Noyer.

Noif: f. *Snow:* ¶Norm.

Noir: m. *Blacke colour; blacking.*

Le noir. *Blacke game; as the wild ſwine, &c.*

Noir: m. noire: f. *Blacke, ſable; darke, obſcure.*

Des noirs cappets; ou chapeaux noirs. *A certaine hearbe whoſe blacke flowers reſemble ſmall hats;* Dioſcorides, *and Plinie, call it* Lonchitis; *but* Mathiolus *proteſts he neuer knew that any man had found it.*

Beſtes noires. *Wild ſwine.*

Biſe noire. *A North-eaſt wind blowing in cloſe weather.*

Monnoye noire. *Braſſe, copper, or yron coyne, vnſiluered.*

Pierre noire. *Blacke Oaker, or the blacke marking-ſtone.*

Veine noire. *Looke* Veine.

Vin noir. *Th'oldeſt, thickeſt, and deepeſt-coloured, red wine.*

Il n'eſt ſi Diable qu'il eſt noir. *He is not ſo bad as he lookes for; he is not ſo curſt, furious, or vntractable, as he ſeemes to be.*

Noire geline pond blanc oeuf: Pro. *A blacke Hen layes a white egge; many a foule woman brings forth a faire child.*

Noiraſtre: com. *Blackiſh, obſcure, duskie, ſootie; ouercaſt.*

Noirault: m. aulde: f. *Swart, browne, dunne, duskie, ſomewhat blacke.*

Noir-beau. *A kind of dog.*

Noir-brun. *A blacke-browne, or darke-browne colour.*

Noir-brun enfumé. *as* Couleur d'Enfer, *(vnder* Enfer.)

Noirceur: f. *Blackneſſe, obſcuritie, darkneſſe.*

Noirci: m. ie: f. *Blacked, blackened; darkened, obſcured, offuſcated, ouercaſt.*

Noircir. *To blacke, blacken; bleach, darken, obſcure, offuſcate, ouercaſt.*

Noirciſſant. *Blacking; darkening, obſcuring.*

Noirciſſement: m. *A blacking; darkening, obſcuring, offuſcating, ouercaſting.*

Noirciſſeur: m. *A blacker, blackener; bleacher, darkener, obſcurer.*

Noirciſſure: f *Blackneſſe, darkneſſe, obſcuritie; ſwartneſſe, blackiſhneſſe, browneſſe; alſo, as* Noirciſſement.

Noirelet: m. ette: f. *as* Noiret.

Noiret: m. ette: f. *Blackiſh, duskie, obſcure, ſootie, ſwart, browne, dunne.*

Noireté: f. *as* Noirceur.

Noireton: m. onne: f. *as* Noiret; *or, A little blacke.*

Noirettes: f. *Blackiſh cliſts; alſo, ſmall Wallnut trees.*

Noir-mordant. *(The name of) a great, and verie venomous blacke Spider.*

Noirté. *as* Noirceur.

Noir-ver: m. *A wilding; or an apple, or peare that is not perfectly ripe:* ¶Norm.

Noiſe: f. *A brabble, brawle, debate, wrangle, ſquabble, chiding, altercation, ſcoulding; a quarell, ſtriſe, oddes, variance, difference, diſcord, or diſagreemēt, in words; alſo, a noiſe, bruit, rumbling, ſlurre, hurrie, coyle, hurliburlie.*

Cercher noiſes pour noiſettes. *To pick a quarell vpon a ſmall occaſion.*

Qui femme a noiſe a: Prov. *He that a wiſe hath ſtriſe hath.*

Noiſelier: m. *A haſel; a haſel nut, or ſmall nut tree.*

Noiſelle: f. *A haſel nut, or ſmall nut.*

Noiſer. *To brawle, chide, ſcould, brabble, ſquabble, wrangle, brangle, fall at odds, or be at variance, with; goe to ſuit, or hold debate, againſt.*

Noiſette: f. *A ſmall nut, or haſel nut; alſo, a Filbeard; alſo, a ſquabbling, or ſmall debate; a contention of little importance.*

Noiſette des Indes. *The drunken Date, called by the Arabians* Fauſel, *and of ſome vſe in Phyſicke.*

Cercher noiſes pour noiſettes. *as vnder* Noiſe.

Noiſeux: m. euſe: f. *Contentious, debatefull, quarelſome, litigious, troubleſome, brabbling, wrangling, moſt vnquiet.*

Noiſif: m. iue: f. *as* Noiſeux.

Noiſille: f. *A ſmall nut, or haſel nut.*

Caſſer la noiſille. *To cog a Die.*

Noiſiller: m. *A haſel, or ſmall nut tree.*

Noiſillier: m. ere: f. *Full of, ſtored with, ſmall nuts.*

Noiſillon: m. *A haſel nut, a ſmall nut.*

Noiſillons des Dattes. *Little Date ſtones.*

Noix: f. *A Wallnut; alſo, the firſt bone of th'inſtep; the buckle bone.*

La noix d'vne arbaleſte. *The nut of a Croſſebow.*

Noix de Cyprés. *A cypres nut, or clog.*

Noix galle, ou de galles. *A Gall; alſo, an Oake-apple.*

Noix Indique. *Th'Indian nut* Cocus *(an excellent fruit.)*

Noix Iuglande. *A Wallnut.*

Noix de Iupiter. *The ſame; called ſo in old time.*

Noix methelle. *A sleepe-procuring nut, or fruit, called by Gerard, the Thorne-apple, or Thornie apple of Peru.*
Noix muscade. *A Nutmeg.*
Noix Persique. *A Wallnut.*
Noix de pin. *A Pine-clog, or Pine-apple; also, a Pinet, the nut, or fruit of the Pine-apple.*
Noix Pontique. *The red Filbeard.*
Noix royale. *A Wallnut.*
Noix vomique. *Nux vomica, or, the vomiting nut: Some hold it to be the fruit of the Spurge* Myrsinites; *others, no fruit, but the root of an hearbe; howsoeuer, it is of a poisonous, deadlie, and stupifying qualitie.*
En cela gist le goust de la noix. *There is the pleasure, therein rests the sport of it; or therein consists th'onely point, or chiefe substance of the matter.*
Nulle noix sans coque: Pro. *No nut without a shell.*
Qui a des noix il en casse, & qui n'en a il s'en passe: Prov. *Nuts are time-trifles; it is a pleasure to haue them, and tis no great losse to want them; for oftentimes their crack doth cost more then their kernells are worth.*
Noix chastaigne. *Th'earth nut, Kipper nut, earth Chestnut.*
Noix prunes. *Plummes that come of a plumme grafted on a Wallnut tree.*
Noleage: m. *as* Nolle.
Nolle: f. *The fraught paid for lading, the fare due for passage, in a ship.*
Nom: m. *A name; the tearme or title, whereby a thing is called; also, a fame, bruit, report; whence,* Il en a le nom.
Au nom de vostre beauté, oserions nous, &c. *By your sweet fauour may we, or, may we for your beauties sake.*
Nombles d' vn cerf. *The numbles of a Stag.*
Nombrable: com. *Numberable, numerable.*
Nombre: m. *A number; a tallie, summe, list, reckoning, account; store, companie, multitude, quantitie of; also (in old French) a Band, Regiment, or Cohort of souldiers.*
Nombre sourd. *Looke* Sourd.
Quatre mille de nombre faict. *Full foure thousand.*
Nombré: m. ée: f. *Numbred; told, reckoned, summed, counted.*
Nombrée. *as* Denombrement; *or, A list, catalogue, register, suruey, of.*
Nombrement: m. *A numbering; reckoning, telling, summing, counting.*
Nombrer. *To number, tell, reckon, summe, count.*
Nombres. *as* Nombles.
Nombreur: m. *A numberer, reckoner, teller, summer, counter.*
Nombreux: m. euse: f. *Numerous, manifold, many; also, consisting of, or directed by, number; whence,* nombreuses loix. *Verses.*
Nombril: m. *The nauell.*
Nombril de mer. *The Sea-nauell; a ruddie, & writhen shell-fish, as hard as a stone.*
Nombril de terre. *The hearbe Sow-bread, Hogs-bread, Swines-bread.*
Nombril de Venus. *Ladies Nauell, great Penniewort, wall Penniwort, Venus garden, Hipwort.*
Nombriller: m. ere: f. *Of, or belonging to, the nauell.*
Ligature nombrillere. *A band wherwith women tie vp their great bellies, and are thereby lightened of a great part of their burthen.*
Nombrillet: m. *A small nauell.*
Nomination: f. *A nomination, or denomination; a calling, naming, cleaping, tearming, or stiling; also, the nominating, choice, or election of a man; th'appointing, or pointing him out, for an imployment.*
Nommé: m. ée: f. *Named, called, cleaped, ecleaped, hight; stiled, entitled, tearmed; minged, mentioned, alledged; nominated, appointed.*
A iour nommé. *On a day certaine.*
A point nommé. *Expresly, of set purpose; also, to purpose, or, at th'appointed time; Looke* Poinct.
Nommée: f. *as* Denombrement; *or, A list, roll, catalogue, register, suruey.*
Nommément. *Namely, by name, particularly, especially, expresly.*
Nommer. *To name; call, cleape, hight, entitle, tearme, stile; also, to ming, mention, alledge, or speake of; also, to nominate, or appoint by name.*
Nommeur: m. *A namer; also, a denominator; the figure thats vnder the line in an Arithmeticall fraction.*
Nomothesie: f. *The making, publishing, or proclaiming of a Law.*
Nompair: m. *Odnesse, or an vneuen number of.*
Nompair. *as* Nompareil; *Also, odde.*
Nompareil: m. eille: f. *Peerelesse, passing, excellent, beyond comparison.*
Nompareille: f. *The name of a delicate peare.*
Nompareillement. *Peerelesly, passingly, surpassingly; excellently.*
Non. (Substan.) vn non de la teste. *A nod that imports a deniall.*
Non. *No, not.*
Non pas? *Art thou not? is it not? &c.*
Non que. *Not onely; much lesse, or, much more.*
Nonain: f. *A Nunne.*
Nonante. *Ninetie; fourscore and ten.*
Nonantiesme. *The ninetieth.*
Nonce: m. *A Nuntio, messenger, tiding-bringer; and particularly, an Embassador from the Pope.*
Noncer. *To tell, declare, relate, report, bring tidings, deliuer newes of; also, to shew, betoken, signifie.*
Nonceur: m. *A reporter, teller, declarer, tiding-bringer, shewer, signifier.*
Nonchalamment. *Heedlesly, carelesly, retchlesly.*
Nonchalance: f. *Carelesnesse, retchlesnesse, heedlesnesse; negligence, idlenesse.*
Nonchalant. *Carelesse, retchlesse, heedlesse; negligent, idle, secure.*
Nonchalemment. *as* Nonchalamment.
Nonchalence: f. *Carelesnesse, retchlesnesse.*
Nonchalent. *as* Nonchalant.
Nonchaloir. *To neglect, or be carelesse of; not to reckon, heed, or accompt of; to liue in securitie.*
Nonchalu: m. uë: f. *Neglected, not heeded, smally tended, little cared for.*
Nonciateur. *as* Nonceur.
Nonciation: f. *A report, relation, message; or, a reporting, relating, newes-telling, message bringing.*
None: f. *The fourth Quarter, or ninth houre, of the day; happening in Summer about foure in th'afternoone; in Winter about two.*
Nones. *The Nones of a Moneth; the dayes next after the Kalends: In March, May, June, and October, there be six, in the rest but foure, of them.*
Nonnie. (Adverb.) *Neuer a bit, not a whit, not at all, by no manner of meanes.*
Nonnain: f. *A Nunne.*
Nonne: f. *A Nunne; also, as* None; *the ninth houre of the day.*

Nonnette: f. *A little Nunne.*
Mesange Nonnette. *A little Titmouse, called the Nunne, because she seemes to weare a Nunne-like fillet about her head.*
Oye Nonnette. *A Brigander.*
Pomme Nonnette. *A kind of small apple thats quickly ripe, and rotten.*
Poule Nonnette. *A little short henne.*
Nonobstant. *Notwithstanding, neuerthelesse, for all that.*
Nonpourtant. *Notwithstanding, neuerthelesse.*
Non-prix: m. *An vnder value, or vnder price; also, a verie small rate, poore value, low price.*
Non-valleur: f. *A disabilitie, or defficiencie; a defect in worth, or want in value.*
Non-valoir: m. *as* Non-valleur.
Non-valoir d'estat. *Looke* Estat.
Nopçage: m. *Mariage, wedlocke; also, the making of mariage; also, a marying.*
Droict de nopçages. *The fee due to Churchmen vpon mariages.*
Nopces: f. *A wedding, bridall, mariage.*
Qui faict nopces, & maison met le sien en abandon: Prov. *Looke* Abandon; *or* Maison.
Tousiours ne sont pas nopces. *A wedding day lasts not alwayes; iollitie, and good cheere continue not for euer.*
Nopcier: m. ere: f. *Nuptiall, bridall, of a wedding.*
Nopcierement. *By way of mariage.*
Nopsage. *as* Nopçage.
Nord: m. *The North, or North-wind.*
Nordest: m. *A Northeast-wind.*
Nore: f. *The wife of a sonne, a daughter in law.*
Normand: m. *A Norman; one of Normandie; (in old time all robbers were called* Normands, *because the Normans had often rauaged, and ouerrun France.)*
Qui fit Normand il fit truand: Prov. *Hee that made a Normand made a begger; (for that people, often fleeced by exactions, was woont to be none of the richest.)*
Norrecquier: m. *A chiefe shepheard, or heardsman, that ouersees, or looks vnto, diuers mens cattell.*
North. *as* Nord.
Nortoest. *The North-west wind.*
Nosocome: m. *A spittle, or hospitall for the diseased.*
Nossieurs. *My maisters.*
Nostradame: m. *A cogger, foister, lyer; conie-catcher, cousener, impostor.*
Nostre. *Ours; our stuffe; belonging to vs.*
Ils sont des nostres. *They be of our side.*
Rien n'est nostre qui ne soit en nous propre: Pro. *No thing, which is not our own, can be said ours.*
Not: m. *A Southerne wind.*
Notable: com. *Notable, known, of mark, easie to be discerned; famous, renowmed; worthie, excellent.*
Notablement. *Notably; worthily, singulerly.*
Notaire: m. *A Notarie; a Scriuener, or Scribe, that onely takes notes, or makes a short draught, of cõtracts, obligations, or other Instruments: these notes he may deliuer vnto the parties that gaue him instructions, if they desire no more; but if they doe he must deliuer them vnto a* Tabellion, *who drawes them at large, ingrosses them in parchment, &c, and keeps a register of thẽ; but this is not generally obserued; for in some townes (& of late yeres in many) the* Notaires *are also* Tabellions; *And in former times the Kings Secretaries haue beene stiled,* Notaires, & Secretaires du Roy.
Notaires Apostoliques. *Are speciall Officers appointed by the Pope, to take Procurations for the resignation of Benefices, and to doe him some other the like seruices, within France.*
Notaires gardes-notes. *Officers appointed within euerie* Bailliage, *and* Siege Royal *(by Edict* Anno *1576) to receiue from the widows, or heirs of deceased Notaries all such notes, draughts, & Records of Instruments as they left behind them; Since that time all Notaries, and* Tabellions *haue beene, by another Edict, made* Gardes-notes.
Notairial: m. ale: f. *Drawne by, or passed before, a Notarie; belonging to th' Office of a Notarie.*
Notamment. *Namely, especially, chiefly, principally.*
Notariacon: m. *The tricke, or iert of a Notaries penne which makes a letter serue for a sillable, or word; as &c for* et cætera, *and such like.*
Note: f. *A note; a marke, signe, token; a pricke, cypher, letter; also, a blot, spot, blemish, touch, aspersion, ill report; also, a note, or tune of Musicke; also, a short obseruation vpon.*
Changer de note. *To alter the mind, purpose, or manner of speech; or, as we say, to turne ouer leafe.*
Il n'entend note. *He conceiues no one iot, he vnderstands neuer a whit, of it.*
Noté: m. ée: f. *Noted, signed; marked, obserued; blotted, spotted, blemished, touched in credit.*
Noter. *To note, signe; marke, obserue, or make a short obseruation on; also, to blot, spot, blemish; defame, reproue, touch in credit.*
Nothe: com. *Bastard, adulterous; counterfeit.*
Notice: f. *Notice, knowledge, aduertisement, acquaintance, vnderstanding.*
Notification: f. *A notification, information, signification, aduertisement.*
Notifié: m. ée: f. *Notified, signified, vnto; aduertised, informed, of.*
Notifier. *To notifie, or signifie, vnto; to aduertise, informe, giue notice, of.*
Notoire: com. *Notorious, euident, well knowne, manifest, open, plaine.*
Notoirement. *Notoriously, manifestly, euidently, openly, that all the world may see, or know, it.*
Notorieté: f. *Notoriousnes, publication, manifestation.*
Notte. *as* Note.
Nou: m. *A knot; also, the knob, or bunch of the throat; also, a vessell of stone like a Funt, holding water, wherein pots, and glasses, are set to coole.*
Nou. A nou. *Swimming, or, by swimming.*
Noüageux: m. euse: f. *Knottie, knobbie; full of knurs, bunches, ioynts.*
Noüailleux. *as* Noüageux.
Noüaine. *Seeke* Neufaine.
Novale: f. *A vine lately planted; a ground newly broken, or ploughed vp; land thats turned from wood, or wild, to be arable.*
Novalité: f. *Innouation; or a renewing.*
Novalitez. *Nouelties, new things.*
Novateur: m. *An innouator; a forger of new things; also, a renewer of old ones.*
Novation: f. *An innouation; also, a renewing.*
Noüe: f. *A little low medow incompassed by, or lying so neere vnto, the water, that it is often subiect to inundations, & euer seemes afloat, and readie to swim; also, a gutter betweene two tiled roofes.*
Noué: m. ée: f. *Tied on, fastened with, a knot; also, all on knots.*
Esguillette nouée. *A charming of the codpeece that restrains a man frõ the vse only of his owne wife, or woman; Looke* Esguillette.

L'her-

L'herbe nouée. *Centinodie, Knotgrasse, Birds-tongue, Bloudwort, Swines-grasse.*
Nouël: m. *(The feast of) Christmas; also, a Christmas Caroll, or song made to the honour of Christ; also, a voice of acclamation, or congratulation vsed by people welcomming such as are gracious with them;* See Noel.
Nouël nouvelet. *The burden of a Christmas Caroll:* ¶Rab.
Novembre. *Nouember.*
Nouëment: m. *A knitting, tying, or fastening with knots.*
Nouëment de jeunes arbres. *The knotting of young trees; their springing, or shooting out from knot to knot, or from ioynt to ioynt.*
Novenaire. *A ninth; or the number of nine.*
Novenaire: com. *The ninth; also, nine.*
Nouër. *To knit; to tie, fasten, or bind with knots; also, to knot (as a tree thats in growing.)*
Il ne peut nouër au bout de l' an les deux bouts de sa serviette ensemble. *He is a cleane Gentleman, or hath nothing left him, by the yeares end.*
Noverce: f. *A stepdame, or stepmother.*
Nouët: m. *A little knot; also, a little linnen bag, or poke, hard tied vp.*
Nouëure: f. *as* Nouement.
Neuëuse: f. *Centinodie, Knotgrasse, Birds-tongue, Bloudwort.*
Nouëux: m. euse: f. *Knottie, knobbie; full of knurres, ioynts, bunches, &c.*
Novice: com. *A nouice, a young Monke, or Nunne; one thats but newly entred into th' Order; also, a yongling, or beginner, in any profession.*
Novimestre: com. *Of nine monethes; or, at nine moneths end.*
Novitiat: m. *A nouice; th' estate of a nouice, or the terme wherein one is in the state of a nouice; also, a beginning, or entrance in any profession.*
Nourri: m. ie: f. *Nourished, fed; nurtured, fostered; nuzled in, brought vp to.*
Fleur de lis au pied nourri d' argent. *Couped, or cut off; (a tearme of Blazon.)*
Nourrice: f. *A Nurse.*
Vn embonpoint de nourrice. *A plumpe, fat, or foggie constitution of bodie.*
Nourrin: m. *The frie, or brood of yong fish, reserued for the storing of a pond, &c.*
Nourrir. *To nourish, feed, sustaine, find; nurture, foster; nuzzle in; breed, or bring vp to.*
Celuy la est bon pere qui nourrit: Prov. *He that maintaines, or keepes a man, may well be tearmed his father.*
Qui veut avoir bon chien il faut qu'il le nourrisse: Pro. *He that will haue a good dog must breed him to it.*
Tel le chié nourrit qui puis mange la courroye de son soulier: Prov. *Looke* Chien.
Nourrissable: com. *Nourishable.*
Nourrissant: m. ante: f. *Nourishing.*
Nourrisse: f. *as* Nourrice.
Nourrissement: m. *A nourishing, feeding, sustaining; a nurturing, fostering; breeding, bringing vp.*
Nourrisseur: m. *A nourisher, feeder, sustainer; a foster father.*
Nourrissier: m. *A Nurses husband, a foster father.*
Nourrisson: m. *A nursling, nurse-child, or nursing child.*
Nourriture: f. *Nourishment, nutriment, sustenance, food, meat; finding, maintenance; also, nurture, or bringing vp; also, cattell, or beasts bred vp about a house; or the breeding thereof; whence;*
Nouritures. *The tending, feeding, or fattening of swine, cattell, or pulleine; also, the commodities, or prouision yeelded by a countrey house towards that part of husbandrie.*
Nourriture passe nature: Prov. *Nurture surpasseth nature.*
Nous. *We, vs.*
Nouveau: m. nouvelle: f. *New; fresh, recent; strange, rare; lately done, or made; vncouth, vnused, vnheard of before.*
Nouveaux acquests. *Looke* Acquests.
Faicts nouveaux. ce sont ceux qui n'ont esté articulez au procez principal; ou encores qu'ils dependent d'iceux, ils ne sont toutesfois les mesmes faicts, ains servent de les esclaircir, & en donner plus ample intelligence.
Le laict nouveau. *Beest, or Beestings.*
Les vingt nouveaux. *A certain lately-erected Court, consisting of twentie Presidents, and (Assistants) Counsellors.*
De nouveau tout est beau: Prov. *Euerie new thing lookes faire.*
De nouveau Seigneur nouvelle mesgnie: Prov. *A new Maister, a new meynie.*
Vieux peché fait nouvelle honte: Prov. *Old sinne breeds new shame.*
Nouveauté: f. *A noueltie; also, newnesse, freshnesse; rarenesse, strangenesse.*
Nouvelan: m. *A new yeare.*
Nouvelet: m. ette: f. *Verie new; or prettie, and new; of late date, of a small standing.*
Nouël nouvelet. *See* Nouël.
Nouvelis. *as* Nouvellis.
Nouvelle: f. *A nouell, newes; tidings; an (vnexpected) message; a strange report; a discourse, or tale vnheard of before.*
Assez en dit qui apporte bonnes nouvelles: Prov. *He spares no words that brings good newes.*
C'est au four, & au moulin ou l'on sçait des nouvelles: Prov. *A common mill, and ouen, affoord much newes.*
Hardiment heurte à la porte qui bonne nouvelle apporte: Prov. *Looke* Hardiment.
Trop tost vient à la porte qui mauvaise nouvelle apporte: Pro. *He that brings ill news comes too soone.*
Nouvellement. *Newly, lately, afresh, not long since.*
Nouvelleté: f. *as* Nouveauté; *also, Nouel disseisin; a new, or late interruption, or impeachment, of possession; Looke* Saisine.
Nouvellis: m. *Fallowes; ground that lies fallow euerie other yeare; or, as* Novales.
Nouzille. *as* Noisette, *or* Noisille.
Noyau: m. *The stone of a Plum, Cherrie, Date, Oliue, &c; also (but lesse properly) the kernell inclosed therin; also, the Nuell, or spindle of a winding staire; also, the mould thats within a peece of ordnance when it is cast; also, the naue of a wheele; also, the brisket of a Deere; whence;*
Fendre au noyau. *To take th' essay of a Deere.*
Noyé: m. ée: f. *Drowned, whirkened, or stifled with; ouerwhelmed in, the water: (A Bowler is said to be* noyé, *when his bowle toucheth th' end of th' Alley, for then it is out of play.)*
Noyé en debtes. *Sunke, vndone, ouer shooes, out at heeles, ouer head and eares, in debt.*
Les bons nageurs sont à la fin noyez: Prov. *Good swimmers are in th' end orewhelmd.*

Noyement: m. *A drowning.*
Noyer: m. *A Wallnut tree.*
Noyer. *To drowne; to whirken, or stifle with water, &c; To ouerwhelme in, or plunge vnder, the water.*
Ce n'est rien, c'est vne femme qui se noye: Prov. *A woman drownes her selfe, no force.*
Qui a à pendre n'a pas à noyer: Prov. *Hee thats borne to be hanged needs feare no drowning.*
Quand vn chien se noye chascun luy offre à boire: Prov. *Looke* Chien.
Noyeraie: f. *A groue, or Orchard of Wallnut trees.*
Noynce. *The knuckle of a finger; (an old word.)*
Noysette: f. *A small nut, or Hasle nut.*
Noysettier: m. *A Hasle, or small-nut tree.*
Noz fieux. *for* mon fits; *My sonne*: ¶Pic.
Nu. *as* Neud.
Le nu d'vne Colonne. *The shaft of a piller, being (for the most part) naked, and bare of any worke.*
Nu. *as* Nud, *Naked, &c.*
Nu à nu. *Meerely, immediately, directly, without mesne, or meanes.*
Nuage: m. *as* Nuée; *or, A thicke, and storme-threatening clowd; also, a representation of th'aire, or of clowdes, in painting; also, a shadowing (with darke colours vpon lighter of the same kind; for if it be with colours of another kind, it is not tearmed* Nuage, *but* Mutation, *or,* Changement.)
Nuage de corbeaux. *A great flight of Rauens, obscuring the skie with their thicke rankes.*
Nuager. *To clowd, beclowd, ouerclowd; to shadow, obscure, ouercast, as with clowds.*
Nuageux: m euse: f. *Clowdie, full of thicke clowds.*
Nuance: f. *A shadowing (with colours of one kind.)*
Nuäux: m. *Clowds.*
Nubile: com. *Mariageable.*
Nubileux: m. euse: f. *Clowdie; ouercast; stormie, tempestuous.*
Nubilosité: f. *A clowdinesse, ouercasting, darknesse of weather.*
Nucque: f. *The nape of the necke.*
Nud: m. nuë: f. *Naked, bare; vncouered, or discouered; beggerlie, poore, without any clothes.*
Nud comme vn ver. *As naked as my nayle (say we.)*
Mettre à nud. *To bare, strip, vncouer; despoyle, or depriue of clothes.*
Mieux vaut vn pied nud que nul: Pro. *A bare foot is better then none.*
On ne peut despouiller vn homme nud: Prov. *A naked man cannot be stript of clothes.*
Nudité: f. *Nuditie, nakednesse, barenesse; beggerie, pouertie.*
Nudosité. *Looke* Nodosité.
Nue: f. *A clowd.*
Il pense que les nues sont pailles d'airain. *Hee thinkes the clowds are brasen spangles; like our; he thinkes the Moone is made of greene cheese.*
Nué: m. ée: f. *Clowded; ouercast, ouershadowed; (in painting) shadowed.*
Nuée: f. *A clowd.*
Peindre es nuées. *To loose time on impossible, or idle attempts.*
Nuement. *Nakedly, barely, beggerly, without means; also, meerely, directly, immediately, without mesne.*
Nuer. *To shadow; to ouercast, ouerclowd.*
Nuesse: f. *Th'extent, or compasse of a feodall, or* censuel *Seigneurie, whereof other* Fiefs, *or* Cens *are held immediately.*
Nugicanoricrepe: m. *An idle singer of lyes, or trifling matters.*

Nuict: f. *The night; also, darknesse.*
Nuict d'vn lievre. *The tract, or pricke of a Hare going to reliefe.*
Harenc de la nuict. *A red Herring.*
Herbe de la nuict. *Looke* Herbe.
En pleine nuict. *In the darkest, or most silent part of the night; when all is husht, when euerie one's asleepe.*
Faire sa nuict. *To sell vp his houshold-stuffe.*
Faire vn trou à la nuict. *To walke, or goe abroad anights; to trauell, or take a iourney by night; also, to slinke, or slip away on a suddaine, or at vnawares.*
La nuict donne conseil: Prov. *Like vnto our, take counsell of your pillow.*
Ce qui se fait de nuict paroist de Iour: Prov. *The Day bewrayes whatsoeuer was done by night; or, the day discouers the harme that night hath done.*
Contre la nuict s'arment les limacons: Prov. *as in* Limaçon.
Nous achetons tout fors le iour, & la nuict: Prov. *We all things buy saue day and night.*
Nuictal: m. ale: f. *Nightlie, by night, of the night.*
Nuictamment. *Nightly; by night, in the night; or, night by night, euerie night.*
Nuictée: f. *The space of a night.*
Nuict egal: m. *Th'Equinoctiall.*
Nuicteux: m. euse: f. *Nightlie, night-bringing; darke, blacke; silent, husht; (as the night.)*
Nuïr. *as* Nuire.
Nuire. *To hurt, offend, indommage, incommodate, annoy, hinder, doe a displeasure vnto.*
Nuisance: f. *Nuisance, hurt, offence, annoyance, harme; dammage, wrong, trespasse.*
Nuisant: m. ante. f. *Hurtfull, harmefull, shrewd, mischieuous, offensiue, noysome; also, hurting.*
Nuisible: com. *as* Nuisant; *or, Likelie to hurt.*
Nuisif: m. iue: f. *as* Nuisant.
Nuitamment. *as* Nuictamment.
Nul: m. nulle: f. *None, not one, not any, no man or thing; also, blanke, idle, friuolous, of no value.*
Nul miel sans fiel: Prov. *No honie without gall.*
Mieux vaut vn pied nud que nul: Prov. *Better halfe a loafe then no bread.*
Ouvrage de commun ouvrage de nul: Prov. *Seeke* Ouvrage.
Nullement. *In no case, at no hand, in no sort, by no meanes, in no wise, not at all.*
Nullité: f. *A nullitie, annihilation, disannulment, nothing.*
Nulluy, & **Nully**. *as* Nul.
Numerable: com. *Numerable, numberable.*
Numereux. *as* Nombreux.
Numero. *The number thats set on euerie Billet in a Lotterie.*
Il entend le numero. *He is throughly informed, or fully acquainted with the matter; he knowes, what will befall, or betide him, beforehand.*
Numerosité: f. *Numerositie, a great number of.*
Numme: m. *A little siluer coyne among the auncient Romanes, worth about three-halfepence* Sterl.
Numulaire: f. *Money-wort, hearbe Two-pennie, Two-pennie grasse.*
Nuncupatif: m. iue: f. *Nuncupatiue.*
Testament nuncupatif. *A Will nuncupatiue; a Will not writtē, but declared in words, before sufficiēt witnesses: (This kind of Will is no more allowed of in France, but abrogated both by Edicts, and by the late-reformed Customes.)*

Nundination: f. *A trafficking in Faires, and Markets.*
Nuptial: m. ale: f. *Nuptiall, brydall, belonging to a wedding.*
Le past nuptial. *That which a Churchman takes for the marrying of a couple.*
Nuque: f. *The nape of the necke; also, the marrow of the backe bone.*
Nutritif: m. iue: f. *Nutritiue, nourishing.*
Nuyct. *Looke* Nuict.
Ny. *Neither, nor; (and sometimes) or.*
Pour vn denier ny moins. *By one pennies expence, or losse I haue not much the lesse.*
Nyaie: f. *An Airie, or neast full of.*
Nyceté. *Looke* Niceté.
Nyche. *as* Niche.
Nyctalope: m. *A night-wandering beast; also, a certaine hearbe that shines, and is seene a farre off, in the night.*
Nymphal: m. ale: f. *Nimphall; of, or belonging to, a Nimphe.*
Nymphe: f. *A Nimphe; also, a little excrescence, or peece of flesh, in the middest of a womans priuities.*
Nymphée: f. *The water Lillie, or water Rose.*
Nymphée grande. *The great water Lillie, whereof there be two kinds, a white, and a yellow one.*
Nymphée petite. *The small water Lillie (of two kinds, as well as the great one.)*
Nymphette: f. *A little Nimphe.*
Nympheux: m. euse: f. *Nimphlie, Nimph-like, of a Nimph, or full of Nimphes.*

O

O *An Aduerbe of calling; or the signe of the Vocatiue Case; whence,* O Pierre retourne, &c.
O. *A Coniunction sometimes vsed in stead of* Auec; *whence,* Venez O moy; I m'en vay O vous.
O. *An Interiection of grieuing, wondering, wishing, anger, exclamation, derision, contempt, &c; and then signifies, Oh, alas, ay me, good Lord; Oh that, pish, fy, tush, &c; Sometimes in speeches of wonder, and mockerie, it is not expressed, but vnderstood; whence,* Le braue homme que voila! L'homme de bien! *in stead of,* O le braue homme! O le meschant!
Obaine. *Looke* Aubaine.
Obedianciers: m. *Foure Church-officers, viz. a Deane, Archdeacon, Almner, and Sexton.*
Obediemment. *Obediently, obsequiously, dutifully.*
Obedience: f. *Obedience; or, as* Obeissance.
Obedient. *Obedient, obsequious, dutifull vnto.*
Obeï: m. ïe: f. *Obeyed; obserued with dutie, yeelded vnto with submission.*
Obeine. *Looke* Aubaine.
Obeïr. *To obey; to obserue dutifully, yeeld vnto submissiuely; to be subiect, obsequious, or dutifull vnto; to doe whatsoeuer another will haue him doe.*
Obeïssamment. *Obediently.*
Obeïssance: f. *Obedience, obeissance; a dutifull obseruing of, an obsequious yeelding vnto.*
Obeïssant: m. ante: f. *Obeissant, obedient; submissiue, obsequious, or dutifull vnto.*
Grande moisson l'obeïssant recueille: Prov. *Seeke* Moisson.
Obel: m. *The white Popler tree.*
Obelisque: m. *An Obeliske; a great, high, and square stone, broad at the bottome, and lessening towards the top like a Pyramides.*
Obelon. *A sallade of sodden Hop-buds.* ¶Rab.
Oberé: m. ée: f. *Indebted.*
Obereau: m. *A hobbie (Hawke;) also, a young minx, or little prowd squall.*
Oberon: m. *The hand-vice, or toole, wherewith a Locksmith holds a key as he files it.*
Obesité: f. *Obesitie; fatnesse, grossnesse.*
Obfusquer. *as* Offusquer.
Obice: m. *A let, hinderance, obstacle, impediment.*
Obicer. *Looke* Obijcer.
Obiect: m. *An obiect; the subiect of the sight; any thing one lookes on directly; any thing that is before the eyes.*
Obiect de tesmoings. *A challenging of witnesses.*
Obiecter. *as* Obijcer.
Obiection. *as* Obiect; *also, an obiection.*
Obier: m. *The Ople, water Elder, marsh Elder, Dwarfe plane, Whitten tree.*
Obijcer. *To obiect, or lay against; to vpbraid, or twit in the teeth with; to reproach, lay to the charge, cast in the dish, of.*
Obit: m. *An Obit, obsequie, buriall, funerall.*
Objurgateur: m. *A chider, a rebuker, a reprouer.*
Objurgation: f. *An obiurgation, chiding, rebuke, reproofe, reprehension, blaming.*
Objurgatoire: com. *Obiurgatorie, reprehensiue, rebuking, chiding.*
Objurguer. *To chide, reproue, rebuke, taunt, reprehend, blame.*
Oblade: f. *A kind of great-eyed, and little-mouthed sea Ruffe, or sea Pearch, hauing a blacke spot on the root of her tayle.* ¶Marseillois.
Oblat: m. *A Souldior, who growne impotent, or maymed in seruice, hath maintenance, or the benefit of a Monks place, assigned him in an Abbey; also, the meanes, or place of a Monke; or of such a souldior.*
Oblat de religion. *A Nouice, a Probationer.*
Oblation: f. *An oblation, an offering.*
Oblectation: f. *Oblectation, delight.*
Oblecter. *To oblectate, reioyce, delight, make sport, giue pastime, yeeld recreation, vnto.*
Obliages. Droict d'ob. *A* Nomine pœnæ, *or fine payed in some places (as within the dominion of* Blois) *by Tenants, who haue not payed their rents, or performed their yearelie duties on their vsuall dayes.*
Obliaige. *as* Obliage.
Oblie. *as* Oublie. ¶Rab.
Obligation: f. *An Obligation, or Bond; also, a beholdingnesse.*
Obligatoire: com. *Obligatorie, obliging, binding.*
Obligé: m. *An Obligor; he thats bound in an Obligation.*
Obligé: m. ée: f. *Obliged, tyed, bound, bounden; beholden, indebted vnto.*
Obligé en rolat. *Subiect vnto the rigor of the Court of a* Bailli.
Obliger. *To oblige; ty, bind; to make bounden, or beholden vnto.*
Qui bien veut payer bien se doit obliger: Pro. *He that will pay well must giue good securitie.*
Oblique: com. *Crooked, oblique, awry; sideling, bowed, winding; trauerse, crosse, ouerthwart, contrarie to straight.*
Sphere oblique. *Looke* Sphere.
Obliquement. *Obliquely, wryly, crookedly, aside, acrosse, a trauers, ouerthwartly.*
Obliquité: f. *Obliquitie, wrynesse, crookednesse.*

Obliteré: m.ée: f. *Obliterated, abolished, worne, blotted, or scraped out.*

Oblivieux: m. euse: f. *Obliuious, forgetfull; also, causing forgetfulneße.*

Oblivion: f. *Obliuion, forgetfulnesse; vnmindfulnesse.*

Obloesion: f. *Sore hurt, much annoyance, great harme.*

Oblong: m. gue: f. *Oblong, somewhat long.*

Obmettre. *Looke* Omettre.

Obnubiler. *To obnubilate, make clowdie, obscure, or darken, as clowds doe the skie.*

Obnunciation: f. *A forbidding of a thing vpon a foreknowledge, coniecture, or likelyhood of the ill successe thereof.*

Obole: m. *A halfepennie; a small coyne worth* vij d Tourn. *also, a halfepennie weight; 12 graines among Apothecaries, and 14 among Mintmen, and Goldsmiths.*

Obole de Gueldres. *A coyne worth* ij s vj d sterl.

Obole de Horne. *Js worth somewhat aboue* xiij d sterl.

Obole du Rhin. *Whereof there be diuers sorts of different value, yet all of them betweene 22, and 27* solz Tourn.

Droict d'obole. *Seeke vnder* Droict.

Obombration: f. *An obumbration, obscurement, shaddow, or shaddowing.*

Obombrer. *To obumbrate, shaddow, obscure.*

Obre. *Bastard blacke Hellebore, Lungwort, Christs-wort, Lyons foot, Lyons claw.*

Obreptice: com. *Obreptitious, stollen, foisted in, conueyed, nimmed, falsely come by.*

Obreption: f. *An obreption; the creeping, or stealing to a thing by craftie meanes; the getting, or obtaining thereof by dissimulation, or priuate cousenage.*

Obreptissement. *By stealth.*

Obrize. Or ob. *Gold perfectly fined, or tryed.* ¶Rab.

Obrophore. *A carrier of light.* ¶Rab.

Obrué: m. ée: f. *Ouerwhelmed; couered, or buried all ouer with earth, &c; drowned, lost, oppressed, confounded, ouercome.*

Obscur: m. ure: f. *Obscure; darke, mirke; duskie, gloomie, mistie, dimme; also, secret, close, misticall, diffused, hard to vnderstand; also, priuate, vnknowne, base, meane, of low parentage, of no reputation.*

Obscurci: m. ie: f. *Obscured; dimmed, darkened; cloaked, hidden, concealed; obnubilated, enwrapped in clowds.*

Obscurcir. *To obscure; darken, dimme, ouercast, or cast a mist ouer; to cloake, hide, conceale; obnubilate, enwrap in clowds.*

Obscurcissement: m. *An obscuring, darkening, dimming, ouercasting, ouershadowing.*

Obscurement. *Obscurely, darkly, dimly, clowdily, duskily; couertly, mistically.*

Obscurité: f. *Obscuritie, darkneße, dimnesse, clowdinesse, duskinesse, an ouercasting; closenesse, couertnesse, diffusednesse; a misticall sence, or hidden meaning in words.*

Obsecration: f. *An obsecration, beseeching, especiall desire, earnest intreatie, heartie prayer.*

Obseques: f. *Obsequies; funeralls, or funerall rites.*

Obsequieux: m. euse: f. *Obsequious, officious, dutifull, seruiceable, obseruant, obedient.*

Observance: f. *Obseruance, dutie, respect, regard; also, an obseruation; a law, discipline, ordinance; fashion, vse, custome.*

Freres de l'observance. *as* Observantins.

Observantins: m. *An Order of gray Franciscan Fryers.*

Observateur: m. *An obseruer, marker, regarder; also, an obseruator, monitor, bill-keeper, in Schooles.*

Observé: m. ée: f. *Obserued, kept, held; heeded, esteemed, regarded; watched, marked.*

Observer. *To obserue, keepe, hold; heed, esteeme, regard; watch, marke, espie, aduise.*

Obsesseur: m. *A besieger, a beleaguerer.*

Obsister. *To withstand, resist; gainesay; impeach, let, stop.*

Obstacle: m. *An obstacle, impeachment, let, hinderance, impediment.*

Obstaclement: m. *A letting, hindering, impeaching; also, a stopping, or shutting vp.*

Obstacler. *To let, hinder, impeach; also, to stop (a doore, window, &c;) to shut vp a house.*

Obstant. *Withstanding, impeaching, letting.*

Non obstant. *Notwithstanding, for all that.*

Obstaqué: m. ée: f. *Hindered, letted, impeached, withstood.*

Obstination: f. *Obstinacie, wilfulnesse, selfe-will; stubbornesse; also, constancie, perseuerance, resolution, in an opinion.*

Obstiné: m. ée: f. *Obstinate; wilfull, selfewillie, opinionatiue; stiff-necked, stubborn; firme, constant, resolute, persisting, determinately bent.*

Obstinément. *Obstinately; wilfully; stubbornly; firmely, resolutely, constantly.*

s'Obstiner. *Stubbornly to persist, or perseuere in; wilfully to harden, set, or bend his thoughts on; to maintaine earnestly, determine absolutely, obstinately to hold tacke.*

Obtemperation: f. *Obtemperation, obedience.*

Obtemperé: m. ée: f. *Obeyed.*

Obtemperer. *To obtemperate, obey; doe the will, follow the direction, be at the commaund of.*

Obtenebrer. *To obtenebrate, obscure, darken.*

Obtenement: m. *An obtaining, acquiring, atchieuing of, attaining vnto.*

Obtenir. *To obtaine, attaine vnto, atchieue, acquire, get.*

Obtenu: m. uë: f. *Obtained; atchieued, gotten, attained vnto.*

Obtenuë: f. *A purchase, acquisition, thing obtained, matter gotten.*

Obtester. *To obtest; coniure; humbly, or heartily to beseech; also, to inuoke, to call to witnesse, or call vpon for succour.*

Obtrectateur: m. *A detractor, deprauer, backbiter, slaunderer.*

Obtrectation: f. *Detraction, deprauation, backbiting, slaundering.*

Obtundre. *To beat, strike, or thumpe; to blunt, or make dull; also, to inculcate, or repeat often; to wearie, or cloy with words.*

Obturateur: m. *A stopper, or shutter vp.*

Obturation: f. *An obturation, a stopping, or shutting vp.*

Obturber. *To trouble, disturbe, disquiet; interrupt.*

Obtus: m. use: f. *Dull, blunt, edgeleße; weakened; without spirit.*

Obtusement. *Obtusely, dully, bluntly.*

Obvention: f. *A meeting with; comming against; happening, or chauncing vnto.*

Obvention testamentaire. *A Legacie bestowed by chaunce, or where it was not looked for.*

Obvier. *To meet with; to resist, or withstand a thing met with; to preuent, stop, forestall.*

Obumbré: m. ée: f. *Obũbrated, ouershadowed, obscured.*

Obumbrer. *To obumbrate, ouershadow, cast a mist ouer, darken, obscure.*

Ocaigne, & Ocaine: f. *Dogs leather; or, a dogs skin well dressed.*

Occasion: f. *An occasion; cause; oportunitie, fit season.*

Occasion trouve qui son chat bat: Prov. *He that would beat his Cat finds a cause for it.*

Occasionnellement. *Occasionally, by occasion.*

Occasionner. *To occasion, or be the occasion of.*

Occiant: m. *as* Occident.

Occiant: m. ante: f. *Killing, slaying, murthering, slaughtering.*

Occident. *The Occident, the West.*

Occidental: m. ale: f. *Occidentall, Westerlie, Westerne.*

Occipital: m. ale: f. *Occipitall; belonging to the noddle, or hinder part of the head.*

Occire. *To kill, slay, murther, slaughter, massacre.*

Occis: m. ise: f. *Killed, murthered, slaughtered, slaine.*

Occision: f. *An occision, killing, slaying, murthering, slaughtering; also, a murther, or slaughter.*

Occultateur: m. *A concealor, or hider.*

Occultation: f. *An occultation, concealing, hiding.*

Occulte: com. *Hidden, close, priuie, couert, concealed, secret, obscure.*

Occulté: m. ée: f. *Hidden, concealed, obscured.*

Occultement. *Hiddenly, priuily, closely, couertly, secretly.*

Occulter. *To hide, conceale, couer, keepe secret, obscure.*

Occupateur: m. *The occupier, possessor, holder, enioyer of a thing which he hath seized.*

Occupation: f. *An occupation, businesse, imployment; also, an occupying, vsing, enioying; a seizure of; also, a disseisin, or vsurpation.*

Occupé: m. ée: f. *Occupied, busied, imployed in; troubled, held, or intangled with; also, woon, seized, vsurped, forcibly taken, violently gotten.*

Occuper. *To occupy; to busie, trouble, imploy; also, to vse, possesse, enioy; also, to win, take, vsurpe by force; to seize on, to disseize one.*

Occuper aucun de. *To accuse, or appeach of; to charge with (an old phrase.)*

Occurrence: f. *An occurrence, or accident; a thing met with, matter happened in the way.*

Occurrent: m. *An occurrent; or, as* Occurrence.

Occurrent: m. ente: f. *Occurrent, accidentall, happening, or comming in the way.*

Occurrer. *To occurre, meet with, come in place, offer it selfe, be in the way; to happen, or fall out on a suddaine.*

Oceane. La mer Oceane. *The Ocean, or maine Sea.*

Oceanique: com. *Of, or belonging to, the Ocean; residing, or liuing in the Maine.*

Oche: f. *A nicke, nocke, or notch; the cut of a Tally; also, a little ground inclosed with a Quick-set hedge, and fruit trees.*

Oché: m. ée: f. *Nicked, nocked, notched; cut as a Tally; also, moued, stirred, wagged, figged, wagled.*

Ocher. *To nicke, nocke, notch; to cut, as a Tally; also, to moue, stirre, fig, wag, wagle.*

Ocieux: m. euse: f. *Idle, quiet, restfull, at ease, at leisure, that hath little to doe.*

Ocre: m. *(Painters) Oker.*

Ocrisse: f. *A scould, shrew, vnquiet or impatient woman.*

Octaëdre. *A bodie, or figure of eight faces.*

Octante. *Eightie, fourescore.*

Octantiesme. *The eightieth.*

Octave: f. *An Octaue; an eighth; a proportion, or the number, of eight.*

L'Octave d'une feste. *The Octaue, eight dayes, on the eighth day, after a holyday.*

Les octaves en seront bien longues. *The blow indeed is giuen, but it may be reuenged a long time hece; or, men are like enough to be long sencible of it.*

Octenaire. *An eight; the number, or a proportion, of eight.*

Octimestre: com. *Of eight moneths.*

Octobre: m. *October.*

Octonaire: com. *Eight, of eight.*

Octostique: f. *A Staffe, or Stanzo of eight verses.*

Octosyllabe: com. *Of eight syllables.*

Octroy: m. *A graunt; a grace; a priuiledge conferred, or suit giuen; also, free will, or good will; also, the graunt of a Subsidie vnto the Prince.*

Deniers d'octroy. *Looke* Denier.

Octroyé: m. ée: f. *Graunted, accorded, condescended vnto; bestowed, or conferred vpon.*

Octroyer. *To graunt, accord, yeeld, consent, or condescend vnto; to bestow, or conferre vpon.*

Assez octroye qui mot ne dit: Pro. *He that sayes nothing yeelds enough.*

Octuple: com. *Eight times doubled, sixteene, twice eight.*

Oculaire: com. *Ocular, perspicuous, euident, apparant; also, belonging to the eye.*

Veine oculaire. *Part of the forehead veine; called so while it accoasts the eye.*

Oculairement. *Perspicuously, euidently, apparantly, before the eyes.*

Oculé: m. ée: f. *Circumspect, soone-spying, cleere-seeing, sightie, quicke of sight.*

Ode. *A way.* ¶Rab.

Ode: f. *Dyers Woad; also, a Poeticall Ode, or Song.*

Odelette: f. *A small, or short Ode.*

Odette. *as* Odelette.

Odeur: f. *An odor, sent, smell, waft; sauor; also, the sence of smelling; also, an inkling, suspition, or doubt of.*

Il ne l'a pas en bonne odeur. *He disgusts him, or distasts him much; he hath no good conceit of him.*

De mauvaise odeur. Telle chose est de m. o. *Such a thing is loathsome, or most vnsauorie; of ill reputation; most lewd, faultie, filthie.*

Odieux: m. euse: f. *Hatefull, odious, loathsome, contrarie to mans nature; also, haynous, detestable, horrible, worthie of hatred.*

Odorant. *as* Odoriferant; *or, smelling, senting.*

Odorat: m. *The sence, or act, of smelling.*

Odoration: f. *as* Odorement.

Odoré: m. ée: f. *Smelt, sented, wafted, vented.*

Odorement: m. *A smelling, senting, wafting, venting; also, a smell, waft, sent, vent.*

Odorer. *To smell, sent, waft, vent.*

Odoriferant: m. ante: f. *Odoriferous, sweet, pleasantly smelling, full of perfume.*

Odorifique: com. *Odoriferous.*

Oé. *Woeh; the voice wherewith Carters vse to stop their horses.*

Oeconomant: m. *The Stewardship, or Controllership of a familie; and particularly, the Stewardship of an Ecclesiasticall liuing, or the Receiuorship of the reuenue thereof, during vacancie.*

Oeconome: m. *The Gouernor, Steward, or Controller of*

of a familie; also, a receiuer of the rents of a Benefice, &c, during vacancie.

Iouïr d'une chose en forme d'oeconome. *To possesse a thing onely as a Gouernour, or Steward thereof, during his owne life.*

Oeconomie: f. *Oeconomie; the gouernment of a familie; the rule, disposition, or managing of houshold affaires.*

Oeconomique: com. *Oeconomicall; of husbandrie, or houshold businesses.*

Oedemateux: m. euse: f. *Full of, or subiect vnto, a flegmaticke, and painelesse tumor, or swelling.*

Oedeme: m. *A painelesse, waterish, and flegmaticke swelling, which pressed downe with the finger, retaynes the impression thereof.*

Oedipodique. Iambe Oedipodique. *A lame, or gowtie leg.* ¶Rab.

Oeil: m. *The eye; an eye; a sight, a looke.*

Oeil d'airain. *A red, fierie, sparkling eye; (Such a one as Lyons, and the leaporous haue.)*

Oeil bigarré. *as* Oeil veron.

Oeil blaffard. *An eye whose Christaline humor is growne white, and almost dryed vp; (an imperfection that befalls old people.)*

Oeil de bœuf. *The hearbe Ox-eye; also, foolish Mathes, vnsauorie white Cotula, white vnsauorie Camomill; also, an out-strouting, or great gogle eye; and, prouerbially, ignorance, or a weake eye; also (in building) such an ouerture as is made in some roofes, and close walls, by a ridge-tyle (or in the forme thereof) to gaine light or ayre from without, or for the voiding of smoake from within.*

Oeil de bouc. *A rolling gogle eye; also, an eye that lookes asquint vpward; an eye whose lid couers halfe of the ball; also, a shell-fish, called a Limpin, or Lempet.*

Oeil de carré. *A squinting side, or leering eye; also, a prowd, surlie, statelie, or big looke.*

Oeil de cerf. *Looke* Cerf.

Oeil de chat. *Purple Snapdragon, Calues snowt (an hearbe;) also, a Cats eye; a sight thats better in the night then by day; also, an out-strouting eye; also, a white stone that glisters like a starre, and casts an azure luster.*

Oeil de chevre. *A whall, or ouer-white eye; an eye full of white spots, or whose apple seemes diuided by a streake of white.*

Oeil d'hypocrite. *An often-twinkling eye.*

Oeil de Iudas. *The Nut, or Fryers peece of a Leg of Mutton.*

Oeil de lievre. *An eye which in sleeping holds the lids open; also, an eye whose vpper lid by conuulsion, or otherwise, is hindered from couering the vpper part of the white.*

Oeil de loup. *A duskie, or darke eye.*

Oeil de mauvais garçon. *as* Oeil de loup.

Oeil de moruë. *A great, and out-strowting (but dull-sighted) eye.*

Oeil de perdrix. *A bright, or orientall rubie Red; also, a kind of Fig.*

Oeil de rat. *A small eye, pinke-eye, little sight.*

Oeil rosti. *A Carbuncle in the eye.*

Oeil de travers. *A squint, or leering eye.*

Oeil veron. *A deprauation of the eyes; when the Christaline humor growes white, or is almost dryed vp in onely one of them; or when they are both of sundrie colours; or when their apples be verie blacke; also, a whall eye; whence the Prouerbe,* Le Cheval à oeil veron est meschant, ou tout bon.

Blanc oeil. Gens aux blancs yeux. *White-liuered, faint-hearted, people.*

Blanc en l'oeil. Il n'a point de blanc en l'oeil. *He is a verie spirit, he hath not a crosse to blesse him with.*

Busche en l'oeil. C'estoit vn busche en son oeil. *That was a log, or beame in his eye; an hinderance to his sight; that cast a mist ouer his vnderstanding.*

Gros oeil. *A scornefull, big, surlie, or angrie looke.*

Mauvais oeil. *Iuie Chickweed, Henne-bit.*

Perle de bel oeil. *A pearle of an excellent colour, or luster.*

'A yeux de cire. *Looke* Cire.

Les yeux plus grands que la panse. *One may sooner, or had better, fill his bellie then his eye.*

L'oeil tendu au bois. *Warily, vigilantly, circumspectly; that feares a surprisall; that lookes verie well about him.*

Il a vn oeil au bois, (ou aux champs) & l'autre à la ville. *He lookes two sundrie wayes, or heeds two seuerall things, at once.*

Il a vn oeil à la poisle, l'autre au chat. *The same; or, as vnder* Poisle.

Faire les yeux; & faire les doux yeux. *Looke* Faire.

Lever l'oeil. Il n'y a homme qui ose lever l'oeil devant luy. *Euerie one stands in wonderfull awe of him; no man dare quitch, or stirre before him.*

Il leur en pend autant en l'oeil. *They are in the like danger; they must one day tast of the same sawce; as much euerie way hangs ouer their (carelesse) heads.*

Servi au doigt, & à l'oeil. *Serued at a becke; diligently attended, excellently wayted on.*

Tenir l'oeil à. *To looke at seriously, view diligently, obserue wistly, giue good heed vnto.*

'A l'oeil malade la lumiere nuit: Pro. *An eye distempered cannot brooke the light; sicke thoughts cannot indure the truth.*

'A cœur dolent l'oeil pleure: Prov. *A weeping eye discouers the sad heart; moist eyes mournefull heart.*

Deux yeux voyent plus clair qu'un: Pro. *Two eyes see better (two wits discerne more) then one.*

L'oeil du maistre engraisse le cheval: Prov. *See* Maistre.

Le cœur ne veut douloir ce que l'oeil ne peut voir: Pro. *What the eye cannot see the heart will not rue.*

Nul ne sçait ce qu'à l'oeil luy pend: Pro. *No man knowes what will befall him, or how neere a mischiefe is to him.*

Orgueil n'a pas bon oeil: Prov. *Pride lookes not well on any.*

Quand les yeux voyent ce qu'ils ne virent oncques, le cœur pense ce qu'il ne pensa oncques: Pro. *New obiects breed new thoughts.*

Qui n'a qu'un oeil bien le garde: Pro. *Let him that hath but one eye keepe it well; let him that hath but one helpe striue to preserue it.*

Toute chose se vend au pris de l'oeil: Prov. *Mans eye doth set a rate on euerie thing.*

Oeillade: f. *An amorous looke, affectionate winke, wanton aspect, lustfull iert, or passionate cast, of the eye; a Sheepes eye.*

Oeilladé: m. ée: f. *Often, or affectionately eyed; looked on wantonly, winked at lasciuiously.*

Oeillader. *To eye often, behold affectionately, winke at lasciuiously, looke on wantonly; to cast a Sheepes eye at, to dart at with a passionate eye.*

Oeilladette: f. *A prettie winke, iert, cast of the eye.*

Oeilladier: m. ere: f. *Belonging to the eye, or looke; also, eying often, affectionately, or wantonly.*
Oeillage de Vin. *The filling vp of leakie Wine vessels.*
Oeillarder. *as* Oeillader.
Oeillé: m. ée: f. *Full of eyes, decked or set thicke with eyes, like a Peacocks tayle; also, filled vp, as a leaking Wine vessell.*
Oeiller les Vins. *To fill vp Wine vessels which haue leaked.*
Oeilleres. Bride à oeilleres. *A bridle with eye-flaps for a fore-horse.*
Oeillet: m. *A little eye; also, an oylet-hole; also, the young bud of a tree, &c; also, a Gilliflower; also, a Pinke.*
Oeillet Dieu. *Rose-Campion (a flower.)*
Oeillet d'Inde. *The Turkie, or Affrican Marigold, or Gilliflower; also, the French Marigold, or Gingioline flower (which is the single kind of the Affrican.)*
Oeillets de Paris. *as* Catherinettes.
Oeillet de Provence. *The ordinarie great, red, and double Cloue-Gilliflower.*
Oeillet de rosette. *A lesse kind of the red Cloue-Gilliflower.*
Oeillet sauvage. *A Pinke; also, the sweet William, &c.*
Oeillet de Turquie. *as* Oeillet d'Inde.
Bois ont oreilles, & champs oeillets: Prov. *Woods haue their eares, and fields their eyes; euerie thing hath some instrument of, or helpe for, discouerie.*
Oeilleté: m. ée: f. *Full of eyes (like ill-prest cheese, or light-wrought bread;) also, full of oylet holes.*
Oeilleton: m. *A Pinke, or small Gilliflower; also, a little bud.*
Oeillier: m. ere: f. *Of, or belonging to, an eye.*
Veine oeilliere. *Seeke* Veine.
Oeillieres: f. *The eye-teeth, or tushes.*
Oesipe: m. *The filth, and sweatie greasinesse of wooll growing on the flanke, and shoulders of a Sheepe.*
Oeson: m. *The weason, or throat-pipe.*
Oesophage: m. *The mouth of the stomack; also, the pipe that reaches from the mouth to the stomacke.*
Oest: m. *The East wind, or coast.*
Oestre Iunonique. *A gad-bee, horse-flye, dun-flye, brimsey, brizze.* ¶Rab.
Oeuf: m. *An egge.*
Oeufs brouillez. *Looke* Brouillé.
Oeufs de Pasques. *Past, or Pasch-egges, egges giuen at Easter; whence;*
Ils s'y attendoient comme à leurs oeufs de Pasques. *They expected it certainely, they looked assuredly, or greedily, for it.*
Donner des oeufs de Pasques à toutes restes. *To bethwacke, belamme, belabor soundly; to lay about him lustily.*
Oeuf des Philosophes. *The vessell wherein Alchymists put the stuffe which they hope will yeeld the Philosophers stone.*
Oeufs des poissons. *The spawne of fishes; whence;*
Harenc aux oeufs. *A full-rowed, or hard-rowed Herring.*
Oeufs à la riblette. *Egges and Collops.*
Couver vn mauvais oeuf. *To hatch an ill egge; to breed an vngracious child; to nourish an vnluckie, or mischieuous designe.*
Faire de ses oeufs poules. *To count his chickens before they be hatched.*
Il n'y fera rien, non plus que le coq sur les oeufs. *He cannot be drawne to attend, or meddle in it.*
Quitter vn bœuf pour prendre vn oeuf. *To quit a great, for the gaine of a small, thing; to change for the worse.*
Tondre sur vn oeuf. *To quarrell without cause, or find a fault where there is none; also, to pick a gaine out of a most bare, or barren commoditie.*
Vn oeuf n'est rien; deux font grand bien; trois c'est assez; quatre c'est tort; cinq c'est la mort: Pro. *One egge is none, two somewhat, three enow; foure be too much, fiue giue a deadlie blow.*
De mauvais corbeau mauvais oeuf: Pro. *An ill bird layes a naughtie egge; lewd creatures breed lewd creatures; as the damme or sire, such is the race.*
Mieux vaut en paix vn oeuf qu'en guerre vn bœuf: Pro. *Better is an egge in peace, then an Ox in warre.*
Noire geline pond blanc oeuf: Pro. *Looke* Noir.
Tel cuide avoir des oeufs au feu qui n'a que les escailles: Pro. *Looke* Escaille.
Vne belle chose est vn oeuf: Pro. *An egg's a beautifull, or goodlie thing.*
Oeuf-molette. *Seeke* Omelette.
Oeuvance. *as* Oeuve; *(at* Blois.)
Oeuve: f. *The rowe, or spawne of a fish.*
Oeuvé: m. ée: f. *Layed, or set on, as an egge; also, spawned.*
Oeuvre: f. *A worke; deed; businesse; labour, trauaile, toyle; also, worke, or workmanship; also, a place, or part of a Parish Church, wherein the Church-wardens, &c, sit together on feastiuall dayes.*
Oeuvre blanche; &, faiseur d'oeuvre blanche. *Looke* Blanc.
Oeuvres fainctes. *Imagerie, or imbossed worke, set on, or appearing but halfe without, a wall.*
Oeuvre de loy. *An actuall dispossession, or transport of aliened Inheritances, Rents, Seruices, &c, suffered, or passed before the Landlord thereof, or his steward; or before other officers of the iurisdiction of the place.*
Oeuvre de singe. *An idle, foolish, lewd, or impure act.*
Bois d'oeuvre. *Great Timber squared, cut out, or fitted for vse.*
Chef d'oeuvre. *A Maister-peece.*
Dedans, ou dehors oeuvre. *Within, or without the walls of a house, &c; (a workmanlie tearme.)*
Maistre des oeuvres. *The Surueyor, or Ouerseer of the Kings workes.*
Maistre des basses oeuvres. *A Jakes-feyer.*
Maistre des hautes oeuvres. *A Hangman.*
Mortes oeuvres. *The outside of a Ship from the wales vpward.*
Mettre toutes pierres en oeuvre. *Looke* Mettre.
'A l'oeure on cognoist l'ouvrier: Pro. *One may discerne a workman by his worke.*
'A bon iour bon oeuvre: Prov. *A goodlie act on a godlie day; or, as we say, the better day the better work; (tis also taken Ironically, and in a contrarie sence) he hath honoured so good a day with a goodlie act indeed; (of one that on a holy day commits a haynous deed.)*
Il n'est oeuvre que d'ouvriers: Pro. *There's no work, but by workmen, rightly done.*
Le cœur fait l'oeuvre non pas les grands iours: Pro. *Tis not long dayes, but willing hearts, that soon dispatch a businesse.*
Tel autheur tel oeuvre: Prov. *Like Author like worke; such as the writer such his booke.*
Of. *(An Interiection expressing a suddaine feare; astonishment, sence of paine, or of disdaine;) Oh, Ah, alas; out, fy, farre be it.*

Offence: f. *as* Offense.
Offencé: m. ée: f. *as* Offensé.
Offencer. *as* Offenser.
Offencible. *Looke* Offensible.
Offendre. *To offend, hurt, mischieue, harme, indommage, doe scathe vnto.*
Offense: f. *Offence, hurt, scathe, harme, wrong, iniurie, dammage, displeasure; also, a crime, fault, offence, trespasse, transgression.*
Offensé: m. ée: f. *Offended, hurt, wronged, iniured.*
Offensement: m. *An offending, displeasing, hurting, wronging, iniuring.*
Offenser. *To offend, hurt, wrong, iniure, abuse, harme, damnifie, doe scathe vnto.*
Offensible: com. *Offencible, hurtfull, indommaging, dangerous.*
Offensif: m. iue: f. *Offensiue, hurtfull, displeasing, troublesome, noisome, or dangerous vnto.*
Offerte: f. *An Offer, an Offering.*
Offertoire: m. *An Offertorie (in the Maße, &c.)*
Offeux: m. euse: f. *Soppie; or full of lumpes, or gobbets.*
Office: f. *An Office; function, magistracie, dignitie, (publicke) charge; also, a mans dutie; also, an office, kindnesse, pleasure, seruice, good turne done one; also, diuine Seruice.*
Offices extraordinaires. *Are those that concerne the* Finances, Aides, Tailles, *and salt Garners.*
Offices ordinaires. *The Offices of ordinarie Iustice, and of the Kings Demaine.*
Causes d'office. *The causes which concerne a Lord* Iusticier.
Greffier d'office; &, Procureur d'office. *A Lord Iusticers Clarke; Atturney, or Proctor.*
Official: m. *An Officiall; a Commissarie, or Chauncelor to a Bishop, &c.*
Officier: m. *An Officer; also, a Magistrate; also, a Sergeant, or Catchpole.*
Officiers d'armes. *Heralds, of all sorts.*
Qui ie sois officier au moins d'un moulin: Prov. *Let me be an Officer though it be but of a Mill: make the King an Officer, and he will soone grow rich; (quoth an old Preacher in* Edward *the sixts time.)*
Officier. *To say Seruice in the Church; also, to work, imploy, or busie himselfe about.*
Officieux: m. euse: f. *Officious, dutifull, seruiceable, diligent, courteous, friendlie, readie at call, willing to doe pleasures, or good offices.*
Officine: f. *A workhouse, or shop.*
Offrande: f. *An Offering.*
Offrant: m. ante: f. *Offering, proffering.*
Au plus offrant. *To him that bids most.*
Offraye: m. *The great water fowle called an Osprey.*
Offre: m. *An offer, proffer; bidding.*
Offrir. *To offer, bid, proffer; also, to present, or exhibit.*
Offuscation: f. *An offuscation; a dimming, obscuring, blackening, darkening.*
Offusqué: m. ée: f. *Offuscated, obscured, blackened, darkened.*
Offusquer. *To offuscate, obscure, blacken, darken; dimme, shadow, cast a mist ouer.*
Oger. *The name of a sharpe tast-pleasing apple.*
Ogive: f. *An Ogiue, or Ogee in Architecture; Looke* Augive.
Ogoesse: f. *An Ogreße, or Gunne-bullet (must be sable) in Blason.*
Ohie: f. *Crazinesse, indisposition, distemper, weakeneße, faintnesse, or feebleneße of the bodie.*
Ohié: m. ée: f. *Crazie, distempered, sicklie, ill-disposed; faint, feeble, weake.*
Ohier. *To distemper, make sicklie or crazie; to weaken, enfeeble, make faint.*
Oho. (Interject.) *Oho? is it euen so? is it so indeed?*
Oignement: m. *An oyle, or ointment; also, an annointing.*
Oignon: m. *An Onyon.*
Oignon de bois. *The wild starrie Jacinth, or Crowtoes.*
Oignon de chien. *Dogs Leeke, the bush Jacinth, or tuft Jacinth; also, as* Porreau de chien.
Oignon fendu. *A Scallion.*
Oignon de mer. *The Squill, or sea Onyon.*
L'oignon du pied. *The (bunchie, or out-bearing) root of the great toe; the fleshie part of the sole of the foot at the root of that toe.*
Oignon sauvage. *The Squill, or sea Onyon; also, the wild field Onyon, Bulbine, wild Bulbus, Corne Leeke, wild starre of Bethlem; also, the hearbe that beares the purple Jacinth* Vaciet.
Oignon sectil. *A Scallion.*
Oignon testu. *The ordinarie garden Onyon.*
Il y a de l'oignon. *There is a pad in the straw, there's somewhat amiße among them.*
Se mettre en rang d'oignon, & ne valoir vn'eschalotte. *To iudge too well of himselfe, to take too much vpon him; to ranke himselfe with, or compare himselfe to, his betters.*
A pain, & oignon trompette, ne clairon: Pro. *See* Clairon.
Apres Pasques, & Rogation, fy de Prestre, & d'oignon: Prov. *After the weeke of Easter, and Rogation, a Priest, and Onyons are abhomination.*
Si tu te trouves sans chapon, sois content de pain & d'oignon: Pro. *If thou want a Capon, fall to bread and an Onyon; or, let not the want of dainties discontent thee.*
Oignoncettes: f. *Ciues, Chiues, rush Onyons.*
Oignonnerie. *as* Oignonniere.
Oignonnet: m. *The Onyon Apple, or Peare.*
Oignonnette: f. *A Scallion; or, a wild Onyon.*
Oignonniere: f. *A Bed, Plot, or Garden of Onyons.*
Oillet. *Seeke* Oeillet.
Oince: f. *A Hawkes Pounce; (and thence) a hooke; and (as in* Rab.*) a hand, or fist; also, the beast called an Ounce, or Linx.*
Oinct: m. *as* Oing.
Oinct: m. oincte: f. *Annointed, greased, besmeared, smeered.*
Oindre. *To annoint, grease, besmeare, smeere.*
Oignez vilain il vous poindra: Pro. *(Like our homelie one) claw a churle by the breech, and he will shite in your fist.*
Charité oingt, & peché poinct: Prov. *Charitie annointeth, sinne annoyeth; or, charitie quiets the heart, sinne afflicts the soule.*
On ne doit pas à gras pourceau le cul oindre: Pro. *We must not grease a fat Sow in the tayle.*
Oing: m. *(Hogs) grease, or seame; smeare.*
Oingtereule: f. *Selfe-heale, Hooke-heale, Sicklewort, Brunell, Prunell, Carpenters hearbe.*
Oingture: f. *An annointing, begreasing, besmearing; also, an ointment.*
En lict de chien n'y a point d'oingture: Prov. *The kennell of a dog smells not of Ciuet.*
Oinze. *An Ounce, or Linx.* ¶Rab.

Oiseau : m. *A bird, a fowle; and (particularly) a Hawke; also, a Hodd; the Tray wherein Masons, &c, carrie their Mortar.*
Oiseau de bec. *A hungrie, or greedie Parasite; one in whom there is nothing but words.*
Oiseau dunette. *A Thrush.*
Oiseau de S.Martin. *A Ring-tayle, or Hen-harme.*
Oiseau de meurte, ou de nerte. *A Mirtle Thrush.*
Oiseau de Paradis. *Looke* Paradis.
Oiseau de proye. *A Hawke, or Kite.*
Langue d'oiseau. *Ashen keyes.*
Pain d'oiseau. *Stone-crop, Stone-hore, Mouse-tayle, wild Prick-madame, Jacke of the Buttrie.*
Parler comme vn oiseau en cage. *To babble, tattle, chatter, talke much to little purpose.*
Oiseau debonnaire de luy mesme se fait: Pro. *The gentle Hawke (halfe) makes, or mannes, her selfe; a well-bred person is of a vertuous disposition, needes not much tutoring, will of himselfe be good.*
L'oiseau gazouille selon qu'il est embecqué: Pro. *A man vsually speakes as his humor moues, gaine leads, or passion vrges him; or (like a good bird) he vtters onely that which he was bid, or taught, to say.*
A tous oiseaux leurs nids sont beaux: Pro. *To euerie bird her neast seemes faire; most men like houses of their owne contriuing.*
D'oiseaux, de chiens, d'armes, & d'amours, pour vn plaisir mille douleurs: Pro. *Looke* Amour, *or* Armes.
Tel oiseau tel nid: Pro. *Like ayerie like Hawke; such as the bird such is her neast.*
Vieil oiseau ne se prend à reths: Pro. *The old (in experience) are not subiect to surprisalls.*
Nid tissu oiseau envolé: Prov. *Tis a signe that the birds are flowen when Spiders build ouer the neast.*
Qui veut prendre vn oiseau qu'il ne l'effarouche: Pro. *Deale gently with the bird thou mean'st to catch; be not too harsh to those thou faine wouldst win.*
Trop tard crie l'oiseau quand il est pris: Pro. *When mischiefes are befallen complaints auaile not.*
Oisel. *as* Oiseau.
Oiseler. *To fall a birding, or flye out at birds, like a giddie, or ill-made Hawke.*
Oiseler vn faulcon sur la grue. *To flesh or fly her vpon, to make or lurcher vnto, the Crane.*
Oiselerie : f. *Fowling, bird-hunting, bird-catching; a flying at, or preying on, birds.*
Oiselet : m. *A little bird.*
Oiseleur: m. *A Fowler, or Bird-catcher.*
Oiseleur: m. eure: f. *Of, or belonging to, a bird.*
Oiselier. *as* Oiseleur; *also, a keeper (or one that hath the charge) of birds, or of fowle.*
Oiseliere: f. *as* Oiselerie; *also, a cage for birds, a coope for fowle.*
Oiseux: m. euse: f. *Lither, sloathfull, sluggish, full of idlenesse; whence;*
Fille oiseuse rarement vertueuse: Prov.
Oisif: m. iue: f. *Lither, lazie, sloathfull, idle, negligent, retchlesse; languishing; that hath but little to doe, or if he had much, would doe but little.*
Fille oisive à mal pensive: Pro. *Looke* Fille.
Oisillon: m. *A young bird, or small bird.*
Il bat le buisson sans prendre l'oisillon. *He beats the bush, and gets not a bird; much fruitlesse paines he takes.*
Oisivement. *Litherly, lazily, sloathfully, idly.*
Oisiveté: f. *Sloath, idlenesse, litherneße, lazineße; negligence, retchlesnesse; also, rest, vacancie; a languishing, or hurtfull ease.*

Oison: m. *A greene-Goose, or young Goose; a Gosling.*
Oison bridé. *A sot, asse, gull, ninnie, noddie.*
La mort aux oisons. *Henbane; also, Hemlocks.*
Pied d'oison. *Goose-foot, wild Orache.*
Fourni d'entendement comme vn oison de creste. *As wise as Waltams Calfe.*
Oison verd bon, grison gueres bon: Prov. *See* Grison.
L'oison n'est pas digne de monstrer les pasquis à l'oye: Prov. *(A checke for young men that presume to teach their elders.)*
Les oisons menent paistre les oyes: Prov. *(Said when subiects gouerne their Princes, children their parents, meane men the Magistrates, and seruants or schollers their maisters; and is a note as well of weakenesse in the Geese, as of sawcinesse in the Goslings.)*
L'oye meine l'oison paistre: Prov. *The Goose leads out the Gosling to the field; (contrarie to the former, and an argument of a well-proportioned gouernment.)*
Oistre. *as* Huistre.
Oistriere. *Looke* Huistriere.
Oleagineux: m. euse: f. *Oylie, full of oyle; also, of an Oliue, or Oliue tree.*
Oleaginité: f. *Oylinesse, or an oylie substance.*
Oleandre. *The Rose tree, Rose Bay, Rose Lawrell, Rose Bay tree.*
Oleastre: m. *A wild Oliue tree.*
Olecrane: m. *The end, or tip of the elbow; also, the elbow it selfe.*
Oleeux: m. euse: f. *Oylie, full of oyle.*
Oliban: m. Olibanum; *Frankincense in drops; (ignorant Apothecaries tearme a kind of Rosen, great Incens, or* Thus; *and the right Incens,* Olibanum; *whereas* Olibanum *(in Greeke* Libanos*) and* Thus *be but one, and the same thing.)*
Oliette: f. *Poppie, Chesbolls, or Cheese-bowles.* ¶Wallon.
Oligarchie: f. *An Oligarchie; or, the absolute gouernment of a few principall men.*
Oligophore. Vin ol. *Weake, or small Wine; such as can beare but little water.*
Olimpiade. *as* Olympiade.
Olivaire: com. *Of an Oliue; like an Oliue.*
Cautere olivaire. *See* Cautere.
Olivastre: m. *A wild Oliue tree.*
Olive: f. *An Oliue; also, as* Canepetiere.
Olivete: f. *A ground, or groue of Oliue trees.*
Olivette: f. *A little Oliue; also, a little Oliue-bitt for a horse.*
Olivier: m. *An Oliue tree.*
Olivier domestic. *The manured Oliue tree.*
Olivier Ethyopic. *The wild Oliue tree of Ethyopia.*
Il a tous ses oliviers courans. *He hath his full swindge or libertie, he doth what he list.*
Olivot: m. *A great Oliue.*
Olle: f. *A seething pot.*
Ollonnes. *as* Aulonnes.
Olmeau: m. *A young, or little Elme.*
Olometre. *An Instrument wherewith all kind of dimẽsions are, or all a thing may be, measured.*
Olonne: f. *Canuas for the sayle of a ship; (as in* Aulonnes;*) and sometimes also the sayle it selfe.*
Olphe. *The Matt-rush, or Matt-weed.* ¶Provençal.
Olybrius: m. *The name of a swaggering Worthie, mentioned in some of the* Romans *(or old, and fabulous Poesies, or Histories) of* France.

Faire l'Olybrius: *To swagger, or play the terrible Roister; to pretend great furie, or talke as if no bodie were able to stand before him.*
Olympe. *Heauen (among Poets.)*
Olympiade: f. *An Olympiade; the space of foure yeares, or of fiftie moneths (each moneth containing thirtie dayes.*
Omaille: f. *Great cattell; as Oxen, Kine, &c.*
Omase: m. *The thicke, and fattie part of a Bullockes paunch; Some also take it for a fat Tripe, or Chitterling.*
Ombelle: f. *A little shadow; also, a fashion of little round fanne; or, as* Ombrelle.
Ombilic. *as* Vmbilic.
Ombilical. *as* Vmbilical.
Ombrage: m. *An vmbrage; a shade; a shadow; also, iealousie, suspition, an incling of; whence;*
Donner ombrage à. *To discontent; make iealous of, or put buzzes into the head of.*
Ombragé: m. ée: f. *Shaded, shadowed; couered; obscured, ouershadowed; also, put into a iealousie, or distrust.*
Ombragement: m. *A shading, or shadowing.*
Ombrager. *To shade, or shadow; to cast a shadow on, or giue shadow vnto; also, to couer, darken, obscure, ouercast; also, as* Donner ombrage à, *in* Ombrage.
Ombrageusement. *Obscurely, darkly, couertly; also, iealously; waywardly, skittishly.*
Ombrageux: m. euse: f. *Shadie, shadowie, couert, full of shade; obscure, darke; also, vmbragious; iealous, suspitious; also, giddie, skittish, bird-eyed, often starting, or starting at euerie feather.*
Ombraire: m. *An Vmbrello, or shadow.*
Ombre: f. *A shadow; also, a shade, or couert; also, a colour, cloake, vale, pretext, or pretence for; also, as* Vmbre.
Combatre son ombre. *To fight with his own shadow; to be angrie to no purpose, or take paines in striuing against no resistance; also, to deuise new matters, and afterwards inueigh against them; also, to reuile, or threaten, the absent.*
Courir apres son ombre. *To runne after his owne shadow; to spend his time verie madly.*
Luicter cõtre les ombres. *as* Combatre son ombre.
Se mettre à l'ombre des bouchons. *To shrowd himselfe vnder the shade of a Taphouse; to slip into a Tauern.*
Sous ombre d'asne entre chien au moulin: Prov. *Looke* Asne.
Il n'y a si petit buisson qui ne porte ombre: Prov. *The least bush hath it shadow; The like is;*
Vn poil fait ombre: Prov. *A haire makes a shadow; the smallest things haue their shadowes;* viz. *their vse, or some ornament.*
Ombré: m. ée: f. *Vmbred, or shadowed; (a tearme of Blason.)*
Ombrelle: f. *An Vmbrello; a (fashion of) round, and broad fanne, wherwith the Indians (and from them our great ones) preserue themselues from the heat of a scorching Sunne; and hence, any little shadow, fanne, or thing, wherewith women hide their faces frõ the Sunne.*
Ombreux: m. euse: f. *Shadowie, shading, full of shade; couert, close.*
Ombriere: f. *as* Ombrelle.
Ombroyer. *To shadow, to cast or yeeld a shadow.*
Omelette: f. *An Omelet, or Pancake of egges; Looke* Aumelette.
Omettre. *To omit; pretermit, baulke, ouerslip, ouerpasse; to neglect, forget; leaue out, leaue vndone.*
Omioteleftes. *Alike-sounding clauses, or closes.*
Omis: m. ise: f. *Omitted, pretermitted, baulked, ouerslipt, ouerpassed; neglected, forgotten; left out, left vndone.*
Omission: f. *An omission; baulking, ouer slip, ouerpassing; forgetting, or neglect of; a leauing out, or letting goe.*
Omitton: m. *as* Aumuce; *a furred Ornament worne by Cannons.*
Omniforme: com. *Of, or hauing, all kind of shapes.*
Omnigene: com. *Of all kinds; also, most kind.* ¶Rab.
Omnimode: com. *Infinite in meanes; of euerie way.*
Omnipotence: f. *Omnipotencie, almightinesse.*
Omnipotent. *Omipotent, almightie, all-able.*
Omopiates: f. *The shoulder-blades.* ¶Rab.
Omphacin. Huile omph. *Oyle made of greene, or vnripe Oliues.*
Omusse. *as* Aumuce.
On. *(Such a Particle as our One, or somewhat more generall, and the signe of a Verbe Impersonall, or impersonally vsed; whence;)* On dit, *men say, people talke, its reported;* &, on le voit par experience; *men see it, or we see it, by experience.*
Onagrier: m. ere: f. *Of a wild Asse.*
Le pas onagrier. *A verie swift pace; (for such a one hath the wild Asse.)*
Onc. *(An Aduerbe of time;) euer, at any time; also, neuer.*
Once: f. *An Ounce, in weight; also, the spotted Ounce, or Lynx.*
L'once de l'année. *A moneth.*
Oncial: m. ale: f. *Of, or belonging to, or weighing as much as, an Ounce; whence;*
Lettres onciales. *Huge letters, great letters.*
Oncle: m. *An Vncle.*
Celuy est biẽ mon oncle qui le ventre me comble: Pro. *He is my neerest friend that fills my bellie; or he is my kindest vnckle who doth feed me.*
Oncles: f. *as* Ongles.
Oncques. *(An Aduerbe of time) neuer.*
Onction: f. *Vnction, an annointing.*
Onction feable. *Seeke* Feable.
Huile d'onction. *The holie, or hallowed Oyle, vsed, by the Church of Rome, in Baptisme, & Extreame Vnction.*
Onctueux: m. euse: f. *Full of Ointments; also, annointing; also, oylie, fattie, greasie.*
Onctuosité: f. *Vnctuositie, oylinesse; greasinesse, fattinesse.*
Ond. D'ond. *Whence; whereby.* ¶Rab.
Iusques à dire d'ond venez vous. *Extreamely, exceedingly, excessiuely, vnmeasurably.* ¶Rab.
Onde: f. *A waue; billow, surge of the sea; also, the tumbling tricke of touching the ground with the hands, and then comming ouer topsie turuie, diuers times together.*
Camelot à ondes. *Water Chamlet.*
Bouillir vne onde. *To boyle a while, or but for one bubble, or a wallop or two.*
Ondé: m. ée: f. *Waued; surging, wauing; also, streaked, wrought, or cut, like waues.*
Ondée: f. *A great and suddaine fall of raine; a gush, or gust, of raine; a powre of raine.*
Ondelé: m. ée: f. *as* Ondé.
Ondeler. *To runne, or powre downe, by waues; or, as* Onder.
Ondelette: f. *A little waue, a small billow.*
Onder. *To waue; to make plaites, or streakes like waues; to worke, or flourish with waues.*
Ondette. *as* Ondelette.
Ondoyant: m. ante: f. *Wauing; surging, floating, swelling as, or with, billowes.*

L'Ondoyante plaine. *The Sea.*
Ondoyé: m. ée: f. *Waued, surged, floated; swolne with billowes.*
Ondoyement: m. *A wauing, surging, floating; a swelling with billowes; also, a dangling, flickering, or gentle mouing, in the wind.*
Ondoyer. *To waue; to surge; to rise in, or swell with billowes; also, to float; flicker, dangle, or moue gently, in the wind.*
Ondoyer vn enfant. *To christen a weake child priuately, or in a chamber.*
Oneraire: com. *Of burthen, for carriage, that may be laden; whence,* Nefs oneraires.
Onereux: m. euse: f. *Onerous, burthensome, heauie, weightie, chargeable.*
`A titre onereux. Acquerir vne maison &c, à titre onereux. *To buy a house, &c, thats lyable vnto an yearelie rent, annuitie, fine, or subiect vnto sundrie duties, or other charges.*
Onglade: f. *A scratch, or paw with, or the print, or marke of, nayles; a nayle-marke.*
Ongle: f. *The nayle (of a reasonable,) the claw, hoofe, or tallon (of an vnreasonable) creature.*
Ongle cabaline. *The hoofe of a horse; also, the hearb Horse-hoofe, Colts-foot, Fole-foot, Bull foot.*
Ongle odorant. Vnguis odoratus. *A long, small, and smooth shell (of a fish) vsed in perfumes.*
Ongle d'une rose. *The nayle, root, or white bottome of the flower of a Rose.*
Goutte sur l'ongle. Boire la goutte sur l'on. *To drinke all but a drop to couer the nayle with.*
Sang aux ongles. Il a du sang aux ongles. *He is resolute, valorous, couragious; there is good mettall, pith, or stuffe, in him.*
Conduire à l'ongle. *To finish, or bring vnto perfection; to leaue no iot vndone of.*
Coniecturant le lion par les ongles. *Ayming at the whole by a little part; or, as vnder* Lion.
Couper les ongles de prez à, & Rongner les ongles à. *To clip ones nayles somewhat neere; to hold him short, to weaken, or disarme him, to take away from him all meanes of doing harme.*
Il s'est rongné les ongles à l'estude de. *He hath beaten his braines exceedingly, or weakened his bodie extreamely, in the studie of, or care about.*
C'est belle bataille de chiens & des chats, chacun a des ongles: Prov. *Faire is the strife when both are arm'd alike.*
Onglé: m. ée: f. *Nayled; hoofed; clawed, talloned, furnished with nayles, &c.*
Onglée: f. *Ache of the fingers ends in extremitie of cold weather; also, a painefull slipping of the flesh from, or swelling of it ouer, the nayle; also, a web in a mans, and the Hawe in a horses, eye.*
Ongler. *To scratch, or marke with a nayle.*
Onglet: m. *A little nayle; hoofe, claw, or tallon.*
Onglons de pourceau. *Hogs-feet singed, then sodden vntill they be verie tender, then broyled on a gridiron till they be verie hard, and then boyled betweene two dishes with veriuice, vineger, pepper, and onyons.*
Onguent: m. *An vnguent, ointment, or oyle; any fat thing fit to annoint with.*
Onguent Apostolorum. *A certaine detersiue salue compounded of twelue Ingredients.*
Es petites boistes met on les bons onguens: Prov. *Men put in little boxes precious ointments; little men haue many times rare gifts.*
Onguentaire: com. *Of, or belonging to, ointments.*
Gland onguentaire. *See* Gland.
Onicocrite: m. *A Iudger of dreames.* ¶Rab.
Onicocritique: com. *Iudging of dreames.*
Oniropole: m. *An expounder of dreames.*
Onitide: f. *Wild Marierome, groue Marierome.*
Onocrotal: m. *A Swan-like bird that brayes like an Asse; (or as* Gouttreuse.)
Onogire. *Loose-strife, Willow hearbe, or hearbe Willow.*
Onomantie: f. *Diuination by names; also, the skill of repeating many names by the art of Memorie.*
Onomatopose: f. *The faining of a name; or a word made by a certaine sound.*
Onothomantie: f. *Diuination by a mans name.*
Onques. *(An Aduerbe of time;) neuer.*
Onques-mais. *Neuer, at no time, nor tyde.*
Onques-puis. *Neuer after, at no time after.*
Onse des doigts. *The fingers ends vnder the nayles.*
Onyche: m. *The Gemme called an Onix.*
Onymantie: f. *Diuination by Oyle, and Wax.* ¶Rab.
Onzain: m. *A small, or base coyne, worth* xj d Tourn.
Onze. *Eleuen.*
Cercher midi ou il n'y a qu'onze heures. *Looke vnder* Midi.
Onziesme. *The eleuenth.*
Opacité: f. *Opacitie, shadinesse, vmbrage, obscuritie, duskinesse, gloominesse, thick-darknesse.*
Opale: m. *The Opall stone.*
Opaque: com. *Duskie, gloomie, obscure, thicke and darke, or thicke-shadowing, blacke.*
Operateur: m. *An Operator, a worker; also, a Quacksaluer, Cheater, Imposter (called so at* Tours.)
Operatif: m. iue: f. *Operatiue, working.*
Operation: f. *An operation; worke; a working, doing, labouring, trauelling.*
Operer. *To operate, worke; labour, trauell; doe; act.*
Ophiase: f. *A sore which fretting the skin of childrens heads, maketh their haire fall off in diuers places; it commonly begins behind, and eats on forward vnto the forhead.*
Ophioctene. *A kind of the many-legd* Scolopendra, *and a mortall enemie to Serpents.*
Ophiogene: m. *The wild Parsenip called* Elaphoboscum, *or Harts fodder.*
Ophite: m. *A kind of marble spotted like a Serpent.*
Ophraye. *as* Orfraye.
Ophthalmie: f. *A (red, and painefull) inflammation of the vppermost skin of the eye, and consequently of the whole eye.*
Ophthalmiste: com. *The vttermost skin of whose eye is inflamed.*
Opiat. *as* Opion.
Opiate: m. *An Opiat; a cordiall Electuarie.*
Opier: m. *The Ople, water Elder, Dwarfe plane, Whitten tree.*
Opilation: f. *as* Oppilation.
Opiler. *Seeke* Oppiler.
Opinant. *Opining, deeming, censuring, deliuering his opinion.*
Conseillers opinans. *The Assistants of a Court.*
Opination: f. *An opination, opining, opinion-deliuering; also, opinion, iudgement, fancie, imagination; fame, reputation.*
Opiné: m. ée: f. *Opined; argued, discussed; censured, deliuered as an opinion.*
Opiner. *To opine; argue; censure; vtter his mind, say what he thinks, deliuer his opinion, or aduice, in.*
On opine. *Sentence is in giuing.*
Opineur: m. *An Opinor; one that deliuers his opinion.*

Opiniastre: com. *Opinionate, opiniatiue, obstinate, wilfull, selfe-willie, wedded to his owne humors, conceited of his owne iudgement, frowardly standing in a wrong, or ill opinion.*

Opiniastre comme vne mule. *As wilfull, or moodie, as a Mule.*

Opiniastrement. *Opiniatiuely, obstinately, wilfully, or as one thats wedded vnto his owne peruerted will.*

s'Opiniastrer. *To be opinionate, wilfull, obstinate; stiffly to maintaine, headily to stand in, or adhere vnto (an ill opinion.)*

Les fievres s'opiniastrerent sur moy. *Very much increased vpon me, or bent or setled themselues to afflict me.*

Opiniastreté: f. *Opiniatiuenesse, wilfullnesse, obstinacie, headinesse; a headstrong maintaining of, or persistance in, (an ill opinion.)*

Opiniastrie, & Opiniastrise. *as* Opiniastreté.

Opinion: f. *Opinion; thought, conceit, imagination; surmise, coniecture, supposall, guesse, weening; also, an opinion, aduise, or saw; and, a censure, sentence, doome, iudgement; also, the prettie game which we call Purposes.*

Autant de testes autant d'opinions. *As many men so many minds; as many humors as heads.*

Opion: m. Opium; *the hardened iuyce of garden Poppie heads.*

Opistographes: f. *Papers written vpon on both sides.* ¶Rab.

Opobalsame: m. Opobalsamum; *the gumme, or liquor which issueth from the wounded Balsame tree; Looke* Basme.

Opobasme. *as* Opobalsame.

Opocalpase: f. *A kind of poyson wherewith Mirrhe is (too often) sophisticated.*

Oportet. *(A Latin Impersonall) it ought; it must; whence;*

Quand oportet vient en place il n'est rien qui ne se face: Pro. *That which must be will be; absolute authoritie, or vrgent necessitie, are excellent workmen.*

Oppilatif: m. *Oppilatiue, obstructiue, stopping.*

Oppilation: f. *An oppilation, or obstruction.*

Oppilé: m. ée: f. *Obstructed, stopped, shut vp.*

Oppiler. *To stop, obstruct, shut vp.*

Opportun: m. une: f. *Timelie, seasonable, fit, right, conuenient; commodious.*

Opportunément. *Opportunely, timely, seasonably; fitly, conueniently; in good time, right in the nicke, iust when it should be.*

Opportunité: f. *Opportunitie; seasonablenesse; fitnesse of time, conueniencie of place; a good occasion.*

Opposant: m. *An Opposant, or Opponent; a resister, withstander; contradictor.*

Opposé: m. ée: f. *Opposed, resisted, withstood; obiected vnto, protested against.*

s'Opposer. *To oppose himselfe; to resist, withstand; gaincsay; to obiect, except, or protest, against.*

Opposite: com. *Opposite, aduerse, in opposition with, oueragainst; placed, put, set, or obiected, against.*

Opposition: f. *Opposition; resistance, withstanding; a crossing, or gainsaying; an obiection, exception, or protestation, against.*

Oppresse: f. *as* Oppression.

Oppressé: m. ée: f. *Oppressed; ouercharged, ouerlayed, weighed downe.*

Oppresser. *To oppresse; ouercharge, quayle, ouerlay, weigh downe, make sinke vnder the burthen of.*

Oppresseur: m. *An oppressor; ouercharger, ouerlayer; extreame dealer; one that sinkes poore people with exactions, or taxations.*

Oppression: f. *Oppression; ouercharging, ouerlaying; an vnreasonable surcharge; a grieuous burthen, taxation, exaction; or the imposing of any of them.*

Opprimer. *as* Oppresser.

Opprobre: m. *A reproach; a defamatorie taunt, rebuke, checke; a disgracefull twit, vpbraiding, reuiling; despightfull rayling.*

Opprobrier. *To reproach; to taunt, rebuke, checke despightfully; disgracefully to vpbraid, cast in the dish, twit in the teeth.*

Oppugnateur. *An oppugnator; assaulter, batterer, besieger; resister; wrong-doer.*

Oppugnation: f. *An oppugnation; assault, batterie; siege; open resistance.*

Oppugné: m. ée: f. *Oppugned; assaulted, battered, besieged; fought, or contended with; openly resisted.*

Oppugner. *To oppugne; batter, assault, besiege; resist, or withstand openly; fight hard, reason eagerly, labor earnestly, against.*

Opter. *To chuse, optate, elect; also, to wish, couet, desire.*

Opthalmie. *as* Ophthalmie.

Option: f. *Option, election, choice; also, a wish, or desire.*

Optique: f. *An Art whereby the reason of sight is knowne.*

Optique: com. *Of, or belonging to, the eye-sight.*

Nerfs optiques. *The sinewes from which the eyes receiue their sight.*

Opulemment. *Wealthily, richly, abundantly.*

Opulence: f. *Opulencie, wealth, riches; plentie, store, or abundance of meanes.*

Opulent: m. ente: f. *Opulent, wealthie, rich, well lyned, abundant in meanes.*

Opulentement. *as* Opulemment.

Opuscule: m. *A little Worke; small Booke, short Treatise.*

Or: m. *Gold.*

Or d'Allemaigne. *A kind of base Gold, the fist part whereof is Siluer.*

Or blanc. *as* Or d'Allemaigne.

Or de Clitie. *The Marigold.*

Or en paille, ou de paillole. *Spangle-Gold, or Gold beaten thinne for Spangles; Looke* Paillole.

Or de pepin. *Round, or massie graines of Gold.*

Or ras. *Smooth Gold, Venice stuffe.*

Or Tholosain. *A dismall, or vnluckie possession; (for euerie one that had it perished.)*

Or traict. *Gold wyre.*

Il est de bas or, il craind la touche. *He is a counterfeit, he feares to be tryed.*

Or est qui or vaut: Pro. *Tis Gold thats worth Gold.*

'A l'or le feu fort, au fort bras la luicte: Pro. *Looke* Bras.

Nul or sans escume. *No Gold without some drosse.*

Dans vne gaine d'or vn cousteau de plomb: Prov. *A base heart vnder a rich habit.*

Fy de plaisirs, d'estats, & d'or, qui de vertu n'a le thresor: Pro. *Looke* Fy.

Or. (Adverb.) *Now; but; on, goe to, well now.*

Or avant. *On forward, on afore there.*

Or bien. *Well now, well then, therefore.*

Or ça. *Now then, or goe to; Or by equiuocation (as in the hastie demaunds of* Grippeminaud;) *Gold here, cast Gold hether.*

Or donques. *Seeing then.*

Or primes. *Now at the length, not before now, but euen now, onely at this time, at this verie instant.*

Or si. *If then, since, or seeing that.*

Or

Or sus. *Goe too,on forward,well then.*
Oracle: m. *An Oracle; a sentence deliuered, an answer giuen, by God.*
Oraculeux: m.euse: f. *Oracle-like,true as the Gospell, infallible.*
Orade: f. *The Guilt-head; a sea-fish.*
Orage: m. *A storme,tempest,orage; outrage.*
Le vent,la tempeste, l'orage monstrent du nocher le courage: Pro. *Looke* Nocher.
Tousiours ne dure guerre,ne orage: Prov. *No violence,nor violent thing,lasts alwayes.*
Orager. *A tempest,or storme to rise.*
Orageux: m.euse: f. *Stormie,tempestuous,raging,outragious.*
Oraison: f. *Orison, prayer; also,a speech, language, discourse,communication; oration.*
Orange: f. *An Orange; also, a kind of pernicious fireball; also, a certaine fowle.*
Orangé: m.ée: f. *Orange-tawnie,Orange-coloured.*
Oranger: m. *An Orenge tree.*
Oraprimes. *as* Or primes.
Orateur: m. *An Orator; Spoakesman,Arguer,Pleader, Aduocate; Embassador.*
Oration: f. *An Oration,or Harang.*
Otatoire: m. *An Oratorie; a Closet,or priuate Chappell to pray in.*
Oratoire: com. *Oratorie,belonging to an Orator; of eloquence.*
Oratoirement. *Orator-like,eloquently.*
Orayn. *whilere.* ¶Picard.
Orbateur: m. *A Gold-beater.*
Orbatu: m. *Leafe-gold.*
Orbe: com. *Blind,sightlesse; wanting, or depriued of, sight; hence also,darke,obscure,without light.*
Coup orbe. *A dry blow; a blow that neither makes ouerture,nor fetches bloud.*
Orbiculaire: com. *Orbicular,circular,globie,compasse, round.*
Orbiculairement. *Orbicularly, circularly, in a round compasse or forme; globe-like.*
Orbiere: f. *A blinding-boord, or head-boord (hung before the eyes of an vnrulie beast.)*
Orbitaire: com. *Belonging,or like,vnto the* Orbite.
Orbité: f. *Orphanisme; lacke of parents; also, want of children; generally,any lacke,or want.*
Orbite: f. *The hole,or seat of the eye; the hole wherein an eye is placed.*
L'orbite d'une poulie. *The mortaise wherein the shiuer of a Pullie runnes.*
Orcanette. *as* Orchanette.
Orchades: f. *Great Ships; also,a kind of great fishes, mortall enemies to Whales.*
Orchal. *as* Archal.
Orchanette: f. *Orkanet,Alkanet,Spanish Buglosse,wild Buglosse.*
Orche. à orche. *On the left hand.* ¶Rab.
Orchenie: f. *A transposing.*
Orches. *as* Orchades. ¶Rab.
Orchestre: f. *The Senators, or Noblemens Place in a Theatre, betweene the Stage,and common Seats; also, the Stage it selfe.*
Ord: m. orde: f. *Filthie,nastie, foule, sluttish; durtie, berayed,ouglie,or loathsome to behold.*
Ordelot: m. otte: f. *Sullied, slubbered, stained, somewhat vncleane.*
Ordement. *Filthily,nastily, sluttishly, durtily,vncleanely, loathsomely.*
Ordi: m. ie: f. *as* Ourdi; *also, fouled,defiled,berayed, begrymed,foyled, slurried, slubbered.*
Ordinaire: m. *An Ordinarie; a Bishop (or his Chauncelor,&c) within his Diocesse; also, an Ordinarie Table,dyet, fare.*
Ordinaire: f. Les Ordinaires de Sorbonne. *Certaine disputations held among Sorbonnists before they commence Doctors.*
Ordinaire: com. *Ordinarie; common,vsuall; also,proper, peculiar, in ordinarie,of ones owne.*
Procez ordinaire. *A ciuill Action,Cause,or Suit.*
Ordinairement. *Ordinarily, vsually,commonly, of custome.*
Ordinateur: m. *An Orderer,Ordainer,Appointer.*
Ordinateur des Thresors. *The Lord high Treasurer of France; called so in* Philip *the faires time.*
Ordinatif: m. iue: f. *Ordinatiue; order-shewing, order-declaring; ordering.*
Ordir. *as* Ourdir; *also,to foule,defile,soyle, beray, bedurt,begryme, slubber,slurrie, sullie; blemish,distaine, inquinate, pollute.*
Ordisseure: f. *as* Ourdisseure; *also,a fouling,defiling, beraying, begryming, slubbering, sullying; distaining, polluting.*
Ordon: m. *A slouen; a filthie fellow; also,the ranke,or rowe which a Reaper hath vndertaken to goe on in.*
Ordonnance: f. *An Ordinance; Edict,Order,Decree, Statute, Institution, Constitution; a Precept,Appointment,Commaundement; also, a right, or due ordering, disposing, digesting,arraying, ranking,or marshalling of things.*
Engin de telle ordonnance. *Of such a bulke,size,or bore.*
Gens d'ordonnance,ou,Gensdarmes des ordonnances. *Looke* Gendarme.
Ordonnateur: m. *An ordainer, enacter, decreer; an orderer,disposer; enioyner,appointer of.*
Ordonné: m.ée: f. *Ordained,enacted, decreed,instituted; ruled,appointed,commaunded; ordered,digested, disposed,marshalled, raunged; arrayed; fitly placed; well furnished, in full equipage; armed, equipped, or fitted at all points.*
Ordonnément. *Orderly, fitly, handsomely, iust as it should be.*
Ordonner. *To ordaine,enact,order,decree; rule,determine; commaund,appoint; ranke,digest,marshall,range, dispose; array, prepare, furnish, prouide of necessaries; arme,equip,or fit at all points.*
Ordonneur: m. *An ordainer,author,enacter,appointer, commaunder; also,an orderer, disposer, marshaller, fit ranker of things.*
Ordonques. *Seeing then.*
Ordoyer. *as* Ordir. *To defile.*
Ordre de Vay. *The name of a verie small apple.*
Ordre: m. *Order; method, fashion; disposition; a rank, file, course, row, continuation; due place, or seat; fit state, or posture; also, the calling, degree, or estate of men; also,an Order,Societie,or Sect of religious men or women; also,a Companie,Fellowship,or Brotherhood of Knights,(tearmed) of the Order,and instituted by a Soueraigne Prince.*
Les ordres,ou les saints ordres. *Priesthood,the Ministerie; or the institution of a Priest,&c; holie Orders.*
Ordre de l'Anonciade. *An Order of Knighthood instituted in the yeare* 1350 *by* Amadeus *Earle of Sauoy.*
Ordre du croissant. *The Order of the halfe Moone,instituted by* René *Duke of Aniou* Anno 1464.
Ordre du S. Esprit. *The Order of the holie Ghost; by* Henry troisiéme, *in the yeare* 1579.

Ordre de S. Estienne. *The Order of S. Stephen; by a Duke of Florence in the yeare 1560.*
Ordre de l'Estoille. *The Order of the Starre; by John King of France in the yeare 1351. Looke* Estoille.
L'Ordre de France. *The Order of S. Michael.*
L'Ordre de la genette. *The Order of the Gennet; instituted long agoe by* Charles Martel *(the grandfather of* Charlemaine) *and now cleane out of date.*
L'Ordre de la Iartiere. *The Order of the Garter; by Edward the third in the yeare 1344.*
Ordre de S. Michel. *The Order of S. Michael; by Lewis the eleuenth in the yeare 1469. (There were two sorts of it; viz.* Le grand, & le petit Ordre; *The Knights of that sort wore a collar of massie gold, of this onely a silke ribbon.)*
Ordre du porcespic. *The Order of the Hedgehog; instituted by Lewis Duke of Orleans, and the brother of Charles the sixt.*
Les Ordres du Roy. *Both the Orders of S. Michael, and of the holie Ghost.*
Ordre de la toison d'or. *The Order of the golden Fleece; instituted by Philip the second Duke of Burgundie, in the yeare 1430.*
Ordre de la Vierge Marie. *The Order of the Virgine Marie; was instituted by John King of France in the yeare 1365.*
Il n'y a point d'ordre d'avoir fait cela. *There was no reason, nor equitie in that act; there was no sence to doe it.*

Ordure: f. *Ordure, filth, durt; nastinesse, impuritie, pollution.*
Il y a de l'ordure dans leurs fleustes. *They are somewhat too blame; all is not right with them; something is amisse among them.*
Truye ne songe qu'ordure: Pro. *A Sow dreames of nought but of durt.*

Oré: m. ée: f. *Prayed unto; besought, implored.*
Le Ieudi, & Vendredi orez. *Holie Thursday, good Friday; Thursday and Friday in the Passion weeke.*
Le Sainct de la ville n'est point oré: Prov. *We seldome craue the helpe of our owne Patron.*

Orée: f. *The side of a River (or a Rivers side;) the sea shore, or strand; the skirt, coast, edge, or border of any place, &c; also, a shower of raine.*

Oreille: f. *An eare; also, attention giuen; also, free, or plausible audience gotten.*
Oreille d'asne. *Comfrey, Knitbacke, Blackwort; Looke* Asne.
Oreilles du cœur. *The Auricles of the hart; two small peeces of flesh growing to the bottome of the heart; and seruing it, as funnels, to receiue bloud from the hollow veine; and as eares, to let in and out the ayre which the lungs haue prepared for it.*
Oreille de Iudas. *The Mushrome, or excrescence called, a Iewes eare.*
Oreille de lievre. *Scorpionwort, or Scorpiongrasse; also,* Buplurum, *or Hares eare; also, a mizzen, or smacke sayle.*
Oreille marine, ou de mer. *A kind of Oyster.*
Oreille d'ours. *Beares-eare; a kind of mountaine Cowslip.*
Oreille de rat. *as* Oreille de souris.
Oreilles d'un soulier. *The latchets of a shooe.*
Oreille de souris. Pilosella, *Mouse-eare; also, a kind of Chickweed, or hearbe resembling Chickweed, called, the right Mouse-eare.*
Conseiller de son oreille. *A Counsellor that hath his Princes eare; or, one whose discourse, or aduice is most plausible to the Princes eare.*
Fer de flesche à oreilles. *A forked, or barbed arrowhead.*
Haut d'oreilles. *Somewhat deafe; thicke of hearing.*
Pendant d'oreille. *A Pendant;* Pendant d'oreille de gibet. *The furniture of a gibbet; a man that hangs on a gibbet, or would become one passing well.*
L'oreille au vent. *Attentiue, listening seriously.*
`A vne oreille. *Said of Wine, thats excellent good; of Taffata, which is but slight, or single.*
Avoir l'oreille de. *To haue at all times free accesse vnto, and a willing attention from; to be a principall fauorite of.*
Il en a iusques aux oreilles. *He is vp to the eares in, or hath his whole fill of.*
Chauver des oreilles. *Looke* Chauver.
Dresser les oreilles. *To list, set, or pricke vp the eares; to prepare, or settle them to attention.*
Sac plein dresse les oreilles: Pro. *A full purse, or fat bribe, commaunds attention.*
Endormir sur l'une, & l'autre oreille. *To sot with ease, or delights; to bring a bed.*
Faire l'oreille sourde. *To be deafe of that eare.*
Mettre le bouquet sur l'oreille à. *To expose vnto sale; See* Bouquet.
Mordre l'oreille à. *See* Mordre.
Partir les oreilles. *To heare both sides.*
Pendre à l'oreille. Autant luy en pend à l'oreille. *He is the more to blame, or hath the more to answere for.*
Rompre les oreilles à. *To trouble with ouermuch, or ouerlowd prating.*
Tirer l'oreille. Ils ne se feronr gueres tirer l'oreille. *They need no long intreatie; they will be easily inuited, soone persuaded, quickly drawne, vnto it.*
`A beau parler closes oreilles: Pro. *Oppose to glosing words a closed eare.*
`A paroles lourdes sourdes oreilles: Prov. *Heedlesse attention vnto hoggish tearmes.*
Bois ont oreilles, & champs oeillets: Pro. *(Wherein the Jewes-eare-Mushrome is the woods eare.) Looke* Oeillet.
Ventre affamé n'a point d'oreilles: Prov. *The hungrie bellie hath no eares.*

Oreillé: m. ée: f. *Eared; well hung, or hangd; which hath great eares.*

Oreiller: m. *A pillow (for the head.)*
Tenir la teste sur l'oreiller. *To slug it, or loll it, a bed; to lye ouerlong in bed; to liue slouthfully, drowsily, retchlesly, carelesly.*

Oreiller. *To hearken, listen, giue eare, or attention vnto.*
Orphée oreilloit les rocs. *Orpheus gaue eares, or hearing, vnto rocks.*

Oreillere: f. *An Earewig.*

Oreillet: m. *An Earing; also, the eare-peece of an helmet, &c; the flap, or peece that couers the eare.*

Oreillette: f. *A little eare; also, an earing, or small toy to hang at the eare.*

Oreilleur: m. *A harkener, or listener.*

Oreilleure: f. *An Earing.*

Oreillier: m. *as* Oreiller.

Oreillon: m. *A little eare; also, the handle, or eare of a porrenger, &c; also, a box, or cuff on the eare; also, an impostume, or swelling about an eare; whence;*
Les oreillons. *The Mumpes; or mourning of the Chine.*
Les oreillons d'un fer de javeline. *The forks, barbs, or iags of the head of a Iauelin.*

Oren-

Orendroit. *Now, or, about this time.*
Orer. *To pray; beseech, implore, desire.*
Ores. *Now, at this time.*
D'ores en avant. *Hence forward, from this time forth.*
Orfanité: f. *Orphanisme; the state of an Orphan.*
Orfanté: f. *as* Orfanité; *Also, barrennesse, want, or depriuation of children.*
Orfaverisé: m. ée: f. *as* Orfavrisé.
Orfaveriser. *To worke Goldsmithes worke, to play the Goldsmith.*
Orfavrerie: f. *as* Orfevrerie.
Orfavrisé: m. ée: f. *Wrought with Goldsmithes worke.*
Orfavriser. *as* Orfaveriser.
Orfe: f. *A kind of daintie Sea-Ruffe, or Sea-Pearch.*
Orfebvre. *Looke* Orfevre.
Orfelin: m. ine: f. *Orphan, fatherlesse and motherlesse, without parents.*
Orfenin. *as* Orfelin.
Orfevre: m. *A Goldsmith.*
Orfevre de la terre. *A Gardener; so tearmed of the excellencie of his worke, wherein he surpasses th'ordinarie Husbandman as farre as the Goldsmith a Blacksmith.*
Orfevré: m. ée: f. *Wrought with Goldsmithes worke.*
Orfevrerie: f. *The Goldsmithes trade, or worke.*
Orfevresse: f. *A Goldsmithes wife, or woman Goldsmith.*
Orfevreux: m. euse: f. *Furnished with, or trauelling in, Goldsmithes worke; also, full of Goldsmithes.*
Orfevrie. *as* Orfevrerie.
Orfrais: m. *Broad welts, or gards of gold, or siluer imbroiderie laid on Copes, and other Church-vestements: In old time the Jackets, or Coat-armours of the Kings Gard were tearmed so, because they were couered with Goldsmithes worke.*
Orfraiz. *as* Orfrais; *also, as* Orfraye.
Orfraye: m. *The great, and greedie water-fowle called an Osprey.*
Orfres: f. *Buds, &c; as* Boutons.
Organe: m. *An Organ, or Instrument wherewith any thing may be made, or done.*
Organique: com. *Organicall, instrumentall, vsed as a meanes.*
Veines Organiques. *Looke* Veine.
Organiste: m. *An Organist; one that vsually playes on a paire of Organs.*
Organiste: com. *as* Organique.
Orgasine: m. *An extreame fit, or expression of anger.*
Orge: m. *Barlie.*
Orge emondé. *Naked Barlie; a kind of Barlie whose huske, when it is ripe, falls from it of it selfe.*
Orge mondé. *The same; also, French Barlie, or pilled and cleansed Barlie; also, pottage, or pap made thereof; Barlie pottage.*
Orge de muraille. *Wild Barlie, purre Barlie, way Barlie, way Bennet.*
Orge paumé. *Beere Barlie, big Barlie, Barlie with the square eare.*
Orge Pelé. *as* Orge mondé.
A grain d'orge. *In a triangle forme.*
Faire leurs orges. *To make their market, or make vp their mouthes.*
L'argent quand l'orge. *One for another (is faire play.)*
Semer vn grain d'orge pour attrapper vn pigeon. *To giue, or loose a little in hope of getting much.*
Orgée: f. *Barlie gruell; Furmentie, or pottage of Barlie.*

Orge-mondé: m. ée: f. *Made of French Barlie, or naked Barlie.*
Orgeol: m. *A long wart resembling a Barlie corne, and growing on th'edge, or corner of an eye-lid.*
Orgie: f. *A fadome.*
Orgies: m. *The Sacrifices of Bacchus.*
Orgoose. Licisque orgoose. *A salt bitch:* ¶Rab.
Orgueil: m. *A rowler, or, a round truncheon laid vnder a great stone, or peece of timber, for the more easie remouing thereof; also, as* Orgeol; *whence the Prouerbe;*
Qui refuse à vne femme enceincte, vn orgueil luy vient à l'oeil.
Orgueil: m. *Pride, swelling disdaine, statelinesse, hautinesse, loftinesse of mind, surlinesse, arrogancie, surquedrie.*
Orgueil n'a pas bon oeil: Prov. *He scuruily lookes that proudly lookes; or, as in* Oeil.
Il n'est orgueil que de povre enrichi: Prov. *There is no pride vnto th'inriched begger.*
Orgueilleusement. *Proudly, surlily, scornefully, arrogantly.*
Orguilleux: m. *as* Orgeol.
Orgueilleux: m. euse: f. *Proud, surlie, swelling; puft vp with a conceit of his owne worth; statelie, hautie, loftie-minded; scornefull, disdainefull.*
Muscle orgueilleux. *A muskle in th'vpper part of the cheeke, neere to the hollow seat of th'eye, which it drawes towards the temples.*
Orgueilleuse semblance monstre folle cuidance: Prov. *An hautie looke argues a fond presumption.*
Deux orgueilleux ne peuvent estre portez sur vn Asne: Prov. *Looke* Asne.
Il n'est si grand despit que de povre orgueilleux: Prov. *A proud begger is the despightfullest creature aliue.*
Orgueilli: m. ie: f. *Growne proud, statelie, surlie, puft vp with pride, swollen with disdaine.*
s'Orgueillir. *To wax proud, grow surlie, become statelie, take much state vpon him.*
Orgues: f. *Organs; wind-instruments; also, Barges for carriage, Westerne Barges; also, a kind of small Artillerie.*
Dire d'orgues. vous dites d'orgues. *You say blew; how say you to that; wisely brother Timothie; true Roger; did am did am.*
Iouër des orgues. *To play the lasciuious wanton, to leacher.*
Oribus. Compere d'oribus. *A superficiall, or hollow-hearted friend, or companion.*
Pouldre d'oribus. *Powder of proiectiõ, or of the Philosophers stone; tearmed thus (in derision, and) because much gold hath beene wasted in the searching for it; thence also, any cousening, or iugling powder.*
Orichal. *as* Archal.
Orient: m. *Th'Orient, East, or East part of the world; the Sunne-rise.*
Oriental: m. ale: f. *Orientall, Easterlie; orient, bright, cleere.*
Orienté: m. ée: f. Maison bien orientée. *A house well set toward th'East; or whose forefront is made Eastward.*
Vne pierre bien orientée. *Verie Orient, or Orientall.*
Oriere: f. *as* Orée.
Orifice: m. *Th'orifice; mouth, brimme, or entrance into, a thing.*
Oriflam. *as* Oriflambe.
Oriflambe. *The great, and holie Standerd, of France;*

borne

borne at first onely in warres made against Infidells; but afterwards vsed in all other warres; and at length vtterly lost in a battell against the Flemings.

Oriflant: m. *An Elephant.*

Origan: m. *Garden Organie, Spanish Origan, wild or bastard Marierome, English wild Marierome.*

Origan de Candie. *Bastard or wild Marierome of Candie.*

Origan commun. *English wild Marierome.*

Origan Heracléen. *Bastard Marierome.*

Origan Onite. *White bastard Marierome.*

Origan sauvage. *Wild Organie, groue Marierome.*

Orige. *Th'Orix; a fierce and cruell wild Goat; of a pale white colour, and a haire falling backwards to his hinder parts, and forward to his headwards; and hauing blacke, vpright, strong, and sharpe-pointed horns, wherewith he often kills the most valiant hunters, or beasts, that pursue, or assault, him.*

Originaire: com. *Originarie, naturall vnto, his from the beginning.*

Les originaires de la ville. *Such as were bred, and borne in the towne.*

Originairement. *Originarily, originally.*

Original: m. *An originall; the first authentick, or true draught of a writing.*

Originalement. *Originally, from the beginning.*

Origine: f. *An originall; a birth, beginning, ofspring; stocke, pedegree, kindred; a ground, cause, head, fountaine, welspring.*

Originellement. *Originally.*

Orillier. *Seeke* Oreiller.

Orillons: m. *The Mumps, or an impostumous swelling behind the eares.*

Orin: m. ine: f. *Golden, of gold.*

Orine. *as* Origine.

Oriol. *as* Oriot.

Orion: m. *A thumpe, dust, cuffe, rap, knocke; also, a number of mischiefes, a multitude of euills; also, a certaine Signe of starres in the firmament.*

Oriot: m. *A Heighaw, or Witwall.*

Oripeau: m. *Base gold, leafe gold, false gold, Orpine, Painters gold; such gold as is laid on hangings, &c, of leather, &c.*

Oripilation. ¶Rab. *Looke* Horripilation.

Orizon. *as* Horison.

Orle: f. *A hemme, seluidge, or (narrow) border; in Blazon, an Vrle, or open border about, and within, a coat of Armes.*

Orlé: m. ée: f. *Hemmed, seluidged; welted, or bordered.*

Orlement: m. *A hemming, seluidging; welting, bordering.*

Orler. *To hemme, seluidge; border; welt th'edges, or sides of.*

Orlet. *A little hemme, seluidge; welt, border.*

Orlure: f. *A hemme, or hemming; seluidge, or seluidging; border, or bordering.*

Ormaire. *as* Armaire.

Ormaye: f. *A groue of Elmes.*

Orme: m. *An Elme tree.*

Orme blanc. *The white Elme, yoake Elme, Hornebeame, hard Beame tree.*

Orme champestre. *Th'ordinarie Elme.*

Orme de montaigne. *The mountaine Elme; or, the great broad-leaued Elme.*

Orme sauvage. *as* Orme de montaigne.

Vn Advocat dessous l'orme. *An obscure Lawyer; a pratling, or pidling Pettifogger.*

Iuge dessous l'orme. *The Judge of a village; an inferiour Judge; Looke* Iuge.

Ormeau: m. *A little, or young, Elme tree.*

Ormeteau. *as* Ormeau.

Orne: f. *The furrow made by a plough; the deepe rut, or tracke made by a cart wheele, in the ground.*

Il conduisoit sourdement cette orne. *Hee carried this businesse verie closely; he handled it so as few had notice, or got any inkling, of it.*

Orné: m. ée: f. *Decked, adorned, trimmed, tricked, garnished, imbellished, beautified, graced; gaily arrayed, gallantly furnished, finely set forth.*

Ornemént: m. *An ornament, grace, beautie, imbellishment; rich, or comelie garnishment, goodlie furnishment, faire attire; also, an adorning, decking, trimming, tricking.*

Ornément. *Neatly, trimly, finely, gallantly, beautifully, gracefully.*

Orneomantie: f. *Diuination by the mouing of birds.*

Orner. *To decke, adorne, trimme, tricke; beautifie, grace, garnish, imbellish; to set out finely, attire gallantly, furnish gaily.*

Ornier: m. ere: f. *Full of ruts, worne with many tracts.*

Orniere: f. *The rut, or tract of a cart wheele, &c.*

Ornithogalon. *Starre of Bethelem (an hearbe.)*

Orobe: m. *Orobus; the bitter Vetch, or Fitch.*

Oroer: m. *as* Oratoire; *An Oratorie.*

Orologeur: m. *A Clocke-maker, Watch-maker, Dyall-maker.*

Oroscope: m. *The Horoscope, or Ascendant, of a Natiuitie; Looke* Horoscope.

Orpeau. *as* Oripeau; *or as*;

Orpel: m. *Siluer and by-gold; a kind of leafe-tinne, vsed in the siluering ouer of trifles for children.*

Orphanité. *as* Orfanité.

Orphe: f. *A kind of daintie sea Ruffe, or sea Pearch.*

Orphée: f. *as* Orphie.

Orphelin. *Seeke* Orfelin.

Orphelinage: m. *Orphanage; the state of an Orphan; a being (young, and) without parents.*

Orphie: f. *The Hornebeake, Hornekecke, Piper-fish, Garre-fish.*

Orpigment: m. *as*;

Orpiment: m. *Orpiment, or Arsenicke; a golden-coloured poison, or drug, found verie deepe in the earth.*

Orpimenter. *To mingle, or colour, with Orpiment.*

Orpin: m. *Orpine, Liblong, or Liue-long; an hearbe; also, Orpine, Orpiment, or Arsenicke; a drug.*

Orpin rouge. *Red Arsenicke; a bright-red colour found in gold, and siluer mines.*

Orprimes. *Looke* Or.

Orque: f. *A Hulke, or huge ship; also, the Ourke, a seamonster, enemie to the Whall; (sometimes) also, the graue, or hell.*

Orteil: m. *A toe.*

Orthodoxe: com. *Orthodox, orthodoxall; of a right faith, true beliefe, sound opinion.*

Orthogoiné: m. ée: f. *Right cornered.*

Orthogonal: m. ale: f *Orthogonall, right cornered.*

Orthopnoïque: com. *One whose light-pipes are so obstructed, or straitned, that he cannot breath but when he holds his necke vpright.*

Ortie: f. *A Nettle; the common Nettle, female Nettle, great Nettle.*

Ortie blanche. *The hearbe Archangell, blind Nettle, dead Nettle.*

Ortie bruslante. *The small Nettle, or small burning Nettle.*

Ortie cendrée. *A kind of the sea Nettle.*
Ortie Grecque. *The Greeke Nettle, Roman Nettle, male Nettle; some also call the small red Nettle so.*
Ortie griesche. *The small stinging red Nettle; or as* Grecque.
Ortie de mer. *The sea Nettle; an ouglie (but verie daintie) fish, which being touched, prickes like a Nettle.*
Ortie morte. *as* Ortie blanche.
Ortie puante. *The stinking blind Nettle, or dead Nettle; a kind of Archangell that smells most filthily.*
Ortie Romaine. *The Romane Nettle, Italian Nettle, male Nettle, Greeke Nettle.*
Ortie rouge. *as* Posterol; *Also, the red Nettle.*
Petite ortie. *The small Nettle, or small burning Nettle.*
Asne d'Arcadie broute chardons, & ortie, quoy que tout chargé d'or: Prov. *Appliable to a rich, and most wretched penie-father; one that all the yeare long bestowes not a bit of good meat on himselfe.*
Ortié: m. ée: f. *Nettled; pricked, or stung with Nettles.*
Ortier. *To nettle, to pricke, or sting with Nettles.*
Ortieur: m. *A nettler.*
Ortigue: f. *as* Ortie de mer.
Ortographié: m. ée: f. *Ortographised, written rightly.*
Ortographier. *To Ortographise; to write, or use, true Ortographie.*
Ortrait. *as* Retraict; *A Priuie, or Jakes.*
Orval: m. *An inconuenience; also, as* Orvale.
Orvale: f. *The hearbe Clarie, or Cleere eye.*
Orvale sauvage. *Wild Clarie, double Clarie, Ocle Christi.*
Oryarris. *as* Hourvaris; *Also, the crie of Huntsmen vnto their dogs, being at a default.*
Orver, & Orvier: m. *A Snake.*
Os: m. *A bone; also, the stone of a Date, Oliue, Peach, Plumme, &c; also, the Garguill, or Dew-claw of a Stag, Bucke, Roe, &c.*
Os barré. *The second part of* Os Ilium, *not so broad as the first, and hauing on each side a large hole.*
Os basilaire. *The Nape, or Nuke-bone; the bone wherby all the parts of the head are supported; some call it the Cuneall bone, because it is, wedge-like, thrust in betweene the bones of the head, and th'vpper Jaw.*
Os Bertrand. *The share-bone; the coniunction of the two great bones whereto the thigh-bones are fastened.*
Os Bregmatis. *Two trianguler bones in th'vpper part of the skull.*
Os de coeur de cerf. *The bone of a Stags heart; is found in the left side thereof (onely betweene the middle of August, and 12 of September) and is good against th'Emrods, and the trembling of the heart.*
Os conjugal. *Th'outward part, or end of the cheeke-bone towards the eare.*
Os corbin. *A certaine hollow bone in the rumpe, or crupper of a Deere.*
Os coronal. *The forhead bone.*
Os du coulde. *Th'vnder, and lesse bone of the cubit.*
Os couloir du nez. *The head-bone, or inner bone of the nose.*
Os cribleux. *as* Os Etmoïde.
Os cuneiforme. *The Cuneall, or fundamentall bone of the head.*
Os Cyboïde. *One of the bones of th'instup.*
Os Eshonté. *as* Os frontal.
Os de l'esperon. *The lesse of the two shanke bones.*
Os Etmoïde. *A bone full of little holes, and seated betweene the forhead bone, and the top of the nose.*
Os de la fesse. *The hip-bone, or huckle-bone.*
Os frontal. *The forhead bone.*
Os furculaires. *The points of the shoulder bones forepart, meeting a little below the necke.*
Os de la greue. *The shinne-bone, or bigger bone of the leg.*
Os de la hanche. *The third part of* Os Ilium; *it selfe consisting also of three parts.*
Os hyoïde. *A bone in the root of the tongue, fashioned like a Greeke Ypsilon.*
Os de la jambe. *as* Os de la greue.
Os des Iles. *Is ioyned to the transuerse processes of the sacred bone; and diuided by Anatomists into three parts; the first whereof (being the highest, and broadest) retaines this name, th'other two are called otherwise.*
Os jougal. *as* Os conjugal.
Os maxillaires. *Th'vpper Jaw bones; those whereinto the teeth are set; in men there are but two of them discerned, in beasts foure.*
Os naviculaire. *The second bone of th'instup; tearmed thus because tis fashioned somewhat like a boat.*
Os occipital. *The noddle bone; of an Ouall forme, and seated in the hinder part of the head.*
Os de l'orbite. *The whole cheeke-bone confining on the bottome, and outside of the eye; or the bone which incloses the eye.*
Os parietal. *A certaine bone in th'vpper, and forepart of the scull, neere to the Coronall suture.*
Os du penillier, ou du penil. *as* Os barré.
Os petreux, ou pierreux. *The bone of the temples.*
Os de la pommette. *The cheeke-bone.*
Os de la pouppe de la teste. *The forhead bone.*
Os du Rayon. *Th'vpper, and bigger of the two bones of the cubit.*
Os sacré. *The great bone whereupon the ridge-bone resteth.*
Os sans nom. *A certaine great bone which containes three others; viz.* Os des Iles, Barré, & de la hanche; *also, the three bones whereby the three great toes are sustained.*
Os scaphoïde. *The skiffe-bone; or as* Os naviculaire.
Os de seiche. *A certaine marrowie, and spungie bone in the backe of the Cuttle fish, vsed by Physitians, and Goldsmithes, for cleansing, and drying purposes.*
Os du sens commun. *The forhead bone.*
Os sesamoïdes. *Certaine little flat bones wherewith the ioynts of the fingers, and toes are filled, setled, and strengthened; their number is vncertaine, and their name they haue of the oylie graine* Sesame, *the which they somewhat resemble.*
Os de la sousgreve. *The lesse bone of the leg.*
Os sphenoïde. *The fundamentall, or Cuneall bone of the head.*
Os spongieux. *The spungie bone; seated in the bottome of the forhead bone, hard aboue the nose; and full of holes like a spunge.*
Os de la temple, ou temporal. *The bone of the temples; a round bone in the side of the head.*
Os zigoma. *The end, or outward part of the cheeke-bone towards the eare; called thus at Paris.*
A vn autre chien avec cet os. *Allure some other with that bait; intice another with that pleasure, treasure, offer.*
Perdre la chair pour les os. *To loose the flesh for the bones;*

bones; to leaue essentiall, for most idle, things.
'A bon chien bon os: Prov. *Looke* Chien.
'A vn bon chien n'escheut onques vn bon os: Pro. *The honester a man is the lesse is his preferment; the worse his lucke.*
Deux chiens ne s'accordent point à vn os: Prov. *Two dogs, and a bone, agree not in one.*
Qui a mangé le lard ronge l'os: Prov. *Let him that hath eaten the best feed on the worst; or, he that hath fondly wasted his best flesh, will be faine, at length, to picke the bones.*
Souvent à mauvais chien tombe vn bon os en gueule: Prov. *The veriest knaue hath oftentimes best lucke.*
Osche, & Oscher. *Looke* Oche, & Ocher.
Oscines: com. *Singing birds; those especially which presage ought by their singing:* ¶Rab.
Oscitation: f. *A gaping, yawning, sloath, idlenesse; negligence, retchlesnesse.*
Osé: m. ée: f. *Dared; presumed; aduentured.*
Oser. *To dare, presume, aduenture; haue the heart, or be so bold as, to doe a thing.*
Oseraye: f. *A groue, or ground of Oziers.*
Osereux: m. euse: f. *Full of; made with, Oziers.*
Oseur: m. *A hater; loather, detester.*
Osier: m. *The Ozier, red Withie, water Willow tree; also, Wicker; also, a basket of Wicker; also, a rod or twig of Ozier, or of any other such pliant wood.*
Franc Osier. *The small Withie, twig Withie, Ozier withie, Spert.*
Osiereux: m. euse: f. *as* Osereux.
Osmonde: m. *Osmund, Osmund the water man, Osmund Royall, water Fearne, S. Christophers hearbe.*
Osmonde royal. *The same.*
Ossailler. *To set, or worke, with bone.*
Ossaillerie: f. *Bone-worke; bone-stuffe; also, a working with bone.*
Ossas: m. *A great thicke bone.*
Ossé: m. ée: f. *Bonie, made of bone.*
Ossec. *as* Lossec.
Osselet: m. *A little bone.*
Osselets. *The game tearmed Cockall, or Huckle-bones.*
Batre le tambour à coups d'osselets. *To play at dice, or huckle-bones on a drummes head.*
Ossemens: m. *Bones; also, the stones of Apricocks, Peaches, Dates, &c.*
Osset. *as* Osselet.
Ossu: m. uë: f. *Bonie, big-boned, full of bones.*
Ost: m. *An Hoast, or Armie.*
Ost banni. *as* Ban & Arriereban.
Aide de l'ost. *Th'assistance a vassall is bound to yeeld vnto his Lord, either by prouiding him of men, or furnishing him with money, when he goes to the warres.*
Seruice de l'ost. *Is (especially) the vassalls personall attendance on his Lord vnto the warres.*
Les Vivres suivent l'ost: Prov. *Looke* Vivres.
Ostade: f. *The stuffe Worsted, or Woosted.*
'A demy ostade. *Cut in panes, &c, like a Spanish leather Jerkin; (a Gascon phrase.)*
Ostadine: f. *Sattin of Cypres.*
Ostage: m. *An hostage, or pledge; a suretie, or gage; Looke* Hostage.
Ostager: m. *One thats deliuered in hostage.*
Ostager: m. *To take in pledge, or for a pledge; to receiue as an hostage.*
Ostarde: f. *A Bustard.*
Osté: m. ée: f. *Taken or carried away, remoued, withdrawne.*
Ostel. *as* Hostel.
Ostement: m. *A remouing, or taking away.*
Ostenseur: m. *Th'index, or hand of an Astrolabe.*
Ostension: f. *A shewing.*
Ostentateur: m. *An ostentator, boaster, bragger, vaunter.*
Ostentation: f. *Ostentation, bragging, boasting, vaunting, cracking.*
Ostentatrice: f. *An ostentatrix, braggardesse, boasting woman.*
Oster. *To remoue, withdraw; pull, take, or carrie away; to put off; bereaue, or depriue of; to lay, or get aside; to discharge, or deliuer; driue, or expell, from.*
Ostez vous de là. *Beware of that, no more of that if you loue me; also, get you hence, lets see your backe.*
Oste-vent: m. *A Porch or Portall contriued, a peece of cloth hung, or set vp, before a doore, to keepe off the wind, &c; also, a penthouse.*
Ostiere: f. *A Spittle, or Hospitall; whence;*
Vn gueux de l'ostiere. *A rogue, vagabond, or Spittle begger.*
Ostize. *A rent henne, &c, paid, or deliuered, in lieu of a dwelling house.*
Ostracisme: m. *Ten years banishment, wherewith the Athenian State allayed th'immoderate power of their great men.*
Ostruce: f. *An Ostridge.*
Otarde: f. *A Bustard.*
Otardeau: m. *A young Bustard.*
Otruche: f. *Maisterwort, false Pellitorie of Spaine.*
Ottelles. *Ottells, or Oates (in Blazon.)*
Ottroy. *Looke* Octroy.
Où. *(accented, an Aduerb) Where, whither, in what place; also, whereas.*
D'où. *Whence; of or from what place; also, whereof; as in this Prouerbe.*
Non d'où tu es, mais d'où tu pais. *Respect not whence thou commest, but whereof thou liuest.*
Ou. *(without accent, a Disiunctiue) Or, or else, either.*
Ou. *in some old Authors is vsed in stead of* Au.
Oüaille: f. *A sheepe.*
Oüaine: f. *A sheath:* ¶Pic.
Oüaire: m. *A great leather bottle, or budget like a bottle, for oyle, or drinke, to be kept, or carried in; (tis commonly made of a Goats skin, and the hairie side sometimes turned inward.)*
Oval: m. ale: f. *Ovall, shaped like an egge.*
Ovale: f. *An Ovall; an egge-like shape, or forme; a peece of worke fashioned like an egge.*
Oüan: m. *A gloue:* ¶Pic.
Oüan. *The last yeare; (an old word.)*
Oüarir. *as* Guarir: ¶Pic.
Ovation: f. *A small triumph granted to a Commaunder, that had gotten a bloudlesse victorie.*
Oüazon. *as* Glazon: ¶Pic.
Oubier: m. *The sap, white, or softest part of wood, subiect to worme-eating.*
Oublayerie: f. *The making of Wafers.*
Oublayeur: m. *A Wafer-maker.*
Oubli: m. *Obliuion, forgetfulnesse.*
Oubliages. *Certaine annuall rents due vnto some particular Canons of* Nostre Dame de Gracay en Berri.
Oubliance: f. *Obliuion, forgetfulnesse.*
Oubliant. *Obliuious, forgetfull; also, forgetting.*
Oublie: f. *A Wafer cake; such a one especially as is sweetened onely with honie; also, the thinne past that serues for the bottomes of Tartes, and March-panes.*

Droict d' oublie. *Is, in some places, a rent Capon hauing a* Douzain,or Sol,*in his mouth.*
Oublié : m.ée : f. *Forgotten, out of mind, out of memorie.*
Oublier. *To forget,put out of mind, blot out of memorie; to fayle in memorie,or in the remembrance of.*
Oublier Dieu parmy tous les Saincts. *Looke* Sainct.
Il est bien fol qui s' oublie : Prov. *He that forgets himselfe's a verie goose.*
Qui bien aime tard oublie : Prov. *Hee that loues heartily forgets not easily; true loue is long a forgetting.*
Oubliette : f. *A dungeon, or close roome,vnder ground for hainous malefactors.*
Oublieur : m. *A Wafer-man,Wafer-baker,or Wafer-maker.*
Oublieux : m. *as* Oublieur.
Oublieux : m.euse : f. *Obliuious, forgetfull,vnmindfull of; alsó,of,or for,Wafers; whence;*
Corbeille oublieuse. *A basket to put,or carrie Wafers in; a Wicker basket.*
Oublition : f. *Forgetfulnesse.*
Ouche. *The name of a fertill vine; also, as* Oche; *also, a spot of ground reserued, neere to a house, for the sowing of Beanes, Pease,or Hempe in.*
Oudre : *A Borrachoe; a great leatherne bottle, or budget like a bottle,made commonly of a Goats skinne,and vsed for the conueying of wine, oyle, &c, through places which cannot be passed by carts; also, as* Ouldre.
Ouë. *as* Oye; *A Goose.*
La petite ouë de viandes. *The paunch, and intralls of edible creatures.*
Oüeille. *as* Oüaille; *A sheepe; whence;*
Chasque oüeille cerche sa pareille : Prov. *Euerie sheepe will haue his fellow; fooles hold there is no comfort but in companie.*
Ouelle : f. *The riuer Smelt, called so at* Roan.
Ovent : m. *A penthouse of cloth,or wood,ouer a window or doore.*
Over. *To lay an egge.*
Oüere. *as* Oüaire.
Oui : m. ouïe : f. *Heard,hearkened,listened vnto.*
Oui-dire. *Report,or heresay.*
Ouï-dire va par ville : Prov. *Tell-tale is the towne Crier; hearesay goeth speedily from doore to doore.*
Ouïltre. *as* Oudre.
Ouïr : m. *Hearing; the sence of hearing.*
Ouïr. *To heare; to hearken, or listen vnto.*
Dieu gard de mal qui voit bien, & n'oit goutte. *would God had me if I conceiue it,or care a iot for it.*
On n'orroit pas Dieu tonner. *The noise is infinite, wonderfull the hurrie; Gods thunder it selfe could not be heard among them.*
Se faisant si bien ouïr en la bouche de. *Shewing so well in, or comming so gracefully from, the mouth of.*
Oy,voy,& de tais, si tu veux vivre en paix : Prov. *Heare, see,and hold thy peace, if thou desire to liue in peace.*
Il n'est point de pire sourd que celuy qui ne veut ouïr : Prov. *No man's more deafe then he that will not heare.*
Qui demande ce qu'il ne devroit il oit ce qu'il ne voudroit : Prov. *He that askes more then he should, heares more then he would.*
Tout ouïr,tout voir, & rien dire, merite en tout temps qu'on l'admire : Prov. *To heare all, see all,and say nought,merits eternall admiration.*
Ouldre. *as* Oudre; *Also, the Orke; a Sea-monster, and the Whalls naturall enemie.*
Oule : f. *A surge,or great waue of the sea; also,a great earthen pot.*
Oulme. *as* Orme; *An Elme.*
Oulot : m. *A kind of brasse,or copper, fit to make Ordnance of.*
Oulque : f. *A Hulke.*
Oultrage : m. *Outrage, excesse, vnreasonablenesse; iniurie,wrong,abuse,insultation,much violence; extreame breach of duetie in what kind soeuer.*
Elle est belle voirement, mais il n'y a rien d' oultrage. *Her beautie though great could ill be spared; faire she is indeed, but no fairer then she should be.*
Ie ne vous demande rien d' oultrage. *My demands are neither vniust,nor vnreasonable.*
Oultragé : m.ée : f. *Outraged,wronged,abused; handled vilely,reuiled filthily.*
Oultragement : m. *An outraging, wronging, abusing.*
Oultrager. *To outrage,wrong,iniure,abuse; lay violent hands on,deale extreamely with,misuse vnreasonably, reuile most spightfully.*
Oultrageur : m. *An outrager, extreame wronger, vnreasonable abuser of.*
Oultrageusement. *Outragiously, excessiuely, most vnreasonably.*
Oultrageux : m. *Outragious, excessiue, vnreasonable, most fell,wrongfull,iniurious.*
Oultrance : f. *Extremitie,excesse,or excessiuenesse; exceedingnesse.*
Combatre à oultrance. *To fight at sharpe,to fight it out,or to the vttermost; not to spare one another in fighting.*
Oultré : m.ée : f. *Pierced,opened,bored, struck through; runne through and through; also, sicklie, vnsound, or consumed in bodie.*
Oultré d' amour. *Farre gone, ouer head and eares, in loue.*
Chevalier oultré. *Runne through; dead, laid along for dead.*
Fleur oultrée. *A fully-withered flower.*
Loy oultrée. Quand quelque different est determiné par enqueste,ou par brief : ¶Ragueau.
Il s'est oultré. *He hath murthered, or laied violent hands on,himselfe.*
Oultre. (Adverb.) *Ouer, beyond, without; more, besides, further; moreouer; on, forwards.*
Passer oultre. *To die.*
Percé d' oultre en oultre. *Runne through and through.*
Oultrebord. *Exceedingly,passing,beyond the bankes,or bounds of.*
Oultrecouler. *To surround,or ouerflow.*
Oultrecuidamment. *Ouer-weeningly,presumptuously, arrogantly.*
Oultrecuidance : f. *An ouer-weening, presumption, pride,arrogancie; too great a conceit of his own sufficiencie.*
Oultrecuidé : m.ée : f. *Ouer-weening, presumptuous, vaineglorious, arrogant, selfe-conceited, or too well conceited of himselfe.*
s'Oultrecuider. *To ouer-weene; to presume too farre on his owne sufficiencie, to thinke too well of himselfe.*
Oultréement. *Through and through; also, extreamely, excessiuely,exceedingly,beyond all measure.*
Oultrefendre. *To cleaue asunder, to pierce cleane through.*

Oultrefendu: m.uë: f. *Clouen asunder, pierced cleane through.*

s'Oultremarcher. *To ouerreach in pacing.*

Oultre-naturel: m.elle: f. *Supernaturall, beyond nature.*

Oultrepasse: m. *An excesse, or transgression; an eminencie, or eminent thing; a surpassing, or passing beyond.*

L' oultrepasse des Advocates. *The best, or most eminent Lawyer; the Paragon of Pleaders.*

Oultrepassé: m.ée: f. *Surpassed, ouerpassed, exceeded, outgone; transgressed; aduanced, proceeded, marched on; runne ouer; carried, or conueied ouer.*

Oultrepassement: m. *A surpassing, exceeding, excelling; an eminencie, ouerpassing, outgoing; also, an aduancement, proceeding, or marching forward.*

Oultrepasser. *To surpaße, exceed, excell, ouerpasse, goe beyond, outgoe; transgresse; runne ouer; also, to aduance, proceed, or passe on; also, to carrie, conuey, or passe ouer.*

Oultrepercé: m.ée: f. *Pierced, thrust, or strucke thorow.*

Oultrepercer. *To pierce, thrust, or strike through.*

Oultreplus: m. *A surplusage, an ouerplus.*

Oultreplus. (Adverb.) *Furthermore, moreouer, besides that.*

Oultrepreux. *Extreamely valiant, hardier then the hardiest.*

Oultrer. *To pierce, open, bore, thrust, or strike through; to runne through and through.*

Oultrer vne iournée. *To fight from morning to night; or to fight a battaile out.*

Ourague: f. *The channell, or conduit, whereby the vrine of an vnborne infant hath passage.*

Ourche. *The game at Tables called Lurch.*

Ourdi: m. ie: f. *Warped; wrought, wouen; also, begun, inuented, in the web; contriued, deuised.*

'A toile ourdie Dieu mande le fil: Prov. *God helps them forward that haue well begun; or, begin to helpe thy selfe, and God will helpe thee: some expound it otherwise of helpe sent (when the vse of it is past) when a businesse is dispatched.*

Ourdir. *To warpe a web of cloth; to lay the warpe thereof, or put it into the loome; to begin a web, to begin to weaue; (hence) also, to inuent, contriue, begin; cause, procure.*

Ourdissant. *Warping, beginning to weaue, or worke; inventing, contriuing; procuring.*

Ourdisseur: m. *A warper; a putter of a web of cloth into the loome; hence also, a beginner, contriuer, inuenter, deuiser.*

Ourdisseure: f. *The warpe of cloth; the threads that runne along in, or make the length of, a web of cloth; also, the warping thereof, or the laying of the warpe; the putting it into the loome; the beginning of a web, and (thence) of any work; a contriuing, inuenting, deuising; procuring.*

Ourlé: m.ée: f. *Hemmed.*

Ourler. *To hemme.*

Ourlet: m. *A hemme; Looke* Orle.

Ourque: f. *An Orke; a great Seafish, the Whalls mortall enemie.*

Ourreler. *as* Ourler. *To hemme.*

Ours: m. *A Beare; also, the Northerlie starres called Charles waine.*

Ours de mer. *A kind of short, vnweldie, and thicke-sheld Lobster, hauing tenne feet armed with as many strong blacke clawes.*

Ail d'ours. *Beares Garlicke, Ramsons, Ramsies, Buckrammes.*

Oreille d'ours. *Looke* Oreille.

Patte d'ours. *Brankursin, Beares-breech; called also by some, Beares-foot, or Beares-claw.*

Oursal: m.ale: f. *Of, or belonging to, a Beare.*

Ourse: f. *A she Beare; also, the sheat, or cable whereby the maine saile is fastened to the Larbord (or left side) of a ship.*

Aller à ourse. *To goe neere a wind.*

Naviger à pogge, & à ourse. *To hold an vncertaine course at sea. Looke* Pogge.

Oursé. *as* Dehousé: ¶Rab.

Ourseau: m. *A little, or young, Beare; a Beare-whelpe, or cub.*

Ourselet: m. *A little Beare.*

Ourset. *as* Ourselet.

Oursette: f. *A young, or little, she Beare.*

Oursillon: m. *A verie little Beare.*

Oursin: m. *The sea Beare; or, a kind of the fish Tunnie.*

Oursin: m.ine: f. *Beare-like, of Beares, belonging vnto Beares.*

Ourson: m. *A Beare-whelpe, the cub of a Beare; also, a little Beare.*

Oursonne: f. *as* Oursette.

Ousclage: m. *That which a contracted man giues to his affianced, or future wife.*

Oustarde. *as* Outarde.

Ousteron: m. *A Reaper, or Mower; a Hind, or hireling, onely for Haruest time, or worke.*

Outarde: f. *A Bustard.*

Outeron. *as* Ousteron.

Outil: m. *A toole, an instrument.*

Meschant ouvrier ne trouvera ia bons outils: Prov. *A bungler cannot find (or fit himselfe with) good tooles.*

Outillemens: m. *Stuffe, mouables, houshold furniture, or implements.*

Outin. *as* Autin.

Outrage, &c. *as* Oultrage, &c.

Outre: m. *The Orke; A kind of huge fish of the sea.*

Outre: f. *A Borrachoe; as* Oudre.

Outre: com. Cocombres outres. *Ouer-ripe, more then ripe, neere-hand spent, past the best.*

Outré: m.ée: f. *Pierced, bored, strucke thorow, run thorow and thorow; Looke* Oultré.

Outre. (Adverb.) *Looke* Oultre.

Outrepasse: m. *An excesse, or eminencie; a surpassing; a transgression; Looke* Oultrepasse.

Ouvé: m.ée: f. *Full rowed, as a fish.*

Ouvert: m.erte: f. *Ouert, opē; patent, euident, apparent; discouered, vncouered, plaine, without colour; also, gaping, wide, broad, large.*

Fief ouvert. *A Fief without seruices performed, or vaßall to performe them; Looke* Fief.

Heaulme doré, & ouvert. *A gilt, and open helmet on a coat of Armes; the marke of a Vicount, Baron, or Chattelain; (who beare it gilt as Knights, to whom the wearing of gilt armour belongs; and open as Captaines, with Visors lift vp, the better to view their troupes.)*

'A huis ouvert. *Plainly, cleerely, fully, wholly; publickly, in open Court.*

Les prisons leur seront ouvertes. *They shall be deliuered, or discharged.*

Tousiours ouvert comme la bourse d' vn Advocat. *Alwayes open like an Aduocates purse.*

Ouvertement. *Ouertly, openly; euidently, apparently, cleerely, plainely; publickly.*
Ouverture: f. *An ouerture, or opening; an entrance, hole, beginning made, path begun or beaten vnto; a motion made; also, an opening, manifestation, discouerie, vncouering.*
L'ouverture des Estats. *Th'assemblie of Parliament men; the beginning of their conference; the first Session.*
Ouverture de fief. *The change of Lord, or of Tenant.*
Ouverture de rachapt. *A fine due (in certaine cases) to the Lord feudal from a new possessor (Lord, or tenant) of an inferiour* fief.
Ouverture de Regale. *The vacancie of a benefice thats subiect vnto* Droict de Regale.
Ouvertures de vendanges. *A beginning of Grape-haruest, appointed or permitted by the Judge of the place.*
Ouvrage: m. *A worke; also, worke; also, workmanship.*
Ouvrage de Marqueterie. *Checker-worke, or Inlaid worke, of sundrie colours.*
Ouvrage Moresque. *Moreske worke; Looke* Moresque.
Ouvrage de commun ouvrage de nul: Prov. *Euerie bodies worke is no bodies worke; that which euerie one can doe is not worth doing; or, as good doe nothing as worke for a multitude.*
Tel ouvrier tel ouvrage: Prov. *Such as the workeman such his worke.*
Ouvragé: m.ée: f. *Wrought with a needle, sowed.*
Ouvrager. *To worke needle-worke, to sow.*
Ouvrant: m.ante: f. *Opening; also, working.*
Ouvré: m.ée: f. *Wrought, laboured, trauelled.*
Ouvrée: f. *The eighth part of a Bourgonian* Iournau; *Looke* Iournau.
Ouvrer. *To worke; to labour, trauell, doe, act; indeuor.*
Il ouvre sagement en cet affaire. *He carries himselfe discreetly in this businesse.*
Le temps ouvre: Prov. *Time workes (or weares) out euerie thing.*
Ouvreur: m. *An opener.*
Ouvrier: m. *A workeman; an Artificer, or handicraftsman; his crafts-maister; & generally, any worker, actor, framer, inuenter, contriuer, deuiser; also, an vndertaker.*
Chaud ouvrier. *(as we say) A hot chapman.*
De main d'ouvrier. *Done workmanly, framed excellently, in all perfection.*
Ouvrier gaillard cele son Art: Prov. *Th'industrious workeman shewes his skill to few.*
Ouvrier mediocre à cheval; ouvrier gentil à l'hospital: Prov. *The meane workman labours hard, & by much light gaine comes to a heauie purse; the skilfull one is (commonly) proud, vnthriftie, or sloathfull; and dies a wretched, or diseased begger.*
Meschant ouvrier ne trouvera ja bons outils: Pro. *Nere will the bungler fit him with good tooles.*
Tel ouvrier tel ouvrage: Prov. *A workman like his worke; or, like workeman like worke.*
'A l'oeuvre on cognoist l'ouvrier: Prov. *The worke bewrayes the man that did it.*
'A l'hospital les bons ouvriers, en dignité les gros asniers: Prov. *Bunglers grow rich, good workemen wretched; the cogging sot gets honour while the cunning workman starues.*
Il est plus d'ouvriers que de maistres: Prov. *There be more workemen then worke-maisters.*
Il n'est oeuvre que d'ouvriers: Prov. *No worke is rightly done but what a workeman does.*
Ouvrier: m.ere: f. *Working, labouring, trauelling; also, prompt, expert, of good dexteritie in a thing; whence;*
Le gerfaut est ouvrier de prendre les oiseaux de riviere. *The Gerfaulcon is apt, able, or accustomed, to prey on riuer fowle.*
Iour ouvrier. *A workie-day, a weeke-day (which is no holy-day.)*
De main ouvriere. *as* De main d'ouvrier.
Ouvriere: f. *A workewoman.*
Ouvrir. *To open; to set open; to disclose, discouer, bewray.*
s'Ouvrir. *To gape, chap, cleaue, riue; to part, burst, or goe asunder, of it selfe.*
Ouvrir les Estats. *To call, assemble, or begin a Parliament.*
Ouvroir: m. *A worke-house, or shop to worke in.*
Ouy: m. ouïe: f. *Heard, hearkened, listened vnto.*
Ouy. *Yes, yea.*
Ouye: f. *Eare, attention, hearing; also, an eare; also, the hearbe called great Sengreene, or great Housleeke.*
Les ouyes de poissons. *The gills of ordinarie fishes; but of huge ones (as Whalls, &c.) the holes wherout they spout water.*
Les ouyes d'vne Violle. *The sound-holes of a Violl.*
Ie n'en ay rien que l'ouye. *I haue it no otherwise then by report, I came to it onely by hearesay.*
Ouystres: f. *Oysters.*
Oxicrat. *Looke* Oxycrat.
Oxidercique: com. *Sharpening, or cleering the sight.*
Oxigone. *A sharpe-pointed angle.*
Oximel: m. *Syrop of vineger (made of honie, water, and vineger.)*
Oximel squillitique. *Hath the iuyce of the Sea-onion added vnto it.*
Oxirrhodin: m. *A liquid medecine of vineger and Rose-water; applied to the heads of the franticke.*
Oxisacre. *Syrop made of vineger and sugar.*
Oxugoine: com. *Sharpe-angled, sharpe-cornered.*
Oxycedre. *Cedar Juniper, the crimson or pricklie Cedar.*
Oxycrat: m. *A potion, or drinke, made of vineger mingled with water.*
Oxymel. *as* Oximel.
Oya. *(An Interiection of wondering) is it possible! &c.*
Oyard: m. *A Gander.*
Oye: f. *A Goose.*
Oye de mer. *A Porpose, (because nosed like a Goose.)*
Oye nonnette. *A Brigander.*
Bec d'oye. *Wild Tansie, Siluer weed; also, the Porpose, or Sea-hog.*
Col d'oye. *The Port, or Vpset of some Bits, made round, and bowing like the necke of a Goose.*
Merde oye. *Goose-turd greene.*
Patte d'oye. *Looke* Patte.
La petite oye. *The giblets of a Goose; also, the bellie, and inwards or intralls, of other edible creatures.*
Pied d'oye. *Goose-foot, wild Orache; an hearb which is also called Swines-bane, because it kills the swine that eat of it.*
Verd d'oye. *A yellowish, or Goose-turd greene.*
Ferrer les oyes. *To spend both time, and labour verie vainely.*

L'oye mene l'oison paistre: Prov. *Carefull parents teach their children how to liue of themselues.*
L'oison n'est pas digne de monstrer les pasquis a l'oye: Prov. *Seeke* Oison.
Les oisons menent paistre les oyes: Prov. *The cart leads the horse; the young instruct the old.*
On plume l'oye sans la faire crier: Prov. *The simple goose complaines not of her plucking; a sillie gull complaines not though you cousen him.*
Peu à peu le loup mange l'oye: Prov. *By little and little the Wolfe deuoures the Goose; by diligence, or degrees a man obtaines his purpose.*
Qui ne fait comme fait l'oye, n'a de sa vie longue ioye: Prov. *(In commendation of the drinking of water)*
Qui mange l'oye du Roy, il en chie la plume cent ans apres: Prov. *He that eats the Kings Goose doth void the feathers an hundred yeares after:* viz. *He that purloynes the Princes treasure payes in th'arrerages (by himselfe, or his heires) one time or another.*
Oye. grand d'oye. *Great store, huge plentie, much abundance:* ¶Rab.
Oyon: m. *A greene Goose, or young Goose.*
Oyre: f. *An oyle-budget; a great leatherne bag, or bottle to keepe, or carrie oyle, &c, in; made, commonly, of a Goats skinne, and the hairie side, oftentimes, turned inward.*
Oyscille. *as* Ozeille.
Oyseler. *Seeke* Oiseler.
Oyson. *as* Oison.
Oyzeau. *Looke* Oiseau.
Oyzelerie: f. *Fowling, bird-catching, birding.*
Oz. *Looke* Os.
Ozane: f. *The name of an apple.*
Ozeille: f. *Sorrell, garden Sorrell.*
Ozeille de brebis. *Small Sorrell, sheepes Sorrell.*
Ozeille petite. *as* Ozeille de brebis; *or, small Sorrell, barren Sorrell.*
Ozeille Romaine. *Roman Sorrell, round Sorrell,* Tours *Sorrell.*
Ozeille sauvage. *Wild Sorrell, sowre Sorrell, the sowre Docke.*
Ozeille de Tours. *as* Ozeille Romaine.
Ozene: f. *A stinking sore, or vlcer in the nose; also, a kind of ranke-smelling Purcountrell fish, that feeds on Oysters, and is fed on by Lampreyes.*
Ozer. *as* Oser.
Ozeraye: f. *A groue of Oziers.*
Ozereux: m. euse: f. *Of Ozier, of Wicker; also, full of Oziers.*
Ozier: m. *The Ozier, water Willow, red Withie tree; also, Wicker; also, a basket, or skip of Wicker; also, a rod, or twig of Ozier, or of any other pliant wood.*
Franc Ozier. *The Ozier Withie, small Withie, twig Withie.*
Oziere: f. *A Withie twig.*
Ozme: f. *A kind of sinke, or pipe, seruing to conuey away filth.*
Ozymel: m. *Oximel; syrrop of vineger; made of honie, water, and vineger.*

P

PAccages: m. *Pastures, pasture grounds, or feeding grounds.*
Pace. mettre in pace. *To burie.*
Pache: f. *A bargain, contract, accord, capitulation, agreement; a couenant, or condition agreed on.*
Pacification: f. *A pacification, quieting, appeasement.*
Pacifié: m. ée: f. *Pacified, calmed, quieted, stilled, appeased.*
Pacifiement: m. *A pacifying, an appeasing.*
Pacifier. *To pacifie, appease, quiet, calme, still.*
Pacifieur: m. *A pacifier, appeaser, peace-maker.*
Pacifique: com. *Pacificous, peaceable; gentle, quiet, calme, still.*
Pacifiquement. *Peaceably, quietly, calmely; gently.*
Pacquet: m. *A packet; a (small) bundle, or fardle; a trusse.*
Il porte son pacquet. *He carries his load about with him; (said of one that is hulch-backt.)*
Pacquette: f. *Honiewort; (an hearbe)*
Pact: m. *as* Pache.
Pactieux: m. euse: f. *Couenanting; contracting.*
Paction: f. *as* Pache.
Pactionné: m. ée: f. *Couenanted, conditioned, indented, promised; bargained, contracted, capitulated, agreed.*
Pactionner. *To couenant, condition; promise, indent; bargaine, cope, contract, capitulate, agree with.*
Pactiser. *as* Pactionner.
Padane: f. *A kind of open bit which giues much libertie to the tongue of a horse.*
Padoen: m. *as* Padoence.
Padoence. *A common pasture.*
Padouen. *as* Padoence.
Padouyr les vns sur les autres. *Neighbours to lead their beasts each into others pastures, or to common one vpon the other.*
Paduentage: m. *Common of pasture in one, or diuers Parishes.*
Paelle: f. *A shouell; a fire-shouell; also, a Peele wherwith bread, &c, is set into an ouen; also, a footlesse Posnet, or Skellet, hauing brimmes like a Bason; a (little) Panne.*
Paelle à bourbe. *A Scauingers shouell; a broad and hollow shouell of wood; such a one as durt is vsually remoued, or taken vp, with.*
Paelle à frire. *A frying-panne.*
Paelle marine. *The Sea-ball; consists of the slender staulks of the hearbe* Alge, *or of peeces of spunges, compacted by the foame of the sea, & by the working therof cast ashore.*
Il ne luy chaut d'avoir paelle puis qu'il n'y a plus que frire. *He takes no care for that which he hath no further cause to vse.*
Tenir la queuë de la paelle. *To haue th'absolute gouernment of, or chiefe dealing in, a matter.*
Qui tient la paelle par la queuë il la tourne là ou il veut: Prov. *He that holds a frying-panne by the taile may turne it which way he list.*
La paelle se mocque du fourgon: Prov. *Said when one friend, or fellow, derides another.*
'A telle paelle tel fourgon: Prov. *One slouen matcht with another.*
Paellerée: f. *A shouell-full, or Peele-full, of.*
Paellette: f. *A little shouell, fire-shouell, Peele, or panne.*
Paellier: m. *The landing-place of a halfe-pace staire; euerie broad (which is commonly euerie fift, or sixt) greese, or step thereof.*
Paellonnet: m. *A small panne, or (footlesse) Skellet.*
Paellonnette: f. *as* Paellonnet.
Paganisme: m. *Paganisme, Heathenisme, Gentilisme; the religion, or state, of the Gentiles.*
Page: m. *A page; a waiting, or seruing boy (in France,*

where he hath often good breeding, he ought to be a Gentleman borne;) thence also, a Taylers boy; and,

Page de navire. *A ship-boy.*

Hors de page; & sorti de page. *Adultus, past breeching, out of his waiting prentiship, growne a tall man, or, a full-growne man; (Huntsmen applie this phrase to a big Leaueret.)*

Page: f. *A page; a side, of a leafe.*

Pageat, & Pageau. *as* Pagel.

Pagel: m. *A little ruddie Sea Breame, which resembles the* Pagre *so neere, as it is often mistaken for a little one; See* Pagre.

Pageot. *as* Pagel.

Pagerot: m. *A (paultrie) little page.*

Pagnon. *The pinnion of a clocke, &c; the nut, in whose notches the teeth of the wheeles doe runne.*

Lanterne à pagnons. *A paire of trundles, or trundle heads; part of a mill; as vnder* Lanterne.

Pagnote: m. *A Bisonian, scoundrell, cowardlie or scuruie souldier; one that hath neither wit, nor courage.*

Pagre: f. *A round-headed, hawke-snowted, red-mouthed, and strong-toothed Sea-Breame, that feeds much on shell-fish; in Summer she is ruddie of colour, in Winter skie-coloured; therin differing from the fish* Pagel, *which is alwayes ruddie.*

Pagrure. *as* Pagul.

Pagul. *The smooth-shelled Cray-fish, tearmed a Grampell, Grit, or Pungar.*

Pagure. *as* Pagul.

Païanisme: m. *Paganisme.*

Païer. *Looke* Payer.

Paignon: m. *A little loafe of bread:* ¶Pic.

Pailerée. *as* Paellerée.

Paillace: f. *A straw-bed; also, a wide vessell made of such stuffe as hiues be of, and somewhat resembling, though not so deepe as, a Bushell.*

Paillard: m. *A lecher, wencher, whoremunger, whorehunter; also, a knaue, rascall, varlet, scoundrell, filthie fellow.*

Paillard: m. arde: f. *Lecherous, whorish, wenching, lasciuious.*

Couleur paillarde. *A pale, bleake, or wan colour; the greene sicknesse.*

Paillard comme vn Moine; &, Paillard comme vn Verrat. *As lecherous as a Goat (say we.)*

Paillarde: f. *A whore, punke, drab, strumpet, harlot, queane, courtezan, callet.*

Paillarder. *To lecher; bitch-hunt it; haunt bawdie houses; also, to tumble in the straw.*

Paillardise: f. *Lecherie, whoredome, venerie, obscenitie, vncleannesse; also, roguerie, knauerie, villanie, wickednesse; any filthie, or beastlie humor.*

Paillasse. *as* Paillace.

Paillé: m. *as* Pailler; *also, straw-colour; also, a Bishops Pall; whence;*

Droict du paillé. *Looke vnder* Droict.

Paille: f. *Straw; also, chaffe; the huske, or hull wherein corne lyeth; also, the first bud of a flower; also, a flaw in a blade, &c; also, a Spangle; See* Pailles.

Paille folle de bled. *Chaffe; the huske wherein corne lyeth; or, as vnder* Fol.

Paille marine. *as* Sagnie.

Cheval de paille. *A horse thats fed with straw in stead of hay; whence the Prouerbe;* Cheval de paille, cheval de bataille.

Couleur de jaune paille. *Straw-colour.*

Loup en paille. *See* Loup.

Or en paille. *Spangle gold; or gold beaten thinne for spangles.*

Rats en paille. *A rumbling, rustling, hurliburlie, confusion, sturre, coyle; or, as in* Rat.

Plus ioyeux que rats en paille. *See* Rat.

Avoir d' autre paille au bec. Il a bien d'autre paille au bec. *He hath other stuffe in him then you are aware of.*

Il y a plus de paille que de grain. *There is more chaffe then corne in him.*

Estre en la paille iusques au ventre. *To enioy all things in great abundance; to liue at verie great ease.*

Faire à Dieu gerbe de paille. *To deceiue, or depriue God of his right, especially in matters of tenthes; Looke* Gerbe.

Mettre la paille au devant de. *To interrupt; to hinder, stop, or stay the speech of.*

Se remplir de foin, ou de paille. *To stop, or fill his guts with any thing, as a horse that wanting hay falls to his straw.*

Rompre la paille avec. *To fall out with a friend, or acquaintant.*

Avec le temps, & la paille l'on meure les mesles: Prov. *In time, and straw are Medlers mellowed.*

De mauvais payeurs foin, ou paille: Prov. *Take any thing thats offered you by an euill debtor.*

Nul grain sans paille: Pro. *No corne without some chaffe.*

Paille-maille. *See* Palemaille.

Pailler: m. *A reeke, or stacke of straw; also, bed-straw; also, the part of an inner Court whereon straw is scattered for fowle to feed on; also, a dung-hill before a barne, or stable doore; whence;*

Vne poule de pailler. *A dunghill henne, a henne thats fed at the barne doore.*

Pailles: f. *Spangles; also, the flakes, or sparkles that flie from hammered, and red-hot yron, &c.*

Il pense que nues sont pailles d' airain. *(Much like to our) He thinkes the Moone is made of greene cheese.*

Paillet: m. ette: f. *Pale-red, pale-claret, flesh-coloured.*

Pailléte. *as* Paillette.

Pailleté: m. ée: f. *Spangled, bespangled.*

Pailleter. *To spangle, to bespangle, to trimme, or decke, with spangles.*

Pailleteur: m. *A Spangle-maker.*

Paillette: f. *A spangle; also, a sparkle.*

Pailleux: m. euse: f. *Strawie; chaffie; also, full of flaws.*

Paillier: m. *A chaffe-heape; or, a place wherein chaffe is kept; also, as* Pailler.

Paillisson. *A small frying-panne.*

Pailliz: m. *A heape of straw, or of chaffe.*

Paillole: f. *A spangle; whence;* Or de paillole. *Spangle gold; or gold thinne-beaten for spangles.*

Paillοté. terre paillotée. *Earth mingled with chaffe, or with straw.*

Paillotes: f. *Spangles; also, plates of Armour.*

Pain: m. *Bread; also, a loafe of bread.*

Pain d'amande. *Almond bread, or bisket made of Almonds; also, Marchpane.*

Pain d'Argus. *Spungie, or light, bread; bread full of eyes.*

Pain d'aveine. *Oaten bread; Jannocks.*

Pain de balle. *Vnranged bread; or, a course bread wherein there is much chaffe.*

Pain benist. *Holie-bread, vsed in Popish Churches.*

Pain benist de la confrairie. *Thumps, thwacks, blows*
Pain benist de la S. Cy. *Wine; or, any good drinke.*
Pain benist d'Escosse. *A sodden sheepes liuer.*
Pain bis. *Browne bread, houshold bread, course bread.*
Pain bis-blanc. *Wheaten bread, or boulted bread.*
Pain de bouche, *as* Pain mollet.
Pain bourgeois. *Crible bread betweene white and browne; a bread (that somewhat resembles our wheaten, or cheat) a loafe whereof is to weigh, when tis baked, 32 ounces.*
Pain de brasse. *A great houshold loafe of course bread, like our Chesloafe.*
Pain de brode. *Browne bread, course houshold bread; a loafe whereof is to weigh 96 ounces, or six pound.*
Pain de Chailli. *A verie white bread (named so of* Chailli *a village) the loafe whereof is to weigh 12 ounces, and to be sold for* 12 d. Paris. *when a* Septier *of wheat is worth* 20 s. Tourn.
Pain chalan. *All kind of countrey-Bakers bread, that of* Gonesse *excepted.*
Pain à chanter. *as* Pain missal.
Pain de Chapitre. *A fine, white, hard-kneaded, and flat manchet, weighing about 16 ounces.*
Pain à cocu. *The smallest, and daintiest kind of red Mushrome; also, as;*
Pain de cocu. *Cuckobread, Stubwort, wood Sorrell, wood Sowre, sowre Trefoile, hearbe* Alleluya.
Pain coquillé. *A kind of hard-crusted bread, whose loaues doe somewhat resemble the Dutch bunnes of our Rheinish-wine houses.*
Pain de Cour. *as* Pain mollet.
Pain farain. *A verie yellow houshold bread, of the better sort, and made in great loaues.*
Pain de fenestre. *Browne bread.*
Pain fraisé. *A Panadoe, of the crummes of stale bread, soaked a while in 2 or 3 changes of water, then boyled in a pipkin with butter, or any other sweet, & fat moisture; or in Capons broath; and often stirred.*
Pain de Gonesse. *A delicate white bread, made in a village called* Gonesse; *whose water is reported to be the chiefe cause of that delicacie.*
Pains d' hostelage. *Looke* Hostelage.
Pain de mesnage. *Ordinarie houshold bread; (for the most part finer then browne, and browner then wheaten.)*
Pain missal. *A Wafer made onely of flower and a little salt.*
Pain mollet. *A verie light, verie crustie, and sauorie white bread, full of eyes, leauen, and salt.*
Pain de moustarde. *A loafe, or ball, of drie, or dried mustard.*
Pain mouton. *Looke* Mouton.
Pain d'oiseau. *Stonecrop, Stonehore, Mousetaile, wild Prickmadam, Pricker, Iacke of the butterie.*
Pain de panniere. *A great white loafe yeelded by the the tenants of* S. Gondon sur Loire *vnto their Lord, yearely, and besides their* Cens.
Pain perdu. *A broath made of wine, Rose-water, and sugar, egges, and bread.*
Le Iour de pain perdu. *Shrouetewsday.*
Pain de la place. *Brown bread, course houshold bread.*
Pain porcin. *as* Pain de pourceau.
Pain de Potensac. *A delicat bread made in a village called* Potensac, *neere vnto* Bourdeaux.
Pain de pourceau. *Hogs bread, swines bread, sow bread; (an hearbe.)*
Pain de Quinque. *See* Quinque.
Pain de rose. *A Rose-cake.*

Pain rousset. *Cheat, or boulted bread; houshold bread made of Wheat and Rie mingled.*
Pain de terre. *The hearbe Sow-bread.*
Gros pain. *Course browne bread.*
Petit pain. *A little loafe of bread; also, spare diet, poore fare, thinne cheere; whence the Prouerb;* Apres grand banquet petit pain. &, faire le petit pain. *To liue neerely, sparingly, nigardly; with a little.*
Au pain, & au cousteau avec. *Verie familiar, verie much conuersant, at bed and at boord, as a companion, or haile-fellow well met, with.*
De mesme pain soupe; &, faire de tel pain soupes. *Looke* Soupe.
Estre en pain; ou hors de pain. *Children to be vnder, or out of, the gouernment of their parents; hence also,* Mise hors de pain. *An emancipation.*
Faire pain separé. *To part housholds; people of one house, or societie, to diet seuerally, or liue by themselues.*
Manger son pain blanc le premier. *To fare well at first and ill at last; or, to spend the best at first in hope the worst will mend.*
Manger son pain en son sac. *To play the snudge, or churle; to eat his victualls priuately, retiredly, or in corners.*
C'est trop mangé d' vn pain en vn lieu. *We haue too much vsed, attended, or vrged, one thing at once.*
Il sçait plus que son pain manger. *He knowes more then th'eating of his bread comes to; he is no child, he is past a babe; his skill is more then ordinarie.*
Mettre le pain en vn four froid. *To put bread into a cold ouen; to imploy things idly, or on that which will not auaile them; or thinke to make vse of things which are of no manner of vse.*
Mettre vn pain au four à. *To doe a man a good (or euill) turne; to put a tricke on him, with a good (or an euill) intention.*
Prendre vn pain sur la fournée. *To get a snatch at his wench thats readie to be maried.*
Quiers tu meilleur pain que de fourment? *Wouldst thou haue better bread then's made of wheat?*
Il veut beaux chiens à peu de pain. *He lookes to be well serued, and yet will giue but little intertainment.*
Pain tant qu'il dure, vin à mesure: Prov. *Eat at pleasure, drinke by measure.*
'A pain, & oignon trompette ne clairon: Pro. *Look* Oignon.
Nul pain sans peine: Prov. *Toyle hath a part in each thing we enioy; or, without some toyle no bread, no benefit.*
Ou pain faut tout est à vendre: Prov. *Where bread is wanting all is to be sold.*
'A l'enfourner on fait les pains cornus (ou cocus: ¶Pic.) Prov. *In the beginning of a cause are faults the sooneft made, and (once made) worst amended; or, the beginning shewes what to presume of the rest.*
'A la faim il n'y a point de mauvais pain: Prov. *Hunger makes any thing tast well.*
Chasque demain apporte son pain. *All dayes produce their owne prouision.*
Ia ne vienne demain qui n'apporte son pain: Prov. *Let the next day produce it owne prouision; or, let him not come next day that now comes vnprouided.*
Croustes de pastez valent bien pain: Prov. *Peeces of pie-crust are as good as bread; or, he doth no wrong that giueth cake for bread.*
De tout s'avise à qui pain faut: Pro. *Necessitie inuented*

ted all good Artes; want more then any thing makes men industrious.

Eau & pain c'est la viande du chien: Prov. *Bread and water is but a dogs dinner.*

Le chat a faim quand il ronge du pain: Prov. *The cat's a hungred when she gnawes a crust.*

Selon le pain il faut le cousteau: Prov. *We must proportion our expence by our meanes.*

Tel a du pain lors qu'il n'a plus de dents: Pro. *Some haue abundance when they cannot vse it.*

Tel grain tel pain: Prov. *Such as the corne such is the bread.*

Vn mesme cousteau me coupe le pain, & le doigt: Prov. *From one thing I receiue both good, and hurt.*

Paincture. *Looke* Peincture.

Paindre. *as* Peindre.

Paineux: m. euse: f. *Breadie, full of bread.*

Paintre. *Looke* Peintre.

Pair: m. *A peere; a paragon; also, a match, fellow, companion; also, a paire, at Cards.*

Pairs. *Vassalls, or tenants holding of a Mannor by one kind of tenure; fellow vassalls, fellow subiects; also, the common Counsellors of incorporate townes haue beene tearmed* Pairs.

Pairs de la Cour; ou Pairs de fief. *Vassalls, or tenants, who sit as Assistants, or Triers in their Lords Courts, (especially when any cause that concerns his inheritance is iudged;) these* Pairs *are finable to the King for all sentences ill giuen in those Courts.*

Pairs de France. *The Peeres of France; in old time, and at their first institution (by Loys le Ieune) were but 12; six Spirituall; viz, the Archbishop of* Rheims, *the Bishops of* Laon, *&* Langres *(who also were stiled Dukes) the Bishops (and Earles) of* Beauvois, Chaalons, *and* Noyon; *and six Temporall ones; viz. the Dukes of Burgundie, Normandie, and* Guienne; *the Earles of Flanders,* Champagne, *and* Tholose: *At this day all the former six continue; and in lieu of the later (whose estates haue beene, at seuerall times, either vnited vnto, or aliened from, the Crowne) there be more then six, either Princes of the Bloud, or the Princes fauourites; created at seuerall times, and equall among themselues (and vnto the first Peers) in all manner of priuiledges.*

Pair, & sequence. *A card-play somewhat like to our Post and paire.*

La Cour des Pairs. *A Court Baron, or Lords Court; and the Parliament of Paris, wherein the Peeres of France may sit as Assistants.*

Veine sans pair. *A branch of the hollow veine, wherby the spaces betweene eight of the lower ribs be nourished.*

I'entends le pair, & la couche. &, Prins au pair, & à la couche. *as in* Couche.

Pair. *Like, alike, equall, matching, euen, meet.*

Pair ou non. *The game called Euen and odde.*

'A pair de. *Like vnto, euen with.*

Aller du pair avec. *To goe ranke in ranke, or cheeke by iowle, with.*

Mettre de pair avec. *To compare, or set in equall ballance, with.*

Paire: f. *A paire, or couple of; also, a bet, or stake; whence;*

Ie m'en vay de paire. *I will not hold the match, I will be vnlaid againe.*

Faire 3 paires de nopces. *To make 3 mariages; and hence, in common speech, they say;* vne paire de Heures, ou de Pseaumes; *A Seruice booke, or Psalter.*

Pairie: f. *A Peeredome of France; also, equalitie of subiects, or vassalls, in tenure, or in estate.*

Pairrie: f. *as* Pairie.

Païs: m. *A Countrey, or Region, Land, Prouince, (natiue) soyle; also, (any) ground, or soyle.*

Païs coustumier. *See* Coustumier.

Païs de droict escrit. *A countrey gouerned by the Ciuile Law.*

Païs de suerie. *The sweating countrey; Cornelius his tub.*

'A travers païs. *Rouing, at randome, at large.*

'A veuë de païs. *Grossely, hastily, at first sight, without certaintie; without any exact, or neere examination.*

Estre bien de son païs. *To be clownish, rude, simple, ignorant.*

Gaigner païs. *To steale on, rid ground, rid way.*

Iecter leurs hommes à païs. *To set their men on land, or ashore.*

Tirer païs. *To flie directly forward; and, in trauelling, to goe on, or, to rid way.*

Qui m'aura perdu ne m'aille cercher en ce païs là. *Let not him that shall happen to loose me looke to find me there.*

Païsage: m. *Paisage, Landskip, Countrey-worke; a representatiō of fields, or of the countrey, in painting, &c.*

Paisant: m. *A peasant, boore, clowne, swaine, hind; a hob, or lob, of the countrey.*

Paisible: com. *Peaceable; quiet, calme, still, gentle, mild, patient.*

Paisiblement. *Peaceably; quietly, calmely, gently, mildly, patiently.*

Paisibleté: f. *Peaceablenesse, tranquilitie, quietnesse, calmenesse, mildneße, gentlenesse.*

Paissage de bestes. *The grazing, pasturing, or feeding of cattell.*

Paisse solitaire. *A certaine black-browne mountaine bird, which resembles a Throstle, or Owsell, and being incaged sings verie sweetly; or, as in* Passe.

Paisseau: m. *A stake, pole, pearch, prop, or stay, wherwith a vine, &c, is held vp; also, the vine so vnderpropped.*

Saulter de treille en paisseaux. *(In discourse) to run giddily, or vncertainly, from one matter to another.*

Paisseler. *To vnderset, or vnderprop with poles, or stakes.*

Paissement. *as* Paissage.

Paissiere: f. *A banke, or causey, held vp, or in, by stakes.*

Paisson: f. *Th'Agistment, or Herbage of woods, or forrests; feeding for cattell therein.*

Paissonner. *Cattell to feed, or brouse, in woods, &c.*

Paissu: m. uë: f. *Fed on, grazed, eaten, by cattell.*

Paistre. *To feed, graze, eat, pasture on.*

Paistre de parolles. *To giue words in stead of money; to delay, put off, or toll on, with faire words.*

La mauvaise garde paist souvent le loup: Prov. *Ill watching often feeds the hungrie Wolfe.*

Les oisons menent paistre l'oye; &, l'oye mene les oisons paistre. *Two contrarie Prouerbes of Confusion, and Order; Looke* Oison.

Paistri, & Paistrir. *See* Pestri, & Pestrir.

Paix: f. *Peace, quiet, rest; a peace, accord, agreement, composition, attonement.*

Homme de paix. *A vassall; Seeke* Homme.

Maison de la paix. *A Court of Iustice; a Law-Court.*

Sergents de la paix. *Ordinarie Sergeants, or Catchpoles, belonging to some Court.*

Villes de paix. *Peaceable, or priuiledged townes; those wherein subiects are bound to keepe the peace, and to end their differences (if they will contend) by Law.*

Tout en paix. *Quietly, stilly, gently, faire and softly.*

La paix est la feste de tous Saincts: Prov. *Peace is all holy mens holy-day.*

Achette paix,& maison faicte: Prov. *Peace, and a house thats built, are to be bought.*

Baston porte paix quant et soy: Prov. *A cudgell breeds the peace of him that beares it.*

Mieux vaut en paix vn oeuf qu'en guerre vn boeuf: &, Mieux vaut servitude en paix que Seigneurie en guerre: Pro. *Better a needie slaue in peace then a wealthie Lord in warre.*

Oy,voy,& te tais, si tu veux vivre en paix: Prov. *Looke* Ouïr.

Peu,& paix don de Dieu: Prov. *A little with peace is a great blessing.*

Qui de tout se taist de tout a paix: Prov. *Hold thy peace and enioy peace; vnseasonable talke is the mother of debate.*

Paix. *(An Interiection inioyning silence) peace, husht, not a word.*

Pal: m. *A pale, stake, or pole; also, a putting to death by a stake thrust (longwayes) through the bodie; much vsed among the Turkes; also, as* Milandre.

Palabre: f. *as* Parole.

Palabreur: m. *A pratler, babler, tatler; an idle or common talker.*

Paladin: m. *A Knight of the round table.*

Il fait bien de son Paladin. *He swaggers, brags, or strouts it mightily.*

Palais: m. *A Palace; a Princes Court, house, or place; also, the house, or Hall, wherin Courts be kept in a town of Parliament; a Guild-hall, Shire-hall, Sessions-house; also, the roofe, or palate of the mouth; also, the tast.*

Palais au Lievre,ou du Lievre. *The smooth Sow-thistle, or soft Milke-thistle, called Hares Lettuce.*

Doctrine du Palais. *Ciuilitie, courtesie, good manners, courtlie behauiour or carriage.*

Escus du palais. *A kind of counters.*

Gens du palais. *Lawyers (of all sorts.)*

Iours de palais. *Court-dayes, sitting-dayes, Hall-dayes.*

Les Poursuyvans au palais. *Suitors, Clients.*

Souris de palais. *An Aduocate, a Pleader; or (most properly) a Pettifogger.*

Faire le palais. *To plead, or argue at the barre.*

Palalalan. *The sound of the French march.*

Palamide: f. *A young Tunnie; also, the Bonito (fish.)*

Palamie: f. *The bloudie rifts; a discase, or impostumation in the roofe of a horses mouth.*

Palatin: m. *A generall, & common appellation, or title, for such as haue any speciall Office, or function in a Soueraigne Princes palace.*

Comte Palatin. *A Count Palatine; (is not the title of a particular Officer, but an hereditarie addition of dignitie, and honor, gotten by seruice done in a domesticall charge; and he whom the Prince appointed to be chiefe Iustice of a whole Prouince hath also beene intitled,* Comte Palatin.*)*

Palatin: m. ine: f. *Of, or belonging to, the palate; whence;* Lettres palatines. *Such letters as be pronounced by the helpe of the palate; as G, T, R, &c.*

Palatinat: m. *A Palinatie; the title, or dignitie of a Count Palatine; also, a Countie Palatine.*

Pale: f. *The fowle called a Shoueler; also, a fire-shouell; also, a shouell; also, th'Indian fig tree.*

Palée: f. *A shouell full of.*

Palefrenier: m. *A Groome of a stable; a Horse-keeper.*

Palefroy: m. *A palfrey; (was in old time, for the most part, understood of a horse for a womans saddle.)*

Palemaille: f. *A game, wherein a round box bowle is with a mallet strucke through a high arch of yron (standing at either end of an alley one) which he that can do at the fewest blowes, or at the nūber agreed on, winnes.*

Palenc: m. *The Pennant; a rope which helpes to hoise vp the boat, and all heauie marchandise, aboord a ship.*

Palerée: f. *A pale full of.*

Palerons des espaules. *The shoulder blades.*

Palet: m. *An yron pestell; also, a small beetle to play at ball with; also, a quoit.*

Paleter du chanure. *To pound, or bruise hempe with a pestle, or beetle.*

Palette: f. *A Lingell, Tenon, Slice, or flat toole wherwith Chirurgians lay salue on plaisters; also, the saucer, or porringer wherinto they receiue bloud out of an opened veine; also, a battle-doore.*

La palette du genouil. *The knee bone, or panne; the whirlebone of the knee.*

Pigeon de palette. *A rough-footed Doue.*

Pal-fer: m. *An yron-headed shouell, spade, or stake, vsed by Gardeners.*

Pali: m. *A pale, or thicke lath; a stake, pole, or pile.*

Paliatif: m. iue: f. *Palliatiue; cloaking, hilling ouer, couering, hiding; shadowing, colouring.*

Cures paliatives. *Cures which haue not searcht to the root, or cause of a disease, but haue brought onely a shew of amendment; as when a wound is closed, and yet festers at the bottome.*

Medecines paliatives. *Medecines which ease for a while, but heale not altogether; or, as in* Cures paliatives.

Paliation. *Seeke* Palliation.

Palicer. *as* Palisser.

Palier. *To palliate; to cloake, to couer, hide, or hill ouer; to shadow, to colour.*

Palifié: m. ée: f. *Impaled, compassed with a pale, defended by a Palisadoe.*

Paligenesie: f. *Regeneration, or, diuersitie of generation.*

Palinodie: f. *A palinodie, recantation, contrarie song, vnsaying of what hath beene said.*

Palinotode: f. *Diuersitie of birth.*

Palis. *as* Pali.

Paliser. *To reueale, publish, bewray.*

Palissade: f. *A palisadoe; a defence, or wall, of pales; also, a hedge-row of sundrie fruit trees set close together.*

Palisse: f. *as* Palissade.

Palissé: m. ée: f. *Palisadoed, staked, or paled about.*

Palisser. *To impale; to inclose with pales, to defend with palisadoes.*

Palisson: m. *A flat yron, or shouell to bake cakes on.*

Paliure: m. *The shrub called Ramme of Libia, or Christs thorne (because it is said he was crowned withall.)*

Pall-allant: m. *A staulking, or strouting braggadochio; or as* Palalalan.

Pallamente: f. *Part of the Orelop, or vpper decke of a Galley.*

Pallares. *A kind of Indian pulse.*

Palle. *as* Pale; *also, as* Palletoc; *also, the beazill, collet, or head of a ring.*

Palle: com. *as* Pasle; *Pale.*

Pallé: m. ée: f. *Partie par-pale; a tearme of Blazon.*

Pallemail. *See* Palemaille.

Pallement. *Palely, bleakly, wanly.*

Paller. *as* Parler. *(an old word.)*

Pallerons des espaules. *The Omeplates, or shoulder blades.*

Palleter. *To scuffle, or fight with; (an old word.)*
Palletie: f. *A scuffling, skirmish, fighting.*
Palletoc: m. *A long, and thicke Pelt, or Cassocke; a garment like a short cloake with sleeues; or such a one as the most of our moderne Pages are attired in.*
Palletoque. *That weareth a* Palletoc.
Pallette: f. *A little shouell; a small peele; also, a shoulder-blade.*
Palleur: f. *Palenesse, wannesse.*
Palliatif. *Looke* Paliatif.
Palliation: f. *A cloaking, couering, hiding, colouring.*
Pallier: m. *as* Palluyer; *also, the landing place of a halfe-pace stayre.*
Pallir. *See* Paslir.
Pallis. *as* Pali.
Pallissade: f. *A Palisado, or defence of pales; also, a Parke, or place impaled.*
Pallissement: m. *Palenesse; or, a waxing pale.*
Pallonneau. *Looke* Palonneau.
Pallourde: f. *A little, narrow, and seldome-gaping Cockle, which we also call, a Palour.*
Palluyer: m. *An Officer which with a shouell vnlades, or lades the salt which is for the Kings store.*
Palmaire: com. *Belonging to, or being in, the paulme of the hand.*
Palmant. *He that bids most rent for a Lease, or money for an Inheritance, which is to be let, or sold.*
Palme: m. *A hand-breadth, foure fingers, or three ynches in measure; also, a shaftment.*
Le grand palme. *Is twelue fingers, or nine ynches; a full spanne.*
Palme: f. *The paulme of the hand; also, the Palme, or Date tree; Looke* Paulme.
Palmée: f. *A bidding of most, or out-bidding of all, for an Inheritance, or Lease.*
Palmer. *To stroake, smooth, lay, or strike downe with the palme of the hand; whence;*
Palmer les cheveux des orgueilleux. *To quell, or abate, the huffe of the prowd.*
Palmier: m. *The Palme, or Date tree.*
Palmier petit. *The little wild Date tree.*
Palmier: m. ere: f. *Of, or belonging to, the Palme tree; also, bearing a branch of Palme.*
Heritage palmier. *An Inheritance exposed vnto sale.*
Palmite: f. *The low, or little wild Date tree.*
Palmule: f. *A Date.*
Palon: m. *The broad end of a (woodden) shouell; or, as* Masserotte.
Palonneau: m. *A peece of a strong rope doubled, & hauing a knot with an eye in the middle of it, whereby it serues to fasten draught horses vnto the thill of a Cart, or carriage.*
Palot: m. *whence;* Tenir palot à. *To hold tacke, or keepe euen with; to hold at euen tearmes.*
Paloüade: f. *A kind of Spanish fish.*
Palourde. *See* Pallourde.
Palper. *To handle gently, feele tenderly, stroake softly, touch gingerly; also, to flatter, soothe, cog, or collogue with, deceiue with faire words.*
Palpitation: f. *A panting, or often beating, as of a throbbing, or affrighted heart.*
Palpiter. *To pant, or throb; to beat, moue, or stirre verie often.*
Palte. *A soft, and delicate Indian fruit, which resembles a great Peare, and hath a stone in stead of a core.*
Palthoc. *as* Palletoc.
Paltoquier. *as* Palletoqué.

Paltret: m. *A Cleaner.* ¶Blesien.
Palu: m. *A fenne, marsh; wet ground, or moore.*
Paludament: m. *A coat-armour, or horsemans coat; a iacket reaching to the knees.*
Paludeux: m. euse: f. *as* Palustre; *or full of marshes, fennes, moores.*
Palvesate: f. *A Targuet-fence, vnder which the souldiors that make approaches, or are vpon entring of a breach, be shrowded.*
Palumbe: f. *A Ringdoue, Stockdoue, Queest, Woodculuer.*
Palustre: com. *Fennie, marsh, marshie, moorish.*
Paluyer. *See* Palluyer.
Pam. *as* Pan; *a spanne.*
Pampe. *Looke* Pampre.
Pamphage. *Eat-all, all-rauening, all-deuouring.*
Pamphredon. *A Hornet, or Ox-flye.*
Pampier: m. ere: f. *Of, or belonging to, a Vine-leafe; also, bearing onely leaues.*
Pampillettes: f. *Spangles.*
Pampre: f. *A Vine leafe, or Vine leaues; also, a young Vine-branch full of leaues.*
Armé de pampre. *Whitled, mellow, cup-shotten, that hath put on armour of pot-proofe.*
Pampré: m. ée: f. *Full of, also, furnished, or couered with, Vine leaues.*
Pamprer. *To fill, furnish, or couer, with Vine leaues.*
Pan: m. *A pane, peece, or pannell of a wall, of Wainscot, of a glasse-window, &c, as* Paneau; *also, a pawne, or gage; also, a spanne; also, a toyle, or hay wherewith wild beasts are caught; also, the skirt of a gowne; the pane of a hose, of a cloake, &c.*
Pans. *Looke after* Panouere.
Panacée: f. *Wound-wort, All-heale; an hearbe.*
Panacée, à pan. *A call vnto meat; like our,* A manger.
Panache. *Looke* Pennache.
Panade: f. *A Panado; crummes of bread (and currans) moistened, or brewed with water.*
Panage: m. *as* Appanage; *also, Pawnage; Mastage for Swine; or the money due to the owner of a wood for the same.*
Panaillon. *See* Penaillon.
Panaiz: m. *A certaine root thats lesse, and ranker, then the ordinarie Parsenip; otherwise resembling it, and oft mistaken for it.*
Panaiz de Macedoine. *The Macedonian Parsenip, whose iuice is much esteemed of by heardsmen.*
Panaiz sauvage. *Hercules Wound-wort, or All-heale; also, the wild Carrot; Some also tearme so, Cow Parsenip, medow Parsenip, Madnep.*
Menus panaiz. *The white Mallow, marsh Mallow, moorish Mallow.*
Panary: m. *A Felon, or Whitlow, at the end of a finger.*
Panax. *as* Panaiz.
Pançart: m. *A Gorbellie, great guts, fat gulch.*
Pancarte: f. *A paper containing the particular rates of Tolls, or Customes due vnto the King, &c; thus tearmed, because, commonly, hung vp in some publicke place either single, or within a frame.*
Pance: f. *The paunch, maw, bellie; also (the fashion of) a great bellied doublet; or the great bellie of a doublet.*
Il avoit les yeux plus grands que la pance. *His eyes were bigger, or worse to please, then his bellie.*
`A pance chaude pied endormi: Pro. *When the bellie is full the bones would be at rest.*
De la pance vient la danse: Pro. *From the paunch comes*

comes your daunce; the bellie glutted sets the legs agog.
Goutte en la hanche fille en la pance: Pro. *Looke* Fille.
Qui a la pance pleine il luy semble que les autres sont saouls: Pro. *He that hath gorged himselfe thinkes all mens mawes be full.*
Rouge visage, & grosse pance ne sont signes de penitence: Pro. *A Swizzers bellie, and a drunkards face are no (true) signes of penitentiall grace.*
Panceron: m. *A great bellie, gulch, or paunch; and particularly, the full-stuffed bellie of a doublet.*
Pancerotte: f. *A little paunch.*
Pancette. *as* Pancerotte.
Panchaïque. Odeur Panchaïque. *The smell of Arabian Frankincense.*
Panchant. *Bowing, leaning, inclining forwards; stooping, or hanging downewards.*
Panché: m. ée: f. *Bent, inclined, or bowed forwards; leaning, declined, hanged downewards; any way stooping.*
Arbre panché. *The ends of whose boughes hang downwards; as some hold all of a tree, whereon a malefactor hath beene hanged, will doe.*
Panchement: m. *A bending, leaning, bowing forwards; an inclining, or hanging downewards; a stooping, a declining.*
De son propre panchement. *Of his owne inclination, from his owne disposition.*
Pancher. *To bend, leane, or bow forwards; to giue, incline, or hang downewards; to stoope, to decline.*
Pançu: m. uë: f. *Gorbellied, great-paunched.*
Pand. *Looke* Pan.
Pandectaire: com. *Containing, or belonging to, all manner of bookes; or bookes that intreat of all matters.*
Pandectes: f. *Pandects; Bookes which containe all matters, or comprehend all the parts of the subiect whereof they intreat.*
Pane. *Looke* Panne.
Pané: m. ée: f. *Breadie, of bread; whence;*
Eau panée. *A Panado, a Mise.*
Paneau: m. *A pannell, of Wainscot; of a saddle, &c; also (in Masonrie) a patterne, mould, or scantling, (made of a thinne boord &c) whereby a stone is cut, and made fit for the place it is to stand in; also, the stone it selfe so cut; whence,* Paneau de doile; *a Cant peece.*
Paneaux. *Old rags, clowts, tatters; also, the hatches, or scuttles of a ship.*
Panegyric: m. *A Discourse, or Oration made in praise of a Prince, or Potentate.*
Panerée: f. *A Pannierfull.*
Paneron: m. *A little Pannier, a small Doßer.*
Panerot: m. *as* Paneron.
Panes. *Red pimples, or freckles on the face.* ¶Langued.
Paneté: m. ée: f. *Made into bread.*
Paneterie: f. *A Pantrie.*
Panetier: m. *A Pantler.*
Panetiere: f. *as* Paneterie; *also, a Shepheards scrip; or the bag, or poke, wherein he puts his victualls.*
Panets, & Panetz. *as* Panaiz.
Paneux: m. euse: f. *Breadie, or full of bread.*
Panic: m. *The Graine called Panicke, and Indian Oatmeale.*
Panic domestique. *Ordinarie Panick.*
Panic sauvage. *Wild Panicke; fit onely to feed birds.*
Panicault: m. *The hundred-headed thistle, field Eringus, Leuant sea-Holme, Champion sea-Hollie.*
Panicault marin. *Sea-Holme, sea-Hollie, sea-Huluer, Eringus.*
S'en aller frotter le cul au panicault. *To spend time idly, lazily, foolishly, or vainly.*
Panice: f. *A suddaine, and madding feare, which comes without any apparant, or knowne, cause.*
Panicle: f. *A little loafe.*
Panier: m. *A Pannier, or Doßer; also, a Pedlers packe; also, a fashion of Trunke made of Wicker couered with the hairie fell of a calfe; much in vse among the iourneying, and warfaring Lords of France, and carried by paires, on either side of a horse one.*
Panier à vesses: C'est le Cul.
Anse de panier. *An Hemycicle, or halfe-circle.*
Les plus meures du panier. *Looke* Meur.
Le pis du panier. *The worst of the matter.*
Ses paniers sont pleins. *She is sped, she is poopt, her panniers be full.*
Chier dans le panier pour le mettre sur la teste. *To disgrace, or dispraise a thing, the sooner to obtaine it; or, kindly to entertaine what he hath formerly contemned.*
Adieu paniers vendanges sont faittes. *(Applyable to any thing whereof we haue no further vse.)*
A chasque mercier son panier: Pro. *Euerie one is to support, or looke vnto, his owne charge.*
Chasque mercier prise ses aiguilles, & son panier: Prov. *Euerie Pedlar thinks well of his packe.*
Petit mercier petit panier: Pro. *See* Mercier.
Qui fait corbeille il fait panier: Pro. *He that can doe, or hath done, one thing, is the apter, or likelier, to do another.*
Qui se mesle d' autruy mestier il trait sa vache en vn panier: Pro. *He that meddles with another mans Trade, milkes his Cow in a Pannier;* viz. *looses his profit, and vndoes himselfe.*
Paniere. Pain de paniere. *See* Pain.
Panifice: m. *Bread-making; the Trade of a Baker; also, bread.*
Panifier. *To make, or bake, into bread.*
Panil. *as* Panic.
Panilliere: f. *The Gryne.*
Panique: com. *Distraught with causelesse feare.* ¶Rab.
Paniz. *Looke* Panic.
Pannader. *A horse to praunce, curuet, or bound; Looke* Se Pennader.
Pannades: f. *The curuettings, prauncings, or boundings of lustie horses.*
Panne: f. *A skinne, fell, or hide; also, a naturall spot on the face.*
Panne de bois. *(Is particularly) the peece of timber that sustaines a gutter between the roofes of two fronts, or houses.*
Panne de gresse. *A leafe of fat.*
Panne de soye. *Stuffe (made of silke;) and particularly, Shag, Plush, or vnshorne Veluet.*
Mettre en panne. *The wind to take a Ship vpon the Stayes; or, as* Bouter vent en penne. *See* Penne.
Panneau. *as* Paneau; *also, a young Peacocke; also, a large Net, or Toyle.*
Pannetier. *as* Panetier.
Pannetiere: f. *as* Panetiere; *also, the dewlap, or brisket of an Ox, Cow, &c.*
Pannicule: m. *A little clowt; also, the skinne wherein a child lyes wrapped in the wombe.*
Pannicule charneux. *The membrane which conducts the vessels throughout the skin of the whole bodie.*

Pan-

Panniere. Pain de pan. *See* Pain.

Pannilliere. *as* Panilliere.

Pannonceau: m. *A Fane, or Weather flag; also, a Pennon; a little flag of Taffata, hauing the Kings, or a Lords, Armes figured in it.*

Pannoyer vn baston; (C'est, le manier en la main) *to wield, or tosse it.*

Panomphée. *Of all Nations, and Speeches.* ¶Rab.

Panoplique: com. *Completely armed, in complete armour.*

Panosse. Vieille panosse. *An old toothlesse hag, a nastie or beggarlie beldame.*

Panouere: f. *A little Dosser, Basket, or Pannier.*

Panoye: f. Le Ieu de la pan. *A game, or kind of wrastling.*

Pans: m. *A kind of large impostumes; also, the Plurall vnto* Pan.

Pansard: m. *A guts, gorbellie, gulch; also, a kind of Turbot called, a Dab.*

Panse: f. *A paunch; Looke* Pance.

Raisins de panse. *Raisins of the Sunne.*

Panser. *To dresse, attend, or looke vnto; Seeke* Penser.

Pansotte: f. *A small paunch.*

Pansseron. *as* Panceron.

Pansu: m. uë: f. *Paunchie, great-bellied, full of guts.*

Pantagone: com. *Fiue-cornered.*

Pantagrueliste. *A Pantagruellist; a merrie Greeke, faithfull drunkard, good fellow.*

Pantagruellion. *Hempe.* ¶Rab.

Pantais: m. *The Pantasse, or Pantais; difficultie of breathing, (in Hawkes, &c.)*

Pantarbe. *A certaine blacke stone which resisteth fire.*

Pantarque. *See* Pancarte.

Pante. *See* Pente.

Panteine: f. *A great Net, or Toyle, vsed for the catching of wild beasts.*

Pantelant: m. ante: f. *Panting, throbbing; beating, or breathing thicke and short.*

Panteler. *To pant, or throb; to beat (also, to breath) short and thicke, or often together.*

Panteller. *as* Panteler.

Pantharbe. *The name of an artificiall Heauen, deuised by one* Ioachas *an Indian Magician.*

Panthelement: m. *A panting, or throbbing; also, a puffing, or fast-breathing; and hence (also) difficultie of breathing.*

Pantheologie: f. *The whole summe of Diuinitie.*

Panthere: f. *A Panther.*

Pantherien: m. enne: f. *Of a Panther; spotted as the Panther; (any way) like a Panther.*

Panthiere: f. *A great swoope-net, or drawing net.*

Panthois. *as* Pantois.

Pantiere. *as* Panthiere *(and the better Ortographie.)*

Pantime: f. *A bundle of raw silke.*

Pantiser. *To breath verie fast; to draw the breath often; to blow thicke and short; or as* Pantoiser.

Pantodiables. *All, or whole diuels.* ¶Rab.

Pantoiment: m. *A panting, or often blowing, by the shortnesse of breath.*

Pantoiment tourmenter. *To vex extreamely; by extreame vexation to shorten the breath, or put out of breath, or make a man scarce able to draw his breath.*

Pantois: m. *Short wind, pursinesse; a frequent breathing, or a difficult fetching of wind by the shortnesse of breath; in Hawkes we call it, the Pantais.*

Pantois: m. ise: f. *Short-winded, oft-breathing, out of breath; pursie, stuffed vp; breathing with difficultie, fetching wind with much adoe.*

Pantoiser. *To breath often, or be short-winded, or be out of breath; also, to breath with difficultie, fetch wind with much adoe.*

Pantomime: m. *An Actor of many parts in one Play; one that can represent the gesture, and counterfeit the speech, of any man.*

Pantoufle: f. *A pantofle, or slipper.*

Porter les souliers en pantoufle. *To tread, or weare his shooes downe at the heeles.*

Pantoufleux: m. euse: f. *Full of pantofles, fit for pantofles.*

Pantoyer. *as* Pantoiser.

Panurge: m. *A slye, craftie, deceitfull companion; an old beaten fox; one that hath experience, or hath been tampering, in most things; also, one that will meddle with, or haue a flirt at, any thing.*

Pao. *as* Par. *By.* ¶Gascon.

Paon: m. *A Peacocke; also, a kind of speckled fish.*

Paon celeste. *A wild Peacocke.*

Paon d'Inde. *A Turkie Cocke.*

Paon reuestu. *Looke* Reuestu.

Paon terrestre. *A tame Peacocke.*

Se Paonnader. *as* Se Paonner.

Paonneau: m. *A young Peacocke.*

Se Paonner. *To brag, or strout it like a Peacocke; proudly to open, or display his feathers; vaingloriously to boast of his outward parts, or faire outside; also (more tollerably) to take a prettie pride in himselfe.*

Paonnesse: f. *A Pea-henne.*

Paonnien: m. enne: f. *Of, or belonging to, a Peacocke; Peacock-like; prowd, or vainglorious, as a Peacocke.*

Paour. *Looke* Peur.

Paovre. *See* Povre.

Paovret. *A poore snake, or sneakesby.*

Paoureusement. *Fearefully, in great feare.*

Papacité: f. *The Papacie, or Popedome; also, Papistrie, Poperie.*

Papafigue: f. *A Gnat-snapper, or Fig-eater; a daintie little bird that resembles a Nightingale.*

Papal: m. ale: f. *Papall; of, belonging to, or like vnto, the Pope.*

Reverence papale. *See* Reverence.

Paparot: m. *Pap; or, a poultice.*

Pape: m. *A Pope, the Pope; (a word which, howsoeuer it be vsed, signifies a father;) also, as* Pappe.

Pape, & puis musnier: Prov. *Fallen from the highest to the lowest estate; or from pompe to pouertie.*

Vn bon pape est vn meschant homme: Pro. *A good Pope is a wicked man.*

Papechieu: m. *A Lapwing, Teewit, blacke Plouer.*

Papefif: m. *The maine course; that part of the maine-sayle whereto the bonnets, or dablers be fastened.*

Papefigue. *as* Papafigue.

Papegau. *as* Papegay.

Papegay: m. *A Parrot, or Popingay; also, a woodden Parrot (set vp on the top of a steeple, high tree, or pole) whereat there is, in many parts of France, a generall shooting once euerie yeare; and an exemption, for all that yeare, from* La Taille, *obtained by him that strikes downe the right wing thereof (who is therefore tearmed,* Le Chevalier;) *and by him that strikes downe the left wing (who is tearmed,* Le Baron;) *and by him that strikes downe the whole Popingay (who for that dexteritie or good hap hath also the title of* Roy, du Papegay, *all the yeare following.)*

Papelard. *An hipocrite, a dissembler; a flatterer.*

Papelarder. *To play the hipocrite; to dissemble, or counterfeit*

terfeit a holinesse; hence, falsely to collogue with; or vse faire words, and barbour foule thoughts.

Papelardie: f. *Hipocrisie, or outward shew of religion; a counterfeiting of zeale in religion; also, flatterie, smooth villanie, false colloguing.*

Papelardise. *as* Papelardie.

Papeligosse. *The countrey of Butterflyes.*

Paperassé: m. ée: f. *Rifled; or often tossed ouer, as the papers of a student.*

Paperasses: f. *Old, dustie, rotten, or often-rifled papers.*

Paperat: m. *A Paper-booke, or Note-booke.*

Papet. *as* Papin.

Papetasié: m. ée: f. *as* Papetassé; *or much fumbled, or often turned ouer, as a bundle of written papers.*

Papetassé: m. ée: f. *Patched, or poorely made vp with paper.*

Papetasser. *To patch, poorely to close, weakely to stop or make vp, as with paper.*

Papeterie: f. *A paper-Mill; also, a paper shop.*

Papetier: m. *A maker, or seller, of paper.*

Papier: m. *Paper; also, the paper-plant, or paper-reed (whereof in old time paper was made.)*

Papier baptistere. *The Church-booke wherein Christenings be recorded.*

Papiers brouillars. *Wast paper, or loose papers, wherein things be written carelesly, disorderly, or at randome.*

Papier iournal. *A Journall, Diarie, or Day-booke; a Register kept, or Commentarie written, of daylie actions, or accidents.*

Papier marchand. *Browne paper (wherein Tradesmen fould vp their wares.)*

Papiers de marchands. *Bills of Accompt, bookes of Reckoning; all sorts of writings which passe through Tradesmens hands.*

Papier raisin. *Grape paper.*

Papier de raison. *A Bill of Accompt, a booke of Reckoning.*

Papier terrier. *A Terrier; a Court-roll, or Catalogue of all the seuerall names, parcells, rents, and seruices belonging to, or yeelded by, the Tenants of a Mannor.*

L'herbe du papier. *The great Egiptian Rush, whereof, in old time, paper, and leaues to write on, were made.*

Vin papier. *White Wine; (called so by some Swizzers.)*

Le papier endure tout: Pro. *Paper indureth all;* *Seeke* Endurer.

Papieter. *Not to eat heartily, to dally with his meat.*

Papifigue: com. *A scorner of the Pope.*

Papille: f. *The nipple, or teat of a womans breast.*

Papillon: m. *A Butterfly; also, a sea-Bat.*

Le grand papillon. *A high Bourlet, or Hood, hauing on either side a large wing, and vsually worne heretofore by the dames of* Lyons.

Alaigre comme vn papillon. *As buxome as a Butterflye.*

Ioye de papillon: Pro. *Short, or momentarie glee; ioy which hardly lasts out a Summer.*

Papillot: m. *A little Butterfly; also, a plague-sore.*

Papillotage: m. *A spatling, or spottinesse; also, the twinckling, glistening, or shaking of spangles, &c.*

Papillotant. *Shewing, or shaking like spangles; glistening, twinckling; also, bespatling, or spotting.*

Papilloté. *as* Papillotté.

Papilloter. *To glisten, twinckle, or shake, like spangles; also, to bespangle, or set with spangles; also, to bespattle, or spot with durt.*

Papillotes: f. *Spangles.*

Papillotte: f. *Thistle-downe, or the soft downe blowne from the tops of flowers by the wind; also, a spangle.*

Papillottes de bouë. *Mirie spots, spatlings, bedashings.*

Il croit que les estoilles sont papillottes. *(Said of an ignorant, and sillie goosecap, that (as we say) thinkes the Moone is made of greene cheese.)*

Papillotté: m. ée: f. *Bespangled; wrought, set, beautified, or made garish, with spangles; also, bespattled, bedashed, spotted, with durt, &c.*

Papillottement: m. *A bespangling; also, a bespattling.*

Papillotter. *as* Papilloter.

Papillotteux: m. euse: f. *All-to-be-spangled; glistening, or set thicke, with spangles.*

Papimanes: com. *Papists; doters on the Pope.*

Papimanie: f. *Papistrie; Popish dotage, or, a doting on the Pope.*

Papin: m. *Pap for children.*

Papoage: m. *Inheritance by kindred, auncient descent.*

Papon: m. *Pap for children:* ¶ Gasc.

Papoal. Biens papoaux. *Which come from an auncestor, or by discent.*

Papoter. *Not to eat heartily, to dallie with his meat.*

Pappa. *Dad; (an infants language.)*

Pappe: m. *Thistle-downe; as* Papillotte; *also, the short, soft, and hairie cotton, or downe which growes on the leaues, and staulkes of some hearbes.*

Paquet: m. *A packet, fardle, bundle, trusse; Looke* Pacquet.

Paqueter. *To packe, trusse, bundle vp.*

Paquette. *See* Pasquette.

Par. *(A Preposition, as the Latine* Per; *signifies;) by, through; of, by reason of; for; on.*

Par ainsi. *Euen so, by this meanes, in that manner; also, wherefore, or therefore, for this cause.*

Par cy: Par là. *This way; that way.*

Par delà. *Seeke* Delà.

Par derriere: Par dessus. *Backward; vpward.*

Par devant. *Before; or, in the presence of.*

Par fois. *Now and then, sometimes.*

Par jour & par nuict. *Both day and night, at all times and tides.*

Par luy. qui est à tout par luy. *That lookes onely to himselfe; or, thats wholly swayed by his owne humors.*

Par mer, & par terre: &, par monts, & par vaux. *In towne and countrey, euerie where, in all places whatsoeuer.*

Par tant. *On this condition; also, therefore.*

Par tel si. *So that, on condition that.*

Par temps. *Seasonably, in verie good time, in a good houre.*

Par temps de guerre; paix, &c. *During the warre, peace, &c; or, while we had warre, peace, &c.*

Au par aller. *At the length.*

De par Dieu soit. *A Gods name be it; God prosper it, or send it good successe.*

De par moy. *By my meanes, or at my intreatie; also, from me; as in,* Ditez luy de par moy: *whence also,* voilà des lettres de par vostre femme; *sent from your wife.*

De par le Roy. *By the Kings appointment, commandement, or authoritie; from the King; (an ordinarie clause in the Proclamations made, and letters written, in his name;) also, with the King; as,* Il a tant de grace, & faveur

faveur de par le Roy. *The King fauours him so much, he is so gracious in his eyes.*

Parabande: f. *The rayle that runnes along on a ranke of Ballisters in a Terrace, &c.*

Parable: com. *Easie to be got, or come by; soone obtained, quickly recouered, readie at hand.*

Parabole: f. *A Parable, similitude, comparison; also, a certaine crooked line made by the cutting of a Cone, or Cylinder.*

Parabrin: m. *A gratulation, or welcome.*

Parachevé: m. ée: f. *(Fully) atchieued, dispatched, performed; accomplished, finished, concluded.*

Parachevement: m. *A (full) atchieuement, performance, riddance, dispatch; a consummation, accomplishment, absolute conclusion or end.*

Parachever. *(Fully) to atchieue, execute, performe, dispatch; finish, consummate, accomplish, make an absolute end of.*

Paraclitique: com. *Defamed, ill-reported of, that hath an ill name.*

Parade: f. *A (boasting) apparance, or shew; a brauado, or vaunting offer; also, a stop on horsebacke.*

Paradis: m. *Paradice, Heauen; a garden, or place, of perfect delight; a heauen on earth.*

Graine de paradis. *The spice called, Graines.*

Oiseau de paradis. *A certaine Egyptian bird, whose feathers dazle, by their glistening lustre, the eyes of such as behold her; also (another) white-bellied, and red-legd bird, thats bigger then a Heron, and beaked like a Parrot; many also call the Indian* Mammuque Oiseau de Paradis.

Pomme de paradis. *An excellent sweet apple that comes of a Peatmayn graffed on the stock of a Quince; some also call so our Honnymeale, or S. Johns apple.*

Paradoxe: f. *A Paradox; a strange, and odd conceit, or assertion, which differs from the common-receiued opinion.*

Paradoxique: com. *Paradoxicall, strange, odd, against common opinion.*

Parafé, & Parafer. *as* Paraphé & Parapher.

Parafernal. *Seeke* Paraphernal.

Parage: m. *Kindred, parentage, linage; also, equalitie of birth, or in bloud; also, coparcenerie, or partition of land among (noble) brothers, or sisters; (vsed onely where homage is due, and ceases after the fourth degree.)*

Haut parage. *Looke* Haut-parage.

Tenir en parage. *To hold part of a fief, as a coheire, or coparcener; or, younger brothers to hold of their elder by homage, and fealtie; which is therefore due vnto him, after partition, because he does homage vnto the Lord Paramount both for their parts, and his owne.*

Parageau: m. *A younger brother, who by partition enioyes part of the land descended from his auncestor.*

Parager: m. *A coparcener; or, as* Parageau.

Parageur: m. *The eldest brother; who by custome hath beene forced to giue equall shares of his auncestors land vnto his younger brethren.*

Paragon: m. *A paragon, or peerelesse one; the perfection, or flower of; the most complete, most absolute, most excellent peece, in any kind whatsoeuer; hence also, a Patterne, or Touchstone whereby the goodnesse of things is tryed.*

Paragonner. *To paragon; equall, match, or compare with; also, to examine, or try the goodnesse of a thing, by comparing it with other (excellent) things.*

Paragraphe: m. *A Paragraffe, or Pill-crow; a full sentence, head, or title of the (ciuill) Law; as much as is comprehended in one sentence, or section.*

Parain: m. *A Godfather; a Suretie in Baptisme.*

Paralelogramme. *A Paralelogramme, or long Square.*

Parallele: m. *A paralell; an equall distance (as) in lines, or circles.*

Paralleles. *The circles, and lines in the Sphere, drawn (with equall distance in euerie part) from the East to the West, and hauing one of the poles for their center.*

Parallele: com. *Paralell, equally distant asunder.*

Paralogizer. *To reason captiously, argue deceitfully, conclude falsely; to reason against reason.*

Paralysie: f. *The Palsie.*

Herbe de paralysie. *The Cowslip, or Oxslip, called also Palsiewort, and pettie Mullein.*

Paralytique: com. *Sicke of, or troubled with, the Palsie.*

Parangon. *as* Paragon; *whence;*

Pierre de parangon. *A Touchstone.*

Parangonneux: m. euse: f. *Full of comparisons.*

Paranniser. *To perpetuate. See* Perenniser.

Paranymphe: m. *An Orator, who a little before the commencement of Doctors, &c. makes a publicke speech in commendation of their honestie, and sufficiencie; also, an ouerseer, or an assistant in the ouersight, or ordering, of Bridall businesses.*

Parapet: m. *A Parapet, or wall breast-high; or defence, in forme of a Penthouse, on the vpper part of a Rampier.*

Paraphe: f. *The flourish, or peculiar knot, or marke set vnto, or after, or in stead of, a name in the signing of a Deed, or Letter; and generally, any such gracefull setting out of a mans hand, or name in writing; also, a subsignature, or signing vnder.*

Paraphé: m. ée: f. *Flourished; graced, or signed with a prettie marke, or knot; also, subsigned; written, or signed vnder.*

Parapher. *To flourish in writing; to grace, or beautifie the hand, or name, with prettie knots; to set a peculiar marke, or knot vnto, or after, or in stead of, a name in the signing of a Deed, or Letter; also, to subsigne; to write, or signe vnder.*

Paraphernal. Biens paraphernaux. *The goods which a wife brings her husband ouer and besides her dowrie, or mariage money; as her bedding, linnen, garments, iewels, &c.*

Paraphernes. *as* Biens Paraphernaux.

Paraphrase: f. *A Paraphrase; an exposition that holds the sence, but changes the words, of the thing expounded.*

Paraphraste: m. *A Paraphrast, or Paraphrasor; one that expounds a Text by other words then it is written in.*

Parappel. *as* Parapet.

Parasangue: f. *Thirtie furlongs; or (about) three, and three quarters, of our miles; a Persian measure.*

Parasceve: f. *A preparation, or preparing.*

Iour parasceve. *Good Friday among Christians; among the Iewes any Friday; when they commonly prouide all things necessarie for the day following, their Sabaoth, whereon they are forbidden all worke.*

Paraseline: f. *A false Moone, or apparance of a Moone.*

Parasite: m. *A Parasite; a trencher-friend, or bellie-friend; a smell-feast, and buffoone at feasts; a clawback, flatterer, soother, smoother for good cheare sake.*

Parasol: m. *as* Ombrelle.

Parastates: f. *The conduits, or passages whereby the seed goes from the kidneyes in the act of generation; or,* two

two kernels which grow at the end of the bladder, and receiue the seed brought vnto them by Vasa deferentia; *also, stones set to, or about, a pillar.*

Parastre: m. *A step-father, a father in law.*

Paravant. *Before, heretofore, in former times.*

Parc: m. *A Parke; a Close, Ground, or Place impaled; also, a Sheepe-fold; also, a Stue, or Fish-pond inclosed.*

Vn parc d'arbres. *A Copse, or Coppice; an impaled, or inclosed groue of trees.*

Chastrer le parc. *Looke* Chastrer.

Parcage: m. *A Parke, or Inclosure; also, an inclosing; also, a foulding (as of Sheepe;) also, a Pound; or as* Parchage.

Parce que. *Because that, for as much as.*

Parcelé: m. ée: f. *Peecemealed; cut, or made, into parcels.*

Parcelle: f. *A parcell; particle, peece, little part.*

'A parcelles. *By degrees, by little and little.*

Par parcelles. *Particularly, by parcels, peecemeale, one peece after another.*

Parchage: m. *Impoundage, or an impounding; also, as* Parcage.

Parchemin: m. *Parchement.*

Parchemin innocent. *Looke* Innocent.

Parchemin vierge. *Parchement made of an abortiue skinne.*

Parcheminerie: f. *Parchment-making; also, the street, or place, wherein Parchement is sold.*

Parcheminier: m. *A Parchement-maker.*

Parciere. Terres baillées à par. *Let out vnto parts, or for part of their crop.*

Parcion. *A coparceners portion.*

Parcité: f. *Parcitie, sparing, scantnesse, neerenesse; frugalitie, thrift, sauing; niggardlinesse.*

Parçon. *as* Parcion.

Parçonnier: m. *A coheire, or coparcener.*

Parcoulé: m. ée: f. *Strayned through.*

Parcouler. *To strayne through.*

Parcourir. *To runne through.*

Parcours: m. *Custome, vsage, auncient proceeding in points of commerce betweene the Townes, or Countries of seuerall Lords.*

Bourgeois de parcours. *Freemen of the Iurisdiction of* Sens *in the marches of* Champaigne, *who by a bare challenge may aduow themselues to be also the Kings freemen.*

Parcreu. *as* Parcru.

Parcroissant: m. ante: f. *Waxing ripe, approaching to perfection; also, growing among.*

Parcroistre. *To ripen, or make an end of growing; to wax perfect, or come to it full pitch; also, to grow among.*

Parcru: m. uë: f. *Full-growne, throughly ripe; mellow, flush; come to perfection, or to a full pitch; also, growne, or sprung vp among.*

Pardé. *as* Par Dieu. ¶Poictevin.

Pardigoince: f. *(The name of) a great, and delicate Plumme.*

Pardil. *A darke-spotted gray colour of a horse.*

Pardon: m. *Pardon, forgiuenesse; remission;* (Se donne par lettres seellees sur double queuë en cire iaune, & au cas qui requiert punition corporelle autre que de mort. ¶Ragueau.) *Wherein it differs from our Pardon some way, and from the French* Remission *euerie way.)*

Les pardons. *The Popes Pardons.*

De grand (ou petit) peché grand (ou petit) pardon: Prov. *Great offences need great pardons; little faults are soone forgiuen.*

Pardonnable: com. *Pardonable, forgiueable.*

Pardonné: m. ée: f. *Pardoned, forgiuen, remitted.*

Pardonnement: m. *A pardoning, remitting, forgiuing.*

Pardonner. *To pardon, forgiue, remit a fault, release a debt, hold excused of.*

Pardonne à tous mais a toy point: Pro. *Pardon all men but thy selfe; or, pardon other mens offences, but punish thine owne.*

Pardonnigere: m. *A Pardon-bearer; one that carries, and makes sale of, the Popes Pardons, vp and downe a countrey.*

Pardonnir. *To sleepe soundly, to take a long, or full sleepe; to take his penniworthes of the pillow; or, to finish, or sleepe out, his sleepe.*

Pardurable: com. *Looke* Perdurable.

Paré: m. ée: f. *Gracefully dressed, dight, arrayed; ordered, or furnished; decked, adorned, garnished; also, hanged with Tapistrie; also, warded, or defended from a blow, &c; and shrowded, or sheltred vnder; also, pared, as the hoofe of a horse.*

Pomme parée. *Ripened in straw, &c; made mellow by art.*

Vin paré. *Wine that is fined, Wine thats readie to be drawne, or drunke.*

Quand la Messe fut chantée si fut la dame parée: Prov. *By that time Masse was done, her Ladiship was dressed.*

Pareade: f. *A certaine fierie-coloured, quick-sighted, and wide-mouthed Serpent, not verie venomous.*

Pareage. *as* Parage; *(an old word.)*

Pareatis. *(The Conclusion of a peremptorie Warrant, or Iniunction; like vnto our) Hereof faile ye not, &c.*

Pare-coup: m. *A ward-blow; or, any thing that serues to keepe off, or put by, a blow.*

Parée. Droict de parée. *Looke* Droict.

Parefrenier. *as* Palfrenier.

Pareil: m. *A match, or fellow, in Gloues, Cuffes, Shooes, &c.*

Qui n'a point son pareil. *A paragon; that hath not his match, that hath no peere.*

Pareil: m. eille: f. *Like, equall, euen, or matching with; mutuall, semblable.*

La pareille. *Like for like, as much for as much, one for another.*

Chasque oüeille cerche sa pareille: Prov. *Euerie sheepe her mate doth seeke; fooles take no comfort but in companie.*

Pareillement. *Likewise, in like manner, semblably, after the same fashion, iust so, euen so, also.*

Parelie: f. *A false Sunne, or apparance of a Sunne.*

Parelle: f. *The hearbe Dockes, or the sharpe-pointed Docke; also, Patience, Monkes Rhubarbe; (a kind thereof.)*

Parelle grande. *The great sharpe-pointed Docke.*

Parelle de marais. *The great water-Docke, or Sorrell; called also water Sorrell, and horse Sorrell.*

Parelle petite. *Ditch Docke, the small water Docke.*

Parelle pointuë. *The (ordinarie) sharpe-pointed Docke.*

Parement: m. *A decking, tricking, garnishing, adorning; a comelie dressing, a gracefull dighting; handsome furnishing, orderlie arraying; also, Arras, Tapistrie, or any costlie Hangings; also, a warding, or defending, in fight; also, a shrowding, or sheltering vnder; also, a paring (of a horses hoofe;) also,* Vne sorte de chair rouge qui vient par dessus la venaison des deux costez du corps d'un cerf.

Cham-

Chambre de parement. *The chamber of Presence.*
Lict de parement. *A womans childbed; also, a bed of State, or, a great Sparuer bed, that serues onely for shew, or to set out a roome.*
Muraille à deux paremens de pierre de taille. *Hauing two courses of, or couered on both sides with, free stone.*
Parence: f. *as* Parure (*in the last sence.*)
Parennité. *Looke* Perennité.
Parensus. Vn par. *A surplusage, ouerplus, remainder;* Le parensus. *The before-named.*
Parent: m. *A kinsman, cousin, allie.*
Parent de Moyse. *A Cuckold. Looke* Moyse.
Parens sans amis, Amis sans pouvoir, Pouvoir sans vouloir, Vouloir sans effect, Effect sans profit, Profit sans vertu, ne vaut vn festu: Pro.
Assez parens assez tourmens: Prov. *Many kinsmen much affliction.*
Qui a mal aux dents a mauvais parents: Prov. *He that is famished hath but ill friends.*
Parentage: m. *Parentage, kindred, affinitie, alliance.*
Parentage d' hanetons. *Kindred intertained for some lecherous respect. Seeke* Haneton.
Parenté: f. *A parentage; linage, bloud, stocke, familie, kindred; also, affinitie, consanguinitie, neerenesse of bloud.*
Bonne amitié seconde parenté: Pro. *A sound friend is a second kinsman.*
Parentelle: f. *Kindred, affinitie, consanguinitie, alliance.*
Parenthese: f. *A Parenthesis.*
Parer. *To decke, tricke, trimme, garnish, adorne, dresse comely, dight gracefully; furnish handsomely, order decently; (also, to prepare, or prouide sufficiently;) also, to hang richly, as a roome with Arras; also, to ward, or defend a blow; whence,* Parer l'escu aux coups de; *to oppose his shield against the blowes of; also, to pare the hoofe of a horse.*
Se parer de. *To couer, shrowd, or shelter himselfe vnder.*
Parer le drap. *To dresse, or smooth cloth with cards made of Tazles.*
Parer l'enlisseure à faire toile. *To starch the yarne whereof Linnen cloth is to be made.*
Parer du fruict sur paille. *To ripen, or mellow fruit in straw.*
Il para sa masse. *He charged, or lift vp, his club.*
Parez vn herisson il semblera baron: Prov. *Tricke vp an Vrchin he will seeme a Baron; good apparrell (as Loue) couers many a fault.*
Parergue: m. *An addition, appendix, accesse; a thing put vnto, though no part of, the matter; any thing that is besides the principall question, point, or purpose in hand.*
Paresol. *as* Ombrelle.
Paresse: f. *Sloath, lazinesse, idlenesse, lithernesse, loytering, sluggishnesse, languishing negligence.*
Paresser. *To laze it, slug it, loyter, liue idly.*
Paresseusement. *Sloathfully, lazily, most idly.*
Paresseux: m. euse: f. *Sloathfull, sluggish, lazie, lither, loytering, most negligent; (and hence) also, dull, slow; cold, vnlustie, languishing.*
Le paresseux aime bien besongne faicte: Pro. *The sluggard loues alife things done to his hand.*
Iamais dormeur ne fit bon guet, ny paresseux ne fit beau faict: Prov. *The sleepie head, and sloathfull hand, watch, and worke, ill alike.*
Paret: m. *A wall.* ¶Langued.

Paretoine: m. *A certaine fattie Painters white.*
Pareure. *as* Parure.
Parfaict: m. cte: f. *Perfected, performed, accomplished, consummated, finished, fully made or done vp; also, perfect, complete, excellent, absolute, singular.*
Parfaictement. *Perfectly, completely, excellently, absolutely.*
Parfaire. *To perfect, performe, consummate, accomplish, finish, end fully, goe through-stitch with, make or doe vp throughly.*
Mal fait qui ne parfait; &, Rien ne fait qui ne parfait: Pro. *He does but ill, or as ill as nothing, who leaues a worke before he ends it.*
Rien n'est bien faict que ce que Dieu parfait: Pro. *Nothing's well done which God hath not a hand in.*
Parfaiseur: m. *A perfecter, accomplisher, finisher, through-doer; a sure card; a performer of what he vndertakes.*
Parfiler. *To spinne all, or spinne throughly.*
Parfin. à la parfin. *At length, at last, in the end, when all is done, when all comes to all.*
Parfois. *Sometimes, now and then.*
Parfondeur: f. *Profunditie.*
Se Parforcer. *To labour, striue, indeauour throughly; to attempt seriously, to doe his best or vtmost.*
Parfournir. *To performe, consummate, accomplish, fulfill; also, to supply, furnish, fill, or make vp.*
Parfum: m. *Perfume, sweet odour.*
Parfumatoire: com. *Perfumatorie, perfuming; vsed in, or for, perfumes; whence,* Canon parfum. *See* Canon.
Parfumer. *To perfume; to sweeten, to giue a delicate sent or smell vnto.*
Pargoys. Cousteau pargoys. *A paltrie little childs knife.*
Parguarir. *To cure soundly, heale throughly.*
Pariage: m. *Equalitie, correspondencie, matching; a due and iust exchange, equall tearmes, like for like, one for another.*
Droict de pariage. *Looke* Droict.
Parier. *To bett, lay, stake downe, at game; also, to breed, ingender, beget, or bring forth, young.*
Parietaire: f. *Pellitorie of the wall.*
Parietaux: m. *(The name of) two bones, which be in the vpper, and fore-part of the skull.*
Parisien: m. enne: f. *Parisien, of Paris; whence;* Matines Parisiennes. *The Massacre of Paris.*
Parisis. *Of Paris; after the Parisien fashion, or computation. Seeke* Livre, & Sol.
Parité: f. *Paritie, equalitie, euennesse, likenesse.*
Paritoire: f. *Pellitorie of the wall.*
Parjure: com. (Subst.) *A periurer, or periured person, a fore-Sworne wretch.*
Parjure: com. (Adject.) *Periured, oath-falsifying, absolutely forsworne.*
Parjurement: m. *Periurie, forswearing, oath-falsifying, faith-breaking.*
Se Parjurer. *To forsweare himselfe; to violate faith giuen; to breake, or falsifie his oath.*
Parlant: m. ante: f. *Speaking, talking, vttering his mind.*
Parlé: m. ée: f. *Spoken, vttered, talked, discoursed of.*
Parlement: m. *A speaking, talking, discoursing; reasoning, arguing; a parleying, communing, conferring, conuersing with; also, a supreame, or soueraigne Court, or Session, of Iustice, established in eight capitall Cities of France; viz.* Paris, Grenoble, Tholose, Dijon, Rouën, Aix, Renes, & Bordeaux. (*In old time, and when*

there was but one of these Courts, it followed the King whither soeuer he went, vntill Philippes de Valois, *(or, as some affirme,* Loys Hutin) *setled it, and made it ordinarie, in* Paris; *after which, other Princes, at seuerall times, established the rest. Before, and about that time,* Tenir le parlement *was as much as* Tenir les Estats *(or to hold a Parliament in England) is at this day.*

Licts de parlement. *Beds that be stuffed with Chestnut leaues; called so of the confused noise yeelded by them when they be stirred, or stird on.*

Parlementer. *To parley, conferre, commune, talke, discourse with.*

Parlementerie: f. *A parley, or parleying, a conference, a communication.*

Parler: m. *Speech, talke, language, vtterance, words.*

Beau parler n'escorche langue: Prov. *Looke* Escorcher.

A beau parler closes oreilles: Pro. *For glosing words well-closed eares.*

On cognoist les balles aux marques des marchãds, & les ames au parler: Pro. *As packs by marks, so wits by words, are knowne.*

Parler. *To speake, talke, declare, say, tell, vtter the mind; to commune, parley, reason, conferre, discourse, conuerse.*

Parler à sa barrette. *To talke roughly vnto, expostulate roundly with, tell plainly of errors committed, or iniuries done.*

Parler bien à. *To beat, vex, chafe, mad with words.*

Parler de quelqu'un en bonne, ou mauvaise bouche. *To commend, or discommend.*

Parler brutif. *To faulter, maffle, famble; to speake as one that hath plummes in his mouth.*

Parler dessous la ceincture. *(A fashion of speech peculiar vnto cheating prisoners.)*

Parler à cheval. *as vnder* Cheval.

Parler entre les dents. *To mutter, murmure, mumble vp his words; to speake like a Mouse in a Cheese.*

Parler doulcement à. *To sooth, flatter, smooth; cog, or collogue with; make faire weather, or giue good words, vnto.*

Parler par escot. *To speake by turnes, to heare one another speake.*

Parler gros. *To swagger, threaten, speake big, vse bugs words; also, to rore; to thunder.*

Parler Latin. *See* Latin.

Parler Latin devant les Clercs, ou Cordeliers. *(We say the same) to speake Latine before Clarks.*

Parler livre. *To speake profoundly, or beyond the vnderstanding of ordinarie men; (Ironically.)*

Parler par livre. *To speake by booke; a Preacher, or Orator to read the most of his Sermon, or Oration.*

Parler en maistre. *To commaund, appoint, bid, inioyne, controwle.*

Parler comme vn oiseau en cage. *To babble, prattle, tattle, chatter; to talke idly; to vse many words to verie small purpose.*

Parler à tastons. *To guesse, or harpe at, to speake at randome, or onely by coniecture.*

Parler à traicts. *Looke* Traict.

S'escoutant parler comme vn porc qui pisse. *Hearing himselfe discourse with the deliberation which a Hog doth vse in pissing.*

Il sçait aller, & parler. *(Said of an industrious, discreet, cunning, and comelie person.)*

Qui a si parle. *He that hath any game let him shew it; (a phrase at Primero, &c.)*

'A peu parler bien besongner: Pro. *Lets haue fewer words, and more deeds; or, good deeds are (commonly) dispatched in fewest words.*

Hardiment parle teste saine: Pro. *The speech of the innocent is confident.*

Il ne parle pas au Roy qui veut: Prov. *Euerie one hath not the Kings eare at commaund.*

Mieux vaut se taire que mal parler: Prov. *Better a silent, then a senceless, tongue.*

Quand d'autruy parler tu voudras regarde toy, & te tairas: Prov. *Let him that meanes to tax another, examine himselfe, and then he will be silent.*

Qui ne parle n'erre: Prov. *He that speakes not, erres not.*

Qui tient boutique doit parler à chascun: Pro. *He that keepes shop must speake to euerie one.*

Qui veut bien parler bien doit pourpenser: Prov. *Let him premeditate, that meanes to speake, well.*

Trop grater cuict, trop parler nuict: Prov. *Excesse, in scratching breedeth smart, in speaking mightie scathe.*

Parleresse. Langue par. *A long tongue, or pratling tongue; a tongue that neuer lyeth.)*

Parlerie: f. *A prattling, tattling, babling, talking.*

Parleur: m. *A speaker, talker, discourser.*

Parlier: m. *A Pleader, Imparler; Atturney.*

Parlier: m. ere: f. *Speaking; in, of, or belonging vnto, speech.*

Parlire. *To read ouer, to read through.*

Parloer. *as* Parloir.

Parloir: m. *A Parlour; also, the Roome out of which Nunnes doe speake (through an Iron grate) vnto the lay people that come vnto them.*

Parloire. *A prattling, or idle discourse.*

Parlouër: m. *A Parliament, or Assemblie of Estates; a publicke conference.*

Parlouër aux Bourgeois. *An Assemblie, Meeting, or common Counsell of Citizens (tearmed so in old time.)*

Parmentier: m. *A Taylor.* ¶Pic.

Parmesan: m. *An inhabitant of* Parma *(in* Italie;) *also, the Cheese Parmesan (made at* Parma.)

Parmi, *or* Parmy. *Among, through, in the thickest of.*

Parnage. *as* Pasnage; *Pawnage.*

Parnombrer. *To number throughly, count all through, reckon all ouer, tell all out.*

Paroccir. *To kill outright, make a full end of, rid out of paine, dispatch out of the way.*

Parodelle: f. *A kind of Cheese-cake.*

Paroi. *as* Paroy.

Paroice. *A Parish; Looke* Paroisse.

Paroir: m. *A Farriers paring-knife, or paring Iron.*

Paroir. *To appeare, or be seene; to peepe out, as the day in a morning, or the Sunne ouer a mountaine; to shew, present, or manifest himselfe.*

Paroisse: f. *A Parish.*

Manches de deux paroisses. *Sleeues of two parishes; viz. whose vpper part is of one kind of stuffe, and the nether of another.*

Paroissien: m. *A Parishioner.*

Parole: f. *A word; a tearme; also, a speech, or saying.*

Avoir la parole fort bonne. *(Vsed, to signifie not so much eloquence, as gracefullnesse, of speech;) to speake out plaine, or without stammering; to goe smoothly, run glibly, passe roundly, on.*

Donner parole. Il avoit secrettement donné parole au Roy. *He had vnder hand offered the King his seruice; or had assured him that he would be for him.*
Humer la parole. *Seeke* Humer.
Des paroles ils vindrent au poil. *From threats they came to effects; from the spending of breath to the spilling of bloud.*
Les paroles font le jeu: Pro. *Words make the game; Oxen by ropes, but men by words, are bound.*
Les paroles ne puent point: Pro. *(Bare) words haue no ill sauor.*
Les paroles du soir ne resemblent pas à celles du matin: Pro. *The euening chat's not like the mornings tattle.*
'A paroles lourdes sourdes oreilles: Prov. *Let th' eares be deafe when words grow rude; harsh tearmes are most vnworthie of attention.*
Bonne parole bon lieu tient: Prov. *A good word hath great acceptation; good language brings it welcome along with it.*
Douce parole n' escorche langue: Prov. *Seeke* Doux.
Douce parole rompt grand ire: Pro. *Fell spleene is quayled by faire speech.*
Longues paroles font les iours courts: Prov. *Long discourses make short dayes.*
Meschante parole iectée va par tout à la volée: Pro. *A bad word quickly flyes abroad; a bad report set once on foot, spreads farre.*
Meschantes paroles ont meschant lieu: Prov. *Bad words find bad acceptance, or are badly intertained.*
'A bon iour bon oeuvre, & bonnes paroles: Prov. *Good workes, and words are fittest for good dayes.*
Parolette: f. *A little word, or speech; but a word or two.*
Parolle. *as* Parole.
Paron. *A damme; an old one that hath young ones.*
Parons. *as* Parens; *Kinsfolkes.*
Paronnel. *The name of a Peare whereof good Perrie is made.*
Paronychie: f. *Whitlo-grasse, Nayle-wort (a weed.)*
Paroximique: com. *Of, or in, the fit of an ague.*
Paroxisme: m. *The returne, or fit, of an ague.*
Paroy: f. *A wall.*
Parpaie: f. *A full payment, or the rest of a payment.*
Parpaigne: f. *A pillar, buttresse, or supporter of stone-work, seruing to beare vp a beame, or summer, in a wall.*
Parpaillon. *as* Parpillon.
Parpaing. *as* Parpaigne.
Parpayer. *To pay throughly, soundly, all.*
Parpeine. *as* Parpaigne.
Parpillon: m. *The little fish called, a Shrimp.*
Parpillottes: f. *Spangles, or Oes.*
Parpin: m. *A great lumpe of stone, vnsquared, or newly cut out of the Quarrey.*
Parquage. *as* Parcage.
Parqué: m. ée: f. *Parked, foulded; impaled, inclosed, hedged, or hemmed in; also, planted, set downe, fixed, or setled in a place; also, strongly incamped.*
Parquer. *To parke, fould; impale, inclose, hedge or hemme in; to compasse about with pales, hedges, walls, &c; also, to soiourne, or stay long, in a place.*
Se parquer. *To plant, set downe, or settle themselues; to pitch their camp, and inclose it with strong defences.*
Il se parque bien. *He defends himselfe exceeding well.*
Parquet: m. *A little Parke, or place impaled; also, the Barre, or Inclosure of a Court of Iustice; sometimes also the Court it selfe; and sometimes, the House, or Hall, wherein tis kept.*
Parquet de jardin. *A Bed, or Border in a Garden.*
Parquetages: m. *Foulds of Hurdles for Sheepe; also, Parkes, or impaled grounds; and particularly, small peeces of salt-marshes, whereinto the sea water is by Salt-makers let, of purpose to be kept vntill the heat of the Sunne haue congealed it.*
Parquoy. *Why? wherefore? also, therefore, for thus, or for which, cause.*
Ie ne t'ay fait, ne dit le parquoy tu me doives faire ce que tu me fais. *I haue giuen you small cause to vse me thus.*
Parrain: m. *A Godfather.*
Parrasine: f. *Stone-Rosin.*
Parricide: com. *A Parricide; a murtherer of his owne father; also, any hainous murtherer.*
Parricider. *To murther his owne father; also, to commit any hainous, or vnnaturall murther.*
Parrin: m. *A Godfather.*
Parrodelle: f. *as* Parodelle.
Parroquet. *as* Perroquet.
Parservir. *To serue throughly, to serue long and well; whence;*
Mal sert qui ne parsert: Pro.
Parsimonie: f. *Parsimonie, sparing, thrift, good husbandrie.*
Parsonnier: m. *A Partener, or Coparcener.*
Parsoy. à parsoy. *Apart, alone, by himselfe; also, from him, by his intreatie or meanes.*
Part: m. *A birth, or bringing forth, as of children; the fruit of a womans wombe; any brood, or litter.*
Part: f. *A part, share, portion, peece; a ioint, limme, quarter; also, a partie, or side; also, a place, coast, or countrey.*
'A part. *Apart, aside, out of the way, out of high wayes; alone, in priuate, secretly, by himselfe.*
Se retirer à part. *To retire, or withdraw himselfe; to get him out of all companie.*
De sa part elle est pucelle. *For all him, or for any thing he hath done, she is a maid.*
En bonne part. Il a le cœur assis en bonne part. *There is great mettall, good stuffe, much vertue, in him.*
Quelque part. *Somewhere, somewhether;* Quelque part que. *Wheresoeuer, or whethersoeuer that.*
Faire la part au plus esloigné; ou, au plus ieune. *To make one but a verie sleight share, to giue him what he list himselfe, or nothing so much as his due.*
L' homme qui a de l' art possede sa part: Prov. *The skilfull gets a share in euerie thing.*
Qui n'y est n'y a sa part: Pro. *He thats not there gets nothing there.*
Partage: m. *A partage, partition, or parting; a sharing, diuiding, or diuision.*
En matiere criminelle n'y a partage. Id est, paribus numero sententijs ea superat que pro reo facit; *or,* Aequo sententiarum numero reus absolvitur.
Partageable: com. *Partible, diuidable.*
Partager. *To part, seuer, diuide, share out.*
Partant. (Partic.) *Parting, departing, going from.*
Partant. *Therefore; on this condition.*
Parterre: m. *A floore; also, a plaine close, or any euen plot, or peece of ground; and hence, a Garden, or the part of a Garden, which consists of beds, and borders of hearbes, and flowers, without any tree among them.*
Parti: m. *A match, bargaine, condition, or offer conditionall; and hence, a marriage, a husband or wife; and, a meanes, fortune, estate; also, a partie, or side.*

Prendre parti. *To bethinke himselfe, to pawse vpon; to be aduised, or take deliberation, in a matter.*

Tenons nous en parti avec le ciel. *Let vs hold quarter, or continue our league, with heauen; let vs hold with religion, cherish deuotion, keepe God on our side.*

Parti: m. ie: f. *Parted, diuided, seuered, distinguished; also, gone, departed.*

Procez parti. *The Court diuided in opinion.*

Partiaire: com. *In parts, for parts, of parts.*

Campagne partiaire. *A Commons, or common Field, (wherein euerie commoner is stinted.)*

Compagnie partiaire. *Companie ingaged together; or whereof euerie one hath a share in the particular suit, or businesse managed by them.*

Mestayer partiaire. *A Farmer which is to yeeld his Landlord a certaine part of the fruits gotten in his Farme.*

Partial: m. ale: f. *Solitarie, priuate, retired, vnsociable, all for himselfe; also, partiall, vnequall, factious, more affected to one then another.*

Partialiser. *To partialize it; to side, bandie, be partiall, or factious; to take parts.*

Partialité: f. *Partialitie, vnindifferencie, siding, factiousnesse; also, a faction.*

Participant: m. *A partner, partaker, or sharer with; a complice, companion, associate, confederate, accessorie, adherent.*

Participant: m. ante: f. *Participant, partaking, or sharing with; adherent, or adhering vnto.*

Participe: m. *A Participle (in Grammar.)*

Participer. *To participate, share, communicate with; also, to partake, or take part with, or take the part of; to adhere, or cleaue vnto.*

Participial: m. ale: f. *Participiall; of, or belonging to, a Participle.*

Participialement. *As a Participle.*

Particularisé: m. ée: f. *Particularized, particularly mentioned; seuered, shared, distinguished.*

Particulariser. *To particularize; to make peculiar, or priuate; to distinguish, or seuer from others; to name specially, to mention particularly.*

Particularité: f. *A particularitie; a speciall, priuate, peculiar, or odd, thing.*

Particulier: m. ere: f. *Particular; priuate, peculiar, proper, ones owne; also, distinct, seuerall, speciall; odd, singular.*

Particulierement. *Particularly, specially, peculiarly; singularly; distinctly, seuerally.*

Partie: f. *A part, share, portion; peece, ioint, member; also, a partie, side, faction; and a match, or set, at game; also, a bargaine, or contract; also, a partie, client, or suitor, in Law; also, an Aduocate, or Counsellor at Law; also, an Accompt; or a head, or summe, in an Accompt.*

Parties. *Parts, conditions, qualities; also, a Taylors Bill.*

Parties casuelles. *Money made of the sale of Offices; also (but lesse properly) all casualties, as Escheats &c, and casuall forfeitures, as fines vpon penall Statutes, forfeitures by vnlawfull Vsurie, &c.*

Partie civile & formée. *He that pursues a criminall action, onely in respect of, or to get some amends for, the wrong done to himselfe.*

Partie civile, & interessée. *The same.*

En partie. *Partly, in part, not altogether.*

Prins à partie. *Sued, accused, or called in question; opposed, withstood, or vndertaken, as an Aduersarie.*

Il plaidoye beau qui plaidoye sans partie: Pro. *He fairely pleads that finds no Aduersarie.*

Vne partie n'est point le tout: Prov. *A part is not the whole; a peecing no perfection.*

Partiere. *as* Partiaire.

Partiment: m. *A parting, diuiding, sundering, seuering; also, a parting, or departing.*

Partir. *To part, sunder, diuide, seuer; also, to part, depart, remoue, or goe from.*

Partir le gasteau. *See* Gasteau.

Partir de la main. *To part from the hand, to set or put on, freely; (a Riders phrase.)*

Partir les oreilles. *To beare both sides.*

Partir du poing. *A Hawke to couet freely; or goe from the hand as soone as she spies her game.*

Le chanteau part le vilain. *See* Vilain.

Ce n'est pas tout de courir, il faut partir à temps: Prov. *A cause must be as well begun seasonably, as followed seriously.*

Partisan: m. *A partner, partaker; associate, confederate; accessorie, adherent.*

Partissement: m. *as* Partiment.

Partisseur: m. *A parter, diuider, sharer, distributor, seuerer, sunderer.*

Partizant. *as* Participant.

Part-prenant: m. *A partaker, sharer; contributor, in a charge to be payed, or seruice to be yeelded; a purchasor that so contributes; and hence;*

Tenir comme part-prenant. *A purchasor to hold part of a fief by contribution with others in the charge, or duties, whereto the whole is lyable.*

Partroublé: m. ée: f. *Extreamely troubled, molested, vexed, annoyed, perplexed.*

Partroublement: m. *An extreame trouble, or sore troubling.*

Partuer. *To kill outright.*

Party. *Looke* Parti; *also, a departure, or departing; a parting, or going away.*

Parvanche. *as* Pervenche.

Parvenir. *To atchieue, attaine, arriue, or come vnto; also, to chieue, thriue, come vp, or come forward in the world.*

Parvis: m. *The Porch of a Church; also (or more properly) the vtter court of a Pallace, or great House.*

Parvité: f. *Smallnesse, littlenesse.*

Parure: f. *A decking, tricking, trimming; also, array, apparrell, attire; also, a Liuerie, or Suit of apparrell.*

Pas: m. *A pace, a step, a stride; a measure of two foot and a halfe; or (as in some places) of three and a halfe; or (as among the old Romanes) of fiue; also, a foot, or footing; also, a pace, gate, or ordinarie traine in going; also, a strait, narrow passage, or strait path; and such a passage kept by one, or moe knights against all commers; and thence also, a Tournay.*

Le pas. *The strait betweene Calis and Douer.*

Pas d'Abbé. *Looke* Abbé.

Pas d'Asne. *Fole-foot, Colts-foot, Horse-foot, Hall-foot, an hearbe; also, a fashion of a Port, or Vpset, in the mouth of a Bitt; also, a certaine Iron ring in the forecastle of a Ship.*

Pas de cheval. *as* Pas d'Asne *(in the first sence.)*

Pas de Clerc. *A foolish tricke, simple part, grosse ouersight, fond pranke.*

Pas d'escrevisse. *A recoyling; a going, or giuing, backe.*

Pas Geometrique. *A fadome; or fiue feet, of foure handfuls to the foot.*

Pas de larron. *See* Larron.
Pas de Lion. *Lions foot, Lions paw, great Sanicle, our Ladies mantle.*
Le pas de la mort. *The path of death; a step vnto it, or, the point of it.*
Trois pas, & vn saut. *The Almond, or Alman, leape.*
Vn pas, & vn saut. *A Pace, and a Leape; a Manage, or Ayre in Horsemanship, tearmed otherwise, the Paßa-salto, or Gallop Galliard.*
Lettres de pas. *Passes, or Pasports.*
Vn faux pas. *A slip, or misse, in footing; and hence, a fault, error, or mistaking; also, a false, or hollow peece of ground that sinkes vnder a mans foot as he goes.*
Mauvais pas. *Ill way.*
Plus viste que le pas. *Exceeding fast, or as fast as his legs would carrie him.*
Aller à pas menu. *To goe nicely, tread gingerly, mince it like a maid.*
Aller le pas. *To pace, or goe a foot pace, to walke faire and softly, or faire and leisurely.*
Courir en deux pas vn saut. *To runne speedily, swiftly, in hast, apace.*
I'auray fait en deux pas & vn saut. *I shall haue dispatched in a trice.*
Entamer le pas. *To begin, or breake the ice; to lead the way, or the daunce; to make an entrie, or ouerture, vnto.*
Fermer le pas à. *To stop the way, to interrupt or stay the proceeding of.*
La Mort l' attend à deux pas pres. *Death is at his elbow, within an ynch of him, readie to seize on him.*
Passer le pas. *To goe the way of all flesh; to dye.*
Plaindre ses pas. *Looke* Plaindre.
Tailler le pas à. *as* Entamer le pas. *To begin vnto.*
Pas à pas le bœuf prend le lievre: Pro. *Step after step the Ox doth catch a Hare; by diligence, and continuance in a direct course the dullest wit comes to great knowledge.*
Pas à pas on va bien loing: Pro. *Step after step goes farre.*
Pas. (*A Particle that euer inforces, or addes weight vnto, a Negatiue;) not at all, no way possibly, by no manner of meanes.*
Non pas? *Art thou not? is it not? are we not? &c.*
Pascage: m. *Grasing, feeding, or pasturing of Cattell.*
Pascal. *as* Paschal.
Paschal: m. ale: f. *Paschall; of, in, or belonging to, the feast of Easter.*
L'Agneau paschal. *The Paschall Lambe; or the Passeouer.*
Paschier: m. *A Pasture Ground; or a Ground thats fit, or serues, for nought but the pasturing of cattell.*
Pascrit: m. ite: f. *Faded, discoloured, dryed, out of season.*
Pasle: com. *Pale, wan, bleake, whitish.*
Les pasles couleurs. *The greene Sicknesse.*
Couleur pasle. *The decayed, vaded, or imperfect yellow colour of Box-wood, &c.*
Paslement. *Palely, wanly, bleakely.*
Pasleur: f. *Paleneße, wannesse, lewneße, bleaknesse, whitishnesse.*
Se Paslir. *To wax pale, wan, bleake.*
Pasinaison: f. *A Crampe; or, as* Pasmoison.
Pasiné: m. ée: f. *Fallen in a swoone.*
Vn Dauphin d' argent pasiné. *Hariant (in Blason.)*
Se Pasiner. *To swoone; to fall into a traunce, or swoone.*
Pasmoison: f. *A swoone, or swoonding; a traunce (caused by an extreame crampe, or conuulsion.)*
Pasnage: m. *Pawnage; Mastage; the money receiued, or profit made, by the Lord of a Forrest for the Agistement, or feeding of Swine with the Mast, or (wherein our pawnage commeth short, and the French is not generall) of Cattell with the herbage, thereof.*
Pasque, ou Pasques. *(The feast of) Easter.*
Pasques closes. *Rogation Sunday.*
Pasque fleurie. *Palme Sunday.*
Pasque de soles. *The same.*
Devoir de Pasques. *A Lambe at Easter, due vnto the Curates of some places from euerie Sheepmaister within their Parishes.*
Oeufs de Pasques. *Paste-egges; egges giuen to children at Easter.*
Donner des oeufs de Pasques à toutes restes. *To thwacke soundly.*
Faire Pasques. *To communicate; or, to receiue the Sacrament.*
Se faire marchand de poisson la vieille de Pasques; &, se faire poissonnier la vigile de Pasques. *To enter into a course, or vndertake an action, in an vnfit, or vnseasonable time.*
Pasques long temps desirées sont en vn iour tost passées: Prov. *The long-desired Passeouer is in a day past ouer.*
Apres Pasques, & Rogatons fy de prestre, & d'oignons: Prov. *Looke* Oignon.
'A Noel au perron, à Pasques au tison: Prov. *At Christmas in the Sunne, at Easter by the fire.*
Pasqueages. *Pastures, or pasture grounds.*
Pasquenade: f. *A Parsenip.*
Pasquerages, & Pasqueraiges. *as* Paschiers.
Pasquerette: f. *A little Daisie.*
Pasques. *Looke* Pasque.
Pasquette: f. *A Daisie.*
Pasquil. *as* Pasquille; *or, as* Pasquin.
Pasquille: f. *A Pasquill; a Libell clapt on a Poste, or Image.*
Pasquin: m. *The name of an Image, or Poste in Rome, whereon Libels and defamatorie Rimes are fastened, and fathered; also, as* Pasquille.
Pasquis: m. *Pastures, or pasture grounds.*
L' Oison n'est pas digne de monstrer les pasquis à l'oye: Pro. *Looke vnder* Oison.
Passable: com. *Passable, tollerable, indifferent, currant enough; also, which may be trauelled through, or passed ouer.*
Passablement. *Paßably, tollerably, indifferently, reasonably, meanely, so so.*
Passade: f. *An almes, beneuolence, or intertainment giuen by, or to, a passenger; also, the manage for combat, or souldiors manage; a gallopping, or managing of a horse forward, and suddainely backe the same way; any course backward, and forward.*
La mer se manie à passades. (*A speech whereby the swift course of the flowing, and ebbing of the sea, on the Sandes, or Washes, is meant.)*
Prendre la passade. *To refresh himselfe, in a long iourney, at a friends house, or elsewhere.*
Passadoux: m. *An Arrow.* ¶Gasc.

Passage: m. *A passage, a strait; a way, path, pace, course; a passing, a gate, going, or winding; also, a passage, entrie, or comming to a place; also, a passe, pasport, safe-conduct, or licence giuen for the free passage, trauell, or transportation of; also, a peece, clause, text, place of, or passage in, a booke; also, musicall diuision, or warbling; and (in Riding) a limitted pace of schoole either forward, or backward.*

Faulcon de passage. *A Passenger.*

Lettre de passage. *A Passe, or Passe-port, &c, (as in* Passage.)

Haut passage. *An Imposition of* vij d *in the pound vpon Woolls, Clothes, Linnen, Canuasses, and other such marchandize.*

Faire le passage. *To prepare fruit (which is to be preserued) for the receiuing of Sugar, by boyling it in cleere water, vntill it be so tender that a pinne pricked into it cannot fetch it vp any height, or hold it vp any while.*

Passager: m. *A Ferryman; also, a passenger, traueller, way-faring man.*

Passager: m. ere: f. *Transitorie, passing, shifting, flitting, vncertaine, vnsteadie, remouing often, euer changing places, most giddie, alwayes gadding vp and downe.*

Colombe passagere. *A Pigeon thats bred betweene a tame, and a wild one.*

Faulcon passager. *A Passenger.*

Nef passagere. *An ordinarie Passage-boat, or Ship.*

Passager. *To passe, proceed, runne, or goe on; to flit, remoue often, euer be shifting of abode, alwayes be gadding vp and downe.*

Passager, & varier la voix. *To warble, or diuide, in singing, &c.*

Passageur: m. *A Ferryman.*

Passagier. *as* Passager.

Passant: m. *A passenger, traueller, wayfaring man.*

Passans. *Passengers, &c; also, the rings through which the cords of a Caueçon passe.*

Les passans d'un boucle. *The two holes of a buckle.*

Passant: m. ante: f. *Passing, going, wending, trauelling along; also, straining; also, passant, currant, verie tollerable.*

En passant. *Sleightly, lightly, cursarily, accidentally, by the way.*

Passature: m. *A strayning; also, the thing thats strayned.*

Passé: m. *Time, accidents, occurrences, or things, past.*

Passe: f. *A Henne Sparrow; also, as* Passerille; *also, the racke of a Crosse-bow; also, the Iron Goale, or Arche, at* Palemaille.

Passe de bois. *The little brambling, or mountaine Spinke.*

Passe de Canarie. *A Canarie bird.*

Passe solitaire. *A little black-browne Owsell (or bird like an Owsell) thats euer alone, or if in any companie, with Sparrowes, among stone walls, or on the tops of houses, where sometime she singeth prettily.*

Arbalestes de passe. *The greatest sort of (rack-bent) Crosse-bowes.*

Biais passe. *A bias gate, or doore, tearmed so by workmen.*

Passé: m. ée: f. *Past, passed, gone; surpassed, exceeded; ouerslipt, omitted; ouergone; also, transported or ferried, carried or conueighed ouer; also, strayned through; also, decayed, farre spent, faded, withered, wrinckled, in the wane, past the best; also, deceased, departed; quite vanished away.*

Passé par les armes. *Shot to death; or, executed by passing the pikes.*

Ie suis passé. *I am gone, or ouercast, I haue throwne ouer, at Bowles, &c.*

On s'en fut bien passé. *One might haue beene without it verie well.*

Passe-caille: m. *See* Cailles.

Passe-chevaux: m. *A Horse-boat.*

Passe-dix. *Such a Game as our Passage.*

Passe-droict: m. *A resignation, or graunt of right; also, a courtesie or fauor done, a gift or salarie bestowed, beyond merit, or aboue ones due.*

Il m'a faict vn grand passe-droict. *He takes not of me the extremitie of Law, he hath dealt verie kindly with me.*

Passée: f. *A passage, course, passing along.*

La passée. *A manner of catching little birds, by sticking lyme-twigs, and placing liue birds in cages, among the boughes of trees, purposely set vp, or such as vsually they passe by.*

Les passées d'un Cerf. *His racke, or passages; the places which he hath gone through, or by.*

Les passées du mois. *The disbursements for Court-Acates omitted, and not set downe, vntill the last day of the month.*

Passefilé: m. ée: f. *Curled, frizled, entrammelled, as out-drawne locks of haire.*

Passe-fillons: m. *Small eare-lockes, or curled lockes drawne out on either side; hence, any frizled lockes, or entrammelled tufts of haire.*

Passefillonné: m. ée: f. *as* Passefilé.

Passe-fin: m. *Excellent fine cloth.*

Passe-fleur: f. *The Passeflower, bastard Anemone, or Windflower; also, red or purple Camomill, red Maths, Rosearubie, Adonis red flower; called Passe flower by the Translator of* Dodoneus.

Passe-martel de temps. *A merrie sport, or pastime, wherewith time (in a time of cares) is driuen away.*

Passement: m. *A passing, pacing, going, an ouerpassing; a transporting, a carrying, or conueying ouer; also, a strayning through; also, a lace, or lacing.*

Passement de tesmoings. *An examination of witnesses.*

Passementé: m. ée: f. *Laced.*

Passementer. *To lace.*

Passementier: m. *A Lace-maker, a Silke weauer.*

Passe-par-tout. Vn p. *A resolute fellow; one that goes through-stitch with euerie thing he vndertakes; one whose courses no danger can stop, no difficultie stay.*

Vne passe-par-tout. *A double key, that opens all the dores in the Court.*

Passe-passe: f. *Heypasse, repasse; a iugling tricke, or tearme.*

Passe-pied: m. *A caper, or loftie tricke in dauncing; also, a kind of daunce, peculiar to the youth of* La haute Bretaigne.

Passe-poil: m. *A snipped, or iagged welt of Taffata, &c, in a garment.*

Passe-pomme: f. *The Pome-paradice, Honny-apple, or Honny-meale; (an apple thats quickly ripe, and quickly rotten.)*

Passe-port: m. *A Passe, Passe-port, or Safe-conduct.*

Elle a son passe-port. *She hath somewhat about her that makes her way wheresoeuer she goes; (Said of a light, and wandering huswife.)*

Passe-porte: f. *A bill of lading.*

Passe-prouesse. *Passing valiant, exceeding valorous, verie*

verie couragious.

Passer. *To passe, wend, goe, walke on afore; to proceed, or hold on a course; also, to flit, remoue, depart from; also, to surpasse, ouergoe, ouerrun, ouerreach, ouertop, ouergrow, surmount, exceed, excell; also, to passe, let goe, suffer, giue way vnto; and, to forget, omit, ouerslip; run sleightly ouer; also, to transport, conuey, or carrie ouer; also, to straine through; also, to decay, fade, wither; decease; vanish away.*

Se passer. *Whence*; Il se passe à peu de chose. *He is contented, he maketh shift, he doth well ynough, he can well ynough away, with a little*: &; De cela ie ne puis passer. *I can by no meanes want it, I cannot be without it*; &, Il a des biens pour se passer. *He hath goods enow to rub on, or to serue his turne, with.*

Passer par l'arc S. Bernard. *To be berayed, or to beray himselfe.*

Passer la capriole. *To cut a caper.*

Passer sa cholere. *To digest his choler, to coole himselfe.*

Passer vne coche. *To driue a coach.*

Passer condemnation. *See* Condemnation.

Passer son droict. *To alien, passe, part with, forgoe, giue ouer, his right.*

Passer son envie. *To satisfie his longing.*

Passer l'esponge sur. *To deface, rase, or blot out.*

Passer par le fil de l'espée. *To kill, slay, slaughter, murther, massacre.*

Passer fortune. *To escape, or auoid, a misfortune.*

Passer par la fenestre. S'ils ne veulent passer par là qu'ils passent par la fenestre. *If they refuse, or will none of that, let them take worse and spare not.*

Passer plusieurs choses par vn Fidelium. *Hastily to shuffle, or huddle vp many things together; to slubber, or sleightly run ouer, a businesse.*

Passe sans flux. *Not a pinne matter; let goe seeing it will be no better.*

Passer par là. *Seeke* Là; *or*, Passer par la fenestre.

Passer en ligne de compte. *To reckon, make account, or giue allowance, of.*

Passer oultre. *To tipe vp the heeles, to die.*

Passer tout oultre. *To passe, or proceed on; to goe through; also, to surpasse, ouerpasse, ouergoe.*

Passer le pas. *To goe the way of all flesh, to die.*

Passer le pied sur la gorge à. *To tread vnder his feet contemptuously, or conqueror-like.*

Passer par les piques. *Looke* Pique.

Passer la plume par le bec à. *To pull a boyes penne through his lips; and thence, to abuse, or vse like a child; also, to amuse, delay, driue off, by trifling pretences, or fond and ouer-familiar trickes.*

Passer procuration. *To grant, yeeld, agree, or giue consent, vnto; also, to appoint an Atturney, or make a letter of Atturney vnto.*

Passer le Rubicon. *To vndertake a great, or hazardous exploit.*

Passer le temps. *To spend his time pleasantly, merrily, contentedly; to passe his dayes in all fulnesse of sensuall contentments; to take his full ease, to studie, or follow nothing but his delights.*

Vous l'eussiez fait passer pur le trou du chat. *You might haue made him crept through the Cat-hole.*

Tout passe par ses tripes comme par le cul du singe. *Nothing is too hot, or too cold for him; nothing doth come amisse vnto him.*

Assez fait qui fortune passe, & plus encor qui putain chasse: Prov. *Looke* Fortune.

Le bonheur tost se passe qui n'en a soing: Prov. *Good lucke vnheeded quickly slips away.*

Quand le chou passe le cep le vigneron meurt de soif: Prov. *When the Cabbidge growes faster then the Vine, there will be a great dearth of Wine.*

Qui passe vn iour d'hyver, il passe vn de ses ennemis mortels: Pro. *A mortall foe he scapes who scapes a Winters day.*

Qui a des noix il en casse, & qui n'en a il s'en passe: Prov. *(Appliable to such indifferent things as we can both spend, and spare.)*

Semelles, & vin passent chemin: Prov. viz. *Rid way apace.*

Passerage. *Dittander, Dittanie, Pepperwort,*

Passerage sauvage. *Cuckoe-flowers, Ladies-smockes, the lesse water Cresse.*

Passerat: m. *A Sparrow.*

Passereau: m. *A Sparrow; (especially the cock; whence the Prouerbe;)*

Passereaux, & moineaux sont de faux oiseaux. *Cocke Sparrowes and (young) Monkes are (much of a disposition) shrewd lechers.*

Passerelles. *as* Passerilles.

Passerille. Raisins passerillez. *Dried, and made Raisins of the Sunne.*

Passerilles: f. *Raisins of the Sunne.*

Passerin: m. ine: f. *Sparrow-like, of, or belonging to, a Sparrow.*

Langue passerine. *The fruit of the Ash, called Ashen keyes, or Kite keyes.*

Passe-rose: f. *The Passe-rose, or Pash-rose; (a great flower.)*

Passeteau: m. *A little Sparrow.*

Passetemps: m. *Pastime, sport, game, recreation, solace, delight.*

Passe-velours: m. *Flower gentle, Veluet flower, Flower-amour, Flower valure; (whereof there bee diuers kinds.)*

Passe-velours branchu. *The branched Flower gentle; which yeelds a white seed, whereas all other kinds haue a blacke one.*

Passe-velours jaulne. *The Gold flower, Gods flower, yellow or golden Steccados, the golden Flore-amour; also, a kind of Marigold thats as big as a Rose, but without any manner of sent.*

Passe-vent. *(An Epithite for a horse) swifter then the wind.*

Passevolant: m. *Th'Artillerie called a Base; also, a hireling whom a Captaine, on Muster dayes, foisteth into his companie; and generally, any such skipiacke, or base nimblesbie.*

Passeur: m. *A Ferrieman, or professed transporter of things ouer a riuer.*

Passibilité: f. *Passibilitie, suffering.*

Passif: m. iue: f. *Passiue, suffering; also, causing passion, or perturbation.*

Debtes passives. *Debts owed, or due by vs, vnto others.*

Passion: f. *Passion, perturbation, trouble, or affliction; also, a motion, disposition, inclination, or affection, of the mind; also, an accident, or symtome concurring with some disease to th'offence, or distemperature, of the bodie; whence;*

Illiaque passion. *Looke* Illiaque.

Nephretique passion. *A paine in the reines, proceeding from a stone, or grauell residing therein.*

Nulle maison sans passion: Pro. *No house without some humour.*

Passionné: m. ée: f. *Passioned, passionate, perturbed, much*

much distempered, or troubled in mind; off the hindges, almost distraught, wellnigh besides himselfe.
Passionnément. *Passionately, passionedly.*
se Passionner. *To grow passionate, or impatient; to distẽper, afflict, or distract himselfe by immoderate passion.*
Passionnerement. *Passionately.*
Passon: m. *A posset.*
Passules: f. *Raisins.*
Past: m. *A meale, repast, refection, feeding; also, meat, victualls, food.*
Le past nuptial. *See* Nuptial.
Pasté: m. *A pie, or pastie; also, a packe (laid) at cards; also, a blurre, scraule, potbooke, or ill-fauoured whimwhau, in writing.*
Pasté en pot. *Minced meat boyled in a pot with a little broath, and hard yolkes of egges, vntill it be halfe consumed.*
Il a descouvert le pasté. *He hath found out the mysterie.*
Crouстes de pastez valent bien pain: Prov. *See* Crouste.
'A celuy qui a son pasté au four on doit donner de son tourteau: Prov. *Giue of thy pie to him that hath a pastie; doe good to him thats able to requite thee.*
Paste: f. *Past, or dough.*
De bonne paste. *Of a good humor, or gentle disposition; an honest, and harmelesse merrie fellow.*
De grosse paste. *Clunchie, churlish, clownish; of rude, homelie, or dull stuffe.*
Ils ont toute la paste entre leurs mains. *They haue got all into their fingers; they haue ingrossed all imployments; the disposition of all rests in their hands.*
Entrer en la paste iusques aux coudes. *To enter, or step farre, into an act, or businesse.*
Mettre la main à la paste. *To assist, or set a helping hand vnto.*
Porter la paste au four. *See* Four.
Rebeluter la mesme paste. *To reexamine, or often to discusse, one matter.*
Rendre paste pour fougasse. *To yeeld a ticke for a tacke, a Jill for a Jacke; to returne a man as good stuffe, or measure, as he brings.*
Pastel: m. *Dyers Woad (of a finer sort then that which is called* Guesde*;) also (the hearbe of whose leaues tis made) garden Woad;* See Guesde.
Pastel sauvage. *Wild Woad; Woad that comes vp of it selfe in grounds wherein the garden Woad hath been sowne; (The translator of Plinie calls a kind of wild Lettuce that growes in woods* Pastel sauvage.*)*
Pastenade: f. *The garden Carrot, or a root like a Carrot (most commonly) of a bloud-red colour; and sometimes of a yellow; but that by Art; some Authors also call the Parsnip thus.*
Pastenade jaulne. *The yellow garden Carrot.*
Pastenade rouge. *The red, or blacke Carrot.*
Pastenade sauvage. *The wild Carrot, called Birdsneast.*
Pastenague. *as* Pastenade: ¶Langued.
Pastenaille: f. *as* Pastenade; *or, more properly, a Parsnip.*
Pastenaille sauvage. *The wild Parsnip, or Madnip.*
Pastenaque: f. *The Forke-fish; a kind of Scate which hath in her taile an indented, and venomous pricke, or sting; also, as* Pastenade.
Pasteur: m. *A Pastor, or Shepheard; one that gouernes, or takes charge of, a flocke.*
Aiguille de pasteur. *Shepheards-needle; an hearbe whereof there be three kinds; Looke* Aiguille.
Bourse de pasteur. *Shepheards-purse, Shepheards-pouch, Picke-purse, Toywood, or Toywort, poore mans Parmacetie, Coose-weed, or Case-weed.*
'A mol pasteur le loup chie laine: Prov. *A gentle Pastor makes the Wolfe cacke wooll.*
Pasteux: m. euse: f. *Doughie; clammie as bread which is dough-baked; soft, or yeelding, as dough.*
Pasticerie. *Looke* Pastisserie.
Pasticier. *as* Pastisier.
Pastilles: f. *Little lumpes, or loaues of wood, &c.*
Pastin: m. *Past; or, a little peece of past, or of dough.*
Pastinage: m. *Past; or past-meat, stuffe made of dough, or past.*
Pastir. *See* Patir.
Pastis: m. *A pasture ground (not inclosed, nor of the better sort, but as our common, or wast, whereon cattell doe but barely liue;) also, pasture, or feeding for cattell.*
Pastissage: m. *A making, or baking of pies, or pastmeats.*
Pastisser. *To make pies, or past-meats.*
Pastisserie: f. *(All kind of) pies, or baked meats; pasterie worke; also, the making of past-meats.*
Pastissier: m. *A pasterer, or pie-maker; also, a maker of past-meats.*
Il a passé par devant l' huis du pastissier. *He is a retchlesse, or carelesse fellow.*
Mestier n'avons de pastissier roigneux: Prov. *Better no pies then pies made with scabd hands.*
Paston: m. *A mash of meale for a horse; also, a certaine past, or mealie ointment that cõforts, or strengthens his hoofe; also, the peece of leather wherewith the toe of a shooe is lined.*
Pastophores: m. *Sacred Priests, reuerend Prelates (among th'auncient Ægyptians.)*
Pastoral: m. ale: f. *Pastorall, Shepheardlie, rurall.*
Baston pastoral. *as* Verge à berger; *especially, water Plantaine.*
Pastorat: m. *A Pastorall Office, or charge.*
Pastoreau: m. *A young, or meane Pastor.*
Pastoureau. *as* Pastoreau; *or, a Pastor.*
Si souhaits fussent vrais pastoureaux seroient Rois: Prov. *If wishes might succeed poore men would Princes be.*
Pastourelle: f. *A Shepheardesse.*
Pastre: m. *as* Pasteur.
Pasturable: com. *Pasturable; which may be turned into, or put vnto, pasture; which may be fed on.*
Pasturage: m. *Pasturage; a pasture ground; also, a grazing, feeding, pasturing in, or eating of, pasture grounds.*
Vain pasturage. *as* Vaine pasture; *or, an eating thereof with cattell.*
Pasture: f. *Pasture, grasse, fodder, grazing, forrage; meat, food, nourishment, sustenance, refection, feeding.*
Pasture de chameau. *Camells hay, Squinant.*
Vaine pasture. *Medowes whose hay, arrable ground whose corne, is got in; held so from S.* Remies *day vnto mid March; also, wast grounds; and generally, any ground thats not inclosed, or lyes vnfenced, and hath neither seed in, nor fruit vpon, it.*
Vive pasture. le temps de la vive pasture. *Is from Michaelmas to Saint Andrewes-tide; or feeding-time in corne grounds, and the season of pawnage, or Agisting of swine in woods (which by our Law is to begin at Holie-rood day, and to end about Martilmas.)*
Folles femmes n'aiment que pour pasture: Prov. *Whores*

Whores loue no longer then they are fed.
Pasturement: m. *A pasturing, grazing, feeding.*
Pasturer. *To pasture, graze, feed; fodder; also, to eat, as grounds with cattell.*
Vain pasturer. *To turne his cattell into, or let them runne in, grounds held* Vaine pasture.
Pasturier: m. *A Grazier.*
Vsagiers vain pasturiers. *Which haue the priuiledge to eat with their cattell grounds held* Vaine pasture.
Pasturon. *as* Paturon.
Patache: f. *A Pinnace.*
Patact: m. *A tacke, clap, knocke, flap, stampe:* ¶Gasc.
Patafle: f. *The size of bread allowed by Authoritie.*
Pataflerie: f. *Fopperie, foolerie, ideotisme, idle trifling.*
Pataque: f. *A Neapolitane coyne worth* 200 Quadrins.
Pataraſſe. *Looke* Petaraſſe.
Patart: m. *A Low-countrey coyne worth a* Sol Tournois; *or the* Stiver, *fiue whereof amount vnto* 6 d. sterl.
Pataut: m. aute: f. *Grosse, corpulent, big, fat.*
Pate: f. *as* Patte; *also, a plate, or band of yron, &c, for for the strengthening of a thing.*
Paté: m. ée: f. *Pawed, broad-footed, or broad at the foot; well vnderlaid.*
Pateade. ¶Rab. *Looke* Pareade.
Patelin: m. *A cogger, colloguer, flatterer, soother, smoother; a cousener; a pratler, or fond dallier; also, a Buffoone, or Vice in a Play.*
Patelinage: f. *A colloguing, flattering, cogging; cousening; a pratling, babling, idle tatling; fond sporting, or dalliance; a buffoonizing, or acting the Vice in a Play.*
Pateliner. *To cog, flatter, sooth, collogue with; to intertaine with idle chat, or vaine dalliance; to cousen, or deceiue with fond-faire words; also, to buffoonize it, or act the Vices part in a Play.*
Patelion. *as* Patelin.
Patelle: f. *The ball, or whirle-bone, of the knee; also, the little shell-fish called a Lympine.*
Pateller. *To chatter, warble, or, as a young bird, record the notes she would learne.*
Patellette de la testiere. *The head-dag; the broad peece of leather that runnes ouer-crosse, or through, the top of a headstall.*
Patene. *as* Patine.
Patenostrages: m. *Beads.*
Patenostre. la p. *The Pater-noster, the Lords Prayer.*
Dire la patenostre à l'envers. *To curse.*
Dire la patenostre du singe. *To didder, or chatter with the teeth.*
Patenostrier: m. *A maker, or seller of beads; also, an hypocrite, &c; as* Patinostrier.
Patent: m. ente: f. *Patent, wide open, discouered; manifest, euident, apparent.*
Patepeluë: com. *Hairie-handed, rough-footed.*
Paterliquer. *To play the father, to be fatherlie.*
Paternel: m. elle: f. *Paternall, fatherlie, of a father, of the fathers side.*
Paternellement. *Paternally, fatherly, father-like.*
Paternité: f. *Paternitie, fatherhood; fatherlinesse, fatherlie goodnesse.*
Pater-noster. *as* la Patenostre.
Pathetique: com. *Patheticall, passionate; persuasiue, affection-mouing.*
Pathetiquement. *Pathetically, passionately.*
Pathologie: f. *That part of Physicke which intreats of the causes, qualities, and differences of diseases.*
Pathologique: com. *Of, or belonging to Pathologie.*
Pathonomique: f. *A necessarie, and vndoubted signe.*
Patible: com. *Patible, passiue, sufferable.*
Patibulaire: com. *Deseruing the gallowes; of, or belonging to, the gallowes.*
Fourche patibulaire. *A gibbet, or gallowes; Looke* Fourche.
Iustice patibulaire. *High Jurisdiction; power to hang offendors; Looke* Pilier.
Signe patibulaire. *A gibbet, or gallowes; a marke, or signe of High Jurisdiction in th'owner.*
Paticier. *Looke* Pastissier.
Paticiere: f. *A Pie-makers wife; or a woman that makes pies, or past-meats to sell.*
Patiemment. *Patiently, mildly, quietly, meekely, obediently; also, resolutely, or constantly.*
Patience: f. *Patience, long sufferance, much abiding; a constancie in bearing, a courage in induring, euill; also, meekenesse, mildnesse, quietnesse, obedience; also, as* la Patiencie.
Patience de Lombard: Prov. *A forced patience.*
Patience passe science: Prov. *Patience passeth science.*
Qui n'a patience il n'a rien: Prov. *He that hath no patience hath nothing.*
Patient. *Patient; suffering, induring, bearing, abiding; meeke, mild, quiet; obedient; also, diseased, hurt, affected, afflicted.*
Au patient demeurent les terres: Prov. *The iust shall inherit the land (sayes the Psalmist.)*
Patienter. *To beare, indure, or attend with patience.*
Patientie: f. *Hearbe Patience, Monkes Rhubarbe.*
Patin: m. *A Pattin, or Clog; also, the footstall of a piller.*
Patine: f. *The Patine, or couer of a Chalice.*
Patiner. *To handle rudely, or carelesly; or to tosse, and turne a (brittle) thing often betweene the fingers.*
Patinostres: f. *Beads.*
Patinostrier: m. *A Bead-maker, &c; as* Patenostrier; *also, beads; or a string, list, or set of beads.*
se Pationner. *Looke* se Passionner.
Patir. *To suffer, indure, beare, sustaine, abide.*
Tu en patiras. *Thou wilt surely smart, or smoake for it.*
Tel en patit qui n'en peut mais: Prov. *Said of one thats punished for another mans fault.*
Patois: m. *Gibridge; clownish language, rusticall speech (or behauiour.)*
Patoüil: m. *A padling, dabling, slabbering; a making foule by much stirring.*
Patoüillard: m. *A padler, dabler, slabberer; one that tramples with his feet in plashes of durtie water.*
Patoüillas: m. *A plash, or puddle.*
Patouille: f. *as* Patrouille *(in the first sence.)*
Patoüillé: m. ée: f. *Slabbered; padled, or dabled in with the feet; also, troubled, or fouled, as liquor by stirring, or by being stirred.*
Patoüiller. *To slabber; to padle, or dable in with the feet; to stirre vp and downe, and trouble, or make foule, by stirring.*
Patriarchat: m. *A Patriarchie, or Patriarkship.*
Patriarche: m. *A Patriarke; a chiefe Father.*
Patriarchie: f. *as* Patriarchat.
Patrice: m. *A Senator of Rome; also, a great Prince; two whereof (sayes a French Author) a full, and absolute King is to haue vnder him; and they two foure Dukes apeece vnder them.*
Patricotage: m. *Wrangling, brangling; idle, or vniust*

contention in words.
Patrie: f. *A mans countrey, or natiue soyle; the Region, or place wherein he was borne.*
Patrimoine: m. *Patrimonie, birthright, inheritance, liuelyhood.*
Patrimonial: m. ale: f. *Patrimoniall; of, or belonging to, the patrimonie, or inheritance of.*
Deniers patrimoniaux. *Looke* Denier.
Fief patrimonial. *A Patrimoniall fief; viz. which descends, or came by descent.*
Patriot: m. *A father, or protector of the countrey, or Commonwealth; also, as* Patriote.
Patriote: m. *A patriote, ones countrey-man.*
Patrociner. *To patrocinate, maintaine, defend, protect, support, vphold.*
Patron: m. *A Patron, Protector, maintainer, defender, supporter, vpholder; also, the Maister of a ship; also, the Lord, owner, or Maister of a house; also, a patterne, sample, example, precedent.*
Patronal: m. ale: f. *Patronall; of, or belonging to, a Patron; done in remembrance, or solemnized in honour, of a Patron.*
Patronnage: m. *Patronage; defence, protection; also, a Patronship.*
Droict de patronnage. *An Aduowson; the right of Seigneurie in, or of presentation vnto, a Benefice; reserued by the Lord, or first giuer of the glebe, thereof; Looke vnder* Droict.
Patronner. *To make, or frame by a patterne; to make the like of; to imitate, or take example by, or follow the precedent of; also, to patronize, take into protection, auow, or allow of.*
Patronymique: com. *Deriued of the Fathers, or Auncestors names.*
Patrouille: f. *A still night-watch in warre; also, a maulkin wherewith an ouen is made cleane.*
Faire la patrouille. *Looke* Faire.
Patrouillé: m. ée: f. *Smeeched, besmeared, begrimed; also, swept, or made cleane with a maulkin.*
Patrouillement: m. *A smeeching, begriming, besmearing; also, a deprauing; also, a sweeping with a maulkin; also, a padling, or puddering, as in the water.*
Patrouiller. *To smeech, begrime, bleach, besmeare; also, maliciously to carpe, taunt, or depraue; also, to sweep, or make cleane with a maulkin; also, to paddle, or pudder in the water.*
Patrouilleur: m. *A smeecher, begrimer, besmearer; also, a malicious carper, or deprauer.*
Patte: f. *The paw, or foot of a beast; also, the footstall of a pillar.*
Patte de chat. *Cats-foot, Alehoofe, Tunehoofe, ground Iuie, Gill creepe by the ground.*
Patte de cheval. *Horse-foot, Colts-foot, Fole-foot, Hall-foot.*
Patte de lion. *Bastard blacke Ellebore, Beares-foot, Setterwort, Settergrasse; also, as* Pied de lion.
Patte de loup. *The Thessalian, and loue-prouoking,* Catanance; *or as*;
Patte louvine. *Yellow, or black, Wolues-bane; most poisonous hearbes.*
Patte d'ours. *Brankursin, Beares-breech; called also by some, Beares-foot, or Beares-claw.*
Patte d'oye. *The fingers, or toes ioyned together; a deformitie in some new-borne children.*
Couché à quatre pattes. *Prostrated, layed groueling.*
Marcher à quatre pattes. *To creep on all foure.*
Patté: m. ée: f. *Pawed, broad-footed.*
Croix pattée. *A crosse Pattie, or crosse Formle (in Blazon.)*
Pattepeluë. *Seeke* Patepeluë.
Pattiner. *To fumble, or handle too much; to hurt, or disorder by much handling.*
Pattouquis: m. *The patting, or pelting sound made by anuile-beating hammers.*
Pattu. *as* Patu.
Patu: m. uë: f. *Broad-pawed, splay-footed, or large footed.*
Naseaux patus. *Wide narrells, great nosethrills.*
Pigeon patu. *A rough-footed Doue.*
Paturon de cheval. *The pasterne of a horse.*
Pau: m. *A stake.*
Pavane: f. *A Pauane.*
se Pavaner. *as* se Pavonasser.
Pavanier: m. *A Pauine-maker; a dauncer of Pauines.*
Paucher les yeux. *Looke* Pocher.
Paucité: f. *Paucitie, fewnesse, little store, small number of.*
Pavé: m. *A pauement; a floore laied with stone, bricke, plaister, &c.*
Batteur de pavez. *A pauement-beater; a rakehell, vnthrift, loose youth, dissolute or debosched fellow; one that walkes much abroad, and riots it wheresoeuer he walkes.*
Pavé: m. ée: f. *Paued; layd, or floored with stone, brick, plaister, &c.*
Pavement: m. *A pauing.*
Paver. *To paue, to floore with stone, &c.*
Pavesade. *as* Pavoisade.
Pavescher. *To shield, shelter, shrowd, couer.*
Paveur: m. *A Pauer.*
Pavide: com. *Timerous, fearefull; quaking at euerie danger, starting at euerie feather.*
Pavidité: f. *Dread, feare, timerousnesse.*
Pavie: f. *A bastard Peach, or fruit like a Peach.*
Pavigeade. *Looke* Pavoisade.
Pavillon: m. *A Pauillion, tent; or Tabernacle; also, the flag borne by an Admirall, or commaunding, ship.*
Le pavillon d'vn lict. *A Canopie for a bed; and sometimes also, the (round) Teaster of some kind of beds.*
Pavis. *as* Pavie.
Paul: m. *Paul (a proper name;) See* Pol; *also, as* Pau.
Paulcer. *as* Pocher.
Paulé: m. ée: f. *Staked, or set with stakes.*
Paulle. *An Italian coyne worth about* 11 d. sterl.
Paulme: m. *as* Palme.
Paulme: f. *The paulme of the hand; also, a ball; (and hence) also, Tennis (play;) also, the Palme tree.*
Paulme de Christ. *Kicke, Ricinus, Palma Christi; an hearbe.*
Paulme Dieu. *The same.*
Frapper en paulme. *To clap, take, or shake by the fist in signe of a full agreement.*
Sifflant en paulme je me rendray à vous. *I will be with you as soone as euer you call; doe but whistle, I am for you.*
Paulmelle: f. *Beere Barlie, big Barlie, Barlie with the square eare.*
Paulpieres: f. *Th'eye-lids; Looke* Paupieres.
Paume. *as* Paulme.
Paumé. Orge paumé. *Beere Barlie, big Barlie, square-eared Barlie, big.*
Teste de cerf bien paumée. *A full-paulmed Stags head.*

Paumée: f. *A clap, stroke, or blow with the hand.* (v.m.)
Paumiere: f. *A woman Tennis-Court keeper.*
Paumon: m. *The Nauell-gall; a horses disease.*
Paumoule: f. *as* Paulmelle.
Pavois: m. *A (great) Shield, or Target.*
Pavoisade: *Any Targuet-fence; especially that of Galleyes, whereby the slaues are defended from the small shot of the enemie.*
Pavoisé: m. ée: f. *Defended, shielded, couered, or armed with a Targuet, or with Targuet-fence.*
se Pavoiser. *To shield, couer, defend, or arme himselfe, as with a Targuet, or Targuet-fence.*
Pavoisier: m. *A Targueteere.*
se Pavonasser. *To strout it; proudly to glorie in himselfe, or set vp his Peacocks feathers.*
se Pavonner. *The same; or (in better, and more tollerable manner) to take a prettie pride in himselfe.*
Pavot: m. *Poppie, Cheesbowls.*
Pavot blanc. *The white seeded garden Poppie.*
Pavot cornu. *Horned Poppie, sea Poppie, yellow Poppie.*
Pavot escumant. *Spatling Poppie, frothie Poppie.*
Pavot des Iardins. *The garden Poppie (of diuers kinds.)*
Pavot noir. *Blacke garden Poppie, or blacke-seeded Poppie, called also, red Poppie; and by some, wild Poppie.*
Pavot rouge. *Corne-rose, wild Poppie; the red flower that growes in corne.*
Pavot sauvage. *as* Pavot rouge.
Pavoiseux: m. *A Targueteere.*
Paupieres: f. *The eye-lids; also, (but lesse properly) the haire that growes on their edges.*
Prise de paupieres. *Looke* Prise.
Pause: f. *A pause; a stop, rest, repose, or stay; a tarriance, demurre, delay.*
Pausement. *Leasurely, faire and softly, with many pauses.*
Paute. *as* Patte: ¶Langued.
Pautoniere. *Looke* Pautonniere.
Pautonnerie: f. *Lewdnesse, knauerie, stubborne roguerie; saucinesse, malapertnesse.*
Pautonnier: m. *A lewd, stubborne, or saucie knaue.*
Pautonniere: f. *A Shepheards scrip; also, a lewd, stubborne, or saucie drab.*
Pauvre. *Seeke* Povre.
Pauvreté. *as* Povreté.
Pauzade: f. *A pausing, resting, reposing; also, a resting seat, or place.*
Pay. *(A silence-imposing Interiection) Peace hoe.*
Payé: m. ée: f. *Payed; requited; satisfied, contented.*
Payelle: f. *A little round panne; also, a little frying-panne.*
Payement: m. *A payment, or paying; a satisfaction.*
Payen: m. *A Pagan, Paynim, Infidell, Heathen man.*
Payennerie: f. *Paganisme, Heathenisme; the sect, or countrey, of Pagans.*
Payenneté: f. *Heathenishnesse.*
Payennie: f. *as* Payennerie.
Payer. *To pay, satisfie, content; requite; reward.*
Payer en gambades. *To make leg-paiments; to runne away in debt.*
Il paye toutes personnes en mesme monnoye. *He vses one forme of speech, or giues one maner of answer, vnto all; also, he vses, or handles euerie one alike.*
Il ne veut ny plaider ny payer. *He will neither plead nor pay; contend nor content; yeeld nor striue.*
Il s'a beau taire de l'escot qui ne paye rien: Prov. *He needs not blame a shot that payes nought towards it; he that will hold his purse may hold his peace.*
La faulx paye les prez: Prov. viz. *Giues them their due.*
Qui bien veut payer bien se doit obliger: Prov. *Looke* Obliger.
Qui pleige paye: Pro. *The suretie (for the most part) payes the debt.*
Payes. les mortes payes. *Looke* Morte-payes.
Payrastre: m. *A stepfather:* ¶Langued.
Payeur: m. *A payer; also, a pay maister.*
De mauvais payeur foin, ou paille: Prov. *Of a decaying, or dishonest creditor take any thing.*
Pays. *Looke* Païs.
Paysage. *as* Païsage.
Pe le quau. *in stead of,* Par le cor: ¶Gasc. ¶Rab.
Peage: m. *Toll; a through-toll, or passage-toll.*
Peageau. *Tollable; of toll.*
Chemin peageau. *Wherein toll may be taken.*
Peager. Seigneur peager. *That claimes, or takes, toll of such as passe through his territorie.*
Peager. *To erect, raise, or impose, a toll.*
Peagerie: f. *Toll-taking; also, a passage whereat, or libertie whereto, toll is due.*
Peagier: m. *A Toll-gatherer.*
Peagier. *as* Peager; *or, Toll-gathering, toll-exacting.*
Chemin peagier. *Wherein toll is gathered, or taken.*
Peau: f. *A skin; fell, hide, or pelt; also, the pill, rind, or paring of fruit; also, a scutchion, or shield charged onely with Argent, or white.*
Peau de vieille. *The name of an apple thats red on th'one side, and white and rugged on th'other.*
La peau luy tient aux costes. *He is clungd, or hide-bound.*
Tous composez d' vne mesme peau. *All whelpes of a litter, or birds of a feather; all of one fashion, affection, disposition.*
Se servir de toutes peaux contre. *To vse all meanes, helpes, or defences; to arme himselfe any way, against.*
Se tenir en sa peau. *To hold himselfe within his limits; to keepe himselfe within the compasse whereto he was borne, or is fit.*
Bon est le lievre dont la peau couste cent sous: Prov. *Looke vnder* Lievre.
Celuy a bon gage du chat qui en tient la peau: Prov. *Looke* Chat.
De mal est venu l' agneau, & à mal retourne la peau: Pro. *Goods badly gotten seldome come to good.*
En la peau de brebis ce que tu veux y escris: Prov. *You may write what you list in a sheepes skin.*
En la peau ou le loup est luy convient mourir: Pro. *He that liues like a Wolfe, should die like a Wolfe.*
Il faut discerner la peau de la chemise: Prov. *Wee must put a difference betweene our skin, and our shirt.*
Le loup mourra en sa peau qui ne l'escorchera vif: Prov. *See* Loup.
Peaucier: m. *A Skinner, Fellmonger, Leather-seller.*
Peaucier: m. ere: f. *Skinnie; of, in, or belonging to, the skinne.*
Muscle peaucier. *The flesh of the face next vnder the skin, whereto it cleaues (in the lips, eye-lids, and forhead) almost inseperably.*
Peaultre: f. *as* Peautre.
Peaussu: m. uë: f. *Skinnie, or thicke-skinned; also, limber, or flaggie, like the loosse skinne of a withered bodie.*
Peautraille: f. *Scrapings, or offalls of skinnes; and hence, a ras-*

a rascall, or base crue of scoundrells.

Peautraillerie: f. *Scuruie old stuffe of skinnes or leather.*

Peautre: f. *The sterne of a ship.*

Peccadille: f. *An escape, little sinne, small fault, veniall offence.*

Peccant: m. ante: f. *Sinning, offending, trespassing; also, offensiue; whence;*

L'humeur peccante. *The corrupt, or corrupting humor in the bodie.*

Peccatrice: f. *as* Pecheresse.

Pece. *as* Perrot; *or, an Oake, or tree of a middle size.*

Peché: m. *A sinne, crime, fault, offence, trespasse, transgression; also, a pot of earth, or stone, &c.*

Contre peché est vertu medecine: Pro. *Vertue's a salue gainst sinne.*

De grand peché grand pardon: &; De petit peché petit pardon: Prov. *As is the fault so must the pardon be.*

Vieux peché fait nouvelle honte: Prov. *Looke* Honte.

Charité oingt, & peché poind: Prov. *Loue couers, hate increases, errours; or, loue is the soules baulme, sin her bane.*

En coffre ouvert le iuste peché: Prov. *An open coffer the theefe excuses.*

Ou richesse est peché est: Prov. *Where wealth is offences are.*

Quand tous pechés sont vieux avarice est encore ieune: Prov. *When all sinnes else be old is auarice young.*

Pecher. *To sinne, offend, trespasse, transgresse, commit a fault, faile in duetie, doe amisse.*

Il peche sagement qui fait folie par conseil: Prov. *He erres discreetly that erres by aduise.*

Pecheresse: f. *A female sinner.*

Pecheur: m. *A sinner, transgressor, offendor, trespassor.*

A grand pecheur esclandre: Prov. *Shame is the lot of sinne.*

Pecile. *A pide, or skude colour of a horse.*

Pecore: f. *A sheepe; and sometimes (more generally) any simple, or sottish beast; whence;*

Va va grosse pecore. *Away thou filthie doult; &;*

Il luy faudroit fendre les pieds, & l'envoyer paistre comme vne pecore. *He is fitter to graze among cattell then to conuerse among men.*

Pecoul: m. *The taile, or arse; and (peculiarly) the staulke, steale, or taile of any fruit:* ¶Langued.

Pect: m. *(sometimes vsed) in stead of* Pis; *the breast, or vdder.*

Pectoncle: m. *A Cockle, or small Scallop.*

Pectoral: m. *A breastplate; petrell; stomacher, or stomack-cloth.*

Pectoral: m. ale: f. *Pectorall; of, or belonging to, the breast; also, breast-curing, breast-comforting, breast-defending.*

Peculat: m. *A robbing of the Princes, or publicke treasure; a conuerting it vnto his priuate vse by theeuerie, vsurie, &c.*

Peculateur: m. *One that robs the publicke treasure; or conuerts it, by indirect meanes, vnto his priuate vse.*

Peculativement. *By robbing of the Princes, or publick treasure.*

Pecule: m. *A stocke, or substance, gotten by priuate industrie, or toyle.*

Peculier: m. ere: f. *Peculiar, priuate, proper, ones owne.*

Pecune: f. *Coyne, money.*

Pecuniaire: com. *Pecuniarie, of money, in coyne.*

Pecunieux: m. euse: f. *Well moneyed, full of money.*

Pedagogie: f. *An instructing, or teaching; th'Office of a Teacher; also, Pedantisme.*

Pedagogisme: m. *as* Pedagogie.

Pedagogue: m. *A Schoolemaister, Instructor, Teacher, Tutor, Pedant.*

Pedales: f. *(A horses) kickings, winsings, yearkings, or flingings out with the heeles.*

Pedanées. Iuges pedanées. *Countrey-Judges, Judges of villages, inferiour Judges.*

Pedant: m. *A Pedant, or ordinarie Schoolemaister.*

Pedanteries: f. *Pedanticall humors, phrase-affectings, inkhorne-tearmes.*

Pedantesque: com. *Pedanticall, inkhornizing, pedantlike.*

Pedantizer. *To pedantize it, or play the Pedant; to domineere ouer lads; also, to inkhornize it.*

Peder. *for* Petter; *To fart:* ¶Rab.

Pederotte: f. *An Opall.*

Pediculaire: com. *Lowsie.*

Pedicule: m. *The staulke of a leafe, or of fruit.*

Pedieux. *A certaine muscle, which issuing from the heele, and going along on th'instup, ends in fiue little gristles, couched each on the side of a toe.*

Pedion: m. *The part of th'instup thats next vnto the toes, and containes fiue bones answerable vnto them.*

Pegade: f. *A glasse-full:* ¶Langued.

Pegase: m. *A Pegasus, or flying horse.*

Pege: f. *Pitch.*

Pegé: m. ée: f. *Pitched, bepitched.*

Pegmate: m. *A stage, or frame whereon Pageants be set, or carried.*

Pegouse: f. *A kind of Sole-fish, that hath eye-like spots on her backe.*

Pehoulle: f. *Sea-coale, or stone-coale.*

Peignarre: m. *A Combe-maker.*

Peigne: m. *A combe; also, as* Metacarpe; *also, as* Parpaigne.

Peigne d'Aleman. *Foure fingers and a thumb.*

Peigne de Venus. *Ladies combe, wild Cheruill, Shepheards-needle, mocke-Cheruill.*

Faire vn peigne. *To flie, auoid, giue the slip, slinke away.*

Faire peigne vuide. *The same.*

Tuer vn mercier pour vn peigne. *To take a sore reuenge of a sleight offence; or, to inflict a great penaltie on a small offendor.*

Iamais teigneux n'aima le peigne: Pro. *Those that are tainted loue no reprehension.*

Peigné: m. ée: f. *Combed.*

Peigner. *To combe.*

Peignerre: m. *A Combe-maker.*

Peigneur: m. *A comber; or as* Peignier.

Peignier: m. *A Combe-maker.*

Peignoir: m. *A comb-case.*

Peignouoir. *The same.*

Peinct: m. cte: f. *Painted, purtrayed, limmed; spotted, speckled; coloured, or set out in liuelie colours; described, delineated.*

Peinctre: m. *A Painter; Pourtrayer, Limmer, Colourer.*

Peincture: f. *A picture, counterfeit, peece of painting; also, painting; th'Art, or act of Painting.*

Sot en bosse, & platte peincture. *An absolute foole, compleat asse, excellent gull, hoydon in graine.*

Le Marbre de soy n'a que faire de peincture: Pro. *Looke* Marbre.

Peinċturer. *To picture, to paint.*

Peindre. *To paint, picture, pourtray, counterfeit, colour, or set out in colours; to delineate, or describe; also, to write.*

Peindre à fraiz. *Looke* Fraiz.

Peindre és nuées. *To attempt impossibilities, or to loose time.*

Cela est pour nous achever de peindre. *There wanteth but that to the filling up of our misfortunes measure; that being once done we are utterly undone.*

Peine: f. *A paine, penaltie, forfeiture, punishment; also, paines, labour, toyle, swinke, travell; indeuor; also, paine, trouble, restlesnesse, affliction, anguish, vexation, carke, thought.*

Peine de faux. *Death; Looke* Faux.

Peine de hart. *Hanging.*

'A peine. *Scant, scarcely, hardly, not without much adoe.*

I'ay peine à le croire. *I can hardly beleeue it.*

C'est grand'peine que d'aller à cheval, & vne mort d'aller à pied: Prov. *A toyle it is to ride, a death to goe on foot.*

C'est grand'peine que d'estre vieux, mais il ne l'est pas qui veut: Prov. *Though it be painefull to be old, yet each one is not so that would.*

Nuls biens sans peine: Prov. *No goods (or good thing) without griefe.*

Nul pain sans peine: Prov. &, Rien sans peine: Prov. *Nor bread, nor ought is gotten without paines.*

Qui d'autruy tromper se met en peine, souvent luy advient la peine: Prov. *Hee that doth labour other to beguile, payes oftentimes full deerely for his wile.*

Peiner. *Looke* Pener.

Peintre. *as* Peinċtre.

Peinture: f. *as* Peinċture.

Pejorer. *To impaire; to make, or grow worse.*

Peis. *as* Poisson; *A fish*: ¶ Gascon; & Provençal; *whence;*

Peis d'auriou. *A Mackerell.*

Peis carpa. *The sea Carpe; See* Carpe.

Peis escome. *The sea Pike, or Spit-fish.*

Peis espase. *The sea Fox, or sea Dog-fish.*

Peis de mesnage. *as* Belenne.

Peis mular. *The huge fish called a Whirlepoole.*

Peis rey. *The Kings fish; or, as* Maigre.

Peis: m. *The breast, &c; as* Pis.

Pel: m. *as* Peau; *also, lome, dawbing, or plaister for the walls of a house.*

Pelade: f. *The falling of the haire.*

Pelage: m. *Hairinesse, haire; also, the colour of the haire.*

Pelain: m. *A Tanners lime-pit.*

Pelamide. *as* Palamide.

Pelard: m. *A round, and pilled, or barked sticke.*

Pelasse: f. *The pilling of the skin; also, the paring of an apple, &c; also, the rinde, or barke of a tree.*

Pelaudé: m. ée: f. *Thwacked, swindged, canuassed, curried; vsed roughly, intreated rudely.*

Pelauder. *To thwack, swindge, belabour, canuasse, cudgell, currie soundly; to vse roughly, intreat hardly, handle rudely.*

Pelauderie: f. *A thwacking, a swindging, a canuassing, or cudgelling; rude handling, hard dealing with, rough intreatie of; also, filthy matter, beastly, or ougly stuffe.*

Peldure. *The name of a certaine hard-skind fig.*

Pele: m. *The boult of a locke.*

Pelé: m. ée: f. *Pild, hairelesse, bauld; also, pilled, flayed; barked.*

Pelegrin. *as* Pelerin.

Pelement: m. *A pilling; a pulling off the haire; a paring, or breaking of.*

Peler. *To bauld, or pull the haire off; also, to pill, pare, barke, vnrinde, vnskinne.*

Il en pelera la prune. *He will smart, or be plagued, for it; he is like to haue the worst of it.*

Aller, & venir font le chemin peler: Prov. *Much travelling makes bad way.*

Nul ne pele son fromage qui n'y ait honte, ou dommage: Prov. *No man pares his cheese without shame, or losse.*

Pelerin: m. *A Pilgrim, Palmer, wanderer, way-faring man; a traueller in a strange countrey; also, a fantasticall, giddie, harebraind, or odde-humored fellow; also, a kind of long-winged, small-trained, and great-headed Faulcon; and (more generally) the Faulcon tearmed a Passenger.*

Dieu sçait qui est bon pelerin: Prov. *God knowes who's a good Pilgrim; the hearts of Pilgrims are best knowne to God.*

Le rouge soir, & blanc matin, font resjouïr le pelerin: Prov. *The euening red and morning gray, are hopefull signes of a faire day.*

Pelerin: m. ine: f. *Peregrine, forraine, strange, wayfaring, wandering.*

Faulcon pelerin. *A Passenger; or, as before in* Pelerin.

Pelerinage: m. *A Peregrination, or Pilgrimage.*

Pelerinant: m. ante: f. *Peregrinating, wandering, or going on Pilgrimage.*

Pelerine: f. *A Pilgrimesse; a woman that goes on Pilgrimage.*

Pelerine de Venus. *A punke, a whore.*

Pelet: m. *A little haire.*

Ie ne l'en estime vn pelet moins. *I thinke not a iot the worse of him for it.*

Pelican: m. *The bird called a Pellican; also, a Snap, or Dog; the toole wherewith Barbers pull out teeth.*

Plication: f. *A depilatorie, or pitchie plaister seruing to pull off haire.*

Pelice: f. *A skinne of furre.*

Pelicé: m. ée: f. *Furred.*

Pelicieux: m. euse: f. Penne pelicieuse. *A dissolute, wanton, or lasciuious penne.*

Pelis: m. *The short wooll, or growth of wooll, vpon sheep which haue beene shorne some little time before, pulled from their fells by the Tawyer, &c.*

Pelisse. *as* Pelice.

Pelisson: m. *A furd petticoat, or frocke; also, a kind of white meat much vsed in* Poiċtou.

Pellage. *Looke* Pelage.

Pelle: m. *The boult of a locke.*

Pelle: f. *as* Paelle; *also (in some parts of France) as* Robbe.

Pellebosse: f. *Loosse-strife, willow hearbe, or hearbe willow.*

Pellerelle: f. *The shooting, or falling of the haire (by disease, or infirmitie.)*

Pellet: m. *The 24 part of a* Prime; *(an exceeding small weight;) Looke* Prime.

Pelleterie: f. *The trade, or shop of a Skinner, Furrier, or Peltmonger.*

Pelletier: m. *A Skinner, Fellmonger, Furrier; whence;*

En fin les regnards se trouvent chez le pelletier: Prov. *At length the subtiltie, and villanie meet with their meed.*

Pellican: m. as Pelican; *also, a vessell of circulation, or extraction; a fashion of Lymbeck.*
Pellicule: f. *A little skinne, a small or thinne rinde.*
Pelliculeux: m. euse: f. *Full of little skinnes, or thinne rindes.*
Pellucide: com. *Bright, shining.*
Pelon: m. *Th'outmost rugged huske of a greene Chestnut.*
Pelorde: f. *A certain little, and thick-sheld Cockle, that liues, and lyes, altogether hid in the mud.*
Pellosses: f. *Bullace; or, little wild plummes.*
Pelote: f. *A (hand) ball, or tennis ball; any little ball to play with; See* Pelotte.
Peloter. *To play at ball; also, to tosse like a ball.*
Peloton: m. *A clue, or (round) bottome of thread, &c.*
Pelotte: f. as Pelote; *also, a small casket to keepe rings in.*
Pelotte marine. *A ball, or little bundle of haire, commonly found among mosse which the working of the sea hath cast ashore.*
Il ioue de moy à la pelotte. *Hee tosses me vp and downe at his pleasure, he bandles me as he lists himselfe.*
Pelourde. as Pelorde.
Pelouse: f. *A Bullace, or Sloe; also, a little hill; also, the lower hazard in a Tennis-court; also, a womans priuities.*
Pelouze. as Pelouse.
Pelu: m. uë: f. *Hairie, full of, rough with, haire.*
Pate peluë. *See* Patepeluë.
Peluche: f. *Shag, plush.*
Peluette: f. *The hearbe Mouse-eare.*
Pelure: f. *The pill, skin, rinde, or paring of fruit; also, the pilling, or white and inner rinde, of trees.*
Pelusse: f. as Pelure, *especially in the last sence.*
Penade: f. *A bounding, prauncing; bragging, vaunting, brauing it.*
Penader. *To bound, praunce; brag, vaunt, braue it; Looke se* Pennader.
Penaillons: m. *Rags, tatters; patches, old clowts.*
Penal: m. ale: f. *Penall, inflicting penalties.*
Penancier. as Penencier.
Penard: m. *A melancholie old man; a selfe-afflicting Menedemus; or a poore abashed fellow, whose head hangs continually downewards, either for shame, or as a true signe of his miserie; also, a feather, or plume of feathers; (and sometimes) also, as the Latine* Penis; *a mans yard.*
Penates. ¶Rab. *Houshold Gods.*
Penault: m. *A Bourgonian measure containing twelue* Quarts.
Penault: m. aude: f. *Abashed, ashamed, out of countenance.*
Pencer. *Looke* Pancher.
Pencher. as Pancher.
Penchon: m. *A declining, or weightie inclining; weightie pressure, or a stooping, or bowing through weight.*
Pend. de guet à pend. *Wittingly, willingly.*
Pendable: com. *Hangable, that deserues hanging, thats fit to be hanged.*
Cas pendable. *A hanging matter.*
Pendage: m. *A hanging.*
Pendant: m. *A pendant; a hanger; any thing that hangeth, or whereat another thing hangs.*
Les pendans d'une bourse. *The strings of a purse.*
Pendant de clef. *A key-clog; or the string whereat keyes are hanged.*
Les pendants d'un Cor. *The strings, and tassells of a Hutchet.*
Pendant d'oreille de gibet. *One that excellently becomes, or would become, a gibbet.*
Elle s'en va par le pendant. *So say they of a purse whose strings are almost worne in peeces; alluding whereto they say likewise of one thats going, or like, to be hanged,* Il s'en va par le pendant.
Pendant: m. ante: f. *Hanging; depending, suspended; stooping, declining, dangling or falling downwards.*
Seau pendant à double queuë. *A Seale hanging by a double labell; and metaphorically, one that hangs on a paire of gallowes.*
Pendant cela. *(Aduerbially;) in the meane while, in the meane time, in the meane season.*
Pendant que. *Whiles, or, the whilest, that.*
Cependant. *Looke* Cependant.
Pendante: f. *A labell pendant.*
Pendard: m. *A rakehell, crackrope, gallowclapper; one for whom the gallowes longeth.*
Pendardeau: m. *A little crackrope, young slipstring.*
Pendement: m. *A hanging.*
Pendentif: m. *The key or scutchion of a vault; that which hangs directly downe in the middle thereof.*
En pendentif. *Steepe-hanging, steepe-downe; or as,* `A dos d'Asne, *vnder* Dos.
Pendereau. as Pendardeau.
Penderie: f. *A hanging.*
Pendesyllable: com. *Of fiue sillables.*
Pendiculation: f. *A pendiculation; or, a stretching in th'approach of an Ague.*
Pendillant: m. ante: f. *Dangling, hanging loossely, or hanging but halfe.*
Pendille. *A thing that hangs danglingly.*
Pendiller. *To hang danglingly, loossely, or but by halues.*
Pendiloches: f. *Jogs, danglings, or things that hang danglingly.*
Pend-oreille. *A Pendant.*
Pendre. *To hang, stoope, incline, or bow, downewards; to hang, dangle, fall, or lye downe, vpon; to hang, depend, rest, or stay, on, to hang ouer, about, or vnto; also, to hang, twitch vp, or strangle, on a paire of gallowes, &c.*
Pendre à l'oreille. *Seeke* Oreille.
Dire pis que pendre. *To reuile, or extreamly raile on.*
Il leur en pend autant à l'oeil. *They are as much subiect vnto this mischief, they are in as great danger euerie way; they must one day drink of the same cup, tast of the same sauce, run the same course.*
Argent fait pendre les gens: Pro. *Money brings many a man to the gallowes.*
Les gros larrons menent pendre les petits: Prov. *as vnder* Larron.
Nul ne sçait ce qu'à l'oeil luy pend: Prov. *No man knowes how neere he is to a mischiefe, or, what miserie may befall him.*
Ou rendre, ou pendre, ou mort d'enfer attendre: Prov. *A thiefe must restore, or be hangd, or looke to be damd.*
Qui a à pendre n'a pas à noyer: Prov. *He thats ordamd to be hangd will neuer be drownd (say we.)*
Qui plus qu'il n'a vaillant despend, il fait la corde à quoy se pend: Prov. *He that dispends more then he hath, makes vp a rope his necke to swath.*
Pendu: m. uë: f. *Hanged; hanging.*
Langue bien penduë. *A smooth, glib, eloquent, or well speaking tongue.*
Procez pendu au croc. *See* Croc.
Relasche de pendu. *A graceleße crackrope, or, one for whom the gallowes grones.*
Pene: m. *The boult of a locke.*

Peneau: m. *A Flag, or Streamer; also, a rag, or tatter; (and in some parts of France) also, a slut, or slatterne.*
Peneliere. *as* Penil.
Penencier: m. *He that after confession made, or a notorious offence committed, enioyneth the confessant, or offendor, his penance.*
Pener. *To trauell, toyle, swinke, labour extreamely, doe his vtmost indeuor, take great paines; also, to vex, trouble, molest, put vnto paine.*
Penetratif: m. iue: f. *Penetratiue, piercing, or entring into, searching, or passing through.*
Penetrer. *To penetrate; pierce, enter, search, or sinke into; also, to passe through.*
Peneusement. *Deiectly, heartlesly; demissely, lowlily; in a dumpe, at a plunge or a nonplus.*
Peneux: m. euse: f. *Deiected, heartlesse, discouraged, dismayed, out of countenance with himselfe, in a pitifull or miserable taking; pitifully complayning, humble, abiect, lowlie, demisse.*
La semaine peneuse. *The Passion weeke.*
Penible: com. *Painfull, toilesome, laborious.*
Penide: f. *A Pennet; the little wreath of sugar taken in a cold.*
Penidial. succre pen. *Fine white sugar whereof Pennets be made; also, the Pennets themselues.*
Penil: m. *A mans, or (most properly) a womans groine.*
Os du penil. *The sharre-bone; or, as* Os barré; *in* Os.
Penillier: m. ere: f. *Belonging to the groine; whence;*
Os penillier. *as* Os du Penil.
Penillons. *Looke* Penaillons.
Peninsule: f. *A Peninsula, or halfe Island.*
Penit: m. *French-wheat, Black-wheat, Bolymong; (a course graine:)* ¶Pic.
Penitence: f. *Penitence, penance, repentance.*
Rouge visage, & grosse pance ne sont signes de penitence: Prov. *Looke* Pance.
Penitencier. *as* Penencier; *or, the Priest, &c, that inioyneth penances.*
On te doit envoyer au penitencier. *Thou hast need to be shriuen; or, thou must be quickly looked to, or else thou wilt be worse then naught.*
Penitencieux: m. euse: f. *Penitentious, verie penitent, most repentant.*
Penitent. *Penitent, repentant, aggrieued at, sorrowing for, troubled in mind with, what he hath done.*
Filles penitentes. *as* Filles repenties, *vnder* Fille.
Pennache: m. *A bunch, or plume, of feathers; also, one great feather bent backe vpon, or couched flatling about, a hat, or cap after th'old French fashion.*
Pennache de boeuf. *A faire paire of hornes.*
Pennache de mer. *Is neither fish, nor plant, but a certaine creature or excrescence of the sea, which at one end resembles a feather, and th'vncouered nut of a mans yard at th'other; and by night shines like a starre.*
Pennade. *as* Penade.
se **Pennader**. *To brag, boast, or braue it; to a proud flourish, or vaine muster of himselfe in publicke; also, to bound, or praunce like a proud horse.*
Pennage: m. *A birds coat, or feathers; also, as* Passage.
Pennarol de Chirurgien. *A Chirurgians Case or Ettuy; the box wherein he carries his Instruments.*
Penne: f. *A quill, or hard feather; a pen-feather; also, the feather of an arrow; also, furre, or furring.*
Pennes. *The rafters on the roofe of a house; called so, because they somewhat resemble the spread wings of a bird.*
Penne de foye. *as* Lobe.
Penne d'un voile: c'est l'aile de la voile enfilée en bouline. *We call it, the Leech of a sayle.*
Bouter vent en penne. *To bring a ship vpon the lee.*
Mettre en penne. *The wind to take a ship vpon the stayes.*
Penneton d'un clef. *The bit, or neb of a key.*
Pennon: m. *A Pennon; Flag, or Streamer.*
Les pennons d'une fleiche. *The feathers of an arrow.*
Pennonceau; ou **Pennoncel**: m. *A Pennon on the top of a Launce; a little Flag, or Streamer.*
Pennule. *(The diminutiue of* Penon.) *A small peece, part of a thing (especially of flesh, or of our bodie) not altogether separated from the whole.*
Penon: m. *A peece, or part of a thing, not altogether separated from it; such as be the laps, or napes of the liuer; called* Penons *by the vulgar of* Languedoc.
Pens. *as* Pensée; *or* Pensement; *whence:*
De guet à pens. *Wittingly, willingly, with premeditation, of set purpose.*
Pensé: m. ée: f. *Thought, weened, deemed, imagined, supposed, coniectured; weighed in mind, perpended, examined, considered of.*
De faict à pensé. *as* De guet à pens.
Pensée: f. *A thought, supposall, coniecture, surmise, cogitation, imagination; ones heart, mind, inward conceit, opinion, fancie, or iudgement; also, the flower Paunsie.*
De guet à pensée. *as* De guet à pens.
Il me vient en pensée que. *My mind giues me, my heart tells me, it comes into my head, that.*
Pensement: m. *as* Pensée; *or, a thinking, weening, imagining; also, a tending, dressing, or looking to; a curing, or Physicking of.*
Penser. *To thinke, weene, deeme, iudge, imagine, suppose, coniecture, surmise; haue an opinion, or be of opinion, that; also, to studie, muse, meditate, consider of; pause, or deliberate vpon; examine, weigh, ponder, perpend, reuolue, or cast, in mind; also, to dresse, tend, looke vnto, haue a care of, prouide for, furnish with all necessaries; also, to dresse, Physicke, applie medecines vnto.*
Penser à soy. *To bethinke himselfe, to call vnto mind.*
Penser ailleurs. *The mind to be vpon somewhat else, the wits to run a wooll-gathering; no way to mind whats gone about.*
Mal pense qui ne repense: Prov. *He thinks not well that thinks of all at once; or thinks not more then once.*
Il est bien tost deceu qui mal ne pense: Prov. *The harmelesse minded man is soone deceiued.*
Le loup sçait bien que male beste pense: Pro. *One knaue can easily ghesse at the drift of another.*
Mettez fol à par soy il pensera: Pro. *Looke* Fol.
Quand les yeux voyent ce que ne veirent oncques le coeur pense ce qu'il ne pensa oncques: Prov. *When th'eyes behold vnwoonted things vnwoonted thoughts possesse the heart.*
Penseresse: f. *A woman that thinketh, imagineth, museth, or careth much.*
Penseur: m. *A thinker, imaginer, supposer; also, one that vses to studie, muse, or deliberate, on matters.*
Penseuse: f. *as* Penseresse.
Pensif: m. iue: f. *Pensiue, heauie, thoughtfull, carefull; also, thinking of; and hence;*
Fille oisive à mal pensive: Prov.
Pensil: m. ile: f. *(Sleightly) hanging.*

Verrue pensile. *A great wart that hangs but by a small thread, or root.*
Pension: f. *A pension, stipend, fee; an yerely payment; also, money payed for the tabling, or boording of children, &c.*
Pensioniste: m. *A Pensioner.*
Pensionnaire: com. *A Pensioner; one that hath, or payeth, an yearely pension; also, a tabler, or boorder; also, a Scholler, who lyes within a Colledge, and is tied, and subiect, onely vnto it; therein differing from* Galloche, *who lying abroad, is at more libertie.*
Pensionné: m. ée: f. *Pensionned, stipended, hired by pension, that takes an yearely stipend.*
Pensiveté: f. *Pensiuenesse, carke, sorrow, heauinesse.*
Pent d'un rets. *A whole pane, peece, or fould of a Net.*
La figure hexagone à six pents. *Hauing six Cants.*
Pentagone: com. *Fiue-cornered.*
Pentametre: m. *A Pentameter, or verse consisting of fiue feet.*
Pentaphylle. *Cinkefoyle, Cinkefield, Fiue-finger grasse, Fiue-leaued grasse.*
Pente: f. *The declining, downeward bent, slopenesse, or slope hanging of a hill, ditch, roofe, &c; also, a peece of hanging; also, an inclining towards a fall.*
Les pentes d'vn lict. *The Valance.*
Donner de pente à. *(In wrastling) to giue an aduantage vnto.*
Penteur: m. *A Penant; the name of one of the ropes which passe ouer the top, or vpper part, of a Mast.*
Penthiere. *as* Panthiere.
Penture: f. *The hindge of a doore.*
Penule: f. *A long cloake fit to be worne in rainie weather.*
Penurie: f. *Penurie, scarcitie, need, necessitie, dearth, lacke, want.*
Peone: f. *Peonie, Kings-bloome, Rose of the Mount.*
Pepelon: m. *The nipple of a dug.*
Pepetiller. *To crackle, or sparkle often.*
Pephage. *Looke* Pamphage.
Pepiant: m. ante: f. *Cheeping, peeping, puling, or crying like a young bird; also, lisping.*
Pepie: f. *The Pip.*
Pepiement: m. *The cheeping, or peeping of yong birds; any such puling noise; also, a lisping, or faultering in speech.*
Pepier: m. *as* Pepiement.
Pepier. *To peepe, cheepe, or pule, as a young bird in the neast; also, to lispe.*
Pepier de soif. *The tongue to peele by reason of an extreame thirst.*
Pepieur: m. *A peeper, cheeper; puler.*
Pepin: m. *A Pippin, or kernell; the seed of fruit.*
Les pepins des raisins. *The stones of grapes.*
Or de pepin. *Looke* Or.
Pepinerie: f. *A Seed plot, Nurserie, Nursing Orchard, or part of an Orchard, wherein the pippins, kernells, or stones of fruit be sowen.*
Pepiniere: f. *as* Pepinerie.
Pepin-percé. *(The name of) a certaine drie sweet apple.*
Pepon: m. *A Pompion, or Melon.*
Pepon Turquois. *as* Pompon Turquois.
Pepré: m. ée: f. *Peppered; seasoned with Pepper.*
Pequatille: f. *A Peccadillo; or as* Peccadille.
Peque: f. *A mare.*
Per: m. *as* Pair; *A Peere; or Paragon; also, a match, make, fellow, companion; also, a paire; at game; also, a game at Cards wherein foure rewes be laid; one for a paire; the second for most of a suit; the third for flush; and the fourth for a sequence.*
Per à compaignon. *A Peere, match, mate, equall fellow, comerade.*
Per ou non per. *The game called Euen and odde.*
Il entend bien son per. *He vnderstands well enough what he goes about.*
Pris à pere à la couche. *as in* Pris.
Peragration: f. *A peragration, going about, wandering through, trauelling ouer.*
Peramese: f. *A Ninth, or a proportion of nine, in Musicke.*
Peratre. *as* Parastre.
Perattendre. *To attend throughly, or seasonably; to attend vntill he haue a fit opportunitie; whence;*
Mal attend que ne perattend: Prov.
Perce: f. *as* Percement, *also, that kind of Loach which hath a prickle neere vnto either of her gills.*
Mettre le vin en perce. *To pierce, or broach wine.*
Percé: m. ée: f. *Pierced, bored, gored, thrust into, or through; transfixed; open, full of holes, or windowes.*
Chaire percée. *A close stoole.*
Perce-fueille: f. *Through-wax, through-leafe; (an hearbe.)*
Percele. *Blew-bottle, Blew blaw, Corne flower.*
Perce-lettre: f. *The little instrument wherewith Secretaries make ouertures for the labells with which they close their letters.*
Percellé: m. ée: f. *Pierced, strucken; ouerthrowne, beaten downe; abated, abashed, appalled; vexed, troubled.*
Percement: m. *A piercing, boring, or goring; a thrusting into, or through.*
Perc'-oreille. *(The worm, or Insect called) an Earewig.*
Perce-pain. *as* Perce-oreille.
Percepceux: m. euse: f. (fruicts percepceus.) *Taken, gathered, receiued.*
Percepierre: f. *(A generall name for most stone-breaking hearbes, but chiefly for those which we call) Saxifrage, and Samphire.*
Percepierre rouge. *Red Saxifrage, Filipendula, Dropwort.*
Perceptible: com. *Perceptible; perceiuable, apprehensible, sensible; also, takeable, gatherable, receiuable.*
Perception: f. *A perception; a perceiuing, apprehending, vnderstanding, also, a gathering, taking, receiuing, of.*
Percer. *To pierce, gore, transfix; thrust into, bore through.*
Percer vne maison. *To breake open, or into, a house.*
Percer le mors. *A horse to thrust his tongue with ease, and at libertie, vnder the Port of his Bit.*
Percet: m. *A Peach.*
Perceu: m. euë: f. *Taken, gathered, receiued.*
Perche: f. *A pearch to hang things, or set Hawkes, on; also, the Pearch-fish; also, the Beame of a Bucks head, and, the broach of a Stags, also, the pearch, pole, or big rod wherwith land is measured; and which though it contain not, all France ouer, one and the same number of feet (for in some places it is 20, in others 22, in others 25, and in others but 18 (the most generall, and most vsuall one) yet is it euery where six fathoms, or* Toises, *the different scantling whereof, causes so great a difference of* Perches, *in seuerall places.*
Les perches d'un bouc sauvage. *The head, or hornes of a wild Goat.*

Perche de mer. *The sea Pearch; a wholesome, rough-find, and tonguelesse, rocke-fish.*
Perché: m. ée: f. *Pearched, placed, or set (as a bird) on a pearch, or on the bough of a tree; also, propped, supported, or underset with pearches, or poles.*
Il l'a perché à vn arbre. *He hath hanged him on a tree.*
Percher. *To set, or put on a pearch; also, to alight; also, to sit, or pearch (as a bird) on a tree; also, to hang, or twitch vp, at a bow; also, as* Percer.
Percheux: m. euse: f. *Belonging to, or full of, pearches.*
Perclorre. *To benumme, strike or make lame, take away the vse of the limmes.*
Perclus de ses membres. *Taken, blasted, striken, benummed, suddenly growne lame, or depriued of the vse, of his limmes.*
Oeil perclus. *An eye that cannot moue because the muskles belonging to it are benummed.*
Perclusion: f. *A blasting, lamenesse, or numnesse in the members.*
Perdable: com. *Loosable; fit, or likelie, to be lost.*
Perdement: m. *A loosing, a forgoing.*
Perdeur: m. *A looser.*
Eschar plaidoyeur est hardi perdeur: Prov. *The miserable pleader is a miserable speeder; the sparing of a fee is often the spoyle of a cause.*
Perdigonne: f. *The name of an excellent plumme.*
Perdition: f. *Perdition, destruction, extreame losse, vndoing, ruine.*
Perdre. *To loose; to cast away; to ouerslip, omit, let goe; also, to marre, spoyle, or spend idly.*
se Perdre. *To perish, to decay; to slip, runne, fall, or goe away.*
Perdre les ambles. il y perdit les ambles. *There was he put beyond his bias, or out of all patience; he knew not how to carrie, or how to containe, himselfe when he came thither.*
Perdre l'instance; & perdre le procez. *To be ouerthrowne, or haue the worse in a, suit; to be cast, or his cause to goe against him.*
Perdre pied. Il y perdoit pied. *There he lost ground; he was put to his shifts, or to his plunges, there.*
Ie n'en perds que l'attente. *Tis but a little tarrying for it.*
'A gens de bien on ne perd rien: Prov. *He that deales with honest men is seldome, or neuer a looser; one looses nought by good men.*
Apres perdre perd on bien: Prov. *One ill lucke succeeds in the necke of another; or, when one begins to loose he leaues not vntill all be gone.*
'A tout perdre il n'y a qu'un coup perilleux: Pro. *One right-set blow would serue to sinke vs all.*
Argent fait perdre gent: Prov. *Looke* Argent.
Asseurement chante qui n'a que perdre: Pro. *And who doth sing so merrie a note as he that cannot change a grote?*
Assez gaigne qui malheur perd: Prov. *He gaines ynough that misses a misfortune.*
En seureté dort qui n'a que perdre: Prov. *He that can loose nought sleepes with great securitie.*
Il faut perdre vn veron pour pescher vn saulmon: Prov. *One must spend a little to gaine much.*
Il ne perd rien qui ne perd Dieu: Prov. *Hee that keepes God to friend can nothing loose.*
Marchand qui perd ne peut rire: Prov. *We say, they laugh that win.*
On ne doit point querir brebis qui se veut perdre: Prov. *A wilfull sinner must not be reclaimd.*
Par trop presser l'anguille on la perd: Prov. *Seeke* Anguille.
Qui perd le sien perd le sens: Prov. *He that looses his wealth looses his wit.*
Qui a à perdre perd tousiours: Prov. *The rich man looses somewhat euerie day; or, he thats ordaind to loose is euer loosing.*
Qui ne retire de sa vache que la queuë ne perd pas tout: Prov. *He that recouers but the tayle of his cow looses not all his cow; better saue a little then loose all.*
Qui preste à l'amy perd au double: Prov. viz. *Both money, and friend.*
Qui tout convoite tout perd: Prov. *He that couets all, keepes, or comes by, nothing.*
Perdreau: m. *A young Partridge.*
Perdriau. *as* Perdreau.
Perdris. *as* Perdrix.
Perdriseur: m. *A Partridger, or Partridge-taker; also, an Officer that hath the commaund of that Game, in France.*
Perdrix: f. *A Partridge.*
La Perdrix des Archers de la garde du Roy. *A sheepes head (wherewith commonly they breake their fasts.)*
Perdrix blanche de Savoye. *as* Arbenne.
Perdrix des champs. *Th'ordinarie Partridge.*
Perdrix gaille, gaule, *or* gaye. *The great browne-bodied, and red-legd Partridge, the French Partridge.*
Perdrix goache. *as* Perdrix griesche.
Perdrix griesche. *Th'ordinarie, or little, Partridge.*
Perdrix grignette, gringette, & grise. *as* Perdrix griesche.
Perdrix maillée. *A Menild, or spotted Partridge.*
Perdrix de mer. *The Sole-fish.*
Perdrix de montaigne. *as* Francolin, *in the last sence.*
Perdrix rouge, ou aux pieds rouges. *The great red-legd Partridge.*
Perdrix des terres neuves. *The Guinnie Henne.*
Oeil de Perdrix. *Looke* Oeil.
Perdu: m. uë: f. *Lost, perished; forlorne, past hope of recouerie, cast away; forgone, omitted, ouerslipped, run, or fallen away; also, lewd, naughtie, wicked, vngracious, or past grace.*
Coup perdu. *See* Coup.
Enfans perdus. *Perdus; or the forlorne hope, of a campe (are commonly Gentlemen of Companies.)*
Fille perduë. *A punke, whore, harlot, common hackney.*
Gens perdus. *as* Enfans perdus; *also, retchlesse, or desperate people.*
'A corps perdu. *Desperately, headlong, without any care at all of his skinne.*
'A pierre perduë. *Hab nab, euen as they fall, one with another.*
Il a perdu sa ceincture. *He hath neither money, nor meanes, left him; all is consumed, all wasted, all gone.*
Bien faict n'est iamais perdu: Prov. *Neuer came losse by doing a good deed.*
Chose perduë est lors cogneuë: Prov. *We know the worth of things when we haue lost them.*
De chose perduë le conseil ne se remuë: Prov. *In vaine we goe to law when things be lost.*
Tout est perdu ce qu'on donne à fol: Prov. *All thats bestowed on fooles is cast away.*
Tout ce que gist en peril n'est pas perdu: Prov. *All is not lost that in some danger is.*

Perduellisme: m. *Treason against Prince, or Countrey.*
Perdurable: com. *Perdurable, perpetuall, euerlasting, aye-during.*
Perdurablement. *Perpetually, euerlastingly, for euer.*
Pere: m. *A father; also, an auncient Monke, or Frier, especially if he be a Confessor; also, a Iesuite, or the Title of a Iesuite.*
Beau pere. *Looke* Beaupere.
Hommes, & peres de la Cour. *as* Pairs.
Ils sont à table aises comme peres. *(Whose bellies being filled their greatest care is taken.)*
'A pere, à maistre, à Dieu tout puissant, nul ne peut rendre l'equivalent: Prov. *No man can doe ynough for his father, maister, and Maker.*
'A pere amasseur fils gaspilleur: Pro. *A warie father hath a wastfull sonne; The like is;*
De pere gardien fils garde-rien: Pro.
Celuy là est bien pere qui nourrit: Prov. *He that doth feed, or foster me, may well be called my father.*
Peré: m. *Perrie; drinke made of Peares.*
Peregrin: m. *A stranger, forrainer, alien, outlander, or outlandish man.*
Peregrin: m. ine: f. *Peregrine, forraine, alien, stranger, outlandish.*
Faulcon peregrin. *A passenger.*
Peregrination: f. *A peregrination, farre iourney, long trauell, pilgrimage.*
Peregriner. *To trauell, take long iourneyes, wander in strange countries, goe on pilgrimage.*
Peregrineux: m. euse: f. *as* Peregrin.
Peregrinité: f. *Strangenesse, outlandishnesse, forrainenesse, forraine speech, habit, custome, behauior, &c.*
Peremption d'instance. *A Nonsuite, or letting a suit fall; a quitting, or forsaking of a cause.*
Peremptoire, & decisif du procez. *A peremptorie rule which determines a cause.*
Peremptoire: com. *Peremptorie, insulting, imperious; absolute; forcible; earnest, that will haue no nay; also, present, sudden.*
Adjournement peremptoire. *A peremptorie summons, after which no day will be giuen, but the cause forthwith proceeded in.*
Peremptoirement. *Peremptorily, imperiously; earnestly; absolutely; presently, suddenly, without further delay.*
Peremptorisé. Heritage peremptorisé. *whose challengers, hauing after summons made default, are no more admitted to prosecute, or continue their claime.*
Peremptoriser. *To peremptorise; to grant, or passe away peremptorily; or (as in* Peremptorisé*) to exclude a challenger after a default made by him.*
Perenne: com. *Perpetuall, continuall, endlesse, ay-during, without ceasing, euerlasting.*
Eau perenne. *Continually running, neuer drie.*
Perennel: m. elle: f. *as* Perenne.
Perenniser. *To perpetuate, eternize, make euerlasting.*
Perennité: f. *Perennitie, eternitie, perpetuitie, euerlastingnesse.*
Perequant: m. *An equall rater, taxer, assessor of others; or, one that gathers head-money.*
Perequant: m. ante: f. *Equalling; also, rating equally.*
Perequation: f. *A perequation; an equalling, or making euen; also, an equall rating, taxation, easement.*
Perfection: f. *Perfection, compleatnesse, accomplishment, absolutenesse; the full ending, or whole finishing, of*
Perfectionner. *To perfect, or bring to perfection; to accomplish, end wholly, finish absolutely.*
Perfigue: f. *A Peare-plumme.*
Perfiguier: m. *A Peare-plumme tree.*
Perflable: com. *Which may be blowne through.*
Perfoliate: f. *Through-wax, through-leafe; (an hearb.)*
Perforatif: m. iue: f. *Boring, piercing, or thrusting through.*
Perfumé: m. ée: f. *Perfumed, sweetened throughly.*
Perfumement: m. *A perfuming.*
Perfumer. *To perfume, sweeten throughly, or giue a sweet sent vnto.*
Perfumeur: m. *A Perfumer.*
Perfums: m. *Perfumes, pleasant fumes, delicate smels, gracious odors.*
Perger. *To proceed, or goe on.*
Pergude. *Perished, lost:* Gasc.
Peri: m. ie: f. *Perished, lost, gone; abolished, annulled, spoyled.*
Peris en croix, en face, ou en pal, &c. *In Crosse, in Fesse, in Pale, &c; a tearme of Blazon.*
Periapte. *A medecine hanged about any part of the bodie.*
Pericarde: m. *The membrane, filme, or slender skinne wherein the heart is wrapped.*
Pericardique: com. *Of, or belonging to, the Pericardium; whence,* Veine pericardique: *Looke* Veine.
Pericharie: f. *Excessiue ioy.*
Periclimene; ou, **Periclymene.** *The Woodbind, or Honie-suckle.*
Pericliter. *To ieopard, hazard, endanger.*
Pericraine: m. *The Pericranion, hairie scaulpe, whole skinne of the scull.*
Perier: m. *The giserne of a Henne, &c.*
Perigée: m. *The point of heauen wherein any Planet is neerest vnto the center of the earth.*
Peril: m. *Perill, danger, ieopard, hazard.*
Tout ce que gist en peril n'est pas perdu: Pro. *All is not lost thats in some hazard.*
Periller. *To perish; also, to be in some perill, or hazard.*
Perilleusement. *Perillously, dangerously.*
Perilleux: m. euse: f. *Perillous, or parlous, dangerous, ieopardous, hazardous.*
Perimer. *To spoyle, abolish, ouerthrow, disappoint vtterly, take away wholly.*
Perinée: m. *The seame, or line that runnes betweene the fundament and cods.*
Periode: f. *A period, perfect sentence, full sence, conclusion, or end; also, a course to a finishing, or the terme wherein a thing is finished.*
Periodic: m. ique: f. *Periodicall; ended, finished, concluded; also, reuolutiue, comming or going by course, or fits.*
Periodiquement. *By periods; endingly, concludingly, or towards a conclusion; also, reuoluingly, by course or fits, or with a continuall, and interchanged course.*
Perioste: m. *The skinne wherewith the ribs be couered; or (more generally) the thinne skinne wherein any bone is couered.*
Peripherée: f. *The circumference, edge, or border of a circle, &c.*
Periphraser. *To paraphrase, vse circumlocutions, expresse one word by many.*
Peripneumonie: f. *Th'inflamation of the Lungs.*
Perir. *To perish, miscarrie, die; decay, consume, wither; to come to ruine, or to naught; to be lost, mard, spoild, cast away.*
Il n'est si bon marinier qui ne perisse: Prov. *The skilfull Sea-man comes at length short home.*

Pe-

Perissable: com. *Perishable, momentarie, looseable, or subiect vnto losse; which by ouer-long keeping will be spoyled, and lost.*
Peristile: m. *A cloister, walking place, or long entrie set about with pillars.*
Peritoine: m. *The inner thinne rind, kell, or skin wherewith the intralls be couered.*
Perjure: com. *Periured, forsworne.*
Perle: f. *A Pearle; an Vnion; also, a Berrie.*
Perle de compte. *A Paragon; an orientall, or faire great Pearle.*
Herbe aux perles. *Pearle-plant, Lichwall Gromell.*
Perlé: m. ée: f. *Rough, rugged, or not smooth; whence,* Dragée perlée *is opposed vnto* Dragée vnie.
Fil perlé. *Hard-twisted thread.*
Teste bien perlée. *Whose Burre is well spotted, and curled.*
Perles: f. *The little spotted Curlings wherewith the Burre of a Deeres head is powdered.*
Perlette: f. *A small Pearle.*
Perlon: m. *A Rochet, Redfish, Gurnard, &c, (tearmed so in* Xaintonge.)
Perlure: f. *as* Perles; *or the Burre it selfe.*
Permanable: com. *Permanent, constant, remaining, durable, abiding.*
Permanent. *as* Permanable.
Permeable: com. *Quickly running, or passing through.*
Permettre. *To permit, suffer, tollerate, beare with, wink at, giue libertie or way, graunt authoritie or power, vnto.*
Permis: m. ise: f. *Permitted, tollerated, suffered, borne with, winked at; also, licenced, or lawfull.*
Permission: f. *A permission, tolleration, sufferance; leaue, licence, allowance;* (Permission s'octroye par le Roy pour vn temps, & tant que bon luy semblera, par lettres patentes addressées aux Maistres des Forrests.)
Permistion: f. *A mixing, mingling, tempering together.*
Permutateur: m. *A barterer, exchanger; alterer.*
Permutation: f. *Permutation, bartering, trucking, exchanging.*
Permuter. *To barter, trucke, exchange.*
Pernicieusement. *Perniciously, pestilently, mischieuously, noisomely, most hurtfully.*
Pernicieux: m. euse: f. *Pernicious, deadlie, mortall, destroying, most dangerous, mischieuous, noisome, hurtfull.*
Pernis. Pierres de pernis. *as* Parpaignes, *or* Perpins.
Perons: m. *Startups, high shooes; fishers boots; also, bags, powtches, or satchels of leather.*
Peroration: f. *A peroration; the conclusion of an Oration, applyed to the humors, or praying the fauors, of the Auditorie.*
Perot. *Looke* Perrot.
Peroximes. *Fits of an ague.*
Perpeigne. *as* Parpaigne; *or* Perpin.
Perpendiculaire: com. *Perpendicular, downe-right, plumpe downe, directly downe.*
Perpendiculairement. *Perpendicularly.*
Perpetrer. *To perpetrate, act, commit.*
Perpetuation: f. *A perpetuation, or perpetuating.*
Perpetuel: m. elle: f. *Perpetuall, eternall, continuall, euerlasting, ay-during.*
Perpetuellement. *Perpetually, eternally, euerlastingly, continually.*
Perpetuer. *To perpetuate, eternize, immortalize, make euerlasting.*
Perpetuité: f. *Perpetuitie, eternitie, immortalitie, endlesnesse, euerlastingnesse.*
Perpetuller. *To tickle; (an old word.)*
Perpetuons: m. *Perpetually-begging Friers.*
Perpins: m. *Perpenders, or perpent stones; stones made iust as thick as a wall, and shewing their smoothed ends on either side thereof.*
Perplex: m. exe: f. *Perplexed; intricate, intangled; vexed, or pestered in spirit, plunged, grauelled, in a maze, at his wits end.*
Perplexement. *Perplexedly, intricately, intangledly, troublesomely.*
Perplexité: f. *Perplexitie; intricacie, intanglednesse; vncertaintie, doubtfulnesse what to doe, or what to determine; and hence also, vexation, perturbation of mind.*
Perprendre. *To seize, or take into his hands ground that lyes wast, or common.*
Perprinse. *as* Perprison.
Perprison: f. *A seizing, or taking into his owne hands (without leaue of Lord, or other) ground that lyes wast, or is vsed in common.*
Perpuce. *as* Prepuce.
Perquisiteur: m. *A diligent searcher, an industrious seeker, a serious inquirer.*
Perquisition: f. *A perquisition, diligent search, or serious inquirie.*
Perresine: f. *Rosin.*
Perrette, & Perrichon. *Womens names, deriued from* Pierre.
Perrie: f. *A Peeredome; the estate, or dignitie of a Peere.*
Perrier: m. *The Ship-Artillerie called, a Fowler.*
Perriere: f. *as* Perrier; *also, a quarrey of stone.*
Perron: m. *An open lodge, passage, or walke of stone raised, some quantitie of staires, directly before the foredore of a great house; also, a square Base of stone, or mettall, some fiue or six foot high, whereon, in old time, Knights errant placed some discourse, challenge, or proofe, of an aduenture.*
A Noel au perron, à Pasques au tison: Prov. *At Christmas warme thee in the Sunne, at Easter by the fire.*
Perroquet: m. *A Parrat; also, the hearbe Aloe, or Sea-aigreene; also, a black-backt, yellow-bellied, and greene-find sea-fish, proportioned somewhat like the Riuer-Pearch.*
Bec de perroquet. *See* Bec.
Graine à perroquet. *Bastard Saffron, wild Saffron, mocke Saffron, Saffron Dorte.*
Perrot: m. *An Oake which hath beene (or might haue beene for the age thereof) twice lopped; also, a mans proper name, being a diminutiue, or deriuatiue of* Pierre.
Perruque: f. *A locke, or tuft of haire.*
Vne fausse perruque. *A Periwig, a Gregorian.*
Perruqué: m. ée: f. *Wearing a locke, or curled tuft; long-haired.*
Perruquet: m. *One that weares an effeminate locke, or frizled tuft of haire.*
Perruquier: m. *A Periwig-maker; also, as* Perruquet.
Perruquiere: f. *A Tyre-maker, or Attire-maker; a woman that makes Perriwigs, or Attires.*
Pers: m. *Peeres.*
Pers: m. Perse: f. *Watchet, blunket, skie-coloured.*
Perscrutation: f. *A through search, diligent inquirie, neere collection, full scanning.*

Perse:

Perse: f. *The piercing of a vessell.*
Persecuté: m. ée: f. *Persecuted, prosecuted; followed with extremitie; vexed, afflicted continually.*
Persecuter. *To persecute, prosecute; follow with extremitie; vex, or afflict continually.*
Persecution: f. *Persecution, prosecution, a cruell following of, extreame pursuit after.*
Perseguier. *as* Persiguier.
Perse-pierre. *See* Perce-pierre.
Perser. *Looke* Percer.
Perseveramment. *Perseueringly, continuingly, constantly, stedfastly.*
Perseverance: f. *Perseuerance, continuance, constancie, a resolute sticking to, or abiding by.*
Perseverant. *Perseuering, persisting, stedfast, constant, continuing to the end in.*
Perseverer. *To perseuer, persist, continue, or abide by; to hold stiffly, maintaine stoutly, stedfastly to remaine in, a good course, or opinion.*
Persicaire. *Dead Arsesmart, dead Culerage, Ciderage, Peachwort.*
Persien. *Persian, of Persia; whence,* Feu Persien. *Looke* Feu.
Persil: m. *Parsely.*
Persil aigrun. *Wild Parseley, great water Parseley, sallade Parseley, Belldars, Bellrags.*
Persil Alexandrin. *Alexanders.*
Persil d'asne. *Asse-Parseley, wild Cheruill, mocke Cheruill, great Cheruill, sweet Cheruill, Mirrhis Cash, or Kex.*
Persil bastard. *Bastard Parseley, Hennes-foot.*
Persil d'eau. *Water Parseley, sallade Parseley; also, as* Persil de marais.
Persil de Macedoine. *Hearbe Alexanders, or Alisaunders; also, rocke Parseley, stone Parseley.*
Persil de marais. *Smallage; or, wild water Parseley.*
Persil de montaigne. *Mountaine Parseley.*
Persil de roc, ou de rocher. *Rocke Parseley, stone Parseley, strange Parseley, true Parseley.*
Persil sauvage. *Wild Parseley.*
Persil vray. *Stone Parseley; (though the least common, yet held the truest, Parseley.)*
Grand persil. *Great Parseley, hearbe Alexanders.*
Gresler sur le persil. *To venture boldly on, or swagger extreamely with, a knowne-weake aduersarie.*
Persin. *as* Persil.
Persister. *To persist, perseuer, continue, hold out, stand to, abide by.*
Persoir: m. *A Piercer.*
Personat: m. *A Place, or Title of honor, enioyed by a beneficed person, without any manner of Jurisdiction, in the Church.*
Personate: f. *The Clote, or great Burre.*
Personier. *See* Personnier.
Personnage: m. *A personage, bodie, person; also, a part in a Play, or part-player; an actor; also, a counterfeit, image, resemblance, of; also, a visard, a false or masking face.*
Vn livre à personnages. *A Dialogue.*
Faict à personnages. *Wrought with Imagerie, or Antickes.*
Personne: f. *A person, wight, creature, bodie; also (with a Negatiue) no bodie.*
Les Meubles suyvent la personne; viz. *are disposed of according to the custome of the place wherein a man dwelled at the time of his death; so that by* Personne *not so much his bodie, as the place of his ordinarie residence, is understood (in the customes of* Amiens, Arras, & Cambray.)
Personnel: m. elle: f. *Personall, in person, bodilie, belonging to the person, or bodie.*
Cour personnelle. *Wherein suitors are to appeare, and plead, in person, and not by atturney.*
Debtes personnelles. *Debts due by a Bill, or Scroll, or vpon a bare promise.*
Tailles personnelles. *Imposed, or leuied by Poll; and whereunto not the land, but the person, of the subiect is lyable.*
Personnellement. *Personally, in person, by presence, bodily, with the bodie.*
Personnerie: f. *A Partnership, or Coparcenership; a contributing, sharing, ioyning, or enioying, with another.*
Personnier: m. *A Partner, in trading; also, a Coheire, or Coparcener; and, a Joint-tenant, or Tenant in common; also, a contributor with others in the payment of taxes, or other publicke duties; also, one that ioynes in an Action, or Suit with another; also, an accessarie, or complice in an offence, or trespasse.*
Personnier: m. ere: f. *Partaking, sharing; contributing; accessarie; ioyning, or enioying, with another.*
Moulin personnier. *A common Mill.*
Perspective: f. *The Perspectiue, Prospectiue, or Opticke (Art.)*
Perspicacité: f. *Perspicacitie; quicke sight, nimble insight, readie apprehension, sharpe vnderstanding.*
Perspicuité: f. *Perspicuitie, cleerenesse, or plainenesse of speech.*
Perspirable: com. *Which may be breathed through.*
Perspiration: f. *A perspiration, or breathing through.*
Perspité: m. ée: f. *Sprinckled, bedeawed, moistened.*
Perstraindre. *as* Perstreindre.
Perstreindre. *To wring, or squeeze hard; also, to course, checke, chide, be verie round with.*
Pour le perstreindre en vn mot. *To be briefe, or make short; to restraine it within, knit it vp in, comprehend it vnder, one word.*
Persuadé: m. ée: f. *Persuaded; moued, induced, exhorted, aduised vnto.*
Persuader. *To persuade; aduise, exhort, moue, induce, vnto; to make beleeue, breed beliefe, put into the head, make sinke into the thought, or mind.*
Persuadeur: m. *A persuader; aduiser, counsellor, mouer, inducer vnto.*
Persuasible: com. *Persuasible, persuadeable.*
Persuasiblement. *Persuadeably.*
Persuasif: m. iue: f. *Persuasiue, persuading, aduising, inducing, mouing.*
Persuasion: f. *A persuasion; aduice, inducement; beliefe.*
Persuasoire: com. *Persuasorie, persuasiue, persuading.*
Pert. Il pert. *of* Paroir; *it appeareth.*
Perte: f. *Losse, dammage, detriment; hinderance; ruine, decay.*
Perte de finance. *Losse of the publicke treasure by a violent robberie; decay of priuat substance by excessiue, or needlesse Vsurie; whence,* Prendre à perte de finance. *Looke* Prendre.
Perte des fruicts. *Is incurred by a vassall, when a Lord hath entred on his land for want of homage, and due seruices done him; the like is;* La pure perte du vassal.

Perte de Veuë. Discours, à p. *Looke* Veuë.
Pertinemment. *Pertinently, properly, fitly, aptly, to purpose.*
Pertinent: m. ente: f. *Pertinent; fit, apt, proper, vnto purpose.*
Pertroubler. *To trouble, or perturbe extreamely.*
Pertuis: m. *A hole.*
Pertuis de l'Araigne. *The centre of an Astrolabe; the hole wherein all the tables thereof are, by a pin or nayle, ioyned together.*
Les pertuis des poelles. *Two trunkes, or gutters of wood, whereby sea-water (for Salt-making) is conueyed from the receptacle called* Forans *vnto those which are called* Viresons.
Les gens qui regardent par vn pertuis. *Monkes, or Fryers (by reason of their Cowles.)*
Faire vn pertuis dedans vn trou. *To doe iust nothing.*
'A tel pertuis telle cheville: Prov. *Looke* Cheville.
Pertuisane: f. *A Partisan, or leading staffe.*
Pertuisanon: m. *A little Partisan.*
Pertuisé: m. ée: f. *Holed, or full of holes.*
Pertuiser. *To make a hole or holes, to bore full of holes.*
Perturbateur: m. *A perturbator, disturber, disquieter, vexer, troubler; an importunate, or busie fellow.*
Perturbation: f. *Perturbation; disturbance, vnquietnesse of mind; a troublesome passion, restlesse affection; an agitation of spirit.*
Perturber. *To perturbe, disturbe, trouble, disquiet, blunder, vex.*
Pervenche: f. *Periwinkle, or Peruincle (an hearbe.)*
Pervers: m. erse: f. *Peruerse, crosse, aukeward, ouerthwart, skittish, froward, vntoward; also, naught, corrupt, mard; wry, skewing.*
Perversement. *Peruersly, crossely, aukewardly, ouerthwartly, frowardly, vntowardly; maliciously; askance, askew, awry.*
Perversion: f. *A peruersion; an vntoward, or ill-fauoured wrying; whence,* Perversion de bouche; *a crampe, or conuulsion, whereby the mouth is drawne awry.*
Perversité: f. *Peruersitie, crossnesse, ouerthwartnesse, aukewardnesse; frowardnesse, harshnesse of disposition; a skittish, giddie, or vntoward humor to doe an vnlawfull, or ill, thing.*
Perverti: m. ie: f. *Peruerted, depraued, corrupted, seduced; maliciously wrested.*
Pervertir. *To peruert, seduce, depraue, corrupt, marre, spoyle; to wrest maliciously, to turne awry, or to a wry course.*
Pervertissement: m. *A peruerting, deprauing, seducing; a false, or malicious wresting of.*
Pervertisseur: m. *A peruerter, deprauer, seducer; a false, or malicious wrester.*
Pervis. *as* Parvis.
Pes. *Looke* Peis.
Pesade: f. *Looke* Posade.
Pesant: m. Le pesant de. *The weight, or burthen of.*
Pesant: m. ante: f. *Weightie, ponderous, heauie, burthensome; also, peising, or weighing.*
Il ne trouve rien trop chaud, ny trop pesant. *He finds nothing too hot, nor too heauie for him; nothing comes amisse vnto him.*
Pesanteur: f. *Weightinesse, ponderositie, heauinesse; also, a weight, burthen, charge.*
Pesanteur de teste. *A dull, or dulling, headache.*
Pesart: m. *The disease called, the Nightmare.*

Peschage: m. *A fishing; or place to fish in.*
Pesche: f. *A fishing; also, the cast, or draught of a fishnet; also, the fish gotten thereby; also, a Peach; whence;*
Pesche blanche. *Our ordinarie white Peach.*
Pesche iaulne. *as* Pesche-coing.
Pesche d'or. *The gold Peach; one of the most delicate kinds of that fruit.*
Pesche rouge, ou sanguine. *The red Peach; the little, round, and ruddie Peach, whose pulpe, neere to the stone, is of a sanguine hue.*
Pesche de Troyes. *An Apricocke; or a small and delicate Peach resembling an Apricocke.*
Pescheable: com. *Fishable, which may be fished in.*
Pesche-amande. *The Almond Peach; a delicate Italian Peach, whose kernell is a verie sweet Almond.*
Pesche-coing. *The Quince-Peach, or yellow Peach, more hard, and more delicate, then any other.*
Peschement: m. *A fishing.*
Pesche-noire. *The blacke Peach.*
Pesche-noix. *The Nut Peach; is of a firme, or hard substance; and not much vnlike, nor much inferior, to the yellow one.*
Pescher: m. *A Fish-pond (for houshold prouision;) also, as* Peschier.
Se mettre en la vigne iusques au pescher. *To be tipled with Wine.*
Pescher. *To fish; to catch fish.*
Pescher en eau trouble. *To fish in troubled waters. Looke* Eau.
Pescher des estourgeons en l'air. *To attempt impossible, or vaine, matters.*
Pescher au maillet. *See* Maillet.
Pescher au plat. *To cut, and carue at pleasure; to take what, and where, one likes.*
Il fait beau pescher en eau large: Prov. *There is no fishing to the sea.*
Il faut perdre vn veron pour pescher vn saulmon: Pro. *Somewhat must be lost that much may be gotten.*
Tousiours pesche qui en prend vn: Prov. *And yet he fishes who catches one; or, he that takes one, may well be said to fish.*
Pescheresse: f. *A fisheresse, a woman fisher.*
Grenouille pescheresse. *The sea-Frog, sea-Toad, or sea-Diuell; a most ouglie fish.*
Pescherie: f. *A fishing; also, a little fish-pond.*
Pescheteau: m. *The sea-Frog, sea-Toad, or sea-Diuell.* ¶Bourdelois.
Pescheur: m. *A fisher, or fisherman; also, the Kingsfisher, called otherwise,* Martinet pescheur.
Tour de pescheur: Pro. *Great hazarding for great matters; whence;*
Il fit vn tour de pescheur. *He exposed himselfe vnto much danger to obtaine a thing of much worth.*
'A grand pescheur eschappe anguille: Prov. *The Eele escapes the cunning fishers hands.*
Pescheux: m. euse: f. *Fishing; or, full of fishing.*
Peschier: m. *A Peach tree.*
Couleur de fleur de peschier. *A Peach colour.*
Pesé: m. ée: f. *Peised, poised, weighed; pondered, considered, examined.*
Pesée: f. *A peising, or weighing; also, poise, or weight.*
Peser. *To peise, poise, weigh; to ponder, perpend, consider.*
Peser sur la plume. *To leane vpon a penne.*
Cela me poise. *That lyes heauie on my stomacke, or exceedingly grieues me.*

Il me pese sur le cœur. *He vexeth me at the heart; I can in no sort abide him, I can by no meanes away with him.*

'A vn chascun son fardeau poise: Pro. *Euerie one is sensible of his owne burthen.*

Mal poise qui ne contrepoise: Pro. *He weighes but ill that weighes not one with another.*

Petite chose de loing poise; &,

Petit fardeau poise à la longue: Pro. *A little trusse farre-carried seemeth heauie.*

Peseur: m. *A peiser, weigher; ponderer.*

Pesle: m. *The boult of a locke.*

Pesle: f. *as* Poile; *whence;*

Il fait le doux Dieu dessous vne pesle. *He behaues himselfe gently, beares himselfe mildly, he is a faire conditioned man; or, he is too nice, quaint, precise; he minces, or simpers it too much.*

Pesle-meslé: m. ée: f. *Pell-melled, confusedly mingled.*

Pesle-mesle. *Pell-mell, confusedly, hand ouer head, all on a heape, one with another.*

Pesles: f. *Thrummes; or that which hangs at the end of a peece of cloth like fringe.*

Pesne: m. *The boult of a locke.*

Peson: m. *A wherue, or wherle to put on a spindle; See* Pezon.

Fusée avec ses pesons. *The small Rundle, or Member of Architecture, called otherwise* Astragale; *and thus called, because it is (commonly) made to resemble many spindles and wherues threaded, or set together.*

Pesqueur. *as* Pescheur. ¶Norm.

Pessaire: m. *A Pessarie; a great Suppositorie made of soft wooll, and fashioned like a finger.*

Pesse. *The Pitch tree; also, a kind of pretious stone.*

Pesseau. *as* Paisseau.

Pesson. *as* Paisson.

Peste: f. *The plague, or pestilence; a death, contagion, infection; also, a pestiferous fellow; one that ruines, or spoyles, others.*

Remede contre la peste par art, fuïr tost & loing, retourner tard: Prov. *Art thus prescribes where plague doth raigne, fly soone and farre, turne late againe.*

Pesteil: m. *A pestle, or pestell.*

Pesteux: m. euse: f. *Plaguie, full of the plague; most pestilent infectious, contagious.*

Pestifere: com. *Pestiferous, pestilent, pernicious, deadlie, infectious, contagious.*

Pestiferé: m. ée: f. *Infected; or, that hath the plague.*

Pestilence: f. *A pestilence, or plague.*

Pestilent: m. ente: f. *Pestilent, plaguie, infectious, contagious.*

Pestilentiel. *Pestilentiall; or, as* Pestilentieux.

Pestilentieux: m. euse: f. *Pestilentious, full of the pestilence.*

Pestiller. *To paddle; or, as* Petiller; *or to patter; to beat thicke and short.*

Pestri: m. ie: f. *Kneaded; wrought as dough.*

Pestri d'eau froide. *Effeminate, cowardlie, white-liuered, without spirit, vigor, mettall; dull, cold, and slack in all he does.*

Pestri de folle farine. *Fond, light, idle, vnprofitable, a trifling fellow.*

Pestrir. *To knead; to worke, settle, or soften (as dough) with the hands.*

Pestrissement: m. *A kneading.*

Pestrisseur: m. *A kneader; a Baker.*

Pestrissure: f. *A kneading.*

Pet: m. *A fart; scape, tayle-shot, or cracke.*

Pet de boulengier. *Such a one as makes the* Bren *to follow.*

Pet en gueule. *The name of an Yew-game.*

Pet de masson. *A fart in syrrup, a squittering fart.*

I'aymeroy autant tirer vn pet d'un Asne mort, que. *I would as soone vndertake to get a fart of a dead man, as &c.*

Chantez à l'asne il vous fera des pets: Pro. *Looke* Asne.

Petacé: m. ée: f. *Peeced, bepatched.*

Petalisme: m. *A forme, or sentence, of banishment among the old Syracusans, writing his name whom they would be rid of in an Oliue leafe.*

Petarade. *See* Petarrade.

Petarasse· f. *A clap, yerke, or stroake on the buttockes; also, the farting of a lustie (and leaping) horse.*

Petard. *as* Petart; *also, a Squib.*

Petardé: m. ée: f. *Petarded, burst open with a Petard.*

Petarder. *To burst open with a Petard.*

Petardier: m. *A Petarder; one that vses, or shoots off, a Petard.*

Petarrade: f. *Gunshot of farting; also, a horses kicking, winsing, or yerking out behind, accompanied, for the most part, with farting.*

Petart: m. *A Petard, or Petarre; an Engine (made like a Bell, or Morter) wherewith strong gates are burst open.*

Petas: m. *A mole, or wart; also, a kind of (Rounciuall) Pease.*

Petasite: f. *Lagwort, Butter-burre (an hearbe.)*

Petaud: m. *A farter; also, a footman.*

C'est la Court du Roy Petaud, ou chascun est maistre: Pro. *Applyable to an Anarchie, or a disordered familie, wherein euerie one may doe what he listeth.*

Petault. *as* Petaud.

Petauristique: com. *Tumbling, vaulting, going vpon ropes, running vpon staues, in the aire.*

Petelement: m. *as* Petelis.

Peteler. *To stampe, trample, or tread hard, vpon.*

Petelis: m. *A stamping, or trampling vpon.*

Peter. *To fart; cracke, let a scape.*

Petereau: m. *A little fart, or Squib.*

Peteuse: f. *A small, and bitter fish of the Riuer* Seine; *as* Bouviere.

Petiere. Cane petiere. *See* Canepetiere.

Petillages: m. *The orders and customes obserued by Marchants in their trading, and custome-paying.*

Petillant. *Crackling; sparkling; also, stamping, or trampling; also, quaking, or shaking.*

Petillement: m. *A cracking, or sparkling; also, a quaking, shaking, panting, throbbing; also, a stamping, or trampling; also, the spitting of a candle, &c.*

Petiller. *To crackle, or sparkle; also, to quake, shake; throb, or pant; beat thicke and short; also, to stampe, or trample.*

La lumiere petille. *The candle sparkles, or spits.*

Vn oeil qui petille. *A sparkling, or often-twinckling eye.*

Petiot: m. otte: f. *Verie little.*

Petit: m. *The whelpe, cub, or puppie, the little one, or young one, of a beast; whence;*

Faire ses petits. *as vnder* Faire.

Petit: m. ite: f. *Little, small; exile, slender; young, prettie; scant, scarce, meane, pettie; low, short.*

Petit bras. *The vpper part of the arme, from the elbow to the shoulder.*
Petit cheval de Dieu. *The little Insect called, a Lady-cow.*
Petits choux. *A kind of puffe-cakes of two sorts; the one round, and plump as an apple; the other also round, but much flatter.*
La petite oye. *The Goose-giblets; Looke* Oye.
Petit pied. *See* Pied.
Petit à petit. *Faire and softly, now one and then one, wiredrawer-like; by leisure, degrees, pawses, little peeces, or parcels.*
Faire le petit. *To bow, encline, or humble himselfe; to lowte it, or beare himselfe lowly; also, to liue meanely, neerely, or poorely; to make no manner of shew in the world.*
Petit à petit on va bien loing: Pro. *Faire and softly goeth farre.*
Petite chose de loing poise; &, Petit fardeau poise à la longue: Prov. *A light thing farre borne heauie growes.*
Petit homme abat grand chesne: Pro. *A low man fells a tall Oke.*
Petite pluye abat grand vent: Pro. *See* Grand.
Les petis ruisseaux font les grandes rivieres: Pro. *Of narrow brookes come nauigable riuers.*
De petit petit, & d'assez assez: Prov. *Of a little take a little, of a mickle mickle.*
De petite chose peu de plaid: Prov. *A sleight cause needeth but sleight canuassing.*
De petit enfant petit dueil: Pro. *Seeke* Enfant.
De petit esguillon poind on bien grande asnesse: Pro. *The little goad pricks on the great she Asse.*
De petit peché petit pardon: Prov. *Small pardon will suffice for a small fault.*
Du petit vient on au grand: Pro. *See* Grand.
En petit buisson trouve on grand lievre; &,
En petite cheminée fait on bien grand feu; &,
En petite maison Dieu à grand part; &,
En petite teste gist grand sens; &,
Es petites boistes met on les bons onguens. *(Prouerbs in commendation of little things.)*
De grands vanteurs petis faiseurs: Pro. *Great boast, and small roast; big words poore worke; the more you talke the lesse you will doe.*
Tel est petit qui boit bien: Prov. *A little man may haue a great swallow.*
Petitement. *Smally, slenderly; scarcely, scantly; meanely, poorely, lowlily; shortly, lowly.*
Petitesse: f. *Smallnesse, littlenesse; prettinesse; exilitie, slendernesse, exiguitie; scarcitie, scantnesse; poorenesse, meanenesse; lowlinesse; shortnesse, lownesse, youngnesse.*
Petiteur: f. *as* Petitesse.
Petition: f. *A petition; suit, request, requirall, demaund.*
Petitoire: m. *A petition; clayme, demaund.*
Petitoire: com. *Petitorie; clayming, demaunding, requiring.*
Action petitoire. *A Clayme; a Writ of right, an action of demaund.*
Petitose: f. *The garbage of fowle; (an old word.)*
Peton: m. *A little foot; also, the slender staulke of a leafe, or of a fruit.*
Mon peton. *My prettie springall, my gentle impe; (any such flattering, or dandling phrase, bestowed by nurses on their suckling boyes.)*
Petoncle: m. *A Cockle, or small Scallop.*
Petonner. *To pat, or tread downe the earth by often stepping, or trampling on it.*
Petoucle. *as* Petoncle.
Petrar: m. *A wild Sparrow, lesse then the tame one.* ¶Orlean.
Petrarquiser. *To Petrarkise it, to write like a passionate louer.*
Petreux. Os pet. *The bone of the Temples; one of the eight bones whereof the skull consists.*
Petrification: f. *A petrification; a making stonie, a turning into stone.*
Petrifié: m. ée: f. *Made stonie, turned into stone.*
Petrifier. *To make stonie, to turne into stone.*
Petrinal: m. *A Petronell, or horsemans peece.*
Petrir. *Seeke* Pestrir.
Petrol: m. Petrole, & Petrolle: f. *as* Naphte.
Petteler. *as* Peteler.
Petulance: f. *Petulancie, malapertnesse, impudencie, sawcinesse.*
Petun: m. *Tobacco.*
Petun femelle. *English Tobacco; the right yellow Henbane; or a small kind of Nicotian.*
Petun masle. *Nicotian, French Tobacco.*
Peu. *(A Participle of the verbe* Paistre*) fed, eaten, repasted, pastured.*
Peu. *(Of the Verbe* Pouvoir) I'ay peu. *I could, or might haue beene able.*
Peu. *(An Aduerbe of quantitie) little, small, scant, scarce, few; a pittance, modicum, small deale, slender companie, almost nothing, or no bodie.*
Peu à peu. *See* Petit à petit.
Peu plus peu moins. *Little more or lesse, thereabouts.*
Peu s'en faut; &, à peu pres. *Almost, wellnigh, verie neere, lacking but little, missing but narrowly, likelie to haue beene.*
Peu souvent. *Seldome, rarely, not verie often.*
Homme de peu. *A worthlesse, poore, or weake-spirited, fellow.*
C'est trop peu d'un. *One is too few; or thats too few by one.*
Tant soit peu. *But verie sleightly, neuer so little.*
Peu de chose ne fait qu'un peu de mal: Prov. *A little thing does but a little harme.*
Peu à peu le loup mange l'oye: Prov. *Bit after bit the Wolfe eates vp the Goose.*
Peu & paix est don de Dieu: Pro. *A little with quietnesse is Gods owne gift.*
De peu de chose peu de prose: Pro. *Little done soone deliuered, little acted quickly vttered.*
Qui peu seme peu prend: Prov. *Of small seeding a small crop.*
Trois beaucoup, & trois peu destruisent l'homme: Pro. viz. *To speake much, and know but little; to spend much, and haue but little; to presume much, and be but little.*
Peucedane: m. *Horse-strong, Hore strange, Sowfennell, Sulpherwort.*
Pevier. Canon pevier. *A Cannon Peuier, or Perrier; See* Canon.
Peuille. *as* Peulle.
Peulle: f. *Before new money be deliuered out of the Mint, an Officer called* L'Essayeur *diuides a peece thereof into foure parts; one he giues to the Maister, a second vnto the Wardens of the Mint; the other two he keepes, and touches, or makes a triall of, one of them: Now each of these parts wrapt vp in a peece of paper, (specifying the quantitie, weight, allay, and day of deliuerie*

uerie out of the coyne) is tearmed Peulle.
Pevoesne: f. *Peonie, Pionie, Kings-bloome, Rose of the Mount; Looke* Pivoine.
Pevoisne. *as* Pevoesne.
Peuplade: f. *A Colonie, or Troope of people, imployed in a Plantation.*
Peuplaye: f. *A Groue of Popler trees.*
Peuple: m. *People; or folke.*
Le menu peuple. *The vulgar, multitude, or meaner sort; the commons, or common people of a Towne, &c.*
Peuple en multitude errant ne nous sert pas de garant: Prov. *The erring multitude is no fit warrant for vs.*
Peuple: m. *The Poplar, or Peplar tree (especially, the blacke one.) See* Peuplier.
Peuple blanc. *The white Poplar, or Abeell tree.*
Peuplé: m. ée: f. *Peopled; populous, inhabited, planted or well stored with folke.*
Peuplement: m. *A peopling; a storing with people.*
Peuplement de vigne. *A furnishing, or storing it with Vine-plants.*
Peupler. *To people, make populous, furnish with people, plant or store with inhabitants.*
Peupleraye: f. *A Groue, or Wood of Poplar trees.*
Peuplier: m. *The Poplar, or Peplar tree; (especially the blacke one.)*
Peuplier des Alpes. *as* Peuplier de Lybie.
Peuplier blanc. *The white Poplar, or Abeell tree.*
Peuplier de Lybie. *The Aspe, or Aspen tree.*
Peuplier de montaigne. *The same.*
Peur: f. *Feare, dread, fearefullnesse, timerousnesse, terror, a fright, or flight.*
Peur Sainct Valier: Prov. *Feare of an approaching mischiefe that breedes effects of a present one; as a man to die (being threatened a death) before any blow be giuen him.*
Qui a peur il est asseur: Prov. *A (warie, and prouident) feare breeds great securitie.*
Qui a peur des fueilles ne doit aller au bois: Pro. *Let him thats skar'd by leaues keepe from the wood.*
Tel menace qui a grand peur: Pro. *Some threaten highly that are ill afraid.*
Peuresie. *In stead of* Pleuresie. *(Rustically.)*
Peureusement. *Fearefully, timerously.*
Peureux: m. euse: f. *Fearefull, timerous, faint-hearted, white-liuered.*
Pezar: m. *A whole Pease, or Beane, stalke.*
Pezart: m. *The Night-mare; (a disease.)*
Pezon: m. *as* Peson; *also, a kind of small coyne; also, (any) small weight.*
Pezze: f. *The Pitch-tree.*
Phagedaine: m. *A kind of vlcerous Canker.*
Phagouë: f. *Looke* Fagouë.
Phaisander. *as* Faisander.
Phalange. *The name of a most venomous Spider; also, a foure-square troope, or batallion of* (8000, *some say* 18000) *souldiors, ranked so as they may incounter the enemie euerie way.*
Phalene. *A small Butterfly, or Moath, which in the night loues to be fluttering about candles.*
Phaleré: m. ée: f. *Barbed, or trapped, as a souldiors great horse.*
Phalerer. *To furnish with Barbes, or (warlike) trappings.*
Phaleres: f. *Barbes, or (warlike) trappings for a horse of seruice.*
Phaleuces: f. *Verses of eleuen sillables.*
Phalot. *as* Falot.
Phanal: m. *The Lanterne of a Gallie, or Ship.*
Phanot. *as* Falot.
Phantasie: f. *A fancie, or fantasie, a conceit, an imagination.*
Phantasié: m. ée: f. *Fancied, or conceiued in mind; fained, imagined, deuised; also, painted, or made, fantastically.*
Phantosme: m. *as* Fantosme.
Pharasse: f. *A Cresset.* ¶Langued. *Looke* Farasse.
Phares: m. *Towers, or high places neere the mouth of a Hauen, &c, wherein continuall nightlie fires, or lights be kept.*
Pharien: m. enne: f. *High, or light, as a watch-tower on the sea-coast.*
Pharique. *A kind of dangerous poison.*
Pharisien: m. enne: f. *Hypocriticall, Pharisie-like.*
Pharmacie: f. *A curing, or medecining with drugs.*
Pharmakeutie: f. *Phisicke which cureth by drugs, or simples.*
Pharmaque: m. *A simple, or drug.*
Pharol: m. *The Lanterne of a Ship, or Gallie.*
Pharot. *The same; also, a Cresset, or paper Lanterne.*
Phaseoles: m. *Phasells, long Peason, Kidney Beanes, Roman or French Beanes, garden Smilax.*
Phaseoles espineux. *The common rough Bindweed.*
Phaseoles peincts. *Particoloured Kidney Beanes.*
Phasioles, & Phasiols. *as* Phaseoles.
Phavier: m. *A Ringdoue, Queest, Coushot, Woodculuer.*
Phée: f. *A Fairie; or one of the Destinies.*
Phéé: m. éée: f. *Fatall, destined, fore-appointed; also, inchaunted, bewitched, forespoken.*
Phelandrion. *Small Burnet Saxifrage; and not medow Rue, as the Parisien Phisitions erroniously hold it to be, sayes* Gerard.
Phengite. *(The name of) a certaine bright stone.*
Phenicé: m. ée: f. *Crimson, or Skarlet, of colour.*
Phenomenes. *Ayrie impressions, or apparitions.* ¶Rab.
Philactere, & Philacterie. *Looke* Phylactere.
Philadelphe: m. *A louer of his brother.*
Philargirie: f. *Loue of siluer, couetousnesse.*
Philibert: m. *A proper name for a man; and particularly, the name of a certaine Bourgonian Saint; whereof;*
Chaine de S. Philibert. *A kind of counterfeit chaine.*
Philippe: m. *Philip; (signifies originally) a louer of horses; also, a valiant, hardie, or warlike person.*
Vn Philippe daller. *A Philips Dollar (a Low-countrey coyne.)*
Philippine: f. *An Edict whereby Philip the Faire assumed to himselfe the absolute bestowing, and dispossall of Regall Benefices.*
Philippus: m. *A golden coyne worth about* iij s *sterl.*
Philippus d'argent. *is worth about* iiij s *sterl.*
Phillyrée: f. *Mocke-priuet; a shrub.*
Philocrise: f. *Loue of gold.*
Philogrobolizé du cerveau. *Intoxicated, astonied, bedunced, at his wits end.*
Philologue: com. *A louer of learning, studie, or discourse.*
Philomesse. *A louer of the Masse.*
Philophanes. *A louer of light.* ¶Rab.
Philosophalement. *Philosophically, according to the rules of Philosophie.*
Philosophe: m. *A Philosopher, a louer of wisedome.*

Huile des philosophes. *Oyle extracted, by distillation, from tiles, or brickes, which haue lyen a good while steeping in verie old oyle.*
Oeufs des philosophes. *Looke* Oeuf.
Philosopher. *To philosophize it; to write, argue, or discourse philosophically.*
Philosopher à la martingale. *See* Martingale.
Philosophie: f. *Philosophie; the loue, or studie of wisdome.*
Philotheamon. *A louer of our gods.* ¶Rab.
Philotime: com. *Ambitious, affecting honor.*
Philotome. *A louer of Passions.*
Philtatodelphe: m. *An excessiue louer (and by consequent a hater) of his brother.*
Philtre: m. *An amorous potion, or loue-procuring medicine; also, the hollow, or gutter of the vpper lip.*
Phiole: f. *A Violl, or small glasse-bottle.*
Phiphre: f. *A Fife, or small Pipe.*
Phisicalement. *Naturally.*
Phissane. *A certaine tumbling tricke; or, a licentious fashion of dauncing, or singing, vsed, in some places, by Buffoons, or the Vices in Playes.*
Phlebotomer. *To let bloud.*
Phlebotomie: f. *Phlebotomie, bloud-letting.*
Phlegmagogue. *A medicine that purgeth flegme.*
Phlegmatique: com. *Phlegmaticke.*
Phlegme: m. *Flegme.*
Phlegme salé. *A most itching manginesse bred by salt flegme.*
Phlegmon. *A Phlegman; a certaine inflammation of the bloud, which causeth a hot, and red swelling; also, a little, and long wart breeding among the haire of the eye-lids.*
Phlegmoneux: m. euse: f. *Swelling with inflammation; also, flegmie.*
Phlegmonné: m. ée: f. *Swollen with hot bloud; or, troubled with a Phlegman.*
Phlomie. *as* Phlymouse.
Phlymouse. *(Rustically, or corruptly) in stead of* Physiognomie.
Phoebe: f. *The Moone.*
Phoenicoptere: m. *A certaine crimson-winged bird.*
Pholade: f. *as* Pelorde. ¶Langued.
Phoque: f. *A sea-Calfe.*
Phougue. *See* Fougue.
Phrene. *The Midriffe.* ¶Rab.
Phrenesie: f. *Frenzie, lunacie.*
Phrigie. *Looke* Phrygie.
Phrontiste. *The first ranke.*
Phrontistere. *The front, or fore-part of a building.*
Phrygie: f. *Phrygian melodie; a kind of tune, or musicke, wherein there seemed to be a diuine furie.*
Phryllelimeuse, & Phryllelimouse. *as* Physiognomie *(barbarously.)*
Phrymeuse, & Phrymouse. *The same.*
Phryson. *A Frizeland horse. Looke* Frison.
Phthiriase: f. *The lowsie euill.* ¶Rab.
Phtise: f. *The Tysicke; an (incurable) vlceration of the lungs, accompanied with a consumption of the whole bodie.*
Phtisique: com. *Tysicall; or, troubled with the Tysicke.*
Phy; &, Maistre phy phy. *Looke* Fy.
Phylaciste: m. *A Gaoler, or Keeper of a Prison.*
Phylacte. *as* Phylaciste.
Phylactere: f. *A prison; also, a (written) preseruatiue against poyson; or as* Phylacterie.
Phylacterie: f. *A scroll of Parchment, with the tenne Commaundements written in it, worne by the Pharisies about their heads, and armes.*
Phylomie, & Phylonomie. *(Vsed corruptly) in stead of* Physiognomie.
Phylosomie, & Phylosonomie. *The same.*
Physetere. *The Whirlepoole (a huge fish.)*
Physicien: m. *A naturall Philosopher.*
Physiognomie: f. *Phisiognomie; a guesse at the nature, or the inward disposition, by the feature, or outward lineaments.*
Physiologie: f. *A reasoning, disputing, or searching out of the nature of things; also, anatomizing Phisicke, or that part of Phisicke which treats of the composition, or structure of mans bodie.*
Physique: f. *Naturall Philosophie.*
Physis: f. *Nature.* ¶Grec. ¶Rab.
Piaffard: m. arde: f. *Braggard, strouting, vaine-glorious, proudly vaunting, fondly brauing it.*
Piaffe: f. *A bragging, strouting, fond brauing of it; a disdainefull carriage, boasting demeanour, vainglorious behauior.*
Piaffer. *To brag, or braue it fondly; to boast, or strout it vainely; to make a vaine-glorious, or foolish muster of himselfe.*
Piaffeur: m. *A braggard, or braggadochio; a strouting, or boasting fop; a proud vaine-glorious cockscombe.*
Piaffeusement. *Braggingly, proudly, vaine-gloriously, stroutingly, vauntingly.*
Piailler. *To cheepe, or cry like a chicke; also, to bib, sip, tiple, or driue away time by drinking.*
Piailleur: m. *A bibber, sipper, wine-swiller; a tipler, bowser, pot-gossip, or Gossip-pint-pot.*
Piaison: f. *A bibbing, sipping, tipling; swilling, immoderate drinking.*
Pialet: m. *Dodder; a weed.*
Pian. Marcher pian. *To march leisurely, goe faire and softly.*
Pianelle: f. *A night-slipper, or choppine, a Pantofle for the chamber.*
Pianelleux: m. euse: f. *Wearing, full of, or belonging to, slippers, or chamber-pantofles.*
Piastre. *A Turkish coyne worth about* iiij s *sterl.*
Piat: m. *A young Pye.*
Piauler. *To peepe, or cheepe (as a young bird;) also, to pule, or howle (as a young whelpe.)*
Piaux: m. *Newly-hatched chickens, or birds.*
Pibale: f. *A young Lamprey.* ¶Bourdelois.
Pible: f. *The pizzle, or yard of a beast.*
Pibole: f. *A kind of Bagpipe.*
Piboleur: m. *A Piper.* ¶Poictevin.
Pic: m. *A Wood-pecker, Hickway, Greenepeake; also, a (Masons) pickax; also, a thrust, foyne, or punch.*
Pic d'Auvergne. *A Wall-pecker.*
Pic de farine. *A Measure which containes about nine of our Pecks; (for it is to weigh 125 pounds.)*
Pic iaulne. *The ordinarie Woodpecker.*
Pic de mer. *A certaine rock-fish, of sundrie colours.*
Pic de muraille. *The small Hickway called, a Wall-pecker.*
Pic rouge. *A Speight, or Specht.*
Pic verd. *The Greene-peake, or ordinarie Woodpecker.*
La Coste à pic; ou, en pic. *A full-deepe shore; a coast of a plumpe, or downe-right depth.* ¶Norm.
Picadilles. *Looke* Piccadilles.
Picardent. *as* Piquardant.

Picardiser. *To Picardize it; to speake, or doe like a Picard.*
Picarel: m. *The small, and white Cackarell fish, whereof the best* Garum, *or pickle is made.*
Pication: f. *A pitching, or bepitching.*
Piccadilles: f. *Piccadilles; the seuerall diuisions or peeces fastened together about the brimme of the collar of a doublet, &c.*
Piccon: m. *A prickle, or small pricke.*
Piccoter. *as* Piquoter.
Piccotin. *See* Picotin.
Picé: m. ée: f. *Pitched, or pitchie.*
Piceastre. *The wild Pitch tree.*
Picée: f. *The Pitch tree.*
Pichier: m. *A Pitcher (pot.)* ¶Langued.
Picmart: m. *A Speight, Woodpecker, Highaw, Hickway.*
Picorée: f. *Picorie; a forraging, ransacking, spoyling of, or preying on, the (poore) countreyman (friend, or foe.)*
Picorer. *To forrage, ransacke, rifle, rob, or prey vpon, the poore husbandman, be he friend, or foe.*
Picoreur: m. *A boothaler (in a friends countrey;) a rauening, or filching souldior.*
Picotage: m. *A pricking here and there; also, a spotting, or speckling.*
Picote: f. *The small Pocks.*
Picoté: m. ée: f. *Spotted, specked, or speckled; also, pricked, or stung often.*
Picoter. *See* Piquoter.
Picoterie: f. *A girding, nipping, or quipping, in speeches; a iarre, odds, or dispute, in words.*
Picoteure: f. *A pricke; a spot; a freckle, or pimple; See* Piquoteure.
Picotin: m. *A (French) Pecke; or, the fourth part of a* Boisseau; *comes to about fiue Pints of our measure; and is vsed onely in the measuring of Oates.*
Picoture: f. *as* Picoteure.
Picquamment. *Prickingly, piercingly.*
Picquant. *See* Piquant.
Picque: f. *A Spade, at Cards; also, as* Pique.
C'est bien rentré de picques noires. *Yea marry sir, now you haue hit it; (Ironically.)*
Picquement, & Picquer. *as* Piquement, & Piquer.
Picqueron: m. *A little Pike; a Iaueline, or Dart; See* Piqueron.
Picque-seiche. *Looke* Pique-seiche.
Picquet: m. *A little Pickax, or Mattocke; also, the peg, or sticke thrust downe into the earth by a Surueyor that measures with cord, or chaine.*
Picqueure. *as* Piqueure.
Picquier: m. *A Pike-man, a Corselet.*
Picquois: m. *A Pickax.*
Picquot: m. *A prickle, or small pricke.*
Picquoté, & Picquoter. *See* Piquoté, & Piquoter.
Picte. *A (French) farthing; the fourth part of the Denier.*
Pictre. *The breast, bosome, or stomacke.*
Picts: m. *The bulke, or pitch of the bodie; (or more properly) as* Pis.
Pié: m. *as* Pied; *a foot, &c.*
Pie: f. *A Pye, Pyannat, Meggatapye.*
Pie ancrouëlle, ou engroüée. *A Waryangle; or, as vnder* Engroüé.
Pie escrayere. *The same.* ¶Savoyard.
Pie griesche. *The same; a rauenous bird, not altogether so big as a Thrush.*
Pie de mer. *The Oliue, or Sea-Pye; a daintie fowle.*
Maigre comme vne pie. *We say (to the same purpose) as fat as a Henne's on the forhead.*
Monté iusques au nid de la pie. *At his full height; as great, rich, or powerfull as euer he can, or will, be.*
Vous ne fustes onques de mauvaise pie couvez. *You are of no ill progenie; you haue no taint of ill breeding in you.*
Pie: f. *Drinke, bowsing, liquor; also, a Goose, the broyled thicke skinne of a peece of Beefe; also, the monstrous appetite of maides, and big-bellied women, vnto Coales, Ashes, Paper, and such other vnnaturall meats.*
C'est vn croque la pie. *He is a notable tosse-pot, or licke-spiggot.*
Pie: com. *Pious, godlie, religious, holie, deuout; mercifull, gentle; also, pied; or blacke and white as a Pie.*
Pie mere de la teste. *Looke* Mere.
Pieça. *A great while since, long agoe; also, heretofore, or in times past.*
Piece: f. *A peece, parcell, part, fragment; morcell; gobbet, lumpe, cantill; share of.*
La piece du chef. *A French Coyfe; the Sattin Coyfe worne now-adayes by diuers of our Ladies, and Gentlewomen.*
Piece de drap. *A whole Cloth (as well as a peece of Cloth.)*
Piece de huict heures. *as* Aloyau; *tearmed so, because the Clarks of the Palace commonly fetch it at the Cookes about eight of the clocke in the morning.*
Piece à pommette. *Looke* Pommette.
Les pieces d'un Procez. *The Bookes, Pleadings, or Copies of Instruments, vsed in a Suit.*
Gens de toutes pieces. *Men of all sorts, and qualities, tag-rag, wise and fooles, rich and poore, one with another.*
La grande piece. *The vpmost, and broadest peece of a Pouldron; or, a broad peece of Armour thats placed betweene the bottome of the helmet, and the Pouldron.*
La haute piece. *The Pouldron.*
En piece. *Of a long time, of a great while.*
Ie n'aurois en piece dit, ne fait, cela. *I would not for any thing haue done, &c, the least part of that.*
'A chef de piece. *In the end, at the length; or, after a long time.*
Il n'y a piece d'eux. *There is not one among them.*
Tout d'une piece. *All of a peece; also, of one whole colour; of onely one colour all ouer.*
Ie ne sçay quelle piece couldre à cecy. *I know not what helpe to apply, what art to imploy, in this; I know not how to remedie, supply, repaire, it.*
Piecette: f. *A shred, bit, mosrell, mammocke; a small parcell, or peece.*
Pied: m. *A foot; a paw; also, a footing, or setting of the foot; also, a* Basis, *or Base; a root, or bottome; a footstall, or foundation; also, the measure of a foot; (for which looke the next Marginall word.)*
Pied d'Alexandre. *Bartrane, or Bertram; Pellitorie of Spaine.*
Pied d'Alouëtte. *Larkes spurre, Larkes claw, Larkes heele, Monkes-hood, Kings Consound.*
Pied de biche. *The end of the Gafle of a Crosse-bow.*
Pieds blancs. *Looke* Blanc.
Pied de canard. *Goose-foot, wild Orache.*
Pied d'un cancre. *The clee, or claw of a Crab.*

Pied de chat. *The port, or vpsett of some bitts, made like the foot of a Cat.*
Pieds chauds. Il a les pieds chauds. *He prattles, tattles, babbles verie much; his tongue neuer stints, neuer leaues, neuer lyes; also, he is lustie, gamesome, frolicke, wanton; also, he is iealous.*
Pied de chevre. *Looke* Chevre.
Pied de colombe. *Doues-foot, Pigeons-foot; a kind of Pinkneedle.*
Pied de coq. *Hedge-fumitorie, Hennes-foot;* Gerard *calls bastard Parseley Hennes-foot, and another calls it* Pied de coq.
Pied de corbin. *Crowfoot, Butter-flower, Kings-cob, Gold-cups, Gold-knops.*
Pied de corneille. *Crowfoot Plantaine, Harts-horne Plantaine, Buck-horne, Harts-horne, Sandwort, hearbe Iuie, hearbe Eue.*
Pieds corniers. *Looke* Pieds-corniers.
Pied droict d'une cheminée, feneſtre, porte, &c. *The iaumb, or iaume of a chimney, &c.*
Pied fourchu. *Any clouen-footed beast; as an Oxe, Hog, Sheepe, &c; also, the toll thats taken vpon the sale of any of them in Markets, or Faires.*
Pied de geline. *Hedge Fumitorie, yellow Fumitorie, Hennes foot; also, as vnder* Geline.
Pied de Griffon. *A Griffons foot; an Instrument wherewith Surgeons draw Moles, or the peeces of a dead child, out of womens wombes.*
Pied gris. *A clowne, boore, hinde, swaine; a countrey hob.*
Pied de jars. *Goose-foot, wild Orache.*
Pied de lievre. *Hares-foot, Hare-foot Trefoile, base Trefoile, rough Clauer.*
Pied de Lion. *Lions foot, Lions paw, Ladies mantle, great Sanicle, Padelion.*
Pied de Loup. *Wolues-claw, Club-mosse.*
Pied de milan. *The hearbe Kites-foot.*
La pied de monnoye. *The ground of reckoning, and for the rate, of money; which was, vntill the yere* 1577, *by* ſolz, *but hath beene euer since by* Eſcus.
Pieds neufs. Faire pieds neufs. *A woman to be deliuered; a horse to cast his hoofes.*
Vn pied de nez. *Great shame, extreame disgrace (or sence of disgrace.)*
Pied d'oiſon. *Goose-foot, wild Orache; called also Swines-bane, because it kills, or meazels, the Swine which eat of it.*
Pied d'oye. *The same.*
Pied de pigeon. *as* Pied de Colombe.
Pied de poulain. *Fole-foot, Colts-foot, Hall-foot, Horsfoot, Bull-foot.*
Pieds pouldreux. *Looke* Pouldreux.
Pied rond. *Any whole-hoofed beast; as a Horse, Cammell, Moyle, Asse, &c; also, the toll thats taken vpon the sale of such beasts.*
Pied de ſtat. *as* Pied-ſtal.
Pied de veau. *Calues-foot, wake-Robin, Ramp, Aaron, Starchwort, Cuckoe-pint, Priests-pint.*
Faire, ou trouſſer le pied de veau. *Looke* Veau.
Colombier à pied. *A round, or square Doue-cote built of stone, &c, from the verie ground.*
Fer à pied. Elle n'a eu fer à pied. *She is vntainted, vndefiled, vnbroken vp.*
Froid aux pieds Avoir froid aux pieds; &, Avoir les pieds froids. *Looke* Froid.
Le grand pied. *The thigh, leg, and foot altogether; tearmed so by Anatomists.*
Haut le pied. S'en aller haut le p. *To flye with lift-vp legs, or as fast as his legs can carrie him.*
Sergent à pied. *A Sergeant, or Officer that arrests, &c, onely within some peculiar Towne, or Towneship.*
Tiers pied. *as* Trepied.
Pied à pied. *By little and little; step after step; one foot before another, by degrees.*
Pied à pied de. *Close by, neere vnto.*
Les pieds au feu. Il ſemble qu'il ait les pieds au feu. *He keepes such a figging that one would thinke his feet were in the fire.*
'A pied coy. *Stilly, softly; also, settledly, reposedly; with a firme, or fast-planted foot.*
'A pied de grue. *In suspence, on doubtfull tearmes; or, not well, or but halfe, settled, like a Crane that stands but vpon one leg.*
'A pied levé. Reſpondre à pied levé. *To answer extempore.*
Au pied levé. Pourſuivre au pied levé. *To follow foot-hot, or hard at the heels.*
Prendre au pied levé. *To snap vp in words; to take verie short, or at all aduantages; to trip a man vnawares, on a suddain, or when he is not prouided; to take things at the worst.*
'A pied de plomb. *Slowly, heauily, dully.*
'A pied de plomb, & de pompe. *The same; also, stately, haughtily, maiestically.*
'A pied tout porté. *Looke* Porté.
'A plein pied. Mettre à plein pied. *To raze, or lay euen with the ground.*
Entre le pied, & le carreau. *In the middest of danger, in the height of affliction.*
Et au pied. *And to his heeles he betooke him, and away he got him; or (more briefely) And away.*
Iuſques à la ſemelle du pied ſeulement. *Sleightly, barely, as little as may be.*
Sur ce pied. *Vpon this ground or occasion, hereupon.*
Sur le plein pied. Mettre ſur le plein pied. *To settle, make sure, make fast.*
Aller de l'un pied ſur l'autre. *To affect, or mince it, in treading.*
Aller du pied comme vn chat maigre. *Looke* Aller.
Cercher cinq pieds en vn mouton. *To look for more then can be had..*
Clocher ſur vn pied. Ie ſçay bien ſur quel pied il cloche. *I know full well his infirmitie, or defects; I know well enough what he ayles, what he lacks.*
Donner pied à. *To set on foot, giue a beginning, make an ouerture, lay a foundation, vnto.*
Donner pied ferme à. *To settle, or giue sure footing vnto.*
Donner du pied à. *To kicke, spurne, contemne, reiect.*
Faire ſelon la jambe le pied. *To doe things orderly; to keepe, obserue, or hold a iust proportion.*
Faucher l'herbe ſous les pieds à. *To supplant, or put the nose out of ioynt; to depriue, or preuent one of a thing which he expected.*
Fendre les pieds. *Looke* Fendre.
Gaigner au pied *To run his countrey, or to run away.*
Iouër à quattre pieds contre. *To kicke, winse, or let fly at with all foure; to contend, or play reakes, against with all his power.*
Marcher de pied en terre. Il ne marche &c. *He is so proud, or so glad, that he knowes not the ground he goes on.*
Mettre ſous pied. *To forgiue, and forget.*
Il me ſe mouche pas du pied. *He is a craftie, subtill, warie whoreson.*

Passer le pied sur la gorge à. *Looke* Passer.

Perdre pied. *To loose ground; or be driuen to a behind-hand (and thereupon, to his shifts.)*

Planté sur le pied gauche. *Setled in an euill posture, or on the wrong side; badly disposed in affection; or ingaged in an vniust cause.*

Prendre pied à. *To regard, heed; build vpon, make reckoning; take notice of; also, to be discontented, or aggrieued, at.*

Rencontrer, ou trouver chausseure à leur pied. *To meet with their matches, or with such as will hold them tacke; also, to light vpon stuffe for their purpose, or that which will serue their turne.*

Saulter à deux pieds sur le ventre à. *Looke* Saulter.

Seicher sur les pieds. *To be in great perplexitie, or in a pecke of troubles. Looke* Seicher.

Tenir pied à. *To keepe play, hold tacke or footing; march ranke in ranke, walke cheeke by iowle, with; also, to tarrie long, or abide by it.*

Tenir pied à boale. *To follow a businesse throughly; to stick hard, or stand close, vnto it (from the play at Ninepinnes, wherein a man must stand where his bowle doth lye.)*

Tenir pied en soulier. Il leur fit tenir pied en soulier. *He curbed them, kept them from raunging, held them in, or in awe.*

Il en tirera pied ou aile. *He will carrie away either leg or wing, either more or lesse, one part or another, of it.*

Le pied saisit le chef. *The floore, or soyle, commaunds the house; he that is Lord of the one may seize the other; (or, he thats owner of the one may owne the other;)* Area enim est pars vel maxima ædificij *(say the Ciuilians;) The customes of* Chalons, Art. 143. *expound this Maxime otherwise; viz. that a man may build his house vpright as high as he will, and compell a neighbor to withdraw any thing that shall hinder him therein, of what continuance soeuer it haue beene.*

'A l'Advocat le pied en main: Prov. viz. *Of Partridges, Phesants, Capons, &c, wherewith they looke to be now and then presented.*

'A l'aise marche à pied qui meine son cheval par la bride: Prov. *Looke* Cheval.

'A panse chaude pied endormy: Pro. *When a man is full, he is fitter to sleepe then to runne.*

Assez escorche qui tient le pied: Prov. *He does ill ynough that helps to doe euill.*

Barbe rase pied ferrat: Pro. *Looke* Barbe.

Bouche fresche, pied sec: Pro. *A coole mouth, and a dry foot (preserue a man long time aliue.)*

Le beau soulier blesse souvent le pied: Prov. *Looke* Soulier.

Mieux vaut vn pied que deux eschasses: Prov. *One foot is better then two stilts.*

Mieux vaut vn pied nud que nul: Pro. *Better a naked, then no foot.*

Mieux vaut glisser du pied que de la langue: Prov. *See* Glisser.

Qui veut aller les pieds nuds ne doit semer des espines: Prov. *He that will bare-foot goe must plant no thornes.*

Selon le pied la forme: Pro. *Fashion your last according to your foot.*

Tenez chaud le pied & la teste, au demeurant vivez en beste: Pro. *The feet and head kept warme, the rest will take lesse harme.*

Pied: m. *A foot, in measure; the length of a foot (twelue ynches) in measuring.*

Pied de bois. *A certaine measure vsed at, and about,* Bourdeaux; *Looke* Pied de ville.

Pied de Clermont. *Is but eleuen ynches long.*

Pied cube. *Is twelue ordinarie feet, and containes euerie way twelue times 144 ynches.*

Pied d'Engoulesme. *Is a sixteenth part longer then the ordinarie foot.*

Pied Geometrique. *Is foure hand-breadthes, or the breadth of sixteene fingers.*

Pied Royal, ou de Roy. *The ordinarie twelue-ynch foot, a foot according to the Standard; containes in square 144 ynches.*

Pied de terre. *Is longer then the ordinarie foot by an eight part in three quarters; and vsed about* Bourdeaux *for the measuring of land.*

Pied de ville. *Exceeds the ordinarie foot by fiue eight parts of an ynch; and is vsed at* Bourdeaux *in the measuring of Timber, Wainscot, and other wood.*

Le petit pied. *A small measure (belike some ynches shorter then the ordinarie foot) which French Masons, and Carpenters vsually carry about them.*

Reduict au petit pied. *Contracted, straitned, stinted; whose plumes are plucked, fortune scanted, meanes withdrawne; that cannot doe as he hath done; that is not the gallant he hath beene.*

'A pied. *By line and leuell, by compasse and measure, proportionably.*

Au pied de. *According to; after the rate, proportion, or scantling of; whence,* Au pied de la lettre; *according to the literall sence, or literally.*

'A tout pied. Ames à tout pied. *Soules of all sizes, spirits for all purposes.*

Tout d'un pied. *Euen, leuell, plaine, without any ascent, or descending.*

Pied-bornier: m. *A tree that serues to diuide seuerall Tenements, or Inheritances.*

Pied-bot: m. *A club-foot, or stub-foot; also, one that hath verie great ankles, or heeles.*

Piedefief. *A fief dismembred, which a vassall may, for his benefit, alien to whom he list.*

Pied-gris: m. *A clowne, hob, hinde, or boore of the countrey.*

Pied-leger. *as* Pied-viste.

Pied-poul: m. *The round-rooted, or Onion-rooted Crowfoot; some also call Purslane so.*

Pieds-corniers: m. *Certaine trees marked out for limits vnto the sale of Wood; or as bounds betweene Groues of Timber-wood, and Copses of Vnderwood; also, trees that diuide seuerall Tenements, or Inheritances.*

Pied-sonnant. *Trampling, or making the ground ring againe with his proud steps.*

Pied-stal: m. *The pedestall, or footstall of a pillar; that whereon it stands an end.*

Pied-terre. *An alighting, or setting foot on the ground; whence,* Cela a mis pied-terre à l'homme; *hath set foot on earth for man.*

Pied-viste: com. *Light-footed, swift of foot.*

Piege: m. *A snare, ginne, or grinne.*

Aujourd'huy en siege, demain en piege: Prov. *To day in pompe, to morrow in prison.*

Pienne. Rose de pienne. *Peonie, Pionie, Kings-bloome, Rose of the Mount.*

Piepou. *as* Pied-poul.

Pier. *To bowse, bib, sip, swill.* ¶Barrag.

Pierigot: m. *as* Manganese.

Pierre: m. *Peter.*

Pierre du Coignet. *A Monkie-like Image of stone in our Ladies Church at Paris, where it was at first set vp, to the disgrace of one of that name, a great aduersarie vnto the Clergie.*

Herbe de S. Pierre. *Sampire, Crestmarin.*

Descouvrir S. Pierre pour couvrir S. Paul. *To borrow of Peter to pay Paule.*

'A la S. Pierre l'hyver s'en va, ou il reserre: Prov. *Looke* Reserrer.

Pierre: f. *A stone; also, the stone.*

Pierre Afrodisiace. *A certaine ruddie white stone.*

Pierre aguisoire, ou, à aguiser. *A Whetstone, or Grindlestone.*

Pierre d'aigle. *An Eagle-stone; a stone found in the neast of an Eagle, and held casefull vnto women in labour.*

Pierre Alabandique. *A certaine bloud-prouoking stone, of a blacke and purple hue.*

Pierre Arabique. *A white stone, cleere, and transparent as glasse, in stead whereof it was in old time vsed.*

Pierre d'Armenie. *as* Verd d'Azur.

Pierre Assienne, ou d'Asso. *A certaine light, and spungious stone (full of yellow streakes, and easie to be broken) whereon there growes a mouldie, or hairie flower, saltish in tast, and good to preserue things in; and therefore haue some imployed it in the imbaulming of dead bodies, (whose superfluous flesh it soone consumes) this, besides the diuers vses thereof in Phisicke, wherein also the stone it selfe is vsed, though with lesse effect then the flower.*

Pierre d'azur. *The Azure stone, called also,* Lapis Lazuli.

Pierre bise. *A certaine hard stone of sundrie colours, and bright as flint, which it somewhat resembles.*

Pierre calaminaire. *See* Calaminaire.

Pierre de Canon. *A Cannon bullet.*

Pierre de castille. *Lyme-stone; called so in some parts of the forrest of* Ardenne.

Pierre à chaux. *Lyme-stone.*

Pierres de colique. *Certaine stones found in the head of the fish* Maigre, *and good against the Collicke (thinkes the vulgar) if they be giuen, but not if they be sold.*

Pierre douce. *The Honnie stone; or, as* Pierre melitite.

Pierre d'eau de mer. *An Agat; or, an Opall; (for it yeelds an Azure lustre.)*

Pierre ematite. *The Bloud-stone.*

Pierres d'escreuisse. *Two whitish stones, found in the heads of some old Creuisses; taken in white Wine, they strengthen the heart; and preuent, or dissolue, the Stone; the powder of them serues also to whiten the teeth.*

Pierres d'esponge. *Certaine stones found in ordinarie spunges; being put in liquor, they melt into a milkie humor; drunken in Wine, they breake the (Kidney-troubling) Stone.*

Pierre d'estanche. *The Bloud-stone.*

Pierre d'estoilles. *The starrie Carbuncle; a precious stone wherein be many golden, and starre-like-shining drops.*

Pierre à feu. *A Marcasite, or Fire-stone; also, a Flint.*

Pierre du fiel de bœuf. *A yellow stone, (sometimes as big, and euer as brittle, as an egge) taken in drinke, it breakes the stone in the bladder, and is verie soueraigne against the Jaundice; being snuft vp in powder, it cleeres the sight, dryes vp the immoderate humors of the eyes, and eases those that haue the falling euill.*

Pierre franche. *The soft, and white, Free-stone.*

Pierre à fusil. *A Flint.*

Pierre galactite. *The milke stone; a certaine white stone, which being pownded, and put into water, becomes of a milkie taste, colour, and consistence.*

Pierre Geodes. *A certaine round stone of the colour of rustie Jron; containes within it a yellowish earth; and is good against inflammations in the priuities.*

Pierre à grain. *A kind of spotted Free-stone.*

Pierre de grison. *See* Grison.

Pierre Hematide. *The Bloud-stone.*

Pierre Herculienne. *A Load-stone.*

Pierre Hieracite. *A kind of Bloud-stone, or stone that staunche th bloud.*

Pierre d'Iris. *The Opall; Seeke* Iris.

Pierre Iudaïque. *A faire white stone, fashioned like an Akorne, and compassed with many equall-distant lines.*

Pierre de laict. *as* Pierre galactite.

Pierre de S. Leu. *An excellent Free-stone, little inferior to the white marble of Italie.*

Pierre de limaçon. *See* Limaçon.

Pierre mariniere. *The Adamant, or Load-stone.*

Pierre marmaride. *A verie hard kind of gray marble.*

Pierre Melitite. *The sweet stone, or Honnie stone; white like the milke stone; and tasting like Honnie.*

Pierre Memphites. *A small stone (oylie, and of diuers colours) wherewith in old time (for now adaies it is not found, or not vsed) members to be cut off were, without any danger, so mortified, as the patient felt no paine in the cutting.*

Pierre menuë. *A kind of Tyle-stone.*

Pierre de Mine. *A Markasite.*

Pierre à miroir. *Looke* Miroir.

Pierre Naxienne. *The Whetstone.*

Pierre noire. *Jeat.*

Pierre Phrygienne. *A certaine pale-coloured, and white-streaked Capadocian stone, vsed in old time by Phisitions, and Dyers; but now out of date, and seldome or neuer found.*

Pierre plombiere. *Lead-oare; or Lead-stone, before it be tryed.*

Pierre de S. Pol. *as* Terre Samienne; *or, a kind of stone found in a certaine Caue in Malta.*

Pierre ponce. *The Pummis stone; the rugged, and spungie substance wherewith Parchment is smoothed.*

Pierre Samienne. *A whitish stone, found among the Samien earth; and of a cooling, and restringent qualitie.*

Pierre sanguine. *A Bloud-stone; Looke* Sanguine.

Pierre scissile. *A yellow stone easie to be cleft, and full of veines, which are spread ouer it like the teeth of a Combe.*

Pierre Selenite. *as* Pierre à miroir; *(for which looke* Miroir.)

Pierre serpentine. *A medicinable stone, whereof there be diuers kinds; some blacke, hard, & heauie; others of a spotted ash-colour; others white, or begirt with white lines: any one of them, hanging about the necke, is held good against headach, & the stinging of venomous beasts.*

Pierre speculaire. *as* Pierre à miroir; *(for which looke* Miroir.)

Pierre de taille. *Free-stone.*

Pierre Thracienne. *A certaine stone, which cast hot into water kindles, into oyle quenches.*

Pierre Thyite. *A greenish stone, which being steeped in liquor yeelds a milkie, or white humor.*
Pierre de tuffe. *A white sand-stone; or a soft and brittle stone, which is easily crumbled vnto sand.*
Pierre vive. *Flint.*
La pierre est eschappée. *My word is past; the dice be cast; the thing is alreadie graunted, and gone.*
C'est vne pierre iettée en son jardin. *This thorne is thrust into his foot; this bone is thrown for him to gnaw on; these words doe touch, and tax him; are meant or directed vnto him, what other shew soeuer they carry.*
Cette pierre tomboit en son jardin. *This blow alighted on his shoulders; this mischiefe was a preiudice, this inuectiue had relation, onely vnto him.*
D'une pierre faire deux coups. *To kill two birds with one stone (say we.)*
Faire de pierres pain. *To make vse, or take aduantage, of any thing.*
Il jette la pierre, & cache le bras. *He does the wrong, and yet will not be seene in't; he giues the blow, and will not be aknowne of't.*
Mettre toutes pierres en oeuvre. *To imploy, or make vse of, euerie thing. (This phrase is also applyable vnto a wench, that suffers any mans stones to grind at her Mill.)*
Remuer toute pierre. *To attempt all courses, try all wayes.*
Pierre en puis n'est pas pourrie: Prov. *Stones rot not in the bottome of a Well; they that rest in fit places languish not.*
Il n'est pas Masson qui pierres refuse: Pro. *He is no Mason who refuseth stones.*
Qui remue les pierres ses doigts casse: Pro. *The busie stone-remouer lames his fingers.*
Pierrerie: f. *A Quarrey of stone; also, stone-worke; also, iewels, or precious stones.*
Pierrette: f. *A little stone.*
Pierreux: m. euse: f. *Stonie; grauellie; rockie.*
La cholique pierreuse. *A paine like the Cholicke, but comming of a stone in the kidneyes.*
Os pierreux. *The bone of the Temples.*
Pierrier: m. *A Cabinet, Casket, Case, or Box for precious stones.*
Pierriere: f. *The same; as also a place wherein stones are gotten.*
Pierriz: m. *Heapes, or walls of dry, or vnmortered stones.*
Pierron. *See* Perron.
Pierrot. *(A diminutiue of* Pierre:) *Piers.*
Pierrote. *as* Pierrette; *or* Pierrotte.
Pierrotte: f. *A small stone; also, a stonie, flintie, or grauellie soyle.*
Pierrou: m. *A certaine base coyne, thats currant about* Avignon.
Piesante: f. *A path, or small way, some two foot and a halfe broad.*
Piesette: f. *A peece, or compartiment; the ioint whereat the players are hanged in the port, or vpsett of a Bitt.*
Pietaille: f. *A footing, or footmanship; also, a footman; also, a troope of footmen.*
Piete: f. *A kind of Spade, or digging Instrument.*
Pieton: m. *A footman; one that trauels on foot; also, a little foot; also, a Pawne at Chests.*
Pietonné: m. ée: f. *Settled, sadned with the feet; often stamped, or trampled on; hard troden downe.*
Pietonner. *To settle, sadden, lay, or beat downe with often treading, stepping, or stamping on.*
Pietonneux: m. euse: f. *Treading thicke and short, often stepping or stamping on the earth.*
Pietre: com. *In bad plight, in bare taking, in ill array, beggarlie, wretched, poore, needie; also, meane, homelie, base, bad; false, counterfeit.*
Pietrement. *Poorely, barely, needily, wretchedly, beggarly; also, falsely, or badly.*
Pietrer. *To stampe on, tread downe, trample vnder the feet.*
Pietrerie: f. *Barenesse, miserie, wretchednesse, needinesse.*
Piette: f. *A Puet.*
Pieu: m. *A stake, or pile; also, the latch of a doore.*
Pieuler. *See* Piuler.
Pieumart: m. *A Wood-pecker, Spight, Hickway.*
Pieur. *Looke* Pire.
Pieusement. *Piously, religiously, deuoutly, holily.*
Pieux: m. euse: f. *Pious, godlie, deuout, holie, religious.*
Pige: f. *as* Pis; *or as* Pinge.
Pigeassé: m. ée: f. *Pied, particoloured.*
Pigeon: m. *A Pigeon, or Doue; also, a fop, cokes, noddie, ninnyhammer.*
Pigeon de palette; &, Pigeon patté; *a rough-footed Doue.*
Pigeon ramier. *A Queest, Cooshot, Culuer, Woodculuer, Blockdoue, Ringdoue.*
Pigeon de Venise. *A kind of Turpentine.*
Pied de pigeon. *Doues foot, Pigeons foot, an hearbe.*
Preneur de pigeons. *A Conycatcher.*
Le pigeon est au colombier. *The Poccard is in his sweating Tub.*
Cela chassera les pigeons du colombier. *See* Colombier.
Semer vn grain d' orge pour attraper vn pigeon. *To giue, spend, or aduenture a little in hope of getting much.*
Pigeon saoul trouve les cerises ameres: Pro. *Said of one who loathes, or derides, his owne ouer-easefull estate.*
La censure tourmente les pigeons laissant aller les corbeaux libres: Prov. *Looke* Censure, *or* Corbeau.
On ne peut d' un pigeon faire vn vif esparvier: Prov. *The sillie Doue good Sparhawke nere will be; (Somewhat to which purpose we say) a man cannot make a Cheuerill purse of a Sowes eare.*
Qui veut tenir nette maison, il n'y faut prestre, ny pigeon: Pro. *He that in a neat house will dwell, must Priest and Pigeon thence expell.*
Pigeonnade: f. *A billing, or Pigeon-like bussing.*
Pigeonneau: m. *A Pigeon, a yong Doue.*
Il a mangé les pigeonneaux. *Said of a man that whizzes, or speakes hoarse.*
Pigeonnelle: f. *A verie young Pigeon.*
Pigeonner. *To catch Pigeons; also, to cheat, cousen, or fetch ouer, a sillie fellow; also, to bill, or kisse like a Pigeon; to giue long, and lasciuious kisses.*
Pigeonnerie: f. *The billing of Pigeons; and hence, a long, and lasciuious kissing.*
Pigeonnet: m. *A young, or little Pigeon.*
Pigeonnier: m. *A Pigeon-house, or Doue-coat; also, a Pigeon-keeper; one that lookes vnto Pigeons; also, the place wherein Poccards be, or put themselues to be, cured.*
Pigmée: m. *A Pigmey, dwarfe, dandiprat, elfe, twatle.*

Pignaresse : f. *A Flax-woman.*
Pignates : f. *Pots, or balls of wild-fire.*
Pignaux de colliers. *The nailes, or prickles of a ban-dogs coller.*
Pigne. *as* Peigne.
Pigneon. *Looke* Pignon.
Pignes. *The gristlie parts of the eye-lids.*
Pignet : m. *The female Pine-apple; also, the Pitch-tree, or wild Pine-tree.*
Pignolat : m. *The preserued kernell of a Pine-apple; or conserue of Pine-kernells.*
Pignolat. Chardon pignolat. *The Teazill, card Tea-zill; Fullers Thistle.*
Pignon : m. *A Finiall, Cop, or small Pinacle on the ridge or top of a house; also, the nut, or kernell of a Pine-apple; also, as* Pagnon.
Il a pignon sur rue. *He is well lined, or well to liue; he may be safely put into the Subsidie.*
Pignoratif : m. iue : f. *Pignoratiue, impledging, ingaging by suretiship, or with a pawne.*
Pignoration : f. *A straining, or distraining; a seising, or taking for a distreße; also, an impledging.*
Pignore. *A distresse; or a thing thats taken Dammage fesant.*
Pignorer. *To distraine; to seise, or take, for a distresse, or in respect of dammage done; also, to impledge.*
Pignoüer : m. *A combe-case.*
Pihourt. *The name of a Mason of* Rennes; *whence;*
Resolu comme Pihourt en ses Heteroclites. *Looke* Resolu.
Pilastre. *A Pilaster, or small Piller; also, th'inflamation, or swelling of the Vvula, growne thereby all of a bignesse.*
Pile : m. *A (footmans) Javelin, or Dart; about fiue foot long, and headed with steele.*
Pilé. *A Suppositarie.*
Pile : f. *A ball to play with, a hand-ball; also, a pile, heap, or stacke; also, the pile, or vnder-yron of the stampe wherein money is stamped; and the pile-side of a peece of money, th'opposite whereof is a crosse; (whence,* Ie n'ay croix ny pile;) *also, the bulke, or bodie of a great tree; also, a funt, or the bowle of a fountaine; also, a great morter, or trough of stone, &c; also, the pile, or whole masse, of weights vsed by Goldsmithes, &c.*
Pile trigone. *A triangle peece of yron to be thrown at a ring, through which he that passes it wins the game.*
Mettre à la pile. *To beat, pound, stampe, crush, break, trounse, course; ruine, spoyle.*
Pilé : m. ée : f. *Pealed, beaten, bruised, crushed, pounded, stamped.*
Pilée : f. *as* Pilement; *A pealing, &c; also, the thing thats pealed.*
Pilement : m. *A pealing, pounding, stamping, braying, beating; a crushing, or bruising.*
Piler. *To peale, pound, stampe, to bray, beat, or breake, in a morter, &c; also, to settle, or sinke; whence,* cette maison pile.
Piler l'eau en vn mortier. *To loose labour; or to imploy it most vainely.*
Piletrigone. *Seeke* Pile.
Pilette : f. *A little ball; pile; bodie of a tree; funt; or morter.*
Pilettes. *Pimples about the nose, or chin.*
Pileur : m. *A pealer, pounder, stamper, brayer.*
Pilier : m. *A Piller.*
Piliers boutans. *Bowing pillers, buttresses, or props wherewith a building is supported.*
Pilier & Carcan. *Is (not much vnlike a Pillorie) an Engine, or Instrument of Justice, for the punishment, & disgrace of offendors; See* Carcan.
Le Pilier de la republique. *The chiefe stay, principall strength, onely supporter, of the Commonwealth.*
Pilier de taverne. *A common tipler; or one that both consumes his owne meanes, and is the meanes of other mens consumption, in Tauernes.*
Iustice patibulaire à deux piliers. *A paire of gallowes, or power to hang offendors on gallowes, that stand on two pillers, belong vnto a Lord* Iusticier; à trois piliers, *to a Lord* Chastelain; à 4 piliers, *vnto a Baron;* & à 6 piliers, *vnto an Earle; (Seeke* Fourche.*)*
Piliforme. *One of the smallest membranes of the eye, before whose glassie humor it stands.*
Pillage : m. *Pillage, bootie, spoyle; a prey.*
Pillard : m. arde : f. *Filching, pilfering, purloyning, sheet-stealing.*
Pillars : m. *Pilferers, filchers, purloyners, henne-stealers; or, such as take (other mens) sheets off hedges.*
Quand les pillars ont pillé, & les pillez sont pillez, les pillez auront du pain, & les pillars mouront de faim : Prov.
Pillastre. *as* Pilastre.
Pille : m. *Seeke* Pile.
Pille : f. *A great morter, or trough of stone, or wood, &c; See* Pile.
Pillé : m. ée : f. *Pilled, rauaged, ransacked, robbed, despoyled, or bereaued of all.*
Quand les pillars auront pillé, &c. *Looke* Pillars.
Pillemaille. *as* Palemaille; *or such a box as our London Prentices beg withall before Christmas.*
Pillement : m. *A pilling, rauaging, ransacking, robbing, rifling; or as* Pillerie.
Piller. *To pill, rauage, ransacke, rifle, rob; make boot, or hauocke of; rauine, or exact from; depriue, or despoyle of all; also, to rub, or rob, at cards.*
Ce qu'assemble pille pille, desassemble tire tirer: Pro. *Looke* Assembler.
Pillerie : f. *A pilling, rauaging, ransacking, robbing, rifling; hauocke, rapine, exaction, spoyle, extortion.*
Pilleur : m. *A piller, a rauager, a ransacker, a rauenous exactor.*
Pillier. *See* Pilier.
Pillolet : m. *Pulicke mountaine, horse Time, wild Time, running Time.*
Pillori : m. *as* Pilori.
Pillorisement : m. *A setting on the Pillorie.*
Pilloriser. *as* Pilorier.
Pillot : m. *A small pile, or heape.*
Pillotage : m. *A piling, or pile-worke, a driuing downe of piles; a foundation, causey, or water-worke made of, or strengthened with, piles.*
Pilloter. *To picke, or take vp here and there; to gather one by one; also, as* Piller.
Pilloterie : f. *A picking or taking vp here and there; a gathering one by one; also, as* Pillerie.
Pilloti. *as* Piloti; *also, a piling.*
Pillule. *as* Pilule.
Piloir : m. *A Pestell.*
Pilon : m. *A Pestell; a pounder, or instrument of pounding; also, a little (footmans) Dart, or Javelin.*
Pilori : m. *A Pillorie; also, a Tumbrell.*
Pilorié : m. ée : f. *Set on the Pillorie.*
Piloriement : m. *A setting, or standing, on the Pillorie.*
Pillorier. *To set, or make stand, on the Pillorie.*
Pilosèlle : f. *Pilosella, Mouse-eare.*

Pi-

Piloselle grande. *Great Mouse-eare; beares a yellow flower.*

Pilosselle petite. *Small Mouse-eare, or broad-leaued Mouse-eare, hath also, a yellow flower; but another kind of this hearbe is called blew Mouse-eare, of the colour of it flower, and is like ynough to be* Fuschius *his little Mouse-eare.*

Pilot: m. *A Pilot, or Steeresman; hee that directs the course of a ship; also, a little (footmans) Iavelin.*

Pilotage: m. *Pilotisme; th'Office, or Art of a Pilot; the the skillfull guiding, or conduction of a ship; also, as* Pillotage.

Piloter. *as* Pilloter; *also, as* Pilotier.

Piloti: m. *A Commaunder, or Water-sledge; the instrument wherewith piles are driuen downe; also, a piling.*

Pilotier. *To play the Pilot; and, to sound the depth of waters with a line, and plummet.*

Pilotis. *as* Piloti.

Pilotisé: m. ée: f. *Piled; founded on, or vnderset with, piles; vnderlayed, vnderpropped, supported.*

Pilotiser. *To pile, or strengthen with piles; to make a foundation of piles; also, to support, vnderlay, vnderset, vnderprop.*

Pilule: f. *A (Physicall) pill; also, a small ball, or bowle.*

Pilure: f. *A pill; whence;*

Vne pilure formentine vne, dragme sarmen me, & la iournée d'une geline, est la meilleure medecine: Prov. *A manchet, cup of wine, and hennes dayes taske, is the best Physicke a sicke man can aske.*

Pimard: m. *A Heighaw, or Wood-pecker.*

Pimbesche: f. *A wilie queane, subtile wench, cunning drab; one that can finely execute her Mistresses knauish deuises.*

Piment: m. *Oake of Ierusalem, or Oake of Paradise; (an hearbe;) also, a kind of wholesome peare.*

Pimente: f. *Spurge Oliue, Widow waile; (a shrub.)*

Pimer. *To quinch, crawle, moue, stirre.*

Pimpant: m. ante: f. *Spruce, compt, picked, neat, gay, fine, trimme.*

Pimpé: m. ée: f. *Sprucified, finified; curiously pranked, comptly tricked vp.*

Pimpenauder. *To pranke, trimme, tricke vp.*

Pimpenelle. *as* Pimpinelle.

Pimper. *To sprucifie, or finifie it; curiously to pranke, trimme, or tricke vp himselfe.*

Pimperneau: m. *A grig, scaffling, spitchcocke, fawson Eele.*

Pimpernelle: f. *Burnet; See* Pimpinelle.

Pimpinelle: f. *Burnet.*

Pimpinelle grande. *Great, or wild Burnet.*

Pimpinelle petite. *Garden Burnet.*

Pimpinelle Saxifrage. *Burnet Saxifrage, great Saxifrage.*

Grosse Pimpinelle. *Great Pimpinell; or, great Saxifrage.*

Pimpompet. *A kind of Game wherein three hit each other on the bumme with one of their feet.*

Pimpreneau: m. *as* Pimperneau; *also, a knaue, rascall, varlet, scoundrell.*

Pimprenelle. *as* Pimpernelle.

Pin: m. *A Pine tree.*

Pin aquatic. *Female Knot-grasse; (a water hearbe.)*

Pin marin. *The sea Pine; of two kinds, a great, and a little one; and both wild ones.*

Pin de montaigne. *The mountaine (wild) Pine.*

Pin sauvage. *The wild Pine; is properly diuided into two kinds; viz. The Mountaine, and Sea, Pine.*

Pinacle: m. *A Pinacle; a Spire.*

Pinard: m. *An exceeding small peece of money.*

Pinart. *The same; also, such a title as is our fellow, &c; whence,* le pinart rencontra frere Adam, &c; *the fellow met Frier Adam, &c.*

Pinasse: f. *The Pitch-tree; also, a Pinnace.*

Pinastre: m. *The wild Pine tree.*

Pinatelle: f. *A copper coyne hauing some small quantitie of siluer in it, and worth about fiue* Liards.

Pinatellier: m. *A coyner of* Pinatelles.

Pinates à feu. *See* Pignates.

Pinaux. *The name of a kind of Grapes.*

Pince: f. *A croe, great barre, or leauer of yron; also, a Pincer; also, a Pinke; also, the view, or footing of a Deere; and (more generally) the tip, or edge of the bottome of a beasts hoofe; that which in treading first touches the ground.*

Pincé: m. ée: f. *Pinched, nipped, or twitched.*

Pinceau: m. *A Pensill; also, a Whitelimers Brush.*

Pinceau de mer. *A shellie reed, or thing like a reed, which at th'one end stickes vnto rocks, at th'other puts out, sometimes, a fishie substance, (wherof it is full) and then resembles a Pensill.*

Pince-maille. *Seeke* Pinse-maille.

Pincement: m. *A pinching, nipping, twitching.*

Pincer. *To pinch, nip, twitch (with the fingers, &c.)*

Pincer sans rire. *Looke* Rire.

Pincersi, & Pincervin: m. *The Linden tree:* ¶Provençail.

Pinces: f. *A paire of Pincers; also, Pinke (flowers.)*

Pinceter. *To pinch thicke; to nip, or twitch often; also, to touch a Lute, &c, nimbly; also, to pull off haires, or moats, with small Pincers.*

Pinche: f. *as* Pince *(in the later sence.)*

Pinchons. *in stead of* Piochons: ¶Rab.

Pinçotter. *To pinch, or nip, often.*

Pindariser. *To affect in speech; or to speak nicely, sprucely, curiously; also, to speake shrilly, or vehemently, as one thats loath his Auditorie should loose a word by him.*

Pine. *as* Quille; *A Kayle; also, a pricke, member, bable.*

Pineau: m. *The seed, or kernell of a Grape; also, a kind of white, and longish grape; whereof;*

Vin pineau. *Excellent strong wine.*

Pinet: m. *Hogs Fennell, sow Fennell, Sulphurewort, Brimstonwort, Horestrong, or Horestrange.*

Pinette: f. *A kind of Cyder made of water mingled with the iuyce of crabs, or wild apples; also, a groue, or wood of Pine-apples.*

Pineux: m. euse: f. *Of or belonging to, also, full of, Pinetrees.*

Pinge: f. *A pillocke, member, bable, &c.*

Pingres. aux p. *A (womanish) play with Iuorie balls.*

Pinguereaux. *A kind of sweet Cherries.*

Pinhadar: m. *A young, or little wild Pine.*

Pinier: m. *The Rosen tree; or any other, whose fruit resembles a Pine-apple; as the great Cedar, Cypresse, &c.*

Piniolat. *as* Pignolat.

Pinne: f. *The shell-fish called a Naker; also, the finne of a fish; also, the broad, and gristlie part of the eare; also, as* Pinge.

Pinne du nez. *The gristle of the nose; the bone wherby the nosetbrills are diuided.*

Pinneux: m. euse: f. *Finnie, full of finnes.*

Pinnophylace: f. *A kind of little Sea-fish.*

Pinnothere. *A little Shell-fish, of the kind of Shrimpes.*

Pin-

Pinnule: f. *A little finne of a fish.*
Pinnules. *The sights belonging to th'Albidada of an Astrolabe.*
Pinocque. *A greene Indian fruit of the bignesse of a Cherrie.*
Pinon. *The pinnion of a clocke, &c; the nut in whose notches the teeth of the wheeles doe run;* Looke Pagnon.
Pinot: m. *The name of a red-stocked, and round-leaued Vine.*
Pinsade: f. *A pinching, or nipping; also, extortion, extremitie, hard or sore dealing.*
Pinse: f. *Looke* Pince.
Pinsegreneur d'Amadis. *A Phrasemonger, spruce discourser, affecting speaker.*
Pinse-maille: com. *A pinch-penie, scrape-good, niggard, miser, penie-father.*
Pinser. *as* Pincer.
Pinses: f. *A paire of Pincers.*
Pinsettes: f. *Nippers, little Pincers.*
Pinsoir: m. *A certaine Engine (made of yron-headed stakes,) wherewith fish is caught.*
Pinson: m. *A Spinke, Chaffinch, or Sheldaple.*
Pinson d'Ardenne. *A Brambling.*
Pinson montain. *The same.*
Pinson royal. *An ash-coloured, and great-headed bird, called otherwise,* Grosbec.
Pinte: f. *A pinte; the French, or Parisien pinte; somewhat lesse then a sixt part short of our Quart; (for in weight it is about 27 ounces, our Quart 32;) and the 288 part of a* Muid; *also, any small wine-pot, or vessell of pewter.*
La pinte de S. Dennis, & de plusieurs autres lieux à l'entour de Paris. *Is halfe as big againe as th'ordinarie one of Paris.*
Appetissement de la courte pinte. *as* Appetissement de mesure. *Looke* Mesure.
Pinteler. *To tipple, or plie the pot.*
Pintelette: f. *A small pinte.*
Pinteur: m. *A tippler, pot companion, spiggot-sucker.*
Pintier: m. *A Pewterer.*
Pinton. *as* Pinteur.
Pinules: f. *Two small tablets in th'Albidada of an Astrolabe, hauing in them two little holes, through which the height of the Sunne, &c, is taken; some call them, the sights of th'Albidada.*
Pioche: f. *A little Pickax, or French Instrument of husbandrie, not much vnlike a Pickax; (and sometimes) also, as* Piot.
Piocher. *To dig, or breake vp the earth with a* Pioche.
Piocheur: m. *A digger, or breaker vp of the earth with a* Pioche; *and (more generally) any such labouring man.*
Piochon: m. *A little* Pioche.
Piolé: m. ée: f. *Spotted, or speckled; whence;*
Riolé piolé. *Gaudie, or pide; also, diuersified, or set out with sundrie colours.*
Piolement: m. *The puling, or cheeping of Sparrowes, or young birds.*
Pioler. *To pule, cheepe, or chirpe, like a Sparrow, or yong bird.*
Piolet de caille. *A Quaile pipe.*
Pioleur: m. *A puler, cheeper, chirper.*
Pion: m. *A certaine great, round, and Bulbus-rooted flower, of one whole colour (though there be of them white ones, red ones, and purple ones;) also, a Bulfinch; also, a young birdling, or neast-bird; also, a small twig, or sprig of a tree; also, a pawne at Chesse; also, an excessiue drinking; whence;*
Mal de pion. *The drunken disease; or a disease that comes by excessiue drinking.*
Pionnier: m. *A Pioner.*
Pionnier: m. ere: f. *Made by, or belonging to, a Pioner; Pioner-like.*
Piorioler. *To diuersifie with variable colours.*
Piot: m. *Drinke, liquor, nippitatie; (clownishly.)*
Pioter. *as* Pioler; *also, to tipple.*
Pioupiou. *Peepe peepe; the voyce of chickins.*
Pipe: f. *A bird-call, or little woodden pipe, wherewith Fowlers doe counterfeit the voyces of the birds they would take; also, the vessell, or measure called a Pipe (vsed as well for corne, as for wine; also, a kind of dizzinesse, or dizzie turning disease, cousen germaine to drunkennesse.*
Pipé: m. ée: f. *Deceiued, cousened, ouerraught, gulled, beguiled.*
Cartes pipées; &, Dez pipez. *False cards, or dice.*
Pipeau: m. *An oaten pipe; a bird-call.*
Pipée: f. *The peeping, or chirping of small birds counterfeited by a Bird-catcher; also, a counterfeit shew, false countenance, dissembling apparance, of sufficiencie, &c.*
La pipée du soir. *Th'edge of th'euening, when the weather freshes, or growes coole.*
Prise des oiseaux à la pipée. *Is thus: a Fowler hid in a thicke bush, or tree, stucke full of lime-twigs, and hauing an Owle fast pearched neere to him, cries like a bird, and pinching a liue one, makes her crie; which others hearing, flie thither to rescue her from th'Owle, and so become intangled.*
Il fait bonne pipée. *He would faine seeme wise, or honest, though he be not.*
Piper. *To whistle, or chirpe, like a bird; also, to cousen, deceiue, cheat, gull, ouerreach, beguile (especially, by false cards, or dice.)*
Piperelle: f. *Gith, Nigella, Bishopswort, Coriander of Rome.*
Piperie: f. *A cousening, deceiuing, beguiling, ouerreaching; a gulling, or cheating.*
Pipet: m. *A small pipe, Fowlers pipe, or bird-call.*
Pipette: f. *The little knot, or tuft, on the top of a cap.*
Pipeur: m. *A whistler, chirper; bird-catcher; also, a cousener, cheater, deceiuer, beguiler; and especially one that vseth false cards, or dice.*
Pipeusement. *Deceitfully, guilefully, couseningly.*
Pipeux: m. euse: f. *Deceitfull, guilefull, cousening, ouerreaching, cheating.*
Pipion. *A Spanish coyne worth about* 18 d. sterl.
Pipis: m. *The whistling, chirping, or peeping of small birds.*
Pippe. *as* Pipe.
Pippeau: m. *A bird-call.*
Pipper. *as* Piper.
Pippeur, & Pippis. *Looke* Pipeur, & Pipis.
Piquant: m. *The point of a Dart, Speare, &c; also, the prickle, or sharpe top of some kind of leaues, as of the Hollie, &c; also, the nose, beake, or stem-end of a ship; also, a kind of pricklie Thistle.*
Piquant: m. ante: f. *Pricking; piercing, thrusting into; stinging, netling; spurring; nipping, quipping, quilting.*
Piquardant. *The name of a Grape that yeelds an excellent white Wine.*
Piquassat. *A speckled Gilloflower:* ¶ Langued.
Pique: f. *A Pike; also, a Pikeman; also, a pike, debate, quarrell, grudge;* Looke Picque.

Pique seiche. *An vnarmed Pikeman.*
Bransler la pique. *To frig.*
Iouër à pique en cul. *See* Cul.
I'ay passé par leurs piques. *I haue beene throughly coursed, or canuassed by them; I haue felt their vtmost efforts; I haue escaped them faire.*
Piqué: m. ée: f. *Pricked; stung, nettled; pierced, or thrust into; nipped, pinched, vexed; ridden, or spurred; also, quilted, or set thick with oylet-holes; also, wrought, or broken vp, with a pickax; also, fastened, planted, or driuen into the ground.*
Pique boeuf: m. *(A nickname for) a clowne, plough-churle, hind.*
Piquement: m. *A pricking; sticking, piercing, or thrusting into; a stinging, or nettling; a spurring; nipping, pinching; vexing; also, a quilting.*
Piquenaire: m. *A Pikeman.* (v.m.)
Pique papier: m. *A Scribe, Scriuener, meane Clerke, base Pettifogger.*
Pique-poule. *The name of a certaine grape.*
Piquer. *To pricke, pierce, or thrust into; also, to nettle, or sting; also, to spurre; also, to ride a horse; also, to nip, cut, quip, taunt, gird; vexe, vrge, exasperate with sharp or biting words; also, to quilt; and thence also, to stiffen a coller, &c; also, to worke, dig, or breake vp, with a pickax; also, to fasten, plant, or set, into the ground.*
Se piquer. *To be titchie, soone offended, quickly moued; (also, to prouoke, or exite himselfe, vnto the doing of a thing;* Se piquer à.*)*
Piquer l'avoine. *To ride a horse verie hard, to make him earne his prouender.*
Piquer les chiens. *To gallop after (and in galloping, to put on) the hounds.*
Le poisson pique. *Begins to haue a tacke, or ill tast; begins to be stale.*
Il ne sent point quand on luy pique la chair. *A phrase appliable both to a lazer; and to a cowardlie, thicke-skinned, or senceless, lozell.*
Qui se fait piquer à tous les pas. *That must be spurred euerie foot; (appliable, from a dull iade, vnto any dullard.)*
Piqueron: m. *A prickle; small pricke, sting, spurre, goad; also, a publicke exactor; a poller, or plumer of the Commonwealth; also, as* Picqueron.
Pique-seiche. *Looke vnder* Pique.
Piquet. *as* Picquet.
Piqueton: *A prickle, as of a thorne, &c.*
Piquette: f. *A sower drinke, or veriuyce, made of wild apples (by the Picards) or of plummes (by the Normands.)*
Piqueu: m. *A pricklie Thistle, tearmed so about* Blois.
Piqueur: m. *A pricker; also, a Rider; and (in hunting) one that on horsebacke pursues the dogs in their full speed.*
Piqueure: f. *A pricking, &c; as* Piquement; *also, a pricke, sting; pinch, cut, quip.*
Piquier: m. *A Pikeman.*
Piquoté: m. ée: f. *Looke* Picoté.
Piquotement: m. *A frequent pricking, or stinging; an often piercing; also, a spotting, peckling, or speckling.*
Piquoter. *To pricke, sting, or pierce often; also, to spot, peckle, or speckle all ouer.*
Piquoteure: f. *A pricke, sting; spot, freckle, speckle; also, as* Piquotement.
Piquoteure de bran de Iudas. *Red pimples rising in the face.*
Piquotte: f. *Small wine, seruants wine; or, as* Piquette.

Piramidal: m. ale: f. *Piramidall; broad beneath, and sharpening vpwards.*
Piramide: f. *A Piramides; any peece of building made broad, and square below, and the higher it goes the smaller growing.*
Piramide d'un trepane. *The little point, or prickle, appearing, or peering out at th'end, or head of a Trepane.*
Pirate: m. *A Pirat, Rouer, Sea-robber.*
Piraterie: f. *Piracie, rouing, sea-robbing.*
Piratique: com. *Piraticall, Pirat-like; of, or belonging to, a Pirat.*
Pirauste. *A Fire-flie; or a worme bred, and liuing in the fire, from which if it bee but a little too farre, it dieth presently.*
Pire: com. *Worse, badder, lewder, naughtier; meaner, vnworthier; of smaller value, of lesse account; (sometimes) also, bad; whence;* Vrayement, voilà que n'est pas pire. *Truely there's no great fault to be found with that.*
Piretre: m. *Hearbe Bartram, bastard Pellitorie, right Pellitorie of Spaine.*
Pirevollet: m. *A whirligig.*
Pirole: f. *Wild Beets; or, th'hearbe Pirola.*
Piromantie: f. *Diuination by fire:* ¶Rab.
Pirope. *as* Pyrope.
Pirot: m. *The Pirot, or Hag-fish; a kind of long shell-fish.*
Pirou: m. *A greene Goose:* ¶Poictevin.
Piroüette: f. *A Whirligig; also, a whirling about, a quick turne often redoubled; and hence, a dauncers turning on the toe.*
Piroüetter. *To whirle, twirle, trill, turne swiftly about.*
Piroüetteux: m. euse: f. *Whirling, twirling, trilling, turning swiftly about.*
Pis: m. *The breast, bosome, or stomacke of a man; the dug, or vdder of a Cow, Yew, she Goat, &c; the brisket of an Oxe, or Beefe; the nauell of a dog.*
Pis. (Adverb.) *Worse; also, worst; whence;*
Au pis aller. *Howsoeuer, be it how it will be, let the worst come to the worst.*
Pisay: m. *as* Pizé.
Piscantine: f. *A kind of small, or well-watered wine.*
Piscine: f. *A fish-pond; also, a poole to water horses, or keepe Duckes, &c, in.*
Pissasphalte: m. *Pissasphaltum; or Pitch mingled with Bitumen, either by accident, or Art; The former is much the better, & comes from* Apollonia *in* Epirus, *where it first comes by that mixture.*
Pissat: m. *Pisse, vrine, lant, stale.*
Pissaulict. *A fusse-ball, puckfusse, puffiste, or bull-fiste.*
Pissé. *Pissed, staled.*
Il a pissé en beaucoup de neiges. *He hath liued many a Winter.*
Pisse-chaude: f. *A burnt P. also, the Venerian flux; the Gonorrhean, or contagious, running.*
Pissement: m. *A pissing.*
Pissenez. serfs pissenez. *The bastards of villaines, or slaues*
Pissenlict: m. *Dandelion, Priests crowne, Monks head, Swines snowt.*
Pisser. *To pisse, to stale, to make water.*
Le laict pisse. *The milke spinnes out of her breasts, or dugs.*
Les bonnes gens, pour cela, ne pisseront pas plus roide. *Will not bee much, or shall bee neuer a whit,*

the better for it.
Pisseux: m.euse: f. *Pissing much, and often; also, full of pisse; whence;*
Lange pisseuse. *A childs pisse-clowt.*
Orange pisseuse. *An Orange full of liquor, or which yeeldeth store of liquor.*
Pissoir: m. *A pissing place.*
Pissolaire: m. *The sheath, or skinne of a horses yard.*
Pisson: m. *A Pipkin.*
Pissoter. *To pisse often.*
Pissotiere: f. *The pissing toole; or, the receptacle of pisse; also, a pissing place; also, the running of a bucking tub.*
Pistaces: f. *Pistachoes, fisticke nuts.*
Pistacher: m. *The Pistacho tree, the Fisticke nut-tree.*
Pistaches. *as* Pistaces.
Pistaulendrier: m. *A mans yard.*
Piste: f. *The strayne, or view of a Deere; the print of any foot.*
Pisté: m.ée: f. *Stamped, pounded, brayed.*
Pisteau: m. *A Pestell.*
Pister. *To bray, pound, or stampe.*
Pistolade: f. *The shot of a Pistoll; the blow giuen by a discharged Pistoll.*
Pistolandier. *as* Pistaulendrier.
Pistole: f. *A Pistoll; a great (horsemans) Dag.*
Pistole de Sancerre. *A Sling.*
Pistolet: m. *A Pistolet; a Dag, or little Pistoll; also, the golden coyne tearmed a Pistolet.*
Pistolier: m. *A Pistoleere; a horseman that serues with a Pistoll.*
Pistolochie: f. *A kind of (the hearbe) long Birthwort.*
Piston: m. *A Pestell, or pounding sticke.*
Canon à piston. *A certaine Bit which giues the tongue libertie without a Port.*
Pistrine: f. *A Bakehouse, or house wherein, before th'inuention of Mills, the Romanes caused their slaues, and vnrulie seruants, to bray all their corne in morters.*
Pit: m. *as* Pis: ¶Breton.
Pitance: f. *Meat, food; acates; victuall of all sorts (bread and drinke excepted.)*
Pitancier: m. *The Manciple, or distributor of victualls, in a Monasterie.*
Pitancier: m.ere: f. *Seruing for a Pittance; of a Pittance.*
Pitaulder. *To behaue himselfe rudely, to play the clowne.*
Pitaulderie: f. *Rudenesse, clownishnesse, vnmannerlinesse, inciuilitie, churlishnesse.*
Pitault: m. *A clowne, boore, swaine, lob, carle, churle, clusterfist.*
Pite: f. *The halfe of a* Maille, *a (French) farthing; also, a Moath, or Mite.*
Pitel: m. *The panne of a close-stoole.*
Piteux: m.euse: f. *Pitifull, mercifull, charitable, tender, gentle, kind; also, wretched, miserable, distressefull, afflicted, in pitifull case, ill taking, wofull estate.*
Vous nous la baillez bien piteuse. *You make vs a homelie relation, you tell vs but a sorie tale.*
Vn piteux medecin fait vne mortelle playe: Prov. *Looke* Playe.
Femme trop piteuse fait sa famille teigneuse: Pro. *A pitifull housewife makes a pitifull houshold; The like is;*
Mere piteuse fait sa fille roigneuse: Prov.
Pitié: f. *Pitie, ruth, compassion, commiseration; charitie, kindnesse, or tendernesse of disposition; also, grace, clemencie, mercifulnesse.*
Pitois: m. *The vermine (or beast) called a Fitch.*
Piton. *as* Piston; *also, an Eye for a curtaine rod, &c; or a pinne of mettall, sharpe at th'one end to enter into wood, &c, & hauing a round eye at th'other for a curtaine-rod, &c, to enter into; and hence;*
Piton à vis. *A skrue with an eye; or such a pinne made skruing at the end where th'ordinarie* Piton *is plaine.*
Pitroy: m. *Durt, mud, mire.*
Pittasse. *whence;* elle faisoit chere pit. *Her behauiour was full of discontentment; or, she chawed her spittle in stead of falling to her vittle.*
Pittouër: m. *A Bittor (corruptly.)*
Pituitaire: com. *Flegmaticke: sniuellie, snottie; slauering.*
Glande pituitaire. *See* Glande.
Pituite: f. *Fleame, sniuell.*
Pituiteux: m.euse: f. *Full of fleame; sniuell, slauering, snot.*
Pityocampe. *A venomous worme that breeds in Pine trees.*
Pive: f. *The fruit of the Pine, or Pitch tree.*
Piverd: m. *A Woodpecker, Hickway, Greenpeake.*
Piugarreau: m. *A great, whitish, and sweetish Cherrie, whose hard pulpe cleaues hard vnto the stone.*
Piuler. *To pule, or cheepe like a little chicken.*
Pivoesne. *as* Pivoine.
Pivoine: f. *Peonie, Pionie, Kings Bloome, Rose of the mount; also, a little blacke-headed, and blacke-taild bird, called a Gnat-snapper; also, a Bullfinch, or Nowp.*
Pivoine femelle. *The female Peonie, whereof there be diuers kinds; as the double, red, and white, Peonies; the maiden or virgine Peonie; and others.*
Pivoine masle. *Male Peonie.*
Pivot: m. *The Piuot, or (as some call it) the Tampin of a gate, or great doore: (a peece of yron, &c, made, for the most part, like a Top, round & broad at th'one end, and sharpe at th'other, wherby it enters into the* Crappaudine; *and serues as well to beare vp the gate (in whose bottome it is placed) as to facilitate the motion thereof. It is also made, sometimes twofold in the vpper part, and nailed vnto both sides of the* Chardonnereau; *and sometimes like a Spindle, sharpe at both ends, th'vpper sticking in the said* Chardonnereau;) *Hence also, the principall Stay, Support, or Piller of a Kingdome, State, Citie, House, or Familie; also, a kind of Vine.*
Pivotter vn huis. *To hang a doore on* Pivots.
Pizé. *whence;* Murailles de pizé. *Earthen walls.*
Placard. *See* Plaquard.
Placardé: m. ée: f. *Fastened, or pasted, as a Siquis, &c, on a post.*
Placart. *as* Plaquard.
Placcar. *as* Plaquard.
Huis qui se ferment à doubles placcars. *Doores which are shut with double locks.*
Place: f. *A place, roome, seat; a space, a stead; also, an Office, Function, Dignitie, Charge; also, a plaine and vnhoused, ground, soyle, or shore; and hence, a spacious plaine, or plot of ground in the middest of a town; and vsed as a Market stead, or as an Exchange for Marchants; or as an Auditorie, for the deciding of controuersies (but then there is a Tribunal, or some open house vpon it;) also, a faire large Court before a Church, or house; also, a Castle, Fort, Fortresse, or Hold; also, a spot, or dapple, on a horse.*
Place mage. *Looke* Mage.
Place marchande. *A Market place, or place of ordinarie bargaining; hence, any free, or indifferent place wherat men may meet, or deale, on euen tearmes.*

Place Maubert. *The Market-stead, and place of execution, for the Vniuersitie of Paris*; *Looke* Maubert.

La place des niais à la table. *Th'vpper end*; *(among the auncient Romanes the best man euer sate in the middest*; *and at this day th'Italians hold the middle place most honourable.)*

Pain de la place. *Browne bread, houshold bread.*

Bien de sa place part qui son ami y laisse: Pro. *He leaues a place well that leaues a friend in it.*

Ceux qui meurent laissent leur place à ceux qui demeurent: Prov. *They that die possessors leaue all to their successors.*

Placé: m. ée: f. *Placed, seated, lodged, settled, fixed, planted.*

Placer. *To place*; *to seat, lodge, plant, settle, appoint a roome vnto.*

Placet: m. *A low stoole*; *also, a short Petition, or Ticket of request, without inscription, and beginning with these words,* Plaise à tel, &c; *(Therein differing from a* Requeste, *which is much longer, and beginnes thus,* Supplie *(naming the Petitioner, which the* Placet *doth not) and specifies in an inscription, the name, and title of him it is presented vnto.)*

Placide: com. *Calme, gentle, quiet, mild*; *peaceable, tractable.*

Placidement. *Gently, quietly, wildly, tractably.*

Placitre. *A faire large Court before a Church, or (great) house.*

Placque: f. *A flat Lingot, or barre of mettall*; *also, as* Patart.

Placque de marbre. *A flat pauing peece of Marble.*

Placque de plomb. *See* Plaque.

Placqué: m. ée: f. *Pargetted, or rough-cast*; *also, clapped, flat, or stucke on*; *laied flat vpon*; *whence*;

Lettres à seel placqué. *Whose seale hangs not by a label, but is applied on the paper, or parchment it selfe.*

Placquer. *as* Plaquer.

Plafagourde: f. *A made word, of some affinitie with our Gixie, Callet, Punke, &c.*

Plage: f. *A flat and plaine shore, or strand, by the sea-side*; *also, a large arme of the sea without any Hauen*; *an open, and shallow Road*; *any flat or shallow, in or neere the sea*; *also, a Climate, Land, Region, Coast, or portion, of the world.*

Plagiaire: m. *One that steales, or takes free people out of one countrey, & sells them in another for slaues*; *a stealer, or suborner of mens children, or seruants, for the same, or the like, purpose*; *(in which sence we tearme him a Stockster*; *) also, a booke-stealer, or booke-theefe*; *one that fathers other mens workes vpon himselfe.*

Plagiaire. Capitaine pl. *That presses, carries, or steales away mens children, or seruants, with a purpose to sell them.*

Plagie: f. *Stealth, or subornation of mens children, and seruants, with an intent to sell them.*

Plaict. *as* Plect.

Plaid: m. *Suit, controuersie, altercation, debate, variance, brabbling, difference, contention, in law*; *also, a plea, or, a pleading*; *also, a Court of pleading*; *Looke* Plait.

Plaid de l'espée. *High Jurisdiction, power or authoritie to punish by the sword.*

Plaids generaux, ou genereux. *Sessions, Assises.*

Les francs plaids. *Wherein the Magistrate, in an extraordinarie course, proceeds against an absent, & vnsummoned offendor, vpon the relation, or accusation of the* Procureur fiscal *(by the customes of* Theroanne.)

Simples plaids, ou querelles. *Looke* Simple.

De petite chose peu de plaid: Prov. *A sleight cause needeth but small arguing.*

En cent livres de plaid n'y pas vne maille d'amour: Prov. *The more law the lesse loue.*

Plaidasserie: f. *Wrangling, pettifogging*; *litigious, or paultrie pleading.*

Plaidé: m. ée: f. *Pleaded, argued, opened*; *also, impleaded before a Judge.*

Plaide-gage. *as* Gage-plege.

Plaider. *To plead, argue, or open, a cause before a Judge*; *also, to sue, contend, goe to law, for, or against.*

Iamais ne gaigne, qui plaide à son Seigneur: Pro. *He neuer thriues, who'gainst his Maister striues.*

Plaidereau: m. *A litigious, or contentious brangler*; *a continuall Suitor*; *one that will goe to Law for euerie trifle*; *one that is neuer out of Law.*

Plaideresque: com. *Lawyer-like.*

Plaiderie: f. *Pleading, arguing, practise*; *also, Suit in Law.*

Plaideur: m. *A Lawyer, Arguer, Pleader*; *also, as* Plaidereau; *whence*;

A plaideur plaideur & demi: Prov. *Said of a knaue well matcht with a worse then himselfe.*

Homme plaideur menteur: Prov. *A Pleader, a lyer.*

Plaidoïer. *as* Plaidoyé.

Plaidoirie: f. *A plea, an argument*; *the pleading, or opening of a cause.*

Plaidoyable: com. *Pleadable, arguable.*

Iours plaidoyables. *Court-dayes, Hall-dayes.*

Plaidoyé: m. *A plea, pleading, argument.*

Plaidoyé de Quaresme prenant. *A bawdie, lasciuious, or wanton argument.*

Plaidoyer: m. *as* Plaidoyé.

Plaidoyer. *To sue, turne Client, goe to Law.*

Il plaidoye bien qui plaidoye sans partie: Prov. *He pleads full well that pleads against none (or hath none to plead against) but himselfe.*

Plaidoyeur: m. *A Pleader*; *a Lawyer*; *also, a Suitor.*

Eschars plaidoyeur est hardi perdeur: Prov. *The sparing Client's willing to be foild.*

Plaie. *Looke* Playe.

Plaignant: m. ante: f. *Plaining, bemoaning, complaining of*; *accusing, blaming, finding fault, with.*

Plain: m. *A plaine*; *a plaine peece of ground, without house, or tree vpon it.*

Le Bois acquiert le plain. *The Lord of a forrest may take in a neighbour-ground, which hath lyen vntilled, or vnused by the space of 30, or 20 yeares, if it be not diuided from the forrest by ditches, meeres, bounds, or other markes.*

Plain: m. aine: f. *Plaine, flat, euen, smooth, without wrinkles, without rubs*; *also, as* Plaint.

De plain. *Presently, immediately, out of hand, without any further proceeding in Law.*

Il ne se tort pas qui va plain chemin: Prov. *Looke* Chemin.

Plaindre. *To plaine, bewaile, bemoane, or make moane for*; *to blame, accuse, expostulate, find fault with, complaine of*; *to grudge, repine, or find himselfe aggrieued, at.*

Plaindre son argent. Ie n'y plainds point mon argent. *I thinke my money well bestowed thereon.*

Plaindre sa despense. *To spare his purse.*

Plaindre ses pas. *To be a niggard of his steps.*

Plaindre sa peine. *To saue labour, not to ouer-worke himselfe*; *or, to repine at the paines he takes.*

Il se plaind de saine teste. *He complaines without cause, or, he is troubled with too much ease.*
Assez demande qui se plaind: Prov. *Ynough demaunds he who of want complaines.*
Chascune vieille son dueil plaind: Pro. *Each beldame of her priuate griefe complaines.*
Femme se plaind, femme se deult, femme est malade, quand elle veut: Prov. *Looke* Femme.
Tel est plein qui se plaind: Prov. *Some how full soeuer they be are neuer contented.*
Tel se plaind qui n'a point de mal: Prov. *Some complaine that feele no paine; or, some, though they feele no hurt, vnquiet are.*
Plaine: f. *A plaine; a spacious peece of (leuell) ground, without either tree, or house, vpon it.*
Plaineure: f. *The superficies; the plaine, leuell, or flat ground of.*
Plaint: m. te: f. *Plained, bewailed, bemoaned, complained of, found fault with, repined at.*
Plainte: m. *A plaintife, complainant, accuser.*
Plainte: f. *A plaint, complaint, moane, lamentation; accusation, expostulation.*
Plaintif: m. *A plaintife, complainant; appeacher, accuser.*
Plaintif: m. iue: f. *Lamenting, moanefull, dolefull, sorrowfull.*
Plaire. *To please, delight; satisfie, content; like, allow, or thinke well, of; seeme good vnto.*
'A Dieu ne plaise, que. *God forbid, that.*
S'il plaist à Dieu. *If God will, if God say amen.*
Ils en ont d'un pleust à Dieu. *They haue not all they would haue, they haue not their full desire.*
Marchandise qui plaist est à moitié venduë: Prov. *Ware that doth please, or that's in request, is alreadie halfe sold.*
Plaisamment. *Pleasantly, merrily, sportfully, ioyfully, delightsomely.*
Plaisance: f. *Mirth, sport, pleasure, delight, game, iollitie, blithenesse, festiuitie, reioycing.*
Plaisant: m. ante: f. *Pleasant, merrie, iocond, blithe, ioyfull, buxome, delightfull, gamesome, recreatiue, sportfull; also, ieasting, bourding, scoffing, flowting.*
Plaisant homme. *(Vsed verie often Ironically, or in euill part) A goodlie fellow sure.*
Plaisanter. *To gibe, ieast, flowt, scoffe, quip merrily, be pleasant with; to play the Jeaster.*
Plaisanterie: f. *Jeasting, merriment, flowting, scoffing, scurrilitie; wittie (but knauish) conceits.*
Plaisanteur: m. *A Jeaster, Buffoone, Parasite, pleasant fellow.*
Plaisir: m. *Pleasure, delight, mirth, ioy, glee; pastime, game, sport, recreation; comfort, solace; delectation, contentment, sensualitie; also, a pleasure, fauour, kindnesse, good turne, friendlie office done; also, the will, appetite, lust; or a full satisfaction of them all.*
'A mon plaisir. *At my will, becke, or commaund; as I list my selfe.*
Pour mon plaisir. *For my minds sake; to please, or satisfie my humor withall.*
De court plaisir long repentir: Prov. *For a short pleasure long repentance.*
Fy de plaisirs, d'estats, & d'or, qui de vertu n'a le thresor: Prov. *Looke* Fy.
Qui plaisir fait plaisir requiert: Prov. *He that doth fauours lookes to be fauoured; one good turne requires another.*

Plait: m. *Suit, controuersie, altercation, debate; also, a plea, or pleading.*
Faire du plait. *To babble, prattle, tattle, keepe a filthie coyle, make a scuruie adoe.*
Il me tient plait. *He holds me tacke, or with a tale; he finds me chat ynough.*
Plameuse: f. *A cuffe, box, or whirret with the fist.*
Plan: m. *as* Plane; masc. *also, the ground-plat of a building.*
Plan. Adverb. *as* Pleinement: ¶Gasc.
Planare. *A Plane tree.*
Planchage: m. *A planking, or boording; also, a floore of plankes; or any thing made of plankes.*
Planchayé: m. ée: f. *Planked, boorded; floored.*
Planchayer. *To planke, boord; floore.*
Planche: f. *A planke, or thicke boord; especially one thats layed ouer a ditch, brooke, or moat, &c, in stead of a bridge; also, a bed, or border, in a garden; also, a pitfall; also, the Till of a Printers Presse, or the shelfe that compasseth the Hose; and generally, any shelfe.*
C'est la premiere planche pour parvenir à vn grand lieu. *This is the first step, readiest course, neerest way, vnto great preferment.*
Faire planche à. *To make way for; to beginne, or breake th'ice, vnto; to lay a ground for, or foundation vnto; also, to forward, further, helpe, assist.*
En pont, en planche, & en Riviere, vallet devant, maistre derriere: Prov. *Looke* Maistre.
Planché: m. ée: f. *Planked, boorded; floored with plankes; closed, or seeled, with boords; also, grounded, fixed, setled, or set fast.*
Planchéer. *To planke; to floore with plankes; to seele, or close, with boords.*
Plancher: m. *A (boorded) floore; also, a seeling of boords; and sometimes (though somewhat improperly) a floore, or bed, of plaister.*
Plancher de vaches. *The ground, the earth.*
Plancher. *To planke; to floore with plankes; to seele, or close, with boords.*
Plancheter. *as* Plancher.
Planchette: f. *A womans stirrup; also, the plate, or bottome of a stirrup whereon the foot resteth; also, a buske.*
Plancheyé: m. ée: f. *Planked; as* Planchayé.
Plancheyer. *as* Planchayer.
Planchier. *as* Plancher.
Plançon. *as* Planson; *or* Planton.
Plane: m. *The great Maple; ordinarily (but erroniously) called, the Sicamor tree.*
Plane: f. *A (Joyners) Plane; (also, a Plaice, or Flooke: ¶Langued.)*
Planer. *To plane; to make smooth, or euen, with a Plane; also, to rase, deface, blot, or put out; also, to plane, as a bird that flies, or houers, without mouing her wings.*
Planetaire: com. *Planetarie, of, or belonging to, the Planets.*
Heures planetaires. *Twelue houres for the day, and as many for the night.*
Planette: f. *A Planet; whereof there bee seuen, bearing the name of seuen seuerall Dieties, because they haue some power ouer earthlie bodies: they bee also called, Wandering starres, because they neuer keepe one certaine place, or station in the firmament.*
Plani: m. ie: f. *Planed, plained, or made plaine; smoothed, leuelled, euened.*
Planier: m. ere: f. *as* Plain; *whence;*

Courtplaniere. *Open house.*
Planier. *To shaue, as a Tanner doth his hides.*
Planir. *To plane, leuell, euen, smooth, make plaine.*
Planisphere: f. *An Astrolabe.*
Planson: m. *A young plant, a sucker, a young tree.*
Plant: m. *as* Plan; *also, the foundation, or ground-worke of a building; also, a planting; or, a quantitie of young trees handsomely ranked together.*
Plantage: m. *A planting, or setting.*
Plantail: m. *as* Plantal.
Plantain: m. *Plantaine, Way-bred.*
Plantain aquatic. *Water Plantaine.*
Plantain grand. *Broad-leaued Plantaine.*
Plantain de marais. *Water Plantaine.*
Plantain de mer. *Sea Plantaine, flowring sea Plantaine.*
Plantain moyen. *Middle Plantaine, hoarie Plantaine.*
Plantain petit. *Ribwort, Ribwort Plantaine, Dogs-rib, Lambes-tongue.*
Long plantain. *The same.*
Plantaire. *The least of the six hinder muskles of the leg, ending in the sole of the foot.*
Plantal: m. *A plant, or set; the science of a tree, or slip of an hearbe, set, or planted.*
Plantars: m. *Willow plants; or great branches, or poles of water-trees, lopped off, and reserued to bee set.*
Plantas: m. *as* Plantement; *also, a place to plant, or set trees in; also, as* Plantat; *or the Plurall thereof.*
Plantat: m. *A plant; and particularly, the branch of a Willow, or other water tree, fit to be planted.*
Plante: f. *A plant, or set; the science of a tree, or slip of an hearbe, set, or fit to be set; also, a vine set of a science, or slip (called so till it be come to it full growth;) also, the sole of the foot.*
Planté: f. *Plentie, store, abundance.*
Arbre trop souvent transplanté ne porte pas fruict à planté: Prov. *The ouer-oft remoued plant's not plentifull.*
Planté: m. ée: f. *Planted, set, setled.*
Planté sur le pied gauche. *Setled on the wrong side; ill disposed in affection; or, that hath vndertaken an vniust, or euill cause.*
Ie y ay bien planté mes seaux. *I haue made a deepe impression into it, I haue set my marke verie fast vpon it; I haue done it surely, soundly, throughly.*
Planteau: m. *A young plant; or, as* Plantal.
Plantemalan: m. *A Caltrop.*
Plantement: m. *A planting, setting; setling.*
Planter. *To plant, set; settle, fix, ground; also, to steale from, giue the slip vnto, slinke out of the companie of.*
Planter à la barre. *Looke* Barre.
Il le planta là pour reverdir. *He left him there to coole his fingers, to picke strawes or daisies, to shift for himselfe; Looke* Reverdir.
En vain plante qui ne clost: Prov. *Looke* Clorre.
Planter: m. ere: f. *In, or belonging to, the sole, or bottome, of the foot.*
Planteur: m. *A planter, a setter.*
Planton: m. *A young plant, or stocke transplanted, and and kept to be graffed on.*
Plantureusement. *Plenteously, abundantly, largely, copiously, fully.*
Plantureux: m. euse: f. *Plenteous, abundant, large, full, copious.*

Planure: f. *A plaine; a large, open, and euen peece of ground.*
Plaquard: m. *A Placard, or Inscription set vp; a Table wherein Lawes, Orders, &c, are written, and hung vp; also, a Bill, Siquis, or Libell stucke vpon a post, &c; also, rough-casting, or pargetting of walls.*
Plaque: f. *A flat Lingot, or barre of mettall; also, a flat pauing peece of Marble, or free stone; also, a plate to naile against a wall, and to set a candle in; a plate-candlesticke.*
Plaques. *Flat peeces of Goldsmithes worke, resembling little flowers, &c; also, parget, rough-cast.*
Plaque de plomb en vn miroir. *The foyle, or steele of a looking-glasse.*
Plaqué: m. ée: f. *Pargetted, rough-cast; also, clapped, pasted, flat, or stucke vpon; layed flat on.*
Plaquement: m. *A pargetting, a rough-casting; also, a clapping, pasting, or sticking on; a laying flat vpon.*
Plaquer. *To parget, or to rough-cast; also, to clap, flat, sticke, or past on; to lay flat vpon; whence;*
Plaquer du passement sur vn habit. *To lace, or set lace vpon a garment.*
Plaques. *Looke* Plaque.
Plasmateur: m. *A Potter; or a maker of earthen Images, &c.*
Plasmation: f. *Potters worke; or the making of Images, &c, of clay, or earth.*
Plasne. *as* Plane; *The great Maple.*
Plassage: m. *A fee payed, in some townes, by Marchants and Tradesmen, for the shewing of their commodities in the Market-place, or publicke streets.*
Plastras: m. *Rubbish; clods, or peeces of old, and drie plaister.*
Plastre: m. *Plaister, morter.*
Plastrer. *To plaister.*
Plastrier: m. *A Plaisterer; a Dawber.*
Plastron: m. *A breast-plate; Armour for the stomacke, or bellie; also, as* Plastre.
Plastronné: m. ée: f. *Breast-plated; armed with a breast-plate.*
Plat: m. *A Platter; or great Dish; also, a Dish of meat.*
Plat de patissier. *A round, and flat footlesse Panne of tinne, wherein pies are kept warme at the ouens mouth, after they be fully baked.*
Plat renvoyé. *A walking meale; wherein one dish going round about the table, euerie guest is his owne caruer.*
Vn grand plat. *A Charger.*
Donner plat. *To bestow victualls.*
Pescher au plat. *Looke* Pescher.
Le plat du bas est tousiours le premier vuide: Prov. *The lowmost dish is alwayes the first emptie; (for commonly the best trencher-men sit lowest.)*
Qui est loing du plat est prez de son dommage: Prov. *We say (more generally) a man thats farre from his good is neere his harme.*
Tout estat, & rien au plat: Prov. *Looke* Estat.
Plat: m. *Flatnesse, or, the flat part of a thing flatted; whence;* Bailler du plat de la langue. *To sooth, flatter, collogue with; A metaphor from a dogs licking; and;*
Frapper du plat d'une espée. *To strike flatling, or with the flat part of a sword.*
Plat: m. ate: f. *Flat, plaine, low; smooth; euen, or leuell with the ground; also, shallow.*

Plat bord. *See* Bord.

Plat païs. *The countrey; also, a vale, dale, plaine, or plaine region, low countrey.*

La besace, ou bourse plate. *An emptie wallet, or purse.*

Maison plate. *(Opposed vnto* Chasteau*) a house which hath neither towers, nor moat; a plaine-built, or plaine countrey, house.*

Pied plat. *A splay foot.*

`A plate cousture. *Rudely, plainly, after the homeliest fashion; also, flatly, fully, vtterly, throughly; as vnder* Cousture.

Platane: f. *The right Plane tree; (a stranger in England.)*

Plateaux: m. *Flat and thinne stones; flakes of stones, &c.*

Fumées en plateaux. *Flat gratiching, fewmishing (or dung) of a Deere.*

Plateforme: f. *A platforme, plot, modell, or draught of a building; also, the foundation thereof; also, a platforme, or square bulwarke; also, a certaine thicke boord in the prow of a ship.*

Platelée: f. *A platterfull, or dish-full, of.*

Plat-escuelle: f. *A deepe dish, or platter.*

Plat-fond: m. *The plaine ground of, or vnder, fretting, or any high-raised worke.*

Platin: m. *A flat; a flat strand, low coast, or low peece of ground, neere vnto the sea.*

Platin de fer. *A cart-clowt of yron.*

Platine: f. *A flat, or thinne peece of wood, or mettall; and hence, a spring-pinne; or a thinne plate of yron, put betweene the end of an yron pinne, and a frame, to keep it the faster; also, as* Patine.

Cautere à platine. *The plate-cauter; See* Cautere.

Platis: m. *A flat, shelfe, or shallow place in the water.*

Platte: f. *A Bleake (fish.)*

Platteaux. *Looke* Plateaux.

Plattebande: f. *A flat band, or bend.*

Platteforme. *as* Plateforme.

Plattiz. *Looke* Platis.

Platuse: f. *A Plaice (fish;)* ¶Langued.

Plau: m. *The South wind.*

Plauder. *Seeke* Pelauder.

Plauton: m. *A clue, or bottome.*

Playe: f. *A wound, bloudwipe, sore cut, gash, incision, hurt; also, as* Plage.

Playe faitte à Iustice. *Tyrannie, or iniustice, curbing, or ouer-ruling iustice.*

Debonnaire Mire fait playe puante: Prov. &; vn piteux medecin fait vne mortelle playe: Prov. *A pitifull Chirurgian makes a pitifull sore.*

Playé: m. ée: f. *Wounded; sore cut, or hurt.*

Player. *To wound, cut, gash, giue a bloudwipe vnto.*

Playt. *as* Plait; *(an old word.)*

Plect, & cheval de service. *Due in some places, and cases, from the vassall to the Lord feudal (as vnder* Service; *) This word is also, in the customes of Britanie, ill printed for* Plaid.

Plect de mortemain. 50 s. *for a* Masure de terre, *due vnto Landlords (in diuers parts of* Poictou*) at the death, or change, of their tenants.*

Plectre: m. *The quill, or bow, wherewith a Citterne, or Violl, is played on.*

Plege: m. *A pledge, a suretie, an vndertaker for.*

Plegement. *as* Pleigement.

Pleger. *To vndertake, be pledge, become suretie, for.*

Se pleger. *To complaine of; to commence a suit, or bring an Action, against.*

Pleger l'emende. *To acknowledge his fault, and pray the fauour of the Court before Iudgement, thereby to lessen his penaltie, or punishment.*

Plegerie: f. *Suretiship; an vndertaking, or answering for.*

Plegeur: m. *A Plaintife in an Action.*

Pleïade: f. *One of the seuen starres.*

Pleige: m. *A Pledge, a Suretie; one that vndertakes, or answers, for another.*

Pleigement: m. *A pledging, vndertaking, or answering, for; also, a complaint preferred, suit commenced, or Action brought, vpon an impeachment, or disturbance, of possession.*

Pleiger. *To be a Pledge, or Suretie, to vndertake, or answer, for; Looke* Pleger.

Qui pleige paye: Prov. *A Suretie's sure to pay.*

Plein: m. *A Plaine; Looke* Plain.

Plein: m. eine: f. *Full; whole, compleat, absolute, large, ample, solide; also, gorged, stuft, replenished, well furnished, stored, fraught, with.*

Pleine. *(Feminine) The same; also, big-bellied, bagd, or great with young; (a word onely for beasts.)*

Pleines armes. *Armes, or a Coat, without difference; belongs to the chiefe, or eldest, of a House.*

Pleine Cour. *A Court Leet, or Baron, whereto a sufficient number of* Pairs, *Assistants, or* Hommes de fief, *be suitors.*

Plein fief. *Looke* Fief.

Pleine nuict. *Darke-night, bed-time, the second watch of the night;* En pleine nuict. *When all was husht, when euerie one asleepe.*

Pleine puissance. *Absolute, Monarchall, or Soueraigne power.*

Plein relief. *Seeke* Relief.

`A plein pied. *Of an euen ground; or with a leuell floore.*

Mettre à plein pied. *To rase; to lay euen, or leuell with the ground.*

Mettre sur le plein pied. *To set full vpon the legs; to settle, or giue sure footing vnto.*

Sain, & plein de vie. *In health, and like to liue.*

Tout plein d'autres choses. *Many other, or, a great sort of other, things.*

Donner le plein & le rond à. *To perfect, consummate, accomplish.*

Tel est plein qui se plaind: Pro. *The wealthie churle complaines of want.*

On lie bien le sac avant qu'il soit plein: Prov. *An emptie sacke will easily be tied; or, as vnder* Sac.

Pleinement. *Fully, wholly, compleatly; absolutely, throughly, soundly; abundantly, largely, amply.*

Plein-fief. *Looke* Fief.

Plein-foncé: m. ée: f. *Spacious, big, full, wide, large; wherein there is stuffe, or scope, ynough.*

Pleintithe. *as* Pleintisse.

Pleintisse: f. *The full scope, or whole compasse of.*

Pleïon: m. *Long straw softened in water, thereby to bee pliant, and fit for the binding of vines, &c.*

Plejure: f. *A pledging; suretiship; vndertaking, or answering for.*

Homme de plejure. *A Pledge, or Suretie; or a vassall who may be a Baile, Pledge, or Suretie for his Lord.*

Plenier: m. ere: f. *as* Planier.

Camelot plenier. *Vnwater Chamlet.*

Plenitude: f. *Plenitude, fulnesse, wholenesse; soliditie, thicknesse, grossenesse.*

Plenté: f. *Plentie, store, abundance, fulnesse, ynough.*
Pleonasmique: com. *Superfluous, redundant.*
Plessé: m. ée: f. *Plashed, as young boughes.*
Plesser. *To plash; to bow, fould, or plait young branches one within another; also, to thicken a hedge, or couer a walke, by plashing.*
Plessis: m. *The plashing of trees; the plaiting, or foulding of their tender branches, one within the other; also, a hedge, or walke of plashed trees, &c.*
Plet. *as* Plaid; *or, as* Plect.
Plethore: f. *Fulnesse, or abundance of good humors in the bodie; also, head-ache by the superfluitie thereof.*
Plethorique: com. *Fat, grosse, corpulent, ouer-full of good humors.*
Plevi: m. ie: f. *Warranted, assured, whose goodnesse, or sufficiencie is vndertaken for.*
Fille plevie. *Promised in mariage; affianced.*
Plevine. *as* Pleuvine.
Pleviner. *To pleuine, warrant, be suretie, giue pledges, vndertake, or promise, for.*
Plevir. *The same*; &, Plevir l'emende; *as* Pleger l'emende.
Pleur: m. *A teare; a trickle; also, weeping, or lamentation.*
Pleurable: com. *Lamentable; fit to be wept, or wailed for.*
Pleurant: m. ante: f. *Weeping, whining, crying, shedding teares; wailing, lamenting.*
Verre pleurant. *Which being ouer-full runnes ouer.*
Pleurard: m. *A weeper, crier, whiner, wailer.*
Pleúre: f. *A thinne, and smooth skinne wherewith th'inside of the ribs is couered.*
Pleuré: m. ée: f. *Wept; whined, cried for; deplored, bewailed, bemoaned.*
Pleurement: m. *A weeping; a crying, whining, shedding of teares; a lamenting, wailing, howling.*
Pleure-pain: m. *A niggardlie wretch; a puling micher or miser; a miserable house-keeper; one whom it grieues to bestow any meat on himselfe, or but a mite on others.*
Pleurer. *To weepe, crie, whine, shed teares; to moane, lament, waile, howle.*
Assez peut pleurer qui n'a nul qui l'appaise: Prov. *He may weepe his eyes out that hath none to appease him.*
Autant pleure mal batu que bien batu. *As much the ill, as the well, beaten crieth; (whence;)*
Mal batu longuement pleure: Prov.
`A coeur dolent l'oeil pleure: Prov. *A weeping eye, a wofull heart.*
Bien courroucé de peu pleure: Prov. *He thats angred agood can hardly weepe.*
Femme rit quand elle peut, & pleure quand elle veut. Prov. *Looke* Femme.
La mere du timide ne sçait que c'est de pleurer: Prov. *The dame whose sonne's a coward seldome weepes.*
Les belles robbes pleurent sur des espaules indignes: Prov. *Faire garments weepe vpon vnworthie shoulders.*
Tel au matin rit qui au soir pleure: Prov. *No glad man knowes how soone he may be sorie.*
Pleuresie: f. *A Pleurisie.*
Pleuretique: com. *Sicke of, or subiect vnto, a Pleurisie.*
Membrane pleuretique. *as* Pleúre.
Pleureur: m. *A weeper, a crier.*
Pleureux: m. euse: f. *Euer weeping, full of teares.*

Pleust à Dieu. *I would to God*; *Looke* Plaire.
Pleuvi: m. ie: f. *as* Plevi; *also, quit, absolued, released.*
Pleuvine: f. *A warrant, warrantie, assurance, vndertaking for, the goodnesse, or sufficiencie of.*
Pleuviner. *as* Pleviner; *also, as* Plouviner.
Pleuvir. *To warrant, assure, vndertake, passe his promise, giue his word, for.*
Pleuvir vne fille. *To affiance a maiden, to promise her in mariage:* ¶Pic.
Pleuvoir. *To raine; Seeke* Plouvoir.
Pli: m. *A plait, fould, lay; bought; wrinkle, crumple; also, a habit, or impression.*
Pli du mitan. *The closing of the middle of a Canonbit.*
Il a prins son pli. *(Said of an obdurate, and incorrigible disposition; or of one in whom a humor, whatsoeuer, is turned to a habit;) he will neuer be other then he is.*
Les Parlemens prindrent divers plis sous tels, & tels Rois; viz. *Tooke diuers formes vnder, got sundrie courses of proceeding from, such and such Kings.*
Pliable: com. *Pliable; fit, or easie, to be foulded, bowed, bent.*
Pliage: m. *A foulding, plying, plaiting, bending, bowing.*
Pliaison: f. *as* Pliement.
Plicature: f. *A foulding, plaiting, bowing, bending.*
Plie: f. *A Plaice (fish, especially, a great one.)*
Plié: m. ée: f. *Foulded, plaited; plied; wried, bent, bowed; wrapped, or put vp; also, wrinkled, or crumpled.*
Pliement: m. *A foulding, plaiting; plying, bending, bowing; turning, wrying.*
Plier. *To fould, plait; plie, bend, bow; turne, wrie; wrap vp; also, to wrinkle.*
Plier ses cartes. *To put vp his cards.*
Plier le coude. *To keepe his elbow in continuall action; to lift the pot often to his head; See* Coude.
Plier le gantelet. *To yeeld, or submit himselfe.*
Mieux vaut plier que rompre: Prov. *Better bow then breake; viz. Better to yeeld vnto good aduice, or the violent sway of the time, then by following his own opinion, or humor, to draw on himselfe a certaine destruction: And of an obstinate, and incorrigible creature they say,* Il rompera plustost qu'il ne pliera; *and yet sometimes it is applied vnto a constant looser, or hazardor, of his life, in defence of a religious, and knowne, truth.*
Plieur: m. *A foulder, plaiter; plier, bender, bower; also, a wrapper, foulder, or putter, vp of.*
Plieur. *(Adiectiuely) Foulding, plaiting; plying, bowing, bending; whence;*
Muscles plieurs. *Two muskles (a great, and a little one) whereby the toes are bowed.*
Plieure. *as* Pliement.
Plieuse: f. *A woman that foulds, plaits; bends, bowes.*
Plinthe: f. *A Plinth, or Slipper; a flat, and square peece of Masonrie, &c. placed sometimes aboue, sometimes below, the footstall (but euer the first of the Basis) of a piller, &c.*
Plion: m. *A kind of stiffe Ozier; See* Butter.
Plionner. *To wrinkle, crumple, frumple, ruffle, disorder, mumble.*
Plis. *as* Pelis; *also, the Plurall vnto* Pli.
Plissé: m. ée: f. *Plaited, foulded, lapped vp; also, plessed, as a tree, &c.*
Plisser. *To plait, fould, lap vp, or one within another;*

ther; (whence) also, to plash.

Plissure: f. *A foulding, or plaiting; also, a fould, plait, lap, wrinkle; also, a plashing, of trees, &c.*

Ploïable. *as* Ployable.

Ploïer. *Seeke* Ployer.

Plomant: m. ante: f. *Pluming; or trying the straightnesse of worke by a plumbe-rule.*

Plomb: m. *Lead; also, a Carpenters plummet, or plomb-line; also, a bullet for a Musket, or Caleeuer; also, as* Plion.

Plomb blanc. *Tinne; or a kind thereof; as* Estaim de glace.

Plomb à chaas. *A kind of plomb-rule, or instrument of copper, &c, whereby (as by the plomb-rule) Masons doe gouerne, and iudge of, the straightnesse, or euennesse of their worke, from top to bottome.*

Plomb de mine. *Blacke lead.* Mine de plomb. *as in* Mine.

Plomb noir. *Ordinarie lead.*

Plomb à rieulle, ou à ruyle. *A Masons plomb-rule.*

'A plomb. *Perpendicularly, downe-right; whence;* La muraille est bien à plomb. *The wall is verie straight, or stands boult vpright; &,* 'A plomb sur. *Direct, or downe-right, vpon.*

'A pied de plomb. *Slowly, dully, heauily, with leaden heeles.*

'A pied de plomb, & de pompe. *The same; and, stately, maiestically, with a Spanish grauitie; Rodomont-like.*

Il a du plomb en teste. *He hath a sad, aduised, or discreet pate of his owne.*

Mis à plomb, & au fin. *Throughly fined, or tried, exactly purified.*

Dans vne gaine d'or vn cousteau de plomb. *(Appliable to the faire outside of a foule inside; or to a pranked coxcombe, or faire foole;) a leaden whittle in a sheath of gold.*

Plombagine: f. *Pure lead turned almost into ashes by the vehemence of the fire: This is th'artificiall* Plombagine, *and comes of lead put into a furnace with gold, or siluer oare, to make them melt the sooner; (by which imployment it gaines some part in the worth of those mettalls;) There is also a naturall, or minerall* Plombagine, *which (as* Mathiolus *thinketh) is no other then siluer mingled with lead-stone, or oare.*

Plombasse: com. *Lead-like, lead-coloured, sallow, bleake, wanne.*

Plombature: f. *Solder of lead, or tinne.*

Plombé: m. ée: f. *Leaded, or tinned; soldered with lead; also, leaden, or leadie; dull, heauie, sad; also, lead-coloured, or blacke and blew after stripes; also, sounded with a leaden plummet; also, marked, or stamped, with lead.*

Plombeau: m. *A plummet; or weight of lead; whence;* Le poids à plombeau. *The Roman beame or Stelleere.*

Le plombeau d'un'espée. *The pommell.*

Plombée: f. *A plummet, or pellet of lead.*

Plombelé. *as* Plombé; *also, bearing lead.*

Plombement: m. *A leading, or tinning; also, a soul-dering; also, a marking of wares, with lead; also, a sounding with a plummet.*

Plomber. *To lead, or tinne; also, to soulder, or colour with lead; also, to marke wares with lead, or set leaden seals, or stamps on them; also, to sound the depth of a place with a plummet.*

Plomber de coups de boulets. *To lead, or turne into lead, with multitude of shot; to bestow more shot on then the skinne can hold.*

Se plomber le sein. *To thump, or beat his own breast.*

Plomberie: f. *A leading; or the leads of a Church, house, &c.*

Plombet. *as* Plombée; *also, the plomb-line, or plomb-rule used by Architects.*

Plombeure: f. *as* Plombement; *whence;* Agraphes de fer à plombeure. *Iron hookes fastened, or soulde-red together, with lead.*

Plombier: m. *A Plummer.*

Plombier: m. ere: f. *Leadie, lead-like, of lead.*

Pierre plombiere. *Lead oare, or lead-stone before it be tried.*

Plomeau: m. *A plummet, or little ball of lead.*

Plomer. *To plumme; a Mason to trie, or iudge of, the straightnesse of his worke by his plomb-rule.*

Plommée: f. *as* Plombée; *or, a weight of lead.*

Traineau à plommée. *Looke* Traineau.

Plommer. *as* Plomer; *or, as* Plomber.

Plongé: m. ée: f. *Plunged; ducked, diued; thrust farre into, ouer head and eares in.*

Plongeant. *Plunging, diuing, ducking; also, thrusting farre into.*

Plongement: m. *A plunging, diuing, or ducking; also, a thrusting farre into.*

Plongeon: m. *The water-fowle called a Ducker; or a generall name for water-fowle which vse to ducke often, or on their weake legs (which they lamely traile after them) can goe but a little.*

Plongeon de mer. *A Puffin.*

Plongeon de riviere. *A certaine fresh-water fowle, that resembles the Puffin.*

Grand plongeon. *A Cormorant.*

Petit plongeon. *A Dydopper, or Arsefoot.*

'A plongeons. *Ducking, plunging; or, by plunges.*

Plongeons. *(The Plurall of* Plongeon; *also) rickes, or stackes of corne.*

Plonger. *To plunge, diue, ducke; runne ouer head and eares, thrust, farre into.*

Plonget. *as* Plongeon; *or particularly, the Dydopper.*

Plongeur: m. *A plunger, ducker, diuer.*

Plorer. *See* Pleurer.

Plot: m. *A blocke:* ¶Bourbon.

Plote. *as* Pelote; *A ball.*

Ploter. *as* Peloter.

Ploton: m. *A clue, or bottome of; also, a low Buffet stoole.*

Plotte. *as* Pelotte.

Plourement: m. *A weeping.*

Plourer. *See* Pleurer.

Ploustre: m. *A Rowler; also, (but somewhat improperly) a Harrow.*

Ploustrement: m. *A leuelling of ground, or breaking of clods with a Rowler.*

Ploustrer. *To leuell ground, or breake clods, with a Rowler.*

Ploustreur: m. *A clod-breaker; or, one that smoothes ground, or breaks clods, with a Rowler.*

Ploutroer: m. *A Rowler; the rowling Instrument where-with ground is leuelled; and clods broken.*

Plouvier: m. *A Plouer.*

Plouviner. *To mizzle, to bedew.*

Plouvoir. *To raine, showre; powre downe wet.*

En hyver par tout pleut, en Esté là ou Dieu veut: Prov. *Raine falls in Winter euerie where, in Summer onely by fauour; (somewhat like wherunto is;)*

Là ou Dieu veut il pleut: Prov.

Tant tonne qu'il pleut: Prov. *Of big words come bloudwipes; after much consultation round execution.*
Ployable: com. *Pliable, bowable, bendable.*
Ployant. *Plying, bowing, bending; arching; foulding.*
Ploye: f. *A bend, bought; vault, arch; also, a bending, bowing; vaulting, arching.*
Ployé: m. ée: f. *Bowed, bent, plied; foulded; arched, vaulted.*
Ployer. *To plie, bow, bend; also, to arch, or vault; also, to fould; Looke* Plier.
Ployer l'amende. Celuy ployoit l'amende, qui en ployant le pan de sa robbe, ou cotte, faisoit amende honorable, & disoit, ie le vous amende: ¶Ragueau.
Pluau: m. *The South wind.*
Plucquoter. *To picke nicely.*
Plumaceau: m. *as* Plumart; *also, a soft fold of linnen laid next aboue the plaister, on a wound.*
Plumage: m. *Feathers; or, as* Plumart; *also, a pluming.*
Plumail: m. *A Goose wing, or duster of feathers; also, a plume of feathers; also, birds, or feathered fowle.*
Plumart: m. *A plume, or bunch of feathers; also, as* Plumail.
Plumassier: m. *A feather-maker.*
Plume: f. *A feather (especially, a soft, or short one;) also, a penne; also (in old French) a plume of feathers; also, casting for a Hawke.*
Alun de plume. *Stone Allum, itching powder; a hard white Allum, or Allum-like simple, which being well pounded, and steeped in water may be spunne into a kind of thread, and matches or candleweekes made of it; and they, once fired, will not out as long as they haue any matter to worke on.*
Relief de plume (&, Rente de plume.) *A rent Capon, Henne, or Chicken, paid for a Reliefe.*
Faict au poil, & à la plume. *Made vnto all kind of sport, practised in all kind of trades, fit for any imployment, good at any game.*
Iecter la plume au vent: & mettre sa plume au vent. *To grow, desperate, retchlesse, carelesse; or, as vnder* Iecter; *or vnder* Vent.
Passer la plume par la bec à. *Looke* Passer.
Vanner les plumes au vent. *To play the foole, to loose time.*
`A dure enclume marteau de plume: Prov. *Seeke* Enclume, *or* Marteau.
Plumé: m. ée: f. *Plumed, plucked, fleeced.*
Plumement: m. *A pluming, or plucking the feathers from; hence also, a fleecing.*
Plumer. *To plume, or plucke the feathers of; thence also, to fleece; to rob, denude, or bare of; to shake out of, all.*
Plumer vne chastaigne. *To pill, or vnbuske, a chestnut; to turne, or take, it out of the rough coat wherein tis bred; which because few can doe easily, or with vnprickt fingers, they say of a man to whom a thing is like to proue costlie, or painefull,* Il en plumera la chastaigne.
On plume l'oye sans la faire crier: Prov. *The sillie Goose complaines not when she's pluckt.*
Plumeteur: m. *A Scribe, Clerke, Penne-man, Scriuener, Penster; one that getteth his liuing by his penne.*
Plumetis: m. *A summarie, or short relation of the substance of a cause, deliuered, in writing, vnto the Judges; also, short, and cursarie notes, or instructions, for the draught of a Pleading, or Euidence, taken from the mouth of a Client (or otherwise) by a Clerke, or Notarie publicke.*
Plumette: f. *A little feather, a small penne.*
Plumeur: m. *A plumer, feather-plucker; fleecer.*
Plumeux: m. euse: f. *Full of pennes, or feathers.*
Pluralité: f. *Pluralitie, or morenesse; more then one of.*
Plure d'une voulte. *The bought, bent, or compasse of a vault.*
Plus. *More.*
`A plus prés. *Within a little.*
Au plus. *At the most;* Au plus prés. *As neere as possible can be;* Au plus tost. *At the soonest.*
Le moins de mon plus. *The most I can, the least I should.*
Non plus. (Ils n'auront qu'un non plus.) *Neither.*
Qui a il plus? *What is behind? what ouerplus remaines there?*
Tant & plus. *Exceeding much, or, as much as may be.*
Qui plus vit plus a à souffrir: Prov. *The longer life the more affliction.*
Pluserois: m. *The name of a (prohibited) fishnet, or fish-destroying engine.*
Plusieur: m. *as* Pluserois.
Plusieurs. *Many, a great number, a great sort.*
Plustost. *Rather, sooner; also, moreouer, or, which is more; also, faster, with more speed.*
Au plustost. *At the most;* &, Au plustost que faire se peut. *With the first, with the soonest; with as much speed as may be.*
Plus-valeur: f. *An ouer-value; a surplusage, ouerplus, remainder; or a thing thats ouer and aboue the value of.*
Plus-valeurs d'estat. *Looke* Estat.
Pluvial: m. ale: f. *Rainie, of raine; like to raine; waterish.*
Pluvier: m. *A Plouer.*
Pluvieux: m. euse: f. *Rainie, much raining, full of raine.*
Pluvine: f. *A Salamander, or Deafe-worme; also, as* Pleuvine.
Pluvir. *Looke* Pleuvir.
Pluye: f. *Raine; also, a Plaice.*
La pluye des mois. *A womans monthlie flux; or the immoderate fall thereof.*
La pluye l'a prins. *He is wet through; he hath taken his liquor throughly.*
Pluye de Fevrier vaut esgout de fumier: Prov. *Februarie raine is th'husbandmans gaine.*
Pluyr. *as* Plouvoir.
Ply. *Looke* Pli.
Plye: f. *A Plaice.*
Poacre: f. *A kind of scab about the nose, or muzzle of a sheepe, gotten by feeding too early in the deawie fallowes, and a verie great hinderance to her feeding.*
Poacre: com. *Looke* Poüacre.
Poale: m. *A stoue, or hot-house; also, as* Poille.
Poale: f. *as* Paelle; *A frying-panne; also, a little panne.*
Poallier: m. *The brasse wherein the stock of a bell rests, or turnes.*
Poalon: m. *A Skillet.*
Poche: f. *A pocket, pouch, or poke; also, a meale-sacke, or corne-sacke; also, a pursenet; also, the fowle called, a Shoueler; also, the crop, or craw of a bird; also, the little narrow, and long Violin (hauing the backe of one peece) which French dauncers, or dauncing Maisters, carrie about with them in a case, when they goe to teach their Schollers.*

Acheter

Acheter chat en poche. *(Like our) to buy a Pig in a poke.*

Il a bien rempli ses poches. *He hath filled his bags, or stuffed his budgets, vp to the top; he hath made good vse of his time, I warrant you.*

La poche sent tousiours l'harenc: Prov. *Corrupted once, we are tainted euer; once get a blot, y'are stained alwayes.*

Poché: m. ée: f. *Poched; thrust or digged out with the fingers; also, blurred.*

Oeil poché. *A blacke, or bloud-shot eye (by a blow, &c.)*

Oeuf poché. *A potched egge.*

Pocheculier: m. *A Shoueler.*

Pochée: f. *A pocket-full, poke-full, sack-full, of.*

Pocher. *To thrust, or dig out with the fingers.*

Pocher le labeur d'autruy. *To poche into, or incroach vpon, another mans imployment, practise, or trade.*

Cet encre poche. *This Inke blurres.*

Pochette: f. *A little pocket; a poke, or little sacke; also, a purse-net.*

Poçon. *Looke* Posson.

Podagre: f. *The Gowt (in the legs, or feet.)*

Podagre de lin. *The weed Dodder; See* Lin.

Podagre: com. *Gowtie-legd.*

Podagreux: m. euse: f. *Full of the Gowt.*

Poderaste, *for* Pederaste. *A Sodomite, boy-louer, or boy-buggerer.*

Podimetrie: f. *Foot-measure, measuring by the foot.*

Poelle: m. *A Stoue, or Hot-house.*

Poëme: m. *A Poeme; a composition, or worke in Verse.*

Poësie: f. *Poesie, Poetrie.*

Poesle: m. *A Stoue, or Hot-house.*

Poesle: f. *as* Paelle.

Poeslier: m. *A Tinker, Brasier, Skellet-maker.*

Poeslon: m. *A Skellet, or Posnet; also, a little Frying-panne.*

Poeste. Homme de poeste. *A yeoman,* Roturier, *vnnoble subiect, vassall, or tenant.*

Poëtastre: m. *An ignorant Poet.*

Poëte: m. *A Poet, Maker, Versifier.*

Bon poëte mauvais homme: Prov. *A good Poet an ill man.*

Poëterie: f. *Poetrie; (an old word.)*

Poëtiquement. *Poetically, Poet-like.*

Poëtiser. *To poetize it; to make Verses.*

Poëtride: f. *A Poetesse.*

Poëtrie: f. *Poetrie.*

Poëtrons: m. *(Ordinarie) yellow Plummes.*

Poevrette. *as* Poivrette.

Poge, ou Pogge: f. *The sheat, or cable which fastens the maine yard, on the right hand of a Ship; whence,* A poge; *at, or on, the right hand.*

Naviger à poge, & à ourse. *To hold an vncertaine course at sea, by reason of contrarie winds, laying tacke aboord sometimes on the right, and sometimes on the left, side of the Ship.*

Pognard: m. *as* Poignard.

Poictevine: f. *A woman of* Poictou; *also, a French farthing, or the fourth part of the* Denier Tournois.

Poictrail: m. *A Petrell for a horse; also, the beame, or summer whereby rafters, or ioists are vpheld.*

Poictreux: m. euse: f. *whence,* Piece poictreuse. *A peece of coyne that rises, bulches, or beares out in the middle, and is flat, or thinne, about the edge.*

Poictrinal: m. *A great, and heauie Petronell; shorter, but of a wider bore, then a Musket.*

Poictrinal: m. ale: f. *Belonging to the breast, or stomack; also, stomacall, breast-comforting.*

Poictrinalier: m. *One that serues with, or vses to shoot in, a great and heauie Petronell.*

Poictrine: f. *The breast, bosome, stomacke; also, a breast-plate, or armour for the breast.*

Poictrine empeschée. *Obstruction of the stomacke; or a drie, and soft Cough (which we call a Sheepes Cough) proceeding thereof.*

Poictrinette: f. *A little breast, prettie bosome.*

Poictrineux: m. euse: f. *as* Poictrinal; *also, as* Poictreux.

Poictron: m. *The arse, nockandroe, fundament.*

Poids: m. *A peise, or weight; also, peise, weight; also, substance, or soundnesse.*

Poids de Marc. *Halfe a pound, or eight ounces; Looke* Marc.

Poids Marchand. *The weight vsed by Marchants, and Tradesmen, is in some (few) places after fourteene, in others after eighteene, but in the most after sixteene, ounces to the pound.*

Poids medecinal. *The weight vsed by Phisitions, &c, is after twelue ounces to the pound.*

Poids de Midy. *One of the Pyrrhenian mountaines, called so, because euer about noone the Sunne shines on it.*

Poids de neuf heures. *Another, called so because the Sunne is euer on it about nine a clocke in the morning.*

Poids du Roy. *Is after sixteene ounces to the pound, eight ounces to the* Marc, *and eight* Gros *to the ounce.*

Gros poids. *Is after 26 ounces to the pound.*

Petit poids. *Troy weight; twelue ounces to the pound.*

Poifaict: m. *Sloath, negligence, idlenesse.* ¶Breton.

Poifaisant: m. *A negligent, sloathfull, or carelesse fellow; one thats euer behind-hand with his businesse.* ¶Breton.

Poignalade: f. *A stab, or thrust with a Poniard.*

Poignalarder. *To stab, or thrust into with a Poniard.*

Poignant: m. ante: f. *Pricking, stinging; also, peeping, or peering out.*

Poignard: m. *A Poinadoe, or Poniard.*

Poignardé: m. ée: f. *Poniarded, stabbed with a Poniard.*

Poignarder. *To poniard, to stab with a Poniard.*

Poignastre. *The Viuer, or little sea-Dragon.*

Poignée: f. *A handfull, fistfull, or gripe of; also, the handle of a sword, or dagger.*

Poignet: m. *The wrist; the ioint thats betweene the hand and the arme; also, a handle.*

Poignet de la chemise. *The wrist-band, or gathering at the sleeue-hand, of a shirt.*

Il a bien foncé le poignet. *He hath gained soundly, he hath gotten sweetly, he hath licked his fingers throughly; (A Phrase often vsed in disgrace of the partie it is applyed vnto, and taxing him of no lesse then theeuerie, or grosse cousenage.)*

Poil: m. *A haire.*

Poil de chat. *A running sore, or tettar, which we also tearme, a Cats haire; also, a Whitlow in the finger.*

Poil folet. *A young mossie beard; also, the first downe, or soft feathers of a young bird.*

Couleur de poil de souris. *A Mouse-colour, or Mouse-dunne.*

Fente en poil. *A cleft in a bone, so little, as it is almost inuisible.*

Velours à deux poils. *Two-pile Veluet.*
Velours a long poil. *Shag, plush; or (most properly) vnshorne Veluet.*
Bas de poil. *Lowlie, or bearing a low sayle; of poore meanes, of small authoritie, that can doe but little any way.*
Eschauffer le poil à. *To irritate, or prouoke vnto anger; also, to bestow a painefull heating on, to bang or bethwacke the skinne-coat of.*
Faire changer de poil. *To reforme by cudgelling, or by seuere courses; (from a Groome, who currying a yong horse throughly, makes the colour of his coat to alter.)*
Fait au poil, & à la plume. *A Generalist; one thats fit for, or can make one in, any imployment, or sport; (from dogs which are good at all kind of Game.)*
Monter sur vn cheval à poil. *To get on a horses bare backe.*
Né à tout le poil (le Diable l'a chié en volant.) *A monstrous Cutter, a terrible Gallant, a horrible braue man.*
Prendre du poil de la beste. *Looke* Beste.
Des paroles ils viennent au poil. *From words they fall to worke, from taunting to knocking.*
Nous prendrons ce nom au poil plus court. *We will vnderstand it more strictly, or in a neerer sence; or in a sence against which least may be sayed.*
Vn poil fait ombre: Pro. *The little haire a shadow casts; the least things haue their vse one way, or other.*
Pour vn poil Martin perdit son Asne: Pro. *Looke* Asne.
En maigre poil a morsure: Pro. *Looke* Morsure.
Le Loup alla à Rome, & y laissa de son poil, & rien de ses coustumes: Pro. *A knaue will returne a knaue from the best place in the world; or as vnder* Loup.
Poilant. *Pilling, paring, barking, taking the rinde, coat, or vpmost crust of.*
Poile: m. *as* Poille; *also, as* Poale.
Poile: f. *A frying-panne; whence;*
Saulter de la poile, & se iecter dedans les braises. *From ill to worse; out of the frying-panne into the fire.*
Poilé: m. ée: f. *Rewed, vneuenly dyed; also, pilled, pared, barked, vnrinded.*
Poiler. *To pill &c, as* Peler; *also, to rew; to dy or colour vneuenly.*
Poille: m. *The square Canopie thats borne ouer the Sacrament, or a Soueraigne Prince, in solemne Processions, or Passages of State; Hence also, a Hearse, Hearse-cloth, or rich cloth, layed ouer the Beere of a dead person; also, a cloth spred, in the Church, ouer a new-married couple; also, an Vmbrello, or great weather-fanne; also, as* Poale.
Poillu: m. uë: f. *Hairie; rugged, or rough by much haire.*
Poilon: m. *A Skellet; or, as* Poeslon.
Poinçon: m. *A bodkin; a punchion; Looke* Poinson.
Poinçonner. *as* Poinsonner.
Poinçonnet: m. *A little bodkin; or punchion.*
Poinçonneux: m. euse: f. *Pricking, as a bodkin.*
Poinct: m. *A point; a pricke; a centre; a period, or full point; a minute, instant, or moment of time; a dram, iot, crum, as little as may be of any thing; also, a stitch in sowing; also, a Stitch in the side; also, the dawning, or breake of the day, twylight; also, the point, principall head, maine proposition, of an Argument; the state, or issue, of a cause; also, the order, trimme, array, plight, health, estate, case, taking, one is in; also, the length, or measure of a man in his stirrup.*
Poinct doré. *A stitching vp of incisions, or wounds, with golden thread.*
Le poinct des pieds. *as* Nadaïr.
Le poinct vertical. *The Zenith, or point of the Firmament which is directly ouer our heads.*
Haut poinct. Honneur au haut p. *Honour in eminence, or of a high pitch.*
Petit poinct. Au petit poinct. *Throughly, soundly, closely.*
Despescher au petit poinct. *Looke* Despescher.
Poinct à poinct. *Throughly; also, fitly, iustly, decently, handsomely, in good order.*
'A poinct. *Aptly, fitly, conueniently, to purpose, in good time, in due season; whence;*
Prendre son à poinct. *To take his fittest oportunitie for; to make his best aduantage of.*
Prendre quelqu' un à son mal à point. *To take one vnprouided.*
Venir tout à poinct. *To come in an excellent season, in pudding time, in the nicke.*
'A poinct nommé. *Fitly, seasonably, at the time prefixed; iust at the time, or at the verie same time; also, expressely, or of set purpose.*
Donner à poinct nommé. *To hit point-blanke, to strike the marke he shoots at.*
De tout poinct. *Quite and cleane.*
En poinct. *In order, in case, in fashion, in array.*
Se mettre en poinct. *To prepare himselfe; to set himselfe in a readinesse.*
En bon poinct; ou, bien en poinct. *Handsome, faire, fat, well liking, in good taking.*
Sur le poinct de. *Readie, or about, to.*
Sur le poinct que. *Then, iust when.*
C'est vn poinct qui trop me poind. *This point too neerely pointeth at me; by this pricke I am ouer-deepely pierced.*
Ils le chaussent à moins de poincts que. *They make his foot, or shoe, of a lesse size then.*
Pour vn poinct Martin perdit son Asne: Prov. *(This* Martin *being Abbot of a Cloister called* Asellus, *and setting ouer the Gate thereof,* Porta patens esto nulli claudaris honesto, *was depriued of his Place for putting a Comma after the word* nulli.)
Tout vient à poinct qui peut attendre: Prov. *He that is patient any thing may compasse.*
Tout vient à poinct qui tient mesnage: Prov. *He that keepes house makes vse of euerie thing.*
Poincte: f. *A bodkin, or nawle; also, a pricke, a goad; a sting; also, the point of a weapon, or toole; also, quicknesse, sharpenesse, subtiltie; an edge; also, vehemence, eagernesse, earnestnesse, the first (violent) brunt of things; also, the middle-sized wax-candle vsed in Churches (the biggest being tearmed* Cierge, *and the least* Bougie.)
Poinctes de houseaux. *Spurres.*
Poincte des morceaux. La premiere p. *The first course, as Sallades, &c.*
La Poincte du nez. *The tip, or end of the nose.*
La Poincte de l'oeil. *The sight of the eye; or the piercing looke, or cast of a liuelie eye.*
La Poincte d'un rocher. *The point, or sharpe top, of a Rocke.*
Chausses en poincte. *Looke* Chausse.
Cul sur poincte. *Vpside downe, topsie turuie, top ouer tayle.*
Chatouilleux à la poincte. *Quicke on the spurre;*

that readily answers the spurre; hence also, titchie, that will not indure to be touched.

Combatre a poincte, & à fendant. *To fight against with point, and edge;* viz. *in all extremitie, by any hurtfull meanes, or way.*

Poursuivre sa poincte. *To follow his thrust (in fencing;) to pursue his aduantage; also, to proscecute his former designes, or courses.*

Poincté: m. ée: f. *Pointed, sharpened at the point; also, stitched; also, quilted.*

Rose poinctée de. *Bearded.* (Blason.)

Poincteler. *To prickle, pricke, or point often; also, to bud, or shoot out.*

Poincter. *as* Pointer.

Poinctille. *Seeke* Pointille.

Poinctiller. *To prickle, or pricke often.*

Poinctu: m. uë: f. *Pointed, sharpe-topped; also, keene, or sharpe at the point.*

Poindre. *To pricke; sting; nettle; bite, vex, fret; spurre, stirre, incite; also, to peepe, or peere out (as a morning Sunne ouer the top of a hill;) whence;*

Incontinent que le iour poindra. *By breake of day.*

Geline qui poind, & ne pond pas. *Looke* Pondre.

Charité oingt, & peché poind: Prov. *Charitie comforteth, sinne afflicteth; charitie supples the heart, sinne wounds the soule.*

Oignez vilain il vous poindra: Pro. *(Applyable to the base ingratitude of a base chuffe, or churle.)*

Qui contre esguillon recule deux fois se poind: Prov. *He doubly hurts himselfe that kickes against a pricke.*

Poinez raclé. C'est vn p. raclé. *Tis a thing resolued, or concluded on, a matter fully determined of.*

Poing: m. *The fist.*

Poing garni. *See* Garni.

Faire de son poing vn maillet. *To make hard shift; or, to be ignorant of the right vse of things; or, sottishly to ouertoyle, or take too much of, himselfe.*

Fol est qui de son poing fait coing: Prov. *See* Coing.

Poinrée: f. *A Peare tree.* ¶Norm.

Poinson: m. *A bodkin; also, a puncheon; also, a stampe, marke, print, or seale; also, a Wine-vessell, containing, in most places, 216 Parisien Pints.*

Poinson d'Ay, & de Champagne. *Containeth 192 Parisien Pints.*

Poinson d'une Tour. *The ball, or middle of the top, of a round Tower; that part whereat all the rafters doe meet in point; that part whereon a weathercocke, &c, is vsually planted.*

Poinsonnade: f. *A pricke, or hole made with a bodkin; also, a stampe, or marke set on with a puncheon, &c.*

Poinsonner. *To pricke, or pierce with a bodkin; to stampe, or marke, with a puncheon, &c.*

Point: m. *Looke* Poinct.

Point. *(An Aduerbe;) not, no one iote, by no meanes, in no manner, not at all.*

Pointade: f. *A pricke, thrust; stitch; or sting.*

Pointe. *as* Poincte.

Pointeler. *Seeke* Poincteler.

Pointer. *To point; or sharpen at the point; or lessen towards the point; also, to pierce, pricke, or sting; also, to stitch, quilt, or counterpoint.*

Pointer vn canon. *To leuell it, or bring it vnto the marke.*

Pointille: f. *A pricke, or prickle; a little nice point; the smallest, or sleightest matter that may be.*

Pointiller. *To prickle, or pricke often; also, to cut, quip, tax, or take exceptions vnto.*

Pointu. *as* Poinctu.

Pointure: f. *A pricke; also, a prickling, or pricking; also, a shooting (as of paine in the bodie;) also, the Gowt in the ioints.*

Poipre: f. *The Purples. Looke* Pourpre.

Poiraisine: f. *Rosin.*

Poiré: m. *Perrie; drinke made of Peares.*

Poire: f. *A Peare.*

Poire d'angoisse. *A choake-Peare; or, a wild soure Peare.*

Poire d'amiot. *A yellow, and hard-skind Peare, whereof excellent Perrie is made.*

Poire de beurée. *The butter Peare; a tender, and delicate fruit.*

Poire de bon Chrestien *(called by some the Eusebian Peare;) a great, and delicate Winter Peare, somewhat resembling the bastard Warden.*

Poire de campane. *as* Poire de Serteau.

Poire chat. *The Cat-Peare; a holesome, sweet-smelling, and sharpe-tasting fruit.*

Poire de chevalier. *The Knight-Peare.*

Poire coing. *The great Quince called, the Peare-Quince, or Quince Peare.*

Poire de conillart. *A soft, and delicate kind of Peare.*

Poire dorée. *The golden Peare; is reasonable big, almost round, and the most delicate of Summer Peares.*

Poire d'eau rose. *The Rose-Peare.*

Poire de l'escuyer. *The Esquire Peare; whereof excellent Perrie is made.*

Poire d'espine. *The thorne-Peare; (ripe in Autumne.)*

Poire d'estranguillon. *A choake-Peare.*

Poire de fin or. *The golden Peare.*

Poire de garde. *A Warden, or Winter Peare; a Peare which may be kept verie long.*

Poire de hastiveau. *A Hasting, or hastie Peare.*

Poire laide bonne. *A certaine ill-looking, but well-tasting, Peare.*

Poire de livre. *The pound-Peare; a verie great Peare.*

Poire à main. *A kind of great Peare which weighes almost a pound.*

Poire de mollart. *A certaine tender, and delicate Peare.*

Poire musquette. *The Muske Peare.*

Poire de nostre Dame. *The Marie Peare, or our Ladies Peare; a reasonable good fruit.*

Poire de parmain. *The Permaine Peare.*

Poire de rateau. *A certaine Peare thats as big as a mans fist.*

Poire de renoult. *A certaine tender, and delicate Peare.*

Poire de rosette. *A soft, and verie delicate Peare.*

Poire de rouseau. *Another; whereof good Perrie may be made.*

Poires sept en gueule. *A kind of small, and soone-ripe Muske-Peares.*

Poire de Serteau. *The Allablaster Peare, Bell Peare, or Gourd Peare.*

Poire superbe. *The Muske-Peare; or water Peare.*

Poire à deux testes. *The two-headed Peare; a yellow, and solide Peare, whereof excellent Perrie is made.*

Poire de verdelet. *The Greening; a tender, and deli-*

delicate *Peare.*
Mords à poire. *The Peare-bit; a bitt whose mouth, or vpset is fashioned like two Peares closed at the smaller ends.*
Il ne le menace point de poires molles. *Tis no trifle, no sleight mischieue, no easie matter, wherewith he threatens him.*
Apres la poire le vin, ou le prestre: Prov. *After a (cold) Peare Wine, or the Priest.*
Qui avec son seigneur mange poires il ne choisit pas des meilleures: Pro. *He that eates Peares with his Lord picks none of the best; (Therefore let him that will eat well eat with his equall.)*
Poire-coing. *The great Quince, called the Peare-Quince, or Quince-Peare.*
Poireau: m. *A Wart; also, as* Porreau.
Poirée: f. *Beets; Looke* Porrée.
Poirier: m. *A Peare-tree.*
Pois: m. *A Pease, or Peason; also, as* Poids.
Pois cerre. *The great Chichling, or flat Pease; or, the great wild Tare, called Pease euerlasting.*
Pois chiches. *Ciches, garden Ciches, Sheepes Cich Pease; Looke* Chiches.
Pois cornu. *See* Cornu.
Pois de gresle. *A haile-stone.*
Pois Massiliens (l'Hippiatrique.) *In stead of,* Seseli de Marseille; *Looke* Seseli.
Pois de merveilles. *Heart-Pease, blacke Winter Cherries, Indian Hearts.*
Pois ramez. *Rounciualls, great Pease, garden Pease, branche Peason, hastie Pease, French Pease, Romane Pease.*
Pois ramiers. *The same.*
Pois à visage. *Fasells, long Peason, Sperage Beanes, French Beanes, Roman Beanes, Kidney Beanes.*
Petis pois. *Field Pease, ordinarie Pease.*
Lard à pois de caresme. *The Bacon-like fish of a Porpose.*
Avalleurs de pois gris. *Good trencher-men, hungrie guts, greedie whorsons; they to whom euerie morsell seemes good, or no morsell comes amisse.*
Esleus, & choisis comme beaux pois sur le volet. *Choice, or daintie peeces; people curiously picked, neatly culled out; (Ironically.)*
Il luy a fait manger des pois verds au veau. *Looke* Veau.
Mon Dieu que tu fais bien le pois verreux. *Thou playest the hypocrite exceeding well.*
Apres la feste & le ieu, les pois au feu: Pro. *When costlie Feasts, and Games are ended, fond wast by thrift let be amended.*
Poisamment. *Heauily, weightily, burthensomely.*
Poisée: f. *A peising, or weighing; or as;*
Poisement: m. *A peising, or weighing; also, weight, or heauinesse.*
Poisillons: m. *A kind of small Pease, or Pulse.*
Poisle: f. *A Skellet; or Frying-panne.*
Le chauderon machure la poisle. *Seeke* Machurer.
Qui a vn oeil à la poisle, l'autre au chat. *That looketh warily, or euery way, about him.*
Poislé: m. ée: f. *Collowed, smeered, bleached, begrymed with soote, or with the touch of a sootie Skellet, &c.*
Poisler. *To collow, smut, smeere, bleach, begryme with the blacke side, or soot of a Skellet, &c.*
Poislier: m. *A Brasier, or Tinker; a Skellet-maker, or Frying-panne maker.*
Poisliers: m. *The posts which vphold the scrue of a Vine-presse.*
Poislure: f. *A collowing, smutting, smeering, besooting.*
Poison: m. *Poison.*
Poisonneux: m. euse: f. *Poisonous, full of poison.*
Poissage: m. *A pitching, or bepitching.*
Poissard: m. *A filcher, nimmer, purloyner, pilferer; one whose fingers are as good as so many lyme-twigs.*
Poissard: m. arde: f. *Pitchie, bepitched.*
Poissé: m. ée: f. *Pitched, bepitched.*
Feux poissez. *Wild fires.*
Poissement: m. *A pitching; or bepitching.*
Poisser. *To pitch, or bepitch.*
Poisseux: m. euse: f. *Pitchie, full of pitch.*
Poissillon: m. *A little, or young, fish.*
Poisson: m. *A fish; also, fish.*
Poisson d'Avril. *A Mackerell; also, a young bawd; a Page turned Pandar.*
Poisson Iuïf. *The (ouglie, and vnluckie) Mallet fish; called so, because headed like a hammer.*
Poisson de mesnage. *as* Belenne.
Poisson S. Pierre. *The Dorce; called also by some of our Fishermen S. Peters fish.*
Poisson royal. *The white Cabot; a delicate fish.*
Poisson sacré. *Looke* Sacré.
Muet comme vn poisson. *As dumbe as a fish.*
Il se retira avec cela qu'il avoit de poisson prins. *He got him away with the shame he had gotten, or with a flea in his eare.*
La sauce ne vaut pas mieux que le poisson. *The sawce is no better then the fish.*
Se faire marchand de poisson la vieille de Pasques. *Looke* Marchand.
Poisson, gorret, & cochin, vie en l'eau, & mort en vin: Pro. *We say, fish must euer swimme twice.*
Le poisson commence à sentir tousiours par la teste: Pro. *The head of a fish is euer tainted first.*
Les gros poissons mangent les petis: Pro. *Justly applyed to the vniust world, wherein the rich deuoure the poore, the strong the weake, the mightie the meane.*
En petite riviere ne se prend gros poisson: Pro. *In poore families, or pettie Townes, great preferment will not be had, much profit cannot be made.*
Ieune chair, & vieil poisson: Prov. *Old flesh, and young fish (is fit for the dish.)*
Il faut hasarder vn petit poisson pour prendre vn grand: Pro. *Hazard a little to gaine much.*
Il ne faut apprendre aux poissons à nager: Prov. *Looke* Nager.
L'hoste, & le poisson passé trois iours puent: Pro. *A guest, and fish at three dayes end grow mustie.*
Qui envoye chetif à la mer n'en rapporte ne poisson, ne sel: Pro. *He that sends a knaue to sea, is sure to loose his venture.*
Poissonnerie: f. *The Fish-market.*
Poissonnet: m. *A little fish.*
Poissonneux: m. euse: f. *Fishie; full of, or abounding in, fish.*
Poissonnier: m. *A Fish-monger.*
Il se fait poissonnier la vigile de Pasques. *Too late he vndertakes that course, or action.*
Poissonnier: m. ere: f. *Fishie; abounding in, or belonging vnto, fish.*
Poissonniere: f. *A Fish-wife, or a woman that sells fish; also, a long Panne to seeth fish in.*
Poissure: f. *A pitching, or bepitching.*
Poisteau: m. *A little bird like a Linnet.*
Poistrir. *as* Pestrir.
Poitral. *See* Poictral.

Poitrir. *Looke* Pestrir.
Poitron: m. *The tayle, arse, bumme; also, a kind of Horse-Plumme.*
Poivre. *Pepper; Looke* Poyvre.
Poivrette: f. *Gith, Nigella, Bishops-wort, Sweet-fauor, S. Catherins flower.*
Poix: m. *Weight; Looke* Poids.
Poix: f. *Pitch.*
Poix blanche de Bourgongne. *Burgundie Pitch; as* Poix Grecque.
Poix blanche de Cordouannier. *White Shoomakers Wax.*
Poix fonduë. *Tarre.*
Poix Grecque. *Greeke Pitch; a light-yellow Pitch, much vsed in plaisters.*
Poix liquide. *Tarre.*
Poix navale. *Ship-Pitch; is scraped from Ships, and then mingled with Wax, and Bay Salt (for Phisicall vses;) also, ordinarie Pitch is by some called* Pix navalis.
Poix picatoire. *A kind of Pitch compounded of Rosen and Pitch.*
Poix resine. *Rosen.*
Poix seiche. *Stone Pitch, ordinarie Pitch.*
Poixement: m. *A pitching, or bepitching.*
Poixer. *To pitch, to bepitch.*
Poix-resine: f. *Rosen.*
Poizage. Droict de p. *A fee due, in some places, to the King for the weighing of commodities with a publike Balance, or Beame.*
Poizer. *Looke* Peser.
Pol: m. *Paule.*
Grace de S. Pol. *See* Grace.
Pierre de S. Pol. *A certaine medecinable stone found in a Maltean caue, wherein (they say) S. Paule preached; some also call the Samien earth so.*
Descouvrir S. Pierre pour couvrir S. Pol. *To build, or inrich one Church with the ruines, or reuenues of another.*
Pol: m. *A Pole; the end, or point of one of the Axletrees, whereon (say Astronomers) the heauens moue.*
Pol Antartique. *The Antarticke, or South Pole; a starre not seene in our Hemisphere.*
Pol Artique. *The North Pole, the North Starre.*
Polaine. *The furniture of a Peece (consisting of diuers peeces) of timber in the prow of a Ship, called,* La Fleche; *also, as* Poulaine.
Polaire: com. *Of, or belonging to, the Poles.*
Estoille polaire. *A starre which maketh the tayle of* Vrsa minor; *called so, because it is the neerest of all others vnto the North Pole.*
Pole: f. *The Sole fish called, a Dogs-tongue, or kind foole.*
Polemoine: m. *Spattling Poppie, frothie Poppie, white Ben; also, the shrubbie Trefoile called, Make-bate.*
Poli: m. ie: f. *Polished, smoothed, burnished, sleeked; also, fine, trimme, neat, spruce, polite.*
Polican. *Looke* Pelican.
Police: f. *Policie; politicke regiment, ciuill gouernment; or as a French Lawyer defines it,* C'est le réglement de la Cité; *or as another,* C'est la forme, & le réglement estably aux choses necessaires à la vie humaine; *whence;*
Droict de police. *Power to make particular Orders for the Gouernment of all the inhabitants of a Towne, or Territorie; this Power (extending chiefely vnto three things, viz. small commodities (as victuals, &c;) Trades, or Occupations; and streetes, or high wayes;) though often challenged by the officers of the King (to whom all generall policie without question belongs) yet is (or should be) enioyed by euerie Lord in France, from the Chattelain vpwards.*
Policé: m. ée: f. *Ordered, gouerned, ruled, aduisedly disposed.*
Policer. *To order, gouerne, rule aduisedly, dispose of wisely.*
Policier: m. ere: f. *Belonging or looking to, taking notice or care of, hauing by office, or in charge, the gouernment, and ordering of, particular matters in a Towne, or Territorie.*
Poliément. *Smoothly, sleekely, brightly, cleanely, neatly, trimly.*
Polieul: m. *Pellamountaine, or Pollie, an hearbe.*
Poligamie: f. *Poligamie; the hauing of many wiues, or of moe then one.*
Poligarchie: f. *A Monarchie diuided into sundrie parts; or such a diuision.*
Poligone: f. *A Geometricall figure that hath many corners.*
Poliment: m. *Smoothnesse, sleekenesse, a glosse, a polished lustre.*
Poliot. *See* Pouliot.
Polipragmon: m. *A Polipragmon, medler, busie bodie.*
Polipus. *Looke* Polypus.
Polir. *To polish; to smooth, sleeke, burnish, brighten, beautifie; to scoure, cleanse, furbish, trim vp, make neat, set a glosse on, giue a lustre vnto.*
Polissable: com. *Polishable, burnishable, furbishable.*
Polissement: m. *A polishing, burnishing, brightening, smoothing, sleeking; a furbishing, or trimming vp.*
Polisseur: m. *A polisher, burnisher; sleeker, smoother; furbisher.*
Polisseure: f. *as* Polissure.
Polissoir: m. *A polisher; a polishers burnishing stone.*
Polissoire: f. *The same.*
Polissure: f. *Polissure, burnishment, smoothneße, sleekeneße, neatnesse, cleanlinesse; also, as* Polissement.
Polisyllable: com. *Of many sillables.*
Politesse: f. *Politeneße; polishednesse; smoothneße, sleekenesse; neatnesse, cleanlineße; trimnesse, briskenesse.*
Politric. *See* Polytric.
Politure. *as* Polissure.
Polles. *Certaine forbidden Engines, or Nets, wherewith fish may be caught.*
Pollisyllabe: com. *Of many sillables.*
Pollu: m. uë: f. *Polluted; defiled, distained; corrupted, dishonested, violated.*
Polluer. *To pollute; soyle, distaine, defile; corrupt, violate, infect.*
Polpe: f. *The pulpe; the brawne of flesh, or fleshie part of the bodie; the substance, or hard pith, of any thing.*
Polsonnets: m. *Two buttons with hookes at their ends, passing through the branch, and holding the water-chayne, of a Bitt.*
Poltron: m. *A knaue, rascall, varlet, scowndrell; also, a dastard, coward; sluggard, lazie-backe, base idle fellow.*
Poltronesque: com. *Knauish, rascallie, base-humored; cowardlie, faint-hearted, cullion-like; lazie, lozellie, sluggish, idle.*
Poltronesquement. *Roguishly, basely, lazily, cowardly, cullion-like.*
Poltronie: f. *Knauerie, vilenesse, baseneße; cowardice, dastardie; sluggishnesse, lazineße; vnworthineße.*

Pol-

Poltroniser. *To pultronize it; to play the knaue, scowndrell; coward; to laze, loll, or slug it.*
Polygamie: f. *as* Poligamie.
Polygone: m. *Knot-grasse, Birds tongue, Swines-grasse, S. Innocents hearbe.*
Polygone femelle. *Female Knot-graße; a water hearbe, seldome found, and of lesse vertue then;*
Polygone masle. *Common Knot-grasse.*
Polygone petit. *Rupturewort,* Herniaria, *Burstwort.*
Polygraphie: f. *A diuers manner of writing.*
Polymixe. *A candle hauing many weekes.*
Polype. *as* Polypus.
Polypeux: m. euse: f. *That hath a* Noli me tangere *in the nose.*
Polyphilie: f. *Affection diuided, loue vnto many.*
Polypode. *Polipodie, Oake-Fearne, Wall-Fearne (which two last names belong vnto two seuerall, yet neerely-resembling, hearbes, called otherwise, Polipodie of the Oake, and Polipodie of the wall.)*
Polypus: m. *The fish Pourcontrell, called also, Manyfeet.*
Polypus chancreux. *The cankerous disease of the nose, commonly called,* Noli me tangere.
Polytric, & Polytrich. *Blacke Venus haire, true Venus haire, Maidens haire, our Ladies haire.*
Polytric doré. *Polytrichon, Gouldilocks, golden Maiden haire, golden Mosse, hairie Mosse.*
Polytric des Officines. *Wall Rue, Rue Maiden haire. white Maiden haire.*
Polytrichon, & Polytricon. *as* Polytric.
Pomardiere: f. *A Farme, or Orchard of apples.*
Poincirade: f. *Balme gentle, hearbe Balme.*
Pomelée: f. *Bearefoot, Setterwort, Settergrasse.*
Pommade: f. *Pomatum, or Pomata (an oyntment;) also, the Pommada, a tricke in vaulting.*
Pommé: m. *Cyder; drinke made of apples.*
Pomme: f. *An apple.*
Pomme d'Adam. *Looke* Adam.
Pomme d'amours. *The raging, or mad, apple; also, the amorous apple, apple of Loue, golden apple.*
Pomme d'anis. *A certaine delicate apple.*
Pomme Appie, ou d'Appie. *An apple thats like a Quince both in smell, and bignesse; and tearmed thus of* Appius Claudius, *who first brought the kind of it from* Peloponesus *vnto Rome.*
Pomme Armeniaque. *An Apricocke.*
Pomme de bois, ou de bosquet. *A Crab, or Wilding; also, the fruit of the Arbute, or Strawberrie tree.*
Pomme de capendu. *See* Capendu.
Pomme de chien. *The Mandrake apple.*
Pomme de claguet. *A firme, iuicie, faire-coloured, and tast-pleasing apple.*
Pomme de coing. *A Quince.*
Pomme de courpendu. *The Short-start, or Shortshanke; an excellent apple.*
Pomme de Cunoet. *A certaine apple, whereof there be two kinds; a sweet, and a tart, one.*
Pomme de Curtin. *A verie sweet yellow apple, whereof excellent Cyder is made.*
Pommes dorées. *Golden apples, amorous apples, apples of loue.*
Pomm' espineuse. *The thorne-apple, pricklie apple, apple of* Peru.
Pomme de belle femme. *The name of a beautifull, sappie, and luscious apple.*
Pomme de Gay. *A sweet apple somewhat bitter, and little bigger then a Wallnut.*
Pomme de Grenade. *A Pomegranet.*
Pomme d'Heroet. *A kind of yellow, and sweet apple, whereof good Cyder may be made.*
Pomme de S. Iean. *S. Johns apple; a kind of soone-ripe Sweeting.*
Pomme de maligre, ou malingre. *The Maligar apple; a sourish fruit.*
Pomme de merveilles. *The male Balsam apple, apple of Jerusalem, Baulme apple.*
Pomme nonnette. *A small apple thats ripe sooner then any other.*
Pomme d'or. *The golden apple, amorous apple, apple of Loue; the Quince hath also beene called,* Pomme d'or.
Pomme de Paradis. *Looke* Paradis.
Pomme de Peru. *The apple of* Peru; *the pricklie, or thorne-apple.*
Pomme poire. *A Peare-apple; a little russet apple; and (as some hold) a Pearemaine.*
Pomme rellet. *The name of a soure apple.*
Pomme de renette. *See* Renette.
Pomme de Rengelet. *A certaine yellow Sweeting.*
Pomme de rougelet. *A kind of soure apple.*
Pomme de rouveau. *A Redding, or Summer Goulding.*
Pomme de savon. *A washing Ball.*
Pomme sauvage. *A Crab, or Wilding.*
Pomme de senteurs. *A Pomander, or sweet Ball.*
Pomme terrestre. *The Mandrake apple.*
Chou à pommes. *A Cabbidge.* ¶Rab.
Pommé: m. ée: f. *Growne round, or like an apple.*
Pommeau: m. *The pommell of a sword, &c.*
Pommeau de la jambe. *The caulfe of the leg.*
Pommeau d'une tour. *The ball of a tower, the centre, or middle of the top thereof; that part whereon the weather-fane, or weather-cock is planted.*
Pommelaye: f. *as* Pomelée.
Pommelé: m. ée: f. *Daple, or dapled; also, round, or plumpe as an apple.*
Temps pommelé. *A curdled season, or skie, wherein the aßembled vapours appeare in thinne, and round flakes.*
Pommelée. *as* Pomelée.
Pommeler. *To grow round, or plumpe like an apple; also, to daple.*
Pommelette: f. *A little apple; also, a Daple.*
Pommelle: f. *The pommell of a sword, &c.*
Pommelu: m. uë: f. *Plumpe, or round, as an apple.*
Pommelure: f. *Plumpenesse, roundneße; also, daplenesse.*
Pommer. *To grow round, or apple-like.*
Pommeraye: f. *An Orchard, an Apple-yard.*
Pommette: f. *A little apple; also, the ball of the cheeke.*
La pommette du nez. *The tip, or end of the nose.*
Piece à pommette. *A little pleasant rowle in the mouth of a Bitt.*
Pommetté: m. ée: f. *Pommetie; (a tearme of Blason.)*
Pommeture: f. *Pommeture; or the being Pommetie.*
Pommeux: m. euse: f. *Full of apples.*
Pommier: m. *An Apple-tree.*
Pommier sauvage. *A Crab tree.*
Pomon. *Looke* Poulmon.
Pompe: f. *Pompe, state, solemnitie, maiestie, sumptuousneße, magnificence, ostentation; also, a Pumpe.*
'A pied de plomb, & de pompe. *With a slow, and statelie gate; or, as vnder* Plomb.
Pomper. *To pumpe.*

Pompes: f. *Armour, called Pullie-peeces, for the knees; also, Bosses.*

Pompette: f. *A pumple, or pimple on the nose, or chinne.*

Pompette d'imprimeur. *A Printers Pumpet-ball; the ball wherewith he beates, or layes Inke on, the Formes.*

Pompeusement. *Pompously, magnificently, solemnely, sumptuously, gorgiously.*

Pompeux: m. euse: f. *Pompous, magnificent, statelie, maiesticall; sumptuous, gorgious, glorious.*

Pompholige: f. *Nil; the light oare, or foyle of Brasse.*

Pompile. *A kind of Pourcontrell fish that swimmeth with her bellie vpwards; also, that kind of Tunnie which followeth ships while they are in the Mayne, and leaues them when they draw towards the shore.*

Pompon: m. *A Pumpion, or Melon.*

Pompon d'hyver. *Our ordinarie Winter Pumpion.*

Pompon succrin. *A Muske Melon.*

Pompon Turquin. *A kind of darke-greene Melon.*

Pomponne: f. *The longest, and smoothest kind of Pumpion.*

Ponant: m. *The West.*

Ponce. Pierre ponce. *A Pumeise stone.*

Ponceau: m. *A little bridge; also, Corne-rose, red Poppie, shadow Poppie.*

Poncel: m. *A little bridge.*

Poncer. *To smooth, polish, rub ouer, with a Pumeise stone.*

Ponceure: f. *A smoothing, polishing, rubbing ouer with a Pumeise stone.*

Poncille: f. *The Assyrian Citron; a fruit as big as two big Leymons; and of a verie good smell, but of a faint-sweet, or wallowish taste.*

Poncire: f. *A Pome-Citron.*

Ponçon: m. *Halfe a Tunne; or, as* Poinson.

Ponctuel: m. elle: f. *Punctuall, distinct, direct, exact.*

Ponctuellement. *Punctually, distinctly, point after point; directly, exactly, throughly.*

Ponderamment. *Ponderously, weightily, heauily.*

Pondereux: m. euse: f. *Ponderous, heauie, weightie, burthensome; massiue, substantiall; of great consequence.*

Ponderosité: f. *Ponderositie, or ponderousnesse, heauinesse, weightinesse, massiuenesse.*

Pondre. *To lay (egges.)*

Elle y peut bien pondre, mais elle n'y couvera pas. *She may soiourne there for a while, but she shall not continue long.*

Geline qui poind, & ne pond pas. *(Said of) an idle, vnprofitable, barren, curst, or scolding, wife.*

Il fait accroire que les lievres pondent, & font des oeufs; *(Applyable to a most notorious lyer;) Seeke* Lievre.

Pondu: m. uë: f. *Layed, as an egge.*

Poneau: m. *A close stoole.*

Ponent: m. *The West; also, the arse, tayle, bumme.*

Poneropole. *The Towne of the wicked.* ¶Rab.

Pongneor. *as* Piqueur; *(an old word.)*

Ponhete. *A kind of Vine.*

Ponneresse. Geline pon. *A laying Henne.*

Ponneuse. *as* Ponneresse.

Pont: m. *A Bridge.*

Pont aux asnes. C'est le pont aux asnes. *(Applyable when such as are ignorant of the true reason, or cause of things, impute them to witchcraft, fortune, &c,) a shift, euasion, helpe at a pinch, for a dunce.*

Pont aux asnes de Logique. *The conuersion of Propositions.* ¶Rab.

Pont de corde. *The netting, or close fight, of a Ship of warre.*

Pont de Gournay. *See* Gournay.

Pont levis. *A draw-bridge.*

Conscience à pont levis. *A verie large conscience.*

Soulier à pont levis. *A shooe hauing a Polonian, or high-raised, heele.*

Pont volant. *The ladder of a ship; the bridge, or ladder, whereby men get aboord her.*

En pont, en planche, & en riviere, vallet devant, maistre derriere: Prov. *Ore waters deepe, and bridges weake or hollow, the man must lead the way, the maister follow.*

Le temps renverse les ponts: Pro. *In time are bridges (all things) ouerthrowne.*

Vn fol dessus vn pont est vn tambour en la riviere. *A foole on a bridge is a drumme in a riuer; Looke* Tambour.

Pontage: m. *Bridge-worke, Bridge-making; also, Pontage, or Bridge-toll.*

Pontail: m. *as* Pont volant.

Pontanage: m. *Pontage; the toll taken for passage ouer a Bridge.*

Ponte: f. *A laying of egges.*

Ponté: m. ée: f. *Bridged; that hath a Bridge ouer it, or belonging to it.*

Pontenage. *as* Pontanage.

Ponthieu. *An Earledome in France, called thus because there be many Bridges in it.*

Pontif, & **Pontife**: m. *A (chiefe) Bishop, or Prelate; also, a Pontificall fellow.*

Pontifical: m. ale: f. *Pontificall, Prelate-like; lordlie, statelie, sumptuous.*

Pontificalement. *Pontifically, lordlily, stately, sumptuously.*

Pontificat: m. *A Prelateship, or Prelacie; a chiefe Bishopricke; the estate, function, or dignitie of a (chiefe) Bishop, or Prelate.*

Pontille: f. *A pricke, or little point.*

Pontique. *Ponticall, or of Pontus, a part of Asia; whence;*

Noix Pontique. *The red Filberd.*

Pontis: m. *A little Bridge.*

Ponton: m. *A Wherrie, or Ferrie-boat; also, a Stilling, or Gauntrie for Caske to stand on.*

Pontonnier: m. *A Ferrie-man.*

Ponts. *The name of a Towne in* Saintonge, *called so of the many Bridges about it.*

Pontueux: m. euse: f. *Bridgie, full of Bridges.*

Popelin: m. *A little finicall darling.*

Popelins. *Soft cakes made of fine flower, kneaded with milke, sweet butter, and yolkes of egges; and fashioned, and buttered, like our Welsh Barrapyclids.*

Popin: m. ine: f. *Spruce, neat, briske, trimme, fine; quaint, nice, daintie, prettie.*

Se **Popiner**. *To trimme, or tricke vp himselfe.*

Popisme: f. *The popping, or smacking sound wherewith Riders incourage, or cherish, their horses.*

Poplitée. *as* Poplitique.

Poplitique. *A large veine in the middle of the thigh; also, a sinew neere to the gartering place, and seruing to turne the leg inwards.*

Populace: f. *The rascall people, base multitude, meaner sort of the vulgar.*
Populaire: m. *The common people, the vulgar.*
Populaire: com. *Popular; people-fauouring, people-pleasing, people-wooing; also, belonging to the people.*
Populairement. *Popularly.*
Populeon. *Popilion, or Pompillion; an ointment made of blacke Poplar buds.*
Populeux: m. euse: f. *Populous, full of people.*
Populo: m. *A Roll, or List of the fees, or augmentation of fees, accruing to the King by the Chauncerie Seale; made, and kept monthly, by one of the 54 Secretaries, or Clarkes of that Court; also, a prettie plump-faced, and cherrie-cheekt boy; or a representation, or picture of such a one; whereupon demaunding how a mans children doe, they say,* Comment se portent vos petis populos?
Populosité: f. *Populositie, abundance of people.*
Populotier: m. *The Clarke of the Chauncerie, who, in his turne, is to make, and keepe the* Populo.
Popyle. *The fish Pourcontrell.* ¶Rab.
Porc: m. *A Porke, Hog, Swyne; also, Porke, or Swynes flesh; also, a hard-skaled sea-fish, resembling a Gurnard; also, as* Bernadet.
Porcs de Dieu. *Bishops, Abbots, and other Prelates, which haue great, and fat Benefices.*
Porc espic. *A Porcupine; See* Porc-espi.
Porcs du Roy. *Financiers, Exchequer men.*
Du porc salé. *Bakon, or Lard.*
Groing de porc. *The head, or vpper part of the shoulder-blade; also, the hearbe Dandelion, Priests Crowne, Piss-abed.*
Homme de porc, & de bœuf. *A clowne, boore, churle, carle; an vnmannerlie, grosse-headed, ill-nurtured hynde.*
C'est vn porc à l'auge. *He feeds like a Hog, or so excessiuely as he is readie to burst withall.*
S'escoutant parler comme vn porc qui pisse. *(In derision of a selfe-affecting Fop;) Looke* Parler.
Le porc a tout bon en soy fors que la merde: Pro. *(Yet is the dung of a Hog an excellent remedie for bloud-spitting; but it must first be eaten, fryed with sweet butter, and some of the bloudie spittle.)*
Porcausou. *Sowsed Hogs flesh.* ¶Rab.
Porceau: m. *A Hog, Porke, Swyne; Looke* Pourceau.
Porcelaine: f. *as* Pourcelaine.
Porcelet: m. *A Pig-hog, or young Hog.*
Porcelet de S.Anthoine. *A Cheslop, or Woodlowse.*
Porcelet farci. *A Pig roasted, or boyled with a pudding in his bellie.*
Porcelette: f. *A shell-fish, called otherwise* Pourcelaine; *also, a kind of little Sturgeon.*
Porc-espi: m. *A Porcupine.*
Porc-espi de mer. *The sea Porcupine; a certaine round fish armed all ouer with prickles.*
Porche: f. *A Porch.*
Porche. *In stead of* Pource; *(an old word.)*
Porchereau: m. *A sea-Hog.* ¶Rab.
Porcherie: f. *A Hogs-stye.*
Porchet: m. *A stake, or pole.*
Porchier: m. *A Hog-beard, or Swyne-beard.*
Porchin: m. ine: f. *Of a Hog, like a Hog; whence;*
Taisson porchin. *A Hog-badger; Looke* Taisson.
Porcille: f. *A sea-Hog.*
Porcin: m. ine: f. *Hoggish, of Hogs, belonging, or like, vnto Hogs.*
Bestes porcines. *Swyne, Hogs.*

Pain porcin. *The hearbe Sow-bread, Swynes-bread, Hogs-bread.*
Porcorau: m. *The mosse, or mossie hearbe, called Liuerwort.*
Pore: m. *A pore; Looke* Pores.
Poreau: m. *A wart; also, as* Cal; *or any corne, or hard skinne, comming by labor on the hands, or feet.*
Porée: f. *as* Porrée. *Beetes; also, pot-hearbes; and thence also, pottage made of Beetes, or with other hearbes.*
Femme lecheresse ne fera ja porée espaisse: Prov. *A lickorous houswife seldome makes thicke pottage.*
On ne fait pas de rien grasse porée: Prov. *Fat broth cannot be made of nothing.*
Pores: m. *Pores; the small, and inuisible holes in the skinne, through which the sweat, and vapours passe out of the bodie.*
Poreux: m. euse: f. *Poric, full of pores; also, feare-full.*
Porfil. *as* Pourfil.
Porfile: f. *The verie middle, or middle line of a mans face, considered from top to bottome; that part whereat a iust diuision may be made thereof.*
En porfile. *Side-wayes;* &, Face representée en porfile. *A halfe-faced, or side-faced, picture.*
Porfiler. *as* Pourfiler.
Porion: m. *The wild Bulbus, wild Onyon, Corne-Leeke, wild Leeke, Bulbine, Starre of Bethlem.*
Porosité: f. *Porinesse, the being full of pores.*
Porositez. *Pores.*
Porphire. *as* Porphyre.
Porphirion: m. *A certaine red-beaked, and long-legd bird, which in drinking seemes to bite the water.*
Porphyre. *Porphirie; a darke-red marble spotted with white; also, an East-Indian, toothlesse, white-headed, and purple-bodied Serpent, whose vomit is most venomous.*
Porque: f. *A Sow.*
Porque: com. *Hoggish; or, Sow-like.*
Porquet: m. *A Porket, or shote Pig; also, young Porke.*
Porquette: f. *A Pig, or young Porke.*
Porracé: m. ée: f. *Greene as a Leeke; of a Leeke; made like a Leeke.*
Porreau: m. *A Leeke; also, a Wart.*
Porreau de chien. *Dogs Leeke, wild Leeke, French Leeke, Leeke of the Vine.*
Porreau sectil, ou tondu. *The cut Leeke, maidens Leeke, blade Leeke, vnset Leeke.*
Porreau testu. *The headed or knobbed Leeke, set Leeke, vncut Leeke.*
Porreau de vigne. *The Leeke of the Vine, dogs Leeke, French Leeke.*
Petit porreau. *as* Porreau sectil.
Bourse liée avec fueilles de porreaux. *A purse thats readie, or easie, to be opened.*
Porrée: f. *The hearbe called Beet, or Beetes; also, as* Porée.
Porrée blanche. *The common white Beet.*
Porrée de chien. *as* Porreau de chien.
Porrée noire. *The blacke Beet; an hearbe, whose boyled root cures all manner of itches; and is good against the stinging of Serpents.*
Porrée de pré. *Hearbe Pyrola, Winter-greene.*
Porrée rouge. *The hearbe called Blite, or Blits; also, the red Beet, Romane Beet.*
Porrette: f. *Maidens Leeke, bladed Leeke, vnset Leeke.*
Vigne porrette. *as* Porreau de chien.

Porreux: m. euse: f. *Porie, full of pores.*
Porriere: f. *A bed of Leekes.*
Porrion. *as* Porion.
Port: m. *A Port, Hauen, or Harbour for Ships; also, carriage, bearing, or bringing; also, custome, fraight, or a fare payed for carriage; also, the carriage, behauior, or demeanour of a man; also, his port, or state; or, the fauour, or good opinion which he hath in the world.*
Maistre des **Ports.** *Looke* Maistre.
Par **port** d'armes. *Violently, in hostile manner, by force of armes, or by maine force.*
Nul vent ne fait pour celuy qui n'a point de **port** destiné: Prov. *No wind serues him that hath no certaine hauen.*
Portache. *as* Procace.
Portage: m. *Portage, carriage, or a carrying; also, the custome, toll, fraight, fare, or fee, payed for carriage.*
Portail: m. *A Portall for a dore.*
Portant: m. ante: f. *Carrying, bearing; also, wearing.*
Le fort **portant** le foible. *One with another, or one helping the other; good and bad, weake and strong, altogether.*
L'un **portant** l'autre. *The same.*
Portatif: m. iue: f. *Portatiue; also, wieldie, or liuelie of bodie.*
Iardin **portatif.** *A fruitfull garden.*
Livre **portatif.** *A pocket-booke.*
Portatisse. *Portatiue, portable, carryable.*
Port'-aubans: m. *Chaine-wales; peeces of wood nayled on both the outsides of a Ship, to keepe them from being worne, or galled by the Shrowdes.*
Porte: f. *A Port, or Gate; a great, or outward, doore; any entrance, or way to enter at; also, a hauther, or eye; also, the port of a sword-hilt.*
La **porte** des champs. *The backe-doore, or field-doore, of a countrey house.*
Droict de **porte**. *Gate-money; a dutie payed by the schollers of Paris at their admission into a Colledge.*
Fausse **porte.** *An inner gate, or doore; also, a posterne gate, or backe doore.*
Veine **porte.** *Looke* Veine.
Donner de la **porte** sur le nez à. *To exclude, shut a doore against, or shut out of doores.*
Tout cela est frappé à la **porte** d'un trespassé. *All thats but losse of time, or labour lost.*
Hardiment heurte à la **porte** qui bonne nouvelle apporte: Pro. *He that good tidings beares full boldly knocketh.*
Les derniers venus ferment les **portes**: Prov. *The last commer latches the doore, maketh all sure.*
Trop tost vient à la **porte** qui mauvaise nouvelle apporte: Prov. *Too soone arriues he that ill tidings hath.*
Porté: m. ée: f. *Carried, borne, conueyed; vpheld, sustained; indured; also, worne; also, hit; whence;*
Ce coup n'a pas **porté.** *This blow hath fayled, or missed.*
'A pied tout **porté**, pour. *Forward, readie, on his way, to.*
Il y est expressément **porté**, que. *There is expresse mention made, or charge giuen, of; thereby it is expressely meant, or signified, that.*
Tout cela s'estoit fort bien **porté**, iusques. *Was passing well handled, or managed; went verie well on, vntill.*

Porte-brandons. *Fierie, flaming, light; whence;*
Ciel **por.** *The starrie Welkin, the cleere Sky.*
Porte-chappe: m. *A Cope-wearer; a Priest, or one that by his place doth often weare a Cope; also, a feast-furnisher; one that hires out all manner of naperie and vessell, & all other prouision whatsoeuer (except victuals) fit for the setting out of a feast.*
Porte-ciel. *Heauen-bearing, Sky-vpholding; (An Epithete for* Atlas.)
Porte-colle. *as* Protecole.
Portée: f. *The burthen, or fruit of a womans wombe; the brood, or litter of a beast; also, the breeding, bearing, or bringing forth of young; also, wit, capacitie, vnderstanding; also, the state, qualitie, condition, or abilitie, of an estate, bodie, &c; also, power, or abilitie to requite; also, a certaine land-measure comprehending 12 cords (of 30 feet to the cord) and vsed most in Burgundie.*
La **portée** d'un Arquebuse. *The reach thereof; or, as farre as it will shoot; whence;*
Sous la **portée** de l'Arquebuse. *Within Caleeuer shot.*
Cela est cause de plus grande **portée.** *That causeth a greater increase of fruits, &c.*
Il n'a plus de sçavoir acquis que ce qu'il en faut pour sa **portée.** *He hath got no more skill then he needs.*
Portées. *The boughes which a Deere bruseth, or beareth downe, with his head in trauersing of thickets.*
Courir vn cerf sur les **portées.** *To pursue a Deere with nose aloft.*
Porte-escritoire: m. *A Notaries boy; one that serues but to carrie his pen and inkhorne after him.*
Port'-espée: f. *A Sword-bearer; one that carries a sword before, or after, another; also, a Bawdricke, or Hanger, for a sword.*
Porte-faix: m. *A Porter; Pedler; Burthen-bearer.*
Porte-flambeaux. Ciel **port.** *The starrie, flaming, or bright Sky.*
Porte-fleurs. *Flourishing, flower-bearing; whence;*
Element **porte-fleurs.** *The earth.*
Porte-fraise: m. *A Rebato, or supporter for a Ruffe; wrought, or imbrodered, and cut into diuers panes.*
Porte-guidon: m. *An Ensigne-bearer vnto a troope of men of Armes.*
Porte-harnois: m. *A Crosse; the crosse-like Pearch whereon an Armor is vsually hanged.*
Porte-haubant. *as* Port'-aubans.
Porte-manteau: m. *A Port-mantue, Cloake-bag, Male; also, the carrier of a Cloake, or a Cloake-bag-carrier.*
Porte-manteau du Roy. *The Kings Cloake-bag-bearer.*
Portement: m. *A carrying, bearing; wearing; supporting, vpholding; also, health, or liking.*
Porte-mors: m. *The cheeke-peece, or cheeke-band, of a Bridle.*
Portente: m. *A prodigious, or monstrous thing.*
Portenteux: m. euse: f. *Prodigious, monstrous, maruelous, astonishing, strange.*
Porte-panier: m. *A basket-carrier; also, a Pedler.*
Porte-parole. *A message-carrier betweene partie and partie.*
Port-peine: com. *Laborious, painefull, paines-taking.*
Porte-piece: f. *A Shoomakers Punch, or Punchion.*

Porte-poche. *A bag-bearer, poutch-bearer, or poke-bearer; he that carries the scrip, or wallet for a companie of beggers.*

Porte-poulet. *A bawde, or carrier of loue-messages.*

Porte-queuë. *A Trayne-bearer to a Prince.*

Porter. *To carrie, or beare; also, to weare; also, to breed, or bring forth; also, to suffer, abide, indure; also, to sustaine, support, vphold; also (at once) to raise, maintaine, and put forward, a doing horse; also (at Tennis) a ball to rise.*

Se porter bien. *To be in good health.*

Se porter bien en vn affaire. *To behaue, or bestirre himselfe well in a businesse.*

Porter son bois. Elle porte bien son bois. *Looke* Bois.

Porter vne chemise blanche à. *To giue a mornings camisado, or a cold pie for a breakfast, vnto; to rowse with a pox, raise out of bed with a vengeance.*

Porter coup. *To hit home, to attaine vnto that it was directed to, or meant for.*

Porter coup à la foy. *To falsifie a promise, or faith, giuen.*

Porter droict contre. *Directly to ayme at, or flye against; to direct it selfe, or goe leuell vnto.*

Porter à deux espaules. *Inconstantly to follow sometimes one, sometimes his enemie; or to be of both sides, but true vnto neither.*

Porter sur ses espaules. *Looke* Espaule.

Porter l'esponge sur. *To deface, blot, put out.*

Porter faux. Ce Ieu porte faux. *This Tennis-court is full of false bounds.*

Porter le flambeau. *Seeke* Flambeau.

Porter la foy. *To doe fealtie.*

Porter des fueilles au bois. *To bestow any thing on them that need it not; or of whom (therefore) he shall haue no thanks for it.*

Porter gré à. *To acknowledge a beholdingnesse vnto.*

Porter Iour. *To be transparent.*

Porter la marotte de. *To be the author, or commaunder of.*

Porter ombre. *To giue, yeeld, or cast a shadow.*

Porter son pacquet. *See* Pacquet.

Porter la paste au four. Il en porta la paste au four. *He bore the blame, or burthen of it; twas he that payed, or smarted, for it.*

Porter vertu. *To be of an excellent nature, or propertie; to haue much vertue in it.*

Ils n'en dirent plus que leurs instructions s'en portoyent. *They sayed no more of it then their instructions gaue them warrant for.*

Il n'est pas si fol qu'il en porte l' habit. *He is not so fond as one would take him for, as outwardly he seemes, or as one would thinke him to be by his outside.*

Qui rien ne porte rien ne luy chet: Prov. *He that carries naught lets nothing fall.*

Portereau: m. *A little, or lesse gate adioyning vnto a greater, for a Palace, or House of State; also, a floudgate, or kind of sluice, whereby the course of a Riuer is diuerted into a gut, on the one side thereof cut out, for the turning of some Mill, &c; also, the name of a street in the Suburbes of* Orleans.

Porte-roolle: m. *A prompter of one that makes an Oration, or acts a part, in publicke.*

Porte-sac. *as* Porte-poche.

Porte-semelle. *The vpper leather of a Pattin; which we now call a* Galoche, *though improperly; for the true* Galoche *(sayes* Nicot*) hath no leather belonging to it.*

Portestrieux. *The plate of a stirrup.*

Porte-tablettes. *A Pedlar; or one that carries Tablebookes, &c, to sell.*

Porteur: m. *A carrier, bearer; bringer, wearer.*

Porteurs de choesne. *Looke* Choesne.

Porteur de Rogatons. *One that carries the Popes Pardons vp and downe a countrey; also, a wandering, and vnlearned Preacher, who bearing about with him some three or foure Sermons in his pocket, and preaching them at seuerall places, gaineth an opinion of great learning among the vulgar.*

Croyez ce porteur. *(The contents, or conclusion of a letter of credit; but vsed sometimes in a contrarie sence for) beleeue the lyer.*

Porteure d'une femme. *A womans burthen, or childbearing.*

Portier: m. *A Porter.*

Portier: m. ere: f. *Carrying, bearing; whence,* Brebis portiere. *A bearing Ewe.*

Portiere: f. *A Porteresse, or woman Porter; also, the boot of a Coach, &c; also, a peece of Tapistrie, &c, hung before a doore; also, the female Salmon; Looke* Bortiere.

Portinal: m. *A Portall.*

Portion: f. *A portion, share, part, parcell, peece, deale, rate; measure, quantitie, proportion.*

Portioniste: m. *A Prebend in a Cathedrall Church.*

Portionné: m. ée: f. *Apportioned, rated, shared; measured out; also, stinted, or whose portion is layed out, or deliuered.*

Portionner. *To apportion, part, share, deale, measure, diuide, rate out.*

Portique: m. *An open Porch, Portall, or walking place before a house, couered ouer head by a roofe borne vp with pillars.*

Portiuncule: f. *An Indulgence obtained (as some report) by* S.Francis, *of the Virgin* Mary, *for the remission of all the sinnes of those, who* (en payant) *came in at one, and went out at another, doore of a Church dedicated vnto her in* Angiers.

Le Portoir des vignes. *The braunch that beares the grapes.*

Portoire: f. *Any thing that helpes to carry another thing; as a Voyder, Skep, Scuttle, Wheelebarrow, &c; and particularly, a vessell somewhat resembling a halfe Tub, wherein grapes be carried on horsebacke from a remote Vineyard.*

La portoire d'une coche. *The space of the doore of a Coach.*

Portoüoire. *A hand-barrow; or, as* Portoire.

Portüeux: m. euse: f. *Full of Ports; belonging vnto a Hauen.*

Portugaise: f. *A Portegue; a golden coyne worth about* iij l. x s. *sterl.*

Portugalle, & Portugaloise. *as* Portugaise.

Porture: f. *A carrying, bearing; wearing.*

La porture d'une brebis. *The little skinne, or filme, wherein a Lambe comes wrapped out of the Ewes bellie.*

Posade: f. *A lighting downe of birds; a laying downe of a burthen; a breathing, resting, or a resting place; also, a stop made by a horse, aduancing withall his foreparts twice, or thrice.*

Estre à la posade. *To pawse, to repose himselfe; to be still; or sit still.*

Pose: f. *A pawse, intermission, stop, ceasing; repose, resting.*

Posé: m. ée: f. *Put, set, layed, pight, placed, fixed, planted, scited, seated, situate; also, temperate, stayed, or settled in humor.*
Posé le cas. *Suppose, allow, put the case.*
Posemént: m. *A putting, setting, pitching, placing, seating, settling, planting.*
Posément. *Settledly, stayedly.*
Poser. *To put, pitch, place; to seat, settle, plant; to stay, or leane on; to set, or lay downe; also, a horse to stop, and aduaunce withall his fore-parts.*
Poser du passement. *To lay it flat;* Le poser à bord rond. *To lay it swelling, or so as no edge thereof can be seene.*
Position: f. *A position; or, as* Posement.
Posque: f. *A potion, or drinke made of vineger and water.*
Possedé: m. ée: f. *Possessed, had, held, enioyed, vsed, occupied.*
Posseder. *To possesse, haue, hold, vse, occupy, enioy.*
Possesseresse: f. *A possesseresse; a woman that possesses, holds, enioyes.*
Possesseur: m. *A possessor, holder, enioyer, vser, owner, of.*
Possesseur de bonne foy. *One that holds a thing by a iust title, as he thinkes.*
Possesseur de mauvaise foy. *A disseisor; one that violently, and wilfully keepes another man from his owne.*
Possesseuse. *as* Possesseresse.
Possession: f. *Possession, vse, occupation, enioyment of; also, wealth, substance, or land possessed.*
Possessoire: m. *A possession, or thing possessed.*
Possessoire: com. *Possessorie, of possession, by way of possession.*
Possibilité: f. *Possibilitie, likelihood.*
Possible: com. *Likelie, possible, that may be.*
Faire son possible. *To doe his vtmost indeauor, to doe as much as he can.*
Posson: m. *The quarter of a* Chopine; *a little measure for milke, veriuice, and vineger, not altogether so big as the quarter of our Pint.*
Poste: m. *A Poste, Currier, speedie messenger; also, a seruant that goes vp and downe about the businesses of Nunnes; also, a rakehell, or Colledge-seruant, thats euer gadding, or ietting abroad.*
Poste de mer. *A great, and swift fish, called in Latin* Dromas; *which name is also, by diuers Authors, giuen to all swift, raunging, and restlesse fishes, as the* Amie, *Bonito, Tunnie, &c.*
Poste: f. *Post, posting, the riding post; as also, the furniture that belongs vnto posting; also, a post, or great stake; also, a broad, and thicke pale, hauing a pike in the bottome, & a hole in the middle for a shot to play through; vsed in approaches vnto a breach.*
Gens de poste. *Yeomen,* Roturiers, *vnnoble vassalls or tenants, ignoble persons.*
'A poste. *Expressely, of set purpose, with premeditation, for the nonce.*
'A ma poste. *Vnto my liking, after my mind, according to my humor, euen as I would haue it.*
Posteau: m. *A poste, or beame.*
Postelé. *as* Poupelé.
Poster. *To post, speed, ride post, make post hast.*
Posteral. *See* Posterol.
Posteres. *The Posteriorums, or hinder parts.*
Posterieur: m. eure: f. *Posterior, hinder, latter, lag, succeeding; inferior.*
Posterité: f. *Posteritie, off-spring; they that are to come of, or will come after, vs.*
Posterol: m. *The red sea-Nettle; an ouglie, and imperfect sea-fish, not much vnlike to a mans bung-hole.*
Postes: f. *Big haile-shot for Herons, Geese, and other such great fowle.*
Posteux: m. euse: f. *Hastie, full of hast, in post hast.*
Posthume: com. *Borne after a fathers death.*
Postidate. *A Post-date.*
Postille: f. *A postill, glosse, compendious exposition.*
Postilleux: m. euse: f. *Much vsing, or louing, to ride post.*
Postillon: m. *A Postillon, Guide, Postes boy.*
Corrompu comme la fesse d'un postillon. *A false lad; one that knowes the world throughly; one that hath drunke of many waters, runne through many dangers; one that hath often passed the pikes.*
Postillonner. *To ride post.*
Postiquer. *To play the vagrant Impostor, wandering Iugler.*
Postiqueries: f. *Cousening sleights, iugling deuises, impostures, tricks of Legerdemaine.*
Postiqueur: m. *A wandering Impostor, a roguing Iugler; a vagrant cousener, cheater, deceiuer.*
Postposé: m. ée: f. *Postposed; set, or left, behind; neglected, omitted.*
Postposer. *To set, or leaue behind; to esteeme lesse, or make lesse account of; to neglect in comparison, omit in regard, of another.*
Postulation: f. *A demaund, suit, request, supplication; also, a complaint, or expostulation.*
Postulé: m. ée: f. *Demaunded, required, sued for; also, admitted, elected, adopted; also, ioyned in office, linked in companie, with.*
Postuler. *To sue, demaund, require; also, to plead, or argue at the Barre; also, to sue, accuse, or complaine of.*
Postules: f. *Wheales, powkes.*
Postuleux: m. euse: f *Full of wheales, or powkes.*
Posturable: com. *Sequestrable, &c; as in* Beste mise en posture.
Posture: f. *The posture, setting, or settling of the bodie in, or before, any action; and hence, the ward, or manner of lying or standing, vsed by fencers; also, the place wherein a horse carries his head, or creast, or the carriage of his head, or creast.*
Beste mise en posture. *Sequestred; left, or bestowed with one, who vndertakes to keepe it safe, and to produce, or present it in Court whensoeuer it shall be called for.*
Pot: m. *A Pot (of what fashion soeuer) is properly a generall name for any small vessell wherein wine, beere, water, &c, readie to be drunke is vsually put; (and yet the French apply it also vnto small vessels, wherein other liquors, and sometimes vnliquid things, are kept;) also, particularly, one of a certaine scantling (verie neere our Gallon;) for iust 400. of them doe make a* Queuë; *also, a round Caske, or head-peece without any creast.*
Pot à deux anses. *An equiuocation; a word, or matter whereof double construction may be made.*
Pot à confitures. *A Comfet-box.*
Pot à l'eau. *A water-pot; and (more particularly) a Lauer, or Yewer.*
Pot de Lion. *A Chafer.*
Pot à pisser. *A Iurdan, Chamber-pot, Pisse-pot.*
Pot à plume. *A feather-pot; an old pot whereinto the French (as we into an old tub) commonly put feathers; and hence the Prouerbe,* Vieil comme vn pot à plume.

Pot pourri. *A pot porride; a Spanish dish of many seuerall meates boyled, or stued together.*
Pot aux roses. *A misterie, secret, hidden matter; a cloake, or couer vnto many knaueries.*
Pot de la teste. *The scalpe, or skull.*
Pot au vin. *The head.* ¶Rab.
Pot de vin. *A pot-full of Wine; also, a reward giuen for good newes brought, lost goods restored, a bargaine well driuen, or in respect of any other acceptable seruice; also, a portion bestowed with a maid in marriage.*
'A pot,& à feu. *At bed and boord, at meat and meale, as one of the house; or, as all of one house; and hence;*
Vivre à pot,& à feu avec. *To keepe companie, haue societie, hold correspondencie, with.*
Aller à l'entour du pot. *To vse many circumstances, to goe about the bush; or, by circuit of words to insinuate that which one dares not plainely deliuer.*
Ils ne font qu'un pot,& vn feu. *They liue continually together.*
Deux pots au feu signifient feste, & deux femmes font la tempeste: Prov. *Two pots a feast presage, two women mickle rage.*
Tel pot tel couvercle: Pro. *Such pot such couer; like will to like, quoth the Diuell to the Collier.*
Il n'y a rien tel qu' un vieil pot à faire la bonne soupe: Pro. *Looke* Vieil.
Potable: com. *Potable, drinkable.*
Potage: m. *Pottage, porridge.*
Potage de la bite. *Beet pottage; also, the oyle of man; an oyle which a woman should not (vnlawfully) tast of.*
Pour tout potage. *When all is done, when all comes t'all; also, for all purposes.*
C'est vn vilain pour tout potage. *This is a notable rascall, a notorious villaine, a verier knaue there liues not.*
Bon gaignage fait bon potage: Prov. *See* Gaignage.
De mauvaise viande on ne sçait faire vn bon potage: Pro. *Ill stuffe will not afoord good worke.*
Potagé: m. ée: f. *Made pottage, reduced into pottage.*
Potager: m. *A by-place in a countrey house, in stead of a Larder, for the laying vp of raw, or cold meates; also, a porridge-bellie, or a great porridge-eater.*
Potager: m. ere: f. *Of, or belonging vnto, pottage.*
Herbes potageres. *Pot hearbes.*
Vie potagere. *Life sustained onely by pottage.*
Vis potagere. *A staire that leades vnto the Larder of a countrey house.*
Potager. *To make pottage; also, to haue in his power.*
Se potager. *To play the good husband, or giue himselfe wholly to husbandrie; to apply his businesse at home.*
Potagerie: f. *Hearbes, or any other stuffe whereof pottage is made.*
Potatif. *Pot-plying, tipling square.*
Pote: f. *The great sea-Nettle; an ouglie fish.* ¶Provenc.
Gens de pote. *as* Gens de poste.
Pote: com. *Clumpse, benummed, or swollen, with cold.*
Poté: m. ée: f. *Plumpe, or plumme, full-round.*
Potée: f. *Brasse, Copper, Tinne, Pewter, &c. burnt, or calcinated; also, a pot-full of any thing.*
Potein. *Lame, or defectiue in a limme, naturally.*
Potelé: m. ée: f. *Plumpe, full, fat, fleshie, plumme.*
Potelée: f. *Fulnesse, or plumpnesse of flesh.*
Potence: f. *A Gibbet; also, a Crutch for a lame man.*
Baston de potence. *The staffe whereat a Ring to be runne at bangeth.*
Potencé: m. ée: f. *Like, or belonging, to a Gibbet, or Crutch; In Blason, potencie; or, as in;*
Champaigne potencée. *A Barre Miere.*
Croix potencée. *A crosse Batune.*
Potentat: m. *A Potentate, great Lord, mightie Personage, powerfull man, in a State.*
Potentiel: m. elle: f. *Strong, forcible, powerfull in operation.*
Cautere potentiel. *A potentiall Cauter; any caustick medicine, or compound.*
Potentille: f. *Wild Tansie, Siluer weed.*
Poterie: f. *A pot-market; also, a Potters shop; also, a place wherein pots are made; also, pot-making.*
Poterne: f. *A Posterne, or posterne gate; a backe-doore to a Fort, &c.*
Potes. *A kind of shining fish made somewhat like a cap; it hath eight feet, and being handled any while, melts like Ice.*
Potestat: m. *A Potestat, principall Officer, chiefe Magistrate.*
Potie: f. *A knot in Woollen cloth; or, a rotten thread, or threads end, readie to fall from cloth.*
Potié. *as* Poupelé.
Potier: m. *A Potter, or Pot-maker.*
Potier d'estain. *A Pewterer.*
Potieux: m. euse: f. *Ouer-daintie, curious, queasie-stomacked, nice; also, peeuish, froward, wayward, pettish, hard to please, content with nothing that is offered, or set before, him.*
Potingues. *Drinking exploits.* ¶Rab.
Potion: f. *A potion; a Phisicall drinke, or drench.*
Potiron: m. *A Mushrome, or Toadstoole; also, a kind of Dolphin-like fish.*
Potonnier. *as* Pautonnier.
Pottée: f. *A potfull of; also, as* Potée.
Pottein. m. *Broken peeces of mettall, or of old vessels, mingled one with another.*
Pottelé. *as* Potelé.
Pottin: m. *Solder of mettall; or, as* Pottein.
Potus: m. *Phisicall potions.*
Pouac. *Faugh; an Interiection vsed when any filthie thing is shewed, or smelled.*
Poüacre. *A filthie scabbinesse on the nose, or about the muzzle of a Sheepe; Looke* Poacre; *also, a kind of Woodland fowle.*
Poüacre: com. *Sniuellie, snottie, rotten, filthie; one that, without respect of any presence, is euer spitting, spattering, or blowing his nose; and hence also, lither, lazie, sloathfull, idle.*
Pouallier. *as* Poallier.
Pouce. *Looke* Poulce.
Poucher. *as* Pocher.
Pouciniere. *Seeke* Poulsiniere.
Poucin: m. *A Chicken.*
Pouctau: m. *The wild Poppie, Corne-rose, red Cornerose.*
Poucyrade: f. *The hearbe called, Baulme.*
Poudre, & Poudroyer. *Looke* Pouldre, & Pouldroyer.
Poudrier: m. *A Gunpowder-maker; also, a dust-box.*
Poveau: m. *The panne of a Close-stoole.*
Pouëe: f. *The ridge of a bed in a Vineyard.*
Poüelle: f. *A Stoue, or Hot-house.*
Pouër. *To mount, ascend, goe vp; or, to hale as Barge-men doe against wind & tide; also, to pile, or heap vp; whence;*
Pouër la vigne. *To raise the beds of a Vineyard into ridges.*
Pouillard: m. arde: f. *Lowsie.*

Pouille : *A part of Naples, whose inhabitants are held verie dangerous in conuersation; whence the Prouerbe;* Compere de la Pouille couste, & despouille.

Blanc de Pouille. *Ceruse, or white Lead.*

Pouiller. *To lowse, to picke out lice, to wait, or looke into, a head, for lice.*

Pouillerie : f. *Lowsinesse; also, beggerie; sluttish, or nastie pouertie.*

Ce n'est que toute pouillerie. *There's no one good, nor faire peece; there's nought but trash, in all his stuffe.*

Pouilles : f. *Lice :* ¶Bourg.

Chanter, ou dire pouilles. *To raile, reproach, reuile, giue most filthie words.*

Pouilleux : m. euse : f. *Lowsie, full of lice; also, beggerlie, of small, or no, meanes.*

Herbe aux pouilleux. *Lice-bane, Lowse-wort, Lowsepowder, Stauesaker.*

Poul : m. *A lowse; also, the Ninmurder, a yellowish bird, and the smallest of birds.*

Poul de mer. *The sea Lowse; a fish thats no bigger then a beane.*

Herbe aux poulx. *as* Herbe aux pouilleux.

Poulaille : f. *Poultrie; Hennes, Chickens.*

Poulailler. *A Henne-house, or Henne-roost.*

Poulaillerie : f. *Poultrie.*

Poulaillier : m. *A Poulter; also, a breeder, or keeper of Poultrie.*

Poulain : m. *A fole, or coult; also, the rope wherewith wine is let downe into a seller; a pullie rope; also, a botch in the groine, a Winchester Goose.*

Pied de poulain. *Fole-foot, Coults-foot, Horse-foot, Hall-foot, (an hearbe.)*

Ce que poulain prend en dompture, il le maintient tant comme il dure : Prov. *The tricks a coult getteth at his first backing, will while he continueth neuer be lacking.*

Rien ne vaut poulain s'il ne rompt son lien : Prov. *The coult that breakes not his halter is not worth a halfepenie.*

Poulainant. *Foling, as a mare.*

Poulaine : f. *Whence;* Souliers à poulaine. *Old fashioned shooes, held on the feet by single latchets running ouerthwart th'instup, which otherwise were all open; also, those that had a fashion of long hookes sticking out at th'end of their toes.*

Ventre à la poulaine. *A gulching, or huge, bellie; a bellie as big as a tunne.*

Poulainement : m. *A foling.*

Poulainer. *(A mare) to fole.*

Poulce : m. *The thumbe.*

Le poulce du pied. *The great toe.*

Poulce, & event, ou vent. *The breadth of a thumbe giuen betweene euerie yard, in measuring.*

A poulce suant. *The same.*

Les poulces à la ceincture. *Idlely, sloathfully, carelesly.*

Mordre les poulces. *To bite his thumbes for anger.*

Poulcée : f. *An inch, or inch-measure; the breadth of a thumbe.*

Poulceon : m. *The 24 part of a* Chopine; *a verie small measure, seldome vsed except it be for the gaging of the little* Demi-sextier, *whereof it maketh a twelfth part.*

Poulcepied : m. *The Pourcontrell, Preke, or many-footed fish.*

Poulcier : m. *as* Poulcée.

Pouldre : f. *Powder, dust.*

Pouldre Agrippine. *Any meat that prouokes, or enables, vnto lust.*

Pouldre blanche. *A powder compounded of Ginger, Cinnamon, and Nutmegs; much in vse among Cookes.*

Pouldre de duc. *A powder made of Sugar and Cinnamon, & hauing (sometimes) other Aromaticall simples added vnto them.*

Pouldre à gripper. *Any luxurious, or lasciuious meat.*

Pouldre de Poussol. *A kind of sand gotte at Poussole, hard by Naples; & vsed in the cutting of Marbles.*

Pouldre rouge. *Precipitate; sublimed, or calcinated, Quickesiluer.*

Il iettera à tous les autres la pouldre aux yeux. *He will outstrip all his competitors, the victorie will without doubt be his; (metaphorically, from the swiftest runner in a sandie race, who to make his fellowes follow aloofe, casteth dust with his heeles into their enuious eyes.)*

Pouldré : m. ée : f. *Powdered, bedusted.*

Pouldrement : m. *A powdering; a turning into powder.*

Pouldrer. *To powder; dust, or bedust; to make, beat, or turne into; to season, sprinkle, or dredge with, powder, or dust.*

Pouldrette : f. *Fine powder, small dust.*

Temps de pouldrette. *The season wherein a husbandman breakes the clods of his plowed land.*

Pouldreux : m. euse : f. *Dustie, full of dust.*

Avoir le pieds pouldreux. *To be of a nimble or actiue constitution, a stragling or wandering disposition; said also of one who being in further debt then he hath will, or meanes, to come out of, playes, for the most part, least in sight.*

Pouldrier : m. *A dust-bag; also, a Gunpowder maker.*

Pouldriere : f. *Dust, or dustinesse.*

Pouldroyement : m. *A puluerising; or powdering; a reducing vnto dust, or into powder.*

Pouldroyer. *To puluerize; to make, or turne into powder, or dust.*

poule : f. *A Henne.*

Poule d'eau. *A Coot, Moorehenne, Fenducke.*

Poule griesche. *A Moorehenne; the henne of the Grice, or Mooregame.*

Poule d'Inde. *A Turkie henne.*

Poule Lombarde. *A Kentish henne, a great henne, a henne of the Game.*

Poule de mer. *A small-mouthed, sharpe-toothed, broad-scaled, little-eyed, rocke-fish; whose finnes bee transparent, and both they, and her whole bodie, powdered ouer with beautifull, and sundrie-coloured spots.*

La poule, & les poulsins. *The seuen starres.*

Cul de poule. *The tops of the fingers, and thumb ioyned, or closed together; also, a hard swelling on th'edge of a Fistula.*

Docte annicheur de poules. *An excellent Cotqueane.*

Courir la poule. *To forrage, ransacke, or rob countrey houses; (from the custome of rauening souldiers, who leaue not a Henne where they come.)*

Faire la poule. *To play the coward.*

Faire de ses oeufs poules. *Looke* Oeuf.

Iamais mauvaise poule ne le couva *He is of a gentle, or gentlemanlie humour; he hath no one iot of ill breeding in him.*

De poules, & de pauvreté on en est bien tost engé: Prov. *Pulleine, and pouertie are quickly increased.*

Le regnard est pris lasche les poules: Prov. *Looke* Regnard.

Le regnard presche aux poules: Pro. *(Sayed when a notable Impostor talks vnto, or treats with, sillie and ignorant people.)*

Par trop trotter la poule, & la femme se perdent facilement: Prov. *Women, and hennes, that gad oremuch, are quickly lost.*

Qui suit les poules apprend à grater la terre: Pro. *He that followes a henne soone learnes to scrape; imitation is, most commonly, too good a Schoolemistresse.*

Tel perd l'appareil d'vne poule à faute d'achepter pour vn liard d'espices: Prov. *Some by the sparing of a little cost, bereaue themselues of daintie sod, and rost.*

Poulemart: m. *A weapon like a Hanger.*

`A fil de poulemart. *With th'edge, or dint of the sword.*

Poulener. *as* Poulainer.

Poulenne. *See* Poulaine.

Poulet: m. *A chicken; also, a loue-letter, or loue-message.*

Veau mal cuict, & poulets cruds, font les cimitieres bossus: Prov. *Raw veale, and chickens, make swelling Churchyards.*

Poulette: f. *A pullet, or young henne.*

Poulie: f. *A pullie.*

Poulier: m. *A Poulter; also, a brood-house, henne-house, or henne-roost; also, as* Bicoque.

Poulinement: m. *A foling.*

Pouliner. *A mare to fole, or bring forth a coult.*

Poulion: m. *A little pullie.*

Pouliot: m. *Penniroyall, Pulial royall, pudding-grasse, Lurkydish.*

Pouliot de Iardin. *Garden Penniroyall, vpright Penniroyall.*

Pouliot de montaigne. *Puliall mountaine, hearbe Masticke, Horse-time.*

Pouliot sauvage. *Wild Penniroyall, Corn-mint, Corncalamint, stinking Calamint.*

Poullailler: m. *A Poulter, or keeper of pullaine; also, as* Poulailler.

Poullarde: f. *The Sea-henne; a fish; Looke* Poule de mer.

Poullart. bled poul. *S. Peters corne.*

Poullaze: f. *Th'Indian Rauen.*

Poulle: f. *Seeke* Poule.

Poullé. Bled poullé. *The wall Barlie, called S. Peters corne.*

Poullier. *as* Poulier.

Poullion: m. *A little pullie.*

Poulmelée: f. *Wild, or bastard, blacke Hellebore, called ordinarily, Beares-foot, Setterwort, and Settergrasse; and by some also, Lungwort.*

Poulmon: m. *The lights, or lungs.*

Poulmon de mer. *A certaine round, spungie, and transparent excrescence, or creature of the sea, which swimming aboue water is the signe of an approaching storme, and taken out of the water seemes dead; but cut into many peeces, they will stirre for two or three daies after.*

Herbe aux poulmons. *The hearbe called Sage of Bethlem, Sage of Ierusalem, spotted Comfrey, and by some also, Lungwort; also, the, the mosse called Lungwort; also, sea Lungwort, Oyster-greene.*

Batre à tout poulmon. *To pant exceedingly, to be almost out of breath.*

Il ne sçait sur quelle fueille de poulmon respirer. *He knowes not whether to addresse himselfe, or how to behaue himselfe; he knowes not what in the world to doe.*

Souffler à tous poulmons. *To blow with might and maine, or with all the force he hath.*

Poulmonnie: f. *The cough, or any infirmitie of the lungs.*

Poulpe: m. *as* Poupe: m. *also, the Pourcontrell, Pricke, or many-footed fish.*

Poulpe musqué. *A kind thereof, whose head yeelds a strong muskie sauor, and is therfore much hunted after by Lampreyes.*

Poulpe: f. *Pulpe; or as* Polpe.

Poulpelé. *Seeke* Poupelé.

Poulpeux: m. euse: f. *Pulpie, or full of pulpe; fleshie, brawnie, pithie.*

Poulpie: f. *The hearbe Purslane.*

Poulpied: m. *The same.*

Poulpitre: m. *A Lecterne, (high) Deske, or Pulpit; also, a Presse for bookes to stand in; also, a Stage, or part of a Theater wherein Players act; also, a roome for Musicians in th'vpper part of a Stage; also, a threshold, or ground-sill; or, as* Marche-pied.

Poulpre. *as* Pourpe.

Pouls: m. *The pulse; the beating, or motion of an Arterie; or th'Arterie so beating.*

Mettre au pouls failli. *To giue a period vnto his pulses beating; to bring to the last gaspe, or vnto the gates of death.*

Poulse: m. & f. *Looke* Pousse: m. & f.

Poulsé: m. ée: f. *Pushed, thrust, iustled, ioulted; inforced, compelled, violently put on; also, driuen, or beaten in; also, turned, as wine, &c.*

Le jeu de dames poulsées. *Draughts.*

Bien poulsé longuement chancelle: Prou. *He that is pushed soundly staggers long; men after blowes or losses great, are long ere they recouer.*

Poulse-avant: m. *Any thing that thrusts another forward; and (more particularly) an Ouerseer, and forwarder of a worke that requires hast.*

Ieu de poulse-avant. *Lecherie.*

Poulsée: f. *as* Poulcée; *also, as* Poulsement; *or as* Poussée.

Poulsement: m. *A pushing, thrusting; ioulting, violent putting on; a driuing, or beating in.*

Poulser. *To push, thrust; inforce, compell, or violently put, on; to driue, or beat in, or on; also, to iustle, or ioult; also, to turne, or be troubled, as wine, &c, by ioulting, &c.*

Poulse poulse. *(Words of incouragement) forward forward, on on.*

Poulser du coude. *Proudly, to shoulder, or elbow euerie one thats next him; or to attempt the displacing, or disappointing of others.*

Poulser a toute haleine. *Seeke* Haleine.

Poulser de sa reste. *Desperately to set his whole rest, or aduenture all; resolutely to imploy his best meanes, or vtmost indeuor.*

Poulser à la roué. *To further, or helpe forward, by all meanes possible.*

Poulser le temps à l'espaule. *To vse delayes; also, to driue off, or passe away, the time vainely; or as he may; or he knowes not, or cares not, how.*

Vn clou sert à poulser l'autre: Prov. *One nayle serues to driue out another.*

Poulsier, & Poulsiere. *as* Pousier, & Pousiere.
Poulsif: m. iue: f. *Pursie, short-winded, breathing with difficultie; also, broken-winded.*
Poulsin: m. *A chicken.*
La poule, & les poulsins. *as vnder* Poule.
Poulsiner. *To hatch, breed, or bring forth, chickens.*
Poulsiniere: f. *The seuen starres.*
Poultis: m. *A little gate, or doore, which ordinarily, accompanies a great one before, or belonging to, a draw-bridge, &c.*
Poultre: m. *A fole, or horse-coult.*
Poultre: f. *A fillie, or mare-coult; also, a beame; and (generally) any peece of timber, thats about a foot, or a foot and a halfe, square.*
Poulx. *as* Pouls.
Pounon. *Seeke* Poulmon.
Poupart: m. *An infant, or young child; also, a meacock, or milkesop; a tender sot that lookes to be alwayes fed with pap.*
Poupe: m. *as* Poulpe: m. *also, the cankerous, and painfull disease of the nose, called* Noli me tangere.
Poupe: f. *The teat of a woman; as also, the dug of a rauenous beast; also, as* Polpe; *also, as* Pouppe.
Poupes de chenilles. *Bunches, or clusters of Caterpillers.*
Poupeau: m. *A little teat, or dug.*
Poupée: f. *A babie; a puppet, or bable; also, the flax of a distaffe; or a distaffe-full of flax, &c.*
Enter en poupée. *To lodge a graffe within a slit made into the top of a stocke; and withall to hood it, as in* Enter en poupine; *Looke* Poupine.
Poupclé: m. ée: f. *Pithie, brawnie, strong, full of pulp; also, plumpe, fleshie, round, fat, well fed.*
Poupelin: m. *as* Popelin; *also, as* Poupon.
Poupetier: m. *A babe-maker, or puppet-maker.*
Poupette: f. *A little babie; puppet, bable.*
Poupier: m. ere: f. *Of, or belonging to, the poope of a ship.*
Vent poupier. *A full, or whole wind, at sea.*
Poupillons: m. *Little teats, or dugs.*
Poupin: m. ine: f. *as* Popin.
Poupine: f. *as* Pompon.
Poupine. *whence,* Enter en p. *as* Enter en poupée; *and to giue it a hood, or couering of straw.*
Poupinement. *Neatly, sprucely, briskly, quaintly, daintily.*
Pouple. *A Popler tree; Seeke* Peuple.
Poupon: m. *An infant, suckling, young babie; also, as* Pompon.
Pouppe: f. *The poope (or hinder part) of a ship.*
Pouppe de filace. *A distaffe-full of flax.*
Os de la pouppe. *Looke* Os.
Avoir vent en pouppe. *To proceed with full sayles; to haue prosperous, or speedie successe in all affaires.*
Pouppée. *as* Poupée.
Poupper. *To dandle, feddle, cocker, cherish much.*
Pour. *(In composition, giuing a word the greater energie) signifies, for, as, as for; on, vpon; because, considering, in respect of; as good, or as much as; in stead, in lieu; or in defence, of; (sometimes) also, against; whence;*
Tous ces charmes se trouverent inutiles pour luy.
Pour estre. *By being; because it is.*
Pour le plus. *At the most.*
Pour vous encore 2 solz. *(in bargaining) Ile haue but two shillings more of you; or, you shall haue it for two shillings more.*
Cette façon estoit nouvelle pour luy. *Was new vnto him.*

Pourbondir. *To bound, leape, or iumpe ouer; also, to manage, or praunce a horse; to make him leape, or bound.*
Pourbouiller. *To parboile throughly.*
Pource: m. *The game called otherwise* Triquetrac.
Pource. *Because, for that cause, therefore.*
Pourceau: m. *A porke, swine, hog.*
Pourceau de mer. *A Sea-hog; a fish that something resembles the land hog, and loues to wallow in mud, as th'other in mire.*
Champignon de pourceau. *The hogs Mushrome, or swines Mushrome; the white, or yellowish Mushrome thats good (if any) to be eaten.*
Fenouil de pourceau. *Hogs Fennell, sow Fennell, Sulpherwort, Brimstonwort.*
Pain de pourceau. *Hogs bread, swines bread, sow bread.*
Queuë de pourceau. *as* Fenouil de pourceau; *and called also (as it) Horestrong, and Horestrange.*
Vin de pourceau. *Looke* Vin.
Gras comme vn pourceau. *As fat as a (frank-fed) hog.*
Semer des roses aux pourceaux. *To throw pearle before swine; to bestow, or cast away excellent things, vpon filthie, sottish, and vnworthie people.*
Pourceau gras rompt sa soute: Prov. *The well-fed hog breakes ope his stie.*
On ne doit pas à gras pourceau le cul oindre: Prov. *We should not grease a fat hog in the taile.*
Reliques sont bien perduës entre pieds de pourceaux: Prov. *Pretious things, in vnworthie hands, are quickly lost; (Others may interpret it otherwise.)*
Si truye forfaict les pourceaux le souffrent: Prov. *Pigs come to lugs for scathe done by the sow.*
Pourcelaine: f. *The Purple-fish; also, the sea Snayle, or Venus shell; (a shell-fish made somewhat like a horne;) also, the hearbe Purslane; whence;*
Pourcelaine cultivée. *Garden Purslane; tame Purslane.*
Pourcelaine de mer. *Sea Purslane.*
Pourcelet: m. *A young, or small hog, a pig-hog; See* Porcelet.
Pourchaille: f. *The hearbe Purslane.*
Pourchas: m. *Eager pursuit, earnest chace after; diligent solicitation, or vehement following, of a matter.*
Pourchasser. *Eagerly to pursue, follow, prosecute, solicite; instantly to seeke, purchase, procure, compasse.*
Qui plus despend qu'il ne pourchasse, il ne luy faut point de besace: Prov. *He that spends more then he gets, needs not a bag, (but a bable.)*
Povre: com. *Poore, needie, bare, beggerlie, penurious; defectiue, scantie, wanting, lacking, hauing but little; also, wretched, miserable, vnfortunate, vnhappie.*
`A povre coeur petit souhait: Pro. *An humble heart breedes homelie wishes.*
`A povres gens menue monnoye: Prov. *Small money satisfies, or serues, the needie.*
Au povre vn oeuf vaut vn boeuf: Prov. *An egge's as much to a poore man as an Oxe.*
Enfans sont richesses de povres gens: Prov. *Looke* Enfans.
Il est povre qui de Dieu est hay: Prov. *Wretched is he who is abhord of God.*
Il est bien povre qui ne voit goutte: Prov. *He that sees nothing 's poore ynough.*
Il n'est si grand despit que de povre orgueilleux: Prov. *The spight of a proud begger is vnmatchable.*

Il n'est orgueil que de povre enrichi: Prov. *Th'inriched beggers pride's without compare.*
La vache du riche velle souvent, celle de povre avorte: Pro. *Looke* Riche.
Le loup emporte le veau du povre: Prov. *Poore men are easily oppressed, vsually preyed on.*
Qui sçauroit les avantures il ne seroit iamais povre: Pro. *(We say) if a man knew when it would raine, he would make hay in faire weather.*
Tant de povres ne sont pas bons à vn huis: Prov. *Many beggers at one doore hinder themselues, & trouble others.*
Povrement. *Poorely, needily, barely, beggerly; miserably, wretchedly; simply.*
Povret: m. ette: f. *A wretch, poore soule, poore snake; or somewhat poore, not too rich, not troubled with abundance, or superfluitie; that hath but from hand to mouth.*
Povreté: f. *Pouertie, penurie, beggerie, barenesse, need, necessitie, want.*
De grasse cuisine povreté s'avoisine: Prov. *Pouertie gets her a house neere prodigalitie; a fat kitchin, and a leane purse grow quickly neighbours.*
De poules, & de povreté on en est bien tost engé: Prov. *Looke* Poule.
En grande povreté n'y a pas grande loyaulté: Prov. *In great pouertie there's no great loyaltie.*
Si jeunesse sçavoit, & vieillesse pouvoit, iamais povreté n'auroit: Prov. *If age had strength, and youth experience, none could for want alledge one iust pretence.*
Pourfendre. *To cleaue through.*
Pourfendu: m. uë: f. *Cleft through.*
Pourfier. *To affirme boldly, assure cōfidently, maintaine, or stand in, peremptorily.*
Pourfil d'un homme. *A mans feature, proportion, shape, outward lineaments; or most properly, the verie middle, or middle line of his face.*
Le pourfil d'une pierre precieuse. *The surface, or superficies thereof.*
En pourfil. *Sidewayes; whence;* visage en pourfil. *as vnder* Porfile.
Pourfiler d'or. *To purfle, tinsell, or ouercast with gold thread, &c.*
Pourfileure, & Pourfilure: f. *Purfling; a purfling lace, or worke; baudkin-worke; tinselling.*
Pourfit. *See* Profit.
Pourfiterolle: f. *A cake baked vnder hot imbers; Looke* Profiterolle.
Pourject. *Looke* Project.
Pourjecter. *as* Projecter.
Pourmenade: f. *A walke.*
Pourmené. *Walked.*
Pourmenée: f. *A walke, or walking.*
Pourmenement: m. *A walking.*
Pourmener. *To walke, to stirre vp and downe.*
Ie le pourmeneray. *I will course him, or keepe him stirring; I will find him worke, or bring him trouble, ynough.*
Pourmeneur: m. *A walker.*
Pourmeneuse: f. *A woman that walkes.*
Pourmenoir: m. *A walke, or walking place.*
Pourneant. *In vaine, for nothing, to no purpose.*
Pourparlé: m. *as* Pourparler: m.
Pourparlement: m. *A treating; a conferring, or talking about the compounding of a difference, or concluding of a bargaine.*
Pourparler: m. *A treatie; conference, talke, or speech had about an agreement to be made, or thing to bee done.*
Pourparler. *To treat, conferre, commune, or talke about matters to be accorded, or concluded.*
Pourpe: m. *The fish Pourcontrell, Preke, or Manyfeet.*
Pourpens: m. *Great thought, care, studie; serious cogitation.*
Pourpensé: m. ée: f. *Throughly considered, seriously thought of, exactly digested, reuolued, perpended, examined.*
Pourpenser. *To bethinke himselfe; throughly to thinke, or consider of; seriously to weigh, perpend, or digest, in the thoughts; exactly to recount, cast, examine, reuolue, in the mind.*
Qui bien veut parler bien doit pourpenser: Prov. *Seeke* Parler.
Pourpied; ou Poupier. *The hearbe Purslane.*
Pourplanté: m. ée: f. *Planted throughout, set all ouer.*
Pourplantement: m. *A planting, or setting all ouer.*
Pourplanter. *To plant, or set, all ouer, throughout, euerie where.*
Pourpoint: m. *A dublet.*
Pourpoint d'escaille. *A Corslet made of plates resembling scales.*
Courir les champs en pourpoint. *To play the madman.*
Doubler le moule du pourpoint. *To feed excessiuely.*
Il y laissa le moule du pourpoint. *See* Moule.
Mis en pourpoint. *Turnd into his dublet, made not worth a groat; robd or depriued of, despoyled or stript out of, all he hath.*
Pourpointerie: f. *A Dublet-makers shop; Dublet-makers row, the street wherein Dublet-makers dwell.*
Pourpointier: m. *A Dublet-maker.*
Pourpre: m. *Purple, purple colour; also, the Purple shell-fish; also, as* Pourpe; *also, the Purples, or a pestilent Ague which raises on the bodie certaine red, or purple spots; also, the Tokens; the blew spots appearing on a bodie thats mortally infected with, or dead of, the Plague.*
Le pourpre au soc, mort d'egal poix balance: Pro. *Death kills, or makes, alike, the rich, and poore.*
Pourpré: m. ée: f. *Of Purple, attired in Purple.*
Pourprendre. *To possesse wholly, to containe on euerie side or euerie way, to hold, or take vp all.*
Pourprins: m. inse: f. *Fully held, wholly contained, possest on euerie side, or euerie way.*
Pourprinse: f. *as* Pourpris.
Pourpris: m. *A close, or inclosure; or one inclosure of diuers roomes, or closes; the whole circuit, compasse, or continent of a ground, house, or place, consisting of many seuerall parcells, rooms, or peeces within one inclosure; whence;*
Le pourpris d'un manoir. *Comprehends all the out-roomes, Courts, Gardens, Orchards, Parke, Wood, or Warren, lying round about, or neere vnto, it; and being within one hedge, ditch, pale, or wall.*
Pourquerre. *To search, or seeke hard after; to solicite, or sue hard for; to procure, purchase, compasse, by all wayes, or meanes.*
Pourquines: f. *A kind of small blacke figs.*
Pourquis: m. ise: f. *Searched, or sought for throughly, sued hard for.*
Pourquoy? *Why? wherefore? whereof, or for what cause?*

Dire pourquoy. *To yeeld a reason, or shew a cause, for.*
Pourreau. *as* Porreau.
Pourri: m. ie: f. *Rotten, putrified; corrupted; tainted.*
Pot pourri. *Looke* Pot.
Le plus grand est le premier pourri: Prov. *The greatest man's the soonest rotten; (perhaps because the much ease, and ill diet, whereto he gaue himselfe, had filled his bodie with corruption.)*
Pierre en puis n'est pas pourrie: Prov. *Looke vnder* Pierre.
Pourrir. *To rot, putrifie; corrupt.*
Pourris: m. *A suppuration; a rotting; a turning out of bloud into healing.*
Pourrissable: com. *Soone rotting, likely to grow rotten.*
Pourrisseur: m. *A rotter; and, particularly, the spotted, broad-headed, small-necked, sharpe-mouthed, and short-tailed Serpent,* Seps; *no bigger then a little Viper; and called thus, because whatsoeuer part of the bodie is stung by her presently rots.*
Pourrissure. *as* Pourriture.
Pourriture: f. *Rottennesse, putrifaction, corruption.*
Poursaillir. *To leape out of, to bound ouer.*
Poursemé: m. ée: f *Sowed throughout, or all ouer.*
Poursemé de rougeolle. *Full of, spotted or powdered all ouer with, the Measells.*
Poursemer. *To sow throughout, or all ouer.*
Poursuir. *as* Poursuivre.
Poursuitte: f. *Pursuit, prosecution, earnest following, eager chase after; also, a suit, or proceeding, in Law.*
Poursuivable: com. *Pursuable.*
Poursuivant: m. *A pursuer, suitor, suer; the follower of a cause; also, a Wooer; (In auncient time a Maister of Requests was also tearmed so.)*
Poursuivant d'armes. *A Herauld extraordinarie, or young Herauld, a Batchler in the Art of Herauldrie; one thats like to be chosen when a place falls.*
Poursuivant: m. ante: f. *Pursuing, prosecuting, following, chasing after; suing for.*
Poursuivi: m. ie: f. *Pursued; followed, or chased hard; sued, prosecuted, persecuted.*
Sans estre poursuivi le meschant prend la fuite: Prov. *The wicked flies though no man follow him.*
Poursuivir. *To follow; also, to walke, or wander from countrey to countrey; (an old word.)*
Poursuivre. *To pursue, prosecute; persecute; eagerly to follow, or chase; earnestly to proceed in, or goe on with.*
Poursuivre à cor, & à cry. *To follow hard, or hatefully; to pursue with all extremitie; to make hue and crie after.*
Poursuivre sa poincte. *To follow his thrust; Looke* Poincte.
Poursuyr. *as* Poursuivir; *or* Poursuivre; *(an old word.)*
Poursuyvant, Poursuyvi, & Poursuyvre. *as* Poursuiuant, &c.
Pourtant. *Notwithstanding, yet for all that, howsoeuer.*
Pourtant que. *Forasmuch as, because that, seeing that.*
Pourtoir. *as* Portoir.
Pourtraict: m. *A pourtrait, image, picture, counterfeit, or draught of.*
Pourtraicture: f. *A pourtraiture; or as* Pourtraict.
Pourtraire. *To pourtray, draw, delineate, paint, counterfeit.*
Il pourtrait fort bien à son pere. *He is verie like his father, he resembles his father verie neere.*
Pourvende: f. *A Prebendrie, the place of a Prebend; (an old word.)*
Pourveoir. *Looke* Prouvoir.
Pourveu: m. *A patent, gift, grant; also, a Patentee, or one thats prouided (by Patent, &c,) of a Bishopricke, or Benefice.*
Pourveu: m. uë: f. *Priuiledged, &c; as* Prouveu.
Pourveu que. *So that, on condition that.*
Pourvoy: m. *A prouision, helpe, remedie.* (v.m.)
Pourvoyance: f. *Prouidence, forecast, foresight.*
Pourvoyant. *as* Prouvoyant.
Pourvoyeur: m. *A Prouidor, or Purueyor.*
Pourvoyeuse: f. *A Prouideresse, or Purueyeresse.*
Pousade: f. *as* Posade.
Poussade: f. *A push, thrust; iustle, ioult.*
Pousse: m. *as* Poussade; *whence;*
De plein pousse. *At once, at one push, thrust, or effort; wholly, all at one time, all together.*
Pousse: f. *Short wind, pursinesse; also, the hinder part of a sowes bellie, or that part whereon her hinder teats are.*
Pousse de bled. *The chaffe of corne.*
Poussé: m. ée: f. *Looke* Poulsé.
Pousse-avant. *as* Poulse-avant.
Poussée: f. *A push, or thrust forward; a putting, or violent wringing, in; also, a ioult, or iustle; also, as* Poulcée.
Poussement: m. *Looke* Poulsement.
Poussepied: m. *The fish Pourcontrell, Preke, or Manyfeet.*
Pousser. *To push, or thrust, &c, as* Poulser; *also, to breath, or fetch wind.*
Pousset de bronze. *The scalie dust that falls from brasse after it hath beene melted, or much beated.*
Pousier: m. *as* Pousiere.
Pousiere: f. *Thicke dust, or dustinesse.*
Qui se laisse jecter de la pousiere dans les yeux. *Looke* Iecter.
D'un sac à charbon ne peut sortir que de la poussiere noire: Prov. *Looke not for ought but coale-dust from coale-sackes; th'infected heart must vnsound stuffe belch out.*
Pousif: m. iue: f. *Pursie, short-winded; also, broken-winded.*
Poussoir: m. *An impulsarie Instrument, vsed by Chirurgians, for the forcing through of a forked arrow head: This Instrument is of two kinds; one hollow, tearmed* Poussoir femelle; *th'other masiue, tearmed* Poussoir masle, ou sourd.
Poussol. Pouldre de Poussol. *See* Pouldre.
Poussouër: m. *Th'yron pinne wherewith Joyners driue out woodden pegs.*
Poustaignade: f. *A brood, neast, or laying of egges; as many as a henne vses to set on at once:* ¶ Langued.
Pousteau: m. *as* Posteau.
Poustelé. *as* Poupelé.
Poutie, & Poutieux. *Looke* Potie, & Potieux.
Poutraiges: m. *Beames; postes.*
Poutre: f. *A beame; also, a fillie, or young mare.*
Poutre dentelée. *A harrow.*
Pouvoir: m. *Power, strength, abilitie, might, force.*
Le pouvoir de la verge. *The Libertie, or Precinct wherein a Sergeant may distraine, or arrest.*
Pouvoir. *To may, or can; to be able; to haue power, force, might, strength.*
Ie n'en puis mais. *I cannot help it, I cannot doe withall, I am no cause of it, it is not long of me.*

Il n'en peut plus. *He hath shot his frie, spent his powder, done the worst or most he can.*

Ainsi va qui mieux ne peut: Prov. *He must doe thus who can no better doe.*

Contre fortune nul ne peut: Pro. *Looke* Fortune.

Qui mieux ne peut à sa vieille retourne: Pro. *When all is done home's homelie.*

Qui quād il peut ne veut, quand il veut il ne peut: Prov. *He that will not when he may, when he would he shall haue nay.*

Tel fait le mieux qu'il peut qui ne fait chose qui vaille: Prov. *Some though they doe their best doe nothing well.*

Poux. *The pulse; Looke* Pouls.

Pouy. *(An Interiection of loathing;) fie.*

Pouyr. Tout n'y sçauroit pouyr. *All cannot goe into, all cannot be held or contained in, it:* ¶Parisien.

Pouzaranque. *A certaine instrument wherewith water is drawne out of garden wells.*

Poy. *as* Peu; *Little; (an old word.)*

Poyle: f. *A stoue.*

Poytois. *as* Putois.

Poyvrade: f. *A seasoning with, or sauce made of, Pepper.*

Poyvre: m. *Pepper.*

Poyvre aquatique. *Culerage, Arse-smart, water Pepper, or water Pepperwort; (an hearbe.)*

Poyvre blanc. *White Pepper; like the blacke in all things but colour, & commonnesse (for there comes not much of it hither;) Th'East Indians vse it in stead of Salt; See* Poyvre verd.

Poyvre d'Espagne. *as* Poyvre d'Inde.

Poyvre Ethiopic. *The husked, or codded Pepper, called in shops* Amomum, & vita longa.

Poyvre Indic, ou d'Inde. *Indian Pepper, Guinnie Pepper, Calecut Pepper; a little, flat, and yellowish seed.*

Poyvre long. *Long Pepper; a blackish, and Catkin-fashioned fruit, consisting of many graines close thrust together.*

Poyvre de montaigne. *Pepper of the Mount; the blacke, and hot-tasting berrie, or graine, of the shrub* Mezereon, *or Spurge-flax.*

Poyvre verd. *as* Poyvre blanc; *Some report that the ordinarie Pepper-berrie gathered while tis greene, &, vnripe, remaines euer white, and is that which we call white Pepper; yet Gerard seemes to allow it a peculiar plant.*

Poyvré: m. ée: f. *Peppered; seasoned with Pepper; also, tasting like Pepper.*

Herbe poyvrée. *Dittander, Dittanie, Pepperwort.*

Poyvrer. *To pepper; to season with Pepper.*

Poyvrette. *as* Poivrette; *Hearbe Gith; some also call so, the Guinnie Pepper plant.*

Poyvrier: m. *The Pepper plant.*

Practic: m. ique: f. *Practicall, practising.*

Practicien: m. *A practiser, or practicioner in Law; a Pleader, Counsellor, Aduocate, Atturney, or Proctor, allowed.*

Practique: f. *Practise, experience; the forme, stile, course of pleading, or of proceeding, in the Law.*

Practiqué: m. ée: f. *Practised, experimented, exercised, vsed, put in vse; dealt with, medled in; also, frequented, much haunted; also (in Architecture) contriued.*

Practiquer. *To practise, exercise, vse, or put in vre; to deale with, or meddle in; to bestow, or imploy himselfe in; also, to frequent, or haunt much; and (in Architecture) to contriue.*

Practiquer argent sur. *To raise, or make money of.*

Pragmaticien. *aunciently, as* Practicien, *at this day.*

Pragmatique Sanction. *Looke* Sanction.

Pragmatizer. *To practise, argue, plead; solicite.*

Praguerie: f. *(The name of) a meeting at* Clermont *betweene Charles the seuenth, & his sonne the Dolphin, who, together with others his subiects, had rebelled against him; Hence, any such league, faction, or ioynt rebellion of subiects against their Soueraigne.*

Prain. *Full-bagd, full-bellied, great with young; (a word applied onely to some kind of beasts.)*

A l'agneler verra on lesquelles sont prains: Prov. *Looke* Agneler.

Prairier: m. ere: f. *Of, or belonging to, a medow, or medow ground.*

Sergent prairier. *A medow-keeper; an Officer that lookes vnto medowes, and watches the hay growing in them.*

Prairie: f. *A medow, or medow ground.*

Pranchette: f. *A womans stirrup, or the plate she hath vnder her foot as she rides.*

Prangeler. *Cattell to chaw their cud in th'afternoone:* ¶Norm.

Praquerie. *as* Praguerie.

Prat. *as* Pré; *A medow.*

Pratique. *as* Practique; *also, a little lace:* ¶Blesien.

Prattique, & Prattiquer. *See* Practique, & Practiquer.

Pré: m. *A medow; a mead.*

La faulx paye les prez: Pro. *The Sithe giues meads their due.*

Toutesfois fut le pré tondu: Prov. *Yet was the medow mowen; Seeke* Toutesfois.

Preage: m. *Medowage; or, a freedome to put cattell into other mens medowes; whence;* Droict de preage; *Looke vnder* Droict.

Prealable: com. *Former, forerunning, before-going; first to be done, discussed, or thought of; which ought to proceed, or fore-goe the rest.*

Au prealable. *as* Prealablement.

Au prealable de. *After the rate of.*

Pour vn prealable. *First and formost; for a beginning, or first worke, before ought else be done, or talked of.*

Prealablement. *First, formost, first and formost, formerly, before all things, ere ought else be discussed, or done.*

Preallable, & Preallablement. *as* Prealable, & Prealablement.

Preallegué: m. ée: f. *Before alledged.*

Preambule: m. *A Preamble, Preface, Prologue.*

Preau: m. *A little medow; and (more particularly) a pleasant greene, greene close, or medow, lying neere a house, and seruing as well for a walke, as for other vses; also, a smooth greene seat vnder an arbor.*

Preaux. *The name of a certaine white, small, and sweet apple.*

Prebende: f. *A Prebendrie.*

Prebender en vn tripot. *To bandie at Tennis.*

Prebstre. *Looke* Prestre.

Precaire. par prec. *as* Precairement.

Precairement. *By intreatie, request, or desire; also, at another mans will and pleasure; or, onely for a while.*

Precaution: f. *A precaution; a forseeing, bewaring, or prouiding for beforehand; also, a premonition, or warning; also, the preuenting of a disease before it come, or the curing of it at first comming.*

Pre-

Precedé: m. ée: f. *Preceded; outstripped, gone or gotten before.*
Precedemment. *Precedently, formerly.*
Precedence: f. *Precedence, or precedencie; a foregoing; place before another.*
Precedent. *Precedent, foregoing, outpassing, outstripping, in ranke before another.*
Preceder. *To precede, surmount, surpasse, excell, goe before.*
Precellence: f. *Precellencie; an excelling, exceeding, surmounting, surpassing.*
Preceller. *To excell, exceed, surmount, surpaße.*
Precepte: m. *A precept, commaundement; lore, document, lesson, instruction; warning, admonition, aduisement.*
Precepteur: m. *A Teacher, Instructor, Tutor, Maister, Gouernour.*
Preception. *as* Precepte.
Preceptorizer. *To teach, instruct, tutorize it; gouerne.*
Preceptrice. *Teaching, instructing, lessoning, admonishing.*
Precesseur: m. *A foregoer; or, as* Predecesseur.
Prechanter. *To prechaunt it; to sing before the rest; or, to begin a song.*
Precieux. *Looke* Pretieux.
Precipitamment. *Headlong, all on a head, or with the head before, hastily, rashly, vnaduisedly.*
Precipitation: f. *Precipitation; headlong rashnesse, desperate hastinesse.*
Precipité: m. *Precipitate; the red, poisonous, or corroding powder of burned Quicksiluer.*
Precipice: m. *A daungerous cliffe, a steepe and vnsteadie place to goe on; a steepe downefall, a downe-right pich, or fall.*
Precipité: m. ée: f. *Precipitated, cast headlong; also, rash, headie, vnaduised.*
Argent vif precipité. *Reduced into Precipitate, burnt into red powder.*
Precipiter. *To precipitate; to throw, tumble, hurle, or cast downe, headlong; also, to deale rashly, proceed hastily, goe vnaduisedly to worke.*
Precipiteux: m. euse: f. *Headlong, foole-hardie, inconsiderate, harebraind, furious, violent, vnaduised, hastie, rash.*
Preciput: m. *Right of birth, eldership, the priuiledge belonging to the eldest.*
Precis: m. ise: f. *Strict, precise, curious, exact.*
Precisément. *Precisely, strictly, exactly, curiously.*
Preclare: com. *Most goodlie, right noble, verie singular, passing, excellent.*
Preclosture: f. *A close, or inclosed ground, lying before a mansion house; or as* Pourpris; *all the ground lying about a house.*
Precogiter. *To precogitate, premeditate, thinke of beforehand.*
Precognition: f. *A precognition; fore-knowledge, prenotion, or former notice, of.*
Precognoissance: f. *The same.*
Precognoistre. *To foreknow; know beforeband, get former notice, haue a foreknowledge of.*
Preconter. *To abate, or defaulke part of a summe due vpon a former reckoning.*
Precordial: m. ale: f. *Belonging to the midriffe; neere to, or about, the heart.*
Precordiaux: m. *The midriffe; also, the heart-strings, or filme of the heart; also, the parts which be neere, or about, the heart: also, the sides of the bellie vnder the ribs; and sometimes also, the whole numbles.*

Predecesseur: m. *A predecessor, auncestor, forefather; one that hath gone, or beene, before vs.*
Predestination: f. *Predestination, fore-appointment.*
Predestiné: m. ée: f. *Predestined, predestinated; ordained, or appointed beforehand, vnto.*
Predestinée fatale. *Fatall destinie; th'vnalterable destination, ordinance, decree, prouidence, or purpose of God.*
Predial: m. ale: f. *Consisting of, growing in, belonging vnto, medowes.*
Predicant. *as* Predicateur; *or a meane Preacher.*
Predicateur: m. *A Preacher, Teacher, Sermon-maker; a reporter, publisher; denouncer of things to come.*
Predication: f. *A Sermon, Preaching; publicke declaration, or denunciation.*
Prediction: f. *A prediction, foretelling, presaging, foresaying.*
Predire. *To foretell, foresay, presage, diuine, prophesie.*
Predisseur: m. *A foreteller, presager, diuine, prophesier.*
Predivination: f. *Diuination, presaging, foreghessing, foreseeing.*
Prediviner. *To diuine, presage, foresee, foreknow, ghesse at beforehand.*
Prée: f. *A medow.*
Préeminence: f. *Preheminence, prerogatiue.*
Préer. *To make medow, lay to medow, turne into medowes.*
Préeslu: m. uë: f. *Preelected, fore-chosen.*
Preface: f. *A Preface, Preamble, Prologue, fore-speech.*
Prefect: m. *A Prefect, President, Principall, or principall Officer.*
Preferable: com. *Preferrable; fit to be esteemed, or aduanced, before others.*
Preference: f. *Preferment, aduancement; account before, place aboue, others.*
Preferer. *To preferre; like better, esteeme aboue, place before, make more account of.*
Prefigé: m. ée: f. *Prefixed; fastened, set, or stucke before; appointed beforehand.*
Prefiger. *To prefix; to fasten, set, or sticke before; also, to appoint beforehand.*
Prefini: m. ie: f. *Determined, appointed, limited beforehand.*
Prefinir. *To determine, appoint, limit beforehand.*
Prefire. *To prefix; to limit, assigne, prescribe, appoint beforehand.*
Prefix. *Prefixed; limited, assigned, prescribed, appointed beforehand.*
Prefixion: f. *A prefixion; fore-appointment, prescription.*
Pregnamment. *Pregnantly; pithily, forcibly, strongly, liuely.*
Pregnant: m. ante: f. *Pregnant, pithie, ripe, liuelie, forcible, strong.*
Raisons pregnantes. *Plaine, apparent, important, or pressing reasons.*
Preguste: com. *A Taster, or Forestaller; one that takes th'essay of meats.*
Prehaster. *To precipitate; to hasten extreamely, or ouer-much.*
Preignant. *as* Pregnant.
Preigne: f. *Bagd, full, with young, with child.*
Preignement. *as* Pregnamment.
Preigneur: f. *A being full-bagd, great with child, or with young.*
Preïr. *To make Medowing of; to turne into Medow.*

Prejudice: m. *A preiudice; a (future) dammage, hurt, hinderance; also, as* Prejugé.
Prejudiciable: com. *Preiudiciall, dammageous, hurtfull, hindering.*
Prejudicier. *To preiudice, hurt, harme, hinder.*
Prejugé: m. *A preiudication, or fore-iudgement.*
Prejugé: m. ée: f. *Preiudicated, fore-iudged.*
Prejugement: m. *A fore-iudgement, or former iudgement; a case ruled in Law; a preiudication, or hurt done to a cause by a Precedent.*
Prejuger. *To preiudicate, preiudge, or foreiudge; to rule, or direct the opinion of Judges by a former iudgement.*
Prelasser. *To carrie himselfe grauely, portly, pompously, magnificently; to strout, or square it like a Prelate.*
Prelat: m. *A Prelate.*
Table de Prelat. *A bountifull, or well-furnished boord.*
Il iure comme vn Prelat. *(A Huguenots comparison.)*
Prelation: f. *Preferment before others in purchasing.*
Prelature: f. *A Prelature, or Prelateship.*
Prele: f. *Small Horse-taile, Tadpipes, naked Shaue-grasse.*
Prelingant: m. *A boasting asse, proud coxcombe, statelie gull.*
Prelude: m. *A Preludium, Preface, Preamble; a flourish before the matter; and in Musicke, voluntarie before a lesson, &c.*
Prematurité: f. *Prematuritie; hastie ripenesse, quicke ripening, forward or timelie growth.*
Premeditation: f. *Premeditation, forethought, or forethinking.*
Premedité: m. ée: f. *Premeditated, forethought of.*
Premediter. *To premeditate, forethinke of, or thinke of beforehand.*
Prémesse. *Looke* Presmesse.
Premices: m. *The first fruits of.*
Premie: m. *A recompence, guerdon, reward.*
Premier: m. ere: f. *Prime, first, formost; principall, chiefe, best.*
Il n'est que les premieres amours: Prov. *The first loue is the fastest, or faithfullest; no loue's like to the first.*
Premier. (Adverb.) *First, at first, the first time; also, before, or aboue, others.*
Premier que. *Rather then, before, or ere, that.*
Au premier. *First and formost; in or at the beginning.*
Tout premier. *First and formost; or, at the very first.*
Qui premier arrive au moulin, le premier doit mouldre: Pro. *He that first comes must first be serued.*
Qui premier prend ne s'en repent: Prov. *He that takes first his hast repents not.*
Premierement. *First; first and formost; with the first, at the verie beginning.*
Tout premierement. *At the verie first, before all other things.*
Premise: f. *A foreplacing, a setting before.*
Premonstré. freres de la prem. *An Order of Friers which weare white habites.*
Premonstré: m. ée: f. *Premonstrated, portended, foreshewed, told, or pointed at beforehand.*
Premourant: m. ante: f. *Dying first, or before another.*
Prenant: m. ante: f. *Taking; putting; apprehending; seising; accepting, receiuing; imbracing; vndertaking; holding, adhering vnto.*
Tenir par prenant. *Looke* Part-prenant.
Prendre. *To take; seise, catch, apprehend, snatch at; receiue, accept of; imbrace, vndertake; also, to cleaue, sticke, adhere, hold fast vnto; also, to put, or put on.*
Prendre barre sur. *To haue th'aduantage, or start of; to be beforehand with.*
Prendre de bec l'un l'autre. *To be at it, by the chaps, or with bitter words.*
Prendre bien. Il leur print bien que. *It was well for them, or they had good fortune, that.*
Prendre vn boeuf par les cornes. *Looke* Boeuf, *or* Corne.
Prendre le bonnet. *To passe Maister of Art.*
Prendre au bric. *To take at aduantage; or, to wrest a hastie word vnto a confession.*
Prendre le cas. pren le cas que. *Admit, suppose, allow we you, that.*
Prendre la Castille pour autruy. *To vndertake another mans quarell.*
Prendre chair. *To battle, get flesh, grow fat.*
Prendre la chevre. *To take in dudgeon, or snuffe; to take the pet, or pepper in the nose.*
Prendre la clef des champs. *To gaine, or take libertie, giue it selfe roome, flie or get out.*
Prendre conclusions. *as vnder* Conclusion.
Prendre le dueil. *To put on mourning apparell.*
Prendre expedition. *To renew a cause hanging, or suspended, in a Court; to bring, or procure a Reuiuor with an especiall request, or clause, for speedie dispatch.*
Prendre le frein aux dents. *To resist Authoritie, as a stubborne iade his rider; obstinately to proceed against all aduise.*
Prendre de gallico. *See* Gallico.
Prendre la garite. *To flie, runne away, slip or take into a lurking hole.*
Prendre de hergne. *A tree to be bred, or grow vp, of a sucker.*
Prendre vn homme ras par les cheveux. *Cruelly to exact, or foolishly to expect, from a man more then he is able to yeeld.*
Prendre honneur d'un escholier. *To get credit, win reputation, by a Scholler.*
Prendre iour pour faire. *To assigne, appoint, or set downe a day for the doing of.*
Prendre langue. *To gaine, or search for, intelligence; to inquire, or learne, how the world goeth.*
Prendre langue entr'eux. *To commune, or conferre together.*
Prendre lettres. *Is (at a certaine Card-play) to aske leaue to giue ouer an vndertaken game.*
Prendre le lievre au Tabourin. *See* Lievre.
Prendre les lions par les jubes. *To act great matters, and greatly hazard himselfe in th'acting.*
Prendre la Lune à belles dents. *To performe impossibilities.*
Prendre la main. *Looke* Main.
Prendre Mars pour Marthe; *And,* prendre Martin pour regnard. *To mistake (things that are somewhat alike) one for another.*
Prendre du pain benist de S. Cy. *To swill vp store of liquor; & sometimes (more generally) to drink wine.*
Prendre Paris pour Corbeil. *Foolishly to mistake most vnlike things, one for another; or greedily to take (in seeming to mistake) a greater for a lesse, thing.*
Prendre parti. *To deliberate, pause, aduise, or bethink himselfe, of.*
Prendre à partie. *To sue, implead, or call in question; to bend, set, or expose himselfe against.*
Prendre à ses perils. Ie le prens à mes perils. *At my perill be it; if it succeed not well I am content to beare the blame, or feele the smart, of it.*

Pren-

Prendre à perte de finance. *To take vp money on great interest, for the paiment of a debt for which lesse is due; Or, to take vp commodities at a high rate, and (for the making of present money) sell them againe dog cheape.*
Prendre pied à. *To reckon, or esteeme, of; build, or ground vpon; heed, or giue credit vnto; also, to be aggrieued, or discontented at; or take exceptions vnto.*
Prendre au pied levé. *To snap at, or take short, in words; to trip on a sudden, or at vnawares; to worke on all aduantages, or make the worst of things.*
Prendre son à poinct. *Look* à poinct, *vnder* Poinct.
Prendre vn rat par la queuë. *To cut a purse.*
Prendre à sa risque. Ie le prens à ma risque. *At my perill, with my danger be it.*
Prendre d'un sac deux moustures. *Looke* Mousture.
Prendre son sel. *To swill, quaffe, caroose; to take in his lading, or his liquor, to the full.*
Prendre à soy. *To assume, or attribute vnto himselfe.*
Prendre terre. *To goe forward, rid ground, get on apace; also, to land, or get ashore.*
Prendre le vent. *To goe vp the wind, to make that way which the wind comes; also, to wind, or follow by the wind, sent, or smell.*
Prendre sans verd. *To surprise, take napping, or at vnawares.*
Se prendre à. *To brawle, quarell, fall out, fight, or contend, with.*
Se prendre à, de. *To accuse, blame, lay the fault, cast th'imputation of, vpon.*
Se prendre de bon biais. Il ne s'y print pas de bon biais. *He tooke not a right course in the matter.*
Se prendre au nez. *To acknowledge a fault, &c; Looke* Nez.
Se prendre au bout du nez. vous vous pourrez prendre au bout du nez. *You may take your selfe by the nose end*; viz. *you are of the number; you are as guiltie, faultie, or farre in, as the rest.*
Ie n'en prendrois pas 10 escus. *I would not take 10 Crownes for it; also, I am as glad of it as if one had giuen me 10 Crownes.*
Il luy en prend comme à. *It fareth, or falleth out, with him as with; (The like is;)*
Il n'en prend pas de ces. *It fareth, or is, not with these.*
Il n'y prend ne n'y met. *It is not his, or for him; his part is least in it, he hath nothing to doe with it; also, he deales not in, or meddles not with, it.*
La pluye le prendra. *He will be well whitled, his cap will be set.*
C'est folie de se prendre aux fémes, & aux bestes: Pro. *T'is a madnes to meddle with women, and beasts.*
Qui a apprins à prendre sçait tard que c'est de rédre: Pro. *The more cunning, & forward one is to take, the more vnapt, & backward he is to restore; or, they that are apt to take are vnwilling to restore.*
Qui d'autruy prend subiect se rend: Prov. *He that receiues a fauour sells his libertie.*
Qui par tout va par tout prend: Prov. *He that goes through gaines throughly; or, he that goeth euerie way getteth euerie way.*
Qui premier prend ne s'en repent: Prov. *He that takes first hath the best; or (being a chuser) cannot repent him that he had it not.*
Qui peu seme peu prend: Prov. *He that sowes little reapes little.*
Vieil oiseau ne se prend à reths: Pro. *Th'old bird is not (easily) intrapped.*
Preneur: m. *A taker; catcher, seiser, apprehender; a receiuer, accepter; vndertaker, imbracer of.*
Preneur de pigeons. *A cheater, cousener, conicatcher*
Prenoncé: m. ée: f. *Foreshewed, foretold, or declared beforehand.*
Prenoncer. *To foreshew, foretell; denounce, or declare beforehand.*
Prent. *as* Preut.
Prenus. Et vbi prenus? *And where will you take, or find them?* ¶Rab.
Preoccupation: f. *A preoccupation, anticipation, preuention; an ouerreaching.*
Preoccupé: m. ée: f. *Preoccupated, anticipated, forestalled, preuented, or taken by preuention; (and hence) ouerraught.*
Preoccuper. *To preoccupate, anticipate, forestall, preuent, or take by preuention; and thence, to ouerreach.*
Preordonné: m. ée: f. *Preordinated, fore-ordained.*
Preordonner. *To preordinate, or fore-ordaine; to determine, enact, appoint, or set downe beforehand.*
Preparatif: m. *A preparatiue, or preparation.*
Preparation: f. *A preparation, or fore-prouision; a preparing; a making or setting of things in areadinesse.*
Preparatoire: m. *A preparatorie.*
Preparé: m. ée: f. *Prepared, made readie; prouided, or ordered beforehand.*
Preparement: m. *A preparing, or prouiding.*
Preparer. *To prepare; prouide; order, dight, make readie for.*
Prepatour: m. *A vineyard, or vine-close for the best, or choicest plants.*
Preplantement: m. *A fore-planting, or former setting.*
Preposer. *To preferre; to put, or set before.*
Preposition: f. *A Preposition (in Grammer;) also, a putting, or setting before.*
Prepostere: com. *Preposterous, vnorderlie, wrong, ouerthwart, altogether from the purpose.*
Preposterer. *To place or set preposterously; to disorder, or turne arsiuarsie; to put the cart before the horse.*
Prepuce: m. *The foreskin, or skin that couereth the head of the yard.*
Prerogative: f. *A prerogatiue, priuiledge, preheminence, great aduantage.*
Prés. *Neere, by, neere by, fast by, hard by, neere vpon, nigh vnto, welnigh, or, as it were touching.*
Au peu prés. *Welneere, almost, in a manner, within a little, or wanting but verie little.*
Au plus prés. *As neere as possibly can be.*
Estre au prés. *To be present, neere, close by, at hand.*
Nous sommes tousiours à vn denier prés. *There is neuer but a pennie winning or loosing betweene vs.*
Presage: m. *A presage, diuining, fore-ghessing, foreshewing; a notice, token, or argument of things to come.*
Presager. *as* Presagier.
Presagiant: m. ante: f. *Presaging, diuining, fore-ghessing, foreshewing, betokening future things.*
Presagier. *To presage, diuine, fore-ghesse, foreshew, foretell; to prophesie of things to come.*
Presagieux. *as* Presagiant; *or full of presages.*
Presbiteral: m. ale: f. *Presbiterall, Priestlie, belonging to a Priest.*
Presbitere: m. *A Parsonage, Vicarage, or Priests house.*
Presbtre. *A Priest; Looke* Prestre.
Presche: f. *A Sermon, Lecture; Preaching.*

Presché: m.ée: f. *Preached; also, preached vnto, instructed, exhorted.*

I'y ay presché sept ans pour vn caresme. *I know it well, or I am well knowne there.*

Il est tout presché qui n'a cure de bien faire: Pro. *He's told ynough that meanes not to doe well; or, too much he's preached to that cares not to be saued.*

Preschement: m. *A preaching; instructing; exhorting, persuading.*

Prescher. *To preach; to teach, instruct; exhort, persuade.*

Le regnard presche aux poules. *Wee say, the Fox preaches, beware your Geese.*

Prescheur: m. *A Preacher.*

De Prescheur qui se recommande en tout temps bon heur nous defende: Prov. *From Preachers who themselues commend, God, and good fortune vs defend.*

Prescience: f. *A prescience, or foreknowledge.*

Prescript: m.ipte: f. *Prescribed; limited, ordained, appointed; also, out of date, or so old, as it can hardly be renewed; whence;*

Vn procez peri, & prescript. *A suit which hath lien so long in the decke, or hung so long by the wall, as it is growne past following.*

Prescription: f. *A prescription; a long possession, or continuance in possession; the course or vse of a thing for a long time; also, a limitation, appointment, rule, or law.*

Prescrire. *To prescribe; to limit; assigne; appoint; ordaine.*

Les procez par escrit receus en la Cour ne se prescrivent point. *May at any time be reuiued, are neuer out of date, or outworne.*

Preseance: f. *Precedence, or precedencie; a first, or former place, ranke, seat; a sitting, or going, before others.*

Presence: f. *Presence; th'aspect, sight, or countenance.*

En la presence de. *Before, before the face, or eyes; in the verie eye of; he himselfe, &c, being by.*

Droict de presence. *Looke vnder* Droict.

Present: m. *A present, gift, offer.*

Present: m. ente: f. *Present; readie; in sight, in view; at hand, hard by; in presence, in his owne person.*

'A tous presents, & à venir. *To all that are and shall be; to all aliue and like to be.*

Par ces presentes. *By these presents, or present letters;* Par la presente. *By th'instant.*

Par le present. *Now, for this time, at this season.*

Presentation: f. *A presentation; a presenting, shewing, representing, setting forth.*

Les presentations. *Th'introductions, or inrollments of bills, or of acts, in a Court, before pleading.*

La presentation nostre Dame. *A holy-day kept by the Church of Rome on the 21 of Nouember.*

Presenté: m.ée: f. *Presented, represented; shewed, offered vnto view; also, offered.*

Presentement. *Presently, quickly, anon, at an instant, at hand, readily, speedily, suddenly.*

Presenter. *To present; represent; shew, bring into presence, offer vnto view; also, to offer.*

Il craint ce coup de telle façon qu'il ne s'y presente pas. *He neuer offers to stop it, or make a stroake at it.*

Presentiment: m. *A prouidence, or fore-feeling; a perceiuing, or vnderstanding of a thing beforehand.*

Preservatif: m. *A preseruatiue, defensiue; counterpoyson, antidote.*

Preservatif: m.iue: f. *Preseruatiue, preseruing.*

Preservé: m. ée: f. *Preserued, saued, kept, shielded, defended.*

Preserver. *To preserue, saue, keepe; defend, shield.*

Presidence: f. *A Presidencie; the place, or Office of a President.*

President: m. *A President; a Iudge in a Court of Parliament, or high Court.*

Le Premier President. *The Lord chiefe Iustice of one of those Courts.*

Presider. *To preside; gouerne, rule, sway, commaund ouer, sit in iudgement on.*

Presidial: m.ale: f. *Presidiall; belonging to a President, or to a Presidiall Court.*

Sieges presidiaux. *Seats, or Courts of Iustice (established about the yeare* 1551 *in diuers good townes of France) wherein ciuile causes (not exceeding* 250 l. Tour. *in money, or* 10 l. Tour. *in rent) are heard, and adiudged, Soueraignly, and without Appeales, or by prouision notwithstanding Appeales.*

Presidialement. *Presidially; within presidiall Iurisdiction, or compasse.*

Presidialité: f. *The Iurisdiction of a Presidiall Court.*

Presidiaux: m. *The Offices of a Presidiall Seat, or Court.*

Presignifié: m.ée: f. *Foreshewed, foretold, signified beforehand.*

Presle. *as* Prele.

Presme: m. *A neere, or next, kinsman by father and mother, or in a direct line.*

Presme d'Esmeraude. *A base, or course Emerauld; whereof there be diuers kinds, some transparent, as the greene Iasper; others of a thicke, or troubled mallow colour.*

Presmesse: f. *Neere kindred, the being next of kinne; or the priuiledge of recouerie, or disingaging of land, due vnto the next kinsman.*

Presomptif: m.iue: f. *Likelie, coniecturall; also, presumptuous.*

Presomption: f. *Presumption, saucinesse, malapertnesse, ouer-boldnesse; also, a presumption, suspition, guesse, coniecture, fore-conceit.*

Presomptions de droict. *Presumptions of right; or (as the Latine)* preiudicia iuris.

Presomptueux: m.euse: f. *Presumptuous; presuming; saucie, malapert, ouer-bold.*

Pres-prenant. Crediteur pr. *An hard, or strict creditor; one that will be satisfied to th'vtmost.*

Presque. *Welnigh, welneere, almost, in a manner; and (with a Negatiue) scarce, hardly.*

Pressant: m.ante: f. *Pressing, inforcing, earnest, vrgent; importunate, vnmannerlie, vnreasonable.*

Presse: f. *A prease, throng, or crowd of people; also, a Presse to Print, or presse things in; also, a kind of greenish, and hard Peach thats long in ripening, and whose pulpe (in some places of a ruddie colour) cleaues hard vnto the stone.*

Vin de grain est plus doux que n'est pas vin de presse: Prov. *Willing dueties are more gracious then such as be extorted.*

Pressé: m. ée: f. *Pressed; squeezed, crowded, thrust hard, or close together; strained, vrged; inforced, constrained; importuned, hard laied to.*

Pressé de son honneur. *That must vntrusse, that must immediately goe to it.*

C'est trop presse. *That is too great extremitie.*

Presseance: f. *Precedence, or precedencie.*

Pressement: m. *A pressing; squeezing, thrusting close together; a straining, vrging, inforcing; an importuning.*

Preser.

Presser. *To presse; to straine, squeeze, crowd, or thrust hard together; also, to vrge, inforce, constraine; be instant vpon, or earnest with; to importune, lay hard vnto; lie heauie on.*

Presser de quelque chose. *To accuse, appeale, or appeach of; to charge home with.*

Trop presser fait le cheval restif: Prov. *Too much vrging makes men desperate, or froward; extreame importuning makes mens friends their enemies.*

Par trop presser l'anguille on la perd: Prov. *Seeke* Anguille.

Pressier: m. *The tree that beares the Peach called* Presse.

Pressif: m. iue: f. *Pressiue; or as* Pressant.

Pressis: m. *Cullisses, or strained meats.*

Pressoir: m. *A presse, or pressor (wherewith the iuyce of things is out-squeezed;) also, the great, and double ventricle made by* Dura mater *in the hinder part of the head.*

De l'arbre d'un pressoir le manche d'un cernier: Prov. *(Like our) from a mill-post to a pudding-pricke.*

Pressoirage: m. *A pressing; also, presse-wine, or wine that is by pressing wrung out of the grapes, alreadie wel drained by that which hath distilled from them; and therefore cut all together before such pressing, thereby to get from them the rest of their moisture.*

Pressoiré: m. ée: f. *Pressed, wrung, strained, squeezed out.*

Pressoirée: f. *A pressing, straining, squeezing out; or the liquor so pressed.*

Pressoirer. *To presse, wring, straine, extort, or squeeze out iuyce, or liquor.*

Pressoireur: m. *A pressor, strainer, squeezer of iuyce, or liquor, out of things.*

Pressoirier: m. *as* Pressoireur.

Pressoüoir: m. *as* Pressoir; *also, a kind of frame wherwith, in France, they trie draught-horses before they buy them.*

Pressurage: m. *as* Pressoirage; *also, the fee thats due to th'owner, or giuen for th'vse, of a cōmon wine-presse.*

Pressure: f. *as* Presure; *also, a pressure, pressing, thrusting, or twindging in of.*

Pressuré: m. ée: f. *as* Pressoiré; *also, milked.*

Pressurer. *as* Pressoirer; *also, to milke a cow, &c.*

Pressurier: m. *A presser, or presse-man; one that works at a wine-presse.*

Visage de pressuirier. *A drunken; crimzon, or high-coloured, face.*

Prest: m. *A loane, or lending of money.*

Prest: m. Preste: f. *Prest, readie, full-dight, furnished, prepared, prouided; prompt, neere at hand; quick, nimble, fleet, wight.*

Prest cōme vn chandelier. *At hand quoth pickpurse.*

Il n'est pas prest de sortir, iusques. *(Threatningly) he is not like to come out, vntill.*

Tel est housé qui n'est pas prest: Pro. *Some, though they booted are, vnreadie are; Looke* Housé.

Viande d'ami est bien tost preste: Prov. *A friends repast is in a trice prepared.*

Prest. *(Aduerbially) as* Prestement.

Prestable: com. *Lendable, which may be lent.*

Prestance: f. *Worthinesse, noblenesse, excellencie, greatnesse; also, a presence, representation, or shew; whence;*

Vn hōme de belle prestance. *A comelie, or personable man; a man of a statelie, and gracefull behauiour.*

Prestation: f. *as* Prest; *a loane; also, a lending; and a paying, or yeelding of dueties, rents, or seruices.*

Presté: m. ée: f. *Lent, and thence, trusted, or let out to a day; also, yeelded, payed; giuen.*

Preste-charitez. *A detractor, or backbiter.*

Prestement. *Promptly, readily, quickly, incontinently, soone, out of hand.*

Prester. *To lend; also, to trust out, or sell vnto dayes; also, to yeeld, affoord, or giue; also, to yeeld, or giue back, as pliant, or soft things.*

Prester l'espaule à. *To helpe, assist, succour, support.*

Du temps qu'on se cachoit pour prester argent. *In th'auntient, and harmelesse age, when people had more care of the borrowers credit then of their owne securitie.*

Au prester Ange, au rendre Diable: Prov. *Some when they would borrow adore, but when they should pay abhorre, a man; The like is;*

Au prester cousin, au rendre fils de putain.

Qui preste à l'ami perd au double: Prov. *He that lends to his friend a double losse incurres.*

Prestere. *A tempest, or whirlewind.*

Prestesse: f. *Readinesse, promptnesse, diligence, quicknesse, nimblenesse.*

Presteur: m. *A lender; also, one that sells vpon trust.*

Presteux: m. euse: f. *Lending, putting out vnto loane.*

Prestiges: f. *Deceits, impostures, delusions, iugling or cousening tricks.*

Prestigiateur: m. *A Jugler, a cousening Inchaunter, a cheating Coniurer.*

Prestitué: m. ée: f. *Prescribed, limited, appointed vnto.*

Prestolant: m. *A Steward, or Ouerseer, a Bailiffe of the husbandrie, or ouer husbandmen; a Surueyor ouer a farme.*

Prest-oreille. *Attentiue, listening, or harkening, lending an eare vnto.*

Prestraille: f. *Bauld shauelings, paultrie Priests; or as;*

Prestraillerie. la p. *Priests; or th'Order of Priesthood; or the whole packe of scuruie Priests.*

Prestal: m. ale: f. *Priestlie, Priest-like, of or belonging vnto Priests.*

Prestre: m. *A Priest.*

Bonnet de prestre. *Spindle-tree, Prick-wood, Prick-timber.*

Coquille de prestre. *Chickweed.*

Couillon de prestre. *See* Couillon.

Couronne de prestre. *His shauen crowne; also, the hearbe Dandelion, Priests-crowne, Pissabed.*

Apres Pasques, & Rogation, fi de prestre, & d'oignon: Prov. *(Belike because in hot weather, which comes quickly after, they stinke both alike.)*

Apres la poire le vin, ou le prestre: Prov. *After a peare wine, or the Priest.*

Bon gré mal gré va la prestre au Sené: Prov. *as vnder* Gré.

Mestier n'avons d'hardi prestre: Prov. *We haue no need of a couragious Priest; valour's a needlesse vertue in a Church-man.*

Qui veut tenir nette maison il n'y faut prestre ny pigeon: Prov. *For (we say) Priests, and Pigeons make foule houses.*

Prestresse: f. *A she Priest; also, a Priests leyman, wench, or whore.*

Prestrise: f. *Priesthood; th'Order, Office, or place of a Priest.*

Prestrot: m. *A little Priest; a Curate, vnder Priest, or Chauntrie Priest; also, a little bird that somewhat resembles a Linnet,*

Presumé: m. ée: f. *Presumed, thought, weened, supposed, imagined.*

Presumer. *To presume, or thinke too well, of himselfe, to*

 arro-

arrogate, assume, or take on him, a great deale more then his due; to ouer-value his owne person, or parts; also, to presume, thinke, weene, imagine, coniecture, suppose.

Presupposé: m. ée: f. *Presupposed.*

Presupposer. *To presuppose; admit, put the case that; imagine, coniecture, weene before-hand.*

Presupposition: f. *A presupposition, or presupposall; an admitting; a coniecture, or weening.*

Presure: f. *The rennet wherewith milke, imployed in cheese-making, is curded.*

Pretendant: m. *One that stands, or sues, or seekes, for a place.*

Pretendant. *Pretending; claiming, challenging; ayming at, suing or putting in for; also, meaning, intending, seeming, making a shew of, giuing a colour for.*

Pretendre. *To pretend; lay claime to, aime at, sue, stand, lay or put in, for; also, to meane, seeme, intend, make a shew of, giue a colour for.*

Pretendre vne chose de son chef. *To deriue his right vnto a thing from the source, or originall thereof.*

Pretendu: m. *A thing for which a pretence, or pretext is made; or whereunto a claime, or challenge is layd; a thing pretended vnto, aimed at, stood for, hoped after.*

Pretendu: m. uë: f. *Pretended; sued, or stood for; wherevnto claime is made; also, intended, seeming, or wherof shew is made.*

Pretente: f. *A pretence; purpose, designement, proiect, intent.*

Preterit: m. ite: f. *Past, ouerpast, ouerslipped, gone, departed, expired.*

Pretermettre. *To pretermit, omit, ouerslip, ouerpasse, leaue, baulke, neglect; forget.*

Pretermis: m. ise: f. *Pretermitted, omitted, ouerpassed, ouerslipped; baulked, neglected.*

Pretermission: f. *A pretermission, omission, ouerpassing, baulking, neglect; forgetting.*

Preteur: m. *A Pretor; a Judge, or Officer of great authoritie among th'auncient Romans.*

Pretexte: m. *A pretext, pretence, couer, cloake, shadow, colour, shew, excuse, for.*

Pretieusement. *Preciously, sumptuously, excellently.*

Pretieux: m. euse: f. *Precious; of great value, much worth, high price; verie sumptuous, excellent, exceeding good.*

Pretoire: m. *The Pauilion, or house of a Pretor; also, the Court wherein he gaue audience to Suitors; also, his Jurisdiction, or the Precinct within which he might exercise it.*

Pretrot: m. *A little bird somewhat resembling a Linnet.*

Preu. *Looke* Preux.

Prevalence: f. *Is th'ouerplus, or that which remaines, of the price of land sold for the paiment of a debt.*

Prevaloir. *To preuaile, gaine, or be the better by; to receiue benefit, assistance, or succour, from; to make vse, or profit of.*

Prevaricateur: m. *A preuaricator, deceiuer, double dealer; a treacherous Atturney, Solicitor, or follower of a cause; one that pleads by couin, or collusion; or hath priuate intelligence with him against whom he pleads; generally, one that in all his proceedings digresseth from truth, reason, and honestie.*

Prevarication: f. *Preuarication; treacherie, double dealing, deceit; couin, collusion, or corruption in pleading; a treacherous continuing of intelligence with an aduersarie; a swaruing from truth, reason, and honestie.*

Prevariqué. *Preuaricated, colluded, treacherously followed, or handled.*

Prevariquer. *To preuaricate, plead by couin, proceed by collusion; to deceiue, deale doubly, or treacherously, with; to betray a cause, wherewith he is trusted, vnto the aduersarie; to swarue, or digresse from truth, and honestie.*

Preudefemme: f. *A chast, honest, modest, vertuous (graue, or discreet) Matron.*

Preudes gents. *Valiant, faithfull, honest persons.*

Preud'homme. *A valiant, hardie, couragious, also, a loyall, faithfull, honest, vertuous (also, a discreet) man; also, the hearbe Clarie.*

Preud'hommie: f. *Courage, valour, prowesse; loyaltie, faithfulnesse; honestie, sinceritie, integritie; good dealing, true meaning.*

Preud'hommier: m. ere: f. *Valiant, couragious; loyall, faithfull; honest, sincere.*

Preveil: m. *An ordinarie meeting of Spinsters, and Youngsters, at a certaine place, where they worke, and make merrie, together.*

Prevenant. *Preuenting, anticipating, outstripping, forestalling.*

Prevenement: m. *A preuenting, anticipating, outstripping, forestalling.*

Prevenir. *To preuent, outstrip, anticipate, preoccupate, forestall; also, to appeach, or call in question.*

Prevention: f. *A preuention, anticipation, preoccupation, forestallment.*

Condamner par prevention: viz. devant que le procez soit faict. *Before th'Indictment be drawne.*

Prevenu: m. *(Is in Law) a preuenting of whatsoeuer may be obiected.*

Prevenu: m. uë: f. *Preuented, outstripped, preoccupated, anticipated, forestalled; also, accused of, charged with, called in question for; whence;* Prevenu en Iustice. *Publickly appeached; called into a Court, or before a Judge.*

Preveu: m. euë: f. *Foreseene, fore-imagined, forecast, perceiued (also, prouided) beforehand.*

Prevoir. *To foresee; fore-imagine, forecast; perceiue a farre off, prouide beforehand; preuent what otherwise would follow.*

Prevost: m. *The Prouost, or President of a Colledge, or Cathedrall Church; also, a principall Magistrate, or Judge in a good towne; also, an vnder Judge of a Prouince; the Judge of a village; or the* Roturiers *proper Judge; (for such as the* Bailli, *and* Seneschal *are among Gentlemen, the* Prevost *is among Yeomen; whose wardships he disposeth of; whose differences he iudgeth of; and on whom (offending) he inflicteth punishments, or penalties; Looke* Prevosts des villes; *) also, an vnder Marshall, or Prouost Marshall.*

Prevost des amendes. *The Collector of all amerciaments, and small casuall rights due vnto the Lord of a Mannor; stiled thus to set a difference betweene him, and th'ordinarie Judge of the Mannor, who is called* Prevost, & Garde, de Iustice.

Prevost d'Eglise. *Is, in a Cathedrall Church, the Deane; or th'Officer which deliuers out victualls vnto the Canons. &c.*

Prevost fermier. *A countrey Prouost, or Officer, who leuies all amerciaments, tolls, & customes, and seises all waifes & strayes, within his Iurisdiction, either to his own vse (as in some places) or for his Lo. (as in the most.)*

Prevost forain. *Is (by the customes of* Senlis*) th'ordinarie Judge of the Prouince; & determines of all Actions reall, or personall; and hath vnder his Jurisdiction all the Churchmen, Gentlemen, Burguers, and others residing, or dwelling within his walke.*

Prevost,& garde de Iustice; *Looke in* Prevost des amendes; *or as*;

Prevost en garde. *A rurall Prouost, or Judge, that keepes either the Kings (inferior) Courts, or those of a Lord* Iusticier; *hath no benefit by any fines, escheates, or amerciaments; and is inferior in all respects vnto a* Bailli.

Prevost de l'hostel; *(Called now adaies,* Le grand Prevost de l'hostel du Roy) *the ordinarie Judge of the Kings houshold; sets rates vpon victualls, and sets downe orders for the gouernment of many other things (especially concerning whores, &c) in all (vnpriuiledged) places within six leagues of the Court.*

Prevost des Marchands à Paris. *The Lord Mayor of Paris; different from the Prouost of Iustice, who is called,* Le Prevost de Paris.

Prevost des Mareschaux. *A Prouost Marshall (who is often both Informer, Judge, and Executioner) punishes disorderlie Souldiors, Coyners, Free-booters, highway robbers, lazie rogues, or vagabonds, and such as weare forbidden weapons.*

Prevost des Monnoyes. *The Prouost of the Mint; the Iudge of controuersies arising by reason of the Mint, or among Mintmen.*

Prevost des Ordres (du Sainct Esprit, & de Sainct Michel;) *The Maister of the Ceremonies in either of the Orders of France; lookes that their Statutes be duly obserued; inquires diligently (and priuately) after their infringers, whom in sleight cases he admonisheth gently, but if their faults be great, he complaines vnto the King; he likewise makes a certificate of the death of euerie Knight, and causes the Clarke of the Order to register it.*

Prevost de Paris. *The ordinarie Iudge of differences betweene the citizens, and all others that reside within the iurisdiction of the* Chastelet *of Paris; the Gouernor generall of the* Police *both of that Towne, and of her seuen daughters (for which looke vnder the word* Fille;) *and of much greater authoritie in his gouernment then the Prouost of other Townes, who be inferior to the Baylifes and Seneschalls thereof.*

Prevost des Ribaulds; *Was in old time the Lieutenant of the* Roy des Ribaulds.

Prevost vicomtal. *The Iudge of a* Chastellenie; *or, as* Prevost en garde.

Prevosts des villes. *Rurall Prouosts, or Judges; are to be present at all Assises held by the* Baillis; *are Judges of the* Police, *take notice of the incorporate trades; and looke to the reparations of the Townes whereto they belong; they likewise receiue the oathes of all Vineyard-keepers; and in Towne-assemblies precede the* Conseillers *of that Iurisdiction, and if the Lieutenant of the Prouince be absent, euer preside; yet are they not to meddle with any causes belonging to the Kings Domaine,* Fiefs, *or* Hommages; *and for their negligence are punishable by the Baylifes.*

Le grand Prevost de France. *as* Prevost de l'Hostel.

Prevostable: com. *Subiect vnto the Iurisdiction of a Prouost, or vnto Marshall law.*

Prevostablement. *By Marshall law.*

Prevostaire: com. *Prouostall, of a Prouost; as a Prouost; subiect vnto the Iurisdiction of a Prouost; and, thence also, criminall.*

Prevostal: m. ale: f. *The same.*

Prevosté: m. *A Prouostship, or Presidentship; the Seat, or Court of a Prouost, or Marshall; also, the precincts, and iurisdiction thereof; also, all sorts of small casuall rights, accruing to a Lord* Iusticier *within his Territories.*

Droict de Prevosté. *The priuiledge of hauing a Prouost, or Marshall, for the keeping of Courts; and leuying of Waifes, Tolls, Estraits, and Amerciaments, &c; belongs to a Lord Baron, or Chattelain, that haue iurisdiction; In some places also, a Passage-toll or Throughtoll is tearmed thus.*

Les sept filles de la Prevosté de Paris. *Looke vnder the word* Fille.

Prevostel: m. elle: f. *as* Prevostaire.

Prevostere: com. *as* Prevostaire.

Prevoyance: f. *Prouidence, foresight, forecast.*

Preut. *First, or first of all.*

En preut, deux, trois, &c: *One, two, three, &c; or* Imprimis; *a word vsed in Inuentories, and Accompts.*

Preuve: f. *A proofe, tryall, essay, experiment, experience; also, reason alledged, authoritie shewed, euidence produced, or testimonie brought, for the proofe, or confirmation of a matter in question.*

'A preuve de marteau. *That will abide the hammering; thats right, sound, solide, good.*

'A la preuve l'on escorche l'asne: Prov. *By prouing, attempting, or laying the hands to, an Asse is flayed;* viz. *a difficultie is compassed; a difference compounded.*

Preux. *Hardie, doughtie, valiant, couragious, full of prowesse; also, loyall, faithfull, sincere, honest, vertuous, worthie; also, discreet, skilfull, readie.*

Les neuf preux. *The nine Worthies.*

Au fils de preux. *The Voice, or Cry of Heralds in honor of a young knight (sonne to a valiant, and worthie father) the first time he presents himselfe, as an assailant, in the Lists.*

Preyer: m. *A kind of Linnet that hath a long, or Larke-like, heele.*

Priant. *Praying, beseeching, requesting, intreating.*

Priapisme: m. *A lustlesse extention, or swelling of the yard.*

Prié: m. ée: f. *Prayed, besought, requested, intreated, desired.*

Priement: m. *A praying, beseeching, requesting, intreating, desiring.*

Prier. *To pray, beseech, intreat, request, implore, desire, craue or beg of, make humble suit vnto.*

Priez vilain, moins il fera: Pro. *The more y'intreat a clowne the lesse heele doe.*

Qui veut apprendre à prier aille souvent sur la mer: Prov. *Much danger breedes deuotion, feare of death teaches religion.*

Priere: f. *A prayer, supplication, intreatie, request, humble suit or desire.*

De mains vuides prieres vaines: Pro. *Emptie hands make idle supplications; he that giues nought, by prayer getteth naught.*

Prieur: m. *A Prior; the head of a Priorie.*

Prieuré: f. *A Priorie, or Fryerie.*

Prieure: f. *A Prioresse; the head of a Priorie of Nunnes.*

Prim: m. *as* Presme.

Prim: m. ime: f. *Prime, forward, or first, principall, chiefe, or soonest; also, as* Prin.

Prime Lune. *The first quarter, or the increase, of the Moone.*

Prim temps. *The Spring.*

Marjolaine prime. *Marierome gentle, sweet Marierome, fine Marierome; also (but lesse properly) Time.*

Filer prim. *To runne thinne, or by little and little.*

Ie veux tailler ma plume plus prime. *I will vse a*

more neat, fine, smooth, eloquent stile; my penne shall runne more glibly along.

Primace: f. *Primacie; excellencie; chiefe rule, highest estate, greatest authoritie; and particularly, an Ecclesiasticall dignitie, or commaund ouer all the Archbishops and Bishops of a Kingdome, or Prouince.*

Primat: m. *A Primat, or Metropolitan.*

Primauté: f. *as* Primace.

Prime. Le p. des chevaliers. *A prime Knight, the Paragon, or flower, of Knights.*

Prime: f. *Primero at Cards; also, the first houre of the day (in Summer at foure a clocke, in Winter at eight;) also, a small Goldsmithes weight, whereof 24 make but one graine.*

Soupes de prime. *Monasticall Browesse; cheese and bread put into pottage; or chopped Parseley strewed or layed together with the fat of the Beefe-pot, on the bread.*

Prime: com. *Thinne, slender, exile, small; also, as* Prim; *whence;*

Cheveux primes. *Smooth, or delicate haire.*

Prime. (Adverb.) *Primely, chiefely; forwardly, soonest, first.*

'A prime. *Whileare, but now, but euen now.*

Retournez vous au prime? *Came you backe no sooner? came you againe but now?*

Prime-barbe. *The downe, or mossie beard on a young mans chinne.*

Primement. *Chiefely, principally, expressely; also, thinly, narrowly; also, exactly, curiously.*

Primerain: m. aine: f. *Earlie, timelie, forward, that springeth, buddeth, or commeth forth with the first.*

Primeroge: com. *as* Primerain; *whence;*

Figues primeroges. *Starued figges, or the first figges that come vpon the tree, which being too forward, commonly thriue not.*

Primerouge. *as* Primeroge.

Primes. Or primes. *Now at the last, onely at this time, not before now, or but euen now.*

Prime-vere: f. *The Spring; also, the Primerose; also, a Cowslip.*

Primeur: f. *Smallnesse, thinnesse, exilitie, slendernesse; also, primenesse, perfection, excellencie; also, forwardnesse.*

Primices: f. *First fruits; the first fruits of the yeare; the firstlings of yearelie fruits.*

Primicial: m. ale: f. *Of, or belonging to, first fruits.*

Primitif: m. iue: f. *Primitiue, the first, which hath no beginning from another.*

Primogeniture: f. *Prime, or first birth; eldership, or the being eldest; the title of the eldest, or first-borne child.*

Primordial: m. ale: f. *Originall, of an off-spring, first rising, beginning from.*

Prin. *Thinne, subtill, piercing, sharpe.*

Prince: m. *A Prince, or Chiefe; a Monarch, Soueraigne, great Lord, great Potentate: Some good French Authors mention six kinds of Princes; the first they stile* Simples Princes; *no better then Magistrates, or Officers of Soueraigntie; such as were the Patriarchs and Judges among the Iewes; the Kings of Lacedemonia; the auncient Kings of France; the first Kings, and (at least in apparance) the first Emperours, of Rome; the moderne Dukes of Venice; and (in* Bodins *opinion) the Emperors of Germanie: The second,* Princes subjects; *owners of Soueraigntie within their owne countries, and yet subiect (one way or other) vnto greater Princes; of which ranke are the Kings protected by the great Turke; those that liue vnder* Prester Iohn; *the ancient Princes of Italie while they acknowledged, and held of the Empire; the ancient Dukes and Earles of Fraunce, while they affoorded their Kings no more then a bare homage, and some small attendance in the warres; the moderne King of Bohemia, and Princes of the Empire: The third,* Princes Seigneurs; *which haue an absolute power ouer the persons, and propertie in the possessions, of their subiects; as had the foure first Monarchs of Assiria, Media, Persia, and Egypt; and as at this day the great Turke,* Prester Iohn, *the Muscouite, and some other such Tyrants haue: The fourth,* Princes Souverains *(more moderate, and commodious for mankind, then the former) enioy an absolute, but publike Soueraigntie, not (much) intermedling with the priuate; of which kind, the later Emperours of Rome, with those of Constantinople, were, and at this day the most of the Kings, and soueraigne Princes of Christendome, are: The fift,* Princes de race, ou du sang; viz. *the children, or off-spring of soueraigne Princes, who by their birth are capable of, or may come vnto, a Crowne; within which branch we may comprehend the eldest sonnes of soueraigne Kings; who not hauing any particular affectation, or accesse, of title by creation (as our Prince) or by donation (as the eldest sonne of France) are tearmed simply* Princes: *The last,* Princes, ou Seigneurs, de Principautez, *doe seeme to deriue their dignitie from certaine auncient, and powerfull vassalls of the Crowne; which hauing, in emulation of the Dukes and Earles of their time, incroached on all rights of Soueraigntie within their owne dominions, and wanting (what the others had) a Title to distinguish them from lesse, or lesse absolute, Lords, verie willingly tooke this vpon them: Since which time the Kings of France reuniting, by seuerall meanes, the Estates of these Vsurpers vnto the Crowne, yet haue beene pleased to continue the name in such of their fauourites as haue sued for it; And at this day some great Lords, which desire to be held Princes, are curious to procure one of their Townes to be made a* Principauté, *and afterwards bestow it, or (at least) the Title of it, on their eldest sonnes: But these are no true Princes, and therefore in all assemblies they be ranked beneath Earles.*

Ieux des princes. *Such sports as are delightfull, or pleasing, to those that vse them.*

Les princes se servent des hommes comme le laboureur des abeilles: Pro. viz. *First take their honey from them, and then smoother, or expell, them.*

Les princes tiennent tousiours leurs comptes, ils ne perdent iamais rien: Prov. *Princes are excellent reckoners, for they seldome loose ought.*

Les princes ne veulent point de servitudes limitez: Pro. *Princes will not be serued on conditions.*

Haine de prince signifie mort d'homme: Pro. *Hee's neere his death thats hated by his Prince.*

Princesse: f. *A Princesse.*

Principal: m. *The Principall, or Head of a Societie; a principall, chiefe, head man, or matter; also, the summe, chiefe knot, maine point, of a matter; also, the principall; the summe in question, or let out vnto vse.*

Principal: m. ale: f. *Principall, soueraigne, most speciall, chiefest, greatest, highest.*

Principalement. *Principally, chiefely, most especially.*

Principauté: f. *A Principalitie; the Estate, or Seat, of a Soueraigne Prince; also, an extraordinarie, and extrauagant Seignorie, bearing, rather then deseruing, the*

the name of this dignitie, and ranked betweene an Earledome, and Vicountie; (Looke in the later end of the word Prince.)

Principe: m. *A Principle, Maxime, ground of Art; also, a beginning, or a beginner.*

Principesque: com. *Princelie, royall, soueraigne.*

Principié: m. ée: f. *Begun, or in breeding.*

Principion: m. *A pettie Prince.*

Prinfief. Le Seigneur de p. *The Lord Paramount; or immediat Lord, of an inheritance charged with rent.*

Pringalle: f. *A fashion of warlike Engine vsed in old time.*

Pringert: m. *A kind of small bird.*

Prins: m. inse: f. *Taken; seised, &c;* Looke Pris.

Prinsault. De pr. *Presently, immediatly, suddainely, at an instant, at the first chop, effort, or iumpe; out of hand.*

Prinsautier: m. *A starter, a nimble iumper.*

Prinsautier: m. ere: f. *Suddaine, quicke, nimble, readie, instant, (quickly) present, at hand.*

Prinse: f. *A taking, seizing; a catching, or laying hold on; Looke* Prise.

Printaner. *To spring, or flourish as the Spring.*

Printanier: m. ere: f. *Earlie, of the Spring.*

Printemps: m. *The Spring, or Spring time.*

Priorité: f. *Prioritie, senioritie, precedencie, auncientnesse, eldership; a being, or going, before others.*

Pris: m. *The price, rate; value; accompt, respect, estimation; worth, of things; also, the prize, reward, or honour got by, kept for, or due vnto, the best deseruer in a Iusts, &c.*

'A pris d'argent. *For money.*

Au pris que. *Euer as.*

'A quelque pris qu'est le bled. *Whatsoeuer it cost me, how deerely soeuer I pay for it.*

Toute chose se vend au pris de l'oeil: Pro. *All things are sold at the price th' eye sets on them.*

Pris: m. ise: f. *Taken; seized, caught, apprehended, receiued, accepted of; imbraced, vndertaken; also, put, or put on.*

Corne prise. *Growne statelie, proud, intollerable.*

Eau prise, & vin pris. *Turned, or curdled; growne thicke, and dead withall.*

Homme bien pris. *Well set, well vnderlayed.*

Pris à coup perdu. *Gotten more by good hap then any great cunning.*

Pris à per & à couche. *Surprised, ouerraught, in danger, met with, euerie way.*

Pris comme le More. Looke More.

Pris du nez. *That hath the Murre, whose nose is stuffed, or stopped with cold.*

Cela a desia pris coup. *Hath alreadie gotten a speeding, or deadlie blow; is brought to that state, that it cannot long subsist.*

Elle a pris sa teste. *She is resolued to doe but what she list.*

Il luy a pris vne verruë. *The giddie worme bites him, the toy hath taken him in the head.*

Les plus rouges y sont pris. Looke Rouge.

Les plus rusez sont les premiers pris: Prov. *The craftiest are the soonest caught.*

Trop tard crie l'oiseau quand il est pris: Pro. *Mischiefes being in, complaints are out of date.*

Prisage: m. *A prisage, prising, praising, rating, valuing.*

Prise: f. *as* Prisage; *also, a taking, seizing; an arrest, or seisure; a catching, a laying hold, or hands on; also, a locke, or hold in wrastling; any aduantage; also, a pike, or quarrell; also, a bootie, or prize; also, the death, or fall of a hunted beast.*

Prise de marres. *A kind of penaltie for the non-payment of* Cens *at the day whereon they are due.*

Prise de paupieres. *The agglutination of the eye-lids; when they cleaue either together, or to the hornie, or coniunctiue membrane, by meanes of some vlcer which hath beene ill cured.*

De belle prise. *Faire, well liking, worth the taking, acceptable or gracious to the eye.*

De bonne prise. *Good, or lawfull prize; also, full ripe, in season, fit to be cropped, gathered, or gotten.*

Corner prise. Cela cornoit prise. *That finished the chase, that made an end of the matter.*

Estre aux prises. *To be closed, locked, or grapled together; to tug one another, to wrastle, or striue with one another.*

C'est vne bonne prise que d'un ieune loup: Prov. *A young Wolfe is a game worth catching.*

Prisé: m. ée: f. *Prised, rated, valued, esteemed.*

Prisée: f. *A prisall, rate, valuation; a prising, rating, valuing.*

Priser. *To prise; esteeme, respect, reckon, accompt of; also, to tax, rate, value, set a price on.*

'A l'hostel priser, & au marché vendre: Prov. *Rate thy commodities at home, but sell them abroad.*

Qui bien se cognoit peu se prise, qui peu se prise Dieu l'avise: Pro. *He that himselfe knowes well, himselfe despises, the selfe-despiser God heeds, and aduises.*

Priserie: f. *A prising, or praising; a rating, or valuing.*

Priseur: m. *A priser, praiser, price-setter; a rater, valuer, taxer.*

Prisine. *Looke* Prime.

Prison: f. *A Prison, Jayle, or Gaole.*

Oncques n'y eut laides amours, ny belle prison: Pro. *There neuer was faire prison, nor foule loue.*

Prisonnier: m. *A prisoner.*

Tous les prisonniers s'en sont fuys de sa bourse. *All manner of pence are flowne out of his purse.*

Priste. *A kind of Whall, or huge fish, whose snowt is verie long, and notched like a Saw.*

Pristine: com. *Former; old, auncient; wonted, accustomed; also, late, or but little past.*

Privaise: f. Lieu ou l'on fait les privez; *or a Pipe, or Funnell, for the voiding of the ill aire of a Priuie.*

Privation: f. *A priuation, depriuing, bereauing, withdrawing of; a want, or wanting; a lacking, or being without.*

Privativement. *Exclusiuely, by way of exclusion, or to the putting out of others.*

Cela luy appartient privativement à tous autres. *Belongeth onely to him, no other hath ought to doe withall.*

Privauté: f. *Priuacie, priuate familiaritie or friendship, inward conuersation or acquaintance.*

Privé: m. *A Priuie, Iakes, house of Office.*

En son privé. *Priuately, secretly, closely, retiredly, within his owne doores, without gadding, or medling, abroad; at his owne home.*

Privé: m. ée: f. *Depriued, reaued, bereft of; also, priuie, close, or secret; also, priuat, familiar, inward, bold with, neere vnto, as one of his owne; tame, gentle, tractable, domesticall; also, ordinarie; homelie; without charge, office, or authoritie in the Commonwealth.*

D'un larron privé on ne se peut garder: Prov. *No creature can auoid the priuie theefe.*

Prive-

Privemént: m. *A depriuing, or bereauing.*
Privément. *Priuily, closely, secretly; priuately, inwardly, familiarly; after an ordinarie fashion.*
Priver. *To depriue, reaue, or bereaue, despoyle of, take from.*
Privilege: m. *A Priuiledge, Libertie, Fraunchise, Licence, Immunitie, Prerogatiue aboue others: A French Lawyer defines it to be,* Vne concession singuliere que le Roy octroye à tousiours par lettres Patentes (qui doivent estre verifiées en la Chambre des comptes.)
Privilegié: m. ée: f. *Priuiledged; exempted from ordinarie dueties, or iurisdiction; out of ordinarie course.*
Cas, ou delict privilegié. *A notable case, or notorious crime, which none but the King, or his Judges, may examine, sentence, or censure.*
Privoité. *as* Privauté.
Prix: m. *Price; Looke* Pris.
Probabilité: f. *Probabilitie, likelihood, apparance of truth.*
Probable: com. *Probable, proueable, which may be proued, likelie, or like to be true.*
Probablement. *Probably, likely, proueably.*
Probableté. *as* Probabilité.
Probation: f. *A probation, proofe; approbation, prouing.*
Probatique. Piscine pro. *A Pond for the washing of the Sheepe that were, by the Law, to be sacrificed.*
Probité: f. *Honestie, integritie, sinceritie, goodnesse, vprightnesse, true dealing.*
Problematique: com. *Problematicall, belonging to a Probleme.*
Probleme: m. *A Probleme; a proposition, position, or sentence, hauing a question annexed vnto it.*
Proboscе: f. *A big snowt, huge nose.*
Proboscide. *The trunke, or snowt of an Elephant.*
Procace: m. *The Post, or Carrier that goeth weekely betweene Rome and Naples.*
Procedé. *Proceeded; passed forth, gone forward; held, continued, or kept on in a course; also, sued, or pursued.*
Proceder. *To proceed, goe forward, passe forth; continue, hold, or keepe on in a course; also, to sue, or pursue.*
Proceder sommairement. *Looke* Sommairement.
Fins de non proceder. *Reasons alledged for the staying of further proceedings in Court.*
Iamais ne gaigne qui procede à son Maistre: Pro. *He neuer thriues that sues his Maister.*
Longuement proceder est à l'advocat vendenger: Pro *Delayes in Law fill Pleaders Barnes.*
Procedure: f. *A procedure; a course, or proceeding; a course of proceeding; a suing, a pursuing.*
Procerité: f. *Height, or length of bodie; tallnesse of stature.*
Procés: m. *A Proces, or Suit; a Case, Cause, Action, Indictment, Matter, in Law; also, debate, strife, suit, altercation, contention; also, the Processe, Apophyse, or out-standing part of a bone.*
Procez mamillaires. *Small teat-like sinewes in the forepart of the braine; th' instruments of the sence of smelling.*
Vn diable en procés. *A notable stirring, vnquiet, or litigious fellow.*
Faire le procés à. *To appeach, or indite; to sit vpon life and death on.*
Son procés est faict. *His cause is readie for Iudgement; also, he is conuicted, or condemned; he is but a dead (but a gone) man.*
Pendre vn procés au croc. *See* Croc.
Perdre son procés. *To be cast in Law.*
De procés ou gist grosse amende, en tous temps bon heur nous defende: Pro. *From suits that subiect be to grieuous fines, good Lord deliuer vs.*
En procés il n'y a point d'amour: Pro. *There is no loue 'tweene lawing aduersaries; or, there is no loue 'mong those that goe to Law.*
Processeux: m. euse: f. *as* Processif; *or full of actions, filled with suits.*
Processif: m. iue: f. *Litigious, debatefull, wrangling, alwayes in suits, euer at Law.*
Procession: f. *A procession.*
Processional: m. ale: f. *Processionall; belonging to, seruing for, a procession.*
Prochain: m. aine: f. *Nigh, neere, next, neighbouring, adioyning, close to, hard by.*
Prochainement. *Neerely, nighly; next, or last.*
Prochaineté: f. *Nighnesse, neerenesse, proximitie, neighbourhood.*
Prochas: m. *A purchase; a pursuit.*
Prochasser. *Looke* Pourchasser.
Proche: com. *Neere, nigh, neighbouring, adioyning, close vnto.*
Prochefief: m. *The* Fief, *or Inheritance thats held of a Lord by a direct, and immediate tenure.*
Procidence: f. *A falling downe of a thing out of it right place.*
Proclamation: f. *A proclamation, a proclaiming.*
Proclamé: m. ée: f. *Proclaimed.*
Proclamer. *To proclame, to publish by proclamation.*
Proclameur: m. *A proclaimer.*
Proclif: m. iue: f. *Inclining, bending; subiect, or inclined, vnto; prone, apt, readie to fall.*
Procours. *as* Parcours.
Procrastination: f. *A procrastination, delay, driuing off from day to day, putting ouer till to morrow.*
Procrastiné: m. ée: f. *Procrastinated, driuen off, or put ouer, from day to day.*
Procrastiner. *To procrastinate, prolong, delay, driue, or put off, deferre from day to day.*
Procreateur: m. *A procreator, begetter, ingendrer, (second) maker.*
Procreation: f. *A procreation, ingendring, begetting.*
Procreatrice: f. *A procreatrix; a mother, or damme.*
Procréer. *To procreate, ingender, beget, breed, make.*
Proculteur. *Vsed sometimes in stead of* Procureur.
Procuration: f. *A procuration; a Warrant, or Letter, of Atturney; a following of another mans businesse by warrant; also, a Visitation executed by an Archdeacon, or some other, as the Bishops Deputie.*
Passer procuration. *To appoint an Atturney, or Deputie; to make one a Warrant, or Letter of Atturney, for the following of his businesse; also, to yeeld, graunt, or agree vnto.*
Procuré: m. ée: f. *Procured, made; solicited.*
Procurer. *To procure, get, purchase, acquire; to solicite, or follow a cause.*
Procureur: m. *A Proctor; an Atturney at Law.*
Procureur fiscal. *The ordinarie Proctor, or Atturney of a Lord high* Iusticier; *who by him prosecutes (within his owne Territories) all causes that either concerne the rights, and dependances of his Seigniorie; or tend to the maintenance of the Peace, and safetie of his vassalls.*
Procureurs d' Hospitaux. *Proctors of Spittles; officers*

officers which receiue the rents belonging to, and almes bestowed on, them.

Procureur d'office, ou de Seigneurie. *The Atturney of a* Moyen Iusticier, *who not hauing any* Fisque, *cannot haue a* Procureur fiscal, *and therefore differs from;*

Procureur de la Seigneurie de la Iustice; *(which is) as* Procureur fiscal.

Prodenou: m. *A rope which compasseth the saile-yard of a Ship.*

Prodigal: m. ale: f. *Prodigall, vnthriftie, riotous, lauish, wastfull, excessiue in expence.*

Prodigalement. *Prodigally, vnthriftily, riotously, lauishly, wastfully.*

Prodigalisé: m. ée: f. *Prodigalized, lauished, wasted, spent riotously, disposed of vnthriftily, squandered away.*

Prodigaliser. *To prodigalize it, spend vnthriftily, wast, lauish, consume, or squander all away.*

Prodigalité: f. *Prodigalitie, riot, vnthriftinesse, lauish, or wastfull expence.*

Prodige: m. *A prodigie; wonder, strange signe, vnnaturall accident, maruelous thing.*

Prodiger. *as* Prodiguer.

Prodigieusement. *Prodigiously; monstrously, wonderfully, most strangely or vnnaturally.*

Prodigieux: m. euse: f. *Prodigious; wonderous, monstrous, most vnnaturall or out of course.*

Prodigue: com. *Prodigall, vnthriftie, lauish, wastfull, riotous, excessiue, or outragious in expence.*

Prodigue, & grand beuveur de vin n'a du sien ne four, ne moulin: Pro. *The drunken spendthrift wasts his best possessions.*

Prodiguer. *To riot, lauish, mispend, play the vnthrift, wast, consume, let flye all he hath.*

Proditeur: m. *A traitor, betrayer; bewrayer, discloser; a treacherous, or disloyall fellow.*

Prodition: f. *Prodition, treason, treacherie, disloyaltie, extreame falsehood.*

Prodrome: m. *The fore-runner, or newes-bringer of another mans comming; a preparer of the way for another; whence;*

Prodromes. *The winds which rise a little before the Dog dayes.*

Production: f. *A production; a proofe, euidence, or testimonie produced in iustification, or confirmation of a cause.*

Produict: m. icte: f. *Produced; yeelded, brought forth; alledged, or shewed, in proofe of.*

Produire. *To produce; yeeld, bring forth; cite bookes, vrge proofes, alledge reasons; also, to furnish with leacherie, to helpe a man to a wench for money; (th' office, and practise of bawdes.)*

Proë. *Looke* Proue.

Proeme: m. *A Proeme, Preface, Prologue.*

Proesme: m. *The same; also, a neighbor.*

Profanateur: m. *A prophaner, violater, vnhallower, of.*

Profanation: f. *A prophanation, or prophaning; a violating, an vnhallowing.*

Profane: com. *Prophane; lay, temporall, worldlie; wicked, vnholie, vngodlie.*

Profané: m. ée: f. *Prophaned; vnhallowed, violated; turned from a holie to a common, from a diuine to an humane, vse.*

Profanement: m. *as* Profanation.

Profanément. *Prophanely; temporally; wickedly, vngodly; worldling-like.*

Profaner. *To prophane, vnhallow, violate; put holie things to vnholie vses.*

Proferer. *To produce, alledge, deliuer; speake, pronounce, vtter.*

Professeur: m. *A professor; a publike Reader in Vniuersities, or Schooles.*

Profession: f. *A profession, facultie, qualitie, vocation, calling; also, an open confession, protestation aduowall, acknowledgement; also, a Reading, or professing in publike Schooles.*

Professoirement. *Professiuely, or by profession.*

Profez: m. *Professed Monkes; or, more generally, such as, hauing made their vowes, are admitted of a religious Order.*

Proficiat: m. *A fee, or beneuolence bestowed on Bishops, in manner of a welcome, immediately after their installments.*

Profilé: m. ée: f. *Wrought, or done, in thread; also, purfled.*

Profit: m. *Profit, gaine, lucre, increase of, aduantage in, estate; commoditie, benefit, vtilitie, cheuissance.*

A profit de mesnage. *Roundly, soundly, throughly, without trifling or dalliance, to purpose, with a witnesse.*

Profit sans vertu ne vaut vn festu: Prov. *Gaine without vertue is not worth a feskue.*

Au despendre gist le profit: Pro. *In spending thrift consists; discreet expence makes many a poore man rich.*

Chascun tire à son profit: Pro. *Euerie one inclines, or hath an eye, to that which may inrich him.*

Profitable: com. *Profitable, gainefull, beneficiall, commodious.*

Hommes profitables. *Vassalls, of whom a Lord both hath his reuenue, and makes other vse to his profit.*

Seigneur profitable. *The possessor, or occupant of an Inheritance; he that, to make the vtmost of it, keepes it in his owne hands.*

Profiter. *See* Proufiter.

Profiterolle: f. *as* Pourfiterolle; *and in the Plurall* (Profiterolles) *be the small vayles, as drinking money, points, pinnes, &c, gotten by a* valet *or* groome *in his maisters seruice.*

Profond: m. de: f. *Profound, high, deepe; of much capacitie, of great receit; secret; vnsatiable, bottomelesse.*

Profondé: m. ée: f. *Deepened; pierced, or searched farre into; pressed, or sunke downe into the bottome of.*

Profondement. *Profoundly, deepely, highly; secretly; vnsatiably; without any bottome.*

Profonder. *To sound, search, pierce, or goe deepe into; to diue, or sinke vnto the bottome of; to presse downe, or put into the deepe.*

Profondeur: f. *Profunditie, profoundnesse, depth, deepenesse; height; vnsatiablenesse.*

Profondité. *The same.*

Profuseur: m. *A powrer out; a profuse, excessiue, lauish, riotous, wastfull spender.*

Progenie: f. *A progenie, off-spring, brood, issue, generation.*

Progenier. *To progenerate, procreate, propagate; breed, beget, ingender, bring forth, young ones.*

Progeniteur: m. *A progenitor, auncestor, forefather.*

Prognostication: f. *A Prognostication, fore-telling, fore-shewing; an argument, or signe, of a future thing; a guessing, by signes, of things to come.*

Prognostique. *as* Prognostication.

Prognostiqué: m. ée: f. *Prognosticated, prophesied, foretold.*
Prognostiquer. *To prognosticate, foreshew, prophesie, foretell.*
Prognostiqueur: m. *A prognosticator, foreshewer, Almanack-maker, fortune-teller, foreteller.*
Progreder. *To proceed, passe on, goe forward, continue in a course begun.*
Progrez: m. *A progression, going forward, passing on, a proceeding, or continuing in a course begun.*
Prohibé: m. ée: f. *Prohibited, forbidden; let, stopped, hindered.*
Prohiber. *To prohibit, forbid; impeach, hinder, not to suffer.*
Prohibeur: m. *A prohibitor, a forbidder.*
Prohibition: f. *A prohibition, inhibition, forbidding.*
Prohibitoire: com. *Prohibitorie, prohibiting, forbidding.*
Project: m. *A proiect, purpose, designement, forecast, intent; also, a modell, or plot of a building made, or delineated, in paper; also, the iutting, out-bearing, or outleaning of a wall, garret, or vpper roome.*
Projecté: m. ée: f. *Proiected, purposed, forecast, forethought of, designed, meant or intended before-hand; also, drawne, delineated, purtrayed.*
Projecter. *To proiect, plot, forecast; purpose, designe, intend; also, to draw, purtray, describe, delineate, proportion, a thing before it be done.*
Projection: f. *A proiection; a casting or throwing forth, a stretching or extending out.*
Proisme. *as* Presme.
Proiation: f. *A pronouncing, vtterance, deliuerie of words.*
Prolectation: f. *A pleasant inticement, a delightsome prouocation.*
Prolepsie: f. *A naturall foreknowledge conceiued in the mind; and hence, a figure whereby we preuent, and auoid, that which another intended to alledge against vs.*
Prolifique: com. *Fruitfull, or breeding apace.*
Prolixe: com. *Prolix, long, tedious; large, abundant, bounteous.*
Prolixement. *Prolixly, tediously, at length, at large; liberally, abundantly, plenteously.*
Prologue: m. *A Prologue, or fore-speech; a preamble to a Play.*
Prolongation: f. *A prolongation, prolonging, drawing out in length; a protraction, demurre, delay.*
Prolongé: m. ée: f. *Prolonged, protracted, or drawne out in length; deferred, put off, delayed.*
Prolongement: m. *A prolonging, protracting, deferring, delaying.*
Prolonger. *To prolong, protract, put or driue off, draw out in length, deferre, delay.*
Prolongeur: m. *A prolonger, protracter, wyre-drawer, delayer.*
Promarginaire: com. *Extended on the margent.*
Prome: m. *A Butler, or Drawer; also, a yeoman of the Larder.*
Promenement: m. *A walking.*
Promener. *To walke; See* Pourmener.
Promesse: f. *A promise; a vow made, or assurance giuen, by word of mouth.*
Belle promesse fol lie: Prov. *Faire promises oblige the foole; or, are no better then fopperies; (for the words* fol lie *equiuocate vnto* folie.)
Prometteur: m. *A promiser.*
Promettre. *To promise; couenant; vow; vndertake, or giue his word, for; also (in bargaining) to offer.*
Promettre sans donner est fol reconforter: Prov. *To promise and giue nought contents the foole.*
Beaucoup promettre, & peu tenir couste peu à entretenir: Pro. *It costs a man but little to say much and doe little.*
Entre promettre, & donner doit on la fille marier: Pro. *Betweene giuing somewhat and promising much, a man may be honestly rid of a daughter.*
Promeu: m. euë: f. *Promoted, aduaunced, preferred.*
Promeu aux ordres ecclesiastiques. *Hauing taken Orders.*
Prominence: f. *A prominence; a standing, iutting, or strouting, out; hence, a Pent-house, &c, in building; and in the bodie, that part of a member which is bigger, or thicker then it fellowes, or those that be next adioyning to it.*
Prominent: m. ente: f. *Prominent; extending, outstretching, iutting out or ouer.*
Promis: m. ise: f. *Promised; vowed; couenanted; giuen by word; also (in bargaining) offered.*
Promiscuë: com. *Promiscuous; confused, mixed without order, mingled without consideration; also, mutuall, indifferent, or without difference, common to many.*
Promiscuëment. *Promiscuously, confusedly; indifferently, without difference, mutually, one with another.*
Promontoire: m. *A Promontorie; a hill which, elbowlike, lies out into the sea.*
Promoteur: m. *A Promooter; also, a Proctor; whence;*
Promoteur d'office. *as* Procureur fiscal.
Promotion: f. *Promotion, aduancement, preferment.*
Promouvoir. *To promote, aduance, preferre.*
Prompt: m. te: f. *Prompt, quicke, speedie, nimble; prepared, readie at hand.*
La plus prompte courtoisie c'est la meilleure: Pro. *A prompt, and willing speed indeareth courtesies; the promptest, and most willing fauor's best.*
Promptement. *Promptly, quickly, speedily, readily, at hand.*
Promptitude: f. *Promptnesse, quicknesse, readinesse; proneuesse, preparation.*
Promptuaire: m. *A Promptuarie, Storehouse; Buttrie, Sellor, Spence.*
Pronateurs: m. *Certaine muscles whereby the hand is bent, or bowed downewards.*
Pronau: m. *A Pulpit; or the place out of which the* Prone *is deliuered.*
Prone: m. *The publication made, or notice giuen, by a Priest vnto his parishioners (when Seruice is almost ended) of the holy daies, and fasting daies in the weeke following; of goods lost, or strayed; of such as desire to be relieued, or prayed for; of Banes of Matrimonie; or of any such thing, besides their prayers, fit for them to vnderstand.*
Prone: com. *Prone; readie, nimble, quicke, wheeme, easily mouing; also, inclined, lying downe or toward, bending or stooping downewards.*
Prononçable: com. *Pronounceable.*
Prononcé: m. ée: f. *Pronounced.*
Prononcer. *To pronounce; expresse, name specially, deliuer out or openly, vtter precisely, denounce plainely, make expresse mention of.*
Prononciation: f. *Pronunciation; plaine vtterance, open declaration, expresse deliuerie, precise mention of; a pronouncing; a denouncing.*

Pronostique. *A presage, or presaging; a foreknowledge, or foreseeing, of; a shrewd, or neere guesse, at.*

Pronube: f. *A bride-maid; or, she that attires the bride, and attends on her vnto the bridegroomes house.*

Pronube. *(Adiectiuely; or as an Epithete, or Adiunct; whence)* Iuno pronube, *assistant, or superintendent at marriages; or, the goddesse of Mariage.*

Propelet: m. *A dapper, neat, spruce, quaint, or compt fellow.*

Propension: f. Vne pro. à. *A propension, or pronenesse; a (naturall) inclination, readinesse, or willingnesse vnto.*

Prophete: m. *A Prophet.*

Prophetie: f. *A Prophesie.*

Prophetique: com. *Propheticall; prophecying; of a Prophet; belonging to a prophecie.*

Prophetizant. *Prophecying.*

Prophetizé: m. ée: f. *Prophecied; presaged, foretold.*

Prophetizer. *To prophecie; presage, diuine, foretell.*

Prophiloctice: f. *An Antidote, a counterpoison; or, that part of Phisicke which concernes the preseruation of the bodie.*

Propice: com. *Propitious, gracious, fauorable; gentle, tractable; well inclined vnto; also, apt, meet, fit, proper, conuenient for.*

'A bon bluteur May propice: Pro. *Looke* May.

Propine: f. *Drinking money, or somewhat to drinke.*

Propitiateur: m. *A propitiator; a reconciler, pacifier, appeaser; one that procures fauor for others.*

Propitiation: f. *A propitiation, or attonement procured; also, a propitiatorie sacrifice.*

Propitiatoire: com. *Propitiatorie; appeasing, pacifying, reconciling, attoning.*

Propitier. *To propitiate, or make propitious; to reconcile, attone, pacifie, appease.*

Proportion: f. *Proportion; a proportion, rate, share; measure, quantitie, size; an equallnesse, or answerablenesse.*

Proportionné: m. ée: f. *Proportioned; equally rated, shared; measured, squared.*

Proportionnellement. *Proportionally, or proportionably; equally, rateably; according to the iust measure, size, quantitie, or qualitie, of.*

Proportionnément. *The same.*

Proportionner. *To proportion; rate, share, square, measure out equally; make one thing answerable, or according, to the other.*

Propos: m. *A purpose, drift, end, intent, meaning, designe, determination; also, talke, speech, discourse, chat, conference, communication; also, aptnesse, fitnesse, conueniencie, seasonablenesse, good season; also, the first Bill which a plaintife puts into a Court.*

'A propos. *Fitly, seasonably, conueniently, commodiously, vnto the purpose, or iust pat.*

'A propos truelle *(followed by)* bon iour Masson. *A prouerbiall phrase, vsed by such, as beginning to quarrell, or expostulate, with others, perceiue on a suddaine some vnexpected thing, the respect or feare whereof makes them as suddainely change, or sweeten, their language.*

Proposé: m. ée: f. *Purposed, intended, meant; determined, decreed; also, proposed, or propounded.*

Proposer. *To purpose, meane, designe, determine, intend; also, to propose, propound, alledge; publish, declare, set, or lay downe, bring out, shew forth.*

Proposer reproches contre. *To challenge, or excep against (a witnesse, &c.)*

Proposeur: m. *A propounder, a proposer.*

Proposition: f. *A proposition; a sentence, or matter propounded; a question, position, or short speech, containing the summe, or substance of that which we intend to proue.*

Proposition d'erreur. *A Writ, or the laying, of Error; Seeke* Erreur.

Propre: m. *Ones proper, or peculiar substance, estate, liuelyhood, condition; ones owne.*

Propre conventionnel. C'est, quand il a esté convenu que les deniers feront imployez en propre heritage; ou quand vn heritage est donné pour estre propre au donataire.

Propre naturel. *Lands, or goods come from a direct auncestor.*

Propre: com. *Proper, peculiar, particular, ones owne; also, fit, apt, meet, conuenient, able for; handsome, seemelie, comelie, well accommodated, vnto the purpose.*

Propres heritages. *Ones auncient inheritance; lands descended, or come vnto him from his auncestors.*

Ce propre iour là. *That verie day.*

Rien n'est nostre n'est que soit en nous propre: Pro. *Nothing can be said ours thats not bred with vs.*

Propre. *(Aduerbially) whence;*

Faict au propre. *Made of purpose, done for the nonce.*

Il se tenoit propre de sa personne. *He kept himselfe neatly, or handsomely.*

Proprement. *Properly, aptly, fitly, iust, meet; conueniently, handsomely, decently, to good purpose.*

Qu'aujourd'huy proprement. *That iust to day, that this verie day.*

Propret: m. ette: f. *Prettie, gentle, feat; neat, spruce, picked, compt, minion, tricksie, trimme.*

Propreté: f. *Fitnesse, aptnesse; prettinesse, neatnesse, handsomenesse, gentlenesse.*

Proprietaire: com. *A proprietarie, an owner.*

Proprietaire: com. *Proprietarie, as an owner.*

Rente proprietaire. *A rent seruice, or fundamentall rent, going with, or annexed vnto, the land.*

Seigneur proprietaire. *The right owner of an inheritance.*

Proprietairement. *In propertie, absolutely, as an owner, as his owne.*

Proprieté: f. *A propertie; proprietie; owing, specialtie in; a iust and absolute power ouer, a freehold in; also, the nature, qualitie, inclination, or disposition of; also, a handsome, or comelie assortment; a fit commoditie, or furnishment; and, a roome or place well accommodated or fitted.*

Propugnacule: com. *A fortresse, bulwarke, strong hold, sure defence.*

Propulsation: f. *A propulsation, repelling, driuing back, chasing forward, putting away.*

Prorata. Au p. de. *Euerie one after the rate, or according to the value, of.*

Proriter. *To prouoke, vrge, excite, exasperate.*

Prorogation: f. *A prorogation, or proroguing; a driuing, or putting off.*

Prorogé: m. ée: f. *Prorogued, prolonged, put off.*

Proroger. *To prorogue, put ouer, driue off; prolong, deferre, delay.*

Proscript: m. *An Outlaw; a man designed, or exposed vnto slaughter; a proscribed, or attainted person.*

Proſcript: m. ipte: f. *Proſcribed; attainted; expoſed, or deſigned vnto ſlaughter; alſo, publikely ſold, or ſet vnto ſale.*

Proſcription: f. *A Proſcription; Attainder; Outlarie; a deſigning, or expoſing vnto ſlaughter; alſo, Portſale, or publike ſale.*

Proſcrire. *To proſcribe; attaint; outlaw; to expoſe, or deſigne vnto ſlaughter; alſo, to publiſh, or proclaime the ſale of.*

Proſe: f. *Proſe; any ſtile which is not Verſe, or Meetre.*

Proſes. *Part of the Maſſe deuiſed by the Abbot of S.* Galle.

De peu de choſe peu de proſe: Prov. *For ſmall matters little ſtriſe; about ſmall things but ſmall adoe.*

Proſelite: m. *A Proſelite; a ſtranger turned to our faſhion, conuerted to our faith.*

Proſenette: m. *as* Proxenete.

Proſerie: f. *A place appointed for the nouriſhment of poore people.*

Proſne. *as* Prone.

Proſner. *A Prieſt to preach, or to pronounce, the* prone; *looke* Prone.

Proſopopée: f. *A diſguiſing; repreſenting of perſons, faining of a perſon to ſpeake.*

Proſpective: f. *The Proſpectiue, Perſpectiue, or Optick Art; alſo, a (bounded) proſpect; a (limitted) view, or ſuruey.*

En proſpective. *Openly, to the view, for a ſhew, to be ſeene.*

Proſperément. *Proſperouſly, ſucceſſiuely, happily, luckily, fortunately.*

Proſperer. *To proſper, thriue, haue or bring lucke; to giue ſucceſſe vnto.*

Proſperité: f. *Proſperitie, happineſſe, good lucke, fortune, or ſucceſſe in.*

Proſtates. *Certaine kernells in the necke of the bladder.*

Proſterné: m. ée: f. *Proſtrated, fallen flat, layed along; foyled, felled, borne, caſt, or ſtrucken downe.*

Proſternement: m. *A proſtrating, or laying along; a felling, foyling, ouerthrowing.*

Proſterner. *To proſtrate, lay flat or along; to foyle, fell, caſt, beare, ſtrike downe.*

Proſtitué: m. ée: f. *Proſtituted, abandoned, ſet to ſale, abuſed, or made common by euerie one that will pay.*

Proſtituer. *To proſtitute, abandon, ſet open to, make common for, euerie one; to play the whore with, or ſubiect vnto the pleaſure of, any man for money.*

Proſtitution: f. *A proſtitution; a ſetting vnto ſale, an abandoning to the vſe of any man for money.*

Proſtration: f. *A proſtrating; a deiection, or falling at the feet of; or, as* Proſternement.

Proſyllogiſme. *A ſecond Syllogiſme prouing the firſt.*

Protecole: m. *The firſt Draught, or Copie of a Deed, Contract, Inſtrument, Euidence; or a ſhort Regiſter kept thereof; alſo, a Precedent for the drawing of a Patent, or Deed; alſo, a booke of ſuch Precedents; alſo, a prompter of one that makes an Oration, or acts a Part, in publike.*

Protecteur: m. *A protector, maintainer, defendor.*

Protection: f. *Protection, ſafegard, publike maintenance, or defence.*

Protectrice: f. *A protectrix, or defendreſſe.*

Protegé: m. ée: f. *Protected, couered, ſhielded, ſaued, defended.*

Proteger. *To protect, ſhield, couer, ſaue, keepe harmeleſſe, defend.*

Protelé: m. ée: f. *Shifted off, put backe, driuen or chaſed away; delayed.*

Proteler. *To ſhift off, put backe, driue or chaſe away; alſo, to delay, deferre, protract.*

Protenotaire: m. *A Pregnotarie, or principall Notarie.*

Proterve: com. *Froward, wayward, peruerſe, curſt, ſnappiſh, peeuiſh; alſo, prowd, ſawcie, malapert, arrogant, impudent.*

Protervement. *Peruerſely, waywardly, frowardly; alſo, prowdly, ſawcily, impudently.*

Protervie: f. *Frowardneſſe, peruerſeneſſe, curſtneſſe, peeuiſhneſſe, waywardneſſe; alſo, pride, ſawcineſſe, malapertneſſe, arrogancie, impudencie.*

Protervité: f. *as* Protervie.

Proteſtant. *Proteſting, denouncing, openly auerring or declaring.*

Proteſtant de trahiſon. *Proteſting, or crying, that he was betrayed.*

Proteſtation: f. *A proteſtation; an open declaration, auerment, or denouncement of an opinion, or purpoſe.*

Proteſté. *Proteſted; openly affirmed, earneſtly auerred, ſolemnly auouched.*

Proteſter. *To proteſt; to affirme earneſtly, auerre ſolemnely, auouch or denounce openly; alſo, to deny the payment of a demaunded debt; or to returne a Bill of debt vnpayed.*

Proteſter de tous deſpens, dommages, & intereſts. *To challenge, demaund, or inſiſt vpon ſatisfaction for his dammages, and a reſtorall of all his coſts and charges.*

Prothocolle, & Protocole. *as* Protecole.

Protodiables: m. *The firſt, or chiefeſt of Diuels.*

Proto-martyre. *The firſt Martyr.*

Protonotaire: m. *A Pregnotarie, principall Notarie, chiefe Scribe; (A title proper, and peculiar to the* Greffier civil de la Cour de Parlement de Paris.)

Prototype: m. *The firſt forme, type, modell, or patterne of.*

Prou, *for* Proufit; *whence;*

Bon prou leur face. *Much good may it doe them; let them follow their owne courſes, or take their owne wayes.*

Prou. *Much, greatly, enough.*

Provature: f. *A kind of greene Cheeſe made in Italie, of the milke of Buffles.*

Prouë: f. *The prow, or forepart of a Ship; alſo, a point aduancing it ſelfe out of a building as the prow out of a Ship.*

Provect: m. cte: f. *Well growne in age, or of good yeares; well ſtudied in an Art; forward, or farre gone, in the courſe of Arts.*

Provençales. *Long ſlops, Marriners long breeches.*

Provende: f. *Prouender; alſo, a Prebendrie.*

Provenir. *To iſſue, come, ſtep, or ſpring forth; to proceed from.*

Proverbe: m. *A prouerbe; adage, old ſaid ſaw, ſhort, and wittie ſaying.*

Proverbial: m. ale: f. *Prouerbiall, of a Prouerbe.*

Prouëſſe: f. *Proweſſe, courage, dowtineſſe, valour, cheualrie; a valiant act, a ſmall action.*

Proufit: m. *Profit, gaine, lucre; increaſe of, or aduantage in, eſtate.*

Proufitable: com. *Profitable, gainefull, commodious, aduantageous.*
Proufitablement. *Profitably, gainefully, commodiously, aduantageously.*
Proufitant. *Gaining, profiting, thriuing by.*
Proufité. *Profited, gained, thriuen by.*
Proufiter. *To profit; get, gaine, or grow rich, by; to doe good vpon; also, to thriue, chieue, increase, grow.*
Proufiterolle. *as* Profiterolle.
Provide: com. *Prouident, heedfull, circumspect, foreseeing, forecasting, warie, carefull, considerate.*
Providemment. *Prouidently, considerately, heedfully, with good forecast.*
Providence: f. *Prouidence, foresight, forecast.*
Proujecter. *Looke* Projecter.
Provignable. *Propagable.*
Provignage. *as* Provignement.
Provigné: m. ée: f. *Set, or planted for breed, nourished for increase; propagated, multiplied, renewed, increased.*
Provignement: m. *A planting, or setting of a stocke, staulke, slip, or sucker for increase; a propagating, multiplying, increasing.*
Provigner. *To plant, or set a stocke, staulke, slip, or sucker, for increase; or (more properly) to couch them downe, or set them double, with both ends appearing aboue the ground; whereby being, within a while, rooted in the middle, they come to yeeld a manifold, or double increase; hence also, to propagate, multiply, get, raise, or breed, many of one; or to renew things out of an old store.*
Provigner des procez. *To breed suit vpon suit, raise one suit out of another; to make worke for Lawyers.*
Provigneur: m. *A planter, or setter (as in* Provigner*) a propagater, breeder, increaser.*
Provin: m. *A stocke, staulke, plant, shute, slip, or sucker planted, or fit to be planted (as in* Provigner*) for increase.*
Province: f. *A Prouince, Region, Countrey, Shire; properly such a one, as hauing beene subdued by force of Armes, is gouerned by a Viceroy, Deputie, or Lieutenant.*
Proviseur: m. *A Purueyor, or prouider.*
Provision: f. *A prouision, purueying, or prouiding for; also, prouision, store, furniture.*
Lettres de provision. *Letters Patents whereby an office, or dignitie is graunted.*
Iuger par provision. *For a time onely, vntill further order be taken, or prouision made.*
Par maniere de provision. *In the meane time, the whilst, or in the meane while.*
Provisional: m. ale: f. *Prouisionall; onely for a season, continuing but for a time; whence;*
Sentence provisionale. *A Sentence implying a limitation, or of force no longer then vntill further order may be taken.*
Provisoire: com. *Prouisorie, conditionall, implying a limitation, including a prouiso; or, as* Provisional.
Proumeu. *as* Promeu.
Proumouvoir. *Looke* Promouvoir.
Provocation: f. *A prouocation, prouoking, egging, vrging, incensing, stirring, inciting.*
Provocatoire: m. *A Prouocatorie; a writing, &c, whereby one is prouoked; a challenge.*
Provoqué: m. ée: f. *Prouoked, vrged, incited, incensed; also, challenged, or defied.*
Provoquement: m. *A prouoking.*
Provoquer. *To prouoke, egge, vrge, moue, stirre, incite, incense; defie, challenge.*
Provoqueur: m. *A prouoker; a challenger.*
Prouvé: m. ée: f. *Proued, tryed; assured, verified; iustified, made good.*
Prouver. *To proue, try, essay; verifie, approue, assure, confirme, iustifie, make good.*
Prouveu: m. *Looke* Pourveu.
Prouveu: m. euë: f. *Prouided or purueyed of, stored or furnished with; also, foreseene, forecast, considered beforehand.*
Prouvoir. *To puruey or prouide for, to furnish or store with; also, to foresee, forecast, beware, take heed, looke to, shift for, consider beforehand.*
Prouvoyance: f. *Purueyance, prouision; foresight, forecast, heed, caution, regard, consideration.*
Prouvoyant. *Prouiding, purueying for; heeding, regarding, looking vnto.*
Proxenete: m. *A Broker, or Huckster; a meane dealer betweene partie and partie.*
Proximité: f. *Proximitie, neerenesse, nighnesse, neighborhood; the next degree of linage, or kindred.*
Proye: f. *A prey, bootie; spoyle.*
Cela n'est pas proye pour ses levriers; *That is no Lettuce for his lips.*
Qui a le vilain il a sa proye: Pro. *He that can seize a churle, commaunds all that he hath.*
Regnard qui beaucoup tarde attend la proye: Pro. *The fox thats long away, for purchase waiteth.*
Proyer. *as* Preyer.
Prudemment. *Prudently, wisely, discreetly, aduisedly, cunningly.*
Prudence: f. *Prudence, discretion, circumspection, aduisednesse, warinesse; cunning, skilfullnesse, knowledge.*
Prudent: m. ente: f. *Prudent, warie, sage, discreet, circumspect, aduised; slye, cunning, skilfull, expert, experienced in many matters.*
Femme prudente, & sage, est l'ornement de son mesnage: Prov. *A woman wise, and prouident, doth beautifie her tenement.*
Prune: f. *A Plumme.*
Prune blanche. *The wheat, or white Plumme.*
Prune de cheval. *A Horse Plumme.*
Prune de Damas. *A Damson, or Damask Plumme.*
Prune sauvage. *A wild Plumme; a Bullace; (as also) a Sloe, or Snag.*
Il en pelera la prune. *He will deerely aby it, he will haue much trouble about it, he wil surely pay, or smart, for it.*
Il ne fait pas bon manger des prunes avec son Seigneur: Pro. *Looke* Manger.
Pruneau: m. *A Prune; or a little Plumme.*
Prunelat: m. *The name of a Vine, or Grape, whereof there be two sorts, the one white the other red.*
Prunelette: f. *A little Plumme.*
Prunelier: m. *The blacke thorne, or Sloe tree.*
Prunelle: f. *A Sloe, or Snag; also, the hearbe called Prunell, or Brunell, Hookeheale, Sicklewort, Carpenters hearbe; also, the ball, or apple of the eye.*
Prunier: m. *A Plumme tree.*
Prunier sauvage. *The Bullace tree.*
Prunier: m. ere: f. *Bearing, or abounding with, Plummes; of, or belonging to, Plummes; louing Plummes.*
Prurir. *To itch, to tickle; to desire lustfully.*
Prurit: m. *An itching, or tickling; a lustfull desire of, or affection vnto.*
Pruyer. *as* Preyer.

Psalme: m. *A Psalme; a song made of, or vnto, God.*
Psalmiste: m. *A Psalmist, a maker of Psalmes.*
Psalmodie: f. *The singing of Psalmes.*
Psalmodier. *To sing Psalmes.*
Psalterion: m. *A Psalterie; a melodious Instrument which resembles a Harpe.*
Psaultier: m. *A Psaulter; a booke of Psalmes.*
Pseaume. *Looke* Psalme.
Pseudonard. *Spike, Lauender, Lauender Spike.*
Pseudonard femelle. *Female Lauender, white Lauender; the smallest Lauender.*
Psilothre: f. *Brionie, Tettarberrie; also, an ointment for the taking of haire away.*
Psoloente. *A kind of lightning whose flash destroyes whatsoeuer it lights on.* ¶Rab.
Ptisane. *as* Tisanne.
Ptoschalazon. *A Polypragmon, medler, busie-bodie.* ¶Rab.
Ptyade: f. *A greenish ash-coloured Aspe, which raising vp her necke and head, spits venome at those whom she cannot reach with her teeth.*
Puamment. *Stinkingly, most vnsauorily.*
Puant: m. ante: f. *Stinking, ranke, vnsauorie, strong; that hath an ill wast, or smell.*
Bestes puantes. *Vermine; or beasts of the chase of the stinking foot; Looke vnder* Beste.
Herbe puante. *Small stinking Fleabane Coniza.*
Debonnaire mire fait playe puante: Prov. *A courteous Surgeon makes a corrupt sore.*
Puanteur: f. *A stinke, stench; rankenesse; a noysome wast, strong sauor, ill smell.*
Puantise: f. *as* Puanteur.
Puberté: f. *Youth; or the age wherein haire begins to grow about the priuities.*
Public: m. ique: f. *Publike, vulgar, common; manifest, euident, apparant, in the eyes of the world.*
Publicain: m. *A Publican, a Tole-gatherer; a Farmer, or leuier of publike reuenue.*
Publication: f. *A publication, diuulgation, manifestation, open discouerie, making of things common.*
Publication d'enquestes. C'est quand les enquestes sont rapportées, & receuës, & que les parties en prennent communication; apres laquelle ils ne sont plus receus à bailler reproches, & obiects de tesmoings. ¶Ragueau.
Publication d'un livre. *The edition, setting forth, or sending abroad, of a booke.*
Publié: m. ée: f. *Diuulged, published, set forth, manifested, made common.*
Publier. *To publish, diuulge, manifest, proclayme, noyse abroad, lay open, set forth, make common, or knowne.*
Publieur: m. *A publisher, cryer, proclaymer.*
Publiquement. *Publikely, commonly, manifestly, openly, all abroad, in the face, or eye of the world.*
Puce. *as* Pulce.
Puceal: m. ale: f. *Virgine, maiden, or maidenlie; of a virgin or maiden, virgin or maiden-like.*
Puceau: m. *A man that hath not lost his virginitie; also, one that with a puffe lights a candle newly put out; also, a kind of Vine.*
Pucelage: m. *Pucellage, virginitie, maidenhead; also, the end of a maidens girdle hanging downe before; also, the hearbe called Periwinkle.*
Puceler. *To corrupt, or deflowre, a maid.*
Pucelle: f. *A maid, virgine; girle, damsell, mother; also, the riuer Pilchard; or, a young, or little Shadfish.*
Pucelle de Marolle. *A crackt peece; a wench that hath got a clap; one that rather goes for a maid then is one.*
Petites pucelles sont ensemble belles: Pro. *Young girles looke faire when they together are.*
Pucher. *To take vp.* ¶Norm.
Pudeur: f. *as* Pudicité.
Pudibunde: com. *Shamefast, bashfull, modest, honest.*
Parties pudibundes. *The priuie parts, or members.*
Pudicité: f. *Pudicitie, chastitie, modestie, puritie, vntaintednesse, cleanenesse of life.*
Pudique: com. *Chast, pure, vntainted, cleane, shamefast, modest, honest.*
Pudiquement. *Chastly, purely, vntaintedly, modestly, shamefastly.*
Pueille. *as* Peulle.
Puël. Bois estans en puël. *Hauing beene lately cut, or lopped.*
Puër la Vigne. *To cut a Vine; or, as* Pouër.
Puerilité: f. *Puerilitie, boyishnesse, childishnesse, trifling, simplicitie.*
Puëtte: f. *A peg in a Hogshead, &c, of Wine; also, the peg-hole.*
Pugnitif: m. iue: f. *Warlike, fighting, contentious, quarrellsome.*
Puinne: f. *Spindle-tree, Prick-wood, Prick-timber.*
Puir. *To stinke, smell ranke, yeeld an ill wast, haue a bad sauor.*
Ce qu'on donne luit, ce qu'on mange puit: Prov. *True bountie consists rather in giuing men meanes then meat; or, as vnder* Luire.
Puis: m. *A Well, a Draw-well; a pit.*
Marier la cave, & le puis. *To mingle wine and water together.*
Pendant que la corde est au puis. *While we haue opportunitie, while occasion serues.*
Pierre en puis n'est pas pourrie: Pro. *Looke vnder* Pierre.
Puis. *(Of the Verbe* Pouvoir;*) I am able, I can.*
Puis. *Then, after, moreouer, furthermore.*
Puis que. *Seeing that, since that.*
Et puis. *Well then, so then; hoe, what sir, how then, what though, what of that, put the case it be so.*
Et puis; qu'en sera il? *After all that, or suppose all that be said, or done, what will follow, or what come of it? (in disdaine.)*
Puisé: m. ée: f. *Drawne vp, taken in, sucked vp; drayned, or drawne dry.*
Puisement: m. *A drawing vp, or out of; a drayning, or drawing dry.*
Puiser. *To draw vp, take in, or sucke out; also, to drayne, or draw dry.*
La Navire puise. *Leakes, or shippes in water apace.*
Puiseur: m. *A drawer, or drayner of water, &c.*
Puisne: f. *as* Puinne.
Puisné. *Punie, younger, borne after.*
Puissamment. *Puissantly, powerfully, mightily, strongly, forcibly.*
Puissance: f. *Puissance, power, or powerfullnesse; force, might, strength; abilitie, possibilitie, wealth, sway, authoritie, iurisdiction; also, a power, armie, or great number of men.*
Puissance de fief. *The power some Landlords haue to redeeme to their owne vses the land sold by their Tenant, by paying vnto the purchaser whatsoeuer he gaue for it, or defrayed about it.*

Puissant. *Puißant, mightie, powerfull, strong, forcible, most able; wealthie, of great meanes or authoritie, swaying where he comes.*
Sergent puissant, & resseant. *Which resides, or dwels within his walke.*
Puitier: m. *A digger, or maker of pits; a Well-maker.*
Puits: m. *as* Puis; *a Well.*
Pulce: f. *A flea; also, the small speckled, or streaked Spider.*
Pulce de mer. *A small vermine in the sea resembling a Shrimpe.*
Pulces musnieres des Hostels-Dieu de Paris. *Lice.*
L'herbe à pulces. *Fleabane, or fleawort;* Looke Pulciere.
Mesurer les sauts des pulces. *To spend, or bestow time verie fondly.*
'A la Saincte Luce du saut d'une pulce: Prov. viz. Le iour croist.
Qui se couche avec les chiens se leve avec des pulces: Prov. *We grow the worse for ill companie: (This Prouerbe is also applyable to such as adhere vnto poore, or hard maisters, from whom no good can be hoped, or drawne.)*
Pulceau: m. *The name of a Vine.*
Pulceux: m. euse: f. *Full of fleas.*
Pulcier: m. ere: f. *Fleaie; of a flea; full of fleas.*
Pulciere: f. *The hearbe Fleawort; also, Fleabane; (The seedes of that resemble fleas; the perfume of this doth kill them.)*
Pulçot: m. *A little flea; also, the worme called a Vine-fretter.*
Pulege: m. *Pennie royall, Puliall royall, Pudding grasse, Lurkydish.*
Pullulant. *Budding, shooting, springing, or sprouting out.*
Pullulé. *Budded, shot, sprung, or sprouted out.*
Pulluler. *To bud, shoot, spring, put, or sprout out.*
Pulmonaire: f. *The hearbe called Lungwort, or Cowslip of Jerusalem; also, the mosse called Lungwort, or wood Liuerwort.*
Pulmonée: f. *as* Poulmelée.
Pulpe: f. *The pulpe, or pith of plants, &c; also, the brawne, or solide and musculie flesh of the bodie.*
Pulpite. *Looke* Poulpitre.
Pulsatil: m. ile: f. *Knocking; beating.*
Pulsatille: f. *Pulsatill, Pasque flower, Paßeflower, Flawflower.*
Pulsation: f. *A knocking, thumping, beating.*
Pulte: f. *A poultice.*
Pulverin: m. *The touch-hole of a peece of Ordnance.*
Pulverizé: m. ée: f. *Pulverized; beaten, or made, into powder.*
Pulverizer. *To pulverize; to reduce, beat, or make, into powder.*
Pulvinaire: m. *A boulster for the bed of a Prince; also, a banketting bed made in the Romane Temples to the honor, and for the ease, of their gods.*
Pulviné: m. ée: f. *Furnished, or boulstered, with cushions, or pillowes.*
Pumice. Pierre pumice. *A Pumeise stone.*
Punais: m. aise: f. *Stinking, ranke or strong of sauor, loathsomely smelling; also, hauing a corrupt, or obstructed nose, and therefore smelling little, or nothing.*
Punaise: f. *The noysome, and stinking worme, or vermine called, a Punie, or the bed Punie.*
Punaise des champs. *The field Punie (is greene) and lesse then the other, but euerie whit as stinking.*
L'herbe aux punaises. *Fleabane, Coniza, Fleabane Mullet.*
Punaisie: f. *Stinke, stench, ranke sauor.*
Punctille. *as* Pointille.
Punction: f. *A pricking, foyning, sticking; stinging; also, a pointing.*
Punctual: m. ale: f. *Punctuall, pointing; also, pricking, or stinging.*
Cautere punctual. *See* Cautere.
Punctuation: f. *A pointing; a marking, or distinguishing by points.*
Punctué: m. ée: f. *Pointed; noted, marked, or distinguished by points.*
Punctuer. *To point; to make points; to note, marke, or distinguish by points.*
Punesie, *for* Pleuresie; *(a rusticall word.)*
Puni: m. ie: f. *Punished, chastised, corrected.*
Punir. *To punish, chastise, correct, inflict plagues on, take vengeance of.*
Punissable: com. *Punishable.*
Punisseur: m. *A punisher, chastiser, corrector.*
Punition: f. *A punishment, chastisement, correction; paine inflicted, vengeance taken; also, a punishing, chastising, correcting.*
Pupe. *The fish Pourcontrell, or Many-feet.*
Pupilaire: com. *Pupillarie, of or belonging to a Pupill.*
Pupilarité: f. *Nonnage.*
Pupile: m. *A Pupill, Ward, Orphan, vnderling, one thats vnder age.*
Pupille. *as* Pupile.
Pupine. *The name of an apple.*
Puput: m. *The bird called a Whoope, or dunghill Cocke; also, a kind of Frog.*
Puputer. *To whoope, or cry like the Whoope.*
Pur: m. ure: f. *Pure; whole, perfect, full, entire, of it selfe; white, faire, cleere, cleane, vnspotted, vncorrupted, neat; thinne, fine, smooth; innocent, simple, honest, vpright, sincere; without mixture, filth; condition, or exception.*
Pure perte du vassal. *An absolute seisure of, or entrie into, the land of a tenant, or vaßall, made by his Landlord.*
Default simple, ou pur. *Looke* Simple.
'A pur, & à plein. *Flatly and plainely, with full authoritie.*
Purée: f. *Sap, iuyce.*
La purée de pois. *Pease strayned, Pease pottage, or the liquor of Pease.*
La purée de Septembre. *Wine.*
Purement. *Purely; neatly, fairely, cleerely; wholly, fully, entirely; sincerely, vprightly; innocently, simply; without welt, or gard; without exception or condition.*
Purer. *To mattar; to grow vnto a head, or mattar; also, to yeeld, or distill mattar.*
Pureté: f. *Puritie, purenesse; neatnesse, fairenesse, clenlinesse, cleerenesse; honestie, sinceritie, integritie, innocencie, intirenesse.*
Purgation: f. *A purgation, purging, cleering, clensing, scowring; a good excuse, full satisfaction, expurgation, iustification.*
Purgatoire: m. *Purgatorie.*
Purgatoire: com. *Purgatorie, purging, clensing, expiatorie, satisfactorie.*
Purge: f. *A purge, purgation, cleering, expiation, iustification, satisfaction; or the indeauor which a delinquent vses to purge himselfe.*

Purgé: m. ée: f. *Purged, cleansed, cleered; iustified; expiated.*
Purgement: m. *as* Purgation.
Purger. *To purge, cleanse, cleere, scowre; expiate, satisfie, remedie, iustifie, excuse fully.*
Purger les arrierages de rentes; les despens, les debtes, les droicts seigneuriaux. *To discharge, or pay them.*
Purger le defaut. *A defendant, or any other, that appeared not at first, to come in by himselfe, or by his Atturney, and offer to answer.*
Purger vne maison, ou heritage. C'est faire sçavoir par proclamations, & affiches, que l'heritage &c, est à purger, & qu'il sera decreté par iustice, afin qu'il soit purgé & deschargé de toutes charges, hypotheques, & empeschemens, autres que ceux qui seront declarez, & receus par sentence. ¶Ragueau.
Purificatif: m. iue: f. *Purificatiue, purifying.*
Purification: f. *A purification, purifying, cleering, clensing, purging, scowring.*
Purifié: m. ée: f. *Purified, cleered, clensed, purged, scowred.*
Purifier. *To purifie, cleere, clense, purge.*
Puron: m. *A botch, powke, or blaine full of ordure, or filthie mattar.*
Purpurin: m. ine: f. *Of Purple, or Purple-like.*
Purulent: m. ente: f. *Mattarie, corrupt, filthie, full of healing, full of ordure.*
Pusillanime: com. *Dastardlie, cowardlie, faint-hearted, white-liuered.*
Necessité rend magnanime le coüard & pusillanime: Pro. *Necessitie, and distresse puts courage into cowards.*
Pusillanimement. *Dastardly, cowardly, without mettall, heart, or courage.*
Pusillanimité: f. *Pusillanimitie, faint-heartednesse, cowardise.*
Pussons: m. *The small greene flyes that lye cluttering vnder the leaues of hearbs, and within a while deuoure them.*
Pustule: f. *A push, blaine, wheale, water-powke, small blister.*
Pustuleux: m. euse: f. *Full of pushes, wheales, blaines, little blisters.*
Putain: f. *A whore, queane, punke, drab, flurt, strumpet, harlot, cockatrice, naughtie pack, light huswife, common hackney.*
Effronté en putain. *As bold, or brasen-faced, as a whore.*
Putain fait comme la corneille, plus se lave & plus noire est elle: Pro. *A queane and Crow alike doe fare, the more they wash the fouler they are.*
Assez fait qui fortune passe, & plus encor qui putain chasse: Pro. *as vnder* Fortune.
Fils de putain ne fit iamais bien: Prov. *Neuer did sonne of a whore doe well.*
Putanier. *as* Putier.
Putasser. *To haunt whore-houses; to vse, follow, or affect whores.*
Putasserie: f. *Whoring, whore-hunting, bawderie, wenching.*
Putassier: m. ere: f. *Whorish, whore-like, of or belonging to a whore.*
Putatif: m. iue: f. *Putatiue, reputed, imaginarie, supposed, esteemed.*
Puteal: m. ale: f. *Deepe as a pit; of a pit.*
Puterbe: m. *An Hermit (or any other) whose breath is tainted by much feeding on hearbes.*
Puterie: f. *Whoring, whoredome, whore-hunting, wenching.*
Putier: m. *A whoremonger, whore-hunter, smell-smocke, wencher.*
Putier: m. ere: f. *Whorish, drab-like, impudent, immodest, light; lasciuious, wenching, whore-hunting.*
Putoir: m. *A stinke, ill sauor, filthie wast, ranke smell; also, as* Putier, *and as* Putois.
Putois: m. *A Fitch, or Fullmart.*
Putput: m. *as* Puput.
Putredineux: m. euse: f. *Full of rottennesse.*
Putrefactif: m. iue: f. *Putrefactiue.*
Putrefaction: f. *Putrefaction, rottennesse, corruption.*
Putrefié: m. ée: f. *Putrified, rotten, corrupted.*
Putrefier. *To putrifie, rot, corrupt.*
Putride: com. *Putride, putrified, rotten, tainted, corrupted.*
Putte: f. *A wench, lasse, girle, modder; (especially one that is no better then she should be.)*
Puy: m. *as* Puis; *A Well; also, a hillocke, or high clot of earth.*
Puye. f. *as* Appuye.
Puyne. *Spindle-tree, Prick-wood, Prick-timber.*
Py: m. *as* Pis; *the breast &c; (an old word.)*
Pyafer, & Pyapher. *Looke* Piaffer.
Pye-pou. *The round-rooted, or Onyon-rooted Crowfoot.*
Pyginé: m. ée: f. *Dwarfie, short, low, little, of a small stature.*
Pylore. *The maw-gut, or stomacke-gut.*
Pyment. *Looke* Piment.
Pynthe. *as* Pinte. ¶Rab.
Pylaride: f. *A fire-fly, or worme bred in the fire, from which if it be kept any while, or remoued any distance, it dies.*
Pyramide. *as* Piramide.
Pyrate: m. *A Pyrate, Rouer, sea-robber.*
Pyraterie: f. *Pyracie, rouing, sea-robbing.*
Pyratique: com. *Pyraticall; of, or belonging to, a Pyrate.*
Pyrethre: m. *The hearbe called Bartram, or Pellitorie; or, the right Pellitorie of Spaine.*
Pyrethre sauvage. *Wild Bartram, wild Pellitorie; also, the hearbe Sneesewort.*
Pyrolle: f. *Pirola, (hearbe) Winter-greene.*
Pyronomie: f. *The art of gouerning, or ordering Alchimisticall fires.*
Pyrope. *A kind of fierie-red Carbuncle (stone.)*
Pyrothecnie: f. *The making of fire-workes.*
Pyrothique: com. *Causticke, and corrosiue.*
Pyrouët: m. *A Shittlecocke.*
Pyrouëtte. *See* Pirouëtte.
Pyrrique. *A souldierlie forme of dauncing in Armour; inuented by* Pyrrhus *King of Macedonia.*
Pyvoine: f. *Pionie, Peonie, Kings bloome, Rose of the mount.*

Q

QVadragenaire: com. *Of fortie yeares.*
Quadragesimal: m. ale: f. *Lenten; of, or belonging to, Lent.*
Quadrain: m. *A Stanzo, or Staffe of foure verses.*
Quadran: m. *A Sunne-dyall.*
Quadrangle: m. *A Quadrangle; a square Plot, or figure hauing foure angles, and foure sides.*
Quadrangulaire: com. *Quadrangular, foure-cornered, foure-square.*

Quadrangule: com. *The same.*
Quadrannier: m.ere: f. *Of foure yeares; also, foure yeares old.*
Quadraturé: m. ée: f. *Square, well growne, well set, almost as thicke as long.*
Quadre. les Quadres de la Lune. *The Quarters of the Moone.*
Quadré: m.ée: f. *Squared; also, fitted, or agreeing, vnto.*
Quadrelle: f. *An Arrow, a Shaft.*
Quadrer. *To square; also, to sute, be fit, agree vnto, stand well with, serue iust in a place.*
Quadrilettre: f. *A word of foure letters.*
Quadrille: f. *A Squadron containing 25 (or fewer) Souldiers.*
Quadrin: m *as* Liard.
Quadrivie: f. *A place where foure sundrie wayes doe meet; also, a way that hath foure seuerall turnings, or partings.*
Quadrupe: com. *Foure-footed.*
Quadruple: com. *Quadruple, foure double, foure-fold, foure times as much.*
Quadruplé: m.ée: f. *Quadruplated; foulded, renewed, repeated foure times ouer; made foure times as much.*
Quadruplement: m. *as* Quadruplication.
Quadrupler. *To fould, renew, repeat foure times; to quadruplate, or make foure times as much.*
Quadruplication: f. *A quadruplication; a renewing, repeating, making foure times ouer.*
Quadruplique du defendeur: f. *A second reioynder; or the third defence made, or writing put into Court, by a defendant.*
Qu'a-huqu'a-ha. *Well or ill, I know not how; here or there, one way or another; also, laboriously, hardly, painefully, with much paine, with great adoe.*
Quai: m. *The key of a riuer, or hauen; also, a piller of Marble, or stone.*
Quaisse: f. *A square woodden chest, such as Armour, or Marchandise is carried in; also, a great, and chestlike partition in garners, to put corne in; also, a Drumme, or (most properly) the barrell, or wood of a Drumme; also, a Scoope, or Ladle, such as Canoniers lade their peeces withall.*
Quaissier: m. *A Chest-keeper; he that keepeth the keyes of the chest wherein publicke Records, or commodities, are kept.*
Qualibre: m. *The bore of a Gunne, or size of the bore; (and hence) also, the size, capacitie, or fashion of any such thing; also, the state, condition, calling, or humor of a man; whence;*
Il n'est pas de mon qualibre. *He is not of my qualitie, ranke, or humor, he is no fit companion for me.*
Qualibré: m. ée: f. *Fit for, or fitted vnto, the bore, agreeing with, or applied vnto the size, of.*
Balotte de fer bien qualibrée. *A bullet of a good size, or seruing for a large bore.*
Qualifié: m.ée: f. *Qualified, intitled, stiled, called, tearmed.*
Qualifier. *To qualifie, tearme, intitle, call, stile.*
Qualité: f. *A qualitie, condition, sort, fashion, manner, degree, state, name, title, function, calling; any circumstance accompanying, or belonging to, a thing.*
Quand. *When, at what time, when as; also, if that, although, howbeit, notwithstanding, all were it; also, seeing that; also, till, vntill, or against the time that.*
Quandoque. Docteur de quandoque. *A dunsicall Doctor.*
Quaneuse: f. *A Mill-hopper.*
Quant à. *As for, as touching, in as much as, in regard of.*
Quant & quant. *Forthwith, incontinently, therewith, by and by.*
Quant & quant vous. *Altogether, together with, in companie of, you.*
Quant est de moy. *For my part, as for me.*
Quant ores. *Albeit, though, although.*
D'icy à quant? *How farre off? how long to? vntill what time?*
Il fait bien le quant à moy. *He stands on verie nice tearmes, he makes verie strange, or daintie of the matter; also, he slackens, relents, growes calme; also, hee hath a good conceit of himselfe, or values a strange opinion of his owne aboue all others.*
Quantes fois. *How often, how many times.*
Toutes & quantes fois; or, Toutes fois & quantes. *As often, as many times, as.*
Quantiesme: com. *Of what number, or which (in number?) in what place, ranke, order?*
Quantité: f. *Quantitie, size, bignesse, greatnesse; a deale, store, plentie, abundance.*
Quanton. *as* Canton.
Quaqueroles: f. *The tawnie Beetles which buzze about by flockes in hay-time; also, the shells of Snayles, &c.*
Quaquet: m. *Prattling, tattling, tittle tattle, prittle prattle, much talke, lowd chat, many words.*
Quaquetant. *Prattling, tattling, babbling, chattering.*
Quaqueté. *Tattled, prattled, babbled.*
Quaquetement: m. *A prating, prattling, babbling, tatling, chattering.*
Quaqueter. *To prate, prattle, babble, tattle, chatter, vse many words.*
Quarantaine: f. *Lent; also, a terme of fortie dayes, during which prayers are, in some places, powred out for the dead.*
La Quarantaine du Roy. *Fortie dayes truce, during which it was not lawfull for a man, in S. Lewis his time, to prosecute any reuenge against the kinsmen, or friends of such as had wronged, or outraged him.*
Quarante. *Fortie.*
Quarantiéme: com. *The fortieth.*
Quarentaine. *as* Quarantaine.
Quaresme: m. *Lent; See* Caresme.
Quaresmeau. Iour quaresmeau. *A Lenten, or fish-day.*
Quarillon. *as* Carillon.
Quarlet: m. *The small Plaice, or fresh-water Plaice; or a kind of broad, and short Plaice.*
Quarme: m. *The Horne beame, Hard beame, Witch Hasell, Yoke tree.*
Quarneau. *as* Creneau.
Quarquan. *See* Carcan.
Quarre: m. *A Square, Quadrant, square figure; any thing that is foure square; and (particularly) a square bed in a Garden.*
Quarré: m.ée: f. *Square, foure-square; squared, made square.*
Quarreau: m. *Is (generally) a little square, or square thing; (particularly) a Diamond, or Picke, at Cardes; also, a square tile, or bricke, fit to paue with; also, a cushion; also, a bed in a Garden; also, a Quarrell, or boult for a Crossebow, or an Arrow with a foure-square head; also, as* Plinthe; *See* Carreau.
Le quarreau de prisons. *The Maisters side.*
Quarrefour: m. *The place in, or part of, a towne whereat*

at fowre streets meet a head.

Par tous les quarrefours de. *Throughout all the foure Quarters, corners, or streets of.*

Quarrelé: m. ée: f. *Paued, floored, or laid with square tiles, or stones; also, soled, or cobled, as a shooe.*

Quarreler. *To paue, lay, or floore, with square tiles, or stones; also, to sole, or coble, a shooe.*

Quarrelet: m. *as* Quarlet; *or as* Carrelet.

Quarreleur: m. *A soler, or cobler of shooes.*

Quarreleure: f. *A pauing, flooring, or laying with square tiles, &c; also, a soling, or cobling of shooes.*

Quarrellage: m. *A pauement of, or pauing with, square tiles, or stones; also, big timber to be sawed into quarters.*

Quarrellé: m. ée: f. *as* Quarrelé.

Quarrément. *Squarely.*

Quarrer. *To square, to make square.*

Se quarrer. *To strout, or square it, looke big on't, carrie his armes a kemboll braggadochio-like.*

Il y quarre le cercle. *as vnder* Cercle; *or, he is therin cleane out of his element; at th'vtmost end of his cunning; he can doe nothing in it hauing puzzled, and grauelled farre greater schollers then himselfe.*

Quarreure: f. *A square; also, a squaring, a making square or broad; also, squarenesse, or breadth.*

Quarrier. *as* Quarrieur.

Quarriere: f. *A highway; a quarrey of stone; a carreere, or course on horsebacke; See* Carriere.

Quarrieur: m. *A Quarrier, or Quarrey-man; a hewer of stones in quarreyes; a plucker of stones out of quarreyes.*

Quarril: m. *The fourth part of a Spanish* Real; *a small coyne worth our three-halfe-pence.*

Quarroy: m. *A great, and broad, highway.*

Le grand quarroy. *The Kings highway.*

Quart: m. *A fourth; a quarter; a fourth part; and particularly, a French pecke, or the fourth part of a* Boisseau; *as also, the fourth part of the value of retailed marchandise, due (sometimes, and in some cases) as a custome vnto the King.*

Quart de Chopine. *The quarter, or fourth part, of a* Chopine; *Looke* Chopine.

Quart d'escu. *A* Teston, *or Quardecue; a siluer peece of coyne worth* 18 d. sterl.

Quart des Sentences. *A part of the Popish Decretalls.*

Quart: m. quarte: f. *The fourth.*

Quart denier. *The fourth pennie, or part of the value of an inheritance* Cottier, *due vnto the Landlord, vpon any sale, grant, or alienation, thereof.*

Quartage: m. *A fourth; or the custome specified in the word* Quart.

Quartagé: m. ée: f. *A fourth part of the price whereof is paied, as a custome, vnto the King.*

Quartaire: m. *The quarter of a pound; also, (as the Roman* Quartarius) *a measure containing about twelue spoonefulls of liquid, and weighing some fiue ounces in drie, things.*

Quartault: m. *The Quarter, or fourth part, of a measure.*

Quarte: f. *A French* Quarte *(almost our pottle;) also, a fourth, in Musicke.*

Quarte d'arpent. *The fourth part of the* Quarteron; *or the 64 part of th'*Arpent.

Quartellée: f. *A certaine quantitie of, or measure for, ground, in* Bourbonnois.

Quartement. *Fourthly.*

Quartenier: m. *Th' Alderman of a Ward in a Towne; or particularly, such an Officer in* Paris, *as th' Alderman is in London; also, in the countrey, an Officer of some resemblance, in his authoritie, with our High Constable; also, the Quarter Maister of a ship.*

Quarteranche: f. *The eighth part of a* Bichot; *a measure for corne.*

Quarterée: f. *as* Boisseau *in some parts of* Bourbonnois.

Qarternier de gensdarmes. *An Officer which hath the charge, or commaund of foure* Gensdarmes. .

Quarteron: m. *A quarter of a pound; also, a quarterne (or the fourth part) of an hundreth; also, a* Pinte, *or little Quart; also, the halfe of an* Emine; *also, a Quarter of the Moone.* (En Languedoc le Quarteron, commun & pour le bled, & pour la terre qui le produit, contient 4 Civadiers, dits aussi boisseaux, divisez par demiz.)

Vn quarteron d'arpent. *Is a quarter of the quarter; or the* 16 *part of th'* Arpent.

Reduict de livres en quarterons. *Extreamely diminished, whereof at the least three parts be spent.*

Quartier: m. *A quarter, coast, part, Region; also, a Quarter, or Ward, in a Towne; also, the quarter of a yeare, of a yard; a Quarter of the Moone; of mutton, &c; the fourth part of any thing thats commonly diuided by quarters; also, a trencher; also, Quarter, or faire war, wherein souldiers are taken prisoners, and ransomed at a certaine rate.*

Quartier de bois. *A Quarter, or square peece of timber.*

Bois de quartier. *Quarters; or timber to make Quarters of.*

Eschalas de quartier. *A square Oaken prop, or supporter, for a vine.*

Avoir vn quartier de la Lune en la teste. *To be giddie, humorous, fantasticall, halfe franticke.*

Entrer en quartier. *To beginne his waiting moneth, &c; also, to get into credit, step into imployment, creep into fauour, come into request, by the disgrace, or discharge, of another; (The like is;)*

Estre en quartier. *To wait, or serue his quarter, moneth, yeare; to be in waiting; and hence, to bee in credit, estimation, good doings.*

Faire quartier neuf, ou faux quartier. *A horses hoofe to riue, or cleaue, from the top to the bottome.*

Faire quartier à part. *To retire aside, or make a partie by himselfe.*

Vn quartier fait l'autre vendre: Prov. *One quarter makes th'other to be sold..*

Quartier. *(Aduerbially) apart, aside.*

Quasi. *Almost, welnigh, welneere, in a manner.*

Quasimodo. *Low Sunday; the next Sunday after Easter.*

Quassation: f. *A shaking, or brandishing; also, a cassation, cassing; breaking, squashing; abrogating, annulling.*

Quassé: m. ée: f. *as* Cassé.

Quasser. *See* Casser.

Quassette: f. *A small casket, box, coffin; frying-panne; trough for birds meat.*

Quasseur: m. *A squasher, breaker; casser, canceller.*

Quassure. *as* Casseure.

Quaternaire. Iours quaternaires. *Euerie fourth day; or euerie foure dayes.*

Quati, & Quatir. *See* Cati, & Catir.

Quatorze. *Fourteene.*

Quatrain: m. *A staffe, or stanzo of foure verses.*

Quatre. *Foure.*

Les quatre temps. *Th'Imber dayes; foure weekes in the yeare appointed for publicke fasts.*

Diablerie à quatre personnages. *Looke* Diablerie.

Quatre-mesnage. *An ill, improuident, or vnskilfull husband; a wast-good, spill-good, or spill-thrift.*

Quatridien: m. *A terme of foure dayes.*

Quatridien: m. enne: f. *Of foure dayes.*

Quatriesme: m. *The fourth pot of, or pennie taken for, wine, &c, retailed; an Imposition first raised by Charles the fift, and continued by some of his successors; and leuiable onely on such wine, &c, as is bought to be retailed; whence;*

Cela est de son cru, il n'en doit point le quatriesme.

Le Quatriesme. *The fourth.*

Quatroillé: m. ée: f. *Diuersified, pide, or breended, streaked with one colour vpon another.*

Quatruplon: m. *A double double Duckate; a peece of gold worth about* 26 s. 8 d. sterl.

Quau. *in stead of* Corps: ¶Lorrainois: ¶Rab.

Quay: m. *A Key of a Hauen, or on a riuer side; the stone wall whereto ships, &c, be fastened; a high banke whereon the water beats and breakes; also, a piller of of stone; or a heape of stones.*

Quayer. *as* Cayer.

Quayre: f. *A little worme that breeds betweene the barke, and wood, of trees:* ¶Bourdelois.

Que. *(A Relatiue of all Genders, and Numbers) that, which, whom, who.*

Que. *(An Interrogatiue of the Singular Number) what, wherefore, how, but what, why, why not, why then?*

Que. *(Sometimes an Aduerbe, sometimes a Coniunction) that, then; in sort, so that; least that, vnlesse; because, to th'end that; but, sauing, except; also, partly, or in part; whence;*

Que bien que mal. *Indifferently, so so, well or ill, one way or other.*

Que cecy; que cela; que si. *As this; as that; as if.*

Non que. *Not onely.*

Il fait que fol. *He playes the foole.*

Il n'est que jeune chair. *There is nothing to young flesh, there's no flesh like the young.*

Il ne se peut garder qu'il ne l'envoye. *Hee must needs send him; he cannot forbeare, or auoid the sending of him.*

Quecas. *as* Quocas: ¶Rab.

Quel: m. elle: f. *What, who.*

Quel qu'il soit. *Whosoeuer, whatsoeuer, what ere, he be.*

Quelle qu'elle soit. *Whatsoeuer; of what ranke or sort, of what greatnesse or humor, soeuer she be.*

Quel. *(Aduerbially)* Ie m'en iray devant recognoistre, quel il fait à Paris. *In what safetie, or state, one may liue at Paris; or whether it be good staying there, or no.*

Quelconque. *Whosoeuer, whatsoeuer.*

Quellement. *How, in what sort, in what manner.*

Tellement quellement. *See* Tellement.

Quelque. *Some, somewhat, any, whosoeuer, whatsoeuer.*

Quelquefois. *Sometimes, now and then, euer and anon; also, euer, or, at any time.*

Quelque part. *(Without addition) somewhere, somewhither; (with addition, or attended on by* Que, *it imports an vniuersalitie of place; as in)* Quelque part que. *Wheresoeuer, whithersoeuer; in or into what place soeuer.*

Quemand. *as* Caimand.

Quemise: f. *The principall ouerture of a melting furnace.*

Quemin: m. *A way:* ¶Pic.

Quemuletier: m. *A Countercharmer, Wizard, or good Witch.*

Quenaille. *as* Canaille.

Quenaise. Droict de quenaise. *The right of Escheatage; whereby an inheritance* Roturier *falls into the Lords hands when the tenant thereof leaues no heires of his bodie behind him:* ¶Breton.

Quenie: f. *A certaine old-fashioned garment, at this day out of fashion; or, as* Squenie.

Quenouille: f. *A distaffe; also, the Feminine line in a succession.*

Quenouilles d'un lict. *The posts of a bed.*

Quenouille rustique. *Wild* Carthamus, *wild bastard Saffron.*

Quenouille sauvage. *The same.*

Contes de la quenouille. *Tales of a tub, old wiues tales.*

Hoir de quenouille. *An Inheritrix, heire female, daughter and heire.*

Tenir de la quenouille. *To hold of, or doe homage to, the smocke; his wife to be his Maister.*

'A la quenouille le fol s'agenouille: Prov. *Fooles kneele to distaues, weake men vnto women.*

Quenouillée de. *A distaffe-full of.*

Quenouillette: f. *A little distaffe; also, a kind of small apple.*

Quens: m. *An old word, signifying a Count, or Earle.*

Quercelle: f. *A Kestrell, Kastrell, Fleingall.*

Quercerelle: f. *as* Quercelle.

Querele: f. *as* Querelle.

Querelé: m. ée: f. *Quarelled with; sued, or called in question, for; also, challenged, or whereto a title is pretended.*

Quereleur. *See* Querelleur.

Querelle: f. *A quarell, pike, brawle, difference, debate; Suit, Action, Processe against.*

Querelle d'Aleman. *An idle, sleight, or drunken contention; a friuolous, or vaine altercation.*

Arrests, ou statuts de querelle. *Iudgements giuen, and entred in cases of possession impeached.*

Sergent de querelle. *A certaine Officer which was vsed in Duelloes, or priuat quarells.*

Simples plaids, ou querelles. *Looke* Simple.

Querellé: m. ée: f. *See* Querelé.

Quereller. *To quarell, wrangle, brawle, brabble, striue, contend with; also, to challenge, lay claime, pretend a right, or title, vnto; sue, or bring an Action, for.*

Querelleur: m. *A wrangler, quareller, brawler, brabbler; an open pretender of right vnto other mens goods; a litigious, or contentious person; a common Barreter.*

Querelleux: m. euse: f. *Quarelsome, brawling, brabbling, litigious, vnquiet, contentious.*

Queri: m. ie: f. *Sought, looked for, inquired after.*

Querimonie: f. *A complaint, wailing, moane-making; a dolefull expressing of aggrieuances.*

Querir. *To looke, search out; seeke, or inquire, after; to goe fetch, call, or send for.*

Quiers tu meilleur pain que de froment? *Wouldest thou haue better bread then's made of Wheat?*

Meschante vie quiert le coing: Prov. *A wicked life affects a corner, or, creepes into corners.*

On ne doit point querir brebis qui se veut perdre: Pro. *The sheepe which will be lost must not be lookt for.*

Que-

Queritant. *Seeking for, searching out, inquiring after.*
Querquois: m. *A quiuer for arrowes.*
Querre. *as* Querir.
Quesne. *Looke* Chesne..
Quesnoy: m. *A wood, or forrest of Oakes.*
Quesse. *as* Quaisse.
Questable: com. *Finable, taxable, as some tenants are at the pleasure of their Lords; also, searchable, seekeable.*
Questal: m. ale: f. *Seruile; holding by Villenage; held by a seruile tenure.*
Questaux: m. *Villeines, the propertie of all whose estate is in their Landlords; so that they can neither deuise by Will, nor alien by bargaine, any part of it.*
Queste: f. *A quest, inquirie, search, inquisition, seeking; also, a demaunding, begging, desiring; also, an Aide giuen, or contribution made, by tenants vnto their Landlords, vpon occasions putting him to an extraordinarie charge (as, for his ransome; towards the mariage of his eldest daughter, &c; tearmed thus, because he is in person to demand it of thẽ; also (within the Jurisdiction of* Acs) *a generall rent, or fine, payed in common, and at once, by all the inhabitants of a Parish, ratably, and according to the iust quantitie of euerie mans land.)*
Queste courant. *An Imposition layed by a Landlord on some kind of tenants, in what season, and at what rates he list.*
Cens à queste. *Which must be demanded by the Lord thereof, or by his Officer.*
Lettres de queste. *A Licence to beg, or to gather almes, in Churches, for the poore.*
Queste-pain: m. *A common begger; or a begging; whence;* Qui est au queste-p. *That is most beggerlie, or the next doore to beggerie, thats growne to a verie low ebbe; thats driuen, readie, or fit, to beg his bread.*
Quester. *To seeke, search, trace, out; quest, hunt, make diligent inquirie after; also, to demaund, or beg, earnestlie; also, to quest, or open, as a dog that seeth, or findeth of his game.*
Quester ses gens. *A Lord to fine, or taxe his vassalls.*
Questeur: m. *A seeker, searcher, inquirer, tracer out of; also, an earnest begger, desirer, demander; also, one that hath a Licence to beg.*
Question: f. *A question, demaund, doubt; controuersie, dispute; proposition; reason; case; also, the Racke, or torture giuen, thereby to wring out confessions.*
Il est ici question de la vie. *This is a matter of life and death; mens liues are hereby brought in question.*
Il n'est pas question de cecy. *It concernes not this; we passe not for this; it is not this we treat of, or are about; it is not this that holds, or troubles, vs.*
Questionné: m. ée: f. *Questioned, examined, demanded or asked of.*
Questionner. *To question, demaund, examine, aske of.*
Questionnette: f. *A small question, sleight demand.*
Questionneur: m. *A questioner, (great) demaunder or asker, inquisitiue companion.*
Questuaire: com. *Gainfull, commodious, profit-bringing.*
Queu: m. *A Cooke; See* Queux.
Queüage: m. *A certaine Impost leuied, in some parts of France, vpon euerie* Queuë, *or Pipe of wine.*
Queuë: f. *A taile, traine, or traile; hence, the stalke, or steale of fruits; the rereward of an Armie; the labell of a Deed; the bable of a man; the close, end, conclusion, or knitting vp of a matter; also, a vessell containing as much as the* Muid *and a halfe;* viz. 54 Septiers, *at eight Parisien Pintes to the* Septier: *This* Queuë *is particularly, tearmed* Queuë Françoise, *for a difference betweene it and* Queuë de Bourgongne, *which is much bigger then it; also, a whetstone.*
Queuë d'arondelle. *A manner of closing, or fastening together of timber, boords, or stones, which resembling a Swallowes, Culuers, or Doues taile, is (also by our workmen) called so.*
Queuë de Bourgongne. *A wine vessell containing (iust as much as the auncient Romanes* Culeus; *or) two* Muids *and a halfe* (viz. 90 Septiers) *of Paris measure.*
Queuë de cheval. *Shaue-grasse, Horse-willow, horsetaile; a water-hearbe (whereof auncient writers haue described but two kinds; (viz. the great Horse-taile, & the little one otherwise tearmed naked Horse-taile, and Shaue-grasse (vsed by Fletchers, &c,) but our moderne Hearbalists haue found out fiue or six kindes more.)*
Queuë de l'hyver. *The season about mid May so tearmed by some.*
Queuë de l'oeil. *The corner of the eye.*
Queuë d'un penon. *The point, or end of a Pennon, which flutters in th'aire.*
Queuë de pourceau. *Sow Fennell, hogs Fennell, Horestrong, Horestrange, Brimstonwort, Sulpherwort.*
Queuë de regnard. *The hearbe called Fox-taile, or tailed Wheat; also, the stopping of a conduit pipe by rootes gotten into it, and growne, in time, so big, that the water hath no roome to passe.*
Queuë de scorpion. *Wartwort, great Tornesole.*
Queuë de souris. *Mouse-taile, Bloud-strange.*
Boutons à queuë. *Long buttons.*
Chausses à queuë de merlus. *Looke vnder* Chausse.
Damoiselle de queuë. *A waiting, or traine-bearing Gentlewoman.*
Demy queuë. *The halfe of the* Queuë (Françoise;) *a Hogshead, or vessell containing* 216 *Parisien Pintes.*
Monsieur sans queuë. *A Maister without any addition; a singlesoled Gentleman; also, a cheater.*
Robbe à queuë. *A traine-gowne.*
Seau pendant à double queuë. *(Is properly) a Seale annexed vnto, or hanging by, a double labell; (metaphorically) one that hangs on a Gibbet.*
Queuë à queuë. *Nose in arse; one close after, one in the necke of, another.*
La queuë entre les jambes. *Vily afraid (as a dog that hath stolne a pudding, &c, and slinkes away with his taile clapt betweene his legs;) also, foully disgraced, much ashamed, or with shame ynough.*
Danse du loup la queuë entre les jambes. *The daunce of lecherie.*
La queuë levée. Il s'en va la queuë levée. *He goes away merrie, iollie, liuelie, well cheered vp; or merrily, iollily, &c.*
A hausse queuë. Elle s'en va à hausse queuë. *Verie fast, or in great hast, she goes; (from the fashion of women, who to make the more hast, tucke vp their clothes behind.)*
Cette queuë n'est pas de ce veau. *This no way belongs vnto, or depends vpon, that.*
La difficulté sera à la queuë. *The hardest will be at last; in the conclusion, or knitting vp, wee shall haue most to doe.*
Brider son cheval par la queuë. *To take a wrong, or contrarie course; to goe most aukwardly, or the contrarie way, to worke.*
Couper la queuë à. *See* Couper.

Couper la queuë au jeu. *To giue ouer a winner.*
Escorcher les anguilles par la queuë. *To doe things disorderedly, aukwardly, the wrong way.*
Faire la queuë. *To play the coward, come or drag behind, march in the rere.*
Frizer la queuë. *To lecher.*
Prendre vn rat par la queuë. *To cut a purse.*
Regarder de la queuë de l'oeil. *To leere, gleeke, or looke askew; to cast a side-glaunce, at.*
Revenu de queuë. *Whose taile is new grown, or come againe: Appliable to an old Cokes, or Callet, growne wanton on a sudden; or, to one, that after a great weakenesse hath recouered his owne, or pickt vp his crummes againe.*
Tenir la queuë de la paelle. *Seeke* Paelle.
Trainer longue queuë. *To be long in doing, or to continue long; to haue a farre reach, bee of great consequence, carrie or traile many things along with it.*
La queuë est pire à escorcher: Pro. *The last is hardest to be done.*
'A la queuë gist le venin: Prov. *Appliable to such as reserue the discouerie, or executiō, of their villanous proiects vnto the conclusion of a businesse.*
'A mauvais chien la queuë luy vient: Pro. *Rakehells thriue better, battle faster, come forward sooner (after a losse) then honester men.*
'A qui est l'asne si le tienne par la queuë: Pro. *Let him that owes th' Asse hold him by the tayle; he that hath a suit to follow, or a thing to keepe, may thinke no Solicitor so good, no watchman so fit, as himselfe.*
Le regnard cache sa queuë: Prov. *The cunning knaue conceales what would discouer him.*
Qui parle du loup on en voit la queuë: Prov. *See* Loup.
Qui ne retire de sa vache que la queuë ne perd pas tout: Prov. *Tis good, when all is going, to saue any little; something, though meane, hath sauor, nothing none.*
Qui tient la paesle par la queuë, il la tourne là ou il veut: Pro. *Those that commaund, or manage, lawes, expound them how they list.*
Vache ne sçait que vaut sa queuë iusques à ce qu' elle l'ait perduë: Prov. *We know not the worth of things till we haue lost them.*
Queüé: m. ée: f. *Tailed, that hath a taile.*
Queuëtte: f. *A little taile, staulke, or steale; the tip of a thing.*
Queus: m. *A whetstone.*
Queuse: f. *A rude lumpe, or masse; as of yron, &c, comming from the furnace, or before it bee wrought into barres.*
Queusser. Que ton car ne se queusse. *To keepe thy cart from being ouerthrowne.*
Queut: f. *as* Queus.
Queute: f. *Small drinke; small beere:* ¶Pic.
Queux: m. *A Cooke.*
Le grand queux de France. *The Maister Cooke, the Kings chiefe Cooke, or chiefe of the Cookes, at Court.*
Queux: f. *A whetstone.*
Queymander. *To beg from doore to doore.*
Qui. *(A Relatiue of all Genders, Numbers, and persons;) Who, which, that, that which, whom, whose, what, any bodie, some bodie.*
Qui ça, qui là. *One here another there, this man here that there; here and there; asunder, in seuerall parts or places.*
Qui que ce soit. *Whosoeuer, or whatsoeuer bee bee; what name soeuer be beareth; what ranke soeuer bee hath, what worth soeuer he is of.*
Ils se feront mal qui ne les departira. *They will mischieue one another if they be not parted.*
Quia. Il est à quia. *He is almost at a nonplus.*
Quiconque. *Whosoeuer, or whatsoeuer.*
Quictance: f. *An acquitiance, release, discharge.*
Quicter. *See* Quiter.
Quid pro quo. *A palpable mistaking, a grosse errour, one for another.*
Quidam. vn q. *An odde, or certaine, fellow.*
Quidditatif: m. iue: f. *Quidditatiue, doubtfull, obscure, full of quirkes, fraught with quiddities; also, contentious, wrangling, litigious.*
Quideau: m. *A Wicker Engine whereby fish is caught.*
Quierchier: m. *The name of a small bird.*
Quietin. *as* Theatin.
Quietude: f. *Rest, calmenesse, tranquilitie, peaceablenesse.*
Quignet: m. *A little corner.*
Quignon: m. *A cantill, gobbet, lumpe, luncheon, good big peece of.*
Quignon de pain. *A corner of a crustie peece of bread; or, the crustie heele of a loafe.*
Quillard: m. *as* Billart.
Quillat: m. *The refining, or touch of gold; or, as* Carat.
Quille: f. *The keele of a ship; also, a keyle; a big peg, or pinne of wood, vsed at Nine-pinnes, or Keyles, &c.*
'A la quille, & au quillard. *At cat and trap.*
On luy a donné son sac, & ses quilles. *Looke* Sac.
Trousser leurs quilles. *To packe vp, or prepare, for their departure.*
Quillebandier: m. *One that playeth much at Nine-pinnes.*
Quillela. *A kind of play like vnto Cat and trap.*
Quilles. *Keyles, or Nine-pinnes.*
Quillevilles: f. *Skirrit roots.*
Quillons de la garde d'un'espée. *The crosse barres of the hilt of a sword.*
Quinaire: m. *An auncient Roman coyne worth about* 3 d. ob. sterl.
Quinaud: m. *An Ape, or Monkie; and hence, a deformed, or euill-fauoured creature.*
Ie l'ay rendu quinaud. *I haue blankt, or graueld him, I haue put him to a nonplus, or to the wall (in disputation.)*
Quinaude: f. *A she Ape, or Monkie; also, an ouglie wench, a Madame Ouglie.*
Quinconcé. vergier quin. *The trees whereof be ranked in equall distance asunder, and directly one ouer against th'other.*
Quine. Faire la quine à. *To mock, or make a mouth at; to point at with the finger.*
Quines. *Two cinks, or fiues, on the Dice.*
Quinette: f. *A crutch; the staffe, or supporter of a cripple; also, a Snite, or Snipe.*
Quinquaille: f. *Chinkes, coyne.*
Quinquailles: f. *Old yron; also, small yron ware; or pedling ware of yron, copper, &c.*
Quinquailler: m. *as* Quinqualier, *or* Quinquallier.
Quinqualier: m. *A paultrie Pedler; also, one that sells, or cries, old yron.*
Quinquallerie: f. *as* Quinquailles; *or, all kind of (small) yron-worke, as Padlockes, Snuffers, Gimmers, or Hindges for doores, &c; sold by Ironmongers.*
Quinquallieur: m. *An Ironmonger; or one that sells all kind of (small) Iron-ware.*
Quinquaneleur: m. *A bankrupt; one that procures, or forces*

forces his creditors to giue him fiue yeares day of payment.
Quinquangle: com. *Fiue-cornered, hauing fiue angles or corners.*
Quinque. Pain de quinque. *Delicate bread made especially against the foure solemne feasts of Easter, S. Peter and S. Paules day, th'Assumption of the Virgine Marie, and Christmas.*
Quinquenaut: m. *A little slinging, and venomous flie, in the Prouinces of* Sologne, & la Beausse.
Quinquenelle. *as* Quinquennelle.
Quinquennelle: f. *A respit, or terme of fiue yeares.*
Faire quinquennelle. *To grow bankrupt; or, as a bankrupt, to procure, in respect of his pouertie or losses, a respit of, or protection for, fiue yeares, during which his creditors can recouer nothing of him.*
Quinquennon. Privilege de q. *A Protection for fiue yeares, granted by the Prince (or his Officers) vnto a debtor, who makes good proofe of the losse, or extreame diminution, of his estate, since the time of the making of the bargaine, whereby he became indebted.*
Quinson: m. *A Spinke, or Chaffinch.*
Quint: m. *A fifth, or fift part; also, as* le quint denier.
Quint datif. *The portion of an inheritance whereof onely a man may dispose, by gift, Will, or otherwise.*
Quint naturel et coustumier. *The portion of younger brethren; being (within the Countie of* Ponthieu, *and in other places) a fift part of all the land their father died seised of, equally diuided among them; yet so, as when any of them dies, his part is to reuert vnto the foure parts enioyed by th'eldest.*
Quint & requint. *Looke* Requint.
Quint viager, ou heredital. *Whereof a man may dispose as of his owne inheritance (by the customs of* Amiens;) *or, the portion of an inheritance* Feodal *belõging to a younger brother (by the customes of* Peronne.)
Quint de vivre naturel. *as* Quint naturel et coustumier.
Droict de quint. *as* le quint denier.
Quint: m. quinte: f. *The fift.*
Le quint denier. *The fift pennie, or part of the price, of land thats sold; payed vnto the Lord of the soyle by the seller in some places, in others by the buyer, and in some others equally by both.*
Quintage: m. *A fift part, or the laying out of the fift part of an inheritance for younger brethren.*
Quintain: m. *French Laune; or, as* Quintin.
Quintaine: f. *A Quintane (or Whintane) for countrey youthes to runne at.*
Les Quintaines, & ban de non vendre vin en detail. *as* Droict de ban à vin.
Quintal: m. *A Quintall, or hundred weight.*
Quinte: f. *as* Quint; *A fift part; also, a fift (or the proportion of fiue) in Musicke, &c; also, a fantasticall humor or veine; a foolish giddinesse of the braine.*
Les quintes d'Angers. *The Territorie, Libertie, Circuit, or extent of countrey, wherein the Prouost, or ordinarie Judge, hath Jurisdiction.*
Il a sa quinte. *He is now in the humor, or in his moods; he hath odde conceits, at this time, in his braine.*
Il est en quinte de faire cela. *He is in the vaine, or a toy hath taken him in the head, to doe that same; he is foolishly affected, or humored vnto it.*
Quintefueille: f. *Cinkfoyle, Fiue-leaued grasse.*
Quintement: m. *A laying, or taking out a fift part.*
Quintement. *Fiftly.*
Quinter. *To lay, or take, out a fift part; also, as* Pancher; *to leane, or hang, at o side.*
Quinter les fiefs. *To diuide a fift part of them among younger brethren.*
Quinter ses heritages. *To dispose of a fift part thereof.*
Quintessence: f. *A quintescence; the vertue, force, or spirit of a thing extracted.*
Quintessencé: m. ée: f. *Exceedingly refined, or purified.*
Quintessencer. *To extract the quintescence, vertue, or spirit, out of a thing; to refine, or purifie exceedingly.*
Quintessencieux: m. euse: f. *All quintescence, full of spirit, exactly fine.*
Quintessentier. *as* Quintessencer.
Quinteux: m. euse: f. *Humorous, fantasticall, toyish, capricious; moodie, waspish; harebraind, giddie headed.*
Quintin: m. *A course kind of Laune.*
Quintil: m. *A rash Judge, or hastie censurer, of other mens writings.*
Quinuneve. En ordre quin. *In Checker forme, or Checker-wise.*
Quinzaine. *A terme, or delay of fifteene whole dayes together, granted, in some cases, by the Judges.*
Sauf quinzaine. *With reseruation of the 15 dayes respit, or terme which he hath gotten.*
Quinze: f. *Fifteene.*
Quinze-vingts de Paris. *An Hospitall wherein three hundred blind people be releeued with bread, lodging, and about iiij. d. a day; besides a priuiledge to beg at certaine Church doores.*
Quinziesme. le q. *The fifteenth,*
Quiquenelle. *as* Quinquenelle.
Quis: m. ise: f. *Sought, looked, searched for; demaunded, asked, inquired after; fetched, gotten.*
Quitance: f. *An Acquitance, Release, discharge.*
Quite: com. *Discharged, quit, freed, released, forgiuen, absolued, set cleere aboord.*
Iouër à quite, ou à double. *To play double or quit, win the mare or loose the haulter.*
Il n'est pas quite qui doibt de reste: Prov. *He is not quit that oweth ought.*
Quité: m. ée: f. *Quitted, forsaken, forgone, remitted, released, yeelded vp, giuen ouer.*
Quitement. *Freely, quietly, peaceably, without let, hinderance, impeachment, or disturbance.*
Quiter. *To quit, forgoe, renounce, yeeld vp, abandon, giue ouer; to void, withdraw, or part, from; to remit, release, discharge, acquit, pardon, forgiue, absolue, dispence with.*
Quiter vn boeuf pour prendre vn oeuf. *To leaue an Oxe for the loue of an egge.*
Quiter la ceincture. *Looke* Ceincture.
Quiter les cendres. *To stirre abroad; or, to quit his idle, base, or vnworthie courses.*
Qui Dieu quite est bien heureux: Prov. *Happie is he whom God absolues.*
Quiterne: f. *A Gitterne.*
Quiteur: m. *A quitter, acquiter, freer, discharger; one that giues an acquittance, or* Quietus est.
Quitté, & Quitter. *as* Quité, & Quiter.
Quitteur. *as* Quiteur.
Quittus: m. *An Acquittance, or* Quietus est.
Qulocul: m. *A dilling, or swillpough; the last, or youngest child one hath.*
Quocas: m. *Shaled nuts:* ¶Rab.
Quocquetier: m. *A Huckster.*
Quolibet: m. *A quirke, or quidditie; also, a ieast, or by-word.*

Vn vieux quolibet. *A moath-eaten adage, or prouerbe; and old said-saw.*
Quoquar: m. *(A childish tearme for) an egge.*
Quoquelicoq: m. *Corne-rose, wild Poppie, red Poppie.*
Quoquemart: m. *A Cauldron, or Chafer, to heat water, &c. in.*
Quote: f. *A quote, or quoting; a marke, or note vpon an article.*
La quote des tailles. *The sessing, or assessing of taxes.*
Quote. la quote partie. *The seuerall portion, or share belonging, or falling, to euerie one.*
Quoté: m. ée: f. *Quoted, marked, noted in the margent; also, taxed, assessed, rated.*
Quoter. *To quote, or marke in the margent, to note by the way; also, to sesse, assesse, tax, rate.*
Quotidien: m. enne: f. *Dailie, returning day by day, happening euerie day, ordinarie, continuall, vsuall.*
Quotiens. Totiens quotiens. *Efisoones, verie often; at pleasure, or as often as he pleases.*
Quotient: m. *The part or portion which, in the diuision of a thing among many, falls vnto euerie ones share.*
Quotizé: m. ée: f. *Taxed, sessed, assessed, rated.*
Quotizer. *To sesse, assesse, tax, rate.*
Quottité: f. *An euen assessement, a rate or totquot imposed; the laying on euerie one his share.*
Quoüat: m. *An vnderling, writling, staruelmg.*
Quoüé: m. ée: f. *Tailed, hauing a taile.*
Froument quoüé. *Foxtaile, tailed Wheat.*
Quoy: m. ye: f. *Quiet, still, peaceable, restfull, ease-affecting, husht, calme.*
Il n'y a pire eau que la quoye: Prov. *Silent, musing, or dreaming spirits are (for the most part) more daungerous, or of a worse composition, then others.*
Quoy. *(Interrogatiue) What? Why? how? what say you? what would you? how say you to this? what would you thinke of it, or doe with it?*
Quoy que. *Whatsoeuer, howsoeuer; notwithstanding, albeit, or although, that.*
'A quoy faire? *To what purpose? for what cause? what to doe?*
De quoy. *Looke* Dequoy.
Avoir de quoy, *or (better)* dequoy. *To be rich, haue somewhat to take vnto, haue wherewithall;* I' ay eu de quoy, mais. *I haue beene able to liue; the time was when I could haue shewed my head among the best of them, or held it as high as another; but.*
Quoyement. *Quietly, stilly, silently, calmely, peaceably.*
Quoyeté: f. *Stillnesse, quietnesse, rest, calmenesse; sobrietie; silence; peaceablenesse.*

R

Rabais: m. *An abatement, deduction, defalcation, diminution, extenuation; an exoneration, remission, discharge; a giuing backe of; also, a fall in price; or a poore rate, or low price, whereto a thing is come.*
Rabaissant. *Abating; abasing, deiecting, taking downe, pulling vnder.*
Se rabaissant bien bas. *Verie humbly, lowly, deiectedly, much disaduowing his owne worth.*
Rabaissé: m. ée: f. *Abated, abased, taken downe, pulled vnder, brought lower.*
Cela luy a bien rabaissé le menton. *That thing hath humbled him, or plucked him downe exceedingly.*
Rabaissement: m. *An abating, diminishing; abasing, deiecting.*
Rabaisser. *To abate; abase, deiect, pull downe, hold vnder, take a hole lower.*
Rabaisseur: m. *An abater; an abaser.*
Raballe: f. *A certaine root, of whose iuyce (mixed with other simples) a prettie sauce is made.*
Rabalter. *To rumble, rattle, or make a terrible noyse, as (they say) spirits doe in some vnfortunate, or vnfrequented houses.*
Rabans: m. *Rope-yards; the ropes, or treble cordes whereby the sayles of a ship are tied vnto the yardes.*
Rabaniste: m. *A dunce; or, one that studies, or is cunning in, the workes of the Rabbies.*
Rabaschement: m. *A rumbling, or a terrible ratling; such as (they say) is made by Hobgoblins in some vnfortunate, or vnfrequented houses.*
Rabascher, & Rabaster. *as* Rabalter.
Rabat: m. *as* Rabais; *also, a beater, the staffe wherwith Plaisterers beat their morter; also, a Rebatoe for a womans ruffe; also, a falling band; also, the retriue in hawking; also, the house, or penthouse of a Tennis-court.*
Vn rabat de bride. *A iob, or checke which a horse giues himselfe with his bridle.*
Le rabat des couvertures des maisons. *The eaues, or eauings; the bottome of the roofe.*
Rabat de manteau. *The cape of a cloke.*
Rabat-joye: m. *A bringer of ill tidings, a teller of ill newes (after the receit of good ones.)*
Rabatre. *To abate, deduct, defaulke, diminish, lessen, extenuate; remit, bate, giue or draw backe; also, a horse to rebate his curuet.*
Rabatre l'attenduë, ou congé. C'est le faire revoquer par comparition subsequente faicte en temps, & lieu.
Rabatre vn congé, ou defaut. *To recall, or disanull them, to make them void.*
Rabatu: m. uë: f. *Rebated, bated, abated, deducted, defaulcated, diminished; giuen, taken, or drawne backe.*
Iouër aux dames rabatuës. *Looke* Dames.
Rabavit: m. *Prickmadame, Sengreene the lesser.*
Rabbais, &c. *as* Rabais.
Rabbatre, & Rabbatu. *as* Rabatre, & Rabatu.
Rabbe. *Looke* Rabe.
Rabbienné: m. ée: f. *Reconciled, made good friends againe.*
Rabbienner. *To reconcile, attone, make friends, bring into good tearmes together, againe.*
Rabdomantie: f. *diuination by twigs, or smalls wands.*
Rabe: f. *A Rape, or Turnep; a round Limosin Raddish.*
Rabiere: f. *A plot, or bed of Rapes, or Turneps.*
Rabilité: m. ée: f. *Reinabled, repaired, reestablished, restored.*
Rabiliter. *To reinable, repaire, amend, reestablish, recouer, restore.*
Rabillage: m. *A repairing, mending, renewing, reforming.*
Rabillé: m. ée: f. *Mended, amended; reformed, corrected, repaired, renewed, trimmed, or dressed vp.*
Rabillecoustrer. *To patch, to mend.*
Rabillement. *as* Rabillage.
Rabiller. *To mend, amend, renew, repaire; correct, reforme; trimme or dresse vp an old thing, thereby making it seeme new.*
Rabilleur: m. *A renewer, mender, amender, trimmer vp of old things.*
Rabin: m. *A Rabbie, or Doctor among the Iewes*

Rabine: f. *A high growne wood; or, as* Bois de haute fustaye.
Rabinique: com. *Rabbie-like, of the Rabbies.*
Rabioles: f. *Turneps* :¶ Provenc.
Rabitué: m. ée: f. *Reaccustomed, reinured, vsed anew; setled againe.*
Rabituer. *To reaccustome, reinure, vse anew; also, to settle againe.*
Rable: m. *A Plaisterers beater; also, the chine, or parts about the chine, of a Deere, &c; thence also, the power or vertue of the backe in venerie, &c.*
Rablé. *Strong-backed, well furnished about the reines; and thence, able for venerie.*
Rablette: f. *A Shrew-mouse.*
Rabobeliné: m. ée: f. *Patched, or peeced againe.*
Rabobeliner. *To patch, or peece againe.*
Rabobelineries: f. *Patches renewed, or patches vpon patches.*
Rabolliere: f. *A Rabbets neast; the hole wherein a Doe Conie keepeth her young ones.*
Rabot: m. *A Joyners Plane; also, a Plaisterers beater.*
Raboté: m. ée: f. *Planed; euened, leuelled, smoothed.*
Rabotement: m. *A planing, euening, leuelling; also, roughnesse, raggednesse, vneuennesse.*
Raboter. *To plane; leuell, make or lay euen; also, to smooth.*
Raboteur: m. *A planer; leueller; smoother.*
Raboteure: f. *A planing; leuelling, laying euen; smoothing.*
Raboteux: m. euse: f. *Rugged, rough; vneuen, craggie, stonie.*
Raboudris: m. *Wraglands; crooked, or misgrowne trees which will neuer proue timber.*
Rabougri. vn rab. *A grub, counterfeit, short or shortnecked crooke backe.*
Rabougri: m. ie: f. *Growne crooked, and low; wrie, mishapen, or imperfect of shape; misgrowne; grubbie, dried vp, shortened more then ordinarie by extraordinarie heat.*
Rabougrir. *To grow crooked, and low withall; to wax mishapen, or imperfect of shape; to become a wragland, or grub; to be shortened, or dried vp by extraordinarie heat.*
Raboullere. *as* Rabolliere.
Rabroüant. *Checking, chiding, schooling, reprouing.*
Rabroüé: m. ée: f. *Checked, chidden, taunted, reproued; dismissed with a sharpe, or sower deniall.*
Rabroüer. *To checke, chide, reproue, taunt, schoole, dismisse with a sharpe, or crabbed answer; speake sowerly, or frowardly vnto.*
Rabroüeur: m. *A sower, or froward reprouer, checker, taunter, censor; an austere companion.*
Rabuser. *To reabuse.*
Racaille: f. *The rascalitie, or base and rascall sort; the scumme, dregs, offalls, outcasts of any companie.*
Raccamusé: m. ée: f. *Squashed, or pashed downe; flattened, beaten or made flat.*
Raccamuser. *To squash, or pash downe; to flatten, beat or make flat.*
Raccointer. *To reaccoint; to make (or grow) once more acquainted with; also, to reconcile.*
Raccoller. *To reimbrace, iterate imbracements, imbrace againe.*
Raccorder. *To reaccord, reconcile, make friends againe.*
Raccorni. *as* Racorny.
Raccornir. *To make hornie, or as hard as horne; also, to wax hornie, or grow hard like horne.*

Raccoupler. *To reunite; to couple, or yoke together againe.*
Raccourci: m. ie: f. *Shrunke, shortened, contracted, compacted; chubbie, trust vp, short and strong, knit well or close together.*
Croix raccourcie. *A crosse Humet, in Blazon.*
Raccourcir. *To shorten, abridge, curtall, contract, compact, shrinke or draw vp, knit or draw close, together.*
Raccourcissement: m. *A shortening, a curtalling, a contracting, or drawing vp close together.*
Raccoustré: m. ée: f. *Mended, repaired, new dressed or trimmed vp.*
Raccoustrement: m. *A mending, repairing, new trimming or dressing vp.*
Rrccoustrer. *To mend, amend, reedifie, repaire, make, trimme, or dresse vp anew.*
Raccoustreur: m. *A mender, a repairer, a renewer; a dresser or trimmer vp of old things; a botcher.*
Raccoustumé: m. ée: f. *Reaccustomed, reinured, brought vp, or into vse, againe.*
Raccoustumer. *To reaccustome, reinure, to renew a custome, to bring vp, or into vse againe,*
Raccueilly: m. ye: f. *Gathered.*
Race: f. *A race; linnage, familie, kindred, house, bloud; litter, brood; sort, kind; also, as* Rape.
Faire race. *To get children; also, to begin, or set vp, a race, or brood, of horses, dogs, &c.*
Noble de trois races. *Noble for three descents, or three manner of wayes.*
Rachais: m. aise: f. *Leane, carrion, scraggie, starueling.*
Rachalander. *To recouer former customes, to get into trade againe.*
Rachapt: m. *A redemtion, redeeming, rebuying, recouerie of a thing sold, by paying that for which it was sold; also, an abilitie, or power to redeeme, or to recouer land in that manner, by being next of kin to the seller; also, a ransome, or paying of ransome; also, a Reliefe; or whole yeares possession, & profit of land, or a summe of mony (as the custom is) due vnto the Lord of whom the land is held by homage, vpon euerie redemption, collaterall descent, exchange, or other change of the tenant.*
Rachapt abonné. *A Reliefe rated vnto the tenant at a certaine price.*
Rachapt rencontré. *A Reliefe vpon a Reliefe; or,* Quand durant l'année du rachapt eschet autre rachapt d'aucune terre tenuë à homage de la terre qui court en rachapt: *In which case though the Lord enioy both, yet it must be no longer then during his yeare in the former.*
Droict de rachapt. *as before in* Rachapt; *also, as* Droict de ventes.
Rachapté: m. ée: f. *Redeemed, recouered, or deliuered, ransomed; brought backe, or bought out, for money.*
Rachapter. *To redeeme; to recouer, or deliuer, to ransome or buy out, for money.*
Rachapter du Seigneur feodal. (Le nouvel acquereur ou vassal) accorder au Seigneur feodal pour retenuë, ou profits de fief, & luy payer les droicts de rachapt.
Rachapteur: m. *A redeemer; a ransomer.*
Rachassé: m. ée: f. *Chased, or driuen, backe againe.*
Rachasser. *To chase, or driue, backe againe.*
Rachasseur: m. *A chaser, or driuer backe againe.*
Sergent rachasseur. *Looke* Sergent.
Rachat. *as* Rachapt.
Rachater. *Looke* Rachapter.
Rachetable: com. *Redeemable; ransomable; recouerable for money.*

Rachetė,& Racheter. *as* Rachapté,& Rachapter.
Racheteur : m. *A redeemer ; a ransomer ; a recouerer of things passed away, for money.*
Rachimburges : m. *Certaine Iudges of causes which were determinable by the Law Salick.*
Racin. *as* Raisin : ¶Langued.
Racine : f. *A root ; also, the spring, source, originall, or cause of a matter.*
Racine creuse. *Hollow root, Holewort, Bulbus fumitorie ; (an hearbe)*
Racine iaulne. *The Carrot root.*
Racine quarrée. *Is(in Arithmetick) a number which multiplied by it selfe yeelds another whole (and square) number ; as 6 doth 36 ; or 10, 100.*
Racine sanguinaire. *A kind of Storks-bill, tearmed Bloudwort, of the propertie it hath to staunch bloud, or cure bloudie wounds.*
Racine sentant la rose. *Rosewort, Roseroot ; an hearb.*
Racine & tout. *Vp, or euen, by the root ; wholly, vtterly, quite and cleane.*
Telle racine telle fueille : Prov. *Such root (we say, such tree) such fruit.*
Racinette : f. *A small root.*
Racineux : m. euse : f. *Rootie, full of roots.*
Raclant. *Scraping ; also, rasping, or grating.*
Racle : f. *A scraper ; a raspe, or grater ; also, th'yron (ring, or) hammer of a doore.*
Raclé : m. ée : f. *Scraped, rasped ; grated.*
C'est vn poinct raclé. *It is a case resolued, a matter concluded of, a thing fully determined.*
Racledenare : m. *A scrape-good.*
Raclement : m. *A scraping ; a rasping.*
Racler. *To scrape ; raspe ; grate ; rake, rub, scrub ; rase.*
A bander & à racler. *By hooke or crooke ; by right or by wrong ; in all extremitie ; Looke* Bander.
Racleresse : f. *A woman that scrapeth.*
Raclet. *(The name of) a foole ; and therefore of little vnderstanding in the Law :* ¶Rab.
Racletorets : m. *Such as rub sweaters in hot bathes, or hot-houses.*
Racleur : m. *A scraper ; a rasper, a grater.*
Racleur de cheminées. *A Chimney-sweeper.*
Racleure : f. *as* Raclure.
Racloir : m. *A raspe, grater, scraper ; also, the strickle wherewith corne is measured ; also, as* Racle.
Le racloir d'un'arquebuse. *The crooked pin of yron scrued into the end of the scowring sticke ; we call it a worme.*
Raclure : f. *A scraping ; rasping ; grating ; raking ; rubbing, scrubbing ; rasure, or a rasing.*
Raclures. *Scrapings, shauings, parings ; offalls, fragments, remnants.*
Racommodé : m. ée : f. *Reaccommodated, mended or fitted anew.*
Racompter. *as* Raconter.
Raconté : m. ée : f. *Told, related, rehearsed, reported.*
Raconter. *To tell, relate, report, rehearse, deliuer.*
Raconteur : m. *A relator, a rehearser, a reporter.*
Racorder. *See* Raccorder.
Racorny : m. ye : f. *Growne hornie, made or become as hard as horne.*
Racourci. *Looke* Raccourci.
Racourir. *To recourse, to recurre, to run towards again.*
Racquette. *as* Raquette.
Racquit. *See* Raquit.
Racrocher. *To wrie or crooke, to make of a hookie forme.*
se Racroupir. *To knit, or draw vp, or gather close together (as a doing horse) his hinder parts.*

Raddouber. *as* Radouber.
Rade : f. *A road, an open harbor for shipping.*
Rade : com. *Quicke, swift :* ¶Pic.
Radeau : m. *A Raft, or float-boat of timber.*
Radial : m. ale : f. *Of, or belonging to, th'vpper, and bigger bone of th'arme.*
Radjancé : m. ée : f. *Readapted, reaccommodated.*
Radjancer. *To reapt, readapt, readiust, reaccommodate.*
Radiation : f. *A rasing, or blotting out ; (a Law tearme ;) also, a radiant brightnesse, as of the Sunne-beames ; or a blazing, shining, glittering ; casting forth of beames.*
Radical : m. ale : f. *Radicall ; of, or from, the root ; belonging to a root.*
Humeur radicale. *Radicall, or naturall moisture.*
Radicalement. *Radically, deepely, vp by the root, from th'originall, from the verie root.*
Radieux : m. euse : f. *Radiant, shining, glittering, blazing, flaring, leaming, full of beames.*
Radis : m. *A Raddish root.*
Radis fendu. *The double Raddish, or many-rooted Raddish.*
Radot. les arbres qui servēt des radots aux maisons. *Which serue, or are good for, the reparation, or mending of houses.*
Radoté. vn vieux radoté. *An old dotard, or doting fool.*
Radotement : m. *Dotage, or a doting.*
Radoter. *To dote, raue, play the cokes, erre grossely in vnderstanding.*
Radoub : m. *as* Radoubement.
Radoubé : m. ée : f. *Patched, botched, peeced, mended.*
Radoubement : m. *A peecing, mending, patching, or botching vp of.*
Radouber. *To peece, mend, renew, patch, or botch vp.*
Radoubeur : m. *A mender, peecer, patcher, botcher.*
Radoüere : f. *A strickle for the measuring of corne.*
Radresse. *A redresse, reformation, amends.*
Radressé : m. ée : f. *Redressed, amended, reformed, corrected.*
Radressement : m. *A redressing, amending, reforming.*
Radresser. *To redresse, amend, correct, reforme.*
Radresseur : m. *A redresser, amender, corrector, a reformer.*
Radvestir. *To readuest, reinuest, reinseisin, put againe into possession.*
Radvestissement : m. *A readuesture, or a readuesting ; a reinuesting, reinseisining.*
Radveu : m. uë : f. *Readuowed ; readuouched, reacknowledged, reapproued, taken into protection againe.*
se Radviser. *To readuise himselfe, take further aduisement, thinke better, or otherwise, of the matter.*
Raduné : m. ée : f. *Assembled, or gathered together.*
Raduner. *To assemble, or gather together.*
Radvouër. *To readuow, readuouch, reacknowledge, reapproue, warrant, or take into protection, againe.*
Raf. il ne leur lairra rif ny raf. *Looke* Rif.
Rafaux : m. *Wild Bores of about two yeares of age, when first their tuskes begin to peere out of their mouthes.*
Rafe : f. *A rifling ; or as* Raffle ; *whence ;*
Faire sa rafe. *To make his hand, or make vp his mouth, by many purchases, or prizes.*
Rafé : m. ée : f. *Rifled ; scraped ; caught, or snatched ; also, slipped away.*
Rafer. *To rifle ; to catch, or snatch ; also, to scrape ; also, to slip away.*
Raffarder. *To raile ; or scoffe at ; (an old word.)*
Raffermi : m. ie : f. *Hardened, or settled anew.*
Raffinage : m. *The refinement, or quintessence of.*
Raffiné : m. ée : f. *Refined, purified.*

Raffinement: m. *A refining, a purifying.*
Raffiner. *To refine; clarifie, purifie; spr ucifie.*
Raffineur: m. *A refiner, purifier, clarifier.*
Rafflade: f. *A gripe, graspe, or violent seisure.*
Par vne rafflade. *At once, all at a clap.*
Faire vne rafflade. *To gripe, catch, or snatch at, seise hastily, graspe violently; also, to scrape, or scratch; also, to rifle.*
Rafflater. *To flatter againe.*
Raffle: f. *A game at three dice, wherin he that throwes all three alike, winnes whatsoeuer is set; also, a rifling; also, the staulke of a bunch of grapes.*
Faire vne raffle. *To rifle, rauage, make hauock, sweep all away before them.*
Iecter vne raffle. *To throw three dice alike, as three aces, &c, to win all; also, to snatch, catch, or scratch.*
Raffler. *To scrape, or scratch; to catch, or seise on, violently; also, to rifle; to rauage, make hauocke, or cleane worke; to sweepe all away.*
Raffoler. *To hurt, or fell againe; also, to bring into a new fooles Paradice, to besot againe.*
Raffusté: m. ée: f. *New stocked; fitted with a new staffe, or stocke; frame, or carriage.*
Raffuster. *To fit, or furnish with a new stocke; staffe, carriage, frame.*
Rafle, & Rafler. *as* Raffle, & Raffler.
Rafreschi: m. ie: f. *Refreshed, cheered, reuiued, put into heart; also, renewed.*
Rafreschir. *To refresh, reuiue, cheere, comfort, put into heart; also, to renew.*
Rafreschissement: m. *A refreshing, or a refreshment; a comforting, reuiuing, cheering vp; a renewing.*
se Ragaillardir. *To be blithe, to wax merrie.*
Ragalice: m. *Lickorice.*
Ragats d'eau: m. *A great floud, inundation, rauage of waters.*
Rage: f. *Rage, furie, madnesse, woodnesse, fiercenesse, terriblenesse, outragiousnesse.*
C'est rage. *Tis a wonder.*
Faire rage. *To be verie briefe, or verie busie; to doe great matters, worke many wonders, keep a great coile, hurrie, sturre.*
Ils firent rage de promettre. *They promised mountaines, or wonderfull matters.*
Qui veut tuer son chien luy met la rage sus: Prov. *He that will hang his dog pretends he's mad.*
Ragement: m. *Toying, dalliance, wantonnesse, lasciuiousnesse.*
Ragencé: m. ée: f. *Readapted, readiusted, reaccommodated.*
Ragencer. *To readapt, readiust, reaccommodate, order anew.*
Rager. *Lasciuiously to toy, dallie, or wantonnize it.*
Rageux: m. euse: f. *Wanton, lasciuious, lustfull.*
Raggrandir. *To greaten, augment, increase, inlarge.*
Ragot: m. *The name of a cunning French begger; who made a booke of all his owne subtilties, and died verie rich (some say worth* 3000 l.) ¶Rab.
Raguiser. *To sharpen anew, or againe.*
Rai: m. *Looke* Ray.
Raïe, & Raïer. *as* Raye, & Rayer.
Raïere: f. *A wrinkle in the face; Looke* Rayere.
Rajeuni: m. ie: f. *Growne young againe.*
Rajeunir. *To grow young againe.*
Raifort: m. *The Raddish, or the Rabone, root (or hearb.)*
Raifort des champs. *Mountaine Raddish, horse Raddish, great Raddish.*
Raifort d'eau. *Water Raddish; (a kind of wild Raddish.)*
Raifort sauvage. *The wild Raddish; also, the water Raddish; (Ruellius affirms, that Elatine, or female Fluellin, is in some parts of France tearmed,* Raifort sauvage.*)*
Grand raifort. *Great Raddish, horse Raddish, mountaine Raddish.*
Fracture faicte en raifort. *A simple fracture (of bones) without any shiuering.*
Raillant. *Jeasting; scoffing at.*
Raillard: m. arde: f. *Jeasting, boording, pleasant, merrie, with; also, flowting, gibing, scoffing, mocking.*
Railler. *To ieast, boord, sport, be merrie, or pleasant, with; to deride, mocke, flowt, scoffe, gibe at.*
Raillerie: f. *Jeasting, boording, sport, merriment; also, a flowt, or scoffe; a flowting, or scoffing.*
Railleur: m. *A ieaster, boorder; mocker, scoffer.*
Raillon: m. *A fashion of three-edged, or treble-bladed dagger, which opens and shuts with a vice.*
Fer de fleche à raillon. *A Shoot-head; a forked, or barbed head.*
Raim: m. *A bough, or branch of a tree.*
Par raim de baston; &, par raim & baston. *A deliuerie, or quitting of possession of land, by the deliuerie of a bough, rod, or sticke that growes thereon.*
Raimceau: m. *A little branch, or bough.*
Rain: m. *as* Raim; *A bough.*
Rain de forests. *The purlues, or skirts, of forrests; the places that be next, or neere adioyning, vnto them.*
Raine: f. *A Frog.*
Raine de buisson. *The hedge Toad.*
Raine verte. *The little venomous green Frog, or Toad.*
Rainette: f. *A little Frog; also, a Pawne at Chests.*
Rainsceau: m. *A little branch, or bough.*
Rainselet: m. *The same.*
Raïolé. *as* Riolé.
Raïon. *as* Rayon.
Raïonné: m. ée: f. *Furrowed; set, or sowne in, furrows; digested into seuerall rankes, rowes, or furrowes.*
Raipaire. *Looke* Repaire.
Raiponce: f. *Rampions, garden Rāpions, the wild Rape.*
Petite raiponce. *Small or little Rampions, wild Rampions.*
Raire. *To shaue.*
Apres raire n'y a que tondre: Prov. *Sheeres after shauing find no worke to doe.*
À barbe de fol on apprend à raire: Prov. *By trimming fooles about the gill, a Barbers prentise learns his skill; or, by doing a thing ill one learns to doe much better; vnseemelie presidents are warnings to the wise.*
Vn barbier rait l'autre: Prov. *One great man, rich man, cunning man, serues anothers turne.*
Rais: m. *The Sunne-beames.*
Rais: m. aise: f. *as* Rasé.
Raise: f. *A path, or furrow, betweene beds in a Garden, or in a tilled ground.*
Raisin: m. *A Grape; also, a Raisin; also, the kernell of a Grape; also, a bunch, or cluster of Grapes.*
Raisins de cabas. *Alligants, or fraile Raisins.*
Raisins chenins. *A kind of great red Grapes, fitter to make medecines, then meat, of.*
Raisins confiz. *as* Raisins de cabas.
Raisins de Corinthe. *Currans, or small Raisins.*
Raisins de Damas. *The best, and greatest kind of Raisins of the Sunne.*
Vn raisin entier. *A bunch, or cluster of Grapes.*
Raisins de lierre. *Ivie berries.*
Raisin de mer. *Sea Grape, sea Raisin, sea Cluster; an hearbe, or little shrub, growing on drie banks neere vnto the sea.*

Raisins de mer. *The frie, or spawne of the Cuttle-fish.*
Raisins d'outre mer. *Red Gooseberries, garden Currans.*
Raisins de panse. *Raisins of the Sunne.*
Raisin de regnard. *Garden Nightshade, pettie Morrell; also, hearbe Paris, One-berrie, True-loue.*
Raisin renversé. *as* Raisin de regnard; *(in the former sence.)*
Il n'est ny figue ny raisin. *He is neither fish nor flesh, there is little or nothing in him.*
Moitié figues, moitié raisins. *Halfe tone halfe tother; and (particularly) betweene ieast and earnest.*
Raisiné: m. *A confection of grapes, made thicke, and eaten with bread, as honie; or as* Raisinnée.
Raisine: f. *Rosen.*
Raisinée. *as* Raisinnée.
Raisineux: m. euse: f. *Full of grapes.*
Raisiniere: f. *The third membrane, or skinne of the eye, (and the first that clothes th'Opticke sinew) wherin the hole is by which we see; also, th'Vuula.*
Raisinnée: f. *A sauce, or confection of delicate, blacke, and ripe grapes, first pressed betweene the hands; then boiled with water and salt; and then strained, & put into earthen vessells, where it will harden like a Marmalade, and keepe verie long.*
Raison: f. *Reason; also, due, right, equitie, iustice; also, knowledge, iudgement, wit, aduice, discretiō, discourse; also, a cause, argument, occasion, consideration; respect, regard; account, reckoning.*
Papier de raison. *A booke of Accounts; or, a bill of Account.*
Avoir raison de. *To get his due, or owne of; to bring vnto an account, or vnto equall tearmes.*
Avoir la raison de. *To take his pleasure, to haue his will, of; or, as* Ranger à raison.
Ie n'ay pas plus de temps que de raison. *I haue but euen a reasonable time; or, I haue no more time then I need.*
Mettre à raison. *To reduce into, or compell vnto, some order; or, as* Ranger à raison.
Regardez si ie ne me mets pas à la raison. *(In a contract, or agreement) See whether I haue not made a faire offer.*
Ranger à raison. *To tame, subdue, reclaime, bring into order, vnto ciuilitie, or to indifferent tearmes.*
Raison est au moulin: Prov. *Looke* Moulin.
Mets raison en toy, ou elle s'y mettra: Prov. *Let reason rule, or it will ouerrule, thee.*
Necessité est la moitié de raison: Prov. *Necessitie hath halfe the force of a reason; a fault which must be made is halfe excused.*
Raisonnable: com. *Reasonable, indifferent, equall, iust, right.*
Raisonnablement. *Reasonably, indifferently, equally, iustly, rightly.*
Raisonné: m. ée: f. *Reasoned, argued; discoursed.*
Loix raisonnées. *Laws grounded on reason, or whose reasons are annexed vnto them.*
Raisonnement: m. *A reasoning, arguing, discoursing, disputing.*
Raisonner. *To reason, argue, discourse, dispute.*
Raiz. *Looke* Rets.
Raiz: m. aise: f. *Shauen, powled neere.*
Raize. *as* Raise.
Rale de cheval. *The Pasterne of a horse.*
Ralenti: m. ie: f. *Slackened, remitted.*
Ralentir. *To slacken; remit, loosen, foreslow, wiredraw, linger, draw out in length; to relent in.*

Ralette. Marchant de ralette. *Treading lightly, or faire and softly.*
se Ralicter. *To fall sicke, or get him sicke to bed, againe.*
Ralle. *as* Rasle.
Rallement: m. *A ratling in the throat.*
Raller. *To rattle in the throat; also, to returne, or goe againe.*
Raller à terre. *To run fast, and close by the ground; (for so does the Rayle.)*
Rallié: m. ée: f. *Rallied, reunited, reassembled, attoned, reconciled, agreed.*
Ralliement: m. *A rallying, reassembling, reuniting; agreeing, attoning, reconciling.*
Rallier. *To rallie, reassemble, reunite, gather dispersed, close disioynted, things together; also, to accord, reconcile, agree, make peace betweene.*
Rallion: m. *An arrow with a forked, or barbed head; a broad arrow.*
Rallumé: m. ée: f. *Reinflamed, kindled, or lighted againe.*
Rallumer. *To light, kindle, inflame, or set on fire againe.*
Ralongé: m. ée: f. *Lengthened, pulled, stretched, or drawne out in length.*
Cerche ralongée. *A certaine Instrument wherwith Masons round, and fashion pillers.*
Ralonger. *To lengthen; to stretch, or draw, out in length.*
Ramadoüer. *as* Amadoüer.
Ramadoux: m. *Th'Indian Rat; enemie to the Crocodile.*
Ramage: m. *Boughes, branches, branching; or any thing that belongs therto; hence, the warbling of birds recorded, or learnt, as they sit on boughes; also, kindred, or linnage; or a branch of a pedegree.*
Velours à ramage. *Branched, or wrought Veluet.*
Ramage: com. *Of, or belonging to, branches; also, ramage, hagard, wild, homelie, rude.*
Chant ramage. *Naturall chaunting, rurall singing.*
Espervier ramage. *A Branchier, a ramage Hawke.*
Ramaigrir. *To wax leane, or fall away, againe.*
Ramaison. *Looke* Ramoison.
Ramanché: m. ée: f. *Rehafted, rehelued; put againe into it right place; reduced vnto fashion, or order.*
Ramancher. *To set a new haft, or handle, vnto; (and hence) also, to reduce vnto fashion, or it former order; and, to put againe in it former place.*
Ramar: m. *The fish called the sea Fox.*
Ramas: m. *A pile, heape, collection, medley, mingle mangle.*
Ramasse: f. *A broome, beesome, or long brush; also, a kind of high sled, or wheelebarrow, whereon trauellers are carried downe certaine steepe, and slipperie hills in* Picmont.
Ramassé: m. ée: f. *Gathered, piled, heaped, collected, or compacted, together; also, carried downe a steepe, or slipperie hill in the sled* Ramasse.
Ramasser. *To pile, heape, gather vp, collect or assemble together; also, to conuey downe a steepe, or slipperie hill in a* Ramasse.
Rambade: f. *The bend, or wale of a Galley.*
Ramberge: f. *A fashion of long ship, or sea-vessell, narrower then a Galley, but swift, & easie to be gouerned.*
Rambure: f. *The name of a sowrish apple.*
Rame: f. *An Oare; also, a reame of paper.*
Gens de rame. *Water-men, Barge-men, Galley-slaues; Rowers.*
`A rame rancade. *Amaine, apace, with all their oares, as fast as they can make, or driue.*
Ramé: m. ée: f. *Boughie, full of boughes, vnderpropped with boughes; also, rowed.*

Balles ramées. *Crosse-barre shot.*
Cerf rainé. *A raine Deere.*
Pois ramez. *Great Pease, garden Pease, hastie Pease, French Pease, Roman Pease.*
Rameau: m. *A branch, a bough.*
La feste des rameaux. *Palme-Sunday.*
Ramée: f. *A thicket; a thick and shadie groue, or copse; also, the shadow of boughes; and an open roome, arbor, or booth, made of boughes; any place thats couered, or ouershadowed, with boughes plashed one within another.*
Ramené: m. ée: f. *Brought backe; returned, reduced; also, retired, or drawne backe.*
Ramener. *To reduce, retire, bring or draw back.*
Se ramener. *A horse to pull in his head, or draw himselfe in, too much.*
Ramener la complainte sur les lieux. *To procure a Judge to heare, and determine a controuersie in the place, or on the land, which it concernes.*
Ramener vne pile. *To cast, or strike, backe a ball.*
Ramentevoir. *To remember, call to memorie, suggest, put in mind of.*
Ramentu: m. uë: f. *Remembred, called to memorie, or to an account, brought into the mind or vnto memorie.*
Ramer. *To row; also, to pricke or sticke full of boughes; to vnderset or vnderprop with boughes.*
Ramerci: m. *A certaine (forbidden) Engine wherewith fish may be caught.*
Ramereau: m. *A young Stockdoue.*
Ramerot: m. *A young, or small Stockdoue.*
Rameur: m. *A Waterman, a Rower.*
Rameure: f. *A rowing; also, as* Ramure.
Rameux: m. euse: f. *Full of branches, or boughes.*
Ramieller. *To vse further inticements, to sweeten once againe.*
Ramier: m. *A Queest, Ringdoue, Coushot, Woodculuer.*
Ramier: m. ere: f. *Of a bough, like a bough, liuing among boughes; whence;*
Coulomb ramier. *The Queest, &c; as* Ramier.
Pois ramiers. *Branch Pease, garden Pease, hastie Pease, French Pease.*
Ramification: f. *A branching; a spreading or diuiding into seuerall branches.*
Ramifié: m. ée: f. *Branched, spread in branches.*
Ramifier. *To branch; to put out, or spread in branches.*
Ramilles: f. *Small stickes, or twigs; little boughes, or branches.*
Raminagrobis: m. *A counterfeit, or counterfeiter of grauitie; a seuere outside of a sleight inside; one that would hide a most vaine and idle heart in an outward austere habit.*
Ramingue: com. *Froward, peeuish; or (as th'Italian* ramengo) *wandering, loytering, rouing about; whence;*
Cheval ramingue. *An inconstant mouing horse; one that keepes not in any direct way; one that holds not any certaine, or setled order in going.*
Ramoderé: m. ée: f. *Moderated, qualified, tempered.*
Ramoderer. *To moderate, qualifie, temper.*
Ramoisin: m. *A seared, or dead branch cut from a tree.*
Ramoisons: m. *Loppings; or the tops of branches lopped off; also, bauens, or bundles therof, or of other small wood, to be imployed either for fires, or in fences, and fortifications.*
Ramoiti: m. ie: f. *Moistened, bedewed, soked, or steeped ouer and ouer.*
Ramoitir. *To moisten, bedew, soke, or steepe ouer againe.*
Ramolles: f. *Past-meats fashioned like Saucidges, and made of the iuyce of hearbs, the yolkes of egges, cheese, and meale seasoned with salt, & boiled in water vntill they float; when, they are taken out of it, and serued vp hot.*
Ramollir. *To soften; or make soft againe.*
Se ramollir. *To soften, slacken, relent, wax gentle, grow tender.*
Ramollissement: m. *A softening, mollifying, making tender.*
Ramon: m. *A broome, or beesome.*
Ramonné: m. ée: f. *Swept with a broome.*
Ramonner. *To sweepe, or make cleane with a broome.*
Ramonneur de cheminée. *A Chimney-sweeper.*
Ramonter. *To lift vp on high.*
Ramortissement. *as* Amortissemeut.
Rampable: com. *Which may be crept on.*
Rampar. *Looke* Rempar.
Rampeau. Droict de ramp. *A priuiledge, or power, to lecher.*
Rampement: m. *A creeping, or crawling along on the ground; also, a climbing.*
Ramper. *To creepe, runne, crawle, or traile it selfe, along on the ground; also, to climbe.*
Ramplaige. *as* Ramplage.
Ramponne: f. *A flowt, scoffe, mocke, gibe, gleeke, ieast broken on.*
Ramponner. *To gibe, flowt, scoffe, deride, mocke, ieast at.*
Ramposne. *as* Ramponne.
Ramson. *as* Rençon; *(an old word.)*
Ramu: m. uë: f. *Branchie; full of branches.*
Ramure: f. *Branchinesse, or a spreading in branches; also, branches.*
La ramure d'un cerf. *A Deeres head well set, or with all his rights; the well-spread head of a red Deere.*
Ramuselé. nez ramuselé. *A thicke and short nose; a bottle nose.*
Ran: m. *A Ramme:* ¶Pic.
Rancade. A rame, ou à voile, rancade. *With all their oares, or sayles; as fast as they can goe.*
Rance: com. *as* Ranci.
Ranche: com. *Hoarse.*
Ranci: m. ie: f. *Mustie, fustie, reasie, restie, tainted, stale, putrified, wasted, stinking, vnsauorie, ill-smelling.*
Rancin: m. *The new hunting of dogs after a default.*
se Rancir. *To putrifie, wax tainted, get a wast, grow mustie, fustie, reasie, restie, stale.*
Rancissure: f. *Mustinesse, fustinesse, reasinesse, restinesse, a taint, stalenesse, putrifaction, vnsauorinesse.*
Ranco. Trotter de ranco. *To walke from ranke to ranke, from one to another.*
Rancoeur: m. *Rankor, hatred, malice, an inward grudge, rankling despight.*
Rancon: m. *A Welsh hooke, or hedging bill; or (most properly) a triple forked weapon about the length of a Partisan.*
Rançon: f. *A ransome; Looke* Rençon.
Rançonné: m. ée: f. *Ransomed, put vnto ransome; also, oppressed, or extorted vpon.*
Rançonner. *To ransome, to put vnto ransome; also, to oppresse, pole, despoyle, exact, or extort most of his substance from.*
Rançonneur: m. *A ransomer; also, an oppressor, or extortioner.*
Rancune: f. *as* Rancoeur.
Randon: m. *The swiftnesse, or force of a strong and violent streame; whence,* Aller à grand randon. *To goe verie fast, or with a great and forced pace.*

Sang respandu à gros randons. *By great gushes, or in great quantitie, at once.*
Randonnée: f. *A swift, or violent course.*
Randonner. *To runne swiftly, violently, as fast as he can.*
Rane: f. *A Frog.*
Rang: m. *A ranke, row, list, file, range, course; place, order, array; also (plurally) the lists of a Justs, or Turnament.*
Vn luth à 16 rangs. *A sixteene-stringd Lute; or a Lute with sixteene strings.*
Au rang de. *Amongst, or in the companie of.*
Mettre sur les rangs. *To make mention, haue speech of; to remember, bring vpon the Stage, or bring in among the rest; also, as;*
Tenir sur les rangs. *To deride, ride, mocke, gibe, scoffe, or ieast at.*
Rangé. *Looke* Rengé.
Rangée: f. *A ranke, file, row.*
Rangée d'avirons. *A banke of oares.*
Ranger. *To range, ranke, order, array, set, sort, place, dispose of, ordaine vnto.*
Ranger à l'estroict. *To driue, or bring vnto a strait.*
Ranger à raison. *To tame, reclayme, ciuilize, bring into temper, vnto reason or order; to ouercome, bring vnder, subdue.*
Se ranger à. *To set, addresse, frame, addict, apply, also, to yeeld, himselfe vnto.*
Se ranger au montoir. *Looke* Montoir.
Rangier: m. *A Raine Deere.*
Ranglier. *The same.*
Ranguillon: m. *The tongue of a buckle.*
Ranimé: m. ée: f. *Reanimated, reincouraged, reuiued, restored vnto life.*
Ranimer. *To reanimate, reincourage, reuiue, put into heart; infuse new vigor, life, or spirit into.*
Ranulaire. Veine ran. *A veine vnder the tongue, opened, or let bloud, for the Squinancie.*
Ranules: f. *The veines which are vnder the tongue; also, the little muskles of that part; so tearmed, because they somewhat resemble the flayed thighes of a Frog.*
Ranulet: m. *A painefull swelling of the veines vnder the tongues of cattell.*
Ranuncule: m. *The Crowfoot, Butter flower, Kings Cob, golden Cup; and (especially a kind thereof) Spearewort, Beanewort.*
Raouler. *Seeke* Rouler.
Rapacité: f. *Rauening, rapacitie, greedinesse; extortion, catching, extreame couetousnesse.*
Rapaire: f. *The dung of a Hare.*
Rapatrier. *as* Repatrier.
Rapé: m. *A verie small wine comming of water cast vpon the mother of grapes, which haue beene pressed; also, the wine which comes from a vessell filled with whole, and sound grapes (diuided from the cluster) and some wine among; which being drawne out, is supplyed by the leauings of good wine, put into the vessell, and reuiued and kept in heart a whole yeare long by the said grapes.*
Rape: f. *A Raspe, or a rough File.*
Rapé: m. ée: f. *Rasped, scraped.*
Rapeau: : m. *as* Rappel; *also, a returne; or a second course, or hurle at Keyles.*
Rapede-nare. *as* Racle-denare.
Rapel: m. *A Lure for a Hawke.*
Rapement: m. *A rasping, hard scraping.*
Raper. *To raspe, or scrape hard; also, to knocke (from the vse of some, to scrape) at a doore, &c.*
Rapetacé: m. ée: f. *Patched, peeced, clowted, mended botched.*
Rapetacer. *To patch, peece, clowt, mend, botch.*
Rapetasser. *The same.*
Rapetissé: m. ée: f. *Diminished, lessened, grown lesse and lesse; also, set in, as a peece of worke.*
Rapetissement: m. *A lessening, diminishing, extenuating; a making or growing lesse and lesse; also, a setting, or standing, in of a peece of worke.*
Rapetisser. *To lessen, diminish, extenuate, make lesse and lesse; also, to set in a peece of worke, or a peece of worke to stand in, beyond it fellowes.*
Rapeur: m. *A Rasper, or hard scraper.*
Raphan. *as* Raifort.
Raphanelle sauvage. *The hearbe Dittanie, Dittander, Pepperwort.*
Raphe: m. *A certaine beast thats shaped like a Wolfe, and spotted like a Panther; also, the name of a Saint; whence;*
Mal de S. Raphe. *A leaprosie, or, the wild scab.*
Raphe: f. *A Raddish; also, a leapers clicket; also, a handfull, or graspfull of; also, the Game at Dice called* Raffle.
Rapher. *as* Raffler.
Raphileux: m. euse: f. *Rugged, rough, knottie, Knobbie; also, full of seames.*
Raphine: f. *The name of a certaine Saint; whence;*
Mal de S. Raphine. *The wild scab.*
Raphler. *as* Raffler.
Rapide: com. *Violent, impetuous, hastie, sudden, swift, vehement; cruell, furious; rauenous.*
Rapidement. *Impetuously, violently, swiftly, hastily, suddenly; rauenously; cruelly, furiously.*
Rapidité: f. *Violent swiftnesse, impetuous hast, vehement or sudden furie; rauenous crueltie.*
Rapiecé: m. ée: f. *Peeced, patched, botched vp.*
Rapiecement: m. *A peecing, patching, botching.*
Rapiecer. *To peece, patch, botch, clowt, mend.*
Rapieceur: m. *A peecer, patcher, botcher.*
Rapiere: f. *An old rustie rapier.*
Rapille: f. *A kind of sand gotten at* Poussole *neere vnto Naples; and vsed in the cutting of Marble.*
Rapine: f. *Rapine, rauine, rauishment, robberie, violent snatching, forcible taking.*
Rapiner. *To rauine, despoyle, rob of, rauish, take violently, snatch greedily, beare away hastily, from.*
Rapineux: m. euse: f. *Rauenous, greedie, violent, couetous, (or violent in couetousnesse,) rauishing, or despoiling of all, or the best things one hath.*
Rapoil: m. *A Shauer, or Barber.*
Rapoule: f. *The Clote, Burre-docke, or great Burre.*
Rappé: m. *Small wine; or as* Rapé.
Rappe: f. *A Game, or Exercise, wherein th' Actors being armed with Gauntlets buffet one another.*
Rappé. *as* Rapé; brouët rappé. *The broth of Chickens and Veale, hauing added vnto it the crummes of white bread, liuers of Pullein, Veriuice, and white Ginger, strained together, and then being boyled againe.*
Rappeau. *as* Rappel.
Rappecon: m. *The sea fish called, a Heauen-gazer.*
Rappel: m. *A repeale, reuocation, recalling; a calling, or fetching backe.*
Rappelé: m. ée: f. *Repealed, reuoked, recalled; fetched, or withdrawne from.*
Rappeler. *To repeale, reuoke, recall, call backe, fetch, or withdraw from.*
Rappeler par bourse. *To redeeme, or to recouer, by the priuiledge of neere kindred, an inheritance which hath*

hath beene sold; giuing for it onely so much as it was sold for.

Rappeler le cochon. *To repeat, or intreat of, his former subiect; to fall into, or come vnto, the matter againe; also, to leaue, or end as he began.*

Rappeller. *as* Rappeler.

Rappes: f. *The Paines; a disease in a horses legs.*

Rappetissement. *Looke* Rapetissement.

Rappez: m. *A kind of Grapes preserued in Must; and serued to the Table as great dainties; Looke* Rapé.

Rappiecé, & Rappiecement. *as* Rapiecé, & Rapiecement.

Rappiecer. *Looke* Rapiecer.

Rappoincté: m. ée: f. *New pointed, or sharpened at the point.*

Rappoincter. *To sharpen the point of, or set a new point on; also, to repaire the losses of, to furnish anew with, to restore to a former estate, to set vp againe; also, to redetermine, redecree; reattone, reconcile; bring into good tearmes againe.*

Rapport: m. *A report, relation, recitall, rehearsall, deliuerie of a tale; also, the returne of a Writ; or that which a Sherife, Sergeant, or other officer, sets downe on the backside of a Writ serued, or otherwise reports of the seruing, or executing, thereof; also, a resemblance, correspondencie, accord, or agreement betweene seuerall things; also, a bearing, yeelding, or bringing forth of fruit.*

Rapport & denombrement. *A suruey; or, as* Denombrement.

Rapport de main pleine; C'est, garnison de la main de Iustice de biens suffisans & valables, pour la somme pour la quelle execution est faicte, sur le rapport du Sergent des biens desia par luy prins sur le debteur; en quel cas il peut avoir recreance, provision, & delivrance d'iceux.

Teste de rapport. *The branch of a Vine that beares the Grapes, is ordinarily a shoot of one that sprung out the yeare before.*

Rapporté: m. ée: f. *Told, reported, related, recited, rehearsed; also, likened or compared with, resembled, referred, applyed, or layed neere vnto; also, fitted, adapted, correspondent, euenly ioyned, iustly applyed; also, brought or carried backe.*

Vers rapportez. *Verses whose words reportingly answer one another; as in,* Pastre, Laboureur, Duc, i'ay peu, besché, soubmis, de rains, de pics, de mains, chevres, champs, ennemis, &c.

Rapporte-nouvelle. Vn r. *A newes-bearer, or tale-carrier; one that takes vp, or hearkens after, any newes, to report them, or make tales out of them.*

Rapporter. *To report, relate, recount, recite, rehearse, tell, deliuer; also, to referre, compare, apply one to; to match, fit, equall one with, another; to lay peece by peece, or one close by another; also, to beare, yeeld, or bring forth fruit; also, to bring, or carrie, backe; also, to represent, as formes, vnto the thoughts, to imprint them therein.*

Rapporter vn procez. *Succinctly, and sincerely to rehearse, and open vnto the Court the principall points of a matter alreadie debated at large by the Councell of both sides.*

Se rapporter à. *To resemble, or agree with; also, to referre, or commit, himselfe vnto.*

S'en rapporter à. *To lay the charge, or care of a businesse on another; whence,* Ie m'en rapporte à celuy, qu'il y prenne garde s'il veut. *I haue rid my hands of it, I will deale no more in it, let him looke to it if he will; and,* Ie m'en rapporte à ce qu'en est; *Let the thing defend, or speake for, it selfe, I neither make nor meddle with it.*

Ou se rapportent, & frappent les rayons. *Where the beames light, or meet.*

Rapporteur: m. *A reporter, a relator, a recitor, a rehearser.*

Rapporteurs de Chancelerie. *Certain officers, which open vnto the Masters of Requests (in that Court) the effect of petitions; and the difficulties, or inconueniences, whereto the Writs, or Letters Patents required by suitors are subiect.*

Rapporteur de proces. *The President, or* Conseillier, *who, when a case hath beene fully argued, and debated by the Councell on both sides, doth open faithfully, and report succinctly, the principall points thereof; immediately after which the Court proceedes vnto Sentence.*

Rapprendre. *To learne ouer againe.*

Raprecy: m. *A reualuation, or new price made, of.*

Rapse: f. *as* Rape; *a Raspe.*

Rapsodie: f. *A Rapsodie; an improper collection, a confused heaping vp, of many sentences.*

Rapt: m. *A rauishing; a violent snatching, taking, or pulling away of.*

Raptacer. *To patch, piece, mend, botch, clowt.*

Raptasser. *as* Raptacer.

Raquaille. *as* Racaille.

Raquamé: m. ée: f. *Imbrodered.*

Raque: f. *Durt; filth, ordure; mud, myre; or, as* Rasque.

Raqué. Vin raqué. *(Perhaps in stead of* Rapé.) *Small, or course Wine, squeezed from the* marc, *or dregs of the grapes, alreadie drayned of all their best moisture.*

Raquedenare: m. *A pinch-pennie, scrape-good, miserable wretch.*

Raquetier: m. *A Racket-maker; also, one that handles a Racket well.*

Raquette: f. *A Racket.*

Raquettes. *The high-sided periwigs, or wires of haire, worne heretofore by Gentlewomen.*

Raquit: m. *A reacquitment, redemption, buying out, a discharge, or extinguishment of rents, &c.*

Raquitable: com. *Redeemeable.*

Raquité: m. ée: f. *Redeemed, bought out.*

Raquiter. *To redeeme, discharge, extinguish, buy out.*

Raquoisé: m. ée: f. *Quieted, stilled, calmed, asswaged, appeased, pacified.*

Raquoiser. *To quiet, still, calme, asswage, pacifie, appease.*

Rare: com. *Rare, seld, vnusuall, geason; thinne, cleere; daintie, precious, excellent.*

Rarefacient. *Making thinne, or scant.*

Rarefaction: f. *A making, or becomming, thinne.*

Rarefier. *To rarifie; to make thinne, or scant.*

Rarement. *Rarely, seldome, vnusually, not often.*

Rarité: f. *Rarenesse, raritie, seldomenesse; thinnesse, scantnesse.*

Ras: m. *The stuffe called Serge.*

Ras de Milain. *The finest kind of bare Serge; or a silke Serge.*

Ras: m. ase: f. *Shauen, cleane shauen, cut close by the ground or bottome; cut quite away.*

Campagne rase. *An euen and plaine field without hillocks, furrowes, or trees.*

Or ras. *Smooth Gold, Venice stuffe.*

Drap d' or ras. *Smooth, or vnfrizeled cloth of Gold.*

Velours ras. *Vncut Veluet.*
Couper tout ras. *To cut cleane off, to sweepe quite away.*
Vouloir prendre vn homme ras par les cheveux. *To require, or exact, of a man much more then he can yeeld.*
Rasant. *Shauing, sheering, paring, or cutting close by the root, or bottome; also, razing, or laying euen by the ground.*
Rascas. Doussin rascas. *The great sea Vrchin.*
Rascase. *as* Doussin rascas; *or (in* Languedoc) *the sea Scorpion.*
Rasche: f. *A scauld, or a running scurfe, or sore (full of little holes) especially in the heads of little children.* ¶Langued.
Rascle: f. *A Partridge (about* Montpellier.)
Rase: f. *A shauing, sheering, powling; and thence, a road into, or a rauaging of, an enemies countrey; Looke* Raze.
Rasé: m. ée: f. *Shauen, cut cleane off, powled close to the skinne; also, razed, or layed euen with, or leuell vnto, the ground.*
Mesure rasée. *Close, neere, or hard measure; stricken measure.*
Raseau: m. *Networke; also, a great flat-bottomd Boat, Barge, or Lighter; or, as* Radeau.
Rasement: m. *A shauing, sheering, striking, or cutting close off; a razing, a laying leuell to the ground.*
Rase-poil: m. *A Barber, a haire-shauer.*
Raser. *To shaue; sheere; cut quite off, close by the root, cleane away; also, to raze, or lay leuell to the ground; also, to touch, or grate, on a thing in passing by it.*
Raser les eaux. *To skimme ouer, to skue or sayle vpon, the water.*
Raser les herbes. *To sit (as the deaw, &c) on hearbes.*
Rasette: f. *The lesse bone of the arme, or leg.*
Rasibus de. *Close or hard vnto, leuell or euen with.*
Rasibus qui bouge? *The word of a certaine Game, wherein one with a staffe strikes all along the top of an open, and vp-standing Hogshead, and thereby makes ducke downe into it another, who is within it.*
Rasier de bled. *A measure containing about foure Bushels.*
Rasle: m. *A rattling in the throat; also, the fowle called, a Ryle.*
Rasle de genest. *The ordinarie Rayle.*
Rasle grand. *The Moorehenne, or small Coot; resembles the ordinarie Coot in all parts but his feet, which be clouen.*
Rasle noir. *The Brooke-Ousell, or Moore-henne.*
Rasle rouge. *The common Rayle.*
Courir comme vn rasle. *To runne verie fast, and close by the ground.*
Rasoir: m. *A Rasour.*
Rasoir de mer. *as* Rason.
Faire la barbe à quelqu'un sans rasoir. *To affront, braue, abuse one.*
'A barbe de fol le rasoir est mol: Pro. *A Goose will brooke any ieast, or put vp any abuse; euery harsh thing hath a gentle touch in his dull conceit.*
'A barbe de fol hardi rasoir: Pro. *Looke* Fol.
Rason: m. *A delicate red-skaled fish in the seas about Rhodes and Malta; tearmed thus, because his backe is fashioned like a Rasour.*
Raspatoire: m. *A Raspatorie, a Raspe, an instrument of scraping.*
Raspé: m. *as* Rapé.
Raspe: f. *A Raspe, or a rough File.*
Raspé: m. ée: f. *Rasped, scraped, grated; filed.*
Raspecon: m. *The sea-fish called (by some) a Heauen-gazer.*
Raspeux: m. euse: f. *Rugged, rough as a Raspe.*
Rasque: f. *The scurfe of a scauld head.*
Rassaillir. *To reassayle, reassault, set on againe.*
Rassasié: m. ée: f. *Filled, saded, satiated, satisfied.*
Rassasiement: m. *A glutting, filling, satiating, satisfying.*
Rassasier. *To fill, glut, sade, satiate, satisfie.*
Rasseant. *Sitting downe againe.*
Rassel: m. *Arsesmart, water Pepper, Killridge, or Culerage (an hearbe.)*
Rassembler. *To reassemble, to rally; also, to set together againe.*
Rasseoir. *To rest, settle, set, or sit, downe.*
Rasserené: m. ée: f. *Made lightsome, cheerefull, cleere, calme.*
Rasserener. *To make lightsome, cheerefull, cleere, calme.*
Rasseurer. *To secure, make sure, confirme, or settle vnto.*
Rassis: m. ise: f. *Setled, stayed, at rest; sober, temperate, well tempered, whose wild oats are sowen.*
Pain rassis. *Stale bread.*
Vin rassis. *Ripe, or fined wine.*
Rassoté: m. ée: f. *Growne sottish, doultish, or childish; fallen into dotage.*
Rassotement: m. *Sottishnesse, dotage.*
Rassoter. *To dote, become doultish, grow fond, vaine, childish, foppish.*
Rasteau: m. *A Rake; also, a Portcullis.*
Rastelé: m. ée: f. *Raked; broken, leuelled, or gathered together, with a Rake.*
Rasteler. *To rake; to breake, leuell, or gather together, with a Rake.*
Rastelier: m. *A Racke, to put Hay &c in; also, the staulke, or steale of a Grape; also, a row of pegs, or woodden pinnes, to hang things on.*
Couvrir leur rastelier. *To couer their gaping mouthes (which otherwise would discouer a thinne, or illfauored sett of teeth.)*
Hausser le rastelier (viz. le bec, ou le nez) à. *Scornfully to cast vp the head at.*
Tout se trouve au rastelier de cuisine: Prov. *All things are, at the length, discouered, or brought vpon the Stage.*
Rastellot: m. *Wild Cheruill, mocke Cheruill, Shepheards needle, Venus Combe, or our Ladies Combe.*
Raston: m. *A fashion of round, and high Tart, made of butter, egges, and cheese.*
Rasue. *as* Resue.
Rasure: f. *A shauing; a close cutting, or striking; also, a razing out of written things; also, the shauings, or scrapings of a thing; whence;*
Rasure d'Aloës.
Rasurier: m. *A Shauer, a Barber.*
Rat: m. *A Rat; also, a Mouse; also, the fish called, a Heauen-gazer; (also, as* Rapt, *in old French.)*
Rat d'Hongrie. *The Hungarian Rat; a little greenish beast which resembles a Weesell, but is no bigger then a Mouse.*
Rat d'Inde. *as* Rat de Pharaon.
Rat de Lasse. *The Lasset Mouse; a beast that beares the Furre which we call Mineuar.*
Rat Liron. *A Dormouse.*
Rat de Montaigne. *as* Marmotaine.
Rat Norique. *The Norican Mouse; bodied like a Weesell, haired like a Hare, and eared like a Mole; she feeds most*

most on Nuts; and (contrarie to other Mice) is easily tamed.

Rat de Nuremberg. *The Rat of Noremberg; coated almost like a Hare, and hauing but two little holes in stead of eares.*

Rat Pannonique. *A small rat of a greenish colour; but otherwise resembling our Weesell.*

Rat de Pharaon. *The Indian Rat; as big as a Cat, and mortall enemie to the Crocodile, whose gaping mouth he creepes into, and getting thence into his bowels, eats them, and kills him.*

Rat de Ponte. *The Pontické Rat, or Mouse; white of colour, and as big as a Squirrell; his tayle (of a fingers length) hauing a verie blacke tip, makes him held, by some, a kind of Ermine, or Ermeline.*

Rat velu. *A Dormouse.*

Oreille de rat. *The hearbe Mouse-eare; also, a kind of Chickweed, or hearbe like Chickweed.*

Yeux de rat. *Small eyes, pinke eyes.*

Rats en paille. *A rustling, foule coyle, hurlyburly, bustling; also, a reuelling, or iollitie; whence;*

Plus ioyeux que rats en paille. *More friske, or liuelie then Rats on a Chaff-heape.*

Prendre vn rat par la queuë. *To cut a purse.*

Les rats se promenent à l'aise là ou il n'y a point de chats: Pro. *The Rats may safely play, when as the Cat's away.*

`A bon rat bon chat: Pro. *Looke* Chat.

Trop tard se repent le rat entre les pattes du chat: Pro. *The Rat can verie ill plead Law when the Cat hath him vnder her paw.*

Rataconné: m. ée: f. *Patched, botched, cobled, clowted.*

Rataconner. *To patch, botch, coble, clowt.*

Rataconnerie: f. *A patching, or botching, a cobling, or clowting.*

Rataconneur: m. *A patcher, botcher, cobler.*

Rataconniculer. *To reiterate leacherie.*

Ratatiné: m. ée: f. *Grubbie, shrunke in, thick and short; Looke* Rattatiné.

Rate: f. *The Spleene, or Milt.*

Ayez bonne rate. *Be liuelie, be merrie, plucke vp your spirits man, be of good cheare.*

Rateau: m. *as* Radeau.

Rateceler. *To clowt, or coble a shooe, &c.*

Ratelant. *Hunting after Mise and Rats; also, howling, or crying, like an Owle.*

Ratelée: f. *A rablement; a fond saw, or saying.*

Sa ratelée du butin. *His share of the bootie.*

En dire sa ratelée. *To speake his mind, blurt out his sentence, deliuer vp his opinion, of the matter.*

Rateler. *To hunt Rats, and Mice as an Owle; also, to howle, skreeke, or cry, like an Owle.*

Ratelier. *as* Rastelier.

Ratelle: f. *as* Rate.

Ratelou: m. *Long Hartwort, or Birthwort, male Birthwort.*

Ratepenade: f. *A Bat, Rearemouse, or Flickermouse; also, a kind of Scatefish; as* Glorieuse.

Ratepenade de mer. *The flying fish; because in colour, and forme of wings it somewhat resembles a Batt.*

Ratepenades. *as* Raquettes.

Ratiere: f. *A Mouse-trap.*

Ratifié: m. ée: f. *Ratified, confirmed, established, warranted, assured vnto.*

Ratifier. *To ratifie, confirme, establish, approue, warrant, assure vnto.*

Ratiocination: f. *A discoursing, discussing, arguing, disputing, reasoning, debating of matters.*

Ratiociner. *To reason, discourse, discusse, dispute, argue, debate.*

Rational: m. ale: f. *Reasonable, indued with reason, hauing the vse, or power, of reason.*

Ratissé: m. ée: f. *Scraped, rasped, grated.*

Ratisser. *To scrape; to raspe; to grate.*

Ratisser le cerveau. *To vex, or perplex the braines.*

Ratissoire: f. *A Raspe; also, a Grater.*

Ratissouër: m. *An yron raspe, rake, or scraper.*

Ratissure: f. *A rasping, or scraping; also, the scrapings of.*

Rat-liron: m. *A Dormouse.*

Ratoir: m. *A Mouse-trap, or a Trap for Rats.*

Ratoire: m. *A Ruptorie; a skinne-breaking oyntment, medicine, or salue.*

Ratoire: f. *The hole in a dore for a Cat to goe in and out at; also, a Mouse-hole; also, as* Ratoir.

Raton: m. *A little Rat (or Mouse;) also, as* Raston.

Ratouëre: f. *A paring shouell; also, a Rat-trap.*

Ratrapé: m. ée: f. *Reintrapped.*

Ratraper. *To reintrap; to catch, or lay hands on once againe.*

Rattaindre. *To reach, or ouertake againe.*

Rattatiné: m. ée: f. *Grubbie, shrunke in, thicke and short; also, as* Renfrongné, ou Rechigné.

Ratte. *as* Rate.

Ratteindre. *To reach, or ouertake once more.*

Ratteint: m. te: f. *Raught, or ouertaken againe.*

Ratteinte: f. *A reaching, or ouertaking once more.*

Ratteloup. *as* Ratelou.

Rattendrir. *To make tender, or soft againe.*

Ratte-volage: f. *A Batt.*

Rattier: m. ere: f. *Sullen, retired, vnsociable, vncompanable, solitarie, strange; also, spleenaticke, or belonging to the Spleene.*

Rattierement. *Sullenly, retiredly, priuately, solitarily, vnsociably, in huggar-muggar.*

Rat-veul: m. *A Dormouse.*

Rature: f. *A raze, or scratch; a razing, or scraping out; a cancelling, or putting out.*

Rature entiere. *A dash, or stroake through a word with a penne.*

Raturé: m. ée: f. *Razed, scraped, effaced, cancelled, blotted, strucke, or dashed, out.*

Ravacher. *as* Ravasser.

Ravage: m. *Rauage, hauocke, spoyle; a violent, and suddaine ransacking, forraying, irruption into; an ouerrunning, or ouerflowing of a countrey, whether by incursion of enemies, or inundation of waters.*

Ravagé: m. ée: f. *Rauaged, spoyled, forrayed, sacked, ransacked, made hauocke of, wasted, ouerflowne, ouerrunne, violently and suddainely.*

Ravager. *To rauage, forray, spoyle, prey vpon, make hauocke of, sacke, ransacke; violently to ouerrunne, suddainely to ouerflow.*

Ravageur: m. *A rauager, spoyler, forrayer, sacker, ransacker, one that makes hauocke of all he can come neere.*

Ravaille: m. *Small fish sold one with another.*

Raval. *as* Ravallement.

Ravallé: m. ée: f. *Deiected, humbled, cast or sunke downe, debased, depressed; lessened or fallen in price; brought low, taken or swallowed downe.*

Ravallement: m. *A deiecting, debasing, depressing, a casting, or sinking, a taking, or swallowing, downe; a falling in price; an humbling, abating, abasing;* bea-

bearing, or pulling downe.

Ravallement de courage. *Faintnesse, or a fainting; faintheartednesse, discouragement, abashment.*

Ravaller. *To pull, cast, bring, or beare, downe; to debase, depresse, deiect; lessen, diminish, abate; bring low, take lower; also, to swallow, or swill downe againe.*

Se ravaller. *To humble himselfe, to stoope, yeeld, condiscend, or vayle bonnet vnto; also, to fall in price.*

Il se ravalla dedans son lict. *He sunke downe, or layed him downe, againe into his bed.*

Ravanel: m. *The Raddish root.*

Ravanille: f. *A little Raddish.*

Ravasser. *To raue, to talke idly.*

Ravasser en dormant. *To sleepe vnquietly, or talke in sleeping.*

Ravauder. *To patch, or botch.*

Ravauderesse: f. *A woman botcher.*

Ravauderie: f. *Botcherie, or botched stuffe.*

Ravaudeur: m. *A Botcher; also, an idle, or ignorant speaker; one that either confounds, or vnderstands not, what he sayes; or one that neither does, nor sayes, ought rightly.*

Ravaudeuse: f. *as* Ravauderesse.

Ravayde: f. *A coyle, or stirre; or, as* Ravage. ¶Orleannois.

Rauder. *as* Roder; *also, to laugh, ieast, be merrie, reuell, riot it.*

Rave: f. *A Rape, or Turnep; the Raddish is also called so in some parts of France, but especially about Paris.*

Rave douce. *The Raddish root.*

Rave forte. *The same; or, as* Raifort.

Rave de Limosin. *A Turnep.*

Rave longue. *The long Rape, or Turnep.*

Rave ronde. *The ordinarie Rape; also, the round Raddish.*

Rave de Savoye. *The Sauoyan Rape, the greatest kind of Turnep.*

Rave sauvage. *The water, and wild, Raddish; also, the wild Rape, or Turnep; some also call Speedwell (or Elatine) so.*

Ce mot sent sa rave. *This word is clownish, or sauors of the clowne.*

Raveforte. *as* Raifort.

Ravel. Bogue ravel. *A little sea-fish, that hath great eyes, a siluer-coloured bellie, a reddish backe and tayle, and all other parts not much vnlike the Cackarells.*

Ravelin: m. *A Rauelin (in fortification.)*

Il y a bien de ravelin en son faict. *All is not well with him, he is much out of square.*

Ravenet: m. *The Raddish root.*

Raverdir. *To wax greene; or to canker, as a brasen vessell thats either not vsed, or ill kept.*

Ravestissement: m. *A readuesting, reinuesture.*

Ravet: m. *The Raddish root.*

Ravette: f. *A little Rape, or Turnep.*

La petite ravette. *The garden Rampion, or wild Rape.*

Raveul: m. *A Dormouse.*

Ravi: m. ie: f. *Rauished, suddainely or forcibly carried away.*

Belle chose est tost ravie: Prov. *Faire things are quickly snatched vp.*

Raviere: f. *A plot, or bed, of Turneps.*

Ravigoré: m. ée: f. *Recouered, restored vnto vigor; cheered vp againe.*

Ravigorer. *To recouer, to restore vnto vigor; to hearten, strengthen, reuiue, cheere vp againe.*

Ravigotter. *To reuiue; or, a halfe-dead man to returne vnto life.* ¶Pic.

Ravine d'eau. *A great floud; a rauine, or inundation of water, which ouerwhelmeth all things that come in it way.*

Ravineux: m. euse: f. *Rauenous, violent, impetuous, like a forcible streame, or inundation of waters.*

Ravir. *To rauish, to snatch away hastily, pull away violently, take away forcibly, beare away suddainely.*

Ravisé: m. ée: f. *Readuised, well bethought of in himselfe, thought better, or otherwise, of.*

Se Raviser. *as* Radviser.

Ravissant: m. ante: f. *Rauishing, rauenous, violent, greedie, swift.*

Ravissement: m. *A rauishing, a rauishment.*

Ravisseur: m. *A rauisher; a violent, or forcible taker; a rauenous, or greedie companion.*

Ravivé: m. ée: f. *Reuiued.*

Raviver. *To reuiue; to returne, or to restore, vnto life.*

Raulet. *The name of a certaine great Peare.*

Ravoir. *To recouer, to haue againe.*

Se ravoir. *To reuiue, recouer, come againe vnto himselfe.*

Ravoire: f. *as* Ravage.

Ravoirer. *(Sometimes vsed) as* Ravoir.

Ravolé: m. ée: f. *Fled backe.*

Ravoler. *To fly backe, to returne flying.*

Rauque: com. *Hoarse; harsh, or vnpleasant of sound.*

Rause: f. *Sedge, Gladen, Glader, Swordgrasse, Sheeregrasse.*

Ray: m. *A ray, or beame of the Sunne; also, a spoke of a wheele.*

Ray de miel. *A honey-combe.*

Rayant: m. ante: f. *Radiant, glittering, shining, blazing, leaming.*

Rayaux: m. *Barres; or long, and narrow peeces of mettall.*

Raye: f. *Ray, Skate, Thornebacke.*

Raye au bec pointu. *The sharpe-snowted (or daintiest kind of) Ray.*

Raye bouclée. *The Rocke-Ray; the Ray whose backe is set thicke with little knurles, not vnlike vnto buckles.*

Raye cendrée. *A kind of smooth Ray; or, as* Coliart.

Raye estelée. *The starrie Skate, the rugged Ray.*

Raye lize. *The smooth Ray, whose finnes are powdered with little specks like Looking-glasses.*

Raye au long bec. *The spotted, long-snowted, or sharp-snowted Ray.*

Raye polie. *The smooth Ray.*

Raye: f. *A ray, line, stroake, row; furrow; also, the spoke, or staffe, of a wheele.*

La raye des arbres. *The graine of Timber, or of Trees.*

La raye du cul. *The nock, fould, or dint betweene the buttocks.*

Tant d'arpents à la raye. *So much arrable land which is to be sowed that yeare.*

Ils sont au bout de la raye. *They haue done as much as they can; they are gone as farre as they are able; they haue no more to doe, or to say.*

Rayé: m. ée: f. *Rased, scraped, crossed, or cleane put out; also, rayed, rewed, streaked, or skored all ouer; also, blazed, or glittered.*

Rayement: m. *A rasing, scraping, crossing, blotting, or putting out; also, a glittering, blazing, flaring, bright shining,*

shining, sending forth of beames; also, a rewing, streaking, or skoring all ouer.

Rayer. *To rase, crosse, blot, scrape, strike, or put out; also, to rew, streake, or skore all ouer; also, to blaze, flare, leame, glitter, shine brightly, send forth beames.*

Se rayer. *To be full of rayes, rewes, or streakes.*

La mamelle ne rayoit que du sang. *Yeelded nothing but bloud; nothing spowted, flowed, issued, or came from it but bloud; hence also,* Il luy fit rayer le sang par le nez.

Rayere: f. *A loope-hole; a long, and narrow cleft in the wall of a Prison, Dungeon, or Tower, whereby light, and ayre (though but verie little) are let into the roomes thereof.*

Les rayeres d'un moulin à eau. *The armes, or starts of the wheele of a water-mill.*

Rayeure: f. *as* Rayement.

Rayfort. *as* Raifort.

Raymolles de blanc de chapon. *The brawne of a Capon, Raisins of the Sunne, and marrow shred all together, then made into little cakes or loaues, and fryed with seame or Hogs sewet, and serued vp with sugar strewed on them.*

Rayolé. *Seeke* Riolé.

Rayon: m. *A furrow; also, a reyne, or drayne for the voiding of superfluous moisture; a water furrow; also, a ray, or beame of the Sunne; also, the spoke, or staffe of a wheele; also, the lesse bone of the arme.*

Rayon de miel. *An honey-combe.*

Rayonnant. *as* Rayant.

Rayonné: m. ée: f. *Furrowed; made, cut out, or plowed vp, into furrowes.*

Rayonner. *To furrow; make furrowes, or make furrowie; also, to radiate, shine, leame, flare, blaze, glitter, yeeld bright rayes, cast forth beames.*

Rayonner des arbres. *To plant, or set trees in furrowes.*

Rayonner la terre. *To plow vp land in furrowes; also, to draine it.*

Rayonneux: m. euse: f. *Full of beames; full of furrowes.*

Raze: f. *The broadest part of the* Omoplate, *or shoulder-blade; verie gristlie, and bending towards the back-bone; also, as* Rase.

Trois razes d'angonnages; *(in stead of* Races*) three kinds of pockie botches.* ¶Rab.

Razé: m. ée: f. *Razed, ruined; shauen, close-cut.*

Raze-forts. *Forts-razing, bulwarks-ouerthrowing.*

Razer. *Looke* Raser.

Razis. *A kind of white oyntment vsed by Surgeons for the drying vp of sores.*

Ré. *Shauen; Looke* Rez.

Re. *Of it selfe hath neither signification, nor vse (other then as a Musicall, or singing Note) In composition, it sometimes alters not the sence; as in* Receler, Recomforter, Remercier, Remonstrer, Repaistre, Reschapper, & Resveiller: *Sometimes it signifies againe; as in* Rechauffer, Relaver, &c; *and backe, as in* Reculer, Rechasser, Repoulser, &c; *and mutually, interchangeably, or backe againe; as in* Rebecquer, Refrapper, Remocquer, Repiquer, &c: *Sometimes it giues an energie to the simple; as in* Reclamer, Redarguer, Redoubter, Reluire, Requerir, Resembler, &c; *and sometimes a contrarie sence; as in* Regorger, Reprouver, Reveler, &c.

Reachet: m. *A redemption, or buying againe.*

Readjourné: m. ée: f. *Readiourned, cited, or summoned once more.*

Readjourner. *To readiourne, to cite or summon againe.*

Readmis: m. ise: f. *Readmitted.*

Readopté: m. ée: f. *Readopted.*

Readopter. *To readopt.*

Reaffle: m. *The diuell.*

Reaffranchi: m. ie: f. *Reaffranchised, made free againe; redeliuered, released once more; also, doubly reclaymed, or tamed; made* franc *in perfection.*

Reagal: m. *(The right)* Aconitum, *or Aconite.*

Reaggravation: f. *A reaggrauation; and (particularly) the last, and most direfull excommunication of offendors.*

Real: m. *A Reall, or Spanish six-pence; also, a kind of the best Sturgeon.*

Real: m. ale: f. *Reall, essentiall; in presence; also, kinglie, princelie, royall.*

Sauce reale. *Venison sawce made of red wine Vineger, whole Cynnamon, Cloues, and Sugar boyled together in a pipkin, vnto the consumption of almost their halfe.*

L'oeil du maistre real engraisse le cheval: Pro. *The horse growes fat whose maister often eyes him.*

Realement. *as* Reaument.

Realgar. *The fume, or smoake of Mineralls.*

Realisation: f. *A realization, a realizing, a making reall.*

Realisé: m. ée: f. *Realized, made reall.*

Realiser. *To realize, to make of a reall condition, estate, or propertie; to make reall.*

Realiser vn contract. C'est le recognoistre par devant le Seigneur dont l'heritage est tenu, ou par devant les officiers de sa iustice; afin d'acquerir droict reel & hypotheque, & pour estre nanti. ¶Ragueau.

Reallegué: m. ée: f. *Realledged.*

Realleguer. *To realledge, to alledge againe.*

Realler. *To returne, to goe againe.*

Reant. *Braying, as a Stag.*

Reaplani: m. ie: f. *New-leuelled, made plaine or euen againe.*

Reappoincté: m. ée: f. *Pointed anew, or new sharpened at the point; also, newly, or againe, agreed.*

Reau: m. *A deepe reyne, or furrow.*

Reaudition: f. *A second hearing; or, a hearing ouer againe.*

Reaument. *Really, essentially, effectually, throughly; assuredly, certainely, verily, in verie deed.*

Rebaigné: m. ée: f. *Rebathed, or bathed againe.*

Rebaigner. *To bathe againe.*

Rebaillé: m. ée: f. *Restored, giuen backe.*

Rebailler. *To restore, giue back, returne a thing that was giuen; giue anew, or againe.*

Rebailler forme à. *To bestow a new shape, or another fashion, on.*

Rebaiser. *To kisse againe.*

Rebaisotter. *To reiterate a frequent kissing; to kisse often and againe.*

Reballier. *To sweepe ouer againe.*

Rebandé: m. ée: f. *Bent; bound; or bandied, againe.*

Rebander. *To bend; bind; or bandie, againe.*

Rebanni: m. ie: f. *Reexiled, againe banished.*

Rebannir. *To reexile, to banish againe.*

Rebanqueter. *To make (or be at) a new, or another, banket.*

Rebaptisé: m. ée: f. *Rebaptised.*

Rebaptiser. *To rebaptise, to baptise the second time.*

Rebarbatif: m. iue: f. *Grimme, sterne, soure; austere, seuere; froward, rude, or harsh of conuersation.*

Rebarboter. *To mutter, or mumble words often betweene the teeth.*
Rebarder vn cheval. *To put on a horses armour, trappings, or furniture againe.*
Rebassiné: m. ée: f. *Often or againe chafed, rubbed, fomented, warmed.*
Rebassiner. *To rub, chafe, beat, foment often, or vntill it be throughly warme.*
Rebaster son asne. *To saddle his Asse againe.*
Rebasti: m. ie: f. *Reedified; repaired.*
Rebastir. *To reedifie, rebuild; repaire.*
Rebatement: m. *A reuerberation, repercussion, repulsing, beating backe.*
Rebatre. *To reuerberate, repell, repulse, beat or driue backe againe.*
Rebaudi: m. ie: f. *Blithe, merrie, buxome, iocond, frolicke; lustie, liuelie, stirring, light.*
Rebec: m. *The fiddle tearmed a Rebeck.*
Visage de rebec. *A chittiface, or sneaksbie.*
Iouër du rebec. *as* Se Rebecquer.
Rebecher. *To dig (the ground) againe.*
Rebecqué. Il a rebecqué contre moy. *He answered me sawcily, replyed vnto me malapertly, withstood me proudly to my teeth.*
Rebecquer. *To giue a pecke for a bob, or to pick againe, as one Cocke at another that pecks him.*
Se rebecquer contre. *Proudly to withstand, resist, contend with, oppose himselfe vnto; to thwart sawcily, answere malapertly; set vp his bristles against.*
Rebeine: f. *A riot, rout, sedition, tumult, vprore; a rebellion.*
Rebelle: com. *Rebellious; wilfull, stubborne, restie, disobedient, that will not be ruled.*
Rebellé: m. ée: f. *Rebelled, reuolted from.*
Rebellement: m. *A rebelling, reuolting, rising against his Soueraigne.*
Rebeller. *To rebell, reuolt from, resist, rise vp against his Soueraigne.*
Rebellion: f. *Rebellion; a publike reuolt; resistance of a lawfull authoritie; stubbornnesse, disobedience, wilfullnesse.*
Rebeluter. *To boult ouer againe.*
Il rebelute ceste mesme paste. *He handles, intreates of, runnes ouer, the selfe-same matter againe.*
Rebender. *To bend againe.*
Rebenir. *as* Rebenistre.
Rebenistre. *To blesse againe, to bestow a new blessing on; also, to hallow, or sanctifie a holie (but prophaned) thing.*
Rebequer. *See* Rebecquer.
Rebetre: f. *A Wrenne.* ¶Norm.
Rebeyne. *as* Rebeine.
Rebigoter. *To play the hypocrite, or superstitious noddie againe.*
Rebindaine: com. *Reuersed, ouerturned, turned vpside downe; whence;*
'A Iambes rebindaines. *With legs wide stragling, and vpwards turned.*
Rebiné: m. ée: f. *Eared, or tilled the second time.*
Rebinement: m. *The second tilth, earing, or breaking vp of land.*
Rebiner. *To plow, till, or eare ground the second time.*
Rebineur des choses accordées. *One that denyes, reuokes, or calls backe, his word; one that withstands, or will not stand vnto, conditions before agreed on.*

Reblanchir. *To white ouer againe.*
Reblandi: m. ie: f. *Soothed, smoothed, sweetned, made gentle, appeased, by faire words.*
Reblandir. *To reblandish; repacifie, reappease; to qualifie, sooth, or smooth againe; to sue, or seeke, vnto a person offended.*
Reblandir le bestail prins en dommage. *To pay for the dammage done by them.*
Reblandir le Seigneur. *A Tenant vpon the seisure of his land for non-payment of rent, &c, to repaire vnto his Landlord, or to his officer, and demaund the true cause thereof; or make him a reasonable, and sufficient offer of satisfaction; or with good words, and in faire tearmes, to excuse his omissions, or defaults of payment, &c, and intreat him to beare yet a while with him.*
Reblandissement: m. *A reblandishment, reblandishing, repacifying, reappeasing; also, an offer of satisfaction, or a request of forbearance, for duties omitted, rents vnpayed, wrongs done.*
Rebobeliné: m. ée: f. *Patched, cobled, mended againe.*
Rebobeliner. *Againe to coble, patch, or mend.*
Rebobelineur: m. *A cobler, patcher, botcher.*
Rebobiné: m. ée: f. *Patched all ouer.*
Rebond: m. *A rebound, a rebounding.*
Rebondi: m. ie: f. *Full, plumpe, fleshie, fat; also, rebounded.*
Rebondir. *To rebound, or leape backe.*
Les viandes nouvelles font rebondir l'estomac: Pro. *The stomacke rises against vncouth meats.*
Rebondissement: m. *A rebounding, or leaping backe.*
Rebondonner. *To put the bung in, or stop with a bung, againe.*
Rebordé: m. ée: f. *Hemmed; bordered, welted, anew.*
Reborder. *To hemme, welt, border, anew.*
Reborner. *To make new bounds for, appoint other limits vnto.*
Reboté: m. ée: f. *Booted againe.*
Reboter. *To boot, or pull on bootes, againe.*
Rebouché: m. ée: f. *Dulled, blunted; also, stopped vp againe.*
Rebouchement: m. *A dulling, or blunting; a stopping vp againe.*
Reboucher. *To dull, or blunt; also, to stop vp againe.*
Cela me rebouche au coeur. *That is against my stomacke, or goeth against my heart.*
Reboucler. *To buckle againe.*
Rebouffer. *Againe to swell, or puffe vp, the cheekes.*
Rebougié: m. ée: f. *Seared anew, or with another size.*
Rebougier. *To seare againe.*
Rebouër: m. Le bas reb. *An Engine wherewith fish is (forbidden to be) caught.*
Rebouillement: m. *A boyling once more, or ouer againe, a second boyling.*
Rebouillir. *To boyle once more, or ouer againe, to boyle the second time.*
Rebouillonner. *To bubble, surge, or wamble often, or ouer againe.*
Reboulé: m. ée: f. *Bowled againe; also, turned downe, or in; shrunke in.*
Rebouler. *To bowle againe; also, to turne downe, or in; to shrinke in.*
Rebourjonnement: m. *A new budding.*
Rebourjonner. *To burgeon, bud, or put out, anew.*
Rebours: m. (Substant.) *The rugged, and high nap of new cloth, raised by certaine yron combes, and then shorne off by the Clothworker.*

Rebours: m. ſe: f. (Adject.) *Croſſe, ouerthwart, wayward, ſurlie; rude, froward; wild, ſauage; vntractable, vnſociable.*

Rebours. 'A reb. (Adverb.) *Arſeward, backward, preposterouſly, oblikely, awry, ouerthwartly, quite contrary, full againſt the courſe, wooll, or haire, inſide out, vpſide downe, cleane kamme.*

Reboursant. *Going arſeward, backward, the wrong way; working againſt the wooll, or haire; turning, or ſtanding inſide outward, or the vpſide downe.*

Rebourſé: m. ée: f. *Diſordered, arſeward, ouerthwart, awry; wrought againſt the wooll, or haire; turned inſide outward, or vpſide downeward; placed, or planted the wrong way.*

'A flot rebourſé. *Vp the water, againſt the tyde, or ſtreame.*

Rebourſer. *To worke againſt the wooll, or haire; ſet, or place the wrong way; turne inſide outward, vpſide downeward; goe arſeward, or backward; take a courſe againſt all courſe.*

Rebourſer chemin. *To returne, or come backe (the ſame way he went.)*

Rebourſer de coeur. *To repent at the verie heart.*

Rebourſer le poil du drap. *To row, or to raiſe the wooll, or nap of cloth.*

Rebourſer vne riviere. *To paſſe vp a riuer; to ſayle, or ſwimme againſt the ſtreame thereof.*

Rebourſoir: m. *The yron combe wherewith Clothworkers raiſe the nap of new cloth.*

Rebouſché: m. ée: f. *as* Rebouché.

Rebouſſé. *as* Rebours (Adject.)

Rebout: m. *A repulſe, foyle, denyall.*

Reboutant. *Repulſing, repelling; denying.*

Rebouté: m. ée: f. *Repulſed, repelled, reiected; foyled; alſo, denyed, refuſed; alſo, taunted, rebuked; alſo, beſtowed, or layed vp, in a conuenient place.*

Reboutement: m. *A repelling, foyling, reiecting; refuſing, denying; taunting, rebuking.*

Rebouter. *To repulſe, foyle, driue backe; repell, reiect; refuſe, deny; alſo, to rebuke, taunt, or take vp; alſo, to beſtow, or lay vp in a conuenient place.*

Reboutonner. *To bud; or button, againe.*

Rebranſler. *To ſhake againe.*

Rebras: m. *A turning vp, a tucking or foulding vpwards or inwards; alſo, a fadome.*

'A double rebras. *Thicke and threefold.*

Vn entendement à double rebras. *An odde head, a notable wit, a terrible pate.*

Manches, ou robbes à double rebras. *Sleeues, or gownes ſo long, or ſo wide, that they may be twice turned, or tucked, vp.*

Rebraſſé: m. ée: f. *Turned, foulded, or tucked vp; alſo, plotted, or contriued anew.*

Bien rebraſſé. *Confidently, audaciouſly; alſo, earneſtly, as one that meant not to dally.*

Vn des plus rebraſſez. *One of the forwardeſt, or buſieſt, of the companie.*

Rebraſſer. *To turne, fould, or tucke vp, the ſleeues, &c; alſo, to plot, contriue, or deuiſe anew.*

Rebriché: m. *A motiue, or aduertiſement in writing vpon an Inqueſt.*

Rebricher. *To make a motiue, or aduertiſement in writing vpon an Inqueſt.*

Rebridé: m. ée: f. *Bridled againe.*

Rebrider. *To bridle againe.*

Rebrillement: m. *A double glittering, or twinckling; a twinckling, or ſparkling reflection.*

Rebriſé: m. ée: f. *Bruiſed, or broken againe.*

Rebriſer. *To bruiſe, or breake againe.*

Rebrocarder. *To retort a ieaſt.*

Rebroïé. *Seeke* Rebroyé.

Rebroſſer. *To returne, to retyre; alſo, to bend; alſo, to turne vp the point, edge, or end, of a thing.*

Rebroſſer la terre. *To breake vp the ground.*

Rebrouiller. *To mingle, or confound anew.*

Rebrouſſé: m. ée: f. *Turned, tucked, bent vpward; alſo, returned, retyred.*

Rebrouſſer. *To turne, or tucke vp the ſleeues; alſo, as* Rebroſſer.

Rebrouſſer chemin. *To turne backe, or to returne the ſame way he came.*

Rebrouſter. *To browſe, or nibble againe.*

Rebroyé: m. ée: f. *Brayed, ſtamped, pownded againe.*

Rebroyer. *To bray, ſtampe, or pownd againe.*

Rebruire. *To reſound; or to make a new rumbling.*

Rebrunir. *To burniſh, or furbiſh anew.*

Rebuglant. *Lowing, bellowing againe; alſo, reſounding.*

Rebugler. *To low, or bellow againe; alſo, to ring, or to reſound.*

Rebus (ou, Equivoques de la peinture à la parole) *be repreſentations of ordinarie, or odde things, accompanied with mottos, or words, which as they ſtand, ſeeme to make a ſentence, but pronounced French-like, and without ſtop, deſcribe the things repreſented: As for example; a foole being painted kneeling, with a horne at his mouth, and the words,* fol age nous trompe *neere him, pronounce them as aforeſaid, and you haue,* fol à genous trompe.

Rebut: m. *The reffuſe, offalls, outcaſts, or leauings of better things; alſo, a foyle, repulſe, reiecting, putting backe.*

Brebis de rebut. *Drapes, Cullings, or Kebbers; old, or diſeaſed ſheepe which be not worth keeping.*

Madame de rebut. *A loathſome queane, raſcallie drab, ouerworne punke, pockie whore; whence,* Les paſles couleurs de Madame de rebut. *The Pocks.*

Rebutable: com. *Reiectable, refuſable; foylable.*

Rebuté: m. ée: f. *Repulſed, foyled, reiected, denyed; alſo, retyred, withdrawne, diſuſed, from.*

Rebutée: f. *A repulſe, foyle; reiection, denyall.*

Rebuter. *To repulſe, repell, foyle, driue, put, or thruſt backe; to reiect, refuſe, deny.*

Recaché: m. ée: f. *Hidden againe.*

Recacher. *To hide againe.*

Recacheter. *To ſeale once more.*

Recalcitrer. *To kicke, winſe, or ſtrike backe with the heeles.*

Recalculé: m. ée: f. *Recalculated, whereof a new calculation is made.*

Recalculer. *To recalculate, or make a new computation of.*

Recamé: m. ée: f. *Imbrodered.*

Recamer. *To imbroder.*

Recancelé: m. ée: f. *Recancelled, cancelled againe.*

Recanceler. *To cancell againe.*

Recanement: m. *The braying of an Aſſe.*

Recaner. *To bray like an Aſſe.*

Recapitulation: f. *A recapitulation; a ſhort rehearſall, a ſuccinct relation, of things alreadie deliuered at large.*

Recapitulé: m. ée: f. *Recapitulated.*

Recapituler. *To recapitulate; rehearſe, relate, make a ſhort repetition of a long diſcourſe.*

Recarder la laine. *To card wooll ouer againe.*

Recargaiſon: f. *A backe-fraught, or the lading of a ſhip home againe.*

Recarreler souliers. *To set new soles on shooes.*
Recassé: m. ée: f. *Cassed, or abolished againe.*
Recasser. *To casse, discharge; abolish againe.*
Recavé: m. ée: f. *Hollowed, or digged into, againe.*
Recaver. *To hollow, or dig into, againe.*
Receindre. *To gird anew.*
Recelation: f. *An extreame concealing, hiding, suppression; couering, or keeping verie close.*
Recelé: m. *as* Recelée.
Recelé: m. ée: f. *Suppressed, close hidden, much concealed, exceedingly dissembled; also, receiued as a stolne thing.*
Recelée: f. *A concealement, suppression, close hiding of; also, a fine of 60 s due to a Lord* Censuel *by the purchasor, which hath not, within eight dayes after the purchase, made him acquainted with it.*
Receléement. *Hiddenly, couertly, closely, most priuily.*
Recelement: m. *as* Recelation; *also, a priuie receiuing of stolne goods.*
Receler. *Closely to hide, couer, conceale, dissemble, suppresse; also, to receiue stolne things.*
Recelleresse: f. *A concealeresse; also, a woman that priuily receiueth stolne goods.*
Receleur: m. *A hider, concealer, suppressor; a secret receiuer of stolne goods.*
Recelle, & Recellée. *as* Recelée.
Recengler vn cheval. *To gird a horse againe.*
Recensé: m. ée: f. *Numbred, told, reckoned; recited, rehearsed, related; mustered, perused, viewed ouer.*
Recensement: m. *A numbring, telling, reckoning vp of; a rehearsing, relating, reciting; also, a mustering, perusing, viewing ouer.*
Recenser. *To number, tell, reckon, relate, recite, rehearse; peruse, muster, view ouer.*
Recent: m. ente: f. *Recent, fresh, new, late, but now come or done.*
Recentement. *Recently, freshly, newly, lately, a little before, soone after.*
Recepé: m. ée: f. *Cut off, or away; also, repaired, mended; or vnderset, (as an vndermined wall) at the bottome.*
Receper tout le bois. *To stocke it vp, or cut it wholly away.*
Receper vne muraille. *To repaire, or mend it at the bottome.*
Recepice. *as* Recepissé.
Recepissé: m. *An Acquittance, Discharge, or Note, acknowledging the receit of a thing.*
Receptacle: m. *A receptacle, store-house, or ware-house; also, a sinke, or sewer; any thing thats fit for the receiuing, or safe-keeping, of things.*
Receptaire: m. *A Receptarie; a note of Phisicall receipts.*
Recepte: f. *A receit; a receiuing, taking, accepting, admitting; the full satisfaction of a debt.*
Receptes generales des finances. *Generall Receits, or places for the receit, of the Kings reuenue; These be* Paris, Chaalons, Amiens, Rouën, Caën, Bourges, Orleans, Tours, Poictiers, Rion, Agen, Tholose, Montpellier, Lyon, Aix, Grenoble, & Dijon: A chascune desquelles sont departies les plus prochaines Receptes particulieres tant du domaine, que des Aides, &c.
Reception: f. *A reception, receit, receiuing; also, an assignation of a place for the receit of money, as at the Exchequer.*
Receptoire: m. *A Receptorie; any place, or vessell, thats fit to receiue.*
Recepveur. *as* Receveur.
Recerceller. *To hoope, or incircle anew; also, to curle, or turne vp, as the haire.*
Recerche: f. *A diligent search, inquisition, examination; a serious groping, feeling, sifting, sounding.*
Cela est de recerche. *That is greatly sought for, often layed for, much hunted after, exceedingly in request.*
Recerché: m. ée: f. *Diligently searched, or examined; much hunted, inquired, or sought after; greatly in request.*
Recercher. *Diligently to search, examine; hunt, inquire, after; earnestly to seeke, looke, sound, feele, grope, for.*
Recercher le bout de la fusée. *To intreat of, or fall into, his former subiect.*
Recercheur: m. *A diligent searcher, examiner, inquirer; feeler, sounder.*
Receu: m. *as* Recepissé.
Receu: m. euë: f. *Taken, receiued, admitted, accepted of.*
Recevable: com. *Receiuable, acceptable, admittable, fit to be taken.*
Monnoye recevable. *Currant money.*
Receveur: m. *A Receiuer.*
Aux receveurs les honneurs, & aux femmes leurs douleurs: Pro. *Looke* Femme.
Recevoir. *To receiue, take, accept, admit of; to intertaine; comprehend, containe.*
Fin de non recevoir. *Reasons for the reiecting of a plea; or for the casting of a cause out of a Court: hereof some be temporall, and dilatorie; some perpetuall, and peremptorie.*
Se faire recevoir par main souveraine. *When a Landlord refuses, without iust cause, the homage and fealtie of his vassall; or when two Lords contend for the tenure of one fief, the vassall (who in the second case is not bound to acknowledge either of them as long as their suit continues) hath his recourse vnto some royall Judge (that vsually deales in feodall causes) and by him may be admitted as amply to all purposes, as if the Lord himselfe had done it: But the Lord must in this case be summoned vnto the admission.*
Recez: m. *Recoylings, retyralls, retreats, goings backe; also, departures or absences from; and hence,* Les Escholes ont leurs recez. *Haue their vacations, or times, wherein schollers be not at them.*
Rechaffaudé: m. ée: f. *Set, or presented, on a scaffold againe.*
Rechaffauder. *To set vp, or set on, a scaffold againe.*
Rechamailler. *To hacke, hew, slash, mall, or charge, afresh.*
Rechaner. *To bray like an Asse.*
Rechange: f. *Shift, change, interchange.*
Doré, & argenté à rechange. *Parcell guilt; or, interchangeably siluered and guilt.*
Robbes de rechange. *Change, or choice of garments; shift of apparrell; seuerall suits.*
Rechangé: m. ée: f. *Shifted, scoorsed, interchanged; also, changed againe.*
Rechangement: m. *A shifting, interchanging, exchanging; also, a changing againe.*
Rechanger. *To shift, interchange, exchange; also, to change againe.*
Rechangeur: m. *An interchanger, or exchanger; a changer againe.*

Rechanté: m. ée: f. *Resounded, or sung againe; also, repeated, reiterated, rehearsed.*
Rechanter. *To sing, ring, or sound, againe; also, to repeat, reiterate, rehearse.*
Recharge: f. *A recharge, surcharge, new charge.*
Ils cannonerent avec telle recharge. *Their Artillerie went off so thicke together.*
Par sa lettre il luy fit nouvelle recharge. *He moued, vrged, or solicited him anew by his letter.*
Rechargé: m. ée: f. *Recharged, charged anew.*
Rechargeoüer: m. *A Spring; the Ginne set for Snites, Woodcocks, &c.*
Recharger. *To recharge; to giue a new charge vnto, a fresh charge on; to redouble a commission, commaund, or assault; also, to resolicite, or to reply.*
Recharger par dessus. *To surcharge, ouercharge, ouerlay; also, to lay ouer, or vpon.*
Rechassé: m. ée: f. *Repelled, retorted, thrust back; chased, or driuen from.*
Rechasser. *To repell, retort, thrust backe; chase, or driue away from.*
Rechatouiller. *To tickle againe.*
Rechaucher. *as* Rechausser.
Rechauffé: m. ée: f. *Heated againe; also, heated; Looke* Eschauffé.
Rechauffement: m. *A heating againe; also, a heating, or putting into heat.*
Rechauffer. *To heat, or warme againe; also, to heat, put into heat, giue warmth vnto.*
Rechauffer vn chien. *To make him lustie, or desirous of the bitch; to bring him into, prouoke him vnto, lust.*
Rechault: m. *A Chafing-dish; also, hot coales, or embers (vsed sometimes in stead, or for want, of a Chafing-dish.)*
Rechaussé: m. ée: f. *New hosed, or shod; hosed, or shod againe; also, couered (as a tree) at the root, foot, or bottome.*
Rechaussement: m. *A new shooing or hosing, a shooing or hosing againe; also, a couering (or new couering) at the root, foot, or bottome.*
Rechausser. *To bestow new hose, or shooes, on;* (Se Rechausser. *To put them on, or put them on againe;) also, to couer at the root, foot, or bottome; whence;*
Rechausser vn arbre. *To lay new earth about the root of a tree.*
Recheance: f. *A possession in trust; the vse or custodie of a thing on condition, or with a prouiso, to restore it.*
Rechef. De re. *Againe, afresh, efisoones, anew.*
Recheminer. *To walke againe.*
Recheoir. *To returne, fall backe or againe.*
Recherche, & Rechercher. *Looke* Recerche, & Recercher.
Rechevillé: m. ée: f. *Pegged, or pinned, anew.*
Recheviller. *To peg, or pinne, anew.*
Recheute: f. *A recidiuation, relapse, new fall.*
Recheuter. *To relapse; to fall backe, or againe.*
Rechiffrer. *To make new ciphers, to reexamine by ciphering, to cipher ouer againe.*
Rechignant. *Powting, frowning, lowring.*
Rechignard: m. *A frowning, lowring, powting, sullen, soure-looking, dogged, or grimme fellow.*
Rechigné: m. ée: f. *Frowning, lowring, soure-looking, powting, sullen, dogged, grimme.*
Rechignement: m. *Grimnesse, frowning, lowring; a powting, sullennesse, doggednesse.*
Rechignément. *Frowningly, grimly, lowringly, with a crabbed, or soure looke.*
Rechigner. *To frowne, lowre, powt, be surlie, looke sullenly, sourely, grimly, doggedly.*
Rechigner des dents. *To gyrne, or grinne like a dog.*
Rechiné, & Rechiner. *as* Rechigné, & Rechigner.
Rechoir. *Looke* Recheoir.
Rechoisir. *To chuse againe.*
Recidive: f. *A recidiuation, relapse.*
Recidivé: m. ée: f. *Relapsed, fallen backe, or againe.*
Recidiver. *To recidiuate, relapse, fall backe, or againe.*
Recimenter. *To cement, or parget ouer anew.*
Reciné: m. *An after-noones nuncheon, or collation; an Aunders-meat.*
Reciner. *To feed betweene dinner and supper; to make an afternoones collation.*
Recipé: m. *A Phisitions Receit; the bill, or ticket whereby he directs the Apothecarie.*
Reciprocation: f. *A reciprocation, returning, mutuall yeelding, or interchanging.*
Reciproque: com. *Reciprocall, mutuall, interchangeable, one for another.*
Reciproquer. *To reciprocate, interchange, returne one for another.*
Recirer. *To put new Wax vnto, to Wax againe.*
Recise. *Hearbe Auens, Bennet, or Blessed.*
Recision: f. *A recision, cancelling, or cutting off.*
Recit: m. *A recitall, rehearsall, narration, declaration.*
Sans faire recit du demeurant. *Omitting the rest.*
Recitateur: m. *A recitor, a repeater, a rehearser, a declarer.*
Recité: m. ée: f. *Recited, repeated, rehearsed.*
Recitement: m. *A reciting, repeating, rehearsing.*
Reciter. *To recite, repeat, rehearse; to declare, or tell ouer againe; also, to cite, adiourne, or summon the second time.*
Reciteur. *as* Recitateur.
Reclaim: m. *A praying in aid of a Superior; a petition, or complaint made vnto a higher power; also, as* Reclain; *or, a bill of Complaint exhibited against a debtor, who being bound in an obligation vnder the Seale Royall, breaketh his promise.*
Reclain. *as* Reclaim; *or, a refusall to pay the contents of an obligation; or (as in some customes) the summe limitted by a Sentence.*
Reclam: m. *as* Reclame.
Reclamation: f. *A contradiction, gainesaying, or crying against; also, a challenge, or demaund; a prosecution, pursuit, or suit in Law; also, an often calling vpon, an earnest crying vnto.*
Reclame: f. *A Soboe, or Heylaw; a lowd calling, whooting, or whooping to make a Hawke stoope vnto the Lure; also, a clayme, or challenge.*
Reclamé: m. ée: f. *Called often or instantly, earnestly cryed vnto; also, repugned, contradicted, gainsayed; exclaimed vpon, complained against; also, sued, prosecuted, pursued; also, demaunded, challenged; owned.*
Reclamer. *To call often, or instantly, to cry vnto earnestly; also, to repugne, contradict, gainesay; exclaime vpon, complaine against; also, to sue, pursue, or prosecute in Law; also, to claime, challenge; demaund; owne.*
Reclamer son homme de corps. *A Lord to prosecute or pursue his villaine which is gone, without his leaue, to reside in a forraine Prouince, or Iurisdiction.*
Recliner. *as* Encliner.

Reclorre. *To shut, or close vp againe; (also, as* Biner, *in* Languedoc.)

Reclos: m. ose: f. *Shut, or closed vp againe.*

Reclouër. *To nayle againe.*

Reclus: m. use: f. *Closely kept in, or shut vp, as a Monke, or Nunne; retyred, solitarie.*

Recocquebillé: m. ée: f. *Snackit, or whose end turnes vpward; whence;*

Nez recocquebillé. *Whose bridge is flat or hollow in the middest, and turnes vp at the end.*

Recogneu: m. euë: f. *Recognized, acknowledged, called vnto remembrance.*

Recognoissance: f. *A recognizing, agnition, acknowledgement; also, a Badge, or Cognisance; also, an acknowledgement of tenure, or that he holds his land of another.*

Recognoissant: m. ante: f. *Recognizing, acknowledging; remembring, or calling vnto mind.*

Recognoistre. *To recognize, agnize, acknowledge, aduow, take notice or acquaintance of; call vnto mind, or memorie; also, to take a precise view of, looke especially or diligently at; also, to acknowledge a tenure, or that he holds of another.*

Il se recognoist à la langue Italienne. *He is well seene, or skilfull, in the Italian.*

C'est vne vache de Barbarie qui ne recognoist que son propre veau; *Looke* Barbarie.

Folie faire, & folie recognoistre sont deux paires de folie: Prov. *To doe euill, and then brag of it, is a double wickednesse.*

Se Recoibler. *To withdraw, or to retire, himselfe.*

Recoiffer. *To dresse or attire (as a woman) her head anew, to put on her coife againe.*

Recoigné: m. ée: f. *Knocked, or wedged, in againe.*

Recoigner. *To wedge, or knocke, in againe.*

Recoin: m. *A corner, by-place, odde hole.*

Recolé: m. ée: f. (Tesmoings recolez) *recalled, and reexamined.*

Recolement de tesmoings. *A reexamination of witnesses (especially when they haue not deposed fully, or plainely, enough) before they be confronted with such as they haue accused: Tis also vsed, sometimes, in tryalls vpon ciuill Actions; howsoeuer, their former depositions are first read vnto them.*

Recoler tesmoings. *To reexamine witnesses, or summon them vnto a reexamination, &c; as in* Recollement.

Recollationné: m. ée: f. *Reexamined by the Originall.*

Recollationner. *To take a new collation; also, to reexamine a copie by the Originall, or one writing by another.*

Recoller. *To glue againe.*

Recollets: m. *A certaine vpstart sect of Franciscan Fryers.*

Recolorer. *To colour anew, to set fresh colours on.*

Recolte: f. *A gathering, reaping, haruest.*

Les soldats ont fait leur recolte. *Haue beene a forraging, haue got in their forrage.*

Recombatre. *To fight againe.*

Recombler. *To add heape vnto heape, to fill vp againe.*

Recomfort &c. *Looke* Reconfort &c.

Recommandable: com. *Recommendable, commendable, praise-worthie.*

Recommandablement. *Recommendably, commendably, praise-worthily.*

Recommandaces: f. *Funerall prayers, or praises.*

Recommandatif: m. iue: f. *Recommendatiue, recommending.*

Recommandation: f. *A recommendation.*

Recommandatoire: com. *Commendatorie, recommendatorie.*

Recommandé: m. ée: f. *Recommended, praised, commended vnto.*

Avoir vne chose pour recommandée. *To haue a care, to make account of.*

Recommander. *To recommend, or commend, vnto; to giue one charge, to commit vnto the care, of; also, to praise, or speake well of.*

Ie me recommande à leurs espaules. *Woe to their shoulders, for they are sure of a cudgelling.*

De prescheur qui se recommande en tout temps bon heur nous defende: Prov. *From begging Preachers fortune still defend vs.*

Recommanderesses: f. *Such women as by commending, and vndertaking for, maids, procure them seruices.*

Recommandeur: m. *A recommendor, commendor, praiser.*

Recommencé: m. ée: f. *Recommenced, iterated, renewed, begun againe.*

Recommencer. *To recommence, iterate, renew, begin afresh.*

Ce sera tousiours à recommencer. *This worke requires so many renewings, as it will neuer be done; or, so may we toyle full hard and be no whit the neerer, or neuer haue done.*

Recommendable &c. *as* Recommandable &c.

Recommuniquer. *To recommunicate, reimpart, conferre with againe.*

Recompense: f. *A recompence, meed, reward, guerdon.*

Recompensé: m. ée: f. *Recompenced, guerdoned, rewarded, remunerated.*

Recompensement: m. *A guerdoning, recompencing, remunerating, rewarding.*

Recompenser. *To recompence, guerdon, remunerate, reward.*

Recompenseur: m. *A recompencer.*

Recomposer. *To recompose, to frame anew.*

Recompter. *To count, or tell ouer, againe.*

Reconciliateur: m. *A reconciler, pacifyer, peace-maker.*

Reconciliation: f. *A reconciliation, pacification, atonement, agreement.*

Reconcilier. *To reconcile, pacifie, attone, agree, make peace, renew loue betweene, bring into fauor againe.*

Reconcilier vne eglise. *To purge, clense, reconsecrate a Church by fasting, prayers, &c.*

Recondamner. *To recondemne, or condemne againe.*

Recondit: m. ite: f. *Hidden, concealed, kept secret.*

Reconduire. *To reconduct, bring backe, lead or guide homeward againe.*

Reconduiseur: m. *A reconductor; a leader, bringer, guider backe, or homeward againe.*

De meschant hoste bon reconduisseur: Pro. *Looke* Hoste.

Reconferer. *To reconferre, or talke of the matter againe.*

Reconfermé: m. ée: f. *Reconfirmed, reinforced, reassured.*

Reconfermer. *To reconfirme, reinforce, reassure.*

Reconfesser. *To reconfesse, or confesse againe.*

Reconfiné: m. ée: f. *Reconfined, banished anew.*

Reconfiner. *To reconfine, or banish anew.*

Reconfisquer. *To reconfiscate, or make a new seisure vnto the Princes, or publike, vse.*

Reconfort: m. *Great solace, or comfort, much consolation.*

Reconforté: m. ée: f. *Much comforted.*

Reconforter. *To comfort, or solace much; to ease, or cheere vp, exceedingly.*

Promettre sans donner est fol reconforter: Prov. *To promise onely does a foole much good; or the foole is fully satisfied with bare promises.*

Reconfronter. *To reconfront, reaccoast, compare once more together.*

Reconfuter. *To reconfute, or confute againe.*

Recongreger. *To reassemble, to rally.*

Reconjuré: m. ée: f. *Reconiured.*

Reconjurer. *To reconiure, to coniure againe.*

Reconnoissable: com. *Acknowledgable.*

Reconquerir. *To resubdue, reconquer, conquer againe, to recouer.*

Reconquerre. *as* Reconquerir.

Reconqueste: f. *A reconquest; a recouerie by conquest.*

Reconquester. *To reconquer, to recouer by conquest; to winne, get, or purchase againe.*

Reconquister. *as* Reconquerir.

Reconsé: m. ée: f. *Hidden, concealed, withdrawne.*

Reconsement: m. *A concealing, hiding, withdrawing.*

Reconser. *To conceale, hide, withdraw.*

Reconsiderer. *To consider, or thinke, better of the matter.*

Reconsigner. *To reconsigne, reassigne, reappoint; reexhibit, vnto.*

Reconsoler. *To recomfort.*

Reconsolidé: m. ée: f. *Reconsolidated, closed vp againe.*

Reconstruire. *To build vp againe.*

Reconsulter. *To reconsult of, take new aduise on.*

Recontemplé: m. ée: f. *Recontemplated, reuiewed.*

Recontempler. *To recontemplate, reuiew.*

Recontester. *To recontest; make new protestation of, or complaint vnto.*

Recontracté: m. ée: f. *Recontracted.*

Recontracter. *To recontract, or passe a new contract.*

Recontraindre. *To reconstraine, to compell againe.*

Reconvaincre. *To reconuince.*

Reconvenir. *To reassemble, reunite; agree anew; also, to fit, or suit passing well; also, to recommence a Suit in Law.*

Reconvention: f. *A new agreement; also, the reuiuing of a Law-suit.*

Reconvertir. *To reconuert.*

Reconvié: m. ée: f. *Reinuited.*

Reconvier. *To reinuite.*

Reconvoquer. *To reassemble, or call together againe.*

Reconvoy: m. *A reconuoy, or attendance backe.*

Reconvoyé: m. ée: f. *Reconuoyed, reconducted.*

Reconvoyer. *To reconuoy, reconduct; bring, or lead, a returner onward on the way.*

Reconvoyeur: m. *A reconuoyer, a reconductor.*

Recopier. *To copie out againe.*

Recoquillé: m. ée: f. *as* Recroquillé; *also, lustie, cranke, peart, in comparison of that he was.*

Recoquiller. *To wrigle, wrythe, turne inward, or into it selfe, like a worme when tis touched, or a gold or siluer thread when tis broken; also, to wind shell-wise; also, to reuiue, wax lustie, grow peart, take heart againe.*

Recoquiller vn livre. *To rumple, or turne vp, the leaues thereof.*

Recoquilleure: f. *A curling, wrything, crooking, turning, or bending inwards; also, a reuiuing, a growing peart, lustie, cranke, a taking heart at grasse.*

Recoquiner. *To fall a begging, to returne to beggerie.*

Record: m. *A Record; a witnesse (that remembers well the thing he witnesses;) also, a testification; also, a repetition, recitall, relation (in Court) of things done.*

Records. *Two persons whom a Sergeant vsed, heretofore, to haue with him (or call vnto him) when he arrested, or serued a Writ on, a man: In the first case, clapping them on the shoulders, he willed them to beare witnesse what he had done; in the second, they signed, together with him, the returne of the Writ; or, if they could not write, he signified in it their names, and presence: These* Records *were to be sufficient, and well-knowne inhabitants of that place; and neither kinsmen, allyes, nor of the household, of the partie that imployed the Sergeant.*

Recordation: f. *A recordation, a remembrance.*

Recordé: m. ée: f. *New-strung; also, testified; also, repeated, recited, related (as a thing thats well remembred;) also, reported, notified, certified.*

Exploict recordé. *Executed by a Sergeant in the presence of* Records, *or two witnesses.*

Recordeler. *To string anew; also, to twyne againe an vntwisted cord, or string.*

Recorder. *To put a new string vnto (or, as* Recordeler;) *also, to testifie; also, to repeat, recite, relate, rehearse; to report, certifie, notifie, make a returne (as a Sergeant of the Writs deliuered vnto him.)*

Se recorder. *To remember, or call to mind.*

Recordeur: m. *A witnesse; one that was present at the deed doing, and remembers it well.*

Recorrigé: m. ée: f. *Recorrected, redressed.*

Recorriger. *To recorrect, reuiew, redresse.*

Recors: m. *A Witnesse, a Record.*

Recors. *Remembring, mindfull of, hauing in mind.*

Recouché. *Layen downe, or layed downe, againe.*

Recoucher. *To lye downe, or get to bed, againe.*

Recouldre. *To sow ouer againe.*

Recouler. *To runne, glide, or slide, backe.*

Recoulourer. *To giue new colour, to add a new dye, vnto.*

Recoupe. La rec. *See* Recoupes.

Recouper. *To cut againe; also, to reply quickly and sharpely vnto a peremptorie demaund, or quip; to returne taunt for taunt, nip for nip, gird for gird; also, to vrge, or lay hard vnto with quipping words, or questions.*

Recoupes: f. *Shreds, clippings, parings, chippings; also, a middle sort of Branne.*

Recoupler. *To couple againe.*

Recourbant. *Bending, or bowing backward.*

Recourbé: m. ée: f. *Bent, or bowed backward.*

Recourbement: m. *A bowing, crooking, bending backward, or againe.*

Recourber. *To bow, crooke, bend backe, or againe.*

Recourir. *To runne hastily ouer; also, to rescue.*

Recourir à. *To runne, recourse, or haue recourse, vnto.*

Recouronner. *To crowne againe.*

Recourquebillé. *as* Recocquebillé.

Recourroucer. *To anger againe.*

Recours: m. *A recourse, refuge, retreat, a returning vnto; (also, an Outcry for goods, or a letting of lands by Outcry; ¶ Wallon;) also, a redresse, remedie, helpe.*

Recours de garantie. *A vouching; a calling of a donor, or seller to warrant, and make good, the graunt or bargaine which he passed.*

Recours reservé. *A reseruation of libertie for one that is condemned, or cast in Law, to seeke his redresse where he thinkes best.*

Monnoye de bon recours. *That passes very currantly.*

Recourse: f. *as* Recours.
Recourser. *To tucke, trusse, or turne vp the garments.*
Recousse: f. *A rescue, recouerie, recouering; a deliuerie from present danger.*
Recousu: m. uë: f. *Sowed againe.*
Recousure: f. *A new sowing, or stitching vp.*
Recouvrable: com. *Recouerable, rescuable, reobtainable; also, gettable, procurable.*
Recouvrance: f. *A recouerie, reobtainment, procurement.*
Recouvré: m. ée: f. *Recouered, reobtained, rescued; also, gotten, procured.*
Recouvrement: m. *A recouerment, recouering, reobtaining; also, a getting, or procuring.*
Recouvrer. *To recouer, to reobtaine, to rescue, to get againe; also, to get, or procure.*
Recouvreur: m. *A mender of slated, or thatched houses.*
Recouvrir. *To couer againe.*
Recoux: m. ouse: f. *Rescued, recouered from an iminent danger.*
Recoy: m. *Rest, quiet, ease.*
Recracher. *To spit againe.*
Recrant. *as* Recreant.
Recreance: f. *A restorall, restitution, giuing backe of; also, a deliuerie of possession; and, a possession giuen in a suit vnto one of the parties (who proues that he enioyed the thing all the yeare before) by Sentence prouisionall, or vpon trust, vntill the cause be determined; also, wearinesse, faintnesse, faint-heartednesse; also, a refreshment, recreation, reuiuing, cheering vp.*
L'Incident de recreance. *A suit wherein the demaundant is bound to forfeit a summe of money, if the thing he sues for proue not his; and the defendant likewise is bound, not to impaire it while the possession is his.*
Recreant. *Tired, toyled, wearied, spent, iaded, out of heart, or faint-hearted, cleane done.*
Recreatif: m. iue: f. *Recreatiue, delightfull, pleasant, sportfull, merrie.*
Recreation: f. *Recreation, pastime, sport, a delightfull or pleasant exercise.*
Recreativement. *Recreatiuely, with recreation, to his recreation, sportfully, delightfully, pleasantly.*
Recreer. *To recreate, refresh, cheere vp, delight, solace, reuiue, please.*
Recremens: m. *Excrements.*
Recrespé. *as* Crespu.
Recrespir vne muraille. *To new-parget a wall.*
Recreu: m. cuë: f. *Tired, wearie, toyled, iaded, spent, out of heart, faint-hearted.*
Iamais François ne furent veus recreus de bien faire: Prov. *Looke* François.
Recreuë: f. *A supplie, or filling vp of a defectiue companie of souldiers, &c.*
Recrever. *To burst againe.*
Recreusé: m. ée: f. *Hollowed againe.*
Recreuser. *To hollow, or make hollow againe.*
Recribler. *To sift ouer againe.*
Recrier. *To crie againe, giue a crie for a crie, answer alowd vnto a lowd demaund.*
Recrimination: f. *A recrimination, an accusation of an accuser, the retorting of a crime.*
Recriminer. *To recriminate, retort a crime, accuse an accuser.*
Recrochu: m. uë: f. *as* Recoquebillé; *or as* Recroquillé.
Recroire. *To beleeue againe; also, to reseise, rearrest; also, to restore, deliuer or giue, backe.*
Recroiser. *To crosse, or cancell againe.*
Recroiset: m. ette: f. *Whence;* Croix recroisette. *A crosse Crosset, or Crosselet (in Blazon.)*
Recroist: m. *A reincrease; a new, or second growth.*
Recroistre. *To reincrease; to grow, or spring vp, againe.*
Recrocquebillage: m. *A hookie crooking, bending, bowing; winding, or turning inwards.*
Recroquebillé, & Recroquevillé. *as* Recroquillé.
Recroquillé: m. ée: f. *Crooked, bent, bending, snackit, retorted; bowing, foulding, or turning; bowed, foulded, wound, or turned, inwards.*
Recroquillement: m. *A crooking, bending, bowing, retorting, turning, winding, or foulding, inwards.*
Recroquiller. *To retort, crooke, bend, bow, turne, fould, or wind, inwards.*
Recroquillonné. *as* Recroquillé.
Recrotter. *To bedaggle, or bedurtie againe.*
Recru. *as* Recreu.
Recrudi: m. ie: f. *Made, or growne, raw.*
Recrudir. *To make (or wax) raw.*
Rectangle: m. *A straight, or euen angle; a corner whose lines are ioyned so, as no part falls out longer, or shorter then other.*
Recte: f. *Right, equitie, iustice, honestie.* (v.m.)
Recteur. *(in* Languedoc, *as in France* Curé) *A Curate, or Parson.*
Recteur de l'Vniversité. *The Rector, the Vicechancelor.*
Rectificateur: m. *A Rectifier.*
Rectification: f. *A rectification, or a rectifying; a correction, purification, separation of pure from vnpure stuffe, by a second distilling, &c.*
Rectifié: m. ée: f. *Rectified; corrected, purified; twice distilled; refined by a second, or by frequent distilling.*
Rectifier. *To rectifie, correct, purifie, purge; to separate the pure, fine, right, from th'impure, grosse, adulterate stuffe, by distillation.*
Rectorerie: f. *A Rectorship, a Vicechancelorship.*
Rectorial: m. ale: f. *Rectoriall, Rector-like; belonging to a Rector, or Vicechancelor.*
Recueil: m. *A collection, gathering, reaping; also, a welcome, or intertainment.*
Recueillant. *Collecting, gathering together; also, intertaining, or welcoming.*
Recueilleur: m. *A Collector, a reaper, a gatherer together.*
Recueiller. *To collect, reape, gather together; also, to welcome, or intertaine.*
Grande moisson l'obeisant recueille: Prov. *Great is the Haruest of th'obedient; they that can yeeld will thriue.*
Recuict: m. cte: f. *Againe, or often, boiled; also, wretched, miserable, niggardlie, miching, pinching, paultrie, dodging.*
Recuire. *To seeth often, or againe; also, to harden, as with ouer-much baking.*
Recuire les carreaux. *To blanch the Copings, or Planchets whereof coyne is to be made.*
Recuire l'or. c'est le passer vn peu sur la braise.
Recuisson: f. *A new seething, or, a seething againe.*
Recuit. *as* Recuict.
Recuitte de laict. *Whay thickned, or curded, by seething; fleetings, wild curds.*
Recul: m. *A recoyle, or giuing backe; also, the hinder part of a thing.*
Reculade: f. *A recoyling, a going, or giuing backe; also, a by-hole, a remote or secret corner.*

Reculant. *Recoyling, giuing backe*; En reculant. *Backward, arseward.*
Reculé: m. ée: f. *Recoiled, repulsed, put or drawne backe; remoued, withdrawne, retired; solitarie, all alone, farre off, out of the way.*
Reculé de son honneur. *Depriued or bereaued of, put or fallen from, the honourable place which he held.*
Tu t'es trop reculé d'icy. *Thou hast beene too long, or too farre, from hence.*
Reculée: f. *A recoyle, retire, going or giuing, backe.*
Reculement: m. *A recoyling, retiring, withdrawing, a giuing backe, a going farre backe, or from, a remouing; also, a refusing, denying, delaying, drawing backe from.*
Reculer. *To recoyle, retire, giue or draw backe, remoue, withdraw, goe from; to deferre, delay, driue off, runne backe, come to no end.*
Reculer pour mieux saulter. *Looke* Saulter.
Il le recula arriere de soy. *He neglected him, respected him not, cast him at his heeles, cared no more for him.*
De cheval qui recule au plustost te deliure: Prov. *Soone rid thee of a horse thats restie.*
Pour neant recule qui malheur attend: Prov. *In vaine he flinches that ill hap attends.*
Qui contre esguillon recule deux fois se poind: Prov. *He's doubly hurt that kickes against a pricke.*
Reculons. A rec. *Recoyling, arseward, giuing backeward; cleane contrarie, quite kamme.*
Gaigner sa vie à reculons. *To liue by going backward*; viz. *by making of ropes.*
Reculorum. A rec. *Backward, behind, or behind-hand; also, forsaken, forgotten, left behind, solitarie, all alone.*
Recultiver. *To till, or plough againe.*
Recupercuté. ¶Rab. *Looke* Repercuté.
Recurer. *To recure, to heale againe.*
Recusant. *Reiecting, refusing.*
Recusation: f. *A recusation, reiection, refusall; a waiuing, or appealing from.*
Recusé: m. ée: f. *Reiected, refused; appealed from.*
Recuser. *To reiect, refuse; waiue, appeale from.*
Recutir. *To circumcise, to clip or cut about.*
Recutit. *Circumcised; clipped or cut about; also, newskinned:* (Quand le prepuce est trop reboulé, le gland demeurant descouvert, on appelle vn tel recutit.)
Recuver. *To tunne, or put into a fat, againe.*
Redaigner. *To redaigne, to vouchsafe once more.*
Redanser. *To daunce againe.*
Redarder. *To retort, or throw back, a Dart.*
Redargué: m. ée: f. *Checked, blamed, reproued, reprehended, controwled.*
Redarguer. *To checke, blame, reproue, reprehend, controwle.*
Redargution: f. *A redargution, checking, reprouing, reprehending, controwling.*
Redater. *To redate, or adde a new date vnto.*
Rede: com. *as* Roide: ¶Gasc.
Reddition: f. *A reddition; a redeliuerie; a restoring, surrendring, yeelding vp, or giuing ouer of.*
Redebatre. *To redebate the matter; to cauill, or brabble about it againe.*
Redebvable: com. *Indebted, in arrerages, beholden, or bound, vnto.*
Redebvable de iurée. *Liable to Juries, or subiect to be sworne thereof.*
Redebvance: f. *A debt, or duetie; or the remainder, or arrerage, of a debt; also, an obligation, or beholdingnesse.*
Redebvances. Ce sont les devoirs, ou charges, es quelles les proprietaires sont tenus envers quelque Seigneur feodal, censuel, rentier, pensionnaire, ou terrageur: ¶Ragueau.
Redebvoir: m. *A double duetie; or as* Redebvance.
Redebvoir. *To owe doubly, to owe againe and againe.*
Redeclamer. *To declaime once more.*
Redeclarer. *To redeclare, to reexpresse, repeat, relate.*
Redecliner. *To redecline, to decline againe.*
Redecorer. *To redecorate, or bedecke againe.*
Rededié: m. ée: f. *Rededicated.*
Rededier. *To rededicate, to consecrate or hallow anew.*
Rededuire. *To rededuct, re diminish, reabate.*
Redefaire. *To vndoe, or defeat againe.*
Redeleguer. *To redelegate, reappoint, giue a new commission vnto.*
Redeliberer. *To redeliberate, redetermine of.*
Redemander. *To redemaund; recall, aske againe earnestly, require often or instantly.*
Redemanger. *To itch againe.*
Redemener. *To stirre, waggle, fig; tosse, tumble, againe.*
Redemeurer. *To stay once more.*
Redemolir. *To redemolish, resubuert, ouerthrow againe.*
Redemourer. *as* Redemeurer.
Redempteur: m. *A redeemer, a ransomer, a deliuerer.*
Redemption: f. *A redemption, redeeming, ransoming; a deliuerie of, a purchasing, or buying out, of.*
Redenoncé: m. ée: f. *Redenounced.*
Redenoncer. *To redenounce; to publish; threaten; or summon anew.*
Redent: m. *A double notching, or iagging, as in the teeth of a saw.*
Redescendre. *To redescend, or goe downe againe.*
Redesfermer. *To open once more.*
Redesfier. *To distrust anew.*
Redesjuner. *To make, or eat, a second breake-fast.*
Redespouiller. *Againe to spoyle, despoyle, vncloth, strip, or bare of.*
Redevable. *See* Redebvable.
Redevaller. *To redescend, let, put, or tumble, downe, againe.*
Redevance. *as* Redebvance.
Redevenir. *To returne, rebecome, or become againe.*
Redevider. *To rediuide, or make a new diuision.*
Redevoir. *as* Redebvoir.
Redhibition: f. *A restitution; or, a legall deliuerie, or giuing backe of a thing vnto him that sold it.*
Redhibitoire. *Whence*; Action red. *An Action which driues him, that hath sold a naughtie thing, to take it backe againe.*
Redicte: f. *A repetition, recitall, iteration, rehearsall.*
Chose bien dite n'a replique, ne redicte: Prov. *Truth well deliuered preuents replies.*
Rediffamer. *To redefame, to slaunder anew.*
Redifier. *Looke* Réedifier.
Redigé: m. ée: f. *Reduced, brought backe, or into; digested, ordered; vrged, or compelled vnto.*
Redigé par escript. *Couched, reported, set downe in writing.*
Rediger. *To reduce; bring backe, or into; vrge, or compell vnto; to ranke, order, digest; couch, or set downe, in writing.*
Redigerer. *To redigest, redigest.*

Re-

Rediiné : m.ée : f. *Redeemed.*
Redimer. *To redeeme, ransome, recouer, buy out.*
Redins : m. *Redding clothes.*
Redire. *To repeat, rehearse, recite, say or tell ouer againe.*
Il n'y aura que redire. *It will find him worke ynough I warrant him.*
Ou il n'y a que redire. *Full, perfect, absolute, exquisite; without fault, without want, without lack; wherin nothing is omitted, no more can be desired then there is.*
Tant redire? *What! so many repetitions? shall mine eares be still cloyed, shall my head be euer beaten, with one tale?*
Redisner. *To dine againe.*
Redistribuer. *To redistribute, or deale backe againe.*
Redite : f. *as* Redicte.
Redition : f. *A restoring, surrendring, yeelding vp, giuing ouer of.*
Redituaires. Moines red. *A sect of Franciscan Friers, which haue lands and reuerewes; therein differing from the Mendicants, or begging Friers, who are to possesse nothing.*
Reditte. *as* Redicte.
Redolent : m. ente : f. *Redolent, fragrant, sweet-smelling, odoriferous, pleasant.*
Redompté : m. ée : f. *Resubdued, or tamed againe.*
Redompteur : m. *A resubduer of.*
Redon : m. *A gift returned; or one thing giuen for another; also, the requitall of an ill by a good, turne.*
Redondage : m. *Grosse, or course meale; grudgions.*
Redondamment. *Redundantly, excessiuely, superfluously.*
Redonder. *To redound, ouercharge, fall vpon, returne backe; light, fall, or breake out; run ouer with fullnesse, abound in excesse.*
Redonner. *To giue backe, to returne.*
Qui du sien donne Dieu luy redonne: Pro. *God rewardeth almes-giuers.*
Redonter. *as* Redompter.
Redorer. *To gild ouer anew.*
Redormir. *To sleepe againe.*
Redormissement : m. *A falling into a new sleepe, a sleeping againe.*
Redouble : m. *A redoublement; double fould, or bought; a redoubling.*
Redoublé : m. ée : f. *Redoubled; often repeated or doubled.*
Redoublement : m. *A redoubling, an often doubling.*
Redoubler. *To redouble; to repeat, or double, often.*
Redoubleur : m. *A redoubler.*
Redoublure : f. *A redoubling.*
Redoubtable: com. *Redoubtable, dreadfull, fearefull, terrible.*
Redoubté : m. ée : f. *Redoubted, feared, awed, dreaded.*
Redoubter. *To dread, redoubt, feare, awe.*
Redoubtillon : m. *A scar-crow; any deuice wherwith birds, &c, are frighted away.*
Redoupier. *A horse to turne diuers times with one breath.*
Redoutant. *Redoubting, dreading.*
Redouter, & Redoutillon. *as* Redoubter, & Redoubtillon.
Redressé : m. ée: f. *Redressed; straightened.*
Redresser. *To redresse, straighten, set or make straight, correct, reforme, amend.*
Reduction : f. *A reduction, reducing, bringing backe, leading or fetching home againe; also, a recouerie, or a reconquest of a lost countrey.*
Reduict : m. *A retrait, or secret place of retirall; also, as* Reduite.
Reduict : m. ácte : f. *Looke* Reduit.
Reduire. *To reduce, bring backe, or vnto; also, to lead forth.*
Reduire à sa memoire. *To remember, or call vnto remembrance.*
Reduire quelqu'un à memoire de. *To remember, or put one in mind of.*
Reduire vn enfant gasté. *To reclaime him.*
Reduire en pouldre. *To make dust, or powder of; to to put or doe into, to pownd or beat vnto, powder.*
Reduisant. *Reducing, bringing backe.*
Reduit : m. *Reduced, brought backe, or into; conducted home againe; also, led forth; also, brought.*
Reduit à l'herbe. *In extreame want, most bare of meanes, in great necessitie; at a verie low ebbe.*
Reduit de livres en quarterons. *Extreamely wasted, whereof at least three quarters be spent.*
Reduit au petit pied. *Looke* Pied.
Reduit au tapis. *Cleane out of meanes, and imployment; (and at play) left a bareboord, whose money is all lost.*
Reduite : f. *A Blockhouse, or little fort.*
Rée. *A faultie, or guiltie person; one that is accused, or arraigned; a defendant in any suit.*
Reedification : f. *A reedification, reedifying, newbuilding.*
Reedifié : m. ée: f. *Reedified, againe built.*
Reedifier. *To reedifie, to build againe.*
Reel : m. *A manner of catching water-fowle.*
Réel : m. elle : f. *Reall, essentiall.*
Tailles réelles. *Which are imposed on, or due by reason of land; which follow the land.*
Réellement. *Really, in verie truth, in verie deed.*
Réement : m. *The braying, or bellowing of a red Deere.*
Reémeré. *as* Remeré.
Réentement : m. *A new graffing, a graffing againe.*
Réenter. *To graffe anew, or againe.*
Réenterrer. *To reenterre; to put into the earth againe.*
Réer. *To bellow, to bray: (In tearmes of hunting we say, that the red Deere bells, and the fallow troytes or croynes.)*
Réestre. *To be renewed, or be againe.*
Refaçon : f. *A second forme, new fashion, reformation.*
Refaçonner. *To reforme, to make of a new, or of another, fashion.*
Refaict : m. ácte : f. *Renewed, repaired, improued, made anew, amended; also, plumpe, fattened, high-fed; swollen, puffed vp, as parboiled meat.*
Chasteau abbatu est à demy refaict : Prov. *Looke* Chasteau.
D'un vilain refaict Dieu nous garde : Prov. *From a churle growne rich good Lord deliuer vs.*
Refaillir. *To faile the second time.*
Refaire. *To repaire, amend, renew, make new; also, to parboyle, or make plumpe by parboyling.*
Se refaire. *To recouer his health, to grow strong, whole, well, in heart, againe.*
Refaire son nez. *To picke vp his crummes againe.*
Robbe refait moult l'homme : Prov. *Good clothes doe much for a man (that would be handsome.*
Refait. *Looke* Refaict.
Refarder. *To paint often, or ouer againe.*
Refascher. *To anger anew.*
Refauché : m. ée : f. *Cut, or mowed, againe.*

Refaucher. *To cut, or mowe neerer, or ouer againe.*
Refect. *as* Refaict.
Refection: f. *A refection, repast, meale; food, sustenance.*
Refections d'une maison. *The reparations of a house.*
Refectouër: m. *A Refectuarie, or Fratrie; the roome wherein Friers eat together.*
Refendre. *To cleaue, to cut againe.*
Refendu: m.uë: f. *Cleft in the middle, or into halues; clouen asunder, or in two.*
Refente: f. *A cleft, slit, or cut (especially) in the middle of a thing.*
Refente de fueilles. *The line, or diuision that runnes along, or appeares in the middle of, leaues.*
Bois de refente. *Cleft wood, such as pales, &c, are made of.*
Referendaire: m. *The Lord Chancelor of France was tearmed so in old time; Now the* Referendaire *is an Officer inferiour to the Maisters of Requests, for whose ease it seems, he & his cōpanions were, at the first, ordained; for they report vnto them th'effect of Petitions preferred vnto, and of Patents that passe out of, the seuerall Chaunceries of France; and are therefore tearmed otherwise,* Rapporteurs.
Referer. *To recite, repeat, rehearse, relate, report.*
Referir. *To smite, or strike againe.*
Refermer. *To close, or shut vp againe.*
Referrer. *To new-shooe a horse.*
Refesser. *To whip, ierke, or scourge againe.*
Refester. *To make a new holy-day.*
Refestier. *To feast againe.*
Refestoyer. *The same.*
Reffe. vne noix reffe. *An hard-sheld nut:* ¶Bourb.
Reffiron: m. *The third gate of the wombe; or the mouth of the matrix, which is cleft acrosse, and not lengthwise, as the Hymen, &c.*
Reffonder. *Looke* Refonder.
Reffort. *as* Raifort.
Reficher. *To fasten againe.*
Refier. *To trust once more.*
Refiger. *To refix, reclose; clot, coagulate, or curdle together againe.*
Refiguré: m.ée: f. *Refigured.*
Refigurer. *To figure, or paint ouer, againe.*
Refiler. *To spinne, or twist anew.*
Reflairer. *To smell, vent, or wind againe.*
Reflamber. *To retort, or beat backe a flame; also, to flame backe, or cast backe flames.*
Reflater. *To flatter anew.*
Reflateur: m. *An egregious flatterer, a palpable clawbacke.*
Reflechi: m. ie: f. *Reflected; bowed, bent, or turned backe.*
Reflechir. *To reflect; to bow, bend, or turne backe.*
Reflefchir. *The same.*
Refleurir. *To flourish againe.*
Refleuter. *To pipe, or whistle often.*
Reflexif: m iue: f. *Reflexiue, reflexing.*
Reflot: m. *An ebbe, or ebbing of waters.*
Refloter. *To flote, or swimme againe; also, to ebbe, or fall, as waters after a floud.*
Reflourir. *as* Refleurir.
Reflux: m. *The ebbe, or ebbing of the sea, or of a riuer, after the tide.*
Refocillation: f. *A refreshing, reuiuing, recomforting, a new heartening.*
Refociller. *To refresh, reuiue, recomfort, recreate, or hearten anew.*
Refomenté: m.ée: f. *Refomented, cherished againe.*
Refomenter. *To refoment, to warme or cherish againe.*
Refoncé: m.ée: f. *Headed againe, as caske; also, plunged, or gone downe to the bottome againe.*
Refonder les despens. *To restore, pay, returne, or giue backe, the costs and charges.*
Refondre. *To cast anew, to melt againe.*
Refondre les gens. *To breed lustie humors in decayed bodies, to make young men of old.*
Refondrement, & Refondrer. *as* Renfondrement, & Renfondrer.
Reforgé: m.ée: f. *New forged, new made, wrought or hammered anew.*
Reforger. *To forge, worke, hammer, anew.*
Reformateur: m. *A reformer, correcter, amender.*
Reformation: f. *Reformation, amendment, correction.*
Reformé: m.ée. f. *Reformed, corrected, amended; also, new-formed, or brought to it former shape.*
Reformez. *Reformists, an Order of Franciscan Fryers.*
Reformer. *To reforme, amend, correct; repaire, bring into better fashion.*
Refort. *Looke* Raifort.
Refouëtter. *To whip, or scourge againe.*
Refouiller. *To search, feele, grope; root, or dig for, anew.*
Refouïr. *To dig into againe.*
Refoulé: m. ée: f. *Dulled, blunted; obtuse; rammed in; troden downe, stamped on againe; also, tyred, wearied, ouerlaboured, foyled, ouertoyled.*
Refoulement: m. *A blunting, dulling; ramming in, treading downe; a tyring, foyling, ouertoyling.*
Refouler. *To dull, blunt; foyle, straine, vex, grieue, tyre, with ouerlabouring; also, to tread vpon againe.*
Refouler le dos d'un cheval. *To gall a horses backe.*
Refouler aux pieds. *To stampe on, or tread vnder foot.*
Refouler la pouldre. *To ramme in the powder.*
Refouller. *as* Refouler.
Refouloir: m. *The Rammer head, wherewith powder is rammed into a Peece.*
Refourbir. *To refurbish, repolish; to smooth, or sleeke vp anew.*
Refournir. *To furnish anew.*
Refourrer. *To furre; also, to thrust in, againe.*
Refourvoyer. *To mistake, roue, erre, stray anew.*
Refractaire: com. *Refractarie, stubborne, wilfull, obstinate, headstrong.*
Refraction: f. *A rebound.*
Refrain d'une balade. *The Refret, burthen, or downe of a Ballade.*
Refraindre. *Looke* Refreindre.
Refrainte: f. *A bridling, refrayning, restraint.*
Refraischi: m. ie: f. *Refreshed, refrigerated; renewed.*
Refraischir. *To refresh, coole, refrigerate, recreate; renew.*
Refranchir. *To leape, or skip ouer againe.*
Refrappé: m. ée: f. *Strucke againe; also, reflected, reuerberated.*
Refrappement: m. *A striking againe; also, a reflecting, or a reuerberating.*
Refrapper. *To returne blowes for blowes, to strike backe or againe; also, to reflect, or to reuerberate.*
Refrein: m. *as* Refrain.
Refreindre. *To bridle, restraine, containe, hold in, keepe vnder, pull backe.*

Se refreindre. *To refraine, forbeare, temper, maister, moderate, himselfe.*
Refrenation: f. *A refraining; a bridling, restraining.*
Refrené: m. ée: f. *Bridled, maistered, moderated; refrained, restrained, kept short, held in.*
Refrener. *To bridle, represse, maister, moderate, restrain, hold vnder, keepe short, pull in.*
Refrequenté: m. ée: f. *Refrequented, rehaunted.*
Refrequenter. *To refrequent, reuisit, rehaunt; vse, or fall to, a former haunt.*
Refreschir. *as* Refraischir.
Refreschissement: m. *A refreshment, refreshing, refrigerating, recreating; renewing.*
Refreschissoir: m. *A small fountaine.*
Refresoté: m. ée: f. *Frizled, curled.*
Refreter vne navire. *To new-rig a ship.*
Refricasser. *To frie againe.*
Refrigerateur: m. *A refrigerator, refresher, cooler.*
Refrigeratif: m. iue: f. *Refrigeratiue, cooling, refreshing.*
Refrigeration: f. *A refrigeration, cooling, refreshing.*
Refrigeratoire: m. *A refrigeratorie, or cooler; the part of a Lymbeck wherin water is put to keepe the rest from being too hot.*
Refrigere: m. *Coolenesse, a refreshment.*
Refrigeré: m. ée: f. *Refrigerated, cooled, refreshed.*
Refrigerer. *To refrigerate, coole, refresh.*
Refriquer. *To rub againe; to renew an old griefe, to rub an old sore.*
Refriquer vne chose iugée. *To reuiue, or set on foot an (old) adiudged suit; to goe about with a matter againe.*
Refrire. *To frie againe.*
Refrisé: m. ée: f. *Frizled, curled; pranked, tricked vp anew.*
Refriser. *To frizzle, curle, pranke, tricke vp, anew.*
Refrissonner. *To quake, or shiuer, extreamely.*
Refroidi: m. ie: f. *Cooled; slackened.*
Refroidir. *To coole, or take away the heat of; to slacken; to calme.*
Se refroidir. *To wax cold, grow calme, become lesse vehement or earnest in.*
Refroidissant. *Cooling; slackening.*
Refroisser. *To breake asunder againe.*
Refroncé: m. ée: f. *Redoubled, much gathered; also, exceedingly wrinkled, crumpled, frumpled; & thence also, frowning.*
Refrongnant. en ref. *Frowningly, frowardly, sullenly, with a sower countenance.*
Refrongné: m. ée: f. *Frowning, surlie, sullen, of a sower looke.*
Refrongnement: m. *A frowning, lowring, sullennesse, a sternenesse, or sowernesse of countenance.*
Refrongner. *To frowne, lowre, looke sternely, sullenly, sowerly, on it.*
Refrotter. *To rub againe.*
Refu: m. *as* Refus; *A refusall; also, the refuse of any thing.*
Refue. *Looke* Resue.
Refuge: m. *A refuge, helpe, succour, a Sanctuarie, shrowd, shelter; a place to flie vnto, a place of safe retrait.*
Refugié: m. ée: f. *Fled, run, resorted vnto for succour, and assistance.*
Refugieux: m. euse: f. *as* Refugié; *or, helpfull, seruing for a refuge, full of refuges.*
Refui: m. uie: f. *Fled from; or fled backe vnto.*
Refuiant. *Flying, shunning, auoiding.*

Refuir. *To flie backe; also, to shun, auoid, eschew, forsake, run from.*
Refuir sur soy. *A Deere to make backe into the couert; a vermine to flie vnto, or keepe within, his earth; (their strengthes.)*
Refuite: f. *A flight or course, a running or flying, backe; also, an euasion, or auoidance.*
Refulger. *To shine, glister, glitter, looke verie bright.*
Refumer. *To dung ouer againe.*
Refus: m. *A refusall, repulse, deniall.*
Qui sont de refus. *The refuse, outcasts, leauings of better things.*
Refusé: m. ée: f. *Refused, denied, reiected, repulsed, neglected, forsaken.*
Refuser. *To refuse, denie, reiect, repell; cast off, renounce, forsake.*
Refuseur: m. *A refuser; denier; a reiecter; forsaker.*
A bon demandeur bon refuseur: Prov. *Looke* Demandeur.
Refutation: f. *A refutation, a confutation.*
Refuté: m. ée: f. *Refuted, confuted, refelled, conuinced; reproued.*
Refuter. *To refute, confute, refell, reproue, conuince, confound by reason.*
Refuyant. *Flying, shunning, eschewing, auoiding.*
Regabeller. *To double a tax, custome, or toll; to impose a new one.*
Regager. *To regage, or wage againe.*
Regaigner. *To regaine; also to gaine doubly.*
se Regaillardir. *Looke* se Ragaillardir.
Regain: m. *A later math, or lateward hay; th'after grasse, or after crop of hay.*
Regal: m. ale: f. *Regall, Royall, Princelie, Soueraigne.*
Regale. *whence,* Droict de Regale. *The Soueraigne Patronage of the Archbishopricks, Bishopricks, Abbeyes, and other Benefices of Royall foundation; due vnto the King of France, and inherent vnto his person, in the right of his Crowne, and therefore not to be transferred, committed, or aliened vnto any other: Hereby hee hath the profits of them during vacancie; and the prouision, collection, and presentation, of successors vnto them. At this day onely three Archbishopricks, and 32 Bishopricks, are subiect vnto it; the rest haue beene, at seuerall times, exempted by speciall priuiledges: In Normandie when diuers Lords are at suit for the Patronage of a vacant Benefice, the King, by this right of* Regale, *enioyes the profits of it vntill the suit be ended, or they agreed.*
La Regale de Theroanne. *The Jurisdiction, or gouernment of* Theroanne, *whereof the Bishop (who onely hath high, meane, and low Justice within it) is the temporall Lord.*
Fief en Regale. *A noble* Fief, *held immediately, and in* Capite, *of the King.*
Regalement. *Regally, kingly, royally.*
Regaler. *(In the customes of* Arthois; Senlis; & Vallois) c'est quand le Seigneur feodal prend, & applique à son profit, les fruicts des heritages de fief, ou Cottiers, à faute de les relever, & droicturer.
se Regaler. *To make as much account, and take as great a care, of himselfe, as if he were a King.*
Regales. des reg. *The musicall Instrument, called Rigolls.*
Regalice: f. *Lickorice.*
Regalisse. *The same.*
Regaliste: m. *One that enioyes, or stands for, a Benefice that is subiect vnto the* Droict de Regale.

Regard:

Regard: m. *A looke, view, sight, aspect; an eye; also, an eye vnto, or eying of; a regard, respect, consideration, of; also, the head of a conduit.*
Pour mon regard. *For my part, as for me; also, for my sake.*
Regardant. *Seeing, eying, beholding, marking, heeding; also, warie, circumspect, vigilant, that lookes narrowly to euerie thing.*
Regardé: m. ée: f. *Eyed, viewed, looked at, beheld, marked, regarded.*
Regardement: m. *A looking, seeing, eying, viewing, beholding; marking, spying, heeding, regarding.*
Regarder. *To looke, eye, see, view, behold; spie, toot at, heed, regard.*
Regarder de gros oeil; &, Regarder de la queuë de l'oeil. *Seeke* Oeil, & Queuë.
De seruiteur qui se regarde donne toy soigneusement garde: Prov. *The seruant proud, and of himselfe respectiue, is in his ductie oftentimes defectiue.*
Quand d'autry parler tu voudras regarde toy, & tu tairas: Prov. *When on another thou wouldst gladly rayle, looke well into thy selfe, thy tongue will quaile.*
Regardeur: m. *A looker, spectator, viewer, eyer, beholder.*
Regardeure: f. *A looke, sight, view, aspect.*
Regardure. *as* Regardeure.
Regarnir. *To regarnish, to new-furnish.*
Regaster. *To spill, or spoyle againe.*
Regazouiller. *To report, or to record, as birds, one anothers warbling.*
Rege: f. *A measure of three foot and a halfe, vsed by Surueyors in the countrey about* Bourdeaux.
Regeance: f. *as* Regence.
Regeiner. *To retorture, to racke once more.*
Regelé: m. ée: f. *Frozen, or ouergrowne with ice, againe.*
Regeler. *To freeze againe.*
Regence: f. *The Regencie, or Protectorship of a kingdome; also, a teaching, instructing, moderating, reading vnto, in Schooles; also, a forme, or lecture, of Schollers.*
Regenner. *To imitate, or counterfeit, neerely.*
Regent: m. *A Regent, Protector, Vicegerent, or Gouernour of a Kingdome during an interraigne, or the minoritie, or absence, of the Prince; also, a Regent, Reader, Teacher, Moderator of a forme in a Colledge.*
Regente: f. *The Regentesse, or Protectresse of a Kingdome.*
Regenté: m. ée: f. *Ruled, gouerned; also, taught, moderated, read vnto, in Schooles.*
Regenter. *To rule, or play the Regent; to gouerne a Kingdome during an interraigne, or in the minoritie, or absence of the Prince; also, to teach, read, or moderate, in Schooles.*
Regercer. *as* Rejarcer.
Regermer. *To bud, or sprowt out againe.*
Regetter. *Looke* Rejecter.
Regi: m. ie: f. *Ruled, gouerned, commaunded, swayed, guided, directed.*
Regimbement: m. *A kicking, winsing, spurning, striking backe with the feet, or heeles.*
Regimber. *To winse, kicke, spurne, strike back with the feet.*
Regimber contre l'esguillon. *To kicke against the pricke (say we in the verie same sence.)*
Ie vous garderay de regimber. *I will fetter you, restraine you, load you soundly, hold you vnder, take off your ouer-keene edge, coole your immoderate heat, keep you from winsing, kicking, outlashing.*

Regimbeur: m. *A winser, kicker, spurner.*
Regime: m. *Regiment, rule, commaund, sway, dominion, authoritie, gouernment.*
Regime de vivre. *An order of diet prescribed.*
Regiment de gens de guerre. *A Regiment of souldiers.*
Region: f. *A Region, Prouince, Realme, Kingdome, coast, countrey, quarter, part, place.*
La region du coeur. *The site, or seat of the heart.*
Regir. *To rule, gouerne, sway, maister, command, Seignorize ouer.*
Regisser. *as* Regir.
Registration: f. *A registring, a recording.*
Droict de registration. *Looke* Droict.
Registre: m. *A Record, Register, memoriall; a booke of remembrances, dayes booke; and (more particularly) a booke of Entries, Acts, Orders, or Decrees.*
Droict de registre: & Droict de registre, ou Contentor. *Looke* Droict.
Reglacer. *To freeze againe; also, to set a new glosse on.*
Reglaner. *To gleane ouer againe.*
Reglement. *See* Reiglement.
Reglisse: f. *Lickorice; Looke* Rigalisse.
Reglisser. *To glide, or slide backe.*
Regluer. *To glew againe.*
Reglure: f. *Seeke* Reigleure.
Regnant: m. ante: f. *Raigning, ruling, gouerning; also, lying about.*
Regnard: m. *A Fox.*
Regnard de mer. *The sea Fox; a long-tailed, and ranke-smelling fish, which in time of danger swallowes vp her young ones, and the feare being passed vomits them vp againe.*
Barbe de regnard. *Goats-thorne,* Tragacantha; *the shrub that yeelds Gum Dragagant.*
La parole du regnard. *A kind of charme.*
Queuë de regnard. *Fox-taile, tailed Wheat; (an hearbe) also, as vnder* Queuë.
Raisin de regnard. *Garden Nightshade; also, the hearbe Paris, One-berrie, True-loue.*
Toux de regnard. *A setled, or old-growne cough, that stickes by a man as long as he liues.*
Vin de regnard. *Such wine as being much drunke of sharpens the wit, & makes the drunkard crafter then he was.*
Coudre la peau du regnard à celle du Lion. *To proceed both craftily, and violently; both by stratagems and strength; or to attempt that by craft which he cannot obtaine by force.*
Crier au regnard l'un sur l'autre. *To raile extreamly one vpon another.*
Escorcher le regnard. *To spue, cast, vomit; (especially vpon excessiue drinking;) either because in spuing one makes a noyse like a Fox that barkes; or (as in* Escorcher*) because the flaying of so vnsauorie a beast will make any man spue.*
Faire le regnard. *as* Regnarder.
Faire vne charruë de regnard. *To loose his time, or bestow it on most fond imploiments.*
Parler regnard. *Looke* Regnaut.
Prendre martin pour regnard. *To mistake resembling things one for another.*
Tirer au regnard. *To cast, vomit, spue.*
Regnard qui dort la matinée n'a pas la langue emplumée: Prov. *Morning sleepers seldome thriue.*
Regnard qui beaucoup tarde attend la proye: Prov. *When Foxes tarrie long they hope for purchase.*

Le regnard cache sa queuë: Pro. *The craftie knaue hides that which would bewray him.*

Le regnard est devenu hermite: Prov. *The Fox an Hermit is become, (beware your Geese good huswiues) appliable also, when a craftie or naughtie fellow reformes himselfe, and growes truely religious.*

Le regnard est pris, lasche les poules: Prov. *Vsed when any dangerous knaue is intrapped, or clapt vp; vsed also, in mockerie of a common wooer, which hauing deceiued many widowes and maids in his time, is at the length ouertaken, and caught by one thats worse then any of them.*

`A regnard regnard & demi: Pro. *Let craft meet, or be matcht, with cunning.*

`A regnard endormi rien ne chet en la gueule: Prov. *Nothing is got by drowsinesse; preferment must be watched, sought, and sued for; it falls not into idle hands, or sleeping mouthes.*

`A la fin le regnard sera Moine: Prov. *Looke* Moine.

En fin les regnards (viz. *their skinnes*) se trouvent chez le pelletier: Prov. *The craftie are at length surprised.*

Il n'y a route que de vieux regnards: Prov. *There is no chase like that of the old Fox; or, no tract so certaine as of aged craft; no path well beaten but by old experience.*

Regnardaille: f. *The generatiō, kind, or brood of Foxes; also, a knot, or crue of subtill knaues.*

Regnarde: f. *A bitch Fox.*

Regnardeau: m. *A Fox cub, a young Fox; a little Fox.*

Regnarder. *To play the Fox; to steale, slip, or slinke, aside, vpō a guiltie conscience, or feare to be taken in the maner; also, to peruert a truth with shifts, trickes, or subtilties.*

Regnarderie: f. *Slinesse, craftinesse, wilinesse; also, a stealing, slipping, or slinking aside, vpon approach of danger, or guilt of conscience; also, a peruerting of the truth with shifts, or craftie lyes.*

Regnardesque: com. *Craftie, wilie, false, Fox-like, full of sleights.*

Regnardiere: f. *A Fox-furred gowne, or garment.*

Regnardise: f. *Fox-like subtiltie, slinesse, wilinesse, craftinesse, falsenesse.*

Regnateur: m. *A raigner, gouernor, absolute ruler.*

Regnatrice: f. *A Queene, a Soueraigne Gouernesse, an absolute Mistresse.*

Regnaut: m. *The language, or barking, of Foxes.*

Parler regnaut. *To speake through the nose.*

Regne: m. *A Realme, or Kingdome; also, a Soueraigne rule; Dominion, Gouernement; also, (the continuance, or manner of that Gouernement) a Raigne.*

Cheval de Regne. *A courser of Naples.*

Regné. *Raigned, ruled, gouerned.*

Regner. *To raigne, rule, gouerne, sway, seigniorize, domineere; to be a King, wield a Scepter, haue Soueraigne authoritie ouer.*

La Terrace regne tout à l' entour du logis. *The terrace lyes, goes, or is contriued, round about the house.*

Regnicoles: com. *Th'actuall inhabitants, or inhabiters of a Kingdome.*

Regnure. *Looke* Renure.

Regobillonné: m. ée: f. *Frolick, merrie, iocond, blithe, in a pleasant humor, in a merrie mood.*

Regodronner. *as* Regoldronner.

Regoldronné: m. ée: f. *New pitched, or tallowed, as a ship; also, new set, or starched, as a ruffe.*

Regoldronner. *To pitch, or tallow, to make tight, a ship; also, to set a ruffe band, againe.*

Regorge: f. *An ouer-full gorge; also, a vomiting, or picking vp thereof.*

Ie leur en bailleray à regorge. *I will ouerglut them with all; I wil feed them, or cramme it into them, vntill they spue againe.*

Regorgé: m. ée: f. *Ouer-glutted, too full gorged, whose stomacke is ouer-charged; also, vomited, cast, or spued vp, as an ouer-full gorge.*

Regorgement: m. *An ouer-glutting, or ouer-charging of the stomacke; any superfluitie, ouerflowing, excesse.*

Regorger. *To ouerglut, or ouercharge the stomacke; to ouerrunne, or ouerflow the bankes; also, to spue, vomit, cast, an ouer-full gorge.*

Regoubillonner. *To make a reare supper, steale an after supper; banquet late anights; also, to be frolicke, blithe, iocond, in a merrie mood.*

Regourmer. *To curbe againe.*

Regouster. *To tast better, often, or againe.*

Regrabellement: m. *A curious, and reiterated sifting of, or search into.*

Regracié: m. *Thanked, or thankefully acknowledged.*

Regraciement: m. *A thankefulnesse, or thankefull acknowledgement.*

Regracier. *To thanke, acknowledge thankefully, yeeld thankes vnto.*

Regraing. *as* Regain.

Regraisser. *To grease ouer againe.*

Regraté: m. ée: f. *Dressed, furbished, scowred, or tricked vp.*

Regratement: m. *A dressing, scowring, furbishing, mending, or tricking vp of old things for sale; huckstrie.*

Regrater. *To dresse, mend, scowre, furbish, trimme or tricke vp, an old thing for sale.*

Regrateur: m. *An huckster; mender, dresser, scowrer, trimmer vp of old things for sale.*

Regratier: m. *as* Regrateur; *whence;*

Regratier de sel, de vivres, &c. *A Regrater, or Ingrosser of salt, &c.*

Regratier. *as* Regracier; *To thanke.*

Regratiere: f. *An Hucksteresse; also, a Regrateresse.*

Regraver. *To graue anew.*

Regravir. *To climbe, or creepe vp, againe.*

Regredillé: m. ée: f. *Frizzled, crisped, curled, intrammelled.*

Regrediller. *To frizzle, or curle the haire, &c, with a hot yron.*

Regredillonné, & Regredillonner. *as* Regredillé, & Regrediller.

Regrés: m. *A resignation of a Benefice, vpon condition, that if during the Resignors life it become voyd by the resignation or death of the Resignee, it shall returne, without further induction, or institution, vnto him: (But this Conditionall Resignation, heretofore in vse, is not at this day allowed of, in France.)*

Regret: m. *Desire, will, affection, stomacke, or humor vnto; also, griefe, sorrow; repentance, forthinking.*

`A regret. *Loathly, vnwillingly, with an ill stomacke, hardly, mauger his head, full sore against his will.*

Regretable: com. *Deplorable, bemonable, bewailable; fit to be repented, or lamented.*

Regreter. *as* Regretter.
Regretté: m. ée: f. *Desired, affected, wished for; also, bewayled, lamented, repented.*
Regretter. *To desire, affect, wish for, looke or long after; also, to bewayle, bemoane, lament, grieue, sorrow, repent, for.*
Regrez. *as* Regrés.
Regrifler. *To claw, paw, scratch, againe.*
Regriller. *To broyle anew vpon a Gridiron.*
Regrimper. *To climbe, or crawle vp againe.*
Regringoté. *Chaunted, quauered, often.*
Regringoter. *To chaunt, warble, or quauer often.*
Regripper. *To gripe, grasple, or snatch againe.*
Regrissé. *as* Renfrongné.
Regrouvi: m. *A starueling, wreckling, writling.*
Reguarir. *To recure, to recouer, to heale againe.*
Regue. *as* Rege.
Reguerdonner. *To reward plentifully, guerdon abundantly.*
Reguerir. *To recure, to recouer.*
Reguetter. *To watch verie narrowly.*
Reguinder. *To hoyse, or lift vp on high againe; also, to beare roomeward, or make backe againe.*
Regule d'antimonie. *A kind of Tinne; or, as* Estain de glace.
Regulier: m. ere: f. *Regular, canonicall, liuing vnder prescript rules.*
Chanoines reguliers. *Regular Canons; tyed vnto greater attendance, and stricter obseruances, then others.*
Regulierement. *Regularly, canonically, orderly.*
Regurgitation: f. *An ouerflowing.*
Regurgiter. *To ouerflow.*
Rehabilitation: f. *A reestablishing, reinnabling, restoring vnto former abilitie.*
Rehabiliter. *as* Rabiliter.
Rehabitation: f. *A reinhabitation, reinhabiting; a returning to a former habitation.*
Rehabiter. *To reinhabite, or dwell againe in.*
Rehabituer. *To settle againe; to begin to vse, accustome, enure vnto againe.*
Rehacher. *To hacke, or chop againe.*
Rehair. *To hate extreamely, or againe.*
Rehaiter. *To reuiue, reioyce, cheere vp exceedingly.*
Rehaler. *To hale, or pull againe.*
Rehanter. *Againe to haunt, or frequent.*
Reharceler. *To harrie, turmoyle, vex againe.*
Reharier. *as* Reharceler.
Rehasarder. *To readuenture, to hazard yet once more.*
Rehaster. *To reaccelerate, or giue new wings vnto.*
Rehaulsé: m. ée: f. *Set higher, or aboue; also, readuanced; also, raised, or vpheld; also, (in painting, &c) reborsed, or heightened; also, imbossed.*
Tapisserie de sayette rehaussée de soye. *Whose ground is say, and worke silke.*
Rehaulsement: m. *A readuancing; also, a raising, a setting higher, or aboue; also, a reborsing, heightening; leeuing, imbossing.*
Rehaulser. *To readuance; to raise or set higher, to place aboue; also, (in Painting, &c) to reborse, heighten; to leeue, to imbosse.*
Rehaussé, & Rehausser. *as* Rehaulsé, &c.
Rehennir. *To neigh, or whinnie often.*
se Reherber. *To get new grasse.*
Reherser. *To harrow ouer againe.*

Reheurter. *Againe to dash, hit, but, or knocke against.*
Rehoché: m. ée: f. *Shaken, wagged, or iogged againe.*
Rehocher. *To shake, wag, or iog, againe.*
Rehonnir. *To shame, or dishonour once more.*
Rehouëment: m. *A new digging about the foot of a vine, &c; or (more generally) a new digging.*
Rehouër. *To dig anew; to alter ground by often digging it; also, to dig or open a plant at the root a second time.*
Rehouser. *To pull on boots once more.*
Rehousser. *To couer with a foot-cloth once againe.*
Rehucher. *To whoope, or call, backe from.*
Rehumecté: m. ée: f. *Moistened, or bedewed once more.*
Rehumecter. *Againe to moisten, or bedew.*
Rehumé: m. ée: f. *Againe supped vp.*
Rehumer. *To sup vp againe.*
Rehurter. *as* Reheurter.
Rejalir. *as* Rejallir.
Rejallir. *To rebound; to leape, skip, iert, spurt, or sprowt (as water) backe, vpwards, against, or againe; also, to reuerberate, or to reflect.*
Rejallissement: m. *A rebounding; a leaping, ierting, spurting backe, or vp, against a thing; also, a reflection, or a reuerberation.*
Rejanner. *To flowt, scoffe, deride, ride.*
Rejaper. *To barke often, or againe.*
Rejarcer. *To riue or cleaue, anew.*
Rejaser. *To babble, or prattle extreamely.*
Rejauger. *To new-gage caske.*
Rejaulnir. *To grow yellow againe.*
Reject: m. *A reiection, a refusall; also, a new putting forth, a casting out againe; also, as* Rejet.
Reject d'arbre. *A young shoot, or sucker, springing out from the root, or foot of a tree.*
Reject de femme. *A diuorse from, or putting away of, a wife.*
Reject de fossé. *The banke of a ditch.*
Fueille de reject. *The leafe that succeeds in the place of another leafe, which hath beene plucked, or beaten downe.*
Rejectable: com. *Reiectable, refusable.*
Rejecté: m. ée: f. *Reiected, expelled, refused; abandoned, forsaken, cast off; also, retorted, or cast backe; also, confuted; also, newly put, or budded, out.*
Rejectement: m. *A reiecting, expelling, driuing or chasing out, putting or casting off; a refusing, forsaking, abandoning, renouncing; also, a retorting, or throwing backe; a confuting, a refelling; also, a new budding, or putting out, as of trees in the Spring.*
Rejecter. *To reiect, expell, put or cast off, driue or chase out; to refuse, abandon, forsake, renounce; also, to retort, or throw backe; also, to refell, or confute; also, to bud, or put out, as trees in the Spring; also, to giue, as timber, &c, in wet weather, &c.*
Rejection: f. *A reiection; or, as* Rejectement.
Rejecton: m. *A young shoot, or sience, that springs from the root, or stocke, of a tree.*
Rejecton de mouches à miel. *A swarme of Bees.*
Rejet: m. *The brimme of the louer of a Doue-coat, whereon the Pigeons alight; also, the iert giuen by a horses legs when he yerkes out behind; also, as* Reject.
Rejettable. *as* Rejectable.
Rejettal: m. *An Engine wherewith small birds are caught.*

Rejetté, & Rejetter. as Rejecté, & Rejecter.
Reifort. as Raifort.
Reigle: f. A rule, canon, order; precept, institution, prescription, instruction; also, a line; square, forme, patterne; method, maner, fashion.
Mieux vaut reigle que rente: Prov. Good gouernement is of more worth then gold.
Reiglé: m. ée: f. Ruled, ordered, gouerned, moderated; directed, held in forme, kept in fashion.
Reiglemént: m. A ruling, ordering, direction, guiding, discipline, gouernment, gouerning; also, a rule giuen by a Judge in a cause; also, the draught of lines by the rule.
Reiglément. Regularly, orderly; moderately; formally, in good fashion.
Reigler. To rule, order, gouerne; temper, moderate; guide, square, direct; to doe things by line and leuell; also, to decree, establish, determine, ordaine; and, to giue a rule in a cause.
Reiglet: m. A little rule, or line; also, a Carpenters Squire.
Regleur: m. A ruler, orderer; moderator; director.
Reigleure: f. as Reiglement; or, a ruling, or drawing by lines; a proceeding by rule and line.
Reiglure. The same.
Reilhage: m. c'est le charrüage, le trainage, & suite de disme.
Reimber. as Redimer.
Reimportuner. To reimportune, or to reimportunate.
Reimposer. To reimpose, to recharge.
Reimprimé: m. ée: f. Printed againe.
Reimprimer. To reimprint, or to print againe.
Reimproperer. To exprobrate, reupbraid, reproach, or blame againe.
Reimputer. To lay a new imputation on.
Rein: m. The kidney.
Reinciser. To make a new incision into.
Reincité: m. ée: f. Reincited; reinuited.
Reinciter. To reincite; reinuite.
Reincliner. To bend, leane, or incline, againe.
Reincorporer. To reincorporate, reintegrate; restore vnto the bodie a part thereof.
Reinduire. To reinduce.
Reine: f. A Queene; Looke Royne; also, a Frog; also, the reine of a bridle.
Reineux: m. euse: f. Lustie, able-bodied, strong-backed, hauing strong reines; also, of, or belonging to, the reines; whence;
Maladie reineuse. The running of the reines.
Reinfecter. To reinfect.
Reinformer. To reinforme, to present with new informations.
Reingerer. To reinsinuate, or thrust in againe.
Reinhumer. To burie againe.
Reinjurier. To reuile, or to wrong againe.
Reinnover. To reinnouate.
Reins: m. The reynes.
Bander aux reins. To bend a crossebow backward.
Reinser. To reinse, to wash.
Reintegrande: f. An Action, or Sentence, for the restorall of a possession, taken from a man either by force, fraud, or any other indirect meanes; And this hath an easie & speedie passage, how vniust soeuer that possession were; for no man is to be his owne caruer, but must recouer his right by Law; (This word was deuised by the Canonists.)
Reintegration: f. A reintegration, reestablishment, full restorall vnto a former estate.
Reintegré: m. ée: f. Reintegrated, reestablished in, fully restored vnto, an estate.
Reintegrer. To reintegrate, reestablish in, restore vnto, his whole estate.
Reintegrer les fruicts. To make restitution of, or giue satisfaction for, them; to make them good.
Reinterpreter. To reinterpret, reexpound.
Reinterroguer. To reinterrogate, reexamine, aske new questions of.
Reinviter. To reinuite, or bid once more.
Rejoindre. To reioyne, reassemble, rally.
Rejouër. To play againe.
Rejouïr. To reinioy, repossesse, haue againe.
Rejouïssance: f. A reinioyment, repossession, reinioying.
Rejouster. To iust againe.
Reiponce: f. as Raiponce.
Reistre: m. A Reister, or Swart-rutter; a German horseman; also, a fashion of long cloake, vsually worne by one of them.
Faict à la Reistre. Made after the new cut, or fashion (especially if there be any grossenesse in it.)
Reiteration: f. A reiteration, a frequent repetition.
Reïteré: m. ée: f. Reiterated, often repeated, often remembred.
Reïterer. To reiterate; (often) repeat, rehearse, renew, remember.
Rejudication: f. A reiudication, a readiudging vnto (c'est quand la chose qui a esté venduë & adiugée publiquement, est derechef mise en criées, & readjugée.)
Rejurer. To sweare againe, to offer a new oath vnto.
Relabouré: m. ée: f. Tilled, or plowed ouer againe.
Relabourement: m. A second tilth, earing, or plowing.
Relabourer. To plough, till, or eare the second time.
Relaict: m. whey.
Relaïer. See Relayer.
Relais: m. A seat, or standing for such as hold Chiens de relais; also, as Armaire; a hole, or box contriued in, or against, a wall.
Champ de relais. Fallowes, or a fallow field; ground thats sowed but euerie other yeare.
Chevaux de relais. Horses layed in certaine places on the highway, for the more hast making, or the ease of those one hath alreadie rid hard on: (In trauelling most of the highwayes of Fraunce, you may (en payant) haue at euerie seuen or eight leagues end fresh horses; so that you leaue behind you those you last rid on, and shew a ticket from the place where you had them: And these are most properly tearmed, Chevaux de relais)
Chiens de relais. Dogs layed for a back-set; such as are held by the side of a long course, to bee bounded after a Deere alreadie pursued by other dogs.
'A relais. Spared, at rest, that is not vsed; or as;
Par relais. By turnes, by change of hands; one resting while another labours, one running while his fellow rests.
Relaisser. To leaue, relinquish, forgoe againe; also, a Hare to squat.
Relancé: m. ée: f. Flung, darted, hurled, backe; also, imprimed, as a Deere; recouered, as a Hare.

Relancer. *To fling, dart, hurle backe, or againe.*

Relancer vn cerf. *To imprime a Stag.*

Relancer vn lievre. *To recouer her, or put her off the squat.*

Relant: m. *Mustinesse, fustinesse, ranknesse, dankishnesse.*

Relant: m. ante: f. *Mustie, fustie, restie, reasie, dankish, vnsauorie.*

Relanteur: f. *as* Relant: m.

Relantir. *To smell mustie, grow fustie, wax restie.*

Relaps: m. se: f. *Relapsed; fallen into an errour which he had recanted, or sicknesse of which he had recouered.*

Relasche: f. *A relaxation; ease, rest, repose, refreshment, recreation, (after labour;) truce, respit, a cessation, intermission, vacation; also, a slackning, loossing, relenting, letting goe.*

Relasche de pendu. *A gracelesse rakehell, or crackrope; one for whom the Hangman waits, the Gallowes grones.*

Relaschement: m. *A reposing, resting, refreshing; a leauing of worke, a making vacation; also, a releasing, loossing, inlarging; also, a relenting, or slackening.*

Relascher. *To slacken, loosse, inlarge, let out; ease, refresh; remit, release; also, to giue backe, forgoe, let goe.*

Relasser. *To wearie extreamely, or againe.*

Relater. *To relate, report, vtter, deliuer; to recite, recount, rehearse; also, to new-lath a building.*

Relateur: m. *A relator, a reporter, a rehearser.*

Relation: f. *A relation, report, recitall; also, the Returne of a Writ; the report made, or account giuen, by an Officer, of the seruing or execution thereof.*

Relaver. *To wash againe, or often ouer; also, to wash (with colours.)*

Relaxation: f. *A relaxation; discharge, inlargement; releasing, acquiting; relenting.*

se Relayans l'un l'autre. *Refreshing, or easing one another by turnes.*

Relayer. *To succeed in the place of the wearie; to refresh, releeue, or ease another by an vndertaking of his taske.*

Relayer coche, & chevaux. *To take new, or fresh horses and coach.*

Relecher. *To licke ouer againe.*

Relegation: f. *A relegation, or exilement, a packing or sending away into banishment.*

Relegué: m. ée: f. *Relegated, banished, exiled.*

Releguer. *To relegate, banish, exile.*

Releu: m. euë: f. *Red ouer againe.*

Relevailles d'une femme. *Th'vprising, or vpsitting, also, the Churching, of a woman.*

Relevé: m. ée: f. *Raised, lift, or set vp, againe; releeued, reuiued, fully restored; also, discharged, freed, or quit of; also, that hath payed his Reliefe.*

Appel relevé. *Sued out; and whereby a suit is remoued, by Writ, from one Court vnto another.*

Cheval bien relevé. *Well raised, or high before.*

Femme relevée. *Churched, or got out of the straw.*

Mineur relevé. C'est quand le Mineur de 25 ans, qui a esté deceu ou circonvenu, est restitué en entier par lettres Royaux interinées en Iustice.

Mineur relevé de bail. C'est quand le baillistre releve le fief de son Mineur, du Seigneur dont il est tenu.

Vne Saincte relevée. *Whose Reliques, or bones are inclosed and shewed aloft, in a shrine.*

Relevé du fumier. *A dunghill Gentleman.*

Il a esté bien relevé. *He hath beene well chidden, or (as we say) taken vp for haulting.*

Relevée: f. *Th'afternoone, or all the time betweene dinner and th'euening; also, a womans Churching; also, a full recouerie of, or vprising after, a sicknesse.*

Relevement: m. *A raising, lifting vp; releeuing, reuiuing, restoring; also, a womans Churching.*

Relever. *To raise or lift vp, to set on foot or afoot, againe; also, to releeue, assist, reuiue, restore.*

Relever vn appel. *To sue or take out, an Appeale; to bring the cause before the Judge appealed vnto.*

Relever droicture. *To pay the Reliefe, and rights due by a tenant vpon his first entrie.*

Relever vn esteuf. *Looke* Esteuf.

Relever vn fief. *To pay a Reliefe; and doe homage for an inheritance; or, to auow, and acknowledge a Landlord vpon any change of Lord, or of tenant.*

Ce fief releve d'un tel. *Is held of such a one.*

Ce fief releve selon la coustume de Touraine. *The Reliefe, right, and dueties thereof are done, payed, and performed, according to the custome of* Touraine.

Relever les vieux fossez. *To cleanse, or scowre them.*

Relever du serment. *To acquit, or discharge of, an oath.*

Fort est qui abbat, & plus fort qui se releve: Prov. *He that, being felled, gets vp of himselfe, does more then he that feld him.*

Releveur: m. *A raiser, or lifter vp; a setter on foot, or afloat againe; also, a releeuer, assister; also, a reuiuor, a renewer.*

Relevoison. Droict de rel. *A yeares rent payed vnto Lords, vpon euerie change of tenants,* Censiers, *or for any estate (in the land they hold) procured by themselues: This is most commonly tearmed,* Relevoison à plaisir.

Relevoison du denier six. *Six pence for each penie of their yerelie Cens, payed vpon euerie change as well as the former.*

Ventes & relevoisons. C'est quand le nouveau vassal relevé de son seigneur feodal, & luy paye certaine somme taxée par la Coustume: ¶Ragueau.

Reliage: m. *A binding, or hooping of caske, &c.*

Relicher. *To licke often, or ouer againe.*

Relié: m. ée: f. *Bound, hooped; handsomely packed, or compacted together.*

Relief: m. *Reliefe; or a releeuing; the raising of a person, or of a thing, fallen; and (particularly) the remedie granted by the Letters Patents of a Soueraigne Prince vnto a subiect incommodated, or fallen into an inconuenience, by the sentence of a Judge, or ill dealing of others; and hence,* Relief d'appel; &, Relief pour minorité: *Also, a Reliefe; a fine due, or profit accruing, to a Landlord vpon certaine changes of his hereditarie tenants; (Looke* Droict de relief, *vnder* Droict; *) also, a place, or thing, raised; & (particularly) raised, or imbossed work; & that which Imbroderers tearme, leeuing; also, rubbidge, or the ruines of ouerthrowne houses; also, the remnant, or offalls, of meat left at a meale.*

Relief d'appel. *An Appeale sued out by Commission from the Chancerie, and from the superior Court appealed vnto, & directed vnto the Judge, or Lord Justicer of the court appealed from, therby to intimate the suit, and proceeding thereof vnto the partie, in respect of whose late recouerie th'Appeale is brought.*

Re-

Relief de bail. *A yeares profit, or value, due vnto a Lord feodall from him that maries a maid, or widow, owner of a* Fief *by any descent, or donation; notwithstanding that she before their mariage haue both paied the Reliefe, and performed all dueties, whereunto her estate was liable; the reason is, the husband comes in as a stranger; and so must both pay a new Reliefe, and doe new homage, as for his owne* Fief: *In some places another Reliefe is also due vpon the death of the husband.*

Relief de bouche. *The acknowledgement of a vassall, or tenant* Cottier, *that he holds his land of a Lord.*

Relief de Chambellage. *A Reliefe due by a husband for an inheritance falling to his wife during her mariage.*

Relief de fief. *Th'acknowledgement of tenure yeelded by a new subiect, or vassall, vnto his Lord.*

Relief à merci. *One yeares profit in three; due by the locall custome of* S. Piat de Seclin sous Lisle.

Relief pour minorité. *Looke* Mineur relevé *(vnder* Relevé.)

Relief de plume. *A rent Capon, Cocke, Henne, or Pullet, giuen in some few places in lieu of a Reliefe.*

Relief de rente. *Due to a Lord vpon the death of his tenant* Cottier.

Droict, ou profit de relief. *See* Droict.

Tels cens tels reliefs. *A whole yeares* Cens *due for a Reliefe, ouer and besides the* Cens *it selfe when it accrues.*

Bas relief. Gentilhōme de bas relief. *A thred-bare, or single soled Gentleman; a Gentleman of low degree.*

Demy relief. à demy r. *Halfe Reliefe, halfe round.*

Plein relief. de plein rel. *Imbossed, or set of in it full proportion.*

Relier. *To bind, or to compact things hādsomely together; also, to hoope, as caske.*

Relievement: m. *as* Relevement; *also, a reliefe, releeving, succor; or money giuen for the reliefe, or succor of.*

Relieur de livres. *A Booke-binder.*

Relieure de livres. *Booke-binding.*

Religieuse: f. *A Nunne.*

Religieux: m. *A Monke or Frier; one thats entred into a religious Order.*

Religieux seculier. *as* Oblat.

Religieux: m. euse: f. *Religious; addicted, consecrated, or belonging, to religion; holie, godlie, deuout.*

Religion: f. *Religion, holinesse, pietie, godlinesse; the worship of God, or of things held sacred; a reuerend, and conscientious affection vnto them, or feare of offending them; also, a Religious house.*

Relimer. *To file, scrape, or shaue often, or vnto a smoothnesse; also, to gleeke againe and againe at.*

Relinquer. *To relinquish, leaue, quit, abandon, forsake.*

Relinqueur: m. *A relinquisher, leauer, quitter, abandoner, forsaker.*

Reliqua: m. *The rest, remainder, ouerplus, arrerage; reliques, remnant, fragments, leauings, of.*

Le reliqua d'une fiebvre. *The remaines, or grudgings of an Ague, after it hath seemed to leaue one.*

Reliquaille: f. *An old remnant, fragment, monument.*

Reliquaire: m. *A coffin, casket, or shrine wherein Reliques be kept.*

Reliquataire: com. *In arrerages, behind-hand; in whose hands there's yet somewhat to be paied; also, left, resting, remaining.*

Reliquateur: m. *One thats behind-hand, or in arrerages; one that yet hath somewhat to pay.*

Reliques: f. *Reliques.*

Reliques sont bien perduës entre les pieds de pourceaux: Prov. *Reliques trod on by hogs are quickly lost; or, Reliques are quickly lost among the feet of hogs; (And may not one iustly wish them lost, rather then in the hands of such hogs as now-a-daies keepe them?)*

Relire. *To read ouer againe.*

Relivrer. *To redeliuer.*

Rellet: m. *The name of a tart apple that hath partie-coloured sides.*

Relods. *as* Relots.

Reloger. *To lodge againe.*

Relots. Droict de relots. *Twentie pence vpon euerie pound of* Lods *and* Ventes, *due vnto a Landlord in purchases made of th'estates of his tenants* Censuels; C'est aussi dix deniers pour livre (en la Chastellenie de Monstrereau ressort de Meaux) quand le vendeur doit avoir son argent franc.

Relouër. *To hire againe.*

Reluicter. *To wrastle, striue, or contend againe.*

Reluire. *To shine, glitter, glister, yeeld a radiant or bright luster.*

Reluisant: m. ante: f. *shining, radiant, glittering, glistering, yeelding a bright luster.*

Remailler. *To peece a broken coat of mayle, or net, with new linkes, or mashes.*

Remaindre. *(A Verbe Impersonall; whence the Prouerbe;)* Beaucoup remaint de ce que fol pense. *Much is behind of that a foole accoūts of; a foole comes euer short of his intentions; fooles thoughts are full of wants, of imperfections.*

Remains. *Remaining, remained, left, behind, left behind.*

Remander. *To remaund, or send for backe againe.*

Remanent: m. *A remnant, residue, rest, remainder.*

Remanger. *To eat againe.*

Remanier. *To handle, or take in hand againe.*

Remanoir. *To remaine, to rest or stay behind.*

Remansilles. *The remnant, remainder, or leauings of.*

Remarchander. *To barraine anew.*

Remarcher. *To march againe, or march backe againe.*

Remarier. *To remarie, or marie againe.*

Remarquable: com. *Remarkable, fit or worthie to be marked.*

Remarqué: m. ée: f. *Marked, noted, heeded, regarded attentiuely; also, marked, or stamped on anew.*

Remarquer. *To marke, note, heed, regard attentiuely; also, to set a new marke or stampe on.*

Remarqueur: m. *A marker, or noter of things.*

Remasché: m. ée: f. *Ruminated; againe or often chawed.*

Remaschement: m. *A ruminating; a chawing often, or againe.*

Remascher. *To ruminate; to chaw often, or againe.*

Remascheur: m. *A ruminator.*

Remassonner. *To build anew.*

Remaudire. *To curse againe.*

Rembade. *as* Rambade.

Remballer. *To repacke, or packe vp againe.*

Rembarquer. *To reimbarke, to put into a ship againe.*

Rembarré: m. ée: f. *Bard vp, kept in, stopped, restrained; also, knocked, thumped; repulsed, repelled, beaten or driuen backe; also, confuted, refelled, conuinced.*

Rembarrer. *To restraine, barre vp, or keepe in; also, to knocke, thumpe; repulse, repell, beat or driue backe; also, to confute, refell, disproue, conuince.*

Rembaucher. *To restore a thing vnto it right place, to set it in order, or into it owne standing, againe.*

Remboister vn os. *To set it, or put it, into ioynt againe.*
Rembouër: m. *An Engine wherewith fish is (forbidden to be) caught.*
Rembourrer. *To stuffe vp againe with flockes.*
Rembourreur: m. *A mender of vnstuffed saddles.*
Rembours. *as* Remboursement.
Remboursé: m. ée: f. *Reimbursed; repayed.*
Remboursement: m. *A reimbursement, a reimbursing; a repayment of money borrowed, or spent.*
Rembourser. *To reimburse; to repay, restore, or giue backe, money spent, &c.*
Il les fit rembourser de tous leurs interests. *He payed them for all their losses, or harmes.*
Il n'y a rien à rembourser tout est à boire. *Spoken ieastingly of a fart let in companie.*
Rembourseur: m. *A reimburser; a repayer.*
Rembraser. *To rekindle, reinflame, put new fire vnto.*
Rembrasser. *To reimbrace.*
Rembre. *To redeeme; (An old word, and yet vsed by some countrey Clerkes.)*
se Rembrider. Cheval qui se rembride. *A horse that armes, or defends himselfe vpon the breast, (by clapping the branches of his Bit against it.)*
Rembrocher. *To spit, or put on a spit againe.*
Rembrouiller. *To reintangle.*
Rembrousser. *Looke* Rebrousser.
Rembusché: m. ée: f. *Reimbushed; lodged, or put among bushes; also, layed or lying, in a new Ambusbuscadoe.*
Rembuschement: m. *A reimbushment; the place wherat wild beasts enter into a thicket after that they haue preyed, or pastured.*
Rembuscher. *To lodge a wild beast among bushes; to driue him into a thicket; also, to lay, or make a new amcadoe.*
Remede: m. *A remedie, redresse, medecine, helpe; also that allay which Goldsmithes, Jewellers, and Money-makers, are permitted to adde vnto th'allowed imbasement of gold, or siluer; as where with a siluer peece of elenen pence value there is a twelfth part of copper allowed to be mingled, the* remede *is about two graines ouer and besides that twelfth. This aduantage they haue gotten vpon allegation, That they cannot precisely hit, or iustly keepe, the scantling required of them by the Law.*
Remediement: m. *A remedying, redressing, healing, helping.*
Remedier. *To remedie, redresse, heale, helpe.*
Remembrance: f. *A remembrance, or mindfulnesse; also, a cause of remembrance; a resemblance, or image of; a thing that beares the forme, or puts vs in mind, of another thing.*
Remembré: m. ée: f. *Remembred, called to memorie.*
se Remembrer. *To remember; to call vnto mind or memorie.*
Rememoration: f. *A remembrance, or a remembring.*
Rememoré: m. ée: f. *Remembred, recorded.*
Rememorer. *To record, remember, call vnto mind.*
Remenacer. *To threaten againe.*
Remenant. *as* Remanent.
Remenement: m. *A bringing backe.*
Remener. *To bring backe.*
Remerciant. *Thanking.*
Remercié: m. ée: f. *Thanked.*
Remerciement: m. *A thanking, or thanks-giuing.*
Remercier. *To thanke, to yeeld or giue thanks vnto.*
Remeré: m. *A redeeming of things morgaged, or sold.*
Grace, ou faculté de remeré. *Is due vnto, or procured by, the sellers next kinsman.*
Remerer. *To redeeme, or buy backe, a thing sold.*
Remesler. *To mingle againe.*
Remesurer. *To measure ouer againe.*
Remettre. *To renew, repaire, reuiue, restore, set vp againe; also, to refer, cōmit, or put vnto; also, to remit, forgiue, pardon, acquit, release; vnto; also, to slacken, or qualifie th'extremitie of; also, to deferre, delay, prorogue, put off.*
Remettez vous en vous. *Come againe vnto, returne againe into, your selfe; bring your selfe home againe.*
Se remettre à sa premiere besongne. *To returne, to fall, set, or giue himselfe, vnto his former imployments.*
Il s'y veut remettre. *He will to it afresh, he will about it againe.*
Remeubler. *To new-furnish with mouables.*
Reminer. *To mine againe.*
Reminiscence: f. *Remembrance (of things which were once before in the mind.)*
Remirer. *To view, see, eye, behold; aime, or leuell at, often, or againe.*
Remis: m. ise: f. *Restored, reuiued, renewed, repaired, set vp againe; also, referred, committed, or put; also, remitted, forgiuen, acquited, released; also, deferred, prorogued, put ouer or off, vnto; also, remisse, cold, slacke, loosse, dull, carelesse, or negligent, in.*
En fin remis vn peu en soy. *Being come gaine vnto himselfe, or hauing somewhat recouered himselfe.*
Remise: f. *A restorall, reuiuement, recouerie, setting vp againe; also, a remitment, acquittance, release; also, a referrence, referring, or committing vnto; also, a slackning, deferring, prolonging, or (as in Law) a delay, or putting off of a cause by consent of parties, and for a certaine time; also, th'alighting of fowle after their second flight; also, the manage, tearmed otherwise,* Passade.
Par remises. *By fits, by turnes, but now and then.*
Remissible: com. *Remittable, pardonable, forgiueable; releasable.*
Remission: f. *A remission, or forgiuenesse; a pardon for an offence which, by the Law, brings death: And hereof some French Lawyers make foure kinds;* viz.
Remission de droict, ou de Iustice. *A Pardon of course; is granted by th'inferior Chanceries (yet in the Kings name) for Manslaughter* se defendendo, *or by chance medley, and for other such offences as the Law may pardon.*
Remission de grace. *A Pardon of grace, or his Maiesties most gracious Pardon (for Homicides, &c, of a more hainous kind) must bee procured from the King himselfe, and out of the great Chauncerie.*
Remission (ou Abolition) generale. *A generall Pardon (with exception) verie like that which is granted in th'end of our Parliaments.*
Remission (ou Abolition) speciale. *A speciall Pardon granted by the King vnto a particular person (in what maner, or by what meanes soeuer) offending.*
Remissionaire: com. *Whose offence is remitted.*
Remmailloter. *To swathe, or swaddle, againe.*
Remmalicer. *To grow more spightfull, or malicious.*
Remmancher. *To put on a new haft, or helue.*
Remocquer. *To mocke, or flowt againe; also, to tow one vessell at the sterne of another.*
Remolin: m. *A feather; a little circle of retorted, or curled haire, on the forhead, creast, or any other part, of a horse.*
Remollitif: m. iue: f. *Mollifying, softening.*

Remolquer. *To draw, or get, off the ground, or out of the grauell; to remoue, set aflote, set cleere; or, as* Remocquer, *in the later sence.*
Remonce. *as* Remonstrance.
Remonstrance: f. *A remonstrance, warning, admonition, reasons giuen, or shewed.*
Remonstré: m. ée: f. *Warned, aduised, admonished; shewed by reasons, or instances; also, chidden, rebuked, reproued.*
Remonstrer. *To warne, admonish; aduertise, aduise; to shew vnto, or set before the eyes; also, to checke, chide, rebuke, reproue.*
Remontages d' artillerie. *Carriages for great Ordnance.*
Remonté: m. *Remounted, or new-mounted, readuanced, relieued, raised vp againe.*
Apres que la marée est remontée. *At a low water; when the tyde is returned, or gone.*
Remonter. *To remount, reascend; readuance; climbe, rise; lift, raise, vp; set, or get on horsebacke, againe; also, to relieue, restore vnto, or set in, a former estate.*
Remordre. *To bite againe; also, to carpe at, or find fault with.*
Remordu: m. uë: f. *Bitten againe; also, carped at, or found fault with.*
Remore: f. *The Suck-stone, or sea-Lamprey; a little fish, which cleauing to the keele of a ship, hinders the course of it.*
Remorfondre. *To take, or grow, cold againe.*
Remorquer. *To hale, or tow along, a ship &c; also, as* Remolquer.
Remors: m. *Diuels bit, Forebit; an hearbe.*
Remors de conscience. *Remorse, the worme, or sting, of conscience.*
Remors de l' estomac. *The vpbraiding of the stomacke.*
Remot: m. ote: f. *Remote, remoued, withdrawne, farre off.*
Remoucher. *To wipe againe.*
Remouillé: m. ée: f. *Wet, or moistened againe.*
Remouillement: m. *A new, or second moistening.*
Remouiller. *To wet, or moisten, once more.*
Remouldre. *To grind againe.*
Remouvoir. *To remoue, retire, withdraw, set aside, put away.*
Rempant: m. ante: f. *Creeping, crawling, or trayling along; also, climbing.*
Ligne rempante. Par vne ligne rempante. *By a leuell, or a well-leuelled line.*
Rempaqueter. *To reimpacke; to make vp into a new packet.*
Rempar: m. *A Rampier; the wall of a Fortresse.*
Remparer. *To fortifie; to inclose with a Rampier.*
Rempart. *as* Rempar.
Rempenner vne flesche. *To new-feather an arrow.*
Remper. *Looke* Ramper.
Remplacé: m. ée: f. *Reimplaced, placed anew, or againe; set in the place, or in stead, of another.*
Remplacement: m. *A reimplacing, or new placing, a laying or setting in another place; also, a putting in the place, or stead, of another.*
Remplacer. *To reimplace; to lay, or place anew; to take out of one place, and set in another; also, to put one thing in the place, introduce one thing in the stead, of another.*
Remplage: m. *A filling or stuffing vp; a replenishing, furnishing, supply of things wanting.*
Rempli: m. ie: f. *Filled, stuffed, replenished, well furnished.*
Ils ont rempli leur cerceau. (*Of mued Hawkes*) *their Sarcells are hard set.*
Remplier. *To lay downe a seame, to turne in a hemme (in sowing of clothes.)*
Remplir. *To fill, or stuffe with; to replenish; throughly to furnish, to supply all wants.*
Remplissage: m. *A filling &c; as* Remplage.
Remplissage de Vins. *Leakage; or the filling vp of Wine-vessells after their leaking.*
Remplissement. *as* Remplage.
Remplisson: f. *A filling, supplying, or furnishing of an emptie place.*
Remploy: m. *A reimployment, as of money, made of one thing, or another.*
Remployer. *To reimploy.*
Remplumer. *To feather anew.*
Ie me remplume. *I begin to recouer my health, wealth, or authoritie; I picke, or gather, vp my crummes againe.*
Rempoigner. *To lay hands on againe.*
Rempoisonner. *To poison, or inuenome anew.*
Rempoissonner. *To furnish againe with fish.*
Remporté: m. ée: f. *Carried or borne backe, brought or got away.*
Remporter. *To carrie or beare backe, to get or bring away from.*
Remprisonner. *To reimprison; to cast into prison againe.*
Remprunter. *To borrow againe.*
Rempson. *as* Rençon. (v.m.)
Remu. Octroier remu. (*In the auncient Customes of Britaine*) *to giue, or agree vnto, a delay in a suit.*
Remuance: f. *A remouance; a frequent mouing, stirring, itching, figging; remouing.*
Remuant: m. ante: f. *Often mouing, stirring, figging; liuelie, nimble, quicke; often remouing, euer flitting, neuer still, or standing.*
Remucrés: m. *Fustinesse; or mouldinesse.*
Remué: m. ée: f. *Moued, stirred; remoued.*
Remuë-mesnage: m. *A stirring, turbulent, vnquiet, seditious person; one that affecteth change, nouelties, innouations.*
Remuëment: m. *A mouing, stirring; remouing.*
Remuër. *To moue, stirre, fig, fidge it; to remoue, or set away.*
Remuër les mains. *To fight hard, lay about him lustily.*
Remuër mesnage contre. *Looke* Mesnage.
Remuër toute pierre. *To attempt all meanes, proue all courses, try all wayes.*
Remuër les serrures. *To be verie busie, to keepe an old coyle, bustling, stirre.*
De chose perduë le conseil ne se remuë: Pro. *See* Conseil.
Qui remuë les pierres ses doigts casse: Prov. *He that remoueth stones crusheth his fingers; he that puts them (into hot, or) vnto hard things (burne, or) bruises them.*
Remuëur: m. *A mouer; a remouer.*
Remuëur de mesnage. *as* Remuë-mesnage.
Remugle. *Mustie, or fustie.*
Remuneration: f. *A remuneration, remunerating, recompencing, rewarding.*
Remuneratoire: com. *Remuneratorie, remunerating.*
Remunerer. *To remunerate, guerdon, recompence, reward.*
Remusseau: m. *A bottome, or clue of thread, yarne, &c.*

Remy: m. *A proper name for a man; and particularly, the name of a Saint, which was the sixteenth Bishop of* Rheims, *and baptised* Clouis *the first Christian King of France: he died in the yeare 545.*

La Sainct Remy. *S. Remyes day; the first day of October, kept holyday in most parts of France.*

Renager. *To swimme backe.*

Renaissance: f. *A new birth.*

Renaissances de forests. *Young trees that come vp after a felling, or cutting of the old ones.*

Renaissement: m. *as* Renaissance; *or, a being new borne.*

Renaistre. *To be borne anew; to rise, grow, spring, or begin, againe.*

Renal: m. ale: f. *Of, or belonging to, the kidneyes.*

Artere renale. *A branch of the great arterie, which enters into the kidneyes, and brings vnto them the serositie of the arteriall bloud.*

Veine renale. *Seeke* Veine.

Renaquer. *To sweare horribly or most idly, to blaspheme, or to renounce, Almightie God.*

Renard. *A Fox; Looke* Regnard.

Renardaille: f. *as* Regnardaille.

Renarde: f. *A Bitch-fox.*

Renardeau: m. *A Fox-cub, or young Fox.*

Renarder. *See* Regnarder.

Renardesque: com. *as* Regnardesque.

Renardier: m. ere: f. *Of, or belonging to, a Fox.*

Renardise: f. *as* Regnardise.

Renasquer. *Looke* Renaquer.

Renavigé: m. ée: f. *Renauigated, sayled backe.*

Renaviger. *To renauigate, sayle backe, or sayle ouer againe.*

Renavrer. *To wound, or hurt againe.*

Renaut. *Looke* Regnaut.

Renchainer. *To reinchaine; to chaine, or bind in chaines, againe.*

Renche. *Looke* Rang.

Rencheoir. *To fall againe.*

Rencheri: m. ie: f. *Growne deerer or higher prised, held or come to a greater rate, then it was at.*

Il fait du rencheri. *He keepes off, holds aloofe, makes it daintie, seemes coy or squeamish; also, he is very churlish, froward, harsh, vntractable, hard to be dealt with.*

Rencherir. *To raise the price of, to make deerer then it was.*

Rencheute: f. *A recidiuation, or new fall.*

Renchier: m. *A Rayne-Deere.*

Renclorre. *To reinclose.*

Renclouër. *To nayle againe.*

Rencocher. *To nocke the second time.*

Rençon: f. *A ransome; that which is payed for the libertie of a prisoner of warre; also, corne giuen backe by a Miller in meale; whence,* Tel musnier faict mauvaise rençon; *yeelds not so much grist, or makes not so much meale, as he should doe.*

Aide de rençon. *Looke in* Aides chevels.

Rençonnement, & Rençonner. *as* Rançonnement, & Rançonner.

Rençonneur: m. *A ransomer; and thence, an oppressor, extortioner, vniust exactor, hard or sore dealer.*

Rencontre: f. *A hap, or aduenture; also, a meeting, or incounter (as of aduerse troopes, which on a suddaine, or by chaunce, fall foule one on the other;) an accidentall getting, obtaining, or lighting on; also, an occurrence; also, an apt or vnpremeditated ieast, conceit, wittie saying.*

Cheval de rencontre. *A horse of seruice, or the value of one, due by a new vassall vnto his new Lord, both falling out to be so by the death of their predecessors within one yeare.*

Mot de rencontre. *An apt or vnpremeditated ieast, &c, as before in* Rencontre.

Nom de rencontre. *A good, acceptable, honest, or happie name.*

Rencontré: m. ée: f. *Incountered, met, occurred with, hit, or light vpon.*

Voilà bien rencontré. *A good and wittie ieast, a fit and quicke reply, beleeue me.*

Ils ont rencontré chaussure à leur pied; *Looke* Chaussure.

Rencontrer. *To incounter, meet, occurre, with; to come to, or light on, casually; also, to speake merrily, wittily, prettily, vnhappily, properly, or to the purpose; to hit vpon a ieast, to make a wittie incounter.*

Deux hommes se rencontrent bien, mais iamais deux montaignes: Prov. *Two men may sometimes meet, but mountaines neuer.*

Rencontreur: m. *A mocker, flowter, giber, ieaster, pleasant companion, facetious person, merrie man.*

Rencourager. *To reincourage.*

Rencuser. *To detect, appeach, bewray, betray.*

Rendable: com. *Rendible, renderable, yeeldable, restorable.*

Rente rendable. *A rent-secke or charge, which may be extinguished, redeemed, or bought out.*

Rendage: m. *A rendering, or yeelding; a restoring, or giuing backe.*

Droict de rendage de chascun ouvrage. *Looke vnder* Droict.

Se Rendebter. *To runne or grow in debt againe.*

Rendement: m. *A rendring, retribution, restoring, yeelding backe.*

Rendenter. *To reindent, or set new teeth vnto.*

Rendez-vous: m. *A Rendeuous; a place appointed for the assemblie, or meeting of souldiors.*

Le rendez-vous d' un' affaire. *The end, or scope of a matter, the drift, or purpose whereto it is directed.*

Renditer. *To reindite, or frame a new Inditement against; also, to demonstrate, manifest, or point at, againe.*

Rendon: f. *Randome, vncertaintie; or, as* Randon.

Se Rendormir. *To fall asleepe againe.*

Rendormissement: m. *A falling asleepe againe.*

Rendouble. *as* Redouble.

Rendouër: m. *A retribution; or the time, or vessell, of restoring.* ¶Rab.

Rendre. *To render, yeeld, giue, or pay, backe; restore, make restitution vnto; also, to yeeld, giue, affoord, assigne, vnto; also, to cause, make, effect, or bring to passe; also, to vomit, spue, or cast vp againe; also, to runne, as a sore, &c.*

Rendre les abbais, ou abbois. *To hold the dogs at a bay; a defence made by a Deere, when he can runne no longer; by a Bore, at his first raising, and before he begin to runne.*

Se rendre à. *To meet with, or at; also, to resort, repaire, come, or get him, vnto.*

Des yeux se va rendre au cerveau. *It reaches, runnes, or goes from the eyes to the braine.*

Ou rendre, ou pendre, ou mort d' enfer attendre: Pro. *Restore, or hang, or looke to be damn'd.*

Au prester ange, au rendre Diable; &, Au prester cousin, au rendre fils de putain: Prov. *Borrowers when they would haue coyne, speake faire, but when they*

they should pay coyne, spit fire.

Qui a appris à prendre sçait tard que c'est de rendre: Pro. *Those that can take best restore worst; or, those that are hastie to take are slow to restore.*

Rendu: m. uë: f. *Rendred; yeelded or giuen backe, restored; also, yeelded, giuen, affoorded, vnto; also, made, effected, or brought to passe; also, vomited, spued, or cast vp againe.*

Renduire. *To reannoint, or besmeare againe.*

Rendurci: m. ie: f. *Reobdurated; made more hard, stiffe, or obstinate, then before.*

Rendurcir. *To reobdurate; to make more hard, or obstinate, then before.*

Reneau: m. *as* Bocque.

Renegat: m. *A renegadoe; one that abiures his religion, or forsweares his profession.*

Reneger. *To snow againe.*

Renes. *Looke* Reines.

Renette: f. *A Game at Tables of some resemblance with our Doublets, or Queenes Game; also, the apple called a Pippin, or a kind thereof.*

Renettoyé: m. ée: f. *Clensed againe, wyped, or scowred anew.*

Renettoyement: m. *A new, or second, clensing.*

Renettoyer. *To clense againe, to wype or scowre ouer, anew.*

Renettoyeur: m. *One that wypes, clenses, or scowres a thing often, anew, or ouer againe.*

Renfardeler. *To packe vp againe.*

Renfermer. *To shut vp againe.*

Renferrer. *To lay new yrons on; also, to strike, or thrust through, againe with a sword &c.*

Renfester vne maison. *To put new ridge-tyles on it, in lieu of the old ones; or to new-roofe it.*

Renfierir. *To make proud, statelie, surlie againe.*

Renfiler vne aiguille. *To thread a needle againe.*

Renflage: m. *A great, or new, swelling.*

Renflamber. *To reinflame.*

Renflammer. *The same.*

Renflé: m. ée: f. *Swelled anew or againe, greatly or doubly swolne.*

Renflement: m. *A new, or double, swelling.*

Renfler. *To swell anew or againe, greatly or doubly to swell.*

Renfoncé: m. ée: f. *New headed, as Caske; whose bottome, or head is new set in; also, hollowed, or sunke in.*

Renfoncement: m. *A new heading of Caske.*

Renfoncemens. (*In Painting*) *hollowings, or sinkings;* (Choses qui semblent estre reculées, & enfoncées;) *or shadowings.*

Renfondré: m. ée: f. *Sunke againe; also, darke, obscure, ouer-shadowed, low-seated, as a hollow bottome.*

Renfondrement: m. *A shadowing, or ouershadowing.*

Renfondrer. *To replunge, or sinke againe; also, to darken, obscure, shadow, ouershadow.*

Se renfondrer. *To sinke in againe.*

Renfonsements. *as* Renfoncemens.

Renfonser. *To driue, thrust, or force backe vnto the bottome; to rebulge, or beat farre into againe.*

Renforcé. *as* Renforci.

Renforcer. *To reinforce, or strengthen againe; to double the force, or strength of.*

Se renforcer. *To gather strength, redouble his force, recouer his former vigor.*

Renforci: m. ie: f. *Reinforced; strengthened or fortified, animated or incouraged, anew; restored vnto force or vigor.*

Renforcir. *as* Renforcer.

Renfort: m. *Aide, supply; abundance, plentie.*

Renfouïr. *To dig againe.*

Renfourner. *To put into the Ouen againe.*

Renfrongné: m. ée: f. *Furrowed, as an angrie brow; wrimpled, crumpled, puckered; frowning, lowring, scowling.*

Se Renfrongner. *To frowne, lowre, scold.*

Se Renfueiller. *To get new leaues, to grow leaued againe.*

Reng: m. *A ranke, &c; as* Rang.

Rengager. *To reingage.*

Rengainer. *To sheath, or put into the sheath againe.*

Renge: f. *A ranke, rew, range.*

Rengé: m. ée: f. *Ranked, ranged, ordered, arrayed.*

Rengée: f. *A play with a ball at nuts, placed on a row.*

Rengelet: m. *The name of a yellow, and sweet apple.*

Rengendré: m. ée: f. *Reingendred, new begotten.*

Rengendrer. *To reingender, to beget againe.*

Rengendreur: m. *A reingendrer.*

Renger. *To ranke, range, order, &c; as* Ranger.

Rengette. *Whence,* Se laisser aller à la rengette. *To giue her selfe a whoorish scope, to suffer her shooe to goe awry.*

Rengier: m. *A Rayne Deere.*

Rengigner. *To bewitch, or deceiue, againe.*

Renglacer. *Againe to take cold, be cold, thicken, or congeale, as Ice.*

Rengloutir. *To reglut, reingulfe, swallow vp againe.*

Rengluer. *To beglue, or belime, againe.*

Se Rengorger. *To hold downe the head, or thrust the chinne into the necke, as some doe, in pride, or to make their faces looke the fuller; we say, to bridle it.*

Rengouffrer. *To reingulfe.*

Rengouler. *To redeuoure.*

Rengourdir. *To benumme, or astonie anew.*

Rengourmer. *To curbe, or keepe in strait subiection; also, to cuffe, knocke, or pash on the mouth; whence;*

Ie te rengourmeray bien le groin. *I will pummell thee soundly; I will make thee hold thy head full low.*

Rengraisser. *To fatten againe.*

Rengraver. *To reaggrauate; reinforce, renew,*

Rengregement: m. *An exaggeration, aggrauating, exasperating, exulcerating.*

Rengreger. *To aggrauate, exaggerate, exulcerate, exasperate, make worse, rub or renew the sore of.*

Rengrenement: m. *A reingraining; a new furnishing, or filling, with graine.*

Rengrener. *To reingraine; againe to furnish, or fill with graine.*

Se Rengrossir. *To wax grosse, or great againe.*

Renhanter. *To new-head a Pike, &c.*

Renhardir. *To reimbolden, reincourage.*

Renhaster. *To put on the spit againe.*

se Renherber. *To get new grasse, to become grassie againe.*

Renhorter. *To reinhort, readuise, require, vnto.*

Renhuiler. *To oyle ouer againe.*

Renjabler. *To new-rigoll a peece of caske.*

Renjanter. *To put new spokes vnto a wheele.*

Renicher. *To nestle anew, to returne vnto his owne home.*

Reniement: m. *An earnest denying, disauowing, disaffirming, abiuring; an ordinarie swearing, or blasphe-ming.*

Renier. *To denie stifly, disaffirme earnestly, disaduow; abiure, forsweare vehemently; also, to sweare (idly, or ordi-*

ordinarily) to blaspheme God.
Renieur: m. *An earnest denyer, disaduower, abiurer, forswearer, of; also, a blasphemer, or an ordinarie swearer.*
Renifler. *To snuffle, or snifter often.*
Rejoindre. *To reinioyne, reordaine vnto, reimpose vpon.*
Renitence: f. *Resistance; a hard thrusting, or indeuouring against.*
Renitent: m. ente: f. *Resisting; indeuouring, labouring, or thrusting against.*
Reniveler. *Againe to measure, or lay euen, with a leuell; againe to sound with a plummet.*
Renn-fane. *The Standart, or Cornet of a troope of horse.*
Rennuyer. *To remolest.*
Renogle: f. *The little greene Frog, or Toad.*
Renoiant. *False of promise.* (v.m.)
Renoircir. *To blacke ouer againe.*
Renoiser. *Againe to brawle, or contend in words.*
Renom: m. *as* Renommée.
Renombrer. *To number, count, reckon, or tell ouer, againe.*
Renommé: m. ée: f. *Renowmed, famous, of much note, of great name, reported or bruited all abroad, exceedingly spoken of.*
Renommée: f. *Renowme, fame, bruit, report, reputation, estimation, a great name.*
Bonne renommée vaut mieux que ceincture dorée: Pro. *A good name graces a woman more (or is of more worth vnto her) then any garment.*
Se Renommer de quelque vn. *To professe, report, or giue out, that he belongs vnto, or depends vpon any one.*
Renoncer. *To renounce, abiure, forsake, abandon, forgoe for euer.*
Renonciation: f. *A renunciation, renouncing, abiuring, forsaking.*
Renoter. *To renote, remarke, to note or marke, againe.*
Renovation: f. *A renouation, renewment, repaire.*
Renouée: f. *Knot-grasse, Swines-grasse, Birds-tongue, S. Innocents hearbe.*
Renouër. *To tye, knit, or linke together againe.*
Renouër vn procés. *To renew, reuiue, patch vp, set on foot, an old weather-beaten, moath-eaten, or disioynted suit.*
Renoüeur de vieilles causes. *A renewer of old suits; a peecer or patcher vp of ruinous causes.*
Renouille. *(Sometimes vsed) for* Grenouille, *a Frog.*
Renouveau: m. *The Spring.*
Renouvée: f. *as* Renouée.
Renouvelant. *Renewing.*
Renouvelé: m. ée: f. *Renewed; new dressed or trimd vp; repeated, begun againe.*
Renouveler. *To renew, repaire, new dresse or trimme vp, redintegrate, reuiue, begin againe.*
Renouvellement: m. *A renewing, repairing, new-trimming vp, reuiuing, beginning againe.*
Renouvelleur: m. *A renewer, repairer, new trimmer vp; reuiuor, beginner againe, of.*
Renouvet: m. *A soone-ripe Apple that is no bigger then a Tennis-ball; also, the Cyder made thereof.*
Rensaisiner. *To repossesse, to giue new seisin vnto.*
Rensemencer. *To sow againe.*
Renserrer. *To shut vp againe.*
Rensevelir. *To burie once more.*
Rentamer. *Againe to cut, open, or breake, vp.*
Rentasser. *To heape, or packe vp againe.*

Rente: f. *Rent; reuenue.*
Rente à l'appreci. *Rent corne, payable in so much money as it might haue beene sold for, on any of the three market dayes, next before the day, whereon it is due.*
Rente censive. *A* Cens, *or quit rent.*
Rente constituée sur heritage. *A rent charge, or a rent-secke, raised vpon, or yeelded out of, an Inheritance.*
Rente constituée à pris d'argent. *An annuitie, or rent, vpon a morgage; a rent raised vpon, or bought for, money; (The rate whereof is, most commonly,* Au denier douze.)
Rente courante. *as* Rente volage.
Rente fonciere. *A rent-seruice, rent-charge, or fee-farme rent; an accession vnto a* Cens, *or chiefe rent; a second charge layed on land vpon a second graunt thereof; called thus, because it euer followes the soyle, and is due vnto the Lord thereof.*
Rente hereditable, ou hereditale, heritable, ou heretiere. *A rent in fee simple.*
Rentes à heritage. *The rents payed out of the Kings demaine in lieu of the Inheritances,* Censuels, ou Roturiers, *which haue beene annexed vnto it.*
Rente noble. *A rent thats due out of a* fief.
Rente proprietaire. *as* Rente fonciere; *tearmed by Ciuilians,* Reditus solaris, fundariusve.
Rente rendable. *Looke* Rendable.
Rentes requerables. *Which, as all rents (not otherwise agreed vpon) must be demaunded on the ground, or at the place, for which they are due.*
Rente roturiere. *Looke* Roturier.
Rente seiche. *Rent secke; tearmed so, not (as ours) because no distresse is incident vnto it, but because it yeelds no profit vnto the Lord of the soyle out of which it issues;* (Car c'est le pension, ou cens annuel, que le subiect impose sur son heritage mouvant d' aucun Seigneur foncier;) *So that it is as well a rent charge as that which we call Rent seck.*
Rente tolerable. *A quit rent, or auncient rent, which cannot be bought out, but must be indured, and payed, by the tenant.*
Rente volage, volante, ou vollant. *A Rent secke, or a Rent charge; any rent thats raised of, or purchased for, money.*
Mieux vaut reigle que rente: Prov. *Better be wise then wealthie, honest then rich; good rule's to be preferd 'fore great reuenues.*
Renté: m. ée: f. Bien renté. *Well rented, of good liuing, of great reuenue.*
Qui sçait mestier il est renté: Pro. *A good Trade is a good reuenue.*
Renter *(for* Réenter) *to graffe againe.*
Renter vn homme. *To giue him rents, or yearelie reuenues.*
Renterrer. *To reinterre, to burie againe.*
Renteux: m. euse: f. *Yeelding rent, charged with rent.*
Rentier: m. *A Tenant; one that payes rent, or (as we say) sits at a yearelie rent; also, a Landlord, or one to whom rent is due; also, a Rent-roll.*
Rentonner. *To tunne, or tune, the second time.*
Rentortiller. *To writhe, or wind about againe.*
Rentraicture: f. *The laying in of a seame with the fingers; also, a drawing of rent cloth; a dearning.*
Rentraieur: m. *A Seamster; or Drawer; or Dearner; a mender of rents in linnen, or woollen clothes.*
Rentrainer. *To traile, or draw, backe.*

Rentraire. *To lay in, or lay downe, a seame; also, to draw, dearne, or sow vp a rent in a garment.*

Rentrayeur. *as* Rentraieur.

Rentré: m. ée: f. *Reentred, returned in, gone in againe.*

C'est bien rentré de picques. *To the purpose I warrant you. (Ironically.)*

Rentrer. *To reenter, to returne in, or goe in againe; also, to speake merrily, or vnhappily; suddainely to come out with a pleasant or wittie conceit; to light on a ieast; also, as* Rentraire.

Rentrer en mesme bourbier. *To fall into the same error againe.*

Rentreur: m. *A drawer of cloth.*

Renvahir. *To reinuade.*

Renveloper. *To reinuelope, reinwrap.*

Renvenimer. *To reinuenome.*

Renverse: f. Coup donné à la ren. *A crosse blow.*

Tomber à la renverse. *To fall backward.*

Renversé: m. ée: f. *Ouerturned, ouerthrowne, turned inside out or vpside downe; peruerted.*

Anguille renversée. *An Eele opened all along, and turned inside out, then well washed, bound vp, and boyled in red Wine, and serued cold, with sawce made of Ginger, Cynnamon, Cloues, Graines, Wine, Vineger, and Veriuice.*

Raisin renversé. *Garden Nightshade, pettie Morell.*

Yeux renversez. *Eyes standing in the head, or decayed eyes.*

Renversemént: m. *An ouerturning, ouerthrowing, euersion, subuerting; also, an inuersion, or turning inside out.*

Renversément. *Inside outward, vpside downe, topsie turuie, backward.*

Renverser. *To ouerturne, euert, ouerthrow; turne vpside downe; also, to inuert, or turne the inside outward.*

Renversure: f. *as* Renversemént.

Renvier. *To reuy, at play.*

Il y renvioit de sa reste. *He set his whole rest, he aduentured all his estate, vpon it.*

Renvoy: m. *A sending backe, a dismission; a referring from one vnto another.*

Renvoy de prisonniers. *A sending of prisoners from one Iudge to another, or from a Court of Parliament vnto some inferiour Iudge.*

Simple renvoy. *A simple dismission; graunted vnto one that being appealed, or called before a superior Iudge, requires to be dismissed to the prosecuting of his suit alreadie begun, before the inferior (his ordinarie) Iudge: Another kind of* Renvoy *(tearmed otherwise* Congé de cour) *is graunted vnto such as are appealed, or called before Iudges that haue no iurisdiction ouer them.*

Faire renvoy. *To dismisse, or send backe; to release, to discharge.*

Faire des renvois. *A Dictionarie &c, to referre you, in one word, vnto another, by the tearmes of, Looke, See, Seeke, &c.*

Renvoyé: m. ée: f. *Dismissed, sent backe, remitted, remanded, returned; referred.*

Renvoyer. *To dismisse, remit, remand, returne, send backe; referre from one to another.*

Se renvoyer l'esteuf l'vn à l'autre. *To shift off, or poast ouer, a thing one to the other; or, to serue one anothers turne withall.*

Cela nous renvoit au devin. *That puts vs to our trumpes; or, we know not, on a suddaine, what to make of it.*

Renure: f. La ren. d'une poulie. *The hollow, or furrow wherein the rope runnes about it.*

Reosté: m. ée: f. *Taken away againe.*

Repaire: m. *A lodging, or haunt; the place whereto one vsually repaires; also, the denne, or couert wherein a wild beast lurkes; also, the dung of a Hare.*

Faulcon de repaire. *A Hagard which euer keepes one certaine stand at night; and hence;*

Cet oiseau n'est de long repaire. *Resorts not much to, or stayes not long in, one place.*

Mauvais repaire. *A place wherein spirits haunt, or walke; also, an apparition, or spirit.*

Repairer. *To haunt, frequent, lodge in, repaire vnto, one certaine place.*

Repaissaille: f. *A feeding, a repast.*

Repaistre. *To feed, nourish, victuall; to giue or take food, nourishment, victuals.*

Repaistre de bayes. *To feede with trifles, or vaine hopes; to intertaine with fibs, or friuolous tearmes.*

Repaistre en Commissaire. *See* Commissaire.

Repaistre les corbeaux. *To feed Rauens, become Rauens food, hang in chaines.*

Il faut que l'herbe soit bien courte quand on ne trouve que repaistre: Prov. *The grasse had need be verie short where nothing's to be nibled.*

Mal de teste veut repaistre: Prov. *(The head smarts for the stomackes emptinesse;) headach refection craues.*

Repaistri: m. ie: f. *Kneaded ouer againe.*

Repandre. *Looke* Respandre.

Reparable: com. *Repairable, amendable, recouerable.*

Reparateur: m. *A repairer, mender, renewer of.*

Reparation: f. *A reparation, amendment, renewing, recouerie of decayed things; also, a full restitution, or satisfaction.*

Reparations. *The repaires, or the reparations, of houses, &c; whereof, sayes a French Lawyer, there be three (generall) kinds; viz.* les necessaires, *without which the thing had fallen downe, or been much the worse;* les vtiles; *by meanes whereof it is greatly improoued;* & les voluptuaires, ou de plaisir; *seruing onely for ornament, and the tenants delight.*

Reparations viageres. *Looke* Viager.

Reparé: m. ée: f. *Repaired, amended, renewed, restored, recouered.*

Reparée: f. *The hearbe called Beets.*

Reparée noire. *Blacke Beets.*

Reparement: m. *A repairing, amending, renewing, recouering, restoring.*

Reparer. *To repaire, mend, renew; recouer, restore.*

Reparer vne iniure. *To make amends, or giue satisfaction, for a wrong done.*

Cela repare bien vn homme quand il parle bien. *Good words improue, grace, or set forth, a man very much.*

Repargner. *Looke* Respargner.

Reparler. *To speake againe.*

Reparoistre. *To reappeare.*

Ie te le feray reparoistre. *I will make thee pay soundly for it.*

Repart: m. *A rediuision, or subdiuision; also, a reply.*

Repartager. *To make a new partition of, to diuide a new.*

Repartement de debtes. *An equall diuiding or sharing of a debtors estate, or of the money made of it, among his creditors.*

Re-

Reparti: m. ie: f. *Subdiuided, rediuided; or diuided into many parts; also, replyed; also, parted againe (as a horse) from the hand.*

Repartie: f. *as* Repart; *also, an answering blow, or thrust (in fencing &c) and thence, a returne of, or answer in speech; a reply.*

Repartir. *To rediuide, or subdiuide; also, quickly to returne a thrust or blow; to answer a thrust with a thrust, a blow with a blow, in fencing, &c; and hence, to reply in speech; also, a horse to part againe from the hand.*

Repas: m. *A repast, meale, refection.*

Repas de chien: Pro. *Hounds fare; nothing but bread and water.*

Repassé: m. ée: f. *Repassed; passed or gone ouer againe; (also, healed, recouered; in old French.)*

Repasser. *To repasse; to passe, or goe ouer againe; also (in old French) to recouer, or grow well againe.*

Repateliner. *To flatter, sooth, cog, or collogue with beyond measure, or againe.*

Repatrié: m. ée: f. *Repatriated, restored vnto his owne home; also, reconciled, or made friends with.*

Repatrier. *To repatriate, or to restore to his owne home; also, to attone, reconcile, make friends againe.*

Mais c'est le repatrier trop loing. *But so we fetch his pettigree too farre.*

Repeigné: m. ée: f. *Often combed, or combed ouer againe.*

Repeigner. *To combe often, or ouer againe.*

Repeindre. *To paint againe.*

Rependre. *To hang vp againe.*

Repensé: m. ée: f. *Seriously considered, aduisedly thought of; reuolued often, discussed much, in the thoughts.*

Repensement: m. *A serious considering, earnest thinking of; a frequent reuoluing, pondering, or examining in the mind.*

Repenser. *To thinke much, muse earnestly, consider aduisedly, of; to examine seriously, ponder duly, often reuolue in the thought.*

Mal pense qui ne repense: Prov. *He thinkes illfauoredly that thinkes not throughly.*

Repentailles: f. *Repentance; or the accidents, or fruits thereof.*

Fiançailles chevauchent en selle, & repentailles en croupe: Pro. *Repentance waits full close on mariage.*

Repentance: f. *Repentance, penitence.*

Repenti: m. ie: f. *Repented, repentant, penitent, repenting.*

Filles repenties. *An Order of Nunnes, which haue beene professed whores.*

Repentin: m. ine: f. *Suddaine; vnlooked for, vnawares.*

Repentir: m. *Repentance.*

Au gibbet le repentir vient trop tard: Prov. *Too late a man repents when the hangman attends him.*

De court plaisir long repentir: Pro. *Looke* Plaisir.

Se **Repentir**. *To repent, forthinke, to grieue at, or be sorrie for, the doing of a thing.*

Qui premier prend ne s'en repent: Pro. *The first taker seldome rues his hast.*

Tel consent qui se repent: Prov. *Some quickly rue their fond consentings.*

Trop tard se repent qui tout despend: Prov. *Looke* Despendre.

Trop tard se repent le rat entre les pattes du chat: Prov. *Too late the Rat cryes had-I-wist when the Cat pawes her.*

Repentiuement. *Penitently, repentingly, with repentance.*

Repercer. *To pierce againe.*

Repercher. *To set on the pearch againe.*

Repercussif: m. iue: f. *Repercussiue, repelling, beating or driuing backe; reuerberating, rebounding; resounding.*

Repercussion: f. *A repercussion, repulsing, beating or forcing backe; a reflection, reuerberation, rebounding.*

Repercuté: m. ée: f. *Repelled, repulsed, beaten or struck backe; reflected, reuerberated.*

Repercuter. *To repell, repulse; force, beat, or strike back; to rebound, reuerberate, reflect; resound.*

Repercutif: m. *A repercutiue; a medicine that repells, or driues, paine from the place whereunto it is applyed.*

Reperdre. *To loose againe.*

Repermis: m. ise: f. *Repermitted; suffered, or tolerated againe; also, newly licenced.*

Repertible: com. *Which may be found, gotten, recouered.*

Repertoire: m. *A Repertorie, List, Roll, Index, Inuentorie, Register.*

Repesché: m. ée: f. *Fished; or fetched out of the water, againe.*

Repescher. *To fish, or fetch out of the water, againe.*

Repeser. *To repeise, to weigh againe.*

Repestrir. *To knead againe.*

Repetasser. *as* Rapetasser.

Repeté: m. ée: f. *Repeated, rehearsed; also, redemaunded, asked or called backe, required, acquired, or fetched, againe.*

Repeter. *To repeat, or to rehearse; also, to redemaund, require, aske, or call backe; also, to returne, recouer, take, or fetch, backe againe.*

Repetition: f. *A repetition, a rehearsall; also, a redemanding, asking, or calling back; a recouerie, taking, or fetching, againe.*

Repeu: m. euë: f. *Fed, filled, satisfied.*

Repeuë: f. *A meale, repast, refection; also, a bait (or baiting place) in an Inne, &c.*

Repeuplement: m. *A repeopling, repopulating, new storing with inhabitants, &c.*

Repeupler. *To repopulate, new-store with people, furnish againe with inhabitants, &c.*

Repeyret: m. *Feuerwort, Earthgall, Centorie the lesse, common Centorie, small Centorie.*

Repicquer. *To pricke, thrust, plant, againe; also, to ride, or spurre, backe.*

Repigeonnement: m. *A budding or sprouting out, a putting forth againe.*

Repigeonner. *To bud, sprout out, put forth, anew.*

Repiler. *To pownd, bray, beat (in a mortar) againe.*

Repincer. *To pinch againe.*

Repionner. *as* Repigeonner; *or to yeeld, or put forth, small twigs, or sprigs.*

Repiquer. *as* Repicquer.

Repisser. *To pisse againe.*

Replaindre. *To complaine anew.*

Replancher. *To planke, to floore or seele with plankes, againe.*

Replantable: com. *Replantable.*

Replanté: m. ée: f. *Replanted, set or planted againe.*

Replantement: m. *A replanting; a new, or another, setting.*

Replanter. *To replant, or set againe.*

Replastrer. *To plaister, or dawbe ouer, anew.*
Replat: m. *A flat, or bottome; the flat part of any thing; also, the alley betweene two beds in a garden; also, the brow of a mountaine, or that part of it which hangeth ouer the rest.*
Replet: m. ete: f. *Replete, full; fat, plumpe, quarrie, corsie.*
Repletif: m. iue: f. *Repletiue, replenishing, filling.*
Repletion: f. *A repletion, replenishing, filling.*
Repletivement. *Repletiuely, fully.*
Repleurer. *To weepe againe.*
Repli: m. *A fould, plait, or bought; a foulding, bowing, winding, or turning in and out.*
Repli de la iambe. *The hamme.*
Le repli d' une lettre. *The fould in the bottome of a Deed wheron we signe, and whereinto the labell is put for the seale.*
Les replis d' une Riviere. *The manifold cranklings, or wriglings made in and out by a Riuer in it course.*
Replié: m. ée: f. *Much foulded, often bowed or plaited, redoubled, turned or winding in and out many wayes.*
Repliement: m. *A redoubling, much foulding, often plaiting or bowing, manifold winding or turning in and out.*
Replier. *To redouble, to bow, fould, or plait into many doublings; to make to turne, or wind in and out verie often.*
Replieur: m. *A redoubler.*
Replieure: f. *A redoublement, a redoubling; or, as* Repliement.
Replique: f. *A reply; second answer; new confirmation of former assertions.*
Chose bien dite n'a replique, ne redite: Pro. *Sound speech preuents replyes.*
Repliquer. *To reply, or answer, vnto.*
Replissé: m. ée: f. *Redoubled, much foulded, often bowed, manifoldly plaited, or plaited againe; also, puckred, or shrunke.*
Replissure: f. *as* Replieure.
Replomber. *To lead; solder; or sound, againe.*
Replonger. *To replunge, to ducke, or diue againe.*
Replouvoir. *To raine againe.*
Reployement: m. *as* Repli; *or, a foulding.*
Repluiner. *To plume, or plucke the second time.*
Reply. *as* Repli; *also, the voiding of the excrements at the mouth; a disease called,* Miserere mei.
Repoindre. *To pricke againe.*
Repoisser. *To pitch ouer againe.*
Repolir. *To repolish, new-furbish.*
Repolon. *The souldiors manage &c; as* Passade.
Reponce. *Rampions; Looke* Raiponce.
Reponcer. *To pounce againe.*
Reponchon. *as* Raiponce.
Repondre. *To lay egges againe.*
Repontique. *Looke* Rheupontique.
Reporté: m. ée: f. *Carried backe, returned, brought againe.*
Reporter. *To recarrie, beare backe, returne; remit, referre.*
Repos: m. *Repose, rest, quiet, ease, peace.*
Terres de repos. *Fallowes.*
Reposade: f. *A rest, or a resting place.*
Faisons reposade. *Let vs rest, sit downe, or take our ease.*
Repose: f. *A Semibreese Rest, in Musicke.*
Reposé. *Reposed, rested; lyen fallow a greatwhile; also, sad, setled, stayed, quiet, graue, discreet.*
Reposée: f. *as* Reposade; *also, the lodge of a Stag, &c.*
Reposément. *Reposedly, quietly, stilly, stayedly.*
Reposer. *To repose, pawse, rest, or stay; to be at quiet, to take his ease.*
Reposer son vin. *To sleepe after hard drinking, to disgest his drinke by sleeping.*
Qui bon vin boit il se repose: Pro. *Good wine breeds quiet rest.*
Qui va il leche, qui repose il seiche: Prov. *The stirrer thriues, the lazie house-Doue pines.*
Repositoire: m. *A storehouse, warehouse, cupboord, counter, place to keepe things in.*
Reposoir: m. *A lodge, mansion; standing; resting place; also, a Stue for fish.*
Les reposoirs d'un escalier. *The rests or landing places of a halfe-pace staire; euerie fift, or sixt &c step, much broader then the rest.*
Reposouër. *as* Reposoir.
Repost. En repost. *Closely, hiddenly, secretly, or as a thing thats well layed vp.*
Repoulsé: m. ée: f. *Repulsed, repelled; foyled; thrust, or driuen, backe.*
Repoulsement: m. *A repulsing, repelling; foyling; a thrusting, pushing, or driuing, backe.*
Repoulser. *To repulse, repell; foyle; thrust, push, force, or driue, backe.*
Repoulseur: m. *A repulser, a repeller; a thruster, pusher, driuer, backe.*
Repoulsoir. *Looke* Repoussoir.
Repous: m. *A pauing; pargetting, or filling with rubble, rubbish, &c.*
Repoussant. *Repulsing, repelling; pushing or forcing backe.*
Repoussé, & Repousser. *as* Repoulsé, & Repoulser.
Repousseur. *as* Repulseur.
Repoussoir: m. *A repulsorie; a thing that repulseth, driueth backe, or pusheth out; and hence, the yron toole wherewith woodden pinnes are thrust out; also, the top of a Pitfall, or Trap set for Foxes, &c.*
Repratiquer. *To practise, or contriue, againe.*
Reprehension: f. *A reprehension, reproofe, rebuke; a blaming, checking, chiding; a controlling.*
Repremiation: f. *A repremiation, a rewarding.*
Reprenant. *Reprehending, reprouing.*
Reprenart: m. *A reprehender, rebuker, reprouer, carper, checker, find-fault, controller.*
Reprendre. *To resume, receiue, take backe, or againe; also, to apprehend, stay, or hold, a fugitiue, &c; also, to reprehend, blame, checke, rebuke, reproue, carpe, controll.*
Se reprendre. *To close, ioyne, or knit againe; also, to cease or breath a little, and after breathing, to begin, or goe to it, againe; also, to take, hold, or get life, as a plant lately transplanted.*
Reprendre le criminel. *(In Law)* ne s'entend faire vn nouveau procés criminel, ains reprendre celuy qui est desia faict.
Reprenons nostre chevre à la barbe. *Let vs backe to our matter againe.*
Repreneur: m. *as* Reprenart.
Represaille: f. *A taking, arresting, or seising on, for a distresse, or pledge; also, a prise, or a reprisall; whence;*
Droict de represailles. *Power giuen, or leaue graunted, vnto a priuate man, which hath beene (or feares to be) robbed, imprisoned, ransomed, or otherwise wronged, by a forraine people, to right (or prouide for) himselfe vpon them, or any of their countreymen.*

Lettres de represailles. *Letters (Patents) of Mart, or Marque; letters authorizing reprisalls; or permitting a priuate man that hath beene wronged by forrainers to right himselfe on them, or theirs as he can.*

Representation: f. *A representation; a shew, resemblance, likenesse, apparance; also, a standing for, or a being presented in the stead of; and hence, the kindred, or neerenesse of a child vnto his father, whose person he represents, and in the right thereof is to inioy that inheritance which, had he liued, should haue beene his.*

Representer. *To represent, resemble, expresse, imitate, act; also, to preuent, offer, exhibit, shew forth.*

Represailles. *Reprisalls; whence,* Droict de represailles; *for which looke vnder* Represaille.

Represser. *To presse againe.*

Represter. *To lend againe.*

Reprier. *To pray often, desire earnestly, require againe.*

Reprimende: f. *A checke, reprehension, reproofe, rebuke.*

Reprimer. *To represse, quell, tame, containe, keepe downe, hold vnder; to bridle, moderate, refraine, restraine.*

Reprimeur: m. *A represser, queller, tamer; bridler, moderator, restrainer.*

Reprin: m. *Branne; or the coursest of meale.*

Reprins: m. inse: f. *Resumed, recouered, taken backe or againe; also, reprehended, reproued, rebuked, checked, blamed; also, closed, ioyned, knit or set together, againe; also, taken or held; also, returned vnto after a pawse, or breath-taking.*

Reprinse: f. *Orpine, Liblong, or Liue-long, an hearbe; also, a resumption, repetition, reiteration; a taking backe, a bringing, or comming, in againe; also, a closing, ioyning, or knitting together of disioynted things; also, a holding, taking, or thriuing of transplanted plants, and the fruit or increase yeelded by any seed or plant; also, a new homage done vpon the change of Lord, or Tenant; also, a turne in the dauncing of a Measure, &c.*

Le comptable fait reprinse de telle somme. *The accomptant reimburses; payes, or allowes, back vnto himselfe such a summe.*

Repris: m. ise: f. *as* Reprins.

Reprise: f. *A resumption; repetition, &c; as* Reprinse.

Reprises de pierre. *Denting peeces of stone.*

`A double reprise. *Doubly hooked; crooking, bending, or turnd inwards, on both sides.*

`A plusieurs reprises. *Sundrie, or many seuerall times; by sundrie, or manie seuerall efforts; falling often vnto that which he formerly left; beginning often there where before he had giuen ouer.*

Repriser. *To set a new rate or price on, to prize againe.*

Reprochable: com. *Reproachable, opprobrious, ignominious.*

Reproche: f. *A reproach, disgrace, defamation, imputation; a blemish, crime, taint, brand, fault; an vpbraiding, twitting, or casting in the teeth; a disabling of; an exception taken, or fault found with.*

Reproché: m. ée: f. *Reproached, disgraced, blemished, branded, tainted; vpbraided, twitted or cast in the teeth with; disabled, excepted against.*

Reprocher. *To reproach; disgrace, blemish, taint; obiect or impute vnto, charge or vpbraid with, lay in ones dish, cast in his teeth, a fault or error committed.*

Reprocher tesmoings. *To disable, challenge, or except against, witnesses.*

Reproduire. *To reproduce, to yeeld or bring forth againe.*

Reprovisionné: m. ée: f. *Furnished with new prouision, refurnished, furnished againe.*

Reprouvable: com. *Reproueable, blameable, condemnable.*

Reprouver. *To reproue, chide, checke, blame, condemne, find fault with, disallow.*

Reptile: com. *Reptile, creeping, crawling; as vermine, plants, roots, &c.*

Republique: f. *The Commonwealth.*

Repudiable: com. *Repudiable, refusable, reiectable, forsakeable.*

Repudiation: f. *A refusall, a refusing.*

Repudié: m. ée: f. *Refused, forsaken, reiected, abandoned, cast off.*

Repudiement: m. *A refusing, forsaking, abandoning, reiecting.*

Repudier. *To repudiate, refuse, forsake, abandon, reiect.*

Repudieur: m. *A refuser, a forsaker.*

Repuë. *Looke* Repeuë.

Repugnance: f. *Repugnancie, contradiction, disagreement.*

Repugner. *To repugne, crosse, thwart, impugne, resist, withstand, contradict, gainesay, disagree from, be opposite vnto.*

Repulluler. *To reburgeon, or bud out againe.*

Repurgé: m. ée: f. *Repurged, clensed anew.*

Repurgement: m. *A new purging, a frequent or iterated clensing.*

Reputation: f. *Reputation, esteeme, regard, account; fame, bruit, renowme, a name.*

Reputé: m. ée; f. *Reputed, held, esteemed, reckoned, accounted.*

Reputer. *To repute, hold, esteeme, reckon, account.*

Requamer. *To imbroder.*

Requarreler. *See* Recarreler.

Requart: m. *The fourth part of a fourth; as of 16 4, of 4 1.*

Requerable. *Searchable; requirable, demaundable, or which must be demaunded; whence;*

Rentes requerables. *Looke* Rente.

Requerant. *Diligently searching, or seeking; also, requesting, or beseeching.*

Vn chien requerant. *A well-nosed, or cold-nosed, hound.*

Requerir. *Diligently to seeke, search, looke for, hunt after; also, to request, intreat, beseech, implore, importune, earnestly to require, pray, or sue vnto.*

Qui plaisir fait plaisir requiert: Prov. *He that does a pleasure lookes to be pleasured; one benefit expecteth another.*

Requerre. *as* Requerir.

Requeste: f. *A request, petition, supplication (in writing; Looke* Placet; *) a desire, demaund, suit, intreatie, prayer, beseeching, inuocation, implorement; also, a search for, an inquirie after; and in hunting, a secke or hooke, againe.*

Requeste d'armes. *A publike challenge.*

Requeste civile. *A Reuiew, Repeale, or Arrest of Judgement, graunted by Letters Patents vpon suggestion, in the Chauncerie, that the Judges haue beene deceiued by false allegations, forged euidences, periured witnesses; or otherwise abused by the cunning, and shifts of the aduerse partie.*

Requeste d'un Oye. *The Goose giblets.*

Maistres

Maiſtres des requeſtes. *The Maiſters of Requeſts; at firſt there were but two, an Eccleſiaſticall, and a lay man; afterwards they came to be fiue; two aſſiſtants to the Chauncellor, and three Petition-receiuers (whereof ſee more in,* Iuges de la porte, *vnder* Iuge.) Anno 1342 *they grew to be ſix; and* Anno 1408 *they increaſed vnto eight; which number* Henry *the third doubling, made them ſixteene. They be* Conſeillers *of the bodie of Parliaments, and of the great Counſell, ouer which, in the abſence of the Iudges, they preſide; as they doe alſo at the Seales of all Parliamentall Chaunceries, where they heare the reports of the* Referendaires: *They alſo take notice of the falſification of Chauncerie Seales; and iudge* (en premiere Inſtance) *all controuerſies ariſing about the Titles of royall Offices.*

Aller aux requeſtes. *To goe, in time of warre, to implore the protection of ſome great perſonage, vpon a feare of being ranſacked by the common ſoldiors: (a ruſticall phraſe.)*

Cela n'eſt plus en requeſte. *Is no more ſought or cared for, no more asked or inquired after.*

Requien: m. *A certaine rauenous, rough-skinned, and wide-mouthed fiſh, which is good meat.*

Requinqué: m. ée: f. *Tricked, ſprucified, or ſmugd, vp.* ¶Pic.

Camus requinqué. *Whoſe flat noſe-end is turned vp.*

Se Requinquer. *To ſprucifie, ſmug, or tricke vp himſelfe.* ¶Pic.

Requint: m. *The fift part of the fift pennie for which a fief hath beene ſold (as of an hundred foure) due, beſides the ſaid fift, vnto the Lord* feodal, *and payed moſt commonly by the purchaſer.*

Requiper. *To arme, equip, furniſh, or make readie, againe.*

Requis: m. iſe: f. *Diligently ſought, ſearched, looked for, hunted after; earneſtly required, beſought, or intreated for; alſo, requiſite, fit, meet.*

Requiſition: f. *A requiſition, requirall, demaund; requeſt, beſeeching, ſuing, or ſeeking to.*

Requiſitoire: m. *A requeſt, or ſuit, vnto.*

Requiſitoire: com. *Inquiſitiue, or full of inquiries; alſo, requiring, requeſting, &c; whence;*

Lettres requiſitoires. *(Oppoſed vnto ſuch as be mandatarie, or of commaund) letters of requeſt, or intreatie.*

Requoy. *Looke* Recoy.

Rere. *To bellow as a Stag, to trout as a Buck.*

Rerefief. *as* Arriere-fief.

Rere-vaſſal: m. *A vaſſall to a vaſſall; a vaſſall that holds of a meſne Lord, or of a vaſſall.*

Rés. *Looke* Rets, & Rez.

Reſacrer. *To reconſecrate.*

Reſaigner. *To let bloud of another veine.*

Reſaillir. *To ſtart backe.*

Reſaiſir. *To reſeiſe, to lay new hold on.*

Reſaiſir, & fournir la complainɛte: C'eſt obtenir lettres pour la remener à effect ſur les lieux.

Reſaler. *To ſalt, or ſeaſon, againe.*

Reſaluër. *To reſalute.*

Reſaper, & Reſapper. *To vnderprop, or vnderſet a wall; to repaire it at the foot, or after it hath beene vndermined.*

Reſarcir. *To mend, reforme, repaire; alſo, to make amends for.*

Reſarcler. *To weed ouer againe.*

Reſaſſer. *To ſift againe.*

Reſavourer. *To taſt, eſſay, try, ſauor of once more, or againe.*

Resbaudir. *To glad, reioyce, exhilerate.*

Resbaudir vn chien. *To incourage, or cheere vp a dog with clapping, whooping, &c.*

Reſchal: m. *Yellow wyre, ſuch as netting for windowes is made of.*

Reſchapper d'une maladie. *To eſcape, or to recouer, of a ſickneſſe.*

Reſchaud: m. *A Chafing-diſh.*

Reſchauffé: m. ée: f. *Heated, or warmed againe.*

Des vieux choux reſchauffez. *An old couple newly married.*

Reſchauffer. *To warme, or heat againe.*

Reſchauffoir: m. *A Chafing-diſh; alſo, a Warming-panne, or Fire-panne, ſuch as is vſed in Barbers ſhops.*

Reſchault. *as* Reſchauffoir.

Reſchier. *To ſhift, or take out of one thing to put into another.*

Reſcindant: m. *A contract which hath been made void by law.*

Reſcindé: m. ée: f. *Cut, or pared off; alſo, cancelled, quaſht, annulled, repealed, fordone.*

Reſcinder. *To cut, or pare, off; alſo, to cancell, quaſh, annihilate, annull, repeale, fordoe.*

Reſciſion: f. *A reſciſion; a cutting, or paring off; a cancelling, annulling, annihilating.*

Reſciſoire: m. *The execution of a* Reſcindant.

Reſclairci: m. ie: f. *New cleered vp, clarified or fined againe.*

Renſconcer. *as* Reſconſer.

Reſconſé: m. ée: f. *Hidden, concealed, withdrawne, cloſe layed vp.*

Reſconſer. *To conceale, hide, withdraw, lay cloſe, put vp.*

Reſcoüable: com. *Reſcuable, recouerable, redeemeable.*

Reſcourre. *To reſcue, take from, free, redeeme, recouer, deliuer.*

Reſcourre vne terre. *To redeeme, diſingage, or buy backe, a peece of land.*

Bien a crié le loup qui ſa proye reſcoult: Pro. *See* Loup.

Reſcouſſe: f. *Reſcue, redemption, deliuerie; reſcous; the reſcuing, or taking of an ingaged thing from.*

Reſcouſſe perpetuelle. Reachet, ou moyen de ravoir, à perpetuité.

Reſcouſſe de rente. *An extinguiſhment, redemption, or buying out of a rent charge.*

Ou il n'y a plus de reſcouſſe. *Deſperate, loſt, gone, paſt hope or helpe, without recouerie.*

Reſcoux: m. ouſſe: f. *Reſcued, redeemed, recouered; freed, taken from, deliuered.*

Rente reſcouſſe. *Rent extinguiſhed, or bought out.*

Reſcreer. *Looke* Recreer.

Reſcript: m. *A reſcript; a writing backe; an anſwer giuen in writing; and hence, the anſwer of a Petition; the returne of a Writ.*

Reſcription: f. *A writing back; an anſwering by letters.*

Reſcrire. *To write backe; to returne an anſwer in writing.*

Reſcrire de ſon exploict. *(A Sergeant) to returne the Writ; or to deliuer in writing how he ſerued it, and what ſucceeded thereon.*

Reſcrit. *as* Reſcript.

Reſeant: m. ante: f. *Reſiant, reſident, continually dwelling, abiding, biding by it; Looke* Reſſeant.

Reſeau: m. *Networke.*

Reſecouër. *To ſhake often, or againe.*

Resection: f. *A resection; a cutting, paring, or shredding off.*

Resée: f. *A Purse-net.*

Reséeller. *To seale againe.*

Reseicher. *To dry againe.*

Reseigner. *To let bloud againe.*

Resemblance: f. *A resemblance; a likenesse, a counterfeit.*

Resemblant: m. ante: f. *Resembling, representing, like vnto.*

Resemblement: m. *A resembling, representing, counterfeiting.*

Resembler *To resemble, counterfeit, represent, be like vnto.*

Il semble à vn larron que chascun luy resemble: Pro. *A theefe imagines euerie one lookes like him.*

Les paroles du soir ne resemblent pas à celles du matin: Pro. *Looke* Parole.

Toutes les femmes se resemblent: Pro. *All women are (in some thing or other) alike.*

Resemer. *To sow againe.*

Se Resentir. *To haue a great smacke, or tast, or to be sensible of; Looke* Se Ressentir.

Resequer. *To pare, cut, or clip off; to shread, or take, cleane away.*

Reserener. *To cleere vp againe.*

Reserrant: m. ante: f. *Restrictiue, stiptick, closing, stopping, binding.*

Reserré: m. ée: f. *Closed, stopped, shut vp; strait, restrained, hard bound, pressed, or thrust together; also, stayed, sober, temperate, that keepes within due limits.*

Reserrer. *To close, bind, stop, or shut vp; also, to presse, squeeze, thrust, or straine hard together; also, to stay, restraine, represse, hold vnder; also, to reinforce it selfe; as in;*

'A la S. Pierre l'hyver s'en va ou il reserre: Pro. *Winter either goes, or growes on, at S. Peters tide.*

Reservatif: m. iue: f. *Reseruatiue, reseruing.*

Reserve: f. *Store; or a reseruation, or keeping of store; also, a reuersion.*

Chose de reserve. *A spare thing; a thing that is more then we need, more then we must (of necessitie) vse; whence;*

Le temps de reserve des principaux affaires. *The time of his vacation, or such time as he could spare, from important affaires.*

Oiseaux de reserve. *Fowle mued vp for the prouision of a house.*

Mettre en reserve. *To lay vp for another day.*

Reservé: m. ée: f. *Reserued, excepted, forprised; also, reserued, kept, or layed vp, for store; also, wise, discreet, stayed, setled, warie, or close, in proceeding.*

Reservéement. *Sparingly, moderately; with reseruation of; euer excepted, &c.*

Reserver. *To reserue, saue, preserue, lay by; keepe for prouision, lay vp for store; also, to except out of a clause, or bargaine; to forprise.*

Reservir. *To serue againe.*

Reservoir: m. *A Closet, or Storehouse; also, a Coope, or Mue for fowle; a Stue, or Pond for fish; any place wherein things are close kept, or safely layed vp.*

Reseul: m. *Networke, netting.*

Residence: f. *A residence, abode, or stay; a continuance, or continuall dwelling at one certaine place.*

Resider. *To reside, stay, continue, abide in, remaine at, one place.*

Residu. Le res. *The residue, rest, ouerplus, remainder, surplusage, arrerage.*

Resignant: m. *A resigner.*

Resignataire: com. *A resignee, or the partie to whom a thing is resigned.*

Resignation: f. *A resignation, resigning, resignment; a surrendring, or yeelding vp.*

Resigné: m. ée: f. *Resigned; surrendred, yeelded or giuen vp.*

Resigner. *To resigne, surrender, yeeld vp, giue ouer; bequeath vnto.*

Resiliment: m. *A leaping, skipping, rebounding, backe; a reuocation of his Deed, Will, &c; a going from his word.*

Resilir. *To leape, skip, rebound, backe; not to rest on, to step or goe from; to reuoke, or disaduow; to forgoe, or giue ouer.*

Resiné: m. *The iuice of Grapes boyled to a consistence of honey, and giuen to children, as our honey, spread on bread; or, as* Raisinnée.

Resine: f. *Rosin.*

Resine Colophonienne. *Dry clarified Rosin; such as we rub Violl-sticks with.*

Resine de Cypres. *A kind of liquid Rosin that resembles the ordinarie Turpentine of the Larch tree; and is in tast verie strong, and biting.*

Resine d'Espagne; frite; & de Grece. *Dry, and clarified Rosin.*

Resine de Lareze. *Common, or ordinarie Turpentine.*

Resine de Lentisque. *Masticke.*

Resine liquide. *Liquid Rosin, common Rosin, Rosin of the Pine tree.*

Resine de Meleze. *Turpentine.*

Resine de sapin. *Frankincense; also, the liquid Rosin thats (erroniously) called in shops, Venice Turpentine.*

Resine de Terebinthe. *The best, and truest kind of Turpentine.*

Resineux: m. euse: f. *Full of Rosin.*

Resiniere: f. *as* Raisiniere.

Resjouï: m. ie: f. *Reioyced, gladded, delighted, cheered vp.*

Resjouïr. *To reioyce, gladden, delight, exhilerate, make merrie, cheere vp.*

Celuy de bon sens ne iouït, qui boit, & ne s'en resjouït: Pro. *The man is sencelesse, and halfe mad, that drinkes good Wine, and yet is sad.*

Resjouïssance: f. *A reioycing; ioy, glee, mirth, gladnesse, pleasantnesse, iocondnesse, cheerefullnesse.*

Resjouïssant: m. ante: f. *Reioycing, delightsome, pleasant, merrie.*

Resipiscence: f. *A returne to vnderstanding; a repentance for, an amendment of, an error; a second thinking wiser then the first.*

Resisiesme: m. *A sixt part of a sixth; as of 36, 6; or of 6 1.*

Resistance: f. *Resistance, opposition, impugning, withstanding; a strife or indeuour against.*

Resisté: m. ée: f. *Resisted, withstood, impugned, oppugned.*

Resister. *To resist, withstand, impugne, repugne, striue, or indeuour against.*

'A quoy mon coeur resiste. *Which goes against my heart, against which my stomacke rises.*

Resixiesme. *as* Resisiesme.

Resixiesmement. *By way of a sixt part out of a sixth.*

Resize. *Hearbe Auens, Benet, or Blessed.*

Resler. *To thaw.*

Reslire. *To read ouer againe.*

Resne: f. *The reine of a bridle.*

Re-

Resolu: m. uë: f. *Resolued, decreed, determined, concluded; fully purposed; wholly bent vnto; constant in; also, resolute, hardie, valiant, stout, vndaunted, dreadlesse, couragious; also, dissolued, loossed, vntyed, vnbound, vndone.*

Resolu comme Pihourt en ses Heteroclites. *Said of one that in a learned companie is forward to speake, or will come in with his vy (as one that would seeme to vnderstand somewhat as well as others, or cares not how little he vnderstand himselfe, so he be not vnderstood by others:) For this* Pihourt, *a Mason of* Rhenes, *finding at* Chasteau-briant *(whither he came to consult, about the making of a Castle, with others) the chiefe workmen of France, who talked of nothing but Obelisques, &c, (which he vnderstood not) to be euen with them, sayd that,* Sans &c, l'Oeuvre ne peut proceder selon l' equipolation de ses Heteroclites; *and so, as he thought, did put them all downe.*

Resoluble: com. *Resolueable; also, dissolueable.*

Resoluëment. *Resolutely, hardily, valiantly, determinately, with full purpose, from a great courage.*

Resolutif: m. iue: f. *Resoluing; dissoluing, vntying, vnloosing, vndoing; also, deciding, or determining.*

Resolution: f. *A resolution, opinion, decision, sentence, decree; a full purpose, a setled intention, deliberation, determination.*

Resommeiller. *To slumber againe.*

Resommer. *To summe, or to summon, againe.*

Resomption: f. *A resumption, repetition, taking backe, assuming or beginning againe.*

Resonder. *To sound againe.*

Resonger. *To dreame againe.*

Resonnamment. *Resoundingly, lowdly, shrilly, melodiously, with good correspondence of voices; Eccho-like.*

Resonnance: f. *A resounding; ringing; melodious Eccho, rebounding sound; a recording, as of birds; also, an accord, agreement, consent of harmonie.*

Resonnant: m. ante: f. *Resounding, lowd recording, sound-reporting, Eccho-making.*

Resonnement. *as* Resonnance.

Resort: m. *Power to take notice of Appeales; or, as* Ressort.

Resort de serrure. *The spring of a locke; See* Ressort de serrure.

Resortir. *To issue, or goe forth, againe, &c; Looke* Ressortir.

Resouffler. *To blow againe.*

Resouhaiter. *To wish once more.*

Resouldé: m. ée: f. *Twice soldered; soldered againe.*

Resoulder. *To solder againe.*

Resouldre. *To loose, dissolue, vntye, vnbind; scatter; melt, resolue, thaw; also, to decree, determine, deliberate, purpose fully.*

Resouper. *To sup againe.*

Resource: f. *A new source, or spring; a recouerie, vpraising, rising againe; Looke* Ressource.

Se Resourdre. *To spring, rise, grow, or get vp, againe; to amend; recouer, come to it former estate, or vigor.*

Resours: m. sourse: f. *Raised, recouered, got vp againe.*

Resouvenances: f. *Memorandums, remembrances.*

Resouvenir. *To be mindfull of, to remember againe.*

Respandement: m. *A spilling, shedding, powring out, scattering or casting abroad.*

Respandeur: m. *A shedder, a spiller.*

Respandre. *To shed, spill, powre out, scatter, or cast abroad.*

Respandu: m. uë: f. *Shed, spilt, powred out, scattered or cast abroad.*

Respardre. *To scatter againe.*

Respargnant: m. ante: f. *Sparing, pinching; warie, thriftie; miserable, hard, neere.*

Respargne: f. *A parcimonie, sparing, thrift, warinesse; neerenesse, hardnesse, miserie.*

De respargne. *Somewhat neerer, scanter, or shorter then needed.*

Respargner. *To spare, or saue.*

Respect: m. *Respect, regard, account; comparison, consideration.*

La Chaire de respect. *The Chaire of Estate.*

Respectable: com. *Respectable, regardable; worshipfull, of note, of accompt.*

Respectatif. *as* Respectif.

Respectif: m. iue: f. *Respectiue, heedie, warie, circumspect, aduised, discreet.*

Respectivement. *Respectiuely, mutually, interchangeably, on both sides, with regard had of one to another.*

Respessir. *To thicken againe.*

Respi: m. *A respite, a delay, a time, a pawsing, or breathing time, a tearme of forbearance or leisure; also (in Law) a Protection of one, three, or fiue yeares, graunted by the Prince, or Magistrate vnto a debtor, vpon great suit made, and cause appearing, for it; Looke* Respit.

Respir: m. *A breath, vent, respiration, blowing.*

Respiration: f. *A respiration, breathing, drawing of breath, venting, blowing.*

Respirement. *as* Respiration.

Respireur: m. *A breather, a respirer.*

Respirer. *To breath, vent, gaspe, take breath againe; also, to pawse, rest, or take his ease.*

Respit: m. *A respite; a delay, a time or terme of forbearance; a pawse, breathing fit; leisure &c; as* Respi.

Acceptation de respit; &, se mettre en ses respits. *Is meant (in some customes) of the feultie, or dutie of a vassall.*

Trois iours de respit vallent cent livres: Prov. *A three dayes respit's worth a hundred pounds.*

Respiter. *To respit; prorogue or put off for a time; to forbeare, to delay.*

Respiter de mort. *To repriue, saue, or deliuer, from death.*

Resplendeur: f. *Resplendencie, splendor, brightnesse; a cleere hue, shining glosse, radiant lustre.*

Resplendir. *To shine, glitter, glister, streame, blaze; to cast a radiant glosse, to yeeld a gallant, or great lustre.*

Resplendissant: m. ante: f. *Resplendent, shining, glistering, radiant, glittering.*

Resplendisseur. *as* Resplendeur.

Respoissir. *To thicken againe.*

Responce. *as* Reponce.

Respondant: m. *A Suretie.*

Respondement: m. *An answering; also, a matching, agreement, correspondencie; a likenesse, concurrence, equalitie.*

Respondre. *To answer; to resolue a doubt or demaund; to vndertake, or be suretie for; also, to match, agree, concurre, hold correspondencie with.*

Respondre par attenuation. C'est quand vn accusé respond aux conclusions contre luy prinses par sa partie civile, & par le Procureur du Roy, ou du seigneur Iusticier, lors qu'il est besoing prendre droict par la confession de l' accusé, laquelle auroit esté communiquée à la partie civile; Ce qui se fait quand le Cas n'est suiect à peine corporelle.

Reſpondre entre deux & az. *Looke* Az.

Qui mal entend, mal reſpond : Prov. *He that miſtakes the queſtion cannot ſpeake to purpoſe; he that conceiues amiſſe anſwers amiſſe.*

Reſpons: m. *The anſwers made by the Clarke, or people, in Seruice time.*

Reſponſadoux. *The ſea-fiſh called, a Heauen-gazer; (deſcribed in* Tapecon.)

Reſponſe: f. *An anſwer; the reſolution of a doubt, or demaund; alſo, a ſuretiſhip, or vndertaking for.*

Reſponſes: f. *Rampions (a ſallade root.)*

Reſponſif: m. *An Anſwer to a Law bill, or, an anſwer in Law.*

Reſponſif: m. iue: f. *Reſponſiue, anſwering, in anſwer, giuing, or making an anſwer.*

Reſponſion: f. *A Suretie, or Suretiſhip; an aſſurance.*

Reſpouſer. *To eſpouſe, or marrie againe.*

Reſſaper. *To repaire a wall, &c, that hath beene vndermined, or broken at the foot.*

Reſſaſié: m. ée: f. *Filled, glutted, ſaded, ſatiſfied.*

Reſſaſier. *To fill, glut, ſade, ſatiate, ſatiſfie.*

Reſſayer. *To reaſſay, reattempt, proue once more.*

Reſſeant: m. ante: f. *Reſiant, reſident; abiding, dwelling continually in.*

Exoine de mal reſſeant. *An eſſoine, or excuſe for the abſence, or not apparance, of one that lyes ſicke.*

Reſſeantiſe: f. *Reſidencie; a continuall dwelling, or abiding in one place.*

Reſſemblable: com. *Much like vnto.*

Reſſembler. *Looke* Reſembler.

Reſſemer. *To ſow againe.*

Reſſentiment: m. *A full taſt, a true feeling, a ſenſible apprehenſion, of.*

Se Reſſentir. *To taſt fully, feele throughly, haue a ſenſible apprehenſion of.*

Se reſſentir des faveurs de. *To be ſenſible of, or fare the better for, the fauors of.*

Se reſſentir d'une iniure. *To remember; to be ſenſible, or deſire a reuenge, of; to find himſelfe aggrieued at, a wrong.*

Il ſe reſſent encor de ſa grande perte. *His great loſſe hath hitherunto ſtucke by him; he ſmarts as yet, he is yet the poorer, by it.*

Reſſie: f. *An afternoones nunchion or drinking, an Aunders meat.*

Reſſimer. *as* Renifler.

Reſſiner. *To make a drinking or collation, to take a repaſt or ſnatch in the afternoone.*

Reſſize. *as* Reſize.

Reſſoigner. *To awe, feare, dread; alſo, to care, carke, take thought.*

Reſſoré: m. ée: f. *Parched, ſcorched, dryed, or burnt vp, by the Sunne.*

Reſſort: m. *The authoritie, prerogatiue, or iuriſdiction, of a (Soueraigne) Court; alſo, the extent, or circuit, of a countrey wherein it hath iuriſdiction, or whoſe inhabitants may repaire, or appeale vnto it; and thence;*

Droict de reſſort. *Abſolute power to take, and determine of, Appeales.*

En dernier reſſort. *Finally, fully, without further appeale, or ſcope left for any appeale.*

Reſſort de ſerrure. *The ſpring of a locke.*

Farce à pluſieurs reſſorts. *A Play wherein many ſeuerall matters are acted, or handled.*

Qui a le reſſort foible. *That wants erection.*

Reſſortir. *To iſſue, or goe forth againe; alſo, to moue of; be tryed by; reſort, recourſe, repaire, be referred, vnto for a full tryall; alſo, to goe directly from a lower to a higher, from a weaker to a ſtronger, from one to another; hence, to appeale vnto; and, to be remoueable, out of an inferior, into a ſuperior, Court.*

Ces choſes reſſortiſſent iugement par devant vn ſage. *Theſe matters are to be determined by a wiſe man.*

Reſſource: f. *A reſource, new ſpring, recouerie, vpriſing, or raiſing againe; alſo, refuge for ſuccour.*

En vieille beſte n'y a point de reſſource: Pro. *Looke* Beſte.

Reſſourdre. *as* Reſourdre.

Reſſuccer. *To ſucke vp, or in, againe.*

Reſſuit: m. itte: f. *Dry or dryed, hard or hardened; without any manner of ſap, or ſoftneſſe.*

Reſſuivre. *To follow againe.*

Reſſuy: m. *The leere of a Deere; the place wherein he lyes to dry himſelfe after he hath been wet by the deaw &c.*

Reſſuyé: m. ée: f. *Dryed, or wiped off, againe.*

Reſſuyer. *To wipe, or dry off, againe.*

Reſtablir. *To reeſtabliſh, reconfirme, ſettle anew in; alſo, to reſtore, giue backe, make good, or make ſatisfaction for, a thing taken.*

Reſtabliſſable: com. *Reeſtabliſhable.*

Reſtabliſſement: m. *A reeſtabliſhing, reconfirming; ſetling anew in; alſo, a reſtoring, giuing backe, making good, of, a ſatisfaction made for, a thing which hath beene taken.*

Reſtaigner. *as* Croupir; *(in the laſt ſence.)*

Reſtancher. *To ſtaunch, or quench, againe.*

Reſtat: m. *A remainder, ſurpluſage, ouerplus.*

Reſtats d'eſtat. *Looke* Eſtat.

Reſtaurant: m. *A reſtoratiue.*

Reſtaurer. *To reſtore, to renew, to repaire, to reinſtall.*

Reſte: f. *A reſt; reſidue, remnant, remainder, ſurpluſage, ouerplus; alſo, a Reſt at Primero, &c.*

A toute reſte. *Extreamely, vehemently, with all his force, out of all meaſure; alſo, whatſoeuer it coſt him; how much ſoeuer he hazard, or lay, on it.*

Faire ſa reſte à. *(In tearmes) to handle rudely, or deale roughly with; to giue a man a beating.*

Renvier de ſa reſte. *Looke* Renvier.

Voici, ou vous voyez, la reſte. *(In anſwer to, How haue you done a great while;) you ſee all that is left of me.*

Reſte. *Except, ſauing, beſide.*

Reſteindre. *To quench, or ſlake, againe.*

Reſtendre. *To reextend, or to reinlarge.*

Reſter. *To reſt, remaine, ſuperabound; be behind, ſuperfluous, ouerplus, or more then ynough.*

Le fol reſte apres la feſte: Pro. *After a feaſt, a foole, is made; wiſe men ſpend not their meanes in feaſting.*

Reſternuër. *To ſneeze againe.*

Reſtibule. Champ res. *as* Retouble.

Reſtif: m. iue: f. *Reſtie, ſtubborne, drawing backward, that will not goe forward.*

Chien reſtif. *A hound which ſeeing his game once hearded, purſues it no further, but ſtayes vntill he be beaten on.*

Reſtifvé: m. ée: f. *Looke* Reſtivé.

Reſtile. Champ reſtile. *Thats ſowed, or beares fruit, euerie yeare.*

Reſtipulation: f. *A waging of Law; a putting in of a a pledge, or gage for the aſſurance of his anſwer vnto an Action, &c.*

Reſtipuler. *To wage Law (as in* Reſtipulation.)

Reſtituer. *To reſtore, returne, render, yeeld or giue back; alſo, to repaire, ſet in his former eſtate or place, make whole againe.*

Restituteur: m. *A restorer; yeelder or bringer backe, repairer or setter vp againe.*
Restitution: f. *A restitution, rendring, yeelding or giuing backe; also, a restoring, repairing, setting vp againe.*
Restivé: m. ée: f. *Made or growne restie; forslowed, protracted; stopped or drawne backe.*
Restivement. *Restily, stubbornely, backwardly, slothfully.*
Restiver. *To stop, draw backe; struggle, be stubborne, play the restie iade.*
Ie ne restiveray point. *I will be forward ynough, I will not lag it, or be left behind.*
Il ne peut restiver au destin. *In vaine he striues against, or thinkes to withstand, his destinie.*
Restor: m. *A recouerie, or remedie against a Vouchee, or any one by whom a man is damnified.*
Restouble. *as* Retouble.
Restouper. *To stop againe.*
Restrainct: m. cte: f. *Restrained, abridged, or shortened of libertie, shut or kept vp, held or closed in.*
Fief restrainct. *A* Fief *that wants, or is not capable of Jurisdiction.*
Restraincte: f. *A restraint, restraining, shortening or abridging of libertie, holding or keeping in.*
Restrainctif: m. *A restrictiue, a stipticke, or binding medecine, or plaister; and particularly, the white of an egge beaten with Rose-water, and applied to preuent the swelling of a part which hath beene drie-beaten.*
Restraindre. *To restraine, straiten or bind in, abridge or shorten of libertie, shut or keepe vp, hold or close in.*
Restrangler. *To strangle againe.*
Restrecir. *To straiten, restraine, shorten, contract, abridge.*
Restrecissement: m. *A straitning, restraining, contracting, abridging.*
Restriction: f. *A restriction, moderation, modification; a restraint of a generalitie.*
Restriller vn cheval. *To currie him ouer againe.*
Restrinction. *as* Restriction.
Restringe. *The Lentiske, or Masticke tree; called so about* Montpellier.
Restudier. *To studie againe, or ouer againe.*
Restuver. *To stue; soake or bath in liquor, warme, againe.*
Restuyer. *To sheath, or shut vp, againe.*
Resvanouir. *To sowne againe.*
Resudant: m. ante: f. *Sweating; also, pithie.*
Resudation: f. *A resudation, sweating, or sweatie dropping.*
Resudé: m. ée: f. *Sweated, swet out of, come from as, or in, a sweat.*
Resuë: f. *An auncient tax, or imposition of foure pence in the pound for marchandise, and 10 s. Tour. vpon euerie Pipe of wine, brought into, or sent out of, the kingdome.*
Resveil: m. *A Hunts-vp, or Morning song for a new-maried wife, the day after the mariage.*
Resveilable: com. *Awakable.*
Resveillé: m. ée: f. *Awaked (in a morning;) rowsed, excited, stirred vp.*
Resveille-matin: m. *Th' Allarum of a watch, or clocke; also, the hearbe called Sunne-spurge, Time-tythimale, and Wartwort.*
Resveille-matin des vignes. *Pettie Spurge, called also Wartwort, and like, in leaues, vnto Sunne-Spurge.*
Beauté de femme fascheux resveille matin: Prov. *A womans beautie reaues (fond) man of rest.*
Resveiller. *To awake; raise from sleepe; rouse, excite, stirre vp.*
Resveiller le chat qui dort. *To rub a hidden sore; to kindle a fire that was neere quenched, stirre vp a mischiefe that was well setled; mention an euill that was almost forgotten.*
Tant dort le chat qu'il se resveille: Prov. *So long the cat sleepes that at length sh' awakes, (appliable to any thing which after long suppression bursteth out.)*
Resveilleur: m. *An awaker; and particularly, a common Bellman, which in the dead of night goes round about a Citie, tinkling, and telling of the houres.*
Resveillon: m. *A meale made late in the night, or long after supper.*
Resuër. *To sweat againe.*
Resver. *To raue, dote, speake idly, talke like an Asse.*
Resverie: f. *A rauing, idle talking, dotage, trifling, follie, vaine fancie, fond imagination.*
C'est resverie. *Tis a dreame, fable, mockerie, ieast, idle tale, which you deliuer.*
Resveur: m. *A dotard, or dreaming fop, a rauing, trifling, fond, or idle cokes.*
Resuivi: m. ie: f. *Followed againe.*
Resuivre. *To follow againe.*
Resul. *as* Reseul.
Resultat: m. *An issue, or successe; also, a resolution taken, or agreement made, vpon a conference, &c; the fruict, or that which comes, thereof.*
Resulter. *To rebound, or leape backe; to hop, skip, moue nimbly backward; also, to rise of, come out of, spring or issue from.*
Resumer. *To resume; to repeat, to take, or beginne againe.*
Resurgir. *To rise, grow, spring vp againe; to recouer a former being; to lift vp his head once more.*
Resurrection: f. *A resurrection, a rising againe.*
Resuscitatif: m. iue: f. *Resuscitatiue, reuiuing, raising vp from death to life.*
Resusciter. *To reuiue, raise, or set vp againe.*
Resusciteur: m. *A reuiuer, a raiser, or setter vp of things decayed, or dead.*
Ret: f. *A net; Looke* Rets.
Retail: m. *A shred, paring, or small peece cut from a thing; also, halfe an Oxgang, or Oxgate, of land.*
Retaillat. *Circumcised:* ¶Rab.
Retaillé: m. *A shred, paring, odde end, peece cut off; a Tailors vailes.*
Retaillé: m. ée: f. *Shred, pared, clipped, cut off.*
Retaillement: m. *A shredding, clipping, snipping, paring, often cutting.*
Retailler. *To shred, pare, clip, snip, cut verie often.*
Retailles. *as* Retailleures; *also, the spalls, or shards; the peeces which flie from stone in the hewing thereof.*
Retailleures: f. *Shreds, clippings, snippings, parings.*
Retaillons. *as* Retailleures.
Retaindre. *To put into a new colour, to re-die, or die againe.*
Retalionné: m. ée: f. *Requited, quitted, satisfied, or payed backe with the like.*
Retapper. *To bung againe.*
Retardé: m. ée: f. *Foreslowed, lingered, slackened, delayed; let, hindered, stopped, impeached, stayed.*
Retardement: m. *A foreslowing, slackening, delaying; impeaching, hindering, staying.*
Retarder. *To foreslow, linger, slacken, delay, stay, stop, let, hinder, impeach, put or hold off.*

Re-

Retargé: m.ée: f. *as* Retardé.
Retargement, & Retarger. *as* Retardement, & Retarder.
Retaster. *To tast againe.*
Retatiné: m. ée: f. *Withered, shrunke in, decayed, old.*
Retaxer. *To tax him that hath taxed vs, to returne one taxation for another.*
Reteinct: m. cte: f. *Died the second time, or died againe.*
Reteindre. *as* Retaindre.
Reteinture: f. *A re-dying, a second or new dying, a dying ouer againe.*
Retenail: m. *An hold, or thing to hold by.*
Retendre. *To stretch out againe.*
Retenеur: m. *A retainer, detainer, withholder.*
Retenir. *To retaine, withhold, stay, keep back; restraine, containe, bridle, hold in; also, to preserue, or maintaine.*
Retenir place pour voir. *To keepe, also, to take vp, a place to see in.*
Retenir par puissance de fief. *A Lord, by the priuiledge of his Seigniorie, to redeeme, or euict, from a purchaser the tenement bought of his vassall.*
Ie retiens apres. *I craue the next:* ¶Rab.
Retenter. *To reattempt, reassay, put vnto hazard againe.*
Retention: f. *A retention, detaining, withholding; a keeping in the hands.*
Retentir. *To resound, to ring againe, to yeeld an eccho, or great sound.*
Lieu ou la voix ne retentit pas. *A dull, dampe, or deafe, place.*
Retentissement: m. *A resounding, or a ringing againe, a rebounding of the voyce, an eccho-like returning of sound for sound.*
Retentissement de harnois. *The clashing of, or the sound yeelded by the slashing on, armour.*
Retentive: f. la ret. *The retaining force of nature whereby food is held in the stomacke vntill it bee fully concocted.*
Il n'a nulle retentive en la bouche. *He hath no hold of his tongue, he cannot forbeare speaking.*
Retentras. Il fait du ret. *He is deafe of that eare, or seemes to listen to somewhat else; or making as if hee had more to listen to, heedes not greatly what one sayes vnto him.*
Retentum. vn ret. in mente Curiæ. *Is when a Court pronounces not a full Arrest, but reserues somewhat to be afterwards ordered.*
Retenu: m. uë: f. *Retained, detained, withheld, stayed backe; restrained, kept in.*
Homme retenu. *A graue, sober, discreet, aduised, well stayed fellow; one whose wild oats are sowne.*
Retenuë: f. *as* Retention; *also, a retinew; also, discretion, staiednesse, aduisednesse; also, a grant in reuersion of an Office in the Kings house.*
Droict de retenuë. *A priuiledge of some Landlords, to redeeme within fortie dayes the land sold by their tenants, paying to the purchaser, besides his reasonable costs and charges, as much as he gaue for it.*
Linagier sur Linagier n'a point de retenuë. *One kinsman cannot recouer the land bought by another: (So that it seemes that neere kinsmen haue, in some cases, the benefit of* Droict de retenuë, *as well as Landlords in others.)*
Plaider par retenuë. (C'est quand les parties ne plaident à vne fois, & à toutes fins;) *To proceed but slackly, by pauses, or by halues.*
Retenuëment. *Sparingly, restrainedly; stayedly, aduisedly.*
Reths. *Looke* Rets.
Retiaire. *Casting a net in fight, therewith to take an enemie.*
Reticence: f. *Silence, concealement, counsell-keeping.*
Retien: m. *A retention; restraint, bridle, holding backe.*
Retier: m. *A Net-maker.*
Retiercement. *By way, or after the rate, of a third out of a third.*
Retiers: m. *A third part of a third, as of nine, three; of three, one.*
Retif. *Looke* Restif.
Retiforme: com. *Fashioned like a net.*
Retinacle: m. *A stay, or hold; any thing whereby another is retained or held backe.*
Retine: f. *The fist thinne membrane of the eye; soft, white, and a nourisher of the glassie humor.*
Retirade: f. *The retrait, or the retiring of an Armie; also, a place of retrait, or of retirall, for defendants behind a breach.*
Retiré: m. ée: f. *Retired, withdrawne, put or got back, pulld or drawne in; also, plucked or taken from; also, harboured, receiued, intertained; also, shot backe or againe.*
Retirée: f. *A retirall, withdrawing, recoyle.*
Retirement: m. *A retiring, withdrawing, recoyling, fetching or putting backe, pulling or gathering in; also, a drawing or comming neere; also, a pulling or plucking away from; also, a priuate harbouring, or receiuing (as of stealers, or of stollen things;) also, a shooting backe, or againe.*
Retirement des nerfs. *The shortening, or shrinking of the sinewes.*
Retirer. *To retire, withdraw; fetch or put backe, pull in, gather vp, recouer, bring or draw backe vnto; also, to shorten, contract, shrinke; also, to take, or plucke from; also, to receiue, harbour, intertaine; also, to shoot backe, or againe.*
Se retirer. *To recoyle, retire, giue backe; to shrinke; to withdraw himselfe.*
Retirer à. *To resemble, be like, or come neere vnto, in face, or fashion.*
Retirer ce qu'on donne. *To giue a thing and take a thing; to weare the diuells gold-ring (say we in a triuiall prouerbe.)*
Retirer son espingle du jeu. *To desist from, to quit, leaue off, giue ouer; to draw his necke out of the coller (say we.)*
Qu'on ne peut retirer. *An irreuocable, or vnrecouerable matter.*
Qui ne retire de sa vache que la queuë ne perd pas tout: Prov. *He that can recouer the least part of his owne, yet looses not all, or is not to neglect it; for better is something, how little soeuer, then nothing.*
Retisser. *To weaue againe.*
Retistre. *The same.*
Retoiser. *To fathome ouer againe.*
Retombe: f. *A false cup, wherein drinke falling into an odde corner, seemes to be drunke vp; also, a flat vault, or a roome thats made vault-wise.*
Retombée: f. *A falling backe; also, a crooking, as of a sickle turned backwards.*
Retombée de humeurs. *A running of humors; or a disease wherin the humors that grieued one place leaue it, and get into another.*

Re-

Retomber. *To fall backe or againe; to fall into a relapse.*
Retondir de toutes parts. *To ring, or to resound all ouer.*
Retondre. *To shaue, or sheere againe.*
Retondu: m. uë: f. *New shauen, clipped, shorne.*
Retorceure: f. *A twining, wreathing, twisting; a wrying, a wresting backe; a retorting.*
Retordement: m. *as* Retorceure.
Retordeur: m. *A twister, twiner; a wrester, a retorter, a wrier, backe.*
Retordre. *To twine, wreath, twist; retort; wrie, wrest backe.*
Retordure: f. *as* Retorceure.
Retorquable: com. *Retortable.*
Retorqué: m. ée: f. *Retorted, wrested backe, writhen backward.*
Retorquer. *To retort, writh backward, wrest backe, to returne violently, to throw or shoot againe.*
Retors: m. orse: f. *as* Retort.
Retort: m. orte: f. *Twisted, twined, wreathed; wrested, or wrung, backe; retorted, violently returned.*
Retorte: f. *A retort, or crooked bodie; a Lymbecke of glasse (varnished or leaded within) for th'extracting of oyle out of wood, and other hard, and drie substances.*
Retouble: m. *A field or ground sowne euerie yeare.*
Retouchement: m. *A second touch, a touching againe.*
Retoucher. *To touch againe.*
Retouiller. *To mingle, meddle, ruffle, puzzle, or confound againe.*
Retour: m. *A returne, returning, comming backe.*
Retour de Matines. *A displeasure done in secret & on a sudden; or the fittest time to surprise a priuate foe;* Looke Matines.
Fustaye qui est sur son retour. *That is some 200 yeres old.*
Avoir retour de. *To play quit, crie quittance, be euen with.*
Tout le retour qu'il en peut avoir. *All the helpe, remedie, or amends, which he can get for, or from.*
Baillez moy mon retour. *Said by such as, hauing paid more then was due, demaund the rest againe; & hence;*
Il me faut deux deniers de retour. *I must haue two pence backe againe.*
Il luy doit cela de retour. *He is beholden to him for that.*
A beau jeu beau retour: Pro. *Round worke, square play, as good returned as came, one good (or bad) turne for another.*
Retourné: m. ée: f. *Returned, come or gone, backe; also, restored.*
Retourner. *To returne, to come or goe backe; also, to restore; also, to giue bootie for a thing exchanged.*
Retourner au champ du bois. Looke Bois.
Retourner ses chasses. *A Hawke (that hath flowne out at her full pitch) to come in againe.*
Retourner à ses moutons. *To resume the subiect from which he hath digressed, to fall in hand with it againe.*
Retourner sa robbe. *To turne his gowne, or coat; to Pernize, or Apostatize it; to play the turne-coat.*
Retourner sur soy. Looke Soy.
Mais n'y retournez plus. *But doe so no more.*
Il n'est chance qui ne retourne: Prov. *All things that haue beene will be; no chance but comes againe.*
Il ne vas pas du tout à honte qui de demie voye retourne: Prov. Looke Honte.
Qui mieux ne peut à sa vieille retourne: Prov. *He that can get no yong, falls backe to his old, stuffe.*
Retracer. *To retrace, or trace backe; to turne often, and the selfesame way, vpon.*
Retracer son los. *Often to repeat his praises.*
Retractation: f. *A retractation; a recanting, reuoking.*
Retracter. *To recant, reuoke, or call backe; also, as* Retraicter.
Retraction: f. *as* Retractation; *also, a retraction; withdrawing; redeeming; also, the crampe.*
se Retrahir. *To retire, or withdraw, himselfe.*
Retraict: m. *An Aiax, Priuie, house of Office; also, a recouerie, redeeming, or drawing backe of things aliened, or ingaged.*
Retraict de barre, ou de Cour *(in the customes of Britanie)* Quand le Iuge du superieur ou de l'inferieur veut cognoistre du delict, ou different: ¶Ragueau.
Retraict censuel, & feodal. *The power a Lord* Censuel, *and* Feodal *haue, to redeeme, euict, or draw backe from a Purchaser th'estates gotten by him of their vassalls.*
Retraict conventionnel. *A couenant, or prouiso in a bargaine, giuing the seller libertie to redeeme the thing he passed (therein resembling our Morgage.)*
Retraict du gobelet. *The Butterie.*
Retraict Lignagier. *A power, giuen by custome vnto the neerest kinsman of one that sells land, to rebuy it within a certaine time (commonly a yeare and a day) for as much as was payed for it; but this must be a kinsman of the stocke, or side, by which the land came to the seller.*
En retraict. *Priuately, retiredly, alone.*
Retraict: m. cte: f. *Retired, withdrawne; drawne backe; straitned, growne narrower, shrunke vp.*
Retraicte: f. *A retrait, retiring, withdrawing; a drawing backe, a returning; also, a place of refuge, of succour, of safegard; also, a straitning, narrowing, or shrinking vp.*
Droict de retraicte. *The power of redeeming, or of buying, land morgaged, ingaged, or sold.*
Retraicter. *To reuise, peruse, ouerlooke, ouersee, runne ouer; also, to handle, repeat, or intreat of, againe.*
Retrainer. *To drag, or draw, backe.*
Retraintif: m. Looke Restrainctif.
Retraire. *To withdraw; draw backe; plucke out or vnto; also, to shrinke, narrow, straiten, draw in; also, to vpbraid, or twit in the teeth.*
Retraire en servage. *To challenge, or auerre, one to be his slaue.*
Retrait: m. aitte: f. *as* Retraict.
Retraitte: f. *as* Retraicte.
Retranchement: m. *An abridgement; abatement; cutting off part of.*
Retrancher. *as* Retrencher.
Retransitif: m. iue: f. *Retransitiue, reflectiue vpon it selfe.*
Retrasser. *as* Retraicter; *also, to amend, correct, reforme, repaire.*
Retrayable: com. *Which may be fetched, or drawne, backe.*
Retrayeur: m. *A redeemer, a fetcher or drawer back of.*
Retrecir. *To straiten, contract, narrow, bind or make strait.*
Retrecissement: m. *A straitning, narrowing, contracting, shortening.*

Retrempé: m. ée: f. *Soaked, or steeped, againe.*
Retremper. *To soake, steepe, or soften in liquor, anew.*
Retrenché: m. ée: f. *Cut, strucke, or chopped, off; diminished, curtalled, lessened, abridged; also, intrenched; inuironed or defended with trenches; lodged in trenches.*
Retrencher. *To cut, strike, or chop, off; to curtall, diminish, lessen, abridge; also, to intrench; to inuiron with, or lodge in, trenches.*
Retresci: m. ie: f. *Straitned.*
Retrescissement. *as* Retrecissement.
Retribuer. *To retribute, restore, yeeld or giue, backe; also, to requite, recompence, reward.*
Retribution: f. *A retribution, requitall, recompence, recompencing, restoring.*
Retroacte. *A former act, proceeding, or dispatch, in Law.*
Retroactif: m. iue: f. *Retroactiue; casting, driuing, relating, backward.*
Retroceder. *To recoyle, retire, giue backe.*
Retrogradation: f. *A retrogradation; a stepping, or going, backe.*
Retrograde: f. *The same; or a step backe.*
Retrograder. *To recoyle, returne, retire, step, or goe, backe.*
Retrouër. *To make new holes into; to pierce, or bore, againe.*
Retroussé: m. ée: f. *Thicke and short, druggellie, trunchion; well trussed, strongly made; also, trussed or tucked vp.*
Oeil retroussé. *A staring eye; an eye, whose lids bee reuersed by some great inflamation; and whose white becomes higher then th'apple.*
Retrousser. *To trusse, or tucke vp.*
Retrouvé: m. ée: f. *Found againe.*
Retrouver. *To find againe.*
Rets: f. *A net.*
Rets admirable. *A certaine narrow skin in the head (made of a part of th'Arterie* Carotide*) which disposes it selfe into the forme of a net, neere to the hole, or passage of the third paire of sinewes; This net is hardly found in a mans head.*
Rets d'aulx. *A little bundle, or double rope of Garlick heads tied together with their leaues.*
Retube: f. *A flat vault, or vault make like the backe of an ouen.*
Retumbée: f. *Looke* Retombée.
Reu: m. *A brooke, small streame, little gullet of water.*
Revanquir. *To reuanquish, resubdue, reouercome.*
Revalider. *To reinforce, improue, raise, or better, the value of.*
Revaloir. Ie te le revaudray. *I will requite, repay, it; or, be as much worth vnto thee as it comes to.*
Revancher. *as* Revencher.
Revangeur: m. *A reuenger.*
Revangeur: m. eure: f. *Reuenging, wreaking.*
Revanner. *To winnow againe.*
Reubarbe: f. *The root called Rewbarb, or Rewbarb of the Leuant; See* Rheubarbe.
Reubarbe des Iardins. *Garden Rewbarb; resembles that of the Leuant, and purges choller, but not so effectually as it.*
Reubarbe des moines. *Hearbe Patience, Monkes Rewbarbe.*
Reve-grand. *(An ironicall illusion to,* Reverend*) much doting.*
Reveille-matin. *as* Resveille-matin.

Reveiller. *Seeke* Resveiller.
Revelation: f. *A reuelation, a reuealing.*
Revelé: m. ée: f. *Reuealed, disclosed, vttered, discouered, manifested.*
Revelement: m. *A reuealing, disclosing, discouering.*
Reveler. *To reueale, disclose, discouer, manifest, vtter.*
Reveleux: m. euse: f. *Wanton, lasciuious, incontinent; shamelesse, impudent, vnrulie, outragious.*
Revenant: m. ante: f. *Returning, reuerting; reuiuing; increasing, rising; comming againe.*
Bois revenant. *Copses or Coppies, young woods.*
Revenche: f. *Reuenge; requitall; returne of as good, or as much as was brought.*
Revencher, soy reven. *To wreake, or to reuenge, himselfe; to returne, or to retort, a displeasure.*
Revendage: m. *A retailing, or selling againe.*
Fermier du revendage du Roy. Entre les mains duquel vn debteur met biens meubles exploictables pour la somme deuë, à fin d'avoir trois semaines de terme pour payer son creancier, & à fin d'avoir main levée de ses biens prins par le sergēt.
Revenderesse: f. *A woman buckster, or bagler.*
Revendeur: m. *A Huckster, a Regrator.*
Revendication: f. *A resuming of, or a reestablishment in, a pretended right.*
Revendre. *To sell againe.*
'A trop acheter n'y a que revendre: Prov. *There's nothing gotten by wares ouer-bought; nor does any man take much ioy in that, which to get hee tooke too much paines.*
Revendu: m. uë: f. *Sold backe, or againe.*
Revengé: m. ée: f. *Reuenged, wreaked.*
Revenir. *To reuert, returne, come backe, or againe; also, to reuiue, or come to himselfe after a trance; also, to swell, rise, or increase, as dough by leauening, or flesh by parboyling; also, to profit, benefit, or yeeld increase; also, to resemble; also, to fit, sute, or agree well with.*
Se revenir. *To come to himselfe againe after a great anger, feare, amazement, or swooning; to recouer, picke vp his crummes, grow well, wax whole, againe.*
Cela me revient bien. *I haue a good conceit thereof, I like it passing well.*
Cela me revient bien au coeur. *It goes to the heart of me; it vexeth, or fretteth me at the verie heart.*
Cela me revient tousiours au ronge. *The same; or, I shall neuer forget it; it will alwayes runne in my mind.*
Il nous revient infinement. *It benefits vs exceedingly.*
Il s'en renvient le mieux qu'il peut. *Hee makes as good shift with, or vse of, it as he can.*
Souvent ils s'en revenoyent, & se mutinoyent. *They turned backe vpon it; they grew sencible of, or into choller vpon, it; or, that made them after fall into mutinie.*
Viande qui revient à la bouche. *Meat that leaues in the mouth an ill tast behind it, or sends it vp thereinto, after it is eaten.*
Reventes. *as* Venterolles; *or, as* Reventons.
Reventons. *A fee due to a Lord* Censuel *(ouer and besides the* Lods, *and* Ventes*) from a purchaser, of land charged with* Cens, *who hath undertaken to discharge the seller of the* Lods *which he for his part, should vpon the bargaine haue paied.*
Revenu: m. *Reuenew; yearelie rents, profits, or incommings.*
Revenu: m. uë: f. *Reuerted, returned, come backe, or againe; also, reuiued, well recouered, or come againe to*

to himselfe; also, swollen, or pufst vp againe.
Revenu de queuë. *Whose taile is new growne (appliable to an old cokes, or callet, growne wanton on a sudden; or to any one which after a great weakenesse hath picked vp his crummes, or is become lustie againe.)*
O que c'est vn homme qui m'est tousiours fort revenu. *Oh how pleasing that mans companie, or conuersation, hath euer beene vnto me.*
Revenuë: f. *Reuenew, rent, &c*; *as* Revenu; *also, a returne, returning, reuerting, or comming againe.*
Revenuë de bois. *The new springing, or putting out of wood after it hath beene lopped, or felled.*
Reveoir. *Looke* Revoir.
Reverable: com. *Reuerend, fit to be reuerenced.*
Reverberation: f. *A reuerberation, reflex, reflection; a repercussion, striking or beating backe.*
Reverberatoire: m. *A reuerberatorie; part of a Lymbecke.*
Reverberé: m. ée: f. *Reuerberated, beaten backe, reflected.*
Reverberer. *To reuerberate, reflect, beat or strike back againe.*
Reverdir. *To flourish, or wax greene, againe.*
Il l'y planta pour reverdir. *He left him in that place without resolution, meanes, or knowledge, to get out of it; also, he ratled him vp with short and sharpe tearms, and suddenly left him to pause on them while, or thinke of them what he listed.*
Reveremment. *Reuerently, with reuerence.*
Reverence: f. *Reuerence, awfull obseruance, worship, honour.*
Reverence papale. *The homage done, or subiection acknowledged, by a Prince vnto a new-elected Pope.*
Reverence Turquesque. *A nod.*
Faire la reverence à. *To arise, giue place, make courtesie, vaile bonnet, vnto; to solicite with cap and knee.*
Reverencer. *To reuerence, respect with an awfull obseruance, worship, honour, adore.*
Reverend: m. ende: f. *Reuerend, venerable, worshipfull, honourable, sacred, graue; also, most respectfull of, or, dutifull vnto.*
Reverender. *as* Reverencer.
Reverential: m. ale: f. *Reuerent, full of reuerence.*
Reverer. *To reuerence, worship, adore.*
Reverifier. *To reuerifie, reconfirme, reapproue, make good againe.*
Reverni: m. ie: f. *as* Verni; *or new glazed ouer.*
Revers: m. *A back blow, clap, stroke, wherrit; or a blow with the backe of a hand, or sword.*
Les revers de fortune. *The crosses of fortune.*
Revers de gouvernail. *The backe of a Rudder.*
Revers de Guysard. ce ne sont pas les revers de Guysard (qui estoyent sans retour.) *These are no such deepe questions, or hard matters; they may be resolued, or answered, well ynough.*
'A revers. *Backward, arsiuarsie, inside outward, vpside downeward, crosse, cleane kamme.*
Revers: m. erse: f. *Strange, vncoth; crosse, harsh.*
Reversailles: f. *The reuersions of, or drinke left in, the Maisters glasses, or draughts, powred together into a pot for the seruants.*
Reuersche. *as* Revesche.
Reverser. *To powre backe, or powre out againe.*
Reversi: m. *A kind of Trumpe (played backward, and full of sport) which the Duke of Savoy brought some ten yeares agoe into France.*
Reversion: f. *A reuerting, returning, or comming back; also, a Reuersion in Law.*
Droict de reversion. *Looke* Droict.
Reversure: f. *The waining, or turning at the top of a land, where one furrow ends, and another begins.*
Reversures. *as* Reversailles.
Revertir. *To reuert, returne, come backe.*
Revertir en quelque lieu, ou avec quelqu'un. *To haunt, frequent, repaire often vnto; to conuerse, accompanie, consort much with.*
Revesche: f. *Course Bayes; Cotton or Frize for lynings.*
Revesche: com. *Harsh, churlish, rude, vntractable, froward; wild, sauage, hagard, vnrulie, fierce.*
Vin revesche. *Hard, sower, tart, vnpleasant wine.*
Reveschérie: f. *Harshnesse, rudenesse, churlishnesse, frowardnesse; wildnesse, sauagenesse, fiercenesse, vnrulinesse.*
Revest: m. *A reinuestment, reinuesture.*
Revestement: m. *An vpper garment, robe, or vestment; also, a reinuesting, reattiring, new-clothing; also, a clothing, attiring, putting on, couering ouer with.*
Revestement de muraille. Ces arbres sont commodes à faire des Lambrunchemens, ou revestemens de murailles. *Are fit, or good to seele, or boord walls withall.*
Revestiaire. *as* Revestiere.
Revestiere: m. *A Vestrie in a Church.*
Revestir. *To reinuest, reattire, cloth or apparell againe; also, to put vpon, or couer ouer with, a garment; to put on an vpper garment; to put garment vpon garment, or one garment ouer another.*
Revestir de quelque terre. *To giue, or put into, possession, to make liuerie and seisin of a peece of ground.*
Revestissement: m. *A reinuestment, or a reinuesting; also, a mutuall, and equall gift made, and passed by publicke Act, betweene two that are ioyned, or allied, by mariage.*
Revestu: m. uë: f. *Reuested, reinuested; inuested; clothed, attired, apparelled, againe; also, clothed or couered all ouer with, wrapped round about in.*
Paon revestu. *A Peacocke flayed, parboyled, larded, and stucke thicke with Cloues; then roasted with his feet wrapped vp to keepe them from scorching; then couered againe with his owne skinne as soone as he is cold, and so vnderpropped that, as aliue, hee seemes to stand on his legs: In this equipage a gallant, and daintie seruice.*
Reveuë: f. *A reuiew, reuiewing, suruey, surueying, ouerlooking; also, a Muster, or the mustering, of an Armie.*
Revifier. *To reuiue, returne vnto life, quicken againe.*
Revigourant. *Adding more strength, giuing more vigour, vnto.*
Revigourer. *To reuigorate, reinforce, adde new vigor, giue new strength, vnto.*
Revirade: f. *A wheeling, or round turne; a backe iert, whirle, whiske, blow, or thrust.*
Revirer. *To whirle often about, to turne againe and againe.*
Se revirer contre son ennimi. *Againe to turne back, or wheele about, vpon an enemie.*
Reviseur: m. *A reuisor, or reuewer.*
Revision: f. *A reuision, reuise, reuiew, reexamination, looking ouer againe.*
Revisit: m. *A reuiew taken by the King of his Officers accounts.*
Revisitation: f. *A reuisitation; or as* Revisitement.
Revisitement: m. *A reuising, reuiewing, recognizing, ouerseeing, ouerlooking againe.*

Revisiter. *To reuise, reuiew; reuisite, recognize; ouerlooke, ouersee, suruey, againe.*
Revisiteur: m. *A reuisor, reuiewer, reuisitor, ouerlooker, ouerseer.*
Revivisienne: f. *A reuiuing, a returning vnto life.*
Revivre: m. *A later math, or crop.*
Revivre. *To reuiue, recouer breath, returne vnto life; to be renewed; to spring or grow vp againe.*
Reume. *The rhewme.*
Reüni: m. ie: f. *Reunited, reioyned, reconciled.*
Reünion: f. *A reunion, reunitement, reconcilement; a new league or coniunction.*
Reünir. *To reunite, reioyne, reconcile, attone.*
Revocable: com. *Reuokable, which may be recalled.*
Office revocable ad nutum. *An Office granted during pleasure.*
Revocation: f. *A reuocation, a reuoking; a countermaund, recalling, recantation.*
Revoguer. *To saile backe, or againe.*
Revoir. *To reuiew, recognize, reexamine; ouerlooke, or ouersee, againe.*
Revol: m. *A flying backe, a returne vpon the wing.*
Revoler. *To flie backe, to returne flying.*
Revolte: f. *A reuolt, a rebellion.*
Revolté: m. ée: f. *Reuolted, rebelled, fallen from; also, returned, or which hath made a new turne.*
Revoltement: m. *A reuolting, rebelling; a quitting, leauing, or falling from; also, a returning.*
Revolter. *To reuolt; rebell; fall, slip, turne, or goe from, leaue, quit, abandon, forsake; also, to returne, or make a new turne.*
Revolu: m. uë: f. *Reuolued; rounded or turned wholly, passed or gone fully about.*
L'an revolu. *The yeare fully ended, runne about.*
Revoluble: com. *Reuoluble, reuoluable; fit or apt to be turned about.*
Revolution: f. *A reuolution; a full compassing, rounding, turning backe to it first place, or point; th'accomplishment of a circular course.*
Revomir. *To vomit againe.*
Revoqué: m. ée: f. *Reuoked, recalled, countermaunded.*
Revoquer. *To reuoke, recall, countermaund, alter, make void.*
Reupe: f. *The dropping of the nose; also, a belch.*
Reupontic: m. *as* Rheupontique.
Reuppe: f. *as* Reupe.
Reupper. *To belch.*
Reüssir. *To issue, rise, or spring out; to succeed, or come vnto good or euill.*
Revulsion: f. *A revulsion, a pulling vp, or plucking away; also, the drawing, or forcing of humors from one part of the bodie into another.*
Reystre. *Looke* Reistre.
Rez: m. *A flat, plaine, leuell ground, floore, bottome; the superficies, or vpper face of a plaine, or leuell peece of ground.*
Rez de chaussée. *The same; or a foundation, bottome, ground; whence;* L'estage de rez de chaussée. *The lowest storie, the storie next to the ground; and,* Le mur est à rez de chaussée. *The foot of the wall stands leuell with the ground thats about it.*
Rez à rez. &, Rez de rez. *Euen or leuell with, close vnto.*
Mettre rez pied rez terre. *To rase, cast or beat downe, lay flat vnto, make euen with, the ground.*
Rez. *Those that are shauen, powled neere, cut close.*
Il ne craint ny les rez ny les tondus. *He is a surlie, rash, or arrogant fellow; he respects no man, cares for no bodie, feares neither one nor other; (from a familie in* Troyes *bearing the surname of* Rez, *and so great in authoritie and means, as it was an ordinarie threat in that towne, to say,* Ie le diray, ou feray sçavoir, aux Rez; *wherwith a good fellow being oftentimes vrged, came out at length with these words;* Ie n'ay que faire des rez, ny des tondus; *alluding to the signification of* rez, *wherewith* Tondus *almost synonymizeth.)*
Rezueil: m. *Networke for the haire; or, a Cawle of networke.*
Rhabarbe: m. *Rewbarb.*
Rhabiller. *as* Rabiller.
Rhabituer. *To reaccustome, reinure.*
Rhagade: f. *A chap, or chawne, comming by cold, &c, in any part of the bodie, but especially in the fundament.*
Rhagadie. *The same.*
Rhainindique. *Th'excellent Indian root called otherwise* Mechoacan.
Rhamne. *The fruitfull white Bramble called Ramme, or Christs thorne.*
Rhapontique. *The least, and worst kind of Rewbarbe, growing in* Pontus.
Rhatimburgs: m. *Select, or expresse Iudges for the decision of all cases that fell within the compasse of the Salick Law.*
Rheteur: m. *A Rhetorician.*
Rhetorique: f. *Rhetoricke; the Art of Eloquence.*
Rhetorique: com. *Rhetoricall, of Rhetoricke; eloquent; whence;* Couleurs Rhetoriques. *Looke vnder* Couleur.
Rhetoriquement. *Rhetorically; eloquently; Rhetorician-like.*
Rhetoriquer. *To Rhetorize it, play the Rhetorician, speake eloquently, argue neatly, plead finely.*
Rhetoriser. *The same.*
Rheubarbe: f. *Rewbarb; and (more particularly) the best and second kinds thereof, brought out of* China, *and out of Barbarie: See* Reubarbe.
Rheume: f. *A rheume, catharre, pose, murre.*
Rheupontique: f. *The worst and least kind of Rewbarbe; growing in* Pontus; *also, the root of great Centorie, called so in diuers Apothecaries shops, but erroniously.*
Rhodais. *The name of a good towne in* Languedoc.
Elle est de Rhodais. *She hath her flowers.*
Rhomb: m. *A Turbot:* ¶Langued.
Rhombe: m. *A spinning wheele, reele, whirle, or turne; also, a figure that hath equall sides, and vnequall angles; as a quarrie of glasse, &c.*
Rhombe girante. *A whirligig, or Top.*
Rhomboïde: f. *A figure hauing vnequall sides, and angles.*
Muscle rhomboïde. *A muskle which drawes backward the shoulder blade.*
Rhon. *as* Rhomb; *also, the shrub Sumacke, Curriers Sumacke, leather Sumacke.*
Rhonboïde. *Almost foure-square; or as* Rhomboïde.
Rhupontique. *as* Rheupontique.
Rhus. *The shrub called Sumacke.*
Riagas. *The poison* Aconitum.
Riant: m. ante: f. *Laughing, geering, fleering.*
Dents riantes. *The foure fore-teeth; so called because in laughing they are commonly discouered.*
Mordre en riant. *Looke* Mordre.
Riard: m. arde: f. *as* Riant; *or continually laughing.*
Ribaine. Ribon ribaine. *Looke* Ribon.

Ribaud,& Ribaude. *as* Ribauld,& Ribaulde.

Ribaudaille: f. *A ruffianlie crue, a roguish companie.*

Ribaudequin: m. *A fashion of huge crossebow (some fourteene or fifteene foot in length) that shot a long arrow feathered with horne, or thinne wood, & is at this day out of vse.*

Ribauderin. *The same.*

Ribaudine: f. *as* Ribaulde; *or, a rascallie queane.*

Ribauld: m. *A rogue, ruffian, rascall, scoundrell, varlet, filthie fellow; also, a ribauld, fornicator, whoremunger, bawdie-house haunter; also, a base fellow, or labouring man, of a big bodie, strong limmes, and hard constitution, a tough whoresonne.*

Le ribauld d'une grappe. *The staulke of a cluster of grapes.*

Roy des ribaulds. *An Officer which, in old time, looked to the vagabonds, & idle persons that haunted the Court; and searched any that came in, to see they had no Armes, or hidden weapons about them; and towards night visited all the chambers in the house, to preuent secret massacres; and thrust out at doores at meale, and bed-time, such as had not their diet, and lodging allowed them; and punished all disorders committed, by the followers of the Court, without the Court gate: This Officer had a gard of Archers attending on him, and a Lieutenant, called* Prevost des ribauds: *In Charles the sixts time the name (too neere a King) was suppressed, and, as some thinke, altered into* Prevost de l'hostel, *of late yeares become,* le grand Prevost de France, & de l'hostel du Roy; *which title Charles the ninth added for more authoritie vnto the Office.*

Ribaulde: f. *A whore, queane, punke, gill, flirt, common hackney, doxie, mort.*

Ribaulder. *To play the ribauld, ruffian, rogue.*

Ribauldise: f. *Ribauldrie, roguerie, ruffianisme, whoring, whore-hunting.*

Ribault. *as* Ribauld.

Ribe: f. *A coast, &c; as* Rive: ¶Langued.

Ribe taillade. *See* Taillade.

Ribes: f. *Red Gooseberries, beyond-sea Gooseberries, garden Currans, bastard Currans.*

Rob de ribes. *Looke* Rob.

Ribettes. *as* Ribes.

Ribier: m. *The red Gooseberrie plant; also, a kind of vine.*

Riblant. *Roauing, ietting, raking, swaggering abroad with weapons to the spoyle, or despoyling, of euerie one he meets.*

Ribler. *To roue, roame, rake, or iet abroad weaponed, and wronging euerie one; to boot-hale, rob, ransacke, prey vpon passengers, or poore countrey people.*

Riblerie: f. *A rouing, ietting, roaming, swaggering; a gadding abroad in armour, to the wronging, ransacking, robbing of passengers, or poore countrey people; a boot-haling; also, a violent course or incursion vpon an enemie.*

Riblette: f. *A collop, or slice of bacon.*

Des oeufs à la riblette. *Egges and collops; or, an Omelet or Pancake of egges, and slices of bacon mingled, and fried together.*

Ribleur: m. *A disorderlie roauer, ietter, swaggerer, outragious reakes-player; a robber, ransacker, boot-haler, preyer vpon passengers, &c.*

Ribon ribaine. *By hooke or crooke, will ye nill ye, whether you will or no.*

Ric à ric. *Quite, wholly, throughly; extreamely; exactly, precisely, in euerie point.*

Ricalde: f. *A gill, flirt, callet; scould; a long-tongued and short-heeled, a light and tatling huswife.*

Ricanant. *Tighying, sporting, dallying, wantonizing it.*

Ricaner. *To giggle, tighie, dallie, wantonize it.*

Ricaneux: m. euse: f. *Tighying, giggling, euer sporting, dallying, or playing the wanton.*

Ricasser. *To giggle, fleere, laugh with a tighie, play the wanton egregiously.*

Richard: m. *Richard; also, the bird called a Jay.*

Fer de richard. *A kind of great yron wire.*

Riche: com. *Rich, wealthie, opulent, well lined, of great meanes, that hath much to take to.*

Riche comme vn ladre. *As rich as a Lazer (who is tearmed rich, either because he gets few children; or because few come to eat on him.)*

'A riche homme n'en chaut qui ami luy soit: Pro. *A rich carle no mans loue respects; or doth not care though no man loue him.*

Homme chiche iamais riche: Prov. *The niggard's nere (in his opinion) rich.*

Il est riche que Dieu aime: Prov. *Rich is the man whom God affects.*

Le plus riche n'emporte qu'un linceul: Pro. *Seeke* Linceul.

La vache du riche velle souvent, celle du povre avorte: Prov. *The rich mans cow is fruitfull, fat, and strong, the poore mans (leane, and ill kept) casts her young.*

Pour devenir bien tost riche il faut tourner le dos à Dieu: Prov. *He that will soone grow rich must God renounce.*

Qui bien gaigne, & bien espargne devient tantost riche: Pro. *He that gets, and spares much, will quickly be rich.*

Richement. *Richly, wealthily, opulently, abundantly.*

Richement mentir. *To lie for the whetstone, or with the best of them.*

Richereau: m. *A wealthie chuffe, rich lobcocke, well-lined boore; one that hath more wealth then wit, more substance then ciuilitie.*

Richesse: f. *Riches, wealth, great substance, meanes, possessions, treasure, fortunes.*

Enfans sont richesses de povres gens. *Store of children is all the wealth poore men can brag of; (yet is that brag but idle if they be idle; Seeke* Enfant.)

Ou richessé est peché est: Prov. *Where riches are sinne is.*

Ricochet. *The sport of skimming a thinne stone on the water, called a Ducke and a Drake.*

C'est la chanson du ricochet. *Tis an idle, or endlesse tale, or song; a subiect whereof one part contradicts, marres, or ouerthrowes, another.*

Ricote: f. *A kind of milke-meat; or as;*

Ricottes: f. *Curds made of whey.*

Ridde: f. *A Flemmish coyne worth about* 5 s. sterl.

Ridde de Gueldres. *Is worth about* 3 s. sterl.

Ridé: m. ée: f. *Wrinkled, wrimpled, crumpled, frumpled, in furrowes like an angrie brow; also, stiffened, or stretched out vnto a stiffenesse.*

Rideau: m. *A curtaine, or cloth-skreene.*

Ridelle: f. *The rayle of a Cart or waine; and more particularly, the vppermost of the three; the middle one being tearmed* fausse ridelle; *and the lowest,* Gisant.

Ridement: m. *A wrinkling, wrimpling, crumpling; also, a stiffening, or stretching out.*

Rider. *To wrinkle, or to wrimple; also (among Mariners) to stiffen, or stretch out vnto a stiffenesse.*
Se rider. *To frowne, lowre, scoule, looke sterne, furrow or wrinkle the forhead, knit the browes.*
Rides: f. *Wrinkles, or furrowes on the face of an old, or angrie person; also, crumples, wrimples; foulds, plaites.*
Ridicule: com. *Ridiculous, vaine, fond, worthie to be laughed at.*
Ridiculement. *Ridiculously, vainely, foolishly.*
Rié: m. *as* Rie.
Rie: f. *A wast; an vntilled or vnhusbanded peece of ground.*
Riéble: m. *Cleauer, Clauer, Goose-share, Loue-man, Goose-grasse.*
Rien. *(without the companie of a Negatiue, signifies as the Latine Res) a matter, thing, some thing, any thing, ought; (but with one either expressed, or vnderstood, signifies) nought, nothing, no whit, not a iot.*
Rien rien. *No no, neither so nor so.*
Ce n'est plus rien que de moy. *I am as good as nothing, or, I am vtterly vndone.*
Elle le haït sur tout rien. *She hates him extreamely, aboue all things, more then she hates all the world besides.*
Encores s'il m'eust donné quelque rien. *Yet, had he giuen me any thing, or neuer so little.*
Me voulez vous rien mander. *Looke* Mander.
Rien n'a qu'assez n'a: Prov. *He nothing hath who (thinkes he) hath not ynough; or, as good haue nothing as not haue ynough.*
Rien n'est bien faict que ce que Dieu parfaict: Prov. &, Rien ne faict qui ne parfaict; *Looke* Parfaire.
Rien n'est si caché qui ne se trouve: Prov. *The closest kept things are at length found out.*
Rien ne peut estre grand qui n'a bon fondement: Prov. *The thing cannot be great that hath no good foundation.*
Rien ne vaut l'assaillant s'il n'est fort, & vaillant: Prov. *In vaine he playes th'assailant who is not strong, and valiant.*
Rien ne vaut la chose sinon ce qu'on la fait valoir: Prov. *Euerie thing is as it is taken; or, conceit sets rates vpon all earthlie things.*
Rien sans peine: Prov. *Looke* Peine.
Aujourd'huy roy demain rien: Prov. *To day a King to morrow (as good as) nothing.*
On ne fait de rien grasse porrée: Prov. *Fat broth cannot without some stuffe be made.*
Qui rien ne porte rien ne luy chet: Prov. *He that beares nothing letteth nothing fall.*
Qui n'a patience n'a rien: Prov. *Looke* Patience.
Qui n'a santé n'a rien: Prov. *He that wants health wants all things.*
Qui n'a suffisance il n'a rien: Pro. *Look* Suffisance.
Qui ne sçait rien de rien ne doubte: Prov. *He that knowes nought of nothing doubts.*
Rien-ne-vaut. *A scoundrell, scumme, rascall; base or worthlesse fellow.*
Riens. *as* Rien. (v m.)
Riere. *Backward, behind; also, with or among; whence;*
Ils ont esté captifs riere les Espagnols. *Among the Spaniards, or in Spaine.*
Riereban. *as* Arriereban.
Rierefief. *A Fief held of a mesne Lord; also, a rent seck, or charge, granted by a vassall out of his* Fief.
Riere-filz: m. *A grand-child.*
Riere-vassal: m. *An vnder vassall, a vassall vnto a vassall.*
Riets. *as* Rie.
Riu: m. *A little brooke, a reyne, or gullet of water.*
Rieulle. *as* Ruille.
Rieur: m. *A laugher.*
Rif: m. *as* Rieu.
Il ne luy lairra rif ny raf. *He will strip, reaue, or depriue, him of all.*
Rifage: f. *A Sowre, lowring, powting, scouling, frowning housewife.*
Rifflarde: f. *A rauenous, or a rifling drab; one that loues, or liues by, the spoyle of them she conuerses with.*
Rifflandouille. *A bellie-god, spoyler of chitterlings, louer of good cheere.*
Rifle: f. *Fire:* ¶Barrag. *whence;*
On n'y a laissé ne rifle, ne rafle. *They haue swept all away; they haue left no manner of thing behind them.*
Rifler. *To rifle, ransacke, spoyle, make hauocke or cleane worke, sweepe all away before him; also, to rauine, or eat greedily.*
Rigalisse: f. *Lickorice.*
Rigalisse fertile. *Common Lickorice.*
Rigalisse sterile. *Barren Lickorice, Hedge-hog Lickorice.*
Rigaud: m. aude: f. *whence;* `A jambes rigaudes. C'est à la renverse, & les jambes en haut; *or, With stradling, and vp-stretcht legs.*
Rigle; & Riglet. *as* Reigle; & Reiglet. (v.m.)
Riglisse: f. *Lickorice.*
Rigolage: m. *A mocking, ieasting, or laughing at.*
Rigolement: m. *as* Rigolage.
se Rigoler de. *To mocke, ieast, laugh at, make himselfe merrie or play the wanton with.*
Se rigoler au soleil. *To sport, solace, or ioyfully to bleake, or spread himselfe in the Sunne, taking a sensuall or wanton felicitie in it.*
Rigolerie: f. *as* Rigolage.
Rigoleur: m. *A common mocker of, or ieaster at; one that battles, or pleases himselfe, in a continuall sporting with, or laughing at, others.*
Rigoreusement. *Rigorously, sternely, austerely, seuerely, in extremitie, without any fauour.*
Rigoreux: m. euse: f. *Rigorous, hard, strict, sterne, extreame, pitilesse, vnmercifull, austere, seuere.*
Rigueur: f. *Rigour, strictnesse, extremitie, austeritie, seueritie, sternenesse.*
Rillon de porc. *as* Graton; *or that part of a hogs intrailes which is like the tripes in an Oxe.*
Rim de vent. *A puffe of wind; or as* Rum.
Rimaille: f. *Paultie meeter, sorrie rime.*
Rimailleur: m. *A meane composer, a sorrie rimer.*
Rimailleuse: f. *An vnlearned, or paultrie Poetesse.*
Rimarde: f. *as* Rimailleuse.
Rimart: m. *An vnlearned, or scuruie rimer.*
Rimasser. *To rime vnlearnedly, to make sorrie meeter.*
Rimasseur: m. *A sorrie rimer, a paultrie meeter-maker.*
Rimasseuse: f. *as* Rimailleuse.
Rime: f. *Rime, or meeter; also, a crannie, chinke, rift, cleft, chap, chawne.*
Rimer. *To rime; to write or speake in meeter.*
Rimette: f. *A little rime, or small riming poesie.*
Rimeur: m. *A rimer, a maker of rimes, a writer in rime.*
Rimeuse: f. *A Poetesse, or woman that makes rimes.*
Rimonner. *To rime, &c; as* Rimer.

Rimoyer. *The same.*
Rimoyeur : m. *A rimer, a meeter-maker.*
Rinceau. *as* Rinseau.
Ringer. *as* Ruminer.
Rinsé : m. ée : f. *Reinsed, as linnen.*
Rinseau : m. *The staulke (or part of the staulke) of a plant; a little bough of a tree.*
Rinsement : m. *A reinsing of linnen clothes.*
Rinser. *To reinse linnen clothes.*
Rinseur : m. *A reinser of linnen.*
Rioge. *as* Mesentere : ¶Langued.
Riolé. *Streaked, rayed; whence,* Riolé piolé; *diuersified with many seuerall colours; or as vnder* Piolé.
Riorte : f. *A with, or band; a or sticke fit to make one.*
Riote : f. *A brabbling, scoulding, brawling, chiding, debate, contention, squaring, altercation; also, as* Riorte.
Rioter. *To chide, brabble, scould, brawle; iangle; debate, square, contend, fall out, in words.*
Rioteux : m. euse : f. *Scoulding, brabbling, brawling, euer chiding, iangling, wrangling; most litigious, or debatefull, neuer quiet.*
Riotte : f. *as* Riorte; *or, the band of a bauen, or fagot; also, as* Riote; *or a small brabble; also, a flimflam, idle discourse, tale of a tub.*
Riottement de chiens. *The yarring, or whurring of dogs, dogs brabbling.*
Ripaille : f. *(Is properly a tearme of warre signifying, pillage; whence,* ripaille necessiteuse, *a needie and rascall companie that liues onely vpon the spoyle; yet is it vsed much for) gluttonie, surfeting, idle expence of money, or of time, in pampering of the bellie :* ¶Norm.
ça ça ripaille, vie de goulus, à la soupe garçons. *(Th'ordinarie speech of such bellie-gods.)*
Riparographe : m. *A writer of trifles, a painter of base or scuruie matters.*
Ripeilleux. *as* Ripilleux.
Ripilleux : m. euse : f. *Craggie, rugged, vneuen, rough.*
Ripopé. Vin rip. *Rascallie hedge wine; bad wine made a great deale worse by much water; or (most properly) the droppings of wine, taken out of the* Bacquet, *or Tub that stands vnder the spigot, and mingled with water by, or for, poore folkes.*
Rippe : f. *The small fish called a Sharpling, Stickle-back, or Banke-stickle.*
Ripperie : f. *A cousening, gulling, cheating, conicatching.*
Rippopé. *as* Ripopé
Ripuaire. *A certaine Law agreeing with the Salicke both in substance, and date.*
Riquaner. *as* Ricaner; *or to bray like an Asse.*
Riqueraque. *Throughly, wholly, quite off or away.*
Feu de riqueraque. *Wild fire.*
Rire. *To laugh, tighie; geere, fleere; mocke, ieast, or scoffe at; make himselfe merrie with.*
Rire à demie bouche. *To laugh disdainfully, or as one that is more angrie then merrie.*
Rire à grosses dents. *From the teeth outward, say we.*
Rire sous leur bonnet; &, Rire sous gorge. *To laugh vnderhand, or in their sleeues.*
Se chatouiller pour se faire rire. *To please or flatter himselfe with trifles, idle hopes, vaine thoughts; or, to coine many sleight or idle ieasts for himselfe to laugh at, if no bodie else will.*
Pincer sans rire. *To gird closely, to giue priuie nips: and,* Iouër à pincer sans rire. *The same; as also, to nimme, filch, purloyne.*
Vous verrez bien rire. *You shall see good laughing.*
Femme rit quand elle peut, & pleure quand elle veut : Prov. *Looke* Femme.
Marchand qui perd ne peut rire : Pro. *Can any man laugh that looses? can any man take pleasure in his losses?*
Tel rit qui mord : Prov. *Some laugh and bite withall; Appliable to an hypocrite, or dissembler, who brings, by his faire words or shewes, confusion to those he conuerses with.*
Tel au matin rit qui au soir pleure : Prov. *Many that were glad in the morning are sad ere night.*
Ris : m. *The graine called Rice.*
Ris : m. *Laughter; or, a laughing, tighying, fleering.*
Ris de chien. *A disloyall, or treacherous geering.*
Ris d'hostelier. *Seeke* Hostelier.
Ris de loup. *The name of a certaine great peare.*
Ris Sardonien. *A forced or causelesse mirth, a laughter onely from the teeth outward; or, a long laughter that ends in sorrow.*
Ris *(The Participle of* Rire) Dequoy il fut bien ris. *whereat good sport was made.*
Risée : f. *A laughter, or laughing; a tighying, or fleering; also, a mocking, flowting, ieasting at.*
Ache de risée. *Crowfoot of the fallow field; or, Crowfoot of* Illiria.
Risible : com. *Fit or worthie to be laughed at.*
Risque : f. *Perill, ieopardie, danger, hazard, chance, aduenture.*
Ie le prens à ma risque. *Hab or nab, at my perill be it, happen how it will.*
Risses chevreaux. *Fat Kids :* ¶Rab.
Rissole : f. *The browneness that is giuen to a thing in the frying thereof.*
Rissolé : m. ée : f. *Fried throughly, or browned all ouer in the frying.*
Rissoler. *To frie a thing vntill it be browne.*
Rissolle : f. *A Iewes eare; or Mushrome thats fashioned like a Demie-circle, and growes cleauing to trees; also, a small and delicate minced Pie, made of that fashion.*
Rit : m. *as* Ris; *Rice.*
Rithmailler. *To rime paultrily, to write or pronounce rime doggerell.*
Rithme : m. *Rime, or meeter.*
Rithmer. *To rime, to make meeter.*
Ritual : m. ale : f. *Rituall, customarie, cerimonious, of or belonging to, rites.*
Rivage : m. *The sea shore, or coast; a water banke, waters side, the sea side.*
Droict de rivage. *Shorage; Looke* Droict.
Rivager : m. ere : f. *Belonging, or neere, vnto a waters side.*
Rivagier : m. *One that dwells neere the waters side.*
Rival : m. *A riuall, corriuall, competitor in loue.*
Rivant. *Riueting.*
Rive : f. *The Sea shore, side, or coast; the banke or side of a Riuer; the brinke, or brimme of a Spring, &c.*
La rive d'un bois. *The skirt, edge, or side of a wood.*
La rive d'un pain. *The side of a loafe.*
Il est plus aisé de se tirer de la rive que de du fond : Prov. *Better may a man get from the brinke then from the bottome; a mischiefe is sooner crushed, a delight more easily cassed, when one is but dipped, then when he is plunged, into it.*

Rivé: m.ée: f. *Riueted, clenched; fastened or turned backe, as the point of a nayle.*

Il luy a bien rivé ses cloux. *See* Clou.

Rivement: m. *A riueting, a clenching,*

River. *To riuet or clench; to fasten or turne backe the point of a nayle, &c; also, to thrust the clothes of a bed in at the sides.*

River vn clou à. *To retort a speech backe vpon; to make a sound replie vnto.*

Riveran: m. *A Ferrie-man or Bote-man; also, a Welsh hooke, or hedging bill made with a hooke at the end; or as;*

Rivereau: m. *The pole with a forke of yron, &c, at the end, wherewith Watermen set forward their boats when they row not; we call it a Bill-hooke.*

Rivereux: m.euse: f. *Frequent, haunting, full of, or belonging to, riuers.*

Faulcon rivereux. *That preyes in marshie places, or on riuer fowle; a riuer Hawke, or Hawke for the riuer.*

Riverotte: f. *A brooke, little streame, small riuer.*

Rivet: m. *The welt of a shooe.*

Tirer au rivet. *Looke* Tirer.

Riviére: f. *A riuer; a streame; also, a certaine apple that yeelds an excellent cyder.*

Les riviéres retournent en la mer: Pro. *Looke* Mer.

En petite riviére ne se prend grand poisson: Prov. *Small towns, or meane families, affoord no great prefirment.*

En pont, en planche, & en riviére valet devant Maistre derriere: Prov. *Looke* Pont.

Les petis ruisseaux font les grandes riviéres: Pro. *Many littles make a mickle; many small parcells ioyned together make vp a great bodie, or bulke.*

Riuler. *To rauell out like silke.* (v.m.)

Rivure. *as* Rivement.

Riz: m. *The graine Rice.*

Rob: m. *The iuyce of blacke Whortle berries preserued.*

Rob de ribes. *The preserued iuyce of red Goose-berries, or bastard Currans.*

Robbe: f. *A robe, gowne, mantle, coat; any long vpper garment; also, the sea Calfe, a fish.*

Robbe d'argent brodée de merde. *A learned text vnlearnedly commented on.*

Robbe courte. gens de robbe courte. *All that professe Armes, hold of the sword, or vsually weare swords.*

Robbe longue. gens de robbe longue. *Lawyers, Clerkes, Professors of Artes, &c.*

Robbe qui sent sa petite ville. *A citizens gowne, a Burguers garment; a ciuile, neat, spruce gowne, or garment.*

Bonne robbe. *A Bona roba; good stuffe, sound lecherie; a round, fat, plumpe wench.*

Accommoder la robbe au petit poinct; Il luy accommoda sa rob. *He set his gowne close to his shoulders, he courst his coat or Jacket soundly.*

Beuvez vn coup ou deux en robbe. *Steale a draught or two vnder your habits.*

Ils ne se sont gueres faict tirer la robbe. *They were soone intreated, easily drawne, to &c.*

Robbe d'autruy ne fait honneur à nulluy: Prov. *A borrowed gowne does well on no mans shoulders; apparell graces none but them that owe it.*

Robbe refait moult l'homme: Prov. *Handsome apparell sets out a man exceedingly.*

Les belles robbes pleurent sur des espaules indignes: Pro. *Great pitie tis to see faire clothes an a clowns backe.*

Fille trop veuë, robbe trop vestuë, n'est pas chere tenuë: Prov. *Looke* Fille.

Ventre de velours robbe de bureau: Prov. *Choyce food, and costlie fare, doe make the backe goe bare.*

Robber. *To rob, steale, purloyne, filch, nimme.*

Robberie: f. *Robberie, theeuerie, stealing, filching, purloyning; prowling.*

Robbeur: m. *A robber; or as* Desrobbeur.

Roberge: f. *A kind of long ship, wherin both sailes, and oares are vsed.*

Robert: m. *Robert (the name;) also, the peare Robert.*

Herbe Robert. *Hearbe Robert; a kind of Storkesbill.*

Le pourpoint de Monsieur Robert. *A Doublet whose forebodie is fine stuffe, and the backe parts course.*

Sauce Robert. *Is made of yolkes of egges, veriuyce, white powder, and a little broth strained together, and serued vp with whole Goose-berries put into it; also, a sauce for hogs feet, of onions, pepper, veriuyce, and vinegar.*

Ie luy bailleray bris contre Robert. *I will giue him bread for his cake, or as good as he brings; I will call him Jacke if he call me Gill.*

Robice: m. *A robbing; or a robberie, felonie, theeuerie; a pilfering act, a theeuish pranke.*

Robille: f. Provision de la rob. *The clothes, rings, Jewels, and attire of a widow, with as much other stuffe as she can carrie, adiudged vnto her vpō her renouncement of her deceased husbands estate.*

Robin: m. *Robin; (a proper name.)*

Bon Robin. *The name of a certaine hearbe.*

Chanson de Robin. *Looke* Chanson.

Robin a trouvé Marion: Prov. *A notorious knaue hath found a notable queane.*

Robin se souvient tousiours de sa fleute: Pro. *A drunkard euer dreames of pots, a miser of his pelfe; the ambitious of greatnesse, the lecher of filthinesse; euery one thinkes most of the thing he affects most.*

C'est la maison Robin de la vallée, ou il n'y a ne pot au feu, ni escuelle lavée: Prov. *Appliable to a needie, and a nastie house.*

Robineries: f. *Pleasant conceits.*

Robinet: m. *A Pipkin; a little Pot; also, the Cocke of a Fountaine, or of a Cesterne; also, the Taps-head.*

Robon: m. *A short gowne; or a side cassocke reaching below the knees.*

La sequele au robon. *Meane Tradesmen poore Marchants; the refuse, or followers of better Citizens.*

Roboration: f. *A strengthening, stiffening, reinforcing, fortifying.*

Roborement. *as* Roboration.

Roborer. *To strengthen, stiffen, fortifie, reinforce.*

Roborin. le bas rob. *as* Remboüer.

Robre: m. *The great Oake, or great Gall tree; the most hard and durable Oake that is.*

Robuste: com. *Strong, tough, sinnewie, pithie, sturdie, mightie, forcible.*

Robustement. *Strongly, toughly, sturdily, forcibly.*

Robusteté: f. *Strength or strongnesse, toughnesse, pithinesse, hardnesse or hardinesse, force, might, abilitie of bodie.*

Roc: m. *A rocke, stonie crag; strong hold; also, a Rooke at Chesse; also, a cradle for a child:* (¶ Bourbon.) *also, the crooked peece of timber that stands on the vtside of the forecastle of a ship; and is tearmed the Knight.*

Sans espargner ny roy, ny roc. *Without mercie, without respect of persons, dealing alike-seuerely with all.*

Rocard. vn vieux roc. *A hoarse mouldichaps, an ouerworne sincaunter, one that can neither whinnie, nor wag the taile.*

Roce. *as* Rosse.

Roch: m. *as* Roche; *also, the name of a Saint, for whom a holy-day is, in some places, kept on the sixteenth day of August.*

Herbe de S. Roch. *Fleawort, Coniza, Fleabane, Fleabane Mullet.*

Desrobber la bosse à S. Roch. *To keepe his hands in vre (as in* Bosse.)

Rochaille: f. *Rockes; rockinesse.*

Rochau: m. *Rocke-fish, any fish that liues among rocks; and particularly, the Cooke-fish, or Sea-thrush; as also, the fish* Cœnus.

Roche: f. *A rocke; a stonie crag or hill.*

Roche bise. *Looke* Bis.

Roche vive. *Such a rocke as is all of stone without any bed, or mixture of earth, or sand among it.*

Il y a bien de l'anguille sous roche. *Therein yet lurks some further matter, there is more in it then the world's aware of.*

Rocher. m. *A rocke.*

La gambade du rocher. *Precipitation, or the being throwne headlong from a rocke.*

Rocher: m. ere: f. *Rockie, of a rocke.*

Rocheray. Colombe rocheraye. *A rocke Pigeon; also, a wild Pigeon, or one thats bred betweene a wild, and a tame one.*

Rochet: m. *A frocke; loose gaberdine, or gowne of canuas, or course linnen, worne by a labourer ouer the rest of his clothes; also, a Prelates Rochet; also, the blurre, button, or blunt yron head, of a tilting-staffe; or, a Tilting weapon hauing a blunt edge, or end.*

Rochier. *as* Rocher.

Rocquer vn enfant. *To rocke a child.*

Rodage: m. *A certaine Toll exacted by some countrey Lords vpon euery waine that passes (though in the high way) neere to their Seigniories, whether it be laden or no; for if it be, they will be paid both for the load, and for the cart.*

Rodanes: f. *A kind of sweet Cherries.*

Rode: f. *The Dorce, or Gold fish.*

Rodé. Qui a rodé le païs. *That hath roamed, wandered, vagabonded it all the countrey ouer.*

Rodelle d'un clou. *The head of a nayle.*

Rodemontade. *Looke* Rodomontade.

Roder. *To roame, wander, vagabondize it, rogue abroad, runne vp and downe, flit here and there, trot all the countrey ouer.*

Roder les rues. *To iet, walke, trot vp and downe the streets (especially anights;) to see the towne serued.*

Roder les yeux. *To roll the eyes vnsteadily, to cast the eyes round about, to looke on euerie side of him.*

Rodeur: m. *A vagabond, roamer, wanderer, streetwalker, highway-beater; a rolling stone, one that does nought but runne here and there, trot vp and downe, rogue all the countrey ouer; an often and vncertaine flitter.*

Rodibiliardique: com. *Fat, or larded with fat.*

Rododaphne. *Oleander, the Rose tree, Rose bay, Rose bay tree; a shrub verie beautifull, and verie full of poyson.*

Rodomontade: f. *A brag, boast, cracke, vaineglorious brauadoe.*

Roëlle: f. *Seeke* Rouëlle.

Rogations: f. *Rogation dayes, the Rogation weeke, the Gang dayes or Gang weeke.*

Apres Pasques, & Rogation sy de prestre, & d'oignon: Prov. *Looke* Oignon; *or* Prestre.

Rogatons: m. *Indulgences, Bulls of pardon, Reliques, &c, borne about the countrey.*

Porteur de rogatons. *Looke* Porteur.

Roger bon-temps. *A mad rascall, a merrie greeke.*

Rognons. *as* Roignons.

Rogue. *The Mesenterium; Looke* Mesentere.

Rogue: com. *Arrogant, proud, presumptuous; malapert, saucie; rude, surlie.*

Roguement. *Arrogantly, proudly, presumptuously; surlily; malapertly, saucily.*

Roide: com. *Stiffe, steadie, firme, stable, strong; sturdie, stubborne; rough, fierce, rude, vnciuile, violent; constant, inflexible; vntractable.*

Roide. *as* Roidement; *Looke* Pisser.

Roidement. *Stifly, steadily, firmely, strongly; sturdily, sternely; rudely, fiercely, roughly; constantly, inflexibly; violently, vehemently.*

Roideur: m. *Stiffenesse, steadinesse, firmenesse; might, strength, force, vigour, power; sturdinesse, rudenesse, roughnesse, vntractablenesse; earnestnesse, violence, vehemencie.*

Roidi: m. ie: f. *Stiffened, hardened; stretched, or bent out.*

Roidir. *To stiffen, harden, straighten, bend or stretch out.*

Se roidir. *To be stifly bent vnto, settled in, resolued of; to frame himselfe vnto a constant, rigid, or vntractable determination, fashion, or humor; also, to be hard frozen, or to grow starke with cold.*

Roidir le jarret. *To shake, or stretch out, the legs, as one thats felled by a deadlie blow.*

Roigne. *as* Rongne.

Roignement: m. *A paring, clipping, shredding, a cutting off or away.*

Roigner, & Roigneux. *Look* Rongner, & Rongneux.

Roignons: m. *The kidneyes.*

Roine. *See* Royne.

Roisons: f. *Rogation weeke or dayes, Gang weeke, or Gate dayes; called so by the vulgar.*

Roitelet: m. *A pettie or poore King; also, a Wrenne.*

Roland. m. *Rowland; a proper name.*

Mort Roland. *Thirst, or a dying of thirst:* ¶Rab.

Faire le Roland. *To brag, boast, cracke; swagger, sweare, teare, stare, fare like a mad-man.*

Rolat. *as* Roule: ¶Bayonnois.

Obligé en rolat. *Subiect vnto the rigour of the Court of a* Bailli.

Rolle, & Rollet. *Seeke* Roule, & Roulet.

Rollier: m. *A Waine-man, or Waggoner; one that in a Waine, or Waggon, carries other mens ware vp and downe.*

Rollon: m. *A rowler, a rowling stone.*

Romain: m. ine: f. *Roman, of Rome.*

Absynthe Romain. *Romā Wormwood, French wormwood, Wormwood gentle, small-leaued Wormwood.*

Espée Romaine. *Looke* Espée.

Laictuë Romaine. *Roman Lectuce, the greatest kind of Cabbadge Lectuce.*

Mente Romaine. *Speare Mint, browne Mint, garden Mints.*

Nielle Romaine. *Gith, Nigella, Bishops-wort, Saint Katherines flower.*

Sauge Romaine. *Balsamint, Costmarie, Alecost*; *as* Mente Romaine.

Romaine: f. *A Roman beame, a Stelleere*; *See* Crochet.

Roman: m. *The most eloquent French, or any thing written eloquently, was tearmed so in old time*; *(of the Roman, or most eloquẽt language) Hence*; Le Roman de la Rose; *The Romant of the Rose: (In the confines of Germanie, and Lorraine the language that is not German is at this day called* Romant.)

Romanesque: com. *Romish, Roman.*

Romans: m. *Beets*: ¶Pic.

Romarin. *Looke* Rosmarin.

Rome: f. *(The citie of) Rome.*

Le loup alla à Rome, & y laissa de son poil, & rien de ses coustumes: Prov. *No place can alter an inueterate lewdnesse.*

Qui fol va à Rome fol en retourne: Pro. *Seek* Fol.

Qui langue a à Rome va: Prov. *He that can speake may trauell any way.*

Romicole: com. *One that affects, or honours, Rome, or the Romish Religion.*

Rommeler. *To rumble, grumble, grunt.*

Rommeny: m. *The furre called Budge.* (v.m.)

Romore. *Seeke* Remore.

Rompable: com. *Burstable, breakable.*

Rompeis: m. *Grounds newly broken vp*; *especially such as either haue neuer, or not within memorie, beene tilled.*

Rompement: m. *A breaking, bursting, pashing asunder, dashing in peeces*; *also, a cancelling, dissoluing, infringing, vndoing.*

Rompe-pierre. *as* Rompierre.

Rompeur: m. *A burster, a breaker.*

Rompeur de chansons. *A continuall interrupter of such as talke more wisely then himselfe.*

Rompierre: f. *The hearbe Saxifrage*; *also, Sampire.*

Rompierre blanche. *White Saxifrage, white Stonebreake.*

Rompierre dorée. *Goldẽ Saxifrage, or Stone-break.*

Rompre. *To burst, break*; *dash, or pash in peeces*; *to pull, rend, or teare asunder*; *also, to casse, cancell, infringe, dissolue, vndoe*; *also, to barre at Dice, &c.*

Rompre l'anguille au genouil. *To performe an impossibilitie.*

Rompre le coup. *To beat or put by a blow, in Fencing, &c.*

Rompre le coup à vne menée. *To diuert, crosse, dissolue, make void, a practise.*

Ie vous romps ce coup là. *I denie you that, or stop you there*; *hoe there neighbour, by your fauour sir.*

Rompre les oreilles à. *To deafe, or molest with ouermuch prattle.*

Rompre la paille avec. *To fall out with a friend, companion, or familiar acquaintant.*

Rompre plustost que plier. *Looke* Plier.

Rompre la teste à. *To wearie, tire, or toyle out with infinit babling*; *to importune, or crie out vpõ ouermuch.*

'A tout rompre. *At the most*; *at the highest*; *at the worst*; *or, when all comes to all.*

Meschant à tout rompre. *An extreame rascall, a most egregious villaine.*

Avarice rompt le sac: Prov. *In striuing to take too much of a thing we spoyle it, and despoyle our selues of all further vse of it.*

Mieux vaut tirer que rompre: Prov. *Better to retch then to breake*; *to yeeld a little then perish altogether.*

Rompture: f. *A rupture*; *breach, breaking, &c*; *Looke* Rompure.

Cas de rompture. *An equall sharing of a bankrupts goods among his creditors*; *In which case, if hee had land subiect vnto rent, the Landlord hath it the first yeare in lieu of his arrerages*; *and after him euerie one, in his turne, hath it his yeare.*

Rompu: m. Bon rompu. *A good companion, good fellow, or (as we say) a good rogue.*

Rompu: m. uë: f. *Burst, broken*; *dasht, or pasht, in peeces*; *pulled, rent, or torne, asunder*; *also, cassed, cancelled, infringed, vndone, dissolued*; *also, burst*; viz. *whose bowells be fallen into his cods.*

Rompu aux affaires. *Practised, much exercised, fully beaten in, well acquainted with, the course of businesses*; *of great experience in the world.*

Rompu de travail. *Harried, wearied, ouer-toyled, cleane beaten out, that hath lost both strength, & health by too much labouring.*

Chemin rompu. Le chemin est tout rompu de gens. *The way is much beaten, or worne by the multitude of passengers.*

Dos rompu. 'A dos rompu. *Doubling, twofold, as if his backe were broken.*

Front rompu. Qui à le front rompu. *An impudent fellow, a shamelesse or brasen-faced companion.*

Gorge rompuë. Crier à gorge rompuë. *Till his mouth split withall.*

Ie m'y suis bien rompu la teste. *I haue extreamely afflicted, perplexed, or troubled my braines withall.*

Rompu-dos. 'A rompu-dos. *as* 'A dos rompuë.

Rompuë: f. *A rout, a discomfiture.*

Rompure: f. *A ruption, rupture, fracture, brack, breach*; *bursting, breaking.*

Ronçay: m. *A Brier-plot*; *a ground or place full of Briers.*

Ronce: f. *A Bramble, or Brier*; *also, a kind of Thornebacke.*

Ronce de cerf. *Rough Bindweed.*

Ronce de chien. *The Brier-bush, or Hep tree*; *or, a great kind thereof, which beares a white flower, and great leaues resembling the soles of mens feet*; *some also call so, the Caper shrub.*

Ronce Ideenne. *A Raspice plant or bush.*

Roncé: m. ée: f. *Hurled*; *or making a whurring noise, as a stone, &c, cast with violence*: ¶Gasc.

Ronceux: m. euse: f. *Bramblie, brierie*; *full of brambles, or briers.*

Ronciere: f. *A bushie close or ground, a place full of brambles or briers.*

Roncey. *as* Ronçay.

Rond: m. *A Sol, or the French shilling (tenne whereof make but one of ours*; *) also, the daunce called a Round*; *whence*;

Ie suis tout saoul, ie dancerois bien vn rond.

Rond: m. ronde: f. *Round, circular, orbicular, compasse*; *full, plumpe*; *also, free, blunt, plaine, open hearted, sincere.*

Muscle rond. *One of the foure muskles which draw vp the nether Jaw*; *and which (particularly) puffes vp the cheeke, and is therfore by the Latine Anatomists called* Buccinator.

Vaisseau rond. *A Ship*; *tearmed thus to make a difference betweene it and a Galley, Foist, Brigantine, &c*; *all which are tearmed*, Vaisseaux longs.

Donner le plein, & le rond à. *To perfect, consummate, accomplish.*

Tenir

Tenir table ronde. *To keepe open house.*
Rondace: f. *A round Targuet, or great Buckler.*
Rondache. *as* Rondace.
Rondacher: m. *A Targuettier; one that serues with a* Rondache.
Ronde: f. *A circle; a compasse, or compassing; the Round (walked) in Garrisons.*
Ronde. *(Aduerbially)* Cent lieuës à la ronde. *A hundred leagues compasse.*
Rondeau: m. *A Scrowle; such as, among Armes or Emblemes, a Deuise or Mottoe is written in; also, a kind of round, and stiffe Pancake.*
Rondeau de pastissier. *A round and flat boord whereon* Pastissiers *doe raise their Past and Pies.*
Rondeau de rime. *A Rime, or Sonnet that ends as it begins.*
Rondeler. *To turne, wind, wheele, goe compasse, cast about.*
Rondelet: m. *as* Rondeau.
Rondelier: m. *A maker of Bucklers, or of round Targuets; also, a souldior that serues with a Buckler; a Targuettier.*
Rondelle: f. *A Buckler, or (little) Targuet; also, the Rochet fish; also, the head of a nayle.*
Rondelle de fer. *A round plate, or band of yron.*
Rondement. *Roundly, circularly, orbicularly; fully, plumply; freely, plainely, bluntly, throughly.*
Rondeur: f. *Roundnesse, globinesse; fullnesse, plumpneße; plainenesse, bluntnesse, free speech, good earnest.*
Rondin: m. *A measure for Corne, or Graine; containing about a* Picotin *and a halfe.*
Rondole: f. *The sea Bat, or Rearemouse of the sea; a flying fish.*
Ronfle: f. *Hand-Ruffe, at Cards.*
Iouër à la ronfle. *To play at hand-Ruffe; also, to snore.*
Vous me remettez à point en ronfle veuë. *You put me shrewdly to my plunges, driue me to the wall, haue me at a bay.*
Ronfler. *To snore, snort, rowt.*
Ronfleur: m. *A snorer, a snorter, a rowter.*
Ronge: m. *A gnawing, fretting, nibling.*
Cela luy reuient tousiours au ronge. *That still doth extreamely vex, or fret him; he cannot forget it, it will neuer from his heart.*
Rongé: m. ée: f. *Gnawne, knapped or nibled off, eaten, fretted, worne away.*
Rongeard: m. arde: f. *Gnawing, knapping, nibling, off; eating, fretting, wearing away.*
Rongement: m. *A gnawing, knapping, or nibling, off; a fretting, eating, or wearing away.*
Ronger. *To gnaw, knap, or nible, off; to fret, eat, or weare away; also, to champe, or chew.*
Ronger vne colere en son esprit. *To fret, vex, or chafe, inwardly.*
Ronger entre les dents. Il faut ronger cela entre les dents sans dire mot. *That must be borne, intertained, or disgested, without contradiction.*
Ronger son frain; *(Much like the former) to bite of the bitt.*
Rongeur: m. *A gnawer, knapper, nibler; fretter.*
Rongne: f. *Scurfe, scabbinesse, the mange.*
Rongné: m. ée: f. *Pared, clipped, shred, cut away; also, circumcised.*
Il s'est rongné les ongles à l'estude de. *Look* Ongle.
Ressembler la monnoye rongnée. *To be vnlearned, or without letters.*
Rongnement: m. *A clipping, paring, shredding; a cutting off, or away.*
Rongner. *To pare, clip, shred, cut, fret, off or away.*
Rongner les ailes à. *To keepe low, hold vnder, hinder from rising; or, as;*
Rongner les ongles à. *To weaken, disarme, or disable (for defence, or offence.)*
Qui fief rongne fief perd. *If a tenant, or vassall, alien part of his* fief, *he forfeits the whole vnto the Lord* Feodal.
Rongnette: f. *A Farriers paring-knife.*
Rongneure: f. *A shred, paring, clipping, remnant, offall, odde end.*
Rongneures. *Shreds, parings, clipping, odde ends; also, wine left in the bottome of a glasse, &c, after a draught.*
Les rongneures du temps que nous desrobbons, & prenons pour nos affaires. *Od, stolne, or vacant times bestowed on our priuate occasions.*
Rongneux: m. euse: f. *Scabbie, mangie, scuruie.*
Cheval rongneux n'a cure qu'on l'estrille: Prov. *A scabbie Jade affects not the Curryeombe; nor a scuruie Jacke any correction.*
Mere piteuse fait sa fille rongneuse: Prov. *A tender-hearted mother breeds a short-heeld daughter.*
Mestier n'avons de pastissier rongneux: Pro. *Looke* Pastissier.
Rongnonner. *To pare, clip, or gnaw by little and little; also, to grumble, murmure, or mutter.*
Rongnure. *as* Rongneure.
Ronsé. Raye ronsée. *A Thornebacke, or rocke Ray.*
Ronsiere: f. *A place full of bryers, a plot full of brambles.*
Ronson. *as* Bondelle.
Ronsoy: m. *as* Ronsiere.
Ronteis: m. *Grounds newly broken vp, especially such as (although they haue lyen a long time lay) either appeare, or be remembred, to haue beene tilled.*
Roole. *Seeke* Roule.
Roolet: m. *Was, in the ciuill warres, a watch-word among the French Clergie, signifying a collection for the pensions of those great Personages, which had vndertaken to protect them; also, as* Roulet.
Roolle. *Seeke* Roule.
Roollé: m. ée: f. *Rowled vp, wrapped or folded inwards, turned round.*
Ropts: m. *Pot-shards.*
Roquau: m. *A gluttonous Rock-fish (of no certaine colour; for there be of them blacke ones, greene ones, red ones, and some of sundrie colours) which makes of grasse a neast in the sea, and therein hatches her spawne.*
Roque: f. *A Rocke; Fort, Castle, Citadell, Block-house, or strong Hold (built on a Rocke.)*
Roquet: m. *as* Rochet.
Roquette: f. *A little Rocke; a small Fort; also, the hearb Rocket.*
Roquette des jardins. *Rocket gentle, garden Rocket, Roman Rocket.*
Roquette sauvage. *Wild Rocket, wall Rocket.*
Roquille de vin. *The quarter of a French (much about our halfe) Pint.*
Rosace: f. *The flower of Brankursine, or Beares-breech; termed so by Ingrauers, &c.*
Rosage. *as* Rosageur.
Rosageur *The shrub Oleander, Nerum, Rose-Lawrell, Rose-tree, Rose-Bay. Rose-Bay tree.*
Rosagine. *as* Rosageur.
Rosaire. *An ordinarie Limbecke for the distilling of Rose-water;*

water; also, a Rosarie, or our Ladies Psalter.

Rosat. Of Roses; whence, Huile rosat; Miel rosat; &c.

Roscignol. as Rossignol.

Rose: f. A Rose; also, the ouglie excrescence of the sea, tearmed the red Nettle; also, a small red-taild fish, not much vnlike a Mennow, but that it hath scales, and is alwayes full-rowed.

Rose Autumnale. The white Muske Rose.

Rose blanche. The ordinarie white Rose.

Roses blanches. as Les Fleurs blanches; vnder Fleur.

Rose de buisson. The brier Rose, hedge Rose, wild Rose.

Rose canine, ou de chien. The wild Rose, or brier Rose (of what kind socuer.)

Rose Damasquine. The white Muske Rose.

Rose de Damas. The same; or the single white Muske Rose, or Damaske Rose.

Rose escarlatine. as Rose incarnate.

Rose franche. The red Rose.

Rose de Hierico. Rose of Jerico, or of Jerusalem; the Heath Rose, our Ladies Rose.

Rose iaulne. The yellow Rose.

Rose incarnate. Our Damaske Rose.

Rose de Iunon. The white Lillie.

Rose muscate; ou musquée. The white Muske Rose.

Rose de nostre Dame. Rose of the mount, Knights Bloome, Peonie, Pionie; also, as Rose de Hierico.

Rose d'outre mer. The garden Mallow, called Hocks, and Holyhocks.

Rose de pienne. Peonie, Pionie, Rose of the mount.

Rose de Provence. The Prouince Rose, the double Damaske Rose.

Rose de Provins. The ordinarie double red Rose.

Rose sauvage. The wild Rose, hedge Rose, brier Rose; also, the Eglantine, or sweet brier Rose.

Camphre en rose. Naturall Camphire, or such as hath not beene touched by fire.

Chapeau, ou chapel de roses. A small, sleight, incompetent, or lesse-then-due, portion giuen a maid to her mariage.

Droict de roses. Looke Droict.

Pot aux roses. A misterie, close matter; secret mischiefe, priuate inconuenience, hidden knauerie.

Racine sentant les roses. Rose-root, Rosewort; an hearbe.

Semer des roses aux pourceaux. To bestow excellent things vpon the vicious that will not, or the ignorant that cannot, make vse of them.

La rose en fin devient vn gratecul: Pro. The fairest Rose ends in a hep; griefe sits on pleasures highest step.

Nulle rose sans espine: Prov. No Rose without a prickle.

Truye aime mieux bran que roses: Prov. Looke Bran.

Roseau: m. A Reed, a Cane; also, a Raft, or Float-boat of timber.

Roseau aromatic. Calamus Aromaticus, the aromaticall Reed.

Roseau Cyprien. Cyprus Cane, Pole Reed.

Roseau des estangs. Reed-grasse, the Burre Reed.

Roseau des Indes. The flowring Reed.

Roseau odorant. as Roseau aromatic.

Estansonner le mensonge d'un roseau. To vphold, or maintaine an vntruth with friuolous excuses, vaine reasons, idle arguments.

Rosée: f. Dew, the dew of Heauen.

Rosée du soleil. Sunne-Dew, Ros solis, Youthwort; an hearbe then moistest, and most couered with dew, when the Sunne lyes hotest on it; In the North parts it is called Red rot (because it rotteth sheepe) and Mooregrasse.

Tendre rosée. A young, tender, delicate lasse.

Rosetique. Vin rosetique. The best kind of Gascon wine, growing within the territorie of Nerac, and there so called of it Vermillion hue.

Rosette: f. Vermillion, Cheeke-Varnish, a bright ruddie colour; also, red Inke to rule bookes with; also, a kind of fine Copper that comes out of Hungarie in rud plates; also, a little Rose; also, the Rose at the end of the cheeke of a bitt, next to the reynes; also, a little rowell of a spurre.

Rosette noire. Latten or Copper whereof Kettles are made; especially such as must not be hammered, but melted.

Poire de rosette. A verie tender, and delicate Peare.

Vin de rosette. Alligant.

Rosier: m. A Rose-tree, Rose-bush, Rose-brier; also, a Garden, Plot, Bed, or Arbour, of Roses.

Rosier sauvage. The wild brier, or hedge brier.

Rosiere: f. A small, yellowish, broad-bellied, or breamelike fish, euer full-rowed. ¶Pic.

Rosillant. Dewie, bedewing, dew-dropping, dewyeelding.

Rosin: m. ine: f. Rosie, red, ruddie, faire, fragrant, Roselike, of or belonging to Roses.

Rosinant. as Rosillant.

Rosinement: m. A bedewing; a falling of dew.

Rosiner. The dew to fall; or to fall, distill, or drop downe as the dew; to dew, to bedew.

Rosineux: m. euse: f. Dewie, full of dew.

Rosle. as Roule.

Rosmarin: m. Rosemarie; also, the hearbe Frankincense.

Rosmarin des iardins. Garden Rosemarie, common Rosemarie.

Rosmarin masle. Rosemarie Frankincense, Libanotis Rosemarie, blacke or white Hart-root.

Rosmarin pointu. Sweet Broome, Heath, Ling.

Rosmarin sauvage. (The red-branched) wild Rosemarie.

Donner du rosmarin. To dismisse, quite put off, giue a flat answer (or denyall) vnto, a wooer.

Rosoyant. Bedewing; also, of a rosie colour.

Rosoyer. To dew, bedew, wet gently, moisten faire and softly.

Vne vapeur qui rosoye. A drisling, misling, mistie raine; or a vapour that houers aloft, and, being not yet come to the substance of a raine, wasts it selfe by drizling.

Rospe: f. A Toad.

Rosse: m. A Iade, a Tit.

Il n'est si bon cheval qui n'en deviendroit rosse. It would anger a Saint, or crest-fall the best man liuing, to be so vsed.

Oncques bon cheval ne devint rosse: Prov. Looke Cheval.

Rosse: f. The Roche-fish; also, a small red-tayld lakefish, not much vnlike a Mennow; also, as Poule de mer.

Rosselet. as Roselet.

Rossette: f. as Marquote; also, a kind of small Dogfish called the sea Cat.

Rossignol: m. A Nightingale; also, a picklocke.

Rossignol d'Arcadie. An Asse.

Rossignols de marais. *So doe they in some places tearme, and cry vp and downe the streets, flayed Frogs.*
Rossignol de muraille. *A Starke, a Red-tayle.*
Rossignol de riviere. *The riuer Nightingale; or, a kind of Kings-fisher that sings verie sweetly.*
Rossignoler. *To record, or sing, like a Nightingale.*
Rossignolesque: com. *Nightingale-like, harmonious, melodious; dolefull, mournefull.*
Rossignolet: m. *A young, or little, Nightingale.*
Rost: m. *Roste, rost-meat.*
Rost de tisserand. *as* Roul; *also, rosted Apples.*
Qui a mangé le rost ronge l'os. *When as the rost-meat is cleane gone, a man must fast or gnaw the bone.*
Rostedom: m. *One that requires, or takes, backe the gift which he bad bestowed.*
Rosti: m. *Rost-meat; Looke* Rosty.
Rosti sanglant. *Is made by dredging with Hares bloud dryed vnto powder.*
Rosti: m. ie: f. *Rosted; tosted; broyled.*
Oeil rosti. *A vehement inflamation of the eye, a Carbuncle in the eye.*
Rostie: f. *A toast.*
Rostir. *To rost; also, to broyle; also, to toast.*
Rostisserie: f. *Rost, rost-meat; also, a kitchin, cookerie, or Cookes shop, wherein meat is vsually rosted.*
Rostisseur: m. *A roster of meat; also, a Cooke that sells, or dresses, none but rost-meat.*
Rostissiere: f. *A rosting Cookes wife.*
Rosty: m. *Rost, rost-meat.*
S'endormir sur le rosty. *Looke vnder* Endormir.
Rot: m. *A belch.*
Rotateurs: m. *Two muscles, a greater and a lesse, which turne about the eye.*
Rote: f. *A great high way in a Forrest; also, a tree growing therein.*
Roteur: m. *A Pond to water Flax, or Hempe, in.*
Rotine. Par rotine. *By rote.*
Rotisserie: f. *as* Rostisserie.
Rotisseur. *as* Rostisseur.
Rotissoir: m. *A Cobiron, or little Racke.*
Rotondité: f. *Rotunditie, roundnesse.*
Rotte: f. *A With, or the band of a Faggot, &c (about* Blois.)
Rotte de cire. *Fiue pound (weight or quantitie) of Wax.*
Rottée de bois. *as* Corde de bois; *or as much wood as will be contained therein.*
Rottement: m. *A belching, or breaking of wind.*
Rotter. *To belch, or breake wind vpwards.*
Rotteur: m. *An Officer that measures* les Rottées de bois *indifferently for the buyer and seller.*
Rottier: m. *as* Routier.
Rottine: f. *An vsuall course, beaten path, ordinarie way.*
Rotule du genouil. *The ball, or whirlebone of the knee.*
Roture: f. *Yeomanrie; the estate, condition, or calling of such as are not of gentle bloud; also, socage, or such an ignoble tenure; also, the land thats held thereby.*
Harnas de roture. *The Plough.*
Heritages en roture. *Land held in socage; or by* Cens, *rent, or other ignoble seruices.*
Roturier: m. *A Yeoman, or Plebeyan; a Ploughman, a Husbandman; any lay man that is no Gentleman.*
Roturier: m. ere: f. *Yeomanlie, Plebeyan, ignoble, vnnoble, base, meane.*
Fief roturier. *Which is held by rent, or* Cens, *or any other ignoble seruice.*
Rente roturiere. *A bare rent charge, or rent secke; also, such a rent as issues out of an inheritance which is no* fief.
Roturierement. *Basely, meanely, ignobly, clownishly, Plebeyan-like.*
Roüable. *as* Rable; *also, an Engine wherewith fish is (forbidden to be) caught.*
Roüage: m. *Wheelage, wheeles, wheeleworke; the furniture of wheeles; prouision of wheeles.*
Roüage d'artillerie. *The carriage of Artillerie.*
Droict de roüage. *Wheelage; Looke* Droict.
Roüaille. *A deuise, or engine wherewith fish is caught.*
Roüaisons: m. *Rogations, Gang-dayes.*
Roüant: m. ante: f. *Wheeling, turning round about; also, light, flitting, vnsteadie; soone passing away.*
Roüart: m. *A Marshall, or Prouost Marshall; an officer that breakes, or sees broken, malefactors on the Wheele; also, the great and strong-boned fish* Rota, *or the Wheele fish.*
Rouce. *as* Ronce.
Rouche: f. *A rush.*
Roucherole: f. *The riuer Nightingale; or a kind of Kings-fisher that sings verie sweetly.*
Rouchet. *as* Rougette.
Roucin. *as* Roussin.
Roucoler. *To croo like a Doue, or Queest.*
Roucoulement: m. *The crooing of Doues.*
Roucouler. *To croo.*
Rouctement: m. *A belching.*
Rouë: f. *A wheele; also, the breaking of all the ioints on a wheele.*
Rouë de compte. *A Notch-wheele in a Clocke.*
Rouë de mer. *The sea-wheele; a huge, round, and monstrous sea-fish.*
Rouë de rencontre. *A Flea-wheele, or the balance-wheele of a Clocke.*
Faire la rouë. *To wheele, goe compasse, turne round, swing or twirle about; (A Peacocke* fait la rouë, *when in the height of his pride he couers himselfe all ouer with his tayle.)*
La maistresse rouë qui tourne le moulin. *That which does all in all.*
Marcher à quatre rouës. Cela marche &c. *That businesse goes roundly, or fast, on.*
Mettre le foin en rouë; viz. *in wind-baulkes, or wind-rowes.*
Pousser à la rouë. *To set forward by all the meanes he can, to assist with might and maine.*
La pire rouë du chariot est celle qui crie le plus fort: Prov. *No man's in companie so lowd as he that can doe least.*
Roüé: m. ée: f. *Broken, or executed, vpon the Wheele; also, wheeled, whurled, or swung, about; also, dapled as a horse.*
Rouëlle: f. *A little flat ring, or wheele of plate, or yron, in horses Bitts; also, a round plate of armour for defence of the arme-hole when the arme is lift vp; and generally, any small hoope, circle, ring, or round thing, thats moueable in the place which it holds.*
Rouëlle du genouil. *The ball, or whirlebone of the knee.*
Rouëlle d'oignon. *A shiue of an Onyon.*
Rouëlle de veau. *The broad end of a leg of Veale, cut round, and diuided from the knuckle.*
Rouëment: m. *A wheeling, or turning round.*
Rouën. Cheval rouën. *A roane horse.*

Rouër: m. Vn rouër. *A wheeling, a compassing, a round turning, a swinging about.*

Rouër. *To wheele, turne round, swing about, goe compasse, draw after him turning; also, to breake vpon the wheele.*

Rouër sur les miseres & calamitez. *To turne vpon the wheele of aduerse fortune.*

Rouësse: f. *The name of a certaine great Peare.*

Rouët: m. *A spinning wheele; any little wheele; also, a Weauers Cloth-beame; also, the locke of an Harquebuse, &c.*

Rouët dentelé. *The cog-wheele of a Mill.*

Mettre au rouët. *To grauell, plunge, lay sore to, put to his last shifts; (from a Hare, which being so farre spent that she can runne no more end-wayes, but is faine to wheele about the dogs, they say of her,* Le lievre est mis au rouët.)

Rouëter. *To turne a (spinning) wheele.*

Rouëtte: f. *A little wheele.*

Rouge d' avoine. *A certaine Peare whereof excellent Perrie is made.*

Rouge: com. *Red, vermillion, bloud-red.*

Rouge bourse. *A Robin-red-breast.*

Rouge grenat; ou grenat rouge. *as vnder* Grenat.

Bestes rouges. *Any kind of Deere, or harmelesse game.*

Gorge rouge. *A Robin-red-breast.*

Monnoye rouge. *Golden coyne.*

Rouge comme vn Cherubin. *Hauing a Fierie facies.*

Le plus rouges y sont pris. *The craftiest, or cunningest of them are intrapped there.*

Rouge visage, & grosse pance ne sont signes de penitence: Prov. *A swagging bellie and a drunken face, are not the signes of a repentant grace.*

Rougeastre: com. *Reddish, ruddie, somewhat red.*

Rouge-bourse. *as* Rouge-gorge.

Rouge-brun: m. *A darke red which Painters lay for a ground to their Vermillion.*

Rouge-clair: m. *An excellent Enammell (made of Gold, Quick-siluer, and the Spirit of Copper) which will not settle on any thing but Gold.*

Rouge-gorge. *The small bird called a Robin-red-breast.*

Rougelet: m. *The name of an Apple.*

Rougement. *Redly.*

Rougeolle: f. *The Meazles.*

Rouget: m. *A Rochet fish; also, a great round Apple that yeelds excellent Cyder.*

Rouget barbé. *The sore Mullet.*

Rougette: f. *The Red-fish; verie like a Gurnard, and by some held to be the same.*

Rougeur: f. *Rednesse.*

Rougir. *To blush, to grow red.*

Rougissant. *Blushing, waxing red.*

Rougnette. *Looke* Rongnette.

Rouhard: m. arde: f. *Crooing, crying, mourning, like a Woodculuer, or Turtledoue.*

Rouhastre: m. *A scuffling, incounter, conflict, contention, bickering, debate.*

Rouille: f. *Rust, rustinesse.*

Rouillé: m. ée: f. *Rustie, full of rust.*

Plus rouillé que la claveure d' un vieil charnier. See Claveure.

Rouiller. *To pummell, or beat about the eares.* (v.m.)

Se Rouiller. *To rust.*

Rouillons: m. *Chichlings, pettie Fitches, or Vetches.*

Rouillure: f. *Rustinesse.*

Rouïr du chanure. *To steepe or water Hempe.*

Rouïsse: f. *The name of a great Peare.*

Rouïssoir: m. *A Pond, or Poole to water Flax, or Hempe in.*

Roul: m. *The stay of a Weauers Loome, hauing teeth of Reed, &c, like a combe.*

Roulant: m. ante: f. *Rowling, foulding vp into a rowle, turning round.*

Chardon roulant. *The hundred-headed Thistle, field Eringus, Leuant sea-Holme, champion sea-Hollie.*

Roule: m. *A Rowle; a List, Inuentorie, Catalogue, Bill, Scrowle, Register, of Names, or of Causes; also, a rowling, foulding, turning, rounding; also, mutabilitie, vnsteadinesse, continuall motion.*

Tour du roule. *The catalogue of causes to be heard that day, deliuered to the Iudges at their sitting downe in Court.*

`A tour de roule. *In course, in order, by turnes, one after another.*

Gaigner le tour du roule. *Which an aduocate is said to doe, when he procures the hearing of a Cause which he is towards (and which is called on in course) to be put off vnto a further day.*

Iouër son roule. *To play his part.*

Roule: f. *The high way for Carts, and Waggons; the Rut, or street, way.*

Rouleau: m. *A Roll of Paper, or of Parchment; also, the round pinne, strutchell, or strickle vsed in the measuring of Corne; and, more generally, any rolling pinne; also, the cloth tearmed Cotton; or a course woollen Stuffe of the making of Cottons.*

Rouleaux. *Long and round Leauers whereon Ships are gotten into a Docke, and launched into the water againe; also (in Architecture) Rolls, Cartridges, or Cartouses.*

Roulement: m. *A rowling, turning, foulding vp or inwards; a rowling, or a running, along.*

Rouler. *To rowle, turne round, fould vp, wrap inwards; also, to rowle along; whence;*

Roule boule. *Runne Bowle; and hence also;*

Il fait beau rouler en esté. *Tis good trauelling by Coach, or driuing of a Cart, in Summer.*

Roulet: m. *A List, Roll, Inuentorie, Catalogue, Scrowle; also, a set speech.*

Bastir, (ou faire) à quelqu'un son roulet. *To prompt, appoint, instruct, or teach one, what he shall speake, or doe.*

Qui sçait bien son roulet. *That knowes his liripoope, thats throughly prouided to speake.*

Roulier: m. *A Carter, Carrier, Wayne-man, Waggonman, that carries other mens things from place to place; generally, any one that guides, driues, or goes with, a Cart, Waggon, &c; also, a Hogs-stye.*

Roulier: m. ere: f. *Whence,* Cheval roulier. *A strong Cart-horse, a lustie tugging Jade.*

Roulis: m. *Great round stakes, or piles.*

Roulle, & Roulleau *as* Roule & Rouleau.

Rouller. *as* Rouler; *also, to driue, or guide a Cart, Waggon, Wayne, &c.*

Roullis. *Looke* Roulis.

Roumarin. *Rosemarie.*

Roupeau: m. *A little Heron which haunteth rockes, and hills, and hath a peake of feathers falling backwards on the hinder part of his head.*

Roupie: f. *An Isicle; or (more properly) the snot, sniuell, or waterie drop that hangs at the nose end in cold weather; also, a Robin-red-breast.*

Coffin à roupies. *A womans Maske.*
Roupieux: m. euse: f. *Snottie, sniuellie, whose nose is euer dropping.*
Il fut bien roupieux. *He was mightily ashamed, or much deceiued.*
Roupille: f. *A Cassocke.*
Rouppeau. *as* Roupeau.
Roupt: m. pte: f. *Broken, burst in peeces.*
Roupte: f. *Looke* Route.
Rovre: m. *The most hard, most strong, and most branchie kind of Oke; also, the great Gall-tree; (a kind thereof.)*
Rous: m. Rousse: f. *Looke* Roux.
Rouseau: m. *A flower which flyes away with the wind like the downe of a thistle; also, the hearbe Water-torch, Cats-taile, red Mace, March Pestill, Douch downe.*
Poire de rouseau. *A verie tender and delicate Peare good to make Perrie of.*
Rousée: f. *as* Rosée.
Rousoyer. *To bedew; to wet gently.*
Roussable: m. *The close roome wherein Herrings are smoaked vntill they be red; Looke* Saurir.
Roussastre: com. *Reddish, or betweene red and yellow.*
Roussau: m. *The name of a Fig.*
Rousse: f. *A red-haired, or freckled, woman.*
Rousseau: m. *A freckled, and red-haired, man; also, the Bittor; or a fowle thats lesse then a Heron, but otherwise resembles her; also, the Crabfish tearmed a Pungar;* (Normand.) *also, a verie tender, and delicate Peare.*
Rousselet: m. *The name of a delicate small Peare.*
Rousselet: m. ette: f. *Reddish, ruddie, somewhat red.*
Rousser. *To groane, or complaine, like a grunting woman, or ouerworne Iade.*
Roussérole: f. *The Riuer Nightingale; a kind of Kingsfisher.*
Roussèt: m. *A little ruddie Dog-fish; also, red wheat, Duck-bill wheat, Normandie wheat.*
Rousset: m. ette: f. *Russet, browne, ruddie, inclining to a darke red.*
Pain rousset. *Cheat or booted bread; houshold bread, made of Wheat and Rye mingled.*
Roussette: f. *A russetin Apple; also, a little Dog-fish, whose ruddie skinne is powdered all ouer with blacke spots; also, a certaine ruddie, or dunne-red bird, no bigger then a Titmouse.*
Rousseurs. *Little, red, wan, or blackish pimples or spots in the face, &c; freckles, or a kind thereof.*
Roussin: m. *A Curtall, or strong German horse.*
Roussin de service. *A horse of Armes, or for the warre; a good strong horse fit to serue on, due to a Lo.* feodal *from euerie vassall (that holds tenne pounds a yeare, or vpwards) once during his life; or in lieu thereof (if there be no certaine rate vsed, or agreed on) the fift part of a yeares Reuenue: The rate of this* Roussin *is* 60 solz Tourn.
Homme mutin, brusque roussin, flascon de vin, prennent tost fin: Pro. *Looke* Homme.
Qui a florin, Latin, & roussin, par tout il trouve le chemin: Prov. *He thats well lyned, well spoken, and well mounted, shall neuer be out of his way.*
Roussiner. *To whinnie after Mares, like a rammish, or lecherous Iade; also, to leape a Mare.*
Roussir. *To wax red.*
Roussoyer. *To wax ruddie, grow reddish.*
Rouste de bois. *A With; or, as* Riorte.

Route: f. *A belch, or belching; also, a rowt, ouerthrow, defeature, discomfiture; the breaking of a troope, or squadron, of men; also, a rutt, way, path, street, course, passage; trace, tract, or footing; also, a rowt, heard, flocke, troope, companie, multitude of men, or beasts; also, a glade in a wood; or, as* Rote.
Routes. *The footing of rauenous, or biting beasts, such as the Wolfe, Bore, Fox, Otter, &c.*
La route d'une branche. *The broken peece of a bough; the truncheon of a broken bough.*
Chascun sa route. *Euerie one in his course, place, order, when his turne or time comes.*
Frapper à la route. *To roose a Deere with a lyme hound.*
Il n'y a route que de vieux regnards: Prov. *Looke* Regnard.
Router. *To belch, or breake wind vpwards.*
Routier: m. *A Ruttier; a directorie for the knowledge, or finding out of courses, whither by sea or land; also, an old traueller, one that by much trotting vp and downe is growne acquainted with most wayes; and hence, an old beaten souldior; one whom a long practise hath made of great experience in, or absolute maister of, his profession; and (in euill part) an old craftie Fox, notable beguiler, ordinarie deceiuer, subtill knaue; also, a Purse-taker, or a Robber by the high way side.*
Routine. *Looke* Rotine, *or* Rottine.
Routte: f. *as* Route; *also, a kind of tumbling or vaulting tricke.*
Routtier. *as* Routier.
Routure. *Looke* Roture.
Routures d'eauës. *Bracks, breaches, pathes, wayes made, or worne out, in rocks by a continuall running, or beating of waters.*
Rouveau. Pomme de rou. *The Ruddocke, Redding, Summer Goulding.*
Rouvieres. *The name of a kind of Oliues.*
Rouvraye: f. *A Forrest, Wood, Groue, or tuft, of strong Okes, or great Gall-trees.*
Rouvre. *as* Rovre.
Rouvroy. *as* Rouvraye.
Roux: m. Rousse: f. *Reddish, ruddie, red-Deere colour, a ruddie or sad yellow, Lyon tawnie.*
Bestes rousses. *All kind of Deere, or harmelesse game.*
Rouy: m. ye: f. *Ouersodden, and wanting liquor in seething; also, steeped or soked in water, as Hempe.*
Roy: m. *A King; also, the chiefe, or head man in a companie.*
Les Roys. *The Epiphanie, or Twelfth day in Christmas.*
Roy d'armes. *A principall Herald, a King of Armes.*
Roy de la Basoche. *Looke* Basoche.
Le Roy Bertault. *A Wrenne.*
Roy de cailles. *A Rayle; or the captaine, and leader of Quayles.*
Roy des merciers. *An officer deputed heretofore by the Lord high Chamberlaine of France to view, or looke vnto, the wares, weights, and measures of those Pedlers, or Shop-keepers that followed the Court: but now the King himselfe appoints him, yet by the title of* Visiteur, *hauing suppressed this, by Edict in the yeare* 1597.
Roy des oyseaux. *The Wrenne.*
Roy des ribaulds. *Looke* Ribauld.
L'Aulne du roy. *The Kings Ell; containes three foot, seuen ynches, and eight lines.*
Couleur de roy. *A title in old time due onely vnto Pur-*

Purple, though vsurped at this day by a kind of bright Tawnie, which we also tearme de roy *colour; and yet some hold, that this comes neerer the true Purple of the Ancients then the moderne one; (Howsoeuer, the Violet is held the French Kings proper colour.)*

La Court du Roy Petaud. *See* Petaud.

La feste des roys. *as* Les Roys.

Mesure de roy. *The Kings measure; which in surueying allowes 22 feet to the Perche (sayes the Author of* La maison Rustique;) *but that proportion is either out of date, or restrained vnto some few places, the more common one being of no more then 20.*

Monnoye de roy. *The Kings money; coyne bearing the French Kings stampe, or made within his dominions.*

Pied du roy. *The ordinarie twelue-ynch foot; a foot according to the Standard.*

Toise de roy. *Is three moderate paces.*

Bailler mornifle à la levre du roy; &, Bailler sur le nez du roy. *To make false money, to counterfeit the Kings coyne.*

Sans espargner ny roy, ny roc. *Equally rigorous, hard, or seuere, vnto all.*

Iouër au roy despouillé. Chascun iouë au roy despouillé. *Where the hedge is lowest euerie one leapes ouer, when a man is falling euerie one helpes him on; a Prince once beaten, growne poore, or otherwise declining, happie is he that can pull a fleece from him, euerie one indeauors by pluming of him to feather their owne neasts.*

Aujourd'huy roy demain de rien: Pro. *Now a King ere long nothing.*

Boy vin en roy: Pro. viz. *Moderately.*

Chascun est roy en sa maison: Prov. *Euerie one is a King in his owne house.*

De meschant homme bon roy: Prov. *Looke* Meschant.

Il ne parle pas au roy qui veut: Pro. *Not euerie one that would, may speake to Kings.*

Que veut le roy ce veut la loy: Prov. *The King and Law haue but one will and pleasure; the Law is wholly gouerned by the King; euen as he will so is it interpreted, so understood.*

Qui mange l'oye du roy il en chie la plume cent ans apres: Prov. *He that eateth a Goose of the Kings doth spue vp her feathers a hundred yeares after; (Applyable to vntrue Exchequer men; and vnto any purloyners of his Treasure, concealers of his Titles, withholders of his Rights.)*

Qui sert le roy il a bon maistre: Pro. *He that serues the King serues a good Maister; or, he needs none else, that hath a King, to Maister.*

Royal: m. *An old coyne of gold, worth about 68 solz.*

Royal de France. *Another of a later stampe, worth* 55 solz Tourn.

Royal: m. ale: f. *Royall, regall, kinglie, princelie, maiesticall.*

Cas royaux. *Looke vnder* Cas.

Chemin royal. *The Kings high way; which, by the customes of* Amiens *and* Boullenois, *is to be 60 foot broad; and by those of* Vallois, *but 30 in erable, and 40 in wooddie grounds.*

Droicts royaux. *Looke vnder* Droict.

Lettres royaux. *Letters Patents.*

Milan royal. *The ordinarie Puttock, or Glead.*

Noix royale. *A Wallnut.*

Pied royal. *A foot according to the Standard; the ordinarie twelue-ynch foot.*

Royalement. *Royally, kingly, princely, maiestically.*

Royaliste: com. *Taking the Kings part, siding with the King.*

Royaulme: m. *A Realme, a Kingdome.*

Royaulme de Suerie. *Cornelius his Tub; or, the sweating kingdome, whereof the Pockie are your onely subiects.*

Le royaulme des Taupes. *The ground, the earth.*

Royaulté: f. *Royaltie, kinglinesse, maiestie, princelinesse.*

Royaume. *as* Royaulme.

Roye: f. *A ray, line, streake, furrow, &c; as* Raye.

Royer. *To raze, blot out, efface, deface.*

Royeu: m. *The Meazles.*

Royne: f. *A Queene.*

La Ceincture de la royne. iij d *vpon a* Muid, *and* iij d *vpon a* Queuë, *of all Wines (that were not gotten in the owners grounds) leuied within Paris, euerie third yeare, to the Queenes vse.*

Roynette: f. *A little, or poore, Queene; also, Maidsweet, Meddow-sweet, Queene of the Meddowes; (an hearbe.)*

Roytelet: m. *A little, or poore, King; also, a Wrenne; also, a thing, like Tynne, found often in Antimonie, and keeping it, moulten, from being transparent.*

Royzelet: m. *A Ginne, or deuise to catch Woodcocks.*

Rozat. *Of Roses.*

Aromatic rozat. *Looke* Aromatic.

Rozelet: m. *A verie small, and beautifull bird, which vseth to sing verie much, and in singing, to flye vp suddainely into the aire, and as suddainely downe againe, into the reeds, or willowes, among which he liues.*

Rozereaux: m. *A kind of Martins, whose skinnes are of much request.*

Ru: m. *A brooke, small streame, or gullet of water; also, a gutter in the middle of a street; also, a cast, hurle, throw, swindge.*

Il entend le ru du baston. *He is a cunning fencer, old-beaten souldior, of much experience in the world.*

Ruade: f. *A horses kicking, winsing, yerking, striking, flinging, flying out with the heeles.*

Ruade seiche. *A dry bob, ieast, or nip; a stroke that crushes, though it cut not.*

Rubarge. *as* Roberge.

Rubefié: m. ée: f. *Rednea, made red.*

Rubeline: f. *A Robin-red-breast.*

Ruben: m. *Ribbon; also, a ribbon; whence;*

Ruben de teste. *A fillet, head-band, haire-lace of ribbon.*

Rubenner. *To decke, trimme, tye, set, or lace with ribbon.*

Rubennier: m. *A ribbon-maker, head-band maker.*

Rubette: f. *A greene earth-Frog, or red Toad; very full of poyson, and of great vse among Witches.*

Rubi. *as* Passefleur; *also, as* Rubis.

Rubicans: m. *The white haires that be scattered here and there vpon the coats of some coloured horses.*

Rubicon: m. *The name of a Riuer in Italie, ouer which* Iulius Cæsar *passed in the beginning of his Expedition against* Pompey; *whence;*

Franchir, ou passer le Rubicon. *To vndertake, or enter into, a great, and dangerous exploit.*

Rubicunde: com. *Verie red, verie ruddie, vermillion, bloud-red.*

Rubie maieur, ou des tainćturiers. *The hearb Madder, red Madder.*

Rubie mineur. *Clauer, Loue-man, Goose-share, Goose-grasse.*

Rubienne: f. *The Red-tayle, or Starke; a small bird.*
Rubis: m. *A Rubie.*
Rubis balay. *A Rubie ballais; a kind of pale, or peach-coloured, Rubie.*
Ruble: m. *An Italian weight of about 600 pound, after 12 ounces to the pound.*
Rublitelle: f. *The halfe of a* Ruble.
Rubrication: f. *A rednesse, or a ruddinesse; also, a making, or waxing red.*
Rubriche. *Rudle, oaker, red lead, red chaulke, red marking stone.*
Rubriché: m. ée: f. *Rubified, made or growne red; also, marked with rudle, red oaker, &c; and written with, or (as a Rubricke) printed in, red Inke; whence;*
Son Kalendrier est rubriché. *Said of a woman that hath her monthlie disease.*
Rubrificatif: m. *A Rubrificatiue; a plaister of so strong, or strongly-drawing simples, that it vlcerates, or (at least) makes red, the place it is applyed vnto.*
Rubrique: f. *A Rubricke; a speciall title or sentence of the Law written, or printed, in red.*
Rubrique Sinopique. *Sinopian red earth; a heauie, massiue, liuer-coloured, and astringent earth, or minerall, which put into water soone moulders, and falls into peeces: This may verie well be the ordinarie Bolearmenie that is, at this day, vsed by manie Surgeons in the staunching of bloud, &c, but is not the true (Orientall) one, redder then it, and not so easily dissolued by water as it.*
Ce nous sera vne rubrique de droict. *This shall be an absolute Law vnto vs; according thereto will we gouerne our selues.*
Ruche: f. *A Bee-hiue; also, an earthen pot, &c, for birds to breed in.*
Ruchée: f. *An Hiue-full.*
Rucher. *To hiue, make hiues, gather honey into hiues.*
Ruchette: f. *A little hiue.*
Ruchot: m. *(A fashion of) a cloke tyed close about the necke, and thence falling downe round about the bodie.*
Rudache. *as* Rondace.
Rude: com. *Rude, rusticall, clownish, boorish, hoblike, lumpish, loblike; blunt, blockish, brutish, barbarous, vnmannerlie, vnciuill, ignorant, home-bred, vntaught; also, curst, soure, surlie, churlish, froward, rigorous, pittilesse, vntractable, vngentle, austere; also, base, plaine, simple, homelie, bungarlie; also, rough, harsh, knottie, rugged, vnsmooth, vnpolished, ill-planed.*
Temps rude. *A stormie, tempestuous, or turbulent season.*
'A rude chien dur lien: Prov. *Curst vsage fits a churlish youth; or, surlie humors must be repressed by soure vsage.*
Rudement. *Rudely, clownishly, vnciuilly, churlishly; sourely, surlily, frowardly, pittilesly, rigorously; basely, plainely, simply; roughly, ruggedly, harshly, bunglarlike.*
Rudenté: m. ée: f. *Wreathed like a Cable.*
Rudenture: f. *A wreath, wreathing, wreathed worke; a border thats wreathed, or of the forme of a Cable.*
Rudepeau: m. *A verie long browne-tawnie Adder, full of scales, and stinking most abhominably.*
Rudesse: f. *Rudenesse, hardnesse, harshnesse, bluntnesse, lumpishnesse, churlishnesse, inciuilitie, surlinesse; roughnesse, curstnesse, frowardnesse, rigor, vntractablenesse, austeritie, sourenesse.*
Rudesse de paroles. *Rude speech, hard words, harsh tearmes, rough language.*
Rudoyement: m. *A chiding, rating, checking, reproaching, reprouing.*
Rudoyer. *To chide, rate, reproach, reproue, checke, tax, take vp, giue ill words to, vse verie hardly in words.*
Rue: f. *Rue, Hearbe Grace.*
Rue de chevre. *Italian Fitch, Goats Rue.*
Rue de muraille. *Wall Rue, Rue Maiden haire, white Maiden haire.*
Rue sauvage. *Wild Rue; (whereof there be diuers kinds) more vehement in smell, and violent in operation, then garden Rue.*
Rue vineuse. *Some hold to be the hearbe called Oke of Jerusalem.*
Rue: f. *A street, in a Towne; also, a causey, or high way (called, in diuers parts of England, a street, and the street way;) also, a Taylors hell, or the place whereinto he casts all his shreds.*
Batre les rues. *To iet, reuell, or swagger vp and downe the streets in the night.*
Rué: m. ée: f. *Beaten or cast down, ruined, ouerthrowne; cast, hurled, flung.*
Ruelle: f. *A little street, a lane.*
La ruelle du lict. *The space betweene the bed and the wall.*
Ruer. *To rush, flye, runne, breake violently in, or vpon; also, to cast, hurle, fling, throw; also, to ouerthrow, subuert, batter, beat or cast downe.*
Ruer vn coup d' estoc à. *To make a thrust, or dart a Rapier, at.*
Ruer coups sur. *To beat extreamely, to poure blowes vpon.*
Ruer en cuisine. Il rue tresbien en cuisine. *He is a good trencher-man, he falls to his victualls eagarly.*
Ruer des pieds. *To kicke, winse, yerke, strike, fling, flye out with the heeles.*
Encores n'a pas failli qui a à ruer: Pro. *He hath not faild thats yet to fling; or, he thats to fling hath not yet failed.*
On ne sçait qui mord ne qui rue: Prov. *One knowes not what may happen, who may hurt him, what mischiefe may in time betide him.*
Ruette: f. *A lane, a little street.*
Rueur: m. *A kicker, striker, winser; a thrower, an ouerthrower.*
Ruffage: com. *Currish, dogged, harsh, churlish.*
Ruffien: m. *A Bawde, a Pandar.*
Ruffienner. *To ruffianize, Pandarize, it; make or set leacherous matches, play the Pandar.*
Ruffiennerie: f. *Ruffianisme, Pandarisme, Bawderie.*
Rufien, Rufienner, & Rufiennerie. *Looke* Ruffien, Ruffienner, & Ruffiennerie.
Rufisque: m. *as* Ruffien.
Rugiment: m. *A roaring, or bellowing.*
Rugine: f. *The Instrument wherewith a Surgeon scaleth bones.*
Ruginer vn os. *To scale (or scrape) a bone.*
Rugir. *To roare, or to bellow.*
Rugissant: m. ante: f. *Roaring, bellowing.*
Rugissement. *as* Rugiment.
Rugisseur: m. *A roarer, a bellower.*
Rugosité: f. *Ruggednesse, wrinklednesse, roughnesse; a crumpling, wrimpling, furrowing, harshnesse to the feeling.*
Rugueux: m. euse: f. *Rugged, wrinkled, wrimpled, crumpled, riuelled, rough, harsh to be felt.*
Ruille; &, Plomb à ruille. *A Masons plumb-rule, or plumb-line.*

Ruin: m. *The grunting of a Hog.*
Ruine: f. *Ruine, wracke, wast, hauocke, spoile; subuersion, desolation, ouerthrow, vndoing, destruction.*
Battre vne ville en ruine. *To shoot at the houses thereof, to batter or breake them downe with great shot.*
Ruiné: m. ée: f. *Ruined, wracked, hauocked, spoyled; subuerted, ouerthrowne, vtterly decayed, vndone.*
Ruinement: m. *A ruining, wracking, spoyling; subuerting, ouerthrowing, vndoing.*
Ruiner. *To ruine, wracke, wast, hauocke, spoyle; subuert, ouerthrow, vndoe, destroy.*
Ruineur: m. *A ruiner, wracker, spoyler, subuerter, ouerthrower, destroyer, vndoer.*
Ruineux: m. euse: f. *Ruinous, falling, declining, ouer-aged, in decay.*
Ruir. *To rore, or to royne, like a Lyon; also, as* Rouïr.
Ruisseau: m. *A brooke, small streame, gullet, current of water.*
Les petis ruisseaux font les grandes riuieres: Pro. *From little streames great riuers haue their swellings.*
Ruisseler. *To streame, runne, trickle, or glide along, like a brooke.*
Ruisselet: m. *A small brooke or gullet; a reane, or gutter of running water.*
Ruissement: m. *A roaring, or Lion-like royning; also, a steeping or watering of Hempe, &c.*
Ruit: m. *The rut of Deere, or Bores; their lust; and the season wherein they ingender; also, a heard of female Deere followed by the male in that season.*
Ruité: m. ée: f. whence, Venaison ruitée. *Thats killed, or gotten in rut-time.*
Rum: m. *The hole, or hold of a ship; also, as* Rumb.
Rumatique: com. *Rhewmaticke; troubled with a Rhewme.*
Rumb: m. *A roombe, or point of the Compasse; a line drawne directly from wind to wind in a Compasse, Trauers-boord, or Sea-card.*
Voguer de rumb en rumb. *To sayle by trauers.*
Voguer par divers rumbs. *Vpon diuers boords, or changes of winds.*
Rume: f. *A Rhewme, Catarrhe; Pose, Murre.*
Rumeur: f. *A rumor, noise, bruit, fame, report.*
Ruminé: m. ée: f. *Ruminated; reuolued, considered, pondered, weighed, examined in the mind.*
Ruminement: m. *A ruminating, or chawing of the cud; also, a deliberating or pawsing on.*
Ruminer. *To ruminate, or chaw the cud; also, to ponder, weigh, examine, consider or thinke of, deliberate or pawse on, reuolue in the mind.*
Rumineur: m. *A ruminator; one that considers or thinkes of, deliberates or pawses on, a matter.*
Runge: m. *The chewing of the cud; or, as* Ronge.
Rupricam. *A bay horse.*
Ruption: f. *A ruption, eruption, bursting, breaking.*
Ruptoire: m. *A ruptorie; a corrosiue, or potentiall cauter.*
Rupture: f. *A rupture, brake, breach, bursting, breaking.*
Ruque. *The name of an Apple that yeelds an excellent Cyder.*
Rural: m. ale: f. *Rurall, rusticall, clownish, countrey-like.*
Fief rural. *An ignoble or base fief; which hath neither moated house, nor any other marke of antiquitie, or gentrie belonging to it.*
Ruscher. *Looke* Rucher.
Ruse: f. *A sleight, wile, stratageme, craftie tricke, subtill part, cunning pranke, shifting deuise.*
Rusé. *Craftie, wylie, subtill, cunning, slye, shifting, deceitfull, false, full of tricks.*
Homme rusé tard abusé: Pro. *The subtill are not easily deceiued.*
Les plus rusez sont les premiers prins: Pro. *He that seekes others to beguile, is ouertaken in his wile.*
Ruséement. *Craftily, cunningly, subtilly, shiftingly, slyly, deceitfully, falsely.*
Ruser. *To beguile, deceiue, shift, vse tricks, deale cunningly, proceed by sleights.*
Rustaude: f. *A churlish, rude, or vnmannerlie baggage.*
Rustauderie. *as* Rusticité.
Rustault: m. *A clowne, boore, churle, hob, hinde, swayne, lobcocke, rude or vnmannerlie lozell.*
Rusterie: f. *as* Rustrerie.
Rustication: f. *Husbandrie, countrey businesse, rurall worke; also, a dwelling in the countrey.*
Rusticité: f. *Rusticitie, rudenesse, clownishnesse, inciuilitie, churlishnesse; homelinesse, plainnesse, ignorance, or ignorant bashfullnesse.*
Rustique: com. *Rusticall, rude, boorish, clownish, hob-like, lumpish, lowtish, vnciuill, vnmannerlie, home-bred, homelie, sillie, ignorant.*
Rustique. A la rust. *as* Rustiquement.
Boire à la rustique. *To drinke vnmeasurably.*
Rustiquement. *Rustically, rudely, boorishly, clownishly, lumpishly, lowtishly, vnmannerly, vnciuilly, ignorantly, clusterfist-like.*
Rustiquer. *To play the clowne, or husbandman; to labour, or till the ground.*
Rustiquerie: f. *Husbandrie, tillage, rurall prouision or stuffe.*
Rustre: m. *A ruffin, royster, hackster, swaggerer; sawcie, paultrie, scuruie fellow.*
Rustre: f. *A lozenge pierced round in the middle; (a tearme of Blason.)*
Rustrement. *Royster-like; sawcily.*
Rustrerie: f. *A roysting, swaggering; roguerie, knauerie; sawcinesse.*
Rut: m. *as* Ru; *a brooke, &c; also, as* Ruit.
Rutiler. *To glister, glitter, shine, glare.*
Ruyer: m. *as* Vicomte; *or* Voyer.
Ruyle: f. *as* Ruille.
Ruyler du plastre avec de l'eau. *To mingle, or moisten, plaister with water.*
Ruylette: f. *A little plumb-rule, or plumb-line.*
Ruze. *Looke* Ruse.
Ruzez. *The turnings, or doublings of a Hare.*
Ry: m. *A little brooke.*
Ryde, & Ryder. *as* Ride, & Rider.
Rym. *as* Rumb.
Ryme. *Ryme, or meeter.*
Rymer. *To ryme, to make meeter.*

S

S. *The letter* S; *also, the marke of a* Sol *in a (written) Reckoning; whence;*
Allonger les SS. *(Falsely) to stretch out an Accompt, or make it rise verie high; to set downe* ff *for* ss, *francs in stead of* sols.
Sabat: m. *A foule coyle, rumbling, dinne, hurrie.*
Sabath: m. *The Sabaoth day, Sunday.*
Sabatique: com. *Of the Sabaoth; keeping the Sabaoth; whence;*
Riviere sabatique. *That runnes six dayes, and the seuenth stands still, or is dry.*

Sabatisme: m. *Holie rest.*
Sabatizer. *To rest, or keepe holie, the Sabboth day.*
Sabe. *New sweet wine boyled vntill it be halfe consumed, and kept for sawces, and seasonings.*
Sabe de coing. *The iuice of Quinces boyled (as aforesaid;) good against a cough.*
Sabé. Haleine sabée. *A fragrant, or sweet-smelling breath.*
Sabech: m. *The little Hawke tearmed, a Musket.*
Sabine: f. *Sauine (a shrub;) also, Hartwort, or Birthwort (an hearbe.)*
Sable: m. *Sand; also, the colour sables, or blacke, in Blason.*
Horloge de sable. *An houre-glasse.*
Sablé: m. ée: f. *Blacked; of a sable hue; also, furred, or inriched, with sables.*
Sablere. *Looke* Sabliere.
Sabliere: f. *The Summer that compasses the top, or vpper part, of a roome.*
Sablon: m. *as* Sable; *Sand; also, great or small grauell.*
Sablon mouvant. *A Quicke-sand; whence,* Il a la teste pleine de sablon mouvant. *His head is full of crotchets, his braine fraught with odde conceits; he hath a running, or a giddie pate of his owne.*
Horloge à sablon. *An houre-glasse.*
Sablonneux: m. euse: f. *Sandie; greetie.*
Sablonniere: f. *A sand-bed, sand-pit, sandie plot; a place full of sand, greet, or small grauell.*
Saboir. *in stead of* Sçavoir. ¶Gascon.
Sabonner; & Saborner. *To agree beforehand, or to be at a certaine rate, with; Looke* Abonner & Aborner.
Sabors: m. *Portholes (for great Ordnance) in ships.*
Sabot: m. *A Top, Gig, or Nunne to whip, or play with; also, a pattin, or slipper of wood; also, a horses hoofe.*
Saboté: m. ée: f. *Turned, or whipped, as a top; also, fashioned like a top; whence;*
Coquille sabotée. *The shell of a Welke, Periwinkle, &c.*
Saboter. *To play at top, or to whip a top.*
Saboulé: m. ée: f. *Rolled, tossed, tumbled with, trodden vnder, the feet; also, tugged, mumbled, or scuffled with.*
Saboulement: m. *A rolling, tossing, tumbling with; a treading vnder, the feet; also, a tugging, or scuffling with.*
Sabouler. *To roll, tosse, or tumble, with; to tread vnder, the feet; also, to tug, mumble, or scuffle with; and hence, to iumble a woman.*
Sabourré: m. ée: f. *Balasted, or whose bottome is filled with grauell, &c.*
Sabourrer. *To balast, or stuffe the bottome of, with grauell; also, as* Sabouler *(in the last sence.)*
Sabrin: m. *The spotted, and skalie Serpent* Hæmorrhoïs, *whereof one being bitten, bleedes, at all the naturall pores, or passages of the bodie, to death.*
Sabuleux: m. euse: f. *Sandie, greetie.*
Saburre: f. *Balast (for shipping) of grauell, or small pibbles.*
Sac: m. *A sacke, wast, ruine, hauock, spoyle; also, a sacke, or sacking, a ransacke, pillage, depopulation, rauaging; and hence;*
'A sac à sac. *The word whereby a Commaunder authorizeth his souldiors to sacke a Place, or People.*
Sac: m. *A sacke, poke, powch, bag; also, as* Intestin borgne; *also, an ill, or ill-digested, humor remaining in a wound (thats healed in apparance) and afterwards turning into an impostume.*
Sacs de charbonniers. *Looke* Charbonnier.
Sac au croc. *A suit vndecided, or, as we say, lying by the wall.*
Sac à vin. *A drunken gulch, or gorbellie; a great winedrinker.*
Cul du sac. Au cul du sac. *At length, in the end, when all is done, when all comes vnto all.*
Freres des sacs. *A certaine Order of begging Friers.*
Gens de sac, & de licol. *Loytering rogues, or vagabonds, &c (as in the next word;) also, begging Friers.*
Homme de sac, & de corde. *A lewd knaue, wicked rascall, gracelesse rakehell, filthie rogue; one thats fit for nothing but to find the executioner worke, whether by drowning him in a sacke, or choaking him with a rope.*
Acheter vn chat en sac. *To buy a Pig in a poake (say we;) to bargaine vnaduisedly, or hand ouer head.*
Se couvrir d' un sac mouillé. *To make a matter the worse by colouring, or excusing, it.*
Donner son sac, & ses quilles à. On luy a donné son sac, &c. *He hath his passport giuen him, he is turned out to grazing; (said of a seruant whom his maister hath put away.)*
Manger son avoine en son sac; *Looke* Avoine; *or as;*
Manger son pain en son sac. *To be churlish, or niggardlie, to snudge or munchion it alone in a corner; also, to spend or imploy good things on a corner, or in too priuate a manner.*
Prẽdre d'un sac deux moustures. *To take double fees; or to make double vse of one thing.*
Servir à sac, & à somme. Qui servent, &c; *Looke* Somme.
Sac plein dresse l'oreille: Pro. *The full purse a full eare procures; the way to good attention lyes by well-filld bags.*
Vn sac percé ne peut tenir le grain: Prov. *A sacke thats torne doth shed it corne; a broken or crackt heart can hold no good thing in it; applyable also to a heart, that pierced with griefe, cannot hold but must vtter it.*
D'un sac à charbon ne peut sortir que de la poussiere noire: Prov. *Nought but blacke dust from Colliers sacks can come; a vicious man will be lewd in his talke.*
Es petis sacs sont les fines espiceries: Pro. *The little head a daintie wit containes.*
Avarice rompt le sac: Prov. *The miser coueting to make his bags hold ouermuch, breakes them, and looses the most of that they had in them.*
Chascun ira au moulin avec son propre sac: Prov. *Each one shall his owne burthen beare.*
Il ne peut sortir du sac que ce qu' il y a dedans; &,
On ne peut tirer du sac que ce qu'y est: Prov. *You can haue no more of a Cat but her skinne; or, there can come no more (no other stuffe) from a man then is in him.*
On ne cache point esguilles en sac: Pro. *A sack's no fit thing to hide needles in; heart-pricking anguish will bewray it selfe.*
On lie bien le sac avant qu'il soit plein: Pro. *A sacke before tis full is well ynough tyed vp; men while they are kept low are easily kept in.*
Sacabribe: m. *A beggars wallet, an Almes-scrip.*
Saccade: f. *A fall or ouerthrow from a horse, a horses casting of his rider; also, a flirt.*
Elle aura la saccade. *She shall be turned ouer.*
Saccader. *To throw, ouerthrow, cast downe; also, to ouerturne a wench.*
Saccagé: m. ée: f. *Sacked, ransacked, rifled, pillaged, ruined, destroyed.*
Saccagement: m. *A sacking, ransacking; ruining.*
Saccager. *To sacke, ransacke, pillage, rifle, ruine, destroy.*
Saccageux: m. euse: f. *Sacking, ransacking.*

Saccamenter. *Looke* Sacmenter.
Saccerelle: f. *A docke for a horses trayne.*
Saccharin: m. ine: f. *Of sugar; as white or sweet as sugar.*
Saccoche: f. *A little sacke, bag, poke, or powch.*
Saccouter à l'oreille. *To round, or whisper in the eare.*
Saceller. *To rub, in bathing, with little bags full of Branne, &c.*
Sacerdoce: m. *Priesthood.*
Sacerdot: m. *A Priest.*
Sacerdotal: m. *Sacerdotall, Priestlie, belonging vnto Priests.*
Sel sacerdotal. *An excellent powder, or compound Salt; (for which looke vnder* Sel.)
Sacmenté: m. ée: f. *Sacked, ransacked, whereof hauock is made; also, hacked, or hewed in peeces.*
Sacmenter. *To sacke, ransacke, make hauocke of; also, to hacke, or hew in peeces.*
Sacotin: m. *Feauerwort, Earth-gall, common Centorie, Centorie the lesse.*
Sacouter. *Looke* Saccouter.
Sacquement: m. *A hastie drawing, a quicke pulling out of a sword, &c; also, a prompt laying of the hand on a sword (in offer of drawing, or in a readinesse to draw;) also, a sacking, ransacking, rifling, making hauocke of.*
Sacquementé. *Looke* Sacmenté.
Sacquer. *To draw hastily, to pull out speedily, or apace.*
Sacquer la main à l'espée. *(An ordinarie, but (sayes* Nicot) *an improper, phrase;) to lay, or clap his hand on his sword (with a purpose to draw it.)*
Il luy sacqua l'espée des mains. *He snatched, or violently pulled, his sword out of his hands.*
Sacquerelle: f. *A docke for a horses tayle.*
Sacraire: m. *A Sextrie, or Vestrie in a Church; also, a priuate Chappell, or Oratorie.*
Sacramentaires: m. *Sacramentaries; Protestants; Huguenots, or Caluinists in the doctrine of the Sacrament.*
Sacre: m. *The dedication of a Church, &c; the coronation of a Prince; the consecration of a Prelate.*
Sacre d'Angers; &, le iour du sacre. Corpus Christi *day.*
Sacre: m. *A Saker; the Hawke, and the Artillerie, so called; also, a rauenous, or greedie fellow, one that makes boot of all he can lay his clutches on; also, an excessiue glutton, or gully-gut; and a spendall, vnthrift, squanderer, extreame rioter (especially in respect of his bellie.*
Sacre d'Egypte. *A kind of Saker that feedes altogether vpon serpents, and carrion; and therefore among the auncient Egyptians the killing of him was accounted felonie.*
C'est vn terrible sacre. *He is a rash, headie, wilfull, or violent fellow; also, he is a monstrous vnthrift, &c; as in* Sacre.
Sacré: m. ée: f. *Sacred, sanctified, made holie; receiued into, inuested with, religious Orders; dedicated, consecrated, or deuoted, vnto religious vses.*
Artere sacrée. *The sacred Arterie; a branch of the great one, which goes vnto the marrow of the* Os sacré.
Feu sacré. *The holie fire; a painefull impostumation, the thinnesse of whose matter giues it a liuelie colour, and makes it almost to shine.*
Huile sacrée. *Oyle of Amber; so called of the excellencie thereof.*
Os sacré. *The sacred bone; the great bone vpon which the ridge-bone resteth.*
Pierre sacrée. *An Altar stone.*
Poisson sacré. *A red-finned sea-fish, called so, because no rauenous or hurtfull fish doth euer swim neere him.*
Veine sacrée. *Looke* Veine.
Sacremens: m. *Mysticall rites, or holie mysteries; and hence, the Sacraments of the Church.*
Sacrer. *To consecrate, hallow, dedicate; inthronize; inuest, install; also, to excommunicate, or outlaw.*
Sacret: m. *The tassell, or male, of a Saker.*
Sacrificateur: m. *A sacrifying Priest, a sacrifier.*
Sacrificatoire: com. *Sacrificatorie, belonging vnto sacrifice.*
Sacrifice: m. *A sacrifice, an offering.*
Sacrifié: m. ée: f. *Sacrificed, offered vp in sacrifice.*
Sacrifier. *To sacrifice, offer sacrifice, or offer vp in sacrifice.*
Sacrilege: m. *A sacrilegious person, Church-robber, stealer of holie or hallowed things; also, sacriledge, or Church-robbing; any hainous, and horrible offence, or offendor.*
Sacrilegement. *Sacrilegiously; most hainously.*
Sacristain: m. *A Sexton, or Vestrie-keeper, in a Church.*
Sacristie: f. *A Vestrie, or Sextrie, in a Church.*
Sadariege: f. *The hearbe Sauorie.*
Sadayer. *To handle gently, or stroke softly; also, to flatter, smooth, cog, or collogue with.*
Sade: com. *Prettie, neat, spruce, fine, compt, minion, quaint.*
Sadément. *Prettily, neatly, sprucely, finely, comptly, quaintly.*
Sadinet: m. ette: f. *as* Sade; *(or a diminutiue thereof.)*
Faire la sadinette. *To mince it, nicefie it, make it daintie, be verie squeamish, backward, or coy.*
Sadrée: f. *The hearbe Sauorie.*
Saffran: m. *Saffron; Looke* Safran.
Saffran bastard. *Bastard Saffron,* Carthamus, *Mock-Saffron, Saffron Dort.*
Saffran sauvage. *Wild Saffron; or, as* Saffran bastard.
Aller au saffran. *To goe downe the weather, to decline or decay verie much in estate.*
Il en est au saffran. *It hath made him bankrupt, his haire is thereby growne through his hat.*
Saffrané: m. ée: f. *Seasoned, or coloured with Saffron; also, blowne vp, fallen bankrupt, or growne deepe in debt.*
Saffranier: m. *A seller of Saffron; also, a bankrupt, one thats blowne vp, or oweth more then he is worth.*
Saffraniere: f. *A Saffron field or plot, a ground sowed with Saffron.*
Saffrenier. *Looke* Saffranier.
Saffreté: f. *Wanton dallying, leacherous ieasting, lasciuious toying; also, rauening, or gourmandizing.*
Saffrette: f. *A wanton, leacherous, or lasciuious trull; a flirt, queane, gixie, pug, punke.*
Safran: m. *as* Saffran; *also, the lining, or backe, of the Rudder of a ship.*
Safrané. *Looke* Saffrané.
Safre: m. *A heauie minerall, which melted with glasse, or some other the like substance (for alone it will not melt) resolues into a blewish water, wherewith glasses, and earthen vessells be painted.*
Safre: com. *Wanton, waggish, toyish, lasciuious, leacherous, full of dalliance; also, rauenous, gluttonous, gourmandizing.*
Femme safre, & yvrongnesse de son corps n'est pas maistresse: Prov. *A wanton, and wine-bibbing dame, her bodie yeelds to open shame.*

Sa-

Safreté. *Looke* Saffreté.
Safrette. *Locke* Saffrette.
Sagapen, & Sagapene, & Sagapin. *The gumme, or hardned aad gummie iuice, of the bruised, cut, or broken root of* Ferula, *or Fennell-gyant.*
Sage: com. *Sage, wise, discreet, aduised, vnderstanding.*
Elle est bien sage. *She is verie honest.* ¶Orlean.
Faire sage de. *To informe, certifie, let to wit, giue to vnderstand.*
Chascun est sage apres le coup: Prov. *An after-wit is euerie bodies wit; any man can tell, after a blow giuen, how it might haue beene auoided.*
En defaut de sage monte vn fol en chaire: Prov. *A foole, for want of better, doth step vp and preach; vndertakes the businesse; vndergoes the charge.*
Femme sage, & de façon de peu remplit sa maison: Pro. *Looke* Femme.
Fols sont sages quand ils se taisent: Pro. *Fooles are held wise as long as they are silent.*
Il n'est si sage qui ne folie aucunes-fois: Prov. *The wisest man doth somtimes play the foole.*
Le plus sage se taist: Pro. *The wisest sayes the least.*
Les plus sages faillent souvent en beau chemin: Prov. *The wisest often erre in plainest matters.*
On revient sage des iours: Pro. *In time one gets experience.*
Vn fol advise bien vn sage: Pro. *A foole may sometimes giue the wise aduise.*
Sagemener. *Looke* Sacmenter.
Sagement. *Sagely, wisely, discreetly, aduisedly.*
Sageraut. *Wise, warie, discreet, well aduised, of great experience.*
Sagesse: f. *Sagenesse, wisedome, knowledge, discretion, vnderstanding.*
Dens de sens, & de sagesse. *The tenne iaw-teeth.*
Mortier de sagesse. *Looke* Mortier.
Voila vne belle sagesse. *That was a worthie wise act; the verie creame of Apolloes braine-panne.*
Mieux vaut vne once de fortune qu'un livre de sagesse: Pro. *An ounce of lucke excells a pound of wit.*
Saget: m. ette: f. *Prettie and sage, indifferently wise.*
Sagette: f. *An arrow, or shaft; also, the Ditch-weed called, Arrow-head, or water-Archer.*
Sagetté: m. ée: f. *Shot, pierced, or transfixed with arrowes.*
Sagetter. *To hit, strike, pierce, transfix, or shoot through with arrowes.*
Saggotter. *To ioult, rudely to shog or shake.*
Sagitale. *Looke* Sagittale.
Sagitelle: f. *The Launcet wherewith a Surgeon openeth veines, and impostumes.*
Sagittaire: m. *An Archer, Bowman, Shooter; and hence, the heauenlie Archer, or Signe* Sagittarius.
Sagittale. Commissure sagittale. *The seame which runnes along on the top of the head, and distinguishes the right side of it from the left.*
Sagmenter. *Looke* Sacmenter.
Sagnie: f. *A bundle of the slender staulkes of sea-grasse, or of other sea-weedes, wrapped close together, and throwne, by the working of the sea, vpon the shore.* ¶Langued.
Sagoin, & Sagouin. *A little Marmoset; and thence, a little crackrope, slip-string, knauish wag, vnhappie lad.*
Sahuc: m. *A Sallow tree, the Goats Willow tree.*
Saic. *Looke* Saye.

Saiffe: f. *The Dace, or Dare fish.*
Saigné: m. ée: f. *Blouded, let bloud.*
Saignée: f. *Phlebotomie, bloud-letting; also, Dogs-grasse, Couch-grasse, Quitch grasse.*
Selon la jambe la saignée: Prov. *Let bloud according to the bodies fullnesse, or strength; subiects, or tenants would not be drawne too dry.*
Saigner. *To bleed; also, to let bloud.*
Saigner du nez. *His heart to faint, or fayle him; cowardly to flinch, fearefully to quayle, at; to clap his tayle betweene his legs, to set vp his crauen feathers (for much bleeding cooles the heart, and he thats cold at the heart must needs be fearefull.)*
Saigner la terre. *To till, or breake vp ground in an vnfit season, as in a verie hard frost.*
Ie vous saigneray d'une autre veine. *I will see what you can say in other matters; I will try, or put you to it, another way.*
Saigneux: m. euse: f. *Bloudie, full of bloud.*
Sailleur: m. *A leaper, iumper, &c; as* Saulteur.
Sailli. *Gone out, issued forth; also, leaped on.*
Saillicoque. *Looke* Salecoque.
Saillie: f. *A sallie, eruption, violent issue, or breaking out vpon; also, a leape, sault, bound, skip, iert; also, an eminence, iutting, or bearing out beyond others; any disordinate excesse, or excessiue out-standing.*
Saillie de maison. *Any out-iutting roome, or part thereof; and particularly, an open gallerie, or terrace made without the wall, or hanging ouer it.*
Saillie de S. Mathurin. *An odde, foolish, humorous, mad, giddie, fantasticall tricke.*
Saillie d'un os. *A Processe; that part of it which, like a knob in a tree, stands out beyond the rest.*
Saillie d'une pierre precieuse. *The imboßement of an enchaced pretious stone.*
Il a fait vne saillie. *He hath runne too much riot; he hath made a foule fault; he was ill ouerseene, or too farre carried by hast, choller, passion, foolish or haire-braind affection.*
Il a les plus plaisantes saillies du monde. *He vses the most prettie, odde, and extrauagant digressions that euer I heard.*
Saillier: m. *A sallie, eruption, digression, extrauagant flying out.*
Saillir. *To goe out, issue forth; appeare aboue, stand out beyond, others; also, to leape, iumpe, bound, skip, hop; also, to ride, or leape one another, as the male doth the female.*
Sain: m. *Seame; the tallow, fat, or grease of a Hog, or of a rauenous wild beast.*
Sain: m. aine: f. *Sound, whole, wholesome, healthfull, safe, in good plight, in good liking.*
Il se plaind de saine teste. *He is troubled with store of good things; he complaines of ease.*
Hardiment par le teste saine: Prov. *The wise, honest, or guiltleße, boldly speake.*
Sainct: m. *A Saint; a (canonized) holie man.*
Sainct de quaresme. *One that liues strictly or deuoutly in Lent, and loosely or prophanely the whole yeare after; also, one that hides himselfe, or is no where to be found.*
Oublier Dieu parmy tous les saincts. *To forget God amongst All-hallowes; amidst many trifling, to neglect his chiefest occasions.*
Le sainct de la ville n'est point oré: Prov. *Men least respect their owne, or that they are vsed to; our well-knowne patrons are the least implored.*

Il n'est miracle que de vieux saincts: Prov. *We credit not reports, or miracles, of a fresh date; antiquitie is of awfull authoritie.*

Il n'y a si petit sainct qui ne desire sa chandelle: Pro. *Looke* Chandelle.

Le fleuve passé le sainct oublié: Prov. *The danger past our vowes are soone forgotten.*

Sainct: m. cte: f. *Holie, sacred, sanctified, godlie, religious, deuout, pure, of perfect or vnspotted life; (and sometimes) also, the contrarie; as,* O le sainct homme, *what a prophane wretch is this.*

Bois sainct. *The wood Gwacum, or Gayac, whereof diet-drinke for the pocks is made.*

Huile sainct. *The oyle vsed by Papists in Baptisme, and Extreame vnction.*

Huile saincte, ou de Sapience. *Looke* Sapience.

La semaine saincte. *The weeke before Easter, the Passion weeke.*

Saincte: f. *A she Saint; a most holie woman.*

Sainctelot: m. otte: f. *Somewhat holie, or Saint-like.*

Sainctement. *Holily, sacredly, godlily, deuoutly, religiously.*

Saincte-n'y-touche. *An hipocrite; an ouer-scrupulous Puritan; one that, fearing to seeme prophane, will not be touched, or dares touch almost nothing.*

Sainct-foin: m. *Medicke fodder, Snayle-Clauer, Spanish Trifolie, horned Clauer.*

Sainement. *Healthfully, soundly, wholly, wholesomely.*

Sainne. *Looke* Seine.

Saint, & Sainte-n'y-touche. *Look* Sainct, & Saincte-n'y-touche.

Sainteur: m. *A certaine rent payed by those that haue beene freed from bondage vnto those that affranchised them.*

Saint-foin: m. *Medicke fodder, Spanish Trifolie, horned or Snayle-Clauer.*

Saintre. Droict de s. *Looke* Droict.

Sainture. *Looke* Ceincture.

Sais: m. *Certaine peeces of yron, whereby the axletree is fastened vnto the bodie, of a Wayne, &c.*

Saisi: m. ie: f. *Seised, layed hold on, possessed of; attached, arrested.*

Saisie: f. *A seisure, arrest, or attachement of goods, &c.*

Saisine: f. *Seisin, liuerie and seisin, possession.*

Cas de saisine. *An Action, or Suit vpon a disseisin, lyes where a man, out of possession a full yeare and a day, had peaceably inioyed within tenne yeares before, either continually, or by times, and the most part of those yeares; in which case the defendant is to continue his possession during the suit: whereas in* Cas de nouvelleté *(which is for a disseisin within the yeare and day) he is to haue the present possession that can shew the last impeachment thereof to haue been receiued by himselfe.*

Droict de saisine. *Looke* Droict.

Saisir. *To seise, lay hold or hands on, take possession of; also, to attach, or arrest.*

Le Mort saisit le vif; &, le pied saisit le chef. *Looke* Mort, & Pied.

Saisissement: m. *A seising, a laying hold or hands on, a taking possession of; also, an attaching, or arresting; also, a suddaine taking with a qualme, or sowne.*

Saison: f. *Season, due time, fit opportunitie; also, a terme, or time.*

Mauvaise est la saison quand vn loup mange l'autre: Pro. *It is a hard yeare when one Wolfe eates another; when one theefe robs, when one pyrate preyes on, another.*

Si le fol ne folie il perd sa saison: Prov. *A foole not fooling is much out of date; or, a foole is most, when he playes least, the foole.*

Saitte: f. *A kind of two-pennie broad Ribbon made of verie course silke.*

Saive. *Looke* Seve.

Salace: com. *Leacherous, lasciuious, lustfull.*

Salacité: f. *Leacherie, lustfullnesse, ranknesse, a prouocation or tickling vnto lust.*

Salade: f. *A Salade, Helmet, Headpeece; also, a Sallet of hearbes, &c; also, the young head of a Deere (long, tender, woollie, and but beginning to braunch) tearmed by our Woodmen, the crossing, or a Deeres head put vp to the crossing.*

Tant de salades. *So many horsemen.*

Qui vin ne boit apres salade est en danger d'estre malade: Pro. *A Sallet without wine is raw, vnwholesome, dangerous.*

Saladier: m. ere: f. *Belonging to, or fit for, a Salade, or Sallet.*

Salage: m. *Saltage; saltnesse; or salt things.*

Droict de salage. *Looke* Droict.

Salaire: m. *A salarie, stipend, pension, hire, wages, fee, pay giuen.*

Salaison: f. *Salt-making, or a trading for salt.*

Salamandre. *A Salamander. Looke* Salmandre.

Salant: m. ante: f. *Salting; powdering or seasoning with salt.*

Marais salans. *Salt marshes; or marshes whereon salt is gathered.*

Salarié: m. ée: f. *Hired, waged, feed; rewarded.*

Salarier. *To hire, wage, fee; giue a stipend, allow pay, vnto; also, to reward.*

Salariser. *as* Salarier.

Salaude: com. *Looke* Sale.

Salcoque: f. *An vncased Prawne.* ¶Normand.

Sale: f. *Looke* Salle.

Sale: com. *Foule, soyled, nastie, sluttish, vncleane, filthie, loathsome, beastlie.*

Le doigt sale. *The middle finger, which we (after the Latines) call the fooles finger.*

Le gris sale. *A darke, or duskie gray.*

Salé: m. ée: f. *Salted, powdered, pickled; also, brackish, or saltish.*

Salecoque: f. *An vncased Prawne.* ¶Norm.

Salément. *Foulely, filthily, nastily, sluttishly.*

Saler. *To salt, powder, pickle; season or corne with salt, steepe or lay in brine.*

Salet: m. ette: f. *Sullied, slubbered, soyled; somewhat nastie, sluttish, or vncleane.*

Saleté: f. *Foulenesse, nastinesse, ordure, sluttishnesse, filthinesse, vncleanenesse, beastlinesse.*

Salette: f. *A little hall; also, the hearb Sorrell, or Souredocke.*

Petite salette. *Pettie Sorrell, sallet Sorrell.*

Saleure. *Looke* Salure.

Saleures. *Salt meats.*

Salez: m. *The Burgonians, called so in old time by the French, mocking them for their controuersies with the Germans touching their Salt-pits.*

Salezart: m. *An arrant or extreame slouen, a filthie or greasie slowch.*

Salfuge: f. *A kind of Serpent thats poisoned by salt.*

Salicoque. *Looke* Salecoque.

Salicor: m. *The hearb Saltwort, Glassewort, Crab-grasse, Frog-grasse.*

Salicorne. *The same.*

Salicots. *Looke* Saligots.

Sali-

Salidure: f. *A little push, wheale, or powke; so called (at its first arising) in* Languedoc.
Saliere: f. *A salt-seller, a table or trencher salt; also, a powdering house; also, the hollownesse, or hollow pit, betweene the blades of the shoulders;* Looke Salliere.
Saliette: f. *Hearbe Sorrell, Sowre-docke, or Greene-sauce.*
Saligot: m. *A slouen, or slouch:* ¶Orleannois.
Saligots: m. *Saligots, water Caltrops, water Nuts.*
Salin: m. *as* Trident; *also, a garner for salt.*
Droict de Salin. *as* Gabelle de sel.
Saline: f. *A salt-pit, or salt-house; a place wherein salt is gotten, or made.*
Salir. *To foule, soyle, sullie, beray, begrime; pollute, make sluttish, defile, or fill with ordure.*
Salisson: com. *A slouen, or slut (at* Tours.)
Salissure: f. *A fouling, soyling, sullying, defiling, beraying, begriming.*
Salival: m. ale: f. *Spittlie, slimie.*
Salivation: f. *A continuall hauing of much spittle in the mouth; or, a drawing of humors to the mouth, and a deliuerie of them from thence in manner of spittle.*
Salive: f. *Spittle; also, a clammie foame, or iuyce; also, the slime of snailes.*
Table sans sel bouche sans salive: Prov. *Appliable to any dull, or vnsauorie thing, which hath no power to excite th'appetite.*
Saliver. *To slauer; to be full of spittle, yeeld much spittle, make a clammie, or slimie foame.*
Saliveux: m. euse: f. *Spittlie, slauering, full of mouth-moisture; yeelding a clammie or slimie foame.*
Saliviere: f. *as* Baverette à babillons.
Sale: f. *A Hall.*
Salle d'audience. *Any Hall, or place, wherein a Soueraigne Court is kept.*
La grande Salle du Palais. *The great Hall of the Palace; that wherin (as in ours at Westminster) most of the Judges doe sit.*
Avoir la salle. *To be whipped in publicke, or (like a breeching boy of a Colledge) publickly in a Hall.*
Salle: com. *Looke* Sale.
Sallebrenaut: m. *A filthie, shitten, stinking, or slouenlie scoundrell; a base, and beastlie companion.*
Sallebreneux: m. euse: f. *Most filthily berayed.*
Salleté. *Looke* Saleté.
Sallette: f. *A little Hall.*
Salli: m. ie: f. *Fouled, soyled, sullied; berayed, begrimed, exceedingly slurried.*
Salliere: f. *as* Saliere; *also, the pit or hole ouer th'eye of a horse; or the bone wherein it is.*
Sallir *as* Salir; *or* Saslir.
Sallisseure: f. *A fouling, soyling, beraying, begriming, defiling.*
Salloir: m. *A salting, or sowcing tub, or table.*
Sallorge. *A sellor, storehouse, or low roome, to keep salt in.*
Salmandre: f. *A Salamander; a spotted Lizard, or beast like a Lizard, which (as old Authors affirme) liues much in the fire, and either is not hurt by it, or within a while quenches it; but the truth is, that although she endure it better then any other beast, yet at length, or if she stay any while in it, it is not quenched by her, but shee consumed by it.*
Salmandre d'eau. *The water Salamander; black-backed, red-bellied, and full of yellow spots.*
Salmigondin: m. *A Hachee; or meat made ordinarily of cold flesh, cut in little peeces, and stewed or boyled on a chafingdish, with crummes of bread, wine, veriuyce, vinegar, sliced Nutmeg, and Orange pills.*

Salmille: f. *The hearbe Cheruill.*
Salmonde: f. *Hearbe Auens, Bennet, or Blessed.*
Salnitre. *Salt-peter candied, or fined vnto the colour, & substance of white Sugar-candie.*
Saloir: m. *A powdering tub, or table.*
Saloppe: com. *A slouen, or slut:* ¶Orleannois.
Saloque. *The South-east wind.*
Salorge: f. *A sellor, low roome, or storehouse, to lay salt in.*
Salouër. *Looke* Saloir.
Salpestre: m. *Salt-peter.*
Salpestré: m. ée: f. *Made of, or mixed with, Salt-peter.*
Salpestreux: m. euse: f. *Full of Salt-peter.*
Salpestrier: m. *A Salt-peter-man, or, Salt-peter-maker.*
Salsature: f. *Looke* Salsitude.
Salseparille: f. *Th'Indian hearbe, or drug,* Sassaparilla.
Salsitif: m. iue: f. *Salt, saltie, or salt-making.*
Salsitude: f. *Saltnesse, brackishnesse.*
Salsugineux: m. euse: f. *Saltie, or smacking of salt.*
Saltereau. *Looke* Sautereau.
Salüade: f. *A salutation, or greeting; and particularly, a volley of great or small shot bestowed on a great person, or worthie friend.*
Salvador: m. *A Sauiour; (drawne from the Spanish.)*
Salvage. Droict de Salvage. *Looke* Droict.
Salvatelle: f. *Th'outward branch of the shoulder veine, falling down, ouer the wrist, vnto the partitiō between the ring finger, and the little one.*
Salvation: f. *A bill, replie, or pleading, which maintains the truth of an account, the depositions of witnesses, or the goodnesse of a deed, reproached, or contradicted by another bill, &c.*
Salubre: com. *Wholesome, healthfull, whole, sound.*
Salubrement. *Wholesomely, healthfully.*
Salubrité. *Wholesomenesse, healthfulnesse, soundnesse,*
Saluë: f. *A volley of shot giuen for a welcome to some great person, &c.*
Salué: m. ée: f. *Saluted, greeted; reuerenced.*
Saluër. *To salute, greet, all-haile, doe reuerence, make a curtesie, send commendations, giue the time of the day, vnto.*
Ils saluërent le promontoire de &c. *They sayled, or passed, by the Promontorie of &c.*
Saluerne: f. *A great carrousing, or drinking cup:* ¶Rab.
Saluëur: m. *A saluter, a greeter.*
Salure: f. *A salting, powdering, pickling; a laying in brine; a seasoning, or corning with salt; also, brine, or pickle.*
Salus. *as* Saluts; *also, a certaine craftie sea-fish, which biteth away the bait, and meddleth not with the hooke.*
Salut: m. *Health, safetie, soundnesse, good plight; also, saluation, safegard, preseruation; also, a greeting, salutation, commendation.*
Salutaire: m. *The health, preseruation, or safegard of.*
Salutaire: com. *Healthfull, wholesome, sound, whole; comfortable; profitable.*
Salutairement. *Healthfully, wholesomely; comfortably.*
Saluta-libenter. vn sàl. *A cogging, flattering, or gleering mate; one that salutes euerie one (but cares for none) he meets.*
Salutation: f. *A salutation, greeting, or courtesie; a reuerencing; a commending himselfe vnto.*
Saluts: m. *An old French Crowne, or coyne, worth about* 5 s. sterl.
Samarré. *Looke* Chamarré.

Sambacin. Huile sam. *Oyle of Jelsomine flowers.*
Sambregoy. par le sam. *A foolish oath, like our Godsbodekin, &c.*
Sambucin. Huile sam. *Oyle of the flowers, or berries of th'Elder tree.*
Same: f. *The Mullet-fish:* ¶Langued.
Samedy: m. *Saturday.*
Samoireau: m. *A great black grape which yeeldeth verie harsh wine.*
Sampongne: f. *A bagpipe, or oaten pipe; also, the bell hanged about the necke of a sheepe, or goat; some call it a Low-bell.*
Sampsuc: m. *The sweet hearbe Marierome.*
Samy. *A silken, or halfe-silk stuffe, which hath a glosse like Satin, and is narrower, but lasteth better, then it.*
Sanable: com. *Healable, curable.*
Sancerre. *The name of a strong towne in* Berry, *held by those of the Religion, and besieged, in the yere* 1573, *by* la Chastre *for the French King; during which siege* 150 *strong vine-labourers did the defendants notable seruice with their slings; whence the Prouerbe;*
Pistoles de Sancerre. *Slings to hurle stones with.*
Sanchet: m. *A pudding:* (Savoyard.)
Sanchet: m. *An old coyne of gold worth about 2 s.* sterl.
Sanctificateur: m. *A sanctifier, a hallower.*
Sanctification: f. *A sanctification, a hallowing.*
Sanctifier. *To sanctifie, hallow, make holie; also, as* Sanifier.
Sanctimoniale: f. *A Nunne:* ¶Rab.
Sanctimonie: f. *Sanctimonie, holinesse, deuoutnesse, religiousnesse; also, the profession of a religious person.*
Sanction: f. *A Sanction, Ordinance, Law, Decree, Statute established.*
La Pragmatique Sanction. *A confirmation of a decree made in the Councell of* Basile, *whereby (among other things established for the reformation of th'Ecclesiasticall State) th'election of Prelates, and collation of Benefices during vacancie, as also the decision of suites concerning them (vsurped some time before by the Court of Rome) was restored vnto the Canons, Priests, or Monkes of the Diocesse: This Confirmation was published by Edict of Charles the seuenth, in the yeare* 1438.
Sanctoron: m. *An hypocrite, or a counterfeiter of Saints.*
Sanctuaire: m. *A Sanctuarie, the Sanctuarie; a Temple Church, or Chappell; a holie or sanctified place.*
Sandal: m. *Saunders; a sweet-smelling wood brought out of th'Indies; also, the stuffe called Sendall.*
Sandal blanc. *White Saunders; Aromaticall, & next in goodnesse vnto the yellow one.*
Sandal citrin. *Yellow Saunders; the tree whereof is bigger, and the wood sweeter, then any other of that kind.*
Sandal rouge. *Red Saunders; the worst kind of Saunders, yeelding, of it selfe, no manner of odour.*
Sandal roux. *Yellow Saunders.*
Sandale: f. *The shooe called a Sandall, or Sendall, open, or fastened with latchets, on th'instup.*
Sandalin: m. ine: f. *Of Sendall, or Saunders.*
Cerat Sandalin. *Looke* Cerat.
Sandarac: m. *The best red Arsenick, or Orpine; a bright Painters red, whereof there be two kinds; one (the right, and better) found in mines of gold and siluer; the other made of burned Ceruse.*
Sandarac des Arabes. *Gumme of Juniper, or of Cypres.*
Sandarache. *Looke* Sandarac.
Sandastre. *A kind of Carbuncle, or burning stone, wherin small golden drops, or sparkles that shine like starres, appeare.*
Sandeau: m. *A Linke, or Torch:* ¶Rab.
Sandouille. *The name of an apple.*
Sanele. *Wild Mustard.*
Sanemonde: f. *Hearbe Auens, hearbe Bennet, or Blessed.*
Saner. *To cure, heale, or make whole; also, to gueld or spey a Sow.*
Sanes. *Parliaments, or generall assemblies; also, two sixes at Dice.*
Sang: m. *Bloud; also, a stocke, race, kindred, linage, parentage, especially of Kings, in which sence we also vse the words, Bloud royall.*
Sang de dez. *Looke* Sang-de-dez.
Sang de Dragon. *Dragons bloud; a gummie iuyce distilling from the Dragon tree wounded, opened, or bruised in the Dog-dayes; also, the hearb called Bloudwort, red Patience, and bloudie Patience.*
Sang de France. *The Bloud royall of France, (wherin this word hath a larger extention, then in,* Les Princes du Sang, *which are onely such of the Kings kinsmen as may come to the Crowne.)*
Sang d'homme. *Atractilis, wild bastard Saffron.*
Iustice à sang. *Meane, or middle Jurisdiction; so tearmed (belike) because the Lord that hath it may by whipping, &c, draw bloud of his offending vassall, but can proceed no further.*
Avoir du sang aux ongles. *To be resolute, forward, valiant; quicke, industrious, diligent.*
Signer de son sang. *Looke* Signer.
Il n'y fait que le sang tout cler. *Hee hath but little skill, or is at the end of his skill, in that.*
Le Bon sang ne peut mentir: Pro. *Good bloud cannot, (the well-bred will not) lie; a noble nature, confronted by wrong, scorne, or any base condition, doth quickly discouer it selfe.*
Sang-de-dez. *Little square-bladed pocket daggers.*
Sanglamment. *Bloudily.*
Sanglant: m. ante: f. *Bloudie, gore, bleeding, imbrued, full of bloud.*
Rosti sanglant. *A dredging with the powder of Hares bloud.*
Sanglantement. *Bloudily, bleedingly.*
Sanglanter. *To bebloud, or make bloudie; to sprinkle, imbrue, or besmeare, with bloud.*
Sangle: f. *A girth, a sengle; also, an auncient meere, or bound, whereby land from land, and house from house, haue beene diuided.*
Il en avoit tout le long des sangles. *He had his full payment (whether in tearmes, or strokes;) also, he had his fill load (whether of the pot, or of the pocks.)*
Sangle: com. *Single; Looke* Sengle.
Sanglé: m. ée: f. *Girt, as a horse, &c.*
Sanglement: m. *A girding of a horse.*
Sangler. *To girth; to fasten, or bind in, with girthes.*
Sangleron: m. *A young wild Boare.*
Sanglier: m. *A wild Boare.*
Le sanglier n'est qu'un hoste: Prov. *The Boare is but a soiourner; for he seldome stayes, any time, within one wood, or forrest, but raunges continually.*
Au cerf la biere, au sanglier le barbier: Prov. *The Stag a coffin, Boare a Barber, needs; or, if thou beest hurt by a Stag prouide a coffin, if by a wild Boare a Chirurgian.*
Sangliere: f. *A wild Sow.*

San-

Sanglot. *Looke* Senglot.
Sanglot de sang. *A lumpe, or clot of congealed, or cluttered bloud.*
Sanglotin : m. *A Boare-pig, or, a little wild Boare.*
Sanglotter. *To yex, or hickock; also, to sob often.*
Sanglout. *Looke* Senglot.
Sanglure : f. *A girding.*
Sang-meslé : m. ée : f. *Whose bloud is stirred, whose colour comes and goes, through a great, or sudden feare, &c.*
Sang-messleure : f. *A disturbing, or stirring of the bloud; a comming and going of colour, by reason of a great, or sudden feare.*
Sangoy. *as much (in rusticall French) as* Sang de Dieu.
Sangreal. *Part of Christs most pretious bloud wandering about the world inuisible (to all but chast eyes) and working many wonders, and wonderfull cures; if we may credit the most foolish, and fabulous Historie of King Arthur.*
Sangsuë : f. *A Horsleech, a bloud-sucker.*
Sangsuër. *To sucke bloud like a Horsleech.*
Sanguificatif : m. iue : f. *Bloud making, turning into bloud.*
Sanguifier. *To conuert, or turne into bloud.*
Sanguin : m. *The purple shrub called Hounds-tree, Hounds-berrie tree, Dog-berrie tree, Gaten or Gater tree.*
Sanguin blanc. *The white barren, or fruitlesse Priuet.*
Sanguin noir. *Our ordinarie Priuet, whose ripe berrie is blacke; or (as* Macaleb*) Pomander Priuet, whose berrie hath a shining blacke hue.*
Sanguin rouge. *as* Sanguin.
Sanguin : m. ine : f. *Sanguine, bloudie, red; of a sanguine complexion; full of bloud.*
Sanguinaire f. *Centinodie, Swines-grasse, Knot-grasse, Birds tongue, S. Innocents hearbe.*
Sanguinaire : com. *Bloudie, gorie, red; bloud-thirstie, cruell.*
Sanguine : f. *The bloud-stone wherewith Cutlers doe sanguine their hilts.*
Sanguine noire. *A certaine scalie, and yron-coloured stone, of the kind of bloud-stones.*
Sanguineral : m. *The little fish called a Mennow.*
Sanguinité : f. *Consanguinitie, kindred, parentage, affinitie, neerenesse of bloud.*
Sanguinolent : m. ente : f. *Sanguinolent, bloudie, full of bloud.*
Sanguisorbe : f. *Burnet, Pimpinell.*
Sanicle : com. *Sanicle, Sanikell, Selfe-heale.*
Sanicle femelle. *Blacke Maisterwort, or Dioscorides his blacke Hellebore; called (vntruely) by the vulgar, Pellitorie of Spaine.*
Celuy qui sanicle a de mire affaire il n'a : &, Qui a du bugle, & du Sanicle, fait au Chirurgien la nique : Pro. *(So great is the vertue, and operation of this hearbe in the closing, and curing of wounds.*
Saniclet : m. *as* Sanicle.
Sanie : f. *Matter; corrupt, or filthie bloud; or, more properly, the serositie, or waterishnesse of bloud, or of other humors; and, the waterie excrement thats yeelded by vlcers, and bred of the same cause.*
Sanie des oreilles. *Eare-wax.*
Sanieux : m. euse : f. *Matterie, corrupt; yeelding, or full of, a filthie moisture.*
Saninier. *Looke* Savinier.
Sannier : m. *A Salter; Salt-seller; Salt-maker.*

Sans. *Sanse, without, besides.*
C'est mon homme sans autre. *Tis the same man I looked for, it is none but he.*
Passe sans flux. *Passe, I am not flush; also, let goe, no matter, not a pinne matter.*
Sansonet : m. *The bird called a Starling, or Stare; also, a little, or prettie and tunable, fart.*
Sansonnet. *The same.*
Sansuë : f. *The water-worme called a Horsleech, or Bloud-sucker.*
Santal. *as* Sandal.
Santé : f. *Health, welfare, soundnesse of bodie: In* Xainctonge *they vse to giue Prawnes vnto diseased persons, and thereupon tearme them,* De la Santé.
De grande maladie vient on bien en grande santé : Prov. *Much comfort after many crosses; long sicknesse often breeds a lasting health.*
Mal dessus mal n'est pas santé : Prov. *Ayle vpon ill cannot be health.*
Point ne faut demander de malade s'il veut santé : Prov. *Aske not a sicke man if he would be sound; make not a question of things questionlesse; doubt not of that which is alreadie resolued.*
Qui n'a santé il n'a rien, qui a santé il a tout : Pro. *He that hath health, hath all things, he that wants it, nothing.*
Santonique : f. *Wormeseed; the seed of holie Wormewood, or Wormeseed-wort.*
Sanuës blanches. *The white wild Colewort.*
Sanut. *as* Canus.
Sanxi : m. ie : f. *Decreed, ordained, enacted, established, ratified; also, forbidden.*
Sanxion : f. *An Act, Law, decree, Statute, Ordinance.*
Sanye : f. *Looke* Sanie.
Saon : m. *A challenge of, or exception against, a witnesse, Juror, &c.*
Saonier : m. *A Salter, one that selleth salt.*
Saonné : m. ée : f. *Challenged, or excepted against.*
Saonnement : m. *A challenging, or excepting against.*
Saonner. *To challenge, or except against, a witnesse, Juror, &c.*
Saoul : m. *A glut, sacietie, fullneße.*
Saoul : m. saoule : f. *Full, glutted, cloyed, saciated, that hath so much of a thing as he is readie to loath it.*
Le Pigeon saoul trouve les cerises ameres : Prov. *The full-stuft maw findes bitternesse in sweet things.*
Qui a la pance pleine il luy semble que tous les autres sont saouls : Prov. *He thats full-bellied thinkes all others full.*
Saoulé : m. ée : f. *Glutted, saciated, filled, cloyed with.*
Saoulement : m. *A glutting, filling, saciating, cloying with.*
Saouler. *To glut, cloy, fill, saciate, giue a gorgefull of.*
On se saoule bien de manger tartes : Pro. *One may well glut himselfe (or, soone haue ynough) in eating Tarts.*
Saouleté : f. *Sacietie, fulnesse, a cloying, glutting, loathing, loathsomenesse.*
Saoulure : f. *The same.*
Sap. Bois de sap. *Deale planke, Deale boords.*
Sape. *Looke* Sabe.
Sapé; &, Saper. *Looke* Sappé; &, Sapper.
Saphene. *The mother veine; runnes ouer th'inner ankle vnto th'instap, and thence to the great toe.*
Saphiques : f. *Saphicks, or Saphicke verses (of eleuen sillables.)*
Saphir : m. *A Saphir stone; also, a bud, or blew pimple on any part of the face.*

Saphre.

Saphre. *Looke* Safre.
Sapience : f. *Sapience, wisedome, discretion, circumspection, warinesse, knowledge of all things.*
Huile de sapience. *Oyle drawne out of tiles, or bricks, which haue beene steeped in verie old oyle.*
Sapin : m. *A Firre tree.*
Sapin femelle. *The Deale tree.*
Bois de Sapin. *Deale planke, or Deale boords.*
Sapine : f. *An open tub, or vessell (of Firre wood, &c,) wherein bottles of wine are vsually set.*
Sapinette : f. *A groue, or wood, of Firre trees.*
Sapineux : m. euse : f. *Firrie, of Firre, full of Firre.*
Sappé : m. ée : f. *Digged, vndermined, opened, cut into or through, as a wall, at the foot.*
Sappement : m. *A digging of a wall, an vndermining, opening, or cutting into it, at the foot; hence also, a supplanting.*
Sapper. *To vndermine, dig into, open, or cut open (as a wall) at the foot; and hence also, to supplant.*
Sappeur : m. *An vnderminer, or miner.*
Sapphir. *Looke* Saphir.
Sappin : m. *A Chiappin, or Spanish Pantofle; monstrous high-soled, and most vsed by women.*
Saquer. *Looke* Sacquer.
Saquerelle : f. *A Docke for a horses traine.*
Sarache : f. *An Albanian fish verie like to th'Anchoua.*
Sarazine. *Looke* Sarrasine.
Sarbacane, *or (which is better)* Sarbataine : f. *A long trunke to shoot in; also, the musicall Instrument called a Sagbut.*
Sarcable : com. *Weedable, fit to be weeded.*
Sarcasme : m. *A biting taunt, bitter ieast, cutting quip, nipping scoffe.*
Sarcelle : f. *The water-fowle called a Teale.*
Sarclé : m. ée : f. *Weeded; grubbed vp with a weeding forke.*
Sarclement : m. *A sarkling, weeding; a grubbing vp with a weeding forke.*
Sarcler. *To weed; to grub, or dig vp weeds.*
Sarclet : m. *A weeding hooke, or weeding forke; made somewhat like a grubbing, or dung, forke.*
Sarcleur : m. *A weeder.*
Sarcloir : m. *Looke* Sarclet.
Sarcocolle : f. *A bitter Gumme which issues from a thornie Persian plant; also, the Wind-rose, or bastard wild Poppie.*
Sarcophange : m. *A stone called Eat-flesh, because it consumes, in fortie dayes, the dead carkasses inclosed within it.*
Sarcotique : com. *Breeding new flesh.*
Sarcueil : m. *A coffin for a dead corps; Looke* Cercueil.
Sardaine : f. *A Pilchard, or Sardine.*
Sardanapalisme : f. *Filthie, and effeminate sensualitie.*
Sarde : f. *A Pilchard; also, a flesh-coloured stone, thats easie to be grauen, and therefore much vsed in Seale-rings.*
Sardelle : f. *The little fish called a Sardell, or Sardine.*
Sardine. *Looke* Sardaine.
Sardoine : m. *The Sardonix; a stone which on th'one side resembles a mans naile, on th'other the* Sarde.
Sardonien. Ris sardonien. *Looke* Ris.
Sarfoët : m. *Looke* Sarfouëtte.
Sarfoüage : m. *A grubbing, digging, or cutting vp of weeds.*
Sarfouëtte : f. *An Instrument, whose yron head, about a foot long, is forked on th'one side, & sharpe on th'other, to grub, or cut vp weeds or noisome hearbs.*
Sarfouïr. *To grub, or cut vp weeds.*
Sarge : f. *The stuffe called Serge.*
Sargette : f. *A fine, or thinne Serge.*
Sargon : m. *The Gilthead, or Goldeney; as some hold; howsoeuer, it is a verie lecherous fish, and often changeth his mate.*
Sargoter. *To shog, ioult, shake, tosse, or thumpe; also, to swiue.*
Sarin : m. *A certaine water-hearbe, which hath a hard root necessarie for Smithes.*
Sarisse. *A long Speare, Launce, Pike, or Javelin, vsed by th'auncient Macedonians.*
Sarlatan : m. *Looke* Charlatan.
Sarment : m. *The twig, or small branch of a vine, &c.*
Se brider de sarment. *To bridle himselfe with a vine-sprig; to be so drunke that he cannot speake.*
Sarmenteux : m. euse : f. *Full of twigs, or small branches.*
Sarmentin : m. ine : f. *Of, or belonging to, a small vine branch.*
Dragme sarmentine. *A draught, or cup, of wine.*
Sarpe : f. *An instrument somewhat resembling a little Bill, and vsed for the lopping of trees, and cutting of other small wood, whereof bauens, and fagots be made.*
Sarpette : f. *A vine-knife, hooked Gardeners knife, small hedging Bill.*
`A pleine sarpette. La vigne qui est à pleine sarpette. *Thats full of, or well furnished with, grapes.*
Sarpillére : f. *A Sarpliar; a peece of canuas, cloth, or other stuffe to wrap, or packe vp wares in.*
Sarpilliere : f. *The same.*
Sarpillon. *Looke* Sarpette.
Sarrabouïte. *Looke* Strabouïte : ¶Rab.
Sarrasine : f. *The hearbe Heartwort, or Birthwort; also, Sarasines Consound, or Comfrey.*
Sarrasson : m. *Fleetings, or hastie curds, scumd from the whey of a new-milke cheese, then thickened with a little milke, or the yolke of an egge, and boyled on a soft fire.*
Sarre : f. *A kind of small peece of Artillerie vsed in old time.*
Sarrer. *Looke* Serrer.
Sarriette : f. *Sauorie, Summer Sauorie.*
Sarriette d'Angleterre. *Winter Sauorie, Timbra, Time-hysop.*
Sars : m. des sars. *Chichlings, yellow wild Fitches.*
Sart : m. *Sea-mosse, Lungwort, Oistergreene.*
Sarteau : m. *The Bell-peare, or Gourd-peare.*
Sartie : f. *A Cocke-boat, or ship-boat; the skiffe belonging to a ship.*
Sartre : m. *A Tailor, or Botcher; a mender of old garments.*
Sarvinien : m. *A fruitfull white vine whose leafe is almost round.*
Sas : m. *A ranging siue, or searce.*
Au gros sas. *Coursly; also, carelesly, sleightly, cursarily.*
Sasle : com. *Looke* Sale.
Saslir. *Looke* Salir.
Sassé : m. ée : f. *Searced, sifted, ranged, boulted.*
Sassefique; *or*, Sassefrique. *Looke* Sassify.
Sassement : m. *A sifting, searcing, ranging, boulting.*
Sasser. *To sift, searce, range, boult.*
Sasse bonne farine sans trompe ne buccine : Prov. *Boult thy fine meale, and eat good past, without report, or Trumpets blast.*
Sasseur : m. *A sifter, searcer, boulter of corne, &c.*

Saſſeures: f. *Siftings; or, that which remaines in a ſiue, range, or ſearce, after that the meale hath beene ſifted from it.*

Saſſefy: m. *Goats bread, Joſephs flower, Starre of Jeruſalem, Noone-tide, Goe to bed at noone.*

Saſſure. *Looke* Saſſement.

Satellite: m. *A Sergeant, Catchpole; or Yeoman of the gard; one that arreſteth, or gardeth a mans perſon.*

Satieté: f. *Satietie, fulneſſe; plentie, content; alſo, a glutting, or cloying.*

Satin: m. *Satin.*

Satirion. *Looke* Satyrion.

Satisfaction: f. *Satisfaction, contentment, a pleaſing; a fulfilling of the deſire, or will; alſo, repaiment; alſo, a purgation, or excuſe.*

Satisfactionnaire: m. *A Preacher of ſatisfaction.*

Satisfactoire: com. *Satisfactorie, ſatisfying.*

Satisfaict: m. cte: f. *Satisfied, contented, pleaſed, payed.*

Satisfaire. *To ſatisfie, content, pleaſe, fulfill the humor or deſire of; to repay, make ſatisfaction; throughly to furniſh, or prouide for.*

Satouilles: f. *Little Lampreyes bred in ſmall freſh-water ſtreames, into which the ſea comes not.*

Satrape: m. *A great Ruler, Commaunder, Potentate, or Peere; the Lieutenant, or Gouernour of a countrey.*

Sattaquer. *Looke* Attaquer.

Saturige: f. *The hearbe Sauorie.*

Saturité: f. *Saturitie, fulneſſe, glutting, plentie, exceſſe.*

Saturnales. *The Feaſts of Saturne, celebrated by th'ancient Painims in December.*

Saturne: m. *Saturne; one of the ſeuen Planets; alſo, lead (among Alchimiſts, &c.)*

Saturnien: m. enne: f. *Sad, ſowre, lumpiſh, melancholie.*

Satyre: m. *A Satyre; a monſter halfe man halfe Goat.*

Satyre: f. *A Satyre; an Inuectiue, or vice-rebuking Poeme.*

Satyriaſe: f. *Pricke-pride, luſt-pride; the ſtanding of the yard; alſo, Priapiſme, a luſtleſſe extenſion, or ſwelling thereof.*

Satyric: m. ique: f. *Satyricall, taunting, inueying, biting, nipping, bitter, ſharpe, rebuking, reprouing.*

Satyrion: m. *Satyrion, Ragwort, Standlewort, Stander-graſſe, Gander-gooſe, Prieſts-pinice, ſweet Cullions, Ladies traces: (The Grecians tearme thus all Bulbus-rooted, and luſt-prouoking, hearbs.)*

Satyrion à deux couillons. *as (th'originall)* Satyrion.

Satyrion à trois couillons. *Triple Orchis, or triple Ladies traces.*

Satyrion à trois fueilles. *Three-leaued Satyrion, Fox-ſtones.*

Satyrion royal. *Satyrion royall, finger Orchis, Palma Chriſti.*

Satyrique. *Looke* Satyric.

Satyriquement. *Satyrically, tauntingly, nippingly, bitingly, railingly, inueyingly, rebukingly, reprouingly.*

Satyrium. *Looke* Satyrion.

Sau: m. *Salt;* ¶Poictevin. *alſo, a ſeller; alſo, an Oxe-houſe, or ſuch like baſe roome in a countrey cottage.*

Savart. *as* Friche.

Savate. *An old ſhooe; alſo, the play called Bob and bit, or Hodman blind.*

Le beau ſoulier devient en fin ſavate: Prov. *Appliable to beautie decayed, or in the wane, by age, &c.*

Savaterie: f. *A cobling, or the trade of a Cobler; alſo, a ſtreet, or place, wherein old ſhooes be ſold.*

Savatier. *as* Savetier; *alſo, the play called Hodman blind.*

Savaton: m. *A ſhooe:* ¶Gaſcon. *alſo, a peece of an old ſhooe.*

Vieil ſavaton. *The Millers thumbe; a fiſh.*

Saubenite. *A ſleeueleſſe yellow coat, or gowne painted all ouer with repreſentations of diuells, and put vpon ſuch as are found guiltie by th'Inquiſition.*

Sauce: f. *A ſauce, condiment, ſeaſoning for meat.*

Sauce barbe Robert. *A ſauce for fried fiſh, or roaſted Conies, made of little Onions fried in butter, veriuyce, vinegar, muſtard, ſmall ſpices, and ſalt, boyled together.*

Sauce blanche. *Is made of blanched Almonds, & the brawne of a boyled Capon pownded together; and then Cloues, Ginger, Cynnamon, Roſe-water, and Sugar, put vnto it.*

Sauce chaude. *Is made of Manchet firſt dried, then ſteeped in vinegar, or veriuyce; and afterwards with long Pepper, white Ginger, Cloues, Graines, and Nutmeg, pownded, and ſtrained.*

Sauce d'enfer. *A ſauce, or condiment made of hogs feet firſt boyled, then broyled, then cut into great flat peeces, then ſcorched on a gridiron, then ſtued in veriuyce with Onions, then ſeaſoned with muſtard, and then boiled in a diſh with hot coales put both vnder, and ouer it.*

Sauce froide. *Another, made of the liuers, and giſerns of chickens boiled with a little bacon, then taken out of their broth and cooled; then white bread ſteeped in vinegar, and greene corne ſtrained together, and Marierome, Parſley, white Ginger, a little Sage, and a good deale of ſalt, added vnto them.*

Sauce reale, & royale: &, Sauce Robert. *Looke* Real; & Robert.

La ſauce ne vaut pas mieux que le poiſſon: Prov. *(Appliable three wayes) the ſauce and fiſh are bad alike; or, the ſauce ſhould not be better then the fiſh; or, the ſauce is ſeldome better then the fiſh.*

Sans ſel ny ſauce. *Inſulſe, vnſauorie, abſurd, without any manner of grace.*

'A chair de loup ſauce de chien: Prov. *Looke* Chien.

Saucer. *To ſauce, to ſeaſon with ſauce; alſo, to dip; whence;*

Il ne ſaucera ſon pain en ma ſouppe. *Hee ſhall not dip his bread in my broth; he ſhall not come neere me, he ſhall haue nothing to doe with me.*

Sauciſſe: f. *A Saucidge; alſo, an Engine couered with leather, and made like vnto, but much greater then, a Saucidge, which writhen by one end between the ſtones of a wall, and fire giuen to it, breakes it downe how ſtrong ſoeuer it be; alſo, an Engine of peeces of wood bound hard together with hoopes of yron in the forme of a Tunne (but much thicker and longer, for a horſeman doth eaſily ſhrowd himſelfe behind it, and fiftie or ſixtie men goe to the rowling of it vp and downe.)*

Sauciſſe de Boulongne. *A Bolonia Saucidge, is made of beefe and leane bacon, in equall quantitie, flayed, and chopped ſmall with halfe as much lard, and ſome Pepper, Ginger, and ſalt; then put into a cleane Oxe gut halfe a foot long, and layd in ſalt for two daies together, and afterwards hung vp in the ſmoake.*

Sauciſſe de Lombardie. *A Lombardie Saucidge, is made of the fleſh of ſodden Capons, and of Partridges, Woodcocks, or ſome riuer fowle, and a little porke with lard chopped ſmall together, and ſeaſoned with whole*

Pepper, salt, and small spice; then put into an Oxe gut, and hung in the smoake; so may it be kept raw two or three yeares; but when you would eat it you must steep it, and afterwards boyle it a good while in wine and water.
Saucisson: m. *A Liuering, or little Saucidge.*
Sauclés. *as* Melet.
Saudenier: m. *A Souldier that taketh pay.* (v.m.)
Save. *Looke* Seve.
Savetier: m. *A Cobler, a Sowter.*
Savetier: m.ere: f. *Of, or belonging to, cobling, or old shooes.*
Saveud. *as* Friche; *whence;* Terres laissées en saveud. *Grounds that lye vnlaboured.*
Saveur: f. *Sauor, smacke, tast, relish; also, pot-hearbes; or seasoning; whence,* mettez la saveur au pot.
Sauf: m. *A limitation of time for the returne of a partie, which vpon his apparance, and th'aduersaries default in Court, hath leaue to be gone.*
Sauf: m. sauve: f. *Safe, sure, sound, whole, vnbroken, without harme or daunger, in good case; also, saued, reserued, excepting, without preiudice vnto; whence, the Phrases,* Sauf mon droict; &, sauf vostre honneur; &, sauf au defendeur son recours; &c.
Saufconduict: m. *A safe conduct, conuoy, pasport, passe; protection, safegard.*
Sauf-respit: m. *Respite of homage, or a time granted by a Lord vnto his vassall for the doing of his homage.*
Sauge: f. *Looke* Saulge.
Saugé: m.ée: f. *Sagie, full of Sage, seasoned with Sage, wherein Sage hath beene steeped.*
Sauger: m. *The name of a sweet and tender apple.*
Saugrenée: f. *A porridge, or meat of Pease and broth halfe boiled, and put into a dish with sops, salt, Saffron, Sallet oyle, and some veriuyce, or vinegar.*
Saugrenu: m.uë: f. *Vntoward, vngainelie, ill-fauoured, insulse, absurd, sottish, or sottishly done.*
Savinier: m. *The Sauin tree, or shrub.*
Saulce. *Looke* Sauce.
Saulcisse. *Looke* Saucisse.
Sauldoy: m. *Branches of Willow cut euerie third or fourth yeare, for poles, and props for vines, &c.*
Saule: m. *A Sallow, Willow, or Withie tree.*
Saule bastard. *The low, or dwarfe Willow.*
Saulgé: m. *Capon sauce, made of Sage.*
Saulge: f. *The hearbe Sage.*
Saulge de bois. *Wood Sage, wild Sage, Garlicke Sage.*
Saulge franche. *Sage royall, small Sage, common Sage.*
Saulge molle, ou de montaigne. *Stachis, wild or yellow Horehound.*
Saulge d'outre mer. *The hearbe Clarie, or Cleere-eye, called by some, beyond-sea Sage.*
Saulge petite. *Small Sage (of a better smell then the great.)*
Saulge Romaine. *Costmarie, Alecost; also, the common garden Mint, speare Mint, our Ladies Mint, browne Mint, Mackerell Mint.*
Saulge sauvage. *Wild Sage, wood Sage, Garlick Sage; also, as* Saulge molle.
Saulge transmarine. *Looke* Saulge d'outre mer.
Grande Saulge. *Great Sage, broad Sage.*
Sans sel ny saulge. *Vnsauorie, insulse, absurd.*
Saulgé: m.ée: f. *Seasoned with Sage; wherein Sage hath beene steeped; Sagie, full of Sage.*
Saulmon: m. *A Salmon.*
Il faut perdre vn veron pour pescher vn Saulmon: Prov. *We must loose a little that we may get much.*
Saulmone de plomb: f. *A great sow of lead.*
Saulmonnée: f. *A great Salmon Trout.*
Saulmonnier: m.ere: f. *Of a Salmon; whence;* Truite Saulmonniere; *A Salmon Trout.*
Saulmonniere: f. *The same.*
Saulmurages: m. *Rubbish of stone, bricke, &c, laied vnder the groundsill, or foundation of a house.*
Saulmure: f. *Pickle; the brine of salt; the liquor of flesh, or fish pickled, or salted in barrells, &c.*
Saulmuré: m.ée: f. *Pickled; kept or condit in pickle, seasoned or mingled with pickle.*
Saulnerie: f. *A Salt-shop, or Garner for salt; a place wherein salt is kept and vented.*
Saulnier: m. *A Salter, Salt-seller, Marchant of salt; also, a Salt-box.*
Sauloye: f. *A plot, or groue of Willowes.*
Saulpiquet. *Looke* Saupiquet.
Saulpouldrer. *To salt, corne or powder with salt, lay in brine or salt.*
Saulpouldrer de sucre. *To powder, bedust, or strew ouer with Sugar.*
Saulsaye: f. *A plot, or groue of Willowes.*
Saulse: f. *Looke* Sauce.
Saulser. *To sauce, to dip in sauce.*
Saulserette, & Saulseron. *A little saucer.*
Saulsiere: f. *A saucer.*
Saulsisse. *Looke* Saucisse.
Saulsissier: m. *A maker of Saucidges.*
Sault: m. *A leape, &c; Looke* Saut.
Saultant: m. ante: f. *Leaping; iumping; skipping.*
En saultant. *By leapes or skips, disorderly, cursarily, scatteringly, leaping from one matter to another.*
Saulté. *Leaped; iumped; bounded, or skipped ouer; whence;*
Aussi tost prest qu'un chien auroit saulté vn eschalier. *Readie in a trice, or, in the turning of a hand; readie ere a dog can haue skipped ouer a stile.*
Saultelement: m. *A bounding, skipping, hopping.*
Saulteler. *To hop or skip, to bound or spring.*
Saultelle: f. *as* Bois debout *(vnder* Bois; *) also, a vine-branch bowed downewards, and the top thereof set into the ground, thereby to get root.*
Saultement: m. *A leaping.*
Saulter. *To leape, iumpe, skip, to spring or bound; also, to rub (at Bowles.)*
Saulter le baston. *Resolutely to passe on, or performe, what must be done.*
Saulter du coq à l'asne. *Seeke* Asne.
Saulter à deux pieds sur le ventre à. *To leape with both feet vpon the bellie of; vtterly, or as much as in him lies, to crush, or confound.*
Saulter de treille en paisseaux. *Idly, or inconstantly to shift, in discourse, from one subiect vnto another.*
Il recule pour mieux saulter. *He goes backe to take burre, or to leape the better; he retires, or withdrawes himselfe, to make his returne the more effectuall.*
Saultereau: m. *A Locust, or Greshopper; also, the Iack of a Virginall, &c; Looke* Sautereau.
Saulterelle: f. *A woman leaper, vaulter, tumbler, dauncer; also, as* Saultereau; *(also, a Shrimpe, or Prawne:* Breton.) *Looke* Sauterelle.
Saulterette: f. *A Shrimpe, or Prawne.*
Saulteur: m. *A leaper, iumper, bounder; also, a vaulter, tumbler, dauncer; also, as* Saultoir.
Saultoir: m. *Saint Andrewes crosse; tearmed so by Heraulds.*

Saulx: f. *The willow, or Withie tree.*
Saulx blanche. *The great white Withie, dunne Withie, goore Withie.*
Saulx Gauloise, ou de Gaule. *The red-barked Withie, or blacke Withie; also, the Spert or Ozier Withie; also, the hearbe called* Agnus castus, *and Abrahams Balme.*
Saulx Grecque. *as* Saulx blanche.
Saulx iaulne. *The Cane withie, or yellow-barked Willow.*
Saulx noire. *The blacke withie, red-barked Willow; called also (by some) the red Spert, or Ozier.*
Saulx viminale. *The same; also, the small Withie, twig Withie, Spert or Ozier Withie.*
Saulx vitelline. *The Cane Withie, or yellow-barked Willow.*
Saume: f. *A she Asse.*
Saumée de bled. *The quantitie of foure* Septiers; *or, the third part of a Parisian* Muid.
Saumée de terre. *A proportion of land containing in square 1600 reedes, and each of those reedes eight spannes in length.*
Saumon: m. *A Salmon.*
Saumonneau: m. *A young, or little Salmon; a Salmon Trout.*
Saumure, & Saumuré. *Looke* Saulmure, & Saulmuré.
Saune: f. *The hearbe called Blite, or Blits; (and some also tearme Helicampanie so.)*
Saunelage. Droict de saun. *The tenth part of goods which are saued from shipwracke, due vnto him that saued them.*
Saunier: m. *A Salter, &c; Looke* Saulnier.
Savon: m. *Sope.*
Terre de savon. *Fullers earth.*
Savonné: m. ée: f. *Soped, or washed in sope; also, frothie like sope-suds, or a lather of sope.*
Savonner. *To sope, or wash with sope.*
Savonnier: m. ere: f. *Of, or belonging vnto, sope.*
Herbe savonniere. *Sopewort, &c; as vnder* Herbe.
Savorade: f. *as* Savorados: ¶Gasc.
Savorados. *A poore kind of pottage extracted only from the iuyce of bare, and hollow bones:* ¶Limosin: ¶Rab.
Savorée: f. *The hearbe Sauorie.*
Savouré: m. ée: f. *Sauorie, that hath a good smacke or tast; also, sauored, or tasted of; also, seasoned.*
Savourer. *To sauor, smack, relish, tast of; also, to season.*
Savoureusement. *Sauorily, tastfully, tastingly, with a good stomacke.*
Savoureux: m. euse: f. *Sauorie, tastfull, tart, well smacking, of a good relish.*
Saupe: f. *A small-headed, little-mouthed, blunt-nosed, large-scaled, vnsauorie, and vnwholesome sea-fish, hauing many golden lines all along from her gills to her taile; and thence, likened by some to the Giltbead; by others mistaken for the fish whereof Stockefish is made.*
Saupiquet: m. *Porke sauce, made of Onions, vinegar, and mustard; also, sauce for a roasted Conie, of Onions, Ginger, veriuyce, and white wine; generally, any kind of tart sauce.*
Saupiqueter. *To sauce, or season; to giue a sharpe tast vnto.*
Saupiqueux: m. euse: f. *Sharpe or tart, as the* Saupiquet; *also, full thereof; seasoned therewith; belonging thereto.*
Saupoudré: m. ée: f. *Salted, corned with salt; also, powdered, besprinkled, or done ouer with powder or dust.*
Saupoudrer. *Looke* Saulpouldrer.
Sauquene: f. *A yong, or small Giltbead:* ¶Langued.

Saur: m. saure: f. *Sorrell of colour; whence;* Harenc saur; *a red Herring.*
Saure: m. *A Sorrell colour; also, a Sorrell horse.*
Saure obscur, ou bruslé. *as* Alezan toustade *(vnder* Alezan.)
Saurel: m. *The bastard Mackerell.*
Saurer. *Looke* Saurir.
Sauret: m. *as* Saure: ¶Langued.
Saurir. *To make Sorrell, or turne into a Sorrell colour; whence;*
Saurir les harencs. *To redden Herrengs; to lay them on hurdles in a close roome, and there smoake them with the dried leaues of Elme, or Oake, or with Tanners barke, vntill they haue gotten their Sorrell hue.*
Saurisseur: m. *A redder of Herrings.*
Saussissier: m. *A Saucidge-maker.*
Saussiere: f. *A saucer, or little sallet dish.*
Saut: m. *A leape, sault, bound, skip, iumpe; also, (at Bowles) a rub; also, an vneuen, or ill pollished part of a pretious stone, which in a curious eye disgraces all the rest.*
Saut de Breton. *A fall vpon the backe, a faire fall giuen one.*
Saut de la carpe. *A turning topsie turuie, or top ouer taile.*
Saut de ferme à ferme. *The manage tearmed a Sault, Capriole, or Goats-leape.*
Saut de hanche. *A comming or turning sidewayes, cleane ouer, without the helpe of any hand.*
Saut de mouton. *A kind of high manage.*
Saut rond. *A turne aboue-ground, in dauncing.*
Mauvais saut. Donner vn mauvais saut. *Looke* Donner.
Trois pas, & vn saut. *The Almond leape.*
Vn pas, & vn saut. *(In manoging) a Passasalto, Gall'op Galliard, Pace and a leape.*
En deux pas vn saut. *Speedily, in a trice, in hast, apace.*
En mesme saut. Moulins estans en mesme saut. *Standing in one leuell, or turned by one height, of water.*
Faire le saut. *To breake, fall bankrupt, run his countrey for debt; also, to leape, or be turned, off an vnpleasing ladder.*
Sauté. *Looke* Saulté.
Sautelle: f. *Looke* Saultelle.
Sautellement, & Sauteller. *Looke* Saultelement, & Saulteler.
Sauter. *Looke* Saulter.
Sautereau: m. *A Grashopper; also, the Jacke of a Virginall, &c.*
Sautereaux de Brie. *The swaines of* Brie *are so tearmed, because they commonly make deepe, and long ditches at the ends of their lands (for the draining of their superfluous moisture) and thereby must leap, if they will passe, ouer them.*
Sautereaux de Verberie. *Looke* Verberie.
Sauterelle: f. *as* Saulterelle; *also, a Masons Instrument, framed like a Squire, yet so, that, as a paire of Compasses, it may be opened, and shut againe at pleasure.*
Sauteur. *Looke* Saulteur.
Sautier: m. *A leaper, iumper, skipper.*
Sautoir: m. *Saint Andrewes Crosse; tearmed so by Heraulds.*
Sautueil. *as* Sautoir.
Sauvage: m. *A wilding apple.*

Sauvage: m. *Sauage, wild, hagard, harsh, vntamed, vnbroken, vnreclaimed.*
Herbe sauvage. *A weed.*
Sauvageau: m. *A wild plant, set, or stocke fit to bee graffed on.*
Sauvagement. *Sauagely, wildly, hagardly, harshly, skittishly.*
Sauvageon. *as* Sauvageau.
Sauvageté: f. *Sauagenesse, wildnesse, vnreclaimednesse, harshnesse, rudenesse.*
Sauvagine: f. *Venison; also, wildnesse; also, ranknesse, or harshnesse of smell, or tast.*
Sauvagine d'oiseaux. *Wild-fowle.*
Sauve: f. *A shoue-net to fish withall.*
Sauvé: m. ée: f. *Saued, secured, preserued, escaped, protected or deliuered from daunger, &c; also, safe, whole, sound, sure.*
Il s'est sauvé par les marets. *He hath cleered, or disingaged himselfe, but by a shamefull meanes, or in an vnworthie manner.*
Sauvegarde: f. *Safegard, suretie, securitie; defence, protection, tuition; also, a Scutcheon, Penon, or Flag charged with the Armes of a Protector, and affixed to the doore of the partie, or on the corner-posts of the Citie, whose protection hee hath vndertaken; also, a Letters Patents of protection; whence;* Lettres de sauvegarde.
Sauvelage. *as* Saunclage.
Sauvemént: m. *A sauing, safe-keeping, securing, protecting, preseruing.*
Sauvément. *Safely, securely, surely, without ieopardie.*
Sauver. *To saue, secure, prescrue, defend, gard, protect, keepe harmelesse.*
Sauveté: f. *Safetie, securitie, assurance, protection, defence.*
Sauve-vie: f *Stone-rue, Wall-rue, white Maiden-haire; some also call it Saxifrage, because it is good against the stone.*
Sauveur: m. *A Sauiour, sauer, preseruer, protector, defender.*
Sauvoir: m. *A flat and close boat (bored full of little holes) for the keeping, and feeding of fish in riuers, &c.*
Sauzin: m. *A kind of Oliue.*
Saxitile: com. *Stonie, grauellie; breeding the stone; also, liuing or lurking among stones.*
Saxifrage: f. *The hearbe Saxifrage, or Stone-breake; (wherof there bee diuers kinds of different shape, sayes Gerard.)*
Saxifrage blanche. *Stone-breake, white or great Saxifrage.*
Saxifrage dorée. *Golden Saxifrage, Golden Stone-breake.*
Saxifrage grande. *Great or white Saxifrage; beares a whitish blossome. (Gerard hath foure such; one which hee calls white Saxifrage, or white Stone-breake; a second called Burnet Saxifrage, which (in his opinion) may also be called great Saxifrage; the third, English Saxifrage; and the fourth described, and tearmed* Saxifraga major, *by* Mathiolus.*)*
Saxifrage jaulne. *Yellow Saxifrage, or Saxifrage with the yellow blossome; vsed (abusiuely) for* Melilot, *or plaister Clauer: Gerard hath a golden Saxifrage, or Stone-breake, but no yellow one; except it be Melilot, which (he sayth)* Fuschius *tearmeth* Saxifraga Lutea.
Saxifrage petite. *Small Saxifrage, or Stone-breake; hath a yellow blossome.*

Saye: m. *A long-skirted Jacket, Coat, or Cassocke.*
Sayete. *The stuffe Sey.*
Sayette: f. *The stuffe Sey; also, as* Saitte.
Sayne: f. *The large fish-net called a Seyne.*
Sayon. *Looke* Saye.
Sbaraglin: m. *An Italian Game at Tables, wherin one addes six to euerie cast he throwes; as, if he cast 12 he playes 18.*
Sbirre: m. *A Sergeant, Catchpole, arresting Marshall, or Officer.*
Scabeau: m. *A Buffit, or ioyned, stoole to sit on.*
Scabelle: f. *The same; or a low Buffit, or ioyned, stoole.*
Scabie: f. *The scab, or scabbinesse.*
Scabieuse: f. *The hearbe called Scabious.*
Scabieuse de brebis. *Sheepes Scabious.*
Grande Scabieuse. *Red-flowred Scabious, Austrian Scabious; also, the great common Scabious.*
Petite Scabieuse. *Small common Scabious,* Mathiolus *his Scabious with the pale blew flower.*
Scabieux: m. euse: f. *Scabbie, scuruie.*
Scabin: m. *A Judge.*
Scabreux: m. euse: f. *Rough, rugged, harsh, knottie, knaggie; skittish, daungerous to be dealt with.*
Scace: f. *A Scatch bit.*
Sçachant. *Knowing, witting, expert in, acquainted with.*
Scaïole: f. *A kind of Allum.*
Scalene: f. *A Triangle, the three sides whereof are vnequall.*
Scalenes. *Certaine necke-muskles, whereby the head is moued, and bent.*
Scalle: f. *A scale, a ladder, a paire of staires.*
Faire scalle. *To ascend, mount, or goe vp vnto; also, to land, or goe ashore.*
Faire scalle en Espagne. *To sayle into Spaine.*
Scalme: m. *A Thowle; the little peg whereby the oare of a Skiffe is staied.*
Scalpelle: m. *A Chirurgians Pen-knife, or Launcet.*
Scameux: m. euse: f. Suture scameuse. *The seame whereby the bone of the temples is vnited with, or diuided from, the scull.*
Scammes: f. *Scales; also, the nailes, or small plates of old-fashioned Haubergeons.*
Scammonée: f. *Scammonie, purging Bindweed.*
Scammonie. *The same.*
Scandale: m. *A scandall, offence, occasion or cause of another mans sinning; also, an imputation, or slander; also, a sturre, tumult, vprore; also, a plummet to sound at sea with.*
Scandaleux: m. euse: f. *Scandalous, offensiue, slanderous.*
Scandalizer. *To scandalize, or offend; to discontent, or giue occasion of dislike vnto; also, to slaunder, defame, or lay an imputation on.*
Scandebec: m. *A kind of Oyster whose fish doth tast somewhat tart.*
Scape: m. *The bodie of a piller betweene the chapter and base.*
Scapellaire: m. *Looke* Scapulaire.
Scaphe: f. *A Skiffe, or ship-boat (all of a peece;) also, as* Niche; *also, a hollow Diall cut into wood, or stone, in the forme of a long bason, & hauing the houre-pinne, or needle in the middle thereof.*
Scaphoïde. Os scaph. *A bone in th'instup made somewhat like a Skiffe, or long bason.*
Scapulaire: m. *A narrow, and square peece of cloth, &c, worne by Monkes ouer the rest of their habit, and falling on both sides from the necke (which goes through*

it by a slit, or hole made for that purpose) downe, almost to the foot.

Scarbillat. *as* Escarbillat.

Scare: m. *A delicate sea-fish (held by some to bee the Gilt-head, or Golden-eye) which cheweth like a beast.*

Scarificateur: m. *A Scarificator, or Scarifier; an Instrument wherein there are 18 sharpe wheeles, the which let goe at once doe scarifie, and make incision, in as many seuerall places.*

Scarification: f. *A scarification or scarifying; a kind of pouncing, sleight opening, or incision making in the skinne with a Fleame, Launcet, or other Instrument, either to giue some issue unto superfluous humors and bloud, or to prepare a place for the better extraction of cupping glasses.*

Scarifier. *To scarifie; to pounce, or sleightly to open or make incision in, the skinne with a Fleame, Launcet, or other Instrument.*

Scariole: f. *Scariole; broad-leaued or garden Endiue, or white Endiue.*

Scariotte. *as* Scariole.

Scarvine: f. *A Pilgrims cloake.*

Scasser. *Looke* Sasser.

Scatophages. *Durt-deuourers, excrement-eaters:* ¶Rab.

Sçavamment. *Skilfully, cunningly, learnedly.*

Sçavant: m. ante: f. *Skilfull, cunning, learned; wise, expert, aduised, of much knowledge, of great experience.*

Sçavantement. *as* Sçavamment.

Sçavoir: m. *Skill, knowledge, cunning, learning; understanding, experience in.*

Quelque sçavoir que soit en l'homme s'il n'a de l'argent l'on s'en mocque: Prov. *The needie learned is but laught at; skill without riches is ridiculous.*

Scavoir. *To know, kenne, wot, understand, conceiue, perceiue, discerne; to haue an insight in, or good acquaintance with; also, to may or can, bee able, haue power.*

Sçavoir sa court. *To be skilfull in courtlie intertainment; See* Court.

Sçavoir bon gré à. *To giue thankes, or acknowledge a beholdingnesse, unto.*

Sçaurions nous boire en vostre verre. *May we, or will you make us, or will you giue us leaue to, drinke in your glasse.*

'A sçavoir. *To wit, that is to say.*

'A sçavoir mon? *Whether or no? whether yea or no?*

Il sçait plus que son pain manger. *Looke under* Pain.

Assez sçait qui sçait vivre, & se taire: Prov. *Hee is cunning ynough that can liue and hold his peace (for he that knowes more knowes too much; and as good know nothing as know lesse.)*

Celuy sçait assez qui vit bien: Prov. *An honest man hath skill ynough.*

Il ne sçait rien qui ne va par villes: Prov. *Hee nothing knowes that knowes not more then his owne.*

Il ne sçait rien qui ne veut bien faire: Pro. *He that will not doe well is ignorant.*

Qui ne sçait rien de rien ne doubte: Pro. *He that knowes nothing nothing doubts of.*

Scede. *A wooden table, whereon, in old time, people writ with chalke.*

Scedule. *Looke* Cedule, *or* Schedule.

Scelerat: m. *A lewd villaine, wicked rogue, ungracious wretch, filthie fellow, naughtie packe.*

Sceleré: m. ée: f. *Lewd, naughtie, wicked, villanous, unhappie, knauish, mischieuous; unnaturall, gracelesse, or ungracious.*

Scelete: m. *The whole coagmentation of bones in their naturall position; also, an Anatomie made thereof; or a carkasse whereof nothing is left but the bones, which we call a Skelton, or Skelton.*

Scenicle. *The little bird called a Siskin.*

Sceptique: m. *One that is euer seeking, and neuer finds; (the fortune, or humor of a Pyrrhonian Philosopher.)*

Sceptre: m. *A (royall) Scepter; also, a Monarchie, kingdome, absolute rule, Soueraigntie in chiefe.*

Sceu: m. *Knowledge, understanding, acquaintance, notice of.*

Sceu: m. euë: f. *Knowne, understood, conceiued, kenned, perceiued.*

Il n'ay sceu luy persuader. *I could not, I had not the power or haue not beene able to, persuade him.*

Schalupe: f. *A Shallop.*

Schede: f. *A schedule, scroll, note, bill, (priuate) writing.*

Schedule: f. *The same; or as* Cedule; *also, a placard, or writing sticke on a post; also, the Returne made by a Sergeant, upon an Adiournement or Arrest;* C'est aussi la memoire qu'un Procureur baille au Greffe, ou au premier Huissier pour l'expedition d'une cause d'appel.

Schelette. *Looke* Scelete.

Schelme: m. *A knaue, rascall, varlet, lewd fellow; (from a German word that signifies wicked.)*

Schine: f. *The linnen cassocke which countrey men weare gathered in the necke like a Surplis.*

Schismatique, & Schisme. *Looke* Scismatique, & Scisme.

Scholarité: f. *Schollership, schollerlinesse, the being a scholler, the place of a scholler.*

Scholastique: m. *as* Escolastre *(in the first sence.)*

Scholastique: com. *Scholasticall, scholler-like.*

Scholiaste: m. *A Scholiast; an expounder of, or glosser upon, a text:* ¶Rab.

Sciage: m. *Saw-dust; or, a sawing; also, cleft wood, as boords, laths, vine-props, &c.*

Sciatique: f. *The Sciatica; a gowtie paine in the hip.*

Sciatique: com. *Of the Sciatica.*

Veine Sciatique. *The Sciatica veine, seated aboue the outward ankle.*

Scie: f. *A Saw.*

Scie de mer. *A kind of Whall which hath a Saw-like snowt.*

Sciemment. *Wittingly, with knowledge.*

Science: f. *Science, learning, learned skill, cunning, knowledge, understanding.*

Vne science requiert tout son homme: Prov. *One Art is imployment ynough for one man.*

Diligence passe science: Pro. *Diligence exceedeth Science.*

Fy de Science, & d'art, qui en raison n'a part: Prov. *Looke* Fy.

Patience passe Science: Prov. *Patience passeth Science.*

Scientement. *Knowingly, wittingly, of set purpose.*

Scientifique: com. *Scientificall, of exceeding skill, infinite learning, wonderfull knowledge.*

Scientique: com. *Most learned, skilfull, cunning, expert, aduised, of great knowledge (especially in ill matters, for which this word is most commonly used.)*

Scier. *Looke* Sier.

Sciette: f. *A little Saw.*
Scieur: m. *A Sawer, or Sawyer.*
Scille: f. *The Squilla, or sea Onion.*
Scillet: m. *The Nut of a (musicall) Instrument.*
Scillitic: m. ique: f. *Of the Squilla, or sea Onion.*
Scinc, & Scinque: m. *The Skinke; a kind of small land Crocodile, diuers parts whereof are of good vse in Physicke.*
Scintillation: f. *A sparking, or sparkling.*
Scintille: f. *A sparke, or sparkle of fire.*
Sintiller. *To sparke, or to sparkle.*
Sciomance. *Diuination by conference with the shadows of dead men.*
Scion: m. *A Scion; a young and tender plant; a shoot, sprig, or twig.*
Scionneux: m. euse: f. *Full of scions, or of shoots; twiggie, spriggie.*
Scipoulle. *The sea Onion.*
Scirre: m. *A hard and almost vnsencible swelling, or kernell, bred between the flesh & skin, by cold, or of thick and clammie flegme.*
Scismatique: com. *A Scismaticke.*
Scisinatique: com. *Scismaticall.*
Scismatiser. *To Scismatise it, or play the Scismatick; to raise a Scisme, or breed a diuision, in the Church.*
Scisme: m. *A Scisme; a diuision in, or from, the Church.*
Scissile: com. *That may be cut or diuided, thats easie to cut.*
Pierre scissile. *Seeke* Pierre.
Scissure: f. *A cleft, cut, cracke, bracke, chap.*
Scissuré: m. ée: f. *Cleft, chapped, cut, cracked, broken, diuided.*
Sciure. *Looke* Sieure.
Sclavine. *as* Esclavine.
Sclirrolique. ¶Rab. *Looke* Shilirhoïque.
Scoffion: m. *A coyfe, cawle, or bead-tire richly set with Jewells.*
Scoletie: f. *A kind of spotted Spider.*
Scolopendre: f. *The Scolopendria, a reddish, many-legd, and venomous worme; also, a certaine fish, which hauing swallowed a hooke, vomiteth her bowells, and rid of it, sucketh them vp againe; also, as* Scolopendrie.
Scolopendrie: f. *Spleenwort, Miltwort, Finger-fearne, Scale-fearne, Stone-fearne.*
Scolopendrie vraye. *The same; called* Vraye, *to make it differ frõ Harts-tongue, or stone Harts-tongue, which is also (falsly) tearmed* Scolopendria.
Scopeterie: f. *A (great) volley of small shot.*
Scordion: m. *Scordium, water Germander, Garlicke Germander.*
Scorie: f. *The drosse, refuse, or scumme of melted, or tried mettall.*
Scorpene: f. *A little darke-greene fish (in the Marsellian sea) which hath certaine weake, but venomous prickles on her backe.*
Scorpion: m. *A Scorpion; also, a kind of small Dag.*
Scorpion de mer. *The sea Scorpion; a red, great-headed, and wide-mouthed fish, which hath but a few, and those verie small, teeth; but in lieu thereof he is armed with many prickles both on his backe, and about his head.*
Scorpion volant. *The flying Scorpion; a rare vermine; and yet* Mathiolus *thinkes that Scorpions may haue wings as well as Ants.*
Herbe aux Scorpions. *Scorpion-wort, or Scorpion-grasse.*

Queuë de Scorpion. *Great Tornesole, Wartewort.*
Scorze: m. *A round Italian corne-measure, 22 whereof goe to the* Ruble.
Scorzon: m. *A short blacke Serpent full of yellow spots; and so venomous & stinking withall, that all vermine feare, and (as much as they can) auoid him.*
Scote. La scote d'une voile. *A Sheat.*
Scotin: m. ine: f. *Difficult, intricate, obscure, full of quirkes and quiddities.*
Scotte. *as* Scote.
Scourgeon: m. *Amell-corne, or Starch-corne; a wild or degenerate Wheat, which is sowne in the Spring, and being ground, yeelds a verie white, but verie light, and little nourishing, meale.*
Scourre. La terre ne se sçait scourre de cette herbe. *The ground cannot ouercome, or bee rid of, this weed.*
Scousse. *Looke* Secousse.
Scripteur: m. *A Writer.*
Scriptule: m. *A Scruple; the third part of a Dramme; Looke* Scrupule.
Scrofulaire: f. *Scrofularia, Pilewort, Figwort, Kernell-wort.*
Scrofulaire majeur. *Great Figwort, or Kernell-wort; Some also call browne Worts, or water Bettonie,* Scrofularia major.
Scrofulaire mineur. *Figwort, Pilewort, little Celandine, or Celandine the lesse.*
Scrofule: f. *The Kings euill; or a Wenne vnder the throat.*
Scrophulaire. *Looke* Scrofulaire.
Scropule: m. *A little sharpe stone falling into a mans shooe, and hindering him in his gate; also, a scruple, doubt, feare, difficultie, care; precisenesse, nicenesse, trouble of conscience; also, a Scruple; a weight amounting vnto the third part of a Dramme.*
Scrupule d'un Arpent. *The 48 part of an* Arpent, *or ten foot square euerie way.*
Scrupuleusement. *Scrupulously, doubtfully, fearefully, nicely, precisely.*
Scrupuleux: m. euse: f. *Scrupulous, doubtfull, fearefull, conscientious, nice, precise.*
Scrutine: f. *A scrutinie, or search.*
Sculpteur: m. *A Caruer, Cutter, Grauer.*
Scutiforme: com. *Fashioned like a Scutcheon, shield-fashion.*
Cartilage scutiforme. *as* Fourchette.
Scybale. *A hard or hardened, turd:* ¶Rab.
Scylle: f. *The sea Onion.*
Scync, & Scynque. *Looke* Scinc.
Scyomantie: f. *Diuination by conference with the shadowes of dead men.*
Scyrrhe. *Looke* Scirre.
Scyrrheux: m. euse: f. *Kernellie, knottie.*
Scytale. *The Scytall; a daungerous Sloe-worme, whose backe is full of variable, & delightfull spots or markes; also, the Shrew-mouse; also, a little round or square sticke full of cyphers.*
Se. *A Relatiue of both Numbers, and euer placed before a Verbe; as in* Il se trompe; *He deceiues himselfe, or is deceiued.*
Seamment. *Fitly, comely, decently, handsomely.*
Seance: f. *Decencie, seemelinesse, handsomenesse, comelinesse, a decorum; also, a roome, seat, or place to sit in; also, a sitting.*
Seant: m. ante: f. *Decent, seemelie, comelie, handsome, gracefull, well suting or fitting.*
Seas. `A Dieu seas. *in stead of* Sois: ¶Gasc. ¶Rab.

Seau:

Seau · m. *A bucket, or water pale; also, a seale, or signet; also, the chiefe* Luminaire *(wreathed, or in works) of wax vsed at funeralls.*
Seau de nostre Dame. *Maries Seale, our Ladies Seale, blacke Brionie, the wild Vine.*
Seau de Salamon. *Salamons Seale, Scala cœli, White wort, White root.*
Seau pendant à double queuë. *A seale hanging at a double Labell; also, one that hangs on a Gibbet.*
I'y ay bien planté mes seaux. *Looke* Planté.
Sebe. *An Onyon:* ¶Langued.
Sebelline. Martre Sebel. *The Sable Martin; the beast whose skinne we call Sables.*
Sebeste, ou Sebestin. *The Sebesten, or Assyrian plum; a small plumme darke-greene of colour, sweet of tast, and of a slimie or clammie substance.*
Sebestier: m. *The Sebesten, or Assyrian plumme tree.*
Sebille: f. *A fashion of woodden bowle vsed in Vintage-time, for the lading, or tunning of new wine, and for the tasting thereof before it be tunned; Looke* Sibille.
Sebu. *The Elder tree.*
Sec: m. *A drie thing; whence;*
Employer le verd, & le sec. *To vse or imploy all the meanes he hath; (from them which to make a fire big ynough, lay on wet wood as well as drie.)*
Sec: m. seiche: f. *Drie, iuycelesse, withered, saplesse, without moisture.*
Pierre seiche. *A stone laid without morter.*
Pique seiche. *An vnarmed Pikeman.*
Rente seiche. *A rent Seck; Looke* Rente.
Son sec. *Course branne; or branne wherein, by extremitie of boulting, not a whit of meale is left.*
Suture seiche. *A fashion of closing wounds; tearmed thus among Chirurgians, because neither flesh, nor skin is pricked thereby.*
'A sec. *(Aduerbially; whence;)* Estre à sec. *To be on drie ground; and thence, to be grauelled, or spent in words or meanes; to haue no more to say.*
Nauiger à sec. Aller aux mas, & aux cordes; *Our Mariners say, to spoone.*
Tirer les vaisseaux à sec. *To tow vessells ashore.*
Sec. (Interject.) *Ware that:* ¶Rab.
Secacul. *A certaine Indian, and Ginger-like root, which eaten (preserued, as euer it is) enables a man vnto venerie: and therefore haue some (erroniously) taken it for the* Eringo, *and others (as wisely) for the Skirret root.*
Seccer. *To saw, or cut asunder; to cleaue, diuide, part.*
Sechabot: m. *The little blacke vermine breeding in puddles, and tearmed a Bulhead.*
Seche: f. *The Sound, or Cuttle-fish.*
Secher. *Looke* Seicher.
Secheron. prez secherons. *High, or drie medowes, such as are neither ouerflowed, nor moistened by any riuer, &c.*
Sechot: m. *A Powt, or Eele-powt.*
Secilienne: f. *The watering chaine of a Bit.*
Seclus: m. use: f. *Secluded, kept or shut vp, from; depriued of.*
Second: m. *A second, or assistant in a single combate.*
Second: m. onde: f. *Second, next after, next vnto the first, inferiour, another.*
Seconde: f. *The 24 part of a Prime; a verie small weight vsed by Goldsmithes, and Jewellers.*
Secondé: m. ée: f. *Seconded, followed next, approached neerest vnto; backed, succoured, assisted.*
Secondement. *Secondly, secondarily, in the secõd place, next after the first.*
Seconder. *To second, follow close or next, approach neerest vnto; also, to backe, helpe, succour, assist.*
Secoüé: m. ée: f. *Shaken, swung, tossed, ioulted, violently moued or stirred.*
Secouëment: m. *A shaking, swinging, tossing, ioulting, violent mouing, iogging, stirring.*
Secouër. *To shake, tosse, ioult, swing, iog, stir vehemently, moue violently.*
Vn Cheual qui secouë son homme. *A horse that trots dagger out of sheath.*
Secouëur: m. *A shaker, tosser, swinger, ioulter.*
Secourable: com. *Succouring, helpfull, comfortable, assisting; readie or willing to releeue.*
Secourcer. *To plucke or tucke vp the coat, &c, for dagging.*
Secourgeon. *as* Scourgeon.
Secourir. *To succour, second, releeue, comfort, back, aid, helpe, assist, further.*
Secours: m. *Succour, a seconding, reliefe, helpe, aid, assistance, comfort, furtherance.*
Secours de Lombardie. *Seeke* Lombardie.
Le secours des Venetiens. *A restoratiue after death, victualls vpon a full repast; offer of helpe, or libertie, to one thats past the worst, or newly gotten out of prison; Looke* Venetien.
Secousse: f. *A ioult, shog, shocke, shake, swing, tosse; a violent iog or swindge, a sudden pull.*
Bailler vne mauuaise secousse à. *To giue a terrible iert, or horrible rush; to worke much mischiefe, or doe a mischieuous turne, vnto.*
Secret: m *A secret, concealement, counsell, mysterie, hidden matter; also, as* Muse.
Secret de deux secret de Dieu, secret de trois secret de tous: Prov. *We onely say, that three may keep counsell when two are away.*
Secret: m. ette: f. *Secret, inward, priuie, close, hidden, concealed, abstruse, darke, mysticall, vnknowne.*
Secretain: m. *The Sexton of a Church.*
Secretainerie: f. *A Sextrie, or Vestrie.*
Secretaire: m. *A Secretarie, Clerke, Remembrancer; whereof (besides those that belong to inferiour Princes, and Lords) there be many immediate, ordinarie, and houshold seruants vnto the French King; tearmed onely,* Secretaires, *or* Secretaires du Roy, *and sometimes* Secretaires du Roy, & de la maison, & couronne de France, *(although in truth they be not Officers of the Crowne:) Of these did Charles the fist institute a Colledge, or Corporation, by the title of,* Le College des Clercs, Notaires, & Secretaires du Roy, & de la maison, & Couronne de France: *At which time there was but sixtie of them, for the writing of all Patents, and dispatches of the Chauncerie; and their intertainment but six shillings* Parisis *a day, besides tenne pounds* Tour. *for their* Droict de Manteaux, *and some pettie fees out of the Chauncerie: But vpon the increase of businesses Lewis, the eleuenth doubled their number; and Henrie the second, in the yere 1554, raised it vnto two hundred, giuing them* 300 l. *wages, in respect of all fees. In the yeare 1570 Charles the ninth ioyned vnto them fortie more; and Henrie the third, in the yeare 1583, foureteene vnto those, allowing them certaine vailes out of the Chauncerie seale, and* 150 l. *wages. Henrie the fourth added vnto all these, first 22, then 23, then nine (intertained at* 300 l. *wages, without any vayles) and in the yeare 1605, twentie six, to whom he assigned* 1000 l. *a yeare (especially for such of them as attended the finances,) And lastly, in the yeare 1608, he made ten more (which haue*

300 l. *wages) in respect of the reunion of his owne demaine vnto the Crowne. The King himselfe is the head of their Colledge; they and their (legitimate) children are ennobled: And besides exemption from all manner of taxations, customes, tolls, impositions, lones, fines of alienation, rights of Seigniorie (for land held of the King;) and a discharge from the* Ban, Arriereban, *Musters, Harbingers,* Estapes, *and Salt-peter-men; and the being fee-free in all Courts of Justice; they enioy many excellent priuiledges.*

Secretaires du cabinet. *The Secretaries of the Closet; such of th'ordinarie (or extraordinarie) Secretaries as the King is pleased to imploy in his priuate, or secret dispatches.*

Secretaires de la chambre du Roy. *The Clerkes, or Secretaries of the Kings Chamber; are of a lower ranke, or, at the least, haue fewer priuiledges, then* les Secretaires du Roy.

Secretaires de la Chancellerie. *The Clerkes of the Chauncerie (whereto all th'ordinarie Secretaries originally belong) are, as some doe hold, most particularly, the foure and fiftie brought in by Charles the ninth, and Henrie the third.*

Secretaires des commandemens; ou d'Estat. *The foure principall Secretaries (who in France doe signe Letters Patents, as well as dispatches of Estate) must haue beene of the Colledge aforesaid; and, vntill of late, were not Officers in ordinarie, but Commissioners, executing their functions, and receiuing their fees, onely during the Princes pleasure.*

Secretaires des finances. *The remembrancers of the Exchequer (deriued from the same source) were likewise but Commissioners, vntill the yere 1605, when they procured themselues, and their successors, th'estate of Officers.*

Secretaire, & Contrerolleur general des guerres. *The Secretarie, or Comptroller generall of the warres, is to keepe a certaine Register, and account of all businesses concerning the leuie, musters, paiments, allowances, increase or decrease, imployment or ingarisoning of the* Gendarmerie, *and other ordinarie souldiers; and, hauing grounded vpon that account his controlment, must, three monethes after euerie yearelie payment, send the same vnto the Chamber of Accounts, and with it a copie of the Rolls of all Musters passed that yeare, that it may be compared with such as shal be deliuered, or sent in by the Treasurer of the warres.*

Secretaires du Roy. *Looke in the word* Secretaire.

Secretariat: m. *A Secretariship; th'Office of a Secretarie, or place wherein he exerciseth it.*

Secrete: f. *A thinne steele cap, or a close scull worne vnder a hat, &c.*

Secretion: f. *A separation or setting apart; also, a thing seperated or set apart, from others.*

Secretrice: com. *Of a separating facultie.*

Secrette: f. *as* Secrete; *also, a fiste (because it is let in secret;) also, a priuate or hidden place.*

Secrettement. *Secretly, inwardly, priuily, closely, hiddenly, darkely, abstrusely, mystically.*

Sectaire: com. *A Sectarie; the ringleader, professor, or follower of a Sect; a seditious, factious, or turbulent person.*

Secte: f. *A sect, or faction; a rout, or troupe; a companie of one (most commonly bad) opinion.*

Sectil: m. ile: f. *Easily cut, soone clouen.*

Porreau sectil. *The cut Leeke, maidens Leeke, bladed Leeke, vnset Leeke.*

Section: f. *A section, cutting; diuision, parting; also, an Anatomie.*

Sects. *as* Ceps: ¶Bourg.

Seculaire. Ieu secul. *Which is played but once euerie age, or 100 yeares.*

Seculariser. *To secularize; to make secular, lay, temporall.*

Secularité: f. *Secularitie, worldlinesse, temporallnesse.*

Seculier: m. ere: f. *Secular, lay, temporall.*

Seculierement. *Secularly, temporally.*

Securidaque: f. *The pulse Axseed, Axwort, Axfitch, Hatchet-fitch.*

Securité: f. *Securitie, retchlesnesse, carelesnesse.*

Sedatif: m. iue: f. *Quieting, asswaging, mitigating, easing, appeasing, stinting.*

Sedenette: f. *The Sea-monster called a Whirlepoole.*

Sedentaire: com. *Sedentarie, euer-sitting, or downe-sitting.*

Iuges sedentaires. *Ordinarie Judges, such as (almost) euerie day sit in Court.*

Seder. *To still, quiet, asswage, qualifie, mitigate, pacifie, appease.*

Sediment: m. *A sitting or setling of dregs, &c, in the bottome of liquor that hath stood.*

Seditieusement. *Seditiously, factiously, mutinously, turbulently.*

Seditieux: m. euse: f. *Seditious, factious, busie, vnquiet, mutinous, turbulent, tumultuous.*

Sedition: f. *A sedition, mutinie, publicke faction, strife, contention, tumult, vprore.*

Sedon. *Looke* Ceton.

Seducteur: m. *A seducer, misleader, deceiuer.*

Seduction: f. *A seduction, seducing, misleading, deceiuing.*

Seduict: m. cte: f. *Seduced, misled, deceiued.*

Seduire. *To seduce, mislead, beguile, deceiue.*

Sedulité: f. *Sedulitie, diligence.*

Séc. *Looke* Soye.

Seel: m. *A Seale, or Signet.*

Seel authentique. *An authenticke, publicke, or approued Seale, such as that of Lords high* Iusticiers; *which notwithstanding was restrained within the limits of the land, and Jurisdiction of the Lord thereof, vntill the yeare 1539; since when an Edict hath gained it allowance, and made it fit to hold plea, in any place, if th'Obligor, at the time of th'obligatiō made, was resident vpon the territorie, or otherwise subiect vnto the Jurisdiction, of the Lord vnto whom it belongs.*

Seel royal. *The Kings Seale for contracts, &c, executorie, and authenticall, within all his dominions.*

Droict de Seel. *Seeke vnder* Droict.

Seellé: m. *A couenant made, or contract passed, betweene partie & partie, vnder seale; also, the sealing of a thing.*

Seellé: m. ée: f. *Sealed.*

Seeller. *To seale.*

Seelleur: m. *A Sealer.*

Seellure: f. *A sealing.*

Seession. faire seession. *To fall bankrupt.*

Seeux. *Looke* Soyeux.

Segaline: f. *A delicate peare thats ripe in August.*

Segle. *Looke* Seigle.

Segnale: com. *Notable, of marke, famous, renowmed.*

Segrarie: f. *A Verderership; or such a like Office of account in forrests.*

Segrayer: m. *A Verderer, or such a like Officer of some authoritie, in forrests.*

Segrayerie: f. *as* Segrarie.

Segregation: f. *A segregation, separation, seuering frō.*

Se-

Segregé: m.ée: f. *Segregated, seperated, seuered, culled or taken out, layed or put apart.*
Segreger. *To segregate, seperate, seuer, put or lay apart, cull or take out, from.*
Segrette: f. *An yron scull, or cap of fence.*
Seguë: f. *Hemlocke, Homlock, hearb Bennet, Kex.*
Seguette: f. *A Caueßon of yron full of teeth, or hauing a sharpe indented edge to the noseward.*
Sehu. *The Elder tree.*
Seïage (des bleds.) *A reaping, or cutting downe (of corne.)*
Sejan. Cheval de Sejan. *A horse that brought ill hap to all that possessed him.*
Seiche: f. *The Sound, or Cuttle fish.*
Seiche poupe. *The Pourcontrell, Preke, or Many-feet.*
Seiche. (*The Feminine to* Sec;) *Looke* Sec.
Seiche-frite. *as* Liche-frite.
Seichemént: m. *A drying, or drayning of moisture; a parching or withering; a pining or wasting away.*
Seichément. *Dryly, barrenly, witheredly, without sap, iuice, or moisture.*
Seicher. *To dry, drayne of moisture; parch or wither; pine or wast away.*
Seicher sur les pieds. *To pine away through fretfullnesse; also, to be in great perplexitie, or much trouble of heart.*
Qui va il lesche, qui repose il seiche: Pro. *The traueller gaines, the loyterer waines; the labouring man gets appetite, but sloath dryes vp the bodie quite.*
Seicheresse: f. *Drought, drynesse, want of moisture, barrenneße.*
Seicheron. *Looke* Secheron.
Seicheur: m. *A dryer; one that layes out things to dry.*
Seicheur: f. *Looke* Seicheresse.
Seides: f. *The bristles, or stiffe haires of a Horse, or Hog.*
Seïer. *To reape or cut downe, as Corne, &c.*
Seieur: m. *A Reaper.*
Seigle: m. *Rye.*
Seigle blanc. *Amelcorne, Starch-corne.*
Seignée: f. *Phlebotomie, bloud-letting.*
Seigner. *Looke* Signer.
Seigneur: m. *A Lord; Sir; Signior; a Maister; a Landlord, or a Lord of Iurisdiction; a Proprietarie, or Owner.*
Seigneurs honoraires. *Titularie Lords; such as haue honour without authoritie; such as (like our English Earles) beare the title, but want the possession, of a place; and such as, in respect of their Title (whatsoeuer) hold not in chiefe, or of the King, but of some other Lord his subiect.*
Seigneurs mediocres. *Are Vidames, Vicounts, and Barons (not holding immediately of the Crowne) and Chattelains.*
Gracieux seigneur. *See* Gracieux.
Grands seigneurs. *Be Dukes, Marqueßes, Earles, and Princes; as also, Vicounts, and Barons, that hold immediately of the Crowne.*
Petits seigneurs. *Lords* Iusticiers, *Lords (onely) of Iurisdiction.*
Vn seigneur de beurre (de feurre, ou de paille) combat, (vainc, ou mange) bien vn vassal d'acier: Prov. *(So great oddes hath a Lord of his tenant, or a Prince of his subiect.)*
Tel seigneur tel chien: Pro. *Such as a maister, such his man will be.*
De tel seigneur telle mesnie; &, De nouveau seigneur nouvelle mesnie: Pro. *Looke* Mesnie.
Aujourd'huy seigneur demain singe ord: Prov. *To day a worthie Lord, to morrow an ape vntoward;* viz. *an absurd imitator of that which he was, or should be.*
Au monde n'y a si grand dommage que de seigneur au fol courage: Prov. *There is no beast like to a wicked Lord.*
C'est folie de manger cerises avec son seigneur: Pro. *Looke* Cerise.
Iamais ne gaigne qui plaide à son seigneur: Prov. *He neuer thriues who with his maister striues.*
On ne doit pas laisser bonne terre pour mauvais seigneur: Prov. *Quit not good land because of a bad Landlord.*
Qui avec son seigneur mange poires il ne choisit pas des meilleures: Pro. *He that eats Peares with his Lord, picks none of the best.*
Qui de ses subjects est hay, n'est pas seigneur de son païs: Prov. *The Lord whose subiects cannot well indure him, finds no place in his countrey to secure him.*
Qui voit la maison de son seigneur il n'y a profit, ny honneur: Pro. *One's not the neerer to esteeme, or wealth, by looking on his Landlords house, or pelfe.*
Tant que le seigneur dort le vassal veille: Prov. *As long as a Lord forbeares to seize his vaßalls land (for want of homage, &c,) the vaßall may lawfully, and without any wrong done to him, enioy it, and take the profits of it.*
Tant que le vassal dort le seigneur veille: Pro. *Seeke* Vassal.
Seigneuriage: m. *Seigniorie, soueraigntie; maisterie, dominion ouer.*
Droict de seigneuriage. *as vnder* Droict; *or,* Ce que revient de bon au Roy outre, & par dessus, le fin qui est en la monnoye, & les frais de la fabrication d'icelle.
Seigneurial: m. ale: f. *Seigniorall, Lordlie, Lord-like, of a Lord, or Landlord.*
Droicts seigneuriaux. Ce sont ceux qui sont deus au Seigneur; comme si c'est fief, la feudalité, droicts, & devoirs; si c'est heritage tenu en censive, les lots & ventes, & le cens, qu'il faut entendre du chef cens qui est deu en signe, & recognoissance de seigneurie portant lots, ventes, & amende.
Seigneurie: f. *Seigniorie, lordship, soueraigntie, maiestie, dominion; absolute sway of, or power ouer; a freehold, full interest, or propertie in, a thing; also, a Lordship, or Mannor; the Iurisdiction, or Territorie belonging to a Lord, &c; also, the societie, or corporation of such as commaund in free Townes; also, an assemblie, or companie of great Lords, and Ladies.*
Seigneurie directe. *The estate of a Landlord; the receiuing of seruices, rents, or* cens *for land.*
Seigneurie privée. *An actuall enioyment of, or an assured propertie in, a thing; a mans particular interest in his owne.*
Seigneurie publique. *Iurisdiction; a superioritie, or authoritie ouer persons, or their possessions.*
Seigneurie souveraine. *(A branch, or species of* La publique) *the soueraigne authoritie of absolute Princes.*
Seigneurie suzeraine. *(Another) the dignitie of a* fief *hauing Iurisdiction; the power of the Lord, or owner of such a* fief.
Seigneurie vtile. *The possession, vse, or occupation of land, for which rents, &c, be paied, or seruices done, to another; the estate of a vassall, or tenant.*

Oncques amour;& seigneurie ne se tindrent compagnie: Prov. *True loue,and lordlinesse neuer held correspondencie; friendship,and lordship agree not long together.*

Plein poing de seigneurie vaut cinq sols l'an: Prov. *Honour without profit is like a six-pennie rent to one that hath nothing else to liue on.*

Seigneurier. *To seigniorize,rule, sway, gouerne, domineere, play the Lord,haue power ouer.*

Seille: f. *A Paile, or Bucket.*

Seillon: m. *A ridge, or (high) furrow; also,the gutter, or hollow furrow made by a plough in the turning of it vp; also,a butt, or land, consisting of diuers of those ridges, or furrowes; also, the narrow trench, reyne, or furrow,left betweene butt and butt for the drayning thereof.*

Seillonné: m. ée: f. *Furrowed; made into furrowes, ridges,butts,&c; also,plowed vp, diuided, cut or clouen asunder,as the sea by a ship.*

Seillonner. *To furrow; to plough, or turne vp into ridges, furrowes; butts; reynes,or narrow trenches; also, to diuide,cut,or cleaue asunder; wherce;*

Seillonner la mer. *To sayle; to cut,or part (as a ship vnder sayle) the waues of the sea.*

Seillonner vne presse de gens. *To make a lane, or giue a furious charge,through a close batallion,or presse of people.*

Seime de vin. *The flower, or coat of wine; the white stuffe that floats on the top of it being in Caske.*

Sein: m. *The bosome; the lap; also, the inward mind,or thought; the height,or depth of the heart, or affection; also,a gulfe,creeke,nooke,angle or arme of the sea,or of a riuer; and, the turning, or hollownesse of a water-banke; also, seame, tallow, or suet; also, a freckle, or mole; also, a signe manuell; or as* Sing, *in the former sences.*

Cette femme a du sein. *This woman wants no dugs, no bulke,no bombast; she is simply vnderlayed.*

Seine: f. *A verie great and long fish-net called,a Seane; also,a circuit,or compasse.*

Seing. *Looke* Sing.

Sejour: m. *A lingering,stay,leisure,delay;also,residence, tarriance, a remaining or soiourning in one place; also, a place of residence, or for abode; a place to soiourne, rest,or stay in.*

Fol de sejour. *An idle fellow, one that hath little to doe.*

Sejourné. *Lingered, soiourned, stayed, remained,resident in a place.*

Vn homme sejourné. *Refreshed by rest, or leisure-taking,and thereby the more fit to returne vnto his former toyle.*

Sejourner. *To soiourne,tarrie, stay,remaine,be resident in; to pawse, linger, delay, take leisure; to intermit either studie,or other imployment; to make holyday; also, to leaue,let stay, giue leisure vnto.*

Seissete: f. *A kind of pale-red wheat.*

Seizain: m. *A quarter of an ounce; or, the 64 part of a pound (weight.)*

Seize. *Sixteene.*

Sel: m. *Salt.*

Sel alcali, ou alkali. *A salt made of the ashes of the hearbe Glassewort,or Saltwort, burned with diuers other hearbes (in lesse quantitie.)*

Sel ammoniac,ou armoniac. *Salt Ammicke; a medicinable drug resembling stone Allum,and found in long flakes vnder the Cyrenian sand.*

Sel gemmé. *A transparent,and shining minerall salt, gotten in* Calabria, *and* Capadocia.

Sel Indien, ou d' Inde. *The onely sugar, which* Dioscorides, *and other auncient writers were acquainted with; distilling of it selfe from the canes, like a gumme, in little peeces, and thus tearmed, because resembling gray salt.*

Sel de Languedoc. *White salt, fine salt.*

Sel de Lezard. *A medicinable, and comfortable salt, comming of a Lizard (in Summer) beheaded,bowelled, stuffed with salt, and layed in a shadie place vntill he be dry.*

Sel marin. *Salt made of Sea-water; or, our ordinarie gray salt.*

Sel mineral. *as* Sel gemmé; *(and yet one kind of it, gotten in the Countie of* Tirolis, *neither shines, nor is transparent,but resembles a reddish Marble.)*

Sel nitre. *Niter; Looke* Nitre.

Sel de pierre. *Salt-peeter; called so by Chymists.*

Sel de Poictou,& de Ponant. *Blacke salt,gray salt.*

Sel sacerdotal. *A powder compounded of two ounces and a halfe of Salt, foure ounces of fine Cynnamon,* Ameos, *Siler Mountaine, Hysope, wild Marierome, and Penniroyall,of each halfe an ounce; all dryed together; this purges the bodie, consumes flegme, stops the cough, clenses the eyes, sweetens the breath, eases the teeth, appeases headache, preserues youth, and giues vigor to old age(if some Phisitions may be beleeued.)*

Sel sel. *An oyle that commeth from Hearbe-salt, or* Sel-alcali, *first calcinated,then beaten to powder,and set on a peece of glasse in a moist cellar.*

Sel viperin. *A medicinable salt, made of a liue Viper, ordinarie salt, honey, and dry figges,inclosed,and with fat earth stopped vp, in a new earthen pot, and then baked in a furnace vnto a consistence of coales.*

Escume de sel. *Sea-foame salt; comes of water left by a tempestuous,and foaming sea in the holes of rockes, and there congealed and turned into salt by the Sunne.*

Fleur de sel. *A brackish foame or skumme that floates on the riuer Nilus,and on certaine Lakes; of colour yellow, fat or oylie of consistence, and vnpleasant in tast; the right (for it is often sophisticated with a kind of red earth) cannot be resolued but in oyle; the false one melts, and looses colour, in water.*

Violet de sel. *A certaine rustie colour which tasteth like to* La Fleur de sel.

Doux de sel. *A fresh-man, shallow,vnaduised,of little experience, a nouice,one thats not acquainted with the course of the world.*

Sans sel. *Fresh, vnsauorie, vnseasoned, foolish, idle, without grace.*

Manger à vn grain de sel. *Seeke* Manger.

Prendre son sel. *To take his liquor soundly.*

C'est vn banquet de diables ou il n'y a point de sel: Pro. *The feast that wanteth salt is fit for deuills.*

Qui envoye chetif à la mer il n'en rapporte poisson, ne sel: Pro. *He that imployes a knaue (or a foole) either looses,or gaines but a little.*

Selenite. *A light,white,and transparent stone, easily cleft into thin flakes,whereof the Arabians, among whom it growes,make their glasse,and glasen windowes.*

Selerin. *Looke* Celerin.

Selle: f. *A saddle.*

Cheval entre deux selles. *A horse of a middle size.*

Selle: f. *A stoole,or seat; (any ill-fauored, ordinarie, or countrey stoole, of a cheaper sort then the ioyned, or buffet-stoole;) also,a (purgatiue) stoole,or the excrement voided at a stoole.*

Selle percée. *A chaire of easement,a close-stoole.*

Selle

Selle à ribauldes,ou à ricaldes. *A Cuck-stoole.*
Assis entre deux selles le cul à terre; &, Il est demeuré entre deux selles à terre.*Betweene two stooles the arse goes to the ground (say we.)*
Seller. *To saddle,as a horse,&c.*
Sellette: f. *A foot-stoole,or low stoole; also,a pad,or saddle for a Cart-horse.*
Sellier: m.*A Sadler; (tearmed also,*Sellier lormier,*because he may vent, or deale for, all kind of Spurriers ware.)*
Selon. *As,euen as, according vnto; in the opinion,like to the fashion,after the rate,or manner,of.*
Selsir. *The rotting Serpent* Seps.
Semaille: f. *Seed sowne; also, a crop,or plants,come vp of seed; also,a sowing; also, sowing or seeding time; also,Gossimeare,or the Cobweb-like exhalations that float in the ayre during hot, and open weather; (In which sence, as also in some of the other,this word is vsed plurally.)*
Semailles d'avoine. *The seed-time for Oates, beginneth about the 15 of March.*
Semailles de febves.*About the 26 of Februarie.*
Semailles de froment. *About the 3 of October.*
Semailles d'orges. *About the 5 of Aprill.*
Semailles de pois. *About the 3 of March.*
Semailles de seigles. *Rye-seed-time,is about the 18 of September.*
Semaine: f. *A weeke.*
Elle a sa male semaine. *She hath her flowers.*
Semainier: m. *One that workes, or does ought, by the weeke.*
Semainier: m. ere: f. *Weekelie,euerie weeke,of or belonging to a weeke.*
Semaises: f. *Great woodden pots,out of which the Germans fill their glasses at meale-times.*
Semaison. *as* Semaille.
Semantiere. *(Vsed in some countries for* Cemetiere) *a Churchyard.*
Semblable: com. *Semblable,like,alike, such,euen such, resembling,according vnto.*
Chascun cerche son semblable: Prov. *Like will to like; all men a make desire.*
Semblablement. *Semblably, likewise, in like sort, in such fashion,after the same manner,also,euen so.*
Semblance: f. *A semblance, shew, seeming, apparance; also, resemblance, likenesse, like forme, alike feature, the same posture or fashion.*
Orgueilleuse semblance monstre folle cuidance: Prov. *A prowd looke shewes the heart's possest with follie.*
Semblant: m. *A shew, seeming, semblance, apparance, countenance.*
Faire semblant. *To seeme,or make as if;* Faire semblant de. *To take notice,or be sencible,of.*
Semblé. *Seemed,made shew of.*
Il t'a ainsi semblé du commencement. *Thou thoughtest so, or wast of that opinion,euen from the beginning.*
Sembler. *To seeme,or make shew of; also,to resemble.*
Il me semble que. *Me thinks,it seemes to me,I am of aduise,or opinion,that.*
Semé: m. ée: f. *Sowed or sowne; also, powdered, set thicke,or couered all ouer,with; also, spread, or published,abroad.*
Cler semé. *Thinne-set, or sowne; rare, seild, scant, scarce.*
Teste de cerf bien semée. *A Stags head which hath all it spillers,rochers,and scrotchers on both sides.*
Qui a semé ces paroles? *Whence comes this rumor, who began or broached it,who was the author of it?*
Semeler. *To sole a shoo,&c.*
Semelle: f. *The sole of a shoo; also, a foot in the measuring of a leape.*
Iusques à la semelle du pied seulement. *Shallowly, sleightly,but a verie little.*
Semelles, & du vin passent chemin: Prov. *Wine is the footmans caroche; a strong foot, and a light head rid way apace.*
Semence: f. *Seed; also, seeding or sowing time; also, a sowing of seed; also, the seed, sperme,or nature of man or beast; and hence, the originall, beginning, chiefe root, principall author, of a thing; also, any thing that is but small, or by reason thereof, but smally accounted of.*
Semence saincte. *Wormeseed.*
Telle semence telle moisson: Prov. *Looke how you sow so shall you reape.*
Semencé: m. ée: f. *as* Semé.
Semencier: m. ere: f. *Of seed,containing seed.*
Sementine: f. *A certaine Peare so called, because it is alwaies ripe about seeding time.*
Semer. *To sow; to set; to powder, or couer ouer with; also, to spread or disperse, to diuulge or publish abroad.*
Semer vn grain d'orge pour attraper vn pigeon. *Looke* Orge.
Semer guerre. *To raise,moue, stirre vp, giue occasion of,warre.*
Semer des roses aux pourceaux.*To strew pearles before Swine.*
On seme les bleds à l'avanture: Pro. *Looke* Bled.
Qui peu seme peu prend: Pro.*Little sow little mow.*
Semestre: m. *A tearme of six monthes.(This word properly belongs to the Parliament of Britaine, halfe the Judges,and Officers whereof doe sit, and attend* par semestre; *viz. full six monthes; which ended, the other halfe succeed, for as long,in their places.)*
Semestre: com. *Of,or for, six monthes.*
Iuges semestres. *Such as attend but euerie other Tearme,or sit but euerie other halfe yeare.*
Semeur: m. *A sower; setter, planter; author, beginner.*
Semidroict: m. *Base,or low Jurisdiction.*
Semillant: m. ante: f. *Wantonly vnquiet, or stirring; euer figging, fidging, or frigging; foolishly restlesse, or remouing from place to place.*
Semillon: f. *A wanton stirring, or strugling; a restlesse figging, fidging,or frigging.*
Seminal: m. ale: f. *Of seed.*
Semoisson. *as* Semaille.
Semole: f. *The fine flower of an excellent fine Italian wheat,ministred by Phisitions in Panadoes & brothes; and some seldome times vsed in bread; euerie way very nourishing.*
Semonce: f.*A bidding,lathing,inuiting; also,a warning, citation, summons.*
Semoncer. *as* Semondre.
Semondre. *To bid,lathe,inuite; also,to summon,warne, cite.*
Semonneur: m. *A Summoner, Citer, Apparitor; also,an inuitor,or bidder of guests.*
Semoule. *as* Semole; *also,ground wheat thats between meale and flower, or hath onely the coursest of the bran sifted from it.*
Sempervive: m. *Houseleeke,Sengreene, Aigreene.*
Sempervive maieur. *Great Houseleeke, Bullockes eye,*

eye, Iupiters beard, Iupiters eye.

Sempervive marin. *Hearbe Aloes, sea Houseleeke, sea Aigreene.*

Sempervive mineur. *Prickmadam.*

Sempervive sauvage. *Spanish Orpine, Orpine of Hungarie, ioynted Orpine.*

Sempiternel: m. elle: f. *Sempiternall, immortall, euerlasting, perpetuall, continuall, aye-during.*

Sempiterneux: m. euse: f. *The same.*

Vieille sempiterneuse. *An euerlasting Hag, a tough or toothlesse trot.*

Sen dessus dessous. *Topsie turuie, vpside downe.*

Senacle. *A height, or storie in a building.*

Senat: m. *A Senat, or Counsell of Citizens.*

Senateur: m. *A Senator, or common Counsellor in a Citie.*

Senaud: m. *A knaue, rascall, varlet; also, a craftie Iacke; or a rich micher, a rich man that pretends himselfe to be verie poore.*

Sené: m. *A Synod, or Assemblie of Curates before their Ordinarie, or Diocesan.*

Bon gré mal gré va le prestre au sené: Pro. *As vnder* Gré.

Sené: m. *Sene; a little purgatiue shrub or plant.*

Sené d'Alexandrie. *Sene of Alexandria; the best kind of Sene.*

Seneçon: m. *The hearbe Groundsell.*

Grand seneçon. *Great Groundsell; hath a stalke two foot high, and furnished with rough, deepe iagged, and whitish leaues.*

Petit seneçon. *The lesse Groundsell;* Gerards *ordinarie, and smooth-leafed Groundsell.*

Senedette: f. *A kind of great Whall, which from the top of her head spowts a huge quantitie of water.*

Senegré: m. *The hearbe, or seed Fenegreeke.*

Senelles: f. *Heps, or Hawthorne berries.*

Sener. *To gueld, or spay a young Bore, &c.*

Senes. *Twelue, or two sixes at dice.* ¶Rab.

Seneschal: m. *A Seneschall; the Prefect, or President, the chiefe Iustice, or Magistrate, of a precinct; and of the same authoritie thats enioyed by the Bailli, from whom he differs in nothing but in name; yet heretofore it seemes he (being in diuers places onely a Iudge to a Lo.* Bas Iusticier) *was little other, or better, then the steward of a particular Mannor.*

Le grand Seneschal de France. *So was* Le grand Maistre *called in old time.*

Seneschaussée: f. *A Seneschallship; the Iurisdiction of a Seneschall, or the precinct within which he gouernes.*

Senesson. *Looke* Seneçon.

Senestre: com. *Sinister; left; (whence,* La main senestre, &c.)

Senevé: m. *Mustard seed, or Senuie seed, whereof mustard is made; also, the hearbe that beares it.*

Senevé blanc. *Common Senuie, field Mustard; beares (in some places) a white flower, and a blackish, or browne seed.*

Senevé de Iardin. *Common Senuie, blacke Mustard.*

Senevé iaulne. *White Mustard, garden Mustard; is leafed like the Turnip; yeelds a yellow flower, and a whitish yellow seed.*

Senevé sauvage. *Wild Mustard, Treacle Mustard; also,* Thlapsia, *wild Cresses, dish Mustard, Bowyers Mustard, churles Mustard.*

Sengle. *as* Sangle; *a girth.*

Sengle: com. *Single, not double, all alone, simple, without addition, of it selfe.*

Senglot: m. *The hickocke; a yexing.*

Sengloter. *Looke* Senglouter.

Sengloteur: m. *One that hath the hickocke; a yexer.*

Senglout. *Looke* Senglot.

Senglouter. *To yex, or haue the hickocke.*

Senicle. *as* Sanicle; *also, the little Siskin (bird.)*

Senné. *The purging plant Sene.*

Senné de Levant. *Sene of the East, Leuant Sene, the best kind of Sene.*

Sens: m. *Sence, wit, conceit, apprehension, vnderstanding, iudgement, reason, knowledge, opinion, thought; also, naturall sence, or feeling; and, a sence, or one of the fiue sences; also, the sence, meaning, or construction of a writing, &c.*

Dents de sens. *The tenne iaw teeth.*

Os du sens commun. *The forhead bone.*

Sens devant, & sens derriere. ¶Rab. *wherein this word either signifies, a smell; or (Imperatiuely, of* Sentir,) *smell; or equiuocates with* Cent, *a hundred.*

A tous sens. *Euerie way, by all wayes or meanes, in any case, whatsoeuer come of it.*

En tous sens. *Euerie way, to all purposes, howsoeuer you take it.*

En tous les deux sens. *On both sides, both wayes.*

Cela est bon sens à eux. *That is wisely done of them, or turnes greatly to their aduantage; and,* Et est bon sens à eux de. *And their best, or safest course is; or, it is wisely done of them, to.*

I'y mettray tous mes cinq sens. *I will imploy my best indeuors in the matter.*

A vn fol avantureux n'est mestier d'avoir sens: Prov. *A foole that is aduenturous needes not to looke about him.*

En amour est folie, & sens: Prov. *Loue is both fond, and wittie; in loue's both follie, and wit.*

En petite teste gist grand sens: Pro. *Within a little sconce, great skill.*

Il est bien fol qui à fol sens demande: Pro. *He that expects a wise part from a foole, is the more foole of the two.*

Nul n'a trop pour soy de sens, d'argent, de foy: Pro. *No person for his owne vse hath excesse of money, wisedome, faith.*

Qui perd le sien perd le sens: Prov. *Looke vnder* Perdre.

Sens. (Adverb.) sens dessous dessus. *Arsie varsie, topsie turuie, top ouer tayle, vpside downe.*

Sens devant derriere. *Preposterously; or, as vnder* Devant.

Sensible: com. *Sencible, feeling, palpable; passionate at; which is, or may be, felt.*

Sensiblement. *Sencibly, palpably, feelingly.*

Sensitif: m. iue: f. *Sensitiue, sencible, feeling, that hath sence or feeling.*

Sensouïre: f. *Excessiue saltnesse of soyle; a vice or fault in land, bred by the noisome slyme of salt marshes.*

Sensualité: f. *Sensualitie, libertinisme, or epicurisme; the pleasing of sence, contentment giuen to the appetite, satisfaction to the flesh.*

S'ensuit. Que s'ensuit il? *what of that? what makes matter? what followes or comes of it?*

Sentant. *Feeling, senting, smelling, venting, winding.*

Sentant son aller de pis en pis. *Seeing he went worse and worse.*

Sentant son coeur. *See* Coeur.

Sente: f. *A hollow path, a narrow (and well beaten) way; Looke* Sentier.

Sen-

Sentement: m. *A feeling; a senting, smelling, venting, winding; tasting, sauouring.*

Sentence: f. *A sentence, or pithie saying; also, a sentence, decree, iudgement, order, or award of a Court; also, an opinion deliuered, or aduise giuen, in a matter.*
De fol Iuge breve sentence: Prov. *The foole hath quickly vttered his thoughts; or, the fooles award is giuen in few words.*

Sententier. *To sentence, adiudge, order, decree, condemne; to giue sentence, deliuer his opinion, pronounce an award.*

Sententieusement. *Sententiously, pithily, grauely, wisely.*

Sententieux: m. euse: f. *Sententious, graue, wise, pithie, solide, full of matter, stuffie, instructiue.*

Senteur: f. *Sent, odor, smelling, sauor.*

Sentier: m. *A path, or way, of a prettie breadth; whence;*
Sentier de Boullenois. *Is, by the customes of that place, to be fiue foot broad.*
Sentier de Bourgongne. *Is to be foure foot, and a halfe.*
Sentier de Clermont, & de Vallois. *Is, by the customes of those places, to be foure foot broad.*

Sentier: m. ere: f. *Of, or in, a path.*

Sentiment: m. *as* Sentement.

Sentine: f. *The sinke of a ship, &c.*

Sentine mere. *A little Salt-boat, or Barke.*

Sentinelle: f. *A Sentinell, or Sentrie; a common souldior appointed to stand, and watch in a certaine place.*
Sentinelle d'amour. *A bawd.*
Lever de sentinelle. *To relieue, withdraw, or take off, a Sentinell; also, to remoue, or dislodge.*

Sentir. *To feele; also, to sent, smell, vent, wind; also, to tast or sauor; also, to heare; also, to yeeld a sent, sauor, or tast; or to sent, sauor, or tast, of; to haue a smacke, touch, or spice, of.*
Sentir son bien. Cela sent son bien. *Thats comelie, seemelie, orderlie, or as it should be.*
Sentir vn peu de boire. *To be a little cupshotten.*
Sentir son Mardi-gras. Cela sent son &c; *is verie licentiously handled, or vttered.*
Sentir la marée. *To looke like a whore.*
Sentir la vieille guerre. *To be of the old stampe; to vse, or be in, an old fashion.*
Sentir sa bonne ville, & sa petite ville. *See* Ville.
Ie me sens de cette cheute. *I smart, or am the worse, for, I feele to my paine, or I am yet sencible of, this fall.*

Sentive: f. *The facultie, vertue, or power of feeling, smelling, &c.*

Sentrille: f. *A kind of fresh-water fish.*

Seoir. *To sit;* Se seoir. *To sit him downe.*
Il se peut seoir sans contredit qui se met là ou son hoste luy dit: Prov. *He needs not feare to be chidden that sits where he is bidden; (The like is;)*
Il se peut bien seoir à table quand le maistre luy commande: Prov. *Well may he sit him downe whom he that may sets downe.*

Sep: m. *The stocke of a Vine; also, as* Estailon.
Les seps. *as* Des Ceps.
Quand le chou passe le sep le vigneron meurt de soif: Pro. *When Cabbages oregrow the Vine, there will be a great dearth of wine.*

Separaison: f. *as* Separation; *also, a baulke, or diuision betweene two lands.*

Separation: f. *A seperation, seuering, sundering, diuision, disiunction, diuorce; a renting, parting, or putting asunder.*

Separatoire: m. *A seperatorie; the Chizell or Instrument wherewith Surgeons cut out the peeces of bones left betweene the holes which they haue bored with a Trepan.*

Separé: m. ée: f. *Seperated, seuered.*

Separément. *Seperately, seuerally, asunder.*

Separer. *To seperate, seuer, part, sunder, disioyne, diuide, vntwine, diuorce, disunite, put asunder.*

Sepe: m. *The Seps; a broad-headed, and sharp-mouthed serpent (of many colours, and about two cubites in length) which rots the bodie he bites.*

Sepedon. *as* Sepe.

Sepmaine: f. *Looke* Semaine.

Sepmainier: m. *as* Dommas.

Sepmainier: m. ere: f. *Weekelie, each weeke, of or in a weeke.*

Sept. *Seuen.*

Septaine: f. *The precinct, bounds, or liberties of a Towne; the compasse of ground, or circuit of countrey, subiect vnto the Iurisdiction thereof.*

Septante. *Seuentie, threescore and tenne.*

Septantiesme. *The seuentieth.*

Septembre. *The month of September.*
Le flot de Septembre. *The great Spring-tydes of the Autumne Equinoctiall.*
Purée de Septembre. *Wine.*

Septembrin: m. ine: f. *Of, or in, September.*
Liqueur septembrine. *Wine.*

Septenaire: m. *A seuenth, a proportion of seuen, the number of seuen.*

Septenaire: com. *Containing seuen, in, of, or belonging to, seuen.*
Par les chainons septenaires. *In euerie seuenth linke.*

Septentrion: m. *The North.*

Septentrional: m. ale: f. *Northerlie, of or in the North.*

Septerée: f. *A* Septier *full of; or, as* Sesterée.

Septiéme, & **Septiémement**. *Looke* Septiesme.

Septier: m. *A certaine Measure; of vse for diuers things, and thereby of diuers sizes; (One, being the least, and vsed by Phisitions, comes but to three ounces in weight.)*
Septier d'avoine. *The* Septier *of Oats, containing 21* Boisseaux.
Septier de bled. *The* Septier *of corne (viz. Wheat, Rye, or Barlie) containes, in most places, two Mines, or twelue* Boisseaux, *or the twelfth part of a* Muid: *In weight it comes to 220 pounds, sayes* Nicot; *but* Vigenere *vpon Liuie makes that the weight onely of Rye; and sayes, that the* Septier *of wheat weighes 240 pounds.*
Septier de charbon. *Containes 21* Boisseaux.
Septier de Moulins. *The* Septier *of* Moulins, *commeth to 16* Boisseaux.
Septier de terre. *Is much about the Arpent.*
Septier de vin. *Containes eight pints.*
Demi septier de bled. *Containeth six* Boisseaux.
Demi septier de vin. *Is but the halfe of a* Chopine, *or a quarter of the French pint.*

Septiesme. *The seuenth.*

Septiesmement. *Seuenthly.*

Septimestre: com. *Of seuen monthes, or at seuen monthes end.*

Septinaire. *Looke* Septenaire.

Septique: com. *Putrifactiue, rotting inwardly; also,* corro-

corrosiue,raising blisters on the skin.
Septirage. *Looke* Stirage.
Septuagenaire: com. *Threescore and tenne yeares old.*
Sept-virat. *The ioint rule, gouernment, or authoritie of seuen men.*
Septuple: com. *Seuen-fold.*
Sepulchral: m. ale: f. *Sepulchrall; of, or in, a sepulcher.*
Sepulchralier: m. *A maker of sepulchers.*
Sepulchre: m. *A sepulcher, tombe, graue, or vault to lay dead coarses in.*
Cheval courant est vn sepulchre ouvert: Prov. *A running horse is an open sepulcher.*
Sepulturable: com. *Buriable; readie, or fit, to be buried.*
Sepulture: f. *Sepulture; a burying, intombing, interring, laying in a graue or in the ground.*
Sepulturer. *To burie, intombe, interre; lay in the ground, or into a graue.*
Sequele: f. *A sequele, following, or consequence, the issue or successe of a thing; also, a great mans trayne or followers.*
La sequele au robon. *Looke* Robon.
Sequence: f. *A sequence at Cards; also, a certaine game that standeth much on sequences.*
Sequences: f. *Answering verses, or verses whereto answer is made, in the Masse.*
Sequenie: f. *A frocke, or loose iacket of canuas, open before, and worne by Porters, &c, ouer the rest of their apparrell.*
Sequent: m. ente: f. *Sequent, following.*
Sequestration: f. *A sequestration; the deliuerie of a litigious thing into the hands of a third indifferent man; or, the seperating of it from the possession of those that contend for it; (of two sorts.)*
Sequestration iudiciaire, ou necessaire. *Which is imposed by the sentence, or authoritie of a Iudge.*
Sequestration volontaire. *Agreed on by mutuall consent of the parties in controuersie: (There be also other kinds of sequestra ion in doubtfull, as well as in controuerted, cases.)*
Sequestre: m. *He into whose hands a thing is sequestred.*
Sequestré: m. ée: f. *Sequestred.*
Sequestrer. *To sequester, or lay aside, to put into an indifferent persons hands.*
Sequin: m. *A small Italian coyne worth about* 10 Quadrins; *also, a golden coyne somewhat more worth then the French crowne.*
Sequinant: m. *The sweet-flowred Rush teamed Squinant, and Camels Hay.*
Ser de laict. *Whay.*
Ser montain. *Siler Mountaine, bastard Loueage.*
Serain: m. *Faire, cleere, calme, or open weather; also, the mildew, or harmefull dew of some Summer euenings; also, the fresh, and coole ayre of the euening; also, the euening.*
Seran: m. *A hatchell, or heach; the yron combe whereon flax is dressed.*
Serancé: m. ée: f. *Hatchelled, or combed, as flax, &c.*
Serancer. *To hatchell flax, &c, to combe, or dresse it on an yron combe.*
Serancier: m. *A flax-man, a hatcheller, or comber of flax.*
Seraph: m. *A Turkish coyne of fine gold worth about a French crowne.*
Seraphin: m. *A Seraphin; a burning, or flame-coloured Angell; also, a kind of Limbeck.*
Seraphique: com. *Seraphicall, celestiall, Seraphinlike; also, firie, or burning.*
Seraphiser. *To sanctifie, consecrate; extoll, magnifie to the heauens.*
Serapin. *as* Sagapen.
Serargent. *(An allusion to* Sergent;*) a scrape-good, penny-father, siluer-hider, money-hoorder.*
Serat. Laict serat. *Milke boyled with Garlicke, and Onyons, and much vsed in Normandie; also, sowre, or sowred milke.*
Serbataine. *Looke* Sarbataine.
Serbin: m. *The crimson, or pricklie Cedar; also, the Rosin that ißueth from the great Cedar.*
Sercifi: m. *The delicate root of the hearb called Goatsbeard, Starre of Ierusalem, Noonetyde, and Goe-to-bed-at-noone.*
Sercler, & Sercleur. *Looke* Sarcler, & Sarcleur.
Sercleure: f. *A sarcling; or weeding.*
Sercueil. *as* Cercueil.
Serée: f. *An euening, euening season, euening tide; also, an euenings taske, worke, art, or exercise; also, a gossipping, or goodfellow-like meeting of neighbours (this night at one, that at another, of their houses) whereto euerie one brings, or sends his dish.*
Serein: m. *Looke* Serain.
Serein: m. eine: f. *Bright, faire, cleere, calme; open; gentle, mild, quiet, peaceable; cheerefull, merrie, pleasant, gracious.*
Sereine: f. *A Mermaid.*
Sereiner. *To cleere, brighten; wax faire, looke cheerefully; make lightsome or pleasant; also, to calme, quiet, pacifie, appease.*
Serenade: f. *Euening Musicke played at the dore, or vnder the window, of a louelie, or beloued creature.*
Serenade d'esprit. *Tranquilitie of spirit.*
Serencer. *Looke* Serancer.
Serene: f. *A Syren, or Mermaid.*
Serene. La goutte serene. *Blindnesse, or extreame dimnesse of sight, caused by the obturation or stopping of the Opticke sinew.*
Serenité: f. *Serenitie, cleerenesse, faireneße, brightnesse, calmenesse, or opennesse of weather.*
Serennade: f. *Looke* Serenade.
Sereux: m. euse: f. *Serous, whayie, waterish; also, louing the euening; and, being in, or neere, the euening.*
Serf: m. *A seruant, seruitor, seruingman; or (most properly) a thrall, slaue, prentice, bondman, villein, drudge to, or base attendant on, another.*
Serfs fonciers. *Looke* Foncier.
Serfs pissenez. *The bastards of slaues, or villeines.* ❡Nivernois.
Serfoët: m. *A weeding hooke, or weeding forke.*
Serfoüé: m. ée: f. *Weeded; grubbed or cut vp with a weeding forke.*
Serfouër. *To weed, to grub or cut vp weeds.*
Serfouëttes: f. *The Instrument wherewith a Gardener grubs or cuts vp weeds; Looke* Sarfouëtte.
Serfs. *An Order of blacke Friers, which thus tearme themselues.*
Serge: f. *The stuffe called Serge.*
Sergeant: m. *A Sergeant; Looke* Sergent.
Sergeant de tonnelier. *The Coopers horse; an yron toole which he vseth in the hooping of Caske.*
Sergeanter, & Sergeanterie. *Looke* Sergeanter, & Sergenterie.
Sergeanteux: m. euse: f. *Sergeant-like, or vsing a Sergeant-like, authoritie.*

Ser-

Sergeantise: f. *Looke* Sergentise.

Sergent: m. *A Sergeant, Officer, Catchpole, Pursuyuant, Apparitor; also (in old French) a footman, or souldior that serues on foot.*

Sergent d'armes. *A Sergeant at Armes; one of those which wait on the King.*

Sergent bastonnier. *An ordinarie Sergeant, or Catchpole in an incorporate Towne.*

Sergent blavier. *as* Sergent Messier, ou Messilier.

Sergens à cheval. *Were, in old time, certaine horsemen inferior to* Les Escuyers, *and seruing for pay in the warres: Now they are officers that ride through all the villages, and fields of the* Ressort, *or* Baillage, *whereto they belong; therein arresting, and doing such other offices, as are performed by the* Sergents à pied *within the principall towne, and the liberties thereof.*

Sergent chevaucheur. *A certaine officer in forrests.*

Sergens dangereux. *Looke* Dangereux.

Sergent de l'espée. Doit tenir les veuës, bailler les assignations, faire les semonces & les commandemens des assises, & faire tenir ce qu'y est iugé, & delivrer par droict les Namps qui sont prins, & iusticier à l'espée & aux armes les malfaicteurs, & fugitifs. ¶Ragueau.

Sergent feodé, fieffé, ou du fief. *An hereditarie Sergeant; hath some kind of Iurisdiction for the recouerie of the* Cens, *Rents, Duties, Customes, Royalties, or feodall Rights, belonging to the Lord of the Seigniorie wherein he resides; and may nominate, and appoint one vnder-Sergeant (and in some places more) to assist, and attend him.*

Sergent fermier. *One that hath farmed the office of a Sergeant (which he is forbidden to doe by the Law.)*

Sergens forestiers. *Officers that may of themselues arrest the persons, and seize the goods, of such as wast, or make hauocke of the Kings woods: Of these there are two sorts;* Les ordinaires, *whose walkes are limitted;* & les traversiers, *which raunge all ouer the forrest; Looke* Traversier.

Sergent franc. *Looke vnder* Franc.

Sergents à masse d'argent. *Sergeants of the Mace:* Ce sont Huissiers de la Chambre du Conseil, ou Audience, en Hainaut.

Sergent messier, ou messilier. *An officer that lookes vnto Corne-grounds, and Vineyards, vntill haruest, and Vintage be fully past.*

Sergens à pied. *The ordinarie Sergeants of a good towne, within which, or the liberties thereof (and not elsewhere) they may arrest, &c, and are to reside.*

Sergent prairier. *An officer that keeps, and looks vnto, medowes, for the preseruation of the hay, and grasse thereof.*

Sergent de querelle. Qui servoit au faict des duels, ou pour les differents des parties: *(But this officer is now out of date.)*

Sergent traversier. *Looke* Traversier.

Sergent à verge. *An ordinarie Catchpole in a good Towne; also, a royall Vsher, or Sergent, who arresting, &c, within his circuit, ought to carrie in his hand a rod, or small Mace, and therewith to touch him whom he doth arrest.*

Sergentaillerie: f. La ser. *Sergeants, Officers, Catchpoles; or a companie of them.*

Sergenter. *To arrest, attache, or summon; to play the Sergeant any way.*

Sergenterie: f. *A Sergeantship; the office, place, or dutie of a Sergeant; also (in the customes of Normandie) a kind of* fief *without Court, or Jurisdiction; or, that seruice which, in our Law, is tearmed* Grand, *or* Petit Sergeantie.

Sergentie, & Sergentise. *as* Sergenterie *(in the former sence.)*

Seri: m. ie: f. *Quiet, mild, calme, still; faire, cleere.*

Seriau. *The same; whence,* Car le iour est seriau. *The Burden of a certaine Christmas Caroll.* ¶Rab.

Serie: f. *The eue of a holie day; also, the euening, or euening-tide.*

Seriens: m. *(An old word;) souldiors that serued on foot.*

Serieusement. *Seriously, verie earnestly.*

Serin: m. *A little singing bird of a light-greene colour, and verie like the Canarie bird other waies; whence;*

Serin de Canarie. *The Canarie bird.*

Serin: m. ine: f. *Silkie; also, as* Serein.

Seringue: f. *A Siringe, or Squirt.*

Seringuement: m. *A squirting; an iniecting, or spurting of liquor by a Siringe.*

Seringuer. *To squirt.*

Seriphie: f. *Sea-Wormewood, called, by some of our countrey women, garden Cypresse.*

Serment: m. *An oath; also, as* Sarment.

Serment de calomnie; &, ser. de fidelité. *See* Calomnie, & Fidelité.

Par mon serment. *By my truth, by the faith I owe to God; or, by the oath I haue taken.*

Sermenteux. *Looke* Sarmenteux.

Sermon: m. *A Sermon, or preaching; an Harang, or Oration, made vnto the people.*

Sermonner. *To preach, to make a Sermon.*

Sermonneur: m. *A Sermon-maker, a Preacher.*

Sermontain: m. *Siler Mountaine, bastard Loueage.*

Serosité: f. *Serositie; the waterishnesse, or thinner parts of the masse of bloud (answering to whay in milke) which floates vpon it after it hath beene let out of a veine; also, the wheyish, or waterish moisture drawne by the kidneyes from all parts of the bodie, and after some concoction tearmed, Vrine.*

Serourge: m. *A brother in law; one that hath married a mans owne, or his wiues, sister.*

Serpaut: m. *Marriage-good; the apparrell, beds, coffers, vessell, cattell, or other houshold-stuffe, or moueables whatsoeuer, giuen in marriage with a sonne, daughter, or cousin.*

Serpe: f. *Looke* Sarpe.

Serpé: m. ée: f. *Towed off ground, set afloat, as a ship by an anchor, or great hooke; also, weighed, as an anchor.*

Serpeger. *To wind, or crankle in and out; to waue, waggle, wrigle, writhe, or to goe wauing, &c, like a serpent.*

Serpeillere. *Looke* Serpillere.

Serpent: m. *A Serpent; a venomous, or poisonous (and footlesse) vermine; also, the male Lamprey.*

Serpent cornu. *The Serpent Cerastes, or the horned serpent; See* Cornu.

Serpent marin. *The sea serpent, resembles a Congar, but hath a sharper beake, or nose, wherewith he suddainely hides himselfe in the sand.*

Ail de serpent. *Wild Garlick, Snakes Garlick.*

Herbe aux serpens. *Vipers hearbe, Snakes Buglosse.*

Il faut tirer le serpent du buisson par la main d'autruy: Pro. *He that will safely liue, must shift off dangers to others; or, dangers cannot be surmounted without helpe.*

Serpentaire: f. *The hearbe Dragons, or Dragonwort.*

Serpentaire aquatique, ou d'eau. *Water Dragons, water Dragonwort.*

Serpentaire masle des Officines. *Snakeweed*, Britannica, *Bistort*.
Grande serpentaire. *Great Dragons or Dragonwort; the ordinarie Dragonwort.*
Petite serpentaire. *Small Dragons; an hearbe like Wake-Robin in all points saue it spots, which are white.*
Serpentant: m. ante: f. *Crankling, wrigling, wigling, crooking, winding, making many turnes.*
Serpente: f. *A Serpent.*
Faire la serpente. *as* Serpenter.
Serpenté. *Wrigled, cranckled, wrythed, turned or wound in and out.*
Serpenteau: m. *A little serpent.*
Serpenter. *To wrigle, wagle, cranckle, wrythe, turne or wind often in and out.*
Serpentin: m. *The vpper part of some Limbecks, made long, and wreathed like a serpent; also, the cocke of an Harquebuze.*
Serpentin: m. ine: f. *Of a serpent, like a serpent, long and wreathed as a serpent.*
Ail serpentin. *Snakes Garlick, wild Garlick.*
Marbre serpentin. *A darke-greene Marble, full of light-greene spots.*
Pierre serpentine. *Looke* Pierre.
Serpentine: f. *A kind of Limbecke, or, as* Serpentin; *also, as* Serpentaire; *also, the Artillerie called a Serpentine, or Basiliskoe.*
Petite serpentine. *Small Dragons; also, Cucko-pint, Wake-Robin, Calues-foot.*
Serper. *To tow a ship off ground, or set her afloat by a great hooke, or ankor fastened vnto another ship thats vnder sayle.*
Serper l'ancre. *To weigh ankor.*
Serpette: f. *A Vine-knife, or Gardeners knife; a verie small hedging, or lopping, bill.*
Serpigine: f. *A rednesse of the skin, accompanied with pushes, and wheales.*
Serpiller. *To packe vp in Canuas, &c; also, to gleane after Grape-gatherers, or cut away from the Vine all the grapes they haue left behind them.*
Serpillere: f. *A Sarpler, or Sarp-cloth; a piece of course Canuas to packe vp things in; also, the course Canuas apron of a Grocer, Chaundler, Painter, Dawber, &c.*
Serpillette: f. *A small Vine-hooke, or Gardeners hooked knife.*
Serpillon. *as* Serpette.
Serpillonnette. *as* Serpillette; *or a verie small one.*
Serpolet: m. *Running Time, wild Time, creeping Time, mother of Time, Puliall mountaine, our Ladies Bedstraw.*
Serpolet sauvage. *Wild creeping Time; of two kinds, the one bearing a white, the other a red flower:* (Gerard *shewes vs no fewer then six kinds of* Serpillum, *all which as he calls wild Times (though with some small, and different additions) so many hold (sayes* Mathiolus) *that euerie* Serpolet *is wild:) Some also tearme Water-mint, and others Balsamint,* Serpolet sauvage.
Serquify: m. *The delicate root of the hearbe Goatsbeard.*
Serrail: m. *The Pallace wherein the great Turke mueth vp his concubines.*
Serrail d'un huis. *The boult of a doore.*
Serran: m. *A certaine fish thats like, but somewhat lesse then, the sea-Pearch; and hath, as it, two stones in his head; called thus about* Marseille.

Serrant: m. *A Greene-finch.*
Serrant: m. ante: f. *Shutting, or locking, vp.*
Serratan. *Looke* Serran.
Serratil: m. ile: f. *Closing, or shutting vp close together.*
Serre: f. *A Hawkes tallon; also, a strait, or narrow pinch; also, a saw; also, the wild Fitch.*
Serres. *A Hawkes tallons; also, wild Fitches; also, the thicke boards whereby the inside of the* Varengues *of a ship are fastened, and held in.*
Tenir en serre. *To restraine, or hold in subiection.*
Serre: com. *Close; whence,* Tenir serre; *to hold himselfe close, to restraine, or keepe in, himselfe.*
Serré: m. ée: f. *Closed, compacted, contracted, thrust vp together, clapped or put neere vnto; restrained; straitned; hard wrung or pressed; fast locked, shut or bound vp.*
Serré de douleurs. *Whose heart is shrunk, or oppressed, with griefe.*
Serré. (*In stead of* Serrément; *whence,*) Dormir fort serré. *To sleepe verie soundly.*
Serre. (*Of the Verbe* Serrer;) *the word whereby souldiors are warned to close themselues, or draw neere together.*
Serrecropiere. Le Ieu de ser. *The close-buttock play; lecherie.*
Serre-front: m. *A head-band, forhead-band, or forhead-cloth.*
Serremént: m. *A closing, compacting, pressing, hardthrusting together; a contracting; vp-shutting, restraining.*
Serrément. *Closely, straitly, narrowly, neere one to another, contractedly, restrainedly, in a little roome.*
Serre-nappe: f. *A cabinet, roome, or chest for the keeking of table-linnen; also, the basket whereinto it is put vp at the taking away.*
Serre-poignet: m. *A griping close-fist, a couetous or close-handed wretch.*
Serrer. *To close, compact, thrust hard, bind fast, force or presse neere together; to locke, shut or put vp, hold or keepe strait; restraine; contract.*
Se serrer. *To goe all on a rucke, or gather himselfe vp close together.*
Serrer le bouton à. *To restraine or keepe short, to hold a strict or hard hand ouer.*
Serrer les ordures. *To sweepe together all the scattered filth of a floore.*
Serrer prés. *To presse mightily, vrge very much, driue vnto a narrow strait, pinch, or plunge; pursue verie neere; also, to be most earnest with, or instant vpon.*
Qui sçait l'art serre la boutique; &, Qui ne sçait l'art serre la boutique: Pro. *Looke* Boutique.
Serres. *as vnder* Serre.
Serre-teste: f. *A border of Goldsmiths worke, &c, worne by gentlewomen vpon their coifes, or hoods.*
Serreure. *Looke* Serrure.
Serriette: f. *The hearbe Sauorie.*
Serrure: f. *A locke.*
Remuer les serrures. *To play the Polypragmon, or busie companion.*
Contre coignée serrure ne peut: Prov. *No lockes hold out against an yron axe; an armed violence forceth any thing.*
Serrurerie: f. *The trade of a Lock-smith; a making of locks.*
Serrurier: m. *A Lock-smith.*
Sert: m. *The first course, or seruice at Table.*
Serte: f. *A kind of flat-bottomed boat vsed in old time.*

Ser-

Servage: m. *Seruitude, slauerie, bondage, thralldome.*
Servans: m. *An Order of blacke Fryers.*
Servant: m. ante: f. *Seruing, attending, waiting on, obseruing, obseruant, obsequious vnto; also, helping, steadding, auailing.*
Fief servant. *A fief thats held by homage and fealtie, of a* fief dominant; *an inferior, or mesne fief.*
Gentilshommes servans. *Gentlemen waiters, those that attend on the King at meale-times.*
Iour servant, & iournée servante. *The day appointed for the hearing, and deciding of a cause.*
Servante: f. *A maid, or woman, seruant (especially of a meane, or inferior, degree.)*
Servantin: m. *The Sole-fish tearmed, a kind foole;* ¶Marseillois.
Serve. *A Stue for fish; also, a Mue for fowle; also, the hearbe Sage.*
Servément. *Seruilely, by villenage, by a seruile or base tenure.*
Servi: m. ie: f. *Serued, obserued.*
Servi de son homage. *That hath receiued his homage in due time.*
Entrer de fief servi. *The homage, &c, due by a tenant at his first entrie, done well enough by another; as by an elder brother for a younger; by a husband for his wife; by a guardian for his pupill, or ward.*
Serviable: com. *Seruiceable, officious, diligent, obsequious; pliant; behoofefull.*
Serviablement. *Seruiceably, officiously, obsequiously, diligently; behoofefully.*
Service: f. *Seruice, attendance; dutie, obedience; also, wages, or hire for seruice; also, diuine seruice, (publike) prayer vnto almightie God; whence;*
La service des morts. *Dirges, Obits, Trentalls, prayers for the dead.*
Service de l'ost. *Looke* Ost.
Service de plaids. *Apparance made, counsell giuen; any attendance yeelded, or seruice done, by a vassall in his Lords Courts.*
Services des vignes. *The pathes, or alleyes, which are made ouerthwart a Vineyard.*
Cheval de service. *A great horse, or horse of seruice; due from a vassall to his Lord* feudal *(or in lieu of him* 60 s Tourn: *as by the customes of* Orleans, Montargis, Chasteauneuf, Chartres, & Dreux; *or* 60 s *and a pennie* Tourn: *by the customes of* Le grand Perche; *or* 100 s Tourn: *as by the customes of* Anjou, *and* Maine;) *And this either once during a Lords, or vassals life, or at euerie change of Lord, and vassall.*
Denier de service. *Looke* Denier.
Beau service fait amis, & vray dire ennemis: Pro. *Dutifulnesse procureth friends, truth enemies; obsequious attendance winneth loue, true and plaine dealing hate.*
Servicial: m. *A glister.*
Serviette: f. *A table napkin.*
Nouër les deux bouts de sa serviette ensemble. *Seeke* Nouër.
Servir. *To serue, attend, wait on, obserue, be obsequious vnto; also, to helpe, stead, auaile, assist, fit ones turne, doe good, be profitable or behoofefull, vnto.*
Servir le fief. *A man to doe homage, fealtie, and all other seruices whereto he is tyed by his tenure.*
Servir son maistre. *To purge, vntrusse a point, goe to the stoole.*
Servir les plaids de son seigneur. *As before, in* Service de plaids.
Se servir de. *To vse, occupie, make a benefit, or take the aduantage, of.*
Se servir de toutes peaux. *as vnder* Peau.
Mal sert qui ne parfert: Pro. *He's but an ill seruant thats not an all-seruant.*
Qui sert commun nul ne le paye, & s'il defaut chascun l'abbaye: Prov. *The seruant of a Comminaltie finds enow to correct his errors, but none to reward his deserts.*
Qui sert dieu il a bon maistre: Pro. &, Qui sert le Roy il a bon maistre: Pro. *Looke* Maistre.
Assez demande qui bien sert: Prov. *Good seruice, of it selfe, demaunds reward.*
Servis: m. *The* Cens, *and other small yearelie rights, or duties, payed by the tenants of Inheritances vnto Lord of the soyle, in acknowledgement of his direct seigniorie.*
Serviteur: m. *A seruant, seruitor, seruing creature, seruing man; an attendant, or waiter.*
Fortune n'espargne ny serviteur, ny maistre: Prov. *looke* Fortune.
Servitude: f. *Seruitude, slauerie, bondage.*
Mieux vaut servitude en paix que seigneurie en guerre: Pro. *Better be peaces vassall, then warfares marshall.*
Servitute: f. *A dutie wherein one peece of ground, and the possessor thereof, is lyable, or subiect, vnto another.*
Hommes de servitute. *A kind of villeins, or seruile tenants, lyable to their Lords taxations while they liue; and when they die, their sonnes must buy their possessions of him, or else he seises, and holds them; and their daughters (if they had no sonnes) must loose the soyle, and take such husbands, and portions, as he is pleased to allot them.*
Servivi: m. *An act, or Certificate of the actuall seruices performed by an officer, who thereupon receiues the wages, and is allowed the priuiledges, due vnto his place.*
Sery: m. *The Shrew-mouse.* ¶Bourguignon.
Sesame: m. *The oylie pulse, or graine* Sesamum.
Sesamin: m. ine: f. *Of* Sesamum.
Sesamoïde. *Bastard Woad; an hearbe of two kinds, a great, and a little one; either of them diuided into two other kinds; viz. the great one into great bastard Woad, and barren Weld; and the little one into small bastard Woad, and Buckhorne Weld, which is* Mathiolus *his little* Sesamoïdes.
Sesamoïdes. Os sesamoïdes. *Looke* Os.
Sesel, & Seseli. *The hearbe Seseli, Seseleos, Hartwort.*
Seseli de Candie. *Seseleos, or Hartwort of Candia.*
Seseli Ethiopique. *Shrub Seseli, Hartwort of Ethiopia.*
Seseli de Marseille. *Marsellian Seseli; large, and broad Cummin.*
Seseli de la Morée. *Hartwort of Peloponnesus.*
Seseli Peloponnesien. *The same.*
Sesne. *The mother of wine; the white or mouldie spots which float on the top of old wine.*
Sesquialtere: com. *One and a halfe, or halfe as much againe; as three in respect of two, &c.*
Sesquin: m. *A kind of base coyne.*
Sesquitiers: m. erce: f. *As much, and a third part more.*
Sessile: com. *Sitting, seeming to sit; easie to sit on; of a low stature.*
Verruë sessile. *A kind of hard, broad, flat, and blackish wart.*

Sesterce: m. *The fourth part of the (auncient) Romane pennie, worth about three halfe pence farthing of our money.*
Sesterée de terre. *The fourth part of a* Saumée; *a measure for land, somewhat lesse then the ordinarie* Arpent.
Sestier. *Looke* Septier.
Sestine: f. *A Sestine, or stanzo of six verses.*
Sete. *The Quitter-bone; A round, and hard swelling vpon the Cornet (betweene the heele, and quarter) of a horses foot.*
Setier: m. *Bristlie, rough, harsh.*
Seton: m. *A rowell; or the rowelling, or roping of a bruised, or strained horse.*
Setton. *The same; also, as* Section.
Setule. *Looke* Sete.
Seu: m. *An Elder tree.*
Seve: f. *The sap, iuyce, or moisture of plants; also, the bleeding of a Vine.*
Seueil: m. *The threshold of a doore.*
Severe: com. *Seuere, austere, sterne; graue; rigorous; rough, sharpe, hard; pitilesse, vntractable, inexorable.*
Severement. *Seuerely, sternely, rigorously; sharpely, vntractably, inexorably.*
Severité: f. *Seueritie, sharpnesse, rigor, austeritie, sternnesse, fiercenesse, vntractablenesse; grauitie.*
Severonde: f. *The eaue, eauing, or easing of a house.*
Seveux: m. euse: f. *Sappie, iuicie, full of naturall moisture.*
Seuil: m. *The threshold of a doore.*
Sevir. *To rage, or be mad at; to be extreamely angred, fierce, eager; to torment extreamely, deale most cruelly with; to tyrannize ouer.*
Seul: m. seule: f. *Sole, single, onely, alone, onely one; meere; singular, seuerall, by it selfe.*
Homme seul est viande aux loups: Prov. *The lonelie man becomes a prey to wolues.*
Fortune ne vient seule: Prov. *One misfortune hales on another.*
Haste ne vient seule: Pro. *Looke* Haste.
Mieux vaut estre seul que mal accompagné: Pro. *Better alone then in ill companie.*
Seule: f. *A threshold; also, a groundsill; or, the peece of timber which compasses the bottome of a roome.*
Seulement. *Solely, onely, but, but onely, by it selfe, alone.*
Seulet: m. ette: f. *Sole, alone, solitarie, priuate, singular, apart from others.*
Seulle. La seulle d'une chartée de foing. *As much (meddow) ground as will beare a load of Hay.*
Seur: m. *An Elder tree; also, a kind of Net, or Engine to catch fish with.*
Seur: f. *A sister; Looke* Soeur.
Seur: m. eure: f. *Sure, safe, sicker, secure, out of danger; fast, assured, certaine; trustie, loyall, faithfull.*
Chiens seurs. *Sure-hunting dogs; those that sticke to their owne, or old, game; those that runne, or hunt their owne.*
Avoir la main seure. *Looke* Main.
Seurant. *Weaning.*
Seurat. *Of Elders; whence,* Vinaigre seurat. *Elder vineger.*
Seure: com. *Sowre, sharpe, tart.*
Seuré: m. ée: f. *Weaned from sucke.*
Seurer. *To weane.*
Seureté: f. *Suretie, safetie, securitie, sureneße; also, a suretie, or securitie.*
En seureté dort qui n'a que perdre: Pro. *Securely sleepes he that hath nought to loose.*
Il n'est pas en seureté à qui ne mescheut oncques: Prov. *He that hath had no ill lucke is in danger.*
Sevronde. *Looke* Severonde.
Seurté. *Looke* Seureté.
Sexagenaire: com. *Threescore yeares old.*
Sexe: m. *A sex, or kind.*
Sextaire: m. *An auncient Romane measure, containing somewhat more then our pint.*
Sexte: f. *The third quarter, or sixt houre of the artificiall day, being about noone all the yeare long; also, a sixt, or proportion of six, in Musicke, &c.*
Sextement. *Sixtly.*
Sexterce, & Sexterée. *as* Sesterée.
Sextier. *Looke* Septier.
Sextule: f. *A weight of foure scruples, or the sixt part of an ounce.*
Seyé: m. ée: f. *Reaped, or cut, as corne.*
Seyer le bled. *To reape, or cut downe corne.*
Seyette: f. *Serge, or Say.*
Seyeur: m. *A reaper.*
Seynale. *as* Salvatelle.
Seyeux: m. euse: f. *Silkie, full of silke.*
Sezain: m. *The toll, or fee thats due for grinding; also, as* Seizain.
Seze. *Sixteene.*
Seziesme: m. *A sixteenth; a sixteenth part.*
Vn sezieme d'aulne. *Three ynches, and (as our Neale of the yard) the least diuision of the French ell, and the least measure for cloth.*
Seziesme: com. *The sixteenth in ranke, number, &c.*
Shilirhoïque. Goutte sh. *A kind of cold Gowt.*
Si. *(Sometimes a Substantiue; whence,)* Par tel si que. *On condition that.*
Il n'a nul si. *He is perfect, without fault or defect, no want or error can be found in him, no blemish or deformitie about him.*
Si. *An Aduerbe, vsed single, and in answere to a negatiue demaund, or speech; whence to,* Vous n'avez pas faict celà; *they answer,* si; *yes forsooth haue I, or yes that I haue; In which sence it hath sometimes also the companie of other words; as in answer to one that tells them, you cannot, or will not doe that, or it will neuer be; they say,* Vous verrez que si; *you shall see that I can or will, or, that it will fall out &c.*
Si. *In the beginning of a speech now and then implies, (among some auncient Authors) a kind of certaintie, or of resolution; as,* si advint en ce iour mesme que le heraut arriva; *Surely it happened the verie same day whereon the herald arriued:* Si voy qu'il nous faudra avoir bataille. *I see for certaine that we must fight.*
Si. *(Ordinarily signifies) if, if so be that, whether; (and) so, in sort, as, euen as: And preceding a Verbe, it imports (many times) a commaund, forcing, or threatning, and before* faut, *a necessitie; as in the two Examples following.*
Si cheminerez vous. *You shall walke whether you will or no; or, walke when I bid you; or, you had best walke.*
Si faut il faire cela. *That must needes be done, or, you must of necessitie doe it.*
Si que. *Whereby, so as, in sort that.*
Si non que. *Sauing that, but that.*
Il avoit vn bel esprit, & si estoit de mauvaise grace. *He had an excellent wit, and yet, &c.*

Il estoit sçavant, & si estoit vaillant aux armes. *He was both learned and valiant, or, learned and valiant withall, or, not onely learned, but also valiant.*

Il n'estoit point clerc, & si n'avoit nulle cognoissance des lettres. *He was neither clarke, nor any way learned.*

Quant à &c, le Grec n'a rien de tel, quant a &, si l'a bien. *The Grecians vse not &c, but & they surely doe.*

Sibi. 'A son sibi. *(as the Latine* sibi.) *To himselfe.*

Sibille: f. *A tunning and tasting dish in the time of Vintage.*

Il a le nez rouge comme la sibille d' un pressoir. *(Fitly applyed to a drunkard; one kind of stuffe dying both his nose, and that dish all of a colour.)*

Sibilot. *(The name of a foole vnto the French* Henry *the third; and thence;) an asse, doult, fop, ideot, ninnie.*

Siboule. *as* Ciboule.

Sibylle: f. *Sybill, one of the tenne* Sybillæ, *famous in their times for prophecying; hence also, a Propheteße, or woman that hath the spirit of prophesie; also, as* Sebille.

Sibyllin: m. ine: f. *Prophecying, of a Sybilla, or Sybillalike.*

Sicap. De leur sicap. *Of their owne head, after their owne fancie, according to their humor.*

Siccité: f. *Siccitie, drynesse, drought, or drouth, want of sap, iuyce, or moisture.*

Siciliane. *Looke* Ceciliane.

Sicilique: f. *A quarter of an ounce.*

Sicinnie: f. *A dauncing, and singing together.*

Sicinnistes: m. *Such as daunce, and sing together; or, as* Siticines. ¶Rab.

Sicnie. *Looke* Sequenie.

Sicot. *as* Bricot.

Sideration. *Looke* Syderation.

Siderite. *The yron-like stone* Siderites, *which, as some imagine, hath power to set men at oddes; also, the Loadstone.*

Sidre: m. *Cider; drinke made of Apples.*

Sie: f. *A Saw.*

Sie de mer. *Looke* Scie.

Sié: m. ée: f. *Sawed, or cut asunder; also, reaped, or cut downe.*

Siecle: m. *An Age; (commonly vnderstood of* 100 *yeares) also, time, or season.*

Sied. Cet accoustrement luy sied bien. *This garment becomes, beseemes, befits, or fits him well.*

Siege: m. *A seat; a chaire, stoole, or bench to sit on; also, a Tribunall, Court, or Throne, the seat of Iustice; the Towne, or Place wherein an ordinarie Court of Iustice is kept; also, the buttockes, arse, fundament, the hinder parts, or part of the bodie whereon we vse to sit; also, the siege of a towne; also, the fish* Gardon.

Aujourd'huy en siege, demain en piege: Prov. *To day a captaine, to morrow a captiue.*

Sieger. Le Parlement siegeoit. *The Parliament (or Court) sate, or was held.*

Le Pape siegeoit 12 ans. *The Pope gouerned, or held his place 12 yeares; (This word being proper to Popes, as* Regner *is for Kings.)*

Siement: m. *A sawing; also, a reaping, or cutting downe of corne, &c.*

Sien: m. *A mans owne; that which he hath in his owne right, that whereof he is absolute maister; or, that which is proper to himselfe.*

Chascun y a mis du sien. *Euerie one hath added somewhat of his owne vnto it.*

Qui perd le sien perd le sens: Prov. *Who looseth his pence forgoeth his sence.*

Sien: m. enne: f. *His, his owne, of or belonging to himselfe.*

Des siens. *Of his faction, side, partie, followers.*

Il ioüe bien des siennes. *He freely playes his prankes, he does euen what he will.*

Siement: m. *A sawing, or cutting asunder; also, a reaping of corne.*

Sienite. *A kind of rich Marble gotten about Thebes.*

Sier. *To saw, or cut asunder (as with a Saw;) also, to reape, or cut downe, corne, &c.*

Sier en arriere: C' est aller le derriere devant; *To shieue, or fall a-sterne; (a tearme of Nauigation.)*

Siefer. *To become, fit, sit on.*

Siette: f. *A little saw.*

Sieu: m. *The suet of Deere, wild Goats, the Roe, &c; also, the grease of Capons, and of such other fowle.*

Sieur: m. *A sawyer; also, a reaper.*

Sieure: f. *Saw-dust, pinne-dust, &c; also, a sawing.*

Sieurel: m. *The bastard Mackarell.*

Sieurie. *Looke* Seigneurie.

Sieuté. Poissons d' une s. *Of one size, or goodnesse.*

Sifflant: m. ante: f. *Whistling; whizzing; hissing.*

Sifflant en paume ie me rendray à vous. *Put but vp the finger I am for you.*

Sifflantement. *Hissingly, with a whistling sound.*

Sifflé. *Whistled; whizzed; hissed.*

Sifflement: m. *A whistling; whizzing; hissing.*

Siffler. *To whistle; whizze; hisse at.*

Sifflerie: f. *A whistle, or whistling.*

Sifflet: m. *A whistle; also, the weason, or wind-pipe.*

Siffleur: m. *A whistler; also, the whistling bird called, a Nowpe, or Bull-finch.*

Sifre. *Looke* Chifre.

Sigillatif: m. iue: f. *Sigillatiue, sealeable, apt to seale; made of wax.*

Sigillé: m. ée: f. *Sealed.*

Signacle: m. *A signe, seale, marke, or character.*

Signal: m. *A signall, signe; token, marke.*

Signale: com. *as* Segnale.

Signalé: m. ée: f. *Notable, famous, renowmed; of note, of marke; (An Italianisme; and deriued from the custome of marking souldiors in auncient Garrisons.)*

Signaler. Se sign. *To make himselfe to be noted, or spoken of; to get himselfe a name.*

Signamment. *Namely, expressely, especially, particularly.*

Signature: f. *A signature, signing, subscribing; a signe manuell, ones hand or marke set vnto a writing; In old bookes (written when but a few could write) it signifies a seale, or sealing.*

Signe: m. *A signe, marke, token, or note; an argument; a presage; a winke with the eye, becke with the hand, nod with the head; also, a pledge, or pawne.*

Vn signe au ciel. *A signe in the Zodiake, a celestiall signe.*

Signe patibulaire. *A Gibbet, or paire of Gallowes.*

Les vertus surmontent les signes: Prov. *Worth exceedeth wonders; example preuailes more then a signe to the conuersion of a sinner.*

Signé: m. ée: f. *Signed, subscribed; marked, branded, noted, stamped on.*

Signer. *To signe, subscribe; marke, brand, set his stampe on, or hand vnto; also, to note; also, to skarre; also, to beckon vnto, or by signes to bid one approach.*

Se signer. *To blesse, or crosse himselfe; to make the signe of the Crosse on some part of himselfe.*

Signer de son sang. *To signe with his bloud; to asure the truth of his promises, or words, by most vehement, faithfull, or effectuall demonstrations.*

Signet: m. *A signet, seale, stampe, marke.*

Signet de Salamon. *Salamons seale,* Scala cæli, *White-root, or White-wort.*

Signeur: m. *A signer, subscriber; marker, brander; stamper; also, a crosser, or blesser.*

Signifiance: f. *A signification, or signifying; a declaring, a betokening; also, an argument, signe, or token of.*

Significance. *as* Signifiance.

Signification: f. *A signification, sence, meaning; a declaration, aduertisement, information.*

Signifier. *To signifie, betoken, shew, note, meane; to declare, denounce, warne, aduertise, informe.*

Haine de prince signifie mort d'homme: Prov. *A Princes hate portends the bane of man.*

Silence: m. *Silence, peace-holding; stillnesse, quietnesse; also, a deauelnesse, or solitarinesse.*

Silenes. *Boxes in Apothecaries shops painted on the outside, with diuers odde figures.*

Silentiaire: m. *A silenciarie, a patron or patterne of silence.*

Silentieux: m. euse: f. *Verie silent, full of silence, most quiet, husht, or still; that vseth to speake but little; where no noyse at all is vsed.*

Siler. *The hearbe Seseli, Seseleos, Hartwort; some also call Spert, or the Osier Withie so.*

Siler de Candie. *Hartwort of Candia.*

Siler de Montagne. *Siler Mountaine, bastard Loueage.*

Sili. *A yellow earth (found in gold and siluer mines) whereof, being burnt, Painters make a kind of Vermillion.*

Siliquastre: m. *Guinnie Pepper, Calecut, or Indian Pepper; also, as* Guainier.

Silique: f. *The huske, or cod of Beanes, Pease, &c; and particularly, the Carob, or Carob Beane cod, the fruit of the Carob tree; also, a poise, among Phisitions, &c, comming to foure graines.*

Siller les yeux. *To seele, or sow vp, the eye-lids; (& thence also) to hoodwinke, blind, keepe in darknesse, depriue of sight; also, to winke, as when one lookes vpon the Sunne.*

Sillon: m. *as* Seillon; *also, a glimpse, or small light.*

Silure: m. *The rauening sheat fish, or Whall of the riuer.*

Simagrée: f. *A wry mouth, or filthie face, the countenance of a Ieaster, or Clowne in a Play, made to prouoke laughter; also, a soure countenance, crabbed visage, vinegar face put on; sorrow dissembled, affliction counterfeited; any hipocriticall shew, looke, or behauior.*

Simbolizer. *Looke* Symbolizer.

Sime. *Looke* Cime, *or* Simme.

Sime. La partie fine du foye. *The massie part of the liuer, that which hath no manner of hollownesse in it.*

Simier de boeuf. *Looke* Cimier.

Similaire: com. *Similar; like, resembling.*

Parties similaires. *Parts (of the bodie) of one substance, and which, although diuided, retaine the name of the whole.*

Similitude: f. *A similitude, comparison; likenesse, resemblance.*

Simiotique. Medecine sim. *That part of Phisicke which intreats of the significant markes of what is past, and what is to come, as well in regard of health, as of sicknesse.*

Simme: f. *The top, or tuft on the top, of a tree; the cop, ridge, or height of a mountaine, &c.*

Simmetrie: f. *Simmetrie, the iust, and mutuall proportion of euerie part in respect of the whole.*

Simmiste: m. *A Secretarie, or priuie Counsellor.*

Simoniaque: com. *A Simonist; one that selleth, or buyeth Church preferments, &c.*

Simonie: f. *Simonie; the buying, or selling of spirituall functions, or preferments.*

Simple. *A simple in Phisicke, a Phisicall drug; also, a single in dauncing.*

Simple: com. *Simple; single, pure, meere, vnmixt, vncompounded, of one sort, of it selfe; also, plaine, round, blunt, sincere, vnfained; harmelesse, innocent, without welt or gard; shallow, vnskilfull, ignorant, foolish; also, rude, homelie, meane, base.*

Simple donation. *An absolute gift; a thing thats giuen without any respect other then of the donces good.*

Simple gagerie. *A bare distraining, without carrying away of the distresse.*

Simple heritier. *An heire by discent, not by legacie or testament.*

Simples plaids, ou querelles. *Sleight suites, or controuersies;* A la difference des demandes, & procez d'importance, & criminels.

Simple vendition. A la difference de celle qui est faicte sous faculté de rachapt; ou de celle qui est faicte sans eschange.

Benefice à simple tonsure. *The place of a Prebend, or Cannon; a Benefice without the charge of soules.*

Default simple, ou pur. *An absolute, or meere default;* S' obtient par le demandeur contre le defendeur, & par l'appellant contre l'intimé.

Amende simple. *The ordinarie, or accustomed amercement of* 5 solz, *or* 7 solz 6 deniers.

Hommage simple. *Looke* Hommage.

Simplement. *Simply, singly, purely, meerely, without mixture; plainely, roundly, bluntly, vnfainedly; harmelesly, innocently; shallowly, vnskilfully; rudely, meanely, basely.*

Simpler. *To cousin, cunnie, gull, deceiue, beguile.*

Simplesse: f. *Looke* Simplicité.

Simplette: f. *A little, simple, or homelie wench; one that is apt to beleeue, and thereby soone deceiued.*

Simpliciste. *as* Simpliste.

Simplicité: f. *Simplicitie, singlenesse, sleightnesse; plainenesse, bluntnesse, rudenesse, homelinesse, harmelesnesse; follie, shallownesse, vnskilfullnesse, ignorance.*

Simpliste: m. *A Simplist, or Herbalist; one that vnderstands, or professes to vnderstand, the nature of simples, of plants, of drugs.*

Simploce: f. *The ending, and beginning of two (next-adioyning) verses with one word.*

Simulachre: m. *The image, picture, or counterfeit of a man or woman; the figure, semblance, resemblance, likenesse, forme, or proportion of any thing represented.*

Simulateur: m. *A dissembler, cogger, glosér, flatterer, hypocrite, fainer, or counterfeiter of that which hee is not, or meanes not.*
Simulation: f. *Simulation, dissembling, cogging, glosing, flatterie, hypocrisie; a colour, or pretence; a fayning, or counterfeiting, of what one is, or meanes not.*
Simulté: f. *A grudge, inward conceit against, priuie hatred or displeasure, gilt ouer with a countenance or shew to the contrarie.*
Sinalles *Looke* Senelles.
Sinapiser. *To reuiue a mortified place, and draw fresh humors and colour vnto it, by a plaister of mustard seed, &c; Hence also, to raise blisters, or bring smart, by such plaisters; and, to besprinkle, dredge, or strew ouer with sharpe, and smarting powder.*
Since: f. *A dish-clowt, shooe-clowt, clowt to wipe downe tables, or to rub the house.*
Sincer. *To wipe, to rub, to make cleane with a clowt.*
Sincere, & Sincerité. *Looke* Syncere, & Syncerité.
Sincopé: m. ée: f. *Cut off.*
Sincoper. *To cut off.*
Sinelles. *Looke* Senelles.
Sineulle: f. *The handle whereby some kind of wheeles, or wheele-like Engines, are turned.*
Sing: m. *A signe, marke, note, character; a superscription, stampe, or signe manuell; also, a spot (of what colour soeuer) on the face, or other part of a new-borne infant; also, a bell, or the sound of a bell; whence,* Tocsing; *an Allarum bell; and;*
Tu n'en as pas fait les sings sonner. *Thou hast not cried it at the crosse, nor made all the world ring of it; thou diddest not greatly publish, or brag of, it.*
Singe: m. *An Ape; also, an imitator, emulator, counterfeiter; also, a windlesse, or draw-beame.*
Singe de mer. *A kind of rough-skinned Ray, whose long, and flat taile somewhat resembles a sword.*
Monnoye de singe. *Mopping, mumping, mowing; also, friskes, gambolds, tumbling tricks.*
Oeuvre de singe. *An idle, foolish, lewd, or impure act.*
Patenostre du singe. *A diddering, or chattering with the teeth.*
Vin de singe. *Looke* Vin.
Branslant les levres comme font les singes de seiour. *Wagging their lips like Apes that haue little to doe.*
Contournant la teste comme vn singe qui avalle pilules. *Wrying his head like an Ape that swalloweth pills.*
Remuant les babines comme vn singe qui cerche poux en teste. *Stirring his chaps like an Ape that looketh a head for lice.*
Tout passe par ses tripes comme par le cul du singe. *Looke vnder* Passer.
Aujourd'huy Seigneur, demain singe ord: Prov. *To day a goodlie Lord, to morrow an ouglie lozell.*
Oncques vieil singe ne fit belle moüe: Prov. *Old age cannot be gracious, comelie, louelie.*
Singeot: m. *A little Ape.*
Singeotte: f. *An ill-fauoured, or Monkie-faced wench, a Madame ouglie, foule slut, looke-like-an-Ape.*
Singeries: f. *Apish trickes, idle toyes; or, as* Monnoye de singe.
Singesse: f. *A she Ape.*
Singeur: m. *An Apish mome, or, a keeper of Apes.*
Singlage: m. *A sayling in, a cutting or diuiding of, the sea; also, a Mariners hire, wages, or intertainment, or, the earnest, or presse-money, giuen him when he is intertained.*
Singlant: m. ante: f. *Sayling, diuiding or cutting the sea; also, whisking, lashing, ierking; whence;*
Verge singlante. *A scutcher, switch, or switcher.*
Voix singlante. *A shrill voyce.*
Singlé: m. ée: f. *Sailed on, cut or diuided, as water by a boat; also, whisked, scutched, lashed, ierked, switched, scourged.*
Singlée: f. *as* Singlement.
Singlement: m. *A sayling, or cutting of the sea by sayling; also, a whisking, lashing, ierking, scutching.*
Singler. *To sayle, to cut the water, with a full wind; also, to whiske, or whizze, like the wind among sayles; and, to switch, lash, whip, ierke, scutch, or scourge with a rod.*
Singler en haute mer. *Looke* Mer.
Singlet: m. *A scutch, lash, whiske, yerke or ierke with a rod, &c.*
Singleure. *Looke* Singlement.
Singularité: f. *Singularitie, excellencie, peerelesnesse; peculiarnesse.*
Singulier: m. ere: f. *Singular, excellent, exquisite, peerelesse, passing others; also, single, one, odde, peculiar, especiall, alone.*
Singulier en ses opinions. *Obstinate, wilfull, opinionatiue.*
Singulierement. *Singularly, excellently, exquisitely, chiefly, onely, peculiarly, especially, aboue other things.*
Sinipion. *A kind of disease peculiar to children.*
Sinissome. *Blessed Thistle,* Carduus benedictus.
Sinistre: com. *Sinister, vnluckie.*
Sinistrement. *Sinisterously, vnluckily; also, in euill part.*
Sinon. *Sauing, except, but onely, vnlesse.*
Sinople: m. *Sinople, greene colour (in Blazon.)*
Sintegne. *A kind of bloudie flix.*
Sinterese: f. *The pricke, or sting of conscience; or as* Synderese.
Sintre. *Looke* Cintre.
Sinueux: m. euse: f. *Bosomie, intricate, crooked, full of hollow turnings, windings, or crinkle crankles.*
Sinuosité: f. *A hollow turning, or winding; a bosomie crooking, or in-bending; an indenting; an intricatenesse.*
Sion: m. *A scion, or shoot, &c, as* Scion.
Sions. *The boisterous incounters of two strong winds, either sidelong, or acrosse.*
Siphach. *Th'inner rind of the bellie, wherewith all the intralls are couered:* ¶Rab.
Siphon. *The cocke, or pipe of a Conduit; the tap, or faucet of a hogshead; also, a funnell, or tunnell; also, a quill, or pipe to sucke wine with:* ¶Rab.
Sire. *Sir, or Maister; A title of honor which, without addition, is giuen onely to the King; but with addition, vnto Marchants, or Tradesmen; (whence,* Sire Pierre, Sire Simon, &c; *) and vnto Knights, (whence,* Sire Chevalier; *) and vnto some few owners of* Fiefs, *or* Seigniories, *(whence,* le Sire de Ponts en Guyenne; *) to whom it was much more cōmonly giuen in old time, (whence,* le Sire du païs, *often vsed to signifie the Lord of the countrey;) And as it appeares by auncient French Histories, and Bookes, all Lords, whether of Territorie, or Iurisdiction, were stiled* Sires.
Siringue: f. *A squirt, or siringe.*
Siringué: m. ée: f. *Squirted, iniected.*
Siringuer. *To squirt, or iniect with a siringe.*
Sirocco, & Siroch. *A South-east wind.*
Sironne: f. *A kind of fomentation.*

Sisalle.

Sisalle. grive sisalle. *A Fieldfare; or a kind of great, and Doue-coloured Thrush, which vsually makes her neast in walls.*
Sisame. *Looke* Sesame.
Siserre: f. *The Throstle, or Mauis:* ¶Lionnois.
Sistolique: com. *Without intermission, in motion:* ¶Rab.
Sistre: m. *A kind of brasen Timbrell.*
Sistre. *The hearbe Spignell, or Spicknell, Mew, Baldimonie, and Bearewort.*
Sit: m. *A site, or seat.*
Sitibond: m. onde: f. *Extreamely athirst.*
Siticines: m. *That sounded Trumpets, or sung vnto Pipes, at Funeralls:* ¶Rab.
Situation: f. *A situation; the seat, site, or standing of a place.*
Situé: m. ée: f. *Situate, or situated, seated, sited, standing, placed.*
Situer. *To situate, site, seat, place.*
Sivé: m. *A broth, or sauce made of th'intralls of a hog; also, broth, or sauce for the forepart of a fried Hare, made of wine, vinegar, veriuyce, hearbes, and spices, & serued with tosts, or sops; also, seame, or swines grease.*
Du sivé d'huistres. *Oyster broth, or broth made of boiled Oisters.*
Sive: f. *A Chiboll, hollow Leeke, Scallion.*
Sivele: f. *A buckle:* ¶Langued.
Sivette: f. *Ciuet; also, a Ciuet Cat; also, a Chiue, or small Chiboll.*
Siviere. *Looke* Civiere.
Sivot: m. *A Scallion, a hollow or vnset Leeke.*
Six. *Six, halfe a dozen.*
Sixain: m. *A sixt, a sixt part, the proportion of six; Hence, a Poeme, or stanzo of six verses; and, the halfe of a* Sol, *a coyne worth six* Deniers, *or somewhat more then our halfepenie.*
Sixener. *To yeeld six for one; also, to come forth by halfe-dozens, or by six and six together.*
Sixiesme: m. *A sixt, or sixt part; a proportion of six.*
Droict de sixiesme. *An yearelie rent of six pence due by euerie affranchised inhabitresse of* Henault *vnto the Earle thereof, in acknowledgement of her former thraldome, and as a gratuitie for her new-gotten freedome.*
Sixiesme: com. *The sixt, or sixth.*
Droict du sixiesme denier. *The sixt penie, or part of the price of aliened land, due (in some places) vnto the Lord of whom it is held.*
Sixte: m. *A sixt, a proportion of six, in Musicke.*
Sizement: m. *A sitting, setling, seating.*
Skelete. *Looke* Scelete.
Smirge: m. *Louage, or Parsley of Macedonia.*
Sobre: com. *Sober, temperate, continent, stayed or setled in humor, well aduised.*
Sobrement. *Soberly, temperately, continently, staiedly; aduisedly.*
Sobressaut: m. *A Sobressault, or Summer-sault; an actiue, or nimble tricke in tumbling, &c.*
Sobresse: f. *as* Sobrieté; *also, actiuitie, or nimblenesse.*
Sobrieté: f. *Sobrietie, temperance, continencie, stayednesse, aduisednesse.*
Sobriqué: m. ée: f. *Pranked, or perfumed.*
Sobriquet: m. *A surname; also, a nickname, or byword; and, a quip or cut giuen, a mocke or flowt bestowed, a ieast broken on a man.*
Soc d'une charruë. *The culter, or share of a plough; also the plough it selfe; whence;*
Le pourpte au soc mort d'egal poids balance: Pro. *Death equalls plough-driuers with purple-wearers.*
Sociable: com. *Sociable, companable, familiar, courteous, gentle, friendlie.*
Societé: f. *Societie, fellowship, consort, companie.*
Socque: f. *A socke or sole of durt, or earth, cleauing to the bottome of the foot in a cloggie way, or in a moist & clayie soyle.*
Sodalité: f. *Sodalitie, fellowship, societie, brotherlie companie.*
Sodomie: f. *Sodomie, buggerie.*
Sodomite: m. *A Sodomite, Ingler, Buggerer.*
Soëf: m. soëfve: f. *Sweet, plausible, delicious, delicate, soote; gentle, courteous, mild; soft, smooth.*
Soëf. *(Aduerbially, & in stead of* Soëfvement;*) whence;*
Le boeuf las marche soëf: Prov. *The wearie Oxe treads gently or gingerly; goes faire and softly.*
Soëfflairant, & Soëffleurant: m. ante: f. *Most fragrant, delicately smelling.*
Soëfvement. *Sweetly, deliciously, smoothly, gently.*
Soëfveté: f. *Sweetnesse, pleasantnesse, deliciousnesse, plausiblenesse; gentlenesse, mildnesse, smoothnesse.*
Soeil du sanglier. *Looke* Sueil.
Socur: f. *A sister.*
Le frere veut bien que sa soeur ait, mais que rien du sien n'y ait: Prov. *The brother would haue his sister thriue by any meanes but by his.*
Soeurette: f. *A little sister.*
Soeurorge. *Looke* Sororge.
Sofistication: f. *A sophistication, or sophisticating; an adulterating, or falsifying.*
Sofistiquer. *To sophisticate, falsifie, adulterate.*
Sogrenu: m. uë: f. *Looke* Saugrenu.
Sogrenuë: f. *A ieast.*
Soiage: m. *The reaping of corne, &c.*
Soie de porc. *The bristles, or stiffe haire, of a hog.*
Soïer. *To reape, or cut downe corne.*
Soïeur: m. *A reaper.*
Soif: f. *Thirst; a drouth, or drought; a desire to drinke.*
Endurer la soif aupres d'une fontaine. *To suffer want in the middest of abundance.*
Il n'a pas soif qui de l'eau ne boit: Prov. *Hee's not athirst that water drinkes not.*
On a beau mener le boeuf à l'eau s'il n'a soif: Pro. *Looke* Boeuf.
Qui mieux aime autruy que soy au moulin il meurt de soif: Prov. *Hee that loues others better then himselfe dies athirst on a Mill-damme.*
Soigner. *To care, heed, regard, attend, see to, prouide for, take paines in, be diligent about.*
Soigneusement. *Carefully, heedfully, diligently, painefully, seriously, laboriously, studiously.*
Soigneux: m. euse: f. *Carefull, heedfull, regardfull, circumspect, attentiue, warie, solicitous, diligent, vigilant, studious, industrious, laborious, painfull, earnest.*
Soil de sanglier. *Looke* Sueil.
Soilure: f. *A galling, or breaking of the skinne by frequent vse, or ouermuch rubbing; some call it a chafegall.*
Soimesme. *Himselfe.*
Soing: m. *Care, studie, diligence, vigilancie, warinesse, heed, regard, attention, circumspectiō, industrie, labour, paines.*
Soir: m. *The euening.*
Nul soir sans iour: Prov. *No dawning without a day.*
Les paroles du soir ne ressemblent pas à celles du matin: Prov. *Ere night our morning stile is chaunged; or, few make at night their mornings promise good.*

Le rouge soir, & blanc matin, &c. *Looke* Matin.
Tel rit au matin qui au soir pleure: Prov. *Some laugh amornings who ere night shed teares.*
Soiré. *Looke* Soireux.
Soirée: f. *The euening, or euening-tide.*
Soireux: m. euse: f. *Of, or in, the euening; late adaies, towards night.*
Soitier: m. *A Silkeman.*
Soitier: m. ere: f. *as* Setier; *also, of, or full of, silke.*
Soiture: f. *A reaping of corne.*
Soixante. *Sixtie, threescore.*
Sol: m. *The soile, ground, land, foundation, or bottome of a place; the floore, or lowest storie of a house; also, the Sunne; whence,* vn Escu sol; *A Crowne of the Sunne; the French Crowne whereon a little Sunne, or Starre, is figured.*
Sol: m. *A Sous, or the French shilling; whereof tenne make one of ours; (But this is to be vnderstood of the* Sol Tournois, *the most generall, and best-knowne* sol *in France; and euer vnderstood when the word* sol *is vsed without addition.)*
Sol Barrois. *Is a sixt part in twentie lesse then the* Tournois, *whereof fourteene are worth twentie of these.*
Sol Bourdelois. *Is worth halfe as much as the* Sol Parisien.
Sols forts. *Looke* Forte monnoye, *vnder* Fort.
Sol de guerre. *A Lorraine coyne of small value.*
Sol neret. *Looke* Neret.
Sol Mansais. *Is worth two* sols Tournois.
Sol Parisien, ou de Paris. *The Parisian* sol; *is as much as the* Tournois, *and a quarter; for twentie of them amount vnto twentie fiue of th'other.*
Sol Tournois. *The tenth part of our shilling, or one part in six better then our penie; the most ordinarie, and most knowne* Sol *in France.*
Il fait de six sols vn teston. *He makes a Noble of nine-pence; (appliable to an industrious thriuer.)*
Il fait de son teston six sols. *(The contrarie, and meant of a riotous vnthrift, of whom we say) He will quickly bring a Noble to nine-pence.*
Solacier. se sol. *To solace, make merrie, recreate himselfe.*
Solacieux: m. euse: f. *Solacious, recreatiue, delightfull, comfortable.*
Solage: m. *as* Solaige; *also, soyle, or good ground.*
Solaige: m. *Sunnage, or Sunninesse; th'eleuation, aspect, force, or power of the Sunne; th'effects of Sunne-shine, vpon a place.*
Solaire de la jambe. *The greatest of the six hinder muskles of the leg, ending in the sole of the foot, the which it serues to extend.*
Solaire: com. *Sunnie, of or belonging to the Sunne.*
Herbe Solaire. *The Marigold.*
Vent Solaire. *An Easterlie wind.*
Solane: m. *The hearbe Nightshade; or as* Solatre.
Solane grand. *Dwale, deadlie Nightshade.*
Solatre: m. *Garden Nightshade, Morrell, pettie Morrell.*
Solatre dormitif. *Sleepie Nightshade.*
Solatre dormitif commun. *Dwale, great Nightshade, sleeping Nightshade.*
Solatre furieux. *Raging Nightshade.*
Sold: m. *A* Sous; *Looke* Sol.
Soldade. 'A la soldade. *Souldier-like; brauely, valiantly; swaggeringly.*
Soldan. *Looke* Souldan.
Soldanelle: f. *Sea Withiewind, sea Bindweed, sea Cole, or sea Caule, sea Bells, sea Folesfoot, Scottish Scuruiegrasse.*
Soldat: m. *A souldier; one that followes the warres.*
Soldat de fortune. *An aduenturer, or voluntarie; one that serues without pay, or charge.*
'A jeune soldat vieil cheval: Prov. *A young souldier would be fitted with an old horse; (both to temper his heat, and to helpe his ignorance.)*
Soldatesque: f. *Souldierie; also, a troupe or companie of souldiers.*
Soldatesque: com. *Souldierlie, of a souldier, souldier-like.*
Soldatesquement. *Souldierly, souldier-like.*
Soldatisé: m. ée: f. *Souldierized, made a souldier, turned souldier.*
Solde. *Looke* Soulde.
Sole: f. *The sole, plant, or vnder part of the foot; (and hence) also, the sole of a stocking, or shooe; also, the Sole-fish; also, the peece of timber called a Girder, or Joyst betweene two Summers.*
Pasque de Soles. *Palmes Sunday.*
Tant d'arpens à la sole. *The proportion of land which is to be sowed that yeare; (In many parts of France they sow euerie yeare but a third part of their arrable.)*
Soleil: m. *The Sunne; also, Gold; called so by Alchimists.*
Soleil de mer. *A certaine fish, or sea-vermine, which resembles a painted Sunne.*
Biens au soleil. *Lands, grounds, leases, cattell, &c; any possessions which lie without doores, and are often beheld by the Sunne; differing therein from money, which he but seldome lookes on.*
Herbe au soleil; &, Herbe du soleil. *as vnder* Herbe.
Rosée du soleil. *The hearbe Sunne-dew,* Ros solis, *Toothwort, called in the North, Red rot, and Mooregrasse.*
Gratant le cul au soleil. *Slothfully, lazily, litherly, carelesly, playing the idle and slouenlie lozell, clawing his breech in the Sunne.*
Ie l'envoyeray bien grater le cul au soleil. *I will send him packing, turne him out a grazing, make him goe shake his eares abroad.*
Le ventre au soleil. Il y demeura le ventre au sol. *He was slaine, or left dead, in that place.*
Il ne laisse dormir sa debte sur le soleil. *Hee suffers not the dayes debt to be vnpayed at night; hee loues to pay readily, loues to be soone out of debt.*
Soleil qui luisarne au matin, femme qui parle Latin, & Enfant nourry de vin, ne viennent point à bonne fin: Prov. *A glaring morne, a woman Latinist, and wine-fed child, make men crie had I wist.*
Tel est le gendre comme le soleil d'hyver: Prov. *Looke* Gendre.
Soleillant: m. ante: f. *Sunning, Sunnie.*
Soleillé: m. ée: f. *Sunned; aired or weathered by, dryed or warmed at, layed in, exposed vnto, the Sunne; also, warme, Sunnie, shining or heating like the Sunne.*
Soleiller. *To Sunne; to aire or weather in, drie or warme at, expose vnto, lay out into, the Sunne.*
Soleilleux: m. euse: f. *Sunnie; open vnto, or lying full in, the Sunne.*
Solennel: m. elle: f. *Solemne (not altogether as we doe commonly vnderstand it, but) annuall, yearelie, ordinarie, woont, vsed, accustomed, done publickly, and at a certaine time.*
Solennellement. *Solemnely; publickly; annually, ordinarily,*

dinarily, vsually, accustomably.
Solennité: f. *A solemnitie, or solemne feast; also, a prescript forme, precise manner, ordinarie custome, vsuall fashion, kept or held.*
Solennization: f. *A Solemnization, or Celebration.*
Solennizer. *To solemnize, celebrate, obserue solemnly, vse reuerently.*
Soler. *To sole (a shooe, or stocking.)*
Solerets: m. *Looke* Sollerets.
Solerre: m. *The East wind.*
Soles. les soles. *The groundsill of a house.*
Soleyé: m. ée: f. *Sunned; aired in, heated by, exposed vnto, the Sunne.*
Solfe: f. *A Solfa; a note in singing.*
Solfié: m. ée: f. *Solfaed; also, distempered.*
Solicitation: f. *A solicitation, or soliciting, a mouing, or importuning vnto; an instant pursuit, the following of a suit.*
Solicité: m. ée: f. *Solicited, importuned, often and earnestly moued; instantly pursued or followed; also, heedfully or carefully looked vnto.*
Soliciter. *To solicite, moue, importune, intreat instantly, pursue earnestly, follow hard; also, to heed seriously, looke verie carefully vnto.*
Soliciteur: m. *A Solicitor, or follower of a cause for another; also, the mouer, importuner, or inciter of another.*
Solicitude: f. *Solicitude, care, carke, thoughtfulnesse; heauinesse, pensiuenesse, fretfulnesse, perplexitie or anguish of mind.*
Solidaire: com. *Solide, whole; in for, liable to, the whole.*
Solidairement. *Solidely, soundly, surely; also, wholly; or (as our Bond-Latine* in Solido*) for the whole.*
Solide: com. *Solide, sound, whole, fast, firme, full, strong, tough, stiffe, hard, sure, pithie, massiue.*
Solier: m. *A sellar, or low garner; also, as* Plancher; *also, as* Soulier.
Solifuge: f. *A kind of Spider, or vermine like a Spider, in the siluer mines of* Sardinia; *tearmed thus, because it euer flies from light.*
Soliseque: com. *Sunne-following.*
Solistime. *Diuinatiō by a falling on the ground of bread giuen vnto chickens:* ¶Rab.
Solitaire: com. *Solitarie, lonely, deauelie, desert, priuate, without companie, all alone.*
Passe solitaire. *Looke* Passe.
Solitude: f. *Solitude, solitarinesse, lonelinesse, priuacie, want of companie, deauelinesse; also, a desert, wildernesse, vncouth and vnhabited place; also, a forlorne, or succourlesse estate.*
Solive: f. *The peece of timber called a Girder, or Joist (betweene two Summers.)*
Soliveau: m. *A little Girder, or Joist.*
Solle. *Looke* Sole.
Sollerets: m. *Supeters; foot-peeces of Armour; Armor for the feet.*
Sollette: f. *A little sole.*
La sollette d'un esperon. *The vnder leather of a spurre.*
Sollier: m. *A sellar, or low garner.*
Sollouoir: m. *A salting, or sowcing tub:* ¶Rab.
Soloecisme: m. *Solecisme, or incongruitie.*
Soloir. *Looke* Souloir.
Sols. *Looke* Sol.
Solsie. *Looke* Soulsie.
Solstice: m. *The Solstice, Sunne-stead, or stay of the Sunne; the longest or shortest day of the yeare; or the season wherein the dayes be at the longest, or the shortest.*
Solsticial; ou, Solstitial: m. ale: f. *Solsticiall; of, or in, the Solstice.*
Solu: m. uë: f. *Loose, free, carelesse, of scope.*
Oraison soluë. *Prose.*
Solvable: com. *Payable, answerable, sufficient, able to pay his debts; also, warranted, or made good.*
Solut. *Loose, &c; as* Solu; *whence;*
Clerc solut. *A lay, or secular Church-man; one thats not tied vnto the Church, nor bound to attend a Cure; Prebend, Canon, Deacon, &c.*
Solutif: m. iue: f. *Solutiue; laxatiue; loosing, dissoluing.*
Solution: f. *A discharge, or paiment; a resolution, or answer; a dissolution, releasing, loosing.*
Solution de continuité. *The diuision of an intire, the opening of a close, thing.*
Solz. *Looke* Sol.
Som: m. *Branne.*
Somate. *A bodie:* ¶Rab.
Somayer. *Looke* Sommayer.
Sombre: com. *Close, darke, clowdie, muddie, shadie, duskie, gloomie.*
Sombre-pres. *Darke-blue; also (of the skie) thinly darkened, or ouerspred with clouds.*
Sombrer. *To darken; also, to dig vp a vineyard, (the first labour done to it) thereby to supple, and soften the soyle thereof.*
Sombriere: m. *A (broad-brimd) hat.*
Somiere: m. *Looke* Sommiere.
Sommade: f. *A horse-load:* ¶Langued.
Sommage: m. *as* Corvée; *or drudgerie, or a drudging seruice.*
Sommaige: m. *The top of a tower, &c.* (v.m.)
Sommaire: m. *A summarie; breuiarie, abridgement, epitome of the whole; a breefe and full collection of words, or things; the summe, substance, chiefe point or knot of.*
Sommaire: com. *Summarie; chiefe, principall, whole, full, all-comprehending; succinct, compendious.*
Vn procez sommaire. *A processe wherein no formalitie, or formall proceeding hath beene vsed.*
Sommairement. *Summarily; succinctly, briefly, compendiously; also, throughly, wholly, fully.*
Proceder sommairement. C'est qu'on dit en droict, de plano; asçavoir qu'on peut traicter à l'extraordinaire, & ou le Iuge se trouve sans attendre le iour de l'ordinaire: Et en cecy ne convient observer les exactes solennitez de droict, ou de pratique, ainsi apres l'adiournement libellé faict à celuy qui est appellé devant le Iuge, les parties doivent estre ouyes sur le champ, sans ministere d'Advocats; & par briefs delais leur doit estre prefix, & ordonné, ce qu'il convient pour parvenir au iugement definitif, sans les appointer, par multiplicité de delais, à faire de longs plaidoïers, ou escritures.
Sommarer. *To plough, or breake vp the earth.*
Sommation: f. *A summe, or, the summing, of money; also, a summoning, or denouncing.*
Sommayer. *To put hoopes vpon hoopes, or, to hoope a vessell with the hoopes called* Sommiers.
Somme: m. *Sleepe, rest.*
Somme: f. *A summe of money, &c; the summe of an account; also, an Arithmeticall product; the summe produced by, or comming of, a number multiplied; also, a (horse) load, or burthen; also, the summe, issue, end, conclusi-*

conclusion, top, height, fulnesse, consummation, perfection of things.

Chevaux de somme. *Sumpter-horses, or Carriers horses.*

Somme toute. *In briefe, to conclude.*

Servir à sac, & à somme. *To hold by vile, or drudging services; to be bound, by his tenure, to till his Landlords ground; to inne his corne and hay; to carrie his wine, and wood, &c.*

Sommé: m. ée: f. *Summed; summarily reckoned; also, summoned, or vouched; also, topped, furnished or couered at the top with; also, come, or growne, to it full height; whence;*

Les pennes d'un faulcon toutes sommées. *Full summed, full growne; and;* Teste de cerf sommée; C'est quand le cerf a tout ce qu'il doit porter.

Sommeil: m. *Sleepe; also, a slumbering.*

Sommeillant: m. ante: f. *Sleeping; sleepie.*

Sommeillard: m. arde: f. *Sleepie, drowsie, sluggish; negligent, slothfull, heauie-headed.*

Sommeiller: m. *A Butler.*

Sommeiller. *To sleepe; to slumber.*

Sommeilleux: m. euse: f. *Sleepie, drowsie, sluggish, heauie-headed, full of sleepinesse, much giuen to sleeping.*

Sommelerie: f. *A Butterie.*

Sommer. *To summe, reckon, or cast vp; to bring to a head, or conclusion; to make a summarie, or collection of; to fill vp to the top; also, to summon, denounce; giue notice of; and to vouch, call vpon, challenge warrantie of.*

Tant travaille, & tracasse l'homme, qu'en fin il se rompt, ou somme: Prov. *A man so long doth toyle and swinke, till vnder his owne charge he sinke.*

Sommet: m. *The top, cop, height, or highest part of a thing; and hence, the ridge, or the roofe of a house; &, the crowne, or noddle of the head.*

Sommette: f. *A little summe, or summarie.*

Sommier: m. *A Sumpter-horse; (and generally any toyling, and load-carrying, drudge, or groome;) also, the peece of timber called a Summer; also, the Sound-boord of an Organ; also, a Trussing-hoope; the double hoope which is next aboue the head-hoope of a peece of caske, and which, being directly ouer the Croes, doth beare more stresse then all the rest of the hoopes.*

Sommiers. *Be also, double hoopes; or hoopes put vpon the hoopes of a vessell, to strengthen them, and to indure, in carriage, all rushes without breaking them; also, the Ensigne-bearers of a marching Armie; tearmed so to put a difference, betweene their toyle, and th' ease enioyed by the Roman Ensignes, who neuer held their Colours but when they were, or were set, in a readinesse to fight.*

Sommission: f. *A submission, an humbling.*

Sommiste: m. *A Summist; an imitator, or vnderstander, of Thomas Aquinas his summes.*

Sommité: f. *as* Sommet; *or, a Summitie, or highnesse.*

Somnifique: com. *Sleepe-causing.*

Morelle somnifique. *Deathes hearbe, sleepie or deadlie Nightshade.*

Somption: f. *A taking, a receiuing.*

Somptüaire: com. *Sumptuarie, of or belonging to cost, breeding or bringing in expence.*

Somptuëusement. *Sumptuously, costly, expensiuely, gorgeously, excessiuely.*

Somptuëux: m. euse: f. *Sumptuous, costlie, expensiue, gorgeous, magnificent, prodigall, excessiue.*

Somptuosité: f. *Sumptuousnesse, costlinesse, huge expence, prodigalitie, superfluitie, excessiuenesse.*

Son: m. *Branne; (and thence) also, the scurfe, or little scales in the head, &c, called Dandarfe.*

Son gras. *Pollard; or, branne that hath some small quantitie of meale among it.*

Son sec. *Looke* Sec.

Son: m. *A sound; voyce, noyse, diane; tune, musicke, melodie.*

Son esclatant. *A great crash, clash, crack, or creaking, a violent clap, a resounding bounce or thumpe.*

C'est le son des cloches. *(Said of a thing that may with ease be diuersified, or altered seuerall wayes.)*

Son: m. sa: f. *His, hers, belonging vnto him or her.*

Sonde: f. *A Mariners sounding plummet; also, a squirt, or siringe; and, an instrument whereby virginitie is tried.*

Aller tousiours la sonde en main. *To proceed aduisedly, to goe warily to worke.*

Sonder. *To sound, proue, trie, feele, search the depth, or bottome of.*

Sondre. *The Linden tree; Looke* Soudre.

Songe: m. *A dreame.*

Songes sont mensonges: Prov. *Dreames are delusions.*

De sot homme sot songe: Prov. *A foolish man hath foolish dreames.*

Songé: m. ée: f. *Dreamed.*

Songeant. *Dreaming, or in a sleepie vision.*

Songeard: m. *A continuall dreamer, or a dreaming fellow.*

Songeard: m. arde: f. *Dreaming, of or in a dreame.*

Songe-creux: m. *One that's in his dumps, or in a brown studie; also, a dreaming, sleepie, or heauie-headed gull.*

Songe-malice: m. *An imaginer of mischiefe, a continuall plotter of villanies.*

Songer. *To dreame; also, to speake dreamingly; also, to plot, contriue, deuise, inuent; imagine.*

Songer creux. *To muse exceedingly, meditate seriously, thinke verie much vpon.*

Tousiours truye songe bran: &, Truye ne songe qu'ordure: Prov. *Looke* Truye.

Songeur: m. *A dreamer.*

Vous me logez (ou vous me mettez bien) chez Guillot le songeur. *You make me search all the corners of my wit; you driue me into a great dumpe, or a great studie.*

Songner. *Looke* Soigner.

Songneusement. *Carefully, thoughtfully.*

Sonnaille: f. *A little bell; and particularly, the bell hung about the necke of a Weather, or heard-beast.*

Sonnaillerie: f. *A tinkling, or the tingling of a little bell.*

Sonnaillier: m. ere: f. *Carrying a bell; whence;*

Mouton sonnaillier. *A Bell-weather.*

Sonnalier. *The same.*

Sonner. *To sound, noise, tune, ring, resound; to ting as a bell, strike as a clocke, chinke or gingle as money; also, to call.*

Sonner les sings; &, sonner la tuile; *Looke vnder* Sing, & Tuile.

Sonnerie: f. *A sounding, tuning, ringing, resounding; a tinging, chinking, gingling.*

Sonnet: m. *A sonnet, or canzonet, a song (most commonly) of 14 verses.*

Sonnette: f. *A little bell, Antham bell, Sans or sacring bell; any small tinging bell; as the bell about the necke of a Bell-weather, &c; whence,* Moutõ à la sonnette.

Attacher la sonnette à l'oreille du chat. *as* Mettre la campane au chat, *vnder* Chat.

'A fol ne faut point de sonnette: Prov. *A foole needs neither bell nor bable; his words, and actions quickly will discouer him.*

Sonoreux: m. euse: f. *Sonorous, lowd, shrill, roring, ringing.*

Sont. Messieurs de non sont. *Imperfect, or pricklesse men.*

Sophie: f. *Wisedome; also, the hearbe called Laxwort, Flixwort, or Flixweed; also, the Dace, or Dare-fish.*

Sophisme: m. *A sophisme, fallacie, tricke of sophistrie; a sophistication; cauill, or quidditie.*

Sophiste: m. *A Sophister; a cunning, or cauilling disputer.*

Sophisterie: f. *Sophistrie; a cunning, or captious arguing.*

Sophistiqué: m. ée: f. *Sophisticated, adulterated, falsified; also, cunningly handled, or cauillingly vttered.*

Sophistiquement: m. *A sophisticating, adulterating, falsifying.*

Sophistiquer. *To sophisticate, falsifie, counterfeit, adulterate, corrupt; also, to play the Sophister, dispute subtilly, argue cunningly; to deceiue.*

Sophistiquerie: f. *Sophistrie, argute cauilling, subtile cunning; also, a sophisticating, adulterating, counterfeiting.*

Soporal: m. ale: f. *Sleepie, of or in sleepe.*

Soporifere: com. *Soporiferous, sleepe-procuring.*

Soprefin: m. *Superfine, thred of gold, or siluer.*

Sor. la pipée du sor. *The season wherein the weather growes cold.*

Sor. Faulcon sor. *A soare Hawke.*

Harenc sor. *A red Herring.*

Sorbition: f. *A supping; also, broth, cale, pottage.*

Sorceler. *To charme, inchaunt, forspeake, bewitch.*

Sorcelerie: f. *Sorcerie, charming, inchaunting.*

Sorcellage: m. *The same.*

Sorcier: m. *A Sorcerer, Charmer, Inchaunter, Wizard.*

Sorciere: f. *A Sorceresse, Inchauntresse, Charmeresse, Hag, Witch.*

Sordide: com. *Sordide; foule, filthie, corrupt, stinking, nastie, sluttish; vile, naughtie, base; also, pinching, miserable, miching, nigardlie, close-handed, full of, or giuen to, paultrie dodging.*

Sordidement. *Filthily, nastily, naughtily; basely, miserably, for (deere) lucres sake.*

Soré: m. ée: f. *Reeked, made red or sorrell, as a Herring by the smoake.*

Sorel: m. *The hearbe Sorrell, or Sowre-docke.*

Sorel du bois. *Stubwort, sowre Trefolie, Cucko-meat, Alleluia, wood Sorrell, wood Sowre.*

Sorer. *To reeke; to drie, or make red (as Herrings) in the smoake.*

Sori. *Looke* Souris.

Soriciere: f. *A Mousetrap.*

Soringue: f. *Eele sauce made of fried Onions, and toastbread steeped in Pease broth, then strayned with wine, vinegar, Cinnamon, Ginger, and other spices, all put into a pot with the Eeles cut into peeces, and (after a little seasoning with Saffron, and salt) throughly boyled.*

Soriser. *To Mouse, or hunt Mice like a Cat; also, as* Sorer.

Sorisseau: m. *A little Mouse.*

Sorissiere: f. *A Mousetrap.*

Sorne: f. *The euening.*

Sorner. *To ieast, boord, frumpe, gull, sell bargaines, speake merrily, talke idly.*

Sornette: f. *A ieast, boord, merrie word, sportfull conceit, pleasant speech; a tale, fib, foist, mockerie, gullerie.*

Sornetteux: m. euse: f. *Full of ieasts, or pleasant conceits; that loues, or vses to tell merrie tales.*

Sororge: m. *A brother in law; the husband of a sister.*

Sororité: f. *Sisterhood.*

Sorrat: m. *A great, short-snowted, sharpe-toothed, and most rauenous Hound-fish.*

Sort: m. *A lot, or lotterie; also, fate, lucke, hazard, fortune, chance, casualtie; also, a charme, incantation, or spell; also, the stocke, or principall of money in banke, or at vse.*

Sortable: com. *Sortable, euen, fit or befitting, sutable, equall, proportionable.*

Sortablement. *Sortably, fitly, befitting, sutably, proportionably.*

Sorte: f. *Sort, manner, forme, fashion, kind, qualitie, condition, calling.*

De sorte que. *So that.*

Chascun demande sa sorte: Prov. *Each to his kind, as words to wind.*

Sorti: m. ie: f. *Issued, gone or burst out; also, deliuered or brought out of; also, furnished, or fitted with.*

Sorti de fil, & d'aiguille. *Fully prouided of all necessaries.*

Sorti de mauvaise femme. *Vnhappily matched, pestered or troubled with an euill wife.*

Sortie: f. *An issue, egresse, going forth.*

Sortilege: m. *Witchcraft, or diuination by lots.*

Sortir. *To issue, sallie, come forth, goe beyond, depart or goe out of; also, to assort, furnish, or fit with; also, to deliuer, or bring, out of.*

Sortir effect. *To succeed, or take effect.*

Sortir des gonds. *To flie off the hindges; to be impatient, violent, ouer vehement, break into outrage or extreame tearmes, forget his duetie or himselfe.*

Sortir hors de propos. *To digresse, wander, extrauagate it, fall from the matter, goe from the purpose.*

Il ne peut sortir du sac que ce qu'il y a dedans: Prov. *You can haue no more of him then there is in him.*

Sosmes: m. *Vassalls, tenants:* ¶Bearnois.

Sot: m. *A sot, asse, dunce, dullard, blockhead, loggerhead, growtnoll, iobernoll, growthead, ioultheat; also, a foole, or vice in a play; and, any fond, vaine, or trifling fellow.*

Va ailleurs cercher ton sot. *Looke for some other to laugh at, I am not the gull you looke for.*

Le fol est sot quant & quant, mais tout sot n'est pas fol: Prov. *The foole is sure ynough a sot, but euery sot's no foole.*

Quand les febves sont flories, les sots commencent leurs folies: Prov. *In Cuckoe-time when Beanes doe flower, the cracke-braind fooles build vp their bower.*

Sot: m. sotte: f. *Sottish, dull, dansicall; grosse, absurd, improper; foolish, fond, vaine, friuolous; wanton, lasciuious.*

De sot homme on n'en peut faire vn bon conte: Prov. *An asse does nothing worth the speaking of.*

De sot homme sot songe: Prov. *The dreames of fops are but meere fopperies.*

Femme sotte se cognoist à la cotte: Prov. *The robes that women doe array, their priuate fooleries bewray.*

Sotart: m. *A noddie peake, wittall, cockscombe, woodcocke, dotterell, ninnihammer*; *or as* Sottart.
Sotbriquet. *Looke* Sobriquet.
Sotiner. *To play the sot.*
Sotise: f. *Sottishnesse, dotage, dulnesse, blockishnesse, absurditie, follie, foppishnesse.*
Sottart: m. *A dunce, foule sot, great asse, blockish luske, foolish lob.*
Sottelet: m. *A little sot.*
Sottement. *Sottishly, blockishly, grossely, absurdly*; *friuolously.*
Sotterie, & **Sottie**. *Looke* Sotise.
Sottiner, & **Sottise**. *Looke* Sotiner, & Sotise.
Sou: m. *Hogs feet in pickle, or souce*; *also, the Sous, or French shilling*; *Looke* Sol.
Soüater. *To partake with, or be a partner in*; *also, to ioyne with, or together, after the manner of countrey peasants, who bring euerie one a horse or two for the making of a teame, which no one of himselfe can furnish.*
Soüaton: m. *A partner, or partaker with*; *also, one that ioynes, or contributes, with his neighbors, to the making vp of a thing for their common vse*; *as in* Soüater.
Soüatter. *Looke* Soüater.
Soubarbe. f. *The part thats betweene the chinne and the throat*; *also, as* Sousbarbe; *and as* Soubride.
Endurer vne soubarbe. *To indure an affront, pocket vp an iniurie, swallow downe a wrong.*
Soubassement de colonne. *The base, or foot of a piller.*
Soubassement de lict. *The bases of a bed; that which hangs downe to the ground at the sides, & feet of some statelie beds.*
Soubastement: m. *A foundation, or ground-worke*; *a low building within the ground for the support of roomes aboue-ground.*
Soubattuë: f. *A surbate*; *or, surbating.*
Soubatture: f. *A surbating*; *or, surbate.*
Soubchanter. *To sing vnder, or after, another*; *to hold the base or ground vnto*; *to follow, in a song of three, or foure parts in one.*
Soubchantre: m. *An vnder-chaunter*; *an Officer in a Cathedrall Church inferiour to the head Chaunter.*
Gardez le soubchantre. *(Said when a man stoopes so low, or straines so hard, that he is in danger to let a fart;) ware crackes hoe.*
Soubcontrolleur: m. *An vnder Controller.*
Soubcurateur: m. *An vnder Gardian*; *one that hath the tuition, or charge of a thing vnder another.*
Soubdain. *Looke* Soudain.
Soubdainement, & **Soubdaineté**. *Looke* Soudainement, &c.
Soubdespensier. *An vnder Cater, or an vnder Clerke of a kitchin.*
Soubdiacre: m. *A Subdeacon.*
Soubelin. vn chat soubelin. *A great or mightie Cat.*
Soubeliné: m. ée: f. *High, loftie, hautie*; *or, extolled, lifted vp, set on high.*
Sougardien: m. *An vnder Warden, vnder Keeper, vnder Gardian.*
Soubhaiter. *Looke* Souhaiter.
Soubhastation: f. *Open sale or portsale, sale of things forfeited, &c. by an outrope, or outcrie.*
Soubhaster. *To make open sale, or portsale of, to sell at an outrope, or outcrie, things forfeited, &c.*
Soubiect: m. *A subiect*; *Looke* Subject.
Soubiect: m. cte: f. *Subiect*; *Looke* Subject.
Soubiection: f. *Subiection*; *Looke* Subjection.
Soublevé: m. ée: f. *Lift, raised, houen or held, vp*; *eased, lightned, helped, supported*; *peised, or weighed with the hand.*
Soublevement: m. *A lifting, heauing, raising, a holding vp*; *an helping, easing, lightning*; *also, a peising, or weighing with the hand*; *also, a commotion, insurrection, vprising.*
Soublever. *To lift, raise, heaue, or hold, vp*; *also, to helpe, aid, ease, lighten, or lessen the burthen of*; *also, to peise, or weigh with the hand.*
Soublin. *as* Soubelin; *whence*, Marte Soub. *a Sable.*
Soub-maistre: m. *An vnder Maister, an Vsher in a Schoole.*
Soubmerger. *to drown, ouerwhelm, sink, boulge, plunge.*
Soubmettre. *To submit, lay vnder, put below*; *vnderset, vnderprop*; *debase, humble, subdue.*
Se soubmettre à. *To vaile bonet, strike sayle, crooch, giue place or obedience, applie himselfe, vnto*; *to come vnder the lee, iurisdiction, or power, of.*
Soubministration: f. *A subministration, an vnder seruice.*
Soubministre: m. *An vnder minister, vnder seruant, vnderling in Office.*
Soubministrer. *To subminister vnto, to minister or serue vnder another.*
Soubmis: m. ise: f. *Submitted, humbled, abased, vnder*; *inthralled, subiected, or yeelded, vnto.*
Soubmission: f. *A submission, humiliation, or humbling*; *a putting, or setting vnder.*
Soubors. *Looke* Sabors.
Soubpenduë: f. *Looke* Souspenduë.
Soubpeser. *To peise, weigh, ponder diligently.*
Soubrecoup: m. *A downe-right blow.* (v. m.)
Soubresault: m. *A Sobresault, or Summer sault*; *a Gamboll, or friske*; *an actiue or nimble tricke in tumbling, &c.*
Soubresaulteux: m. *A Tumbler*; *or, one that fetcheth many an odde, or nimble friske.*
Soubride: f. *A checke, twitch, ierke, or iob giuen to a horse with his bridle*; *also, as* Sousbarbe.
Soubriquet. *Looke* Sobriquet.
Soubrire. *To smile.*
Soubris: m. *A smile, or smiling.*
Soubs. *Vnder, &c*; *Looke* Sous.
Soubs-acazement, & **Soubs-acazer**. *Looke* Soubzacazement, &c.
Soubs-agé: m. ée: f. *Vnder age, not yet of yeares.*
Soubs-aide: m. *An vnder Aid*; *the Aid which tenants pay vnto their mesne Lord, towards that which is due both by him, and them vnto the Lord Paramount.*
Soubsarrenter. *To let out at an vnder rent, to let goe at a low yearelie rate.*
Soubscelerier: m. *An vnder Butler, or a Yeoman of the sellar.*
Soubscription: f. *A subscription, or subscribing.*
Soubscrire. *To subscribe.*
Soubs-fiefver. C'est bailler en arrierefief partie de son fief: ¶Ragueau.
Soubsigner. *To subsigne, subscribe, set his handmarke, or signe manuell vnder.*
Soubslevement: m. *Looke* Soublevement.
Soubs-majeur: m. *(Is in some townes) a Magistrate of authoritie, or dignitie, next vnto the Maior.*
Soubs-maistre: m. *An vnder Maister*; *or, an Vsher in a Schoole.*
Soubs-manant: m. *A tenant, vassall, or subiect vnto a Lord*; *(an old* Picard *word.)*
Soubson, & **Soubsonner**. *Looke* Souspeçon, & Souspeçonner.
Soubspoictrine: f. *The flanke-peece, or bottome of the brisket of an Oxe, &c.*

Soubstenable,& Soubstenance. *Look* Soustenable, & Soustenance.
Soubstenant: m. *An vnder tenant; a tenant vnto a tenant, or to a mesne Lord; also, as* Soustenant.
Soubstenement. *Looke* Soustenement.
Soubstenir,& Soubtenir. *Looke* Soustenir.
Soubterrain: m.aine: f. *Which is vnder the ground, or within the earth.*
Soubterrer. *Looke* Sousterrer.
Soubtraire. *To withdraw; nimme, purloyne, filch closely, conuey away priuily; also, to subducc, peruert, allure, intice, toll away.*
Soubtrayant: m.ante: f. *Subtracting, withdrawing; nimming, purloyning, closely filching; subducing, alluring, inticing away.*
Soubz. *Beneath; vnder; Looke* Sous.
Soubzacazement: m. *A dead* Fief, *rent secke, mesne, or vnder rent.*
Soubzacazer. *To raise a new rent secke, new seruices, or a new* Cens *vpon the letting, or aliening of land alreadie so rented, or liable to seruices, or vnto* Cens.
Soubzacazeur: m. *One that raises, &c; as in* Soubzacazer.
Soucens,& Soucensier. *Look* Surcens,& Surcensier.
Souche: f. *The stock, trunke, or bodie of a tree; a log; also, the maine stock, or direct line of a pedegree, progenie, or familie; also, as* Souchet; *or the root of the wild, or English Galingale.*
Souche commune. *The descent of many brothers or cousens, from one father, mother, grandfather, or grandmother.*
Tant que tige fait souche, elle ne branche iamais. *Looke* Tige.
Souchet: m. *Ciperous, or Galingale; a Bull-rush whose root smells verie sweetly; also, as* Souchon; *also, a kind of Imposition.*
Souchet de bois. *Set-foyle, Tormentill; an hearbe.*
Souchet d'Inde. *Indian Galingale; whose root resembles Ginger, and which in shops is tearmed* Curcuma.
Souchet Romain. *Sweet Ciperous.*
Souchette: f. *A little stocke, trunke, or log.*
Soucheux: m.euse: f. *Full of stocks, logs, or stumps.*
Souchon: m. *The stumpe of a tree, &c.*
Souci: m. *Care, carke, thought; regard, heed; perplexitie, anxietie, or trouble of mind; also, a Marigold; (for which looke* Soulsi.)
Enfans sans souci. *Carelesse children, retchlesse fellowes, dissolute companions; those that care not how much they wrong themselues, & abuse others; also, a certaine rakehellie generation of Iuglers, or Tumblers.*
Soucicle. *as* Soucie.
Soucie: f. *A little yellowish bird, hardly as big as a Wren, and called, by some, a Ninmurder; (Looke* Soulsie.)
Soucier. *To infect with cark, to afflict with cares; whence;*
Ce temps soucie le monde. *This vnseasonable weather doth trouble the world;* viz. *doth vexe, and hinder the most that would be abroad.*
Se soucier. *To care, heed, regard, reckon or make account of, prouide or take thought for, be diligent, curious, or earnest about; vex, perplex, trouble, or disquiet himselfe withall.*
Ceux qui ne se soucient depuis le nez en amont. *Men that care onely for the present, men that prouide but from hand to mouth.*
Soucieux: m.euse: f. *Carefull, thoughtfull, solicitous, much perplexed.*
Soucille: f. *Th'vnder-lid of the eye.*

Soucy: m. *The Marigold.*
Soudain: m.aine: f. *Sudden; vnwares, vnpremeditate, vnlooked for; quicke, swift, hastie, speedie.*
Soudainement. *Suddenly, at vnawares; in a trice, in the twinkling of an eye, ere you can haue said, this; hastily, swiftly, speedily, incontinently, by and by.*
Soudaineté: f. *Suddennesse, hast, great speed, quicknesse, violence.*
Soudan: m. *(In th'Ægyptian, and Morish tongues, doth signifie) a King, Prince, or Soueraigne; a Souldan.*
Soudard. *Looke* Soldat.
Soude. *Looke* Soulde.
Souder. *To soulder.*
Soudespensier: m. *An vnder Cater; or, an inferiour Clerke of a kitchin.*
Soudiacre: m. *A Subdeacon.*
Soudic: m. *An auncient title for a great Lord, or Noble man.*
Soudre. *The Linden tree.*
Soudre: com. *Ouglie, deformed, most foule, loathsome to looke on.*
Soudre. *To loosse, &c; Looke* Souldre.
Souduire. *To seduce.*
Souduis: m.ise: f. *Seduced.*
Souduisant: m.ante: f. *Seducing.*
Souduiseur: m. *A seducer; (old words.)*
Soudure: f. *A souldering; Looke* Souldure.
Souëf. *Looke* Soëf.
Souëfflairant: m.ante: f. *Most fragrant, sweetly smelling.*
Souëffleurer. *To sweeten, perfume, bemuske, imbaulme.*
Souër. *To bring a Boare vnto the Sow; (whence,* ne faittez souër la truye; *Let her not haue the Boare;) also, to gueld, or splay a Sow.*
Souëvement. *Sweetly, smoothly, mildly, pleasantly.*
Souffire. *Looke* Suffire.
Souffle: m. *Ones breath, wind, blast, or breathing; also, a small gale, puffe, gust, or flaw of wind.*
Ce sont souffles. *These are but idle words, fond brags, vaine tearmes, paultrie tales.*
Soustenir le souffle à. *To maintaine, support, vphold, or hold in breath.*
Soufflé: m.ée: f. *Breathed, blasted, blowne, puffed out; also, sounded, or winded on a horne, &c.*
Soufflemboyau: m. *A Pudding-maker:* ¶Rab.
Soufflement: m. *A blowing, strong breathing, puffing out; a winding of a horne, &c.*
Souffler. *To blow, breath (strongly,) puffe out, send forth blasts; to sound, or wind, as a Cornet, horne, &c; also, to kisse behind.*
Soufflez. *(The Imperatiue of this Verbe; vsed scorningly, or in derision) Tis but a ieast, there is no such matter; or, he brags most vainly, prates most fondly; his words are but wind, his boasts little other then smoake.*
Il souffle. *He playes the Alchimist.*
Souffler au bassin. *To make present paiment, giue readie money for.*
Souffler les choux en dormant. *To puffe, or blurt out puffes, in sleeping.*
Souffler à l'encensoir. *Looke* Encensoir.
Souffler aux estoupes. *To labour a matter while the time serueth; to assist in season, helpe in time.*
Souffler les fourmis dans leurs fourmillieres. *Looke* Fourmilliere.
Souffler en l'oreille de. *To round, or whisper in the eare.*
Soufflet: m. *A paire of bellowes; also, a box, cuffe, or whirret on th'eare.*

Souffleté: m. ée: f. *Often puffed, or blowne; also, cuft, or clapt on the eare.*
Souffleter. *To puffe, or blow often; also, to cuffe, box, or clap on the eare.*
Souffleteur: m. *A cuffer, boxer, buffeter.*
Souffleteux: m. euse: f. *Blowing often, or puffing violently; also, readie, or apt to puffe.*
Soufflеur: m. *A blower, puffer, breather; also, the Whale tearmed (otherwise)* Gibbar.
Vn souffleur par derriere. *A Prompter.*
Souffleux: m. euse: f. *Often puffing, much blowing.*
Souffrance: f. *Sufferance, forbearance, patience, tolleration, induring, abiding; also, need, pouertie, scarcitie, penurie.*
Souffrance du Seigneur donnée au vassal. *Respit of homage; or the Lords permitting of a tenant to enioy his estate before hee haue done him homage; which to the tenant is as auailable as if hee had formally done it.*
Articles tenus en souffrance. *Time giuen vnto an Accomptant (Receiuor) for the producing of some acquittance (of no great moment) wanting to the perfection of his account; as also, when it is found that he hath done his indeuor (though it be not sufficient) for the bringing in of moneyes that be due.*
Souffre. *Looke* Soulfre.
Souffreter. *To be in great need, or penurie, to pinch it.*
Souffreteux: m. euse: f. *Penurious, needie, poore, wanting, wretched, in a miserable case.*
Souffrette: f. *Need, penurie, pouertie, scarcitie, want of necessarie meanes.*
Souffrir. *To suffer, beare, tollerate, abide, indure.*
Se souffrir de. *To forbeare the doing of.*
Qui plus vit plus a à souffrir: Prov. *The longer we liue the more we haue t'indure.*
Si truye forfaict les pourceaux le souffrent: Prov. *Children are punisht for their parents faults.*
Soufre. *Looke* Soulfre.
Sougorge. *Looke* Sousgorge.
Souhait: m. *A wish, or desire.*
Qui vient à souhait. *A happie successe of hopes, a prosperous issue of expectation; a matter that falls out pat, or euen as one would haue it.*
Si souhaits furent vrais pastoureaux seroyent Rois: Prov. *If wishes might preuaile poore shepheards would be Kings.*
'A povre coeur petit souhait: Pro. *The poore mans heart hath low thoughts, meane desires.*
Vin sur laict c'est souhait, laict sur vin c'est venin: Prov. *Milke before wine I would twere mine, milke taken after is poisons daughter.*
Souhaitable: com. *Wishable, desirable, fit to be longed or looked for.*
Souhaité: m. ée: f. *Wished, coueted, longed for, much desired.*
Souhaiter. *To wish, desire, long for, couet after.*
Souil de sanglier: m. *The soile of a wild Boare; the slough, or mire wherein he hath wallowed.*
Souillard: m. *A Scullion, or kitchin boy; also, the name of a dog, betweene which, and a bitch called* Baude, *the race of the* Bauds *(white, and excellent hounds) was begun.*
Souillarderie: f. *Sluttishnesse, nastinesse, greasinesse; the habit, state, or exercise of a Scullion.*
Souillé: m. ée: f. *Soiled, slurried, durtied, smutched, berayed, distained, blemished, contaminated.*
Souillement: m. *A soyling, slurrying, durtying, smutching, beraying, begriming.*
Souiller. *To soyle, slurrie, durtie, smutch, beray, begrime, defile, blemish, distaine.*
Se souiller. *(Of a swine) to take soyle, or wallow in the mire.*
Souillon: m. *A Scullion, or drudge in a kitchin; (and thence) also, a greasie, filthie, nastie, or slouenlie fellow.*
Souillonne: f. *A drudge, or kitchin wench.*
Souillonnerie: f. *Scullionerie, drudgerie; slouenrie, nastinesse, greasinesse.*
Souillure: f. *Soyle, filth, nastinesse, greasinesse, durtinesse, pollution, sluttishnesse.*
Souisse: m. *A Swisse, or Swizer.*
Soulacier. *To solace; comfort, recreate, make merrie.*
Soulagé: m. ée: f. *Eased, lightened; recreated, comforted.*
Soulagement: m. *An easement or easing, a lightening of toyle, a lessening of paine; a comforting, recreating, cheering vp.*
Soulager. *To ease, lighten, lessen the paines or griefe of; to recreate, solace, comfort, cheere vp.*
Il la soulage a le bras, ou, du bras. *He led, held, or bore, her vp by the arme.*
Soulas: m. *Solace, comfort, consolation, contentment, ease, recreation.*
Nul soulas mondain sans helas: Prov. *No worldlie comfort without crosses, or corrasiues.*
Soulasser, & Soulassier. *Looke* Soulacier.
Soulci: m. *Care, thought, heed, studie, regard, carke, anxietie, trouble, perplexitie, vexation of mind; also, a Marigold; Looke* Souci.
Soulcicle, & Soulcide: f. *The little yellowish bird called a Ninmurder.*
Soulcie: f. *The same; also, a Marigold.*
Soulcier. *Looke* Soucier.
Soulcieux: m. euse: f. *Solicitous, carefull, thoughtfull, perplexed, much in dumps.*
Sould: m. *Souldiers lendings, intertainment, or pay; (an old word.)*
Souldan. *Looke* Soudan.
Souldart: m. *A souldier.*
Soulde: f. *Saltwort, Glassewort, Crab-grasse, Frog-grasse, (an hearbe;) also, pay, intertainment, or lendings for souldiers; also as* Soulte.
Ils sont tousiours à la chasse des souldes. *They are euer hunting after intertainment, they greedily & continually pursue the scraps of bountie.*
Souldé: m. ée: f. *Souldered; consolidated.*
Souldée: f. *as* Sould.
Soulder. *To soulder; consolidate; close, or fasten together.*
Souldeur: m. *A Soulderer.*
Souldeure: f. *A souldering.*
Souldoyer: m. *A Souldier; one that fights, or serues, for pay.*
Souldoyer. *To intertaine, pay, giue wages or lendings vnto, Souldiers.*
Souldre. *To loosse, vnfold, expound, resolue, cleere, or soile, a doubt, &c.*
Qu'ay ie à faire, ne que souldre avec toy? *What haue I to doe with thee?*
Souldure: f. *A souldering; and particularly, the knot of soulder which fastens the lead of a glasse window.*
Soulet: m. ette: f. *Sole, alone, priuate, solitarie, without companie:* ¶Langued.
Soulever. *Looke* Soublever.
Soulfre: m. *Sulpher, Brimstone.*
Soulfre artificiel; ou contrefaict. *Artificiall Brimstone, or Brimstone made with fire.*

Soulfre iaulne. *as* S.contrefaict; *and yet some call so the naturall one, because it is yellow within.*

Soulfre naturel,ou vif. *Naturall Sulpher; ash-coloured without,yellowish within,and glistening,or shining like a Gloworme.*

Soulfreux: m. euse: f. *Sulpherie, full of brimstone.*

Soulfriere: f. *A Sulpher pit or mine; the place wherein brimstone is gotten,or made.*

Soulfureux. *as* Soulfreux.

Soulier: m. *A shooe.*

Soliers à bec de cane. *Looke vnder* Bec.

Soulier cambrez. *Polonian shooes, high and hollow heeled shooes,*

Souliers à clique corde. *Shooes open at the heeles.*

Souliers à pont-levis. *as* S. cambrez.

Souliers à poulaine. *Shooes open on the foot,and tied ouer th'instap with a latchet.*

Souliers à trepointe renversée. *Turnouers.*

Tenir pied en soulier. *To keepe within his limits, to be continent, stayed,aduised.*

Le beau soulier blesse souvent le pied: Prov. *The goodlie shooe doth often hurt the foot; (little know you where this new shooe wrings me, quoth* Metellus *to a friend of his.)*

Le beau soulier devient en fin savate: Pro. *(So beautie endeth in deformitie.)*

`A telle forme tel soulier: Pro. *Like leauen like past; such as the shooe such is the last.*

Le trou trop ouvert sous le nez fait porter souliers deschirez: Prov. *The hole too open vnder the nose, breeds tattered shooes,and ragged hose.*

Soulier: m. ere: f. *Fit for,or belonging vnto,a shooe.*

Souloir. *(A Verbe which, besides this Infinitiue, hath onely th'Imperfect tense of the Indicatiue mood; viz.* Ie souloye, tu soulois, il souloit, &c;) *to bee wont, or accustomed; to vse verie commonly, doe verie often.*

Soulphre. *Looke* Soulfre.

Soulphrer. *To besulpher,to mingle with,or make of, Sulpher; to powder,or bestrew with Brimstone.*

Soulphriere. *Looke* Soulfriere.

Souls: m. *A Sous,or the French shilling; Looke* Sol.

Soulsi: m. *The Marigold, Ruds.*

Soulsi aquatique, ou d'eau. *The yellow Willowhearbe, Looste-strife, water Willow.*

Soulsie: f. *as* Soulsi; *also,as* Soucie.

Moineau à la soulsie. *Looke vnder* Moineau.

Soulte: f. *Souldiers wage,pay, or intertainment;* C'est aussi, en matiere d'eschanges, le retour que l'on baille pour la plus-valeur d'un heritage; *whence,* Eschange de terre sans soulte. *Land exchanged without boot, without any paiment ouer, without any ouerplus paid, without any money giuen in regard of inequalitie,or in consideration of oddes; land exchanged onely for land.*

Soulte mobiliaire. *A returne,or amends in mouables, or in money,made by a coheire,or coparcener that hath a greater,to him that hath a lesse, part in the land then he should haue.*

Sou-maistre: m. *An Vsher in a schoole.*

Soumettre. *Looke* Soubmettre.

Soupape: f. *The stopple of a Baloone; also, the Supper, or Sucker of a Pumpe.*

Soupçon: f. *Suspition, doubt, feare, iealousie, diffidence, misdeeming, distrust.*

Soupçonnable: com. *Suspectable.*

Soupçonner. *To suspect, feare, doubt, distrust, be iealous of, haue little confidence in.*

Soupçonneux: m. euse: f. *Suspitious, diffident, doubtfull, or distrustfull.*

Soupe: f. *A sop; a peece of bread in broth,or in browis; also,pottage,or broth (wherein there is store of sops,or sippets;) also, browis.*

Soupe aux aulx. *Garlick broth,or browis; is made of Garlick sodden in white wine with marrow, sops of bread, a Partridge, Cloues, Ginger, a little Cinnamon, and good store of Sugar.*

Soupe despourveuë. *Browis, or sops of bread steeped in water, salt, and Parsley, which haue beene boyled toger, & the Parsley fried with butter before the boiling.*

Soupes de levrier; & soupes de prime. *Seeke* Levrier, & Prime.

Soupe vermeille. *A dish,or sauce made of red wine, vinegar, and Cinnamon, strained together, and boiled with marrow; & then, with small peeces of Chickens, Pigeons,or Partridges, well sugared, and serued in.*

Soupe en vin. *Medicke fodder, Snayle Clauer.*

Yvre comme vne soupe. *As drunke as a sop,or toast.*

De mesme pain soupe; &, On luy a fait de tel pain soupes. *Said when a babler is put downe with words, a lyer confuted by his owne allegations, a deceiuer ouerraught, a quareller cudgelled, or a proud scab ouercrowed.*

Il ne saucera son pain en ma soupe. *Looke* Saucer.

De la main à la bouche se perd souvent la soupe: Prov. *Many a bit miscarries betweene the hand, and the lip; we often loose things when wee almost enioy them.*

Soupé. *Supped,or, hauing supped.*

Soupendre. *To hang on,or ouer; to iuttie or beare out, to stand or leane beyond; also, to build vpon arches, pillers, vaults, &c.*

Soupenduë: f. *A penthouse; iuttie,or, part of a building that iuttieth beyond, or leaneth ouer, the rest; also, a hanging, or building vpon, or ouer; a iuttying, or a leaning, out or beyond; Looke* Surpenduë.

Soupente: f. *The same (in the first sence.)*

Souper: m. *A supper.*

Souper de Marchand. *A large, or plentifull supper, eaten,or made.*

Qui garde son disner il a mieux à souper: Pro. *He that keepes his dinner hath the more to his supper; he that spares while he's young may the better spend when hee's old.*

Qui tost vient à son hostel mieux luy en est à son souper: Prov. *He that comes earlie to his Inne hath much the better supper.*

Souper. *To sup.*

Ou nous avons disné nous souperons. *We will end where we begã, or hold on the course wherin we begã; or keep, in this businesse, the order we vsed in th'other.*

Mal soupe qui tout disne: Prov. *Looke* Disner.

Soupeser. *To peise, weigh, ponder.*

Soupeser vn dard. *Violently to shake and (thereupon) hurle, a dart.*

Soupoictrine: f. *Looke* Soubspoictrine.

Soupoultreau: m. *An vnder-beame.*

Souppe. *as* Soupe.

Souppendre. *Looke* Soupendre.

Souppenduë. *Looke* Soupenduë.

Souppier: m. *A sopper,or browis-bellie; one that is euer dipping his bread in the beefe-pot.*

Soupple: com. *Supple, limber, tender, pliant, nimble flexible, easie to be bent.*

Soupplesse: f. *Supplenes, pliantnes, flexiblenes, actiuitie, nimblenes; & hence also, a feat of actiuitie, a tumbling tricke.*

Souppous. *Looke* Supposts.
Souquenie: f. *A Canuas Iacket, frocke, or Gaberdine; such a one as our Porters weare.*
Source: f. *A source; head, originall, beginning, of; a spring, well-head, well spring; a seminarie; race, of-spring.*
Sourcé: m. ée: f. *Sourced, sprung or begun from; also, originally drawne from, taken from the source of.*
Sourcens; &, Sourcensier. *Looke* Surcens; &, Surcensier.
Sourcer. *To source, to spring; to begin; to issue, or draw it originall from.*
Sourchelons: m. *The Frounce; a Hawkes disease.*
Sourcicle. *The Ninmurder; a yellowish, and verie small bird.*
Sourcier: m. *A Sorcerer.*
Sourcil: m. *An eye-brow; also, the ridge of haire growing thereon; also, a frowning, surlie, or sowre countenance.*
Sourcilier: m. ere: f. *Of, or on, the eye-browes.*
Sourciller. *To moue the eye-browes vp and downe.*
Sourcilles: f. *The eye-browes.*
Sourcilleux: m. euse: f. *Hauing verie great eye-brows; also, frowning, or looking sowrely on it; surlie, or proud of countenance; also, raised, aduanced, or lift vp on high.*
Sourd: m. *The Salamander.*
Sourd: m. sourde: f. *Deafe, hard of hearing, or, that cannot heare; also, listlesse, vnattentiue, heedlesse; also, dumme, without dinne or noise; (whence, in moist weather, they say that a Tennis-court is* sourd; *) and solide, or without sound, as a full bodie, or vessell well filled; also, dull, insensible, vnsauorie; also, darke, priuie, priuate, secret, vnder-hand.*
Aspic sourd. *(The Aspe, sayes Gesner, by reason of her exceeding drought is accounted deafe; but that one Aspe is deafer then another I read not.)*
Lanterne sourde. *A theeues Lanterne; the blacke Lanterne of yron which theeues, & other priuate night-walkers vse to carrie about them.*
Nombre sourd. *A surd number; a number whereof a perfect square cannot be made.*
Teincture sourde. *The coursest kind of dying, with nought but hearbes.*
Sourd comme vn tapis. *As deafe as a doore-nayle (say we.)*
Il n'est point de pire sourd que celuy qui ne veut ouïr: Prov. *No man's worse deafe then he that will not heare.*
Sourdant. *Springing vp, rising or arising, from.*
Sourdastre: com. *Deafish, thicke of hearing.*
Sourdault. *Somewhat deafe, thicke of hearing.*
Sourdement: m. *A rising, arising, springing vp, appeaپearing out of.*
Sourdement. *Deafely; also, vnattentiuely; also, priuately, vnder-hand, in huggermugger, without any din or noise; also, dully, insensibly.*
Sourdent: m. *The stumpe of a broken tooth.*
Sourdesse: f. *Deafenesse.*
Sourdeté: f. *The same.*
Sourdin: m. ine: f. *Deafish, thicke of hearing.*
Sourdine: f. *A Sourdet; the little pipe, or tenon put into the mouth of a Trumpet, to make it sound low; also, a Sordine, or a kind of hoarse, or low-sounding Trumpet.*
A la sourdine. *Priuately, secretly, closely, without much dinne, or noise.*
Sourdise: f. *Deafenesse.*
Sourdon: m. *A kind of little shell-fish.*
Sourdoyant. *Rising, issuing, springing out or vp; mounting, arising, appearing aboue; also, raising.*
Sourdre. *To rise, issue, spring, boyle, come, out or vp; to mount, arise, ascend, appeare, or shew it selfe aboue; also, to raise, or put vp; whence they say when a Hawke is a wing, or lyes for game,* Qu'on luy sourde des oiseaux.
Souretier: m. *A Rat-catcher; a Mouser, or catcher of Mice.*
Sourge. Laine S. *New shorne, vnwashed, or greasie wooll; wooll that is yet full of it owne grease.*
Sourgeon: m. *The young shoot, or tender and vp-shooting plant of a tree; also, the spring of a fountaine; or the rising, boyling, or spouting vp of water in a spring.*
Souriceau: m. *A little, or young Mouse.*
Souricier: m. *A Mouser, or Mouse-catcher.*
Souricier: m. ere: f. *Of Mice; whence;* Vermine souriciere; *Mice.*
Souriciere: f. *A Mousetrap.*
Sourien: m. enne: f. *Mousing; louing Mice; hunting after Mice.*
Souris: f. *A Mouse; also, the sinewie brawne of th'arms; also, an Engine whereby a draw-bridge, downe, is hindered from being pulled vp againe.*
Souris araigneuse. *A shrew Mouse.*
Les souris du Palais. *Aduocates, Counsellors, Pleaders, Pettifoggers.*
Oreille de souris. *The hearbe Pilosella, or Mouse-eare, &c; Looke* Oreille.
Queuë de souris. *Mouse-taile, Bloud-strange.*
La souris qui n'a qu'une entrée est incontinent happée: &, Tost attrapée est la souris qui n'a pour giste qu'un pertuis: Prov. *(So ill a Protector is Improuidence.)*
De grand desseing vne souris: Prov. *(as the Latine* Parturiunt montes &c; *) All that mountaine proues but a molehill.*
Sourisseau: m. *A little or young Mouse.*
Sourisson. *The same.*
Sourte. *Looke* Soutte.
Sous. *Vnder, beneath, at the bottome of.*
Sous terre. *Vnder-hand, priuily, in huggermugger.*
Faire tout sous soy. *A child to beray himselfe.*
Sousbarbe: f. *as* Soubarbe; *also, the throat-band of a bridle.*
Endurer vne sousbarbe. *To indure an iniurie.*
Sousbride: f. *as* Sousbarbe, *in the later sence; also, as* Soubride.
Souschambriere: f. *A kitchin wench, or drudge to a house.*
Souschanter. *To sing vnder, to hold the base, or ground vnto; or as* Soubschanter.
Sousclavier: m. ere: f. *Vnder the Kannell bone.*
Artere sousclaviere. *The ascendant branch of the great Arterie.*
Muscle sousclavier. *One of the muskles which, in the fetching of breath, dilate, and stretch out, the breast.*
Veine sousclaviere. *Looke* Veine.
Souscoeur: m. *The Pericardium, or thinne skin wherby the whole heart is couered.*
Sousgorge d'une bride. *The throat-thong, or throat-band of a bridle.*
Sousgrewe: f. *The lesse bone of the leg; also, the calfe of the leg.*
Sousleuement, & Sousleuer. *Look* Soubleuement, & Soubleuer.
Souspape: f. *as* Soupape.

Souſpeçon: f. *Suſpition, iealouſie, diffidence, doubt, feare, diſtruſt, miſtruſt.*

Souſpeçonné: m. ée: f. *Suſpected, miſtruſted, bad in iealouſie.*

Souſpeçonner. *To ſuſpect, feare, doubt of, diſtruſt, miſtruſt, haue in a iealouſie.*

Souspeçonneuſement. *Suſpitiouſly, iealouſly, doubtfully, diſtruſtfully.*

Souſpeçonneux: m. euſe: f. *Suſpitious, doubtfull, diffident, iealous, diſtruſtfull.*

Souſpendement: m. *A hanging or leaning ouer; a iuttying or bearing out.*

Souspendre. *Looke* Soupendre.

Souspendu: m. uë: f. *Hanging, or hung ouer; iuttied, or ſet out beyond.*

Vne deſmarche ſouſpenduë. *A ſtealing pace.*

Souſpenduë: f. *as* Soupenduë; *alſo, as* Surpenduë, *eſpecially in the laſt ſence.*

Souſpente. *Looke* Soupenduë.

Souspeſé: m. ée: f. *Peiſed, weighed, pondered.*

Souspeſer. *To peiſe, weigh, ponder diligently; Looke* Soupeſer.

Souſpir: m. *A ſigh; alſo, a ſhort breath; alſo, a Minime reſt in Muſicke.*

Demy ſouſpir. *A Crochet reſt.*

Au dernier ſouſpir. *At the laſt gaſpe.*

Souſpirable: com. *Fit to bee ſighed for, worthie of moane.*

Souſpirail. *as* Souſpiral.

Souspiraillé: m. ée: f. *Hauing holes, vents, open windowes, or other paſſages, for aire to come in and out at.*

Souſpiral: m. *An ouerture, or paſſage for aire or breath to come in and goe out at; a vent, or breathing hole; Hence, the tunnell of a chimney; the window of a ſellar; the mouth of a caue, or denne.*

Souſpirement: m. *A ſighing.*

Souspirer. *To ſigh; alſo, to deſire vehemently.*

'A coeur dolent la bouche ſouſpire: Prov. *Sighes in the mouth, ſorrow at the heart.*

Souſplié: m. ée: f. *Bent, or bowed vnder, ſubiect vnto.*

Souſſigner. *Looke* Soubſigner.

Souſte. *A prop, ſtay, or treſle of wood.*

Souſtenable: com. *Suſtainable, ſupportable, abideable.*

Souſtenance: f. *A prop, ſupport, ſtay, maintenance.*

Souſtenant (de balance.) *The cheekes of a balance; the two vpright peeces betweene which the needle plaieth.*

Souſtenant de bride. *The cheeke-peece of a bridle.*

Souſtendrons: m. *The ſides of the bellie vnder the ſhort ribs.*

Souſtenement: m. *A ſuſtaining, ſupporting, vpholding, maintaining; induring, abiding.*

Souſtenir. *To ſuſtaine, ſupport, vphold, ſtay or beare vp; alſo, to indure, tollerate, abide; alſo, (in ſinging) to hold a note; and (in manage) to keepe a horſe, being riſen, from comming too ſoone to the ground.*

Souſtenir & abſtenir. *Looke* Abſtenir.

Souſternery. *She that giues ſucke to a new-borne child for two or three dayes, and vntill the mothers milke be fit for it*: ¶Provençal.

Sousterré: m. ée: f. *Put, laid, or buried vnder, or within, the ground.*

Souſterrer. *To put, lay, burie vnder, or within, the ground.*

Souſtien: m. *The firſt bill which a Plaintiffe puts into a Court.*

Souſtraire. *Looke* Soubtraire.

Soutane: f. *A long and looſſe coat, or caſſocke, ſuch as Church-men weare vnder their gownes.*

Soute: f. *as* Soutte; *alſo, a franke, or hogs-ſtie; whence;* Pourceau gras rompt ſa ſoute: Prov. *(Appliable to the vnrulie humors of pampered, or high-fed creatures.)*

Souteſt. *as* Pericraine.

Soutre. *Looke* Soutte.

Soutte: f. *A binne to keepe bread in; alſo, the roome of a ſhip, wherein the prouiſion-bisket is laied.*

Souvenance: f. *Memorie, remembrance; alſo, a Ring with many hoopes, whereof a man lets one hang downe when he would be put in mind of a thing.*

Souvendier: m. *The hearbe Cichorie.*

Souvenir: m. *A remembrance.*

Souvenir. *To remember, put in mind, bring to the memorie of.*

Se souvenir. *To remember, haue in memorie, call to mind.*

Il ſouvient touſiours à Robin de ſes fleutes: Prov. *Looke* Robin.

Souvent. *Often, many times.*

Souvenu: m. uë: f. *Remembred, called to mind or memorie.*

Souverain: m. *A Soueraigne; one that acknowledges no ſuperior; (and yet in old time a Preſident of Iuſtice, or any in Office aboue others, was tearmed ſo.)*

Souverain: m. aine: f. *Soueraigne, Princelie, chiefe, principall, paſſing, excellent, high, notable, ſingular.*

Souverainement. *Soueraignely, Princely, chiefely, principally; moſt highly, notably, ſingularly, excellently.*

Souveraineté: f. *Soueraigntie, principalitie, higheſt authoritie, chiefe gouernement, ſupreme power.*

Droicts de Souveraineté. *Are generally ſix;* viz. *Th'enacting of, and diſpenſing with, Lawes; the creating of Officers; the making of warre, and peace; the hauing of* le dernier reſſort de la Iuſtice; *the coyning of money; and the raiſing, or impoſing thereof; whereunto ſome adde, Confiſcation for Hereſie, Treaſon, &c; the granting of Priuiledges, Faires, Markets, and Letters of Mart;* la Regale; *right vnto all wreckes, and ſhipwrackes; an intereſt in th'abſolute fealtie, and homage of the ſubiect; power to naturalize forrainers, legitimate baſtards, ennoble* Roturiers, *or peaſants; a tenth in all manner of mines that haue beene, or ſhall be, opened throughout all France; and diuers other Royalties.*

Soy. *Him, himſelfe; her, herſelfe.*

Retourner ſur ſoy. *To returne the ſame way he came.*

Soye: f. *Silke; alſo, hogs briſtles.*

Appliquer ſoye ſur ſoye. *To lecher.*

Meſler la ſoye avec le fleuret. *To iumble good and bad together.*

Soyer. *To reape corne.*

Soyes: f. *Is, in the throats of ſwine, a diſeaſe that ſtifles them, if it be not preſently cured; alſo, as* Sais.

Soyeux: m. euſe: f. *Silkie; briſtlie; full of ſilke or of briſtles.*

Soymeſme. *Himſelfe.*

Soytier: m. ere: f. *Of ſilke, or dealing with ſilkes.*

Spadaires: m. *An Order of white Friers which weare on their habites a repreſentation of two red ſwords.*

Spadaſin; *or,* **Spadaſſin**: m. *A cutter, hackſter, ſwaggerer, ſwaſh-buckler.*

Spal-

Spalmer. *To breeme and graue, or make cleane a ship.*
Sparaillon: f. *The purple fish; (not the purple shell-fish, but a kind of small Guilt-head, or yellow Sea-breame, which hath a blacke spot on her tayle.)*
Spargirie: f. *Alchymie; extraction of quintessences.*
Spargirique: com. *An Alchymist, or extractor of quintessences.*
Spargitide. Terre spar. Terra sigillata, *Lemnian earth.*
Spariée: f. *A sea-wrecke; or, as* Varech.
Sparte: m. *as* Sparton.
Sparton: m. *Spanish broome, or bastard Sparish broome, whereof bands to tye Vines, and (as in old time) roapes for shipping, may be made; also, Matweed.*
Spase, ou peis Espase. *The sea-fox, or fox dog-fish; ash-coloured on the backe, and white on the bellie; little mouthed, but sharpe-toothed; shorter, and thicker bodied, but hauing a longer tayle, then any other dog-fish; for that (somewhat like a short, and crooked sword-blade) is longer then her bodie.* ¶Gascon.
Spasmatique: com. *Troubled with a crampe, or a conuulsion.*
Spasme: m. *The crampe; a conuulsion, shrinking, or plucking vp of the sinewes.*
Spasmé: m. ée: f. *Crampped; or, as* Spasmatique.
Spasmeux: m. euse: f. *Full of the crampe; or, conuulsiue, cramp-breeding.*
Spatieusement. *Spaciously, widely, amply, largely, broadly.*
Spatieux: m. euse: f. *Spacious, roomie, wide, large, ample, broad.*
Spatule: f. *The slice wherewith a Surgeon spreadeth salues, &c.*
Spaze: f. *A sword; and as* Spase. ¶Gasc.
Speans d'une vache. *A Cowes duddes.*
Speautre. *Looke* Espeautre.
Special: m. ale: f. *Speciall, particular, proper, peculiar, chiefe, especiall.*
Specialement. *Especially, namely, chiefely, particularly, peculiarly.*
Specieux: m. euse: f. *Specious, goodlie, faire, gracefull in apparance, outwardly beautifull, honourable in shew.*
Specifier. *To specifie, particularize, declare, signifie, denote.*
Specifique: com. *Speciall, particular.*
Specifiquement. *Specially, particularly.*
Spectable: com. *Visible, worthie the seeing, noteable, goodlie, renowmed.*
Spectacle: m. *A spectacle; a publike sight, shew, pageant, play.*
Spectateur: m. *A spectator, beholder, on-looker.*
Spectatrice: f. *A spectatrix; a woman that giues a (publike) thing the looking on.*
Spectre: m. *An Image, or Figure, seene either truly, or but in conceit; (thence) also, a spirit, ghost, vision, apparition, fantasme.*
Speculaire: com. *Cleere, transparent; also, helping the sight.*
Pierre speculaire. *as* Pierre à miroir, *vnder* Miroir.
Speculateur: m. *A speculator, contemplator, obseruer, considerer; watcher, viewer, beholder.*
Speculation: f. *Speculation, contemplation; a considering, or obseruing; a viewing, watching, or spying out from a high place.*
Speculatrice: f. *A speculatrix; a contemplatiue, obseruing, aduised, or watchfull woman.*
Speculer. *To speculate, contemplate, obserue, consider, search out; behold seriously, watch hard; looke or see farre, espie a farre off.*
Spelonque: f. *A hole in a rocke; a wild beasts denne.*
Speltre: m. *as* Espeautre.
Spengitide. ¶Rab. *Looke* Sphengitide.
Spermatique: com. *Spermatick; containing, or full of, sperme.*
Veine spermatique. *Looke* Veine.
Spermatiser. *To spermatize; to shed, eiect, or iniect sperme.*
Sperme: m. *Sperme, seed, nature, generatiue moisture.*
Spet: m. *A slender, long, rauenous, great-eyed, sharpe-nosed, crooked-toothed, white-bellied, blackish-backt sea-fish, called by some the Spit-fish, and by others (because it somewhat resembles a Pike) the sea-Pike.*
Sphacelé: m. ée: f. *Mortified by inflamation.*
Sphaceler. *To mortifie by inflamation.*
Sphatule. *Looke* Spatule.
Sphengitide. *Transparent.* ¶Rab.
Sphenoïde. Os sphen. *The cuneall bone.*
Sphere: f. *A sphere, circle, rundle, bowle; any round figure, or thing.*
Spheres. *The round knobs on the borders of some French-hoods.*
Sphere droicte. *That sphere wherein one sees both the Poles vnder his horizon, the Equator standing iust ouer his head.*
Sphere oblique. *An oblique sphere; that wherein one of the Poles is raised aboue our horizon, and the other hidden vnder it.*
Spherique: com. *Sphericall, orbicular, globe-like, round.*
Sphicie: f. *A kind of spider like a great Waspe.*
Sphinge: m. *The Sphinga, or Sphinx; an Indian, and Ethyopian beast, rough-bodied like an Ape (of the kind whereof he is) yet hairelesse betweene his necke, and breast; round, but out, faced; and breasted like a woman; his vnarticulate voice like that of a hastie speaker; more gentle, and tameable then an ordinarie Ape, yet fierce by nature, and reuengefull when he is hurt: hauing eaten meat ynough, he reserues his chaps-full to feed on when he feeles himselfe hungrie againe.*
Spicaire. *Roman Spike, or Lauender.*
Spicquenard: m. *The hearbe Spikenard.*
Spinal: m. ale: f. *Of, or in, the chine, or back-bone.*
Spinale medulle, ou mouëlle. *The marrow of the back-bone; deriued from the braine, and like a maine stocke, from which all the sinewes vnder the head doe grow.*
Spinelle: f. *A kind of verie red Gurnet.*
Spineux. *as* Espineux.
Spinul: m. *A splent in a horses leg.*
Spique: f. *Spike, Lauender, Lauender Spike.*
Spiquenard: m. *The hearbe Spikenard.*
Spiquenard vulgaire. *Lauender Spike.*
Spiracle: m. *A breathing hole; a hole to let ayre, breath, or smoake in and out; also, a hole that euaporates a strong, or pestilent ayre; a damp-hole.*
Spiracle: com. *Giuing breath, breathing life, infusing spirit into.*
Spiral: m. ale: f. *Circling, wreathing about, winding or turning round.*
Spire: f. *A rundle, round, or circle; a turning or winding compasse; the coyling, or making vp of a Cable; also, a Quadrant, or Square in the bottome of a Pillar.*
Spiriteux. *Looke* Spirituëux.

Spirituel. La Chapelle blanche spirituel d'Anjou; viz. *within the dioces, or spirituall Iurisdiction, of* Anjou.

Spirituel: m. elle: f. *Spirituall, ghostlie, diuine; ecclesiasticall.*

Spiritueux: m. euse: f. *Spirituall, breathfull, breathing, in life; giuing life; also, quicke, liuelie, vigorous, full of spirit.*

Spirole: f. *A kind of small Artillerie.*

Splanade: f. *A plaine, champian countrey, leuell ground, euen plot.*

Splendeur: f. *Splendor, light, shining, luster, glistering, brightnesse; also, bountie, noblenesse, excellencie; also, honor, glorie, renowme.*

Splenitique: com. *Troubled with the spleene; also, of, or in, the spleene; whence;*

Artere splenitique. *Seeke vnder* Artere.

Splenique: com. *Of, or in, the milt, or spleene.*

Veine splenique. *The spleene veine; one of the six branches of the liuer veine; or, as* Veine splenitique, *vnder* Veine.

Spode: m. *The heauier foile, soot, or oare of Brasse, gathered on the floores of melting-houses.*

Spodizateur: m. *One that maketh Spode, or getteth soot, &c, from Brasse, by trying, or melting it.*

Spodon de canne. *Artificiall, or counterfeit Spode, made of the rootes of reedes, and Ox-bones burned.*

Spoliateur: m. *A spoyler; stripper, despoiler; theefe, robber; pyrate.*

Spoliation: f. *A spoyling; despoyling, stripping; depriuing of.*

Spoliatrice: f. *A spoyling, or despoyling woman; a wench that liues on the spoyle.*

Spolier. *To spoyle; despoyle, strip, ransacke, rob, vnrobe; to depriue, or bereaue of; to disseise.*

Spolin: m. *A kind of gold, or siluer thread.*

Spolentes. *Looke* Ploloente. ¶Rab.

Sponde. 'A sponde. *Sidewaies, or edgelong.*

Spondilles, ou Spondyles. *The knuckles, or turning ioynts of the chine, backe, or neck-bone; also, the heads of Artichokes; also, the vnsauorie, or ill-tasting oysters* Gaideropes.

Spongethere: f. *A certaine little sea-fish, which resembles the sea-spider, and is said to guard, and gouerne the spunge.*

Spongieux: m. euse: f. *Spungie; light, pust vp; full of small holes, or eyes, like a spunge.*

Os spongieux. *The bone* Ethmoïdes, *placed in the top, or vpper part of the nose.*

Spongiosité: f. *Spunginesse, or spungiousnesse; a spungie lightnesse.*

Sponseur: m. *A voluntarie promiser, vndertaker, or suretie for another.*

Spontane: com. *Voluntarie, of free will; naturall, not forced; without helpe, or constraint.*

Spontanement. *Voluntarily.*

Sporte: f. *A fashion of hand-basket, or frayle with handles, vsed for market-imployments; also, the load of a Cammell, or Moyle, comming to 375 pounds, after 16 ounces to the pound.*

Sportule: f. *Money, or meat giuen ordinarily by Princes to the people, or vnto their followers; (most properly the former) boord-wages, or a pecuniarie allowance in lieu of dinner and supper; also, the fee giuen by a Clyent vnto his Counsellor; also, a little maund, or hand-basket.*

Spouilleresse. *as* Espouilleresse.

Spurrie: f. *Spurrie, or Franke; a Dutch hearbe, and an excellent fodder for cattell.*

Spyrate. ¶Rab. *A kind of flux in the fundament; or, more properly, as;*

Spyrathe. *The dung of a Sheepe, or Goat.*

Squadron: m. *A squadron; a square troope, or band, or battaile of souldiors; also, in euery companie, the troope thats vnder the command of a Corporall.*

Squaranchon: m. *The smooth-shelled Crayfish tearmed a Pungar, Grit, or Grampell.*

Squelette. *Looke* Scelete.

Squenente. *Looke* Squinant.

Squenie: f. *The Frocke, long Iacket, Coat, or Cassocke (most commonly) of Canuas, worne outmost, or ouer all other clothes, by Porters, Carters, Horse-keepers, Peasants, &c.*

Squille: f. *The Squill, or sea-Onyon; also, a Prawne, Beard, Shrimp; or, a generall name for all fishes of that kind.*

Squille commune. *Our ordinarie sea-Onyon; lesse in forme, and weaker in operation then* Dioscorides *his* Scilla, *which* Mathiolus *holds to be onely that which growes on the sea-coasts of Spaine.*

Squilles d'os. *Little scales, or splints of broken bones.*

Squillin: m. *Vineger sharpened by the sea-Onyon, or Scallion.*

Squillitique: com. *Of, or seasoned with, or wherein there is, the sea-Onyon.*

Squinade. Cancre squin. *The long-legd, and rough-coated Crabfish, tearmed by some, a Fryll.* ¶Marseillois.

Squinance: f. *The Squinancie, or Squinzie; a disease.*

Squinant: m. *The sweet rush tearmed Squinant, and Cammels Hay.*

Squinaude. *Looke* Squinade.

Squine. Bois de squine. *The knottie, and medicinable root of an Indian, or Chinean bullrush.*

Squiopetins: m. *An Order of Augustine Fryers.*

Stabilité: f. *Stabilitie, stedfastnesse, firmenesse, surenesse, constancie, fastnesse.*

Stable: com. *Stable, firme, sure, stedfast, immoueable, constant, assured.*

Stacte; or, Myrrhe stacte. *Looke* Myrrhe.

Stade: m. *A race for men, or horses to runne in; also, a proportion, or measure of ground, whereof there be three sorts; viz. the Italian, containing 125 paces; the Olympicke, of 120 paces; and the Pythick, of 200 paces; all after fiue feet to the pace.*

Stafilade: f. *A lash, or thwacke with a stirrup-leather.*

Stagnant. Eau stagnante. *The water of ponds, pooles, motes, or ditches; water that runnes not, standing water.*

Stalle. *A seat, or stall to sit on.*

Stanbouque: f. *The wild Goat Ibex; Looke* Ibice.

Stance: f. *A station; a lodging, dwelling, or abiding place; also, a pawse, or stay; also, a stanzo, or staffe of verses.*

Stangue d'un'ancre. *The staffe of an Anchor.*

Stanguette: f. *The eye of the branch of a Bit.*

Staphisaigre. *Stauesaker, Licebane, Lowse-wort, Lowse-powder.*

Staphisaigre sauvage. *Wild Licebane.*

Statere: m. *An Athenian coyne of siluer, weighing halfe an ounce; also, a coyne of gold worth about* xvj s iiij d.

Statere: f. *A Roman, or Goldsmiths ballance; Troy-weight.*

Statif: m. iue: f. *Standing, pitched, or set.*

Station: f. *A station, stand, standing place, or pawse; also,*

a place of resort, abode, or stay; a mansion, dwelling, abiding, staying; also, a road, or bay for shipping.
Stationnaire: com. *That hath a standing, or place of abode, appointed him; also, stationarie, setled, standing.*
Stationné: m. ée: f. *Set or setled, planted or pitched, in a place, appointed a place to stand in.*
Stationner. *To set or settle, plant or pitch, in a place; to appoint a standing vnto.*
Statuaire: m. *A Statuarie, Stone-cutter, Statue-maker.*
Statuaire: f. *(The art of) Stone-cutting, or Statue-making.*
Statuë: f. *A Statue; a standing, or massiue Image of mettall, yuorie, or stone.*
Statuer. *To establish, enact, ordaine; assigne, appoint; pitch, plant, settle, or set fast; purpose, determine, iudge, or thinke assuredly of.*
Stature: f. *Stature, pitch, height, or proportion of bodie.*
Statut. Arrests, ou statuts de querelle. *Judgements giuen, and entred in cases of impeached possession.*
Statutaire. Amende stat. *as* Amende coustumiere; (Au stil de Liege.)
Steatome: m. *An impostume whose mattar is like fat, or tallow.*
Steccade: f. *A place railed in for a Combat, or Lists.*
Stechados. *Steckadoe or Stickadoue, Cassidonia or Cast-me-downe, French Lauender, or the sweet flower thereof.*
Stellage. Droict de stellage. *Toll-corne, and Toll-salt; a dish-full vpon euerie* Septier *of either sold within* Buillon; *due to the Duke thereof.*
Stellagier: m. *A Toll-gatherer for the Duke of* Buillon.
Stellingues: m. *Libertines; for so did the Saxons, vpon libertie of conscience graunted them by* Lotharius *the Emperor, tearme themselues.*
Stellion: m. *The spotted, or starrie Lizard Stellio; also, an enuious fellow; or one that cannot indure another should be the better by him; from the Stellio, which hauing (as he doth halfe-yearelie) cast his skin (a soueraign remedie for the falling sicknesse) presently deuoures it, to depriue mankind of it.*
Stellionat: m. *A cousening, a counterfeiting of marchandise; an vniust or deceitfull gaining; a malicious or fraudulent bereauing another of his money, wares, due prouision, or bargaine.*
Stentoré: m. ée: f. *whence,* Voix Stentorée. *A huge voice, such a one as the Grecian* Stentor *had.*
Stercorin: m. ine: f. *Excrementall, turdie.*
Stereometrie: f. *The measuring of solide bodies.*
Sterile: com. *Sterile, barren, fruitlesse.*
Sterilité: f. *Sterilitie, barrennesse, vnfruitfullnesse.*
Sterlin: m. *The 24 part of an ounce; or 28 graines, and foure fifts of a graine; a weight among Iewellers.*
Sternomantie: f. *Diuination by a mans breast.*
Sternutatoire: m. *A sneezing medicine, or powder.*
Sterometrie: f. *Looke* Stereometrie.
Sterpi. *as* Courtilliere.
Sticines: m. *Fluters, or Pipers.* ¶Rab.
Sticonomantie: f. *Diuination by words written on the barkes of trees.*
Stier: m. *as* Septier. ¶Bourguignon.
Stigmatizé: m. ée: f. *Branded, marked, burnt with a hot yron; defamed, infamous.*
Stigmatizer. *To brand, burne, or marke with a redhot yron; also, to defame openly, disgrace publikely.*
Stil: m. *The stile, vse, course, or forme of pleading, or of proceeding in Law.*
Stile: m. *Looke* Style.
Stilé: m. ée: f. *Well acquainted with; long trayned, much practised in; enured, or vsed vnto.*
Stillatoire: com. *Stilling, distilling, dropping.*
Stillicide: m. *The dropping of a houses eaues.*
Stillitique. Vinaigre stil. *Wherein the prepared sea-Onyon hath beene steeped.*
Stimulateur: m. *A pricker forward; a prouoker, egger, vrger, instigator, inciter.*
Stimulation: f. *A pricking or spurring forward; a prouoking, egging, instigating, vrging.*
Stimulatrice: f. *A stimulatrix, an instigatrix.*
Stimule: m. *A goad, pricke; sting; spurre; an vrging, egging, inciting; an instigation, or violent motion vnto.*
Stimuler. *To pricke, instigate, incite, spurre forward.*
Stinc: m. *The shinne bone; also, a kind of small fish.*
Stince. ¶Rab. *as* Scinc.
Stipal. Fief stipal. *Which descends to a direct heire; or still continues in the possession of those which are of the maine stocke of a familie.*
Stipendié: m. *A stipendiarie, or hireling.*
Stipendié: m. ée: f. *Hired, waged, intertained with wages.*
Stipendier. *To hire, wage, intertaine.*
Stipicité: f. *Stipicitie, costiuenesse, obstruction.*
Stipoule: f. *The sea-Onyon.*
Stippes, Droict de stippes, & nobis; &, Droict de vins, & stippes. *Looke vnder* Droict.
Stiptique. *Stipticke, restrictiue; stopping.*
Stipulant. *Couenanting, requiring.*
Stipulateur: m. *A stipulator; he that intending to bind another by words, asketh him whether he will giue, or doe, such a thing or no.*
Stipulation: f. *A stipulation; a couenant, promise, bargaine, agreement; a demaunding of the performance of couenants; a bond for the payment of money, or performance of couenants.*
Stipulé: m. ée: f. *Required according to law; bargained, contracted, conditioned, couenanted.*
Stipuler. *To stipulate; to require a thing in ordinarie tearmes of Law; also, to couenant, or promise effectually.*
Stirage: m. *Toll, or custome due to the King, &c, vpon euerie* Septier.
Stocfiz: m. *Stockfish.*
Stoechados. *French Lauender, Steckadoe, Stickadoue, Cassidonie, Cast-me-downe.*
Stole: f. *A stole; a long robe, gowne, or garment, reaching to the ankles, or heeles.*
Stomacal: m. ale: f. *Stomacall, cordiall; of or in the stomacke; hurting, or helping the stomacke.*
Mot stomacal. *Earnest, comming from the heart; also, vttered in choller.*
Stomachique: com. *Of, or in the stomacke; or sicke at the stomacke.*
Veine stomachique. *Looke* Veine.
Stomaqué: m. ée: f. *Angrie or angred, put into a chafe, moued vnto choller.*
Stoques. *A borrowing, or taking vp, money vpon interest; whence,* Faire stoques. *So to borrow.*
Storax. *The sweet Gumme Storax.*
Storax calamite. *The best kind of Storax, brought from Aleppo, and kept in canes, or the leaues of reedes.*
Storax liquide. *Liquid Storax; as* Myrrhe stacte (*vnder* Myrrhe.)

Stra-

Strabouïte: m. *A squint-eyed fellow; also, one whose actions, as well as eyes, are awry.*
Stradiot. *as* Estradiot.
Strambot: m. *A Jyg, Round, Catch, countrey Song.*
Strangulation: f. *A strangling, stifling, choaking.*
Strangulation de la matrice. *The suffocation of the Matrix.*
Strap. ¶Rab. *Looke* Seraph.
Stratagematique: com. *Stratagemicall, full of stratagems; of, or like to, stratagems.*
Stratageme: m. *A stratageme; a wittie tricke, or shift in warre.*
Strepite: m. *A noyse, dinne, or bruit; a cracking, creaking, rumbling, rustling.*
Strette: f. *A pinch, nip, wrinche, twindge, gird.*
Strident: m. ente: f. *Crashing, clashing, creaking.*
Strié: m. ée: f. *Chamfered, channelled, made full of gutters, or holes.*
Strieure: f. *A chamfering, channelling, furrowing in stone, or timber.*
Strin: m. *A bastard Dyamond.*
Stropes: m. *The loopes whereby the oares of a Skiffe, &c, doe hang, or hold, to the Thowles.*
Strophe. *The fretting of the guts, or belly-ache.*
Strophule: f. *The Kings euill.*
Stropier. *To lame, or mayme.*
Structure: f. *A structure; fabricke, frame, composition, building; a proportionable ordering, fit couching, seemelie compacting of things together.*
Strumosité: f. *The swelling of the throat.*
Stryge. *A Scriche-owle.*
Stuc: m. *A fine, and shining Potters clay; also, a compounded morter or clay made of lime, sand, paper, and other materialls; verie fit for Jmagerie.*
Studieux: m. euse: f. *Studious, painefull, earnest, carefull; desirous or greedie of; addicted or deuoted vnto.*
Stupeur: f. *Stupor, numnesse, vnsencibleneſſe, dullneße, astonishment, astoniedneße.*
Stupide: com. *Stupide, benummed, sencelesse; dull, blockish, lumpish; amazed, appalled, astonied.*
Stupidement. *Sencelesly, dully, blockishly, lumpishly; with much amazement.*
Stupidité. *Stupiditie, sencelesnesse; dullneße, blockishnesse; astonishment, amazement.*
Stygial: m. ale: f. *Of, in, or belonging to, the Stygian lake.*
Stygien: m. enne: f. *Stygian; or as* Stygial; *whence;*
Femme stygienne. *A most fell, cruell, or diuellish queane.*
Stygieux. *as* Stygial.
Styl: m. *as* Stil.
Style: m. *The pinne of a paire of writing tables; also, a stile; a vaine, forme, or manner of indicting; also, the strict forme, order, or course obserued in iudiciall pleadings, and proceeding.*
Choses qui sont de style. *Things which haue an ordinarie passage, or proceeding; things of course.*
Faillir au style. *To commit an error in pleading.*
Stylet: m. *A Stiletto; the small, and sharpe-pointed dagger, forbidden in many townes of Jtalie.*
Stylobate: f. *The footstall of a Pillar; or the whole frame of the lower part thereof.*
Styptique: com. *Styptick, restrictiue, astringent, costiue, binding.*
Styrax. *Looke* Storax.
Su: m. *The South; also, an Elder tree.*
Su. *as* Sus.
Suader. *To persuade, aduise, moue, induce by reasons.*
Suadeur: m. *A persuader, aduiser, mouer, inducer.*
Süages: m. *Sweatings; or, things which procure sweating.*
Suaire: m. *The peece of linnen wherein the face of a dead man is wrapped; also, a hand-kercher, or linnen cloth to wype on.*
Suais. *Looke* Suays.
Süant: m. ante: f. *Sweating.*
A poulce süant. *By ynch, or thumbe-measure; the breadth of a thumbe giuen betweene euerie yard in measuring.*
Suaseur: m. *A persuader, inducer, aduiser.*
Suasif: m. iue: f. *Persuasiue; able, or fit to persuade.*
Suasion: f. *A persuasion, aduise, exhortation.*
Suasoire: com. *Suasorie, persuading.*
Suave: com. *Sweet, pleasant, palate-pleasing, delicious; smooth; courteous, gentle, meeke, soft.*
Suavement. *Sweetly, deliciously; softly; smoothly; gently, courteously.*
Suavité: f. *Suauitie, sweetnesse, deliciousnesse; softnesse, smoothneße; courtesie, gentlenesse, meekenesse.*
Suays: m. *A kind of frogs which be seene onely in some parts of France.*
Subalterne: com. *Subalterne, secundarie, vnder, inferior, subiect vnto others.*
Subarbe: f. *The museroll, or nose-band of a bridle, &c.*
Subaudition: f. *Part of a mans meaning expressed, and the rest vnderstood; or, such an expressing.*
Subcostale: f. *A thin, and smooth skin, which clothes the inner side of the ribbes, and couers the vitall parts contained within the bulke.*
Subdelegation: f. *A subdelegation, or substitution.*
Subdelegué: m. ée: f. *Subdelegated, substituted.*
Subdeleguer. *To subdelegate, substitute, appoint another vnder him; or to referre ouer a busineße, &c, committed.*
Subdial: m. ale: f. *All-open, wholly discouered; without the house, abroad in the ayre.*
Subdiviser. *To subdiuide; to make a second diuision, or a diuision of a diuision.*
Subelin. Martres subelinnes. *Sable-Martins; the best kind of Martins.*
Subet: m. *A Lethargie.*
Subhastation: f. *An Outrope, Outcry, Portsale; or the selling of things by Outrope, &c: (The auncient Romans vsed (especially in time of warre) to hold their Outcries vnder a kind of speare, or iauelin.)*
Subhasté: m. ée: f. *Sold, or passed away, by Outcry.*
Subhaster. *To passe away goods by Outcry, or Portsale; to sell things publikely to them which will giue most.*
Subiacent: m. ente: f. *Subiacent; vnder-lying.*
Subiect: m. *A subiect, vassall; vnderling; seruant, thrall; and particularly the peasant, who being bound, by his tenure, to pay scot and lot vnto his Lord, is not bound to follow him to the warres without pay.*
Qui de ses subiects est haï n'est pas seigneur de son païs: Pro. *Poore is the Prince thats hated by his subiects; as good loose all his countrey as their hearts.*
Vn seigneur de paille vainc bien vn subiect d'acier: Pro. *A Lord of straw subdues a slaue of steele.*
Subiect: m. ecte: f. *Subiect, vaßall, vnder; seruant, thrall; obedient; lyable vnto; gouerned by; vnder the iurisdiction of.*
Subiect aux biens. *Couetous;* à sa bouche. *Jntemperate;* à ses fantasies. *Fantasticall, &c.*
Subiection: f. *Subiection, thraldome, seruitude; obedience,*

dience; restraint, limitation.
Subier: m. *The Corke-tree; the tree whose barke is Corke.*
Subinfeudation: f. *A subinfeoffing; the creating of an vnder tenure, or tenancie in fee.*
Subioindre. *To subioyne, adde or put vnto, bring or set vnder.*
Subit: m. ite: f. *Swift, quicke, hastie, speedie; suddaine, vnthought of, vnlooked for.*
Subitain. *Looke* Soudain.
Subitement. *Swiftly, quickly, speedily, in a trice, out of hand, by and by; suddainely, at vnawares.*
Subjugation: f. *A subduing, taming, yoking, or bringing vnder obedience.*
Subiugé: m. ée: f. *Tamed, subdued, vanquished, brought vnder the yoke of obedience.*
Subiuguer. *To subdue, vanquish, tame, bring into subiection, or vnder the yoke.*
Subler. *To whistle; to whizze.*
Sublet: m. *A whistling, or whizzing noise.*
Sublim. *as* Sublime, *or* Sublin.
Sublimation: f. *A sublimating, raising, or lifting vp; also, a sublimation, distillation, or extraction.*
Sublimatoire: m. *A sublimatorie; an instrument, or vessell, of sublimation.*
Sublimé: m. Sublimatum, *or Sublimie, Arsenick, Ratsbane.*
Sublime: com. *Sublime, high, loftie, haughtie, honourable, statelie.*
Sublimé: m. ée: f. *Raised, exalted, aduanced vnto dignitie; also, sublimated, or mixed with Arsenicke; also, sublimed, extracted, or distilled.*
Argent sublimé. *Mercurie subtilized by the Limbecke.*
Sublimément. *Loftily, highly, haughtily, statelily, honourably.*
Sublimer. *To raise, aduance, exalt, set vp on high; also, to sublimate, or mingle with Arsenick; also, to sublime, distill, extract, or subtilize by distilling.*
Sublimité: f. *Sublimitie, loftinesse, haughtinesse, highnesse, statelinesse.*
Sublin: m. ine: f. *High, sublime, loftie, haughtie; also, refined, most fine, exquisite, excellent.*
Submergé: m. ée: f. *Submerged, plunged or sunke vnder, whirkened or ouerwhelmed in, boulged or ouerflowne by, the water.*
Submerger. *To submerge; to plunge or sinke vnder, whirken or ouerwhelme by, dip, drowne, or boulge in, the water.*
Submersion: f. *A submersion, plunging, sinking, ouerwhelming, drowning, boulging.*
Subministrateur: m. *A subministrator, an vnder-furnisher, an inferior officer.*
Subministration: f. *A subministration, (inferior) seruice, vnder-hand supply.*
Subministré: m. ée: f. *Subministred, serued vnder, supplyed or furnished vnder-hand.*
Subministrer. *To subminister, or serue vnder; also, to furnish or supply (vnder-hand, or vnder another.)*
Submirmilant. ¶Rab. *as* Submurmurant.
Submis. *Looke* Soubmis.
Submurmurant. *Murmuring, muttering, mumbling to himselfe.*
Subornation: f. *A subornation, or suborning; the making, instructing, or bringing in of a false witnesse; also, a corrupting, peruerting, deprauing.*
Subornement. *as* Subornation.
Suborner. *To suborne; to make, prepare, instruct, foist or bring in, a false witnesse; also, to depraue, corrupt, peruert, persuade or allure vnto lewdnesse.*
Suborneur: m. *A suborner of witnesses; a corrupter of others.*
Subrecart: m. *An assistant, or associate; one whom a Judge calleth to sit with him; one whom Phisitions, for an important cure, or consultation, chuse to ioyne with them.*
Subredorade: f. *A great Guilt-head, or the greatest of Guilt-heads.*
Subreptice: com. *Subrepticious, or surrepticious; foisted, or falsely crept in; supposed; indirectly come by.*
Subreptif: m. iue: f. *Subreptiue; or, as* Subreptice.
Subreption: f. *A subreption; supposition, foisting or false creeping in; also, a filching, purloining, or stealing away.*
Subreptivement. *Subrepticiously, priuily, vnder-hand, pilferingly, by stealth, by false meanes.*
Subricant. *Looke* Subrecart.
Subrogation: f. *A subrogation, substitution, deputation, appointing another in the roome of.*
Subrogé: m. ée: f. *Subrogated, substituted, deputed, appointed in the roome of another.*
Subroger. *To subrogate, substitute, depute, or appoint in the roome of another.*
Subrogué. & Subroguer. *as* Subrogé, & Subroger.
Subsecutif: m. iue: f. *Subsecutiue; consequent; immediately following or depending on, succeeding in the necke of.*
Subsecutivement. *Subsequently, consequently, immediately, hard at the heeles of.*
Subside: m. *Helpe, aid, assistance, reliefe, succour; also, a subsidie.*
Subsidiaire: com. *Subsidiarie, succouring; assistant; sent, or giuen to the aid of.*
Subsidiairement. *Subsidiarily, helpingly, by way of succour.*
Subsidier. *To lay subsidies on.*
Subsistence: f. *Subsistence, continuance, abode, remaining, a standing to, or by, it.*
Subsister. *To subsist, abide, remaine, stand his ground, keepe or continue his place.*
Substance: f. *Substance, matter, stuffe.*
Substancier. *To sustaine, feed, nourish, fatten, stuffe with matter, fill with substance.*
Substanté. & Substanter. *Looke* Sustenté, &c.
Substantifique: com. *Substantiall, or substance-yeelding.*
Substantieux: m. euse: f. *Substantiall, stuffie.*
Substitu: m. *A Substitute; a Deputie, Vicegerent, Lieutenant.*
Substitué: m. ée: f. *Substituted, deputed, ordained or put in the place of another.*
Substituer. *To substitute, ordaine, depute, appoint, place, or put in the roome of another.*
Substitut: m. *A substitute.*
Substitution: f. *A substitution, or deputation; the appointing, or placing of one in the roome of another.*
Substraction: f. *A substraction; a withdrawing or taking away from; a diminution of.*
Subterfuge: m. *A subterfuge; a shift; a priuie slip, craftie euasion, cunning escape; a corner or hole to slip into, or slinke out at.*
Subterrain: m. aine: f. *Thats vnder the earth.*
Subtil: m. *A kind of small gold or siluer thread.*
Subtil: m. ile: f. *Subtill, craftie, wilie, wittie, cunning.*
Subtilement. *Subtilly, wittily, cunningly, craftily.*
Subtiliant: m. ante: f. *Extenuating, subtilizing.*

Subtiliation: f. *A subtiliation, or subtilizing.*
Subtilier. *To subtilize, extenuate, make thinne, fine; lesse or more slender; also, to plot, inuent, contriue, deuise; imagine, muse.*
Subtilisement: m. *A subtilizing.*
Subtiliser. *To subtilize; to make thinne, fine, small.*
Subtiliseur: m. *A subtilizor.*
Subtilité: f. *Subtiltie, wittinesse; craft, cunning.*
Subtilizer. *Looke* Subtilier.
Subvenir. *To helpe, aid, succour, assist, relieue, maintaine.*
Subventané: m. ée: f. *Windie, full of wind, that hath nothing but wind in it.*
Subvention: f. *Subuention, helpe, aid, reliefe, succour; also, a subsidie.*
Subvention de procez. *An imposition of* 100 s Tourn: *vpon euerie Action thats aboue, and* 40 s *vpon euerie one that is vnder,* 100 *pounds.*
Subversion: f. *A subuersion, ruine, ouerthrow.*
Subverti: m. ie: f. *Subuerted, ouerturned, ruined, ouerthrowne, destroyed.*
Subvertir. *To subuert, ouerturne, destroy, ruine, ouerthrow.*
Subvertisseur: m. *A subuerter, ouerturner, ouerthrower.*
Suc: m. *Sap, iuice, moisture.*
Succarin: m. ine: f. *Of sugar; Looke* Succrin.
Succeder. *To succeed, follow, ensue, haue issue, come to, or come to passe; also, to inherite.*
Succelent. *Looke* Succulent.
Succement: m. *A sucking.*
Succentriné: m. ée: f. *Verie finely searsed.*
Succenturieux: m. euse: f. *Supplying the number, filling vp the place, of one that is absent, or dead.*
Succer. *To sucke.*
Succeron: m. *A certaine little, and long-nosed vessell of earth, whereby young infants are suckled, or fed.*
Succes: m. *Successe, issue, euent, the end, or falling out of a matter; hap, lucke.*
Successeur: m. *A successor, succeeder, follower.*
Successif: m. iue: f. *Successiue, belonging to succession.*
Succession: f. *Succession; inheritance; a succeeding, or following in the place of another.*
Par succession de temps. *In time; in tract, processe, or continuance of time, after some dayes or yeares.*
Successivement. *Successiuely, one after another.*
Succez. *Looke* Succes.
Succif: m. iue: f. *Sucking; or, which may be sucked.*
Succinctement. *Succinctly, compendiously, shortly, briefely.*
Succion: f. *A sucking.*
Succocitrin. *Looke* Cicotrin.
Succombé: m. ée: f. *Ouercharged, ouercome; fayled, or fallen downe through faintnesse.*
Succomber. *To faile, faint, fall or lye downe, vnder a burthen; to yeeld, giue way; be subdued, ouercharged, ouercome.*
Succot. *Full of iuice.*
Succoté. *Sucked gently, and smackingly; also, kissed often.*
Succoter. *To sucke gently, and smackingly; also, to kisse often.*
Succotrin: m. *An extraordinarie fine searse; also, as* Cicotrin.
Succotriné: m. ée: f. *Searsed verie finely.*
Succré: m. ée: f. *Sugred, sugrie.*
Succrin: m. ine: f. *Sugrie, of sugar, mingled or seasoned with sugar, sweet as sugar.*
Alun succrin. *Allum compounded of Rosewater, whites of egges, and roche Allum; vsed much by some women for the clensing, or whitening of their faces.*
Succulent: m. ente: f. *Succulent, sappie, moist, full of iuice.*
Succussation: f. *A hard shaking, a ioulting, a violent iogging.*
Sucement: m. *A sucking.*
Sucer. *To sucke.*
Suceron: m. *Looke* Succeron.
Sucher. *The same.* ¶Picard.
Suçotant. *Greedily, or gently, and smackingly, sucking.*
Sucre: m. *Sugar.*
Sucre penidial. *Fine and white sugar whereof Penets &c, are made; also, the Penets themselues.*
Sucré: m. *whence,* Faire le sucré. *Looke vnder* Faire.
Sucré: m. ée: f. *Sugred; sugrie; sweet as, or sweetened with, sugar.*
Sucrée: f. *A nice, quaint, squeamish, or precise wench; whence;*
Faire la sucrée. *To mince it, or make it goodlie; to shew her selfe verie coy.*
Sucrier: m. *A Comfet-maker.*
Sucrin. *Looke* Succrin.
Suction: f. *A sucking.*
Sud: m. *The South.*
Sudorifique: com. *Procuring, or causing sweat.*
Suée: f. *A sweat, or sweating.*
Sueil: m. *The threshold of a doore; also, the soyle of a wild Bore; the mire wherein he commonly walloweth.*
Suëment: m. *A sweating.*
Suër. *To sweat.*
Suërie: f. *A sweating.*
Le Païs de suërie. *Cornelius his Tub; a countrey frequented by the Pockie.*
Süest: m. *The Southeast wind.*
Suetolt: m. *The lumpe, puddle, sea-Owle; (an ouglie fish.)*
Suëtte: f. *The sweating sicknesse; also, a kind of small Dace, or Dare fish.*
Suëur: m. *A sweater.*
Suëur: f. *Sweat.*
Suëux: m. euse: f. *Sweating; taking great paines.*
Suffire. *To suffice, content, satisfie, giue enough vnto, be sufficient for.*
Suffisamment. *Sufficiently, fully, enough, with good satisfaction.*
Suffisance: f. *Sufficiencie, enough, fullnesse, plentie, abundance, the belly-full; satisfaction, contentment.*
Qui a suffisance il a prou de bien, qui n'a suffisance n'a rien: Prov. *He thats content, of riches hath great store, but he thats discontented is most poore.*
Suffisant. *Sufficient, enough, full; able, of worth.*
Sufflegan. ¶Rab. *A Suffragan.*
Suffocation: f. *A suffocation, stifling, strangling, whirkening, choaking.*
Suffoqué: m. ée: f. *Suffocated, stifled, choaked, whirkened, smoothered, whose breath is stopped.*
Suffoquer. *To suffocate, smoother, choake, stifle, stop the breath of.*
Suffragant: m. *A Suffragant, or Suffragan, a Bishops deputie.*
Suffrage: m. *A suffrage, voice; consent, fauour; good word, in an election.*
Suffumigation: f. *A suffumigation; a smoaking, or fuming*

ming vnder; the smoake which is, from vnder a stoole, receiued into the bodie, for the diseases of the guts, fundament, or matrix.

Suffusion: f. *A suffusion, or powring vpon; a spreading abroad.*

Suffusion des yeux. *A pinne, or web in the eyes.*

Suggerer. *To suggest, prompt, or put in mind of; also, to minister, giue, yeeld, find, furnish, or allow, vnto.*

Suggestion: f. *A suggestion, prompting, telling, inducement, putting in mind of.*

Suggillation, & Suggiller. *as* Sugillation, &c.

Sugillation: f. *A blacke and blue marke or spot on the face, &c, by a blow; also, the bloudshot of an eye; also, reproach, deprauation, slaunder; detractation.*

Sugillé: m. ée: f. *Marked with blacke, and blue spots; also, nipped, taunted, galled, reproued; blemished, reproached, depraued.*

Sugiller. *To make blacke and blue with strokes; also, to nip, taunt, gall, reproue maliciously, reproach, blemish, depraue.*

Suject, ou Sujet. *Looke* Subject.

Suiection. *Looke* Subiection.

Suier: m. *The Elder tree.*

Suif: m. *Tallow, suet, substantiall fat.*

Visage de suif. *A tallow face; bleake visage, pale countenance.*

Suiffe. *The Deale tree, a kind of Firre; (also, the Dace fish; or as* Vandoise. ¶Lionnois.)

Suil: m. *The threshold of a doore.*

Suille: com. *Hoggish.*

Suin: m. *The Elder tree.*

Suin de laine. *The filth, greasinesse, or oylinesse of sheepes wooll before it be washed.*

Suin de verre. *Sandeuer; the fattie substance floating on glasse when it is red-hot in the furnace, and which being cold is as hard as stone, yet brittle, and easily broken.*

Suineux: m. euse: f. *Greasie, oylie, or filthie, as the vnwashed wooll of sheepe.*

Suinter. *To giue, yeeld, or sweat, as stones against moist weather.*

Suite: f. *A suit, or pursuit, &c; as* Suitte.

Suites. *The cods of a wild Bore.*

Suitte: f. *A chase, pursuit, prosecution of, suit against; also, a sequele, issue, consequent, or consequence; also, a succession, continuance, or vnintermitted course of things; also, the trayne, attendants, or followers of a (great) person; the companie he drawes along with him.*

Suitte en acquisition, ou saisie; est, quand le creancier, ores que l'hypotheque luy manque, ne laisse de suyvre la chose saisie sur son debteur, soit contre celuy qui l achetée par apres, ou contre celuy qui l'a saisie.

Suitte par hypotheque; c' est quand vn creancier suit son hypotheque ou contre l'acquereur, ou contre le creancier posterieur. ¶L'Oiseau.

Droict de suitte de bestes; de disme; & de gens, ou de personnes serves. *Looke vnder* Droict.

Serfs de suitte. *Such as (like our villeins regardant to a Mannor) must not depart out of their Lords dominion or Territorie; or if they doe, he may pursue them whethersoeuer, and compell them to returne.*

Bourse n'a suitte. *When a tenant workes in the tythegrounds of a forreine Lord with hired cattell; or when he himselfe is hired to worke in them for mony, his Lord can haue no aduantage against him by his priuiledge of* Suitte de disme; *(for which looke vnder* Droict.)

Meuble n'a point de suitte par hypotheque; viz. l'acquereur du meuble hypothequé n'en peut estre inquieté: Et, la suitte, & ordre d'hypotheque n'a lieu aux meubles entre plusieurs creanciers ausquels ils sont hypothequez. ¶L'Oiseau.

Suittes. *Looke* Suites.

Suivamment. *Consequently, afterwards.*

Suivant: m. *A follower.*

Les suivants. *The Maisters of Requests, tearmed so in old time.*

Le plus proche suivant du degré. *The next full kinsman, or the next heire.*

Suivre. *Looke* Suyvre.

Sul: m. *An Elder tree.*

Sulphureitez: f. *Sulphurie things.*

Sulphureux: m. euse: f. *Sulphurous, full of sulphure.*

Sulphurin: m. ine: f. *Sulphurie, of sulphure.*

Suls: m. *An Elder tree.*

Vn Canon de suls. *A kex; or, a hollow stick, or branch of Elder; or, a Pot-gunne made thereof.*

Sultan: m. *A Sultan, or Souldan; a King, Prince, or Soueraigne; also, a Turkish coyne of gold worth about* vj s vj d *sterling.*

Sultane: f. *as* Soutane; *also, a Sultanesse; or soueraigne Princesse.*

Sultanin. *A Turkish coyne of gold worth about* vij s vj d *sterling.*

Sumach. *Sumacke, Curriers Sumacke, leather Sumack; (a shrub.)*

Sumach de cuisine. *The berrie, or fruit of that shrub, vsed heretofore in stead of salt, especially in sawces; whence, as it seemes, we call it, meat Sumacke, and sawce Sumacke.*

Sumelle. *Looke* Semelle.

Sumerger. *To sinke, submerge, ouerwhelme, drowne.*

Sumettre. *Looke* Soubmettre.

Sumis: m. ise: f. *Submitted, humbled, subiected, or yeelded vnto.*

Sumptüaire. *Looke* Somptüaire.

Sumptuosité: f. *Sumptuousnesse, great costlinesse, wastfullnesse, excessiue expence.*

Superabondance: f. *Superabundance, superfluitie, excesse, ouermuch.*

Superabonder. *To superabound, exceed, be excessiue, tend to superfluitie.*

Superbe: com. *Prowd, high-minded, arrogant, surlie, disdainefull; haughtie, loftie, statelie, sumptuous; magnificent, maiesticall.*

Supercedé: m. ée: f. *Surceassed, left off, giuen ouer.*

Articles supercedez. *Parts of an accompt neither allowed, nor vtterly reiected, vpō the accomptants humble suit for a further day to bring in some principall acquittances, or peeces of importance; which day if he slip, he falls into arrerage, and an Execution is presently awarded against him.*

Superceder. *To surceasse, leaue off, giue ouer.*

Supercession. *Looke* Supersession.

Supercherie: f. *Supercherie; foule play; an iniurie, wrong, affront, brauado, assault, on a suddaine, or vpon great aduantage;* (vn mauvais tour à l'impourveu;) *also, a superfluitie, ouerplus, or ouercharge.*

Supereminence: f. *Supereminence, prerogatiue, excellencie aboue others.*

Superengendrez. *Children begot at seuerall times by superfetation.*

Superer. *To vanquish, ouercome, surmount, passe, exceed, excell.*

Supereroguer. *To superarogate, giue ouerplus, doe more then needs, or is required.*

Superfetation. *Looke* Superfoetation.
Superficie: f. *The superficies, or surface; the outside, or outmost part of a thing.*
Superficiel: m. *The same.*
Superficiel: m. elle: f. *Superficiall, outward, exterior, vtmost.*
Ventre superficiel. *as* Epigastre.
Superficiellement. *Superficially, outwardly.*
Superflu: m. *A superfluitie, ouerplus, excesse.*
Superflu: m. uë: f. *Superfluous, profuse, excessiue, ouermuch.*
Superfluité: f. *Superfluitie, excesse, profusenesse, an ouerplus, more then needs.*
Superfoetation: f. *A superfétation, or second conceiuing; a breeding of young vpon young.*
Superfoeter. *To conceiue a second time; to breed young vpon young.*
Supergurgiter. *To ouerflow (an Inkhornisme in* Rabelais.)
Superieur: m. eure: f. *Superior, vpper, higher, better, former, elder, senior.*
Superimposer. *To superimpose, surcharge, or charge anew; to lay new impositions on things alreadie taxed.*
Superimposition: f. *A superimposition, or surcharge; an imposition vpon an imposition.*
Superintendance: f. *Superintendancie, a principall ouersight, gouernment, or care ouer.*
Superintendant: m. *A Superintendent; a principall ouerseer.*
Superintendant des finances. *The Superintendent, or chiefe* Intendant *of the Exchequer; is, in all points of authoritie, equall with the Lord high Treasurer of France (an Officer of long time out of date;) yet is he but a Commissioner, whereas the Treasurer was an officer of the Crowne.*
Superiorité: f. *Superioritie, preheminence, eldership, senioritie.*
Superlatif: m. iue: f. *Superlatiue, exceeding, passing, of the highest degree; also, loftie, statelie, haughtie, all on the huffe.*
Superlatiuement. *Superlatiuely, exceedingly, in the highest degree; also, loftily, haughtily, in a huffe.*
Supernater. *To swimme aboue, aloft, or ouer, to float on; also, to ouerflow.*
Supernaturel: m. elle: f. *Supernaturall, metaphisicall, aboue nature.*
Supernaturellement. *Supernaturally.*
Supernel: m. elle: f. *Supernall, high, chiefe, aboue.*
Supernellement. *Supernally, highly, on high, from aboue.*
Supernumeraire: com. *Supernumerarie, ouer and besides the iust or prefixed number, superfluous, redundant, ouerplus.*
Superscription: f. *A superscription, inscription, title.*
Supersedé: m. ée: f. *Surceased, &c; Looke* Supercedé.
Supersession: f. *A surceasing, leauing off, giuing ouer; and in Exchequer matters, the suspension of an Accompt vpon the Accomptants humble suit for a further day to bring in some principall Acquittance, or Instrument for his full discharge; which if hee faile to doe, he is forthwith seuerely proceeded against.*
Superstitieusement. *Superstitiously, ouerscrupulously, ceremoniously, curiously.*
Superstitieux: m. euse: f. *Superstitious, ouerscrupulous, too ceremonious, more curious about, or fearefull of, a (diuine) thing then needs.*
Superstition: f. *Superstition; excesse of scruple or ceremonie in matters of religion, idle worship, vaine reuerence; a superfluous, needlesse, or ill-gouerned deuotion.*
Supinateur: m. *A muscle in the wrist, seruing to turne the palme of the hand vpwards.*
Suppedité: m. ée: f. *Throughly supplyed, furnished, or ministred vnto; also, fully subdued, vanquished, or trodden on.*
Suppediter. *To supply throughly, furnish sufficiently, giue or minister enough vnto; also, to vanquish, ouercome, subdue, tread or bring vnder.*
Suppied: m. *A footstoole, or any thing set vnder the foot for the better setling, or stay thereof.*
Suppied d'orgues. *The footstoole, or pedalls to a paire of Organs.*
Supplanté: m. ée: f. *Supplanted, rooted, or tripped vp; ouerthrowne, trodden vnder foot; also, preuented, beguiled, or beguiled by preuention.*
Supplanter. *To supplant, root or trip vp, foyle or put vnder foot; also, to preuent, beguile, deceiue, or deceiue by preuenting.*
Suppléer. *To supply, furnish, close, fill, or make vp.*
Supplément: m. *A supplement, supply, supplying; a furnishing, filling, or making vp of defectiue numbers, emptie roomes, void places, &c.*
Supplesse: f. *Suppleneße, plyablenesse, actiuitie, nimblenesse.*
Suppliant: m. *A suppliant, petitioner, humble suitor.*
Suppliant: m. ante: f. *Suppliant, beseeching.*
Supplication: f. *A supplication, prayer, humble request or suit; also, a little packet of grapes wrapped vp in figleaues one by one, and thereby lasting, at the least, two yeares.*
Supplice: m. *Punishment, chastisement, correction, torment.*
Nul vice sans son supplice: Pro. *No vice without its punishment; or, each vice is to it selfe a punishment.*
Tel vice tel supplice: Prov. *Like paine shall chastice thine excesse to that wherein thou didst transgreße.*
Supplier. *Humbly to pray, petition, intreat, request, beseech, or be suitor vnto.*
Suppliment. *Looke* Supplement.
Support: m. *Support; a prop, or stay; fauour, maintenance; helpe, succour, assistance.*
Supportable: com. *Supportable, tollerable, beareable.*
Supportation: f. *A supportation; bearing, abiding; a boulstering, succouring, assisting.*
Ce qui soit dit avec supportation; viz. *by fauor, or vnder correction.*
Supporté: m. ée: f. *Supported, sustained, boulstered, borne with, or vp; fauored, assisted, succoured; tollerated, suffered, indured.*
Supporter. *To support, sustaine, stay or beare vp; to boulster, fauor; assist, succour; to tollerate, indure, abide, or beare with.*
Supposé: m. ée: f. *Suppôsed, imagined, meant, vnderstood; also, vnderset, or put vnder; and suppositious, suborned, foisted, or put in for another; whence;*
Enfant supposé. *A changeling.*
Supposé que. *(Aduerbially; or as an absolute Ablatiue;) albeit, although, notwithstanding, or howsoeuer that.*
Supposement: m. *A supponing, or putting of a thing vnder*

vnder another; a suborning, foisting, forging, thrusting of bad stuffe among, or in lieu of, that which is good.

Supposer. *To suppone; to put, lay, or set vnder; to suborne, forge, counterfeit, foist or thrust in false things among, or in stead of, true; also, to suppose, imagine, meane, vnderstand, more then's expressed.*

Supposer vn enfant. *To change a child.*

Supposeur: m. *A suborner, foister, forger, counterfeiter.*

Suppositoire: m. *A Suppositarie; made of honey, and salt boyled vnto the consistence of paste, and fashioned somewhat like a finger.*

Suppost: m. *A Deputie, one that is put in the roome of another; a suborned, counterfeit, forged, or foisted-in peece; also, a disciple, or scholler; also, an inferior, or vnder officer in a Court of Justice.*

Vn suppost du diable. *A limme of the diuell.*

Quelque bon suppost vous le dira. *Some good fellow or other will tell it you.*

Suppression: f. *Suppression, a suppressing or holding downe; a concealement; a stopping, or staying.*

Supprimé: m. ée: f. *Suppressed, held downe, kept vnder; hidden, concealed; stopped, retained, restrained; suffocated; base, low, soft; short.*

Supprimer. *To suppresse, represse, oppresse; hold vnder, keepe downe; conceale, hide; stop, retaine, restraine vnlawfully; suffocate; humble.*

Suppuratif: m. iue: f. *Suppuratiue, mattaring, drawing to a head, causing to mattar.*

Suppuration: f. *A suppuration, or mattaring; a gathering to a mattarie head; also, a breaking and clensing thereof.*

Suppuré: m. ée: f. *Suppured, growne mattarie; resolued into mattar; also, voided, or drained of such mattar; fully clensed.*

Suppurer. *To suppure; a byle, or impostume to become soft, resolue into mattar, or grow to a mattarie head; also, to breake, and void, or draine it; fully to clense it.*

Supputation: f. *A supputation, account, reckoning, supposition, coniecture, surmise.*

Sur: m. *The South.*

Sur: m. sure: f. *Sowre, sharpe, eagar, tart.*

Sur. *On, vpon, ouer, aboue; before; at, by, hard by, toward, about; also, touching, or concerning.*

Avoir vn ieu sur. *To haue a game with.*

Surabonder. *To superabound, redound, exceed, ouerflow.*

Surachapt: m. *An ouerbuying; a bargaine too deerely bought, or for which too much hath beene giuen.*

Suracheter. *To ouerbuy, pay too deerely, giue too much for.*

Suradjouster. *To giue vantage, adde more, put moreouer.*

Suragé: m. ée: f. *Decrepite, ouer-old, growne farre in yeares.*

Sural: m. ale: f. *as* Sur; *or, sowrish.*

Surale: f. *A great veine vnder the bought of the knee; Looke vnder* Veine.

Surandoillier: m. *The beankler, or second branch of a Deeres head; Looke* Surendouiller.

Surannation: f. *A growing old, stale, or aboue a yeares date; and, a cause not followed or called on, a sentence, commission, or command not executed, within the yeare and day.*

Suranné: m. ée: f. *Aboue a yeare passed or old, of more then one yeares date or age; also, stale, past the best, ouerworne with yeares.*

Suranner. *To passe, or exceed the compasse of a yeare; to be of more then one yeares date or age; also, to heape yeares vpon yeares, grow stale, wax verie old.*

Suranter. *To graffe, settle, or fasten vpon.*

Surattendre. *To goe faire and softly before, to slacke his pace that another may ouertake him; to attend or stay for, not altogether, but in passing easily forward; also, to attend, or wait too long.*

Qui bien attend ne surattend: Prov. *He that expects good lucke stayes not too long; or, he that waits to good purpose ouerwaits not.*

Suravancer. *To aduance too farre, or vpon.*

Surbaigné: m. ée: f. *Bathed, bedewed ouer.*

Surbaissé; *whence,* Voute surbaissée. *A flat vault, or arche.*

Surbandé: m. ée: f. *Bound, welted, or garded ouer.*

Surbastir. *To build vpon.*

Surbatture: f. *A surbating.*

Sur-belheur: m. *The name of a certaine tart Apple.*

Surboire. *To drinke vpon, or drink more then is needfull after, meat.*

Surceance. *Looke* Surseance.

Surcens: m. *A* Cens *raised vpon a* Cens; *a second rent, or* Cens *created vpon the alienation of land* Censuel; *as when a tenant* Censier *passes away his estate with reseruation of a rent or* Cens *to himselfe, besides that which was formerly due, and is still to be payed, vnto the Lord.*

Surcense: m. *as* Surcens.

Surcensier: m. *One that charges land with a new, or second* Cens.

Surcensier: m. ere: f. *whence,* Rente surcensiere. *as* Surcens.

Surcharge: f. *A surcharge, or new charge; a charge vpon a charge, load vpon a load, burthen vpon burthen.*

Surcharger. *To surcharge; ouerload, ouerburthen; or, lay load vpon load, burthen vpon burthen.*

Surciel: m. *The tester of a cloth of State, &c; the part thereof which hangs, commonly in a square forme, ouer the Princes head.*

Surconcevoir. *To conceiue young vpon young; or, as* Superfoeter.

Surcot: m. *An vpper kirtle; or garment worne ouer a kirtle.*

Surcottier: m. *The tenant vnto a* Cottier; *he to whom a* Cottier *hath let his land for a Rent, or* Cens.

Surcottiere: f. *Land, or an estate in land, held of a* Cottier *by Rent, or* Cens.

Surcouvert: m. te: f. *Couered ouer.*

Surcouvrir. *To couer ouer.*

Surcrest: m. *A crest vpon a crest; an vpper top, or crest.*

Surcrez. *as* Surcroist.

Surcroist: m. *A surplusage, ouer-measure, vantage, addition, amends; also, an ouer-growing, a rising or springing vpon.*

Surcroistre. *To ouergrow; to rise or spring vp on.*

Surculeux: m. euse: f. *Full of hard shootes, slips, or sprigs.*

Surdastre: com. *Deafish; somewhat deafe, hard or thicke of hearing.*

Surdité: f. *Deafenesse.*

Surdoré: m. ée: f. *Gilt ouer.*

Surdorer. *To gild ouer.*

Surdoreur: m. *A gilder ouer.*

Surdoreure: f. *A gilding ouer.*

Sureau: m. *An Elder tree; Looke* Suseau.

Sureau aquatic. *The water Elder, Whitten tree, Ople tree, Dwarfe-plane tree.*

Sureau de marais. *The same; or marish Elder.*
Sureau de montaigne. *The mountaine Elder, the wild Elder.*
Surelle: f. *Sorrell.*
Suremplir. *To fill vp, or to ouerfill.*
Surendouiller, ou Surentouiller: m. *The royall of a Stag, the Beancler of a Bucke; the second branch on either of their heads.*
Surer. *Looke* Seurer.
Sureté: f. *Suretie, safetie, securitie, assurance.*
Surface: f. *The surface; the superficies or vpper part, the first shew or outward face, of things.*
Surfaire. *To ouerprise, to hold at an ouer-deere rate.*
Surfaiseur: m. *One that ouerpriseth his ware.*
Surfaix: m. *A surfengle, or long girth.*
Surflorir. *To blossome vpon the fruit, or to bloome or blossome after the first blossomes are vaded.*
Surflot: m. *The rising of billow vpon billow, or the interchanged swelling of seuerall waues.*
Surflotter. *To floate or swimme vpon.*
Surfoncier: m. ere: f. *whence,* Rente surfonciere; à la difference de la premiere rente fonciere, qui est la plus ancienne, & premierement creée.
Surfondu: m. uë: f. *Melted away; also, powred vpon.*
Surfondre. *To melt away; also, to powre vpon.*
Surfriser. *To frizle ouer, to curle vpon.*
Surgallion: com. *A slouen, or slut (at* Blois.)
Surgeon. *Looke* Sourgeon.
Surgeonner. *To shoot out, spring, spurt vp.*
Surgermé: m. ée: f. *Sprung vp, spred abroad.*
Surgetté: m. ée: f. *Ouercast.*
Surgi: m. ie: f. *Arriued, come to shore, or neere the shore.*
Surgidoir: m. *as* Surgidoire.
Surgidoire: f. *A road, gulfe, or bosome of the sea, for shippes to ride in; (sometimes also the opposite, a Promontorie, Cape, or Bay of land entring into the sea; belike because they alwaies affoord a riding for ships;) also, the hole, or hollow of an impostume, or mattarie sore.*
Surgir. *To arriue, take land, goe ashore; or to ride, or draw neere the shore.*
Surgissant: m. ante: f. *Arriuing, comming to shore; or riding, as a ship, neere the shore.*
Surgissement: m. *An arriuing, taking land, going ashore; or a riding, or drawing, neere the shore.*
Surguinder. *To hoise vp on high.*
Surhasté: m. ée f. *Precipitated, ouerhastened; hastened vnseasonably, or before it time.*
Surhaster. *To precipitate, ouerhasten; hasten vnseasonably or before it time.*
Se surhaster. *To make too much hast, or more hast then good speed.*
Surhausser. *To hoise, raise, or lift vp on high.*
Se surhausser. *To swell, rise, increase.*
Suriect: m. *A couering, or ouercasting.*
Droict de suriect. *Power to adde vnto the last price thats offered at an Outcry.*
Suriectement: m. *An ouercasting, or casting vpon.*
Suriecter. *To ouercast, or cast vpon.*
Surillustre: com. *Superexcellent, most illustrious, exceedingly renowmed.*
Surimposition: f. *A surcharge; an ouer-great imposition, or, an imposition raised vpon an imposition.*
Surintendance: f. *Superintendencie, an ouerseeing.*
Surintendant: m. *A superintendent, an ouerseer.*
Surion. *Looke* Sourgeon.
Surlié: m. ée: f. *Tyed ouer, bound vpon.*
Surlier. *To tye ouer, to bind vpon.*
Surluire. *To shine, or cast a great light vpon.*
Surmaçonner. *To build vpon, or ouer.*
Surmanger. *To eat vpon, or immediately after, a meale; to eat more, to ouer-eat.*
Surmarcher. *To tread, or goe vpon.*
Surmeule: f. *An vpper Mill-stone.*
Surmesure: f. *Ouer-measure, too great measure.*
Surmontable: com. *Surmountable, surpassable, exceedable; subduable.*
Surmonté: m. ée: f. *Surmounted, surpassed, exceeded; subdued, vanquished, ouercome.*
Surmontement: m. *A surmounting, surpassing, exceeding; subduing, ouercomming.*
Surmontement des ioues. *A chuffie out-standing, or swelling of the cheekes, beyond all due, and comelie proportion.*
Surmonter. *To surmount, surpasse, get before; goe beyond; to subdue, vanquish, ouercome.*
Surmoust: m. *New or sweet wine.*
Surmulet: m. *A sore Mullet; or, the great sea-Barbell.*
Surnager. *To float, swimme aloft, ouer, or vpon.*
Surnaissance: f. *An ouergrowth, or growing vpon.*
Surnaissant. *Growing ouer, or vpon; succeeding.*
Surnaistre. *To grow ouer, or vpon; to succeed of.*
Surnom: m. *A surname.*
Surnommé: m. ée: f. *Surnamed.*
Surnommer. *To giue a surname vnto.*
Surnoyer. *To ouerdrowne, ouerwhelme; oretop, ouergrow.*
Suroest: m. *The Southwest wind.*
Suroindre. *To annoint vpon, or ouer.*
Suronder. *To float vpon the waues.*
Surop. *Looke* Syrop.
Suroreiller. *To round, or whisper in the eare.*
Suros: m. *A bonie, and vicious excrescence, growing about the cornet of a horses foot (and then called a ringbone) or vpon his shinne-bone (and then called a knot, or knob.)*
Surot. *as* Suros.
Surpasser. *To surpasse, goe beyond, exceed, surmount, excell.*
Surpayer. *To pay too deerely for.*
Surpeau: f. *An vpper skinne.*
Surpelis: m. *A Surplis.*
Surpendant: m. ante: f. *Hanging ouer, or vpon.*
Surpendre. *To hang vp, ouer, or vpon.*
Surpendu: m. uë: f. *Hanged vp, ouer, or vpon.*
Clef surpenduë. *Looke vnder* Clef.
Surpenduë: f. *A iettie; an out-iutting roome, &c, as* Soupenduë; *also, a roome, or false floore to lay wood in, gained betweene a cellar, (for that purpose made the deeper) and the roome which is next aboue it.*
Surpente: f. *The same in the first sence; or, as* Soupenduë.
Surpoids: m. *Ouerweight, or weight aboue iust weight; the ouerplus of weight put into the scole of a balance, and making it weigh downe, or ouerweigh that which is in the other scole.*
Surpepon: m. *A great Melon, or Pumpion.*
Surplis: m. *A Surplis.*
Surplus: m. *A surplusage, remainder, ouerplus.*
Au surplus. *(Aduerbially) besides, ouer, aboue, ouer and besides, ouer and aboue, moreouer, furthermore.*
Surpoil: m. *as* Serpaut.
Surpoinct: m. *Spech grease; an oylie grease scummed fron*

from peeces of lickored leather sodden in water for that purpose.

Surpoiser. *To ouerweigh, or weigh downe, a thing weighed with it.*

Surpoix. *Ouerweight;* *Looke* Surpoids.

Surposte: f. *A hurt vpon the Cornet of a horses foot, by crossing one foot ouer another.*

Surprendre. *To surprise; to take napping, tardie, at vnawares, in a trip, in the manner, in the deed doing; also, to preuent, intercept, or ouertake; also, to beguile, supplant, circumuent, ouerreach.*

Surpreneur: m. *A surprisor; oppressor; ouerreacher, cheater, cousener, craftie dealer.*

Surprins: m. inse: f. *Surprised; tripped, taken napping, or tardie; or in the manner; found in the deed doing; also, preuented, intercepted, or ouertaken; also, beguiled, ouerraught, supplanted, circumuented; also, oppressed, or hard layed to on the suddaine.*

La nuict nous a surprins. *Night is stolne vpon vs, or hath ouertaken vs, ere we were aware.*

Surprinse: f. *A surprisall, or suddaine taking; an assaulting, or comming vpon, a man ere he is aware; a tripping, taking tardie, finding in the manner; also, a tricke, fallacie, subtiltie, cauill, shift, euasion; a deceitfull quirke, or quidditie vsed by a cunning Pettifogger.*

Surpris: m. *Too great a price; a price exceeding the worth of that for which it is demaunded, or bidden.*

Surquanie: f. *Looke* Souquenie.

Surquerir. *To question too busily with.*

Surreptice: com. *Surrepticious, &c;* *Looke* Subreptice.

Surreption: f. *Looke* Subreption.

Surrester. *To rest, or pawse vpon.*

Surrogation. *Looke* Subrogation.

Surrogué: m. ée: f. *Surrogated, substituted, appointed in the roome of another.*

Surroguer. *To surrogate, substitute, place, depute, or appoint in the roome of another.*

Sursaillant: m. ante: f. *Ouerpeering; leaping on, or ouer; springing, or spurting ouer.*

Sursaille: f. *as* Sursault; *also, a leaping on, or ouer; also, an ouerpeering, or ouergrowing.*

Sursaillir. *To leape on, or ouer; also, to ouerpeere, ouergrow, spring or spurt vp ouer; also, to start vp suddainly, as one thats awaked by a great noise, &c.*

Sursangle: f. *A sursengle, or long girth.*

Sursault: m. *A suddaine starting, or surprise that makes one start.*

En sursault. *In a start, vnawares, on a suddaine.*

Sursaulter. *To leape, or spring ouer; to leape, or iert out on a suddaine; also, to start.*

Sursaut, & Sursauter. *as* Sursault, & Sursaulter.

Surseance: f. *A surceasing, or giuing ouer; a pawse, intermission, delay.*

Surseant: m. ante: f. *Surceasing, or giuing ouer; pawsing, intermitting, delaying; also, as* Resseant.

Surselle: f. *A broad, and great band, or thong of strong leather, &c, fastened on either side of a thill, and bearing vpon the pad, or saddle, of the thill-horse: About London it is called, the Ridge-rope.*

Sursemé: m. ée: f. *Sowen, or strewed vpon; also, measeld as a Hog.*

Sursemer. *To sow, strew, or sprinkle vpon.*

Sursemeur: m. *A sower, or strewer.*

Sursemeur de noises. *A make-bate, firebrand of contention, quarrell-breeder, dissention-sower.*

Sursemure: f. *The measeldnesse of Hogs.*

Surseoir. *To surcease, pawse, intermit, leaue off, giue ouer, delay or stay for a time.*

Sursis: m. ise: f. *Surceased, intermitted, left off, giuen ouer, stayed or delayed for a time.*

Sursomme: f. *Ouer-weight, an ouer-heauie burthen; whence;*

La sursomme abbat l'asne: Pro. *An extreame burthen swayes the sillie Asse.*

Sursoulte: f. *Too much boot giuen in an exchange, &c.*

Sursoyer. *as* Surseoir.

Sursueil: m. *The vpper sill, or head-peece of a doore; the peece of timber that lyes ouer a doore.*

Surtaux: f. *An ouer-cessing, ouer-rating, hoisting, surcharging, in the Subsidie booke, &c.*

Surtaxé: m. ée: f. *Ouer-cessed, hoisted, surcharged.*

Surtissu: m. uë: f. *Wouen, or whipt ouer with.*

Surtomber. *To fall ouer, or vpon.*

Survaleur: f. *Ouer-value.*

Surveille: f. *The day before the eue of a (great) holyday.*

Survenance: f. *An accident, hap, chaunce, vnexpected occurrence.*

Survenant: m. ante: f. *Happening, chauncing, occurring, befalling.*

Survendre. *To ouersell.*

Survenement: m. *Looke* Survenuë; *or, a happening, chauncing, befalling; and, a relieuing, helping, succouring.*

Survenir. *To happen, chaunce, fall out, light, befall, step in vnlooked for, occurre or come on a suddaine; also, to relieue, helpe, succour.*

Survenu: m. uë: f. *Happened, chaunced, light, fallen out, befallen, stept in vnlooked for, occurred or come on a suddaine; also, relieued, helped, succoured.*

Survenuë: f. *An accident, or vnexpected occurrence; a stepping, or comming, in vnlooked for; a suddaine lighting on, or falling into, companie.*

Surverser. *To powre vpon.*

Survestement: m. *An vpper garment.*

Survestir. *To put aloft vpon, or couer ouer with, a garment.*

Survivance: f. *A suruiuancie, suruiuing, outliuing; also, a remainder after a life.*

Survivance d'office. *A resignation of an Office, not absolute, but implying a condition, that the Resignor may, if he will, enioy it wholly during his life, and otherwise dispose of it if he happen to suruiue the Resignee.*

Survivant: m. *A suruiuor, outliuer, ouerliuer.*

Survivant: m. ante: f. *Suruiuing, outliuing.*

Survivre. *To suruiue, outliue, ouerliue, remaine after others.*

Survoler. *To flye ouer.*

Survoleter. *To flicker, or houer ouer.*

Survuidé: m. ée: f. *Emptied out of one vessell into another.*

Survuider. *To emptie out of one vessell into another.*

Sus. *On, vp, vpon, ouer, aboue.*

Sus avant. *On before, forward there hoe.*

Susan: m. *A yeare and day past; or the passing of a yeare and day, without performing that which should haue beene done within it.*

Susanné: m. ée: f. *Looke* Suranné.

Susanner. *as* Suranner.

Susat. *Of Elder, or Elder flowers; whence,* Vinaigre susat. *Elder Vineger.*

Susbarbe d'une bride. *The nose-band of a bridle.*

Susbout. (Adverb.) *Vp, an end.*
Suscept: m. *A subiect, or one that liues vnder the protection of another.*
Susceptible: com. *Susceptible, capable.*
Suscet. *as* Suscept.
Suscitateur: m. *A raiser, awaker, inciter, prouoker, stirrer vp.*
Suscitation: f. *A suscitation, awaking, raising, inciting, or stirring vp.*
Susciter. *To suscitate, awake, raise, quicken, kindle, incite, stirre vp.*
Susciteur: m. *A raiser, awaker, kindler, quickener, inciter, stirrer vp.*
Susclavier: m. ere: f. *Vpon the kannell bone; whence;*
Veine susclaviere. *The second maine ascendant branch of the hollow veine.*
Suscouche: f. *The Night-mare.*
Suseau: m. *An Elder tree; Looke* Sureau.
Suseau bas. *as* Suseau femelle.
Suseau femelle. *Wallwort, Danewort, Bloudwort, dwarfe Elderne.*
Petit suseau. *The same.*
Susespineux: m. euse: f. *Resting vpon the backe-bone; whence;*
Muscle susespineux. *A muscle whereby the arme is raised, or drawne vpwards.*
Suslambris: m. *The vpper seeling of a house, &c.*
Suspect: m. ecte: f. *Suspected, doubted, mistrusted, had in iealousie.*
Suspection: f. *Suspition, iealousie.*
Suspend. *as* Suspens.
Suspendre. *To suspend; remoue, depose, depriue, discharge for a time; also, to deferre, delay, keepe in doubt, hold off with vncertaine tearmes.*
Suspendu: m. uë: f. *Suspended; deposed, remoued, or discharged for a time; also, deferred, put off, delayed, held in suspence.*
Suspens. *Doubtfull, vncertaine, in suspence.*
Suspensif: m. iue: f. *Suspensiue, suspending, onely for a time.*
Suspension: f. *A suspension, or suspending; a deposall, remoue, or discharge, onely for a time.*
Suspensoire: com. *Hanging, dangling, swinging; suspensorie, in suspence.*
Suspensoires. *Certaine cords, or strings (hanging from the bedstead) for a sicke man to take hold of, and beare vp himselfe with, when he would remoue, or alter his lying.*
Suspied. (Adverb.) *vp, or afoot.*
Sustenté: m. ée: f. *Sustained, fed, nourished; maintained; comforted.*
Sustenter. *To sustaine, feed, nourish, find; maintaine; comfort.*
Sustentifique: com. *Sustaining, feeding, nourishing, maintaining.*
Sus-test: m. *The Pericranion, or skinne that couers the skull.*
Susteste d'une bride. *The head-peece of a bridle.*
Sus-ventre. *as* Epigastre.
Susuest: m. *A Southwest wind.*
Sutin: m. *The sweating sicknesse.*
Suture: f. *A suture, or seame; a sowing, ioyning, or fastening together.*
Suture coronale. *The coronall suture; a seame which compasses the forhead, or forepart of the head in forme of a halfe circle.*
Suture Lambdoïde. *A suture in the hinder part of the skull, toward the bottome whereof it begins, and ends when it meets with the* Sagitale.
Suture Mendeuse. *The suture, whereby the bone of the temples is diuided from the scull.*
Suture sagitale. *The seame which running straight on in the top of the scull, diuides the right side from the left, and (sometimes) descends euen to the nose.*
Suture scameuse. *as* Mendeuse.
Suture seiche. *A closing vp of wounds (especially in the face) by gluing on either side thereof a peece of indented cloth, whose points answering one another, are gently drawne together with needle and thred.*
Suture sphenoïde. *A false suture in the end, or bottome of the noddle, whence it passes vnder the* Os coniugal, *and ends neere the ends of the Coronall suture.*
Suvereau: m. *The great bastard Mackarell.* ¶ Marseillois.
Suye: f. *Soot of a chimney; any bleach.*
Suye d'Encens. *Soot of Incense, burnt (of purpose for the soot) in a close pot; of an abstersiue, and cooling propertie; clenses, and fills vp the vlcers, and appeases the heats and inflamations, of the eyes.*
Suye des Peintres. *Painters soot; a corrosiue, and astringent stuffe gotten in Glasse-houses.*
Suyer: m. *An Elder tree.*
Suyn de laine. *Looke* Suin.
Suyne: f. *A precious stone found in some Serpents.*
Suyte: f. *A chase, pursuit, prosecution of suit against; also, the traine, attendants, or followers of a (great) person; the companie he drawes along with him; also, a sequele, issue, consequent, or consequence; also, a succession, continuance, or vnintermitted course of things; Looke* Suitte.
Suyvamment. *Successiuely, consequently, afterward.*
Suyvant: m. *A follower, one of the traine of.*
Suyvant: m. ante: f. *Following, succeeding, ensuing.*
Suyvre. *To follow, goe after, attend or wait on; imitate, or counterfeit; chase, or pursue; succeed, or ensue:* (En la vendition on dit qu'on suit la chose, quand on la demande à vn tiers detenteur non obligé personnellement à la rendre. l'Oiseau.)
Suyvre le broust. *Looke* Broust.
Suyvre ses coups. *To prosecute, or second a beginning.*
Suyvre la fortune. *To take, or adhere vnto, the stronger side.*
Suyvre les lopins. *To hunt after good cheere; to prostitute himselfe, on all base conditions, vnto his owne appetite.*
Qui suit les poules apprend à grater la terre: Pro. *See* Grater.
Qui bons lopins mange bons lopins le suyvent: Prov. *Prouision followes them that vse to fare well; where best meat's eaten markets are best serued.*
Suzeau. *Looke* Suseau.
Suzerain: m. *Soueraigne (yet subalterne) superior (but not supreame) high in iurisdiction (though inferior to the highest.)*
Suzeraineté: f. *Soueraigne (but subalterne) iurisdiction, superior (but not supreame) power; high or chiefe authoritie, subiect or inferior, to the maiestie of Kings.*
Suzerains: m. *High and mightie Lords hauing vnder them many vassalls, were tearmed so in old time; and at this day the Kings principall Judges haue sometimes this title bestowed on them.*
Sybilot: m. *Looke* Sibilot.
Sycomantie: f. *Diuination by Figge-leaues.*
Sycomore: m. *The Sycomore, Figge-Sycomore tree, Mulberrie Figge-tree.*

Sycomore bastard. *as* Sycomore d'Italie.
Sycomore de Chypre. *The Cyprian Sycomore; a great tree almost like the Poplar, but leaued like the Elme; it beares foure times a yeare, but the fruit ripens not vntill it haue beene slit, and haue yeelded at that slit a milkie iuyce.*
Sycomore d'Egypte. *as* Sycomore d'Italie.
Sycomore d'Italie. *The Bead tree, th'Italian Lote or Nettle tree; yeelds a fruit, of whose stones (for want of better things) beades are made.*
Sycophage: com. *A Fig tree:* ¶Rab.
Sycophantin: m. *A sycophant, buffoone, parasite, claw-backe, tale-bearer, smell-feast.*
Syderal: m. ale: f. *Starrie, of or belonging to, the starres.*
Syderation: f. *Tree-plague; a blasting in trees by great heat and drought; also, a sudden taking, or benumming of a limme, followed by a totall putrifaction, and vtter destruction thereof.*
Syderé: m. ée: f. *Tempered, and forged by the course and constellation of the starres.*
Syer. *Looke* Sier.
Syllable: f. *A sillable.*
Syllogisme: m. *A (Logicall) Syllogisme.*
Syloatique. ¶Rab. *Huge, mightie.*
Symbole: m. *A token, badge, or signe to know one by; a secret, priuate, and mysticall note; a short and intricate ridle or sentence; a passport; a shot; a collation; also, an vniforme consent or concurrence of sundrie opinions; also, the summe of our Beleefe; the Creed.*
Symbolizant: m. ante: f. *Symbolizing, sympathizing.*
Symbolization: f. *A symbolization, or symbolizing; a mutuall agreement in opinion, humor, and manners; a sympathizing.*
Symbolizer. *To symbolize, or sympathize; to concurre in opinion, iumpe in conceit, agree in humors or manners, with.*
Symmetrie: f. *Simmetrie; a iust, and mutuall proportion of each part in respect of the whole.*
Symmetrié: m. ée: f. *Well proportioned, in iust symmetrie.*
Symmistre: m. *A Secretarie, or priuie Counsellor.*
Symmiste: m. *A fellow, or colleague in a (sacred) profession.*
Sympathie: f. *Sympathie; a symbolizing; naturall consent, or combination; mutuall passion, affection, disposition; a fellow-feeling.*
Sympathiser. *To sympathize, or haue a fellow-feeling of, to iumpe with in passion, consent with in affection, agree with in disposition.*
Symphise: f. *A naturall, and vnmouing vnion of two bones.*
Symphonie: f. *Harmonie, tunable singing, &c, a consent in tune.*
Symplegade: f. *An imbracing, or clipping; and thence also, a whirlepoole, or swallowing gulfe.*
Symposiarque: m. *The Maister, or Ouerseer of a feast; a feast-maker.*
Symptome: m. *A symptome; an affect, passion, or accident accompanying a disease; a sensible griefe ioyned therewith; as with an Ague the headache, &c; generally, whatsoeuer happens to a liuing creature against or besides nature, as sicknesse, & th'inward causes, and accidents thereof.*
Syn. *Looke* Suin.
Synagogue: f. *A Sinagogue, assemblie, congregation.*
Synanchie: f. *The Squinzie, or Squinancie.*
Synanthrose: f. *A close coniunction of bones without any visible motion.*
Syncere: com. *Sincere, pure, perfect, intire, sound; vncorrupted, iust, vpright, honest, open-hearted, plainely dealing.*
Syncerement. *Sincerely, purely, intirely, soundly, vncorruptly, iustly, vprightly, plainely, without fraud or guile.*
Syncerité: f. *Sinceritie, integritie, soundnesse, intirenesse, honestie, puritie, cleanenesse, vprightnesse, plainnesse, true-heartednesse.*
Syncope: f. *A cutting away; also, a sowning, or swounding.*
Syncopization: f. *A cutting away; also, an often swounding.*
Syncopizer. *To cut away; also, to sowne, or swound.*
Syncretisme: m. *The ioyning, or agreement, of two enemies against a third person.*
Syncrisme: m. *A thinne, and spreading ointment, or medecine.*
Synderese: f. *The remorse, or pricke of conscience; that part of the soule which opposeth it selfe vnto sinne.*
Synderique. Nerfs Synderiques. *Binding sinewes.*
Syndic: m. *A Sindicke, Censor, Controller of manners; also, an Atturney, or Agent for a Commonwealth, or Comminaltie.*
Syndicable: com. *Subiect vnto examination, censure, or controllment.*
Syndicat: m. *Th'Office of a Syndicke, &c.*
Syndiquer. *To examine, censure, or controll mens conuersations or courses.*
Synochite. *A stone whereby (as Magitians affirme) the dead be raised.*
Synodal: m. ale: f. *Synodall, of a Synode, enacted in a Synode.*
Synode: m. *A Synode, or assemblie of Ecclesiasticall persons.*
Synonime. *A Synonima; a word hauing the same signification which another hath.*
Synonimer. *To make two words beare one sence.*
Synople. *Sinople; Greene, in Blazon.*
Synterese. *Looke* Synderese.
Syntre. *Looke* Cintre.
Syparathe. *The dung of a Goat, or Sheepe:* ¶Rab.
Syphon. *Looke* Siphon.
Syre. *Sir; Looke* Sire.
Syringuant. *Squirting, iniecting into.*
Syringue: f. *A Siringe, a squirt.*
Syringué: m. ée: f. *Squirted, or iniected, as liquor with a Siringe.*
Syringuer. *To squirt, or iniect with a Siringe.*
Syroch. *Looke* Siroch.
Syron: m. *Looke* Ciron.
Syrop. *Sirrop, or a syrrup; also, a slimie, and blackish humor in the stomacke of a new-borne infant, the most whereof it corrupts, if it be not euacuated before the youngling sucke.*
Syrop vignolat. *Syrrup of the vine, wine.*
Syrte. *A quicksand, or shelfe of sand in the sea, or in a riuer.*
Systole: f. *The motion, or lifting vp of the heart, and Arteries; also, the shortening of a long vowell.*
Sytorpé. *Cut off:* ¶Rab.

T

TA. *The Feminine of* Ton; *Thy.*
Tabarre: m. *A long riding cloke, or garment.*

Tabellion: m. *A Notarie publicke, or Scriuener, allowed by authoritie to ingrosse, and register priuate contracts, and obligations: Therein differing from* Notaire *(as in the word* Notaire*) more generally, then that (as in the opinion of* Nicot*) the* Notaire *does the Office of both in Cities, and Townes of respect, and the* Tabellion *onely in Boroughes, and Villages: And yet they are very often confounded, and taken for one, and the same (sayes* Ragueau;*) And their Offices are (sayes another) at this day made, or growne one.*

Tabellionnage. *Th' Office of a* Tabellion; *the place wherein hee ingrosses, and registers priuate contracts.*

Droict de Tabellionnage. *as vnder* Droict; *also, a halfepenie in the pound for contracts of the sale of land, &c, exceeding the value of* 15 l. Tour. *due to the King within the Libertie of* Sens.

Tabellionné: m. *The Office, Function, or Art, of a* Tabellion.

Tabellionné: m. ée: f. *Drawne at large, ingroßed, registred by a* Tabellion.

Tabellionner. *A* Tabellion *to draw, ingrosse, or record a deed.*

Tabernacle: m. *A Tabernacle, pauillion, tent, or hall; also, a shed, shelter, or little shop of boords; also, a gaudie Cabinet, Box, or Chariot to set, keepe, or carrie Images in.*

Tabian. laict Tab. *The milke of* Tabia, *a place in Italie, verie healthfull for such as are in a consumption:* ¶Rab.

Tabide: com. *Consuming, wasting, languishing, pining away; also, welneere all melted, or wasted.*

Tabifié: m. ée: f. *Wasted, consumed, rotted, putrified; also infected, poisoned, corrupted.*

Tabifier. *To wast, consume, putrifie, rot; infect, poison, marre, corrupt.*

Tablage: m. *A tabling or boording; also, a table, or great boord.*

Tablature d'un Luc. *The bellie of a Lute.*

Table: f. *A table; a long and square boord; a table, or boord to eat on; the table, or counter of Bankers, and Marchants; the Table, or Index of a booke; also, a Chesse-boord, or that whereon we play at Tables; also, a (square) plate of mettall; also, food, fare, diet, victualls, meat and drinke; In Law, the Fief, demaine, whole Seigniorie, or intire bodie of estate in land, belonging to a Lord, &c; whence,* Mettre, & vnir, en sa Table, &c.

La table d'un Luc. *The bellie of a Lute.*

Tables rabbatuës. *The Queenes Game, Doublets.*

Table ronde. *Open house-keeping; also, a merrie meeting, or feasting together of friends, and allies; also, a little round boord wheron the* Pastissiers *carrie their Pies, and Tarts from place to place.*

Diamant en table. *A square table Diamond.*

Il est à table & n'ose manger. *Either he is a coward and dare not, or a pinch-crust and will not, fall to the meat thats before him.*

Revenir à la table de l'aisné. *The part of a younger brother, or of his issue (deceased without naturall heirs) to reuert, or escheat vnto the eldest.*

Tenir table. *To banquet, or feast it euerie day in his house.*

Tenir bonne table. *To keepe a good table, to fare well.*

Tenir longue table. *To sit long at meat.*

Table d'Abbé; ou de Prelat: Pro. *A plentifull, or well-furnished boord.*

Table sans sel bouche sans salive: Prov. *An vnlearned discourse is (commonly) as vaine, as meate without salt's vnsauorie.*

Table vaut escole notable: Prov. *Table-discourse is an excellent Schoolemaister.*

De grosse table à l'estable: Prov. *Excessiue housekeeping makes Gentlemen turne Groomes.*

Ronde table oste le debat: Prov. *Round tables take away contention; one being as neere his meat as another.*

Tableau: m. *A picture; a table whereon things be painted, or written; a writing table; memoriall, register.*

Tablée: f. *A table-full of.*

Tables. *Playing Tables; Looke* Table.

Tablette: f. *A little table, or boord; also, a childes horne-booke.*

Tablettes. *Writing tables; also, the scales of a Hawks legs; also, Losenges, ministred in Physick.*

Tablier: m. *A Chesse-boord, or Table to play on; also, an Apron; also, a long, and large table-cloath; also, a tabler, or boorder.*

Tablier de Notaire. *A Scriueners shop, or booth.*

Tabouler. *To make a great noise or troublesome dinne; or, to knocke lowd and fast, like a Cooper in the hooping of caske.*

Taborlan: m. *A mightie Prince, or Potentate; or, a name of state, and dignitie (perhaps from Tamberlaine.)*

Tabour: m. *A Drumme; also, a Tabor.*

Batre le tabour à coups d'osselets. *To play at Dice on a Drummes head.*

Tabourasse: f. *A Drumme, or Tabor.*

Tabourder. *To play on a Drumme, or Tabor; (& thence) also, to rap, or knocke.*

Tabourdeur: m. *A Taborer, or Drummer.*

Tabourement: m. *A Drumming; also, a rapping, knocking, or thumping (as on a Drumme) at a doore, window, or other thing of wood; also, the noise, or dinne thats made thereby.*

Tabourer. *To drumme; also, to rap, knocke, or thumpe (as on a Drumme) at a wooden window, doore, &c; also, to strike, or bumpe on the Posteriorums.*

Tabouret: m. *A pinne-pillow, or pinne-case; also, a cushion stoole, or little low stoole for a woman or child to sit on; also, the flat base, or foot of a piller, resembling such a stoole; also, the hearbe Toywort, Caseweed, Pickpurse, Shepheards-purse.*

Taboureur: m. *A Drummer, or Taborer; also, a thumper, bumper, knocker; whoremunger.*

Tabourin: m. *A Tabor; also, a Drumme; and a little Drumme; also, the Drumme, or Drummer belonging to a Companie of footmen; also, a Timpanie in the bellie.*

Tabourin de Basque. *A kind of small, and shallow Drumme, or Tabor, open at the one end, and hauing the barrell stucke full of small bells, and other gingling knacks of lattin, &c, which, together with the Taborers fingers on the other end thats couered, make (in the ears of children and sillie people) a prettie noyse.*

Tabourin de guerre. *Is properly, the Drumme.*

Tabourin des oreilles. *A certaine skinne, or filme within the eares; thin, the more easily to receiue sounds and aire from without; yet strong, thereby to resist outward annoyances; and drie, the better to resound.*

Chausses à tabourin. Ce sont chausses enflées de bourre, & grosses comme vn tambour.

Prendre le lievre au tabourin. *To performe impossible matters; See* Lievre.

Ce qui est venu par la fleute s'en retourne avec le tabourin: Pro. *Looke vnder* Fleute.

Ta-

Tabouriner. *To play on a Tabor; also, to drumme or strike vp a Drumme.*

Tabourinesse: f. *A woman that playes on a Tabor, or strikes vp a Drumme.*

Tabourinet: m. *A Drumme, or Tabor for a child; a little Drumme, or Tabor; also, a little roome contriued in the corner of a square hall with Tapistrie, or boords.*

Mener au tabourinet. *To inueagle, allure, lead by the nose, draw whither, or to what, he list.*

Tabourineur: m. *A Taborer; one that playes on a Tabor.*

Tabourineuse. *as* Tabourinesse.

Tabouriniere. *The same.*

Tabourne. *as* Tadorne.

Tabouter. *as* Tabuter.

Tabureau: m. *A mocker, or scoffer.*

Tabut: m. *Trouble, turmoile, disquiet, molestation.*

Fagoteur de tabus. *A seditious, turbulent, or troublesome fellow.*

Ce vilain ne vaut pas le tabut. *Is not worth the beating, or not worth the paines one must take in the beating of him.*

Tabuter. *To ioult, butt, or push; to trouble, disquiet, molest, infest; not to let alone one that would faine be in quiet.*

Tac: m. *A kind of rot among sheepe; also, a Plague-spot, or Gods-token on one that hath the Plague; also, as* Tal; *also, the name of a strange disease (raging in the yeare 1411) wherein the patient lost both rest, and appetite; feeling, whensoeuer he did eat, a fit of an Ague; often coughing; euer trembling; and voiding, vpon his amendment, great store of bloud at his mouth, nose, and fundament.*

Herbe du tac. *Lungwort, wood Liuerwort.*

Tacconnet. *as* Taconne.

Tache: f. *A spot, staine, blemish; mole, naturall marke; also, a reproach, disgrace, disreputation, blot vnto a mans good name.*

Taches de fumier. *Buds, or hard and bluish pimples, breaking out on the face.*

Taché: m. ée: f. *Spotted, blotted, stained, blemished; disgraced.*

Tacher. *To spot, blot, staine, blemish; disgrace; also, as* Tascher.

Tacheté: m. ée: f. *Spotted, speckled, marked.*

Tacheter. *To spot, speckle, marke.*

Tachette: f. *A little spot, blot, staine, blemish.*

Tacheture: f. *A spot, specke, or speckle; also, a spotting, speckling, marking.*

Tacite: com. *Silent, still, husht, quiet; secret, couert, inward; holding his tongue, saying nothing; let passe without mention, passing on without any noyse.*

Tacitement. *Silently, stilly, quietly, secretly, couertly, priuily, inwardly, without noise, without any words.*

Taciturne: com. *Silent, secret, holding his peace, vttering little, vsing few or no words of.*

Taciturnité: f. *Taciturnitie, secretnesse, or secrecie, silence, counsell-keeping.*

Tacle: m. *Any (headed) shaft, or boult, whose feathers be not waxed, but glued on.*

Tacon: m. *A little Salmon; or more properly, a kind of small, and delicate Trout, caught in a riuer that passes by* Clermont en Auvergne.

Taconne: f. *The hearba Fole-foot, Horse-foot, Coultsfoot, Hall-foot.*

Taconner vn soulier. *To cobble, clowt, or set a patch on it.*

Taconnet: m. *as* Taconne.

Tacroux: m. ouse: f. *Sunne-burnt; growne verie bleake, or swart, by being all day in the Sunne; also, extreamely couetous, or miserable.*

Tadorne. *A black-headed, and whitishbodied waterfowle, make somewhat like, but bigger then, a Ducke.*

Taffetas: m. *Taffata.*

Taffetas chenillé. *Stript Taffata.*

Taffetas à gros grain. *Silke Grogeram.*

Taffetas mouscheté. *Tuffe-taffata.*

Taffetas velouté. *The same.*

Taforée: f. *A horse-boat; a great flat-bottomed boat, or ship to carrie horses in.*

Tahon: m. *A Brizze, Brimsee, Gadbee, Dunflie, Oxeflie.*

Tahon marin. *The sea Brizze; a kind of worme found about some fishes.*

Tahou. Poire de Tahou. *A small peare whereof excellent perrie is made.*

Taïe: f. *A great grandmother:* ¶Pic. *also, as* Taye.

Taige. *A kind of vine:* ¶Rab.

Tail. *as* Taillade: ¶Langued.

Taillable: com. *Taxable, subiect or liable vnto taxes, which may be taxed; also, paying taxes.*

Heritages taillables. *Held by villeines, or by Villenage; by seruile tenants, or by a seruile tenure.*

Taillablier. Seigneur tail. *A Lord that taxes, or may taxe his tenants; or to whom taxe is due from them.*

Taillade: f. *A cut, slash, gash; a slit; a launcing, or slitting.*

Taillade: com. ¶Langued. *as* Tailladé; *whence;*

Ribe taillade. *A full-deepe shore; a shore, or side of a water of a plumpe, and downe-right depth.*

Tailladé: m. ée: f. *Cut, slashed, gashed, slit, launced, incisioned.*

Taillanderie: f. *The smithie, or shop of a* Taillandier.

Taillandier: m. *A maker of Hatchets, hedging Bills, Axes, Chopping Kniues, and such other great cutting Instruments, or tooles of yron.*

Taillandier: m. ere: f. *Cutting, or snipping off.*

Taillant d'un ferrement. *Th'edge of a toole.*

Taillant: m. ante: f. *Cutting, slitting, hacking, gashing, nicking, notching, indenting, ingrauing; also, fashioning, or proportioning.*

Taille: f. *A cut, slit, gash, notch, nicke; any incision; also, a cutting, slitting, gashing, notching, indenting, nicking; ingrauerie, caruing; also, a iag, or shred; also, a tallie, or score kept on a peece of wood; also, the sharpenesse, keenenesse, or edge of a weapon, or toole; also, the proportion, size, or stature of man, or beast; also, the Tenor part in singing, &c; also, as* Bois taillis; *also, a tax, &c; (Looke the next marginall word.)*

Taille douce. *Looke vnder* Doux.

Pierre de taille. *Free stone.*

Vin de la seconde taille. *Wine that comes of the last pressing, after the best of the grape hath beene squeezed out;* (car taille se prend pour la coupeure du marc du vin, estant sur le pressoir, quand on le veut serrer derechef: ¶Nicot.)

Avoir bonne taille. *A Tailor to cut a garment handsomely, or fitly for such as are to weare it.*

Cocher sur la grosse taille. *(As wee say) to lay it on, (take it off who as will;) to spend, or borrow, exceeding much.*

Il n'est de taille pour estre si mal traitté. *He is not a man to be so abused; he is not fit to beare, or not likelie to brooke, such iniuries.*

De toute taille bon levrier: Prov. *There are good and bad, valiant and cowardlie, strong and weake, of all*

all shapes and sizes.

Taille: f. *A taske, or tax; a tallage, tribute, imposition:* (Les Tailles ne sont point deuës de devoir ordinaire, ains ont esté accordées durant la necessité des affaires seulement, *sayes* Ragueau.) *In old time they were permitted (onely) in foure cases;* viz. Nouvelle chevalerie; mariage de filles; voyage d'outre mer; & captivité: *Since they haue been commonly leuied in time of war; and at length Charles the seuenth made them ordinarie.) Diuers French Lords haue a* Taille *from some of their vassalls, or tenants, as well as the King hath his from onely some of his subiects; I say onely some; because all Gentlemen (of a Gentlemanlie profession) all Clergie men; the Presidents, and* Conseillers *of Soueraigne Courts; the Maisters of Requests, and Secretaries, of the Kings houshold; the Secretaries, or Clerkes of the Chauncerie; the Gouernours, graduate Schollers, and diuers Officers, of Vniuersities; the Burguers, and inhabitants of many great Townes; and some Officers, and others by speciall priuiledge, are exempted from it.*

Taille abonnée, ou abournée. *For which the tenant is at a certaine yerelie rate with his Lord.*

Taille franche. *Due, in th'aforesaid foure cases, by freeholders,* ou ceux qui tiennent heritages en franchise à devoir d'argent.

Taille iurée. *Looke* Iuré.

Taille mixte. *Is imposed on a mans house, and makes liable vnto it all his goods in what place, or part soeuer they be.*

Taille mortaille. *Which is leuied of villeines, or seruile tenants, yearely, and at the reasonable pleasure of the Lord, or as he and they can agree.*

Tailles personnelles. *Personall taxes; are imposed vpon the persons of men, according to their meanes.*

Tailles reelles. *Reall taxes; are imposed, not on the persons, but on their possessions, the which they follow; and proportioned vnto the rates set downe in a* Censuel *description, or suruey of them: nor are they tied onely to immouables; for the mouables (as Marchandise, and commodities) whereof gaine is made, are subiect vnto them.*

Droict de taille. *Looke vnder* Droict.

Ville, & taille. C'est la septaine, & le territoire de la ville.

Taillé: m. ée: f. *Cut, sliced, slit, gashed, slashed, hacked; nicked, notched, ingrauen, indented; also, made, fashioned, proportioned; also, guelt, or speyed; also, taxed, assessed.*

Taillé d'avoir du mal. *Destined, or borne to be miserable.* Taillé d'avoir du pire. *Likelie to get the worse.*

Taillé de l'avoir. *Like ynough, or in good forwardnesse to haue it.*

Besongne taillée. *The hands full, ynough to doe, as much as one can turne him to;* Laissant leur besongne ia taillée. *Leauing their worke alreadie cut out, their businesse begun, their labour halfe done.*

Taille-bacon: m. *A clunch, clowne, boore; one that vsually feeds on nought but Beanes and bacon.*

Taille-boudin. *Captaine cut-pudding.*

Taille-bras: m. *A hackster, arme-slasher, cutter, swaggerer, swash-buckler.*

Taille-canton: m. *as* Taille-bras.

Taille-fer: m. *The surname of the old Earles of* Engoulesme; *so tearmed because William the second Earle thereof, cloue, with his sword, at one blow, an armed Captaine downe to the stomacke.*

Taillement: m. *A cutting, slicing, slitting, hacking, slashing; nicking, notching, indenting; caruing, ingrauing; also, a guelding, or speying.*

Tailler. *To cut, slit, slice, hew, hacke, slash, gash; nicke, snip, notch, indent; carue, graue; also, to gueld, or spey; also, to tax, impose taxes on, leuie tributes of.*

Tailler de la besongne à. *Looke* Taillé.

Tailler vn marc. *To cut off the edges, or sides of the mother of Grapes (alreadie hard pressed, and which will runne no more) and throw those cuttings into the middle of the presse, there to receiue, with the rest, another squeeze.*

Il est bien veau qui veau taille: Prov. *He is a calfe that calues-flesh cutteth; (A fit answer to a Butcher that calls a man Calfe.)*

Taillerin: m. *A slice of.*

Taille-sebe. *as* Courtilliere.

Taille-vent: m. *A wind-cutter; an idle, or fond swaggerer.*

Tailleur: m. *A cutter, slitter, hewer, hacker, slasher; Caruer, Grauer.*

Tailleur d'habits. *A Taylor.*

Desieuné, ou morceau, de tailleur. *A plumme.*

Tailleure. *as* Taillure.

Taillis: m. *A Hachee; or made dish of Creuises, the flesh of Capons, Chickens, or Veale, bread, wine, salt, veriuyce, and spices; also, a kind of gellie.*

Taillis. Bois taillis. *A copse, groue, vnderwood; such wood as is felled, or lopped euerie seuen or eight yeres.*

Tailloir: m. *A trencher, or trencher plate; also, the vppermost square of the Chapter of a piller.*

Mettre le çol sur le tailloir. *To lay his head vpon the blocke.*

Taillon: m. *A little slice; cut, or gash; also, a great chipping knife; also, a tax raised by Henrie the second,* Anno 1549, *towards the increase of the pay of the* Gensdarmes *(who vsually lay billeted in villages) and to enable them to pay their hosts for whatsoeuer they had of them: Whereby poore countrey men got at the first, a little ease; but not long after they became as much oppressed by their vnrulie guests as euer; and yet they still payed, and still doe pay, both* Taille, Taillon.

Taillonné: m. ée: f. *Cut by slices, bits, or parcells.*

Taillonneux: m. euse: f. *Full of slices, parcells, little bits.*

Taillouer. *as* Talloir.

Taillure: f. *A cutting, slicing, slitting, slashing, snipping, nicking, notching, indenting; caruing, or grauing; also, a slice, cut, slit, slash, &c.*

Tainturier: m. *A Dier.*

Taïon: m. *A great grandfather:* ¶Pic. *also, an Oake of three loppings, or of 60 yeares growth.*

Taire. *To be silent, mumme, husht, quiet, still; to hold his peace, vse no words of, make no noyse; conceale, keepe secret, or vnto himselfe.*

Taire, & faire sont requis par mer, & par terre: Prov. *Be doing still, and cease to talke, whether by sea, or land thou walke.*

Bien dire fait rire, bien faire fait taire: Prov. *Wee laugh at goood words, but admire good deeds.*

Fols sont sages quand ils se taisent: Prov. *Fooles passe for wise men while they silent are.*

Le plus sage se taist: Prov. *The wisest man speakes least.*

Mieux vaut se taire que mal parler: Prov. *Better no words then words vnfitly placed.*

Oy, voy, & te tais, si tu veus vivre en paix: Prov. *Looke vnder* Ouïr.

Quand d'autruy parler tu voudras, regarde toy, & te

te tairas: Prov. *When on another thou wouldst raile, behold thy selfe, thy tongue will quaile.*

Qui de tout se taist de tout a paix: Prov. *He that holds his peace of, is at peace with, all men.*

Tairir. *as* Tarir; *To drie up.*

Tais: m. *A potshard; also, a scull, or scalpe; also, a shell, or great scale.*

Taiser. *Looke* Taire.

Taisible: com. *Still, silent, quiet, husht.*

Taisiblement. *Silently, quietly, stilly.*

Taisson: m. *A Gray, Brocke, Badger, Bauson; of two kinds.*

Taisson chemin. *The dog Badger; footed, and snowted somewhat like a dog; blacker, and longer-legd then the* Porchin; *feeds on flesh, and carrion; and voyds his ordure farre from his earth; whichhe makes (either in a tough soyle, or in some rocke) both deeper, and narrower, then the other doth his.*

Taisson porchin. *The hog Badger; is footed, & snowted like a swine; feeds on roots, and fruits; and dungs in the mouth of his earth, which hee, commonly, makes in a sandie, or light soyle: he sleepes verie much, and is thereby much fatter, & (for such as can eat of him) better meat then th'other.*

Tal: m. *Oyle extracted from the berries of the Crimzon, or pricklie Cedar.*

Talaires: m. *Mercuries winged shooes.*

Talare: com. *Reaching, or hanging downe to the heeles, or ankles.*

Talc: m. *A tender and transparent stone, which indures extreame heat, and cold, without breaking, and hath beene heretofore vsed in stead of glasse.*

Talemouse. *as* Talmouse; *also, a cuffe, or dash on the lips.*

Talemouser. *To cuffe, or dash on the lips; also, to vex, harrie, trouble, toile, molest.*

Talent: m. *A talent in money; of diuers sorts; one worth about* 175 l. sterl. *another* 291 l. *and a noble; and another* 400 l. *also, will, desire, lust, appetite, an earnest humor vnto.*

Talenté: m. ée: f. *Verie desirous of, eager vpon, earnest after.*

Taleoles: m. *Shiuers, or slices of a sticke, or of a root.*

Tales. *Dice; also, the game tearmed Cockall.*

Talion: m. *A paine equall to harme done, a punishment counteruailing the offence committed; one bad turne for another.*

Talle: f. *as* Thale; *also, a shoot, sprig, bud.*

Tallemellier: m. *A hedge-baker.* (v.m.)

Taller: m. *The coyne tearmed a Dollar.*

Taller. *Looke* Thaller.

Tallevas: m. *A large, massiue, and old-fashioned Target, hauing in the bottome of it a pike, whereby, when need was, it was stucke into the ground.*

Tallut. *as* Talus.

Talmouse: f. *A Cheese-cake; a Tart, or cake made of egges, and cheese.*

Taloche: f. *A bob, or a rap ouer the fingers ends closed together.*

Taloché: m. ée: f. *Rapped, or bobbed ouer the fingers ends.*

Talon: m. *The heele, a heele.*

Talon du gouvernail. *The bottome of the backe of a rudder.*

Le talon d'un soulier. *The heele-part of the sole.*

Chausser les talons à. *To course, pursue neere, giue hard chase vnto.*

Iouër des talons. *To shew a faire paire of heeles, betake him to his legs, runne away.*

Talonné: m. ée: f. *Kicked, spurred, or strucken with the heeles; also, hard chased, hotly followed, neerely pursued.*

Talonnement: m. *A kicking, spurring, striking, or beating with the heeles; also, a hard chasing, neere pursuing, close following; also, a digging with the heeles in the sides of a horse.*

Talonner. *To kicke, spurre, strike, or beat, with the heeles; also, to chase hard, follow hotly, pursue closely, tread on the heeles of; also, to spurgall, or to ride digging with the heeles into a horses sides.*

Talonneux: m. euse: f. *Vsing, or hauing heeles.*

Talonniere: f. *A treading on or downe, a spurring or striking with, the heele.*

Talque. *as* Talc.

Talu: m. uë: f. *Slope, sloping, slopewise, aslope.*

Maison taluë. *A house whose bottome is fenced from the raine that falls off the eaues, by water-tables, or boords, set off from the wall.*

Talvassier: m. *A long lowt or lubber, fond luske or slimme, foolish or vnfashioned loggerhead.*

Taluër. *To slope, to set, cut, or make aslope.*

Talure: f. *The blue marke of a blow, bruise, or hurt.*

Talus: m. *A slope, sloping, slopenesse, or slopinesse; also, the sloping side, or descent of a hill, banke, or causey; (and sometimes) also, the banke, or causey it selfe; also, the head-hoope of a peece of caske; also, a great furrow in ploughing.*

Fossé en talus. *A narrow-bottomed, and wide-mouthed ditch.*

Talusant: m. ante: f. *Sloping, made or descending aslope.*

Talut, & Taluz. *as* Talus.

Taluzer. *To build, or make aslope.*

Tam: m. *Blacke Brionie, our Ladies Seale, the wild Vine.*

Tamaridin. *as* Tamarind.

Tamarin. *as* Tamaris.

Tamarind: m. *A small, soft, and darke-red Indian Date, of a laxatiue propertie, and a good purger of the heat of choller.*

Tamarinde: f. *The Indian Date tree.*

Tamaris: m. *Tamariske; a shrub, or small tree, red-barked, and leaued like Heath.*

Tamaris sauvage. *Wild Tamariske; is lesse then the other, and beares no fruit at all; some also call thus, Heath, Ling, or Hather, because it resembles the wild Tamariske.*

Tambour: m. *A Drumme; also, a Tabor.*

Batre le tambour avec les dents. *To didder, or chatter with the teeth for cold.*

Prendre les lievres au son du tambour. *Seeke* Lievre.

Vn fol dessus vn pont c'est vn tambour en la Riviere: Prov. *A foole on a bridge is a Drumme in the riuer; viz. makes it resound by his madde thumping, leaping, or dauncing ouer it.*

Tambrays. *as* Estambres.

Tambu: m. *The bastard Pepper plant called Bettle, or Betre, sometimes (but improperly) taken for the Indian Leafe.*

Tamis: m. *A searce, or boulter; (also, a strayner) made of haire.*

Tamisé: m. ée: f. *Searced, or boulted; also, strained through a searce.*

Tamiser. *To searce; to boult; also, to passe or straine through a searce.*

Tamoulenant. *Pondering, musing, studying.*

Tampon : m. *A bung, or stopple.*
Colin tampon. *See* Colin.
Tan : m. *The barke of young Oake, wherewith (being small beaten) leather is tanned; also, as* Tahon; *also, as* Tam; *also, furie, enragednesse, frenzie, madnesse.*
Moulin à tan. *A Tanners mill.*
Tanaisie : f. *The hearbe Tansie.*
Tanaisie sauvage. *Wild Tansie, Siluer hearbe.*
Tancer. *Looke* Tanser.
Tanche : f. *A Tench (fish.)*
Tançon : f. *A chiding, checking, rebuking, reprouing.*
Tandiment. *as* Tandis *(at* Blois.)
Tané : m. ée : f. *Tanned; also, troubled, molested, irked, wearied, ouertoyled; also, swart, sallow, duskie, or tawnie of hue, as things which haue beene tanned, or people which are ouertoyled.*
Tanée : f. *The hearbe Feauerfue; or a male kind thereof (held by some, but improperly, a third kind of Mugwort) which expelleth wormes, dissolueth windinesse; and, as an enemie to the stone, prouoketh vrine to come.*
Tanelliere : f. *The Worme-fretter; a worme which maketh holes in the sides of ships.*
Taner. *To tanne; also, to die into a tawnie; also, to trouble, irke, molest, harrie, ouertoile.*
Tanerie : f. *as* Tannerie.
Tanesie : f. *The hearbe Tansie; Looke* Tanaisie.
Taneur : m. *A Tanner.*
Taneuse : f. *A Tanners wife, or woman which tannes.*
Tangible : com. *Tangible, touchable.*
Tangueurs : m. *Looke* Tanqueurs.
Taniere : f. *A denne, caue, burrow; the lurking hole of a wild beast.*
Tanné : m. ée : f. *Tawnie; also, duskie, swart, sallow.*
Mastines tannées. *Oughe or ill-coloured bitches, fell and ill-fauoured queanes.*
Tannée : f. *The hearbe Tansie.*
Tanner. *Looke* Taner.
Tannerie : f. *Tanning; the Art, or act of Tanning; also, a Tanne-house, or place wherein leather is tanned.*
Tanneur : m. *A Tanner.*
Tanquard : m. *A Tankard:* ¶Rab.
Tanqueurs : m. *Such as carrie ashore stuffe, or persons, out of ship-boats.*
Tansé : m. ée : f. *Chidden, checked, rebuked, reproued.*
Tansement : m. *A chiding, checking, rebuking, reprouing.*
Tanser. *To chide, rebuke, checke, taunt, reproue, take vp.*
Tanson : m. *A chiding, checking, brawling, scoulding with; a taunting, rebuking, reprouing.*
Tansonnier : m. ere : f. *Chiding, or full of chiding.*
Tant. *So, as, so great, so much, or so many; as well, as deere, or as worthie; in sort, in such manner.*
Tant & si fort. *Vntill, so long as, in as much as, so much that.*
Tant & plus. *Mainly, hugely, mightily, infinitely, as much as may be.*
Tant seulement. *Onely.*
Tant soit peu. *How little soeuer; or, neuer so little.*
Tant soit peu trop. *A thought too much, or (at bowls) too hard.*
Tant pour tant. *Ratably, proportionably, mutually, one for another.*
'A tant. *Thus, by this, hereupon or thereupon, this or that done; therewithall; at length; immediately after.*
Ne tant ne quant. *Neuer a iot, nor one nor another, not one whit.*
Si tant est. *If so be that, or, if it happen that.*
Douze escus tant sous. *Twelue Crowns odde mone;,*
300 tant d'escus: 300 *and odde Crownes.*
Tantan : m. *The bell that hangs about the necke of a cow, &c.*
Tante : f. *An aunt; also, a tent; also, a hanging of Tapistrie, &c.*
Tantiesme : m. *whence;* Le tantiesme du mois. *Such a day certaine of the moneth.*
Tantinet : m. vn tan. *A little, small deale, poore quantitie, neuer so little.*
Tantost. *Anon, forthwith, immediately, presently, incontinently, by and by; also, one while, sometimes, now and then.*
Tantouiller. *To tumble, to wallow, to welter, in.*
Taon. *as* Tahon.
Tapecon : m. *The Heauen-gazer; a scalelesse sea-fish (of the bignesse of a foot) hauing a wide mouth, and a great head, on whose top his eyes (wherewith he lookes directly vpward) are placed.*
Tape-coué : m. *A taile-knocker, bellie-bumper, hairebeater, extreame lecher.*
Tapeinois. *as* Tapinois.
Taper. *To tap, or strike:* ¶Pic. *also, to stop.*
Taphorée : f. *as* Taforée.
Tapi : m. ie : f. *Hidden; lurking, lying close; low crooched, scowked, squatted, dowked or ducked downe.*
Tapinaudiere : f. *A denne, or lurking hole.*
Tapinet : m. *The same; or, a secret corner, a starting hole.*
Tapineux : m. euse : f. *Lurking, secret, couert, hidden, close.*
Tapinois, en tap. *Crooching, lurking, skowking, lying close and still, ducking for feare of being seene; also, couertly, closely, secretly.*
Contenu en tapinois. *Held low, kept vnder.*
Tapir. *To hide, conceale, couer, keepe close.*
Se tapir. *To hide, or couer himselfe; to crooch, lurke, squat, or ducke vnder, to lye close, for feare of being seene.*
Tapir des pieds contre la terre. *To make holes in the ground by hard stamping on it.*
Tapis : m. *Tapistrie, hangings, &c, of Arras.*
Sourd comme vn tapis. *As deafe as an Image in a painted cloth.*
Il demeura maistre du tapis. *He got the spurres; became commaunder of the place; woon the crowne, honour, victorie.*
Mettre sur le tapis. viz. en deliberation.
Reduict au tapis. *At an extreame low ebbe of fortune; cleane out of request, imployment, or meanes; and in game, that hath lost all his money, thats brought to the bare boord.*
Tapissant. se tap. *Hiding, or couering himselfe; crooching, lurking, ducking, squatting.*
Tapissement : m. *A hiding of himselfe; a lurking, squatting, lying close, a crooching, skowking, or ducking downe; also, a furnishing with Tapistrie.*
Tapisser. *To hang, or furnish with Tapistrie; also, to work Tapistrie worke; also, as* Tapir.
Tapisserie : f. *Tapistrie.*
Tapissier : m. *A Tapistrie-maker, or one that worketh in Tapistrie.*
Tapon : m. *A bung, or stopple.*
Taponnus. *A made name for a dunce; or in stead of* Pontanus: ¶Rab.
Tappecon. *As* Tapecon.
Tapper. *whence;* Iouër au tapper. *To play at Spannecounter.*

Tapper. *To tap, strike, hit, bob, clap; also, to bung, or stop with a bung.*
Tappi. *as* Tapi.
Taquain: m. *as* Taquin.
Taquain. (Adverb.) *Suddenly, or at the same instant.*
Taquet: m. *A brace, or peece of wood nailed against a post, &c, to keepe another from shaking, or slipping; also, the clapper of a mill.*
Taquet. *as* Taquain (Adverb.)
Taquette. *whence;* Besongner à la taquette; *To work hard, or eagerly; to sit at it:* (¶Orleannois.)
Taquin: m. *A niggard, miser, micher, penie-father, pinch-crust, hold-fast; also, a Porter, or any such base companion.*
Taquinerie: f. *Sordide miserie, wretched miching, base pinching.*
Tar: m. *A kind of Weesell.*
Tarabin tarabas. *An Interiection of interruption, like our, pish pish tut tut, &c.*
Tarabuster. *See* Tabuter.
Taraire. *as* Tariere.
Tarande: f. *The beast called a Buffe.*
Tarantole: f. *The most venomous Spider* Tarantola; *called so of the Neapolitan Citie* Taranta, *neere vnto which there be more of them then in any other part of Italie.*
Tarascon. *A towne in* Provence *seated vpon the* Rhosne, *iust ouer against another towne, called* Beaucaire; *whence;*
Entre Beaucaire, & Tarascon ne paist ny brebis, ny mouton: Prov. *For that great riuer drownes vp all the ground thats betweene them.*
Taravelle: f. *A Gardeners setting yron.*
Tarault. *as* Tariere; *also, as* Tarots.
Tarc. *A kind of Tarre, wherewith sheepe are marked, and (for some scabbie diseases) annointed.*
Tard: m. tarde: f. *Tardie, late, slack, tedious, lingering, long in comming.*
Tard. (Adverb.) *Late, lately, tardily, slackly, lingeringly.*
Qui tard veut ne veut: Pro. *He that will not quickly will not at all.*
Qui bien fait tard est reprenable: Pro. *A good turn that is done too late, is subiect vnto blame, and hate.*
Tardance: f. *A tarriance, lingering, delay, loitering, long staying in a place.*
Tardé: m. ée: f. *Tarried, stayed, deferred, delayed.*
Tardelet: m. ette: f. *Latish; or, somewhat tardie, slow, tedious.*
Tardement. *Tardily, lately, lingeringly, tediously.*
Tarder. *To tarrie, stay, demurre, abide long; deferre, linger, foreslow, delay; to stop, let, hinder, slacken, put off, hold backe, withhold.*
Il me tarde que. *I thinke long till.*
Quoy que fol tarde iour ne tarde: Prov. *Though the foole tarrie day-light tarries not.*
Tard-fleury: m. *A verie sweet apple of the bignesse of a Tennis-ball.*
Tardif: m. iue: f. *Tardie, slow, slacke, lingering, remisse; backward, lateward, long in comming; dull, vnweldie, lither, lazie.*
Tardité. *Tarditie; or as* Tardiveté.
Tardivement. *Tardily, slackly, remisly, slowly, dully, vnweldily, lazily, litherly.*
Tardiver. *To linger, foreslow, slacke, delay, wire-draw it, loyter, or stay long in a place.*
Tardiveté: f. *Tardinesse, loitering, slacknesse, lingering, delay, tediousnesse; backwardnesse, coldnesse, remissnesse, dulnesse, lazinesse, vnweldinesse.*
Tardoune. *Looke* Tadorne: ¶Rab.
Tare: f. *Losse, diminution, decay, impairement, want, or wast in Marchandise, &c, by the exchange, or vse thereof; also, the allay, or imbasement of gold or siluer coynes.*
Il n'est cheval qui n'ait sa tare: Prov. *He is liuelesse who is faultlesse.*
Taré: m. ée: f. *Defectiue, wasting, drossie, corrupt; outcast, hurtfull, dãmageous, which none possesseth without hinderance, or losse; whose vse counteruailes not the charge one is at about it; also, worme-eaten, or full of holes.*
Tarefranc: m. &, Tarefranche: f. *as* Glorieuse.
Tarelet: m. *A little Augar.*
Tarelle: f. *An Augar.*
Tareronde: f. *The Forke-fish; a kind of Scate which hath in her taile an indented, and venomous pricke.*
Targe: f. *A kind of Targuet, or Shield, almost square, & much in vse along the Spanish coast lying ouer against Affrick, from whence it seemes the fashion of it came.*
Il n'a escu ny targe. *Looke vnder* Escu.
Targé: m. ée: f. *as* Tardé; *also, couered, shielded, shrowded vnder.*
Targement: m. *A tarrying, lingering, delaying, long staying; also, a couering, shielding, or shrowding vnder.*
Targer. *as* Tarder *(Among old Authors;) also, to shield, couer, shrowd vnder.*
se Targer d'une raison. *To arme, fortifie, defend, or excuse, himselfe by a reason.*
Targette: f. *A kind of snacket, or haspe, wherwith casemates, &c, are closed.*
Targon: m. *The hearbe Tarragon.*
Targue. *as* Targe.
Targué: m. ée: f. *Shielded; armed, or couered with a Targuet.*
Tari: m. ie: f. *Dried vp, drained of naturall moisture; withered, without any manner of sap.*
Tarier: m. *The bird called a Bunting.*
Tariere: f. *An Augar.*
Tariere à boiste. *A Wimble.*
Tariffe: f. *Wast paper to bind vp small wares in; also, Arithmetick, or the casting of accounts.*
Tarin: m. *A little singing bird, hauing a yellowish bodie, and an ash-coloured head.*
Tarir. *To drie, soake, wither vp; to draine of naturall moisture.*
Tarle: m. *A wood-worme, or wood-moath.*
Tarlé: m. ée: f. *Worme-eaten.*
Tarmées: f. *Thick magots; or short and hairie wormes, oftentimes breeding in the fundaments of horses; also, wood-wormes.*
Tarots: m. *A kind of great cards, wheron many seuerall things are figured; which make them much more intricate then ordinarie ones.*
Tarquet: m. *A kind of little dog, or hound, vsually kept by Ladies, and Gentlewomen.*
Tarracier: m. *as* Terrassier.
Tarré: m. ée: f. *Hauing an ouerture, or hole; or as* Taré.
Tarse de l'oeil. *The gristle whereon the haire of the eyelids groweth.*
Tarse du pied. *The first part of the foot next to the leg, and answerable to the wrist of the hand; containes, or consists of, seuen bones.*
Tartaire: m. *A Tartarie Faulcon.*
Tartarasse: f. *A Tortoise.*
Tartare. *Tartar; Looke* Tartre.
Tartarin: m. *The water-bird called a Kings-fisher.*

Tartarot: m. *A Barbarie Faulcon; or rather as* Tartaire.

Tarte: f. *A Tart.*

Tarte Bourbonnoise. *A mire, bog, slough, deepe and durtie place.*

Tarte Iacobine. *A Tart made of fat cheese, the yolkes of egges, sweet butter, Suger, and salt, all mingled, and layed in past, together.*

Tarte rouge. *Another made of apples steeped in red wine, Sugar, Powder-Cynnamon, and sweet butter; then strained, and laid in past.*

Payer la tarte de sa nativité. *To make a feast, or banquet on his birth-day.*

On se saoule bien de manger tartes: Prov. *Sweets quickly breed sacietie.*

Tartelages: m. *Tarts; meats like vnto Tarts; or, things that belong to, or be fit for, Tarts.*

Tartelette: f. *A little Tart.*

Tartelle; ou, Tartenelle: f. *A Whirligig.*

Tartinages. *as* Tartelages.

Tarton-raire. *Cutwort; a beautifull, and extreamely-purging French shrub, or shrub-like hearbe.*

Tartre: m. *Tartar, or Argall; the lees or dregs that sticke to the sides of wine-vessells; hard and drie like a crust; sound, and so close compacted, that you may beat it vnto powder.*

Tartriere: f. *A Jag; the Spurre-rowell-like instrument wherewith Pastissiers make indented iags; also, a Tartpanne.*

Tarugue: f. *An Indian beast which hath hanging eares; liueth alone, and without any trouping, among rockes; and breeds a kind of Beazer stone.*

Tas: m. *A heape, a pile, a bundle; a deale, sort, rabble, companie, troupe.*

Tas de charge. *The root of a vault; the stones whereby it is begun, or which doe serue as foundations to all the seuerall branches thereof.*

Tasche: f. *A taske.*

En bloc, & en tasche. *Tag and rag, all together, one with another.*

Tasché: m. ée: f. *Indeuored, laboured, attempted, essayed, gone about; also, tasked.*

Taschement: m. *An indeuoring, labouring, attempting, essaying; also, a tasking.*

Tascher. *To indeuor, labour, attempt, essay, offer, or goe about, to doe a thing; also, to taske, or appoint a taske vnto.*

Ie n'y taschois point. *A did it not of purpose.*

Tasse: f. *A bole, or cup to drinke in; also, a tuffe of grasse; also, a bag, or pouch.*

Tasse de foing. *A bundle, or trusse of hay.*

Tassé: m. ée: f. *Heaped, piled; made vp into trusses, or bundles.*

Tasser. *To heape or pile vp; to make into trusses, or bundles.*

Tassette: f. *A little cup; also, the skirt of a garment; & the tasse of an Armor (in which sence it is most commonly vsed plurally) also, the hearb Shephcards-purse, Pickpurse, Toywort, poore mans Parmacetie.*

Tassot: m. *A Newt, or Aske.*

Tastement: m. *A tasting; or essaying; also, a handling, feeling, touching; a groping for.*

Taster. *To tast; or take an essay of; also, to handle, feele, touch, or grope for.*

Taste-vin: m. *A Broker for Wine-marchants, a Winecunner.*

Taston. *whence;* Aller à tastons. *To feele, or grope along as he goes.*

Les manches à tastons. *The sleeues drawne out with puffes.*

Parler à taston. *To speake by ghesse or coniecture, onely to harpe at the matter.*

Tastonnant. *Feeling, groping; handling, touching, stroking.*

Aller tastonnant. *as* Aller à tastons.

Tastonnement: m. *A groping, feeling; handling, touching, stroking.*

Tastonner. *To feele, grope; touch, handle, stroke.*

Tate-vin. *Looke* Taste-vin.

Tatin: m. *A little, small quantitie, poore deale.*

Tatou: m. *A kind of long-tailed Hedge-hog, which in stead of a pricklie, hath (somewhat like the Tortoise) a skalie coat, whereinto, in times of danger, he drawes vp himselfe.*

Tavaillole: f. *A Cushion-cloth; or a good big peece of linnen (commonly wrought) and seruing as a couer for night-clothes, &c, or to the bag wherein they be kept.*

Tavaïolle. *as* Tavaillole; *(and the better word.)*

Tavan: m. *A Brizze, &c; as* Tahon: ¶Langued.

Tavan de mer. *The sea Brizze; resembles a big Cheslop, and hath sixteene feet, each whereof is armed with a hooke, or crooked nayle: This vermine lodging himselfe vnder the finnes of the Dolphin, and Tunnie, &c, afflicts them as much as the land Brizze doth an Oxe.*

Tavayole: f. *Looke* Tavaïolle.

Taudir. *To couer boothes in Faires &c, with canuas, or with raw cloth, &c.*

se Taudir. *To couer, shrowd, shelter, hide himselfe, to skowke, or ducke, vnder.*

Taudis: m. *The roofe, or vault of a house; any shrowd, or shelter made roofe-wise; and thence, a Targuetfence, or a defensiue engine, vnder which approaches are made, or breaches entred, by souldiers; also, a Taylors boord, or stall; also, the couer of a booth, or stall; also, a foule, sluttish, vnhandsome, or vndressed roome.*

Vn taudis tout chargé de vaisselle d'or. *A Cupboord of golden plate; or a Goldsmithes booth, or stall, set thicke therewith.*

Tavelé: m. ée: f. *Spotted, speckled, mennelled.*

Taveler. *To spot, or bespeckle; to marke with spots of sundrie colours.*

Tavelle: f. *A small edging lace; a Crowne-lace.*

Tavellement: m. *A spotting, or speckling, a marking with spots of sundrie colours.*

Tavelliere: f. *The little worme called a Wood-fretter.*

Tavelure: f. *as* Tavellement.

Taverdette: f. *A kind of plague.*

Taverne: f. *A Tauerne; is also (in some few places no better then) a victualling house.*

Taverneage: m. *The penaltie inflicted on a Vintner, or Wine-drawer, that hath sold his wine at a higher rate then was set him by the Magistrate.*

Taverneur: m. eure: f. *Frequenting Tauernes.*

Taverneux: m. euse: f. *as* Taverneur; *also, full of Tauernes.*

Tavernier: m. *A Vintner, Tauerne-keeper, Wine-drawer; also (in some places) a Victualler, of whom (as in our Tauernes of London) one may haue meat, and drink for his money.*

Le Tavernier s'enyvre de sa taverne: Prov. *Looke* Enyvrer.

Taverniere: f. *A woman that keepes, or haunts, a Tauerne; a woman that sells, or swills, much wine.*

Taves: f. *Red pimples, or freckles on the face.*

Tau-

Taulache: f. *A little Targuet, or Buckler.*
Taulpe: f. *The little beast called a Mole, or Moldewarp.*
Fourmage de taulpe. *Heauie, or sad cheese.*
Royaume des taulpes. *The earth.*
Fouilleur des taulpes. *A Mole-catcher.*
Fouïr aux taulpes. *To decease, to die.*
Taulpetier: m. *A Mole-catcher.*
Taulpin. franc taulpin. *A trained man, or souldier, made of a husbandman; also, a chuffe, boore, swaine, hind.*
Taulpiniere: f. *A Molehill, or hole; Seeke* Taupiniere.
Tauné. *Looke* Tanné.
Taupe: f. *A Mole; Seeke* Taulpe.
Taupiere: f. *An impostume, or soft swelling in the head, wherein it makes a hole somewhat like that which a Mole roots in the ground.*
Taupiniere: f. *A Molehill, or hole.*
Taupiniere d'assassinateurs. *A denne of murtherers.*
Taure: f. *Small Lunarie, small Moonewort.*
Taureau: m. *A Bull; also, the signe* Taurus.
Mener la genisse au taureau. *To bring the Heyfer to the Bull; to sell a virginitie, prostitute a maid; or (any way) to bring a wench to a mans bed.*
Boy le vin comme roy, boy l'eau comme taureau: Prov. *Drinke little wine, and much water; or, drinke wine moderately, water abundantly.*
Taureliere: f. *A Cow that affects, or longs for, the Bull.*
Taurillon: m. *A young, or little Bull.*
Taute: f. *A Calamarie, or Sleeue-fish; resembles the sea Cut, or Cuttle fish, and being skared, powres out a red liquor; also, a roller, or a round truncheon, laid vnder a great stone, &c, the more easily to remoue it.*
Tauter. *To lay a roller, &c, vnder a heauie thing, the better to remoue it.*
Tautte, *as* Taute.
Taux: m. *A taxation, or estimation; a taxing, assessing, rating, or prizing of things.*
Il en aura le taux du Iuge. *He will sure, and soone ynough, beare of it to his cost; he will surely be paid, or soundly be beaten, for it.*
Tauxation: f. *A taxation, taxing, rating, assessing, setting downe a certaintie in.*
Tauxe: f. *as* Taux.
Tauxer. *To tax, rate, assesse, make a certaine estimate of, set a certaine price or scantling on; to allow costs and charges vnto.*
Tauxeur: m. *A rater, taxer, assessor, prisor, praisor.*
Taxaté d'un despens. *A taxation of th'expences in, or charges of, a suit.*
Taxation. *as* Tauxation.
Taxe: f. *as* Taux.
Taxé: m. ée: f. *Taxed, rebuked, checked, reprehended, reproued; disparaged, disabled; also, assessed.*
Taxer. *To tax, checke, taunt, rebuke, reprehend, reproue; disgrace, disable, disparage; also, as* Tauxer.
Taye: f. *Any filme, or thinne skinne; as that which is left by Butchers, on th'inside of a breast of Veale, quarter of Lambe, &c; and hence, a pin or web in th'eye, a white filme ouergrowing the eye; also, the wooddie skin wherby the kernell of a wallnut is almost quartered; also, the sappie heart, pith, or middle, of a Pine tree, diuided into slices, and vsed by some of the poorer French, in stead of candles.*
Vne taye d'oreiller. *A Pillowbeere.*
Dure taye. *Th'outward skinne of the braine; the double skinne whereby it is couered, and kept from being hurt or touched by the skull.*

Tayeux: m. euse: f. *Skinnie, filmie; full of skinnes, or filmes; also, troubled with a pin, or web in the eye.*
Tayon: m. *A grandfather; also, an Oake of 60 yeares growth.*
Te. *(The Pronowne) thee.*
Té. *A voyce which is vsed by the French when they call a dog.*
Tect: m. *The roofe, or couer of a house; also, a stye, or house to keepe hogs, or geese in.*
Tede: f. *The fat pith, or heart of the Pine tree, called by some the Torch tree; tis also (and most properly) the whole stocke thereof turned heart, or of so fat and rosinie a substance, that lights may be (and by the clownes of* Auvergne *are) made of it.*
Tei. *as* Té; *a voyce whereby dogs be called.*
Teigne: f. *Scurfe, or a hot scabbinesse, on the head; the scurfe of a scauld pate; also, the weed Strangle-tare, Tenentare, Tine, Strangleweed, Choakweed, Choakfitch; also, a Moath.*
Teigne de lin. *Dodder.*
Teigne de thym. *Laced Time, Dodder Time.*
Teigneux: m. euse: f. *Scuruie, scauld-pated.*
Herbe aux teigneux. *Butter-burre.*
Troix teigneux, & vn pelé. *A messe, or small troupe of scuruie, or paultrie fellowes:* ¶Rab.
Femme trop piteuse fait sa famille teigneuse: Pro. *A tender housewife makes a tainted houshold.*
Iamais teigneux n'aima le peigne: Pro. *No scauldpate will the combe indure.*
Teille: f. *The rind, or pilling of hempe, &c.*
Teiller. *To pill, strip, scale, or shale hempe, &c.*
Teillet. *as* Tillet.
Teinct: m. *A tincture, die, staine; complexion, colour, hue; also, Shoomakers blacke; Looke* Teint.
Teinct: m. cte: f. *Died, stained, coloured, imbued.*
Teincture: f. *A tincture, dying, staining, colouring; also, the stuffe wherewith, or colour whereof, a thing is dyed.*
Teincture sourde. *Looke vnder* Sourd.
Teinturerie: f. *A die-house.*
Teincturier: m. *A Dier.*
Herbe aux teincturiers. *Madder.*
Teincturiere: f. *A Diers wife; or, a woman Dier.*
Teindre. *To die, staine, colour, imbue, dip in colour.*
Teint: m. *as* Teinct; *a die, &c; whence;*
Ioye au coeur fait beau teint: Pro. *Hearts-ioy giues to the face a beauteous tincture; a cheerefull conscience cleeres the countenance.*
Teinter. *To twang, like the string of a hard-bent bow.*
Teinture, &c. *as* Teincture, &c.
Tel: m. telle: f. *Such, like, resembling, such like.*
Il n'y a quelque chose de tel. *There is no such matter.*
Entre tels tel deviendras: Prov. *Among such thou wilt be such; their cōpanie will make thee like them; or, among such be such; fit thy selfe to thy companie.*
Telamons: m. *Great ships; also, supporters, or supporting Images in buildings.*
Telant. vin telant. *Thicke, or clammie wine; wine that ropeth.*
Tele: f. *as* Toile.
Teleniaban. *Manna:* ¶Rab.
Telephion. *Orpin, Liblong, Liue-long; or most properly, that kind thereof which is called ioynted Orpin, Spanish Orpin, and Hungarian Orpin.*
Telier: m. *A Linnen Weauer.*
Teline: f. *as* Flion: ¶Langued.
Tellement. *So, in sort, in such wise, in that fashion.*
Tellement quellement. *Indifferently, reasonably, so so, not too well.*

Telline: f. *as* Flion: ¶Langued.
Telon. *as* Tiretaine.
Tember; &, Tembut. *The bastard Pepper, called Betle, or Beter.*
Temeraire: com. *Rash, hastie, hare-braind, headlong, foole-hardie, ouer hazardous, incõsiderate, vndiscreet, more forward then needs, more aduenturous then hee should be.*
Temerairement. *Rashly, hastily, too hazardously, in a headlong course, at randome, at rouers, at all aduentures.*
Temereément. *as* Temerairement.
Temerité: f. *Temeritie, rashnesse, hastinesse, foole-hardinesse, vnaduisednesse, indiscretion, want of due consideration.*
Temperance: f. *Temperance, moderation, sobrietie; the meane betweene the extremities of appetite, and affection.*
Temperature: f. *A temper, temperature, tempering; a meane, moderation, qualification, orderlinesse.*
Temperé: m. ée: f. *Temperate, moderate, sober, orderlie, forbearing, refraining, meane-obseruing, of good temper, without any excesse; also, tempered.*
Temperemént: m. *A tempering, moderating, ordering, gouerning, restraining.*
Temperéement. *Temperately, moderately, soberly, measurably, orderly.*
Temperer. *To temper, moderate, qualifie; gouerne, order; allay, asswage; forbeare, spare, abstaine, refraine from; to mingle discreetly, measure equally, keepe a meane.*
Temperie: f. *Temperatenesse of weather.*
Tempes. *Looke* Temples.
Tempestatif: m. iue: f. *Turbulent, contentious, troublesome, vnquiet, seditious; euer iarring, wrangling, scoulding, brabling.*
Tempestatiuement. *Turbulently, tumultuously, troublesomely, contentiously, seditiously, wranglingly.*
Tempeste: f. *A tempest, storme, bluster, boisterous weather.*
Deux pots au feu signifient feste, & deux femmes font la tempeste: Prov. *Looke vnder* Femme; *or* Feste.
Tempesté: m. ée: f. *Stormed, blustered; tossed, vexed, hurried, harried; taken, or ouertaken with, broken or ouerthrowne by, a tempest.*
Tempester. *To storme, bluster, keepe a horrible coyle or stirre, raise a tumult, be in an vprore; to tosse, hurrie, harrie, torment, vex, turmoyle; also, to chafe extreamly at.*
Tempesteux. *as* Tempestuëux.
Tempestuëux: m. ëuse: f. *Tempestuous, blustering, stormie, troublesome, vnquiet.*
Temple: m. *A Temple, a Church.*
Temples: f. *The temples; the sides of the head betweene the eyes, and eares.*
Templettes: f. *Fillets, or head-bands for women; also, Jewells hanging vpon their forheads by bodkins thrust into their haire.*
Temporal: m. ale: f. *Of, or in, the temples; whence;* Veine temporale. *Seeke vnder* Veine.
Temporalles. *Coat-armors; or Heraulds coats.*
Temporaux: m. *The muskles by which the temples are moued.*
Temporel: m. elle: f. *as* Temporal; *also, temporall.*
Temporisé: m. ée: f. *Temporized.*
Temporisement: m. *A temporizing; an obseruing, or following of the time; also, a lingering, or protracting of time.*
Temporiser. *To temporize it; to obserue, agree with, applie himselfe, to the time; to liue as the time goes, or according to the time; also, to linger, delay, protract the time.*
Temporiseur: m. *A temporizer, time-seruer, protracter of time.*
Temporiseux: m. euse: f. *Temporizing, time-seruing, lingering, protracting of time.*
Tempre. *Quickly, shortly, soone, suddenly.*
Temprement. *Apace; or as* Tempre.
Tempre-meure. Elle est tem. *(Said of a maid) she is full ripe, or mariageable.*
Temps: m. *Time, season; while, opportunitie, leasure; weather.*
Le temps advenir. *Hereafter.*
Le temps des besongnes. *Haruest, or reaping time; so tearmed by husbandmen.*
Temps de forgas. *Looke vnder* Forgas.
Temps de pouldrette. *The season wherein the husbandman is to breake the clods of his plowed lands.*
Les quatre temps. *The foure Imber weekes.*
Bon temps. *Prosperitie; also, merriment, or time passed in merriment.*
Bon temps mau temps. *Howsoeuer the world goes, whatsoeuer come of it; also, one with another.*
Avec le temps. *In time, in th'end, at length.*
En temps & lieu. *Fitly, in good season, as it should bee.*
En peu de temps. *Shortly, quickly, ere long, within a while.*
Par temps. *Seasonably, in good time.*
Avoir son temps. *A woman to haue her flowers.*
Faire son temps. Il a faict son temps. *He is growne old, or out of date.*
Faire le guet au temps. *To obserue, and make vse of worldlie occurrences.*
Cela se faisoit au temps jadis. *Thats stale, or obsolete; thats quite out of vse, cleane out of date, altogether out of fashion.*
Gaigner le temps. *To prolong, or draw out the day; to win time.*
Galler le bon temps. *To liue merrily, blithly, iocondly; licentiously, sensually, luxuriously.*
Hausser le temps. *To tipple hard, or tipple vnto drunkennesse; to sit long tipling, and yet not thinke it long.*
Passer le temps. Il passe le temps. *Hee liues at his ease, or takes pleasure ynough in this world; he giues himselfe all fulnesse of sensuall contentment.*
Pousser le temps à l'espaule. *To vse delayes, &c; as vnder* Espaule.
Le temps n'est pas tousiours en bonne disposition: Prov. *Time is not alwayes fauourable; or, all times bee not good for all things.*
Le temps ouvre. *Looke* Ouvre.
Le temps vient, va, & passe, fol qui ne le compasse: Pro. *Time commeth, goeth, and away doth passe, he that obserues, or weighes it not's an asse.*
Avec le temps, & la paille l'on meure les mesles: Pro. *Time and straw doe make greene Medlers, which are as hard as stones, as soft as roasted apples: we must attend with hope times operation; The like is;*
Avec le temps l'on moissonne: Prov. *In time our corne is ripe, our haruest gotten.*
Ingratitude asseiche les fonts, & le temps renverse les ponts: Prov. *Vnthankfulnesse dries bounties springs, and bridges time to ruine brings.*
Tenable: com. *Holdable, fit to be held or kept.*
Tenacement. *Fastly, cleauingly, surely, holdingly.*

Tenacité: f. Tenacitie; fast keeping, sure holding, strait retaining; hardnesse, niggardlinesse, miserie, sparing; also, constancie, steadfastnesse; also, clamminesse.

Tenaillade: f. A plucke, twitch, or stroake with a paire of pinsers.

Tenaille: f. A paire of pinsers.

Tenaillé: m. ée: f. Plucked out, or taken hold of, with pinsers; also, whose flesh is pinched, or torne off with hot pinsers.

Tenaillement: m. A plucking out, or taking hold of with pinsers; also, a pinching, or tearing off, of the flesh with hot pinsers.

Tenailler. To pull out, plucke off, take hold of, with pinsers; also, to pinch, or teare the flesh off with hot pinsers.

Tenais: m. The slip of a plant.

Tenaisie: f. The hearbe Tansie.

Tenamment. Fastly, cleauingly, holdingly, close together.

Tenant: m. A miser, snudge, niggard, pinchpenie, penifather; a sparing, hard, or neere snudge; a close-handed, or couetous hold-fast; also, the side, or limit on the side, of a house, or peece of ground; also, a defendant in a Just, or Turnament; any one that withstands another, or holds, & makes good a place against him; also, a cōtinuall course, or vnintermitted continuance, of things; whence;

Tout d'un tenant. All together; &; Tout en vn tenant; Together, in one, all as one.

Tenant: m. ante: f. Holding, keeping, detaining; also, bounding or abutting on, next or neere adioyning vnto.

Le Roy tenant son lict de Iustice. Sitting in the throne of Justice.

Tenar de la main. A certaine muskle whereof the greatest part of the palme of the hand consisteth.

Tencer. Looke Tanser.

Tenche: f. A Tench.

Tenche de mer. The sea Tench, a rock-fish made like the riuer Tench, but of sundrie colours, and verie tender when she is dressed.

Tendant. Bending, stretching, reaching, giuing forward, making towards; tending, inclining, drawing neere vnto.

Tendelet: m. The tilt, or couer, of the poope of a galley; the cloth wherewith it is couered.

Tendineux: m. euse: f. Of, or full of, a Tendon.

Tendon: m. A Tendon, or taile of a muskle; a bloudlesse instrument of motiō, consisting partly of the sinew, and partly of the ligament, and fibers, which issue confusedly from the bellie of a muskle.

Tendre. To tend; bend; reach, extend, stretch out, spread or display; to pitch; incline, or giue forwards; approach, or make towards; goe on, or draw neere vnto; also, to indeuor, goe about, labour to get or come by; also, to tender, or offer vnto.

Tendre à fin de non receuoir. To oppose th'entrie, or admittance of his aduersaries plea, or processe.

Tendre le giron en la Iustice. (A defendant) comparoir à l'assignation qui luy a esté baillée, & accorder au demandeur ses fins, & conclusions.

Tendre les mains. To beg, or aske for mercie.

Tendre aux oiseaux. To lay, or set nets, &c, for birds.

Il n'a veine qu'y tend. He hath no fancie nor humor vnto it, he minds or meanes nothing lesse.

Qui à aise tend aise luy faut: Pro. He that prouides for his ease doth often loose it; or, he that cares for his ease is often crost in't.

Qui à asne tend à asne vient: Pro. He quickly may, that needs will, be an asse; or, at any time hee speedes that would be an asse.

Tendre: com. Tender; young; soft, supple, gentle, plyant; mercifull, tractable, soone induced, easily drawne vnto; also, nice, nesh, puling, delicate, effeminate.

Tendrelet: m. ette: f. Somewhat tender, &c.

Tendrement. Tenderly; softly, supplely, pliantly; gentlely, tractably; neshly, delicately; gingerly.

Tendret: m. ette: f. A little tender, soft, supple; gentle, tractable; nesh, delicate.

Tendreté: f. Tendernesse, softnesse, supplenesse; gentlenesse, tractablenesse; neshnesse, effeminacie, delicatenesse.

Tendreur: f. as Tendreté.

Tendrieres: f. Chaps, rifts, or chawnes on the nipple of a womans breast.

Tendrillons: m. Tendrells, little gristles.

Tendrineux: m. euse: f. Full of tendrells, or of slender gristles.

Tendron: m. A tender, nesh, delicate, or effeminate fellow; also, a cartilage, or gristle; also, a tendrell, or the tender branch, or sprig of a plant.

Tendronneux: m. euse: f. Gristlie, full of gristles, or of tendrells.

Tendu: m. uë: f. Tended; bent; raught, extended, stretched out; spred, or displayed; pitched; inclined, or made towards; tendered, or offered vnto; layed, or set for.

Tenebres: f. Darknesse, obscuritie, dimnesse; also, the seruice vsed in Popish Churches the three dayes next before Easter; whence; Les trois jours de tenebres; be those three dayes.

Tenebreux: m. euse: f. Tenebrous, darkesome, obscure, full of darknesse, or of obscuritie.

Tenebrions: m. Night-spirits, Hobgoblins, such as loue, and liue in, continuall darknesse: ¶ Rab.

Tenement: m. A countrey, territorie, or lands possessed, or held absolutely; also, a tenemēt, inheritance, or lands held in fief, by Cens, or a chiefe rent.

Tenementier: m. A tenant, or farmer.

Tenesme: m. A great desire, deuoid of power, to purge.

Teneur: m. The Tenor part in Musicke.

Teneur: f. The tenor, content, stuffe, or substance of a matter; also, a continuall order, state, fashion, race, course; an vnstopping, or vnintermitted continuance of things without any change in the manner thereof.

Tenie: f. A fillet, head-band, or haire-lace; also, a kind of brow, or iuttying in a piller.

Tenir. To hold, haue, keepe, enioy, possesse; take; detaine, withhold; reserue, retaine; also, to beare, vphold, support, sustaine, maintaine; also, to performe, effect, obserue, make good; also, to let, stop, hinder, impeach; gouerne, keepe in order, bridle, restraine; also, to iudge, deeme, account, repute, esteeme; also, to cleaue, cling, adhere, sticke fast, lye close, or sit sure, vnto.

Tenir adverti de. To giue notice or intelligence of.

Tenir des basses marches. To hold of the smocke, his wife to be his maister.

Tenir le bec en l'eau. To delay, or dallie with; Looke vnder Bec.

Tenir la bride haute à. To awe, restraine, keep short, hold in.

Tenir bon. To be firme, or constant in a matter; to continue or persist in it, to hold or stand to it, without any flinching or shrinking.

Tenir bon à quelqu'un. To hold him play.

Tenir son coeur. To malice inwardly, to beare a grudge vnto.

Tenir coup à la besongne. Seeke vnder Coup.

Tenir court. *To restraine, curb, keepe short.*
Tenir de court. *To presse, vrge, lay hard, or follow close, vnto.*
Tenir vn enfant sur le fons. *To Christen a child.*
Tenir l'Eschiquier. *To sit, or keepe a Court, in th'Exchequer.*
Tenir son estat à. *To giue maintenance vnto.*
Tenir à fable. *To esteeme, or account of, as a fable.*
Tenir fief. *To possesse a feodall inheritance.*
Tenir en fief. *Looke vnder* Fief.
Tenir de la Lune. *To be inconstant, variable, or changeable, as the Moone; also, to bee a little franticke.*
Tenir le livre. Il veut tousiours tenir le livre. *Hee talks continually, or so much as no bodie else can speak for him.*
Tenir le main à: &, Tenir la main pour. *Looke vnder* Main.
Tenir le marché faict. *To stand to his bargaine.*
Tenir le menton à. *To support, vphold, beare vp; whence the Prouerbe;* Celuy peut hardiment nager à qui l'on tient le menton.
Tenir à la mer. *To worke or sayle against the tide, or current of the sea.*
Tenir la mule à. Il luy fit tenir la mule. *He ouerruled, ouerswayed, or ouer-maistered him; also, he made him tarrie his leasure, or daunce attendance on him.*
Tenir la plaidoirie. *To keepe, or hold, a Court.*
Tenir pied à. Ie ne leur tins beaucoup de pied. *I gaue them not much consent, assistance, or countenance; also, I stayed not long with them; I held them not tack, or play, any while.*
Tenir pied à boule. *To applie his businesse throughly, to hold hard or stand close vnto it.*
Tenir pied en soulier. *Looke vnder* Soulier.
Tenir la queuë de la paelle. *To rule, sway, or dispose of a businesse; to haue the chiefest dealings, or most authoritie, in it; and hence the Prouerb;* Qui tient la queuë de la paelle il la tourne là ou il veut.
Tenir sur les rangs. *To deride, mocke, flowt, ieast at, make himselfe merrie with.*
Tenir serre. *To keepe in, to hold himselfe close, to restraine himselfe.*
Tenir table. *Looke vnder* Table.
Tenir teste. *To stand vnto it.*
Tenir tort. *whence;* Il sçait bien le tort qu'il nous tient; *He knowes well ynough the wrong he does vs.*
Tenir au vent. *To sayle verie neere a wind.*
se Tenir. *To beare, or carrie himselfe; also, to abide, continue, remaine;* se Tenir de; *To forbeare.*
se Tenir à vn denier. *To sticke at, or dodge about, a penie.*
se Tenir debout. *To stand, or stand vpright.*
se Tenir fort. *To presume, relie, or build vpon; to trust vnto, haue confidence in.*
se Tenir sur le bon bout; &, sur le haut bout. *Looke vnder* Bout.
Faire tenir quelque chose à. *To conuey, or send a thing vnto.*
Se faire tenir. *To be lustie, play the gallant, &c, as vnder* Faire.
'A cela ne tienne. *For that not a pin matter, let that be no hinderance, let it not sticke vpon that.*
Il tient à luy que. *Tis long of him, or hee is the onely cause, that.*
Il tient tant de moy. *He presumes, relies, depends so much vpō me; he hath that trust or cōfidence in, that hold or assurance of, me.*
Il ne tient qu'à cela. *There needs, or wants but that; that done will serue the turne; that done our taske is done.*
Il se tint fort par le nez de ce refus. *He forbore all he could to seeme sencible of this refusall; also, as vnder* Nez.
Ie n'en voudrois pas tenir dix escus. *(Vsed vpon an accident, or occurrence that pleaseth) I wold not for 10 Crownes it were otherwise; or, I am as glad as if one had giuen me tenne Crownes; (but vpon any other occasion) I would not take ten Crownes for it; and thence also;*
Ils n'en eussent pas voulu tenir vn denier moins. *They would not haue taken a penie lesse for it; also, they made themselues as sure of it as if they had held it.*
Ie sçay bien à qui m'en tenir. *I know well ynough whom to thanke, or whom I am beholden to, for that.*
Ou vont ils tenir? *Whither goe they to keepe, dwell, soiourne, remaine, abide?*
Ou ils n'ont que tenir. *Where they haue nothing to take hold of, where there is nothing that makes for them.*
Sans cela ils n'auroient que tenir. *Without that they knew not what shift to make, what course to take; they knew not how to earne their bread, or what in the earth to doe.*
Tout ce que ie vous dis ie le tiens de luy. *I haue all that I tell you from him, I heard all that I tell you of him.*
Vous ne m'y tenez pas. *You haue me not there as yet, you haue not got so much from, or out of, me.*
Qui tient se tienne: Prov. *He that holds let him hold still; or, let him that hath a hold keepe it.*
Mieux vaut vn tenez que deux vous l'aurez: Pro. *Better one bird in the hand then two in the bush.*
Tenon: m. *A tenon; the end of a rafter, &c, put into a morteise, &c.*
Tenons. *The vice nayles wherewith the barrell of a peece is fastened vnto the stocke; also, the (leatherne) handles of a Targuet.*
Tenre. as Tendre: Pic.
Tenser. *To chide; Looke* Tanser.
Tensif: m. iue: f. *Bending, or stiffe-bent.*
Tentation: f. *A temptation, tempting, proofe, essay, prouing, assaying.*
Tentative: f. *The posing (for the passing) of Graduates; a probation, or examination of such as are to take a degree.*
Tentatoire: f. *A proofe, essay, offer, attempt.*
Tente: f. *A tent, or pauilion; also, an open booth for a Pedler, &c; also, a tent for a wound.*
Tenté: m. ée: f. *Tempted; essayed, tried, proued, sounded, tasted; also, prouoked, or moued (vnto euill.)*
Tentement: m. *A tempting; an essaying, trying, prouing, sounding, tasting, attempting; also, a suggesting, prouoking, or mouing (vnto euill.)*
Tenter. *To tempt; to proue, trie, sound, essay, tast, attempt; also, to suggest, prouoke, or moue (vnto euill.)*
Tenteresse: f. *A tempteresse, a woman that tempts.*
Tenteur: m. *A tempter, prouoker; attempter, essayer.*
Tenthredon. *A kind of flie.*
Tentier: m. *A tent-keeper; or one that liues in a tent.*
Tentissement: m. *A ringing, resounding, tinkling, tingling.*
Tenture: f. *A tending; bending, reaching; stretching, spreading, extending, displaying; pitching.*
La tenture d'une chambre. *The hanging of, or a suit of hangings for, a chamber.*

Tenu:

Tenu: m. uë: f. *Held, kept, had, enioyed, possessed, retained, reserued, detained, withheld; borne, supported, vpheld; performed, effected, obserued; stopped, hindered; bridled, restrained; iudged, reputed, esteemed; bound, or beholden vnto.*

`A toy n'a pas tenu. *Thou wert no hinderance, thou gauest no impediment, broughtest no impeachment; it was not long of thee. And,* S'il n'eust tenu à toy. *Without thee, had it not beene for thee.*

On luy avoit tenu si avant la liberté, de. *He had so much libertie giuen him, or men had so long suffered him, to.*

Tenuë: f. *Hold; apprehension; performance; also, a Tenure in Law.*

Femme de proüesse, & de tenuë. *That will say and hold, that is as good as her word.*

Homme qui n'a point de tenuë. Cet homme n'a point, &c. *There is no certainetie in his speeches, no constancie in his actions; we cannot build any way vpon him.*

Tenuë: com. *Thin, slender, sleight, fine; weake; leane, gaunt; little, spare, small.*

Tenuëment. *Thinly, slenderly, sleightly; weakely; leanely, gauntly; smally, poorely.*

Tenuité: f. *Tenuitie, thinnesse, exilitie, sleightnesse, finenesse; leannesse, gauntnesse, slendernesse, scantnesse.*

Tenure: f. *A tenure; a hold, or estate in land.*

Tenure brisée. *A dissëisin.*

Tenure: com. *as* Tenuë.

Tenurement. *as* Tenuëment.

Tenuret: m. ette: f. *Somewhat slender, thin, sleight; verie little, scant, small.*

Tenureté: f. *Looke* Tenuité.

Tephramantie: f. *Diuination by ashes blowne, or cast, vp into the aire.* ¶Rab.

Tepidité: f. *Luke-warmenesse.*

Terapeutique. *as* Therapeutique.

Terbenthin: m. *The Turpentine tree.*

Terbenthine: f. *Turpentine; Looke* Terebinthine.

Terçage: m. *A third breaking, or digging vp of the ground.*

Terceau: m. *A quantitie of wine taken by some Lords vpon euerie vessell belonging to their vassalls; who if they broach any before, or before notice thereof giuen to the Lord, or his officers, loose* 60 s Tourn.

Tercéer. *To till, breake, or dig vp the ground a third time.*

Tercer. *as* Tercéer.

Tercot: m. *A little ash-coloured, and long-tongued bird, called a Wry-necke.*

Terebentine. *as* Terebinthine.

Terebinthe: f. *The Turpentine tree.*

Terebinthine: f. *Turpentine; the Rosin, or Gumme of the Turpentine tree: (This is the right Turpentine, whereas that which is commonly sold for such, is the liquide Rosin of the Larch tree.)*

Terebinthine de Venise. *Turpentine of Venice, right Turpentine; (In the shops of England, and Germanie, the liquid Rosin taken from the barke of young Firre-trees is falsely called,* Terebinthina Veneta.)

Terelle. *as* Tarelle.

Tereniaban. *Liquid Manna; of the colour, and consistence of honey.*

Terges: f. *Little Images of Saints made on peeces of painted paper, or leather, and worne, like brooches, in the hats of the youths of the parish, at publick meetings, or on solemne dayes.*

Tergiversation: f. *Tergiuersation; a flinching, withdrawing, shifting, slinking, or shrinking backe; a hafting, dodging, paultering, or paultrie excusing; a Nonsuit in Law.*

Tergiversateur: m. *A flincher, shrinker, starter, hafter, dodger, paulterer; one that is nonsuited, or withdrawes a suit, but with a purpose to begin anew.*

Tergiverser. *To flinch; to shift, slinke, or shrinke backe from; to dodge, paulter, hagle, or haft; to wrangle; excuse, deny; withdraw a suit, fall to a Nonsuit; run back, but not giue ouer.*

Teriere: f. *An Augur.*

Teriz: m. *A kind of long-heeled Linnet.*

Terme: m. *A terme, time, or day; also, a tearme, word, speech; also, a Pillar fashioned, at the vpper end, like an arme-lesse man or woman; and (more generally) any arme-lesse Image: also, a crosse way; also, a great high way; also, a stone, bound, limit, mere, diuiding land from land.*

Estre en termes. Et sommes nous en ces termes? *What? are we at this point, are we come to this passe?*

Mis en termes. *Discussed, examined, deliberated of, or fallen into deliberation.*

Tenir terme. Quel terme il tient. *What face he sets on it, what countenance he shewes in it.*

Le terme vaut l'argent. *The terme is worth my money; a Prouerbe wherewith diuers, that haue borrowed much vpon long dayes, are apt to flatter themselues, hoping that somewhat may, in the meane while, occurre to their further benefit, or full discharge.*

Il n'y a terme qui passe par delà celuy de frere: Pro. *No title goes beyond the deere name of a brother.*

Termement: m. *The appointing, or setting downe of a certaine terme, or time.*

Terminaison: f. *A termination.*

Termination: f. *A determining, finishing, ending; also, a limitting, or bounding.*

Terminé: m. ée: f. *Determined, ended, finished; bounded, limitted; also, ending, finishing; limitting, bounding.*

Terminer. *To determine, finish, end; limit, bound.*

Termoyer. *To appoint a terme, assigne a time, limit or set a day.*

Ternaire: com. *Of three, or of a third.*

Ternenaire. *A number containing many threes.*

Terner. *To throw a tre, or three.*

Terni: m. ie: f. *Wan, lew, pale, bleake, sallow, discoloured, of a duskish or deadlie hue; whose luster is lost, or verie much decayed.*

Yeux ternis. *Dull or dead eyes; eyes that are growne heauie, or be nothing so quick, liuelie, or piercing, as they haue beene.*

Ternier: m. *The small Hickway, tearmed a Wall-pecker.*

se Ternir. *To wax pale, wan, lew, bleake, discoloured, or sallow of colour; to loose, or decay much in, it former luster.*

Ternisseur: m. *A bleaker, blemisher, discolourer.*

Ternissure: f. *Palenesse, bleakenesse, wannesse, leadennesse of colour; a sallow, duskish, or deadlie hue.*

Terrace. *as* Terrasse; *also, a Terrace, or high, and open Gallerie.*

Terrage: m. *Field-rent, countrey toll; which is (if in the tenants Graunt, or Lease, there be no certaine rate set downe) the twelfth sheafe, or bundle of all sorts of Corne, Flax, Hempe, and Fruit gotten on a tenement; onely the profits and increase of Meddowes, Woods, and Vineyards are exempted, vnlesse there be a speciall custome,*

custome, or condition to the contrarie.

Disme, & terrage à deux mains. *Looke vnder* Main.

Terragé. Terre terragée. *Land held by the title, or lyable to the payment, of countrey toll.*

Terrageal: m. ale: f. *whence,* Grange terrageale. *A Barne for the receit, or keeping, of countrey toll.*

Seigneur terrageal. *A Lord that receiues* Terrage *from his tenants.*

Terrageau. *as* Terrageal, *or* Terragier.

Terrager. *To hold, or let out, lands for which* Terrage *is due; also, to sort, or lay out the fruits belonging thereto.*

Terrageresse. Grange terrageresse. *as* Grange terrageale.

Terragerie: f. *Field-rent; or, the hauing of, or holding by, field-rent.*

Terrageur: m. *One that hath* Terrage, *or field-rent.*

Terragier: m. *The tenant that yeelds, or payes his Lord field-rent.*

Terragier: m. ere: f. *Held, or holding, by* Terrage.

Terraignol: m. *A horse thats hardly raised from the ground.*

Terrain: m. *(Forced) earth, land, soyle; or, a heape thereof.*

Terrantole. *as* Tarantole.

Terrasse: f. *A plot, platforme, fort, or bulwarke; also, a banke, heape, or hillocke, of earth; also, a Pond-head; also, as* Terrace; *also, an earthen panne.*

Terrassé: m. ée: f. *Felled, ouerthrowne, or cast downe, to the earth; also, floored.*

Terrassement: m. *An ouerthrowing, or casting downe, to the earth; also, a flooring, the laying of a floore, with earth; and the strengthning of the inside of a wall with a banke, &c, of earth.*

Terrasser. *To fell, ouerthrow, or cast downe, to the earth; also, to lay, or make a floore of earth, &c.*

Terrasser vne muraille par dedans la ville. *To rampire, strengthen, or fill vp the inside of a wall with earth.*

Terrassier: m. *An ignorant, or home-bred clowne; one that neuer stirred off his owne dunghill.*

Terrau: m. *Mould, soyle, fat earth; also, as;*

Terraul: m. *A Plot, or Bulwarke of earth; also, a heape of earth; also a seat of earth in an Arbor; also, as* Terrau.

Terraut. *as* Terraul.

Terre: f. *Earth, Ground, Land, Soyle; also, a Mannor, Farme, Close, Field, peece of Ground; also, a Land, Region, Prouince, Countrey; also, the world, or the whole earth.*

Terre Ampelite. *A blackish earth, which broken, resolues into oyle: In old time they annointed Vines withall, thereby to destroy Caterpillers, and other vermine wherewith they were infested.*

Terre de l'arnage. *A whitish clay, or fat earth, whereof, in old time, Goldsmiths melting pots were made.*

Terre de Beauvois. *A certaine earth whereof pots, or vessells may be made.*

Terre Blesienne. Terra sigillata, *or* Lemnia; *found sometimes neere vnto* Blois, *and therefore so tearmed.*

Terre de Chio. *A white ash-coloured earth, which is gotten in the Island* Chio; *and which being vsed as a washing ball, makes a smooth, cleere, and well-coloured skin.*

Terre Cimolienne. *A medicinable earth, whereof there be two sorts, one white, the other purplish; the best of both feeles cold, and fattie; some call it Fullers earth.*

Terre à degraisser. *Fullers earth.*

Terre Eretrienne. *An astringent, and refrigeratiue earth, whereof there be two kinds, one exceeding white, the other ash-coloured.*

Terre Guerinienne. Terra sigillata. (*A medicinable earth.*)

Terre à laver. *Fullers earth.*

Terre Melie, ou Melienne. *A rough, and ash-coloured earth, which being tasted of, bites, and dryes, the tongue like Allum; and is vsed for the clensing of the bodies outside, whereto it giues a liuelie, and gracious hue.*

Terre d'ombre. *Beyond-sea Azur; an earth found in siluer mines, and vsed by Painters for shadowings.*

Terre Pharmacite. *as* Terre Ampelite.

Terre Pnignite. *A gluie, and ash-coloured earth, which is good to coole hot hands.*

Terre de S. Porcin. *as* Terre de l'arnage.

Terre Samienne. *A white, light, soft, moist, and gluie earth, which drunke in water, is good against poyson, and the impoysoned biting of venomous beasts.*

Terre de savon. *Fullers earth.*

Terre seellée. *The medicinable earth called,* Terra sigillata.

Terre Selinusienne. *A white, shining, and brittle earth, which quickly melts in liquor, and is an excellent skowrer of the skin.*

Terre de Venise. *A white earth, or clay, vsed by Potters.*

Terre Verde. *Borax, greene earth; also, a kind of tough greenish clay, whereof the best earthen vessells be made.*

Terre à vigne. *as* Terre Ampelite.

Enfans de la terre. *Worldlings; Looke vnder* Enfant.

Mau de terre. *The falling sicknesse.*

Terre à terre. *Euen by, close vnto, the ground.*

Manege de terre à terre. *A manage more low, and more quicke then the ordinarie gallop, or curuet.*

Sous terre. *Vnder hand, in huggar muggar.*

N'avoir ny de terre iaulne, ny de la blanche. *To haue neither gold nor siluer; to be in a verie poore, or miserable case.*

Faire de la terre le fossé; &, De terre d'autruy remplir son fossé. *Looke* Fossé.

Il ne marchoit de pied en terre. *He was so glad that he could stand on no ground, or felt not the ground he went on.*

Mettre à terre; en terre; & par terre. *Looke vnder* Mettre.

Prendre terre. *To proceed, goe forward, rid ground, get on apace; also, to land, or get ashore.*

Terre chevauchée est à demy mangée: Pro. *Farre-off land oft rid to halfe spends it selfe; The like is;*

Terre loing de soy n' apporte que flascons, & bouteilles: Pro.

De bonne terre bon tupin: Prov. *Good earth good pipkins yeeldeth.*

Nulle terre sans guerre: Pro. &, Qui a terre si a guerre: Prov. *No land without Law; no contentment without contention.*

Telle terre telle cruche: Pro. *See* Cruche.

Aujourd'huy en terre demain enterré: Pro. *To day on the earth, to morrow in it.*

On ne doit pas laisser bonne terre pour mauvais seigneur: Pro. *Good land must not be left because of a bad Landlord.*

Pour laver ses mains on n'en vend pas sa terre: Prov.

Prov. *Not clenlineſſe but coſtlineſſe makes men to ſell their lands.*

Tant vaut l' homme tant vaut ſa terre : Prov. *So worthie as a man is makes he the things belonging to him.*

Terreau: m. *Mould, ſoyle, fat earth.*

Terregarde. Matiere de ter. *A controuerſie about the meeres, or bounds of land.*

Terre-né: m. ée: f. *Borne, begotten, or bred of the earth.*

Terreneufviers. *New-found-landers, new-found-land-men.*

Terre-plein: m. *A platforme of earth ; or, the earth which is rampired, and filled vnto the inſide of a bulwarke, or wall.*

Terrer. *To terrifie, deterre, feare, skare, affright.*

Terreſtre: com. *Terreſtriall, earthlie ; liuing on, or belonging to the earth.*

Terreſterrité, & Terreſtreté: f. *Earthlineſſe, worldlineſſe ; alſo, an earthlie light, luſt, or appetite.*

Terre-tremble: m. *An earthquake.*

Terreur: f. *Terror, feare, dread, gaſtlineſſe, horror.*

Terreux: m. euſe: f. *Earthie, earthlie, of earth, full of earth.*

Terrible: com. *Terrible, dreadfull, moſt fearefull ; gaſtlie, fell, horrible, moſt cruell.*

Terriblement. *Terribly, dreadfully, moſt fearefully ; gaſtfully, horribly, moſt felly.*

Terribler. *To make terrible, or make a terrible ſhew.*

Terrien: m. *A man of meanes or poſſeſſions, a landed man.*

Terrien: m. enne: f. *Terrene, earthlie, conſiſting or ſauouring of earth.*

Terrier: m. *The hole, berrie, or earth of a Connie, or Fox ; alſo, a little hillocke ; alſo, as* Papier terrier ; *alſo, fat earth, mould, or ſoyle.*

C'eſt vne toux de regnard qui vous menera au terrier ; viz. au ſepulchre.

Terrier: m. ere: f. *Of earth, or ſoyle.*

Papier terrier. *The Court-roll, or catalogue of all the names of a Lords tenants, and of all the rents they pay, and ſeruices they owe, him.*

Terriere: f. *A Terrier, or Augar.*

Terrin: m. *as* Terraſſe.

Terrine: f. *An earthen pot, or panne ; and particularly, a panne (of earth, &c) for a Cloſe-ſtoole.*

Territoire: m. *A territorie ; the compaſſe, or continent of land or countrey belonging to a Citie, Towne, Pariſh, Lordſhip, or Mannor.*

Territoire d' un Iuge ; comprend tout le reſort. ¶L'Oiſeau.

Terroir: m. *Soyle, ground, or land ; alſo, as* Territoire.

Terron: m. *Soyle, manure, dung fully incorporated with the earth.*

Tertiane: f. *A tertian Ague.*

Tertre: m. *A little hill ; a hillocke, or barrow.*

Terue: com. *Thin, ſlender.*

Terzerol: m. *A mizzen, or poope-ſayle.*

Teſme: m. *A theame, argument, poſition, propoſition.*

Teſmoignage: m. *A teſtimonie, witneſſe, depoſition, euidence.*

Teſmoigné: m. ée: f. *Teſtified, witneſſed.*

Teſmoigner. *To teſtifie, witneſſe ; depoſe.*

Teſmoing: m. *A witneſſe, teſtis, teſtifier ; a deponent, or one that giues in euidence.*

Teſmoings. *(Are ſometimes) a mans teſticles, or ſtones.*

Teſmoing paſſe lettre: Pro. *Seeke* Lettre.

Teſniere. *as* Taniere: f. *A denne.*

Teſſeré: m. ée: f. *Squared, or made foureſquare like a dye.*

Teſſon: m. *A Gray, Brocke, or Badger ; (Looke* Taiſſon ;) *alſo, a little potſhard.*

Teſſonneau: m. *A young, or little Badger.*

Teſſons d'un preſſouër. *The ſide-boords of a preſſe.*

Teſt: m. *The ſcalpe, or ſcull of the head, &c ; Looke* Teſts.

Teſtable: com. *Teſtable ; that can make a Will ; that may be deuiſed by Will.*

Teſtament: m. *A Teſtament, or Will ; alſo, the wit, conceit, vnderſtanding ; head-furniture.*

Elle ſçait bien tout le vieil teſtament, & le nouveau. *She hath throughly learnt her lyripoope.*

Graſſe cuiſine maigre teſtament: Prov. *A fat kitchin a leane Will ; great houſe-keepers often die beggars.*

Teſtamentaire: com. *Teſtamentarie, of a Will or Teſtament.*

Teſtard: m. *The Pollard, or Cheuin fiſh ; alſo, the little blacke water-vermine called, a Bullhead.*

Teſtard: m. arde: f. *Headie, ſelfewillie, headſtrong, obſtinate.*

Teſtarderie: f. *Headineſſe, obſtinacie, ſelfewillineſſe.*

Teſtateur: m. *A teſtator ; one that hath made a Will.*

Teſte: f. *A head, pate, skonce, nole, coſtard, noddle ; alſo, headineſſe, obſtinacie, ſelfewillineſſe.*

Teſte d'un anneau. *The beazill, or collet, that part wherein the ſtone is ſet.*

Teſte d'un'armée. *The front, or forepart of an Armie.*

Teſte d'Aſne. *The Gull, Bullhead, or Millers thumbe ; (a little fiſh.)*

Teſte de boeuf. *An Oxehead, ioulthead, &c ; as vnder* Boeuf.

Teſte de cerf. *His hornes ; which we alſo call his head.*

Teſte de chien. *Looke vnder* Chien.

Teſte creuſe. *A ſhallow braine, addle head, idle aſſe.*

Teſte groſſe. *Looke hereafter, in* Groſſe teſte.

Teſte de grue. *Pinkneedle, Shepheards bodkin, Storks bill, Cranes bill, Hearons bill ; (an hearbe.)*

Teſte de Linotte. *A light head, ſhittle pate, giddie braine.*

Teſte de Moine. *A kind of blunt, and round-noſed Porpoſe ; alſo, the hearbe Dandelion, Monkes-hood, Prieſts crowne, Piſſe-abed.*

Teſte de More. *A Moores head ; and by conſequent, any blacke, or blackiſh head ; whence,* Cheval teſte de More. *A Roane horſe with a blacke face ; alſo, the Knights, a crooked peece of timber in the fore-caſtle of a ſhip ; thus tearmed, becauſe the vpper part thereof is now & then faſhioned like a Moores, or Sarracenes, head.*

Teſte de mouſche. *Looke vnder* Mouſche.

Teſte d'un pennon. *That part thereof which compaſſes, or holds by, the handle, or ſtaffe.*

Teſte de rapport. *Looke* Rapport.

Teſte d'une roſe. *The bud, or bottome of a Roſe.*

Teſte ſaine. *A ſound, or iudicious head ; an honeſt, or innocent heart ; both which are confident ; and thereupon the Prouerb,* Hardiment parle teſte ſaine.

Teſte de veau. *Calues ſnowt, Snapdragon, Lyons ſnap ; (an hearbe.)*

Teſte de vedel. *A ninniehammer, ſot, ſillie fellow.*

Teſte verte. *A young, raſh, wild-headed, or haire-braind cocks-combe.*

Crinons en teste. Il a beaucoup de crin: en la teste. *His head is full of crickets, or crochets; much troubled, or perplexed; he beates it exceedingly about some odde matter or other: Hence the Prouerbe,* Crinons en teste gastent la feste; *to signifie how vnfit, and vniust a man, in that mood, is to intertaine, or accompanie his friends, which would faine be merrie.*

Le derriere de la teste. *The noddle, or nape of the necke; the seat of the memorie; whence,* Il a le derriere de la teste vn peu large. *He hath but a bad memorie.*

Feu en la teste. Il a du feu en la teste. *He is verie chollericke, furious, or courageous; he will carrie no coales.*

Grillons en la teste; &, Tintouïns en la teste. *as* Crinons en teste.

Grosse teste. Il a vne grosse teste. *He is a ioulthead, or iobernoll; he hath more head then wit; he hath a dull, heauie, or grosse head of his owne: But when* teste *is before* grosse, *these words haue another signification; as,* Il n'a pas la teste si grosse. *His capacitie is not so large, his vnderstanding not so great, his insight into matters not so deepe.*

Mal de teste. *The headach; also, iealousie.*

Mercure en la teste. *Seeke* Mercure.

Os de la teste. *Is properly the forhead bone.*

Teste à teste. *Face to face, cheeke-by iowle, fellow-like, euen with, affront, one ouer against the other.*

`A teste baissée. *Desperately, furiously.*

`A sa teste: *As pleaseth him, of his owne head; after his owne fancie, according to his lust or liking, euen as he would haue it.*

La teste levée. *Boldly, daringly, confidently, with head lift vp aloft, holding vp his head.*

Avoir bonne teste. Il a bonne t. *He is hardie, stout, valiant:* Elle a bonne t. *She is maisterfull, curst, shrewd; a virago, or scold.*

Avoir la teste bien faicte. *To be iudicious, learned, discreet.*

Avoir la teste prez du bonnet. *Looke vnder* Bonnet.

Avoir vne teste. *To be wilfull, headie, selfewillie; to be obstinately bent vnto.*

Baisser la teste. *Looke* Baisser.

Bransler la teste. *To shake the head; a gesture denoting mockerie, or contempt; (We say of one that shaketh his head, it seemes he is not verie well pleased.)*

La teste luy bransle. *Said of one thats in a great feare, or that hath taken a pot too much.*

Donner de la teste. *To butt, or iurre; also, to runne his head against.*

Il ne sçait ou donner de la teste. *He knowes not whither to turne or betake himselfe, he knowes not what to doe.*

Faire teste à. *To resist, or withstand.*

Faire hon de la teste. *To seeme loath, or shew himselfe vnwilling, to doe a thing.*

Ie ne feray que ma teste. *I will doe no more then I thinke good, I will doe but what pleases me.*

Hocher de la teste. *Looke* Hocher.

Laver la teste à. *To chide, reproue, taunt, or checke verie bitterly.*

Mettre en teste à. *To persuade, suggest, moue, or induce vnto; to put into the head, present vnto the conceit of; also, to oppose, or set against, to confront with.*

On luy mettra la teste aux pieds. *He must be beheaded, he must loose his head.*

Ie y partis pour vne teste. *I ought to haue a share therein as heire, or coparcener; (for* Teste, *in matters of succession, is taken for an heire; whence, if there be three or foure, they say,* Ils sont tant de testes; *and if one of them die, and leaue many children, they say that altogether,* Ils font vne teste; viz. *are to haue among them the part which he had, or should haue had.)*

Se plaindre de saine teste. *To complaine of health, or ease.*

Prendre sa teste. Elle a prins sa teste. *She is grounded in wilfullnesse, of a setled obstinacie, resolued to doe but what she list.*

Rompre la teste à. *To trouble, vex, or wearie with extreame babbling.*

Tenir teste. *To stand vnto it.*

Autant de testes autant d'opinions: Prov. *As many men so many minds: The like is;* Autant d' hommes autant de testes.

En petite teste gist grand sens: Pro. *Within a little head great wit.*

Grosse teste & prim col, c' est le commencement d'un fol: Prov. *Call him a foole, and feare no checke, whose great head stands on slender necke.*

'A laver la teste d'un asne on ne perd que le temps, & la lexive: Pro. *Seeke* Asne.

Le poisson commence à sentir tousiours par la teste: Pro. *Fish euer begins to taint at the head; the first thing that's deprau'd in man's his wit.*

Le ventre emporte la teste: Prov. *The bellie ouerbeares the head; Seeke* Emporter.

Telle beste telle teste: Pro. *Such as the beast such is his head; a good, or bad nature hatches good, or bad intentions.*

Tenez chaud le pied, & la teste, au demeurant vivez en beste: Pro. *Keept head and feet warme for the rest, thou must resolue to liue a beast;* (viz. *to eat, and drinke no more then will doe thee good.)*

Testelette: f. *A little head.*

Tester. *To make a Will; to deuise, bequeath, or conuey by Will.*

Testicule: f. *A testicle, or stone.*

Testicule de chien. *Dogs testicles, dogs cullions, dogs stones, bastard Satyrion, Standlewort, Adders-grasse.*

Testier: m. ere: f. *Headie, ruling or possessing the head.*

Testiere: f. *Is generally any kind, or fashion of headpeece; but particularly, a Scull, Sallet, or steele cap; also, the crowne of a hat; also, the head-stall of a bridle; also, a horse-collar.*

Testiere d' un boeuf. *The yoaking of an Oxe by the head.*

Testification: f. *A testification, testimonie, witnessing, witnesse-bearing; a prouing, or confirming, by a witnesse.*

Testifié: m. ée: f. *Testified, witnessed, proued or confirmed by witnesses.*

Testifier. *To testifie, witnesse, beare record; proue by testimonie, confirme by witnesses.*

Testimoniale. *A Testimoniall.*

Teston: m. *A box, or cuffe giuen by the knuckles of a closed fist; also, a Testoone; a piece of siluer coyne worth* xviij d *sterling.*

Il fait de son teston six solz; &, Il fait de six solz vn teston. *Two Prouerbes applyable to a bad, and a good husband.*

Testonné: m. ée: f. *Curled, frizled, entramelled.*

Testonner. *To curle, entramell, frizle.*

Testonner la bourre. C'est la batre, *(thereby to make it the more soft, or supple.)*

Tests: m. *The scaulpe, or scull of the head; also, a potshard,*

shard, or the peece of a broken pot; also, the hard shell of a Crab, Tortoise, &c.
Testu: m. *The Pollard, or Cheuin; also, the Cod-fish.*
Le testu d'un masson. *A Masons hammer.*
Testu: m. uë: f. *Testie, headie, headstrong, wilfull, obstinate; also, headed, or hauing many heads.*
Chardon testu. *The hundred-headed thistle, field Eringus, Leuant sea Holme, champion sea Hollie.*
Femme testuë. *A domineering, or maisterfull housewife; one that (at least) would be her husbands maister; one that hath too much head.*
Tetard. Grand tetard. *A great sucker, a child that sucketh much.*
Tetasse: f. *A long, swagging, flaggie, withered, and filthie dug; whence,* Avallé en tetasse de vieille. *Hanging downe like the wrinckled, and ouglie breast of an old hag.*
Tetassier: m. ere: f. *Duggie, hauing great or long dugs.*
Tete: f. *A teat, pap, dug.*
Teté: m. ée: f. *Sucked as a dug; Looke* Tetté.
Teter. *To sucke a dug.*
Tethe. *as* Tette.
Tethine: f. *A little teat, pap, or dug.*
Tethye: f. *A certaine deformed excrescence (being neither fish, nor plant) of the sea.*
Tetin: m. *The nibble, or nipple of a dug.*
Du tetin en hors. *From his infancie.*
Tetine: f. *as* Tette; *also, an instrument of glasse, wherewith new-deliuered women get out their beest, or first grosse milke out of their breasts.*
Tetineux: m. euse: f. *Duggie, or hauing great dugs.*
Tetons. *Little teats, or dugs.*
Tetrade: f. *A quaternitie, or messe; the proportion, or number of foure.*
Tetradique: com. *Of, or belonging to, foure.*
Degrez tetradiques. *Which haue betweene euerie foure steps one broad one, called by our workmen the landing place.*
Tetragnathe. *A white, rough-legd, and most venomous spider.*
Tetragnatic. *as* Tetragnathe.
Tetragone: com. *Quadrangle, or of foure corners.*
Tetrahil, ou Tetrahit. *The Judaicall hearbe, called otherwise, Glidewort.*
Tetrasyllabe: com. *Of foure syllables.*
Tetrique: com. *Rude, harsh, vnpleasant, rough, sowre, crabbed, froward, crosse, hard to away with.*
Tette: f. *A teat, pap, dug, breast.*
Tetté: m. ée: f. *Sucked; drawne, or milked by a young one.*
Il a tetté de bon laict. *He hath beene well bred; there is much worth, or much good stuffe, in him.*
Tettée: f. *One sucking, a childs meale, as much as it will sucke at once.*
Tetter. *To sucke a dug.*
Tetthe, & Tetther. *as* Tette, & Tetter.
Tetthons. *Looke* Tetons.
Tevot: m. *A cowardlie braggadochio; one that will say much more then he dare doe.*
Teur: m. *A lattise-like couer of horse-tayle haire, in many doubles, vpon the narrow boord, whereon Clothworkers doe sheere their clothes.*
Texte: m. *A Text; the originall words, or subiect of a booke, &c, whereon Comments, or Discourses, are sometimes made.*
Textuel: m. elle: f. *Of, or in, a text.*
Iuges qui sont bons textuels. *Learned, text-readie, good booke-men, such as can readily cite all the bookes which are in a Case.*
Texture: f. *A texture, contexture, web, or weauing; composition, worke, frame.*
Tez. Le tez de la teste. *The scalpe, or skull of the head.*
Tezez. ¶Rab. *Shauen, or bald fellowes; or, as* Niais, *younglings, fops, fondlings.*
Thacor. *A scab, or pile in the fundament.* ¶Rab.
Thagadie. *Looke* Rhagade.
Thairir. *as* Tarir. *To wither.*
Thalasié: m. ée: f. *Sea-sicke.*
Thalasse. *The sea.* ¶Rab.
Thale: f. *A Greene; or, as* Talle.
Thalent. *Looke* Talent.
Thaller. *Corne to bud, shoot out their tops, or begin to eare.*
Thalmud: m. *The Jewish* Thalmud; *a superstitious and blasphemous Booke, or Law, deuised by their Rabbies, and of great authoritie among them.*
Thalmudiste: m. *A Thalmudist; a student, or professor of the superstitions contained in the* Thalmud.
Thamarinde. *as* Tamarinde.
Thapsie: f. *The stinking, or deadlie Carrot.*
Tharir. *Looke* Tarir.
Thassot: m. *A Newte, or Aske.*
That: m. *A Salamander.*
Thaumaste. ¶Rab. *A wonderer.*
Theatins: m. *The Theatins; a sect of Priests, in credit about Pope* Clement *the seuenths time, and of more antiquitie, by some few yeares, then the Iesuits.*
Theatral: m. ale: f. *Theatrall; of, belonging to, or done in, a Theater.*
Theatre: m. *A Theater; a publike Play-house; an halfe-round house wherein people sit to behold publike Playes, or Games.*
Theïe: f. *An Aunt.* ¶Pic.
Theïon: m. *An Vncle.*
Thelemite: m. *A Libertine; one that does what he list.*
Theme: m. *A theame; also, the Bill put into a Court by a plaintife.*
Theologal: m. ale: f. *Theologall; belonging to Diuinitie, or Diuines.*
Vin Theologal. *Notable good, and strong Wine; or, the best Wine, of what kind soeuer.*
Theologalement. *Theologically, diuinely.*
Theologastre: m. *A small or simple Diuine; a smatterer in Diuinitie.*
Theologie: f. *Theologie, Diuinitie; the profession, or studie of holie things.*
Theologien: m. *A Theologian, Diuine, professor of Diuinitie.*
Theomaches: m. *Warriors against the gods, as the old gyants are fained to haue beene.*
Theophaine. *The Epiphanie, or Twelfth day in Christmas.*
Theophile: com. *Louing God.*
Theorie: f. *Theorie, contemplation, deepe studie; a sight, or beholding, speculation.*
Theorique: f. *The same; and, the knowledge of an Art without practise.*
Therapeutique: com. *Curing, healing; whence;*
Medecine therapeutique. *That Phisicke, or part of Phisicke, which prescribeth remedies for the curing of diseases, and recouerie of health.*
Theraputrice. *The same.* ¶Rab.
Therbenthine. *as* Terebinthe.
Theriacal: m. ale: f. *Treacle, of Treacle.*

Theriaque: m. *Treacle.*
Theriaque des Alemans. *The iuice of Gineper berries extracted according vnto Art.*
Thermes: m. *Arme-lesse Images, &c; as in* Terme.
Thermes: f. *Hot bathes; or waters which be naturally, and continually, warme.*
Thesaurier, & Thesauriser. *as* Thezoriser.
These: f. *A generall question, argument, or position; also, as* Tede.
Thesorisé: m. ée: f. *Threasured vp; hoorded as threasure.*
Thesorisement: m. *A threasuring vp; a hoording of threasure.*
Thesoriser, & Thesorizer. *To threasure vp; to hoord, or gather threasure.*
Theumulle: f. *A Coat armor, or horsemans coat, worne by a Prince, or Generall on a day of battaile.*
Theutonique: com. *Teutonicke, German, Allman.*
Alliance Theutonique. *The Companie, or Corporation of the Hanse marchants.*
Theze. *as* Tede.
Thezoriser. *To hoord, or gather threasure; to threasure vp, to lay vp threasure.*
Thibauld. *Theobalde; a proper name for a man.*
Thie *as* Tede.
Thielles. *Ayrie inflamations.* ¶Rab.
Thierri *Theoderick; a proper name for a man.*
Thilibié. *Whose stones be worne, or wasted away.*
Thimbre. *The hearbe Sauorie.*
Thimbrée. *Looke* Thymbrée.
Thinnicule. *The fish Tunnie.*
Thiphaine. *The Epiphanie, or Twelfth day.*
Thiriaque: f. *Treacle.*
Thlasié. *Hauing bruised or broken stones.*
Thoë. *A kind of strong, swift, and short-legd Wolfe, rough-coated in Winter, bare in Summer, and a great friend vnto men, whom he defends, and fights for, against other mankind wild beasts.*
Thomas, *for* Estomac. ¶Rab.
Thon: m. *A Tunnie fish.*
Thonneu. *as* Tonlieu, *or* Toulieu.
Thonnieu. *Whence,* Droict, ou Gabelle de thonnieu. *A certaine toll, or impost, leuied to the Duke of* Buillons *vse, vpon euerie Tunne, and Hogshead of wine, or other drinke sold, in grosse, within his dominions, or transported out of them.*
Thonnine: f. *The backe, or backe-parts, of a Tunnie.*
Thorachique: com. *Belonging to the breast, or stomacke.*
Artere, & Veine thorachique. *Looke* Artere, & Veine.
Thore: m. *A certaine thicke and round circle, or member about a Pillar.*
Thore f. *The hearbe Wolues-bane; also,* Napellus, *or Monks hood: both of one poysonous kind.*
Thouiller, & Thouilleur. *as* Touiller, & Touilleur.
Thrasonien: m. enne: f. *Boasting, prowd, insolent, Thraso-like.*
Thresor: m. *Threasure, store of coyne, wealth, riches, abundance; and particularly, the (French) Kings ordinarie reuenue, or demaine; Looke* Finance.
Thresor des chartres. *The Rolls; or any place wherein publike Records (especially such as concerne the King) are kept.*
Le Thresor de garde. *The Chamber of a Citie; or, a threasure neuer touched but vpon most vrgent occasions.*
La Chambre du thresor. *Looke* Chambre.

Thresorerie: f. *A Treasurership; the office, or place of a Threasurer; also, a Threasurie, the place wherein threasure is kept.*
Thresorier: m. *A Threasurer; whereof there be diuers sorts (as here, so) in France.*
Thresorier de l'argenterie. *The Threasurer of the Kings ordinarie Wardrobe, who payes for his Maiesties apparrell, and for that which is allowed vnto his pages, and Gard.*
Thresorier de la Chambre aux deniers. *The Threasurer, or Paymaister for the diet, and for the implements (as linnen, vessell, &c) belonging to the diet, of the Kings House.*
Thresorier des Chartres. *The Maister of the Rolls; or, more properly, an officer that keepes all the Euidences concerning the Kings threasure.*
Thresorier du Domaine. *The Receiuer Generall of the Kings demaine; as also of all moneyes made by the legitimation of bastards, naturalizing of strangers, and ennobling of* Roturiers.
Thresorier de l'Espargne. *The Threasurer (somewhat resembling our Chauncellor) of the Exchequer; was at the first but one, made by* Francis *the first, and appointed to be aboue the Receiuers generall, for the bringing in, and laying vp, of all such* finance *as should be left in their hands, after the defrayment of the ordinarie charges, and extraordinarie necessities, of the Realme:* Henry *the second (his sonne) made two of them, and appointed them to serue by turnes; one his yeare, for the which he receiued 2000 pounds sterling wages; the other (who onely made vp his accompts for the yeare before) hauing but halfe as much. The Office, at the first institution, was not vendible; but being made alternatiue, it became extreamely subiect to the ordinarie Office-disease of France.*
Thresoriers extraordinaires, ou de l'extraordinaire des guerres. *Threasurers, or Paymaisters for the foot-Regiments; of two sorts, either generall ones, which are but foure; or particular and prouinciall ones, which be diuers; all alternatiue, and waiting euerie yeare by turnes.*
Thresoriers de France. *The Threasurers of France; at first there was but one, an officer of the Crowne, and called the great (or high) Treasurer of France: Afterwards,* Philippe de Valois *made a second,* Charles *the fift a third, and* Charles *the sixt a fourth; which number continued vntill the raigne of* Henry *the second, who, at one clap, made 16; a proportion, though great, yet verie moderate, in respect of the multitude brought in by his successors, and continued to these times, wherein there be aboue 200; (viz. 10, or 12 in euerie* Generalité;) *which finger no money, but looke that the Kings demaine be husbanded, his rents gathered, his houses, &c, repaired, his debts gotten, and his moneyes brought in, to his most aduantage: And although they be not officers of the Crowne (as the first high Threasurer was) nor generall throughout the Realme (howsoeuer stiled* Thresoriers de France, & Thresoriers Generaux, & Generaux des finances) *as the foure auncient* Thresoriers *were, yet are their Titles verie specious (the better to make money of) their Places held honorable, their Authoritie great, and their Priuiledges many.*
Thresorier de la maison du Roy. *The Threasurer of, or Paymaister for, the houshold; payes onely all houshold officers, and seruants their pensions, and wages.*
Thresorier des menus. *The keeper of the priuie purse; an officer which hath allowed him ten crownes*

a day for the Kings extraordinarie, and idle expences.
Thresoriers ordinaires (ou de l'ordinaire) des guerres. *The Paymaisters for the* Gensdarmerie.
Thresorier des parties casuelles. *The Threasurer for all such moneyes as be raised by the sale of Offi-*
Aujourd'huy thresorier demain tresarriere: Prov. *Looke* Tresarriere.
Thresorillon: m. *A little threasure.*
Thriacle: m. *Treacle; See* Theriaque.
Thriacleur: m. *A maker, or seller of Treacle; also, a Mountebanke, Impostor, Drug-seller, Quack-saluer.*
Thriaque. *as* Theriaque.
Thringle. *Looke* Tringle.
Thrombes de sang. *Clots, or clutters of congealed bloud.*
Throne: m. *A Throne, a royall Seat.*
Thrubal. ¶Rab. *A Trumpettor.*
Thun: m. *The fish called a Tunnie.*
Thunine: f. *as* Thonnine; *or; as* Tun.
Thym: m. *The hearbe Time; also, a certaine kernell in the kannell bone of man, or beast; also, a kind of wart within a womans priuities.*
Thymbre: f. *Winter Sauorie, Pepper Hysop.*
Thymbrée: f. *Fish-Mint, Water-Mint, Brooke-Mint; and (by some) also, Balsamint, or Balme-Mint.*
Thymelée: f. *Spurge-Flax, mountaine Widow-wayle.*
Thymique. Veine thy. *Looke* Veine.
Thymoxaline. *A composition of Time, Pennyryall, Rue, dry barlie meale, salt, water, and vineger; good against the gowt, ventosities, and weakenesse of the stomacke, and a good euacuator of grosse, and blacke humors.*
Thyn: m. *as* Thon.
Thynnuncule. *A little Tunnie fish.*
Thyon: m. *The Bunting; (a bird.)*
Thyphaine. *The Twelfth-day in Christmas.*
Tiare: f. *A round and wreathed Ornament for the head (somewhat resembling the Turkish Turbant) worne, in old time, by the Princes, Priests, and women of Persia.*
Tiburon: m. *A kind of sea-Calfe, in the Indian sea.*
Tichous: m. *Little cakes made of egges, and flower, with a little butter (and sometimes cheese among) eaten ordinarily with sugar and Rosewater.*
Ticq: m. *as* Tiquet; *(in the last sence.)*
Ticque torche lorgne. *Voices or words, whereby, as by our thwicke thwacke, &c, a beating, or cuffing with the fists, &c, is expressed.*
Ticquet. *as* Tiquet.
Tictac. *Ticke-tacke, a Game at Tables.*
Tie. *as* Tede.
Tiede: com. *Luke-warme, neither hot nor cold, betweene hot and cold; also, faint, slow, remisse, or backward in a matter.*
Tiedéer. *as* Tieder.
Tiedement. *Luke-warmely; faintly, backwardly.*
Tieder. *To warme, to make luke-warme, put some warmth into, giue a little heat vnto.*
Tiedeté: f. *Warmenesse, luke-warmenesse.*
Tiedeur: f. *Warmth; also, moistnesse, or moist warmth.*
Tiedi: m. ie: f. *Warmed, a little heated; also, bathed in, or bedewed with, teares.*
Se Tiedir. *To wax warme, grow luke-warme; also, to bath, or bedew, himselfe in teares.*
Tien: m. enne: f. *Thine, belonging to thee.*
Tien-main: m. *A stay for the hand along the wall of a staire.*
Tiens-le-bien: m. *A Crians; the long lune or line which is tyed vnto a Hawkes leg, to keepe her from flying away at her first luring.*
Tierçage: m. *A third earing, tilth, or culture of ground.*
Tierce: f. *The 24 part of a* Seconde; *a maruellous little, (and the least) weight vsed by Jewellers.*
Tierce. L'heure des tierces. *The second quarter, or third houre, of the artificiall day; in Summer eight of the clocke, in Winter tenne.*
Tierce. *whence,* Fievre tierce. *A tertian ague; Looke* Tiers, *whereof this is the feminine.*
Tiercé: m. ée: f. *Ploughed, or eared the third time; also, raised, or increased a third part euerie yeare.*
Tiercé de. *In the third place; (a tearme of Blason.)*
Paroles tiercées. *Broken or vnperfect language, disiointed speeches, halfe words.*
Tiercelet: m. *The Tassell, or male of any kind of Hawke, so tearmed, because he is, commonly, a third part lesse then the female.*
Vn tiercelet de Iob. *An exceeding patient man.*
Tiercelin: m. *Sarcenet.*
Tiercelin Plomb tiercelin. *Lead mingled a third part with white and fine, the other two with course and blacke, stuffe.*
Tiercement: m. *A third ploughing, or earing; also, an adding of a third part vnto a summe; or the rising, or increasing a third in value euerie yeare; also, a certaine inferior officer in a ship, &c.*
Tiercement. *Thirdly.*
Tiercer. *To plough, till, or eare the ground a third time; also, to rise, or increase a third part in value; as in euerie yeare, from v s the first, to vij s vj d the second, x s the third, &c.*
Tiercer le cens. C'est quand pour vingt solz de cens le subiect doit au seigneur censuel trente solz pour le profit de cens. ¶Ragueau.
Tiercerets. m. *Certaine crosse branches on the outside of a vault.*
Tiercerons. *The same.*
Tiercet: m. *A Song of triple Stanzoes, or Stanzo of three verses.*
Tierciere: f. *The vessell, or measure called a Tierce.*
Tiers: m. *A tierce, third, third part, or thirden-deale; also, as* Harle; *also, a kind of play somewhat like our Barly-breake.*
Tiers en ascendant *(in the valuation of Offices) is as much as a halfe; whence, if an Office be worth 2000 pounds, the* Tiers en ascendant *is held to be 1000 pounds.*
Droict de tiers & danger. *Looke* Danger.
Tiers: m. erce: f. *Tertian; third, the third.*
Droict de tiers denier. *Looke* Droict.
Escheoir, tomber, ou venir, en main tierce. *A noble or free Inheritance, bought by a* Roturier, *to come by discent vnto a third* Roturier *(the purchasor being the first, and both he and his next-succeeding heire hauing done homage for it;) In which case it may be parted among heires in the same manner as it should haue been, had it continued still in the hands of a Gentleman.*
Tiers-pied. *as* Trepied.
Tiers-poinct: m. Voute poinctuë comme à tiers-poinct. *Raised a little higher then the hemicicle, or halfe-circle.*
Tieu tieu Margot. *The voice of countrey people calling their Kine vnto them.*
Tieul, *for* Tel. *Such; (an old word.)*
Tifé, & Tifer. *as* Attiffé, & Attiffer.
Tiffer. *The same; also, to tifle with the fingers, or busie the hands long about a thing, to the end it may be done well, or to the good liking of him that does it.*

Tige: f. *The staulke, or stemme of an hearbe; also, the maine stocke of a Familie, or Pettigree; whence;*
Tant que tige fait souche elle ne branche iamais. *As long as there be any heires of an elder Prince of the bloud, the younger cannot haue the Crowne.*
Tigette: f. *A little staulke, or stemme.*
Tigname. *Red Stirax; an aromaticall Indian wood vsed by Perfumers.*
Tigne. *as* Teigne.
Tigneux. *Looke* Teigneux.
Tignon: m. *A scurfe, or scalinesse of the skin.*
Tigre: m. *A Tiger.*
Ialoux comme vn tigre. *Extreamely iealous; (for so is that beast reported to be.)*
Tigreau: m. *A young, or little Tiger.*
Tigresque: com. *Tiger-like; fierce, cruell, violent, swift, sauage.*
Accoustré à la tigresque. *Horribly beaten or bescratched, cruelly handled.*
Tigresse: f. *A Tigresse, a she Tiger.*
Tigrin: m. **ine**: f. *Of a Tiger; like a Tiger; cruell, fierce, violent, swift.*
Tigrique: com. *as* Tigrin.
Til: m. *The Line, Linden, or Teylet tree; Seeke* Tillet.
Tiles. *The small moats of dust appearing, and wauing vp and downe, in the Sunne-beames which come into a roome at the crannies, or holes of walls, &c.*
Tilet: m. *A ticket, billet, or little note.*
Tilier: m. *as* Tillet; *the Linden tree.*
Tillac: m. *The Orelop, or Arloup; or, more generally, the hatches of a ship.*
Tillaquer. *To boord, or floore the Orelop of a ship.*
Tille: f. *The rinde, or pilling of Hempe, &c; also, the fruit of the Linden tree; also, a kind of Wimble.*
Tillé: m. **ée**: f. *Pilled, or shaled, as Hempe.*
Tiller. *To pill, or shale Hempe.*
Tillet: m. *The Line, Linden, or Teylet tree; also, a ticket, billet, or little note.*
Tillet femelle. *The female Line tree, called in some places, the broad-leafed Elme.*
Tillet masle. *The male Line tree; the timber whereof is yellowish, and more knottie, hard, and substantiall, then that of the female, which is whitish, plaine, smooth, and soft in the handling and cutting.*
Tilleul. *as* Til.
Tilleux: m. **euse**: f. *Knobbie, scalie, rough, rugged.*
Tillier: m. *The Linden tree.*
Tiltre: m. *A tittle; a small line drawne ouer an abridged word, to supply the letters wanting; also, a title, or inscription; also, a title, name, surname, or addition of dignitie; also, a title vnto land, &c; also, an Euidence, Deed, or Instrument, of Purchase, &c; also, a brace of dogs layed in a place to be let slip at a Deere as he passeth by; also, the rate, value, or degree of goodnesse of gold, and siluer; the highest of the first being 24 graines, and of the second 12 d; but to be wrought by Goldsmithes, &c, at 23 graines three quarters the one, and 11 d 10 graines the other.*
Timble. *A Coat-armor, or coat of Armor; or as* Tymbre; *(an old word.)*
Timbon. *A kind of brasen Drumme.*
Timbre: m. *A Colledge-bell; or the Hall-bell of a Colledge, or Cloister; also, the bell of a little Clocke; also, a great Tub; also, the stone bason, trough, or vessell at the foot of a Fountaine; also, the creast, or cognisance, thats borne vpon the helmet of a coat of Armes: This in the opinion of our Blasonners, who call it a Timber, and deriue it from the Germane* Timmer; *whereunto* Nicot *seemes agreeable, as to the sence, in his,* Timbre qu'on met sus vn Heaulme; *and* Vigenere *vpon* Liuie, *in his,* Il portoit au timbre de son cabasset vne figure de poisson; *yet* L'Oiseau, *a late, and learned writer, appropriates it (in his Booke* des Ordres) *onely to the Helmet.*
Vn timbre de Martres. *A certaine quantitie, or number, of Martins skins.*
Timbré. Armoiries timbrées. *Timbered, creasted; adorned with a creast, or with a mantle, helme, creast, &c; or (onely) insigned with an Helmet.*
Cerveau mal timbré. *An idle, ignorant, or ill-furnished braine; a wit that wanteth fit, or due ornaments.*
Timbrer. *To timber; to creast; to furnish, or adorne with a creast, or with a mantle, helme, and creast (as one of our latest Blasoners expounds it;) or (onely) to garnish, or insigne it with an helmet.*
Timide: com. *Timerous, fearefull, awfull, bashfull, faint, cowardlie, white-liuered.*
La mere du timide ne sçait que c'est de pleurer: Pro. *The mother of a fearefull sonne knowes not what tis to weepe.*
Timidement. *Timorously, fearefully, cowardly, bashfully.*
Timidité: f. *Timiditie, timorousnesse, fearefullnesse, faintheartednesse, cowardlinesse, bashfullnesse.*
Timon: m. *The beame, or draught tree of a wagon, &c; also, the staffe, or handle (which we call the whip) of the Rudder, or sterne of a ship.*
Timoré: m. **ée**: f. *Frighted, skared, put into a feare.*
Timpan. *Looke* Tympan.
Timpanisé. Bastiment timp. *Hauing a gable-end.*
Timper. *To tingle, to make ring or sound, &c; as* Tinter. ¶Rab.
Tin: m. *Tinne; also, a tinging; whence;*
Les oreilles me font tin. *Mine eares tingle, or glow.*
Tiné: m. *A Colestaffe, or Stang; a big staffe whereon a burthen is carried betweene two on their shoulders.*
Tine: f. *A Stand, open Tub, or Soe, most in vse during the time of Vintage, and holding about foure or fiue pailefulls, and commonly borne, by a Stang, betweene two.*
Tinée: f. *A Stand full, or Soe-full.*
Tinel: m. *A houshold, or familie; also, the roome wherein all the seruants of a familie dine and sup; also, as* Tine.
Tinet: m. *The Whall tearmed a Horlepoole, or Whirlepoole; also, as* Tine.
Tinette: f. *A little Stand, Soe, or Tub; a bathing tub.*
Tiniez: m. *Long white rockes lying vnder water in the sea.*
Tinne. *as* Tine.
Tinole: f. *A little Soe, Tub, Stand, &c.*
Tinon: m. *A little Soe; a Stand, or small open Tub.*
Tintalorisé. *Grimme, frowning, froward.*
Tintamarre: f. *A clashing, or crashing, a rustling or gingling noise, made in the fall of wooдden stuffe, or vessels of mettall; also, a blacke* Santus; *the lowd wrangling, or iangling outcryes of scoulds, or scoulding fellowes; any extreame or horrible dinne.*
Tintamarré: m. **ée**: f. *Crashing, gingling; wrangling, iangling; extreame-dinne-making.*
Tinté. *Tinged, tingled, rung, resounded; towled.*
Tintement: m. *A tinging, ringing, tingling; towling; resounding, cleere-sounding.*
Tinter. *To ting, ring, tingle; to towle; to resound, or sound cleere.*
Les oreilles me tintent. *Mine eares tingle, or glow.*
Tinthimal. *as* Tithymale.

Tintillant: m. ante: f. *Tinging, ringing, tingling; tolling; resounding.*
Tintimale. *as* Tithymale.
Tintin: m. *The tinging, or tolling of a bell; also, the warble, or song of a Nightingale.*
Tintiner. *To ting, or toll, a bell.*
Tintoïns. *Looke* Tintouïns.
Tinton: m. *The burthen of a song; also, the ting of a bell; also, a kind of dance.*
Tintoner. *To ting, or toll often; to glow, tingle, dingle.*
Tintouïn: m. *A ringing, singing, or tingling in the head, about the eares; also, great care, anxietie, or trouble of spirit; whence;*
Il a beaucoup de tintouins en la teste. *His thoughts are verie much busied, his pate sore troubled, braine extreamely puzled; his head is full of proclamations, perplexitie, dinne.*
Tintouïner. *as* Tintoner; *also, to resound in the eare; and to trouble, puzle, or perplex the braine.*
Tinture: f. *Red wine, or Aligant; (belike because it staines.)*
Tiphaine: f. *The Epiphanie, Twelfth day.*
Tipher. *as* Tiffer.
Tiphoine. *as* Tiphaine; (Rustiquement.)
Tipule: f. *A water-spider; a spider which runnes on the water without sinking.*
Tique: f. *The vermine called a Ticke.*
Tiquet: m. *as* Tique; *or, a little Ticke; also, the hearbe Kicke,* Ricinus, Palma Christi; *also, a disease which on a suddaine stopping a horses breath, makes him to stop, and stand still.*
Au tiquet. *In an exceeding strait or extremitie, at his wits end, not knowing further what to say or doe.*
Prés du tiquet de la mort. *Neere his last gaspe, readie to breath his last.*
Tiqueté: m. *Ticketted, or appointed by ticket.*
Tirace. *Looke* Tirasse.
Tirade: f. *A draught, pull, plucke; shot, or shoot; a drawing, pulling; shooting.*
Tirage: m. *Draggage; or, a drawing, haling, pulling, plucking, towing, tugging.*
Droict de tirage pour le sel, ou pour le Vin. *Looke vnder* Droict.
Tirailler. *To rend, or teare in peeces.*
Tiran: m. *Any string, lace, line, or cord, which pulled at one end, closes at the other the thing it is fastened vnto; Hence,* Les tirans d'une bourse; &, les tirans d'un chaperon de faucon; *the strings wherewith they are shut.*
Tirans: m. *as* Trayans.
Tirant: m. ante: f. *Drawing, &c; Looke* Tirer.
Tirasse: f. *A Drag-net for Partridges, &c; also, the strap of a boot.*
Tirassé: m. ée: f. *Dragged, pulled, haled, towed along, or towards.*
Tirasser. *To drag, pull, hale, tow along, or towards.*
Tire: f. *A draught, pull, plucke, twitch, tug, lug; stretch, retch; also, a shot, or shoot, hurle, fling, throw, cast, pitch; also, a tire; a stroke, hit; kicke, yarke; iert, ierke, twang, twing; also, a reach, gate, course, or length and continuance of course; also, the drawing out of a womans gowne sleeues with Cobweb-lawne, &c.*
'A tire d'aile. *By force, with might of wing; also, with long and much flight, or flying.*
'A tire & à aire. *Quite and cleane; Looke* Aire.
Tout d'une tire. *All in one length, continually, or continuedly; at once, at one iert, all together; without stop, intermission, or delay.*

Tiré: m. ée: f. *Drawne, haled, dragged, towed, pulled, plucked, lugged; trayled along, or towards; also, stretched, retched; also, shot, hurled, throwne, cast, flung; also, moued, induced, persuaded; also, wrested, extracted, or forced from; also, shot, or slaine, with a Pistoll, &c; also, drawne, pourtrayed, delineated.*
Tiré de loing. *Farre fetched.*
Bien tiré. *Well drawne; also, neat, spruce, fine, tricksie, trimme.*
Tire-balle. *An Instrument wherewith Surgeons draw bullets out of the bodie.*
Tirée: f. *as* Tire.
Tirée d'oeil. *The sight, view, looke, or glaunce of the eye.*
Tirebourre: f. *A worme, or skrue; the Instrument wherewith a charged Cannon is vnladen.*
Tire-feu: m. *A medicine, or plaister for the drawing of fire, or extreame heat, out of a wound, &c.*
Tire-fiens: m. *A Drag wherewith dung is taken vp, vpon the remoue of a dunghill.*
Tire-fleiche: f. *An Instrument wherewith Surgeons draw arrowes out of the bodie.*
Tirefond de Chirurgien. *A Surgeons Terebra, or Piercer; an Instrument which he puts vnto diuers vses.*
Tirefond de tonnelier. *A Coopers Turrell; the Augar wherewith he boreth holes.*
Tirelaines: m. *Cloke-twitchers; rogues which in the night-time lurke about the corners of streets, to snatch away the clokes of such as passe by them.*
Tire-laisse: m. *A forgoing of a new-taken hold; a speedie restorall, or giuing backe, of a thing seised as his owne, but prouing another mans.*
Tire-lardon: m. *A lickorish, or greedie fellow.*
Tire-larigaud. Boire à tire-la. *To carowse lustily, quaffe extreamely.*
Tirelire. *A Christmas box; a box hauing a cleft on the lid, or in the side, for money to enter it; vsed in France by begging Fryers, and here by Butlers, and Prentices, &c; also, the warble, or song of a Larke.*
Tirelirer. *To warble, or sing like a Larke.*
Tirelupin: m. *A catch-bit, or captious companion; a scowndrell, or scuruie fellow.*
Tirelyre. *as* Tirelire.
Tirement: m. *A drawing, haling, dragging, trayling, towing; pulling, plucking, twitching, along, or towards; also, a retching, or stretching; also, a shooting, darting, flinging, hurling, throwing; also, a wresting, exacting, or forcing from; also, a drawing, delineating, pourtraying; also, a yerking, ierting, kicking; also, a going along, or making towards.*
Tire-pance. 'A tir. *Hold bellie hold, or till the bellie cracke withall.*
Tire-pied: m. *A Shoomakers stirrup.*
Tire-pierre. *A Surgeons Instrument, made like a toothpicker at the one end, like a hooke at the other; and vsed for the drawing of stones, &c, out of the bladder, &c, or bullets, &c, out of the bodie.*
Tire-poil: m. *A haire-plucker; an instrument, medicine, or plaister, for the plucking away of haire.*
Tirer. *To draw, drag, trayle; tow, hale; pull, plucke, lug, tug, twitch; bring, lead, along, or towards; also, to stretch, retch, dilate, extend, wiredraw; also, to dart, shoot, sling, fling, hurle, cast, throw, pitch fromwards; also, to shoot one with a Pistoll, &c; also, to take, extract, wrest, or force from; also, to yerke, winse, fling, or flye out with the heeles; also, to wend, goe, trauell, make along or towards; also, to draw, delineate, or pourtray; also, to resemble, or draw neere vnto.*

Tirer des armes. *To fence.*
Tirer arriere. *To giue or fall backe, to retire.*
Tirer à l'auiron. *To row hard, to tug at an Oare.*
Tirer au baston. *To striue, contend, struggle, wrastle; also, to fight, or deale blowes; whence,* Tandis qu'ils tiroient au baston. *Whilest that they bickered, or layed about them.*
Tirer les chausses. *To tipe vp the heeles, to dye.*
Tirer au cheurotin. *Looke* Cheurotin.
Tirer au collier auec. *To striue, contend, wrastle hard with.*
Tirer à consequence. *To make an example, or precedent of.*
Tirer la couuerte de son costé. *To pull the Couerlet vnto his side;* viz. *all dealings, or gaines vnto him, and his.*
Tirer de dessous l'aile. *To purloyne, steale cunningly, filch priuily from.*
Tirer l'eau. *To leake, or let in water.*
Tirer l'eau à son moulin. *Looke vnder* Eau.
Tirer l'espaule. *To shrinke in the necke, or lift vp the shoulders, as one that hath no liking of, or fancie to, a matter.*
Tirer son espingle du ieu. *To flinch, or slinke away in an extremitie, to slip his necke out of the collar.*
Tirer à faute. *To misse, in shooting.*
Tirer à la fin. *To be at the last cast, lye a dying, approach vnto his end.*
Tirer des flancs. *A horse to strike often at his owne bellie.*
Tirer du foing aux chiens. *To spue, vomit, cast his gorge.*
Tirer la laine. *To snatch a cloake off a mans backe, and runne away withall.*
Tirer la langue sur. *Scornefully to put out the tongue at.*
Tirer hors ligne. *To summe vp, &c; as vnder* Ligne; *also, to expresse, mention, set downe.*
Tirer à la main. *A horse to presse vpon the hand, or striue to get forward, and goe faster then he should.*
Tirer l'oreille. *Seeke* Oreille.
Tirer païs. *(In hunting) to runne his countrey; or, to flye directly forward; (in trauelling) to goe on, rid ground, gaine way.*
Tirer la quintaine. *To runne at the Quintaine.*
Tirer au regnard. *To spue, cast, vomit.*
Tirer le rideau. *To display, manifest, make apparent; also, to conclude, or shut vp.*
Tirer au riuet. *To sow like a Shoomaker; also, to plucke as much from one as from another.*
Tirer la robbe. *Looke* Robbe.
Tirer le serpent du buisson. *To performe a difficult, or dangerous exploit.*
Tirer son vent. *To fetch his breath.*
Tirer les vers du nez à. *To pumpe, or draw secrets out of, to vndermine.*
Tant que le vaisseau peut tirer. *As long as it will runne, or hath any thing in it.*
Le ventre luy tire. *His bellie strouts, retches, or is readie to cracke, by fullnesse.*
Chascun tire à son profit: Pro. *Euerie one lookes after his owne profit, or inclines vnto that which is likelie to bring him in gaine.*
Mieux vaut tirer que rompre: Prov. *Better to bow then to cracke, to bend then to breake.*
On ne peut tirer du sac que ce qu'y est: Pro. *Looke vnder* Sac.
Pour bien tirer il faut prendre visée: Prov. *To doe things well we must consult aduise.*
Qui bien tire deux en a: Pro. *Who pulls amaine does rend in traine; he that plucks hard gets two.*
Ce qu' assemble pille pille, desassemble tire tire: Pro. *What hath beene got by miserie and pillage, comes to be subiect to vnthriftie spoylage.*
On touche tousiours sur le cheual qui tire: Pro. *The free drag-horse is alwayes ouerraught.*
Tiret: m. *A little draught, pull, plucke, twitch, tug, &c, as in* Tire; *also, a little stroke, or tittle in writing.*
Tiretaine: f. *Linsie-wolsie; or a kind thereof, worne ordinarily by the French peasants.*
Tireur: m. *A drawer, puller, plucker, haler, lugger, tugger, tower; a shooter, darter, caster, hurler, flinger; a retcher, stretcher, extender, lengthener, wire-drawer.*
Tireur à l'auiron. *A Rower.*
Tireur de laine. *A Teyser of wooll; also, as* Tire-laine.
Tirin. *as* Tarin.
Tirofageur: m. *A cheese-eater.* ¶Rab.
Tiroir: m. *A ring, or any other thing, on the outside of a doore, seruing to pull it to, or shut it after one that goes out.*
Tirouër: m. *Tiring for Hawkes; also, a Drawer vnder a Table, or Cupboord; also, as* Tyrouër.
Tiroüoir. *The same; or, as* Tiroir.
Tirse: f. *The dart, or iauelin of Bacchus.*
Tisanne: f. *Ptisanne, Barlie water.*
Tison: m. *A fire-brand.*
'A Noel au Perron; à Pasques au tison: Pro. *Warmth at Christmas, cooth at Easter; the fire which Christ-tide spareth Easter spendeth.*
Tisonner. *Often to stirre firebrands, or lay them close together.*
Tisserand: m. *A Weauer.*
Tisserande: f. *A woman Weauer.*
Tisseure: f. *A weauing; or, as* Tissure.
Tissier, & Tissiere: f. *as* Tisserand, & Tisserande.
Tissotier: m. *A Weauer.*
Tissu: m. *A bawdricke, ribbon, fillet, or head-band, of wouen stuffe.*
Tissu: m. uë: f. *Wouen; plaited, interlaced, wound one within another.*
Tissure: f. *A weauing; or plaiting; an interlacing; also, the woofe, or west; the thread which crosseth stuffe, or goeth ouerthwart it in the weauing; also, any wouen stuffe; but especially cloth of gold, siluer, silke, &c.*
Tistre. *To weaue; also, to plait, infould, enwrap, interlace one within another.*
Titan. Le Titan. *(Poetically) the Sunne.*
Titanique: com. *Belonging, or, like to the Sunne.*
Force Titanique. *Huge, mightie, Giant-like force.* ¶Rab.
Titeller. *To ting, or tingle, as a (little) Bell.*
Tithymale: m. *The hearbe Spurge, Tithymale, Wolues-milke.*
Tithymale Amygdaloïdes. *as* Tithymale Characias: *or the second kind thereof.*
Tithymale Caryites. *Myrtle Spurge, female Spurge.*
Tithymale Characias. *Wood Spurge, or male Spurge.*
Tithymale Cyparissias. *Cypresse Spurge, Pine-Spurge; or (as* Mathiolus *thinkes) small Esula.*
Tithymale Dendroïdes. *Tree Spurge; growes among stones, and rockes, to a tree-like height.*
Tithymale femelle. *Myrtle Spurge, female Spurge, Phisicke Spurge.*

Tithymale Helioscopius. *Sunne Spurge, time Tithymale.*
Tithymale Leptyphyllos. *Small-leafed Spurge.*
Tithymale marin. *Sea-Spurge, sea-Wartwort.*
Tithymale masle. *Wood Spurge, male Spurge, Almond Spurge.*
Tithymale Myrsinites, & Myrtien. *as* Tithymale femelle.
Tithymale Paralius. *Sea-Spurge, Wolues-milke, sea-Wartwort.*
Tithymale Platyphyllos. *Broad-leafed Spurge.*
Tithymale suyvant le soleil. *as* Tithymale Helioscopius.
Titillation: f. *A tickling.*
Titillé: m. ée: f. *Tickled.*
Titiller. *To tickle; to stirre, touch, or moue with delight.*
Titrac: m. *The fashion, or order of a thing.*
Titre. *Looke* Tiltre.
Titubant: m. ante: f. *Tripping, stumbling, staggering; faultering, stutting, stammering; also, quiuering, doubtfull, wauering.*
Titubation: f. *A tripping, stumbling, staggering; a faultering, stutting, stammering; a quiuering, trembling, doubtfullnesse, wauering.*
Titulaire: com. *Titular; hauing a title; consisting of titles, or onely in title.*
Tochere. *Fearne, brakes; or a fearnie ground.* ¶Rab.
Tocque: f. *as* Toque.
Tocqué: m. ée: f. *Coyffed.*
Tocquement: m. *as* Toquement.
Toffe: f. *as* Touffe; *also, a plant called Spunge of the Riuer.*
Toffu: m. uë: f. *Looke* Touffu.
Toge: f. *A gowne; long robe, or garment.*
Togue. *as* Toge.
Tohu. *Confusion.* ¶Rab.
Toict: m. *The roofe, or couer of a house; also, the house it selfe.*
Toile: f. *Cloth, linnen cloth; also, a staulking horse, of cloth, &c; whence,* Chaffer à la toile; *also, the cawle, or kell within the bellie; also, as* Peritoine.
Toile de araigne. *A Cobweb.*
Toile baptiste. *A strong, and verie white (but course) Cambricke, whereof Nunnes make their vayles.*
Toile de Cambray. *Cambricke.* d'Hollande; *Holland.*
Toile Gautier. *See* Gautier.
Toile de maison; &, Toile de mesnage. *A good strong huswiues, or houshold, linnen cloth.*
Iour de toile. *A Court day, day of Pleading, Hall day.*
Vn penitent de quatre aulnes de toile. *A small, or sleight repentant (God he knowes.)*
A toile ourdie Dieu mande le fil: Pro. *Seeke* Fil.
Toiles: f. *Toyles; or, a Hay to inclose, or intangle, wild beasts in.*
Toilette: f. *A Toylet; the stuffe which Drapers lap about their clothes; also, a bag to put night-clothes, and buckeram, or other stuffe to wrap any other clothes, in.*
Toillé. *as* Touillé.
Toinin: m. *(A diminutiue of Anthoine) Tonie.*
Toisage: m. *A fadoming; or the measuring by fadomes.*
Toise: f. *A fadome; a measure containing six feet in length; This is the most ordinarie* Toise, *howsoeuer the Kings be seuen foot and foure ynches; and some of particular places longer, some lesse.*
Toise des bois & forests. *The fadome for woods, and forests; is (by the customes of* Orleans*) fiue foot and a halfe long.*
Toise de Bourgongne. *The Burgonian fadome, is seuen foot and a halfe.*
Toise de charpentier. *The Carpenters fadome, is as the fadome for woods, &c.*
Toise cube. *The square fadome, or a fadome in square, containes all ouer 216 feet.*
Toise de Masson. *The Masons fadome, is (as the ordinarie one) six foot long.*
Toise des Mesureurs de terres, & vignes. *The Surueyors fadome, is but fiue foot long.*
Toise de Roy. *The Kings fadome, is, among Architects, three moderate paces; and among Surueyors, seuen feet and foure ynches.*
Toiser. *To fadome, or measure by fadome.*
Toiseur: m. *A fadomer.*
Toison: m. *A fleece of wooll; the whole wooll of a sheepe.*
Tolerable: com. *Tollerable, sufferable, indifferent, reasonable; that may be borne, indured, abidden.*
Rente tolerable. *An auncient rent which cannot be extinguished, nor bought out, but must be borne, & payed.*
Tolerablement. *Tollerably, sufferably.*
Tolerance: f. *Tolleration, sufferance, permission, induring, patience, forbearing.*
Tolerer. *To tollerate, suffer, permit, beare with, winke at, indure, abide.*
Toliban: m. *A Turbant, or Turkish hat.*
Tollart: m. *An executioner, a hangman; and hence, the Prouost Marshalls attendants be (in disgrace) oftentimes called* Tollarts.
Tollere. *A Turkish coyne worth about* iiij s *sterling.*
Tollet. *A Thowle, &c, as* Scalme.
Tollieu. *as* Toulieu.
Tollin: m. *The toll taken by a Miller.*
Tollir. *To remoue, take away; disannull, abrogate, cancell, abolish, make void.*
Tollu: m. uë: f. *Taken, remoued, lift, or carried, away.*
Tolopan. *as* Turbant.
Tolte: f. *A taking, exaction, leuie.*
Tombant: m. ante: f. *Falling, or tumbling downe, alighting vpon.*
Tombant levant. *Well or ill, hittie missie, here or there, one way or other.*
Tombe: m. *A Gurnard fish.*
Tombe: f. *A tombe; a tombe-stone, or graue-stone.*
Tombé: m. ée: f. *Fallen, tumbled downe or into; light vpon.*
Tombeau. *A tombe, graue, sepulcher.*
Tombement: m. *A falling, or tumbling downe; a lighting vpon.*
Tomber. *To fall, or tumble downe, or into; also, to light vpon.*
Tomber de l'eau. *To pisse, or make water.*
Tomber à faux. *Looke* Faux.
Attendre le gland qui tombe. *(An ordinarie person) to liue in expectation of profit, or preferment, at Court.*
Ie crains fort, ou tombera cecy. *I greatly feare the successe, or issue of this matter;* &, ou veulent tomber ces belles parolles. *I doubt me no good will come of this glozing.*
Qui chope, & ne tombe adiouste à ses pas: Prov. *The man that trips, and falls not, gaines a step.*
Vn meschant vaisseau iamais ne tombe de la main: Pro. *The best things runne more hazard then the worst; ill vessells neuer, good ones often, fall.*
Tombereau: m. *A Tumbrell, or Dung-cart.*
Tombereaux de Verberie. *Looke* Verberie.
Tomberel. *as* Tombereau.

Prendre les perdris au tomberel; viz. *by tunnelling.*
Tomberelée: f. *A tumbrell full, the load of a tumbrell.*
Tombier: m. *A Tombe-maker.*
Tombir. *To make a noise with stamping, or trampling; to rustle, or hurrie, like the feet of many gallopping horses.*
Tombissement: m. *A stamping, or trampling noise; the rustling, or hurrie of running horses feet.*
Tome: m. *A Tome, or Volume; part of a Booke, or Worke, in one volume.*
Tome: f. *A traine with a lame and disarmed Heron, for the making of a young Faulcon.*
Tomin: m. *Six-pennie weight, or the weight of a Spanish Reall.*
Ton: m. *A tune, or sound; also, the Tunnie fish.*
Ton: m. ta: f. *Thy, belonging to thee.*
Tondailles: f. *A sheepe-sheering, or the feast made thereat.*
Tondelet: m. *(A fashion of) Bases for a horseman, or one that rides.*
Tonderesse: f. *A woman that sheereth, or shaueth.*
Tondeur: m. *A sheerer, clipper, powler, shauer; barber; vermine-snipper.*
Tondeur de draps. *A Shearman, or Clothworker.*
Tondeur de nappes. *as* Escornifleur.
Tondeuse: f. *The wife of a Clothworker, or Barber; also, a woman which liues by sheering of cloth, or cutting of haire.*
Tondoison. *as* Tonsure.
Tondre. *To sheere, clip, cut, powle, nott, pare round; sweepe cleane, or cleere away.*
Tondre sur vn oeuf. *To accuse truth of falsehood, charge vertue with vice, find a fault where there is none; also, to make a commoditie of any thing, how bare socuer it be;* whence, Ils trouveront à tondre sur vn oeuf.
Si ie ne fais cela qu'on me tonde. *Let me be baffled if I doe not that.*
Aprez raire n'y a que tondre: Prov. *Sheeres vpon shauen places doe no good; nought's to be got where all's alreadie gone.*
Tondu: m. *Shorne, clipped, powled, notted, cut, pared round.*
La fesse tonduë. *One that is bare-breecht, or hath not a rag to couer his tayle withall; also, a notable wencher; or, as* Fesse-tonduë.
Il a esté tondu de son entreprise, ou de sa brigue. *He hath failed of his purpose, or lost his suit.*
Il ne craint ny les rez ny les tondus. *Looke* Rez.
Toutesfois fut le pré tondu. *Yet was the meddow mowen; the businesse ended.*
Tondu-ras. *Close-shauen, leuelled, or layed euen with.*
Tondure: f. *as* Tonsure.
Tonlieu: m. *Toll due vnto the Lord of a Faire or Market, for the sale, or standing of cattell, and other commodities in it.*
Tonne: f. *as* Tonneau; *also, an arbor.*
Tonneau: m. *A Tunne; or (generally) any great vessell, or peece of Caske for Wine, &c; as a Tunne, Pipe, Hogshead, &c; also, a Tunnell for Partridges.*
C'est d'un autre tonneau. *This is of another straine, or pitch of conceit.*
Tonneler, & Tonneleur. *Seeke* Tonneller, & Tonnelleur.
Tonnelet: m. *A little Tunne, or small peece of Caske.*
Tonnelier: m. *A Cooper.*
Tonnelieu. *as* Tonlieu.
Tonnelle: f. *A Tunnell, or staulking horse for Partridges; also, a round Arbor, or an Alley couered round with the interlaced branches of a Vine, &c; from;*
Tonnelles. *The tender branches of trees plashed, or interlaced together as they grow.*
Tonneller. *To take Partridges with a Tunnell, or staulking horse.*
Tonnelleur: m. *A Tunneller; a Taker of Partridges with a Tunnell.*
Tonner. *To thunder.*
On n'orroit pas Dieu tonner. *The noise, or dinne they made was most extreame; a thunder clap could not haue beene heard among them.*
Quand il tonne en Mars nous pouvons dire helas: Prov. *We say that, Winters thunder is Summers wonder.*
Tant tonne qu'il pleut; &, Tant tonne, & vente, que pluye descend: Pro. *So much it thunders that at length raine falls; Looke* Plouvoir.
Tout ce que tonne ne nous estonne point: Pro. *All that does thunder makes vs not to wonder.*
Tonnerre: m. *Thunder.*
Apres gros tonnerre force eau sur la terre: Prov. *After a furious thunder much raine the earth doth blunder.*
Tonnereux: m. euse: f. *Full of thunder, thunder-like, thundering.*
Tonnine: f. *A meat made of Tunnie; or, as* Thonnine.
Tonnoirre: m. *Thunder.*
Tonsilles: f. *Certaine kernells at the root of the tongue, subiect vnto inflamations, and swellings, occasioned by the falling downe of humors from the head.*
Tonsture. *as* Tonsure.
Tonsure: f. *A sheering, clipping, powling, notting, cutting, or paring round; also, the shauing, or shauen crowne of a Priest;* whence, Tonsure clericale; &;
A simple tonsure. *Such Clergie men as are but meerely Clarkes, not hauing taken Orders, nor vndertaken the charge of soules; of which ranke are Prebends, Canons, Deacons, &c.*
Alleguer sa tonsure. *A Priest, challenging the priuiledge of his Orders, to appeale from the ciuill Iudge vnto his Ordinarie.*
Tonsuré: m. ée: f. *Sheered, clipped, powled; also, shauen;* whence;
Clercs tonsurez. *Shauelings, full Priests.*
Tonsurer. *To clip, sheere, powle, nott; also, to shaue.*
Tonture: f. *as* Tonsure.
Topase: f. *A topase, stone.*
Topiaire: f. *The making of Images in, or Arbors of, Plants.*
Topiquer. Se top. *To be titchie, or apt to take offence at; also, to oppose, contest with, bandie against.*
Topiques: m. *Topicks; bookes, or places of Logicall inuention; also, remedies (as plaisters, &c) applyed vnto vnsound parts of the bodie.*
Topiqueur: m. *An acute arguer, or disputer; or, an inuentor of Logicall, and probable arguments.*
Topographe: m. *A describer of places.*
Topographie: f. *The description of a place.*
Toppe. Terre estant en toppe. *Wast (because vnhusbanded, or vntilled) ground.*
Toque: f. *A (fashion of) bonnet, or cap (somewhat like our old Courtiers veluet cap) worne ordinarily by schollers, and some old men.*
Toque d'or, ou d'argent. *Plated cloth of gold, or siluer; a kind of tinsell, or stuffe that is striped with gold, or siluer.*

Toquement: m. *as* Toque; *also, the wearing of, or furnishing the head with, a* Toque; *also, a clapping, hitting, or knocking against.*

Toquer. *To put on a* Toque; *to furnish or attire the head therewith; also, to clap, knocke, or hit against; also, to iumble a woman.*

Toquesing: m. *An Allarum bell; or the ringing thereof.*

Toquet: m. *A little* Toque; *or a kind of bonnet not so large as the* Toque, *worne most by children.*

Torasse: f. *A low and little-bodied Cow, which couets the Bull more then other kine, and neither giues much milke, nor brings many calues.*

Torce. *as* Torse.

Torche: f. *A Linke; also, the wreathed clowt, wispe, or wad of straw, layed by wenches betweene their heads, and the things which they carrie on them; also, the heart, or pith of a Pine, or of any Rosen-yeelding tree; also, as* Torchon de paille, *in the later sence.*

Torches. *as* Fenons.

Torche de fonte. *A fashion of great Linke (made all of wax, and without staffe, or handle) borne anights before great persons, by their Pages, &c.*

La torche au poing. *With as much shame as may be; or, as in* Amende honorable.

Torche lorgne. *Words, like our thwicke thwacke, expressing a liberall and free dole of blowes; also, here and there, without discretion, at randome.*

Torché: m. ée: f. *Wiped, made cleane.*

Torche-bouche. Banquet à tor. *Which costs a man nothing, or whereat he nothing payes.*

Torche-cul: m. *A wispe for the tayle.*

Torche-culatif: m. iue: f. *Taile-wiping.*

Torche-pot: m. *The bird called a Nut-iobber.*

Il resemble au torche-pot. *He is his wiues Maister, or dare schoole her when she doth amisse; (from the propertie of the cocke Nut-iobber, which beateth his henne when she hath wandered any long time from him.)*

Torcher. *To wipe, or make cleane; also, to buffet, or cuffe with the fists.*

Torcher à autruy le cul de sa chemise. *To helpe a man (but as he could haue holpen himselfe) onely by his owne meanes; (Looke vnder* Chemise; *) The like is;*

Torcher le nez de sa manche. *To pay a man with his owne money; to giue him an apple out of his owne Orchard, a loafe of his owne batch, a pig of his owne Sow.*

Torcheux: m. euse: f. *Full of Linkes; of a linke; linke-like; seruing for a linke.*

Torchon: m. *A rubber, a wiper, a shooe-clowt.*

Torchon de paille. *A wispe of straw; also, a handfull, or small bundle thereof; as much as a Thatcher layes at once.*

Torcionné: m. ée: f. *Wrested, wrinched, violently writhen.*

Torcis de vermillons. *A wreathed bunch of small wormes.*

Torcol: m. *The little ash-coloured, and long-tongued bird, called a Wrie-necke.*

Torcollet: m. *The same.*

Torcu. *A certaine vnluckie bird, of a browne, or (as in some places) of a white colour.*

Torculaire: com. *Belonging to the tunnell of the braine; whence;* Veine torc. *Looke* Veine.

Tordement: m. *A wreathing, twisting, twining; wringing, wresting; a crisping, or curling.*

Tordille: f. *A fleabitten, menniled, or spotted colour of horses, dogs, &c.*

Tordoir: m. *The bedder, or vnder stone of an oyle-mill, or presse.*

Tordre. *To wreath, twine, twist, writhe, bend or turne round, wind in, whirle about; hence also, to crispe, or curle; also, to wring, wrest, wrinch.*

Tordre le col à. *To make a wrie necke, or cast a wrie looke, at; to scorne, contemne, despise.*

Tordre le nez à. *To make a nose of wax of; to wrest, wrie, manage, turne, at pleasure.*

se Tordre & fourvoyer. *To goe aside out of the way.*

Ne faire que tordre, & avaller. *To make brick walls of his cheekes, to swallow his meat halfe chawed, to rowle it once about his (paued) mouth, and then let it downe.*

Femme qui son alleure tord; &c; Prov. *Looke vnder* Femme.

Il ne se tort pas qui va plain chemin: Prov. *Hee that goes on plaine ground spraines not his foot; mischiefe attends those that take rugged wayes.*

Tore: f. *Broad-leaued Wolues-bane; or as* Thore.

Toreau: m. *A Bull; Seeke* Taureau.

Toret: m. *A small Wimble*

Torment: m. *Torment, or torture; extreame affliction, great vexation, hellish anguish, horrible paine; Looke* Tourment.

Tormente: f. *A tempest, or storme of wind at sea.*

Les tormentes des procez. *The troubles, or troublesome vexations, attending on suits.*

Tormenté: m. ée: f. *Tormented, tortured, excruciated; extreamely vexed, grieued, afflicted; horribly tossed.*

Tormenter. *To torment, racke, torture, excruciate; grieue or afflict extreamely, put vnto horrible paine; also, to tosse, as a raging sea doth a ship.*

Tormentille: f. *Tormentile, Setfoile (an hearbe.)*

Tormentine: f. *Turpentine.*

Tornadot: m. *A returne of Dowrie; the giuing back of a womans portion.*

Torné. *as* Tourné.

Torne-dos. *Looke* Tourne-dos.

Torner. *To turne, alter, change, &c; as* Tourner.

Tornerost: m. *A Turne-spit.*

Tornes. *as* Tournes.

Tornesol: m. *Turnesole, Heliotropium, Wartwort.*

Tornier. *Often to stagger, or turne round, like a Stag thats drunke with brouzing in May; also, to beat vp and downe, or flie round, thereby to deceiue the dogs that pursue him.*

Torpille: f. *The Crampe-fish; a fish that benummes the hands of such as take, or touch, it.*

Torpin. *as* Torpille: ¶Marseillois.

Torque: f. *A small groue, or tuft of wood, growing by it selfe.*

Torqué: m. ée: f. *Writhen, wreathed; wound in, wrapped about.*

Torquer. *To writhe, wreath; wind in, wrap about.*

Torqueure: f. *A wreath; wreathing; place or thing writhen; and particularly, the wreath whereby the foot of a graffe is preserued from the iniurie of weather.*

Torrefié: m. ée: f. *Scorched, parched, toasted; dried by the fire, or in the Sunne, and then done to dust.*

Torrefier. *To scorch, parch, toast; to drie, & afterwards doe vnto dust.*

Torrent: m. *A torrent, land floud, fall of waters from a hill, caused by raine, or snow; a swift streame running with a great, and violent sweepe.*

Torrentin: m. ine: f. *Belonging to, or abiding in, torrents, or swift and violent streames.*
Torride: com. *Torride, scorched, burned, parched; also, dried, or dried by the extremitie of heat.*
Zone torride. *The torride, or firie Zone; a circle, or certaine breadth in the firmament, vnder which, by reason of exceeding heat, few people inhabit.*
Torrillon d'un Canon. *The middle of a Canon, or the wreath, or band about the middle part of it.*
Torrion: m. *A great tower.*
Tors. m. torse: f. *Wreathed, or twined; also, wrested, wrinched, wrung; bowed, crooked, wried, awrie.*
'A tors & à travers. *Ouerthwartly, here and there, to and fro, without any manner of regard.*
Il s'est tors. *He is wandered, or gone out of the way.*
Torse: f. *A wreath; also, a wrest, wrinch; wrythe, wrying; a bending, wandring, or going out of the way.*
Torsement: m. *A wreathing; also, a wresting, wrinching; writhing, wrying; a bending, straying, wandering, or going out of the way.*
Torsion: f. *A writhing, wrying, wresting; griping, wringing.*
Torsionnairement. *as* Tortionnairement.
Torsure: f. *as* Torsement.
Tort: m. *Wrong, iniurie, hurt, offence, dammage, displeasure.*
'A tort. *Wrongfully, vniustly, vnworthily.*
'A tort ou à droict. *By hooke or crooke, by right or wrong, by one meanes or another.*
I'ay tort. *I am to blame*; I'ay le tort; *My cause is naught, I am in the wrong.*
Torteau: m. *A Pancake; or as* Tourteau.
Torteaux. *Torteauxes, and by old Blazonners, Wastells; must be round, whole, and of some colour, not of mettall; therein to make them differ from Besants.*
Tortelle: f. *Banke Cresses; some also call so, the Rape Chadlocke, or Charlocke; others, wild Mustard; others, Rocket gentle, and Rocket gallant; but erroniously; for these hearbes onely resemble it.*
Tortellées: f. *The curled toppings of the haire.*
Tortement. *Crookedly, wryly, crosly.*
Tortice. *as* Tortisse *(the feminine to* Tortis; *) whence,* Veines tortices; *crooked, or crankling veines.*
Torticoler. *To writhe, or wrie the necke.*
Torti col'y. *A wrie-necked fellow.*
Tortillé: m. ée: f. *Wreathed, twined; curled; wryed; also, gnawne, or chawed in peeces.*
Tortillemens. *Wreathes, wreathings, knots, curlings.*
Tortiller. *To wreath, twine, twist, to twirle, or wind about; Hence also, to curle, or tie on many knots; also, to wrinch, or to wry.*
Tortillon: m. *A little wreath; also, a curled locke of haire; also, the twirle, or twirling tendrell of a vine; and generally any double thing writhen, twirled, wound or twisted together, or one within another.*
Tortillonné: m. ée: f. *Wreathed; wound vp; curled; twisted, twirled, twined.*
Tortillonner. *To wreath, twine, twirle, twist, curle.*
Tortionnaire: com. *Wrongfull, vniust, or vniustly wrested; hard, cruell, seuere.*
Tortionnairement. *Wrongfully, vniustly; crookedly, hardly, cruelly.*
Tortionnier: m. *An Extortioner.*
Tortipé: m. *A splay-foot; a shaling, or splay-footed fellow.*
Tortis: m. *A wreath; a garland.*
Toris cavez. *Crooked pathes, turning wayes.*
Tortis de cire. *A wreathed Linke, or great candle of wax; most in vse about Candlemas.*
Tortis: m. isse: f. *Writhen, writhing, crooked, or crooking.*
Tortiz. *Lime, or loame which hath straw chopt into it:* ¶Gasc.
Torterelle: f. *A Turtle Doue.*
Tortouëre: f. *A hunting pole.*
Tortu: m. uë: f. *Crooked, awrie, bent, bowed; writhing, twining; wrying, crooking; winding in and out, turning often, full of crinklecrankles.*
Tortuë busche fait droict feu: Prov. *(So comes a crooked thing to be good for something.)*
Tortuë: f. *A Tortoise.*
Tortuë de bois. *A land Tortoise, garden Tortoise, wood Tortoise.*
Tortuemént: m. *A crooking, bowing, bending, wrying, writhing, often turning, winding in and out.*
Tortuément. *Wryly, crookedly, crookingly, wryingly, writhingly.*
Tortuëusement. *Most wryly, crookedly, crookingly, wryingly, writhingly.*
Tortuëux: m. ëuse: f. *Full of crookednesse or crookings, full of turnings, windings, crinklecrankles.*
Tortugue. *as* Tortuë.
Tortuosité: f. *A crookednesse, a crooking, bending, winding in and out, a crinkling or crankling.*
Torture: f. *Torture, torment, a racke, or a racking.*
Torturé: m. ée: f. *Tortured, tormented, racked; also, wrested or made crooked, wrythed or wried aside.*
Torturer. *To torture, torment, racke; also, to wrest, writhe, wry aside.*
Torty colly. *See* Torti-colly.
Torve: com. *Grimme, sterne, fell, spightfull, frowning, lowring, vnpleasantly looking.*
Tost. *Quickly, presently, suddenly, swiftly.*
Parler tost. *To speake thicke, or fast, or (as we say) nine words at once:* ¶Orleannois.
Plus tost. *Looke* Plustost.
Qui tost donne deux fois donne: Pro. *He that giueth quickly giueth twice; or, he giues as good as twice, that giues things in a trice.*
Tostée: f. *A toast of bread:* ¶Pic.
Totage: m. *The whole summe, substance, matter of; the whole, all.*
Total: m. *The totall, or whole summe.*
Totalement. *totally, wholly, vtterly, absolutely, throughly, in all sorts, altogether.*
Totalité: f. *A totalitie, the vttermost penie, the totall, or or whole summe.*
Totene. *The Sleeue, or Calamarie fish:* ¶Marseil.
Totiens quotiens. *as in* Quotiens.
Totinge. *as* Totage: ¶Rab.
Totum. *A kind of game with a whirlebone.*
Toüaige: m. *Towage; the towing of a ship by boats, or at the sterne of another ship.*
Toüaille: f. *A Towell.*
Toüasse: m. vn gros tou. *A lumpish, ignorant, or vnmannerlie clusterfist.*
Toüassier: m. ere: f. *Clownish, rude, ignorant, vnmannerlie, lumpish.*
Touc: m. *A sinke, or filthie gutter:* ¶Breton.
Touchant. *Touching, handling; also, concerning, as concerning, as for, about.*
Touche: f. *A touchstone; and thence, a triall; as also, the allay, or goodnesse of mettall; also, a fescue; also, a penne, or pinne for a paire of writing tables; also, a stop or fret in a Musicall Instrument; also, a hit, or venie at fence.*

Tou-

Touche de bois. *A boult; a little thicke groue or tuft of high trees, especially such a one as is neere a house, and serues to beautifie it, or as a marke for it.*
Bois de touche. *The same.*
Il est de bas or, il craint la touche. *His cause, or conscience, naught, makes him auoid all triall.*
Touché: m. ée: f. *Touched, felt, handled; also, stricken, blasted; hit; inspired; also, driuen, as a beast; also, brought, as money, vnto.*
Nous avons touché sur les articles. *We haue onely mentioned, or spoken lightly of, the Articles.*
Touchement: m. *A touching, feeling, handling; also, a striking, blasting; hitting; inspiring; also, a driuing of beasts, &c; a bringing of money vnto.*
Toucher. *To touch, feele, handle; to approach, concerne, or come neere vnto; also, to strike, hit; blast; inspire; also, to driue beasts, &c; or bring money vnto.*
Il toucha la main entre leurs mains. *He layed his hand betweene theirs; or, he gaue them his hand, and promise, that he would be theirs.*
Il leur toucha à tous la main. *He tooke euerie one of them by the hand;* &, Il leur toucha en la main; *He tooke them by the hands, as desiring to be better acquainted with them.*
Des yeux il touche iusques au cerveau. *It reacheth, or goeth from the eyes to the braine.*
On touche tousiours sur le cheval qui tire: Prov. *The forward horse is alwayes most put on.*
Toucheur: m. *A toucher, feeler, handler.*
Toucheur d'asnes. *An Asse-driuer.*
Touchon: m. *A little touch-stone.*
Toudi. *as* Tousiours: ¶Pic.
Toue: f. *A little, long, shallow, and flat-bottomed boat.*
Touër. *To tow a ship; to bring her along tied vnto boats, or at the sterne of another ship.*
Touffe de bois. *A boult; a tuft of trees growing neere a house, and seruing for a marke, or grace, vnto the seat thereof.*
Touffe de cheveux. *A tuft, or locke of curled haire.*
Bois de touffe. *as* Touffe de bois.
Touffeau: m. *as* Touffe; *or a little tuft.*
Touffillon: m. *A small tuft, or locke; boult, or groue.*
Touffu: m. uë: f. *Tuffie, thicke growing, thick of boughs, growing close together.*
Touillaut: m. *A scuruie troublesome fellow; or as* Touilleur.
Touillé: m. ée: f. *Filthily mingled, pestered, or shuffled together; also, durtied, besmeared, berayed, smeeched, begrimed; whence;*
Avoine touillée croist comme enragée: Prov. *In mirie ground Oats grow as if they were mad.*
Touillement: m. *A filthie mingling, beastlie confounding, ill-fauoured shuffling together; also, a durtying, beraying, besmearing, begriming.*
Touiller. *Filthily to mix, or mingle; confound, or shuffle together; to intangle, trouble, or pester by scuruie medling; also, to bedurt, begrime, besmeare, smeech, beray.*
Touilleur: m. *A Polipragmon, filthie medler, shuffling or troublesome fellow; one that marres things by a beastlie mingling of them.*
Touillon: m. *A Scullion; or a filthie, greasie, nastie, or slouenlie fellow; also, a clowt to wipe shooes, or make cleane vessell, withall.*
Toulieu: m. *Toll of Markets, and Faires.*
Toulte: f. *An exacting, or extorting of Subsidies.*
Tounine: f. *as* Thonnine; *or* Tonnine.
Toupeau: m. *A tuft, or tassell of silke, &c; a flocke, or locke of wooll.*
Toupet: m. *A tuft, or topping; a womans haire layed out on her forhead, or temples, and called her goldilockes; also, a horses foretop; also, a tuft, or tassell of silke, &c.*
Toupiant: m. ante: f. *Whirling about like a gig.*
Toupie: f. *A gig, or casting-top; also, the shell-fish called a Welke, or Winkle.*
Toupier. *To turne, or cast a top; also, to whirle about like a top.*
Toupil: m. *as* Toupie.
Toupillon: m. *A little gig, or casting top.*
Toupillonnet: m. *A verie small top; or stopple.*
Toupin: m. *A stopple for a bottle, &c.*
Toupon: m. *A stopple.*
Tour: m. *A turne, round, circle, compasse, wheeling, revolution, circumuolution, vicissitude, interchangeable course of things; also, a turne, bout, or walke, as (we say) in Powles; also, the turne, course, ranke, place, or order, wherein a man is or stands; also, a deed, act, worke, part, good or bad Office, good or ill turne; also, a feat, pranke, tricke, sleight, shift, deuise; also, a spinning wheele; also, a Turne, or Turners wheele; or as* Tournoir; *also, a Turnepike, or Turning-stile; and the open turning box in the wall of a Nunnerie, wherby the sisters vnseeing, and vnseene, receiue in, and deliuer out, commodities; also, the Rooke at Chests; also, the breadth of fiue fingers in measure; also, a fashion of killing Deere, &c, by riding gently neere them, and hauing* en croupe *some Bowman, who may with aduantage, and on a sudden shoot at them.*
Tour de Basche, ou de Basque. *Nimble knauerie.*
Le tour de baston. *The fees, or vailes comming in to an Officer, ouer and besides his ordinarie wages.*
Il sçait bien le tour du baston. *He is a craftie, subtile, or cunning fellow; hee knowes well ynough the trickes, and sleights of the world.*
Tour de bec. *A kisse.*
Tour de bras. A tour de bras. *With maine strength, or, with confident authoritie.*
Tour de guerre, ou de vieille guerre. *Seeke vnder* Guerre.
Tour du Labyrinthe. Il fait le tour du Labyrinthe. *He treads a Maze; he is runne into an endlesse Laborinth; or, he toyles extreamely, and yet is neuer the neerer; also, he falls againe, after many digressions, or much adoe, into his former argument.*
Tour le lict. *A close, or whole curtaine, incompassing a fashion of bed, that (commonly) wanteth a testerne.*
Tour de mulet. *A iadish tricke.*
Tour de pescheur. *A daungerous aduenturing for great matters.*
Tour du roule: &, à tour de roule. *Seeke* Roule.
Ie ne leur donneray ny, tour ny attainte. *I will not touch, or handle them; I will not approach, or come neere them.*
Faites vn tour iusques icy. *Make a step hither.*
Chascun a son tour: Prov. *Euerie one hath his time, or turne.*
Chascun à son tour: Prov. *Euerie one in his time, ranke, or turne.*
Tour: f. *A Tower.*
Touraille: f. *A Kill, or Kilne to drie mault, &c, on.*
Tourban. *as* Turban.
Tourbe: f. *A troupe, rout, crue, rabble; prease, crowd, thrust, throng, clutterment of; also, trouble, stirre, businesse, debate, ruffling.*
En tourbe. *By flockes or multitudes; with confused voy-*

voyces; all, or verie many, at once; trouping, or crowding together.

Tourbiginaux: m. *Wreathes of old ropes, dipped in greaſe and pitch, and to be burnt in Creſsets.*

Tourbillon. les tourbillons d'une fleuve. *Th'eddie, whirling, round turning, of a ſtreame.*

Tourbillons de teſte. *The turning, or ſwimming of the braine; or a giddineſſe comming thereof.*

Tourbillon de vent. *A whirlewind; alſo, a guſt, flaw, berie, ſudden blaſt, or boiſterous tempeſt, of wind.*

Tourbillonner. *To whurle about like a whirlewind; to deale boiſterouſly, or ſweepe all away before it.*

Tourbillonneux: m. euſe: f. *Full of whirlewinds, like a whirlewind, whurling about as a whirlewind; boiſterous, raging, outragious.*

Tourchon: m. *as* Torchon; *or as* Torche, *in the ſecond ſence.*

Tourd: m. *A Thruſh; or a generall name for the Thruſh, Throſtle, and Fieldifare.*

Tourd de mer. *The ſea Thruſh; a certaine rock-fiſh not much vnlike a Pearch, or Tench; of ſundrie kinds, and each of diuers and ſundrie colours.*

Tourdelle: f. *The great Thruſh, or Fieldifare.*

Tourdion: m. *A turning, or winding about; alſo, a tric e, or pranke; alſo, the daunce tearmed a Round.*

Tourdre: m. *as* Tourd; *a Thruſh.*

Touré: m. ée: f. *Towred, full of, graced or furniſhed with, Towers.*

Tourelle: f. *A Turret, a ſmall Tower.*

Tourelle à cul le lampe. *A ſmall out-iuttying garret, or Tower like a garret, on the top of a wall.*

Touret: m. *A Throſtle, or Mauis; alſo, a Drill, the Inſtrument wherewith holes are made into mettall, &c; alſo, the chaine which is at the end of the cheeke of a Bit; alſo, the annelet, or little ring whereby a Hawkes Lune is faſtened vnto the Jeſſes.*

Touret de nez. *A Muffler.*

Tourette: f. *A Turret, or ſmall Tower.*

Tourier: m. *The keeper of a Tower; a watchman in a Tower; alſo, a Goaler.*

Touriere. *Looke* Tourriere.

Tourillon: m. *An inner Verrill; the round plate of yron whereby a peece of wood, often turned on, is preſerued from wearing, and burning.*

Tourillon du bras. *The head, or top of the arme where it is ioyned with the ſhoulder blade.*

Tourment: m. *Torment, or torture.*

Aſſez parens, aſſez tourmens: Prov. *Many kinſmen much trouble; we ſay (with ſome difference) many kinſmen few friends.*

Tourmente. *Looke* Tormente.

Tourmentine: f. *Turpentine.*

Tournaille: f. *A crooked turning, or winding in and out.*

Tournay: m. *A Tourney.*

Tournayer. *Looke* Tournoyer.

Tourné: m. ée: f. *Turned; rounded; changed, altered, conuerted; alſo, tranſlated; alſo, bending or inclining towards; alſo, giuen in exchange, or to boot; alſo, returned; (alſo, amazed, or aſtoniſhed:* ¶Breton.)

Croiſſans tournez. *In-creſsants; Creſſants turned inwards.*

Nez tourné à la friandiſe. *Looke vnder* Nez.

Il à tourné en mes flancs. *It was I that bore him; ſayed by a mother of her child; either becauſe, as Phyſitians report, the child hauing beene eight monethes in the wombe, ſhifts from the one ſide thereof to the other; or becauſe at his comming out he turnes (of himſelfe, or by the Midwiues helpe) his heeles vpwards.*

Tourne bouler. *To turne round.*

Tourne-bride. *A returne, or turning backe.*

Tourne-dos: m. *A turne-backe, run-away, coward.*

Tournée: f. *whence;* Par tournées; *Euerie one in his turne or courſe, ranke or place.*

Tourne-fol: m. *A turning ſtile.*

Tourne-lict: m. *as* Tour de lict *vnder* Tour.

Tournelle: f. *A Turret, or little Tower; (See* Tourrion; *) alſo, a Parliamentall Court for criminall cauſes, whereon the Judges of the other Courts doe ſit by ſeuerall turnes.*

Tourne-main: m. *The turning of the hand; whence;* Dans vn tourne-main; *In a trice, on a ſudden, before you can ſay, this.*

Tournement: m. *A turning; rounding; reuolution; a conuerting, changing; exchanging; tranſlating; a bending, or inclining towards.*

Tournement de teſte. *The turne-about ſickneſſe; a giddineſſe, or dizzineſſe, a ſwimming of the head.*

Tourneployer. *To turne, wind, bend, or bow which way ſoeuer one will haue it.*

Tourner. *To turne; conuert, alter, change; exchange, giue in exchange, or to boot; alſo, to tranſlate; alſo, to round or make round; alſo, to make ſowre; alſo, to returne; alſo, to bow, bend, or incline.*

Tourner la charruë contre les boeufs. *To ſet the cart before the horſe (we ſay;) to doe a thing prepoſterouſly; alſo, to alter ones talke, or anſwer from the purpoſe, thereby to ſtop, or ſuppreſſe, an argument bandied before.*

Tourner court. *See* Court.

Tourner fueillet. *To change a cuſtome, alter a wont; or, (as we ſay) turne ouer a new leafe.*

Tourner ſa jaquette. *To turne his coat; viz. Breake his faith and oath; or quit his religion, opinio, or Prince, and follow another, or a contrarie one, for what reſpect ſoeuer.*

Tourner les truyes au foing. *To anſwer from the matter, or as if hee knew not what demaund was made.*

C'eſt la Maiſtreſſe rouë qui tourne le moulin. *See* Moulin.

Il nous reſte quelqu'autre moulin à tourner. *There's yet a further matter to be bandied, looked vnto, done.*

Bon charron tourne en petit lieu: Prov. *A skillfull Coachman turnes in a ſmall roome; Looke* Charron.

Tournerie: f. *A turning; alſo, Turners worke, or turners ware.*

Tournerot: m. *A turne-roaſt, or turne-ſpit.*

Tournes en eſchange, ou partage de biens. *as* Soulte.

Tourne-ſoleil: m. *Torne-ſole, Heliotropium.*

Tournet: m. *A ſmall turning rundle, or ring, in the mouth of a Bit, &c.*

Tournette: f. *A Rice, or Yarwingle to wind yarne on.*

Tourne-vent: m. *A faſhion of penthouſe, or portall ſet before a doore, for the keeping of wind out of a roome; alſo, a Horſe, or mouable Louer, of mettall, on the top of a chimney, or houſe.*

Tournevirer. *To whirle, or whurre about.*

Tourneure: f. *A turning; alſo, any thing that turnes, or makes a thing ſowre; as leauen doth bread, runnet milke, &c.*

Tourniquet: m. *The pinne of a* Vielle; *that which the* Vielleur *turnes with his hand as he playes.*

Tour-

Tournoir: m. *A Turne, turning wheele, or Turners wheele, called a Lathe, or Lare; also, the vice, or winch of a Presse.*

Tournois: m. *A French penie; the tenth part of a penie Sterling; which rate it holds in all other words (as the* Sol, *or* Livre) *whereunto it is ioyned.*

Tournoy: m. *A Turney, or Turnament; also, as* Tournoir.

Tournoyant. *Rowling, wheeling, turning round, fetching a compasse, vsing an vncertaine course.*

Tournoyement: m. *A rowling, wheeling, turning round, fetching a compasse, going about; a staggering course, vncertaine gate, reeling, dizzinesse, giddinesse; also, an enuironing, or incompassing; also, a vsing of circumstances; also, a turneying.*

Tournoyer. *To rowle, wheele, turne round, fetch a compasse, goe about; also, to reele, stagger, make indentures; vse an vncertaine course; also, to enuiron, incircle, incompasse; also, to vse shifts, or circumstances, without comming at all to the point; also, to goe about, or spie on euerie side, the meanes of preuailing with, or attempting on, a thing; also, to turney, iust or fight in a Turney.*

Tournure. *as* Tourneure.

Tourrelé: m. ée: f. *Towerie, tower-like, begirt or incompassed with towers.*

Tourrier: m. *The keeper of a tower; a Goaler of prisoners which be in a tower.*

Tourriere: f. *The Nunne which attends on the* Tour, *or turning box in the wall of a Nunnerie.*

Tourrion: m. *A small Turret (lesse then the* Tournelle, *and commonly made off the wall by iuttying, whereas* Tournelle *is euer boult vpright.)*

Tourte: f. *A Turtle Doue; also, a great loafe of houshold or browne bread (called so in* Lionnois, *and* Dauphiné;) *also, the made-dish which we call a Florentine; also, a Trundle head of a Mill.*

Tourteau: m. *A cake (made, commonly, in hast, and of lesse compasse then the* Gasteau; *) also, a little loafe of houshold, or browne bread; also, a Pancake; also, a wreath of pitched cord for a Cresset; also, the Crabfish tearmed a Pungar.*

`A celuy qui a sa paste au four on doit donner de son tourteau: Prov. *Be not a niggard vnto him thats able to requite thee.*

Tourtelle: f. *See* Tortelle.

Tourterelle: f. *A Turtle, or Turtle Doue.*

Tourtillon: m. *A verie little loafe of houshold bread; or a small* Tourteau.

Tourtoire: f. *A hunting pole; also, any yron toole (with a woodden handle) wherewith a Cooper notches, and drawes on, the principall hoopes of caske.*

Tourtourain: m. *The nature of the Turtle.*

Tousé: m. ée: f. *Shorne, clipped, powled, cut, notted, pared round.*

Touser. *To sheere, &c; as* Tondre.

Tousjours. *Alwayes, euer, still, perpetually, continually, for euer and euer, euermore.*

Nous avons trois tousjours. *Howsoeuer, or as hard as the world goes, yet we haue three.*

Toussaincts. la T. *All-Saints day, Allhallowday.*

Toussant. *Coughing.*

Tousser. *as* Tousir.

Tousseur: m. *A cougher.*

Tousir. *To cough.*

Toustade. Alezan toust. *A burnt sorrell; a darke-red colour like wood scorched, or mettall burnt, in the fire.*

Tout: m. *(Substantiuely.) an all, a totall or whole summe; any, or euerie thing.*

C'est mon tout. *Tis all, tis th'onely, or chiefest thing I relie on.*

Qui tout convoite tout perd: Pro. *He that couets, looses, euerie thing.*

Qui tout me donne tout me nie: Prov. *He that giues me, denies me, all I demaund; a thing thats easily granted is in effect denied.*

Qui de tout si taist de tout a paix: Prov. *Looke* Paix.

Tout: m. toute: f. *All, the whole, whatsoeuer, euerie iot or whit.*

Toutes & quantes fois. *As often as.*

`A tout le poil. *whence,* Né à tout le poil. *Seeke vnder* Poil.

De tout point. *Quite and cleane.*

Vne science requiert tout son homme: Prov. *One Art well learnt takes vp a mans whole time.*

Tout. (Adverb) *whence;* Tout ainsi; *Euen as, euen like, as it were, as much as, to as great effect or purpose as, none otherwise then.*

Tout autant. *as* Tout ainsi.

Tout beau. *Soft and faire, not too fast, ynough I say.*

Tout à coup. *Suddenly, at once, at one blow.*

Tout à faict. *Wholly, throughly, altogether, vtterly, indeed, quite and cleane.*

Tout à l'heure. *At the verie instant.*

Tout fin. *Hard by, neere hand, euen verie now; whence,* Tout fin à Noel; *Verie neere Christmas; &c.*

Tout fin mere nu; *All discouered, all ouer naked, or (as we say) starke-bellie naked.*

Tout incontinent. *Presently, straightway, out of hand, by and by.*

Tout maintenant. *But euen now.*

Tout outre. *Throughout, through and through; wholly, in euerie respect.*

Tout à point *Fitly, opportunely, seasonably, in as good time as may be.*

Tout tant. *All that euer:* Sur tout tant; *Especially, chiefly, all other occasions layed apart.*

Tout à traict; &, Tout d'un mesme traict. *Looke vnder* Traict.

Tout vray. *Most certaine, most true.*

`A tout. *With; sufficiently, wholly, throughly; also, neuerthelesse, notwithstanding.*

`A tout jamais. *For euer and euer.*

`A tout rompre. *At the most, highest; or worst; when all comes to all; come of it what come will.*

Du tout. *Throughly, vtterly, quite and cleane, altogether.*

Par tout. *Throughout, into euerie place or thing, euewhere, euerie whither; whence the Prouerbe;* Qui par tout va par tout prend.

Et fut tout besoing à eux de se retirer. *And it was best, most needfull, or high time, for them to retire.*

Il est tout presché qui n'a cure de bien faire: Pro. *ynough he's preacht vnto thats carelesse of well doing: or, too much hee's preacht vnto that meanes not to amend.*

Toute-bonne: f. *The hearbe Clarie, or Cleere-eye; also, good Henrie, or All-good.*

Toute-bonne des jardins. *Garden Clarie.*

Toute-bonne sauvage. *Wild Clarie, Ocle Christi.*

Toutesfois. *Yet, but, albeit, although, howbeit, neuerthelesse, notwithstanding.*

Toutesfois & quantes. *As often.*

Toutesfois fut le pré tondu: Pro *Maugre their stir*

yet was the medow mowed; 'gainst all our hopes, their wills, the businesse ended.

Tout feu. *All-fire; the name of a valley neere* Estampes, *thus tearmed because much infested by robbers.*

Touton: m. *Part of a womans priuities.*

Tout-puissant. *Almightie, all-able.*

Toux: f. *A cough.*

Toux de regnard. *The Foxes cough; a rooted, or old-growne cough, which waits on a man to his graue.*

Touzelle: f. *Fine Wheat, white Winter Wheat; a kind of smooth Wheat, which hath an vpright stalke, and a verie white graine.*

Toxaint: m. *An Allarum-bell; or, the ringing thereof.*

Toy. *Thee; thou.*

Toye de plomb. *A web of lead.*

Toymesme. *Thou thy selfe, thy verie selfe.*

Tozelle. *as* Touzelle.

Trabe d'un ancre: m. *The beame, or staffe of an Anchor.*

Trabée: f. *A purple and imbrodered cassocke, or robe worne by Kings, or great personages, vnder their mantles of Estate.*

Trabuchet. *Looke* Trebuchet.

Trac: m. *A tracke, tract, or trace; a (frequent) footing, beaten way or path; also, a trade, or course.*

Trac de bataille. *The traine, prouision, or followers of an armie.*

Tout à trac. *Plainly, roundly, frankly, flatly; wholly, throughly, outright, altogether.*

Tracanard: m *See* Traquenard.

Tracas: m. *Much trotting, or hurrying vp and downe; hence also, toyle, trouble, turmoile.*

Tracassé: m. ée: f. *Hurried, tossed; tugged, tewed; spoiled, ouerworne, or misused, by much remouing.*

Tracasser. *To trot, raunge, roame, hurrie much vp and downe; to toyle, moyle, or labour (in going) like a horse; also, to tug, tew, spoyle, misuse, make hauocke of.*

Tant travaille, & tracasse l'homme, qu'il se rompt, ou somme: Prov. *So long a man toyles that at length he tires.*

Tracasserie: f. *A restlesse trotting, raunging, roaming, hurrying vp and downe; a busie, or needlesse trauell, tugging, or toyling out of himselfe.*

Tracasseur: m. *A restlesse trotter, or hurrier vp and downe; a fond busie bodie; one that toyles, or trauells much to verie little purpose.*

Trace: f. *A trace, footing, print of the foot, step, footstep; also, a path, or tract.*

Les traces d'un sanglier. *The tract, heeles, or tallons of a Boare.*

Tracement: m. *A tracing, inquisition, following, or hunting after by the foot.*

Tracer. *To trace, follow, pursue, inquire, seeke out, hunt after, by the foot; also, as* Trasser; *whence;*

Tracer vne harengue. *To minute, or make the first draught of, an Oration.*

Nature fait chien tracer: Prov. *The hound by nature's taught to hunt.*

Tracette: f. *A little trace, tract, or footing.*

Traceure: f. *as* Trace; *or as* Tracement.

Traceux: m. euse: f. *Tracing out, following the tract, or footing of.*

Trache. *A cluster of fruites (as of Apples, Peares, &c;) growing together.*

Tracher. *as* Tracer; *(Rustically.)*

Trachet: m. *as* Trache; *or, a little cluster.*

Trachiartere. *The pipe of the lungs; one of the three principall Arteries in mans bodie; begins at the Larinx, end at the lungs; & is th'instrument of the voice, and of breathing.*

Trachie. *as* Trachiartere; *or, the windpipe.*

Traction: f. *A draught, or extraction, a drawing out.*

Tradiment: m. *Treacherie, betraying, treason.*

Traditif: m. iue: f. *Traditiue, or of tradition; whence;*

Science traditive; *a Science deliuered by word of mouth from father to sonne; or, continued, or left vnto posteritie, by tradition.*

Traditive: f. *A method of teaching, or of speaking.*

Traduire. *To translate out of one tongue into another.*

Traduit: m. te: f. *Translated.*

Trafique: f. *Trafficke, trade, commerce, or intercourse of marchandizing; also, cousening, deceit, ouerreaching.*

Trafiquer. *To trafficke, trade, occupie, vse, commerce, deale in marchandise; also, to cousen, deceiue, beguile, ouerreach.*

Trafiquerie: f. *A trafficking; also, marchandise, ware, or stuffe to trafficke with; also, a deceiuing, beguiling, ouerreaching.*

Trafiqueur: m. *A trafficker, trader, marchant, occupier, dealer in the world; also, a cousener, deceiuer, ouerreacher.*

Tragedie: f. *A Tragedie; a statelie Play whose conclusion is dolefull, and doubtfull.*

Tragée. *Looke* Dragée.

Tragelaphe: m. *The great, and blackish Deere called, a Stone-bucke, Deere-Goat, or Goat-hart, because conceiued betweene a Buck-goat, and the Hind.*

Traget: m. *as* Traject.

Tragique: com. *Tragicall, tragicke, of or belonging to Tragedies, Tragedie-like; bloudie, deadlie, dolefull, dismall.*

Tragiquement. *Tragically; dolefully, dismally.*

Tragon: m. *The hearbe Tarragon; also, Amelcorne, or Starch-corne.*

Tragoncée: f. *as* Tragon.

Traguetter. *See* Trajetter.

Trahi: m. ie: f. *Betrayed, treacherously dealt with.*

Trahi trahi. *Is in auncient Authors a crie of warre, importing as well feare as treason; as when an Armie fighting in front was on a sudden charged in the reere by a troupe of vnexpected enemies; or in the forcing of a Garrison: We may English it with a double, surprised, inclosed, forced, or taken.*

Trahir. *To betray, or deale treacherously with.*

Trahison: f. *Treason, treacherie, a betraying; also, any lewdnesse, villanie, or disloyaltie.*

Bois de la trahison. *The name of a wood neere vnto* Saint Germain en Laye, *the branches of whose trees cast into the water, sinke like stones, and lopped off, nothing doth afterwards come out in the place of them.*

Frapper en trahison. *To strike a man behind his backe, or ere he be aware*

Traiclou: m. *The toole wherwith Shoomakers pull their tackes out.*

Traict: m. *A Dart, Arrow, or Shaft; also, a shot, or shoot; (and thence, a nip, taunt, quip, cut;) also, a draught, line, streake, or stroake made by a penne, or pensill; (and thence, the forme, shape, figure, feature, lineaments of the face, or bodie, or of any other thing;) also, length, drawing out, prolonging of, leasure in, things; also, the whole, course, progresse, or proceeding of a matter; also, a subtile, or ingenious tricke, part, act, pranke, shift; also, a draught of drinke; also, a teame-trace, or trait; the cord or chaine that runnes between the horses, &c; also, the draught-tree of a Caroche, &c; also, a lime, or line wherein a Bloud-hound is led, and stayed in his pursute.*

Vn traict du laict d'une beste. *A meales milke.*
Cheval de traict. *A drag-horse, or draught-horse.*
Gens de traict. *The bow-men, or small shot, of an Armie.*
Franc au traict. *Looke* Franc.
Par traict de temps. *In tract of time, at length, in time, one time or another.*
Tout à traict. *Easily, faire and softly, by leasure.*
Tout d'un mesme traict. *At once, all vnder one.*
Parler à traicts. *To speake leasurely, soberly, softly, by pauses, without hast.*
Tirer vn traict sus la lie. *Seeke* Lie.
Du dire au faict y a grand traict: Prov. *There is 'tweene (most) mens word and deed, great space, and but a little speed.*
Traict: m. cte: f. *Drawne, pulled out; prolonged; also, pliant.*
Or traict. *Gold wire.*
Traictable: com. *Tractable, pliant, facile, intreatable, courteous, gracious.*
Traicte: m. *A treatie; a league, agreement, or alliance, talked of (as also, one that is concluded on) betweene Princes, &c; also, a Treatise, Pamphlet, small booke, or part of a booke.*
Traicte: f. *A draught, prolonging, or drawing out in length; also, a course, trace, way, iourney, progresse, proceeding; also, a transportation, outward vent, or shipping ouer; and, an Imposition vpon commodities exported; whence;*
Droict de traicte. *as vnder* Droict; *also, that which is due to the King, and to the Maister of the Mint vpon the coyning of money.*
Traicté: m. ée: f. *Treated, intreated of; intertained, handled, vsed; made, contracted, agreed on.*
Traictement: m. *A treating, intreating; intertayning, vsing, handling; a contracting, or concluding of a treatie.*
Traicter. *To treat, intreat, intertaine, vse, handle, tend or looke vnto; to deale in, or meddle with; to discourse, debate, or make mention of; also, to couenant, or contract with.*
Traicter à la fourche. *Looke* Fourche.
Traictif. nez traictif. *A prettie long nose; a nose of a gracefull length.*
Traictis: m. isse: f. *whence;* Traictisses mains. *Long, and slender hands.*
Traictoire de tonnelier. *as* Tourtoire *(in the later sence.)*
Traject: m. *A ferrie; a passage ouer.*
Trajectaire: m. *A Ferrie-man; also, one that tumbles through a hoope held vp; also, a Jugler, Imposter, Cousener.*
Trajecter. *To ferrie, transport, passe, conuey, or carrie ouer from shore to shore; also, to send, thrust, transferre, put, or cast through.*
Trajectoire: m. *The cannon, or taile of a perfuming funnell.*
Trajectoire: com. *Casting, thrusting, putting, sending, passing, transporting, conueying through, or ouer.*
Trajetter. *as* Trajecter.
Traigne: f. *The sea Dragon, Viuer, Quauiuer:* ¶ Marseillois.
Traillant. *Reeling, or winding yarne; also, trayling a Deere; hunting him vpon a cold sent, or with a lime-hound.*
Traille. *Vsed sometimes in stead of* Treille.
Trailler. *To reele, or wind yarne; also, to trayle a Deere, or hunt him vpon a cold sent; as also, to hunt, or pursue him with a lime-hound.*
Traine: f. *The woofe, or west in weauing; also, a garment of course cloth; also, a plot, practise, conspiracie, deuise.*
Trainer. *To weaue; also, to plot, contriue, practise, conspire, deuise.*
Train: m. *A (great mans) traine, retinue, or followers; also, the traine, or hinder part of a beast; also, the pace of a horse, or moyle, &c; also, the trace, way, or course, taken by a wild beast, or made of purpose for it; also, any way, course; worke, dealing, trade, practise, trafficke vsed, or entred into; also, a crupper for a loaden horse, &c; also, a sled, a drag or dray without wheeles.*
Le train de devant d'une coche. *The fore-wheeles of a Coach.*
Le train de guerre. *Warfare.*
Le train de practique. *The stile, or forme of pleading, or of proceeding, in a Court.*
D'un train. *Together, at on clap, at once.*
En bon train. *In a good forwardnesse.*
Mener le train de quelqu'un. *To doe any mans businesse for him.*
Mettre en train. *To make a motion, breake the ice; introduce or bring in, set in the way.*
Se mettre en train. *To set forward, or take his way; also, to bring himselfe into practise, put himselfe in vre.*
De grand train à l'estrain: Pro. *From a great traine into the straw.*
Trainacer. *as* Trainer.
Trainage: m. *Trainage; or, as* Droict de suitte de Disme, *vnder* Droict.
Trainant: m. ante: f. *Trayling, dragging, drawing after.*
Trainant la vie. *Liuing sorrily, or but from hand to mouth; also, leading an irksome, or wearisome life.*
Trainard: m. *as* Traine-gain.
Trainard: m. arde: f. *as* Trainant; *also, crawling, or creeping along close by the ground.*
Trainassé: m. ée: f. *Dragged, or trailed along.*
Trainasser. *To drag, or traile along.*
Trainasserie: f. *A traine, traile, or long taile; also, a trailing, or dragging along.*
Traine: f. *A sled; a drag, or dray without wheeles; also, a drag-net, or draw net.*
Traineau: m. *as* Traine; *also, draggage, or carriage.*
Traineau à plommée. *A Stelleere; a Roman, or Venice beame, for the weighing of things.*
Trainée: f. *A traine for a Wolfe, or any other such wild, and rauenous beast; also, as* Trainement.
Trainegain: m. *A draw-latch, lazie companion, slouenlie lowt; one that trailes the scabberd of his sword after him, or weares it so low, and so loossely, that it drags on the ground as he goes.*
Traineller. *To trammell for Larkes.*
Trainement: m. *A trayling, dragging, or drawing along; also, a creeping, crawling, or running close by the ground.*
Traine-pieds: m. *One that lazily, or weakely, trailes his legs after him.*
Trainer. *To traile, drag, draw, carrie or lead after him; also, to be throwne vp and downe, as a thing thats not well layed vp.*
Se trainer. *To creepe, or crawle along close by the ground.*

Trainer son Lien. *See* Lien.

Trainer longuement. *To be long sicke of a disease, to languish a great while.*

Trainer longue queuë. *To continue long, or be a great while, in doing; also, to be of great consequence, haue a farre reach, carrie full many things along with it.*

Trainer sa parole. *To speake dreamingly, draylingly, draw-latch-like; also, to smooth, claw, gloze, flatter, fawne on, collogue with; (for commonly such as wire-draw their speech are notable dissemblers.)*

Trainercsse. *whence;* Bonnettes traineresses. *The drablers for a Saile.*

Trainiere: f. *Common Trefoile, three-leaued grasse, Irish Shamrocks, Cockheads, Suckles, Honisuckles.*

Trainoir: m. *A sled; a drag, or dray without wheeles.*

Trainon: m. *A drag-net, or dray-net for fish.*

Trainquenailles: m. *Scoundrells, ragamuffins, base rascalls, flabergudgions.*

Traïon: m. *The teat, or nipple of a cowes vdder.*

Traiot: m. *A milking Pale, or Piggin.*

Traire vne vache. *To milke, or draw milke from, a Cow.*

Traistre: m. *A traitor; a treacherous, or disloyall person; also, a naughtie-packe; a lewd, or wicked fellow.*

Traistreau: m. *A young, or little traitor.*

Traistrement. *Traiterously, treacherously, most disloyally, or faithlesly.*

Traistreusement. *The same.*

Trait. *Looke* Traict.

Traite: f. *A draught, or drawing out in length; also, a course, trace, progresse, or proceeding; also, a transportation, vent outward, shipping ouer, and an Imposition vpon commodities exported, or so transported; See* Traicte.

Traite de bleds; &, Traite foraine. *Looke* Bled; & Forain.

Traité & Traiter. *See* Traicté, & Traicter.

Traitif *as* Traictif.

Trainail: m. *A Trammell, or net for Partridges.*

Tramaillé: m. ée: f. *Treble-mailed; or wouen, bound, or insnared by treble mashes, or mailes.*

Tramailler. *To weaue, bind, fasten, or insnare by threefold mashes, or mailes.*

Tramer: m. *A Weauer.*

Tramblotis: m. *A trembling.*

Trame. *as* Traime.

Tramé: m. ée: f. *Wouen, contriued.*

Trameau: m. *A kind of Drag-net, or Draw-net for fish; also, a Trammell net for fowle; also, a sled, or dray, without wheeles.*

Tramer. *To weaue, to contriue.*

Trameter. *To continue a suit, or hold on a pursute.*

Trameul: m. *A Mill hopper.*

Tramillon: m. *A kind of little Drag-net, or Drawnet for fish.*

Tramois: m. *Meslin of Oats, and Barlie mingled.*

Tramontain: m. aine: f. *Northerlie, comming from, or dwelling in, the North.*

Tramontaine: f. *The North; North-wind, or starre.*

Tranchaison. *as* Trenchée.

Tranchant. *Looke* Trenchant.

Tranche: f. *A kind of pruning knife, or instrument, vsed by Gardeners; also, a slice of any thing.*

Tranchefile. *Seeke* Trenchefile.

Tranchelion: m. *A notable trencher-man:* ¶Rab.

Tranche-montaigne: m. *A swash-mountaine, terrible swash buckler, horrible swaggerer.*

Tranche-plume: f. *A Penknife.*

Trancher. *Looke* Trencher.

Tranchet d'un Cordoüannier. *A Shoomakers paring, or cutting knife.*

Trançon: m. *A truncheon; also, a little peece of.*

Trangle. *as* Tringle.

Tranquille: com. *Calme, vntroubled, without surges, quiet, still, husht, peaceable, peacefull.*

Tranquillement. *Calmly, quietly, stilly, peaceably, without any manner of trouble.*

Tranquiller. *To calme, still, quiet, pacifie, appease.*

Tranquillité: f. *Tranquilitie, stillnesse, calmenesse, quietnesse, peaceablenesse; a calme; rest.*

Tranquilliter. *as* Tranquiller.

Transacteur: m. *A transactor, dayes-man, accorder, match-maker.*

Transaction: f. *A transaction, accord, agreement, attonement.*

Transailles: f. *Corne sowed in the Spring, as Barlie, Oates, &c.*

Transalpin: m. ine: f. *Forrein, Italian, beyond the Alpes, on the further side of the mountaines.*

Transanimation: f. *Pythagoras his* Metempsycosa; *or the passage of the soule from one bodie to another.*

Transcendant. *Transcendant, surmounting, surpassing, exceeding.*

Transchangement: m. *An alteration, or changing ouer into another qualitie, or nature.*

Transcoulation: f. *A gliding, slipping, running, a drilling, trilling or trickling, through.*

Transcoulé. *Glid, slid, slipped, runne, trilled, trickled, strained through; also, set packing, pumped, or let run out.*

Transcouler. *To glide, slide, slip, runne, trill, or trickle, (also, to straine) through; also, to set packing, to pumpe, or let runne, out.*

Transcrire. *To transcribe, to write or copie out.*

Transcrit: m. ite: f. *Transcribed, written out, copied forth.*

Transcrivain: m. *A Transcriber, a bare copier out of other mens writings.*

Transe: f. *Extreame feare, dread; anxietie, or perplexitie of mind; also, a traunce, or sowne; a great astonishment, amazement, or appallment.*

Dormer en transe. *To be dog asleepe, to be in a deepe or dead sleepe.*

Transenter. *To graffe out of one stocke into another; to take a graffe out of one stocke, and set it in another.*

Transferé: m. ée: f. *Transferred, transmitted, posted or passed ouer vnto.*

Transfiguration: f. *A transfiguration, or transformation.*

Transfigurer. *To transfigure, transforme, turne out of one shape into another.*

Transfondre. *To powre, deriue, or passe out of one vessell into another; to transferre, to transpose.*

Transformation: f. *A transformation; a change of forme, an alteration of shape.*

Transformer. *To transforme, alter, change, turne out of one shape into another.*

Transfretter *Hastily to passe ouer, or along.*

Transfuge: m. *A runne-away; one that runnes to, and sides with, a publicke enemie.*

Transfuyard: m. *as* Transfuge.

Transglou-

Transgloutir les morceaux. *Greedily to swallow downe his meat halfe chawed.*

Transgresseur: m. *A transgressor, trespasser, sinner, offendor.*

Transgression: f. *A transgression, trespasse, misdeed, offence; also, a digression.*

Transi: m. ie: f. *Fallen into a traunce, or sowne; whose heart, sence, or vitall spirits faile him; astonied, amazed, appalled; halfe dead.*

Transi de froid. *Benummed, or stunnied with cold.*

Transiger. *To accord, agree, come to a point, fall to an end, or attonement.*

Transissement: m. *A sowning, a falling into a traunce or sowne.*

Transitoire: com. *Transitorie, momentarie, fraile, fading, flitting, soone passing away.*

Translaté: m. ée: f. *Translated.*

Translater. *To translate; to turne out of one language into another; also, to reduce, or remoue from one place vnto another.*

Translateur: m. *A translator.*

Translatice: com. *Translaticious, translatiue; transposed, transferred; also, transitiue, or flitting.*

Translation: f. *A translation; also, a remoue, or a remouall; whence;*

La translation S. Martin. *The Translation of Saint Martin; a holy-day (kept in some places) the fourth of Julie.*

Transluire. *To be transparent, to shine, or bee bright, through.*

Transmarché: m. ée: f. *Transported, or sent packing into farre, and forreine countreyes; also, passed, or shifted out of one countrey into another.*

Transmarchement: m. *A transporting; a sending into farre, or forreine countreyes; also, a passing, remouing, or shifting out of one countrey into another.*

Transmarcher. *To transport, or packe away into farre and forreine parts; also, to passe, remoue, or shift out of one countrey into another.*

Transmettre. *To transmit, or passe ouer vnto another; to send from one place to another; to giue, or let a thing from himselfe to others.*

Transmigration: f. *A transmigration; a flitting, a shifting of aboad, a changing of place.*

Transmigrer. *To flit, shift aboad, change place, depart further off, goe from one dwelling vnto another.*

Transmis: m. ise: f. *Transmitted, sent away; passed, giuen, let goe, posted ouer to another.*

Transmissible: com. *Transmittable.*

Transmontain: m. aine: f. *Forreine; or, dwelling beyond the mountaines (whereby, most commonly, th' Alps are vnderstood.)*

Transmontane. *as* Tramontane.

Transmuër. *To change, or alter ouer.*

Transmutation: f. *A transmutation, alteration, change.*

Transompt: m. *as* Transumpt.

Transon: m. *A truncheon, or peece of.*

Transparent: m. ente: f. *Transparent, through-shining, or which may be seene through.*

Transpasser. *To passe, or goe through; also, to passe ouer.*

Transpercer. *To pierce, thrust, or strike through.*

Transpirable: com. *Transpirable, easie to breath out or through.*

Transpiration: f. *A transpiration, euaporation, breathing through.*

Transplacer. *To transplace, remoue, place or put ouer.*

Transplantation: f. *A transplantation; a remouing, or setting in another place.*

Transplanté: m. ée: f. *Transplanted.*

Transplantement: m. *A transplanting.*

Transplanter. *To transplant; remoue, plant, or set in another place.*

Transplanteur: m. *A transplanter.*

Transpontin: m. *A ship-ladder; also, a little bridge ouer a ditch.*

Transpontin: m. ine: f. *Outlandish, ouer-sea.*

Transport: m. *A transport, or transportation; a remouall, a carrying ouer, or out of one place into another.*

Droict par transport. *A right, or title by assignement, or meane conueyance.*

Transporté: m. ée: f. *Transported; carried or conueyed ouer; also, remoued out of one place into another; also, distraught, rauished, beside himselfe; whence;* Tu as l'esprit transporté; *Thy wits runne a wooll-gathering.*

Transportement: m. *A transporting.*

Transporter. *To transport; carrie or conuey ouer, remoue from one place to another; also, to transferre, and to flit, or shift places.*

Se transporter. *To flit, or shift his place; to remoue, wend, goe.*

Se transporter quelque chose. *To attribute or draw vnto himselfe, to take or applie to his owne vse, any thing.*

Transporteur: m. *A transporter.*

Transposé: m. ée: f. *Transposed.*

Transposer. *To transpose; translate, remoue.*

Transposition: f. *A transposition; translation, remouall out of one place into another.*

Transvasation: f. *A turning, powring, shifting, remouing out of one vessell into another.*

Transvasé: m. ée: f. *Turned, powred, shifted out of one vessell into another.*

Transvasément: m. *as* Transvasation.

Transvaser. *To turne, powre, shift, remoue out of one vessell into another.*

Transubstantiation: f. *Transubstantiation, alteration or change of substance.*

Transubstantier. *To transubstantiate, to alter the substance of.*

Transversaire: com. *Trauers, crossing, or crosse-wise, ouerthwart.*

Muscle transversaire. *A certain muskle which draws the head aside.*

Transversal, & Transversel. *as* Transversaire.

Transumpt: m. *A transumpt, or exemplification; the copie of a Record.*

Trantaner. *as* Trantraner.

Trantin: m. *A peece of coyne worth a French penie, or better.*

Trantrac: m. *The lowd resounding, or sound, of a Hunters horne.*

Trantran. *The same.*

Trantraner. *To wind a horne verie lowd, to make it rattle.*

Trape: f. *A trap, or trap doore; (also, a boord; ¶* Champenois.*)*

La trape des cieux. *The windowes of heauen.*

La trape d'embas. *A Pitfall, or trap made like a Pitfall; also, a trap-doore in a lower roome, or which opens into a dungeon, or deepe hole; also, a womans &c.*

Trape de feu. *A fire-panne, or panne for coles.*

Trape: com. *Square, quarrie, big set, strong made, well knit, well squat, well timbered, well pitched or trust together (but low withall.)*
Trapelle: f. *A little trap.*
Trapercer. *as* Transpercer.
Trapeze. *whence;* Figure trapeze. *Vnequally sided and cornered, broader on th'one side then on the other, of vnequall breadth.*
Muscle trapeze. *The muskle whereby the shoulder-blades are drawne vpwards.*
Trappan: m. *A Stone-cutters Drill; the toole where-with he bores little holes in Marble, &c.*
Trappe: f. *as* Trape; *also, a certaine trip, or tricke in wrastling.*
Trappelle: f. *A little trap; a Mouse-trap.*
Trappu: m. uë: f. *Thick, and short; or as* Trape: com.
Trapusse: f. *A trap.*
Traquenard: m. *A racking horse or guelding, a hack-ney.*
Traquenarderie: f. *A racking, or shuffling pace.*
Traquet: m. *The bird called a Bunting; also, the clack, or clapper of a mill.*
Trascendant. *as* Transcendant.
Trasle: f. *A Thrush, or Fieldfare.*
Traslier: m. *A kind of the barren Skarlet Oake.*
Trasser. *as* Tracer; *also, to delineate, score, trace out; or to draw the first (rude) lines of a picture, &c.*
Trasses: f. *The slot, view, or footing of a Deere, &c; (Looke* Trace.)
Trasseure: f. *A streake, line, dash, or score, made with a penne, or pensill; also, a tracke, trace, path, footing; or as* Tracement.
Trastravat: m. *A horse thats crosse-trauersed;* viz. *hath two ouerthwart white feet.*
Trau. *as* Trou: ¶Wallon.
Travail: m. *Trauell, toyle, teene, labour, businesse, pains-taking; trouble, molestation, care; also, the frame whereinto Farriers put vnruie horses when they shooe, or dresse them.*
Vn homme de grand travail. *A verie painfull man.*
Travaillant. *Laborious, painefull, industrious, diligent.*
Travaillé. *Trauelled, toyled, laboured, much busied, or exercised in; troubled, molested, vexed, or wearied with.*
Ioye triste coeur travaillé: Pro. *Th'aggrieued heart makes heauie cheere.*
Travaillement: m. *A trauelling, toyling, moyling, swinking, labouring; molesting, harrying, trou-bling.*
Travailler. *To trauell, swinke, labour, toyle, moyle, take paines, or busie himselfe in; also, to exercise, hold occu-pied, set on worke; harrie, wearie, vex, trouble, tur-moyle, disquiet, infest.*
Travailler en bourdican. *Looke* Bourdican.
Tant travaille, & tracasse l'homme qu'il se rompt, ou somme: Prov. *So long a man toyles, and trots vp and downe, that at the length he bursts, or falls flat downe.*
Travaison: f. *A floore, or frame of beames; or of thicke plankes, whereby one roome, or chamber is diuided from another; also, a single beame, or thicke planke.*
Travat: m. *A horse which is trauersed;* viz. *hath two white feet on the right, or left side.*
Travée: f. *A Bay of building; the space, and length, be-tweene the maine beames of a roome; or betweene two beames, or the two walls thereof; in breadth about twelue foot, in length betweene nineteene & twentie.*
Travelot: m. *A double quarter, or small beame.*
Travelure: f. *as* Travaison; *or, a frame of beames.*
Travers: m. *A Toll Trauers; due by vassalls vnto their Lord, vpon the transportation of their mouables, com-modities, or wares, out of his territorie, by what pas-sage, or way soeuer (our Lawyers define it to be, Toll thats payed for passing ouer a priuate mans ground;) also (but not so properly) a passage toll, or through-toll.*
Vn travers de nez. *A flirt, or cut, ouerthwart the nose.*
Travers: m. erse: f. *Crosse, crosse-wise, thwart, ouer-thwart; ill placed, out of order.*
Travers. De travers. (Adverb.) *Acrosse, crosly, ouer-thwartly; whence;*
Paroles de travers. *Nips, quips, taunts, girds; thwar-tings, crosse or ouerthwart words.*
Regarder de travers. *To leere, to looke askew at, or a-wry vpon; to behold with a fell, sterne, angrie, frow-ning, or despightfull eye.*
Travers. *(Preposition.)* 'A travers païs. *At randome, at rouers, roamingly.*
Traversain: m. aine: f. *Crosse, lying or layed acrosse, o-uerthwart, oblique, awry, crooked, sidelong.*
Les plumes traversaines d'un oiseau. Celles qui vont, & se couchent par travers: ¶Nicot.
Traversan: m. *A crosse rafter, or quarter; an ouerthwart planke, or boord.*
Traversant: m. ante. f. *Trauersing, crossing, thwarting, lying acrosse, or athwart ouer.*
Chevaux traversans. *Are due vnto the Lords feodall of* Poictou, à l'ouverture des fiefs; *or, in lieu of them, a certaine summe agreed on betweene them and their vassalls: These horses, as it seemes, be inferiour vnto Steeds, or horses of seruice.*
Traverse: f. *A crosse-way, or by-lane, which leads out of the highway; (An old French Lawyer defines it,* Vn chemin, qui traverse d'un village en autre, & qui doit contenir, comme les plus des Coustumiers sont d'accord, jusques à vingt, ou vingt-deux pi-eds:) *a house in a street which leanes, or iutties out further then those that be about it; also, a crosse, crosse blow, thwart, cuffe, misfortune, trouble, disturbance, let, barre, hinderance, in the course of a suit, or busi-nesse.*
Bois de traverse. *A size of billets, which be lesse then the* Bois de moule.
Iecter quelque mot à la traverse. *To cast out a word.*
Venir à la traverse. *To come on the contrarie side, or directly against; to come along in the way of.*
Traverse: com. Oeil traverse. *A leering, or side eye, or cast of an eye.*
Traversé: m. ée: f. *Trauersed, crossed ouer; also, pier-ced, or strucke, through; and hence also, wet through, or (as we say) to the skinne.*
Cheval traversé. *A thicke, broad-set, well-trussed, short-made horse.*
Traversement: m. *A thwarting, a going ouer-thwart, a crossing ouer; also, a piercing or striking through.*
Traverser. *To thwart or goe ouerthwart, crosse or passe ouer; also, to strike or pierce through.*
Traverseux: m. euse: f. *Ouerthwart, crosse, froward.*
Traversier: m. *Such a Ferriboat as is guided by a rope fastened vnto a post, &c, on either side of a riuer; also, a transome, crosse beame, ouerthwart rafter, peece of timber, planke, or boord; also, the wine vessell, called otherwise,* Poinson.

Traverſier: m. ere: *Croſse or croſſing, thwarting, ouerthwarting, lying ore-croſse, layed acroſſe ouer.*

Sergents traverſiers. *Extraordinarie Raungers, or Officers of a Foreſt; wherein they haue no certaine walke aſſigned them, but are to viſit all the parts of it, and certifie what abuſes are committed, what waſt made, in it.*

Traverſin: m. *A croſſe-beame, or peece of timber, in a ſhip, &c; alſo, a bed-boulſter.*

se Travestir. *To diſguiſe, or ſhift, his apparell; to maske it, or take on him another mans habit; to play the counterfeit.*

Traumatique: com. *A Vulnerarie; any oinment, or ſalue thats fit, or good, for wounds.*

Travoiſon: f. *A frame, ſeeling, or floore made with beames, or thicke plankes.*

Travonaiſon: f. *An arched frame, ſeeling, or floore of beames, &c.*

Travonizer la muraille, &c. *To arch, or floore it ouer with a frame of beames, &c.*

Travonner. *as* Travonizer.

Travouil: m. *A Ricc; or, a turning reele.*

Trayans: m. *The wires which are placed in the fore-part of an arched, or old faſhioned Organ; and ſerue to ſtop, or open the Pallets thereof.*

Traye: f. *A kind of Thruſh.*

Trayer: m. *A milking Pale, or Piggin.*

Trayne, & Traymeau. *A kind of drag-net for fiſhing.*

Trayne: f. *A great round poſt, or peece of timber, like to an apple-tree; alſo, as* Traine.

Trayneau: m. *as* Traineau.

Trayne-guain. *Looke* Trainegain.

Trayons: m. *The teats, or duds of a Cow.*

Treau de Saffran. *A bed of Saffron.*

Treboufet: m. *A kind of ſweet wine.*

Trebuchant. *Tripping, ſtumbling, ſlipping downewards.*

Eſcu trebuchant. *Which beares downe the balance, or is much more then weight.*

Trebuchement: m. *A ſtumbling, tripping, ſlipping, or falling downe; alſo, an offending, miſdoing, or miſtaking.*

Trebucher. *To ſtumble, or trip; to ſlip (and thereby ſometimes) to fall downe; alſo, to offend, miſdoe, miſtake; alſo, to ouerweigh, or beare downe by weight; as, in a balance, a heauier thing doth a lighter.*

C'eſt tout vn de cheoir, & de trebucher: Prov. *There's but little difference betweene ſtumbling, and tumbling.*

Il vaut mieux trebucher vne fois que tousjours chanceller: Prov. *Better at once to fall outright then euermore to ſtagger; Looke* Chanceller.

Trebuchet: m. *A pitfall for birds; a pit, with a trap doore, for wild beaſts; alſo, a paire of gold weights; alſo, an old-faſhioned Engine of wood, from which great, and battering ſtones were moſt violently throwne.*

Trece. *Looke* Treſſe.

Tref: m. *The beame of a houſe; alſo, a Tent, or Pauillion of ſtrong canuas; alſo, a kind of ſayle in a ſhip; whence;*

'A plein tref. *With full ſayle.*

Treffle: m. *Trefoile, Clauer, Three-leaued graſſe; alſo, a Club at Cards.*

Treffle aigre. *Wood Sorrell, wood Sowre, Alleluya, Stubwort.*

Treffle bas. *Hares-foot, rough Clauer.*

Treffle bitumineux. *as* Treffle puant.

Treffle au limaçon. *Snaile Clauer, horned Clauer, horned Trefoile, medow Fother.*

Treffle odoriferant. *Sweet Trifolie, garden Clauer, Scillat Clauer.*

Treffle des prez. *Common Trefoile, medow Trefoyle, Suckles, Cockheads.*

Treffle puant. *Smelling Clauer, Treacle Clauer, Pitch Trefoile, ſtinking Trefoile, Clauer gentle.*

Treffle ſauvage (jaulne.) *Wild yellow Trefoile, wild yellow Lotus.*

Treffle vraye. *the right Trefoile; or as* Treffle puant.

Grand Treffle. *Spaniſh Trifolie, Medicke Fother, Snayle Clauer; alſo, great Trefoile, winged Clauer; and, (in the opinion of ſome) horned Clauer.*

Petit Treffle jaulne. *Pettie Clauer, ſmall Trefoile, ſlone Trefoile.*

Treffoncier. *as* Tresfoncier.

Treffond. *as* Tresfond; *and, ground with the crop yet growing vpon it.*

Trefont de Tonnelier. *A Coopers Turrell; the Augar wherwith he maketh holes:* ¶Norm.

Tregenier: m. *A Salter; or, one that ſelleth ſalt (as ſome here) out of carts, &c.*

Trehu. *as* Treu.

Treillage: m. *Grates, croſſe-barres, Lattice-worke; Arbors; a rayling.*

Treille: f. *An Arbor, or walke, ſet on both ſides with vines, &c, twining about a* Treillis, *or latticed frame.*

Saulter de treille en paiſſeaux. *To run (without cauſe or conſcience) from one ſubiect vnto another.*

Treillé: m. ée: f. *Grated, or latticed; ſupported or vnderſet with, held vp or in by, growing or twining about, lattices, croſſe-barres, or grated frames.*

Treiller. *To grate, or lattice; to ſupport or vnderſet by, compaſſe or hold in with, croſſe-barres, or latticed frames.*

Treillis: m. *A Trellis; a lattice before a doore, hole, or window; a grate ſet thicke with croſſe-barres of wood; any lattice, or (wodden) grate; any latticed, or grated frame.*

Treilliſſé: m. ée: f. *Croſſe-barred, latticed, grated (with wood.)*

Treilliſſer. *To lattice, croſſe barre, grate (with wood;) to hold vp, or hemme in, by lattices, croſſe-barres, grates.*

Treine. f. *as* Trene; *alſo, a Dorman, or great beame.*

Trelis. *Looke* Treillis.

Treluire. *To gliſter, or ſhine verie bright.*

Tremail: m. *Barlie, Oates, & Fitches, mingled together.*

Tremaille: f. *A Trammell, or net for Partridges.*

Tremaillé: m. ée: f. *Treble-mailed; whence,* Alier tremaillé; *A Trammell net, or treble net, for Partridges, &c.*

Tremblant. *Trembling, ſhiuering.*

Tremblant entre cuir & chair. *See* Cuir.

Tremblante de moulin. *A Mill hopper.*

Tremblaye: f. *A groue of Aſpes.*

Tremble: m. *An Aſpe, or Aſpen tree.*

Tremble: f. *The* Torpedo, *or Crampe-fiſh.*

Tremblement: m. *A trembling, ſhiuering, diddering, ſhaking, or quaking.*

Trembler. *To tremble, ſhiuer, didder, quake, ſhake.*

Faire trembler le lard au charnier. *To terrifie, or affright (ſenceleſſe or weake people) with big words.*

Trembloer: m. *The Sound-boord of a Muſicall Inſtrument.*

Tremblotement: m. *An often trembling; a quaking, diddering; panting.*

Trembloter. *To tremble, quake, pant (often;) to shiuer, or didder.*

Tremblotis: m. *as* Tremblement; *or as* Tremblotement.

Treme. *Looke* Traime.

Tremeau: m. *as* Trumeau; *or a hough, or leg of Beefe.*

Tremegiste: m. *An excellent Maister (of* Trismegiste, *an excellent Philosopher:)* ¶Rab.

Tremeiller. *To quake, to quauer, to wag.*

Tremés. Bled tremés. *Looke* Bled.

Tremeur: m. *A great feare, or dread; a trembling, shaking, or quaking (thereby.)*

Tremeze. *A kind of Rie sowed in the Spring.*

Tremie de moulin. *The Mill-hopper.*

Tremoise: f. *The Scate called the Crampe-fish:* ¶Bourdelois.

Tremouille. *as* Tremie.

Tremoussement: m. *A violent quaking, shrugging, or trembling; also, a sudden starting, or liuelie stirring.*

Tremousser. *To tremble, shrud, shrug, shiuer, quake, extreamely, or vpon an extreame feare; also, to totter exceedingly; also, to start suddenly, stirre sprightfully.*

Tremoy: m. & **Tremoye**: f. *as* Tremail.

Trempe: m. *Houshold wine, or small wine made, for the seruants, of water, and the grounds or bottomes of good wine.*

Trempe: f. *The temper of a weapon; also, a dipping; steeping; seasoning, tempering; also, the temperature, disposition, or composition of the mind; the mood, humor, or temper wherein it is.*

Trempé: m. ée: f. *Dipped; moistened, wet; steeped, soaked; seasoned, tempered.*

Trempez en sang. *In bloud; imbrued, or distained with bloud.*

Apres avoir trempé longuement en prison. *After a most strict, and tedious imprisonment; after that hee had lien a long time by it.*

Temprement: m. *A dipping; moistening, wetting; steeping, soaking; seasoning, tempering.*

Tremper. *To dip; moisten, wet, soake, steepe; season, temper, supple in liquor, &c.*

Trempette. *A sop, or sippet.*

Trempeur: m. *A dipper; wetter, moistener; soaker, steeper; seasoner, temperer.*

Trempis: m. *Filthie water wherein raw things haue beene dipped, steeped, or soaked.*

Tempoir: m. *The pit wherein Tanners doe soake their hides after they haue beene in their lime-pit.*

Tremuë de moulin. *A Mill-hopper.*

Tren: m. *An Instrument (somewhat like an Eele-speare) wherewith Marriners doe strike, and kill, fish at sea.*

Trenchaison: f. *A gripe, or a wring, as of the Chollicke, &c.*

Trenchaisonner. *To wring or gripe like the Cholicke, &c.*

Trenchant: m. *The edge of a weapon, or toole; also, cutting, sharpenesse, keenenesse.*

Trenchant: m. ante: f. *Cutting, sharpe, keene, well-edged; slicing, hewing, thwiting off, or asunder.*

Escuyer, & *(in old time)* valet, trenchant. *A Caruer.*

Trenche: f. *as* Tranche.

Trenché: m. ée: f. *Cut off, or asunder; sliced, carued; hacked, or hewed in peeces.*

Laict trenché. *Milke which is turned, and halfe curded.*

Trenchée: f. *A trench; also, a fretting, wringing, or griping in the bellie, or lower parts; the wormes, or bellie-ache.*

Trenchées de S. Mathurin. *Madde moods, Bedlam fits.*

Trenchefile: f. *The head-band of a booke; also, a snaffle; or the mouth of a snaffle, or watering Bit; also, the trench, or trenching of a Crossebow string; that part thereof whereinto the neb of the arrow entreth.*

Trenchefile de soulier. *The cording, or binding of the inside of the heele, or ties.*

Trenchement: m. *A cutting, slicing; caruing; hacking, or slashing in peeces.*

Trenche-montaigne. *as* Tranche-montaigne.

Trencheoir: m. *A Trencher.*

Trenche-plume. *A Penknife.*

Trencher. *To cut; carue; slice, hacke, hew; to thwite off, or asunder.*

Trencher du grand. *To take a great deale of state vpon him.*

Trencher le mot. *To speake briefely and properly, to answer quickly and shortly.*

Il en faut trencher la broche. *Th'expectation thereof is to be preuented, or cut off.*

Trenchet de cordoüannier. *A Shoomakers cutting-knife.*

Trenchoir. *as* Trencheoir.

Trene. *A threefold rope, cord, string, or twist, called by Marriners, a Sinnet.*

Trenne. *as* Trene.

Trenné. Chanure trennée. *Twisted, or made into a threefold rope.*

Trenou: f. *A great raumpe, or tomboy.*

Trense. *as* Transe.

Trentain: m. *A thirtieth or thirtie, the nũber of thirtie.*

Trentaine: f. *as* Trentain.

Trente. *Thirtie.*

Trente-costes: m. *A gangerell, slimme, long luske, lank loobie.*

Trentiesme. *The thirtieth.*

Trepan: m. *A Trepane; an Instrument hauing a round, and indented edge, wherewith Chirurgians open a fractured skull, and by the helpe of a Leuatorie (within it) raise vp the crushed, and depressed parts thereof, and take out peeces of bones, and clotted bloud.*

Trepané: m. ée: f. *Trepaned.*

Trepanation: f. *A trepaning; a round opening of the skull with a Trepane.*

Trepaner. *To trepane; to open, or bore holes in the skull with a Trepane.*

Trepasser. *To passe ouer, not to mention.*

Trepé: m. ée: f. *Trampled on, troden vnder foot.*

Trepelu: m. *A poore tattered rogue; a base, bare, and beggerlie wretch.*

Trepelu: m. uë: f. *Poore, bare, beggerlie; paultrie, base, vnworthie.*

Treper. *To hop, skip, trip or foot it vp and downe; also, to stampe, trample on, tread vnder foot.*

Trepidation: f. *Trembling, terrour, feare.*

Trepied: m. *A Treuet.*

Trepier: m. *A place whereat three or foure sundrie streets, or highwayes doe meet a-head.*

Trepigné. *Trampled, daunced; often troad on.*

Trepigner. *To trample; hop, skip, daunce; tread often vpon.*

Trepillard: m. arde: f. *Skipping, hopping, dauncing, stirring; traumping or trampling on.*

Trepiller. *as* Treper.

Trepiné. *as* Trepigné.

Trepis de bestes. *A trampling, or often treading on by the feet of beasts.*

Tre-

Trepointe. Souliers à trep. renversée. *Turne-ouers.*

Tres. *A Particle, or vndeclinable word, neuer vsed but in composition, and then, for the most part, adding to that which it precedes the superlatiue energie of thrice, most, excellently, exceedingly, passing, or aboue all others, &c; In which sence being applyable to manie Verbes, and to the most Adiectiues, and Aduerbes, (which are in their originall, and due places expounded) I haue purposely omitted all, except foure or fiue, of them; it being an easier matter for simple Readers to find out the meaning of the rest, by the application of them to these few, or by the generall direction of this Rule, then for me to please the iudicious, by stuffing vp (though with some warrant of example) much Paper with needlesse repetitions.*

Tresabonescient. *Most wittingly, most earnestly, or in exceeding great earnest.*

Tresacertes. *Throughly, in great earnest, as much, or as farre as may be.*

Tresalant: m. ante: f. *Scorching, parching, drying vp by extreame heat.*

Tresalé: m. *A scorching, parching, extreame drynesse or drought by an extreame heat.*

Tresalé: m. ée: f. *Scorched, parched, vtterly dryed vp, or drayned of moisture, by extreame heat.*

Tresaler. *To scorch, parch, dry or be dryed vp, drayne or be drayned of all manner of moisture, by extreame heat.*

Tresarriere. *Exceedingly backward, verie farre behindhand; whence;*

Aujourd'huy thresorier, demain tresarriere: Pro. *No man knowes what his last accompt will be; or, no rich man knowes how poore he soone may be.*

Tresbuchant, & Tresbucher. *as* Trebuchant, & Trebucher.

Trescheur. (*whence,* Vn Lion enclos en vn double trescheur;) *A Tracke, or Tresseur (in Blason.)*

Treseau: m. *A shocke, stowke, halfe-thraue, rowke, or heape of sheaues in a corne-field; also, halfe a quarter of an ounce in the weight of ware, or marchandise.*

Tresfoncier: m. iere: f. *Proper, fundamentall, bred with, or grounded in; also, thats owner of, or belongs vnto, the soyle.*

Seigneur tresfoncier. *The Lord of the soyle; he in whom the propertie (in whomsoeuer the possession) thereof is;* (Ce mot a lieu en cas de roture, *sayes* Nicot.)

Tresfond: m. *The soyle of land; and, as* Treffond.

Tresine, & Tresmer. *as* Traime, & Traimer.

Tresmousser. *To bring forth abundance of Mosse; also, as* Tremousser.

Tresne. *as* Trene.

Tresnon: m. *A three-fold wreath, cord, rope, string.*

Tresor, & Tresorier. *Looke* Thresor, & Thresorier.

Trespas: m. *A death, dying, or decease; a departure out of this world; also, a passage; whence;*

Trespas de Loire. *A kind of Passage-toll, or Custome payed at Passages ouer the* Loire.

Trespassant: m. *A Passenger.*

Trespassé: m. ée: f. *Dead, deceassed, departed this life; also, exceeded, ouerpassed.*

Il pisse pour les trespassez. *An equiuocation; for it may either signifie the dead (vpon whose graues the Papists vse to sprinkle holie water) or haue relation vnto* Traicts passez; *draughts of drinke alreadie swallowed downe.*

Tout cela est frappé à la porte d'un trespassé. *Looke* Porte.

Trespasser. *To die, decease, depart this life; also, to ouerpasse, exceed; passe on, or ouer.*

Trespasser son serment. *To breake, or goe from, his oath.*

Trespecer. *To pull, or teare into many peeces; (an old word.)*

Trespercé: m. ée: f. *Transpierced, pierced through.*

Trespercer. *To pierce, or strike, through.*

Tresque. *Exceeding much.*

Tresquer. *To daunce; (an old word.)*

Tressaillir. *To start; also, to leape, hop, or skip; liuely, sprightfully, or apace; to iert, or spring vp; also, to ouerleape, and to leape ouer.*

Le coeur luy tressaut. *His heart leapes, or pants, for ioy, &c.*

Tressault, & Tressaut: m. *A start, or starting; a springing, liuelie ierting, sprightfull skipping vpwards; also, a leape, or leaping, ouer.*

Tresse de cheveux. *A tresse, or locke of haire.*

Tressé: m. ée: f. *Plaited, wouen, or made into tresses.*

Tresseau. *The name of a fertile Vine.*

Tresser. *To plait, weaue, or make into tresses.*

Tressette: f. *A little tresse, or locke.*

Tresteau. *Looke* Treteau.

Trestous. *All, each, or euerie one, not one excepted, not one to be spared.*

Treteau, & Tretteau. *A tresle for a Table, &c; also (as* Chevalet) *a kind of racke, or stretching torture.*

Treu: m. *as* Trou; *a hole.* ¶Picard. *also, the toll, or custome payed vnto Lords, for salt, and other commodities, or marchandise, carried along by their dominions; and generally, any toll, tax, or imposition.*

Le Droict de treu accoustumé. *Looke* Droict.

Treüage: m. *as* Treu.

Trevercin: m. *A kind of marble, or marble-like stone.*

Treves: f. *Truce; a limitted cessation from warre.*

Treves brisées ou enfraintes. *The breach, or violation of a graunted Protection.*

Treufle. *A Club at Cards; Looke* Treffle.

Vn Nez d'az de treufles. *A flat bottle nose.*

Treuil. *as* Trieule.

Trevisaine. La Danse Tre. *Lecherie.*

Treul: m. *A Wine-presse; or (more generally) any Presse.*

Treule: f. *A little fish-net for Stues, and small Ponds.*

Trezain: m. *A thirteene-pennie peece; a coyne of base mettall worth* xiij d Tourn.

Trezain: m. *A thirteenth; whence;*

Le trezain du pain. *Vantage of bread; the thirteenth loafe giuen by Bakers vnto the dozen.*

Treze. *Thirteene.*

Trezeau. *Looke* Treseau.

Trezeine de bois: f. *Thirteene billets, or logs; or as much wood as a man can carrie.*

Trezeler. *To make vp sheaues of corne into shocks; also, to exclayme, or to rayle, on.*

Treziesme: m. *A thirteenth; also, the thirteenth pennie, or part, of the money for which land is sold, in many places payed, vnto the Lord* feodal, *by the seller (if there be no couenant to the contrarie;) also, the thirteenth sheafe due vnto Lords for some kinds of countrey Toll.*

Treziesme de Vin. *The thirteenth pot, or pennie of the price of retayled Wine, due in some places vnto the Lord of the Iurisdiction, or Soyle.*

Treziesme: com. *The thirteenth.*

Le treziesme denier. *as* Treziesme *in the second sence.*

Triacle: m. *Treacle*; *See* Theriaque.
Triaclerie: f. *The making of Threacle*; *also, an imposture, deceit, sophistication.*
Triade: f. *A tre*; *or, a third.*
Triage: m. *Choice*; *a culling, or picking out from among others.*
Triages de forests. *The seuerall diuisions, walkes, or parts, of Forests.*
Triangle: m. *A triangle, or three-cornered figure.*
Triangulaire: com. *Triangular, three-cornered, of three corners.*
Muscle triangulaire. *The triangular muscle whereby the hanch, or flanke is bowed.*
Tribaille: f. *The Poultrie.*
Triballer. *To wagle, or dangle vp and downe; to goe dingle dangle, wig wag.*
Triballeur: m. *A Poulter.*
Tribart: m. *A short Cudgell.*
Tribe. *Looke* Tribu.
Tribort. *The starre-boord, or the right side, of a ship.*
Tribouil: m. *Trouble, vexation, molestation*; *(an old word.)*
Triboule-mesnage: m. *An ill, or vnskilfull husband, one that marres, or confounds, his owne businesse.*
Triboulet: m. *A Triblet*; *the toole whereon Goldsmiths and Clock-makers put Rings, and little wheeles, when they file, or otherwise worke, them*; *also, as* Triboullet.
Triboulller. *To shog, or iog, like a Cart, &c, in an vneuen way*; *and hence also, to iumble, disorder, or set out of order, any thing.*
Triboullet: m. *as* Triboulet; *also, a slouenlie fellow, one that vsually weares his hose vngartered, and shooes vntyed*; *also, the name of a famous foole belonging to King* Francis *the first*; *and thence, any fop, cokes, ridiculous ninniehammer, or laughing-stocke.*
Tribu: f. *A Tribe*; *Companie, Band, Ward, Canton, or Hundred, in a Citie, or Countie.*
Tribulation: f. *Tribulation, affliction, anguish, paine, trouble, griefe.*
Tribule (aquatic.) *The water Caltrop, Saligot, water-Nut.*
Tribule terrestre. *The land Caltrop, or Saligot.*
Tribun: m. *A Tribune of the people among the auncient Romans.*
Tribut: m. *Tribute*; *a generall tax, or subsidie raised vpon the goods of subiects.*
Tributaire: com. *Tributarie, tribute-paying.*
Tric: m. *A word whereby Printers doe signifie, that they giue ouer working.*
Tricdondaines: f. *as* Triquedondaines.
Trichard: m. arde: f. *Cousening, cheating, deceiuing, beguiling.*
Tricher. *To cousen, cheat, beguile, deceiue, play false, vse false tricks.*
Tricherie: f. *(whence, as it seemes, our trecherie) cousenage, deceit, a cheating, a beguiling.*
Tricheur: m. *A cousening companion.*
Tricheuse: f. *A cousening queane.*
Trichiase: f. *A disease comming vnto nurses paps by drinking downe a haire*; *also, a small, and inuisible cleft about the back-bone, running out in length, and oftentimes causing death*; *also (in horses) a vicious inuersion of the vpper eye-lid, to the trouble of the vnder one, and torment of the whole eye.*
Trichoterie: f. *as* Tricoterie.
Tricon: m. *Is (at Cards) that which we now call, a Gleeke of Kings, Queenes, Knaues, &c*; viz. *three of them in one hand together.*
Tricoter. *To knit.* ¶Orleannois.
Tricoter la pureté de l'or, &c. *To alter, change, allay, or imbase it.*
Tricoterie: f. *Cousenage, cheating, trecherie, deceit, in the following of a suit, &c.*
Tricoteur: m. *A knitter.* ¶Orl.
Tricoteur de procez. *A contriuer, or canuaser of suits*; *a Pettifogger*; *a craftie, or cousening Lawyer.*
Tricoteuse: f. *A knitter, a woman that knits.* ¶Orl.
Tricotter, & Tricotterie. *as* Tricoter, & Tricoterie.
Tricouse: f. *as* Triquehouses.
Trictrac: m. *The inside, or playing-side of a paire of Tables*; *also, the Tables themselues*; *also, the Game Ticktacke at Tables*; *also, the clattering noise made by Table-men, &c.*
Tride. Carriere tride. *A strong, and speedie mouing of a horse in his carriere.*
Trident: m. *Neptunes three-forked Mace*; *and thence, any weapon, toole, or instrument made of that fashion, or hauing three teeth.*
Trie: f. *A choice, culling, or picking out.*
Trié: m. ée: f. *Chosen, culled, or picked out from among others.*
Triege: com. *Strong, lustie, able-bodied (from the Spanish* Cavallo de triego, *a lustie horse*; *or from the custome of Spaniards, to feed their best horses of seruice with Wheat.)*
Triennal: m. ale: f. *Triennall, of three yeares.*
Trier. *To picke, chuse, cull out from among others.*
Trieule d' un puis. *The round beame about which the cord of a Well doth turne.*
Trifere: f. *A certaine compound, and delicious Electuarie, called thus of a Greeke word, which signifieth sumptuous.*
Trifourché: m. ée: f. *Treble-forked*; *three-fold.*
Trigaut: m. *An intricator, intangler, perplexer of a businesse*; *one that by tricks, or sleights makes it hard to be decided*; *and (more generally) one that is full of shifts, or sleights.*
Triglyphes: m. *Trigliphes*; *hollow grauings like three short gutters, or furrowes, on Compartiments, or Borders in Masonrie.*
Trihoris, ou Trihory: m. *A kind of British, and peasantlie daunce, consisting of three steps, and performed, by those hobling youthes, commonly in a round.*
Trikatiste: com. *Spitting fire.* ¶Rab.
Triller. *To put on a new shirt, &c, and weare it vntill it be growne easie, or soft.*
Trillon: m. *The ninth place in Numeration, and a hundred millions in number.*
Trilly d'Allemaigne. *Fine Buckeram waued like water-Chamlet.*
Trimestre: com. *Of three moneths.*
Trine: com. *Tripled, compounded or made of three.*
Tring'e: f. *A Curtaine-rod*; *and more generally, a peece of round yron, or wire, of the grossenesse of a Curtaine-rod, vsed for the ioyning of stones, or timber, and for the hanging vp of things*; *also, a flat sticke, or lath-like peece of wood.*
Tringue: f. *A drinking*; *also, as* Tringle.
Trinité: f. *The holie Trinitie.*
Herbe de la Trinité. *The Paunsie, hearbe Trinitie, Hearts-ease, loue in idlenesse, two faces vnder a hood*; *some also call so the hearbe Harefoot, or Harefoot Trefoile.*
Trinquamaille. *See* Trinquemaille.

Trinqueballer les cloches. *To iangle, or to ring bels vntuneably, and too much.*
Trinquemaille: f. *Such a box as Players take money in at their doores.*
Trinquer. *To drinke, to quaffe, to carowse.*
Trinquerie: f. *A drinking, quaffing, carowsing.*
Trinquet: m. *Is properly the top, or top-gallant, on any Mast; the highest sayle of a ship.*
Triochite. *Triple-stoned.*
Triolaine: f. *A list, file, series; rabble, continuall or continued cluttermen.*
Triolet: m. *Meddow Trefoile, common Trefoile, three-leafed grasse.*
  Triolet aromatique. *Sweet Trefoile, garden Clauer.*
  Triolet des chevaux. *Melilot, plaister Clauer.*
Triollet. *as* Triolet.
Triomphal: m. ale: f. *Triumphall, of or belonging vnto triumphes.*
Triomphamment. *Triumphantly, triumphingly, in triumph.*
Triomphant. *Triumphant, triumphing.*
Triomphe: m. *A triumph; a pompous, and publike shew.*
Triomphe: f. *The Card-game called Ruffe, or Trump; also, the Ruffe, or Trump at it.*
Triomphé. *Triumphed.*
Triomphement: m. *A triumphing; also, a trumping at Cards.*
Triompher. *To triumph; or greatly to reioyce; also, to trumpe at Cards.*
Trion: m. *Choice or picked graine, cleane corne.*
Tripaille: f. *A quantitie of tripes, or guts.*
Tripailleries: f. *All kind of tripes.*
Tripe: f. *A Tripe; (In which sence it is most vsed plurally;) also, the bellie, or paunch; also, Valure, Irish Tuftaffata, Fustian an apes.*
  Les tripes d'un fagot. *The smallest stickes in a faggot.*
  Tripe de moruë. *The bellie, or stomacke of the* Moruë, *which dryed, and then layed in water, becommeth soft againe, and is ordinarily sold in Lent by it selfe.*
  Il a la tripe grosse. *(Said of) a Gorbellie, Swagbellie, Gulch, fat Guts.*
  Le tout pour la tripe. *All for the bellie.*
  Tripe pleine ne combat bien, ny ne fuit bien: Prov. *He thats full-bellied neither fights, nor flyes, well.*
Tripelle. *as* Tripoly.
Triper. *To tread or stampe on, to trample vnder the feet.*
Triperie: f. *A Triperie; a market, street, or shop wherein tripes are vsually sold.*
Tripetter. *To trip, or foot it nimbly in dauncing.*
Triphere. *as* Trifere.
Tripied: m. *A Treuet.*
Tripier: m. *A Tripe-seller; also, a gorbellie, gulch, great guts; also, as* Tripied.
Tripiere: f. *A Tripe-wife.*
  Cousteau de tripiere (qui coupe des deux costez.) *One that, in a faction, holds correspondencie with both sides, rather to hurt them both then to helpe either.*
  Iniurieux en tripiere. *Scolding like a Butter-whore.*
  Langue de tripiere. *A rayling tongue.*
Triple: m. *A Triple; also, Galliard-time, in Musicke.*
Triple: com. *Triple, threefold.*
Triplé: m. ée: f. *Tripled, trebled.*
Triplement: m. *A tripling, or making threefold.*
Tripler. *To triple, or make threefold.*
Triplication: f. *A tripling, a thricefolding or doing; a multiplying by three.*
Triplique: f. *A second reply, or the answer of the plaintife vnto the defendants Reioinder.*
Tripliquer. *To make a second reply; or a plaintife to answer vnto the defendants Reioinder.*
Tripolion. *Serapions Turbith, sea Starrewort, Hogsbeanes, blue Camomill, blue Daisies.*
Tripoly: m. *Tripoly; a stone with the powder whereof Lapidaries doe smooth, or polish their iewels.*
Tripot: m. *A Tennis-court.*
Tripotage: m. *A confused iumbling, or hudling of things together, a confusion.*
  Fais tellement ton tripotage que tu ne m'y mesles point. *Handle this thy fond businesse, or bargaine so, as I be not drawne into it.*
Tripoté: m. ée: f. *Bandied, or tossed to and fro, as a ball at Tennis; also, confusedly iumbled, hudled, bungled, or slubbered ouer.*
Tripoter. *To play at Tennis; to bandie, or tosse to and fro, as a ball at Tennis; also, confusedly to iumble, or hudle together; illfauoredly to bungle, or slubber ouer.*
Tripoteur: m. *A bungler; a confounder of his owne worke, or businesse; a slubberer ouer of things; a hudler, or shuffler of them together.*
Tripotier: m. *A great haunter of Tennis-courts.*
Trippe. *as* Tripe.
Tripper. *as* Triper.
Triqué: m. ée: f. *Seuered from, or culled out of, the rest.*
Triquebalarideau: m. *A toy, trifle, nifle; a thing of no worth.*
Triquedondaines: f. *All kind of superfluous trifles vsed, or vsually bought, by women; hence, any trash, nifles, or paltrie stuffe; and, a rascallie companie, or crue of scowndrels.*
Triquehouse: f. *A boot-hose; or a thicke hose worne in stead of a boot.*
Triquemadame: f. *Prickmadame, Sengreene the lesser.*
Triqueniques: f. *Trash, trifles, nifles, paltrie stuffe, things of no value.*
  Argumens de triqueniques. *Vaine, fond, sleight arguments.*
  Monsieur de triqueniques. *A gentleman of straw, a thred-bare gentleman.*
Triquetrac. *as* Trictrac.
Triquetre. *A Triangle.*
Triquette: f. *A whirlygig.*
Triquotter. *To knit as stockings, &c; also, as* Tricher.
Trisayeul: m. *A great great grandfather.*
Triscacifte: com. *Exceeding ill, or thrice threefold ill.* ¶Rab.
Trissage: m. *Germaunder, English Treacle; (an hearbe.)*
Trissyllabe: com. *Of three syllables.*
Triste: com. *Sad, pensiue, grieued, heauie, discontented, melancholicke, wofull, dolefull, sorrowfull; also, graue, austere, sowre, harsh.*
  Triste comme vn bonnet de nuict sans coiffe. *As melancholicke as a coyfelesse nightcap.*
Tristement. *Sadly, pensiuely, sorrowfully, wofully, dolefully; grauely, austerely, sowrely.*
Tristesse: f. *Sorrow, griefe, sadnesse, pensiuenesse, melancholie, discontentment, wofullnesse, dolefullnesse.*
Tristeur: f. *as* Tristesse.
Trisulque: com. *Hauing three edges.*

Trituration: f. *A crumming, crumbling, breaking, or grinding small.*

Trituré: m. ée: f. *Crummed, crumbled, broken, or ground small.*

Triturer. *To crumme, crumble, breake, or grind small.*

Trivial: m. ale: f. *Triuiall, common, homelie, ordinarie, vsuall, sleight, of small worth.*

Yeux triviaux. *Eyes that be intentiue, or earnestly cast, three or foure seuerall wayes at once.*

Trivialitez: f. *Triuialities; triuiall, sleight, common, homelie, ordinarie matters.*

Triule. *as* Trieule.

Troc. *Looke* Troq.

Trocanters: m. *Two processes, or bunches towards the top of the thigh-bone; a great one (and the greatest of the whole bodie) standing outward; a lesse, and lower, standing inward.*

Troché. *whence,* Teste de cerf trochée. *Troched, or whose top is diuided into three or foure small branches.*

Trochée: f. *A cluster of apples, &c; a bunch of nuts, &c, growing close together vpon one bough.*

Trochelle: f. *A certaine instrument of torture vsed in the Inquisition-house.*

Trochet: m. *as* Trochée; *also, a kind of small, white, and sweet apple.*

Trocheure: f. *The troching on the top of a Deeres head; or, the top troched; as in* Troché.

Trochile: m. *A Wrenne; also, a little water-fowle which vsually picketh the teeth of Crocodiles; also, a little wreathed band, or member in Pillars.*

Trochisque: m. *A Trochiske, or Trosque; a little rundle, or cake, whereinto diuers medicinable things be reduced, the better to be kept, and the readier to be vsed.*

Trochisqué: m. ée: f. *Made like, or into, a Trochiske.*

Trocisque. *as* Trochisque; *also, a staulke.*

Trocisqué: m. ée: f. *Reduced, or made into the forme of a Trochiske.*

Troesne: m. *Priuet, Primprint.*

Trofée. *Looke* Trophée.

Trognic: m. ique: f. *Scoffing, mocking, flowting, deriding.*

Trognon: m. *The stocke, stump, or trunke of a (branchlesse) tree.*

Troignon. *as* Trognon; *also, the core within fruit.*

Trois. *Three.*

Monsieur de trois au boisseau, ou de trois à vne espée. *Looke* Monsieur.

Secret de trois secret de tous: Prov. *As good let all, as three, men know a thing.*

Troisiesme. *The third.*

Trokalazou. *Looke* Ptoschalazon. ¶Rab.

Troller. *Hounds to trowle, raunge, or hunt out of order.*

Trollerie: f. *A trowling, or disordered raunging, a hunting out of order.*

Trombe: f. *A round and hollow ball of wood, hauing a peake like a casting-top, and making a great noise when it is cast as a top.*

Tromble: f. *The Cramp-fish, tearmed otherwise* Torpille.

Trompe: f. *A Trump, or Trumpet; also, a writhen, and brazen Hunters horne; also, a top; also, the shell-fish called, a sea-Top; also, the snowt of an Elephant; also, the pump of a ship; also, a closet, or such a like roome, built out of a wall with a hanging bottome like th'end of a trũpet.*

Il n'a pas le fouët pour mener cette trompe. *He is too weake for such a wench.*

Il y a plus de trompeurs que de trompes: Pro. *Looke* Trompeur.

Sasse bonne farine sans trompe, ne bucine: Prov. *Enioy thine owne good things without much talking of them.*

Trompé: m. ée: f. *Deceiued, cousened, beguiled, cheated, circumuented, ouerraught.*

Tromper. *To cousen, deceiue, beguile, delude, circumuent, cheat, ouerreach.*

Tromper vn corbeau à bouche beante. *To beguile or depriue a greedie fellow of a thing which he gaped for; or (much more properly) to bring him into a fooles Paradice; and, by commending, to get from him that, which otherwise he would not, or in discretion he should not, by any meanes haue parted with.*

Qui d'autruy tromper se met en peine, souvent luy en advient la peine: Pro. *Looke* Peine.

Tromperie: f. *A craft, wile, fraud, fallacie, deceit, cousenage, delusion, circumuention, ouerreaching, imposture, sophistication, tricke of legerdemain.*

Trompeter. *To trumpet, or sound a Trumpet.*

Trompeteur: m. *A Trumpetter.*

Trompette: m. *as* Trompeteur.

Trompette: f. *A Trumpet; also, the Needle-fish, Garre-fish, Horne-beake, Horne-fish, or Piper-fish; tearmed thus, because her beake doth somewhat resemble a Trumpet.*

Il est bon cheval de trompette. *He feares no noise, big words affright him not.*

`A pain, & oignon trompette ne clairon: Pro. *Warre is seldome heard of in bare, and barren places; poore men may, if they list, liue quietly, and peaceably at home.*

Trompetté: m. ée: f. *Trumpetted, or noised abroad; published, or proclaymed with sound of Trumpets.*

Trompetteur: m. *A Trumpetter.*

Trompeur: m. *A deceiuer, beguiler, cousener, cheater, conycatcher, fraudulent dealer.*

`A trompeur trompeur & demy: Prov. *Applyable vnto a knaue, ouer-raught, or ouer-matched by a knaue.*

Il y a plus de trompeurs que de trompes: Pro. *The world is fuller of trumperie then of trumpetting.*

Trompeusement. *Deceitfully, couseningly, cautelously, fraudulently.*

Tron: m. *A peece of a thing; or, as* Tronc.

Tronc: m. *The trunke, stocke, stemme, bulke, or bodie of a tree, &c, without the boughes; also, a trunke, or headlesse bodie of man or beast; also, the poore-mans box in Churches; also, the Boat called a Lighter.*

Troncation: f. *A truncation, trunking, mutilation, cutting off.*

Tronche: f. *A great peece of timber; or, as* Tronc.

Tronché: m. ée: f. *Stocked, growne a stocke, or in the stocke.*

Troncher. *To stock, or yeeld a stock, or grow in the stock, as a tree.*

Troncher les grains. *Many staulks, or eares to spring from one root of corne.*

Tronchet: m. *A truncheon; a little trunke, stocke, or stemme.*

Tronchou: m. *A certaine blew-backt, siluer-bellied, and smooth-skind flat fish, without skales.*

Troncir. *To cut or breake off, or in two, or into peeces.*

Tronçonné: m. ée: f. *Trunked; lopped, or cut off; made headlesse, branchlesse, memberlesse; mutilated, maymed.*

Tronçonnement: m. *A trunking; lopping, cutting off; a making headlesse, branchlesse, memberlesse; a mutilating, or mayming.*

Tronçonner. *To trunke; lop, cut off; to make headlesse, branchlesse, memberlesse; to mutilate, or mayme.*

Tronçonneur: m. *A trunker, or lopper; a cutter of things into truncheons, or lumpes.*

Trondel: m. *The trundle, or trundling of a ball, &c.* ¶Pic.

Trondeler. *To trundle as a ball, &c; or, as* Rondeler. ¶Pic.

Trone. *Looke* Throne.

Trongne: f. *The face, aspect, looke, visage, countenance.*

'A la trongne cognoist on l'yvrongne: Prov. *Two things a drunkard doe disclose, a fierie face, and crimson nose.*

Bonne bouche bonne trongne: Prov. *A temperate mouth breedeth a fresh complexion; or, a well-shap'd mouth makes all the face shew faire; or, a silent mouth settles the countenance.*

Trongné. *Of the face; also, from the teeth outward; also, mocking, mowing, or making faces at.*

Trongneux: m. euse: f. *Making, yeelding, or shewing a sowre countenance.*

Trongnon: m. *as* Trognon.

Tronqué: m. ée: f. *Trunked, cut off, cut in two, or into peeces.*

Tronquemént: m. *A trunking, stocking, or cutting off.*

Tronquément. *Peecemeale, with whole peeces cut off; also, lamely, or by halues.*

Tronquer. *To trunke, to stocke; to cut off, in two, or into peeces.*

Tronson: m. *A truncheon, or little trunke; a thicke slice, luncheon, or peece cut off.*

Tronsonner. *Looke* Tronçonner.

Trop. *Too much, ouermuch, superfluous, or superfluitie of, excesse, more then needs; also, much, greatly, mainly, mightily.*

Trop est trop; &, Trop n'est point bon: Pro. *Too much is too much; and, too much is good for nothing.*

Assez y a si trop n'y a: Prov. *Enough there is where too much is not.*

Nul n'a trop pour soy de sens, d'argent, de foy: Pro. *Looke* Sens, *or* Foy.

Trophée: m. *A Trophie; a signe or token of victorie; any spoyles gotten from a conquered enemie, and kept, or hangd vp, as monuments of the conquest.*

Tropique: m. *A Tropicke, or Circle in the firmament, whereunto the Sunne once comming, either descends, or ascends, as being at the highest, or lowest; and hence it is that there be two Tropicks.*

Tropique de Cancer, ou d'Esté. *Is about the 12 of June, when the Sunne (at the highest) enters into the first point of* Cancer.

Tropique de Capricorne, ou d'hyver. *Is about the 12 day of December, the Sunne then (at the lowest) entring into the first point of* Capricorne.

Troppeller. *To troope, or flocke together.*

Troq: m. *A trucke or trucking, bartering, swabbing, an exchange of one thing for another.*

Troquer. *To trucke, chop, swab, scoorse, barter, change, exchange one thing for another.*

Troquet: m. *A kind of small, white, and sweet apple.*

Trosseau: m. *A trusse, packet, bundle, fardle.*

Trossel: m. *as* Trosseau.

Trosse-queue: f. *A docke for the traine of a horse.*

Trosser. *Looke* Trousser.

Trot: m. *The trot of a horse.*

Troter, & Troteur. *Looke* Trotter, & Trotteur.

Trotier: m. ere: f. *Trotting, or which trotteth; also, gadding, or wandering much vp and downe; as in the Prouerbe,* Fille fenestriere, & trotiere rarement bonne mesnagiere.

Trotiere: f. *A raumpe, fisgig, fisking buswife, raunging damsell, gadding or wandering flirt.*

Trotigner. *To trip it, trample fast, or trot thicke and short; also, to gad, runne, roame, trot much to and fro, or vp and downe.*

Trotté: m. ée: f. *Trotted.*

Trotter. *To trot like, or as, a horse; also, to gad, or goe much abroad.*

Trotter de ranco. *To passe from ranke to ranke, to runne from one to another.*

Trotteresse. *as* Trotiere.

Trotteur: m. *A trotter; also, an earth-planet; a roamer, gadder, wanderer vp and downe.*

Trottier. *as* Trotteur.

Trottouër: m. *A boord in the louer of a Douecoat for Pigeons to alight on; also, the Seat, or Tribunall of a Iudge; also, babling, or pratling (in Pedlers French.)*

Trottres: f. *Low tresles to heighten coffers withall.* ¶Orleannois.

Trou: m. *A hole, narrow passage, or issue; and thence also, a pore in the bodie; and the bung-hole, fundament, nock-androe.*

Trou de chou, de Lentisque, &c; *(In stead of* Tronc) *the stemme, or staulke of a Cabbage, &c.*

Trou Madame. *The Game called Trunkes, or the Hole.*

Trou d'une rets. *The mash of a net.*

Trou d'un soufflet. *The Gullet mouth, or nose of a paire of bellowes.*

Trou de la Sybille. *The arse-hole.*

Avoir à chasque trou vne cheville. *To haue an answer for euerie obiection, a solution for euerie question, an excuse for euerie fault, or a colour for euerie error.*

Faire vn trou à la nuict. *To walke, or goe abroad a-nights; to trauell, or take a iourney by night; also, to slinke aside, or slyly to be gone before he be missed, or suspected to stirre.*

Faire vn pertuis dedans vn trou. *To doe iust nothing.*

Le trou trop ouvert sous le nez fait porter souliers deschirez: Prov. *Gluttonie breedes pouertie; the mouth too open makes men weare torne shooes.*

Se Troüant. *Holing, or growing full of holes.*

Trouble: m. *Trouble, disquiet, molestation, disturbance, turmoyle; a sedition, tumult, hurliburlie; a stirre, coyle, or broyle; also, a let, barre, stop, impeachment, hinderance.*

Trouble: com. *Thicke, muddie, vnsettled, pudlie, darke, foggie, ouercast, obscure.*

Pescher en eau trouble. *To fish in troubled or thicke water; to seeke for gaine out of other mens broyles, or losses.*

Vin trouble ne brise dents: Pro. *Thick wine breakes no mans bones; sweet things goe downe without a shoo-horne.*

Troublé: m. ée: f. *Troubled, disturbed, disquieted, molested, turmoyled; also, letted, stopped, impeached, hindered.*

Trouble-feste: m. *A vaine, or importunate buffoone; or any one who by idle chat, or vnseasonable chiding, offendeth, or cloyeth, such as would be merrie.*

Troublement: m. *A troubling, busying, disturbing, disquieting; letting, impeaching, hindering.*

Troubler. *To trouble, disturbe, turmoyle, busie, hurrie, disquiet, molest; to marre, disorder, confound; dismay; also,*

also, to barre, stop, let, hinder, impeach.

Troüée: f. A gap, or muset in a hedge.

Se Troüer. To hole, to grow full of holes, musets, or gaps.

Trougne. Looke Trongne.

Troupe: f. A troupe, crue, rout, rable, throng, or multitude of people, &c.

Troupeau: m. A flocke, heard, or droue of cattell; also, a heape, or bundle.

Oster les chiens pour venir à bout du troupeau. The watchfull dog to kill, that he the flocke may spill; or (as a sentence) the way a flocke to spill, is watchfull dogs to kill.

Sottes filles à marier sont fascheux troupeaux à garder: Pro. A combrous cattell maidens proue, when their greene sicknesse growes of loue.

Troupelet: m. A little troope, rowt; flocke, heard.

Troupet. In stead of Toupet. ¶Rab.

Trouppe, & Trouppeau. as Troupe, & Troupeau.

Trousse: f. A Quiuer for arrowes; also, a cousening tricke, blurt, flampant; also, as Tresse.

Droict de trousse. Looke vnder Droict.

Troussé: m. ée: f. Trussed, or tucked vp; twitched vp; also, spoyled, cast away, vndone, ouerthrowne.

Sans cela il estoit troussé en male. Seeke Male.

Trousseau: m. A Trussell; the vpper yron, or mould, thats vsed in the stamping of coyne; also, a (little) trusse, fardle, bundle, or bunch; also, as Serpaut.

Trousse-galant: m. Stoope-Gallant; a kind of plague wherewith the richest, and strongest are the soonest infected, and once infected, dead within two or three dayes: (This Plague raged in Puy, a part of Auvergne, about the yeare 1546; and such another (or at the least one of the name) in England not long agoe.)

Troussel. as Trousseau.

Trousse-queue: f. A docke for a horses trayne.

Trousser. To trusse, tucke, packe, bind or gird in, plucke or twitch vp; also, to plow ground sleightly a little before it be sowne.

Trousser leurs quilles. Ils pensoient à trousser leurs quilles. They thought of, they prouided or prepared for, their departure.

Trousser vn verre de Vin. To quaffe, or fetch, off a glasse of Wine.

Trousseure: f. as Troussoire; also, a trusse vsed by such as are burst.

Troussis: m. A tucke, or tucking vp in a garment.

Troussoire: f. A belt, or girdle.

Troussure: f. as Trousseure.

Trouvage: m. A finding; inuenting, deuising; lighting on.

Trouvé: m. ée: f. Found; deuised, contriued, inuented; had, gotten, obtained.

Il s'est bien trouvé de la foire. He hath made a good market, he hath sped verie well.

Tu as bien trouvé ton homme de 10000 escus (Ironically) I am a like man indeed to haue 10000 crownes.

Tu luy as bien trouvé la veine. Thou hast hit him right; thou hast toucht him to the quicke.

Trouvement: m. A finding, inuenting; lighting on.

Trouver. To find; inuent, contriue, deuise; light on, meet with, take in the manner; also, to get, obtaine, procure.

Trouver à dire. To lacke, want, or misse the things we had before.

Trouver bon. To allow or approue of, to hold or thinke it good.

Trouver vne boule. To hit a bowle.

Trouver la febve au gasteau. Looke Febve.

Trouver à tondre sur vn oeuf. To picke matter out of a barren subiect, or meanes out of a bare imployment.

Se trouver à tel lieu. To be, be present, or appeare, at such a place.

Ie ne trouveray rien mauvais de vous. I will take nothing ill at your hands.

Le diable vous en fairoit bien mal trouver. The diuell were in it if you should not be well withall; or, you must needs be well withall I trow.

Tu t'en trouveras bien. Thou wilt speed, or thriue, well withall.

Qui bien fera bien se trouvera: Pro. We say of one that does a good and charitable deed, He will find it in another world.

Tout se trouve au rastelier de cuisine: Prov. Looke Rastelier.

Trouverre: m. An ordinarie Poet, Rimer, Versifier, Ballade-maker. (vieil mot.)

Trouveur: m. A finder, inuenter, contriuer, deuiser.

Trouveuse: f. An inuentrix; or a woman that findeth ought.

Tru: m. as Trüage; or, as Treu.

Trüage: m. A toll, custome, tax, imposition.

Truan. as Truand.

Truand: m. A common beggar, vagabond, rogue, a lazie rascall, an vpright man; also, a knaue, scowndrell, varlet, filthie or lewd fellow.

Qui fit Normand il fit truand: Pro. He that a Normand made a beggar made; (for the Normands haue beene more fleeced, and harried then any people subiect vnto the Crowne of France.)

Truand: m. ande: f. Beggarlie, rascallie, roguish.

Cens truans. Double Cens payed by Purchasers (within the dominion of Soesmes, which belongs vnto Blois) for the first yeare onely, in lieu of all Lods, and Ventes; and generally, any dead or bare Cens, which yeeld no further profit vnto the Lords thereof.

Truandaille: f. A crue of rascallie beggars, a rabble of lewd rogues.

Truande: f. A filthie beggarlie queane; a Doxie, or Mort.

Truandeau: m. A young rascall, rogue, beggar.

Truander. To beg, or cant; to play the rogue, or liue like a rogue; to carrie himselfe most basely, scuruily, vnworthily; also, to oppresse, wrong, abuse.

Truandise: f. Beggarie, canting, begging; roguerie, knauerie, cousening, villanie.

Truble: m. A little fish-net for Stues, and small Ponds; also, the water fowle called, a Shouelar.

Truc: m. A blow, or thwacke. ¶Gasc. also, the popping, or sound of the lips, wherewith we vse to encourage a horse.

Ie vous grupperay au truc. I shall take you napping, or catch you as you goe by.

Trucheman: m. A Trucheman, an Interpretor.

Truchemander. To interpret, or play the interpretor, to serue as an interpretor vnto, to mediate by interpretors, or by interpretation.

Truchement. as Trucheman.

Trucheran. The hearbe S. Iohns wort.

Trucheter. To sneeze.

Truculent: m. ente: f. Truculent, cruell, threatfull of countenance, terribly looking.

Truege: f. The Dorce, or Gold-fish; (Looke Truette;) ¶Marseillois.

Trueie. as Truege.

Truelle: f. A Trowell.

'A propos truelle. *See* Propos.
Truellée: f. *A trowell-full; or, a clap, flat, or flamp with a Trowell.*
Truelleur: m. *A Troweller; a Plaisterer, or any one that workes with a Trowell.*
Truette: f. *The Dorce, or Gold-fish; called thus, or* Truege, *because she is as greedie, and rauenous as a Sow.*
Trufemande: f. *Female Sothernwood, mountaine Sothernwood, great Sothernwood.*
Truffant bourdant. *Betweene ieast and earnest.*
Truffe: f. *A gibe, mocke, flowt, ieast, gullerie; also, a Saligot, or water-Nut; also, a most daintie kind of round and russet root, or rootie excrescence, which growes in forests, or dry and sandie grounds, and within the ground, but without any stalke, leafe, or fiber annexed vnto it.*
Truffer. *To mocke, deride, flowt, ieast or gibe at; also, to nod, or shake the head, as those doe that approue not the thing they heare.*
Truffette: f. *A gibe, ieast, flowt, mockerie; also, a little* Truffe.
Truffeur: m. *A mocker, flowter, giber, ieaster.*
Truffler. *as* Truffer.
Trufle: f. *as* Truffe *(in the second, and third sence.)*
Truie. *as* Truye.
Truine: f. *The fish Tunnie.*
Truite: f. *A Trowt.*
Truite franche; &, royale; &, saulmonniere. *The Salmon Trowt.*
Trulle: m. *A part of the Imperiall Palace of Constantinople, wherein matters of State were ordinarily discussed, and dispatched.*
Trulle: f. *The fowle called a Shouelar.*
Trumeau de boeuf. *A knuckle, hough, or leg, of Beefe.*
Trumeau de Veau. *as* Rouëlle de Veau.
Trupelu. *as* Trepelu.
Trupet: m. *A lock, or foretop of haire.*
Truquar. ¶Gasc. *To knocke, or fight.* ¶Rab.
Trut. *(An Interiection importing indignation,) tush, tut, fy man.*
Trut avant. *A figs end, no such matter, you are much deceiued; also, on afore for shame.*
Truye: f. *A Sow; also, a warlike engine vsed in old time for the beating downe of walls; also, a kind of Game.*
Truye de mer. *The Porpose, or sea-Hog.*
Honteux comme vne truye qui emporte vn levain. *Looke* Honteux.
Entendre autant en quelque chose comme fait truye en espices. *That is iust nothing.*
Tourner les truyes au foin. *To answer from the matter.*
Truye aime mieux bran que roses: Prov. *The Sow had rather lye in dung then on a bed of Roses.*
Truye ne songe qu' ordure; &, Tousiours truye songe bran: Pro. *Base minds haue alwayes base, and beastlie thoughts; their wishes, proiects, dreames, are like themselues.*
Si truye forfaict les pourceaux le souffrent: Pro. *If the old Sow doe a fault and men abhorre it, her young, and harmelesse Pigs are punisht for it.*
Truyes. *as* Truyettes.
Truyette: f. *A young, or little Sow.*
Truyettes: f. *The markes of shin-burning; the red scorches, or spots on burnt shins.*
Trycher, & Trycherie. *as* Tricher, & Tricherie.
Trye. *Looke* Trie.

Trygonne: f. *A kind of Scatefish.*
Tu autem. Vous en sçaurez le tu autem. *You shall know the point, head, or knot of the matter; or, you shall vnderstand all the storie, the whole matter it selfe.*
Tube: m. *A Conduit-pipe; also, the hollow of the backbone, or the pipe through which the marrow thereof doth runne.*
Tubercle: m. *The small rising or swelling of a wheale, push, powke, or pimple; also, a push, or wheale.*
Tuberculeux: m. euse: f. *Swelling like a push, or wheale; also, full of pushes, powkes, or wheales.*
Tubereux: m. euse: f. *Swelling, bunchie, knobbie.*
Tuberositez: f. *Tuberosities, swellings; bunches, wennes; knobs; knots.*
Tubilustre: m. *A day whereon the Trumpets dedicated vnto sacrifices were hallowed, and the Trumpetters with water purged.* ¶Rab.
Tubule: m. *A little Conduit-pipe, or hollow reed.*
Tucquet: m. *A little hill, or hillocke, a little ascent or rising of ground.*
Tudey. *(Fondly) for* Vertu Dieu. ¶Lorrainois.
Tué: m. ée: f. *Killed, slaine, murthered, massacred.*
Tue-chien: m. *The hearb Dogs-bane; also, medow Saffron, wild Saffron.*
Tue-loup: m. *The hearbe Wolues-bane.*
Tue-loup iaulne. *Yellow Wolfe-bane, plaine Wolfebane, Heath Crowfoot.*
Tuement: m. *A killing, slaying, massacring.*
Tuer. *To kill, slay, murther, massacre; also, as* Tutoyer.
Tuer le feu. *To quench, or put out, the fire.*
Tuer vn mercier pour vn peigne. *To do great harme vpon a small occasion.*
Il en tuera dix de la chandelle, & vingt du chandelier. *He will doe wonders (Ironically.)*
Tel tue qui ne pense que blesser; &, Tel cuide frapper qui tue: Prov. *The wounding mind hath oft a murthering hand; a hurt intended with death is ended.*
Tuerie: f. *A slaughter, killing, occision, massacre, murther.*
Tueur: m. *A killer, slayer, murtherer, massacrer.*
Tuf: m. *A kind of white-sand, or soft and brittle stone, oftentimes couering, or lying in flakes on, good soyle.*
Tufeux: m. euse: f. *Couered with, or full of,* Tuf.
Tuffe: m. *A footman, or souldior seruing on foot.* (vieil mot.)
Tuffe. Pierre de tuffe. *as* Tuf.
Tuffeau. *as* Tuf.
Tuffiere: f. *A bed of* Tuf; *the ground, or Quarrie wherein it is gotten.*
Tugnicien: m. *Looke* Tunicien.
Tugure: m. *A cottage, or countrey house, a shepheards coat, shed, or bullie.*
Tugurion: m. *as (or a little)* Tugure.
Tuïau. *Looke* Tuyau.
Tuile: f. *A tile.*
Sonner la tuile. *To ring, or knocke to dinner, by striking on a sonorous kind of tile; a phrase vsed among the* Capucins, *onely in some places; for in others they haue Bells (as we in our Colledges) or Plates of yron, for the same purpose.*
Tuileau: m. *A little tile, or broken tile.*
Tuilerie: f. *A tile-kill, or place wherein tiles be made; also, tiling, or tiles.*
Tuileur: m. *A tiler, or a tile-maker.*
Tuileux: m. euse: f. *Full of tiles.*
Tuilleau. *See* Tuileau.
Tuillette: f. *A little tile; also, a wedge, or lingot of gold, or siluer.*

Tuillier: m. *A Tiler.*
Tuilot: m. *A tile-shard, a broken tyle, or peece of a tyle; also, a little tyle.*
Tuition: f. *Tuition, protection, defence, gard.*
Tulbant: m. *as* Turbant.
Tuleau. *See* Tuileau.
Tulebute: f. *The pipe of a fountaine, or gutter.*
Tulipan: m. *The delicate flower called a Tulipa, Tulipie, or Dalmatian Cap; and by some (though not so properly) Lillie Narcissus.*
Tulippe. *as* Tulipan.
Tumbe, & Tumber. *Looke* Tombe, & Tomber.
Tumbe. *The great sea-Dragon, or Quauiuer; also, the Gurnard, called so at* Roan.
Tumbereau: m. *A Tumbrell.*
Tumefié: m. ée: f. *Swollen, or made to swell; puffed vp.*
Tumefier. *To make to swell, or puffe vp.*
Tumeur: f. *A tumor, swelling, rising, or puffing vp of the flesh.*
Tumulte: m. *A tumult, vprore, sedition, broyle, ruffling, stirre, insurrection, commotion, hurlyburly.*
Tumultuaire: com. *Tumultuarie, rash, disordered, hudled vp in hast, ruffled or shuffled vp on a suddaine, done with more speed then heed, more feare then aduisement.*
Tumultuairement. *Tumultuarily, rashly, disorderedly, in hast, on a suddaine, with much feare, without any aduisement.*
Tumultueusement. *Tumultuously, turbulently, seditiously, most troublesomely, in a terrible vprore, with a great hurrie or stirre.*
Tumultueux: m. euse: f. *Tumultuous, turbulent, seditious, mutinous, most troublesome, full of stirre, broyles, businesse, all on a hurrie, or in a hurlyburlie.*
Tunal: m. *The Indian Fig-tree.*
Tunicien: m. *A Barbarie Faulcon; and particularly, that Faulcon, which is gotten in the countrey about* Tunis.
Tunicis. L'herbe de tunicis. *Frothie or spatling Poppie; also, the hearbe that beareth sweet Williams.*
Tunique: f. *A Coat-armor; and generally, any sleeuelesse long Iacket, or Coat; also, a thinne coat, or skinne couering the eye, &c.*
La tunique agnelette. *as* Agneliere.
Tuph: m. *as* Tuf; *also, rubbish.*
Tupin: m. *A pipkin, or earthen pot.*
De bonne terre bon tupin: Pro. *Good cloth of good wooll; good stuffe good garments yeeldeth.*
Turaulx: m. *Old Mole-hills, or hillocks raised by Moles, &c, and ouergrowne with grasse.*
Turban: m. *A Turbant; a Turkish hat, of white and fine linnen wreathed into a rundle; broad at the bottome to inclose the head, and lessening, for ornament, towards the top.*
Turbateur: m. *A troubler, disturber, disquieter.*
Turbation: f. *A trouble, or troubling; a disturbance, molestation, disquieting.*
Turbe: f. *as* Tourbe; *also, a troope (consisting at the least) of tenne witnesses; two such troopes being required to the approuement of an vnwritten custome, and for the exposition of a written one.*
Turbentine: f. *Turpentine.*
Turbet: m. *The name of a little apple, a graffe whereof doth streighten the crooked stocke whereon it is set.*
Turbin: m. *The shell-fish called a Welke, or Winkle.*
Turbine: m. *A tempest, whirlewind, boisterous wind, or storme.*
Turbiné: m. ée: f. *Fashioned like a Top, sharpe at the bottome, and broad at the top.*
Turbit: m. *Seraphions Turbith, sea Starrewort, blue Daisie or Camomill, Hogs-beanes.*
Turbit des Apothicaires. *Turbith of the shops, white Turbith.*
Turbit bastard. *The root of the stinking Carrot, and of the Spunge Esula; both too often sold, by couseners, for the true Turbith.*
Turbit blanc. *White Turbith, Turbith of the shops, the best Turbith, which is the root of the Syrian, or Antiochian Scammonie; also, the reddish hearbe Alypum, or Alypia; talked of, but not otherwise named, by our English Herbarist.*
Turbit faux. *The root of the deadlie, or stinking Carrot.*
Turbit noir. *Blacke Turbith, Quacksaluers Turbith,* Esula maior.
Turbit de la Pouille. *as* Turbit bastard.
Turbot: m. *The Turbot fish.*
Turbulent: m. ente: f. *Turbulent, blustering, stormie, tempestuous; troublesome, vnquiet, contentious, busie, seditious.*
Turbulenter. *To bluster, hurrie, storme; vex, turmoyle, disquiet.*
Turc: m. *A Turke.*
Herbe au Turc, ou du grand Turc. *Rupturewort, Burstwort.*
Turc: m. que: f. *Turkish, of Turkie; belonging to a Turke; also, Turkeis-like; whence;*
Couleur Turque. *Azure, Sky-colour, the colour of a Turkeis-stone (betweene a blue, and an Azure.)*
Turcée de raisins. *A cluster of grapes.*
Turci: m. *A causey, rampire, or banke for the keeping backe, or holding in, of waters.*
Turcie: f. *as* Turci; *also, the raising of a banke, rampier, or causey, for the holding in, or keeping backe, of waters.*
Turcot: m. *The little ash-coloured, and long-tongued bird, called a Wrynecke.*
Tureaux: m. *as* Turaux.
Turelureau. Mon tur. *My pillicocke, my prettie knaue.*
Turgent: m. ente: f. *Swelling, rising, puffing vp, strouting out.*
Turgon: m. *A kind of red Beets which haue neither sent, nor sauor.*
Turguet: m. *A little Wimble; also, Amelcorne, or Starchcorne, tearmed particularly,* Double turguet.
Turlupin: m. *A grub, mushrome, start-up, new-nothing, man of no value.*
Turnne. *as* Truffe *(in the last sence.)*
Turonde: f. *A round pellet, or peece of dough, paste, or bread, wherewith fowle is crammed; also, a Hawkes casting.*
Turpe: com. *Foule, ouglie, filthie, dishonourable, vnhonest.*
Turpitude: f. *Turpitude, filthinesse, or a filthie act, ouglinesse, deformitie; lewdnesse, dishonestie.*
Turpot: m. *A certaine peece of timber (whereof there be foure, two in the prow, and two in the poope) of a ship, fastened vnto the* Varengues, *and seruing, among other things, to keepe the artillerie from recoyling too farre backe.*
Turquesque: com. *Turkish, Turke-like, of, or belonging to, the Turkes.*

Reverence Turquesque. *A nod with the head.*
Turquet. *as* Turguet.
Turquie: f. *Turkie.*
Bled de Turquie. *Turkie corne, or Turkie wheat; of diuers kinds, and colours.*
Turquin. *as* Couleur Turque (*vnder* Turc;) *or* Couleur Turquine (*vnder* Couleur;) *also, a kind of dark-greene Pumpion.*
Turquois: m. oise: f. *Turkish; whence,* Arc Turquois. *The Turkish Long-bow.*
Turquoise: f. *A Turqueis, or Turkish-stone.*
Turrement: m. *A violent shocke, ioult, or iurring, as of an Engine of batterie against a wall.*
Turse. *as* Turcée.
Tursie. *as* Turcie.
Turturelle: f. *A Turtledoue.*
Turumber. *An auncient Arabian word, signifying the finest sort of sugar.*
Tusé: m. ée: f. *Pounded, brayed, beaten, or bruised in a mortar.*
Tute: f. *A hole, or berrie made by a Conie.*
Tutelaire: com. *Tutelarie, garding, protecting, patronizing, defending.*
Tutele: f. *Wardship; gardianship, the custodie of a child vnder age; also, tuition, defence, protection, safegard.*
Tuteur: m. *A Tutor, Gardian, Ouerseer.*
Tuthie: f. *Tutie; a medecinable stone, or dust, said to be the heauier soyle of Brasse, cleauing to the vpper sides, and tops of Brasse-melting houses: and such doe ordinarie Apothecaries passe away for Tutie; although the true Tutie be not heauie, but light and white like flocks of wooll, falling into dust as soone as it is touched; this is bred of the sparkles of brasen furnaces, whereinto store of the minerall Calamine, beaten to dust, hath been cast.*
Tuthie Alexandrine. *The best kind of artificiall Calamine, tearmed by Phisitions,* Botryitis.
Tutoyer. *To thou one.*
Tutrice: f. *A tutrix, or tuteresse; a defendresse, or gardianesse.*
Tutsan: m. *Tutsan, Parke-leaues; (an hearbe.)*
Tutuyer. *as* Tutoyer.
Tutye. *Looke* Tutie.
Tuyau: m. *A pipe, quill, cane, reed, canell.*
Tuyau de bled. *A straw, or staulke of corne.*
Tuyau de mer. *A red sea-worme found among rocks, inclosed in a white, round, and (on the outside) rugged pipe, or shell.*
Enter en tuyau. *as* Enter en canon. *See* Canon.
Tyberiade: f. *A Topographe; the modell, or draught of a place, called so of a booke of that name, composed by* Bartholus *the Lawyer; who was the first that graced his works with such figures.*
Tygre. *Looke* Tigre.
Tymbale. *A Timbrell; or, a little brasen drumme to daunce by.* ¶Langued.
Tymbon. *A kind of brasen drumme.*
Tymbre, & Tymbré. *Looke* Timbre, & Timbré.
Tymbrée: f. *Fish-Mint, water-Mint, brooke-Mint.*
Tympan: m. *A Timpan, or Timbrell; also, a Taber; also, the Gable-end of a house; also, a Printers Timpane; that whereon he layes the sheet, or leafe thats to be printed; also, the great wheele of a Crane; also, a Mill-wheele that taketh, and yeeldeth water in turning.*
Tympan d'une campanelle. *The broad-end of a Campanell.*
Tympan dentelée. *The cog-wheele of a Mill.*
Tympane. *Looke* Tympanne.
Tympaner. *To play on a Timpan, Timbrell, or Taber.*
Tympaniser. *as* Tympaner; *also, to defame, slaunder, traduce.*
Tympaniste: m. *A Timpanist; a player on a Timpan, &c; also, one that hath a Timpanie.* ¶Rab.
Tympanne: m. *The pannell, or flat square on the top, or head of a pillar.*
Tyn. *The hearbe Time.*
Tyne. *Looke* Tine.
Typhaine: f. *The Epiphanie, or Twelfth day in Christmas.*
Typhe. *Water-Torch, Cats-tayle, Reed Mace, Ditch Downe, the marsh beetle or pestle.*
Typher. *Looke* Tifer.
Typholope. *A kind of hard-skinned Blind-worme, or Slow-worme, which is not verie venomous.*
Typhones. *Great, or violent whirlewinds.* ¶Rab.
Tyran: m. *A Tirant; a cruell King, Lord, Ruler; a violent Gouernor.*
Tyranneau: m. *A pettie Tyrant.*
Tyrannie: f. *Tyrannie, Lordlie crueltie, a violent or bloudie Gouernment.*
Tyranniquement. *Tyrannously, cruelly, bloudily.*
Tyrannizer. *To tyrannize, or play the Tyrant.*
Tyrasser. *Looke* Tirasser.
Tyrepet: m. *A great farter.* ¶Rab.
Tyrer. *Looke* Tirer.
Tyromantie: f. *Diuination by a Cheese.*
Tyrouër: m. *Is, in a Violin, or small Fiddle, the flat peece behind the bridge whereto the strings be fastened; also, as* Tirouër.
Tyrse. *The dart, or iauelin of* Bacchus.
Tyrsigere: com. *Iuie-bearing, or decked with Iuie.*

V

VA. *(Is the second Person of the Imperatiue Mood of the Verbe* Aller*) goe, goe thy wayes, get hence, get thee gone; also (the third Person of the Present tense of the Indicatiue Mood; whence,* Il va;*) he goes, wends, walkes on; Tis also vsed sometimes as a Substantiue; whence;*
Vn va cy va là. *One that is sent vp and downe on errands.*
Vn va par tout. *The same; also, a quicke or nimble fellow; one that dispatches his worke apace; one that soone rids way.*
Vacabons: m. *Vagabonds, rogues.*
Vacant: m. *The reuenue of a Benefice during vacancie.*
Vacant: m. ante: f. *Vacant, emptie, void; at leisure; without vse, or imployment; without owner; whence;*
Biens vacans. *Wayfes, strayes; a purse, or treasure found; any land, or thing, which is without owner.*
Vacarme: f. *A battaile, or fight; and, the rustling noyse made by armor, or armed men, in a battaile; also, a suddaine inuasion or assault, or the boisterous hurrie it goes with; also, a tumultuous garboyle, hurlyburlie, sturre, coyle.*
Vacation: f. *A vacation, vacancie, leisure, ceasing from labor; also, a trade, art, handicraft, profession, vocation, calling.*
Vache: f. *A Cow; also, Neats-leather; also, a heape of new-made salt.*

Vache de Beard. *A base coyne worth about* vj d Tourn.

Vache de Foix. *The name of an auncient coyne, which bore on it the stampe of a Cow, the armes of the old Earles of* Foix.

Vache de mer. *A kind of daintie Thornbacke, hauing a pointed beake.*

Il a mangé de la vache enragée. *He hath drunke of many waters, passed many pikes, tryed many experiments; he hath beene well practised in, or beaten vnto, the course of the world; also, as vnder* Manger.

Le Diable sera bien aux vaches. *There will be an old stirre, hurrying, hurlyburly.*

Vache de Barbarie qui ne recognoist que ses propres veaux: Pro. *Applyable to one that either simply knowes not, or churlishly cares not for, more thē her own.*

Vache de loing a laict assez: Pro. *Things farre-fetcht are held most sufficient; the further a thing is brought, the better we thinke of it.*

Vne vache prend bien vn lievre: Prov. *A Cow may catch a Hare (as vnder* Lievre.)

La vache du riche velle souvent, celle du povre avorte: Prov. *The rich mans Cow (well-fed) does often calfe, the poore mans casts hers, & thriues worse by halfe.*

Vache ne sçait que vaut sa queuë iusques à ce qu' elle l'ait perduë: Prov. *The want, more then the vse, indeares the worth of good things; we know our friends best when we want them most.*

Aussi tost meurt vache comme veau: Pro. *The skipping Calfe, and wanton Lambe, are often kill'd before their damme.*

Qui se mesle d' autruy mestier il trait sa vache en vn panier: Pro. *He that with other mens trades will be medling, doth most-an-end loose the fruit of his pedling.*

Qui ne retire de sa vache que la queuë ne perd pas tout: Prov. *He looses not his whole auayle, that of his Cow saues but the tayle.*

Vachelette: f. *A verie little Cow.*

Vacherie: f. *A heard of kyne; also, a Cow-house, or stable for kyne.*

Vachette: f. *A little Cow; also, as* Vache de Foix.

Vachier: m. *A Cow heard, or Cow-keeper.*

Hier vachier huy chevalier: Pro. *One thats raised, on a suddaine, from a base, to an honorable, calling.*

Vaciet: m. *The blue or purple Jacinth, or Hiacinth, tearmed by some, Crow-toes.*

Vacilé, & Vacilement. *as* Vacillé, & Vacillation.

Vaciler. *See* Vaciller.

Vacillation: f. *A reeling, staggering, wagging, stirring, wauering, an inconstant mouing.*

Vacillé. *Reeled, staggered, wagged, wauered.*

Vaciller. *To reele, totter, stagger, wag, shake, wauer, be loose, vnsure, vnconstant, moue or stirre inconstantly.*

Vacuité: f. *Vacuitie, voidnesse, emptinesse, hollownesse.*

Vade. *Passe (at Primero, &c.)*

Vagabond: m. *A vagabond, roamer, faitour, earth-planet, wandering idlesbie, ranging or gadding rogue.*

Vagabonder. *To gad, wander, stray, roame, raunge, vagarie, vagabond it; to flit hither and thither, goe from coast to coast, loyter vp and downe.*

Vageux. *Looke* Vagueux.

Vagine: f. *A sheath, scabberd, case, couering; also, the hose, or cod of corne.*

Vagir. *To cry like a little child.*

Vague: f. *A waue, sourge, or billow of water.*

Vague: com. *Void, emptie; wast, idle; also, faire, beautifull, cleere, bright; also, wandering, flitting, raunging, oft remouing; whence;*

Fievre vague. *The fits whereof doe hold an vncertaine course.*

Vaguer. *To wander, vagarie, gad, raunge, roame, flit, remoue often from place to place.*

Vagueur. *Flitting, floating, or full of waues, as the sea, &c.*

Vagueux: m. euse: f. *The same; or wauie, full of waues.*

Vaillamment. *Valiantly, valorously, couragiously.*

Vaillance: f. *Valiancie, valor, courage.*

Vaillant: m. *A mans whole estate, or worth; all his substance, meanes, fortunes.*

Qui plus qu'il n'a vaillant despend, il fait la corde à quoy se pend: Pro. *He that feares not to spend more then he hath, sets, at the least, one foot in th' hangmans path.*

Vaillant: m. ante: f. *Valiant, hardie, couragious; also, right honest, of much worth.*

Rien ne vaut l'assaillant s'il n'est fort, & vaillant: Pro. *In vaine men goe t'assayle, when force, or courage fayle.*

Vaillantise: f. *Valiantnesse, couragiousnesse, hardinesse.*

Vain: m. aine: f. *Vaine; emptie, void; frustrate; friuolous, idle, trifling, fond, without purpose; also, faint, weake, feeble, forcelesse.*

Vaine pasture. *Looke* Pasture.

Terre vaine. *A wast ground; or, a ground which hath neither seed in, nor fruit vpon, it.*

Terre vaine, & place vuide. *Which hath neither building on it, nor garden in it.*

Vsagiers vain pasturiers. *Looke* Pasturier.

Vain. *(Aduerbially;) whence,* En vain. *In vaine, idly, to no purpose.*

Vain pasturer. *To turne cattell into, or let them runne among, such grounds as be held* Vaine pasture.

Vaincre. *To vanquish, ouercome, subdue, foyle, ouermaister, surmount; also, to conuince, or put downe by reason, or in reasoning.*

Vaincu: m. uë: f. *Vanquished, ouercome, subdued, foyled, ouer-maistered, surmounted; also, conuinced, or put downe by reason, or in reasoning.*

Vainement. *Vainely, friuolously, to no purpose, idly, fondly, foolishly; also, faintly, weakely, feebly.*

Vaineté: f. *as* Vanité.

Vainqueresse: f. *A vanquishing or victorious woman, a conqueresse.*

Vainqueur: m. *A vanquisher, ouercommer, conqueror, victor, subduer.*

Vair: m. *A rich furre of Ermines powdered thicke with blue haires; also, the grayish colour of some eyes; also, that which our Blasonners call Verry.*

Menu Vair. *Mineuer; the furre of Ermines mixed, or spotted, with the furre of the Weesell called* Gris.

Vairé: m. ée: f. *Verry; diuersified with argent and azure.*

Vairie. *as* Vayrie.

Vairole. *as* Verole.

Vaisseau: m. *A vessell (of what kind soeuer.)*

Vaisseau circulatoire. *A Limbecke, or Stillitorie.*

Vaisseau contenant, ou corpulent. *The lower part of a Limbecke, that which holds the stuffe which is to be distilled.*

Vaisseau long. *A Galley, Foist, or Brigantine, called so to make a difference betweene them, and a Ship, which is* Vaisseau rond.

Vaisseau d'un navire. *The bulke, bellie, or bodie of a ship.*

Vaisseau d'une riviere. *The channell of a riuer.*

Double vaisseau. *A cauldron,or kettle full of hot water; or,as* Bain de Marie.
Qui veut tirer quelque chose de ce vaisseau il luy faut donner du vent. *He that will get ought from this cokes,must commend,or collogue with,him.*
En vaisseau mal lavé ne peut on vin garder: Prov. *In vncleane Caske wine will not keepe.*
Vn meschant vaisseau iamais ne tombe de la main: Pro. *That oft proues best which we loue least; a course glasse neuer falls vnto the ground.*
Vaisselle: f. *Vessell (of any sort;) also,Plate.*
Val: m. *A vale,valley,dale.*
Du mont à val. *From the top to the bottome.*
Par monts,& par vaux. *Euerie where, in all places whatsoeuer.*
Promettre monts, & vaux. *To promise Gods Cope, mountaines of gold,impossibilities.*
Valable: com. *Valuable,in force,of value.*
Valdimonie. *A day of apparance; or a promise of, or bond for,apparance at a certaine day.*
Valée: f. *A valley; a vale,or dale; See* Vallée.
Valence: f. *as* Vaillant: m.
Valentianes. Par val. *By fits,by turnes; but slowly forward.* ¶Rab.
Valeriane: f. *Garden Valerian,Capons-tayle,Setwall.*
Valeriane moyenne. *Great wild Valerian.*
Valeriane petite. *Small wild Valerian.*
Grande Valeriane. *Garden Valerian; also, great wild Valerian.*
Valerienne: f. *as* Valeriane.
Valet: m. (Quasi va-lez son maistre;) *a groome, yeoman, or houshold seruant of the meaner sort : In old time it was a more honorable title; for all young gentlemen,vntill they came to be eighteene yeres of age, were (as at this day Batchelers in Britaine are) tearmed so; besides, those that waited in the K. Chamber (and who were, for the most part, Gentlemen) had no other title then of* Valets de chambre, *vntill that* Francis *the first, perceiuing such as attended him to be no better then* Roturiers, *brought in, aboue them, another sort, and caused them to be stiled,* Gentilshommes de sa chambre: *presently after which the Title of* Valet *grew into disesteeme,and is,at the length,become opposite vnto that of* Gentilhomme; *Looke* Varlet.
Valet d'Aoust. *A hind,or hireling,onely for Haruesttime.*
Valet à bras. *A groome, hind,or seruant in a mechanicall office; a Labourer.*
Valet de chambre. *A chamberlaine; a groome of, or waiter in,the bed-chamber; See* Valet.
Valet de Constantinople. (*In the Historie of* Villehardouin) autant que Prince.
Valet de cuisine. *An vnder-Cooke; a scullion, or kitchin drudge.*
Valet du diable (qui fait plus que l'on luy commande;) *an ouer-officious seruant;one thats more busie then he is bidden to be.*
Valet d'Escolier. *A Subsisor,or Seruant (in ordinarie) vnto a Scholler.*
Valets de la feste. *A kind of Morrisdauncers,attired like fooles,and hauing, as ours, their legs gartered with bells.*
Valet d'huis. *A log, blocke, or peise of mettall, &c, hanging by a rope on one side of a doore,and seruing to shut it too presently after such as goe in,or out,at it.*
Valet de Iustice. *A Sergeant, Officer, Catchpole.*
Valet de Picques. *The knaue of Spades.*
Valet trenchant. *A Caruer.*
Vin des valets. *Looke* Vin.
Ce que maistre donne, & valet pleure ce sont larmes perdues: Pro. *Why should a groome grudge at his maisters bountie ?*
Cheval faict,& valet à faire:Pro. *Chuse a horse made, a seruant to be made.*
Contre disner appert valet: Pro. *Wer't not for meat I should not see my man (sayes the ill-serued maister.)*
De grand maistre hardi valet: Prov. *A maisters greatnesse breedes him hardie seruants; the might of Lords addes mettall to their men.*
En pont, en planche, & en riviere valet devant, maistre derriere: Pro. *Looke vnder* Maistre.
Valetaille: f. *A rascallie crue of campe-following boyes, or drudges; also,a companie of groomes,or meaner seruants.*
Valeter. *Basely to obserue, attend or wait on, play the drudge or groome; to stoope, crouch, deiect, or submit himselfe too much.*
Valeton: m. *A boy-seruant,a young or little groome.*
Valetté: m. ée: f. *Made verie common, or so common, that meane seruants haue it vp; groome-ridden, prostituted vnto the vse of groomes.*
Valetudinaire: com. *Sicklie,queasie,crasie,subiect vnto infirmities.*
Valeur: f. *Value,worth,worthinesse; rate, price.*
Valeure: f. *The valure,value,rate,or price,of.*
Valeureusement. *Valorously, valiantly, couragiously.*
Valeureux: m. euse: f. *Valorous, valiant, hardie, couragious.*
Validation: f. *A strengthening,inforcement,confirming; an establishing,a ratifying.*
Valide: com. *Valide, strong,weightie,forcible,of worth, or value,that can doe much.*
Validé: m. ée: f. *Strengthened, inforced, confirmed; made worthie, or of worth; established,authorized,ratified.*
Valider. *To strengthen,confirme,inforce,make good; ratifie,establish, giue weight,or authoritie vnto.*
Vali-dire: m. Vn Val. *A footman,or seruant, onely for errands.*
Validité: f. *Validitie,weight, strength, force.*
Valier. *The name of a Saint; whence,* Peur S. Valier; *More feare then harme; or, a falling, by ouermuch feare, into the mischiefe, or danger feared; as when a man, thats threatned a hanging, dyes before he be turned off the ladder; for so,as the report goes,this Saint did.*
Valise: f. *A Male,Clokebag,Budget; Wallet.*
Valitude: f. *Health, strength, good liking,welfare.*
Vallant: m. *as* Vaillant: m.
Vallée: f. *A valley,vale,bottome,dale.*
Chevaucher la chevre en la vallée. *Looke* Chevre.
Apres grande vallée rude montée: Pro. *After great rest much toyle; after much ease great paine.*
Apres grande montée grande vallée: Prov. *They that the highest climbe the lowest fall.*
Vallet: m. *A groome,&c; Looke* Valet.
Vallet à bras. *A labourer; a labouring seruant; a groome,hind,or seruant in a mechanicall office.*
Valletaille,& Valleter. *See* Valetaile, & Valeter.
Valleton: m. *as* Valeton; *also (in some auncient Authors) a bastard.*
Vallidation, & Vallider. *as* Validation, & Valider.
Vallois: m. *A kind of Net, wherewith fish is (forbidden to be) caught.*
Vallon: m. *A little valley; a dale.*

Valoir: m. *Value, worth; rate, price.*
Non valoir d'estat. *Looke* Estat.
Valoir. *To be worth; as much worth, or as worthie, as; to countervaile, counterpeise, or answer in value; to be of equall esteeme, or goodnesse with; also, to profit, serue, be good for; and to merit, or deserue.*
Cela vaut faict, ou la chose vaut faicte. *The matter is neere an end, or as good as done.*
Couste & vaille. *Fall it out how it will, whatsoeuer come of it; at what rate, or hazard soeuer; also, no matter what it cost so as it be good.*
I'en vaus bien vn autre. *I am as fit for it, or worthie of it, as another.*
Se mettre en rang d' oignon, & ne valoir vn' eschalotte. *Seeke* Oignon.
C'est argent qu'argent vaut: Pro. *As good haue money-worth as money; that which is worth coyne is as good as coyne.*
Les choses valent autant qu' on les fait valoir: Pro. *Things are as they are esteemed of; or, are esteemed of as they are set forth; The like is;*
Rien ne vaut la chose sinon qu'on la fait valoir: Prov. *A thing is worth no more then it's set out for; things without shew, out-setting, praise, or vse, are nothing worth.*
Vn homme ne vaut sinon qu' il se fait valoir: Pro. *As thou of thine owne selfe doest deeme, so other men will thee esteeme.*
Les cousteaux de Iean Colot, l'un vaut l'autre: Pro. *See* Colot.
Tant vaut l' homme tant vaut sa terre: Prov. *A good, or bad man makes good, or bad, the things belonging to him.*
Tout bois vaut busches: Pro. *The worst wood's good ynough to make logs of; or, the worst wood yeeldeth fuell for the fire.*
Valois. *as* Vallois.
Valvasseur. *See* Vavasseur.
Valve: f. *A foulding, or two-leafed doore, or window.*
Valuë: f. *Value, worth, goodnesse.*
Valvule: f. *A flap in the inside of the mouth of a vessell; which keepeth the liquor it containes from running, ierting, or gushing, out.*
Valvules du coeur. *Eleuen small open gates, or entries in the heart, whereby passage is giuen to the bloud and spirits that come vnto it from the veines, and arteries.*
Van: m. *A Vanne, or winnowing Siue; (made of Ozier, and rather like a Scallop shell then our Siue.)*
Vandanger. *Looke* Vendanger.
Vandoise: f. *The Dace, or Dare-fish; also, a Witch, or Hag.*
Vanereau: m. *A young Lapwing.*
Vaner, & Vaneur. *as* Vanner, & Vanneur.
Vanger. *Looke* Venger.
Vangeron: m. *A little red-finned fish in the Lake of Geneua.*
Vanier. *as* Vannier.
Vanité: f. *Vanitie, trifling, lightnesse, inconstancie, fondnesse; also, emptinesse.*
Vanné: m. ée: f. *Vanned, or winnowed; also, coursed, schooled, canuassed; also, scoffed, mocked, flowted, played vpon, ridden, derided.*
Vanneau: m. *A Lapwing.*
Vanner. *To vanne, or winnow (not much in our manner, letting the corne fall from the siue to the ground; but, more commonly, shogging it with both hands against the thigh, to make the chaffe come aloft of the corne, and then sweeping so much of it off with a wing, &c, as the wind hath not carried away;) also, to course, chide, canuasse, bayt, schoole; or, to mocke, flowt, ride, play vpon; or to rake vp, scoffingly, the faults or imperfections of others.*
Vanner sa farine au vent. *To spend his meanes, or substance on toyes.*
Vanner sa plume au vent. *To play the foole, or loose his time.*
Vannerie: f. *as* Venerie; *a hunting, &c.*
Vannet: m. *A Lapwing; also, as* Coquille *(in Blason.)*
Vanneur: m. *A vanner, or winnower of corne; also, a chider, schooler, bayter.*
Vanneure: f. *A winnowing; also, a chiding, bayting, schooling; and, a scoffing, mocking, deriding.*
Vannier: m. *A Siue-maker; a Basket-maker.*
Vannures: f. *Winnowings, or siftings of corne.*
Vanoyer. *To vanish, disappeare, come to nought; also, to be vaine, or play vaine parts.*
Vantance: f. *A vaunt, brag, boast; or, as* Vanterie.
Se Vanter. *To vaunt, brag, boast, glorie, cracke.*
Tel a necessité qui ne s'en vante pas: Prov. *Necessitie doth pinch them most, who of their wants doe shame to boast.*
Vanterie: f. *A vaunting, bragging, boasting, ostentation, cracking, glorying.*
Vanterolles. *as* Venterolles.
Vanteur: m. *A vaunter, bragger, cracker, boaster.*
De grands vanteurs petis faiseurs: Prov. *Great boasters small roasters; the fairest chimneyes yeeld out the least smoake.*
Vanteux: m. euse: f. *Vaunting, cracking, bragging, boasting, full of ostentation.*
Vapeur: f. *A vapor, fume, exhalation, hot breath, steaming, reeking.*
Vapide: com. *Wastie, or wasted; that sends vp an ill fume, that yeelds a stinking vapor.*
Vaquane: f. *The vacancie of a Benefice.*
Vaquant. *as* Vacant.
Vaquer. *To be at leisure, cease from labour, desist from working; also, to attend, apply, bestow time on, giue the mind, or bend his studie, vnto; also, to be vacant, emptie, void, without.*
Var. *as* Bar.
Varandé: m. ée: f. *Well dryed, and seasoned, as a Herring thats readie to be barrelled.*
Varander. *To dry, and season Herrings for the barrell.*
Varangues: f. *The ribs, or floore-timbers, of a ship.*
Varaville: f. *The name of a greene sweet apple, which is fashioned like an egge.*
Varech: m. *A sea-wracke, or wrecke; all that is cast aland by chaunce, or tempest; or that comes so neere the land, that a man on horsebacke may reach it with his launce.*
Varene: f. *A flat valley; or, a plaine betweene two hills.*
Varengues. *as* Varangues.
Varenne: f. *A reddish earth, whereof the moulds of Founders, and ouens of Potters be ordinarily made; and hence;*
Varennes. *Leane, and dry grounds, fit onely to beare Oats, and Rye.*
Varenneux: m. euse: f. *Sterill, dry, leane.*
Varesque. *as* Varech.
Variable: com. *Variable, changeable, mutable, wauering, fickle, inconstant, flitting.*
Variation: f. *A variation, change, mutation, differing from that it hath beene.*

Varice: m. *A crooked veine swelling with corrupt bloud in the temples, bellie, or legs.*

Varicqueux: m. **euse**: f. *The veines of whose temples, &c, be swollen with corrupt bloud; also, stradling, striding, going wide asunder.*

Varier. *To varie, change, alter, disguise; to square, differ, disagree, write, or speake diuersly; to diuersifie; to make of seuerall fashions or colours.*

Varier en la teste. *To wag, or waggle with the head; to haue a giddie head.*

Il varie. *He holds not steadily; his hand shakes, quauers, or wauers.*

Varieté: f. *Varietie, change, choice, diuersitie; ficklenesse, inconstancie, mutabilitie.*

Varig: m. *Flag, Sword-grasse, Corne-flag.*

Varin: m. *A wooden Engine consisting of two vices, and a skrue, and seruing to lift vp great peeces of timber, or of Artillerie.*

Varinet: m. *A little* Varin.

Varioles: f. *The small Pockes.*

Variqueux. *as* Varicqueux.

Varlet: m. *A Groome, &c; as* Valet; *also, a younker, stripling, youth; as in the Prouerb;*

Autant se prise beau varlet que belle fille: Prov. *The smirking youth as much himselfe esteemes, as doth the Nimph who beautie fairest seemes.*

Varletaille. *as* Valetaille.

Varleter; &, **Varleton.** *as* Valeter; &, Valeton.

Varre. *A certaine long Italian measure.*

Vasche. *Looke* Vache.

Vase: m. *A vessell.*

Vase: f. *as* Vaze; *mud, or owze.*

Vasois: m. *A shore, or place oft ouerflowed with water, and thereby full of owze, or mud.*

Vasquine: f. *A Kirtle, or Petticoat; also, a Spanish vardingale.*

Vasquinier: m. *A maker of Kirtles, Petticoats; or Spanish vardingales.*

Vassal: m. *A vassall, subiect, tenant; properly such a one as holds his land of another by Knights seruice, or by homage and fealtie; and is thereby tied to attend his Lord in person to the warre, or to send one with him in his stead, or to allow him money for the hiring of one; all at his owne charge: (And therefore in the auncient Romanes,* Vassal *is taken for the contrarie to* Souldoyer; *(who receiued pay) as also for any Gentleman whatsoeuer;) Also, a slaue, or bondman.*

Vn Seigneur de beurre (de feurre; ou de paille) combat (vainc, ou mange) bien vn vassal d'acier. *A Prouerbe expressing the great aduantage a Lord hath of his subiect, or tenant.*

Tant que le vassal dort le Seigneur veille. *A Lord hauing entred into his vassalls land for want of homage, or due seruices, may lawfully enioy it, and the whole fruits of it, vntill he haue receiued his due.*

Tant que le Seigneur dort, le vassal veille. *Looke* Seigneur.

Vassaudie: f. *as* Vasselage.

Vassausie: f. *The right which a Soueraigne, or Landlord pretendeth to haue ouer his vassall, or tenant.*

Vasselage: m. *Vassellage, or subiection; the duetie, or estate of a vassall: (In th'auncient* Romans *tis vsed for valour, and a valiant or worthie deed.)*

Vasselage actif. *Fealtie.*

Vasseur: m. *as* Vassal; *or a villein.*

Vastadour: m. *A Pioner, or digger; also, a mender of highwayes.*

Vastation: m. *A wasting, spoyling, ransacking, destroying.*

Vaste: com. *Vast, huge, wide, broad, large, burlie, spacious; also, desolate, desert, vninhabited, wild.*

Muscle vaste. *One of the foure muskles whereby the thigh is bent.*

Vastibousier: m. *A luske, lubber, loggerhead, lozell, hoidon, lobcocke.*

Vastines: f. *Wast grounds, as deserts, rockes, sands, &c; (an old word.)*

Vaticinateur: m. *A Prophet, Soothsayer, Diuiner, foreteller of things to come.*

Vaticination: f. *A prophecying, diuining, foretelling, soothsaying.*

Vaticiner. *To prophesie, diuine, soothsay it, coniecture at, foretell of, things to come.*

Vatton: m. *The latch of a doore; also, a leauer.*

Vau: m. *A vale, or valley; See* Val.

Vavasseur: m. *A Valuasor, or Vauasour; a Lord that held of some Duke, Marquesse, or Earle; and (at least among vs) was in degree inferior to a Baron; a Mesne, or Mesne Lord; or as* Arrierevassal; *also, a villeine.*

Vavassorie: f. *A Valuasserie; th'estate, land, or territorie of a Vauassor, Mesne Lord,* Arrierevassal; *or villeine.*

Vavassourie: f. *The same.*

Vauche. *The hearbe called Periwincle.*

Vaucrer. *To raunge, roame, vagarie, wander, idle it vp and downe.*

Vaucrer. *A ship to float, or waue vp and downe, to hold an vncertaine course at sea, to sayle whither wind and tide will carrie it.*

Vauderoute. s'en fuïr à vaud. *To flie amaine; or to run headlong along.*

Mettre à vauderoute. *To put wholly, or vtterly to flight.*

Vaudeville: f. *A countrey ballade, or song; a Roundelay, or Virelay; so tearmed of* Vaudevire, *a Norman towne, wherin* Olivier Bassel, *the first inuẽter of them, liued; also, a vulgar prouerbe; a countrey or common saying.*

Vaudre. *A kind of vessell for Rhenish wine.*

Vauldeville. *See* Vaudeville.

Vauldrée: f. *A maulkin.*

Vaulneant: m. *A good-for-nought; a rakehell, raskall, scoundrell, retchlesse or idle companion.*

Vaultour: m. *A Vulture, Geire, Gripe, or Grap; (a rauenous bird.)*

Cataplasme de chair de vaultour avec les vifs. *A plaister of warme guts.*

Vaultrait: m. *as* Vaultre.

Vaultre: m. *A mungrell betweene a hound, and a mastiffe; or of a size betweene the* Allan *and great countrey curre; fit for the chase, or hunting of wild Beares, and Boares.*

Vaultrer. *To hunt with a* Vaultre.

Vaultrey: m. *A kennell, or hunt of* Vaultres.

Vaultroy: m. *A wild Boare; or more properly, as* Vaultre; *or, a Lime-hound for the wild Boare.*

Vautour, *as* Vaultour.

Vayer: m. &, **Vayrie.** *as* Voyer; &, Voyerie.

Vaze: m. *A vessell.*

Vaze: f. *Owze, mud, soft durt in the bottome of water.*

Vbiquité: f. *An vbiquitie; a being in euerie place, or euerie where.*

Vbir. *To reare; to make thriue, or grow, by good vsage, or good fare.*

Vce: f. *as* Sourcil.

Veau: m. *A Calfe, or Veale; also, a lozell, boydon, dunce, iobbernoll,*

iobbernoll,doddipole; also,a baulke vntilled betweene two lands,or furrowes.

Veau de disme. *A notable sot,or blockhead, a notorious lobcock.*

Veau marin,ou de mer. *The Seale,or sea Calfe.*

Fievre de veau. *Trembling vpon fullneße; or, an indisposition vpon surfeting.*

Pied de veau. *Calues-foot,Ramp,Aaron,Wake-Robin, Starch-wort,Priests Pint.*

Teste de veau. *Calues-snowt, Snap-dragon, Lions-snap.*

Faire,ou trousser le pied de veau. *To make an vntowardlie,or clownish leg; or, clownishly to lift vp the leg in dauncing,&c.*

C'est vne vache de Barbarie qui ne recognoist que son propre veau. *Looke* Vache.

Cette queuë n'est pas de ce veau. *This effect proceeds not from that cause; or, this is no part of, or dependant on,that thing.*

Il luy a fait manger des pois verds au veau. *He hath cheated him finely, he hath so fetched him ouer that he cannot perceiue it.*

Tu n'as non plus d'arrest qu'un jeune veau. *Thou art as wanton,giddie,or vnstayed, as a milch calfe.*

Veau mal cuict,& poulets cruds font les cimitieres bossus: Prov. *Young meat raw-drest makes church-yards grow bulch-backt.*

Aussi tost meurt vache comme veau: Prov. *As soone the young,as old,goes to the pot.*

Il est bien veau qui veau taille: Prov. *See* Tailler.

Le loup emporte le veau du povre: Pro. *The Wolfe makes his feast of the poore mans beast.*

Veaurre: f. *The fleece of a Ramme.*

Veautrant. *Wallowing.*

Veautrement: m. *A wallowing,tumbling, rowling vp and downe in the mire.*

se Veautrer en la bouë. *To wallow,tumble,rowle,turne (lying)vp and downe in the mire.*

L'esprit se veautre. *The mind reuolues,casts about,or is diligently imployed.*

Veautreur: m. *A wallower,or tumbler in the mire.*

Veautroir: m. *A puddle,or slough wherin hogs doe vse to wallow.*

Vedat: m. Bois vedat. *Looke* Bedat.

Vedeau: m. *A Beadle; such a one as vshers with his Mace,the Vicechancellor, or principall Officer, of an Vniuersitie.*

Vedel: m. ¶Gasc. *A Calfe,a Veale; whence;*

Teste de vedel. *A calfe,blockhead,or sillie fellow.*

Vedelle: f. *A sucking calfe,a calfe thats fid with milke.*

Vedet: m. *A lubber, boydon,lobcocke, lozell, ioultbead, iobbernoll,doddipole.*

Vedette: f. *A Sentrie,or Court of gard, placed without a fort,or campe; and more generally, any high place from which one may see afarre off.*

La vedette d'une gallere. *The top of the mast; or the part of a Galley from whence the furthest discouerie may be made.*

Vedille: f. *The nauell-string of a new-borne infant.*

Vée: f. *Labour,toyle, paines,trauell; (an old word.)*

Veé: m.ée: f. *Forbidden; whence;* Chose veée est plus desirée: Prov. *We couet most what we are most forbidden.*

Véeurs: m. *Witneßes,or assistants in a view,or suruey of land:* ¶Norm.

Vef: m. *A widower.*

Vef: m. vefve: f. *Widow, widow-like, of or belonging to a widow.*

Vefvage: m. *Widowhood,the state of a widow.*

Vefve: f. *A widow; Looke* Veufve.

Vefve d'honneur. *A woman that hath lost her good name.*

Vegade: f. *A draught; a turne,or bowt; whence;*

Vne vagade. *Once,or one time.*

Vege: m. *A kind of water tree,or shrub.*

Vegetable: com. *Vegetable, fit or able to liue; hauing, or likelie to haue, such life, or increase in growth, as plants,&c.*

Vegetal: m. ale: f. *Vegetall; hauing or giuing a(plant-like) life, increase,budding,or growing.*

Vegetatif: m. iue: f. *Vegetatiue; liuelie,quicke, fresh, growing,or giuing life,quicknesse,growth,increase.*

Vegetation: f. *A giuing of life,increase,or growth vnto; a quickening; refreshing, or comforting; a making strong.*

Vegeter. *To quicken, refresh, giue life, growth,or increase vnto; also, to grow, bud, or put forth,as plants.*

Vegettes: f. *Vegetatiue,or growing parts.*

Veguade. *as* Vegade.

Vegué. *as* Beguer: ¶Bearnois.

Vehemence: f. *Vehemence,eagarnesse,earnestnesse,violence, force, fierceneße.*

Vehement: m. ente: f. *Vehement,eagar,earnest,fierce, violent, sharpe, vrgent; maine, forcible,strong.*

Vehementement. *Vehemently.*

Veher. Iuge veher. *A Judge of meane, or base Jurisdiction.*

Veherie: f. *Meane,or base Jurisdiction.*

Vehicule: m. *A carriage; a cart,waine, charriot, wagon; any such instrument,or engine of carriage.*

Vejete: com. *Liuelie,iollie, fresh, frolicke, full of spirit, of mettall,of life.*

Vejetter. *as* Vegeter.

Veillant: m. ante: f. *Waking, watching, wakefull, or watchfull, vigilant,heedfull,circumspect,carefull.*

Veille: f. *A Vigile,or Wake; the Eue of a holy-day.*

Veillement: m. *A waking,or watching; an heedfull, or carefull attending.*

Veiller. *To wake,watch,lie awake, abstaine from sleepe; to be vigilant, heedfull, diligent, carefull; studiously to attend.*

Assez veille qui bien fait: Prov. *He that does well, watches ynough.*

Vn ami veille pour l'autre: Prov *A friend is watchfull, and doth arme himselfe to keepe his friend from harme.*

Veillere: f. *Withwind,Bindweed,Hedge-bells.*

Veillottes: f. *The best,and sweetest kind of Acornes, or mast,growing on the small Oke* Esculus.

Veine: f. *A veine in the bodie,a pulse; (yet euerie veine is not a pulse,though euerie pulse bee a veine;) also, a veine of the earth,or of mettall,&c, in the earth; also, a veine or stile of writing; a veine or conceit in versifying,&c.*

Veines adipeuses. *Two veines, a right (sometimes a branch of the right kidney veine)and a left,one(euer a branch of the descendant trunke of the hollow veine) which particularly nourish the fat, and skinne thats about the kidney, and generally breed fat in those parts which they runne by.*

Veine aiscellaire. *as* Veine axillaire.

Veine Arterieuse. *One of the fiue principall veines of mans bodie, issuing from the right ventricle of the heart,the bloud whereof it carries vnto the lungs for their nourishment.*

Veine auriculaire. *The eare veine; Seeke* Auriculaire.

Veine axillaire. *Looke* Axillaire.

Veine basilique. *(Called by our Anatomists) the liuer veine; issues from the* Sousclaviere, *and is diuided into two branches, a deepe and a superficiall one; the later whereof being neere the inward processe of th'arme, and verie neere the skinne, is diuided into other two;* viz. *a lesse which runnes into the head veine, and together with it makes the* Mediane; *whilest the greater passes along by th'elbow vnto the hand, & there makes the* Salvatelle.

Veine borgne. *as* Coecale.

Veine cave. *The hollow veine; a great veine issuing from the thickest part of the liuer, & then diuided into two maine branches, and they into many others.*

Veine cephalique. *The head veine; or, a third branch of* la Sousclaviere; *passes betweene the muskle* Deltoïde, *and that of the breast, and goes vnto the bought of the elbow, where it diuides it selfe into two brāches; the lower, and lesse, going along th'inner part of the arme, ioynes with a branch of* la basilique, *and together with it makes the* Mediane; *the higher, and greater, seated in the outside of the elbow, yeelds on both sides many branches, the greatest whereof meets with* la Basilique, *and together with it makes* la Salvatelle.

Veine cervicale. *The veine of the braines; a fourth branch of* la Sousclaviere; *passes by the crosse processes of the neck ioynt vp to the filme or thinne skinne which is next the braine, and there ends.*

Veine coecale. *The blind veine; a second branch of* la Mesenterique; *runnes vnto the blind gut, and there ends in many branches.*

Veine commune. *The common veine; or as* Mediane.

Veine coronale. *The crowne veine; a branch of the spleene veine, so tearmed because it enuirons the heart in manner of a crowne.*

Veine corporelle. *See* Corporel.

Veine crurale. *The thigh veine; a great veine which issues from the trunke descendant of the hollow veine.*

Veine cystique. *A small, and sometimes double sometime single, branch of the* Port *veine, whence it mounts vnto the necke of the gall, and there diuides it selfe into two branches.*

Veines diaphragmatiques. *The midriffe veines; two seuerall branches of the hollow veine, from which they runne vnto the midriffe, and there end.*

Veines emulgentes. *Looke* Emulgent; *or as* Renales.

Veines epigastriques. *An outward, and an inward branch of the flanke veines, both which after diuers passages, at length ioyne themselues vnto those that belong to the dugs.*

Veine epiploïque dextre. *The second branch of the spleene veine; goes vnto the* Epiploon, *and the gut* Colon; *also, a fourth branch of the spleene veine, which ending towards the vpper part of the* Epiploon, *is called* Epiploïque, *but with the addition of* Posterieure.

Veine Espauliere. *The shoulder veine.*

Veine frontale. *The forhead veine; a third branch of the outward throat veine, whence mounting by the bottome of the nether iaw, it comes vnto the lips and the nose, & from thence ascends by the inside of the eye vnto the middle of the forhead.*

Veine gastrepiploïque. *See* Gastrepiploïque.

Veine gastrique. *The bellie veine; a branch of* la Porte, *from which it descends vnto the hollow part, and backeside, of the ventricle; there is also another, called* la petite gastrique; *which is the first branch of the spleene veine, and goes vnto the right side of the ventricle.*

Veine hederiforme. *Seeke* Hederiforme.

Veine hemorrhoïdale. *The first branch of the* Mesenterique; *which runnes vnto, and ends at, the* Colon *& straight gut; sometimes it issues from the spleene veine.*

Veine hepatique. *The liuer veine.*

Veine honteuse. *A fift branch of the flanke veines; besloweth it selfe among the priuie parts of women, & on the outward skinne of the yard, and cods of men.*

Veine humerale. *The Humerall, or shoulder veine.*

Veine hypogastrique. *The third branch of the flank veines, and is it selfe diuided into diuers branches; the first whereof runne vnto the yard, bladder, and straight gut, and thence to the bottome of the fundament; others vnto the matrix; and others, after a long course, goe downe almost vnto the hamme.*

Veine jartiere. *The garter, or gartering, vein; a fourth branch of the thigh veine, from which it descends among the backe muskles of the thigh, vnto the bought of the hamme, where it gets this name.*

Veines Iliaques. *Th'Iliacke, or flanke veines; two maine descendant branches of the hollow veine, a right and a left one, from either of which fiue others issue; the right one is opened against the dropsie, & other diseases of the liuer; the left one for the passion of the spleene.*

Veine intercostale. *The fourth branch of the trunke ascendant of the hollow veine: It feeds three distances betweene th'vpper ribs.*

Veine intestinale. *A fourth branch of* la Porte, *from the posterior, and right, part whereof it issues, and communicates it selfe sometimes vnto the hungrie gut, and sometimes to the* Douze doigtier.

Veines jugulaires. *The two throat, or necke, veines;* viz. *an outward one (the first diuision of* la Sousclaviere) *which is sometimes double, and mounts along the sides of the necke vnto the bottome of the head, where it is diuided into fiue branches; And an inward one (the second branch of* la Sousclaviere) *which ascends along by the windpipe vnto the bottome of the braine, and is there diuided into two branches.*

Veines labieres. *The lip veines, whereof there be two on each inner side both of the vpper, and vnder lip.*

Veine lumbaire. *The veine of the loynes; the fourth branch of the descendant trunke of* la Cave, *diuided neere vnto it source into diuers parts, all which bestow themselues among the foure ioynts of the loynes.*

Veine mammale. *A third branch of* la Sousclaviere; *double, an inward, and an outward, one, distributed among the parts of the breasts.*

Veine matricaire. *The matrix veine; or a veine that runnes along the flanke neere to the reynes.*

Veine mediane. *The middle, common, or black veine, compounded of the two lesse branches of the liuer, and head veines, and running along the middle of the arme almost vnto the wrist, where it passes in the forme of an* Y *into the hand: there is likewise another of this name vnder th'instup.*

Veines meseraïques. *as* Mesenteriques.

Veines mesenteriques. *Two veines; one, a branch of* la Porte, *ends at the* Mesentere; *but is formerly diuided into three branches, whereof th'other is the third, and called so because it likewise ends at the* Mesentere, *in some 14 or 15 branches.*

Veine musculeuse. *The first branch of the flanke veines;*

veines; tearmed thus, because it communicates it selfe with diuers muskles about the bellie, and loynes.

Veine nasale. *The nose veine, seated betweene the nosethrills.*

Veine oculaire; ou, oeilliere. *Th'eye veine; that part of the forhead veine which runnes along by the inside of the eye.*

Veines organiques. *as* Veines Iliaques.

Veine pericardique. *The second branch of the* Sousclaviere, *whence it runs vnto the* Pericarde, *and there ends.*

Veine popletique. *The hamme veine; as* Iartiere.

Veine porte. *The port, or carrying veine; seated in the liuer by diuers rootes, the which, at length, ioyne in one stocke, or trunke, and so passe forth into the ventricle, spleene, gall,* Mesentere, *and other parts of the bodie.*

Veine ranulaire. *The first branch of the outward throat veine; ascends vnto the tongue, and parts in two vnder each side thereof.*

Veines renales. *The kidney veines; two thicke, and and short branches of the descendant trunke of the hollow veine; a right, and a left one, diuided into 7 or 8 others (when they come neere the kidney, into the substance whereof they enter;) there is likewise another of this name seated vnder th'instup.*

Veine sacrée. *The second branch of the flanke veine, running to the* Os sacré, *and thereupon getting this name.*

Veine salvatelle. *Is made of the two bigger branches of the liuer, and head veines, from which it runnes through the wrist into the hand, and vnto the root, or diuision of the third, and little fingers.*

Veine sans pair. *A third branch of the hollow veine, out of the right side whereof it runnes to nourish the spaces betweene eight ribs.*

Veine saphene. *The mother veine; the first branch of the thigh veine, consisting of two diuisions; the one inward, which ends among the inner kernells of the thigh; the other more outward hath three branches, the first ends in the skinne of the thigh, the second goes but vnto the knees, the third vnto the muskles of the leg, whence running along aboue the inner ankle (where it is most opened, and knowne by this name) it comes vnto the sole of the foot, and there ends.*

Veine sciatique. *The Sciaticke veine; a branch of the thigh veine, which descends downe the leg vnto th'outward ankle, where it is commonly opened for the Sciatica, and thereupon gets this name.*

Veine seynale. *as* Veine salvatelle.

Veine sousclaviere. *One of the two maine ascendant branches of the hollow veine, diuided into six parts.*

Veine spermatique. *The third branch of the trunke descendant of the hollow veine.*

Veine splenatique. *The spleene veine; one of the two maine branches of* la Porte, *from which it runnes vnto the spleene, and there ends diuided into fiure parts.*

Veine stomachique. *The stomack veine; runnes vnto the hollow part of the ventricle, and there ends in two branches.*

Veine surale. *One of the two maine branches of the thigh veine, most eminent in the bought of the knee, from whence it bestowes, and looses, it selfe among the muskles of the calfe of the leg.*

Veine susclaviere. *The secōd maine ascendāt branch of the hollow veine, diuided into three branches.*

Veine temporale. *The veine of the temples; opened for the Megrum, paine of the eares, and extraordinarie watering of the eyes.*

Veine thorachique. *The breast veine; the sixth branch of* la Sousclaviere; *is diuided into two others, both which bestow themselues among the muskles of the* Thorax.

Veine Thymique. *The first branch of* la Sousclaviere; *goes vnto the fag-peece, or kernell which is vnder the Kannell bone.*

Veine torculaire. *The second branch of the outward throat veine, from which it ascends by the inside of the scull vnto the braine, which it moistens, and feeds.*

Veine vmbilicale. *That whereby an infant in the wombe receiueth nourishment, and which, it being borne, doth close it selfe, and serueth as a ligament to settle the liuer vnto the nauell.*

Laisser la lancette dans la veine. *To fill a man with doubts, and leaue him vnresolued; to bring him into trouble, and then to abandon him; or, to begin to remedie a mischiefe, and, presently, (of malice, or negligence) to giue ouer so good a beginning.*

Il n'a veine qu'y tend. *He hath no manner of humor vnto it.*

Tu luy as bien trouvé la veine. *Thou hast hit him right.*

Veiné: m. ée: f. *Veined, or full of veines.*

Veinelette: f. *A verie little veine.*

Veinette: f. *A little veine.*

Veineux: m. euse: f. *Veinie, full of veines.*

Artere veineuse. *Looke* Artere.

Veinu: m. uë: f. *Veinie; or as* Veineux.

Vejove: m. *A wicked spirit; a god that can doe hurt, & will doe no good.*

Veirat: m. *The Mackerell fish.*

Velà. *as* Voilà.

Velar: m. *The hearbe called banke Cresses, and by some wild Mustard (but not so properly;) others improperly call the Rape Chadlocke, or Charlocke, so.*

Veleure: f. *Shag, hairinesse, nappinesse.*

Veleux: m. euse: f. *Full of, or abounding in, calues.*

Velin. *as* Venin; *also, vellam; whence;*

Velins. *Smooth peeces of fine parchment, or of vellam.*

Vellé: m. ée: f. *Calued.*

Veller. *To vaile, couer, &c; as* Voiler; *also, to calue.*

La vache du riche velle souvent, celle du povre avorte: Prov. *The rich mans cow doth often calfe, the poore mans oft miscarries.*

Vellication: f. *A plucking, pulling, lugging; also, a carping at, a deprauing, or detracting from.*

Velocité: f. *Velocitie, speed, swiftnesse, fleetnesse, quicknesse, nimblenesse.*

Velours: m. *Veluet.*

Velours figuré. *Branched Veluet.*

Velours à fond de satin pourfilé. *Figured Satin.*

Velours à long poil. *Vnshorne Veluet.*

Tripe de velours. *Valure, Mocke-veluet, Fustian an Apes.*

Ventre de velours robbe de bureau: Prov. *Much bellie-cheere, & daintie fare, doth make the garments poore and bare.*

Velous. *as* Velours.

Velouté: m. ée: f. *Veluetted, of Veluet, clad, or couered with Veluet.*

Cuir velouté. *Frize leather.*

Taffetas velouté. *Tuffe-taffata.*

Veloutier: m. *A maker of Veluet.*

Veloux. *as* Velours.

Velu: m. uë: f. *Hairie, shag, nappie, or of a high nap, full of haire, rough with haire.*
Couverture veluë. *An Irish Rug, Mantle, Cadow.*
Herbe veluë. *Cudwort, Cudweed, Cottō weed, Chaffe-weed.*
Veluate. *as* Veluoté.
Veluette: f. *Pilosella, Mouse-eare.*
Veluoté: m. *Speed-well, female Fluellin.*
Veluté. *as* Velouté.
Venaison: f. *Venison; the flesh of (edible) beasts of chace; as the Deere, wild Boare, &c; also, the fat of their flesh; whence;*
Le sanglier a chargé sa venaison. *The Boare is very fat: and,* Il a trois doigts de venaison; *He is three inches fat.*
Toute chair n'est pas venaison: Prov. *All dishes are not dainties; or as vnder* Chair.
Venal: m. ale: f. *Vendible, sale, salable, set or let vnto sale, that may be hired or had for money; that will doe any thing for money.*
Venalement. *Vendibly, salably, sellably.*
Venalité: f. *Venalitie, vendiblenesse; a being salable; a letting or setting vnto sale.*
Venant. *Comming, arriuing; happening; growing.*
Vendable: com. *as* Vendible.
Vendange; *(or better)* **Vendenge**: f. *Vintage, vine-haruest, grape-haruest, grape-gathering, wine-making; and the season wherein it is made; (In all which sences this word is, for the most part, vsed plurally;) also, grapes, or the fruit of vintage.*
Cuideur de vendenge. *as vnder* Cuideur.
Adieu paniers vendenges sont faittes. *Farewell good fellowes, we haue no further need of you, or vse for you; our turne's alreadie serued; our businesse done.*
Vendengé: m. ée: f. *Cut, gathered, and made into wine, as grapes.*
Vendengeoire: m. *The basket, scuttle, or pannier whereinto grapes are gathered.*
Vendenger. *To cut and gather grapes for wine, to make wine of grapes; to performe, or finish his vintage, (wherof this word comprehends all the parts.)*
Vendengeret: m. ette: f. *Belonging to, or seruing for, vintage.*
Vendengeur: m. *A Vintager, or vine-reaper; a cutter or gatherer of grapes, in vintage.*
Vendengeuse: f. *A woman thats hired, &c, in vintage time, to cut, or gather grapes.*
Venderesse: f. *A woman that selleth.*
Vendeur: m. *A seller.*
Vendeuse: f. *as* Venderesse.
Vendible: com. *Vendible, sellable, sale, alienable.*
Vendiquer. *To vendicate; to claime, or challenge.*
Vendition: f. *A sale or selling.*
Droict de venditions. *Looke vnder* Droict.
Vendoise: f. *A Dace, or Dare-fish.*
Vendre. *To sell, make sale of, set to sale; to alien or passe away for money, &c:* (Vendre en beaucoup des anciennes ordonnances signifie, Bailler à ferme. ¶ l'Oiseau.)
'A l'hostel priser, & au marché vendre: Prov. *Set prices on thy things at home, but passe them away abroad.*
Fille qui prend elle se vend: Prov. *A maid by taking sels her libertie; or, the maid that wooers proffered gifts doth take, a wanton bargaine will be drawne to make.*
Ou pain faut tout est à vendre: Prov. *A man will sell all rather then be starued.*
Pour laver ses mains on n'en vend pas sa terre: Prov. *It is no great cost to be cleanelie.*
Toute chose se vend au pris de l'oeil de l'homme: Prov. *Mans eye doth rule the price of euerie thing.*
Vn quartier fait l'autre vendre: Prov. *One peece doth helpe to passe away th'other.*
Vendredi: m. *Friday.*
Vendredi oré; Sainct; &, le grand vendredi. *Good Friday.*
Vendu: m. uë: f. *Sold, made sale of, set to sale; aliened, or passed away, for money, &c.*
Chose qui plaist est à demi venduë: Prov. *Ware that is pleasing to th'eye is passed away by and by.*
Marchandise offerte est à demi venduë: Pro. *Ware that is offered yeelds but halfe a price; we say, proffered ware stinkes.*
Venduë: f. *as* Vente.
Vené. *as* Veiné.
Venefique: com. *Venomous, poisonous, contagious.*
Venelle du lict: f. *The space betweene a bed, and the wall; and (when there is such a space) the beds side next vnto the wall.*
Il est bien apparenté, mais c'est au costé de la venelle. *He is of a good house, but yet he came in at the window.*
Venenosité: f. *Venomednesse, venomousnesse.*
Vener. *To hunt.*
Venerable: com. *Venerable, reuerend, honourable.*
Veneration: f. *Veneration, reuerence, awe, worship, honour.*
Venerie: f. *A hunt, or hunting; also, a hound-house, or kennell for hounds.*
Venerien: m. enne: f. *Belonging to Venus; also, addicted, or giuen to venerie; lecherous, lasciuious.*
Veneur: m. *A Hunter, or Huntsman; also, a kind of Spider, tearmed thus because he is euer in chase of one prey or other.*
Grand Veneur de France. *The great Huntsman of France; an Officer of the Crowne, whose Jurisdiction extends onely to the ruling of courses, and iudging of causes, that concerne hunting in forests; but in old time (when hee was called,* le grand forestier de France) *he had also as much authoritie as the Great Faulconer, and the* Maistre des eaux & forrests, *enioy at this day.*
C'est vne chasse ou le veneur est prins. *Looke* Chasse.
Vengé. *Auenged, wreaked, reuenged.*
Vengeance: f. *Vengeance, reuengement; punishment.*
Venger. *To wreake, reuenge, auenge, take vengeance of.*
Se venger en vn fief, ou heritage. *A purchaser of rent issuing generally out of land in diuers Mannors, or* fiefs, *to auow, & declare, that he will haue it onely out of one of them:* Car lors le Seigneur d'iceluy fief en a les ventes, ou bien peut vser de puissance de fief: ¶ Ragueau.
Tel pense venger sa honte qui l'accroist: Prov. *Some that doe thinke to couer their shame, discouer it; some weening to redeeme their shame, increase it.*
Vengeresse: f. *A reuengeresse, an auengeresse.*
Vengeron: m. *A Dace, or Dare-fish.*
Vengeur: m. *A reuenger, auenger, punisher of wrongs.*
Venim: m. *Venome; any thing that impoisoneth, or infecteth outwardly by touching.*
'A la queuë gist le venim: Pro. *The last, is commonly the worst, part of a practise, &c.*
Venimeux: m. euse: f. *Venomus, full of venome.*
Venir. *To come; arriue, approach, draw neere vnto; to proceed, issue, be deriued, from; to spring, proue, grow; also,*

also, to happen, chance, or fall out.

Venir bien. Cela luy vient bien. *That fits, becomes or agrees well with, him:* le compte vient bien; *The reckoning falls out right.*

Venir à bien. *To succeed or fall out well, to turne vnto good.*

Venir entre la bourse, & les deniers. *To preuent, forestall, wipe the nose of, come betweene and home; A law-phrase, vsed most when the next kinsmã to a seller of land, redeemes it, and disappoints another that had, with the purchasers consent, vndertaken it, and made sure account of it.*

Venir à bout de. *To accomplish, performe, bring to passe, atchieue, compasse, attaine vnto; also, to rule, or ouerrule.*

Venir devant. *To preuent, or forestall; to come, or appeare, before.*

Venir au devant. *To meet, or come to meet, with.*

Venir de dire. Ce qui ie viens de dire. *That which I did but euen now deliuer:* Comme ie viens de dire; *As I said verie lately; or, as I told you but now.*

Venir à ses droicts. *Looke vnder (the first)* Droict.

Venir à la loy. *To be receiued, or admitted, vnto the waging of his Law.*

Au mieux venir. *At the best, how well soeuer it fall out, come the best of it that can.*

Des paroles ils viennent au poil. *From words they fall vnto blowes.*

Il eut l'allée pour le venir. *He had his trauell for his paines; he returned as emptie, or poore, as he came.*

Il ne demeure pas trop qui vient: Prov. *He that comes at the length stayed not too long.*

Quand beau vient sur beau beau perd sa beauté: Prov. *When one faire colour is layed on another their beautie is vtterly confounded.*

Qui vient est beau, qui apporte encores plus beau: Prov. *A mans presence doth much, but his purse doth more.*

Qui tost vient à son hostel mieux luy en est à son souper: Prov. *Looke* Hostel; *or* Souper.

Tant crie on Noel qu'il vient: Prov. *So long is Christmas called for that it comes; a constant importunitie at length preuailes.*

Tout vient à poinct qui peut attendre: Prov. *He that can wait long shall haue a good houre.*

Venise: f. *Ceruse, white lead (wherewith some women paint.)*

Venitiens: m. *Venitians; the citizens of Venice.*

Le secours des Venitiens (trois iours apres la bataille.) *After meat mustard; after death a potion; after iudgement giuen our Counsell at leasure to attend our cause.*

Venne: f. *A fizzle, or small fyste.*

Venneur: m. *A fizzler, or fyster.*

Vennier: m. *A kind of Pedler, or seller of old yron stuffe.*

Venredi. *Looke* Vendredy.

Vent: m. *A wind; a blast, gale, puffe, gust, flaw, or berrie, of wind; also, a vent, smell, sent, aire, breath, vapor; also, a brute, rumor, noise, report.*

Vent d'amont. *An Easterlie wind.*

Vent d'aval. *A West South-west wind; or a Westerlie wind that somewhat inclines to the South.*

Vent d'Aurom. *A South wind.*

Vent à la boline. *A side wind at sea.*

Vent cardinal. *A principall, or direct wind; as East, West, &c.*

Vent collateral. *A side wind; as North-west, South-east, &c; or a quarter wind, at sea.*

Vent coulis. *The wind, or ayre that commeth into a roome by a hole, crannie, or creuice; held verie vnwholesome.*

Vent derriere. *A fore-wind at sea.*

Vent d'embas; & fueillu. *A Westerlie wind; or as* Vent d'aval.

Vent de Galerne. *A North-west wind.*

Vent Grec. *A North-east wind.*

Vent hautain. *The Southerne wind.*

Vent de Levant. *The East wind.*

Vent marin; meridional; ou de midi. *A South wind.*

Vent occidental. *The West wind.*

Vent oriental. *The East wind.*

Vent pluau. *A Southerne wind.*

Vent de ponent. *A Westerne wind.*

Vent en pouppe. *A fore-wind at sea; and thence, ease, prosperitie, good successe, the world at will, euerie thing as one would haue it.*

Vent à quartier. *A quarter wind, betweene a fore-wind, and a side wind.*

Vent septentrional. *The North wind.*

Vent solaire. *The East wind.*

Herbe du vent. *The Wind-flower; so called because it neuer opens but when the wind blowes.*

Avoir vent. Ie n'en ay eu vent ne voix. *I neuer heard a word, nor had any notice, of it.*

Avoir le vent de. Il en a eu le vent. *He hath got an inkling, he is come by the knowledge, of it.*

Batu de mauvais vent. *Crost by a contrarie, or malignant thwart; whom fortune breathes maliciously vpon.*

Donner voile à tous vents. *Looke vnder* Donner.

Emporté du vent. Il se laisse emporter du vent. *He runnes on freely, carried vpon the wings of his owne conceit; also, he is inconstant, light-headed, variable, of a changeable humor.*

Autant en emporte le vent. *So much breath is wasted, so many speeches lost; Looke* Emporter.

Estre au dessus du vent. *To flourish, liue in prosperitie, be all aflaunt or a hoight.*

Estre au dessus du vent de. *To get the wind, aduantage, vpper hand of; to haue a man vnder his lee; The like is;*

Estre sur vent. *To be in the wind, or haue the wind, of;* Estre sous vent; *To be to the leeward, or vnder the lee, of.*

Faire voile à tout vent. *To follow the fashions, or sway of the time, how often soeuer they alter.*

Fendre le vent. *To runne his countrey.*

Iecter son vent. *To breath his last; to giue vp the ghost.*

Iecter la plume au vent. *To grow carelesse, let the world runne; weigh not how matters passe, which way he goes, what course he takes, what thing he does; The same is;* La plume jectée au vent; *carelesly, or that way the staffe falls; (from those which being irresolute, or without designe, cast feathers into the aire, and goe on the way they flie.)*

Mettre sa legitime au vent. *Fondly to passe or make away with, riotously to consume or squander away, his whole portion, all that he hath.*

Mettre la plume au vent. *as* Iecter la plume au vent.

Prendre le vent. *To goe vp, or against, the wind; also, to vent, or wind; to follow, or draw towards by the wind, sent, or smell of.*

Tenir

Tenir au vent. *To beare hard with, or sayle verie neere to, a wind.*
L'aureille au vent. *Listeningly, attentiuely.*
Tout d'un vent. *At one breath, all at once.*
Vie fouet, & au vent. *Auant &c; as vnder* Foüet.
I'ay veu d'autres vents venter. *I haue seene better, or other dayes; I haue knowne when the time, or state of things, hath beene other then it is.*
On a veu d'aussi grand vent venter (sans abbatre les maisons.) *We haue heard of as many brags made, or threats vsed, and yet nothing, or no hurt, done.*
Qui veut tirer quelque chose de ce vaisseau il luy faut donner du vent. *He that will draw ought out of his Peece, must giue him vent; viz. must collaude, or collogue with, him.*
Le vent, la tẽpeste, & l'orage monstrent du nocher la courage: Pro. *Crosses are the touchstones of courage.*
Vent au visage rend l'homme sage: Prov. *Aduersities teach a man wit.*
Nul vent ne fait pour celuy qui n'a point de port destiné: Prov. *No wind can blow him to good whom Destinie will not harbour.*
Les mal-vestus devers le vent: Pro. *He that worst may the candle holdeth; or as vnder* Mal-vestu.
Qui est sur la mer ne fait pas des vents ce qu'il veut: Pro. *The Mariner can make no winds; or, the Sayler cannot haue what winds he will.*
Ventail: m. *A childish toy of a card cut acrosse, like the sayles of a wind-mill, and put with a pinne vnto th'end of a sticke, and so held into the wind, which makes it to twirle verie fast about.*
Ventaille f. *The breathing part of a helmet; the sight of the beauer.*
Ventailles du ciel. *The windowes, or floud-gates, of heauen.*
Ventau: m. *as* Ventail; *also, a Fanne.*
Vente: f. *A sale, or selling; an alienation, or passing away for money, &c.*
Vente extraordinaire de bois. *A sale of timber, or of great and high trees:* Vente ordinaire de bois; *a sale of copse-wood, vnderwood, or small wood.*
Ventes. *A fine for alienation: viz. (for the most part) 20 d. in the pound, or the twelfth part of the price of land sold, due sometimes vnto the Lord feodal, but more commonly to Lords* Censuel, *of whom it is held; and paied, in some places, by the purchaser, in others, by the seller, and in others, betweene them both: The French Lawes, and customes, doe often ioyne with this another dutie, called* Lods, *which comes to as much more.*
Ventes, & gants; ventes, & honneurs; ventes, & issuës. *Looke vnder* Droict.
Si boute tel feur telle vente. *The thing is sold euen as it was bought, it goes away as it came; or, no matter, tis well ynough, let it be how it will be.*
Venté. *Blowne, puffed.*
Venteler. *To breath, or blow a soft gale; also, to waue, houer, wauer; also, to ayre, in the wind; also, to vanne or winnow corne; and to tosse or canuasse to and fro; to turne out of one hand into another.*
Ventelet: m. *A little wind; a small puffe, gentle gale, coole blast, of wind.*
Ventelle. *as* Ventaille.
Venter. *The wind to blow, or puffe.*
I'ay veu d'autres vents venter. *Looke vnder* Vent.
On a veu d'aussi grand vent venter. *We haue knowne as great a wind as this without any house blowne downe; (In answer to one that speakes big words, but is valiant in nothing but words.)*
Tant vente qu'il pleut: &, Tant tonne, & vente que pluye descend: Prov. *This wind will haue raine; bloud-wipes often follow big words.*
Venter. se Venter. *To brag; Looke* se Vanter.
Venteroles; *or* Venterolles. Droict de vent. *A certaine fine due to a Landlord frõ the purchaser that undertakes to discharge his selling tenant of all fines; Looke* Droict.
Venteux: m. euse: f. *as* Vanteux; *also, windie, full of wind; as light, or as swift, as the wind.*
Ventier. *whence,* Marchand ventier; Asçavoir, de ventes de bois.
Ventilation: f. *A ventilation, breathing or gentle blowing; also, a wauing, or houering in the ayre; a winnowing, or airing in the wind; also, an estimation, valuation, prizing.*
Ventiler. *To gather wind, &c; as* Venteler; *also, to estimate, prize, value.*
Ventoir: m. *as* Ventail.
Ventelin: m. *A verie small wind.*
Ventose: f. *A cupping glasse.*
Ventoser. *To cup, or applie cupping glasses.*
Ventosité: f. *Ventositie, windinesse.*
Ventousé. *as* Ventose; *also, a vent in caske.*
Ventousé: m. ée: f. *Cupped with a cupping glasse; also, vented.*
Ventre: m. *The bellie, paunch; wombe.*
Ventre de bureau. *One that feeds grossely, or eates none but course meats.*
Ventre goy. *(Corruptly, or clownishly) for* Ventre Dieu.
Ventre inferieur. *The bellie from the bulke to the priuities.*
Ventre moyen. *The bulke, breast, or stomacke; all that part which the ribs inclose.*
Ventre à la poulaine. *A gulch, big-bellie, gorbellie, swag-paunch, bundle of guts.*
Ventre superficiel. *as* Epigastre.
Ventre superieur. *The head, so called by Anatomists.*
Haut ventre. *The stomacke.*
Mal de ventre. *The wormes; or bellie-ache; a fretting, wringing, or griping in the bellie.*
Sur le ventre. *Groueling.*
Estre en la paille iusques au ventre. *To be fully accommodated, easefully lodged, plentifully furnished, both for vse, and delight.*
Faire bon ventre. *To loosẽ the bellie, to make soluble.*
Mettre le coeur au ventre. Cela luy mit le coeur au ventre. *That heartened, cheered, or comforted him; that made him take heart at grasse.*
Saulter à deux pied sur le ventre à. *Looke* Saulter.
C'est le ventre ma mere. *I will come no more there, I will doe no more so.*
Il y demeura le ventre au soleil. *He left his guts there, he was there knockt in the head.*
Ventre affamé n'a point d'oreilles: Prov. *Hunger no eare to reason yeeldeth.*
Ventre de velours robbe de bureau: Prov. *Looke* Velours.
Le ventre emporte la teste: Prov. *Th'appetite often ouerrules the wit; or, as vnder* Emporter.
En petit ventre grand coeur: Prov. *A great stomack oft lodges in a little one.*
Il n'est horologe plus iuste que le ventre: Prov. *No clocke more iust, or true, then the bellie; or, the bellie is best dyall, to giue all things their triall.*
La verge ennoblist, & le ventre affranchist. *(A Proverbe, or Principle in the French Lawes) Children are*

by their father ennobled, and by their mother infranchised; but this is not alwayes so.

Ventrée: f. *A bellie-full; or, more particularly, the burthen or load of a womans bellie; the child wherewith she goes; also, the cholicke, bellie-ache, or griping of the bellie (especially in horses.)*

Succeder par ventrées. *To succeed by venters; or land to be diuided among the issue a man hath by diuers wiues, or venters.*

Ventrelet: m. *A little bellie.*

Ventresque: f. *Is, generally, th'offalls, intralls, inwards, guts, or paunch of an (edible) creature; as a calues pluck, a hogs haslet, a sheeps gather, &c; but particularly, the bellie (which is the daintiest) part of a Tunnie.*

Ventricule: m. *The ventricle; the place wherein the meat sent from the stomacke is disgested; some call so the stomacke it selfe; others expresse by it th'*Epigastre.

Ventricules du coeur. *The ventricles of the heart; two large holes, one on the right, th'other on the left, side thereof; that, the greater, and closed within a slender flesh, containes the naturall bloud, this, of a harder substance, containes the bloud wherewith our Arteries be nourished; and thereupon that is called, the bloudie, this the spirituall, ventricle.*

Ventricule posterieur du cerveau. *The hinder ventricle, or tunnell of the braine; the seat of the memorie.*

Ventriere: f. *A bellie-band for a draught horse.*

Ventripotent. *Ventripotent, big-paunch, bellie-able, huge-guts:* ¶Rab.

se Ventrouiller. *as* Se veautrer.

Ventru: m. uë: f. *Paunchie, great bellied, gorbellied, full-bellied, all-guts, all-bellie.*

Venture. *as* Adventure.

Venu. *Come, arriued, approached, or drawne neere vnto; proceeded, issued, or deriued from; sprung, prouen, growne; happened, chanced, betided.*

Le dernier venu est le mieux aimé. Le dernier venu ferme la porte. &, Les derniers venus sont les maistres: Prov. *Looke* Dernier.

Venuë: f. *A comming, arriuall, approach; a passage, accesse; increase, groweth, growing or comming on; also, a vennie in fencing; also, a turne, tricke, iert, or ierke.*

La venuë des arondelles. *The comming in of Swallowes, about the 22 of March.*

Attendre la venuë du boiteux. *Looke* Attendre.

Tout d'une venuë. *Without any diuision, all of one peece; all of one shape, size, making; also, at once, at a clap, at the same time, by the same meanes; while his hand is in, or while he is at it.*

Venus: f. *Venus; one of the seuen Planets, the day or morning starre; also, the Goddesse of lust; or lust, venerie, wantonnesse, vnchastnesse, lecherie; also (among Alchymists) the mettall Copper.*

Cheveux de Venus. *Venus haire, our Ladies haire, blacke maiden-haire, true maidens haire (an hearbe).*

Pour Venus advienne Barbet le chien. *Losse, or ill lucke, betide him: an imprecation, or spightfull wish, relating to the play at huckle-bones, wherein he that turns vp Venus (figured on one side of the bone) doth winne; whereas he that turnes vp the dog, doth loose.*

Veoir. *To view, see, looke, perceiue, behold, ouersee, suruey; prie, spie; marke, note, heed, obserue, regard; examine, search into, consider of, deuise, or find some meanes for.*

Voici, ou, vous voyez la reste. *Looke* Reste.

Voila qui est bon. *Why this is good, well, braue.*

'A le veoir. *To see to, or he seemed.*

Ne voici pas vne brave response? *Is not this a goodlie answer thinke you?*

Il m'est à veoir, que. *Me thinkes, or it seemes vnto me, that.*

Il n'a rien que veoir en, ou sur, cela. *He hath nought to doe with that, it concernes him not, he is not to meddle withall.*

Qui voit enfant, il voit neant: Prov. *He that an infant seeth, nothing seeth.*

Qui voit la maison de son Seigneur, il n'y a profit ny honneur: Prov. *Looke* Seigneur.

Tout voir, tout ouïr, & rien dire, merite en tout temps qu'on l'admire: Prov. *To heare, and see, and nought to say, deserues to beare the bell away.*

Il est bien povre qui ne voit goutte: Prov. *He that wants eyes may well be tearmed poore.*

Quand les yeux voyent ce que ne veirent oncques, le coeur pense ce qu'il ne pensa oncques: Pro. *New obiects in the eyes, new thoughts in the heart.*

Tels sont huy qui demain ne verront pas: Pro. *To day a man, to morrow none.*

Ver: m. *A worme.*

Ver coquin. *A certaine worme bred in a mans head, and making him cholericke, humorous, and fantasticall when it biteth; also, the Vine-fretter, or Diuels Goldring.*

Vers courts. *Arse-wormes; little round wormes which breed in the ends of our guts.*

Ver volant. *A Ringworme, or Tetter.*

Mal de ver. *The Farcie in a horse.*

Mort aux vers. *Wormeseed, or Wormeseedwort.*

Nud comme vn ver. *We say, bare as a birds arse; poore as Job.*

Tirer les vers du nez à. *as vnder* Tirer; *or, to creep into a mans most inward conceits; to fetch out of him the verie secrets of his heart.*

Tout estat est viande aux vers: Pro. *All States are wormes acates.*

Ver. Menu ver. *Looke vnder* Vair.

Veracée: f. *The fulnesse, or full measure of, a certaine vessell (somewhat like a Porrenger) wherein* Caillebotes *are vsually put.*

Veraire: m. *The hearbe called Hellebore (especially the blacke one.)*

Veraire blanc. *White Hellebore, Lingwort, Neesewort; of whose root Neesing powder is made.*

Veraire noir. *Blacke Hellebore, Christs wort, Christs root.*

Verangenes. *Mad apples, raging apples.*

Verart, & Veratre: m. *as* Veraire.

Verbal: m. ale: f. *Verball, of words, onely in words, according to the word.*

Appellation verbale. Se plaide verbalement, & se peut juger sur le champ en l'audience; à la difference du procez par escript, qui se distribuë, & juge en la chambre sur les enquestes, & productions des parties.

Procés verbal. *A verball answer made by a partie before a Iudge; or, more generally, a verball report (made by Judge, or partie) of all the parts, and pleadings of a suit; also, the Returne, or answer of a Sergeant vpon an Execution, &c.*

Verbalement. *Verbally, by word of mouth.*

Verbasce: m. *Mullein, Higtaper, Torches, Haresbread, Woolblade, Longwort, Bullocks Longwort.*

Verbe: m. *A (Grammaticall) Verbe.*

Verbe: com. *Stout, hautie, stomackfull.*

Verbenique: f. *Veruine, Pigeons grasse, Holy-hearbe, Junoes teares, Mercuries moist-bloud; Look* Verveine.

Ver-

Verberie. *The name of a Burrough within the Duchie of* Valois, *and in the highway betweene* Senlis, *and* Compiegne; *whence*;
Sautereaux, ou tombereaux de Verberie. *The boyes of that Burrough, tearmed so because they are woont, for the sport of passengers (giuing them some small peece of money) and without any hurt vnto themselues, to tumble from the top to the bottome of a hill that is there-by.*
Verck. menu verck. *as* Menu vair, *vnder* Vair.
Verd: m. *A greene, or greene colour; a greene bough, greene Carpet, greene thing; also, greenenesse.*
Verd d'asur. *A certaine blewish greene stone, found in Mines of Copper which be mingled with siluer, and an excellent purger of melancholie.*
Verd de chevre. *A kind of sand, whereof Painters make their greenes.*
Verd de flambe. *A greene colour made of the bruised leaues of the Flower de luce.*
Verd gay. *A Popiniay greene.*
Verd de glayeul *as* Verd de flambe.
Verd de gris. *Verdigrease, a Spanish greene.*
Verd d'oye. *Gooose-turd greene; a greenish yellow; or a colour which is betweene a greene and a yellow.*
Verd de terre. *A kind of greene minerall chaulke, or sand.*
Verd de vessie. *Sap-greene; a greene made of Buckthorne berries.*
Employer le verd, & le sec. *Looke* Sec.
Prendre sans verd. *To take napping or vnprouided, surprise on a sudden or at vnawares; (A phrase deriued from the sport, or sportfull agreement (vsed in some parts of France) which binds him thats taken without a greene leafe about him, to forfeit somewhat.)*
Verd: m. verde: f. *Greene; fresh, new; flourishing, youthfull, in prime, liuelie, pithie, sturdie, strong; also, rawly tart or sharpe, as vnripe fruit, or wine, &c.*
Cuir verd. *A raw hide.*
Huis verd. *A peece of Tapistrie, or Darnix, hanging before a doore.*
Lict verd. *A couch, or bed of ease.*
Oeil verd. *A gray eye.*
Teste verde. *An inconsiderate, vnexperienced, rash, or hare-braind noddie.*
Donner de verdes. Il nous a donné de bien verdes. *He hath gulled vs extreamely, he hath told vs many a lowd lye.*
Mettre entre deux verdes vne meure. *To iumble good and bad, ripe and raw, together; or for the better passing away of bad things to put some few good ones among them.*
Verdales: f. *A kind of grapes.*
Verdalle: f. *A Dunneck, or Hedge-sparrow.*
Verdastre: com. *Greenish, or somewhat greene.*
Verdelet: m. *The tender, and delicate peare, called a Greening.*
Verdelet: m. ette: f. *Prettie and greene; onely beginning to be greene, but young, not yet ripe; also, a little raw, tart, sharpe.*
Verdement. *Greenely; freshly, newly; flourishingly; youthfully, lustily, strongly, sturdily; also, rawly, sharply, sowerly.*
Verdere, & Verdereule: f. *The little bird called a Yellow-hammer, or Yowlring.*
Verderie: f. *Th' Office of a Verderer in a Forest.*
Verderis: m. *Verdigrease.*
Verdet: m. *The same; called also, Spanish greene.*
Verdeur: f. *Verdure, greenenesse; also, a raw, or naturall sowrenesse in wine, fruits, &c; Looke* Verdure.
Verdureux: m. euse: f. *Somewhat greene.*
Verdier: m. *A Verderer, or Ouerseer of a forest; a Judge or Officer (next in authoritie vnto the* Maistre des Eaux & forests) *who commaunds all the Raungers, Woodwards, Foresters, &c, and punishes their & other mens disorders, in cases not exceeding the penaltie, or forfeiture, of 60 s.* Tourn: *Also, the little singing bird called a Greenefinch; also, the little venomous greene Toad; also, a Gardener, or Orchard-keeper.*
Verdillon: m. *An vnripe, or sowre grape.*
Verdir. *To flourish, or wax greene.*
Verdon: m. *A Dunneck, Dike-smowler, Hedge-sparrow.*
Verdondaine, & Verdondille *(fained & fond oaths)*
Verdot: m. otte: f. *Greenish, a little greene; yong, raw, or not yet ripe.*
Verdoyant: m. ante: f. *Flourishing, full of greenenesse; liuelie, youthfull, strong.*
Verdoyer. *To flourish; to be greene, young, lustie, youthfull, strong.*
Verdrier: m. *The Gold-hammer, Yellow-hāmer, Yowlring.*
Verducade: f. *A Closet; a hiding hole, or corner.*
Verdugalle: f. *A Vardingall.*
Verdun: m. *The little Rapier, called a Tucke; also, as* Verdrier; *or as* Verdon.
Verdure: f. *Verdure, greenenesse, or greene things, as hearbs, greene boughes, &c; also, as* Verdeur.
Ouvrage de verdure. *Forest worke; or flourisht worke, wherin gardēs, woods, or forests be represented.*
Verdurer. *To make, or become greene.*
Verdurier: m. Verduriere: f. *An hearb-man, or woman; one that furnishes a house with such greene things as be in season.*
Vere. *as* Voire: ¶Norm. ¶Rab.
Verecond: m. de: f. *Demure, shamefac'd, bashfull, modest.*
Veresque: f. *A wrecke of the sea.*
Veret: m. *A little worme; or, a kind of little worme; also, as* Gueret *(in the first sence.)*
Vereux: m. euse: f. *Wormie, full of worms; also, wormeatē; & thence, faultie, failing, in decay; Look* Verreux.
Vergadelle: f. *A pond-fish, like vnto, but lesse then, the* Saupe.
Vergaland: m. *A lustie yonker.*
Vergay. brouët vergay d'anguille. *Broth made of Eeles boiled in small peeces with Parsley, tosted bread, Saffron, and Ginger.*
Vergaye: f. *A kind of daunce.*
Verge: f. *A rod, wand; sticke, small staffe; a whisker, switch, or scutcher, to ride with; a twig, sprig, small or single branch; also, a Sergeants verge, or mace; also, a yard; also, the sayle-yard of a ship; also, a plaine hoope, or gimmall, ring; also, a rood of land; also, the rod wherwith a Thatcher fastens his straw to the roofe.*
Verge à berger. *The Tazle, Teazle, Fullers Thistle, Venus bason; also, water Plantaine.*
Verge dorée. *The hearbe called Golden rod.*
Verges à nettoyer. *A brush.*
Verge d'or. *as* Vergee doré; *also, a gold ring.*
Verge de pasteur, ou pastoral. *as* Verge à berger.
Verge sanguine. *The Hounds tree, Dog-berrie tree, Pricke-timber tree.*
Le pouvoir de la verge, & sergenterie. *The libertie, or precinct, wherein a Sergeant may arrest, &c.*
De telles verges ils sont tous batus. *They are all sick of that disease.*

Mettre la main à la verge. *To dispossesse himselfe of an inheritance in presence of his Landlord, or of his Officer, by the deliuerie of a rod, or little sticke, to him he passes it to.*

La verge ennoblit,& le ventre affranchit.*The gentleman ennobles his child, a free woman enfranchises hers; Looke* Ventre.

Vergé: m.ée: f. *Made of rods,or twigs; also, streaked with long,and rod-like rayes; also,worme-eaten.*

Vergée: f. *A yard of,the length of a yard in; also,a yard-land,or,a rood of land.*

Verger: m. *A Verger; one that beares a Verge before a Magistrate, &c.*

se Verger. *To be rewed, or streaked all ouer.*

Vergeteux. *as* Vergeux.

Vergette: f. *A small rod, or wand; a twig, or sprig; also,a boyes play with rods or wands pecked at a heape of points.*

Des vergettes. *A brush.*

Vergettons: m. *Small twigs,or sprigs.*

Vergeux: m.euse: f. *Roddie, full of rods; of a rod, rod-like.*

Vergier: m. *An Orchard; also,as* Verger.

Vergilies: f. *The seuen starres.*

Verglacer. *To freeze vpon raine.*

Verglas: m. *Frost, or a freezing, presently after a misling raine, wherby the ground seemes in a manner glazed; also,a glazing vpon a wall; or a painting that represents,and stands for,glaße.*

Verglassant. vent verglas: *A sharpe freezing,or sleeting wind.*

Vergne. *Th'Aller,or Alder tree.*

Vergobert: m. *A Maior,or Burgomaister.*

Vergongne: f. *Shame, bashfulnesse, blushing; also,the priuie parts.*

Vergongner. *To shame, to make ashamed, to disgrace, or dash out of countenance.* se Vergongner. *To blush, or be ashamed at, to be out of countenance with.*

Vergongneux: m.euse: f. *Shamefull, shame-fac'd, bashfull,blushfull,demure,modest; also,shamelesse,impudent, brasen-fac'd, past shame.*

Vergue: f. *The sayle-yard of a ship; whence;* Vergues hautes; *with hoised sailes, or sayle-yards (Sayed of a ship that hath weighed anchor,and wants but wind to be gone with.)*

Veridique: com. *Truth-telling.*

Ver-jettons. *as* Vergettons.

Verification: f. *A verification,verifying,auerring,approuing.*

Verifié: m. ée: f. *Verified,auerred, approued, confirmed,made good.*

Verifier. *To verifie,auerre,approue,cõfirme,proue true, make good.*

Verin: m. *as* Varin.

Verineux: m. euse: f. *Full of, troubled with, gnawne by,wormes.*

Verisimilitude: f. *Likelihood, possibilitie, resemblance of truth.*

Veritable: com. *True, sincere, vpright, a man of his word.*

Veritablement. *Verily,truely,certainely;without faile, doubt,or question.*

Verité: f. *Veritie,truth,sooth,verie deed.*

Franche verité. *(Looke* Franc; *) whence;* Comparoir à la franche verité: &,Tenir veritez; &, Tenir,ou Avoir, verité speciale. *A Sessions, or priuie Sessions.*

Grande dispute la verité rebute: Pro. *Wrangling contention is truthes preuention; The like is;*

Par trop debatre la verité se perd: Prov. *Too much debating makes truth to be lost.*

Verjus: m. *Veriuyce; especially that which is made of sowre, and vnripe grapes; also,the grapes whereof it is made.*

Verjus miellé. *Three parts of grape-veriuyce, and one of clarified honie incorporated,or well mingled together.*

Estre mis au verjus. *To be trounst,or courst.*

Verm: m. *A worme:* ¶Auvergnois.

Vermeil: m. *Vermillion,ruddinesse,a beautifull red.*

Vermeil: m.eille: f. *Vermillion,ruddie,reddish,claret, of a cleere or beautifull red.*

Soupe vermeille. *Looke* Soupe.

Vermeiller. *To root for wormes,like a hog.*

Vermeillet: m.ette: f. *Somewhat ruddie,prettie and red.*

Vermeilleur: m. *A rooter,or digger for wormes.*

Vermeillon, & Vermeillonner. *as* Vermillon, & Vermillonner.

Vermelet: m. *A verie little worme.*

Vermeniers: m. *Vermine; or as* Verminiere.

Vermerie: f. *Wormes.*

Vermet: m. *A little worme.*

Vermiculaire: f. *Wild Prick-madame, great Stone-crop,Worme-grasse.*

Vermiforme: com. *Fashioned like a worme.*

Vermiformes. *Two worme-resembling parts of the* Cervelet.

Vermiller. *To worme,to root for wormes.*

Vermillon: m. *Vermillion; a ruddie colour made of Brimstone and Quicksiluer; also,as* Chermes; *also,a little worme.*

Arbre de vermillon. *The Skarlet Oke, or Skarlet Holme Oke.*

Vermillonné: m.ée: f. *Made ruddie,painted red; of a Vermillion hue.*

Vermillonner. *To paint, or make Vermillion, or of a Vermillion hue; also,to blush,or wax red.*

Vermine: f. *Vermine; also, little beasts ingendred of corruption and filth; as Lice,Fleas, Ticks,Mice, Rats; and (most particularly) wormes.*

Vermineux: m. *The name of a certaine Spider whose bodie is full of spots.*

Vermineux: m.euse: f. *Wormie,or full of vermine.*

Herbe vermineuse. *Moath Mulleine.*

Verminiere: f. *A worme-hill; or a place neere a countrey house,wherin wormes are,of purpose,bred for pulleine.*

Vermisseau: m. *A little worme.*

se Vermoulir. *To grow worme-eaten,mouldie,rotten.*

Vermoulissure: f. *A being worme-eaten, or full of worme-holes; rottennesse; mouldinesse.*

Vermoulu: m.uë: f.*Worme-eaten,full of worme-holes, rotten; mouldie.*

Verne. *as* Vergne.

Vernedé. *A certaine charme, or charming prayer, for the tooth-ache.*

Vernicer. *as* Vernisser.

Vernillage. ce n'est que vernillage. *(Speaking of the starching of two or three bands at a time) this is but a pidling.*

Vernilles: f. *Nifles,trifles,things of nothing,or no value.*

Vernis: m. *Varnish; (made of Linseed oyle and) the Gumme of the Juniper tree.*

Vernis liquide. *Tarre.*

Vernissé : m.ée : f. *Varnished; slecked, or glazed ouer, with Varnish.*
Vernisser. *To varnish, to sleeke, or glaze ouer, with Varnish.*
Verny. *as* Vernis.
Verole : f. *The small Pockes.*
La grosse verole. *The Neapolitane disease, called by vs the French Pockes, though not verie iustly, the Spaniards hauing first brought it out of the Indies into Christendome, and bestowed it among the French, their enemies, at the siege of Naples, in the yeare 1528.*
Veroleux : m.euse : f. *Pockie, full of the Pockes.*
Verolique : com. *Pockie, of or belonging to the Pockes.*
Veron : m. *The little fish called a Menow.*
Il faut perdre vn veron pour pescher vn Saulmon : Prov. *A man must loose a feather to win a Goose; a small, to come by a great, matter.*
Veron. *whence;* Oeil veron; *Looke vnder* Oeil.
Veronique : f. *The hearbe Fluellin, Speed-well, Pauls Betonie, Ground-heele; also, a representation, image, picture, counterfeit, likenesse of; also, a sheet which, many beleeue, a woman of that name brought to wipe Christ withall when he did sweat; which sheet is yet shewed, as a Relique, at Rome.*
Veronique femelle. *Fluellin the female; or Speedwell bearing a yellowish flower.*
Veronique masle. *The male Speed-well, or Paules Betonie (the Author of the* Theatre d'Agriculture, *sayes it beares a reddish, or purple flower; Gerard hath six kinds thereof; and the first, which he calls* Veronica vera, & major, *comes neerest vnto the Frenchmans description.)*
Verrat : m. *A tame Boare; also, a Mackerell.*
Paillard comme vn verrat. *(Said of an extreame lecher.)*
Verrate : f. *A Sow.*
Verre : m. *Glasse; a drinking glasse.*
Droict de verre. *Looke vnder* Droict.
'A grand homme grand verre : Prov. *A great man cannot vse a little glasse; men should be fitted in things of much vse.*
Verrerie : f. *A Glasse-house.*
Verretre : m. *A mans yard:* ¶Rab.
Verreux : m.euse : f. *as* Vermineux; *also, worme-eaten, corrupted, putrified; also, hot, cholericke, hastie; light-headed, odde-humored, hare-braind.*
Faire le pois verreux. *To play the hypocrite; to seeme seeme more honest then he is; (as many worme-eaten Pease doe seeme a great deale sounder then they be.)*
Verri : m.ie : f. *Shining, or transparent, like glasse.*
Parchemin verri. *Cleere Parchment, virgine Parchment.*
Verrier : m. *A Glazier; also, a Glasse-maker; also, a frame to set glasses in.*
Verriere : f. *A glasse-window; and, a peece of glasse wherewith a thing is incompassed, or couered; also, a Glasse-house; and the furnace wherein glasse is melted.*
Verrin : m.ine : f. *Glassie, or of glasse; whence;* Medicament verrin; *a blackish medecine, or salue, made of burnt glasses, and good against the stone.*
Verrine : f. *as* Verriere.
Verrouil : m. *A boult for a doore, &c.*
Verrouiller. *To boult a doore.*
Verrucaire : f. *The hearbe Wartwort, or Turnesole; some also call Gumme succorie so, because the seeds thereof, in powder, take away warts.*
Verruë : f. *A wart.*
Verrüeux : m.euse : f. *Wartie, full of warts.*
Cichorée verrüeuse. *Yellow Gumme Succorie.*
Verruque : f. *as* Verruë; *also, a hillocke, or knap of a hill.*
Verry : m. *A mouldie cheese when it is greene; or any liquid thing which gathers a greene mouldinesse.*
Vers : m. *A verse.*
Vers. *Towards, vnto, neere to or by; at, with; before, or in presence of; also, against.*
Versal. *whence;* Lettres versales; *Text letters; or great letters; such as* Rex *in a Patent, &c.*
Versane : f. *A diuision, or part of a plowed ground, amounting to some 200 paces in length.*
Versatil : m. ile : f. *Quickly turning, easily turned, or powred out.*
Versé : m.ée : f. *powred, or turned, out; spilt, or shed forth; ouerturned, ouerthrowne.*
Verseau. *Aquarius; one of the twelue Signes of the Zodiacke.*
Verselet : m. *A little, or short verse.*
Versement : m. *A powring out, or vpon; a spilling, or shedding.*
Verser. *To powre, turne, put, out, or vpon; to shed, or spill; also, to conuerse with.*
Verser à boire à. *To fill drinke for.*
Verser vn chariot. *To wault, ouerturne, or ouerthrow a chariot; whence the Prouerbe;* Il n'est si bon chartier qui ne verse; *The best that driues, will sometimes wault, a cart.*
Verser de l'huile sur le feu. *Looke* Feu.
Verser par terre. *A horse to throw his rider.*
Verset : m. *A versicle, or short verse.*
Verseur : m. *A powrer; shedder, spiller; ouerturner, ouerthrower.*
Versificateur : m. *A versificator, versifier, maker of verses.*
Versifier. *To versifie, to make verses.*
Versure : f. *The taking vp of money to pay debts with; whence;* Faire versure; *To make shift; or to trouble one for the satisfying of another; or (as we say) to borrow of Peter to pay Paule.*
Versures. *The remainder, or leauings of draughts powred out of late-drunke-in cups, or glasses, into some vessell standing vnder the cupboord, &c, for that purpose.*
Vert : m. *as* Verd : m. *also, the apple called a Greening.*
Vert : m.verte : f. *Greene; Looke* Verd.
Vertaper. *To stop with a bung:* ¶Orlean.
Vertau : m. *A stopple, or bung; also, as* Vertoil.
Vert-de-gris : m. *Verdigrease.*
Vertebre : f. *A turning ioynt, or ioynt wherein the bones meet so as they may turne; as in the buckle-bone, &c.*
Vertement. *as* Verdement.
Vertemoulte. Droict de vert. *Looke vnder* Droict.
Vertevelles : f. *The great hindges of a gate.*
Vertical : m.ale : f. *Verticall; wauering, inconstant, apt to change or turne; also, standing right ouer the head.*
Cercle vertical. *The Verticall circle; a circle of the Azimuth which comes from the Zenith to the Horizon.*
Poinct vertical. *The Zenith, or point of the firmamēt which is directly ouer ones head.*
Vertige : f. *A dizzinesse, giddinesse, or swimming in the head; a disease wherein the patient thinkes that all things turne round.*
Vertigieux : m.euse : f. *Giddie, dizzie, turning round; or troubled with the swimming of the braine.*
Vertigineux. *as* Vertigieux.
Vertiginosité : f. *A giddinesse, dizzinesse, or swimming of the head or braine.*

Vertigné: m.ée: f. *Worme-eaten.*
Vertiller. *To swell, or increase, as womens breasts doe when the matricall veins are stretched by the menstruall bloud.*
Vertillons: m. *The whirling, round turning, or eddie of a water.*
Vertir en quelque lieu. *To haunt, frequent, or be conuersant in, a place.*
Il n'y sçauroit vertir. *He cannot fadge with, he cannot abide, or frame himselfe to.*
Vertjus. *as* Verjus.
Vertoeil: m. *A kind of greenish brasse, whereof great Ordnance is made.*
Vertoil: m. *The wherue, or whirle of lead belonging to a spindle.*
Vertu: f. *Vertue, goodnesse, honestie, sinceritie, integritie; worth, perfection, desert, merit; also, valour, prowesse, manhood; also, energie, efficacie, force, power, might; also, a good part or propertie, a commendable qualitie.*
Les vertus surmontent les signes: Pro. *Look* Signe.
Contre peché est vertu medecine: Prov. *Vertuous must he be who of sinne cur'd will be; or, let him, that of sinne would recouer, to vertue recourse.*
Vertuëusement. *Vertuously, honestly, manfully, worthily.*
Vertuëux: m.ëuse: f. *Vertuous, honest, sincere; manfull, valiant; worthie; thats furnished with good parts, and qualities.*
Vertugadin: m. *A little Vardingale.*
Vertugalle: f. *A Vardingale.*
Vertugoy. *for* Vertu dieu.
Vertumal: m.ale: f. *Changeable at pleasure, to be altered at will, or when one list.*
Vervaine. *as* Verveine.
Veruë: f. *A brawling, frapling, iangling, iarring; also, an odd humor in a man; a worme in the head, or brizze in the taile; whence;*
Il luy a pris vne verruë. *He is growne verie fantasticall, humorous, giddie-braind; the worme pricks him, the toy hath taken him, in the head.*
Verveil: m. *A Sweepe-net, or Drag-net.*
Verveine: f. *Veruein, Holie hearbe, Junoes teares, Pigeons grasse, Mercuries Moist-bloud.*
Verveine basse. *Holie Verueine, creeping Verueine; or as* Verveine femelle.
Verveine femelle. *Female Verueine, base or flat Verueine, creeping Verueine, holie Verueine.*
Verveine masle. *Male Verueine, straight or vpright Verueine, common Verueine.*
Verueleux: m.euse: f. *Moodie, humorous, fantasticall, giddie headed, hare-braind.*
Vervelles: f. *Varuells for a Hawke; also, as* Vertevelles.
Verveul. *as* Verveil.
Ver-volant: m. *A Ringworme, or Tettar.*
Vesce: f. *The pulse called Fitch, or Vetch.*
Vesce noire. *The Tare, or bitter Fitch.*
Vesce sauvage. *Strangle-tare, Tine, wild Fitch; or the small wild Vetch, or Fitchling.*
Vesceron: m. *Strangle-tare, Tine, the wild Fitch.*
Vescu. *Liued.*
Vesé. *Looke* Vezé.
Vesialere. Fermance vesialere. *A kind of Officer, or Magistrate, within the Jurisdiction of* la Solle.
Vesicaire: f. *Red Nightshade, Alkakengie, Winter Cherries.*
Vesicatif: m.iue: f. *Blistering, blister-raising.*
Vesicatoire: m. *A vesicatorie; a cupping glasse, or any sharpe ointment, cataplasme, or plaister, which hath power to draw humors outward, exulcerating the skinne, and raising little blisters on it.*
Veller. *To calse; See* Veller.
Vesner. *To fizzle.*
Vesperies: f. *Euening exercises, or disputations, among the Sorbonists.*
Vesperisé: m.ée: f. *Chidden, checked, taunted, schooled, reuiled, railed on; also, mocked, flowted, ieasted at, ridden, derided.*
Vesperiser. *To checke, taunt, schoole, chide, reuile; also, to mocke, flowt, ieast at, ride, or deride.*
Vespertin: m.ine: f. *Of the euening, done in an euening.*
Vespre: m. *The euening.*
Il n'est si grand iour que ne vienne vespre: Prov. *The longest day is ended by an euening.*
Vesprée: f. *The euening tide, or season.*
Vespres: f. *Euen-song, or Euening prayer.*
Vespres Siciliennes: Prov. *The Sicilian Euensong; mischiefes done, or death inflicted, in a place, and time, of imagined securitie; (from a generall massacre of the French, made on a sudden, and throughout Sicilie (whereof they were ouer-insolent Maisters) by the incensed Islanders, on Easter day (*Anno 1282*) and about fiue of the clocke in the afternoone.)*
Vessaille: f. *A fysting; or a crue of fysting slouens, or sluts.*
Vesse: f. *A fyste; also, as* Vesce.
Vesse de loup. *The dustie or smoakie Toadstole, called a Fusse-ball, Pucke-fusse, Bull-fyste, Puffyst, Wolues fyste.*
Panier à vesses. C'est le cul.
Vesseron: m. *as* Vesceron.
Vesseur: m. *A fyster, a stinking fellow.*
Vesseuse: f. *A fysting housewife.*
Vessie: f. *A bladder; also, a blane, or blister; also, a kind of brasen Stillitorie, the pipe whereof is cōueyed through a vessell of water, and afterwards yeelds the distilled liquor into the Recipient.*
Vessies d'orme. *Certaine blisters, or little bladders (full of a slimie, or clammie, liquor) in some Elme leaues.*
Croire que vessies sont lanternes. *To beleeue that the Moone is made of a greene cheese.*
Vessié: m.ée: f. *Beblistered, or full of blisters.*
Vessier: m. *A fyster.*
Vessier. *To blister.*
Vessiere: f. *as* Vesseuse.
Vessiette: f. *A little bladder, or blister.*
Vessifiant: m. ante: f. *Causing one to fyste.*
Vessifier. *To breed a fyste, to make breake wind, or let a fyste.*
Vessigons: m. *Windgalls in a horses legs.*
Vessir. *To fyste, to let a fyste.*
Vest: m. *A Liuerie and seisin made vnto a purchaser, in some places by the seller, but in most by the Lord* Foncier *or* Censier *of whom the land is held.*
Droict de vest. *Looke vnder* Droict.
Vestales: f. *The Vestall virgines, the Nunnes of the Heathenish Romans.*
Vestement: m. *A vestment, vesture, weed, garment, habit, array, attire, apparell, cloathing, sute of cloathes.*
On croit d'un fol bien souvent qu'il soit clerc pour ses vestemens: Prov. *Discreet cloathes often passe a foole for a wise man.*

Vesteure: f. *A vesture; or, as* Vestement.
Vestiaire: m. *The Vestrie in a Church.*
Vestige: m. *A step, footstep, tracke, trace, marke, signe, or token of a footing.*
Vestir. *To clothe, array, apparrell, attire, decke, enrobe, suit with, put on a suit of clothes; also, to vest, invest, inseisin, giue possession of, make liuerie and seisin vnto.*
Vests, *for* Va; *goe thou.* ¶Pic. ¶Rab.
Vestu: m. uë: f. *Clad, clothed, yclad, arrayed, apparrelled, attired, suited, enrobed, couered; vested, inuested, inseisined, put into possession of.*
Long vestu. *An auncient peece of coyne, worth about* ij s vj d *sterling.*
Vesture: f. *A clothing, arraying, apparrelling, attiring, enrobing, suiting, couering; also, a vesting, inuesting, or putting into possession of; also, as* Vestement.
Vetade: f. *The filletted Cockle; smooth, broad, and exceeding hard, shelled.*
Veterinaire: m. *An old beaten souldior; one that hath serued long in a place, or office.*
Vetiller. *To tickle, &c, as* Fretiller; *also, to trifle.*
Vetilles: f. *Tarriers to play with; also, nifles, trifles, things of no value.*
Vettoine: f. *The hearbe Betonie.*
Veu: m. *A vow; a solemne promise, or protestation; also, a request, prayer, desire.*
Veu: m. euë: f. *Viewed, seene, perceiued, beheld, ouerlooked, surueyed; marked, heeded, obserued, regarded; examined, searched into, considered of.*
Boule veuë; &, Iouër à boule veuë. *See* Boule.
Ronfle veuë. Vous me remettez à point en ronfle veuë. *You haue me at a vantage, hold me at a bay, put me to my shifts, force me to quit, or abandon all.*
Avoir veu boire. *A ieasting speech whereby they signifie that a man is drunken.*
Il a veu le loup. *His voice is growne hoarse, or he hath lost his voice, on a suddaine; See* Loup.
Il est veu du Roy. *The King doth grace, or fauour him.*
Veu. (Adv.) *Considering, seeing, in respect of; whence,*
Veu la facilite qu'est en luy, veu son impudence; &, veu qu'il ne vient point, &c.
Veuë: f. *The sence, act, or instrument of seeing; the eyes, or their function; the glaunce, or the reach thereof; a view, looke, sight, aspect, regard; a prospect; also, the suruey of a house, or peece of ground; also, the viser of a Helmet; also, a light, or ouerture for light; whence;*
Veuës mortes. *Close, or vncasemated windowes.*
Droict de veuë. *Power to get light vnto a house by a window, or ouerture, made into a neighbors.*
Droict de veuës. *The same; as also, to damme vp those of his that offend me; or to compell him to remoue, or take away that which impeaches mine.*
Veuë à veuë. *Face to face, right oueragainst.*
'A veuë de païs. *At randon, roaming, at rouers, at large; without exact examination, or certaine proofe.*
Discours à perte de veuë. *Vast, extrauagant, or wandering discourses; tales without order or end.*
Aller à la veuë. *To goe harbour a Stag, or lodge a Bucke.*
Veuf: f. *A widow; Looke* Vef.
Veufvage: m. *Widowhood.*
Veufve: f. *A widow.*
Droict de veufve. *A widowes due, or part in moueables (ouer and besides her iointure, or dower) viz. her best gowne, her marriage ring and iewels, her bed fully furnished, and certaine other houshold-stuffe: By the customes of* Lalleuë *in* Artois, *the suruiuor (man or woman) takes by this priuiledge, onely the best peece of euerie kind of houshold-stuffe.*
Veuilles: f. *The clasping tendrels, or small twyning sprigs of a Vine.*
·Veule: com. *Weake, faint, infirme, vnsound, ouertoyled with heat and labour; also, hollow, loose, or light about a thing.*
Vexateur: m. *A vexer, afflicter, tormentor.*
Vexation: f. *Vexation, torment, extreame griefe, trouble, or disquiet.*
Vexé: m. ée: f. *Vexed, afflicted, tormented, turmoyled, extreamely grieued, or disquieted.*
Vexer. *To vex, afflict, or torment; extreamely to grieue, trouble, disquiet.*
Vezarde: f. *A great feare, dread, horror.* ¶Rab.
Vezé. C'est vn gros vezé. *A gulch, gorbellie, fat guts.*
Veze: f. *A Bag-pipe.* ¶Poictevin.
Iouër de la veze. *To play on the Bagpipe; also, to fizle.*
Vezées. Bille vezées. *Looke* Bille-vezées.
Vezeur: m. *A Bagpiper.* ¶Poictevin.
Vezie: f. *A Carbuncle, or blaine-sore.*
Vezon: m. *The arse, tayle, breech.* ¶Norm.
Vgne. *The name of a Vine.*
Vi: m. *Wine (so tearmed about* Montpellier.)
Viable: com. *Liueable, likelie to liue.*
Viage: m. *as* Vsufruict; *also, a liuing.*
'A viage. *For life.*
Viager: m. *A tenant for life.*
Viager: m. ere: f. *For life, during life.*
Quint viager. *See* Quint.
Rente, ou pension viagere. *A rent-charge, or annuitie bought for money; called so, because it may also be redeemed, or extinguished, by money.*
Reparations viageres. Ce sont menuës reparations, pour l'entretenement de l'heritage, hors les quatre gros murs, poultres, & entieres couvertures, & voultes.
Viager. *To enioy during life, to haue an estate for life in.*
Viagerement. *During life, onely for life.*
Viagier. *as* Viager; *or, as* Vsufruictier.
Viaige: m. *A tenant for life.*
Viaire: m. *The face, looke, aspect, visage, countenance; also, an annuitie, or yearelie pension, for life.*
Viande: f. *Meat, food, sustenance, victuals, viands, acates (especially of flesh.)*
La viande creuse. *Wenches, trulls, two-legd beasts.*
Viande d'ami est bien tost preste: Prov. *Meat in a friends house is (or is thought) soone readie; Looke* Ami.
La viande semond les gens: Pro. *Well-cooked meats inuite the stomacke.*
De mauvaise viande on ne sçait faire vn bon potage: Pro. *No man can make of ill acates good cale.*
Tout estat est viande aux vers: Prov. *Wormes prey, by times, on all Estates.*
Viander. *(A word peculiar to red Deere) to feed; also, as* Fianter.
Viandier: m. ere: f. *Of, or belonging to, meat.*
Viandy: m. *The pasture, or ground wherein a Deere feeds; also, the meat which he feeds on.*
Viateur: m. *A traueller, passenger, wayfaring man.*
Vibailli: m. *A Vice-Baylife, or vnder-Steward; an officer that (in some Prouinces) examines, and punishes malefactors.*
Vibrequin: m. *A Wimble.*

Viburne: m. *as* Viorne; *or, onely the wayfaring tree.*

Vicaire: m. *A Vicar, or Vicegerent; also, the Tenant, or Incumbent, who in the right of a Corporation, or Church, is to pay duties, or doe seruices, vnto the Lord of the land.*

Grand vicaire. *A Vicar generall; or an officer whom a Bishop imployes for the disposition of such Benefices as be in his gift.*

Vicairie: f. *A Vicaredge; or, as* Vicariat.

Vicariant. *Gadding, raunging, roaming, trotting vp and downe the countrey.*

Vicariat: m. *A Vicarship, the place of a Vicar; also, a Vicegerencie.*

Vicarier. *To raunge, roame, gad, or trot vp and downe a countrey.*

Vice: m. *A vice, fault, sinne, offence, villanie, roguerie, lewdnesse, naughtinesse, corruption, blemish, defect, imperfection, default.*

Au vis le vice: Prov. *Mans face often tells what vice in him dwells.*

Nul vice sans son supplice: Pro. *All vices haue their plagues attending on them.*

Tel vice tel supplice: Pro. *Such as the crime such the correction.*

Vice-admiral: m. *A Viceadmirall.*

Vice-chancelier: m. *A Vicechancelor.*

Vice-conte: m. *A Vicount; Looke* Vicomte.

Vice-conte: f. *A Vicountie, a Vicountship; Looke* Vicomté.

Vice-gerent: m. *A Vicegerent; a Deputie, or Lieutenant.*

Vice-roy: m. *A Viceroy, or Deputie vnto a King; he that in his absence representeth his person, and gouerneth his kingdome.*

Vicié: m. ée: f. *Viciated, mard, corrupted, infected, defiled; blemished, imperfect, vnsound.*

Vicier. *To viciate, marre, corrupt, infect, spoyle, blemish, defile.*

Vicieusement. *Viciously, lewdly, corruptly, faultily.*

Vicieux: m. euse: f. *Vicious, lewd, bad, wicked, sinfull, naughtie, roguish, villanous; filthie, corrupt; erronious, imperfect, vnsound.*

Vicinité: f. *Vicinitie, neighborhood, nighnesse, proximitie, neerenesse.*

Vicomte: m. *A Vicount; was at the first the Deputie, or Lieutenant, of an Earle, in some towne wherein he could not reside himselfe; or by the King made gardian of a Countie, vntill he had furnished it with an Earle: These Vicounts had but* la moyenne Iustice, la haute *being reserued by, or for, the Earles themselues (and therefore in most of the customes of* la Gaule Belgique *that Jurisdiction is hitherunto stiled,* Vicomtiere;) *howsoeuer, they were at first but Officers; and, euen at this day, the* Prevosts, *or* Iuges *of Normand villages are tearmed* Vicomtes. *Now it is to be presumed, that when the Earles of Prouinces, &c, vsurped a proprietie in their charges, the Vicounts, not to be behind them, did the like in those townes, and villages which they gouerned. There be at this day three or foure sorts of them; first those that, holding immediately of the Crowne (as the* Vicomte de Turenne, *and but a few others) are to be ranked among great, or high Lords, and before any Barons: then those that, holding of the King as of Counties reunited to the Crowne; or holding of Counties lately created, or not yet reunited (and being thereby in the qualitie of* Arrierevassaux de la Couronne) *are no better then meane Lords, and precede onely those Barons that either but equall, or be inferior vnto, them in Tenure: Lastly, those (in Picardie, Flanders, and elsewhere) that hauing not hitherunto beene able to compasse more then a meane Jurisdiction, and therefore not meriting the place, or esteeme, of absolute Lords, are not qualified* Vicomtes, *but barely, and in difference from the rest,* Seigneurs Vicomtiers.

Vicomté: f. *A Vicountie; the dignitie, territorie, or estate of a Vicount; also, meane Jurisdiction.*

Vicomtier: m. ere: f. *Of a Vicount, Vicountlike; also, enioying, or belonging to, meane Jurisdiction.*

Chemin Vicomtier. *Looke* Chemin.

Vicon. Mon petit vicon. *My little pricke, or pillicocke.*

Victimaire: m. *One that sold a beast for sacrifice; or, one that assisted the sacrificer in the killing, and dressing thereof.*

Victoire: f. *Victorie, conquest, a subduing, or vanquishing, the vpper hand of an enemie.*

Victorial: m. ale: f. *Victoriall, of or belonging to victorie.*

Victoriat: m. *The fourteenth part of an ounce.*

Victorien: m. *A conqueror, vanquisher, subduer, ouercommer.*

Victorienne: f. *A victoresse, a victorious or vanquishing woman.*

Victorieux: m. euse: f. *Victorious, triumphant, conquering, vanquishing.*

Victuailles: f. *Victualls, food, commons, dyet, prouision for the bellie.*

Vicugne. *A hornelesse wild beast in* Peru, *of whose wooll the Indians make excellent Couerlets.*

Vidame: m. *A Vidame; was originally the Judge of a Bishops temporall Iurisdiction, or such an Officer to him as the* Vicomte *was to the* Comte: *but in processe of time, of an Officer he became a Lord, by altering his office into a fief, held of the Bishopricke he belonged vnto: So that, euen to this day, the estate of all* Vidames *dependeth of some Bishopricke, or is annexed vnto the Temporalities thereof; and therefore they be no better then* Seigneurs mediocres, *although the first of that ranke; and in all other priuiledges and rights equall to Vicounts, with some aduantage of credit in respect of High Iurisdiction, which those haue vsurped, by degrees, vpon their Earles, and these had, at the first, by the gift of their Bishops.*

Vidimé: m. ée: f. *Confirmed, approued, ratified; the goodnesse whereof is, after examination, warranted.*

Vidimer. *To confirme, approue, or warrant the goodnesse of a thing, after an examination thereof.*

Vidimus de lettre. *An examination of a Copie by the originall, signed by a Secretarie, Register, Notarie, or Clarke.*

Viduité: f. *Widowhood, the estate of a widow.*

Vie: f. *A life, or liuing; whole age, or time; also, the direct way into a hauen, or barre.*

Arbre de vie. *The sweet tree, called also by vs, the tree of life.*

Huile de vie. *The (most excellent) oyle of Vitrioll.*

La vie de dix. *As much as would serue tenne.*

C'est toute ma vie. *Tis all I haue to liue on.*

De l'une & l'autre vie. *Liuing both on land, and in the water.*

Il est François pour la vie. *He is French to the death.*

Iour de ta vie. *Neuer, not as long as thou liuest.*

Vie n'est pas seur heritage: Prov. *Life is no sure (no true) inheritance.*

Bonne

Bonne vie embellit; & attrait bonne fin: Pro. *Good life imbellishes, and ends in blisse.*
De meschante vie les bonnes loix sont venuës: Pro. *Ill liues occasioned good Lawes.*
Il n'est vie que de coquins; &, Il n'est vie que de coquins quand ils ont assemblé leurs bribes: Pro. *Our countrey Fidlers haue a song which begins thus; Of all Occupations a beggar is the best, for when he is wearie, he may lay him downe and rest, &c.*
Il n'est vie que d'estre bien aise: Pro. *All happinesse, consists in quietnesse, of life.*
Il n'est vie que de faire bonne chere, mais la fin n en vaut rien: Prov. *(Whether you consider the stuffe it turnes into, or the end it brings one to.)*
Ioyeuse, & riche vie pere, & mere oublie: Pro. *Contentment and wealth gotten, makes father, and mother forgotten.*
Meschante vie quiert le coing: Prov. *Lewdnesse affecteth corners.*
Telle vie telle fin: Prov. *Such as his dealing was his death.*
Vie vie. *(An Aduerbe of incouraging, or commaunding;) On, on apace, goe on, away, forward, make hast, march march, quickly, speed it my hearts.*
Vie fouët & au vent. *Auaunt, packe, be gone.*
Viedaze: m. *The member of an Asse; also, an old dunce, doult, blockhead, noddie, ninnyhammer.*
Viedazer le nez à. *To play with the nose of; to baffle, abuse, flowt, make a foole of; also, to trouble, vex, molest.*
Vieil: m. eille: f. *Old, aged, auncient, stale, decrepit, in yeares; Looke* Vieux.
La vieille guerre. *See* Guerre.
Faict à la vieille mode. *Made rudely, of a grosse forme, of a fashion thats quite out of fashion.*
Vn vieil chien iamais ne iappe en vain: Pro. *An old dog barketh (we say biteth) sure.*
Vieil oiseau ne se prend a reths: Pro. *The old birds care auoides the snare.*
Depuis que la brebis est vieille le loup la mange bien: Prov. *The sheepe is neuer too old for the Wolfe; how tough soeuer she be he eats her well.*
Il n'est chasse que de vieux chiens: Pro. *There is no hunter to the old dog; no searcher to experience.*
Il n'est miracle que de vieux saincts: Pro. *Wonders of old are most authenticall.*
Il n'y a rien tel qu'un vieil pot à faire la bonne soupe: Pro. *No pot makes so good pottage as the old one.*
On n'aura ja bon asne vieil: Prov. *An old Asse is good for nothing.*
Oncques vieil singe ne fit belle mouë: Pro. *Th' old Monkey neuer made well-fauored mowe.*
Vieillard: m. *An old, or aged, man.*
Mieux vaut l' ombre d' un sage vieillard que les armes d'un ieune coquard: Pro. *A wise old man may doe more with his shade, then can a young cokes with his glistering blade.*
Vieille: f. *An old, or aged woman; also, as* Vielle *in the later sence; or, as* Poule de mer.
Peau de vieille. *The name of an Apple.*
Chascune vieille son dueil plaind: Pro. *See* Plaindre.
La necessité fait trotter la vieille: Pro. *Need addes new life, strength, quicknesse, to old age.*
Qui mieux ne peut à sa vieille retourne: Prov. *He that can haue no young, makes much of his old, stuffe; old serues the turne where young will not be had.*

Vieillement. *Oldly, agedly, auncienily.*
Vieillesse: f. *Eld, or old age.*
Ieunesse oiseuse vieillesse disetteuse: Prov. *A lazie youth, a lowsie age.*
Si ieunesse sçavoit, & vieillesse pouvoit, iamais povreté n'auroit: Prov. *If youth were cunning, and age able, poorenesse would soone be but a fable.*
Vieilli: m. ie: f. *Become old, growne auncient, stept farre into yeares.*
Vieillir. *To wax old, become aged, grow in yeares.*
Vieillissement. *as* Vieillement.
Vieillot: m. otte: f. *Elderlie, somewhat old.*
Vieilly. *as* Vieilli.
Vielle: f. *A rude, or harsh-sounding Instrument of Musicke, vsually played on by base Fidlers, and blind men; also, the sea-Thrush, or particularly that kind thereof which hath a sky-coloured head, greenish backe, ruddie head, and purple finnes.*
Ils accorderent tresbien leurs vielles ensemble. *They iumbled their fidles passing well together; (but this phrase hath a further (filthie) sence.)*
On ne fait pas à grands coups douce vielle: Prov. *Not great, but apt, stroakes make sweet Musicke.*
Vielleur: m. *One that vsually playes on, or gets a rascallie liuing by playing on, a* Vielle, *and thence, any base, or beggarlie Fidler.*
Vierge: f. *A virgin, maid, maiden; also, the signe in the Zodiake tearmed Virgo.*
Vierge: com. *Virgin, pure, cleere, prime, vnbroken, vntainted, vndefiled, vntouched.*
Huile vierge. *The first (and best) oyle that comes out of the presse, or from a stillitorie.*
Miel vierge. *Virgins honey; the honey which, of it selfe, and without any pressing distills from the combe.*
Or vierge. *Gold vnmelted, or vntryed; Gold that comes whole from it veine, or mine.*
Parchemin vierge. *Virgin Parchment; Parchment made of an abortiue skin.*
Poix vierge. *The first pitch that issues out of the Pitchtree.*
Terre vierge. *Ground that is whole, or vnfoyled; good ground that was neuer plowed, or broken vp.*
Viet-dase, & Vietz-daze. *Looke* Viedaze.
Vieuté. *as* Vileté.
Vieux. *Old, aged, ancient, stale, decrepit, in yeares (Looke* Vieil; *to which it is also the Plurall.)*
Vieux peché fait nouvelle honte: Prov. *Old sinne begets new shame.*
Vin vieux, ami vieux, or vieux, sont loüez en tous lieux: Pro. *The praise of old wine, friends, and gold, is in all places often told.*
C'est grande peine que d' estre vieux, mais il ne l' est pas qui veut: Pro. *A noysome thing it is to be old, yet no man can be so that would.*
En esperance d' avoir mieux, tant vit le loup qu'il devient vieux: Pro. *The Wolfe so long hopes his estate to mend, that (without helpe) his life's growne neere an end.*
Vif: m. vive: f. *Quicke, liuing, aliue, in life; also, quick, liuelie, sparkling, spurting, light, nimble, full of life.*
Vive pasture. *Looke* Pasture.
Donation entre vifs. *A deed of Gift executed in the donors life time.*
Eau vive. *Running water, Spring water.*
Herbage vif. *Looke* Herbage.
Pierre vive. *Flint.*
Roche vive. *An entire rock; a rocke, without mixture of earth, all stone.*

Le mort execute le vif; &, Le mort saisit le vif. *(Principles of Law;) for which looke* Executer, & Mort.

Vif-argent. *Quick-siluer.*

Vif-argent vulgal. *A kind of base Quick-siluer made of dung, and hay.*

Vif-argentin: m. ine: f. *Quick-siluerie, of Quick-siluer.*

Vif-gage: m. *A pawne of land, for the profits whereof he vnto whom it is pawned is accomptable.*

Vifs. Les vifs: m. *The intrayles, or guts; whence,* Cataplasme de chair de vautour avec les vifs; *Looke vnder* Cataplasme.

Vighier: m. *The Captaine of a watch;* ¶Langued: *or, as* Viguier.

Vigilamment. *Vigilantly, wakefully, watchfully, circumspectly, charily, warily.*

Vigilance: f. *Vigilancie, wakefullnesse, watchfullnesse; circumspection, warinesse.*

Vigilant. *Vigilant, wakefull, watchfull; also, warie, prouident, circumspect, that looketh well about him.*

Vigile: f. *A Vigile; the Eue of a holie, or solemne day.*

Vigle. *See* Bigle.

Vignages. Droict de vign. *Looke vnder* Droict.

Vigne: f. *A Vine; the plant that beareth Grapes.*

Vigne bastarde. *The wild (Grape-bearing) Vine.*

Vigne blanche. *Brionie, white Brionie, Tettarberrie; also, Brionie of* Mexico, *or of* Peru.

Vigne noire. *Blacke Brionie, our Ladies Seale, the wild Vine.*

Vigne porrette. *The Leeke of Vines, wild Leeke, dogs Leeke, French Leeke.*

Vigne sauvage. *as* Vigne bastarde; *also, the wild Vine, called otherwise, blacke Brionie, and our Ladies Seale.*

Se mettre dedans la vigne iusques au pescher. *To step ouer head and eares into a Vineyard; to steepe his head, or wit in a Wine-tub.*

Il faut acheter vigne deserte: Prov. *Buy an vndressed Vineyard; (so mayest thou fashion it according to thine owne humor.)*

L'eschalas fait tomber la vigne: Prov. *(Applyable when he, that should protect or support a man, is the cause of his ruine.)*

Vigneron: m. *A Vine-dresser, or Vineyard-keeper; one that works in, or lookes to, a Vineyard.*

Quand le chou passe le sep le vigneron meurt de soif: Pro. *Looke* Sep.

Vigneronne: f. *A woman that workes in a Vineyard, or dresses a Vine.* (Le lier, esbourgeonner, & redresser sont les façons de la vigneronne; du vigneron le tailler, houër, biner, tercer. ¶Nicot.)

Vignette: f. *A little Vine; also, as* Coulevrée blanche; *also, the hearbe called French Mercurie.*

Vignettes. *Vignets; branches, or branch-like borders, or flourishes, in Painting, or Ingrauerie.*

Vignettement: m. *A vignetting; a bordering or flourishing with the branches of Vines, or other Plants.*

Vignetter. *as* Vignotter.

Vignetterie: f. *A vignetting; a bordering or flourishing with branches, leaues, flowers, &c.*

Vignoble: m. *A Vineyard.*

Vignol: m. *A kind of great shell-fish.*

Vignolant: m. *as* Vigneron.

Vignolette: f. *A little Vine.*

Vignot: m. *as* Vignol.

Vignotter. *To make vignets; to border or flourish with the branches of Vines, or of other Plants.*

Vignottes. *as* Vignettes.

Vigoureusement. *Vigorously, lustily, strongly, toughly, sturdily, forcibly, effectually.*

Vigoureux: m. euse: f. *Vigorous, lustie, liuelie, strong, tough, sturdie, forcible, effectuall.*

Viguerie: f. *A Prouostship, or Justiceship; the office of a* Viguier; *or, the Precinct wherein he commaunds.*

Vigueur: f. *Vigor, strength, force, toughnesse, courage, liuelinesse, efficacie.*

Viguier: m. *The ordinarie Iudge of a countrey Towne; or such a Magistrat in* Languedoc, *as the* Prevost *is in the rest of France.*

Vil: m. ile: f. *Vile, abiect, base, low, meane, homelie, simple, worthlesse; good cheape; of small price, little value, no accompt.*

Vilain: m. *A villaine, slaue, bondman, seruile tenant;* C'est l'homme serf, ou qui tient heritage de serve condition, ou mortaillable d'aucun seigneur, *sayes* Ragueau, *(who likewise affirmes, that the Gentlemen of France tearme* vilains *all Farmers, Husbandmen, Plowmen, and generally all yeomen, how free soeuer their condition, or tenures be: and that countrey Gentlemen tearme so all Citizens, Burguers, & Inhabitants of walled Townes:) Hence also, a churle, carle, boore, clowne; and, a miser, micher, pinch-pennie, penny father; and, a knaue, rascall, varlet, filthie fellow; any base-humored, ill-borne, and worse-bred hinde, cullion, or clusterfist: also, the Cheuin, or Pollard fish (called so because it feedes vpon nothing but filth;) also, a kind of Hagard Faulcon.*

Estant en son vilain. *Being in the suds, or sullens, swelling with his ordinarie dogged, or surlie humors.*

Vilain affamé demi enragé: Pro. *A starued clowne is halfe a mad man; when victualls faile, all temper failes, him.*

Vilain enrichi ne cognoist parent, ny ami: Pro. *The base clowne that hath got a little pelfe, knowes neither friend, nor kinsman, (nor himselfe.)*

Les vilains s'entretiennent, les nobles s'embrassent: Pro. *Clownes are but cold, the gentle kind, in mutuall conuersation.*

Le vilain ne sçait qu'esperons valent: Prov. *Base people know not the worth of good things.*

D'un vilain refaict Dieu nous garde. *Looke* Refaict.

De grand vilain lourde cheute; &, De grand vilain grand flac: Pro. *A great or mightie knaue, a mightie fall will haue.*

Oignez vilain il vous poindra: Prov. *The base vnthankfull chuffe returnes bad offices for good.*

Priez vilain moins il fera: Pro. *The more you pray a slaue the lesse you preuaile.*

Connin, & vilain avec la main: Pro. *See* Connin.

Il n'est danger que de vilain: Prov. *The (incensed) churle is a most dangerous beast.*

Le Chanteau part le vilain: Pro. *When villeines by birth or estate (who for the most part are tenants in common) doe meane to part their possessions, they diuide a lumpe of bread, and giue each to other a peece thereof; Hence is this Prouerb applyable to those base fooles, that fall out with their best friends for trifles, or victualls.*

Qui a le vilain il a sa proye: Pro. *Looke* Proye.

Si tu veux cognoistre vn vilain baille luy la baguette en main: Prov. *If thou a knaue, or churle wouldst faine bewray, giue him authoritie, let him beare sway.*

Vilain: m. aine: f. *Villanous, vile, base, filthie, sordide, lewd, bad; vnworthie, churlish, niggardlie; also, as* Vilein.

Vilainement. *Villanously, vilely, basely, niggardly, churlishly, scuruily, filthily.*
Vilainer. *as* Vilener.
Vilané. *as* Vilené.
Vilbrequin: m. *A Wimble.*
Vilein: m. eine: f. *Seruile, base, vile, drudging, villeinlike, held by villenage; also, as* Vilain.
Vilenaille: f. *A pack of scowndrels, rascals, base abiects, scuruie fellowes; the dregs, riffraffe, offscum, of the people.*
Vilené: m. ée: f. *Defiled, soyled, besmeared, begrymed; also, disgraced, dishonored, blemished in reputation; also, berated, reuiled, rayled on.*
Ils m'eussent vilenez s'ils m'eussent peu ioindre. *They had done me some roguerie or other, if they could haue raught me.*
Vilener. *To soyle, defile, besmeare, begryme, beray; baffle, abuse, disgrace, blemish the reputation of; also, to berate, reuile, rayle on.*
Vilenie: f. *Villanie, vilenesse, roguerie, knauerie, lewdnesse; filth, nastinesse, ordure, impuritie, scuruinesse; miching, baseneße, niggardlinesse, couetousnesse, churlishnesse.*
Laide vilenie. *Slaunderous, reproachfull, disgracefull, defamatorie tearmes; words which will beare an Action.*
Vilenot: m. *A little villeine; or one that is somewhat churlish; also, a clowne, peasant, boore, hob, or hinde of the countrey.*
Vileté: f. *Vilenesse, basenesse, worthlesnesse, paultring, scuruinesse; also, cheapenesse.*
Vilette. *as* Villette.
Vilipender. *To vilipend, set little by, contemne, despise, disable, disesteeme; also, to defame, slaunder, traduce, giue an ill report of.*
Village: m. *A village; a countrey towne, consisting of many houses ioyned together; therein to differ from* Hameau *(a hamlet) which consists but of a few, and those either scattered, or not verie neere together.*
Mais suis-ie pas de mon village? *But am not I a clowne, or a sillie fellow?*
Villageois: m. *A countreyman, husbandman, ploughman, farmer, clowne, hob, hinde, swaine, boore.*
Villain. *See* Vilain.
Villanelle: f. *A countrey daunce, round, or song.*
Villanie. *as* Vilenie.
Villaquerie: f. *Villanie, roguerie, rascalitie, skowndrellisme.*
Villatique: com. *Countrey-like; of, or belonging to, the countrey.*
Ville: f. *A Towne; an incorporate, or inclosed Towne; a Citie; also, the long oagar tearmed by our Coopers, a Turrell.*
Villes de paix. *Looke* Paix.
Ville aux Roix. *The citie of* Blois; *tearmed so, because the French Kings doe oftentimes soiourne, and their children be commonly brought vp, within it.*
Ville & taille. *The territorie, or precincts of a towne.*
La ville est gaignée. *(Prouerbially) the victorie is gotten, our suit obtained, our cause woon.*
Avoir vn oeil au bois l'autre à la ville. *To haue an eye on all sides of him, to looke verie warily about him.*
Elle a tousiours quelque commission par la ville. *Sayed ieastingly, or in disgrace, of a gadding housewife.*
Qui sent sa bonne ville. *A courteous, and ciuill person, or part.*
Robbe qui sent sa petite ville. *A neat, spruce, cleanebrushed gowne, or garment.*
A l'entrée de la ville est le commencement des maisons: Pro. *Looke* Maison.
Il ne sçait rien qui ne va par villes: Prov. *He that goes not abroad knowes nothing.*
Le sainct de la ville n' est point oré: Prov. *The townes peculiar Saint is not prayed to; for helpe that may be had at home we care not.*
Selon la ville les bourgeois: Prov. *Like to the towne the townesmen are.*
Tant de villes tant de guises: Pro. *As many seuerall customes as countrie townes.*
Villebrequin: m. *A Wimble.*
Villein. *as* Villain.
Villenage: m. *Villenage; or any base, and seruile tenure; hence also,* Socage tenure; *or, as* Censive.
Villenaille. *as* Vilenaille.
Villenot: m. *A little villaine, clowne, or swayne; or, as* Vilenot.
Villes de la Vigne: f. *The tendrells, or twyning sprigs, of a Vine.*
Villette: f. *A little Towne, or Citie; also, a little Turrell, or Coopers oagar.*
Villiere: f. *as* Veillere.
Villon: m. *A cousener, conycatcher, cunning, or wittie rogue; a nimble knaue; a pleasant theefe; (for such a one was* Francois Villon, *whose death a halter suited to his life;) also, a kind of weed wherewith bands to tye Vines are made.*
Villonner. *To cousen, cheat, conycatch, play the cunning or wittie rogue; the nimble knaue, the pleasant theefe.*
Villonnerie: f. *A cousening, or conycatching; wittie or cunning roguerie; nimble knauerie; pleasant or merrie theeuerie.*
Villote: f. *A cocke of hay.*
Villoter. *To runne, trot, rogue, roame, raunge; gad, or gossip it from one towne to another.*
Villoteur. *as* Villotier.
Villotier: m. *A vagabond, land-loper, earth-planet, continuall gadder from towne to towne.*
Villotier: m. ere: f. *Towne-bred, home-borne; of, or belonging to, the towne onely.*
Villotiere: f. *A gadding houswife, wandering fisgig, raunging flirt; one that does nothing but runne a gossipping from one towne to another; also, a Bawd.*
Vilonage. *as* Villenage.
Vimaires: f. *Stormes, tempests, any boisterous, and hurtfull weather; inundations, and breaking out, of waters; ruines of buildings; mischieues done by earthquakes, or thunderclaps; any such fearefull, or dommageous accidents, which no reason can foresee, no foresight preuent; Lawyers tearme them* Vis maior.
Vimeres. *as* Vimaires.
Viminal: m. ale: f. *Apt to wind, or bind, as twigs or oziers; also, belonging thereto.*
Saulx viminale. *Looke* Saulx.
Vimpilon: m. *A holie-water sprinkle.*
Vin: m. *Wine.*
Vin ardant. *Aquauite.*
Vins de Bourgongne. *All wines which grow aboue the bridge of* Sens, *in* Auxerrois, Beaune, *and other countries, whose commodities are sent downe by the riuer* Yonne.
Vin des clers. *Fees for expedition; somewhat, aboue ordinarie fees, for the Clarks to drinke.*
Vin de coipeau. *New wine quickly made fit to be drunke, by Beechen chips first boyled then dryed, and af-*

terwards put into the vessell.

Vin de commeres. *Palate wine, sweet and pleasant wine.*

Vin cuict. *Wine boyled on the fire to a certaine thicknesse, and then put into vessells, and reserued for sweet sawces.*

Vin de despense. *Small, houshold, ordinarie, or seruants, wine.*

Vins François. *The wines which grow, or are made, below the bridge of* Sens.

Vin de Lion. *Strong, and headie wine; or, such wine as makes the drinker a swaggerer.*

Vin du marché. *The charge which contractors are at with the witnesses, or confirmers of their bargaine.*

Vin miellé. *Honied wine, bastard, Metheglin, sweet wine; any drinke thats made of honey, and wine.*

Vin muscat. *Muscadell, or Muscadin.*

Vin noir. *Looke* Noir.

Vin papier. *White wine called so by some Switzers.*

Vin de porceau. *Which makes the drunkard to sleepe, vomit, and tumble him in his vomit.*

Vin de pressoirage. *Looke* Pressoirage.

Vin de regnard. *The wine that sharpens, or sets an edge on, the drunkards spirit, making him more subtill, or cunning, then he is, at anytime, sober.*

Vin de singe. *Wine which makes the drinker (or drunkard) pleasant, wanton, or toyish.*

Vin des valets. *Spending pence, extraordinarie vayles or gifts; odde money bestowed on a mans ordinarie seruants, ouer and aboue the summe due, or agreed on.*

Droict de vin, ou de vins, &c. *Looke* Droict.

Entrée de vin és villes closes. *Looke* Entrée.

Pot au vin. *A mans head.*

Pot de vin. *A summe of money; a reward, or gift; also, the dowrie giuen with a maid in marriage.*

Souppe en vin. *The hearbe Meddicke fodder, Snayle-Clauer.*

Avoir son vin. 'A cett' heure il aura son vin. *He will now be tickled, or haue his full payment; he neuer met with his match till now:* Elles ont eu leur vin. *Those wenches haue had it to a haire; viz. a full tast of the sap which they hold most sauorie; (for the bestowing of wine being a principall courtesie in intertainments betweene man and man, is fittest to expresse the other liquor which in courtesie a man giueth a woman.)*

Couper le vin. *See* Couper.

Entrer en vin. *To enter into a drunken match, to fall a drinking.*

Estre sur le vin. *To tast, also, to loue, wine verie well.*

Faire iambes de vin. *To take in store of liquor before the vndertaking of a iourney; to supple his legs, by soaking his head, in wine.*

Mettre de l'eau dedans leur vin. *Looke vnder* Mettre.

Reposer son vin. *To sleepe after a carousing, to disgest his wine by sleeping.*

Vin de grain est plus doux que n' est pas vin de presse: Pro. *Willing seruice, though but small, is more acceptable, then much extorted dutie.*

Le vin n'a point de chausure; &, le vin va sans chausses: Prov. *Wine wanteth, or goeth without, breeches; viz. bewrayeth a mans infirmities, or worst parts; layeth open his shame, or layeth him open to shame.*

Vin pour saveur, drap pour couleur: Pro. *Let wine good sauor, cloth fresh colour, haue; so wine be sauorie, no matter how it looke.*

Vin sur laict c'est souhait, laict sur vin c'est venin: Prov. *Looke* Souhait.

Vin trouble ne brise dents: Prov. *Wine though it be thicke yet breakes it no mans teeth.*

Bon vin bon vinaigre: Pro. *Good wine is made good vineger; good things transform'd retaine part of their worth.*

Bon vin mauvaise teste: Pro. *Good wine breeds many a brable.*

Boy vin en Roy; viz. *temperately*: Pro.

Apres bon vin bon cheval: Prov. *After a man hath drunke hard he dare any thing.*

Qui vin ne boit apres salade est en danger d'estre malade: Pro. *He that wine drinkes not after a (cold) sallate, his health indangers (and does wrong to his pallate.)*

Qui bon vin boit il se repose: Prov. *Looke* Reposer.

Apres la poire le vin, ou le prestre: Prov. *After a (cold) Peare either drinke wine to concoct it, or send for the Priest to confesse you.*

En vaisseau mal lavé ne peut on vin garder: Prov. *Wine in ill-washed Caske will not be kept.*

Femme, argent, & vin, ont leur bien, & leur venin: Prov. *Wine, money, and the female brood haue properties both bad, and good; are (as th' are vsed) bad, or good.*

Homme mutin, brusque roussin, flascon de vin, prennent tost fin: Pro. *The person turbulent, a liuelie steed, and cup of wine, come to an end with speed.*

Il ne faut pas enquerir d' ou soit le vin, mais qu'il soit bon: Pro. *No matter whence wine came so it be good.*

Il ne sçait que c'est de vendre vin qui n' attend de May la fin: Prov. *Against good husbandrie he hath offended, that sells his wines before May be full ended.*

Le boeuf salé fait trouver le vin sans chandelle: Prov. *The salt-beefe eater needs no candle to light his drinke the way to his mouth.*

On ne cognoist pas le vin aux cercles: Prov. *Looke* Cercle.

On ne doit point mentir en vin: Prov. *Somewhat like the Latine,* In vino veritas, *or an aduise to make it good; and then may be rendered thus; when men are drunke they should not lye, because in wine is veritie.*

Pain tant qu'il dure, vin à mesure: Prov. *Eat bread at pleasure, drinke wine by measure: A Precept which the French obserue in the first (howsoeuer in the second) part; for no people eat more bread, nor haue better bread to eat, then they.*

Semelles & du vin passent chemin: Pro. *Looke* Semelle.

Vinade: f. *The vse, and worke of two yoake of Oxen, or of a Cart, all the time of Vintage.*

Vinage: m. *A Phisicall wine, or a decoction of hearbes in wine, to be drunke for the curing of vlcers, and wounds.*

Droict de vinage. *Looke* Droict.

Vinaigre: m. *Vineger.*

'A nez frotté de vinaigre. *Of a sharpe conceit, or foresight, of a quicke apprehension; a metaphor from Huntsmen, who to make their dogs quick-sented, rub their noses with vineger.*

Ie le feray chier vinaigre. *I will make him starke mad.*

Vinaigrette: f. *Sorrell sawce.*

Vinaigrettes. *Sallets, or sawces, which be seasoned with much vineger; any hearbs, or fruits in pickle.*

Vinaigrier: m. *A Vineger-man, or Vineger-maker; also, a Vineger glasse, violl, or bottle.*
Vinatier: m. *A Barberrie tree; or the Barberrie it selfe.*
Vincibosse: m. *Woodbind, Caprifolie, Hony suckle.*
Vincent. *Vincent, a mans name; and particularly, the name of a Saint, for whom, in some places, a holyday is made the 22 of Januarie; whence the Prouerbe;*
'A la S. Vincent si l'hyver s'engrine, si l'attends. *If the wind blow sharpe on S. Vincents day, looke for a cold later part of a Winter.*
Vindicatif: m. iue: f. *Vindicatiue, reuenging, wreakefull, auengefull.*
Vindice: f. *Reuenge, auengement, vengeance, punishment.*
Vindicte: f. *as* Vindice.
Vindiquer. *To redeeme, deliuer, exempt, saue from; also, to reuenge, auenge, wreake.*
Vindre. *A kind of long Hooke, or Crampiron, full of notches.*
Viné: m. ée: f. *Seasoned with, or for the holding of, wine; also, tunned as wine.*
Vinée: f. *The fruit, or profit of a Vineyard; a crop of Grapes; whence;*
Avoir bonne vinée. *To find a good Vintage, to gather or get in store of wine.*
Vinenotte. *as* Vivelotte.
Viner. *To season with, or for the holding of, wine; also, to tunne wine.*
Vinet: m. *Small or thinne wine, hedge wine.*
Vinetier: m. *as* Vinotier; *also, the Barberrie tree.*
Vinette: f. *Sorrell, or Sowre-docke; also, the Barberrie, or Barberrie tree.*
Vinetteux: m. *A Vintner; but in* Rabelais *the name of a Cooke.*
Vineux: m. euse: f. *Winie, of wine, full of wine, proceeding from wine.*
Vingeron. *as* Vengeron.
Vingt. *Twentie; a skore.*
Vingtain, & Vingtenier. *Looke* Vintain, & Vintenier.
Vingtiesme: m. *A twentieth, or twentieth part of; whence,* Droict de vingtiesme. *Looke* Droict.
Vingtiesme. *The twentieth.*
Vinoble. *as* Vignoble.
Vinot: m. *as* Vinet; *also, a kind of little Peare, the Perrie whereof doth tast like wine.*
Vinotier: m. *A Vintner, Tauerner, Wine-seller.*
Vinotier: m. ere: f. *Of, or belonging to, wine; also, bringing, or yeelding wine.*
Vintain: m. *A twentieth; or a twentieth part of.*
Vintenier: m. *The Corporall to a foot-companie.*
Vin-verjus: m. *Veriuice, made of wild, or vnripe, Grapes.*
Vioge: com. *Lustie, liuelie, cranke, frolicke.* ¶Norm.
Violable: com. *Violable, infringible, breakeable; deflowrable, defilable, pollutable.*
Violant. Le gris violant. *Mallow-flower colour; or, a colour betweene a Grey, and a Violet.*
Violat. *Of Violets.*
Violateur: m. *A violator; infringer, transgressor; a corrupter, defiler, deflowrer; wrong-doer, abuser.*
Violation: f. *A violation, or violating; a breaking, transgressing, infringing; also, a corrupting, defiling, deflowring; wronging, misusing, abusing.*
Viole. *as* Violle; *also, a Gilliflower; whence;*
Viole iaulne. *The Winter Gilloflower, or Wallflower.*

Violé: m. ée: f. *Violated; broken, transgressed, infringed; corrupted, defiled, deflowred; wronged, misused, abused.*
Violement: m. *A violating; or, as* Violation.
Violemment. *Violently, impetuously, forcibly, compulsiuely, vehemently, fiercely, ragingly.*
Violence: f. *Violence; impetuousnesse; vniust force, or compulsion; wrong; rashnesse, fiercenesse; vehemencie.*
Violent: m. ente: f. *Violent, impetuous, vehement; forcible, compulsiue; raging, fierce.*
Violenté: m. ée: f. *Violated, or violented; vsed or handled violently; forced.*
Violentement. *as* Violemment.
Violenter. *as* Violer; *also, to force, or breake into by force.*
Se violenter soy mesme. *To vse violence against, lay violent hands on, himselfe; to murther himselfe.*
Violer. *To violate; infringe, transgresse; to marre, corrupt, defile, deflowre; to wrong, hurt, misuse, abuse.*
Violet: m. *as* Violette; *a Violet-colour.*
Violet de sel. *A certaine rustie colour brought from the salt-pits of Germanie, and of a brackish tast.*
Violet: m. ette: f. *Violet of colour.*
Violette: f. *A Violet; also, a Gilliflower; also, Violet-colour; also, as* Luette; *whence,* Violette abaissée. *The falling of the Vvula.*
Violette arborée. *The vpright Paunsie, or Hearts-ease.*
Violette d'Automne. *The Paunsie, or Hearts-ease; also, the Calathian Violet, blue haruest Lillie, Autumne Bell-flower, Haruest-bell.*
Violette blanche. *The white Violet; also, the white flocke Gilloflower; also, the timely-flourishing Bulbus Violet.*
Violette de caresme. *as* Violette de Mars.
Violettes de Damas. *Damaske Violets, or Gilloflowers, rogues Gilloflowers, close sciences.*
Violettes de Dames. *Dames Violets, &c, as* Violettes de Damas.
Violettes herbuës. *Pinkes, or small Honesties.*
Violette iaulne. *The Wall-flower; the yellow, or Winter Gilloflower.*
Violettes de Marie. *Marians Violets, Couentrie Bells, Couentrie Rapes; of the kind, qualitie, and (almost) the forme of Throatworts, or Canterburie bells.*
Violette de Mars. *The ordinarie Violet, March Violet, Garden Violet, sweet Violet.*
Violettes des Matrones. *as* Violettes de Damas.
Brune violette. *A kind of darke Purple of the colour of an Amethist.*
Clere violette. *A Murrey; or (as some hold) a light Red.*
Violier: m. *A Fidler, or common Musition, that playes on a Violin; also, a Violet root, or plant; also, a Flower-pot; also, the crowne of Ozier, &c, which they set ouer pots of Gilloflowers, to strengthen the staulkes thereof.*
Violier des murailles. *The plant that beares the Wall-flower, or Winter Gilloflower.*
Violle: f. *A (Musicall) Viol, or Violin.*
Violon: m. *A Violin, or little Violl.*
Viorne: f. *The Hedge-plant called, the Trauellers ioy; also, the Hedge-tree called, the Way-faring tree; (both verie common in Kent;) also, a shoot, or sprig putting vp from the root of a tree.*
Viotrant. *as* Veautrant. ¶Rab.
Viouche: com. *Of long life; or, as* Vioge, *liuelie, &c, (an old word.)*
Vipere: f. *The Serpent called a Viper.*

Herbe aux Viperes. *Vipers hearbe, Snakes Buglosse, Vipers Buglosse, wild Buglosse the lesse.*
Vipereau: m. *A young, or little Viper.*
Viperiere: f. *as* Herbe aux Viperes.
Viperillon: m. *A young, or small Viper.*
Viperin: m. ine: f. *Viperous, of a Viper.*
Sel viperin. *Looke vnder* Sel.
Viquerie: f. *as* Vicairie; *or, as* Viguerie.
Virade: f. *A whirling, or swift turning about.*
Carte, ou Charte virade. *The Dutch Card-game called, Hocke.*
Viraire. *Looke* Veraire.
Vire: f. *The arrow called a Quarrell; vsed onely for the Crosse-bow.*
Virebrequin: m. *A Wimble.*
Virecots: m. *Little bundles, or packets of grapes made vp in Fig-leaues, and thereby long kept.*
Virelay: m. *A Virelay, Round, freemans Song.*
Virelis: m. *A Periwinkle; or, as* Nerites.
Virement: m. *A veering, whirling, wheeling, round turning, frisking about.*
Virer. *To veere, turne round, wheele or whirle about.*
De quelque costé que le bast vire. *Howsoeuer things be carried, which way soeuer the world waggeth.*
Mau de terre te vire. *The foule euill take, or choake, thee.*
Vire-soli. *as* Herbe au soleil.
Vireson: m. *One of the last, and least receptacles for the sea-water, whereof salt is made.*
Vireton: m. *A little Quarrell; or, a fashion of arrow-head, thats turned, or made, like a skrue.*
Virevolte. *as* Virevoulte.
Virevolter. *Looke* Virevoulter.
Virevoulte: f. *A veere, whirle, round gamboll, friske, or turne.*
Virevoulter. *To veere, whirle, turne or wheele round about, fetch many a friske about.*
Virevouste. *as* Virevoulte.
Vireur: m. *A veerer, or whirler, a round turner, or turner of things often about.*
Vireurs d'aumelettes. *Pancake-turners, Omelet-makers; Looke* Aumelette.
Vireux: m. euse: f. *Ranke, strong-smelling, rammish of sauor; also, poysonous.*
Virgeal. *as* Virginal.
Virginal: m. ale: f. *Virgine-like, maidenlie, belonging to a virgin or maid.*
Huile virginal. *Virgines oyle; the oyle which of it selfe, and without any pressing, comes from Oliues.*
Laict virginal. *See* Laict.
Virgineux: m. euse: f. *as* Virginal.
Virginité. *Virginitie, maidenhead, or maidenhood.*
Virgule: f. *A little rod, yard; streake; and thence also, a comma.*
Virgulte: m. *A bunch of young, and tender shootes; a companie of sprigs, or sprouts growing together.*
Viridique: com. *Looke* Veridique.
Viril: m. ile: f. *Virile, manlie, manlike, manfull, male; bold, stout, couragious, valiant; strong, substantiall, pithie; graue.*
Virilement. *Manly, manfully; boldly, stoutly; pithily, substantially; grauely.*
Virilité: f. *Virilitie, manlinesse, manfullnesse; strength, vigor; stoutnesse, courage; also, a mans genitalls.*
Virlis. *as* Virelis.
Virole: f. *An yron ring put about the end of a staffe, &c, to strengthen it, and keepe it from riuing.*
Virolet: m. *as* Ventail, *a boyes windmill; also, a shittlecocke; also, an arrow-head; also, a sword with an indented edge; also, a piercer; also, a mans yard.*
Virollé: m. ée: f. *Bound about with an yron ring, or hoope.*
Virollette: f. *A sword with an indented edge.*
Viron. *(Vsed in some parts of France) as* Environ.
Vironnant: m. ante: f. *Veering, enuironning, turning or winding about.*
Vironner. *To veere, enuiron; turne, goe, or wind about.*
Virulence: f. *Stench, ranknesse, rammishnesse; poison, venomousnesse.*
Vis: m. *The visage, &c, as* Visage.
Vis à vis. *Face to face; directly opposite, right ouer against.*
Au vis le vice: Pro. *Our faults may be read in our faces; our visage telleth what our vices be.*
Vis: f. *The vice, or spindle of a Presse; also, a winding staire.*
Vis brisée. *A staire which hauing four or fiue steps vpright, then turnes, and hath as many forward another way.*
Vis S. Gilles. *A fashion of winding staire, thats vaulted all vnder the steps.*
Vis à iour. *Another consisting of many steps, and yet so contriued, that a man may from the highest discerne the lowest.*
Visa. *A word written by the Lord Chauncelor on the backside of Edicts, and Charters, to signifie his examination, and approbation of them; tis also vsed by the Patrons of Benefices, or by Ordinaries, or Diocesans, for the allowance, or in the behalfe, of such, as come into Spirituall Cures, &c, by Prouision.*
Visadmiral: m. *A Viceadmirall.*
Visage: m. *The visage, face, looke, cheere, countenance, aspect of a man.*
Visage d'appelant. *A sad, heauie, pittifull, or cheerelesse looke.*
Visage de bois faict à. *A doore shut against.*
Visage de preslurier. *A mustulent, or maumsie face.*
Visage de rebec. *A sneake-bill, sharp-nose, chitiface.*
Faux visage. *A Maske, or Visard.*
Homme à deux visages. *A dissembler, or double-dealer; one that seldome keepes promise, or is neuer as good as his word; whence the Prouerbe;*
Homme à deux visages n'agrée en villes, ne villages. *A man that hath a double visage is neither lou'd in towne, nor village; dissembling is a hatefull sinne.*
Mot à deux visages. *A word of a doubtfull sence, or double vnderstanding; an equiuocation.*
Pois à visage. *Looke* Pois.
Vent au visage: Pro. *Aduersitie, crosses; Looke vnder* Vent.
Couché sur son visage. *Layed groueling.*
Rouge visage, & grosse pance, ne sont signes de penitence: Prov. *He that a red face hath, and swollen guts, his bodie vnto pennance little puts.*
Visant. *Ayming, leuelling at.*
Visc: m. *Missell, Misseltoe, Misseldine; also, Birdlime (which is commonly made of Misseltoe.)*
Visceral: m. ale: f. *Inward, of or from the bowels.*
Viscide: com. *Clammie, cleauing, Birdlime-like.*
Viscidité: f. *Viscidit̃ie; or, as* Viscosité.
Viscosité: f. *Viscositie; a Birdlime-like slyminesse, clamminesse, or cleauing.*
Visduché: f. *A Vice-Duchie, or Vice-Dukedome.*
Visée: f. *A leuelling, or ayming at with the eye; also, a leuell, or ayme taken.*
Il ne tiroit iamais sans visée. *He neuer shot at randon.*

Pour bien tirer il faut prendre visée: Prov. *Take ayme with thy sight if thou meane to shoot right; ere thou thy arrow doe let fly, let th' hand be guided by thy eye; he that will preuayle must proceed by aduise.*
Viseneschal. *as* Vibailli; *or, an vnder steward.*
Viser. *To ayme, or leuell at with the eye; also, to regard, or heed.*
Qui vise loing, iamais ne rend son coup heureux: Pro. *as vnder* Coup.
Tousiours ne frappe l'on pas ce à quoy l'on vise: Pro. *One alwayes gets not that he aspires vnto.*
Viseur: m. *An aymer, or leueller.*
Visible: com. *Visible, discernable, euident, apparant.*
Visiblement. *Visibly, discernably, euidently.*
Visiere: f. *The viser, or sight of an helmet.*
Visiere meurtriere. *A Port-hole for a murthering Peece in the forecastle of a ship.*
Vision: f. *A vision, sight, apparition, fantasie; also, a viewing, or perusing.*
Visitation: f. *A visitation, visiting; view, suruey, ouerseeing.*
La visitation de nostre Dame. *The feast of the Visitation of our Ladie, celebrated, among the Papists, on the second of July.*
Visité: f. *as* Visitation.
Visiter. *To visit, or goe to see; to view, suruey, ouerlooke, ouersee.*
Visiteur: m. *A visitor, searcher, ouerseer.*
Le grand visiteur de France. *The great Visitor of France: is no Officer of the Crowne, nor (how great soeuer his Title be) more then a bare minister of Justice; being subiect vnto the ordinarie Judge of the place wherein he visits, and of himselfe determining nothing: In old time he was called* Le Roy des Merciers, *which Title the last King changed into this,* Anno 1597.
Visine: m. *A Willow, or Wicker twig.*
Visqueux: m. euse: f. *Viscous, clammie, cleauing, birdlyme-like.*
Esprit visqueux. *A captious wit.*
Viste: com. *Swift, quicke, flightie, speedie, nimble, suddaine, hastie.*
Viste en besongne. *Readie, or quicke, at worke; fit, or apt for a suddaine dispatch; also, craftie, subtill, sly, warie.*
Plus viste que le mot. *In lesse time done then spoken of; done before one could haue said, this.*
Viste-courant. *Swift, or light of foot; that seemes to fly as he runnes.*
Vistement. *Quickly, speedily, readily, swiftly, nimbly; hastily, suddainely, immediately, incontinently.*
Vistempenard: m. *A Duster made of a Fox-taile fastened vnto a staffe.*
Vistempenardé: m. ée: f. *Dusted, or flapped with a Fox-tayle; also, raggedly, vilely, or basely attired.*
Vistesse: f. *Swiftnesse, quicknesse, lightnesse, nimblenesse, speed, hast, suddainesse.*
Visual: m. ale: f. *Visuall, of or belonging to the sight; also, carried by the sight, or extending as farre as the eye can carrie it.*
Visuel: m. elle: f. *Giuing, or causing sight; also, as* Visual *(in the later sence.)*
Visum visu. ¶Rab. *as* Vis à vis.
Visure: f. *The side betweene the vpper leather, and the sole of a corked shooe; the rand of a shooe.*
Vit: m. *A mans yard; a beasts pizle.*
Vit de caille. *A Rayle.*
Vit de chien. *as* Vit de prestre.
Vit de coq. *A Woodcocke.*
Vits de gouvernail. *The Pintles, or yron hooks whereby the sterne of a ship doth hang.*
Vit de mer. *An ouglie creature, or excrescence, like to the end of a mans yard.*
Vit de prestre. *Priests-Pintle, hearbe Aaron, Cuckoe-Pintle, Wake-Robin, Rampe.*
Vit volant. *as* Pennache de mer.
Vitailler. *To handle, dallie, or play with, a P.*
Vital: m. ale: f. *Vitall, liuelie, likelie to liue; also, bringing, breeding, maintaining, or preseruing, life.*
Vitault: m. *A great toole, or, one that hath a good toole; also, a flattering word for a young boy, like our, my prettie pillicocke; whence,* Mon vitault.
Vite: f. *A womans &c.*
Vitellin: m. ine: f. *Of or belonging to the yolke of an egge.*
Cholere vitelline. *A kind of choller bred by a rotten or vnnaturall heat, and resembling, both in colour and consistence, the yolkes of egges.*
Saulx vitelline. *Looke* Saulx.
Vitette: f. *A verie little pricke, bable, member.*
Vitez. *The shrub Agnus castus, Abrahams Balme, Chasttree, Hemp-tree.* ¶Rab.
Vitier. *Looke* Vicier.
Vitieux. *as* Vicieux.
Vitrage: m. *Glasse, Glasse-worke, or Glasing worke.*
Vitre: f. *Glasse, or a Glasse-window.*
Vitres. *The squares, or mashes of a racket; (from the resemblance they haue with quarries of Glasse.)*
Vitré: m. ée: f. *Glased; couered or done ouer with glasse; also, glazed, or varnished as the inside of an earthen vessell.*
Vitreau: m. *A Glasse-window.*
Vitrée: f. *The bird called a Whittayle.*
Vitreole: f. *Small Withywind, Hedgebells, Bindweed; also, the blacke purging Bindweed.*
Vitrer. *To glase; to stop, couer, or doe ouer, with glasse; also, to varnish the inside of a vessell of earth, &c.*
Vitrerie: f. *A glasing, or Glasse-making.*
Vitreux: m. euse: f. *Glassie, of Glasse, full of Glasse; cleere, transparent, or brittle as Glasse.*
Humeur vitreuse. *The glassie humor in the (hinder part of) the eye.*
Vitrice: m. *A stepfather, or father in law.* ¶Rab.
Vitrier: m. *A Glasier, or worker in Glasse.*
Vitrification: f. *Glassinesse, or the making of Glasse.*
Vitrifier. *To turne, or make into Glasse.*
Vitriol: m. *Vitrioll, Copperose; also, Pellitorie of the wall.*
Vitriol d'Allemagne. *German Vitrioll; worse then the Roman, as hauing somewhat of yron in it.*
Vitriol d'Hongrie. *Hungarie Vitrioll; naturall (and thereby the best) Copperose.*
Vitriol Romain. *Roman Vitrioll; Copperose; made of such like stuffe as glase is.*
Vitriole. *as* Vitreole.
Vitriolique: com. *Like Vitrioll, of Copperose.*
Vitte: f. *A womans &c.*
Vitulos. *The last word of a Latine Psalme of Mercie, which beginning with the word* Miserere, *hath bred the phrase,* Tu auras du miserere iusques à vitulos, *for one thats to be whipped extreamely, or a long time.*
Vituperable: com. *Vituperable.*
Vituperation: f. *A vituperation, or dispraising.*
Vitupere: m. *Dispraise, discommendation; disparagement; reprehension, blame.*
Vituperé: m. ée: f. *Vituperated; dispraised; blamed.*

Vituperer. *To vituperate, dispraise, discommend; reproach, disparage, dishonour, blame, reprehend, find fault with.*

Vitupereur: m. *A dispraiser, discommender; disparager, disgracer; blamer, fault-finder.*

Vitus. *whence,* Mal S. Vitus. *Looke* Mal.

Vivace: com. *Liuelie, lustie, strong, vigorous; nimble, actiue, quicke; full of life, mettall, spirit; also, of long life.*

Vivacité: f. *Viuacitie, liuelinesse, lustinesse, vigor, strength; spirit, mettall; actiuitie, quicknesse, nimblenesse; iollitie, gaynesse of humor.*

Vivacité d'esprit. *Wittinesse, quicknesse of apprehension, sharpnesse of conceit.*

Vivandier: m. *A Victualler, Suttler, Prouaunt-men.*

Vivant: m. *whence,* De son vivant. *In his life-time, while he liued.*

Vivant: m. ante: f. *Liuing, breathing, aliue, in life.*

Homme vivant mourant. *Looke* Homme.

Vive: f. *The Quauiuer, or sea-Dragon.*

Vivelle: f. *A huge kind of Whall in the Indian seas.*

Vivelote, ou Vivelotte; *whence,* Droict de v. *The dower which is due to the widow of a* Cottier, *or tenant of* Mainferme.

Vivement. *Liuelily, quickly, lightly, sprightfully, vigorously.*

Vivenote, ou Vivenotte. *as* Vivelote, &c.

Vivifiant: m. ante: f. *Quickning, life-giuing.*

Vivifier. *To quicken, or giue life vnto.*

Vivifique: com. *Which quickeneth, or giueth life.*

Vivoter. *To liue poorely, barely, needily, or but from hand to mouth; to make hard shift for a liuing; to keepe the wolfe from the dore.*

Vivre: m. *A liuing, meanes, maintenance; meat, food, sustenance; any thing whereon we feed, or liue.*

Vivres. *Victualls; acates.*

Quint de vivre naturel. *See* Quint.

Les vivres suivent l'host: Prov. *Victualls follow the Campe; where store of companie is victualls will be.*

Vivré: m. ée: f. *(in Blason;)* Il fortoit d'or à la bande vivrée d'argent. *A bend Viurie.*

Vivre. *To liue, haue life, be aliue; to lead, or spend a life; to breath.*

Vivre en beste. *(In the Prouerbe,* Tenez chaud le pied & la teste, au reste vivez en beste;*) to eat moderately, or no more then will serue the turne.*

Vivre à la Carlonne. *To vse a homelie, rude, or plaine course of proceeding; to liue grossely or plainly, to deale open-heartedly.*

Vivre à discretion. *To liue at what rate they list, to pay for their dyet what they list.*

Vivre par estapes. *Looke* Estape.

Vivre à ses heures. *To liue regularly, to keepe a temperate, or set dyet; to prescribe to himselfe a certaine forme of, or time for, his ordinarie feeding.*

Se vivre. *In stead of,* se paistre. *To feed, or victuall, himselfe.*

Assez ieune qui povrement vit: Pro. *Enough he fasts that barely feeds.*

Celuy sçait assez qui vit bien: Prov. *He that liues well enough hath skill enough.*

Il est bien fol qui cuide tousiours vivre: Prov. *He that thinkes to liue euer is an Asse.*

L'un meurt dont l'autre vit: Prov. *That which preserues one man poysons another.*

Qui vit à compte, il vit à honte: Pro. *See* Compte.

Qui a honte de manger a honte de vivre: Prov. *Shame to eat, and cease to liue; A taxation of vnseasonable bashfullnesse, and not much vnlike our,* Spare to *speake and spare to speed.*

Qui bien veut mourir bien vive: Prov. *He that desires to dye, let him liue well.*

Qui plus vit plus a à souffrir: Pro. *The longer life the greater griefe.*

Viz: f. *as* Vis.

Vlceraire: f. *Crowfoot; also, Horehound; (hearbes.)*

Vlceratif: m. iue: f. *Vlceratiue, vlcerating, vlcer-breeding.*

Vlceration: f. *An vlceration; a making or growing vlcerous, a drawing to an vlcer.*

Vlcere: m. *An vlcer; a raw scab; a running, or mattarie sore.*

Vlcere ambulatif. *Seeke* Ambulatif.

Vlcerer. *To vlcerate, exulcerate; exasperate; raise a blister; make a raw scab, draw to a running sore.*

Vligineux: m. euse: f. *Wet, plashie, sobbie, full of water; full soaked, or growne soft, by a long abode in water.*

Vlmeau: m. *A young Elme.*

Vlne: f. *An Ell, or fadome; also, a cubit.*

Vlophone. *A venomous glue, or clammie substance, made of Misseltoe berries; some call so the blacke Cameleon thistle, whose root is also venomous.*

Vlpic: m. *Great, or wild Garlick.*

Vltime: com. *Last, lag, finall, extreame; the furthest, or furthermost.*

Vltion: f. *A reuenging, auenging, taking vengeance of; a punishing.*

Vlulement: m. *A howling, or yelling.*

Vmbelle de fenouil. *The vmble, or the round tuft, or head wherein the seed thereof growes.*

Vmbilic: m. *The nauell, or middle, of.*

Vmbilical: m. ale: f. *Vmbilicall, belonging to the nauell; whence,* Veine vmbilicale. *Seeke* Veine.

Vmble: m. *The Geneua Trout, or Salmon; found in the Lakes of Sauoy.*

Vmble chevalier. *A kind of fresh-water Trout, or Salmon, bigger then the ordinarie* Vmble.

Vmbragé, & Vmbrager. *Looke* Ombragé, & Ombrager.

Vmbre: f. *as* Ombre; *also, an Omber, or Grayling; a fish (not much vnlike the* Maigre.*)*

Vmbre de riviere. *A big-bellied, sharp-nosed, toothlesse, delicate, and wholesome Trout, found in the lakes, and riuers of* Auvergne, *and* Savoy.

Vmbrette: f. *A little Omber, or Grayling fish.*

Vmbrine: f. *A great-eyed, round-tongued, small-toothed, and holesome sea-fish, which hath certaine barres ouercrosse her backe, and growing often to the bignesse of a* Maigre, *is sometimes taken for it.*

Vmbroyer. *To be in the shadow; also, to cast, or yeeld a shadow.*

Vn: m. vne: f. *One, a; In the plurall sometimes vsed for some; whence,* Les vns; *some of them; and,* vnes verges; *some rodds.*

Deux pour vn. *The Snyte-knaue; tearmed so, because two of them are worth but one good Snyte.*

En avoir d'une. *To be gulled, or to swallow a gudgeon.*

Donner d'une. *To tell a lye; to giue a lurch, or dry list; to gull, or make a foole of.*

L'un portant l'autre. *One with, or for another; good and bad together.*

Commun n'est pas vn: Pro. *See* Commun.

Qui n'en a qu'un, n'en a point: Prov. *(Meant of Cocks, Bulls, &c, and sometimes alledged by lasciuious women) as good haue none as haue no more but one.*

Vnanime: com. *Of one mind, heart, will, consent, accord; agreeing fully together.*
Vnanimement. *With one mind,&c; with full consent, or agreement.*
Vnde. *Looke* Onde.
Vndé. *as* Ondé; *also,in Blason,vndie,or wauie.*
Vndecimestre. *Of eleuen moneths.*
Vndiculation: f. *A wauing, or water-worke, in Imagerie, or caruing.*
Vndimie: f. *as* Oedeme.
Vnguent. *Looke* Onguent.
Vnguenteux: m. euse: f. *Full of oyntments,or salues; oylie, greasie, fattie.*
Vni: m. ie: f. *Iust,euen, equall, plaine; smooth; also,vnited, or ioyned together.*
Vnicorne: f. *An Vnicorne.*
Vniement: m. *An euenning,equalling, planing; a making iust,or leuell,with another.*
Vniément. *Equally, euenly, plainely, smoothly, iust one with another.*
Vniesme: com. *The first; the one, or onth.*
Vniforme: com. *Vniforme; of one forme, proportion, shape, or fashion.*
Vniformement. *Vniformely, with one order, in one manner.*
Vniformité: f. *Vniformitie; agreement in forme, proportion, shape, fashion,manner, order.*
Vniment: m. *An vniting,ioyning,or knitting together.*
Vniment. *With one accord.*
Vnion: f. *An vnion,or vnitie; a league, peace, consent, agreement,attonement.*
Vnipare: com. *Breeding, or bringing forth, but one at once.*
Vnique: com. *Single, singular, one,onelie, alone; entire; especiall.*
Vniquement. *Singly, singularly, entirely; chiefely, especially; onely,alone.*
Vnir. *To vnite,ioyne,annex or knit vnto, make one of.*
Vnisonnant: m. ante: f. *Sounding alike, according, or agreeing in sound, of one and the same sound.*
Vnisonnement. *All with one sound, voice, accord; in good harmonie.*
Vnisson: f. *An vnison; an one; an onelynesse, or lonelynesse; a single, or singlenesse.*
Vnité: f. *An vnitie, singlenesse, concord, agreement, attonement; an vnion, vniting,or ioyning of things together.*
Vnivers. L'vn. *The vniuerse, or vniuersall world.*
Vniversel: m. elle: f. *Vniuersall,common,generall,belonging to all.*
Vniversellement. *Vniuersally, generally, wholly,altogether.*
Vniversité: f. *Vniuersitie,vniuersalitie, generallnesse; also,an Vniuersitie.*
Vnivoque: com. *Simple, of one onely sence,or signification.*
Vnziesme: m. *An eleuenth; a rate,or proportion of eleuen.*
Vnziesme: com. L'vn. *The eleuenth in number.*
Voarre: m. *A glasse; or glasse.*
Voarrerie: f. *A Glasse-house.*
Voarrier: m. *A Glasier; or Glasse-maker.*
Voarriere: f. *A Glasse-window; also,as* Voarrerie.
Vocable: m. *A word, a tearme.*
Vocabulaire: m. *A Vocabularie,Dictionarie,world of words.*
Vocal: m. ale: f. *vocall; belonging to, or consisting in, the voice; also,well-tuned,that maketh a distinct sound; and,resounding,or that hath a lowd voice.*
Oiseau vocale. *A bird which may be taught to speake.*
Vocale: f. *A vowell.*
Vocalizé: m. ée: f. *Vowelled,made a vowell.*
Vocation: f. *A vocation,a calling.*
Vociferation: f. *A vociferation,exclamation, braying, lowd crying.*
Vociferer. *To exclaime,bray,cry out,cry alowd.*
Vociter. *To call often.*
Voeu: m. *A vow, religious promise,deepe or deuout protestation.*
Vogue: f. *Vogue, sway, swindge; authoritie, power; a cleere passage, as of a ship in a broad sea.*
Vne vogue de faveur de peu de durée. *A geere of fauor, momentarie grace.*
Voguement: m. *A sayling forth,or forward; a parting or passing along vnder sayle.*
Voguer. *To sayle forth, or forward; to set sayle, hoyse vp sayles, put forth vnto the sea; to part or passe along vnder sayle.*
Vogue avant. *On a Gods name,on forward,on afore.*
Vogue la gallere. *See* Gallere.
Voici. *See here,looke here,behold here.*
Voicture, & Voicturier. *See* Voiture, & Voiturier.
Voïe. *See* Voye.
Voïer. *Looke* Voyer.
Voilà. *Looke, see, loe, behold, there.*
Voilà ce que ie demande. *Why thats the thing I aske.*
Ie croy que voilà le plus propre. *This is, as I thinke, the fittest.*
Voile: m. *A Vayle; (vsed by Nunnes, widowes, or churched women:) also, a curtaine or other cloth to couer, or lay ouer, a thing.*
Voile: f. *The sayle of a ship; also, a sayle, or ship; whence,* 200 voiles; *200 ships, or sayle of ships.*
`A voile desployée. *With sayles displayed; hastily, speedily, furiously; with might and maine, as fast and as much as one can.*
`A voile rancade. *See* Rancade.
Friand à la voile. Navire friand à la voile. *A ship that goes exceeding well and swiftly, an excellent sayler.*
Donner (ou faire) voile à tous vents. *To sayle with, or be carried by, euerie wind; to doe alwayes as others doe; also, to be transported by euerie windie motion of his owne vaine thoughts.*
Faire voile. *To set sayle, to make out to sea, &c.*
Voilé: m. ée: f. *Vayled; attired in, or couered with, a vayle; also, professed, as a Nunne; also, furnished with sayles.*
Voiler. *To vayle; to couer with, or attire in, a vayle; also, to make a Nunne of; also, to excuse, ouershadow, hide, conceale.*
Voilier: m. ere: f. *Of a sayle, hauing sayles.*
Voir: m. *Truth, a true tale or matter, sooth.* (v.m.)
Voir. *To see; Looke* Veoir.
Voire. *But, yea but; surely, certainely; verily, indeed; forsooth; also.*
Voire Dea. *(Ironically) yes forsooth, yea ywis, much, as though, in my tother hose.*
Voire voirement s'il n'estoit point ainsi. *As though forsooth it were not so; or by your fauor sir it was euen so.*
Il s'est mocqué de moy, voire il m'a batu. *He mocked me, yea and beat me to; or, he gaue me both quips and cuts, both mockes and stroakes, to boot.*
Voirement. *Surely, certainely, verily; forsooth; indeed.*

Voirie: f. *Iurisdiction,&c*; *as* Iustice; *whence*; Grande voirie. *Meane Iurisdiction*; *or as,* La moyenne Iustice; &, simple voirie. *Base, or low Iurisdiction.*

Voirie: f. *A way, path, road, or street*; *also, the laystall of a towne*; *the place whereon all the dung, and filth of a towne is layed, or vnloaden*; *(In which sence it is much vsed plurally.)*

Gens de voirie. *Scauingers, dung-farmers, goldfiners.*

Voiriefier. Allez voiriefier. *A Parisien equiuocation vpon* Allez vous y fier; *trust to it if you list*; *and vsed in detestation of a filthie, or dunghillike thing.*

Voirre: m. *Glasse.*

Voirre dormant. *Looke vnder* Dormant.

Voirré: m. ée: f. *Glassie, of glasse.*

Voirrier: m. *A Glasier.*

Voirriere: f. *A glasse window*; *glasse-worke.*

Voirrin: m. ine: f. *Glassie, of glasse*; *also, transparent.*

Voirrine: f. *as* Voirriere.

Voirrinier: m. *A Glasier*; *a Glasse-maker*; *a worker in glasse.*

Voise, voisent. Qu'il s'en voise; qu'ils s'en voisent. *Let him, or them, goe.*

Voisin: m. *A neighbor.*

Bien a en sa maison qui de ses voisins est aimé: Pro. *He that hath neighbors loue liues well at home.*

Bon advocat mauvais voisin: Pro. *The best Lawyer is the worst neighbor*; *those that know most are worst to dwell by.*

Qui a bon voisin a bon matin: Pro. *He that hath a good neighbor gets good words.*

Tenir ne faut pour bon voisin vn ami de table, & de vin: Pro. *Trencher friends are seldome good neighbors*; *they will feast it, but not fast it with you*; *or when your prouision fayles them, their companie fayles you.*

Voisin: m. ine: f. *Neighbouring, or neere vnto*; *hard by, not farre off*; *also, verie like vnto.*

Voisinage: m. *Neighbourhood, nighnesse, neerenesse.*

En mauvais voisinage se loge on: Prov. *The poorest swad affoords a pad: ill neighbours may be lodg'd among.*

Voisinal: m. ale: f. *Neighbouring, or neighbourlie.*

Chemin voisinal. *as vnder* Chemin.

Tesmoings voisinaux. *Which dwell neere the land, &c, in controuersie.*

Voisinance: f. *Neerenesse, neighborhood.*

Voisiné: m. Ceux du voisiné. *The neighbors, or those that dwell thereabouts.*

Voisine: f. *A she neighbour*; *whence the Prouerb*; Pour grasse que soit la geline, elle a besoing de sa voisine; *The fattest henne within the coope, without good neighbours will soone droope.*

Voisiner. *To be neighbour, nigh, neere, or adioyning, vnto*; *also, to gossip it, or goe to visit neighbours.*

Voistrer. *Looke* Veautrer.

Voiture: f. *Carriage, portage, fraight, loading*; *also, a load, Carte-full, or Cart-full.*

Voituré: m. ée: f. *Carried by Cart, &c.*

Voiturer. *To carrie by Cart, Waine, Wagon, &c.*

Bien voiturer sa viande. *Throughly to disgest, (or, as we say, to shake downe) his meat by trauell, or exercise.*

Voiturier: m. *A Carrier (especially by Waine, or Wagon) a Waine-man, or Wagon-man.*

Voix: f. *A voyce*; *a sound, noise, tune, word, crie*; *a repercussion of th'aire*; *talke, bruit, report.*

Avoir voix en chapitre. *To be heard attentiuely and with respect*; *to be of authoritie, or beare some sway, in a publike assemblie.*

Ie n'en ay eu vent, ny voix. *I neuer heard the least word of it.*

Vol: m. *A flight, or flying*; *a quicke running, speedie passage, hastie course*; *also, a robbing, or stripping by the high-way side*; *also, a Lure, in Blason.*

Le vol du chapon. *Is by the customes of* Clermont, Orleans, Berri, le Perche, Blois, Romorantin, Leuroux, & Trembleui, *an* Arpent; *by those of* Chasteauneuf, *an* Arpent *and a halfe*; *by those of* S. Aignan, Chabris, & Auvergne, *a* septerée; *and by those of* Anjou, *and* le Maine 320 *single paces, of the ground lying next vnto, or about, a Gentlemans Mannor house, or principall messuage*; *with which (in default of a competent garden) it euer falls vnto the share of the eldest heire.*

Volage: com. *Light, giddie, shittle-headed*; *inconstant, fickle, humorous, flitting*; *shallow-braind, inconsiderate, rash.*

Appel volage. *Looke* Appel.

Rente volage. *A rent raised of, or purchased for, money.*

Volagement. *Lightly, giddily, inconstantly, fickly*; *humorously*; *rashly.*

Volageté: f. *Lightnesse, giddinesse*; *humorousnesse, inconstancie, ficklenesse*; *inconsideration, rashnesse.*

Volant: m. *The sea-Bat, or Reremouse of the sea*; *a flying fish*; *also, the sayle of a Windmill*; *(also, a cloke*; *and a Capon, or other peece of Pullein*; *in the language of Rogues*; *also, a Shittlecocke.)*

Volant: m. ante: f. *Flying, swiftly-passing, fast running*; *momentarie, flitting*; *subiect to remoue often, or to frequent remoues.*

Camp volant. *A flying campe, a campe of light-horsemen for ordinarie roades.*

Pont volant. *The ladder of a ship.*

Rente volant, ou volante. *A Rent-seck, rent-charge*; *or, any rent thats raised of, or bought for, money.*

Volante: f. *A loose Ierkin, or Cassock, a Mandilion.*

Volatil: m. ile: f. *Flying*; *fleeting, or flitting.*

Volatiliser. *To fly, flicker, flit, wauer.*

Vole: f. *The palme, or hollownesse of an halfe-open hand*; *the ioint, or muscle vnder the thumbe.*

Volé: m. ée: f. *Fled*; *also, robbed, pilled, spoyled.*

Volée: f. *A flight, or flying*; *also, a whole flight, flocke, or companie of birds*; *and, a brood of fowle of one season.*

`A la volée. *Rashly, vnaduisedly, inconsiderately*; *at randome, at rouers, at all aduentures, euen as it chaunces, falls out, happens.*

Perdre la volée pour le bond. *To loose, or let slip, an oportunitie, in hope that it will returne.*

Que de bond que de volée. *More by meere hap then any good cunning*; *or, by one course or another, what by one meanes and another.*

Meschante parole iectée va par tout à la volée: Pro. *See* Parole.

Volement: m. *A flying*; *fleeting, flitting*; *speedie running, swift passing.*

Le Voler. *A certaine tricke vsed in prisons for the drawing of drinking mony from new-come guests.*

Voler. *To flye*; *take a flight, be on wing*; *runne swiftly, passe away quickly*; *fleet, or flit speedily*; *also, to rob, rifle, strip, despoyle of all.*

Voler à faulte. *A hawke to loose, or misse her flight.*

Voler de haute aile; & voler sans ailes. *Looke* Aile.

Ie ne vole point sur la gorge. *I vse not to exercise presently after meat.*

Faire bourre voler. *To play much at Tennis; also, to vse much any costlie game, or pastime.*

Tel pense voler qui ne sçauroit bouger: Prov. *Looke* Bouger.

Volerie: f. *A robberie; robbing, ransacking; a violent road wherein all goes to wracke; also, a place ouer a stage which we call the Heauen.*

Volet: m. *A cloth spread on the ground for the picking of corne; also, a shut, or woodden window to shut ouer a glasse one (as* Contre-fenestre; *) also, a flight, or light shaft; also, a shittle-cocke; also, a boord, or planke.*

Esleus, & choisis comme beaux pois sur le volet: &, Triez sur le volet. *Choice peeces, picked stuffe.*

Voleter. *To flicker, or flutter; to flie thicke, moue the wings often; wauer with the wings.*

Voleur: m. *A flier; also, a robber, or highway theefe; & an inroder, or a road-maker.*

Voleuse: f. *A woman that flies; or robbes.*

Volier: m. *A great cage, or coope wherein birds haue roome ynough to flutter.*

Voliere: f. *as* Volier; *or (more generally) a cage, or coop for fowle; also, a Doue-coat standing on pillers; therein differing from* Colombier à pied; *and of a meaner qualitie (or for meaner persons) then it.*

Vollatiliser. *See* Volatiliser.

Voller. *To get neuer a tricke, at cards:* ¶Rab.

Vollicre. *as* Voliere.

Volontaire: com. *A voluntarie; one that serues, or does any thing, without pay, or compulsion.*

Volontaire: com. *Voluntarie, willing, free, of it selfe, of his owne accord; also, prone, readie, forward, apt to thinke, or execute a thing put into his head; also, wilfull, that does what likes him best, or whatsoeuer comes in his head.*

Volontairement. *Voluntarily, willingly, promptly, readily, freely, without procurement or compulsion, of his owne accord.*

Volonté: f. *The will, mind, list; heart, consent, meaning, affection, humor, desire.*

Bonne volonté. *Willingnesse, freenesse, readinesse, owne accord or good will; also, absolute will and pleasure; whence,* Ie me rends, faites de moy vostre bonne volonté: viz. *Whatsoeuer you thinke good.*

'A la mienne volonté, que. *I would to God, or I pray God, that.*

Volonteux: m. euse: f. *Wilfull, selfewillie, wedded to his will; swaied by the throng, or caried by the streame, of his owne (intemperate) humors.*

Volontiers *willingly, readily, freely, gladly, at ease, with delight.*

Voltant: m. ante: f. *Bounding, curuetting; also, turning.*

Volte: f. *A round; or turne; and thence, the bounding turne which cunning riders teach their horses; also, a Tumblers gamboll, or turne; whence;*

Volte en arriere. *A backe turne; a ierting, or wheeling backward, lighting againe on the feet; and,* Volte en avant; *(the contrarie) a turning ouer forward.*

Prendre la volte de Londres, &c. *To goe to Londonwards, or towards London.*

Volter. *To vault, or tumble; also, to bound, or curuet; also, to turne, or make turne.*

Voltigeant: m. ante: f. *Vaulting, or tumbling; also, curuetting, or managing in a (narrow) circle.*

Voltigement: m. *A vaulting, or tumbling; also, a curuetting, or managing in round.*

Voltiger. *To vault, or tumble; also, to curuet, or manage in a (narrow) circle.*

Voltoline: f. *The name of a vine.*

Volubilité: f. *Volubilitie; an easie rolling, or glib turning; and thence, vnsteadinesse, or an inconstant mouing.*

Voluble: f. *Withiwind, Bindweed, Roapweed.*

Voluble: com. *Voluble; easily rolled, turned, or tumbled; Hence, fickle, inconstant, variable, wauering, often flitting, or changing; and, glib, nimble, rolling, alwayes running, euer turning.*

Volume: m. *A volume, tome, booke, or seuerall part of a booke; also, the bulke, size, quantitie, or largenesse of a thing.*

Voluntaire, & Voluntairement. *See* Volontaire, & Volontairement.

Volunté: f. *as* Volonté.

Volupté: f. *Pleasure, voluptuousnesse, sensualitie, worldlie delight.*

Voluptueusement. *Voluptuously, sensually.*

Voluptueux: m. euse: f. *Voluptuous, fleshlie, sensuall, carnall, wholly deuoted to worldlie delights.*

Volute: f. *The rolling shell of a Snayle; also, the writhen circle, or curle tuft that hangs ouer, or sticks out of the chapter of a piller, &c; and is tearmed by our workmen a Rowle, Cartridge, or Carthouse.*

Vomique: f. la vom. *A secret, and daungerous imposthumation full of matter.*

Vomique: com. *Vomiting; whence,* Noix vomique; *the vomiting nut, or fruit; See* Noix.

Vomir. *To vomit, spue, cast, parbreake.*

Vomissement: m. *A vomiting, or spuing.*

Vomitif: m. *A Vomitiue, or Vomitorie; any thing that prouokes vomiting.*

Vomitoire: m. *as* Vomitif.

Vorace: com. *Rauenous, deuouring, swallowing, gluttonous, consuming.*

Voracité: f. *Voracitie, rauening, gluttonie, deuouring, swallowing, excessiue or greedie feeding.*

Vorage: m. *A gulfe, whirlepoole, quagmire; a swallowing or vnsaciable depth.*

Vortillement des fleuves. *as* Vortillons.

Vortillons: m. *The eddie, whirling, round turnings in a streame.*

Vos. *the plurall to* Vostre.

Vostre: com. *Your, yours, belonging to you.*

Vote: m. *A vow.*

Vou: f. *A daughter in law, a sonnes wife:* ¶Gasc.

Vouade. *as* Bouade.

Vouchement: m. *A vouching in law.*

Voucher. *To vouch; to cite, pray in aid, or call vnto aid, in a suit:* ¶Norm.

Voüé: m. ée: f. *Vowed; religiously promised, or protested; also, giuen, bequeathed, betaken, or deuoted, vnto.*

Voüer. *To vow; promise or protest; also, to giue, bequeath, betake, or deuote vnto; whence,* Voüer au Diable, &c.

Voüer arbre à arbre. *To ioyne, or glue tree to tree, boord vnto boord, &c.*

Voüerie: f. *as* Voirie; *Iurisdiction.*

Voüeur: m. *A wooer, or suter vnto a woman.*

Vouge: m. *A Hunting, or Hunters staffe; a Boores speare.*

Voulant. Bien vo. *Well-willing, friendlie or affectionate, vnto.*

Voulceure: f. *A vaulting, arching, bowing, crooking; or, a vault, arch, bought.*

Voulenteux. *as* Volenteux.

Vouloir: m. *A will, mind, fancie, affection, humor; wish, desire; meaning, purpose, intent.*

Vouloir. *To will; couet, wish, desire; meane, mind, purpose, intend.*

En vouloir. *whence;* 'A qui en voulez vous? *What ayles you? who hurts you? or, whom doe you stomacke? who haue you a quarell to? with whom doe you meane to brabble? Sometimes also the contrarie; as,* l'heur vous en veut; *fortune fauours you; (but in this sence it is not often vsed.)*

Dieu le vueille. *God grant, God send it, or I pray God it fall out so.*

Ie le veux bien. *With all my heart; I am well content, or pleased withall.*

Il ne nous donne qui ne veut. *No man is constrained to giue vs; any man may chuse whether he will giue vs or no; The like is;* Il y va veoir qui veut; *He that will, he that hath a mind to it, any one, may goe and see it.*

Si les dez ne vous veulent. *If the dice runne not to your mind, on your side; or as you would haue them.*

Que veut le Roy ce veut la Loy: Prov. *The Law makes good her Princes expositions.*

Qui quand il peut ne veut, quand il veut il ne peut: Prov. *Looke* Pouvoir.

Qui tard veut ne veut: Prov. *A delay imports a deniall; and he that driues one off with words, doth meane to let him haue nought but words.*

Voulrie: f. *Th'authoritie which a father and mother haue ouer their child; also, the house, or dwelling of a father.*

Voulsure: f. *as* Voulceure.

Voulte: f. *A vault, or arch; also, a vaulted, or embowed roofe.*

Voulté: m. ée: f. *Vaulted, arched; bowed, or bending on all sides downeward; also, crooke-backed, or hulch-backed.*

Voulter. *To vault, arch, bow; crooke, or bend (on all sides) downeward.*

Voulteur: m. *A maker of vaults, or of arches.*

Voultis: m. *The seeling of a roome.*

Voulture: f. *A vaulting, or arching.*

Voulu. *willed, wished; coueted, fancied, desired, affected; meant, intended, purposed.*

Vous. *You.*

Voussé: m. ée: f. *Vaulted, arched.*

Vousure: f. *as* Voulture.

Voute. *as* Voulte.

Voutoyé: m. ée: f. *Vaulted, arched, bowed.*

Voutrer. *Looke* Veautrer.

Vouture: f. *as* Voulture.

Voyable: com. *Visible, perceiuable, seeable, subiect vnto the view.*

Voyage: m. *A voyage, iourney, peregrination; also, (among Diers) a heating, or copper-full, of liquor.*

Voyagement: m. *A voyaging, trauelling, iourneying.*

Voyager. *To trauell, iourney, goe a voyage.*

Voyager en Cornoüaille. *To be a cuckold; or to haue his head horne-graffed at home while his feet are plodding abroad.*

Voyagere: f. *A trauelling, or way-faring woman.*

Voyageur: m. *A traueller, a way-faring man.*

Voyant. *viewing, seeing, perceiuing, beholding.*

Voy-cy. *Looke, see, behold, here.*

Voye: f. *A way, path; street, causey; properly such a one as is about 16 foot broad; also, a meane, manner, fashion; order, course, rule, method; also, the carriage or portage of a thing; also, a load, or cart-full of; and, in the plurall* (Voyes) *the view, or footing of a Stag; whence;*

Courir vn cerf sur les voyes; *Dogs to hunt, or pursue a Stag, with noses to ground.*

Par voye. *as* à clere-voyes; *or so farre set asunder that one may easily looke betweene them.*

Par voye de faict. *Looke* Faict.

Tout d'une voye. *All at once; or, all vnder one.*

Accueillir sa voye vers. *To trauell, wend, or goe, towards.*

Mettre en voye. *To set packing, going, or agate; to put forward, or into the way.*

Il ne va pas du tout à honte qui de demye voye retourne: Prov. *Himselfe with shame he will not staine to goe, that hath turn'd back againe; he that hath once a course abandond hath not the face againe to stand on't.*

Voyelle: f. *A vowell.*

Voyer: m. *A Surueyer, or Ouerseer of highwayes, (and punisher of the offences committed therein;) also, the Surueyor of the publicke workes, and buildings belonging to a towne, who, in some places, likewise appoints meeres and bounds vnto bordering lands; and orders the lights, gutters, and sinkes of neighbouring houses; and limits vnto those that build in a street, their ground and scope of iuttying; and lookes that the streets, and highwayes be not straitned, or incombered by stalls, seats, stayres, shoring of houses, &c; and lastly, Scauinger-like, giues order that they be made cleane: Also, a Gentleman that hath some Jurisdiction (though not altogether so much as the* Iusticier) *within his territorie; whence;*

Gros voyer. *as* Moyen Iusticier; &, Simple voyer. *as* Le bas Iusticier.

Le grand Voyer de France. *The great Surueyor of France; is but a meane Officer, how great soeuer this title, or the person that holds it, be.*

Voyerie: f. *Jurisdiction; whence,* Grande Voyerie; *as* La moyenne Iustice; *(vnder* Iustice;*)* &, Simple voyerie; *Base, or low Jurisdiction.*

Voyes d'un cerf. *Looke* Voye.

Voy-là. *See, looke, behold, there.*

Voyrement. *Surely, verily, indeed, forsooth.*

Voyrie. *as* Voyerie.

Voyture, & Voyturier. *as* Voiture, & Voiturier.

Vpe: f. *The bird called a Whoope, or dunghill Cocke.*

Vrac. Hareng vrac. *A Herring well seasoned, and seasonably imbarrelled.*

Vranopetes. *Goers to heauen:* ¶Rab.

Vraque. *The pipe, or passage whereby a wombe-infants vrine is carried from it.*

Vraques. *The name of certaine ropes, or tackling, which belong vnto sayles.*

Vray: m. *A truth; whence;*

'A vray dire perd on le ieu: Prov. *The fairest gamester alwayes looseth most: he that to Truth himselfe a prentise ties, will speed worse then the knaue that vseth lyes.*

Beau service fait amis vray dire ennemis: Prov. *Faire seruice friends, true plaineneße foes, procures.*

Tout vray n'est pas bon à dire: Prov. *All that is true is not to be told.*

Vray: m. vraye: f. *True, vnfained, sooth, iust, right; sure, certaine, vndoubted; vnsoisted, vnmingled, naturall, of it selfe.*

Ce sont les pires bourdes que les vrayes: Prov. *The truest are the worst (because the bitterest) ieasts.*

Vraybis; & Vraybot. *for* Vrayement.

Vrayement. *Truely, in truth, in sooth, indeed, verily, certainly, surely, iustly, rightly, unfainedly, in good faith.*
C'est vrayement bien dict à toy. *Thou hast hit the naile on the head; thou hast now strucken it dead; (Ironically.)*
Ouy vrayement. *Yea sure, true Roger, wisely brother Timothie; (Ironically; yet is it vsed sometimes otherwise; as in)* Ouy vrayement ie le nie; *Yea truly, or, for my part, I denie it vtterly.*
Vraysemblable: com. *Probable, likelie, like or seeming to be true.*
Vraysemblance: f. *Probablenesse, or likenesse of truth.*
Vrbain: m. *Vrban; a proper name for a man.*
Vrbanie: f. *as* Vrbanité.
Vrbanité: f. *Vrbanitie, ciuilitie, courtesie, affabilitie, gentlenesse; good behauiour, seemelie carriage, a handsome fashion, a comelie grace, a prettie and pleasant manner of ordinarie discourse.*
Vrbec: m. *The Vine-fretter, or Diuells Gold-ring; a worme.*
Vrderis. *as* Verdegris.
Vre: m. *The huge-bodied, hulch-backed, short-horned, and red-eyed wild Oxe; called the Vre-oxe.*
Vreder. *To runne hastily.*
Vrelepingue: m. *A drinke-spiller:* ¶Rab.
Vreniller. *To pisse, or void vrine:* ¶Rab.
Vrge. *in stead of* Vrne: ¶Rab.
Vrgent: m. ente: f. *Vrgent, vrging; hard or sore pressing, straining, forcing, importunate, earnest.*
Vrille: f. *A Gimlet, or Piercer.*
Vrilles: f. *Hooke-like edges, or ends of leaues (called by some of our workemen Scrolls, and) sticking out in the vpper parts of pillers, and of other peeces of Architecture.*
Vrillonner vne cable. *To coyle a cable, to wind or lay it vp round, or in a ring.*
Vrinaire: com. *Of, or belonging to, vrine; also, vrinall-like.*
Vrinal: m. *An Vrinall; also, a Iordan, or Chamber-pot.*
Vrinal: m. ale: f. *Of vrine.*
Vrine: f. *Vrine, lant, stale, chamber-lye, pisse.*
Ie voudrois bien voir de leur vrine. *I would gladly see what there is in them, what stuffe they be made of, or what they are able to doe.*
Vriner. *To vrine, pisse, make water, stale.*
Vriner vne cable. *To coyle a cable.*
Vrineux: m. euse: f. *Full of vrine; sauoring, or smelling of vrine.*
Vrinier: m. *A conduit passing to the middle of the nauell, and carrying away the vrine of an infant while it is in the wombe.*
Vris: m. *A rime, or white frost vpon trees.*
Vrne: f. *A narrow-necked pot, or pitcher of earth, to fetch, or keepe water in; also, a vessell wherinto the Roman Pretor did put the names of such as were to be elected, or tried, by lot; also, a coffin, or vessell wherein the ashes of the dead were preserued.*
Vroesne. *The hearbe Woodbind.*
Vrsin: m. *The sea Vrchin; so called about* Marseille.
Vrsin: m. ine: f. *Beare-like; of a Beare.*
Vsage: m. *Vsage; vse, wearing, imployment, occupation, fruit, profit, possession; also, woont, custome, guise, manner, fashion; and, practise, exercise, experience, habit, enurement; acquaintance, familiaritie, conuersation with; also, interest, or vsurie; also, a right of Pasture, and Pawnage, & of taking wood for necessarie vses, in a forest belonging to the King, or some other Lord; This Right is enioyed by diuers, and in diuers manners; for some may take timber for their building; others haue onely fire-boot, and hedge-boot; some take it throughout the forests, and as much as they need; others are limited both place, and quantitie: Some hold it as a* fief; *others by rent, or* Cens; *lastly, some haue it onely for their liues; and others but for yeares; Howsoeuer, they can neither sell, giue, transferre, nor passe ouer, in any manner, that which they haue.*
Vsages. *Common pastures, woods, or vnderwoods;* (Rabelais *vses (or his Printer misuses) this word for* Vases.)
Vsager: m. *as* Vsagier.
Vsager: m. ere: f. *Common, for euerie bodies vse; whence;*
Femme vsagere. *A common whoore.*
Vsagier: m. *A customarie tenant.*
Vsagier de bois. *One that hath common of Pasture, Pawnage, or wood for his necessarie vses, in another mans wood; as in* Vsage.
Vsance: f. *Vsance, vse, vsage.*
Vsé: m. ée: f. *Vsed, occupied, worne, imployed; possessed, enioyed; wasted, consumed; accustomed, practised, enured.*
Vsement: m. *A vse, vsing, vsage, guise, custome; also, a wearing, possessing, wasting, consuming.*
Vser. *To vse; to weare, occupie, imploy; wast, consume, spend; accustome, practise, exercise, enure vnto; possesse, enioy, take the vse, reape the profit, of.*
Vser de force. *To deale by force, to take by violence.*
Vser de redictes. *To repeate or iterate the same things often.*
Vous n'en deussiez vser ainsi en mon endroit. *You should not handle, or deale with, me so; you should not beare your selfe towards me in that manner.*
Vsité: m. ée: f. *Vsuall, customable, common, ordinarie; vsed, wonted, accustomed, practised, exercised, skilfull, cunning, experienced in.*
Vsiter. *To vse, practise, accustome, enure, exercise, trade in.*
Vsucaption: f. *Three yeares possession in a Moueable (which in Law counteruayles a prescription;) or more generally, any prescription, or long possession; or the winning of a thing thereby.*
Vsuelles: f. *Pastures, and wooddie grounds, belonging in common vnto diuers townships.*
Vsufructuaire. *as* Vsufruictier.
Vsufruict: m. *The vse, and profit (but not the property) of goods, with th'owners consent.*
Vsufruictier: m. *One that hath the vse, and reapes the profit, of a thing, whereof the propertie resteth in another.*
Vsuraire: com. *vsurious; taken, or giuen for interest or vse.*
Vsure: f. *The wearing or occupation of a thing; also vsurie, vse, interest.*
Vsurier: m. *An Vsurer.*
Vsurpateur: m. *An vsurper of, an incroacher on, another mans right.*
Vsurpation: f. *An vsurpation, or vsurping; an vniust, or often vsing.*
Vsurpatrice. *An vsurpatrix; a woman that vsurpeth.*
Vsurpé: m. ée: f. *vsurped; often, or vniustly vsed.*
Vsurper. *To vsurpe; to seise, or incroach on, another mans right; also, to vse much, often to mention.*
Vtagues; *or* Vtaques: *as* Estaques. ¶Rab.
Vtensile: m. *An vtensile; any implement, necessarie, vsefull*

vsefull toole, or houshold stuffe.

Vtensilé. Bien vten. *Throughly furnished with vtensiles.*

Vterin: m. ine: f. *Of the bellie or wombe; of one and the same wombe or bellie; borne of one mother, or damme.*

Herbes vterines. *Hearbes which be good for the Mother.*

Vtile: com. *Gainefull, beneficiall, profitable, commodious, aduantagious; also, expedient, necessarie, seruiceable, good, conuenient.*

Vtile domaine. *Th'estate of a vassall in th'inheritance which he holds of his Lord; so tearmed because hee hath onely a profitable, not a direct, interest in it.*

Seigneur vtile. *An occupant, or occupier of land; he that possesses, and receiues the fruits of, an inheritance, for which rent, or* Cens, *are payed, or seruices done.*

Seigneurie vtile. *The vse, occupation, or possession of a fief, or inheritance.*

Vtilement. *Profitably, gainefully, beneficially, commodiously; with great aduantage, to good purpose.*

Vtilité: f. *Vtilitie, commoditie, profit, gaine, benefit, cheuissance, aduantage.*

Vtopie: f. *An imaginarie place, or countrey.*

Vtrin. *as* Vterin.

Vuaine: f. *A sheath:* ¶Pic.

Vuan: m. *A gloue:* ¶Pic.

Vuaranion. *as* Garagnon; *(an old word.)*

Vuard; &, Vuarder. *as* Gard; &, Garder: ¶Pic.

Vuaresque: m. *A wrecke, or ship cast away; or the right of Admiraltie, whereto it belongs.*

Vuarisons. Advestures, & vvar. *Corne, grasse, or other fruits growing, or standing; or vncut, vngot, vngathered.*

Vuarlouque: com. *Squint eyed, skenning, askew-looking:* ¶Pic.

Vuaudrée: f. *A maulkin, or the clowt wherewith an Ouen is made cleane:* ¶Pic.

Vuayves: f. *Waifes; casualties; things which be left, abandoned, escheated, or vnowned.*

Vvedde. *Weld, Woad, garden or tame Woad:* ¶Pic.

Vvée. Membrane Vvée. *The grapie membrane of the eye; Looke* Membrane.

Vueil. *as* Vouloir; *Will.*

Vuel. *See* Venel.

Vuele. *as* Veule *in the later sence.*

Vuerp: m. *A deliuering, or giuing ouer vnto; also, a duetie of* 12 d. Paris. *paied by a purchaser vnto the Sherifes for their presence when possession is, by the seller, deliuered vnto him.*

Vuerpi: m. ie: f. *Deliuered, yeelded, or giuen ouer vnto.*

Vuerpir. *To deliuer, yeeld, or giue ouer vnto.*

Vueuil; ou, Vueul. *as* Vouloir; *Will.*

Vuidange: m. *A voidnesse, emptinesse, inanitie, vacuitie; a voyding, emptying, euacuation, eiection; also, the decision of a controuersie.*

Vuidanges d'une ville. *The laystall of a towne; or the place wherein Scauengers, and Gold-finders emptie their filthie carts.*

Vuidangier: m. ere: f. *Emptying, voyding, euacuating.*

Vuide: m. *A wast; a void, or emptie space; a wide, or vast roome.*

Vuide: com. *Void, emptie, wast, vast, wide, hollow; deuoyd, without, free of, exempt from, not combered or troubled with.*

'A bast vuide. *Looke* Bast.

Vuides chambres font les Dames folles: Pro. *Womens freedome breeds their follie; when they are left alone all modestie is gone.*

De mains vuides prieres vaines: Prov. *They that giue nought get nought; th'emptie-handed pray in vaine.*

Le plat du bas est tousiours le premier vuide: Pro. *The lowest dish is euermore first emptie; (belike because it is (most commonly) furnished the worst, and fed on the best.)*

Vuidé: m. ée: f. *Voyded, emptied, euacuated; exhausted; purged, cleansed; hollowed; auoyded; also, decided, determined, dispatched, made an end of; also, drawne, as* Pulleine, *&c.*

Ce point sera tantost vuidé. *Will quickly be resolued, or cleered.*

Vuide-main: m. *A quitting, yeelding, rendering, or giuing vp of.*

Vuidement: m. *A voyding, emptying, euacuating; exhausting; hollowing; purging, cleansing; deciding, determining, dispatching, ending.*

Vuider. *To void, euacuate, emptie; exhaust, hollow; purge, cleanse; auoyd; also, to cleere, determine, decide, resolue, dispatch; rid of, make an end of.*

Vuider ses mains. *To yeeld, render, giue vp, deliuer ouer; quit, rid his hands of; also, to pay readie money for things bought publickly, or assigned by publicke Order.*

Vuider la maison, ou mestairie. *A tenant, or farmer to goe out of, or giue vp, against his will, the tenement he tooke, or thought to haue kept, for a longer time.*

Vuider les poulets. *To draw them, to draw out their guts.*

Vuideté: f. *Voidnesse, emptinesse, hollownesse; inanitie, vacuitie, euacuation.*

Vuideur: m. *A voyder, emptier, euacuater.*

Vuideure: f. *as* Vuidement.

Vuiho: m. *as* Cocu: ¶Pic.

Vuilles: f. *The tendrells, or twining sprigs, of vine-branches.*

Vulgaire: m. *A kind of great mall, or hammer wherewith, in old time, gates were broke open.*

Vulgaire. le vul. *The vulgar, common people, many-headed multitude.*

Vulgaire: com. *Vulgar, common, publicke; ordinarie, triuiall, vsuall, or much vsed.*

Vulgairement. *Vulgarly, commonly; ordinarily, triuially.*

Vulgal. *whence;* vif argent vulgal. *The basest kind of Quicksiluer, made of dung and hay.*

Vulneraire: com. *Vulnerarie, healing wounds, belonging vnto wounds.*

Vulpin: m. ine: f. *Fox-like, of a Fox.*

Vulturne: m. *The North-east wind.*

Vulve: f. *The wombe-pipe, or priuie passage; the way, or entrance into the wombe; also, the matrix, mother, or wombe it selfe.*

Vvule: f. *The Vuula, or palate of the mouth.*

Vuydange. *as* Vuidange.

Vuyde: Vuydé; &, Vuydement. *as* Vuide: Vuidé; &, Vuidement.

Vuyder; &, Vuydeté. *Looke* Vuider; &, Vuideté.

Vyt. *as* Vit.

Vytaut; &, Vytte. *as* Vitaut; &, Vitte.

Vz: m. *Vse, vsage, custome, woont.*

X

XEnomanes. ¶Rab. *A traueller.*
Xilaloë. *Lignum Aloes.*
Xilobalsame: m. *The wood of the Balsame tree.*

Y

Y. *(A Relatiue, or Aduerbe of Relation) vnto him, it, or them; thereto, or thereunto; also, there, or thither.*
Dieu vous y aide. *(To one that sneezeth) God blesse you.*
Ie ne sçauroy que vous y faire. *I should not know how to helpe you, or what to doe for you, in it.*
Il y a esté trois iours. *He hath beene three dayes about it.*
Il se nommoit Philippus, & y fut souvent appellé. *And was often called so.*
Puis que pisseurs y a: &, Puis que de nos marottes y a. *Seeing that we are speaking of pissers, &c.*
Yeble: m. *Wallwort, Danewort, Dwarfe Elderne.*
Yeose. *as* Yeuse.
Yeuse. *The Holme Oke, barren Skarlet Oke, French Oke.*
Yeux. *(The Plurall to* Oeil*) Eyes; Looke* Oeil.
Yf: m. *The Yew tree.*
Ymagé. *Looke* Imagé.
Ypreau: m. *The Elme tree.*
Yraigne. *as* Araigne.
Ysard: m. *The Shamois, or wild Goat of whose skin Shamois leather is made.*
Yssé: m. ée: f. *Hoised, lift vp.*
Ysser. *To hoise, or lift vp.*
Yssir. *To issue; to come, goe, or flow forth.*
Yssuë: f. *An issue; going out, comming forth; also, as* Issuë.
Yve: f. *as* Ive; *also, (in old French) water.*
Yver: m. *Winter; Looke* Hyver.
Yvernade: f. *A wintering.*
Yvernal: m. ale: f. *Fit for, of or belonging to, the Winter.*
Yverner. *To winter, to spend or passe away the Winter; also, to dig, or dresse a vineyard in Winter.*
Yvoire: m. *Ivorie, Elephants tooth.*
Yvoirin: m. ine: f. *Of Ivorie, like Ivorie.*
Yvraison: f. *Drunkennesse; or, th'act of drunkennesse;* (Yvrongnerie *being the vice, or vse thereof.)*
Yvraye: f. *The vicious graine called Ray, or Darnell.*
Yvraye sauvage. *Red Darnell, wall Barlie, way Bennet.*
Yvre: com. *Drunken, cupshotten, tipsie, whitled, flusht, mellow, ouerseene, whose cap is set, that hath taken a pot too much, that hath seene the diuell.*
Yvre de laict caillé. *Tipled by a small matter; whose weake braine is distempered, or ouerturned, by weake drinke.*
Yvre comme vne soupe. *Looke* Soupe.
Yvrosse: f. *Drunkennesse; also, as* Yvrongnesse.
Yvrongne: m. *A drunkard.*
'A la trongne cognoist on l'yvrongne: Prov. *A drunkard is by his rich face discerned.*
Yvrongner. *To be drunke, or to drinke drunke; to swill or carouse vnmeasurably.*
Yvrongnerie: f. *Drunkennesse; (the vice, custome, or habit of drunkennesse.)*
Yvrongnesse: f. *A drunken woman, a drunken sow.*
Femme safre, & yvrongnesse, de son corps n'est pas maistresse: Prov. *We say, A drunken Tnuc hath no Porter.*
Yvrongnet: m. ette: f. *Somewhat drunken, ouerseene, or too blame; a little out of the way.*
Yvroye. *as* Yvraye.

Z

ZAffre. *A kind of exceeding drie sand, or grauell; or as* Safre.
Zagaye: f. *A fashion of slender, long, and long-headed Pike, vsed by the Moorish horsmen.*
Zaguille. *as* Zagaye.
Zain: m. *A horse thats all of one (darke) colour, without any starre, spot, or marke about him; and therby commonly vicious.*
Zalas. *Alas:* ¶Rab.
Zanit: m. *A Vice to a Tumbler, &c; or in a Play.*
Zarzeparille: f. *The medicinable plant called* Zarzaparilla, *or (corruptly)* Sassaparilla, *and rough Bindweed of* Peru.
Zebedée: f. *A double Damaske Rose.*
Zec: m. *Reed to thatch houses with.*
Zecchin: m. *A Venetian coyne of gold, worth about 5* s. sterl.
Zedoaire: f. *The root of* Anthora, *or wholesome woluesbane, called also, Monkes-hood or Helmet-flower, and Aconits mithridate; And this doe some stile* Zedoaire d'Auicenne: *Others call worme-seed* Semen Zedoariæ, *or Zedoar-seed.*
Zedoaire de Serapion. *An East-Indian root which resembleth ginger, but is more bitter in tast, and better in smell, then it, though not so strong in eyther as it.*
Zein *as* Zain.
Zelateur: m. *A zealous, or iealous person.*
Zelatif: m. iue: f. *zealous, or iealous.*
Zele: m. *Zeale; earnest affection, loue, enuy, emulation; extreme care, exceeding desire to doe a thing.*
Zelé: m. ée: f. *Zealous, iealous; feruent, earnest, or affectionate, in extremitie.*
Zeler. *To be zealous, or iealous of; to emulate, or enuy; to affect extremely; to haue an exceeding care of, or desire vnto.*
Zelotopie: f. *Iealousie.*
Zelote: com. *Iealous, or zealous.*
Zelotype. com. *as* Zelote.
Zenith: m. *Our Zenith; or the point of the firmament which is directly ouer our heads.*
Zephyre: m. *the West-wind.*
Zero: m. *A Cypher in Arithmetick; a thing that stands for nothing; whence;*
Se reduire au Zero. *To bring himselfe to th'wallet; to ruine his fortunes, to spend or consume all.*
Zest: m. *The thicke skin, or filme whereby the kernell of a wall-nut is diuided.*
Il ne vaut pas vn Zest. *He is not worth a dodkin, straw, rush, a pinnes head, the taking vp.*
Zest. *A voice resembling, or expressing the noise made by a ierk, stripe, yarke, thwack, &c.*
Zibelline: f. *The Sable Martin.*

Zigome. *The outward part, or end of the cheeke-bone towards the eare; so tearmed by the Anatomists of Paris.*
Zimiech: m. *A kind of Eagle which preyes vpon the Crane, and other lesse fowle.*
Zin; ou Zint. *The twang, or twanging sound of the string of a hard-bent bow.*
Zinzembre. *Ginger.*
Zinziberine: f. *Powder of Ginger.*
Zivette. *Looke* Civette.
Zizanie: f. *Ray, Darnell.*
Zizolin: m. *Gingioline colour.*
Zoaire. *Looke* Zedoaire.
Zodiaqué: m. *The Zodiacke; a broad circle in the firmament, in which the 12 Signes are placed, and vnder which the Planets moue.*
Zoette: f. *An Owle, or Howlet; called so about* Avignon.
Zon: m. *The whiske, or sound of a switch, rod, or wand; also, a iert, lash, box, blow.*
Zone: f. *A girdle; also, a Zone; or, a certaine breadth from North to South, bounded out by some of the globes principall circles; Of these breadths there be fiue; one extreame hot and fierie; two most cold and euer frozen; and two which be, for the most part, mild and temperate, or betweene both.*
Zoophore: m. *A painted, or carued girdle, or border about a Porch, or Piller.*
Zoophytes: m. *Such things as be partly plants, & partly liuing creatures; as Spunges, &c.*
Zoucet: m. *The little water-fowle called a Dabchicke, or Die-dopper.*
Zubelines. Martes zub. *Sables.*
Zummach. *The Eagle that hath on her head, or backe, a kind of whitenesse; which is a certaine signe of her perfect goodnesse.*

FINIS.

Briefe Directions for such as desire to learne the French Tongue:

And first, of the Vowels, and Diphthongs.

A A Is to be sounded fully, as in this English word all; not as we sound it in stale ale.

E E, when it is thus accented é, whether in the middle or in the end of a word, is called é Masculine, and sounded out, as in the Latine word docére. Otherwise it is called e Feminine, and is to bee sounded imperfectly as the second sillable of Facere, Or as in this English speech, Is he come? If two or three, e, bee in the end of a word, the first are Masculines, the last is e Feminine, as destinée, creée.

E, In the same sillable before N or M is to be sounded like a, as enfance, the first sillable like the second: Except mien, tien, sien, bien, chien, rien, and some others; and enerver and the like, wherein e is not sounded in the same sillable with n.

I I, Is to be sounded like ee in English in feeble or meeke. So must you sound amitié: &c.

O O, Before N or M hath the sound of oo in our English word Moone. So must you pronounce the French word mon, comme on dit, commencement, &c.

V V, Is sounded as if you would whistle it out, as in the word, a Lute.

I, and V, are consonants when they are put before other vowells, as with the Latines, as jalousie, vive le Roy. V also standing before R is sometimes a consonant, as vray, not u-ray.

Dipthõgs Ai The Dipthong ai is to be sounded as it is written, in the end of the Aorist of the first Coniugation, as j'aimay. Secondly, if a vowell follow it, as j'aye, ayons, ayant. Thirdly, if ll follow it, as toüaille. Otherwise it is alwayes sounded like é Masculine, as j'ay, j'aimeray, like j'é, j'émeré.

Ao The Diphthong ao, in the word saoul, is to be pronounced Sou, by omitting the prepositiue vowell. But in these words paon, tahon, faon, the Subiunctiue vowell is omitted, and they are sounded pan, tan, fan.

Au The Diphthong au is to be sounded like o, as wee pronounce it in saying Pauls crosse; so sound aux paux like os pos.

Apostrophus. Apostrophus taketh away a vowell out of a word of one sillable, when it standeth before another word beginning with a vowell; as, L'eglise for la eglise; L'obelon for le obelon; So we say S'il for si il.

Synalæpha. Synalæpha taketh away the sound, but not the bodie, of e feminine before a word beginning with another vowell, as mon pere & ma mere ont disné, reade mon per & ma mer ont disné. If a Verbe end in a or o, and il or on follow it, wee put in the sound of the letter t; as for parle il, parlet il, for dira on, dirat on.

Diæresis Diæresis is when two points ouer a vowell diuide it from another vowell, as bouë, queuë, reade bou-e, queu-e, not bo-ue, que-ue.

Of Consonants:

THe generall rule of Consonants is, that if a word end in a consonant, and the word following begin with another, the finall consonant of the word going before is not to bee sounded, as tout ce qui luit n'est pas or, reade it thus, tou ce qui luy ne pas or,

Except
1. The word end in a liquide l, m, n, r, as mon pere, not mo pere. Howbeit l is not to be sounded in the word il, as il faut, reade it i faut.
2. The word end in c, as avec moy, not ave moy.
3. The word end in f, as le bœuf d'Angleterre.
4. The word end in g, as le ioug de Christ est legier.
5. The word end in q, as vn coq d'Inde.
6. There follow any point, , ; : ? !.

C, with a taile thus ç is to bee sounded like s, as garçon, pleça, like garson pieſſa. Secondly ch is pronounced like sh, as cheval like sheval. Except in proper names, as Chanaan, and these foure appellatiues, Cholere, Chorde, Eschole, Cichorée. Thirdly c before t is not to be sounded, as faict, dicton, like fet, ditton. Ç Ch

G, Ioyned with n is to be sounded through the nose, as you sound n, in the English word onion: So pronounce the French oignon, and Espagnol like Spaniard in English. These syllables gua, gue, gui, are to be sounded like ga, ge, gi, as in guaine, guerre, guise: Except the proper names Guise, Guillaume, and the Verbe Esguiser. G

L, In the middest of a word is not to bee sounded, as aultre, oultre, like autre, outre. In the end of these words, fol, mol, col, sol, is to bee sounded like u, as fou, mou, &c. If il come after e or ai, it is to bee sounded like ll in the English word Scullion, or Collier. So must you sound Sillon, toüaille, as though it were written after ll, Sillion, toüirillie. L

M, In the end of words is to be sounded like n, as nom, faim, dam, temps, like non, fein, dan, tans. M

N, Is not to be sounded in the third person plurall N

Nnnn that

that endeth in ent, *as* ilz aiment, ilz parlent, *reade* iz aimet, &c.

Q Q. *In* qua, que, qui, *is to be sounded like* ka, ke, ki; *as* quatre, querir, quiter; *like* katre, kerir, kiter.

RS R, *and* S, *in the beginning of words, or next vnto some other Consonant, are to bee sounded out; more strongly when they be double, as in* guerre, *and* poisson; *and as gently, single, and betweene two vowells; as in* guere, *and* poison; *the tongue in the former giuing onely a touch to the palate, and sounding the later as if it were a Z.*

S, *Preceding a Consonant within a word, is either fully to be suppressed (as in the most naturall French words) or fully to be sounded: As first in all proper names, as* Auguste, &c; *Except in* Basle, *the citie* Basil; Crespin, Crispinus; Christ, *(although now the most pronounce the* s *in it)* Escosse, Hierosme; *(whereunto Beza, and Bellot, adde* Cosme, *though it seeme by the same Analogie as fit to pronounce* s *in that from the word* Κόσμιον, *as* Erasme *from* Ερασμιος.)

Secondly, in all words ending in isme; *as* Iadaisme; *except* Abisme, *and the Deriuatiues thereof.*

Thirdly, in names of Sects; as Atheiste, Anabaptiste, &c.

Fourthly, in all words that signifie the fashion of people; as, A la Moresque, Greguesque, Barbaresque, &c.

And particularly in the words following (whereunto sundrie others may bee added, which comming from the Latine, retaine the latine pronunciation.)

A

Accoster, *when it signifieth to approach; but whẽ it signifieth to prop vp, the* s *is not to be sounded.*
Annaliste.
Aposter.
Apostolique; *though in* Apostre *the* s *bee suppressed.*
Apostume.
Artiste.
Asperges, & Asperger.
Astres.
Attester.

B

Basque.
Baste.
Bastille.
Bastion.
Bastonnades: *and yet in* Baston *the* s *is not to be sounded.*
Bestialitẽ, & Bestiole; *howbeit that in* Bestail, Beste, & Bestelette, *the* s *bee not sounded.*
Birrasque.
Biscaye.
Biscuit.
Blasphemer.
Bosquet.
Brusque.

C

Cameristes.
Caustique.
Celeste.
Chasteté.
Circonstance.
Cisternes.
Clistere.
Costiller.
Contester.
Contrescarpe.
Crotesque.

D

Damasquiner.
Desastre.
Debusquer.
Desesperer.

E

Embuscade.
Enregistrer.
Escabeau.
Escabreux.
Escalade.
Escamper.
Escarbillat.
Escarbot.
Escargot.
Escarlatin; *yet in the word* Escarlate *the* s *is not sounded.*
Escarpins.
Escarcelle.
Escopeterie.
Escoüade.
Espace.
Espece.
Esperance.
Esprit.
Esquadron.
Estafier.
Estase.
Estamet.
Estimer.
Estocade.
Estomac.
Estrade.
Estradiots.
Estrapade.
Estropiat.
Evangeliste.

F

Festin, *but yet in* Feste *you must not sound* s.

G

Gastadour.
Gestes.
Gaspiller.

H

Herboriste.
Histoire.

I

Improviste.
Inceste.
Investiture, *and yet in the Verbe* Vestir *the* s *is not to be sounded.*
Iuristes.
Iusques.
Iusquiame.
Iustice.

L

Lansquenets.
Legiste.
Liste.
Limestre.
Leste.
Lustre.

M

Masque.
Mastic.
Menstrual.
Ministre.
Miste.
Monstre, *when it signifieth a monster: but when it signifieth a muster of souldiours, the* s *is not sounded.*
Mosquet.
Mosquée.
Moustache.
Moustele.
Muscade.
Muscadet.
Muse.
Muscles.

N

Non obstant.

O

Obelisque.
Ostade.

P

Pensionistes.
Pastorelle; *but in* Pastoureau, *and* Paistre, s *is not to bee sounned.*
Pasquil.
Pastel.
Pastenades.
Peste.
Pisteau.
Poste.
Postillon.
Postiles.
Presque; *though* Sereius *doth not pronounce* s.
Proscrire; *but in* Escrire, *and* Descrire, *you must not sound* s.

Q

Question.

R

Reste.
Rustre.
Rustaud.

S

Sequestre.
Sinistre; *yet in* Senestre *you must not pronounce* s.
Suspendre.

T

Tempestatif; *yet in* Tempeste *the* s *is not to be sounded.*
Testament.
Teston.
Testonner.

V

Vestiaire.
Vistempenard, &c.

T, In

T *in the word* et *is neuer pronounced, as* vous et moy, *like* vous e moy.

X *in the end of a word is to bee sounded like* s, *as* paix, prix, *like* pais, pris: *in the middest, like* z; *as* dixiesme, diziesme. *But in these words,* Soixante, Lexiue, Bruxelles, Complexion, *it is to be sounded like* ss, *as* Lessiue, Complession, &c. *In other words that come from the Latine, it retaineth its sound; as* Zeuxe, excuse.

Accent the last syllable, vnlesse it be e *feminine, as* amoúr, aprés, demaín. *Note this moreouer, that the taking away of a letter causeth the vowell that goeth before it to be pronounced long, and consequently serueth to distinguish betweene words of like sound, as* teste *an head, and* tete *a breast,* mastin, *a mastiue, and* matin *the morning, &c.*

Of a Nowne.

Nownes are commonly joyned with Articles. { Le *and* vn *are for the masculine,* / La *and* vne *for the feminine.* } Plur. *les.*

The declining of Nownes is made by Prepositions, the Accusatiue case being alwayes like the Nominatiue, and the Ablatiue like the Genetiue.

These Articles serue

In the singular number to the
- *Genitiue case*: De le *before a vowell, as* de l'immortel. Du *before a consonant, as* du roy.
- *Datiue case*: A le *before a vowell, as* à l'immortel. Au *before a consonant, as* au roy.

In the plurall number to the
- *Genitiue*: Des, *as* des hommes, *of men.*
- *Datiue*: Aux, *as* aux hommes, *to men or to the men.* A les, *as* à les femmes, *to the women.* A des, *as* à des femmes, *to some women.*
- *Ablatiue*: Aux, *as* aux champs, *in the fields.* Des, *as* des cieulx, *from the heauens.* Es, *as* es deserts, *in the wildernesses.*

Declining of Nownes.

	Masc.		Masc.
Sing.	*Nom.* vn, *or* le roy.	Plur.	*Nom.* les roys.
	Gen. d'vn, *or* du roy.		*Gen.* des roys.
	Dat. à vn, *or* au roy.		*Dat.* aux roys.
	Accus. vn, *or* le roy.		*Accus.* les roys.
	Vocat. ô roy, *or* ô le roy.		*Vocat.* ô roys.
	Ablat. à vn roy, *or* du roy.		*Ablat.* des roys.

	Femin.		Femin.
Sing.	*Nom.* vne, *or* la femme.	Plur.	*Num.* les femmes.
	Gen. d'vne, *or* de la femme.		*Gen.* des femmes.
	Dat. à vne, *or* à la femme.		*Dat.* aux femmes.
	Accus. vne, *or* la femme.		*Accus.* les femmes.
	Vocat. ô femme.		*Vocat.* ô femmes.
	Ablat. d'vne, *or* de la femme.		*Ablat.* des femmes.

Forming of the plurall number.

The Plurall number is formed from the Singular, by putting to s *or* z, *as* roy, roys, lettré, lettrez; *except words that end in* s, x, *or* z, *whose Singular and Plurall are one; as* le païs, *and* les païs; le faix, *and* les faix; le filz, *and* les filz.

Words ending in l, *change* l *into* ux; *as* cheval, chevaux; cheveul, cheveux; mal, maux; metal, metaux; *Except these irregulars,* ciel, cieux; celuy, ceux; oeil, yeux; vieil, vieux; genouil, genoux.

Words ending in a consonant, in the Plurall lose the sound of their consonant; Grec, Grecs; *as if it were* Gres; *except they end in a* liquide; *as* bal, bals; nom, noms; don, dons; jour, jours.

Genders of Nowns Substantiues.

1 *Nownes are all of the Masculine gender, except* 1. *the names of women, & offices to them belonging; as* mere, nourrice; *names of fruits; as* vne poire; *of cities; as* Clermont, Marseille.

2 *Substantiues in* é *Masculine; as* bonté; *except* blé, congé, clergé; *and such as come from Latine words in* atus; *as* Duché, Comté, marché.

3 *Substantiues in* e *Feminine, as* grace; *Except words comming from Masculines & Neuters in Latine, as* pere, livre, titre; office, sacrifice. *Yet these are Feminines,* lexiue, responce; image, rage, table, fable.

4 *Substantiues in* eur, *as* douceur; *except* pleur, labeur, heur, *with his compounds,* bonheur, malheur.

5 *Nownes in* on, *as* affection, prison, chanson; *except* horion, tison; *and words ending in* sson, *as* poisson.

6 *Substantiues in* u, virtu, tribu; *except* festu.

7 *Nownes in* ix, *as* paix, voix, noix, poix, *for pitch; except* prix.

8 *These are also Feminines,* mercy, loy, peau, soif, clef, nef, faim, mois, nonnain, putain, fin, façon, leçon, mer, toux, tour *for a tower, otherwise not;* brebis, perdris, lument, forest, dent, part, hart, mort, cour.

Some Nownes changing their signification, change also their Gender; as le temple, *a Temple,* la temple, *the temple of the head;* vn livre, *a booke,* vne livre, *a pound;* le manche, *the helue or handle,* la manche, *the sleeue.*

Of Adjectiues.

ADiectiues forme the feminine gender, by putting to e feminine, as hault, haulte, caché, cachée; except it end in e feminine, for then it is common to both genders, as homme or femme honorable, l'eau trouble.

Exception.

1 ADiectiues in c, turne c into ch, as sec, seche, except Grec, Grecque, Duc, Duchesse, Clerc, Clergesse.

2 Words in eau change eau into elle, as beau, belle, puceau, pucelle, nouveau, nouvelle.

3 Words in eux make the feminine in euse, as piteux, piteuse, Roux maketh rousse, faulx, faulse, doulx, doulce, frais, fraische.

4 Words in f change f into v, as brief, brieve, restif, restive, pensif, pensive.

5 Words in eur make the feminine in euse, as flateur, flateuse, menteur, menteuse, iureur, iureuse, pecheur maketh pecheresse.

6 These double their consonant, bas, basse, bon, bonne, net, nette, quel, quelle, tel, telle, bel, belle. Where note also, that bel is put before a vowell as bel homme, beau before a Consonant as beau garçon. So nouveau is put before the Substantiue, as le nouveau Testament, feminine nouvelle: but neuf, and the feminine neuve, after the substantiue; as le College neuf.

The comparatiue is made by plus, and the superlatiue by tres, as docte, plus docte, tresdocte. Except (for the Comparatiue) in bon, meilleur, tresbon; mauvais, pire, tresmauvais. Petit, moindre or pluspetit, trespetit.

Of a Pronowne.

IE, tu, jl, jlz, are put when the Verbe is expressed; as, je chante, tu jouës, jl frappe, jlz ont. But moy, toy, luy, eux, are put when the Verbe is not expressed; as, qui ha fait cecy? who hath done this? answere moy, not je; toy, not tu. So, Qui ha fait cela? answere luy or eux; not jl or jlz. je is thus declined.

Nom. Ie *or* moy.	Plur.	*Nom.* nous.	*So decline* tu *plur.* vous, *and* soy *in both numbers. Nominat. is wanting. Gen.* de soy. *Dat.* à soy, &c.
Gen. de moy.		*Gen.* de nous.	
Dat. à moy *or* me.		*Dat.* à nous.	
Accus. moy *or* me.		*Accus.* nous.	
Ablat. de moy.		*Ablat.* de nous.	

Nom. Il *or* luy.	Plur.	*Nom.* Ilz, eulx, ou leur.
Gen. de luy.		*Gen.* d'eulx, de leur.
Dat. à luy *and* luy.		*Dat.* à eux, leur, leurs.
Accus. le *and* luy.		*Accus.* ilz, eulz, les.
Ablat. de luy.		*Ablat.* d'eux, leurs.

Luy. Leur. Luy, is common to both genders, and signifieth to him, or her; as ma mere m'ha demandé, & je luy ay respondu. Leur likewise signifieth to them in both genders, as je leur ay baillé, I gaue it them, both men and women. But leur with an article is a Nowne possessiue, as le leur, theirs. Eux is sometimes put for soy the reciprocall, as ilz ont tous biens communs entre eux, for entre soy.

Ce, Cest. Ce and Cest this, plur. ces. Ce before a Consonant, as ce garçon. Cest before a vowell, as cest homme.

Celuy, Cestuy, Iceluy. Celuy, that man; cestuy, this man; iceluy, the same man, plur. ceux and iceux, femin. celle and icelle, are thus placed in a sentence. Celuy goeth before; qui and iceluy repeateth it as its relatiue, as celuy qui seme mauvaise semence, iceluy recueille mauvais grain. He that soweth ill seed, that man gathereth ill graine.

Mesme. Mesme, is ioyned to Nownes and Pronownes, and is as much as selfe in English, as l'homme mesme, the selfe same man; moy mesme, my selfe; luy mesme, himselfe.

Y. Y is sometimes a Relatiue
- Of place, signifying both in, and to, a place; as il y est, he is there; j'y vay, I goe thither.
- Of the thing mentioned; as tu y pourvoiras, thou shalt take care of it.

In this speech, il y ha, there is, or there are, the auxiliar Verbe ha is put for est.

En. En, is a Relatiue sometimes
1 Of place, and signifieth frō thence; as j'en vien, I come from thence.
2 Of the person or thing mentioned; as, ha-il vn pere, or du papier? hath he a father, or hath he any paper? ouy il en ha, yea, he hath one, or he hath some.

Mon, ton, son. These Possessiues, mon, ton, son, noz, voz, are put when the Substantiue is expressed; as mon livre, my booke, noz livres, our bookes. But mien, tien, sien, nostres, vostres, are put without the Substantiue, hauing alwayes an Article ioyned with them; as, à qui est ce livre? whose booke is this? we may either say, il est à moy, or else, c'est le mien, it is mine, les nostres. Noz amis, & les vostres, our friends, & yours.

Of a Verbe.

VErbes with the French are onely of three kinds. Actiues, whose Preterperfect tense is formed by j'ay, as j'ay aimé. 2 Passiues, which all along are formed by je suis, as je suis aimé. Imp. j'estoys aimé, &c. 3 Newters, whose Preterperfect tense is formed by je suis, as je suis allé. Moodes and tenses are the same with the Latins, except the Aorist, which thē is to be vsed in the French, Italian, & Spanish, when we find the same fitly vsed in our English, such as are, I went, I ran, I rode, I sate, &c.

The Coniugations, togither with their forming, are to be seene in the Table of the Verbes hereunto adioyning.

☞ A Table

Concerning the forming of the Tenses. The Imperfect of the Indicatiue is formed from the first person plurall of the Present changing ons in oy, *as* chantons, je chantoy. *The first and second persons plurall in the present of the Optatiue, and in the Imperfect of all Moods, interpose* i, *in all Coniugations, as,* Aimions, aimassions, amerions.

The second of the Imperatiue, is from the first of the Indicatiue of all Coniugations, as Di tu, reçoy tu,&c. *The third from the third plurall of the same tense, by taking away* nt, *as* ilz donnent, qu'il donne,&c. *Some be irregular, as* qu'il face, qu'il sache, *from* sont, *and* sçavent.

The Present of the Optatiue, from the third of the Imperatiue euermore. The Imperfect from the second singular of the Aorist, tu leus, je leusse.

The Imperfect of the Subiunctiue from the Future of the Indicatiue, by changing ay in oy, *as* j'aymeray. j'aymeroy,&c.

The Participle Present from the first plurall of the present of the Indicatiue, changing ons, *in* ant, *as* bastissons, bastissant.

A Verbe Passiue.

A *Verbe Passiue is made by putting the Participle of any Verbe to the persons of the Verbe* je suis, *as* je suis, tu es, il est aimé, nous sommes, vous estez, ils sont aimez. *Imperfect.* j'estoy aimé, nous estions aimez,&c.

Note also, that the third persons in both numbers are passiuely to bee rendred, when se *is set before them, as* il se fait, *it is done,* ilz se sont, *they are made.*

A Verbe Impersonall

1 *Actiue is made by putting* il *before the third person, as* il convient, il convenoit, il fault, il falloit, il fallust, il ha fallu, il faudra,&c. *Such are these* il neige, *it snoweth,* il gresle, *it haileth,* il Gele, *it freezeth,* il regele, *it thaweth,* il avesprit, *it waxeth night,* il plut, *it raineth.*

2 *Passiue is made by putting* on, *or* lon, *before the third persons singular of Verbes Actiues, as* on dit, dicitur, *it is said, or men say,* on aime, amatur, *men loue,* on aimoit, on aimast,&c.

The Anomala or irregular Verbes *of the first Coniugation.*

Aller, to goe. OF *the first Coniugation there is onely one auxiliar Verbe,* Aller, *to goe. Present tense.* Ie vay *or* je vois, tu vas, il va, nous allons, vous allez, ils vont. *Imperf.* I'alloy, tu allois. &c. *Aorist.* I'allay, tu allas, &c. *Preterit.* Ie suis allé, tu es allé. *Plusquam Perfect.* I'estoye allé, &c. *Futur.* I'iray, tu iras, il ira, nous irons, vous irez, ils iront. *Imperat.* Va tu. Qu'il aille, *or* qu'il voise, allons, allez, qu'ils aillent, *or* qu'ils voisent. *Optat. Pres.* Dieu vueille que j'aille *or* voise; tu ailles *or* uoises, il aille *or* voise, nous allions, vous alliez, ils aillent *or* voisent. *Imperf.* I'allasse, tu allasses, il allast. *Perf.* Que je soye allé, tu soys allé. *Plusquam Perfect.* Que je fusse allé. *Futur.* Que j'aille cy apres. *The Preterimperfect. of the Subiunctiue,* Quand j'iroye, tu iroys, il iroit, nous irions, vous iriez, ils iroyent.

Martin Caucius, Fol. 48. *doth further obserue, that the word* doint *is an irregular third person from the Verbe* Donner, *as* Dieu vous doint bon jour; *as* Plautus *vseth* Duit *for* det: *And* Terence *saith,* Dij tibi dignum factis exitium duint. Andria Act.4.Scen.1. *So likewise,* Iamais Dieu ne me pardoint, s'il n'est ainsi.

The irregulars of the second *Coniugation.*

Assaillir, to assault. P*Res.* I'assau, tu assaus, il assault; *or according to* Iohn Serrcius, j'assaille, tu assailles, *and* nous assaillons. *Aorist.* I'assaille. *Pret.* I'ay assailly. *Fut.* I'assailliray, *Caucius.* I'assaudray. *Serreius.*

Benir, or Benistre, to blesse *Pres.* Ie beni, is, it, nous benissons,&c. *Pret.* I'ay benit.

Bouillir, to boyle. *Pres.* Ie bou, tu bous, il bout, nous bouillons. *Aorist.* Ie boullu *or* boully, ils bouillirent. *Pret.* I'ay boulu. *Fut.* Ie bouilleray *or* boudray.

Courir, to runne. *Pres.* Ie cour, tu cours. *Aorist.* Ie courru. *Pret.* I'ay couru. *Fut.* Ie couriray, *and also* je courray.

Couvrir, to couer. *Pres.* Ie couvre, nous couvrons. *Aorist.* Ie couvry. *Pret.* I'ay couvert. *Fut.* Ie couvriray.

Cueillir, to gather. *Pres.* Ie cueil *or* cueille, *or* je cus, tu cueilles, nous cueillons. *Aorist.* Ie cueilly. *Pret.* I'ay cueilly. *Fut.* Ie cuilleray.

Dormir, to sleepe. *Pres.* Ie dors, tu dors, il dort, nous dormons. *Aorist.* Ie dormi. *Pret.* I'ay dormy. *Fut.* Ie dormiray.

Faillir, to faile or misse. *Pres.* Ie fau, nous faillons. *Aorist.* Ie failly. *Pret.* I'ay failly. *Fut.* Ie fauldray.

Farcir, to stuffe. *Pres.* Ie fars, nous farçons. *Aorist.* Ie farçy. *Pret.* I'ay farçy.

Ferir, to strike. *Pres.* Ie fier, nous fierons. *Aorist.* Ie feru, *or according to* Caucius, je feris. *Pret.* I'ay feru. *Fut.* Ie feriray *or* je fierray.

Fuir, to fly. *Pres* Ie fuy, tu fuys, nous fuyons.

Gesir, to lye in. *Pres.* Ie gi, tu gis, nous gisons. *Aorist, according to* Caucius, je gesy. *But* Stephanus *and* Serreius *will haue it to be* je jeu. *Pret.* I'ay jeu, *and also* gesy. *Fut.* Ie gesiray.

Haïr, to hate. *Pres.* Ie haï, tu haïs, nous haions *and* haïssons. *Aorist.* Ie haï. *Pret.* I'ay haï. *Fut.* Ie haïray.

Issir, to goe forth: whence commeth reussir, to succeed well. *Pres.* I'issis, tu issis.(*Howbeit* Caucius *saith it wanteth the singular number.*) *Plural.* Nous ississons; *or, as* Caucius, *and some others,* nous issons, vous isses, ils issent. *Aor.* I'issis. *Pret.* I'ay issu. *In steed of this Verbe we commonly vse* Sortir.

Mentir, to lye. *Pres.* Ie ments, nous mentons. *Aorist.* Ie menty.

Mourir, to die. *Pres.* Ie meurs, meurs, nous mourons, ils meurent. *Aorist.* Ie mouru. *Preterit.* Ie suis mort. *Fut.* Ie mourray.

Offrir, to offer. *Pres.* I'offre, tu offres, nous offrons. *Aorist.* I'offri. *Pret.* I'ay offert

Ouir, to heare. *Pres.* I'oy, tu oys, nous oyons. *Aorist.* I'ouy. *Preter.* I'ay oui. *Fut.* I'ouiray *or* j'orray.

Ouvrir, to open. *Pres.* I'ouvre *or* j'euvre, nous ouvrons. *Aorist.* I' ouvri. *Preterit.* I'ay ouvert.

Partir, when it signifieth *To diuide or part. It hath its Present*, je parti, tu partis, nous partissons. *To depart or goe away. It hath its Present*, je pars, tu pars, nous partons.

Puir, to stinke. *Pres.* Ie pu, tu pus, nous puons. *Aorist.* Ie pu. *Fut.* Ie puëray.

Querir, or Querre, to goe fetch, *Pres.* Ie quiers, tu quiers nous querons, vous querez, ils quierent. *Aorist.* Ie quis. *Pret.* I'ay quis. *Fut.* Ie querray. *In like manner forme*, acquerir & requerir. *Howbeit*, Caucius *doth forme the Aorist*, Ie requeru. *Pret.* I'ay requeru. *But it is better*, I'ay requis.

Repentir to repent, *Pres.* Ie me repents, tu te repents, nous nous repentons. *Aorist.* Ie me repenti. *Preterit.* Ie me suis repenti. *Fut.* Ie me repentiray.

Saillir, to leape. *Pres.* Ie sau, nous saillons. *Aorist.* Ie sailly. *See* Assaillir.

Secourir, to succour *Pres.* Ie secours, nous secourons. *Aorist.* Ie secouru. *Pret.* I'ay secouru. *Fut.* Ie secouray.

Sentir, to feele *Pres.* Ie sens, nous sentons. *Aorist.* Ie senty. *Pret.* I'ay senti.

Servir, to serue. *Pres.* Ie sers, nous servons. *Aorist.* Ie servy.

Soubvenir, to remember. *It is coniugated Impersonally. Pres.* Il me soubvient. *Imperf.* Il me soubvenoit. *Aorist.* Il me soubvint. *Perif.* Il m'est soubvenu, *Fut.* Il me soubviendra.

Soubvertir, to ouerthrow. *Pres.* Ie soubvers, nous subvertons. *Aorist.* Ie soubverti.

Souffrir, to suffer. *Pres.* Ie souffre, nous suffrons. *Aorist.* Ie souffri. *Perf.* I'ay souffert,

Sortir to goe forth *Pres.* Ie sors, nous sortons,

Tenir, to hold. *Pres.* Ie tiens, nous tenons, ils tiennent. *Aorist.* Ie tins, nous tinsmes, vous tinstes ils tindrent. *Pret.* I'ay tenu, *Fut.* Ie tiendray.

Toussir to cough, *Pres.* Ie tousse, nous toussons, *as if it were of the first Coniugation.*

Tollir, an old verbe to take away. *Pres. According to* Caucius. Ie toul, tu touls, il toult, nous tollons, ils toulent. *Pret.* I'ay tollu *or* tolly.

Venir, to come. *Pres.* Ie vien, nous venons, ils viennent. *Aorist.* Ie vins nous vinsmes, vous vinstes, ils vindrent. *Pret.* Ie suis venu. *Fut.* Ie viendray. *Imperat.* Vien tu, qu'il vienne.

Vestir, to cloth. *Pres.* Ie vest, tu vests, nous vestons. *Aorist.* Ie vesti. *Perf.* I'ay vestu. *Fut.* Ie vestiray.

The irregulars of the third *Coniugation*

Apparoir, or Apparoistre, to appeare. *This Verbe hath a double forming, as* 1 *Pres.* I'apparoy, nous apparoissons, *Imperf*, I'apparoissoy, *Aorist*, Ie paru, 2 *Pres*, I'apper, tu appers, nous apperons, ils apperét, *Imperf*, I'apparoye. *Aorist*, j'apparu, *Fu.* I'apparoistray,

Appercevoir, to perceiue. *Pres*, I'appercoy, nous appereeuons, ils apperçoivent, *Aorist*, I'apperçeu, nous apperçeusmes, *Fut* I'apperçeuray, *Imperat*, Apperçois, qu'il apperçoiue, *So coniugate* Conçevoir, reçevoir, deçevoir,

Challoir, to care for *It is coniugated impersonally*, Il me chault, il me challoit, il me challust, il m'ha challu, il me chaudra, *or* chaura, *according to* Stephanus,

Cheoir, to fall. *Pres.* Ie che, tu ches, nous cheons, ils cheent. *Aorist.* Ie cheu. *Pret.* Ie suis cheu, *Fut.* Iecherray.

Douloir, to grieue. *Pres.* Ie me deul, nous nous doulons *or* dueillons, ils se deulent. *Imperf*, Ie douloy *or* deuloy. *Aorist.* Ie me doulu, *Fut*, Ie me dueilleroy, *Imperat*, Dueille qu'ils deulent, *Particip*, Dolent,

Debvoir, to owe: *Pres.* Ie doy, nous devons, ils doibvent, *Aorist*, Ie deu, *Pret*, I'ay deu. *Fut.* Ie debvray. *Particip.* Debvant.

Mouvoir, to moue. *Pres.* Ie meu, nous mouvons, ils mouvent *or* meuvent. *Aorist.* Ie meu. *Pret.* I'ay meu. *Fut.* Ie mouvray.

Pouvoir, to be able. *Pres.* Ie puis *or* peux, tu peulx, il beult, nous pouvons, ils peuvent. *Aorist.* Ie peu. *Pret* I'ay peu. *Fut.* Ie pourray, *Optat*, *Pres*, Ie puisse, *Imperf.* Ie peusse,

Ramentevoir, to call to minde. *Pres.* Ie ramentoy, nous ramentevons, ils ramentoivent. *Aorist.* Ie ramentu. *Pret.* I'ay ramenteu. *Fut.* Ie rementevray.

Recevoir, to receiue. *Pres.* je reçoy, nous reçevons. *Aorist.* je reçeu *Fut* je recevray.

Scavoir, to knowe. *Pres.* Ie sçay, nous sçavons. *Aorist*, Ie sçeu. *Pret.* I'ay sçeu, *Fut* Ie sçauvray *or* sçauray. *Imper.* saches, qu'il sache, sachons, sachez, qu'ils sachent. *Particip. Pres.* sachant *or* sçavant. *Pret* sçeu.

Seoir, to sit. *Pres.* Ie sie, tu sies, il sied, nous seons, ils seent. *Aor* Ie si, tu sis, il sid. *Pret.* I'ay sy, *or* je me suis assis. *Fut.* Ie serray. *Imperat.* See *or* sies, qu'il see *or* sie. *Opt. Pres.* Que je sie. *Imperf.* Ie sisse. *Part. Pres.* Seant *Perfect.* Sis *Likewise* asseoir. je m'assie, &c.

Souloir, to be wont. *Pres.* Ie suis accoustomé, tu es accoustumé, il est accoustumé, nous soulons, vous soulez, ils soulent. *Imperf.* Ie souloy, tu souloys: *the other Tenses it borrowed from the verb* accoustumer, *as Pret.* Ie suis accoustumé, &c.

Valoir, to be worth. *Pres.* Ie vau, tu vaulx, il vault, nous valons, vous valez, ils vaillent. *Aorist.* Ie valu. *Pret.* j'ay valu. *Fut.* Ie vauldray. *Imperat.* Vaulx qu'il vaille

Vouloir, to be willing. *Pres.* Ie vueil *or* je veux, nous voilons, ils veulent. *Aorist.* Ie voulu. *Pret.* I'ay voulu. *Fut.* je vouldray. *Optat.* je vueille, nous voulions, il vueillent. *Imperf.* je voulusse *or* voulisse, *saith* Pilot, *or rather* voussisse, *saith* Caucius, *as* Le Roy ne pouvoit trouver gens qui y voussissent aller. Theatre du monde, *fol*, 120.

The irregulars of the fourth *Coniugation.*

Absouldre, to absolue. *PRes.* I'absous, nous absolvons, ils absolvent. *Aorist.* I'absouls *or* j'absolu, il, absulurent. *Pret* j'ay absouls *or* abselu. *Fut.* j'absouldray.

Apprendre to learne. *Pres.* I'appren. nous apprennons. *Aorist.* j'appris. *Pret.* j'ay apprins. *Fut.* j'apprendray.

Ardre, to burne. *Pres.* I'ars, nous ardons. *Aorist.* j'ardi. *Pret.* je suis ards. *Particip.* Ards.

Attaindre, to attaine vnto. *Pres.* I'attain, nous attaignons, ils attaignent. *Aorist.* I'attaigni, tu attaignis, ils attaignirent. *Pret.* je suis attaint. *Fut.* j'attaindray.

Attendre, to wait for. *Pres.* I'attends, nous attendons. *Aorist.* j'attendy. *Pret.* I'ay attendu. *Fut.* j'attendray.

Battre, to beat. *Pret.* je ba, nous battons, *Aorist* je batti. *Pret.* j'ay battu, *Fut* je battray.

Pres.

Boire. *Pres.* Ie boy, nous beuvons, ils beuvent or beuvent. *Aorist.* Ie beu. *Pret.* I'ay beu. *Fut.* Ieboiray, ou beuvray.

Bruire, to make a noise. *Pres.* Ie bruy, nous bruyons. *Aorist.* Ie bruy. *Pret.* I'ay bruit. *Fut.* Ie bruiray.

Braire, to bray. *Pres.* Ie bray, nous brayons, &c.

Ceindre, to gird. *Pres.* Ie ceins, nous ceignons. *Aorist.* Ie ceigny. *Pres.* I'ay ceint. *Fut.* Ie ceindray.

Clorre, to shut. *Pres.* Ie clo, nous cloons; *in stead whereof, saith* Stephanus, *we vse* Fermons.

Conclure, to conclude *Pres.* Ie conclu, nous concluons. *Aorist.* Ie conclu.

Confire, to sauce. *Pres.* Ie confi, nous confisons, ils confisent. *Aorist.* Ie confis. *Pret.* I'ay confit.

Contraindre, to constraine. *Pres.* Ie contrains, nous contraignons. *Aorist.* Ie contraigny, ils contraignirent. *Pret.* I'ay contraint. *Fut.* Ie contraindray.

Coudre, to sew. *Pres.* Ie cou, or couds, *according* to Pilot, nous cousons. *Aorist.* Ie cousy or cousu. *Pret.* I'ay cousu. *Fut.* Ie coudray.

Craindre, to feare. *Pres.* Ie crains, nous craignons, ils craignent. *Aorist* Ie craigni, *say* Bellot *and* Pilot, ils craignirent or craindrent. *Pret.* I'ay craint. *Fut.* Ie craindray.

Croire, to beleeue. *Pres.* Ie croy, nous croyons. *Aorist.* Ie creu. *Pret.* I'ay creu. *Fut.* Ie croyray. *Imperat.* Croy, qu'il croye.

Croistre, to grow. *Pres.* Ie croy, nous croissons. *Aorist.* Ie cru. *Pret.* I'ay cru. *Fut.* Ie croistray.

Cuire, to seeth. *Pres.* Ie cuy, nous cuisons. *Aorist.* Ie cuysi, *sayeth* Caucius.

Descēdre, to descend. *Pres.* Ie descends. *Aorist.* Ie descendi. *Pret.* I'ay descendu. *Fut.* Ie descendray.

Destruire, to destroy. *Pres.* Ie destruy, nous destruissons. *Aorist.* Ie destruisi, ils destruisirent.

Dire, to say. *Pres.* Ie di, nous disons, vous dites, ils disent or dient. *Aorist.* Ie di *Pret.* I'ay dit. *Fut.* Ie diray. *Imperat.* Dis, qu'il dise, or die.

Duire, to content. *Pres.* Ie dui, nous duisons. *Aorist.* Ie duisy, ils duirent or duisirent. *Pres.* I'ay duit. *Fut.* Ie duiray. *Likewise* conduire, deduire, induire.

Entendre, to vnderstand. I'entends, j'entendi, j'ay entendu, j'entendray.

Escrire, to write. I'escri, nous escrivons. *Aorist.* I'escrivi. *Pret* I'ay escrit. *Fut.* I'escriray.

Eslire, to chuse. I'esly, nous eslisons. *Aorist.* I'esleu. *Pret.* I'ay esleu. *Fut.* I'esliray.

Espandre, to spill or shed. I'espands, nous espandons. *Aorist.* I'espandy. *Pret.* I'ay espandu. *Fut.* I'espandray.

Espardre, to scatter. I'espars, nous espardons. *Aorist.* I'espardi. *Pret.* I'ay espars. *Fut.* I'espardray.

Espraindre, to squeeze out I'esprains, nous espraignons. *Aorist.* I'espraigny, ils espraindirent. *Pret.* I'ay espraint. *Fut.* I'espraindray. *Likewise coniugate* esteindre, *to quench.* I'esteings, nous esteignons, &c.

Faire, to make or do. Ie fay, tu fais, il fait, nous faisons, vous faites, ils font. *Aorist.* Ie fi or fei, nous fismes. *Pret.* I'ay fait. *Fut.* Ie firay. *Imper.* Fay, qu'il face, faisons, faites, qu'ils facent. *Opt. Pres* Ie façe, tu façes, il façe, nous faςions, vous faciez, ils façent.

Feindre, to faine. Ie feins, nous feignons. *Aorist.* Ie feigni nous feignismes, ils feignirent. *Pret.* I'ay feint.

Fendre, to cleaue. Ie fends, nous fendons. *Aorist.* Ie fendi, ils fendirent. *Pret.* I'ay fendu. *Fut* Ie fendray *Likewise* Fondre, *to melt*, je fons: *Aorist.* Ie fondu, ils fondurent.

Frire, to frie. Ie fri, nous frions. *Aorist.* Ie fri. *Pret.* I'ay frit. *Fut.* Ie friray.

Ioindre, to ioyne. Ie joing, nous joignons. *Aorist.* Ie joigny, nous joignismes, ils ioindrent or joignirent. *Pret.* I'ay joint. *Fut.* Ie joindray.

Lire, to read. Ie li, nous lisons, vous lisez. *Aorist.* Ie leu. *Pret.* I'ay leu.

Luire, to shine. Ie lui, nous luisons. *Aorist.* Ie luisy, nous luisismes, ils luirent.

Mettre, to put. Ie mets, nous mettons. *Aorist.* Ie mis, nous mismes, ils mitent. *Pret.* I'ay mis. *Fut.* Ie mettray.

Mordre, to bite. Ie mords, tu mords, il mord, nous mordons. *Aorist.* Ie mordi, nous mordismes, ils mordirent. *Pret.* I'ay mordu.

Morfōdre to chill. Ie me morfonds. *Aorist.* Ie me morfondi, ils se morfondirent.

Mouldre, to grinde. Ie mou or meu, nous moulons. *Aorist.* Ie moulu. *Pret.* I'ay moulu. *Fut.* Ie mouldray.

Naistre, to be borne. Ie nay, nous naissons. *Aorist.* Ie nasqui. *Pret.* Ie suis né. *Fut.* Ie naistray.

Nuire, to annoy. Ie nui, nous nuisons, ils nuisent. *Aorist.* Ie nui, and nuisy, nuisismes, ils nuisirent. *Pret.* I'ay nuit. *Fut.* Ie nuiray.

Occire, to kill. I'occis; nous occions, *and* occisons, ils occisent. *Aorist.* I'occi. nous occismes, ils occirent *Pret.* I'ay occis. *Fut.* I'occiray.

Oindre, to annoint. I'oings, nous oignons, *Aorist.* I'oigny, nous oignismes, ils oindrent. *Pret.* I'ay oint. *Fut.* I'oindray.

Paistre, to feed. Ie pais. nous paissons. *Aorist.* Ie peu, nous peusmes, ils peurent. *Pret.* I'ay peu, *Fut.* Ie paistray.

Paroistre to appeare. *See* Apparoir *in the third Coniugation.*

Pendre, to hang. Ie pends, nous pendons. *Aorist.* Ie pendi, nous pendismes, ils pendirent. *Pret.* I'ay pendu. *Fut.* Ie pendray.

Perdre, to lose. Ie pers, nous perdons. *Aorist.* Ie perdi, ils perdirent. *Pret.* I'ay perdu.

Plaire, to please. Ie plai, nous plaisons. *Aorist.* Ie pleu, nous pleusmes, ils pleurent. *Pret.* I'ay pleu. *Fut.* Ie plairay.

Pleindre, to cōplaine Ie me pleigns, nous pleignons. *Aorist.* Ie me pleigny, nous pleignismes, ils pleindrent. *Pret.* Ie me suis pleint. *Fut.* Ie me pleindray.

Peindre, to paint. Ie peins, nous peignons. *Aorist.* Ie peigni, ils peindrent. *as in* Pleindre.

Poindre, to pricke. Ie poings, nous poignons. *Aorist.* Ie poigni, nous poignismes, ils poignirent.

Pondre, to lay an egge. Ie pon, nous ponnons, *or* pondons, *which is lesse in vse. Aorist.* Ie ponnu. *or* pondu. *Some say*, Ie ponnis. *whence commeth the* 3. *Plurall*, Ils pondrent. *Pret.* I'ay ponnu. ¶ Caucius *will haue it*, j'ay pu, *which is verie irregular.*

Prendre, to take, Ie prens, nous prennons. *Aorist.* Ie prins, *or* pris, nous prinsmes, ils prindrent. *Pret.* I'ay pris, *Fut.* Ie prendray.

Raire, to shaue. Ie ray, nous rayons, *or* rasons, ils rasent. *But for this they vse the Verbe* Raser. *Pret.* I'ay raiz, *or* rez. *whence seemeth to come that aduerbiall speech*, Rez terre, *gliding by the earth*,

Respondre: to answer. Ie responds, nous respondons. *Aorist.* Ie respondi, ils respondirent. *Pret.* I'ay respondu. *Fut.* Ie respondray.

Rire, to laugh. Ie ri, tu ris, nous rions. *Aorist.* Ie ri, nous rismes, ils rient. *Pret.* I'ay ri. *Fut.* Ie riray.

Rompre, to breake. Ie romps, il rompt, nous rompons. *Aorist.* Ie rompy, il rompirent. *Pret.* I'ay rompu, *Fut.* Ie rompray.

Ie

Semondre, to summons, or inuite. Ie semonds. *Aorist.* Ie semondi, ils semondirent. *Pret.* I'ay semondu.

Souldre to loose. Ie sou, nous soluõns, *or* solvons *according to* Caucius: ils soudent, *or* soluẽnt. *Aorist.* Ie solus. *Pret.* I'ay solu. *Likewise* Absouldre, *to absolue, sauing that it makes its Preterfect.* I'ay absoult, *and the Optat. Pres.* I'absolue; *as* Dieu te absolve.

Suffire, to suffice. *It is formed Impersonally.* Il suffist, il suffisoit, il suffist, il ha suffi, il suffira.

Suivre, to follow. Ie suy, nous suivons. *Aorist.* Ie suivy. *Pret.* I'ay suivy, *or according to* Caucius, l'ay suit. *Fut.* Ie suivray.

Taire, to hold ones peace. Ie tay, *or* je me teus, nous taisons. *Aorist.* Ie me teu. *Pret.* Ie me suis teu. *Fut.* Ie me tairay.

Tendre, to tend. Ie tends, nous tendons. *Aorist.* Ie tendi. *Pret.* I'ay tendu.

Teindre, to die. Ie teigns, nous teignons. *Aorist.* Ie teigny, ils teignirent. *Pret.* I'ay teint. *Fut.* Ie teindray.

Tistre, to weaue. Ie ti, nous tissons. *Aorist.* Ie tissy, ils tiffirent. *Pret.* I'ay tissu. *Fut.* Ie tistray.

Tondre, to pole. Ie tonds, nous tondons. *Aorist.* Ie tondi, ils tondirent. *Pret.* I'ay tendu.

Tordre, to wrest. Ie tords, nous tordons. *Aorist.* Ie tordi, ils tordirent. *Pret.* I'ay tordu, *or* j'ay tords. *Fut.* Ie tordray.

Traire, to draw, or to milke. Ie tray, nous traions, *or* treons. *Aorist.* Ie traï, ils traïrent. *Pret.* I'ay trait. *Likewise the compound* Pourtraire, *to limme: howbeit for* Traire *they vse* Tirer.

Vaincre, to ouercome. Ie vaincs, *or* vainqs, nous vainquons. *Aorist.* Ie vainqui. *Pret.* I'ay vaincu.

Vivre, to liue. Ie vis, nous vivons. *Aorist.* Ie vesqui. *Pret.* I'ay vescu. *Fut.* Ie vivray.

Of the indeclinable parts, Aduerbs, Coniunctions, Prepositions, and *Interjections.*

These parts, saith Pilot, *may easily be omitted, and therefore I will sleightly passe them ouer, obseruing onely the hardest, and those which seldome occurre.*

Adverbes.

Of Time. Auprime, *or* auprimes. *Now instantly; as it were,* nunc horâ primâ.

Cipricimi. *Presently, suddenly, as it were,* cy pris, cy mis, *here taken, and here hanged.*

Doresenavant. *From hence forward.* Entretemps, *or* ce pendant. *In the meane time.*

Guere, *or* gaire. *Much. This word is neuer put without a Negatiue, as* Il n'y a guere, *for* Il n'y ha moult de temps. *There is not much time past since, or not long since.*

Huy. *whence come.* Aujourd'huy. *To day.* Meshuy. *A while agone.*

Onques. *Euer. It is alwaies put with a Negatiue, as* Ie ne vi onques. *I neuer saw.*

Pieça, *as it were,* piece ha. *Long agone; or, It is a good peece, or space of time since.*

Of Place. Ens. *within. as* ceans, *for* cy ens; *here within;* Leans, *for* li ens; *there within.*

Fors, *for* hors. *as* fors que cela; *Except that, for* hors mis cela. *As in Gloucestershire they likewise say, Out-set that, for except that.*

Illec. *There.* Vis a vis. *Ouer against.*

Of Affirming. C'est mon. *It is true; or, yea indeed; as much as* vrayement. *Sometimes it is an Interrogatiue, as* μῶν *in Greeke; as* asçavoir mon s'il le feroit. *To wit whether he would doe it yea or nay.* Voire. *Yea.*

Of denying. Nani, *or* nenny, *or* Nanin. *No.*

Hola, *or* hau. *To which they commonly answer.*

Of calling Plaist il? *what is your pleasure?*

Of wishing. Pleust a Dieu, *or* à la mienne volonté. *I would to God.*

Of exhorting. O avant. *Forward, forward.* Sus, orsus. *Goe to.* Lala. *There there.*

Of Numbring. Fois, *which is alwayes added to some Noune of number, as* vne fois; *once, or one time;* deux fois, *twice.*

Of quantitie. Beaucoup, *or* moult. *Much, or a faire deale.* Prou, *from the Latine word* Probè, *signifying much; as when they say,* Vir probè doctus; *a man very learned.* Bon prou leur face. *Much good may it doe them. And in this sence they vse* bien *and* fort, *as the Latines haue their* valdè *from* validè. Homme bien sçavant, *or* fort docte. *A man very learned:*

Conjunctions:

Copulatiues. Et, *which neuer soundeth* t *neether before Consonant, nor Vowell.* Ainsy que; *euen as.* C'est à sçavoir; *namely; or, that is to wit, that is to say.*

Davantage. *Moreouer.*

Conditionalls. Si. *If.* Sinon que. *But that, or except that.* Pendant que, *or* tandis que. *Whiles that.*

Discretiues, or Aduersatiues. Combien que, *or* jaçoit que. *Albeit that.* Ains, *or* ainçois. *Yea rather.* Toutesfois. *Notwithstanding.* Neantmoins. *Neuerthelesse. These which* Ramus *makes Discretiues,* Stephanus *will haue to bee Aduersatiues.*

Disjunctiues. Ou, *either; when it is put without an accent; for when it is accented it is, saith* Serreius, *an Aduerbe of place; as* où est il? *where is he?*

Illatiues or Rationals. Dont. *whereupon.* Doncq, *or* Doncques. *Then, therefore.* Partant. *Wherefore.*

Causalls. Car. *For; from the Greeke* γὰρ Parce que, *or* pour autant que. *For as much as, &c.*

Paepositions.

Apres, *after.* Arriere, *beyond.* Chez, *at; as* chez nous, *at our house.* Chez euz, *at their house.* Deça, *on this side.* Dela, *on that side, or beyond.* Dessus, *vpon.* Dessoubs, *vnder.* Vers, *or* envers, *towards.* Iusques, *vntill.* Selon, *according to, &c.*

Inter-

Interjections.

OF lamenting. Las, helas, *alas.* *Of silencing.* It. *as with the Latines. The rest I purposely omit.*

Syntaxis of Nounes.

A*Diectiues, especially those that sign fie colour, are put after their Substantiues, as* vin blanc, vin clairet, pain bis. *These are set before the Substantiues,* bon, beau, belle; nouveau, nouvelle; mauvais, petit; *as* petit homme, mauvaise femme.

The *Adiectiue agreeth with his Substantiue in Gender*; *as* mon pere, ma mere. *Yet if the Substantiue begin with a vowell, they put an Adiectiue Masculine before it, as* mon espée, mon hostesse: *Except* m'amie, *or if the word begin with* h, *when it is sounded with aspiration, as* ma hauteur.

When two Substantiues come together, the later is put in the Genitiue case, as L'argent du Prince est sujet à la pince. *Sometimes one of the Substantiues is taken away by Elleipsis, as* à la Sainct Iean, la Toussaincts, *where the word* Feste *is vnderstood.*

Adiectiues of desiring, or plentie, or carefulnesse, and their contraries gouerne a Genitiue case, as riche d'argent, nonchalant de son prouffit.

Comparatiues gouerne a Genitiue case, as la face n'est plus grande de demy pied. *Sometimes* que *serueth to the Cōparatiue, as* plus blanc que neige.

Of Verbes.

T*He Infinitiue with an Article becommeth a Noune Substantiue, as* le boire estaint la soif, *for* le boisson.

When two Verbes come together, the later is the Infinitiue Mood, as je veulx aimer. *Sometime the principall Verbe is vnderstood, as* les mastins de courir, & nous d'aller apres. I. commencerent, & nous commenceasmes.

The Nominatiue case goeth before the Verbe. Except the question be asked, as iray je? *shall I goe?* as-tu? *hast thou?*

The Accusatiue followeth the Verbe, j'aime mon maistre: *except* me, te, se, le, luy, leur, nous, vous; *as* tu te prises, il se tourmente, je luy diray, je leur escriray: *Except it be the Imperatiue Mood, as* battezle. Moy, toy, soy, *are also put after the Imperatiue Mood, as well for the Datiue as the Accusatiue, as* di-moy leve-toy.

Me, te, se, *are put before the particle* en, *especially before Verbes Neuters, signifying mouing to a place, as* je m'en vay, va t'en, fui t'en, ilz s'en sont allez. *Sometimes a Verbe hath two Pronounes before it, as* vous vous corroucez fort, *one the Nominatiue, the other the Accusatiue case; or else the Verbe is placed betweene them, as* Comme vous portez vous? *Sometimes there are three, as* vous vous en irez vous?

Some Verbes being construed with an Infinitiue Mood, cause it to be rendred passiuely, as je vous feray batre, *I will make you beaten*; faites faire chemin, *cause roome to be made*; je le vei mettre en prison, *I saw him put in prison.*

The Verb aller *is elegantly construed with a Participle, as* il s'en alloit disant. I. il disoit; il s'en va mourant. I. il meurt.

A Participle added to je suis, *to make a Preterperfect tense, may varie both Gender and Number, as* je suis venu; elle est venuë; nous sommes venus. *But being added to* j'ay, *it changeth not its termination, as* j'ay disné, elle ha disné, nous avous disné. *Yea if a Substantiue goe before the Nominatiue case and the Verbe, the Participle following is rendred passiuely, and agreeth in Gender and Number with that Substantiue, as* les graces que Dieu nous ha données; les corps que la mer ha engloutis.

Of Adverbes.

N*E the negatiue is alwayes accompanied with* point, *or* pas; *as* il n'y est point, *or* pas, *hee is not there at all. And without either of these words it is equiualent, to an affirmatiue,* il est plus sçavant que ne sont ses compagnons, *he is more learned then are his fellowes.*

Dont *is a Particle of Relation, and signifieth as much as* de que, de quoy, du quel, desquels; *as* j'ay le livre dont vous parlez, *I haue the booke of which you speake.*

Of Prepositions.

The Preposition à
1 *Standing betweene two Substantiues, maketh the later an Adiectiue, as* hōme à cheval, *an horseman,* homme à pied, *a footman*, escuelle à oreillons, *a Porrenger, or a dish with eares.*
2 *Standing before a Denominatiue, it signifieth as much as after the fashion, as* à la Francoise, *after the French fashion*; à la Todesque, *after the Dutch fashion. So* en *is vsed as* vivre en beste, *to liue after the manner of a beast*; traité en Prince, *intertained like a Prince.*
3 *Is put after an Adiectiue signifying aptnesse, or nimblenesse, as* viste à l'esteuf, *nimble at the ball.*

The Prepositions de *&* du
1 *Standing before a Substantiue, it signifieth either matter, as* bague d'or, *a gold ring; or the instrument, as* batre de verges, *to beat with rods*; iouër de l'espinette, *to play on the Virginalls.*
2 *It is put after Adiectiues signifying dexteritie, as* habile de la plume, *skilfull at his pen*; habile du pied, *actiue, or swift of foot.*
3 *Standing before the Infinitiue mood, it is Englished* to, *as* je vous prie de faire cela, *I beseech you to doe that.*
4 Du *standing before a Substantiue signifieth part of any thing, and is E lished* some, *as* d des poissons, *so*

Devant *is construed with* que *before an Infinitiue*, *as* Devant qu'aller, *before wee goe*. Apres *with the Preterperfect tense of the Infinitiue mood*, *as* apres avoir receu vos lettres, *after the receiving of your letters*.

Aupres, Arriere, à lentour, *gouerne a Genitiue case*, *as* aupres du feu, *neere the fire*, arriere de nous, *behind vs*, à l'entour de soy, *round about himselfe*.

Conjunctions.

Comme *is vsed for* comment; *as* comme vous portez vous? *how doe you*.

Que *is diuersly Englished*; *as* qu'est ce que de l'homme? *what is man?* Si j'estoye que de luy, *if I were as he*; qu'est ce à dire cecy? *what is this, or how call you this?* Qu'en est il, *what matter is it?*

FINIS.